The Reader's Companion to American History

The Reader's Companion to American History

Eric Foner and John A. Garraty, Editors

Sponsored by the Society of American Historians

Houghton Mifflin Company
Boston

Copyright © 1991 by Houghton Mifflin Company

For information about permission to reproduce selections from
this book, write to Permissions, Houghton Mifflin Company,
2 Park Street, Boston, MA 02108.

Library of Congress Cataloging-in-Publication Data

The Reader's companion to American history / Eric Foner
and John A. Garraty, editors.
    p.   cm.
Includes bibliographical references and index.
ISBN 0-395-51372-3 : $35.00
1. United States — History — Encyclopedias.   I. Foner, Eric.
II. Garraty, John Arthur, 1920–   .
E174.R43 1991 91-19508
973'.03 — dc20 CIP

Printed in the United States of America

RMT 10 9 8 7 6 5 4 3 2 1

Contents

Tables and Maps

Contributors

Daniel Aaron
Harvard University

John Algeo
University of Georgia

Tyler Anbinder
University of Wyoming

David L. Anderson
University of Indianapolis

Margo Anderson
University of Wisconsin — Milwaukee

Marilyn Arnold
Brigham Young University

Cindy Sondik Aron
University of Virginia

Leonard J. Arrington
Salt Lake City, Utah

Dore Ashton
The Cooper Union

James Atlas
New York Times

Steven Gould Axelrod
University of California, Riverside

Beth Bailey
Barnard College

Richard Allan Baker
Historical Office,
United States Senate

Randall Balmer
Columbia University

James M. Banner, Jr.
Washington, D.C.

Lois W. Banner
University of Southern California

C. Robert Barnett
Marshall University

William L. Barney
University of North Carolina
    at Chapel Hill

Richard A. Bartlett
Florida State University

Rosalyn Fraad Baxandall
State University of New York,
College at Old Westbury

Bernard W. Bell
University of Massachusetts
    at Amherst

Thomas Bender
New York University

Richard Bensel
Center for Studies of Social Change,
New School for Social Research

Ira Berlin
University of Maryland
    at College Park

Aaron Berman
Hampshire College

Richard B. Bernstein
Papers of John Jay

Jeff E. Biddle
Michigan State University

Robert Bishop
Museum of American Folk Art

Karen J. Blair
Central Washington University

David W. Blight
Amherst College

John Bodnar
Indiana University
   at Bloomington

Patricia U. Bonomi
New York University

Alan Brinkley
Columbia University

David Brody
University of California, Davis

Hugh Brogan
University of Essex

D. Lydia Brontë
The Phelps-Stokes Fund

Paul Brooks
Lincoln Center, Massachusetts

Dee Brown
Little Rock, Arkansas

Richard D. Brown
The University of Connecticut

Robert V. Bruce
Madbury, New Hampshire

Stuart Bruchey
Columbia University

Borgna Brunner
Cambridge, Massachusetts

Paul M. Buhle
Oral History of the American Left,
Tamiment Library, New York University

Edwin G. Burrows
Brooklyn College,
City University of New York

Richard L. Bushman
Columbia University

Robert H. Canary
University of Wisconsin — Parkside

Albert H. Cantril
Cambridge, Massachusetts

Elizabeth Capelle
New York, New York

Mark C. Carnes
Barnard College

Clayborne Carson
Stanford University

Gerald Carson
Newtown, Pennsylvania

Dan T. Carter
Emory University

Joan E. Cashin
Rutgers University
   at Camden

Richard D. Challener
Princeton University

Clarke A. Chambers
University of Minnesota
   at Twin Cities

John Whiteclay Chambers II
Rutgers University

Alfred D. Chandler, Jr.
Harvard University

Joyce E. Chaplin
Vanderbilt University

Robert W. Cherny
San Francisco State University

Norman H. Clark
Olympia, Washington

Catherine Clinton
Harvard University

Edward M. Coffman
University of Wisconsin — Madison

John Y. Cole
Library of Congress

Wayne S. Cole
University of Maryland
   at College Park

Susan Keselenko Coll
New Delhi, India

Blanche Wiesen Cook
John Jay College and the Graduate School,
City University of New York

Nancy F. Cott
Yale University

Edward Countryman
University of Warwick

Robert D. Cross
University of Virginia

Tom D. Crouch
National Air and Space Museum,
Smithsonian Institution

Robert M. Crunden
The University of Texas
   at Austin

Noble E. Cunningham, Jr.
University of Missouri
   at Columbia

Richard N. Current
Natick, Massachusetts

Barbara Ritter Dailey
Watertown, Massachusetts

David J. Danelski
Stanford University

Allen F. Davis
Temple University

Warren Dean
New York University

Alexander DeConde
University of California, Santa Barbara

Andrew Delbanco
Columbia University

J. Bradford De Long
Harvard University

John D'Emilio
University of North Carolina
   at Greensboro

Morris Dickstein
Queens College,
City University of New York

Susan J. Douglas
Hampshire College

Thomas Dublin
State University of New York
   at Binghamton

Melvyn Dubofsky
State University of New York
   at Binghamton

Ellen Carol DuBois
University of California, Los Angeles

David C. Duke
Marshall University

Richard S. Dunn
University of Pennsylvania

Thomas J. Dunnings, Jr.
Tarrytown, New York

Alice Echols
University of Michigan

R. David Edmunds
Indiana University
   at Bloomington

Abraham S. Eisenstadt
Brooklyn College,
City University of New York

Robert Ellsberg
Orbis Books

Everett Emerson
University of North Carolina
at Chapel Hill

Charles A. Fecher
Baltimore, Maryland

Robert H. Ferrell
Indiana University
at Bloomington

Leon Fink
University of North Carolina
at Chapel Hill

Anita Finkel
New York, New York

Gilbert C. Fite
University of Georgia

Thomas Fleming
New York, New York

James J. Flink
University of California, Irvine

Eric Foner
Columbia University

Robert Booth Fowler
Madison, Wisconsin

R. France
Westbrook, Maine

William W. Freehling
The Johns Hopkins University

Joshua B. Freeman
Columbia University

Frank Freidel
Harvard University

Paul A. Freund
Harvard Law School

Lynn Garafola
New York, New York

Mario T. García
Yale University

Lloyd C. Gardner
Rutgers University

John A. Garraty
Columbia University

Roger L. Geiger
Pennsylvania State University

Arthur Gelb
New York, New York

Barbara Gelb
New York, New York

William E. Gienapp
Harvard University

Timothy J. Gilfoyle
Loyola University of Chicago

Jacqueline Goggin
W. E. B. Du Bois Institute,
Harvard University

Warren Goldstein
State University of New York,
College at Old Westbury

Lawrence Goodwyn
Duke University

John Steele Gordon
North Salem, New York

Linda Gordon
University of Wisconsin — Madison

Arthur A. Goren
Columbia University

Elliott J. Gorn
Miami University

Lewis L. Gould
The University of Texas
at Austin

Henry F. Graff
Columbia University

Otis L. Graham, Jr.
University of California, Santa Barbara

Jack P. Greene
University of California, Irvine

Robert L. Griswold
University of Oklahoma

Richard Griswold del Castillo
San Diego State University

Allen Guttmann
Amherst College

Michael R. Haines
Colgate University

Alonzo L. Hamby
Ohio University

William H. Harbaugh
University of Virginia

Earl N. Harbert
Northeastern University

Neil Harris
The University of Chicago

Robert L. Harris, Jr.
Cornell University

William C. Harris
North Carolina State University

Ellis W. Hawley
University of Iowa

Dolores Hayden
University of California, Los Angeles

Samuel P. Hays
University of Pittsburgh

David Healy
University of Wisconsin — Milwaukee

Carolyn G. Heilbrun
Columbia University

Steve Joshua Heims
Jamaica Plain, Massachusetts

John M. Hemphill II
Williamsburg, Virginia

Karen Hess
New York, New York

Christine Leigh Heyrman
University of Delaware

Patricia Hills
Boston University

Cindy Himes
Towson State University

Darlene Clark Hine
Michigan State University

Arnold R. Hirsch
University of New Orleans

Joan Hoff
Indiana University
    at Bloomington

Stanley C. Hollander
Michigan State University

J. S. Holliday
Carmel, California

David A. Hollinger
University of Michigan

Thomas C. Holt
The University of Chicago

Ari Hoogenboom
Brooklyn College,
City University of New York

Olive Hoogenboom
Brooklyn, New York

Reginald Horsman
University of Wisconsin — Milwaukee

A. E. Dick Howard
University of Virginia Law School

Daniel Walker Howe
University of California, Los Angeles

Michael D. Hummel
The Victoria College

Akira Iriye
Harvard University

Peter Iverson
Arizona State University

Kenneth T. Jackson
Columbia University

D. Clayton James
The Virginia Military Institute

Rhodri Jeffreys-Jones
University of Edinburgh

Francis Jennings
The Newberry Library

Robert W. Johannsen
University of Illinois
    at Urbana-Champaign

Patricia Condon Johnston
Afton, Minnesota

David A. Jones
University of Pittsburgh

Alvin M. Josephy, Jr.
Greenwich, Connecticut

Michio Kaku
The Graduate School and University Center,
City University of New York

Joseph Kastner
Grandview, New York

David M. Katzman
University of Kansas

Morton Keller
Brandeis University

David M. Kennedy
Stanford University

Randall Kennedy
Harvard Law School

Alice Kessler-Harris
Rutgers University

Thomas Kessner
Kingsborough Community College
    and the Graduate School,
City University of New York

Alexander Keyssar
Duke University

Rashid I. Khalidi
The University of Chicago

Frances Arick Kolb
Marlborough, Massachusetts

Peter Kolchin
University of Delaware

Richard B. Kowall
New York, New York

Hilton Kramer
New Criterion

Marc W. Kruman
Wayne State University

Allan Kulikoff
Northern Illinois University

Glenn W. LaFantasie
Woodrow Wilson International
    Center for Scholars

Walter LaFeber
Cornell University

Ellen Condliffe Lagemann
Teachers College,
Columbia University

Ann J. Lane
University of Virginia

Daniel J. Leab
Seton Hall University

Edward F. Leddy
Tarleton State University

Gretchen Lemke-Santangelo
Berkeley, California

Thomas C. Leonard
University of California, Berkeley

Gerda Lerner
University of Wisconsin — Madison

M. X. Lesser
Northeastern University

J. C. Levenson
University of Virginia

Susan Levine
Carrboro, North Carolina

Sanford Levinson
School of Law,
The University of Texas
    at Austin

Leonard W. Levy
The Claremont Graduate School

Leonard P. Liggio
George Mason University

Patricia Nelson Limerick
University of Colorado
    at Boulder

Kathryne V. Lindberg
Harvard University

Arthur S. Link
Princeton University

Jean Lipman
Carefree, Arizona

Laurie Lisle
Sharon, Connecticut

Guy Logsdon
Tulsa, Oklahoma

Priscilla Long
Seattle, Washington

Kip Lornell
Smithsonian Institution

Robert W. Love, Jr.
United States Naval Academy

Paul R. Lucas
Indiana University
    at Bloomington

Christine A. Lunardini
New York, New York

Russell Lynes
New York, New York

Nicholas B. Maher
Chicago, Illinois

Bruce J. Mann
Oakland University

Jack D. Marietta
University of Arizona

Martin E. Marty
The University of Chicago

Geraldine Maschio
University of Kentucky

Elaine Tyler May
University of Minnesota
    at Twin Cities

Lary May
University of Minnesota
    at Twin Cities

Benjamin McArthur
Southern College of Seventh-Day Adventists

Frank D. McConnell
University of California, Santa Barbara

Richard P. McCormick
Rutgers University

Drew R. McCoy
Clark University

Thomas K. McCraw
Harvard Business School

Robert S. McElvaine
Millsaps College

Eric L. McKitrick
Columbia University

Linda O. McMurry
North Carolina State University

James M. McPherson
Princeton University

Russell R. Menard
University of Minnesota
    at Twin Cities

Donna Merwick
University of Melbourne

Robert Middlekauff
University of California, Berkeley

Steven Mintz
University of Houston
    at University Park

Michael M. Mirabito
Ithaca College

James C. Mohr
University of Maryland
    at Baltimore County

Eric H. Monkkonen
University of California, Los Angeles

Regina Morantz-Sanchez
University of California, Los Angeles

H. Wayne Morgan
The University of Oklahoma

Leonard Moss
State University of New York
    at Geneseo

Eleanor Munro
New York, New York

Paul L. Murphy
University of Minnesota
    at Twin Cities

David F. Musto
Yale School of Medicine

Gary B. Nash
University of California, Los Angeles

Steve Neal
Chicago Sun-Times

Donald Nieman
Clemson University

Linda L. Nieman
Graduate School and University Center,
City University of New York

John Niven
The Claremont Graduate School

Tim Page
Newsday

Beverly Wilson Palmer
Pomona College

Phyllis Palmer
The George Washington University

Herbert S. Parmet
Queensborough Community College
    and the Graduate School,
City University of New York

Thomas G. Paterson
The University of Connecticut

James T. Patterson
Brown University

Tiffany R. L. Patterson
Spelman College

Allan Peskin
Cleveland State University

Edward Pessen
Baruch College and the Graduate School,
City University of New York

Robert Peters
University of California, Irvine

Donald Pizer
Tulane University

Elizabeth H. Pleck
Center for Research on Women,
Wellesley College

Forrest C. Pogue
Arlington, Virginia

Nicholas Christopher Polos
University of La Verne

Jeffrey Potter
East Hampton, New York

L. A. Powe, Jr.
School of Law,
The University of Texas
    at Austin

Howard N. Rabinowitz
University of New Mexico

Albert J. Raboteau
Princeton University

Benjamin G. Rader
University of Nebraska — Lincoln

Nicol C. Rae
Florida International University

Jack N. Rakove
Stanford University

Arnold Rampersad
Princeton University

Jonah Raskin
Sonoma State University

James A. Rawley
University of Nebraska — Lincoln

Leo P. Ribuffo
The George Washington University

Martin Ridge
The Huntington Library

Frank W. D. Ries
University of California, Santa Barbara

Phyllis Rose
Wesleyan University

Rosalind Rosenberg
Barnard College

David Rosner
Baruch College and the Graduate School,
City University of New York

Robert I. Rotberg
Lafayette College

Vicki L. Ruiz
University of California, Davis

Robert Allen Rutland
Charlottesville, Virginia

Nancy Ruttenburg
University of California, Berkeley

Robert W. Rydell
Montana State University

Nick Salvatore
Cornell University

Dana D. Nelson Salvino
Louisiana State University

Jeffrey T. Sammons
New York University

Miles David Samson
Columbia University

Martha Saxton
New York, New York

Ronald Schaffer
California State University, Northridge

Frederick Schauer
Kennedy School of Government,
Harvard University

Arthur M. Schlesinger, Jr.
Graduate School and University Center,
City University of New York

Ellen W. Schrecker
Yeshiva University

Stanley K. Schultz
University of Wisconsin — Madison

Robert D. Schulzinger
University of Colorado

Bernard Schwartz
New York University

Jordan A. Schwarz
Northern Illinois University

Nathan A. Scott, Jr.
University of Virginia

Stephen W. Sears
Norwalk, Connecticut

Richard B. Sewall
Yale University

Peter Shaw
New York, New York

James P. Shenton
Columbia University

Suzanna Sherry
University of Minnesota Law School

Martin J. Sherwin
Tufts University

Susan Shillinglaw
San Jose State University

Barbara Sicherman
Trinity College

Fred Siegel
The Cooper Union

Marcia B. Siegel
New York University

Stephen A. Siegel
DePaul University Law School

Joel H. Silbey
Cornell University

Kathryn Kish Sklar
State University of New York
  at Binghamton

Henry Clay Smith
West Tisbury, Massachusetts

Jean R. Soderlund
University of Maryland
  at Baltimore County

Jonathan Soffer
Columbia University

Lee Soltow
Ohio University

Sally Sommer
New York, New York

Marlene A. Springer
East Carolina University

Darren Marcus Staloff
New York, New York

Bruce M. Stave
The University of Connecticut

David L. Stebenne
Columbia University

Judith Stein
City College,
City University of New York

Anders Stephanson
Columbia University

James Brewer Stewart
Macalester College

Catharine R. Stimpson
Rutgers University

Ronald H. Stone
Pittsburgh Theological Seminary

John F. Stover
Purdue University

Susan Strane
New York, New York

Susan Strasser
The George Washington University

Jean Strouse
New York, New York

Sterling Stuckey
University of California, Riverside

Charles Süsskind
University of California, Berkeley

Richard Sylla
New York University

Richard F. Taruskin
University of California, Berkeley

Graham D. Taylor
Dalhousie University

William R. Taylor
State University of New York
  at Stony Brook

Jon C. Teaford
Purdue University

Richard S. Tedlow
Harvard Business School

Carroll F. Terrell
The National Poetry Foundation

Athan G. Theoharis
Marquette University

Emory M. Thomas
University of Georgia

Barbara L. Tischler
Barnard College

John Toland
Danbury, Connecticut

Alan Trachtenberg
Yale University

Hans L. Trefousse
Brooklyn College and the Graduate School,
City University of New York

Allen W. Trelease
University of North Carolina
    at Greensboro

Barbara M. Tucker
Eastern Connecticut State University

Mark Tucker
Columbia University

Joseph S. Tulchin
Woodrow Wilson International
    Center for Scholars

Robert Twombly
City College,
City University of New York

Melvin I. Urofsky
Virginia Commonwealth University

Frank E. Vandiver
Texas A&M University

Alden T. Vaughan
Columbia University

Albert J. von Frank
Washington State University

Edward Wagenknecht
West Newton, Massachusetts

Linda Wagner-Martin
University of North Carolina
    at Chapel Hill

Bennett H. Wall
University of Georgia

Joseph Frazier Wall
Grinnell College

James D. Wallace
Boston College

Kenneth W. Walpuck
Queensborough Community College,
City University of New York

Ronald G. Walters
The Johns Hopkins University

Susan Ware
New York University

Wilcomb E. Washburn
Washington, D.C.

Harvey Wasserman
Greenpeace

Russell F. Weigley
Temple University

Bernard A. Weisberger
Chicago, Illinois

Deborah Welch
Elon College

Jacqueline Bograd Weld
New York, New York

William Welling
New York, New York

Dennis Wepman
Bronx, New York

Jon Wiener
University of California, Irvine

Sean Wilentz
Princeton University

Mira Wilkins
Florida International University

Patrick G. Williams
Columbia University

William Appleman Williams
Waldport, Oregon

Charles Reagan Wilson
University of Mississippi

Christopher P. Wilson
Boston College

Laurie Wilson
New York University

Nancy Woloch
Barnard College

Gordon S. Wood
Brown University

Peter H. Wood
Duke University

Harold D. Woodman
Purdue University

Robert Wooster
Corpus Christi State University

Gwendolyn Wright
Columbia University

Irwin Yellowitz
City College,
City University of New York

Robert L. Zangrando
The University of Akron

Larzer Ziff
The Johns Hopkins University

Hiller B. Zobel
Cohasset, Massachusetts

Contributors of Unsigned Entries

Jeanie Attie
Barbara J. Bennett
Richard B. Bernstein
Borgna Brunner
Elizabeth Fortson
Joanne B. Freeman
Michael S. Green
Owen Gutfreund

Elizabeth Hovey
Tony Kaye
Kevin Kenny
Amy Mittelman
Alice N. Nash
Becky M. Nicolaides
Sandra Opdycke
Mike Sappol

Jonathan Soffer
Kathleen Spencer
Gary Stone
Midori Takagi
Vernon Takeshita
Cecile Rhinehart Watters
Marc Weiss
Patrick G. Williams

Staff

Publisher: Jonathan P. Latimer
Managing Editor: Borgna Brunner
Developmental Editor: Paul Bernabeo
Editorial Assistants: Richard Blow, Lauren Byrne, Jennifer L. Crawford, Maggie May, Rebecca A. Parker,
  Jonathan Soffer, Kathleen Spencer, Margaret M. Waters, and Marike Westra
Copyeditor: Cecile Rhinehart Watters
General Index and Cross-references: Cecile Rhinehart Watters
Index of Contributors: Joseph P. Pickett
Fact-checkers: Manya S. Chylinski and Hanna Schonthal
Proofreaders: Kathryn Blatt, Alice Carmen, Philip G. Holthaus, Karen Hughes, and Nancy Phinney
Production and Manufacturing Manager: Christopher Leonesio
Production Supervisor: Patricia McTiernan
Senior Art and Production Coordinator: Margaret Anne Miles
Manufacturing Supervisor: Greg Mroczek
Database/Word Processing Supervisor: Miriam E. Palmerola
Word Processing Operators: Lawrence Annucci, Edward Coleman, Cary Hawkins Doran, Bruce E. Frost II,
  and Donna Whiting
Design: Margaret Ong Tsao and Ann Stewart
Cartography: Sanderson Associates

Introduction

An encyclopedia, the dictionary tells us, is a reference work containing articles on a variety of topics, arranged alphabetically. Our *Reader's Companion to American History* certainly fits this description. But it is much more than a place to look up the date when Millard Fillmore was president of the United States, or to get a brief rundown on the causes, course, and consequences of the War of 1812, or to find out what the "Ashcan school" was, or to settle a bet about whether Alaska is the forty-ninth or fiftieth state. As its title suggests, this is primarily a *reader's* encyclopedia, a book to be read for enjoyment and — like the famous encyclopedia of the eighteenth-century philosophes — for enlightenment. We believe that this work offers a fresh, up-to-date overview of the main themes and significant personalities that have made up the American experience, presented in a manner that will engage the interest of a broad public.

Of course, nearly all encyclopedias are enlightening in one way or another. But most are meant to be used mainly for reference; like dictionaries and telephone books, they are sources where people can locate information on a subject they want to know more about. Individuals have been known to read through the vast *Encyclopaedia Britannica* from beginning to end. There are even said to be some who enjoy working their way systematically through a telephone book. But doing so is like winning a pie-eating contest or climbing the stairs to the top of the Empire State Building. The pleasure, if there is any in such an accomplishment, is in having done it, not in the doing. Put differently, the whole of the typical encyclopedia is no more than the sum of its many parts.

The Reader's Companion to American History, on the other hand, offers those who consult it a great deal more than a series of discrete facts and ideas. While keeping in mind the necessity of allowing readers to locate essential information easily, we have tried to bring out the relationships between topics separated from one another not only geographically and in time but in most encyclopedias by the vagaries of alphabetical or chronological organization. Scattered through our book, for example, are articles on Bacon's Rebellion, which occurred in 1676, the New York City draft riots that erupted during the Civil War, and a number of other civil disturbances. But there is also a general article on "Rebellions," which puts all these uprisings and a number of others into a single context that makes the significance of the individual uprisings clearer. These longer articles are intended to function as windows into the American past. They are meant to show relationships, to explain as well as describe, to be interpretive essays rather than mere compilations of data.

The word *history* has two quite different meanings. *History* can mean both "what happened" in the past and what people who experienced or otherwise learned about past events have said or written about them. No one can describe "what happened" even in a small area and during a brief time. Too much is going on at once, even in the life of an individual, for a complete description to be possible, let alone comprehensible. Historians impose order on the past by selecting those elements of what happened that are relevant to their purposes. Like sculptors, they explain meaning and create understanding as much by what they leave out as by what they include. Give ten sculptors identical blocks of marble and the same model and no two of their statues will be exactly alike. Ask ten historians to write about the same subject and their accounts will be equally individual.

No one knows better than a practicing historian that the past is more complex than any narrative can suggest and that the order historians impose on it to make it comprehensible is an artifice, not true reality. Indeed, one of the most exciting experiences that historians encounter in their work is the discovery of significant connections between superficially unrelated data. In this encyclopedia, we have tried to make this experience available to readers by giving them a sense of how the pursuit of knowledge about the past is not a matter of following a guide from point A to point B but rather an open-ended exploration, full of unexpected discoveries and sudden insights.

To build this concept into our book we have commissioned three types of articles. Some closely resemble the short entries in conventional encyclopedias. They contain essential information about specific topics and events. There are, for example, entries on every presidential election, and each provides the name and party affiliation of the candidates for president and vice president, the main issues of the campaign, and the popular and electoral votes. These short articles have been written by Columbia University graduate students and recent Ph.D.'s under our supervision.

The second type of article makes up the heart of the encyclopedia. These are longer, interpretive essays on broad topics. They have been written by authorities on the subjects and offer incisive introductions to the key periods, concepts, and themes that have made up the American past. Each of these essays directs the reader to other entries, long and short, that elaborate on aspects of the subject at hand.

A third group of articles is composed of biographies. Although these, which are also written by authorities, include such essential facts as

the dates of the subject's birth and death, they are based on the assumption that users of an encyclopedia designed to be read for pleasure will profit more from reading an expert's overall estimation of the person's significance than a dry recitation of dates and facts. There are articles on all the presidents and on the more historically significant vice presidents, for example, and these add depth and detail to both the short and long entries. A reader may not know a great deal about President Millard Fillmore, but someone looking him up will find a biographical account of his career and that can lead to such articles as the essays on American nativism and the Whig party, as well as the major essays about the presidency, the vice presidency, and so on.

In a one-volume encyclopedia, needless to say, it has been impossible to cover American biography fully. The famous *Dictionary of American Biography* describes the careers of 18,110 Americans, but it requires twenty-eight large volumes to do so. We have had to be much more selective. First of all we have limited ourselves to persons readers are likely to come across either because of the positions they held or because of the significance of their achievements. Thus, we have included all the presidents — even Millard Fillmore.

The biographical entries, however, move well beyond the most familiar government officials. We have made a special effort to include women and members of minority groups, partly because such people have often been neglected in encyclopedias, but more because the rapidly expanding body of knowledge about the history of women and minorities means that readers are ever-more likely to run across unfamiliar names and because so many of our longer essays deal with subjects in which women and minorities have played important roles. Of course, we could have profitably included many more people than we have found room for, but we are confident that each individual represented has made a critical contribution to American life, whether in politics, the arts, sports, business, entertainment, or some other endeavor.

Examples of how the different kinds of articles relate to one another come to mind almost at random. One is the essay on twentieth-century art, which is buttressed by short entries on the Armory Show, abstract expressionism, and pop art and by the biographical sketches of such artists as Jackson Pollock, Willem de Kooning, Louise Nevelson, and Jasper Johns. Another is the two essays on American feminism, linked to the entries on the Seneca Falls Convention and women's organizations as well as sketches of such leaders of the feminist movement as Susan B. Anthony, Betty Friedan, and Gloria Steinem. American labor history is dealt with here in longer essays on such topics as strikes, domestic work, and indentured servitude, biographies of figures like Eugene V. Debs and Samuel Gompers, and shorter entries on various labor organizations. The longer essays on the institution of slavery and slave rebellions are linked to other entries on cotton, the plantation system, and abolitionism, and biographies of figures ranging from John C. Calhoun to Frederick Douglass.

To further aid readers in pursuing their interests in larger subjects and digging more deeply into topics of special interest, the book contains, besides the cross-references and the bibliographic suggestions that follow all the signed articles, an elaborate index. For example, all persons who are mentioned in the interpretive essays have been indexed even if no formal biographical article on them has been included. Readers seeking information about such persons will be introduced to important aspects of their careers, though not necessarily to a detailed account of their lives. Thus, in different ways, hundreds of individuals central to the American experience are discussed either in their own right or in articles on broad topics. We have tried particularly to focus on persons whose activities span apparently separate aspects of American life and on topics that interact with others that seem superficially unconnected. Anyone looking into the essays on the Civil War may be drawn into subjects as diverse as, among many others, the development of railroads, philanthropy, conservatism, and feminism.

We have avoided having articles overlap but have not tried to keep our authors from inadvertently disagreeing with one another. This reflects our commitment to producing an *interpretive* encyclopedia rather than a purely factual volume and our refusal to impose a single stance on our many contributors. Each author is an authority in the field of his or her contribution, and each has been given a free hand in interpretation.

Apart from providing readable, enlightening articles on the myriad themes that make up the American experience, this encyclopedia offers a lens through which to view the study and writing of American history today. In the past two decades, the scholarly investigation of the American past has undergone a profound transformation. Conventional political history, once the structure through which accounts of the past was organized, has largely been eclipsed by the rise of the "new social history," dedicated to studying the day-to-day lives of ordinary Americans and rescuing groups like African-Americans, women, and others from neglect.

Nonetheless, the "old" and "new" histories are not mutually exclusive, and the articles in *The Reader's Companion to American History,* like the contributors themselves, reflect the best of both. Here one will find the presidents, political parties, and major national political issues, as well as articles on economic history, American literature, and other well-established topics. But we have also devoted attention to such recent preoccupations as family life, social mobility, and the history of race relations, and we have tried to be sensitive to the ways in which rapidly expanding fields like African-American history have reshaped our understanding of the American past. Our biographical selections reflect the heterogeneity of the American population, just as our contributors — young and old, black and white, male and female — reflect the historical profession's diversity today. All the writers, however, are committed to the premise that underlies this effort — that making history accessible to a broad public is essential if our profession is to remain a source of collective self-understanding.

The Society of American Historians, which has sponsored *The Reader's Companion,* is devoted to the writing of history as literature and thus to encouraging historians to write for the broad public interested in reading about our nation's past. Its officers are members of the Advisory Board of our encyclopedia, and we editors and many of our contributors are Fellows of the organization.

The society brings together academic and independent historians and encourages both to combine in their work the scientific pursuit of accuracy and truth with the literary qualities that make the best histories works of art. The annual Parkman Prize of the society, named in honor of the great nineteenth-century American historian Francis Parkman, is awarded to the book that best achieves this combination. Its Nevins Prize, sponsored by a group of publishers particularly interested in good history, is named after Professor Allan Nevins, one of the founders of the society and a twentieth-century exemplar of its objectives. This prize is awarded annually to the author of the doctoral dissertation in American history that best reflects both scholarly and literary qualities.

As historians we are committed to the idea that history is an art as well as a science but that making history interesting to nonspecialists does not require either simplifying or embellishing past events. As editors of *The Reader's Companion to American History* we have encouraged all our contributors to keep the goals of the society in mind. We wish to thank them and also Jonathan Latimer, the publisher of Houghton Mifflin's Reference Division, Borgna Brunner and Paul Bernabeo, who have served as managing editors of our project, Cecile Rhinehart Watters, who copyedited the volume, and others at Houghton Mifflin, whose professionalism and enthusiasm have made the task of completing the encyclopedia far more enjoyable than we had any right to expect. Jonathan Soffer served effectively as researcher and as coordinator of the short entries. The authors of short entries are listed separately, but we wish to give special thanks to Michael S. Green, Elizabeth Hovey, Amy Mittelman, Sandra Opdycke, and Jonathan Soffer, each of whom contributed a substantial number. Finally, we want to express our gratitude to Larry Shapiro, executive editor of Book-of-the-Month Club, and to Byron Hollinshead, chairman of the Americana Group, who was convinced that an encyclopedia such as this should be undertaken and that the Society of American Historians should sponsor it.

Eric Foner
John A. Garraty

A

ABLEMAN V. BOOTH

This Supreme Court case in 1859 asserted the supremacy of federal law and federal courts over the states. It also showed the depth of northern abolitionists' anger over the Fugitive Slave Act of 1850 and the *Dred Scott* decision and the lengths to which they would go in their fight against the peculiar institution.

In 1854, abolitionist editor Sherman M. Booth was arrested for violating the Fugitive Slave Act when he helped incite a mob to rescue a black fugitive from Wisconsin federal marshal Stephen V. R. Ableman. Booth appealed to the state supreme court, which ruled the federal law unconstitutional and ordered Booth's release. When Ableman turned to the federal courts, the Wisconsin Supreme Court affirmed Booth's release and again declared the Fugitive Slave Act of 1850 unconstitutional.

The case went to the U.S. Supreme Court. According to Chief Justice Roger B. Taney's opinion, state courts had no power to review or interfere with federal laws. Taney still was anathema to the North for his actions in the *Dred Scott* case two years before. But the Supreme Court, although it was divided along sectional lines, was unanimously opposed to this use of John C. Calhoun's doctrine of nullification, even though it had been invoked by northern antislavery forces for purposes completely opposed to Calhoun's.

See also Abolitionist Movement; Nullification Controversy.

ABOLITIONIST MOVEMENT

From the 1830s until 1870, the abolitionist movement attempted to achieve immediate emancipation of all slaves and the ending of racial segregation and discrimination. Their propounding of these goals distinguished abolitionists from the broad-based political opposition to slavery's westward expansion that took form in the North after 1840 and raised issues leading to the Civil War. Yet these two expressions of hostility to slavery — abolitionism and Free-Soilism — were often closely related not only in their beliefs and their interaction but also in the minds of southern slaveholders who finally came to regard the North as united against them in favor of black emancipation.

Although abolitionist feelings had been strong during the American Revolution and in the Upper South during the 1820s, the abolitionist movement did not coalesce into a militant crusade until the 1830s. In the previous decade, as much of the North underwent the social disruption associated with the spread of manufacturing and commerce, powerful evangelical religious movements arose to impart spiritual direction to society. By stressing the moral imperative to end sinful practices and each person's responsibility to uphold God's will in society, preachers like Lyman Beecher, Nathaniel Taylor, and Charles G. Finney in what came to be called the Second Great Awakening led massive religious revivals in the 1820s that gave a major impetus to the later emergence of abolitionism as well as to such other reforming crusades as temperance, pacifism, and women's rights. By the early 1830s, Theodore D. Weld, William Lloyd Garrison, Arthur and Lewis Tappan, and Elizur Wright, Jr., all spiritually nourished by revivalism, had taken up the cause of "immediate emancipation."

In early 1831, Garrison, in Boston, began publishing his famous newspaper, the *Liberator,* supported largely by free African-Americans, who always played a major role in the movement. In December 1833, the Tappans, Garrison, and sixty other delegates of both races and genders met in Philadelphia to found the American Anti-Slavery Society, which denounced slavery as a sin that must be abolished immediately, endorsed nonviolence, and condemned racial prejudice. By 1835, the society had received substantial moral and financial support from African-American communities in the North and had established hundreds of branches throughout the free states, flooding the North with antislavery literature, agents, and petitions demanding that Congress end all federal support for slavery. The society, which attracted significant participation by women, also denounced the American Colonization Society's program of voluntary gradual emancipation and black emigration.

All these activities provoked widespread hostile responses from North and South, most notably violent mobs, the burning of mailbags containing abolitionist literature, and the passage in the U.S. House of Representatives of a "gag rule" that banned consideration of antislavery petitions. These developments, and especially the 1837 murder of abolitionist editor Elijah Lovejoy, led many northerners, fearful for their own civil liberties, to vote for antislavery politicians and brought important converts such as Wendell Phillips, Gerrit Smith, and Edmund Quincy to the cause.

But as antislavery sentiment began to appear in politics, abolitionists also began disagreeing among themselves. By 1840 Garrison and his followers were convinced that since slavery's influence had corrupted all of society, a revolutionary change in America's spiritual values was required to achieve emancipation. To this demand for "moral suasion," Garrison added an insistence on equal rights for women within the movement and a studious avoidance of "corrupt" political parties and churches. To Garrison's opponents, such ideas seemed wholly at odds with Christian values and the imperative to influence the political and ecclesiastical systems by nominating and voting for candidates committed to abolitionism. Disputes over these matters split the American Anti-Slavery Society in 1840, leaving Garrison and his supporters in command of that body; his opponents, led by the Tappans, founded the American and Foreign Anti-Slavery Society. Meanwhile, still other foes of Garrison launched the Liberty party with James G. Birney as its presidential candidate in the elections of 1840 and 1844.

Although historians debate the extent of the abolitionists' influence on the nation's political life after 1840, their impact on northern culture and society is undeniable. As speakers, Frederick Douglass, Wendell Phillips, and Lucy Stone in particular became extremely well known. In popular literature the poetry of John Greenleaf Whittier and James Russell Lowell circulated widely, as did the autobiographies of fugitive slaves such as Douglass, William and Ellen Craft, and Solomon Northrup. Abolitionists exercised a particularly strong influence on religious life, contributing heavily to schisms that separated the Methodists (1844) and Baptists (1845), while founding numerous independent antislavery "free churches." In higher education abolitionists founded Oberlin College, the nation's first experiment in racially integrated coeducation, the Oneida Institute, which graduated an impressive group of African-American leaders, and Illinois's Knox College, a western center of abolitionism.

Within the Garrisonian wing of the movement, female abolitionists became leaders of the nation's first independent feminist movement, instrumental in organizing the 1848 Seneca Falls Convention. Although African-American activists often complained with reason of the racist and patronizing behavior of white abolitionists, the whites did support independently conducted crusades by African-Americans to outlaw segregation and improve education during the 1840s and 1850s. Especially after the passage of the

1850 Fugitive Slave Law, white abolitionists also protected African-Americans threatened with capture as escapees from bondage, although blacks themselves largely managed the Underground Railroad.

By the later 1850s, organized abolitionism in politics had been subsumed by the larger sectional crisis over slavery prompted by the Kansas-Nebraska Act, the *Dred Scott* decision, and John Brown's raid on Harpers Ferry. Most abolitionists reluctantly supported the Republican party, stood by the Union in the secession crisis, and became militant champions of military emancipation during the Civil War. The movement again split in 1865, when Garrison and his supporters asserted that the passage of the Thirteenth Amendment abolishing slavery made continuation of the American Anti-Slavery Society unnecessary. But a larger group led by Wendell Phillips, insisting that only the achievement of complete political equality for all black males could guarantee the freedom of the former slaves, successfully prevented Garrison from dissolving the society. It continued until 1870 to demand land, the ballot, and education for the freedman. Only when the Fifteenth Amendment extending male suffrage to African-Americans was passed did the society declare its mission completed. Traditions of racial egalitarianism begun by abolitionists lived on, however, to inspire the subsequent founding of the National Association for the Advancement of Colored People in 1909.

Blanche Glassman Hirsh, *The Feminist Abolitionists* (1978); Benjamin Quarles, *The Black Abolitionists* (1970); James Brewer Stewart, *Holy Warriors: The Abolitionists and American Slavery* (1986).

JAMES BREWER STEWART

See also American Colonization Society; Civil War; *Dred Scott* Case; Emancipation Proclamation and Thirteenth Amendment; Free-Soil Party; Fugitive Slave Law; Gag Rule; Kansas-Nebraska Act; Liberty Party; Quakers; Radicalism; Republican Party; Second Great Awakening; Slavery; Underground Railroad; *and entries for individual abolitionists.*

ABORTION

Abortion has been practiced in the United States since the founding of the Republic, but both its social character and its legal status have varied considerably. Through the early decades of the nineteenth century, Americans regarded abortion primarily as the recourse of women wronged by duplicitous suitors or pregnant as the result of illicit relationships, though records exist of married women having abortions. Americans tolerated the practice, which had long been legal under colonial common law and remained legal under American common law, provided the pregnancy was terminated before quickening: the first perception of fetal movement by the woman. Quickening generally occurs near the midpoint of gestation.

As married women moved to lower their fertility rates after 1830, abortion became a widespread practice in the United States. Abortionists advertised in the daily press and pharmaceutical firms competed in a lucrative market of purported abortifacients. Women spoke to each other and to their doctors in straightforward terms about their abortions. When physicians estimated American abortion rates in the 1860s and 1870s, they used figures strikingly close to those of the 1960s and 1970s: approximately one abortion for every four live births.

In the middle decades of the nineteenth century several state legislatures began to restrict the increasingly common practice of abortion. Some lawmakers feared for the safety of women undergoing abortions. Others reacted negatively to what they considered indecent advertising. Concerned about falling birthrates, many opposed all forms of fertility control, not just abortion. But the greatest pressure for legal change came from the American Medical Association (AMA), founded in 1847.

Led by Horatio Robinson Storer, a Boston physician, the AMA and its affiliated medical societies worked in state capitals throughout the nation during the 1860s and 1870s to outlaw abortion at any stage of gestation, except when doctors themselves determined the procedure to be necessary. Though the physicians put forward scientific, social, and moral arguments, their professional aspirations to upgrade and regulate American medical practice also loomed large. The legal status of abortion was altered by state legislatures after the Civil War not in a religious context but in the context of who would be allowed to do what to whom in the practice of medicine.

The antiabortion laws and legal decisions of the second half of the nineteenth century, though seldom and selectively enforced, drove the practice of abortion underground. Substantial numbers of women, especially immigrant women with limited access to other (also illegal) methods of fertility control, nonetheless continued to have abortions. Surveys conducted under the auspices of the AMA and the federal government confirmed the persistence of widespread abortion in the United States through the 1930s.

By the late 1950s significant portions of the population began to call for repeal of the regulations that proscribed abortion. Nineteenth-century concerns about female health had been undermined by reliable data demonstrating that early abortions under proper conditions were actually safer than normal births. Nineteenth-century alarms about the dwindling national birthrate had been replaced by twentieth-century fears of overpopulation. Nineteenth-century commitments to life of any sort under any conditions were being questioned as a result of heightened sensitivities to what was called the quality of life. Even so, three additional factors stood out.

First was a profound shift in the role of American women. Abortion had always been a women's issue, but not until the 1960s did significant numbers of women address it in an overtly public and political fashion. Control over their own reproductive processes, including the right to terminate an unwanted pregnancy, became for many women one of the fundamental demands of modern feminism. Second was a perception of inequality. While the wealthy and well connected arranged discreet abortions under favorable conditions, the poor and the unsophisticated often suffered. Third was an almost complete reversal of opinion within the medical establishment. By 1967, according to a national survey, 87 percent of American doctors favored liberalization of the antiabortion laws that their professional predecessors had fought to enact a century earlier.

During the late 1960s and early 1970s, several states moved to modify or repeal their antiabortion statutes. In the legislative battles of that period, however, and in countless legal and political confrontations since, the antiabortion laws of the nineteenth century found vehement modern defenders. Foremost among the latter was the Roman Catholic church, which denounced abortion under any circumstances. Several fundamentalist and evangelical Protestants agreed, as did a diverse coalition of other Americans, including some concerned about the dramatically shifting public and political role of American women and many uneasy with what they considered to be deteriorating moral standards on many fronts. Whereas most Americans in the nineteenth century had considered early abortion on a continuum with contraception, these twentieth-century groups considered abortion at any point in gestation a form of murder.

In January 1973 the Supreme Court in *Roe* v. *Wade* ruled that women, as part of their constitutional right to privacy, could choose to terminate a pregnancy prior to the point at which the fetus reached a stage of development that would allow it to survive outside the womb. This ruling, and its subsequent refinements, effectively struck antiabortion laws from state criminal codes and returned the United States, in a rough sense, to standards functionally similar to those of the early Republic.

After the *Roe* decision, abortion became a divisive and intensely emotional public issue. One side applauded and defended the decision; the other sought to reverse it altogether or to undercut it severely by the application of restrictions or principles they considered transcendent in this matter. Both houses of Congress divided on the issue. The Hyde Amendment of 1976, passed over a presidential veto and sustained by the federal courts, essentially eliminated federal funding for abortions. Members of Congress opposed to the practice blocked foreign aid to programs alleged to be tolerant of abortion in other countries. Federal judicial nominees were questioned closely by both sides about their views on abortion.

As debate over abortion intensified during

the 1980s, both sides strengthened their national organizations. One side emphasized each woman's right to make reproductive decisions for herself; the other emphasized the right to life of the unborn. When a challenge to the *Roe* decision came before the Supreme Court in 1989, hundreds of thousands of citizens from both sides demonstrated and counterdemonstrated in the streets of Washington, D.C., in an effort to influence public and judicial opinion. That case, *Webster* v. *Reproductive Health Services,* also generated a record-breaking number of friend-of-the-court briefs, as organizations of many sorts sought to place their views about abortion before the justices.

In the *Webster* decision the Supreme Court sustained its fundamental ruling in *Roe,* but encouraged the separate states to reconsider political solutions to the many practical and secondary questions posed by abortion policy. Political parties found the Court's charge difficult to deal with. Republican presidents Ronald Reagan and George Bush both opposed abortion, and most Democratic officeholders favored reproductive choice. But by 1990 neither major party was anywhere near unanimity on the issue, which seemed to cut across generational, educational, and religious lines more clearly than it did across political party lines.

Kristin Luker, *Abortion and the Politics of Motherhood* (1984); James C. Mohr, *Abortion in America: The Origins and Evolution of National Policy, 1800–1900* (1978).

JAMES C. MOHR

See also Birth Control; *Roe* v. *Wade.*

ABSTRACT EXPRESSIONISM

Abstract expressionism, the most influential and original movement in American art, developed in New York City in the 1940s and 1950s. It first gained public attention in 1951 with an exhibit at the Museum of Modern Art and became the dominant international style after another MOMA exhibit, The New American Painting, toured Europe in 1958–1959. The emergence of the movement shifted the capital of the art world from Paris to New York.

Abstract expressionists, who are sometimes called the New York school, conveyed the artist's vision through abstraction unfettered by the familiar and commonplace associations inherent in representational art. Characterized by the monumental scale of its canvases, the movement distinguished itself from earlier modern painting through its metaphysical ambitiousness. As three of its proponents declared in 1943, "only that subject matter is valid which is tragic and timeless." Influenced by surrealism's attention to the irrational and subconscious and adopting cubism's reductive techniques, the abstract expressionists forged a new art that permitted form, line, and color to act as the pure conductors of emotion, myth, and symbol.

Of the various terms describing the divergent styles within the movement, the most common are action painting and color-field painting. Action painting relies on the energy and power of line, often splattered or dripped onto the canvas. Color-field painting is typified by a single image or unified expanse of color. Included among the abstract expressionists are Willem de Kooning, Robert Motherwell, Franz Kline, Mark Rothko, Barnett Newman, Adolph Gottlieb, Arshile Gorky, and its most famous member, Jackson Pollock.

See also Painting and Sculpture.

ACHESON, DEAN

(1893–1971), secretary of state, 1949–1953. Always a controversial figure, Acheson, a lifelong Democrat, broke with the early New Deal policies of Franklin D. Roosevelt when that president took the United States off the gold standard. He returned to government at the outset of World War II and served in various high-level positions in the Department of State.

At the outset of the cold war, Acheson, now under secretary of state in Harry S. Truman's administration, took charge of a White House briefing of congressional leaders on what became the Truman Doctrine. Until then, the legislators had not been overly impressed with the urgency of the need to pick up Great Britain's role in supporting Greece and Turkey. The under secretary painted a stark picture of Soviet communism poised at the intersection of three continents, ready to spread through the Mediterranean area down into Africa, westward into Europe, and eastward into the Middle East. At the conclusion of his remarks, Republican senator Arthur Vandenberg, chairman of the Senate Foreign Relations Committee, told Truman he would support the plan if it was put to Congress in those terms.

Despite his key role in the development of the containment policy, Acheson quickly became the target for Republican criticism of Truman's foreign policies. In part this was a reaction to Acheson's personality — he could be devastatingly acerbic. Fed up with criticism of American commitments to Europe, Acheson described his antagonists as "re-examinists." They reminded him, he said, of the farmer who pulled up his crops every morning to see how they were growing. But it was also a reaction to the twin setbacks of 1949: the Russians' developing the atomic bomb and the "loss" of China to communist-led forces. Republicans merely took advantage of the national sense of malaise to attack the steward of American foreign policy. Acheson made matters worse with his statement that he would not turn his back on Alger Hiss, convicted of perjury in connection with charges that he had passed documents to Soviet agents in the 1930s. Senator Joseph R. McCarthy focused much of his attention on Acheson's supposed role as protector of "card-carrying communists" in the Department of State, describing him as "this pompous diplomat in striped pants, with a phony British accent."

Nevertheless, Acheson survived these attacks and with the passing of time became a figure much admired in conservative circles. In typical fashion, he titled his memoirs *Present at the Creation,* a reference to all that had been accomplished in establishing the cold war bastions of the West.

His defense of American foreign policy in the 1960s and his criticism of third world nations now put him at odds with liberal critics of the Vietnam War. He was never much in sympathy with revolutionaries, he said. Yet it was Acheson who advised President Lyndon B. Johnson in March 1968 that he must find a way out of the war. The Joint Chiefs of Staff, he said,

had been leading the country down the primrose path with overly optimistic predictions. His controversial statements continued to the end of his life, when he defended Richard Nixon against press attacks. The national press, he insisted, simply must stop destroying presidents.

Gaddis Smith, *Dean Acheson* (1972).

LLOYD C. GARDNER

See also Anticommunism; Cold War; Truman Doctrine.

ACLU

See American Civil Liberties Union.

ADAMS, ABIGAIL

(1744–1818), writer and First Lady. Abigail Adams's talent as a correspondent has won her a high place in American letters. Born in Weymouth, Massachusetts, she was descended from many well known New England families. Self-educated, she read widely and studied French. In 1764, at age nineteen, she married a young lawyer, John Adams, and moved to his home in Braintree, where she stayed through the Revolution. There she raised four children, Abigail, John Quincy, Charles, and Thomas Boylston. Another child died in infancy.

In the 1770s, John Adams became involved in revolutionary politics. He served as a delegate to the Continental Congresses and in other wartime posts. During his frequent absences, Abigail Adams ran the household and family farm, engaged in business enterprises, purchased land, and dealt with tenants. In 1784, she joined John in Europe, where he was the American minister to Great Britain. During his terms as vice president and president (1789–1801), she lived in New York, Philadelphia, and Washington, and thereafter in Quincy, Massachusetts.

Abigail Adams may have found her calling as a correspondent during her courtship in the 1760s or, more likely, during her wartime separation from her husband. For over four decades, she wrote letters to him and to her children, relatives, and friends. As a writer she chose the form most natural to eighteenth-century women, for whom publication was rarely an option. Letter writing was not only a form of communication but a mode of self-definition and a way of relating to the larger society. An avid reader, Abigail devoured literature, history, and political philosophy. Despite her lack of training, phonetic spelling, and often faulty grammar, she perfected her style and excelled at her craft. "My pen is always freer than my tongue," she wrote to John in 1775. "I have wrote many things to you that I suppose I never could have talked."

Her letters provide a window on eighteenth-century life, private and public. They reveal Abigail's roles as wife, parent, and friend; her domestic and social activities; her opinions and observations. They also convey her zeal for politics, her intense interest in national affairs, and her avid patriotism. "Our country is as it were a Secondary God, and the first and greatest parent," she wrote to Mercy Warren in 1776. "It is to be perferred [sic] to parents, to wives, children, Friends and all things the Gods only excepted." Her wartime correspondence with John Adams combined personal messages, local news, and political commentary. In March 1776, she vented a complaint about the legal subjection of married women. "I desire you would Remember the ladies, and be more generous and favourable to them than your ancestors," she wrote in a jesting tone. "Do not put such unlimited power into the hands of the Husbands."

In her later years, Abigail remained a strong partisan of John Adams and a staunch supporter of her successful oldest son, John Quincy Adams, who was elected president in 1824. In 1840, her grandson, Charles Francis Adams, published 114 of her letters and edited for an 1876 volume the wartime correspondence between John and Abigail Adams.

L. H. Butterfield et al., eds., *The Book of Abigail and John: Selected Letters of the Adams Family, 1762–1784* (1975); Lynne Withey, *Dearest Friend: A Life of Abigail Adams* (1981).

NANCY WOLOCH

See also Adams, John; Adams, John Quincy.

ADAMS, HENRY

(1838–1918), historian and writer. As a fourth-generation member of one of America's most distinguished families, Henry Adams was born into history, which became a determining influence on his long but undramatic life. Childhood visits to grandfather John Quincy Adams in the White House and family tales of great-grandparents John and Abigail Adams first served to personalize the facts and dates he studied at school. During the Civil War, he witnessed history in the making as secretary to his father, Charles Francis Adams, minister to the Court of St. James.

Rather than becoming a maker of history, however, Henry, a master of English prose, chose to write about it. His classic account of self, *The Education of Henry Adams* (privately printed, 1907; published, 1918), today remains his most popular work; yet his finely crafted letters, essays, and especially *Mont-Saint-Michel and Chartres* (privately printed, 1904; published, 1913) retain a specialized appeal, as, to a lesser degree, do his novels, *Democracy* (1880) and *Esther* (1884). Adams's reputation as a historian derives chiefly from the nine-volume *History of the United States of America during the Administrations of Thomas Jefferson and James Madison* (1889–1891), a pioneering study of intellectual and documentary history that focuses on the years between the presidencies of the two Adamses.

Henry Adams also introduced both the seminar method and the Germanic rigor of the Ph.D. degree to Harvard during his seven-year stint as a faculty member and editor of the prestigious *North American Review*. Dissatisfied with both roles, however, he moved to Washington, D.C., where he conducted research for the *History*. From that base, he launched one travel expedition after another during the remaining years of a highly independent life. In 1885, his domestic comfort was shattered by the suicide of his wife, Marian ("Clover") Hooper Adams, a tragedy that drove him deeper into seclusion. Notable among his few intimates were the colorful geologist Clarence King; the politically ambitious John Hay, biographer of Abraham Lincoln; and the reigning beauty Elizabeth Cameron, who was unhappily married to a much older senator and who filled an idealized role of heroine in Adams's later life.

Adams believed in the possibility of a truly "scientific" history, founded on such models as physics or mathematics. Yet his *Education* also declared that "Chaos was the law of nature; Order was the dream of man." In fact, his most ambitious goal as a thinker and writer was never simply prescriptive; instead, he sought to understand history in the largest possible way. Concluding his *History,* Adams insisted that although "the traits of American character were fixed" by 1815, any final test of the results "required another century of experience." Not surprisingly, such high ambition often led him to express pessimism and disappointment, especially in terms of personal "failure." Nevertheless, he succeeded most admirably as a writer. He used the exercise of composition to escape from excessive introspection and, even more, to instruct and provoke his readers, hoping they might reach even higher levels of intellectual performance than he had displayed.

William H. Jordy, *Henry Adams: Scientific Historian* (1952); J. C. Levenson, *The Mind and Art of Henry Adams* (1957); Ernest Samuels, *Henry Adams* (1989).

EARL N. HARBERT

See also History and Historians; Literature.

ADAMS, JOHN

(1735–1826), lawyer, revolutionary theorist and leader, diplomat, first vice president and second president of the United States. Adams, raised on a farm in Braintree (later Quincy), Massachusetts, was the first in his family to attend college — Harvard — and its first professional man — a lawyer. Beginning in 1765 Adams, living part of the time in Boston with his wife, Abigail, and their children, opposed British revenue measures and their enforcement by the military. He did so as a moderate, never joining in demonstrations or publishing inflammatory rhetoric in the manner of his cousin Samuel Adams or fellow lawyer James Otis.

In 1765 Adams drew up the Braintree In-

structions, a widely disseminated argument against the Stamp Act, which he also opposed in his "Dissertation on Canon and Feudal Law." In 1770, following the Boston Massacre, Adams, on the principle that the accused always has the right to a vigorous defense, was willing to defend the British troops who had fired on the Boston crowd. But in 1774, after the Boston Tea Party and the British Coercive Acts, he came out for independence.

Adams had already been a Massachusetts legislator and one of the colony's delegates to the First Continental Congress when at the Second Congress he emerged as the leading advocate of independence. His *Thoughts on Government* (1776) set forth a design whereby the colonies could govern themselves as independent states. Typically, this blueprint was moderate in tone, but its publication was a radical step toward independence.

Adams's best-known contribution to independence was his indefatigable support in favor of the issuance of a formal declaration of independence. Neither an orator nor an adept forger of political alliances, Adams moved men and events with his earnestness and lawyerly thoroughness of argument. Thomas Jefferson described him as a "colossus"; other delegates called him "the Atlas of Independence." By 1778 he had served on more committees than any other member, simultaneously acting as a virtual one-man war department.

From 1778 to 1788 Adams served as a diplomat in France, the Netherlands, and England. He secured Dutch loans, chaired the commission that concluded a peace treaty with England, and ended as ambassador to the English court, where he was received by George III, the king against whom he had helped lead a revolution.

Returning to America after the adoption of the U.S. Constitution, he stood out as a public figure well respected for his *Defence of the Constitutions* (1787–1788), a three-volume commentary on political systems favoring the bicameral legislature just adopted for the new United States, partly on the model of the Massachusetts State Constitution he had drafted in 1779. His political conservatism linked him to the Federalist party, but Adams consistently held himself aloof from its counsels.

Adams was elected vice president under George Washington and then served as president from 1797 to 1801. His presidency was marred by the threat of war with France and by the Alien and Sedition Acts, not proposed by Adams but signed by him. After a single term, Adams was defeated by Thomas Jefferson. Adams was deeply hurt by the voters' rejection, which reflected the view that he had grown increasingly conservative, especially as evidenced by his low opinion of human nature in his *Discourses on Davila* (1790–1791). Resentfully, he retired to Quincy and refused all public involvements.

Beginning in 1812 he was reconciled with Jefferson, who had been a friend in Europe, and began with him a correspondence that is now regarded as a monument of the American enlightenment. Adams's philosophical spirit, sometimes submerged by politics, reasserted itself as he argued the limitations of human nature in a more balanced and memorable way than in any of his published works. Adams died on the same day as Jefferson: July 4, 1826, the fiftieth anniversary of independence, a coincidence taken by contemporaries as a sign of divine approval of the American experiment.

L. H. Butterfield et al., eds., *The Adams Papers* (1961–); Peter Shaw, *The Character of John Adams* (1976).

PETER SHAW

See also Adams, Abigail; Boston Massacre; Conservatism; Continental Congresses; Elections: 1789, 1792, 1796, 1800; Federalist Party; Paris, Treaty of (1783); Revolution; Stamp Act. *For events during Adams's administration, see* Alien and Sedition Acts; XYZ Affair.

ADAMS, JOHN QUINCY

(1767–1848), sixth president of the United States, diplomat, congressman, U.S. senator, and secretary of state. As the eldest and most gifted son of John Adams, second president of the United States, Adams enjoyed many opportunities that prepared him for later public service.

In 1802 Adams was elected a U.S. senator from Massachusetts as a Federalist, but he was too independent of mind to follow a regular party line. During the international tensions that arose from the Napoleonic Wars, he supported the policies of the Jefferson administration. His stand, contrary to the position of his party, resulted in his replacement as senator. He resigned, however, before the end of his term, only to be appointed to a series of important diplomatic posts. He was one of the American commissioners who arranged for the Treaty of Ghent that ended the War of 1812. As secretary of state, he drafted the Monroe Doctrine and acquired Florida from Spain for the United States.

He was the New England candidate for the presidency in 1824, but neither he nor any of the other candidates commanded the electoral majority the Constitution required. Therefore the election was decided by the House of Representatives, each state casting one vote. Henry Clay threw his support to Adams, who was then elected over Andrew Jackson. When Adams made Clay his secretary of state, the disapproving Jacksonians accused the president of entering into "a corrupt bargain" with Clay. From then until the end of his administration, Adams was the target of highly charged partisan abuse.

Adams was probably the most experienced and intelligent of all American presidents, but his ideas about the role of the national government in developing the nation were too far in advance of then current economic thinking. An advocate of national planning that would have extended to a federally funded system of internal improvements, canals, turnpikes, and the like, Adams also proposed the establishment of a national university and recommended substantial government support for scientific investigation. As part of his program of national planning, Adams favored a protective tariff. He also supported a national banking system that would provide uniform currency and regulate credit. These policies were to a considerable degree an extension of Alexander Hamilton's ideas, especially in economic affairs, but they were more visionary and less class-oriented in other areas of public responsibility. They were, in addition, a formative influence on the evolution of Whig party doctrine. His first message to Congress that introduced his policies stands as a brilliant state paper. But his administration, bedeviled by partisan attack, must be accounted a failure. Savagely attacked as an aristocrat and a quasi Federalist, Adams lost his reelection bid to Andrew Jackson in 1828.

In 1831, Adams was elected to the U.S. House of Representatives. Although no abolitionist, he battled single-handedly against a southern-dominated House for the right to present petitions from antislavery groups. Subjected to a gag rule and threatened with censure and even expulsion, Adams persisted in his efforts to defend a constitutional right. Finally, in 1844, Congress repealed its gag rule and the right of petition was restored. In many ways Adams's congressional record as a champion of civil rights was the crowning point of his long career in public service.

S. F. Bemis, *John Quincy Adams and the Union* (1956); George Dangerfield, *The Era of Good Feelings* (1952).

JOHN NIVEN

See also Adams-Onís Treaty; Corrupt Bargain; Elections: 1824, 1828; Monroe Doctrine.

ADAMS, SAMUEL

(1722–1803), American revolutionary political leader. The son of a Boston merchant and maltster, Adams was a 1740 graduate of Harvard College where he publicly defended the thesis that it is "lawful to resist the Supreme Magistrate, if the Commonwealth cannot be otherwise preserved." Adherence to this principle was ever afterward a central theme in his career.

After failing as a brewer and newspaper publisher, Adams found that his chief preoccupation, politics, was his true calling. Following lengthy experience in Boston town affairs, he rose to prominence in the Massachusetts assembly during the opposition to the Stamp Act in 1765. An organizer of Boston's Sons of Liberty, he played a key role from 1765 until the end of the War of Independence in Patriot opposition to what Adams believed was a British plot to destroy constitutional liberty.

Adams's contributions to the independence movement were many and varied. During the 1760s and 1770s he frequently wrote polemical articles for the Boston newspapers, and he recruited talented younger men — Josiah Quincy,

Joseph Warren, and his second cousin John Adams, among others — into the Patriot cause. It was Samuel Adams who conceived of the Boston Committee of Correspondence and took a leading role in its formation and operations from 1772 through 1774. He was among those who planned and coordinated Boston's resistance to the Tea Act, which climaxed in the famous Tea Party, and he later worked for the creation of the Continental Congress, helping propel it into supporting Massachusetts in the crisis.

From 1774 through 1781 Adams represented Massachusetts in the Continental Congress, where his industry, stamina, realism, and commitment made him one of the handful of "workhorses" who served year in and year out on numerous committees. Although Adams's influence in state and national affairs waned during the 1780s, he was elected to the Massachusetts convention on the ratification of the Constitution, which he was ultimately persuaded to support even though it contradicted some Whig principles. But, as in the past, he remained wary of centralized governmental power and never became part of the Federalists, the dominant party in Massachusetts.

After serving as John Hancock's lieutenant governor from 1789 to 1793, Adams succeeded to the governorship at Hancock's death. Although he opposed Jay's Treaty with England in 1795, he was thrice reelected before infirmity led him to retire in 1797. Three years later, when Thomas Jefferson was elected to the presidency over his cousin John, Samuel congratulated the Virginian on the triumph of democratic republicanism.

Samuel Adams was a revolutionary of great self-discipline and patience. "We cannot make events," he believed. "Our business is wisely to improve them." After his death, one colleague likened him to John Calvin, "cool, abstemious, polished, refined," although Adams was "more inflexible, uniform, consistent" than the Genevan reformer. Avoiding all social pretension and cultivating ascetic manners, Adams embodied an austere Puritan republicanism that was seen as exemplary in 1775, but became archaic by the 1790s. Uniformly respected, though not always liked, Samuel Adams was, in John Adams's words, "born and tempered a wedge of steel to split the knot of *lignum vitae*" that bound America to Britain.

Pauline Maier, "A New Englander as Revolutionary: Samuel Adams," in Pauline Maier, *Old Revolutionaries: Political Lives in the Age of Samuel Adams* (1980); John C. Miller, *Sam Adams: Pioneer in Propaganda* (1936).

RICHARD D. BROWN

See also Boston Tea Party; Committees of Correspondence; Continental Congresses; Revolution; Sons of Liberty; Stamp Act.

ADAMS-ONÍS TREATY

The Adams-Onís Treaty (1819), also known as the Transcontinental Treaty, solved two problems. Citizens of Georgia wanted the United States to purchase eastern Florida from Spain because Seminole natives frequently raided the state and then retreated to the Spanish territory. Spain wanted to establish the boundary between Mexico and the Louisiana Purchase before too many American settlers moved into the area. John Quincy Adams, secretary of state under President James Monroe, negotiated the treaty with Luís de Onís of Spain.

Because independence movements in Spain's other colonies demanded attention, Onís was willing to sell eastern Florida. Despite the Spaniard's initial insistence on his country's rights to much of the lands involved, Adams secured a boundary between the Louisiana Purchase lands and the Texas territory that was extremely favorable to the United States. The boundary was set at the western bank of the Sabine, Red, and Arkansas rivers to the Continental Divide. From that point the line followed the forty-second parallel west to the Pacific Ocean. Spain also gave up all claims on the Oregon territory.

The purchase of Florida for a mere $5 million (paid directly to citizens with claims against the Spanish government) assured the treaty's popularity in the United States, but Adams considered establishing the western boundary his most important diplomatic feat. The treaty was finally signed and ratified in 1821.

See also Expansion, Continental and Overseas.

ADDAMS, JANE

(1860–1935), settlement house founder and peace activist. Addams, one of the most distinguished of the first generation of college-educated women, rejected marriage and motherhood in favor of a lifetime commitment to the poor and social reform. Inspired by English reformers who intentionally resided in lower-class slums, Addams, along with a college friend, Ellen Starr, moved in 1889 into an old mansion in an immigrant neighborhood of Chicago. Hull-House, which remained Addams's home for the rest of her life and became the center of an experiment in philanthropy, political action, and social science research, was a model for settlement work among the poor. Addams responded to the needs of the community by establishing a nursery, dispensary, kindergarten, playground, gymnasium, and cooperative housing for young working women. As an experiment in group living, Hull-House attracted male and female reformers dedicated to social service. Addams always insisted that she learned as much from the neighborhood's residents as she taught them.

Having quickly found that the needs of the neighborhood could not be met unless city and state laws were reformed, Addams challenged both boss rule in the immigrant neighborhood of Hull-House and indifference to the needs of the poor in the state legislature. She and other Hull-House residents sponsored legislation to abolish child labor, establish juvenile courts, limit the hours of working women, recognize labor unions, make school attendance compulsory, and ensure safe working conditions in factories. The Progressive party adopted many of these reforms as part of its platform in 1912. At the party's national convention, Addams seconded the nomination of Theodore Roosevelt for president and campaigned actively on his behalf. She advocated woman's suffrage because she believed that women's votes would provide the margin necessary to pass social legislation she favored.

Addams publicized Hull-House and the causes she believed in by lecturing and writing. In her autobiography, *Twenty Years at Hull-*

House (1910), she argued that society should both respect the values and traditions of immigrants and help the newcomers adjust to American institutions. A new social ethic was needed, she said, to stem social conflict and address the problems of urban life and industrial capitalism. Although tolerant of other ideas and social philosophies, Addams believed in Christian morality and the virtue of learning by doing.

Because Addams was convinced that war sapped the reform impulse, encouraged political repression, and benefited only munition makers, she opposed World War I. She unsuccessfully tried to persuade President Woodrow Wilson to call a conference to mediate a negotiated end to hostilities. During the war she spoke throughout the country in favor of increased food production to aid the starving in Europe. After the armistice she helped found the Women's International League for Peace and Freedom, serving as president from 1919 until her death in 1935. Vilified during World War I for her opposition to American involvement, Addams a decade later had become a national heroine and Chicago's leading citizen. In 1931, her long involvement in international efforts to end war was recognized when she was awarded the Nobel Peace Prize.

Allen F. Davis, *American Heroine: The Life and Legend of Jane Addams* (1973); Daniel Levine, *Jane Addams and the Liberal Tradition* (1973).

ELIZABETH H. PLECK

See also Progressivism; Settlement Houses.

ADVERTISING

Advertising as we know it today began during the last quarter of the nineteenth century. If an advertising agent working on the account of a product such as Quaker Oats cereal in about 1900 were to have been transported forward in time to 1925, the challenges, choices, and risks he faced would have been in many respects familiar. If the same agent had been transported backward to 1875, that could not be said. Advertising agencies were relatively unknown then, and those that existed had ill-defined responsibilities. The mix of products for which they were placing advertisements was quite different from that on the market at the turn of the century. Quaker Oats itself had not yet been invented. Thus, the history of advertising in America falls into two eras separated at about this turning point.

To begin with, we should define advertising. It is mass communication an advertiser pays for in order to convince a certain segment of the public to adopt ideas or take actions of benefit to the advertiser. During the past century, large American manufacturers have played a leading role in developing this craft, but in earlier years, leadership in terms of design and creativity lay elsewhere.

In the eighteenth century, Great Britain boasted the most advanced advertising. Handbills and trade cards proclaiming in extravagant terms the excellence of sundry products and services were common. Among the items being sold, few if any caused more excitement than the New World itself. Signs and handbills touting its wonders were so ubiquitous in London that Richard Hofstadter has observed that America was conceived amidst "one of the first concerted and sustained advertising campaigns in the history of the modern world." Daniel J. Boorstin believes that such promotion may have had a significant impact on the speed of emigration and has wondered about the impact on American civilization of the fact that "there was a kind of natural selection here of those people who were willing to believe advertising."

Advertising was a well-established practice in the late colonial and early national periods in America, but these advertisements were neither as appealing to the eye nor as cleverly crafted as were their counterparts in England. The type was so illegible that Benjamin Franklin observed: "If you should ever have any secrets that you wish to be well kept, get them printed in [the] papers." Moreover, the United States was a predominantly rural nation. Its farmers may not have been totally self-sufficient, but they produced more of their own food, clothing, and household items than did urbanites. Thus, more Americans focused on production for survival than on consumption for pleasure. With a sparse, predominantly rural population and without an efficient system of transportation and communication, the country had neither the need for nor the means of concerted national advertising campaigns.

Most advertising during the early national and antebellum periods was repetitious and unimaginative. Writing of the pioneer merchants on the middle border, historian Lewis Atherton observed that "in general the early advertising was dreary, matter of fact reading, served a limited purpose, and was completely devoid of . . . customer appeal. . . . one advertisement was like all others."

There were advances in American advertising in the larger cities during the 1820s and 1830s with improvements in printing technology and a change in advertising philosophy. James Gordon Bennett, Sr.'s, *New York Herald* and other New York penny press newspapers prided themselves on speaking directly to the mass public in understandable and accessible terms, and they wanted their advertising to have the same appeal. In 1848, Bennett began changing the *Herald*'s advertisements every day, making them news just like the editorial matter.

The precursors of advertising agencies also date from this period. By the 1840s, Volney B. Palmer was listing his "coal and advertising" agency in New York City's business directory. The very description of the business — coal and advertising — illustrates how undifferentiated advertising was in those days.

Modern advertising really began in the 1880s, when new methods of manufacturing led to greatly increased output and decreased costs for the producers of consumer goods. Advances in packaging technology meant that products could be packaged at the plant rather than shipped to a wholesaler who traditionally broke bulk and put his own name on them. Moreover, the telegraph network was in place and the continent had been crisscrossed by a network of railroads, bringing its farthest reaches within the purview of the incipient consumer culture.

Prior to the 1880s, the American marketing system had been characterized by an intricate set of wholesalers, jobbers, and other middlemen whose most important function was to buy in large lots and sell in smaller ones. In this age, the wholesaler was king. But in the new era of the 1880s, the importance of the packaged goods manufacturer greatly increased. What manufacturers could package at their own plant, they could brand. What they could brand, they could advertise. What they could distribute nationally, they could advertise nationally. This, Daniel A. Pope has written, "necessitated the growth of advertising agencies and dictated their activities" and also "tipped the balance in advertising from information (however specious much of it had been) to persuasion."

National advertisers provided the media and advertising agencies with a new set of clients whose standards of conduct were far higher than those preceding them. The most widely advertised consumer products through most of the nineteenth century had been patent medicines — nostrums for which their purveyors made extravagantly false claims. But the new companies, although not always innocent of misstatements, depended upon repeat-purchase behavior and thus upon building a bond of trust with the consumer. To do this, they had to eschew blatant falsehoods.

As late as 1893, according to Pope, more than half of a sample of over a hundred firms spending more than fifty thousand dollars annually on advertising were patent medicine manufacturers, whose advertisements were often of the "cancer cure" variety. His list of the largest national advertisers some twenty years later showed a sharp contrast. Most of these firms were not "medical messiahs" but manufacturers of food, consumer chemicals like soap and cosmetics, and consumer durables like automobiles and auto accessories.

For these new firms, advertising served many purposes:

- The introduction of new products, ranging from inexpensive items like bottled cola to consumer durables such as the automobile.

- The introduction of products already on the market to new consumers, like those entering adulthood and immigrants.

- The suggestion of new uses for products already on the market and the repositioning of products. Coca-Cola, for example, began as something close to a medicine. It was said to "revive and sustain," and to cure headaches. By the 1920s, the beverage's quality as a refreshment and "fun food" was being emphasized.

◻ The management of the distribution system. Manufacturer advertising could pressure distributors into stocking products because advertising created consumer demand. A consumer might feel more loyalty to a heavily advertised brand like Coca-Cola than to a particular soda fountain and thus not patronize a fountain that did not carry Coca-Cola.

For the consumer product marketer, advertising became the marketing analogy to assembly-line production techniques. It was systematized mass salesmanship, which became a key weapon in the arsenal of companies seeking to create and build brands.

With the new mix of advertising clients and the new conception of advertising came a host of changes in the trade that sharply differentiated twentieth-century practice from the previous era. Among the most important changes were those in the areas of copywriting, research, and source of compensation.

Through most of the nineteenth century, the principal function of the nation's advertising agencies was to buy space in publications at wholesale and sell it to advertisers at retail. In 1892, the N. W. Ayer and Son agency in Philadelphia hired its first full-time copywriter to write the advertisement itself. Soon after, Albert Davis Lasker of the Chicago agency of Lord and Thomas greatly boosted the prestige of the copywriting function within the agency. He founded the "reason why" school, which held that an advertisement had to give the customer a specific reason (perhaps a more accurate description would be "rational-sounding excuse") to purchase a product. This approach contrasted with the bulk of previous copy, which had often consisted of an announcement accompanied by disconnected and incredible claims to excellence.

Modern business corporations and advertising agencies make a major effort to research the projected and actual impact of their advertising.

Research at agencies dates back at least to 1879, when Ayer undertook its first such project. Since then agencies, their clients, and independent market research firms — often assisted by marketing academicians and economists — have spent large sums to determine advertising's effectiveness.

Advertising agencies have always been intermediaries between advertisers and the mass media. During much of the nineteenth century, it was unclear whom the agency represented. Was it primarily a seller of media space or a seller of a manufacturer's product? In the twentieth century, the answer has been the latter. Agencies sell products by buying space or time and are compensated by manufacturers.

The most visible change in advertising in the past hundred years has resulted from the new technology of broadcasting. Initially, many thought that advertising over the "ether" would never be accepted by the public because it would constitute an obnoxious intrusion into the home of the owner of a radio set. And even if it did not prove unacceptable on grounds of taste, many felt that radio advertising should be prohibited as a matter of public policy. When he was secretary of commerce, Herbert Hoover said at a conference on radio in 1922 that it was "inconceivable that we should allow so great a possibility for service to be drowned in advertising chatter." By the end of the decade, however, advertisers and their agents had come to realize radio's possibilities. With its drama and immediacy, radio could convey their message directly to the consumer who would not need to purchase a publication or even be literate.

In the 1950s came television, which was commercialized in the United States to an exceptional degree. American advertisers had more minutes to telecast more commercial messages to more market segments (including children) than anywhere else in the world. Through television, advertisers could demonstrate the use of their product and present well-known figures to praise it. As had been the case with radio, those companies that first exploited the commercial potential of television reaped lavish rewards.

Advertising has been heavily criticized on a variety of counts. Economists have charged that advertising distorts competition by raising barriers to the entry of new firms into an industry and by distracting the consumer from price. Sociologists have complained that advertising barges into the home with pseudopopulist rhetoric ("We do it all for you") that in fact encourages a starkly materialistic approach to the world and promotes an ethos suggesting that what one possesses is more important than who one is. The historian of the content of advertising copy Roland Marchand has shown how advertisements adopt various clichés and parables whose relationship to a sensible evaluation of a product's benefits is tenuous at best. Indeed, much advertising copy conveys a message that, if not false, is not really true either.

Consumer advocates have accused advertising of victimizing children too young to tell the difference between a sales pitch and disinterested advice, and they have assailed what they view as its offensiveness to the elderly, to minorities, and to women. Educators, journalists, and others have often voiced disapproval of advertising: a "torrent of mendacity, imbecility, and bilge" was how author Bernard De Voto characterized it some years ago.

Among advertising's critics are the corporations that pay for it. Witness the following complaint: "I know that half of my advertising budget is wasted. The problem is that I don't know which half." This quip, attributed to John Wanamaker, Frank W. Woolworth, and Lord Leverhulme among others, has gained a permanent place in advertising lore and illustrates the degree to which advertisers themselves, despite the vast sums spent on research, remain skeptical about how effective their advertising dollars really are.

It is, however, worth noting that disingenuous as it often has been, advertising is first of all about persuasion. It has, therefore, been historically far less important in command economies than it has been in market economies. For all its many faults, relative freedom to advertise is an emblem of a more general economic and social freedom. Perhaps it is part of the price we pay for that freedom.

Paul W. Farris and John A. Quelch, *Advertising and Promotion Management: A Manager's Guide to Theory and Practice* (1983); Daniel A. Pope, *The Making of Modern Advertising* (1983); Richard S. Tedlow, *New and Improved: The Story of Mass Marketing in America* (1990).

RICHARD S. TEDLOW

See also Federal Trade Commission; Radio and Television.

AEC

See Atomic Energy Commission.

AFFIRMATIVE ACTION

The term *affirmative action* is applied almost exclusively to the use of racial, ethnic, or gender preferences in allocating a variety of social benefits. The groups receiving such benefits, such as African-Americans, Native Americans, or women, are assumed to have been victims of systematic discrimination in the past. Thus, a program explicitly benefiting white males as a group would not for most people be an example of "affirmative action"; rather, it would be seen as unconstitutional — as invidious discrimination against nonwhites or women.

The Supreme Court has considered the constitutionality of affirmative action in a number of cases involving such issues as admission to educational institutions, job hiring and promotion, exemption from ordinary seniority-bound job-layoff rules, award of public building contracts, and award of licenses for radio and television stations by the Federal Communications Commission. The constitutional question can be simply stated: does the Constitution, which prohibits government from denying "equal protection of the law," always ban the use of racial, ethnic, or gender criteria in the allocation of social benefits? No one has ever argued that the Constitution prohibits classification as such; almost all laws, in fact, classify and select certain categories of persons for beneficial or negative treatment. Is there, then, something special about racial, ethnic, or gender classifications that make them different in kind from those based on, say, state residence, athletic ability, or status as a veteran, to offer only three common examples of benefit-conferring classifications that are almost never treated as instances of affirmative action?

The constitutional debate was best set out in

the first important construction by the Supreme Court of the meaning of the equal protection clause of the Fourteenth Amendment, *Strauder* v. *West Virginia* (1880). West Virginia had prohibited African-Americans from serving on juries, and the Court had little trouble deciding that that was unconstitutional. But Justice William Strong's opinion explaining the decision pointed in conflicting directions. On the one hand, he stated that the Fourteenth Amendment "was designed to assure to the colored race the enjoyment of all the civil rights that under the law are enjoyed by white persons. . . . It ordains . . . that *the law in the States shall be the same for the black as for the white*" (emphasis added). This language easily leads to the argument made most memorably by Justice John Marshall Harlan in his famous dissent in *Plessy* v. *Ferguson* (1896) that the "Constitution is color-blind" and, presumably, invalidates any laws based on racial criteria. (To the extent that later generations treated ethnicity and gender as basically similar to race, the arguments became the same in regard to these other classifications, though relatively few in fact argue that the Constitution should be read to require a gender-blind society. This article focuses on the problems raised by racial preferences.)

Justice Strong, however, emphasized throughout his opinion that the protection provided by the Fourteenth Amendment was against "unfriendly action" by the government directed at newly freed, but still often victimized, African-Americans. One could read Strong's opinion as suggesting that the Constitution might tolerate "friendly" racial classifications, ones that do not imply inferiority, but are aimed at increasing the participation of a formerly "subject race" in all aspects of American society. What makes affirmative action *affirmative*, after all, is that it is designed to help a formerly discriminated-against group and thus conforms with the deep purposes of the Fourteenth Amendment.

The conflicting messages of Strong's opinion became crucial following the adoption of various racial preference plans, resulting from the civil rights movement of the 1960s, and their emphasis on the necessity of ensuring African-Americans entry into institutions from which they had been excluded. One response, seen in the Civil Rights Act of 1964, was to prohibit racial discrimination by private businesses. Another was the adoption, by both businesses and governments, of "friendly" preferences designed to integrate African-Americans into the work force. Did such programs violate either the statute or, in the case of governmental programs, the Constitution?

Subsequent courts have reached different and often confusing conclusions in various cases. The first major case dealing with affirmative action, *Bakke* v. *University of California* (1978), involved the use by a state medical school of racial preferences in admissions. There was no majority opinion in the *Bakke* case. The most important opinion was that written by Justice Lewis Powell. He found the particular program unconstitutional because it established a rigid quota, but he indicated that it did not violate the Constitution to pay "some attention" to race in deciding whom to admit. Similarly divided courts in later cases struck down the use of racial preferences in deciding which employees of a school system could be laid off first in times of economic decline, but, on the other hand, upheld the imposition of hiring quotas on a state highway patrol that had been guilty of egregious discrimination in its hiring practices.

An added source of complexity (or confusion) is the different level of freedom accorded the state and federal governments in regard to affirmative action. In the 1980 case of *Fullilove* v. *Klutznick,* the Supreme Court upheld a federal program that required that minority-controlled businesses be preferred in awarding certain contracts. But, in 1989, the Court held that Richmond, Virginia, could not require that 30 percent of its building contracts be awarded to minority contractors. The Court stated in effect that the Fourteenth Amendment limits the states' use of racial preferences more strictly than it does the federal government's. A 5–4 majority in a 1990 case applied this argument to uphold a program of the Federal Communications Commission that favored minority-owned radio and television stations in awarding broadcasting licenses. Many commentators have found this distinction between state and national governments less than persuasive, and the replacement of Justice William Brennan, the author of the 1990 case, by Justice David Souter has led some to wonder if it will survive. All that can be predicted with any degree of confidence is that the controversy will continue, probably indefinitely, into the future.

Marshall Cohen, Thomas Nagel, and T. M. Scanlon, eds., *Equality and Preferential Treatment* (1977); Michael Rosenfeld, *Affirmative Action and Justice: A Philosophical and Constitutional Inquiry* (1990); Thomas Sowell, *Preferential Policies: An International Perspective* (1990).

SANFORD LEVINSON

See also Civil Rights Movement; Feminist Movement; Racial Desegregation.

AFL

See American Federation of Labor.

AFRICAN METHODIST EPISCOPAL CHURCH

See A.M.E. Church.

AFRICA-U.S. RELATIONS

Africa significantly influenced the Americas from the sixteenth century, when slaves from West Africa began to be transported first to Spain's colonies and then to Portuguese Brazil from Zaire and Angola. English slavers soon joined in the business, carrying tens of thousands of slaves to the West Indies and, subsequently, to the English mainland colonies. By 1800 nearly one million black slaves from Africa lived in the new American nation.

Seagoing merchants from New England, and later from the Mid-Atlantic colonies, were acquainted with West Africa from the early eighteenth century. As time passed, a brisk trade developed. African slaves, gold, copper, and ivory were exchanged for textiles, tobacco, rum, sugar, canned meat, guns, and hatchets. After the slave trade was outlawed by Congress, the mills of Massachusetts continued to supply parts of Africa as distant as Kenya and Tanzania with the rough cotton cloth that is still known, in upcountry East Africa, as *amerikani*. The first U.S. consulate south of the Sahara was established in Zanzibar in 1837 to foster trade. It was followed by consulates in Cape Town, Gabon, and Liberia.

Americans knew the coasts of Africa well by the nineteenth century, and a few helped make inner Africa better known to the West. Paul Belloni du Chaillu was responsible for mapping the interior of Gabon and bringing gorillas to the attention of Europeans and Americans. The most famous American of this era was Sir Henry Morton Stanley, a Welsh-born orphan who fought on both sides of the U.S. Civil War and went to Africa as a journalist for the *New York Herald*. He covered the British punitive expedition to Ethiopia in 1868 and then "found" the great Scottish explorer David Livingstone in Ujiji, on the shores of Lake Tanganyika, in 1871. These journalistic coups were followed in 1874–1877 by his epic journey from Zanzibar to Lake Victoria and westward to the mouth of the Congo River. In so doing, he inaugurated the last phase of Europe's imperial conquest of Africa.

Although the United States took no other direct part in the scramble for Africa, slavery involved America inextricably with the fate of the continent. As early as 1714, Americans interested in the "Negro question" and opposed to slavery suggested that all "men of color" should be removed beyond the borders of the colonies. Nearly a century later, Thomas Jefferson favored a similar scheme. In 1816 the American Colonization Society was formed to help slaves resettle in Africa. From 1820 to 1847 the society repatriated slave volunteers, in the process conquering the small portion of coastal West Africa that became the Republic of Liberia in 1847. Under an octoroon émigré from Virginia, Joseph Jenkins Roberts, Liberia became almost an unofficial colony of the United States. Its constitution denied indigenous Africans equal rights with the mostly lighter-skinned ex-slaves.

Representatives of the United States attended the conference in Berlin in 1884–1885 that sanctioned the occupation of sub-Saharan Africa by the powers of Europe, but American territorial and commercial ambitions were focused then on the Caribbean, the Pacific, and Asia.

The United States was again active regarding Africa after World War I. The creation of the

League of Nations and its mandatory system owed much to President Woodrow Wilson; at the Versailles conference, he prevented the outright annexation of the former German colonies in Africa by Britain, France, and South Africa. After World War II, the United States again came to play an important role in Africa. Its representatives to the Trusteeship Council of the United Nations were among those responsible for accelerating the independence of former mandates like Tanganyika (now Tanzania), Togo, and Cameroun.

But America's greatest impact on black Africa throughout the first half of the twentieth century was made by private missionaries and educators. No other nation sent so many denominations and orders to evangelize and teach Africans. Black Americans were often in the forefront of this movement, their influence penetrating deep into the interior of southern and central Africa. Mainstream groups like the Baptists and millennial sects like the Jehovah's Witnesses were important.

Many Africans who later led their own independent nations were trained in American seminaries and universities. When the African National Congress (ANC) was formed in South Africa in 1912, several of its leaders were lawyers, ministers, and physicians who had studied in the United States. John Chilembwe, an American-educated churchman, fomented a rebellion against British-controlled Nyasaland (Malawi) in 1915, and other American-linked religious separatists were blamed for disturbances elsewhere in Africa.

America's official consciousness of black Africa began with the presidency of John F. Kennedy. Colonialism was in flight, and Kennedy was squarely behind those who had won or were about to win their freedom. Washington during this period was wide-eyed in its hopes for democracy in Africa. It was generous in its grants of aid and technical assistance and engaged in covert intervention to prevent the new nations from tying themselves to the Soviet Union.

During this period the independence of black African nations emboldened the black power movement in the United States. The ex-

ample and the rhetoric of the new governments encouraged black Americans, just as black power in the United States subsequently helped stimulate the rise of a black consciousness movement in apartheid-ridden South Africa. In many ways the ideological forebears of the African movements of independence and black power were the same: both Marcus Garvey's back to Africa crusade of the 1920s and the Pan-African Congresses of the 1920s to 1940s. Many of the Africans who led the Congresses and later became national leaders in West Africa had been schooled in the United States and had incorporated its social and political values.

No greater contribution to strengthening the bonds between America and Africa was crafted than by Kennedy's Peace Corps, which from its inception forged strong people-to-people ties between two very different cultures. By 1989, three thousand volunteers were living in twenty-seven African countries.

Since the Kennedy era, U.S. aid levels have dropped dramatically, to $850 million of nonmilitary aid in 1989. Some of Kennedy's successors, like Presidents Richard M. Nixon and Gerald Ford, aligned the United States with Portugal (which had colonies in Africa until 1974–1975) and South Africa. Although major efforts were made during the presidency of Jimmy Carter to wrest Namibia from South Africa and assist Rhodesia's transition to independence as Zimbabwe (in 1980), President Ronald Reagan's administration had markedly cool relations with black Africa. Nearly all the nations on the continent perceived the United States during this period as pro–South Africa and at best ambivalent about the freedom struggle there.

"Constructive engagement," as the American policy was known, depended more on friendship with the apartheid rulers of South Africa than on backing the ANC. Only at the very end of the Reagan administration was this policy reversed, with the passage of legislative sanctions against South Africa. Such pressure and the military stalemate in Angola between Cuban and South African combatants also led, by 1988, to a long-sought, U.S.-brokered agreement to end South African intervention in Angola and withdraw thirty-five thousand Cuban soldiers and technicians from that country. In 1989 this agreement permitted South Africa to begin giving up control over Namibia, and for the United Nations to begin overseeing Namibia's transition to independence, which became a reality in March 1990.

Peter Duignan and Lewis H. Gann, *The United States and Africa: A History* (1984); Thomas J. Noer, *Cold War and Black Liberation: The United States and White Rule in Africa, 1948–1968* (1985).

ROBERT I. ROTBERG

See also American Colonization Society; Black Nationalism; Garvey, Marcus; Missionaries; Peace Corps; Slavery; Triangular Trade.

AGRICULTURE

Agriculture was the most important economic activity in America from the founding of Virginia in 1607 to about 1890. Although farming declined rapidly in relative economic importance in the twentieth century, U.S. agriculture continued to be the most efficient and productive in the world. Its success rested on abundant fertile soil, a moderate climate, the ease of private land ownership, growing markets for farm produce at home and abroad, and the application of science and technology to farm operations.

The first settlers, finding that European agriculture could not easily be transferred to the new environment, adopted the Indian practices of raising corn, squash, tobacco, and other crops. From the beginning corn, grown in all the colonies, was the leading food crop. Tobacco, which was exported to earn foreign exchange, was raised mostly in Virginia and Maryland.

In New England, farmers on small acreages raised corn, oats, and rye, vegetables and fruits, and livestock, especially cattle and sheep. In the central colonies of New York, Pennsylvania, and New Jersey wheat was the major crop. Farmers there were also heavy producers of livestock and animal products, as well as fruit and vegetables. Most farmers in early America were largely self-sufficient, producing enough for their family needs, but also some surplus for sale.

Agriculture from Maryland southward was more specialized and commercialized than in the North. Corn was the main grain and food crop, but tobacco, rice, and indigo were the principal export crops. Farmers grew tobacco in Virginia as early as 1612, and production expanded rapidly. Rice, introduced into South Carolina in 1685, soon became a major commercial crop in that colony and later in Georgia. The plantation system was developed in connection with the production of tobacco and rice, with black slaves providing much of the labor by the late seventeenth century. Cotton was grown for home use in the late eighteenth century, but because it was difficult to extract the seeds it did not become an important commercial crop until after the invention of the cotton gin by Eli Whitney in 1793.

Farmers then used crude hand tools made of wood, sometimes with iron parts. Plows too might have an iron facing on the cutting edge. Planting, weeding, and harvesting were done by hand labor.

Significant changes in farming began to occur at the beginning of the nineteenth century. Between the American Revolution and the Civil War, tens of thousands of farmers surged westward to settle on the rich lands of the Ohio and Mississippi valleys. There a grain-livestock empire gradually took shape that was unequaled anywhere in the world. In the South farmers and planters pushed into Alabama and Mississippi and as far west as Texas, establishing a vast cotton kingdom and backcountry of mainly self-sufficient farmers. By 1860 the nation had 2,044,077 farms. Agricultural expansion was encouraged by removal of Indians from choice farmlands, liberal public land policies, development of canal and rail transportation, demand for food and fiber in the growing towns and cities, increasing exports, and especially improved farm machinery.

One of the greatest advances made in agriculture before the Civil War was the shift from human to animal power and the use of new labor-saving machines. Besides the cotton gin, innovations such as iron and steel plows, reapers, threshing machines, grain drills, corn and cotton planters, and iron harrows and cultivators became common. These implements were drawn by oxen and horses. In 1800, it took fifty-six man-hours to grow and harvest an acre of wheat but only thirty-five man-hours in 1840.

Meanwhile, agricultural reformers advised farmers to rotate their crops, conserve the soil, use fertilizers, adopt new crops, improve livestock breeds, and use the latest machinery. Although a few farmers practiced soil conservation by rotating crops or growing legumes, most simply plowed up new lands when the fertility of their fields declined. Of the three main components of production — land, labor, and capital — land was the cheapest, so it made economic sense in the short run to exploit the soil to the fullest.

By 1860 the nation's 2 million farms were producing a remarkable abundance. In that year, farmers grew 838 million bushels of corn, 172 million bushels of wheat, and large quantities of other grains, plus 5.4 million bales of cotton, millions of pounds of tobacco, and a great variety of fruits, vegetables, and other crops. Livestock numbers ran into the millions.

Farmers continued to supply many of their own needs, but increasingly they were selling their produce, much of it abroad, and buying manufactured goods. In 1860 farm products made up 82 percent of the country's exports. These exports, especially that of cotton, were highly important because they earned foreign exchange for investment in American manufacturing and transportation. Moreover, agriculture supplied the raw materials for some of the nation's leading manufactures such as textiles and food products. In brief, agriculture was a powerful engine behind American economic development in the first half of the nineteenth century.

Following the Civil War, agricultural expansion accelerated at an even faster pace as hundreds of thousands of farmers migrated to the Great Plains and the Rocky Mountain and West Coast states. With the end of slavery, blacks became sharecroppers on hundreds of thousands of small farms in the South. Between 1860 and 1916, the number of farms rose from slightly over 2 million to 6.4 million, and farm acreage more than doubled from 407 million to 879 million acres. Farm machines for planting, cultivat-

ing, and harvesting were steadily improved and some new machines such as the steam tractor were introduced. With larger acreages and better machinery the production of corn, wheat, cotton, tobacco, and other crops continued to increase tremendously.

By World War I the nation's agriculture had settled into regional patterns. Farmers in the Northeast concentrated on dairying, poultry raising, and producing fruits and vegetables for the growing urban markets. In the Midwest, corn, oats, and barley were the leading grain crops, which supported a thriving hog and cattle business. Dairying was highly important in the upper midwestern states of Minnesota, Wisconsin, and Michigan. The Great Plains from Texas to the Canadian border became the country's breadbasket with wheat as the main commercial crop, supplemented by a strong livestock economy.

Agriculture in the Rocky Mountain states centered around cattle and sheep raising and the production of wheat and irrigated crops such as sugarbeets and alfalfa. In eastern Washington and Oregon wheat was the principal grain crop, but those states also raised large quantities of apples, peaches, pears, other fruits, and vegetables. California farmers produced a great variety of products, including wheat, vegetables, fruit, nuts, and after World War II, cotton and rice. Much of the agriculture in the Far West depended on irrigation. In the South cotton was the main cash crop from the Carolinas to Texas until after World War II. Tobacco, sugarcane, and rice continued to be the other leading commercial crops in the region.

Although American agriculture was extremely productive, most farmers were not prosperous. Part of the problem was that farmers produced raw materials and exchanged them for more expensive manufactured goods. The terms of trade were unfavorable for farmers. In 1900 income per worker in agriculture was only $260 annually compared to $622 for nonagricultural workers. Tenancy increased from 25 to 35 percent between 1880 and 1900. It was especially high throughout the South where hundreds of thousands of black and white farmers worked as tenants and sharecroppers with little prospect of ever owning a farm or making a decent living. Between 1900 and the end of World War I, however, farmers experienced better times. The demand for farm commodities increased, land values rose, and during part of the period, farm prices went up faster than nonfarm prices. The first two decades of the twentieth century became known as the golden age of American agriculture.

Then in 1920 the postwar deflation hit farmers extremely hard as agricultural prices dropped much further than nonfarm prices. Arguing that farmers suffered unfairly from the cost-price squeeze, farm spokesmen began campaigning for federal farm relief. There was plenty of precedent for congressional action on behalf of farmers. In 1862 Congress had passed three basic laws to assist farmers — the Homestead Act, the Morrill Land Grant Act, which provided federal aid to set up agricultural and mechanical colleges, and an act establishing the Department of Agriculture. Later Congress enacted credit and cooperative marketing legislation to help farmers.

None of these laws, or others, however, solved the problem of low returns to farmers or the disparity between agricultural and nonfarm prices. It was not until 1933 that Congress passed the Agricultural Adjustment Act that inaugurated a wide range of federal programs to support the prices of basic agricultural commodities, encourage soil conservation, and subsidize exports. The New Deal programs continued through the rest of the century without major modifications. Government payments to farmers in 1934 totaled $134 million; by 1961 they had increased to $1.5 billion, and by 1987 to $22 billion.

By the 1930s agriculture was undergoing still more fundamental changes through advances in technology and the application of science to farming. The gasoline tractor, which came into general use in the 1920s and 1930s, brought the horse age in farming to a close shortly after World War II. The development of bigger and better machines, like the grain combine harvester and the mechanical cotton picker, continued to reduce the amount of labor needed in agriculture.

A second aspect of the revolution was the widespread use of chemicals for fertilizer, insecticides, and herbicides, and a third phase involved the breeding of better crop strains, such as hybrid corn, and the development of improved livestock. Other dramatic changes included confined hog and poultry production, contract cattle feeding, artificial breeding, and better control of crop and livestock diseases. Major shifts occurred in regional output. Many southern farmers abandoned cotton after World War II and turned to soybeans, poultry, and cattle. Cotton growing moved westward where West Texas, Arizona, and California producers grew the crop under irrigation.

These and other developments combined to increase agricultural productivity dramatically without the need to increase acreages. The amount of land in farms stayed at about 1 billion acres between 1930 and 1980. For example, corn production increased from 20 bushels an acre in 1930 to about 110 bushels half a century later. Annual milk production per cow rose from 4,622 to 12,147 pounds in the same period. A new crop, soybeans, surged to prominence after 1930, and by 1981 farmers were producing slightly more than 2 billion bushels annually.

Even before productivity rose so sharply, American farmers grew a constant surplus, so that a large portion of their output had to be exported. In 1980 one-third of farm production was sold abroad, and agricultural exports made up about 20 percent of the country's overseas sales.

By the end of the twentieth century some new trends were emerging in agriculture. These included organic farming and the reduced use of chemicals in response to health and environmental concerns. Some producers practiced no-till farming to lower costs and conserve the soil. The effects of biotechnology or genetic engineering to increase crop and livestock production were also being felt. With larger and more powerful machines and scientific methods, farmers were able to cultivate more land and handle more livestock with less labor. Consequently, after 1940 there was a sharp increase in the average size of farms and a rapid decline in the number of farmers. In 1940 there were 6.1 million farms averaging 215 acres in size. By 1980 only 2.4 million farms remained, but the average size was 431 acres. Despite the growing size of farms, the great majority of American agriculture remained in the hands of family farmers. There were large plantations in the South and some huge agricultural corporations elsewhere, but at the end of the twentieth century over 90 percent of the nation's farms were still in the hands of family operators.

In 1930 some 30 million Americans lived on farms, or 25 percent of the population. By the 1980s the number of people living on farms had declined to 5.7 million, or less than 2.5 percent. Throughout U.S. history farming had been an important economic activity, but it had also been a distinctive way of life for millions of Americans. Many people held to the Jeffersonian ideal that farming was a superior way of life and that farmers were better people than urbanites. Farming and rural life had become romanticized, mainly by nonfarmers, most of whom had never made a living on the farm. By the end of the twentieth century, however, agriculture had become a business that required skilled labor, capital, and good management and was an activity with which very few Americans had any direct contact. Shifting from a labor-intensive to a capital-intensive industry, commercial agriculture had become a specialized business. Much of the nation's farm production and distribution was in the hands of large agribusiness firms. Nevertheless, some of the ideas, traditions, and values associated with farming and the rural way of life still prevailed in a society that had become predominantly urban.

Gilbert C. Fite, *American Farmers, The New Minority* (1981); John T. Schlebecker, *Whereby We Thrive: A History of American Farming, 1607–1972* (1975).

GILBERT C. FITE

See also Carver, George Washington; Chavez, Cesar; Cotton; Cotton Gin; Dust Bowl; Farmers' Alliance; Granger Movement; Homestead Act; McCormick, Cyrus; Morrill Land Grant Act; Plantation System; Public Land Policy; Southern Tenant Farmers' Union; Tobacco; Whitney, Eli.

AIR FORCE

See Armed Forces.

AIRPLANES

See Aviation.

ALABAMA CLAIMS

The *Alabama* claims were brought by the United States against Great Britain for the damage caused by several Confederate warships built in Liverpool during the Civil War, most notably the commerce raiders *Alabama* and *Florida*. The British Foreign Enlistment Act of 1819 forbade the construction and outfitting of foreign warships. The Confederates evaded the letter of this law during the early years of the war by various ruses and managed to purchase a number of cruisers. After these vessels were completed, they destroyed or captured more than 250 American merchant ships and caused the conversion of 700 more to foreign flags. By the end of the war, the U.S. Merchant Marine had lost half its ships. The subsequent demands for compensation took the title of the vessel that had done the most damage — *Alabama*.

Most historians now believe that the raiders' worst effect was on the U.S. Merchant Marine, which never regained its prewar standing, rather than on the actual course of the war. But at the time many Americans believed that the raiders had indeed lengthened the war. British and U.S. diplomats worked out the Johnson-Clarendon Convention of 1869, recommending a commission to review the *Alabama* claims, but this proposal met overwhelming defeat in the Senate, where Charles Sumner, chairman of the Foreign Relations Committee, spoke passionately against it. He maintained that the British were accountable not only for private citizens' losses but for all the costs of the war after Gettysburg, on the grounds that the Confederates were defeated by then except for their maritime operations. He proposed a compensation of $2 billion and recommended the cession of Canada as well.

Diplomacy resumed nevertheless, and in

1871 Secretary of State Hamilton Fish negotiated the Treaty of Washington, calling again for an arbitration panel. This time the proposal was accepted on May 8. The arbitrators met in Geneva in 1871–1872. They dismissed the "indirect" claims for war costs but granted the full amount of private compensation requested, $15 million.

See also Civil War.

ALAMO

The Alamo was the site of a legendary battle in Texas's struggle for independence from Mexico (1835–1836). Texans had been chafing under the Mexican government, which legislated against slavery, allowed the military to intrude upon civil affairs, and was chronically unstable. In December 1835, a volunteer Texan force drove government troops out of San Antonio and settled in around the Alamo, a mission compound adapted to military purposes after the 1790s. In January 1836, Mexico's president, Gen. Antonio López de Santa Anna, concentrated forces south of the Rio Grande. Sam Houston, the commander of Texas's armies, ordered San Antonio abandoned, but troops under James Bowie and William B. Travis chose to remain. They were joined by others, notably the "Tennessee boys" led by Davy Crockett.

When Santa Anna's army reached San Antonio, Travis, in full command because Bowie had fallen ill, declared from within the Alamo, "*I shall never surrender or retreat. . . .* VICTORY OR DEATH." The latter increasingly became the more likely prospect. The Mexican force has been estimated at from 2,400 to over 5,000, the Alamo's defenders numbered only about 185, and Santa Anna declared he would give no quarter. On March 6, after thirteen days of siege, the Mexicans stormed the citadel. It took three assaults and close combat to overcome the insurgent garrison. Apparently, only one Texan combatant survived — José María Guerrero, who persuaded his captors he had been forced to fight. Noncombatants — women, children, and a black slave — were also spared. "Best estimates" of Mexican dead have ranged from six hundred to nearly sixteen hundred.

Both the Texan and the Mexican decisions to fight at the Alamo have been criticized on military grounds. But the battle gave the insurgent cause its martyrs and its battle cry. Shouting "Remember the Alamo!" Texans overwhelmed a Mexican force six weeks later at San Jacinto (April 21, 1836). There, Santa Anna was captured and independence won.

See also Texas Revolution and Annexation.

ALASKA PURCHASE

In 1866, the Russian government offered to sell Alaska to the United States. Russia had held the territory since 1741, but by the mid-nineteenth century, British and American settlers were pressing Alaska's southern border, increasing the likelihood of territorial quarrels. Furthermore, the Russian treasury was short of funds. Accordingly, Baron Edouard de Stoeckl, the Russian minister to the United States, was instructed in December 1866 to negotiate the sale. He and Secretary of State William H. Seward worked out a treaty under which the United States would purchase Alaska for $7.2 million in gold. Seward initially offered $5 million, an amount Stoeckl was empowered to accept. But Stoeckl correctly judged that the secretary would agree to a higher figure because of Seward's passionate commitment to American expansion as well as his wish to conclude the matter while Congress was still in session. Stoeckl received final approval of the treaty terms from his government on March 30, 1867.

When it became clear that the Senate would not debate the treaty before its adjournment on March 30, Seward persuaded President Andrew Johnson to call the Senate back into special session the next day. Many Radical Republicans scoffed at "Seward's folly," although their criticism appears to have been based less on the merits of the purchase than on their hostility to President Johnson and to Seward as Johnson's political ally. Seward mounted a vigorous campaign, however, and with support from Charles Sumner, chairman of the Senate Foreign Relations Committee, won approval of the treaty on April 9 by a vote of 37–2.

For more than a year, as congressional relations with President Johnson worsened, the House refused to appropriate the necessary funds. But in June 1868, after Johnson's impeachment trial was over, Stoeckl and Seward revived the campaign for the Alaska purchase. Combining public appeals and private persuasion (including bribes to a number of key Republicans), they won a favorable vote on July 14. With the purchase of Alaska, the United States acquired an area twice as large as Texas, but it was not until the great Klondike gold strike in 1896 that Alaska came to be seen generally as a valuable addition to American territory.

See also Expansion, Continental and Overseas; Seward, William H.

ALBANY CONGRESS

Representatives of seven colonies of British North America met in Albany, New York, in 1754, at the outbreak of the French and Indian War. The Board of Trade, the organ of the British government responsible for the colonies, called the congress to unify the colonists in the face of the threat of war.

The Albany Congress is most famous for the Albany Plan of Union, drafted by Benjamin Franklin. The Albany Plan provided for a federal union of the mainland colonies under the British Crown. The legislature of each colony would elect representatives to a Grand Council, apportioned according to the size of the colony and administered by a president-general appointed by the Crown. This "general government" would have the power to make peace or war, as well as primary financial and command responsibility for defense, Indian relations, and regulation of frontier settlement. The Grand Council could make laws and levy taxes for these two purposes. Franklin enjoined his proposed government to make the taxes "such as may be collected with the least inconvenience to the people; rather discouraging luxury, than loading industry with unnecessary burdens."

The Albany Plan, though adopted by the Albany Congress, never went any further. Most of the individual colonies preferred to keep their decentralized governments. The plan remained important as a model and precedent for the joint action of the mainland colonies in the American Revolution.

See also Revolution.

ALBANY REGENCY

The Albany Regency was an influential cadre of New York Democratic leaders of the Bucktail faction of their party, starting around 1817. It was so called because it maintained the political presence of Martin Van Buren in New York's state capital while he was serving in Washington, D.C. Regency members William L. Marcy, Azariah C. Flagg, Benjamin F. Butler, Silas Wright, and John A. Dix had long political careers, but Edwin Croswell, editor of the *Albany Argus,* was at least as influential. As allies of Van Buren, they arrayed themselves against the state's governor, DeWitt Clinton. Van Buren saw parties as a legitimate vehicle for winning elections based on issues, not as earlier political leaders did, as factions created solely on the basis of some principle. Andrew Jackson benefited from the Albany Regency's lasting influence. When Van Buren and the Regency supported Jackson for the presidency, the campaign did much to create the Democratic party.

See also Van Buren, Martin.

ALCOHOL

See Prohibition and Temperance.

ALCOTT, LOUISA MAY

(1832–1888), author. Alcott spent her early years in and around Boston, where her transcendentalist father, Bronson, wrote, lectured, and established short-lived experimental primary schools. Her mother, Abigail May, was an early and ardent abolitionist and involved in many contemporary issues including feminism, dietary reforms, and the causes of poverty. Alcott grew up surrounded by the writers and activist friends of her parents such as Henry David Thoreau, Ralph Waldo Emerson, Theodore Parker, the Peabody sisters, William Lloyd Garrison, Orestes Brownson, and Margaret Fuller. Although Alcott associated transcendentalism with impracticality and fuzzy thinking, she was deeply affected by the abolitionist cause. Her active role in her mother's struggles with the family's poverty caused by Bronson's economic vagaries led Alcott to feminism. For reasons of health and temperament, she manifested her allegiance with the suffrage movement more in her writings than in public.

Alcott began writing as an adolescent, publishing her first story, "The Rival Prima Donnas," in a theatrical paper. She called the story, which featured two actresses pitted against one another professionally and personally, "rubbish" and followed it quickly with *Flower Fables,* fairy stories she had written for Emerson's daughter, Ellen. These tales illustrated the theme that hard work, self-denial, and patience can win love from even the chilliest heart.

These beginnings indicate the two directions Alcott's work would take. On the one hand, she wrote, enthusiastically and often pseudonymously, colorful and improbable stories for grown-ups about unrequited or tragically misdirected love, jealousy, vengeance, and retribution. On the other hand, she wrote, more slowly and with less gusto, moral stories for children, which illustrated the principles of *Flower Fables.* As she matured, these works also contained lessons for women about transcending their roles as mothers and housekeepers by becoming doctors, writers, or charity workers.

In the winter of 1862–1863 Alcott went to Washington, D.C., as a nurse in Dorothea Dix's newly established service. She washed, fed, and tended wounded soldiers until, after only a few weeks, she fell ill. In accordance with army medical practice she was given large doses of calomel, an emetic containing mercury, which rendered her a semi-invalid for the last two decades of her life. She returned home to convalesce. In the following years she wrote her most exciting pseudonymous thrillers as well as *Hospital Sketches,* a humorous account of her nursing experiences.

In 1868, following an often repeated suggestion of her father, who had an exceptionally strong influence on her life, she wrote *Little Women.* It was a heartwarming and rigidly moral

account of her difficult childhood and her strenuous efforts to cope with her rebellious thoughts and feelings while growing up in a large, poor family, guided unsteadily by an improvident idealist. The success of *Little Women* was immediate and lasting. Alcott dismissed it and its many sequels (*Good Wives, Little Men, Jo's Boys, Eight Cousins, Rose in Bloom,* and *Under the Lilacs*) as "pap" for the young, but she enjoyed some aspects of her success including the comforts and the trips to New York and Europe it provided her and her family. Her health deteriorated, and she died at the age of fifty-five, four days after the death of her eighty-eight-year-old father.

Louisa May Alcott, *Plots and Counterplots,* ed. Madeleine Stern (1977).

MARTHA SAXTON

See also Feminist Movement; Literature; Transcendentalism.

ALGER HISS CASE

In August 1948, Whittaker Chambers, a former Communist appearing before the House Un-American Activities Committee, charged that Alger Hiss, president of the Carnegie Endowment for International Peace, was a Communist spy. Chambers claimed that he and Hiss had belonged to the same espionage ring and that Hiss had given him secret State Department documents. Chambers later repeated these charges on "Meet the Press."

Hiss, a Harvard-educated lawyer and a prominent Washington figure, had been responsible for Far East affairs for the State Department and had played a significant role in the planning for and development of the United Nations. He responded to Chambers's charges by suing him for slander. Chambers then produced copies of the secret documents, saying he had hidden them in a pumpkin in a field near his farm. Since the statute of limitations for an espionage charge had expired, the government prosecuted Hiss for perjury. His first trial ended in a hung jury; at the second he was found guilty and sentenced to five years in prison.

The Hiss case played an important role in the domestic controversies over the cold war and

McCarthyism. Supporters of Hiss believed that Chambers was a liar and that the incident was an attempt to discredit the New Deal and social reform. Chambers and his followers, for their part, always stressed the communist threat to the United States.

See also Anticommunism; Espionage.

ALI, MUHAMMAD

(1942–   ), boxer and spokesman for the Nation of Islam. The increasing militancy of African-American politics during the 1960s coincided with the transformation of Olympic gold medalist Cassius Marcellus Clay into Muhammad Ali, the most controversial and widely known of all heavyweight boxing champions. Born into a black working-class family in Louisville, Kentucky, Clay experienced the racial restrictions that fueled the civil rights protests of the late 1950s and 1960s. As a youngster, he resented being named after a white man, albeit an abolitionist. When he read news of the 1955 racial murder in Mississippi of Emmett Till, a black youngster about his age, he reacted angrily, hurling stones at an UNCLE SAM WANTS YOU poster.

He learned to box while a teenager, and his exceptional skills quickly became evident. By 1959 he had won a national Golden Gloves championship. Following his success as a member of the 1960 U.S. Olympic boxing team, he signed a professional contract with Louisville promoters and soon became a contender for the heavyweight boxing crown. Brashly outspoken about racial issues, he also bragged about his pugilistic ability, often proclaiming, "I am the greatest." His facile rhymes and sometimes accurate knockout predictions attracted the attention of boxing fans.

As he was perfecting his boxing and promotional skills, he became affiliated with the Nation of Islam, an all-black religious group, often labeled the Black Muslims, led by Elijah Muhammad. He became close friends with the Nation's best-known spokesman, Malcolm X, but remained loyal to Elijah Muhammad after Malcolm's 1964 break with him. Recognizing that the Nation of Islam was notorious because of its advocacy of black self-defense and racial separat-

ism, Clay kept his affiliation with the group secret until February 1964, when he defeated Sonny Liston and became heavyweight champion. He then announced his religious ties and stated that he had rejected his "slave" name in favor of the new name Muhammad Ali.

For a decade thereafter, Ali remained at the center of controversy. Many reporters and boxing officials continued to refer to him as Cassius Clay and some even demanded that his title be withdrawn. The hostility increased when he refused in 1967 to be inducted into the army, citing the fact that his religion forbade him from doing so. Government officials were unwilling to accept his claim that he was a lay Islamic minister, especially when he made clear his lack of sympathy for the war in Vietnam. "I ain't got no quarrel with the Vietcong," he explained. Although he indicated that he was simply responding to religious imperatives, Ali became a widely admired symbol of black pride and militancy because of his consistent unwillingness to back down in the face of threats from white authorities. Stripped of his title after being indicted for refusing induction, he was later convicted and sentenced to five years in prison. In June 1970, however, the Supreme Court overturned his conviction. In 1974, Ali gained further vindication when he defeated George Foreman and regained the title that had been taken from him.

Although Ali's activities in the years after 1974 were not as controversial as they had once been, he remained an internationally known public figure. After his retirement from boxing during the late 1970s, he developed Parkinson's syndrome, a condition that severely restricted his once extensive public-speaking activities.

Muhammad Ali, with Richard Durham, *The Greatest: My Own Story* (1975); Henry Hampton and Steve Fayer, *Voices of Freedom: An Oral History of the Civil Rights Movement from the 1950s through the 1980s* (1990).

CLAYBORNE CARSON

See also Spectator Sports.

ALIEN AND SEDITION ACTS

The Alien and Sedition Acts were passed by Congress in 1798 in preparation for an anticipated war with France. Interpreting the prominent participation of immigrants in the Republican opposition party as evidence of a relationship between foreigners and disloyalty, Federalists championed tighter restrictions for foreigners and critics of their policies.

The Naturalization Act of 1798 increased the residency requirement for American citizenship from five to fourteen years, required aliens to declare their intent to acquire citizenship five years before it could be granted, and made persons from "enemy" nations ineligible for naturalization. The act consequently deprived Republicans of an important source of political support. Aliens were specifically affected by two other acts, which authorized their deportation if they were deemed "dangerous to the peace and safety of the United States" and their wholesale incarceration or expulsion by presidential executive order during wartime.

Under the Sedition Act, even the rights of American citizens were curtailed by prohibiting assembly "with intent to oppose any measure . . . of the government" and made it illegal for any person to "print, utter, or publish . . . any false, scandalous, and malicious writing" against the government.

Armed with these statutes, Federalists attempted to suppress Republican opposition on the basis of ideological differences — most successfully prosecuting newspaperman Thomas Cooper and Republican congressman Matthew Lyon. These controversies provoked the first probing of the constitutional limits on free speech, the press, and the rights of an organized political opposition. When Thomas Jefferson became president, enforcement of the Alien and Sedition Acts ended. The sedition and incarceration provisions of the acts, however, were resurrected during later wars.

See also Bill of Rights; Freedom of Speech; Freedom of the Press; Immigration; Nativism.

ALLEN, RICHARD

(1760–1831), African-American religious leader and reformer. As a shaper of thought and builder of institutions, few of his white contemporaries matched the accomplishments of Allen in the postrevolutionary period. At age twenty, only a few months after purchasing his release from slavery, he was preaching to mostly white audiences and converting many to Methodism. At twenty-seven, he was one of the founders of the Free African Society of Philadelphia, probably the first autonomous organization of free blacks in the United States. Before he was thirty-five, he had become the spiritual leader of what grew into Philadelphia's largest black congregation — Bethel African Methodist Episcopal Church. Over a long lifetime, he founded or served as officer in many other organizations designed to improve the lives of African-Americans. Although he had no formal education, he became an accomplished writer of sermons, tracts, addresses, and remonstrances.

Born a slave in the family of a prominent Philadelphia lawyer and officeholder, Benjamin Chew, Allen was sold with his family to a farmer near Dover, Delaware, in about 1768. It was here, in 1777, that Allen experienced a religious awakening through the preaching of itinerant Methodists shortly after most of his family had been sold again. Three years later he contracted to purchase his freedom.

Supporting himself as a woodchopper, brickyard laborer, wagon driver, and shoemaker, Allen, by 1783, had fixed the course of his life through his frequent itinerant preaching. In 1786, the Methodists in Philadelphia called him to preach to black members of their flock.

In Philadelphia, Allen founded Mother Bethel, a black Methodist church that opened its doors in 1794, and the independent African Methodist Episcopal (A.M.E.) church in 1816. Between those years, he established schools for black youth and mutual aid societies to free black Philadelphians from dependence on white charity. He wrote pamphlets and sermons attacking the slave trade and slavery and became a leader in almost every African-American institution in the city.

His twenty-year battle with the white Methodist church, which led to a final separation in 1817, was a vital phase in the African-American struggle in the North to get out from under the controlling hand of white religionists. The A.M.E. church, with Allen as its first bishop, allowed former slaves to forge an Afro-Christianity that spoke in the language and answered the needs of a growing number of northern and, later, southern blacks. For decades, the church helped heal the scars of slavery and facilitated the adjustment of black southern migrants to life in the North.

In his later years, Allen was drawn to the idea of colonization — in Africa, Haiti, and Canada — as an answer to the needs of blacks facing discrimination and exploitation as freed persons. The capstone of his career was leadership at the first meeting of the National Negro Convention Movement, an umbrella organization that launched coordinated reform efforts among black Americans.

Carol V. R. George, *Segregated Sabbaths: Richard Allen and the Rise of Independent Black Churches, 1760–1840* (1973).

GARY B. NASH

See also Abolitionist Movement; A.M.E. Church; Black Churches; Free Negroes, 1619–1860.

A.M.E. CHURCH

Stirred into action by the Great Awakening of the 1740s, white evangelical Protestants began proselytizing black Americans. The most successful of these were the Methodists. Their program of systematic evangelism and their emphasis on a "near" rather than "distant" God, self-help, liberation from sin through conversion, and lively preaching and singing — along with John Wesley's denunciations of the evils of slavery — proved tremendously effective in attracting converts among slaves and free people of color.

By the time of the Revolution, blacks formed substantial minorities in congregations in Philadelphia, Baltimore, and New York, and a majority in Charleston. But given the contradiction between the Methodist gospel of a Christianity transcending race and class, and the prejudices among white adherents against black people, tensions soon developed.

In November 1787, white elders attempted to relegate black Methodists to a newly built gallery in Philadelphia's St. George's Methodist Church. Richard Allen, an ex-slave and charis-

matic lay preacher, and several others refused to sit in segregated seats. They began praying at the altar rail. When white trustees attempted to remove them, Allen and others founded Bethel church and, in 1816, the African Methodist Episcopal church (A.M.E.), the first independent, black-run Protestant denomination. With Allen as its bishop, the church took on philanthropic and educational endeavors in the black community and in Canada, Haiti, the British West Indies, and West Africa. It was active in the abolitionist movement, especially in opposing the American Colonization Society and other colonization schemes. Prior to the Civil War, the A.M.E.'s strength lay in the Mid-Atlantic region and the Midwest; its expansion in slave states was hampered by repressive slave codes. After the Civil War, the A.M.E. church spread widely throughout the South.

See also Allen, Richard; Black Churches.

AMENDMENTS, CONSTITUTIONAL

See Bill of Rights; Constitution.

AMERICA FIRST COMMITTEE

The America First Committee was organized in July 1940 to oppose American intervention in World War II. The committee built a considerable following, particularly in the Midwest. Some America Firsters actively supported the Nazis, but more — like the committee chairman, Gen. Robert E. Wood, head of Sears, Roebuck — were businessmen who considered neutrality the only way to keep America safe and prosperous. Some also feared that organizing for war would give the federal government and their archenemy, President Franklin D. Roosevelt, even more power than the New Deal already had. Other committee members were old-line progressives like Senators Gerald P. Nye and Burton K. Wheeler, who associated pressure for aid to Great Britain with the international financial interests they believed had drawn the country into World War I.

America First's most noted spokesman, Charles A. Lindbergh, said flatly that U.S. intervention in Europe would be useless. With the fall of France, Britain apparently close to defeat, and a Nazi attack on the United States not inconceivable, he argued that the only way to save the country was to stay out of a hopeless battle in Europe and concentrate on defending the American way of life at home. Although Lindbergh's increasingly extreme remarks — some with strong tones of anti-Semitism — antagonized many, his high public standing did attract followers to the movement. Within a year, America First had established more than 450 chapters, building a membership of several hundred thousand.

But the tide of public opinion was moving against isolationism; the committee was able to prevent neither the reelection of Roosevelt in 1940 nor congressional approval of the Lend-Lease agreement to assist Britain in the spring of 1941. The Japanese attack on Pearl Harbor, December 7, 1941, was the final blow, destroying the last hope that Americans could protect their country by remaining neutral.

See also Isolationism.

AMERICA IN THE BRITISH EMPIRE

Among the European Atlantic states, England was notably slower than Spain, Portugal, or France to become interested in the New World. The early Tudor monarchs did very little to encourage exploration. And when English adventurers during the reign of Elizabeth I (1558–1603) finally began to reconnoiter the North American coast and to plunder Spanish shipping in the Caribbean, they operated as private entrepreneurs, with minimal support or supervision from the Crown. Queen Elizabeth mobilized large armies at great expense to conquer Ireland, but she made no equivalent investment in America. Instead, she granted Sir Walter Raleigh the authority to colonize at his own expense — and he failed at Roanoke in 1584–1587.

Under James I (1603–1625) and Charles I (1625–1649), the English established a dozen permanent colonies in America, but the home government paid little heed to any of these ventures. The settlement of Virginia was undertaken in 1607 by a privately financed joint stock company. Although the Crown took direct control of the colony in 1624, it provided no real supervision. A number of other colonies — such as Barbados and Maryland — were started by individual proprietors who managed their settlements as semifeudal principalities. And the Puritans who founded the New England colonies openly challenged the Crown. They had come to America in order to get away from Charles I's rule, and they set up religious and political institutions in repudiation of the establishment at home. Thus each English plantation in the early seventeenth century was essentially autonomous. And because the pioneer settlers were free to do as they pleased, the Caribbean, Chesapeake, and New England colonies developed distinctive regional characteristics, many of which are still observable today.

In the 1640s, with king and Parliament absorbed in civil war at home, the English colonists in America achieved maximum independence. In New England, the four chief colonies formed a military confederation and conducted their own foreign policy. In the West Indies, the Barbados planters entered into a lucrative partnership with the Netherlands, selling their sugar to Dutch traders in exchange for thousands of African slaves.

During the 1650s and 1660s, the English government finally began to play a more active role in American colonial development. Parliament passed a series of Navigation Acts, designed to exclude the Dutch from trading in English America and to channel the shipment of all Chesapeake tobacco and Caribbean sugar to the mother country. Lord Protector Oliver Cromwell (1653–1658) seized the Spanish island of Jamaica in 1655, and Charles II (1660–1685) seized the Dutch colony of New Netherland in 1664. But the king handed over this colony to his brother, the duke of York, and permitted other court favorites to establish proprietary colonies in the Carolinas and Pennsylvania. By the mid-1670s, only seven of the twenty English colonies in America were under direct Crown control. In the royal colony of Jamaica, the governor was conducting his own privateering war against

Spanish commerce. In the royal colony of Virginia, the governor was nearly overthrown in a rebellion led by Nathaniel Bacon. In Puritan New England, the colonists ignored the Navigation Acts and fought a long and bloody Indian war — King Philip's War — without bothering to consult the home authorities.

Faced with this evidence of colonial chaos and disobedience, the royal government from 1675 onward made serious efforts to regulate the American colonies and establish an imperial system. A colonial office was finally created, and agents were dispatched to America to enforce the Navigation Acts. In the 1680s, energetic royal governors with military experience pressured the legislative assemblies of Virginia and Jamaica into granting permanent tax revenues, and Massachusetts lost its chartered powers of self-government.

The trend toward centralized authority accelerated under James II (1685–1688), who aimed at a Spanish style of viceregal colonial administration. His most spectacular innovation was to combine seven colonies into a single unit, the Dominion of New England, which was ruled by a royal governor backed by troops and unimpeded by a representative assembly. James's authoritarian style, however, proved to be as unpopular and ineffectual in the colonies as at home. The Glorious Revolution in England in 1688 spread to America in 1689. The colonists in Boston and New York City dismantled the Dominion of New England and asked the new king William III to restore their lost privileges.

The postrevolutionary reorganization of the American colonies in the 1690s proved to be of great importance. It established a new imperial formula that for sixty years satisfied all interested parties reasonably well but then failed disastrously in the 1760s and 1770s. The royal policymakers under William III (1689–1702) and Anne (1702–1714) abandoned James II's autocratic mode while retaining his policy of central planning and administration. They were much influenced by strategic considerations. From 1689 to 1713, Britain was almost continuously at war with France, and the Crown invested heavily for the first time in American military and naval operations, particularly in the Caribbean.

Many of the royal governors in America during these years were military men, who tried zealously to enforce orders from home. A number of previously self-governing or proprietary colonies, including Massachusetts and Maryland, were brought under direct royal rule. A new supervisory body, the Board of Trade and Plantations, was created in 1696, and in this same year Parliament legislated the most comprehensive of its Navigation Acts, which effectually tied colonial commerce to the mother country.

London was now the acknowledged imperial entrepôt. On the fringes of the empire the North American and Caribbean colonies settled into a mutually beneficial trading partnership, in which merchants in Boston, New York, and Philadelphia supplied food and timber to the sugar islands in exchange for molasses and rum. In 1707 England entered into political union with Scotland, which further strengthened the empire by opening the colonies to Scottish talent; by the 1760s, Glasgow merchants were surpassing London merchants in the Chesapeake tobacco trade.

Yet the reorganized British imperial system represented a compromise. The colonists accepted their dependent and provincial status while preserving a great deal of local autonomy. Although the Board of Trade wanted to abolish all proprietary governments in America, it failed to do so. And mutual jealousies between Crown and Parliament discouraged the Crown from initiating any policies in America that required legislative enforcement, beyond the strictly commercial regulations established by the Navigation Acts.

During the reigns of George I (1714–1727) and George II (1727–1760), the home authorities administered the American colonies in a deliberately low-key style until the renewal of war with France in the 1740s and 1750s. The Board of Trade instituted no policy changes. The royal ministers who made colonial appointments were more interested in exercising patronage than in rewarding talent. The governors they sent to America were hard-pressed to combat colonial assemblies with rising pretensions to power. These were years of enormous population growth and economic expansion in America and of self-conscious efforts by the provincial colonists to acquire fashionable British consumer goods and to adopt British cultural standards in education, religion, and the law.

Yet psychologically the transatlantic gulf was widening rather than shrinking. Most of the new eighteenth-century immigrants to the colonies came from Ireland, Germany, and Africa rather than from England and Scotland. The Americans developed a political outlook emphasizing fear of centralized power and corruption that the ruling elite at home dismissed as old-fashioned and irrelevant. And though transatlantic trade was booming as never before, most Britons retained an indifferent and condescending attitude toward their distant colonial cousins.

It was against this background that Britain entered into another long war with France, one that lasted from 1740 to 1763. Both nations had extensive colonial holdings in America, developing at asymmetrical rates. While the thirteen mainland British colonies were growing far more rapidly than French Canada, the British sugar colonies in the West Indies were being overtaken by their French rivals. In consequence, the merchants in the British mainland colonies felt increasingly constricted by British commercial regulations and sought to do business with the French sugar planters. The British sugar interest, having strong political leverage at home, tried to block this competition by getting Parliament to legislate the Molasses Act of 1733, which taxed French molasses prohibitively — but the northern merchants countered by trading illicitly with the French, even during wartime.

Fighting between the two imperial powers broke out in America in the 1740s. At first they sparred inconclusively, but the combat gradually intensified. The French alarmed the mainland colonists by invading Pennsylvania and New York in 1755–1757. The British responded to this challenge by mounting a massive and decisive counterattack. Under the dynamic leadership of William Pitt, the home government abruptly terminated its low-key management of American affairs. Mobilizing an unprecedented war effort with generous parliamentary subsidies to the colonies, a large expeditionary army, and a powerful fleet, the British not only conquered French Canada but also captured every major French island except St. Domingue in 1759–1763. Indeed, they gained so much territory that at the 1763 peace conference they returned Guadeloupe and Martinique to France, largely at the insistence of the British sugar planters who continued to fear new competition.

Ironically, the smashing imperial victory over France in 1757–1763 undermined the political compromise that had been worked out in the 1690s and led directly to the breakup of the British Empire in America in 1763–1783. George III (1760–1820) and his ministers felt unable to revert to their traditional hands-off policy. They wanted to retain a military presence in North America in order to govern their new French subjects and to manage restive Indian tribes. And they expected the colonists to help cover the increased costs of imperial administration, since the Crown was now saddled with a huge war debt. The American colonists, on the other hand, saw an opportunity in the 1760s to enlarge their already extensive political and economic liberties. With the removal of the French military threat, they saw less need than ever for centralized imperial government, and they refused to accept responsibility for the king's war debt.

The transatlantic gap between British and American political expectations was suddenly revealed to be very large, and spokesmen for the two sides were unable to communicate and unwilling to negotiate effectively. When George Grenville secured parliamentary passage of the Stamp Act in 1765, the colonists refused point-blank to pay this new tax. They insisted that the colonial assemblies had the exclusive right to raise revenue and that Parliament's sole imperial function was to regulate commerce. Although the royal government acceded to pressure from the British merchant community and repealed the Stamp Act in 1766, Parliament declared that it had full power to legislate for the colonies "in all cases whatsoever." Britons and Americans had now staked out irreconcilable interpretations of their imperial relationship.

The ideological impasse of 1765–1766 quickly triggered civil war within the empire. As George III's ministers kept trying to levy taxes in America, a rebel movement gained momentum in the thirteen mainland colonies, driven by petitions and riots and boycotts and intercolonial congresses. But the Americans were by no means united in rebellion. As the crisis deepened, many people in the mainland colonies chose to remain loyal to the Crown. The rebel cause attracted little support in the island colonies, where imperial protection was much more highly prized than political freedom. And in the mother country, as Lord North's ministry veered toward open war with the rebels in 1775, most Britons — including the merchants who had pressed for repeal of the Stamp Act in 1766 — heartily endorsed the home government's decision to preserve centralized imperial authority.

The American War for Independence turned out to be a longer and more difficult struggle than either the royalists or the rebels anticipated. The British, although they generally beat George Washington's amateur troops in pitched battle, were unable to conquer the rebel army or to occupy the rebels' far-flung territories. And the rebels, being allergic to taxes and suspicious of central planning, were poorly equipped to sustain an effective war effort. The turning point in the war came when the rebels entered into alliance with the French whom they had fought in 1757–1763. At the peace conference of 1783, the British accepted the breakup of their empire by recognizing the political independence and territorial sovereignty of the newly created United States of America.

Jack P. Greene, *Peripheries and Center: Constitutional Development in the Extended Polities of the British Empire and the United States, 1607–1788* (1986); Alison Gilbert Olson, *Anglo-American Politics, 1660–1775: The Relationship between Parties in England and Colonial America* (1973).

RICHARD S. DUNN

See also Chesapeake Colonies; Colonial Economy; Colonial Government and Politics; Colonial Wars; French and Spanish Settlements; Middle Colonies; New England Colonies; Proclamation of 1763; Revolution; Southern Colonies.

AMERICAN CIVIL LIBERTIES UNION

During and after World War I the federal government prosecuted antiwar protesters and aliens thought to be subversive. Responding to Attorney General Mitchell Palmer's attack on civil liberties during the red scare of those years, the American Civil Liberties Union (ACLU) was formed in 1920 by a group that included Clarence Darrow, Felix Frankfurter, Jane Addams, Helen Keller, Norman Thomas, and John Dewey. Roger Baldwin, the first director of the ACLU, served from 1920 to almost 1950.

The ACLU was involved in a number of well-known legal cases including the Scopes "monkey" trial in 1925, the defense of the Scottsboro Boys in 1931, and the right of children of Jehovah's Witnesses to refuse to salute the flag because of religious beliefs in 1936, as well as many revolving around free-speech issues.

Although the ACLU was usually aligned with the Left, Baldwin had Communists, including Elizabeth Gurley Flynn, a personal friend, expelled from the national board in 1940. In another controversial act the ACLU defended the right of Nazis to march in Skokie, Illinois, during the 1970s.

AMERICAN COLONIZATION SOCIETY

The American Colonization Society, founded in 1817, grew out of efforts by a Presbyterian minister from New Jersey, Robert Finley. It was typical of many benevolent societies of the period. Being concerned with social order and desirous of eventually ending slavery, colonizationists saw the emigration of blacks as a solution to what was thought to be the dual problem of freeing blacks and the incompatibility of the races. The movement received a good amount of support in the Upper South and represented a first stage for many abolitionists. Although William Lloyd Garrison and other activists ultimately rejected the gradual approach of colonizationists, the movement maintained its appeal for moderates, among them Abraham Lincoln.

In 1822 the American Colonization Society established Monrovia (later Liberia) on the west coast of Africa. Over the next forty years the society settled some twelve thousand African-Americans in that country. Although the society existed until 1912, after 1860 it functioned primarily as the "caretaker" of the settlement in Liberia.

See also Abolitionist Movement; Expatriates and Exiles.

AMERICAN DILEMMA, AN

In 1938 the Carnegie Corporation commissioned Gunnar Myrdal, a Swedish economist, to direct a two-year study of the condition of African-Americans. To assist him Myrdal employed forty-eight writers and researchers including Ralph Bunche and Kenneth B. Clark. Published in two volumes in 1944, *An American Dilemma: The Negro Problem and Modern Democracy* has had an impact even beyond its sale of 100,000 copies.

The work depicted the ever-widening gap between the American principle of equality and the reality of African-American lives. Myrdal argued that discrimination in the South was due less to prejudice on the part of whites than to the failure of municipal authorities, including the police and the courts, to enforce the Constitution. He predicted, however, that the democratic principles inherent in the legal system would triumph. Racism would eventually disappear. Writing at a time when a majority of African-Americans still lived in the South, Myrdal underestimated the entrenched nature of discrimination in the North and thus was highly optimistic about the ability of America to resolve its racial problems.

An American Dilemma played a role in undermining discrimination when the Supreme Court cited the work as a footnote to its 1954 decision, *Brown* v. *Board of Education of Topeka,* outlawing school segregation. In arguing that "separate but equal" encouraged feelings of inferiority, the decision noted "And see generally Myrdal. An American Dilemma."

See also Brown v. *Board of Education of Topeka;* Bunche, Ralph; Racial Desegregation; Segregation.

AMERICAN FEDERATION OF LABOR

The American Federation of Labor (AFL) was organized as an association of trade unions in 1886, growing out of an earlier Federation of Organized Trades and Labor Unions founded in 1881. The AFL's president, Samuel Gompers (who served nearly every year until 1924), was convinced that unions open to workers of all types of skills within a given industry — called industrial unions — were too diffuse and undisciplined to withstand the repressive tactics that both government and management had used to break American unions in the past. The answer, he believed, was craft unions, each limited to the skilled workers in a single trade. According to Gompers's "pure and simple unionism," labor should not waste its energies fighting capitalism; its sole task was to hammer out the best arrangement it could under the existing system, using strikes, boycotts, and negotiations to win better work conditions, higher wages, and union recognition.

Applying this philosophy to politics, the AFL refused to ally itself with the Socialist party or with independent labor parties. Instead, Gompers argued that labor should "reward its friends and punish its enemies" in both major parties. After 1908, the organization's tie to the Democratic party grew increasingly strong, but the AFL continued to concentrate on political protection for unions, rather than seeking social change through legislative action.

By 1904, the AFL claimed 1.7 million members. Although the union represented only the more privileged members of the country's work force, it gained increasing influence as the recognized voice of American labor. Its membership declined between 1904 and 1914 in the face of a concerted open-shop drive by management but rose again during World War I, when unions were given considerable government protection. By 1920 the AFL had nearly 4 million members.

After the war, however, business resumed its union-busting activities, and the AFL lost ground throughout the 1920s.

By the time the New Deal opened the door again to organized labor, the AFL — now led by William Green (president, 1924–1952) — was facing increasing dissension within its ranks. Craft unions had proved ineffective as a way of organizing the huge industries, such as auto, rubber, and steel, that now dominated the economy. Many in the AFL believed that only industrial unions fit the modern pattern of production. In 1935 John L. Lewis led the dissenting unions in forming a new Committee for Industrial Organization within the AFL. This group, which became the Congress of Industrial Organizations (CIO), grew so powerful that the AFL expelled the ten CIO unions in 1937. The AFL and CIO continued as separate organizations during World War II but were reunited in 1955.

The AFL-CIO was now the nation's dominant labor organization, but this achievement was already being undermined by changes in the American economy and work force — most notably, the growing loss of jobs in the manufacturing sector where unions had been strongest. In 1945 nearly one-third of American workers belonged to a union; by 1990 the proportion had fallen to less than one-fifth.

See also Congress of Industrial Organizations; Gompers, Samuel; Labor; Lewis, John L.

AMERICAN INDEPENDENT PARTY

The American Independent party (AIP) was organized in 1968 by the followers of Governor George C. Wallace of Alabama. Four years earlier, Wallace had scored well in several Democratic primaries, but had been persuaded to withdraw so as not to compete with the Republican nominee, Barry Goldwater. In 1968 the AIP was established to promote his candidacy. The new party was less a national organization than a loose affiliation of local groups; indeed, the party appeared under six different names in various states. Nevertheless, Wallace's followers managed to get his name on the ballot in every state, and he mounted a powerful campaign,

muting the explicit racism of his earlier days and stressing more general themes: Americanism, local choice, public order, and contempt for the "pointy-headed intellectuals" and bureaucrats who, he claimed, were losing the Vietnam War and surrendering to "welfare chiselers, hippies, and anarchists" at home. Right-wing groups responded to this message, but so did many ordinary working people. By September 1968, Wallace's standing in the polls had risen to 21 percent; it seemed possible that AIP votes might prevent either major party from winning the election.

But in October the tide began to turn, starting when the AIP vice-presidential candidate, former Air Force chief of staff Curtis E. LeMay, used most of his first campaign speech to stress the utility of nuclear war. Wallace's increasingly venomous confrontations with hecklers lost him voters, as did a massive campaign launched by labor unions to bring their members back to the Democratic party. In November, the AIP carried five states (all in the Deep South), but won only 13 percent of the vote. In 1969, a split within the AIP created a new American party. Although Wallace began 1972 with solid wins in several Democratic primaries, he was still keeping his third-party options open when he was paralyzed by a gunshot attack in May. The American party offered to nominate him; when he refused, they selected John Schmitz, a member of the John Birch Society. Schmitz won only 1 million votes in 1972, compared to Wallace's 9 million in 1968. By 1976, Wallace had returned to the Democrats, and many of the old AIP members had joined the right wing of the Republican party.

See also Wallace, George C.

AMERICAN PARTY

See Know-Nothing Party.

AMERICAN REVOLUTION

See Revolution.

AMERICAN SYSTEM

Following the War of 1812, a new nationalism emerged in the United States. Henry Clay's "American System" was a neofederalist program of a national bank, a tariff to promote and protect domestic industry, and congressionally financed internal improvements. Clay, John C. Calhoun, and John Quincy Adams helped fashion this new political agenda, which promised to meet the needs of all sections.

Until 1832 Congress was able to pass high tariffs without meeting much opposition, and in 1816 the Second Bank of the United States received a twenty-year charter. Only internal improvements, a critical element of the nationalist program, did not fare well. Although President James Madison approved the building of the National Road, he maintained that the Constitution did not authorize the use of federal funds for local projects.

The nationalism embodied in the American System hastened the demise of the Federalist party and ushered in the Era of Good Feelings, but the rise of a new party and indeed a new party system ultimately doomed this broad vision of the scope of the federal government. The victory of Andrew Jackson in the 1828 presidential election marked the emergence of newly articulated principles of laissez-faire, individualism, and sectional autonomy.

See also Clay, Henry; National Road.

AMERICAN WOMAN SUFFRAGE ASSOCIATION

This group resulted from the divisions in the women's rights movement of the late nineteenth and early twentieth centuries. It grew out of the New England Woman Suffrage Association, formed in 1868 to focus exclusively on obtaining the franchise. It was opposed to the policies of Elizabeth Cady Stanton and Susan B. Anthony, who broke with their abolitionist and Republican supporters, accusing them of emphasizing black civil rights at the expense of women's rights.

When Stanton and Anthony led the forma-tion of the National Woman Suffrage Association in 1869, the New England group reacted by creating the American Woman Suffrage Association (AWSA) to work for the inclusion of women in the Fifteenth Amendment. Founded in Cleveland in November 1869, the AWSA was led by such longtime abolitionists and women's rights advocates as Lucy Stone, Julia Ward Howe, and Thomas Wentworth Higginson. It accused the Stanton-Anthony group of diverting attention from the suffrage issue by scattering its efforts among broader social reforms. The AWSA convinced the Republican party to include a reference to women's suffrage in its 1872 convention platform, although the party did not pursue the issue later.

Putting aside their differences, the American and National Woman Suffrage associations united in 1890, forming the National American Woman Suffrage Association (NAWSA). It continued to seek the franchise, but it changed tactics, now arguing that giving women the right to vote would not be a threat to women's "separate sphere." With a boost from progressive reforms, changes in the workplace during World War I, and a final concerted drive, the NAWSA succeeded in 1919; the Nineteenth Amendment took effect in time for the 1920 election.

See also National American Woman Suffrage Association; National Woman Suffrage Association; Suffrage.

AMISTAD CASE

In 1839, fifty-three illegally purchased African slaves being transported from Cuba on the ship *Amistad* managed to seize control of the vessel. They killed two crew members and ordered the remainder to head for Africa. But by altering course at night, when the position of the sun did not reveal the ship's course, they sailed in a northeasterly direction. Eventually, the *Amistad* was intercepted by an American brig off the coast of Long Island. The two Spaniards who had enslaved the Africans were freed by the Americans, and the slaves were imprisoned. President Martin Van Buren, along with many newspaper editors, favored extraditing the Africans to Cuba. But abolitionists and other northern sympathizers won an American trial for them.

At a hearing in Hartford, a federal district court judge ruled that the Africans were not liable for their actions because they had been enslaved illegally. The case then proceeded on appeal to the Supreme Court, where former president John Quincy Adams, defending the Africans, argued that they should be granted their freedom. The Court agreed, ruling that since the international slave trade was illegal, persons escaping should be recognized as free under American law.

See also Slavery.

ANDERSON, MARIAN

(1902–), contralto. Eight years after Jackie Robinson broke the infamous color line in professional baseball, contralto Marian Anderson made her debut at New York's Metropolitan Opera House on January 7, 1955. Her successful performance of the role of Ulrica, the soothsayer, in Giuseppi Verdi's *Un ballo in maschera* paved the way for singers of color to appear at the Met and other major houses in the United States. According to *Variety*, "Miss Anderson — like Joshua, but more quietly — had fought the battle of Jericho and at last the walls had come tumbling down."

Anderson's Metropolitan performance came late in her career, after years of acclaim as a solo performer and a champion of racial equality. A native of Philadelphia, she studied and performed there prior to winning a competition that led to a performance with the New York Philharmonic Orchestra in 1925. She sang extensively in the United States and made her London debut in 1930. After performing in Europe, she sang in Town Hall in New York City to critical acclaim in 1935.

But it was a scheduled performance at Constitution Hall in Washington, D.C., in the spring of 1939 that brought Anderson's voice and her color to the attention of a broader public. Denied the right to perform in the hall by the Daughters of the American Revolution, Anderson, with the public support of Eleanor Roosevelt who resigned from the DAR in protest, sang instead to an audience of seventy-five thousand at the Lincoln Memorial. The public outcry over the DAR's action, particularly at a time when the United States was supporting the fight against Nazi doctrines of racial supremacy, brought this issue of justice to the forefront of public attention.

Anderson's Metropolitan Opera career lasted only one year, as her voice had lost some of its exceptional power by the time she appeared on the operatic stage in the United States. But she continued to perform works from the operatic repertoire along with lieder and African-American spirituals in concert.

Anderson performed at the White House for the Roosevelts in 1936 and again in 1939 for the king and queen of England. She performed for the Eisenhower family and served on the Advisory Committee on the Arts that contributed to the realization of the National Cultural Center in Washington, D.C., later named the John F. Kennedy Center for the Performing Arts. Anderson received the Presidential Medal of Freedom from John F. Kennedy in 1963 and a Congressional Gold Medal in 1978. She established a scholarship fund to assist young artists in 1972 and was the first recipient of New York City's Human Rights Award named in honor of Eleanor Roosevelt (1984). Anderson's reputation rests not only on the quality of her voice but also on the dignity with which she asserted her right to be heard.

Marian Anderson, *My Lord, What a Morning: An Autobiography* (1956); Kosti Vehanen, *Marian Anderson: A Portrait* (1941; rev. ed., 1970).

BARBARA L. TISCHLER

See also Music; Racial Desegregation.

ANGLO-AMERICAN RELATIONS

See America in the British Empire; Great Britain–U.S. Relations.

ANTHONY, SUSAN B.

(1820–1906), women's rights leader. Anthony was born in Adams, Massachusetts. Her father, a Quaker, was excluded from his meeting when he married her mother, a Baptist, and Susan, while much affected by her Quaker background, was also shaped by the proud independence this exclusion gave her family. In the depression of 1837, the family's economic security was shaken, and Anthony became a teacher, the only profession open to middle-class women. She never married and was a lifelong self-supporting woman. Her most distinctive contribution to the early women's rights movement was her appreciation of the importance of economic independence to women's emancipation.

In 1851, while visiting in nearby Seneca Falls, New York, Anthony met Elizabeth Cady Stanton, who had organized the first women's rights convention in 1848. Together they led the women's rights movement for the next half century. They first tried to organize a women's temperance society, but that reform proved too church-bound for their feminist concerns. In 1854, they turned to the creation of a women's rights movement per se. While Cady Stanton wrote articles and declarations to legislatures, Anthony discovered her own special genius, the organization of women into a sustained political movement. From 1854 to 1860, she circulated petitions demanding married women's rights to property, wages, and the custody of their children in the event of a divorce, and all women's rights to the suffrage. In 1860, all but the vote were secured by New York's landmark Married Women's Property Act.

The Civil War and its aftermath had a tremendous impact on Anthony and Cady Stanton. At first they believed that women's rights agitation should be suspended during the crisis. Indefatigably active, however, they organized the National Women's Loyal League to demand the constitutional abolition of slavery (and incidentally the emancipation of women). After the war, they expected that congressional Republicans would enfranchise women along with the freedmen, but were horrified to discover that the Fourteenth and Fifteenth Amendments did not give women the vote. In response, they severed their ties with old abolitionist allies and organized an independent woman suffrage society, an action with which many other women's rights leaders disagreed.

Without a family to divide her interests and more inclined than Cady Stanton to dedicate herself to a single issue, Anthony spent the rest of her life working for the vote. Believing that women should be enfranchised by federal, not state action, she annually pressed woman suffrage on Congress. As the range of women's public activities grew, she educated college women, "social purity" activists, and women's club members in the necessity of gaining the vote. To this end, she effected an alliance of sorts with the dynamic leader of the Woman's Christian Temperance Union, Frances Willard. This conflicted with the militant secularism of Cady Stanton, and though their personal bond remained strong, their activities diverged in their final years.

Anthony did not live to see the constitutional enfranchisement of women, but she had helped establish the conditions for victory. She set aside old hurts and encouraged the reunification of the suffrage movement in 1890. She nurtured a second generation of suffrage leaders, treating them virtually as kin. So totally did she merge her personal fate and that of the suffrage movement that dedication to "the cause" and love of "Miss Anthony" became indistinguishable. In 1900, she retired from the presidency of the National American Woman Suffrage Association, but remained active to the end. The respect accorded her was even stronger after her death, and devotees honored her memory long after the vote had been won and the names of other suffrage leaders forgotten.

Ida Husted Harper, *The Life and Work of Susan B. Anthony,* 3 vols. (1898–1908); Alma Lutz, *Susan B. Anthony: Rebel, Crusader, Humanitarian* (1959).

ELLEN CAROL DuBois

See also Feminist Movement; Married Women's Property Acts; National American Woman Suffrage Association; National Woman Suffrage Association; Stanton, Elizabeth Cady; Suffrage; Willard, Frances.

ANTICOMMUNISM

Anticommunism dominated American domestic politics in the late 1940s and 1950s, when it was transformed by the cold war from a right-wing to a mainstream ideology. It was composed of many strands, each with its own definition of the communist menace and its own formula for combating it. The American Communist party also had a hand in shaping the opposition it encountered. Although never a serious threat to the nation's security, the party's ideological submission to the Soviet Union and its penchant for clandestine activities seemingly justified the campaign against it. But the scope of that campaign went far beyond the needs of national security. Political conservatives took advantage of the party's association with a wide range of social reforms to mount an attack on the entire Left and on the legacy of the New Deal.

The social unrest that followed World War I coincided with the founding of the Communist party and precipitated the first wave of explicit anticommunism, the red scare of 1919–1920. This crackdown, like earlier outbreaks of political repression, focused on foreigners and labor unions. Immigration officials rounded up and tried to deport thousands of foreign-born radicals, and many employers used red-baiting to break strikes. The repression succeeded, and, during the 1920s, neither the American Communist party nor the rest of the Left had any significant influence.

But in the following decade, the onset of the Great Depression and the rise of Adolf Hitler spurred the party's growth. In accordance with an international Communist policy known as the Popular Front, the party tried to create a broad coalition against fascism. By muting its revolutionary rhetoric and supporting President Franklin D. Roosevelt and the New Deal, it attracted many middle-class idealists. Others joined the party to organize labor unions or stop Hitler. As a result, it was easy for right-wing opponents of the social changes of the 1930s to attack them as a Communist plot. But such charges had little impact. Many Americans, though never tempted to become Communists themselves, nonetheless tolerated the party.

That toleration disappeared in 1939 when, as a result of the Nazi-Soviet pact, the Communist party opposed Roosevelt's foreign policy and the Popular Front disintegrated. Liberals, who until then had defended Communists against the Right, turned against the party themselves, transforming anticommunism into a more widespread enterprise. Labor unions, universities, private organizations, and governments at every level ousted Communists from their ranks. A broader purge would certainly have occurred had Hitler's invasion of Russia in June 1941 not changed the Soviet Union into an American ally.

The coming of the cold war resuscitated domestic anticommunism and made it central to American politics. Because of the Communist party's connection to the Soviet Union, it was now seen as a threat to national security. A consensus developed based on several key assumptions: that all Communists owed their primary loyalty to Moscow; that they unblinkingly followed the party line; and that they would, whenever possible, work to subvert the American system. There was just enough substance to these charges to make it possible for this otherwise unrealistic image of American Communism to gain currency and fuel the demand for its exposure and elimination.

Although the campaign against communism took place on every level, the most effective initiatives came from the federal government. In 1947, the Truman administration promulgated a loyalty-security program that barred Communists or people who associated with Communists from government jobs. At the same time, the Department of Justice brought criminal prosecutions to bear on the party. It tried to deport foreign-born Communists and, in 1948, indicted and convicted the party's top leaders under the Smith Act, a 1940 law prohibiting the "teaching and advocating" of subversive doctrines. Several hundred Communists went to jail. Congressional committees, especially the House Un-American Activities Committee (HUAC), investigated supposed Communist subversion throughout American society. The Supreme Court, despite the serious constitutional issues involved, placed few restrictions on the anticommunist campaign. This official activity legitimated a witch-hunt. Politicians, abetted by sympathetic journalists and other interested parties, used the charge of Communist infiltration to implement agendas that often bore little or no relation to national security.

As the anticommunist campaign spread, the civil liberties of many people were threatened. This occurred primarily because of the widespread belief that communism so endangered the nation's security that the rights of individuals, especially of those supposed to be Communists, could be ignored. The structure of the anticommunist campaign, with its two-stage procedure of first exposing and then punishing alleged subversives, diffused responsibility for the repression. Official authorities like HUAC and the FBI usually handled the first stage by identifying the tainted individuals, and employers usually handled the second by firing them.

The party's insistence on secrecy made the exposure of its members the central feature of the anticommunist crusade. Because Communists had been part of a larger political movement that encompassed an entire constellation of left-wing causes and organizations, investigators assumed that all participants in the larger movement belonged to the party as well. Reactionary and overzealous investigators expanded the definition of what constituted a communist activity until it came to include anything from appreciating the paintings of Pablo Picasso to speaking out for the Bill of Rights.

Anticommunism was used for partisan purposes as well. The Republican party sought to capitalize on a few cases of alleged Communist infiltration of the New Deal. Ambitious politicians like Joseph R. McCarthy asserted that the Democrats had been "soft" on communism and had "lost" China after the war. There was no truth in these charges, but they put the Democrats on the defensive and, especially after the Korean War broke out in June 1950, made them afraid to challenge the anticommunist crusade and the abuses that accompanied it.

By the late 1950s, the furor had subsided. Zealots and opportunists like McCarthy had given anticommunism a bad name. And it was clear that the enfeebled and internally divided Communist party was no threat to national security. But the crusade had taken a toll. Not only had thousands of people lost their jobs, but political dissent had almost disappeared — an ironic result at a time when the United States was combating communism throughout the world in the name of freedom and democracy.

David Caute, *The Great Fear: The Anti-Communist Purge under Truman and Eisenhower* (1978); Kenneth O'Reilly, *Hoover and the Un-Americans* (1983).

ELLEN W. SCHRECKER

See also Alger Hiss Case; Army-McCarthy Hearings; Cold War; Communist Party; Conservatism; Federal Bureau of Investigation; House Un-American Activities Committee; John Birch Society; McCarthy, Joseph R.; Oppenheimer, J. Robert; Radicalism; *Rosenberg* Case; *Sacco-Vanzetti* Case.

ANTIFEDERALISTS

The Antifederalists were persons who opposed ratification of the U.S. Constitution in 1787–1788. This group had been known during the Revolution as Federalists, because they favored a federation of relatively autonomous states rather than the more centralized system advocated by the Nationalists. During the debate over the Constitution, however, the Nationalists began calling themselves Federalists and their opponents became known as Antifederalists.

The Antifederalists conceded that the central government needed more power than it had under the Articles of Confederation, but they argued that the Framers of the Constitution had gone too far, giving the president too much power, setting up federal courts that would encroach on the more responsive local system, and creating a Congress so small that it would exclude humbler officeholders and make it difficult for politicians really to know or represent their large constituencies. In the end, they predicted, the state governments would wither away, leaving a national government so removed from local conditions that it would have to rule by force rather than consent. In seeking to insulate national decision making from the tyranny of local majorities, the Antifederalists argued, the Framers had opened the door to another kind of tyranny, in which centralized power would be expanded and abused.

The Antifederalists seem to have had about the same number of adherents as the Federalists, but they were weak in urban areas and as a group had far less influence and political sophistication. Also, they were in the difficult position of acknowledging the need for changes in the Articles of Confederation while objecting to the particular changes proposed. Finally, partly by luck and partly through the Federalists' skill, eight states (out of the necessary nine) had already ratified the Constitution by the time the states controlled by the Antifederalists began their debates. In the end, only Rhode Island and North Carolina voted against ratification. The one point on which the Antifederalists prevailed was the need for a set of constitutional amendments to guarantee individual liberties; their arguments helped ensure the prompt passage of the Bill of Rights soon after the new Congress convened.

See also Ratification of the Constitution.

ANTI-IMPERIALIST LEAGUE

The Anti-Imperialist League was founded in November 1898 to oppose America's territorial expansion, especially the acquisition of the Philippine Islands. In October 1899, the original organization became the New England chapter of a national American Anti-Imperialist League, based in Chicago.

The league opposed the annexation of Hawaii, the passage of the peace treaty ending the Spanish-American War (which included the United States' acquisition of the Philippines), and the military campaign against the Filipino rebels. It pressed its case through meetings, petitions, pamphlets, and speeches. Most league members favored American economic expansion, but they argued that the country's economic goals could be better achieved through free trade than through political domination. Imperialism, they maintained, was unjust, ineffective, and unnecessary. They drew a dramatic

contrast between America's proud history as the land of liberty and its brutal repression of the Filipinos' struggle for independence. Such militaristic tyranny, they argued in their national platform, would ultimately have repercussions at home as well, eroding the country's "fundamental principles and noblest ideals."

The league had a diverse membership, including such respected public figures as Carl Schurz, Charles Francis Adams, Mark Twain, and E. L. Godkin, but it failed to develop a mass following. Its own fragmentation became evident in the election of 1900, when members found themselves unable to agree on whether to support or oppose the reelection of President William McKinley. By 1901, with McKinley back in office and the collapse of Emilio Aguinaldo's resistance in the Philippines, the Anti-Imperialist League had lost its significance, although the concerns it articulated about America's role as a world power would recur over the succeeding decades.

See also Expansion, Continental and Overseas.

ANTI-MASONS

The Anti-Masonic party, the first third-party movement in the United States, arose in response to the disappearance of William Morgan, shortly after his release on September 12, 1826, from a Canandaigua, New York, jail. Morgan had threatened to publish a book divulging the secrets of Freemasonry; opponents of the order asserted that a conspiracy among Masons had led to his arrest on trumped-up charges and subsequently to his being kidnapped and murdered.

The Anti-Masonic movement grew rapidly, drawing its initial following from farmers and skilled craftsmen — many of them with ties to evangelicalism and the temperance movement. They maintained that the Masonic order's secrecy, rituals, and aristocratic character posed a threat to republican democracy. Anti-Masonry also provided a vehicle for rural people to express their antipathy to the cities, and for ordinary people to voice their resentment of the powerful leaders, many of them Masons, who dominated the nation's public affairs. From western New York, the movement spread through New England, the Mid-Atlantic states, and Ohio and Michigan. Anti-Masons elected a governor of Rhode Island in 1833, controlled Vermont and Pennsylvania for several years, and played a significant part in local politics in both Massachusetts and New York.

In 1831, the Anti-Masonic party nominated William Wirt to run for president; in the process, it became the first American political party to select a presidential candidate by means of a national convention and the first to adopt an official party platform. Wirt carried only one state (Vermont) in 1832, but the party continued to grow, offering an increasingly general program of reform. As it expanded, it came to be dominated by new members more impelled by personal ambition or by a general opposition to the Jacksonian Democrats than by Anti-Masonry. At its second and final convention (1835), the Anti-Masonic party approved a slate for 1836 identical to that of the new Whig party, and thereafter it disappeared into the Whig coalition.

During its brief career, however, Anti-Masonry had played an important part in northeastern politics and had helped launch the careers of such leaders as William Lloyd Garrison, William H. Seward, Thurlow Weed, and Thaddeus Stevens.

See also Elections: 1832; Fraternal Societies; Third Parties.

ANTI-SALOON LEAGUE

Congregationalist minister and temperance activist Howard Hyde Russell started the Anti-Saloon League of Ohio in 1893. One of his recruits was Wayne Wheeler, a recent graduate of Oberlin who became the organization's chief administrator for a quarter of a century. The Ohioans merged with a similar group in Washington, D.C., to form the national Anti-Saloon League in 1895.

Under Wheeler's leadership, the league focused on one issue at a time, avoiding partisanship: its unofficial motto was "It is better to be united in a bad fight than divided in a good one." It won prominence when it helped unseat

Myron Herrick, Ohio's Republican governor and one of the league's foes, in 1905. The league organized at the grass-roots level, working through churches and carefully questioning politicians about their views on temperance and then endorsing or opposing them accordingly, no matter what their stands on other issues, their party affiliation, or their progressivism. Unlike other such groups, the Anti-Saloon League worked with the two major parties rather than backing the small Prohibition party.

Wheeler and the Anti-Saloon League had considerable national influence. The league concentrated on lobbying legislatures on behalf of antiliquor laws and were especially successful in the South. Wheeler helped draft both the Eighteenth Amendment, which enacted national Prohibition in 1919, and the Volstead Act, which created the machinery to enforce it. The league's lobbying contributed to the passage of these measures, and its resources defended them in the courts. But when the Democrats nominated the antiprohibition Alfred E. Smith, governor of New York, for president in 1928, the league became tied more closely to the Republican party. With the death of Wheeler, the rise of Franklin D. Roosevelt, and the end of Prohibition in 1933, the Anti-Saloon League faded in importance.

See also Prohibition and Temperance; Volstead Act.

ANTISLAVERY MOVEMENT

See Abolitionist Movement.

ANTITRUST MOVEMENT

To the average American in the last two decades of the nineteenth century, economic and political life seemed to be moving out of control. In a country that valued independent entrepreneurs, rural self-sufficiency, and middle-class religious values, politics seemed to be growing corrupt and opportunities for leading a morally satisfying life were becoming fewer. Economic power was clearly concentrating into small groups that were not open to the average citizen. A feeling of impotence in the face of these perceptions led to numerous movements for reform; antitrust was one of these.

Trusts had emerged as sensible ways of rationalizing economic life. Basic industries needed dependable supplies, means of transportation, markets, and banking connections. Competing local, state, and federal jurisdictions interfered with efficient business practice without providing firm legal guidelines specifying which practices were illegal, unethical, or merely inevitable. In order to survive fierce competition after the Civil War, businesses were soon negotiating agreements that froze competitors out of markets and enabled surviving firms to raise prices. Certain companies, such as Standard Oil, set the pace: ruthlessly buying out or forcing out its competition in the production of oil, it was soon in a position to charge whatever it wanted for its products. Independent businesses and consumers were both at risk. Industries that dealt with the company, most obviously the railroads, especially felt threatened, for so large a customer could intimidate those who supplied it with goods or services. Politicians soon got the message that something had to be done or the American way would be in danger.

Agitation against the trusts grew in the 1880s and resulted in the Sherman Antitrust Act (1890). Its first two provisions made illegal "every contract, combination in the form of trust or otherwise, or conspiracy, in restraint of trade or commerce among the several States, or with foreign nations," and declared that "every person who shall monopolize, or attempt to monopolize . . . any part of the trade or commerce among the several States, or with foreign nations," was guilty of a misdemeanor. The law was vague and unclear, and never defined what a "trust" or a "monopoly" was. It seemed yet another example of congressional irresponsibility, substituting rhetoric and ritual for meaningful reform. The courts soon made hash of any effective application: cases against the whiskey and sugar trusts were thrown out. The pattern of many reforms of the Progressive Era was being set: economic forces led to problems unknown a few decades earlier; agitation by those who were hurt in some way led to political debate and the enactment of a statute; and the courts, in their leisurely way, made sure that few businesses suffered in practice. In America, economic activity had divine sanction in all but the most egregious cases, and the protection of property took legal precedence over any sense of damage to the community as a whole.

Theodore Roosevelt, like most Americans, was both proud and fearful of successful trusts. They represented something new and native in modern life and were premonitions of a wider American role in world affairs. To him, some trusts were good and some were bad. Good trusts were run by gentlemen who were often his friends and contributors to Republican campaigns; with their capital concentrations and huge markets they could pour new products into an ever greater democracy: electric lights, farm machinery, and automobiles, to select almost at random, were on the way, promising a more bountiful life for all. Bad trusts were those whose leaders were greedy financiers interested in private profit regardless of consequences, thus undermining the public sense of moral and decent behavior.

Roosevelt was no radical, but he knew when conditions were getting out of hand. Eager for favorable publicity and preferring a conservative approach that would preempt a more destructive, radical reform, he authorized his attorney general in 1902 to file suit against a huge and growing railway trust, the Northern Securities Company. In 1904, in a narrow 5–4 vote, the Supreme Court backed him up, effectively overruling its own earlier decisions and issuing a significant public warning against certain industrial combinations. Businessmen, always easily shocked, were publicly outraged at such restrictions on their liberties; the public seemed delighted. In practice, the impact was mostly cautionary and journalistic: the Court in effect had warned businessmen to be careful. The decision also encouraged numerous articles by muckrakers eager to expose the "money trust," the "meat trust," the "patent medicine trust," and the rest.

Roosevelt instituted a reasonable number of other prosecutions, and his successor, William Howard Taft, began even more. But few critics were happy, and in 1914 Woodrow Wilson asked for further controls on interlocking directorates and an interstate trade commission with enhanced regulatory authority especially over railways, as well as clearer definitions of what precisely was illegal. He won the Federal Trade Commission Act to regulate unlawful trade practices and the Clayton Antitrust Act, which tightened some of the loopholes in the Sherman Act. This legislation specifically prohibited pricing agreements that restrained trade, outlawed interlocking directorates in large corporations, and made it illegal for a firm to acquire stock in a competitor.

Once again, these reforms were more public relations than substance, and court interpretations gutted any meaningful effect. Little of substance occurred during the 1920s. Not until late in the New Deal, under the direction of Thurman Arnold, once one of antitrust policy's sharpest critics, did antitrust revive as an issue. It remained alive, well funded, and occasionally effective through the 1970s. In the 1980s, during the presidency of Ronald Reagan, public faith in antitrust reached an all-time low, with few prosecutions being initiated and others being abandoned. Even the vogue of the leveraged buyout, which threatened the independence of many industries throughout the economy, and the bad publicity surrounding the issuing of so-called junk bonds, failed to stir the public or the regulators to antitrust activity.

As America entered the 1990s, antitrust remained a possibility rather than an actuality in the minds of both politicians and businesspeople. In a world where competition often spoke Japanese or Korean, antitrust seemed almost quaint. Some of its victories, such as the one that broke up American Telephone and Telegraph, seemed quixotic at best, confusing consumers and raising the phone bills of most citizens, all in an effort to restrain a company that seemed to be a model of public service. But the mere existence of an antitrust division probably prevented numerous unhealthy combinations and modified the practice of many others. In a complex society, it plays a small but important role as a lingering progressive conscience, cautioning business leaders against excessive behavior.

Thomas K. McCraw, *Prophets of Regulation* (1984); H. B. Thorelli, *Federal Antitrust Policy: The Origination of an American Tradition* (1955).

ROBERT M. CRUNDEN

See also Federal Trade Commission; Muckrakers; Roosevelt, Theodore; Taft, William Howard; Wilson, Woodrow.

ARAB-U.S. RELATIONS

See Middle East–U.S. Relations.

ARCHITECTURE

From its colonial and Native American origins unto the present day, American architecture has been exceptionally complex, both in the multiple traditions from which it has drawn and in the variations of style and public response it has produced. Architecture has also been caught up in the commercial domain. Major commercial buildings — business blocks and department stores in the nineteenth century, office towers and shopping malls in the twentieth — dominate the public domain of most cities. There has been no official patronage of certain firms for governmental commissions. Instead architects compete for most jobs; they must sell their skills and new ideas to the public; and they constantly vie with builders, who still produce the bulk of new housing and commercial buildings in this country. Efforts to promote hegemonic styles and master architects, though continually asserted, have never fully prevailed.

When the first European settlers arrived in the New World, some two hundred nations of Native Americans had already developed their own architectural traditions. The pueblo, hogan, longhouse, and tipi remain evocative images. Likewise, the colonialists' Spanish mission and the clapboard-sided New England dwelling of the seventeenth century endure as romantic prototypes in many parts of the country, suggesting a synthesis of local cultures into an idealized homogeneous society — a recurring theme in American cultural history.

The New England and Spanish colonies at first required settlements to be grouped in towns, close to a central plaza or meetinghouse square for governmental and religious structures, reinforcing social and architectural homogeneity. In time the abundance of land and the social constraints of these societies spun off new settlements and eventually isolated farmsteads. All the same, architecture remained a significant social act that reinforced community ties, even in the sparsely settled southern colonies. The planning and construction of a major building, whether an aristocratic home or a parish church, involved considerable deliberation, time, and effort on the part of many people.

By the time of the Revolution the American colonies still had no trained architects. Journeymen carpenters designed and built most structures, but gentlemen amateurs often undertook their own estates, following the English tradition that regarded architecture as one of the refined arts. Both groups looked to English architectural books and builders' guides for counsel. They adapted the fashion of neoclassicism to their own circumstances, usually building in wood and simplifying the detailing in a style we have come to call Federal. Especially admirable was the work of Boston's Charles Bulfinch.

Thomas Jefferson envisioned his major architectural works — Monticello (1772, 1789–1809), the Virginia State Capitol (1785–1796), and the University of Virginia (1817–1826) — as prototypes for the new nation. Looking to Enlightenment ideals of social reform, Jefferson believed that the right environment could uplift minds and promote civic virtue. The nation's first professional architect, the English émigré Benjamin Latrobe, aspired to similar ideals, hoping that moral purpose would enhance professional prerogatives. He designed the Bank of Pennsylvania (1798–1800) and the Baltimore Cathedral (1804–1821), but he was even more appreciated for his engineering skills, most evident in the Philadelphia water system (1798–1801).

The early nineteenth century witnessed an extraordinary rate of urbanization, with a plethora of new banks, exchanges, public markets, and commercial buildings. Despite the absence of any form of public regulation, distinct districts appeared, including elegant blocks of colonnaded row houses and the first multifamily tenements and lodging houses. A greater homogeneity of styles was visible, in both dwellings and public buildings; yet variations in details, materials, and even the arrangement of blocks maintained the particularity of cities such as Savannah, Charleston, Baltimore, Boston, and Cincinnati.

Among the buildings that attracted the most attention were asylums — prisons, orphanages, almshouses, mental hospitals, and the like — now removed to the outskirts of cities where it was possible to have a carefully controlled environment. John Haviland's Eastern State Penitentiary in Philadelphia (1823–1826), with its radial arrangement of cell blocks around a central control station, was one of the first instances of American architecture influencing European design.

A belief in reform through the environment also fueled the park movement, beginning with the rural cemeteries of the 1830s and culminating in Frederick Law Olmsted's majestic Central Park (1857–1880). The parks provided a respite within the commercial city, a place designed for leisure, recreation, nature, and social intermixing. Olmsted, a major figure in American intellectual and reform circles, elaborated the idea of landscaped "parkways" to connect a coordinated park system, most notably the Emerald Necklace for the city of Boston, designed with Charles Eliot (1889). Some of Olmsted's numerous other commissions suggest the wide range of late-nineteenth-century residential settings which saw moral purpose in planned natural beauty: Riverside, Illinois (1868), a bucolic suburb outside Chicago; Riverside Drive, New York (1888); Stanford University (1888); and Vandergrift, Pennsylvania (1895), a planned factory town for the Apollo Steel Company.

What Olmsted accomplished in site planning, others parlayed into architectural design. A distinctive and original American architectural fashion — later named the Shingle Style — emerged in the suburban and resort work of such architects as Henry H. Richardson, William Ralph Emerson, and Willis Polk. Residences were self-consciously individualized, combining diverse materials and architectural elements with a rambling floor plan. Post–Civil War industrialization allowed this style to proliferate, with the factory production of building materials and ornament, inexpensive pattern books with abundant illustrations, and electric streetcars to facilitate commuting. Yet stylistic diversity persisted. These same decades also produced museums, libraries, and sumptuous homes in the manner of Renaissance palazzi or medieval castles — the most grandiose by Richard Morris Hunt and the firm of McKim, Mead, and White.

Business districts were being transformed by another architectural innovation, similarly the product of technological advances and artistic creation: the skyscraper. Beginning in the 1880s, architects and engineers in Chicago and New York began to experiment with new framing systems to achieve greater height, as well as an appropriate elevation for these taller buildings — at first only ten and then soon twenty stories high. The contrast among these buildings soon produced a new way of experiencing cities, captured in the term *skyline*, first used in *Harper's* in 1896 to describe Lower Manhattan. Louis H. Sullivan designed the most stunning compositions, clarifying a tripartite elevation, much like an enormous Greek column, and Daniel Burnham's name became synonymous with the corporate office, whereby scores of variations on a basic prototype were built in cities around the country.

At the turn of the century private business organizations prodded municipalities to build majestic civic centers. Washington, D.C., underwent such a change in 1902, epitomizing the fascination with comprehensive urban design. In San Francisco, Denver, Chicago, and dozens of other cities, large and small, the City Beautiful movement commissioned Beaux-Arts museums and libraries alongside new city halls for the governments espoused by progressive reformers.

Businesses undertook other major changes on their own initiative, generating new kinds of commissions for architects. In Detroit, Albert Kahn almost single-handedly transformed the American factory into a sprawling industrial plant for automobile assembly lines. John Nolen and Ernest Flagg experimented with planned industrial towns and model tenement buildings. Movie houses and theaters evoked new flights of fantasy, especially the creations of Rapp & Rapp, Thomas Lamb, and Joseph Urban. Art Deco or "moderne" detailing enlivened department stores and other buildings oriented toward consumers.

Architectural debate still focused on the proportions and style of the façade, hoping to find a "correct" formula. The diversity of taste and opinions became manifest in the 1922 competition for the Tribune Tower in Chicago. Over 250 entries were submitted, with the winning design a Gothic fantasy by Howells & Hood.

New York's zoning regulations of 1916 suggested the need to control the height and use of buildings, protecting the public interest and assuring investors of future stability. The result was a new skyscraper style in which a series of set-backs maximized light and air. As commercial buildings grew larger, they also accommodated more activities. This process of coordinated concentration culminated in three blocks of intricate spaces for varied uses at New York's Rockefeller Center (Reinhard & Hofmeister with Harvey Wiley Corbett and Raymond Hood, 1927–1935).

In 1932 a seminal exhibition, Modern Architecture, at New York's Museum of Modern Art sought to establish a new canon. This austere, functional approach, supposedly anonymous and oblivious to the traditions of place, came to be called the International Style. A minor part of the exhibition (Lewis Mumford was curator) alluded to housing reform, a central aspect of modernism in Europe. Under the impetus of the New Deal, the government produced a range of modern buildings, usually designed under the auspices of federal agencies, including the TVA complexes in Appalachia, WPA service buildings across the country, Greenbelt towns, and PWA housing projects — of which Oskar Stonorov and Albert Kastner's Carl Mackley Houses in Philadelphia (1932–1934) were the most ambitious.

At the end of World War II a cooler, more anonymous imagery characterized American skyscraper design, largely derived from the modernist aesthetic of Ludwig Mies van der Rohe. The "glass box" epitomized the corporate world of business, including architectural offices such as Skidmore, Owings, and Merrill. The latter firm produced Lever House in New York (1952), the Crown Zellerbach Building in San Francisco (1959), and the Hancock Center (1970) and the 104-story Sears Tower (1974) in Chicago.

Similar themes also characterized residential design. Developers platted winding streets for vast suburban enclaves in the 1920s. Such settlements often adhered to a historical style such as the Spanish or English colonial, as well as covenants and zoning restrictions that proscribed certain ethnic groups or commercial activities. Among the best-known planned communities were the Country Club District outside Kansas City (Edward Tanner for J. C. Nichols, 1922), Sunnyside Gardens in Queens (Stein & Wright for the City Housing Corporation, 1924–1928), and Radburn, New Jersey (Stein & Wright, 1928–1929). Critics admired the combination of architectural, social, and environmental controls, especially the separation of automobile and pedestrian thoroughfares and the distinctive shopping district.

Even more rationalized, large-scale development characterized architecture and building after World War II. The Urban Renewal Act of 1954 provided federal funds for acres of new luxury apartments, office buildings, and convention centers in downtown blighted areas. The prototypical suburb of Levittown, New York, used mass production techniques to produce thousands of identical versions of each year's model home. Entire new towns like Reston, Virginia, and Columbia, Maryland, orchestrated a mixture of housing types and recreational facilities. Victor Gruen's vast mall at Southland, outside Minneapolis (1956), brought suburban shopping and social life under one air-conditioned roof, with abundant parking all around.

The postwar era brought celebrity to several architects, the most revered being Frank Lloyd Wright. Beginning in the Midwest with his early-twentieth-century prairie houses and culminating with the Guggenheim Museum in New York (1956–1959), Wright's long career encompassed virtually every region and building type, as well as continual innovations in both technology and design. Two other "expressionistic" ar-

chitects of the era also deserve mention. Eero Saarinen's work involved monumental corporate structures, including the General Motors Technical Center outside Detroit (1948–1956) and the TWA Terminal at Kennedy Airport (1956–1962). Louis Kahn represents the more intellectual side of architectural heroism during the 1960s, both in his somewhat stirring but rather opaque statements and in his major commissions: the Richards Medical Research Building in Philadelphia (1957–1961), the Salk Institute at La Jolla (1959–1965), and the Kimball Art Museum in Fort Worth (1966–1972).

Architectural pluralism now became more pronounced than ever. As skyscrapers reached new heights, they displayed an extraordinary variety of colors and ornamental motifs. The reuse of historical buildings became a common spectacle — notably in "festival marketplaces" such as Boston's Quincy Market (built by Alexander Parris in 1826, adapted for the Rouse Company by Benjamin Thompson & Associates in 1974–1978). Robert Venturi's buildings and writings celebrated American popular culture in all its diversity.

Perhaps the most significant example of architecture in the 1980s was New York's Battery Park City. Stanton Eckstut's design guidelines, developed in 1979, broke from the modernist megastructure that had been proposed a decade earlier. Instead he looked to the existing city, adopting its most successful architectural elements, landscaped spaces, and street grid to provide a sense of continuity; a variety of architects and developers were then brought in, so that buildings would display a rich diversity of responses to the architectural controls. The result, in the best of the American architectural tradition, was both exuberant and well planned, romantic and modern.

William H. Jordy and William H. Pierson, Jr., *American Buildings and Their Architects*, 4 vols. (1972–1980); Leland M. Roth, *A Concise History of American Architecture* (1979); Gwendolyn Wright, *Building the Dream: A Social History of Housing in America* (1981).

GWENDOLYN WRIGHT

See also Balloon-Frame House; City Planning; Housing; Johnson, Philip; Levittowns; Pei, I. M.;

Suburbanization; Sullivan, Louis H.; Urbanization; Wright, Frank Lloyd.

ARMED FORCES

The most important historical influence shaping the armed forces of the United States has been the abruptness of their transition from a merely peripheral involvement in international politics to a center-stage role of dauntingly large responsibilities.

Through most of its history, the U.S. Army and the colonial forces that preceded it were not instruments of foreign policy but tools for the domestic task of protecting settlements against the North American Indians. When World War II broke out in Europe in 1939, the army was still mainly deployed for constabulary tasks, patrolling the Mexican border and policing colonial subjects in the Philippine Islands. Until nearly the end of the nineteenth century, the navy similarly was less an instrument of foreign policy than a device for showing the flag in support of private American business ventures around the world. Although the navy began to take on diplomatic significance sooner than the army, neither of the armed forces was prepared by its history for sudden elevation during World War II to international preeminence.

The military institutions of the United States have their roots in the militia systems of the British colonies before 1776. Because of dangers posed by the Indians and the rival colonial powers, all the colonies that were to form the United States except Quaker Pennsylvania compelled their citizens to become part-time soldiers under universal military service laws applying to males of appropriate age. (Even Pennsylvania created a voluntary militia in 1755 and made military service virtually compulsory in 1775.) The deficiencies of a part-time soldiery for campaigns extended in time or geography led to supplementing the militia with the British regular army, beginning on an important scale in 1755, early in the French and Indian War.

Thus the United States inherited from the colonial era a dual military tradition of citizen-soldiers and regulars. The United States established a standing army modeled on the British regulars, first in the Continental army of the revolutionary war, growing out of legislation of the Second Continental Congress of June 14, 1775. This army was almost completely disbanded by the Confederation Congress on June 2, 1784, but the next day Congress authorized the creation of a new, albeit small force that the government of the Constitution inherited in 1789 and that became the nucleus of the Regular Army. The United States also accepted the compulsory-service militia legacy, particularly with the Second Amendment to the Constitution, which went into effect in 1791.

For defense against foreign enemies, it was intended that the militia would be mobilized to reinforce the Regular Army, which remained small throughout the nineteenth century; it numbered fewer than twenty-five thousand as late as the eve of the Spanish-American War of 1898. Much of the time, however, Americans perceived the Regular Army and the militia less as complementing each other than as rivals. From the military dictatorship that followed the English Civil War, from the English Whig ideology that regarded standing armies as inherent threats to liberty, and from the memory of the vexatious quartering of British regulars in America after the French and Indian War, which helped precipitate the Revolution, American politics derived an anti-standing-army tradition.

But Indian troubles along with friction with Great Britain and France during the French Revolution and the Napoleonic Wars prevented the anti-standing-army tradition from prevailing altogether. Furthermore, the compulsory-service militia declined before the Civil War because a rhetorical preference for citizen-soldiers over professionals became an insufficient motive for enforcing universal military training once the Indian frontier had receded westward. The rivalry between citizen-soldiers and professionals remained alive, however, as volunteer militia companies sprang up all over the United States in the first half of the nineteenth century. These companies achieved a remarkable vitality, and their drill competitions became a vehicle for expressing rivalries among towns and cities before the heyday of organized athletics.

Possessing such military forces, both the secessionist and the loyal states had the means to begin the Civil War in 1861, the volunteer companies providing the core of both armies. They were later supplemented by conscription, in what became the first American war of mass armies, over 2 million men eventually serving in the Union forces and some 750,000 in the Confederate forces. The Regular Army of the United States, only about 16,000 strong when the Civil War began, found itself playing only an inconspicuous role in the war.

The role was not unimportant, however, for the Regular Army had been growing increasingly professional. The U.S. Military Academy at West Point, founded in 1802, had after the War of 1812 added to what was essentially an engineering curriculum a solid foundation of schooling in tactical practice and strategic thought. The West Point influence encouraged officers to continue their studies after graduation, and some visited Europe to observe armies there. By the Civil War, both armies were commanded, organized, and administered with considerable professional skill largely by officers drawn from the Regular Army.

After the war, the emphasis on educated professionalism as a criterion of officership intensified. Gen. William Tecumseh Sherman, commanding general of the army from 1869 to 1883, was a vigorous exponent of military education and encouraged the formation of schools for the various combat arms to advance the professional education of their officers beyond West Point's undergraduate curriculum.

The navy also took steps toward refining officer professionalism. At the U.S. Naval Academy, founded at Annapolis, Maryland, in 1845, the technical mastery of seamanship took priority over military study, which the navy had little need for until the Civil War. Its single-ship duels in the Quasi-War with France in 1798–1800 and the War of 1812, its commerce-raiding in the latter war, and its major peacetime function of showing the flag required little strategic or military insight. But the blockading and capturing of Confederate ports and, after the war, the first intimations of American participation in world politics provided the impetus for establishing the Naval War College at Newport, Rhode Island, in 1884.

The War College helped transform the navy from a loose collection of individual ships into coordinated squadrons organized around battleships and designed to contend for command of the seas against potential enemies. Although the navy could not yet challenge the preeminence of the British Royal Navy, its transformation had progressed far enough by 1898 to achieve spectacular successes in the war with Spain.

Although the army had preceded the navy in developing officer professionalism, by 1898 it was lagging behind. After the Civil War, it mostly reverted to its constabulary role and waged occasional small wars against the Indians. The closing of the frontier brought with it a sense of directionlessness. After the war with Spain, Secretary of War Elihu Root strove to reorganize the army for a role in advancing American world power, by improving the command system through the General Staff Act of 1903 and establishing the Army War College in Washington the same year. Nevertheless, the fact that large-scale participation in battle in World War I was delayed until its final six weeks suggests how little the army was prepared for its role on the world stage.

The navy had taken another step ahead of the army when the Naval Act of 1916 set the goal of building a navy second to none. The Washington Naval Treaty of 1922 gave international confirmation to the parity of the U.S. Navy with the British Royal Navy, with the Imperial Japanese Navy ranking a close third. Japanese dissatisfaction with this rank, however, was among the factors that led the American and Japanese navies to spend the 1920s and 1930s planning for a war for naval mastery of the Pacific. On the American side, a conspicuous feature of the planning was the rise in strategic importance it accorded to the U.S. Marine Corps; to wrest mastery of the western Pacific from the Japanese, numerous islands would have to be conquered to serve as intermediate bases, and to that end the marines made amphibious assault their specialty.

The performance of the armed forces in World War II was highly impressive, especially given the recency of their preparation for the exercise of first-rank military power. The marines assaulted the Pacific islands with exemplary efficiency. The navy operated effectively at distances no steam-powered navy had ever mastered. The Coast Guard, which in wartime moves from the Department of the Treasury into the navy, contributed much to antisubmarine warfare. The army, embarrassed by its performance in World War I, had engaged during the interwar years in economic mobilization planning that helped American industry become the economic bulwark of the entire Allied coalition.

For all that, the American performance in World War II also displayed difficulties inherited from the nation's military past, some of which still persist. The historic tensions over the appropriate orientation of the army gave it a strategy and a force structure not entirely consistent with each other. The strategy called for an overwhelmingly powerful invasion of German-occupied Europe as early in the war as possible. After that strategy was invoked on June 6, 1944, however, an army still designed primarily for mobility found itself not well suited for prolonged large-scale combat and for absorbing heavy casualties, and the German army was able to hold the Americans and British to lengthy stalemates.

The tendency for ground fighting to degenerate into costly deadlock encouraged experimentation with the Army Air Forces' offer of a cheaper way to victory through strategic bombing of the enemy's economic and urban centers. Such bombing against Germany was remarkably successful when in 1944–1945 it was concentrated on the synthetic petroleum industry, imposing a paralysis that would have compelled Germany to surrender even if it had not been invaded. But strategic bombing inevitably entailed the killing and maiming of civilians, contrary to the international law of war; and it hardened the national conscience, so that attacks on civilians became increasingly acceptable. By March 1945 the Army Air Forces were routinely bombing Japanese cities not only to eliminate particular industries but to wreak total destruction, a process that culminated in the atomic bombing of Hiroshima and Nagasaki in August 1945.

The atomic bombs precipitated Japan's surrender, so that American strategic bombing had produced a second triumph. Thus it is not surprising that when the postwar cry for demobilization rapidly broke up the armed forces that had peaked at some 12 million men and women at the close of the war, national security policy began to rely almost solely on atomic weaponry. In keeping with the resulting emphasis on air power, the U.S. Air Force became a separate service under the National Security Act of 1947, and an Air Force Academy was established in Colorado and an Air War College in Alabama. The three services were federated in the Department of Defense in 1949.

The post-1945 reliance on nuclear weapons yielded to the demonstration in the Korean War of 1950–1953 that such weapons were unsuitable for use in limited wars. Accordingly "conventional" military strength was revived at levels that have been maintained ever since except for expansion during the Vietnam War of 1965–1973. By 1989, the army had 800,000 active soldiers with 850,000 in the National Guard and reserves; the navy, 590,000 active sailors with 200,000 reserves; the marines, 190,000 members with 50,000 reserves; and the air force, 600,000 active personnel with 275,000 in the Air National Guard and reserves.

Yet the conventional forces did not fight either the Korean or the Vietnam War with exemplary success. The army in particular has never resolved its historic dilemma of whether to prepare mainly for large-scale war or for smaller campaigns. After its experience in World War II, it was restructured for a sustained struggle in Europe against the Soviet Union; but the wars it actually fought were of a different kind. Meanwhile the rapid diversification of sizes and varieties of nuclear weapons encouraged planning for their limited, "tactical" use, though this entailed the danger of escalation into a nuclear holocaust.

By 1990 the armed forces were faced with a very different predicament: the cold war seemed to be ending. If it did, there would end also the central purpose that had sustained them for more than a generation, the focus on the Soviet Union as a major military rival. Should this central purpose be lost, it would be only the latest in a series of nearly revolutionary dislocations for the armed forces since the 1940s.

These dislocations had included the full integration of blacks in the armed forces. After serving in the colonial and revolutionary war forces, blacks had been officially excluded from the army and the marines — though tolerated by the navy — until the Civil War. Then they served in segregated units, often relegated to menial labor, until an executive order of President Harry S. Truman on July 26, 1948, integrated the armed services; it was not completely implemented, however, until the Korean War.

The dislocations also encompassed the acceptance of women into the armed forces. Women were admitted as nurses and as navy "yeomen (F)" to the number of 11,000 in World War I, and on a much larger scale but still in auxiliary units in World War II, reaching a peak strength of 271,000 out of some 12 million. By 1989 women numbered 251,000 of the active-duty personnel and were almost fully integrated, although still for the most part barred from combat. The rapid expansion of their numbers coincided with the end of the military draft on January 27, 1973, which signified yet another jarring change. Accustomed since 1940 to drawing men from the compulsory Selective Service System, the armed forces now had to learn how to recruit enough volunteers. This change still causes debate reaching to the fundamental issue of the responsibilities of democratic citizenship.

Amid much change, however, one important fact remains. The fears of the Founding Fathers that the military must be a threat to liberty have never materialized. In the early years, such fears revolved around a military coup d'état. After World War II, the fears were more subtle, envisaging a subversion of democracy through the immensely enhanced influence of a permanently large military establishment in alliance with the industrial interests that supplied it. Throughout, however, the armed forces have remained faithful to an apolitical acceptance of civilian supremacy. Never have they posed a substantial threat to a stable democracy.

Allan R. Millett and Peter Maslowski, *For the Common Defense: A Military History of the United States, 1607–1983* (1984); Geoffrey Perret, *A Country Made by War: From the Revolution to Vietnam — the Story of America's Rise to Power* (1989).

RUSSELL F. WEIGLEY

See also Conscientious Objection; Conscription; Draft Riots; Mahan, Alfred Thayer; Nuclear Weapons: Origins and Legacy; *and entries for individual wars, military leaders.*

ARMORY SHOW

The Armory Show, the informal title of the International Exhibition of Modern Art held at New York's Sixty-ninth Regiment Armory in 1913, was the country's most influential exhibit of painting and sculpture. Attended by 300,000 in New York and at subsequent traveling exhibits in Chicago and Boston, its purpose was to introduce the work of antiacademic artists from both sides of the Atlantic "usually neglected by current shows."

One-third of the sixteen hundred pieces were by European artists, and it was the avant-garde nature of these European entries rather than the largely conventional American majority that was responsible for the exhibit's controversial reception and historic impact. The Armory Show surveyed modern movements that included impressionism, postimpressionism, fauvism, and cubism. It provoked furious debate. Marcel Duchamp's cubist painting, *Nude Descending a Staircase,* inspired the much-quoted comparison to "an explosion in a shingle factory," and in Chicago effigies of Henri Matisse and Constantin Brancusi were hanged.

Exposing American provincialism, the Armory Show introduced the public to modernism and spawned American collecting on an international level. The exhibit's further effects, however, surfaced only gradually. Most modern art remained suspect in the eyes of the public. Museums resisted housing it, and another thirty years would pass before it had much impact on American painting and sculpture.

See also Painting and Sculpture.

ARMS

See Dueling; Guns and Gun Control.

ARMSTRONG, LOUIS

(1900–1971), trumpeter and singer. A product of New Orleans's rich musical culture, Armstrong took up the cornet in his early teens and was soon playing in parades with the Colored Waifs' Home band and in local nightspots. His tutor on the instrument was Joseph "King" Oliver, who later asked Armstrong to join his Creole Jazz Band in Chicago in 1922. Armstrong made his first recordings with this ensemble the following year, but since he played second cornet to Oliver's lead, he rarely can be heard soloing.

In 1924 Armstrong married pianist Lillian Hardin and went to New York to join Fletcher Henderson's orchestra. With this ensemble he established himself as a brilliant soloist whose virtuosity and rhythmic dynamism set new standards for instrumental jazz performance. His reputation increased through a series of recordings made in Chicago between 1925 and 1928 with groups of New Orleans musicians variously titled Louis Armstrong's Hot Five or Hot Seven. On such records as *Struttin' with Some Barbecue, Potato Head Blues* (both 1927), and *West End Blues* (1928), the young Armstrong displayed the hallmarks of a fully formed trumpet style and a mature musical conception; his purity of tone, dazzling speed, daring breaks, rhythmic drive, and startling imagination were unprecedented and, to some extent, remain unequaled.

Armstrong also emerged as a singer on the Hot Five and Hot Seven recordings, a role that he would assume more and more in the years ahead. When fronting his own orchestra in the 1930s and early 1940s, or when appearing with his All Stars, a small, New Orleans–styled combo, from 1947 until 1971, Armstrong alternated between singing in his characteristically husky voice and taking trumpet solos with the same penetrating sound and rhythmic assurance that marked his recordings of the twenties.

Gradually Armstrong — known to many by his nickname "Satchmo" — developed his stage persona as a genial performer of popular songs ("Mack the Knife," "Hello, Dolly") and New Orleans standards. This image eclipsed his earlier radical innovations in jazz. But Armstrong himself may not have seen a great dividing line in his career nor perceived a conflict between the roles of artist and entertainer. Coming from a city whose musicians traditionally valued direct emotional expression more than innovation for its own sake, and from a generation of jazz mu-

sicians who functioned, by and large, as popular entertainers, Armstrong carved out a career typical for his place and time. The extraordinary aspects came from the profound impact he made on other musicians, the joy he brought to listeners the world over, and the sincerity, dignity, and love of life he conveyed in all his performances.

Louis Armstrong, *Satchmo: My Life in New Orleans* (1954; reprint, 1986); Max Jones and John Chilton, *Louis: The Louis Armstrong Story, 1900–1971* (1971).

MARK TUCKER

See also Jazz; Music.

ARMY-McCARTHY HEARINGS

The Army-McCarthy hearings dominated national television from April to June 1954. A subcommittee of the Senate Committee on Government Operations was seeking to learn whether Senator Joseph R. McCarthy had used improper influence to win preferential treatment for Pvt. G. David Schine, a former member of the senator's staff who had been drafted. McCarthy countercharged that the army was trying to derail his embarrassing investigations of army security practices through blackmail and intimidation.

The congressional hearings were among the first to be televised, and they captured national attention because of McCarthy's notoriety. The camera made clear his methods and manner, greatly weakening his popular support and leading to his censure by the Senate on December 2, 1954.

The word *McCarthyism* has become synonymous with the practice of publicizing accusations of treason and disloyalty with insufficient evidence.

See also Anticommunism; McCarthy, Joseph R.

ARNOLD, BENEDICT

(1741–1801), Continental army general and traitor. Arnold was born in Norwich, Connecticut, the son of a merchant, who had married into Connecticut aristocracy but failed in business, took to strong drink, and was unable to support the family. Apprenticed to his mother's cousins, Arnold nevertheless managed to free himself to fight in the French and Indian War. He then entered business for himself.

The American Revolution tapped Arnold's capacities for leadership and gave him the fame he craved, but it also provided an outlet for his greed and selfishness. He joined in the war as head of a Connecticut militia company, and upon receiving news of the Battles of Lexington and Concord, he marched the group to Boston. But not wanting to join in a siege, he participated instead in the American attempt to capture Fort Ticonderoga. It was Ethan Allen and his Green Mountain Boys, however, who took the fort, depriving Arnold of the glory a victorious command would have brought.

Arnold's next effort demonstrated his strong will and immense talent as a leader. The expedition against Canada, one part of which he led, would have taxed the abilities of any man. The main part of the drive carried his force of about a thousand men through the Maine wilderness, hampered by driving rainstorms, flooding rivers, and nearly impassable forests. They reached Quebec and joined in an unsuccessful assault on the night of December 30, 1775, under Gen. Richard Montgomery. Arnold was wounded in the battle and forced to retire.

When, in 1777, British general John Burgoyne led his forces into the New York wilderness, Arnold was with Horatio Gates, the commander of the opposing American army. Arnold did not get along with Gates, and after expressing his disapproval of the general's plans, he was ordered to the rear. He did not remain there for long but joined in the Battle of Bemis Heights on October 7, 1777. Here he performed brilliantly with the dash and recklessness that made his troops love him.

Wounded again, he was given command of Philadelphia in June 1778 after the British evacuation of the city. There his combativeness embroiled him in clashes with other commanders, and his acquisitiveness led to corruption in his command. A court-martial followed, and he was in effect cleared of most of the charges, though not all. Gen. George Washington issued a reprimand, which angered him and probably played a part in his decision to sell himself to the enemy.

Arnold, whose first wife had died, was married again, this time to nineteen-year-old Peggy Shippen of an important Philadelphia family. She took part in the conspiracy to betray West Point, where Arnold had taken command in August 1780. The plot had begun in Philadelphia the year before and was discovered in September 1780. Arnold first contacted the British in May 1779. His motives were personal, not political: he was greedy, always looking for money, and hard-pressed to keep up a style of life he could not really afford. He also resented what he took to be a lack of appreciation by Congress and the government of Pennsylvania, which questioned his administration of Philadelphia. He chose Joseph Stansbury, a Loyalist shopkeeper in Philadelphia, to convey his messages to the British general Sir Henry Clinton, who relied on Maj. John André, his adjutant general, to handle negotiations. Arnold's demands for payment varied, but in August 1780 Clinton agreed to £20,000 if Arnold's betrayal led to the capture of West Point and three thousand troops. The plot was discovered when André, carrying incriminating papers, was seized September 23, 1780, by New York militia near Tarrytown while he attempted to return from a meeting with Arnold. Arnold fled to General Clinton in New York City and an army he expected would honor his talents. He was disappointed, however, for he never received a major command. His new masters did not trust him.

After the war he lived for a short time in New Brunswick but went to England in 1791 where he died ten years later. Since 1780, Arnold's name has been synonymous in the United States with betrayal and treason.

James Thomas Flexner, *The Traitor and the Spy: Benedict Arnold and John André* (1953; 2nd ed., 1975); Carl Van Doren, *Secret History of the American Revolution* (1951).

Robert Middlekauff

See also Revolution.

ARTHUR, CHESTER A.

(1829–1886), twenty-first president of the United States. Born in Vermont, Arthur graduated from Union College in Schenectady, New York, and taught school before moving to New York City, where he was admitted to the bar in 1854.

An antislavery Whig, Arthur joined the Republican party at its birth. He was appointed engineer in chief on the New York governor's military staff in 1861 and then became quartermaster general of New York because of his honesty and efficiency. He served until the Republicans lost the governorship in 1862. After the Civil War, Arthur helped build Roscoe Conkling's political organization as collector of the Port of New York, where he was responsible for collecting two-thirds of the nation's tariff revenue. Arthur mastered the tariff laws and within the limits imposed by the spoils system brought some efficiency to the customhouse. Nevertheless, President Rutherford B. Hayes removed him from office in 1878, believing that partisan considerations were his central concern.

Out of office but not out of politics, Arthur became chairman of the New York Republican State Committee and in 1880 was nominated for the vice presidency to balance the ticket headed by James A. Garfield. The Republicans won the election, but after Garfield was assassinated, Arthur became president in September 1881.

To the surprise of his many detractors, Arthur was an able chief executive. In damning him as a mere machine politician, his critics ignored the fact that he was an intelligent man who had run the largest federal office in the country. Despite a tendency to procrastinate, Arthur grew in the presidency and was able to meet its demands. He never became a born-again civil service reformer, but preferred instead an efficient partisan government service to one selected by open competitive examinations. It took the Republican defeat in state and congressional elections in 1882 to induce him to support the Pendleton Civil Service Reform Act (1883), the most important legislation passed during his administration. Drawing on his expertise, Arthur condemned the existing tariff. But when he failed to convince Congress to make the 20 to 25 percent reduction his tariff commission advocated, he signed the aptly named "Mongrel" Tariff into law (1883). Arthur vetoed the outrageous pork-barrel rivers and harbors bill of 1882 (a thinly disguised raid on the Treasury), only to see Congress pass it over his veto. He signed legislation excluding Chinese laborers from the United States, supported appropriations to modernize the navy, and personally supervised a sumptuous refurbishing of the White House.

Arthur was a dandy in dress and a gourmand at the table, but he was neither happy nor healthy when president. He grieved over the death in 1880 of his wife and suffered the debilitating effects of Bright's disease, particularly after 1882. As part of his effort to hide his condition from the public, he did nothing to stop those striving to nominate him in 1884. Their efforts failed, however, partly because he lacked charisma and partly because he was too much of a spoils politician to win reform support, yet too sound an administrator to suit party regulars.

Justus D. Doenecke, *The Presidencies of James A. Garfield & Chester A. Arthur* (1981); Thomas C. Reeves, *Gentleman Boss: The Life of Chester Alan Arthur* (1975).

ARI HOOGENBOOM

See also Chinese Exclusion Act; Civil Service Reform; Elections: 1880; Tariff.

ARTICLES OF CONFEDERATION

(1781–1788), the first written constitution of the United States, superseded by the Constitution in 1788. From the beginning of the American Revolution, Congress felt the need for a stronger union and a government powerful enough to defeat Great Britain. During the early years of the war this desire became a belief that the new nation must have a constitutional order appropriate to its republican character. A fear of central authority inhibited the creation of such a government, and widely shared political theory held that a republic could not adequately serve a large nation such as the United States. The legislators of a large republic would be unable to remain in touch with the people they represented, and the republic would inevitably degenerate into a tyranny. To many Americans their union seemed to be simply a league of confederated states, and their Congress a diplomatic assemblage, representing thirteen independent polities.

The impetus for an effective central government lay in wartime urgency, the need for foreign recognition and aid, and the growth of national feeling. Altogether six drafts of the Articles were prepared before Congress settled on a final version in 1777. Benjamin Franklin wrote the first and presented it to Congress in July 1775. It was never formally considered. Later in the year Silas Deane, a delegate from Connecticut, offered one of his own, which was followed still later by a draft from the Connecticut delegation, probably a revision of Deane's.

None of these drafts contributed significantly to the fourth version written by John Dickinson of Pennsylvania, the text that after much revision provided the basis for the Articles approved by Congress. Dickinson prepared his draft in June 1776; it was revised by a committee of Congress and discussed in late July and August. The result, the third version of Dickinson's original, was printed to enable Congress to consider it further. In November 1777 the final Articles, much altered by this long deliberative process, were approved for submission to the states.

By 1779 all the states had approved it except Maryland, but prospects for acceptance looked bleak, because claims to western lands by other states set Maryland in inflexible opposition. Virginia, the Carolinas, Georgia, Connecticut, and Massachusetts claimed by their charters to extend to the "South Sea" or the Mississippi River. The charters of Maryland, Pennsylvania, New Jersey, Delaware, and Rhode Island confined those states to a few hundred miles of the Atlantic. Land speculators in Maryland and these other "landless states" insisted that the West belonged to the United States, and they urged Congress to honor their claims to western lands. Maryland also supported the demands because nearby Virginia would clearly dominate its neighbor should its claims be accepted. Eventually Thomas Jefferson persuaded his state to yield its claims to the West, provided that the

speculators' demands were rejected and the West was divided into new states, which would be admitted into the Union on the basis of equality with the old. Virginia's action persuaded Maryland to ratify the Articles, which went into effect on March 1, 1781.

Not all issues had been settled with ratification, however. A disagreement over the appointment of taxes forecast the division over slavery in the Constitutional Convention. Dickinson's draft required the states to provide money to Congress in proportion to the number of their inhabitants, black and white, except Indians not paying taxes. With large numbers of slaves, the southern states opposed this requirement, arguing that taxes should be based on the number of white inhabitants. This failed to pass, but eventually the southerners had their way as Congress decided that each state's contribution should rest on the value of its lands and improvements. In the middle of the war, Congress had little time and less desire to take action on such matters as the slave trade and fugitive slaves, both issues receiving much attention in the Constitutional Convention.

Article III described the confederation as "a firm league of friendship" of states "for their common defence, the security of their liberties, and their mutual and general welfare." This league would have a unicameral congress as the central institution of government; as in the past, each state had one vote, and delegates were elected by state legislatures. Under the Articles, each state retained its "sovereignty, freedom, and independence." The old weakness of the First and Second Continental Congresses remained: the new Congress could not levy taxes, nor could it regulate commerce. Its revenue would come from the states, each contributing according to the value of privately owned land within its borders.

But Congress would exercise considerable powers: it was given jurisdiction over foreign relations with the authority to make treaties and alliances; it could make war and peace, maintain an army and navy, coin money, establish a postal service, and manage Indian affairs; it could establish admiralty courts; and it would serve as the last resort on appeal of disputes between the states. Decisions on certain specified matters — making war, entering treaties, regulating coinage, for example — required the assent of nine states in Congress, and all others required a majority.

Although the states remained sovereign and independent, no state was to impose restrictions on the trade or the movement of citizens of another state not imposed on its own. The Articles also required each state to extend "full faith and credit" to the judicial proceedings of the others. And the free inhabitants of each state were to enjoy the "privileges and immunities of free citizens" of the others. Movement across state lines was not to be restricted.

To amend the Articles the legislatures of all thirteen states would have to agree. This provision, like many in the Articles, indicated that powerful provincial loyalties — and suspicions of central authority — persisted. In the 1780s — the so-called Critical Period — state actions powerfully affected politics and economic life. For the most part, business prospered and the economy grew. Expansion into the West proceeded and population increased. National problems persisted, however, as American merchants were barred from the British West Indies and the British army continued to hold posts in the Old Northwest, American territory under the Treaty of Paris. These circumstances contributed to a sense that constitutional revision was imperative. Still, national feeling grew slowly in the 1780s, although major efforts to amend the Articles in order to give Congress the power to tax failed in 1781 and 1786. The year after the failure of 1786, the Constitutional Convention met in Philadelphia and effectively closed the history of government under the Articles of Confederation.

Merrill Jensen, *The Articles of Confederation: An Interpretation of the Social Constitutional History of the American Revolution, 1774–1781* (1940); Jack N. Rakove, *The Beginnings of National Politics: An Interpretive History of the Continental Congress* (1979).

ROBERT MIDDLEKAUFF

See also Continental Congresses; Philadelphia Convention; Republicanism.

ARTS

See Architecture; Dance; Literature; Music; Painting and Sculpture; Theater.

ASHCAN SCHOOL

The Ashcan school of art evolved during the early years of the twentieth century in New York City. The core of the movement was formed by "the Eight" — Robert Henri, Arthur B. Davies, Maurice Prendergast, Ernest Lawson, William Glackens, Everett Shinn, John Sloan, and George Luks — a diverse group of painters opposed to academism who exhibited together in 1908. Another central figure, George Bellows, joined the movement later. Their rebellion against academic art led several to play key roles in organizing the iconoclastic Armory show (1913) and in founding the Society of Independent Artists (1917).

Conservative in style, the Ashcan paintings were revolutionary in content. Departing from the staid portraiture and genteel landscapes of the nineteenth century, the artists focused on urban scenes, particularly those exposing the shabbier aspects of city life. Their intent, however, was not muckraking social commentary but the portrayal of urban vitality. Four of the original members had begun their careers as newspaper illustrators, and their paintings exhibited the gritty realism, informality, and rapid execution of visual reportage. With such unprepossessing titles as *The Wrestlers, The Shoppers,* and *Hairdressers' Window, Sixth Avenue,* their paintings captured spontaneous moments in everyday events.

Also known as the New York Realists, they were reviled by critics as the "revolutionary black gang" and the "apostles of ugliness." The other, originally pejorative label — Ashcan school — became the standard term for this first important American art movement of the twentieth century.

See also Painting and Sculpture; Progressivism.

ASIA-U.S. RELATIONS

Since around 1500, the countries and peoples of Europe (and later the United States) and the rest of the world have met, collided, and influenced one another, in the process transforming not only themselves but also the international order. Both Americans and Asians have played major roles in this transformation.

When Americans achieved their independence, the new nation defined itself as an entity willing and capable of defending itself, as an economic system with expanding territorial and commercial horizons, and as a social order characterized by certain values and proclivities. It fitted into the international order also at various levels: it was a military presence in a world consisting of military powers, an economic organization participating in global commercial activities, and a culture exemplifying such principles as freedom and human rights in an international community that had lost a sense of cultural unity.

What was the relevance of Asia to such a nation? The countries of Asia had defined their own identities and their own world system. They were less military than economic entities; their armed power, compared with the West's, was designed primarily for maintaining domestic order, whereas their resources (population, minerals, agricultural products, manufactured goods) in combination surpassed those in Europe. Culturally, East Asian countries subscribed to a Confucian tradition, which, though it had gone through as much transformation as Christianity, provided legitimacy to political authority and social order. In other parts of Asia, Buddhism, Hinduism, and Islam played a similar role.

The West and the non-West came into more extensive contact in the late eighteenth century than earlier, and the contact deepened steadily thereafter. Western countries' superior military technology and organization enabled them to establish their outposts overseas; the Industrial Revolution facilitated, and also necessitated, the penetration of non-Western markets; and the new democratic ideology as well as the religious fervor that accompanied both the Industrial Rev-

olution and the Democratic Revolution led thousands of Westerners to travel and proselytize abroad to save non-Westerners from their "moral darkness."

The initial American encounter with Asia had little of the military character. The country's independence, security, or power did not depend on anything happening in Asia or on establishing some control in that part of the world. The United States did have a small squadron in Asian waters, and more ships were added as occasion demanded. In the mid-nineteenth century, American naval power impressed itself upon Chinese, Japanese, and Koreans, and already Hawaii was being developed as a key base. Still, the role of the gunboats was primarily to protect Americans in Asia — merchants, consuls, and missionaries — not to entrench American power in that part of the world. Rarely did Asians feel threatened by America, as distinguished from Britain, Russia, or France. The two expeditions to Japan undertaken by Commodore Matthew C. Perry (1853, 1854) may have been an exception, but they were diplomatic missions to persuade the Japanese to render assistance to shipwrecked American whalers and to consent to the coming of some American merchants. As such they were more an economic and a cultural phenomenon than a military, strategic one.

Americans from the very beginning were conscious of the economic opportunities in Asia. Initially their role was that of broker. American sailors and merchants took European goods to Asian ports and returned with teas, silks, and chinaware. There was little that the United States itself produced that could be marketed in Asia, and for this reason the American-Asian trade was never as important as that with other regions during most of the nineteenth century. Quick fortunes were made, to be sure, by New England merchants or by consular officials (Townsend Harris was a conspicuous example) who took advantage of the differential rates of exchange between gold and silver or invested heavily in the opium trade. But these were transient phenomena, and the trade with Asia was only a small fraction of America's overall commerce. Still, the lure of the Asian (especially Chinese) market was always there, and this, more than any strategic calculations, served to keep that part of the world alive in the American consciousness. Ultimately, this lure was part of the process of the West's industrialization, which increased its share of the world manufacturing output from 29 percent in 1800 to 86 percent in 1900, whereas Asia's declined from 57 to 10 percent. Here clearly was an opportunity not to be overlooked. Americans, either as shippers or as manufacturers, wanted to be part of the process that was creating a global economic system.

It was, nevertheless, in the cultural realm that the American presence in Asia became most conspicuous. Far more than as a potential market, Asian countries invited Americans culturally. Culture, defined anthropologically, refers to "structures of meaning" that serve to establish a community or social order among individuals. Why American culture produced men and women eager to traverse the oceans in order to transform other cultures is a fascinating question, and even more intriguing is the primacy of Asia in this endeavor. There was something in Asian culture that persuaded Americans that they had a mission to reach out there and help change it. Protestant missionaries constituted a constant stream going out to Siam, Burma, China, Japan, and Korea, and their number at the end of the nineteenth century amounted to over three thousand. They were joined by educators, scientists, explorers, and others who taught young men and women of Asia or served Asian governments as advisers. Precisely because the United States did not maintain a significant military or commercial presence in Asia, the thousands of private individuals educating Asian children, preaching Christianity, and advising local governments on projects ranging from the writing of a constitution to the building of a railway defined U.S.-Asian relations as primarily cultural. It cannot be said that they Americanized Asia; rather, they played a part in the Westernization of many Asian countries. Still, in such areas as women's education or in combating "feudal" customs like footbinding, concubinage, or idolatry, Americans in Asia made a crucial contribution.

So far the story has been unidirectional. The contact between America and Asia did not have as much impact upon the former as on the latter. This began to change in the last years of the nineteenth century, and in the present century America's destiny has become more and more affected by developments in, and activities by, Asian countries.

One already sees this in the Spanish-American War of 1898. Although originating in Cuba, the war involved the United States in the Philippines where insurgents were struggling for liberation from Spanish rule. American naval operations against the Spanish fleet in Manila made it virtually impossible for U.S. forces to stand aloof from internal events. Similarly, political crises in Hawaii following the overthrow of the monarch in 1893, coupled with Japanese ambitions there (Tokyo wished to protect its immigrants in the islands), forced America's hand. The resulting annexation of the Philippines and Hawaii signaled the intrusion of faraway developments upon American national life.

American security now became partially dependent upon the geopolitical situation in Asia and the Pacific, especially Japan's rapid naval buildup, penetration of the Asian continent, and alliance (in 1902 and thereafter) with Britain. By the same token, the growth of the United States as a naval and colonial power had serious strategic implications for Japan. To simplify the complex evolution of U.S.-Japanese competition that eventuated in the war of 1941–1945, the uneasy balance (from around 1900 to the First World War) in the Pacific was followed by the emergence of the two countries as the hegemonic naval powers in the Pacific, each developing war plans against the other. But at the Washington and the London naval conferences of 1921–1922 and 1930, they decided to check the arms race and build a more stable relationship on the basis of reduced naval forces. This changed again during the 1930s, when Japan augmented its military power and sought to establish a greater measure of control over the Asian continent than it had before, and the United States slowly but firmly resisted these moves and rebuilt its own forces. The confrontation that came in 1941 pitted a nation trying to establish control over China, Southeast Asia, and the western Pacific against another that stood in its way and was reinforcing its power in Hawaii, the Philippines, and (through military advisers and aid) China.

In the meantime, economic relations between America and Asia had become much closer. Although American trade continued to be largely oriented toward Europe, Asia did begin to play an increasingly important role as a market for industrial products, cotton, kerosene, and wheat. American exports to China and Japan expanded phenomenally during and following the First World War, accounting for over a third of these countries' imports in the 1920s. The United States, in turn, provided a good market for Asian commodities. American purchases of silk and silk goods composed the largest portion of Japan's export trade. The deepening interdependence was further promoted by the infusion of American capital and technology, both badly needed for Japanese industrialization as well as for China's reconstruction after the country had been devastated by internal strife following the fall of the Manchu dynasty in 1911.

These economic ties did not disappear in the 1930s during the world depression. If anything, because of the economic crisis, Americans became even more interested in Asian markets, and the Chinese continued to count on American capital and technology. The Japanese imported increasing quantities of American trucks, aircraft, and oil. In the end, however, economic relations became incorporated into the power-level relationship, with the United States anxious to help China resist Japanese aggression, while Japan decided to free itself from its dependence on America by creating an East Asian "coprosperity sphere." Thus in the story leading up to the Japanese attack on Pearl Harbor on December 7, 1941, economics played a symbolic role; Japan was opting out of a relationship of interdependence for an autarky, while the United States insisted on an "open door" in Asia and the Pacific, free from Japanese military domination.

During this period the cultural aspect continued to be of real importance to all countries involved. Americanization of Asia proceeded apace; educators, doctors, engineers, and other experts flocked to China as it belatedly began its modernization programs. The U.S. government as well as private institutions invited thousands of students from China, and these students, upon returning home, became agents of cultural transformation. There were fewer American teachers in Japan or Japanese students in America, but American influence was conspicuous through hundreds of movies shown in Japanese cities, in political ideologies that affected the movement for democratization during the 1920s, and in popular entertainment areas such as baseball, jazz, and dance halls. These instances of Americanization did not abate in China or in Japan throughout the 1930s; only on the eve of Pearl Harbor did Japanese authorities ban (not totally successfully) the showing of American films or the sale of American books.

American society and culture, too, came under some Asian influence, although it was much more limited in scope. Most important was the presence of Asian immigrants in the United States. Although composing less than one-tenth of 1 percent of the American population, Chinese and Japanese immigrants and their offspring, especially on the West Coast and in Hawaii, helped transform the physical and cultural landscape of these lands. Their impact often aroused American hostility and gave rise to racist propaganda. One should also note the beginning, after the First World War, of Asian studies in the United States. Serious attempts were made in the interwar years to train young Americans in the study of Chinese and Japanese history and politics. They joined Chinese and Japanese students and scholars in the United States as bridge builders, and they continued to serve in that capacity even during the Pacific war as the nation called on them to interpret Japanese behavior, translate Chinese documents, or otherwise prepare for a more stable pattern of U.S.-Asian relations after the war.

The history of these relations since 1945 shows a continuity with past patterns. Economically and culturally, Americans and Asians have vastly expanded their interconnections, whereas in the strategic area there have been as many twists and turns as there were before the war. Japan, defeated and demilitarized, was now an insignificant factor, and even after it regained its sovereignty in 1952, its security was defined within the framework of an alliance with the United States. China, however, emerged as America's antagonist as the communist leadership, establishing a new regime in 1949, entered into an alliance with the Soviet Union. The U.S.-Chinese antagonism developed into a major confrontation in Korea where their forces collided in 1950, and in Vietnam where Chinese-assisted Vietminh and American-supported South Vietnamese fought a long war till the latter's defeat in 1973. Both these wars pitted American power in defense of the status quo against forces in Asia determined to challenge it.

In the meantime, European colonialism steadily receded, to be replaced by independent countries in South and Southeast Asia. But these countries, as well as China and the two Koreas, were no less committed to augmenting military power than the United States, with the result that the whole region of Asia and the Pacific became increasingly militarized. At the same time, however, geopolitical considerations led America and China to come together, to create between them some sort of balance so that together they might check the growth of Soviet power. Compared with the situation before the war, it is clear that the United States was far more extensively involved in Asia militarily and strategically. In that process, tens of thousands of Americans were killed, even while millions of Chinese, Koreans, and Vietnamese suffered losses of life, property, and economic resources.

Fortunately, this has not been the only story of postwar Asian-U.S. relations. Since World War II the whole region has witnessed real economic growth. Starting from the devastation wrought by the war, the countries of Asia have registered the most rapid economic growth of any part of the world. During the 1980s the region's share in the world's output increased from 10 to 20 percent. Undoubtedly, the United States has contributed to this development, first through the postwar programs of rehabilitation assistance, then by providing capital and technology for industrialization, and, perhaps most crucial, by purchasing huge quantities of Asian products. All this has created greater economic interdependence than was ever dreamed of. Some, especially manufacturers and labor unions in the United States, worry about excessive interdependence, which they interpret as America's becoming more and more dependent on Asian manufactured products and on Asian capital as well. But any drastic change in the near future is unlikely.

Of even greater significance has been the cultural interconnectedness. Postwar Asian countries, whether one is talking of defeated Japan occupied by American forces or of China cautiously opening its doors to American visitors, have been infused with American cultural influences, ranging from fast foods and movies to ideas of democracy and human rights, from popular sports to scholarly treatises. For their part, Asians have made themselves conspicuous in American society through their sheer numbers — there are now more Asian immigrants and refugees coming to the United States than from any other part of the world — as well as their activities as grocers, restaurateurs, artists, scholars, and just plain neighbors. Asians now compose more than 2 percent of the American population, and they have already made some significant entry into the worlds of American business, law, academia, and the mass media. This, too, is a culmination of earlier trends, although the extent to which American society has been Asianized would never have been dreamed of by prewar generations.

In the course of two centuries Americans and Asians have contributed to promoting contact between the West and the non-West, in the process transforming themselves as well as the world. The West has become more Asian, and the non-West more American. That is the ultimate significance of the history of American-Asian relations.

Michael H. Hunt, *The Making of a Special Relationship: The United States and China to 1914* (1983); Akira Iriye, *Across the Pacific: An Inner History of American–East Asian Relations* (1967).

Akira Iriye

See also Chinese Exclusion Act; Dollar Diplomacy; Gentleman's Agreement; Japanese-American Relocation; Korean War; Open Door Policy;

Philippines; Spanish-American War; Vietnam War; World War II.

ASSOCIATION (1774)

The Association of 1774, created by the First Continental Congress on October 20 of that year, arose in response to the Quebec Act and the so-called Coercive Acts, all passed by Parliament in the spring of 1774. The Association committed the American colonies to a boycott of trade with Great Britain until these laws were repealed. As Association members, the colonies agreed not to import goods from Great Britain, Ireland, or the West Indies or East India tea from anywhere in the world and to end American participation in the slave trade. If these actions failed to lead to repeal, the Association would move in September 1775 to prohibiting exports to Great Britain, Ireland, and the West Indies. To reduce the impact of nonimportation, the colonies agreed to support domestic industry, especially wool manufacture, and to encourage "frugality, economy, and industry" among their citizens. Profiteering from shortages was prohibited. The Association empowered an elected committee in each community to make periodic inspections and publicize its findings, so that violators of the agreement could be condemned and ostracized.

The nonimportation, nonconsumption, nonexportation agreement was seen by many Patriots as the last alternative to armed rebellion. Many believed that the economic pressure of suspending trade would arouse British public opinion, forcing a repeal of the contested laws. Through the winter of 1775, the program gradually took shape. Creating the machinery for enforcement moved the colonies further into the realm of self-government, and the elected committees opened opportunities for public office-holding for many outside the communities' traditional leadership. Public support of the agreement was fairly consistent, although episodes of noncompliance in the major ports led to numerous clashes and occasional violence. By April 1775, the plan was in operation in twelve of the thirteen colonies, but the outbreak of fighting at Lexington and Concord ended this last effort to express the colonies' resistance economically and politically rather than through force of arms.

See also Coercive Acts; Quebec Act; Revolution.

ASTAIRE, FRED

(1899–1987), dancer and actor. Astaire first performed as a child in vaudeville with his sister, Adele, and later the team was very successful on Broadway. In 1933, Astaire, now performing alone, made his first film, *Flying Down to Rio,* for RKO. It was an immediate success, and he went on to make forty more movie musicals. After 1958 he produced and directed four award-winning television musical specials, appeared in numerous television acting roles, wrote an autobiography, and played in straight acting roles in eight films. Astaire's dancing and choreography were sophisticated, the technique always hidden by his debonair charm as a performer. Astaire films continue to be shown throughout the world, and his dancing has come to be associated with the best of the American style, admired by such classical artists as Rudolf Nureyev and Mikhail Baryshnikov.

Known as a perfectionist, Astaire created some of his finest dances in collaboration with dance director Hermes Pan, although he also worked with choreographers like Roland Petit, Eugene Loring, and many others. A musician as well as a dancer, Astaire was able to oversee musical arrangements, making sure they were tailored to fit the needs of the dancing. His most famous partnership was with Ginger Rogers. If others of his partners, like Eleanor Powell, Rita Hayworth, Cyd Charisse, and Vera Allen, were technically better dancers, it was Rogers whose persona and movements seemed to fit with Astaire's in beautiful complement. The image of the two locked in an embrace, twirling across a highly polished floor, came to symbolize ideas about dance and romance for many in their audiences.

Astaire made the dance number the culmination of the plot, and by giving dance the honored position, he turned movie dancing into a fine art. He always directed his own dance numbers and tended to create within certain genres — like the romantic ballroom dance, tap competitions, tap solos, and solos with props. It was said that he could dance with anyone — and anything. One of his famous dances involving props is "Say It with Firecrackers" (*Holiday Inn,* 1942, Paramount), in which he sets off firecrackers, smoke, and small explosive charges with his feet. Another is a mad duet with a drum set in "Nice Work If You Can Get It" (*Damsels in Distress,* 1937, RKO).

Astaire made many innovations in the filming of dance, including filming the entire body of the dancer and capturing the dance's continuity by filming it from beginning to end in a single take. In love with movement, Astaire said that either the camera would dance — or he would. An example of his use of camera movement is his well-known dance in *Royal Wedding* (MGM, 1951) in which he appears to dance on the walls and ceiling of a room; actually, the entire room and the camera were turning around him in a kind of gigantic squirrel cage.

It is a testament to Fred Astaire's artistry that no matter how clever the devices, they were always made to serve the dance, for he never sacrificed integrity for the special effect. He is still the finest director of dance on film, and his contributions to the art as well as his own dancing on film remain unparalleled.

John Mueller, *Astaire Dancing: The Musical Films* (1985).

SALLY SOMMER

See also Dance; Movies.

ASTOR, JOHN JACOB

(1763–1848), fur trader, businessman, and real estate investor. Astor began life as one of twelve children of a poor German butcher and died the richest man in America. The making of a great fortune was the aim and purpose of Astor's life, and he accomplished it by dominating the American fur trade and investing his profits in the real estate of burgeoning New York City. Shortly before his death, Astor was asked if he would have done anything differently with his life. He

is supposed to have replied that his only regret was not having bought all of Manhattan.

Astor was born in the small town of Waldorf, near Heidelberg, Germany. At twenty he followed his older brother Henry to New York, arriving with hardly a penny. He became a clerk to a fur trader and mastered that business quickly. His employer was impressed with Astor's intelligence and energy and entrusted him with more and more responsibilities, including buying furs upstate and selling them in London.

Before long Astor was operating on his own account and prospered at once. He began putting his profits into Manhattan real estate, investing nearly $7,000, a large sum of money in those days, between 1789 and 1791. Astor's strategy was to buy, very cheaply, land that lay far beyond the developed area of the city and then to wait for the city's rapid growth to reach his lots. In 1803, for instance, he paid $25,000 for seventy acres located more than an hour's ride north of what were then the city's physical limits. By the 1870s the land was worth $20 million to the Astor family. Today the area is known as Times Square.

Because China was an excellent market for furs in 1800, Astor entered the China trade and earned large profits from it, often as much as $50,000 from a single voyage. In 1808 he established the American Fur Company to exploit the newly acquired Louisiana Purchase and the Pacific Northwest. He built a trading post at the mouth of Oregon's Columbia River in 1811, naming it Astoria. This grand scheme fell apart when one of Astor's ships was lost at sea and the War of 1812 cost him the support of his allies in Canada. It was Astor's one great failure.

Regardless, Astor turned the War of 1812 to good account when he made the federal government, desperate for cash, a large loan, paying only about forty cents on the dollar for government bonds. As always it was the increase in his fortune that mattered to Astor; patriotism did not deter him from driving any but the hardest of bargains.

By the end of the 1820s Astor had a near monopoly of the American fur trade, but he realized that because of the vagaries of fashion and rising costs, the trade was becoming less profitable. He sold out all his fur interests in 1834 and spent the last fourteen years of his life speculating in New York real estate.

When Astor died in New York, he left an estimated $40 million, a sum several times larger than any other American fortune of the day. He left nearly all of it to his son, but gave $400,000 to establish the Astor Library, one of three that would later merge to form today's great New York Public Library.

Kenneth W. Porter, *John Jacob Astor, Business Man* (1931); David Sinclair, *Dynasty: The Astors and Their Times* (1984).

JOHN STEELE GORDON

See also Robber Barons.

ATLANTIC CHARTER

President Franklin D. Roosevelt and Prime Minister Winston Churchill of Great Britain issued the Atlantic Charter after a conference aboard USS *Augusta* at Placentia Bay, Newfoundland, on August 9, 1941. Originally designed to rally support for the war effort, it later became a blueprint for the postwar world.

The charter announced that the signatories sought no additional national territory and recognized the right of all peoples to choose their own form of government and to approve any territorial changes that might affect them. It also guaranteed all nations the right to trade and navigate anywhere in the world and called for international cooperation to promote improved labor standards, economic advancement, and social security. The object was to make sure that "all the men in all the lands may live out their lives in freedom from fear and want." Finally, Churchill and Roosevelt called for the disarmament of the Axis powers, pending the establishment of a "permanent system of general security," a system later codified by the United Nations Charter.

See also World War II.

ATOMIC ENERGY

See Nuclear Power.

ATOMIC ENERGY COMMISSION

The Atomic Energy Commission (AEC), established by the Atomic Energy Act of 1946, was given a monopoly on the development of nuclear energy. David E. Lilienthal, previously head of the Tennessee Valley Authority, was its first chairman. In 1954, revisions of the Atomic Energy Act allowed private industry to participate in the development of nuclear technology and gave the AEC regulatory powers in the areas of public health and safety and national security as related to nuclear energy. Because the dual tasks of the AEC — regulation and promotion — often came into conflict, Congress separated the two functions.

Throughout the 1960s and 1970s the nuclear energy industry grew larger, leading to greater work loads for the regulators. Reaction against this growth and the fact that one agency both created and regulated the industry prompted passage of the Energy Reorganization Act of 1974, which replaced the AEC with the Nuclear Regulatory Commission and the Energy Research and Development Administration.

See also Nuclear Power.

ATOMIC WEAPONS

See Nuclear Weapons: Origins and Legacy; Hydrogen Bomb.

AUDUBON, JOHN JAMES

(1785–1851), artist and ornithologist. Audubon was a self-taught naturalist and artist who became the most famous of all nature painters after he had failed as a businessman. The illegitimate son of a French sea captain, he was born in Santo Domingo (now Haiti) and brought up in France where, as a schoolboy, he made rudimentary drawings of the local birds. He immigrated to the United States at the age of eighteen and set up as a storekeeper on the Kentucky frontier. But he became more and more absorbed in watching, studying, and drawing America's birds, and this distraction, along with unlucky investments, sent him into bankruptcy in 1819.

Largely through his own observations, he

had made himself a first-rate field ornithologist. His understanding of birds, along with his talent as a draftsman, gave his drawings and paintings a full-bodied, dramatic reality that made the stiff profiles of other bird artists seem lifeless and archaic. Working as a teacher and itinerant painter — and with the help of his wife, Lucy, who showed a storybook loyalty to her often difficult husband — he saved enough money to undertake publication of his work. In 1826, unable to find support at home, he went to Europe where his paintings delighted the English and impressed the French. His birds, an English critic wrote, "in their motion and at rest, in their play and in their combats, singing, running, beating the air, skimming the waves . . . are real and palpable images of the New World." In Paris, the eminent scientist, Georges Cuvier, declared that the paintings were "the greatest monument ever erected by art to nature."

A natural salesman and showman, Audubon played the role of the American woodsman for the English, walking around London in his fringed leather jacket, slicking his hair with bear grease, telling romantic stories of the frontier. This was playacting, but Audubon was an expert huntsman and rifleman, at home in the wilderness and with the Indians whom he amused by playing his fiddle and flute around their campfires. An innate elegance and an animated mind put him at ease with the English upper classes on whom he relied to subscribe to his work. In a dozen extraordinary years, he completed and published his *Birds of America* with its 435 life-size, elephant folio engravings (done by a gifted craftsman, Robert Havell). He sold about a hundred sets in England and some seventy-five in the United States, where his European success made him a kind of hero. Back in America in 1838, he published a smaller octavo edition of *Birds,* which opened his work to a wide public, and with his son, John Wodehouse, did paintings for a companion work, *The Viviparous Quadrupeds of North America.*

Visionary in his ambition, Audubon was single-minded and methodical in his working methods. He traveled all over the United States to observe and collect birds, measured and dissected them, made careful field sketches. All this, in the final paintings, gave his birds an authentic presence, enhanced by the direct colors and the natural backgrounds (some of which were done by other artists). His voluminous and invaluable field notes were published as *Ornithological Biography.*

Although sometimes criticized for being inaccurate and overly dramatic, Audubon's paintings are ornithologically honest, faithful to nature and to the basic object of any zoological illustration, which is to present an identifiable image of the subject. It is nature, of course, that dictates Audubon's art, but his monumental work suggests, just as much, that Audubon's art often dictates to nature.

Alice Ford, *John James Audubon* (1965); Francis Hobart Herrick, *Audubon the Naturalist* (1938).

JOSEPH KASTNER

See also Painting and Sculpture.

AUSTIN, STEPHEN F.

(1793–1836), colonizer and "Father of Texas." Born in Virginia, Austin moved with his family to Missouri in 1798 but spent most of his life on the farthest edges of the western frontier.

The economic collapse that followed the panic of 1819 changed the direction of Austin's life. When the family's ventures, including a bank and lead mines, failed, Austin moved to Arkansas where he held a territorial judgeship, and his father, who had become a Spanish subject when he first moved to Missouri, turned his attention to Spanish Texas. In December 1820, Moses Austin traveled to San Antonio, where he obtained permission to colonize three hundred American families in Texas. He died, however, before he was able to recruit the colonists.

Although he lacked enthusiasm for his father's scheme, Stephen Austin acceded to his father's dying wish and dedicated himself to the fulfillment of the colonization plan. In 1822 he established the first authorized American settlement on Texas's Gulf coast, along the rich bottomlands of the Brazos, Colorado, and Bernard rivers. When Mexico won its independence from Spain, the validity of Austin's Spanish grant was brought into question. Austin carried his case to Mexico City, where, after a year of uncertainty, he received not only confirmation of his grant but also broad political powers over the colonists. He continued to influence local governmental affairs after Texas was united with the Mexican state of Coahuila. Under the terms of Mexico's liberal colonization policy, which Austin helped draft, he expanded his settlement by an additional nine hundred families. Although contracts were drawn by the Mexican government with other *empresarios* (as the colonizers were called), Austin was the most successful. He was largely responsible for a law that allowed slaves to be brought into Texas even though Mexico had abolished slavery, and he was instrumental in providing Texas with a judicial system. In 1831–1832, he served as a member of the Coahuila and Texas legislature. The growth and stability of the early American settlements in Texas was primarily due to Austin's energy, foresight, and good relations with the Mexican government. He developed a land system, dealt with the Indians, mapped the area, encouraged economic development, established schools, and promoted commerce with the United States.

When he moved to Texas, Austin had become a Mexican citizen and always remained loyal to Mexico. Although he tried to stand aloof from the revolutionary movements that afflicted the Mexican republic, he was ultimately drawn into them. In 1832, he supported Santa Anna in the latter's effort to overturn the central government, and in the following year, he became involved in the movement to create a separate state government in Texas. Although he doubted the expediency of the movement, he was chosen to carry the appeal to the Mexican capital. Not only was he not successful, but upon his arrival in Mexico City he was thrown into prison for over a year. When Austin returned to Texas in 1835, he was drawn into the Texas Revolution.

After a trip to the United States to secure support for the new Texas Republic, he was defeated by Sam Houston for president. At the time of his death, Austin had accepted appointment as Texas's secretary of state. Although Texans had often expressed their impatience with Austin's caution, his temporizing attitude toward the Mexican authorities, and his sense of loyalty to Mexico, he was revered following his death as one of Texas's founding fathers.

Stephen F. Austin, *Papers,* ed. E. C. Barker, 4 vols. (1924–1928); Eugene C. Barker, *The Life of Stephen F. Austin, Founder of Texas, 1793–1836* (1925; reprint, 1968).

ROBERT W. JOHANNSEN

See also Mexico-U.S. Relations; Texas Revolution and Annexation.

AUTOMOBILES

Although the automobile was to have its greatest social and economic impact in the United States, it was initially perfected in Germany and France toward the end of the nineteenth century by such men as Nicolaus Otto, Gottlieb Daimler, Carl Benz, and Emile Levassor.

The 1901 Mercedes, designed by Wilhelm Maybach for Daimler Motoren Gesellschaft, deserves credit for being the first modern motorcar in all essentials. Its thirty-five-horsepower engine weighed only fourteen pounds per horsepower, and it achieved a speed of fifty-three miles per hour. But as late as 1909, with the most integrated automobile factory in Europe, Daimler employed some seventeen hundred workers to produce fewer than a thousand cars per year.

Nothing illustrates the superiority of European design better than the sharp contrast between this first Mercedes model and Ransom E. Olds's 1901–1906 one-cylinder, three-horsepower, tiller-steered, curved-dash Oldsmobile, which was merely a motorized horse buggy. But the Olds sold for only $650, putting it within reach of middle-class Americans, and the 1904 Olds output of 5,508 units surpassed any car production previously accomplished. The central problem of automotive technology over the first decade of the twentieth century would be reconciling the advanced design of the 1901 Mercedes with the moderate price and low operating expenses of the Olds. This would be overwhelmingly an American achievement.

Bicycle mechanics J. Frank and Charles E. Duryea of Springfield, Massachusetts, had designed the first successful American gasoline automobile in 1893, then won the first American automobile race in 1895, and went on to make the first sale of an American-made gasoline car the next year. Thirty American manufacturers produced 2,500 motor vehicles in 1899, and some 485 companies entered the business in the next decade. In 1908 Henry Ford introduced the Model T and William C. Durant founded General Motors.

The new firms operated in an unprecedented seller's market for an expensive consumer goods item. With its vast land area and a hinterland of scattered and isolated settlements, the United States had a far greater need for automotive transportation than the nations of Europe. Great demand was ensured, too, by a significantly higher per capita income and more equitable income distribution than in European countries.

Given the American manufacturing tradition, it was also inevitable that cars would be produced in larger volume at lower prices than in Europe. The absence of tariff barriers between the states encouraged sales over a wide geographic area. Cheap raw materials and a chronic shortage of skilled labor early encouraged the mechanization of industrial processes in the United States. This in turn required the standardization of products and resulted in the volume production of such commodities as firearms, sewing machines, bicycles, and many other items. In 1913, the United States produced some 485,000 of the world total of 606,124 motor vehicles.

The Ford Motor Company greatly outpaced its competitors in reconciling state-of-the-art design with moderate price. *Cycle and Automobile Trade Journal* called the four-cylinder, fifteen-horsepower, $600 Ford Model N (1906–1907) "the very first instance of a low-cost motorcar driven by a gas engine having cylinders enough to give the shaft a turning impulse in each shaft turn which is well built and offered in large numbers." Deluged with orders, Ford installed improved production equipment and after 1906 was able to make deliveries of a hundred cars a day.

Encouraged by the success of the Model N, Henry Ford was determined to build an even better "car for the great multitude." The four-cylinder, twenty-horsepower Model T, first offered in October 1908, sold for $825. Its two-speed planetary transmission made it easy to drive, and features such as its detachable cylinder head made it easy to repair. Its high chassis was designed to clear the bumps in rural roads. Vanadium steel made the Model T a lighter and tougher car, and new methods of casting parts (especially block casting of the engine) helped keep the price down.

Committed to large-volume production of the Model T, Ford innovated modern mass production techniques at his new Highland Park, Michigan, plant, which opened in 1910 (although he did not introduce the moving assembly line until 1913–1914). The Model T runabout sold for $575 in 1912, less than the average annual wage in the United States. By the time the Model T was withdrawn from production in 1927, its price had been reduced to $290 for the coupe, 15 million units had been sold, and mass personal "automobility" had become a reality.

Ford's mass production techniques were quickly adopted by other American automobile manufacturers. (European automakers did not begin to use them until the 1930s.) The heavier outlays of capital and larger volume of sales that this necessitated ended the era of easy entry and free-wheeling competition among many small producers in the American industry. The number of active automobile manufacturers dropped from 253 in 1908 to only 44 in 1929, with about 80 percent of the industry's output accounted for by Ford, General Motors, and Chrysler, formed from Maxwell in 1925 by Walter P. Chrysler. Most of the remaining independents were wiped out in the Great Depression, with Nash, Hudson, Studebaker, and Packard hanging on only to collapse in the post–World War II period.

The Model T was intended to be "a farmer's car" that served the transportation needs of a nation of farmers. Its popularity was bound to wane as the country urbanized and as rural regions got out of the mud with passage of the 1916 Federal Aid Road Act and the 1921 Federal Highway Act. Moreover, the Model T remained basically unchanged long after it was technologically obsolete. Model T owners began to trade up to larger, faster, smoother riding, more stylish cars. The demand for basic transportation the Model T had met tended increasingly in the 1920s to be filled from the backlog of used cars piling up in dealers' lots as the market became saturated.

By 1927 replacement demand for new cars was exceeding demand from first-time owners and multiple-car purchasers combined. Given the incomes of the day, automakers could no longer count on an expanding market. Installment sales had been initiated by the makers of moderately priced cars in 1916 to compete with the Model T, and by 1925 about three-quarters of all new cars were bought on time. Although a few expensive items, such as pianos and sewing machines, had been sold on time before 1920, it was installment sales of automobiles during the twenties that established the purchasing of expensive consumer goods on credit as a middle-class habit and a mainstay of the American economy.

Market saturation coincided with technological stagnation: in both product and production technology, innovation was becoming incremental rather than dramatic. The basic differences that distinguish post–World War II models from the Model T were in place by the late 1920s — the self-starter, the closed all-steel body, the high-compression engine, hydraulic brakes, syncromesh transmission, and low-pressure balloon tires. The remaining innovations — the automatic transmission and drop-frame construction — came in the 1930s. Moreover, with some exceptions, cars were made much the same way in the early 1950s as they had been in the 1920s.

To meet the challenges of market saturation and technological stagnation, General Motors under the leadership of Alfred P. Sloan, Jr., in the 1920s and 1930s innovated planned obsolescence of product and put a new emphasis on styling, exemplified in the largely cosmetic annual model change — a planned triennial major restyling to coincide with the economics of die life and with annual minor face-liftings in between. The goal was to make consumers dissatisfied enough to trade in and presumably up to a more expensive new model long before the useful life of their present cars had ended. Sloan's philosophy was that "the primary object of the corporation . . . was to make money, not just to make motorcars." He believed that it was necessary only that GM's cars be "equal in design to the best of our competitors . . . it was not necessary to lead in design or to run the risk of untried experiments." Thus engineering was subordinated to the dictates of stylists and cost-cutting accountants. General Motors became the archetype of a rational corporation run by a technostructure.

As Sloanism replaced Fordism as the predominant market strategy in the industry, Ford lost the sales lead in the lucrative low-priced field to Chevrolet in 1927 and 1928. By 1936 GM claimed 43 percent of the U.S. market; Ford with 22 percent had fallen to third place behind Chrysler with 25 percent. Although automobile sales collapsed during the Great Depression, Sloan could boast of GM that "in no year did the corporation fail to earn a profit." (GM retained industry leadership until 1986 when Ford surpassed it in profits.)

The automobile industry had played a critical role in producing military vehicles and war matériel in the First World War. During World War II, in addition to turning out several million military vehicles, American automobile manufacturers made some seventy-five essential military items, most of them unrelated to the motor vehicle. These materials had a total value of $29 billion, one-fifth of the nation's war production.

Because the manufacture of vehicles for the civilian market ceased in 1942 and tires and gasoline were severely rationed, motor vehicle travel fell dramatically during the war years. Cars that had been nursed through the depression long after they were ready to be junked were patched up further, ensuring great pent-up demand for new cars at the war's end.

Detroit's Big Three carried Sloanism to its illogical conclusion in the postwar period. Models and options proliferated, and every year cars became longer and heavier, more powerful, more gadget-bedecked, more expensive to purchase and to operate, following the truism that large cars are more profitable to sell than small ones. Engineering was subordinated to the questionable aesthetics of nonfunctional styling at the expense of economy and safety. And quality deteriorated to the point that by the mid-1960s American-made cars were being delivered to retail buyers with an average of twenty-four defects a unit, many of them safety-related. Moreover, the higher unit profits that Detroit made on gas-guzzling "road cruisers" were made at the social costs of increased air pollution and a drain on dwindling world oil reserves.

The era of the annually restyled road cruiser ended with the imposition of federal standards of automotive safety (1966), emission of pollutants (1965 and 1970), and energy consumption (1975); with escalating gasoline prices following the oil shocks of 1973 and 1979; and especially with the mounting penetration of both the U.S. and world markets first by the German Volkswagen "bug" (a modern Model T) and then by Japanese fuel-efficient, functionally designed, well-built small cars.

After peaking at a record 12.87 million units in 1978, sales of American-made cars fell to 6.95 million in 1982, as imports increased their share of the U.S. market from 17.7 percent to 27.9 percent. In 1980 Japan became the world's leading auto producer, a position it continues to hold.

In response, the American automobile industry in the 1980s underwent a massive organizational restructuring and technological renaissance. Managerial revolutions and cutbacks in plant capacity and personnel at GM, Ford, and Chrysler resulted in leaner, tougher firms with lower break-even points, enabling them to maintain profits with lower volumes in increasingly saturated, competitive markets. Manufacturing quality and programs of employee motivation and involvement were given high priority. The industry in 1980 undertook a five-year, $80 billion program of plant modernization and retooling. Functional aerodynamic design replaced styling in Detroit studios, as the annual cosmetic change was abandoned. Cars became smaller, more fuel-efficient, less polluting, and safer. Product and production were being increasingly rationalized in a process of integrating computer-aided design, engineering, and manufacturing.

The automobile has been a key force for change in twentieth-century America. During the 1920s the industry became the backbone of a new consumer goods–oriented society. By the mid-1920s it ranked first in value of product, and in 1982 it provided one out of every six jobs in the United States. In the 1920s the automobile became the lifeblood of the petroleum industry, one of the chief customers of the steel industry, and the biggest consumer of many other industrial products. The technologies of these ancillary industries, particularly steel and petroleum, were revolutionized by its demands. The automobile stimulated participation in outdoor recreation and spurred the growth of tourism and tourism-related industries, such as service stations, roadside restaurants, and motels. The construction of streets and highways, one of the largest items of government expenditure, peaked when the Interstate Highway Act of 1956 inaugurated the largest public works program in history.

The automobile ended rural isolation and brought urban amenities — most important, better medical care and schools — to rural America (while paradoxically the farm tractor made the traditional family farm obsolete). The modern city with its surrounding industrial and residential suburbs is a product of the automobile and trucking. The automobile changed the architecture of the typical American dwelling, altered the conception and composition of the urban neighborhood, and freed homemakers from the narrow confines of the home. No other historical force has so revolutionized the way Americans work, live, and play.

In 1980, 87.2 percent of American households owned one or more motor vehicles, 51.5 percent owned more than one, and fully 95 percent of domestic car sales were for replacement. Americans have become truly auto-dependent. But though automobile ownership is virtually universal, the motor vehicle no longer acts as a progressive force for change. New forces — the electronic media, the laser, the computer, and the robot probably foremost among them — are charting the future. A period of American history that can appropriately be called the Automobile Age is melding into a new Age of Electronics.

James J. Flink, *The Automobile Age* (1988); David L. Lewis and Lawrence Goldstein, eds., *The Automobile and American Culture* (1983).

JAMES J. FLINK

See also Ford, Henry; Iron and Steel Industry; Model T Ford; Oil Industry; Sit-Down Strikes; Suburbanization; Vacations and Resorts.

AVIATION

Americans have always been fascinated by the possibility of flight. On June 24, 1784, only seven months after Pilatre de Rozier and the Marquis D'Arlandes became the first human beings to fly, thirteen-year-old Edward Warren rose above the streets of Baltimore aboard a balloon constructed by Peter Carnes, a lawyer and tavern keeper from Maryland. During the next century, balloons became a familiar sight, but the gaily decorated gasbags were captives of the wind. Navigating in air with the freedom of the birds came only with the invention of the airplane.

During the 1890s Octave Chanute and Samuel Pierpont Langley helped set the stage for achieving winged flight. In 1896, Langley, the secretary of the Smithsonian Institution, launched a series of large, steam-powered model aircraft on flights of up to three-quarters of a mile over the Potomac River. Several months later, Chanute, a civil engineer, led a band of assistants into the dune country east of Chicago, where they flew a series of manned gliders, including an advanced biplane.

Wilbur and Orville Wright, the proprietors of a bicycle shop in Dayton, Ohio, wrote to Langley and Chanute in 1899–1900, requesting information on aeronautics and announcing their decision to conduct their own tests. They made the world's first powered, sustained, and controlled flights with a heavier-than-air flying machine at Kitty Hawk, North Carolina, on December 17, 1903. Unwilling to risk unveiling their technology without the protection of a patent and a contract for the sale of airplanes, the Wrights did not make their flights in public until 1908. By that time, photographs and descriptions of their machine had inspired other pioneers to follow their lead.

Glenn Hammond Curtiss, a motorcycle builder from New York, emerged as their most important American rival. Flying in a competition in France in 1909, Curtiss won the first James Gordon Bennett trophy competition with a speed of forty-six miles per hour. In spite of the Wrights' legal efforts to curb his activity, Curtiss had, by 1914, established himself as the most successful of all American aircraft manufacturers.

American aeronautical hegemony was short-lived, however. With war looming, European leaders were quick to recognize the military potential of the technology and to encourage its development by sponsoring speed, altitude, and distance competitions, establishing aerial units in their armed forces, and creating laboratories to conduct research and development programs.

During World War I, the nation that had given birth to the airplane only fourteen years before scarcely qualified as a third-rate aeronautical power. American pilots flew into combat aboard airplanes designed and, for the most part, manufactured in Europe. In spite of some success in the production of training craft and engines, the performance of the fledgling aircraft industry was disappointing.

Postwar congressional investigations underscored the problems of a limited market and high research and development costs faced by airframe and engine manufacturers. Recognizing the growing importance of the airplane to national defense and prestige, federal officials took a series of steps between 1915 and 1940 designed to strengthen and regulate the aviation industry.

Established by Congress in 1915, the National Advisory Committee on Aeronautics (NACA) conducted programs of research and development that by 1925 had demonstrated the value of basic research. Technical reports issued by the agency introduced U.S. aircraft designers to a host of improvements, including revolutionary airfoils; improved propellers, engines, and instruments; and various streamlining techniques. Specialists experimented with wing flaps and other high-lift devices and explored innovative construction techniques and new materials.

American engineers made use of the information provided by the NACA, university researchers, and organizations dedicated to flight research. By the 1930s, a new generation of low-wing, streamlined, all-metal airplanes were flowing off their drawing boards. Aircraft like the Boeing 247, the Douglas DC-3, and the Sikorsky, Martin, and Boeing flying boats marked the return of the United States to a position of world aeronautical leadership.

Congressional leaders had taken steps to ensure that there would be a market for the new airplanes. The Kelly Air Mail Act of 1925 authorized the use of private companies for the delivery of air mail. Most American airlines trace their lineage back to contract mail carriers; postal subsidies were an important source of income during the years when paying passengers were few and far between.

The government also regulated commercial aviation. The Air Commerce Act of 1926 created a Bureau of Aeronautics within the Commerce Department, which had limited regulatory authority and was charged with establishing aids to aerial navigation. The Civil Aeronautics Act of 1938 and the Civil Aeronautics Board and Civil Aeronautics Administration (1940) worked to improve passenger safety, route markings, and air traffic control systems.

The time between the wars was the golden age of American aviation. The products of companies like Lockheed, Boeing, Douglas, and Northrop were instantly recognizable by small boys from coast to coast. The pilots who flew higher, faster, and farther — fliers like Charles Lindbergh, Amelia Earhart, Jimmy Doolittle, Wiley Post, Richard Byrd, and Howard Hughes — were the heroes of what everyone referred to as the air age.

The airplane, an instrument of commerce, also gave birth to total war during the years 1939–1945. Traditional definitions of the battlefield lost their meaning in an age when fearful destruction could be rained on the enemy's heartland. Attacks from the sky directed against Guernica (1937), Nanking (1937), Warsaw (1939), Pearl Harbor (1941), and a hundred other places climaxed with the destruction of Hiroshima and Nagasaki by atomic bombs in 1945. From the great carrier battles of the Pacific to the fierce combat fought four miles up in the sky over Europe, the products of American aircraft builders carried the day.

Traditional piston-engine, propeller-driven aircraft technology reached its height during the Second World War. But far more revolutionary was the turbojet engine, which opened the way to much higher speeds. After the war the pressure of international tension between the United States and the Soviet Union led to increased defense spending and a drive for supremacy in the field of aerospace technology. The steady flow of military funding for flight research and development resulted in a string of technological triumphs, from the first faster-than-sound flight by the Bell X-1 in 1947 to the launch of the first successful U.S. satellite by a modified army ballistic missile in 1958.

The real impact of the airplane on the postwar world, however, came in the field of commercial transportation. By 1950 the airliner was well on the way to replacing the railroad and the ocean liner as the primary means of long-distance travel. The entry of the first turbojet airliners into scheduled service in 1952 literally accelerated the pace of the air transport revolution. The first three decades following the end of World War II were especially good years for the American airframe and engine industry, with the jet-propelled products of Boeing, McDonnell-Douglas, Lockheed, and other U.S. firms dominating the international air routes.

The result of the postwar air transport boom was nothing short of a social revolution. Regional and local airlines and air freight operations joined the giant international air carriers to create an aerial network linking every corner of the globe. The economic, social, and political consequences included the creation of global markets, opportunities for global travel undreamed of a generation before, and increasing cultural homogeneity.

For U.S. carriers, however, the era of

growth and optimism came to an end in the 1970s, as the industry became plagued by a seemingly endless stream of problems. The airlines suffered from labor unrest at every level from the cockpit to the control tower, corporate mismanagement, airport congestion, skyrocketing fuel costs, increasingly crowded skies, and public concern over issues ranging from safety and service to air and noise pollution.

Industry leaders also had to accommodate to a changing political environment. The proponents of the Airline Deregulation Act of 1978 hoped to encourage competition and increased efficiency by decreasing government controls and abolishing the Civil Aeronautics Board, for forty years the principal regulatory agency in the field of commercial aviation.

Initially, the measure did attract new competitors into the field and led to lower ticket prices. But deregulation brought with it a new set of difficulties. Increasingly congested hub airports, circuitous routing, greater passenger crowding, the loss of service to small towns, discriminatory and rapidly changing fare structures, longer working hours for flight crews, and the temptation to risk operating with narrower safety margins were but a few of the problems the industry struggled with.

Beyond its importance to national defense and the movement of freight and passengers around the globe, the aerospace industry became the single most important factor driving technological advance in a wide variety of fields. The great breakthroughs in materials science and technology, electronics, and computer sciences were inextricably linked to the needs of aviation and space flight. In eight short decades after Kitty Hawk, the aerospace enterprise changed the world in myriad ways and enormously expanded our vision of the possible.

Roger Bilstein, *Flight in America, 1900–1983* (1984); C. H. Gibbs-Smith, *Aviation: An Historical Survey* (1985).

Tom D. Crouch

See also Armed Forces; Earhart, Amelia; Lindbergh, Charles A.; Wright, Wilbur, and Wright, Orville.

AWSA

See American Woman Suffrage Association.

B

BACON'S REBELLION

Long-standing tensions between small freeholders and the elite of the Virginia colony burst suddenly into the open in 1676. The elite had previously remained united to maintain its hold on the best lands of the colony and other privileges. That changed, however, in April. Free men who lived along the James River had become convinced that Governor William Berkeley's plans to protect them from Indian assaults were inadequate and decided to mount their own campaign, which Nathaniel Bacon, a wealthy planter, agreed to lead. Bacon and his men made few distinctions among Indian tribes, killing friends and foes alike.

Governor Berkeley invited Bacon to come to Jamestown, but Bacon's demand for a commission convinced the governor that Bacon posed a greater threat to the colony than the Indians. The men under Bacon's command were former indentured servants who had received land grants after completing their indentures. Virginia's elite had long feared that the grievances of free men, servants, and slaves would boil over into open rebellion. Berkeley therefore charged Bacon and his men with treason.

When Bacon arrived in Jamestown with five hundred men on June 6, he was arrested. Then, having reestablished his authority, the governor pardoned Bacon. But Bacon was not appeased. He and several of his men confronted the governor and demanded a commission and authorization to recruit an army. Berkeley agreed and fled to the Eastern Shore. Bacon spent three months raising volunteers and plundering the estates of Berkeley loyalists.

Ironically, Berkeley made fears of a class revolt a self-fulfilling prophecy. He promised freedom to servants who joined his ranks in an unsuccessful attempt to raise troops to return to Jamestown. Bacon made the same offer to the servants and slaves of Berkeley's supporters. After degenerating into random plundering, Bacon's Rebellion ended with his death on October 26, probably of dysentery. When British ships arrived with men to restore order, all Bacon's men, except eighty slaves and twenty servants, surrendered.

See also Rebellions; Southern Colonies.

BAKER, ELLA

(1903–1986), civil rights activist. Baker was born in Virginia and at the age of seven moved with her family to Littleton, North Carolina, where they settled on her grandparents' farm — land they had worked as slaves. Her aunt was a midwife and her mother active in the church, so Baker grew up around women engaged in community work. Her mother prodded her into attending Shaw University in Raleigh, from which she graduated in 1927.

Baker hoped to attend graduate school but first went to New York City to live with family. The Great Depression dashed her hopes of higher education, and she became involved in community activities. By 1932 she had become national director of the Young Negroes Cooperative League, a branch of the Works Progress Administration (WPA). She also worked during this period as a waitress, a factory worker, and a journalist.

In 1938 Baker became a field secretary in the South with the National Association for the Advancement of Colored People (NAACP). Her rapport with southern rural folk, her willingness to talk *with* rather than *at* her potential recruits, gave Baker an edge in the NAACP's campaign for members. But by 1946 she was decidedly out of step with the conservative male ministerial leadership of the organization; her blunt manner, deep, booming voice, and formidable presence were disturbing to ministers accustomed to more docile "sisters." When a niece required care, Baker took the girl back with her to New York City and resigned from her NAACP post, ostensibly for personal reasons. Many urged her to voice her concerns about egocentric leadership within the organization, but she refused to fuel dissent and reaffirmed her loyalty by serving as president of the Manhattan NAACP in 1954.

Baker returned South to work with the Southern Christian Leadership Conference (SCLC) established during the Montgomery bus boycott of 1955–1956 and headed by Martin Luther King, Jr. Following sit-ins at lunch counters in Greensboro, North Carolina, in February 1960 she organized a youth leadership meeting for Easter weekend at her alma mater. Hundreds responded to her call. Baker engineered the conference so that students controlled the agenda, defying the established black leaders who attempted to coopt the activists. Baker thus helped the students establish an independent network, the Student Non-Violent Coordinating Committee (SNCC). Shortly thereafter, she quit SCLC to work with SNCC, being more in tune with its collectivist, nonhierarchical leadership. During the struggle for voting rights in the South, Baker remained at the core of the movement, delivering the keynote address at the 1964 Jackson convention of the Mississippi Freedom Democratic party — formed in protest against the segregated mainstream political parties.

Baker remained active well into the 1970s, and, indeed, in her seventies and eighties, she was fighting for liberation in Africa, struggling against racial intolerance in America, and working for many organizations and causes, especially in Harlem. She was a source of wisdom for her old comrades and an inspiration for the young.

"Ella Baker," in G. J. Barker Benfield and Catherine Clinton, eds., *Portraits of American Women* (1991); Ellen Cantarow and Susan O'Malley, *Moving the Mountain: Women Working for Social Change* (1980).

CATHERINE CLINTON

See also Civil Rights Movement; National Association for the Advancement of Colored People; Southern Christian Leadership Conference; Student Non-Violent Coordinating Committee.

BAKER, JOSEPHINE

(1906–1975), performer and civil rights activist. Born and raised in poverty in the black ghetto of St. Louis, Baker left home at thirteen to tour on the southern vaudeville circuit. By fifteen she had joined the company of *Shuffle Along,* a musical comedy by Noble Sissle and Eubie Blake, which was the twenties' most successful black theatrical enterprise. She played with great skill the comic chorus girl, the one at the end of the line too dumb to remember the words and too uncoordinated to keep up with the others. When *Shuffle Along* closed, Baker appeared in Sissle and Blake's next Broadway production, *Chocolate Dandies*. She was noted in New York as a comedienne, often wearing blackface makeup in the minstrel show tradition.

This seemed likely to be her destiny, but in 1925, she joined the cast of *La revue nègre* in Paris. Baker danced bare-breasted and became an immediate star. Next, at the Folies Bergère, she danced the Charleston and the shimmy in skimpy outfits, including a skirt of bananas that became her signature costume. Repeatedly cast as the local girl with whom the French colonist falls in love, she seemed the perfect object for colonialist fantasies, sexy yet good-natured. Although she was introducing American jazz dancing to Europe, many saw her not as an American but as a representative of French colonial

Africa — so much so that she was made queen of France's Colonial Exposition of 1931 until it was pointed out to the organizers that America was no French colony.

Gradually Baker transformed herself into a glamorous European star. Her act, comparable to that of other French music hall performers, did not present her as stereotypically black. But when she tried to project this persona in New York's Ziegfeld Follies in 1935, she was a flop — America was not ready for a glamorous black star. She returned to France and became a citizen when she married a Frenchman in 1937.

During World War II, Baker worked for Charles de Gaulle's Free French, providing cover for a military intelligence officer and later serving as a spokesperson for the cause in North Africa. For her work, she was awarded the Croix de Guerre and the Medal of the Resistance.

In her later years, she developed into a masterful nightclub performer, singing as well as dancing. Increasingly she used her celebrity as a platform for civil rights activities in the United States. On a 1951 American tour she insisted on a nondiscrimination clause in her contracts, effectively integrating nightclubs across the country. Through a much-publicized incident at New York's Stork Club, she focused attention on discrimination against blacks in restaurants and nightclubs. And by taking up the cause of Willie McGee, a black man sentenced to death for raping a white woman, she helped increase the public's awareness of race-based inequalities of punishment.

Baker adopted twelve children of different races and nationalities, seeking thereby to demonstrate the possibility of interracial harmony. She made the children the centerpiece of a large entertainment complex built around her country home in the Dordogne, though in the process, she went bankrupt.

Baker was the first black woman to achieve international stardom. Her success in Europe was a source of joy and inspiration to many African-Americans, and her example encouraged some to look to France for life beyond the color bar. When Baker, who continued to perform all her life, died at sixty-nine, she was given a state funeral as a war hero.

Phyllis Rose, *Jazz Cleopatra: Josephine Baker in Her Time* (1989; paperback ed., 1991).

PHYLLIS ROSE

See also Expatriates and Exiles; Jazz; Musical Theater.

BAKER V. CARR

Baker v. *Carr* (1962) was a Supreme Court case involving the apportionment of seats in state governing bodies. Tennessee was using sixty-year-old district boundaries in electing members of its legislature, despite the fact that they no longer reflected the true distribution of the population. By keeping old election district boundaries, it allotted rural citizens greater proportional representation than their counterparts in the growing cities. Not only did outdated apportionment ease the reelection of incumbent legislators; it also conveniently watered down the voting power of ethnic minorities and blacks who lived in the cities (often the only blacks permitted to vote). The number of Memphis voters electing one state representative was ten times the number of voters electing a representative in a rural district.

The Court had formerly considered state apportionment a "political question," better resolved by the legislative branch. "Courts ought not to enter this political thicket," it ruled in *Colegrove* v. *Green* (1946). In his 1962 majority opinion, however, Justice William J. Brennan, Jr., declared that a case involving "a political right" did not necessarily hinge on "a political question." Courts could direct that district boundaries be redrawn to ensure citizens political rights, but where the lines would be drawn should be resolved politically by the elected branches. By implying the unconstitutionality of apportionment schemes of many states, the case prompted a flood of lawsuits contesting legislative districting. In resolving these later cases, the Court eventually established the principle of equal representation: "one man, one vote."

See also Suffrage.

BALANCHINE, GEORGE

(1904–1983), choreographer and founder-director of the New York City Ballet. Born in St. Petersburg and a graduate of the former Imperial Theatrical School, Balanchine created his first dances in the experimentalist era that followed the Russian Revolution. From the first, he was recognized as a major talent, provocative and avant-garde in his reworking of classical movement. In 1924, he left Russia permanently and in the next decade choreographed for émigré companies, including Diaghilev's famed Ballets Russes and his own Les Ballets 1933.

In 1934, at the invitation of Lincoln Kirstein, the department store heir and jack-of-all-arts who now became his indefatigable patron, Balanchine settled in the United States. Initially, their efforts to establish a permanent American company met with little success, although the School of American Ballet, founded soon after Balanchine's arrival, survived to become the country's most influential training academy, which it remains today. The organization of the Ballet Society in 1946 and, two years later, of the New York City Ballet brought a happy reversal of fortune. With a permanent company at his disposal, Balanchine now embarked on the adventure that secured his position as the foremost choreographer of twentieth-century ballet.

The Balanchine style that emerged in the 1940s and 1950s rested firmly on classical technique, even as it wed this technique to distinctly modernist concerns. Although Balanchine choreographed a number of story ballets (his 1954 *Nutcracker* started the rage for this Christmas entertainment), his greatest works dispensed with narrative and scenery. Abstract, embedding their themes in daring and original images, they insisted on the primacy of movement in the creation of dance meaning. Thus, in *Theme and Variations* (1947), *Symphony in C* (1948), and *Gounod Symphony* (1958), he honored classical style by transforming it: speeding it up, complicating it, ridding it of inessentials. Balanchine's "leotard" ballets, so-called because the dancers wore practice clothes, proved even more revolutionary. Stark, anguished, set to music by Hindemith, Stravinsky, and Webern, they charted new territory in their exploration of sexuality. Created in the postwar years, *The Four Temperaments* (1946), *Agon* (1957), and *Episodes* (1959) remain powerful statements of modernity.

Balanchine's influence over American ballet has been immense. Under his direction, the New York City Ballet became a great international company. He gave his works freely to American regional companies, especially those directed by former NYCB dancers, thereby creating a body of work analogous to a national repertory. He left a definitive mark on ballet technique, stressing speed and definition, especially in the use of the legs and feet, characteristics now associated with American ballet generally. "Ballet is woman," he was fond of saying, and in countless roles, he displayed his mastery of the female dance and his ability to develop female talent, above all the slim, musical, technically accomplished "Balanchine ballerina." He formed many outstanding dancers, including Lew Christensen, Maria Tallchief, Tanaquil LeClerq, Melissa Hayden, Edward Villella, Allegra Kent, Jacques D'Amboise, Gelsey Kirkland, Merrill Ashley, and Suzanne Farrell, regarded by many as his last and greatest muse.

Lincoln Kirstein, *The New York City Ballet* (1973); Bernard Taper, *Balanchine: A Biography,* rev. ed. (1984).

LYNN GARAFOLA

See also Dance.

BALDWIN, JAMES

(1924–1987), African-American novelist and social critic. Born in Harlem, Baldwin grew up poor and unhappy, especially after his mother's marriage in 1927 to a domineering fundamentalist minister from New Orleans who seemed to hate his stepson. As a boy, he read prodigiously. He also became, in his teens, a junior minister whose oratory attracted a growing congregation. He subsequently lost his faith, however, and left Harlem to work in New Jersey. His experience of racism and segregation there drove him to Greenwich Village where he found a somewhat more congenial racial climate and more opportunities for writing.

In 1947, Baldwin began his literary career with book reviews in the *Nation* and *New Leader* and attracted attention with an article on black-Jewish relations and a short story in *Commentary*. Seeking greater personal freedom, he moved to Paris in 1948. In his essay "Everybody's Protest Novel," about Harriet Beecher Stowe's *Uncle Tom's Cabin* and Richard Wright's *Native Son,* he questioned the use of fiction to advocate social change. In 1953, Baldwin published his first novel, the largely autobiographical *Go Tell It on the Mountain.* Set in Harlem, the book recounted the difficulties of his adolescence and his struggles with his stepfather. *Notes of a Native Son* (1955), a collection of essays, commented skillfully on racism in America, and his novel *Giovanni's Room* (1956) was one of the boldest treatments of homosexuality in American literature to that time.

In 1956, Baldwin returned home to observe the burgeoning civil rights movement. A long trip through the South resulted in a series of highly rhetorical essays, which, collected in *Nobody Knows My Name* (1961) and *The Fire Next Time* (1963), led to his recognition as a major American essayist and a leading critic of racism. Between these books came *Another Country* (1962), a sensational, best-selling novel about racism, love, and sexuality. The three books established Baldwin as an international celebrity, sought out by the press and traveling among homes in France, Turkey, and the United States.

In 1964, his controversial drama *Blues for Mister Charlie,* about one of the most heinous crimes of the civil rights era, ran for 150 performances on Broadway. Some critics found it complex, but others thought it confused and propagandistic. Another play, *The Amen Corner,* first staged in 1955 and revived on Broadway in 1968, drew on his religious background and left unsettled the question of his competence as a dramatist. His later novels, none of which achieved the success of his earlier work, included another study of the sixties in America, *Tell Me How Long the Train's Been Gone* (1968), the best-selling *If Beale Street Could Talk* (1974), and perhaps his most ambitious book, *Just Above*

My Head (1979). The last, especially, testified to Baldwin's continuing fascination with homosexuality and with the place of music, especially gospel, in black culture; it also reflected the less confrontational attitude of his later years. His nonfictional writing was collected in *The Price of the Ticket* (1985).

Especially in his earlier novels and essays, Baldwin brought to the often turbulent American discussion of race an almost unsurpassed understanding of its various psychological nuances and consequences. His complicated sense of himself as an artist, a black American, a homosexual, and a man of religion (even after he lost his faith) was well served by high intelligence, distinct literary ability, and a will toward love, peace, and reconciliation in spite of the rage and bitterness that racism inspired. His best work continues to afford keen insights into perhaps the most intractable of American social problems.

John W. Roberts, "James Baldwin," in Trudier Harris and Thadious M. Davis, eds., *Dictionary of Literary Biography* (1985), 33:3–16; Fred L. Standley, "James Baldwin," in J. M. Brook, ed., *Dictionary of Literary Biography (Yearbook, 1987)* (1988), 219–225.

ARNOLD RAMPERSAD

See also Literature.

BALLET

See Dance.

BALLINGER-PINCHOT CONTROVERSY

The Ballinger-Pinchot controversy was a dispute during the Taft administration in 1909 between Secretary of the Interior Richard A. Ballinger and the head of the Forestry Service in the Department of Agriculture, Gifford Pinchot. An appointee and personal friend of William Howard Taft's predecessor, Theodore Roosevelt, Pinchot was a passionate conservationist who, along with the previous secretary of the interior, James A. Garfield, had helped carry out Roosevelt's policy of withdrawing millions of acres from the public domain. These policies had antagonized many western senators and their constituents, who wanted the land kept available for mining, lumber, and grazing leases. Ballinger, a Taft appointee, had, in his previous position at the General Land Office, shown sympathy for the westerners' point of view.

Soon after taking office, Ballinger identified a group of water-power sites, totaling a million acres, which Garfield and Pinchot had made unavailable for leases by designating them as ranger stations. Arguing that their actions had been improper, Ballinger returned the land to the public domain. Pinchot immediately launched a crusade against Ballinger. He spoke against him in public meetings and supported the claim of Louis Russell Glavis, the new commissioner of the General Land Office, that Ballinger had improperly overlooked collusion in the settlement of certain Alaskan land claims during his tenure in the Land Office. Pinchot also provided most of the information for two articles in *Collier's* magazine attacking Ballinger. These actions caused Taft to dismiss him.

In the investigation that followed, Ballinger was exonerated, but Pinchot's close identification with Roosevelt and with the popular cause of conservation attracted wide sympathy, especially among the insurgent Republicans in Congress, helping to set the stage for the Progressives' bolt from the Republican party in 1912.

See also Conservation and Environmental Movements; Public Land Policy.

BALLOON-FRAME HOUSE

In 1833, a breakthrough in building technology revolutionized the construction of private homes, making them affordable to middle- and low-income families and ultimately allowing the proliferation of suburbs nationwide over the next 150 years. This innovation was the balloon-frame house.

Home construction previously was arduous and expensive. Houses were built using stout pieces of lumber fitted together with heavy joints. For example, the traditional New England frame house was built using hardwood beams connected with mortise-and-tenon joints fastened by hand-cut dowels or hand-wrought nails. An entire frame wall was fitted on the ground and then lifted into place by a crew of about twenty laborers. These homes were durable but expensive and unwieldy to construct, requiring much labor and the expertise of skilled craftsmen.

Then the balloon frame was developed, making its first appearance in Chicago. Partially a result of the incipient industrialization occurring in the young nation, the balloon frame was based on much lighter precut two-by-four-inch studs positioned sixteen inches apart and held together by factory-produced nails. Although light, the frame was very strong and able to withstand heavy winds, since the stress was spread over a large number of studs. The factory production of nails and mill cutting of standardized lumber reduced costs and increased availability of materials to individual builders. These houses were constructed quickly and easily, requiring only two workers using basic carpentry techniques. The method allowed many urban workers in America to build their own homes, in contrast to Europe where traditional construction techniques kept the rates of homeownership low for most of the nineteenth century.

Over the next few decades, home building was transformed from a specialized craft into an industry, as entrepreneurs produced house plan pattern books and even prefabricated building materials in mass quantities based on the balloon-frame method. Throughout the country, single-family homes became affordable to Americans who were previously unable to purchase what had been a luxury. Balloon-frame construction has persisted, with most homes today, whether stucco, wood, stone, or brick, based on this method.

See also Architecture; Housing; Suburbanization.

BANCROFT, GEORGE

(1800–1891), historian, politician, diplomat. Bancroft won both popular success and critical acclaim with the 1834 publication of the first volume of his *History of the United States of Amer-*

ica. The tenth volume (1874) brought the narrative up through the success of the American Revolution. None of his other works has the stature of the *History;* his last, *Martin Van Buren* (1889), is little more than a campaign biography published forty-five years too late, and his first, *Poems* (1823), demonstrates only that Bancroft was wise to choose history as his muse.

As a politician, Bancroft was a Jacksonian Democrat; as a historian, he believed in progress, Providence, and an innate American will to liberty and self-government. His convictions found expression in rhetorical set pieces scattered throughout the *History* and also affected its structure, as Bancroft concentrated on those features of the colonial era that prefigured later events. Beliefs so in tune with the romantic nationalism of the Jacksonian era helped make him a best-seller in his own century but have led some modern readers, less receptive to historical presentism and purple prose, to underestimate his virtues as a historian.

In 1820, Bancroft, a graduate of Harvard, was one of the first Americans to obtain a doctorate in Germany, where he studied at Göttingen under the historian August Heeren who thought that history was a science and must always be based on primary sources. Bancroft's books reflect his mastery of primary sources, with later editions including European sources to which he gained access as a diplomat.

Although his father was a prominent Unitarian minister in Massachusetts, Bancroft himself was not a success in the pulpit in his few trials after his return from Germany. After a brief career as a schoolmaster, he devoted himself primarily to history and politics. His popularity as a historian helped make him an asset to his party, and his involvement with public affairs helped enrich his understanding of politics past. Bancroft held the important patronage post of collector of the Port of Boston (1838–1840) and played an important role in the nomination of James K. Polk in 1844. As secretary of the navy (1845–1846) under Polk, he helped establish the U.S. Naval Academy. He was especially happy as U.S. minister to Great Britain (1846–1849) and Prussia (1867–1874). During the Civil War, he was a War Democrat and supported Lincoln in 1864. He delivered the memorial oration on Lincoln to a joint session of Congress in 1866.

Bancroft received many honors: he was granted floor privileges in the U.S. Senate in 1879 and was elected president of the fledgling American Historical Association in 1886. Nevertheless, he was something of an anachronism as both statesman and scholar in his later years. His real place is with an earlier period, when historical scholarship was still a branch of literature. His special gift was for the narrative synthesis needed to make a long and complicated story into an intelligible whole.

Russel B. Nye, *George Bancroft, Brahmin Rebel* (1944; reprint, 1972).

ROBERT H. CANARY

See also History and Historians; Literature.

BANKING

Not banks but merchants were the sources of money and credit in the colonial period of American history (1607–1783). It was only after independence that the first commercial bank received a charter of incorporation — the Bank of North America, in 1781. British merchant banking houses stood at one end of a long chain of credit that stretched to the American frontier. They gave short-term (less than a year) credits to American merchants who then extended them to wholesalers of their imports, and the wholesalers passed them on to both urban and rural retailers — country stores and wandering peddlers.

When the Constitution went into effect in 1789 the nation boasted three commercial banks, the Bank of North America, chartered by Congress at the behest of Robert Morris, the superintendent of finance, and two state banks, those of Massachusetts and New York. The primary function of these and later commercial banks was the making of short-term loans, which they did either by issuing their own bank notes or by creating a deposit in the name of the borrower (opening an account to the person's credit) and dispersing checks to draw against it. Since the bank notes were promises to pay specie to the bearer on demand, banks had to maintain adequate reserves in order to do so. Defining adequacy, however, was no easy task, and numerous banks were forced into bankruptcy because they had overexpanded their loans and discounts.

Conservatism was the hallmark of the earliest commercial banks. The thinking of the time favored the establishment of a single quasi-governmental bank in each state that would operate in the public interest under private management. The overriding fear of political leaders was that excessive numbers of banks or loans too much in excess of specie reserves would hobble the taxing and spending functions of government by swamping the economy in depreciated paper. Political leaders also recalled very well the wild inflation resulting from unrestrained governmental issues of continental and state bills of credit (paper money) during the Revolution, and in the Constitution they barred the states from issuing them.

The management of the first Bank of the United States (BUS), chartered by Congress in 1791, reflected these concerns. Although the BUS was a large commercial bank providing loans to the private sector as well as to government, its board of directors managed the institution in a highly conservative manner. Balance sheets for the years 1792–1800 reveal a generally high degree of success in maintaining the Bank's specie reserves. The ratio between bank notes in circulation and specie holdings was quite small.

Growing population and trade, however, created a need for comparable growth in the volume of money and credit — for a policy of accommodation rather than restraint. Sharp increases in the number of state banks and in their authorized capital stock represented a response to this need. During the life of the first BUS (1791–1811) banks chartered by the states increased in number from 5 to 117, and their combined capital stock went from $4.6 million to almost $66.3 million.

The British raid on Washington in 1814 induced banks throughout the country (except in New England) to suspend specie payments. The bank note currency circulated at a variety of dis-counts from place to place, and since the government was compelled to accept it for taxes and imposts, the public finances became so disordered as to threaten the operations of the federal government. It was in this context of nationwide inflation and governmental derangement that Congress decided to charter a second BUS (1816–1836). The expectation was that the institution would be able to force the state banks to resume specie payments and restore soundness to the currency.

The Bank's success in achieving those objectives is mainly attributable to its president Nicholas Biddle (1823–1836). The mechanism was simple. The nation's currency was largely made up of bank notes, most of it placed in circulation by state banks, so payments made to the federal government were likely to be in that form. And far more payments were made to that government than to any other transactor of business in the nation. In consequence, the government deposited large quantities of state bank notes in the BUS and its branches, which therefore were creditors of the state banks and as such could insist on payment in specie. This threat, or its implementation, induced the state banks to keep their loans and discounts within bounds, which in turn enabled them to redeem their notes in specie at par.

But the BUS could not succeed equally well in both its fiscal and its monetary functions. If, as a great commercial bank, larger than any other and receiver of the government's deposits as well, it could succeed in maintaining sound money, it could not at the same time make available to the expanding population and economy the credit that was needed. The nation's money was good, but there was not enough of it. Wholesale price indexes for all commodities from 1790 to 1860 reveal a long-term downward drift that commenced in 1820 and lasted till the eve of the Civil War, a drift that was interrupted only by speculative surges in the mid-1830s and mid-1850s. The policy of restraining credit expansion in the interests of monetary stability was the wrong policy for the times.

Not surprisingly, that policy was vigorously opposed by political forces determined not to renew the Bank's charter. Although the "bank war" (1829–1832) between the administration of President Andrew Jackson and the supporters of the Bank had other elements — most notably, Jackson's deep conviction that hard money rather than paper was the only sound money and that the economic power of the Bank threatened democratic government — it was Secretary of the Treasury Roger B. Taney's belief in free competition that led him to stop the deposit of government funds in the Bank in 1833. Moreover, he objected to the Bank's power to restrain the country's economic development. The enactment of the Free Banking Act by New York in 1838 and later by other states reflected the same views. Previously, the states had granted charters to banks only by special legislative acts that were semimonopolistic in nature.

Meanwhile, since the government had stopped depositing its funds (mainly state bank notes) in the BUS, that institution lost its power to influence the volume of business done by the state banks. Freed of restraint, the latter increased in number from 506 in 1834 to 901 in 1840 and 1,601 by the time of the Civil War. Some of these "pet" banks were for a while selected depositories of federal funds, but in the main those funds were deposited at sub-treasury offices in major cities. These offices represented an effort in the 1840s and 1850s to establish an independent system that would separate the operations of the U.S. Treasury from any connection with the banks. The effort was unsuccessful, however. The system fell far short of the purposeful influence over money and credit that a central bank would have been able to exercise. The vacuum created by the federal government's withdrawal was later filled by the large Wall Street banks.

The effort to divorce government from the banking system came to an end in 1862 because of the chaotic condition of the currency caused by the government's need to finance the costs of the Civil War. The National Bank Act of 1863 invited state banks to take out federal charters, thereby becoming known as national banks. Each was required to buy government bonds in an amount equal to one-third of its paid-in capital stock. The bonds had to be deposited with the U.S. Treasurer, who then turned over to the

bank bank notes equal to 90 percent of the current market value of the bonds. To discourage undue credit expansion the act required national banks to keep reserves not only against their bank notes but also against their deposit liabilities. The amount of reserves depended on the size and location of the national banks. Small "country banks" had to maintain reserves of at least 15 percent of their notes and deposits. Reserves for large banks in "reserve cities" and for the "central reserve city" of New York were 25 percent (in 1887 Chicago and St. Louis were added to the category of central reserve cities).

The growth of the national banking system was slow until Congress imposed a prohibitive 10 percent tax on state bank notes in 1865. By the late 1860s the new system covered about three-fourths of the nation's banking resources. The triumph was a brief one, for state banks possessed advantages over national banks — the latter being prohibited by law from making loans on real estate, for example. By the early 1870s the deposits of nonnational commercial banks roughly equaled those of national banks and from then until through the 1980s the deposits of the two classes of banks remained about equal in size.

Other disadvantages, indeed defects, of the new system proved more important. Arbitrary limits placed by the law on the quantity of national bank notes that could be issued were soon removed by the Resumption Act of 1875, but the scheme by which the notes were apportioned by Comptroller of the Currency Hugh McCulloch resulted in a maldistribution injurious to the less populous states of the South and Midwest (the less advanced states needed more rather than less currency because of the ability of more developed ones to use checks and other credit instruments for business transactions). A more serious defect resulted from the pyramiding of reserves in the national banks of New York City, but even more important was the system's inability to do anything about periodic shortages of cash and credit. The entire system was based on cash reserves and the total amount of cash could not be quickly altered. What was lacking was a central institution that could hold the reserves of the commercial banks and, above all, could increase those reserves. It was in response to these needs that Congress passed the Federal Reserve Act in December 1913.

Instead of setting up a single powerful central bank, however, the act divided the nation into twelve districts and established a regional central bank in each. The nine-member boards of directors of the district Federal Reserve banks are subject to the direction of a seven-member Board of Governors appointed (since 1935) by the president and sitting in Washington. The system's prime instrument of governance is its Open Market Committee, which meets about every three weeks to determine the monetary policy mix it believes best calculated to promote economic growth while dampening inflationary pressures.

Although far from infallible, these determinations are highly influential because most of the country's banking resources are subject to the board's regulations. (National banks were required by law to become members of the system.) Member banks — now classified as "reserve city" and "other" banks — are required to keep their reserves in the Federal Reserve Bank of the district in which they are located. The amount of reserves may range, for reserve city banks, between 10 and 22 percent of their demand deposits, and for "other" banks, between 7 and 14 percent. By raising or lowering percentages within these ranges the Board of Governors can either discourage or encourage member bank credit expansion.

But this is a blunt instrument that is seldom used. More sensitive are two other techniques available to the Fed. One is known as "open market operations," which consist of purchases or sales of government securities by the manager of the system's Open Market Committee, a vice president of the Federal Reserve Bank of New York. Purchases automatically increase and sales decrease the reserves of the member banks, thus permitting loan expansion or compelling contraction, respectively. The other involves altering the interest rate charged on loans and advances by Federal Reserve banks to member banks. These techniques affect the quantity of money and its cost — factors of great importance to the investment decisions of business managers, and hence to the tone of the national economy.

The present-day powers of the Federal Reserve System owe much to legislation enacted in response to the system's inability to prevent widespread bank failures in the early years of the Great Depression. (President Franklin D. Roosevelt's initial reaction to the failures was to issue an executive order in March 1933 temporarily suspending banking activities throughout the country and forbidding dealings in gold. No bank could reopen for business until its condition had been examined by the secretary of the treasury — in the case of member banks of the Federal Reserve — or by state authorities — in the case of state-chartered nonmember banks. Congress then followed with a law designed to get at the roots of the failures.)

The Glass-Steagall Banking Act of 1933 established the Federal Deposit Insurance Corporation and required all members of the Federal Reserve System to insure their deposits. The act also increased the authority of the twelve Federal Reserve district banks to control the amount of credit extended to their members and prohibited the payment of interest on demand deposits to discourage outlying banks from sending large sums to New York — where they might feed speculation in securities by being re-lent on the call loan market. In addition, the act required that banks belonging to the Federal Reserve divorce themselves from their security affiliates — necessitating that they choose between deposit and investment banking — and empowered the Federal Reserve Board to regulate bank loans secured by the collateral of stocks or bonds. Finally, partners or executives of security firms were barred from serving as directors or officers of commercial banks. For more than half a century this legislation secured bank depositors from loss. Regretfully, massive failures in the nation's savings and loan institutions in the late 1980s — many of them tinctured by fraud and mismanagement — revealed deficiencies in federal deposit insurance, requiring both a huge federal bailout of more than $150 billion and structural changes in the insurance program. At the beginning of the 1990s the latter had not yet been provided.

Milton Friedman and Anna J. Schwartz, *A Monetary History of the United States, 1867–1960* (1963); Bray Hammond, *Banks and Politics in America from the Revolution to the Civil War* (1957).

STUART BRUCHEY

See also Bank of the United States; Bank War; Independent Treasury; Specie Circular.

BANK OF THE UNITED STATES

The Bank of the United States was established in 1791 to serve as a repository for federal funds and as the government's fiscal agent. Initially proposed by Alexander Hamilton, the First Bank was granted a twenty-year charter by Congress in spite of the opposition of the Jeffersonians to whom it represented the dominance of mercantile over agrarian interests and an unconstitutional use of federal power. The Bank, based in Philadelphia with branches in eight cities, conducted general commercial business as well as acting for the government. It was both well managed and profitable, but it won the enmity of entrepreneurs and state banks, who argued that its fiscal caution was constraining economic development. Others were troubled by the fact that two-thirds of the bank stock was held by British interests. These critics, working with agrarian opponents of the bank, succeeded in preventing renewal of the charter in 1811, and the First Bank went out of operation.

Soon, however, problems associated with the financing of the War of 1812 led to a revival of interest in a central bank, and in 1816, the Second Bank of the United States was established, with functions very much like the first. The Second Bank's initial years were difficult, and many felt that its mismanagement helped bring on the panic of 1819. Popular resentment led to efforts by several states to restrict the Bank's operations, but in *McCulloch* v. *Maryland* (1819), the Supreme Court held that the Constitution had granted Congress the implied power to create a central bank and that the states could not legitimately constrain that power.

This decision did not settle the controversy, however. State banks and western entrepreneurs continued to criticize the Bank as an instrument of federal control and of eastern commercial interests. In 1832, Senator Henry Clay, a longtime supporter of the Bank, was running for president against Andrew Jackson, who was up for reelection. Clay persuaded the Bank's president, Nicholas Biddle, to apply early for rechartering, thus injecting the issue into the campaign. Congress approved the renewal, but Jackson (who distrusted banks) vetoed it, campaigned on the issue, and took his electoral victory as a mandate for action. Starting in 1833, he removed all federal funds from the Bank. When its charter expired in 1836, the Second Bank ended its operations as a national institution. It was reestablished as a commercial bank under the laws of Pennsylvania, where it continued to operate until its failure in 1841.

See also Banking; Bank War; Jackson, Andrew; *McCulloch* v. *Maryland*.

BANK WAR

The Bank War was the name given to the campaign begun by President Andrew Jackson in 1833 to destroy the Second Bank of the United States, after his reelection convinced him that his opposition to the bank had won national support. (The Second Bank had been established in 1816, as a successor to the First Bank of the United States, whose charter had been permitted to expire in 1811.) In 1832, Jackson had vetoed a bill calling for an early renewal of the Second Bank's charter, but renewal was still possible when the charter expired in 1836; to prevent that from happening, he set out to reduce the bank's economic power. Acting against the advice of congressional committees and over the opposition of several cabinet members, and after replacing two resistant secretaries of the treasury with a more amenable appointee (Roger Taney), Jackson announced that, effective October 1, 1833, federal funds would no longer be deposited in the Bank of the United States. Instead, he began placing them in various state banks; by the end of 1833, twenty-three "pet banks" (as they were popularly known) had been selected.

The president of the Bank, Nicholas Biddle, anticipating Jackson's actions, began a counter-move in August 1833; he started presenting state bank notes for redemption, calling in loans, and generally contracting credit. A financial crisis, he thought, would dramatize the need for a central bank, ensuring support for charter renewal in 1836. In fact, Biddle's campaign appears to have had less effect than either his supporters or his detractors believed at the time, but the Bank War became a matter of intense debate in Congress, in the press, and among the public. Deputations of businessmen descended on Washington, complaining about business conditions and seeking an end to the Bank War, while administration spokesmen argued that Biddle's capacity to disrupt the economy only highlighted the dangers of a central bank. The federal deposits were not returned to the Second Bank, and its charter expired in 1836. President Jackson had won the Bank War.

See also Banking; Bank of the United States; Jackson, Andrew.

BANNEKER, BENJAMIN

(1731–1806), African-American scientist. Banneker was the country's first important black scientist, and his accomplishments were vital to abolitionists combating late-eighteenth-century claims of innate African inferiority. The son of free African-Americans, Banneker lived his entire life on the Maryland tobacco farm he inherited from his father. His mechanical and scientific genius appeared early. Although he had received only a few winters' education at a country school, he constructed a striking clock of hand-carved wooden parts. This feat of untutored craftsmanship — he had never seen such a clock — brought him local fame.

At about age fifty-seven, Banneker borrowed astronomical instruments and texts from a Quaker neighbor, George Ellicot. Working alone, he soon grasped the principles of calculus and spherical trigonometry that were necessary to construct an astronomical almanac — a virtually unheard-of feat of self-education. This accomplishment led to plans by abolition societies in Pennsylvania and Maryland to publish Banne-

ker's almanac as a testimony to the intellectual capabilities of Africans.

In 1791, the surveyor appointed to lay out the boundaries of the District of Columbia employed Banneker as his assistant. This appointment was, in itself, used to advantage in the campaign to undermine the arguments about blacks' mental inferiority. In a reference to ruminations about African inferiority in Thomas Jefferson's *Notes on the State of Virginia*, one newspaper reported the appointment of Banneker, "an Ethiopian whose abilities as surveyor and astronomer already prove that Mr. Jefferson's concluding that that race of men were void of mental endowment was without foundation."

After three months of surveying in the field, Banneker returned to preparing an almanac for 1792. It was the manuscript of this volume that he sent to Secretary of State Jefferson, along with a letter that represents one of the most effective protests against slavery written by an African-American in the early national period. Although he was a retiring and extremely modest man, Banneker, in this letter, was at pains to counter Jefferson's reflections on African inferiority. He also reminded Jefferson of his stated belief that "all men are created equal" — an "invaluable doctrine" that Jefferson was violating "in detaining by fraud and violence so numerous a part of my brethren under groaning captivity and cruel oppression." Jefferson's ambiguous reply declared his wish to "see such proofs as you exhibit, that nature has given to our black brethren, talents equal to those of the other colors of men." He ignored Banneker's strictures about continuing to hold slaves, however.

Banneker's first published almanac included a biographical sketch by one of his chief sponsors, James McHenry, who indicated that the issuing of the almanacs was part of the political program of a group of abolitionists, many of them Quakers. McHenry described Banneker's achievements as evidence that "the powers of the mind are disconnected with the colour of the skin." At least twenty-nine editions of his almanacs appeared between 1791 and 1796 in Philadelphia, Baltimore, Wilmington, Petersburg, Trenton, and Richmond.

Banneker continued to compute the astronomical calculations for his almanacs until 1804, although no almanacs were published after 1797. When he died in 1806 on his farm, he was known throughout the United States and abroad as the "African astronomer."

Silvio A. Bedini, *The Life of Benjamin Banneker* (1984).

GARY B. NASH

See also Abolitionist Movement; Free Negroes, 1619–1860; Science and Technology.

BARBARY WARS

The Barbary states (Morocco, Algeria, Tunis, and Tripolitania) were small kingdoms, nominally under the rule of the Ottoman Empire but actually autonomous. Pirates from these states, during the seventeenth and eighteenth centuries, harassed merchant shipping in the Mediterranean and nearby Atlantic Ocean, selling their booty and enslaving or ransoming the prisoners. Although the British navy could have wiped out the pirates, Great Britain chose instead to let them remain as a threat to its maritime rivals, while purchasing protection for itself with a modest annual tribute.

Until the Revolution this arrangement protected American ships as well, but with independence, the United States began to suffer substantial losses from raids. There was some talk of an international military action, but Congress was unwilling to invest the necessary funds. Instead, a treaty with Morocco (June 28, 1786) guaranteed payment of an annual tribute; by 1797, similar treaties had been made with the other Barbary states. The latter agreements held until 1815, but in 1801 the pasha of Tripoli increased his demands and, being refused, declared war against the United States on May 14. President Thomas Jefferson, who had opposed the initial Tripolitan agreement, responded by sending warships to the Mediterranean. Sustained action began in 1803 under the leadership of Comdre. Edward Preble. In February 1804, Lt. Stephen Decatur became a hero by retaking and destroying the *Philadelphia,* a U.S. frigate Tripolitania had captured a few months earlier. An extended blockade ended the Tripolitan War, and the peace treaty (June 4, 1805) stipulated no further tribute payments.

During the War of 1812, the dey of Algiers declared war on the United States, claiming insufficient tribute. An Algerine expedition was launched on May 10, 1815, under Captain Decatur. After his prompt capture of two enemy ships, a treaty was signed on June 30, guaranteeing the future security of U.S. vessels without the payment of tribute. Similar agreements were soon made with Tunis and Tripolitania, and U.S. ships suffered no further attacks.

BARNUM, PHINEAS T.

(1810–1891), showman, impresario, and author. Barnum, who was born poor of Yankee stock in rural Connecticut, grew up with a burning desire to make good. After various false starts in speculative business ventures, his career prospered when he took over the tour of a former slave, Joice Heth, who claimed to be more than 160 years old and to have been George Washington's nurse. Barnum's gift for publicity enabled him to make profits where others had failed, and as Joice Heth's manager he hit on the technique of encouraging disbelief as well as credulity. A temperance advocate, the only liquid that he enthusiastically purchased was printer's ink, for he was an early master of incessant and ingenious advertising.

After the Joice Heth affair, and a few setbacks in his career, Barnum toured the United States in the 1840s and 1850s with a series of fabled show business attractions, from the amiable midget Tom Thumb to the Swedish soprano Jenny Lind. He also opened the most successful private museum of curiosities in the country, after purchasing two rival institutions. There, on Broadway in New York City, Barnum's American Museum drew thousands annually to see its fossils, specimens, historical relics, what were then called "freaks of nature," and performances in the "lecture room." Barnum proved just as adept at gauging popular taste in western Europe; he brought his attractions to Britain and the Continent, exploiting royal favor as he had glorified democratic opinion.

Making, then losing, then making again a

fortune, Barnum also dabbled in business, in lecturing, in real estate (both in Bridgeport, where he lived, and in the Far West), in politics (he was an abolitionist, a Republican, and an unsuccessful candidate for Congress), and in literature. His books included *Humbugs of the World* and a much amended autobiography, expanded annually after he brought out his first edition in mid-career, as well as various other texts that he hawked as part of his entertainments.

In the early 1870s, already famous and wealthy, Barnum became involved with circus management. Within a few years he was running the "Greatest Show on Earth," perfecting, with the help of his younger partner, James A. Bailey, the three-ring, touring railroad circus. He continued to seek out and purchase extraordinarily popular attractions, ranging from the elephant Jumbo, the great attraction of the London Zoo that Barnum imported over the protests of Queen Victoria, to the notorious "White Elephant" of Siam.

At his death Barnum could claim to be one of the most celebrated living Americans, a pioneer in the creation of mass amusements, who not only had revolutionized their presentation and publicity but had also produced a philosophy of life to justify them. Moralizer and moralist both, Barnum laid claim to delivering his compatriots from the "thrall" of puritanism and in so doing became a cultural hero of the first importance. His posthumous fame, however, rested largely on the immense popularity of his circus enterprise.

Neil Harris, *Humbug: The Art of P. T. Barnum* (1973; reprint, 1989); A. H. Saxon, *P. T. Barnum: The Legend and the Man* (1989).

NEIL HARRIS

See also World's Fairs.

BARTON, CLARA

(1821–1912), founder of the American Red Cross. Barton was born in Massachusetts and worked briefly as a schoolteacher. She became a clerk in the U.S. Patent Office in 1854, but lost the job when the Democrats won the presidency in 1856.

With the outbreak of the Civil War, Barton saw the need for an efficient organization to distribute food and medical supplies to the troops. The network, Barton believed, had to be disentangled from the bureaucracy of the War Department and the U.S. Sanitary Commission. Her work of soliciting and distributing supplies and nursing the wounded was grueling and endless. She once complained to a friend, "I cannot tell you how many times I have moved with my whole family [the Army] of a thousand or fifteen hundred and with a half hour's notice in the night." Her efforts, however, were much appreciated at battle sites, especially Antietam and Fredericksburg. At war's end she set up an office to sort out the difficult business of locating and identifying prisoners, missing men, and the dead buried in unmarked graves. But the strain of her work took its toll, and she was ordered to Europe by her doctor for a rest cure in 1869.

While abroad Barton came into contact with the International Committee of the Red Cross. She participated in relief efforts during the Franco-Prussian War in 1870–1871, but was forced into temporary retirement by ill health in 1872. After recovering, she campaigned to establish an American branch of the Red Cross, despite government resistance arising from fears of foreign entanglements. The U.S. Senate, after years of lobbying, finally ratified the Geneva Convention in 1882, forming the American Association of the Red Cross. Barton became its president. Her subsequent domestic program was impressive. The Red Cross provided relief at the Johnstown, Pennsylvania, flood in 1889 and after hurricanes in the Sea Islands off the southeastern coast in 1893. The organization also marshaled support for international campaigns, sending supplies to Russia during a famine in 1892 and to Armenia in 1896.

Barton, at the age of seventy-seven, distinguished herself again, this time in Cuba during the Spanish-American conflict. But her presence on the battlefield called her methods into question and widened a rift between the national Red Cross and its local chapters. Barton was unwilling to delegate responsibility and her inability to do so was a drawback sustained within the ranks of the Red Cross. Her inflexibility forced her to resign in 1904 from the organization she had founded and built. Barton nevertheless remained active and involved in relief work until her death at the age of ninety-one. Her energy and commitment to humanitarian causes over a forty-year period has made her a household name, a symbol of charitable self-sacrifice.

Elizabeth Brown Pryor, *Clara Barton: Professional Angel* (1987).

CATHERINE CLINTON

BARUCH, BERNARD M.

(1870–1965), businessman called "adviser to presidents." Baruch, a minor adviser to Woodrow Wilson, Franklin D. Roosevelt, Harry S. Truman, and Dwight D. Eisenhower, was a giant influence upon Democratic congressional leaders between 1918 and 1948. A man of great wealth gained from speculation on Wall Street, Baruch was a superb publicist whose influence with the press furthered the causes he favored, such as anti-inflation policies.

He was chairman of the War Industries Board (WIB) in 1918, economic adviser to President Wilson at the Versailles Peace Conference of 1919, and an éminence grise with Democratic lawmakers from 1926 to 1932, helping to formulate the bipartisan consensus that passed President Herbert Hoover's antidepression program in 1932. Baruch's influence upon the New Deal was indirect in that President Roosevelt respected his power. Rexford Tugwell, a New Deal brain truster recalled Roosevelt's telling him that "Baruch owned — he used the word — sixty congressmen." It was that apparent power that compelled Roosevelt to add Baruch's crony, Hugh S. Johnson, to the brain trust during the 1932 campaign. Johnson later became head of the National Recovery Administration, a peacetime version of the War Industries Board. Later, Roosevelt told Secretary of Labor Frances Perkins that Baruch had "lots of influence on the Congress still. . . . He helps out tremendously in keeping the more wild members of Congress, the Southern members of Congress . . . reconciled."

A conservative opposed to New Deal welfare state legislation, Baruch nevertheless rationalized the New Deal as a humane and political necessity, and Roosevelt shrewdly saw to it that Baruch's influence was represented in industrial and agricultural recovery programs. The Agricultural Adjustment Administration was modeled on the cooperation strategy of the WIB and was led by George Peek, another WIB veteran and Baruch crony. Yet neither Johnson nor Peek lasted out Roosevelt's first term. Although by 1936 Baruch was only on the fringes of power, his support for the repeal of the undistributed profits tax in 1938 dealt a heavy blow to New Deal tax policy.

Baruch's influence with Congress endured, and in addition Eleanor Roosevelt and various New Deal administrators respected his views on rearmament to meet the rise of fascism in Europe and Asia. To symbolize his disagreement with the lack of speed and comprehensiveness of Roosevelt's preparedness program during 1938–1941 (and his exclusion from its policymaking and administration), Baruch told reporters that his Washington office was a park bench in Lafayette Square across the street from the White House. During World War II — while in his seventies — he was at the height of his fame as "adviser to presidents" and the "park bench statesman."

President Truman put aside his personal dislike of Baruch and appointed him chairman of the U.S. delegation to the U.N. Atomic Energy Commission, where he presented the "Baruch Plan" for creating an international atomic energy development authority. Truman hoped that Baruch would sell the idea to Congress and the American public, but the Soviets rejected it. An advocate of stabilization planning so as not to distort the economic system during a war, Baruch deplored Truman's unwillingness to resort to price controls during the Korean War. In 1952, although he had been a Democrat most of his life, Baruch endorsed Dwight D. Eisenhower for president.

Bernard M. Baruch, *The Public Years* (1960); Jordan A. Schwarz, *The Speculator: Bernard M. Baruch in Washington, 1917–1965* (1981).

JORDAN A. SCHWARZ

See also World War I.

BASEBALL

One of America's most distinctive spectator sports, baseball seems always to have lived more in myth than in history. Children in England and the United States had been playing variants of the game — known also as rounders, one o' cat, and base — for years when, in 1845, some young men in Manhattan organized themselves into the Knickerbocker Base Ball Club and wrote down the rules of the game they were playing. Twenty years later dozens of baseball clubs in New York and Brooklyn, and their journalist brethren, had made what they called the "national pastime" more popular than cricket, and the metropolis had become the country's first baseball powerhouse.

As baseball clubs were transformed into entertainment businesses and instruments of civic boosterism, so grew their need for first-rate players who could attract paying crowds. The remarkable undefeated season of the nationally touring Cincinnati Red Stockings in 1869 paved the way for baseball's full-blown professionalization in the 1876 formation of the National League of Professional Base Ball Clubs. Although distinctions between players and their clubs (now really small businesses) had been hardening for years, the National League formalized the division — which has continued until the present. Baseball soon outdistanced other spectator sports in popularity and contributed to the sports boom of the 1880s and 1890s.

Late nineteenth-century baseball resembled the Gilded Age business world. Owners moved the clubs frequently, while rival leagues — essentially small cartels — sprung up and competed for players and spectators. The National League either defeated its opponents outright or incorporated them into a subordinate national structure of minor leagues. Not until 1901 was the National League forced to accept the American League, the only other surviving major league.

Leagues controlled access to spectators by granting franchises. Owners and leagues controlled the players through labor practices that combined elements of chattel slavery (the infamous reserve rule) and freewheeling industrial capitalism: blacklisting, fines, salary limits and reductions, even the use of Pinkerton spies.

The reserve clause, initiated in 1879 and inserted into every player's contract, gave his employer the right to reserve his services for the following year, and every subsequent year, unless the player was traded, sold, or released from his contract. Players fought the reserve rule, most notably when the Brotherhood of Professional Base Ball Players launched its own Players' League in 1890. When the players' financial backers sold them out to the National League, baseball owners triumphed and ruled organized baseball virtually unchallenged for eighty-five years. They were aided by a series of bizarre Supreme Court rulings that baseball was not interstate commerce and therefore not bound by federal antitrust law.

In 1975 an arbitrator ruled that the reserve clause applied for only one year and players, as "free agents," regained their negotiating power; salaries quickly reached unheard-of levels. Owners retaliated in 1981 but were soundly defeated by a players' strike. Then in the late 1980s they conspired (illegally, an arbitrator held) to limit salary offers to free agents.

After a twenty-year period of franchise movement, league expansions, and the creation of divisions within leagues, baseball became organizationally stable again in the late 1970s. Attendance grew dramatically throughout the 1980s, as more people attended major league baseball games (over 50 million per year at the end of the decade) than at any other time in the game's history.

Baseball has been America's most popular sport for so long mainly because it has successfully straddled some of the nation's most important cultural divisions. Though it was born among the respectable working class and sporting middle class, the game's cultural antecedents lay in the boisterous street culture of saloon-based volunteer fire companies, militias, theater partisans, street gangs, and political factions.

The National League explicitly appealed to more middle-class audiences by requiring its teams to charge fifty cents, ban the sale of alcohol, and refuse to play on Sundays. The rival American Association appealed to immigrant and working-class audiences by charging a quarter, selling liquor, and playing Sunday ball.

Despite the outrage with which baseball officials and writers treat baseball's occasional betting scandals (in 1865 and 1877 as well as more famously in the 1919 "Black Sox" scandal and the 1989 banishment of Pete Rose), the game has never been completely free of the sporting underworld of gambling and lowlife. Even though they are men with extraordinarily disciplined athletic skills, ballplayers — like most professional entertainers — frequently behave badly off the field. Alongside the game's reputation as an upright, all-American pastime, its culture continues to have a whiff of the unrespectable.

Baseball has also had an archaic aura throughout most of its history — the heyday of modern industrializing America. It enshrined craft excellence at precisely the time industrialists were destroying craft production. As the traditional foundations of manhood were subjected to enormous strains, the mostly young men who played baseball worried about devoting so much time to a child's game and tried to distinguish their "manly sport" from "boyish play." Although baseball's origins are urban, its myth is powerfully, stubbornly rural. While city populations swelled in the late nineteenth century, and mass entertainment was born at places like Coney Island, baseball fans flocked to watch a game featuring individuals, isolated and surrounded by the green grass of ball*parks*.

Fans — driven by memories of timelessness, of a pointless game taken with great seriousness, of individual heroism that serves the team — seek an emotional past in the game. That is why they dislike the fact that players make money for playing baseball and why they usually prefer myth to history.

It is also why fans identify so strongly with a home team, frequently throughout their lives. The game internalizes the play of home and away: danger abroad, the safety of "home." Baseball owners have skillfully promoted their businesses by relying on (sometimes creating) rivalries within and between cities and towns. The presumptuously named World Series, base-

ball's postseason showcase begun in 1903, effectively built on league loyalties as well. For partisans of the New York Yankees and Brooklyn Dodgers in the 1940s and 1950s, such rivalry was additionally charged by class, racial, and ethnic identification.

Baseball's history has been intimately linked to the development of the press and media. Sportswriters were some of the game's key early promoters. In the 1920s radio created a national, immediate audience for Babe Ruth's home run feats. As televised baseball concentrated spectators' attention on the major leagues in the 1950s and 1960s, most of the minor leagues collapsed. The largest source of concentrated income in the game, television both fueled and shaped the business of baseball. Indoor stadiums, astroturf, divisions within leagues, the designated hitter, World Series schedules, and lights at Wrigley Field were all due to the demands and power of television.

Baseball had never been a racially integrated sport, though a few blacks played in the major leagues until the color line hardened and forced them out in the late 1880s. African-American ballplayers and entrepreneurs organized their own loosely structured touring teams, and the 1920s saw the formation of Negro Leagues. Some of the finest ballplayers played in these leagues, which reached their peak in popularity at the end of World War II.

The major league color barrier was breached in 1947 by the careful planning and daring of Brooklyn Dodgers general manager Branch Rickey and the courage, self-control, and baseball skill of Jackie Robinson, whom Rickey invited to pioneer with his team. Robinson's talents and legendary aggressiveness made him into one of the best second basemen who ever played the game.

Currently, baseball is integrated in that there are large numbers of African-American and Latin players; it is not unusual for a starting lineup to have a minority of whites. Still, the higher echelons — managers, general managers, and owners — are almost completely white, and there are many fewer African-American catchers and pitchers than there are outfielders and first basemen.

Bill James, *The Bill James Historical Baseball Abstract* (1988); Roger Kahn, *The Boys of Summer* (1973); Lawrence S. Ritter, *The Glory of Their Times: The Story of Baseball's Early Years Told by the Men Who Played It* (1966).

Warren Goldstein

See also Mays, Willie; Rickey, Branch; Robinson, Jackie; Ruth, Babe; Spectator Sports.

BATTLES

See Alamo; Indians; Pearl Harbor, Attack on; Tet Offensive; *entries for individual wars.*

BAY OF PIGS INVASION

The Bay of Pigs affair was an unsuccessful invasion of Cuba on April 17, 1961, at Playa Girón (the Bay of Pigs) by about two thousand Cubans who had gone into exile after the 1959 revolution. Encouraged by members of the CIA who trained them, the invaders believed they would have air and naval support from the United States and that the invasion would cause the people of Cuba to rise up and overthrow the regime of communist Fidel Castro. Neither expectation materialized, although unmarked planes from Florida bombed Cuban air bases prior to the invasion. Cuban army troops pinned down the exiles and forced them to surrender within seventy-two hours.

The Eisenhower administration planned the Bay of Pigs attack, training anti-Castro Cubans in Guatemala and obtaining permission from Nicaraguan dictator Anastasio Somoza to launch the invasion from Puerto Cabezas on Nicaragua's Atlantic coast. After some hesitation, President John F. Kennedy allowed it to go forward.

At first, the State Department denied any direct links to the exiles. The true American role did not become public until a few days after the invasion. President Kennedy assumed full responsibility for what he admitted was a mistake. Nonetheless, he refused to negotiate a settlement of America's differences with the Castro regime.

Before and after the invasion, the United States promoted the expulsion of Cuba from the Organization of American States, attempted an unsuccessful diplomatic quarantine, and stopped all Cuban exports from entering the United States. Economic and diplomatic estrangement remained American policy toward Communist Cuba for the indefinite future.

See also Anticommunism; Caribbean-U.S. Relations.

BEARD, CHARLES A., and BEARD, MARY R.

(Charles: 1874–1948; Mary: 1876–1958), historians and social activists. The Beards, passionately independent-minded social critics, were both born and raised in Indiana and met as college students at DePauw University in the 1890s. They married in 1900 and departed for Oxford University in England, where Charles had begun studying the year before and helped found Ruskin Hall, in which evening and correspondence courses were offered to working-class people. Throughout their lives as scholars, both believed that learning was sterile unless it was aimed at progressive social change, an approach that crystallized during their two-year sojourn in England where they absorbed the thinking of cooperative socialists. Mary, influenced by Emmeline Pankhurst (soon to become renowned for suffrage militance), focused her interests on the problems of women workers and on their acquiring the vote as a remedy.

The couple returned to New York City in 1901 and enrolled in graduate school at Columbia University, Mary remaining only briefly. Charles earned a Ph.D. (1904) in political science and was hired as lecturer in history; in 1907 he was appointed to a new chair in politics and government.

Policymaking, constitutional change, and municipal reform absorbed both Beards during the 1910s. Concentrating on votes for women from 1910 to 1917, Mary was a prime mover in the militant Congressional Union, which became the National Woman's party; she also wrote an overview, *Women's Work in Municipalities* (1915). Charles, a leader at the New York Bureau of Municipal Research, produced an astounding ten books in history and political science between 1904 and 1919, in addition to many shorter pieces. Joining the swell of the "New History" at Columbia and influenced by iconoclastic works in political science and economics by Arthur Bentley, Edwin Seligman, and James Allen Smith, he shattered academic complacency with *An Economic Interpretation of the Constitution of the United States* (1913), which analyzed the Founders' motives according to their economic interests rather than their abstract political principles. This and his further works, such as *Economic Origins of Jeffersonian Democracy* (1915), were seen as muckraking attempts to unveil the underlying engines of politics; they became classics of a non-Marxist economic interpretation of history.

A fervent, witty, and magnetic teacher, and a principled defender of free speech, Charles Beard resigned from Columbia in 1917 to protest the university's failure to reappoint several professors who opposed U.S. involvement in World War I. (He himself supported the American war effort.) Thereafter the couple were unaffiliated with any institution of higher education, although Charles remained prominent in academic circles and was president of the American Political Science Association in 1926 and the American Historical Association in 1933.

In 1927 the Beards published their acclaimed two-volume *The Rise of American Civilization*, a work, said Richard Hofstadter, that "did more than any other . . . of the twentieth century to define American history for the reading public." The couple also collaborated on *America in Midpassage* (1937) and *The American Spirit* (1942), as well as three textbooks. Amid increasing renown for her work with her husband, Mary Ritter Beard emerged in the 1930s as an insistent spokeswoman for the importance and utility of women's history. She published *On Understanding Women* (1931), an overview of women's part in Western civilization and edited two collections of documents. Between 1935 and 1940 she headed an (ultimately unsuccessful) effort to found a World Center for Women's Archives. A pioneering thinker "obsessed" with the history of women from her suffragist days, she had an ambivalent relation to the feminists of the 1930s and 1940s. She scorned their view that

men had dominated women through history and contended instead for recognition of woman's force in constructing civilization, a view explicated in *Woman as Force in History* (1946).

During the 1930s Charles Beard turned increasingly to international relations. Distressed with the failure of World War I to achieve world peace or end imperialism, he directed his efforts toward preserving U.S. neutrality and encouraging rational domestic economic planning during the depression crisis. In *The Open Door at Home* (1934), *The Idea of National Interest* (1934), and *Giddy Minds and Foreign Quarrels* (1939), he expressed these concerns, which culminated in his opposition to U.S. entry into World War II and the writing of his last (harshly criticized) works, *American Foreign Policy in the Making, 1932–1940* (1946) and *President Roosevelt and the Coming of War* (1948). Although outspoken noninterventionists, both Beards were vigorous antifascists; nonetheless, Charles was vilified during the war for his views. His advocacy of an engaged practice of history, symbolized in his presidential address to the American Historical Association in 1933, "Written History as an Act of Faith," came under fire as a result.

After Charles Beard died in 1948, Mary Beard lived for another decade, writing two more books, *The Force of Women in Japanese History* (1953) and *The Making of Charles A. Beard* (1955). Both controversial public figures, the Beards are best remembered as distinguished historians whose purposeful readings of the past were intended to change the present and future.

Nancy F. Cott, *A Woman Making History: Mary Ritter Beard through Her Letters* (1991); Ellen Nore, *Charles A. Beard: An Intellectual Biography* (1983).

NANCY F. COTT

See also Feminist Movement; History and Historians; Progressivism.

BEECHER, CATHARINE

(1800–1878), educator and writer. Older sister of Harriet Beecher Stowe and Henry Ward Beecher, and eldest child of Lyman Beecher, Catharine Beecher in the 1840s was the best-known member of her large and prodigiously active family. Her life was shaped by the same issues that governed theirs: the transformation of American religious life from Puritan to evangelical values, the national crisis over slavery, western migration and settlement, and profound changes in middle-class American domestic life.

Resisting her father's powerful religious influence, Beecher directed her creativity into more secular channels. Yet throughout her long career as an educator of women, an advocate for the feminization of the teaching profession, and a publicist for women's power in family life, she invoked religious sanctions for the innovations she promoted.

Beecher never really enjoyed teaching, but like many American women in the nineteenth and early twentieth centuries — especially those who did not marry — she used it as a means of obtaining economic independence and as a route to other forms of social influence. For example, her first school, Hartford Female Seminary, became well known for its stirring religious revivals in the 1820s, which Beecher herself helped lead. Her success as an educator reflected the enormous increase in common schooling that accompanied the tremendous growth in American population and its geographic expansion during the first half of the nineteenth century. Although the main reason women replaced men as teachers in the nation's common schools was their willingness to work for lower wages, Beecher's writings, such as *An Essay on the Education of Female Teachers* (1835) and *The Duty of American Women to Their Country* (1845), turned necessity into a virtue by extolling the superior ability of women teachers to produce moral citizens.

Catharine Beecher also became well known as a commentator on changes taking place in middle-class American family life. She expanded her constituency beyond the schoolroom to the parlor with such writings as *Letters to Persons Who Are Engaged in Domestic Service* (1842), *The Evils Suffered by American Women and American Children: The Causes and the Remedy* (1846), *The True Remedy for the Wrongs of Women* (1851), *Letters to the People on Health and Happiness* (1855), and, above all, her often reprinted *Treatise on Domestic Economy* (1843). Her name became synonymous with the expansion of women's power within the domestic sphere. Some scholars have called this "domestic feminism," since it advocated women's control of their bodies and their immediate life circumstances. Predictably, she opposed women's activism in the public domain, particularly in the antislavery movement.

A complex figure embodying many internal contradictions, Beecher, as a single woman, exemplified the possibilities for personal autonomy available in the nineteenth century to women who never married. Yet despite all her domestic advice, and despite her effort to construct a retirement home on the campus of a school she founded in Milwaukee, she was never able to maintain a home of her own. This rendered her autonomy problematic for her and for the family members with whom she lived. Nevertheless, within these constraints Catharine Beecher helped her contemporaries see new social and political significance in women's talents as teachers and homemakers.

Jeanne Boydston, Mary Kelley, and Anne Margolis, eds., *The Limits of Sisterhood: The Beecher Sisters on Women's Rights and Woman's Sphere* (1988); Kathryn Kish Sklar, *Catharine Beecher: A Study in American Domesticity* (1973; paperback ed., 1976).

KATHRYN KISH SKLAR

See also Education.

BELL, ALEXANDER GRAHAM

(1847–1922), inventor and speech teacher. Bell owes his immortality to his having been the first to design and patent a practical device for transmitting the human voice by means of an electric current. But Bell always described himself simply as a "teacher of the deaf," and his contributions in that field were of the first order.

Bell, who was born in Edinburgh, Scotland, was educated there and at the University of London. He also studied under his grandfather, Alexander Bell, a noted speech teacher. He taught elocution, assisted his father, also a speech teacher and noted phonetician, and taught at a school for the deaf in England, using his father's methods. In 1870, Bell immigrated with his parents to Canada.

Two years later he established a school for the deaf in Boston, Massachusetts, and the following year became a professor in speech and vocal physiology at Boston University. While teaching he experimented with a means of transmitting several telegraph messages simultaneously over a single wire and also with various devices to help the deaf learn to speak, including a means of graphically recording sound waves.

In 1874 the essential idea of the telephone formed in his mind. As he later explained it, "If I could make a current of electricity vary in intensity precisely as the air varies in density during the production of sound, I should be able to transmit speech telegraphically." Two years later he applied for a patent, which was granted on March 7, 1876. On March 10, the first coherent complete sentence — the famous "Mr. Watson, come here; I want you" — was transmitted in his laboratory.

Many others had worked to develop a practical telephone (the word itself was coined as early as 1849), and in all some six hundred suits were filed against Bell's patent. But it was ultimately upheld and he became a very rich man, in part thanks to his father-in-law, Gardiner G. Hubbard, who organized the first Bell Telephone Company. That firm evolved in the next few decades into the Bell Telephone System owned by the American Telephone and Telegraph Company (AT&T).

In later years Bell experimented with a means to detect metal in wounds and with a vacuum-jacket respirator that led to the development of the iron lung. He helped bring Thomas A. Edison's phonograph to commercial practicality and experimented with hydrofoil boats and with airplanes as early as the 1890s.

With the wealth derived from the telephone, Bell was able to assist the careers of other scientists. He also founded and helped finance the journal *Science,* today the premier American scientific journal, and the National Geographic Society.

While constantly engaged in scientific experiments, Bell crusaded tirelessly on behalf of the deaf, encouraging their integration into society with the help of lip-reading and other techniques. In 1890 he founded the Alexander Graham Bell Association for the Deaf.

He died in 1922 at his summer home on Cape Breton Island, Nova Scotia. People throughout North America were urged to refrain from making phone calls during his burial so that telephones would remain silent as a tribute.

Robert V. Bruce, *Bell: Alexander Graham Bell and the Conquest of Solitude* (1973).

JOHN STEELE GORDON

See also Science and Technology.

BELLOW, SAUL

(1915–   ), novelist. In 1984, when Bellow returned to his hometown of Lachine, Quebec, and spoke at a ceremony in his honor, the mayor described him as "le plus grand écrivain de notre epoque" — a claim that few would dispute. The only American writer ever to win three National Book Awards, the Pulitzer Prize, and the Nobel Prize (1976), Bellow stands in a line of succession to William Faulkner and Ernest Hemingway, both Nobel laureates and, in their own idiosyncratic ways, representatives of the American realist tradition. What distinguishes Bellow from these predecessors is the international character of his fiction: he is the first American to incorporate the great nineteenth-century European realists in his work. An heir of Isaac Babel and Isaac Bashevis Singer as well as of his fellow Chicagoan Theodore Dreiser, Bellow is unique — a Jewish-American writer who has transcended both identities and become a figure in world literature.

Born in Lachine to Russian immigrants, Bellow was nine when his family moved to Chicago. After graduating from Northwestern University in 1937, he studied for a semester at the University of Wisconsin before returning to Chicago. There he found employment with the New Deal Federal Writers' Project, compiling biographies of midwestern novelists and poets. In the early forties he taught at Pestalozzi-Froebel Teachers College in Chicago and in 1943 went to work for

Mortimer Adler, indexing ideas for Adler's *Syntopicon*.

Bellow's first novel was *Dangling Man* (1944), a slender book written in the form of a journal about a disenchanted young man in Chicago awaiting induction into the army. It was followed by *The Victim* (1947), a grim novel that chronicled the tribulations of a Jewish office worker in New York who finds himself shadowed and hounded by a bullying anti-Semite. These books were stiff, well wrought, earnest — Bellow later referred to them as his M.A. and his Ph.D. — and they established his reputation in the New York literary world. But they gave little indication of the profuse, exuberant novels that were to follow.

In Europe on a Guggenheim in the late forties, Bellow stumbled upon the voice that would sustain *The Adventures of Augie March.* "All I had to do was to be there with buckets to catch it," he recalled. Published in 1953, the novel won Bellow his first National Book Award.

Three years later came *Seize the Day,* Bellow's terse masterpiece about the fragile fortunes of Tommy Wilhelm, a loser adrift on New York's Upper West Side; and in 1959, *Henderson the Rain King,* a manic, picaresque novel that tracks the gigantesque Eugene Henderson through an Africa that Bellow had never seen. But it was with *Herzog* (1964) that he obtained the position of preeminence he has occupied ever since. However entertaining as a chronicle of its hero's marital vicissitudes, the book is primarily a novel of ideas. Herzog is at work on a volume of essays about romanticism, and the novel is energized by his tireless and high-flown theorizing. In his subsequent novels — *Mr. Sammler's Planet* (1969), *Humboldt's Gift* (1975), and *The Dean's December* (1982) — Bellow became increasingly ruminative; his cerebral protagonists, suffused with what Sammler calls "earth-departure objectivity," are less obsessed with their private dramas than with the human condition. "The job, once and for all," declares Charles Citrine in *Humboldt's Gift,* "was to burst from the fatal self-sufficiency of consciousness and put my remaining strength over into the Imaginative Soul."

Bellow's extraordinary range — his book of

reportage about Israel, *To Jerusalem and Back* (1976), and his numerous uncollected lectures and essays — demonstrates a knowledge of history and an erudition unrivaled in American literature. He possesses, in the words of Irving Howe, "the most powerful mind among contemporary American novelists" and the most powerful imagination.

Mark Harris, *Saul Bellow: Drumlin Woodchuck* (1981).

JAMES ATLAS

See also Literature.

BENNETT, JAMES GORDON, SR., BENNETT, JAMES GORDON, JR.

(Senior: 1795–1872; Junior: 1841–1918), editors and newspaper publishers. James Gordon Bennett roared into the small, tidy world of American newspaper journalism brandishing his pen like a Highland claymore, and when he was through, it was a combative arena that he dominated. Born in Scotland, Bennett was an outsider in his own culture — a seminary-educated Catholic who extended his education by voracious reading, especially in the emerging romantics. He immigrated to the United States in 1819, lean and hungry, and began to earn a living as a teacher and swift, forceful writer on assorted cultural, economic, and political topics for newspapers in Charleston and New York City.

In 1835, after a stint as Washington correspondent for the *New-York Courier and Enquirer,* Bennett founded the *New-York Herald* on a capital of five hundred dollars, initially serving not only as editor-owner but as the entire staff. The *Herald* appeared daily (a relatively new practice at the time) and sold for a cent a copy (an even newer idea that Bennett did not invent but built on brilliantly). Most daringly, the *Herald* aimed at self-support through a large circulation and advertising at a time when papers lived only through subsidies by political parties or the expensive subscriptions of a limited business clientele. Bennett broke new ground by filling the paper with hitherto-disdained news from police courts, sporting fields, theaters, and other sources that appealed to "the great masses of the community." But the *Herald* also featured first-rate coverage of national and international events, and it both reported and made use of the latest technological innovations just as fast as Bennett could reinvest his growing earnings. By 1860 great steam presses were daily stamping out up to fifty thousand copies of each day's paper, and each edition, well written and well illustrated, was full of the latest news gathered by telegraph, mail trains, and ocean steamers.

The dynamo of the whole enterprise, however, was Bennett. He combined Byronic vanity and canny pragmatism, wrote daily first-person editorials delivering abrasive opinions on everything, and unblushingly declared himself the "Napoleon of the newspaper," the man who had infused it with "life, glowing eloquence, philosophy, taste, sentiment, wit, and humor." Though castigated, horsewhipped, and boycotted at first, he was also irresistibly read, and on his retirement in 1867, the *Herald*'s annual profits were estimated at $400,000. Bennett did not create the social circumstances that generated a democratic readership, but his combination of genius and brass was ideally suited to Jacksonian era journalism.

After Bennett died, his son followed somewhat erratically in his footsteps. Young Bennett had been educated abroad and returned to the United States to serve in the navy during the Civil War and, at war's end, to take over the paper. He continued the senior Bennett's lavish spending on circulation-building enterprises. For example, he sent Henry M. Stanley to find David Livingstone in Africa, and he financed an exploring expedition in Arctic waters. But he lacked his father's curiosity and zest for newspapering's day-in and day-out combination of grind and theater. In 1877, after a domestic scandal, he moved back to Europe. He kept pumping money into the *Herald* but also withdrew prodigal sums to spend on his private pleasures, especially speed. He raced yachts and horses, and when they came along, balloons, airplanes, and automobiles. In the 1890s the *Herald* was outstripped in New York by its brassier young rivals, William Randolph Hearst's *Journal* and Joseph Pulitzer's *World*. After Bennett's death the debt-burdened *Herald* was merged in 1922 with the bitterest rival of its early years, the *New York Tribune*.

Oliver Carlson, *The Man Who Made News: James Gordon Bennett* (1942); Don C. Seitz, *The James Gordon Bennetts, Father and Son* (1928); Bernard A. Weisberger, *The American Newspaperman* (1961).

Bernard A. Weisberger

See also Magazines and Newspapers.

BERLIN, IRVING

(1888–1989), popular songwriter. Born Israel Baline in Russia, Berlin came to the United States in 1893 and received his first music lessons from his father, a cantor. The young Berlin performed on the streets of New York's Lower East Side and as a singing waiter in Chinatown before taking a job as a song plugger. His first published song was "Marie from Sunny Italy" (1907), and it was a printer's error on the cover of the sheet music that gave him the "nom de musique" of Berlin.

Berlin achieved success as a performer in musical revues, which were a popular form of theatrical and musical entertainment in the United States during the years around World War I. He sang his own songs in *Up and Down Broadway* (1910) and composed the music for the *Ziegfeld Follies* of 1911, 1919, 1920, and 1927. "Alexander's Ragtime Band," for which Berlin wrote both words and music, became an instant hit, and he composed the music for *Watch Your Step* (1914), a show that featured popular dancers Vernon and Irene Castle. He continued to compose musical revues, some of which were performed in New York's Music Box Theater, which he helped build. His famous song "Easter Parade" was composed for the revue *As Thousands Cheer* in 1933. World Wars I and II gave Berlin the inspiration for two of his most popular revues, *Yip, Yip, Yaphank!* (1918), which included the song "Oh, How I Hate to Get Up in the Morning," and *This Is the Army* (1942).

A self-taught pianist and composer, Berlin published more than fifteen hundred songs. Many were written for musical films that showcased such entertainers as Bing Crosby and Fred

Astaire. He wrote the scores for *Top Hat* (1935) and *Holiday Inn* (1942), which includes "White Christmas," one of his best-known songs. Ethel Merman helped popularize many Berlin songs in *Annie Get Your Gun* (1946) and *Call Me Madam* (1950). In 1939, Berlin published "God Bless America," for which he wrote both words and music.

Just as Berlin's music captured the ear of Americans, it was often heard at the White House. He played and sang informally for Franklin D. Roosevelt and his guests after one of the president's fireside chats in 1941. The composer wrote "It Gets Lonely in the White House" in 1948 to commemorate Harry Truman's election, and he used the song in a later show, *Mr. President* (1962). His output included love songs, dance numbers, and humorous pieces that appealed to Americans' desire for the singable melodies and upbeat lyrics. Berlin joined a cast of stars who performed at a special banquet on May 24, 1973, for more than six hundred prisoners of war recently returned from Vietnam. Gerald Ford awarded Berlin the Presidential Medal of Freedom on January 10, 1977, in recognition of his long career and contribution to the popular culture of the United States.

Laurence Bergreen, *As Thousands Cheer: The Life of Irving Berlin* (1990); David Ewen, *The Story of Irving Berlin* (1950); M. Freedland, *Irving Berlin* (1974).

BARBARA L. TISCHLER

See also Jazz; Music; Musical Theater.

BERLIN BLOCKADE

The Berlin blockade was an attempt in 1948 by the Soviet Union to limit the ability of France, Great Britain, and the United States to travel to their sectors of Berlin, which lay within Russian-occupied East Germany. The agreement after World War II to divide Germany and Berlin into occupation zones, with Berlin located deep in the Russian zone, had come out of the Yalta Conference in February 1945 and had included no arrangements for access to Berlin. Since then, the relationship between the Soviet Union and the West had deteriorated steadily, as reflected in disputes at the United Nations, Winston

Churchill's Iron Curtain speech in March 1946, growing emphasis in U.S. foreign policy on containment of Russian expansion, Soviet hostility toward the Marshall Plan, and growing Western commitment to establishing a separate capitalist West Germany.

In late 1947, discussions on Germany broke down over Soviet charges that the Allies were violating the Potsdam Agreement, and on March 20, 1948, the Soviets withdrew from the Allied Control Council administering Berlin. Ten days later, guards on the East German border began slowing the entry of Western troop trains bound for Berlin. On June 7, the Western powers announced their intention to proceed with the creation of West Germany. On June 24, arguing that if Germany was to be partitioned, Berlin could no longer be the single German capital, the Soviets stopped all surface travel between West Germany and Berlin.

Within the United States there was some sentiment for accepting the Soviet logic; many were reluctant to risk war over maintaining ties to their recent enemies, the Berliners. But the Truman administration was convinced that losing Berlin would mean losing all of Germany. After a military challenge was considered and rejected, the Berlin airlift was initiated. Over the next 321 days, Western fliers made 272,000 flights into West Berlin, delivering thousands of tons of supplies every day. The effort gained wide public sympathy, and on May 12, 1949, the Soviets, concluding that the blockade had failed, reopened the borders. East and West Germany were established as separate republics later that month.

See also Cold War; Germany-U.S. Relations.

BERNSTEIN, LEONARD

(1918–1990), conductor, composer, pianist, author, and educator. Bernstein, born in Lawrence, Massachusetts, showed musical talent at a young age. He graduated from Harvard University, where he studied with Edward Burlingame Hill and Walter Piston, and continued his studies with Fritz Reiner at the Curtis Institute in Philadelphia. During the summers of 1940 and 1941, he worked at Tanglewood with Serge

Koussevitzky, who became his mentor. In 1943, he became assistant conductor of the New York Philharmonic. On November 14, 1943, Bernstein stepped in for the ailing Bruno Walter to conduct a nationally broadcast Philharmonic program. His vigorous, charismatic, and thoroughly prepared performance brought him overnight fame.

Bernstein's First Symphony, subtitled *Jeremiah,* was chosen by the New York Music Critics' Circle as the best new American orchestral work of 1943–1944. That same season, his ballet, *Fancy Free,* with choreography by Jerome Robbins, was introduced by the Ballet Theater at the Metropolitan Opera House. Its success led Robbins and Bernstein to use the scenario as the basis for the musical *On the Town,* which ran for more than a year on Broadway. In 1954, Bernstein composed his only film score, the brooding, expressionist music for *On the Waterfront.*

In 1957, Bernstein's masterpiece, the musical *West Side Story,* written with Stephen Sondheim, opened on Broadway to extraordinary critical and popular acclaim. The same year, he was appointed co-conductor, with Dimitri Mitropoulos, of the New York Philharmonic. In 1958, he was named music director and chief conductor, positions he held until 1969, whereupon he was appointed conductor laureate for life. After leaving the Philharmonic, Bernstein remained active as one of the most successful guest conductors in the world.

Bernstein had a profound effect on American music. As the first world-class musician in America to build a career in the United States, he brought a new respect to American musical endeavor. His influence on younger artists cannot be overemphasized.

As a conductor, Bernstein was at his best in the subjective, passionate literature of the romantic and modern eras, and he had a special affinity for the works of Gustav Mahler, whose music he did much to popularize. He was a champion of American music, especially the relatively conservative work of such men as Aaron Copland, William Schuman, and Roy Harris. His podium manner was balletic and demonstrative; some found it flamboyant.

Bernstein wrote three symphonies, four musicals, a violin concerto, an idiosyncratic theatri-cal Mass (1971), and two interrelated operas, *Trouble in Tahiti* (1950) and *A Quiet Place* (1983), as well as other minor pieces. His lighter works are generally considered to be his most successful; Bernstein's "serious" music tends toward the ponderous.

A gifted pianist, he recorded Copland's Piano Sonata, as well as concertos by Mozart, Beethoven, and Ravel, which he conducted from the keyboard. Through the televised New York Philharmonic "Young People's Concerts," which reached millions of viewers, Bernstein became perhaps the most influential music teacher in history. He published several books, the best of which is *The Joy of Music* (1959), a spirited, informal introduction to the art.

Joan Peyser, *Bernstein: A Biography* (1987); Paul Robinson, *Bernstein* (1982).

TIM PAGE

See also Music; Musical Theater.

BERRY, CHUCK

(1926–   ), rock musician and composer. "If you tried to give rock 'n' roll another name, you might call it 'Chuck Berry,' " John Lennon of the Beatles once said. At the height of Berry's popularity, in the last half of the fifties, other singers had more hits, but no one had more influence. During the sixties the Beatles and the Rolling Stones played a dozen of his songs note for note, and Bob Dylan acknowledged his debt to Berry as a lyricist.

Berry was born in St. Louis into a lower-middle-class black family. He served three years in reform school on a robbery conviction, earned a certificate in hairdressing and cosmetology, and then took a job on an auto assembly line to support his wife and children. By 1953 he was leading a three-piece blues group, which played on weekends. In 1955, his first hit, "Maybelline," reached the top ten after being plugged by New York disc jockey Alan Freed, who earned royalties on it by listing himself as the song's coauthor — an example of whites exploiting black musicians and of the pervasive corruption in the music industry at that time.

Berry's greatest hits recounted teenage experiences and frustrations, but also conveyed the fun of adolescent rebellion. "School Day" (which reached the number 3 spot on the *Billboard* charts in 1957) complains about teachers and in retrospect seems to prophesy the student rebellion of the sixties: "Close your books, get out of your seat / Down the halls and into the street." "Sweet Little Sixteen" (number 2 in 1958) presented the breathless world of a young rock fan. The autobiographical "Johnny B. Goode" (number 8 in 1958) provides a classic treatment of the small-town-boy-makes-good theme — in this case, as a rock 'n' roll star. The *Voyager I* spacecraft, heading out toward distant galaxies, includes among its messages to other worlds a recording of "Johnny B. Goode."

In 1959, at the peak of his creativity and popular success, Berry was convicted under the Mann Act and went to prison for two years. He had few hits after that. In 1972, touring as an "oldies" act, he finally reached number 1 on the charts with "My Ding-a-ling," a forgettable novelty song. Its success only underscored the fact that none of his classic records ever sold as well as those of white crooners like Pat Boone.

As a rock lyricist, Berry was among the best. His lyrics convey an immense, childlike delight in linguistic play, cataloging the fun and frustrations in the lives of white teenagers. That these lyrics were the work of a black man in his thirties makes them especially remarkable. As a guitarist, wrote Robert Christgau, Berry's style featured a "limited but brilliant vocabulary of guitar riffs that quickly came to epitomize rock 'n' roll. Ultimately, every great white guitar group of the early sixties imitated Berry's style."

In 1987 he published a widely praised autobiography. A 1988 feature film, *Hail! Hail! Rock 'n' Roll*, available on home video, documents his career.

Chuck Berry, *Chuck Berry: The Autobiography* (1987); Robert Christgau, "Chuck Berry," in Jim Miller, ed., *The Rolling Stone Illustrated History of Rock & Roll* (1980).

JON WIENER

See also Music.

BETHUNE, MARY McLEOD

(1875–1955), educator, civil rights leader, presidential adviser, and founder of black women's clubs. Bethune was born in Mayesville, South Carolina, the fifteenth child of former slaves. More fortunate than her many siblings, she entered the local Presbyterian Mission School for Negroes, and with the help of scholarships, part-time jobs, and familial sacrifice she was able to attend, from 1888 to 1894, Scotia Seminary (now Barber-Scotia College) in Concord, North Carolina. Aspiring to work as a missionary in Africa, she studied at the Moody Bible Institute in Chicago, graduating in 1895. The Presbyterian Mission Board, however, turned down her application for a missionary post.

Undaunted, McLeod returned south where she secured a series of teaching positions in Georgia and South Carolina. She married Albertus Bethune and in 1899 bore a son, Albert McLeod Bethune. Her husband died soon afterward.

Convinced that education was the most powerful weapon in the fight against black powerlessness and racial subordination, Bethune settled in Daytona, Florida, where she founded, in October 1904, the Daytona Literary and Industrial School for Training Negro Girls. Reflecting on her work years later, Bethune recalled, "The school expanded fast. In less than two years I had 250 pupils. . . . I concentrated more and more on girls, as I felt that they especially were hampered by lack of educational opportunities." In 1923, however, she agreed to merge with Cookman Institute, a Methodist school for Negro boys, forming the Bethune-Cookman College.

Bethune's pioneering work in black education earned national acclaim. In many respects she was as formidable a fund-raiser as Booker T. Washington. Like him she adhered to an educational philosophy that stressed teacher preparation, industrial training and domestic arts, good manners, and Christian virtue. She soon attracted the attention of white political leaders, serving as adviser on black education and racial affairs in the Coolidge administration. From 1936 to 1945, under the New Deal's National Youth Administration, Bethune served as director of the Division of Negro Affairs. She well understood the need for blacks to marshal political power and acquire advanced education as strategies in the ongoing struggle for equal rights.

In 1935 she founded and served as president, until 1949, of the National Council of Negro Women (NCNW) — the largest and most resilient federation of black women's organizations. The NCNW proposed to collect, interpret, and disseminate information concerning the activities of black women. The leaders also desired "to develop competent and courageous leadership among Negro women and effect their integration and that of all Negro people into the . . . life of their communities." To work toward these ends, NCNW leaders founded the *Aframerican Woman's Journal,* dedicated to achieving "the outlawing of the Poll Tax, the development of a Public Health Program, an Anti-lynching Bill, the end of discrimination in the Armed Forces, Defense Plants, Government Housing Plants and finally that Negro History be taught in the Public Schools of the country."

Bethune is a pivotal figure in twentieth-century black women's history. Her life and work formed a major link connecting the social reform efforts of post-Reconstruction black women to the political protest activities of the generation emerging after World War II.

James J. Flynn, *Negroes of Achievement in Modern America* (1970), 228–234; B. Joyce Ross, "Mary McLeod Bethune and the National Youth Administration: A Case Study of Power Relationships in the Black Cabinet of Franklin D. Roosevelt," in John Hope Franklin and August Meier, eds., *Black Leaders of the Twentieth Century* (1982), 191–219.

DARLENE CLARK HINE

See also Education.

BILL OF RIGHTS

The roots of the Bill of Rights — the first ten amendments to the U.S. Constitution — lie deep in Anglo-American history. In 1215 England's King John, under pressure from rebellious barons, put his seal to Magna Carta, which protected subjects against royal abuses of power. Among Magna Carta's more important provisions are its requirement that proceedings and prosecutions be according to "the law of the land" — the forerunner of "due process of law" — and a ban on the sale, denial, or delay of justice.

In response to arbitrary actions of Charles I, Parliament in 1628 adopted the Petition of Right, condemning unlawful imprisonments and also providing that there should be no tax "without common consent of parliament." In 1689, capping the Glorious Revolution (which placed William and Mary on the throne), Parliament adopted the Bill of Rights. Not only does its name anticipate the American document of a century later, the English Bill of Rights anticipates some of the American bill's specific provisions — for example, the Eighth Amendment's ban on excessive bail and fines and on cruel and unusual punishment.

The idea of written documents protecting individual liberties took early root in England's American colonies. Colonial charters (such as the 1606 Charter for Virginia) declared that those who migrated to the New World should enjoy the same "privileges, franchises, and immunities" as if they lived in England. In the years leading up to the break with the mother country (especially after the Stamp Act of 1765), Americans wrote tracts and adopted resolutions resting their claim of rights on Magna Carta, on the colonial charters, and on the teachings of natural law.

Once independence had been declared, in 1776, the American states turned immediately to the writing of state constitutions and state bills of rights. In Williamsburg, George Mason was the principal architect of Virginia's Declaration of Rights. That document, which wove Lockean notions of natural rights with concrete protections against specific abuses, was the model for bills of rights in other states and, ultimately, for the federal Bill of Rights. (Mason's declaration was also influential in the framing, in 1789, of France's Declaration of Rights of Man and the Citizen).

In 1787, at the Constitutional Convention in Philadelphia, Mason remarked that he "wished the plan had been prefaced by a Bill of Rights." Elbridge Gerry moved for the appointment of a committee to prepare such a bill, but the delegates, without debate, defeated the motion. They did not oppose the principle of a bill of rights; they simply thought it unnecessary, in light of the theory that the new federal government would be one of enumerated powers only. Some of the Framers also were skeptical of the utility of what James Madison called "parchment barriers" against majorities; they looked, for protection, to structural arrangements such as separation of powers and checks and balances.

Opponents of ratification quickly seized upon the absence of a bill of rights, and Federalists, especially Madison, soon realized that they must offer to add amendments to the Constitution after its ratification. Only by making such a pledge were the Constitution's supporters able to achieve ratification in such closely divided states as New York and Virginia.

In the First Congress, Madison undertook to fulfill his promise. Carefully sifting amendments from proposals made in the state ratifying conventions, Madison steered his project through the shoals of indifference on the part of some members (who thought the House had more important work to do) and outright hostility on the

Bill of Rights

Amendment I

Congress shall make no law respecting an establishment of religion, or prohibiting the free exercise thereof; or abridging the freedom of speech, or of the press; or the right of the people peaceably to assemble, and to petition the government for a redress of grievances.

Amendment II

A well-regulated militia being necessary to the security of a free State, the right of the people to keep and bear arms shall not be infringed.

Amendment III

No soldier shall, in time of peace, be quartered in any house without the consent of the owner, nor in time of war, but in a manner to be prescribed by law.

Amendment IV

The right of the people to be secure in their persons, houses, papers, and effects, against unreasonable searches and seizures, shall not be violated, and no warrants shall issue but upon probable cause, supported by oath or affirmation, and particularly describing the place to be searched, and the persons or things to be seized.

Amendment V

No person shall be held to answer for a capital, or otherwise infamous crime, unless on a presentment or indictment of a grand jury, except in cases arising in the land or naval forces, or in the militia, when in actual service in time of war or public danger; nor shall any person be subject for the same offense to be twice put in jeopardy of life or limb; nor shall be compelled in any criminal case to be a witness against himself, nor be deprived of life, liberty, or property, without due process of law; nor

shall private property be taken for public use without just compensation.

Amendment VI

In all criminal prosecutions, the accused shall enjoy the right to a speedy and public trial, by an impartial jury of the State and district wherein the crime shall have been committed, which district shall have been previously ascertained by law, and to be informed of the nature and cause of the accusation; to be confronted with the witnesses against him; to have compulsory process for obtaining witnesses in his favor, and to have the assistance of counsel for his defense.

Amendment VII

In suits at common law, where the value in controversy shall exceed twenty dollars, the right of trial by jury shall be preserved, and no fact tried by a jury shall be otherwise reexamined in any court of the United States, than according to the rules of the common law.

Amendment VIII

Excessive bail shall not be required, nor excessive fines imposed, nor cruel and unusual punishments inflicted.

Amendment IX

The enumeration in the Constitution, of certain rights, shall not be construed to deny or disparage others retained by the people.

Amendment X

The powers not delegated to the United States by the Constitution, nor prohibited by it to the States, are reserved to the States respectively, or to the people.

part of others (Antifederalists who hoped for a second convention to hobble the powers of the federal government). In September 1789 the House and Senate accepted a conference report laying out the language of proposed amendments to the Constitution.

Within six months of the time the amendments — the Bill of Rights — had been submitted to the states, nine had ratified them. Two more states were needed; Virginia's ratification, on December 15, 1791, made the Bill of Rights part of the Constitution. (Ten amendments were ratified; two others, dealing with the number of representatives and with the compensation of senators and representatives, were not.)

On their face, it is obvious that the amendments apply to actions by the federal government, not to actions by the states. In 1833, in *Barron* v. *Baltimore,* Chief Justice John Marshall confirmed that understanding. Barron had sued the city for damage to a wharf, resting his claim on the Fifth Amendment's requirement that private property not be taken for public use "without just compensation." Marshall ruled that the Fifth Amendment was intended "solely as a limitation on the exercise of power by the government of the United States, and is not applicable to the legislation of the states."

The Civil War and Reconstruction brought, in their wake, the Fourteenth Amendment, which declares, among other things, that no state shall "deprive any person of life, liberty, or property, without due process of law." In those few words lay the seed of a revolution in American constitutional law. That revolution began to take form in 1947, in Justice Hugo Black's dissent in *Adamson* v. *California.* Reviewing the history of the Fourteenth Amendment's adoption, Black concluded that history "conclusively demonstrates" that the amendment was meant to ensure that "no state could deprive its citizens of the privileges and protections of the Bill of Rights."

Justice Black's "wholesale incorporation" theory has never been adopted by the Supreme Court. During the heyday of the Warren Court, in the 1960s, however, the justices embarked on a process of "selective incorporation." In each case, the Court asked whether a specific provision of the Bill of Rights was essential to "fundamental fairness"; if it was, then it must apply to the states as it does to the federal government. Through this process, nearly all the important provisions of the Bill of Rights now apply to the states. A partial list would include the First Amendment's rights of speech, press, and religion, the Fourth Amendment's protection against unreasonable searches and seizures, the Fifth Amendment's privilege against self-incrimination, and the Sixth Amendment's right to counsel, to a speedy and public trial, and to trial by jury.

The original Constitution has been amended a number of times — for example, to provide for direct election of senators and to give the vote to eighteen-year-olds. The Bill of Rights, however, has never been amended. There is, of course, sharp debate over Supreme Court interpretation of specific provisions, especially where social interests (such as the control of traffic in drugs) seem to come into tension with provisions of the Bill of Rights (such as the Fourth Amendment). Such debate notwithstanding, there is no doubt that the Bill of Rights, as symbol and substance, lies at the heart of American conceptions of individual liberty, limited government, and the rule of law.

Irving Brant, *The Bill of Rights: Its Origin and Meaning* (1965); Robert A. Rutland, *The Birth of the Bill of Rights, 1776–1791* (1955).

A. E. DICK HOWARD

See also Black, Hugo; Constitution; Freedom of Speech; Freedom of the Press; Ratification of the Constitution; Madison, James; Mason, George; Philadelphia Convention.

BIRTH CONTROL

"Birth control" was an early-twentieth-century slogan, but it has become the generic for all forms of control of reproduction. In popular usage it refers particularly to contraception, but in fact its historical practice cannot be separated from that of abortion. Attempts to control reproduction have characterized virtually every society of which we have records. In ancient societies these methods ranged from the magical to the highly effective and included coitus interruptus, spermicidal douches, homemade pessaries designed to obstruct the opening of the cervix, and abortions. With the spread of agriculture and the economic advantages of large families, religious and in some cases secular law increasingly restricted birth control, with the result that there appears to have been an increase in reliance on abortion while contraceptive technology and use declined. Both practices were legal in the United States until the mid-nineteenth century.

Starting in the 1830s, a state-by-state drive to prohibit abortion developed and was largely successful by 1880. It was spurred by a backlash against the women's rights movement that reflected anxieties about women deserting their conventional position as mothers, and by professionalizing physicians eager to restrict their competition from "irregular" practitioners, many of them offering abortion services. Then in 1873 all birth-control information was specifically included within the definition of the obscene and was therefore barred from interstate commerce by the federal Comstock Act. Nevertheless the steady decline of the U.S. birthrate in the nineteenth century suggests that some traditional birth-control methods were widely used despite legal prohibition, notably, abortion, coitus interruptus, and douches.

Although birth control is ancient, political movements for birth control are modern, arising in opposition to the prohibitions that began in the early nineteenth century. There were several movements. The first, neo-Malthusianism, appearing in England in the early nineteenth century, sought to increase the standard of living among the poor by reducing births. But the common view that America was underpopulated gave neo-Malthusianism little support in the United States.

Stronger in the United States were birth-control programs rooted in antebellum reform movements, both secular and religious. They advocated birth control to control population, to prevent the spread of hereditary disease, to improve the hereditary "stock" (early versions of eugenics), to liberate women from reproductive drudgery, and sometimes to permit greater sexual freedom. In the 1820s, neo-Malthusian ideas were integrated into the experimental socialism associated with Robert Dale Owen and feminist Frances Wright. These secular socialists were soon joined by religious radicals who also promoted birth control, but in different forms. The Second Great Awakening had given rise to a "perfectionist" mode of thought — heretical in relation to orthodox forms of Protestantism because it emphasized the possibility of perfecting earthly life. Also committed to improving women's condition and public health generally, these religious socialists rejected contraception as artificial and instead tried to effect birth control by changing the nature of sexual activity itself. For example, the Oneida community in the 1840s, ruled autocratically by John Humphrey Noyes, practiced male continence, a regimen in which men refrained from ejaculation altogether, and reproductive sex was practiced only by couples appointed by Noyes for the purpose of breeding superior people. He and his supporters believed that male continence not only built self-discipline but heightened sexual pleasure. In the second half of the century, "Free Lovers" further developed these noncontraceptive forms of birth control, recommending withdrawal or sexual activity other than intercourse. Feminist socialist physician Alice Stockham designed a sexual system called "Karezza" that required both men and women to avoid orgasm and, she believed, intensified and prolonged pleasure.

Women's rights advocates shared the view that the discipline and self-control required by noncontraceptive birth control was in itself liberating. By the 1870s, a flourishing feminist movement transformed this tradition of thought into a new political demand, with the slogan "voluntary motherhood." Nineteenth-century feminists continued to oppose contraception and abortion, which, they feared, would further license predatory male sexual aggression. Instead they recommended abstinence. Their proposals and rhetoric have been considered prudish, and there is some truth in this characterization, since they were expressing many women's negative experiences of heterosexual sex; yet viewed in their historic context, they can also be characterized as spokeswomen for women's sexual liberation. They understood that women could not find and defend their own sexual desires until they gained the power to reject men's. At the Free Love edges of the feminist movement, some advocated greater sexual experience and pleasure for women, whereas more mainstream women's rights advocates tended to emphasize the dangers of licentious sexuality. Their arguments for abstinence as a form of birth control thus had two meanings: one was voluntary motherhood, opposition to coercive childbearing; the other was voluntary sex, opposition to men's traditional prerogatives of demanding sexual submission from wives. Moreover, some voluntary motherhood advocates developed a critique of male sexuality, prefiguring much that late-twentieth-century feminists argued regarding the obsessiveness and dominance embedded in much of what men experience as sexual desire. Unlike their neo-Malthusian predecessors, voluntary motherhood advocates were not concerned with population size or with working-class power; they were resolutely pro-motherhood and, far from challenging the Victorian romanticization of motherhood, they manipulated it to increase women's power.

At the turn of the century a conservative reaction against voluntary motherhood agitation set in, focused on the "race suicide" alarm popularized by President Theodore Roosevelt. Race suicide moralists propagandized against the "selfishness" of women who avoided their maternal duties by using birth control, deploying racist fears (in a period of heavy immigration) that "WASP" dominance would be undermined by the high birthrates of those of "inferior stock."

In the first decades of the twentieth century a renewed birth-control movement arose among feminists associated particularly with the Socialist party and the Industrial Workers of the World (IWW) and took a militant turn in demanding the legalization of contraception. As urban radicals grew more daring sexually, they discovered the use of vaginal diaphragms in Europe. Emma Goldman of the IWW and Margaret Sanger of the Socialist party visited clinics in Holland where women were fitted with diaphragms. When these two women adopted civil

disobedience as a means of dramatizing the issue in the United States, distributing prohibited leaflets about contraception and opening illegal birth-control clinics, the Left leadership remained uninterested, but rank-and-file women responded with enthusiasm. Between 1914 and 1918 birth-control leagues developed in every major city of the United States. When these activists offered contraceptive information and services, they were deluged with clients. When they were arrested, their political defenses publicized contraception and created an even more avid demand for it.

Shortly after World War I the birth-control mass movement subsided, victim of the strongly conservative mood that followed the war. The leader of the main national birth-control organization, Margaret Sanger, shifted political strategies, downplaying the earlier association of reproductive control with women's rights and seeking instead a compromise: legalizing contraception at physicians' discretion. Birth-control leaders also emphasized the eugenic arguments popular for several decades, but now in more overtly racist ways, building on fears of high immigrant and black birthrates to support the case for legalization of contraception. The adoption of statutes providing for forcible sterilization of the feeble-minded, "degenerates," and some other groups by many states (with especial alacrity in the southern states) was also part of this redefinition of the function of birth control. This compromise was the basis for significant hostility to birth control among many twentieth-century African-Americans.

The World War II period produced two new birth-control movements: Planned Parenthood and population control. These were distinct but related. The Planned Parenthood organization, dating from 1942, renewed the campaign for the legalization and promotion of contraception, arguing primarily that birth control promoted family stability. Unlike the profamily backlash of the race suicide alarm, these family planning advocates asserted that marital adjustment must rest on a permissive attitude toward sex without fear of conception. Planned Parenthood, unlike the voluntary motherhood movement, endorsed unlimited marital sex and did not raise issues of women's sexual exploitation. In its domestic campaigns, the organization promoted small families and planning. In its international aspects, it argued a renewed neo-Malthusianism: it advocated population control as a cure for poverty. By 1960 population control had become such an unchallenged ideology in the United States that many used the phrase interchangeably with the earlier *birth control.*

In the late 1960s the renewed women's liberation movement again changed the terms of understanding of reproduction-control politics. The women's movement viewed birth control as part of an overall campaign for women's self-determination and began to distinguish that goal from those of family planning or population control. This orientation was influenced by the introduction of birth-control pills in 1960, which were mass-marketed so successfully that within a year 1 million women in the United States were using them. The "pill" had a twofold effect: its availability accustomed a generation of women to sex without fear of reproduction, and feminist exposure of its health dangers and discomforts, some of them hidden by the great pharmaceutical companies that were reaping vast profits from this new market, decreased women's trust in professionals and sparked a powerful women's health movement.

Intrauterine devices (IUD) were mass-marketed from the late 1960s, and women's experience with them further increased feminist conviction that the FDA, the agency responsible for reviewing the safety of drugs and medical devices, could not be relied on to protect women. The Dalkon Shield IUD caused at least twenty deaths and hundreds of thousands of severe infections and injuries, often creating permanent sterility or other damage. In a victorious class-action suit brought by the victims, its manufacturer, A. H. Robins, was shown to have ignored warnings of the dangers from its own staff. The result did not necessarily help the cause of birth control, however, as nearly all forms of IUD, including those with good safety records, were removed from the U.S. market.

The feminist campaign coalesced around the issue of abortion. The campaign for legal abortion in the 1960s began not with feminists but with civil libertarians and physicians, and the Supreme Court decision in *Roe* v. *Wade* in 1973 continued the tradition of defending physicians' discretion. The women's movement began to insist on a broader program, supporting reproductive self-determination and criticizing forced sterilization, unsafe contraception, and unnecessary hysterectomies and cesarean sections. This movement had considerable impact, forcing governments to adopt regulations for informed consent in sterilization procedures, for example.

In response a widespread antiabortion movement arose, organized first by the Catholic hierarchy but soon becoming more ecumenical and receiving support notably from fundamentalist Protestants. It remains a largely religious movement. Unlike the nineteenth-century antiabortion movement, which spoke explicitly of prohibiting abortion in order to enforce women's domesticity, the late-twentieth-century movement, known by the slogan "right-to-life," defined itself as defending the rights of fetuses.

By 1990 abortion had become perhaps the most controversial political issue in the country. Some conservative courts and state legislatures had sharply limited the right to abortion, especially among the poor, by establishing or encouraging prohibitions on public funding. In its 1989 *Webster* decision the Supreme Court enlarged the area in which state legislatures were allowed to restrict abortion. A new and safer hormonal abortifacient developed in France, known as RU-486, had not found a U.S. marketer because of fear of antiabortionists' retaliation.

Birth control was also implicated in a range of other controversial social and political issues in the 1980s, notably high teenage out-of-wedlock pregnancy rates and AIDS. Some responded to these problems by calling for increased public education about and availability of birth-control and prophylactic devices, and the antiabortion lobby continued to argue that the emphasis should be on chastity instead. The vision of mid-century civil libertarians that birth control might become a private issue in which no government action is necessary seems distant from the late-twentieth-century situation.

Linda Gordon, *Woman's Body, Woman's Right: A Social History of Birth Control in America* (1976; rev. ed., 1990); James Mohr, *Abortion in America: The Origins and Evolution of National Policy* (1978); Rosalind Pollack Petchesky, *Abortion and Woman's Choice: The State, Sexuality, and Reproductive Freedom* (1984; 2nd ed., 1986).

LINDA GORDON

See also Abortion; Family; Feminist Movement; Goldman, Emma; *Griswold* v. *Connecticut;* Marriage; *Roe* v. *Wade;* Sanger, Margaret; Second Great Awakening; Stanton, Elizabeth Cady; Wright, Frances.

BIRTHRATE AND MORTALITY

Every modern, economically developed nation has experienced the demographic transition from high to low levels of fertility and mortality. America is no exception. In the early nineteenth century, the typical American woman had between seven and eight live births in her lifetime and people probably lived fewer than forty years on average. But America was also distinctive. First, its fertility transition began in the late eighteenth or early nineteenth century at the latest. Other Western nations began their sustained fertility declines in the late nineteenth or early twentieth century, with the exception of France, whose decline also began early. Second, the fertility rate in America commenced its sustained decline long before that of mortality did. This contrasts with the more typical demographic transition in which mortality decline precedes or occurs simultaneously with fertility decline. American mortality did not experience a sustained and irreversible decline until about the 1870s. Third, both these processes were influenced by America's very high level of net inmigration and also by the significant population redistribution to frontier areas and later to cities, towns, and suburbs.

One particular difficulty for American historical demography is lack of data. During the colonial period, there was neither a regular enumeration nor vital registration. Some scholars, however, have conducted family reconstitutions and other demographic reconstructions using genealogies, parish registers, biographical data, and other local records, so we do know something about vital rates and population characteristics. In 1790, of course, the federal government commenced the decennial U.S. census, which has been the principal source for the study of population growth, structure, and redistribution, as well as fertility prior to the twentieth century. But vital registration was left to state and local governments. Massachusetts was the first state to institute continuous recording of births, deaths, and marriages, beginning in 1842 (some individual cities had registered vital events earlier), but the entire nation was not covered until 1933.

For the colonial period, we know more about population size than other matters, since the British colonial authorities did conduct some enumerations. The population of the British mainland colonies increased from several hundred non-Amerindian individuals in the early seventeenth century to about 2.5 million (2 million whites and about half a million blacks) in 1780. Birthrates were high, ranging between over forty and over fifty live births per one thousand people per annum. The high fertility of American women attracted comment from late eighteenth-century observers, including Benjamin Franklin and Thomas Malthus. Mortality rates were probably moderate, with crude death rates ranging from about twenty per one thousand people per annum to over forty. We know a good deal about mortality rates in New England, somewhat less about the Middle Colonies, and least about the South. But apparently mortality was lower from Pennsylvania and New Jersey northward, and higher in the South. Life expectancy at birth ranged from the late twenties to almost forty.

Information on America's demographic transition becomes more plentiful for the nineteenth and twentieth centuries. The accompanying table provides summary measures of fertility and mortality for the period 1800–1980. They include, for fertility, the crude birthrate, the child-woman ratio (based solely on census data), and the total fertility rate; and, for mortality, life expectancy at birth and the infant mortality rate. The results are given for the white and black populations separately because of their very different social, economic, and demographic experiences.

The table indicates the sustained decline in white birthrates from at least 1800 and of black fertility from at least 1850. Family sizes were large early in the nineteenth century, being approximately seven children per woman at the beginning of the century and between seven and eight for the largely rural slave population at midcentury. The table also reveals that mortality did not begin to decline until about the 1870s or so. Prior to that, death rates fluctuated, being affected by periodic epidemics and changes in the disease environment. There is some evidence of rising death rates during the 1830s and 1840s. The table also shows that American blacks had both higher fertility and higher mortality relative to the white population, although both groups experienced fertility and mortality transitions. For example, both participated in the

rise in birthrates after World War II known as the baby boom as well as the subsequent resumption of birthrate declines in the 1960s.

Conventional explanations for the fertility transition have involved the rising cost of children because of urbanization, the growth of incomes and nonagricultural employment, the increased value of education, rising female employment, child labor laws and compulsory education, and declining infant and child mortality. Changing attitudes toward large families and contraception, as well as better contraceptive techniques, have also been cited. Recent literature suggests that women were largely re-

Fertility and Mortality in the United States, 1800–1980

Year	Birthrate[a]		Child-Woman Ratio[b]		Total Fertility Rate[c]		Expectation of Life[d]		Infant Mortality Rate[e]	
	White	*Black[f]*	*White*	*Black*	*White*	*Black[f]*	*White*	*Black[f]*	*White*	*Black[f]*
1800	55.0		1342		7.04					
1810	54.3		1358		6.92					
1820	52.8		1295		6.73					
1830	51.4		1145		6.55					
1840	48.3		1085		6.14					
1850	43.3	58.6[g]	892	1087	5.42	7.90[g]	38.9		217.4	
1860	41.4	55.0[h]	905	1072	5.21	7.58[h]	40.9[k]		196.9[k]	
1870	38.3	55.4[i]	814	997	4.55	7.69[i]	44.1		176.0	
1880	35.2	51.9[j]	780	1090	4.24	7.26[j]	39.6		214.8	
1890	31.5	48.1	685	930	3.87	6.56	45.7		150.9	
1900	30.1	44.4	666	845	3.56	5.61	49.6		120.1	
1910	29.2	38.5	631	736	3.42	4.61	51.9		113.0	
1920	26.9	35.0	604	608	3.17	3.64	57.4	47.0	82.1	131.7
1930	20.6	27.5	506	554	2.45	2.98	60.8	48.5	60.1	99.9
1940	18.6	26.7	419	513	2.22	2.87	65.0	53.9	43.2	73.8
1950	23.0	33.3	580	663	2.98	3.93	69.1	60.8	26.8	44.5
1960	22.7	32.1	717	895	3.53	4.52	70.7	63.6	22.9	43.2
1970	17.4	25.1	507	689	2.38	3.07	71.7	65.2	17.8	30.9
1980	14.9	22.1			1.75	2.32	74.4	68.1	11.0	19.1

a. Births per 1000 population per annum. b. Children aged 0–4 per 1000 women aged 20–44. c. Total number of births per woman if she experienced the current period age-specific fertility rates throughout her life. d. Expectation of life at birth.
e. Infant deaths per 1000 live births per annum. f. Black and other population for 1920 and later. g. Average for 1850–1859.
h. Average for 1860–1869. i. Average for 1870–1879. j. Average for 1880–1884. k. For the total population.

Sources: U.S. Bureau of the Census, *Historical Statistics of the United States* (U.S. Government Printing Office, 1975); U.S. Bureau of the Census, *Statistical Abstract of the United States, 1988* (U.S. Government Printing Office, 1987); Ansley J. Coale and Melvin Zelnick, *New Estimates of Fertility and Population in the United States* (Princeton University Press, 1963); Ansley J. Coale and Norfleet W. Rives, "A Statistical Reconstruction of the Black Population of the United States, 1880–1970: Estimates of True Numbers by Age and Sex, Birth Rates, and Total Fertility," *Population Index* 39, no. 1 (Jan. 1973): 3–36; Michael R. Haines, "The Use of Model Life Tables to Estimate Mortality for the United States in the Late Nineteenth Century," *Demography* 16, no. 2 (May 1979): 289–312.

sponsible for much of the birthrate decline in the nineteenth century — part of a movement for greater control over their lives. The structural explanations fit the American experience since the late nineteenth century, but they are less appropriate for the fertility decline in rural areas prior to about 1870. The increased scarcity and higher cost of good agricultural land has been proposed as a prime factor, although this is controversial. The standard explanations do not adequately explain the post–World War II baby boom and subsequent baby bust. More complex theories, including the interaction of the size of generations with their income prospects, tastes for children versus material goods, and expectations about family size, have been proposed.

The mortality decline since the late nineteenth century seems to have been the result particularly of improvements in public health and sanitation, especially better water supplies and sewage disposal. The improving diet, clothing, and shelter of the American population over the period since about 1870 also played a role. Specific medical interventions beyond more general environmental public health measures were not statistically important until well into the twentieth century. It is difficult to disentangle the separate effects of these factors. But it is clear that much of the decline was due to rapid reductions in specific infectious and parasitic diseases, including tuberculosis, pneumonia, bronchitis, and gastrointestinal infections, as well as such well-known lethal diseases as cholera, smallpox, diphtheria, and typhoid fever. Nineteenth-century cities were especially unhealthy places, particularly the largest ones. This began to change by about the 1890s, when the largest cities instituted new public works sanitation projects (such as piped water, sewer systems, filtration and chlorination of water) and public health administration. They then experienced rapid improvements in death rates. As for the present, rural-urban mortality differentials have converged and largely disappeared. This, unfortunately, is not true of the differentials between whites and blacks.

Maris A. Vinovskis, ed., *Studies in American Historical Demography* (1979); Robert V. Wells, *Uncle Sam's Family: Issues in and Perspectives on American Demographic History* (1985).

MICHAEL R. HAINES

See also Birth Control; Epidemics; Medicine; Population.

BLACK, HUGO

(1886–1971), political leader and associate justice, U.S. Supreme Court. Constitutional experts have lionized Black, contending that he was "one of a handful of great judges in American history, second only to John Marshall in his impact on the Constitution." And indeed Black left a deep impression on the nation's fundamental document. This seems remarkable in light of his rural Alabama origins and controversial prejudicial career.

Black first practiced law in Birmingham and served as a police court judge and county prosecutor there before entering the U.S. Senate in 1927. His campaign was aided by his brief membership in the Ku Klux Klan. In the Senate he became a strong supporter of the New Deal and a tenacious, even ruthless senatorial investigator, particularly of the economically powerful. When Franklin D. Roosevelt appointed him to the Supreme Court in 1937, critics objected because of his KKK past; but on the Court he proved to be an active constitutional populist.

Black's two fondest constitutional hopes were to achieve federal enforcement of the national Bill of Rights against the states through the Fourteenth Amendment and to bring about a First Amendment absolutism that would prohibit any restrictions on freedom of speech and press. Prior to 1925, the federal government had not been authorized to enforce the provisions of the federal Bill of Rights against state governments. If citizens of New York, for example, were being denied free speech by the state, their only recourse was to the New York State Constitution. They had (to use lawyers' language) "no federal remedy" since the U.S. Bill of Rights limited only the federal government. To Black's disappointment, however, the Court agreed to incorporate federal rights against the states only on a selective basis. As to the First Amendment rights ("preferred freedoms," as Black saw them), they were strengthened and became the core of a freer, more democratic society.

Black's career on the Court went through two phases. Until 1953, his opinions were frequently liberal dissents, although in 1952 he wrote the majority opinion in the steel seizure case, voiding President Harry S. Truman's emergency takeover of the industry. Here, he demonstrated his constitutional literalism by reaffirming the separate and limited roles of the three branches of the federal government.

After the appointment of Chief Justice Earl Warren in 1953, Black's commitments to the protection of civil liberties and civil rights became majority positions. His 1946 call for reapportionment was now accepted as the Court moved to the "one-man, one-vote" principle. His strong commitment to religious liberty played a key role in the development of the First Amendment's religious guarantees, as his Jeffersonian view of the "wall of separation" between church and state prevailed, especially in his controversial school prayer ruling. His reading of the First Amendment was accepted by the majority, as seen in the limitations the Court developed to constrain the use of libel and obscenity laws. As to political speech, he argued with increasing success for virtually unlimited expression "whether or not such discussion incites to action, legal or illegal."

Although critics charged that he was making the Court an active agent of reform, Black did not consider himself a judicial activist. He did not condone judges exercising personal judgment in constitutional adjudication. Rather, he insisted that the Constitution be interpreted literally. Thus, while he was prepared to apply most of the procedural provisions of the Fourth through the Eighth Amendments to the states, he interpreted the Fourth's limitation on unreasonable search and seizure restrictively, generally accepting law enforcement actions. When other justices sought to create new rights, Black balked, rejecting the notion that the Constitution contains general guarantees of privacy, or "natural rights," beyond those expressly articulated in the text.

In the final analysis, Black was a people's justice. His opinions were clear and moving, and his commitments were to a constitutional order that would extend "liberty and justice for all."

Gerald T. Dunne, *Hugo Black and the Judicial Revolution* (1977); Tinsley E. Yarbrough, *Mr. Justice Black and His Critics* (1988).

PAUL L. MURPHY

See also Bill of Rights; Supreme Court.

BLACK CHURCHES

During the colonial period, the Christianization of slaves was erratic and generally ineffective until the 1740s. Then evangelical revivals began to attract significant numbers of black converts, largely because they enabled the lower classes, including slaves, to pray and preach in public. In the emotional fervor of the revival meetings whites and blacks preached to and converted one another. Baptists and Methodists licensed black men to preach, and by the 1770s some black ministers, slave as well as free, were pastoring their own congregations. Black churches in the South were subject to restrictions intended to prevent unsupervised slave assemblies. But despite occasional white harassment, southern black churches survived and provided a limited religious independence. In the antebellum years, Christianity spread gradually among the slaves. Some attended church with whites or under white supervision, but the majority had little if any access to formal church services. Nevertheless slaves often conducted their own religious meetings, with or without their owners' consent. They developed a distinctive Christianity in which blacks figured as God's chosen people awaiting their exodus from American bondage. The spirituals, which expressed the slaves' religious traditions, were also a way of transmitting these traditions to future generations.

In the North, the abolition of slavery gave blacks more leeway to exercise their religious preferences. Roused by discriminatory treatment in white-dominated churches, blacks in Philadelphia founded two influential churches, Bethel African Methodist and St. Thomas African Episcopal in 1794. Bethel's pastor, Richard Allen, and St. Thomas's pastor, Absalom Jones, both former slaves, exercised civic leadership in the black community in Philadelphia. Over the next decade, separate black congregations sprang up in free black communities across the North. In 1816, the first major black denomination, the African Methodist Episcopal (A.M.E.) church, was formed under the leadership of Richard Allen. Because the church was the only institution that African-Americans controlled, it served as the primary forum for addressing their social and political, as well as religious, needs. Many of the leading black activists in the abolition movement were ministers. And when the first National Negro Convention was organized in 1830, it met at Bethel A.M.E. church in Philadelphia with Richard Allen presiding.

Black churches were overwhelmingly Protestant because blacks had little contact with Roman Catholicism outside of Maryland and Louisiana. Some blacks did become Catholics, however, and because other religious orders refused black candidates, two communities of black nuns were founded — the Oblate Sisters of Providence in 1829 and the Holy Family Sisters in 1842. The first black American priest, James Augustine Healy, was ordained in 1854.

Black church membership was predominantly female, but its clergy was exclusively male since black women were barred from ordination until the twentieth century. Exceptional laywomen preachers like Jarena Lee and Amanda Berry Smith were approved as traveling evangelists by the A.M.E. church, but women were not allowed to head congregations. Women led home prayer meetings and served on auxiliary, missionary, and Sunday school boards.

The first Americans to embark on foreign missions were two Virginia-born black Baptists. In the 1780s, George Liele established churches in Jamaica, and David George founded congregations in Nova Scotia and Sierra Leone. With support from the American Colonization Society, the A.M.E. missionary Daniel Coker sailed to Sierra Leone in 1820 and the black Baptist Lott Carey began work in Liberia in 1821. The A.M.E. church also established missions in Haiti and Canada.

During the Civil War, northern missionaries headed South in the wake of the Union armies to organize schools and churches among the former slaves. The increase in southern members enlarged the size of northern black denominations and made them national in scope. When Reconstruction opened electoral politics to black participation, ministers took active roles, and several were elected to state and national office. Subsequently, violence and disfranchisement drove blacks out of politics and relegated black leaders primarily to the church.

In the late nineteenth century, worsening race relations prompted some black Americans to encourage large-scale emigration to Africa. One of the most forceful proponents of emigration was A.M.E. bishop Henry McNeal Turner, whose ordination of South African ministers contributed to the development of an independent African church movement. Few black Americans emigrated, but the belief in pan-African unity inspired prominent black clergy like the Episcopalian Alexander Crummell, a former missionary to Liberia, to preach that it was the divinely appointed destiny of African-Americans to convert Africa to Christianity.

Black church membership at the end of the century stood at 2.7 million out of a population of 8.3 million. Baptists constituted the largest denomination. In 1895, they formed the National Baptist Convention, Inc., which split into two branches twelve years later. As time passed, new Holiness and Pentecostal churches disrupted older black denominations by emphasizing doctrines of sanctification and speaking in tongues. A black preacher, William J. Seymour, led the 1906 Azusa Street Revival in Los Angeles that gave rise to Pentecostal churches across the nation.

Beginning in the 1890s and mounting steadily during and after World War I, rural southern blacks migrated to cities in the North as well as the South. Larger city churches, like Abyssinian Baptist in New York and Olivet Baptist in Chicago, developed extensive social services to assist the newcomers. Migrants strained the resources of existing urban churches and transported rural congregations into the small home and storefront churches that proliferated in the growing ghettos. Urbanization also presented new religious alternatives. Catholicism attracted significant numbers of blacks, primarily because of parochial schools. Esoteric versions of Judaism and Islam flourished, asserting that Christianity was a religion exclusively for whites. Charismatic religious leaders like Father Divine gained followers with promises of health and happiness in this world as well as the next.

Twentieth-century urbanization and modernization challenged the black church as a conservative and apolitical institution. At the same time, black intellectuals celebrated and romanticized the religious culture of the black folk. Despite secular competition, the church retained a strong influence in black social, cultural, and political life. Secular organizations, such as the Universal Negro Improvement Association and the National Association for the Advancement of Colored People depended heavily upon the support of local ministers and churches, as did the civil rights movement of the 1950s and 1960s. The career of Martin Luther King, Jr., epitomized for many the religious basis of the political struggle for racial equality, and two decades later, Rev. Jesse Jackson's campaigns for the presidency demonstrated the organizational strength of the black churches.

In the 1960s and 1970s black militants claimed that Christianity was incompatible with black identity and power. Some were attracted by the separatist ideals of the Nation of Islam as articulated by Malcolm X. In response, some black clergy formulated a black theology that emphasized liberation from oppression as the central gospel message. Recently, black women theologians have condemned sexism in the church. The black church is no longer the only institution in which black Americans exercise control. The authority of the church, according to some social analysts, has weakened, especially among the urban poor, but statistically black church membership has remained high.

C. Eric Lincoln and Lawrence H. Mamiya, *The Black Church in the American Experience* (1990); Albert J. Raboteau, *Slave Religion: The "Invisible Institution" in the Antebellum South* (1978).

ALBERT J. RABOTEAU

See also Allen, Richard; A.M.E. Church; Jackson, Jesse; Jones, Absalom; King, Martin Luther, Jr.; Religion.

BLACK CODES

Southern laws called Black Codes were passed in the aftermath of emancipation in order to control the newly freed black labor force. Mississippi and South Carolina passed the first and toughest measures late in 1865, and other southern states soon followed. Their provisions varied from state to state, but typically they stipulated that freedpeople could rent land only in rural areas — a means of keeping them on the plantations. All blacks were required to sign contracts for employment each January for the coming year. Those who quit in the middle of a contract lost any wages they had earned to that point and were subject to arrest for vagrancy — defined simply as not working. Punishments for vagrancy included fines, forced labor, whipping, or sale for a year's labor. The freedpeople were banned from "insulting" whites and preaching without a license. The Black Codes also tried to regulate sexual behavior and to force women who wished to be homemakers to return to the field.

These codes had effects beyond their impact on the everyday lives of their black victims. The northern public reacted angrily. To end Andrew Johnson's Presidential Reconstruction, which had allowed these measures to be enacted, Congress passed the Civil Rights Act of 1866 over Johnson's veto, defining the freedpeople's civil rights. Later, Congress approved the Fourteenth Amendment and imposed military rule to counter these southern efforts to subvert Reconstruction.

See also Reconstruction.

BLACK EXODUS, 1879

During the Exodus of 1879, an estimated twenty thousand Afro-Americans migrated from southern states to Kansas. Ever since the Civil War, former slaves had been moving west, particularly to Kansas, where, encouraged by promoters like Benjamin ("Pap") Singleton, a number of black colonies had been established. These early black migrants fared reasonably well.

Then, in 1879, the slow westward stream became a flash flood. Advertising by the railroads and land promoters helped encourage the Exodus, but worsening conditions for blacks in the South played a larger part. With the end of Reconstruction, white supremacists had regained power, causing some to fear that slavery might be reestablished. A sense of impending doom, combined with an idyllic picture of life in the West, evolved into a millenarian vision of Kansas as the new Promised Land. During the spring of 1879, hundreds and then thousands of black families from all over the South joined the Kansas Fever Exodus.

Most of the "Exodusters" managed to reach Kansas, but their huge numbers and relative penury overwhelmed the resources of the various charitable organizations set up to assist them. Few had enough money to start farming; most had to turn to wage labor, and some became destitute. Public attitudes toward them hardened.

By 1880 the Exodus had ended. News of the first Exodusters' problems, the growing efforts by Kansans to discourage further immigration, and the difficulties of winter travel all broke the momentum. Kansas's black population continued to grow, but slowly. In 1880, southern Democrats in Congress produced a committee report blaming the migration on enticement by Republicans and promoters. But it seems clear that, whatever the attractions of the West, the Exodus of 1879 was primarily a desperate reaction to the economic and political repression faced by Afro-Americans in the South.

See also Black Migration; Internal Migration; Reconstruction.

BLACK GHETTOS

In historical terms, the rise of the black ghetto — a massive, geographically continuous, isolated place of almost exclusively black residence and institutional life — is a recent phenomenon. Scattered enclaves of free blacks, fugitives, and slaves existed in the less desirable sections of antebellum southern towns, and refugees uprooted by the Civil War hastened their growth. But nowhere in the United States could anything resembling the modern black ghetto be found in 1880. Its emergence occurred in stages; the first occupied the half century between 1880 and 1930, and the second — after a brief respite early in the Great Depression — extended from 1935 to at least 1970.

This pattern stemmed from a series of dramatic demographic shifts. The movement of black populations from rural to urban areas and from the South to the North and West, and the evolution of American cities and the rise of the suburbs each played an instrumental role. The coming of World War I, the subsequent cutoff of European immigration, and the northern cities' demand for unskilled labor spurred a heavy black migration that continued through the 1920s. The United States' mobilization for World War II and the postwar economic boom later provided an even stronger impetus for movement, and the largest decennial black migration from the South occurred between 1940 and 1950. Overall, between 1940 and 1970, more than 4 million blacks left the region; where 77 percent of all American blacks lived in the South on the eve of World War II, only 53 percent did so thirty years later.

This movement was part of a larger phenomenon that encompassed the South as well — the urbanization of African-Americans. In 1880 only 12.9 percent of the blacks in the United States lived in urban areas, and it was not until 1950 that a majority did (whites had reached that benchmark a generation earlier). Ten years later, blacks were more highly urbanized than whites. The twentieth-century movement of blacks into American cities coincided, moreover, with a white exodus out of the city and into the suburbs.

The century following 1880 thus witnessed the emergence and maturation of the modern urban ghetto in the United States. The march toward stringent residential segregation began in the postbellum South where blacks frequently represented 40 percent or more of urban populations. No southern city possessed a single, all-encompassing ghetto, but many towns had several clusters of black residents, frequently located on the urban periphery, surrounding a largely white core. Antebellum black neighborhoods that contained institutional supports (particularly churches and schools) and the camps established for freed slaves during the Civil War often served as the bases for black territorial expansion. Southern ghettoization in the nineteenth century was limited, however, by economic, technological, and spatial constraints. Despite the hostility of the dominant white population, these compact southern towns lacked the capacity to disperse and sort out their populations by either class or race. Moreover, southern race relations during the slave era and its immediate aftermath demanded close contact within a hierarchical system. Social — not spatial — distance governed relationships across the color line.

The vast expanses of almost exclusively black settlement that exploded on the national scene during the riotous 1960s were twentieth-century northern creations. On the eve of the great migration of southern blacks, northern cities, proportionately, held infinitesimal black populations. As was the case in the South, they lived in scattered clusters. With the rapid increase in black population, however, larger, more densely settled black neighborhoods developed. The blacks' disproportionate poverty and cultural affinities, and even the actions of some progressive reformers who tried to serve them on a segregated basis, contributed to their residential isolation. But there is no question that white hostility, vented as rapidly industrializing metropolises obliterated their old, compact "walking cities," radically altered the use of urban space and tangibly expressed the desire to subordinate and control the new black presence.

Racial zoning ordinances, appearing first in the South, were declared unconstitutional by the Supreme Court in 1917 (*Buchanan* v. *Warley*). They were quickly supplanted, however, by the widespread use of racially restrictive covenants, which proved popular between the wars and were upheld by the Supreme Court in 1926 (*Corrigan* v. *Buckley*). Day-to-day business practices further buttressed such legalistic restrictions and

were even more instrumental in creating the pattern of residential segregation. Local real estate interests, lending institutions, and "improvement" associations acted as so many gatekeepers, steering blacks into all-black areas and preserving the homogeneity of white neighborhoods. Violence remained the ultimate sanction that prevented blacks from enjoying unfettered residential mobility. An early twentieth-century wave of urban racial rioting that became particularly severe during the "red summer" of 1919 heralded the emergence of the modern ghetto.

It was the second era of ghetto formation, however, that produced the vast concentrations of urban blacks that generated the "long, hot summers" of the 1960s. During this period, the federal government facilitated the persistence of high levels of residential segregation. Between 1935 and 1950, it displayed an intense color consciousness and insisted upon discriminatory practices as a prerequisite for support from such new agencies as the Federal Housing Administration (FHA). Combined with the slum clearance, urban renewal, public housing, and highway construction programs of the 1950s and 1960s, such initiatives encouraged and subsidized white flight to the suburbs, helped strip older towns of their middle classes, and practically ensured that blacks would remain locked in economically weakened central cities.

Beginning in 1948, the federal government moved haltingly toward a color-blind stance on housing issues. First came the Supreme Court decision (*Shelley* v. *Kraemer*) that rendered restrictive covenants unenforceable. That was followed by John F. Kennedy's 1962 executive order that placed a partial ban on discrimination in federal housing programs, the 1964 Civil Rights Act, and the 1968 Fair Housing Act that extended the prohibition of discrimination to include virtually all housing. The real estate industry, lenders, and advertisers all fell under the sweep of the law, although enforcement remained problematic and the legacy of earlier policies could not be easily overcome.

The 1980 census, consequently, counted fourteen cities with black populations of at least 200,000. Geographically, they spread across the North (New York, Chicago, Detroit, Philadelphia, and Cleveland), the South (Houston, New Orleans, Memphis, Atlanta, and Dallas), the border states (Washington, D.C., Baltimore, and St. Louis), and the West (Los Angeles). Together, these metropolitan giants contained nearly 10.4 million blacks, or approximately 40 percent of all black Americans in 1980. Every measurement for these major population centers reveals consistently high levels of segregation that remained fiercely resistant to change down to 1970. Most striking was the rising level of segregation found in each of the southern cities as they became more like their northern counterparts. The economic modernization of the South and the dismantling of the Jim Crow system by the civil rights movement were accompanied by a rapid separation of urban blacks and whites, although there has been some moderation in these trends since 1970, particularly in smaller cities.

The establishment of substantial, segregated urban black communities gave rise to new economic, social, political, and intellectual forces within those communities. The intensive concentration of a host of urban ills was most immediately apparent. Although not all ghetto residents shared such experiences or characteristics, these environments limited access to quality education and health services while fostering endemic poverty, poor housing, high rates of crime, and behavioral patterns often detrimental to self-improvement. In recent years, a so-called underclass distinguished by chronic dependence, a disproportionate number of female-headed households, and high rates of teenage pregnancy has emerged. Increasingly isolated from a deindustrializing economy that demands skills they do not possess in jobs they cannot reach from the central city, the underclass is finding itself distanced as well from a growing black middle class that has fled the poorest neighborhoods for more comfortable, if still largely segregated, quarters. Such spatial separation has traditionally reflected social, ideological, and political differences in American urban history, but the implications of this movement have yet to be seen. If the dismal material circumstances of the ghetto have been improved for some and escaped by others, it shows no signs of disappearing and may now present the dual problems of race and

poverty in more concentrated form than ever before.

But the ghetto produced more than the "tangle of pathology" that has often been associated with it. It was also a self-sustaining institutional and cultural entity that nourished the social and intellectual networks that made the flowering of a Harlem Renaissance possible, and it provided the personal freedom that permitted blacks to pursue their own strategies in coping with modern America. Ideologically, the movements for self-help, race pride, and black nationalism found a natural home there.

The initial era of ghetto formation subsequently gave rise to the militant "New Negro" and to the literary and artistic outpouring that placed New York's Harlem in the vanguard of African-American cultural expression. The ghetto provided a mass base that sustained Marcus Garvey's Universal Negro Improvement Association (UNIA), an organization of racial protest and assertion that, along with such new institutions as the *Chicago Defender,* gave prideful voice to those now able to rally on their own turf. The move into the industrial economy also produced leaders such as the Brotherhood of Sleeping Car Porters' A. Philip Randolph, whose March on Washington movement helped initiate a new era of black-led protest in the 1940s. The civil rights revolution itself gained important momentum from urban black concentrations in Montgomery and Birmingham, Alabama, where the numbers, resources, leaders, and key institutions (especially churches) could be marshaled against the Jim Crow system. And a wave of "ghetto rebellions" in the 1960s dramatized the failure to extend the gains of the civil rights era to the urban North.

Perhaps most significantly, concentrations of urban blacks have provided political bases for an increasing number of black officeholders. Beginning with the election of Oscar DePriest from Chicago's Black Belt in 1928, and continuing with the elevation of Chicago's William L. Dawson, New York's Adam Clayton Powell, Jr., and Detroit's Charles Diggs, Jr., in the 1940s and 1950s, a growing post-Reconstruction black presence was reestablished in the Congress of the United States. More recent advances have come on the state and local levels, with black mayors — beginning with Gary, Indiana's, Richard Hatcher and Cleveland's Carl Stokes in 1967 — occupying center stage. These successes, however, have reified black consciousness without demonstrably altering the conditions that called forth protest and political mobilization. Whether politicians shepherding their voters, black businesses catering to a concentrated black clientele, ministers tending their flocks, or ordinary citizens occupying a zone of social familiarity, the ghetto has produced a class that could view its dispersal only with grave misgivings. There was thus irony in the freedom born of restriction. Alone, the forces emanating from within these increasingly complex black settlements could not determine the future development of the ghetto; there were larger economic, social, and political forces at work. And they rendered less clear, and perhaps more painful, the choices confronting urban blacks after World War II.

The ghetto concept has also been used to describe the experience of European ethnics when they crowded the industrial centers of the Northeast and Midwest in the era of mass immigration (1880–1920). But though ethnic clustering was unmistakable, the black and immigrant experiences remained different. Even if black communities could, perhaps, approximate the high transiency rates detected in the foreign quarters, such appellations as "Little Italy," "Polonia," and "Jewtown" described geographic areas more accurately viewed as ethnic amalgams than monoliths. None of the European-based communities displayed the homogeneity that was imposed upon black neighborhoods by the mid-twentieth century. Moreover, the European nationalities began their tenure in urban America in ethnic enclaves and dispersed with time — a communal trajectory literally the opposite of that traveled by blacks. And though a welter of inner-city pathologies stalked whites as well as blacks, the immigrant "ghetto" was surrounded by permeable membranes rather than virtually impenetrable race-based barriers.

Indeed, as late as 1910, recently arrived southern and eastern European immigrants (such as Russian Jews, Poles, and Italians) did display measurably higher degrees of residential segregation from native whites than did blacks. By 1930, however, with the trends of migration, assimilation, and isolation running in opposite directions for white ethnics and African-Americans, their situations were reversed. Continued improvements in the social and economic status of whites and the rush of suburbanization that followed World War II further depressed the degree of white ethnic segregation even as black isolation reached peak levels. White ethnic communal and kinship networks survived, moreover, in the age of the automobile and the telephone, without the benefit of intense geographical concentration. Sources of comfort and preparation for life in America — and advantageously located in an age when unskilled industrial jobs crowded the city core — the early ethnic communities hardly seem to have been "ghettos" in the sense that most blacks would understand that term.

The most recent immigrants to urban America, Asians and Hispanics, also entered host cultures where their limited economic resources and minority status evoked more suspicion than empathy. Yet, segregation studies reveal that the separation of blacks and whites remains much more severe than that distancing the newest ethnics from the majority population. Arriving in large numbers during the United States' stunning era of post–World War II economic expansion and rapid urban decentralization, Hispanics and Asians never became as segregated as African-Americans and, more importantly, their communal paths now seem to be following those of the European ethnics more closely than that of the blacks. Nationally, in 1980, calculations of "average black isolation" remained 2.5 times that of Hispanics and ten times that of Asians. Indeed, at present rates of decline, it would take more than a half century for blacks to reach the level of segregation presently experienced by Hispanics and Asians. The degree of racial isolation, the historical record of restriction, and the relative permanence of the barriers all argue that the "ghettos" encompassing white ethnics, Hispanics, and Asians remain fundamentally different from that which is associated with urban black America.

Nowhere are these differences more apparent than in the emerging anomalous position of the growing black middle class. The most mobile segments of that class have been denied the role played by their earlier white ethnic counterparts. As the older immigrant communities dispersed, those who enjoyed some measure of economic success led the movement and eased the transition into the American mainstream for those who trailed them. Economically advantaged blacks, however, have undertaken that outward push with different results. Unlike other groups, indicators of social and economic status for blacks bear no clear relation to levels of suburbanization or segregation. Black economic achievement and material well-being have not heralded the disappearance of those "assimilated" blacks as was the case with their ethnic competitors; and the plight of those left in the poorest neighborhoods seems hardly advantaged by such successes. The relative weights assigned to continued discrimination, the legacy of past practices, and the centripetal pull of African-American cultural communities in sustaining this pattern remain open questions. The uniqueness of the African-American experience, however, is clear.

Arnold R. Hirsch, *Making the Second Ghetto: Race and Housing in Chicago, 1940 to 1960* (1983); Kenneth L. Kusmer, *A Ghetto Takes Shape: Black Cleveland, 1870–1930* (1976).

ARNOLD R. HIRSCH

See also Black Migration; Civil Rights Movement; Garvey, Marcus; Harlem Renaissance; Housing; Internal Migration; Segregation; Suburbanization; Urban Bosses and Machine Politics; Urbanization.

BLACK HAWK

(1767–1838), Sac Indian leader. "We always had plenty. Our children never cried with hunger; our people were never in want." This was Black Hawk's idealized memory of his early years. He was born in Saukenuk, a village of the Sac (or Sauk) Indians in Illinois. The lands provided ample crops, which the men supplemented through hunting, trading, and the spoils of war.

By 1803 Black Hawk had gained fame through his exploits in battle. But Lt. Zebulon Pike's exploratory push into the upper Mississippi valley that year signified the end of an era for the Sacs and their allies, the Foxes. Soon the Indians were debating whether to accommodate or resist the advance of the whites' frontier. One group, headed by another Sac, Keokuk, argued for accommodation, but Black Hawk fiercely opposed such a policy. He was confirmed in his convictions when Americans convinced Sac and Fox representatives in 1804 to sign a treaty they little understood.

Black Hawk, who sympathized with Tecumseh's efforts to forge a pan-Indian confederacy, sided with the British in the War of 1812. In August 1814, he assisted the British in routing the American forces of the young Zachary Taylor and was disappointed when the British ended the war. But after a brief battle with the Americans in May 1815, he too gave up fighting.

The next decade witnessed a steady decline in the fortunes of the Sacs and Foxes. White population pressures forced the Indians to adhere to the treaty of 1804 and abandon their old territory. By the end of the 1820s, all had been forcibly removed and the lands sold by the state at public auction.

Black Hawk kept returning to the land even after it had been sold. He and his followers ventured back in the summer of 1830 without a major confrontation and announced their intention to return the next year. But when the Indians claimed the land in June 1831, they were confronted by hundreds of soldiers who forced them to evacuate and sign an agreement. They were never again to return to Saukenuk and Keokuk was to be their spokesman.

Black Hawk spurned this unhappy armistice, and in a subsequent conflict between the Foxes and the Menominees, some of the Foxes sought his assistance. The smoldering resentment of the younger men fired Black Hawk's spirit: he would go back to his homeland and show the Americans and Keokuk he could not be vanquished.

This resistance only provoked the tragic conflict known as the Black Hawk War. From April until August 1832, Black Hawk and his followers fought, but the American military, swollen by volunteers including miners, farmers, and even a young lawyer named Abraham Lincoln, was too much for them. Black Hawk's defiant trail ended on August 3 in Wisconsin with the death of dozens of his people. He escaped but was later turned in.

He lived for six more years. He had his portrait painted and received much attention during a trip east in 1833. But he had to acknowledge Keokuk as the leader of the Sacs and Foxes, and the days of plenty became but a distant memory.

Even in death Black Hawk suffered indignity. His corpse was exhumed by a white man and his bones sold to an Iowa museum for public display. They were lost in a fire that engulfed the building in 1853.

Black Hawk, *Black Hawk: An Autobiography,* ed. Donald Jackson (1955); William T. Hagan, *The Sac and Fox Indians* (1958).

PETER IVERSON

See also Indians.

BLACK HAWK WAR

The Black Hawk War (1832) put down the last armed Indian resistance in the territory north of the Ohio River and east of the Mississippi. Early in the nineteenth century, whites started moving into what is now the state of Illinois. This movement precipitated numerous clashes with the Indians, and U.S. government officials sought to move the Indians out of the path of settlement.

In 1804, a treaty of questionable validity decreed that the Sac and Fox Indians move west of the Mississippi. Some refused, however, and soon after the War of 1812 one leader, Black Hawk, denounced the treaty and proclaimed the Indians' determination to retain their land. After years of skirmishes, the whites forced a new treaty on Black Hawk in 1831, which compelled the Indians to leave.

The next spring, however, Black Hawk returned with four hundred braves and their families, hoping to gain additional support from other tribes. When little help materialized, he prepared to sue for peace, but when the whites murdered one of his emissaries, he attacked again, defeating a much larger force. Fleeing into what is now Wisconsin, he was pursued by a newly formed army of volunteers assisted by the Sioux. A final battle took place at the Bad Axe River. Although Black Hawk raised a white flag, the attackers shot most of his band — men, women, and children. Black Hawk escaped to the Winnebagos, but they surrendered him to the whites. After a year of imprisonment, he returned to the remnants of his people in Iowa. The defeat of Black Hawk removed the last obstacle to white settlement in the Old Northwest.

See also Indians.

BLACK MIGRATION

Migration has been one of the defining characteristics of black life in the United States since the forced migration of African slaves to the New World. Major movements before the Civil War included the Atlantic slave trade, the extension of slavery to the Mississippi Valley (1820–1850), the manumission and escape of slaves to freedom in the North, the movement of free people of color from the South to the North and Canada, and the immigration of small numbers of black Americans to Africa.

During and after the Civil War emancipated men and women moved to secure their freedom. At the same time many northern free blacks went south as soldiers, and other black men and women traveled south to teach and help lead communal institutions. The Exoduster movement (1877 to 1881) during which forty thousand to seventy thousand African-Americans left the former slave states for Kansas was the first grass-roots movement out of the South. Blacks, in protest against the loss of political rights, sought equality and opportunity in the West. Then and later, the "Talented Tenth" — educated African-American leaders — fled the rise of Jim Crow and moved northward. Others considered emigration, but only a few ever returned to Africa.

The onset of the Great Migration — the mass movement of black people from the rural areas of the South to the cities of the North — came in the 1890s, as black men and women left to settle in eastern coastal cities such as Philadelphia and New York. The single largest movement of African-Americans occurred during World War I when approximately 500,000 people moved from the rural and small-town South into the cities of the North and the Midwest. The steady migration out of the South lasted until the 1970s; from 1916 through the 1960s, more than 6 million black people made the move. In the 1970s and 1980s, however, more black people moved to the South than left, part of a general population shift to the Sunbelt. When migration out of the South ebbed in the 1960s, the urban North and West became the focal point of black life. And even in the South, a majority of African-Americans lived in cities.

The Great Migration was a grass-roots, leaderless movement. All the migrants — male laborers, women domestics, families — made individual decisions to move. Nonetheless, the deterioration of the quality of life of southern blacks in the two decades prior to World War I, coupled with a labor shortage in the industrial North, stimulated the migration. In the South, the rise of Jim Crow, the disfranchisement of black voters, and the spread of lynchings and other mob violence against blacks provided strong impetus for individuals and families to move. Widespread flooding and the infestation of cotton by the boll weevil created additional economic woes in the rural South.

For the first time, the North needed southern blacks. Before World War I most northern factories had barred blacks, and few other well-paying positions were open to them. But the war in Europe stretched American industrial capacity to its limits at the very time that European immigration, which had exceeded 1.2 million in 1914, dropped sharply to 100,000 in 1918. Many businesses now hired anyone they could get, and black men and white women found new jobs and industries open to them. Although most blacks obtained only semiskilled and service jobs and their wages were usually lower than those received by white men and women for the same work, they nevertheless earned far more than they could in the South.

The Great Migration differed from previous migrations in that it was a movement directly from the rural South to the urban North. Railroads and black sleeping car porters were an important link between rural black communities and northern cities. Pullman porters on the Illinois Central Railroad distributed the *Chicago Defender,* a black newspaper, on their trips south and facilitated the migration of fellow blacks to Chicago. In the cities of the North, vast black ghettos appeared. Chicago's black population grew from 44,000 in 1910 to 110,000 in 1920.

Not all northerners welcomed the migrants, and white violence against blacks became common. Major race riots occurred, as in East St. Louis in 1917, when white rioters killed thirty-nine African-Americans. There were more than twenty major race riots in 1919. In Chicago a riot turned into a race war, as black workers and returned veterans fought back. After five days, federal troops were called in; twenty-three blacks and fifteen whites were dead.

In the nineteenth and early twentieth centuries African-American leaders frequently debated the wisdom of migration. Two decades apart, Frederick Douglass and Booker T. Washington advised black people to stay in the South. During World War I, on the other hand, Robert Abbott of the *Chicago Defender* and others among the new, business-oriented, black middle class urged black southerners to come northward.

Southern counties and cities attempted to prevent the outmigration. But those who moved were exercising their mobility as free people and demonstrating their optimism about the future. Wrenching themselves from church and community in the South, they ventured into the unknown to escape oppression and create opportunities for themselves. Black migration has been inseparable from protest. Often powerless and with no other means of redress, blacks found mobility the only way to improve their lives. This was true of runaways during slavery, of free people of color before the Civil War, of newly emancipated slaves during the Civil War, and of the Exodusters to Kansas. And it was the thrust behind the Great Migration. The more recent "reverse" migration from North to South has been inspired, in part, by a desire to escape the social disintegration — high unemployment, inferior schools, crime, drugs — in many northern ghettos.

In reshaping their own lives, then, blacks have also reshaped the United States, and urban black culture has come to be recognized as an important component of modern America.

James R. Grossman, *Land of Hope: Chicago, Black Southerners, and the Great Migration* (1989); Nicholas Lemann, *The Promised Land: The Great Black Migration and How It Changed America* (1991); Nell I. Painter, *Exodusters: Black Migration to Kansas after Reconstruction* (1988); William M. Tuttle, Jr., *Race Riot: Chicago in the Red Summer of 1919* (1970).

DAVID M. KATZMAN

See also Black Exodus, 1879; Internal Migration; Reconstruction; Slavery; Underground Railroad; World War I.

BLACK NATIONALISM

Classical black nationalist theory holds that blacks must unite, gain power, and liberate themselves. As these goals were being articulated by free blacks in antebellum America, blacks held in slavery were generating their own culture. But most free blacks did not understand that the development of an autonomous slave culture was a force that challenged white dominance, and the few who did failed to relate this development to liberation theory.

Journalist and physician Martin R. Delany, for example, did recognize that African slaves arrived in America knowing how to cultivate rice, cotton, and tobacco and possessing skills that were used in workshops and animal husbandry on slave plantations. But he failed to incorporate this insight systematically in his theory. Other free black nationalists, however, did not recognize the skills brought to America by Africans, nor did they appreciate the art that slaves were creating within their culture. Thus they failed to respond to Frederick Douglass's recognition that slave art reflected African values. He realized that the slaves' music was an ironic mixture of sadness and joy that helped them confront their predicament and noted that it derived directly from their African heritage. In later years, jazz and blues would draw on this same emotional and spiritual legacy.

But whatever the degree of understanding of slave culture by nationalists, none thought whites would permit blacks to build a political system of their own in America. Consequently, they resolved that real freedom for their people would not come until the African motherland was redeemed. In his *Appeal to the Colored Citizens of the World,* published in 1829, David Walker advanced this and other principles on which nationalists would build. He denounced the avarice that he thought motivated Europeans in their relations with one another and with people of color. But he did not consider whites by nature an enemy. If they were willing to atone for their crimes, reconciliation was possible.

Henry Highland Garnet, an ex-slave and disciple of Walker, thought racism resulted mainly from whites having seen blacks in a low condition for so long. In his "Sidney" letters, which began appearing in the late 1830s, he brilliantly pursued this argument, contending that as blacks struggled to improve their condition, whites would be won to their cause. Moreover, he insisted that the oppressed would have to liberate themselves or they would never be truly free, a position with which Delany agreed. Delany, however, thought the problem was greater, for he was convinced that blacks would never have enough white friends in America to make real freedom possible. Their only hope, he observed a few years before the Civil War, was for some to build a powerful black state elsewhere that would win respect for blacks who remained in America. Nevertheless, like most antebellum nationalists, he persisted in opposing every sign of racism.

The government's abandonment of black rights during and after Reconstruction made it evident to nationalists that their people needed not only self-reliance but, more sorely than ever, power. Douglass stated this as well as anyone ever had: "No man can be truly free whose liberty is dependent upon . . . others, and has himself no means in his own hands for guarding, protecting, defending, and maintaining that liberty. . . . The law on the side of freedom is of great advantage only when there is power to make that law respected."

After Garnet immigrated to Africa where he died in 1882, Delany and Bishop Henry M.

Turner became the dominant figures on the nationalist scene. Alexander Crummell, who had spent years in Africa seeking to advance both Christianity and the cause of black emigration from the United States, joined them as a major force in nationalist circles toward the end of the century. It was Turner, however, who took the lead in back-to-Africa agitation.

Crummell was an important influence on W. E. B. Du Bois, who worked with whites while advocating a conception of freedom that he thought would fulfill the needs, spiritual and material, of his people and, indeed, of all humanity. Opposed to class privilege, Du Bois upheld values of cooperation sacred to Walker and Garnet. But his socialist preferences were not shared by Marcus Garvey, who in the 1920s built a mass movement based on black capitalism and a return to Africa. Garvey's emphasis on color distinctions, however, placed his nationalism outside the classical tradition.

In the 1930s, Paul Robeson raised nationalist theory to new heights. With his command of African languages, folklore, and anthropology, Robeson propounded a conception of culture that recognized the self-generative activity, largely African in origin, that had produced the spirituals and prepared the way for blues and jazz. Despite such achievements, he was convinced that black culture was being strangled in America, that it could truly flower only when values were the issue, not the color of one's skin. No narrow nationalist, Robeson regarded Africa as an artistic and spiritual frontier on which problems common to humanity might be worked out, and he urged his people to search for values there that might, in combination with the technology of the West, advance that process.

In the 1950s and 1960s the most prominent nationalist organization was the Lost-Found Nation of Islam, which had been established in Detroit in the 1930s and was quietly rehabilitating many blacks from society's "lower depths." Although Elijah Muhammad was its head, it was the charisma and articulate rage of Malcolm X, his chief aide, that captured the attention of black people as a whole, broadening the influence of the organization. Its preoccupation with race, however, rather than broader human values, was at sharp variance with classical nationalist thought. In 1964, with his influence growing in the civil rights movement, Malcolm X left the Nation.

Respect for Malcolm X and a growing sense of white America's reluctance to share real power with blacks led the Student Non-Violent Coordinating Committee (SNCC), a pivotal force in the civil rights movement, to urge blacks to rely on themselves to secure freedom—hence, the organization's call for black power in 1966. Like Malcolm, SNCC looked to the independent nations of Africa as a source of inspiration and support. But SNCC failed to ground black power in the best of the nationalist tradition, and black nationalism was left in disarray even as its standard was being raised by the flower of America's black youth.

Harold Cruse, *The Crisis of the Negro Intellectual* (1967); Sterling Stuckey, *Slave Culture: Nationalist Theory and the Foundations of Black America* (1987).

STERLING STUCKEY

See also Black Power; Cuffe, Paul; Delany, Martin R.; Douglass, Frederick; Du Bois, W. E. B.; Garvey, Marcus; Malcolm X; Robeson, Paul; Student Non-Violent Coordinating Committee; Walker, David.

BLACK POWER

Black power is an umbrella term used to describe the more militant aspects of the late 1960s civil rights movement. The term gained popularity in 1966 when Stokely Carmichael, a leader of the Student Non-Violent Coordinating Committee, used it in a series of speeches. It became a rallying cry for young urban black males who felt increasingly alienated from the civil rights leadership of Martin Luther King, Jr.; his nonviolent ideology, they believed, relied too heavily on the largesse of the white establishment. The main thrust of the civil rights movement, with its concentration on eliminating segregation and winning the right to vote in the South, had largely ignored the economic problems of blacks in the northern urban ghettos.

As a political idea, black power derived from

a long tradition of black nationalism dating back to the nineteenth century. Such figures as Marcus Garvey and, more recently, Malcolm X had asserted that black communities should strive for self-determination rather than integration and had the right to retaliate against violent attack. Although associated in white eyes with violence, black power mostly referred to black self-reliance, racial pride, and economic and political empowerment.

National conferences on black power were held annually beginning in 1966. The increasingly radical and separatist resolutions agreed upon at these gatherings called for, among other things, a boycott of the military draft by blacks, self-defense training for black youths, and the partition of the country into separate black and white nations. But many others attracted to the concept sought to increase the numbers of black-owned businesses and black officeholders rather than pursuing extreme separatism. Although black power advocates achieved only a few of their goals, the idea remained a powerful one in modern black America.

See also Black Nationalism; Civil Rights Movement.

BLACKWELL, ELIZABETH

(1821–1910), physician, reformer, and medical educator. Blackwell was the first woman to receive a medical degree in the United States or Europe. She was also active in moral reform, an interest that antedated her attraction to medicine. In part this was due to her remarkable family, English immigrants who moved to America when Elizabeth was eleven and immersed themselves in Christian perfectionism and reformist activity. Elizabeth's brothers, Henry and Samuel, supported antislavery and women's rights: the former married the feminist Lucy Stone and the latter married Antoinette Brown, the first formally ordained woman minister in the United States. Sister Emily also became a physician, and another, Anna, a poet and translator.

Studying medicine did not come easily to Blackwell, but she longed for engrossing, ennobling activity. When a woman friend, dying of cancer, urged that her own situation would have been eased immeasurably by the attendance of a woman doctor, Blackwell determined to make medicine her calling.

She was forced to study privately for several years while she searched for a school that would train her. Geneva Medical College in upstate New York finally accepted her after a reluctant faculty hinged her admission on the unanimous agreement of the student body, and the men, partially as a practical joke, voted her in without protest. After receiving her degree in 1849, she studied in Paris and London, returning to New York City in 1851 to hang out her shingle.

Ignored by medical colleagues and mistrusted by patients, she found her first years lonely and discouraging. In 1856 she was joined by her sister Emily and Marie Zakrzewska, both of whom had recently graduated from Western Reserve Medical School. The following year the three expanded Blackwell's dispensary into a hospital, the still-extant New York Infirmary for Women and Children. A decade later came the hospital's medical school for women, an institutional showcase that trained hundreds of women doctors before merging with Cornell in 1899.

Blackwell was an eloquent spokesperson for the women's medical movement in the United States and England, where she settled permanently in 1869. These years saw her concentrate increasingly on medical reform. Her holistic approach to disease led her to believe that the physician must not merely cure but bring about scientific social reform. Sharing with many feminists of the time the belief that women innately possess a higher moral sense than men do, she saw their role in medicine as integral to the proper and healthy progress of the profession as a whole. All physicians, she believed, must display the nurturing qualities she termed "the spiritual power of maternity" and should monitor medical progress so that it would not violate moral truth.

At the end of her career she became progressively more uncomfortable with the new medical reductionism inspired by advances in bacteriology and laboratory medicine. When she died, her moralism appeared anachronistic to a younger generation of physicians turning with mounting enthusiasm toward the apparent objective absolutes of laboratory science and technocratic care.

Elizabeth Blackwell, *Pioneer Work in Opening the Medical Profession to Women* (1895; reprint, 1977); Regina Morantz-Sanchez, *Sympathy and Science: Women Physicians in American Medicine* (1985).

REGINA MORANTZ-SANCHEZ

See also Feminist Movement; Medicine.

BLAINE, JAMES G.

(1830–1893), politician and secretary of state. Blaine was one of the most popular, influential, and controversial political leaders of the late nineteenth century. He was instrumental in shifting the Republican party from the ideological issues of the Civil War to the economic and organizational appeals of the years 1877 to 1893. Born in Pennsylvania, Blaine attended Washington and Jefferson College and then taught in Kentucky at the end of the 1840s. He became a follower of the Whig leader from that state, Henry Clay. He moved to Maine during the 1850s, entered the newspaper business, and joined the young Republican party. Elected four times to the state legislature, he served as Speaker before moving on to the U.S. House of Representatives in 1862.

Blaine spent the next thirteen years in the House, including six years as Speaker between 1869 and 1875. He was identified with the moderate "Half-Breed" Republicanism that opposed the "Stalwart" faction of his bitter enemy Roscoe Conkling of New York. In general, Blaine believed that his party had to overcome its identification with the Civil War, pursue business-oriented policies such as the protective tariff, and build a national organization that would give the Republicans majority status.

Blaine was elected to the Senate in 1876 and became a leading candidate for the Republican presidential nomination. Then a scandal over an Arkansas railroad that he had allegedly aided as Speaker and the disclosure of documents known as the Mulligan Letters tarnished his reputation. Friends called him the "Plumed Knight" of American politics, but he was not nominated. In 1880 he supported James A. Garfield, spoke out for the protective tariff, and helped the party to victory. Garfield named him secretary of state, but the brief presidency that followed limited Blaine's accomplishments.

Blaine was nominated for the presidency by the Republicans in 1884. Although he campaigned vigorously, he could not overcome the lingering questions about his honesty and lost to the Democratic candidate, Grover Cleveland. (The celebrated "Rum, Romanism, and Rebellion" incident was not a significant element in his narrow defeat.) During the next four years, Blaine continued to champion the tariff and emphasize the Republican organization. He campaigned for Benjamin Harrison in 1888 and became secretary of state again in 1889. He pursued better relations with Latin America through the Pan-American Conference of 1889 and advocated reciprocal trade agreements and the annexation of Hawaii. Worsening relations with the president and his failing health caused Blaine to resign in June 1892 and make a futile challenge to Harrison's renomination.

Blaine's celebrated popularity did not long outlast his death in 1893. He was, however, the key figure in the organizational history of the Republican party between 1870 and 1890. His advocacy of the tariff and his stress on party unity were important elements in the quest for a national electoral majority that dominated the Republicans during the last quarter of the nineteenth century.

H. Wayne Morgan, *From Hayes to McKinley: National Party Politics, 1877–1896* (1969); David S. Muzzey, *James G. Blaine: A Political Idol of Other Days* (1934).

LEWIS L. GOULD

See also Elections: 1884; House of Representatives; Republican Party.

BLEEDING KANSAS

Said to have been coined by Horace Greeley's *New York Tribune,* the label "Bleeding Kansas" was first fixed on that strife-ridden territory by antislavery publicists. The opening of the Kansas and Nebraska territories in 1854 under the principle of popular sovereignty provoked a protracted political crisis in both Kansas and the nation at large. Rival governments had been established in Kansas by late 1855, one backed by proslavery Missourians, the other by antislavery groups. Although the Pierce and Buchanan administrations recognized the former, Republicans as well as a number of northern Democrats deemed it a fraud imposed by Missouri "border ruffians." Civil conflict in Kansas accompanied the political polarization. The volatility to be expected of a frontier area was compounded by the activities of parties interested in the slavery issue — both the Missourians and the northerners who reputedly shipped free-state settlers and armaments to the region.

Hostilities between armed bands seemed imminent in late 1855 as well over a thousand Missourians crossed the border and menaced Lawrence, a free-state stronghold. On May 21, 1856, ruffians actually looted that town. In response, John Brown orchestrated the murder several days later of five proslavery settlers along Pottawatomie Creek. Four months of partisan violence and depredation ensued. Small armies ranged over eastern Kansas, clashing at Black Jack, Franklin, Fort Saunders, Hickory Point, Slough Creek, and Osawatomie, where Brown and forty others were routed in late August.

John W. Geary, appointed territorial governor in September, managed to cool the "border war" with the aid of federal troops. But Kansas had hardly ceased bleeding — as became apparent in 1858 with the Marais des Cygnes massacre of five free-state men and pronounced disorder in several counties. Although Kansans in that year once and for all rejected the proslavery Lecompton constitution, such violence continued on a smaller scale into 1861.

See also Abolitionist Movement; Brown, John; Kansas-Nebraska Act.

BLUE LAWS

State and local regulations banning various activities on Sundays are called "blue laws." The origin of the term is uncertain. It has been said variously to have originated in the color of the paper on which a code of laws for the early New Haven, Connecticut, colony was printed or to have derived from the concept of being "true blue" to the law. Whatever the origin, these measures, which are based on the biblical injunction against working on the Sabbath, have been traced back to fourth-century Rome, when Constantine I, the first Christian emperor, commanded all citizens, except farmers, to rest on Sunday. The first blue law in America was enacted in the Virginia colony in the early 1600s and required church attendance.

About three-fourths of the states still carry on their books laws imposing some kind of Sunday restriction on such activities as retail sales, general labor, liquor sales, boxing, hunting, or barbering, as well as polo, cockfighting, or clam digging. These laws have been challenged in federal courts as a violation of the Sherman Antitrust Act and the First Amendment guarantee of freedom of religion. The Supreme Court has upheld them, starting with *McGowan* v. *Maryland* (1961), ruling that though the laws originated for religious reasons, the state has a right to set aside a day of rest for the well-being of its citizens.

Nevertheless, Sunday blue laws have declined since the 1960s. A number of states have repealed them, and many municipalities have long ignored those still on their books, simply choosing not to enforce them.

BOK, EDWARD

(1863–1930), editor of the *Ladies' Home Journal*. In 1870, when Edward was six years old, the Bok family left a comfortable life in the Netherlands to immigrate to the United States. When his family suffered financial reverses, Edward quit school after six years to go to work. By his early teens, however, he was visiting and corresponding with famous literary, religious, and political figures, including presidents of the United States. And before the age of twenty, this born entrepreneur was publishing a magazine and syndicating articles nationally.

In 1889, Bok accepted an offer from Cyrus H. K. Curtis to become editor of the *Ladies'*

Home Journal; the two built the *Journal* into the world's most widely circulated magazine. During Bok's reign, from 1889 to 1919, the *Journal* led the industry, making many innovations, including high-quality illustrations and printing techniques, a different cover for each number, and extensive marketing research. In addition, the *Journal*'s policy of reporting accurate circulation figures served as the basis for new federal regulations in this area.

Balancing his personal principles with the demands of advertisers and the interests of subscribers was usually not a problem for Bok. His intellectual and artistic tastes harmonized closely with those of his middle-class readers in everything from fashions, home design, and etiquette to literature and secular ethics. It is unclear whether the magazine was reflecting opinion or molding it — probably both.

Nevertheless, Bok occasionally risked offending some of his subscribers and advertisers in order to champion causes he favored. The most significant of these were a crusade against patent medicines, a campaign promoting frank sex education for children by their parents, and a series advocating progressive educational reforms. During World War I, the *Journal* worked closely with federal agencies to enlist women's support on the home front.

On one major issue, however, Bok's personal views became anachronistic; that issue, ironically, was women's role in society. Early in his tenure, Bok assailed the New Woman, insisting that women's proper sphere was the home and entreating them to fulfill their divinely ordained roles as wives, mothers, and homemakers. But American women did not listen; indeed, during these years they made more advances than at any earlier time. To maintain his magazine's popularity, Bok had to yield. By the early teens he had ended his attacks on the New Woman and was publishing articles and short stories praising her. During World War I, the *Journal*'s endorsement of female employment in industry erased the final vestiges of genteel womanhood from the magazine. This shift was testimony to the magnitude of the shift in the public's perception of woman's place in society as well as to Bok's expediency.

In retirement, Bok was justifiably proud of his role in improving the quality of American magazines, advancing the reforms he had crusaded for, molding middle-class attitudes, and supporting the war effort. He was not proud, however, that when the American woman had brazenly stepped down from her pedestal, he had given her a helping hand.

Edward William Bok, *The Americanization of Edward Bok: The Autobiography of a Dutch Boy Fifty Years After* (1920); Salme Harju Steinberg, *Reformer in the Marketplace: Edward W. Bok and "The Ladies' Home Journal"* (1979).

MICHAEL D. HUMMEL

See also Feminist Movement; Magazines and Newspapers.

BONNIN, GERTRUDE

(1876–1938), Yankton Sioux writer and pan-Indian activist. Bonnin, or Zitkala-Sa, was the author of *Old Indian Legends* (1901) and *American Indian Stories* (1921), and a leader in the first twentieth-century political pan-Indian movement, the Society of American Indians (1916–1919). She also founded and served as president of the National Council of American Indians (1926–1938). Zitkala-Sa rose to national prominence in the early decades of the twentieth century as a proponent of cultural pluralism and Indian self-determination in defiance of long-prevailing government acculturation policies. Almost alone among both Indian and white Progressive Era reformers, she rejected the efforts of well-meaning but ethnocentric government and philanthropic assimilationists who sought to "save" the Indian. Throughout her life she demanded American recognition of the continuing viability of Indian societies and an Indian identity.

Zitkala-Sa kept the reform pan-Indian movement alive in the decades between the demise of the Society of American Indians in the 1920s and the formation of subsequent organizations. The National Council of American Indians, which she founded in 1926, identified crucial land and resources issues facing Indian peoples while developing techniques to attract public attention. Throughout the 1920s, she worked with the General Federation of Women's Clubs to establish their nationally active Indian Welfare Committee. She participated in an investigation of government abuses endured by Oklahoma Indian peoples and wrote much of the final report published in 1924, *Oklahoma's Poor Rich Indians: An Orgy of Grant and Exploitation of the Five Civilized Tribes — Legalized Robbery.* In her congressional lobbying and persistent use of the media, Zitkala-Sa stressed the critical importance of maintaining intact reservations as cultural centers for future generations. The National Council had some success in organizing Indian voting blocs in Oklahoma and South Dakota.

Equally important, Zitkala-Sa contributed to emerging definitions of tribalism and Indian identity. Committed to national reform, she spent the last twenty years of her life in Washington, D.C. Yet she returned often to South Dakota, always identifying herself as a Yankton Sioux woman with full rights and obligations to participate in Yankton affairs. As increasing numbers of Indian peoples were compelled to live apart from the reservations in the twentieth century, Zitkala-Sa fought to establish and preserve the strength of tribal identities and responsibilities for these people, even as she fought to protect the Indian land base as a perpetual cultural homeland.

Above all, Zitkala-Sa worked for the right of Indian peoples' self-determination. She vehemently opposed all government-mandated policies, refusing to distinguish between old Bureau of Indian Affairs ethnocentrism and enlightened policy reforms put forward by Franklin D. Roosevelt's Indian commissioner John Collier. The Indian Reorganization Act (or Wheeler-Howard Act) passed by Congress in 1934 ended allotment in severalty and sought to promote cultural pluralism by guaranteeing Indian peoples' rights to traditional religion, education, and tribal government. While Collier organized regional meetings of Indian leaders to discuss the act, he did not always take their advice. An often stubborn man, he and Zitkala-Sa clashed when he rejected her attempts to guide his actions. As a result, these one-time reform allies became bit-

ter enemies as Zitkala-Sa publicly opposed Wheeler-Howard and devoted the last years of her life to persuading many Indian peoples to reject this policy in tribal referenda. Zitkala-Sa's opposition to Collier blinded her to the needed reforms Wheeler-Howard represented, but at the cost of impeding tribal unity and promoting factionalism, especially among the Sioux.

These shortcomings do not diminish the contributions Zitkala-Sa made in serving as national spokesperson for self-determination and the values of Indian cultures in the early twentieth century. Her collection of stories and the autobiographical account of her school days at White's Manual Institute in Wabash, Indiana, and later at Earlham College contained in *Old Indian Legends* and *American Indian Stories,* her many articles found in pan-Indian and popular journals and newspapers of those years, and the volume of her correspondence with the Bureau of Indian Affairs contained in the National Archives continue to provide insight into the struggle of Indian peoples in the early twentieth century to protect their heritage while developing a modern Indian identity.

Hazel Hertzberg, *The Search for an American Indian Identity: Modern Pan-Indian Movements* (1971); Zitkala-Sa, *American Indian Stories* (1921; reprint, 1985).

DEBORAH WELCH

See also Indians.

BOONE, DANIEL

(1734–1820), frontiersman and Kentucky pioneer. Daniel Boone is the most widely known of American frontiersmen. He served as the model for James Fenimore Cooper's Leatherstocking, and his adventures inspired incidents in hundreds of works of fiction. Even Lord Byron mentioned him in *Don Juan.* Without Boone the history of Kentucky would have been much different.

Boone was born near Reading, in Berks County, Pennsylvania, the son of hard-working but adventurous Quaker parents. He learned some blacksmithing but had very little formal education. Daniel appears to have been a scrappy lad who loved hunting, the wilderness, and independence. When his parents left Pennsylvania in 1750 bound for the Yadkin valley of northwest North Carolina, Daniel went along willingly.

There, on the cutting edge of the frontier, he was able to indulge his hunting prowess and love of the wilderness. In the following years he served as a wagoner with Gen. Edward Braddock's ill-fated expedition to Fort Duquesne in 1755; married a neighbor's daughter, Rebecca Bryan, in 1756; and in 1758 is believed to have been a wagoner with Gen. John Forbes who was hacking out the road to Fort Duquesne, which he rebuilt as Fort Pitt (now Pittsburgh). Back in North Carolina, Daniel purchased land from his father but never seriously engaged in farming; he loved to roam. In 1763 he and his brother Squire journeyed to Florida, although for unknown reasons they did not stay.

Boone's fame rests primarily upon his exploration and settlement of Kentucky. He was first in eastern Kentucky in 1767, but his expedition of 1769–1771 is more widely known. With a small party Boone advanced along the Warrior's Path into an Edenic region. When the time came for the party to return he remained behind in the wilderness until March 1771. On the way home, he and his brother were robbed by Indians of their deerskins and pelts, but the two remained exuberant over the land known as "Kentuck."

So much did Daniel love that "dark and bloody ground" that he tried to return in 1773, taking forty settlers with him, but the Indians drove them back. The next year he went again into the region carrying a warning of Indian troubles to Governor John Murray Dunmore's surveyors. Even as Judge Richard Henderson was concluding the Treaty of Sycamore Shoals (March 1775) by which much of Kentucky was sold to his Transylvania Company, Boone was hacking out the Wilderness Road. As soon as he reached his destination, he began building Boonesboro, one of several stations (forts) under construction at that time.

For the next four years — through 1778 — Boone, a captain in the militia, was busy defending the settlements. His leadership helped save the three remaining Kentucky stations, Boonesboro, Logan's (St. Asaph's), and Harrodsburg. These were stirring years of ambushes (such as Blue Licks in 1778), captures (Boone was seized but escaped from the Shawnees), rescues, and desperate defenses.

Although he was highly respected and served in the Virginia assembly, Boone was not a good businessman and he lost his Kentucky lands. In September 1799, he set out for Missouri where a son had preceded him. He settled in the Femme Osage valley where he continued to hunt and roam until his death. Twenty-five years later his remains and those of his wife were returned to Kentucky for burial.

Daniel Boone was helped to immortality through the writings of John Filson, whose *The Discovery, Settlement and Present State of Kentucke* included an appendix containing "The Adventures of Col. Daniel Boon [sic]." The book was widely read in England and Europe as well as in America, and Boone became the model of the American frontiersman. But even if he had not been cast as a heroic figure in *Kentucke*, residents of Kentucky would still honor him as that state's frontier hero.

John Bakeless, *Daniel Boone* (1939; reprint, 1989); Lawrence Elliott, *The Long Hunter: A New Life of Daniel Boone* (1976).

RICHARD A. BARTLETT

BORAH, WILLIAM E.

(1865–1940), U.S. senator. Born near Fairfield, Illinois, Borah "went West" as a youth, spent several months at the University of Kansas, passed the easy Kansas bar, and headed for Seattle. But he got off the train at Boise, Idaho, and stayed. He ran for local office as a Republican and bolted momentarily to the Democrats in 1896, but thereafter he never strayed from the Republican fold. His role as prosecutor in a trial of three union leaders accused of killing former governor Frank Steunenberg, which he lost to Clarence Darrow, propelled him into the Senate in 1907, where he remained until his death.

The Lion of Idaho, a burly, leonine figure, was a great orator. He managed criticisms without personal rancor, so that even his enemies, such as President Woodrow Wilson, admired him. He possessed a way of catching the desire of the people of the United States for moral positions and often convinced them that words were better than actions, which doubtless made many people feel good.

Borah's essence, however, was contrariness, although he disguised it with his oratorical and moral periods. President Calvin Coolidge supposedly observed, when gazing out of a White House window and seeing the senator ride by on a horse, that it was remarkable that horse and rider were both going in the same direction. Although he entered the Senate as a devotee of Theodore Roosevelt, Borah often opposed him, notably in 1912 when he refused to join the Bull Moose party. He enthusiastically voted for war in 1917 and with equal enthusiasm became an "irreconcilable" over the Versailles treaty and League of Nations, believing they would entangle the United States in the toils of European politics; he said he wanted the League twenty thousand leagues under the sea. In the 1920s he pushed for naval limitation and the Kellogg-Briand Pact. In 1929 he supported Herbert Hoover for president and then turned against him. He voted for New Deal legislation but adamantly opposed Franklin D. Roosevelt on foreign policy, reversing his 1917 stance in favor of entering World War I and going over to isolationism. In the summer of 1939 he even predicted that a second world war was unlikely: he flatly told the president there would be no war, basing his judgment on an obscure and, of course, unreliable private intelligence digest published in London that he had happened to read.

It is insufficient, however, to categorize Borah as a nineteenth-century idealist, unable to adjust to the twentieth, for his views fit no categories. On domestic issues he seems to have been a progressive if allowance is made for his anticonservation and free-silver views, the result of his state's interests. On foreign policy he was a theorist only, evident in the fact that he served as chairman of the Foreign Relations Committee in the late 1920s and took all sorts of international positions, but never found time to travel outside the continental United States.

Robert James Maddox, *William E. Borah and American Foreign Policy* (1969); Marian C. McKenna, *Borah* (1961).

ROBERT H. FERRELL

BOSSES, POLITICAL

See Urban Bosses and Machine Politics.

BOSTON MASSACRE

The Boston Massacre occurred on March 5, 1770. A squad of British soldiers, come to support a sentry who was being pressed by a heckling, snowballing crowd, let loose a volley of shots. Three persons were killed immediately and two died later of their wounds; among the victims was Crispus Attucks, a man of black or Indian parentage. The British officer in charge, Capt. Thomas Preston, was arrested for manslaughter, along with eight of his men.

The British troops had been billeted in Boston in October 1768 after repeated requests from British customs officials, who had been harassed and intimidated because of their efforts to enforce the Townshend Acts. Numerous clashes between the soldiers and the citizenry resulted. The killings of March 5, promptly termed a "massacre" by Patriot leaders and commemorated in a widely circulated engraving by Paul Revere, aroused intense public protests and threats of violent retaliation. This pressure caused Lieutenant Governor Thomas Hutchinson to withdraw the troops to an island in the harbor.

In an effort to demonstrate the impartiality of colonial courts, two Patriot leaders, John Adams and Josiah Quincy, volunteered to defend Captain Preston and his men. The prosecution produced little evidence, and Preston and six of the soldiers were acquitted; two others were found guilty of manslaughter, branded on the hand, and released. Although many Patriots criticized the verdicts and the anniversary of the Boston Massacre became a patriotic holiday, the removal of troops from Boston and the repeal of all but one of the contested import duties resulted in a lowering of tension in the years following the incident. Nevertheless, Governor

Hutchinson's reluctant removal of troops from Boston under threat of insurrection dramatized the impotence of imperial power as it was then constituted when faced with organized local resistance.

See also Revolution.

BOSTON TEA PARTY

The Boston Tea Party of December 16, 1773, took place when a group of Massachusetts Patriots, protesting the monopoly on American tea importation recently granted by Parliament to the East India Company, seized 342 chests of tea in a midnight raid on three tea ships and threw them into the harbor. This action, part of a wave of resistance throughout the colonies, had its origin in Parliament's effort to rescue the financially weakened East India Company so as to continue benefiting from the company's valuable position in India. The Tea Act (May 10, 1773) adjusted import duties in such a way that the company could undersell even smugglers in the colonies. The company selected consignees in Boston, New York, Charleston, and Philadelphia, and 500,000 pounds of tea were shipped across the Atlantic in September.

Under pressure from Patriot groups, the consignees in Charleston, New York, and Philadelphia refused to accept the tea shipments, but in Boston, the chosen merchants (including two of Governor Thomas Hutchinson's sons as well as his nephew) refused to concede. The first tea ship, *Dartmouth,* reached Boston November 27, and two more arrived shortly thereafter. Meanwhile, several mass meetings were held to demand that the tea be sent back to England with the duty unpaid. Tension mounted as Patriot groups led by Samuel Adams tried to persuade the consignees and then the governor to accept this approach. On December 16, a large meeting at the Old South Church was told of Hutchinson's final refusal. About midnight, watched by a large crowd, Adams and a small group of Sons of Liberty disguised as Mohawk Indians boarded the ships and jettisoned the tea. To Parliament, the Boston Tea Party confirmed Massachusetts's role as the core of resistance to legitimate British rule. The Coercive Acts of 1774 were intended to punish the colony in general and Boston in particular, both for the Tea Party and for the pattern of resistance it exemplified.

See also Revolution.

BOURKE-WHITE, MARGARET

(1904–1971), photographer. Bourke-White is best remembered for her classic photo-essays depicting such topics as American and Soviet industry, the depression-ridden American South, the "look" of two wars in Europe and Korea, the half-crazed victims of Buchenwald, and Gandhi in India.

Bourke-White studied photography with pictorialist Clarence White while attending Columbia University for one semester. Afterward she attended two midwestern colleges, was married and divorced, and then received a B.A. from Cornell in 1927. After opening a studio in Cleveland, she assumed the name Bourke-White (her mother's and father's surnames) and attracted attention for her photographs of steel making. In 1929, Henry Luce brought her to New York to become a photographer for his new magazine, *Fortune.* Luce once accompanied her on an assignment portraying the working life of an industrial city (South Bend, Indiana) and taught her a lesson she never forgot: pictures must be beautiful, but should also convey facts.

Bourke-White wrote a number of books about her assignments, illustrated with her photographs, and an autobiography, *Portrait of Myself.* She collaborated with her one-time husband Erskine Caldwell and John La Farge on other books. Attracted to heights, she shot photographs from a myriad of military and commercial aircraft and airships.

By all accounts Bourke-White was an "insistent individualist" possessing "extraordinary courage." Also characterized as "hard driving" and determined to get "exactly the picture she wanted," she often organized, lighted, and posed her pictures to the frustration of many she photographed. A *Life* magazine reporter recalled how in 1947 she "brutally" posed starving Sikh refugees too fearful to complain, ordering them "to go back again and again" for a photograph that now appears statuesque and essentially without emotion. But her coworker Alfred Eisenstaedt wrote in 1969 that she possessed "the ideal attitude" of a photojournalist: "At the peak of her distinguished career," she "was willing and eager as any beginner on a first assignment. She would get up at daybreak to photograph a bread crumb, if necessary." And another coworker Carl Mydans remembered her saying: "Sometimes I could murder someone who gets in my way when I'm taking a picture. I become irrational. There is only one moment when a picture is there, and an instant later it is gone — gone forever."

She recalled in later years one such episode. On the night of the stock market crash in 1929, she was taking advertising photographs in a Boston bank, but worried vice presidents kept getting in her way. She realized later she was probably the only photographer inside a bank that fateful night. She always regretted the picture she had missed: the expression on the faces of the bank executives "frantically" running about.

Vicki Goldberg, *Margaret Bourke-White* (1986); Jonathan Silverman, *For the World to See: The Life of Margaret Bourke-White* (1983).

WILLIAM WELLING

See also Photography.

BRADFORD, WILLIAM

(1590–1657), governor of Plymouth Colony. Born of substantial yeomen in Yorkshire, England, Bradford expressed his nonconformist religious sensibilities in his early teens and joined the famed Separatist church in Scrooby at the age of seventeen. In 1609 he immigrated with the congregation, led by John Robinson, to the Netherlands. For the next eleven years he and his fellow religious dissenters lived in Leyden until their fear of assimilation into Dutch culture prompted them to embark on the *Mayflower* for the voyage to North America.

The Pilgrims arrived in what became Plymouth, Massachusetts, in 1621 with a large number of non-Separatist settlers. Before disembarking, the congregation drew up the first New World social contract, the Mayflower Compact, which all the male settlers signed.

Bradford served thirty one-year terms as governor of the fledgling colony between 1622 and 1656. He enjoyed remarkable discretionary powers as chief magistrate, acting as high judge and treasurer as well as presiding over the deliberations of the General Court, the legislature of the community. In 1636 he helped draft the colony's legal code. Under his guidance Plymouth never became a Bible commonwealth like its larger and more influential neighbor, the Massachusetts Bay Colony. Relatively tolerant of dissent, the Plymouth settlers did not restrict the franchise or other civic privileges to church members. The Plymouth churches were overwhelmingly Congregationalist and Separatist in form, but Presbyterians like William Vassal and renegades like Roger Williams resided in the colony without being pressured to conform to the majority's religious convictions.

After a brief experiment with the "common course," a sort of primitive agrarian communism, the colony quickly centered around private subsistence agriculture. This was facilitated by Bradford's decision to distribute land among all the settlers, not just members of the company. In 1627 he and four others assumed the colony's debt to the merchant adventurers who had helped finance their immigration in return for a monopoly of the fur trading and fishing industries. Owing to some malfeasance on the part of their English mercantile factors and the decline of the fur trade, Bradford and his colleagues were unable to retire this debt until 1648, and then only at great personal expense.

Around 1630 Bradford began to compile his two-volume *Of Plymouth Plantation, 1620–1647*, one of the most important early chronicles of the settlement of New England. Bradford's history was singular in its tendency to separate religious from secular concerns. Unlike similar tracts from orthodox Massachusetts Bay, Bradford did not interpret temporal affairs as the inevitable unfolding of God's providential plan. Lacking the dogmatic temper and religious enthusiasm of the Puritans of the Great Migration, Bradford steered a middle course for Plymouth Colony between the Holy Commonwealth of Massachusetts and the tolerant secular community of Rhode Island.

William Bradford, *Of Plymouth Plantation, 1620–1647,* with notes and introduction by Samuel Eliot Morison (1952).

DARREN MARCUS STALOFF

See also Mayflower Compact; New England Colonies.

BRADLEY, OMAR

(1893–1981), U.S. Army general. Bradley was the first member of his 1915 West Point class to receive a star. Much of his rapid advance he owed to Gen. George C. Marshall, under whom he served four years as professor of tactics at the Infantry School and one year as an assistant in the War Department. Jumping him from lieutenant colonel to brigadier general in 1940, Marshall made Bradley head of the Infantry School, gave him a second star in 1941, and in succession appointed him commanding general of the Eighty-second and Twenty-eighth divisions. Impressed by Bradley's success as a planner, Marshall sent him to North Africa early in 1943 to be Gen. Dwight D. Eisenhower's "eyes and ears." Soon Bradley commanded the U.S. Second Corps in clearing the enemy from the American sector of Tunisia. As a corps commander under Gen. George S. Patton's Fifth Army, Bradley played a key role in the thirty-eight-day conquest of Sicily in the summer of 1943.

Early in preparations for the 1944 invasion of Normandy, Marshall selected Bradley to command the First Army, which he later directed in the D-Day landings and Normandy campaign. When Patton was sent with the Third Army to assist in the breakout from France several weeks later, Bradley became the Twelfth Army Group commander, with Gen. Courtney Hodges's First and Patton's Third armies under his command. He led this force in a rapid dash across northern France and Belgium to the German frontier. Slowed by rugged terrain and supply shortages, Bradley's forces were hard hit in the Ardennes area in mid-December. When the German ad-

vance made it necessary for him to hand over to British field marshal Bernard Montgomery command of the American forces north of the German penetration, Bradley used Patton's army to restore his lines in the south. His renewed drive in February forced the Germans back across the Roer and led to seizure of a bridge across the Rhine in early March. In April Bradley's Army Group, now consisting of the First, Third, Ninth, and Fifteenth armies, led a massive drive through central Germany to the Elbe and beyond, to link up with the Russians at Torgau on April 25 before pushing into Czechoslovakia at the war's end.

President Harry S. Truman after World War II picked Bradley to head the Veterans' Administration in its difficult job of arranging demobilization, hospital care, education, and housing for returning troops.

When General Eisenhower retired as chief of staff in 1948, Bradley assumed the post until he became the first chairman of the Joint Chiefs of Staff, a position made necessary by the recent unification of the armed forces. Soon involved in supporting military operations in Korea, Bradley was caught up first with getting additional forces to MacArthur and then in the controversy between the Far East commander and Washington over policy. Bradley and the Joint Chiefs supported the president. Bradley became the last five-star general upon his elevation to chairman of the Joint Chiefs. He retired in 1953.

Bradley's disdain for military pomp and his concern for the welfare of the individual soldier won him acclaim as "the soldiers' general." Marshall praised his ability to organize great forces and his skill in devising bold plans. Eisenhower called him "a master tactician" and predicted that the quiet, almost diffident general eventually would be considered "America's foremost battle leader."

Omar N. Bradley, *A Soldier's Story* (1951); Omar N. Bradley and Clay Blair, *A General's Life: An Autobiography* (1983).

FORREST C. POGUE

See also Armed Forces; Korean War; World War II.

BRADY, MATHEW

(1823?–1896), photographer. In his portraits of prominent Americans in the late 1840s and 1850s and in the camp and battlefield views made under his aegis during the Civil War, Mathew Brady helped define a role for American photographers as historians of contemporary life. Although he operated a camera himself only infrequently — he was hampered by poor eyesight — he shaped, more effectively than any of his contemporaries, an identity for photography as a force in American society, politics, and culture.

In 1839, the same year Louis-Jacques-Mandé Daguerre announced his invention of photography in Paris, the young Brady arrived in New York City from his upstate New York home where he had been born to Irish parents. After a brief stint as a clerk in the A. T. Stewart department store and a few years as a manufacturer of jewelry cases (including cases for daguerreotypes), he opened a daguerreotype portrait studio at the corner of Broadway and Fulton streets in 1844. In the growing competition among professional daguerreotypists Brady became expert in advertising himself and attracting prominent sitters. "Brady of Broadway" became the most widely recognized and admired photographic trademark of the antebellum era.

The inaugural issue of the *Photographic Art-Journal* in 1851 described him as the "fountainhead" of the young profession of portrait photography. In the same year he was awarded one of three gold medals for daguerreotypes at the Crystal Palace Exhibition in London (the other two also went to Americans). In the 1850s his trade, now including paper prints, expanded rapidly; he moved his gallery into more sumptuous quarters uptown and in 1858 opened a branch in Washington, D.C. With his portraits of public figures appearing regularly as engravings in the national press, Brady had immense influence on the times. His famous Cooper Union portrait of Abraham Lincoln during the presidential campaign of 1860 contributed in no small way to making Lincoln a popular figure.

But Brady's greatest success lay in his organization of a corps of Civil War photographers who followed the armies and produced an incomparable firsthand record of the war years. The pictures he acquired and published represent one of the greatest collective depictions in photography of a major historical event. Brady, however, never recovered from the loss of the private fortune he invested in this project, and his career declined precipitously during the Gilded Age. When he died in 1896 he was close to destitution.

Although he made no profit from it in his lifetime, his collection of Civil War pictures, including many antebellum portraits of prominent figures of the war years, finally made its way into national archives, where it remains the chief source of visual information about the period and the war. Interest in Mathew Brady revived in the 1930s, and his work exerted a major influence on the documentary movement in photography in the depression era.

James D. Horan, *Mathew Brady: Historian with a Camera* (1955); Dorothy Meserve Kunhardt and Philip B. Kunhardt, *Mathew Brady and His World* (1977).

ALAN TRACHTENBERG

See also Photography.

BRAIN TRUST

The "brain trust" was the name given to a diverse group of academics who served as advisers to President Franklin D. Roosevelt. The group, first suggested in March 1932 by Roosevelt's legal counsel Samuel Rosenman, included Raymond Moley, Rexford Tugwell, and Adolf Berle of Columbia University, attorney Basil O'Connor, and later Felix Frankfurter of Harvard Law School. These men played a key role in shaping the New Deal. Although they never met as a group after Roosevelt's inauguration, most of them served in official posts during his presidency.

The brain trust offered Roosevelt a wide range of approaches for dealing with the Great Depression. He in turn welcomed their ideas in his constant search for new paths. Refusing to adhere to a single ideological approach, Roosevelt would usually pick and choose among their proposals. Although the brain trusters represented a variety of ideologies, they shared a basic, somewhat self-justifying belief that organized intelligence could restore the political, economic, and social health of society. They abandoned the Wilsonian belief that the classical society of small competitors could be re-created and turned instead to structural economic reform that accepted big business. All espoused some sort of government-business cooperation, but beyond this they differed. For example, Moley emphasized business initiative, Tugwell favored a state-administered economy, and Berle believed businesses could be compelled to alter their ways without forceful government intervention.

The term *brain trusters*, often applied to all New Dealers, was used disparagingly by opponents who believed that intellectuals in government were steering the country toward socialism or communism.

See also New Deal.

BRANDEIS, LOUIS D.

(1856–1941), lawyer, reformer, and associate justice, U.S. Supreme Court. Born in Louisville, Kentucky, Brandeis attended the Harvard Law School and shortly after graduation opened a practice in Boston with Sam Warren, a law school classmate. At a time when industrialization was revolutionizing legal work, Brandeis was one of the first to recognize that clients needed advice prior to acting in order to avoid expensive litigation and problems with regulatory agencies. By the end of the century, Brandeis had become one of the most sought-after lawyers in the country.

By then, however, he had shifted his interest from the practice of law to reform. Like many Progressives, he believed that industrialization and monopoly limited individual opportunity and corrupted the political system. He started his reform efforts locally, opposing corrupt traction franchises in Boston. He then moved to the state level, where he demonstrated the traits that made him so effective. He not only exposed the high rates insurance companies charged workers

for limited coverage but came up with a solution — savings bank life insurance — which he saw through to its establishment in 1907.

Brandeis gained a national reputation as the "People's Attorney," for his then-unique trait of defending public causes without a fee. In *Muller* v. *Oregon* (1908), he pioneered a new type of appellate legal brief, emphasizing economic and social evidence rather than legal precedents. The "Brandeis brief" became the prototype for later reform litigation.

Between 1908 and 1916 Brandeis devoted himself almost entirely to reform work, such as exposing the Taft administration's bungling in the Ballinger-Pinchot affair. In 1912 he met Woodrow Wilson and helped him formulate for the 1912 presidential campaign the New Freedom program, with its emphasis on competition, in response to Theodore Roosevelt's call for extensive governmental regulation of business. Brandeis also headed the American Zionist movement, which by 1919 he had made into the largest Jewish organization in the country.

In 1916 Wilson named Brandeis to the Supreme Court. In his twenty-three years on the bench, he earned a reputation as the greatest legal craftsman of his era. Although he often dissented, his carefully argued opinions were in practically every instance eventually adopted by later courts.

Brandeis's ideas affected many areas of law, but his greatest contributions involved privacy and the application of the Bill of Rights. In *Olmstead* v. *United States* (1928), a decision upholding wiretapping, he entered an eloquent dissent arguing for the first time that a constitutional right of privacy exists. A few years earlier he had argued that the Fourteenth Amendment's due process clause applied the First Amendment's guarantee of free speech to the states.

Throughout the conservative domination of the Court in the 1920s and early 1930s, Brandeis led the liberal minority in maintaining that state legislatures and Congress had the right to experiment in response to changing socioeconomic conditions. This doctrine of judicial restraint and deference to the legislative branch in economic matters became accepted by the entire Court in the 1940s.

Philippa Strum, *Louis D. Brandeis: Justice for the People* (1984).

MELVIN I. UROFSKY

See also Ballinger-Pinchot Controversy; *Muller* v. *Oregon*; New Freedom; Progressivism; Supreme Court.

BRITAIN-U.S. RELATIONS

See Great Britain–U.S. Relations.

BRITISH EMPIRE

See America in the British Empire; Great Britain–U.S. Relations.

BROTHERHOOD OF SLEEPING CAR PORTERS

The Brotherhood of Sleeping Car Porters was founded in 1925 by A. Philip Randolph and others. It was the nation's first African-American union. The new union faced opposition from their employer, George Pullman and the Pullman Company, supporters of Booker T. Washington, and craft unionists. Although the head of the American Federation of Labor (AFL), William Green, supported the brotherhood's efforts, the Hotel and Restaurant Employees International claimed jurisdiction over the porters. The union did not receive an international charter until 1936, however.

In 1937 the Pullman Company gave the Brotherhood its first contract, which met some of the union's long-standing demands. It granted a reduction in the number of hours worked, a wage hike, job security, and union representation.

Ultimately the union became more prominent for its work in civil rights. Beginning in 1934 Randolph, its president, spoke at every AFL convention and called for the integration of blacks in the labor movement. From his position in the AFL and, after 1960, as leader of the Negro American Labor Council, Randolph fought for black people's rights. He led the March on Washington of 1941, which caused President Franklin

D. Roosevelt to create the Fair Employment Practices Committee in an effort to prevent thousands of African-Americans massing in the nation's capital. Twenty years later Randolph and the brotherhood were also in the forefront of the 1963 March on Washington.

See also Labor; Marches on Washington: 1941, 1963; Randolph, A. Philip.

BROWN, JOHN

(1800–1859), abolitionist and insurrectionist. Born in Torrington, Connecticut, Brown spent his boyhood in Ohio, where he mingled from the first with dedicated opponents of slavery. While his professional life featured a series of business failures, his family responsibilities grew even as his abolitionist principles deepened.

In 1855, after assisting the escape of several slaves, Brown and his five sons moved to Kansas just after that territory had been opened for the possible expansion of slavery by the Kansas-Nebraska Act. Joining the struggle there between proslavery and Free-Soil settlers, Brown appointed himself "captain" of the antislavery forces on Osawatomie Creek. (The struggle arose out of a long-standing disagreement between North and South over slavery's expansion that had its roots in the framing of the Constitution.) When proslavery forces sacked the "free state" town of Lawrence, guerrilla warfare ensued. The success of the proslavery guerrillas inspired Brown, with four of his sons and two other accomplices, to murder five reputedly proslavery settlers who lived along Pottawottamie Creek. Justifying his action as obedience to the will of a just God, Brown soon became a hero in the eyes of northern extremists and was quick to capitalize on his growing reputation. By early 1858 he had succeeded in enlisting a small "army" of insurrectionists, including three of his sons, whose mission was to foment rebellion among the slaves.

Brown had toyed with the idea for years, but it took form after a meeting of Brown and his followers in the free black community of Chatham, Ontario, in the winter of 1858. He proposed to provoke a black insurrection through armed intervention in northern Virginia, thereby establishing a stronghold to which escapees could flee and from which further insurrection might be spawned. Meanwhile, mounting frustration over the failure to achieve peaceful emancipation made many abolitionists receptive to Brown's violent approach. Some of them, known subsequently as the "secret six" — Franklin Sanborn, Thomas Wentworth Higginson, George Luther Stearns, Gerrit Smith, Samuel Gridley Howe, and Theodore Parker — were aware of his intentions and became his financial supporters. Others, however, contributed funds and good wishes while remaining studiously ignorant of Brown's exact plans. Early in 1859, he rented a farm near Harpers Ferry, Virginia (now West Virginia), collected weapons and his "army," and on October 16 with twenty-one followers attacked and occupied the federal arsenal in Harpers Ferry. Quickly surrounded by militia commanded by Col. Robert E. Lee, Brown's position was overrun, ten of his followers were killed, and Brown himself was wounded and captured.

News of the raid electrified the North and outraged the white South. Brown was tried and convicted of treason. He conducted his defense with extraordinary astuteness, conveying to supporters and sympathizers the appearance of a powerfully inspired and selfless religious martyr. Popular expression of support for Brown was widespread in the North (the best remembered of which is Henry David Thoreau's "Plea for Captain John Brown") before he was hanged on December 2, 1859. In the South, his execution did little to allay spreading fears of slave insurrection and a growing conviction that northern opponents of slavery would continue to stimulate insurrection. Many analysts then and since have concluded that Brown's raid did much to hasten the coming of the Civil War.

Richard O. Boyer, *The Legend of John Brown* (1973); Steven Oates, *To Purge This Land with Blood: A Biography of John Brown* (1970).

JAMES BREWER STEWART

See also Abolitionist Movement; Bleeding Kansas; Kansas-Nebraska Act; Slavery.

BROWNSVILLE AFFAIR

The Brownsville Affair was the name given to an incident in August 1906, when a group of about twelve black soldiers from the Twenty-fifth U.S. Infantry, in retaliation for discriminatory treatment by local citizens, shot off their guns in Brownsville, Texas, killing one resident. The soldiers then returned unobserved to their base at nearby Fort Brown. When none of the men in three black companies would confess or identify the culprits, President Theodore Roosevelt, on November 5, ordered that all 167 of them be given dishonorable discharges. Among those discharged were 6 Medal of Honor winners.

The president received considerable praise for his action from the South but was widely criticized in the North. The action had political significance because nearly all black voters at that time were supporters of the president's Republican party. When the matter was debated in Congress in January 1908, most of the Republicans condemned Roosevelt's action, and the Democrats defended it. This controversy intensified the strained relations between Roosevelt and Congress.

President Roosevelt's order was finally reversed in 1972, when the secretary of the army cleared the soldiers of guilt and changed their discharges from dishonorable to honorable.

BROWN V. BOARD OF EDUCATION OF TOPEKA

This unanimous decision handed down by the Supreme Court on May 17, 1954, ended federal tolerance of racial segregation. In *Plessy* v. *Ferguson* (1896) the Court had ruled that "separate but equal" accommodations on railroad cars conformed to the Fourteenth Amendment's guarantee of equal protection. That decision was used to justify segregating all public facilities, including schools. In addition, most school districts, ignoring *Plessy*'s "equal" requirement, neglected their black schools.

In the mid-1930s, however, the National Association for the Advancement of Colored People (NAACP) challenged school segregation in a series of court cases. In these the Court required "tangible" aspects of segregated schools to be equivalent. The rulings prompted several school districts to improve their black students' schools. Then the NAACP contested the constitutionality of segregation in four regions. Each of the school districts involved had improved the tangible aspects of its black schools, but *Brown* brought segregation, per se, squarely before the Court. In the unanimous decision Chief Justice Earl Warren rejected the *Plessy* doctrine, declaring that "separate educational facilities" were "inherently unequal" because the intangible inequalities of segregation deprived black students of equal protection under the law. A year later, the Court published implementation guidelines requiring federal district courts to supervise school desegregation "on a racially nondiscriminatory basis with all deliberate speed."

See also Racial Desegregation.

BRUCE, BLANCHE K.

(1841–1898), black political leader and U.S. senator. Although he was born a slave in Virginia, Blanche Bruce's childhood was relatively benign, and he shared a tutor with his master's son. He spent most of his youth in Missouri, where his master moved the family in 1850. When Missouri abolished slavery during the Civil War, Bruce established in Hannibal the first school for blacks in the state. After the war, he studied briefly at Oberlin College and then went south, settling in Bolivar County in the Mississippi Delta. A man of magnificent physique and handsome countenance, he possessed the manners of a Chesterfield.

Bruce became involved in Reconstruction politics as a Republican organizer among the freedmen on plantations, and in 1870 he was selected sergeant-at-arms of the Mississippi state senate. In 1871 he won election as sheriff of Bolivar County and then was appointed county superintendent of education. He made the Bolivar County public school system, although racially segregated, a model for biracial cooperation in the formation of free public schools. He also became a relatively large landowner in the Delta.

Despite the strong opposition of most Mis-

sissippi whites to the Reconstruction rights of blacks, Bruce succeeded locally in harmonizing various political elements and reducing white-planter opposition to Republican control. With a foot in both the radical and the moderate Republican camps, he won election to the U.S. Senate in 1874. He was the second black to serve in the Senate and the first to serve a full term. After taking his seat in March 1875, he served on Senate select committees on Mississippi River improvements and the Freedman's Bank; he chaired the latter committee. On the Senate floor, he usually maintained a low profile, but after the violent overthrow of Republican rule in Mississippi in 1875–1876, he pressed vigorously for the appointment of a committee to report on political conditions in the state and recommend action for the protection of Republicans. Although the Senate created such a committee, the House of Representatives blocked congressional action on its report.

After Reconstruction Bruce adopted an accommodationist stance toward conservative or Democratic control of the South. He became attentive to intraparty politics and the struggle over federal appointments in Mississippi. Along with black leaders John R. Lynch and James Hill, Bruce controlled the Mississippi Republican party and the state's federal patronage during the late 1870s and most of the 1880s. After the expiration of his senatorial term in 1881, he continued to live in Washington and supported his family with earnings from minor federal appointments as well as from his Mississippi plantation.

Despite the failure of Reconstruction, Bruce continued to subscribe to the idea that the best hope for the freedmen was their assimilation into white society. He therefore opposed the black migration movements to Kansas and Liberia during the late 1870s, which caused him to lose favor among many African-Americans. His formula for the freedmen's progress inclined more and more toward the self-help doctrine, and he stressed education as the means for their obtaining equality. His popularity in the black community revived during the 1890s, culminating in a strong but unsuccessful movement to secure his appointment to William McKinley's cabinet in 1897.

As a leader of his race during and after Reconstruction, Bruce perhaps pursued too conservatively and too optimistically the objectives of political equality, fundamental civil rights, and education for blacks. But by choosing to ignore the hardening racial practices of late-nineteenth-century America, Bruce avoided the despair that eventually drove many of his race to accept the separate-but-equal doctrine contained in Booker T. Washington's philosophy.

William C. Harris, *The Day of the Carpetbagger: Republican Reconstruction in Mississippi* (1979); Howard W. Rabinowitz, ed., *Southern Black Leaders of the Reconstruction Era* (1982).

WILLIAM C. HARRIS

See also Black Exodus, 1879; Reconstruction; Republican Party; Washington, Booker T.

BRYAN, WILLIAM JENNINGS

(1860–1925), Democratic party leader and secretary of state, 1913–1915. Born in Illinois, Bryan inherited from his parents an intense commitment to the Democratic party and a fervent Protestant faith. After graduating from Illinois College and Union Law School, he married and, seeing no political future in Illinois, moved to Nebraska in 1887. In 1890, when the new Populist party disrupted Nebraska politics, Bryan won election to Congress; he was reelected in 1892. In Congress, he earned respect for his oratory and became a leader among free-silver Democrats. In 1894 he led Nebraska's Democrats to support the state Populist party.

Bryan electrified the 1896 Democratic convention with his stirring Cross of Gold speech favoring free silver and thereby captured the presidential nomination. Also nominated by the Populists, Bryan agreed with their view that government should protect individuals and the democratic process against monopolistic corporations. "The Boy Orator of the Platte" traveled eighteen thousand miles and spoke to thousands of voters, but lost; William McKinley's victory initiated a generation of Republican dominance in national politics. Bryan's 1896 campaign, however, marked a long-term shift within the Democratic party from a Jacksonian commitment to minimal government toward a positive view of government.

During the Spanish-American War, Bryan served as a colonel in a Nebraska regiment, but after the war, he condemned McKinley's Philippine policy as imperialism. Nominated again by the Democrats in 1900, Bryan hoped to make the election a referendum on imperialism, but other issues intervened, including his own insistence on free silver and attacks on monopolies. McKinley won again.

After his defeat, Bryan launched a newspaper, the *Commoner* (based on his nickname "the Great Commoner") and made frequent speaking tours. Although he was a superb orator, he was neither a deep nor an original thinker. He used the *Commoner* and the lecture circuit to affirm equality, to advocate greater popular participation in governmental decision making, to oppose monopolies, and to proclaim the importance of faith in God. "Shall the People Rule?" became the watchword of his third campaign for president, in 1908, when he lost to William Howard Taft.

In 1912, Bryan worked to secure the Democratic presidential nomination for Woodrow Wilson, and when Wilson won, he named Bryan secretary of state. As secretary, Bryan promoted conciliation, or cooling-off, treaties, in which the parties agreed that, if they could not resolve a dispute, they would wait a year before going to war and would seek outside fact-finding. Thirty such treaties were drafted.

When the European war broke out in 1914, Bryan, like Wilson, was committed to neutrality. But he went beyond Wilson in advocating restrictions on American citizens and companies to prevent them from drawing the nation into war. When Wilson strongly protested Germany's sinking of the *Lusitania*, Bryan resigned rather than approve a message he feared would lead to war.

Thereafter, Bryan worked for peace, prohibition, and woman suffrage, and he increasingly criticized the teaching of evolution. In 1925, he joined the prosecution in the trial of John Scopes, a Tennessee schoolteacher charged with violating state law by teaching evolution. In a famous exchange, Clarence Darrow, defending Scopes, put Bryan on the witness stand and revealed his shallowness and ignorance of science and archaeology. Bryan died soon after the trial ended.

Robert W. Cherny, *A Righteous Cause: The Life of William Jennings Bryan* (1985); Paolo E. Coletta, *William Jennings Bryan*, 3 vols. (1964–1969).

ROBERT W. CHERNY

See also Elections: 1896, 1900, 1908; Populism; *Scopes* Trial.

BUCHANAN, JAMES

(1791–1868), fifteenth president of the United States. Born in Pennsylvania of prosperous Scotch-Irish parents, Buchanan graduated from Dickinson College and became a highly successful lawyer. He began his political career as a Federalist, and after serving in the Pennsylvania legislature, he was elected to Congress in 1820. When the Federalist party collapsed, he joined the Andrew Jackson bandwagon and became an important Democratic leader in Congress. After a brief stint as minister to Russia, he was elected in 1834 to the Senate, where he served for a decade. Plodding and unimaginative, he was a loyal party man who strongly sympathized with the South on the slavery issue.

In 1844 he helped carry Pennsylvania for James K. Polk and was rewarded by being named secretary of state. Overriding Buchanan's ingrained caution, Polk assumed the dominant role in shaping foreign policy, although Buchanan's studious habits and tact made him a useful subordinate in handling the Texas and Oregon controversies. He pushed the administration's unsuccessful effort to acquire Cuba, a goal he reaffirmed in the notorious Ostend Manifesto (1854).

After unsuccessful bids for the Democratic presidential nomination in 1848 and 1852, he accepted an appointment in 1853 as minister to Britain. Since he was out of the country; he was not associated with the Kansas-Nebraska Act or the ensuing turmoil in Kansas, a fact that helped him win the Democratic presidential nomination in 1856. With strong support from the South, he was elected in November.

Buchanan's presidency was mired in contro-versy. Upholding the southern view that a territorial legislature could not prohibit slavery, he secretly influenced the Supreme Court's controversial *Dred Scott* decision by privately pressing a northern justice to vote with the southern majority against the legality of the Missouri Compromise; the onslaught of a depression in the fall of 1857 and his opposition to northern-sponsored economic legislation further undermined his administration; his expansionist foreign policy recklessly exacerbated sectional tensions; and he presided over the most corrupt administration in the nation's history before the Civil War. But his worst blunder was endorsing Kansas's admission as a slave state under the Lecompton constitution in violation of his earlier pledge for a fair vote. Buchanan's course disrupted the Democratic party, badly weakened it in the free states, and greatly strengthened the sectional Republican party. Aided by Buchanan's actions, the Republican party easily triumphed in 1860.

In the ensuing secession crisis, Buchanan desperately sought to avoid precipitating a war. The resignation of a majority of the cabinet and their replacement by staunch Unionists strengthened Buchanan's resolve, and he steadfastly refused to recognize the legality of secession or to surrender remaining federal property in the South. Eventually the administration worked out informal agreements to preserve the status quo at Forts Sumter and Pickens, and with a sigh of relief, he turned the problem over to his successor. He took no active part in politics during the war and died in 1868.

The last of a series of presidents who dealt ineptly with rising sectional tensions, Buchanan had neither the vision nor the talent to defuse the crisis. Although he was devoted to the Union, his one-sided pro-Southern policies were disastrous for the Democratic party and the nation. Few presidents have entered office with more experience in public life, and few have so decisively failed.

Philip S. Klein, *President James Buchanan: A Biography* (1962); Roy F. Nichols, *The Disruption of American Democracy* (1949).

WILLIAM E. GIENAPP

See also Democratic Party; Elections: 1856; Ostend Manifesto. *For events during Buchanan's administration, see* Brown, John; *Dred Scott* Case; Lincoln-Douglas Debates; Secession.

BUCKLEY, WILLIAM F., JR.

(1925–), conservative editor and writer. Buckley was born the son of a Texan engaged in the oil business in Mexico and Venezuela. The Buckley children had Latin American nurses and French governesses and spoke Spanish and French fluently.

On his father's advice, Buckley read the works of Albert Jay Nock, a family friend and legendary prophet among the emerging anti–New Deal Right. Buckley was strongly influenced by Nock's commitment to high culture. Unlike the "new conservatives" who emphasized challenging communism by building democracy and the welfare state, Buckley preferred Nock's term *individualist* and believed that communism could best be met by American economic growth based on reducing regulation and taxes.

Buckley first gained national attention with *God and Man at Yale* (1951), published a year after his graduation from that university. The book attacked the liberal bent of American college courses and the professoriat's ideology. Buckley also founded the Intercollegiate Society of Individualists.

In November 1955 Buckley launched the *National Review,* and until his retirement as editor-in-chief in 1990, he and the magazine were virtually synonymous. Within a year of the *Review*'s founding, its conservatism faced a test over the momentous events of 1956. In response to Nikita Khrushchev's February 1956 speech demythologizing Joseph Stalin, *Review* contributor James Burnham declared it to represent a real thaw, but other editors attacked it as a Soviet ruse. Although Buckley did not agree with Burnham, he supported his right to publish in the *National Review,* which led to the resignation of several editors.

In the 1950s and early 1960s Buckley deplored the conformism and apathy on college campuses and published *Up from Liberalism* (1959) to challenge this attitude. Dominant pro-

gressive philosophy, he said, "cannot care deeply, and so cannot be cared about deeply."

Also in the sixties, Buckley took strong exception to Pope John XXIII's encyclical *Mater et Magistra* (1961), objecting that it focused attention on social as well as moral issues. Among American Catholics, Buckley's views on political and economic issues were widely discussed. According to John B. Judis, "Buckley urged the Church to allow married priests; he refused to follow the Church in opposing contraception and divorce; and he applauded the call of Vatican II for tolerance toward other religious beliefs and practices."

Although the *National Review* was founded as a reaction against the Eisenhower administration's moderate policies, Buckley has consistently supported Republican presidential candidates. In 1965, he ran for mayor of New York City, receiving almost 12 percent of the vote. This prefigured the campaign for the U.S. Senate in New York, in which his brother, James Buckley, was elected as the Conservative party candidate. Buckley's positive relations with the Nixon and Ford administrations blossomed into overwhelming approval of the Reagan administration. Buckley's celebrity status (derived partly from his television program) as well as his political views admitted him to the limited social list of Nancy Reagan's White House.

An accomplished sailor, harpsichordist, and author of best-selling spy novels, Buckley is something of a Renaissance man. His erudition, stylishness, and range of talents have made him one of the most respected voices in the conservative movement.

William F. Buckley, Jr., *Did You Ever See a Dream Walking?* ed. Leonard Levy and Alfred Young (1970); Frank S. Meyer, *In Defense of Freedom* (1962).

LEONARD P. LIGGIO

See also Conservatism.

BULL MOOSE PARTY

See Progressive Parties: 1912, 1924, 1948.

BUNCHE, RALPH

(1904–1971), scholar, statesman, and U.N. under secretary general. Bunche was the first black person to win the Nobel Peace Prize, awarded in 1950. Born in Detroit, Michigan, Bunche and his sister were orphaned in 1915 and were reared by their grandmother in Los Angeles.

A brilliant, industrious student, Bunche graduated from Jefferson High School in 1922 as class valedictorian but was barred from the honor society because of his race. He would be reminded of this insult years later when the West Side Tennis Club in New York denied membership to him and his son. After he lodged a complaint, the club relented because of his international prominence. He refused to join the club, however, because its exception was based on his personal prestige rather than on the principle of racial equality. Bunche noted that "no Negro American can be free from the disabilities of race . . . until the lowliest Negro . . . is no longer disadvantaged because of his race."

In 1927 Bunche graduated from the University of California at Los Angeles, where he had excelled both in and outside the classroom. He wrote for the school newspaper, won oratorical contests, was sports editor of the yearbook, played guard for three years on the basketball team, and became Phi Beta Kappa. He then entered Harvard University, where in 1934 he became the first African-American to earn a Ph.D. in government and international relations. While completing his doctoral studies, Bunche joined the faculty at Howard University, where he established and chaired the political science department and served as special assistant to Howard's president. He organized the Joint Committee on National Recovery to lobby Congress for black participation in New Deal programs and to fight against racial discrimination in New Deal agencies. He also helped form the National Negro Congress to arouse blacks to work for social and economic progress and to unite black and white workers.

For Bunche, the so-called Negro problem in America was rooted more in economic and class conflict than in racial antagonism. He was one of Gunnar Myrdal's six staff members for the study of race relations that resulted in the monumental two-volume *An American Dilemma* in 1944. Bunche wrote extensive memoranda on black politics, organizations, leadership, and ideology for the study.

After the United States entered World War II, Bunche took a leave of absence from Howard and joined the Office of Strategic Services as senior social scientist for research on Africa and other colonial areas. Given his doctoral research on colonial administration, he was the foremost American authority on colonialism in Africa. In 1944, he moved to the State Department, where he supplied advice on dependent territories for U.S. representatives to the Dumbarton Oaks Conference and the meetings that established the United Nations. Bunche helped draft the trusteeship provisions of the U.N. Charter and assisted in organizing the Division of Trusteeship at the United Nations, becoming its director in 1947.

That same year, he became secretary to the U.N. Special Committee on Palestine and acting mediator in 1948 after the assassination of the first mediator, Count Folke Bernadotte of Sweden. Bunche earned high praise from all quarters for his deft handling of the armistice negotiations that ended the Arab-Israeli conflict in 1949 and won him his Nobel Peace Prize. He became the U.N. under secretary general in 1955 and directed U.N. peacekeeping missions in the Suez in 1956, in the Congo in 1960, and in Cyprus in 1964.

An indefatigable advocate of human rights at home and peace abroad, Bunche was given the NAACP's Spingarn Medal, its highest honor, in 1949. He served on the NAACP's board of directors for twenty-two years. In 1937, he walked his first picket line for civil rights in Washington, D.C.; he later participated in the 1963 March on Washington and in the 1965 Selma to Montgomery march for voting rights. In 1953, the American Political Science Association elected him president in recognition of his scholarship and mediation of international conflict, and President John F. Kennedy, in 1963, bestowed upon him the nation's highest civilian award, the Medal of Freedom.

Robert L. Harris, Jr., "Ralph J. Bunche and Afro-American Participation in Decolonization," in Robert A.

Hill, ed., *Pan-African Biography* (1987); Peggy Mann, *Ralph J. Bunche: UN Peacemaker* (1975).

ROBERT L. HARRIS, JR.

See also American Dilemma, An; Marches on Washington: 1941, 1963; National Association for the Advancement of Colored People; Racial Desegregation.

BURGER, WARREN

(1907–   ), lawyer and chief justice, U.S. Supreme Court. Burger attended the University of Minnesota and evening law classes at the St. Paul College of Law. He joined one of St. Paul's leading law firms and within five years had become a partner, specializing in corporate and real estate work. His work as floor manager for Harold Stassen's 1948 bid for the Republican presidential nomination caught the attention of other party leaders, including Herbert Brownell and Richard M. Nixon, and in 1953 Brownell appointed him assistant attorney general for the Civil Division. His legal competence and political conservatism won him respect within the Eisenhower administration.

Burger decided to return to private practice, but in 1956 Eisenhower nominated him to the Court of Appeals for the District of Columbia Circuit, considered by many the second most important court in the federal system. In the thirteen years he served on that court, Burger established a reputation as an articulate conservative who opposed the liberal tendencies of the Warren Court and of the majority on his own bench. In many areas, however, it would be fairer to characterize him as a progressive, willing to change with the times but in a thoughtful rather than a precipitous manner. He espoused, for example, a strong view of constitutionally protected privacy and personal autonomy, but articulated it in terms more familiar to conservatives than to liberals.

On one subject, however, Judge Burger increasingly stood apart from his brethren. The Warren Court's "due process revolution" increased the rights accorded to accused persons, and Burger, in opinions and speeches, argued that the law had tilted too far in favor of criminals. One of these speeches caught Nixon's at-

tention; Burger appeared to be just the sort of person to carry out Nixon's campaign promise to put the Court back on a proper conservative path. On May 21, 1969, the president nominated Burger to succeed Earl Warren as chief justice of the United States.

Burger served from 1969 to 1986. During that time he proved unable to *lead* the Court, as Warren had done, or to influence its jurisprudential drift. It became one of the most factious courts in history, and Burger could not move it doctrinally to a more conservative position. In the one area where the Court did move to a more conservative stance, the rights of accused persons, the Warren Court had already begun that process by 1965.

But in such areas as separation of church and state, freedom of speech, federal power, and right of privacy, the Court remained fairly consistent with earlier doctrine. Despite some fears from liberals, the Burger Court continued the Warren Court's uncompromising stand against de jure segregation and approved affirmative action plans. The Court also handed down a number of decisions that undermined traditional discriminatory patterns against women.

Burger himself seemed to have no set voting pattern and often joined a majority only in order to be able to assign the opinion. Thus, although he originally opposed the decision in the 1973 abortion case, *Roe* v. *Wade,* he signed on with the majority to control who wrote the final opinion. Burger's major opinion was that handed down in the Nixon tapes case, which reasserted the judiciary's primacy in interpreting constitutional issues.

When he retired at the end of the October 1985 term, commentators gave him high marks for overhauling and modernizing the administrative apparatus of the federal court system, but poor grades as a chief justice. He apparently left no doctrinal legacy.

Herman Schwartz, ed., *The Burger Years: Rights and Wrongs in the Supreme Court, 1969–1986* (1987).

MELVIN I. UROFSKY

See also Supreme Court.

BURR, AARON

(1756–1836), vice president of the United States, revolutionary, soldier, and adventurer. Burr's life began in the age of George II and ended in that of Andrew Jackson. But he achieved his notoriety during little more than a decade of his middle years.

The son of one Princeton president and the grandson of another (Jonathan Edwards), Burr studied at Princeton himself. During the Revolution he was a staff officer under George Washington, participated in the invasion of Canada, and commanded a regiment. He was close to the organizers of the Conway Cabal of 1777–1778, in which discontented officers surrounding the Franco-Irish volunteer Thomas Conway sought to replace Washington as commander in chief with Horatio Gates, the victor of Saratoga. Burr also supported Gen. Charles Lee when Washington dismissed Lee after the Battle of Monmouth. Leaving the army in 1779, he completed his law studies, practiced in New York City, and served one term in the state assembly. At this point his opinions were close to those of Alexander Hamilton.

Burr became the New York attorney general in 1789 and was elected to the U.S. Senate two years later. In 1796 he received thirty electoral votes for the presidency. Returning to the assembly, he parlayed his political following in New York City into the Republican vice-presidential nomination in 1800. At the time the Constitution required presidential electors to cast two votes each for the presidency: whoever came second became vice president. The Republican electors cast their votes for both Jefferson and Burr with the result that they tied. The election then went to the House of Representatives, where Jefferson finally won after thirty-six ballots. Burr did not openly subvert Jefferson's candidacy, but he resented Hamilton's decision to support Jefferson instead of himself, a fellow New Yorker.

Burr was never close to Jefferson, and in 1804 he was rejected for a second vice-presidential term. His major task during his incumbency was to preside at the impeachment trial of Justice Samuel Chase of the Supreme Court. As he prepared to leave the vice presidency he sought the governorship of New York, but once again Hamilton blocked him. Burr took Hamilton's continuing political opposition as a personal insult and challenged him to a duel. It took place at Weehawken, New Jersey, on July 11, 1804. Hamilton fell mortally wounded after firing his own pistol into the air. After Hamilton died Burr fled to Virginia and went into hiding.

By this time Burr had begun to entertain visions of winning fame and power in the West. With Gen. James Wilkinson and agents of Britain and Spain he entered on a series of nebulous intrigues to detach Mexico from Spain, and perhaps Trans-Appalachia from the United States. But the plans were exposed in 1806 and Burr was arrested on charges of treason.

Chief Justice John Marshall presided at his trial in 1807. The trial was notable for its intensely partisan quality and for its twofold constitutional significance. The first was Jefferson's refusal to appear in response to a subpoena, which asserted the independence of the presidency from the courts. Marshall's narrow construction of the constitutional law of treason was the second. Burr was acquitted.

Burr then went to Europe, where he continued his schemes. He returned to the United States in 1812 and practiced law in New York until his death. Burr was an intensely ambitious and highly intelligent man. But he was also deeply cynical and had a way of attaching himself to others of the same sort.

Milton Lomask, *Aaron Burr: The Years from Princeton to Vice President, 1756–1805* (1979); Dumas Malone, *Jefferson the President: Second Term, 1805–1809* (1974).

EDWARD COUNTRYMAN

See also Dueling; Elections: 1800; Hamilton, Alexander; Revolution.

BUSH, GEORGE

(1924–   ), forty-first president of the United States. Bush is the latest if not the last Bull Moose, one of those elite easterners who renew their spirit and make a career in the West. He was born in Milton, Massachusetts, the son of

Prescott Bush, an investment banker and U.S. senator. Bush easily imbibed the values of his parents and teachers at Phillips Andover Academy: propriety, service, and an Episcopalian version of muscular Christianity. A navy pilot in the Pacific in World War II, he was shot down and narrowly escaped death. Afterward, he graduated from Yale University, married, and moved to Texas to learn the oil business.

Bush took quickly to such Texas ways as pitching horseshoes and eating chicken-fried steak, but he remained a devout Episcopalian, socialized with other transplanted Ivy Leaguers, and used family connections to finance his petroleum exploration and equipment companies. Ultimately settling in Houston, he ran unsuccessfully for the U.S. Senate in 1964, but won a House seat in 1966. In Congress he opposed most Great Society legislation but voted for some civil rights measures.

After losing another Senate race in 1970, Bush served in succession as ambassador to the United Nations, where he enjoyed verbal duels with the Soviet delegate; chairman of the Republican National Committee, where he defended Richard Nixon during the Watergate scandal; U.S. representative to the People's Republic of China, where he established enduring ties with Communist leaders; and director of the Central Intelligence Agency, where he tried to improve morale and public relations. In 1980, running as a moderate, Bush lost the Republican presidential nomination to Ronald Reagan but was then nominated and elected as vice president.

Bush had slight influence on policy while serving as vice president. He apparently had no advance knowledge of the illegal diversion of funds in the Iran-Contra scandal. His loyalty, propriety, and boyish enthusiasm led critics to label him a "wimp," but they underestimated his ambition, shrewdness, and occasional unscrupulousness. He wooed the Republican Right, established himself as Reagan's heir apparent, and won the presidency in 1988. In the campaign he echoed Richard Nixon's earlier appeals to the "silent majority," questioned Democratic opponent Michael Dukakis's patriotism and commitment to fighting crime, and exploited racial fears.

Bush abandoned these demagogic tactics after the election, perhaps because he privately found them embarrassing, but certainly because he preferred to govern by consensus. Indeed, the first years of his administration called to mind not Nixon or Reagan but Ford (whom Bush had served in two posts) and Eisenhower (who was a friend of his father's). Key appointments went to Washington and Wall Street insiders. Bush enjoyed high approval ratings, though the long-range consequences of Reagan era fiscal policies and precipitous deregulation posed potential threats to the economy. Like his fellow moderate Republicans, Eisenhower and Ford, Bush pursued both détente with the Soviet Union and a policy of old-fashioned intervention in the third world, as the invasion of Panama and declaration of an international "drug war" illustrated. In 1990–1991, while proclaiming the advent of a "new world order," Bush organized an international coalition and sent 540,000 American troops to liberate Kuwait after an Iraqi invasion. Appropriately, he displayed in the cabinet room a portrait of Theodore Roosevelt, the first Bull Moose to wield a big stick.

George Bush, with Victor Gold, *Looking Forward* (1987); Fitzhugh Green, *George Bush: An Intimate Portrait* (1989).

LEO P. RIBUFFO

See also Elections: 1980, 1984, 1988.

C

CAGE, JOHN

(1912–), composer and philosopher of music. As a composer and writer on aesthetics, John Milton Cage, Jr., has been among the most influential voices contributing to the development of new music and, indeed, of new definitions of music itself. A native of Los Angeles, Cage studied in Europe and New York before returning to the West Coast as a composer and accompanist for the Bonnie Bird dance company in Seattle. His longtime collaboration with dancer and choreographer Merce Cunningham began in Seattle in the late 1930s, and writing for dance has been an important aspect of his work for more than fifty years.

Cage's early music incorporated experiments with the twelve notes of the chromatic scale. His interest in rhythmic freedom and the tonal possibilities of nontraditional instruments led him to compose many pieces for percussion in the late 1930s and early 1940s. He also experimented with the "prepared piano," whose keys produced uncharacteristic sounds because of the metal, wood, and other objects placed on the strings; the piano was then played by striking the keys in the usual manner or by striking, plucking, or strumming the strings inside. Prepared piano performances met with mixed audience reactions, but composers were excited by his extension of the traditional parameters of music. By 1949, Cage's prepared piano pieces were being performed at Carnegie Hall, and he had received a Guggenheim Fellowship and recognition from the National Institute of Arts and Letters.

Cage next became interested in Eastern philosophy and Zen Buddhism, and ideas of indeterminacy and chance entered into his thinking about music. Much of his work from the 1950s and 1960s suggested that music should not be controlled by the composer but should come from the environment as well as a score. Works whose sounds could be performed in any order or pieces such as "4′ 33″ " in which the performers sit silently on stage and the music consists of whatever sounds happen in the environment reflect Cage's conviction that "everything we do is music."

In 1967, Cage brought together dancers, mimes, singers, rock musicians, jazz performers, and pianists to perform simultaneously to the accompaniment of slide and light shows. The result was "Musicircus," an event rather than a composition. This experiment was followed by "HPSCHD" (1967–1969), composed with Lejaren Hiller, which consisted of simultaneous performances of computer-modified works by several composers along with fifty-one electronic tapes directed at the audience through fifty-one speakers.

Cage's experimental works may incorporate words from a James Joyce novel or popular nineteenth-century music or the sounds generated by plants. He has also used computer technology to create random selections of notes and rhythms. Not surprisingly, some have considered him a charlatan, but increasingly, his work has been recognized as innovative and challenging, and his ideas have influenced other composers and earned him numerous awards. He was elected to the American Academy of Arts and

Sciences in 1978 and received a Mayor's Award of Honor for Arts and Culture in New York City in 1981.

Stephen Husarik, "John Cage and Lejaren Hiller, HPSCHD, 1969," *American Music* 1, no. 2 (Summer 1983); Virgil Thomson, "Expressive Percussion," in *The Art of Judging Music* (1948).

BARBARA L. TISCHLER

See also Music.

CALDER, ALEXANDER

(1898–1976), artist and inventor of the mobile. Calder, who was born in Lawnton, Pennsylvania, grew up in an art environment. His grandfather had been a sculptor and both his parents were artists. Thus the family moved in art circles, and home was always a studio.

After graduating from high school in 1915, he had decided to become an engineer and entered Stevens Institute of Technology in Hoboken, New Jersey, graduating with a degree in mechanical engineering. In 1923 Calder attended drawing classes at a public night school in New York, and in the fall he entered the Art Students League, where he continued to study for the next three years.

Calder's early training as an engineer was responsible for the impressive precision of his sculptural works, a precision that is evident in everything he made. He was so at ease with various techniques that many people find a casual look to even the most complex and monumental of his works.

Calder was one of the most versatile of the twentieth-century artists. His works include paintings in oil and gouache, drawings, lithographs, jewelry, tapestries, toys, stage sets, and sculpture in bronze, wood, and wire. An elaborate miniature circus, which he began in his twenties, is on permanent display at the Whitney Museum of American Art and now rivals in public interest the great mobiles and stabiles. Its combination of spontaneity and playfulness characterizes much of his work.

Calder, however, is most famous for his mobiles (the name was coined by Marcel Duchamp), which, through the random designs they create while in motion, are performers as well as pieces of art. This invention inaugurated the now popular concept of art in motion. Another of his innovations, the stabile (the name coined by Jean Arp), is, as the word implies, stationary; it is nevertheless similar to his mobiles. In this case, the spectator moves around the sculpture to observe its changing, interacting elements.

A fun-loving, modest man with many friends, Calder was serious in his approach to his art on whatever scale — from a brass necklace or a child's toy to a monumental stabile. But his enjoyment in the process of making these things and the direct manner in which he approached his work is always evident. He once remarked, "I feel an artist should go about his work simply with great respect for his material. . . . simplicity of equipment and an adventurous spirit are essential in attacking the unfamiliar and unknown. . . . Disparity in form, color, size, weight, motion, is what makes a composition." The word *motion* is significant here since it was he who freed sculpture from its base.

Universal has often been used to characterize Calder's broad appeal: in his own words, "The underlying sense of form in my work has been the system of the Universe, or part thereof." Notable for their originality, vitality, grace, and power, his works are in public and private collections throughout the world. All reflect his particular blend of creative imagination and technical assurance.

Alexander Calder, *An Autobiography with Pictures* (1966); Margaret Calder Hayes, *Three Alexander Calders* (1977); Jean Lipman, *Calder's Universe* (1976).

JEAN LIPMAN

See also Painting and Sculpture.

CALHOUN, JOHN C.

(1782–1850), preeminent spokesman for the slave-plantation system of the antebellum South, U.S. representative, secretary of war, senator, vice president, and secretary of state. A nationalist at the outset of his political career, Calhoun was one of the leading War Hawks who maneuvered the unprepared United States into war with Great Britain in 1812. After the Treaty of Ghent that ended that conflict, Calhoun was responsible for establishing the Second Bank of the United States, and he wrote the bonus bill that would have laid the foundation for a nationwide network of roads and canals if President James Madison had not vetoed it.

A candidate for the presidency in 1824, Calhoun was the object of bitter partisan attacks from other contenders. Dropping out of the race, he settled for the vice presidency and was twice elected to that position. But after Andrew Jackson's assumption of the presidency in 1829, Calhoun found himself isolated politically in national affairs.

At first he supported the Tariff of 1828, the so-called Tariff of Abominations, but responding to his constituents' criticism of the measure and believing that the tariff was being unfairly assessed on the agrarian South for the benefit of an industrializing North, Calhoun drafted for the South Carolina legislature his *Exposition and Protest.* In this essay he claimed original sovereignty for the people acting through the states and advocated state veto or nullification of any national law that was held to impinge on minority interests. He later developed the argument in his two essays *Disquisition on Government* and *Discourse on the Constitution,* presenting the classic case for minority rights within the framework of majority rule. A moderate during the nullification crisis of 1832–1833, Calhoun joined with Henry Clay in working out the Compromise Tariff.

By then he had resigned from the vice presidency and had been elected a senator from South Carolina. For the rest of his life he defended the slave-plantation system against a growing antislavery stance in the free states. He continued his strident defense of slavery even after he joined the Tyler administration as secretary of state. In that position he laid the groundwork for the annexation of Texas and the settlement of the Oregon boundary with Great Britain. Reelected to the Senate in 1845, he opposed the Mexican-American War because he felt American victory would result in territorial concessions that would place the Union at jeopardy. Similarly he opposed the admission of Cal-

ifornia as a free state, and the free-soil provision in the Oregon territorial bill. In his last address to the Senate, he foretold the disruption of the Union unless the slave states were given adequate and permanent protection for their institutions.

Calhoun, along with Daniel Webster, Henry Clay, and Andrew Jackson, dominated American political life from 1815 to 1850. A tall, spare individual, Calhoun was a gifted debater, an original thinker in political theory, and a person of broad learning who was especially well read in philosophy, history, and contemporary economic and social issues. His public appearance as the so-called Cast Iron Man was belied by his personal warmth and affectionate nature in private life.

John Niven, *John C. Calhoun and the Price of Union* (1988); Charles M. Wiltse, *John C. Calhoun,* 3 vols. (1944–1951).

JOHN NIVEN

See also Nullification Controversy; Secession; War Hawks.

CALIFORNIA GOLD RUSH

See Gold Rushes.

CAMPAIGNS, PRESIDENTIAL

See Elections.

CAMP DAVID ACCORD

The Camp David Accord between Egypt and Israel negotiated in September 1978 led to normalization of diplomatic relations between Egypt and Israel for the first time since Israel was declared an independent state in 1948. The agreement consisted of a general "Framework for Peace in the Middle East," based on a five-year transitional period of civil self-rule for Palestinians in the West Bank and Gaza. This framework required the agreement of other Middle Eastern nations and was never implemented, but a "Framework for the Conclusion of a Peace Treaty between Egypt and Israel" was fulfilled.

In it, Israel agreed to return territory captured from Egypt in the Six-Day War. In return, Egypt recognized Israel as a nation, the first Arab country to do so.

The Camp David Accord took its name from the American presidential retreat at Camp David, Maryland, outside Washington, D.C. There, for two weeks, President Jimmy Carter mediated between Israel's prime minister Menachem Begin and Egyptian president Anwar Sadat. The agreement is considered probably Carter's greatest achievement as president.

See also Carter, Jimmy; Middle East–U.S. Relations.

CANADA-U.S. RELATIONS

Two phrases exemplify the ambiguous historical relationship between Canada and the United States: "the undefended border," a rhetorical staple of the early twentieth century emphasizing the relatively peaceful political relations and close economic linkages between the two countries, and Canada as "a mouse next to an elephant," coined by Canadian prime minister Pierre Trudeau in the 1970s, focusing on the disparity of political and economic power in the relationship.

Relations between the United States and British North America from the American Revolution to Canadian confederation in 1867 was marked by tension over territorial issues and less abrasive but still uneasy economic relations. At the outset of the Revolution, Americans tried unsuccessfully to invade Quebec, which was subsequently used as a base for British counterattacks. At the Paris peace conference in 1782–1783, boundary settlements were complicated by Britain's decision to resettle refugee Loyalists in present-day Ontario and the Maritime Provinces, creating an enduring bastion of anti-American sentiment in the early years of the Republic. Rivalry between American settlers and British-backed Indian tribes in the Ohio Valley aggravated border tensions, culminating in an American invasion of Ontario in 1812 that was blocked by the Loyalist militia and British regulars.

After the War of 1812, improved Anglo-American relations led to the demilitarization of the Great Lakes and the movement of American settlers into Ontario, paralleled by a migration of French Canadians from Quebec to work in New England textile mills. But tempers flared again after 1837 over American sympathies with rebellious elements in Quebec and Ontario, and rivalry between lumberjacks along the Maine–New Brunswick border. The latter was settled by the Webster-Ashburton Treaty of 1842, and another boundary dispute, between Americans in the Columbia River valley and the Hudson's Bay Company in Oregon Territory, was resolved in 1846.

Trade between the United States and British North America was limited by Britain's preferential system in the early nineteenth century. When Britain dismantled its mercantile system after 1846, however, its North American colonies looked south, and the Elgin-Marcy Treaty, a reciprocal trade agreement affecting agricultural products and raw materials, was negotiated in 1854. The onset of the American Civil War imperiled these growing linkages: U.S. suspicions of Britain's pro-Southern sympathies were intensified by Confederate use of British North America as a base for raids on American shipping and border settlements. After 1865, similar concerns were aroused north of the border as Irish Fenians raided Ontario and New Brunswick from U.S. bases. Meanwhile, protectionist elements in the U.S. Congress successfully agitated against renewal of the reciprocity treaty in 1866. This deterioration and demands in Congress for annexation of British North America strengthened the case of advocates of unification in the debates over Canadian confederation, which was achieved in 1867.

Toward the end of the century political relations improved in tandem with Anglo-American rapprochement: during the Alaska boundary controversy of 1903, for example, Britain prevailed on Canada to accept a compromise solution. Although coordinating its foreign policies with Britain up to the 1930s, Canada negotiated bilaterally with the United States on specific issues, such as use of common waterways and fisheries through a joint commission. The major steps toward direct political cooperation came in World War II: the Ogdensburg Agreement, negotiated by Franklin D. Roosevelt and Canadian prime minister Mackenzie King, established a Permanent Joint Board of Defense, and the Hyde Park Agreement coordinated economic war mobilization of the two countries. These linkages were forged anew in the cold war: Canada joined NATO in 1949 and contributed troops to U.N. forces in Korea. More specific bilateral ties took shape in this period as well: defense production–sharing agreements were renewed, the St. Lawrence Seaway was developed cooperatively, and Canada permitted placement of U.S. radar networks across the northern territories, culminating in the joint North American Air Defense Command (NORAD) in 1957.

Economic relations progressed in the same direction between 1867 and 1960, although not without periods of friction and debate among Canadians over long-term costs and benefits. Canadian efforts to renew reciprocal trade after 1870 were rebuffed, and in 1879 Canada adopted a "National Policy" instituting protective tariffs for industry and constructing an "all-Canadian" railway to the Pacific Coast. A new reciprocity agreement drafted in 1911 was stillborn when the Canadian government that negotiated it was defeated in an election. But despite this setback, Canadian-American trade increased and by the mid-1920s surpassed Anglo-Canadian commerce. Meanwhile, American direct investment in Canada's resource and manufacturing sectors grew, stimulated in part by Canada's National Policy tariffs; here also American investment exceeded that of Britain by 1930.

The trade rivalries incident to the Great Depression temporarily slowed the trend toward closer economic ties, but reciprocal trade agreements in 1935 and 1938 significantly reduced commercial barriers in agriculture and natural products. Canada's postwar participation in the General Agreement on Tariffs and Trade (GATT) led to mutual reductions of tariff restrictions on industrial products. Proposals for a Canadian-U.S. customs union in 1948, however, were not pursued.

During the 1960s these close political and economic linkages came under more critical scrutiny, particularly in Canada. The U.S. government objected to Canadian trade with Communist China and Cuba and many Canadians opposed the arming of missiles located in Canada with nuclear warheads. During the Vietnam War, Canadian leaders criticized U.S. policies and allowed American draft resisters to flee to their country. Friction widened into a more general critique in Canada of the degree of American influence. By the mid-1970s, concerns over alleged American domination of Canadian energy resources and industry and the pervasiveness of the U.S. media in Canada led to measures to limit foreign investment, particularly in the oil industry, develop trade links beyond North America, and establish an arm's-length posture toward the United States. After 1984, however, relations became less contentious. The Canadian government, alarmed by growing protectionist sentiment in the United States, negotiated a Free Trade Agreement that took effect in 1989.

The debate in Canada over this agreement reflected the historical ambivalence of Canadians toward the United States. While supporting collective security and acknowledging mutual cultural and political traditions as well as the economic benefits of access to U.S. markets and capital, Canadians remained wary of the prospects of close integration with their neighbor. To this day, Canadian nationalism defines itself largely in terms of the cultural characteristics that distinguish Canadians from Americans.

John B. Brebner, *North Atlantic Triangle: The Interplay of Canada, the United States and Britain* (1945); Norman Hillmer, ed., *Partners Nevertheless: Canadian-American Relations in the Twentieth Century* (1989); Reginald C. Stuart, *United States Expansionism and British North America, 1775–1870* (1988).

GRAHAM D. TAYLOR

See also Fenian Brotherhood; Paris, Treaty of (1783); War of 1812.

CANALS

See Erie Canal; Panama Canal; Transportation Revolution.

CARDOZO, BENJAMIN

(1870–1938), lawyer and associate justice, U.S. Supreme Court. Born in New York, Cardozo attended Columbia College and Law School but left without taking a law degree. He pursued in essence the calling of a barrister, that is, serving as counsel to other lawyers. He soon gained a reputation as a "lawyer's lawyer," especially in complicated commercial cases.

President William Howard Taft offered Cardozo a federal district judgeship, but Cardozo was supporting his two sisters and declined because of the meager salary. In 1913, however, reformers secured his election as a judge on the Supreme Court of New York, the lowest court in the state system. Within six weeks Governor Martin Glynn named him to the state's highest court, the Court of Appeals, on which he served for the next sixteen years, the last six as chief judge.

The "lawyer's lawyer" soon became the "judge's judge," and he made the Court of Appeals the second most distinguished tribunal in the land. Especially in commercial law, Cardozo's opinions carried great weight in New York and throughout the country. His decision in the landmark case of *McPherson* v. *Buick Motor Co.* (1916) changed the very nature of product liability law. Abolishing the old rule of privity, by which only those with a direct contractual relationship to the manufacturer could sue on a defective product, Cardozo made manufacturers directly liable to the consumer.

If lawyers and judges appreciated his legal skills, scholars esteemed his insights into forces that affected both judging and the law. Legal realists argued that a variety of nonlegal matters determined judicial decision making, an idea heretical to those who believed that judges did no more than proclaim established legal truths. In his classic Yale lectures, *The Nature of the Judicial Process* (1921), Cardozo explicitly declared that many factors influenced how judges decided cases. He also argued that rules of law should be judged not by their antiquity or logic but by the extent to which they contributed to society's welfare.

On the retirement of Oliver Wendell Holmes in 1932, President Herbert Hoover was besieged with demands that he name Cardozo to the Supreme Court. With two New Yorkers — Charles Evans Hughes and Harlan Fiske Stone — already on the bench, Hoover feared that a third would create a geographical imbalance. Senator William Borah of Idaho calmed the president's fears; Cardozo, he said, belonged to Idaho as much as to New York.

On the bench Cardozo joined the liberal bloc of Louis D. Brandeis and Stone. In his six terms he showed promise of becoming one of the Court's great justices, but he died before he could leave a significant corpus of opinions. One decision, however, *Palko* v. *Connecticut* (1937), determined the debate over the application of the Bill of Rights to the states through the Fourteenth Amendment. Cardozo argued that not all the guarantees of the first eight amendments applied to the states, only those that constituted "the very essence of a scheme of ordered liberty." This left it in the hands of judges to decide which rights fit the definition and which do not. In the 1940s, Justice Felix Frankfurter successfully carried on Cardozo's call for selective incorporation over Justice Hugo Black's demand for total incorporation.

Beryl H. Levy, *Cardozo and the Frontiers of Legal Thinking* (1969).

MELVIN I. UROFSKY

See also Supreme Court.

CARIBBEAN-U.S. RELATIONS

Even before American independence, the Caribbean region was an important source of slaves and a major market for the farm surpluses of the thirteen colonies, accounting for about a third of U.S. exports before 1815. From then on the trade level steadily dropped, undermined by the decline of West Indian sugar production. The United States always had other concerns about the region, however. The bloody slave revolt in Haiti that preceded its independence in 1804 made U.S. leaders fearful of black rebellion in their own country, and they refused diplomatic ties with Haiti until 1862. The Monroe Doctrine

(1823) announced American opposition to further European colonization in the New World, reflecting concern that the breakup of Spain's American empire would tempt stronger powers to scavenge in the wreckage. Fears lingered that Puerto Rico and Cuba, still in Spanish hands, might fall to great-power ambitions. Almost all the earlier presidents hoped to acquire Cuba, but Spain rebuffed purchase offers in 1848 and 1853 by southern expansionists who wanted to make Cuba a slave state.

Transit routes across the Central American isthmus also interested Americans, especially after the 1848 acquisition of California and the discovery of gold there. The 1850 Clayton-Bulwer Treaty with Britain stated that any future isthmian canal should be jointly controlled. But interest in the isthmian routes faded after completion of a transcontinental railroad system.

The American Civil War diverted attention from Caribbean initiatives, but in 1869–1870 President Ulysses S. Grant vainly sought Senate approval for the request of the president of Santo Domingo (later the Dominican Republic) for annexation. A private French project to build a Panama canal aroused a sharper reaction: President Rutherford B. Hayes insisted that any such canal must be under American control (even a British partnership was now unpopular in the United States). Washington's alarm lessened when the French company went bankrupt in 1888.

Beginning in 1895 a Cuban revolt against Spain brought guerrilla warfare and widespread suffering to that island. A skillful Cuban propaganda campaign caused the American public and Congress to favor Cuban independence, the one concession Spain rejected. The mysterious 1898 explosion of the battleship *Maine* in Havana mobilized sentiment for war with Spain, which broke out that year.

During the four months' war, U.S. forces occupied Puerto Rico and fought a short campaign in eastern Cuba. The peace treaty gave Puerto Rico to the United States and left Cuba free of Spanish control, but under American military occupation. Congress's war resolutions had included a promise not to annex Cuba. Ultimately

the Platt Amendment of 1901 established a protectorate — the United States retained extensive controls over Cuba's government and had the right to intervene if order broke down — and U.S. occupation ended the next year.

Having acquired bases in Cuba and Puerto Rico, U.S. policy now focused on an isthmian canal. Under pressure from Washington, Great Britain gave up its right to share in a canal project. Panama, a province of Colombia, became the preferred site, and Panamanians were dismayed by Colombia's rejection of a canal treaty with the United States. In 1903 Panama declared its independence, and U.S. naval forces promptly appeared to overawe the Colombians. President Theodore Roosevelt began government construction of the canal in 1904, and it was completed in 1914.

The Panama Canal was soon defined as a place of unique strategic importance, and Washington henceforth viewed the entire Caribbean as a security zone. But local tendencies toward revolution and defaulted government debts often invited European interventions of which Germany's were most suspected of sinister designs. Between 1898 and 1917 the United States built a system of regional control. Troops returned to Cuba (1906–1909) under the Platt Amendment's right of intervention; revolts in Nicaragua drew in U.S. forces in 1910 and 1912; and a cycle of revolutions in Haiti resulted in American military occupation from 1915 to 1934. Protests of European creditor states at the threatened bankruptcy of the government of Santo Domingo brought a U.S. takeover of the Dominican customs service in 1905; political violence there led to another full-scale occupation (1916–1924). American marines became a routine factor in Caribbean politics, as did general U.S. oversight of the region's affairs.

Fears of European threats dimmed after World War I, and a period of U.S. retrenchment in the Caribbean followed, though marines were embroiled in the Sandino War (1927–1932) in Nicaragua. President Franklin D. Roosevelt's Good Neighbor policy marked a pause in the use of force in the Caribbean. Even so, America imposed a settlement after a Cuban revolution in 1933. The abrogation of the Platt Amendment in

1934 ended formal U.S. controls over Cuba, but left the United States still dominant in that country's affairs. In general, Washington favored Caribbean governments that maintained stability, even harsh dictatorships like those of Anastasio Somoza in Nicaragua and Rafael Trujillo in the Dominican Republic. World War II brought closer U.S.-Caribbean cooperation, as every Caribbean state joined the wartime alliance.

Early cold war perceptions that the Caribbean was safe from the "red threat" soon changed, and long-standing alliances with right-wing dictators were supplemented by active anti-Marxist measures. The rise of a leftist government in Guatemala prompted fears of Soviet influence, which ended with the regime's overthrow in 1954 by a Guatemalan exile force organized by the Central Intelligence Agency (CIA). Similarly, after 1959 Fidel Castro's leftist government in Cuba faced a hostile United States. By 1961 Castro was allied with the Soviet Union, and the CIA had prepared a Cuban exile force, hoping to duplicate its Guatemalan success. The Bay of Pigs invasion was a fiasco, however, embarrassing President John F. Kennedy while convincing Castro that a U.S. invasion was imminent. In October 1962 a U.S. spy plane discovered Soviet missile bases under construction in Cuba. The ensuing superpower crisis seemed to threaten nuclear war, but ended with Soviet withdrawal of the missiles and a U.S. pledge not to invade Cuba. Since then U.S.-Cuban diplomatic communication has resumed but relations are chilly.

A revolt in the Dominican Republic in 1965 raised new though unproven charges of a Marxist takeover and this time U.S. troops, not locals raised by the CIA, invaded to seize control. After this, however, the familiar pattern of using local proxies for armed incursions returned. In 1979, revolutions in Nicaragua and El Salvador released new leftist forces in Central America, while U.S. authorities still struggled to block Caribbean Marxist movements. President Ronald Reagan moved in 1981 to assist right-wing rebels or regimes in Central America, and in 1983 U.S. forces invaded Grenada to oust a Marxist government. A new CIA-created army

began a civil war in Nicaragua that failed to dislodge the Marxist Sandinista government. By 1990 the Contra revolt seemed to have collapsed, but an election in that year saw the Sandinistas peacefully ousted by a non-Marxist coalition.

American interests in the Caribbean included commercial, ideological, and strategic elements. At times of international tension, as during the two world wars or the cold war, strategic factors predominated, though ideological elements were also important at such times and during the opening years of this century. In more relaxed eras economic interests, first in a Caribbean export market, later in U.S.-owned enterprises in the region, gained in relative weight. Prominent among the latter were the United Fruit Company and large American sugar concerns in Cuba and the Dominican Republic. The use of military intervention declined between the two world wars, reflecting reduced security fears and a conscious effort to work through other means. The cold war years again saw direct U.S. intervention and added the use of local CIA-raised proxy forces.

By the 1980s, U.S. domination had been challenged in Cuba and Central America. In Puerto Rico, whose status changed from colony to self-governing commonwealth in 1952, a vigorous independence party labored to improve its minority position. Panama moved toward full control of its canal under a 1977 treaty providing for final turnover by the year 2000. But a U.S. invasion of Panama in 1989 ousted the regime of Manuel Noriega, who was accused of complicity in the region's booming drug trade. All the while unrest, discontent, and poverty brought Cuban, Haitian, Dominican, and Central American immigrants to the United States in unprecedented numbers, almost a million Cubans alone arriving in the three decades after 1959. Much had changed, but the unstable Caribbean was still an area of special concern to the United States.

Lester D. Langley, *Struggle for the American Mediterranean* (1976); Lester D. Langley, *The United States and the Caribbean, 1900–1970* (1980).

DAVID HEALY

See also Bay of Pigs Invasion; Good Neighbor Policy; Iran-Contra Affair; Monroe Doctrine; Ostend Manifesto; Panama Canal; Platt Amendment; Puerto Rico; Spanish-American War; Triangular Trade.

CARNEGIE, ANDREW

(1835–1919), industrialist and philanthropist. Andrew Carnegie's awesome prowess in getting wealth and giving it away enriched his adopted nation even more than himself. The circumstances of his boyhood fostered both passions. His mother exemplified the proverbial thrift and enterprise of his native Scotland. The plight of his father, a weaver whose skill was made worthless by new machinery, brought home the pain and humiliation of poverty. But money was not the sole concern of Carnegie's family; his father and uncles were zealous in the cause of political democracy and social justice. When Andrew was twelve, the family set out for America, the land of promise for both material ambition and social idealism.

Kin and countrymen in the new land smoothed the Carnegies' way and led them to Pittsburgh, well fitted by natural resources and river transport to soar with American industry in its rocketing takeoff. Young Andrew rose with it. As a bright, alert, cheerful telegrapher he won the favor of Thomas A. Scott, a high official of the Pennsylvania Railroad. At twenty-four, Scott's protégé became superintendent of the western division of the railroad. With Scott's help in the form of a loan, advice, and influence, Carnegie was already making money in stocks, and by his thirties he was a wealthy investor, promoter, and entrepreneur in a variety of enterprises. During the depression of the seventies, with properties cheap and the Bessemer process coming into its own, Carnegie concentrated all his resources and energies in the making of steel. He hired the best people in steel technology and plant management, shrewdly held on to absolute control of his enterprise the better to plow back profits into capital improvements, and outgeneraled all his rivals in the field. By applying the coordinating and cost accounting techniques he had learned from the Pennsylvania Railroad,

holding down wages and salaries, keeping up with the latest technology, and "hard-driving" both his men and his furnaces, he held costs to a minimum and prices below his competitors', thereby capturing an ever-growing share of the market and maximizing return on plant investment. By his sixties, having vertically integrated his holdings from ore to finished products, he dominated the American steel industry, which he had done much to make first in the world. When he sold out to the Morgan-created United States Steel Corporation in 1901 for $250 million in U.S. Steel bonds, he found himself one of the world's richest men.

But despite his wealth-getting, his wage-cutting, and his responsibility for a bloody labor dispute at his Homestead plant in 1892, Carnegie had not forgotten his heritage of concern for social justice. In his 1889 article "Wealth," he gloried in the cheap steel his leadership had given the American consumer but also proclaimed the moral duty of all possessors of great wealth to plow back their money into philanthropy with the same judgment, zeal, and leadership they had devoted to getting rich. And he lived up to that precept, paying for thousands of library buildings, setting up trusts and foundations, endowing universities, building Carnegie Hall in New York and the Peace Palace at The Hague, and much more. He once wrote that the man who dies rich dies disgraced. He had some sins to answer for, and it took him a while, but in 1919 at eighty-three Andrew Carnegie died in a state of grace by his own agnostic definition.

Harold C. Livesay, Andrew Carnegie and the Rise of Big Business (1975); Joseph F. Wall, Andrew Carnegie (1970).

ROBERT V. BRUCE

See also Frick, Henry Clay; Homestead Strike; Iron and Steel Industry; Libraries and Museums; Philanthropy; Robber Barons.

CAROLINA, FUNDAMENTAL CONSTITUTIONS OF

See Fundamental Constitutions of Carolina.

CARPETBAGGERS

Northerners who moved south after the Civil War were called "carpetbaggers" by critics who claimed they carried all of their possessions in one bag (luggage made of carpeting). Actually, most were educated people, ranging from business and political leaders to former soldiers. Some northern blacks, whose greater experience with freedom sometimes put them at odds with the goals of the newly freed people, also went south after the war.

Many carpetbaggers sought to invest in abandoned or repossessed lands and in partnerships with planters. Although at times they met with violence, ostracism, or derision because of their racial views, most capital-starved southerners seeking to rebuild their economy accepted them eagerly. At the height of Radical Reconstruction in 1867, some were also active in political and social reform. Because few southerners joined the Republican party, carpetbaggers won the lion's share of southern political offices.

The carpetbaggers sought to modernize the southern economy through railroad building and other internal improvements. After the Compromise of 1877, many of them, who had relied upon federal patronage, returned to the North or moved quietly into southern society.

See also Reconstruction.

CARS

See Automobiles.

CARSON, RACHEL

(1907–1964), writer, biologist, and environmentalist. A trained scientist and an eloquent writer, Rachel Carson did much to shape attitudes toward the natural world. Born in Springdale, Pennsylvania, in a family of modest means, she shared from childhood her mother's love of books and feeling for the beauty and mystery of nature. At Pennsylvania College for Women (later Chatham College) she first majored in English, but switched to biology, thanks to a brilliant teacher in that field. It was the merging of these two powerful currents — the imagination and insight of a creative writer with a scientific passion for fact — that goes far to explain the blend of beauty and authority that made her books so successful. After graduating with honors, she won a scholarship to Johns Hopkins University, where she earned an A.M. in zoology. Most important to her career were the summers she spent at the Marine Biological Laboratory at Woods Hole, Massachusetts. She felt a strong emotional response to the sea, which she had hitherto known only in books. Henceforth it would shape her career.

When her father died suddenly in 1935, she took a job as an aquatic biologist with the U.S. Bureau of Fisheries (later the Fish and Wildlife Service). An article for the *Atlantic Monthly* led to her first book, *Under the Sea Wind* (1941). During World War II she wrote conservation bulletins for the government and later a series of booklets on wildlife refuges. Meanwhile she had been working on a book that would make her known throughout the world. Published in 1951, *The Sea Around Us* became an immediate bestseller, won numerous honors and literary awards, and was translated into thirty-two languages. At last financially independent, she could devote full time to writing. Her next book, *The Edge of the Sea* (1955), was a biological counterpart of its predecessor.

Rachel Carson's last book, *Silent Spring* (1962), became one of the most influential books of the last half of the twentieth century. Ever since the end of World War II, when the insecticide DDT came on the market, she had been concerned about the dangers inherent in the uncontrolled use of nonselective and persistent poisons: their effect on wildlife, on human life, and on the environment as a whole. Reluctantly, she decided to speak out.

The result was a book showing how modern society has been poisoning the earth on a worldwide scale. Violently attacked by the agricultural chemical industry, *Silent Spring* was officially endorsed by President John F. Kennedy's Science Advisory Committee and in retrospect was given a major share of credit for initiating the modern environmental movement. "A few thousand words from her," wrote a newspaper editor, "and the world took a new direction."

Paul Brooks, *The House of Life: Rachel Carson at Work* (1972); Frank Graham, Jr., *Since Silent Spring* (1970).

PAUL BROOKS

See also Conservation and Environmental Movements.

CARTER, JIMMY

(1924–   ), thirty-ninth president of the United States. When Carter took the oath of office in 1977, he inherited a nation divided by the social turmoil of the 1960s and disillusioned by the cynical political practices of the Nixon White House. Within minutes after his inauguration, Carter left his heavily armored limousine and, holding hands with his wife, Rosalyn, walked the parade route to the cheers of spectators. Carter's stroll down Pennsylvania Avenue seemed to symbolize the end of one era and the beginning of another. In retrospect, however, the Democratic victory in 1976 was a historical anomaly in an era of Republican domination of the presidency.

Carter, the son of a Georgia landowner and businessman, was part of the first generation of moderate southern politicians who emerged in the aftermath of the civil rights movement. His term as Georgia governor (1971–1975) was a modest success, marked by an emphasis upon governmental reorganization and aggressive actions to end racial discrimination. Still, it hardly seemed a springboard to the White House, and his announcement in December 1975 that he would seek the presidency evoked incredulity or amusement from most knowledgeable political observers.

But they underestimated Carter. American voters were disgusted by the Watergate revelations of corruption, and they responded warmly to the soft-spoken southerner with his perpetual smile and his often repeated promise: "I'll never lie to you." His moderate economic views, his commitment to civil rights, and his background as a southerner helped him assemble a coalition of traditional Democrats, blacks, and southern whites who had become increasingly alienated from the Democratic party. Carter narrowly defeated incumbent Gerald Ford with 50.1 percent of the vote.

Carter's administration was not without achievements. The drive and focused intelligence that carried him to the White House made it possible for him to push through (by one vote) the Panama Canal Treaty in 1978 and to broker a peace agreement between Israel's Menachem Begin and Egypt's Anwar Sadat in the fall of 1978.

But failures in domestic and foreign policy overshadowed these accomplishments. He had been elected as an outsider, and he often proved inept in dealing with his own party. He also seemed unable to mobilize public support for his policies of restraint and sacrifice.

He was dogged, too, by events beyond his control: the energy crisis that triggered double-digit inflation, the fall of the shah and the seizure of hostages in Iran, and the chill in Soviet-American relations following the Soviet invasion of Afghanistan. In retrospect, many of the crises Carter confronted were insoluble, but his style of hands-on management led a restive American public to hold him personally responsible for failure. The seizure of American hostages proved his final undoing. Americans' increasing frustration over the nation's inability to effect their release focused upon Carter. When an attempted rescue ended in ignominious failure in 1980, his fate as president was sealed. He went down to a smashing defeat at the hands of Ronald Reagan.

In 1986 Carter founded the Carter Center of Emory University, an institution devoted to mediating international conflict and ameliorating health problems in the world's developing nations. In a departure from the usual quiet retirement of presidents, Carter played an active role in numerous diplomatic and domestic efforts after leaving office.

Jimmy Carter, *Keeping Faith: Memoirs of a President* (1982); Erwin C. Hargrove, *Jimmy Carter as President: Leadership and the Politics of the Public Good* (1988).

DAN T. CARTER

See also Elections: 1976, 1980. *For events during Carter's administration, see* Camp David Accord; Iran Hostage Crisis; Middle East–U.S. Relations; Panama Canal; Strategic Arms Limitation Talks.

CARVER, GEORGE WASHINGTON

(c. 1864–1943), black educator and agricultural researcher. Carver was one of the best-known African-Americans of his era. Growing mainly from his research on peanuts, his rise to fame created myths and obscured much of the true nature of his work. His humble origins were part of his appeal to publicists who made him a national folk hero. He was born in the Missouri town of Diamond. His mother and older brother were the only slaves of Moses and Susan Carver, successful, small-scale farmers. His mother disappeared, presumed kidnapped by slave raiders, while George was an infant. He became both free and orphaned at about the same time.

The childless Carvers raised him and his brother as their own children. Being a sickly child, George was not required to do hard labor but helped around the house. Very early his intellect and knowledge of nature awed those around him, but he was not allowed to attend the neighborhood school because of his color. Thus at a young age he began a series of moves through the Midwest, seeking more education. He supported himself cooking, doing laundry, and homesteading before finally enrolling at Simpson College in Indianola, Iowa, in 1890.

At Simpson Carver majored in art, but a teacher convinced him to transfer to Iowa State College to study agriculture. By the time he completed a master's degree in agriculture in 1896, Carver had impressed the faculty as an extremely talented student in horticulture and mycology as well as a gifted teacher of freshman biology. Had he been white, he probably would have stayed at Iowa and concentrated on research in one of those fields. Instead he accepted an offer from Booker T. Washington to head the agricultural department at the all-black-staffed Tuskegee Institute in Alabama.

For nearly twenty years (1896–1915) Carver labored in the shadow of Washington. He taught classes and operated the only all-black agricultural experiment station, but he proved inept at administration, provoking frequent clashes with the principal. He was engaged, however, in some of his most significant work — seeking solutions to the burden of debt and poverty that enmeshed landless black farmers.

Carver's research and innovative educational extension programs were aimed at inducing farmers to utilize available resources to replace expensive commodities. He published bulletins and gave demonstrations on such topics as using native clays for paints, increasing soil fertility without commercial fertilizers, and growing alternative crops along with the ubiquitous cotton. To enhance the attractiveness of such crops as cow peas, sweet potatoes, and peanuts, Carver developed a variety of uses for each. Peanuts especially appealed to him as an inexpensive source of protein that did not deplete the soil as much as cotton did.

Carver's work with peanuts drew the attention of a national growers' association, which invited him to testify at congressional tariff hearings in 1921. That testimony as well as several honors brought national publicity to the "Peanut Man." A wide variety of groups adopted the professor as a symbol of their causes, including religious groups, New South boosters, segregationists, and those working to improve race relations. Some white publicists exploited Carver's humble demeanor and apolitical posture to provide a "safe" symbol of black advancement; many, however, seem to have been genuinely captivated by his compelling personality. Carver's fame increased and led to numerous speaking engagements, taking him away from campus frequently.

By the late 1920s Carver had abandoned both teaching and agricultural plot work. He continued to advise peanut producers and others, always refusing to accept compensation. Much of his time was devoted to lecture tours of white college campuses, sponsored by the Commission on Interracial Cooperation and the YMCA. With his warm personality he cultivated close personal relationships with dozens of young whites, opening their eyes to racial injustice, and continued to serve as a mentor and father figure to black students.

Carver never made a significant contribution to scientific theory, and he developed no commercially feasible new products. His ideas of sustainable agriculture based on renewable resources were out of step with his times, but perhaps not with the future. His early work enriched the lives of countless sharecroppers, and later in life he was a potent source of inspiration as a symbol of African-American achievement.

Gary R. Kremer, *George Washington Carver in His Own Words* (1987); Linda O. McMurry, *George Washington Carver: Scientist and Symbol* (1981).

LINDA O. MCMURRY

See also Agriculture; Washington, Booker T.

CASSATT, MARY

(1844–1926), painter and printmaker. Cassatt, born in Pittsburgh and raised in Philadelphia, was the first American woman artist to achieve eminence comparable with that of her male contemporaries, in her case, Winslow Homer, John Sargent, and Thomas Eakins.

During her lifetime, educational and professional options hitherto closed to women gradually opened. Female students attended art schools and a few, like Cecelia Beaux, enjoyed careers. But Cassatt pushed her opportunities further by moving to Paris, then the center of avant-garde experiment, and enthusiastically accepting the influence of Edgar Degas and other impressionists.

A five-year family sojourn in Europe during her childhood prepared her for expatriate life. After studies at the Pennsylvania Academy of the Fine Arts in Philadelphia, she returned to Paris in 1866, determined, she wrote, to make herself "a professional." Excluded by gender from the traditionalist École des Beaux Arts, she took lessons where her eye led: at the Louvre, in private studios, and in the *plein air*. The Franco-Prussian War sent her home briefly (where she tried to market her copies of religious works), but by 1872 she was back in Europe, submitting paintings to the yearly Salons and continuing her informal studies, this time of the Italian mannerist Antonio Correggio and, in Spain, Diego Velázquez.

The turning point came in 1875 when she saw Degas's pastels in a Parisian gallery. The sight, she wrote, "changed my life." Degas had already noticed her work in a Salon exhibition and soon invited her to join the Independents, parent group of the impressionists. Cassatt's abandonment of Salon-style painting was permanent, although this aesthetic breakthrough was not accompanied by social liberation. Her parents and sister moved to Paris to provide her with a homelike ambience and, in time, subject matter for many of her figure studies.

Cassatt's work falls into three categories. From the 1870s to the mid-1880s, she focused on female family members at the tea table, at the opera, and the like, under the clear but assimilated influence of Degas and impressionism. In 1889 and the early 1890s, she found her own theme in monumentally conceived, dazzlingly gestural oils and pastels of mothers with children. Also between 1889 and 1891, she produced drypoint color prints of exceptional virtuosity and grace, in the spirit of Japanese woodblocks. Less well known is her ambitious mural, *Modern Woman,* painted for the Woman's Building of the 1893 Columbian Exposition in Chicago and thereafter destroyed.

As far as is known, Mary Cassatt had few intellectual or emotional ties in France outside her expatriate circle. Such social confinement may have been a factor during her late years when, insulated from and disdainful of the new currents of modernism, she gradually abandoned her art and instead chose to help her old friends, the H. O. Havemeyers of New York, assemble their important impressionist and old master collection.

Still, a supporter of women's suffrage and deeply affected by the horrors of World War I, Cassatt became an iconic figure in her old age, when European and American notables made pilgrimages to her country home, the Château de Beaufresne outside Paris. She was named a chevalier of the Legion of Honor in 1904.

Nancy Hale, *Mary Cassatt* (1975); Nancy Mowll Mathews, *Mary Cassatt* (1987).

ELEANOR MUNRO

See also Expatriates and Exiles; Painting and Sculpture.

CATHER, WILLA

(1873–1947), writer. Although known best as a novelist of the American prairie, Cather also published at least sixty short stories, numerous essays and articles, and two different editions of a volume of poems. Having achieved notable popularity at the peak of her career in the 1920s, she was viewed by many in the 1930s as an old-fashioned writer who ignored the pressing social issues of her time and relapsed into a more congenial past.

A revival of interest in Cather and her work began with the publication of several biographies in the early 1950s and accelerated as the women's movement gained momentum in the late 1960s and 1970s. New readers, attuned to issues of women's abilities and contributions, became aware that Cather's life was an exceptional one for a woman of her time. Moreover, they realized that her art, though espousing traditional values, was boldly innovative in conception and design. And it was central to the American experience.

As a participant in the great westward movement, Cather was uniquely qualified to write of pioneer life in the Midwest. Born in the hilly farm country near Winchester, Virginia, she moved with her parents to begin a new life in the sparsely settled frontier of Webster County, Nebraska. Accustomed to the more genteel lifestyle of Virginia, the Cather family soon moved into nearby Red Cloud, but not before young Willa had become acquainted with many pioneer families, most of them European immigrants.

Cather always believed that it was with her second novel, *O Pioneers!* that she hit, as she said, the "home pasture" and launched her career as a novelist. It was then she was certain that she had made the right decision in leaving an important editorial position with the muckraking *McClure's* magazine to strike out on her own. Encouraged by Sarah Orne Jewett, she devoted full time to her art and turned to a subject she knew firsthand — pioneer life in late-nineteenth-century Nebraska. Her fourth novel, *My Ántonia,* is a memorable eulogy of a pioneer woman whom Cather had known as a child and whom she revered all her life. One of the first to dare to use such unlikely material in fiction, Cather captured the imagination of a wide range of readers who were struck by the truth of her portraiture and the lyricism of her prose. Her appeal was not to the thrill seekers or the professional litterateurs.

Endowed with a special sense of the past and its value in the present, Cather wrote several novels that may be regarded as "historical." Most notable are *Death Comes for the Archbishop* and *Shadows on the Rock,* the former an account of the firm establishment of the Catholic ministry in New Mexico Territory and the latter an account of early colonial life in Catholic Quebec. In both Cather depicts admiringly the civilizing influence of Old World culture, particularly French culture, on the rugged frontier of the New World.

Although some recent historians have faulted Cather for what they regard as inaccurate portrayals of certain historical figures, her defenders have pointed out that a writer of fiction may interpret and alter historical fact to suit the needs of her art. When such debates have long been forgotten, Cather's fiction will remain as a landmark in artistic accomplishment and a revelatory tribute to the people whose lives shaped some vital aspects of America's past.

Mildred R. Bennett, *The World of Willa Cather* (1961); James Woodress, *Willa Cather: A Literary Life* (1987).

MARILYN ARNOLD

See also Literature.

CATHOLIC CHURCH

See Roman Catholic Church.

CATT, CARRIE CHAPMAN

(1859–1947), woman's suffrage leader. The triumph of woman's suffrage in the United States in 1920 was very much the work of Carrie Catt. A brilliant strategist, she was twice president of the National American Woman Suffrage Association (NAWSA), first from 1900 to 1904 and then in the dramatic final years of the struggle, from 1915 to 1920.

Catt, born Carrie Lane in Ripon, Wisconsin, spent most of her youth in Iowa, where she went to college. She became a teacher and then superintendent of schools in Mason City in 1883. This was an unusual achievement for a woman of that day, but no great surprise to those who knew her. Bright, resilient, and self-confident, she never acceded to conventions that made no sense to her.

In 1885 Catt married newspaper editor Leo Chapman, but he died in California soon after, leaving her far from home with no resources. Eventually she landed on her feet but only after some harrowing experiences in the male working world. In 1890 she married George Catt, a wealthy engineer. Their marriage allowed her to spend a good part of each year on the road campaigning for woman's suffrage, a cause she had become involved in in Iowa in the late 1880s.

Catt rose rapidly in suffrage ranks. Over time she became a close colleague of Susan B. Anthony, who selected Catt to succeed her as head of the NAWSA. Catt led the movement over the next twenty years, struggling against great odds and many frustrating setbacks. In Catt's approach to politics, organization was the watchword and she was superb at it. From her first endeavors in Iowa in the 1880s to her last in Tennessee in 1920, Catt supervised dozens of campaigns, mobilized numerous volunteers (1 million by the end), and made hundreds of speeches. She made skilled use of communication and publicity, fashioning disciplined campaigns and building a highly effective machine.

Catt believed it was woman's natural right to participate in politics on an equal basis with men. If women could vote, she argued, they would become a force for world peace and would help improve the conditions of life for themselves and their children. Above all, she was concerned with women's dignity. Angry that women had no control over their lives, she felt that political participation would give them a voice in decisions affecting them, enhancing their dignity as human beings.

One of Catt's overriding goals was that of world peace, a cause she pursued throughout her life. Another was that the political process should be rational and issue-oriented, dominated by citizens, not politicians. To that end, she founded the League of Women Voters in 1920. It remains something of a monument to her ideals, devoting itself to issues and placing what it considers the public interest over partisan politics. Catt was proud of her role in this organization until the end of her life.

Robert Booth Fowler, *Carrie Catt: Feminist Politician* (1986).

ROBERT BOOTH FOWLER

See also Feminist Movement; League of Women Voters; National American Woman Suffrage Association; Suffrage.

CCC

See Civilian Conservation Corps.

CENSUS

Every ten years, the U.S. government takes a census of the American population. The first census, in 1790, found that the population encompassed 3.9 million people. The census has been conducted regularly ever since, and the American population now approaches a quarter billion.

In 1787 the Constitution mandated a decennial census as a mechanism to determine the number of representatives each state would have in the House of Representatives. The apportionment, based on a head count of the population, separated the free and the slave and excluded "Indians not taxed." The "representative population" was to be determined by summing the number of free persons and three-fifths of the slaves. Originally, direct taxes were also to be allocated among the states according to population.

The United States has been one of the most diverse and demographically dynamic nations in the history of the world. It has seen high rates of growth, rapid settlement patterns, sharp demographic transitions, and major migrations, all in the context of a racially and ethnically diverse population. These patterns have made the decennial census and reapportionment very important in American political and, more recently, economic and social life. Each decade the census triggers increased or decreased power or resources for a given geographic region. Over time, the census has also come to be used to interpret the success or failure, or "virtues or vices," of various regions, peoples, and ways of life.

The major events in the history of the census are therefore intimately connected to the nation's development. The census has grown in scope and in technological and administrative sophistication through the years. The particular character and timing of the changes and innovations have been rooted in the specific social and political controversies that concerned Americans at the time. From 1790 to 1860, for example, the American population grew at the rate of 30–35 percent a decade, and the decennial census recorded the rapid territorial expansion that shifted political power westward and fueled the sectional conflict between North and South.

Between 1790 and 1840, assistants to U.S. marshals canvassed their districts and asked each household head how many people in the home fell into particular demographic categories. The figures were aggregated in the field; the secretary of state merely totaled the results he received and reported them to Congress. During these years the number of questions grew from six to over seventy.

But after the 1840 census a controversy over the accuracy of the data emerged. The census seemed to indicate extraordinarily high rates of insanity for northern free blacks. Southerners suggested the data showed that blacks were unsuited to freedom. Northerners charged the data were flawed. The data were not changed, but Congress reformed the census-taking machinery in 1850. It mandated an individual-level census, new questions — for example, on occupation and nativity — and the creation of a large, temporary Census Office in Washington to tabulate and publish the data. After 1850, separate schedules were used to obtain statistics on population, agriculture, manufactures, mortality, and addi-

tional social characteristics. The volume of published data increased dramatically.

After the Civil War, the Thirteenth Amendment abolished the three-fifths compromise and led to congressional concern about the role of the census in Reconstruction. In an attempt to force the South to enfranchise the freedmen, Section 2 of the Fourteenth Amendment mandated that Congress deny representation to states in proportion to the adult male citizenry that was disfranchised. The 1870 census collected data on the number of male citizens over twenty-one and the number denied the right to vote. Congress revamped the machinery for the 1880 census and gave the census superintendent control of the appointment of local supervisors and enumerators.

Rapid urban growth and dramatic European immigration were the dominant demographic characteristics of the period from the Civil War to World War I. In 1890 the census superintendent reported the closing of the frontier. The census that year introduced machine tabulation to speed up data processing and permit more detailed cross-tabulations. In 1902, the Census Bureau became a permanent agency in the Department of Commerce and Labor; it remains today in the Commerce Department.

The 1920 census revealed that a majority of the population now lived in urban areas. Congress restricted immigration in 1924 and used census-based apportionments of the national origins of the population to determine the quotas of immigrants who would be admitted. Because members of Congress from rural areas resisted the loss of political power during these years, Congress, for the only time in the history of the Republic, failed to pass a reapportionment bill. But in 1929, recognizing that a constitutional crisis could result if seats were not reapportioned, Congress passed a prospective reapportionment bill for the 1930 census. It also removed the requirement for equally sized congressional districts, however, thus allowing most states to distribute the seats to maintain rural political dominance. Legislative malapportionment remained the norm in the United States until the one-person, one-vote Supreme Court decisions of the 1960s restored the connection between accurate census counts of local areas and political representation.

In the meantime the census was redirected to measure the economic and social situation of Americans. During the depression of the 1930s, the bureau began to measure unemployment and income. It introduced the sample census and a housing census in 1940 and developed the first nondefense computer (UNIVAC) to process the 1950 census. Since the New Deal, Congress has made increasing use of the grant-in-aid system to assign federal funds to state and local areas on the basis of demographic formulae, many of which are determined by census data. By 1970, the bureau had dispensed with most of the enumerators in favor of a mail census. In 1990, the bureau introduced the TIGER (Topographically Integrated Geographic Encoding and Referencing) system to map the addresses of the entire nation by computer.

Census data are now employed in a wide variety of settings in addition to the original use for legislative apportionment. The data are used by members of Congress, legislators, and policymakers to plan and evaluate programs and to allocate funds to other units of government; by researchers and marketers to construct sampling frames and to obtain authoritative information on Americans; by lobbyists and advocates for interest groups to advance the goals of their constituents; and by the courts and agencies enforcing civil rights laws to measure compliance.

Census categories and classifications saturate the nation's political and social discourse. Americans conceptualize, measure, and evaluate the health and well-being of their society in terms of census data. The data and classifications from the occupational inquiries, for example, formed the basis for defining and evaluating the shape of the American class structure and potential for social mobility. Over the past two hundred years, the bureau's racial and ethnic classifications have highlighted or submerged the existence of racial or ethnic communities within the United States.

Not surprisingly, therefore, Americans have created a "census politics." Constituencies ranging from politicians to academic researchers to community leaders regularly urge the Census Bureau to provide more and better data to suit their needs. Recently, the most contentious of these debates involved the differential undercount of racial and ethnic minorities, primarily in poor urban areas.

Census officials have always found it harder to count some groups than others in the population. These include individuals without a settled residence or with more than one residence, people suspicious of government (for example, undocumented immigrants), and people living in nonstandard housing situations (overcrowded units or squatter housing). Since missing some people results in less political representation and government funding for their local areas, the courts have ruled that the Census Bureau violates the Fourteenth Amendment rights of uncounted individuals. Under court pressure, the bureau instituted a large-scale postenumeration survey (PES) in July 1990 to evaluate the complete count. The bureau may decide to adjust the April 1990 complete count if the PES results in conjunction with the census provide a better estimate of the American population.

Margo Anderson, *The American Census: A Social History* (1988); Patricia Cline Cohen, *A Calculating People: The Spread of Numeracy in Early America* (1982).

MARGO ANDERSON

See also Population.

CENTENNIAL EXPOSITION

To celebrate the one-hundredth anniversary of the Declaration of Independence, the United States held its first international exposition. After ten years of planning, the exposition opened on May 10, 1876, in Fairmount Park, Philadelphia, and ran for over five months. Nearly 10 million people attended.

The exposition covered over 450 acres, and more than thirty thousand exhibitors from the thirty-eight states and fifty nations participated. The exhibits were placed in seven categories, most of which reflected the predominantly industrial orientation of the exhibition: mining and metallurgy, manufactured products, science and education, machinery, agriculture, fine arts, and horticulture. The exposition demonstrated that industrial America had come of age and provided relief to citizens weary of the scandals of the Grant administration.

See also World's Fairs.

CENTRAL AMERICA–U.S. RELATIONS

See Latin America–U.S. Relations.

CENTRAL INTELLIGENCE AGENCY

In 1947 congressional legislation reorganized the Department of Defense and created the Central Intelligence Agency (CIA) and the National Security Council. The CIA grew out of the wartime Office of Strategic Services. Its major functions are to gather foreign strategic intelligence and counterintelligence and to engage in covert political activity. Statutes have provided a great deal of leeway and secrecy to the organization's operations. A director who is also the president's chief intelligence officer heads the CIA.

Since its inception the CIA has engaged in several unsuccessful covert operations that were actually counterproductive. One involved a U-2 espionage plane that was shot down over the Soviet Union in May 1960, aborting a scheduled summit meeting; another was the invasion of Cuba at the Bay of Pigs in April 1961, which ended in disaster. Such failures and the excesses of the Watergate era led, in the 1970s, to congressional investigations. Hearings held by Senator Frank Church of Indiana and others revealed that the CIA had plotted assassinations of foreign leaders, interfered in the domestic politics of Chile and other sovereign states, and spied on Americans at home in violation of its legislative charter.

During Ronald Reagan's presidency the CIA and Director William Casey attempted to finance illegal covert operations in Nicaragua through the sale of arms to Iran in exchange for American hostages being held throughout the Middle East. The ensuing scandal, known as the Iran-Contra affair, resulted in a major congressional investigation and court trials of a number of the principals.

See also Bay of Pigs Invasion; Espionage; Iran-Contra Affair; U-2 Affair; Watergate Scandal.

CHAPLIN, CHARLIE

(1889–1977), actor, director, screenwriter, producer, and composer. Born in London to music-hall performers, Chaplin had a wretched childhood. His father abandoned the family, and his mother was increasingly unable to work. Chaplin first went on stage at age five. After a period of destitution he made his mark as a juvenile, touring with a Fred Karno comedy company in England and the United States. During an American tour in 1912–1913, Chaplin, one of the troupe's leading comedians, signed with filmmaker Mack Sennett's Keystone Company.

At first Chaplin played supporting roles in Sennett's comedy shorts. In 1914 he made over thirty short films and after the first dozen began to write and direct his own material. He created the character of "the tramp," which became one of the most popular figures in movie history. The "little fellow," as Chaplin called him, is a remarkably winning combination of cockiness, sentimentality, and slapstick.

Over the next years Chaplin refined the character, achieving fame and fortune. Keystone had paid him $175 a week; when he signed with Mutual in 1916, it was for $10,000 per week plus a bonus. The twelve Mutual two-reelers he made during the next two years are among his best work: films like *The Adventurer* and *The Immigrant* are dazzlingly creative and hilarious. In 1918 he signed a million-dollar contract with First National. Among the resulting films was his first feature, *The Kid* (1921), an extraordinary critical and box-office success.

In 1919 Chaplin joined with Mary Pickford, Douglas Fairbanks, and D. W. Griffith to found United Artists. Chaplin's first film for United Artists, *A Woman of Paris* (1923), which he wrote and directed, was an unsuccessful attempt at sophisticated drama. Many consider the second film he made for the company, *The Gold Rush* (1925), his masterpiece. The tramp's adventures in the film strikingly portray the universal fallibility of men and women through tragicomic situations that touch on bathos and are never far from hilarity, as in the eating of a boot by a starving Chaplin as if it were gourmet food. A 1952 poll of world film critics judged it the second best film ever made.

At first, Chaplin resisted talking pictures. In *City Lights* (1931) and *Modern Times* (1936) his only concessions to sound were musical scores he composed and conducted, and in the latter film, a gibberish song sung by him. *Modern Times* marks the last appearance of "the tramp."

Chaplin's popularity in America declined during the 1940s and early 1950s. His films were less winning. He first spoke dialogue in *The Great Dictator* (1940), an uneven attack on fascism; *Monsieur Verdoux* (1947) satirized mass murder; and *Limelight* (1952), his last American film, was an old-fashioned tear-jerker. Sensationalistic divorces from teenage brides had eroded the public's affection for him in the 1920s. But his popularity plummeted during and after World War II as a result of trumped-up paternity suits and the left-leaning political positions he championed.

In 1952 U.S. authorities voided Chaplin's reentry permit while he was en route to Europe. He settled in Switzerland and did not return until 1972, when he received a special Academy Award. Other honors of his last years included a knighthood in 1975. In a bizarre episode after his death, his body was stolen from its grave in 1977 in Vevey, Switzerland, but recovered the next year.

Chaplin's work was uneven. Many of his later films were flawed, but his "little fellow" became a lasting part of American, indeed, world culture.

Charles Chaplin, *My Autobiography* (1964); Charles J. Maland, *Chaplin and American Culture* (1989); David Robinson, *Chaplin: His Life and Art* (1985).

DANIEL J. LEAB

See also Movies.

CHARLES RIVER BRIDGE V. WARREN BRIDGE

Decided by the Supreme Court in 1837, this case encouraged economic development in transportation and other public facilities. In 1785 Massa-

chusetts granted a charter to the Charles River Bridge Company to build a bridge over the Charles River between Boston and Charlestown and to collect tolls for its use. Then in 1828 the legislature granted a charter to the Warren Bridge Company to build another bridge less than three hundred yards from the first. The Warren Bridge would be turned over to the state and become a free bridge after tolls had paid its cost. The first company sued, arguing that its charter "by implication" gave it the exclusive right to operate a bridge at that point over the river and that the charter granted to the Warren Bridge Company was prohibited because the Constitution stated that "no state shall enter into any . . . Law impairing the Obligation of Contracts" (Art. I, Sec. 10).

Chief Justice Roger B. Taney, speaking for the majority, stated there was no "implied" obligation that prevented the state from building another bridge even if it "diminished the amount" of the tolls. "No exclusive privilege" had been granted to the proprietors of the first bridge. Such a grant would jeopardize progress. "The whole community . . . have a right to require that the power of promoting their comfort and convenience, and of advancing the public prosperity, by providing safe, convenient, and cheap ways for the transportation of produce and the purposes of travel, shall not be construed to have been surrendered . . . by the State, unless it shall appear by plain words that it was intended to be done." Taney declared that "the object and end of all government is to promote the happiness and prosperity of the community by which it is established." The Constitution reserved to the states "power over their own internal police and improvement, which is so necessary to their well-being and prosperity."

CHAUTAUQUA MOVEMENT

The chautauqua movement grew out of summer Sunday school institutes held by the Methodist Episcopal church during the 1870s. At a camp meeting in 1873, Bishop John H. Vincent proposed that secular as well as religious education be offered at these institutes. The next summer, the Chautauqua Assembly was established at Lake Chautauqua, New York, offering adult education in both science and the humanities. Thousands came to eight-week sessions to hear lectures by many of the period's most eminent politicians, authors, artists, and scientists, as well as to enjoy the entertainments and festive atmosphere of the gatherings.

In 1878 William Rainey Harper (later president of the University of Chicago) added a course of home reading, which spread the chautauqua movement nationwide. Soon after the turn of the century, "traveling chautauquas" were organized by commercial lecture bureaus, with tent shows moving from town to town during the summer offering lectures and entertainment. These were very successful for two decades, but they began to lose audiences after World War I, and the movement ended about 1924. The assembly continued at Chautauqua for many years, but never regained the popularity of earlier days.

See also Vacations and Resorts.

CHAVEZ, CESAR

(1927–   ), executive director of the United Farm Workers. Born in Yuma, Arizona, to immigrant parents, Chavez moved to California with his family in 1939. For the next ten years they moved up and down the state working in the fields. During this period Chavez encountered the conditions that he would dedicate his life to changing: wretched migrant camps, corrupt labor contractors, meager wages for backbreaking work, bitter racism.

His introduction to labor organizing began in 1952 when he met Father Donald McDonnell, an activist Catholic priest, and Fred Ross, an organizer with the Community Service Organization, who recruited Chavez to join his group. Within a few years Chavez had become national director, but in 1962 resigned to devote his energies to organizing a union for farm workers.

A major turning point came in September 1965 when the fledgling Farm Workers Association voted to join a strike that had been initiated by Filipino farm workers in Delano's grape fields. Within months Chavez and his union became nationally known. Chavez's drawing on the imagery of the civil rights movement, his in-

sistence on nonviolence, his reliance on volunteers from urban universities and religious organizations, his alliance with organized labor, and his use of mass mobilizing techniques such as a famous march on Sacramento in 1966 brought the grape strike and consumer boycott into the national consciousness. The boycott in particular was responsible for pressuring the growers to recognize the United Farm Workers (UFW; renamed after the union joined the AFL-CIO). The first contracts were signed in 1966, but were followed by more years of strife. In 1968 Chavez went on a fast for twenty-five days to protest the increasing advocacy of violence within the union. Victory came finally on July 29, 1970, when twenty-six Delano growers formally signed contracts recognizing the UFW and bringing peace to the vineyards.

That same year the Teamsters' union challenged the UFW in the Salinas valley by signing sweetheart contracts with the growers there. Thus began a bloody four-year struggle. Finally in 1973, the Teamsters signed a jurisdictional agreement that temporarily ended the strife.

Believing that the only permanent solution to the problems of farm workers lay in legislation, Chavez supported the passage of California's Agricultural Labor Relations Act (the first of its kind in the nation), which promised to end the cycle of misery and exploitation and ensure justice for the workers. These promises, however, proved to be short-lived as grower opposition and a series of hostile governors undercut the effectiveness of the law.

After 1976 Chavez led the union through a major reorganization, intended to improve efficiency and outreach to the public. In 1984 in response to the grape industry's refusal to control the use of pesticides on its crops, Chavez inaugurated an international boycott of table grapes.

For thirty years Chavez tenaciously devoted himself to the problems of some of the poorest workers in America. The movement he inspired succeeded in raising salaries and improving working conditions for farm workers in California, Texas, Arizona, and Florida.

Jacques E. Levy, *Cesar Chavez: Autobiography of La Causa* (1975); Dick Meister and Anne Loftis, *A Long Time Com-*

ing: The Struggle to Unionize America's Farm Workers (1977).

RICHARD GRISWOLD DEL CASTILLO

See also Agriculture; Labor.

CHEROKEE NATION V. GEORGIA

By refusing to consider *Cherokee Nation* v. *Georgia* (1831), the Supreme Court denied self-government to a Native American tribe. Prior to 1831, the federal government treated tribes as foreign entities in conducting official interactions with them. In an effort to keep their tribal lands, the Cherokee living within Georgia turned to farming and ranching. They also wrote a constitution and laws reflecting some aspects of U.S. law. The state of Georgia declared all the Cherokee laws void, prompting that nation to appeal to the Supreme Court. Chief Justice John Marshall wrote the opinion dismissing the case, saying that Indian tribes were "domestic dependent nations" and could not turn to the Supreme Court. The case's dismissal allowed Georgia to strip the tribe of its governmental forms.

A year later, however, in *Worcester* v. *Georgia* (1832), Marshall wrote that the "laws of Georgia can have no force" in Cherokee territory. He then established the doctrine that the national government alone could conduct Native American affairs. President Andrew Jackson and John Marshall locked horns on the issue. After *Worcester,* Jackson remarked, "John Marshall has made his decision. Now let him enforce it." Georgia instead enforced its laws on the Cherokee tribe.

See also Indians.

CHESAPEAKE COLONIES

In the middle of the seventeenth century, a resident complained that the Chesapeake "is reported to be an unhealthy place, a nest of Rogues, whores, desolate and rooking persons; a place of intolerable labour, bad usage and hard Diet." Such circumstances, partly true of early Virginia, were an inauspicious beginning for England's first region of permanent settlement on the North American mainland and a misleading harbinger of the Chesapeake's eighteenth-century prominence and prosperity.

English interest in the Chesapeake area had begun in the late sixteenth century as a prospective outpost for attacking Spanish ships, as a possible source of precious metals and semitropical crops, as a presumably congenial location for English settlement and conversion of the Indians, and, perhaps, as the eastern terminus of a transcontinental passage. By the early seventeenth century, when English explorations farther north and south proved disappointing, England's imperialists focused on the Chesapeake area as the most promising site for British colonization. The formation of the Virginia Company of London in 1606 led the following year to England's outpost at Jamestown and eventually to the extensive settlement of Virginia and Maryland.

Although the Jamestown colony survived, it failed for several decades to accomplish any of its avowed objectives. The outpost, moreover, was lethal to its settlers, expensive to its investors, and intermittently at war with its native neighbors. Major problems were the colonists' lack of appropriate skills and the company's inability to send necessary supplies. As a garrison against attacks and simultaneously a self-supporting work force, the first colonists should have been predominantly soldiers, farmers, and laborers. Instead they were a hodgepodge of workers with irrelevant skills and posturing lesser gentry. Matters improved only slightly with additional recruits and supplies: time and again the wrong people and wrong things arrived. As England's first major experiment in American colonization, the Chesapeake was a trial-and-error disaster.

The mortality rate in the early years reflects the colony's problems. From an initial population of approximately 105 at its founding in 1607, the number dropped to 50 at the end of the first year; new arrivals swelled the ranks to nearly 400 by the summer of 1609, but a year later the number was down to 90. A few settlers had returned to England, but most of the population loss came from persistent diseases and Indian retaliation for encroachment and forced contributions of food. The deadly pattern continued well into the 1620s and abated only gradually thereafter. Even after 1624, when Virginia came under direct Crown control and Maryland (settled in the 1630s) was administered by a benign proprietor, the Chesapeake compared poorly in healthfulness, orderliness, and overall prosperity to New England and, in some respects, to the British Caribbean.

Maryland, founded a generation after Jamestown, learned from Virginia's mistakes. Lord Baltimore's colony began with more realistic expectations and better planning and accordingly enjoyed relative health and tranquillity in its early years. It also attracted a more dedicated group of colonists. As a haven for Roman Catholics (though they were a minority in the colony from the outset), Maryland appealed to families with intentions of staying the course rather than to single men with expectations of quick profits and an early departure. But Maryland's golden age was brief; as Virginia gradually gained stability, Maryland succumbed to internecine strife. For most of the seventeenth century, the two British colonies suffered internal friction and hostility not only with neighboring Indians but often with each other.

The Chesapeake's economic vitality began with John Rolfe's introduction of a superior species of tobacco from Trinidad in 1612. The imported plants (*Nicotiana tabacum*) flourished in the Tidewater's soil and climate; soon a tobacco craze hit Virginia that undermined efforts to grow other crops, even for local use. The early settlers of Maryland followed suit. By midcentury, the Chesapeake colonies were exporting large and profitable tobacco cargoes, and their prosperity thereafter rose and fell with fluctuations in the international market.

Tobacco profits dramatically increased the demand for labor. When early hopes that the Indians would work for the English proved ephemeral, a system of indentured labor (whereby one worked usually for four or five years in exchange for passage to America and all necessities during the period of service) was linked to head rights of fifty acres of land (sometimes one hundred acres in Maryland) to anyone who paid a person's passage to the colony. This system provided a temporary solution to the labor shortage; it also encouraged the amassing of huge estates by men rich enough to obtain scores of head rights. But the number of indentured immigrants was always inadequate, and the ex-servants often became tobacco growers themselves, thus increasing the demand for servants. And as good farming land became scarce, the ex-servants increasingly formed a disgruntled frontier subculture — landless, restless, and armed — that culminated in Nathaniel Bacon's uprising in 1676 in Virginia. Moreover, the demand for field-workers skewed the sex ratio heavily toward male immigrants, which gave the Chesapeake a heavy (about five to one) male preponderance during most of the seventeenth century. Indentured servants remained an important part of the Chesapeake labor force throughout the colonial era, but by the late seventeenth century they were no longer its core. In the eighteenth century, Maryland imported substantial numbers of British convicts as bound laborers, usually with terms of seven years, but again the supply fell short of the need.

Slavery was the solution. In both Virginia and Maryland, the shift to imported African slave labor began early but did not reach major proportions until the last quarter of the seventeenth century, when a growing demand for labor coincided with a slackening of the supply from England and an expansion of the Atlantic slave trade. By the second quarter of the eighteenth century, black labor predominated, although white workers continued to hold most of the skilled positions on the tobacco plantations until acculturated slaves took over those roles as well. Whites of all socioeconomic classes increasingly eschewed labor in the fields, as a caste system based on pigmentation became a hallmark of Chesapeake society. By the eve of the American Revolution, African-Americans constituted nearly 40 percent of the region's non-Indian population.

In both Virginia and Maryland, leadership in the eighteenth century came from the planters and their associates — merchants and lawyers — though the roles often overlapped. The plantocracy dominated both houses of the legislatures, the local governments, the colonial militias, and the church vestries. A few families, most notably in Virginia, set the tone for a society that emulated the English landed gentry's style and influence. But unlike its English counterparts, the Chesapeake aristocracy depended on a single-crop economy based on vast landholdings and black bondsmen. Even toward the end of the eighteenth century, when falling tobacco prices and exhausted soil encouraged a more diversified economy, tobacco and slaves remained central to the colonial Chesapeake, and the plantocracy retained its remarkable homogeneity and hegemony. The power of the plantocracy took on new meaning in the 1760s and 1770s when the struggle with the mother country highlighted a remarkable cadre of articulate and energetic leaders whose national prominence lasted far beyond the revolutionary era.

Wesley Frank Craven, *The Southern Colonies in the Seventeenth Century, 1607–1689* (1949); Gloria Lund Main, *Tobacco Colony: Life in Early Maryland, 1650–1720* (1982); Edmund S. Morgan, *American Slavery, American Freedom: The Ordeal of Colonial Virginia* (1975).

ALDEN T. VAUGHAN

See also Bacon's Rebellion; Colonial Culture; Colonial Economy; Colonial Government and Politics; Colonial Wars; Indentured Servitude; Indians; Plantation System; Slavery; Tobacco.

CHICAGO SEVEN

The Chicago Seven were political radicals accused of conspiring to incite the riots that occurred during the Democratic National Convention in Chicago, August 21–26, 1968. There were originally eight defendants: David Dellinger, a pacifist and chairman of the National Mobilization against the War; Tom Hayden and Rennie Davis, leaders of the Students for a Democratic Society (SDS); Abbie Hoffman and Jerry Rubin, leaders of the Youth International Party (YIP); John Froines and Lee Weiner, local Chicago organizers; and Bobby Seale, cofounder of the Black Panther party.

Except for the Panthers, who were uninvolved from the start, all the groups represented had planned massive demonstrations during convention week. But with the withdrawal of their principal target, President Lyndon B. Johnson, as a candidate for reelection and Chicago mayor Richard Daley's increasingly threatening public statements about maintaining order, the appeal to "come to Chicago" became more muted. In the end, some ten thousand or so demonstrators gathered — enough to trigger a week of violent confrontations with the police, including one later termed by a federal commission a "police riot."

The five-month trial of the Chicago Eight began in September. While Weathermen (an SDS splinter group) proclaimed "Days of Rage" in the streets outside, the prosecution stressed the defendants' provocative rhetoric and subversive intentions. William Kunstler — lawyer for all the defendants except Seale — attributed the violence to official overreaction rather than conspiracy and brought singers, artists, and activists into court to explain what the demonstrators found troubling about American society. Prosecutor Thomas Foran and Judge Julius Hoffman clashed continually with the defendants. In particular, Seale's manner of conducting his own defense led to his spending three days in court bound and gagged; his case was then declared a mistrial, and he was sentenced to four years for contempt of court. The Chicago Eight thus became the Chicago Seven. In February 1970, five of the seven were found guilty, but an appeals court overturned the convictions in the fall of 1972, citing Judge Hoffman's procedural errors and his overt hostility to the defendants.

See also Daley, Richard; Elections: 1968; Hoffman, Abbie; New Left; Students for a Democratic Society.

CHIEF JOSEPH

See Joseph (Chief Joseph).

CHILD, LYDIA MARIA

(1802–1880), abolitionist and author. Child grew up among the educated elite of Boston. At the age of twenty-two she published her first novel and became a member of the prestigious

Boston Athenaeum. She continued to write while teaching school, and in 1826 her interests fused: she started *Juvenile Miscellany,* the first periodical for children in America. Shortly thereafter she married David Child, whose checkered career as lawyer, editor, and reformer did not endear him to her conservative family.

During this period Child did some of her most popular domestic writing and earned an international reputation, especially with the popular advice manual *The Frugal Housewife* (1829). *Good Wives* (1833) and *The History of the Condition of Women in Various Ages and Nations* (1835) were ambitious biographical studies that reflected her serious commitment to women's rights. She also became an ardent abolitionist. In her antislavery jeremiad, *An Appeal in Favor of That Class of Americans Called Africans* (1833), she proclaimed her allegiance to the cause of immediate emancipation. This declaration cost her the popular following her writings had won. The Boston literary establishment considered her a radical, and she was turned out of the Athenaeum.

Child, however, followed her own conscience. She was sidetracked from public activities in 1837 when her husband decided to raise sugar beets to replace sugarcane, a product of slave labor. But in 1841 she left their farm where they lived in little more than a shack and ventured alone to New York City to edit the *National Anti-Slavery Standard.* Her editorial style was deemed too meek by antislavery activists, and she resigned in 1843. She then supported herself by churning out newspaper columns and writing for periodicals; her *Letters from New York* (1843–1845) recaptured some of the audience she had lost earlier. When her husband arrived in New York in 1843 (and tried his hand at the *Standard* before he was forced to resign in 1844), she asked her lawyer to separate their financial affairs, because, she said, "to pump water into a sieve for fourteen years is enough to break down the most energetic spirit. I must put a stop to it or die."

The Childs were estranged for nearly a decade but returned to Massachusetts in 1850. After another failed attempt at farming, they moved in with her father in Wayland. Child seemed reconciled now to her marriage. Although she regretted having no children, she wrote that David "serves me for husband and 'baby and all.' " She wrote religious histories, antislavery tracts, a novel (*Romance of the Republic* about mulattoes in New Orleans), and a book on the plight of Indians. She also helped Harriet Jacobs publish her compelling autobiography, *Incidents in the Life of a Slave Girl* (1861). Child published a final volume, *Aspirations of the World,* two years before her death, but she never fully regained the popularity of her early years.

Jane Pease and William Pease, *Ladies, Women, and Wenches* (1990); Jean Fagan Yellin, *Women and Sisters* (1990).

CATHERINE CLINTON

See also Abolitionist Movement; Literature.

CHILDHOOD

Children in the colonial period were seen as beings who should adopt adult behavior and assume adult responsibilities as soon as possible. They were dressed as adults as early as age seven or eight. By age ten children often lived with other families and worked for them as hired laborers or servants. The American Revolution, which produced so many changes in political and social life, encouraged families in the new nation to become more egalitarian. The family, magazine articles advised, should be a less authoritarian institution. Children had needs of their own; they were individuals, not simply the property of their parents. Stories and advice literature urged parents to reason with their children rather than scold or beat them.

European and British philosophers were influential in shaping these attitudes toward child rearing. John Locke held that the child's mind was an empty slate upon which parents and instructors could write their lessons. Jean-Jacques Rousseau believed that children were by nature innocent beings who should enjoy a carefree period before having to assume adult responsibilities. Both Locke and Rousseau rejected the concept of "infant depravity," the Calvinist belief, widely held in colonial America, that the infant was born tainted by the original sin of Adam and Eve.

By the middle of the nineteenth century these changes in the view of children had spread from the elite to the urban (and largely Protestant) middle class. Books, magazines, poetry, and fiction were written especially for children. Parents eagerly read advice books about how best to rear children. Merchants began offering dolls, trains, and other children's playthings, and stores specializing in games, toys, and children's goods opened in larger cities. The attitude toward children's early learning also changed. As late as the 1830s and 1840s, infant schools in the North included children as young as three, and reading at an early age was encouraged. Elizabeth Palmer Peabody established the first formally organized kindergarten in Boston in 1860. Influenced by German experiments, Peabody sought to offer children learning activities, such as clay modeling and paper cutting, rather than specific instruction in reading or writing. The former activities, she argued, stimulated the educational development of the child.

The American Revolution, which preached the ideal of equality and opposed hierarchy and tyranny in any form, had also helped give greater recognition to women as mothers. Their status was elevated both because of the belief in equality and also because of their new role in educating children to become virtuous citizens of the young Republic. Women, it was asserted, were the moral guardians of the home. By the middle of the nineteenth century, industrialization, too, had enhanced the importance of the mother in the home. Wives of the middle class were no longer needed to tend a loom or make straw hats for market. Their husbands became more preoccupied with business matters, and mothers came to spend an increasing amount of time attending to their children.

The mother, considered the naturally affectionate parent, became the emotional center of the family. Nothing was more sacred than the bond between mother and child. Because more attention was to be devoted to the individual child, mothers sought to have fewer children. Among earlier generations of parents, whipping had been a common form of punishment, with some striving to break a child's will by the age of two or three. As the supposedly gentler sex, mothers now were exhorted to use "gentler" measures of punishment; they should mold their children's behavior, not break their will, and resort to spanking — hitting the child with one's hand, not a stick or rod — only as a last measure.

Although urban middle-class families could prosper without having to put their children to work, for most families a child was still a necessary and valuable economic asset. The vast majority of American families lived on farms and depended on the labor of every family member. By the age of six or seven, farm children had specific responsibilities. By ten or twelve, sons were working at men's tasks and daughters were helping their mothers with cooking, washing, spinning, and milking.

The responsibilities of slave children resembled those of white children of farm families. By the age of ten or twelve, however, slave daughters as well as sons were sent to work in the fields from sunup to sundown. Thus, slavery imposed a special physical burden on slave girls.

In cities, the child whose father was absent or unable to provide for the family had to run errands, scavenge for coal, and help the mother, who took in laundry, cared for boarders, or did sewing or piecework in the home. Young boys sold newspapers or became street peddlers. Children of the poor often did not attend school regularly or dropped out at an early age.

Employed to tend spinning machines in textile mills, children were among America's first industrial workers. They remained an important part of the work force in the textile industry as late as the early twentieth century; by 1900, 13 percent of textile workers were under sixteen. Industry preferred hiring children for unskilled tasks because they could be paid less than adults. Parents sent the young to work because they needed their wages to supplement the family income.

In the Progressive Era reformers advocated a variety of measures, from establishing children's playgrounds to setting age limits on their employment. As early as the 1850s some states had enacted compulsory school attendance laws;

progressive reformers now helped pass further legislation requiring students to remain in school until a minimum age. The reformers' ideal of the affectionate family was widely adopted among families with modest means.

In the twentieth century, the nineteenth-century idea of the child-centered family continued. American parents valued children highly and placed their hopes for the future in them. Children benefited from living in more prosperous times and in more comfortable homes and from advances in health care and sanitation, and the eradication of such childhood diseases as polio, meningitis, and smallpox. Meeting the needs of children, even inventing new ones, became an important element of the consumer economy. Many children had their own rooms, took music or tennis lessons, and spent part of the summer at camp.

Children of the poor also participated in the consumer society: they might own toys or television sets, and attend summer camp. But like children in colonial society, they often assumed adult responsibilities, such as caring for younger siblings, at an early age. Poverty took its toll on their health and educational prospects. Children of the poor were often underweight and malnourished; they rarely saw a dentist. Despite laws prohibiting child labor, children of migrants often picked crops at very low wages or worked many hours in illegal sweatshops. Schooling was compulsory until age sixteen. But many of these children attended school irregularly and dropped out without graduating from high school.

Throughout the twentieth century Americans believed that the main job of the family was the proper rearing of children. Parents were still expected to provide their children with moral guidance and to oversee their education and training for an occupation. But while these functions remained much the same, the American family itself underwent many changes. Since the 1960s the employment of mothers with young children had increased dramatically, teen pregnancy soared, and divorce rates rose; single-parent households, usually headed by mothers, were becoming more common. Many critics worried that these changes endangered the family's traditional function of raising children because parents were either too busy or too "disconnected" to provide their children with proper supervision and guidance.

The greatest cause for concern was that children had become the poorest Americans. They were often the victims of parental drug use, abuse and neglect, poverty, and inadequate health care and schooling. To remedy these problems required government funding for education and social welfare programs. But Americans not among the poor seemed to balk at increased spending for programs that would benefit other people's children, distinguishing between the protection and comfort they wanted for their own children and a decent standard of living for all youngsters. One reason for this attitude was the absence of an effective political lobby on behalf of child welfare. Because children did not vote, and their advocates could not apply the political pressure of other special interests, politicians were able to ignore children's needs. Another reason was that the United States, with its tradition of individualism and opposition to government intervention in the family, had never developed a full-fledged welfare state, which provided the kind of family support, medical care, and child care programs common in West European countries. Americans debated whether the social problems of children were mainly a parental or community responsibility. Advocates of child welfare, who believed that society should provide children with a minimum standard of decent living, called for an expansion of the poverty programs of the 1960s, such as Head Start (early childhood education for poor children), nutrition programs, and pediatric care for children of the working poor.

Robert H. Bremner, ed., *Children and Youth in America: A Documentary History* (1970–1974); Steven Mintz and Susan Kellogg, *Domestic Revolutions: A Social History of American Family Life* (1988).

ELIZABETH H. PLECK

See also Child Labor; Family; Spock, Benjamin.

CHILD LABOR

The minimal role of child labor in the United States today is one of the more remarkable changes in the social and economic life of the nation over the last two centuries. In colonial America, child labor was not a subject of controversy. It was an integral part of the agricultural and handicraft economy. Children not only worked on the family farm but were often hired out to other farmers. Boys customarily began their apprenticeship in a trade between ages ten and fourteen. Both types of child labor declined in the early nineteenth century, but factory employment provided a new opportunity for children. Ultimately, young women and adult immigrants replaced these children in the textile industry, but child labor continued in other businesses. They could be paid lower wages, were more tractable and easily managed than adults, and were very difficult for unions to organize.

The educational reformers of the mid-nineteenth century convinced many among the native-born population that primary school education was a necessity for both personal fulfillment and the advancement of the nation. This led several states to establish a minimum wage for labor and minimal requirements for school attendance. These laws had many loopholes, however, and were in place in only some states where they were laxly enforced. In addition, the influx of immigrants, beginning with the Irish in the 1840s and continuing after 1880 with groups from southern and eastern Europe, provided a new pool of child workers. Many of these immigrants came from a rural background, and they had much the same attitude toward child labor as Americans had in the eighteenth century.

The new supply of child workers was matched by a tremendous expansion of American industry in the last quarter of the nineteenth century that increased the jobs suitable for children. The two factors led to a rise in the percentage of children ten to fifteen years of age who were gainfully employed. Although the official figure of 1.75 million significantly understates the true number, it indicates that at least 18 percent of these children were employed in 1900. In southern cotton mills, 25 percent of the employees were below the age of fifteen, with half of these children below age twelve. In addition, the horrendous conditions of work for many child laborers brought the issue to public attention.

Determined efforts to regulate or eliminate child labor have been a feature of social reform in the United States since 1900. The leaders in this effort were the National Child Labor Committee, organized in 1904, and the many state child labor committees. These organizations, gradualist in philosophy and thus prepared to accept what was achievable even if not theoretically sufficient, employed flexible tactics and were able to withstand the frustration of defeats and slow progress. The committees pioneered the techniques of mass political action, including investigations by experts, the widespread use of photography to dramatize the poor conditions of children at work, pamphlets, leaflets, and mass mailings to reach the public, and sophisticated lobbying. Despite these activities, success depended heavily on the political climate in the nation as well as developments that reduced the need or desirability of child labor.

During the period from 1902 to 1915, child labor committees emphasized reform through state legislatures. Many laws restricting child labor were passed as part of the progressive reform movement of this period. But the gaps that remained, particularly in the southern states, led to a decision to work for a federal child labor law. Congress passed such laws in 1916 and 1918, but the Supreme Court declared them unconstitutional.

The opponents of child labor then sought a constitutional amendment authorizing federal child labor legislation. Congress passed such an amendment in 1924, but the conservative political climate of the 1920s, together with opposition from some church groups and farm organizations that feared a possible increase of federal power in areas related to children, prevented many states from ratifying it.

The Great Depression changed political attitudes in the United States significantly, and child labor reform benefited. Almost all of the codes developed under the National Industrial Recovery Act served to reduce child labor. The Fair Labor Standards Act of 1938, which for the first time set national minimum wage and maximum hour standards for workers in interstate commerce, also placed limitations on child labor. In effect, the employment of children under sixteen years of age was prohibited in manufacturing and mining.

This success arose not only from popular hostility to child labor, generated in no small measure by the long-term work of the child labor committees and the climate of reform in the New Deal period, but also from the desire of Americans in a period of high unemployment to open jobs held by children to adults.

Other factors also contributed in a major way to the decline of child labor. New types of machinery cut into the use of children in two ways. Many simple tasks done by children were mechanized, and semiskilled adults became necessary for the most efficient use of the equipment. In addition, jobs of all sorts increasingly required higher educational levels. The states responded by increasing the number of years of schooling required, lengthening the school year, and enforcing truancy laws more effectively. The need for education was so clear that Congress in 1949 amended the child labor law to include businesses not covered in 1938, principally commercial agriculture, transportation, communications, and public utilities.

Although child labor has been substantially eliminated, it still poses a problem in a few areas of the economy. Violations of the child labor laws continue among economically impoverished migrant agricultural workers. Employers in the garment industry in New York City have turned to the children of illegal immigrants in an effort to compete with imports from low-wage nations. The recent liberalization of the federal government's rules concerning work done at home also increases the likelihood of illegal child labor. Finally, despite the existing laws limiting the number of hours of work for those still attending school, some children continue to labor an excessive number of hours or hold prohibited jobs. Effectiveness in enforcement varies from state to state. Clearly, the United States has not yet eliminated all the abuses and violations, but it has met the objective of the child labor reformers and determined by law and general practice that children shall not be full-time workers.

Walter Trattner, *Crusade for the Children: A History of the National Child Labor Committee and Child Labor Reform in America* (1970).

IRWIN YELLOWITZ

See also Childhood.

CHINA-U.S. RELATIONS

See Asia-U.S. Relations.

CHINESE EXCLUSION ACT

The Chinese Exclusion Act of 1882 was the first significant law restricting immigration into the United States. Those on the West Coast were especially prone to attribute declining wages and economic ills on the despised Chinese workers. Although the Chinese composed only .002 percent of the nation's population, Congress passed the exclusion act to placate worker demands and assuage prevalent concerns about maintaining white "racial purity."

The statute of 1882 suspended Chinese immigration for ten years and declared the Chinese as ineligible for naturalization. Chinese workers already in the country challenged the constitutionality of the discriminatory acts, but their efforts failed. The act was renewed in 1892 for another ten years, and in 1902 Chinese immigration was made permanently illegal. The legislation proved very effective, and the Chinese population in the United States sharply declined.

American experience with Chinese exclusion spurred later movements for immigration restriction against other "undesirable" groups such as Middle Easterners, Hindu and East Indians, and the Japanese. The Chinese themselves remained ineligible for citizenship until 1943.

See also Asia-U.S. Relations; Immigration; Nativism.

CHISHOLM V. GEORGIA

This 1793 case prompted the Eleventh Amendment to the Constitution after the Supreme Court ruled that it was appropriate for citizens of one state to sue another state. Two citizens of South Carolina sued the state of Georgia in the Supreme Court for confiscating certain property. Their suit rested on the Constitution's description of the Court's jurisdiction as including all cases "between a State and citizens of another State." Georgia contested the Court's jurisdiction, and its lawyers refused to appear in court. In response to this challenge to the Court's authority, Chief Justice John Jay's opinion said such suits should be heard. He declared that it would "far deviate from the plain path of equality and impartiality" to allow a state to sue a citizen of another state (as in criminal proceedings) and deny the out-of-state citizen a forum to sue the state.

Despite clear constitutional support for the opinion, it was an unpopular limitation on state sovereignty. Immediately, the Eleventh Amendment was proposed to prohibit federal courts from hearing citizens' suits against other states. It was ratified within five years. Courts eventually allowed suits against officials of other states, sidestepping the amendment.

See also Constitution.

CHRISTIAN SCIENCE

Christian Science, a homegrown American religious and medical sect, was founded by Mary Baker. She suffered from a variety of ailments — lung, liver and stomach problems, backaches, colds, fevers, "nervousness," and "depression" — and had tried a variety of remedies, including dietary cures and homeopathy, when in 1862, she traveled to Portland, Maine, to receive treatment from Phineas Parkhurst Quimby, a healer. After Quimby effected a cure through his system of massage, encouragement, and "mental healing," she became his student and associate.

Shortly after Quimby's death in 1866, she slipped and fell on an icy street. Confined to bed and given little chance of recovery, she began reading the Bible. After a period of solitary meditation, she was overwhelmed by the idea that her life was in God and that God was the only life. From this revelation followed her healing; she got out of bed, dressed, and walked out of her sickroom, to the amazement of those in attendance.

In 1875, Mary Baker published *Science and Health* (in later editions, *Science and Health with Key to the Scriptures*), the founding text of Christian Science. In it, she asserted that "all is mind and there is no matter," death and sickness are only illusions, and that everything emanates from God and is perfect — healing comes from the true understanding of these doctrines.

Two years later she married Asa Gilbert Eddy, one of her students. In 1879, the Church of Christ, Scientist, was founded and in 1881 ordained Mrs. Eddy its minister. After some dissension within the ranks, the original church dissolved and in 1892, Mrs. Eddy founded the First Church of Christ, Scientist, of Boston, also called "the Mother Church."

Practically from its inception, Christian Science was embroiled in controversy in the form of disputes over Eddy's authority, and lawsuits challenging the claims and efficacy of Christian Science healing practice and the originality of Eddy's doctrine. Competition from rival mental healing sects (called "New Thought") — some of which derived their theories from Eddy's own texts — led to further contention. Despite these difficulties, Christian Science and related doctrines spread widely in the late nineteenth and early twentieth centuries, forming an alternative, especially popular among women, to both established religion and orthodox medicine.

See also Eddy, Mary Baker; Religion.

CHURCH AND STATE

In American religious and legal history, the terms *church* and *state* refer to the religious communities in their relation to the civil order. Strictly speaking, the two terms do not seem applicable to the United States. They derive from the situation in the Middle Ages, when there was but one ecclesiastical body in the Western world, the Catholic church obedient to Rome. There was in each case only one political authority — for example, the Holy Roman Empire — which was often expressed by a single local sovereignty. All citizens and observers would know exactly what the terms *church* and *state* referred to.

In the United States, however, the circumstances differ vastly. Where, the analyst must ask, is "the church" in a nation of so many churches? To what does one refer when no single church is to have preference over any other, and no one of them is to be legally established, as the church was through the Middle Ages and ordinarily even after the sixteenth-century Reformation in Europe? As for "the state," it happens that ecclesiastical bodies must relate to local, state, and national authorities alike, so some other term referring to these plural realities ought to be in place.

Nevertheless, despite the diversity of references or, in more common language, the pluralism of American life, the terms *church* and *state* have become common, even normative. Although all the American Founders used the terminology, no one did more than Thomas Jefferson to frame the context in which it is used. The author of the Declaration of Independence, a determined fighter for religious freedom, wrote in 1802 while president of the United States to some New England Baptists that the nation had erected "a wall of separation between church and state."

The metaphor of the wall was attractive, but it has obscured more than it has illuminated the actual situation in America. More appropriate is the language used thirty years later by an aging James Madison. Madison had been associated with Jefferson in the struggles in Virginia to win religious freedom and had a major hand in drafting the U.S. Constitution and the Bill of Rights with its First Amendment support of churchly disestablishment and religious freedom. Madison spoke of a *"line* of separation between the rights of religion and the Civil authority." In other words, he conceived more of a distinction than a wall.

In fact, throughout two centuries of national existence, all sorts of relations between religious bodies or individuals and civil authorities have developed. They occurred against the background of the inheritance most European colonists brought with them. Whether Anglicans who settled the southern colonies and there established their Church of England or Puritan Protestants who, rebelling against the Church of England, came to the northern colonies to be free to establish their own Congregational churches, most of them reverted to medieval models. They wanted but one "church" (theirs) to exist in each colony, which became the "state." This existence meant *establishment,* a term referring to the fact that financial, legal, and honorific privileges were to be extended to that one church and all others were to be seen as dissenters, tolerated at best and persecuted at worst.

Thus it was that at some time or other, nine of the thirteen colonies had an establishment. The founders of Rhode Island were the exceptions in the North. Chiefly Baptist in outlook, they drew Madison's line boldly and decisively, and permitted all churches and believers virtually equal status, always independent of the state. In the Middle Colonies, William Penn and the founders of Pennsylvania created a Quaker colony, but they were determined that the many faiths represented there should have equal rights and that none should depend upon the civil authority for support. Other Middle Colonies took the same course.

Eventually dissent grew so strong, commercial interests were so handicapped by the policies of religious monopoly, and philosophies encouraging toleration developed so extensively that establishments became ineffective and personal religious freedom grew. After decisive struggles for separation in colonies like Virginia, it became clear to the Framers of the Constitution that there dared be no national establishment of religion. For that reason, when drafting the First Amendment, they came up with a classic sixteen-word formula: "Congress shall make no law respecting an establishment of religion, nor prohibiting the free exercise thereof."

That sentence was open to many interpretations, and the story of religion in America often revolves around them. From 1789 to 1940 the U.S. Supreme Court almost never took up or decided cases on the basis of it. But after 1940 it applied the Fourteenth Amendment guarantees that the rights assured by Congress be assured in all states when the Court made decisions about religion. Although the Court has not acted consistently and has not always described its rationales well, it has set out to minimize governmental involvement in supporting religious institutions in any direct sense and has worked strenuously to assure the greatest possible freedom of citizens to exercise religion or to be nonreligious. The two clauses of the First Amendment often seem to be at war with each other; in prohibiting establishment, for instance, the Court rules out religious practices and teachings in public schools, thus promoting a pattern that some assertive religious people claim limits their free exercise of religion in tax-supported schools.

The United States has never lived with a solid wall of separation between church and state. For instance, by granting tax exemption to the property of religious organizations, the state and national governments in effect are favoring religious institutions and granting them a financial boon. The vast majority of citizens support such a policy. Similarly, there are tax-supported military and legislative chaplaincies. Still, despite the inevitable and necessary confusions and blurrings of the distinctions, most citizens favor the First Amendment resolution and want church and state to be "separate" even as the government shows what one justice called "wholesome neutrality" in respect to the churches.

John T. Noonan, Jr., *The Believer and the Powers That Are: Cases, History, and Other Data Bearing on the Relation of Religion and Government* (1987); John F. Wilson, *Church and State in America: A Bibliographical Guide*, Vol. 1, *The Colonial and Early National Periods* (1986), and Vol. 2, *The Civil War to the Present Day* (1987).

MARTIN E. MARTY

See also Bill of Rights.

CHURCHES

See Religion.

CHURCH OF JESUS CHRIST OF LATTER-DAY SAINTS

See Mormons.

CIA

See Central Intelligence Agency.

CIO

See Congress of Industrial Organizations.

CITIES

See City Government; City Planning; Urbanization.

CITY GOVERNMENT

Rapid expansion and precipitous decline, social conflict, and demands for ever-increasing public services have all characterized the history of the American city. Chicago grew from a trading post to a metropolis of 1.5 million inhabitants in a single lifetime; Detroit was an industrial boomtown in the early twentieth century but the corroding buckle of America's Rustbelt fifty years later. In the mid-nineteenth century Irish and German migration to America's cities posed unprecedented demands and ignited new tensions; one hundred years later millions of blacks moved to the urban core, again transforming urban life.

American city government was responsible for coping with these rapid changes. Although often maligned as corrupt and incompetent, mayors and city councils in the nineteenth century struggled to handle the needs of growing populations desiring more and better police, fire, water, and sewer services. Their successors in the late twentieth century faced rioting, fiscal crisis, and inner-city abandonment and attempted to maintain cities as viable places of work and residence. Throughout American history city government has faced formidable challenges, and lawmakers have tinkered with the mechanism of urban rule to ensure it could meet those challenges.

The rulers of America's small colonial cities devoted much of their time to the regulation and promotion of commerce; they guaranteed standard weights and measures, fixed prices, and supervised wharves, ferries, markets, and fairs. By the mid-eighteenth century, however, municipal governments were focusing increasing attention on such services as fire protection and street lighting, and throughout the colonial era city ordinances attempted to eliminate such nuisances as livestock running through the streets. With only night watches and some volunteer fire companies, municipal work forces remained small well into the nineteenth century. Although the demand for street improvements and better fire protection mounted and municipal taxing powers expanded during the first decades of the nineteenth century, American city government was still a modest operation.

All this changed in the mid-nineteenth century. In the 1840s and 1850s one city after another created professional police forces patrolling the streets both night and day, and during the 1850s and 1860s the largest municipalities replaced the volunteer fire brigade with paid full-time firefighters. Meanwhile, some cities were financing the creation of school systems, libraries, and the first large-scale municipal parks. Moreover, municipalities were assuming responsibility for building waterworks and constructing the first comprehensive sewer systems. One consequence of this great leap in the provision of services was a rise in taxes and municipal indebtedness. For example, between 1845 and 1875 Boston's per capita municipal expenditures soared from $8.29 to $42.92 and that city's debt rose from $784,000 to over $27 million.

Responding to this seeming orgy of spending, many taxpayers cried corruption and urged reform. Although rising taxes and debt purchased many needed services, there was enough evidence of malfeasance in public office to anger these concerned citizens. Moreover, middle-class taxpayers viewed with suspicion the rise of political organizations that sought the votes of seemingly uneducated and ill-bred immigrants and offered city jobs to these newcomers from Europe. In the eyes of many native-born, middle-class taxpayers, the city appeared to be falling into the hands of vulgar Irish Catholic aldermen who sought only to line their pockets.

The best-publicized gang of malefactors was New York City's Tweed Ring, a coterie of Democratic politicians associated with the Tammany Hall faction and named for Boss William Tweed. By encouraging contractors to overcharge the city and kick back some of the profits to politicians, the Tweed Ring spent $13 million to construct a courthouse originally estimated to cost $250,000; a prominent reformer claimed that this structure's cornerstone "was conceived in sin, and its dome, if ever finished, will be glazed all over with iniquity." Another outraged businessman declared that "there is not in the history of villainy a parallel for the gigantic crime against property conspired by the Tammany Ring."

Equally disturbing to many middle-class Americans was the willingness of urban politicians to ignore the drinking, gambling, and prostitution that seemed to be corrupting the lower classes and threatening the moral tone of the nation. During the 1890s New York City's Rev. Charles Parkhurst led a well-publicized crusade against the Tammany organization's tolerance of such sin, attacking the ruling Democratic politicians as "a lying, perjured, rum-soaked, and libidinous lot," "polluted harpies that, under the pretence of governing this city, are feeding day and night on its quivering vitals." Throughout the late nineteenth century moral laxity and political thievery were the twin indictments against the political leadership of the country's largest cities. Many middle-class Americans believed that politicians of little breeding were profiting from city projects and compounding their sins by betraying the city to purveyors of evil.

This litany of complaints about corruption and immorality distracted many voters from the great accomplishments of city government during the second half of the nineteenth century. Municipal engineers were providing cities with the most extensive and modern water and sewer systems in the world, guaranteeing middle-class Americans the comfort and convenience of the indoor flush toilet and bathtub. New York City, Chicago, Boston, and a multitude of smaller cities were employing the finest landscape architects to create beautiful parks for harried urban dwellers. Newly created public libraries offered knowledge and enjoyment for millions of city residents. Mud and manure might have been all too evident along the city streets and police might have been pocketing bribes from gamblers rather than upholding moral standards, but a corps of the ablest engineers, park designers, and librarians were providing municipal services unequaled in the Western world.

Nevertheless, in the minds of most middle-class Americans, the bad in city government outweighed the good. President Andrew D. White of Cornell University labeled American city government the "worst in Christendom," and by the beginning of the twentieth century many believed a major restructuring of urban rule was necessary to secure businesslike, efficient municipal government. Thus a number of cities adopted the commission plan of government, which replaced the mayor and council with a small board of commissioners, each elected at large and each responsible for a single area of municipal administration. At-large election weakened the power of the neighborhood politician whom middle-class reformers associated with the corner saloon and the immigrant masses. Moreover, under the new plan voters could easily identify and punish those responsible for shortcomings in city services. If sewers backed up and flooded basements, the electorate could deny the commissioner of public works another term in office, and if cash was missing from the city treasury, voters could hold the commissioner of public finance accountable when they cast their ballots. Yet the commission plan did not provide for a single chief to coordinate the work of the various commissioners, and this shortcoming led to the creation of the city manager scheme. Under this plan an elected city council determined basic policy and appointed a professional, nonpartisan city manager who was in charge of the day-to-day operation of the municipality. Although most of the largest cities did not opt for this plan, during the second and third decades of the twentieth century hundreds of smaller communities and suburban municipalities hired city managers.

Other reforms in structure and procedure also were popular among citizens seeking an honest, effective government. Critics of corruption urged adoption of nonpartisan elections, new methods of municipal accounting, a civil

service system for city employees, and state constitutional amendments to halt state legislative interference in municipal affairs. City governments were creations of the state legislatures with no powers but those granted by the state. Now the cry was for home rule and greater local control of municipal operations. Together with the commission and manager plans these reforms were all attempts to overhaul the machinery of government and achieve the administrative efficiency popularly associated with the modern business corporation.

Structural changes, however, did not satisfy some reform crusaders of the early twentieth century. These leaders sought reform that supposedly would help the "little guy" who suffered from misrule of the cities. According to such mayors as Detroit's Hazen Pingree, Toledo's Samuel Jones, and Cleveland's Tom Johnson, streetcar companies operating under franchises granted by the city councils were charging extortionate fares and providing poor service. Moreover, leaders like Jones and Johnson claimed that crackdowns on saloons penalized working-class patrons of those establishments while city governments too often ignored the large-scale thievery of public utility magnates. Jones wrote that government must cease to be "an instrument of the cunning few for the purpose of plundering the poor," and a vital step toward this goal would be municipal ownership of public utilities. Throughout the nation there were growing demands for city operation of electric, gas, and streetcar companies, and the periodic renegotiation of franchises ignited bitter debate, with proponents of municipal ownership attacking greedy tycoons and advocates of private enterprise brandishing charges of rampant socialism. The result was increased regulation of public utilities by state commissions, but municipal ownership made only modest headway.

By the 1920s, however, the automobile was freeing many city dwellers of their bondage to the hated streetcar companies. It was also accelerating the flow of population beyond the central-city limits to newly developing suburban municipalities. One consequence was the political fragmentation of urban America with scores of city governments sharing authority within a single metropolitan area. The number of municipalities in suburban St. Louis County, Missouri, for example, soared from twenty-one in 1930 to forty-one in 1940 to eighty-three in 1950. An older central city such as St. Louis included manufacturing and retailing, working-class housing and middle-class residences. Thus its municipal government was a compromise among diverse interests, not totally satisfying to any. Yet the suburban municipalities were most often small homogeneous units offering government tailored to one fragment of metropolitan society. Upper-middle-class suburbs adopted stiff zoning ordinances excluding undesirable businesses and maintained public schools that emphasized preparation for college. Industrial suburbs offered manufacturers low taxes and a tolerant attitude toward pollution. Given the choice between inclusive central-city government and exclusive suburban rule, most Americans who could afford to opted for the latter.

Yet such fragmentation posed formidable problems. It fostered inequity, with some municipalities enjoying excellent services and others poor services; in some communities the tax burden was light but elsewhere it was heavy. Moreover, this multitude of municipalities posed an obstacle to metropolitan planning and cooperation. To achieve regional planning of facilities and services required delicate negotiation among a myriad of governments that too often proved impossible. Some southwestern cities such as Phoenix, San Diego, Albuquerque, and Houston continued to annex outlying tracts, thus limiting the problem of fragmentation. In a few other communities such as Nashville and Indianapolis the consolidation of the city and county likewise ensured some degree of metropolitan unity. But in an increasing number of metropolitan areas, especially in the Northeast and Midwest, fragmentation was becoming the general rule.

With residents and business migrating outward to suburban municipalities, central-city governments were too often left with a decaying tax base. Slum housing and vacant factories were commonplace in the central cities, and these structures added little to municipal treasuries. To enhance city tax rolls the federal government launched an urban renewal program in 1949, granting money to municipalities to encourage the reconstruction of the urban core. Yet rebuilding proceeded slowly and offered no quick cure for central-city ills. Meanwhile, poor migrants from the American South and Latin America supplanted more affluent residents, imposing new demands on local welfare services and schools. And by the 1960s municipal employees were resorting to protests and strikes to force higher wages from city governments. With the tax base shrinking, service demands mounting, and municipal employees expecting more in their paychecks, fiscal crisis loomed for many older central-city governments. Federal aid and creative bookkeeping saved some cities from disaster in the late 1960s and early 1970s. But the virtual bankruptcy of New York City in 1975 and the default of Cleveland in 1978 made the municipal fiscal crisis front-page news. Layoffs of municipal employees and a series of austerity budgets followed, yet in the 1980s the fragmentation of local government in America continued to ensure a patchwork of metropolitan units, some rich and some poor, some struggling and some thriving.

Melvin G. Holli, *Reform in Detroit: Hazen S. Pingree and Urban Politics* (1969); Jon C. Teaford, *The Unheralded Triumph: City Government in America, 1870–1900* (1984).

JON C. TEAFORD

See also Black Ghettos; Corruption; Education; Fire Departments; Internal Migration; La Guardia, Fiorello; Libraries and Museums; Police Forces; Public Transportation; Suburbanization; Tammany Hall; Tweed Ring; Urban Bosses and Machine Politics; Urbanization.

CITY PLANNING

Americans since the seventeenth century have planned their cities primarily as containers for business. In one sense, all cities are planned environments, the cumulative results of contemporary decisions about physical uses of land and the residential distribution of people. Those decisions sometimes emerged from the blueprint of a formally drawn plan; other times they reflected the individual desires of real estate builders and developers. Not every scheme for growth and change in the past embodied the breadth of possibilities mentioned in a formal twentieth-century city plan — land-use zoning, transit and recreational facilities, street layouts, public works, and the like. Yet nearly all those of either private citizens or governments aimed at shaping an environment for the profitable and, if possible, pleasant conduct of economic activities.

Customarily the Spanish, French, Dutch, and English colonizers drew up formal town and city plans well in advance of settlement, or in their absence, they legislated plans shortly thereafter. Decades before the planning of America's earliest city — St. Augustine, Florida (1565) — the Spanish Crown declared, "One of the most important things to observe is that . . . the places chosen for settlement . . . be healthy and not swampy, good for unloading goods. . . . Towns newly founded may be established according to plan without difficulty." The Dutch trading company that founded New Amsterdam in 1625–1626 (renamed New York when it came under British control in 1664) sent with the settlers explicit plans. Although it expanded in a haphazard fashion until the middle of the eighteenth century (a practice repeated in western towns and cities in the nineteenth century), what became the nation's largest city began as a planned environment.

The English joint stock corporations that settled the Chesapeake Bay area and later New England intended from the outset to populate the wilderness with planned towns. Especially in New England, colonizers usually built their communities based on plans pioneered in Ulster Province in Ireland. Philadelphia (1682–1683), perhaps the most successful English colonization project in the New World, also was the most thoroughly planned. Proprietor William Penn ordered preparation of a minutely detailed plan after explaining that "our purpose is . . . to erect and build one principal town; which by reason of situation must in all probability be the most considerable for merchandize, trade and fishery in those parts."

Community, not the wilderness, was the point of departure for colonial America. Whether in Virginia or Massachusetts, Georgia or Pennsylvania, the town (and, far more often than not, the planned town) was the characteristic mode of settlement. Jamestown (1607), New Haven (1638), Charleston (1680), Annapolis (1695), Williamsburg (1699), Mobile (1711), New Orleans (1722), Savannah (1733), St. Louis (1762–1764), and Louisville (1779), among others, were examples of town planning in the New World. It was in these early towns and cities that colonywide and then national unity had its origins.

In physical layout, the only significant exception to the characteristic gridiron pattern of streets crisscrossing at right angles interrupted occasionally by an open square was the plan for the new nation's capital city, Washington, D.C., prepared by the French architect Pierre L'Enfant in 1791. L'Enfant overlaid the gridiron's unrelieved monotony with fifteen major public squares connected by broad, tree-lined avenues along diagonal lines. His monumental plan finally became reality a little over a century later, in 1901, when a Senate-appointed agency, the McMillan Commission, received unanimous government approval for an updated and expanded version of L'Enfant's vision.

A town-designing and city-making mania gripped the imaginations of nineteenth-century Americans. The period of most rapid urban growth in the nation's history occurred between 1820 and 1860. Americans were intent on packaging a continent; land speculation in the North, the South, and particularly the West was rampant. City building was the chief activity of real estate speculators and many territorial governments. Federal land law after the Northwest Ordinance of 1787 ensured that town promotion would prove the most profitable means of expansion westward. Plans for prospective communities in the West poured forth from the 1830s on, although many never saw the light of day. Both imagined and actual towns, however, shared in common the gridiron. That physical layout, which still stamps the shape of late-twentieth-century urban America, even in the newer cities of the Sunbelt, gained wide acceptance from the New York City Commissioner's Plan of 1811. That plan locked Manhattan's growth northward into an unrelieved gridiron that ignored topography. The justification, explained the chief surveyor, was that it facilitated the "buying, selling and improving of real estate." The results, in New York City and elsewhere, were intensification of congestion, creation of physically similar and ugly communities across the nation, and the ignoring of public health considerations.

Besieged by pressures of rapid population growth and mounting evidence of urban mental, moral, and physical health problems, a variety of reformers confronted the deterioration of the cities' physical environment. They deliberately worked to construct a new urban culture built on the foundations of planning for present needs and future growth. At least four new professions emerged to challenge urban problems and to champion new technologies as solutions — the sanitarians, municipal lawyers, landscape architects, and municipal engineers.

Between the 1840s and the 1880s local and national leaders created the sanitarian profession, beginning with men such as Boston's Lemuel Shattuck and John H. Griscom whose *Sanitary Conditions of the Laboring Population of New York* (1845) set the tone for subsequent reports on the health and ill-health of the cities. Relying on current although inaccurate medical theories, sanitarians lobbied against epidemic diseases, filthy streets, unhealthy disposal of garbage and human and animal wastes, air pollution caused by industrialization, and the slum housing that had sprung up for both native and foreign immigrant poor. By the 1870s a new organization, the American Public Health Association (1872), had developed to promote vigorously city planning ideas, practices, and legislation.

Aiding the sanitary campaigns was the emergence of a new body of urban law, the creation of the municipal corporation, and efforts to devise a legal tool — the police power — that allowed some public interest control over private property rights. Although bitterly contested, the new legal body grew, as exemplified by John F. Dillon's *Treatise on the Law of Municipal Corporations,* which expanded from one volume in 1872 to five in the last edition in 1911. The U.S. Supreme Court finally capped generations of efforts to expand the police power in a 1926 land-

mark case, *Village of Euclid* v. *Ambler Realty Co.,* that legitimated the right of communities to zone land for business, industrial, and residential purposes.

Concurrent with sanitary crusades and legal innovations was the new profession of landscape architecture. Frederick Law Olmsted and then other practitioners reshaped urban America by promoting a public parks movement and by planning romantic suburbs for wealthy urbanites eager to escape the growing congestion of industrializing cities. First in New York City with Olmsted's appointment (1858) to oversee construction of Central Park, and then in cities across the nation, the new professionals permanently altered the physical and social geography of urban America. In 1899 they formed their own national organization, the American Society of Landscape Architects.

Central to growing public acceptance of planning were new public works technologies of water supplies, sewage disposal, and street paving, all shepherded by the emerging profession of municipal engineers from the 1870s on. Virtually the only problems successfully attacked by late-century city leaders were those treatable by engineering expertise. Mortality rates plunged sharply in cities serviced by such projects. By century's close, although much remained to be accomplished, American urbanites enjoyed the highest standards of public services in the world. Engineers crafted a supposedly nonpartisan professional bureaucracy that, by the early years of the twentieth century, stood for all that Progressive Era government reformers most admired — businesslike efficiency and skill in the management of urban affairs. Engineers dominated the new governmental structures — the city commission and the city manager — created by reformers determined to end the alleged corruption of city bosses and political machines.

Nineteenth-century planning efforts culminated in the construction of the "White City" for the World's Columbian Exposition held in Chicago in 1893. Under the direction of Olmsted and noted Chicago architect Daniel H. Burnham, the city (if real it would have housed over 200,000) physically expressed in one locale all that planners had struggled to achieve over the previous six decades. It spurred a City Beautiful movement that led to preparation of comprehensive plans in cities around the nation during the twentieth century's early years, one that reached full stride in the massively detailed *Plan of Chicago* (1909), prepared by Burnham for a local business organization, the Commercial Club. That same year the First National Conference on City Planning gathered a broad cross section of people concerned about urban problems who pressed for a new profession "to make city planning the social and economic factor it ought to be." Eight years later the American Institute of Planners appeared.

By the 1920s, the older currents of planning thought and practice had merged to form a nascent corps of city managers and an embryonic profession of city planners. An innovative planning model, ignored by official planning agencies and opposed by most urban businesspeople, emerged from the formation of the Regional Planning Association of America that endorsed a "new towns" movement of small and socially integrated communities. After the *Euclid* decision, the decade's end saw three-fifths of the nation's urban population living under some type of zoning controls. Planning's victory appeared assured. It was not. From then to the present, zoning and planning principally have served urban business interests.

During the 1930s, for the first time, federal policies began to remake the face of urban America as city governments turned to Washington for aid. The Home Owners Loan Corporation (1933) rescued a million home owners from debt foreclosure. The Federal Housing Administration (1934) initiated a process that over the next thirty years stripped central cities of millions of white middle-income families, boosting peripheral growth by making it less expensive to live in newly built suburbs while, at the same time, ensuring core concentration of low-income minority families through deliberate policies of racial exclusion from the suburbs. To move moderate-income families from urban slums, the Resettlement Administration proposed construction of over two thousand socially innovative greenbelt towns outside major cities; it built three, eventually selling them to private developers. The Wagner-Steagall Act (1937) inaugurated attempts to encourage cities to construct low-income public housing units by promising federal support to supplicant local housing authorities. The 100,000 units built by the outbreak of World War II perpetuated the government's policy of racial apartheid by segregating white and black families.

The Housing Act of 1949 resurrected the public housing program and promised "a decent home and a suitable living environment for every American family," a promise repeated in every piece of federal urban housing legislation through the last major one in 1968 and consistently honored in the breach. Aimed at eradicating urban slums, the 1949 act undercut its own good intentions by introducing federal support of urban redevelopment, renamed urban renewal in the 1954 Housing Act. Between 1937 and the early 1960s, only 10 percent of the needed stock of public housing arose through federal funding. Having invaded the province of city planning, Washington spent with abandon, but not on the poor. Mayors, bankers, and real estate interests found federal funding of urban renewal planning far more profitable than expenditures on low-income families. Central city slums fell before the onslaught of federally funded bulldozers. Gleaming office towers, civic centers, and apartment projects for middle- and upper-income citizens replaced the slums. The urban business community thrived while the black and white poor suffered from becoming denizens of the movable slums that cropped up elsewhere in the least profitable sections of cities. Another federal program, the Interstate Highway Act (1956), compounded the problems of the poor and hastened white flight to the suburbs by making the central city accessible to professionals who worked there during the day and fled to leafy suburbs at day's end. The automobile and the freeway had triumphed; federal policies, however well intentioned, had sealed the fate of urban America.

The last significant bow of Washington toward the planning of cities came in 1965 with the creation of a new cabinet-level office, Housing and Urban Development (HUD). That agency principally has served the interests of the urban financial communities. From the "long, hot summers" of the mid-sixties' race riots through the lean years of the 1970s and 1980s, the federal government has turned an increasingly deaf ear toward the plight of all urbanites except the well-to-do.

From the seventeenth century to the present, the cycle has come full circle. Despite generations of efforts by planning reformers enthusiastic about solving the physical, social, and moral problems of urban America, cities remain as they began. They are containers for business, boasting vastly improved physical environments, to be sure, but they function as centers for the conduct of economic activities, not as humane habitats meant to enrich the lives of most of their citizens.

John W. Reps, *The Making of Urban America: A History of City Planning in the United States* (1965); Stanley K. Schultz, *Constructing Urban Culture: American Cities and City Planning, 1800–1920* (1989).

STANLEY K. SCHULTZ

See also Architecture; Black Ghettos; City Government; Housing; Progressivism; Public Transportation; Suburbanization; Urban Bosses and Machine Politics; Urbanization.

CIVILIAN CONSERVATION CORPS

Formed in March 1933, the Civilian Conservation Corps (CCC) was one of the first New Deal programs. It was a public works project intended to promote environmental conservation and to build good citizens through vigorous, disciplined outdoor labor. Close to the heart of President Franklin D. Roosevelt, the CCC combined his interests in conservation and universal service for youth. He believed that this civilian "tree army" would relieve the rural unemployed and keep youth "off the city street corners."

The CCC operated under the army's control. Camp commanders had disciplinary powers and corpsmen were required to address superiors as "sir." By September 1935 over 500,000 young men had lived in CCC camps, most staying from six months to a year. The work focused on soil conservation and reforestation. Most important,

the men planted millions of trees on land made barren from fires, natural erosion, or lumbering — in fact, the CCC was responsible for over half the reforestation, public and private, done in the nation's history. Corpsmen also dug canals and ditches, built over thirty thousand wildlife shelters, stocked rivers and lakes with nearly a billion fish, restored historic battlefields, and cleared beaches and campgrounds.

Although professing a nondiscriminatory policy, the CCC failed to give a fair share of work to blacks, especially in the South where local selection agents held sway. But in spite of rigid segregation and hiring quotas, black participation reached 10 percent by 1936.

In all, nearly 3 million young men participated in the CCC. The army's experience in managing such large numbers and the paramilitary discipline learned by corpsmen provided unexpected preparation for the massive call-up of civilians in World War II.

See also Conservation and Environmental Movements; New Deal.

CIVIL RIGHTS MOVEMENT

Because large segments of the populace — particularly African-Americans, women, and men without property — have not always been accorded full citizenship rights in the American Republic, civil rights movements, or "freedom struggles," have been a frequent feature of the nation's history. In particular, movements to obtain civil rights for black Americans have had special historical significance. Such movements have not only secured citizenship rights for blacks but have also redefined prevailing conceptions of the nature of civil rights and the role of government in protecting these rights. The most important achievements of African-American civil rights movements have been the post–Civil War constitutional amendments that abolished slavery and established the citizenship status of blacks and the judicial decisions and legislation based on these amendments, notably the Supreme Court's *Brown* v. *Board of Education of Topeka* decision of 1954, the Civil Rights Act of 1964, and the Voting Rights Act of 1965. Moreover, these legal changes greatly affected the opportunities available to women, nonblack minorities, disabled individuals, and other victims of discrimination.

The modern period of civil rights reform can be divided into several phases, each beginning with isolated, small-scale protests and ultimately resulting in the emergence of new, more militant movements, leaders, and organizations. The *Brown* decision demonstrated that the litigation strategy of the National Association for the Advancement of Colored People (NAACP) could undermine the legal foundations of southern segregationist practices, but the strategy worked only when blacks, acting individually or in small groups, assumed the risks associated with crossing racial barriers. Thus, even after the Supreme Court declared that public school segregation was unconstitutional, black activism was necessary to compel the federal government to implement the decision and extend its principles to all areas of public life rather than simply in schools. During the 1950s and 1960s, therefore, NAACP-sponsored legal suits and legislative lobbying were supplemented by an increasingly massive and militant social movement seeking a broad range of social changes.

The initial phase of the black protest activity in the post-*Brown* period began on December 1, 1955. Rosa Parks of Montgomery, Alabama, refused to give up her seat to a white bus rider, thereby defying a southern custom that required blacks to give seats toward the front of buses to whites. When she was jailed, a black community boycott of the city's buses began. The boycott lasted more than a year, demonstrating the unity and determination of black residents and inspiring blacks elsewhere.

Martin Luther King, Jr., who emerged as the boycott movement's most effective leader, possessed unique conciliatory and oratorical skills. He understood the larger significance of the boycott and quickly realized that the nonviolent tactics used by the Indian nationalist Mahatma Gandhi could be used by southern blacks. "I had come to see early that the Christian doctrine of love operating through the Gandhian method of nonviolence was one of the most potent weapons available to the Negro in his struggle for

freedom," he explained. Although Parks and King were members of the NAACP, the Montgomery movement led to the creation in 1957 of a new regional organization, the clergy-led Southern Christian Leadership Conference (SCLC) with King as its president.

King remained the major spokesperson for black aspirations, but, as in Montgomery, little-known individuals initiated most subsequent black movements. On February 1, 1960, four freshmen at North Carolina Agricultural and Technical College began a wave of student sit-ins designed to end segregation at southern lunch counters. These protests spread rapidly throughout the South and led to the founding, in April 1960, of the Student Non-Violent Coordinating Committee (SNCC). This student-led group, even more aggressive in its use of nonviolent direct action tactics than King's SCLC, stressed the development of autonomous local movements in contrast to SCLC's strategy of using local campaigns to achieve national civil rights reforms.

The SCLC protest strategy achieved its first major success in 1963 when the group launched a major campaign in Birmingham, Alabama. Highly publicized confrontations between nonviolent protesters, including schoolchildren, on the one hand, and police with clubs, fire hoses, and police dogs, on the other, gained northern sympathy. The Birmingham clashes and other simultaneous civil rights efforts prompted President John F. Kennedy to push for passage of new civil rights legislation. By the summer of 1963, the Birmingham protests had become only one of many local protest insurgencies that culminated in the August 28 March on Washington, which attracted at least 200,000 participants. King's address on that occasion captured the idealistic spirit of the expanding protests. "I have a dream," he said, "that one day this nation will rise up and live out the true meaning of its creed — we hold these truths to be self-evident, that all men are created equal."

Although some whites reacted negatively to the spreading protests of 1963, King's linkage of black militancy and idealism helped bring about passage of the Civil Rights Act of 1964. This legislation outlawed segregation in public facilities and racial discrimination in employment and education. In addition to blacks, women and other victims of discrimination benefited from the act.

While the SCLC focused its efforts in the urban centers, SNCC's activities were concentrated in the rural Black Belt areas of Georgia, Alabama, and Mississippi, where white resistance was intense. Although the NAACP and the predominantly white Congress of Racial Equality (CORE) also contributed activists to the Mississippi movement, young SNCC organizers spearheaded civil rights efforts in the state. Black residents in the Black Belt, many of whom had been involved in civil rights efforts since the 1940s and 1950s, emphasized voter registration rather than desegregation as a goal. Mississippi residents Amzie Moore and Fannie Lou Hamer were among the grass-roots leaders who worked closely with SNCC to build new organizations, such as the Mississippi Freedom Democratic party (MFDP). Although the MFDP did not succeed in its attempt to claim the seats of the all-white Mississippi delegation at the 1964 National Democratic Convention in Atlantic City, it attracted national attention and thus prepared the way for a major upsurge in southern black political activity.

After the Atlantic City experience, disillusioned SNCC organizers worked with local leaders in Alabama to create the Lowndes County Freedom Organization. The symbol they chose — the black panther — reflected the radicalism and belief in racial separatism that increasingly characterized SNCC during the last half of the 1960s. The black panther symbol was later adopted by the California-based Black Panther party, formed in 1966 by Huey Newton and Bobby Seale.

Despite occasional open conflicts between the two groups, both SCLC's protest strategy and SNCC's organizing activities were responsible for major Alabama protests in 1965, which prompted President Lyndon B. Johnson to introduce new voting rights legislation. On March 7 an SCLC-planned march from Selma to the state capitol in Montgomery ended almost before it began at Pettus Bridge on the outskirts of Selma, when mounted police using tear gas and wielding clubs attacked the protesters. News accounts

of "Bloody Sunday" brought hundreds of civil rights sympathizers to Selma. Many demonstrators were determined to mobilize another march, and SNCC activists challenged King to defy a court order forbidding such marches. But reluctant to do anything that would lessen public support for the voting rights cause, King on March 9 turned back a second march to the Pettus Bridge when it was blocked by the police. That evening a group of Selma whites killed a northern white minister who had joined the demonstrations. In contrast to the killing of a black man, Jimmy Lee Jackson, a few weeks before, the Reverend James Reeb's death led to a national outcry. After several postponements of the march, civil rights advocates finally gained court permission to proceed. This Selma to Montgomery march was the culmination of a stage of the African-American freedom struggle. Soon afterward, Congress passed the Voting Rights Act of 1965, which greatly increased the number of southern blacks able to register to vote. But it was also the last major racial protest of the 1960s to receive substantial white support.

By the late 1960s, organizations such as the NAACP, SCLC, and SNCC faced increasingly strong challenges from new militant organizations, such as the Black Panther party. The Panthers' strategy of "picking up the gun" reflected the sentiments of many inner-city blacks. A series of major "riots" (as the authorities called them), or "rebellions" (the sympathizers' term), erupted during the last half of the 1960s. Often influenced by the black nationalism of Elijah Muhammad and Malcolm X and by pan-African leaders, proponents of black liberation saw civil rights reforms as insufficient because they did not address the problems faced by millions of poor blacks and because African-American citizenship was derived ultimately from the involuntary circumstances of enslavement. In addition, proponents of racial liberation often saw the African-American freedom struggle in international terms, as a movement for human rights and national self-determination for all peoples.

Severe government repression, the assassinations of Malcolm X and Martin Luther King, and the intense infighting within the black militant community caused a decline in protest activity after the 1960s. The African-American freedom struggle nevertheless left a permanent mark on American society. Overt forms of racial discrimination and government-supported segregation of public facilities came to an end, although de facto, as opposed to de jure, segregation persisted in northern as well as southern public school systems and in other areas of American society. In the South, antiblack violence declined. Black candidates were elected to political offices in communities where blacks had once been barred from voting, and many of the leaders or organizations that came into existence during the 1950s and 1960s remained active in southern politics. Southern colleges and universities that once excluded blacks began to recruit them.

Despite the civil rights gains of the 1960s, however, racial discrimination and repression remained a significant factor in American life. Even after President Johnson declared a war on poverty and King initiated a Poor People's Campaign in 1968, the distribution of the nation's wealth and income moved toward greater inequality during the 1970s and 1980s. Civil rights advocates acknowledged that desegregation had not brought significant improvements in the lives of poor blacks, but they were divided over the future direction of black advancement efforts. To a large degree, moreover, many of the civil rights efforts of the 1970s and 1980s were devoted to defending previous gains or strengthening enforcement mechanisms.

The modern African-American civil rights movement, like similar movements earlier, had transformed American democracy. It also served as a model for other group advancement and group pride efforts involving women, students, Chicanos, gays and lesbians, the elderly, and many others. Continuing controversies regarding affirmative action programs and compensatory remedies for historically rooted patterns of discrimination were aspects of more fundamental, ongoing debates about the boundaries of individual freedom, the role of government, and alternative concepts of social justice.

Taylor Branch, *Parting the Waters: America in the King Years, 1954–1963* (1988); Clayborne Carson, *In Struggle:*

SNCC and the Black Awakening of the 1960s (1981); Hugh Davis Graham, *The Civil Rights Era: Origins and Development of National Policy* (1990); Steven F. Lawson, *Running for Freedom: Civil Rights and Black Politics in America since 1941* (1990).

CLAYBORNE CARSON

See also Black Ghettos; Black Power; *Brown* v. *Board of Education of Topeka;* Congress of Racial Equality; Freedom Rides; Freedom Summer; Jackson, Jesse; King, Martin Luther, Jr.; Malcolm X; Marches on Washington: 1941, 1963; National Association for the Advancement of Colored People; Racial Desegregation; Segregation; Southern Christian Leadership Conference; Student Non-Violent Coordinating Committee; Wallace, George C.

CIVIL SERVICE REFORM

With the extension of democracy and the rise of mass-based political parties in the Jacksonian era, civil servants were expected to contribute time and money ("political assessments") to electioneering. For many of them, organizing the electorate and looking after the interests of their patrons were more important than their ordinary tasks. The party out of power recruited people who hoped success in the forthcoming election would lead to a government job, for to the victors belonged the spoils of office. When in the 1840s and 1850s the rival Whig and Democratic parties won every other election, the spoils system triumphed. Frequent rotation in and out of office decimated the career service, and efficiency suffered. The spoils system reached its zenith during the Civil War with incoming Republicans in 1861 dismissing Democrats both as political enemies and as possible traitors.

The Civil War both expanded and strained the civil service, and agitation for its reform began in December 1865 with legislation introduced by Representative Thomas A. Jenckes of Rhode Island. Borrowing heavily from British precedents, Jenckes proposed that appointments to nonpolicymaking positions be made from among those candidates who did best on a competitive examination open to all and impartially administered by a civil service commission. The bill also required that entrance to the service be at the lowest level and promotions be determined by competitive examinations. Congressmen, however, were reluctant to pass the Jenckes bill because they feared it would devastate party organization and eliminate executive dependence on them for recommendations of constituents for appointments.

Civil service reform lacked mass support but attracted a social and intellectual elite that thought of itself as "the best people." Many had joined the Republican party during the antislavery crusade and had been awarded patronage, primarily in the diplomatic corps. They tended to be lawyers, editors, clergymen, professors, and businessmen (with mercantile and financial rather than industrial interests), who came from established New England families, lived in the Northeast, and were laissez-faire in their outlook. By 1867 they felt excluded from politics and perceived post–Civil War America as indulging in an orgy of political corruption. They recognized that the Jenckes bill would enhance their influence while crippling the power of the spoils politicians. Farmers and laborers were indifferent to reforms, and politicians were usually hostile to them, although some politicians who were out of power embraced reform to cripple hostile party organizations.

President Ulysses S. Grant adopted but quickly abandoned civil service reform, whereas his successor, Rutherford B. Hayes, consistently if pragmatically supported reform. Hayes depoliticized the New York Customhouse and encouraged reform in the New York Post Office.

Realizing that Hayes's innovations could be dropped by his successors, reformers in 1880 organized a Civil Service Reform Association to secure legislation to make reforms permanent. Their bill was adopted by Democratic senator George H. Pendleton of Ohio. President James A. Garfield actually began to dismantle Hayes's reforms before he was assassinated by a man said to be a deranged office seeker in 1881. Civil service reformers exploited his death by convincing the public that the spoils system was responsible for his murder.

Neither Chester A. Arthur, the new president, nor Congress backed the Pendleton bill until after the Republicans were decisively defeated in the election of 1882. Both parties then courted reformers and their votes. Republicans wished to use reform to freeze their partisans in office, and Democrats wanted to use it to neutralize the civil service. A bipartisan majority passed the Pendleton Civil Service Reform Act in January 1883, which established a merit system administered by a bipartisan Civil Service Commission in federal offices with more than 50 employees (about 14,000 out of 130,000 civil servants). The Democrats eliminated the restriction of entrance to the merit system at the lowest level, and westerners and southerners added a requirement that appointees be apportioned among the states according to population. The bill also outlawed political assessments of civil servants by other federal officers, although the Republicans preserved "voluntary" contributions.

The Pendleton Act transformed the civil service and profoundly affected the organization of political parties. The merit system expanded as presidents extended it in order to freeze their partisans in place. By 1900 workers were becoming professionalized, better educated people were being recruited, local political considerations were giving way to national concerns, and political influence was being replaced by business interests. Civil servants no longer financed political campaigns or did party work.

During the Progressive Era civil service reform efforts were directed at developing good management practices to achieve economy and efficiency. Extensive rule changes in 1903 and the adoption of a retirement system in 1923 accelerated the trend toward a career service, and by the 1920s, 80 percent of the service (560,000 in 1922) operated under merit system rules.

The Great Depression and World War II disrupted this trend. Franklin D. Roosevelt's New Deal created many agencies, and their staffs, appointed outside the merit system, brought ideas and energy as well as chaos to the service. In 1938, however, new rules were adopted that set up personnel sections in all departments coordinated by the Civil Service Commission and extended the merit system to include 90 percent of the nation's 1.8 million employees. When World War II expanded the civil service (to 3.8 million by 1945) the merit system was virtually abandoned. But it was revived at the war's end, and administrators deplored the inflexibility and new procedures — primarily required by the Veterans Preference Act (1944) — that made it difficult to remove incompetents.

In 1949 a bipartisan commission headed by former president Herbert Hoover recommended that personnel matters be further decentralized but coordinated by the Civil Service Commission, that hiring procedures be simplified, and that workers receive higher, uniform salaries. These suggestions were adopted, but veterans' groups prevented any change in veterans' preference. Unfortunately the Hoover Commission's suggestion, also adopted, that the chair of the Civil Service Commission advise presidents and attend cabinet meetings weakened the watchdog function of the bipartisan Civil Service Commission.

The exposure of corruption in the Watergate scandal under Richard M. Nixon stimulated further reform. President Jimmy Carter's Civil Service Reform Act of 1978 was the most sweeping reform legislation since 1883. It abolished the Civil Service Commission and split its functions among an Office of Personnel Management (handling 2.1 million of the 2.8 million civil servants), a Federal Labor Relations Authority to oversee labor-management relations, and an independent quasi-judicial Merit System Protection Board. Legislation, however, is only as effective as the people who administer it, and some of President Ronald Reagan's appointees had a devastating impact on the civil service, particularly in the Department of Housing and Urban Development, where they were unsympathetic to needy citizens while lining the pockets of corrupt partisans.

Civil service reform is "unfinished business." Machinery to achieve a depoliticized civil service and a responsive bureaucracy has yet to be devised. With each succeeding administration disagreeing over the proper proportions of politics, security, and self-direction in the public service, there will always be a need for civil service reform.

Ari Hoogenboom, *Outlawing the Spoils: A History of the Civil Service Reform Movement, 1865–1883* (1961); Paul P. Van Riper, *History of the United States Civil Service* (1958).

Ari Hoogenboom

See also Arthur, Chester A.; Hayes, Rutherford B.; Spoils System.

CIVIL WAR

I. Causes and Results

"Of the American Civil War it may safely be asserted that there was a single cause, slavery," wrote historian James Ford Rhodes in 1913. Although historians today would not put it quite so starkly, Rhodes's basic point remains valid.

In the decades since 1913 various schools of historiography have advanced other interpretations of the war's causes. The progressive historians emphasized the widening economic gulf between the North and South. Cultural and social historians stressed the contrast between the civilizations and values of the two regions. But revisionist historians denied the existence of any fundamental economic or social conflicts. They pointed instead to self-serving politicians who created and then exploited the false issue of slavery's expansion into new territories to whip up sectional passions and get themselves elected to office.

Few historians today subscribe to either the progressive or the revisionist interpretation in unalloyed form. To be sure, conflicts of interest occurred between the agricultural South and the industrializing North. But issues like tariffs, banks, and land grants divided parties and interest groups more than they did North and South. The South in the 1840s and 1850s had its advocates of industrialization and protective tariffs, just as the North had its millions of farmers and its low-tariff, antibank Democratic majority in many states. The Civil War was not fought over the issue of tariff or of industrialization or of land grants. Nor was it a consequence of false issues invented by demagogues. It was fought over profound, intractable problems that Americans on both sides believed went to the heart of their society and its future.

In this sense the "two civilizations" thesis

comes closest to the mark. As a lawyer in Savannah, Georgia, expressed it in 1860, "in this country have arisen two races [i.e., Northerners and Southerners] which, although claiming a common parentage, have been so entirely separated by climate, by morals, by religion, and by estimates so totally opposite to all that constitutes honor, truth, and manliness, that they cannot longer exist under the same government." What lay at the root of this separation? Slavery. It was the sole institution not shared by North and South. The peculiar institution *defined* the South. "On the subject of slavery," declared the *Charleston Mercury* in 1858, "the North and South . . . are not only two Peoples, but they are rival, hostile Peoples."

Two of the North's foremost political leaders echoed this point in the same year. Slavery and freedom, said Senator William H. Seward of New York, are "more than incongruous — they are incompatible." The collision between them "is an irrepressible conflict between opposing and enduring forces, and it means that the United States must and will, sooner or later, become either entirely a slaveholding nation, or entirely a free-labor nation." Abraham Lincoln, in a famous speech, declared that "'a house divided against itself cannot stand.' I believe this government cannot endure, permanently half *slave* and half free."

But why could it not so endure? After all, in 1858 it had done so for seventy years. To be sure, slavery had been a source of contention at the Constitutional Convention, at the time of Missouri's admission into the Union in 1821, in the debates between abolitionists and slavery's defenders especially in the 1830s, at the time of Texas's admission as a state in 1845 and the subsequent war with Mexico, and on numerous other occasions. But compromises palliated these conflicts; the Republic endured. What made the rhetoric of 1858 different? What split the Republic in 1861? The answer lies mainly in the schism generated by the *expansion* of slavery.

The Missouri Compromise of 1820 had seemed to settle this matter by dividing the territory acquired in the Louisiana Purchase between slavery and freedom at the latitude of 36°30' (with Missouri as a slave-state exception north of that line). But the conquest from Mexico of vast new regions in the Southwest following the annexation of Texas as a slave state reopened the question in 1846. With the support of nearly all Northern congressmen, the House of Representatives passed over unanimous Southern opposition the Wilmot Proviso stating that slavery should be excluded from all territory acquired by the Mexican War. Southern strength in the Senate was sufficient to defeat the proviso there. And that was the point. With the Union comprising fifteen free states and fifteen slave states in 1848, the South could block in the Senate any measures threatening slavery. But if only free states were to be admitted in the future, the South would eventually become a helpless minority in all branches of government. Slavery would be doomed by Northern hostility.

What explained the growing Northern hostility to slavery? Since 1831 the militant phase of the abolitionist movement had crusaded against bondage as unchristian, immoral, and a violation of the republican principle of equality on which the nation had been founded. The fact that this land of liberty had become the world's largest slaveholding nation seemed a shameful anomaly to an increasing number of Northerners. "The monstrous injustice of slavery," said Lincoln in 1854, "deprives our republican example of its just influence in the world — enables the enemies of free institutions, with plausibility, to taunt us as hypocrites." Slavery degraded not only the slaves, argued Northerners opposed to its expansion, by demeaning the dignity of labor and dragging down the wages of all workers; it also degraded free people who owned no slaves. If slavery goes into the territories, declared abolitionists, "the free labor of all the states will not. . . . If the free labor of the states goes there, the slave labor of the southern states will not, and in a few years the country will teem with an active and energetic population." The contest over expansion of slavery into the territories thus became a contest over the future of America, for these territories held the balance of power between slavery and freedom.

The South accepted the gauntlet flung down by the Free-Soil movement. Proslavery advocates countered that the bondage of blacks was the basis of liberty for whites. Slavery *elevated* all whites to an equality of status and dignity by confining menial labor and caste subordination to blacks. "If slaves are freed," said Southerners, whites "will become menials. We will lose every right and liberty which belongs to the name of freemen." The fear that emancipation would degrade whites to the level of black slaves explains why most of the Southern whites who owned no slaves (70 percent of all whites) supported the institution. They agreed with slave owners that slavery must be allowed in the territories, for such expansion might increase their own chances of acquiring slaves.

This question became the dominant political issue of the 1850s. Southerners led several filibustering expeditions into Cuba, Mexico, and Nicaragua to try to gain control of these regions in order to annex them to the United States as slave states. Southern Democrats used their domination of the party, which in turn controlled the federal government during most of the decade, to make annexation of Cuba a party policy (but Spain refused to sell its colony). Southern Democrats and their Northern allies passed the Kansas-Nebraska Act in 1854, which repealed the Missouri Compromise's restriction on slavery north of 36°30′ in Louisiana Purchase territories. The outraged Northern response led to the founding of the Republican party as a coalition of Free-Soilers, Northern Whigs, and those Northern Democrats who were fed up with Southern domination of their party. Tensions were exacerbated in 1857 when the Southern-dominated Supreme Court handed down its *Dred Scott* decision, which declared

The Divided Nation—Slave and Free Areas, 1861

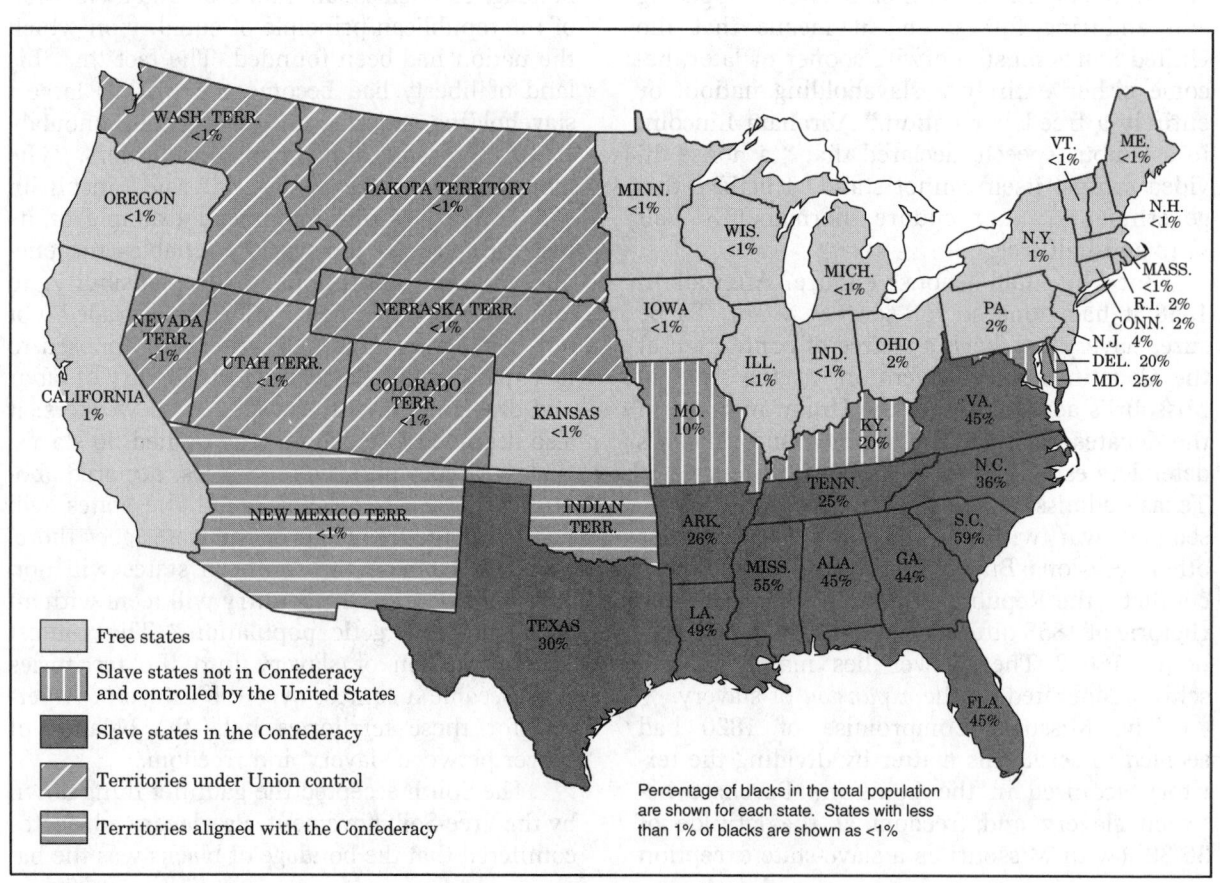

slavery legal in all territories. During the remainder of the decade, the territory of Kansas echoed with the gunfire of strife between pro- and antislavery settlers. Out of the Kansas conflict came John Brown with his vision of a holy war to free the slaves, which culminated with his attack on Harpers Ferry, Virginia, in 1859.

These events were flash points in the increasing polarization of North and South over slavery. When Lincoln won the presidential election in 1860 without winning a single electoral vote and with scarcely any popular votes in the slave states, Southerners knew they had lost control of the government. A Northern antislavery party would dominate the future. Slavery was doomed if the South remained in the Union. So seven slave states seceded (followed by four more after the firing on Fort Sumter) and formed the Confederate States of America.

Still, that did not inevitably mean war. If the new Lincoln administration and the Northern people had been willing to accept secession, the two halves of the former United States might have coexisted in an uneasy peace. But most Northerners were not willing to tolerate the dismemberment of the United States. This would create a fatal precedent whereby "any minority [would] have the right to break up the Government at pleasure," declared Northern newspapers and political leaders. The government would become "a rope of sand" and "our thirty-three States may resolve themselves into as many petty, jarring, and hostile republics. . . . Our example for more than eighty years would not only be lost, but it would be quoted as a conclusive proof that man is unfit for self-government."

Lincoln intended to maintain the federal garrison at Fort Sumter in Charleston Bay as a symbol of national sovereignty in the Confederate states, in the hope that a reaction toward Unionism in those states would eventually bring them back. To forestall this happening, the Confederate army attacked Fort Sumter on April 12, 1861. This was the spark that ignited four years of war in which at least 620,000 American soldiers lost their lives — nearly as many as in all the other wars this country has fought *combined*. The destruction wrought in the South by the

Civil War was devastating. It killed one-quarter of the Confederacy's white men of military age and destroyed two-fifths of Southern livestock, half of the farm machinery and a similar proportion of factories and railroads, and two-thirds of Southern wealth. The Civil War was the great trauma and tragedy of American history.

But it was also a great triumph of nationalism and freedom. The war resolved the two fundamental problems left unresolved by the Revolution of 1776, problems that had preoccupied the country for four score and nine years down to 1865. The first was the question whether this fragile republic would survive in a world of monarchs and emperors and dictators or would follow the example of most republics through history (including many in the nineteenth century) and collapse into tyranny or fragment in a dreary succession of revolutions and civil wars. Northern victory in the Civil War settled that question: the United States would survive as a single nation with a republican form of government. Since 1865 no state or region has tried to secede. The second problem left unresolved by the Revolution was slavery, which had divided the country from the beginning. The Civil War abolished the institution and freed 4 million slaves. What still remained unresolved in 1865 were the meaning and dimensions of that freedom — issues that continue to concern Americans today.

James M. McPherson, *Battle Cry of Freedom: The Era of the Civil War* (1988); David M. Potter, *The Impending Crisis 1848–1861* (1976).

JAMES M. McPHERSON

See also Abolitionist Movement; Bleeding Kansas; Brown, John; Crittenden Compromise; Democratic Party; *Dred Scott* Case; Kansas-Nebraska Act; Lincoln, Abraham; Missouri Compromise; Republican Party; Secession; Slavery; Wilmot Proviso.

II. Strategies and Tactics

In military terminology, *tactics* is the handling of troops on the battlefield. The definition of *strategy* is usually divided into two parts: national strategy, which is the shaping of a nation's political goals in time of war, and military strategy, which is the use of armed forces to achieve those goals.

The Confederacy's national strategy in the Civil War was to defend its political independence and territorial borders. This goal remained constant throughout four years of war, but the military strategies devised to achieve the goal fluctuated. The initial Southern military strategy consisted of what might be described as a "dispersed defensive." Numerous small contingents of troops were dispersed around the circumference of six thousand miles of land and water borders of the Confederacy in the hope of blocking enemy invasions at any and all points. Some of these troops were stationed in forts along the seacoast and on rivers; others were organized in small mobile armies that defended key rail junctions, mountain passes, or river crossings on or near the Confederate border. This proved to be an unwise use of the South's limited military manpower (which was only one-third of the Union potential), for by fragmenting its forces the Confederacy risked a breakthrough at one or more crucial points by larger enemy forces. This was precisely what happened in the winter and spring of 1862, when Northern armies and river navies breached Southern defenses dispersed along a four-hundred-mile line in Tennessee and Kentucky with breakthroughs at Fort Henry, Fort Donelson, and Island No. Ten on the Tennessee, Cumberland, and Mississippi rivers.

Yet though militarily unsound, the dispersed defensive was politically necessary. Confederate regiments were recruited and organized by the states, whose governors retained some control over them even after they were incorporated into the Confederate army. The governors of, say, South Carolina and Arkansas were unwilling to send most of their regiments to crucial points in Virginia or Tennessee if this would leave their own states unprotected. The political allegiance of states was almost as important to Confederate national survival as the military defense of the Southern heartland. Thus Jefferson Davis and his military leaders could never wholly abandon the dispersed defensive. Substantial numbers of troops remained scattered in several quiet sectors instead of concentrated in the most active and threatened theaters (mainly Virginia and Tennessee) until 1864, when Union conquests had shrunk Confederate territory to the point where most Southern troops were perforce concentrated into the Army of Northern Virginia and the Army of Tennessee.

But even earlier, Southern strategists had used interior lines of communication to combine scattered forces into a larger army that could meet an invading Union army on even or nearly even terms. Joseph Johnston brought most of his small army from Winchester to Manassas Junction to combine with P. G. T. Beauregard's force in July 1861 to win the Battle of Manassas. Robert E. Lee likewise brought Thomas J. (Stonewall) Jackson's army from the Shenandoah Valley in June 1862 to join with the Army of Northern Virginia to drive George B. McClellan's besieging force away from Richmond. After the losses of Forts Henry and Donelson in Tennessee, Gen. Albert Sidney Johnston ordered Confederate detachments from Louisiana, Arkansas, and Alabama as well as those driven from Kentucky and Tennessee to concentrate at Corinth, Mississippi, where they launched the counteroffensive that almost won the bloody Battle of Shiloh.

These modifications of the dispersed defensive became known in the Confederate lexicon as an "offensive-defensive" strategy. What this meant was that although the Confederate *national* strategy remained defensive, it could sometimes best be achieved by an offensive military strategy — by attacking the enemy in Confederate territory, as Lee did in the Seven Days Battles and as Johnston did at Shiloh, or by invading enemy territory, as Braxton Bragg and Lee did in September 1862 and Lee did again in June 1863.

Large risks inhered in this offensive-defensive strategy. One was the danger that Union forces would move into the vacuum created by the departure of troops from one place to concentrate in another. The transfer of first-line Confederate regiments from Louisiana to Corinth in March 1862, for example, left New Orleans defended by only two forts, a makeshift navy, and raw militia. These were no match for the Union army-navy task force that fought its way up the Mississippi to Vicksburg during April and May, capturing New Orleans and gaining control of most of the vital Mississippi Valley. Another risk of the offensive-defensive strategy was the possibility of defeat and destruction of an army far from its home base. This danger was especially acute for Confederate armies, which did not have the logistical capacity to operate in enemy territory for an extended period. Thus Lee risked the loss or crippling of his army after the Battles of Antietam and Gettysburg.

The timidity and caution of opposing commanders enabled Lee to bring his battered army back to Virginia on these occasions. But thereafter, Confederate armies were too weak for effective employment of an offensive-defensive strategy, though John B. Hood tried it once more with the Army of Tennessee in November 1864 — with disastrous results. The virtual destruction of Hood's army in the Battles of Franklin and Nashville seemed to confirm the necessity for a less aggressive strategy that would minimize one's own casualties and maximize the enemy's. This was a strategy of attrition, which became the principal Confederate strategy in 1864. In Virginia and Georgia, Lee and Joseph Johnston stood on the entrenched defensive, forcing enemy armies to attack or carry out difficult flanking maneuvers, trading space for time in the hope that high Union casualties and prolonged stalemate would convince the Northern people to give up the attempt to conquer the South because the human and material cost was too high. It almost worked, owing to tactical changes introduced by rifled weapons and trenches.

The Confederate strategy of attrition was a matter of tactics as well. In the military campaigns of 1864 the opposing armies seldom lost contact with each other. Fighting or maneuvering in the presence of the enemy was almost continuous, merging battlefield operations (tactics) with campaign maneuvers (strategy). The Napoleonic tactics taught in American military schools and employed in the Mexican War were becoming obsolete in the age of rifled muskets and artillery. These tactics involved close-order assaults by troops bunched in lines of two or three ranks or in dense columns in order to mass firepower and impact. This worked reasonably well in the era of the muzzle-loading, smooth-bore musket and bayonet. The effective (i.e., accurate) range of the smoothbore musket was at most a hundred yards, and a good soldier could get off two shots a minute. Heavy close-order assaults often succeeded because of the short range of defensive fire before attackers reached the defenders' line. But the development of rifled muskets in the 1850s increased the effective firing range of an infantryman to four or five hundred yards, and the range of an expert sharpshooter to nearly twice as far. This vastly strengthened the defense against close-order assaults. Civil War soldiers by 1863 also learned to entrench whenever they came into contact with the enemy because of the added protection this provided against long-range rifled muskets and rifled artillery. Old-fashioned cavalry charges became suicidal because enemy fire could cut down men and horses long before the shock of their charge could break a defensive line. The Civil War thus produced the evolution of dismounted cavalry tactics, as well as looser infantry assault tactics, which amounted to large-scale skirmishing, flank attacks, and the like. Although commanders on both sides continued to order close-order assaults until virtually the end of the war, thus providing an example of how tactics lagged behind technology, these assaults became increasingly suicidal, especially for Union attackers running up against Confederate trenches, which by 1864 were almost as elaborate as those on the western front in World War I.

What kind of Union strategy could overcome the vastly increased strength of defensive warfare? The Northern national strategy was to preserve the territorial and governmental integrity of the United States. At first this meant restoring the Union as it had existed before 1861 by suppressing the insurrection that had gained control of eleven states. This seemed to require a military strategy of limited war: defeat the armies of the insurrectionists and arrest their leaders, in order to enable the Unionists (whom Northerners in 1861 assumed to be the silent majority in most Southern states) to regain control and bring the states back into the Union. This strategy worked well in the border states of Maryland, Missouri, and Kentucky, which were kept in the Union with the aid of military force despite the Confederate allegiance of a substantial minority of their citizens. It worked also in Virginia west of the Alleghenies, where Northern troops helped the Unionist majority form the new state of West Virginia.

But elsewhere the silent majority of Unionists remained largely a myth. By 1862, therefore, Union strategy evolved to a second stage: conquest of Confederate territory. This too seemed to result in great success. In Tennessee and the lower Mississippi Valley, Union arms conquered and occupied fifty thousand square miles of territory in the spring of 1862 while McClellan's Army of the Potomac swept up the Virginia peninsula and stood poised to capture Richmond. But then the Confederate offensive-defensive onslaught recaptured some of this territory and knocked Union armies back on their heels.

It became clear that so long as Southern armies retained striking power, the Confederacy would remain a viable state. Thus in 1863 Northern military strategy evolved to a third phase: destruction of Confederate armies. Ulysses S. Grant captured one whole army at Vicksburg and badly crippled another at Chattanooga; Lee's army limped home to Virginia badly hurt after Gettysburg.

But the Confederacy still lived, its armies sustained by the will of the population to resist and to continue producing the sinews of war. By 1864 Union strategists recognized that it was not enough to conquer territory and cripple enemy armies; they must destroy the resources and capacity of the Southern people to wage war. Gen. William T. Sherman saw this most clearly. "We are not only fighting hostile armies," he wrote, "but a hostile people." In Sherman's march through Georgia and South Carolina in 1864–1865 and in the campaigns of other Union armies elsewhere, Northern forces burned and destroyed railroads, factories, farms — anything that could feed and supply Confederate armies as well as the civilian population, to break their will and ability to continue the war.

This worked. It had been foreshadowed in 1861 by the Union naval blockade to restrict Confederate imports of war matériel and by the Lincoln administration's adoption of an emancipation policy in 1862 to uproot the South's labor force and convert it to a Union labor and fighting force. By 1863 several hundred thousand former slaves had become free people within Union lines, and the Union army had begun the process that ultimately recruited 180,000 of them to fight for the Union — and freedom. This crippled a crucial Southern resource for waging war and added a powerful resource to the Northern strategic effort. Sherman's destruction of all Southern resources was a logical extension of these policies. It was a strategy of total war that by 1865 overcame the South's defensive tactics and strategy of attrition by totally destroying the Confederacy's capacity to continue fighting. In several respects, therefore, the tactics and strategy of the American Civil War foreshadowed those of the two world wars in the twentieth century.

Paddy Griffith, *Rally Once Again: Battle Tactics of the American Civil War* (1989); T. Harry Williams, *Lincoln and His Generals* (1952).

JAMES M. McPHERSON

See also Copperheads; Davis, Jefferson; Emancipation Proclamation and Thirteenth Amendment; Grant, Ulysses S.; Jackson, Thomas J. (Stonewall); Lee, Robert E.; McClellan, George B.; Sanitary Commission; Sherman, William Tecumseh.

III. Foreign Relations

The Confederacy's principal goals in foreign policy were to obtain diplomatic recognition and material assistance from European countries. The Union's main diplomatic objective was to prevent this. In the end the South failed to achieve diplomatic recognition or British aid in breaking the Union blockade. But foreign assistance and sympathy did contribute in a minor way to the Confederate war effort. Both the Union and the Confederacy focused their diplomatic activities primarily on Britain, the world's foremost industrial and naval power whose lead other nations would follow.

On April 19, 1861, President Abraham Lincoln proclaimed a blockade of Confederate ports. By 1863 the Union navy had built up its force sufficiently to make this blockade effective, seriously curtailing the export of cotton and the imports of war matériel the agricultural South needed to supply its armies. But when, in 1861, the blockade was still little more than nominal, Southerners pursued one of their objectives by placing an embargo on cotton exports, reasoning from what has been termed "the King Cotton illusion." Aware that textiles were the most important industry in Britain (and almost as important to the economy of France) and that 80 percent of Britain's raw cotton came from their fields, Southerners believed that by withholding the 1861 crop from export they would compel British intervention to break the blockade in order to obtain cotton. They miscalculated. The 1859 and 1860 cotton crops had been so large that British mills had enough on hand to carry them into 1862, and the war boom in arms trade and shipping to both the Union and the Confederacy took up part of the slack in the British economy caused by a slowdown in textiles. In any case, the world's richest and most powerful nation was not likely to submit to economic blackmail. Moreover, many working-class leaders and their middle-class allies in Britain sympathized with the Union, thinking it was fighting for democracy and the dignity of labor against a society dominated by slaveholders. After the Emancipation Proclamation, it became even less likely that Britain would side with the South.

Confederate diplomats tried to convince British leaders that the Union blockade in 1861–1862 was so leaky that under international law it should be considered a "paper blockade" and therefore illegitimate. Such arguments fell on deaf ears. As a naval power, Britain relied on blockades in time of war and did not want to create an antiblockade precedent that might boomerang on the Royal Navy in a future conflict. Hence the British government recognized the Northern blockade as legal, and British blockade-runners seized and confiscated by the

Union navy could expect no help from their government.

One crisis associated with the blockade, however, almost ruptured relations between the United States and Britain: the *Trent* affair. On November 8, 1861, the USS *San Jacinto* stopped the British packet *Trent* on the high seas near Cuba and captured James Mason and John Slidell, Confederate diplomats on their way to London and Paris, respectively, to seek diplomatic recognition. The British government considered this a violation of international law and demanded an apology and the release of Mason and Slidell. Public opinion in the North and in England rose to fever pitch while Southerners watched with high hopes that a war would break out between Britain and the United States. But President Lincoln and Secretary of State William H. Seward cooled the crisis by releasing Mason and Slidell, and Britain dropped the demand for an apology.

Confederate hopes for diplomatic recognition rose again in the summer of 1862. Southern armies were on the offensive, having won several small battles in Tennessee and two big ones in Virginia. This convinced some European leaders that the North could never conquer the South. And, too, the cotton shortage was beginning to hurt. The British and French governments discussed the possibility of jointly offering to mediate a peace on the basis of Confederate independence, planning to recognize the Confederacy if the Lincoln administration rejected the offer.

As Southern armies invaded Maryland and Kentucky in September 1862, European governments awaited the outcome. When Union forces turned back the invasions at Antietam and Perryville, Britain dropped the idea of mediation. As things turned out, this was the closest the South came to gaining diplomatic recognition.

One other issue exacerbated Anglo-American relations. Confederate agents contracted with private British shipyards to build fast, sleek warships to prey on American merchant vessels. This was a violation of British neutrality laws, but forged papers and lax British enforcement allowed some of these ships to put to sea. Two of them, the CSS *Alabama* and css *Florida,* sank or captured nearly one hundred American merchant ships. Union protests did not stop these and other commerce raiders from putting to sea but did prevent the culmination of an even more egregious and dangerous violation of British neutrality. In 1863 the Laird shipbuilding firm in Liverpool built for the Confederate navy two armor-plated warships fitted with seven-foot iron spikes at their prow for ramming enemy vessels. Designed for use against the blockade, these powerful ships would surely have occasioned a diplomatic breach between Britain and the United States if they had gone to sea. At the last minute, however, the British government seized and detained them.

In this as well as other diplomatic crises, the painstaking, skillful efforts of the American minister to Britain, Charles Francis Adams, did much to ensure the success of Union foreign policy, which in turn played an important role in Northern victory.

D. P. Crook, *Diplomacy during the American Civil War* (1975); Brian Jenkins, *Britain and the War for the Union,* 2 vols. (1974, 1980).

JAMES M. MCPHERSON

See also Alabama Claims; Confederate States of America; Cotton; Great Britain–U.S. Relations; Seward, William H.

CLAY, CASSIUS

See Ali, Muhammad.

CLAY, HENRY

(1777–1852), statesman. Leader of the Whig party and five times an unsuccessful presidential candidate, Clay played a central role on the stage of national politics for over forty years. He was secretary of state under John Quincy Adams, Speaker of the House of Representatives longer than anyone else in the nineteenth century, and the most influential member of the Senate during its golden age. In a parliamentary system, he would have undoubtedly become prime minister.

Clay's personal magnetism made him one of America's best-loved politicians; his elaborate scheming made him one of the most cordially hated. Through it all he displayed remarkable consistency of purpose: he was a nationalist, devoted to the economic development and political integration of the United States.

As Speaker of the House in 1812, Clay was one of the "War Hawks," men who believed that war with Great Britain was necessary to preserve the overseas markets of American staple producers. But Clay also served as a negotiator at the Ghent peace conference, and for the rest of his life pursued conciliation at home and abroad. Although a slaveholder, Clay disapproved of slavery as a system; he advocated gradual emancipation and the resettlement of the freed people in Africa. He defended, unsuccessfully, the right of the so-called Five Civilized Tribes of Indians to their lands. He warned that annexation of Texas would provoke war with Mexico and exacerbate tensions between North and South, and he opposed the war when it came. He consistently fostered good relations with Latin America.

The centerpiece of Clay's statecraft was an integrated economic program called "the American System." This envisioned a protective tariff, a national bank jointly owned by private stockholders and the federal government, and federal subsidies for transportation projects ("internal improvements"). Public lands in the West were to be sold rather than given away to homesteaders so the proceeds could be used for education and internal improvements. The program was intended to promote economic development and diversification, reduce dependence on imports, and tie together the different sections of the country.

The American System became the chief plank in the platform of Clay's Whig party, which was formed in opposition to the Democratic party of Andrew Jackson, creating "the second party system." Whigs were found in all parts of the country, but especially among the prosperous classes, in areas wanting government economic aid, and among Protestant religious bodies that hoped a strong government would further their agenda of moral reform.

Clay was called "the Great Compromiser" because he played a major role in formulating the three landmark sectional compromises of his day: the Missouri Compromise of 1820, the Tariff Compromise of 1833, and the Compromise of 1850. Coming from the border state of Kentucky, he was predisposed toward moderation when sectional conflicts were involved. His main objective was to avoid a civil war. But in this, as in so many of his more immediate goals, he was defeated.

Clay never became president, and his Whig party disappeared shortly after his death. But its successor, the Republican party, put many features of the American System into operation. In the long run, his economic and political vision of America was largely fulfilled.

Clement Eaton, *Henry Clay and the Art of American Politics* (1957); Glyndon G. Van Deusen, *The Life of Henry Clay* (1937).

DANIEL WALKER HOWE

See also American System; Compromise of 1850; House of Representatives; Missouri Compromise; Nullification Controversy; Senate; Tariff; Texas Revolution and Annexation; War Hawks; War of 1812; Whig Party.

CLEMENS, SAMUEL

See Twain, Mark.

CLEVELAND, GROVER

(1837–1908), twenty-second and twenty-fourth president of the United States. Cleveland studied law in Buffalo, New York, and became a leading lawyer there, but for over twenty years he was unknown outside that city. His rise to the presidency was phenomenal because of its rapidity and because he was so lacking in qualities deemed essential for Gilded Age politicians. Brutally honest, frugal with public money, undramatic, ungracious, and obstinate, Cleveland was admired for his enemies rather than his friends. He was the only victorious Gilded Age presiden-

tial candidate lacking a military career, and he was a bachelor. He possessed a contrariness that appealed to reformers.

Receiving the Democratic nomination for mayor of Buffalo in 1881, Cleveland defeated the corrupt Republican organization. By thwarting attempts to raid the city's treasury, he earned the title "Veto Mayor" as well as the gubernatorial nomination in 1882. In the contest that followed, he attracted independent reformers and triumphed over a divided Republican party. As governor, Cleveland distanced himself from Tammany Hall. A factionalized Democratic party, united by his reform image, gave him its presidential nomination in 1884. After a vituperative campaign, which pitted Cleveland's personal morals (he was possibly the father of an illegitimate son) against the questionable public morals of the Republican nominee, James G. Blaine, Cleveland carried New York by eleven hundred votes and won the election.

Unable to delegate responsibility, Cleveland immersed himself in the minutiae of the presidency. He studied applications for pensions and jobs, weeding out the undeserving and incurring the wrath of veterans and politicians. He conscientiously administered the Civil Service Reform Act and late in his term made permanent his appointees by extending the merit system to cover them. Cleveland signed the Indian Emancipation (Dawes) Act (1887) and the Interstate Commerce Act (1887) but shaped no major legislation. Although he called for tariff revision, he failed to fight effectively for it. Marrying his twenty-two-year-old ward, Frances Folsom, in the White House was his most popular act. Running for reelection in 1888 on the tariff issue, he lost to Benjamin Harrison.

He did defeat Harrison four years later, however. But he had scarcely taken office when the panic of 1893 signaled the onset of a severe economic depression that made his second term a disaster. Believing that agitation for "free silver" had caused the depression in 1894, Cleveland convinced a reluctant Congress to repeal the Sherman Silver Purchase Act and negotiated unpopular bank loans in order to keep the United States on the gold standard. Having thus alienated western and southern farmers, he outraged labor by intervening on the side of the railroads during the Pullman strike of 1894. In foreign affairs he was an anti-imperialist; he refused to annex Hawaii and forced Great Britain to arbitrate a boundary dispute with Venezuela. Cleveland so angered Democrats that they repudiated him and adopted "free silver" in 1896, only to suffer a resounding defeat at the polls. Ironically the virtues that had elected Cleveland failed to help him lead his party or the country.

Allan Nevins, *Grover Cleveland: A Study in Courage* (1933); Richard E. Welch, Jr., *The Presidencies of Grover Cleveland* (1988).

ARI HOOGENBOOM

See also Elections: 1884, 1888, 1892; Mugwumps. *For events during Cleveland's administrations, see* Civil Service Reform; *Coin's Financial School;* Coxey's Army; Dawes Severalty Act; Depressions; Hatch Act; Interstate Commerce Commission; Pullman Strike; Tariff; Tenure of Office Act; *United States* v. *E. C. Knight Co.*

CODY, BUFFALO BILL

(1846–1917), western scout and showman. Anyone interested in the history of the American West must eventually reckon with the life and legacy of William F., "Buffalo Bill," Cody. A master of show business, Cody confirmed American and European audiences in their conviction that the real West was a place of glory and adventure, an enormous space reserved for the equestrian exercises of Indians, cowboys, and outlaws.

With his buckskin outfits and sharpshooting skills, Cody was by no means a frontier fake. Born in Iowa, he moved with his family to Kansas in 1854 and, following his father's early death, began a long occupational odyssey. He worked as a messenger for the freighting firm of Russell, Majors, and Waddell; he served as a scout for the U.S. Army; he killed buffalo to feed workers on the Union Pacific Railroad; he guided celebrities on hunting expeditions; he tried his hand at mining, at ranching, and at townsite development.

In 1872, the flexible Cody added "actor" to his list of occupations, appearing on stage in a frontier melodrama in Chicago. In 1883, Cody departed from the limitations of stage plays and launched his open-air Wild West Show. For thirty years, the show toured the United States and Europe.

Featuring horses and riders in a variety of displays, the Wild West Show held equal appeal for American crowds and European royalty, with England's Queen Victoria a particular fan. Although the down-to-earth project of transporting, feeding, sheltering, outfitting, and organizing cowboys, Indians, sharpshooters, advance men, laborers, cooks, managers, horses, and even buffalo may well have been the show's most impressive feat, audiences were riveted by the evocation of another, less practical world — a world of parades, races, and reenactments of stagecoach robberies and Custer's Last Stand. Over time, the show added events and participants beyond the framework of the American West, with the staging of the Charge at San Juan Hill and the creation of the Congress of Rough Riders of the World, including Russian, French, German, British, Arab, Argentinian, Mexican, Cuban, Hawaiian, and Filipino riders.

Marketing both himself and his show, Buffalo Bill Cody traded heavily on the authentic adventures in his personal history. He had in truth been a child of the West and a genuine scout and hunter. But the necessary theatricality of the Wild West Show, the flourishes of dime novelists using Cody as their main character, and Cody's own creative habits as an embellisher of his autobiography soon made the line dividing authenticity from illusion an impossible one to trace. Accordingly, depending on the interpreter's perspective, the Wild West Show was a trick and a fraud in its distortions of western reality or an innocent diversion, of considerable mythic power, from the mounting pressures of urban industrial life.

Although the show brought in substantial revenue, Cody spent his last years in financial uncertainty, drained in particular by unwise investments in an Arizona mine. At the time of his death in Denver, his unsuccessful struggle for financial stability had forged yet another link in the chain that made Buffalo Bill Cody, both intentionally and unintentionally, a key representative of the fortunes of the American West.

David H. Katcive et al., *Buffalo Bill and the Wild West* (1981); Joseph G. Rosa and Robin May, *Buffalo Bill and His Wild West: A Pictorial Biography* (1989).

PATRICIA NELSON LIMERICK

See also Cowboys.

COERCIVE ACTS

The Coercive Acts were four laws passed by Parliament in the spring of 1774 to punish Massachusetts for its continuing resistance to parliamentary rule (in particular, the Boston Tea Party). Although some leaders like Lord Chatham and Edmund Burke advised against the measures, King George III and most of Parliament were determined to restore imperial authority in the colonies. Massachusetts was widely believed in England to be the focal point of American resistance, and it was felt that the Restraining Acts (as they were officially titled) would quash rebellion at the source while setting an example to the other colonies.

The Boston Port Bill declared Boston Harbor closed until the East India Company and the customs office had been reimbursed for their Tea Party losses. The Administration of Justice Act permitted British soldiers and Crown officials in Massachusetts to be tried in England rather than in provincial courts if they were charged with a capital crime committed while quelling a riot or collecting revenue. The Massachusetts Government Act virtually annulled the colony's charter, significantly curtailing town meetings and changing most high elective offices in the province to appointments by the king or governor. The Quartering Act (the only one applicable to all the colonies) legalized billeting troops in people's homes.

Like earlier efforts to assert imperial power, the Coercive Acts heightened rather than quieted colonial resistance. Indeed, the colonists grouped these laws with the Quebec Act and called them the Intolerable Acts. To coordinate resistance, the First Continental Congress was convened in Philadelphia, September 1774. Besides declaring the Coercive Acts unconstitutional and hence nonbinding, the Congress formed an Association to enforce economic sanctions against Britain and urged Massachusetts to withhold taxes from the royal government until the acts had been repealed. Repeal did not come, however, until 1778 (as part of Britain's unsuccessful effort to prevent an American alliance with France), and by then it was too late; the United States was committed to independence.

See also Association (1774); Quartering Acts; Revolution.

COIN'S FINANCIAL SCHOOL

Throughout the late nineteenth century the nature of the American financial structure was the subject of contentious debate. By the 1890s, gold-based and silver-based currency represented distinct political as well as monetary philosophies. The Coinage Act of 1873 introduced a currency based on gold alone. The Sherman Silver Purchase Act of 1890 restored limited bimetallism, but was repealed owing to the erosion of Treasury funds after the crash of June 1893. By mid-1894 the American economy was in deep depression, and calls for some kind of monetary inflation mounted. In the midst of unprecedented social strife, William Hope Harvey published *Coin's Financial School.* It quickly became the quintessential expression of the free-silver philosophy.

Capitalizing on rural distrust of the urban East and of British monetary power, Harvey denounced attempts to restrict bimetallism as a conspiracy against farmers and debtors. Such attempts, he charged, were designed to enrich eastern financiers controlled by London. The appeal of the book lay in its simple, accessible style and its graphic cartoons. The eponymous hero, youthful and uncorrupted, lectured financiers and politicians, many of them real-life figures, on the errors of their ways. The depression, he argued, was caused by reliance on gold monometallism, which restricted the money supply and lowered prices. Free and unlimited coinage of silver was the only solution. Printed in cheap paper editions, *Coin's Financial School* quickly sold a million copies. Without it, William Jennings Bryan could never have struck so receptive a chord in his Cross of Gold speech in 1896.

COLD WAR

"Cold war" is the term given to the competition, conducted through means short of direct military conflict, between the United States and the Soviet Union since World War II. Its roots go back to the 1890s when, after a century of friendship, Americans and Russians became rivals over the development of Manchuria. Russia, unable to compete industrially, sought to close off and colonize parts of East Asia, while Americans demanded open competition for markets. In 1917, with the Bolsheviks' triumph in Russia, the rivalry turned intensely ideological. The Soviets feared that the United States, as the most powerful capitalist nation, sought to overthrow their communist system. The communists' success in consolidating power, their confiscation of U.S. property, and the possibility that their revolution would spread to Europe, Asia, and perhaps even the Western Hemisphere created deep American fears. Diplomatic relations between the United States and the Soviet Union did not exist between 1917 and 1933. They became allies only after both were attacked by the Axis in 1941.

The alliance was a temporary aberration in the post-1890s relationship. Even during the war the Soviets bitterly disagreed with their American and British partners over military tactics and postwar plans. President Franklin D. Roosevelt feared that Soviet dictator Joseph Stalin might again make a separate settlement with Germany, as indeed the Soviets had in 1918 and 1939. The fear of such a German-Russian deal haunted, and shaped, U.S. policy during and long after the war.

Disagreements over postwar plans first centered on Central and Eastern Europe. Having lost 20 million dead in the war and twice suffered German invasion through Poland in thirty years, Stalin's Soviet Union was determined to use its Red Army to control Poland, dominate the Balkans, and destroy Germany's capacity to start another war. The United States, led after April 1945 by President Harry S. Truman, was equally determined to shape the postwar world according to principles laid down by Roosevelt after 1941: self-determination (in such nations as Poland), equal economic access (as in the Balkans), and a rebuilt capitalist Europe that could again serve as a hub in world affairs. Such a Europe required a healthy Germany at its center. Truman could advance these principles with an economic juggernaut that produced 50 percent of the world's industrial goods and military power that rested on a monopoly of the new atomic bomb. Stalin nevertheless clamped his control over Eastern Europe between 1945 and 1947. Winston Churchill condemned him for cordoning off the new Russian empire with an "iron curtain." When Truman finally refused to give Stalin large amounts of West Germany's industrial plants as war reparations, the dictator first stripped East Germany, which he controlled, and then sealed it off as a communist state.

The post-1945 cold war began in Europe, but it quickly spread. In 1945–1946 Stalin demanded some control over Turkey's Dardanelles Strait, which would allow Soviet passage from the Black Sea to the Mediterranean. Churchill had earlier recognized Stalin's claims, but now the British and Americans forced the Soviet leader to pull back. In 1946, when Red Army units refused to leave Iran (which the three Allies had occupied since 1942), Truman forced a showdown that some feared might lead to a military confrontation. Stalin again retreated, but he simultaneously announced his refusal to cooperate with the new international agencies — the World Bank and the International Monetary Fund — that were created to ensure an open, capitalist, international economy. In Greece, communist-led insurgents threatened to overthrow the corrupt, British-led, monarchical government. The insurgents were helped by communist Yugoslavia, not the Soviet Union. When, however, the British told Truman in February 1947 that they lacked the resources to provide more help, the president rallied Americans by warning them in his Truman Doctrine speech of

March 1947 that they would have to spend $400 million immediately to protect "free" peoples against "totalitarian" regimes. By successfully helping Greece, Truman also set a precedent for U.S. aid to regimes, no matter how regressive, who pleaded that they were threatened by communism. American policy moved from State Department officer George Kennan's argument that the Soviets had to be "contained" using "unalterable counterforce at every point," until "either the breakup or the gradual mellowing of Soviet power" occurred. Kennan provided the policy and Truman the political rallying cry, to fight what columnist Walter Lippmann called in 1947 "the cold war."

The focus returned to Western Europe in 1948. The American Marshall Plan began to pump $12 billion into that part of Europe, which included a West Germany made up of the U.S., French, and British occupation zones. Stalin, fearing a revived Germany, responded by blocking western access to Berlin, which was deep within the Soviet zone although subject to four-power control. Military confrontation loomed, but Truman held West Berlin by flying supplies in over the blockade during 1948–1949. Now committed to ensuring Europe's security, Truman joined eleven other nations in 1949 to form the North Atlantic Treaty Organization (NATO), America's first "entangling" European alliance in 170 years. Stalin countered by tying together the economies of Eastern Europe in his version of the Marshall Plan, exploding the first Soviet atomic device in August 1949, and (after fierce negotiations) signing an alliance with the new communist China in February 1950.

Confronted by these Soviet successes and a growing Western economic crisis, U.S. officials quickly moved to escalate and expand their containment policy. In a secret 1950 document, NSC-68, they proposed to strengthen their alliance systems, quadruple defense spending, and convince Americans to fight this costly cold war. Truman also ordered the development of a hydrogen bomb. In early 1950 came the first U.S. commitment to save Vietnam from communist forces, plans to form a West German army, and proposals for a peace treaty with Japan that would guarantee long-term U.S. military bases.

Some observers (including Kennan) believe that the Japanese treaty led Stalin to approve a plan by communist North Korea to invade U.S.-supported South Korea on June 25, 1950. A united communist Korea could neutralize U.S. power in Japan. To Stalin's surprise, Truman committed U.S. forces and obtained help from the United Nations to drive back the North Koreans. The Soviets, boycotting the U.N. Security Council because it would not admit communist China, could not veto Truman's action. The president, making a historic error, allowed his forces to go to the Chinese-Korean border. China responded with human-wave attacks in November 1950 that decimated the U.N. armies. Fighting stabilized along the thirty-eighth parallel, which had separated the two Koreas, but Truman now faced an implacably hostile China, a Sino-Soviet partnership, and a defense budget that had quadrupled in eighteen months.

In 1953, the new president, Dwight D. Eisenhower, moved to end the war (accomplished with a shaky armistice) and cut the federal budget. He reduced military spending by one-third but continued to fight the cold war effectively. Possessing great nuclear superiority, he faced down Soviet threats to intervene in the Middle East during 1956 and in West Berlin between 1958 and 1961. He used the Central Intelligence Agency (CIA) to overthrow governments that he suspected were turning procommunist in Iran (1953) and Guatemala (1954). In 1958 he sent troops into Lebanon to maintain its pro–United States stance, and between 1954 and 1961 he dispatched economic aid and 695 military advisers to build an independent South Vietnam.

In the meantime, a new Soviet leader, Nikita Khrushchev, was also broadening Moscow's policy by establishing new relations with India and other key neutrals. He increased Soviet power by developing a hydrogen bomb and, in 1957, by launching the first earth satellite. Khrushchev formed an alliance with Cuba after Fidel Castro's successful revolution in 1959. To stabilize his European position, Khrushchev created the Warsaw military pact in 1955 (to counter West German rearmament) and built the Berlin Wall in 1961 (to stop Germans from leaving the communist East).

Other events mark 1956 to 1962 as the first major cold war turning point. In 1956, Khrushchev had to use tanks to ensure continued control of Hungary and Poland. Sino-Soviet ties frayed to the breaking point in these years. Eisenhower's control of his own camp was also imperiled. In 1956 he had to force his two closest allies, Great Britain and France, to retreat from a badly planned invasion with Israel intended to seize the Suez Canal from Egypt. The West Europeans developed their own nuclear forces as well as an economic Common Market (joined by the British in 1971) to be less dependent on Washington. American economic competitiveness faltered in the face of Japan's and West Germany's challenges. American nuclear superiority grew, but in 1962 this led Khrushchev to place missiles in Cuba. President John F. Kennedy, backed by a superior military force, induced the Soviets to retreat. In return, Kennedy promised not to invade Cuba (as he had in 1961 when his Cuban exile forces were destroyed at the Bay of Pigs). After this brush with nuclear war, the two leaders banned nuclear tests in the air and underwater after 1963. But the Soviets also undertook a huge military buildup.

The postwar world dominated by the two superpowers was now transformed into a pluralistic world of decolonized African and Middle Eastern nations and of surging nationalism in Latin America and Asia. Both superpowers tried to control this new world. President Lyndon B. Johnson landed 22,000 troops in the Dominican Republic in 1965 to prevent the unlikely emergence of another Castro. Under Leonid Brezhnev, the Soviets used force in 1968 to destroy a Czechoslovakian reform movement. But elsewhere the two leaders suffered defeats. Johnson stationed 575,000 troops in South Vietnam to prevent its supposed domination by China. He also feared that Vietnam's fall would lead to dominolike communist successes in Southeast Asia. The president, however, not only failed to defeat communist forces, but his costly policy further weakened the U.S. economy. Brezhnev could neither stop bloody clashes between Soviet and Chinese troops along their common border nor bolster a USSR economy that was declin-

ing, in part because of heavy military expenditures.

In 1972–1973 the superpowers sought each other's help. After making a surprise trip to China (his "China card"), President Richard Nixon signed the SALT I treaty with Brezhnev to limit costly strategic weapons. They also agreed to respect newly emerging nations' independence and to strengthen U.S.-Soviet economic ties. This détente was short-lived. During outbreaks in the Middle East, Chile, and Angola, the two nations competed with each other for influence. The economic pact was so emasculated by the U.S. Congress that Brezhnev repudiated it in 1975. President Jimmy Carter tried to place another cap on the arms race with a SALT II agreement in 1979, but his efforts were undercut by other events that year: the Iranian Revolution that destroyed a pro–United States regime; the Nicaraguan Revolution, aided by Cuban and Soviet supplies; and, above all, Brezhnev's invasion of Afghanistan in late 1979 to save a shaky pro-Moscow regime.

In 1980 Ronald Reagan defeated Carter by promising to loosen governmental restraints on the marketplace, increase military spending, and confront the Soviets everywhere. Reagan spent $2.2 trillion for the military over eight years and imposed economic sanctions to protest Brezhnev's crackdown on Poland. Military spending and structural economic problems transformed Americans from the world's leading creditor in 1981 to its leading debtor by 1985. Relations between the United States and the Soviet Union worsened until the tension rivaled that of the worst days of the cold war in the late 1940s.

The tension finally lessened after Mikhail Gorbachev assumed power in Moscow during 1985. Realizing that the Soviet economy was collapsing, he made such major concessions in the areas of conventional forces, nuclear weapons, and removing internal controls (e.g., concerning emigration) that Reagan agreed to arms and economic agreements. In 1989 Gorbachev pulled stalemated Soviet forces from Afghanistan and announced that "the postwar period is over." After some hesitation, the George Bush administration in Washington agreed that the world had "clearly outgrown" the post-1945 superpower "clash." Both powers had actually begun losing control of the international arena in the late 1950s and, especially, the 1970s. Their competition in newly emerging areas wound down after both suffered disasters.

The ideological struggle also lessened as Gorbachev supported reforms through *perestroika* (economic restructuring), *glasnost* (openness), and more democracy within the communist bloc. George Bush meanwhile had to live, however reluctantly, with communist regimes in China, Cuba, and Angola. By 1990, Europe, long divided between Warsaw Pact and NATO alliances, became fragmented and unpredictable. In the East, Gorbachev's policies and the communists' economic failures resulted in the sudden overthrow of communist regimes in Poland, Hungary, Czechoslovakia, Romania, and East Germany. In the West, policymakers were reconsidering the future of both the European Economic Community and NATO in light of Germany's reunification. Fractured by rising nationalist and ethnic demands, Europe began to spin out of the superpowers' orbits. Forty-five years (and, indeed, more nearly a century) of costly competition was climaxing in a world that neither Russians nor Americans could control.

Thomas J. McCormick, *America's Half-Century: U.S. Foreign Policy in the Cold War* (1989); Joseph L. Nogee and Robert H. Donaldson, *Soviet Foreign Policy since World War II* (1988).

WALTER LAFEBER

See also Bay of Pigs Invasion; Berlin Blockade; Détente; Hydrogen Bomb; Kennan, George; Korean War; Lippmann, Walter; Marshall Plan; Middle East–U.S. Relations; North Atlantic Treaty Organization; Strategic Arms Limitation Talks; Truman Doctrine; Vietnam War.

COLLEGES

See Education.

COLONIAL CULTURE

Writing in 1782, J. Hector St. John de Crèvecoeur tried to define "the American, this new man." He was, Crèvecoeur argued, "neither a European nor a descendant of a European" but an "American, who, leaving behind all his ancient prejudices and manners, receives new ones from the new mode of life he has embraced, the new government he obeys, and the new rank he holds." Crèvecoeur presumed that America was a melting pot, that the environment created a homogeneous American culture, with similar values, beliefs, and social practices. Such cultural uniformity is inherently plausible. After all, most white colonial Americans worked the soil, enjoying the fruits of their labor, and practiced similar Protestant faiths. Moreover, they believed in private ownership of the means of production by individual cultivators. Generations of scholars, following the lead of Frederick Jackson Turner in the early twentieth century, argued that free and open land on the frontier created an American people whose identity was shaped by the independence land ownership provided and whose ideology was characterized by individualism, democracy, and equality of opportunity.

Colonial cultures, however, were far less uniform than Crèvecoeur imagined. The women and men who peopled early America — Native Americans, Africans, East Anglians, Welsh, Germans, Dutch, among many others — invented conflicting popular cultures, meshing the beliefs and practices of their birthplaces with the demands of the American environment and the cultures of their neighbors. Indians and Africans, a substantial part of the colonial population, have been ignored in models of cultural uniformity. Even white Protestant immigrants created diverse cultures. While sharing a common religious vision, Puritans and Anglicans, Baptists and Quakers, differed vehemently in the particulars of their faiths. In America, without the pressure of a strong Anglican established church, the particularities of each group were accentuated. By the end of the seventeenth century, the main lines of most of American popular cultures could be clearly seen.

Notwithstanding continuing cultural differences among ethnic groups, there was some cultural convergence in the eighteenth century, a tendency for division among white colonists between a popular culture of the vast majority and

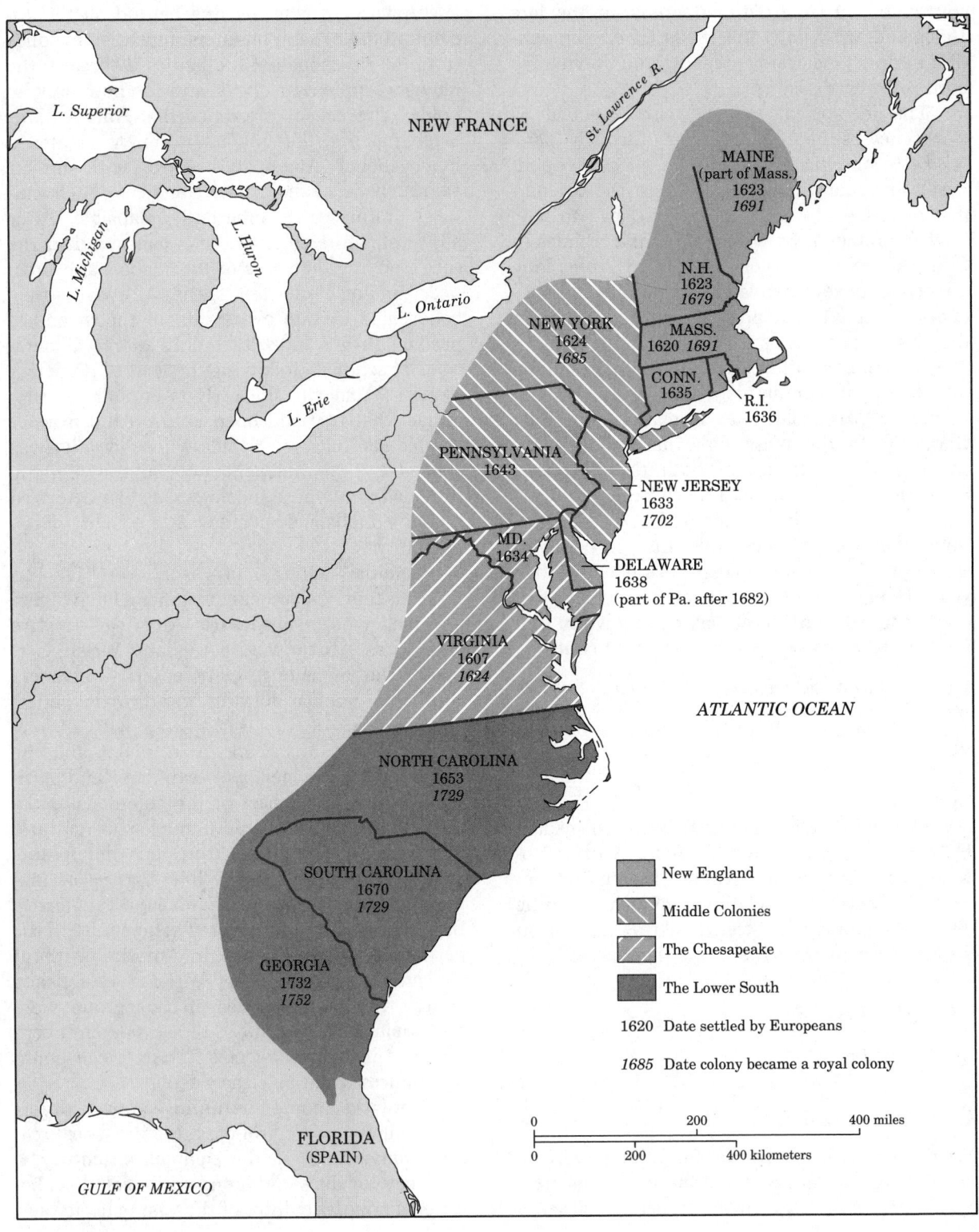

NEW FRANCE

St. Lawrence R.

L. Superior

L. Michigan

L. Huron

L. Ontario

L. Erie

MAINE
(part of Mass.)
1623
1691

N.H.
1623
1679

MASS.
1620 *1691*

NEW YORK
1624
1685

CONN.
1635

R.I.
1636

PENNSYLVANIA
1643

NEW JERSEY
1633
1702

MD.
1634

DELAWARE
1638
(part of Pa. after 1682)

VIRGINIA
1607
1624

ATLANTIC OCEAN

NORTH CAROLINA
1653
1729

SOUTH CAROLINA
1670
1729

GEORGIA
1732
1752

FLORIDA
(SPAIN)

GULF OF MEXICO

New England

Middle Colonies

The Chesapeake

The Lower South

1620   Date settled by Europeans

1685   Date colony became a royal colony

0		200		400 miles

0	200	400 kilometers

a high culture of the ruling few who emulated their peers in England. Such cultural convergence within social classes had several sources. Waves of evangelical revivalism touched every colony at different times between the 1730s and 1780s, democratizing and personalizing religion, Christianizing the unchurched everywhere. Newly rich merchants, great planters, and lawyers received similar educations, built mansions in the English manner, and indulged in conspicuous consumption far beyond the reach of middling farmers.

The development of vernacular cultures in the colonial era depended upon two contrasting geographic facts: widely dispersed settlement and concentrated ethnic enclaves. Even on the eve of independence, most Americans — Indians and settlers alike — lived in isolated farm neighborhoods or villages, separated from neighbors a few miles away by almost impenetrable forests. Most were surrounded by people like themselves: Iroquois lived with Iroquois, Germans settled in Pennsylvania villages, East Anglians dominated many New England towns. Under such circumstances, contrasting popular cultures could flourish. An examination of three cultural indicators — forms of agriculture, patterns of social order, and family and gender mores — before colonization and after American settlement among Indians, New Englanders, white Virginians, and backcountry residents will suggest the ways that the interplay of received culture and environment made new popular cultures. Such an analysis, however, hardly exhausts the diversity of cultures in early America, ignoring, for example, African-Americans in the Chesapeake colonies and coastal South Carolina; Quakers, Dutch, and Scots in the Middle Colonies, and various Germanic ethnic groups. Moreover, there were class conflicts in all the seventeenth-century colonies that common regional cultures did little to hide.

Despite extraordinary differences among groups of Native Americans, they shared some general cultural similarities. Indians insisted upon communal ownership and sovereignty over land; temporary "ownership" came with use. Eastern Woodland Indians, with the exception of those living in the far Northeast, prac-

ticed subsistence agriculture, growing corn and vegetables to feed themselves, using extensive slash-and-burn techniques. Each year, men burned stubble and underbrush; then women did the planting, hoeing, and harvesting of crops. The work of women provided the vast majority of the food the tribes ate. Although they sometimes paid corn as tribute to chiefs, there was minimal exchange of agricultural goods beyond the community. While women farmed and cared for children, men hunted or went to war. Men killed animals for meat and skins (for clothing) for the community as well as pelts to trade with whites. Indians maintained social order through governance by tribal elders; although men made most decisions about war and peace, women participated in some tribes, such as the Iroquois. But white settlement profoundly affected Indian cultures. Indians traded with the first colonists, exchanging furs and corn for iron goods and cloth. As settlers farmed land, chasing animals away, and as they conquered the Indians' lands, Native Americans either had to move west to preserve their cultures or accommodate to the market economies and male agriculture of the whites.

English colonists left East Anglia in the 1630s for New England to escape depression in the cloth trade and to create a covenanted society free from Anglican persecution. Mostly middling textile workers and farmers, they traveled in family groups. Once in New England, communal leaders readily formed communities and distributed land confiscated from Indians among the inhabitants by social rank, holding some land in common for future generations. Communal land thereby became private property, a pattern very different from that of Indians. After all the land had been distributed, those without left to found new communities. Using family labor, New England farmers grew crops for subsistence, trading small surpluses at local markets to pay for taxes and consumer goods. They devised a complex system of local exchange of labor and goods between area families. These exchanges were predicated upon a division of labor in which men farmed and governed while women — considered subservient — gardened, cared for children, and acted as deputy husbands when their spouses were away. A strong sense of order pervaded the society: mutual obligations were expected to tie parents and children together, and when they overstepped communal norms, they faced discipline from church or town; disreputable outsiders were forced to leave the community.

English immigrants to the Chesapeake region in the mid-seventeenth century left highly stratified societies in London and the south of England to find greater economic opportunities. The migrants, mostly poor agricultural and urban wage laborers, had worked in London or Bristol or on large rural estates, producing grain for the market. Three-quarters of them, almost all men, came as indentured servants; once they arrived they cultivated tobacco for English markets and corn for subsistence. Everyone, free and servant, male and female, performed agricultural labor. After initial distribution of land by grant, sale, and headrights (acreage given for every adult brought to the colony), a capitalist land market developed. Despite the original widespread ownership of land, Chesapeake gentlemen soon built vast estates, which they populated with servants and (later) slaves. Given the high death rate and the relatively late age of marriage in the region (servants could not marry until they were free), widows, orphans, and complex families with step- and half-siblings became common, breaking down patriarchal authority in the family, and allowing orphans' courts to replace the father.

When slaves began to replace servants as laborers in the tobacco fields after 1680, Chesapeake culture was transformed. With more laborers, white women no longer had to cultivate tobacco; and with increasing life expectancy and lower ages of marriage among whites, male patriarchal authority increased. Africans, and especially their descendants, created their own culture with African and European elements, forming complex cross-plantation communities and intense extended families in the slave quarters. Within this bicultural society, with its strict class and racial boundaries, gentlemen gained political hegemony, insisting upon the liberty to rule others — their slaves, servants, families, and white social inferiors. Acquiescing in gentry rule, poorer planters expected occasional credit from gentlemen and legal support for their dominance over their own families.

The last major group of European migrants during the colonial era came from Scotland, Ulster, and the north of England during the middle half of the eighteenth century and moved to the back parts of the American colonies, from Pennsylvania to Georgia. Mostly herdsmen, cottagers, and traditional tenants, they moved to avoid proletarianization in regions of rapid capitalist transformation. They took with them a culture constrained by generations of conflicts along the borders of England that instilled a distrust of authority and an insistence upon honor and personal integrity. Since they moved to a frontier similar to their homeland, they could invent new societies reflecting their culture. Access to or ownership of land and the open range together provided them with the means of subsistence that was quickly disappearing in their homelands. Men and women shared all agricultural labor in the mountains and valleys they settled, yet each man maintained control over his wife and family through tradition, intimidation, and violence. Fathers instilled in sons pride and independence; mothers trained daughters to be industrious and subservient to men. Insisting upon limited government, they personally attacked anyone who challenged enjoyment of their property, sometimes banding together in vigilante groups.

Waves of evangelicalism that swept over the colonies from the late 1730s to the 1780s dissolved some of these cultural differences. Starting in New England in the 1730s, they spread to the Middle Colonies in the 1740s and to the South in the 1760s and 1770s. Evangelical preachers insisted upon the spiritual equality of all people, whatever their origin, class, race, or gender. All could participate in the direct, experiential religion they mandated. Ordinary people — small farmers in the Chesapeake, urban craftsmen (masters and journeymen), blacks — interpreted spiritual equality in secular terms, allowing the free people among them to contest the hegemony of the wealthy ruling class of merchants and great planters. Widespread participation in evangelical religion provided ordinary rural Americans with a common language, thereby mitigating differences between ethnic groups.

Once whites had expropriated millions of acres of Indian land, vast areas were open to whites for settlement. By the early eighteenth century, farm families, the majority of colonists, came to expect land ownership. Out of this expectation, a yeoman ideology developed throughout the colonies. Land provided farmers with a social and political identity. Small landowners insisted upon the right to secure land tenure, arguing that they had earned ownership through their own labor. This homestead ethic was sustained in a series of conflicts that covered nearly every colony from New York to South Carolina between the 1730s and the 1770s. Whenever landlords, creditors, or venal colonial officeholders challenged the farmer's title, insisted upon early collection of debts, raised taxes, or failed to protect them from Indians or bandits, one of these conflicts resulted.

Notwithstanding continuing differences and the persistence of colonial loyalties, a high culture that transcended local peculiarities began to develop in the early eighteenth century. This high culture was predicated upon the rise of hereditary fortunes in every colony and the sustained dominance of these families in high political office. Men of wealth educated their sons at colonial colleges or in England, where students not only met their peers from other colonies but gained a taste for the writings, theater, and consumption patterns of wealthy English families. They made sure their daughters knew all the genteel female skills, from music to sewing. Thus the rich became "cultivated," building large houses, adorning their homes with the most fashionable furnishings, holding genteel assemblies, and patronizing the arts. Wherever a gentleman traveled in the colonies, he was sure to find similarly cultivated men.

The cultures of early America were complex. By the mid-eighteenth century class similarities among farmers and gentlemen pointed toward consolidated class cultures. But ethnic differences, transformed by varying economic uses colonists made of the American environment, persisted. American farmers continued to grow different crops with different forms of labor; women gained some rights in the North, but none in the South. Regional differences, within class cultures, would have a profound effect on American politics, leading ultimately to civil war.

David Hackett Fischer, *Albion's Seed: Four British Folkways in America* (1989); Carolyn Merchant, *Ecological Revolutions: Nature, Gender, and Science in New England* (1989).

ALLAN KULIKOFF

See also Chesapeake Colonies; Childhood; Family; Great Awakening; Indians; Literature; Middle Colonies; Music; New England Colonies; Painting and Sculpture; Slavery; Southern Colonies; Theater.

COLONIAL ECONOMY

The American colonial economy was export-driven, although by far the largest share of output was consumed internally. English merchant-capitalists financed the settlement of American colonies, hoping that they would gain profits from their investments. Notwithstanding the English navigation laws, which attempted to ensure the profits of English capital by restricting American manufacturing and mandating the markets for exports of colonial crops, colonists sought self-sufficiency, not only growing most of their own food but making many of the crude tools they used in production. Colonial economic development should be seen as the result of both foreign commerce and dynamically growing local economies.

Joint stock companies, founded by English merchants and landlords, financed the initial conquest of New England and the Chesapeake colonies. Expecting profits from the riches of the New World, these investors wound up merely paying the colonists' bills. Ultimately, after several decades of experimentation, colonists discovered that agricultural goods (corn, wheat, tobacco, rice, indigo, naval stores) were in great demand in England and Europe. By the mid-seventeenth century, trade under England's umbrella was mutually beneficial: the English navy protected colonial commerce, and colonists gained a guaranteed market in England and access to English and Scottish credit and manufactured goods; the English gained markets for manufactured goods, profits from the sale of colonial staples on the Continent, and interest payments on the credit they extended.

Although a majority of free and indentured white colonial migrants came from towns (where they had been artisans and wage laborers), the colonies were overwhelmingly agricultural. As many as four-fifths of all colonists, including their families, servants, and slaves, were farmers. Most of the rest provided such essential services for farm communities as shopkeeping, blacksmithing, or carpentry. Such behavior suggests that urban people sought the independence that farming entailed. At first, however, there was remarkably little land available to colonists to farm. During the seventeenth century, the Indian "menace" restricted quantities of land available for exploitation, but after disease and warfare decimated Indian populations, millions of "widowed" acres awaited cultivation.

A few towns developed in the eighteenth century — Boston, New York, Philadelphia, Charleston — but they served mostly to collect agricultural goods from the countryside and disperse English manufactured goods to farmers. Such commercial activity, bounded by rural needs, not only employed merchants but also such artisans as coopers and shipbuilders. As trade grew, town populations increased, and the internal life of towns (newspapers, government, petty shopkeepers) rose as well. But since most manufacturing and credit came from England, towns stayed small. Philadelphia, the largest town, and its suburbs counted less than forty thousand people on the eve of the Revolution.

Each colonial region developed its own peculiar economy. Staple export economies, using unfree indentured or slave labor, developed in the southern colonies. Booming tobacco prices in the 1620s led Virginia planters to export the crop, and production spread throughout the Chesapeake region (Maryland, Virginia, and adjacent North Carolina) before the end of the century. Notwithstanding lower prices and slow diversification of crops, most planters in that region still exported tobacco on the eve of the Revolution. After experimenting with livestock production and naval stores, planters in coastal South Carolina (perhaps aided by the skills of their slaves) took up rice cultivation, developing large plantations that persisted through the colonial era. Farmers in southern mountains and valleys, however, produced mostly grains and livestock, and entered the export economy only gradually.

The northern colonies developed more diversified economies, relying less upon the export of staples. Northern frontier settlers engaged in the fur trade, but that trade diminished rapidly because of overhunting. Although some New England farmers exported grain and livestock, many could barely feed themselves and their families. New Englanders therefore turned to alternative occupations, trading with the West Indies and developing vigorous fishing, small manufacturing, and shipbuilding industries. Farmers in the Mid-Atlantic, in contrast, sent flour and grain (wheat, corn) to the West Indies in great quantities from the beginning of colonization, thereby encouraging the growth of Philadelphia and New York. Nonetheless, many of these farmers participated in grain commodity markets only in occasional years of high prices until the 1760s and 1770s, when wars and crop failures in Europe opened new markets in southern Europe for grain, enticing farmers to greater market production.

Farm operators relied heavily upon their families for labor. While fathers and older sons cleared land and planted, cultivated, and harvested grain or other staples, mothers and older daughters operated the dairy and vegetable gardens. The greater the level of staple production, the higher the likelihood that farm operators had access to labor beyond the family. The great majority of farm families in New England owned few slaves and infrequently hired wage laborers, but wealthy men in the Mid-Atlantic colonies (including Quakers before the 1770s) owned slaves and indentured servants in some numbers. Although Chesapeake planters at first used English and Irish indentured servants, by the early eighteenth century a significant (and increasing) minority of southern tobacco planters and nearly all rice planters owned slaves.

Notwithstanding the importance of international market exchange to the colonies, farm families, especially in the North, invented a complex system of local "gift" exchange, which sheltered them, to a degree, from the vagaries of the market. Farm women and farm men traded labor for goods or goods for goods (fieldwork for corn, mutual help with the harvest, eggs for wool, weaving for spinning), expecting eventual repayment in kind, but charging no interest. Such neighborliness permitted households to procure food and cloth that they could not produce themselves. Families with insufficient resources to participate in such exchange networks had to sell their labor or personal goods to feed and clothe themselves.

The American colonies, affected by the vagaries of the North Atlantic economy, experienced booms and busts, much like England. Nonetheless, the colonial economy grew cumulatively at a slow rate. Starting with few possessions, typical colonials owned goods worth $1,150 (1976 dollars) in 1650. After a century of slow growth (.3–.4 percent annually), average colonists owned property valued at over $1,500; a quarter of a century later, after faster growth (.5 percent), per capita wealth reached almost $1,800.

Average growth rates and income and wealth levels obscure both increased prosperity and great poverty among Americans. Between two-thirds and three-quarters of white male farmers owned the land they cultivated; they and their families enjoyed not only the fruits of their labors but progressively higher levels of consumption of consumer goods (amenities like ceramic plates and knives and forks) over the eighteenth century. But many other families were poor, and nearly a quarter of all Americans were enslaved and consumed very little. Moreover, inequality in property ownership among free people had been high since the outset of settlement, and probably grew somewhat more concentrated in older regions over the eighteenth century, with the wealthiest tenth of the population owning between one-third and two-thirds of the total wealth.

Alice Hanson Jones, *Wealth of a Nation to Be: The American Colonies on the Eve of the Revolution* (1980); John J. McCusker and Russell R. Menard, *The Economy of British America, 1607–1789* (1985).

ALLAN KULIKOFF

See also America in the British Empire; Indentured Servitude; Plantation System; Slavery; Tobacco.

COLONIAL GOVERNMENT AND POLITICS

During the last two decades of the sixteenth century, the English Crown granted various proprietors and chartered companies authority to establish colonies in America. These grants formed the basis for an extraordinary devolution of political authority from the English Crown to separate polities in the New World. In the following century, this process led to the creation on the North American continent of twelve colonies stretching from South Carolina north to New Hampshire. In 1713, the British wrested Nova Scotia from the French, and in the early 1730s a group of government-sponsored trustees established Georgia.

Except for New Hampshire and Nova Scotia, both of which were started under the direct supervision of the Crown, these colonies were private ventures little supervised by the English. The welter of institutions devised by their sponsors to govern the colonies varied enormously. By the late seventeenth century, however, most of their political systems were roughly similar. This development was largely the result of the gradual conversion, between 1624 and 1729, of the majority of the colonies into royal provinces, but it also occurred in the private colonies — the three proprietaries, Maryland, Delaware, and Pennsylvania, and the two corporate colonies, Connecticut and Rhode Island. This pattern was clearly derived from English political institutions. The governorship, the colonial equivalent of the Crown, was filled by appointees, except in Connecticut and Rhode Island, where it was elective. As the chief representatives of Britain, governors were responsible for enforcing British trade laws and carrying out other directives. As viceroys of the Crown, they were invested with its vast prerogative powers, powers that in theory extended well beyond those exercised by the Crown itself in Britain following the restrictions imposed after the Glorious Revolution of 1688–1689.

As chief executives, governors were responsible for executing colonial laws, administering justice, and appointing most administrative and judicial officers. As commanders in chief, they were responsible for provincial defense and diplomatic relations with the Indians and the other colonies. As one of three branches of the legislature, they had veto power over all laws and took an active role in the legislative process. Finally, they held the exclusive power to grant lands from the enormous royal or proprietary domains.

The governor's advisory councils took on the functions performed in Britain by the Privy Council and the House of Lords. Like the former, they served as an advisory body whose approval was required for most executive actions, and in a few colonies they acted as a superior court. Like the latter, they constituted in every colony except Pennsylvania after 1701 an upper house of the legislature whose consent was necessary for the passage of laws. In three colonies these bodies were elected by the lower houses of the legislature. Elsewhere, they were composed of usually twelve royal or proprietary appointees.

The lower houses of the colonial assemblies were the equivalents of the British House of Commons. Composed of elected representatives from local constituencies, they were the primary instruments for the expression of political demands. Though limited in the royal colonies and Pennsylvania by the requirement that all statutes be sent to Britain for review, their lawmaking powers were as extensive in their spheres as was that of the Commons in Britain, and their consent was required for all taxes.

Variations among colonies were greatest at the level of local government. Everywhere, in the English fashion, justices of the peace operating through local courts had primary responsibility for the administration of justice. For handling other areas of local administration, three main systems emerged. From North Carolina north to New York and in Nova Scotia, the county was the central unit of local government and was administered by county courts composed of justices of the peace appointed by the governors. In South Carolina and Georgia, the parish was the main component and was overseen by parish officers, all of whom were appointed by governors. In the four New England colonies, the town was the primary local unit and was administered by selectmen and other officials elected (usually annually) by a town meeting.

Colonists expected remarkably little from government. Budgets and taxes were low; paid full-time officials few; civil, judicial, and police establishments small, part-time, and unprofessional; and military establishments temporary. Hence, politics provided little scope for the active involvement of citizens. Outside New England, where some town offices were elective as were some provincial offices in Connecticut and Rhode Island, only representatives to the lower houses were not appointed, and the franchise was limited to independent property-owning adult males. Because property was relatively easily available, however, a large majority (up to 80 to 90 percent) of free white males in most colonies could expect to acquire enough property to meet suffrage requirements.

For several generations in most colonies, politics was relatively primitive. Leadership and institutional structures were weak and undefined, levels of political expertise and socialization low, and political consciousness undeveloped. Under such conditions, public life was volatile, and would-be leaders jockeyed with one another for power, wealth, and prestige. In a few places for brief periods, this primitive politics of competition resulted in the triumph of restrictive oligarchies.

Beginning in the 1720s and 1730s, these primitive forms gave way to traditional modes more like those of Britain. The hallmarks of this new type of politics were the muting of fundamental issues that divided the body politic, the dominance of broad elites who were roughly representative of or sensitive to the needs and interests of all important segments of free society, and the reduction of political strife to relatively low levels. In the few colonies in which these conditions could not be sustained and levels of conflict remained high, notably New York and Rhode Island, a more modern type of polity began to emerge around 1750 with the development of semipermanent political parties.

However politics developed, public life everywhere after 1720 became more settled. Levels of political socialization and consciousness rose, and institutional and leadership structures became more sharply articulated. Civil disorder was rare and tended to be confined to particular situations: when a political system failed to perform its expected functions; political leaders did not act on issues deemed important by a significant section of the population; strong contending parties disagreed over some fundamental issue, such as land titles or currency; or the traditional rights and privileges of the community seemed threatened.

For the most part, however, the limited coercive powers of colonial polities, their small scale, their extreme susceptibility to constituent demands, a generally high degree of constituent trust in leaders, and a new level of civility in the public arena all helped to channel conflict into publicly acceptable forms. These factors promoted a conception of politics as an accommodative process in which the broad body of the people normally deferred to the leadership and decisions of an increasingly expert community of experienced elite politicians.

Bernard Bailyn, *The Origins of American Politics* (1968); Leonard W. Labaree, *Royal Government in America* (1930).

JACK P. GREENE

See also America in the British Empire; Chesapeake Colonies; Middle Colonies; New England Colonies; Southern Colonies.

COLONIALISM, BRITISH

See America in the British Empire.

COLONIAL WARS

In the late seventeenth century, North America was dominated by England, France, and Spain. For the next century and beyond, these European powers were repeatedly engaged in war, and each time war broke out, their colonies in America were swept into the conflict, as were the Indians, on one side or the other.

Despite the fact that the European settlements in America were separated in most places by vast areas of wilderness, Spanish, English, and French colonists mistrusted and feared one another, often with good reason. Canadian and New England fishermen competed on the Grand Banks in the North Atlantic, as did colonial fur traders and their Indian allies everywhere from Spanish Florida to Hudson Bay. English Protestants detested the French and Spanish because they were Catholics, and they tended to blame them for their troubles with the Indians, usually *without* good reason.

Nevertheless, all but the last of the colonial struggles were small-scale, tiny in comparison to the conflicts in Europe that triggered them. The English colonists tended to name the wars after their monarchs; these were other people's wars, not their own. They named the European War of the League of Augsburg (1689–1697) King William's War and the War of the Spanish Succession (1702–1713) Queen Anne's War. King George's War (1740–1748) was their name for the War of Jenkins' Ear against Spain and the War of the Austrian Succession against France.

The fighting in these conflicts consisted mainly of surprise attacks on frontier settlements and raids on strong points such as Port Royal in Nova Scotia, Fort Louisbourg on Cape Breton Island off the mouth of the St. Lawrence River, and St. Augustine and other Spanish posts in Florida. The colonies were mere pawns in these wars; though casualties at times were heavy, relatively few Americans participated in the fighting and those who did were militiamen, not regular army soldiers. Colonists had almost no influence on the peace settlements. For example, the New Englanders who captured Fort Louisbourg during King George's War were dismayed when the British returned the fort to

France under the terms of the Treaty of Aix-la-Chapelle.

The French and Indian War (1754–1763) was a different affair — different in size, in how it started, in how it was fought, and in its significance. By 1750 fur traders and land speculators in Pennsylvania and Virginia were becoming interested in the lands beyond the Appalachian Mountains, a region long claimed by France. When the French built a line of forts south from Lake Erie to the headwaters of the Ohio River in what is now western Pennsylvania, Governor Robert Dinwiddie of Virginia sent a young surveyor named George Washington to protest. Washington returned in January 1754 with word that the French refused to withdraw. Dinwiddie then sent him back with 150 armed men, but this little army was defeated by a larger French force.

The British government then sent 1,400 Redcoats commanded by Gen. Edward Braddock to Virginia to drive the French out of the disputed territory. In July 1755, however, Braddock's army, accompanied by a small colonial force under Washington, was ambushed by the French and Indians in the forest south of Fort Duquesne. Braddock was killed and the remnants of his expedition driven back into Virginia. What the historian Lawrence Henry Gipson named the Great War for the Empire had begun. In 1756 the conflict spread to Europe and eventually to Asia, with the British, in alliance with Prussia, opposing Austria and Spain as well as France.

In North America the war went badly for the Anglo-American armies at first, despite the fact that they vastly outnumbered the French. The tide turned, however, after William Pitt became virtual prime minister of Great Britain in 1757. Realizing that control of an entire continent was at stake, Pitt committed masses of troops, powerful fleets, and huge sums to the contest, and he found and swiftly promoted talented officers, most notably James Wolfe and Jeffrey Amherst, to top commands. Wolfe and Amherst recaptured Fort Louisbourg in the summer of 1758, and the next year the British mounted a three-pronged drive that resulted in the capture of Fort Niagara in the west, Fort

Crown Point at the southern end of Lake Champlain in New York, and Quebec on the St. Lawrence. In July 1760 Montreal was captured and the last French resistance in Canada collapsed.

British victories elsewhere in the world followed and in 1763 what was known by Europeans as the Seven Years' War ended with the signing of the Peace of Paris. Canada and all of North America east of the Mississippi River, including Spanish Florida, became British territory.

For the English colonists the triumph appeared to open a new era of peace and prosperity. Gratitude to the British was universal. British soldiers had borne the brunt of the fighting, and Britain had paid most of the cost of maintaining their own troops and the large numbers of colonials who took up arms. A Massachusetts town was named after General Amherst, and Fort Duquesne, the capture of which had frustrated Washington and Braddock in the 1750s, was renamed Fort Pitt.

How, within a decade, this universal spirit of admiration and loyalty was replaced by scorn and revolution has long been a subject of historical investigation. Changes in British policy, particularly Parliament's attempt to tax the colonies, was surely the chief cause of the change. But the roots of the break can be located in the relations of British and American soldiers during the war. As Fred Anderson points out in *A People's Army,* a work based on diaries kept by American soldiers during the war, these relationships were far from harmonious. The Americans admired the courage and professional skills of the Redcoats, but they were shocked by their profanity and lewdness and horrified by the imperiousness and brutality of their officers, who could condemn a man to death for refusing to obey an order and who thought nothing of administering hundreds of lashes to soldiers caught gambling. (By provincial law no Massachusetts soldier could be sentenced to more than thirty lashes.) When Patriot leaders denounced British tyranny after the Stamp Act and in later crises, ex-soldiers found the charge easy to believe.

For their part British officers characterized colonial troops as dirty, cowardly, and disorganized, "the world's worst soldiers." They used them mostly for fatigue duty and as camp guards. This belief explains why, for example, Gen. Thomas Gage assumed that "rebels" would run at the very sight of Redcoat bayonets and marched his men in close ranks against entrenched Patriots at the Battle of Bunker Hill in 1775.

Such opinions reflected the degree to which English and colonial values and traditions had diverged, and they suggest that separation of the two societies was not merely possible but probably inevitable.

Fred Anderson, *A People's Army* (1984); H. H. Peckham, *The Colonial Wars* (1963).

JOHN A. GARRATY

See also America in the British Empire; Indians; Seven Years' War.

COLONIES

See America in the British Empire; Chesapeake Colonies; French and Spanish Settlements; Middle Colonies; New England Colonies; Southern Colonies.

COLUMBIAN EXCHANGE

Upon the arrival of the Europeans to North America in 1492, there began a massive transformation in the global ecosystem resulting from the exchange of flora, fauna, and disease between the Old World and the New. This interchange of native life-forms was called the Columbian Exchange by historian Alfred Crosby in his book of that title.

Centuries of geographic isolation had led to the divergent evolution of flora and fauna in North America and Europe. In the New World, Europeans encountered indigenous plant foods, often cultivated by Native Americans, such as potatoes, beans, squash, and maize (corn), probably the world's most important cereal crop. These plants carried back to Europe so enriched nutrition in the Old World that they stimulated major population explosions. To America, Europeans introduced crops like wheat, rice, bananas, sugar, and wine grapes, many serving as cash crops for export by the colonists. Europeans also brought a number of domesticated animals to the New World, including horses, cattle, pigs, sheep, and fowl, producing mixed results for the Indians since the animals destroyed their croplands but also served as valuable sources of food, clothing, and energy.

Disease was another dimension of the Columbian Exchange, with catastrophic consequences for Native Americans who for centuries were an isolated population and thus lacked adequate immunities for diseases introduced by Europeans. Eruptive fevers, like smallpox and measles, proved deadly and often wiped out over half of entire tribes. The European microbe was the ultimate conqueror of America, more than any act of war. In turn, Europeans fell prey to the New World disease of syphilis, generating widespread social and biological effects.

The long-term consequences of the Columbian Exchange were mixed. It created enormous increases in food production and human populations, but it also destroyed the ecological stability of vast areas, increased erosion of the land, and led to the extinction of many life-forms.

See also Indians.

COMMERCE

See Economic Growth; International Commerce.

COMMITTEES OF CORRESPONDENCE

Committees of Correspondence were the American colonies' first institution for maintaining communication with one another. They were organized in the decade before the Revolution, when the deteriorating relationship with Great Britain made it increasingly important for the colonies to share ideas and information. In 1764, Boston formed the earliest Committee of Correspondence, writing to other colonies to encourage united opposition to Britain's recent stiffening of customs enforcement and prohibition of American paper money. The following year New York formed a similar committee to keep the other colonies notified of its actions in resisting the Stamp Act. This correspondence led to the holding of the Stamp Act Congress in New York City. Nine of the colonies sent representatives, but no permanent intercolonial structure was established. In 1772, a new Boston Committee of Correspondence was organized, this time to communicate with all the towns in the province, as well as with "the World," about the recent announcement that Massachusetts's governor and judges would hereafter be paid by — and hence accountable to — the Crown rather than the colonial legislature. More than half of the province's 260 towns formed committees and replied to Boston's communications.

In March 1773, the Virginia House of Burgesses proposed that each colonial legislature appoint a standing committee for intercolonial correspondence. Within a year, nearly all had joined the network, and more committees were formed at the town and county levels. The exchanges that followed helped build a sense of solidarity, as common grievances were discussed and common responses agreed upon. When the First Continental Congress was held in September 1774, it represented the logical evolution of the intercolonial communication that had begun with the Committees of Correspondence.

See also Revolution.

COMMON SENSE

The political pamphlet *Common Sense* was published in 1776 calling for American colonists to rebel against the British monarchy and proclaim their independence. Its author was Thomas Paine who had recently arrived in Philadelphia from England. Called by historian Bernard Bailyn "the most brilliant pamphlet written during the American Revolution, and one of the most brilliant pamphlets ever written in the English language," it helped persuade the majority of colonists, who had hoped for a peaceful resolution of differences with England, to take the path of revolution.

Paine used the liberal ideals of John Locke and radical criticisms of aristocratic government to press the case for liberty. The colonists had a

mission of greatness, he said, to rebel against "a violent abuse of power" and throw off tyranny. "The cause of America is in a great measure the cause of all mankind. . . . We have it in our power to begin the world over again. . . . The birth-day of a new world is at hand." The pamphlet also demonstrated the practical advantages to the colonists of independence from the mother country. It had a phenomenal sale of some 120,000 copies in the first three months and 500,000 copies in 1776.

While a soldier in the revolutionary army, Paine followed *Common Sense* with *The Crisis,* a series of inspiring political pamphlets. The first began with the famous lines: "These are the times that try men's souls: The summer soldier and the sunshine patriot will, in this crisis, shrink from the service of his country; but he that stands it now, deserves the love and thanks of man and woman. Tyranny, like hell, is not easily conquered."

See also Paine, Thomas; Revolution.

COMMONWEALTH V. HUNT

In *Commonwealth* v. *Hunt* (March 1842), Chief Justice Lemuel Shaw of the Massachusetts Supreme Court held that it was not inherently illegal for workers to organize a union or try to compel recognition of that union by means of a strike.

Three years earlier, the Boston Journeymen Bootmakers' Society had called a strike against all employers who insisted on hiring nonunion bootmakers. Although members were not charged with violence or with intending to destroy the employers' businesses, seven of the union leaders were indicted for criminal conspiracy. All were found guilty in city court in October 1840. On appeal, Chief Justice Shaw reversed the municipal ruling, on the ground that seeking to induce one's fellow workers to join a union was not illegal unless the methods used to accomplish that aim were unlawful. Shaw held that, since no contracts were broken, the bootmakers' refusal to work for particular employers was simply the legal exercise of their "acknowledged right to contract with others for their labor," even if it might have the indirect effect of impoverishing those employers.

Later judges were more prepared than Shaw to find unions' methods for enforcing recognition to be illegal, but the *Commonwealth* v. *Hunt* decision had set an important precedent in establishing the concept that seeking to compel recognition of a union did not in itself constitute a conspiracy.

See also Labor.

COMMUNISM

See Anticommunism; Cold War; Communist Party; Soviet-American Relations, 1917–1945.

COMMUNIST PARTY

Following the Bolshevik Revolution in Russia, the Socialist party, then the largest institution on the American left, split into factions. The Communist party emerged as an organization of those who identified with the new Soviet state and wished to adopt Leninist forms of organization — a tightly knit, secretive body following an ideology dictated by its leadership. Although it became involved in a number of labor conflicts, such as the textile workers' strike in Gastonia, North Carolina, the Communist party for most of the 1920s was a tiny sect, isolated from the mainstream of American life.

The Great Depression changed this, as the party became an active participant in movements for unemployment relief, civil rights for blacks, and union organizing. In 1935, as part of Joseph Stalin's support of the fight against fascism, the world Communist movement, including the party in the United States, began to cooperate with the noncommunist liberal left. As part of this Popular Front strategy, the party cultivated a broader appeal, achieving considerable influence and popularity. But the Popular Front ended with the signing of the Nazi-Soviet nonaggression pact in 1939.

Once the United States and the Soviet Union became allies in World War II, the party's fortunes revived, and it reached a peak membership of about 100,000. But the outbreak of the cold war in the postwar period led to the stigmatizing of Communists as domestic agents of a foreign enemy. During the McCarthy period, the party became the subject of intense repression. Many members in unions, universities, and the labor movement lost their jobs. In 1949, the Justice Department prosecuted the eleven top leaders of the party for violation of the Smith Act of 1940, which made it illegal for anyone "to teach and advocate the overthrow and destruction of the United States government by force and violence." After a long trial all eleven were convicted on October 14 and sentenced to prison terms. Their convictions were upheld by the Supreme Court in the case of *Dennis et al.* v. *United States* (1951), with two justices dissenting because of the free-speech issues involved. Another 126 members of the party — who composed the second level of leadership — were then prosecuted also. Dozens of others who were aliens were rounded up for deportation. With its leaders in prison and other members subjected to various degrees of persecution, the party was on the defensive and many of those left in its ranks went underground.

Nikita Khrushchev's 1956 speech revealing Stalin's crimes further weakened the party, leading to an exodus of many who had remained members during the McCarthy years. When political radicalism revived in the 1960s, the party had little to do with it, although some individuals were active in the civil rights and student movements.

See also Anticommunism; Radicalism.

COMPROMISE OF 1850

Divisions over slavery in territory gained in the Mexican War were resolved in the Compromise of 1850. It consisted of laws admitting California as a free state, creating Utah and New Mexico territories with the question of slavery in each to be determined by popular sovereignty, settling a Texas–New Mexico boundary dispute in the former's favor, ending the slave trade in Washington, D.C., and making it easier for southerners to recover fugitive slaves. The compromise was the last major involvement in national affairs of Senators Henry Clay of Kentucky, Daniel Webster of Massachusetts, and John C. Calhoun of South Carolina, all of whom had had exceptional careers in the Senate. Calhoun died the same year, and Clay and Webster two years later.

At first, Clay introduced an omnibus bill covering these measures. Calhoun attacked the plan and demanded that the North cease its attempts to limit slavery. By backing Clay in a speech delivered on March 7, Webster antagonized his onetime abolitionist supporters. Senator William H. Seward of New York opposed compromise and earned an undeserved reputation for radicalism by claiming that a "higher law" than the Constitution required the checking of slavery. President Zachary Taylor opposed the compromise, but his death on July 9 made procompromise vice president Millard Fillmore of New York president. Nevertheless, the Senate defeated the omnibus bill.

Senator Stephen A. Douglas of Illinois then split the omnibus proposal into individual bills so that congressmen could abstain or vote on each, depending on their interests. They all passed, and Fillmore signed them. The compromise enabled Congress to avoid sectional and slavery issues for several years.

See also Abolitionist Movement; Calhoun, John C.; Clay, Henry; Douglas, Stephen A.; Slavery; Webster, Daniel.

COMPROMISE OF 1877

In order to settle the contested 1876 election, a bargain was struck that also ended Reconstruction. Democrat Samuel J. Tilden led Republican Rutherford B. Hayes in popular votes, and 184–165 in the electoral college, but fraud and violence in South Carolina, Florida, and Louisiana, and questions about an Oregon elector's eligibility, left 20 electoral votes in doubt. Splitting over each state's contradictory returns, the Democratic House and Republican Senate created a fifteen-member electoral commission of ten congressmen and five Supreme Court justices, divided by party, with one independent, Justice David Davis. When Davis declined to serve, Re-

publican Joseph Bradley replaced him, and the commission gave Hayes all 20 votes, prompting a Democratic filibuster.

Representatives of the candidates and parties then negotiated a compromise through correspondence and at a meeting at Washington's Wormley House. The South would accept Hayes's election, back Republican James A. Garfield for House Speaker, and protect black rights; Republicans would provide federal aid for internal improvements, patronage, and, especially, home rule. But Garfield was defeated for Speaker, the government failed to subsidize improvements, and Hayes dispensed patronage and followed existing policy by removing federal troops from the South. The final southern Republican governments, all in the disputed states, collapsed, leading to the Democratic Solid South and violence and discrimination toward blacks.

See also Elections: 1876; Reconstruction.

CONFEDERATE STATES OF AMERICA

Formed in February 1861, the Confederate States of America was a republic composed of eleven Southern states that seceded from the Union in order to preserve slavery, states' rights, and political liberty for whites. Its conservative government, with Mississippian Jefferson Davis as president, sought a peaceful separation, but the United States refused to acquiesce in the secession. The war that ensued started at Fort Sumter, South Carolina, on April 12, 1861, and lasted four years. It cost the South nearly 500,000 men killed or wounded out of a population of 9 million (including 3 million slaves) and $5 billion in treasure.

The Confederacy's eastern military fortunes went well for the first two years, with major victories at First Manassas (Bull Run), "Stonewall" Jackson's Valley Campaign, and the Seven Days' Battles, where Gen. Robert E. Lee took command of the main eastern army in June 1862 and cleared Virginia of federal troops by September. His invasion of Maryland was checked at Sharpsburg (Antietam) in mid-September, and he returned to Virginia, where he badly defeated federal forces at Fredericksburg and Chancellorsville. The main western Confederate forces — commanded by Generals Albert Sidney Johnston, P. G. T. Beauregard, and Braxton Bragg — suffered defeats at Forts Henry and Donelson and Shiloh in Tennessee, and at Corinth, Mississippi, but they held that flank through 1862.

Davis formed his government at the first Confederate capital in Montgomery, Alabama. The Confederacy's Permanent Constitution provided for presidential item veto, debating seats for cabinet members, and six-year terms for the president and vice president (the president was ineligible for successive terms); it prohibited the foreign slave trade and forbade Congress from levying a protective tariff, giving bounties, or making appropriations for internal improvements.

After initial problems, Davis's government grew stronger as he learned to use executive power to consolidate control of the armed forces and manpower distribution. But some Southern governors resisted Davis's centralization and tried to keep their men and resources at home. Although Davis used authority effectively, the insistence on preserving states' rights plagued him constantly. Vice President Alexander H. Stephens, an early dissident, for example, sulked in his native Georgia and finally urged its secession from the Confederacy.

But nothing gave the government more trouble than its poverty. There was only $27 million worth of specie in the Confederacy, and money remained scarce. A federal blockade gradually shrank Southern foreign trade and drained financial reserves. Christopher G. Memminger, treasury secretary, followed conservative policies. A campaign to raise funds through a domestic loan in February 1861 lagged; a $50 million loan drive launched in May did little better. Finally Congress resorted to a "produce loan," which allowed planters to pledge produce as security for bonds. Although initially popular, this expedient also failed.

The next resort, paper money, stimulated inflation, and on April 24, 1863, Congress passed the toughest tax law ever seen in the South. Rates were increased, an income tax was authorized, and a profits tax was imposed on farm products; farmers and planters were subjected to a tax-in-kind, which required them to contribute one-tenth of their annual crop yield to the government. This unpopular law did not solve the financial problems, however. In mid-1863, Memminger proposed taking one-third of the currency out of circulation. Congress resisted, but finally, in February 1864, it passed a funding act that created a brief drop in inflation, which soon yielded to a price-and-money spiral that presaged bankruptcy. An 1863 foreign loan for $15 million through the Erlanger Bank in France realized only about $9 million in purchasing power.

Then the government resorted to such desperate measures as impressment of private produce, livestock, machinery, and transportation equipment, which brought limited relief to the armies but endless enmity for what was seen as a "despotic" government. The failure to tax land, cotton, and slaves earned cries of "a rich man's war and a poor man's fight" and sapped morale behind the lines.

The Confederacy never won the loyalty of the black population. Some free blacks volunteered for Southern ranks but were rejected. Federal invaders liberated slaves, and fear of insurrections sapped Southern strength in the last two war years.

Keeping the ranks of the armies filled became difficult as casualties mounted and enthusiasm faded. In April 1862, Congress, on the advice of Davis, passed the first draft law in American history, which took into Confederate service all white men between eighteen and thirty-five. Liberal exemptions (including one white exemption for every twenty slaves owned) weakened the law. But the courts upheld it and most people accepted it as necessary, an attitude that persisted even after February 1864, when the age limits were extended to seventeen and fifty and substitutes were prohibited. In March 1865 blacks finally were enrolled in Confederate ranks, but very few served.

Taxation, impressment, and conscription — these were the hallmarks of a tough administration. President Davis pursued centralization much as Abraham Lincoln did — laissez-faire policies could not win a modern war. The lessons learned in management, sacrifice, fortitude, and logistics would change the South permanently.

Supplying and moving the armed forces became the main work of many in the South, and new methods of procurement, storage, and distribution were developed. Railroads were essential to the mass movement of men and matériel, of ordnance and medicine, and of civilian refugees from occupied areas. Congress passed laws nationalizing rail lines, sequestering space on blockade runners, and controlling commerce. Industrial development had lagged in the antebellum South, and now Congress encouraged industrialization by siphoning manpower and money to companies producing war goods. A minor industrial miracle occurred in the Confederacy: a nation with minuscule manufacturing capacity acquired foundries, powder works, rolling mills, arsenals enough to sustain nearly a million troops and ships enough to scare American merchantmen. The chief of ordnance, Gen. Josiah Gorgas, a Pennsylvanian and genius of logistics, supplied Rebel munitions to the end.

Gorgas, an advocate of blockade running, oversaw the building of small, fast ships capable of eluding federal coastal patrols. Blockade running was a very successful venture: at least 600,000 rifles were imported, plus large quantities of cannon, saltpeter, lead, clothing, coffee, and medicines. Highly profitable, blockade running produced heroes, villains, and millionaires — and sustained the Rebels.

Davis's foreign policy centered on gaining recognition by Great Britain and France. Napoleon III wanted a Confederate victory but hesitated to act without the British. Many Britons sympathized with the Confederates, but the working class supported Lincoln's Emancipation Proclamation. Judah P. Benjamin, Confederate secretary of state, hoped that an embargo on "King Cotton" would force help from textile-producing countries. But each time recognition was almost at hand, military reverses chilled prospects. The issue remained with the Rebel soldiers: when they won, independence came close; when they lost, nothing else mattered.

And they lost almost steadily after the first terrible week of July 1863. Defeats at Gettysburg and Vicksburg cost fifty thousand men and seventy thousand arms. After that week, long retreats began in the East through the Wilderness, Spotsylvania, Cold Harbor, Petersburg; in the West from Chickamauga, Lookout Mountain/Missionary Ridge, Atlanta, to Franklin and Nashville, Tennessee, which led to Lee's surrender at Appomattox and Joseph E. Johnston's at Durham Station, North Carolina.

Sustained for a while by Davis's offensive-defensive strategy, Confederate armies were finally defeated by attrition, the country behind them exhausted and drained. The surprise is not that they lost but that they persisted for four arduous years.

E. Merton Coulter, *The Confederate States of America, 1861–1865* (1950); Frank E. Vandiver, *Their Tattered Flags: The Epic of the Confederacy* (1975).

FRANK E. VANDIVER

See also Civil War.

CONFEDERATION, ARTICLES OF

See Articles of Confederation.

CONGRESS

See House of Representatives; Senate.

CONGRESS, LIBRARY OF

See Library of Congress.

CONGRESSES, CONTINENTAL

See Continental Congresses.

CONGRESS OF INDUSTRIAL ORGANIZATIONS

The Congress of Industrial Organizations (CIO) was founded in response to the failure of the American Federation of Labor (AFL) to organize unskilled workers in mass production industries. At the 1934 AFL convention, a move to organize these workers lost when only 30 percent of the members voted for the measure. After failing again in 1935, John L. Lewis, head of the United Mine Workers, Sidney Hillman, leader of the Amalgamated Clothing Workers, David Dubinsky of the International Ladies Garment Workers Union, and representatives of the Textile Workers and the Typographers unions formed the Committee for Industrial Organization. It was expelled from the AFL in 1936 and became the CIO in 1938.

The National Industrial Recovery Act of 1933, section 7A, which gave workers the right to organize and bargain collectively, provided an impetus to unionization in the 1930s. The CIO's major organizing tactic was the sit-down strike, which was quite successful: CIO membership reached 2,654,000 by 1940.

John L. Lewis was the first president of the CIO. Responding to the passage of the Taft-Hartley Act in 1947 and the election of a Republican president in 1952, the AFL and the CIO merged in 1955.

See also Labor; Lewis, John L.

CONGRESS OF RACIAL EQUALITY

The Congress of Racial Equality (CORE) was founded on the University of Chicago campus in 1942 as an outgrowth of the pacifist Fellowship of Reconciliation. For the next two decades, CORE introduced a small group of civil rights activists to the idea of achieving change through nonviolence, but during these years, its chapters were all in the North and its membership predominantly white and middle class. In 1955 CORE went into the South and provided nonviolence training to demonstrators during the Montgomery, Alabama, bus boycott. Soon thereafter, CORE hired a small staff to work in the South.

The group first drew national attention in 1960 with its active support of the sit-in movement at lunch counters that refused to serve blacks. Symbolic of the organization's new direction was the appointment in February 1961 of James Farmer, as CORE's first black national director. A few months later, CORE organized the first Freedom Ride to desegregate interstate transportation facilities. Although the riders

were attacked so brutally in Alabama that they were unable to continue, more than a thousand participants, black and white, carried on Freedom Rides during the summer.

Starting in late 1961, voter registration became the new civil rights priority, and CORE focused on Florida, Louisiana, and South Carolina. At this time many civil rights workers were beginning to feel that black political power, not integration, offered the best hope for achieving racial equality. Although CORE did not abandon its commitment to racial understanding — it was, for instance, a cosponsor of the March on Washington in August 1963 — it placed increasing emphasis on black autonomy. Pessimism about integration was reinforced by the wave of beatings and murders that met the voter registration projects and by CORE's expanded work in the North, which shed new light on the depth and intransigence of racial discrimination in the United States. In early 1966, Farmer, a pacifist and longtime advocate of racial integration, was replaced as national director by Floyd McKissick, who had become committed to black separatism. Thereafter, as a primarily black organization, CORE continued to press for political and economic justice for blacks while also lending its voice to the rising antiwar movement.

See also Civil Rights Movement.

CONSCIENTIOUS OBJECTION

Conscientious objectors are those who, for political and religious reasons, oppose war. Their opposition may take several forms: refusing to serve in the military, to register for the draft, to pay war taxes, or to contribute labor and resources to any war effort.

Prior to the American Revolution, most conscientious objectors belonged to "peace" churches. Quakers, Brethren, Mennonites, Rogerenes, and Schwekenfelders — all of whom opposed war as a matter of Christian principle — were among the first European colonists of North America, and conflict between white settlers and Native Americans provided the first test in the New World of their beliefs. Members of peace churches who refused to fight or help build fortifications were persecuted by Puritans who considered war against Native Americans the "Lord's Revenge."

By the mid-1600s some colonies had exempted Quakers and other members of peace churches from military service. Other colonies, however, were less tolerant, fining or imprisoning citizens who refused to serve in militias or maintain forts. During the French and Indian War, for example, colonial governments forced them to pay for substitutes or face property confiscation.

During the American Revolution, anti-British forces expected conscientious objectors to help provision troops and raided the property of those who refused. Moreover, as the army's need for soldiers increased, some pacifists were forced into service.

During the War of 1812 American political leaders considered national conscription to supplement state militias, but Daniel Webster successfully argued before Congress that such a measure would be unconstitutional. Thus, conscription remained a matter for individual states to decide. Peace church members continued to resist military service and to refuse payment of fines or war-related taxes. As a consequence many, such as pacifists in Baltimore, had their property confiscated by local authorities.

By the 1830s peace had become a political as well as a religious issue. Such organizations as the American Peace Society and the New England Non-Resistance Society linked Christian ethics, abolition of slavery, and pacifism. In 1846, both groups led an organized campaign against the Mexican War. In his essay on civil disobedience, Henry David Thoreau, a representative of political pacifism, presented his rationale for refusing to pay war taxes, and his subsequent imprisonment became a classic example of nonviolent resistance as a means of social change.

During the Civil War, Congress enacted the first federal conscription legislation, requiring all male citizens between the ages of twenty and forty-five to serve in the military if called. The act provided no exemptions for conscientious objectors, but excused from service anyone who paid three hundred dollars. Draft riots erupted among poorer citizens, who could not afford the fee, in protest against the class bias implicit in the legislation. In July 1863 white workers in New York protested the draft by destroying the central recruiting station, factories, transportation lines, and the homes of wealthy citizens. The rioters, viewing African-Americans as the cause of the war, also attacked and killed black citizens. Similar protests erupted in the cities of Boston, Newark, Toledo, and Troy, New York. Quakers, too, objected to commutation fees and, in 1864, pressured Congress into passing the first national legislation allowing members of peace churches to perform alternative service. The law also exempted those whose beliefs forbade any form of service or commutation payment. Confederate conscription legislation initially exempted peace church members who provided substitutes or paid a fine, but these exemptions were eliminated as the need for conscripts increased. In the South, as well as the North, overzealous officers, enlistees, and civilians subjected some objectors to forced service and physical abuse.

During World War I only members of recognized peace churches were granted noncombatant alternatives to military service. Those who belonged to religious sects without a traditional antiwar stance, who opposed war for political reasons, or who refused any form of compulsory service were forcibly inducted, court-martialed, and sentenced to terms in military camps and prisons. Of the 500 objectors who were court-martialed, 17 received death sentences and 142, life terms. Although none of the death sentences were carried out and other terms were reduced, physical abuse in military camps was common. Guards subjected objectors to compulsory exercise, cold showers, solitary confinement, inadequate rations, and cruel punishment. One young man who refused to wear a uniform contracted pneumonia and died. His body, dressed in a uniform, was sent home to his parents.

The majority of World War I objectors were Quakers, Mennonites, Molokans, Seventh-Day Adventists, Jehovah's Witnesses, Brethren, and members of other peace churches. There were also smaller numbers of political objectors, including socialists, anarchists, members of the International Workers of the World, and non-aligned radicals. Social worker Jane Addams, anarchist leader Emma Goldman, and Socialist party founder Eugene Debs were outspoken supporters of conscientious objectors and of the First Amendment rights of all Americans to voice opposition to war. The government and most citizens, however, viewed all objectors as subversive radicals and silenced the antiwar position along with other dissenting voices by suspending constitutional rights to freedom of the press, speech, and assembly. Goldman, along with several thousand suspected alien "subversives," was deported without formal trial under the Alien Act of 1918. Debs, charged with violating the Espionage Act of 1917 for giving an antiwar speech, was sentenced to ten years in prison. The Espionage Act, strengthened by the Sedition Act of 1918, virtually destroyed the American Left through government-sanctioned censorship of its press and prosecution of its leadership.

During the Second World War, the Selective Training and Service Act of 1940 exempted from military service those who "by reason of religious training and belief" opposed war and mandated alternative service in work of "national importance." Objectors who accepted alternative service worked in civilian public service camps on conservation projects, staffed mental hospitals, or volunteered to be human guinea pigs in government-sponsored experiments on diet, endurance, and the transmission and control of malaria, hookworm, typhus, and infectious hepatitis. Objectors received no pay or benefits and had to rely upon families and churches for support.

Those who refused to register for the draft, opposed compulsory service, or failed the test for religious conviction were sentenced to prison. Most imprisoned objectors were Jehovah's Witnesses, but roughly a thousand were radical pacifists affiliated with the War Resisters League, the Catholic Worker movement, or the Socialist party.

Approximately four hundred African-Americans also refused to serve in the military in World War II. Some belonged to the Nation of Islam, which viewed the war as a "white man's conflict." Others refused to serve in a Jim Crow army or to fight for a country that denied basic democratic freedoms to its black citizens.

During the Vietnam War, Selective Service denied exemption to conscientious objectors whose views were "essentially political, sociological, or philosophical." But that war, unlike World War II, was widely viewed as unjust, and the number of political objectors far outnumbered those who held deep religious convictions. Moreover, objectors had a great deal of public support. By the mid-1960s, the peace movement had become a politically powerful and broad-based coalition of radical pacifists, civil rights advocates, nonpacifist anti-imperialists, liberals, and members of the traditional peace churches. This coalition not only helped objectors file for exemption but encouraged those who were denied objector status to resist induction. By the end of the war, 50,000 conscientious objectors had fled the country or assumed false identities in the United States. An estimated 250,000 never registered, and another 110,000 burned their draft cards. High levels of noncompliance with the draft, mass opposition to the war, and declining military morale ultimately forced the government to end its involvement in Vietnam.

Following the Vietnam War, many Quakers, members of other religious groups, and radical pacifist organizations such as the War Resisters League, advocated nonpayment of taxes allocated for military use and the creation of an alternative Peace Tax Fund. In the 1980s, with the reinstatement of draft registration, these organizations supported a new generation of conscientious objectors who refused to register. Tax resistance and nonregistration — both federal offenses — became the central forms of American conscientious objection.

Robert Cooney and Helen Michalowski, eds., *Power of the People: Active Nonviolence in the United States* (1987); Lawrence S. Wittner, *Rebels against the War: The American Peace Movement, 1933–1983* (1984).

GRETCHEN LEMKE-SANTANGELO

See also Addams, Jane; Conscription; Day, Dorothy; Debs, Eugene V.; Draft Riots; Goldman, Emma; Quakers; Thoreau, Henry David.

CONSCRIPTION

The term *conscription* has an unpleasant connotation to Americans who prefer the word *draft* whenever they speak of compulsory military enrollment. Temporary, selective drafts have played a periodic and often substantial part in obtaining America's wartime armies.

The draft has been characterized by two traditions in America. One is that it has often contributed, along with voluntarism, to raising forces of short-term citizen-soldiers in time of international tension and war. (In contrast, the regular standing army is composed of long-term volunteers.) The other tradition has been an ongoing opposition to conscription by pacifists, libertarians, and opponents of particular wars. This is not surprising in a pluralistic society that emphasizes individual liberty and religious freedom.

The English colonists brought to America the county militia system of universal short-term military training and service under local officers. In the eighteenth century, however, most colonies turned for their expeditionary forces to ad hoc units, composed of volunteers and an occasional draftee or a legally hired substitute. In the French and Indian War, Massachusetts's provincial units were more than 90 percent volunteers, primarily young men in their late teens or early twenties who enlisted, as do most wartime volunteers, for a combination of economic, religious, or patriotic reasons, or because of social pressure or a desire for adventure.

In the American Revolution, the new state governments assumed the colonies' authority to draft men, through county militia officers, for their short-term militias. They extended it to the long-term state units of the Continental Army, but they denied Gen. George Washington's request that the central government be empowered to conscript. As the initial volunteering subsided, most states boosted enlistment bounties and held an occasional draft, producing more hired substitutes than actual draftees. Although some dissenters suffered, several states recognized Quaker and other religious conscientious objectors. In contrast to the largely middle-class, short-term militia, the long-term volunteers and substitutes of the Continental Army were mainly poor youths, white and black, who were indentured servants, laborers, unemployed drifters, recent immigrants, or the sons of marginal farmers.

The Constitution adopted in 1789 gave Congress the "power to raise and support armies," but it neither mentioned nor prohibited conscription. The Framers left that issue to the future, although most of them believed that the United States like Britain would enlist its men rather than conscript them, and would pay for its armies through the power to tax.

Since threats to the country's national security in the nineteenth century were generally limited or sporadic, Americans built a two-army tradition. The small Regular Army, a peacetime constabulary and wartime cadre, was obtained exclusively by voluntary enlistment. The wartime armies of citizen-soldiers, from the Indian wars of the 1790s through the Spanish-American War of 1898, were composed primarily of ad hoc wartime units of volunteers, locally raised and led but federally financed and directed. Units of the so-called U.S. Volunteers were distinct from the U.S. Army and the militia, later called the National Guard.

Although some states drafted men during the War of 1812, James Madison's administration was unable to enact national conscription (which Daniel Webster, a Federalist opponent, denounced as an attempt at "Napoleonic despotism"), and it was not until the Civil War that the need to sustain massive armies brought a taste of national conscription to America. With a smaller population to draw upon, the Confederacy adopted the draft in 1862, eventually applying it to white males seventeen to fifty years of age. In all, 21 percent of the 1 million Confederate soldiers were conscripts. But by violating individual liberty and states' rights and by including unpopular class-bound occupational exemptions such as for overseers on large plantations, the Confederate conscription act engendered much discontent and considerable resistance.

In the North, following some state drafts in 1862, Congress adopted a selective conscription law in 1863 applicable to males twenty to forty-five. Avoiding unpopular occupational exemptions, the lawmakers authorized draftees to escape personal service by hiring a substitute or paying the government a commutation fee of three hundred dollars, which, although equal to a worker's annual wages, was less than the current price of substitutes. Peace Democrats claimed it was a "rich man's war but poor man's fight," and when military provost marshals began conscripting, thousands evaded or actively resisted the draft. Bloody draft riots then erupted in New York City.

Northern authorities also increased enlistment bounties and actively recruited immigrants and southern blacks (ultimately, 25 and 10 percent, respectively, of the Union army). In 1864 Congress did away with commutation, but allowed drafted religious pacifists to provide alternative service or contribute to a hospital fund. Four federal drafts produced only 46,000 conscripts and 118,000 substitutes (2 and 6 percent, respectively, of the 2.1 million Union troops). The draft was credited, however, with prodding volunteers and, equally as important, with encouraging the reenlistment of battle-trained veterans.

Not until World War I did the United States rely primarily upon conscription. The Selective Service Act of 1917 was adopted in large part because a civilian-led "preparedness" movement had persuaded many Americans that a selective national draft was the most equitable and efficient way for an industrial society to raise a wartime army. Woodrow Wilson overcame considerable opposition, particularly from agrarian isolationists in the South and West and ethnic and ideological opponents of the war in the North, to obtain the temporary wartime draft.

The 1917 draft law prohibited enlistment bounties and personal substitution, but did authorize deferments on the grounds of dependency or essential work in industry or agriculture. It allowed religious conscientious objectors (COs) to choose noncombatant service within the military. The law was implemented through a Selective Service System, composed of a national headquarters — commanded by a major general — and some four thousand local draft boards staffed by civilian volunteers who decided on the induction or deferment of particular individuals within overall national guidelines.

In 1917 and 1918, Selective Service registered and classified 23.9 million men, eighteen to forty-five, and drafted 2.8 million of them. In all, 72 percent of the wartime army of 3.5 million troops was raised through conscription.

There was no repetition of the Civil War draft riots. Aside from a few violent episodes and a number of antidraft demonstrations, opposition was expressed mainly through criticism and evasion. Between 2 and 3 million men apparently never registered, and 338,000 (12 percent of those drafted) failed to report when called or deserted after arrival at training camp. In addition, 64,700 registrants sought CO status. Of the 20,900 COs drafted into the army, 4,000 refused to participate in any military role, and 450 "absolutists" were sent to prison. In 1918, the U.S. Supreme Court unanimously held that national conscription was constitutional.

In World War II, the fall of France in 1940 led Congress to adopt the nation's first prewar conscription act as a result of a campaign headed by old preparedness leaders. The draft was to run through 1945, but because of intense opposition from pacifists, isolationists, and others, the draftees (aged twenty-one to thirty-five) were obligated to serve only one year, and service was restricted to the Western Hemisphere and U.S. territories. In August 1941, however, Congress, by a one-vote margin (203–202) in the House, voted to keep the one-year draftees in the Army beyond their term. After Pearl Harbor, the lawmakers removed all remaining restrictions and extended the draft to men aged eighteen to thirty-eight (and briefly to forty-five) for the duration. Approximately 10 million men were drafted through the Selective Service System, and nearly 6 million enlisted, primarily in the U.S. Navy and Army Air Corps.

There was some discontent. Some 72,000 registrants applied for CO status, of whom 25,000 entered the army in noncombatant service, another 12,000 went to civilian work camps, and 20,000 had their claims rejected. Ultimately, 6,000, the majority of them Jehovah's Witnesses, were imprisoned. Some antidraft incidents in Chicago and other cities stemmed from protest by African-Americans against discrimination and segregation in the armed forces. Draft evasion did not disappear. The Justice Department investigated 373,000 alleged evaders and obtained convictions of 16,000.

The draft did not end with World War II. Except for a brief hiatus between 1947 and 1948, it helped maintain throughout the cold war a sizable number of men in the armed forces (a mix of volunteers, conscripts, and draft-induced volunteers). During the Korean War, 1.5 million men, eighteen to twenty-five, were drafted; another 1.3 million volunteered, primarily for the navy and air force. Discontent led to an increase in COs (the percentage of inductees exempted as COs grew to nearly 1.5 percent, compared to .15 in each world war). Some 80,000 draft evasion cases were investigated.

Conscription became one of the many casualties of the Vietnam War. After President Lyndon B. Johnson committed American ground troops in 1965, draft calls soared from 100,000 in 1964 to 400,000 in 1966, enabling U.S. forces there to climb from 23,000 military advisers in 1964 to 543,000 troops by 1968.

Although draftees were only a small minority (16 percent) in the American armed forces, they made up the bulk of the infantry riflemen in Vietnam (88 percent by 1969) and accounted for more than half the army's battle deaths. Because of student and other deferments, the draft and the casualties fell disproportionately upon working-class youths, black and white. African-Americans, 11 percent of the U.S. population, accounted for 16 percent of the army's casualties in Vietnam in 1967 (15 percent for the entire war).

Opposition mounted along with the rising draft calls and casualty rates. Supported by an antiwar coalition of students, pacifists, clergy, civil rights and feminist organizations, and many other liberal and radical groups, a draft resistance movement grew in strength. It generated demonstrations, draft-card burnings, sit-ins at induction centers, and break-ins and destruction of records at a dozen local draft boards.

Between 1965 and 1975, faced with well over 100,000 apparent draft offenders, the federal government indicted 22,500 persons, of

whom 8,800 were convicted and 4,000 imprisoned. As the Supreme Court expanded the criteria from religious to moral or ethical objections, CO exemptions grew in relation to actual inductions from 8 percent in 1967 to 43 percent in 1971 and 131 percent in 1972. Between 1965 and 1970, 170,000 registrants were classified as COs.

The most common form of draft "protest" was evasion. Of the 26.8 million young men who reached draft age between 1964 and 1973, 16 million (60 percent) did not serve in the military. Of those who avoided service, 15.4 million received legal exemptions or deferments, and perhaps 570,000 evaded the draft illegally. Among illegal draft evaders 360,000 were never caught, another 198,000 had their cases dismissed, 9,000 were convicted, and 4,000 sent to prison. In addition, an estimated 30,000 to 50,000 fled into exile, mainly to Canada, Britain, and Sweden.

With the draft so controversial, Congress came under increased pressure either to reform it or to eliminate it. Supported by many conservatives, Gen. Lewis B. Hershey, the director of Selective Service since 1941, blocked any changes until 1969, including the 1967 recommendations for equity and national uniformity from a presidential commission headed by former assistant attorney general Burke Marshall. President Richard M. Nixon, after criticizing the draft in his 1968 campaign, ended new occupational and dependency deferments, instituted an annual draft lottery among eighteen-year-olds (beginning in December 1969), removed General Hershey, and appointed a commission, headed by former secretary of defense Thomas Gates, which in 1970 recommended an All-Volunteer Armed Force (AVF) with a stand-by draft for emergency use.

Nixon reduced draft calls while gradually withdrawing U.S. troops, but his dispatch of American units across the border into Cambodia in 1970 led to massive public protests. Only reluctantly did Congress in 1971 extend the draft for two more years. The lawmakers also eliminated student deferments and voted a massive ($2.4 billion) pay increase for the lower ranks in order to achieve an AVF by mid-1973. During the

1972 election campaign, Nixon cut draft calls to 50,000 and stopped forcing draftees to go to Vietnam. On January 27, 1973, the day a cease-fire was announced, the administration stopped drafting, six months before induction authority expired on July 1, 1973.

Compulsory draft registration, which President Gerald Ford suspended in 1975, was resumed in 1980 by President Jimmy Carter in reaction to the Soviet invasion of Afghanistan. President Ronald Reagan extended it in 1982 and prosecuted a few of those who refused to register (estimated at 500,000 between 1980 and 1984).

Although it retained considerable support, the AVF of 2.1 million (including 775,000 in the army) remained controversial. It came under criticism for drawing disproportionately from lower socioeconomic groups, particularly nonwhites. There were also concerns about the comparatively high financial cost of the All-Volunteer Force.

John Whiteclay Chambers II, *To Raise an Army: The Draft Comes to Modern America* (1987); George Q. Flynn, *Conscription and American Culture, 1940–1973* (1992); Stephen M. Kohn, *Jailed for Peace: The History of American Draft Law Violations, 1658–1985* (1986).

JOHN WHITECLAY CHAMBERS II

See also Armed Forces; Conscientious Objection; Draft Riots; *and entries for individual wars.*

CONSERVATION AND ENVIRONMENTAL MOVEMENTS

The conservation movement of the first half of the twentieth century and the environmental movement that arose after 1950 had symbolic and ideological relationships but quite different social roots and objectives. The first emphasized natural resources as commodities to produce material goods; the second focused on resources — air, water, and land — that would enhance the quality of life.

The conservation movement grew out of a concern for the depletion of water, forests, minerals, and soils. Many deplored the rapid exploitation of these resources, fearing that they would soon be exhausted. They called for more efficient management to sustain the yield of renewable resources on a permanent basis and enable nonrenewable resources to last longer.

Key objectives of the movement were the construction of dams to conserve water for irrigation, navigation, and hydroelectric power production and, in the process, store flood waters and prevent flood damage; the management of forests on a sustained-yield basis; the reduction of soil erosion to foster permanent farm productivity; and the restoration of fish and game populations for fishing and hunting.

These policies emerged in the late nineteenth century, developed rapidly during the presidential administration of Theodore Roosevelt (1901–1909), and took on new life in the 1930s during the presidency of Franklin D. Roosevelt. In that decade funds to combat the depression were spent on large-scale dam and reservoir projects; the Civilian Conservation Corps constructed roads in the national parks and forests; fish and wildlife protection moved ahead rapidly.

Alongside but subordinate to these ventures was the movement to establish national and state parks in order to enhance the quality of the human environment by protecting natural areas. The first national park was Yellowstone (1872); after a number of other parks were created, the National Park Service was formed in 1916 to administer them.

The initial impetus for the environmental movement was the growing interest in outdoor recreation in a more natural environment. This led to the creation of the National Wilderness Preservation System (1964), the National Trails System (1968), and the National Wild and Scenic Rivers System (1968) and to a public purchase program in the Land and Water Conservation Act (1964). By 1989 the wilderness system, the most dramatic result of these measures, had reached 90 million acres.

These programs set a direction in resource management different from the conservation focus on efficient development of material resources. In wilderness areas no timber was to be cut and no roads built; wild and scenic rivers were to remain free-flowing with no dams built in them. The programs meant that resources were now prized for their aesthetic rather than their material value.

The environmental movement gave rise to a new appreciative use of wildlife as an object of observation rather than of hunting. This led to a federal endangered species program, nongame wildlife programs fostered by the states, a heightened interest in habitat for wild plants and animals, and a focus on biological diversity of wild resources.

In the environmental era a new interest arose in curbing pollution — first air and water pollution in the 1950s and 1960s and then the pollution from toxic chemical wastes in the 1970s and thereafter. A host of new laws, federal, state, and local, were intended to protect drinking water, contain the spread of pesticides and other toxic chemicals, and clean up the air, rivers, lakes, and oceans. These programs emphasized a healthy as well as an aesthetically pleasing environment. Environmental health policies had long stressed the purification of drinking water to prevent contagious disease. Now they were expanded to reduce exposure to pollution, including harmful chemicals in the workplace.

Public support for environmental objectives grew steadily over the years, as charted by public opinion surveys and membership in citizen organizations such as the Sierra Club, the Wilderness Society, the National Wildlife Federation, and the National Audubon Society. After 1970 many new organizations were formed, often to address specific problems such as scenic rivers, hiking trails, billboard removal, pesticide control, energy efficiency, mineral extraction on public lands, and solid waste management. These organizations expanded their activities from national legislative lobbying to include initiating legal actions and participating in administrative proceedings; in the late 1970s they began to work in electoral campaigns for members of Congress; and in the 1980s they became involved in state environmental affairs. This growth was a result of slow and persistent change rooted in the new attitudes, interests, and values of the American people.

Both the conservation and environmental movements focused on the management of public resources; hence they were deeply involved in the formation of public policy and debates over how land, air, and water should be used — for private or public objectives. But there were also differences. The conservation movement, which arose out of the interests of technical experts and managers in reducing waste in production, had a limited popular base. The environmental movement, in contrast, arose out of broad public interests in improving the quality of life and thus had widespread support. It was an integral part of the increasing citizen participation in American public affairs during the last half of the twentieth century.

Stephen Fox, *John Muir and His Legacy: The American Conservation Movement* (1981); Samuel P. Hays, *Beauty, Health and Permanence: Environmental Politics in the United States, 1955–1985* (1987); Samuel P. Hays, *Conservation and the Gospel of Efficiency: The Progressive Conservation Movement, 1890–1920* (1959).

SAMUEL P. HAYS

See also Ballinger-Pinchot Controversy; Carson, Rachel; Civilian Conservation Corps; Public Land Policy.

CONSERVATISM

The Reagan presidency has been hailed as the high point of twentieth-century American conservatism. But writing while Ronald Reagan was at the peak of his popularity, George Will shocked his fellow American conservatives by arguing that in America "there are almost no conservatives, properly understood," and he continued, "The conservatism for which I argue is a European conservatism." Will's polemic led conservative Charles Kessler to ask in a famous article, "Is Conservatism Un-American?" What place can there be for a homegrown conservatism, Kessler wondered, in an America that was founded "not only as a democratic country given to the love of the new, but a modern country conceived in the spirit of progress?"

This conservative soul-searching bears a striking resemblance to the long-standing debate over "why there is no socialism in America." Both are a response to "American exceptionalism." Unlike European liberals and radicals who had to fight feudalism to obtain political liberty, Americans were, politically speaking, "born equal." In America the (white male) individual was neither held down by a powerful state nor restrained by encrusted social institutions like a national church or a nobility.

A uniquely American form of conservatism first arose in opposition to the nation's sense of boundless optimism about human nature under democracy. And for roughly the first two hundred years of the Republic, conservatism was defined politically and culturally by its fears of the political excesses, economic egalitarianism, and cultural vulgarity generated by a democratic society shorn of any aristocratic restraints.

The success of the Revolution drove the nation in a dramatically democratic direction. Not only did the most conservative elements, the Loyalists, flee, but the Revolution released a rapidly flowing river of participatory political energy. This produced an outpouring of legislation — much of it, like debtor relief and paper money laws, threatening to both property ownership and economic stability.

Frightened nationalists like James Madison spoke of the danger of majoritarian tyranny and "elective despotism" insofar as local majorities set the economic rules. Madison and his fellow Federalists, painfully aware of the fact that all earlier democracies had been destroyed by class struggle, proposed a new constitution to wrest political control from the legislative majorities at the state level. Madison hoped that it would filter out local passions and allow men of standing to rise to political control.

The Antifederalists, proponents of local democracy and opponents of the new Constitution, decried the Federalist attempt to make the United States "be like other nations." But John Adams, informed by a Calvinist sense of human sinfulness, responded with what is perhaps the signature phrase of early-nineteenth-century conservatism: "There is no special providence for Americans." He argued that "to expect self-denial from men, when they have the majority in their favor and consequently power to gratify themselves, is to disbelieve history and . . . the Word of God, which informs us that the heart is deceitful above all things and desperately wicked."

Fears of mass tyranny deepened as the generation of the Founding Fathers was displaced by party politicians, who frankly represented the self-interest of a population undeterred by deference to their social betters and driven by ambition. Andrew Jackson became the tribune of these men. He insisted, contrary to Madison, that "the first principle of our system" is that the majority is to govern. The voice of the people was to be equated with the voice of God. Outside of the Virginia and South Carolina Tidewater, Jacksonian democracy politically routed the Whig heirs of Federalism. It reduced the conservatism of the Founding Fathers to a literary temperament kept alive by writers like James Fenimore Cooper who warned that "the true theatre of a demagogue is a democracy."

The Tidewater conservatism of the Old South was born of a resentment based on slaveholding and race. The region's grandees resented the economic development of the up-country and the threat it posed to both their status and their slaves. Their proponents, like Beverley Tucker, produced a maddening mixture of what might be called "free-market chivalry." Tucker sought to restore "that beautiful harmony in which Power is gentle & Obedience liberal & the will of the superior prevails." The social basis for southern conservatism was destroyed in the Civil War, but echoes of its call for hierarchical harmony continued to resonate well into the twentieth century.

But in rapidly industrializing post–Civil War America, the Whig politics of property, organized to protect wealth from the democratic "mob," underwent an extraordinary transformation. "What it did," writes Louis Hartz, "was to smash the 'mob' into a million bits, so that the fierce acquisitive passion, instead of being expended against property, would be expended against itself in the quest for property." From roughly the end of the Civil War to the onset of the New Deal, there was a right wing in American politics but nothing, literary tendencies aside, that could be described as "conservative" as the term is commonly understood. The right wing turned against government in the name of that oxymoron laissez-faire conservatism and feared the state as an instrument of majoritarian reform. This came to be called "the American (as opposed to European) Way."

State action, said social Darwinists like William Graham Sumner, threatened the natural social processes that produced prosperity through inequality. State action to regulate business or protect workers from injury was said to be the equivalent of European socialism and thus a threat to civilization itself. Or as John D. Rockefeller, Jr., explained it, the rise of big business was merely the working out of a law of nature and law of God. In the Gilded Age "the inequalities of nature would be allowed to run their full course."

If laissez-faire conservatism had simply been a device whereby the robber barons of the Gilded Age used the language of Jeffersonian antistatism to justify a very un-Jeffersonian inequality, it would not have been nearly so pervasive or enduring. Rather it drew on that part of the American individualist psyche that has found all institutions, let alone the state, a suffocating danger. This created what Irving Howe has called "a politics that dares consider . . . whether society is necessary." The hero of Sumner's essay "The Forgotten Man" (a forerunner of the "Silent Majority"), a lower-middle-class taxpayer who desires nothing so much as a chance to "make it," is sure that the state will serve only to choke off his avenues of opportunity through taxation and regulation.

Fittingly, the courts, America's least conspicuous and least democratic branch of government, became the guardian of laissez-faire conservatism in its conflict with the sometimes "populist" legislatures. The "professional" guardians of the Constitution became the counterweight to the "amateur" democrats of the legislature. The post–Civil War Supreme Court led by Justice Stephen Field reshaped the Fourteenth Amendment (designed to ensure due process for the freed slaves) into an instrument of laissez-faire. In the *Slaughterhouse* cases of 1873, Field suggested that the very idea of economic regulation was un-American. And in the *Pollock* income tax case of 1895, progressive economic policy was denounced as "socialistic" and

"communistic." The Supreme Court saw itself as fashioning the Constitution into a bulwark "behind which private rights and private property may shelter themselves and be safe" from "the will of the majority." In short, for conservatives the only good legislature was an adjourned legislature.

According to what came to be known as "constitutional morality," legislation supporting the right to unionize or limiting children's working hours was an un-American form of group privilege. Laissez-faire conservatism reached its intellectual apogee in the 1920s. A critic complained that by 1924 you didn't have to be a radical to be denounced as un-American: "according to the lights of Constitution worship you are no less a Red if you seek change through the very channels which the Constitution itself provides."

In Europe conservatism was based on hereditary classes; in America it was based on hereditary religious, ethnic, and racial groups. The GOP, a largely Protestant party, looked upon itself as the manifestation of the divine creed of Americanism revealed through the Constitution. To be a conservative, then, was to share in a religiously ordained vision of a largely stateless society of self-regulating individuals. This civil religion, preached by President Herbert Hoover, was shattered by the Great Depression and the usurpation of the government by an "alien" power, Franklin D. Roosevelt, in league with "un-American," that is, unexceptionalist ideas.

Conservatives were traumatized by their fall from grace. Diminished in place and prestige, they consoled themselves with bizarre conspiracy theories and cranky accusations of communist infiltration. Overwhelmed and resentful, they did not so much address the disaster of the depression as yearn for the days when they were able to run their towns, their businesses, and their workers in the manner to which they had been accustomed. Then, in 1940, just when it seemed they had Roosevelt on the ropes, World War II revived and extended his presidency.

At war's end conservatives unleashed their frustrations. On the one hand, postwar popular conservatism was based on an anticommunist hysteria that antedated the antics of Senator Joe

McCarthy. Politics for the McCarthyites was not so much a matter of pursuing material interests as a national screen on which to project their deepest cultural fears. And on the other, it represented the fervent desire for normalcy that characterized the Eisenhower years. After two decades of war and depression, the American people, said an astute politician, "have been through a lot of experiments, and they want a rest." Significantly for the conservative future the postwar years saw the first buds of a conservative intellectual flowering with the publication of Frederich von Hayek's *The Road to Serfdom,* an eloquent reformulation of laissez-faire doctrine that appealed to America's antibureaucratic instincts.

The conservative political revival began inauspiciously with Barry Goldwater's 1964 landslide defeat for the presidency. Goldwater, a fervent believer in American uniqueness, captured the Republican party for its "restorationist" wing of young political activists who wanted to return to pre–New Deal America. Like their left-wing counterparts, these young militants, inspired in part by the *National Review* and its editor, William F. Buckley, disdained New Deal welfarism with its compromises and paternalism. But this new conservatism did not so much win the country over to its perspective as board the empty ship of state vacated by a 1960s liberalism that had self-destructed. Conservatism triumphed because New Deal liberalism was unable to accommodate the new cultural and political demands unleashed by the civil rights revolution, feminism, and the counterculture, all of which was exacerbated by the Kulturkampf over Vietnam.

Ever since the 1930s, shrewd conservatives had dreamed of uniting social and economic conservatives under one tent. At first they failed, in part because of the religious and ethnic divisions between the small towns and the city slums. But as these antipathies subsided and race became the storm center of American politics, the Republican restorationists realigned American political and intellectual life. They forged a coalition with southerners and street-corner conservatives in opposition to a liberalism increasingly defined in terms of cultural permissiveness and government-sponsored mobility for blacks. As New Right leader Paul Weyrich put it bluntly: "We talk about issues people care about, like gun control, abortion, taxes and crime. Yes, they're emotional issues, but that's better than talking about capital formation."

Near the end of the Reagan presidency conservatives were shaken by the publication of Alan Bloom's *The Closing of the American Mind.* Bloom, writing from the perspective of an antimodern European conservative, looked at the economic dynamism unleashed by Reaganism and pronounced it defective. Vulgar America, he argued, could never live up to a conservatism based on the good, the true, and the beautiful, properly understood.

Russell Kirk, ed., *The Portable Conservative Reader* (1982); George Nash, *The Conservative Intellectual Movement in America* (1976); Clinton Rossiter, *Conservatism in America* (1962).

FRED SIEGEL

See also Anticommunism; Buckley, William F., Jr.; Federalist Papers; Federalist Party; Isolationism; Republican Party; Robber Barons; *Slaughterhouse* Cases; Social Darwinism; Whig Party.

CONSTITUTION

The document that emerged from the Philadelphia Convention of 1787 has become the longest-lived national constitution in the world, fulfilling Chief Justice John Marshall's vision that it was "meant to endure for ages to come, and to meet the various crises of human affairs" (*McCulloch* v. *Maryland,* 1819). It was the product of a sense of urgency and of mission, solid preparation, secret debate that allowed open-mindedness and compromise, and a body of delegates who in the aggregate possessed both a command of political philosophy and much practical experience under state constitutions and the Articles of Confederation.

Despite some serious deficiencies, revealed most notably in the crisis of the Civil War, the Constitution has served at once as a symbol of national unity and the continuity of basic ideals amid change, as a supple (but not mushy) framework of government, and as a binding code of supreme law. Its grant of powers and its constraints on power are addressed to governmental action, national and state, not to private conduct. The latter is reached by legislation enacted pursuant to the specific constitutional grants of power to Congress, together with the vital auxiliary "necessary and proper" clause. The design of the whole is to maintain a government that is effective, adaptable, and safe for the rights of its people. The principal features of the Constitution that contribute to this end may be set out under four heads.

1. *Republican form of government.* The Framers feared both the despotism of a monarch and the tyranny of a fixed popular majority. For the central problem of a republic, the design of the electoral process, they adopted a series of provisions calculated to filter the popular will through a screen of minds deemed virtuous and wise. Thus the president would be chosen by electors in the several states or, failing a majority, by the House of Representatives. Senators would be chosen by the state legislatures, and qualifications to vote for members of the House would parallel, state by state, their own prescribed qualifications for the suffrage.

All this has given way before the rise of political parties and a steady movement toward a more inclusive and direct electorate. Indeed, if there is any recurring theme in the constitutional amendments since the Bill of Rights of 1791, it is the enlargement of the franchise. The Seventeenth Amendment (1913) provided that members of the Senate be elected by popular vote. The Fifteenth Amendment (1870) enfranchised blacks; the Nineteenth (1920), women; and the Twenty-third (1961), residents of the District of Columbia in presidential elections. The Twenty-fourth (1964) outlawed the poll tax or other tax as a condition of voting, and the Twenty-sixth (1971) enfranchised eighteen-year-olds. In addition to access, the effectiveness of the ballot was increased by the Supreme Court's one-person-one-vote decision requiring electoral districts within a state to be approximately equal in population; this was based on the equal protection guarantee of the Fourteenth Amend-

ment, which to then had not been thought to embrace political rights (*Baker* v. *Carr,* 1962). The reform of districting gave increased political weight to the growing suburban areas, and increased voter eligibility and registration enhanced the influence of black and other minority groups in the cities. James Madison's model of counterbalancing, moderating forces has been strengthened by these and other unforeseen developments, not least the sustained operation of a two-party system.

Despite Madison's strong warning against "factions" in the famous Tenth Federalist Paper, a two-party system has ironically served to mitigate further divisions: each party, to maximize its appeal, is a haven for a congeries of political and social interests. This pattern is only indirectly the result of constitutional provisions. A multitude of ideological parties is discouraged by the single-member districts for the House; proportional representation, which would foster such multiplicity, is incompatible with that model. Moreover, without any constitutional compulsion, the states have opted for the "unit rule" for presidential elections, whereby the total electoral vote allotted to the state is awarded to the winner, rather than apportioned by districts or by proportions of the popular vote. In thus maximizing its strength in the counting of electoral votes, each state contributes to the two-party pattern, which in turn avoids the multiple divisions in many democratic countries that typically require the formation of coalition governments. In the United States the coalitions are formed before the election.

2. *Separation of powers.* It is commonly said that the Constitution establishes a national government of three branches — legislative, executive, and judicial — whose separation is mandated to prevent an all-powerful consolidation of functions. From the beginning, however, there has been an admixture of powers — checks and balances — that serves the same end, the safeguarding of people's liberty. The president's veto power, congressional override, the president's nomination of federal judges, and the senatorial consent required for the appointment of the highest officials and for the ratification of treaties made by the president are all embedded in

the document itself. As Justice Louis D. Brandeis explained, "The doctrine of the separation of powers was adopted by the Convention of 1787, not to promote efficiency, but to preclude the exercise of arbitrary power. The purpose was not to avoid friction, but, by means of the inevitable friction incident to the distribution of the governmental powers among three departments, to save the people from autocracy" (*Myers* v. *United States,* 1926).

The problems of coping with giant enterprise and with a multitude of complex commercial and financial practices, as well as the need for technical expertise and continuity of policy, prompted the creation of independent agencies, starting with the Interstate Commerce Commission in 1887 and proliferating ever since, most dramatically during the New Deal period under President Franklin D. Roosevelt. The danger of consolidated powers within these agencies is recognized in the effort to keep apart in an agency's bureaucracy the functions of rule making, enforcement, and adjudication.

In foreign affairs, the growing exercise of presidential power, particularly in times of crisis, from World War II to the Vietnam conflict, has provoked efforts to demarcate the spheres of executive authority, on the one hand, and legislative participation and oversight, on the other. The War Powers Act of 1973, passed over President Richard M. Nixon's veto, is the product of such efforts. The courts were drawn into the murky area of presidential war powers over the economy in wartime in the steel-seizure controversy during the Korean War, but whether they will accept arbitral authority in more direct foreign policy decisions or will regard these as "political" questions for resolution outside the courts remains an issue for the future. Perhaps for purposes of judicial control a line can be drawn between actions that affect primarily the prerogatives and sensibilities of the contesting branches of government, like a duty to consult when each side possesses political leverage, and those actions that directly affect the liberty and rights of individuals, like a call to military service abroad in an undeclared war.

3. *Federal system.* Like the separation of powers, the allocation of powers between the national and state governments was meant to be a safeguard against undue concentration in one sphere of authority. The Civil War and the postwar amendments augmented the national role; the amendments in effect nationalized the Bill of Rights. They altered, but did not obliterate the federal system. The development of the national-state distribution of powers, as with the separation of powers, has been marked by flexibility rather than an either-or ordering. The Constitution itself designates few powers as exclusively national: naturalization, bankruptcy laws, taxation of imports and exports. Others, by their nature, must be exclusive, like the borrowing of money on the credit of the United States. Nor is there a list of powers reserved to the states; these are residual, as declared by the Tenth Amendment. The demarcation of the great powers that are the engine of government, notably the regulation of commerce and the taxing and spending power, was left to be worked out by congressional and state legislative assertions of authority and by Supreme Court review in cases and controversies coming before it in ordinary litigation.

The expansion of national power over the economy, whether through acts of Congress or judicial denials of state power, was legitimized and shaped by the opinions of Chief Justice Marshall. This movement, interrupted by the Court a century after Marshall, resumed when President Roosevelt's Court reorganization plan of 1937 was proposed and the major New Deal legislation was finally upheld. In 1895 the Sherman Antitrust Act was held incapable of reaching a combination of sugar refiners that controlled 90 percent of production because production was deemed not to be commerce, and in 1918 a similar fate befell the federal law prohibiting the shipment of child-made goods. But federal regulation of agricultural production was sustained in 1942, as was the application of the Fair Labor Standards Act to the operations of a motel in 1964. If interstate commerce feels the pinch, as Justice Robert Jackson put it, it does not matter where the squeeze occurs.

Taxation, too, has had wide scope. The so-called Madisonian view would limit Congress to spending in support of powers expressly granted, whereas the Hamiltonian view placed no such limit on the power to tax and spend for the general welfare. Not until 1937, when the Social Security Act was sustained, did the Supreme Court explicitly put the issue at rest, in favor of the broader view. "General welfare" has become virtually a political, not a juridical, concept.

It should be remembered, however, that a political check does exist. The members of Congress represent states and localities, and although their perspective is not identical with that of local leaders, their caretaking function cannot be disregarded in the formation of policy. In part, at least, this dual loyalty is responsible for creative patterns of cooperative federalism, including direct relations between the national government and cities.

4. *Safeguarding personal rights.* The foregoing features of the Constitution represent an internal, structural, self-executing design to protect and preserve civil liberties. But the original Constitution, the Bill of Rights, and the post–Civil War amendments, in particular the Fourteenth (1868), contain express prohibitions on governmental action, federal or state, that ultimately depend on judicial interpretation and enforcement. These safeguards could be given a narrow reading, confined to the circumstances at the time of their adoption, but here too history has shown that though we are tethered to the words of the Constitution we are not shackled by them. Indeed, the evolving protection of individual rights and equality of treatment has become the central focus of constitutional law and the dominant subject of Supreme Court review. Throughout its history the Court has emphasized different aspects of the constitutional order at different periods. Before the Civil War the Court created a nationwide common market, largely through its view of the commerce power. Later it fostered the autonomous growth of business enterprise through its concept of economic "liberty" and a substantive, not simply procedural, reading of the due process clauses in the Fifth and Fourteenth Amendments.

At times the Court, giving a formal rather than realistic meaning to liberty, seemed to forget the old common-law maxim that a necessitous person is not a free person, as well as the homely truth that the freedom of the whale is the death of the minnow. The clash between the popular will and a majority of the Supreme Court became especially acute during the Progressive Era, and it came to a head, as noted, in the constitutional crisis of the New Deal. As the role of government in a welfare state has grown, so also has judicial scrutiny of the procedures, criminal, civil, and administrative, employed in governing. Now the cutting edge of constitutional law is at the line between individual autonomy (confusedly called a right of privacy) and the asserted need for social control.

Besides the judicial responses to the needs and aspirations of society, adaptation and change can be brought about by formal amendment. There have been remarkably few. Of the twenty-six that have been adopted through the difficult process required by Article V, the first ten are essentially part of the original document, since the ratification process produced a virtual commitment to draw up a set of prohibitions addressed to the new national government, and three, the Thirteenth, Fourteenth, and Fifteenth, marked the ending of the Civil War.

The remaining thirteen introduce predominantly structural changes. Note has already been taken of the successive enlargements of the voting franchise. Remarkable too is the paucity of amendments to override decisions of the Supreme Court: the Eleventh, to recognize sovereign immunity from suit in the federal courts, and the Sixteenth, to enable Congress to enact an income tax. The reluctance to add amendments is illustrated by several recent efforts. The failure to adopt the Equal Rights Amendment was mainly due to a perception that it was no longer essential, in light of the favorable decisions under the equal protection guarantee. The failure of a budget-balancing proposal evidently reflected a judgment that the subject was too complex to lend itself to a place in the Constitution. The failure of a flag-burning proposal to emerge from Congress reflected a sentiment that its object was too inconsequential practically and that symbolically it would send to later generations and to other nations a wrong message about tolerance of dissent.

New proposals for structural change are being discussed in response to the problem of collaborative government when the Congress and the executive branch are of different party allegiances. These ideas, which adapt certain features of parliamentary-cabinet government, include making members of Congress eligible for cabinet or subcabinet posts and four-year terms for members of the House, whose election would coincide with presidential elections. Action on such proposals, barring an intractable stalemate in government, will probably have to await the twenty-first century.

Archibald Cox, *The Court and the Constitution* (1987); David P. Currie, *The Constitution of the United States: A Primer for the People* (1988); Leonard W. Levy and Kenneth Karst, eds., *Encyclopedia of the American Constitution,* 4 vols. (1986).

PAUL A. FREUND

See also Bill of Rights; Equal Rights Amendment; Federalist Papers; Freedom of Speech; Freedom of the Press; Judicial Review; Philadelphia Convention; Ratification of the Constitution; Supreme Court. *(For the text of the Constitution, see appendix.)*

CONSTITUTIONAL CONVENTION

See Philadelphia Convention.

CONSTITUTIONAL UNION PARTY

This short-lived political group was a haven in the election of 1860 for Whigs and Know-Nothings unwilling to join northern or southern Democrats or the Republicans. Its members nominated for president John Bell of Tennessee, a border-state Whig and large slaveholder who had opposed the Kansas-Nebraska Act and the Lecompton constitution, and for vice president Edward Everett, president of Harvard University and a former secretary of state and Cotton Whig in the Fillmore administration, on a platform of "the Union as it is and the Constitution as it is."

The Constitutional Union party had its genesis in Democratic divisions over the Lecompton constitution, the collapse of the Whigs, and the problems of the American, or Know-Nothing party. The Whigs' collapse had left anti-Democratic southerners adrift without a political party. Senator John J. Crittenden of Kentucky, Henry Clay's successor in border-state Whiggery, set up a meeting among fifty conservative, pro-compromise congressmen in December 1859, which led to a convention in Baltimore on May 9, 1860. The Constitutional Unionists nominated Bell.

Bell and Everett ran a lackluster campaign, winning only 39 of the possible 303 electoral votes. They carried the three border slave states of Virginia (15), Kentucky (12), and Tennessee (12). Bell and many other Constitutional Unionists later supported the South during the Civil War, and the party and its purpose disappeared.

See also Civil War; Elections: 1860.

CONTINENTAL CONGRESSES

The First Continental Congress met in Philadelphia, September 5–October 26, 1774, to develop a common colonial response to the Coercive Acts recently passed by Parliament. An advisory council rather than an empowered legislature, the Congress (as it came to be called) included delegates from twelve of the American colonies; Georgia did not participate. Congress advised each colony to form a militia, organized an association to enforce strict economic sanctions against Britain, and recommended that Massachusetts, the focus of the Coercive Acts, form an independent government. After issuing addresses to the king and to the British and American people, the delegates agreed to meet again in May 1775 if their grievances had not been resolved.

By the time the Second Continental Congress convened in Philadelphia, fighting had taken place at Lexington and Concord. Congress quickly assumed responsibility for coordinating the rebellion, starting with the raising of a Continental army. A year later Congress took the final step toward separation by officially adopting the Declaration of Independence on July 4, 1776.

For the next five years, Congress continued

to direct the war and to administer the central government, although military events forced it to move from city to city. Its efforts were hampered by its inability to raise funds or to take other significant action without near-unanimity among the individual states. The Articles of Confederation (finally ratified 1781) perpetuated the wartime balance of power, keeping the central government politically and financially dependent on the states. Yet Congress did manage to prosecute the war successfully and could point to a number of other important achievements, including the Northwest Ordinance, the complicated balancing of state-federal financial accounts, and the creation of the first federal departments. In campaigning for the new Constitution in 1787, the Federalists stressed the impotence and ineffectiveness of the existing government. But though this criticism was not without merit, Congress under the Articles had played a critical part in laying the foundations for the new Republic.

See also Morris, Robert; Revolution.

CONTRACEPTION

See Birth Control.

CONVENTIONS

See Party Conventions; Philadelphia Convention; Seneca Falls Convention.

COOKERY

According to a study by Dr. Paul A. Fine, a psychological consultant to major food corporations, the diet of the "American mainstream" consists of "Oreos, peanut butter, Crisco, TV dinners, cake mix, macaroni and cheese, Pepsi and Coke, pizzas, Jell-O, hamburgers, Rice-a-Roni, Spaghetti-O's, pork and beans [canned], Heinz ketchup and instant coffee." One might add hot dogs, ice cream, tacos, and diet soda, perhaps, but his findings remain as valid today as in the 1970s when they were presented to the American Medical Association.

Yet there is a traditional American cookery,

and it is a magnificent tapestry of which the warp is English, with wondrous shadings and strands of color from myriad influences: Native American, African, French, Dutch, West Indian, Spanish, and German, among the early ones.

In the beginning, American cookery was Native American. All products were natural; fish and game were plentiful; the aroma of their cooking mingled with that of wood fires; food that was not eaten fresh was dried or smoked. Although the settlers brought many new products from the Old World, along with radically different cooking methods, some aspects changed but little for a century or so. William Byrd, in *Natural History of Virginia* (1737), described the country as "the Newly Discovered Eden" and was lyrical over the quality and array of fruits and vegetables that were being grown: "beautiful cauliflower . . . very large and long asparagus of splendid flavor . . . watermelons and fragrant melons," as well as all sorts of squash, pumpkins, beans, apples, apricots, pears, plums, quinces, cherries, walnuts, and many more. In *History and Present State of Virginia* (1705) Robert Beverley described Native American cookery in some detail. He too was enthusiastic about the quality and variety of produce and observed that before the English had come, fish were so plentiful that children could take them with pointed sticks. So things had already started to change. Still, as late as 1780, the Englishman Samuel Pegge was able to write that "*American* fruits are exceedingly odoriferous . . . to us *Europeans* . . . [so that] our fruits appear insipid to them, for want of odour."

Native American influence on colonial cookery was incalculable, but primarily in terms of kinds of produce, leading off with maize, which the settlers dubbed *Indian corn,* or simply *indian.* The Native Americans taught them how to grow it and how to prepare it for storage; they learned how to roast young ears and how to make popcorn; and they observed that cornmeal could be made into cakes, wrapped in leaves, and baked in the ashes. But peoples historically are highly conservative about food, particularly basic foods, so that at the beginning, maize was accepted only out of necessity. The English came to love it, however, and they adapted their own traditional recipes for hearth cakes, puddings, and the like, to cornmeal, which could be substituted for ground oats. The flavor was different but the method was identical. Thus Americans have johnny cakes (from *jannock,* an old English word for oat bread), boiled and baked Indian puddings, and other dishes, all made by English recipes but using Indian corn. This use of maize is the most important and original aspect of American cookery, and because Mexican recipes have entered the cuisine as well, the nation has an extraordinarily rich repertory of corn dishes. They are more American than apple pie.

Two other important groups of indigenous vegetables were easily accepted. Various *Cucurbitae,* the group to which squash and pumpkins belong, had been known in Europe since classical times; recipes for pumpkinlike gourds appear in fourteenth-century manuscripts. The specific American varieties were new to the settlers, but not strange. And the American bean, *Phaseolus vulgaris,* although not related to the broad bean of Europe nor to any other, resembled it sufficiently to be immediately accepted. The French early developed improved varieties of this American bean, so that well into the nineteenth century, the term *French bean* referred to the young edible pod, or string bean, in both English and American sources.

Other plants of American origin, such as potatoes, tomatoes, peanuts, chocolate, vanilla, and *Capsicum* peppers, came into use somewhat later, partly because they originated far away to the south, often coming to the colonies by wildly circuitous routes, and also because they seemed strange to Europeans. That said, the use of all of them, the tomato particularly, was far earlier than many writers claim.

Acceptance of American edible animals and birds was easier. Some were "new," but many were reassuringly similar to European species. The uniquely American turkey had come to Elizabethan England by way of Spain, so that its presence in Massachusetts did not seem remarkable to the Puritans when they held their first Thanksgiving feast.

Contrary to conventional wisdom, seventeenth-century English cookery was very fine, making skillful use of aromatic herbs and wine.

Whatever the faults of American cookery today, they cannot be blamed on that legacy, as admirably demonstrated in cookbooks and surviving family manuscripts. Most of the books are known to have circulated in the colonies, and a number of manuscripts came over, notably one inherited by Martha Washington, a brilliant example of early seventeenth-century English cookery. This is the lineage of *The Virginia House-Wife* (1824) by Mary Randolph; indeed, she may have known the work. She presents the same sophisticated cookery with wine and herbs, the same lovely custards, and the same breads and cakes baked in the brick oven. She also gives recipes for some forty vegetables and often echoes Hannah Glasse's admonition in *The Art of Cookery* (London, 1747), far and away the most popular cookbook in the colonies: "Most People spoil Garden Things by over boiling them. All Things that are green should have a little Crispness, for if they are over boil'd they neither have any Sweetness or Beauty." But the Virginia work also includes the un-English use of maize, pumpkin pie, West Indian recipes specifically attributed, seventeen recipes calling for tomatoes, recipes collected by her sister in Cádiz, turnip greens "boiled with bacon in the Virginia style," and above all, the African influence — in short, an eclectic, aromatic cuisine, authentically American. (It may be objected that this represents upper-class cookery. But the poor have always eaten badly — they still do — and their cookery is ill-recorded.)

It was the African presence in the South that accounts for the near mythic reputation of southern cookery as distinguished from that of the North. Many of the products that have characterized southern cookery came from Africa, or by way of Africa or the West Indies and the slave trade: okra or gumbo, black-eyed peas, benne seeds (sesame), eggplant, sorghum, watermelon, and, ironically, the peanut, which had early traveled from its native Brazil to Africa in the slave trade. The American sweet potato reminded blacks of the African yam. And there is the long association of African-Americans with rice. Rice is indigenous to Africa — as well as to India and the Malay Archipelago — and had been the staple of many slaves brought from

West Africa so that their expertise in rice culture might be used in the new rice lands of South Carolina.

Southern food is soul food. African-American women did the cooking, and they imbued southern cookery with heady aromas; even English recipes, dictated by the mistress, developed unsuspected nuances in the hands of those cooks. And they brought their own recipes, most dramatically hoppin' John, rice and black-eyed peas, which to this day is a signature dish of South Carolina, even among whites. The African-American way of cooking rice "Carolina style" became the paradigm of rice cookery, so much so that rice companies today exploit the name, as well as depictions of African-American cooks, as logos. This rice kitchen was recorded by Sarah Rutledge in *The Carolina Housewife* (1847). Rice came to be grown in many states, but nowhere else did such a rice kitchen develop except to some extent in Georgia and, of course, New Orleans with its distinctive Creole cuisine, a unique blend of French, Spanish, African, and Native American influences.

It is not possible here to detail all influences, even important ones. It must suffice to say that the great chowders and baked bean dishes of New England, the hearty fare of the Germans in Pennsylvania, and the Dutch *olykoeks* (doughnuts) and cole slaw of New York, for example, are familiar to most Americans.

Immigrants to the American heartland brought their cookery with them. Nearly all came westward from the Atlantic seaboard states, as did all but a handful of American cookbooks published before 1870. Life on the frontier left little time for fancy cooking, yet there is a recipe for Southern Rice in *Buckeye Cookery* (Minneapolis, 1880) signed "Mrs. P. F. Morey, Charleston, S.C.," and one for Okra Gumbo in *The Kansas Home Cook-Book* (Leavenworth, 1886) — these in addition to less surprising recipes such as one for New England Johnny Cakes.

The annexation of parts of Mexico and succeeding waves of immigration added further scintillating accents to the tapestry of American cookery: Mexican, Italian, Portuguese, Bohemian, Scandinavian, Russian, Latin American, Greek, Polish, Jewish, Chinese, and many oth-

ers. It is primarily those demographic patterns of settlement that account for regional variations in American cookery.

In cities and prosperous farming regions the quality of food and cooking tended to be good well into the nineteenth century. Then the Industrial Revolution began to transform it, beginning with the canning industry. Cookbooks reflected the change by calling for ever longer cooking times for greens, for example. When milling of wheat was centralized and speeded up, the new flour was so lifeless that yeast was unable to make bread dough rise properly unless it was hyped up with sugar. The taste of American bread, remarked upon by early travelers, declined, so more sugar was added, and food writers were enlisted to defend it. New processing, new fertilizers, breeding for hardiness and shelf life, even improvements such as refrigeration, all conspired to suppress flavor. Major staples produced in distant areas replaced the freshness of local produce. As is often said, these changes have made it possible to eat strawberries and tomatoes in January — with a near total loss of flavor. Indeed, the strawberries of June and the tomatoes of August suffered a similar fate. (It is to be noted that many cookbook authors routinely recommend the use of canned *imported* tomatoes in cooking, rather than fresh ones.)

The quality of cooking suffered along with the produce. Recipes in cookbooks appearing since the turn of the century, especially those for bread and salads, show the doses of sugar increasing almost decade by decade to replace lost flavor. The old cookbook writers, themselves fine cooks, were replaced by home economists like Fannie Farmer (1896 on) adapting the dish to the product. At the same time, many ersatz products, such as Crisco, margarine, and Jell-O, were coming on the market and being touted by the new food writers. The break with earlier generations, and the pressure to conform and cut corners, the influence of advertising and marketing, and finally the movement of women out of the kitchen and into paid jobs all took their toll.

The microwave oven, designed primarily to reheat frozen precooked food, became a fixture in a majority of kitchens. The family meal itself became something of a myth. The dominant pattern of American eating became the snack — on the run, at the desk, before the television set, between meals. Meanwhile, concerns about health and about contaminants in food, such as pesticides, hormones, and antibiotics, led to waves of dietary fads based on changing nutritional theories — good fats and bad fats, good fibers and bad fibers, and so on. Not only packages but also cookbooks and even some restaurant menus listed calories, lipoproteins, and soluble fibers.

Amid all this, a genuine interest in good food and the environment developed a countervailing trend. Interest in exotic cuisines has made it possible to find products that previously were all but unavailable, such as leeks, shallots, wild and cultivated mushrooms. Organic gardening, revival of heirloom varieties of fruits and vegetables, revival of farmers' markets, small-scale output of honest breads, old-fashioned cheeses, wines, and beers, all have found new practitioners and willing customers. Even large companies have found it profitable to cater to these tastes. The palate survives, and with it a craving for traditional foods.

John L. Hess and Karen Hess, *The Taste of America* (1977; 3rd ed., 1989); *Martha Washington's Booke of Cookery,* transcription and commentary by Karen Hess (1981); Mary Randolph, *The Virginia House-Wife* (1824; facsimile ed., introduction by Karen Hess, 1984); Sarah Rutledge,*The Carolina Housewife* (1847; facsimile ed., introduction by Anna Wells Rutledge, 1979).

KAREN HESS

COOLEY, THOMAS

(1824–1898), jurist, first chairman of the Interstate Commerce Commission. Cooley was born on a small farm in upstate New York, the tenth of fifteen children. From his parents Cooley acquired a devout Protestant faith and a love of literature and history. Despite meager circumstances, Cooley attended three years of high school before apprenticing with a lawyer. When he was nineteen, Cooley moved to the Michigan frontier. There he became a nationally respected law teacher, scholar, judge, and administrator,

whose contributions to the University of Michigan Law School, the Michigan Supreme Court, and the Interstate Commerce Commission helped establish the prestige of those institutions. His central contribution to American law, however, was *A Treatise on the Constitutional Limitations Which Rest upon the Legislative Power of the States of the American Union* (1868), the most popular and influential constitutional law treatise of the late nineteenth century. *Constitutional Limitations* was the first treatise to formulate "due process of law" as a broad protection of property and liberty of contract. The treatise served as a basic authority for the Fourteenth Amendment's elaboration during the early *Lochner* era, when the judiciary began using the due process clause to void social welfare legislation.

Accordingly, historians have considered Cooley a seminal proponent of laissez-faire constitutionalism, but this assessment is wide of the mark. Cooley drew his constitutional views from two sources: the principles of Jacksonian democracy and the common law tradition. From these he derived a commitment to private property, equal rights, and political liberty and an aversion to corporate privileges.

Cooley's landmark treatise illustrates this Jacksonian–common law constitutionalism. He balanced a chapter advocating substantive due process with chapters supporting extensive police power regulation of private property and limited contract clause protection of corporate charters. Another seminal chapter urged expanded First Amendment protection of speech and press.

Cooley's constitutionalism is shown also by his work on the Michigan Supreme Court. In his opinions, he drew from the common law to set distinct limits on government power, but he did so to prevent corporations from using their influence to receive government largess or to violate the public trust. Cooley urged clear separation between the spheres of public and private activity to prevent railroads from using public credit and tax revenues to finance their development; to prevent manufacturing companies from using eminent domain to acquire mill sites; and to prevent businessmen and lawyers from using libel law to deter newspaper investigations of their activities.

Cooley's work on the Interstate Commerce Commission (ICC) illustrates the same perspective. He interpreted the ICC Act as authorizing the commission to regulate railroad rates, but only to lower them, never to raise them. Cooley also opposed judicial review of the commission's rate determinations. He saw rate making as an instance when common law due process did not require judicial process. (Eventually, the federal courts rejected these positions.)

Thus Cooley's constitutionalism was not dedicated simply to limited government and the protection of property. Although he believed the economic system generally should be free from state control, he also believed that government should closely regulate enterprises that possessed legal privileges not equally available to all citizens. Essentially, Cooley envisioned society as it was in the Age of Jackson: composed of small-scale entrepreneurs disciplined by a self-regulating market. He never understood that late-nineteenth-century technology was making large-scale, market-dominating corporations the normal form of economic endeavor and rendering the traditional common law an anachronism.

Consequently, Cooley's lot was to restate the constitutional principles of pre–Civil War America in an urbanizing and industrializing era without successfully addressing the emerging contradiction between its commitment to limited government and its distrust of corporate enterprise. By so doing, he unwittingly laid the groundwork for corporate America's claim to freedom from government regulation.

Alan Jones, *The Constitutional Conservatism of Thomas McIntyre Cooley* (1987); Phillip Paludan, *A Covenant with Death* (1975), chap. 10.

STEPHEN A. SIEGEL

See also Constitution; Interstate Commerce Commission.

COOLIDGE, CALVIN

(1872–1933), thirtieth president of the United States. Coolidge presided over an era of governmental frugality and probusiness policies that were popular at the time but later regarded as misconceived.

Born in Plymouth Notch, Vermont, Coolidge graduated from Amherst College in 1895 and three years later established a law practice in Northampton, Massachusetts. A conservative Republican, he rose rapidly in politics, serving successively as city councillor and solicitor (1899–1902), state legislator (1907–1909), mayor (1910–1911), state senator (1912–1915), lieutenant governor (1916–1918), and governor (1919–1921). In 1919 he gained national prominence by intervening to restore order during a Boston police strike and in 1920 was the surprise nominee of his party for vice president. Coolidge was noted for his cautious reserve, public taciturnity, and pronounced frugality, but he was also a competent administrator, a skillful manipulator of the media, and a man devoted to career and family.

As Warren G. Harding's vice president (1921–1923), Coolidge did little. But when Harding's death in August 1923 made him president, he moved quickly to neutralize the effects of the Harding scandals, control the party machinery, and secure the 1924 presidential nomination for himself. In November 1924, he was easily elected, receiving 54 percent of the popular vote and 382 electoral votes to 136 for Democrat John W. Davis and 13 for Progressive Robert M. La Follette. His victory seemed to confirm both the appeal of his public image and the popularity of the conservative policies that he claimed were responsible for a growing national prosperity. In the domestic policy sphere, he helped secure further cuts in federal taxes and expenditures, maintain a high protective tariff, reorient regulatory policy along probusiness lines, and block the McNary-Haugen scheme for raising farm income by dumping agricultural surpluses abroad. In foreign affairs, he accepted the guidance of his secretaries of state, Charles Evans Hughes and Frank B. Kellogg, and continued the search for improved international relations through mechanisms operating outside the League of Nations. Among his administration's diplomatic achievements were the Dawes Plan for scaling down German reparations, the Stimson accords for pacifying Nicaragua, and the Kellogg-Briand Pact outlawing war.

In 1927 Coolidge announced that he would not run for president again, and in March 1929 he returned to Northampton. There he busied himself with writing his autobiography and a daily newspaper column entitled "Thinking Things over with Calvin Coolidge."

Throughout his tenure, Coolidge remained a remarkably popular president. But the Great Depression brought his policies into disrepute, and most historians now regard him as having been overly complacent and inactive, lacking in vision, and ill·equipped to deal with the period's emerging problems. In the conservative 1980s he became a hero in some quarters, but scholarly revisionism has been limited largely to more positive assessments of his rhetorical, political, and public relations skills.

Claude M. Fuess, *Calvin Coolidge* (1940); Donald R. Mc-Coy, *Calvin Coolidge* (1967); William Allen White, *A Puritan in Babylon* (1938).

ELLIS W. HAWLEY

See also Conservatism; Elections: 1920, 1924.

COOPER, JAMES FENIMORE

(1789–1851), novelist and historian. Son of a Federalist judge, Cooper was expelled from Yale for a dangerous prank. He then joined the navy but resigned his commission to marry. He converted to Jeffersonian principles, but then tried to live as an eighteenth-century gentleman while the fevers of Jacksonian democracy swept the land. At the height of his popularity as a novelist, he took his family to Europe, and during his seven-year stay, he wrote a fascinating assessment of his native land, *Notions of the Americans* (1829), and gathered the materials for four travel books. *A Letter to His Countrymen* (1834) was a bitter attack on American provincialism. Upon his return in 1833 he retreated to Cooperstown and plunged into a series of lawsuits designed to force the townspeople to respect the sanctity of private property and truth in journalism. *The American Democrat* (1838), designed as a textbook for high school students, lectured Americans on their political and social responsibilities.

By the time of his death Cooper had developed an international reputation as America's "national novelist," but he was also a keen observer of the political and cultural life of his nation, an accomplished controversialist, and a fine naval historian. His studies of naval history included *The History of the Navy of the United States of America* (1839), *The Cruise of the Somers* (1844), and *Lives of Distinguished American Naval Officers* (1846).

But it is for his fiction that Cooper is best known, especially for the mythic sweep and power of his five Leatherstocking novels (*The Pioneers,* 1823, *The Last of the Mohicans,* 1826, *The Prairie,* 1827, *The Pathfinder,* 1840, and *The Deerslayer,* 1841). The Leatherstocking series represents, in D. H. Lawrence's words, "a *decrescendo* of reality, and a crescendo of beauty," but all his novels engaged historical themes and helped to form the popular sense of American history and romantic historiography in the nineteenth century.

In his second novel, *The Spy* (1821), Cooper adapted the historical romance of Sir Walter Scott to an array of themes suggested by the American Revolution: the legitimacy of the rebellion, the enfeebling arrogance of British officers, the random violence of paramilitary groups of self-proclaimed patriots, the patriarchal benevolence of Washington as the "father of his country," and the cultural centrality of the outcast spy of the title, Harvey Birch. It was an immediate success and, together with Washington Irving's *The Sketch Book* (1820) and William Cullen Bryant's *Poems* (1821), was cited as evidence that American culture had begun to produce a worthwhile democratic art.

For his next novel, *The Pioneers,* he drew on his experience growing up in the frontier village of Cooperstown to investigate what it meant to inherit the American history of conflict over possession of the landscape, setting the claims of Native Americans, British Loyalists, American Patriots, roaming hunters, and forest-clearing farmers against each other. If the novel wistfully resolves all these conflicts in the marriage of the children of all the contending parties, it nevertheless succeeds brilliantly as a thoroughly *American* fiction, not least in its invention of the Leatherstocking, Natty Bumppo, Cooper's essential American hero. Other novels similarly (and sometimes as successfully) engaged American history. *The Wept of Wish-ton-Wish* (1829) was set in Connecticut in the period of King Philip's War; the "Littlepage Trilogy" (*Satanstoe, The Chainbearer,* and *The Redskins,* 1845–1846) chronicled events of the Anti-Rent Wars in New York (1839–1846) virtually as they occurred.

The weaknesses of Cooper's fiction are famous. James Russell Lowell called attention to Cooper's undemocratic class consciousness and to the limitations of his female characters: "And the women he draws from one model don't vary, / All sappy as maples and flat as a prairie." Mark Twain hilariously skewered the excesses of Cooper's romanticism in "Fenimore Cooper's Literary Offenses" (1895). Moreover, all his fictions reflect Cooper's didactic concern to educate his audience in the requirements of democracy, and he could be oppressively schoolmasterish. But his characters (including women) are often more richly developed than is usually recognized and compose a remarkable gallery of American types. The novels also constitute a record of American life and society and at their best present a richness, depth, and complexity that was unsurpassed in American fiction before the works of Hawthorne and Melville.

James Franklin Beard, ed., *The Letters and Journals of James Fenimore Cooper,* 6 vols. (1960–1968); John P. McWilliams, *Political Justice in a Republic: James Fenimore Cooper's America* (1972).

JAMES D. WALLACE

See also Literature.

COPLAND, AARON

(1900–1990), composer and writer about American music. Often called the "dean of American composers," Copland referred to himself simply as a "good citizen of the Republic of Music." He filled both roles during his lifetime and many of his pieces are considered paradigms of American music by the public. His popular ballet scores are still regularly performed, as is *Lincoln Portrait.* His "Fanfare for the Common Man" has been flattered by imitation in film scores, commercials, and music for the Olympics.

Copland studied piano in his native Brooklyn and by 1917 had become a modernist in reaction to the more traditional aesthetic of his harmony and composition teacher, Rubin Goldmark. From 1921 to 1924 Copland studied at the American Academy at Fontainebleau with Nadia Boulanger. On his return to the United States, he contributed articles to *Modern Music,* participated in the League of Composers, and in 1928 founded (with Roger Sessions) the Copland-Sessions Concerts. During the 1920s, Copland incorporated the rhythms, instruments, and blue notes of jazz into some of his compositions.

For a brief period in the mid-1930s Copland was associated with the Composers' Collective and wrote for the *New Masses.* He promoted singable music for workers, and his marching song "Into the Streets, May First" (text by Alfred Hayes) won the 1934 *New Masses* song competition. His opera for children, *The Second Hurricane* (1936), and the *Outdoor Overture* (1938), composed for New York City's High School for Music and Art, are examples of his commitment to making American music accessible to a wide audience.

Copland incorporated folk and popular music into such "Americanist" works as the scores for the ballets *Billy the Kid* (1938), *Rodeo* (1942), and *Appalachian Spring* (1943–1944), which portray episodes from American regional history. Copland also traveled to Latin America during these years and utilized the rhythmic and melodic patterns he heard there in several pieces. His film scores, which reflect a variety of styles, helped liberate composers from the rut into which much movie music had fallen. The *Lincoln Portrait* (1942), for orchestra and narrator, incorporates popular tunes from Lincoln's time along with the president's own speeches and writings. This patriotic work was scheduled for performance at the inauguration of Dwight D. Eisenhower in 1953 but was withdrawn because of congressional accusations that Copland had been a "communist sympathizer" in the 1930s.

In the fifties and sixties, Copland abandoned the self-conscious Americanism of the previous period and returned to the modernism of his 1920s music. An interest in the twelve-tone scale influenced *Connotations* (1962), composed for the opening of Philharmonic Hall in New York's Lincoln Center, and *Inscape* (1967), which he wrote for the 125th anniversary of the New York Philharmonic Orchestra. But the *Duo* for flute and piano (1971) and other works of the seventies returned with a fresh perspective to the harmonies and sound, if not the direct quotation from familiar songs, characteristic of Copland's music of the 1930s and 1940s.

Copland, who headed the composition faculty at the Berkshire Music Center at Tanglewood from 1940 to 1965, was much honored in his career. He received a Pulitzer Prize in 1945 and an Oscar in 1949. In 1964, he and soprano Leontyne Price became the first musicians to receive the Presidential Medal of Freedom. Queens College of the City University of New York established the Aaron Copland School of Music in 1982.

Arthur Berger, *Aaron Copland* (1953); Aaron Copland and Vivian Perlis, *Copland: 1900 through 1942* (1984).

BARBARA L. TISCHLER

See also Music.

COPLEY, JOHN SINGLETON

(1738–1815), painter. Born of Irish immigrants in Boston, Copley received little formal artistic training. His widowed mother's marriage in 1748 to Peter Pelham, a London-trained engraver, introduced Copley to portraiture through Pelham's European engravings. Pelham's death in 1751 forced the impoverished youth to set himself up as a fledgling artist. Painting in the colonies at this time consisted almost wholly of portraiture of prominent families or commercial signs, both usually executed by poorly trained, itinerant artist tradesmen. Copley with studious meticulousness slowly refined his natural ability, assimilating technique through observing the work of other local artists, especially Robert Feke and Joseph Blackburn. His mastery of his art through trial and error, combined with his superlative ability to convey the sitter's character, made him by his mid-twenties a prominent artist well patronized by the prosperous merchant class attracted by the linear, insightful verisimilitude of his style.

A portrait of his half brother Henry, *Boy with a Squirrel,* submitted to London's annual exhibition of the Society of Artists in 1766, brought great acclaim and invitations from both Joshua Reynolds, then president of the Royal Academy, and the American-born painter Benjamin West to work in Europe. In 1769 he married the daughter of a rich Tory merchant and soon purchased a twenty-acre farm on Boston's Beacon Hill. It was not until 1774, with political unrest and violence escalating in Boston, that Copley, the most accomplished painter in the colonies, heeded the repeated urgings of Reynolds and West and departed for London. Immediately he embarked on a tour of Italy, Germany, and Holland, studying and copying the old masters, ardently imitating them in preference to his own painfully worked out technique.

His family joined Copley in London in 1775, and his career prospered. Although continuing to paint portraits, he increasingly turned his attention to grand history painting, which was at the time deemed to be of higher aesthetic significance. The first of these, *Watson and the Shark* (1778), brought Copley membership in the Royal Academy. His rise to wide public acclaim in England was epitomized by the successes of *The Death of Chatham* (1779–1781), portraying the recent death in Parliament of the American sympathizer William Pitt; *The Death of Major Pierson* (1782–1784); and *The Repulse of the Floating Batteries at Gibraltar* (1788) — all of which were exhibited privately to enormous crowds of paying spectators.

But, embittered and unsettled by personal tragedies and a wide economic downturn in the 1790s and increasingly alienated from both colleagues and connoisseurs because of his irascible, vindictive personality, Copley's ability to capture critical acclaim and patronage deteriorated. His work after 1800 grew superficial, losing the lucidity and directness that had so informed his earlier paintings. Although he remained in England and worked constantly, he painted no more innovative canvases.

Throughout the nineteenth century Copley's fame derived from having been an American who had achieved prominence in England. Not until the twentieth century did the clarity and force of his American portraits and their independence from mannered European idealization win wide critical appreciation.

James T. Flexner, *John Singleton Copley* (1948); Jules D. Prown, *John Singleton Copley* (1966).

RICHARD B. KOWALL

See also Expatriates and Exiles; Painting and Sculpture.

COPPERHEADS

The Copperheads, or "Peace Democrats," vexed Abraham Lincoln and the Republicans during the Civil War, campaigning against the war as a failure and opposing many military appropriations. The term *Copperheads* apparently came from the habit of some midwestern, hard-money Democrats of wearing copper pennies around their necks. Like most Democrats who supported the war, the antiwar Copperheads were opposed to the emancipation of the slaves. They were unhappy with the war effort, and reflecting their Jacksonian heritage, they disliked Republican economic policies, especially a national banking system.

The most notorious Copperhead was Clement Vallandigham, an Ohio congressman who gave up his seat to campaign for peace. In 1863, the writ of habeas corpus having been suspended, Gen. Ambrose Burnside had Vallandigham arrested; Lincoln released him, but exiled him into Confederate territory. He made his way north by ship and then across Canada. He ran for governor of Ohio in 1863, but lost, as did many Copperheads in state elections that year, in the wake of northern victories at Gettysburg and Vicksburg.

Still, the Copperheads retained some power. With Confederate agents, they subsidized several Democratic papers throughout the war, as well as freeing prisoners and capturing ships. They opposed the Democratic nomination of Gen. George McClellan for president in 1864 because he refused to accept their demands for an immediate peace; but they still had enough standing in the party to force the selection of Ohio Copperhead George Pendleton as the vice-presidential candidate. Their actions lent added credence to the Republican party's postwar use of the "bloody shirt" to charge Democrats with disloyalty.

See also Civil War; Elections: 1864.

CORE

See Congress of Racial Equality.

CORRUPT BARGAIN

"Corrupt bargain" refers to charges by partisans of Andrew Jackson that John Quincy Adams and Henry Clay conspired to deny Jackson the presidency when the election of 1824 was thrown into the House of Representatives.

After an acrimonious campaign involving Jackson of Tennessee, Adams of Massachusetts, Clay of Kentucky, and William H. Crawford of Georgia, Jackson received the largest popular vote (43.1 percent to Adams's 30.5 percent). In the electoral college, Jackson led, with ninety-nine votes to eighty-four for Adams, forty-one for Crawford and thirty-seven for Clay. Because no candidate held an electoral college majority, the House of Representatives had to choose between the two leaders, with each state delegation having one vote. Clay decided the issue by throwing his considerable influence in the House to Adams.

In late January 1825, before the House vote, a Philadelphia newspaper charged that Adams had offered Clay an appointment as secretary of state in return for his support. Clay demanded an investigation, but his accusers failed to appear. The charge was serious because of the widespread belief at the time that presidential candidates should not campaign or make deals to obtain office. When, after being elected, Adams did name Clay secretary of state the "corrupt bargain" charge was made.

See also Elections: 1824.

CORRUPTION

American political corruption — the betrayal of an office or duty for some consideration — may seem to be a subject uniquely blessed with opportunities for historical research and controversy. Yet it has never commanded significant scholarly attention, thanks chiefly to several vexing problems of definition and interpretation. First, *corruption* is simply a catchall for specific abuses — bribery, graft, extortion, nepotism, ticket-fixing — each of which, arguably, has a distinct history. Second, given the decentralization of American political institutions, it is also arguable that the history of corruption on the national level would differ appreciably from that on the state or municipal level, and which of these histories would throw more light on the political system is open to question: a scandal in Washington may matter less than chronic payoffs to city health inspectors. Finally, as Walter Lippmann once remarked, the history of corruption is really the history of reform — of those occasions when corruption is alleged, discovered, and attacked. Working with evidence almost always supplied by hostile sources is a daunting challenge to historical objectivity.

These caveats notwithstanding, a case can be made for dividing the history of American corruption into three broad periods. The first extends from the beginning of European settlement in North America through the American Revolution, the second from the early nineteenth through the early twentieth centuries, and the last from roughly the Great Depression to the present.

Prior to the American Revolution, the most spectacular examples of corruption center on the colonial governors — a dreary succession of royal and corporate placemen whose chief concern was grabbing as much as they could before returning home. Most assumed they had every right to do so. Capt. Samuel Argall, deputy governor of Virginia from 1617 to 1619, boasted openly of his intention to "make hay whilst the sunne doth shine, however it may fare with the generality." No less audacious was Governor Benjamin Fletcher of New York (1692–1698), who took protection money from pirates, shook down Indian traders, bilked the customs, padded military payrolls, and stole funds raised to pay the provincial debt. "To recount all his arts of squeezing money both out of the publick and private purses would make a volume instead of a letter," grumbled one of Fletcher's contemporaries.

Advancing hand in glove with proconsular venality was the willingness of colonial merchants and customs officials to work around the Acts of Trade and Navigation by which Britain regulated imperial commerce. For importers and exporters in every coastal city, the difference between success and failure often came down to whether they could evade this or that duty, get a better price for their wheat in, say, the French West Indies, or produce a manifest for twenty barrels of molasses when there were thirty below deck. By 1765, according to one estimate, systematic smuggling, graft, extortion, and bribery in the colonies cost the British Treasury £700,000 a year. Attempts were made from time to time to clean things up, but defiant juries and mercenary judges — one of whom remarked "that in his opinion the Nicetyes of the Law ought not to be observed" — invariably got in the way.

Still another source of political corruption in the colonies was the profitability of land speculation. Angling for a share of the apparently endless supply of American land, investors and politicians on both sides of the Atlantic left a trail of chicanery, inside dealing, favoritism, and outright theft that even now staggers the imagination. The "Walking Purchase" of 1737, by which Pennsylvania authorities tricked native peoples out of most of their lands west of the Delaware River, is only one of many scandalous examples. For suitable considerations, George Cornbury, sometime governor of New York, handed out grants the size of entire English counties; his Hardenburgh Patent ran to an amazing 2 million acres, larger than Connecticut.

The banality of this corruption mocked a widespread belief that the New World had once afforded pristine sanctuary from the evils of the Old. Around the middle of the eighteenth century, restoring this American purity in fact became an issue of major religious and political significance in the colonies. Its growth fed, and in turn fed upon, charges by politicians and pamphleteers of the British opposition that corrupt ministerial "influence" — patronage, bribery, and graft — had neutralized Parliament as a bulwark of English liberty.

Barricading the new nation against corruption thus proved one of the revolutionary generation's most critical tasks. The institutional solution, elaborated in the 1787 federal Constitution, linked the preservation of liberty to a system of checks and balances that limited executive power and buttressed legislative autonomy. If the corrupt influence that destroyed Parliament could never be eradicated, in other words, at least its career might be obstructed and its effects blunted. But so great a task demanded more than constitutional tinkering. Ultimately, the only enduring safeguard against political corruption in a republic was the personal "virtue" of its citizens — not just honesty, but a willingness to sacrifice selfish interests for the good of the whole.

This way of defining and dealing with corruption gradually lost its edge, however. The early Republic proved comparatively free of the systematic corruption that had so distressed Americans earlier, but rampant factionalism in state and national affairs during the 1780s and 1790s punctured the hope of rallying virtuous citizens around a single definition of the public good. Thomas Jefferson, James Madison, and Albert Gallatin, among others, predicted that Federalist financial policies would cause massive corruption. But after his election in 1800, Jefferson's conciliatory policies appeared to confirm that the old ways of thinking about corruption no longer applied.

Beginning around the 1820s, a new chapter opened in the history of American political corruption. Rapid westward expansion, urbanization, and the advent of industrialization vastly increased the importance of government at all levels — not merely as a short-run source of lucrative contracts, franchises, and licenses but also as the source of the laws of property and exchange that would promote the accumulation of capital. Liberal economic and social thought, riding the crest of a new spirit of competitive in-

dividualism, obliterated the old republican ideal of self-sacrifice for the common good. Concurrently, political parties, once taken as evidence of corrupt executive influence, gained acceptance as the means to manage elections, negotiate conflicts of interest and opinion, mark the boundaries of legitimate dissent, and regulate access to power.

Corruption nourished by these changes permeated the executive and legislative branches of the federal government throughout the nineteenth century, peaking in the scandals that rocked the Grant administration in the mid-1870s. What most aroused concern, though, was corruption identified with municipal and state governments — focal points of business pressure for concessions and privileges, and nurseries of the great nineteenth-century political machines. Its characteristic form, pioneered by New York's Tammany Hall, was a web of understandings between party leaders, officeholders, and businessmen willing to cut corners. In return for getting out the vote, the machine received exclusive control of government appointments and programs — the spoils of office. Its placemen returned a fixed percentage of their salaries to the organization, along with a cut of whatever bribes, kickbacks, and the like they could devise. The resulting stream of "boodle" (a lush new vocabulary of corruption was being created, too) then passed down to county and district leaders, ward heelers, and precinct captains. They completed the cycle by distributing the gifts and favors that ensured voter loyalty to the organization on election day.

Responding to this epidemic of graft, bribery, extortion, and electoral fraud, reformers again took up the cudgels against corruption. Some, like E. L. Godkin, Charles Eliot Norton, and Henry Adams in the 1870s and 1880s, expressed upper-class outrage; others, above all the progressives of the pre–World War I era, spoke to the worries of the middle classes. Both agreed on the fundamentals. Unlike their eighteenth-century predecessors, who had associated corruption with undue executive "influence" over legislative bodies, they affirmed the beneficial role of political parties and did not question the capitalist system. The remedies they instituted were correspondingly moderate: civil service legislation to place government jobs beyond the reach of spoilsmen; immigration restrictions to curb the power of big-city bosses; federal and state laws mandating direct primaries and restricting or regulating corporate campaign contributions; and, overall, a trend toward government by nonpartisan professionals sitting on commissions, bureaus, boards, and agencies that could not be controlled by party bosses.

After World War I, and most noticeably after World War II, patterns of corruption and reform in the United States shifted yet again. One change was the demise of the political machines. What happened is a subject of controversy, although the prevailing wisdom emphasizes the advent of the "welfare state" under the New Deal, which deprived the machines of popular support and made them easy pickings for organized crime. Another change was the apparent decline of federal-level bribery, graft, extortion, and the like between the 1920s and the 1960s. Warren G. Harding's administration suffered from Teapot Dome and other depredations of the "Ohio Gang." Revelations of corruption likewise embarrassed Presidents Harry S. Truman and Dwight D. Eisenhower. From time to time members of Congress, too, have run afoul of the law. But Franklin D. Roosevelt's twelve years in the White House were untroubled by major scandals. So were the Kennedy and Johnson administrations.

More to the point, the 1960s and 1970s witnessed a legislative offensive against corruption that is virtually without parallel in American history. Prompted by a 1964 probe into the activities of Robert G. ("Bobby") Baker, secretary to the Senate majority, both houses of Congress created Select Committees on Standards and Conduct to prepare codes of ethics for their members. Limitations on campaign contributions by individuals and corporations were established by the 1971 Federal Election Campaign Act (FECA). When the Watergate scandal of 1972–1974 revealed massive illegal corporate and personal contributions to President Richard M. Nixon's 1972 campaign, Congress responded by tightening FECA and creating the Federal Elections Commission. In 1977, moreover, both

the Senate and House acted to close loopholes in their own codes of ethics and passed the Foreign Corrupt Practices Act, prohibiting gifts or payments to foreign officials by American companies. The 1978 Ethics in Government Act imposed stringent financial disclosure requirements on federal officeholders and authorized special prosecutors (now referred to as "independent counsel") to investigate all charges of corruption against them. By 1987 it had been used eight times, twice to consider charges against President Ronald Reagan's attorney general Edwin Meese.

Nationwide, there was a striking increase in the number of state and local officials charged under federal law with corrupt practices of one kind or another — from two hundred or so every year in the middle 1970s to nearly five hundred in 1986 alone, according to Justice Department figures. Prosecutors found corruption particularly widespread in New York, Chicago, Philadelphia, Washington, and Boston.

There are indications, on the other hand, that congressional codes of conduct have done little to alter patterns of corruption on Capitol Hill. The "Koreagate" scandal of 1976–1978 revealed dozens of congressmen who had taken money or gifts from agents of the South Korean government; the House managed to reprimand only three of its members, and the Senate took no action at all. In the "Abscam" scandal of 1978–1980, FBI agents posing as Arab sheiks found numerous public officials willing to accept money for help with immigration authorities; six representatives and one senator were convicted of bribery. In the "Wedtech" scandal of 1986–1989, payoffs by a military contractor led to the conviction of two representatives and dozens of other figures on charges of racketeering, tax evasion, bribery, fraud, grand larceny, and perjury. All told, no fewer than twenty members of the One Hundredth Congress have been accused of misconduct, ranging from sexual harassment to misuse of campaign contributions, bribery, and tax evasion. Corruption also made new inroads into the White House during Reagan's presidency. Between 1981 and 1989, dozens of high-ranking Reagan appointees were charged with wrongdoing. They included, besides Attorney General Meese, Labor Secretary Raymond J. Donovan, the first member of a president's cabinet to be indicted while in office, and Franklyn ("Lyn") Nofziger, one of Reagan's key advisers. Donovan was subsequently acquitted; Nofziger was convicted of illegally lobbying the executive branch on behalf of private clients, among them the Wedtech Corporation, but his conviction was reversed on appeal.

The Supreme Court meanwhile placed new impediments in the way of prevention and prosecution of corruption. In *Buckley* v. *Valeo* (1976) and *First National Bank of Boston* v. *Bellotti* (1978), the Court struck down certain long-established state restrictions on individual and corporate campaign contributions on the grounds that they violated First Amendment guarantees to free speech. In *Federal Election Commission* v. *National Conservative Political Action Committee* (1985), the Court likewise voided limitations on campaign spending by political action committees (PACs). Perhaps more important, its decision in the 1987 case of *McNally* v. *United States* blunted the use of mail-fraud statutes to prosecute state and local officials for corruption. Dozens of prior convictions and ongoing prosecutions were said to have been jeopardized as a result.

Another, contemporary trend, altogether new in its scope and magnitude, is the spread of corruption financed by the stupendous resources of the illegal drug "industry" — gross sales of which neared the $120 billion mark in 1988, far exceeding the combined profits of the nation's five hundred largest industrial corporations. According to some authorities, payoffs to police, judges, and other officials have brought about the effective disintegration of law enforcement in many parts of the United States. If that is so, then this constitutes corruption of a kind and on a scale for which there are simply no precedents in American historical experience.

EDWIN G. BURROWS

See also City Government; Civil Service Reform; Crédit Mobilier of America; Hatch Act; Iran-Contra Affair; Police Forces; Progressivism; Republicanism; Spoils System; Tammany Hall; Teapot Dome Affair; Tweed Ring; Urban Bosses and Machine Politics; Watergate Scandal.

COTTON

References to phenomena that make up the "fabric of history" are usually metaphorical, but in the case of cotton, the fiber truly did help weave the fabric of American history. Cotton was, above all, a crucial factor in the nation's economic development. But cotton cultivation was also a source of conflict (racial, sectional, and between social classes) before the Civil War, and after the war, cotton fields and factories engendered debate over the extent to which the federal government could change society and the economy through centralized planning.

Cotton was grown in the New World and in Asia for centuries before Europeans settled in America. English colonists first cultivated cotton to make homespun clothing. Production significantly increased when the American Revolution cut off supplies of European cloth, but the real expansion of production came with the rising demand for raw cotton from the British textile industry. This led to the development of an efficient cotton gin as a tool for removing seeds from cotton fibers in 1793. The breeding of superior strains from Mexican cotton and the opening of western lands further expanded production. (During the early 1800s, the center of production moved south and west, from cotton's early national cradle in South Carolina and Georgia to the black belt of Alabama and Mississippi.) Production rose from 2 million pounds in 1791 to a billion pounds in 1860; by 1840, the United States was producing over 60 percent of the world's cotton. The economic boom in the cotton South attracted migrants, built up wealth among the free inhabitants, encouraged capitalization of investments like railroads, and facilitated territorial expansion.

Cotton also contributed to the national economy. The crop comprised more than half the total value of domestic exports in the period 1815–1860, and in 1860, earnings from cotton paid for 60 percent of all imports. Cotton also built up domestic capital, attracted foreign investment, and contributed to the industrial growth of the

North. In the early 1800s, northeastern merchants began channeling commercial profits into industrial production of cloth (using southern cotton). These early textile factories and the concomitant growth of the working class created political and social problems in the new Republic; reactions ranged from fears about the fragmentation of the polity into distinct economic classes to celebrations of free labor as the strongest foundation for the nation.

Just as cotton mills revealed the problem of inequality among white Americans, cotton fields expressed the racial inequality inherent in black slavery. The relation of cotton to slavery is complex. Except in the Upper South slavery was not declining in the 1790s. The crop was, therefore, not responsible for perpetuating slavery where it already existed, though it certainly was responsible for the continuing expansion of the institution westward. Whites' acceptance of black slavery, combined with their gradual removal of southern Indians from cotton lands, demonstrated the extent to which they assumed that the political and economic liberties of whites were inversely related to those of people of color.

By the 1830s, the South's political economy — resting on cotton and slaves — was a key factor in sectional tension between North and South. The possibility that cotton cultivation would continue to move west and the prospect that new slave states would thereafter enter the Union were the most significant causes of this tension. Although slavery was not necessary for growing cotton (three-quarters of southern whites held no slaves, and much of the South's cotton was produced by free workers), southern whites assumed that slavery was an efficient method of increasing production, and they wanted to take slaves wherever cotton might be grown. They believed that their continuing to use slaves to grow cotton in new, western territories was their right. Northern whites assumed otherwise and sought to curtail the expansion of slavery in the nation. Although slavery alone was not the cause of the Civil War, controversy over whether the South's peculiar institution would continue expanding (and over the role of the federal government in regulating its expansion) was central to the impending crisis.

After the war, cotton cultivation provided new debate over the role of the federal government in economic affairs. Although declining in overall importance in the American economy, cotton production actually expanded after 1865. Out of the disarray that followed emancipation, southern landowners constructed new forms of servitude — tenantry and sharecropping. These coercive institutions (involving the extension of goods or credit to rural inhabitants in exchange for their labor) controlled poor whites as well as newly freed blacks. Rural poverty, overproduction, and the resulting low prices for cotton all contributed to the South's postwar stagnation. The region's woes increased after 1894 with the arrival of the boll weevil, which savaged cotton crops.

The Great Depression exacerbated the South's chronic poverty. But the proposed cure — federal supervision of agriculture — provoked controversy. Federal intervention had begun with the creation of the U.S. Department of Agriculture, especially its Extension Service (1914), which attacked the problem of the boll weevil with federal funds and agents. Intervention continued with the New Deal, after Franklin D. Roosevelt created the Federal Emergency Relief Administration and its rural unit, the Agricultural Adjustment Administration (AAA). The AAA drafted monetary incentives to landholders for reducing production of cotton, in hopes of raising the crop's price. Responding to this experiment with centralized power, critics on the Right complained of its invasive meddling with the market, while critics on the Left pointed out that the truly impoverished — tenants and sharecroppers — gained little from the program. Indeed, although southern landholders reduced the acreage of their cotton fields by 30 to 50 percent, there was no parallel decline in tenantry — the most glaring manifestation of rural poverty — as planners had hoped there would be. Federal policy, in fact, probably worsened conditions for sharecroppers and tenants.

After the 1930s, cotton cultivation moved farther west, especially into Texas and California. This shift began a trend toward "agribusiness" — large estates dependent on mechanization — a trend that accelerated after World War II. In the meantime, many rural southerners left farming for the textile industry as cotton mills closed in the Northeast and reopened in the old cotton South. Cotton's contribution to the domestic textile industry weakened, nonetheless, because of increased importation of foreign textiles and increased use of synthetic fibers. The South's calls for tariffs to regulate foreign competition formed a new chapter in the continuing debate over federal regulation of the economy. And western cotton cultivation, because of its dependence on irrigation, raised new questions about its potentially destructive effects on the environment.

Stuart Bruchey, *The Wealth of the Nation: An Economic History of the United States* (1988); Pete Daniel, *Breaking the Land: The Transformation of Cotton, Tobacco, and Rice Cultures since 1880* (1985); Gavin Wright, *The Political Economy of the Cotton South: Households, Markets, and Wealth in the Nineteenth Century* (1978).

JOYCE E. CHAPLIN

See also Agriculture; Cotton Gin; Plantation System; Slavery; Textile Industry.

COTTON GIN

Invented by Eli Whitney in 1793, the cotton gin was a machine for removing the seeds from cotton balls. It revolutionized the southern economy and helped perpetuate slavery. Except in the Sea Islands of South Carolina and Georgia, southern planters could grow only short-staple cotton. The fibers of this variety stuck to the seeds, and it was expensive to remove them by hand. Whitney's gin (for engine) consisted of a cylinder with rows of wire teeth rotating in a box. The teeth caught the fibers, and a second cylinder, rotating in the opposite direction, pulled cotton from the wires.

A person operating a gin could clean fifty times as much cotton in a day as one working by hand. Whitney made little money from his invention because his machine was so easy to copy. The real beneficiary was the South and its economy. Cotton production and prices rose quickly and remained at consistently high levels. Because cotton could now be cultivated throughout most of the region, the South became the

world's leading cotton supplier, becoming closely tied to the British textile industry. The gin also revitalized slavery, which had been largely stagnant since the spurt of abolitionist sentiment during the Revolution, and dashed the hope of many Founding Fathers that the institution would soon die out.

See also Cotton; Whitney, Eli.

COUGHLIN, FATHER CHARLES E.

(1891–1979), Catholic priest, radio personality, and political activist. Coughlin is not the only Catholic priest to have become an important political figure in America. But at the peak of his public career he was surely the most influential, and at its sordid conclusion he was perhaps the most menacing.

Coughlin was of Irish descent and spent his childhood in Hamilton, Ontario, where from an early age he was immersed in the institutions of the Catholic church. Ordained as a priest in 1916, he taught in Catholic schools for several years and in 1926 moved to Royal Oak, Michigan (a suburb of Detroit), to serve as pastor of a new church, the Shrine of the Little Flower. The small parish generated little money and faced an active Ku Klux Klan; Coughlin set out immediately to combat both problems by broadcasting his sermons over a local radio station in hopes of attracting attention, sympathy, and financial support. His magnetic radio personality quickly won him enormous popularity, and by 1930 his "Golden Hour of the Little Flower," broadcast over the CBS radio network, was attracting as many as 40 million listeners.

By then, Coughlin had turned his attention from religious to political issues. His radio broadcasts became attacks on the gold standard, Wall Street, international bankers, and what he described as the rapacious nature of modern capitalism. After 1932, they became tributes to Franklin D. Roosevelt as well. The president, he said, was the salvation of the nation, and he attempted to build a close personal and political relationship with him. But Coughlin was intensely ambitious, and he soon grew impatient both with what he considered the slow pace of New Deal monetary reform and, equally important, with the modest role he was allowed to play within the administration. By 1934, Roosevelt and Coughlin were drifting apart, and the following year Coughlin launched his own political organization — the National Union for Social Justice — and gradually turned it into a vehicle for challenging the president. In 1936, the group spearheaded the formation of the Union party, a loose confederation of dissident organizations that nominated William Lemke, an obscure North Dakota congressman, as its presidential candidate. Coughlin promised to retire from the airwaves if the Union party ticket did not attract at least 9 million votes. When Lemke polled only a little over 900,000, Coughlin ceased broadcasting for a short time. Early in 1937, however, he returned.

By now, Coughlin was passionate in his hatred of Roosevelt, and his radio sermons attacked the New Deal as a communist conspiracy and an incipient dictatorship. In 1938, he added a harsh anti-Semitism (almost completely absent from his earlier career) to both his broadcasts and his newspaper, *Social Justice*. He also began expressing sympathy for the fascist regimes of Hitler and Mussolini. Although Coughlin retained a devoted following, his new extremism drove away most of his traditional supporters; in 1940, no longer able to afford radio time, he ceased his broadcasts. Two years later, in the aftermath of Pearl Harbor, he obeyed the orders of his bishop and abandoned all political activities. He continued as a parish priest until 1966.

Alan Brinkley, *Voices of Protest* (1982); Charles J. Tull, *Father Coughlin and the New Deal* (1965).

ALAN BRINKLEY

See also Elections: 1936; Roman Catholic Church.

COURT-PACKING PLAN

The Court-packing plan (as the judicial reorganization bill was called by its opponents) was submitted to Congress by President Franklin D. Roosevelt on February 5, 1937, shortly after his landslide reelection. Although Roosevelt presented his plan as a simple organizational reform, he was clearly motivated by the consistent opposition that New Deal legislation had been encountering in the federal courts, most notably the Supreme Court's recent invalidation of such laws as the National Industrial Recovery Act, the Railroad Retirement Act, and the Agricultural Adjustment Act. The president proposed that the federal judiciary be expanded by adding one new judge for each sitting justice over the age of seventy; a total of fifty new judgeships could be created, including a maximum of six on the Supreme Court. The bill also included other measures to streamline judicial action.

Roosevelt's proposal met with fiery opposition. Many accused the president of seeking to subvert the Constitution and destroy the independence of the judiciary. Even some of those sympathetic to the president's purposes felt that the changes he sought should be made only by constitutional amendment. In addition, Roosevelt antagonized potential supporters within his own party by refusing to consult with them on the bill or consider changes in it. In March, the president launched a personal campaign on behalf of his proposal, arguing that national progress was being blocked by the prejudices of the Court majority and that his plan would restore, rather than threaten, the balance of power among the three branches of government.

Pressure for passage of the bill was weakened by the retirement of one conservative Supreme Court justice; by the death of Senator Joseph Robinson, who had been leading the fight for the plan; and by the fact that several major pieces of New Deal legislation (including the Social Security Act and the National Labor Relations Act) were upheld by the Court between March and May 1937. In August, the Judicial Procedure Reform Act was passed instead, incorporating some of the president's recommendations but leaving the number of federal justices unchanged. Over the next four years, a combination of deaths and retirements enabled Roosevelt to make seven appointments to the Court.

See also New Deal; Supreme Court.

COURTS

See Judiciary Act of 1789; Supreme Court.

COWBOYS

"When you call me that, *smile*," the hero said to the bad man in that first of thousands of cowboy novels, Owen Wister's *The Virginian*. Even before that book's publication in 1902, the cowboy had become a part of the American psyche. Something there was about him — tall in the saddle, alone, facing danger, one man against nature's vast, treeless plains and humanity's outlaws — that appealed to people and made the cowboy a folk hero, a half-real, half-mythological symbol of the American West.

Predecessors of the cowboy date back to colonial times. In western Massachusetts, in the uplands of the Carolinas, in Florida, and across the northern, red clay hills of Georgia and Alabama, cattle-raising societies existed long before the Great Plains had been cleared of buffalo. It was in Florida that much of the protocol involving branding evolved. Yet the cattle industry of the Southeast never attracted national attention. The herders never became heroes. They remained little known and were recognized for what they were — illiterate, unmounted trespassers on the public domain, drifting from grazing ground to grazing ground, trailing their beasts to markets at Ohio River towns or to Savannah or Jacksonville.

The cowboy of myth and reality had his beginnings in Texas. There cattle grew wild with few natural enemies; by the end of the Civil War there were an estimated 5 million of them. It was then that the cowboy entered his twenty-year golden age, 1866–1886, the era of the open range and the great cattle drives.

The incentive was the high price of beef up North, where Union armies had exhausted the supply and the urbanizing East provided a ready market. A steer worth four dollars in Texas was worth forty dollars in the North. The economics did not escape the Texans. Beginning in 1866 they began moving long lines of longhorns northward, with the primary destination being the railhead at Sedalia, Missouri. Indians and farmers who resented cattle trampling their crops and spreading the dreaded Texas fever protested their passage. Outlaws stole the cattle and were not averse to killing the men driving them.

Texans searched for a route with better grass and fewer Indians, farmers, and desperadoes. When railroads inched across the plains, new trails, among them the Chisholm, Western, and Loving, veered westward to intercept them. Cattle towns such as Abilene, Wichita, Ellsworth, Caldwell, and Dodge City enjoyed a brief heyday of prosperity and violence. Later trails headed on north to Ogallala, Cheyenne, Glendive, and Miles City. By 1886 the open-range cattle business had spread throughout the Great Plains and had merged with earlier cattle enterprises in Colorado, Idaho, Washington, Utah, Nevada, Arizona, and California.

The men who worked the cattle in the treeless expanses of the West, at least one-fourth of them blacks, became known as cowboys. The image of the courageous, spirited horseman living a dangerous life carried with it an appeal that refuses to disappear. Driving a thousand to two thousand cattle hundreds of miles to market; facing lightning and cloudbursts and drought, stampedes, rattlesnakes, and outlaws; sleeping under the stars and catching chow at the chuckwagon — the cowboys dominated the American galaxy of folk heroes.

Even their dress inspired envy. The cowboys' hats were high-crowned with wide, floppy rims, practical for protection from the sun's glare, useful as a cup with which to scoop up water or, folded over, as a pillow. The bandana handkerchief tied around the neck could be lifted to cover mouth and nostrils from dust. Originally the collarless shirt and trousers were nondescript, of flannel or wool. A vest was often worn; it gave some protection from cold winds and also had a number of useful pockets, one of which held Bull Durham tobacco and cigarette papers. The boots with heels two inches high, the better to rest in the stirrups or dig into the ground while roping a calf, may have appeared exotic to a dude, but they were absolutely practical. The stock saddle's design traced all the way back to the Moors of North Africa, having come to the American cowboy by way of the Spanish and Mexicans. Chaparejos, or chaps, served a valuable purpose when a cowboy had to chase after a steer into a patch of thorny mesquite. A bridle, a lariat, and, during the cattle drives, probably a well-balanced six-shooter completed the cowboys' outfit.

Ranchers staked out homesteads often centered in a cottonwood grove, with ample water nearby; they grazed their cattle over thousands of acres of public domain. Barbed wire, a web of railroads throughout the Great Plains, and enforcement of federal land laws all put an end to the open-range cattle industry and the great trails. By the mid-1880s prudent cattlemen realized that the industry was overexpanded, the Great Plains overgrazed, and the price of beef declining.

The dry summer of 1886 followed by the terrible winter of 1886–1887 destroyed what remained of the original industry. The open range was ended. Blooded cattle were brought in to improve the stock. The cowboy who hated to work unmounted was often reduced to riding a haymow, mending fences, and applying medicines to sick cattle. Where once he had herded cattle up the trails to Abilene or Dodge, he now ran the line — the water divide between his ranch and his neighbor's. There was still the semiannual roundup when cowboys representing several ranches rendezvoused and rode great circles, rounding up all the cattle they could find. They were then herded to a central place where cowboys from each ranch cut out its beasts and drove them back to the home range.

Glorified in thousands of novels and hundreds of motion pictures, the American cowboy is so mythologized that the reality and the legend are almost inseparable. Yet the reality is that the cowboy still exists because his work is essential to the industry. In many areas of the American West he still rides a horse, though he may carry it in a horse trailer behind his pickup truck to the point where the road gives out and a horse becomes indispensable. He may survey the ranchman's spread in a small airplane that he pilots, and he may help his employer determine with a computer matters of feed, weight, and salability. But he still dresses like a cowboy because the garb is practical; he understands cattle and horses and gazes out upon the treeless expanse just as his predecessors did. His work and his workplace, in spite of encroaching population, are still there.

David Dary, *Cowboy Culture: A Saga of Five Centuries* (1981); Joe B. Frantz and Julian E. Choate, Jr., *The American Cowboy: The Myth and the Reality* (1955); Philip Ashton Rollins, *The Cowboy* (1922; rev. ed., 1936).

RICHARD A. BARTLETT

COXEY'S ARMY

Following the panic of 1893, the United States was plunged into a severe economic depression. In response to growing economic distress and mass unemployment in the winter of 1893–1894 Jacob Sechler Coxey, a populist leader in Massillon, Ohio, proposed a recovery program. Congress should enact a large increase in the amount of legal tender currency in circulation, he argued. The extra money could be spent on public works, thereby providing jobs for the unemployed.

To bring his plan to the attention of Congress and the public, Coxey enlisted the support of Carl Browne in California and decided to send Washington a "living petition" — a vast army of the unemployed masses. Coxey and Browne formed an organization called the Commonweal of Christ, and left Massillon on Easter Sunday, March 25, 1894, leading an "army" of 100 followers. They hoped to attract a further 100,000 en route and to arrive in the capital for a massive demonstration on May Day. In the event, Coxey arrived in Washington on April 30 leading an army of 500. He and the other leaders were arrested and the army rapidly disbanded.

But Coxey's army had inspired the formation of other larger "industrial" armies on the Pacific Coast and elsewhere, the largest in Los Angeles and San Francisco. Overcoming the resistance of the railroad companies, federal marshals, the U.S. Army, and judicial injunctions, 1,200 members of these armies made it through to Washington in the course of 1894. Although Coxey had failed to achieve his legislative objectives, he had succeeded in publicizing the plight of the unemployed and in encouraging them to organize.

See also Depressions.

CRANDALL, PRUDENCE

(1803–1890), educator and abolitionist. Prudence Crandall, director of the first private boarding school for black girls in New England, was born into a Quaker family in Hope Valley, Rhode Island, and spent most of her childhood in the prosperous village of Canterbury, Connecticut. The second of four children, Prudence received a superior education at the New England Yearly Meeting School in Providence, Rhode Island. She taught school for a brief time in Lisbon and Plainfield, Connecticut, before returning to Canterbury.

In 1831, with the assistance of the town fathers, Crandall opened the Canterbury Female Seminary in a large house on the village green. The school thrived until she granted the request of Sarah Harris, a black servant girl, to attend classes. When the parents of her white students threatened to withdraw their daughters, Crandall conferred with Boston abolitionist William Lloyd Garrison, editor of the *Liberator,* and decided to close her school and reopen it as a school for black girls.

Her main opponent was Andrew T. Judson, Canterbury town clerk, lawyer, political aspirant, and neighbor. Judson circulated petitions against the school in sixteen towns, which resulted in the passage of the so-called Black Law of May 24, 1833. The law made it illegal to teach, board, or harbor black people seeking education who were not legal inhabitants of Connecticut without first obtaining permission from the town authorities.

When she was arrested, Crandall refused to pay bail and embarrassed her enemies by spending a night in the county jail. The case came to trial in August 1833 and ended with a hung jury. Her lawyers based their defense on Article IV, Section 2, of the U.S. Constitution, which guarantees that the rights of citizens in one state are to be respected in other states. Three months later another jury pronounced her guilty after Connecticut Supreme Court Judge David Daggett instructed them that black people were not citizens according to the Constitution. On appeal to the Connecticut Supreme Court of Errors in July 1834 the case was dismissed on a technicality. The Black Law was repealed in 1838.

Daily life for the more than twenty students at the school was punctuated by incidents of vandalism and harassment. Rocks were thrown through windows, a well was fouled with manure, and once the building was set afire. Shopkeepers refused to serve the girls and the local Congregational church turned them away. A mob assault on the house during the night of September 9, 1834, finally convinced Crandall that she could no longer ensure the safety of her students and she closed the school.

After her marriage to Calvin Philleo, a conservative Baptist minister, in 1834, she lived in Troy Grove, Illinois, where she homesteaded, taught school, and agitated for women's rights and temperance. In 1876, two years after her husband's death ended their chronically unhappy marriage, she moved with her widowed brother Hezekiah to Elk Falls, Kansas.

The poverty of her last years was alleviated somewhat in 1886 when a campaign by citizens of Canterbury and celebrities including Mark Twain resulted in an annual pension of four hundred dollars. She also received a formal apology from the state of Connecticut. A believer in spiritualism, she died peacefully in January 1890.

Philip S. Foner and Josephine F. Pacheco, *Three Who Dared: Prudence Crandall, Margaret Douglass, Myrtilla Miner — Champions of Antebellum Black Education* (1984); Susan Strane, *"A Whole-Souled Woman": Prudence Crandall and the Education of Black Women* (1990).

SUSAN STRANE

See also Abolitionist Movement; Education.

CRANE, STEPHEN

(1871–1900), writer. Crane, the son of a Methodist minister and a leader in the Woman's Christian Temperance Union, grew up in Port Jervis, New York, which became the small town of his boyhood memory, just as the hunting and fishing country of Sullivan County became a (tame) kind of wilderness memory for him. His early, somewhat fantasized *Sullivan Country Sketches* and his late, partly realistic *Whilomville Stories* drew on these resources.

In 1883 Crane moved with his widowed mother to Asbury Park, New Jersey, where a few years later he was to work as a reporter for his brother's news agency. After a semester at Lafayette College, he transferred to Syracuse University in 1891. Writing and baseball were more interesting to him than his studies, and he left college at the end of the term. That summer he met Hamlin Garland, whose popular lectures on realism and impressionism helped shape his literary ideal — a "personal honesty" about the world as seen "with his own pair of eyes."

Crane began his career in New York, where doing sketches of the slums helped him write his first novel, *Maggie: A Girl of the Streets* (1893). After searching old soldiers' narratives in vain for "how they *felt* in those scraps," he put vivid inner detail into *The Red Badge of Courage* (1895). Since he sold the novel outright, his chief benefit from its critical and popular success was his winning journalistic commissions like the one that took him to the West and Mexico in 1895. While he was in Mexico, his first book of poems, *The Black Riders,* came out, containing eerie visions and succinct parables in free verse that he liked for giving his "ideas of life as a whole."

Crane's best work is his short fiction. In his later novels, he often mixed his fine honesty with the banalities of genteel fiction, but in his short stories he used conventions of vulgar entertainment like the Wild West tale. He could brilliantly exaggerate and ironically deflate. He wrote in a clean simple prose that he would suddenly, unpredictably illuminate with vivid, expressive touches, like the monstrous imaginings that go with the young soldier's battles with fear in *The Red Badge.*

Late in 1896, Crane went to Florida en route to cover the Cuban revolution. On January 2, 1897, he was aboard the *Commodore* when it sank a few hours out of Jacksonville. The thirty-hour ordeal that followed is the basis of his greatest story, "The Open Boat," a tale of endurance, comradeship, and deep realization of the contingency of things.

Back in port, Crane was cared for by Cora Taylor, proprietress of the Hotel de Dream, who then accompanied him to the Greco-Turkish War as the "first woman war correspondent" and afterward settled with him in England as "Mrs. Stephen Crane." In the autumn and winter of 1897–1898 he wrote a series of short stories, among them "The Bride Comes to Yellow Sky" and "The Blue Hotel." But short stories, even great ones, could not support the Crane household. Debts and anxiety mounted.

When the Spanish-American War broke out, Crane tried to enlist in the navy but, failing that, signed on as a correspondent. After the war, he lingered in Havana until year's end with both his health and his finances deteriorating.

Upon returning to England, he enjoyed literary recognition from the public and from such friends as Joseph Conrad and Henry James. Despite worsening tuberculosis, he managed to finish a second volume of poems, a volume of Cuban stories, his Whilomville tales, and a good deal of hackwork before he died in 1900, deeply in debt.

Crane's gift for misadventure continued beyond his death. Thomas Beer's *Stephen Crane* (1923), the earliest biography, has been discredited, and the letters that are quoted there, unless independent evidence survives, cannot be taken as authentic.

John Berryman, *Stephen Crane* (1950); Stanley Wertheim and Paul Sorrentino, eds., *The Correspondence of Stephen Crane* (1988).

J. C. LEVENSON

See also Literature.

CRAZY HORSE

(c. 1842–1877), Teton Sioux military leader. Since his violent and controversial death, Crazy Horse, or Tashunka Witko, has become almost a mythical figure of the Great Plains Indian wars. The place and date of his birth are uncertain, but he was probably born in the early 1840s near Bear Butte on the Belle Fourche River in South Dakota. His father was a medicine man of the Oglala subtribe, his mother a Brulé. There has been much speculation about the origin of the name Crazy Horse, but most historians now agree that his father had the same name. As a youth he was known as Curly, but acquired the father's name after proving himself in combat.

He was below average height, his body lithe,

his hair and complexion lighter than that of most Indians. Various photographs bear his name, but most have been discredited, and probably none is genuine. Except for his last days near Fort Robinson, Nebraska, he was out of reach of frontier photographers.

His first encounter with U.S. soldiers was on the old Oregon Trail, July 25, 1865, at Platte Bridge, where he acted as a decoy to draw soldiers out of their defenses. During the following year, when soldiers marched up the Bozeman Trail to build forts, Crazy Horse honed his skills as a guerrilla fighter and studied the ways of his military adversaries.

In December 1866, when the Sioux and Cheyenne combined to challenge Fort Phil Kearny, Crazy Horse's daring as a leader of the decoy warriors brought Lt. Col. William J. Fetterman and eighty men into an ambush that became known as the Fetterman massacre.

During the following decade, Crazy Horse joined Sitting Bull in an unyielding determination to defend the Black Hills and resist reservation control. When the U.S. Army mounted a three-pronged military operation in 1876 to drive the "free" Plains Indians onto reservations, Crazy Horse confronted the column led by Gen. George Crook at Rosebud Creek, June 17. He concentrated his warriors against weak spots in Crook's lines, fighting hand to hand at times to win the day.

After the battle, the victors rode over to the Little Bighorn to join Sitting Bull's large encampment of Sioux and Cheyenne. On the twenty-fifth, Gen. George A. Custer's column attacked the camp, and Crazy Horse and Gall, a chief of the Hunkpapa Sioux, led their warriors in a pincers attack that quickly enveloped Custer's divided cavalry and wiped it out.

Other military forces pursued the Indians, eventually driving Sitting Bull into Canada. Crazy Horse and his followers attempted to hold out in remote areas of the Yellowstone country, but soldiers hunted them relentlessly. On May 6, 1877, he gave himself up and spent the summer near Fort Robinson, awaiting the assignment to a reservation that had been promised him for surrendering.

The events affecting Crazy Horse during that long summer were imbued with elements of classical tragedy. Deceptions, betrayals, and false rumors engulfed him. He was disliked by some of the older Indian leaders, and because of his popularity among the young warriors, rumors spread that he was planning an outbreak. When on September 5 he was arrested, he offered no resistance at first. But when he saw that he was to be locked in a guardhouse, he struggled with his captors and was stabbed to death. From the day of its occurrence this incident has been described in several versions, all adding to the mystique of Crazy Horse.

Robert A. Clark, ed., *The Killing of Crazy Horse: Three Eyewitness Views*, with commentary by Carroll Friswold (1978); Mari Sandoz, *Crazy Horse: The Strange Man of the Oglalas* (1942).

DEE BROWN

See also Custer, George Armstrong; Indians; Sitting Bull.

CRÉDIT MOBILIER OF AMERICA

The Crédit Mobilier scandal of 1872–1873 damaged the careers of several Gilded Age politicians. Major stockholders in the Union Pacific Railroad formed a company, the Crédit Mobilier of America, and gave it contracts to build the railroad. They sold or gave shares in this construction to influential congressmen. It was a lucrative deal for the congressmen, because they helped themselves by approving federal subsidies for the cost of railroad construction without paying much attention to expenses, enabling railroad builders to make huge profits. When the *New York Sun* broke the story on the eve of the 1872 election, Speaker of the House James G. Blaine, a Maine Republican implicated in the scandal, set up a congressional committee to investigate.

The House censured two of its members who were involved in the scandal: Oakes Ames of Massachusetts and James Brooks of New York. But the affair also tarnished the careers of outgoing vice president Schuyler Colfax, incoming vice president Henry Wilson, and Representative James A. Garfield, all of whom were implicated (although Garfield denied the charges and was subsequently elected president). Probably hurt most of all was Blaine, who was accused of writing the "Mulligan letters" about his corrupt actions. Blaine denied all wrongdoing, but charges of corruption swirled around him throughout his career, probably keeping him from becoming president. The scandal also showed how corruption tainted Gilded Age politics, and the lengths railroads and other economic interests would go to assure and increase profits.

See also Corruption.

CRIME

Crime is antisocial conduct for which punishment may be imposed in the name of the state. Crimes can be classified according to their nature: violent personal crimes, such as murder and rape; property offenses, such as burglary and theft; and public welfare or moral infractions, such as gambling, intoxication, and promiscuous sexuality. Usually, those in the first group are thought to be more serious than those in the second and are therefore punished more severely. Today, in Western culture, the third group is perceived as the least serious, but two hundred years ago, moral infractions such as consensual sodomy could be punished by death.

When the United States was founded, punishments for crimes ranged from public mockery, such as being fastened to a pillory, to being put to death. Dunking an offender in water as punishment for a moral offense was common. Nathaniel Hawthorne's *The Scarlet Letter* confirms the use of extended social embarrassment as punishment for bad morals: Hester Prynne wore a red letter A, for adultery, embroidered on her dress.

Witchcraft is an example of a crime that was directly associated with Satan, an idea the Puritans brought with them from England. In theory, a woman became a witch by sleeping with the devil. In practice, innocent but socially outcast women were targeted as witches by clerics who used the accusation to keep churchgoers in line. (Some colonial women who believed they were witches actually practiced witchcraft.) Convicted "witches" faced death by hanging in America (burning in Europe), although this crime was difficult to prove. Persons accused of witchcraft and some other crimes were tortured into "confessing." The confession was frequently used to justify the imposition of ghastly punishments in the guise of preparing the accused to receive religious absolution thought necessary for entry into heaven following execution. Thus, crimes were confused with sins and punishment confused with blessings.

Such was the realist interpretation of crime up to the Enlightenment in the eighteenth century and the publication in 1764 of the book *Of Crimes and Punishment* by the Italian Marchese di Beccaria. The nineteenth century saw advances in technology plus new and idealistic theories in penology. Previously, jails had been built of stone and were designed to hold prisoners only temporarily, as they awaited trial and eventual execution. The development of light iron and later steel permitted the construction of multitiered cells for long-term confinement in densely populated prisons. During most of the nineteenth century imprisonment at hard labor was imposed in the belief that years of physical toil would restore to a prisoner his lost moral fiber. Convict labor also was cheap and convenient in the new Republic. In a utilitarian era, prisoner labor was instrumental in erecting many public buildings, particularly new prisons. The more cells available the more people the courts sentenced to fill those cells, a process that continues today, perhaps unfortunately, although politicians convince themselves new prisons are necessary to meet the need.

Also in the nineteenth century, in both America and England, the concept of professional police forces emerged from utilitarian political thought, such as that of Jeremy Bentham. Police were employed, first in large cities and later in small towns, to maintain public order by means of crime prevention and deterrence. In the meantime, the Industrial Revolution taking place in America resulted in large amounts of goods being shipped between major cities that were increasingly populated by immigrants. Robbery of these goods and of banks became the crime that attracted the most attention throughout the West. Within America's cities, crimes flourished among occupants of densely populated neighborhoods, housing people whose native languages and cultures were strange to one another. Vice offenses also proliferated as newcomers struggled to earn a living and take their place in the mainstream of American society.

A population receptive to the early psychological theories of Sigmund Freud and others came to view some criminal offenders as being *sick* rather than bad. This followed the "discovery" of the asylum as a place where one who is mentally ill could be treated instead of punished. Eventually, during the first half of the twentieth century, techniques of behavior modification came into use to alter the personalities of prisoners as well as mental patients, signaling the age of rehabilitation. Efforts to obtain planned change in the behaviors of offender populations have achieved only marginal success, however. Sexual deviates, particularly violent ones, for example, seem unresponsive to conventional behavior modification techniques and remain high recidivist risks.

After World War I, controversy surrounded the consumption of alcohol. The Eighteenth Amendment (1918) and the Volstead Act (1919) criminalized the sale though not the consumption of alcoholic beverages. During the decade and a half of Prohibition, although alcoholic consumption declined overall, many Americans consumed more than they did before or after simply because it was forbidden. The smuggling of illegal alcohol, or bootlegging, became a big business dominated by ethnic groups who rose to the entrepreneurial occasion in the American spirit of free enterprise. It was at this time that one such group, the Sicilian Mafia, became most powerful of all, attracting much attention in the movies and newspapers.

The United States after World War II became concerned about communist aggression and, particularly, domestic subversion. The Federal Bureau of Investigation, which had gained a reputation tracking and apprehending gangsters during Prohibition, became a major investigative agency, using computer technology to standardize its fingerprint files together with a state-of-the-art crime laboratory and National Crime Information Center. Known as NCIC, the center maintains files on criminals and stolen property, particularly items, such as automobiles, that bear serial numbers. Auto theft became and remains the nation's most commonly perpetrated serious crime, costing the insurance industry and consumers many millions of dollars annually.

The Korean War introduced American servicemen to opium and its derivatives, such as heroin, and addiction to drugs besides alcohol burgeoned in the 1950s, 1960s, and 1970s, becoming a national disaster by 1988. Cocaine joined heroin as a serious substance abuse product in the 1970s and 1980s. The government's ban on the importation of illegal drugs failed to stem the incoming tide or the domestic trafficking of these dangerous commodities, largely because demand for them rose so high among Americans. What the public wants, it gets, or so it seems, regardless of the price it must pay. The Mafia apparently controlled access to most narcotic drugs and in the process contained drug trafficking to specific neighborhoods until the federal government destroyed much of its leadership in the 1980s. The result has been capricious distribution of synthetic narcotic drugs such as China White and impure mixtures such as crack that have increased the addict population and turned formerly peaceful neighborhoods into war zones. A strong Mafia, unhappily, had its uses, it seems, in regulating the distribution of drugs and settling disputes among drug dealers.

America's most famous criminologist, Indiana University's Edwin H. Sutherland, articulated in 1949 what he termed white-collar crime, including as examples embezzlement, stock frauds, and violations of antitrust laws by businesses. Prosecutions of white-collar offenders were rare until the 1980s, when many respected stock brokerage houses on New York City's Wall Street, some of their key executives, and even television evangelists were convicted of fraudulent transactions. Heated debate continues over whether the nonviolent offender requires incarceration. The same sort of controversy exists as to whether fines discriminate against the poor and whether forced restitution (financial compensation paid by an offender to a victim) unreasonably injures an offender's family by reducing its assets and income.

Aside from experiments by the federal government and some states with sentencing major drug dealers to imprisonment for life without possibility of parole, the overall thrust in penology since World War II has been to achieve the reintegration of most prisoners by returning them to society rapidly. Thus, actual sentences served may be much shorter than those pronounced. Early release from prison conditioned upon good behavior, known as parole, may occur upon completion of one-third of a sentence. First-time offenders or repeat nonviolent criminals tend to be placed on probation, or conditional release, with no imprisonment at all. Prisons are very expensive to build and maintain. Contemporary penologists tend to agree that, far from rehabilitating offenders, imprisonment hardens them, turning the nonviolent into vicious criminals and novice petty offenders into sophisticated career criminals. Lawful employment is difficult for an ex-convict to obtain. Only a small segment of the prison population requires confinement to protect the public. Incarceration of the rest serves no useful purpose, and it becomes counterproductive when subjected to a cost-benefit analysis. For one thing, prolonged imprisonment destroys the typical prisoner's family, escalating the risk that his children will become delinquent and follow in his footsteps, other opportunities having been denied them.

Explaining criminality continues to be an exercise in futility, as it has been historically. Nineteenth-century Italian criminologist Cesare Lombroso devoted years to trying to identify genetic causes of criminal behavior, without much success. His positivist criminology was popular at the turn of the twentieth century but declined thereafter. Most American criminologists have concentrated on psychological or sociological explanations of crime and delinquency, with many favoring the latter.

Naturalist criminology as a school of thought stresses Freud's view of the importance of the mother-child relationship especially in the early months after birth when psychosexual dysfunctions may be set into motion. This viewpoint influenced the formation of the insanity defense during the nineteenth century, the diminished criminal responsibility theme more recently, and the overall effort to rehabilitate convicts using behavior modification techniques.

Pragmatic criminology, a product of the Chicago school of sociology at the beginning of the twentieth century, looks to offenders' life experiences not only between parents and children or among siblings but also among members of peer groups, particularly in school. This viewpoint emphasizes that crime is learned by predelinquent children as they interact with others who are significant to them as role models. When role models favor criminal behavior, children follow their lead; when they are law-abiding, so will be the children who respect them. Sociological explanations of crime were consolidated by Sutherland in his theories of differential association.

Radical analytic criminologists have looked upon crime as a matter of semantics. They maintain that a dominant social class defines as criminal any behavior that threatens their power over the less privileged. Marxism is a factor in this viewpoint. One flaw in this proposition is that ordinary people share an opposition to crime along with the wealthy and powerful. Moreover, ordinary people are elected to the public bodies that make laws. The fact is crimes are perpetrated by a cross-section of society, rich and poor, dumb and smart. Simple explanations are insufficient.

Some contemporary criminologists still search for the genetic explanation of criminality that eluded Lombroso. An extra Y chromosome may be a factor inducing a small number of males to become abnormally violent, yet that would not seem to explain dishonesty. New technologies for sequencing DNA may help scientists identify and study genetic factors that may influence criminal and noncriminal behavior. In addition, DNA sequencing can link organic matter (blood, skin, sperm) found at a crime scene to the perpetrator of the crime with a certainty as high as 34 billion to one. Technology is continuing to improve law enforcement, but courts seem reluctant to recognize the value of some new technologies, such as DNA sequencing.

Finally, there is the existential view of crime, which holds that we are frail human beings who are strangers in a strange land, and strangers even to ourselves from time to time. We profess common values — life is sacred, property sacrosanct — but what we believe in theory we do not always practice. Crime in this view reflects what life is all about — uncertainty. Given a particular convergence of circumstances, not always foreseeable, human behavior can be monstrous, collectively, as in warfare, or individually, as in crime. Crime, like warfare, is part of life and not always predictable or preventable, much less redressable.

Thus, in two centuries attitudes toward crime have evolved from a realist tendency to explain crimes, as well as natural disasters, as examples of God's wrath, to an idealist acceptance of human blame for crime with its implication that the causes of crime can be understood and its incidence reduced, to an existentialist outlook that sees crime as an inescapable part of the human condition.

David A. Jones, *History of Criminology: A Philosophical Perspective* (1987); Edwin H. Sutherland and Donald R. Cressey, *Principles of Criminology* (1986).

DAVID A. JONES

See also Corruption; Crédit Mobilier of America; Drugs; Espionage; Federal Bureau of Investigation; Guns and Gun Control; Lynching; *Miranda* v. *Arizona;* Police Forces; Prohibition and Temperance; Prostitution; Salem Witch Trials; Teapot Dome Affair; Volstead Act; Watergate Scandal.

CRITTENDEN COMPROMISE

This was an unsuccessful effort to avert the Civil War during the winter of 1860–1861. Senator John J. Crittenden, a Kentucky Whig and disciple of Henry Clay, proposed six constitutional amendments and four resolutions. The amendments made major concessions to southern concerns. They forbade the abolition of slavery on federal land in slaveholding states, compensated

owners of runaway slaves, and restored the Missouri Compromise line of 36°30′, which had been repealed in the Kansas-Nebraska Act. One amendment guaranteed that future constitutional amendments could not change the other five amendments or the three-fifths and fugitive slave clauses of the Constitution. Crittenden's proposals also called for the repeal of northern personal liberty laws. Aware of congressional divisions, Crittenden urged that his plan be submitted to a nationwide vote.

Despite considerable popular support for Crittenden's compromise, Congress failed to enact it. Although incoming secretary of state William Seward, viewed by southerners as a radical on slavery, backed the plan, most Republicans agreed with President-elect Abraham Lincoln, who opposed it.

See also Civil War; Slavery.

CROCKETT, DAVY

(1786–1836), frontiersman, folk hero, congressman, and Alamo defender. Crockett's biographers say there were two Crocketts. *David* was the historic one, the frontiersman and congressman martyred at the Alamo. *Davy* was the mythical frontiersman who became a bigger-than-life folk hero glorified in several books and a series of almanacs.

The historic David Crockett was born of a pioneer family living on the Nolichucky River in east Tennessee. The family followed the patterns of western settlement, moving three times by the time David was twelve. Later, as a young man with a family of his own, Crockett continued this westward movement until he settled in extreme northwest Tennessee. In 1813, following a massacre by Creek warriors of the occupants of Fort Mims in southwest Alabama, Crockett enlisted in the Tennessee militia. He participated in a massacre of Indians at Tallussahatchee in northern Alabama, but returned home when his enlistment was up; he was not present at the decisive Battle of Horseshoe Bend (March 27, 1814) when the Creeks were defeated. During his second enlistment, begun September 18, 1814, he joined Andrew Jackson's forces at Pensacola; but, discharged again, he returned home, missing the Battle of New Orleans.

Crockett was a natural leader. He advanced from justice of the peace to two terms in the Tennessee legislature. He was elected to Congress in 1827 and 1829 as a Democrat. Then he broke with Jackson over a number of issues and was defeated in 1831; in 1833 he returned to Congress, this time as a Whig. In 1835 he was again defeated. Disgusted, he is quoted as saying, "You can all go to Hell and I'm going to Texas." True or not, he did leave Tennessee in November 1835, and subsequently appeared in east Texas, ostensibly looking for land upon which to settle. Controversy surrounds his reason for going to the Alamo. He was there when it was attacked, however, and he died when it fell.

David Crockett was clearly an outstanding frontiersman, a successful Tennessee politician, and a colorful congressman, but these attributes alone would not have earned him lasting fame. His record in Congress was not good: most of the legislation he favored failed to pass. Even as a defender of the Alamo he should have attracted no more fame than the other fallen heroes.

But his frontier lingo and tall stories attracted the attention of journalists. Books about *Davy* Crockett, the "ring-tailed roarer" from Tennessee, sold well. Beginning with a pseudo-biography in 1833, followed by his own autobiography in 1834 (written with the aid of Thomas Chilton), a plethora of Davy Crockett books and almanacs appeared over the next two decades. They claimed to be true stories about *David* Crockett. Narrated in frontier lingo and revealing the cruelty, bigotry, and racism of the frontier, they related the bigger-than-life adventures of a frontier superman. The half-horse, half-alligator hero, touched with the snapping turtle, who could wade the Mississippi and leap the Ohio and whip his weight in wildcats became a part of American folklore. Rediscovered by Hollywood in the 1940s and 1950s, and by television to the present day, *Davy* Crockett, if not *David,* seems assured of immortality.

Thus, *David* Crockett — outstanding frontiersman, excellent hunter, good family man, leader of men, and politician with integrity —

became the epitome of the rough, unwashed, dangerous West of Jacksonian America. Motion pictures and television have revived him as a frontier superhero for twentieth-century audiences. Their portrayal of him as a courageous, patriotic, fair, and kind frontiersman may be closer to the real *David* Crockett than the bigoted, racist, and cruel *Davy* Crockett depicted in earlier works.

David Crockett, *A Narrative of the Life of David Crockett of the State of Tennessee: A Facsimile Reproduction with Annotations and Introduction by James A. Shackford and Stanley F. Folmsbee* (1946); Michael A. Lofaro and Joe Cummings, eds., *Crockett at Two Hundred: New Perspectives on the Man and the Myth* (1989); John B. Shackford, *David Crockett: The Man and the Legend* (1956).

RICHARD A. BARTLETT

See also Alamo.

CUFFE, PAUL

(1759–1817), philanthropist, merchant, and sea captain. The son of a former slave father and Indian mother, Paul Cuffe was born on the island of Cuttyhunk, Massachusetts, near the commercial port of New Bedford. Later persuaded "that commerce furnished to industry more ample rewards than agriculture," he prepared himself for that field by becoming proficient in mathematics and navigation.

Keenly opposed to discrimination against his people, Cuffe championed their cause with an intensity that might be expected of a less successful man. But his wealth was no shield against racism, and his problems reveal as much about its long arm as about the difficulties encountered by a black person in America. A nationalist and Quaker, he was shaped by the major currents of his era. The concerns of his people did not alone define his interests, but they were at the center of his life and accounted for much of his influence. It was through his efforts that blacks were granted the right to vote in Massachusetts in 1783.

Most of Cuffe's life was spent in Westport, a Quaker enclave in southwestern Massachusetts where, in 1797, he bought a farm for $3,500. He had earned his fortune from whaling and trade in the Americas and Europe. He owned shares, over a period of time, in up to ten ships, and the financial support of the Friends and their doctrine figured in his success as a businessman. They captained some of his ships and, like him, believed that the virtues of the countinghouse, such as industry and frugality, were pleasing in the sight of God. Cuffe's faith was a factor in his using a substantial portion of his wealth to help others, building a school when the community failed to do so and contributing to the raising of a new Friends meetinghouse in Westport.

Cuffe's interest in Africa stemmed in part from his father's having been born there. The success he achieved as a black captain with black crews was evidence of the black expertise thought essential to the redemption of Africa. His voyage there in his own ship in 1815 with emigrants from America and his financial success anticipated ideals later associated with black nationalists from Henry Highland Garnet to Marcus Garvey. And this complex man, like Bishop Henry M. Turner later in the century, was certain enough of his own vision to risk association with the American Colonization Society, whose motives regarding the return of blacks to Africa were highly suspect in black leadership circles.

Paul Cuffe, though working for the uplift of his people, accepted support from white allies, and though struggling for black rights in America, assisted in the regeneration of Africa. He made an impact on his time sufficient to begin a tradition, and that, perhaps, is his greatest legacy. In September 1817 large numbers of people were present at his funeral in Westport. He was buried in the Friends cemetery there.

Sheldon Harris, *Paul Cuffe: Black America and the African Return* (1972); Henry Noble Sherwood, "Paul Cuffe," *Journal of Negro History* 8 (April 1923).

STERLING STUCKEY

See also American Colonization Society; Black Nationalism; Free Negroes, 1619–1860; Quakers.

CUISINE

See Cookery.

CULTURE, COLONIAL

See Colonial Culture.

CUMBERLAND ROAD

See National Road.

CUMMINGS, E. E.

(1894–1962), poet, autobiographical novelist, painter. As the son of Edward Cummings, a Unitarian minister who had been executive secretary of the World Peace Foundation, Cummings fit naturally into literary and classical studies at Harvard. There he collected data and sharpened the irreverent wit that would yield such lines as "The Cambridge ladies live in furnished souls, . . . They speak of God and Longfellow, both dead." Following the latest trends in art, he moved to New York in 1916 and became a cubist painter of some note, exhibiting two paintings in the Society of Independents Show (1919), where Marcel Duchamp's infamous "readymade" porcelain urinal debuted. In Cambridge and in New York's bohemian Greenwich Village, and later in Paris, he befriended many poets and artists, most notably Hart Crane and Gertrude Stein, and worked at his writing.

In his earliest collection, *Tulips and Chimneys* (1923), he was both iconoclastic and Emersonian (that is, individualistic yet secretly religious), punningly playful and transcendentally depressed about the relationship of the individual to society, the artist to "mostpeople." Emulating European avant-gardist syntactic dislocations and visual poetry, "e. e. cummings," whose unique signature of typed lowercase letters adopted in 1923 signals his idiosyncrasy, is perhaps best known for typographical distortions, neologisms, and surprising juxtapositions of free and fixed verse forms, high- and lowbrow allusions.

More stunningly than his hundreds of short poems or the infamous Charles Eliot Norton Lectures at Harvard, *i: six nonlectures* (1952–1953), his autobiographical war narrative, *The*

Enormous Room (1922), and his satire/travelogue of Soviet bureaucracy, *eimi* (1933), show the range of emotional responses of an alienated and powerless — if selfish and ethnocentric — American individualist to the world's absurd economic and political institutions. Quite differently from the realism of contemporaneous antiwar action novels, *The Enormous Room* depicts the humor and horror at the margins of World War I. In the close quarters of a concentration camp, with sundry foreigners, criminals, corrupt guards, and his American friend, B (John Slater Brown), the narrator only half ironically employs allegorical names and religiophilosophical concepts adapted from John Bunyan's *Pilgrim's Progress*.

Like all of Cummings's art, *The Enormous Room* wobbles among serious psychological sketches, a proto-beatnik fascination with lower-class or marginal camaraderie, and an elitist send-up of American bourgeois values. For example: "The great American Public has a handicap which my friends at La ferte did not as a rule have — education. Let no one sound an indignant yawp at this. I refer to the fact that . . . there is and can be no authentic art until the bons trucs (whereby we are taught to see and imitate on canvas and in stone and by words in this so-called world) are entirely and thoroughly and perfectly annihilated by that fast and painful process of Unthinking which may result in a minute bit of purely personal Feeling. Which minute bit is Art."

Banished, for the most part, from academe and serious criticism by Edmund Wilson's characterization of Wallace Stevens as "master in a particular vein" and Cummings as "precisely not," as well as Allen Tate's 1932 "heresy of unintelligence," his works nevertheless lead an underground life and enjoy great popularity. If critics reject him for a general irreverence, for writing mere typographical gimmickry, or for his proto–cold war caricature of the Soviet Union, his poems remain accessible, memorable, and of historical interest.

KATHRYNE V. LINDBERG

See also Expatriates and Exiles; Literature.

CUOMO, MARIO

(1932–   ), governor of New York (1983–   ). The first Italian-American governor of New York, Cuomo burst on the national political scene in the 1980s, a decade dominated by the conservatism of Ronald Reagan. Perhaps the most gifted and inspiring political speaker of his generation, Cuomo quickly became the great hope of the Democratic party, which had won only one presidential election since 1964.

Cuomo was born in a room above the family grocery store in the polyglot New York neighborhood of South Jamaica, Queens, only a few years after his parents had arrived in the United States from southern Italy. His ethnic background, which led to his feeling the sting of discrimination when he was rejected by leading Manhattan law firms, is one of the three wellsprings of Cuomo's character. Another is his competitiveness, evidenced by his fling with minor league baseball as well as his legal representation of groups of citizens in conflicts with the city. But despite his relish for competition, Cuomo's reputation came to be that of a masterful conciliator as he worked out compromises in seemingly intractable disputes over public housing projects. These roles put Cuomo in the spotlight and led him into politics, where his craving for contests could best be combined with his other basic motivations, a religious-based compassion and a calling to serve others.

His early political ventures were unsuccessful. Particularly galling was his 1977 loss to Edward Koch in the New York City mayoral race. Were it not for his competitive nature and his desire to serve, this defeat might have marked the end of his political career. But in the 1982 election for governor, Cuomo overcame the heavily favored Koch to win.

Cuomo's keynote address to the 1984 Democratic National Convention in San Francisco did more to promote a political reputation than had any oratory since William Jennings Bryan's Cross of Gold speech in 1896. Speaking, at the very peak of Reaganism about the societal and family values that were at the heart of the Democratic party, Cuomo brought tears to the eyes of even cynical politicians.

As governor, Cuomo enjoyed at first the benefits of a booming regional economy, which helped him increase spending at the same time that he was reducing tax rates. Although political foes labeled him "soft" on crime because of his opposition to the death penalty, he embarked on the largest prison-building program in the state's history. And though a deeply religious Catholic personally opposed to abortion, he nevertheless took the position that the state should not deny a woman's right to make her own decision on this most personal matter.

In 1986 Cuomo was reelected by the greatest margin in the history of New York gubernatorial races. He was the clear front-runner for the 1988 Democratic presidential nomination, but startled the political world in early 1987 by declaring his noncandidacy. For more than a year thereafter, however, he kept interest high by refusing to close the door to a possible draft.

Cuomo's second term as governor was marred by a major downturn in the economy of the Northeast, reversing the happy circumstances of his first years in office. But despite massive budget problems, Cuomo remained so formidable in 1990 that the Republicans had difficulty finding anyone to run against him, and most political observers once more had him at the top of their lists of Democratic presidential prospects.

Mario M. Cuomo, *Diaries of Mario M. Cuomo: The Campaign for Governor* (1984); Robert S. McElvaine, *Mario Cuomo: A Biography* (1988).

ROBERT S. MCELVAINE

CUSTER, GEORGE ARMSTRONG

(1839–1876), Civil War cavalry commander and Indian fighter. Born in New Rumley, Ohio, Custer entered West Point in 1857. Upon graduation in 1861 he was assigned immediately to duty as an aide to Gen. George McClellan. Next he drew a cavalry assignment, and his boldness in battle brought rapid promotions. At twenty-three he was the youngest brevet brigadier general in the Union army. While on furlough he met and soon married Elizabeth Bacon, who was

to play a significant role in shaping his career and perpetuating his memory.

When the war ended, Custer was returned to the permanent rank of captain. After serving several months in Texas, he was commissioned a lieutenant colonel and assigned to the Seventh Cavalry Regiment based at Fort Riley, Kansas. Accompanied by Elizabeth, he reported for duty early in 1867. Under Gen. Winfield Hancock's command, Custer led the Seventh Cavalry in several skirmishes against Indians in Kansas and Nebraska. Soon after the campaign closed, his uxoriousness came near to ending his career. Instead of remaining with his troops at Fort Wallace as ordered, he made a hasty journey to Fort Riley to see Elizabeth. As a result he was suspended for one year.

In 1868 Gen. Philip Sheridan replaced Hancock and soon arranged for Custer's reinstatement. That November, after raiding Black Kettle's Cheyenne village, he was in trouble again for leaving the field without searching for a missing reconnaissance unit that had been ambushed and slain. Among other activities during the next six years, Custer wrote *My Life on the Plains* in which he attempted to justify his actions, and in 1874 he violated the treaty of 1868 by taking an expedition into the Indians' sacred Black Hills where gold was discovered. The gold rush that followed created intense Indian hostility and precipitated the government's decision to confine all northern Plains tribes to reservations.

In 1876, under command of Gen. Alfred Terry, Custer led the Seventh Cavalry as one force in a three-pronged campaign against Sitting Bull's alliance of Sioux and Cheyenne camps in Montana. During the morning of June 25, Custer's scouts reported spotting smoke from cooking fires and other signs of Indians in the valley of the Little Bighorn. Disregarding Terry's orders, Custer decided to attack before infantry and other support arrived. Although scouts warned that he was facing superior numbers (perhaps 2,500 warriors), Custer divided his regiment of 647 men, ordering Capt. Frederick Benteen's battalion to scout along a ridge to the left and sending Maj. Marcus Reno's battalion up the valley of the Little Bighorn to attack the Indian encampment. With the remainder of the regiment, Custer continued along high ground on the right side of the valley. In the resulting battle, he and about 250 of his men, outnumbered by the warriors of Crazy Horse and Gall, were surrounded and annihilated. Reno and Benteen suffered heavy casualties but managed to escape to a defensive position. Since that day, "Custer's Last Stand" has become an American legend. The battle site attracts thousands of visitors yearly.

Throughout his career, Custer exhibited a reckless temperament that kept him in almost constant trouble with superior officers. Yet his courage has rarely been questioned. In life he was a flamboyant man who attracted ardent admirers and severe critics. In death it has been the same. His wife, Elizabeth, through her publications and lectures during the half century she survived him, did much to create the image of a *beau sabreur* that still persists. Probably more words, pro and con, have been written about George Armstrong Custer than any of his military contemporaries of comparable rank.

Evan S. Connell, *Son of the Morning Star* (1984); Robert M. Utley, *Cavalier in Buckskin: George Armstrong Custer and the Western Military Frontier* (1988).

DEE BROWN

See also Crazy Horse; Indians; Sitting Bull.

D

DALEY, RICHARD

(1902–1976), Chicago political leader. The grandson of Irish immigrants, Daley was the nation's dominant big-city mayor in the second half of the twentieth century and a major force in the national Democratic party. Launching his political career in 1936, Daley was elected to the Illinois House of Representatives and then advanced to the state senate in 1938, where he served as Democratic minority leader from 1941 through 1946. He was also the deputy controller of Cook County from 1936 through 1949 and was named Illinois state revenue director in 1949. In these positions, Daley gained a keen understanding of government and a mastery of budgets and revenue sources.

Daley moved into the Chicago Democratic machine's hierarchy in 1947 with his election as ward committeeman of the Southwest Side's Eleventh Ward. Working behind the scenes, he engineered the ouster of Col. Jacob M. Arvey as Democratic chairman following Republican victories in the 1950 elections. In 1953, Daley took over the chairmanship of the Cook County Democratic Central Committee, which he forged into the strongest political organization in the country. As party chairman, Daley challenged and defeated Mayor Martin Kennelly in the 1955 Democratic primary and then won the first of six mayoral terms in the general election.

For twenty-one years, Daley presided over city government and the Democratic organization in his dual role as mayor and party chairman. He cultivated alliances with organized labor and industry that contributed to Chicago's renaissance at a time when other northern industrial cities were declining. He helped build the world's largest airport and tallest office building, a lakefront convention center, a governmental complex that would later bear his name, a Chicago campus for the state university, expressways, and mass transit lines.

Daley was among John F. Kennedy's key supporters in the 1960 presidential election, providing him with the delegates who helped him win a first-ballot nomination and a massive Chicago vote that delivered Illinois for Kennedy in his narrow victory over Richard M. Nixon. Daley hosted the 1968 Democratic National Convention at President Lyndon B. Johnson's request. Daley's national reputation was seriously tarnished as the result of violence between anti–Vietnam War demonstrators and Chicago police. Ironically, Daley had been a private critic of the Vietnam War and had urged Johnson to withdraw U.S. forces. In 1972, Daley was dealt another blow when the Democratic National Convention refused to seat his Illinois delegation because of noncompliance with new selection rules. In 1976, Jimmy Carter said that Daley's endorsement clinched his first-ballot nomination for the presidency, but Daley failed to deliver Illinois for Carter in the election.

Blacks were a major component of the Daley coalition, providing him with his winning margin in his two closest mayoral elections. But his relationship with them deteriorated in the turbulent hours after Dr. Martin Luther King's assassination when Daley issued a shoot-to-kill order in the wake of riots and looting on the city's West Side. He later resented the challenge to his authority as party chairman by black Democratic politicians.

A series of court rulings against political patronage diminished Daley's clout in his final term, and his political organization declined further in the decade after his death. Richard M. Daley, his eldest son, was elected mayor of Chicago in April 1989.

Bill Gleason, *Daley of Chicago* (1970); Mike Royko, *Boss: Richard J. Daley of Chicago* (1971).

STEVE NEAL

See also Chicago Seven; Urban Bosses and Machine Politics.

DANCE

I. Theatrical Dance

American theatrical dance, like the nation itself, has always been fueled by a mixture of native and imported elements, noble and crass goals, individuals, institutions, and traditions, all in a flux of accommodation and competition. Its history is a constant interplay between popular culture and high culture, with infusions of exotica, technology, and aesthetics. Repeatedly, it becomes more refined and stratified, only to be invaded, rethought, and reinvigorated by new influences. If it is unstable, it is also dynamic. A fusion of many styles and forms, it is distinctive everywhere for the high energy and versatility of its practitioners, its belief in the ability of movement to communicate.

Although historians usually date American dance from the end of the nineteenth century, when indigenous institutions and artists of stature began emerging, there was never a time when dance did not figure in public celebrations, entertainments, and spectacles. The earliest settlers were aware of Native American ceremonials and dances. Despite the Puritans' condemnation of dancing on moral grounds, social dancing flourished in colonial times, as did religious and patriotic pageantry. Early theatrical entertainments included displays of folk dancing (clogs, jigs, and hornpipes), acrobatics, feats of balance on the tightrope, pantomimes, and sketches descended from the Italian commedia dell'arte. The first known "ballet" in America was a Harlequin-Scaramouche pantomime, arranged in 1735 by an English dancing master, Henry Holt, who had opened a school in Charleston, South Carolina, the year before.

Even in Europe, ballet was still a century away from anything like an independent existence, and the ballets brought to America by English, French, and Italian companies during the revolutionary and postrevolutionary periods were appended to operettas, operas, and pantomimes. Dancing also found its way into circuses and variety shows, where independent acts, recitations, and divertissements were presented without theme or plot to unify them. The first famous American dancer, John Durang, was essentially a variety artist — an actor, acrobat, rope dancer, and blackface comic whose specialty was the hornpipe.

Durang began his career in Philadelphia with the Old American Company, one of the earliest theatrical troupes. Founded in 1784, this enterprising unit presented its own shows until 1796 and attracted important foreign visitors as well. Dancers with increasingly rigorous training brought the emerging romantic ballet from the Continent. In the populist wake of the French and American revolutions, ballets now depicted peasant life instead of centering on gods and goddesses, symbols of the nobility. *La Forêt Noire,* the first of these pastorales to reach America, was performed in Philadelphia and other cities in 1794–1795. Jean Baptiste Francisqui, trained in the French Académie de la Danse, staged some 125 ballet-pantomimes, adaptations of light opera, and *ballets villageoises* during his years in the United States from 1793 to 1808. Francisqui, like other itinerant ballet masters, worked in theaters up and down the Atlantic seaboard. He founded an opera-ballet company and a successful dancing school in New Orleans around 1799.

La Fille Mal Gardée was staged in 1828. When Paul Taglioni began an American tour in 1839 he gathered a corps de ballet in New York to put on the first complete *La Sylphide* and other ballets. Marius Petipa, who later shaped the style of Russian classicism as ballet master in St. Petersburg, visited New York in 1839. Forming a ballet company, he mounted *La Tarentule* and two other productions. The great Fanny Elssler enjoyed a phenomenal success with American audiences on an extended tour in 1840–1842.

The year 1837 saw the joint debut in Philadelphia of two American ballerinas, both trained by P. H. Hazard, formerly a member of the Paris Opera corps de ballet. Augusta Maywood pursued a long and successful career in Europe, principally in Italy, where she became known as a dramatic ballerina in the tradition of Fanny Elssler. Mary Ann Lee studied with Elssler's partner, James Sylvain, learned some of Elssler's roles, and had a distinguished career dancing and staging French ballets. She danced the first American Giselle, in Boston in 1846, partnered by George Washington Smith, the first American male classic dancer. Smith's fifty-year career spanned ballet, opera, and circus, and he taught social and Spanish dancing as well as ballet.

Whereas dancing masters and ballet productions showed middle-class Americans how to behave with gentility, even artistry, the popular stage showcased physical skills, specialty dancing, and comedy. Minstrel shows crystallized as a variety form around the 1840s. The stock characters, an interlocutor who introduced the acts and two comic end men, framed a wide variety of skits, songs, and dances. Tap dancing, a highly individualized and virtuosic composite form derived from the dances of African slaves and northern European step dances, flowered in the minstrel shows. William Henry Lane, known as Master Juba, became famous in America and England for the speed and variety of his rhythms and the ingenuity of his improvisations. Tap and other black dance styles became firmly implanted in the American musical theater, and they can be said to underlie nearly all popular dance today.

Theatrical spectacle comprising ballet, pageantry, melodrama, and scenic effects reached a climax in 1866 with the production of *The Black Crook* at Niblo's Gardens in New York. This extravaganza, frequently imitated, was a fixture on the American stage for the rest of the century. Because there were few permanent organizations capable of presenting full ballet productions, ballet remained a high-toned addition to spectacle or an appendage of opera until the twentieth century, while *The Black Crook* engendered an avid taste for all kinds of bizarre and sensational entertainments. With the exception of prestigious foreign artists, dancers could work professionally only on the popular stage — music halls, burlesque, and vaudeville — and they were stigmatized as immodest and immoral. Through the 1920s, when the book musical emerged, vaudeville shows featured "eccentric," acrobatic, tap, and toe dancing, comic and character dance sketches, adagio teams and ballroom dancers, skirt dancing, artistic or interpretive dancing, and specialty numbers in various ethnic styles.

Although stage dancers' reputations were suspect, amateur dancing and parlor theatricals enjoyed widespread respectability. Together with dress reform, women's education, and physical culture, a form of aesthetic recitation spread across the country. Called Delsarte, after François Delsarte, the French elocution teacher who devised it, the system combined rhythmic but decorous gymnastics with gestures indicating specific emotions. Delsarte recitals featured women declaiming poetry and imitating Greek statues, and community pageants were adorned with tableaux that represented famous historical or literary events.

Because it combined physical activity of the whole body with poetic feelings of unimpeachable virtue, Delsarte opened the way for expressive, nonballetic stage dancing. Ruth St. Denis learned Delsarte from her mother. She began on the variety stage as a skirt dancer, manipulating the flounces of her costume to make enticing designs. But wishing to do more artistic work, she merged her interests in the spiritual and the exotic. Her 1906 program of interpretations of India (*Radha, The Incense,* and *The Cobras*) launched her on an impressive career in Europe. After returning to America, she founded the Denishawn school (1915–1930) with her partner Ted Shawn. Loie Fuller, another American with serious intentions, combined skirt dancing with dramatic lighting, and her serpentine imagery captured the spirit of the art nouveau movement in Paris.

The other great pioneer of the expressive or interpretive dance, later called modern dance, was Isadora Duncan. Born into a semirespectable San Francisco family, she too tried the commercial stage but soon began to interpret serious music in her own way. Appearing barefoot, in Greek-inspired tunics, on a platform with simple drapes for a backdrop, she created a sensation in Europe. She developed a system of training children in a "natural" style of dancing. Although Duncan's American appearances were clouded by her outspoken socialist sympathies and by her audiences' lingering puritanism, her uninhibited approach to dance as an art inspired generations of American dancers.

While Duncan and St. Denis insisted that dancing could be a serious art form, the popular stage reached its height. Florenz Ziegfeld's elaborate *Follies* revues, beginning in 1907, transformed the ensemble into a chorus of beautiful women in flamboyant costumes who did not dance much but posed à la Delsarte or impersonated flowers, vegetables, or musical instruments. During the 1920s Ned Wayburn, borrowing from the formula of the famous Tiller Girls in London, added precision kicks, turns, and gestures to the chorus line routines. Classically trained dance directors like Albertina Rasch and Chester Hale incorporated steps from the ballet vocabulary, called "fancy dancing," in their numbers. The most ambitious of the Broadway dance masters, Gertrude Hoffmann, had studied the new Russian ballets that were sweeping Europe and had mounted imitations in New York before Serge Diaghilev's Ballets Russes arrived in 1915 with the real thing.

By the end of World War I, Americans were smitten with the stars and glamour of ballet. Touring Russians began to settle and open schools: Michel Fokine in New York, Adolf Bolm in Chicago, and others across the country. But it was not until Lincoln Kirstein persuaded George Balanchine to come to America in 1934 that American ballet emerged as a distinct entity. Although trained in St. Petersburg's Imperial Theatrical School, Balanchine had novel and independent ideas. With a small company of cohorts, he left Russia in 1924 and joined Diaghilev. After the impresario's death in 1929 Balanchine sought a company where he could continue his experiments. Kirstein provided this through his personal fortune and wealthy American connections. With the School of American Ballet providing a pool of dancers, whenever opportunities arose Balanchine formed a company and produced ballets. Between times, he choreographed for other ballet and opera companies, on Broadway, and in the movies, until the establishment of the New York City Ballet in 1948. Balanchine's achievement was to extend both the range and the metaphoric power of ballet by rejecting the pomp and display of the Imperial style and extending the lexicon of classicism — steps, form, and virtuosic bodies — with contemporary shapes and energies.

The other great indigenous company was founded in 1940 by Lucia Chase and Richard Pleasant. The Ballet Theater (now called American Ballet Theater) initially had three main stylistic themes: the Russian classics, dramatic modernism under the English choreographer Antony Tudor, and ballets about American life, American energies. This last agenda was filled most prominently by Jerome Robbins and Agnes de Mille. Ballet Theater became a major interpreter of the classics during the 1960s and 1970s with its policy of featuring foreign guest stars such as Carla Fracci, Erik Bruhn, Natalia Makarova, and, later, Mikhail Baryshnikov, who directed the company during the 1980s.

Concurrently, another group of dancers thought American dance should have nothing to do with what they considered the decadent and undemocratic European ballet. Martha Graham, Doris Humphrey, and Charles Weidman were trained in the Denishawn school but became convinced that Denishawn's glamorous dances, based loosely on mythology and Asian theatrical forms, were foreign to the American sensibility. Together with Helen Tamiris, and with Hanya Holm, who brought the German modern dance of Mary Wigman to New York in 1933, they developed movement and choreography that legitimized the idiosyncratic, the idealistic, and the body-centered approach to personal style. Their progeny has included Paul Taylor, Alwin Nikolais, José Limón, Alvin Ailey, and Merce Cunningham.

The next turning point in American dance occurred in the mid-1960s with the establishment of large-scale state and federal funding for the arts. The Ford Foundation's allocation of a multimillion-dollar grant to the School of American Ballet and several affiliated regional organizations in 1964 consolidated Balanchine's leadership of the ballet field. The New York State Theater opened in 1964 as the home of the New York City Ballet in Lincoln Center, a model for arts complexes around the country. With government support of dance companies and touring opportunities, and the presentation of dance on television, dance in the 1970s gained a visibility never before experienced by the so-called stepchild of the arts.

Serious choreographers working in the musical comedy field (Balanchine, de Mille, Robbins, Holm) had begun the process of raising standards there. As classical and modern dancing merged in the popular theater, the hostilities between the two forms also broke down. Today a dancer must have balletic training for strength and stretch, modern training for speed and flexibility. Ballet companies such as the Dance Theater of Harlem and the Joffrey Ballet perform an eclectic repertory of old and new, contemporary and classic dances. Perhaps the most original and successful contemporary choreographer, Twyla Tharp, has deliberately merged modern dance and ballet in her choreography, in the kinds of dancers she works with, and in the companies for which she creates.

Experiments generated by countercultural ideas in the 1960s and 1970s have also influenced mainstream dance. Merce Cunningham and composer John Cage questioned the authoritarian, personalized choreographic approach of modern dance, and in 1951 Cunningham began using chance devices to structure the movement and the placement and timing of movement in the performing space. This, along with other strategies for dislodging the audience's preconceptions, gave the dance stage a new and challenging set of possibilities.

The so-called postmodern generation that followed Cunningham, centered at first on the experimentation of the Judson Dance Theater, discarded not only conventional order and organization but most of the theatrical properties of dancing itself, in a concerted purging and rehumanizing of the form. Their collages, minimalism, and environmental adventures soon evolved into complex theatrical choreography again. By the 1980s, the attitudes and range of stage dancing had come closer to everyday life, and Americans, preoccupied with health, exercise, and sports, were pushing everyday life closer to dancing.

Paul Magriel, ed., *Chronicles of the American Dance* (1948; reprint, 1978); Marcia B. Siegel, *The Shapes of Change: Images of American Dance* (1979; reprint, 1985).

Marcia B. Siegel

See also Astaire, Fred; Baker, Josephine; Balanchine, George; Duncan, Isadora; Graham, Martha; Musical Theater; Robbins, Jerome; Theater; Ziegfeld, Florenz.

II. Social Dance

The history of American social dance goes far beyond the importation of European dance forms. Most striking in its three-hundred-year evolution has been the Africanization of the European dance sensibility. Although colonial America was marked by a pluralism of immigrant groups and Native Americans, the two major traditions that provided the cornerstone of American dance have been Western European and West African dance styles.

The fusion took place slowly during the colonial era and most of the nineteenth century; then the pace picked up. The late 1890s was the dawn of the jazz age, and the worldwide popularity of American vernacular dance turned the twentieth century into a golden period for that art. Choreography for social dance has always been democratically contributed by thousands of participants who devised the steps and styles, and in bursts of creativity, invented hundreds of dances from the silly to the sublime.

Dances that originated in African-American communities spread first to the nation and then to the world — like the Cakewalk, Turkey Trot,

Charleston, Lindy Hop (a.k.a. Jitterbug, Jive), Rock 'n' Roll, Electric Boogie, Breaking, and Rap/Funk. With the commercial export of American pop culture to the world, especially after the 1920s, American dance has become the most influential.

Until the twentieth century, dances tended to move from a rural to an urban setting, but after 1900 that trend reversed. In part the result of rural migration to the city, dances were born in ghetto neighborhoods, and then, cleansed of anything sexually suggestive, they were adapted to the ballroom and from the ballroom, were transferred to the stage. As new dances replaced older ones, the older forms were performed by older dancers in situations where it was important to reinforce traditional values (an inaugural ball, for example). As the formal elements of European dance were relaxed, their rhythms became syncopated; as the African elements became diluted and formalized, their rhythms became more regular.

Between the 1600s and 1800s in America, Africans adopted aspects of European dance for their use (i.e., partner relationships and dance patterns). Traditionally, in African dance, men dance with men, women with women. But in the New World, Africans began to move as male-female couples in European figure dances like the quadrille (a suite of dances performed in a square pattern by couples). But if the formal patterns were distinctly European, the steps, syncopations, and hip motions were distinctly African. By the 1850s that trend began to reverse, and European-Americans copied African-American dance styles — a practice that still prevails.

Dancing was popular in colonial America wherever religious sanctions were not imposed to curb it. From the 1700s to the late 1800s there was a progression from minuets and country dances to cotillions and quadrilles. Dance activity was layered because different kinds of dances were appropriate to different situations. For example, the wealthy, who looked to Europe as their cultural and social model, imported European figure dances like the minuet (a dance of highly ritualized, courtly manners) or more spritely country dances and quadrilles. All were

complex dances (well-known patterns determined how and where the dancers moved) that displayed dancing skills and graceful deportment and were taught by professional dancing masters.

Ingredients of those country dances (basically English) and quadrilles were democratized and Americanized into square dances. Now a caller called out the figures, steps, and instructions *during* the dance in rhythmic speech-song, making complex figure dances accessible to everyone and eliminating the need for a dancing master.

Regional dances like Irish step dances, Scotch-Irish jigs, German reels, Dutch chimney dances, and sailors' competitive hornpipes reflected ethnic traditions. Into this category fell the great families of African dances that stressed individual improvisation, percussive accompaniments, and call-and-response song and movement styles — the vernacular Juba, and its sister form, the religious Ring Shout, animal dances like the Buzzard Lope, funeral and processional strut dances, and seasonal dances.

Although these New World forms had much in common with their Old World progenitors, they were no longer identical. Changed by environmental and social conditions, they were synthesized into a strong new hybrid style of music and dance. The coincidental appearance in the New World of step dances from disparate cultural traditions provided a flexible form around which a national style might coalesce.

If early America had a preferred dance, it was the jig. This step dance, which emphasizes quick dexterous footwork and rhythms, was popular throughout Europe and subsequently in America. The jig was nothing if not flexible. Performed on- and off-stage, it could be a solo, couple, or group dance; it was danced by people from different classes and economic strata, cut across racial lines, and was performed in the ballroom, on the frontier, and on the stage. Complementary to it were African step dances in which the feet stamped, slid, chugged, and beat the ground rhythmically. Because they seemed similar, Europeans labeled these African dances "jigs," and when African and European elements combined into performance forms such as the Buck, Clog, and Jig, these exhibition dances parented the American tap dance. Most important, this new hybrid jig opened up social dance to the possibilities of individualism and improvisation — two qualities that would distinguish American social dance.

In the 1800s the Waltz arrived from Europe, followed by galops, mazurkas, polkas, the redowa, and schottische brought by the new waves of European immigrants who arrived in the 1800s. Balls became public affairs, more public ballrooms were built, and dances became egalitarian events with strangers in attendance, in contrast to the smaller, private parties of the previous centuries. Individualism invaded the ballroom. Instead of couples moving in harmony as interlocking parts of larger patterns, they now twirled independently across the floor.

Contact took the form of games. The German was an enormously popular — and odd — suite of dances and games led by a master of ceremonies to encourage a continual changing of partners. One example (there were hundreds) from the 1890s began with eight seated ladies, each with one piece of candy. Each lady's partner selected two other men to kneel before her with their mouths open and eyes closed. Choosing, she put candy in one's mouth and danced (waltzed) with the other. Then her first partner, along with the one given the candy, could select new partners from the circle.

It was with the Cakewalk in the 1890s that the first indigenous African-American dance became a national dance fad and then spread to Europe. According to slaves' oral histories, the Cakewalk began around 1850 on the plantations. In its characteristic high-kneed strut walk, it was meant to parody the solemn decorum of the white masters as they promenaded, two by two, in the formal marches that opened their balls. The formality and simplicity of their walk made it irresistible to satirize — and it resonated with the slaves' own processionals, usually funeral dances. When the masters saw the new Cakewalk, they were delighted, encouraging competitions among neighboring plantations and adopting the dance as their own, apparently unaware of its satiric origins. Sheet music from 1890 to 1907 reveals how popular this dance became in

America. In 1904 it received the validation of aristocratic society when the Prince of Wales learned it from the team of Williams & Walker (Burt Williams and George Walker were famous black performers who were a comedy team as well as theatrical producers).

After the Cakewalk, a rash of rollicking "animal" dances became popular in 1907–1914. Originating in the United States, these dances, like the Turkey Trot, Kangaroo Hop, and Grizzly Bear, spiced the vocabularies of the couple dance by incorporating gestures and steps from African animal dances — elbows flapped, heads pecked, and dancers hopped like bunnies.

In the 1920s, the Charleston (which probably evolved in black neighborhoods in Charleston, South Carolina, a decade earlier) was introduced to white audiences in Noble Sissle and Eubie Blake's *Runnin' Wild* in 1922. The Charleston broke American social dance free of European styles once and for all. It brought the African-American aesthetic into dominance with flying kicks and the rambunctious swinging of oppositional limbs, the rubber-legging, the pigeon-toeing grinding footwork, the shimmying shoulders, hip twists, and slapped buttocks (Black Bottom and Spank the Baby). Most important, through its vivacious syncopations and free-wheeling, solo improvisations, it was a prototype of an American vernacular jazz dance. By 1924, the Charleston had become the rage first in Paris and then in the rest of Europe, as audiences were beguiled by the elegant Josephine Baker.

In 1928 another American classic, the Lindy Hop, burst on the scene (named after Charles Lindbergh's flight across the Atlantic, it is commonly known as the Jitterbug in white communities). The Lindy reflected the pace and frenetic attitude of the big city, and at Harlem's Savoy Ballroom, it was taken to an extraordinary level of performance. In the early 1930s, responding to the rising speed and volume of big band swing music, the Lindy took to the air, and women were tossed and thrown by their partners like limp dolls. Initially through radio, records, movies, and newsreels and then through American G.I.'s during World War II, the Lindy was spread throughout the world. It had a long life and adapted to many kinds of music. There was the Mambo Lindy and the Bebop Lindy, and then, during the 1950s, the Jitterbug changed tempos and accents once again and adapted to rock 'n' roll music.

By the early 1960s, the Lindy was fading. Rock 'n' roll became rock, and the Twist enjoyed brief popularity. A social revolution was in the making, and during the civil rights era, in dances like the Watusi, Monkey, Frug, Jerk, Hitchhike, and Pony, males and females danced face to face as solo improvisers. An infusion of American interpretations of Africanisms was apparent not only in the dances' names but in movements of rippling spines, hip rotations, and hand-jive gestures that pantomimed little narratives.

The 1970s opened with the Hustle (careful examination reveals the Lindy Hop cut down to half-time) and closed with the eruption of Hip Hop and its panoply of musical (rap), graphic (graffiti), and dance expressions. Breaking and Electric Boogie developed in New York City's boroughs of the Bronx and Brooklyn during the late 1970s, and Popping and Snapping flowered in California. The structures and contents of all these dances reinforced, once again, the power of popular African-American music and movement. They used improvisation, magic circles, call-and-response patterns, competition, acrobatics, undulations, slides, complicated body and foot rhythms (polyrhythmic and polymetric), pantomime, and movement quotes from well-known popular culture artifacts and from television.

In the 1990s, there are few named dances. The prevailing free style combines many different styles and is described by musical types of funk/reggae/house/club/rap. Older ballroom and regional dance forms are kept alive at dance studios and by special dance clubs, and at weddings, formal charity balls, and government functions. European couple dances like the Waltz and Foxtrot continue to be performed.

Like contemporary American popular music, popular dancing tends to be percussive. Dances do not sweep across the floor in large group patterns. Dancers remain rather stationary, the feet stomping, sliding, hopping, while the arms punch the air or swing in counterpoint.

Movements are centered in pelvic rotations, the torso is handled as a multi-unit instrument with supple spine, shimmying shoulders, and swiveling hips. Knees are bent, heads circle and bob. The dance floors are crowded, bodies are close, yet the dancers move as individuals. The younger generation of American club dancers move in casual circles that randomly arise then disintegrate and are sexually mixed or not. Male-female partnerships are in constant flux.

Dancing in America tends to be age-specific, perhaps a national rite of passage; fourteen- to twenty-five-year-olds engage in the most dance activity. It is a testament to their inventiveness that American social dance continues to be an almost international language of movement that speaks to young people throughout the world.

Joseph E. Marks III, *America Learns to Dance* (1957); Richard Nevell, *A Time to Dance: American Country Dancing from Hornpipes to Hot Hash* (1977); Marshall and Jean Stearns, *Jazz Dance: The Story of American Vernacular Dance* (1964).

SALLY SOMMER

DARROW, CLARENCE

(1857–1938), labor and criminal lawyer, reformer, and social critic. Notable for his courtroom skills and his wide-ranging concern over the maladjustments in society, Darrow acted as attorney for the defense in nearly two thousand courtroom battles. He was successful at persuading juries in the years before World War I to consider sympathetically the social context of the bitter struggle then going on between capital and labor. In 1911, however, when he felt compelled to advise two labor leaders, the McNamara brothers, to plead guilty to the bombing of the antiunion *Los Angeles Times,* the labor movement repudiated him and he had to rebuild his practice.

Darrow then entered into a second career in the field of criminal law. Victories in a series of spectacular trials, many of them desperate cases, made him a national figure, especially his defense of Richard Loeb and Nathan Leopold in Chicago in 1924. The teenaged defendants had kidnapped and killed a young boy for thrills. By introducing psychiatric evidence, a novelty at the time, and invoking a sense of pity for the inscrutable human predicament, Darrow cast a spell over the courtroom. His plea for mercy, which took over two days to deliver, resulted in a verdict of life imprisonment rather than the death penalty. Today Darrow is best remembered for his role in the so-called monkey trial held at Dayton, Tennessee, in 1925 in which he defended a schoolteacher, John T. Scopes, who was charged with violating a law banning the teaching of evolution in the public schools. His relentless grilling of his opponent, William Jennings Bryan, on his literal interpretation of the Bible, drew international attention.

Darrow also wrote extensively — short stories and novels, essays on literary themes, and works on crime and penology. He wrote an engaging and pastoral account of his rural birth and early youth at Kinsman in northeast Ohio. The liberal and free-thinking outlook of his poor but intellectually active parents, he wrote, colored his later life.

After a somewhat sketchy education, which included a year at Allegheny College and a year at the University of Michigan Law School, Darrow was admitted to the Ohio bar in 1878. After a few years of practice in small Ohio towns, he moved to Chicago in 1888, his home for the rest of his life. There he developed associations important to his career and thought with John Peter Altgeld, the governor of Illinois, Henry George, the author of *Progress and Poverty,* and Henry Demarest Lloyd, publicist and pioneer muckraker.

In his later years Darrow became widely known on the lecture platform where he advanced with wit and passionate advocacy his views on such troublesome issues as capital punishment, Prohibition, prison reform, evolution, the relationship of science to society, and the philosophic problem of free will versus determinism. As a convinced materialist, Darrow's outlook on religion was in the skeptical tradition of Robert G. Ingersoll, although he preferred a conversational, colloquial style to the florid rhetoric of the orator. Darrow was a man of brilliant talents and many paradoxes in whom cynicism and compassion, pessimism and a zest for life,

were mingled. During his long and colorful career, he served both the poor and the powerful, but never the strong at the expense of the weak.

Kevin Tierney, *Darrow* (1979); Arthur Weinberg and Lila Weinberg, *Clarence Darrow: A Sentimental Rebel* (1980).

GERALD CARSON

See also Scopes Trial.

DARTMOUTH COLLEGE V. WOODWARD

In this early contract clause case, *Dartmouth College* v. *Woodward* (1819), the Supreme Court established substantial protection for the charters of institutions and businesses. Dartmouth College was established according to a charter written by the colonial governor of New Hampshire and granted by King George III in 1769. The charter provided for a self-perpetuating board of trustees to oversee the school. In 1816 the state legislature revised Dartmouth's charter, creating a new and different board of trustees. The original trustees sued but lost in the New Hampshire courts.

Enter Daniel Webster, a graduate of Dartmouth and spokesman for remnants of the Federalist party. He argued before the Supreme Court that the college's original charter should not be subject to the political whims of the state. "It is, sir, as I have said, a small college, but there are those who love it." Chief Justice John Marshall wrote the Court's opinion, which held that New Hampshire could not change the board of trustees. The Constitution's contract clause provided that no state could impair the obligation of contracts. This language protected the charter as a contract between New Hampshire and the college.

See also Constitution.

DARWINISM, SOCIAL

See Social Darwinism.

DAVIS, JEFFERSON

(1808–1889), politician and president of the Confederate States of America. Davis had an impressive political career before he became president of the Confederacy, but he was appointed, not elected, to many of the offices he held in his antebellum career. His limited experience with electoral politics was a handicap to his presidency, and, perhaps more important, he lacked the personal qualities that made Abraham Lincoln a successful president.

Raised on the Mississippi frontier, Davis's life was shaped by his brother Joseph, who was twenty-four years his senior. Joseph Davis made a fortune as a lawyer and planter, and he played a paternal role in Jefferson's life for many years. After Jefferson graduated from West Point and served in the army, Joseph gave him a plantation and the slaves to farm it. In the 1840s, Joseph managed the plantation so that Jefferson could go into politics.

Jefferson Davis became a staunch states' rights Democrat and champion of the unrestricted expansion of slavery into the territories. He was elected to the U.S. Congress in 1845 — his only successful electoral campaign — and then was appointed to the Senate after he became a hero while serving in the army during the Mexican War. In the Senate he opposed the Compromise of 1850, particularly the admission of California as a free state. In 1851 he resigned from the Senate to run unsuccessfully for the Mississippi governorship. In 1853, President Franklin Pierce appointed Davis secretary of war. Davis served ably in this office and in 1857 reentered the Senate, where he continued to advocate the spread of slavery into the territories. During the secession crisis, he resigned from the Senate and in 1861 was chosen by acclamation to be the Confederate president.

Davis worked very hard at his presidential duties, concentrating on military strategy but neglecting domestic politics, which hurt him in the long run. He could not manage congressional opposition as successfully as Lincoln, nor could he inspire the southern public as Lincoln did his public in the North. Davis was also a poor judge of people, unlike Lincoln. The Confederate president protected incompetents, such as Braxton Bragg, and he did not make use of talented men he disliked, such as Joseph E. Johnston. In April 1865 the Union armies finally surrounded Richmond, and Davis and his family fled the city for the Deep South, only to be captured in Georgia in May.

Davis's life after the war was bleak. Charged with treason, he went to prison in Fort Monroe, Virginia, where he remained for two years. In prison his physical and emotional health deteriorated, and he was never the same after he was released in May 1867. He and his family traveled abroad for two years. When he returned to America, he had trouble making a living. He worked for an insurance company in Memphis, but the company went bankrupt, and when he published a history of the Confederacy, it did not sell well. He lived off the charity of friends and relatives until his death in New Orleans in 1889. He refused to take the oath of allegiance to regain his citizenship, which was restored only posthumously by the U.S. Congress in 1978.

Clement Eaton, *Jefferson Davis* (1977); Paul D. Escott, *After Secession: Jefferson Davis and the Failure of Confederate Nationalism* (1978); Haskell M. Monroe, Jr., et al., *The Papers of Jefferson Davis* (1971–).

JOAN E. CASHIN

See also Civil War; Confederate States of America.

DAWES PLAN

The Dawes plan was prepared in 1924 by a committee of the Allied Reparations Commission as a way of stabilizing the Germany economy and systematizing the repayment of Germany's World War I reparations to the Allied countries. In 1921, the Reparations Commission had agreed that Germany must pay billions of dollars to the Allies. Germany defaulted in less than a year and was granted a twelve-month moratorium. Before the moratorium had expired, however, France and Belgium instituted their own method of collecting reparations by seizing Germany's principal industrial center, the Ruhr. Devastating inflation in Germany followed; by

September 1924 the mark had become almost worthless. The deterioration of the German economy concerned the United States both because of its general impact and because Americans were intent on recovering nearly $10 billion loaned to Allied countries during and immediately after World War I. These nations in turn needed the reparations to fund their debt payments to the United States.

The Dawes Committee, created to resolve the problem, had two representatives each from Belgium, France, Italy, and Great Britain as well as two Americans, Owen D. Young and the chairman, Charles G. Dawes. Their proposal, submitted on April 9, laid out a new more manageable schedule for German reparations payments, linked to an elaborate system of new taxes in Germany, stabilization of the German currency on the gold standard, the reorganization of the Reichsbank under Allied supervision, and, most important, massive American loans. The loans made possible German payments to the Allies, who in turn repaid their debts to the United States. The plan went into effect in September and did enable Germany to resume paying reparations. In 1929, the Young plan negotiated a lower reparations bill, based on a reduction in Allied war debts to the United States. With the Hoover moratorium on all intergovernmental debts in 1931, both reparations and war-debt payments virtually ended.

See also World War I.

DAWES SEVERALTY ACT

The Dawes General Allotment (Severalty) Act, February 8, 1887, converted all Indian tribal lands to individual ownership in an attempt to facilitate the assimilation of Indians into the white culture. Pressure for a reform in Indian policy was triggered by Helen Hunt Jackson's book, *A Century of Dishonor* (1881), which chronicled the unjust treatment American Indians had received at the hands of the federal government. Indian Rights associations sprang up across the country, and consensus grew that Indians must be helped to become full members of American society. The reformers saw the tradi-

tional patterns of Indian culture as the principal obstacle to meaningful citizenship; their first task, they believed, was to end the nomadism and isolation of reservation life. The new law was thus tailored to attack a central institution of Indian culture, common ownership of tribal lands.

Under the Dawes Act, Indian tribes lost legal standing, and tribal lands were divided among the individual members. In exchange for renouncing their tribal holdings, Indians would become American citizens and would receive individual land grants — 160 acres to family heads, 80 acres to single adults. Even these grants were qualified, however; full ownership would come only after the expiration of a twenty-five-year federal trust. (In 1906, the Burke Act waived the remaining trust for all Indians judged competent to handle their property independently.)

The Dawes Act significantly undermined Indian tribal life, but did little to further their acceptance into the broader society. In addition, the law severely reduced Indian holdings; after all individual allocations had been made, the extensive lands remaining were declared surplus and opened for sale to non-Indians. In 1887, the tribes had owned about 138 million acres; by 1900 the total acreage in Indian hands had fallen to 78 million. This policy was not reversed until 1934, when the Indian Reorganization Act asserted the importance of perpetuating Indian cultural institutions and permitted surplus lands to be returned to tribal ownership.

See also Indians.

DAY, DOROTHY

(1897–1980), Catholic journalist, peace activist. As founder of the Catholic Worker movement, Dorothy Day joined a conservative religious piety with radical political convictions. Although her pacifism provoked criticism, in later years she was widely admired as a heroic, even holy woman, uncompromisingly committed to social justice and the cause of the poor. She left a deep impact on the American Catholic church.

Having grown up in a newspaper family in

Chicago, Day was attracted to journalism and the progressive cause at an early age. She left college in 1916 to work for a number of socialist and left-wing journals in New York City. She was active in antiwar circles during the First World War and was jailed for demonstrating on behalf of women's suffrage. After the war she passed some restless years as part of New York's literary and political avant-garde.

A turning point in her life came in 1927 with the birth of a daughter, an experience so filled with joy and mystery that it prompted her conversion to the Roman Catholic church. The conversion itself, as she later described it in her autobiography, *The Long Loneliness,* was a painful process, involving not only separation from the child's father but alienation from many of her radical friends, for whom the Catholic church represented a bastion of conservatism. She herself was left wondering how to reconcile her political commitment with her religious faith.

The solution came in 1932 when she met Peter Maurin (1877–1949), a self-educated French philosopher of peasant background. He inspired her to establish a Catholic newspaper addressed to workers. The result was the *Catholic Worker,* launched in May 1933 in the heart of the depression. From the start the paper reflected a radical, anticapitalist perspective rooted in the Bible, Catholic social teaching, and a personalist, communitarian philosophy. Around the newspaper a community emerged combining the "works of mercy" — feeding the hungry and sheltering the homeless in "houses of hospitality" — with direct action on behalf of peace, labor, civil rights, and other causes. Catholic Worker communities proliferated around the country, united by a similar faith expressed in voluntary poverty, the works of mercy, action for peace and justice, and solidarity with the poor. According to Day, "The mystery of the poor is that they are Jesus, and what we do for them we do for him."

Day's pacifism was her most controversial position, but perhaps also her most enduring contribution. It influenced such figures as Thomas Merton, Daniel Berrigan, and successive generations of Catholic peace activists. In the 1950s and 1960s she was frequently jailed for acts of civil disobedience. For this she was often criticized, even by those who admired her service to the poor. After her death in 1980, however, she was widely credited with having restored the ideal of gospel nonviolence to a place of honor within the Catholic church.

Robert Ellsberg, ed., *By Little and By Little: The Selected Writings of Dorothy Day* (1983); Jim Forest, *Love Is the Measure: A Biography of Dorothy Day* (1986).

ROBERT ELLSBERG

See also Conscientious Objection; Radicalism; Religion; Roman Catholic Church.

D-DAY

D-Day was the code word designating June 6, 1944, the day for the invasion of the Cotentin Peninsula in Nazi-occupied Normandy by Allied forces during the Second World War. The invasion was the largest amphibious landing in history. Within one week of D-Day, the Allies had landed, in the face of hostile obstacles, 326,000 men, 50,000 vehicles, and over 100,000 tons of supplies — a technical miracle. The landing established a firm beachhead in Normandy from which the Allied armies swept across France, liberating Paris on August 25, 1944. Ultimately, armies of the Western Allies linked up with the Red Army on the Elbe River on April 25, 1945, for the final defeat of Germany.

Under the overall direction of Supreme Allied Commander Dwight D. Eisenhower, Gen. Omar Bradley commanded the U.S. First Army, which invaded Utah and Omaha beaches, while the British Twenty-first Army Group, commanded by Gen. Bernard Montgomery, and Gen. Brian Dempsey's British Second Army hit Gold, Juno, and Sword beaches. Gen. Matthew Ridgway's 82nd Airborne and Gen. Maxwell Taylor's 101st Airborne landed by parachute and glider behind the German lines and linked up with the armies advancing from the beaches. The heaviest fighting occurred on Omaha.

The British and American navies enjoyed complete superiority in the English Channel, but landing soldiers faced concrete-hardened machine-gun emplacements and hostile artillery fire coming from higher ground. Against these they were supported by tactical bombers and ship-to-shore bombardment.

Part of the success of D-Day lay in the numerical superiority of the Allied forces. Technical ingenuity — such as the invention of landing craft capable of carrying tanks, the construction of an entire prefabricated port to replace the ports destroyed by the Nazis, and the use of PLUTO, a flexible, ever-advancing pipeline for gasoline — helped translate Allied industrial might into military victory.

See also World War II.

DEBATES, LINCOLN-DOUGLAS

See Lincoln-Douglas Debates.

DEBS, EUGENE V.

(1855–1926), labor organizer and socialist. Debs grew up in the small midwestern city of Terre Haute, Indiana, where his parents, Alsatian immigrants, operated a grocery store. In 1875 he was elected secretary of the Terre Haute lodge of the Brotherhood of Locomotive Firemen. His intelligence and commitment, coupled with his conservative outlook (he argued against participation in the nationwide railroad strikes of 1877), attracted the attention of the brotherhood's leaders. By 1881, he was national secretary of the brotherhood, increasingly its spokesman on labor issues, and its most tireless organizer. Simultaneously, Debs entered politics as a Democratic candidate for city clerk in 1879. First elected over Republican and Greenback-Labor party candidates, Debs was overwhelmingly reelected in 1881. Four years later, he was elected to the Indiana State Assembly with broad support from the wards of Terre Haute's workers and businessmen.

During the 1880s Debs's ideas began to change. At first a firm proponent of organization of workers by their separate crafts, he resisted the industrial organization implicit in the efforts of the Knights of Labor and ordered his members to report to work during the Knights' 1885 strike against the southwestern railroads. But his year-long involvement (1888–1889) in the strike against the Chicago, Burlington, and Quincy Railroad altered these views. He now thought craft organization divisive, a hindrance to working people's efforts to secure fair wages and working conditions. And concentrated corporate power, he argued, had a debilitating effect on the political rights and economic opportunity of the majority of Americans. By 1893 he had resigned his position as secretary of the brotherhood and begun organizing an industrial union of railroad workers, the American Railway Union (ARU).

The ARU's 1894 strike against the Pullman Company of Chicago marked a second turning point in Debs's thinking. The unified power of railroad management working intimately with federal authorities broke the strike. Federal troops occupied Chicago, federal injunctions prevented communication between ARU locals, and federal judges sentenced Debs and other activists to jail terms. Debs emerged from this experience with two convictions. He questioned the ultimate ability of trade unions to combat successfully capital's economic power and, after the 1896 elections, looked upon socialism as the answer to working people's problems.

Between 1900 and 1920 Debs was the Socialist party's standard-bearer in five presidential elections. In 1912, in a four-way race with Woodrow Wilson, Theodore Roosevelt, and William Howard Taft, he received 6 percent of the vote — his highest total ever. Between campaigns, Debs was a tireless speaker and organizer for the party, and he traveled the nation defending workers in their strikes and industrial disputes. Although many workers enthusiastically applauded Debs's vision, relatively few endorsed his political program. He conducted his last campaign for president as prisoner 9653 in the Atlanta Federal Penitentiary while serving ten years for his opposition to World War I. He received nearly a million votes. As the American Socialist party fragmented in the aftermath of the Bolshevik Revolution, Debs remained with the party he had led for so many years. Upon his death he was buried in Terre Haute, his home throughout his life.

Nick Salvatore, *Eugene V. Debs: Citizen and Socialist* (1982).

NICK SALVATORE

See also Conscientious Objection; Elections: 1912, 1920; Labor; Socialism; Socialist Party.

DEBT

See National Debt.

DECLARATION OF INDEPENDENCE

On June 7, 1776, Richard Henry Lee proposed a resolution to the Continental Congress stating that "these United Colonies are, and of right ought to be, free and independent States." Four days later Congress appointed a committee to draft a declaration embodying the intent of the resolution. The committee, consisting of Thomas Jefferson, John Adams, Benjamin Franklin, Roger Sherman, and Robert R. Livingston, pressed on Jefferson the task of writing their report. On June 28 the committee submitted to Congress "A Declaration by the Representatives of the United States of America, in General Congress Assembled." The Congress passed Lee's original resolution on July 2, thus deciding in favor of independence, but took three days to debate and amend the committee's draft declaration before approving it on July 4. "The Unanimous Declaration of the 13 United States of America" (the Continental Congress never officially called it the Declaration of Independence) was engrossed on parchment, and on August 2 every member present signed it, the remaining members signing later.

The separation of Lee's resolution for independence from Jefferson's declaration suggests the prescience of Congress. It recognized that more was required on this auspicious occasion than a simple statement of withdrawal from the British Empire. The world was watching and a "decent respect to the Opinions of mankind" required a statement of causes and principles. Fortunately, Jefferson did not fail them. The declaration presents in brief compass the fundamental premises of American nationhood: "that all men are created equal, that they are endowed by their creator with inalienable rights," and "that to secure these rights, governments are instituted among men, deriving their just powers from the consent of the governed."

Looking back more than two hundred years later, the reader focuses on these brief phrases in the declaration and wants to know where they came from and what they meant. A few scholars have claimed that Jefferson relied heavily on a handful of eighteenth-century Scottish philosophers, notably Francis Hutcheson, for many of the key ideas. More believe that John Locke exercised a predominant influence over Jefferson's thinking; many of the words in the opening paragraphs of the declaration closely resemble passages from Locke's *Two Treatises of Government.* Jefferson himself did not credit any particular philosopher but claimed his aim was to "place before mankind the common sense of the subject" and to make the declaration "an expression of the American mind." For the document to serve its purpose, Jefferson had to draw together ideas in common currency, whatever their source. The declaration is a powerful and incisive summary of Whig political thought to which Locke and many others had contributed.

The most perplexing word in the declaration is *equality.* How could the slaveholders in Congress have embraced an idea so out of keeping with the realities of bound labor in America? Jefferson and the committee implicitly recognized the contradiction by including in the original draft a charge that the king had "waged a cruel war against human nature" by assaulting a "distant people" and "captivating and carrying them into slavery in another hemisphere." Although Jefferson deflected guilt from the colonists to the monarch, the words offended southern delegates, especially those from South Carolina, who were unwilling to countenance any acknowledgment that slavery violated the "most sacred rights of life and liberty." The price of their endorsement of the declaration was removal of the slavery passage, foreshadowing the repeated compromises with slavery that were made after independence was achieved. The word *equality* remained, however, and eventually, after immense cost to the nation and thousands of blighted lives, it triumphed over the slave power.

The significance of the declaration's fundamental principles came to be understood only as American history unfolded. At the time, Congress was as concerned with the charges brought against the king as with ideas of political philosophy. The list of his tyrannical acts constitutes the bulk of the declaration, and Congress devoted more attention to amending these charges than polishing the statement of principles. The indictment of the king assumed importance because the colonists previously had directed their criticism against Parliament or the king's ministers, not against the king himself. Protests against royal government customarily began with an assertion of loyalty to the monarch. He was the friend of the people amid their many enemies. In constitutional terms, the most radical revolutionaries asked only that the king treat their assemblies as the sovereign legislatures for the colonies, just as Parliament was for England. They never questioned his right to rule.

To turn on the king after 1774 was a sharp reversal, yet necessary before independence could be complete. It was a difficult turn to make. England waged war on the colonies for fourteen months after April 19, 1775, before the colonists could bring themselves to make the final break. During all that time they referred to the troops as "ministerial," as if the Crown's bureaucracy, not the king, waged the war. One principle inhibited criticism of the king himself, the idea that the king could do no wrong. Even if the policies came from his mouth or pen, it was assumed as a necessary fiction of state that malicious ministers had deceived him, not that he had acted out of ill will toward his people.

That idea was so strong that it took much evidence to the contrary to persuade people that George III endorsed the oppressive policies of his ministers and favored severe measures against the colonists. By August 1775, he was using his personal influence to persuade the Privy Council to declare the colonies in open rebellion. Through the fall he urged the "most decisive exertions" to put an end to the disorders. On December 22, 1775, he signed the American Prohi-

bition Act into law, forbidding all commerce with the colonies. He explicitly put the Americans outside of his protection, thus, according to the principles of monarchical government, ending their obligation of allegiance.

Thomas Paine's *Common Sense,* published in January 1776, crystallized the growing sense that George III was a "royal brute" who merited disdain rather than allegiance. Even then many held back, but by June 1776 the preponderance of opinion was that the last tie with Britain, allegiance to the monarch, had been broken not by his loyal American subjects but by the king himself. Jefferson noted in the declaration that "mankind are more disposed to suffer while evils are sufferable" than to abolish accustomed forms of government. "But when a long train of abuses and usurpations pursuing invariably the same object, evinces a design to reduce them under absolute despotism it is their right, it is their duty to throw off such government."

It was the purpose of the declaration to demonstrate that the history of the king was a "history of repeated injuries and usurpations, all having in direct object the establishment of an absolute tyranny." By showing the king to be a traitor to his people, the colonists rightfully dissolved the last political bonds with Britain and assumed a "separate and equal station" among nations of the earth. Although looking back we turn most frequently to the noble enunciation of political principles, at the time perhaps the primary purpose of the Declaration of Independence was to achieve release from Britain by indicting the British king for treason against his American subjects.

Carl Lotus Becker, *The Declaration of Independence: A Study of Political Ideas* (1922); Garry Wills, *Inventing America: Jefferson's Declaration of Independence* (1978).

Richard L. Bushman

See also Common Sense; Continental Congresses; Jefferson, Thomas; Revolution. *(For the text of the Declaration of Independence, see appendix.)*

DEFENSE

See Armed Forces.

DEISM

Deism, a European religious and philosophical movement, was influential in eighteenth-century American thought. It described a world order based on human reason rather than divine revelation. God was viewed as the "first cause" who had established an ordered universe controlled by immutable laws that functioned without miracles or other divine intervention. Human beings had to rely on reason to know God's existence and their own moral duties. This radical development in religious thought was prompted by new philosophical methods, frustration with doctrinal controversies, new political and social theories, and a revolution in the empirical sciences led by Isaac Newton.

Although deism appealed to the individualism and optimism of many eighteenth-century American political and social thinkers, it was popular only among upper-class intellectuals. American deists ranged from the moderate anticlericism, rational morality, and political liberalism of Thomas Jefferson and Benjamin Franklin to the much less common militant deism of Ethan Allen and Thomas Paine, who called for an abolition of traditional religion. The one unifying factor in the different versions of deism was a readiness to question traditional revealed religion.

See also Religion.

DE KOONING, WILLEM

(1904–   ), painter. Considered by many art historians a *chef d'école* of the moment in American art history called abstract expressionism, de Kooning himself would never concede that he belonged to any movement or school. Like other painters whose stylistic evolution occurred during the Great Depression when a lively debate ensued among artists working in the Federal Art Project under the WPA, de Kooning abjured received ideas about painting. Throughout his career, he challenged even his own assumptions.

When he arrived in the United States as an illegal immigrant in 1926, de Kooning had already had eight years of conventional training at the Rotterdam Academy of Fine Arts and Techniques and had made intelligent appraisals of the great modernists, including his countryman Piet Mondrian. He carried with him a culture that informed his painting no matter how vigorously he challenged himself and his colleagues. Both de Kooning and his closest ally in the new movement germinating in New York — the Armenian-born Arshile Gorky — fed their painting impulse with insights gained equally from the old masters and from modern painters such as Matisse, Picasso, Mondrian, and Miró. Gorky's example (he unabashedly rehearsed several styles gleaned from Picasso and Miró before he evolved his own) was important to de Kooning, who slowly moved from tentative explorations of cubist and surrealist modes to a singular, free style.

His first one-man exhibition in 1948 was an event of considerable moment: he showed an audacious group of black and white abstractions rendered with enamel house paints in which tightly organized spaces were articulated in sweeping strokes. Shortly after, in such monumental works as the six-by-eight-foot *Excavation* (1950; Chicago Art Institute), de Kooning established an autographic idiom that was identifiably abstract — that is, whispers of organic forms were sublimated — and expressionist in its freely brushed, sweepingly animated technique. Along with Jackson Pollock, with whom he had been friendly since the early 1940s, de Kooning was regarded as a pioneer of a new painterly idiom for which the terms *gestural* and *informal* were often invoked. In 1953, de Kooning surprised his appreciative public with an exhibition of heavily brushed, bluntly frontal images grouped under the title *Woman,* in which what had earlier been only cryptic allusions to human shapes became explicit. These shocking images, which de Kooning himself compared to the Venus of Willendorf, were proof of his extraordinary freedom from all strictures.

Thereafter, his spirited brush moved to capture ideas of figures, landscapes, and what he called the "Byzantine" image of urban New York, offering scores of younger artists a model of technical and moral freedom. Known first as a painter's painter, de Kooning is now recognized throughout the world as the old master of abstract expressionism.

Thomas B. Hess, *Willem de Kooning* (1959); Harold Rosenberg, *Willem de Kooning* (1974).

DORE ASHTON

See also Abstract Expressionism; Painting and Sculpture.

DELANY, MARTIN R.

(1812–1885), abolitionist, author, and politician. A nineteenth-century Afro-American leader, Delany was a gadfly of many talents and considerable controversy. He is principally remembered as an early black nationalist and an architect of emigration to Africa, endeavors that have obscured the many other remarkable features of his career.

Delany was born free in Charlestown, Virginia (now West Virginia), the son of a slave and a free black woman. He grew up knowing his African ancestry; one of his grandfathers was a Mandingan prince and the other a Golah village chieftain. Delany achieved a solid education in Pittsburgh, where his family had moved in 1831. There he gained his first experience in abolitionism, temperance reform, and the Underground Railroad. In 1843 he married Catherine Richards, the daughter of a member of the Pittsburgh black elite; all their seven children were named for famous blacks.

For a short time Delany published a newspaper, the *Mystery,* and in 1847–1848, he served as coeditor and agent of Frederick Douglass's newspaper, the *North Star.* His friendship with Douglass became strained over ideology and strategy, prompting Douglass's famous comparison, "I thank God for making me a man, but Delany thanks him for making him a *black* man." In 1850–1851 Delany attended medical school at Harvard. After white students protested his presence, he was asked to leave, but before this bitter experience he amassed enough knowledge to enable him to practice medicine periodically.

Delany's discouragement with the persistence of slavery and racism prompted him to move his family to Chatham, Ontario, in the 1850s and to organize emigrationist conventions in both the United States and Canada. In 1859 he went to West Africa, touring Liberia and the Niger River valley, investigating sites for colonization, and negotiating a treaty for the use by Afro-American settlers of a portion of Yorubaland (modern Nigeria). The depth of Delany's discontent is captured in his two major writings: *The Condition, Elevation, Emigration and Destiny of the Colored People of the United States, Politically Considered* (1852), a book that recommended emigration for blacks and sketched a nationalist consciousness; and a novel published serially in 1859, *Blake, or the Huts of America,* the story of a free Afro-Cuban who, after being kidnapped in America, begins to organize an international slave insurrection. Delany was a dedicated activist, but his leadership style was often authoritarian, and his thought was sometimes as rooted in class interests as it was in race. He viewed emigration as a genuinely new start for American blacks, but also as moral regeneration for Africa, to be led by enlightened Afro-Americans.

Delany garnered considerable support for his African venture, but when the Civil War broke out he switched his attention to recruiting black troops in Massachusetts, Rhode Island, and Connecticut. In 1865 he was commissioned a major in the Union army, the first black field officer in the war. He recruited two regiments of ex-slaves, and at the war's end he stayed in South Carolina, working diligently for the Freedmen's Bureau for three years and then entering state politics. But he became increasingly disenchanted with Radical Reconstruction, especially its political corruption. He then championed southern home rule and eventually became an active supporter of the ex-Confederate, antilabor, white supremacist Wade Hampton, the Democratic candidate for governor of South Carolina. Delany's misadventures in Reconstruction politics found him once again interested in Liberian emigration in the late 1870s. After his death, he remained relatively unknown until young black nationalists in the 1960s, looking for their ideological origins, resurrected the memory of his pre-1861 career.

Cyril E. Griffith, *The African Dream: Martin R. Delany and the Emergence of Pan-African Thought* (1975); Nell

Irvin Painter, "Martin R. Delany: Elitism and Black Nationalism," in Leon Litwack and August Meier, eds., *Black Leaders of the Nineteenth Century* (1988), 149–171.

DAVID W. BLIGHT

See also Abolitionist Movement; Black Nationalism; Free Negroes, 1619–1860; Civil War; Freedmen's Bureau; Reconstruction.

DeMILLE, CECIL B.

(1881–1959), film director and producer. DeMille may well have been the most important filmmaker of the first half of the twentieth century. Yet his work is rarely mentioned by film critics or historians. Rather, his importance lies elsewhere. Starting in 1914, he helped found a major studio, Paramount Pictures, and produced and directed during the next forty years more than seventy films that grossed over $750 million. His original production and remake of *The Ten Commandments* were the top-grossing films of the twenties and fifties, respectively. By the end of his career he had presided over the industry's major trade associations and served as vice president of the Bank of America. Claiming to be a man with a "keen sense of civic responsibility," he was an anti-union Republican and an anticommunist who sought to mobilize American films in the cold war era to save free enterprise and democracy around the world. During his career, he received numerous honorary degrees and national awards, and two public schools in California were named for him.

DeMille saw his work as an extension of duties handed down to him by his family. Unlike other early filmmakers, such as D. W. Griffith or the studio magnates of immigrant Jewish stock who came from poor backgrounds, DeMille was the son of a well-to-do eastern family that traced its ancestry in America back to the seventeenth century. His father had been an Episcopalian priest, but in the 1890s joined with the Broadway impresario David Belasco to create plays catering to the New York wealthy. In this environment, Cecil and his brother turned to acting, producing, and writing plays advocating a "social revolution through drama."

DeMille entered the movie industry just as it was creating the first mass audience in the United States. He became known for addressing through his films the fears surrounding the rise of the new consumer culture and the moral revolution of the twenties. In film after film, his characters belonged to those classes whose ancestors had helped found a nation on notions of Anglo-Saxon superiority and concepts of economic freedom. Yet his men and women felt trapped in urban offices or Victorian homes. To alleviate their boredom, they turned to nightclubs or amusement parks where the classes and sexes mingled, and the New Woman and dances like the Charleston challenged the old order of self-denial and public virtue. DeMille's films proposed leaving undisturbed the old code of Anglo-Saxon virtue dominating public life, but instead altering private life. The family would satisfy the desires for new relationships between men and women, and the yearnings for consumer pleasures.

During the next three decades, DeMille joined other filmmakers in merging the new popular culture with nationalism. His films' protagonists struggled to reform the country, contain rebellions, and counter the hedonism of the day. In the more placid fifties, films like *The Ten Commandments* and *Samson and Delilah* were filled with metaphors signifying triumph over the Golden Calf and Godless external enemies, the latter not too different from his perception of the Soviet Union.

Summing up in 1958 the spirit animating his work for over half a century, DeMille recalled that his mother had persuaded her husband to leave the ministry for the "wider pulpit" of the stage. Their son's films had been seen by over 3 billion people and had inspired numerous leaders to identify with the new "American way" of abundance. Truly, said DeMille, this achievement had fulfilled his mother's "prophecy."

Lary May, *Screening Out the Past: The Birth of Mass Culture and the Motion Picture Industry* (1983); Gene Ringgold and DeWitt Bodeen, *The Films of Cecil B. DeMille* (1969).

LARY MAY

See also Movies.

DEMOCRACY IN AMERICA

This work remains one of the classic, most-quoted studies of the nineteenth-century American mind and way of life, although its views reflect its author's upper-class biases. Alexis de Tocqueville and Gustave de Beaumont, both French aristocrats, arrived in New York from France in May 1831 to study the American prison system for the French government. They spent nine months touring the country, recording their impressions not only of its penal system but also of its society, economy, and political system. After returning to France in February 1832, they wrote their report on prisons, and Beaumont wrote a novel about American race relations. But it is Tocqueville's work that is remembered.

Tocqueville wrote, "In America, men are nearer equality than in any other country in the world." By that, he meant that whatever class distinctions existed in American society were not due to government decree because everyone had equality of opportunity. Tocqueville analyzed the religious and social views of Americans, differing conceptions of the role of government, and the tragedy of the forced migration of the Choctaw Indians. But he also glossed over or ignored completely poverty, sexual inequality, and the plight of the slaves. Still, his work remains an insightful portrait of Jacksonian America.

See also Foreign Views of America.

DEMOCRATIC PARTY

The Democratic party began to assume its modern form during the intense political conflict that divided Americans after the War of 1812. Over the next decade, as the party's organization developed, Democrats argued that they were combating Federalist efforts to impose an aristocratic, centralized government on the American people. The conflict between centralizers and egalitarians, Democrats declared, went back to the Hamiltonian efforts in the 1790s to erect a powerful national authority, threatening to individual liberties.

These Democrats, unlike their Jeffersonian predecessors, accepted the inevitability and legitimacy of popular political conflict and believed that political parties were the best means to handle that conflict. Although the Democrats did not originate conventions, platforms, and highly institutionalized campaigning, they brought these features of the party system to a new level. The leaders of this organizational revolution were Martin Van Buren, James K. Polk, Franklin Pierce, and a few others.

There was plenty to stimulate their efforts. Regional, ethnoreligious, and economic fault lines ran throughout American society, dividing Democrats from Whigs. The core of the Democratic party's support lay in southern slave plantations, farms of all sizes in every part of the nation, and immigrants in the urban centers of the eastern seaboard. Whigs also drew support from these groups and from the commercial classes throughout the nation (a group that also included some Democratic supporters). What distinguished the parties were their cultural and ideological perspectives. Democrats tended to be drawn from the "outsider" groups in Anglo-Saxon society: the Scots-Irish, Presbyterians, and other nonconforming religious and ethnic groups, who had long been in conflict with the dominant groups in the British Isles. They feared a powerful government and were hostile to the aggressive commercialism of the dominant Anglo-Saxons.

All this gave the Democrats the air of an egalitarian party challenging the nation's ruling elite. The role played by the party's leader, Andrew Jackson, in these efforts differed from earlier ideas of political leadership. He conveyed, by words and deeds, a few simple truths about republican purity and democratic striving and served as the symbol of a Democratic crusade against greed, unfairness, and the domination of a manipulative elite.

By the presidential election of 1836, the Democrats had developed an effective national organization. Thereafter, they moved beyond mere organization and created a powerful partisan culture, energetically cultivated by armies of party activists. By 1840, voters were surging to the polls in unprecedented numbers, and they continued to do so in subsequent elections. The Democrats were the primary advocates of this new culture, and their constituents reacted with almost religious fervor. Democrats worshiped, it was said, at "the shrine of party." It was indispensable, its members believed, to everything that went on in American politics.

From the mid-1830s to the Civil War, the Democrats were the nation's majority party, usually controlling Congress, the presidency, and many state offices. But they suffered their first significant disruption in the electoral realignment of the mid-1850s. A surge of Irish and German Catholic immigration provoked powerful reactions among many northern Democrats, as well as Whigs. Fears for the future of the "Protestant nation" led to the creation of the Know-Nothing party, which drew much support from Democrats. At the same time, the unwillingness of many Democratic leaders to take a stand against slavery was increasingly seen as a prosouthern position that unfairly permitted slaveholders to prevail in more and more of the nation's territories and to dominate national policy when Democrats were in power. This resentment of the South grew out of a succession of party decisions that, by accommodating increasingly aggressive slaveholder demands, sought to maintain both party and national cohesion. A new Republican party shrewdly played on the nativism and antisouthern sentiment to build a movement to resist southern and Catholic "assaults" on the American nation. The result was a significant political realignment.

The Democrats' second important era lasted from the Civil War into the 1890s. The party of Grover Cleveland and Samuel J. Tilden echoed the antigovernment rhetoric of the Jacksonians. After stumbling badly during the Civil War when one segment of the party advocated making peace with the Confederacy, the Democrats returned to national competitiveness. Partisan loyalties, planted in the 1840s and nourished by the events of the 1850s and the Civil War, kept thousands faithful in election after election. In the aftermath of war and Reconstruction, southern whites who had not been Democrats earlier now came over in massive numbers. The Solid (Democratic) South became a major feature of the American political landscape in the last years of the nineteenth century. But the Democrats' persistent immigrant and Catholic aura and their toleration of the most reactionary elements in the South were significant barriers to any improvement in the party's national situation.

The Democrats lost electoral ground once again in the 1890s when, under the leadership of William Jennings Bryan, the old rural and southern-western core of the party recaptured its egalitarian ethos. The Bryanites reiterated familiar themes about the unfair manipulation of government power for the benefit of a selfish industrial elite dominating the Republican party, as its forebears had dominated the Federalists and Whigs. At the same time, Bryanites were more willing than their party ancestors to use government power to restore balance within the system, especially to help the commercial-agricultural sector sinking under a worldwide price depression. They coupled this, however, with an antiurbanism that seemed hostile to the other core Democratic constituencies — immigrants and Catholics. The latter were growing in numbers and importance. Not all the urban political machines that developed from the 1850s onward were Democratic, but a significant number were. They brought renewed vigor to the party's electioneering and organization and attracted new voters to the polls. They were repelled by Bryan's parochial echoing of the past, the nature of his policies, and his denunciations of them. Their lack of support for the Bryanites lay behind the party's reverses in the decade after the 1896 election.

What was most significant about the Democrats' rise to importance was its approach to government power. Urban Democrats remained traditionally suspicious of the use of government authority to enforce conformity in such matters as prohibition, a particular school curriculum, or the promotion of a distinct brand of Americanism. But, like the Bryan wing, they believed that government could have a benign function, such as maintaining decent living conditions and providing direct help to those in need — in short, dealing with the dislocations caused by the industrial and urban revolutions.

Woodrow Wilson straddled both wings of the party as he rose to prominence after 1910. Deeply rooted in the party's traditional core, he was much affected by a progressive reformism dedicated to using the powers of government to meliorate the ruptures in the social and economic system. Elected president because of a Republican split in 1912, Wilson called for a New Freedom, which echoed traditional American (and Democratic) individualism, as well as a commitment to use government to promote that individualism against the forces manipulating the system for their own narrow ends. During his first term, there was an expansion of federal authority over the nation's financial system and some willingness to use national power to improve working and living conditions at the lower reaches of the social scale. Wilson's reformism was limited, but his presidency suggested some important shifts among the Democrats.

The world situation after 1914 raised divisive questions about the Democrats' approach to foreign policy matters. Associating the Republicans with excessive nationalism, the Wilsonians adopted a liberal internationalism and commitment to collective security to maintain world stability and promote American interests. That commitment was defeated in the fight over the League of Nations after World War I. That fight and the tensions associated with U.S. involvement in the war also led to another significant party reverse. Irish Democrats, German voters, and many others reacted against Wilson's commitment to Great Britain and the range of controls imposed on economic life during the war. Losing the presidential elections of 1920 and 1924, the party reached new lows in popular support and legitimacy.

Throughout the 1920s, while southern and agrarian forces retained significant party power, the Democrats' urban-immigrant wing, with its different values and commitments, continued its rise to power. Party divisions deepened as a result, especially in Al Smith's presidential efforts in 1924 and 1928 which split the party wide open. Democratic power was renewed only by the economic depression after 1929. The Demo-

cratic administration under Franklin D. Roosevelt in 1933 proved willing to use national power to confront depression conditions. At first primarily interested in stimulating economic activity, the New Deal came to adopt elements of the social welfarism of the party's urban and progressive wings.

The Roosevelt administration spawned a revolution in national politics. The electoral surge to the party was immense, particularly at the lower end of the social scale. Those who came over, and those who had always been there, developed a loyalty to FDR's Democratic party that did not let up even after his death in 1945. During and after World War II, the Democrats expanded their commitment to use government to assuage social ills. They argued that the promotion of equality of opportunity and the provision of a level of economic security demanded vigorous government spending and authority — not intermittently in response to emergencies but permanently, as a legitimate function of federal policymaking. The shift from the once hallowed Democratic commitment against government power could not have been more profound.

The Democrats had rarely been attractive to American blacks. The party's earlier pro-South stance had not been forgotten. But the New Deal, though not color-blind, had shared government largesse with blacks in need, and Roosevelt in the 1930s became an object of devotion in the black community comparable to Abraham Lincoln. His successors, albeit hesitatingly at first, committed themselves increasingly to what ultimately became a civil rights revolution, which, in turn, completed the transformation of the party. As its black constituencies increased in size into the 1960s and their leaders assumed positions of political power, Democratic presidents, from John F. Kennedy to Lyndon B. Johnson, sought to meet the needs of blacks through federal programs.

These changes bred much tension within the party between the early thirties and the sixties. At first, southern Democrats, through their influence in party councils and the congressional seniority system, served as a brake on the pro-black movement. But they began to lose power in the 1940s to the growing urban wing. In response, some restive southerners finally bolted their political home. Their support of the Dixiecrats in 1948, of the Republicans in the 1950s and early 1960s, and of George Wallace in 1968 proved to be way stations in their passage out of the Democratic party, contributing to the party's difficulties in presidential elections after 1948.

In the 1960s, missteps in foreign policy and a backlash against the welfare state at home added to the Democrats' problems. Persistent prosperity through the sixties led some to question the continuation of government spending for welfare. The aggressive demands of the civil rights movement, widely supported by the Democratic leadership and some of the party's core constituencies, and the outbreak of student protest against the Vietnam War rendered party leaders less and less able to cope with the discordance. The party was increasingly dominated by eastern urban liberal Democrats, who projected a humane, technological, and often upper-middle-class viewpoint. In addition, blacks and third world ethnic groups filled up the party spaces once occupied by southern whites and eastern European and Irish ethnic groups. The latter were still around, sometimes important in state parties, but increasingly less influential in national party councils.

Powerful antiparty breezes, which were blowing through American politics generally, also contributed to the Democrats' situation after the mid-1960s. New technologies, such as television, changed the way politics was played. There was a decline in the vigor of party organizations and the importance of the party in campaigns, elections, and the setting of policy. The rising levels of education contributed to an ebbing of the tribal commitments that had bonded groups to their party homes. Voting participation sagged, even as individual advocacy groups became more potent and forcefully pressed their demands regardless of their impact on the party as a whole. An open politics, carried on in front of television cameras, was not conducive to the kinds of compromises traditionally framed in "smoke-filled rooms" that had ensured party unity. These factors had an impact on all parties, but the Democrats seemed less able to cope with the new political world. Defeated in every presidential election but one from 1968 to 1988, they retained control of Congress not so much because of voters' party loyalty as because of loyalty to long-serving individual members of Congress. The disintegration that characterized American politics found Democrats unable to come to terms with a personalist ethos that foreswore collective discipline and asserted individual authority over organizational and community loyalties.

Dewey Grantham, *The Life and Death of the Solid South* (1988); Robert Rutland, *The Democrats: From Jefferson to Carter* (1979).

JOEL H. SILBEY

See also Civil Rights Movement; Civil War; Dixiecrat Party; Jacksonian Democracy; Know-Nothing Party; Liberalism; New Deal; New Freedom; Urban Bosses and Machine Politics; *and entries for individual party figures.*

DEPRESSIONS

The Great Depression

The years since the United States became an industrial economy have seen one Great Depression, that of 1929–1941. Whether assessed by the relative shortfall of production from trend or by the duration of slack production, the Great Depression was of an order of magnitude larger than any others. Thus this essay breaks chronological order and considers it first.

It is straightforward to narrate the slide of the United States into the depression. The 1920s saw a boom as firms invested in capacity and consumers bought durable goods on credit in quantity for the first time. The boom was the result of optimism: businesspeople and economists believed that the newly born Federal Reserve would stabilize the economy and that the pace of technological progress guaranteed rising living standards and expanding markets. The Federal Reserve's attempt in 1928 and 1929 to raise interest rates to discourage stock speculation brought on an initial recession. Caught by surprise, firms cut back their own plans for further purchase of producer durable goods, and firms making producer durables cut back production; out-of-work consumers — and those who feared they might soon be out of work — cut back purchases of consumer durables, and firms making consumer durables faced falling demand as well.

Businesspeople, economists, and politicians — most memorably Secretary of the Treasury Andrew Mellon — expected the recession of 1929–1930 to be self-limiting. Earlier recessions had come to an end when the gap between actual and trend production was as large as in 1930. They expected workers with idle hands and capitalists with idle machines to try to undersell their still at-work peers. Prices would fall. When prices fell enough, entrepreneurs would gamble that even with slack demand production would be profitable at the new, lower wages. Production would then resume.

Instead, falls in prices during the depression set in motion further contractions in production, which triggered additional falls in prices. With prices falling at 10 percent per year, investors calculated that they would earn less profit investing now than if they delayed investment until the next year when their dollars would stretch 10 percent further. Banking panics and the collapse of the world monetary system cast doubt on the value of everyone's credit and reinforced the belief that now was a time to watch and wait. The slide into the depression — with increasing unemployment, falling production, and falling prices — continued throughout President Herbert Hoover's term (1929–1933).

There is no fully satisfactory explanation of why the depression happened when it did. If such depressions were always a possibility in an unregulated capitalist economy, why weren't there many great depressions in the years before World War II? Milton Friedman and Anna Schwartz argued that the Great Depression was the consequence of an incredible and unlikely sequence of blunders in monetary policy. But those controlling economic policy during the early 1930s saw themselves as following the same gold-standard rules of conduct that had been followed before. Why hadn't obedience to the rules of conduct led to similar blunders earlier?

At its nadir, the depression paired individual rationality with collective insanity. Workers were idle because firms would not hire them to work their machines; firms would not hire workers to work machines because they saw no market for goods; and there was no market for goods because workers had no income to spend. George Orwell's powerful account of the depression in Britain, *The Road to Wigan Pier,* speaks of watching "several hundred men risk their lives and several hundred women scrabble in the mud for hours . . . searching eagerly for tiny chips of coal" in slagheaps so they could heat their homes. For them, this arduously gained "free" coal was "more important almost than food." And all around them the machinery they had previously used to mine in five minutes more than they could gather in a day stood idle.

Workers who kept their jobs — even with reduced hours — and financiers whose money was invested in bonds prospered during the depression. Their incomes in dollars dropped, but prices dropped even more: the baskets of goods they could buy increased. Farmers, workers who lost their jobs, and entrepreneurs who had bet their money on continued prosperity were the big losers of the depression. Production was a third less than normal and the distribution of income shifted toward those who kept steady employment or who had invested their wealth conservatively. As a result, at the nadir the standard of living of losers taken all together was perhaps half of what it had been in 1929.

No large-scale social insurance programs compensated the losers from the depression during Hoover's term. In contrast to Europe, the United States had no effective system of unemployment insurance to cushion job loss. The federal government's only significant action before the New Deal was the veterans' bonus — granted over Hoover's objection. State governments, with limited abilities to tax, could not come close to finding the resources to significantly cushion the decline in living standards of the unemployed.

Recovery began with the inauguration of Franklin D. Roosevelt. The two initial planks of the New Deal — the abandonment of the gold standard with a concomitant attempt to force the dollar price of gold and other commodities up, and the National Industrial Recovery Act (later declared unconstitutional) with its explicit aim of keeping competition from pushing wages and prices down — broke the expectation of further deflation. The end of deflation caused a mini–industrial boom. Output slowly increased and unemployment slowly decreased throughout the New Deal.

Although the shift in expectations brought about by the announcement of the New Deal deserves credit for breaking the downward slide, it may be the case — such arguments are still controversial — that the New Deal hindered the recovery as well. New Deal spending was by and large not deficit spending: each dollar Harry Hopkins funneled into relief was matched by a dollar removed from private-sector pockets by taxation, causing little if any rise in aggregate demand. The alliance of the New Deal with organized labor may have led to policies biased toward maintaining the real incomes of those still employed, perhaps at the expense of the unemployed in the late 1930s.

Social democracy came to America in the New Deal. The fact that the Great Depression was the impetus for the leftward shift had an impact on the form of the post–World War II American welfare state. In Europe social democracy had an egalitarian bent: it was to level the income distribution as well as insure citizens against the market. In America the major programs — Social Security and unemployment insurance — were built up as *insurance* in which individuals on average got what they paid for. They were not tools to shift the distribution of income. And the prolabor framework set up by the National Labor Relations Board was of most use to relatively skilled and well-paid workers with secure job attachments who could use the legal machinery to share in their industries' profits; it was of less use to the ill-paid without secure attachment.

Railroad Cycles and Earlier Depressions

The years between the Civil War and the 1890s saw the great railway booms. In 1870 and 1871 U.S. railroad construction reached its first post–Civil War peak. The number of miles of operated railroad in the United States, then around fifty thousand, grew at about 12 percent per year. The construction of six thousand miles of railroad track each year employed perhaps one-tenth of America's nonfarm paid labor force and half of the production of America's metal industries. But four years later, railroad construction had collapsed. In 1875, operated railroad mileage grew at only 3 percent. Railroad construction employed less than 3 percent of America's nonfarm paid labor force and required perhaps 15 percent of the production of America's metal industries.

It is hard to attribute such spasms of construction to independent disturbances in finance: railroad finance *was* then more or less the sole business of Wall Street. By default such depressions appear to have been driven by waves of optimism about future growth followed by recognition of overbuilding and contraction until the economy had grown enough that it seemed that shipping by rail was a railroad's and not a farmer's market.

Such waves must have been difficult to absorb. Each wave required an expansion of capacity in iron and steel for rails, timber for ties, equipment for locomotives and cars, furniture to equip the cars to carry passengers on the new lines, and so on — and most important the redirection of 1 million workers to railroad construction. As the wave passed, suppliers and workers would have to find new markets and new jobs. The dislocation generated may well have been extreme and severe. But we know little about how it was accomplished or about what workers who built railroads in 1871 were doing in 1875.

Before the railroad cycles our quantitative knowledge is even more limited. Our inability to track workers from job to job, coupled with the agricultural nature of American life then, leaves us unsure of the quantitative rhythm of the economy in earlier years. Was the presidency of Martin Van Buren marked by a deep depression, with widespread unemployment and lowered living standards? Or was it a mere deflation — a lowering of prices without consequence for working Americans whose nominal wages were matched by reduced prices — that impoverished only the vocal and politically influential class of merchant-entrepreneurs? My guess is that pre–

Civil War depressions were closer to the second, but I am far from sure.

Financial Panics and Depressions, 1890–1930

The fifty years before the Great Depression saw no depression of remotely similar magnitude. Whether those that did occur were worse than they have been since World War II remains disputed; given our limited quantitative knowledge, it is likely to remain so. That depressions before 1929 were more painful is, however, clear. Those who lost their jobs had no welfare state to cushion them. Individual states had sketches of a future welfare system, but such embryonic systems did not have the resources to cope with episodes of widespread unemployment. Extended families, friends, and local benevolent associations must have provided support for those who lost their jobs, so that, for the most part, they were fed and housed. American cities during depressions at the turn of the century were centers of poverty and want, but apparently not of mass near-starvation.

Depressions before 1929 by and large had different causes from post–World War II depressions. The 1921 recession aside, there was no Federal Reserve to risk high unemployment to reduce inflation. The typical pre-1929 depression had its origin in the United States' gold standard links with the London-centered world economy. The panic of 1907 and depression of 1908 followed a recession in Great Britain during which the Bank of England raised interest rates to pull gold to London, leaving the United States short of currency to be paid out to farmers and middlemen during the shipment of the fall harvest to the East.

The gold standard appears also in the depression of the 1890s. The possibility that "free silver" might sweep American politics made investors and financiers uneasy. Relative to what they would earn if they kept their cash, investments, and capital in London, a free-silver victory and subsequent devaluation might well have cost them a third of their wealth as measured by the international yardstick of the gold standard. Perhaps the free-silver movement was powerful enough to cause capital flight, investment shortfall, and depression, but not strong enough to secure devaluation and monetary expansion to reduce the debt burdens of farmers and create a booming labor market for urban workers. The United States thus got the worst of both worlds: it suffered the disadvantages of being on the gold standard without reaping the gold-standard advantage of keeping financiers confident and investing.

Post–World War II Depressions

The Great Depression did create a new orthodoxy in politics: the government was now considered responsible for maintaining a high level of production. Government deficits in recessions were seen as signs that the government was boosting demand to avoid another Great Depression. Confidence in this commitment to maintain spending helped, perhaps as much as the commitment itself, to keep the post–World War II era free of great depressions. Instead, the bias of the government seemed to be to risk an acceleration in inflation rather than to take even a tiny chance of severe depression. Over the decades, this pro-inflation bias intensified and became generally anticipated.

As a result, the United States in the postwar years experienced only three minidepressions — the slowdown in growth during the second Eisenhower administration, the OPEC shock (1974–1975), and the Paul Volcker depression (1979–1982). All were deliberately caused by governments that momentarily gave priority to reducing inflation at the cost of unemployment, but even such governments were unwilling to push contraction too far. Postwar America coped with these minidepressions relatively well in the sense of providing comparatively generous unemployment insurance and income support to the "deserving unemployed" — those who had previously held secure, higher-wage jobs. It did less well at supporting those unemployed who had not previously been in the middle-class circle.

Milton Friedman and Anna J. Schwartz, *A Monetary History of the United States* (1963); Herbert Stein, *The Fiscal*

Revolution in America (1969); Peter Temin, *Lessons from the Great Depression* (1989).

J. BRADFORD DE LONG

See also Coxey's Army; Government and the Economy; New Deal; Unemployment; Welfare and Public Relief.

DESEGREGATION

See Racial Desegregation.

DÉTENTE

Détente (a French word meaning release from tension) is the name given to a period of improved relations between the United States and the Soviet Union that began tentatively in 1971 and took decisive form when President Richard M. Nixon visited the secretary-general of the Soviet Communist party, Leonid I. Brezhnev, in Moscow, May 1972. Both countries stood to gain if trade could be increased and the danger of nuclear warfare reduced. In addition, Nixon — a candidate for reelection — was under fire at home from those demanding social change, racial equality, and an end to the Vietnam War. The trip to Russia, like his historic trip to China a few months earlier, permitted him to keep public attention focused on his foreign policy achievements rather than his domestic problems. Nixon's trip to China had also heightened the Soviets' interest in détente; given the growing antagonism between Russia and China, Brezhnev had no wish to see his most potent rivals close ranks against him.

On May 22 Nixon became the first U.S. president to visit Moscow. He and Brezhnev signed seven agreements covering the prevention of accidental military clashes; arms control, as recommended by the recent Strategic Arms Limitation Talks (SALT); cooperative research in a variety of areas, including space exploration; and expanded commerce. The SALT treaty was approved by Congress later that summer, as was a three-year agreement on the sale of grain to the Soviets. In June 1973, Brezhnev visited the United States for Summit II; this meeting added few new agreements, but did symbolize the two

countries' continuing commitment to peace. Summit III, in June 1974, was the least productive; by then, the SALT talks had ground to a halt, several commercial agreements had been blocked in Congress because of Soviet treatment of Jews, and the Watergate investigation was approaching a climax. Nixon's successor in the talks, President Jimmy Carter, supported SALT II, but also pressed a military buildup and a human rights campaign, which cooled relations between the countries. With the election of Ronald Reagan, who emphasized military preparedness as the key to Soviet-American relations, détente as Nixon had envisioned it came to an end.

See also Cold War.

DEWEY, GEORGE

(1837–1917), naval hero. Although George Dewey was taken to the public heart for his martial triumphs, he was inept and ineffective in the tumultuous political arena. His career was marked by the tension between the popular desire to celebrate war heroes and the deep American distrust of power and authority.

Born in Vermont, Dewey went to Annapolis in 1854 and had the good fortune to become a commissioned officer in April 1861, the month of Fort Sumter and the outbreak of the Civil War. He served competently in Adm. David Farragut's successful New Orleans and Vicksburg campaigns, learning lessons of boldness and resoluteness that he put to good use decades later in Manila Bay. His career bogged down in the decades after 1865, along with the rest of his generation of naval officers. Then in the late nineties the gathering confrontation with Spain over Cuba reopened the doors of opportunity. Dewey had good social and political contacts, among them his fellow Vermonter Senator Redfield Proctor and Assistant Secretary of the Navy Theodore Roosevelt. They supported him in his successful quest to become commander of the Far Eastern Squadron — the chosen instrument in the American plan to attack the Spanish fleet at Manila Bay in the event of war.

Although he had spent only four of the past twenty years at sea when appointed in 1897,

Dewey expeditiously smashed the much weaker, incompetently handled Spanish warships at Manila in the spring of 1898. His soon-mythic order to his chief gunner — "You may fire when you are ready, Gridley" — caught the flavor of his performance. (So, too, did the less than impressive record of his gunners: 142 hits of 5,859 shells fired.)

No ideological imperialist — "Our government is not fitted for colonies. . . . We have ample room for development at home," he once observed — Dewey nevertheless convinced himself that the Filipinos wanted to come under American sovereignty. He lent his considerable weight to the fateful American decision to replace Spain as the ruler of the Philippines. Nevertheless, here as in the rest of his career he tried to avoid taking a controversial part in public affairs.

The popular response to Dewey's victory reflected the pent-up desire for glamour and glory that had been a major factor in the declaration of war against Spain. He returned home to great popular acclaim, and Congress in 1899 elevated him to the new rank of admiral of the navy. He quickly caught the attention of Democrats seeking an alternative to William Jennings Bryan for the forthcoming 1900 rematch with President William McKinley.

After much hesitation, Dewey announced his candidacy. But he had recently married a social-climbing Catholic widow and made the politically injudicious decision to deed to her the Washington home given to him as a gift of the people. When he then announced that "since studying the subject, I am convinced that the office of President is not such a very difficult one to fill," his candidacy became an object of derision and quickly petered out.

During the remainder of his career he chaired the General Board of the Navy, created in March 1900 to work on potential war strategy. Dewey's stronger qualities again emerged. Although he did not join them, he assured a full and fair hearing to younger officers seeking to modernize the navy. He died in January 1917, a few months before the United States entered the war that put an end to the world in which his career had run its course.

Ronald H. Spector, *Admiral of the New Empire: The Life and Career of George Dewey* (1984); Richard S. West, *Admirals of American Empire: The Combined Story of George Dewey, Alfred Thayer Mahan, Winfield Scott Schley, and William Thomas Sampson* (1971).

MORTON KELLER

See also Philippines; Spanish-American War.

DEWEY, JOHN

(1859–1952), philosopher and educator. Dewey was a world-renowned founder of pragmatic philosophy and theoretician of progressive education. His voluminous writings dealt not only with philosophy and education but also with politics, art, and current events. He was a founder and the first president of the American Association of University Professors, an organizer of the New School for Social Research in New York City and of the American Committee for Cultural Freedom, an officer of the American Civil Liberties Union, and a trustee of Hull-House; he also chaired the commission that investigated Leon Trotsky's Moscow trial. Throughout his long career, Dewey was engaged with scholarly and public concerns that were shared by many of his contemporaries. He was once described as "the most profound, most complete expression of American genius."

Born and reared in Burlington, Vermont, Dewey graduated from the University of Vermont in 1879. Thereafter, he taught school for two years before enrolling for graduate study at the Johns Hopkins University in Baltimore, where he imbibed the reverence for empirical, hypothesis-testing science that was the staple of conversation at the new university. This attitude was critical in turning Dewey away from abstract approaches to philosophy, as were the reform interests of Harriet Alice Chipman, a student at the University of Michigan, where Dewey taught from 1884 until 1894 (with one year, 1888–1889, at the University of Minnesota). Chipman became Dewey's wife in 1886. (She died in 1927, and Dewey married Roberta Lowitz Grant in 1946.)

Dewey's eagerness to find ways to relate philosophy to contemporary concerns was an important source (as were his own children) for his interest in education, and, during the ten years he served on the faculty of the University of Chicago (1894–1904), this interest became a primary one. Dewey presided over the university's work in philosophy, psychology, and education and was director of the university's Laboratory School. His most important educational writings, *The School and Society* (1899) and *Democracy and Education* (1916), grew out of observations made at this time. It was during the Chicago period that Dewey developed a conception of education as an experimental science capable of guiding individual and community growth and of illuminating problems of associated life, or democracy.

Dewey left Chicago in 1904 to become a professor of philosophy at Columbia University. His prolific writings set forth a functionalist conception of psychology, in which intelligence is portrayed as a constantly changing capacity that develops through continuous interaction between people and their environment, and a liberal, instrumentalist conception of democracy, in which public problems are seen as requiring continuous, ever-widening discussion among citizens. The test of a democracy, Dewey believed, is the degree to which all people likely to suffer the consequences of a decision have participated in the making of that decision.

During his years at Columbia, Dewey achieved fame of a kind rare for such a reticent, often rumpled philosopher. He visited Japan, China, Turkey, and the Soviet Union, but, after 1904, New York remained his home. The optimism and emphasis upon education as both schooling and, more important, a mode of democratic politics that was so characteristic of his thought was essential in all that he wrote and said in his long life. Dewey's greatness as a thinker was inseparable from a consistency of perspective across specialized domains and over time combined with an unusual agility in applying that perspective to an extraordinary array of life's momentous and more mundane concerns.

Neil Coughlan, *Young John Dewey: An Essay in American Intellectual History* (1972); George Dykhuizen, *The Life and Mind of John Dewey* (1973).

ELLEN CONDLIFFE LAGEMANN

See also Education; Progressivism.

DICKINSON, EMILY

(1830–1886), poet. During her lifetime, Emily Dickinson, though known to a few, hardly existed as a national figure. Only ten of her poems found their way into print, all anonymously. There was a flurry of interest during the decade of the 1890s occasioned by the publication of three slim volumes of selections (1890, 1891, and 1896). But the editing during the next half-century was erratic and piecemeal. It was not until 1955 that her entire corpus of 1,775 poems appeared, carefully edited, with variants. The *Letters* followed (1958), giving, at last, adequate and reliable material for a just estimate of her work. The event, historic in our cultural history, gave rise to much reevaluation and intensified research. It continues unabated.

Not that she had gone unnoticed till then. The flurry of the 1890s showed, among other things, a significant discrepancy between the popular appeal of her poetry, demonstrated by eleven reprintings of the first volume in a single year, and the cautious, mixed reception by the critics. The reviews, generally, recognized her originality and imaginative power but deplored her stylistic eccentricities — her approximate rhymes, jolting rhythms, strained syntax, bizarre imagery, symbol, metaphor. Her first reviewer (Arlo Bates), though sympathetic, called her poems "half barbaric." But it was just such qualities that attracted a new generation of poets — imagists, symbolists, metaphorists — in general, those who responded to a new voice and its capacity to refresh the language. She has been translated into at least six languages (including Japanese, which readily appropriates her often haiku-like manner), and studies of her life and work appear from all quarters of the globe.

The facts of her life are few and simple, the interpretations many and complex. She was born in Amherst, Massachusetts, at the time a small farming town with a college and a hat factory; she seldom left it, and she died there. After a year at Mount Holyoke, her growing sense of poetic vocation led to ever deeper concentration and the privacy of her home.

Her reclusiveness has been variously explained — a frustrated love affair, a tyrannical father, an inadequate mother, religious perplexities, failure to publish, the limits imposed upon women in her time. But, as with the attempts to categorize her poetry — is she a transcendentalist? a mystic? a romantic? a metaphysical? a meditative? was she pessimistic? optimistic? a believer? a disbeliever? — no single theory is adequate. Her range is wide, her "voices" many; her heights are high, her depths deep. One of the most private of major poets, she was of little help in answering these questions. Yet, as the studies proliferate, her once "half barbaric" poems become available to an ever-widening public and her place in the pantheon of world poets ever more secure.

Jay Leyda, *The Years and Hours of Emily Dickinson* (1960); Richard B. Sewall, *The Life of Emily Dickinson* (1974).

RICHARD B. SEWALL

See also Literature.

DISARMAMENT

See Strategic Arms Limitation Talks.

DISCOVERY OF AMERICA

See Exploration of North America.

DISEASE

See Epidemics.

DISNEY, WALT

(1901–1966), filmmaker and show-business entrepreneur. Disney's phenomenal career exemplifies the way modern popular culture has affected many aspects of twentieth-century life, from entertainment to civic institutions to nationalism. Starting as the creator and producer of short cartoons in 1928, Disney turned ten years later to making feature-length animated films that became very successful with American audiences. In World War II his company served as an agent of defense mobilization, with the result that such cartoon characters as Mickey Mouse and Donald Duck became known around the world. At the end of his life he controlled his own studio, had expanded into television production, and had received thirty-one Academy Awards and several medals from Congress. His face has graced a postage stamp and civic groups all over the nation have named schools in his honor. By the 1970s vast amusement parks, like his original Disneyland constructed in 1955 in Anaheim, California, had spread to Florida, Japan, and France, testifying that the Disney touch appealed to the popular imagination in other nations as well.

Disney's father was a small contractor and farmer in Illinois who gave his family a strict Protestant upbringing. Like many others who would gain success in Hollywood, young Walt appears to have rebelled against a parental code that abjured play and leisure. As a teenager he turned to imitating Charlie Chaplin's tramp at vaudeville amateur hours and became an animator of cartoons in Kansas City. Shortly afterward he went to Hollywood and created his first film cartoon featuring Mickey Mouse. In the midst of the depression, Disney gained widespread fame with *The Three Little Pigs,* which proffered the theme of hard work to counter the threats embodied in the "Big Bad Wolf." In 1938 he began to make animated feature-length films that drew on characters from children's stories, such as Snow White and the seven dwarfs, Bambi, Cinderella, Pinocchio, Brer Rabbit, and Uncle Remus. The Disney characters appeared in World War II training films for American troops across the world.

After 1945 Disney's influence came to permeate popular culture. In the wake of the class conflicts of the 1930s and the war, he supported numerous conservative causes hostile to unions, the welfare state, and communism, and developed a series of products that reinforced a cultural vision of social harmony. The Disney studio, its business managed by his brother, Roy, expanded into television, documentaries, clothing, and amusement parks. In the 1950s they built Disneyland, a vastly profitable enterprise where patrons entered a spotlessly clean world and embarked on a journey that showed history less as a story of crisis and trials than as a continuous unfolding of the progressive dreams that had dominated national life since the nineteenth century. The first stop was Main Street, U.S.A., and the last was Tomorrow Land, U.S.A. On that excursion, children and adults were assured that the great fears of modern life — race relations, consumerism, technology, uncontrolled nature, internationalism — could be translated into an optimistic panorama of progress. Disney saw this utopian vision as the culmination of his lifework. Shortly before his death in 1966, he said, "I hate to see downbeat pictures. . . . I know life isn't that way, and I don't want anyone telling me it is." Clearly millions of his fans agreed, and their adulation made him one of the most popular figures in postwar American culture.

Diane Disney Miller, as told to Pete Martin, *The Story of Walt Disney* (1957); Richard Schickel, *The Disney Version* (1968).

LARY MAY

See also Movies.

DIVORCE

Despite their belief that the family was the basis of political and ecclesiastical authority, seventeenth-century Puritans held that marriage was a civil contract that could, under certain circumstances, be broken. Divorce was permissible on several grounds, including adultery, long absence, and cruelty, but such grants were rare and reflected the gender hierarchy that pervaded all of social life. In principle, both men and women could receive divorces on the ground of adultery, but in keeping with the sexual double standard, men were the chief beneficiaries of this law. In Massachusetts between 1692 and 1786, half of all male petitioners (50 of 101) named adultery as their sole grievance and 70 percent received divorces; no woman petitioned for divorce solely on the ground of adultery until 1774, and only 6 did so in the next twelve years. In the South, only separations were legal, a reality that left colonial women yoked to their

more powerful husbands. On the other hand, although only a few hundred colonial men and women actually obtained divorces, thousands simply deserted their spouses, suggesting more marital conflict than the low divorce rate for the period suggests.

But divorce laws and procedures gradually changed in ways that benefited women. In the revolutionary era, wives found courts more receptive to their complaints about adultery, and in the early nineteenth century, state legislatures expanded the grounds of divorce, including most significantly, intemperance and cruelty. The change fueled the expansion of female divorce petitioners over the course of the century: by 1900 about two-thirds of all divorces went to women, and by 1929, 44 percent of divorces granted to women were on the ground of cruelty. Nor was the definition of cruelty static: during the nineteenth century, it came to embrace the idea of "mental cruelty" as a sufficient reason for divorce. Again, women were the chief beneficiaries of the change. But although thousands of women received divorces on the grounds of cruelty or desertion (the most common late-nineteenth-century complaints), they seldom received child support or alimony. Women did, however, gain increasing access to child custody over the course of the nineteenth century as new cultural emphases on the importance of motherhood and childhood predisposed courts to award children of "tender years" to their mothers. For some women, then, divorce brought freedom and independence; for others, merely new obligations, difficulties, and dependencies.

Divorce finally became a major social issue in the late nineteenth and early twentieth centuries because of a huge expansion in the divorce rate. In 1880 only one of every twenty-one marriages ended in divorce; in 1916 that figure was one of every nine. The surging divorce rate prompted a protracted debate over the cultural meaning of divorce. Feminists and liberals could see no reason stringent divorce laws should stand in the way of freedom and happiness, but a diverse group of conservatives saw in the legal dissolution of families a prelude to social disorder and a sign of female selfishness. While the former hoped to widen access to divorce, the latter called for tougher divorce laws and a dose of traditional morality to reduce the flow through the divorce courts.

Although conservatives failed to enact a uniform divorce code, they did manage to abolish omnibus clauses, restrict the rights of remarriage, and impose stricter residency requirements on divorce seekers. Nevertheless, these conservative measures did nothing to stem the tide of women and men seeking to end their marriages. Although there were short-term fluctuations, the divorce rate rose slowly in the 1920s, dropped off in the early years of the depression, and then rose steadily in the late 1930s before soaring during World War II. Destroying conservative efforts to reduce the divorce rate were rising romantic and sexual expectations within marriages, heightened tensions over finances and the use of leisure time, growing female opportunities for economic self-support, increasingly expansive definitions of cruelty, the adoption in some states of "irreconcilable differences" as a ground for divorce, and a marked shift toward consensual divorce.

Explanations and remedies for divorce proliferated. Conservatives reiterated their emphasis on moral breakdown and female selfishness; feminists, the need for women to escape the heavy hand of patriarchy; and progressives, the impact of wider social change on family stability. As early as 1910 and continuing until the 1940s, many family experts rejected these explanations and put forth a psychological alternative. Divorce seekers found themselves described as neurotic, abnormal, and infantile. Among professionals, divorce was widely viewed as stemming from immaturity and psychological instability. Rather than seeking changes that might reduce marital stress or simply accepting the inevitability of divorce, reformers instead emphasized curing the neuroses that lay behind divorce. Not surprisingly, the agent of cure — a patriarchal legal system acting as a therapeutic agent — was ill suited for the task. Family courts, social work investigations, reconciliation sessions, and counseling services often devolved into a form of therapeutic intervention that satisfied neither the interests of the couple nor those of the state.

The divorce rate reached an all-time high in 1946 and then declined before leveling off in the 1950s and early 1960s. But beginning in the mid-1960s, it again began to rise dramatically, fueled by ever-higher marital expectations, a vast expansion of wives moving into the work force, the rebirth of feminism, and the adoption of no-fault divorce (that is, divorce granted without the need to establish wrongdoing by either party) in almost every state. These factors all made marital stability more problematic.

The last factor, although hailed as a progressive step that would end the fraud, collusion, and acrimony that accompanied the adversarial system of divorce, has had disastrous consequences for women and children. Presupposing an equality between husbands and wives that has no basis in reality, no-fault divorce has left women and their dependents in an unenviable position. Statistically, men's standard of living rises sharply in the first years following divorce, whereas women's and children's plummets, a situation brought about by men "cashing out" on home sales and by inadequate alimony awards and child support payments. No-fault's seeming equity does not take into account the fact that women find it difficult to compete in a job market characterized by gender segregation and persistent discrimination; moreover, many have been out of the job market for years and are often poorly equipped to earn their own living. Women with small children are especially handicapped. By contrast, divorcing husbands take with them the assets of education, degrees, professional certifications, their good business name, and preference in a segmented labor market. Freed from direct family responsibilities, divorcing husbands can often concentrate on improving their financial situation.

America's divorce rate signifies less a disillusionment with the institution of marriage — the high remarriage rate among the divorced contradicts such a conclusion — and more the consequences of loading marriage with high expectations. Over the last two centuries, American men and women have come to expect material, psychological, emotional, and sexual satisfaction from their marriages. When these expectations are not met, divorce is a logical recourse in a society dedicated to individual happiness. Divorce, then, is likely to remain a prominent feature of American family life. The task before lawmakers and courts is to accept this fact and to make spousal and child support awards that will ensure some measure of parity in the living standards of divorced men and women.

Roderick Phillips, *Putting Asunder: A History of Divorce in Western Society* (1988); Lenore J. Weitzman, *The Divorce Revolution: The Unexpected Social and Economic Consequences for Women and Children in America* (1985).

ROBERT L. GRISWOLD

See also Family; Marriage.

DIX, DOROTHEA

(1802–1887), social reformer. Born into a family of modest means in rural Maine, Dix spent her early years with family members in Boston. She opened her own dame school there in 1821. During these years she published a primary reader in science, *Conversations on Common Things* (1824), and *Hymns for Children* (1825). Her pupils were the children of influential Bostonians, including William Ellery Channing, who became her sponsor as well as friend. She spent a winter with his family in the Virgin Islands in 1830–1831 in an effort to restore her failing health. In 1836 her condition had so deteriorated that she abandoned teaching and went to England for a prolonged visit. During her time abroad Dix traveled in British reform circles, which stimulated her interest in humanitarian causes.

She returned to Boston in 1837 and lived on the income from an inheritance. For a time she neither fulfilled her early promise as an educator nor sought other outlets for her abilities. But in 1841 she visited a Cambridge jail to teach a Sunday school class and was shocked to encounter mentally incompetent women — or "lunatics," as their jailer called them — confined with common criminals in unsanitary cells. Dix's pleas to the local court combined with a newspaper campaign against these conditions resulted in reforms. Channing and philanthropist Samuel Gridley Howe championed Dix's cause, as she undertook a survey of poorhouses and jail facilities throughout the state of Massachusetts.

When Dix reported what she had found to the legislature, the government responded with a plan for separate facilities for the mentally ill. After her success in Massachusetts, she turned her attention to other states.

From the Mid-Atlantic states of Pennsylvania, New York, and Rhode Island to the Gulf states of Mississippi and Alabama, from the Upper South of Maryland and Kentucky to the interior of Tennessee and Ohio, Dix found everywhere shameful conditions and neglect of the mentally ill. Her campaign spurred legislatures into appropriating funds to establish and improve state hospitals. Overcoming her initial reluctance, Dix became an effective speaker. She campaigned tirelessly, demanding that criminals be separated according to the seriousness of their crimes and that prisoners be offered education. Her work led to the establishment of a school for the blind in Illinois in 1848. Eventually she abandoned these state-by-state crusades and lobbied for federal reforms.

The Civil War interrupted these activities, and in 1861 she was appointed superintendent of nurses for the Union army. Although there was some friction over her imperious style, Dix successfully trained a legion of young women to serve during wartime. When she retired after the war she shifted her interests to the defeated South.

Dix in no small way fostered a revolution in mental health care. Although she threw herself into many other campaigns (for orphanages, for example), she remains best remembered for the central role she played in forcing the government to reckon with the problem of widespread mental illness. During her lifetime, the number of state mental hospitals grew from a handful of custodial centers to over 120 thriving medical facilities where the insane received sympathetic professional treatment.

CATHERINE CLINTON

DIXIECRAT PARTY

In 1948, the Democratic National Convention was splintered by debate over controversial new civil rights planks that had been proposed for addition to the party platform. Adoption of the planks, urged by a group led by Hubert Humphrey of Minnesota, was resisted by delegates from southern states. In the middle, trying to hold together the New Deal coalition he had inherited from Franklin D. Roosevelt, was President Harry S. Truman. As a compromise, he was prepared to settle for the adoption of only those planks that had been in the 1944 platform. But Truman's own civil rights initiatives, including the formation of the Committee on Civil Rights and the Fair Employment Practices Commission, had advanced the civil rights debate to a new level, and he could not turn the clock back. The planks were adopted, prompting thirty-five southern Democrats to walk out. They formed the States' Rights party, which came to be popularly known as the Dixiecrats.

Meeting in Birmingham, Alabama, the Dixiecrats nominated South Carolina governor Strom Thurmond as their candidate for president. In the November election, Thurmond carried four states: Alabama, Louisiana, Mississippi, and South Carolina. He received well over a million popular votes, and his thirty-nine electoral votes represented more than 7 percent of the total.

The Dixiecrat episode was one of the most significant third-party efforts in America's history. Truman won reelection, but the strong showing put forth by the Dixiecrats signaled impending changes in electoral politics. It was the most visible sign of the postwar erosion of the New Deal coalition.

See also Elections: 1948; Racial Desegregation; Third Parties.

DOLLAR DIPLOMACY

Dollar diplomacy is the term used to describe America's efforts — particularly under President William Howard Taft — to further its foreign policy aims in Latin America and the Far East through the use of economic power. President Theodore Roosevelt laid the groundwork for this approach in 1905 with his Roosevelt Corollary to the Monroe Doctrine, maintaining that if any nation in the Western Hemisphere appeared po-

litically or fiscally so unstable as to be vulnerable to European control, the United States had the right and obligation to intervene.

Taft continued and expanded this policy, starting in Central America, where he justified it as a means of protecting the Panama Canal. In 1909 he attempted unsuccessfully to establish control over Honduras by buying up its debt to British bankers. In Nicaragua, American intervention included funding the country's debts to European bankers but also involved participating in the overthrow of one government and the military support of another. In addition, the State Department persuaded four American banks to refinance Haiti's national debt, setting the stage for further intervention in the future.

Dollar diplomacy was also pursued in China, where Taft's secretary of state, Philander C. Knox, became convinced in 1910 that America's free access to trade there was threatened by European financing of the new Hukuang Railroad. With some difficulty, the Taft administration arranged for American bankers to be included in the project and then prevailed on J. Pierpont Morgan to create an American syndicate for the purpose. Taft was also concerned about Russian and Japanese railroad activities in Manchuria and managed to persuade American bankers to join a six-power consortium that would give China the money instead.

This approach to foreign policy was repudiated by President Woodrow Wilson within a few weeks of his inauguration in 1913. Although he did not abstain from Caribbean intervention, dollar diplomacy was no longer an explicit national policy.

See also Asia-U.S. Relations; Latin America–U.S. Relations; Roosevelt Corollary; Taft, William Howard.

DOMESTIC WORK

From the founding of the country until the mid-twentieth century, domestic work was the largest female occupation in the United States. The number of women engaged in such work was not counted until the 1870 census, when it was reported that 52 percent of employed women worked in "domestic and personal service," probably the normal level from the time of the Revolution until the end of the nineteenth century (when 1.5 million women listed the job). The proportion declined to 28 percent of employed women in 1920 and 18 percent in 1940, the last time the job led the list of women's occupations. After World War II, the percentage declined rapidly to 5.1 percent in 1970 and 2.5 percent in 1980. Women stopped being domestics because new jobs, especially clerical work, appeared. Work once done at home, such as cooking food or tending children, moved outside to restaurants and day-care centers.

The history of domestic work reflects changes in domestic ideologies and household technologies. The American Revolution occurred at a moment when homes were beginning a century-long transformation. Colonial homes produced goods; neighborhood girls helped the housewife with her unending work of cooking, spinning yarn, sewing clothes, and making butter, cheese, and bread in return for room and board and an apprenticeship in these skills. In the new nation, a growing class of well-to-do, urban housewives bought many of the products that rural households made for themselves and typically oversaw the work of a young live-in servant, who cooked, cleaned, laundered, served meals, and helped care for children. (These young single women often faced their first sexual assaults or temptations from the men in the house where they worked as domestics.) By the end of the century, the housewife expected her single live-in servant (two, in larger homes) to master the appliances made possible by new public water, gas, and electric lines, sewer systems, and commercial laundries, freeing the mistress for civic work in temperance, literary, garden, or political clubs.

The workers who adapted from "help" to "service" were rural women seeking city wages. From the 1840s through the turn of the century, a majority of first-generation Irish teenagers worked as live-in domestics. They dwarfed the numbers of northern free black women, who were often pushed to the fringes of hard, live-out, specialized tasks like laundry or heavy spring cleaning. Irish women became so identi-fied with the job that domestics were generically known as Bridgets or Biddys into the 1920s, but first- or second-generation German and Scandinavian single women often found employment in live-in domestic service, too.

In the pre–Civil War South, the wives of plantation owners continued to direct home production similar to that of prerevolutionary northern women and were responsible for social rituals and their slaves' health care. Much of the physical labor entailed in the mistress's jobs, however, was assigned to slaves. Slave women and children, often pulled from field labor, spun thread and wove fabric, cooked and served meals, washed dishes and clothes, swept floors, cleaned furniture, made beds, and provided deferential service available only to the wealthiest non-slave-owning families — fetching and carrying, and fanning and dressing the white family. Slave women notoriously faced sexual demands from their owners as well.

In the early twentieth century, rising higher education for women, coupled with shattered family fortunes in the South and increased consumption in the North and West, led more middle-class women to enter the job market. Although these wives needed someone to care for their home and family, fewer women felt compelled to live in as domestic workers. By the 1920s, most such workers were older women who lived in their own homes, worked by the day, and supported dependents.

Domestic work remained a low-status job, but now it was identified with women of color, whose concentration in domestic work increased as African-American, Mexican-American, and American Indian women migrated from farms to urban centers and white women moved into other occupations. In 1920, 46 percent of African-American women workers were domestic workers; in 1930, 53 percent; and in 1940, 60 percent. (Even when industrial and clerical jobs opened up further during World War II, it was mostly white women who increasingly escaped domestic work, so that by 1944, black women made up over 60 percent of all domestic workers.)

The most common form of domestic work by the 1980s was day-cleaning, often contracted for with commercial companies employing a labor force of older white and African-American women, or immigrant women from Mexico, Latin America, or the West Indies. Most white Americans who were listed as domestic service workers were teenage baby-sitters.

Throughout its history, then, domestic work was a job for the society's lowest-status women: the very young or very old; racial minorities; rural immigrants or migrants escaping poverty; single women in search of housing; and women coerced into service, first in slavery and later to obtain immigration papers. The few men working as cooks, chauffeurs, or valets were also of low status, as the predominance of African-American men, or Chinese men in late-nineteenth-century California, indicates.

Domestic workers' powerlessness, or the identification of the occupation with housework — seen as nonwork — may explain why the path to regulating this job like others was so slow. Excluded from New Deal laws, such as the Wagner Act (1935), the Social Security Act (1935), and the Fair Labor Standards Act (1937), domestic workers were denied protections for union organizing (of which there were many local examples between the 1860s and the 1960s), retirement and unemployment insurance, and maximum hour and minimum wage regulation. Domestic workers did not gain Social Security retirement coverage until 1951, and they came under Fair Labor Standards protection only in 1974. The remnants of the once huge tribe of domestic workers gained legal respect as workers at the moment of the job's virtual demise.

Faye E. Dudden, *Serving Women: Household Service in Nineteenth-Century America* (1983); David M. Katzman, *Seven Days a Week: Women and Domestic Service in Industrializing America* (1981); Phyllis Palmer, *Domesticity and Dirt: Housewives and Domestic Servants in the United States, 1920–1945* (1989).

PHYLLIS PALMER

See also Housework; Indentured Servitude; Slavery; Women and the Work Force.

DOUGLAS, STEPHEN A.

(1813–1861), member of Congress and presidential candidate in 1860. Born in Vermont, Douglas studied law in Canandaigua, New York, before moving to Illinois in 1833, where he became involved in politics. As a youth he had been captivated by Andrew Jackson, and it was as a Jacksonian that he built his career. He played an important part in the organization of the Democratic party in Illinois, introducing such new devices as party committees and nominating conventions and pushing for party regularity and discipline. He enjoyed a lasting popularity among the small farmers of the state, many of whom had migrated from the border South, and he used his popularity to establish a tightly knit Democratic organization.

After holding several state offices, Douglas ran for Congress in 1837, losing by the narrow margin of thirty-five votes. Six years later, he was elected to the House of Representatives, where he sat for two terms. In 1847, he was elected U.S. senator, a position he held until his death in 1861.

Douglas was involved in every major issue to come before the nation during his years in Washington. As chairman of the House and Senate Committees on Territories, he developed a strong interest in the West. One of his first legislative proposals was a program that included territorial expansion, the construction of a Pacific railroad, a free land (homestead) policy, and the organization of territorial governments. "You cannot fix bounds to the onward march of this great and growing country," he declared. He believed in America's unique mission and manifest destiny, was a leading proponent of Texas annexation, demanded the acquisition of Oregon, and supported the war with Mexico. A man of great energy and persuasive power, standing only five feet four inches tall, Douglas became known as the Little Giant.

When slavery became a divisive political issue during the Mexican War, Douglas's romantic nationalism faced a new challenge. Fearing that the issue might disrupt the Republic, he argued for the doctrine of popular sovereignty — the right of the people of a state or territory to decide the slavery question for themselves — as a Union-saving formula. He led the fight in Congress for the Compromise of 1850. Four years later, he incorporated the doctrine in the Kansas-Nebraska Act, thus repealing the Missouri Compromise of 1820. Douglas's hopes for the country suffered a setback when the act aroused bitter opposition from northern antislavery elements, who eventually formed the Republican party.

During the 1850s, he continued to fight for popular sovereignty in Congress and in Illinois, where the state election campaign of 1858 was highlighted by his famous debates with Abraham Lincoln. He blamed the agitation over slavery on abolitionists in the North and disunionists in the South, trying to find a middle way that would preserve the Union. Slavery, he believed, must be treated impartially as a question of public policy, although he privately thought it was wrong and hoped it would be eliminated some day. At the same time, he saw in popular sovereignty an extension of local self-government and states' rights and charged his opposition with seeking a consolidation of power on the national level that would restrict individual liberty and endanger the Union.

Douglas's popularity waned as the party system foundered on the slavery question. Proposed as the Democratic candidate for president in 1852 and 1856, he did not win his party's nomination until 1860, when it was too late. With his party hopelessly divided and a Republican elected to the presidency, he fought strenuously to hold the sections together with a compromise on the slavery issue, but to no avail. Following the firing on Fort Sumter in April 1861, he pledged his support to the northern cause and urged a vigorous prosecution of the war against the rebels. He died in June, however, worn out from his exertions and broken in spirit.

Robert W. Johannsen, ed., *The Letters of Stephen A. Douglas* (1961); Robert W. Johannsen, *Stephen A. Douglas* (1973).

ROBERT W. JOHANNSEN

See also Compromise of 1850; Freeport Doctrine; Kansas-Nebraska Act; Lincoln-Douglas Debates; Popular Sovereignty.

DOUGLAS, WILLIAM O.

(1898–1980), associate justice, U.S. Supreme Court. Douglas served longer on the Court (1939–1975) and wrote more opinions and more dissents than any justice before or since. He was an academic founder of the influential legal realist movement, probably the finest New Deal administrator as chairman of the Securities and Exchange Commission, and an internationalist. He aspired to the presidency, but turned down an offer of the vice-presidential nomination in 1948. He was an ecologist years before the term was generally known. In his later years, when American youth proclaimed you couldn't trust anyone over thirty, he was a political hero on college campuses. He had an extraordinary intelligence, an excessive work ethic, the ability to see larger issues when contemporaries could not, and the willingness, maybe even the need, to be different. Underlying his character were the experiences of his youth when he had lived in poverty and had battled the effects of polio.

Douglas had an integrated judicial philosophy based on the belief that the Bill of Rights existed "to keep government off the backs of the people" — even in times of severe crisis. Douglas and Hugo Black stood alone during the McCarthy era in dissenting from the Court's decisions sustaining the loyalty-security measures. Unlike Black, however, Douglas's view of appropriate dissent was not narrow, and he easily accommodated the novel tactics of civil rights and antiwar activists to his First Amendment positions. His reputation as an uncompromising defender of the individual rests on his First Amendment opinions, especially his classic dissents in the Smith Act convictions of the Communist party leaders (*Dennis et al.* v. *United States,* 1951) and a jailhouse sit-in case (*Adderly* v. *Florida,* 1966).

Douglas looked upon work as having a constitutional dimension, believing it was essential for a person's fulfillment. Like other New Dealers, he believed that governments had to exert control over the economy; yet he distrusted bureaucracies, whether corporate or governmental, saying they would create "a nation of clerks." For Douglas, all individuals, regardless of race, religion, or status, were entitled to all the rights that the privileged, by virtue of their money, traditionally enjoyed, a view that eventually paved the way for the Court's controversial 1973 abortion decision, *Roe* v. *Wade*.

Douglas was a complex, driven man who changed significantly over the years. Until he was fifty, he was so politically attuned that Franklin D. Roosevelt made him the youngest Supreme Court nominee in over a century and he was a serious candidate for the presidency. Yet by the time he was seventy, he had become known for his injudiciousness and disdain for convention. He was a man with few friends (he publicly called his generation "bankrupt") and four wives (the last two in their early twenties), who faced a serious, albeit unsuccessful, impeachment attempt by Richard Nixon and Gerald Ford.

Despite eventual acceptance of many of his constitutional positions, Douglas has a mixed reputation because of his extrajudicial activities and his seeming scorn for lawyerlike analysis. Most believe he could have been an all-time judicial great, but few hold that he achieved his potential. Whatever the evaluation, his personality and varied interests ensure that there will never be another like him.

James Simon, *Independent Journey: The Life of William O. Douglas* (1980).

L. A. POWE, JR.

See also Securities and Exchange Commission; Supreme Court.

DOUGLASS, FREDERICK

(1818–1895), abolitionist, writer, and orator. Douglass was the most important black American leader of the nineteenth century. Born Frederick Augustus Washington Bailey on Maryland's Eastern Shore, he was the son of a slave woman and, probably, her white master. Upon his escape from slavery at age twenty, he adopted the name of the hero of Sir Walter Scott's *The Lady of the Lake*. Douglass immortalized his years as a slave in *Narrative of the Life of Frederick Douglass, an American Slave* (1845).

This and two subsequent autobiographies, *My Bondage and My Freedom* (1855) and *The Life and Times of Frederick Douglass* (1881), mark his greatest contributions to American culture. Written as antislavery propaganda and personal revelation, they are regarded as the finest examples of the slave narrative tradition and as classics of American autobiography.

Douglass's life as a reformer ranged from his abolitionist activities in the early 1840s to his attacks on Jim Crow and lynching in the 1890s. For sixteen years he edited an influential black newspaper and achieved international fame as an orator and writer of great persuasive power. In thousands of speeches and editorials he levied an irresistible indictment against slavery and racism, provided an indomitable voice of hope for his people, embraced antislavery politics, and preached his own brand of American ideals. In the 1850s he broke with the strictly moralist brand of abolitionism led by William Lloyd Garrison; he supported the early women's rights movement; and he gave direct assistance to John Brown's conspiracy that led to the raid on Harpers Ferry in 1859.

Rhetorically, Douglass was a master of irony, as illustrated by his famous Fourth of July speech in 1852: "This Fourth of July is *yours*, not *mine*. You may rejoice, *I* must mourn," he declared. Then he accused his unsuspecting audience in Rochester, New York, of mockery for inviting him to speak and quoted Psalm 137, where the children of Israel are forced to sit down "by the rivers of Babylon," there to "sing the Lord's song in a strange land." For the ways that race have caused the deepest contradictions in American history, few better sources of insight exist than Douglass's speeches. Moreover, for understanding prejudice, there are few better starting points than his timeless definition of racism as a "diseased imagination."

Douglass welcomed the Civil War in 1861 as a moral crusade against slavery. During the war he labored as a propagandist of the Union cause and emancipation, a recruiter of black troops, and (on two occasions) an adviser to President Abraham Lincoln. He viewed the Union victory as an apocalyptic rebirth of America as a nation rooted in a rewritten Constitution and the ideal of racial equality. Some of his hopes were dashed during Reconstruction and the Gilded Age, but he continued to travel widely and lecture on racial issues, national politics, and women's rights. In the 1870s Douglass moved to Washington, D.C., where he edited a newspaper and became president of the ill-fated Freedman's Bank. As a stalwart Republican, Douglass was appointed marshal (1877–1881) and recorder of deeds (1881–1886) for the District of Columbia, and chargé d'affaires for Santo Domingo and minister to Haiti (1889–1891).

Brilliant, heroic, and complex, Douglass became a symbol of his age and a unique voice for humanism and social justice. His life and thought will always speak profoundly to the meaning of being black in America, as well as the human calling to resist oppression. Douglass died in 1895 after years of trying to preserve a black abolitionist's meaning and memory of the great events he had witnessed and helped to shape.

David W. Blight, *Frederick Douglass' Civil War: Keeping Faith in Jubilee* (1989); Waldo E. Martin, *The Mind of Frederick Douglass* (1984).

DAVID W. BLIGHT

See also Abolitionist Movement; Free Negroes, 1619–1860; Lynching; Reconstruction; Segregation; Slavery; Suffrage.

DRAFT

See Conscription.

DRAFT RIOTS

On March 3, 1863, in the midst of the Civil War, Congress passed a conscription law making all men between twenty and forty-five years of age liable for military service. The attempt to enforce the draft in New York City, on July 13, ignited the most destructive civil disturbance in the city's history. Rioters torched government buildings and, on July 15, fought pitched battles with troops. Conservative contemporary commentators, concerned about an anti-Union plot,

claimed that 1,155 people were killed. In fact, about 300, over half of them policemen and soldiers, were injured, and there were no more than 119 fatalities, most of them rioters.

A majority of the rioters were Irish, living in pestilential misery. The spark that ignited their grievances and those of other workingmen and women was the provision in the law that conscription could be avoided by payment of three hundred dollars, an enormous sum only the rich could afford. In a context of wartime inflation, black competition for jobs, and race prejudice among working people, particularly the Irish, New York's blacks were chosen as scapegoats for long-accumulated grievances. Many innocent blacks were slain and their homes sacked. A Colored Orphan Asylum was razed. In this intersection of ethnic diversity, class antagonism, and racism lay the origins of the draft riots.

See also Conscription.

DRED SCOTT CASE

This convoluted case (1857), both a cause and an effect of sectional conflict, contributed to antebellum political and constitutional controversy. It also made Chief Justice Roger B. Taney seem a satanic figure to contemporary antislavery activists and many later historians.

Dred Scott, a black slave, and his wife had once belonged to army surgeon John Emerson, who had bought him from the Peter Blow family of St. Louis. After Emerson died, the Blows apparently helped Scott sue Emerson's widow for his freedom, but lost the case in state court. Because Mrs. Emerson left him with her brother John Sanford (misspelled Sandford in court papers), a New York citizen, Scott sued again in federal court, claiming Missouri citizenship. Scott's lawyers eventually appealed to the U.S. Supreme Court.

Originally, Justice Samuel Nelson was to write a narrow opinion, arguing that the case belonged in the state, not a federal court. But northern antislavery justices John McLean of Ohio and Benjamin R. Curtis of Massachusetts planned to dissent, arguing that Scott should be freed under the Missouri Compromise because he had traveled north of the 36°30′ line, whereas the Court's southerners wanted to rule the compromise unconstitutional. Among several opinions, Taney's was both the most important and the most tortuous. He ruled that blacks, slave or free, could not be citizens (Curtis showed this to be counter to precedent). Nor could Scott have become free by traveling north of the Missouri Compromise line; slavery, Taney said, could not be banned in the territories. Six justices agreed that Scott was not a citizen, but disagreed over whether a freed slave could become a citizen. Nelson concurred in the ruling but not in its reasoning, and McLean and Curtis dissented.

Republicans assailed the decision, which they saw as an attempt to destroy their nascent party. Democrats divided over the *Dred Scott* case. Stephen A. Douglas ended up opposing it as counter to his doctrine of popular sovereignty. President James Buchanan's supporters considered it a final answer to the sectional controversy, although they were unaware at the time that Buchanan had influenced Justice Robert Grier of Pennsylvania to join the southern majority so that it would look less like a sectional decision. The *Dred Scott* case remained the subject of noisy constitutional and historical debate and contributed to the divisions that helped lead to Abraham Lincoln's election and the Civil War.

See also Slavery.

DREISER, THEODORE

(1871–1945), author. Dreiser was the foremost American literary naturalist and author of two of the most significant works of early-twentieth-century American fiction, *Sister Carrie* (1900) and *An American Tragedy* (1925). He was raised in a large and poor Catholic family (his father was German-born) in various Indiana towns. After arriving in Chicago in his teens, he worked at menial jobs ranging from stock clerk to laundry truck driver until he broke into newspaper reporting in 1892. After almost a decade of successful work as a reporter in St. Louis and Pittsburgh, as an editor of the New York magazine *Ev'ry Month,* and as a free-lance magazine writer

in New York, Dreiser in late 1899 began his first novel, *Sister Carrie.* Set in Chicago and New York, the work is remarkable for its amoral yet sympathetic portrayal of the role of female sexuality in the rise of its heroine and for its rendering of the complex union of chance, character, and place in the fall of its male protagonist, Hurstwood. Although *Sister Carrie* was published, its publisher failed to promote the work because of its contents — an incident that Dreiser and such later supporters as H. L. Mencken made infamous as an example of the power of puritanical ideas in America.

Dreiser went into a decline after the publication of the novel (his unsuccessful marriage to Sara White in 1898 contributed to his breakdown), and it was not until 1904 that he again took up literary work. He edited a magazine in New York and then, in 1910, wrote his second novel, *Jennie Gerhardt* (1911). There followed a remarkable decade and a half of literary productivity, during which Dreiser published fourteen substantial books of fiction, plays, autobiography, travel writing, sketches, and philosophical essays. Among the most important of these books were the first two novels of his Cowperwood trilogy, *The Financier* (1912) and *The Titan* (1914), which recount in great detail the rise to power of a ruthless late-nineteenth-century American financial tycoon. This period was capped by Dreiser's masterpiece, *An American Tragedy,* a novel based on an upstate New York murder some twenty years earlier. *An American Tragedy* powerfully expresses Dreiser's naturalistic conviction that many individuals are so severely conditioned by the circumstances of their parentage and social background that they have little responsibility for their natures or actions. The work is also a striking indictment of the American myth of success, since its protagonist, Clyde Griffiths, is disastrously impelled by the myth to pursue wealth and position despite his lack of strength and ability.

Dreiser always thought of himself as a man of ideas — he had been deeply affected, for example, by Herbert Spencer's evolutionary thought and by Freud's theories — and he devoted the last two decades of his life to philosophical speculation. But like many American writers of the late 1920s and the 1930s, he was also increasingly drawn into social activism and support of the far Left. These interests culminated not long before his death in his joining the Communist party in 1945 and completing his long-delayed last two novels, *The Bulwark* (1946) and *The Stoic* (1947), works in which he expressed his final ideas about the relationship of spirit to matter in humanity and in the universe.

Donald Pizer, *The Novels of Theodore Dreiser: A Critical Study* (1976); W. A. Swanberg, *Dreiser* (1965).

DONALD PIZER

See also Literature.

DRUGS

Drugs have never been absent from American life, but the type and level of use have varied over time. Legal responses to drugs were profoundly influenced by the evolving interpretation of the U.S. Constitution, which, until the twentieth century, reserved to the states the police powers to regulate the health professions and drug availability. The result was a generally free economy in drugs until late in the nineteenth century when an ineffective patchwork of state antidrug laws were enacted.

Excluding alcohol and tobacco, opium was the major mood-altering substance available to Americans in the eighteenth and nineteenth centuries. Crude opium, the dried juice of the poppy, has been available for millennia, and from it various medicines have been concocted. Alcoholic extracts of opium include laudanum and paragoric; extraction with acetic acid was known as black drop or Quaker's opium. Opium prepared for smoking was closely linked in popular thought with Chinese immigrants.

About 10 percent of crude opium is the alkaloid morphine, its most powerful mood-altering ingredient. Morphine was isolated from opium in 1805 by the German pharmacist F. W. A. Sertuerner, although commercial production did not begin for about two decades. It was first produced in the United States in Philadelphia during the 1830s. The impact of the purified active ingredient was enormous. Morphine could be taken by mouth, as were crude opium compounds, but it could also be dusted into wounds, sprinkled on blistered skin, and after the development of the hypodermic syringe and needle, injected into the body's tissues with a powerful effect. Heroin, a derivative of morphine, was commercially introduced by the Bayer Company in 1898.

The extraction of purified active ingredients and their direct injection into the body marked a fundamental change in the relationship of drugs to society. After popularization of the hypodermic syringe in the 1860s, the use of opiates rose by the 1890s to a per capita level rivaled only by that of the early 1970s. Initially, physicians thought morphine by injection was a protection against addiction because the amount required for a given level of pain relief was less than when the drug was taken by mouth. That this erroneous belief persisted for about two decades illustrates the difficulty even trained observers have when evaluating new procedures. By the beginning of the twentieth century physicians were being widely blamed for having created addicts through careless prescribing. Both public and professional pressure thereafter led to extreme caution in the provision of pain relief to patients.

Another drug in use for centuries was contained in the coca leaf, which people living in the growing regions of the high Andes chewed as a way to obtain more energy and endurance. Cocaine was isolated from coca leaves in 1860 by A. Niemann of Vienna. An alcoholic extract was introduced shortly thereafter by Angelo Mariani as Vin Mariani, a tonic that proved popular until about the turn of the century. Testimonials from such celebrities as Thomas Edison, as well as a gold medal from Pope Leo XIII, came to Mariani for his coca extracts. Coca-Cola was modeled after Vin Mariani except that the alcohol was removed to make it a temperance beverage. Cocaine was removed from the soft drink about 1900.

Cocaine became available commercially in the 1880s and rapidly found favor with the public. The drug was taken in many forms, including hypodermic injection. Initially, there were no restrictions on its sale or distribution. And as in the case of morphine, many physicians believed that cocaine was harmless and so advised the public.

Over a decade passed before concern about cocaine began to outweigh the assurances of safety. Due to cocaine's ability to stimulate violence and paranoia, the reaction against the drug was dramatic and changed the acclaimed tonic into an extremely feared substance by 1900. Americans, too, along with their other social concerns of the Progressive Era, were growing increasingly worried about narcotics being surreptitiously included in patent medicines (easily available through mail-order houses) and about their being wrongly prescribed or overprescribed by physicians.

Some were also uneasy about opium smuggling into the newly acquired Philippine Islands. Partly because of this concern, but also to curry favor with the Chinese government, the United States convened the Shanghai Opium Commission in 1909. The thirteen nations assembled considered ways to help China with its opium problem, and although the conclusions were vague and not binding, the commission paved the way for an international conference, also called by the United States, which met two years later at The Hague. In January 1912, The Hague Opium Treaty, which also proposed to regulate cocaine, was completed by the dozen nations represented and submitted to all the world's powers for ratification.

The Harrison Narcotic Act of 1914 was the United States' implementation of The Hague treaty. The act's restriction took the form of a tax, and its purpose was to stop careless prescribing and easy availability of opiates and cocaine. This attempt to establish a national antinarcotic law controlling the health professions encountered serious constitutional impediments, however, and was not upheld by the Supreme Court as a legal prohibition of simple addiction maintenance until 1919.

The laws against narcotics at the local, state, and national levels early in the twentieth century reflected a strong antagonism to drug use. By 1937 intolerance and fear of drugs had reached such dimensions that the Marijuana Tax Act was passed with little debate. As use of drugs decreased, punishment increased until by

1955 the death penalty for providing heroin to anyone under eighteen was added to federal statutes. Narcotic use retreated to the margins of American society.

But, beginning in the 1960s, drugs became increasingly popular for recreational use, particularly among young people. The favored drug was marijuana, but hallucinatory substances such as LSD and peyote, depressants such as barbiturates, and opiates, particularly heroin, were also widely used. The clash between the extremely punitive laws that had evolved since the Harrison Act and the large number of new drug users led to softened penalties and a coalescence of federal drug laws under the Comprehensive Drug Abuse Act of 1970.

Toleration of drug use continued to rise until it reached a peak about 1978. Popular music and such entertainments as rock concerts and movies often glorified and sanctioned drug use. Campaigns to legalize drugs argued that they were harmless and that legalization would end black markets and reduce crime. They achieved a de facto decriminalization of marijuana for the user, but eradication and interdiction campaigns persisted.

After the late 1970s fear of drug use rose while toleration of drugs decreased, partly as a result of observation of the effects of drug use. Extensive antidrug campaigns were conducted in the media and by activist groups collectively termed "the parents' movement." The Reagan administration strongly supported the antidrug mood and First Lady Nancy Reagan introduced the motto of the antidrug movement, "Just say no."

During the 1980s the use of cocaine, especially a conveniently inhalable form called crack, reached alarming levels, and by 1989 public opinion polls were reporting that Americans believed that drugs were the most serious problem facing the nation. Increased homicides, violence, and damage to fetuses of crack-using pregnant women were common allegations. The fear of lifelong damage to children of drug-using mothers created a new concern in the war on drugs. In 1986 and 1988 increasingly severe federal antidrug laws were enacted as Republicans and Democrats vied over who was the more opposed to drug use. Between the 1960s and the 1980s attitudes had once again shifted: toleration turned into intolerance and a hope that some drug use might be beneficial gave way to a growing conviction that any drug use was damaging.

DAVID F. MUSTO

See also Corruption; Crime.

DU BOIS, W. E. B.

(1868–1963), historian, sociologist, writer, and civil rights activist. Du Bois was the foremost African-American intellectual of the twentieth century. Born in Great Barrington, Massachusetts, Du Bois knew little of his father, who died shortly after his birth, but he was socialized into an extended family network that left a strong impression on his personality and was reflected in his subsequent work. Educated at Fisk University (1885–1888), Harvard University (1888–1896), and the University of Berlin (1892–1894), Du Bois studied with some of the most important social thinkers of his time and then embarked upon a seventy-year career that combined scholarship and teaching with lifelong activism in liberation struggles.

Interspersed with his teaching career at Wilberforce and Atlanta University were two stints as a publicist for the National Association for the Advancement of Colored People (NAACP), of which he was a founding officer and for whom he edited the monthly magazine, the *Crisis*. He resigned from the NAACP in June 1934 in a dispute over organizational policy and direction. He believed the depression dictated a shift from the organization's stress on legal rights and integration to an emphasis on black economic advancement, even if this meant temporarily "accepting" segregation. But after teaching at Atlanta University, he returned in 1944 as head of a research effort aimed at collecting and disseminating data on Africans and their diaspora and putting issues affecting them before the world community. Renewed disputes with the NAACP caused him to be dismissed in 1948.

During the 1950s Du Bois was drawn into leftist causes, including chairing the Peace Information Center. The center's refusal to comply with the Foreign Agents Registration Act led to his indictment with four others by a federal grand jury in 1951. All five were acquitted after a highly publicized trial, but the taint of alleged communist association caused him to be shunned by colleagues and harassed by federal agencies (including eventual revocation of his passport) throughout the 1950s. In 1961, Du Bois settled in Ghana and began work on the *Encyclopedia Africana,* a compendium of information on Africans and peoples of African descent throughout the world. Shortly thereafter he joined the American Communist party and became a citizen of Ghana, where he died in 1963.

During Du Bois's prolific career he published nineteen books, edited four magazines, co-edited a magazine for children, and produced scores of articles and speeches. Perhaps his most outstanding work was *Souls of Black Folk* (1903), a poignant collection of essays in which he defined some of the key themes of the African-American experience and the dominant motifs of his own work.

He clashed on occasion with other black leaders over appropriate strategies for black advancement, notably Booker T. Washington (whose strategy of accommodation and emphasis on industrial education for blacks he rejected) and Marcus Garvey (whom he considered a demagogue, although they shared a commitment to Pan-Africanism and the liberation of Africa). Du Bois's own approach was an eclectic mix of scientific social analysis, which led him eventually to Marxism, and a romantic evocation of the poetry of black folk culture, which is reflected in his nationalist sympathies and Pan-Africanist organizational efforts. Above all Du Bois sought to place African-American experience in its world historical context. Out of this mix evolved his dual projects of building an African socialism and publishing a unifying work of scholarship on the African diaspora.

Manning Marable, *W. E. B. Du Bois: Black Radical Democrat* (1986); Arnold Rampersad, *The Art and Imagination of W. E. B. Du Bois* (1976).

THOMAS C. HOLT

See also Anticommunism; Black Nationalism; Literature; National Association for the Advancement of Colored People; Niagara Movement; Washington, Booker T.

DUELING

Dueling first became relatively common in America during the Revolution, encouraged by the wartime instability of American society and the presence of European officers well versed in the rules of the code duello. Young army officers, often from the same social class as common foot soldiers, yearned for ways to prove their superiority and gain acceptance into America's upper class. Dueling provided a standard of conduct and an ideology from which the masses were excluded — the rules of the code duello and the ideals of honor and reputation.

Although most duelists fought in secluded areas to avoid prosecution under the law, dueling relied on public knowledge. Challenging an opponent to a duel was a public demonstration of one's right to claim admission to a superior social class. Its theatrical rituals and risks publicly demonstrated bravery, political and social loyalties, and a willingness to risk death rather than face dishonor.

The code duello provided instructions for duelists, including the appointment of seconds to communicate between the disputants and the formalities of issuing a challenge. As dueling became increasingly common, more sophisticated rules developed, offering ways to settle disputes, maintain honor and reputation, and avoid the field of honor. Once two men took the field against each other, however, each was honor-bound to attempt to kill the other.

During the early nineteenth century, with the increasing sophistication of the American legal system and, specifically, libel and slander laws, the practice of dueling declined. Public clamor over the death of renowned statesman Alexander Hamilton — the result of a duel with Vice President Aaron Burr (1804) — led to the demise of dueling in the northern states. Dueling lingered the longest in the South — an area with unique social hierarchies entrenched in the institution of slavery.

See also Burr, Aaron; Hamilton, Alexander.

DULLES, JOHN FOSTER

(1888–1959), Wall Street lawyer and secretary of state. Dulles, grandson of one secretary of state (John Foster) and nephew of another (Robert Lansing), served Dwight D. Eisenhower in that capacity from January 1953 until his death, from cancer, in 1959. An international lawyer and senior partner in the prestigious Wall Street firm of Sullivan and Cromwell, he built a modest reputation in the twenties as an authority on the tangled issue of Allied war debts and German reparations. Long an unreconstructed Wilsonian, Dulles opposed American involvement in Europe in the thirties on the grounds that the victors of 1919 had ignored Woodrow Wilson's call for "peaceful change" and sought only to preserve the harsh features of the Versailles settlement.

Dulles emerged during World War II as the principal lay spokesman for the Federal Council of Churches in its effort to promote the proposed United Nations. But at the same time, as a protégé of New York governor Thomas E. Dewey, he was also emerging as a leading proponent of the foreign policy views of the eastern wing of the Republican party. Senator Arthur Vandenberg and he were the architects of postwar bipartisan foreign policy. By the late forties he was a Republican adviser, and later consultant, to the Truman administration and in that capacity negotiated the Japanese peace treaty in 1950–1951.

But by 1952 partisanship and policy differences led him to become one of Harry S. Truman's and Dean Acheson's most acerbic critics, especially on Far Eastern policy. His well-publicized article in *Life* magazine condemned the containment policy of the Truman administration as merely a negative attempt to restrain Soviet expansionism and demanded a new policy of boldness that would restore the initiative to the United States. During the 1952 campaign he called stridently not only for the "rollback" of Soviet gains in Eastern Europe but also for the "unleashing" of Chiang Kai-shek.

As secretary of state Dulles was often portrayed as the stern Presbyterian moralist who made speeches condemning atheistic communism and threatening massive retaliation. For many historians he was the very model of the "cold warrior," a reductionist whose rhetoric intensified the ideological gulf between East and West. Moreover, since Eisenhower was perceived as a chief executive who reigned but did not govern, Dulles was regarded as *the* architect of American foreign policy.

Later it became evident that Eisenhower was an activist and that his foreign policy was a joint creation, not simply the work of his secretary of state. Declassified documents, moreover, indicated that Dulles was far more complex and flexible than previously thought. He considered the possibility of genuine negotiations with the Soviets, recognized the process of change in post-Stalinist Russia, did not always regard neutrality as immoral, and, above all, was prudent and cautious on atomic issues. Despite the campaign rhetoric of 1952, he, in effect, accepted the underlying postulates of containment, and his stewardship of American foreign policy deserves to be remembered more for what it preserved from the Truman-Acheson heritage than for its innovations. And despite the furor over massive retaliation and the crises over Suez, Dien Bien Phu, and Lebanon, Dulles was adept at crisis management and presided over a six-year period during which the United States was, at least technically, at peace.

Richard D. Challener, "John Foster Dulles: Theorist/ Practitioner," in L. Carl Brown, ed., *Centerstage: American Diplomacy since World War II* (1990); John Lewis Gaddis, *The Long Peace: Inquiries into the History of the Cold War* (1987).

RICHARD D. CHALLENER

See also Cold War; Eisenhower, Dwight D.; Elections: 1952.

DUNCAN, ISADORA

(1877–1927), dancer and choreographer. Born in San Francisco, Duncan grew up in a freethinking family headed by her mother, a follower of Robert Ingersoll. From the city's thriving Bohemia, Duncan absorbed the cult of nature, Hellenism, and belief in the semidivinity of the body that became tenets of her artistic credo. Other lasting influences were Delsartism, a system of movement that linked gestural expression with mental states, and the "new gymnastics," which stressed flexibility, coordination, and balance and was aligned with the feminist movements for dress and health reform.

After a brief stint in the commercial theater, Duncan embarked on a career as a solo concert artist, first in New York and then in Europe, where she arrived in 1900 and spent the better part of her life. In London and Paris, she created her first important dances, idylls rooted in Grecian themes and performed to composers like Mendelssohn, Gluck, and Chopin. She quickly found an audience among artists and intellectuals who appreciated her striking originality — her daring use of concert music, her open expression of physicality (enhanced by bare feet and body-revealing tunics), her creation of an idiom that owed nothing to the technique and tradition of ballet.

Although she occasionally choreographed for groups, her greatest works were solos she created for herself. Duncan was a charismatic performer, exceptionally musical and with a gift for coaxing emotion from pure movement and gesture. Her vocabulary was simple, but she had a magnificent sense of space and an intuitive understanding of its psychological organization. She knew the value of stillness and made a virtue of weight. Abandoning corsets, she discovered the "crater of motor power" in her articulate and liberated torso.

Duncan's personal life was as unconventional as her dancing. A believer in free love, she had numerous liaisons and bore her two children, by Gordon Craig and Paris Singer, out of wedlock. She spent money like water, running up bills others usually paid. Her politics, always radical, took a socialist turn during World War I when she discovered the poverty of New York's Lower East Side. In 1921, at the invitation of Anatoly Lunacharsky, the Soviet commissar of enlightenment, she went to Moscow, where she established a school and married the poet Sergei Essenin. Duncan's last American tour, in 1922–1923, was filled with scandal; in Boston, baring her breast and waving a red scarf, she cried,

"This is red! So am I!" In 1927, it was a scarf, caught in the moving wheel of a flashy Bugatti, that broke her neck. Her lively, if not always accurate autobiography, *Ma Vie,* was published posthumously.

Although her art died with her, Duncan's influence on contemporaries was enormous. In Europe, especially, she set off a wave of "interpretative" dancers who flooded theaters, salons, and concert halls up to the 1930s. Ironically, in view of her loathing for the *danse d'école,* elements of her style were absorbed into the period's "new ballet." Regarded as a founding mother of American modern dance, she left to future generations a legacy of daring and unconventionality — art as an act of heroic self-creation.

Frederika Blair, *Isadora: Portrait of the Artist as a Woman* (1986); Isadora Duncan, *My Life* (1927).

LYNN GARAFOLA

See also Dance.

DU PONT, ALFRED I.

(1864–1935), industrialist, banker, and philanthropist. Du Pont was the great-great-grandson of the noted French physiocrat Pierre Samuel du Pont de Nemours, and the great-grandson of Eleuthère Irénée du Pont, founder of the E. I. du Pont de Nemours gunpowder company in Wilmington, Delaware. His parents both died in 1877, leaving the thirteen-year-old Alfred and his four siblings to be raised by their du Pont elders.

After receiving his education at Phillips Academy (Andover) and the Massachusetts Institute of Technology, du Pont returned to the Brandywine to begin his apprenticeship in the family powder mills. Within ten years he was generally recognized as the best "black powder man" in America, and his many patented inventions for corning and glazing powder greatly improved both the efficiency and the safety of the mills. Upon the death of Eugene du Pont, president of the company, in 1902, none of the three senior du Pont partners wished to succeed him. They were prepared to sell the family's century-old company to their major competitor when Alfred boldly announced that he would take over the company. His surprised elders agreed to this proposal providing that Alfred share the management with his cousins, T. Coleman du Pont and Pierre Samuel du Pont II.

Under the able direction of the three, the company was modernized and greatly expanded, achieving by 1910 a virtual monopoly within the gunpowder industry. Although his own expertise was largely in the field of black powder, Alfred, as general manager of all du Pont production, was one of the first to urge that the company diversify and find other commercial uses for its cellulose research than that of high explosives.

Alfred's divorce from his first wife and his marriage to his cousin Alicia precipitated a bitter family feud that culminated in a struggle between Pierre and Alfred for control of the company after T. Coleman du Pont put his shares up for sale. The victorious Pierre forced Alfred out of the company in 1916, although Alfred remained the second largest stockholder.

At loose ends after his ouster, Alfred entered politics, largely to thwart the political ambitions of his hostile cousins. He destroyed the old du Pont machine that had for many years dominated Delaware politics, and although he never held public office himself, he was largely instrumental in bringing progressive reforms to Delaware, including a statewide old-age pension system.

At the urging of his third wife, Jessie Ball du Pont, whom he had married following Alicia's death in 1920, du Pont moved to Florida in 1926. There he created a second empire with the purchase of thousands of acres of pineland in the Florida panhandle, the establishment of a chain of banks, and the promotion of research to make southern pine suitable for paper production. He thus helped rejuvenate the economy of the state, which had been stricken by the collapse of the land boom and the devastating hurricane of 1926.

Alfred du Pont died at his winter residence, Epping Forest, in Jacksonville, Florida, on April 29, 1935. In his will he provided that his entire estate of $40 million would upon the death of his wife go to the Nemours Foundation for the treatment of crippled children and the care of the indigent elderly of Delaware and Florida. Under the trusteeship of his wife and her brother, Edward Ball, the value of the estate increased to over $2 billion by the time of Ball's death in 1981, making it one of the largest philanthropic foundations in the nation.

Marquis James, *Alfred I. du Pont: The Family Rebel* (1941); Joseph Frazier Wall, *Alfred I. du Pont: The Man and His Family* (1990).

JOSEPH FRAZIER WALL

See also Philanthropy.

DUST BOWL

The Dust Bowl was the name given to the Great Plains region devastated by drought in 1930s depression-ridden America. The 150,000-square-mile area, encompassing the Oklahoma and Texas panhandles and neighboring sections of Kansas, Colorado, and New Mexico, has little rainfall, light soil, and high winds, a potentially destructive combination. Ranchers and farmers in the nineteenth and early twentieth centuries, driven by the American agricultural ethos of expansion and a sense of autonomy from nature, aggressively exploited the land and set up the region for ecological disaster. Most early settlers used the land for livestock grazing until agricultural mechanization combined with high grain prices during World War I enticed farmers to plow up millions of acres of natural grass cover to plant wheat. When drought struck from 1934 to 1937, the soil lacked the stronger root system of grass as an anchor, so the winds easily picked up the loose topsoil and swirled it into dense dust clouds, called "black blizzards." Recurrent dust storms wreaked havoc, choking cattle and pasture lands and driving 60 percent of the population from the region. Most of these "exodusters" went to agricultural areas first and then to cities, especially in the Far West.

In response, the federal government mobilized several New Deal agencies, principally the Soil Conservation Service formed in 1935, to promote farm rehabilitation. Working on the lo-

cal level, the government instructed farmers to plant trees and grass to anchor the soil, to plow and terrace in contour patterns to hold rainwater, and to allow portions of farmland to lie fallow each year so the soil could regenerate. The government also purchased 11.3 million acres of submarginal land to keep it out of production. By 1941 much of the land was rehabilitated, but the region repeated its mistakes during World War II as farmers again plowed up grassland to plant wheat when grain prices rose. Drought threatened another disaster in the 1950s, prompting Congress to subsidize farmers in restoring millions of acres of wheat back to grassland.

The Dust Bowl prompted a cultural response from artists like Dorothea Lange, Woody Guthrie, and John Steinbeck, who lamented the American economic ethos that had created the disaster. To them, the Dust Bowl signified the final destruction of the old Jeffersonian ideal of agrarian harmony with nature.

See also Agriculture.

DYLAN, BOB

(1941–   ), singer and composer. The most influential American singer and composer of popular music in the sixties was born Robert Zimmerman in Duluth, Minnesota, and grew up in Hibbing, a mining town in northern Minnesota where his father ran a hardware store. Zimmerman attended the University of Minnesota and in 1960 arrived in New York's Greenwich Village as Bob Dylan, an aspiring folksinger and songwriter. He modeled himself at first on Woody Guthrie. But his second album, *The Freewheelin' Bob Dylan* (1963), marked his emergence as the voice of his generation, a fierce nonconformist and passionate critic of racism, injustice, and war.

Dylan's engagement with the civil rights movement in 1962–1963 led to his topical protest songs that also succeeded as art. "Blowin' in the Wind," his best-known song, was allusive and beautiful; it became an anthem of the civil rights struggle. During the 1962 Cuban missile crisis, he wrote "A Hard Rain's A-Gonna Fall," which conveyed a sense of terror with its chilling poetic images. At twenty-two, Dylan had brought his personal vision and political commitments together with a power and a beauty that neither he nor anyone else would later equal in popular music.

Another Side of Bob Dylan (1964), his next album, stunned his fans. He dismissed social issues and sang personal songs that expressed, among other feelings, considerable bitterness toward women. It was the first of his several transformations, viewed by many fans as a betrayal: after abandoning protest for personal songs, he would abandon folk for rock, then rock for country, and then Judaism for born-again Christianity.

Dylan's mid-sixties rock was exuberant, tumultuous, hallucinogenic: *Bringing It All Back Home* and *Highway 61 Revisited* (1965) captured an enormous audience. His lyrics consisted of long strings of wild, poetic images, sung with his unique phrasing and unmistakable nasal voice. "Like a Rolling Stone," the most enduring and triumphant song of this period, passionately expressed the frustrations of sixties' youth and gave voice to their cheerful defiance. It marked the high point of Dylan's role as spokesman for a generation.

In 1966 Dylan broke his neck in a motorcycle accident, and his subsequent music never equaled his earlier work. *John Wesley Harding* (1968), the first album after his accident, abandoned raucous rock for a quieter, more personal sound: "All Along the Watchtower" expressed a new commitment to truthfulness and seriousness; "I'll Be Your Baby Tonight" was a tender love song. But his next albums declined steadily.

Blood on the Tracks (1975) marked a long-awaited comeback — his first number 1 album, followed by a second, *Desire* (1976). Once again he sounded passionate and engaged. In 1979 he changed course again, declaring himself a born-again Christian: *Slow Train Coming* was self-righteous and lacking in Christian charity. He returned to Judaism in 1983. A five-record set, *Biograph* (1988), summed up his musical career after 1960.

If Dylan had died in his 1966 motorcycle accident, he would have achieved mythic status. Critics and fans since that time have intermittently declared "Dylan's back!" Nevertheless, none of his subsequent albums rivaled the poetry and power of his earlier work, which stands as an eloquent expression of the political and the personal in rock music.

Anthony Scaduto, *Bob Dylan* (1973); Robert Shelton, *No Direction Home: The Life and Music of Bob Dylan* (1987).

JON WIENER

See also Music.

E

EAKINS, THOMAS

(1844–1916), painter, photographer, and teacher. Eakins, Philadelphia-born, was a painter of scientific bent, an urban provincial in the American materialist tradition, whose restricted life in an uncongenial postbellum society forced him into lonely concentration on the question of what authentic art should be. He rejected conventional painting of his time for what he considered its structural flaws and false emotion. Instead, he sought to paint the human figure in space with factual accuracy and genuine feeling. Before committing himself to art, he had considered careers in surgery and singing and never really put those options aside: his major portraits are of men of medicine and women vocalists. And his lifework consisted of profound, even obsessive, study of anatomy and perspective, two systems of nature that, properly understood and put to use, afford power to heal the body or to inspire empathetic response in an audience.

The son of a master calligrapher, Eakins grew up among intellectuals and artists, many of whom he would later paint. After a four-year stint at the École des Beaux Arts in Paris, he returned to Philadelphia for good. There, isolated from both fashionable and avant-garde art movements, burdened by psychological conflicts, and mostly unappreciated, he pressed his research into the structure of bodies through dissection and into perspective through his own system of measurements. These disciplines he taught at the Pennsylvania Academy of the Fine Arts and elsewhere. In the early 1880s, his interest in human and animal mobility led him to experiments in photography inspired by Eadweard Muybridge.

Eakins's early studies were of his own family members in their heavily curtained drawing room. After his mother's death, he took his bearings outdoors with meticulous studies of friends sculling and sailing on local waters. Then in 1875, he produced a work so singular that his public reputation was ruined. *The Gross Clinic* is a monumental work centered on a portrait of a surgeon midway through an operation. Thoughtful, even world-weary, he stands by the patient among black-coated assistants. Blood fills the incision and stains the hands of the doctor and his assistants. Various levels of interpretation suggest themselves today, but to an audience only a decade away from the surgical barbarities of the Civil War, the effect was "sickening." Intended for the Centennial Exposition of 1876, the painting was rejected and was hung instead in an outlying mock-up of an army hospital. In 1878, Philadelphia's Jefferson Medical College bought it for two hundred dollars. Today it is acknowledged as one of the masterpieces of nineteenth-century art.

Eakins once wrote, "my honors are misunderstanding, persecution and neglect," and his later work reflects both disappointment and obstinate dedication. He painted a *Crucifixion,* an odd subject for an artist of Quaker background. He made a number of arcadian studies of nude youths. His portraits show single figures deep in thought, posed with awkward naturalness in shadowed space. Most were rejected by the sitters as unflattering. In 1887, he painted an aged Walt Whitman. A second surgical tableau, *The Agnew Clinic,* though milder in spirit, was no less attacked than the first one. Only in the next generation did his work begin to win respect, first by painters of the New York Ashcan school. Robert Henri, one of that group and an influential teacher and writer, called Eakins "one of the very great men in all American art," a judgment history accepts today.

Lloyd Goodrich, *Thomas Eakins,* 2 vols. (1982); Elizabeth Johns, *Thomas Eakins: The Heroism of Modern Life* (1983); Barbara Novak, *American Painting of the Nineteenth Century* (1969).

ELEANOR MUNRO

See also Painting and Sculpture.

EARHART, AMELIA

(1897–1937), aviator. Earhart symbolizes the fascination that aviation held for Americans in the 1920s and 1930s. Like Charles Lindbergh, she became a national celebrity because of her exploits in the air. Her modest demeanor and short, tousled hair made her a perfect heroine for a media-conscious age. Her public career lasted less than a decade (from 1928 to 1937), but she used her fame to promote two causes dear to her: the advancement of commercial aviation and the advancement of women.

Earhart's entire life had a certain restless quality. By 1928, she had found a calling of sorts as a social worker in Boston who flew in her spare time. When New York publisher George Palmer Putnam asked if she wanted to be the first woman to fly the Atlantic, she readily agreed. The June 1928 flight from Newfoundland to Burry Port, Wales, made her an instant celebrity, although she was quick to note that she had been merely a passenger, "a sack of potatoes," who kept the log. When she soloed the Atlantic in 1932, another first for women, she proved to the world and, more important, to herself that 1928 had not been a fluke.

After the 1928 flight, Earhart turned her hobby of flying into a paying career. As a lecturer, author, and airline industry vice president, she preached her message that flying would soon be an accepted part of everyday life. Many of her widely publicized flights — the 1932 transatlantic crossing, her 1935 solo from Hawaii to California, the 1937 round-the-world attempt — hastened the introduction of commercial air routes. Her career was managed by Putnam, whom she married in 1931 in what was as much a business relationship as a love match. Earhart kept her own name professionally and made no plans to have children. She continued to identify herself publicly with feminism and served as the first president of the Ninety-Nines, an organization of women pilots.

Amelia Earhart had a poet's appreciation of flight, and she flew because she wanted to, which to her individualistic mind-set was the best reason of all. She was delighted when Purdue University, where she had served as aviation consultant and counselor on careers for women since 1935, presented her with a Lockheed Electra so advanced she dubbed it "the flying laboratory." Now she could fulfill her ambition to fly around the world. The first attempt in March 1937 ended prematurely when her plane crashed on takeoff in Hawaii. A second attempt began two months later, now following a west-to-east direction. On July 2, 1937, during the hardest leg, a 2,556-mile segment from New Guinea to a tiny speck in the mid-Pacific called Howland Island, Earhart and her navigator, Fred Noonan, disappeared.

The circumstances of Earhart's "popping off" (her matter-of-fact phrase) have been a source of speculation ever since. Was she on a spy mission for Franklin Roosevelt? Did she land on a desert island and become a Japanese prisoner? The weight of evidence suggests that her plane ran out of fuel somewhere near Howland Island and sank quickly. But given the aviator's hold on the popular imagination, the search for Amelia Earhart continues.

Amelia Earhart, *Last Flight* (1937), arranged by George Palmer Putnam from material and dispatches filed before her death; Mary S. Lovell, *The Sound of Wings* (1989).

SUSAN WARE

See also Aviation.

EASTMAN, CRYSTAL

(1881–1928), lawyer, antimilitarist, feminist, socialist, and journalist. Eastman has been one of the United States' most neglected leaders. Although she wrote pioneering legislation and created long-lasting political organizations, she disappeared from history for fifty years.

Known for her vigorous spirit and splendid oratory, Eastman sought to extend the contours of women's power and achievements beyond all "preconceived ideas of what was fit or proper or possible." Six feet tall and athletic, she graduated from Vassar in 1903, received an M.A. in sociology from Columbia in 1904, and was second in the class of 1907 at New York University Law School.

Social work pioneer and journal editor Paul Kellogg offered Eastman her first job, investigating labor conditions for the Pittsburgh *Survey* sponsored by the Russell Sage Foundation. Her report, *Work Accidents and the Law* (1910), became a classic (reprinted in 1970) and resulted in the first workers' compensation law, which she drafted while serving on a New York State commission. She never considered workers' compensation a substitute for safe working conditions, however, and continued to campaign for occupational safety and health while working as an investigating attorney for the U.S. Commission on Industrial Relations during Woodrow Wilson's presidency.

During a brief marriage, Eastman lived in Milwaukee and managed the unsuccessful 1912 Wisconsin suffrage battle. The experience further radicalized her. When she returned east in 1913 she joined Alice Paul, Lucy Burns, and others in founding the militant Congressional Union, which became the National Woman's party. After women won the vote, Eastman and three others wrote the Equal Rights Amendment introduced in 1923. One of the few socialists to endorse the ERA, she warned that protective legislation for women would mean only discrimination against women. Eastman claimed that one could assess the importance of the ERA by the intensity of the opposition to it, but she felt that "this is a fight worth fighting even if it takes ten years."

During World War I Eastman poured her vast energies into the peace movement. She founded the Woman's Peace party and was president of the New York branch. Renamed the Women's International League for Peace and Freedom in 1921, it remains the oldest extant women's peace organization. Eastman also became executive director of the American Union against Militarism, which lobbied against America's entrance into the European war and more successfully against war with Mexico in 1916, sought to remove profiteering from arms manufacturing, and campaigned against conscription and imperial adventures. When the United States entered World War I, Eastman organized the National Civil Liberties Bureau to protect conscientious objectors: "To maintain something over here that will be worth coming back to when the weary war is over." Though never appropriately credited as a founder of the organization, which became the American Civil Liberties Union, she was the attorney in charge.

Eastman had married British poet and antiwar activist Walter Fuller in 1916 with whom she had two children, and worked with him until the end of the war, when he returned to England to find work.

After the war, Eastman organized the First Feminist Congress in 1919; co-owned and edited a radical journal of politics, art, and literature, *The Liberator,* with her brother Max; and commuted between London, to be with her husband, and New York, where she was blacklisted and thus rendered unemployable during the red scare of 1919–1921. During the 1920s her only paid work was as a columnist for feminist journals, notably *Equal Rights* and *Time and Tide.* Until her death in 1928, Crystal Eastman worked for world peace, economic security, and feminism. Aware that "life was a big battle for the complete feminist," she was nevertheless convinced that the complete feminist would someday achieve total victory.

Blanche Wiesen Cook, ed., *Crystal Eastman on Women and Revolution* (1978).

BLANCHE WIESEN COOK

See also American Civil Liberties Union; Conscientious Objection; Feminist Movement; Socialism.

EASTMAN, GEORGE

(1854–1932), inventor, manufacturer, and philanthropist. Born at Waterville, New York, Eastman left school at age fourteen to help support his widowed mother and two sisters as an errand boy in a real estate office. He became interested in photography as a youth, and while working as a bookkeeper in a Rochester bank, he perfected a process for making dry plates in his home studio. In 1880, without quitting his job, he established the Eastman Dry Plate Company with partner Henry A. Strong in the loft of a factory building. So rapidly did this business grow that Eastman left the bank to devote himself full-time to the fledgling photography firm in September 1881.

During the next decade, Eastman transformed photography from a laborious and costly art into an easy, inexpensive hobby enjoyed by millions. In 1884, he replaced cumbersome glass plates with a paper-backed roll film which he invented and marketed through the reorganized Eastman Dry Plate and Film Company. Four years later, he introduced the hand-held Kodak; loaded with film sufficient for one hundred photographs, it produced round pictures two and one-half inches in diameter. "You push the button — we do the rest," Eastman advertised. After snapping a hundred pictures, the amateur photographer returned the loaded camera to the factory where the photos were processed and the camera reloaded.

In 1889 Eastman applied for a patent for celluloid film, which provided the foundation for an entirely new and unforeseen industry — moving pictures. Three years later, after developing daylight-loading film, the firm was reorganized as the Eastman Kodak Company; in 1901 it became the Eastman Kodak Company of New Jersey, capitalized at $35 million. To minimize his competition, Eastman bought out many rivals, acquired patent rights from others, and made exclusive contracts with his wholesale and retail dealers. By 1928, the year the company

perfected color photography for motion pictures, Eastman Kodak was the largest manufacturer of photographic supplies in the world, producing everything required by amateur, commercial, scientific, and motion picture photographers.

Eastman's phenomenal success was rooted in continuing scientific research, cost-efficient manufacturing methods, and a loyal labor force. He was one of the first American manufacturers to employ full-time research chemists; he pioneered large-scale production at low costs for a world market; and he introduced profit-sharing and stock-option plans for employees. At the time of his death, the company operated manufacturing plants in Rochester, New York, Kingsport, Tennessee, and England, France, Germany, Australia, and Hungary. The main plant at Kodak Park, Rochester, spread over 480 acres and employed nineteen thousand people.

Eastman never married, and his philanthropies, including bequests, totaled more than $75 million. His primary beneficiary was the University of Rochester, to which he contributed $35 million for the Eastman Theater, the School of Music, the School of Medicine and Dentistry, and the College for Women. Lesser sums were donated to the Massachusetts Institute of Technology and the Hampton and Tuskegee institutes. His hobbies included big-game hunting and growing orchids, and he advocated a calendar based on thirteen months of twenty-eight days. Long in poor health, he took his own life at age seventy-seven. The note he left read: "My work is done. Why wait?"

Carl W. Ackerman, *George Eastman* (1930).

PATRICIA CONDON JOHNSTON

See also Photography.

ECONOMIC GROWTH

By "economic growth" economists mean, in the first place, annual increases in the nation's total output of goods and services — its national product. Gross national product (GNP) does not take into account the wastage of the machinery and other capital goods used in production. Net national product (NNP) makes allowances for capital replacements. Although NNP includes final consumer goods and services, it counts only net additions to capital goods. It is therefore a better measure of real growth than GNP. The reason only final consumer goods are included is that care must be taken to avoid double counting; the output of bread is included, but the output of wheat used to produce the bread is not.

The monetary equivalent of national product — national income — can be measured in various ways. One is to measure it as the "value added" by economic activity in agriculture, manufacturing, mining, and so on. (Value added is calculated by summing output at producers' prices and deducting the cost of the fuel and raw materials used to produce the output.) Another way is to measure it as the aggregate value of the final products of the economy. Still another is to total the incomes accruing to persons supplying different productive factors (such as wages and salaries, profits, rents). Each of these approaches yields the same total, provided a consistent scheme of valuation is used. The component detail of each, however, illuminates different facets of the process of production, distribution, and consumption of the nation's output, and each serves a different use.

Changes in national income may be measured either in current prices — the prices that prevailed during the year in which the economic activity took place — or in constant prices — the prices of a given year, for example, those of 1929, which then serve as a base. In a study of financial developments or market trends the former is often preferable. But if the purpose is to analyze change in consumer levels of living or national productivity, the latter is more appropriate. For purposes of studying economic growth, therefore, it is constant price measurement that is desirable.

There are two additional requirements for the measurement of economic growth if the purpose is to calculate change in material welfare. A nation's rate of growth must be divided by the size of its population in order to find the rate per capita; if an increased number of people is required to produce an increase in the amount of goods and services produced, no one is better off than before. On the other hand, high levels of both population and output growth, even without corresponding growth in per capita output, bespeak an economy's ability to sustain large increases in population, and this is of interest to students of the sources of national influence and power. A final point: the increase in output should not be a temporary one, such as might follow a year of unusually good harvests. Nor should it merely represent an upward movement in the business cycle. Economic growth is *sustained* growth, secular in duration rather than cyclical.

In the output data of various countries scholars have found growth cycles (often called "long swings") of varying lengths, some of them 10 years long, others 60 years, and still others even 100 years. In the data of American history the most common long swing, named the "Kuznets cycle" after its discoverer, the Nobel Prize–winning economist Simon Kuznets, ranges between 10 and 20 years. A swing is a change in the *rate* of growth. During a long swing there occurs an expansion phase, followed by a period of continued growth at a retarded rate, culminating in depression. In the 124-year period between 1814 and 1938, nine long swings have been found, averaging 14 years in duration. In the expansion phase of these swings GNP grew at an average rate of about 6 percent, followed by retardation averaging 2 percent. During the depression phase, the rate of growth was extremely low or, ceasing altogether, negative.

Except for agriculture, the pace of growth of nearly every kind of economic activity registered advances during the expansion phase. Long swings occurred in the growth of population, labor force, immigration, transport development, internal migration, geographical settlement, urbanization, residential construction, the prices of common stocks, railroad bond yields, the money supply, commodity prices, and still other economic variables. Long swings, it should be emphasized, took place not in the *total volume* of output (which has risen without significant interruption, except for the 1930s, since the 1870s) but rather in the *rate of increase* of that total. Almost always, total output has risen, but at rates that accelerate and then decline. It is these alternations between acceleration and retardation that characterize the long swings of economic growth. America's growth has proceeded in a series of great surges, followed by periods of much slower growth, and so has the growth of a number of other industrial countries.

Whether or not long swings characterized growth in the earlier years of the nation's history seems impossible to know. Decennial census returns of output in the various sectors of the economy provide the most reliable source of information on which estimates of growth rates can be based and even these returns are incomplete before 1870. Not until 1840 did census takers include agriculture, which was then and for a number of decades afterward the main provider of incomes in the United States. Investigators of the quantitative records for the years before 1840 are compelled to work in the half-light of what has been called a "statistical dark age." For the long colonial period (1607–1783) the light is even dimmer.

It is certain, however, that economic growth in the sense of increased population and output took place during the colonial years. From 105 colonists aboard the three small ships carrying English settlers to Virginia in 1607, the population grew to an estimated total of over 2 million by 1770, and by the time of the first federal census in 1790, it was nearly twice as large. Even if each person provided only enough food and clothing for his or her own subsistence, its imputed value would imply a huge expansion in total output. And available data on exports of tobacco and other commodities for a number of years in the eighteenth century enlarge that output even more. What historians do not know is whether or not growth per capita took place, and if so, by how much. Data on the size of houses and their furnishings in the later years, along with other supportive evidence, argue that the standard of living also rose. If so, and however slowly, growth in output per capita must also have occurred.

The quantitative remains of the early decades of independence are somewhat more satisfactory but still so fragmentary that conclusions about economic growth are little more than "guesstimates." Making the most of the available evidence, Paul A. David posits the existence of three long swings between the 1790s and the Civil War. He finds in each a period of surge. In the first, the surge covers the years from the early 1790s to about 1806 and is associated with a large increase in the volume of foreign trade after the outbreak of the French Revolution and the Napoleonic Wars. In the second long swing the surge lasts from the early 1820s to about 1834 and is linked with early manufacturing development. In the third, identified with continuing industrialization, the surge commences in the latter half of the 1840s and runs its course before the firing on Fort Sumter. Although David believes that none of the surges involved a break in the secular growth rate, Robert E. Gallman is of the opinion that a "gradual acceleration took place over a very extended period of time." Both scholars reject the hypothesis of W. W. Rostow that a dramatically abrupt transition from low to high rates of change, or "take off into self-sustained economic growth," took place in the latter 1840s.

Viewing a longer segment of American history, from 1840 to 1960, Simon Kuznets has illuminated the phenomena of growth from a perspective that permits comparison with the records of a number of other countries. During that 120-year span the American population grew at an average annual rate of about 2.2 percent, GNP at 3.6 percent, output per capita at 1.6 percent, and product per worker at 1.4 percent. As a result of these growth rates, the population in 1960 was about 10.5 times as large as in 1840, the labor force almost 13 times, per capita product over 6 times, and product per worker over 5 times as large.

Surviving statistical data from the United Kingdom, France, Germany, Russia, and Japan range from 79 years for Japan to 117 years for the United Kingdom. The first result of a comparison between these countries and the United States is that the annual rate of growth of population in the latter was much higher than in any of the others. Compared with 2.2 percent in the United States, the rates of others ranged from 1.2 percent for Japan to 0.2 percent for France. Except for Japan alone, population growth rates in all the others were no more than half that of the United States.

Second, the annual rates of growth of product per capita for the United States and for the European countries were not greatly different. (The rates range from 1.9 percent for Russia, for a period reaching back to 1760, to 1.2 percent for the United Kingdom, back to 1841.) The American rate was 1.6 percent. The Japanese rate, for the period 1880–1960, was distinctly higher, 2.8 percent. Were data available to permit comparisons between the United States and these countries over the same length of time — all the way back to 1840 — the averages for the other countries would be lower, including that of Japan. Finally, the rate of growth of GNP in the United States was higher than for the European countries, by amounts ranging from one-fifth to twice as high. This result naturally follows from the fact that the United States' roughly equivalent rate of growth of per capita product was combined with a much higher rate of growth of population.

The American performance was exceptional. In his *Essay on the Principle of Population* (1798) Thomas Malthus offered a grim assessment of the consequences that would follow an increase in output. Population would respond by growing and would consume the additional output, reducing the level of living to what it had been before. The pressure of population on resources seemed relentless to Malthus, and he expected that war, pestilence, and starvation would provide the means of reducing it. American history offered testimony of a different kind: it was possible to have it both ways — more people and more resources, too. Technological advances would enable developed countries throughout the world to respond similarly to Malthus's predictions.

In the closing decades of the twentieth century the American economy, as before, alternated between periods of expansion (for example, 1963–1968, 1976–1980, 1983–) and contraction (for example, 1969–1970, 1974–1975, and 1980–1982), without, however, sinking into a deep and prolonged depression like those of the 1870s and 1930s (although some of the contractions — now called recessions — were severe, for example, those of 1974–1975 and 1980–1982). Built-in stabilizers put in place by President Franklin D. Roosevelt's New Deal in the 1930s — for example, old age and survivors' and unemployment insurance — provided cushions during periods of falling demand. The uses of monetary and fiscal policies, too, were far better understood than before.

Nevertheless, the prospects of long-term economic growth are beset by problems far more grievous than those of earlier years. Although these problems are too numerous and complex for exploration here — they include a massive federal debt, large annual budget and trade deficits, and relatively low rates of domestic saving and investment in research and development — we can single out one because of the substantial effect it exerts on economic growth.

In recent years the rate of increase in manufacturing productivity — measured as output per unit of labor and capital combined — has been slowing down. From an annual average of 3.4 percent between 1948 and 1960 the rate fell to 2.3 percent from 1966 to 1973, to 1 percent from 1973 to 1977, and to 0.4 percent between 1977 and 1978. In 1979 and 1980 growth stopped altogether and productivity actually declined. Since then small recoveries have not overcome the long-term downward trend.

The late nineteenth- and twentieth-century successor to Great Britain as the "workshop of the world," the United States now finds its competitive edge dulled in the international marketplace while at the same time faced with intensified foreign competition at home. Indeed, by 1980 foreign-made goods were competing with more than 70 percent of those manufactured in the United States. Addressing this condition, and the budget and trade problems with which it is intimately connected, will be one of the great challenges of the 1990s and beyond.

Stuart Bruchey, *The Roots of American Economic Growth: An Essay in Social Causation* (1965); Simon Kuznets, *Modern Economic Growth: Rate, Structure and Spread* (1966); Simon Kuznets, *Postwar Economic Growth: Four Lectures* (1964).

STUART BRUCHEY

See also Depressions; Government and the Economy; Industrial Revolution; Tariff.

ECONOMIC MOBILITY

See Mobility, Social and Economic.

ECONOMY

See Colonial Economy; Economic Growth; Government and the Economy; National Debt.

EDDY, MARY BAKER

(1821–1910), founder of the Christian Science church. Born near Concord, New Hampshire, Eddy was a frail, emotional woman whose first husband died six months after their marriage. She returned home and gave birth to a son, but plagued by a spinal problem, she abandoned the child (although she helped him financially as an adult). Despite her illness, Eddy in 1853 was married again, this time to a philandering, itinerant dentist whom she divorced in 1873.

Eddy recovered her health in 1862, when she was treated by Phineas Parkhurst Quimby of Portland, Maine. Quimby did not deny that illness existed but claimed that its cause was often in the mind of the sufferer. Although primarily interested in results, he wrote out his theories (calling one manuscript "Christ or Science"), which Eddy studied and copied.

Devastated when Quimby died in 1866, Eddy gradually realized she could proclaim his healing message. Estranged from her family and without financial resources, Eddy published *Science and Health* (1875), the handbook of the Christian Science movement. Asserting that mind could triumph over illness, the book made a religion of Quimby's theories, which Eddy now claimed as her own. In the 381 revisions that followed, Eddy gradually altered Quimby's teachings and linked them to portions of the Bible. She denied the reality of illness and death, claiming they were not of the "Father Mother God" who created everything. When they appeared ill, Christian Scientists were to seek help from their own practitioners, not medical doctors. (Perhaps because Eddy had bad teeth and wore glasses, she banned neither dentists nor optometrists.) A believer in demonology, Eddy blamed problems, even deaths, including that of her third husband Asa Gilbert Eddy, on the "Malicious Animal Magnetism" of former disciples.

Eddy was an inspired teacher and an energetic, effective organizer. She formed the Christian Science Association in 1876, chartered the Church of Christ (Scientist) the next year, and in 1881 the Massachusetts Metaphysical College, which granted degrees for nearly a decade. For a fee of three hundred dollars (Eddy was undoubtedly the highest paid teacher of her day) believers attended lectures and became teachers and healing practitioners. The trainees (mostly women) brought new believers to the movement, particularly after 1883 when the monthly *Journal of Christian Science* began to publicize their triumphs. Eddy, who valued good publicity, established in 1898 the weekly *Christian Science Sentinel* and in 1908 the daily *Christian Science Monitor.*

Among the most famous women in America during the last two decades of her life, she inspired loyalty in her disciples, but repeatedly clipped the wings of potential rivals. Burdened by everyday problems and harassed by defecting followers, Eddy in 1887 went into semiretirement. Relieved from routine administration, she tightened her control by creating "the Mother Church" with a self-perpetuating board of directors. Retreat made it possible for her to appear the saint her followers envisioned. Her emotional outbursts, her consulting with doctors and taking morphine to relieve the pain of kidney stones, and her paranoia were less noticed. She left the bulk of her $2.5 million estate to her church, which, despite unfavorable publicity, had grown to nearly 100,000 members.

Ernest Sutherland Bates and John V. Dittemore, *Mary Baker Eddy: The Truth and the Tradition* (1932).

OLIVE HOOGENBOOM

See also Christian Science; Religion.

EDISON, THOMAS A.

(1847–1931), inventor. Thomas Edison made a lasting mark on the daily lives of Americans by what he did and on their minds by the way he did it. From his boyhood he exemplified what they liked to believe about their society and destiny. His small-town birthplace, Milan, Ohio, was bypassed by the railroad and fell into decline, his family's fortunes with it. As a boy Edison lost much of his hearing, and his formal schooling was fragmentary. Yet he surmounted those handicaps in the Horatio Alger hero's mode of pluck and luck, peddling candy and newspapers to railroad passengers, and prefigured another hero of boys' novels, Tom Swift, by setting up a small lab for electrical experiments in a baggage car. Chance thus endowed him with the makings of a surefire myth, the equivalent of Lincoln's log cabin remodeled for the new age of exuberant technology.

Electricity, which in that day chiefly meant telegraphy, had long fascinated Edison, and his frequenting of railroad stations prompted him to make telegraphy his calling, since the range of his hearing encompassed the chatter of the instruments. Journeymen telegraphers were given to wandering, and young Edison's irrepressible tinkering, together with his taste for unnerving practical jokes, hurried him along from job to job. Thus in 1868 he arrived in Boston, the de facto capital of American science and technology, where he turned full-time inventor. The electrical shop of Charles Williams, which catered to inventors, gave him, as it did Alexander Graham Bell soon after, the facilities and skilled workmen needed to put ideas into practice. But unlike Bell, Edison in 1869 saw still greater financial opportunity in New York. There and in New Jersey over the next twenty years he astonished the world with a series of epoch-making inventions unequaled by any one individual before or since, notably his quadruplex telegraph, carbon-button telephone transmitter, phonograph, electric light, and system of electrical generation and distribution. Ultimately more than a thousand patents bore his name (though not all were primarily of his creation).

As notable a concept as any was the "invention factory" he created in the pastoral setting of Menlo Park, New Jersey, in 1876. Owing something perhaps to the Williams shop, it was a pioneering, independent, self-sustaining research and development center. Staffed with brilliant technicians and trained theoretical scientists, the Menlo Park establishment was too narrowly profit-oriented to be classed with the twentieth-century research labs of corporate giants like American Telephone & Telegraph and General Electric, with their quasi-academic ambience. On the other hand, Menlo Park, unbeholden to any established industry, was not inhibited from calling whole new industries into being. Edison was hailed as "the Wizard of Menlo Park."

Edison, however, yielded to the temptation of organizing and directing some of the new enterprises. Clumsier in entrepreneurship than in invention, distracted by the demands of management, and his inventive genius ebbing with age, Edison produced no breathtakingly fundamental inventions after the 1880s (although his team did much to develop motion pictures). Still, his persona did not fade with his performance. More than half a century after his death, his image remains incandescent in the public's memory, and his work stands as a bridge between the era of the independent inventor and that of corporate, government, and academic research and development.

Matthew Josephson, *Edison* (1959); Wyn Wachhorst, *Thomas Alva Edison: An American Myth* (1981).

ROBERT V. BRUCE

See also Science and Technology.

EDUCATION

I. Education to 1877

American education developed from European intellectual traditions and institutions transplanted to the New World and modified by contact among different colonial groups and between new settlers and indigenous peoples. Of the European groups that settled in North America, the English majority had the most influence on education. Especially in New England but increasingly throughout the thirteen colonies, the English language, laws, and customs came to define colonial educational practice. In addition, English Protestantism set the mold for colonial educational aspirations. Piety combined with devotion to vocation became the aim of education for the individual, and social perfectionism combined with an aggressive evangelicism became the aim of education for the community as a whole.

Throughout the seventeenth and eighteenth centuries, the family was the most important institution of both socialization and education. Families in the New World tended to be nuclear and patriarchal in organization, with educational relationships following scriptural prescriptions. Fathers were responsible for the education of their offspring and for that of apprentices and indentured servants living in their households. With the assistance of their wives and other relatives, they provided instruction in reading, usually from a primer or the Bible, as well as in practical skills for earning a living. They also sought to instill a sense of duty and moral rectitude through exhortation, example, and discipline. Throughout the seventeenth century and for much of the eighteenth, families fulfilled many functions: they were factories, farms, schools, religious centers, hospitals, jails, and almshouses. In consequence, education was intimately associated with most economic and social activities.

The first formal schools appeared in the 1630s. The Boston Latin School, established in 1635, is usually considered the first town-supported school with a continuous history. It established a pattern of local control that was further strengthened by passage in Massachusetts of the "old Deluder Satan Act" of 1647, which required every town of at least fifty households to hire a teacher of reading and writing and those of one hundred or more households to establish and operate a grammar school as well. Intended to advance literacy so that all could possess "knowledge of the Scriptures," the act expressed the colonists' concern to preserve learning amid the wilderness conditions of their communities.

Church-sponsored schools were organized in many of the colonies during the seventeenth century. In 1638, a school supported by the Dutch West India Company and affiliated with the Dutch Reformed Church was opened in New Amsterdam; in 1689, the Friends Public School was founded by the Quakers in Philadelphia. Schools such as these enrolled students from a variety of backgrounds and provided a free elementary education to poor children, thereby serving an important public function. Beginning in the eighteenth century, private tutors and pay-per-lesson teachers also offered instruction in such subjects as Latin, French, arithmetic, dancing, and drawing.

Schooling beyond the elementary level was available first in grammar schools and, increasingly after 1700, in private academies. The first incorporated academy was probably one planned by Benjamin Franklin and chartered in Philadelphia in 1753. Some academies were small and local; others drew students from a wide area and taught a broad curriculum, which could include Latin, Greek, arithmetic, English, the modern languages, algebra, history, and the practical arts of navigation, agriculture, surveying, and pedagogy. Some academies were coeducational; others served only one sex. Although a few public high schools were opened before the Civil War, private academies were the predominant mode of postelementary education for both sexes.

Although the initial institutional infrastructure of American education was in evidence by the time of the Revolution, the establishment of the new nation had a significant impact on the purposes and content of education. Because the welfare of the new Republic would depend on the loyalty, vision, and skill of its citizens, the teaching of "republican virtues" now became a central goal. This new purpose was evident in the texts used in the common schools, which described George Washington and others of the nation's statesmen in heroic terms. It was evident as well in a new emphasis on teaching American pronunciation and spelling, people widely concurring in Noah Webster's claim that "as an independent nation, our honor requires us to have a system of our own, in language as well as government." And it was evident, finally, in the new importance assigned to the education of young women, who were now recognized as "republican mothers" to whom would fall the responsibility for instructing the next generation in the civic virtues deemed essential to the national welfare. Education after the Revolution increasingly became for many Americans the preferred instrument of social policy.

Almost all the half million African-Americans in the colonies at the time of the Revolution were slaves. In a few instances, religious groups established schools for them. One of the earliest was sponsored by the Church of England's Society for the Propagation of the Gospel in New York City, where between 1704 and 1722 a minister named Elias Neau taught school three times a week for Indians, poor whites, and blacks. Because the Quakers opposed slavery, they tended to be the most outspoken advocates of freedom and education for African-Americans. Led by Anthony Benezet, they organized the Philadelphia African School in 1782, separate African free schools thereafter appearing in other cities as well. The Boston public schools were the first to be integrated by law in 1855. Although generally denied schooling, enslaved blacks in the South sometimes managed to learn to read and write. Despite ever-more-stringent slave codes, which made it illegal to teach blacks reading and writing, whites sometimes provided instruction. In addition, slaves taught themselves to read from primers, Bibles, and books stolen or borrowed from white owners, and literacy skills acquired earlier through the teaching of Quaker and Anglican missionaries continued to be transmitted covertly within slave quarter communities from one generation to another. Thus, roughly 5 percent of the slave population was literate at the time of the Civil War.

During the first half of the nineteenth century, the percentage of white children enrolled in school increased dramatically. Although school going had been widespread in New England among both boys and girls by the end of the colonial period, now the practice spread throughout the Midwest. (Public schooling existed but did not become generally available in the South until the end of the nineteenth century.) Aggregate national school enrollment rates for whites between the ages of five and nineteen rose from 35 percent in 1830 to 50.4 percent in 1850 and 61.1 percent in 1870.

Increased school enrollments derived from the establishment of common schools in newly settled regions as well as the founding of more and more academies throughout the nation. Because the proportion of the population that was foreign-born increased dramatically, half of New York City's residents by 1855 were foreign-born and the percentages were also high in other urban areas. Combined with increasingly evident differences between social classes, these circumstances prompted some to argue that more schooling was needed to eradicate foreign influences and to inculcate the training necessary for economic productivity and democratic self-discipline.

At the same time, a number of technological and economic developments made it possible to support more schools and to serve more students for longer periods of time. New printing methods made textbooks relatively inexpensive to produce. Combined with sales techniques adopted from the pamphlet distribution campaigns of evangelical Protestant organizations like the American Tract Society, these economies made it possible to disseminate schoolbooks much more widely than before. More important, young women eager for a measure of independence and some relief from domestic life between their years as daughters and their years as wives were ready to staff the nation's proliferating schoolrooms. They were presumed by "nature" to be suited to teaching and, owing to a lack of other opportunities for paid work outside the home, they were willing to work for low wages. As a result, they provided an inexpensive pool of labor to staff the enlarging educational apparatus. The number of male teachers in Massachusetts decreased 44.3 percent between the 1830s and the 1880s while the number of female teachers increased 156.3 percent. Female teachers in Massachusetts during this period were paid less than half of what male teachers made.

Finally, the antebellum extension of public schooling was encouraged by one of the most popular reform campaigns of the nineteenth century — the so-called common school movement. Actually a congeries of distinct but affiliated state campaigns, the common school movement involved shifting coalitions of men and women, most of them Congregationalists or Presbyterians, Whig by political persuasion, and professional by occupation. Horace Mann, Catharine Beecher, and Henry Barnard were among the best-known leaders of the campaign.

Common school reformers, who often referred to themselves as the "friends of education," favored the extension of elementary schooling to all white children. To achieve that goal, they lobbied for public control of schools, with state authorities assuming increasing responsibility for the support and oversight of local common schools; and they advocated the improvement of teaching through the establishment of normal schools and other institutions of teacher training. In line with Whig advocacy of increasing industrialization, they argued that schooling was necessary for the economic development of the nation, thereby inaugurating the now traditional argument that school reform and economic prosperity were related. In addition, they claimed that common schooling would foster equality between social classes and prevent "intemperance, avarice, war, slavery, [and] bigotry." Relying upon millennialist rhetoric familiar to nineteenth-century audiences, common school reformers formulated the arguments necessary to make the extension of schooling a popular cause. By the time of the Civil War, schools had been established where they had not existed before, and their calendars, curricula, and finances had been regularized. Thanks to the efforts of the friends of education, an increasing number of state legislatures authorized the creation of state boards of education, and this significantly advanced the systematization of education under public auspices, even though the early boards had little power beyond the authority to gather and publish information.

The antebellum period was also one of college founding. By 1831, 46 colleges were listed in the *American Almanac;* by 1850, 119 were listed by the census; and by 1876, 356 colleges and universities were listed by the U.S. Bureau of Education. More important, since only some 5 percent of the population attended college, the antebellum period marked the zenith of the lyceum, where adults could hear lectures on history, science, and literature from the likes of Ralph Waldo Emerson, and of the agriculture fair and exposition, which brought information about new seeds, techniques of animal husbandry, and methods for canning and baking to towns and villages across the United States. Newspapers proliferated now and were filled with practical advice on farming and homemaking for rural families and with international and national news organized, written, and commented upon by editors like Horace Greeley who saw themselves as educating their readers about the pressing issues of their day.

Institutions such as these were vital in extending and reinforcing the instruction offered to children in the nation's schools. Although the Civil War brought an end to the easy mix of culture, entertainment, and education that had marked the early national period, that mix had established very high levels of literacy among the white male and female populations of the United States. According to the census, the literacy rate among the white adult population was about 90 percent in 1860, a rate higher than that of Scotland, Germany, England, France, Ireland, or Italy.

During the Civil War, schooling was disrupted for many whites, and many schools, especially in the South, were destroyed; but the war also inspired the founding of schools for blacks even before the Emancipation Proclamation of 1863 and the establishment of the Freedmen's Bureau in 1865. After the war, northern philanthropists joined with federal agencies to open additional schools, and blacks in local communities across the former slave states banded together to organize and operate their own Sabbath schools and "native schools." Understanding the degree to which educational deprivation had been a mark of enslavement, newly freed blacks were eager for learning. By the 1870s, about a quarter of school-age ex-slaves were enrolled in public schools, and many more attended intermittent classes held elsewhere. As white planters regained control of state governments, however, the educational gains of the Reconstruction era were brought to an end. For blacks more than for any group in the United States, equality in and through education remained an elusive goal.

Lawrence A. Cremin, *American Education: The Colonial Experience, 1607–1783* (1970) and *American Education:*

The National Experience, 1783–1876 (1980); Carl F. Kaestle, *Pillars of the Republic: Common Schools and American Society, 1780–1860* (1983).

ELLEN CONDLIFFE LAGEMANN

See also Beecher, Catharine; Crandall, Prudence; Freedmen's Bureau; Lyceums; Mann, Horace; McGuffey's *Reader*.

II. Education since 1877

By the 1870s, public schools had been established throughout the United States. During the next fifty years, however, there was a movement toward more schooling for more students. In part, this was a result of the development of public high schools. Although such schools had existed since the early nineteenth century, they began to enroll a significant proportion of young people only at the turn of the century. In 1890, 4 percent of the nation's youth between fourteen and seventeen years of age enrolled in school, a figure that rose by 1930 to 47 percent. Reflecting the realization that schooling was an alternative to early employment, the social worker Florence Kelley observed that the most effective compulsory education law was a child labor law. By 1918, all states had some form of compulsory school attendance.

At the same time that schooling was being extended upward, it was moving downward to encompass more and more young children. Never constant, the age of school entry declined as kindergartens were added to an increasing number of school systems. Developed by the Prussian educator Friedrich Froebel, kindergartens were intended to teach children between the ages of three and seven to work, to cooperate with one another, and to appreciate the spiritual unity of all things. Kindergartens spread rapidly in the United States. Initially operating under private auspices, the first kindergarten that was part of a public school system was opened by Susan Blow in St. Louis, Missouri, in 1873; more than four thousand kindergartens were in operation by 1898. Acceptance of the idea of early childhood education programs was encouraged by such influential American educators as the psychologist G. Stanley Hall, who was a critical figure in the child study movement that began in the 1890s, and the psychologist and philosopher John Dewey, whose early writings focused attention on the need to organize schools in harmony with the interests and capacities of children. At a time of significant immigration and heightened concern with urban poverty, early childhood education became a favorite project of many philanthropic organizations and social settlements.

The increasing school going that resulted from the development of high schools and kindergartens was associated with a trend toward greater comprehensiveness in the purposes schools were expected to serve. Nowhere was this more evident than in reports published by the National Education Association (NEA) about high school curricula. Defined in 1893 as primarily college preparatory institutions that should offer students a rigorous academic core curriculum, high schools had become multifunctional institutions by 1918. In that year, the NEA's *Cardinal Principles of Secondary Education* argued that high schools should provide instruction in seven basic areas: health, family life, vocation, citizenship, the worthy use of leisure time, ethical character, and "fundamental processes" like reading and writing. As high schools broadened in purpose, students began to be divided into academic and vocational tracks, depending on apparent ability and career expectation. Guidance, which often involved the use of newly developed intelligence tests, became a school function distinct from teaching. During the years between 1890 and 1930, the junior high school was also developed as an institution, one of its primary purposes being to provide the testing and counseling necessary to place youngsters in the tracks or streams they would follow throughout their high school years.

At the turn of the century, a trend toward centralizing the control of schooling emerged. Centralization developed at several levels. It was first evident in the governance of city school systems. Typically, coalitions of professionals and "good government" reformers lobbied for the organization of central boards of education. They were to replace or supervise local boards and be responsible for overseeing school construction, teacher recruitment and promotion, and pupil progress. Although presented as a corrective to inefficiency and graft, centralization often served to consolidate the power of old established urban elites who were being increasingly challenged by large numbers of newly arrived immigrants. A study of changes in school governance in twenty-eight cities between 1870 and 1920 found that as local school boards were superseded by central agencies, wage earners lost representation (they were not represented on central boards), and professional groups and businessmen gained representation.

Centralization of control increased within school buildings at this time, too. One could see this in the growth of supervisory positions. Between 1890 and 1920, for example, the number of supervisors in the Boston public schools increased from 7 to 159; in New York City, from 235 to 1,310; and in Cleveland, from 10 to 159. As supervision became a function separate from teaching, teachers lost some of their autonomy. Questions about curriculum, schedules, and standards were increasingly dealt with in "the central office."

Throughout the first decades of the century, however, many teachers continued to work in rural schools, where they remained in charge of their own classrooms; sometimes, too, a classroom still served as a one-room school. Generally young (twenty-five was the average age of teachers in 1910), female, and native-born, such teachers had typically finished four years of school beyond the elementary level and received salaries of five hundred dollars a year. Many left teaching to marry; of those who remained, some stayed in the same classroom throughout their careers.

If centralization was far more evident in urban than in rural areas, centralization at the national level touched all areas. This was a result of the establishment of new institutions that were concerned with questions of educational policy nationwide. In the early years of the twentieth century, for example, newly chartered philanthropic foundations like the Carnegie Foundation for the Advancement of Teaching began to set standards for the curriculum and for student promotion and graduation. Although

foundations did not have the power to enforce standards, many schools adopted them voluntarily in order to obtain foundation grants. Increasingly, too, national testing organizations like the Educational Testing Service and the College Board fostered reliance upon national standards, in the process themselves becoming centralizing agencies in education.

The establishment of national testing and standardizing agencies and many other turn-of-the-century developments in schooling were related to the growing faith in and reliance upon science. During the early years of the century, scholars such as Edward L. Thorndike at Teachers College, Columbia University, and Charles Hubbard Judd at the University of Chicago took the lead in developing the field of educational psychology, which was, in turn, a central component in the newly emerging science of education. Such a science was necessary to the professionalization of the proliferating specialized fields that emerged with the extension of schooling — for example, curriculum, guidance, educational administration. It became an important part of teacher training and was essential to the development of testing and the "scientific management" of schools. Belief in science was a hallmark of the progressive movement in education, as was advocacy of centralization, an expansionist view of school functions, and a preference for more child-centered pedagogies. The progressive school reformers were responsible for many of the educational innovations institutionalized between 1870 and 1920.

In the South, the progressive movement perpetuated and helped justify the separate and unequal schools that had developed for blacks and whites. Despite post–Civil War Radical dreams for universal schooling, the tax-supported common school systems established by Reconstruction governments were segregated by race and separated by significant disparities in financing, facilities, and curricula. Subsequently, the progressive campaign for increased school funding and broadened school curricula, led by northern businessmen, philanthropists, religious leaders, and professionals working in collaboration with their white counterparts in the South, sanctioned these arrangements. Convinced that education meant economic progress, the progressive coalition in the South advocated vocational training for blacks and gained significant financial support for vocational programs from northern philanthropic foundations like the Rockefellers' General Education Board, the Phelps-Stokes Fund, and the Peabody and Slater funds. Although they were successful in securing increased funding and improved facilities for schools, the progressives did not succeed in lessening the disparities between white and black schools. Thus, while school appropriations rose in every southern state between 1900 and 1930, gaps between the amounts available for whites and blacks widened. Equally important, while curricula for whites broadened to include both vocational and academic subjects, curricula for blacks tended to narrow, jettisoning earlier aspirations to academic excellence and focusing almost exclusively on vocational and character training.

The trend toward increasing school enrollment that began in the 1870s continued throughout most of the twentieth century. Indeed, in the fifty years after World War I, enrollments in schools and colleges tripled while the total population doubled. Although the Great Depression resulted in a narrowing of school curricula and unemployment for many teachers, it facilitated increases in school attendance; and although World War II caused temporary enrollment declines among men of high school and college age, it was followed by steady gains in school attendance. As a result of growing demand the late 1940s and the 1950s were periods of national shortages in education with teachers and classrooms both in short supply.

From the 1940s through the 1960s, the nation's schools were often involved in divisive public questions concerning the rights of minorities, the nature of citizenship, and the implementation of democratic ideals. Many of these questions were litigated in cases that made their way to the U.S. Supreme Court. At issue were the use of public moneys in parochial schools and the legality of school prayers, which concerned the separation of church and state, and cases focusing on racial segregation, which, after separate schools were ruled inherently unequal

in *Brown* v. *Board of Education of Topeka* (1954), addressed the problem of what remedies were required to overcome de jure and de facto segregation.

The role the Supreme Court played in educational policy from the 1940s on (some observers called the Court a national school board) foreshadowed a generally more prominent role for the federal government in the formulation and implementation of educational policy. Although questions of religion and race long delayed legislation directing federal aid to the nation's public schools, the Elementary and Secondary Education Act was finally passed in 1965. Known as ESEA, the act provided assistance to school districts with large numbers of disadvantaged students, thereby advancing the educational strategy essential to President Lyndon Johnson's War on Poverty. It also helped establish enduring expectations concerning the responsibility of the federal government to support education. While some believed this responsibility should be assumed by the government's providing financial aid to the states and localities, others believed it should be fulfilled through personal advocacy. President Ronald Reagan argued the latter position in the 1980s, as did Secretary of Education William J. Bennett. However the role was defined, the emergence of federal involvement was one of the most important post–World War II developments in education.

The expectation that schooling should fulfill crucial public functions sometimes led to significant shifts in policy. For example, a wave of school reform swept the nation after the Soviet Union launched *Sputnik*, the first earth satellite, in 1957. In response to fears that the Soviets were ahead of the United States in science and engineering and might therefore win the cold war, schools were asked to teach more mathematics and science, often using materials and pedagogies designed with the most gifted students in mind. Similarly, as the U.S. economy floundered in the late 1970s and early 1980s and Japanese businesses outpaced their American counterparts, there was a new perception of crisis, which was dramatized by the 1983 report, *A Nation at Risk*. Having shifted toward more egalitarian goals after the alarm over *Sputnik* waned, school reformers now returned to the earlier emphasis on high levels of academic achievement and special attention to the gifted, and an "excellence" movement emerged again. Illustrating the fluctuation that had characterized education policy since 1945, however, concern shifted once again in the middle 1980s, with some attention being directed to the problems of poverty, homelessness, and drug addiction that made school achievement difficult. Increasingly, too, there were efforts both to increase local control of schools through school-based management and to foster parent involvement through school-choice plans. Long established as the social institution Americans looked upon to foster economic progress, promote equality, and address urgent social problems, by the late 1980s the public schools were overwhelmed with the tasks thrust upon them.

Marvin Lazerson, ed., *American Education in the Twentieth Century: A Documentary History* (1987); David B. Tyack, *The One Best System: A History of American Urban Education* (1974).

ELLEN CONDLIFFE LAGEMANN

See also Brown v. *Board of Education of Topeka;* Chautauqua Movement; Dewey, John; Great Society; Kelley, Florence; Philanthropy; Progressivism; Racial Desegregation; Segregation; Settlement Houses.

III. Higher Education

American higher education, which provides the widest access to postsecondary education in the world, is a decentralized system of public and private institutions coordinated by informal means. Through a combination of growth and pluralism, the system has responded slowly, but surely, to changes in American society.

The country's first college, Harvard (founded in 1636), was an institution of the Protestant Reformation and combined civic and religious functions within a theocratic Puritan society. It was supported primarily by the colony and gifts, along with some student charges. Civic and religious leaders were its overseers. The college offered a liberal education in order to pro-

vide learned ministers for the colony. They studied Latin, Greek, and largely Aristotelian philosophy in a pious environment that included twice-daily church services. The founding of the College of William and Mary (1693) by Anglicans and of Yale College (1701) by Connecticut Congregationalists repeated the model of a Reformation college.

This mold was broken when the College of New Jersey (later Princeton) was chartered in 1746. As a Presbyterian college in what was now a religiously mixed society, it adopted a policy of toleration. All the colonial colleges soon conformed to this approach. On the eve of the American Revolution nine colleges were instructing 731 students, almost half of them at Harvard and Yale.

By that date the American college had assumed an enduring form. Students were admitted whenever they acquired sufficient skills in Latin and Greek, and they went through four years of study as a unified class. The first two years were heavily devoted to Latin and Greek, and the third and fourth included a sampling of philosophy (metaphysics, ethics, logic), history, and natural science. The curriculum grew more secular over time with the inclusion of science, especially Newtonian mechanics. The chief practical emphasis was public speaking or oratory. The students were taught largely by tutors, themselves recent graduates who stayed with a class all four years. Each new college sought to construct a hall where students and tutors could live and attend class. The elites of colonial society sent their sons to the colleges, but there were also some poorer students, typically the sons of farmers who had been trained by local ministers. College was seen as preparation for the professions and for careers in public life.

Independence set off a new wave of college foundings. North Carolina and Georgia led the way in establishing state institutions, but the denominational college remained the dominant form. Even the strongest provincial colleges, like Harvard and Yale, soon lost their territorial monopoly and their public subsidies. In 1819 the Supreme Court decision in the *Dartmouth College* case secured private colleges against state interference. This did nothing to help state institu-

Colonial Colleges

Date	Original Name	Religious Affiliation	Name Today
1636	Harvard College	Congregational	Same
1693	College of William and Mary in Virginia	Anglican	College of William and Mary
1701	Yale College	Congregational	Same
1746	College of New Jersey	Presbyterian	Princeton University
1751	Philadelphia Academy[a]	Nonsectarian	University of Pennsylvania
1754	King's College	Nonsectarian (Anglican direction)	Columbia University
1764	Rhode Island College	Baptist	Brown University
1766	Queen's College	Dutch Reformed	Rutgers University
1769	Dartmouth College	Congregational	Same

a. Founded in 1740 as the Academie and Charitable School of the Province of Pennsylvania; chartered as a college in 1755.

Note: A number of other colleges and universities (including the University of Delaware, Dickinson College, St. John's College, and Washington and Lee) claim a prerevolutionary date, but they were founded as secondary schools and did not become colleges until considerably later. Only those listed above were established as colleges before 1776.

tions. The competition from denominational colleges, refracted through statehouse politics, deprived them of public support, with few exceptions, until well after the Civil War.

The tenor of American higher education changed after 1800. The ideas unleashed by the French Revolution — rationalism, atheism, radical republicanism — were anathema to the conservative clergymen who governed the denominational colleges. Their fears were exacerbated by a wave of student riots, and they responded by strengthening discipline and avoiding current intellectual concerns.

In the two generations before the Civil War higher education lost its sense of purpose. The dead languages on which it concentrated, Greek and Latin, were neither taught well nor learned competently. Classical civilization and literature were ignored; instead, random excerpts from classical authors were translated as examples of grammar. New subjects had to be squeezed into the last two years of the curriculum and were treated with extreme superficiality. Since all members of a class took the same courses — a cardinal principle — neither specialization nor advanced study was possible.

Dissatisfaction abounded, but efforts to introduce serious scholarship or to establish degree courses in the sciences made little progress. Responding to such initiatives, the Yale Report of 1828 gave a magisterial defense of the classical curriculum. It argued that expanding the powers of the mind through mental discipline was the chief goal of college and that this could best be accomplished by studying Latin and Greek. Acquiring knowledge (the "furniture of the mind") was relegated to a subordinate role — advanced learning had no place in the American college.

These arguments would stand for another generation, but the rigidity of the old-time college owed more to its acceptance by the elites of American society. They considered a college education to be an emblem of the professional classes and saw little reason for change. In eastern cities, at least, attending college remained an exclusive privilege: New York City, with 500,000 people, had two colleges that enrolled 241 students in 1846. Paradoxically, colleges were far more popular near the frontier.

Denominational colleges continued to proliferate as the country expanded westward. Local boosters, eager to enhance the reputations of their towns, and perhaps their land values, promoted colleges; and they were assisted by the zeal of competing denominations. By 1860 there were 217 colleges in the country, 60 percent of them in the Midwest or Southwest. Most were small, impecunious, and faithful to the classical curriculum. Although only 1 percent of white males attended, their proliferation indicated a degree of popular support.

Away from the population centers, where most colleges were located, they served a variety of purposes. Their preparatory classes provided considerable local education, and the colleges themselves gave rural people the verbal skills needed for urban occupations. Their spread kept American higher education open and growing.

The monopoly of the old-time college was slightly diminished in the generation before the Civil War. At Harvard and Yale separate "scientific schools" were established to teach subjects that did not fit into the classical curriculum. Yale awarded the first American Ph.D.'s in 1861, and the University of Michigan under Henry Tappan modernized its curriculum, introducing a scientific degree and a master's degree. Similar efforts by Francis Wayland at Brown failed, however.

After the Civil War, the principal types of higher education took form: agricultural colleges, institutes of technology, colleges for women, and universities appeared. The old-time colleges became liberal arts colleges. One of the critics of the latter, Congressman Justin Morrill of Vermont, felt that the country needed education for the "industrial classes," those who were engaged in the productive economy. In 1862 he sponsored the Morrill Land Grant Act, which gave each state land to support a college that would teach agriculture and the mechanical arts but "without excluding other scientific and classical studies." The Morrill Act had two profound effects. It created a nationwide network of state-sponsored colleges and universities, and by stipulating that both practical and academic subjects be taught, it united them in the same institutions. Such parity did not occur in European universities, nor had it been attempted at Harvard or Yale. By linking university education with the productive economy, this forced marriage contributed greatly to the relevance and expansiveness of American higher education. Before 1890, however, the land-grant colleges were struggling institutions that received little help from their states, so that initially they did not appreciably widen access to higher education, as is commonly believed.

The curricular reformation of the college was led by President Charles W. Eliot of Harvard (1869–1909). From the outset of his presidency he began to dismantle the classical curriculum, emphasizing and expanding elective courses. The new system allowed students to follow their interests and aptitudes; it undermined the old pedagogy based on memorization and recitation; and most important, it encouraged scholarship by allowing faculty to specialize and offer advanced courses. Eliot was also responsible for reforming professional education. The Harvard schools of law and medicine employed full-time faculties and required entering students to be college graduates.

In 1876 came another momentous development: Johns Hopkins University became the country's first institution to emphasize research and graduate education, in imitation of the universities of Germany. Its success in fostering advanced learning was a direct challenge to higher education, and American universities took up the challenge in the 1890s. The decade began with the appearance of new models of research universities in Stanford (1891), Chicago (1892), and a rejuvenated Columbia. But the form that the American university would eventually take was typified by Harvard. There the senior faculty of the college also served as the graduate faculty of arts and sciences — graduate education and research in the American university would be built upon the undergraduate college. From 1890 to World War I, a rapid growth in undergraduate enrollment allowed both private and state universities to enlarge their faculties, add professional schools, and cultivate scholarship and research.

During this age, what a contemporary called the fourteen "great American universities" enrolled one of every five students. They established standards for admissions and curricula that other institutions were obliged to meet. But for all their scholarly ambitions, the universities remained beholden to their undergraduate colleges for income, whether from tuition, state appropriations, or alumni gifts. The undergraduates, in turn, were more attracted by extracurricular activities than by the advanced electives offered by their professors. From the 1890s to the 1920s undergraduates were increasingly concerned with athletics and the social side of college life.

After World War I the private universities found it desirable to limit their growth and instituted a process of selective admissions based upon social as well as academic criteria. The "Ivy League" schools became more socially exclusive. State universities, on the other hand, continued to expand, and new types of institutions grew even more rapidly. During the 1920s normal schools were upgraded to postsecondary teachers' colleges in most states. They were joined by public junior colleges, which made the first two years of college available locally. In cities, too, some colleges and universities began to cater to large numbers of students on a part-time basis; such students were likely to study vocational courses like business. Much of the growth of American higher education resulted from nonaffluent students who were seeking to move ahead socially and occupationally.

This diversity among institutions allowed higher education to serve a growing portion of the population. In 1890 about 3 percent of the age group attended college. From then until World War I, rates of college attendance roughly doubled and then doubled again between the wars. Because of population growth, actual enrollments increased almost tenfold between 1890 and 1940.

Growth accelerated after World War II, aided by the G.I. bill. In 1948 the number of federally supported ex-servicemen studying was equal to the total enrollment of 1940. When this wave subsided in the early 1950s, a fourth of young Americans were attending college, a level two-thirds higher than that of 1940.

The most far-reaching change of the postwar era was large-scale federal funding of university research. During the interwar years the universities had become accustomed to receiving support for research from private foundations, but during World War II the government sponsored research on campus and continued these projects after 1945. This support dwarfed that available before the war. The new research funding came from federal agencies for purposes related to their particular missions rather than to further the growth of academic knowledge. Despite university complaints, this system did not change until after the Soviets launched *Sputnik* in 1957. Then the need to match the achievements of Soviet science galvanized the government into investing vast resources in graduate education and university research. The National Institutes of Health and the National Science Foundation surpassed the Department of Defense and the Atomic Energy Commission as the largest federal funders of academic science, and the emphasis shifted markedly to disinterested basic research. Funds were also abundant for research facilities and institutional support. These commitments peaked in the late 1960s, the golden age for university science.

The number of students more than doubled during the 1960s. Much of this growth was achieved by the expansion of state systems and especially by the proliferation of community colleges. The high priority given to higher education by state and federal lawmakers, and by the public generally, brought prosperity but not contentment to American campuses.

The first disturbances occurred over the integration of southern universities early in the 1960s. The first black student at the University of Mississippi had to be protected by federal marshals and riots greeted the first at both Mississippi and the University of Georgia. Georgia Tech, however, succeeded in integrating peacefully. Black students established only a token presence at southern universities during the 1960s, but those pioneers paved the way for significant numbers in the 1970s.

Students for a Democratic Society (SDS), the first New Left group, composed its theoretical manifesto, the Port Huron Statement, in 1962; the free speech movement rocked Berkeley in 1964; and by 1966 the anti–Vietnam War movement was a fixture on campuses. The resulting turmoil caused an internal revolution: colleges and universities abandoned almost all control over the personal lives of their students. This reversed a fundamental tenet of American higher education — that college residence should explicitly shape the moral development of students. Politically, the student rebellion increasingly looked beyond the campus, opposing the war and the "establishment" and championing its own conception of social justice. The conflict that closed Columbia in the spring of 1968 touched off a cycle of violent confrontations. In 1970 National Guardsmen at Kent State in Ohio fired into a crowd of students, killing four, and police at Jackson State in Mississippi fired into a dormitory, killing two, the worst atrocities in American academic history.

The changed national mood of the sixties in and toward higher education marked the end of fiscal expansion. Retrenchment became the watchword of the 1970s as institutions faced mounting costs and inflation. Providing greater access to underprivileged and underrepresented groups displaced research and graduate education as the nation's top priority. The centerpiece of this effort was the 1972 legislation that established a federally funded system of need-based student aid. With financial help available and local campuses proliferating, virtually all qualified individuals had at least the opportunity for postsecondary study, even though social, cultural, and economic factors continued to affect who would actually attend. In 1970 women constituted 40 percent of all students — the same proportion as in 1910. But by the end of the decade they had become the majority.

After 1975 American higher education for the first time ceased to exhibit meaningful growth. These steady-state conditions promise to persist until early in the twenty-first century, but the times have not been unkind to higher education. The dominant theme has been privatization. Public funding of higher education has had a low priority, and the strongest institutions financially have been those able to increase revenues through higher tuitions and fund-raising. Federal student aid has survived repeated challenges but nevertheless has lost some value to inflation. These trends have reinforced the quality differences inherent within the system. Private industry has been the fastest expanding funder of university research, but the universities themselves and governments have also sought to mobilize academic science to sharpen the competitiveness of American industry.

Higher education now touches the lives of at least half of American young people. Colleges and universities are gatekeepers to desirable occupations. Their prominence makes them a target for critics who would have them transform the culture, values, and social patterns of American society. The system of higher education, however, reflects both the strengths and the weaknesses of American society. The national reluctance to raise taxes has been compensated for by a vibrant and diverse nonprofit sector. The low value placed on academic attainment, which affects the preparation and performance of college students, has not hindered the development of the world's finest system of graduate education and research. The decentralized, pluralistic character of the system has allowed diverse institutions to respond to different social needs. American higher education offers students, more fully than any other country, opportunities throughout their lifetimes, and despite inefficiencies and an ineluctable need for improvement, it manages better than most to provide personal fulfillment for individuals and the skills demanded by a productive economy.

Roger L. Geiger, *To Advance Knowledge: The Growth of American Research Universities, 1900–1940* (1986); Frederick Rudolph, *The American College and University: A History* (1962); Laurence R. Veysey, *The Emergence of the American University* (1965).

ROGER L. GEIGER

See also Dartmouth College v. *Woodward;* G.I. Bill; History and Historians; Hutchins, Robert Maynard; Kent State Incident; Morrill Land Grant Act; New Left; Racial Desegregation; Social Sciences; Student Non-Violent Coordinating Committee; Students for a Democratic Society.

IV. Women's Education

The state of women's education in America has always reflected public attitudes toward learning in general and women in particular. In colonial times, formal learning had a low priority. Girls' education typically took place at home, where they learned to perform household tasks and, occasionally, to read. Apprenticeship provided vocational training in housewifery. Indenture contracts might specify that apprentices be taught "to reade the English tongue." Only a minority of girls attended New England's primary schools or the dame schools that also taught children to read. Few girls learned writing or arithmetic, and only the daughters of the well-to-do had access to further education. By the mid-eighteenth century, young women in cities might attend "adventure schools," some of which taught academic subjects, such as writing, geography, or French. Most offered an array of "accomplishments," such as drawing, enameling, and fancy needlework.

Late in the century, Quaker and Moravian schools established "female departments." But few colonial women had access to any formal schooling, and female literacy lagged behind that of men. At the end of the colonial era, less than half of the women in New England, the most educationally advanced of the colonies, could sign their names on wills, compared to 80 percent of the men. Female literacy elsewhere, measured by their ability to sign their names, was even lower. An indeterminate number of women probably learned to read but not to write.

In the wake of the American Revolution, interest in women's education rose among the elite, and the first "female academies," modeled on private secondary schools for boys, appeared. The new academies were strongly defended by their proponents. Girls' education, said Connecticut school founder Sarah Pierce, would "vindicate the equality of female intellect," and Massachusetts essayist Judith Sargent Murray argued that education would inculcate "elevation of soul" and "reverence of self." Benjamin Rush, a trustee of the Young Ladies Academy in Philadelphia (1787), stressed women's family roles in the new Republic. Academic training, he said, would make women better wives and household managers, and as mothers, they would teach their sons "the principles of liberty and government."

During the early nineteenth century, advances in women's education narrowed the literacy gap between men and women. A major step toward female literacy was the rise of public primary schools, or common schools. Boys and girls learned reading, writing, and arithmetic in these mostly one-room institutions, with seating segregated by sex. More boys than girls attended, and enrollment and literacy rates varied by region. At mid-century in New England, 81 percent of boys under twenty attended some sort of school, and 75.7 percent of girls. Only 3.6 percent of white women were illiterate, about the same proportion as among men. In the southeastern states, less than half of the northern proportions of school-age persons attended school, and 23 percent of white women could not read or write, nor 14 percent of white men. Literacy rates among free blacks were far lower and similarly skewed by region, though not by gender.

Female academies also multiplied rapidly in the early nineteenth century. Typically, these were boarding schools that catered to the daughters of the emerging middle class. They offered a combination of primary and secondary schooling, plus religious training and the accomplishments. Some, like the school that Sarah Pierce opened in her home in 1792, won widespread reputations; by 1827, her Litchfield Female Academy was enrolling over one hundred students each year from around the Northeast and farther afield.

The antebellum female seminary, a more advanced institution than the academy, admitted older students who could pass examinations. Scorning the classes in accomplishments, seminaries adopted features of the male college curriculum such as classics and sciences. Some of the leading women educators and their seminaries included Emma Willard, Troy Seminary (1821); Catharine Beecher, Hartford Seminary (1823); Zilpah Grant, Ipswich Seminary (1828); and Mary Lyon, the influential Mount Holyoke Seminary (1837).

Although Willard's proposal in 1819 that the New York legislature fund advanced education for women never made headway, academies and seminaries won community support. Their graduates helped make teaching a women's profession. At Mount Holyoke, a model for many other schools, alumnae often became teachers. Many Troy Seminary graduates taught in the common schools and founded some two hundred on the Troy plan. Catharine Beecher mounted a campaign in the 1840s to send eastern teachers to staff new schools in western towns. By 1860, three out of four teachers in Massachusetts were women, and by the end of the century, women predominated as schoolteachers nationwide.

In the late nineteenth century, public secondary education expanded women's opportunities. The first public high school for girls opened in Worcester, Massachusetts, in 1824 and several more appeared in New England and New York. To distinguish themselves from academies, girls' high schools tested applicants for entrance and gave regular examinations. Their two-to-four-year-course of study featured English, languages, algebra, history, and science. At mid-century, single-sex schools gave way to less costly coeducational public high schools. In 1850 there were under 80 such schools, in 1870, 170, and in 1900, 6,005. By 1920, students attended over 14,000 public high schools and some 2,000 private secondary schools, usually single-sex institutions.

From 1870 on, the majority of high school graduates were female, and by 1900, girls outnumbered boys in private secondary schools and far outnumbered them in public high schools. The proportion of the school-age population that attended secondary school surged upward, rising from 2 percent in 1870 to 17 percent in 1920. The growing number of women high school graduates provided a labor pool for schoolteaching and new white-collar jobs in offices.

The expansion of secondary education for women nurtured demands for higher education. The first women college students had been accepted in 1837 at Oberlin College in Ohio; they enrolled in a "female department" and received special degrees. Antioch (1852) also accepted women. After the Civil War, an era of college founding began. Excluded from the older elite male colleges like Harvard, Yale, Brown, and Columbia, many women attended the new women's institutions. The first, Vassar (1865), was followed by Wellesley (1875), Smith (1875),

Bryn Mawr (1884), and a number of others. Bryn Mawr's first president, M. Carey Thomas, became the most prominent woman educator of this era. Mount Holyoke attained collegiate status in 1888. A pioneer black women's college, Spelman in Atlanta, opened in 1881 as a seminary. New coordinate colleges, single-sex schools affiliated with men's universities, included Barnard at Columbia (1889) and Radcliffe at Harvard (1894).

The rapid expansion of higher education in the late nineteenth century also provided coeducational options. Since male enrollment did not keep pace with the founding of new colleges, many of these institutions welcomed women. Some women attended Swarthmore (1864), Boston University (1873), Stanford (1885), and the University of Chicago (1892). The largest number of women college students, however, attended state universities, which were fostered by the Morrill Land Grant Act of 1862. By 1870, eight state universities in the West and Midwest admitted women, and Cornell (1865) accepted them in 1872. Black institutions founded in the late 1860s, such as Howard University, were also coeducational. By 1900, over one hundred coeducational colleges and universities had been founded.

As higher education expanded, women's proportion of the college population rose swiftly. In 1870, when 1 percent of college-age Americans attended college, 21 percent of these were women. In 1910, 5 percent of college-age people attended, 40 percent of them women. These figures caused concern. In 1873, Dr. Edward Clarke, a Harvard trustee, had contended that higher education would ruin women's health and reproductive capacity. Then after women proved able to survive their college years, the "marriage question" arose. According to statistics gathered at the end of the nineteenth century, fewer women college graduates married, and those who did bore fewer children than their less-educated peers. This disparity did not end until well into the twentieth century, when college attracted far larger numbers of women. The high proportion of women in college around 1900 provoked a backlash. Some institutions responded by ending coeducation, altering curricula to appeal to men, segregating classes by sex, or separating women into special divisions or academic programs.

The first generation of women college students in the late nineteenth century had their own concern: "After college, what?" Some graduates joined the Association of Collegiate Alumnae (1881), which discussed academic issues and promoted women's education. (In 1921 the ACA became the American Association of University Women.) Some of the early alumnae attended law schools and medical schools, and others became academics; in 1910, women made up 1 percent of American lawyers, 6 percent of physicians, and 20 percent of college faculty members. Larger numbers of graduates entered fields dominated by women such as schoolteaching, social work, and library work. Noncollege women attended normal schools, nursing schools, or secretarial schools. By 1910, 52 percent of social workers were women, as were 79 percent of librarians, 83 percent of stenographers and typists, 93 percent of nurses, and about 66 percent of teachers.

After 1920, as college enrollments expanded, women's share of the student population began to shrink. Women made up 47 percent of college students in 1920, but their percentages dropped for the next five decades. From 1930 on, although the absolute numbers of women students and faculty members rose, the proportion of faculty members who were female declined, as did the share of doctorates granted to women. The rise of the research university tended to exclude women academics.

But during the 1960s, the number of women college students doubled, and the feminist movement of the late 1960s and 1970s rekindled women's educational ambitions, inspired new efforts to achieve educational equity, and changed institutional policies. During the 1970s, higher educational institutions that once excluded women, such as all-male colleges and the military service academies, turned to coeducation. Federal law now prevented sex discrimination in university policies and procedures. Hundreds of institutions established programs in women's studies, an academic by-product of the feminist movement. Expansion of state university systems, growth of community colleges, and acceptance of older students also helped increase female enrollment. During the 1980s, when about a third of all college students were twenty-five or older, women became a majority of the college population.

Issues concerning women's education that have arisen since the 1970s include sexual stereotyping in textbooks and curricula, funding of programs and scholarships for women athletes, debates over the relative merits of single-sex and coeducational schools, implementation of affirmative action programs at educational institutions, and causes of gender disparities in widely used scholastic aptitude tests.

Barbara Miller Solomon, *In the Company of Educated Women: A History of Women and Higher Education in America* (1985); Thomas Woody, *A History of Women's Education in the United States,* 2 vols. (1929).

NANCY WOLOCH

See also Beecher, Catharine; Midwives; Morrill Land Grant Act.

EDWARDS, JONATHAN

(1703–1758), theologian and philosopher. No American has affected the course of American religious history more profoundly than Jonathan Edwards. Not only did he give religious experience in America a distinctive evangelical turn, still evident in the spiritual awakenings and moral crusades that sweep the country from time to time; he also forged a rational and inventive account of American Puritanism.

Edwards entered Yale before he was thirteen, graduated first in his class, and wrote speculative papers on spiders, atoms, rainbows, being, and the mind. He stayed on to study for the ministry and became head tutor — president, in effect — of the college in 1724. Five years later he succeeded his grandfather Solomon Stoddard as pastor of the Congregational church in Northampton, Massachusetts. For twenty-three years he labored to shore up Puritan orthodoxy and evangelical Christianity against a rising tide of liberalism in theology and rationalism in philosophy. He published *A Faithful Narrative* (1737) about the "surprising" conversions in his parish, including that of a four-year-old; *Sinners in the Hands of an Angry God* (1741), the most famous imprecatory sermon of the Great Awakening: "The God that holds you over the pit of hell, much as one holds a spider, or some loathsome insect, over the fire, abhors you, and is dreadfully provoked"; *Some Thoughts concerning the Present Revival* (1743), a spirited defense of the Great Awakening in general and the "high and extraordinary transports" of his wife in particular; and *Religious Affections* (1746), a psychological study of "true" religion that has become a handbook for evangelicals. But there was growing unease about his pastoral authority in Northampton and, in 1750, in a dispute over qualifications for church membership, his congregation dismissed him. For the next seven years Edwards ministered to the Housatonic Indians and a handful of frontier settlers in Stockbridge, Massachusetts, and composed his *summa theologica* — *Freedom of the Will, Original Sin, The Nature of True Virtue,* and *The End of Creation.* In 1758 he became president of the College of New Jersey (now Princeton) but died shortly after his inauguration.

The central issue of Edwards's theology was the problem of free will: if God determines everything, how can people have free will? In *Freedom of the Will* he argues that the question is misplaced. Borrowing in part from John Locke's *Essay concerning Human Understanding* (1690), Edwards insists that as long as one has the power to choose and, in choosing, to act, one is free. And the person who acts freely is responsible for those acts and so merits praise and reward, blame and punishment.

That conclusion led Edwards to *Original Sin* and its problem of the imputation of Adam's sin, a problem he solves through the philosophical notion of identity and his theory of continued creation. That God created the first man as the first of men implies that Adam and the children of Adam constitute a "oneness" or identity and that they share his nature, his apostasy, and his guilt. That God created Adam and his nature prior to his apostasy and his guilt implies that the same order obtains in the children of Adam, that sharing his nature, they follow the steps of

his fall. But God not only creates being; he preserves and upholds it in time. Hence, the first creation differs from the last "only circumstantially," and the first apostasy from the last not at all.

Two dissertations published posthumously celebrate the absolute sovereignty of God with joyful praise. In *The Nature of True Virtue* he wrote that since God is infinite being it "must necessarily" mean that true virtue "radically and essentially" consists in "love to God." All else — love of family, neighbors, community, country — is "secondary" and "inferior." Still, these natural dispositions are "useful and necessary" to society, even though they "leave the divine being out." *The End of Creation* centers on the primary relationship between human beings and God. God diffuses his fullness, beauty, and holiness and "makes himself his end." God seeks our good, because in seeking it he seeks himself. It is nothing but another reminder that the end for which God created the world is God.

Perry Miller, *Jonathan Edwards* (1949).

M. X. LESSER

See also Evangelicalism; Great Awakening; Puritanism; Religion.

EIGHT, THE

See Ashcan School.

EIGHTEENTH AMENDMENT

See Prohibition and Temperance.

EINSTEIN, ALBERT

(1879–1955), physicist. Einstein was born in Ulm, Germany, and grew up in Munich, in a family of independent-minded, nonpracticing Jews. Little is known about his childhood. Because he was slow in learning to speak — he was not fully fluent even at the age of nine — he was at various times thought to be mentally retarded. Some experts have speculated that he was dyslexic. A headmaster once told his father that what Einstein chose as a profession wouldn't matter, because "he'll never make a success at anything." At six he began learning to play the violin and became a gifted amateur violinist, maintaining this skill throughout his life.

Einstein attended the Luitpold Gymnasium in Munich, which he disliked intensely for its authoritarianism. He was deeply interested in physics and mathematics and read eagerly in both subjects. Ultimately he rebelled, leaving Luitpold at fifteen without receiving his diploma.

Without a gymnasium diploma, Einstein could not enter a German university, so he enrolled in the Swiss Federal Polytechnic School in Zurich. He was so impressed with the democratic atmosphere of Switzerland that he formally renounced his German citizenship at the age of sixteen; in 1901 he was granted Swiss citizenship, which he retained for the rest of his life.

After graduating he held several teaching jobs and became a technical assistant in the Swiss Patent Office in Berne, where he remained for six years. The job's great advantage, he later said, was that it gave him time to think about physics.

Between 1901 and 1904 Einstein published five papers on physics. In one he virtually proved the existence of molecules, solely by the use of theory; in another he showed that light is both a wave and a particle. In his sixth paper, "On the Electrodynamics of Moving Bodies," published in the summer of 1905, he established the outline of his special theory of relativity. His arguments radically revised existing concepts of electromagnetism, light, and the behavior of moving bodies as set forth in Newtonian physics. Einstein contended that the speed of light is constant, and that nothing in the universe can travel faster than light. If the velocity of light is constant, then all motion and even time itself must be relative to it. If objects could approach the speed of light, their age, mass, and size would appear very different to a stationary observer than if the objects were moving at slower speeds. A clock nearing the speed of light would slow down; if it reached the speed of light, time would stand still. Many of his contentions have been confirmed by subsequent experiments.

Atomic clocks in spacecraft orbiting the earth, for example, run a fraction of a second more slowly than clocks on earth.

In the fall of 1905, Einstein published another short paper in which he proposed the famous equation, $E = mc^2$: the energy in matter is equal to its mass multiplied by the square of the velocity of light. This equation explained how stars, like our own sun, can emit large amounts of light while losing very little mass; and it anticipated the splitting of the atom and the construction of the atom bomb thirty-five years later.

After receiving his doctorate from the University of Zurich in 1905, Einstein taught there and elsewhere until 1913, when he accepted a professorship in Berlin. There he established an Institute of Physics. He took up the question of gravity in his next major publication in 1916, "The Foundations of the General Theory of Relativity." One expert called it "the greatest feat of human thinking about nature." Whereas Newton had seen gravity as a universally present force, Einstein described it as a characteristic of matter. He proposed that gravity affected light just as it did matter and outlined both new structural laws and new laws of motion. The validation of the general theory was provided in 1919 by two English astronomical expeditions mounted to test its hypotheses by photographing an eclipse of the sun. When word was received that their results were positive, Einstein became the most famous scientist in the world overnight.

During the twenties, Einstein became more identified with his Jewish roots and worked to prevent another world war. In 1933, troubled by the swelling tide of anti-Semitism in Germany, he accepted an invitation to the Institute for Advanced Studies at Princeton, New Jersey, where he remained for the rest of his life.

Einstein's scientific work from this point was devoted to his effort to create a unified field theory, linking electromagnetism and light. Although such a theory eluded him, and other scientists proclaimed it impossible, he persisted with characteristic stubbornness. He consulted for the navy on the Manhattan Project during World War II, an action that went against his pacifist grain but seemed essential at the time because of the war's menace.

Nigel Calder, *Einstein's Universe* (1979); Ronald W. Clark, *Einstein: The Life and Times* (1974).

D. LYDIA BRONTË

See also Manhattan Project; Science and Technology.

EISENHOWER, DWIGHT D.

(1890–1969), supreme commander of Allied forces in Europe during World War II, chief of staff of the U.S. Army, and thirty-fourth president of the United States. Eisenhower's personal leadership qualities were crucial in fusing an enormous fighting force made up of disparate armies and egocentric leaders. He brought those same talents to the White House, where he concentrated on his role as a national unifier.

Eisenhower, born in Denison, Texas, and raised in Abilene, Kansas, graduated from West Point in 1915. He served as a captain in the First World War and worked under Gen. Douglas MacArthur in the Philippines from 1936 until 1939, afterward spending a brief period in Washington with the Office of Chief of Staff. After Pearl Harbor he commanded U.S. forces in Great Britain, leading the invasions of North Africa and Italy in 1943. The confidence of Prime Minister Winston Churchill and President Franklin D. Roosevelt in his abilities resulted in his appointment as supreme commander of Allied forces in Western Europe, with responsibility for planning the cross-channel invasion of France on D-Day.

Among the best-regarded World War II military leaders, Eisenhower was appointed chief of staff in 1945, succeeding Gen. George C. Marshall. His subsequent service as president of Columbia University in 1948 was brief; by 1951 he was back in uniform as supreme commander of the North Atlantic Treaty Organization.

But pressures on "Ike" to run for president followed him to Europe. Leaders of both political parties tried to enlist the popular war hero, but Eisenhower was a Republican by heritage and personal disposition. He relinquished his NATO command in the spring of 1952 to compete for that party's nomination. He won it and the election with relative ease.

Eisenhower's two-term presidency, scorned at first by liberals and specialists as unresponsive and lethargic, came to be seen later as an artful example of holding the line against contemporary political and social forces. Only with great reluctance did he force the racial integration of Little Rock's high school in 1957. Eisenhower contained the Republican right wing, winning it over to internationalism, while pursuing cold war policies that largely continued the Truman legacy. He and his secretary of state, John Foster Dulles, dealt with conflicts in different parts of the world, most notably Southeast Asia, via mutual security treaties and covert military intervention. They were cautiously wary of Soviet leader Nikita Khrushchev and his overtures toward détente. (These collapsed, however, with the shooting down of an American U-2 spy plane over the Russian heartland in 1960.)

Eisenhower did not have much success in his efforts to trim the military budget, the central concern of his farewell address on January 17, 1961. But he had managed to keep intact the major reforms and institutions inherited from the New Deal and, at the same time, produce three balanced budgets. The leadership that seemed timid and uncreative at the time was later described by historians as adroit management of a not-so-placid decade.

Stephen E. Ambrose, *Eisenhower: Soldier, General of the Army, President-Elect, 1890–1952* (1983) and *Eisenhower, the President* (1984); David Eisenhower, *Eisenhower at War, 1943–1945* (1986).

HERBERT S. PARMET

See also D-Day; Dulles, John Foster; Elections: 1952, 1956; North Atlantic Treaty Organization; World War II. *For events during Eisenhower's administration, see* Anticommunism; Army-McCarthy Hearings; *Brown* v. *Board of Education of Topeka;* Cold War; Middle East–U.S. Relations; Racial Desegregation; *Rosenberg* Case; U-2 Affair.

ELECTIONS

1789

The first presidential election was held on the first Wednesday of January in 1789. No one contested the election of George Washington, but he remained reluctant to run until the last minute, in part because he believed seeking the office would be dishonorable. Only when Alexander Hamilton and others convinced him that it would be dishonorable to refuse did he agree to run.

The Constitution allowed each state to decide how to choose its presidential electors. In 1789, only Pennsylvania and Maryland held elections for this purpose; elsewhere, the state legislatures chose the electors. This method caused some problems in New York, which was so divided between Federalists who supported the new Constitution and Antifederalists who opposed it that the legislature failed to choose either presidential electors or U.S. senators.

Before the adoption of the Twelfth Amendment, each elector cast two votes for president. The candidate with a majority won the presidency, and the runner-up became vice president.

Most Federalists agreed that John Adams should be vice president. But Hamilton feared that if Adams was the unanimous choice, he would end in a tie with Washington and might even become president, an outcome that would be highly embarrassing for both Washington and the new electoral system. Hamilton therefore arranged that a number of votes be deflected, so that Adams was elected by less than half the number of Washington's expected unanimous vote. The final results were Washington, 69 electoral votes; Adams, 34; John Jay, 9; John Hancock, 4; and others, 22.

1792

As in 1789, persuading George Washington to run was the major difficulty in selecting a president in 1792. Washington complained of old age, sickness, and the increasing hostility of the Republican press toward his administration. The press attacks were symptomatic of the increasing split within the government between Federalists, who were coalescing around Treasury Secretary Alexander Hamilton, and Republicans, forming around Secretary of State Thomas Jefferson. James Madison, among others, convinced Washington to continue as president by arguing that only he could hold the government together.

Speculation then shifted to the vice presidency. Hamilton and the Federalists supported the reelection of John Adams. Republicans favored New York governor George Clinton, but Federalists feared him partly because of a widespread belief that his recent election to the governorship was fraudulent. In addition, the Federalists feared that Clinton would belittle the importance of the federal government by retaining his governorship while serving as vice president.

Adams won relatively easily with support from New England and the Mid-Atlantic states, except New York. Only electoral votes are recorded here, because most states still did not select presidential electors by popular vote. Nor was there a separate vote for president and vice president until the Twelfth Amendment took effect in 1804. The results were Washington, 132 electoral votes (unanimous); Adams, 77; Clinton, 50; Jefferson, 4; and Aaron Burr, 1.

1796

The 1796 election, which took place against a background of increasingly harsh partisanship between Federalists and Republicans, was the first contested presidential race.

The Republicans called for more democratic practices and accused the Federalists of monarchism. The Federalists branded the Republicans "Jacobins" after Robespierre's faction in France. (The Republicans sympathized with revolutionary France, but not necessarily with the Jacobins.) The Republicans opposed John Jay's recently negotiated accommodationist treaty with Great Britain, whereas the Federalists believed its terms represented the only way to avoid a potentially ruinous war with Britain. Republicans favored a decentralized agrarian republic; Federalists called for the development of commerce and industry.

State legislatures still chose electors in most states, and there was no separate vote for vice president. Each elector cast two votes for president, with the runner-up becoming vice president.

The Federalists nominated Vice President John Adams and tried to attract southern support by running Thomas Pinckney of South Carolina for the second post. Thomas Jefferson was the Republican standard-bearer, with Aaron Burr as his running mate. Alexander Hamilton, always intriguing against Adams, tried to throw some votes to Jefferson in order to elect Pinckney president. Instead, Adams won with 71 votes; Jefferson became vice president, with 68; Pinckney came in third with 59; Burr received only 30; and 48 votes went to various other candidates.

1800

The significance of the 1800 election lay in the fact that it entailed the first peaceful transfer of power between parties under the U.S. Constitution: Republican Thomas Jefferson succeeded Federalist John Adams. This peaceful transfer occurred despite defects in the Constitution that caused a breakdown of the electoral system.

During the campaign, Federalists attacked Jefferson as an un-Christian deist, tainted by his sympathy for the increasingly bloody French Revolution. Republicans (1) criticized the Adams administration's foreign, defense, and internal security policies; (2) opposed the Federalist naval buildup and the creation of a standing army under Alexander Hamilton; (3) sounded a call for freedom of speech, Republican editors having been targeted for prosecution under the Alien and Sedition Acts; and (4) denounced deficit spending by the federal government as a backhanded method of taxation without representation.

Unfortunately, the system still provided no separate votes for president and vice president, and Republican managers failed to deflect votes from their vice-presidential candidate, Aaron Burr. Therefore, Jefferson and Burr tied with 73 votes each; Adams received 65 votes, his vice-presidential candidate, Charles C. Pinckney, 64,

and John Jay, 1. This result threw the election into the House of Representatives, where each state had one vote, to be decided by the majority of its delegation. Left to choose between Jefferson and Burr, most Federalists supported Burr. Burr for his part disclaimed any intention to run for the presidency, but he never withdrew, which would have ended the contest.

Although the Republicans in the same election had won a decisive majority of 65 to 39 in the House, election of the president fell to the outgoing House, which had a Federalist majority. But despite this majority, two state delegations split evenly, leading to another deadlock between Burr and Jefferson.

After the House cast 19 identical tie ballots on February 11, 1801, Governor James Monroe of Virginia assured Jefferson that if a usurpation was attempted, he would call the Virginia Assembly into session, implying that they would discard any such result. After six days of uncertainty, Federalists in the tied delegations of Vermont and Maryland abstained, electing Jefferson, but without giving him open Federalist support.

1804

The 1804 election was a landslide victory for the incumbent Thomas Jefferson and vice-presidential candidate George Clinton (Republicans) over the Federalist candidates, Charles C. Pinckney and Rufus King. The vote was 162–14. The election was the first held under the Twelfth Amendment, which separated electoral college balloting for president and vice president.

The Federalists alienated many voters by refusing to commit their electors to any particular candidate prior to the election. Jefferson was also helped by the popularity of the 1803 Louisiana Purchase and his reduction of federal spending. The repeal of the excise tax on whiskey was especially popular in the West.

1808

Republican James Madison was elevated to the presidency in the election of 1808. Madison won 122 electoral votes to Federalist Charles C.

Pinckney's 47 votes. Vice President George Clinton received 6 electoral votes for president from his native New York, but easily defeated Federalist Rufus King for vice president, 113–47, with scattered vice-presidential votes for Madison, James Monroe, and John Langdon of New Hampshire. In the early stages of the election campaign, Madison also faced challenges from within his own party by Monroe and Clinton.

The main issue of the election was the Embargo Act of 1807. The banning of exports had hurt merchants and other commercial interests, although ironically it encouraged domestic manufactures. These economic difficulties revived the Federalist opposition, especially in trade-dependent New England.

1812

In the 1812 contest James Madison was re-elected president by the narrowest margin of any election since the Republican party had come to power in 1800. He received 128 electoral votes to 89 for his Federalist opponent De-Witt Clinton, the lieutenant governor of New York. Elbridge Gerry of Massachusetts won the vice presidency with 131 votes to Jared Ingersoll's 86.

The War of 1812, which had begun five months earlier, was the dominant issue. Opposition to the war was concentrated in the northeastern Federalist states. Clinton's supporters also made an issue of Virginia's almost unbroken control of the White House, which they charged favored agricultural states over commercial ones. Clintonians accused Madison, too, of slighting the defense of the New York frontier against the British in Canada.

In the Northeast Madison carried only Pennsylvania and Vermont, but Clinton received no votes south of Maryland. The election proved to be the last one of significance for the Federalist party, largely owing to anti-British American nationalism engendered by the war.

1816

In this election Republican James Monroe won the presidency with 183 electoral votes, carrying every state except Massachusetts, Connecticut, and Delaware. Federalist Rufus King received the votes of the 34 Federalist electors. Daniel D. Tompkins of New York was elected vice president with 183 electoral votes, his opposition scattered among several candidates.

After the bitter partisanship of the Jefferson and Madison administrations, Monroe came to symbolize the "Era of Good Feelings." Monroe was not elected easily, however; he barely won the nomination in the Republican congressional caucus over Secretary of War William Crawford of Georgia. Many Republicans objected to the succession of Virginia presidents and believed Crawford a superior choice to the mediocre Monroe. The caucus vote was 65–54. The narrowness of Monroe's victory was surprising because Crawford had already renounced the nomination, perhaps in return for a promise of Monroe's future support.

In the general election, opposition to Monroe was disorganized. The Hartford Convention of 1814 (growing out of opposition to the War of 1812) had discredited the Federalists outside their strongholds, and they put forth no candidate. To some extent, Republicans had siphoned off Federalist support with nationalist programs like the Second Bank of the United States.

1820

During James Monroe's first term, the country had suffered an economic depression. In addition, the extension of slavery into the territories became a political issue when Missouri sought admission as a slave state. Also causing controversy were Supreme Court decisions in the *Dartmouth College* case and *McCulloch* v. *Maryland,* which expanded the power of Congress and of private corporations at the expense of the states. But despite these problems, Monroe faced no organized opposition for reelection in 1820, and the opposition party, the Federalists, ceased to exist.

Voters, as John Randolph put it, displayed "the unanimity of indifference, and not of approbation." Monroe won by an electoral vote of 231–1. William Plumer of New Hampshire, the one elector who voted against Monroe, did so because he thought Monroe was incompetent. He cast his ballot for John Quincy Adams. Later in the century, the fable arose that Plumer had cast his dissenting vote so that only George Washington would have the honor of unanimous election. Plumer never mentioned Washington in his speech explaining his vote to the other New Hampshire electors.

1824

The Republican party broke apart in the 1824 election. A large majority of the states now chose electors by popular vote, and the people's vote was considered sufficiently important to record. The nomination of candidates by congressional caucus was discredited. Groups in each state nominated candidates for the presidency, resulting in a multiplicity of favorite-son candidacies.

By the fall of 1824 four candidates remained in the running. William Crawford of Georgia, the secretary of the treasury, had been the early front-runner, but severe illness hampered his candidacy. Secretary of State John Quincy Adams of Massachusetts had a brilliant record of government service, but his Federalist background, his cosmopolitanism, and his cold New England manner cost him support outside his own region. Henry Clay of Kentucky, the Speaker of the House of Representatives, and Andrew Jackson of Tennessee, who owed his popularity to his 1815 victory over the British at the Battle of New Orleans, were the other candidates.

With four candidates, none received a majority. Jackson received 99 electoral votes with 152,901 popular votes (42.34 percent); Adams, 84 electoral votes with 114,023 popular votes (31.57 percent); Crawford, 41 electoral votes and 47,217 popular votes (13.08 percent); and Clay, 37 electoral votes and 46,979 popular votes (13.01 percent). The choice of president therefore fell to the House of Representatives. Many politicians assumed that House Speaker Henry Clay had the power to choose the next president but not to elect himself. Clay threw his support to Adams, who was then elected. When Adams subsequently named Clay secretary of state, the

Jacksonians charged that the two men had made a "corrupt bargain."

John C. Calhoun was chosen vice president by the electoral college with a majority of 182 votes.

1828

Andrew Jackson won the presidency in 1828 by a landslide, receiving a record 647,292 popular votes (56 percent) to 507,730 (44 percent) for the incumbent John Quincy Adams. John C. Calhoun won the vice presidency with 171 electoral votes to 83 for Richard Rush and 7 for William Smith.

The emergence of two parties promoted popular interest in the election. Jackson's party, sometimes called the Democratic-Republicans or simply Democrats, developed the first sophisticated national network of party organizations. Local party groups sponsored parades, barbecues, tree plantings, and other popular events designed to promote Jackson and the local slate. The National-Republicans, the party of Adams and Henry Clay, lacked the local organizations of the Democrats, but they did have a clear platform: high tariffs, federal funding of roads, canals, and other internal improvements, aid to domestic manufactures, and development of cultural institutions.

The 1828 election campaign was one of the dirtiest in America's history. Both parties spread false and exaggerated rumors about the opposition. Jackson men charged that Adams obtained the presidency in 1824 through a "corrupt bargain" with Clay. And they painted the incumbent president as a decadent aristocrat, who had procured prostitutes for the czar while serving as U.S. minister to Russia and spent taxpayer money on "gambling" equipment for the White House (actually a chess set and a billiard table).

The National-Republicans portrayed Jackson as a violent frontier ruffian, the son, some said, of a prostitute married to a mulatto. When Jackson and his wife, Rachel, married, the couple believed that her first husband had obtained a divorce. After learning the divorce had not yet been made final, the couple held a second, valid wedding. Now the Adams men claimed Jackson was a bigamist and an adulterer. More justifiably, administration partisans questioned Jackson's sometimes violent discipline of the army in the War of 1812 and the brutality of his invasion of Florida in the Seminole War. Ironically, Secretary of State Adams had defended Jackson at the time of the Seminole War, taking advantage of Jackson's unauthorized incursion to obtain Florida for the United States from Spain.

1832

Democratic-Republican Andrew Jackson was reelected in 1832 with 688,242 popular votes (54.5 percent) to 473,462 (37.5 percent) for National-Republican Henry Clay and 101,051 (8 percent) for Anti-Masonic candidate William Wirt. Jackson easily carried the electoral college with 219 votes. Clay received only 49, and Wirt won the 7 votes of Vermont. Martin Van Buren won the vice presidency with 189 votes against 97 for various other candidates.

The spoils system of political patronage, the tariff, and federal funding of internal improvements were major issues, but the most important was Jackson's veto of the rechartering of the Bank of the United States. National-Republicans attacked the veto, arguing that the Bank was needed to maintain a stable currency and economy. "King Andrew's" veto, they asserted, was an abuse of executive power. In defense of Jackson's veto, Democratic-Republicans labeled the Bank an aristocratic institution -- a "monster." Suspicious of banking and of paper money, Jacksonians opposed the Bank for giving special privileges to private investors at government expense and charged that it fostered British control of the American economy.

For the first time in American politics, a third party, the Anti-Masons, challenged the two major parties. Many politicians of note participated, including Thaddeus Stevens, William H. Seward, and Thurlow Weed. The Anti-Masonic party formed in reaction to the murder of William Morgan, a former upstate New York Freemason. Allegedly, some Masons murdered Morgan when he threatened to publish some of the order's secrets. The Anti-Masons protested Masonic secrecy. They feared a conspiracy to control American political institutions, a fear fed by the fact that both the major party candidates, Jackson and Clay, were prominent Masons.

The Anti-Masons convened the first national presidential nominating convention in Baltimore on September 26, 1831. The other parties soon followed suit, and the convention replaced the discredited caucus system of nomination.

1836

The election of 1836 was largely a referendum on Andrew Jackson, but it also helped shape what is known as the second party system. The Democrats nominated Vice President Martin Van Buren to lead the ticket. His running mate, Col. Richard M. Johnson, claimed to have killed Indian chief Tecumseh. (Johnson was controversial because he lived openly with a black woman.)

Disdaining the organized politics of the Democrats, the new Whig party ran three candidates, each strong in a different region: Hugh White of Tennessee, Senator Daniel Webster of Massachusetts, and Gen. William Henry Harrison of Indiana. Besides endorsing internal improvements and a national bank, the Whigs tried to tie Democrats to abolitionism and sectional tension, and attacked Jackson for "acts of aggression and usurpation of power." Democrats depended on Jackson's popularity, trying to maintain his coalition.

Van Buren won the election with 764,198 popular votes, only 50.9 percent of the total, and 170 electoral votes. Harrison led the Whigs with 73 electoral votes, White receiving 26 and Webster 14. Willie P. Mangum of South Carolina received his state's 11 electoral votes. Johnson, who failed to win an electoral majority, was elected vice president by the Democratic Senate.

1840

The election of 1840 has been called the first modern political campaign because of the way image and merchandising were employed. The Democrats nominated President Martin Van Buren, whom many Americans blamed for the economic problems associated with the panic of 1837. They officially chose no running mate owing to the unpopularity of incumbent Richard Johnson, but party regulars supported him as the candidate anyway.

Aware that Van Buren's problems gave them a good chance for victory, the Whigs rejected the candidacy of Henry Clay, their most prominent leader, because of his support for the unpopular Second Bank of the United States. Instead, stealing a page from the Democratic emphasis on Andrew Jackson's military exploits, they chose William Henry Harrison, a hero of early Indian wars and the War of 1812. The Whig vice-presidential nominee was John Tyler, a onetime Democrat who had broken with Jackson over his veto of the bill rechartering the Second Bank.

Studiously avoiding divisive issues like the Bank and internal improvements, the Whigs depicted Harrison as living in a "log cabin" and drinking "hard cider." They used slogans like "Tippecanoe and Tyler too," and "Van, Van, Van / Van is a used-up man" to stir voters. Harrison won by a popular vote of 1,275,612 to 1,130,033, and an electoral margin of 234 to 60. But the victory proved to be a hollow one because Harrison died one month after his inauguration. Tyler, his successor, would not accept Whig economic doctrine, and the change in presidential politics had little effect on presidential policy.

1844

The election of 1844 introduced expansion and slavery as important political issues and contributed to westward and southern growth and sectionalism. Southerners of both parties sought to annex Texas and expand slavery. Martin Van Buren angered southern Democrats by opposing annexation for that reason, and the Democratic convention cast aside the ex-president and front-runner for the first dark horse, Tennessee's James K. Polk. After almost silently breaking with Van Buren over Texas, Pennsylvania's George M. Dallas was nominated for vice president to appease Van Burenites, and the party backed annexation and settling the Oregon boundary dispute with England. The abolitionist Liberty party nominated Michigan's James G. Birney. Trying to avoid controversy, the Whigs nominated anti-annexationist Henry Clay of Kentucky and Theodore Frelinghuysen of New Jersey. But, pressured by southerners, Clay endorsed annexation, although concerned it might cause war with Mexico and disunion, and thereby lost support among antislavery Whigs.

Enough New Yorkers voted for Birney to throw 36 electoral votes and the election to Polk, who won the electoral college, 170–105, and a slim popular victory. John Tyler signed a joint congressional resolution admitting Texas, but Polk pursued Oregon, and then northern Mexico in the Mexican War, aggravating tension over slavery and sectional balance and leading toward the Compromise of 1850.

1848

The election of 1848 underscored the increasingly important role of slavery in national politics. Democratic president James K. Polk did not seek reelection. His party nominated Senator Lewis Cass of Michigan, who created the concept of squatter, or popular, sovereignty (letting the settlers of a territory decide whether to permit slavery), with Gen. William O. Butler of Kentucky for vice president. Antislavery groups formed the Free-Soil party, whose platform promised to prohibit the spread of slavery, and chose former president Martin Van Buren of New York for president and Charles Francis Adams, the son of President John Quincy Adams, of Massachusetts for vice president. The Whig nominee was the Mexican War hero, Gen. Zachary Taylor, a slave owner. His running mate was Millard Fillmore, a member of New York's proslavery Whig faction.

Democrats and Free-Soilers stressed their views of slavery, and Whigs celebrated Taylor's victories in the recent war, although many Whigs had opposed it. For his part, Taylor professed moderation on slavery, and he and the Whigs were successful. Taylor defeated Cass, 1,360,099 to 1,220,544 in popular votes and 163 to 127 in electoral votes. Van Buren received 291,263 popular votes and no electoral votes, but he drew enough support away from Cass to swing New York and Massachusetts to Taylor, assuring the Whigs' victory. With the Taylor-Fillmore ticket elected, the forces had been set in motion for the events surrounding the Compromise of 1850. But Van Buren's campaign was a stepping-stone toward the creation of the Republican party in the 1850s, also committed to the principle of "Free Soil."

1852

The 1852 election rang a death knell for the Whig party. Both parties split over their nominee and the issue of slavery. After forty-nine ballots of jockeying among Senator Lewis Cass of Michigan, former secretary of state James Buchanan of Pennsylvania, and Senator Stephen A. Douglas of Illinois, the Democrats nominated a compromise choice, Franklin Pierce of New Hampshire, a former congressman and senator, with Senator William R. King of Alabama as his running mate. The Whigs rejected Millard Fillmore, who had become president when Taylor died in 1850, and Secretary of State Daniel Webster and nominated Gen. Winfield Scott of Virginia, with Senator William A. Graham of New Jersey for vice president. When Scott endorsed the party platform, which approved of the Fugitive Slave Law of 1850, Free-Soil Whigs bolted. They nominated Senator John P. Hale of New Hampshire for president and former congressman George Washington Julian of Indiana for vice president. Southern Whigs were suspicious of Scott, whom they saw as a tool of antislavery senator William H. Seward of New York.

Democratic unity, Whig disunity, and Scott's political ineptitude combined to elect Pierce. "Young Hickory of the Granite Hills" outpolled "Old Fuss and Feathers" in the electoral college, 254 to 42, and in the popular vote, 1,601,474 to 1,386,578.

1856

The 1856 election was waged by new political coalitions and was the first to confront directly the issue of slavery. The violence that followed the Kansas-Nebraska Act destroyed the old political system and past formulas of compromises.

The Whig party was dead. Know-Nothings nominated Millard Fillmore to head their nativist American party and chose Andrew J. Donelson for vice president. The Democratic party, portraying itself as the national party, nominated James Buchanan for president and John C. Breckinridge for vice president. Its platform supported the Kansas-Nebraska Act and noninterference with slavery. This election saw the emergence of a new, sectional party composed of ex-Whigs, Free-Soil Democrats, and antislavery groups. The Republican party opposed the extension of slavery and promised a free-labor society with expanded opportunities for white workers. It nominated military hero, John C. Frémont of California for president and William L. Dayton for vice president.

The campaign centered around "Bleeding Kansas." The battle over the concept of popular sovereignty sharpened northern fears about the spread of slavery and southern worries about northern interference. The physical assault by Congressman Preston S. Brooks of South Carolina on Senator Charles Sumner of Massachusetts on the floor of the Senate heightened northern resentment of southern aggressiveness.

Although the Democratic candidate, Buchanan, won with 174 electoral votes and 1,838,169 votes, the divided opposition gained more popular votes. The Republican party captured 1,335,264 votes and 114 in the electoral college, and the American party received 874,534 popular and 8 electoral votes. The Republicans' impressive showing — carrying eleven of sixteen free states and 45 percent of northern ballots — left the South feeling vulnerable to attacks on slavery and fearful the Republicans would soon capture the government.

1860

The election of 1860 resulted in southern secession and Civil War. At the Republican convention, front-runner William H. Seward of New York faced insurmountable obstacles: conservatives feared his radical statements about an "irrepressible conflict" over slavery and a "higher law" than the Constitution, and radicals doubted his moral scruples. Hoping to carry moderate states like Illinois and Pennsylvania, the party nominated Abraham Lincoln of Illinois for president and Senator Hannibal Hamlin of Maine for vice president. The Republican platform called for a ban on slavery in the territories, internal improvements, a homestead act, a Pacific railroad, and a tariff.

The Democratic convention, which met at Charleston, could not agree on a candidate, and most of the southern delegates bolted. Reconvening in Baltimore, the convention nominated Senator Stephen A. Douglas of Illinois for president and Senator Herschel Johnson of Alabama for vice president. Southern Democrats then met separately and chose Vice President John Breckenridge of Kentucky and Senator Joseph Lane of Oregon as their candidates.

Former Whigs and Know-Nothings formed the Constitutional Union party, nominating Senator John Bell of Tennessee and Edward Everett of Massachusetts. Their only platform was "the Constitution as it is and the Union as it is."

By carrying almost the entire North, Lincoln won in the electoral college with 180 votes to 72 for Breckenridge, 39 for Bell, and 12 for Douglas. Lincoln won a popular plurality of about 40 percent, leading the popular vote with 1,766,452 to 1,376,957 for Douglas, 849,781 for Breckenridge, and 588,879 for Bell. With the election of a sectional northern candidate, the Deep South seceded from the Union, followed within a few months by several states of the Upper South.

1864

The contest in the midst of the Civil War pitted President Abraham Lincoln against Democrat George B. McClellan, the general who had commanded the Army of the Potomac until his indecision and delays caused Lincoln to remove him. The vice-presidential candidates were Andrew Johnson, Tennessee's military governor who had refused to acknowledge his state's secession, and Representative George Pendleton of Ohio. At first, Radical Republicans, fearing defeat, talked of ousting Lincoln in favor of the more ardently antislavery secretary of the treasury Salmon P. Chase, or Generals John C. Frémont or Benjamin F. Butler. But in the end they fell in behind the president.

The Republicans attracted Democratic support by running as the Union party and putting Johnson, a pro-war Democrat, on the ticket. McClellan repudiated the Democratic platform's call for peace, but he attacked Lincoln's handling of the war.

Lincoln won in a landslide, owing partly to a policy of letting soldiers go home to vote. But the military successes of Generals Ulysses S. Grant in Virginia and William T. Sherman in the Deep South were probably more important. He received 2,206,938 votes to McClellan's 1,803,787. The electoral vote was 212 to 21. Democrats did better in state elections.

1868

In this contest, Republican Ulysses S. Grant opposed Horace Seymour, the Democratic governor of New York. Their respective running mates were Speaker of the House Schuyler Colfax of Indiana and Francis P. Blair of Missouri. The Democrats attacked the Republican management of Reconstruction and black suffrage. Grant, a moderate on Reconstruction, was accused of military despotism and anti-Semitism, and Colfax, of nativism and possible corruption. Besides criticizing Seymour's support for inflationary greenback currency and Blair's reputed drunkenness and his opposition to Reconstruction, the Republicans questioned the wartime patriotism of all Democrats.

Grant won the popular vote, 3,012,833 to 2,703,249, and carried the electoral college by 214 to 80. Seymour carried only eight states, but ran fairly well in many others, especially in the South. The election showed that despite his popularity as a military hero, Grant was not invincible. His margin of victory came from newly enfranchised southern freedmen, who supplied him with about 450,000 votes. The Democrats had named a weak ticket and attacked Reconstruction rather than pursuing economic issues, but revealed surprising strength.

1872

President Ulysses S. Grant ran against *New York Tribune* editor Horace Greeley in 1872. Greeley headed an uneasy coalition of Democrats and liberal Republicans. Despite Greeley's history of attacking Democrats, that party endorsed him for the sake of expediency. The vice-presidential candidates were Republican senator Henry Wilson of Massachusetts and Governor B. Gratz Brown of Missouri.

Disaffected by Grant administration corruption and the controversy over Reconstruction, Greeley ran on a platform of civil service reform, laissez-faire liberalism, and an end to Reconstruction. The Republicans came out for civil service reform and the protection of black rights. They attacked Greeley's inconsistent record and his support of utopian socialism and Sylvester Graham's dietary restrictions. Thomas Nast's anti-Greeley cartoons in *Harper's Weekly* attracted wide attention.

Grant won the century's biggest Republican popular majority, 3,597,132 to 2,834,125. The electoral college vote was 286 to 66. Actually, the result was more anti-Greeley than pro-Grant.

1876

In 1876 the Republican party nominated Rutherford B. Hayes of Ohio for president and William A. Wheeler of New York for vice president. The Democratic candidates were Samuel J. Tilden of New York for president and Thomas A. Hendricks of Indiana for vice president. Several minor parties, including the Prohibition party and the Greenback party, also ran candidates.

The country was growing weary of Reconstruction policies, which kept federal troops stationed in several southern states. Moreover, the Grant administration was tainted by numerous scandals, which caused disaffection for the party among voters. In 1874 the House of Representatives had gone Democratic; political change was in the air.

Samuel Tilden won the popular vote, receiving 4,284,020 votes to 4,036,572 for Hayes. In the electoral college Tilden was also ahead 184 to 165; both parties claimed the remaining 20 votes. The Democrats needed only 1 more vote to capture the presidency, but the Republicans needed all 20 contested electoral votes. Nineteen of them came from South Carolina, Louisiana, and Florida — states that the Republicans still controlled. Protesting Democratic treatment of black voters, Republicans insisted that Hayes had carried those states but that Democratic electors had voted for Tilden.

Two sets of election returns existed — one from the Democrats, one from the Republicans. Congress had to determine the authenticity of the disputed returns. Unable to decide, legislators established a fifteen-member commission composed of ten congressmen and five Supreme Court justices. The commission was supposed to be nonpartisan, but ultimately it consisted of eight Republicans and seven Democrats. The final decision was to be rendered by the commission unless both the Senate and the House rejected it. The commission accepted the Republican vote in each state. The House disagreed, but the Senate concurred, and Hayes and Wheeler were declared president and vice president.

In the aftermath of the commission's decision, the federal troops that remained in the South were withdrawn, and southern leaders made vague promises regarding the rights of the 4 million African-Americans living in the region.

1880

The election of 1880 was as rich in partisan wrangling as it was lacking in major issues. Factional rivalry in the Republican party between New York senator Roscoe Conkling's Stalwarts and Half-Breed followers of James G. Blaine resulted in a convention in which neither Blaine nor the Stalwart choice, former president Ulysses S. Grant, could gain the nomination. On the thirty-sixth ballot, a compromise choice, Senator James A. Garfield of Ohio, was nominated. Stalwart Chester A. Arthur of New York was chosen as his running mate to mollify Conkling's followers. The Democrats selected Civil War general Winfield Scott Hancock, a man of modest abilities, because he was less controversial than party leaders like Samuel Tilden, Senator Thomas Bayard, or Speaker of the House Samuel Randall. Former Indiana congressman William English served as Hancock's running mate.

In their platforms, both parties equivocated on the currency issue and unenthusiastically endorsed civil service reform, while supporting generous pensions for veterans and the exclusion of Chinese immigrants. The Republicans called for protective tariffs; the Democrats favored tariffs "for revenue only."

In the campaign, Republicans "waved the bloody shirt," ridiculed Hancock for referring to the tariff as a "local question," and quite possibly purchased their narrow but crucial victory in Indiana. Democrats attacked Garfield's ties to the Crédit Mobilier scandal and circulated the forged "Morey Letter" that "proved" he was soft on Chinese exclusion. Turnout was high on election day (78.4 percent), but the result was one of the closest in history. Garfield carried the electoral college, 214–155, but his popular majority was less than 10,000 (4,454,416 to Hancock's 4,444,952). Greenback-Labor candidate James Weaver garnered 308,578 votes. Outside the southern and border states, Hancock carried only New Jersey, Nevada, and 5 of 6 California electoral votes.

1884

This race, marred by negative campaigning and corruption, ended in the election of the first Democratic president since 1856. The Republicans split into three camps: dissident reformers, called the Mugwumps, who were opposed to party and government graft; Stalwarts, Ulysses S. Grant supporters who had fought civil service reform; and Half-Breeds, moderate reformers and high-tariff men loyal to the party. The Republicans nominated James G. Blaine of Maine, a charismatic former congressman and secretary of state popular for his protectionism, but of doubtful honesty because of his role in the scandal of the "Mulligan letters" in the 1870s. His running mate was one of his opponents, Senator John Logan of Illinois. This gave Democrats a chance to name a ticket popular in New York, where Stalwart senator Roscoe Conkling had a long-running feud with Blaine, and they took advantage of it. They chose New York governor Grover Cleveland, a fiscal conservative and civil service reformer, for president and Senator Thomas Hendricks of Indiana for vice president.

The campaign was vicious. The Republican reformers and the traditionally Republican *New York Times* opposed Blaine. When it became known that Cleveland, a bachelor, had fathered a child out of wedlock, Republicans chanted "Ma! Ma! Where's my pa? Gone to the White House, Ha! Ha! Ha!" But the furor died down when Cleveland acknowledged his paternity and showed that he contributed to the child's support. Blaine alienated a huge bloc of votes by not repudiating the Reverend Samuel Burchard, who, with Blaine in attendance, called the Democrats the party of "Rum, Romanism, and Rebellion." Cleveland defeated Blaine by a very close margin, 4,911,017 to 4,848,334; the vote in the electoral college was 219 to 182, with New York's 36 votes turning the tide.

1888

In 1888 the Democratic party nominated President Grover Cleveland and chose Allen G. Thurman of Ohio as his running mate, replacing Vice President Thomas Hendricks who had died in office.

After eight ballots, the Republican party chose Benjamin Harrison, former senator from Indiana and the grandson of President William Henry Harrison. Levi P. Morton of New York was the vice-presidential nominee.

In the popular vote for president, Cleveland won with 5,540,050 votes to Harrison's 5,444,337. But Harrison received more votes in the electoral college, 233 to Cleveland's 168, and was therefore elected. The Republicans carried New York, President Cleveland's political base.

The campaign of 1888 helped establish the Republicans as the party of high tariffs, which most Democrats, heavily supported by southern farmers, opposed. But memories of the Civil War also figured heavily in the election. Northern veterans, organized in the Grand Army of the Republic, had been angered by Cleveland's veto of pension legislation and his decision to return Confederate battle flags.

1892

The Republican party in 1892 nominated President Benjamin Harrison and replaced Vice President Levi P. Morton with Whitelaw Reid of

New York. The Democrats also selected the familiar: former president Grover Cleveland and Adlai E. Stevenson of Illinois. The Populist, or People's party, fielding candidates for the first time, nominated Gen. James B. Weaver of Iowa and James G. Field of Virginia.

The main difference between the Republicans and the Democrats in 1892 was their position on the tariff. The Republicans supported ever-increasing rates, whereas a substantial wing of the Democratic party pushed through a platform plank that demanded import taxes for revenue only. The Populists called for government ownership of the railroads and monetary reform, confronting these issues in a way the two major parties did not.

Cleveland, avenging his defeat of 1888, won the presidency, receiving 5,554,414 popular votes to Harrison's 5,190,801. Weaver and the Populists received 1,027,329. In the electoral college Cleveland, carrying the swing states of New York, New Jersey, Connecticut, and Indiana, garnered 277 votes to Harrison's 145.

1896

In 1896 the Republican nominee for president was Representative William McKinley of Ohio, a "sound money" man and a strong supporter of high tariffs. His running mate was Garret A. Hobart of New Jersey. The party's platform stressed adherence to the gold standard; western delegates bolted, forming the Silver Republican party.

The Democratic party platform was critical of President Grover Cleveland and endorsed the coinage of silver at a ratio of sixteen to one. William Jennings Bryan, a former congressman from Nebraska, spoke at the convention in support of the platform, proclaiming, "You shall not crucify mankind on a cross of gold." The enthusiastic response of the convention to Bryan's Cross of Gold speech secured his hold on the presidential nomination. His running mate was Arthur Sewall of Maine.

The Populists supported Bryan but nominated Thomas Watson of Georgia for vice president. Silver Republicans supported the Democratic nominee, and the newly formed Gold Democrats nominated John M. Palmer of Illinois

for president and Simon B. Buckner of Kentucky for vice president.

Bryan toured the country, stressing his support for silver coinage as a solution for economically disadvantaged American farmers and calling for a relaxation of credit and regulation of the railroads. McKinley remained at home and underscored the Republican commitment to the gold standard and protectionism. The Republican campaign, heavily financed by corporate interests, successfully portrayed Bryan and the Populists as radicals.

William McKinley won, receiving 7,102,246 popular votes to Bryan's 6,502,925. The electoral college votes were 271 to 176. Bryan did not carry any northern industrial states, and the agricultural states of Iowa, Minnesota, and North Dakota also went Republican.

1900

In 1900 the Republicans nominated President William McKinley. Since Vice President Garret A. Hobart had died in office, Governor Theodore Roosevelt of New York received the vice-presidential nomination. The Democratic candidates were William Jennings Bryan of Nebraska for president and Adlai E. Stevenson of Illinois for vice president.

Bryan campaigned as an anti-imperialist, denouncing the country's involvement in the Philippines. Delivering over six hundred speeches in twenty-four states, he also persisted in his crusade for the free coinage of silver. McKinley did not actively campaign, relying on the revival of the economy that had occurred during his first term.

In the election McKinley won wide support from business interests. Bryan was unable to expand his agrarian base to include northern labor, which approved of McKinley's commitment to protective tariffs. Foreign policy questions proved unimportant to most voters. McKinley was elected, receiving 7,219,530 popular votes to Bryan's 6,358,071. In the electoral college the vote was 292 to 155.

1904

This race confirmed the popularity of Theodore Roosevelt, who had become president when

McKinley was assassinated, and moved Democrats away from bimetallism and toward progressivism.

Some Republicans deemed Roosevelt too liberal and flirted with nominating Marcus A. Hanna of Ohio, who had been William McKinley's closest political adviser. But the party easily nominated Roosevelt for a term in his own right and Senator Charles Fairbanks of Indiana for vice president. Democrats divided again over gold and silver, but this time gold won out. The party nominated conservative, colorless New York Court of Appeals judge Alton Parker for president and former senator Henry Davis of West Virginia for vice president.

Parker and his campaign attacked Roosevelt for his antitrust policies and for accepting contributions from big business. His having invited Booker T. Washington for a meal at the White House was also used against him. William Jennings Bryan overcame his distaste for Parker and his supporters and campaigned in the Midwest and West for the ticket. Playing down bimetallism, he stressed moving the party toward more progressive stances.

Parker gained some support from the South, but Roosevelt won 7,628,461 popular votes to Parker's 5,084,223. He carried the electoral college, 336 to 140, with only the South going Democratic.

1908

After Theodore Roosevelt declined to run for reelection in 1908, the Republican convention nominated Secretary of War William Howard Taft for president and Representative James Schoolcraft Sherman of New York as his running mate. The Democrats chose William Jennings Bryan for president for the third time; his running mate was John Kern of Indiana.

The predominant campaign issue was Roosevelt. His record as a reformer countered Bryan's reformist reputation, and Taft promised to carry on Roosevelt's policies. Business leaders campaigned for Taft.

In the election Taft received 7,679,006 popular votes to Bryan's 6,409,106. Taft's margin in the electoral college was 321 to 162.

1912

In 1912, angered over what he felt was the betrayal of his policies by his hand-picked successor, President William Howard Taft, former president Theodore Roosevelt sought the Republican nomination. When the party chose Taft and Vice President James Sherman at the convention, Roosevelt bolted and formed the Progressive party, or Bull Moose party. His running mate was Governor Hiram Johnson of California. After forty-six ballots the Democratic convention nominated New Jersey governor Woodrow Wilson for president and Thomas R. Marshall of Indiana for vice president. For the fourth time the Socialist party nominated Eugene V. Debs for president.

During the campaign Roosevelt and Wilson attracted most of the attention. They offered the voters two brands of progressivism. Wilson's New Freedom promoted antimonopoly policies and a return to small-scale business. Roosevelt's New Nationalism called for an interventionist state with strong regulatory powers.

In the election Wilson received 6,293,120 to Roosevelt's 4,119,582, Taft's 3,485,082, and nearly 900,000 for Debs. In the electoral college Wilson's victory was lopsided: 435 to 88 for Roosevelt and 8 for Taft. The combined vote for Taft and Roosevelt indicated that if the Republican party had not split, they would have won the presidency; the total cast for Wilson, Roosevelt, and Debs spoke to the people's endorsement of progressive reform.

1916

In 1916 the Progressive party convention tried to nominate Theodore Roosevelt again, but Roosevelt, seeking to reunify the Republicans, convinced the convention to support the Republican choice, Associate Justice Charles Evans Hughes. The Republicans selected Charles Fairbanks of Indiana as Hughes's running mate, but the Progressives nominated John M. Parker of Louisiana for vice president. The Democrats renominated President Woodrow Wilson and Vice President Thomas R. Marshall.

The Democrats stressed the fact that Wilson had kept the nation out of the European war, but Wilson was ambiguous about his ability to continue to do so. The election was close. Wilson received 9,129,606 votes to Hughes's 8,538,221. Wilson also obtained a slim margin in the electoral college, winning 277 to 254.

1920

After a generation of progressive insurgency within the Republican party, it returned in 1920 to a conservative stance. The party's choice for president was Senator Warren G. Harding of Ohio, a political insider. Governor Calvin Coolidge of Massachusetts, best known for his tough handling of the Boston police strike of 1919, was the vice-presidential nominee.

The Democratic party nominated James M. Cox, governor of Ohio, and Franklin D. Roosevelt of New York, assistant secretary of the navy in the Wilson administration. Democratic chances were weakened by President Woodrow Wilson's having suffered a stroke in 1919 and his failure to obtain ratification of the League of Nations treaty. The Socialist party nominated Eugene V. Debs, imprisoned for his opposition to World War I, and Seymour Stedman of Ohio.

A bedridden Wilson hoped the 1920 election would be a referendum on his League of Nations, but that issue was probably not decisive. If anything, the election was a strong rejection of President Wilson and an endorsement of the Republican candidate's call for a "return to normalcy."

Harding's victory was decisive: 16,152,200 popular votes to Cox's 9,147,353. In the electoral college only the South went for Cox. Harding won by 404 to 127. Although still in prison, Debs received more than 900,000 votes.

1924

The Republican nominees for president and vice president in 1924 were President Calvin Coolidge and Charles G. Dawes of Illinois. President Warren G. Harding had died in 1923.

Disaffected progressive Republicans met under the auspices of the Conference for Progressive Political Action and nominated Robert M. La Follette for president. The new Progressive party chose Senator Burton K. Wheeler of Montana for vice president. The platform called for higher taxes on the wealthy, conservation, direct election of the president, and the ending of child labor.

In choosing their candidates the Democrats were faced with polar opposites. Alfred E. Smith of New York was the epitome of the urban machine politician, and he was also Catholic; William G. McAdoo was a Protestant popular in the South and West. A deadlock developed; on the 103rd ballot the delegates finally settled on John W. Davis, a corporation lawyer, and Charles W. Bryan of Nebraska, the brother of William Jennings Bryan.

The Republicans won easily; Coolidge's popular vote, 15,725,016, was greater than that of Davis, 8,385,586, and La Follette, 4,822,856, combined. Coolidge received 382 electoral votes to Davis's 136. La Follette carried only his home state, Wisconsin, with 13 electoral votes.

1928

The Republican presidential nominee in 1928 was Secretary of Commerce Herbert Hoover of California. Charles Curtis of Kansas was his running mate. The Democrats nominated Alfred E. Smith, governor of New York, and Senator Joseph T. Robinson of Arkansas.

The Eighteenth Amendment (Prohibition) and religion — Al Smith was Catholic — dominated a campaign that was marked by anti-Catholicism. Hoover firmly supported Prohibition, whereas Smith, an avowed wet, favored repeal. Many Americans found the urban and cultural groups that the cigar-smoking Smith epitomized frightening; Hoover seemed to stand for old-fashioned rural values. The Republican campaign slogan promised the people "a chicken for every pot and a car in every garage."

The election produced a high voter turnout. The Republicans swept the electoral college, 444 to 87, and Hoover's popular majority was substantial: 21,392,190 to Smith's 15,016,443. The Democrats, however, carried the country's twelve largest cities; the support for Smith in urban America heralded the major political shift to come.

1932

In 1932, the third year of the Great Depression, the Republican party nominated President Herbert Hoover and Vice President Charles Curtis. Although Hoover had tried to respond to the crisis, his belief in voluntarism limited his options.

The Democratic party nominated Franklin D. Roosevelt, the governor of New York, for president and Senator John Nance Garner of Texas for vice president. The platform called for the repeal of Prohibition and a reduction in federal spending.

During the campaign Hoover defended his record, his commitment to a balanced budget, and the gold standard — a backward-looking stance, given that the number of unemployed stood at 13 million. Roosevelt made few specific proposals, but his tone and demeanor were positive and forward-looking.

The Democrats won the election in a landslide. Roosevelt received 22,809,638 popular votes to the president's 15,758,901 and took the electoral college by 472 votes to 59. The voters' rejection of Hoover and his party extended to both houses of Congress, which the Democrats now controlled.

1936

In 1936 the Democratic party nominated President Franklin D. Roosevelt and Vice President John Nance Garner. The Republican party, strongly opposed to the New Deal and "big government," chose Governor Alfred M. Landon of Kansas and Fred Knox of Illinois.

The 1936 presidential campaign focused on class to an unusual extent for American politics. Conservative Democrats such as Alfred E. Smith supported Landon. Eighty percent of newspapers endorsed the Republicans, accusing Roosevelt of imposing a centralized economy. Most businesspeople charged the New Deal with trying to destroy American individualism and threatening the nation's liberty. But Roosevelt appealed to a coalition of western and southern farmers, industrial workers, urban ethnic voters, and reform-minded intellectuals. African-Ameri-

can voters, historically Republican, switched to FDR in record numbers.

In a referendum on the emerging welfare state, the Democratic party won in a landslide — 27,751,612 popular votes for FDR to only 16,681,913 for Landon. The Republicans carried two states — Maine and Vermont — for 8 electoral votes; Roosevelt received the remaining 523. The unprecedented success of FDR in 1936 marked the beginning of a long period of Democratic party dominance.

1940

In 1940 President Franklin D. Roosevelt won an unprecedented third term by a margin of nearly 5 million: 27,244,160 popular votes to Republican Wendell L. Willkie's 22,305,198. The president carried the electoral college, 449 to 82. The new vice president was Secretary of Agriculture Henry A. Wallace, chosen by the Democrats to replace the two-term vice president John Nance Garner who no longer agreed with Roosevelt about anything. Charles A. McNary was the Republican candidate for vice president.

The major issue facing the American people in 1940 was World War II. This fact had determined the Republican choice of Willkie, who was a liberal internationalist running as the candidate of a conservative isolationist party. Although Willkie did not disagree with Roosevelt on foreign policy, the country chose to stay with an experienced leader.

1944

By the beginning of 1944, in the middle of World War II, it was clear that President Franklin D. Roosevelt planned to run for a fourth term, and this shaped the coming campaign. Democratic party regulars disliked Vice President Henry A. Wallace; eventually they persuaded Roosevelt to replace him with Senator Harry S. Truman of Missouri.

Although Wendell Willkie, the nominee in 1940, was initially the front-runner in the Republican race, the party returned to its traditional base, choosing conservative governor Thomas E. Dewey of New York. Republicans had hoped that Governor Earl Warren of California would accept the vice-presidential nomination, but he declined. The party then turned to John W. Bricker.

The president won reelection with results that were similar to those of 1940: 25,602,504 people voted for Roosevelt and Truman, and 22,006,285 voters gave their support to Dewey. The electoral vote was 432 to 99.

Franklin D. Roosevelt was the issue in 1944: his health — the sixty-two-year-old suffered from heart disease and high blood pressure — his competence as an administrator, and his stand on communism and the shape of the postwar world. At issue also was whether any president should serve four terms. The Democrats and the president were vulnerable on all these points, but the American people once again chose the familiar in a time of crisis: "Don't change horses in midstream" was a familiar slogan in the campaign.

1948

President Harry S. Truman, who had succeeded President Roosevelt after his death in 1945, stood for reelection on the Democratic ticket with Alben Barkley of Kentucky as his running mate. When the Democratic convention adopted a strong civil rights plank, southern delegates walked out and formed the States' Rights party. The Dixiecrats, as they were called, nominated Governor Strom Thurmond of South Carolina for president and Fielding Wright for vice president. A new left-leaning Progressive party nominated former vice president Henry A. Wallace of Iowa for president with Glen Taylor, a senator from Idaho, as his running mate. The Republican slate consisted of two prominent governors: Thomas E. Dewey of New York and Earl Warren of California.

Although polls and conventional wisdom predicted a Dewey victory, Truman campaigned vigorously as the underdog, making a famous whistle-stop tour of the country aboard a special train. Results were uncertain to the last minute. A well-known photograph shows Truman the day after the election smiling broadly and holding aloft a newspaper with the headline DEWEY WINS! The paper was wrong: Truman had re-

ceived 24,105,812 popular votes, or 49.5 percent of the total; Dewey, 21,970,065, or 45.1 percent. Thurmond and Wallace each received about 1.2 million votes. The Democratic victory in the electoral college was more substantial: Truman beat Dewey 303 to 189; Thurmond received 39 votes, and Wallace none.

1952

When President Harry S. Truman declined to run for a third term, the Democratic convention nominated Governor Adlai E. Stevenson of Illinois for president on the third ballot. Senator John Sparkman of Alabama was chosen as his running mate.

The Republican fight for the nomination was a conflict between the isolationists, represented by Senator Robert Taft of Ohio, and the more liberal internationalists, who backed World War II general Dwight D. Eisenhower, then president of Columbia University. Eisenhower won the nomination. Richard M. Nixon, an anticommunist senator from California, was the vice-presidential candidate.

Popular discontent with Truman's handling of the Korean War, charges of corruption in his administration, an inflationary economy, and a perceived communist threat worked against Stevenson. He was also confronted with Eisenhower's immense personal popularity — I LIKE IKE! the campaign buttons proclaimed — and the voters' belief that he would swiftly end the war. A scandal regarding Nixon's campaign fund threatened briefly to cost him his place on the ticket. But an emotional speech he delivered on television featuring his wife's "good Republican cloth coat" and his dog, Checkers, saved him.

Eisenhower's victory was the largest of any candidate's to that time: he received 33,936,234 popular votes and 442 electoral votes to Stevenson's 27,314,992 popular votes and 89 electoral votes.

1956

Despite suffering a heart attack and abdominal surgery during his first term, President Dwight D. Eisenhower was nominated by the Republicans for a second term without opposition. Although Richard M. Nixon had been a controversial vice president and many Republicans felt he was a liability, he was also renominated. For the second time the Democrats chose former governor Adlai E. Stevenson of Illinois; his running mate was Estes Kefauver of Tennessee.

Foreign policy dominated the campaign. Eisenhower claimed responsibility for the country's being prosperous and at peace; Stevenson proposed ending the draft and halting nuclear testing. The Suez Canal crisis, occurring in the final weeks of the campaign, created a sense of emergency, and the country responded by voting strongly against change.

Eisenhower won with 35,590,472 votes to Stevenson's 26,022,752. His margin was 457 to 73 in the electoral college.

1960

In 1960 the Democratic party nominated John F. Kennedy, a senator from Massachusetts, for president. Senator Lyndon B. Johnson of Texas was his running mate. The Republicans nominated Vice President Richard M. Nixon to succeed Dwight D. Eisenhower, who was prohibited from running for a third term by the recently adopted Twenty-second Amendment. The Republican nominee for vice president was Senator Henry Cabot Lodge, Jr., of Massachusetts.

Although much of the campaign centered on style rather than substance, Kennedy stressed what he claimed was a "missile gap" between the United States and the Soviet Union. Kennedy was Catholic, and though religion was not a major issue, it had considerable influence on many voters.

Kennedy won the presidency by a popular margin of less than 120,000, receiving 34,227,096 votes to Nixon's 34,107,646. The race was not as close in the electoral college where Kennedy got 303 votes to Nixon's 219. Kennedy was the first Catholic and the youngest person to be elected president.

1964

The Democrats nominated Lyndon B. Johnson who had succeeded to the presidency upon the assassination of President John F. Kennedy.

Johnson, the first president from the South since Andrew Johnson, had been Democratic leader of the Senate. Senator Hubert H. Humphrey of Minnesota, a longtime liberal, was nominated as Johnson's running mate. The Republicans chose Senator Barry Goldwater of Arizona for president and Congressman William E. Miller of New York for vice president.

In the campaign, conducted in the midst of the escalating Vietnam War, Goldwater, an ultraconservative, called for the bombing of North Vietnam and implied that the Social Security system should be dismantled. President Johnson campaigned on a platform of social reform that would incorporate Kennedy's New Frontier proposals. Despite the country's deepening involvement in Vietnam, the president also campaigned as the candidate of peace against the militaristic Goldwater.

Johnson won a decisive victory, polling 43,128,958 popular votes to 27,176,873 for Goldwater. In the electoral college he received 486 votes to Goldwater's 52.

1968

The Vietnam War, the civil rights movement, and protests tied to both combined in a tumultuous year to cause a tight, unusual election closely linked to these issues. Opposition to the war moved Senator Eugene McCarthy of Minnesota to enter the Democratic race, followed by Senator Robert F. Kennedy of New York, both with strong support from liberal constituencies. On March 31, 1968, in the wake of the Tet offensive, President Lyndon B. Johnson announced that he would not seek reelection. This prompted Vice President Hubert H. Humphrey to announce his candidacy. Kennedy won the California primary, but immediately thereafter, he was assassinated by Sirhan Sirhan.

Humphrey then pulled ahead and was nominated for president, with Senator Edmund Muskie of Maine for vice president. The party convention in Chicago was marred by bloody clashes between antiwar protesters and the local police. In comparison, the Republican race was less complicated. Former vice president Richard M. Nixon completed his political comeback by winning the presidential nomination. He chose

Governor Spiro Agnew of Maryland as his running mate. The conservative American Independent party nominated Governor George Wallace of Alabama, a segregationist, for president, and Air Force general Curtis LeMay of Ohio, who advocated using nuclear weapons in Vietnam, for vice president.

Nixon campaigned for law and order and said he had a "secret plan" to end the war. Wallace was highly critical of Supreme Court decisions that had broadened the Bill of Rights and of Great Society programs to rebuild the inner cities and enforce civil rights for blacks. Humphrey supported most of Johnson's policies, but late in the campaign he announced he would seek to end American involvement in Vietnam. It was not quite enough to overcome Nixon's lead in the polls. Nixon received 31,710,470 popular votes to 30,898,055 for Humphrey and 9,466,167 for Wallace. Nixon's victory in the electoral college was wider: 302 to 191 for Humphrey and 46 for Wallace, the latter from the South.

1972

In 1972 the Republicans nominated President Richard M. Nixon and Vice President Spiro Agnew. The Democrats, still split over the war in Vietnam, chose a presidential candidate of liberal persuasion, Senator George McGovern of South Dakota. Senator Thomas F. Eagleton of Missouri was the vice-presidential choice, but after it was revealed that he had once received electric shock and other psychiatric treatments, he resigned from the ticket. McGovern named Sargent Shriver, director of the Peace Corps, as his replacement.

The campaign focused on the prospect of peace in Vietnam and an upsurge in the economy. Unemployment had leveled off and the inflation rate was declining. Two weeks before the November election, Secretary of State Henry Kissinger predicted inaccurately that the war in Vietnam would soon be over. During the campaign, a break-in occurred at Democratic National Headquarters in the Watergate complex in Washington, D.C., but it had little impact until after the election.

The campaign ended in one of the greatest landslides in the nation's history. Nixon's popular vote was 47,169,911 to McGovern's 29,170,383, and the Republican victory in the electoral college was even more lopsided — 520 to 17. Only Massachusetts gave its votes to McGovern.

1976

In 1976 the Democratic party nominated former governor Jimmy Carter of Georgia for president and Senator Walter Mondale of Minnesota for vice president. The Republicans chose President Gerald Ford and Senator Robert Dole of Kansas. Richard M. Nixon had appointed Ford, a congressman from Michigan, as vice president to replace Spiro Agnew, who had resigned amid charges of corruption. Ford became president when Nixon resigned after the House Judiciary Committee voted three articles of impeachment because of his involvement in an attempted cover-up of the politically inspired Watergate break-in.

In the campaign, Carter ran as an outsider, independent of Washington, which was now in disrepute. Ford tried to justify his pardoning Nixon for any crimes he might have committed during the cover-up, as well as to overcome the disgrace many thought the Republicans had brought to the presidency.

Carter and Mondale won a narrow victory, 40,828,587 popular votes to 39,147,613 and 297 electoral votes to 241. The Democratic victory ended eight years of divided government; the party now controlled both the White House and Congress.

1980

In 1980 President Jimmy Carter was opposed for the Democratic nomination by Senator Edward Kennedy of Massachusetts in ten primaries. But Carter easily won the nomination at the Democratic convention. The party also renominated Walter Mondale for vice president.

Ronald Reagan, former governor of California, received the Republican nomination, and his chief challenger, George Bush, became the vice-presidential nominee. Representative John B. Anderson of Illinois, who had also sought the nomination, ran as an independent with Patrick

J. Lucey, former Democratic governor of Wisconsin, as his running mate.

The two major issues of the campaign were the economy and the Iranian hostage crisis. President Carter seemed unable to control inflation and had not succeeded in obtaining the release of American hostages in Tehran before the election.

Reagan won a landslide victory, and Republicans also gained control of the Senate for the first time in twenty-five years. Reagan received 43,904,153 popular votes in the election, and Carter, 35,483,883. Reagan won 489 votes in the electoral college to Carter's 49. John Anderson won no electoral votes, but got 5,720,060 popular votes.

1984

In 1984 the Republicans renominated Ronald Reagan and George Bush. Former vice president Walter Mondale was the Democratic choice, having turned aside challenges from Senator Gary Hart of Colorado and the Reverend Jesse Jackson. Jackson, an African-American, sought to move the party to the left. Mondale chose Representative Geraldine Ferraro of New York for his running mate. This was the first time a major party nominated a woman for one of the top offices.

Peace and prosperity, despite massive budget deficits, ensured Reagan's victory. Gary Hart had portrayed Mondale as a candidate of the "special interests," and the Republicans did so as well. Ferraro's nomination did not overcome a perceived gender gap — 56 percent of the women voting chose Reagan.

Reagan won a decisive victory, carrying all states except Minnesota, Mondale's home state, and the District of Columbia. He received 54,455,074 popular votes to Mondale's total of 37,577,185. In the electoral college the count was Reagan, 525, and Mondale, 13.

1988

Although Vice President George Bush faced some opposition in the primaries from Senator Robert Dole of Kansas in 1988, he won the Republican nomination by acclamation. He chose

Senator Dan Quayle of Indiana as his running mate. The Democrats nominated Michael Dukakis, governor of Massachusetts, for president and Senator Lloyd Bentsen of Texas for vice president. Dukakis had faced strong competition in the primaries, including the Reverend Jesse Jackson and Senator Gary Hart of Colorado. Hart withdrew from the race following revelations about an extramarital affair, and party regulars and political pundits perceived Jackson, a liberal and an African-American, as unlikely to win the general election.

Once again the Republicans were in the enviable situation of running during a time of relative tranquillity and economic stability. After a campaign featuring controversial television ads, Bush and Quayle won 48,886,097 popular votes to 41,809,074 for Dukakis and Bentsen and carried the electoral college, 426 to 111.

ELECTORAL COLLEGE

The electoral college is the method stipulated in Article II, Section 1, of the Constitution for electing the president and vice president. Originally each state chose electors equal in number to its representatives and senators. The electors voted for two candidates each, at least one of whom had to be from another state. The person receiving the most votes became president with the runner-up becoming vice president. If no person received a majority, the House of Representatives was to choose the president and vice president from the three leading candidates.

The election of 1800, in which Thomas Jefferson and Aaron Burr were tied in the electoral vote, resulted in passage of the Twelfth Amendment (1804). Electors now cast separate votes for president and vice president; in the event of ties the House of Representatives is to choose the president and the Senate the vice president.

Modern critics note that the electoral college has several potentially dangerous flaws. For example, a president can be elected with a majority of electoral votes, even though his or her opponent has won a majority of popular votes; this last happened in 1888. Reformers have urged that the electoral college be abolished in favor of direct popular vote for president and vice president, or that the electoral votes of each state be allotted to the candidates in proportion to the popular vote they receive rather than the present winner-take-all system. Defenders of the electoral college reject the dangers as exaggerated and insist that the system has worked far better than one might expect.

See also Elections; Presidency; Vice Presidency.

ELLINGTON, DUKE

(1899–1974), composer, bandleader, and pianist. Born Edward Kennedy Ellington in Washington, D.C., Ellington developed his keyboard skills by listening to local black ragtime pianists; he composed his first piece, "Soda Fountain Rag," around 1915. A successful professional musician by the early 1920s, he left Washington in the spring of 1923 for New York, which was his home base for the rest of his life. Between December 1927 and 1931 his orchestra held forth at Harlem's Cotton Club, where regular radio broadcasts, together with an active recording schedule, helped him establish a nationwide reputation.

In such compositions as "Black and Tan Fantasy" (1927), "Mood Indigo" (1930), "Solitude" (1934), and "Echoes of Harlem" (1935), Ellington emerged as a distinctive composer for his ensemble, employing the rhythms, harmonies, and tone colors of jazz to create pieces that vividly captured aspects of the African-American experience. At the same time he sought to broaden jazz's expressive range and formal boundaries in such extended works as *Reminiscing in Tempo* (1935), *Black, Brown, and Beige* (1943), and *Harlem* (1951).

An essential feature of Ellington's composing method was to write with specific instrumentalists in mind, often drawing them into the creative process by building entire pieces out of their musical ideas. This practice began in the 1920s, with Ellington drawing inspiration from such players as saxophonists Johnny Hodges and Otto Hardwick, trumpeters Bubber Miley and Cootie Williams, and trombonist Joseph Nanton. Another important contributor to the Ellington orchestra's sonic identity was the composer and arranger Billy Strayhorn, who worked closely with Ellington from 1939 until his death in 1967. Strayhorn was responsible for the band's famous theme, "Take the A Train" (1941), and in later years collaborated with Ellington on such projects as *Such Sweet Thunder* (1957) and the *Far East Suite* (1966).

During the 1930s Ellington began the pattern of regular touring — including trips to Europe in 1933 and 1939 — that he maintained throughout his career. His orchestra performed in concert halls, nightclubs, and theaters, with Ellington appearing before the public as a composer and songwriter, entertainer, bandleader, and eventually global ambassador of American music.

Although many saw Ellington primarily as an exponent of big-band jazz, his compositional achievements, prolific output (estimated at over fifteen hundred works), and expressive range set him apart from others in the field. He wrote scores for musicals, films, television, and ballet and in the 1960s produced a series of sacred concerts combining his orchestra, choirs, vocalists, and dancers. Ellington was successful, as few others have been, in reconciling the practical function of a popular entertainer with the artistic aspirations of a serious composer. His rich legacy consists of hundreds of recordings, his many pieces that have entered the standard repertory, and his musical materials now preserved in the Duke Ellington Collection at the Smithsonian Institution.

Stanley Dance, *The World of Duke Ellington* (1970; reprint, 1981); Duke Ellington, *Music Is My Mistress* (1973).

MARK TUCKER

See also Jazz; Music.

ELLISON, RALPH

(1914–), essayist and novelist. As a cultural historian and novelist, Ellison has had since 1952 an extraordinary influence on European-American and African-American literature. Born and raised in Oklahoma and trained at

Tuskegee Institute as a symphony composer, Ellison has successfully managed to reconcile his folk and classical cultural heritages. Before a fateful Harlem meeting with Richard Wright in 1937, he had already been educated in the rich oral ethnic forms of his region. Besides the rhythms, imagery, and poetry of the vernacular, Oklahoma City, a southwestern center of jazz, was vibrant with the blues during his boyhood. But in school, young trumpet-playing Ellison was also drilled in military and classical music.

Ellison realized his boyhood dream of becoming a renaissance man. He has been a freelance photographer, jazz musician, vice president of the National Institute of Arts and Letters, a member of the American Academy of Arts, a trustee of the John F. Kennedy Center for the Performing Arts, and a professor at New York University. He has received such prestigious awards as the Russwurm, the Medal of Freedom, and the Chevalier de l'Ordre des Arts et Lettres.

He peppered his conversations, lectures, and writings with anecdotes that revealed his humble origins, professional relationships with celebrated, culturally diverse artists, and a strong sense of bicultural rather than black cultural nationalist identity as an American writer of African descent. More highly respected by his peers than by younger black students and writers, Ellison was as much at home in a Harlem barbershop as in a Harvard lecture hall.

In synthesizing the best conventions of his bicultural heritage, Ellison was inspired by Eliot's *The Waste Land.* It was Wright, however, who discussed the art of fiction with the young college dropout and guided him to Conrad, James, and Dostoyevsky; Wright who introduced him to Leadbelly and Marxism in the same evening; and Wright who acted as midwife for his first publication. Subsequently, on the strength of a single novel, a couple of collections of essays, and nearly two dozen stories, Ellison won acclaim as a major American author and influenced the assumptions and methodologies of contemporary critical theories of African-American literature.

The superb integration of surrealism and folklore in his best short stories, "Flying Home" and "King of the Bingo Game," anticipate the irony and parody of his epic novel *Invisible Man* (1952). In a poll by *Book Week,* it was judged "the most distinguished single work" published in America between 1945 and 1965. Its complex time structure, spacious setting, nameless ethnic protagonist, allegorical and legendary characters, rites of passage, ironic theme, and ritualistic use of music and language suggest that Ellison drew on African-American folklore and the Western epic tradition to render his vision of the historical odyssey of blacks in America to define themselves. Eight excerpts from a second novel that Ellison began in 1953 have been published in journals; the best of these is "And Hickman Arrives."

The most significant essays in *Shadow and Act* (1964) and *Going to the Territory* (1986), which sparkle with the same wry wit and wisdom, are essentially cultural and autobiographical. These pieces celebrate Ellison's efforts to reconcile his double consciousness by drawing on his indigenous ethnic culture for standards, role models, and rites of passage. The essays have three general themes: African-American music, the complex relationships of folklore to literature, and those between African-American and European-American cultures. Convinced "that the most authoritative rendering of America in music is that of American Negroes," Ellison argues that the music is a unique blend of European and African cultural expression. And his argument in *Shadow and Act* that the possibilities for formal literature are infinite for writers who draw on the techniques and spirit of the slave songs, blues, jazz, and black vernacular has had a profound influence on critical studies of African-American literature. *Shadow and Act,* like *Invisible Man,* has become a standard college text.

Kimberly W. Benston, ed., *Speaking for You: The Vision of Ralph Ellison* (1987); Robert G. O'Meally, *The Craft of Ralph Ellison* (1980).

BERNARD W. BELL

See also Literature; Wright, Richard.

EMANCIPATION PROCLAMATION AND THIRTEENTH AMENDMENT

Slavery was "an unqualified evil to the negro, the white man, and the State," said Abraham Lincoln in the 1850s. Yet in his first inaugural address, Lincoln declared that he had "no purpose, directly or indirectly, to interfere with slavery in the States where it exists." He reiterated this pledge in his first message to Congress on July 4, 1861, when the Civil War was three months old.

What explains this apparent inconsistency in Lincoln's statements? And how did he get from his pledge not to interfere with slavery to a decision a year later to issue an emancipation proclamation? The answers lie in the Constitution and in the course of the Civil War. As an individual, Lincoln hated slavery. As a Republican, he wished to exclude it from the territories as the first step to putting the institution "in the course of ultimate extinction." But as president of the United States, Lincoln was bound by a Constitution that protected slavery in any state where citizens wanted it. As commander in chief of the armed forces in the Civil War, Lincoln also worried about the support of the four border slave states and the Northern Democrats. These groups probably would have turned against the war for the Union if the Republicans had made a move against slavery in 1861.

But the president's role as commander in chief cut two ways. If it restrained him from alienating proslavery Unionists, it also empowered him to seize enemy property used to wage war against the United States. Slaves were the most conspicuous and valuable such property. They raised food and fiber for the Southern war effort, worked in munitions factories, and served as teamsters and laborers in the army. Gen. Benjamin Butler, commander of Union forces occupying a foothold in Virginia at Fortress Monroe on the mouth of the James River, provided a legal rationale for the seizure of slave property. When three slaves who had worked on rebel fortifications escaped to Butler's lines in May 1861, he declared them contraband of war and refused to return them to their Confederate owner. Here was an opening wedge for emancipation, and

hundreds of such "contrabands" voted with their feet for freedom by escaping to Union lines in subsequent months. By 1862 the trickle had become a flood. Some Union commanders gave them shelter and protection; others returned them to masters who could prove their loyalty to the United States. In August 1861 Congress passed a confiscation act that conferred "contraband" status on all slaves who had been used in direct support of the Confederate war effort. In March 1862 Congress enacted a new article of war forbidding army officers to return fugitive slaves to their masters. Before the war was a year old, therefore, the slaves themselves had taken the initiative that forced Northern authorities to move toward making it a war for freedom.

Most Republicans had become convinced by 1862 that the war against a slaveholders' rebellion must become a war against slavery itself, and they put increasing pressure on Lincoln to proclaim an emancipation policy. This would have comported with Lincoln's personal convictions, but as president he felt compelled to balance these convictions against the danger of alienating half of the Union constituency. By the summer of 1862, however, it was clear that he risked alienating the *Republican* half of his constituency if he did not act against slavery.

Moreover, the war was going badly for the Union. After a string of military victories in the early months of 1862, Northern armies suffered demoralizing reverses in July and August. The argument that emancipation was a military necessity became increasingly persuasive. It would weaken the Confederacy and correspondingly strengthen the Union by siphoning off part of the Southern labor force and adding this manpower to the Northern side. In July 1862 Congress enacted two laws based on this premise: a second confiscation act that freed slaves of persons who had engaged in rebellion against the United States, and a militia act that empowered the president to use freed slaves in the army in any capacity he saw fit — even as soldiers.

By this time Lincoln had decided on an even more dramatic measure: a proclamation issued as commander in chief freeing all slaves in states waging war against the Union. As he told a member of his cabinet, emancipation had become "a military necessity. . . . We must free the slaves or be ourselves subdued. . . . The Administration must set an example, and strike at the heart of the rebellion." The cabinet agreed, but Secretary of State William H. Seward persuaded Lincoln to withhold the proclamation until a major Union military victory could give it added force. Lincoln used the delay to help prepare conservative opinion for what was coming. In a letter to journalist Horace Greeley, published in the *New York Tribune* on August 22, 1862, the president reiterated that his "paramount object in the struggle *is* to save the Union, and is *not* either to save or destroy slavery." If he could accomplish this objective by freeing all, some, or none of the slaves, that was what he would do. Lincoln had already decided to free some and was in effect forewarning potential opponents of the Emancipation Proclamation that they must accept it as a necessary measure to save the Union. In a publicized meeting with black residents of Washington, also in 1862, Lincoln urged them to consider emigrating abroad to escape the prejudice they encountered and to help persuade conservatives that the much-feared racial consequences of emancipation might be thereby mitigated.

One month later, after the qualified Union victory in the Battle of Antietam, Lincoln issued a preliminary proclamation warning that in all states still in rebellion on January 1, 1863, he would declare their slaves "then, thenceforward, and forever free." January 1 came, and with it the final proclamation, which committed the government and armed forces of the United States to liberate the slaves in rebel states "as an act of justice, warranted by the Constitution, upon military necessity." The proclamation exempted the border slave states and all or parts of three Confederate states controlled by the Union army on the grounds that these areas were not in rebellion against the United States. Lincoln had tried earlier to persuade the border states to accept gradual emancipation, with compensation to slave owners from the federal government, but they had refused. The proclamation also authorized the recruitment of freed slaves and free blacks as Union soldiers; during the next 2½ years 180,000 of them fought in the Union army and 10,000 in the navy, making a vital contribution to Union victory as well as their own freedom. Emancipation would vastly increase the stakes of the war. It became a war for "a new birth of freedom," as Lincoln stated in the Gettysburg Address, a war that would transform Southern society by destroying its basic institution.

Meanwhile Lincoln and the Republican party recognized that the Emancipation Proclamation, as a war measure, might have no constitutional validity once the war was over. The legal framework of slavery would still exist in the former Confederate states as well as in the Union slave states that had been exempted from the proclamation. So the party committed itself to a constitutional amendment to abolish slavery. The overwhelmingly Republican Senate passed the Thirteenth Amendment by more than the necessary two-thirds majority on April 8, 1864. But not until January 31, 1865, did enough Democrats in the House abstain or vote for the amendment to pass it by a bare two-thirds. By December 18, 1865, the requisite three-quarters of the states had ratified the Thirteenth Amendment, which ensured that forever after "neither slavery nor involuntary servitude . . . shall exist within the United States."

Ira Berlin et al., eds., *Freedom: A Documentary History of Emancipation 1861–1867*, Ser. 1, Vol. 1, *The Destruction of Slavery* (1985); John Hope Franklin, *The Emancipation Proclamation* (1963).

JAMES M. MCPHERSON

See also Civil War; Lincoln, Abraham; Slavery.

EMBARGO ACT OF 1807

This act was passed by Congress to protest British and French interference with American neutral shipping during the Napoleonic Wars.

Although the wars created a huge demand for goods, each side attempted to block the other's trade. In the spring of 1806 the British navy began to blockade Continental ports, and in reply, Napoleon, in the Berlin and Milan decrees, prohibited trade with the British Empire. The British retaliated with Orders in Council blocking all neutrals from trading with France and its allies. At that time France controlled most of continental Europe.

Before these acts, the British navy had already interfered with American shipping by stopping ships to draft sailors from their crews — a practice called "impressment." The British claimed they were impressing British subjects, but often American citizens were taken.

After the Orders in Council and Napoleon's decrees, British and French warships hunted American merchantmen with impunity. Ever cost-conscious, President Thomas Jefferson had built small, cheap gunboats intended to protect the coast rather than vessels capable of protecting American shipping against the European powers. Although lucrative war profits offset shipping losses, European attacks became intolerable to American national pride.

Jefferson responded by imposing the embargo, which prohibited all exports. Since foreign ships would be forced to depart empty, the act also effectively limited imports. The president hoped that economic pressure would persuade the British and French to moderate their maritime policies. Further, he believed that keeping ships in American ports would prevent further violations of national honor. Instead, the embargo caused costly disruptions of the American economy and forced no concessions. American merchants evaded it just as they had ignored British trade restrictions before the Revolution.

In the last days of Jefferson's presidency, Congress replaced the Embargo Act with the almost unenforceable Non-Intercourse Act of March 1809, which prohibited trade only with Great Britain and France. Finally, in May 1810, Macon's Bill No. 2 removed all restrictions on commerce, but continued to bar foreign warships. The bill also empowered the president to reapply the ban on trade with either Britain or France if the other ceased to violate American neutral rights. After the passage of Macon's Bill, trade soon rebounded to prewar levels. The basic problem of violation of American sovereignty remained unsolved, however, and would lead to the War of 1812 with Great Britain.

See also Impressment Controversy; War of 1812.

EMERSON, RALPH WALDO

(1803–1882), essayist and poet. A central figure in the history of ideas in America, Emerson attacked the sterile rationalism and materialism of his age and encouraged a new generation to find "an original relation to the universe." His romantic advocacy of self-reliance, based on a notion of the "god within," diminished the authority of institutions and traditions and empowered the self. As the central figure in the movement known as transcendentalism, he had an immediate and personal influence on Henry David Thoreau, Margaret Fuller, Bronson Alcott, and Theodore Parker, among others, and his writings on philosophical and aesthetic subjects strongly influenced the work of such major American authors as Nathaniel Hawthorne, Herman Melville, Walt Whitman, and Emily Dickinson.

Emerson was educated at the Boston Latin School and Harvard College and prepared for the Unitarian ministry at Harvard Divinity School. He served as minister at Boston's Second Church from 1829 to 1832, when he resigned over his refusal to administer Communion. Already a widower, in frail health, and unsure of his future, he traveled to Europe, where he met notable literary figures, including Thomas Carlyle with whom he carried on a correspondence for almost fifty years. He returned to the United States in 1833 and began his lecturing career.

In his first book, *Nature* (1836), a transcendentalist manifesto, Emerson distinguished between the Me (the soul or immaterial self) and the Not-Me (the external world, including nature and one's own body), arguing that the universe is so constructed as to make the Not-Me a subordinate representation of the Me. Influenced by Platonic idealism, Emerson gave primacy to the spiritual over the material, but argued that the two realms were not radically disjoined (as he felt Americans believed) but rather corresponded symbolically, point for point, as if in a kind of mirror. Emerson developed these and related ideas in various lectures, including his American Scholar address (1837) and his Divinity School address (1838), and in two volumes of *Essays* (1841 and 1844). At the time, his antitraditional views were regarded as both difficult to understand and, in their antinomian emphasis on self-reliance, dangerous to established institutions, especially the church. Still, his ideas and his poetic, aphoristic style attracted a devoted following among the younger generation, including the members of the Transcendental Club, and he won increasing popular respect as his lectures and books reached ever-larger audiences. In addition to collections of essays, he published *Poems* (1847) and *May-Day* (1867).

Emerson's writings bore the stamp of the Calvinist and Unitarian culture of his ancestors, present to him through much of his life in the person of his Aunt Mary Moody Emerson, who helped raise him after his father died in 1811. She instilled a love of nature in her city-bred nephew, impressed on him the value of an unceasing self-culture, and taught him to admire the poetry of John Milton and William Wordsworth. The writings of Samuel Coleridge and Carlyle led him early to an admiration of the riches of German romantic thought. Later, while editing the *Dial*, an important literary journal, he became interested in the "ethnical scriptures" of India and China and in the poetry of Persia. For all these many and varied influences, though, he never lost the distinctive New England texture of his early thought. His writings, including his voluminous journals, are central documents of American romanticism.

Gay Wilson Allen, *Waldo Emerson* (1981); B. L. Packer, *Emerson's Fall* (1982); Stephen E. Whicher, *Freedom and Fate: An Inner Life of Ralph Waldo Emerson* (1953).

ALBERT J. VON FRANK

See also Literature; Transcendentalism.

ENGLAND-U.S. RELATIONS

See Great Britain–U.S. Relations.

ENTAIL

This is the name given to the legal status of a landed estate when its ownership is restricted through inheritance to biological descendants of the original grantee in order to maintain its size. Originally practiced in New York and the South, entail was abolished, along with primogeniture (inheritance by only the eldest son), throughout the United States before 1800. The practice of protecting large estates through restrictions on inheritance was brought from England, but owing to the vast abundance of available rich land in America, workers and tenants could obtain their own land, and large holdings became less profitable. Also, descendants of landowners could turn to the challenge of earning even greater wealth through their own efforts, and inheritance of large holdings was no longer the major path to wealth.

Abolition of entail and primogeniture was part of a general reform movement that included the grant to married women of the right to control their own property and the disestablishment of churches.

See also Primogeniture.

ENVIRONMENTAL MOVEMENTS

See Conservation and Environmental Movements.

EPIDEMICS

The health of Americans through the centuries has been shaped by the shifting nature of economic, social, and political life. In particular, epidemic diseases have been affected by such factors as the isolation of rural communities, the development of an economy based on commerce, the growth of large cities, extremes of poverty and wealth, and changing housing and work conditions.

In the seventeenth century, the relative isolation of many colonies tended to limit the impact of epidemics, in contrast to conditions in crowded European cities. But by the end of the eighteenth century, an extensive commercial economy combined with a growing, increasingly urbanized, and poor population made epidemics a much greater threat to Americans. Epidemic disease, once a local phenomenon circumscribed by the relative lack of mobility among rural communities, began to sweep through the nation along well-established trade routes. By the middle of the nineteenth century, the crowded and increasingly poor urban centers experienced death rates that were as high as those in Europe. Cholera, dysentery, tuberculosis, and other waterborne and airborne infectious conditions became endemic in such cities as New York, Boston, Philadelphia, and New Orleans.

One example of the close connection between health and geographical and social conditions is the experience of seventeenth-century colonists in Massachusetts. Studies have revealed an extraordinarily healthy population as measured by statistics on average length of life, mortality and morbidity rates, and infant mortality. Male residents of the first settlements lived into their seventies and eighties while their English counterparts were dying in their mid-thirties. Similarly, colonial women in the Massachusetts Bay Colony who escaped death during childbirth also lived long lives.

Although yellow fever and malaria, both mosquito-borne diseases, were widely reported in seventeenth-century New England, their impact on the colonists of Jamestown was far greater. The first generations of settlers in the Virginia colonies were plagued by malaria, yellow fever, and other epidemics. The prevalence there of early death, infirmity, and infertility led historian Edmund Morgan to entitle one of his essays about the region "Living with Death." The initial lack of commitment to establishing permanent colonies in Virginia helps explain both the dearth of women among the first generations of colonists and their inability to avert starvation leading to their susceptibility to epidemic diseases. (The sickle-cell trait among African-Americans is associated with greater resistance to malaria. Some have argued tenuously that this relative ability to withstand malaria helps account for the introduction of slavery in the American South.)

Smallpox, an acute viral disease that disfig-

ures its victims, was perhaps the most fearsome illness of the colonial period. Introduced to the Americas by European colonists, the disease had an especially devastating effect on Native Americans who, because of their lack of contact with the virus, had virtually no immunity to it. While English and Spanish settlements were periodically swept by epidemics that caused varying degrees of distress, Native American populations throughout the colonies were all but wiped out. John Duffy, in *Epidemics of Colonial America,* quotes a letter written by a settler of South Carolina in 1699: smallpox "swept away a whole neighboring [Indian] nation, all to 5 or 6 which ran away and left their dead unburied." Duffy also reports that an "epidemic in 1738 killed one half of the Cherokee Indians" near Charleston. In a horrifying instance, some U.S. Army units in the nineteenth century gave blankets used by smallpox and measles victims to Indian tribes, thereby destroying their communities and slowing resistance to western expansion.

In some early epidemics it was observed that a technique called "variolation" practiced by African-American slaves appeared to be effective in protecting blacks from the worst ravages of the diseases. The focus of intense public and religious debate in the early eighteenth century, the technique consisted of transplanting scabs or pus of smallpox victims into open wounds of healthy individuals. These people then developed a mild set of symptoms and thereafter immunity. This technique was adopted by European-Americans and helped in the development of inoculation and vaccination as effective preventives.

Epidemics became national in character with the development of extensive coastal and river trade in the eighteenth and early nineteenth centuries. Earlier, local outbreaks had been devastating but limited geographically. But by the 1790s, linked epidemics ranged up and down the East Coast in such cities as Philadelphia, New York, and Boston. Often understood in religious or moral terms, epidemics were thought to be forms of godly retribution for sins of the individual or the community.

In the nineteenth century a number of new waterborne and airborne diseases swept through the growing cities of the nation. Cholera, a disease that caused severe dehydration through acute diarrhea, made dramatic and fearsome appearances in 1832, 1848, and 1865. In the absence of sewage systems, clean water, systematic street cleaning, pure food and milk, and effective methods for preserving or freezing meats, diphtheria and whooping cough, fevers and flu — all present to varying degrees in earlier periods — became constant threats to babies and young children in the nation's filthy urban centers. By the second half of the century, death and disease rates in American cities had climbed substantially and Americans' average length of life was now no better than that of Europeans.

Tuberculosis, perhaps the most pervasive and deadly disease in the West, became the focus of intense concern as its primary symptom, coughing and spitting, took on a seemingly dangerous aspect in the crowded, poverty-stricken urban environments of the late nineteenth century. Despite the fact that incidence of the disease probably peaked in the middle years of the century and that it declined as a major cause of mortality after the 1880s, efforts of public health professionals and charity workers to combat the illness continued for several decades.

In the twentieth century, infectious diseases still accounted for vast suffering among urban and rural populations alike. In 1918–1919, the worldwide pandemic of influenza reached the United States, causing about 400,000 deaths, by far the most devastating epidemic in American history. In the next few decades, diphtheria, whooping cough, measles, and mumps continued to exact a high toll among children. But public health attention began to turn increasingly to chronic, noninfectious illnesses such as cancer, heart disease, and stroke.

With the advent of sulfa drugs, penicillin, and antibiotics in the decades following the Great Depression, both the medical profession and the public believed that infectious diseases would soon cease to be a major threat to Americans. The polio epidemic of the 1950s was fearsome, but the promise of the new "wonder drugs" seemed to be confirmed with the vaccines developed by Jonas Salk and Albert Sabin.

Ironically, the very successes of the postwar decades in the development of technological medical innovations left the nation mostly unprepared for the new scourge of the 1980s, acquired immune deficiency syndrome, or AIDS. Health departments were underfunded and understaffed, and a generation of public health and medical practitioners had come of age believing that medical science and technology could protect Americans from any widespread epidemic. Also, the fact that the 1970s was marked by a fiasco in which millions of dollars were spent on the development and distribution of a vaccine for a swine flu epidemic that never materialized undermined the nation's ability to mobilize against the disease. And because AIDS primarily affected gay men and intravenous drug users — both subject to widespread biases — some accused government and research scientists of deliberate inaction or at least of reluctance to undertake massive programs to combat the latest American epidemic.

The nature of epidemics and the public's response to them changed greatly over time. Once simply local problems perceived to be of divine origin, epidemics became national in scope and understood in medical terms. But the reaction to a given disease was often still influenced by society's perceptions of its victims.

Judith Leavitt and Ronald Numbers, eds., *Sickness and Health in America,* 2nd ed. (1985); Charles Rosenberg, *The Cholera Years* (1987); Barbara Rosenkrantz, *Public Health and the State* (1973).

DAVID ROSNER

See also Birthrate and Mortality; Medicine; Salk, Jonas.

EQUAL RIGHTS AMENDMENT

The Equal Rights Amendment (ERA), which would provide for the legal equality of the sexes, was first proposed by the National Woman's party in 1923. In its most recent form the amendment declared, "Equality of rights under the law shall not be denied or abridged by the United States or any State on account of sex." The amendment was approved by the requisite two-thirds vote of the House of Representatives in October 1971 and by the Senate in March 1972. Spurred by the revival of feminism in the late 1960s and 1970s, the ERA received much early support as thirty states ratified it within one year of its Senate approval. But it ultimately failed to achieve ratification by the required thirty-eight states, even though the deadline for ratification was extended to June 30, 1982. The defeat of the ERA was spearheaded by Phyllis Schlafly and her organization Stop ERA, which benefited from the conservative backlash that gained momentum in the mid-1970s. Nonetheless, despite its defeat, public support for the amendment never fell below 54 percent, and as late as 1976 support for its passage was included in the platforms of both major political parties.

See also Feminist Movement.

ERIE CANAL

The Erie Canal, an engineering marvel of its time, was a product of New York's political scene and its prosperity. Gouverneur Morris first advocated a waterway to link the Hudson River and Lake Erie in 1800, and a surveyor laid out a route in 1809. In 1815, former New York City mayor DeWitt Clinton pushed the idea, in part to rebuild his political career. In 1817, the legislature authorized construction under the auspices of a canal commission headed by Clinton. The commission helped elect Clinton to several terms as governor, to the chagrin of his rival Martin Van Buren.

Construction of the canal went smoothly. Part of it was operating by 1820, and by 1823 boats could go from the Hudson to Rochester. The Erie Canal was finished in 1825. The first boat traveled from Buffalo to New York City, with ceremonies held in both cities. The canal caused freight costs to fall sharply, and New York City and river towns like Buffalo, Rochester, and Syracuse boomed. Politically, the canal split Democrats and Whigs over how to pay for improvements and maintenance, but helped unite the Albany Regency against the Whigs.

See also Transportation Revolution.

ESPIONAGE

George Washington was already a devotee of military intelligence when he assumed command of the Continental army. While serving as a British officer in the French and Indian war, he had ruefully noted the benefits that accrued to the French through their alliance with the natives of the North American forests. Small parties of white men, he observed, were not "so dexterous at skulking as Indians; and large parties will be discovered by their spies early enough to have a superior force opposed to them."

By employing such tactics in the revolutionary war, Washington prevailed against overwhelming military odds: his deployment of spies and his wise evaluation of the information they brought in helped him keep his nationalist guerrilla soldiers out of reach of the enemy and intact as a fighting force. The events of these years began to shape the American attitude toward espionage and spies. There were verifiable tales of true heroes: Nathan Hale on the American side, and Maj. John André on the British. Equally, the mercenary treachery of Benedict Arnold made a deep impression on the American mind.

Although some of the main lineaments of espionage are discernible in the earliest days of the Republic, developments in the nineteenth century were slow. Absorbed by the challenges of their own continent and heeding the isolationist advice of Presidents Washington, Thomas Jefferson, and James Monroe, Americans saw no need to practice systematic international intrigue, or even to defend themselves against it.

To be sure, some nineteenth-century Americans engaged in espionage. Stories abound about the exploits of secret agents in the Civil War. Belle Boyd was only seventeen when federal soldiers burst into her Virginia home, enraging her to such a degree that she variously resorted to homicide, espionage, and charm on behalf of the Confederacy. Although arrested several times between July 1862 and the spring of 1864, she escaped severe retribution, obtaining a pardon from President Abraham Lincoln on one occasion and marrying her jailer on another. Yet, the tale is more redolent of glamour than of competence. Neither side developed an effective espionage or counterespionage network in the course of the war.

Many Americans remained suspicious of espionage in the 1890s. One reason was the ill repute of the Pinkerton National Detective Agency, an organization that had occasionally served the federal government. For the "Pinkerton men" had spied on labor unions and, in 1892, were involved in a notorious shoot-out with striking workers at Andrew Carnegie's showpiece steelworks at Homestead, Pennsylvania. Another reason was the White House's habit of evading congressional scrutiny by using secret agents to conduct unofficial diplomacy. Following the acquisition of Hawaii in this manner, Senator George Hoar of Massachusetts secured passage of a resolution stating that a presidential spy "could be in no sense an officer of the United States."

Yet America was on the eve of a long run of success in the counterintelligence field. In the Spanish-American War of 1898, Spain set up a spy network in Montreal under the leadership of Ramón de Carranza. But John E. Wilkie, a Chicago businessman with a weakness for loud bow ties, had just been put in charge of the U.S. Secret Service, and he soon mopped up the "Montreal spy ring." In World War I, Franz von Papen — a future chancellor of Weimar Germany — organized a spy and sabotage ring. The Secret Service and fledgling FBI eliminated it. In the 1930s, the FBI was effective against Nazi agents in both the United States and South America. So far as we know, neither the Russian KGB nor any other foreign intelligence agency has ever effected a serious penetration of the CIA.

The Japanese attack on Pearl Harbor on December 7, 1941, surprised the defending forces, a circumstance that suggested a need for improved U.S. facilities for the collection and analysis of intelligence. In the course of World War II, the Office of Strategic Services attempted to meet these needs and also established for itself a covert operational role. In 1945, the traditional American distrust of espionage resurfaced, and the world's first superpower was temporarily shorn of a large-scale intelligence capability. But on July 26, 1947, Section 102 of the National Security Act established the CIA, the world's first democratically sanctioned secret service.

Fear of foreign espionage for a while far exceeded reservations about an American "police state." In 1950, former State Department official Alger Hiss went to prison after being accused of spying for the Soviet Union. In 1953, the married couple Julius and Ethel Rosenberg died in the electric chair in Sing Sing prison, having been convicted of passing atomic secrets to the Russians. The evidence in both these cases is suspect, and it is possible that Hiss and the Rosenbergs were at least partly innocent. But this was the McCarthy era, and their respective trials were patently unfair. In the name of freedom, American judges and juries had impaired the very liberties they were supposed to be defending.

In due course, a strong reaction set in, at some cost to the intelligence agencies. Liberals, who took exception to the involvement of the FBI in some of the McCarthyist excesses, became even more vehement in their denunciations when they learned about the bureau's harassment of Martin Luther King, Jr., and the civil rights movement in the 1960s. Cold war calumny abroad added to the furor. Presidents had begun to rely on the CIA's covert operational capabilities to produce quick fixes — most notoriously, the overthrow of the democratically elected, if leftward-leaning, governments of Guatemala and Chile in 1954 and 1973, respectively. After the failure of the 1961 Bay of Pigs venture, an attempt to overthrow Fidel Castro in Cuba, the CIA became increasingly vulnerable to criticism.

Nevertheless, the intelligence community retained widespread respect and support for several reasons. In contrast to the FBI's J. Edgar Hoover, Allen Dulles, the 1950s' CIA director, had refused to cooperate with Senator Joseph McCarthy, a stand that won his particular agency well-deserved support. With the passage of time and the declassification of documents, it also emerged that both the CIA and military intelligence had issued sound warnings about the unsatisfactory progress of the Vietnam War. Even more important, the intelligence community's "Soviet estimate" has, in general, been sound, a circumstance that helped protect America and its allies from Soviet attack and prepare the groundwork for arms agreements in the Nixon, Carter, and Reagan administrations. In 1975, vigorous congressional investigations into their agencies shook many intelligence officers, but in fact they prepared the way for some confidence-boosting reforms, such as the ban on assassination as an instrument of state policy.

In the 1980s, the intelligence agencies were indirectly involved in an illegal scheme to sell weapons to Iran and divert the profits into the pockets of the Contra resistance movement in Nicaragua. The Iran-Contra affair reminded many Americans that espionage remained a dirty game. They still had reason to retain some of their old ambivalence, even if they could claim to have recovered from their nineteenth-century antipathy to espionage.

Rhodri Jeffreys-Jones, *The CIA and American Democracy* (1989); Nathan Miller, *Spying for America: The Hidden History of U.S. Intelligence* (1989).

RHODRI JEFFREYS-JONES

See also Alger Hiss Case; Arnold, Benedict; Central Intelligence Agency; Federal Bureau of Investigation; Iran-Contra Affair; Pinkertons; *Rosenberg* Case; U-2 Affair.

ETHNICITY

The term *ethnicity* as used by historians to mean "the character or quality of an ethnic group" is of recent origin, first appearing in the *1972 Supplement* to the *Oxford English Dictionary*. A more extended definition was given in the 1973 *American Heritage Dictionary:* "1. The condition of belonging to a particular ethnic group; 2. Ethnic pride." It has become a term susceptible to varying meanings. Nowhere is this more apparent than the extent to which ethnicity has become the foundation for the reinterpretation of the American immigrant experience.

Traditionally, American immigration was discussed in terms of "Anglo-conformity," and "the melting pot," both processes that assumed the rapid assimilation of the immigrant into the prevalent American culture shaped by English colonial settlement. Implicit in this view was the subordination of the cultural norms, mores, and assumptions brought by other immigrant groups. Marcus Lee Hansen, an early historian of immigration, asked, did the original American settlers make "a bad blunder, when consciously or unconsciously they decreed that one literature, one attitude toward the arts, one set of standards should be the basis of culture?" This question set the agenda for the reexamination of immigration within the context of ethnicity.

What made American immigration extraordinary was and is its sheer scale. Although the primary source in the colonial and the early federal periods was the British Isles, even then, significant minorities came from the Netherlands and the Rhine valley. What historians have defined as the "push-pull factors" explained why immigrants left their homelands and what attracted them to America. The underlying constant was economic pressures at home, particularly affecting the landless, the underemployed, and the unemployed. When combined with rapid population growth, the impetus for departure became overwhelming. But other currents, such as the search for religious tolerance and escape from political oppression, also played a role.

It is noteworthy that some early immigrant groups such as the Mennonites and the Amish remained stubbornly attached to a religious identity that set them off from the mainstream. They also persisted in their use of German, known as Pennsylvania Dutch (from *deutsch*). But the predominantly British character of colonial immigration set the terms of future assimilation. The core American culture that took shape in the first two centuries was a blend of English, Scottish, and Welsh ethnicity. At its heart stood the English language, English common law, and Protestantism. As self-defined natives, the Anglo-Americans saw other newcomers as a danger to their revolutionary and republican identity, which they thought added a uniquely American dimension to their British inheritance. A central concern was whether a different religion or ethnicity would preclude assimilation. It cemented the nativist conviction that the successful absorption of newcomers required the obliteration of their ethnicity.

One intriguing aspect of ethnicity was the extent to which immigrants made religion a primary dimension of their identity. This took on major significance with the huge influx of Catholic Irish between 1846 and 1855. Driven by the "potato famine," close to a million and a half Irish poured into northeastern ports. Traditional Protestant assumptions about the reactionary nature of Catholicism were combined with ancient English prejudices against the Irish to make the newcomers seem irredeemably alien. The Irish response was to accentuate their group-consciousness. Their Catholicism provided a counter to nativist pressure. Nowhere was this more evident than in the development of a parochial school system to counteract the Protestant bias of the public schools. The process was reinforced by the arrival during the same period of over a million Germans, who did not accept the superiority of English over German. Wherever Germans and Irish settled, ethnic communities intent upon preserving their culture, traditions, and language appeared.

Pressure to restrict immigration was balanced by America's need for labor. Economic growth and immigration complemented each other. But as native workers saw it, the newcomers drove down wages and worsened labor conditions. The immigrants also stratified the working class along ethnic lines, as the newest arrivals tended disproportionately to gravitate toward the lowest kinds of employment. The experience repeated itself as subsequent arrivals propelled earlier arrivals upward economically. Continuing immigration had the further ironic effect of transforming previous arrivals into natives.

The sheer numbers who immigrated to America between 1840 and 1924 were staggering — some 37 million. Their overwhelmingly European origin was overshadowed by their diversity of language, religion, mores, customs, and culture. Even within Catholicism, the difference in religious practices among ethnic groups obliged the church hierarchy to organize national parishes. The dominant Irish clergy had to accommodate ethnic priorities. Efforts to make English the language of common church parlance led to threats of schism. When faced with the subordination of Polish to English, for example, a significant number of Poles defected to form the Polish National Catholic church. By the end of the nineteenth century, Catholic leaders were preoccupied with the task of creating out of the diversity of European Catholicism a distinctly American Catholicism. In a sense, a counterassimilation emerged to resist both the divisiveness inherited from Europe and the pull of the dominant Protestant ethos.

Departure from the old country did not end immigrants' interest in the affairs of their homelands. For many, the United States provided a base from which to mount efforts to overturn the old order at home. European authorities infiltrated immigrant organizations to keep tabs on potential revolutionary agitation. Britain had good reason to suspect that Irish-Americans were the main source of support for the Fenians in the nineteenth century and the Irish Republican Army (IRA) in the twentieth. The Czechoslovak republic was in significant measure founded in the United States. Key Bolsheviks such as Leon Trotsky and Nikolay Bukharin were residing in New York when the Russian Revolution began in 1917. Cuban exiles found Miami a convenient base from which to mount opposition to their nemesis Fidel Castro. Perhaps no aspect of ongoing interest in the affairs of another country is more significant than the key role American Jews have played in support of Israel.

Cohesive ethnic communities provided the social, economic, and political environments within which new arrivals began the process of integrating into the larger American society. For first-generation immigrants, these ethnic villages provided a transitional environment in which familiar norms were sustained. An infrastructure of businesses designed to meet their everyday needs created an economic mobility that was independent of the host society. In many former ethnic urban enclaves businesses still survive that continue to cater to the descendants of those who called them home. Another powerful anchor for these settlements was the sprawling industrial factories that provided immigrants with employment. But the diversity of their origins proved a formidable obstacle to worker organization.

America's twentieth-century industrial labor force was drawn from central, eastern, and southern Europe. Between 1900 and 1910 almost 6 million immigrants arrived from Italy, Russia, and Austria-Hungary. Their brawn was complemented by skills necessary to the textile, garment, mining, construction, and other heavy industries. In the silk industry of Paterson, New Jersey, for example, a combination of English, French, and Italian labor was essential to growth. Coal mining witnessed a progression from Welsh, English, and Irish miners to Slavic. The booming New York garment industry owed much of its existence to the Jewish workers who fled the Russian Pale at the end of the nineteenth century. Their ranks were supplemented by Italian seamstresses and then those from the Caribbean. A massive rejuvenation of garment production took place in the late twentieth century as Chinese workers flooded into America. A significant number of immigrant workers were women whose earnings were essential to their family's survival.

Over time, as the sources of immigration shifted, the children and grandchildren of earlier arrivals gradually assimilated into the dominant culture, and the seemingly monolithic solidarity of ethnic communities eroded. The emphasis on endogamous relations deteriorated as marriage across ethnic lines became the norm. The vast majority of Americans were increasingly of mixed ethnicity. The preeminence of the English language confirmed Anglo conformity. A new idea, the "melting pot," emerged, which viewed Anglo dominance as a transitory stage to a new American identity fused from all races, religions, and nationalities. But less evident was the stubborn retention of the unique characteristics of the seemingly submerged ethnicities. A cultural pluralism steadily permeated the homogeneous values that "natives" insisted were essential to the American identity. As ethnics dispersed, hyphenated societies proliferated. As early as 1843 Jewish-Americans had organized B'nai B'rith to protect their interests. Irish Catholics, confronted on their arrival with the Protestant Irish

Orange societies, responded with the Ancient Order of the Hibernians. Germans developed the Turnvereins, an athletic, social group derived from the Czech and Slovak Sokols. Italian-American doctors created the Morgagni Medical societies and family associations provided Chinese with social and financial aid. Ethnics had assimilated, but they retained networks that advanced their political and socioeconomic interests.

The nearly unlimited admission of immigrants that largely prevailed until World War I gave way to a deepening drive to limit their numbers when the war ended. Public doubts about whether the United States could assimilate "undesirable" immigrants climaxed in the Immigration Act of 1924, which established national quotas. The lifeblood of ethnic communities dwindled to a mere trickle. The act reduced the number of immigrants to be admitted annually to 164,677, divided by quota almost exclusively among European countries. Eighty-six percent of the total was allotted to northwestern Europe, closing the door to the "new immigrants." The Great Depression further inhibited immigration and World War II practically ended it. For entry-level jobs the United States turned to domestic sources such as Puerto Ricans and southern blacks. It introduced the question of race into assimilation. Foreshadowed was the impending influx of Asians, Africans, and Latin Americans. What had been a bias toward Europeans shifted in 1964 with the reallocation of quotas favoring third world countries.

Immigrants from Asia encountered a different reception than Europeans. The treatment of Chinese immigrants in the nineteenth century had culminated with the Chinese Exclusion Act of 1882. The resident Chinese-American population steadily declined afterward as only a handful were allowed entry. But those who were in America created the distinctive, secluded worlds of urban Chinatowns, where it was possible for Chinese-Americans to maintain a measure of autonomy. The unofficial exclusion of Japanese was officially confirmed in 1924 when they were denied a quota. The tenuous nature of their presence was grimly revealed when in 1942 they were consigned to detention camps during

World War II. The segregation of blacks and the confinement of Native Americans to reservations effectively denied people of color the benefits of assimilation. But these policies came apart as the postwar overthrow of colonial empires obliged the United States to deal on a basis of equality with the citizens of the newly independent nations.

African-Americans had a long history of opposition to efforts that denied them assimilation. In the aftermath of World War II, a surging challenge to Jim Crow discrimination at all levels eroded the foundations of black separation. Employment, education, and public transportation and facilities were protected by federal and state laws guaranteeing racial equality; the black consciousness movement of the 1960s brought to the fore a militant leadership that proclaimed "black is beautiful." From the long-quiet reservations, Native Americans insisted that they receive recognition for their distinctive cultures. Japanese-Americans demanded apologies and compensation for their oppression during World War II. In short, the message was that assimilation had to be color-blind. What had once been a European civilization was becoming a world civilization.

The entry of Africans, Asians, and Latin Americans after 1965 added over 5 million legal immigrants to the population. More than a million Cubans and Vietnamese were admitted under special political refugee provisions. Calculations of the number of illegal immigrants have run between 3 and 10 million drawn primarily by the prospect of economic opportunity. The composition of the American population has been steadily altered as Americans born in Europe dwindled in number. Concern for the dominance of the English language and the cultural impact of immigrants reemerged as resident Americans wondered how these changes would affect them. How best to prepare immigrant children to use the new language had traditionally been the sink-or-swim approach. In the 1960s, a call for bilingual education to ease the transition to English resulted in extensive programs using the immigrants' languages as a bridge. But the process gave rise to the question of whether bilingualism was a temporary or a permanent situation. Many ethnics, particularly Spanish speakers, insisted that their language share equality with English. The appearance of multilingual signs, ballots, applications, and formal notices created a conviction among natives that English be declared the official language, as if that were the test of how fully immigrants embraced their new nationality.

The complex historical origins of the newcomers are evident in their ethnic enclaves. What is also clear is that the American identity is still in the making and that the process is far from over. And non-Americans comment with awe at the remarkable ability of the United States to fuse from diversity a consensus that is an ever-changing mosaic.

Thomas J. Archdeacon, *Becoming American: An Ethnic History* (1983); Stephan Thernstrom, Ann Orlov, and Oscar Handlin, eds., *Harvard Encyclopedia of American Ethnic Groups* (1980).

JAMES P. SHENTON

See also Immigration; Nativism.

EVANGELICALISM

The visits of George Whitefield, an Anglican itinerant preacher, to the American colonies in the 1730s and 1740s triggered a widespread evangelical revival known as the Great Awakening. This was the first major evangelical flowering in America. Whitefield built upon and knit together disparate revivals in the colonies — the pietistic awakenings among the Dutch in the Raritan Valley of New Jersey, the revival in Jonathan Edwards's congregation in Northampton, Massachusetts, and the sacramental seasons among the Scots-Irish Presbyterians in the Middle Colonies. Evangelicalism in America has largely retained characteristics emphasized by the Great Awakening — the centrality of conversion, the quest for an affective piety, and a suspicion of wealth, worldliness, and ecclesiastical pretension.

Eighteenth-century evangelicals, known as New Lights, helped shape American culture in the revolutionary era and beyond. Evangelicals generally lined up with the Patriots during the Revolution, and evangelical leaders joined Enlightenment deists in an unlikely alliance to press for religious disestablishment. The Second Great Awakening in the early nineteenth century stoked the revival fires once again in New England, western New York, and the Cumberland Valley. Each region made its own contribution to antebellum evangelicalism. The revival fervor in New England gave rise to benevolent and reform societies such as the temperance movement, the female seminary movement, prison reform, and abolitionism. The era's leading evangelical preacher, Charles Grandison Finney in western New York, believed that his "new measures" would precipitate revival, and he emphasized the role of human volition in the salvation process. American evangelicalism ever since has eschewed Calvinist notions about predestination in favor of Finney's doctrines exalting the individual's ability to "choose God" and take control of his or her spiritual destiny.

In the South, the revival functioned as a civilizing force in a society of widely scattered settlements, prodigious alcohol consumption, and notoriously rowdy behavior. Circuit riders, a product of the organizing genius of American Methodism, brought religion to the people; Baptists, the other major religion of the South, ordained their own ministers without regard for clerical education. Camp meetings, still a fixture of southern religion, lured thousands for socializing, preaching, conversion, and spectacular displays of religious enthusiasm. Evangelicalism has left its mark on southern culture — witness the persistence of backwoods camp meetings and baptisms, evangelical revivals, and public prayers at school events.

The social reforming impulse emanating from Protestantism in the North, however, soon clashed with southern mores. Evangelicalism in the antebellum South came to be identified with the social order, since southern evangelicals saw themselves at odds with northern abolitionists over the issue of slavery. Southern evangelicalism turned inward and became increasingly insular in the face of attacks from the North. The sectional conflict divided denominations before it sundered the Union, thereby creating institutional schisms that, in some instances, still fester.

The Emancipation Proclamation removed the one adhesive, abolitionism, that had united northern evangelicals, so that after the Civil War evangelicalism in the North began to dissipate in a flurry of theological controversies and denominational disputes. The publication of Charles Darwin's *The Origin of Species* in 1859 had gone virtually unnoticed amid the sectional tensions, but after the war evangelicals began to recognize its implications for literalistic interpretations of the Bible. American Protestants, especially in the North, waged fierce battles over biblical inspiration. Conservatives, notably A. A. Hodge, B. B. Warfield, and the theologians at Princeton Seminary, reasserted the divine inspiration and inerrancy of the Bible, while liberal theologians such as Charles A. Briggs at Union Theological Seminary took a less rigid view.

The industrialization and urbanization of American culture in the decades following the Civil War exaggerated the divide within American Protestantism. In the face of urban squalor and the frustrated ambitions for a Protestant empire, disappointed evangelicals adjusted their eschatology. No longer did they believe that their efforts could bring about the millennium; instead, they adopted an interpretive scheme of the Bible called dispensational premillennialism that insisted Christ would come at any moment to "rapture" the true Christians from the earth and unleash his judgment against a sinful world. While evangelicals retreated to dispensationalism and despaired of social reform, their liberal counterparts embraced the Social Gospel, which held that God redeems not individuals only but sinful social institutions as well.

Evangelicals and liberals clashed again in the 1910s and 1920s. Two tycoons, Lyman and Milton Stewart of Union Oil in California, financed the publication of a series of pamphlets called *The Fundamentals,* which outlined what the writers regarded as the essentials of orthodoxy: biblical inerrancy, the virgin birth, Christ's atonement and resurrection, the authenticity of miracles, and dispensationalism. These "five points of fundamentalism" became the focus of doctrinal struggles in the 1920s, with the "fundamentalists" (hence the name) defending the doctrines against the "modernists" or liberals.

With rare exceptions, the fundamentalists lost those struggles for power within Protestant denominations; though some stayed within mainline churches, others left to form independent churches or denominations. An even larger defeat came in 1925 in Dayton, Tennessee, at the Scopes "monkey trial." Although fundamentalists, represented in the courtroom by William Jennings Bryan, won the case against John T. Scopes (his conviction was later overturned on a technicality), fundamentalists lost badly in the court of public opinion. The merciless lampoons of H. L. Mencken and other journalists covering the trial portrayed fundamentalists as uneducated country bumpkins, a stereotype that, unfairly, persists to this day.

After the 1920s, fundamentalists, perceiving that American culture had turned against them, retreated from public life, but they did not disappear. Instead, they set about building a huge subculture of churches, denominations, Bible institutes, colleges, seminaries, Bible camps, mission societies, and publishing houses that provided the foundation for their resurgence in the 1970s. Half a century after the *Scopes* trial and coincident with the presidential campaign of Jimmy Carter, a Southern Baptist Sunday school teacher, evangelicals, especially southerners, began to reassert themselves in the public arena. Although they deserted Carter for Ronald Reagan in 1980, evangelicals, led by preacher-activists like Jerry Falwell and Pat Robertson (who would mount a campaign for the Republican presidential nomination in 1988), have made their presence felt in American politics.

Despite some general surprise over this political activism, evangelicals in recent years have merely reclaimed their historic place in American public discourse. The return of evangelicalism to public life has also served gradually to erode popular perceptions of evangelicals as backward and somehow opposed to technology and innovation. Evangelicals, in fact, have consistently been pioneers in mass communications — the open-air preaching in the eighteenth century, which prefigured the Patriot rhetoric during the Revolution; the Methodist circuits on the frontier, which anticipated grassroots political organizations; the adroit use of broadcast media in the twentieth century, from the radio preachers of the twenties to the televangelists of the seventies, which provided a model for such masters of political communication as Franklin D. Roosevelt and Reagan.

Evangelicalism — from the revival tradition of the eighteenth and nineteenth centuries to the militant fundamentalism of the 1920s to pentecostalism with its emphasis on speaking in tongues and other gifts of the Holy Spirit — is deeply imbedded in American life, in part because of its promise of easy salvation, intimacy with God, and a community of fellow believers. In 1925 H. L. Mencken, no friend of evangelicals, remarked that if you threw an egg out of a Pullman window almost anywhere in America, you would hit a fundamentalist. Pullman cars are all but obsolete now; fundamentalists remain a strong force in American life.

Randall Balmer, *Mine Eyes Have Seen the Glory: A Journey into the Evangelical Subculture in America* (1989); George M. Marsden, *Fundamentalism and American Culture: The Shaping of Twentieth-Century Evangelicalism: 1870–1925* (1980); Timothy L. Smith, *Revivalism and Social Reform in Mid-Nineteenth-Century America* (1957).

RANDALL BALMER

See also Edwards, Jonathan; Graham, Billy; Great Awakening; Missionaries; Religion; *Scopes* Trial; Second Great Awakening; Social Gospel.

EVOLUTION, TEACHING OF

See Scopes Trial.

EXECUTIVE BRANCH

See Presidency; Vice Presidency.

EXODUS, BLACK

See Black Exodus, 1879.

EXPANSION, CONTINENTAL AND OVERSEAS

The thirteen colonies that became the United States were on the cutting edge of the expansion of England that created a global political economy ultimately known as the British Empire. Born of the expansionist impulses that had led to the conquest of Wales, Ireland, and Scotland, the United States itself became an empire that equaled, indeed surpassed, the greatest projections of British power. Today, more than two centuries after independence, the sun never sets on American territory, properties owned by the U.S. government and its citizens, American armed forces abroad, or countries that conduct their affairs within limits largely defined by American power.

The first U.S. census, conducted in 1790, asserted ownership of 891,364 square miles of the North American continent. Much of that acreage was also claimed by Native American societies, and various European powers contested marginal areas. Today, the fifty states total 3,623,420 square miles, and the directly ruled overseas possessions bring the total to 3,630,254. The United States also maintains military bases in thirty-five nations and enjoys military usage agreements with several others. Corporations, banks, other associations, and individuals are estimated to own between $233 and $260 billion abroad. By any standard, the United States is today an empire that extends its economic, political, and military power around the globe.

Such impressive expansion in just over two hundred years cannot be explained in simple terms. The American empire, to quote Winston Churchill's remark about the British Empire, "did not just grow like Topsy," nor was it the creature of any single urge (say, power or greed) or dream (to save the world) or fear (of being conquered). It is more useful, rather, to think about American expansion in terms of the changing interactions among ideology, economics, military strategy, and domestic politics.

The early pressures for expansion across the continent emphasized the desire for land for agriculture, natural resources (wood, water, minerals, fossil fuels), and markets for those products. The gradual development of manufacturing, the related need for a continental infrastructure of transport, growth of a merchant marine, and the financial profits of all these activities combined to increase such pressure. The advocates of each of the expansionist objectives developed their particular explanations of why outreach was necessary.

At the same time, those interest group ideologies began to be integrated in a general ideology of expansion. That process and the resulting overview developed from religious as well as secular origins. The theological arguments were drawn from the *Gospel of Matthew* and adapted to America as early as 1630 by John Winthrop: "Men shall say of succeeding plantacions: the Lord make it like that of New England: for wee must Consider that wee shall be as a Citty upon a Hill, the eies of all people upon us." And some two centuries later, in 1850 after the war against Mexico, Herman Melville echoed that justification for continental and maritime expansion: "We Americans are the peculiar, chosen people — the Israel of our time; we bear the ark of the liberties of the world. . . . God has predestined . . . the rest of the nations must be in our rear."

The secular argument for expansion was also expressed very early, perhaps most explicitly by Thomas Paine in his 1776 pamphlet *Common Sense:* "We have it in our power to begin the world again." Whatever Paine's fluctuating relationship with religion, that formulation echoed Winthrop as well as John Locke's earlier proposition that "in the beginning America was the world." Thus it remained for James Madison (with some help from his friend Thomas Jefferson) to develop the most sophisticated and powerful secular explanation of the need for expansion.

First in letters and then publicly during the debate over ratification of the Constitution, Madison argued that the only way to sustain a republican government was to provide a surplus of resources and social space. The logic comes down to us in the present as the assertion that social peace and civil government depend upon enlarging the pie rather than arguing over the shares of a constant pie. Expansion (read "growth" in our time) is necessary to avoid class conflict and to provide for population growth. Jefferson cut through to the heart of the matter in a slightly different way: without expansion it would be necessary to redivide the existing property for each new generation (which even in his time implied a communitarian redistribution of property). Both men were candid. "This form of government," wrote Madison in 1787, "in order to effect its purposes, must operate not within a small but an extensive sphere." Having secured

Westward Expansion, 1800–1860

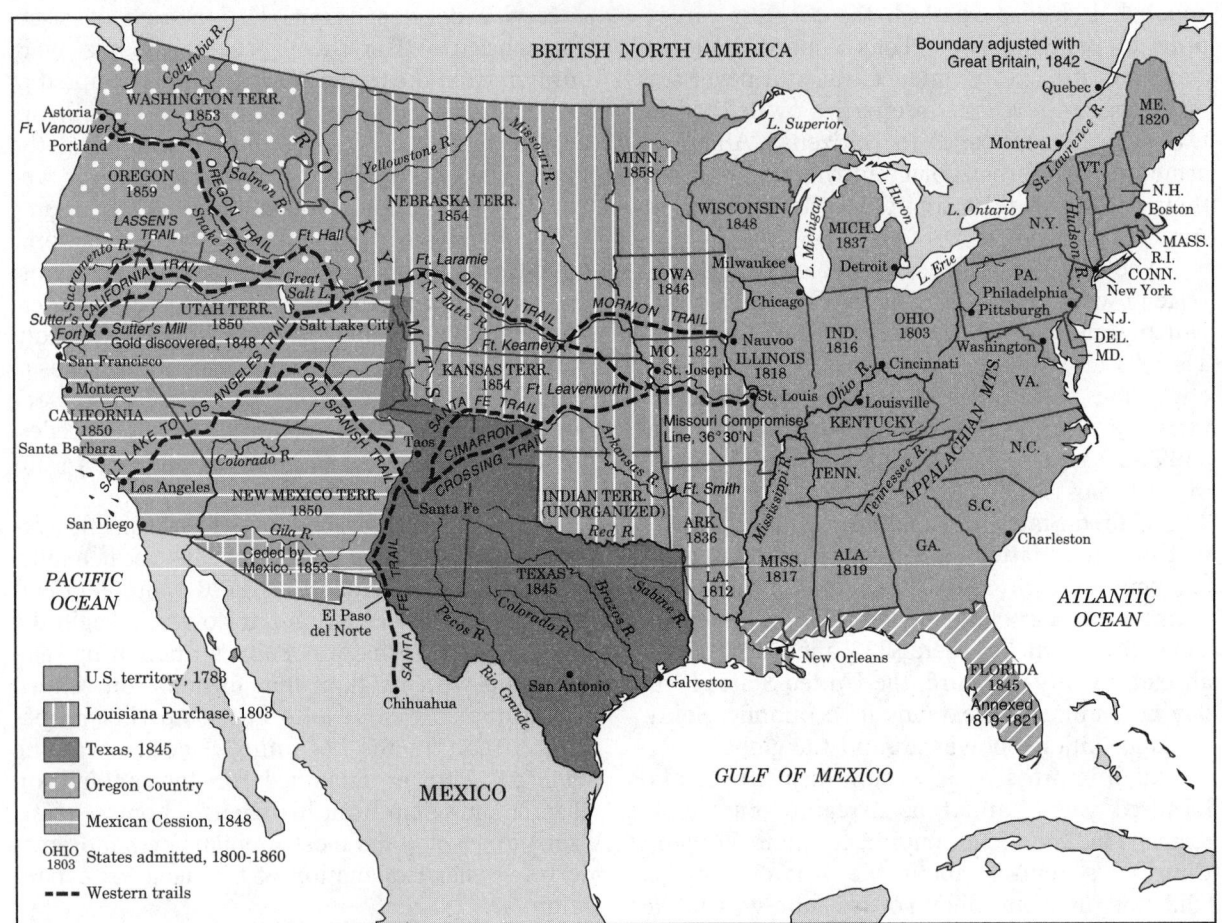

American access to the Pacific through the Louisiana Purchase (1803), Jefferson summed it up in 1809: "I am persuaded no constitution was ever before as well calculated as ours for extensive empire and self-government."

Within that consensus, however, the politics were never neat and rational. The arguments over which kind of expansion for which particular interests, and over the order of priorities, continued to bedevil American leaders. And the religious and secular concerns about spreading the light from the City upon a Hill and beginning the world again raised questions about the obligations toward the other peoples conquered in the process of extending truth and freedom. Finally, the military problems of furthering and defending an ever-larger system confounded the best minds. Those matters were at the center of American politics during the continuing battle

to subjugate the Native American cultures and the debates on the Louisiana Purchase, the war of conquest against Mexico, and whether or not to allow the slave-owning states to find their own way to salvation.

Those issues were not resolved by the North's victory in the Civil War. Indeed, the moral and practical questions of how best to rule and transform or regenerate a defeated enemy and to restore a marketplace economy were dramatized with wrenching force. At the same time, the rapid maturation of the industrial political economy in the North posed its own economic, social, and military challenges.

The new industrial leaders faced the same problem of markets for their booming production as had their agricultural predecessors. And like them, they concluded that overseas markets would be the answer.

Many perceptive, shrewd, or moralistic minds labored to adapt that idea to a program to solve the industrial problems. As in earlier times, the particular arguments offered were integrated in popular terms by a few charismatic leaders such as Theodore Roosevelt and Woodrow Wilson. They advocated overseas expansion in order to sustain economic prosperity, to maintain domestic social peace and welfare, and to fulfill the American mission to reform the world.

Roosevelt insisted, for example, that it was "of the utmost importance" that the United States secure "the commanding position in the international business world . . . especially at a time when foreign markets are essential." He added that it would be necessary to "exercise an international police power" from time to time. Wilson had a different style, but his points were the same. "If America is not to have free enterprise, then she can have freedom of no sort whatever. . . . We need foreign markets." Later he said, "the world must be made safe for democracy."

Such language revealed the inherent logic both of the concept of America as the City upon a Hill and of the capitalist marketplace political economy. Problems and solutions were externalized: opposition was either misguided or evil and had to be overcome. Thus rival capitalist powers, as well as anticapitalist revolutions, were viewed as dangers to be thwarted. That outlook guided the response of the great majority of Americans toward the policies and actions of Germany and Japan in the late 1930s, and also toward the Soviet Union and anticapitalist revolutions after World War II. Each of those nations and social movements was perceived as a threat to the economic, political, ideological, and military well-being and security of the United States.

From the end of the revolutionary war, however, that expansionist consensus was periodically challenged by conservatives as well as liberals and radicals on moral and pragmatic grounds. Those who opposed the proposed constitution during the debate of 1786–1787, for example, argued that it would create a political system calculated for empire and thus lead to the ultimate subversion of meaningful democracy at home. One can fairly say that they understood Madison's argument and its implications.

Similar criticism was offered against the continuing conquest of Native Americans, the purchase of the Louisiana Territory, and, even more militantly, the War of 1812 (particularly in New England and among groups in the seaboard South). Anti-imperial sentiment reached a climax in opposition to the war of conquest against Mexico. Its essence was best captured on July 4, 1821, by Secretary of State John Quincy Adams: "America goes not abroad in search of monsters to destroy. . . . She might become the dictatress of the world; she would no longer be the ruler of her own spirit."

Although the anti-imperial movement was a latent factor in northern opposition to the Civil War, it did not become a serious force in politics again until the war against Spain led to expansion into Cuba and the Philippines (1898–1903). But it did succeed in turning policy away from classic colonialism, and it was a factor in the successful opposition to Woodrow Wilson's proposal to involve the United States (through the League of Nations) in a sustained effort to make the world safe for democracy. The anti-imperial outlook continued to exert significant influence on American policy during the 1920s and 1930s.

The war against the Axis powers, however, and the subsequent perceived threats from Russia and revolutionary movements effectively undercut that influence. The next major effort by the anti-imperialists came during 1947–1948 when an unusual combination of anticommunist conservatives led by Senator Robert Taft and noncommunist liberals and radicals led by Henry A. Wallace tried to slow the revived momentum of imperialistic policies. The effort failed.

It can be argued with some force that the anti-imperial outlook contributed significantly to the widespread support for President Dwight D. Eisenhower. He was far less a militant crusader than Harry S. Truman, and in particular the latent if unorganized opposition to Truman's arbitrary intervention in Korea correctly viewed Eisenhower as an advocate of a less enthusiastic and bellicose approach to reforming the world in the image of America.

As an intellectual and political movement,

Territorial Expansion of the United States

Territory	Date Acquired	Square Miles	How Acquired
Original states and territories	1783	888,685	Treaty with Great Britain
Louisiana Purchase	1803	827,192	Purchase from France
Florida	1819	72,003	Treaty with Spain
Texas	1845	390,143	Annexation of independent nation
Oregon	1846	285,580	Treaty with Great Britain
Mexican Cession	1848	529,017	Conquest from Mexico
Gadsden Purchase	1853	29,640	Purchase from Mexico
Alaska	1867	589,757	Purchase from Russia
Hawaii	1898	6,450	Annexation of independent nation
The Philippines	1899	115,600	Conquest from Spain (granted independence in 1946)
Puerto Rico	1899	3,435	Conquest from Spain
Guam	1899	212	Conquest from Spain
American Samoa	1900	76	Treaty with Germany and Great Britain
Panama Canal Zone	1904	553	Treaty with Panama (returned to Panama by treaty in 1978)
Corn Islands	1914	4	Treaty with Nicaragua (returned to Nicaragua by treaty in 1971)
Virgin Islands	1917	133	Purchase from Denmark
Pacific Islands Trust (Micronesia)	1947	8,489	Trusteeship under United Nations (some granted independence)
All others (Midway, Wake, and other islands)		42	

however, the anti-imperialists did not begin to reassert themselves until President John F. Kennedy intervened to overthrow Cuba's revolution, which led to the missile crisis with the Soviet Union. But they exerted only marginal influence on policy until the intervention in Vietnam became a major war. What came to be called by expansionists the "Vietnam syndrome" was actually the revival of traditional anti-imperialism, and it played a crucial role in the withdrawal from Vietnam and the reluctance to engage in further interventions around the world.

Under Presidents Ronald Reagan and George Bush, however, the pendulum swung back. The Reagan administration, until blocked by Congress, supplied money and equipment to the Contras who were trying to overthrow the Marxist government in Nicaragua; secret efforts to continue funneling money to them culminated in the Iran-Contra affair. Reagan also sent U.S. military forces into Grenada to check the threatened expansion of communism there and bombed Libya in an effort to reduce its alleged support of international terrorism. Under Bush, the United States invaded Panama to remove Manuel Noriega from power. And when Iraq under Saddam Hussein invaded and annexed Kuwait, the United States assembled and led a multinational coalition in a full-scale war to reclaim the country. "We've licked the Vietnam syndrome!" Bush declared. Thus the historical confrontation between the two conceptions of America's place in the world continued to be played out.

Edward McNall Burns, *The American Idea of Mission: Concepts of National Purpose and Destiny* (1957); Lloyd Gardner, *Architects of Illusion: Men and Ideas in American Foreign Policy, 1941–1949* (1970); Albert K. Weinberg, *Manifest Destiny: A Study of Nationalist Expansionism in American History* (1935).

WILLIAM APPLEMAN WILLIAMS

EXPATRIATES AND EXILES

Thomas Danforth, a Massachusetts lawyer who was exiled because of his loyalty to the British Empire during the American Revolution, complained in 1783 from his new home in London that he was "near his fortieth year, banished under pain of death, to a distant country, where he has not the most remote family connection." He was "cut off from his profession . . . and in a great degree from social enjoyments." Loyalists such as Danforth represented the earliest and one of the largest groups of Americans to live outside their homeland as expatriates or exiles. Many other groups would follow.

Several hundred thousand Americans have likely been exiles or expatriates. The two terms are often used interchangeably, but *expatriates* are individuals who have chosen to live in a foreign country, and *exiles* are individuals who have been forced to leave their homeland. True exiles have been few in the American experience; most Americans who have left the nation did so as expatriates. Some have left for purely personal or family reasons, others because they objected to certain social or political conditions in the United States.

Between sixty thousand and eighty thousand Loyalists, out of a population of 2.5 million, fled the country during and after the American Revolution. They were true exiles, many having endured the confiscation of their property, humiliation at the hands of former friends, and relocation to distant, often unwelcoming places. Thousands went to England, the Maritime Provinces of British North America, and the West Indies. More than half came from New York, Massachusetts, and South Carolina, but every state contributed a share.

Some Loyalists were British officials, like Thomas Hutchinson of Massachusetts, or back-country residents who relied on British authority as a counterweight to the political power of the coastal elite. Others believed the rebellion would be crushed by the British military or considered it an illegal attack upon legitimate authority.

Most went to the Canadian provinces, but between seven thousand and eight thousand went to England. There they spent much time and energy seeking positions within the British government, often without success, and lobbying for continuation of the war against the rebellion. Loyalists wanted, above all, to justify their decision. They wrote histories of the Revolution, arguing that it lacked legitimacy and widespread support and that its leaders were cruel and dishonest. But, in this first American lost cause, they remained outsiders in their land of birth and in England as well.

The most famous lost cause in American history led to a second group of expatriates when leaders of the failed Confederacy, fearful of postwar political conditions, emigrated. Judah P. Benjamin, the Confederate secretary of war and secretary of state, moved to England and became a successful lawyer. Gen. Jubal Early and a few others went to Canada and still others to Japan, Australia, and Egypt.

The largest number, however, moved to Central and South America. Mexico appointed Confederate admiral Matthew Fontaine Maury as commissioner of immigration, and he helped attract some two thousand ex-Confederates who established the colonies of Carlota and Cordova between Mexico City and Vera Cruz. Honduras, Jamaica, and Cuba also drew southern whites in the aftermath of war. Between twenty-five hundred and four thousand southerners set up agricultural colonies in Brazil where slavery was still legal. The Brazilian government encouraged this movement by offering cheap land and appointing immigration agents to aid the migrants. Most of the Brazilian expatriates returned to the South in the 1870s, but several hundred remained. Americana, Brazil, is still home to four hundred or so descendants of these expatriates; Jimmy Carter visited the community during his presidency in the late 1970s.

The first large-scale black American emigration also grew out of the slavery issue and focused on Africa and Canada. The American Colonization Society, formed in 1816, wanted to relocate American blacks in Africa as a way of dealing with the problem of slavery. The society founded Liberia specifically as a black American colony, and a few thousand ex-slaves moved there. This, however, was a white-sponsored movement and was widely criticized by blacks themselves. Black leader Frederick Douglass opposed black emigration altogether, although other leaders, such as Martin R. Delany, promoted black-sponsored African emigration.

Canada was also a destination for blacks before the war. It was the terminus of the Underground Railroad; escaped slaves followed the North Star, which thereby gained mythic meaning. About forty thousand went to Canada, settling in the new agricultural communities of Wilberforce, Dawn, the Refuge Home Society, and Elgin. Over half went as a result of the Fugitive Slave Act (1850), which required northerners to cooperate in capturing runaway slaves, and the Supreme Court's *Dred Scott* decision (1857), which denied citizenship to blacks.

After the Civil War, worsening race relations, southern agricultural depressions, and northern ghetto life caused some African-Americans to entertain hopes of drastic change through immigration to Africa. Several hundred South Carolina blacks went to Liberia in 1878, and disciples of Henry McNeal Turner, a black spokesman for African-American nationalism, carried emigrants to different areas of Africa in the first decade of the twentieth century. Alfred C. Sam, a Ghanaian, launched a movement in Oklahoma that led thousands of blacks to Houston in 1914, after which many of them journeyed on to Liberia on his ship the S.S. *Liberia*.

In the late nineteenth century, another group joined the ranks of expatriates: American painters. James McNeill Whistler, Mary Cassatt, Theodore Robinson, John Singer Sargent, Frank Duveneck, and William Merritt Chase were among the most important members of this group. These artists were often repelled by the opulent materialism and vulgarity of the Gilded Age and fled to Paris, the international art center of this era. Whistler and Sargent eventually moved to London, and other artists became a part of the Munich, Germany, art colony. Some painters stayed in Europe permanently, but others eventually returned.

Henry James, perhaps the most famous American literary expatriate, shared much with these artists. He divided his time between Europe and the United States in the 1860s and early 1870s, before settling permanently in London in 1876. He left his native land for the cosmopolitanism of Europe and the opportunities it afforded to write of the domestic affairs and fashionable lives of the leisure class. His writings explore the experience of expatriation and the differences between cultures, often portraying provincial Americans facing a complex world. He became a British citizen in 1915.

Although artistic and literary expatriates of the post–Civil War era were small in number, they tied American culture more closely to European currents. The same was true of the "Lost Generation" writers of the 1920s, who may be the best known of all American expatriates. Among the reasons for their departure was what their chronicler Malcolm Cowley called their rootlessness. Children of the well-off bourgeoisie, they had gone off to college, where they learned of a wider world and broke their ties with home.

But World War I was the main reason these expatriates left America. Many had served as ambulance drivers attached to the French forces before the United States entered the war. Among them were Ernest Hemingway, John Dos Passos, Julian Green, William Seabrook, E. E. Cummings, Harry Crosby, Sidney Howard, Louis Bromfield, Robert Hillyer, and Dashiell Hammett — a who's who of literary figures of the era and all of them future expatriates. Disillusionment after the war added to their distrust of idealism and tradition.

They had returned to the United States at war's end, but in the early 1920s their discontent led many back to Europe. They disliked postwar American culture, seeing its social mores as moralistic, standardized, and vulgarized. They saw themselves as creative artists living in a business civilization devoted to the worship of materialism. Europe represented ancient wisdom, a place of history and of refinement. They went there hoping to discover new creative energy, to become a part of an emerging modernist culture.

The lives of the Lost Generation expatriates offer appealing images: the cafés of Paris, the coffeehouses of Vienna, the cabarets of Berlin, the bullfights of Pamplona. But theirs was a religion of living for art, and after a few years abroad most decided they could practice their new religion at home as well as in Europe: Europe, too, they claimed, had been conquered by the business civilization. Exposure to Europe had made them feel less culturally inferior, and they became homesick, as Cowley wrote, longing for "a Kentucky hill cabin, a farmhouse in Iowa or Wisconsin, the Michigan woods."

Europe also nurtured African-American expatriates. It offered the same attractions that drew other Americans, but for blacks it represented something more: a cultural environment free of the racial obsessions of American society. After World War I, France, in particular, had the reputation of welcoming black Americans, and writers, artists, entertainers, and intellectuals found a refuge there. Writer Richard Wright, entertainer Josephine Baker, and jazz musicians Arthur Briggs, Benny Carter, and Dexter Gordon were only a few of the prominent African-Americans who found a home in France.

In the 1920s, too, a Jamaica-born, charismatic black man, Marcus Garvey, was reviving the back-to-Africa idea but now as a mass movement among blacks. Garvey had founded the Universal Negro Improvement Association in 1914 in the British West Indies, with the goal of promoting black equality through independence from white society. He formed a Harlem chapter soon after coming to the United States in 1916. Garvey's steamship company, the Black Star Line, sent the migrants to Africa, but Liberia refused to cooperate, fearing Garvey wanted to take control of that nation. He soon was in trouble with the American government for misuse of funds from his investors and was deported to Jamaica in 1927.

Garvey's expulsion from the United States ended that particular movement, but Africa throughout the twentieth century continued to attract prominent American black intellectuals, including W. E. B. Du Bois, who spent his last years in the newly independent nation of Ghana. Pan-Africanism was a theme in the Harlem Renaissance of the 1920s and in the black freedom movement of the late 1960s, leading some American blacks, including Stokely Carmichael, to emigrate there.

In the 1930s another group of Americans were attracted by a European society, but this time it was not the artistic world of Western Europe but the brave new communist world of the Soviet Union. The Great Depression impelled American socialists to seek a radical alternative to capitalism, one that the Soviet Union seemed to represent. By the early 1930s the Soviet economy was expanding, and its culture offered innovations that appealed to intellectuals. Social scientists were attracted to the possibilities of a planned society, and political scientists predicted an appealing fusion of democracy and socialism. Americans who immigrated to the Soviet Union saw that nation as fundamentally different from other societies. As historian Richard Pells has written, to radical American writers of the 1930s "the Soviet Union was ultimately not a country but a state of mind."

John Reed, who traveled to the Soviet Union in 1917 to observe the revolution, was the first of a long line of American journalists, social scientists, novelists, and poets to go there. The Soviet government assiduously courted American visitors and showed off their model factories and collective farms. Among those who emigrated were Marxist ideologues who saw the Soviet Union as the testing ground for the theory of working-class revolution, noncommunist socialists who admired the Soviet experiment in social and economic planning, engineers and workers targeted by Soviet recruiters, and writers who believed that the new society valued their work. After serving a prison sentence for anticonscription activities in World War I, the anarchist Emma Goldman was deported to Russia in 1919. She remained there for three years before leaving over differences with the Bolshevik government. The number of those living in Russia was no more than a few thousand at its height in the early 1930s.

By the late 1930s, though, disillusionment had set in, as Joseph Stalin increasingly appeared to be a new version of the czar. In 1934 he had begun the show trials and executions in his bloody purge of thousands of high-level officials and bureaucrats. Many socialists condemned the terrorist campaign, as well as his foreign policy that accommodated European fascists. Well before 1940 the flow of American sympathizers to the Soviet Union had virtually ended, and many had returned home. Later, during the cold war, those who had spent time in the country were subject to harassment and worse for their expatriation.

The most recent group of American expatriates dates from the Vietnam War era. Some twenty-five hundred to three thousand draft resisters sought asylum in Canada (mainly in Toronto) and Scandinavia. Deserters from the military, mostly in Europe, established a community in Sweden in 1967, when that country granted asylum to four disaffected servicemen off the aircraft carrier *Intrepid*.

Expatriation during the 1960s sometimes involved a broad questioning of American institutions and materialistic values, particularly on the part of middle-class youth. But the draft was the major reason many who opposed the war chose expatriation. The high point of the movement came in the late 1960s, as the number of American troops in Vietnam steadily increased. When the draft ended in the early seventies and American forces were gradually withdrawn, both protest against the war and expatriation because of it declined. In contrast to draft resisters, who tended to be middle class, the military deserters in exile typically came from poor or working-class families, volunteers who joined the military for financial reasons and then left the ranks as transfer to Vietnam loomed.

Jimmy Carter's first act as president, in January 1977, was to pardon those individuals convicted of criminal law violations because of peaceful opposition to the Vietnam War. Those who had fled the United States rather than face charges were free to return without fear of prosecution, and many did so, although some had made permanent lives abroad. Military deserters were not pardoned.

American expatriates and exiles, then, have sought sanctuary in other lands for many reasons — economic, political, intellectual, cultural, personal, and ethnic. Many struggled with their estrangement, some choosing permanent expatriation, others eventually returning. "I am not now, and never will become — at least, not by my own desire — an expatriate," said African-American writer James Baldwin while living in France in the 1960s. "For better or for worse, my ties with my country are too deep, and my concern is too great." Baldwin was typical of Americans who fled their homeland. Alienated from it, they continued to ponder its meaning for clues to their identity.

David Caute, *The Fellow-Travellers: Intellectual Friends of Communism* (1973); Malcolm Cowley, *Exile's Return: A Literary Odyssey of the 1920s* (1934); Ernest Dunbar, *The Black Expatriates: A Study of American Negroes in Exile* (1968); Eugene C. Harter, *The Lost Colony of the Confederacy* (1985); Mary Beth Norton, *The British-Americans: The Loyalist Exiles in England, 1774–1789* (1972).

CHARLES REAGAN WILSON

See also American Colonization Society; Underground Railroad; *and entries for individual expatriates.*

EXPLORATION OF NORTH AMERICA

The first attempt by Europeans to colonize the New World occurred around A.D. 1000, when the Vikings sailed from the British Isles to Greenland, established a colony, and then moved on to Labrador, the Baffin Islands, and finally Newfoundland. There they established a colony named Vineland (meaning fertile region) and from that base sailed along the coast of North America, observing the flora, fauna, and native peoples. Inexplicably, after a few years Vineland was abandoned.

Although the Vikings never returned to America, their accomplishments became known to other Europeans. Europe, however, was made up of many small principalities whose concerns were mainly local. Europeans may have been intrigued by the stories of the feared Vikings' discovery of a "new world," but they lacked the resources or the will to follow their path of exploration. Trade continued to revolve around the Mediterranean Sea, as it had for hundreds of years.

But between 1000 and 1650 a series of interconnected developments occurred in Europe that provided the impetus for the exploration and subsequent colonization of America. These developments included the Protestant Reformation and the subsequent Catholic Counter-Reformation, the Renaissance, the unification of small states into larger ones with centralized political power, the emergence of new technology in navigation and shipbuilding, and the establishment of overland trade with the East and the accompanying transformation of the medieval economy.

The Protestant Reformation and the Catholic church's response in the Counter-Reformation marked the end of several centuries of gradual erosion of the power of the Catholic church as well as the climax to internal attempts to reform the church. Protestantism emphasized a personal relationship between each individual and God without the need for intercession by the institutional church. In the Renaissance, artists and writers such as Galileo, Machiavelli, and Michelangelo adopted a view of life that stressed humans' ability to change and control the world. Thus, the rise of Protestantism and the Counter-Reformation, along with the Renaissance, helped foster individualism and create a climate favorable to exploration.

At the same time, political centralization ended much of the squabbling and fighting among rival noble families and regions that had characterized the Middle Ages. With the decline of the political power and wealth of the Catholic church, a few rulers gradually solidified their power. Portugal, Spain, France, and England were transformed from small territories into nation-states with centralized authority in the hands of monarchs who were able to direct and finance overseas exploration.

As these religious and political changes were occurring, technological innovations in navigation set the stage for exploration. Bigger, faster ships and the invention of navigational devices such as the astrolabe and sextant made extended voyages possible.

But the most powerful inducement to exploration was trade. Marco Polo's famous journey to Cathay signaled Europe's "discovery" of Chinese and Islamic civilizations. The Orient became a magnet to traders, and exotic products and wealth flowed into Europe. Those who benefited most were merchants who sat astride the great overland trade routes, especially the merchants of the Italian city-states of Genoa, Venice, and Florence.

The newly unified states of the Atlantic — France, Spain, England, and Portugal — and their ambitious monarchs were envious of the merchants and princes who dominated the land routes to the East. Moreover, in the latter half of the fifteenth century, war between European states and the Ottoman Empire greatly hampered Europe's trade with the Orient. The desire to supplant the trade moguls, especially the Italians, and fear of the Ottoman Empire forced the Atlantic nations to search for a new route to the East.

Portugal led the others into exploration. Encouraged by Prince Henry the Navigator, Portuguese seamen sailed southward along the African coast, seeking a water route to the East. They were also looking for a legendary king named Prester John who had supposedly built a Christian stronghold somewhere in northwestern Africa. Henry hoped to form an alliance with Prester John to fight the Muslims. During Henry's lifetime the Portuguese learned much about the African coastal area. His school developed the quadrant, the cross-staff, and the compass, made advances in cartography, and designed and built highly maneuverable little ships known as caravels.

After Henry's death, Portuguese interest in long-distance trade and expansion waned until King John II commissioned Bartolomeu Dias to find a water route to India in 1487. Dias sailed around the tip of Africa and into the Indian Ocean before his frightened crew forced him to give up the quest. A year later, Vasco da Gama succeeded in reaching India and returned to Portugal laden with jewels and spices. In 1500 Pedro Álvares Cabral discovered and claimed

Brazil for Portugal, and other Portuguese captains established trading posts in the South China Sea, the Bay of Bengal, and the Arabian Sea. These water routes to the East undercut the power of the Italian city-states, and Lisbon became Europe's new trade capital.

Spain's imperial ambitions were launched by Christopher Columbus. Born in Genoa, Italy, around 1451, Columbus learned the art of navigation on voyages in the Mediterranean and the Atlantic. At some point he probably read Cardinal Pierre d'Ailly's early fifteenth-century work, *Imago mundi,* which argued that the East could be found by sailing west of the Azores for a few days. Columbus, hoping to make such a voyage, spent years seeking a sponsor and finally found one in Ferdinand and Isabella of Spain after they defeated the Moors and could turn their attention to other projects.

In August 1492, Columbus sailed west with his now famous ships, *Niña, Pinta,* and *Santa María.* After ten weeks he sighted an island in the Bahamas, which he named San Salvador. Thinking he had found islands near Japan, he sailed on until he reached Cuba (which he thought was mainland China) and later Haiti. Columbus returned to Spain with many products unknown to Europe — coconuts, tobacco, sweet corn, potatoes — and with tales of dark-skinned native peoples whom he called "Indians" because he assumed he had been sailing in the Indian Ocean.

Although Columbus found no gold or silver, he was hailed by Spain and much of Europe as the discoverer of d'Ailly's western route to the East. John II of Portugal, however, believed Columbus had discovered islands in the Atlantic already claimed by Portugal and took the matter to Pope Alexander II. Twice the pope issued decrees supporting Spain's claim to Columbus's discoveries. But the territorial disputes between Portugal and Spain were not resolved until 1494 when they signed the Treaty of Tordesillas, which drew a line 370 leagues west of the Azores as the demarcation between the two empires.

Despite the treaty, controversy continued over what Columbus had found. He made three more voyages to America between 1494 and 1502, during which he explored Puerto Rico, the Virgin Islands, Jamaica, and Trinidad. Each time he returned more certain that he had reached the East. Subsequent explorations by others, however, persuaded most Europeans that Columbus had discovered a "New World." Ironically, that New World was named for someone else. A German geographer, Martin Waldseemüller, accepted the claim of Amerigo Vespucci that he had landed on the American mainland before Columbus. In 1507 Waldseemüller published a book in which he named the new land "America."

More Spanish expeditions followed. Juan Ponce de León explored the coasts of Florida in 1513. Vasco Núñez de Balboa crossed the Isthmus of Panama and discovered the Pacific Ocean in the same year. Ferdinand Magellan's expedition (in the course of which he put down a mutiny and was later killed) sailed around the tip of South America, across the Pacific to the Philippines, through the Indian Ocean, and back to Europe around the southern tip of Africa between 1519 and 1522.

Two expeditions led directly to Spain's emergence as sixteenth-century Europe's wealthiest and most powerful nation. The first was headed by Hernando Cortés, who in 1519 led a small army of Spanish and Native Americans against the Aztec Empire of Mexico. Completing the conquest in 1521, Cortés took control of the Aztecs' fabulous gold and silver mines. Ten years later, an expedition under Francisco Pizarro overwhelmed the Inca Empire of Peru, securing for the Spaniards the great Inca silver mines of Potosí.

In 1535 and 1536 Pedro de Mendoza went as far as present-day Buenos Aires in Argentina, where he founded a colony. At the same time, Cabeza de Vaca explored the North American Southwest, adding that region to Spain's New World empire. A few years later (1539–1542) Francisco Vásquez de Coronado discovered the Grand Canyon and journeyed through much of the Southwest looking for gold and the legendary Seven Cities of Cíbola. About the same time Hernando de Soto explored southeastern North America from Florida to the Mississippi River. By 1650 Spain's empire was complete and fleets of ships were carrying the plunder back to Spain.

The impulse for exploration was further fueled by the European imagination. The idea of "America" antedated America's discovery and even Viking exploration. That idea had two parts: one paradisiacal and utopian; the other savage and dangerous. Ancient tales described distant civilizations, usually to the west, where European-like peoples lived simple, virtuous lives without war, famine, disease, or poverty. Such utopian visions were reinforced by religious notions. Early Christian Europeans had inherited from the Jews a powerful prophetic tradition that drew upon apocalyptic biblical texts in the books of *Daniel, Isaiah,* and *Revelations.* They connected the Christianization of the world with the second coming of Christ. Such ideas led many Europeans (including Columbus) to believe it was God's plan for Christians to convert pagans wherever they were found.

If secular and religious traditions evoked utopian visions of the New World, they also induced nightmares. The ancients described wonderful civilizations, but barbaric, evil ones as well. Moreover, late medieval Christianity inherited a rich tradition of hatred for non-Christians derived in part from the Crusaders' struggle to free the Holy Land and from warfare against the Moors.

European encounters with the New World were viewed in light of these preconceived notions. To plunder the New World of its treasures was acceptable because it was populated by pagans. To Christianize the pagans was necessary because it was part of God's plan; to kill them was right because they were Satan's or Antichrist's warriors. As European powers conquered the territories of the New World, they justified wars against Native Americans and the destruction of their cultures as a fulfillment of the European secular and religious vision of the New World.

While Spain was building its New World empire, France was also exploring the Americas. In 1524, Giovanni da Verrazano was commissioned to locate a northwest passage around North America to India. He was followed in 1534 by Jacques Cartier, who explored the St.

Lawrence River as far as present-day Montreal. In 1562 Jean Ribault headed an expedition that explored the St. Johns River area in Florida. His efforts were followed two years later by a second venture headed by René de Laudonnière. But the Spanish soon pushed the French out of Florida, and thereafter, the French directed their efforts north and west. In 1608 Samuel de Champlain built a fort at Quebec and explored the area north to Port Royal, Nova Scotia, and south to Cape Cod.

Unlike Spain's empire, "New France" produced no caches of gold and silver. Instead, the French traded with inland tribes for furs and fished off the coast of Newfoundland. New France was sparsely populated by trappers and missionaries and dotted with military forts and trading posts. Although the French sought to colonize the area, the growth of settlements was stifled by inconsistent policies. Initially, France encouraged colonization by granting charters to fur-trading companies. Then, under Cardinal Richelieu, control of the empire was put in the hands of the government-sponsored Company of New France. The company, however, was not successful, and in 1663 the king took direct control of New France. Although more prosperous under this administration, the French empire failed to match the wealth of New Spain or the growth of neighboring British colonies.

The Dutch were also engaged in the exploration of America. Formerly a Protestant province of Spain, the Netherlands was determined to become a commercial power and saw exploration as a means to that end. In 1609, Henry Hudson led an expedition to America for the Dutch East India Company and laid claim to the area along the Hudson River as far as present-day Albany. In 1614 the newly formed New Netherland Company obtained a grant from the Dutch government for the territory between New France and Virginia. About ten years later another trading company, the West India Company, settled groups of colonists on Manhattan Island and at Fort Orange. The Dutch also planted trading colonies in the West Indies.

In 1497 Henry VII of England sponsored an expedition to the New World headed by John Cabot, who explored a part of Newfoundland

European Explorations in America

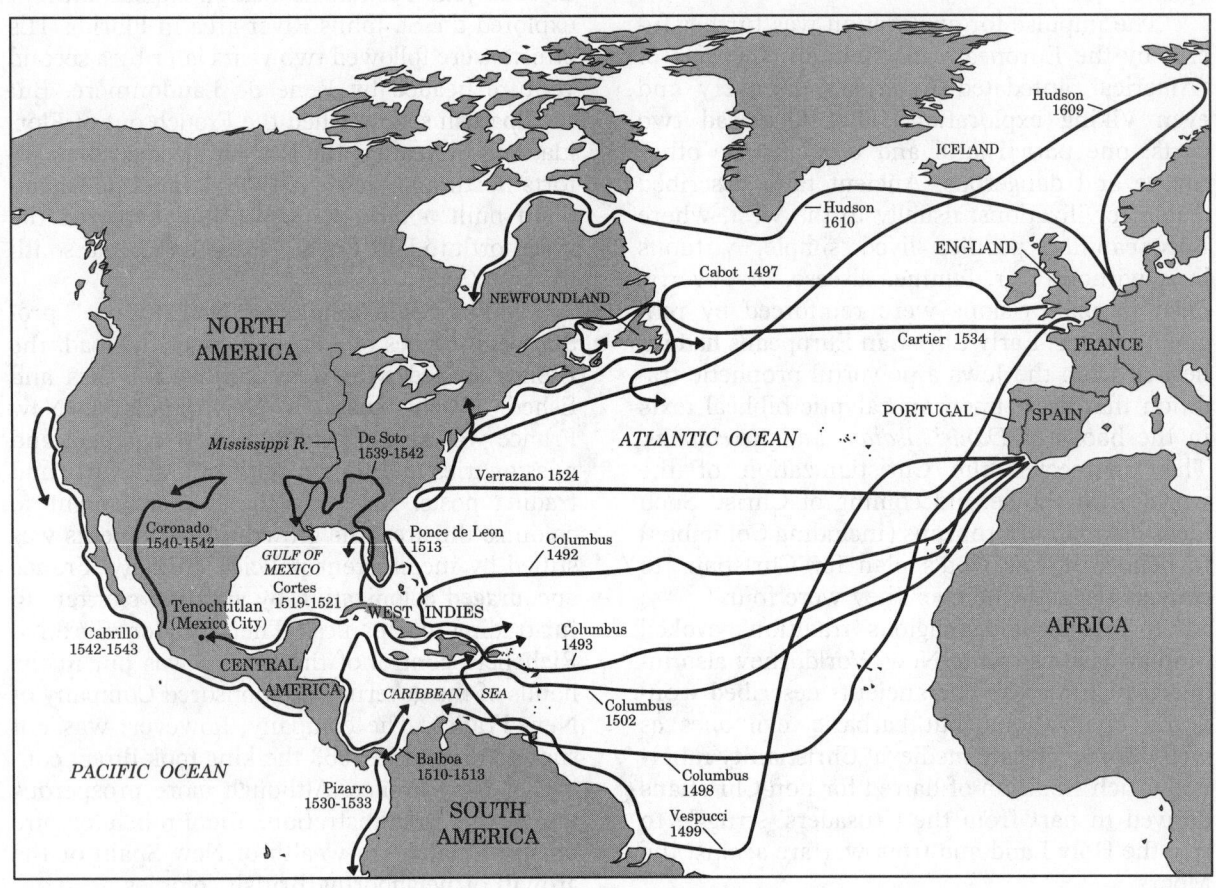

and reported an abundance of fish. But until Queen Elizabeth's reign, the English showed little interest in exploration, being preoccupied with their European trade and establishing control over the British Isles. By the mid-sixteenth century, however, England had recognized the advantages of trade with the East, and in 1560 English merchants enlisted Martin Frobisher to search for a northwest passage to India. Between 1576 and 1578 Frobisher as well as John Davis explored along the Atlantic coast.

Thereafter, Queen Elizabeth granted charters to Sir Humphrey Gilbert and Sir Walter Raleigh to colonize America. Gilbert headed two trips to the New World. He landed on Newfoundland but was unable to carry out his intention of establishing military posts. A year later, Raleigh sent a company to explore territory he named Virginia after Elizabeth, the "Virgin Queen," and in 1585, he sponsored a second voyage, this time to explore the Chesapeake Bay region. By the seventeenth century, the English had taken the lead in colonizing North America, establishing settlements all along the Atlantic coast and in the West Indies.

Sweden and Denmark also succumbed to the attractions of America, although to a lesser extent. In 1638 the Swedish West India Company established a settlement on the Delaware River near present-day Wilmington called Fort Christina. This colony was short-lived, however, and was taken over by the Dutch in 1655. The king of Denmark chartered the Danish West India Company in 1671, and the Danes established colonies in St. Croix and other islands in the cluster of the Virgin Islands.

Samuel Eliot Morison, *The European Discovery of America: The Northern Voyages, A.D. 500–1600* (1971); John H. Parry, *The Spanish Seaborne Empire* (1966; 2nd ed., 1980); David B. Quinn, *England and the Discovery of America, 1481–1620, from the Bristol Voyages of the Fifteenth Century to the Pilgrim Settlement at Plymouth: The Exploration, Exploitation, and Trial-and-Error Colonization of North America by the English* (1974).

PAUL R. LUCAS

See also French and Spanish Settlements.

F

FAIR DEAL

In his January 1949 State of the Union message President Harry S. Truman characterized his legislative agenda as providing a "Fair Deal" for all Americans. Building upon the New Deal legacy of reform, Truman advocated full employment legislation, an increase in the minimum wage, economic assistance for farmers, extension of Social Security, and enactment of antidiscrimination employment practices based upon the wartime Fair Employment Practices Committee. The president had previously mentioned these points and called for national health insurance, federal aid to education, and government support for housing in a message to Congress shortly after he took office in 1945. He also advocated antilynching and anti–poll tax legislation.

A coalition of Republicans and southern Democrats in Congress blocked most of Truman's Fair Deal, although the Employment Act of 1946 committed the federal government to the goal of full employment. After Truman's upset victory in 1948, Congress responded by increasing the minimum wage from forty cents to seventy-five cents an hour and extending Social Security benefits to an additional 10 million people. The Housing Act of 1949 provided for slum clearance and construction of 800,000 housing units for the poor. By 1950, however, the president's focus had shifted toward foreign affairs, primarily the Korean War.

See also Truman, Harry S.

FAIRS

See Centennial Exposition; World's Fairs.

FAMILY

For over three centuries, Americans have bemoaned the decline of the family. Even in Puritan New England, community elders decried the growing fragility of marriage, the selfishness of parents, and the rebelliousness of children. Nevertheless, the American family has endured by adapting to changing economic and social environments.

In colonial times, the family was the basic unit of society. It educated children, cared for the elderly and infirm, transferred occupational skills to the young, and functioned as the economic center of production. All members participated in the family's support. Wives cooked, laundered, spun yarn, wove cloth, and made clothing. They gardened, milked cows, brewed beer, harvested fruit, kept chickens, and preserved food. Children had work responsibilities before age seven.

All individuals were required to live within a family. In Puritan New England, bachelors and single women paid special taxes and were forced to enter existing households as a boarder or servant; married couples who lived apart from each other were fined.

Seventeenth-century Americans conceived of the family as a hierarchical unit — a "little commonwealth" — in which the father was endowed with patriarchal authority. He alone sat on a chair (others sat on benches, chests, or stools). Child-rearing manuals were addressed to him. Legally, his consent was necessary for his children to marry, and his control over inheritance kept grown sons dependent, often unable to set up their own households for years. Three colonies made it a capital offense for children to curse or strike their fathers.

Love was not considered a prerequisite for marriage. Ministers advised the young to choose a spouse on grounds of property, religion, and family interest, not on the basis of physical attraction or romantic love. It was assumed that love would follow marriage. Relations between spouses tended to be formal and reserved. Husbands commonly referred to their wives as their "dear child" and wives addressed their husbands as "sir" or "mister."

Attitudes toward children differed sharply from those of today. New England Puritans considered newborn infants to be embodiments of guilt and sin and many parents sought to break their child's willfulness by physical beatings or by taking them to see corpses or hangings. Boys and girls were often "fostered out" between the ages of seven and fourteen as servants or apprentices. Death rates among children were much higher than those today. In New England, one child in ten died during the first year in healthy areas and three in ten in less healthy regions. Birthrates were also high: over half of all New England children had nine or more siblings.

During the early colonial era there was no prototypical "American" family. Native Americans, Afro-Americans, and white colonists in the Chesapeake region, for example, established family patterns that differed markedly from those in the northern colonies.

More than 240 Native American groups inhabited what is now the United States, each with its own pattern of family and kinship. Some, like the Iroquois-speaking groups of the eastern woodlands, practiced matrilocal residence in which husbands joined their wives' households and resided in longhouses, large rectangular structures accommodating about ten families. Algonquin-speaking groups, who also lived in the East, had variable residence patterns — spouses might join the husband's or the wife's family — and usually inhabited wigwams, dome-shaped structures for one or two families. Most Plains Indians lived in extended families of two or three generations, occupying earth- or sod-covered lodges or tipis of buffalo skin. In the Southwest, many Pueblo Indians also lived in extended households, which consisted of female relations and their husbands, sons-in-law, and maternal grandchildren residing together in a multistoried communal structure. Diversity, then, was the hallmark of Native American family life with patterns shaped by economic and sociopolitical circumstances.

Afro-Americans, during the seventeenth century, had few opportunities to establish a stable, independent family life. Most lived on plantations with fewer than ten slaves. These units were so small and widely dispersed and the sex ratio so skewed that it was very difficult for the individual to find a suitable spouse. A high death rate meant that many slaves did not live long enough to marry, or if they did, their marriages were usually brief. In the early eighteenth century, however, slaves could more readily find spouses and establish families as the number of Africans imported into the colonies increased sharply, the average size of plantations grew, and life expectancy rose.

Seventeenth-century white colonists in Maryland and Virginia also suffered from a high death rate and a sharply skewed sex ratio. In Virginia, death broke half of all marriages before the seventh wedding anniversary. Two-thirds of all children lost a parent before their eighteenth birthday and one-third lost both parents. At the end of the century, family life in the Chesapeake stabilized as the death rate fell, life expectancy rose, and the imbalance of the sexes eased.

Toward the end of the eighteenth century, family life underwent far-reaching changes. Parental control over children's sexual behavior weakened, and illegitimacy rates rose sharply as did the proportion of brides pregnant on their wedding day. Children acquired greater leeway in selecting a spouse. Marriage was increasingly conceived not as a property arrangement but as an emotional bond involving mutual esteem, mutual friendship, and mutual confidence.

Spouses displayed affection more openly, calling each other "honey" or "dear." Parents also became more interested in their children's development, viewing them as special creatures with unique needs — evident in the proliferation of children's books, games, toys, and furniture. Child-rearing ideals shifted from suppressing a child's innate sinfulness to instilling a capacity for self-government through such techniques as evoking guilt or withdrawing love.

The family's social and economic significance declined, and institutions such as almshouses, schools, and businesses assumed many traditional family functions. At the same time, the family acquired new significance as a refuge from the materialistic world of commerce and as a shelter for higher moral and spiritual values — a "haven in a heartless world."

It was in the early nineteenth century that a new division of domestic roles appeared with the husband as breadwinner and wife as full-time homemaker and mother. Inside their "separate sphere" of domesticity, women were valued not as laborers but as nurturers. In stark contrast to the colonial conception of women as devious, sexually voracious, and mentally and physically inferior to men, a "cult of domesticity" now glorified motherhood, associated women with piety, purity, and spirituality, and declared that their child-rearing role would determine the success or failure of America's democratic experiment. More parents kept their children home into their late teens, instead of sending them out at the age of seven or eight to work as servants or apprentices. By the middle of the century, the family vacation had appeared, as did a series of new family-oriented celebrations such as the birthday party, the Thanksgiving feast, and decoration of the Christmas tree.

But the white middle-class family was only one of a number of distinctive families that coexisted in nineteenth-century America. Slaves forged a distinctive family and kinship system that helped them survive the effects of material deprivation and physical violence. Slavery placed severe pressures upon black families. The women were vulnerable to sexual exploitation by masters and overseers and sales often broke up families. During the Civil War, nearly 20 percent of ex-slaves reported that an earlier marriage had been forcibly broken. Nevertheless, Afro-Americans within slavery managed to establish strong and durable kin ties. Despite legal prohibitions, most slaves married, and ties of the immediate family stretched outward to a network of extended kin. Although these marriages lacked legal sanction, most slaves established de facto arrangements that were often stable over long periods of time. Whenever children were sold to a neighboring plantation, blood relatives and strangers took on the functions of parents. The strength of the family was revealed vividly after abolition when thousands of freedmen roamed the South, struggling to reunite families that had been separated by sale, and many couples formalized their marriages.

Immigrant and working-class Americans also created their own durable family systems. For these families, earnings were low and full-time, year-round employment was a rarity. Given inadequate public and private charity, the family and kin group was the only reliable source of assistance. Working-class people accepted the necessity of a cooperative family economy in which all members contributed to the family's support. Wives did piecework in the home or took in laundry or rented rooms to boarders. Children under the age of fifteen earned as much as 20 percent of a working-class family's income.

At the end of the nineteenth century many Americans feared that the family was disintegrating. Three momentous developments contributed to the sense of crisis: a declining birthrate, a rising divorce rate, and mounting evidence that younger women were no longer content to remain within their "sphere of domesticity."

Between 1800 and 1900, the birthrate fell 40 percent overall and even more sharply among the middle class. At the century's beginning, a typical wife gave birth to her first child at twenty-three and bore children every two years until menopause; in 1900 she bore her last child at thirty-three. The birthrate dropped in part because children, in an increasingly commercial society, were no longer economic assets who could be employed in household industries or bound out as apprentices and partly because many women were eager to break the unending cycle of pregnancy, birth, and nursing. The sharp rise in the divorce rate also generated anxiety. Despite efforts late in the century to restrict divorce by reducing legal grounds and lengthening residence requirements, the rate jumped fifteenfold between 1870 and 1920. A further source of alarm was the changing role of women. Increasing numbers were going to college, joining women's organizations, and taking jobs outside the home.

Many educators, scholars, and social workers responded to these developments by popularizing a new ideal — the "companionate family," which emphasized equal rights, sexual attraction, and companionship. Spouses would be "friends and lovers," parents and children, "pals." To achieve this ideal, influential groups recommended liberalized divorce laws, marriage counseling, sex education, access to birth-control information, and permissive child-rearing practices that stressed affection and encouraged self-expression rather than self-control. The full impact of this new ideal was delayed by the Great Depression and World War II, but the concept resurfaced after the war.

In the meantime, during the depression, unemployment or part-time work, lower wages, and demands of needy relatives tore at the fabric of family life, forcing many to share living quarters with relatives, delay marriages, and put off having children. The divorce rate fell, for the simple reason that fewer people could afford one, but the rate of desertion soared. By 1940, over 1.5 million married couples were living apart. Families sought to cope by pooling incomes and planting gardens, canning food, and making clothing. Children took part-time jobs and wives earned supplementary income by taking in sewing or laundry, setting up parlor groceries, or housing lodgers.

World War II also subjected the social order to severe strain. During the war, one-sixth of the nation's families suffered prolonged separation from sons or fathers. Five million "war widows" ran their homes and cared for children alone, and thousands went to work in war industries.

Wartime migration added to the strain, as more than 15 million civilians moved about in search of work. Families faced a severe shortage of housing and a lack of schools, hospitals, and child-care facilities. These stresses contributed to a dramatic upsurge in the divorce rate and to severe problems among the young. Tens of thousands became unsupervised "latchkey" children, and rates of juvenile delinquency, venereal disease, and truancy all rose.

The next decade witnessed a sharp reaction to the stresses of the depression and war. The divorce rate slowed and couples married earlier than their parents had. Women bore more children, at younger ages, and closer together than in the past. As the housing shortage eased, millions of people moved to new single-family homes in the suburbs.

Since 1960, the American family has undergone further radical changes. In little more than a decade, the divorce rate doubled, as did the proportion of working mothers; the number of single-parent households tripled; the number of couples living together outside of wedlock quadrupled; and the birthrate fell by half. Forces for change have included a massive influx of women into the work force, propelled by a rapidly rising cost of living; increased control over fertility, which has permitted many women to pursue careers more readily; heightened emphasis on self-gratification and self-fulfillment, which has helped reduce the stigma attached to divorce; and the rise of feminism, which has challenged the idea that child care and housework are the apex of a woman's accomplishments and her sole means of fulfillment.

Black families have experienced particularly intense strain. In 1960, 21 percent of black families were headed by women and 24 percent of black children were born outside of marriage. By the end of the 1980s, nearly half of all black children lived in female-headed households, more than half were born outside of wedlock, and over half were growing up in poverty. Low wages, unstable jobs, high levels of unemployment, and welfare policies that permitted many states to deny benefits to two-parent households contributed to the breakup of many impoverished families.

Carl N. Degler, *At Odds: Women and the Family in America from the Revolution to the Present* (1980); Steven Mintz and Susan Kellogg, *Domestic Revolutions: A Social History of American Family Life* (1988).

STEVEN MINTZ

See also Abortion; Birth Control; Birthrate and Mortality; Childhood; Divorce; Domestic Work; Feminist Movement; Housework; Marriage; Women and the Work Force.

FARMERS' ALLIANCE

The Farmers' Alliance moved to the forefront of the agrarian revolt in the 1880s, as farmers in the South and West found it increasingly difficult to survive economically. The post–Civil War deflation caused farm prices to fall, and farmers sank deeper into debt. Thousands lost their land. Two principal groups emerged: the National Farmers' Alliance (Northern Alliance) in the plains states, and the National Farmers' Alliance & Industrial Union (Southern Alliance) centered in Louisiana, Texas, and Arkansas. The Southern Alliance was particularly strong; its thousands of suballiances supported a network of cooperatives, traveling lecturers, and newspapers, all promoting a powerful sense of group solidarity. Increasingly, the Alliance members focused on the entrenched economic and political interests they felt were combining to deny farmers a decent living. By 1888, the Alliance had 250,000 members. Its list of demands included government control of transportation and communication and a "subtreasury" scheme for agricultural credit, as well as reforms of currency, land ownership, and income tax policies. Meanwhile the Northern Alliance was placing increasing emphasis on the free coinage of silver.

Efforts were made in 1889 to bring the two Alliances and the Knights of Labor into a coalition of "producing classes," as well as to cooperate with the Colored Farmers' Alliance, but sectional, racial, and organizational loyalties overrode the groups' common interests. Soon the Southern Alliance began organizing nationwide on its own, ultimately reaching into forty-three states. As it became clear that their cooperatives could not succeed without legislative changes, and as major-party politicians whom they had supported proved undependable once in office, the Alliance took the lead in creating a new farm-labor party, the People's (Populist) party in 1892. The Populist platform that year repeated nearly all the Alliance demands, and although the defeat of the Populists in 1896 finished both the party and the Alliance, many of the reforms they had advocated were adopted over the next half century.

See also Agriculture; People's Party; Populism.

FARMING

See Agriculture.

FASHION AND STYLE

During America's first three centuries, women's fashions in physical appearance and in dress followed European models. This dependence reflected the seventeenth- and eighteenth-century colonial status of the United States and its secondary international position during the nineteenth century. Women's styles were set especially in Paris, which gained a reputation for elegance with the rise by the 1850s of powerful dress designers, mostly male, beginning with Charles Worth, known as the originator of the Parisian haute couture. In the case of male attire, the center shifted from Europe to England as early as the eighteenth century. This change was occasioned by the popularity of the country-gentleman sports tradition as well as by the power of the British Empire and its middle-class entrepreneurs.

By the 1830s, the era of Jacksonian democratic attitudes, even the less well-to-do in the United States attempted to follow high style and pored over style plates printed in wide-circulation women's magazines like *Godey's Lady's Book,* established in 1830. In 1850, novelist Maria McIntosh noted that foreign travelers praised American political institutions while finding appalling the ubiquitous finery women wore. "I do not think I ever saw so large a proportion of highly dressed women," observed English writer John Robert Godley in 1844. Foreign travelers noted that workers had abandoned the prerevolutionary, preindustrial practice of trade-specific garb, making it difficult to differentiate among classes in public places. The matter of gender, however, was different. As men adopted the simple dark suit appropriate to a regimented business society (which has remained standard male garb to the present), women's dress became ever more fanciful and confining. After the postrevolutionary popularity of a long straight style bound under the bosom (known as *empire* because of its origin during the years of the Napoleonic Empire), women in the 1820s returned to the bell-shaped silhouette of the ancien régime. With the invention of the bent steel hoop in the mid-1850s, the skirt's dimensions reached extreme proportions, as women among the well-to-do vied for prominence in that intraclass competition that fashion often inspires.

Fashion in women's dress is characterized by constant small changes in decoration and design, leading slowly to changes in general style and silhouette. Thus the bell shape peaked in the mid-1860s, to be superseded by a straight front line with a pile of material over the buttocks known as a bustle. This silhouette remained dominant until the 1900s. In 1899, in *The Theory of the Leisure Class,* Thorstein Veblen presented the principle that, while the pursuit of wealth demanded middle-class men's full attention, their wives became decorated objects, displaying in their dress a capitalist "conspicuous consumption."

More than this, however, fashions in dress, especially when coupled with fashions in physical appearance, reflected a complex of cultural conventions. Thus the bell-shaped silhouette as the ideal of dress was accompanied by the ideal of the small, thin body type as well as delicate facial features and a pale skin reflective of Victorian domesticity and repressive sexual attitudes. Concomitantly, the popularity of tight lacing to achieve the smallest possible waist related to women's oppression. On the other hand, when combined with bust enlargers, or "falsies" (similarly popular throughout the century), tight lacing also related to the countervailing desire of women to appear sexually attractive to men.

Moreover, all these features reflected the universal drive to appear wealthy and leisured and thus of upper-class status: women who worked could severely corset their bodies only with difficulty, and white skin and a delicate look was the luxury of those who remained indoors and inactive.

By the 1860s the diminutive ideal of womanhood had given way to a weightier model. The voluptuous woman, with large bosom and bustle-accentuated hips, reflected both the concerns of doctors about women dieting strenuously to achieve slimness and the increased prominence of immigrant and middle-class groups for whom weight was a sign of prosperity. Another factor was the mid-century rise to popularity of variety theater and burlesque actresses whose bodies reflected the sensuality of stage and demimondaine subcultures, which had long celebrated the fleshy odalisque. Thus, from the 1860s to the 1890s, women who would later be called "fat" were considered beautiful.

Throughout the nineteenth century, ethnic, religious, and communal groups created their own fashions in dress and physical appearance in contradistinction to the elite, designer-dictated modes. Quakers and Shakers wore simplified versions of the bell-shaped dress, without padding or underpinnings, made of homespun fabrics in subdued colors. Catholic and Orthodox Jewish women covered their heads and wore clothing that concealed the body. Working women, farm women, and slave women on plantations also wore simple dresses or often the cast-off clothing of those more affluent. Upon occasion garish dress constructed from out-of-date styles could represent a sartorial rebellion against class oppression, as in the case of the pre–Civil War New York City "Bowery Girls," many of whom were dressmakers' assistants. By and large, however, most women owned little clothing, and even the better-off hired seamstresses each year to remodel old clothing rather than make new attire. Commercial ready-made clothing began to appear in the 1830s in the form of cloaks for women and pants and jackets for men, but not until after the Civil War, with its heavy demand for uniforms, was standardized sizing achieved. This innovation created the basis for the extensive ready-made clothing industry late in the century.

Dress reformers criticized the cost and restrictiveness of the dominant styles throughout these years. In 1850 women's rights advocates Elizabeth Cady Stanton and Amelia Bloomer designed a simplified bell-shaped dress, ankle-length and worn over pantaloons. But both they and others who wore the costume abandoned it after a few years because of vehement public protests, particularly directed against the pantaloons, widely viewed as sexually suggestive. Dress reform thereafter was pursued primarily by moderates like Jane Croly, editor of the popular *Demorest's Monthly,* and groups within the women's clubs and the Woman's Christian Temperance Union. But the general force of nineteenth-century feminism, women's increasing entry into the labor market (especially in white-collar occupations like clerical work), and the growing popularity of participant sports combined to create a demand for simplified, alternative clothing styles.

By the 1860s women on New York City streets were wearing jacketed dresses modeled after male suits. Thirty years later, these styles had evolved into the shirtwaist, the man-tailored blouse that became emblematic of the clerical working woman and that bore considerable resemblance to the kinds of blouses women now wore for sports like tennis and especially bicycling, which became a craze among all classes in the 1880s and 1890s. The 1890s also witnessed the advent of the "New Woman." This popular descriptive phrase was widely regarded as symbolic of the overturning of Victorian social repression and of the achievement of new freedoms for women in areas like education, law, and other professions. Personified in the popular drawings of Charles Dana Gibson, the "Gibson Girl" as the New Woman was tall, athletic, and self-confident. Her look was also patrician, and, although often shown in sports dress, she was never depicted as a working woman.

In many ways the new styles were an outgrowth of the process of modernization, of that force that seems everywhere to operate in the direction of secularization, standardization, and simplicity. But in particular, the styles became associated with the United States and its drive for leisure and the practical. In keeping with the nation's growing international status in an age of imperialism, the Gibson Girl was the first beauty model created in the United States to gain international recognition. Moreover, the fluidity of the American class structure in contrast to European rigidities (and in contradistinction to the principle that fashion always originates among the elites) was underscored by the origin of the shirtwaist among working women and its spread upward through the other classes.

The 1890s were the truly revolutionary years in the matter of dress and the desirable "look." Developments set in motion then were gradually worked out in succeeding decades. Skirts became shorter and tight lacing was abandoned; in the early 1920s the "flapper," with her slim, boyish body, short hair, and insouciant manner, became the new model of beauty, embodying the personal independence and social rebelliousness of the decade. Yet, although often presented as a model of freedom, the flapper actually was hemmed in by restrictions, reflective of the ambiguous position of feminism in the interwar years. The dominant beauty standards called for heavy makeup and a thin body, which required strict dieting. Fashion also dictated a bosomless body line best achieved by binding the breasts, thus often destroying muscular structure. In addition, the celebration of youth that had long been a feature of American fashion became a near-fetish in the 1920s. Advertising and the commercialized culture of beauty reached their early maturity and based their sales appeals on valorizing an evanescent stage of life. Finally, the continuation of the beauty contest, already popular by the 1900s, focused women's competitive spirit on their bodies, in contrast to men, who competed in business and sports.

From the 1930s through the 1980s, styles in dress and physical appearance continued to reflect cultural trends. During the depression and the Second World War, the look for women was one of greater maturity, including heavier bodies, longer skirt lengths, fuller facial features, and shoulder pads, adopted from standard male tailoring. A nation in crisis seemed to look to its women to provide security. The postwar era, however, returned to the glorification of youth, not as rebels but as adolescent consumers and innocent mothers-to-be. The line of the dress returned to the bell-shaped silhouette it had not had for fifty years, and the popularity of blonde hair, always a symbol of purity and easily achieved through hair dye, became a major advertising success. The film star Marilyn Monroe, combining earthy sexuality with childlike innocence, became the era's major beauty exemplar.

The radicalism and feminism of the 1960s, however, brought extremely short skirts and a rebellion against consumerism that took the form of the adoption of a natural look for women without makeup or artificially curled hair. Most important, the sixties' rebelliousness ended the dominance of the Anglo-Saxon look, preeminent throughout the history of the nation, as more Mediterranean, Asiatic, and African-American looks were taken up by the media and fashion magazines as acceptable models. The 1960s also witnessed the end to the dominance of Hollywood films as the primary creators of cultural beauty standards, and the rise to prominence of television and the appearance of a host of new magazines directed to specific, often newly affluent markets. Yet in the same decade a vogue for extreme thinness, which continued through the 1980s, was partially responsible for an epidemic of anorexia nervosa among adolescent women. These strains of extreme individualism also nurtured a narcissism that, by the 1980s, had resulted in the appearance of "yuppies" (young upwardly mobile professionals), prey to advertising's manipulations and major consumers of expensive cosmetics and designer clothes.

Still, American inventiveness, casualness, and love of leisure continued throughout the century to produce simplified types of dress that both found their own markets and influenced the mode. In particular, workmen's blue jeans and coveralls as well as a wide variety of sports clothing became popular garb, peaking in the 1980s in sequined T-shirts, made of nonelite cotton, for day and evening wear. Unisex styles in sportswear reflected broader cultural trends of equal rights among men and women. The rise of major American designers, like Claire McCardell who challenged the Parisian hegemony over high fashion, begun in the 1930s, led in the 1980s to the internationalization of fashion, with major centers in New York and Los Angeles. As the center of the entertainment industry and with its combination of aesthetic daring, relaxed morality, and consistent class and subculture interaction, Los Angeles had become a new mecca for fashion leaders.

Lois W. Banner, *American Beauty* (1983); Valerie Steele, *Fashion and Eroticism: Ideals of Feminine Beauty from the Victorian Era to the Jazz Age* (1985).

LOIS W. BANNER

FAULKNER, WILLIAM

(1897–1962), novelist. Considered by many critics to be America's greatest writer, Faulkner wrote novels and stories that are drenched with a sense of history's (and the South's) agonies. He was born in Mississippi to a distinguished family and in high school was a mediocre student whose main interest was football. An older friend introduced him to avant-garde literature, and he soon preferred reading and attempting to write to working in his grandfather's bank. In 1918 he enlisted in the Canadian air force, hoping to see action in World War I, but the war ended before he completed flight training.

Faulkner published his undistinguished first novel, *Soldier's Pay,* in 1926. In his third novel, *Sartoris* (1929), he hit his stride, creating his fictional realm, Yoknapatawpha County, and a southern family full of foolhardy, suicidally defiant men and suffering, caring women. In his next novels he enlarged this portrait of a South wracked by grief and defeat, clinging to old values while struggling to embrace the harsh rationality of modern capitalist America. Faulkner married this historical imagination to a profound humanism and a readiness to experiment with a wide range of fictional techniques. His books are full of convoluted time sequences and interior monologues, exploring his characters' deepest drives and unrecognized anxieties.

Although some critics and reviewers praised

his talent, for twenty years Faulkner's novels sold poorly. He made his living with straightforward stories written for magazines and stints as a Hollywood screenwriter. In 1944 Faulkner's career was apparently at a dead end. He seemed doomed to be regarded as a regional writer with a very small following. He was out of step with the social realism and left-leaning ideology that had dominated fiction in the preceding decade.

In 1946 an astonishing reversal of fortune began. Viking Press published *The Portable Faulkner* with a prescient foreword by critic Malcolm Cowley, asserting that Faulkner was a writer exploring universal themes. In 1948 he was elected to the prestigious National Academy of Arts and Letters and in 1949 was awarded the Nobel Prize for literature. In the next ten years he collected a National Book Award and two Pulitzer Prizes. Abandoning his reclusive life in Oxford, Mississippi, he toured as a lecturer and became a writer in residence at the University of Virginia. Affluence enabled him to take up fox hunting and other pleasures of the southern gentleman. He died from injuries from a fall from a horse, a denouement a Faulknerian narrator would have appreciated.

His last book, *The Rievers,* published a month before his death, is a nostalgic look at Yoknapatawpha County in 1905. Near its close, Lucius Priest, a young man who is just beginning to grasp the power of the past, asks his grandfather if he can somehow forget the embarrassing, humiliating events of the story. The old man replies with words that sum up Faulkner's enduring contribution to American literature and our sense of history. "Nothing is ever forgotten," the grandfather says. "Nothing is ever lost. It's too valuable."

Richard P. Adams, *Faulkner: Myth and Motion* (1986); Joseph Blotner, *Faulkner: A Biography,* 2 vols. (1974); David Mintner, *William Faulkner: His Life and Work* (1980).

Thomas Fleming

See also Literature.

FBI

See Federal Bureau of Investigation.

FCC

See Federal Communications Commission.

FEDERAL BUREAU OF INVESTIGATION

The Federal Bureau of Investigation (FBI), the investigative arm of the Department of Justice, was created in 1908 by Attorney General Charles J. Bonaparte over the initial opposition of Congress who feared political abuse of such powers.

During and after World War I, the FBI investigated draft resisters, violators of the Espionage Act of 1917, and alien residents suspected of radicalism. This kind of surveillance marked a shift away from criminal investigations toward individuals thought to be domestic security threats, a group including such diverse figures as Jane Addams and Fiorello La Guardia. Such misuse of the FBI's powers led to reorganization in 1924. The bureau received orders not to engage in wiretapping or to investigate the political activities of individuals. J. Edgar Hoover, appointed director, professionalized the bureau, placing appointments and promotions on a merit basis and developing new crime-fighting techniques.

Despite the ban on political surveillance, World War II and the cold war prompted a wide expansion of security investigations. Under the guise of national security the FBI amassed over thirty-five thousand linear feet of files on individual citizens. Following the death of Hoover and the Watergate scandal in which it was involved, Congress and the attorney general again issued guidelines designed to prevent such abuse. In the late 1970s the FBI shifted its investigations toward organized and white-collar crime.

See also Anticommunism; Espionage; Hoover, J. Edgar.

FEDERAL COMMUNICATIONS COMMISSION

The Federal Communications Commission (FCC), an independent executive agency formed to regulate interstate and foreign communications, was established under the Communications Act of June 19, 1934. This body replaced the former Federal Radio Commission. The new commissioners were responsible for telephone communication as well as radio; supervision of telegraph and television was added in subsequent years. The FCC assigns broadcasting frequencies, makes all decisions regarding the granting, modification, or revocation of broadcasting licenses, and generally is expected to protect the public interest in matters of communications. The scope of FCC activities expanded significantly when the ceiling it had set in 1948 on the number of American television licenses was lifted; the number of stations soon increased from 108 to more than 2,000, including nearly 250 noncommercial stations. The commission has seven members, each serving a seven-year term; they are appointed by the president with the consent of the Senate.

The FCC's role in representing the public's interest began to be questioned more aggressively as the nation's communications network matured. A congressional investigation in February 1958 led to the resignation of one commissioner over graft in the granting of television licenses. Three years later, FCC chairman Newton Minow stirred a national debate by declaring television "a vast wasteland." In 1964, court rulings forced the FCC to grant the public a larger voice in its consideration of license renewals. The quality and propriety of television watched by children also became a matter of concern. The deregulatory policies of President Ronald Reagan's administration in the 1980s gave broadcasters a freer hand, as did the growth of relatively unregulated cable television, but by the end of the decade, discussion had turned again to the need for closer FCC supervision.

See also Radio and Television.

FEDERAL CONVENTION

See Philadelphia Convention.

FEDERALIST PAPERS

These are a series of eighty-five letters written to newspapers in 1787–1788 by Alexander Hamilton, James Madison, and John Jay, urging ratification of the Constitution.

After a new Constitution, intended to replace the ineffectual Articles of Confederation, had been hammered out at the Philadelphia Convention, it was agreed that it would go into effect when nine of the thirteen states had approved it in ratifying conventions. There ensued a nationwide debate over constitutional principles, and the press was inundated with letters condemning or praising the document, among them these articles, signed "Publius."

The three men — chief among them Hamilton, who wrote about two-thirds of the essays — addressed the objections of opponents, who feared a tyrannical central government that would supersede states' rights and encroach on individual liberties. All strong nationalists, the essayists argued that, most important, the proposed system would preserve the Union, now in danger of breaking apart, and empower the federal government to act firmly and coherently in the national interest. Conflicting economic and political interests would be reconciled through a representative Congress, whose legislation would be subject to presidential veto and judicial review. This system of checks and balances and the Constitution's clear delineation of the powers of the federal government — few, limited, and defined, as Madison put it — would protect states' rights and, as they saw it, individual rights. The ultimate protection of individual liberties had to wait for later passage of the Bill of Rights, for these men, as their arguments made plain, distrusted what Madison called "the superior force of an interested and overbearing majority." Many of the constitutional provisions they praised were intended precisely to dampen democratic "excesses."

The articles, written in the spirit both of propaganda and of logical argument, probably had little influence on public opinion of the day. Nevertheless, the essays, published in book form as *The Federalist* in 1788, have through the years been widely read and respected for their masterly analysis and interpretation of the Constitution and the principles upon which the government of the United States was established.

See also Ratification of the Constitution.

FEDERALIST PARTY

The Federalist party was one of the first two political parties in the United States, and thus in the world. It originated, as did its opposition, the Democratic-Republican party, within the executive and congressional branches of government during George Washington's first administration (1789–1793), and it dominated the government until the defeat of President John Adams for reelection in 1800. Thereafter, the party unsuccessfully contested the presidency through 1816 and remained a political force in some states until the 1820s. Its members then passed into both the Democratic and the Whig parties.

Although Washington disdained factions and disclaimed party adherence, he is generally taken to have been, by policy and inclination, a Federalist — and thus its greatest figure. Influential public leaders who accepted the Federalist label included John Adams, Alexander Hamilton, John Jay, Rufus King, John Marshall, Timothy Pickering, and Charles Cotesworth Pinckney. All had agitated for a new and more effective constitution in 1787. Yet, because many members of the Democratic-Republican party of Thomas Jefferson and James Madison had also championed the Constitution, the Federalist party cannot be considered the lineal descendant of the pro-Constitution, or "federalist," grouping of the 1780s. Instead, like its opposition, the party emerged in the 1790s under new conditions and around new issues.

The party drew its early support from those who — for ideological and other reasons — wished to strengthen national instead of state power. Until its defeat in the presidential election of 1800, its style was elitist, and its leaders scorned democracy, widespread suffrage, and open elections. Its backing centered in the commercial Northeast, whose economy and public order had been threatened by the failings of the Confederation government before 1788. Although the party enjoyed considerable influence in Virginia, North Carolina, and the area around Charleston, South Carolina, it failed to attract plantation owners and yeoman farmers in the South and West. Its inability to broaden its geographic and social appeal eventually did it in.

Originally a coalition of like-minded men, the party became publicly well defined only in 1795. After Washington's inauguration in 1789, Congress and members of the president's cabinet debated proposals of Alexander Hamilton, first secretary of the treasury, that the national government assume the debts of the states, repay the national debt at par rather than at its depressed market value, and charter a national bank. Secretary of State Thomas Jefferson and Congressman James Madison rallied opposition to Hamilton's plan. Yet not until Congress debated the ratification and implementation of Jay's Treaty with Great Britain did two political parties clearly emerge, with the Federalists under Hamilton's leadership. Federalist policies thenceforth emphasized commercial and diplomatic harmony with Britain, domestic order and stability, and a strong national government under powerful executive and judicial branches. Washington's Farewell Address of 1796, prepared with Hamilton's assistance, can be read as a classic text of partisan Federalism as well as a great state paper.

John Adams, Washington's vice president, succeeded the first president as an avowed Federalist, thus becoming the first person to attain the chief magistracy under partisan colors. Inaugurated in 1797, Adams tried to maintain his predecessor's cabinet and policies. He engaged the nation in an undeclared naval war with France; and, after the Federalists gained control of both houses of Congress in the 1798 elections, he backed the infamous and Federalist-inspired Alien and Sedition Acts.

In addition to a widespread public outcry against those laws, Adams met with mounting attacks, especially from the Hamiltonian faction of his own party, against his military priorities. When Adams, as much to deflect mounting Democratic-Republican opposition as to end a war, opened diplomatic negotiations with France in 1796 and reorganized the cabinet under his own control, the Hamiltonians broke with him. Although his actions strengthened the Federalist position in the presidential election of 1800, they were not enough to gain his reelection. His party irreparably split and he on his way to retirement, Adams was nevertheless able to conclude peace with France and to secure the appointment of moderate Federalist John Marshall as chief justice. Long after the Federalist party was dead, Marshall enshrined its principles in constitutional law.

In the minority, Federalists at last accepted the necessity of creating a system of organized, disciplined state party organizations and adopting democratic electoral tactics. Because their greatest strength lay in Massachusetts, Connecticut, and Delaware, the Federalists also assumed the aspects of a sectional minority. Ignoring ideological consistency and a traditional commitment to strong national power, they opposed Jefferson's popular Louisiana Purchase of 1803 as too costly and threatening to northern influence in government. Largely as a result, the party continued to lose power at the national level. It carried only Connecticut, Delaware, and part of Maryland against Jefferson in 1804.

That defeat, the party's increasing regional isolation, and Hamilton's untimely death that same year threatened the party's very existence. Yet strong, widespread opposition to Jefferson's ill-conceived Embargo of 1807 revived it. In the 1808 presidential election against Madison, the Federalist candidate, Charles C. Pinckney, carried Delaware, parts of Maryland and North Carolina, and all of New England except Vermont. The declaration of war against Great Britain in 1812 brought New York, New Jersey, and more of Maryland into the Federalist fold, although these states were not enough to gain the party the presidency.

But Federalist obstruction of the war effort seriously undercut its newfound popularity, and the Hartford Convention of 1814 won for it, however unjustly, the stigma of secession and treason. The party under Rufus King carried only Connecticut, Massachusetts, and Delaware in the election of 1816.

Although it lingered on in these states, the party never regained its national following, and by 1828, it was dead. Its inability to accommodate early enough a rising, popular democratic spirit, often strongest in towns and cities, was its undoing. Its emphasis upon banking, commerce, and national institutions, although fitting for the young nation, nevertheless made it un-

popular among the majority of Americans who, as people of the soil, remained wary of state influence. Yet its contributions to the nation were extensive. Its principles gave form to the new government. Its leaders laid the foundations of a national economy, created and staffed a national judicial system, and enunciated enduring principles of American foreign policy.

James M. Banner, Jr., *To the Hartford Convention: The Federalists and the Origins of Party Politics in Massachusetts, 1789–1815* (1970); Linda K. Kerber, *Federalists in Dissent: Imagery and Ideology in Jeffersonian America* (1970).

JAMES M. BANNER, JR.

See also Adams, John; Alien and Sedition Acts; Elections: 1796, 1800, 1804, 1808, 1816; Hamilton, Alexander; Hartford Convention of 1814; Marshall, John.

FEDERAL RESERVE SYSTEM

See Banking.

FEDERAL THEATRE PROJECT

The Federal Theatre Project (FTP) was one of five public works programs for artists and writers created in 1935 by the New Deal Works Progress Administration (WPA). This was the first time the federal government subsidized the arts on such a vast scale. The FTP's purpose was twofold: to provide relief work for theatrical artists that utilized their talents and to make their work widely available to ordinary Americans, thus democratizing "high culture."

The FTP was the most controversial and short-lived of the WPA's arts projects. Hallie Flanagan, former head of Vassar College's Experimental Theater, served as director and shaped the FTP into a forum for experimental theater committed to creating public awareness of contemporary issues. They produced a range of plays from Shakespeare to Sinclair Lewis's *It Can't Happen Here* and T. S. Eliot's *Murder in the Cathedral*. Sixteen black theater units were established. Their most notable production, staged in Harlem, was an all-black version of *Macbeth* set in Haiti. The FTP also produced the "Living Newspaper," dramatizations combining newsreel, radio, and stage techniques that focused on contemporary social issues, such as slums and public utilities. The FTP employed actors, playwrights, directors, producers, composers, and technicians, including such notables as Orson Welles, Arthur Miller, John Huston, E. G. Marshall, and John Houseman.

The FTP gave many Americans their first opportunity to attend live theater. It sent companies on tour to smaller cities and also staged children's plays, puppet shows, radio dramas, and circuses. About 30 million people attended these productions in the four years of the FTP's existence.

In the late 1930s, the FTP came under attack by the House Un-American Activities Committee, which was conducting a larger investigation into propaganda activities. The FTP was accused of communist leanings and of providing a forum for New Deal propaganda. Congress abolished the FTP in 1939 because of this controversy and as part of a general abandonment of the New Deal.

See also New Deal.

FEDERAL TRADE COMMISSION

The Federal Trade Commission (FTC), established in 1914 as part of President Woodrow Wilson's effort to combat trusts, is an independent regulatory agency charged with ensuring free and fair competition among the nation's businesses (except for banks and common carriers, which are supervised by other agencies). Its five members are appointed to seven-year terms by the president, but a Supreme Court ruling in 1935 established that, once appointed, they cannot be dismissed by the president. The FTC was initially intended to carry out its regulatory functions primarily through economic planning, serving as a clearinghouse of information, publicizing examples of unfair competition, and advising the president and Congress on needed legislation. (These functions are similar to those of the earlier Bureau of Corporations, which it absorbed, but the FTC was given considerably more

power than the bureau to do its work, including unprecedented access to corporate records and the right to issue cease-and-desist orders.)

In the years since its creation, however, an increasing portion of FTC work has come to involve enforcement rather than planning; dozens of statutes have made the commission an enforcing agent, giving it responsibility for monitoring gas utilities, preventing unfair price discrimination, reviewing corporate mergers, and maintaining standards for advertising, packaging, and labeling. Because of staff constraints and because court decisions have somewhat reduced its investigatory powers, the FTC does much of its enforcement by working out voluntary industry-wide agreements, but it has also brought numerous court suits for unfair business practices. In 1982, complaints to Congress about the FTC from businesses and the medical profession led to a defeat of the agency's usual three-year authorization. Since that time, its funding has been on a year-to-year basis.

See also Antitrust Movement.

FEDERAL WRITERS' PROJECT

The Works Progress Administration (WPA) was a New Deal agency created in 1935 to provide jobs for the unemployed through public works. A small but significant portion of WPA funds were used to support several controversial public works projects in the arts, marking the first time in American history that the federal government granted substantial subsidies to writers and artists. The Federal Writers' Project (FWP) was one of these programs.

Under the direction of former journalist and theater director Henry Alsberg, the FWP gave jobs to thousands of unemployed writers, who produced about a thousand publications centered on American topics. These included now classic state, city, and regional guides, a 150-volume Life in America series, which included studies of ethnic groups like *The Italians of New York* and *The Negro in Virginia,* and various collections of folklore. Workers also conducted an extensive series of interviews with some two thousand former slaves, a priceless historical resource. The FWP employed a number of now well-known writers, such as Conrad Aiken, Saul Bellow, Ralph Ellison, and John Cheever, and many received crucial support for their budding careers. The young Richard Wright spent his spare time while working for the FWP writing *Native Son*. The agency also employed many unknown, self-described writers, such as former teachers and librarians in need of work.

The FWP always operated in the face of public skepticism. Many Americans questioned whether writing was the sort of work deserving public aid. In 1939, Congress required that local sponsors provide 25 percent of the funds for the FWP to continue. Every state met the requirement. The Federal Writers' Project ceased when the WPA was terminated in 1943.

See also New Deal.

FEMINIST MOVEMENT

I. From Its Origins to 1960

The history of American feminism — the self-conscious desire to achieve sexual equality — began soon after the Revolution, when women's rights tracts first appeared in print. Citizens of the late eighteenth century might read Englishwoman Mary Wollstonecraft's treatise on *Vindication of the Rights of Woman* (1792) or Judith Sargent Murray's essays in New England magazines. Both authors urged increased independence for women through access to education. The egalitarian spirit that pervaded their works reappeared in many ways over the next two centuries.

During the early nineteenth century, women participated in numerous efforts to improve women's status, defend their interests, and increase their rights. Educators, such as Emma Willard, Mary Lyon, and Catharine Beecher, promoted advanced training for women in female academies and seminaries. Thousands of women in the 1830s and 1840s joined moral reform societies, organized to end licentiousness, seduction, and prostitution. Female temperance societies strove to save abused wives and families from drunken spouses. Individual reformers

spoke out for women's rights. Scottish radical Frances Wright, a follower of Robert Owen, addressed eastern audiences on women's need for equal education, legal equality, and divorce rights. Another Owenite, Ernestine Rose, campaigned for married women's property rights. Author Margaret Fuller led "conversations" among Boston women devoted to "woman and her rights." Among women in the antebellum North, the "woman question" became a lively issue.

The first women's rights movement emerged in part from women's sense of alliance with one another and their shared discontents. It arose also from their experience in reform, especially antislavery. William Lloyd Garrison's wing of abolition, the American Anti-Slavery Society (1833), welcomed women into its ranks and introduced them to politics. Fervent campaigners, such as Philadelphia Quaker Lucretia Mott, Sarah and Angelina Grimké of South Carolina, and Abby Kelley of Massachusetts, served as organizers and lecture agents. But their activism evoked disputes about women's role in public life. Forced to defend their right to speak to audiences of both men and women, the Grimké sisters became advocates of sexual equality. "The investigation of the rights of the slave has led me to a better understanding of my own," Angelina Grimké declared in 1836. Younger women in abolitionist circles, such as Elizabeth Cady Stanton and Lucy Stone, learned political tactics and absorbed the Garrisonian ideology of human rights.

The first women's rights meeting, at Seneca Falls, New York, in 1848, capitalized on women's antislavery experience. Called by Mott and Stanton, who had met at an 1840 antislavery convention in London, and some Quaker friends, the convention attracted about three hundred women and men. One-third of the participants signed a "Declaration of Sentiments," modeled on the Declaration of Independence and drawn up by Stanton. The declaration denounced the "absolute tyranny" of men and presented resolutions demanding equal rights for women in marriage, education, religion, employment, and political life. This manifesto channeled a diffuse array of grievances into an agenda to change women's lives. The call for the vote, the most controversial resolution, directly challenged male dominance. Unlike the others, which were unanimously adopted, it won approval by a bare majority only after strenuous efforts by Stanton and abolitionist Frederick Douglass.

During the 1850s, the new women's rights movement promoted its broad agenda through annual conventions. Its leaders waged legislative campaigns to attain married women's property rights and worked independently to rouse support. Susan B. Anthony canvassed New York State, organizing meetings and seeking recruits. But limited by its abolitionist affiliation, the movement was unable to expand its small following. During the Civil War, women's rights leaders maintained their antislavery stance. After the Emancipation Proclamation of 1863 made abolition of slavery a Union war goal, they organized the National Women's Loyal League to support the Union war effort, promote the Thirteenth Amendment, and press for woman suffrage.

The immediate postwar years proved a crucial period for women's rights. The controversial issue of black political rights — and debate over the Fourteenth and Fifteenth Amendments — quickly made woman suffrage the most prominent of women's demands. Women's rights leaders formed the Equal Suffrage Association of 1866 to strive for both black and woman suffrage and joined a referendum campaign on these issues in Kansas in 1867. But in that state, male abolitionist support for woman suffrage dwindled. Alienated from their former allies in the antislavery movement, Stanton and Anthony began to campaign independently. Through their publication *Revolution,* financed by the eccentric Democrat George Francis Train, they promoted a broad spectrum of women's rights — equal suffrage, equal pay, marriage reform, more liberal divorce laws, and "self-sovereignty." They denounced the Fifteenth Amendment, which enfranchised only black men and which other women's rights leaders endorsed. In 1869, two rival suffrage movements emerged. The New York–based National Woman Suffrage Association (NWSA) led by

Stanton and Anthony, accepted only women and opposed the Fifteenth Amendment. The Boston-based American Woman Suffrage Association (AWSA), which included men, supported black suffrage as a step in the right direction. Among its leaders were Lucy Stone and Julia Ward Howe.

The new woman suffrage associations followed separate paths for two decades. The NWSA campaigned for a federal woman suffrage amendment, but made no progress. The AWSA published the *Women's Journal* and waged state campaigns, but lost all state referenda. By 1890 only Utah and Wyoming had enfranchised women. Although women had acquired partial voting rights (in local elections or school board elections) in nineteen states, equal suffrage remained elusive. Meanwhile a larger "woman movement" developed. Women's clubs, which started in 1868, multiplied. The clubs promoted self-education through cultural discussions, and after their federation in 1892, turned their attention to civic affairs. Black women's clubs, which also federated in the 1890s, supported racial causes, discussed women's issues, and worked on philanthropic projects. The huge Woman's Christian Temperance Union attracted members by the thousands. Under the leadership of Frances Willard, many members supported woman suffrage. Other women became involved in the campaign for higher education, the establishment of women's colleges, and the promotion of women into the professions.

Although suffragists won no major victories, the growing woman movement provided a potential constituency. The ranks of women activists increased in the Progressive Era with the emergence of new women's organizations devoted to reform. Such endeavors as the settlement movement, the National Consumers League (1899), the Women's Trade Union League (1903), and the women's peace movement abetted the suffrage crusade. By taking part in public affairs, women reformers helped legitimize suffragist claims. Advocates of the ballot had always combined demands for sexual equality (women deserved the vote) with arguments based on sexual difference (women would bring special qualities to politics). During the progressive years, suffragist rhetoric tilted toward an emphasis on the good that women would do for society if enfranchised.

In 1890, the rival women suffrage organizations united in the National American Woman Suffrage Association (NAWSA) and began the long path toward victory. Under the leadership of Anna Howard Shaw (1904–1915) and Carrie Chapman Catt (1900–1904, 1915–1920), the NAWSA ran a propaganda crusade and campaigned in the states. In its final decade, the suffrage movement built up the momentum that had thus far eluded it. By now, the ballot symbolized all the rights for which women had campaigned. During World War I, conflict arose between the NAWSA and Alice Paul's more militant National Woman's party, which waged hunger strikes and picketed the White House. In 1919, Congress at last approved woman suffrage and in August 1920, the Nineteenth Amendment was ratified by the states.

In the last decade of the suffrage campaign, the word *feminism* first came into use. Its appearance marked a watershed dividing the long suffrage crusade from modern feminism. During the course of the struggle for suffrage, the ballot had assumed paramount importance, obliterating the once-broad agenda of women's rights. To Susan B. Anthony, suffrage had been "the pivotal right, the one that underlies all other rights." Modern feminists envisioned a new type of emancipation embracing political equality, economic independence, liberation from convention, and changed relations between the sexes. "All feminists are suffragists, but not all suffragists are feminists," one adherent explained in 1913. Modern feminism embodied paradoxes. Its supporters stressed, variously, women's equality with men and differences from men. They advocated both individualism and gender solidarity. Similar contradictions had long been evident among feminists, from Elizabeth Cady Stanton to Charlotte Perkins Gilman, whose *Women and Economics* (1899) energized turn-of-the-century activists.

With suffrage achieved, the contradictions within feminism led to conflicts among feminists. These conflicts emerged in the 1920s, a high point of feminist activity. The suffrage movement remobilized for future battles. The NAWSA became the League of Women Voters, which sought to educate women about politics and maintained a nonpartisan stance. Disputes erupted between the National Woman's party, which proposed an Equal Rights Amendment (ERA; 1923), and reform-minded activists in the League of Women Voters and other women's organizations, which opposed it. An ERA, the reformers claimed, would vitiate laws protecting women workers. Adding to the conflict within the movement was the apparent failure of woman suffrage to change politics. Women failed to vote as a bloc, support women candidates, or effect reforms. Passage of the Sheppard-Towner Act of 1921, which provided funds for maternal and child health clinics, represented the sole legislative triumph of the suffrage movement. Another set of problems was loss of constituency, failure to connect with the next generation, and diversion of feminist energies into careerism or new causes, such as birth control. Finally, feminists of the 1920s might face attacks for trying to dismiss sex differences or, alternately, for dwelling on them and fostering "sex antagonism."

The spirit of social reform dominated women's work in public life during the 1930s. Women who filled important posts in the New Deal — the circle of women around Eleanor Roosevelt — came from the reform-minded wing of the women's movement. Like Labor Secretary Frances Perkins and Mary W. Dewson, head of the Women's Division of the Democratic party, they had experience in settlements, women's clubs, and social welfare, and they opposed the National Woman's party position on an ERA. Often staunch defenders of women's interests, they described themselves as reformers, not feminists.

The feminist movement reached a low ebb during the 1940s and 1950s. Now aging or retiring, the veterans of the last feminist wave were not replaced by newcomers. Old organizations shrank and vanished or else lost their feminist drive. The remnant of the National Woman's party, the only group still committed to sexual equality, had little influence. World War II undermined women's egalitarian goals. During the war, women won attention as workers in defense industries, but in public life women had little impact on policymaking. The postwar era represented a nadir of feminist history. Characterized by suburbanization, consumerism, and the baby boom, the 1950s constituted a domestic decade. Mass culture emphasized women's family roles, disparaged career women, condemned working mothers, and labeled feminism a form of deviance.

Yet the 1950s saw some important developments that would contribute to the revival of feminism. One was the rapid expansion of higher education. Although the proportion of women among college students fell during the postwar years, their numbers kept rising. This meant a far larger constituency of educated women, always the nucleus of feminist movements. Another major development was the steady, incremental increase of women, notably married women, in the postwar labor force. The rising number of working wives reflected the impact of birth control; women now completed their families at younger ages. It also reflected the postwar growth of the middle class. Among upwardly mobile Americans, the desire to maintain a middle-class lifestyle began to legitimize the two-income family. These developments set the stage for a feminist revival in the 1960s.

Nancy F. Cott, *The Grounding of Modern Feminism* (1987); Ellen Carol DuBois, *Feminism and Suffrage: The Emergence of an Independent Women's Movement in America* (1978); William L. O'Neill, *Feminism in America* (1969; 2nd ed., 1989).

NANCY WOLOCH

See also American Woman Suffrage Association; Equal Rights Amendment; League of Women Voters; Married Women's Property Acts; National American Woman Suffrage Association; National Woman Suffrage Association; National Woman's Party; Seneca Falls Convention; Suffrage; *and entries for individual feminists.*

II. From 1960 to the Present

The revival of feminism in the sixties is often dated from the appearance of Betty Friedan's *The Feminine Mystique.* This 1963 best-seller found a receptive audience among middle- and upper-class women whose experiences Friedan captured. Although her book was important for its challenge to the ideology of domesticity, other factors also contributed to the reemergence of feminism. Unprecedented numbers of married women were being drawn into the job market — albeit on unequal terms — as the service sector of the economy expanded and consumerism fueled the desire of many families for a second income. Both the growing numbers of women graduating from college and the availability of the birth-control pill (which accelerated the already noticeable decline in the birthrate) further encouraged women's entry into the work force. By the early sixties the contradiction between the realities of paid work and higher education, on the one hand, and the still pervasive domestic ideology, on the other, could no longer be reconciled. Equally important in sparking feminist consciousness were the oppositional movements of the sixties, particularly the black freedom movement, which was a source of inspiration and a model for social change for second-wave feminists.

The new feminism emerged from two groups of educated, middle-class, predominantly white women. The National Organization for Women (NOW) consisted mainly of politically moderate professionals; those who stressed women's liberation were younger, more radical women and typically veterans of the black freedom movement and the New Left. For the former, John F. Kennedy's establishment of the President's Commission on the Status of Women (PCSW) in 1961 and Title VII of the Civil Rights Act of 1964, which prohibited employment discrimination on the basis of race, sex, religion, and national origin, were important catalysts for change. The PCSW, with Eleanor Roosevelt as chair, was charged with the task of documenting the position of American women in the economy, legal system, and the family. Its 1964 report uncovered such pervasive sex discrimination that many commissioners were shocked. Most states also convened commissions that similarly documented widespread sex discrimination. It was at the third national meeting of the state commissions in 1966 that NOW was born. Angered by the failure of the newly created Equal Employment Opportunity Commission (EEOC) to enforce the anti–sex discrimination provision of Title VII, twenty-eight women (including Friedan) formed the organization to pressure the government into challenging sex discrimination.

Like the NAACP after which it was modeled, NOW adopted a legalistic and assimilationist approach to achieving women's equality. Rather than challenging their subordination in domestic life, the feminists of NOW committed themselves to fighting for women's integration into public life. Early debates in NOW concerned the group's advocacy of abortion rights and the Equal Rights Amendment (ERA). Indeed, when NOW accorded top priority to the ERA in its 1968 Bill of Rights, women from the United Auto Workers (out of whose offices the first NOW mailings had been sent) were pressured to resign from NOW because of their union's opposition to the amendment. From the moment the ERA was first discussed by feminists in 1920, it had caused enormous divisiveness; many feared that its passage, by invalidating legislation protective of women, would lead to worsening work conditions for them. This time around, however, opposition to the ERA from progressive and feminist quarters evaporated quickly when it became clear that the courts and the EEOC were already interpreting Title VII as invalidating protective legislation. Indeed, the women of the United Auto Workers rejoined NOW two years later when their union endorsed the amendment.

Over the years NOW's membership became more heterogeneous and its political stance more daring. Although its primary commitment to the ERA continued, especially after the election of Eleanor Smeal as its president in 1977, NOW supported even more controversial issues, including lesbian and gay rights, an issue it had earlier skirted. The ERA ratification effort tripled NOW's membership (210,000 members by 1982), but its ultimate failure in 1982 deflated the organization's spirit and its numbers. The ERA campaign had been important in keeping alive public discussion of sex discrimination, but NOW's focus on the amendment had diverted attention from such pressing problems as child care, abortion rights, and the feminization of poverty.

Within a year of NOW's formation white women involved in the black freedom movement and the New Left began meeting in small groups to discuss sexism within the radical movement. In contrast to the Old Left, which gave token support to the struggle against male chauvinism, neither the New Left nor the black movement directly addressed the question of female inequality. But the New Left's efforts to expand political discourse to include personal relations (encapsulated in the slogan "the personal is political") unintentionally fueled feminist consciousness as it encouraged women to define housework, relationships with men, and sex in political terms. Moreover, despite the sexism they encountered, women through their work in these movements developed new skills and confidence, as they defied conventional norms of femininity. Important as well was their exposure in the black movement to assertive black women — both older community leaders and the younger activists — whose behavior was at odds with the ideology of domesticity.

Although they sometimes worked with NOW, these women's liberationists opposed NOW's moderate politics and its emphasis on legal equality on the grounds that this policy ignored women's subordination in the family and that it encouraged women's integration into a class- and race-stratified system rather than seeking to dismantle that system. Deeply skeptical of achieving substantive change through reform, they disagreed with NOW's focus on electoral politics, legislation, and lobbying. Instead, like other sixties' radicals, they sought a movement that would maximize individual participation and lead to a radical restructuring of society.

If women's liberationists were united in their opposition to NOW's liberal feminism, they found themselves in disagreement over two issues: (1) the proper relationship between their fledgling movement and the larger radical movement and (2) the source of women's oppression. Some women (who were called politicos and later identified themselves as socialist-feminists) argued that the two movements should be closely connected: socialism would achieve women's liberation. Others (who called themselves radical feminists) maintained that the women's movement should be entirely independent: capitalism was not the sole source of male dominance nor socialism its remedy. This schism often resulted in separate organizations in larger cities.

The arguably most far-reaching and provocative analyses of male supremacy were propounded by radical feminists such as Shulamith Firestone, Kate Millett, and Ti-Grace Atkinson, who, following Simone de Beauvoir, maintained that gender exists as a social construct, not a biological fact. They were the first to criticize marriage, the nuclear family, normative heterosexuality, violence against women, and sexist health care. By the early seventies both socialist-feminists and liberal feminists had come to agree with much of their analyses.

In the mid-seventies radical feminists became concerned less with confronting male dominance than with building a women's counterculture where "male" values would be banished and "female" values nourished. In this shift, they were following a course taken by some radicals of the sixties. Socialist-feminists who had organized a network of women's liberation unions in many cities found these unions attacked by sectarian leftists who believed that feminism was diverting women from the more important class struggle. As a consequence, socialist-feminism exists primarily in the academy as a theoretical tendency. The liberal feminists of NOW, benefiting most from the refocusing of radical feminism and the attenuation of socialist-feminism, became the recognized voice of feminism. By 1975 the women's movement as a whole was facing a formidable backlash, one that was orchestrated by the Right but did not lack female adherents. The antifeminists exploited women's fears that feminism would encourage male irresponsibility and female vulnerability and would eliminate male protection of women, especially wives.

Each strand of feminism had drawbacks. Liberal feminism's emphasis on the liberating nature of work ignored the realities of the jobs held by most American women. Radical feminists' contention that gender is the primary con-

tradiction impeded their efforts to reach beyond their white, middle-class base. Socialist-feminists often spoke a language too abstract and jargon-filled to appeal to most women. As one of them, Barbara Ehrenreich, conceded, in trying to "fit all of women's experience into the terms of the market," socialist-feminists were at times "too deferential to Marxism."

Nevertheless, the women's movement probably accomplished more profound and lasting changes than the other radical movements of the sixties:

- Although the increase in the number of women elected to Congress from 1975 to 1988 has been slight — from 19 to 27 — the number of women elected to state legislatures has doubled in the same period, from 604 to 1,261.

- Women's rights to work and to equal pay are generally no longer arguable. Because sex segregation in the work force has preserved the wage differential, however, feminists have pioneered a new concept — that of comparable worth for jobs of equal skill and expertise. By 1987 more than forty states and seventeen hundred local governments had taken steps to implement the comparable-worth policy.

- The number of women in professional occupations and in professional and graduate schools has risen dramatically. For example, in the late 1980s one-quarter of all new graduates of law, medical, and business schools were women, compared to 5 percent twenty years earlier. Most colleges and universities have established women's studies programs, and feminist scholars produced some of the most significant work to come out of the academy in the seventies and eighties.

- Feminist efforts to reverse the law's traditionally punitive stance toward victims of rape and domestic violence have been fairly successful. In cases of rape, most states now prohibit evidence regarding a woman's past sexual history and no longer require corroboration in the form of a witness or proof of resistance. Moreover, many police departments have adopted new policies for investigating rape and domestic violence.

☐ Because feminists have regarded abortion rights as vital to women's self-determination, they have played a key role in abortion's decriminalization and in subsequent efforts to keep it legal.

☐ The movement's critique of the nuclear family and compulsory heterosexuality has eliminated much of the stigma attached to remaining single and has made it easier for lesbians and gay men to live "outside the closet."

☐ Most important, the movement has brought about a rethinking of gender that has resulted in far less constricting cultural definitions of maleness and femaleness.

Future prospects depend upon the movement's ability to acknowledge women's differences — both those rooted in race, class, and sexual preference and those arising from different political perspectives. Although it was black women's example that originally helped inspire white women's liberationists, few black women became involved in the early women's movement. Their noninvolvement had many sources, but crucial were white feminists' dichotomization of race and gender, their hostility to the family (traditionally a refuge from racism for blacks), and their idealization of paid work as liberating for women — all of which were at odds with the lived experience of most black women. Since the mid-seventies growing numbers of women of color have joined the feminist movement, and it is from within that they have criticized white feminists' tendency to speak of "women" as a single concept and to analyze gender in isolation rather than in relation to other systems of oppression. How the movement responds to this challenge in the future will determine whether or not it becomes truly multiracial.

Also emerging in the eighties as a divisive issue was the question of pornography. Some feminists, contending that pornography causes violence against women, campaigned for legislation that would effectively eliminate much of it.

Other feminists opposed such efforts on civil libertarian grounds and criticized as well the antipornography feminists' critique of pornography as "male"; they argued that this unintentionally fortifies the traditional distinction between "good" and "bad" women. These "sex wars" did not follow the familiar fault lines of the past; indeed, the salient categories of the late sixties and seventies (radical feminism, socialist-feminism, and liberal feminism) were far less useful for understanding feminist politics in the eighties.

On another issue, some feminists questioned whether mandating equality in circumstances of inequality might not in some cases have deleterious consequences for women: they called for an equality that acknowledges or includes difference. But as other feminists noted, arguments rooted in female difference have usually been invoked by conservatives wishing to maintain gender inequality. It remained to be seen how successfully "equality with difference" could be pursued.

Alice Echols, *Daring to Be Bad: Radical Feminism in America, 1967–1975* (1985); Sara Evans, *Personal Politics: The Roots of Women's Liberation in the Civil Rights Movement and the New Left* (1970).

ALICE ECHOLS

See also Abortion; Education; Equal Rights Amendment; Friedan, Betty; National Organization for Women; Steinem, Gloria; Women and the Work Force.

FENIAN BROTHERHOOD

The Fenian Brotherhood, founded in New York City by John O'Mahony in 1858, was a sister organization to the Irish Revolutionary Brotherhood organized in Dublin by James Stephens in the same year. Its aim was to rid Ireland of English rule by providing American money and manpower to encourage insurrection. By 1865 it had attracted 250,000 followers, many of them Civil War veterans, and an Irish Republican government on the American model had been set up at Philadelphia.

Fenianism, however, also spawned dissident

factions hoping to benefit from Anglo-American conflict by attacking Canada. On April 12, 1866, an attempt to seize the Canadian island of Campobello in the Bay of Fundy was thwarted at Eastport, Maine. The British and American navies cooperated in intercepting a shipment of arms, and U.S. troops under Maj. Gen. George Meade forced the Fenians gathered at Eastport to disperse. On June 1, Col. John O'Neill defeated a Canadian militia company before retreating to Buffalo. O'Neill's second foray into Canada, on May 25, 1870, was easily repelled. Stephens, fleeing from the threat of arrest in Ireland, arrived in New York on May 10, 1866. Denouncing the attacks on Canada, he ousted O'Mahony from the leadership of the movement and reasserted the goal of insurrection on Irish soil alone. Betrayed by police informants, this goal ended in small sporadic rural uprisings on March 5–6, 1867. Fenianism collapsed in both countries, but Irish nationalism had taken on an irrevocable American dimension.

FERRARO, GERALDINE

(1935–   ), congresswoman and Democratic candidate for vice president, 1984. Born in Newburgh, New York, Ferraro was the youngest child of Dominick Ferraro, an Italian immigrant, and Antonetta Ferraro. When she was eight, her father died, and the family moved to the Bronx, where her mother found work sewing beads. Ferraro graduated from Marymount Manhattan College in 1956. After a stint as legal secretary, she taught elementary school in Queens while attending Fordham Law School. Upon her graduation in 1960, she married businessman John A. Zaccaro.

During the 1960s, Ferraro raised three children and practiced law occasionally at her husband's real estate office. In 1974, her cousin Nicholas Ferraro, then district attorney of Queens, helped her get a job as an assistant district attorney. In this capacity, she headed a victims' bureau that dealt with child abuse, sex crimes, and crimes against the elderly. (She retained her maiden name in her professional life to honor her mother.)

When the congressman from her district re-tired in 1978, Ferraro sought the Democratic nomination for his seat and won the primary. She then defeated an opponent with Republican and Conservative party backing and won reelection in 1980 and 1982. In the House, Ferraro served on the Post Office and Civil Service, Public Works and Transportation, and Budget committees. When the Democratic party altered its delegate selection rules in 1980, she devised a plan under which elected Democrats and party officials attended conventions as "superdelegates." In January 1984, she became chair of the Democratic Platform Committee.

At the Democratic National Convention in July 1984, presidential nominee Walter Mondale selected Ferraro as his running mate. When the convention confirmed his choice she became the first woman vice-presidential nominee of a major party. Reasons for Mondale's historic decision included Democratic hopes of capitalizing on a "gender gap" in voting patterns, pressure from the National Organization for Women to select a woman candidate, and sentiment within the party that such a candidate would signify equal opportunity for all. Democrats also hoped that as a Catholic and an Italian-American, Ferraro might appeal to blue-collar, ethnic voters who had been defecting to the Republicans in recent elections.

No sooner had the campaign started than a furor arose over whether Ferraro would reveal her family finances, beyond the income tax statements required by law. This meant a public airing of her husband's business dealings before the press. Although Ferraro met the challenge with poise, the unexpected controversy did not help the Democratic cause in the campaign.

In the election, Republicans Ronald Reagan and George Bush defeated the Mondale-Ferraro ticket with 58.8 percent of the popular vote and an electoral college sweep. The Republicans also won 57 percent of women's votes. After the election, Ferraro returned to the practice of law.

Geraldine Ferraro, *My Story* (1985).

NANCY WOLOCH

See also Democratic Party; Elections: 1984; Vice Presidency.

FIELD, MARSHALL

(1834–1906), Chicago "Merchant Prince" and philanthropist. Field's life was a typical Horatio Alger story. Born on a farm in Conway, Massachusetts, Field enjoyed a meteoric career that paralleled the development of the West after the Civil War and the rise of urbanization. When he died of pneumonia in New York City, he was a multimillionaire. Although Deacon Davis, his first employer, said that the shy Marshall was not suitable for commerce, Field moved to Chicago in 1856 and entered the dry goods business. By 1882 he had bought out Leiter of Field, Palmer, and Leiter, changed the firm's name to Marshall Field and Company, weathered the panic of 1873 and the Great Chicago Fire, and cashed in on Chicago's rapid population growth as the railroad center of America.

As Field prospered, he began to manufacture his own merchandise in factories all over the world (Spain, Germany, Italy, Australia, and China). Field adopted a strict cash system, separated his wholesale from his retail business, and concentrated on "The Store — The Grand Emporium" in Chicago. He advertised heavily in newspapers and instituted a one-price policy, citywide deliveries, high-quality merchandise, and a liberal return policy. The store became a fashionable social center with modern dining rooms, a theater ticket office, a "give-the-lady-what-she-wants" policy, and artistic window displays.

Field's powers of concentration plus his eight "basic rules" (such as never borrow, never speculate, always pay cash) were the foundation stones of his success. Along with the Armours, Pullmans, and McCormicks, "Silent Marsh" provided the leadership that created a national market in the West for standardized goods.

Field paid his lower echelon of workers less than the going rate, but his remarkable ability to choose capable subordinates helped build his merchandising empire. Field, however, made his own decisions. Sadly, his family life did not match his business success. At twenty-nine he impetuously married Nannie Douglas Scott and had two children. It was not a happy marriage, and she died in France in 1896. His happiness was also marred by the death of his son in an accidental shooting. But he built a marble palace on Prairie Avenue, Chicago's "street of the stately few," and in 1904 married the beautiful Mrs. Arthur Delia Caton.

Field hated unions, and the National Guard was called "Marshall Field's boys" by Chicago's labor leaders after he supported the use of federal forces against Pullman railroad strikers in 1894. An odd mixture of Adam Smith's "laissez-faire man" and the Good Samaritan, Field subscribed heavily to the Chicago World's Fair (1893) and gave money to charities, the University of Chicago, and the Field Museum of Natural History.

John Tebbel, *The Marshall Fields: A Study in Wealth* (1947); Robert W. Twyman, *The History of Marshall Field & Company* (1954).

Nicholas Christopher Polos

See also Libraries and Museums; Philanthropy; Pullman Strike.

FIFTEENTH AMENDMENT

See Suffrage.

FILLMORE, MILLARD

(1800–1874), thirteenth president of the United States. Unlike most presidents, Fillmore knew poverty as a boy. Of old New England stock, he was born in western New York, where his father scraped out a living as a tenant farmer. In his youth he received only a limited education before being apprenticed as a clothier. His prospects brightened when he was offered the chance to read law with a local judge; after moving to Buffalo, he continued his legal training and in 1823 was admitted to the bar.

In 1828 Fillmore was elected to the New York legislature as an Anti-Mason and served three terms. He eventually joined the Whig party and served four terms in the U.S. Congress. As chairman of the Ways and Means Committee, he played a leading role in framing the tariff of 1842. Deciding to retire from Congress in 1844, he was selected as the Whigs' gubernatorial candidate but was narrowly defeated. In 1848, while serving as state comptroller, he received the Whig vice-presidential nomination and was elected in November.

Despite his support for President Zachary Taylor's policies, Fillmore had little influence in the new administration, and in 1850, after much hesitancy, he backed Henry Clay's compromise proposals rather than the president's plan for settling the sectional conflict. When he became president following Taylor's death in July, Fillmore, displaying rare decisiveness, threw his influence behind the compromise movement in Congress. By September, he had signed the various compromise measures into law, and in his annual message in December, he hailed them as a final settlement of the sectional controversy.

As part of his plan to purge the Whig party of its radicalism, Fillmore began removing opponents of the compromise from federal office. This ill-considered policy deepened party divisions and precipitated a bruising struggle for the 1852 presidential nomination. Fillmore was at best a reluctant candidate: though eager for the popular endorsement that the nomination would convey, he believed that no Whig could win in 1852. Despite Fillmore's strength in the South, the Whig convention eventually nominated Winfield Scott, who suffered a crushing defeat.

At the end of his term, Fillmore returned to Buffalo. He remained politically active and in 1855 joined the secret nativist American party, which nominated him for president in 1856. Hoping to transform the party into a national, conservative organization, Fillmore downplayed nativism in the campaign and emphasized the Union issue instead. His candidacy alienated both antislavery forces and fervent nativists, and he finished a distant third in the election.

Following his defeat, Fillmore devoted his energies to civic affairs. Alienated from the Republican party, which was controlled by his personal enemies, he opposed the Lincoln administration during the war and sympathized with Andrew Johnson in his clash with congressional Republicans during Reconstruction.

Although honest and hardworking, Fillmore manifested a habitual lack of self-confidence that significantly limited his political effectiveness. He was a pompous, colorless individual who rose far beyond his ability, and as such he left only a limited mark on his generation.

Robert J. Rayback, *Millard Fillmore: Biography of a President* (1959); Elbert B. Smith, *The Presidencies of Zachary Taylor and Millard Fillmore* (1988).

WILLIAM E. GIENAPP

See also Anti-Masons; Elections: 1848, 1856; Know-Nothing Party; Nativism; Whig Party. *For events during Fillmore's administration, see* Compromise of 1850; Fugitive Slave Law.

FILM

See Movies.

FIRE DEPARTMENTS

The history of the fire service in the United States begins in New Amsterdam (later New York), when Director-General Peter Stuyvesant appointed four fire wardens in 1648. Similar legislation followed in Boston in 1653, and this city purchased its first fire engine in 1654. Philadelphia secured an engine in 1719, and New York in 1731.

Early efforts at fire prevention and extinction relied on chimney laws, bucket brigades, simple ladders, and hand-pumped engines imported from Europe, all manned by loosely organized volunteers. Actual fire companies and departments, however, were active in Boston, New York, and Philadelphia early in the eighteenth century. Benjamin Franklin, George Washington, and Thomas Jefferson, as well as other prominent men, were among the ranks of these early volunteers.

Alarms of fire in the early period were given verbally and by rattles, gongs, and bells. The fire alarm telegraph system, with its distinctive fire boxes, developed gradually. Today there are paid dispatchers, radio pagers, the Emergency 911 telephone network, and voice-activated emergency response system street boxes.

The labor of firefighting was divided from the beginning. Hose companies supplied water to the engines and they, in turn, applied it to the fire. Hook and ladder companies were responsible for rescue, ventilation, and overhaul. It is much the same today. Similarly, the helmets, turnout coats, boots, axes, and so on used today closely resemble their predecessors.

Despite their energy, skill, enthusiasm, and dedication, volunteers in large cities were unable to control major fires. A typical example is New York: large portions of the city were destroyed in 1776, 1835, and again in 1845. Even so, the volunteers stubbornly defended their system and hand-drawn equipment against the critics.

By the mid-nineteenth century, urban volunteer fire departments in this country had reached their zenith. They were well organized and, for the most part, effective firefighting forces. But they were also excessively large, racked by dissension and rowdyism, and unwilling to adopt the new technology of the steam engine. This resistance to change, well-publicized fights, and pressure from insurance companies and influential citizens led to the end of the volunteer system in large cities. Politics, ethnic tension, greater fire risks, increasing population, and a decline in the quality of membership were also factors in the change from volunteer to professional firefighters. The transition was not an easy one, however, and the volunteers sometimes fought with their paid successors. In New York the problem was exacerbated by the traditional practice of using nonfiremen, or "runners," to augment the regular force of some three thousand men. These runners, of dubious character and intensely loyal to individual companies, were often only too ready to engage in fights with rival companies. Responding to criticism of the new steam engines by most of his contemporaries, Cincinnati's chief engineer, Miles Greenwood, reportedly said that steamers didn't get drunk or throw brickbats. He apparently felt their only drawback was that they couldn't vote.

With a successful self-propelled steam engine in service ("Uncle Joe Ross"), Cincinnati instituted the first paid department in 1853. New York followed in 1865 and Philadelphia in 1871. It should be noted, though, that many former volunteers filled the ranks of these early departments. Elisha Kingsland, long a volunteer, served as New York's first paid chief engineer.

A paid department, however, did not guarantee that major fires could be quickly and suc-cessfully controlled. Witness the devastating fires that occurred in Chicago, 1871; Boston, 1872; Baltimore, 1904; and San Francisco, 1906. Nevertheless, paid departments did offer the following advantages: a constant labor force, modern equipment, greater discipline and efficiency, selective response, and improved alarm systems.

Twentieth-century firefighters, both volunteer and paid, benefited from three technological advances: the internal combustion engine, radio communication, and self-contained breathing apparatus (SCBA). As technology advanced, however, risks also increased. The large fires of yesterday were certainly dangerous, but they were not fueled by toxic chemicals, petroleum distillates, and radioactive material, sometimes in a skyscraper setting. As a result, two distinctively modern firefighting units have evolved in large cities: hazardous materials and high-rise. Some departments also have rescue units, fire boats, and ambulance service.

Fire protection in the United States today is provided by volunteer and paid firefighters, male and female, acting both separately and in concert. Volunteer departments greatly outnumber paid ones at present, but the fire service continues to change. In many suburban and rural areas, volunteer departments are in peril. Recruiting and retaining members is becoming increasingly difficult because of the high cost of housing, strict training requirements, population mobility, and distant employment. The coming decades will bring more paid departments, greater reliance upon female firefighters during the day, and increased interdepartmental cooperation via the mutual aid system.

Another factor that affects today's firefighter is the keen competition for the taxpayer's dollar; regrettably, this often revives the old rivalry between volunteers and professionals. Municipal governments and their constituents are faced with the huge costs of apparatus and equipment, insurance, and building maintenance. Volunteer departments have traditionally provided low-cost fire protection, but it remains to be seen if they can continue to do so.

Twentieth-century firefighters, like their early counterparts, endure extremes of heat and cold, enjoy parades, and curse false alarms. Having adopted the cross worn by the medieval

Knights of Malta as their emblem, they also continue to save lives and property on a daily basis.

Donald J. Cannon, general ed., *Heritage of Flames* (1977); Paul C. Ditzel, *Fire Engines, Firefighters* (1976); Dennis Smith, *Dennis Smith's History of Firefighting in America* (1978).

THOMAS J. DUNNINGS, JR.

FIRST AMENDMENT

See Bill of Rights; Freedom of Speech; Freedom of the Press.

FITZGERALD, ELLA

(1918–), singer. Born in Newport News, Virginia, and raised in Yonkers, New York, Fitzgerald was discovered in 1934 when she won an amateur night contest at the Apollo Theater in Harlem. She made her professional debut in 1935 with Tiny Bradshaw's band at the Harlem Opera House and later that year became the vocalist with drummer Chick Webb's orchestra.

Fitzgerald's appearances with Webb brought the singer widespread exposure through remote radio broadcasts and such recordings as *A-tisket, A-tasket* (1938) and *Undecided* (1939). She also made records with Benny Goodman, Teddy Wilson, and groups under her own nominal leadership. When Webb died in 1939, Fitzgerald continued to front the band until 1942 when she launched a solo career.

In the late forties Fitzgerald became associated with Norman Granz's Jazz at the Philharmonic concerts, touring widely in this context both in the States and abroad and building an international reputation as one of the preeminent vocalists in jazz. A series of Great American Songbook recording projects in the late fifties and early sixties established her also as a superior interpreter of standards; these records, made for Granz's Verve label and often featuring arrangements by Nelson Riddle, revealed Fitzgerald's artistry of phrasing and delivery, with improvisatory excursions often taking a backseat to straightforward lyrical statements. They also exhibited a broader emotional range and deepening tone quality, as on albums devoted to George and Ira Gershwin (1959) and Jerome Kern (1964). Other records — like the Harold Arlen songbook (1960–1961) featuring arrangements by Billy May — displayed Fitzgerald's buoyant rhythmic sense and unfailing swing that characterized her first recordings with Webb in the 1930s.

After the 1950s Fitzgerald maintained a steady schedule of touring, often appearing with an accompanying trio but also taking part in festivals where she might perform with ensembles of varying sizes. Recordings from live performances show her unparalleled mastery of scat singing, as she constructs long, inventive improvisations that steadily mount in intensity and that often take considerable musical risks (especially large leaps and rapid-fire runs). A good example can be heard in her extended scat solo on *St. Louis Blues* from a concert in Rome recorded April 25, 1958 (first issued in 1988).

Fitzgerald's main achievements as a singer lay in her consistently high performing standards sustained over a fifty-year period, her authority as an interpreter of American popular song, and her outstanding abilities as a jazz improviser.

Sid Colin, *Ella: The Life and Times of Ella Fitzgerald* (1986); Henry Pleasants, *The Great American Popular Singers* (1974).

MARK TUCKER

See also Jazz; Music.

FITZGERALD, F. SCOTT

(1896–1940), novelist, chronicler of the jazz age. Born in St. Paul, Minnesota, Fitzgerald had the good fortune — and the misfortune — to be a writer who summed up an era. The son of an alcoholic failure from Maryland and an adoring, intensely ambitious mother, he grew up acutely conscious of wealth and privilege — and of his family's exclusion from the social elite. After entering Princeton in 1913, he became a close friend of Edmund Wilson and John Peale Bishop and spent most of his time writing lyrics for Triangle Club theatrical productions and analyzing how to triumph over the school's intricate social rituals.

He left Princeton without graduating and used it as the setting for his first novel, *This Side of Paradise* (1920). It was perfect literary timing. The twenties were beginning to roar, bathtub gin and flaming youth were on everyone's lips, and the handsome, witty Fitzgerald seemed to be the ideal spokesman for the decade. With his stunning southern wife, Zelda, he headed for Paris and a mythic career of drinking from hip flasks, dancing until dawn, and jumping into outdoor fountains to end the party. Behind this façade was a writer struggling to make enough money to match his extravagant lifestyle and still produce serious work. His second novel, *The Beautiful and the Damned* (1922), which recounted an artist's losing fight with dissipation, was badly flawed. His next, *The Great Gatsby* (1925), the story of a gangster's pursuit of an unattainable rich girl, was close to a masterpiece.

The Fitzgeralds' frenetic ascent to literary fame was soon tinged with tragedy. Scott became an alcoholic and Zelda, jealous of his fame (or in some versions, thwarted by it), collapsed into madness. They crept home in 1931 to an America in the grip of the Great Depression — a land no longer interested in flaming youth except to pillory them for their excesses. The novel with which he had grappled for years, *Tender Is the Night,* about a psychiatrist destroyed by his wealthy wife, was published in 1934 to lukewarm reviews and poor sales. Fitzgerald retreated to Hollywood, a defeated and more or less forgotten man. He made a precarious living as a scriptwriter and struggled to control his alcoholism. Miraculously he found the energy to begin another novel, *The Last Tycoon* (1941), about a complex gifted movie producer. He had finished about a third of it when he died of a heart attack. Obituaries generally dismissed him.

Not until the early fifties did interest in Fitzgerald revive, and when it did, it became a veritable scholarly industry. A closer look at his life and career reveals a writer with an acute sense of history, an intellectual pessimist who had grave doubts about Americans' ability to survive their infatuation with the bitch goddess success. At the same time he conveyed in his best novels and short stories the sense of youthful awe and hope America's promises created in many people. Few historians have matched the closing lines of *The Great Gatsby,* when the narrator reflects on how the land must have struck Dutch sailors' eyes three hundred years earlier: "For a transitory enchanted moment man must have held his breath in the presence of this continent, compelled into an aesthetic contemplation he neither understood nor desired, face to face for the last time in history with something commensurate to his capacity to wonder."

Matthew J. Bruccoli, *Some Sort of Epic Grandeur* (1981); Arthur Mizener, *The Far Side of Paradise* (1951; rev. ed., 1965).

THOMAS FLEMING

See also Expatriates and Exiles; Literature.

FLETCHER V. PECK

Fletcher v. *Peck* (1810) was the first Supreme Court review of the contract clause in Article 1, Section 10, of the Constitution forbidding states from impairing contracts. The Court ruled that a state grant was a kind of contract and could not be unilaterally withdrawn. In 1795, after speculators had spread bribes liberally around the Georgia statehouse, the legislature granted them lands on the frontier. This "Yazoo grant" outraged Georgia voters, who turned most of the incumbents out of office in the next election. The next legislature promptly repealed the Yazoo grant. Speculators who had bought Yazoo land tested the validity of the repeal in *Fletcher* v. *Peck.*

Chief Justice John Marshall wrote that the state's grant was an executory contract, and a succeeding legislature could not cancel it without violating the Constitution's contract clause. The Court could not consider the first legislature's corrupt motivations without establishing a precedent for the judicial branch having the power to determine the appropriateness of legislation, another violation of the Constitution. As a Federalist, Marshall had no doubt that the Constitution was adopted to protect property from the actions of potentially volatile legislatures; the contract clause was a bulwark of that protection. He wrote that the Framers and ratifiers had wanted to shield people and "property from the effects of those sudden and strong passions. . . . The restrictions on the legislative power of the States are obviously founded in this sentiment."

See also Constitution.

FLYNN, ELIZABETH GURLEY

(1890–1964), agitator and organizer for the Industrial Workers of the World and Communist party activist. In an era when street life and mass strikes were important in people's lives, Flynn's notoriety was like that given to media stars today. In major strikes in Lawrence, Massachusetts, and Paterson and Passaic, New Jersey, "the Rebel Girl," as she was called, agitated among and led immigrant workers. A great orator, Flynn saw labor court trials as important aspects of organizing, and so participated in fights for free speech in Missoula, Montana (1908), and Spokane, Washington (1909–1910). She brought to the attention of the general public the case of Sacco and Vanzetti, which was already at issue in the Italian community. The case involved her for seven years (1919–1926). She organized the Workers' Defense League to fight for the victims of the post–World War I red scare and was one of the founders of the American Civil Liberties Union (ACLU). (The ACLU ousted her in 1940 because she was a member of the Communist party, but reinstated her posthumously in 1976.)

Flynn's life was both illustrious and stormy. Born to radical Irish immigrants, she grew up in the poverty of the South Bronx. After a brief marriage she left her husband and lived most of her life with her mother and sister, who raised her son.

Reacting to fatiguing labor battles, left-wing faction fights, and an unhappy love affair with the anarchist organizer Carlo Tresca, Flynn retreated from the labor struggle during the years 1928–1937. But in 1937, she joined the Communist party and rose quickly in the organization, joining the national board in 1938. Actually she was only a figurehead and rarely dissented from the party line. Having come in at the top, instead of rising through the ranks, Flynn always felt uncomfortable in the party. Nevertheless, she was one of its most popular speakers and publicists; two to four times a week for twenty-six years she wrote a column for the *Daily Worker*. But her constituency consisted of rough-and-tumble miners and immigrant workers, and she preferred militant organizing to bureaucratic and reform work.

Flynn was indicted and convicted with other party leaders under the Smith Act, which made it illegal to advocate the overthrow of the government by force. With flair and eloquence she defended herself in a nine-month trial. While awaiting jail in 1955 she wrote *Rebel Girl,* an account of her early life. She was sentenced to three years in the Alderson Federal Penitentiary and served from January 1955 through May 1957. After her release she published a memoir, *Alderson Story.*

In 1961, Flynn became the first female national chair of the Communist party. She ran for the New York State Assembly, headed the Women's Commission, and traveled abroad. She died in the Soviet Union where she had gone to write and rest and was given an elaborate state funeral.

Rosalyn Baxandall, *Words on Fire: The Life and Writings of Elizabeth Gurley Flynn* (1987); Elizabeth Gurley Flynn, *The Rebel Girl, an Autobiography: My First Life (1906–1926)* (1955).

ROSALYN FRAAD BAXANDALL

See also American Civil Liberties Union; Anticommunism; Communist Party; Industrial Workers of the World; Labor.

FOLK ART

It is necessary to suspend the criteria with which academic art is usually considered to understand the work of American folk artists. The subtleties of elaborate composition, mastery of technique, and sophisticated organization are only occasionally the concerns of the folk artist, although they are often unconsciously achieved.

In her introduction to the exhibition catalog *The Flowering of American Folk Art* (1974), Alice Winchester writes: "One may look for, and find, originality of concept, creativity of design, craftsmanly use of the medium, and flashes of inspiration, even genius. Folk art makes its appeal directly and intimately, even to people quite uninitiated into the mysteries of art."

Certainly the early settlers in the New World colonies had little concern for the qualities of fine art. A portrait for them was a pictorial document that indicated a significant position of power and wealth within the community. At the same time, it recorded the sitter for future generations. This notion of art, as social icon and economic indicator, was repeated in the Hudson River Valley where, in the early eighteenth century, the rich merchants and planters dominated every aspect of colonial life between New York City in the south to Albany in the north.

The first real appreciation of American folk art began during the 1920s when artists, returning from World War I, began to search for what was American about American art. Since that time, collectors and scholars have attempted to identify and classify the naive art that at different times has been called by such diverse terms as *amateur, artisan, pioneer, popular, primitive,* and *provincial*. The confusion about this vast body of work, which for the most part was executed by self-trained artists in a state of relative artistic innocence, is not surprising, for the art falls into several broad categories based upon medium and type.

Oil and tempera paintings on canvas and board, watercolors on paper and cardboard, drawings, sketches, and pastels are the mediums most often encountered. Portraits, silhouettes, landscapes, pinprick pictures, calligraphic drawings, wall murals, furniture decoration, coach decoration, shop signs' fireboards, overmantel paintings, and theorems on paper, velvet, and silk are but a few of the types of art that are included in the catchall term *American folk painting*. Folk sculpture, also multifaceted, includes such diverse objects as carved gravestones, both painted and carved signs, weathervanes and whirligigs, ships' figureheads and nautical orna-

ments, scrimshaw, waterfowl and fish decoys, religious carvings, pottery, carousel and circus carvings, and chalkware ornaments. All may reasonably be considered folk art.

Regardless of the medium, several characteristics consistently appear in folk art. In the best examples there is a combination of naturalness and simplicity, resulting in a directness that has come to be much admired by contemporary art historians, critics, and collectors.

Some scholars have spent much of their lives studying American folk art, and nearly all have arrived at their own definitions. Perhaps the most pertinent was developed by Mary Childs Black, first director of the Museum of Early American Folk Arts in New York: "The genesis, rise, and disappearance of folk art is closely connected with the events of the nineteenth century when the disappearance of the old ways left rural folk everywhere with an unused surplus of time and energy. People were free to invent and make simple things for their own pleasure in each household and in each village, until the rise of industrial production toward the end of the nineteenth century. Folk art occupies the brief interval between court taste and commercial taste." Definitions used by other scholars support Black's theories in general, and it is possible to derive from them a consensus of the qualities usually associated with great folk art. Such words as *freshness, directness, simplicity,* and *imaginative* frequently occur in writings on the subject.

For many years it was generally thought that the folk artist was essentially anonymous, itinerant, and untrained, but research has altered these views. A number of artists have been identified, such as the Massachusetts painter Rufus Hathaway, the Hudson Valley artist Gerardus Duyckinck, the youthful Benjamin West who flourished in Pennsylvania prior to an illustrious career in England, and Sheldon Peck who worked first in Vermont and later moved with the frontier to western New York.

During the 1790s Rufus Hathaway traveled on horseback as an itinerant painter. After marrying, he entered the medical profession and practiced for some twenty-seven years in Duxbury. Gerardus Duyckinck was a member of a family of painters who established themselves in the early eighteenth century in New York City. He and several relatives executed portraits and were well known for painted and decorated furniture. Like many young, self-taught artists, Benjamin West looked at English and European prints for the design sources for many of his landscapes. At thirteen years of age Edward Hicks entered apprenticeship with a coach maker. Soon after the turn of the nineteenth century he became a partner in a Milford, Pennsylvania, coach-making and painting business and in time painted street signs and shop and tavern signs. A jack-of-all-trades, he also executed decorative paintings on furniture, fireboards, and clock faces. Later his success was such that he required assistance, and when writing his memoirs, he noted, "I am now employing four hands, besides myself, in coach, sign and ornamental painting, and still more in repairing and finishing carriages, and I think I should find no difficulty in doubling my business." Not all of the folk artists, then, were itinerant, and more important, a good many had the advantage of at least basic artistic training.

In 1839 the *Knickerbocker* enthusiastically heralded a new age: "We have seen the views taken in Paris by the 'Daguerreotype' and have no hesitation in avowing that they are the most remarkable objects of curiosity and admiration, in the arts, that we have ever beheld. Their exquisite perfection almost transcends the bounds of sober belief. . . . There is not an object even the most minute, embraced in that wide scope, which was not original; and it is impossible that one should have been omitted. Think of that!"

Think of that indeed! Few American artists, even those who earned their living by painting portraits, realized that this new process would ultimately drive many of them from their profession. As the use of the camera spread, folk artists found it increasingly difficult to defend their less-than-realistic creations. Some simply abandoned the profession. Others, such as E. S. Field, acquired training in the new invention and used the camera to photograph their subjects. They then painted over the image. This saved the sitter the tedium of posing for several sessions.

In recent decades the folk arts have come to a new prominence. The Museum of American Folk Art in New York City has been at the forefront of folk-art scholarship, presenting national and international exhibitions, engaging in an ambitious publishing program, including a quarterly magazine, the *Clarion,* and conducting far-reaching educational programs.

The field in some ways has been redefined in recent years as well. The pioneer collectors steadfastly refused to acknowledge that naive artists working in our own time are capable of creating works of art of enduring quality. Now, however, interest in contemporary folk art is widespread, and as the efforts of the modern-day folk artists gain credibility with collectors, museums, and the academic world, new definitions for the field will have to be devised.

There are two types of contemporary folk expression that are of great interest to the modern-day collector. The first, and probably the most universal, is called "memory" painting. Generally older, self-taught artists record scenes from their early life and in the process document a way of life that was rural, less complex, and free from the changes wrought by improved communications and transportation in America during the twentieth century. Their idyllic renderings have immense popular appeal. Probably the best known of these twentieth-century artists are Grandma Moses, Mattie Lou O'Kelley, and Kathy Jakobsen.

A separate contemporary category of folk art is the raw, expressive, seemingly childlike efforts of artists like Howard Finster, Will Hawkins, and Thornton Dial, who are related to contemporary art at least as much as they are to folk art. They represent an individual vision that reflects the artist's concern with oneself, one's place in society, and one's highly personal point of view. These somewhat eccentric, self-taught painters and sculptors are referred to as "outsider" artists or "isolate" artists. Though their work is created outside of the traditions generally associated with folk artists, many of their pieces will endure and add significantly to the patchwork of naive creativity in America in the twentieth century.

Robert Bishop, *American Folk Sculpture* (1974); Robert Bishop and Patricia Coblentz, *Folk Painters of America*

(1979); Jean Lipman and Alice Winchester, *The Flowering of American Folk Art: 1776–1876* (1974).

ROBERT BISHOP

See also Painting and Sculpture.

FOOTBALL

American football descends from a rowdy medieval game in which, typically, the men, women, and children of one village attempted to kick, throw, or carry a ball across fields and streams to the fiercely defended portals of another village's parish church. By the nineteenth century, British schoolboys and university students had tamed the mayhem into something approximating modern soccer and rugby. Americans had occasionally played some forms of the premodern game, but the first intercollegiate contests occurred November 6, 1869, when Rutgers defeated Princeton in soccer by a score of 6–4, and May 15, 1874, when Harvard and McGill played to a scoreless tie in rugby.

As the game evolved, rugby's scrum became American football's scrimmage (1880) and the unique system of downs and measured yardage was introduced (1882). Other distinctive elements, like the forward pass, date from the early twentieth century. Many innovations were suggested by Yale's Walter Camp, an enormously successful coach whose teams, led by famed Lee McClung and Walter "Pudge" Heffelfinger, had nine undefeated seasons between 1883 and 1898. Camp wrote the rule books, named the "All-America" teams, and spoke tirelessly of the game's contributions to "character."

By the end of the nineteenth century, football had become the most popular and also the most controversial intercollegiate sport. The rituals associated with "the big game" were in place. Faculties struggled to control the game (and to save students from a "win at all costs" attitude that threatened the code of fair play). The intensity of competition had led to widespread and occasionally fatal violence on the field. When abolition of the game seemed a likely response to public dismay, President Henry MacCracken of New York University convened an emergency conference that led in 1906 to the formation of the National Collegiate Athletic Association (NCAA).

Rules set down by the NCAA reduced the level of violence but failed to solve such problems as unethical recruitment. The Carnegie Foundation documented widespread abuses in 1919, but the NCAA's inability to temper a "win at all costs" attitude bothered few. In the 1920s players like Harold "Red" Grange of Illinois and coaches like Notre Dame's Knute Rockne were heroes to millions who never went to college.

Professional football, born in the 1890s, came to maturity under the leadership of George Halas, principal founder of the National Football League (NFL; 1920). A hint of the NFL's industrial origins remains in the name Green Bay Packers. The college game was racially integrated in the nineties (in the North), but the NFL remained segregated until 1946, when Kenny Washington and Woody Strode played for the Los Angeles Rams. Blacks became almost four times as numerous in the NFL as in the census returns, but residual racism continued to "stack" gifted black players — like O. J. Simpson — as ends and rushers while whites — like Johnny Unitas and Joe Montana — starred as quarterbacks (and garnered lucrative endorsement contracts). Black players led the way to the exuberant exhibitions of gleeful triumph that have replaced the reserved modesty once thought appropriate for gridiron heroes. Played on artificial turf in a domed stadium with a razzle-dazzle electronic scoreboard, accompanied by the antics of sexually enticing cheerleaders, touted by booster-commentators who assure the world that the players have come to play, football has become the nation's favorite spectacle.

In the postwar period, the spectacle has been experienced more often on television than in situ. Under Roone Arledge, ABC Sports led the way with programs like "Monday Night Football." In negotiating with the networks, NFL commissioner Alvin "Pete" Rozelle proved a hard bargainer. After he persuaded Congress to waive the antitrust laws and allow a merger of the NFL and the rival American Football League (1966), football attracted viewers by the millions — enough to win the professionals a $50 million television contract (which has since become a multiyear billion-dollar agreement).

To recoup their outlay, the networks charge advertisers upward of $500,000 a minute. Franchises have multiplied, spread geographically, and soared in value. The players' salaries, comparable in the 1920s to those of ordinary workers, rose dramatically to rival those of rock stars.

Television's largess changed the nature of the college game as well. Unsatisfied with the NCAA's distribution of television income and with the NCAA's limitations on the number of nationally televised games, the University of Georgia sued for the right to negotiate its own contracts and was upheld in a 1984 decision by the Supreme Court. That year dissident schools within the NCAA formed the College Football Association in order to deal directly with the networks. Increasingly, the most successful schools, like Notre Dame, have demanded the right to sign separate contracts. As the rewards for success (i.e., winning) have grown greater and the penalties for failure (i.e., losing) have become more severe, athletic directors and football coaches have been tempted to recruit academically unqualified athletes and to break NCAA and university rules in order to keep them eligible. The stakes have become so high that some players have turned to anabolic steroids to enhance their already awesome performance and to increase their chances for an NFL career.

In many regions, especially in the South, high school football has become as fiercely competitive as the college and the professional games. The "rites of fall" are a demonstration of adolescent masculinity and an instrument of communal solidarity. High school coaches have begun to feel the pressures long felt by college and professional coaches; they too have begun to recruit and to "red shirt" (i.e., to encourage athletes to spend an extra year in school in order to gain size and strength).

But despite the continual controversy over big-time sports, fans scramble for season tickets, and Super Bowl Weekend has, since its inauguration in 1967, become a centerpiece of American popular culture. Numbered in Roman numerals, the Super Bowl is reminiscent of antiquity's grandiose amusements. And football has never been played so well. For most fans,

this, and not the abuses of the game, is what counts.

Allison Danzig, ed., *Oh, How They Played the Game* (1971).

ALLEN GUTTMANN

See also Spectator Sports.

FORD, GERALD

(1913–   ), thirty-eighth president of the United States. Ford served in the House of Representatives from the Fifth District of Michigan beginning in 1949 and was elected minority leader in 1965. Under the provisions of the Twenty-fifth Amendment, President Richard M. Nixon chose him in 1973 to be vice president following the resignation of Vice President Spiro T. Agnew. Upon the resignation of Nixon himself in the face of likely impeachment, Ford became president on August 9, 1974. He named as his vice president Nelson A. Rockefeller, former governor of New York, thus completing the only unelected presidential team in American history.

Ford had no clear-cut political agenda, pledging only to end the "long national nightmare" provoked by the Watergate affair. A month after becoming president, he startled the nation by granting Nixon an unconditional pardon for any offenses he may have committed against the United States. A storm of protest arose, amid cries that a deal had been struck. No one has made the allegation stick, although Ford and Nixon were in constant negotiations before and after Ford took the presidential oath. Ford, keenly sensitive to the lingering suspicions, has insisted that his sole aim was to help heal the wounds of the nation. With poor timing, he announced only a few days after the pardon his amnesty proposal for Vietnam draft resisters and evaders. Unlike Nixon, they would have to meet conditions.

Ford presided over the evacuation of U.S. personnel from Vietnam, which he ordered in April 1975. Because he was linked to this withdrawal, he was destined to have no notable strength in foreign affairs. Although he claimed credit for the Helsinki Accord in which the Soviet Union renounced its right to keep its satellite states in line by military intervention, the true effect was to recognize at last Soviet domination of the eastern bloc nations. Possibly, however, the Helsinki Accord helped restrain the Soviet Union from intervening when citizens in communist countries overthrew their governments in 1989.

In domestic affairs Ford's initiatives were few. A volunteer anti-inflation program, called by its acronym WIN (Whip Inflation Now), was widely derided as inadequate. When New York City fell into dire financial straits, Ford was unmoved. A now-famous headline in the *New York Daily News* — FORD TO CITY: DROP DEAD — helped underscore his apparent insensitivity to the national significance of the city's plight. In the presidential campaign of 1976, he aroused sympathy but not much support. In the election, his loss to Jimmy Carter was widely interpreted as completing the fall of the Nixon administration, for he had retained as his own staff most of Nixon's appointees.

Possessed of an open personality, Ford was perceived as a straight-shooter. He was "Mr. Nice Guy," unpretentious but unimaginative. A splendid athlete (he had been an outstanding college football player), he sometimes seemed more comfortable talking about sports than about the intricacies of public policy. He could never live down Lyndon B. Johnson's cruel quips, which stuck like Velcro (e.g., "The trouble with Jerry Ford is that he used to play football without a helmet").

Ford's wife, Betty, broke fresh ground for a First Lady by her forthrightness on controversial and personal matters. She championed abortion rights and the Equal Rights Amendment; expressed uncommon understanding for some of the new norms of young people's behavior, including premarital sex and the use of marijuana; and went public about her mastectomy, her drinking problem, and her entry into psychiatric treatment.

Ford was deeply pained that he could not vindicate his presidency at the polls. He must remain satisfied to be remembered as a congressional president whose historic role it was to mop up the dregs of the two most damaging episodes in the history of the modern White House, the Watergate affair and the Vietnam War.

Betty Ford, with Chris Chase, *The Times of My Life* (1978); Gerald R. Ford, *A Time to Heal* (1979); Edward L. and Frederick H. Schapsmeier, *Gerald R. Ford's Date with Destiny: A Political Biography* (1989).

HENRY F. GRAFF

See also Elections: 1976; Strategic Arms Limitation Talks; Watergate Scandal.

FORD, HENRY

(1863–1947), industrialist. Ford did not invent the automobile, but he developed design concepts and production techniques that allowed its manufacture in such volume and at such cost as to bring it within reach of the average wage earner. It can be said that he, more than any other individual perhaps, invented the twentieth century.

Ford was born on a farm near Dearborn, Michigan. From his earliest days he displayed a marked mechanical aptitude, and all his life he delighted in working with machinery. In 1879 he became an apprentice in a machine shop in Detroit, repairing watches at night to make ends meet.

In the early 1890s he began experimenting with the new internal combustion engine and in 1896 produced his first car, built in the garage of his home. In 1903 he established the Ford Motor Company with twenty-eight thousand dollars in capital provided by others. Profitable from the first, it became much more so when he introduced the Model T in 1908.

As Ford developed his production ideas, fully introducing the assembly-line principle in 1913, the price of the Model T dropped steadily. In 1908 the company made 10,607 cars and sold them for $850 apiece; in 1916 it manufactured 730,041 priced at only $360. Originally Ford held a quarter of the firm's stock, but by 1920 he had become the sole owner of one of the largest industrial enterprises on earth. In 1927, when the last of more than 15 million Model T's was produced, the company boasted undistributed earnings of nearly $700 million along with billions more in plant and equipment.

In 1914, when industrial workers were averaging about eleven dollars a week, Ford announced that his employees would be paid five dollars for an eight-hour day. His purpose was not only to motivate his workers to endure the drudgery of the assembly line but to bring his automobiles within their economic reach. The policy made Ford famous around the world, and it seemed for a time that he might have a political career.

Once an industrial revolutionary, in his later years Ford became set in his ways. He refused to make changes in his production system, his automobiles, or his labor policies, even when the need and the market signals were clear. Finally, a plummeting market share left him no choice but to shut down production of the Model T and retool to produce the Model A. Other automobile companies, especially General Motors, took advantage of the hiatus, and the Ford Motor Company never regained its once overwhelming dominance.

Ford, a mechanical genius, was otherwise ignorant, narrow, and naive. He published many scurrilous anti-Semitic articles and fought unionization with every weapon at his disposal, including a private police force. Nor would he allow modern management techniques to interfere with his autocratic ways. By the mid-1930s the company was riven by factions, and no one was really in charge at all. A decade later the Ford Motor Company, once the most prodigious engine of wealth creation in the American economy, was on the brink of ruin, losing a million dollars a day.

Two years before his death, his family finally forced him to cede control to his grandson, Henry Ford II.

Peter Collier and David Horowitz, *The Fords: An American Epic* (1987); Allan Nevins and Frank Ernest Hill, *Ford,* 3 vols. (1954–1963).

JOHN STEELE GORDON

See also Automobiles; Model T Ford.

FOREIGN INVESTMENT

See International Investment.

FOREIGN RELATIONS

See Africa-U.S. Relations; Asia-U.S. Relations; Canada-U.S. Relations; Caribbean-U.S. Relations; Cold War; Foreign Views of America; France-U.S. Relations; Germany-U.S. Relations; Great Britain–U.S. Relations; Latin America–U.S. Relations; Mexico-U.S. Relations; Middle East–U.S. Relations; Soviet-American Relations, 1917–1945.

FOREIGN VIEWS OF AMERICA

Before the 1776 Revolution the British colonies in North America were of limited interest to the rest of the world. Britain regarded its possessions as mere adjuncts of its polity; other European empires saw them only as potential threats; to the migrants who were steadily making their way across the Atlantic, whether from the British Isles, the Rhineland, or elsewhere, the colonies were at most a place of religious refuge or economic opportunity (for Africans, not even that); they hardly amounted to an idea. With the coming of the Revolution all was changed. The old attitudes remained, but new political and ideological considerations transformed the context in which they were expressed.

For Europeans, the shift in the balance of power that the Revolution accomplished and that had been the object of the French government's intervention in the War of Independence was the least of the consequences of the great uprising. A new power had suddenly emerged, but it was the new principles of government according to which the United States was organized that really mattered. The dreams, the philosophy, and the political program that the leaders of the Age of Enlightenment had been developing for two generations were suddenly being realized by a new race of men (as they were famously hailed by Michel de Crèvecoeur). A wave of enthusiasm rushed across Europe: even England felt it. *America,* from being a term in geography describing the whole New World, acquired an ideological meaning, and from then on was taken (except by the inhabitants of the Spanish and Portuguese empires) to refer primarily to the extraordinary Republic where reason and liberty were apparently sovereign, bringing in their train all the blessings of peace, prosperity, and civilization.

The French philosophes hailed the new commonwealth enthusiastically. They pored over the state constitutions, the Declaration of Independence, the Articles of Confederation, and, when the 1787 Constitution was promulgated, that too. They were much encouraged in their efforts by such visitors as John Adams and Thomas Jefferson, by the prestige of George Washington, and, above all, by the words and deeds of Benjamin Franklin. The birth of the United States seemed a proof that reform, even of the boldest kind, could be achieved at not too great a cost; and bold reform, they were more and more convinced, was what their own country needed most.

It could not last. The French Revolution destroyed, with so much else, this naive cult of America. For one thing, it drove tens of thousands of French men and women into exile: liberals and conservatives, revolutionaries and royalists, businessmen, intellectuals, and princes of the blood. Those who made their way to Philadelphia and New York discovered that there were many things they did not like about the United States, and many things in France, however badly the nation had treated them, that they missed acutely. From being vaguely idealistic about the brotherhood of man and the unimportance of political boundaries, they became conscious nationalists. Then, for many of them, the revolutionary promise had proved a grievous deception: progress turned out to be a much chancier business than the American example had led them to believe. And they now thought that the destiny of the world was not, after all, going to be worked out in North America. Whatever their other views, it gave them a pang of pride to believe that it was France and the French who were showing the way forward to humanity: 1776 now seemed a mere anticipation of the much more fundamental challenge of 1789. Most of them went home as soon as they could (though not Mr. Jefferson's friend, du Pont de Nemours) and remembered America only as an odd, amusing episode in their adventurous lives.

Yet the idea of America never entirely died.

The tradition of interest in the United States has been continuous in France from the eighteenth century to the present, which in part explains the immediate success of Alexis de Tocqueville's *Democracy in America,* published in 1835. Thanks to the tradition, his readers found his ideas and information reassuringly familiar: they quickly picked up the tune. And although, in the rest of Europe, the experience of the French Revolution and the Napoleonic Wars had closed most minds to liberal ideas, associated as they were with French aggression, in one country at least belief in the possibility of peaceful progress still gained ground, in spite of setbacks, as if the French Revolution had never happened. In Britain the need to adjust government and society to a new age, in which knowledge, wealth, and power were becoming more widely diffused, was increasingly acknowledged; the present was anxiously scanned for clues to the future. The French route to modernity was contemptuously rejected on grounds both of nationalism and common sense, but the American way (so much closer to British traditions) demanded examination. Not surprisingly, then, Tocqueville's success in Britain was as great as it was in France and the United States.

But even before Tocqueville's book appeared, a recognizable literary form had established itself — British travelers' tales about America. Volumes of diaries, letters, and reminiscences poured onto an eager market, a market by no means exclusively made up of persons thinking of emigrating. All such writers acknowledged the energy and prosperity of the United States, but two schools of interpretation were quickly established. The earlier consisted of those writers (such as Capt. Frederick Marryat, Mrs. Frances Trollope, Charles Dickens) who emphasized the vulgarity, conceit, and money-grubbing philistinism of the Yankees and rejected the American model. Somewhat later came those (Leslie Stephen, Anthony Trollope, Goldwin Smith) who found much in America to praise. Anti-Americanism has never quite died out in Britain, but the pro-American tradition early proved the stronger and reached its nineteenth-century climax with the publication of James Bryce's *American Commonwealth* in 1888. Bryce differed from Tocqueville in many respects, but to a striking extent his message to the English was the same as Tocqueville's message to the French: that American democracy was a valid and successful political experiment, the details of which could not, perhaps, be precisely duplicated in European conditions, but that nevertheless was an inspiring and instructive example for all liberals. This theme was to be effectively restated in the twentieth century by such writers as Denis Brogan (*The American Political System,* 1933), Raymond Aron, and Jean-François Revel (*Without Marx or Jesus,* 1972). Jean-Jacques Servan-Schreiber (*The American Challenge,* 1976) followed rather in the tradition of Michel Chevalier (*Society, Manners, and Politics in the United States,* 1836) by emphasizing the economic rather than the political lessons of the American way.

But if in the late twentieth century the heirs of the philosophes could still draw encouragement from the United States, a very different tradition has long possessed the heirs of the Jacobins. It reached maturity in 1848, the year of the revolutions, with the publication of the *Communist Manifesto.* Socialism's belief in the reality and prime importance of class war, and the necessity of revolutionary overthrow of all existing institutions, inexorably made it anti-American. Karl Marx himself, however, perhaps partly in recognition of America's great popularity with the industrial working class in England, was distinctly pro-American, particularly during the Civil War, when he apparently supported the North. But one of the essential Marxist beliefs was that liberal democracy was merely a mask for the tyranny of capital, and as the Industrial Revolution raced ahead in the United States it became impossible for socialists to see America as an exception to the general laws of historical development. The brutality of the American capitalists did nothing to contradict this opinion. Such events as the Haymarket massacre, the Homestead lockout, and the Colorado miners' strike in 1913–1914, which was defeated by the use of federal troops, emphatically confirmed it, and so did the red scare of 1919, when socialists were driven from public life by the grossest legal chicanery.

Meanwhile two events of prime historical importance had once more changed the way the world looked at the United States. Both occurred in 1917. One was the Bolshevik Revolution, which gave the Left a new utopia to study, dream about, and quarrel over; the other was America's entry into the First World War.

Before the war only the Central American republics, and occasionally Britain, had had to reckon with American nationalism. But the war, itself the product of competing European nationalisms, so challenged the interests of the United States (now grown to a great power) that it had to act in their protection, the only questions being, How were those interests to be defined? How were they to be defended? For the rest of the century America, willy-nilly, was to be the leading actor on the world stage, and from the start this brought it into collision with other nationalisms. The two world wars, which devastated its competitors, greatly strengthened America's economy. And through the instrumentality of dime novels, popular music, and, above all, Hollywood, a picturesque and melodramatic myth of America began to dominate European popular culture.

Between the world wars, then, the foreign perception of the United States was exceedingly complex. According to Lenin the United States embodied "state monopoly capitalism," but even he was impressed by the Taylor system of industrial management. Bertolt Brecht was not immune to the charm of America even as he satirized it (especially in *The Rise and Fall of the City of Mahagonny*). The more or less simultaneous rise to power of Adolf Hitler and Franklin D. Roosevelt dramatized the contrast between dictatorship and democracy in a way that revived some of the glamour of liberalism after a long period of shabby retreat and betrayal. Next, the entry of the Soviet Union and the United States into the war against Hitler created the momentary illusion that there was no longer a fundamental distinction between the liberal and socialist traditions. To the innocent it seemed as if the future of the world was safe in the hands of a permanent partnership between the two friendly giants.

So the disillusionment caused by the cold war was acute. It induced much of the European

Left to swallow the communist view of America almost whole, and from leftist circles in Paris and London, as well as Moscow, anti-Americanism spread through much of Africa and Asia. American popular culture was spreading too, but it could not counteract the fact that U.S. foreign policy, dominated by the cold war, was actively counterrevolutionary. As, one by one, the old colonial empires dissolved, Americans liked to think that their country had shown the way, by its own revolution, to the anticolonial movement: in each new postcolonial leader it thought to find a George Washington. This was delusion. Most of the regimes that sought a close relationship with the United States came to a bad end; others were clients of the Soviet or Chinese communists; still others, such as Jawaharlal Nehru and Gamal Abdal Nasser, deliberately sought to be neutral in the cold war and paid the price in U.S. hostility.

The folly of American policy completed this process of alienation. The involvement in Vietnam came near to convincing a generation of the world's youth — the first in history, thanks to modern communications, to have much the same interests and tastes everywhere, all of them thoroughly Americanized — that the communist thesis was correct, and America was nothing but the last imperial power.

Yet in the end the cold war destroyed Russia's standing, too. If the anticommunist crusade came to seem a fraud, sustained only to safeguard the profits of big business and to keep the American Right in power, the pretensions of the Soviet Union came to seem no better. The long, slow, bitter process of de-Stalinization, though initiated by the Soviet leadership itself, confirmed everything the Americans had ever said about the horrors of communism and its economic imbecility. Both superpowers faced enormous internal difficulties as the last decade of the twentieth century opened, and the ideological prospect was as murky as any other. But it did seem that almost every nation had come to yearn, however hopelessly, for a political order that recognized personal rights and freedoms, the freedom of the market, and effective representative government. To that extent the values of the Declaration of Independence seemed to be triumphing worldwide. The myth of America, it may reasonably be claimed, was showing astonishing staying power.

David Paul Crook, *American Democracy in English Politics, 1815–1850* (1965); Durand Echeverria, *Mirage in the West: A History of the French Image of American Society in 1815* (1957).

Hugh Brogan

See also Africa-U.S. Relations; Asia-U.S. Relations; Canada-U.S. Relations; Caribbean-U.S. Relations; Cold War; *Democracy in America;* France-U.S. Relations; Germany-U.S. Relations; Good Neighbor Policy; Great Britain–U.S. Relations; Latin America–U.S. Relations; Mexico-U.S. Relations; Middle East–U.S. Relations; Revolution; Soviet-American Relations, 1917–1945.

FORTUNE, T. THOMAS

(1856–1928), journalist and civil rights leader. In the late nineteenth and early twentieth centuries Fortune was the most prominent black journalist in America. Born a slave in Marianna, Florida, Fortune discovered politics and journalism as a youth. His father, Emanuel, was a Reconstruction politician in Florida; the younger Fortune worked as a page in the state senate and learned the printer's trade at a Jacksonville newspaper. His meager formal education included Freedmen's Bureau schools in Florida and one year as a preparatory student at Howard University.

Fortune moved to New York City in 1881, where over the next two decades he achieved fame as the militant and maverick editor or owner of a newspaper named first the *Globe,* then the *Freeman,* and finally the *New York Age.* A largely self-taught writer and orator of eloquence, Fortune lived with the label "Negro agitator" well before the much-publicized disputes between the followers of Booker T. Washington and W. E. B. Du Bois. Fortune demanded enforcement of black civil rights and attacked the growing wave of indifference toward the plight of southern freedmen, a position he explored in his *Black and White: Land, Labor, and Politics in the South* (1884).

Fortune led the effort to create the National

Afro-American League in 1889. After four years of faltering support, the league collapsed but re-emerged in 1898, again with Fortune at the center, as the National Afro-American Council. The meager achievements of the league and the council should not diminish their role as precursors of the Niagara Movement, the NAACP, and other civil rights organizations in the twentieth century. Fortune's modern legacy also includes his advocacy of the term *Afro-American* for his people rather than *Negro* or *colored*. He believed it was the most accurate term, arguing that blacks were "African in origin and American in birth."

Fortune's political allegiances were more paradoxical. He intermittently supported and excoriated the Republicans during his career, abandoning them over their betrayal of racial equality in 1888 and endorsing Grover Cleveland, the Democrat, for president. Even more complex was Fortune's long relationship with Booker T. Washington. The powerful Tuskegee president secretly financed Fortune's under-funded newspaper. Fortune's militance seemed to be the antithesis of Washington's accommodationism, but the two men had in common their origins and their belief in black economic self-determination. Fortune assisted Washington in creating the National Negro Business League and loyally served him as a ghost writer. But alliances with the Wizard of Tuskegee were risky business; Fortune had serious financial problems and hoped that Washington's influence would bring him a political appointment. Instead, this slippery political path led to his condemnation by followers of Du Bois, severe bouts with alcoholism, and abandonment by Washington. Fortune sold his interest in the *Age* and experienced a nervous breakdown in 1907.

After many years of apparent destitution, he recovered in the 1920s, inspired by though never a complete convert of Marcus Garvey, to edit Garvey's journal, the *Negro World*. Fortune's tragic life ended in 1928, but not before the pioneer activist had joined the ranks of Washington's critics, apologized for his ideological waywardness, and observed that "all along the way I have shaken the trees and others have gathered the fruit."

Emma Lou Thornbrough, *T. Thomas Fortune: Militant Journalist* (1972).

DAVID W. BLIGHT

See also Du Bois, W. E. B.; Garvey, Marcus; Washington, Booker T.

FOUR FREEDOMS

The catchphrase *Four Freedoms* refers to the four "essential human freedoms" outlined by President Franklin D. Roosevelt in his State of the Union message of January 6, 1941: freedom of speech, freedom of religion, freedom from want, and freedom from fear of armed aggression.

Roosevelt stressed that these freedoms should be guaranteed throughout the world: they would become the basis of a secure world order. Although Roosevelt stopped short of asking Congress to enter the Second World War at that time, his Four Freedoms speech did promise America's "full support" for the Allied cause. On August 14, 1941, President Roosevelt and British prime minister Winston Churchill confirmed the Four Freedoms as joint war aims in the Atlantic Charter.

See also Atlantic Charter; World War II.

FOURTEEN POINTS

President Woodrow Wilson listed Fourteen Points as World War I aims in an address to a joint session of Congress on January 8, 1918.

The first five points announced general principles for a peace settlement: "Open covenants of peace, openly arrived at" should replace the secret diplomacy practiced in Europe before and during the war. There should be freedom of the seas in peace and war. Barriers to international free trade should be ended, armaments should be reduced, and colonial claims should be adjusted, balancing the interests of colonial populations and the great powers.

Eight points concerned territorial adjustments: the return of lost territory to Russia, a guarantee of Belgium's independence, the restoration of Alsace-Lorraine to France, and readjustment of Italian frontiers "along clearly recognizable lines of nationality." In addition, the peoples of Austria-Hungary should have the "freest opportunity of autonomous development," and the boundaries of the Balkan states should be rearranged "along historically established lines of allegiance and nationality." Turkey's independence should be preserved, but "autonomous development" for non-Turkish portions of the Ottoman Empire and an international passage through the Dardenelles should be guaranteed. Serbia and Poland should be given access to the sea, and Poland should also be given independence.

Finally, the Fourteenth Point called for creating "a general association of nations" with power to guarantee each nation's territorial integrity and sovereignty.

See also World War I.

FRANCE-U.S. RELATIONS

In colonial North America dynastic, religious, and ethnic rivalries frequently produced bloodshed between Protestant British and French Catholic settlers, leading them to fight four wars between 1688 and 1763, until in the Seven Years' War Great Britain ejected the French from continental North America. When the British colonies revolted, France retaliated by secretly supplying them with guns and other supplies.

After Congress declared independence in July 1776 its agents in Paris recruited officers for the Continental Army, notably the Marquis de Lafayette who served with distinction as a major general. Despite a lingering distrust of France, the agents also requested an alliance. After readying their fleet and being impressed by the American victory at Saratoga in October 1777, the French in the following February concluded treaties of commerce and alliance that bound them to fight Britain until American independence was assured.

Later a fleet and an army commanded by the Comte de Rochambeau arrived in the United States. At the crucial victory of Yorktown in October 1781 French forces outnumbered Americans. In the peace negotiations between the

Americans and the British in Paris in 1783 the American commissioners, Benjamin Franklin, John Adams, and particularly John Jay, suspected the French of a willingness to sacrifice the American interest in the western territory extending to the Mississippi River and of being hostile to American fishing rights off Newfoundland. Hence, with Benjamin Franklin and John Adams, Jay violated the spirit of the alliance by directly bargaining with the British. Nevertheless the allies cooperated to produce a favorable treaty. In all, the French contribution to American independence was decisive.

Six years later the revolution that toppled the Bourbon monarchy dissipated some of the American warmth for France. In February 1793, at war again with Britain, France viewed George Washington's policy as partial to the enemy. It also regarded as hostile Jay's Treaty of November 1794 between Britain and America. To overcome this resentment John Adams in 1797 sent a special mission to Paris. When Charles Maurice de Talleyrand-Périgord, the French foreign minister, demanded a bribe, Adams exposed the episode, known as the XYZ Affair, and two years of hostilities at sea, or the Quasi-War, followed. It ended in September 1800 with the Treaty of Morfontaine which rid the United States of the "entangling" French alliance.

At the same time First Consul Napoleon Bonaparte regained the Louisiana Territory from Spain, leading Thomas Jefferson to consider war to prevent French control of the Mississippi River. Fortunately, because of an insuppressible slave rebellion in St. Domingue, among other reasons, Bonaparte's North American plans collapsed. To keep Louisiana out of British hands in an approaching war he sold it in April 1803 to the United States for $15 million. In their warfare the French infringed on American maritime rights but less than did the British. So in 1812 the United States declared war on Britain and fought indirectly as an ally of France.

In 1834 when Andrew Jackson demanded payment for property destroyed during the Napoleonic Wars, France severed diplomatic relations. When tempers cooled, cordiality and modest cultural exchanges resumed, as in visits to the United States by Gustave de Beaumont and

Alexis de Tocqueville, the author of *Democracy in America* (1835). During the Civil War the Union believed that Napoleon III favored the Confederacy. Furthermore, he intervened in a civil conflict in Mexico. Abraham Lincoln opposed the French occupiers and through judicious use of threat pressured them to leave in March 1867.

In subsequent years the fundamentals of the relationship changed. The United States, rising to the status of a great power, came to overshadow France. All during this period the friendship remained firm — as symbolized by the Statue of Liberty, presented in 1884 as a gift to the United States from the French people. In 1906 when Germany menaced France over Morocco, Theodore Roosevelt sided with the French. During the First World War the United States again sympathized with France and joined it as a cobelligerent. In the peacemaking, however, though sharing major objectives, the two countries clashed over particulars such as debts, reparations, and restraints on Germany.

Nevertheless, during the interwar years, the two nations remained friendly. Beginning in the twenties American intellectuals, painters, writers, and tourists were drawn to French art, literature, philosophy, theater, cinema, fashion, wines, and cuisine. In turn, American novelists such as William Faulkner and numerous filmmakers influenced French life.

In 1928 the two nations sponsored the Kellogg-Briand Pact outlawing war, and in the thirties both supported democracies against dictatorships and favored capitalism over communism. In the Second World War Americans again favored France in opposition to Germany. Franklin D. Roosevelt aided the French with money, munitions, and supplies. This friendliness changed, however, when defeated France in June 1940 established a fascist regime at Vichy. After the United States entered the war its forces attacked Vichy's bases in North Africa.

In the postwar years both cooperation and discord persisted. The United States helped revive the French economy with Marshall Plan aid and in 1949 again became a formal ally through the North Atlantic treaty, but it disapproved of French efforts to regain control over former colonies in Africa and Southeast Asia. In 1954, for instance, Dwight D. Eisenhower refused to intervene in Vietnam to save besieged French forces at Dien Bien Phu.

Both countries opposed the Soviet Union in cold war confrontations but went through another crisis in 1956 when French, British, and Israeli forces attacked Egypt and Eisenhower forced them to withdraw. After Charles de Gaulle became president he clashed with Americans over France's building of her own nuclear weapons, Britain's admission to the European Economic Community, and France's role in the North Atlantic Treaty Organization (NATO).

While no major crises marred the following decades, the two nations differed over the waging of the Vietnam War, in part because French leaders were convinced that the United States could not win. In the eighties the two nations cooperated on most international matters, though at the end of the decade popular opinion within each differed on the desirability of a reunified Germany.

Despite the rifts, the often ambiguous relationship remained stable and remarkably friendly. The two countries continued to share a democratic tradition and to respect each other's culture and way of life.

Henry Blumenthal, *American and French Culture, 1800–1900: Interchanges in Art, Science, Literature, and Society* (1975); Jean Baptiste Duroselle, *France and the United States: From the Beginnings to the Present*, trans. Derek Coltman (1976); Marvin H. Zahniser, *Uncertain Friendship: American-French Diplomatic Relations through the Cold War* (1975).

ALEXANDER DeCONDE

See also French and Spanish Settlements; Jay's Treaty; Kellogg-Briand Pact; Louisiana Purchase; Revolution; Statue of Liberty; XYZ Affair.

FRANKFURTER, FELIX

(1882–1965), legal educator and associate justice, U.S. Supreme Court. Frankfurter, the only naturalized American to serve on the Supreme Court, arrived in New York in 1894 from Vienna, Austria. He graduated from Harvard Law

School in 1906 after compiling an exceptional record. Because he was Jewish, he received no offers from private law firms commensurate with his talents, so he accepted an offer to assist the young Henry L. Stimson, who had just become the U.S. attorney in New York. Stimson took Frankfurter to Washington with him in 1911 when he became secretary of war in the administration of William Howard Taft. Frankfurter remained in Washington until 1914, when he joined the faculty of Harvard Law School. He performed important government service during World War I and participated in the Versailles Conference afterward.

Throughout the 1920s, Frankfurter was influential both as a law professor and as an active participant in public debates of the day, most notably in the controversy surrounding the conviction and subsequent execution of the anarchists Sacco and Vanzetti in Massachusetts. By 1933 Frankfurter had become a trusted adviser and confidant to the new president, Franklin D. Roosevelt, although he rejected an invitation to become solicitor general of the United States. Frankfurter preferred to remain at Harvard, where he could identify bright young lawyers and encourage them to join New Deal agencies in Washington.

One of Frankfurter's mentors was Justice Oliver Wendell Holmes, Jr., who argued that courts should, with rare exceptions, defer to the decisions made by legislatures and the Congress. Frankfurter agreed. He was especially critical of the Court for striking down much New Deal legislation in 1935–1936.

Roosevelt named Frankfurter to the Supreme Court in 1939, to succeed Justice Benjamin Cardozo. Although some anti-Semitic opposition was voiced, his appointment was generally well received, especially by liberals who looked forward to Frankfurter's becoming the intellectual leader of a "Roosevelt Court."

Frankfurter and other Roosevelt-appointed justices agreed that the new regulatory state being established by the New Deal (and in many states by their legislatures) was constitutional. But they disagreed sharply over whether the Court should similarly acquiesce to the victimization of unpopular political minorities by ma-

joritarian legislatures. Frankfurter wrote a controversial opinion in *Minersville School District* v. *Gobitis* (1940), upholding Pennsylvania's right to punish Jehovah's Witness schoolchildren whose religious beliefs prevented their pledging allegiance to the American flag. (The Court reversed itself in *West Virginia State Board of Education* v. *Barnette* [1943], over his sharp dissent.) Thereafter, Frankfurter, though a major figure on the Court, was regularly challenged by Hugo Black, William O. Douglas, and others who thought the Court should play a more active role in protecting minorities and otherwise monitoring the fairness of the political process. Indeed, Frankfurter's last important opinion was a dissent in *Baker* v. *Carr* (1962), objecting to the Court's willingness to assess the fairness of legislative districting.

Liva Baker, *Felix Frankfurter* (1969); Michael Parrish, *Felix Frankfurter and His Times: The Reform Years* (1982).

SANFORD LEVINSON

See also Baker v. *Carr;* Holmes, Oliver Wendell, Jr.; New Deal; *Sacco-Vanzetti* Case; Supreme Court.

FRANKLIN, BENJAMIN

(1706–1790), newspaperman, scientist, inventor, philosopher, politician, and diplomat. Born in Boston, the son of a soap maker, Franklin was apprenticed to his printer brother James at twelve. He was soon contributing witty essays to James's newspaper under various pen names.

In 1723 he moved to Philadelphia and launched the *Pennsylvania Gazette,* which rapidly became the most successful newspaper in the colonies. His *Poor Richard's Almanack,* which he published from 1733 to 1758, was studded with wry aphorisms Franklin borrowed from numerous sources and frequently rewrote. He helped launch projects to pave, clean, and light Philadelphia's streets and founded the American Philosophical Society, the first circulating library in America, and an academy that grew into the University of Pennsylvania. In 1743 he invented a heat-efficient stove to warm houses. Retiring from newspapering in 1748, he turned to the study of electricity. His observations, including his famous experiment with a kite to verify the identity of electricity and lightning, won him world fame.

Already a leader in Pennsylvania's politics, Franklin went to England in 1757 to represent the colony in its quarrel with the descendants of William Penn. He remained there until 1775, becoming agent for several other colonies and de facto ambassador for all thirteen. At first a strong believer in the value of a united empire, he grew disillusioned with England's corrupt politics and aristocratic society, though he made lasting friendships with many prominent men. In 1765 American objections to the Stamp Act caught him by surprise, but he quickly joined the opponents. His testimony before Parliament helped persuade the members to repeal the measure.

Thereafter Franklin's antagonism to Britain's determination to tax Americans deepened. He helped purloin letters of Massachusetts's governor, Thomas Hutchinson, calling for "an abridgment of what are called English liberties." Sent to Boston, these caused a political sensation. He returned to America in 1775 and stunned many of his friends and relatives, in particular his son William, the royal governor of New Jersey, by saying he was for independence. William shocked his father in turn by becoming a Loyalist.

Franklin worked with Thomas Jefferson on the Declaration of Independence and served in the Continental Congress before sailing in 1776 to become ambassador to the court of Louis XVI. Dressing as a humble Quaker, he became a figure of myth and romance to a rapt French public. His popularity made it difficult for the king's wary government to resist the treaty of alliance they signed in 1778, rescuing the faltering Revolution from bankruptcy. For the next five years, Franklin was a pivotal figure on the European side of the struggle. He soothed French doubts about America, extracted loans, urged influential English friends to push for an early peace, and finally negotiated, with John Jay and John Adams, a separate treaty that won, among many concessions, the Northwest Territory and the trans-Allegheny West.

He returned to America in 1784. Although few of his ideas, such as a unicameral legislature, were adopted at the Philadelphia Constitutional Convention in 1787, Franklin played a major role in the compromises that created the final document. His last public act was a memorial to Congress urging the abolition of slavery, which he signed shortly before his death. That farewell gesture epitomizes the mature Franklin, a far more complex and significant figure than the simplistic image of the success-hungry young businessman in his *Autobiography*. In many ways Americans have yet to grasp the full range of his accomplishments as a Founding Father.

Thomas Fleming, *The Man Who Dared the Lightning* (1971); Leonard Larabee et al., eds., *The Autobiography of Benjamin Franklin* (1964); Claude Ann Lopez, *Mon Cher Papa: Franklin and the Ladies of Paris* (1966).

THOMAS FLEMING

See also Constitution; Continental Congresses; Declaration of Independence; Deism; Paris, Treaty of (1783); Philadelphia Convention; Revolution.

FRATERNAL SOCIETIES

The term *fraternal society,* used interchangeably with *fraternal order,* refers to voluntary associations that feature elaborate secret initiations. Some orders provide a simple form of life insurance; nearly all exclude women. Nowadays the most important fraternal societies are the Freemasons, Independent Order of Odd Fellows, Knights of Pythias, and the Benevolent and Protective Order of Elk.

Fraternal orders were once a significant — some observers believed characteristic — aspect of American society. Alexis de Tocqueville was struck by the "immense assemblage" of voluntary associations, including fraternal orders, in antebellum America. Henry David Thoreau complained that America was "dwindling" into a nation of "odd-fellows."

The origins of fraternal orders are obscured by a tangle of implausible legends and dubious histories. Nineteenth-century Freemasons claimed to be heirs of a tradition extending back to the founding of King Solomon's temple. Historians of the Knights of Pythias made a case that Pythagoras was the first Pythian, despite the awkward fact that the order apparently had been founded in Washington, D.C., in 1864. The Improved Order of Red Men, established in the 1830s, claimed descent from the Sons of Liberty of the American Revolution.

Without doubt, the Freemasons were entitled to claim that they were the nation's oldest order. But contrary to the claims of some enthusiasts, Freemasonry originated in London in the early 1700s as a stonemasons' trade guild. The order soon became a club for tradesmen, merchants, and a few much-celebrated noblemen. In the 1730s and 1740s a handful of Masonic lodges were established in coastal towns in America. Although these lodges were dominated by a mercantile elite, some tradesmen were admitted, such as Benjamin Franklin who, as a young printer, became grand master of Pennsylvania Freemasons in 1734.

Freemasonry became associated with patriotism during the Revolution, largely because George Washington and many of his generals belonged to the order. This patriotic association was strengthened when Washington took his oath of office as president upon a Masonic Bible.

Despite the order's association with the Founding Fathers and its profession of universal brotherhood, American officials refused to recognize the legitimacy of black Freemasons, who in 1775 had been admitted to a lodge composed mostly of Irish soldiers stationed in Boston harbor. The leader of the blacks, Prince Hall, subsequently received a dispensation from English officials and established African Lodge No. 459. Black Freemasonry, usually called Prince Hall Freemasonry, became popular among middle-class blacks.

During the early 1800s the number of Masonic lodges multiplied rapidly. The order especially appealed to an emerging middle class of lawyers, commercial farmers, and independent tradesmen, many of whom were growing impatient with orthodox religion and established political elites. Tensions between Masonic leaders and the conservative ministry smoldered until 1826, when a disgruntled ex-Freemason, William Morgan, announced his intention of publishing the secret Masonic rituals. Morgan was abducted by Freemasons and was never seen again. What

happened to him has never been fully explained. Twenty-six Masons were indicted on murder and related charges. Only six came to trial; four were convicted of conspiracy and sentenced to terms ranging from several months to two years in jail. When it became known that many of the jurors and prosecutors were Masons, as was Governor DeWitt Clinton of New York, a coalition of ministers and opportunistic politicians formed to suppress the order. The Anti-Masonic party became the first significant third party in American politics.

Though short-lived as a political movement, Anti-Masonry generated intense public pressure and forced thousands of members to renounce the order and hundreds of lodges to relinquish their charters. By best estimate membership declined from 100,000 in the mid-1820s to 40,000 a decade later. Many renouncing Freemasons flocked into the Odd Fellows.

Odd-Fellowship originated in late-eighteenth-century Great Britain among industrial workers who sought to mitigate the effects of the Industrial Revolution and the English Poor Laws. The order assisted members in dire circumstances and provided them a decent burial. In 1819 English immigrants established the first American lodge of Odd Fellows in Baltimore. During its early decades the order met in taverns and functioned as little more than a drinking society. But the influx of ex-Freemasons during the 1830s and 1840s completely transformed American Odd-Fellowship. This "new and more refined" group, as one nineteenth-century historian described them, gained control of the order, raised fees beyond what most workers could afford, banned liquor from meetings, launched a program to build "temples," and wrote and performed elaborate successions of initiatory rituals. By the 1850s Freemasonry, having just begun to recover from the Morgan debacle, adopted a similar program.

During the last third of the nineteenth century, fraternal orders, featuring reform and ritual, proliferated among the urban middle classes. By 1900 there were more than three hundred orders; total fraternal membership exceeded 6 million. Ambitious clerks, businessmen, and politicians used the orders to cultivate contacts and establish ties with clients and like-minded people elsewhere. Others found satisfaction in the exotic rituals, which provided a religious experience antithetical to liberal Protestantism and a masculine "family" vastly different from the one in which most members had been raised.

Partly to attenuate women's complaints about the secrecy, the cost of membership, and the time members spent away from home, most orders supported creation of ladies' auxiliaries. The Odd-Fellows established the Daughters of Rebekah (1851), and Freemasons, the Order of the Eastern Star (1869).

Early in the twentieth century, however, many young middle-class men, preferring the recreational clubs and service organizations such as Rotary and Kiwanis, refused to follow their fathers into the lodge. Robert and Helen Lynd, in their study of Muncie, Indiana, in the 1920s, reported that "the great days of the lodges have vanished." Aggressive recruitment policies and relaxed admission standards temporarily masked the weakness of most lodges. But the onset of the Great Depression brought about the collapse of the institutional foundations of the fraternal movement as members could no longer afford to pay dues and thousands of lodges, unable to meet mortgage payments, went bankrupt. The major orders together lost nearly a million members; hundreds of others passed out of existence entirely.

After World War II, social activities, philanthropy, and community service took precedence over the rituals, which were abbreviated or occasionally abandoned. Most orders languished and increasingly became identified in the public mind with the televised antics of Jackie Gleason's Ralph Kramden, member of the fictional Loyal Order of Raccoons. In recent decades, however, Freemasonry has gained many new adherents, especially from among white-collar workers and immigrants.

Mark C. Carnes, *Secret Ritual and Manhood in Victorian America* (1989); Dorothy Ann Lipson, *Freemasonry in Federalist Connecticut, 1789–1835* (1977).

MARK C. CARNES

See also Anti-Masons.

FREEDMEN'S BUREAU

Congress created the Bureau of Refugees, Freedmen, and Abandoned Lands in March 1865. Its responsibilities included the provision of food, shelter, and medical aid for the destitute, the education of freedpeople, the establishment of free labor arrangements in former plantation areas, and the securing of justice for blacks in southern legal proceedings. Early on, bureau commissioner Maj. Gen. Oliver O. Howard and assistant commissioners for various states tried to resettle a portion of the freed population on the 850,000 acres of abandoned and confiscated southern land, but President Andrew Johnson's policy of pardoning large numbers of erstwhile Confederates and restoring their land frustrated this project. The bureau thenceforth focused on compelling freedpeople to accept plantation work on a wage labor basis. The contract labor system quickly gave way, however, to various sharecropping and tenancy arrangements in large parts of the South. The bureau's education policy was more successful. Working with private aid societies, it had helped establish nearly three thousand schools by 1869. It contributed, too, to the founding of black colleges and normal schools.

In the summer of 1866, Congress extended the life of the Freedmen's Bureau over Johnson's veto, but it always lacked adequate funds and never fielded more than nine hundred agents. Moreover, by 1867, the bureau's administrators were trimming its legal agencies, its contract supervision, its medical network, and its relief activity. General Howard believed that blacks would be better served if the states were compelled to deal with them as part of the general citizenry rather than their continuing as wards of the federal government. By 1869, Congress had ended all the bureau's work except education, which continued into 1870, and help for black veterans, which survived until 1872.

Although a significant number of its agents and officials were not especially zealous in their defense of black interests, the bureau's activities nevertheless were supported by most of the freed population and roundly loathed by white southerners.

See also Reconstruction.

FREEDOM OF SPEECH

The modern American conception of freedom of speech derives from the principles of freedom of the press (mainly in the context of political criticism) and freedom of religion as they developed in England, starting in the seventeenth century. The arguments of John Milton and others on the importance of an unlicensed press, and of John Locke and others on religious toleration, were the precursors to the idea of freedom of speech, although also relevant is the much narrower concept of "freedom of speech" as an immunity for prosecution for anything said in the course of parliamentary debate.

By 1791, when the First Amendment was ratified, the idea of "freedom of speech" was sufficiently entrenched that it became the primary language of the amendment, with "freedom of the press" being added to ensure that written and printed as well as oral communication was protected: "Congress shall make no law ... abridging the freedom of speech, or of the press." Still, the focus both in law and in political discussion at the time was on printed political argument, whether in newspapers or the kinds of tracts distributed by men like Thomas Paine.

The period from 1791 to the early twentieth century saw almost complete judicial noninvolvement in free speech and free press questions, and public discussion was devoted largely to free press rather than free speech ideas. But when the Supreme Court actively began in 1919 to concern itself with judicial enforcement of the First Amendment, it was in the context not of newspapers or magazines or books but of speakers, or occasionally pamphleteers, who were protesting American involvement in the First World War or promoting anarchist, socialist, or syndicalist causes. Although the convictions were upheld and the speakers imprisoned in cases involving the now-forgotten figures Charles T. Schenck, Jacob Abrams, and Jacob Frohwerk, as well as prominent ones such as Eugene V. Debs, the Supreme Court's language in those cases has had an enduring effect. In upholding the convictions of Schenck, Frohwerk, and Debs, Justice Oliver Wendell Holmes, Jr., enunciated the principle of the "clear and present danger," according to which, to justify regulation, the harms resulting from speech had to be greater in likelihood and immediacy than harms of other varieties. And in dissenting from the conviction of Abrams, Holmes developed the notion of the "marketplace of ideas," which has dominated public understanding of the importance of freedom of speech.

The development of freedom of speech for the next forty years was also dominated by Supreme Court protection of largely oral and frequently socially marginal communicators, of whom the most important were the Jehovah's Witnesses. In case after case in the 1930s, 1940s, and 1950s, they challenged restrictions on their proselytizing activities and won in the Supreme Court and in the lower courts with sufficient frequency that their victories established in legal doctrine and public consciousness the principle that even annoying, intrusive, and offensive speech is to be protected by the courts and tolerated by the public as incidental to an open society.

Contemporary understandings of freedom of speech, however, owe even more to developments in the 1960s, during which first civil rights protesters and then objectors to the Vietnam War found the courts upholding their activities against governmental efforts to restrict them. Increased public acceptance of such activities followed. In this respect, the modern protection of freedom of speech is partly fortuitous, for the protection of civil rights demonstrators, paraders, and picketers in the 1960s was largely an adjunct to judicial protection of the civil rights movement generally. Nevertheless, the First Amendment principles developed to further the civil rights movement remained in place to be used for other speakers promoting other causes.

The most important manifestation of this transfer started in the late 1960s, when the Supreme Court with some consistency recognized the right of speakers in the "public forum" to articulate ideas that not only were in opposition to established military and political authority but also were highly likely to offend unwilling listeners or viewers. In the late 1960s and early 1970s, the Court protected with some frequency those who desecrated the American flag, who displayed offensive language, such as obscene words on an article of clothing, and who conveyed messages often as likely to be harmful as they were offensive. Operating on the assumption that underregulation of even harmful speech was the only way in an imperfect world to protect against the overregulation of harmless speech, the Court went from the protection of Vietnam protesters to the protection of the speech of groups such as the Ku Klux Klan. Indeed, it was the Klan case of *Brandenburg* v. *Ohio* that in 1969 established the current extraordinarily strict understanding of the Holmesian idea of "clear and present danger." Speech leading to violence or other unlawful activities can be restricted only if the ensuing lawless activity is likely to be "imminent" and even then only if the speaker has explicitly urged that activity. By 1977 it was considered an "easy case" when the U.S. Court of Appeals for the Seventh Circuit, sitting in Chicago, upheld the right of the American Nazi party to march in a community (Skokie, Illinois) heavily populated by Holocaust survivors, a decision the Supreme Court refused to review.

Legal doctrine has not always translated into public understanding or freedom in fact, but here the result of a large number of Supreme Court cases protecting even harmful and offensive speech in the public forum, and narrowing to virtual disappearance the legal definition of "obscenity," has created an environment in which the presence of unpleasant speech is taken for granted by most of the public, whether they agree with that state of affairs or not. There will, of course, continue to be disputes about the actual boundaries of this very broad principle, but the legacy of the Jehovah's Witnesses, of the civil rights movement, and of the Vietnam protesters is one that is unlikely to be very much narrowed, in large part because the legacy of the red scare of 1919 and the McCarthy era of the late 1940s and early 1950s is one whose avoidance also influences current understanding.

Harry Kalven, Jr., *A Worthy Tradition: Freedom of Speech in America* (1988); Richard Polenberg, *Fighting Faiths: The Abrams Case, the Supreme Court, and Free Speech* (1987).

FREDERICK SCHAUER

See also Bill of Rights; Freedom of the Press.

FREEDOM OF THE PRESS

Any discussion of freedom of the press must distinguish freedom in fact from legal freedom. The principle of freedom of the press as a constraint on government actions against the press can differ from the amount of freedom the press actually exercises at a given time. On the one hand, various social, political, and economic forces may serve to make the press freer in fact than it is in law. Conversely, those same forces may substantially curtail the exercise of a legal freedom.

This article addresses only the development of the principle of freedom of the press, according to which government control of the press is subject to political, legal, or constitutional constraints greater than those applicable to other forms of government action. In this sense of freedom of the press, the principle in the United States evolved from English thought. Anticensorship themes had been sounded early in the seventeenth century, but the work that had the most lasting influence was John Milton's *Areopagitica: A Speech for the Liberty of Unlicensed Printing to the Parliament of England* (1644). Although Milton argued only for elimination of licensing in advance of publication and did not object to prosecution thereafter, and although the freedom he advocated did not extend to Catholics and others he viewed as beyond the pale, his eloquent objection to what we now call "prior restraint" has had lasting influence.

English pleas for freedom of the press increased in the early part of the eighteenth century. Among the most prominent were John Trenchard and Thomas Gordon's pseudonymous *Cato's Letters,* which went beyond Milton in arguing against prosecutions for seditious and criminal libel as well as against licensing. These and similar writings had great influence in the colonies, and the arguments exemplified by *Cato's Letters* surrounded the trial in 1735 of John Peter Zenger, the most important colonial precursor to later American developments.

Zenger was the publisher of the *New York Weekly Journal,* which had printed harsh criticisms of Governor William Cosby of the Province of New York. Zenger was prosecuted for seditious libel, and consistent with the law at the time the jury was instructed to consider not whether the work was actually seditious (an issue then considered a matter of law for the judge and not one of fact for the jury) but only the questions of whether Zenger had published the work and whether it referred to Cosby. Nevertheless, the jury disregarded these limitations and acquitted Zenger. That acquittal represented the assertion of popular power against the monarchy, in contrast to the modern understanding of freedom of the press as protection against popular control as much as against particular government officials.

Against this background there remains controversy about the intention underlying the First Amendment, which provides that "Congress shall make no law . . . abridging the freedom of speech, or of the press." Although a common understanding takes this to embody an intention to eliminate the law of seditious libel, there is strong evidence that the amendment (as well as similar provisions in various state constitutions) was intended to embody the Miltonian idea, also found in Blackstone's *Commentaries,* that only prior restraints like licensing were to be prohibited, with prosecutions for seditious libel untouched by the new Bill of Rights.

As a matter of constitutional law, these issues were not settled until well into the twentieth century, although political discourse, as shown by the negative reaction to and ultimate repeal of the Sedition Act of 1798, gradually assimilated the view that not only licensing but also subsequent punishment of the press for criticizing government and its officials were inconsistent with the view of the press as an institutionalized counterweight to government power. This political understanding, which grew sporadically throughout the nineteenth century, was supported by the development of the common law privilege of fair comment, which substantially limited the availability of civil libel actions against the press for criticizing governmental officials.

Still, it remained possible for Justice Oliver Wendell Holmes, Jr., to note as late as 1907 that whether the First Amendment prohibited anything other than a prior restraint remained an open question. When the Supreme Court in 1919 started to put teeth into the First Amendment, it increasingly held that that protection went far beyond prohibiting prior restraints. But the historical legacy remains, for prior restraints are the least justifiable form of restriction on the press. When the Court in 1931 in *Near v. Minnesota* held impermissible an injunction against a defamatory scandal sheet called the *Saturday Press,* it established a virtually insurmountable legal standard for attempts to license the press or to enjoin publications in advance. This standard had its most famous application in 1971, when in a widely publicized decision (*New York Times Co.* v. *United States*) the Supreme Court held that government attempts to restrain the publication of the Pentagon Papers was constitutionally impermissible, despite government claims that publication would impede the military's efforts in Vietnam, and despite the fact that the documents then in possession of the *New York Times* and other newspapers had been unlawfully removed from the Defense Department. This case established the principle that prior restraints are for all practical purposes impossible to justify.

By the time the case had been decided, however, the press had also become essentially free from subsequent punishment. In 1936 the Supreme Court struck down a punitive tax on the press that Louisiana governor Huey Long had imposed in retaliation for criticism. And in 1964, in a case that transformed the nature of press freedom in the United States, the Court decided that libel actions based on criticism of public officials (and subsequently all public figures) could not be maintained unless the official was able to show not only that the criticism was factually false but that it had been published with prior knowledge of its falsity. This is such an enormous burden that the press now is largely free from fear of criminal punishment or civil liability based on reporting or commentary on matters of public concern.

As a result, arguments about freedom of the press have turned away from questions of punishment to questions of press privileges and press access. The arguments now commonly concern whether journalists shall be immune from subpoenas or search warrants seeking to discover the products of their investigation, and whether the press shall have access to government information not otherwise available to the public. Although the Supreme Court has largely rejected these arguments as First Amendment claims, the arguments have often persuaded legislatures to enact shield laws, which grant partial immunities from subpoena, and open meeting or freedom of information laws, which give the press greater access to details about governmental actions. Although it is inevitable that the press will always want more information and the government will always want to provide less, the current press freedom in the United States is such that much that happens in government is more widely known and subject to criticism than anywhere else in the world.

Leonard W. Levy, *Emergence of a Free Press* (1985); Norman L. Rosenberg, *Protecting the Best Men: An Interpretive History of the Law of Libel* (1986).

FREDERICK SCHAUER

See also Bill of Rights; Freedom of Speech; Zenger Trial.

FREEDOM RIDES

The Freedom Rides were organized by the Congress of Racial Equality (CORE) to test the effectiveness of a 1960 Supreme Court decision, *Boynton* v. *Virginia,* which prohibited racial segregation in public areas that served interstate travelers.

On May 4, 1961, a small interracial group of CORE members traveling in two buses challenged southern segregated rest rooms, waiting rooms, and restaurants in bus terminals between Washington, D.C., and New Orleans. On May 14, they were attacked by a mob outside Anniston, Alabama. The first bus was set on fire, and as passengers left the burning vehicle, some were beaten. The event drew national and international attention to the race conflict. Attorney General Robert F. Kennedy provided police escorts for the riders, and they continued to other cities. Nevertheless, they met with violence again in Birmingham and later in Montgomery.

The initial Freedom Rides furthered desegregation in terminals throughout the South and demonstrated that civil rights victories in the Deep South were possible. A Freedom Ride Coordinating Committee was created to organize more rides, and by the end of the summer about a thousand riders had participated. These later Freedom Riders attracted less publicity.

The importance of the tactic declined as civil rights organizations such as CORE, the Student Non-Violent Coordinating Committee, and the Southern Christian Leadership Conference shifted the direction of the movement toward voter registration and its greater potential for long-term political gains.

See also Civil Rights Movement; Racial Desegregation.

FREEDOM SUMMER

Freedom Summer was a 1964 voter registration project in Mississippi, part of a larger effort by civil rights groups such as the Congress on Racial Equality (CORE) and the Student Non-Violent Coordinating Committee (SNCC) to expand black voting in the South. The Mississippi project was run by the local Council of Federated Organizations (COFO), an association of civil rights groups in which SNCC was the most active member. About a hundred white college students had helped COFO register voters in November 1963, and several hundred more students were invited in 1964 for Freedom Summer, a much-expanded voter registration project.

On June 15, 1964, the first three hundred arrived. The next day, two of the white students, Michael Schwerner and Andrew Goodman, both from New York, and a local Afro-American, James Chaney, disappeared. Although their badly beaten bodies were not discovered for six weeks, certainty that they had been murdered swept the country and helped precipitate the passage of a long-pending civil rights bill in Congress. In Mississippi, the murders shook the project profoundly. Surrounded by threats and violence, the workers resented the lack of federal protection and the slowness of the investigation. Distrust grew between white and black workers; would the public outcry have been the same, some asked, if all three victims had been black?

The Mississippi project did establish fifty Freedom Schools to carry on community organizing, but it managed to register only twelve hundred Afro-Americans. Another blow came in August when, with the acquiescence of party liberals and civil rights leaders, the Democratic National Convention refused to seat a protest slate of delegates elected through COFO's Mississippi Freedom Democratic party.

The events of Freedom Summer deepened the division between those in the civil rights movement who still believed in integration and nonviolence and others, especially young Afro-Americans, who now doubted whether racial equality was achievable by peaceful means. The civil rights movement continued to be active, but after 1964, it began to lose the hopeful solidarity that had infused its earlier years.

See also Civil Rights Movement.

FREE NEGROES, 1619–1860

In 1860, roughly half a million free people of African descent resided in the United States. Known alternately as free Negroes, free blacks, free people of color, or simply free people (to distinguish them from post–Civil War freedpeople), they composed less than 2 percent of the nation's population and about 9 percent of all blacks. Although the free black population was increasing during the antebellum years, it was growing far more slowly than either the white or the slave population, so that it was a shrinking proportion of American society.

But free Negroes were important far beyond their numbers. They played a pivotal role in society during slave times and set precedents for both race relations and relations among black people when slavery ended. Their status and treatment were harbingers of the postemancipation world. Often the laws, attitudes, and institutions that victimized free blacks during the slave years — political proscription, segregation, and various forms of debt peonage — became the dominant modes of racial oppression once slavery ended. Similarly, their years of liberty profoundly influenced the pattern of postemancipation black life. They moved in disproportionate numbers into positions of leadership in black society when slavery ended. For example, nearly half of the twenty-two black men who served in Congress between 1869 and 1900 had been free before the Civil War.

Although free Negroes have been described as more black than free, they were not a monolithic group. They can be best understood from a regional perspective, for by the nineteenth century three distinctive groups of free Negroes had developed: one in the northern, or free states, a second in the Upper South, and a third in the Lower South. Each had its own demographic, economic, social, and somatic characteristics. These differences, in turn, bred different relations with whites and slaves and, most important, distinctive modes of social action.

The American Revolution transformed the North from a slave to a free society, greatly enlarging its free Negro population. Although slavery died hard in the northern states, postrevolutionary emancipation ensured that eventually all northern blacks would be free. To their number were added numerous immigrants from the South, most of them fugitive slaves. In 1860, about a quarter of a million blacks, slightly less than half of the nation's free Negroes, lived in the free states. But universal emancipation left them in much the same conditions as before. Slaves in the North had been disproportionately urban in residence, black in color, and unskilled in occupation. Free Negroes followed that pattern, becoming in fact more urban and unskilled during the antebellum years, as they increasingly migrated to cities and found themselves pushed out of artisan trades by European immigrants.

Nevertheless, postrevolutionary emancipation allowed blacks certain rights. Because the abolition of slavery freed northern whites from the fear of slave revolts, they did not look upon every gathering of blacks as the beginning of a revolution. They limited the political rights of free Negroes, but they allowed them to travel freely, organize their own institutions, publish newspapers, and petition and protest. Black men and women transformed these liberties into a powerful organizational and political tradition. From Richard Allen to Frederick Douglass, their primary mode of social action was organizing institutions to protect themselves from the rigors of the white world and to demand an end to slavery.

As in the North, the free Negro in the Upper South was largely a product of the American Revolution. But in this region the ideas and events of the revolutionary era only loosened the fabric of slavery by increasing manumission, self-purchase, and successful suits for freedom. Nevertheless, the free black population grew rapidly, so that by 1810 the Upper South contained nearly 100,000 free Negroes, who composed about 8 percent of the black population in the region and almost 60 percent of free blacks in the United States. Thereafter repression slowed the growth of their numbers, and the proportion of free blacks living in the region declined.

The free Negro population in the Upper South was the product of two patterns of manumissions. The first and most important occurred on a large scale and was indiscriminate and rooted in ideological and economic changes; the second, smaller and more selective, originated in personal relations between master and slave. The first wave of manumissions produced a population that, like the slave population, was largely rural and black in color. To the extent, however, that postrevolutionary emancipation was selective — masters choosing whom they would free — it produced a free Negro population that was more skilled and lighter in color than that of the North. In the course of the nineteenth century, manumission became even more selective, so that free people of the Upper South became increasingly skilled in occupation, urban in residence, and light in skin color. The absence of large-scale European immigration to the slave states and a long-standing reliance on black labor allowed these blacks to enjoy a higher economic standing than those in the free states. In cities like Nashville and Richmond, a quarter to a third of free Negro men practiced skilled trades.

But if the presence of slavery helped elevate their economic status, it severely limited their opportunities for political or communal activism, for southern whites looked upon free Negroes as the chief inspiration and instigators of slave unrest. Whites not only prevented blacks from voting, sitting on juries, and testifying in court but also barred them from traveling without permission and meeting without the supervision of whites. These constraints circumscribed their political and organizational opportunities. No black newspapers were published and no black conventions met in the South. There were no southern counterparts of Allen or Douglass. Black churches, schools, and fraternal societies were fragile organizations, often forced to meet clandestinely. With limited political outlets, blacks poured their energies into economic opportunities and, as tradesmen and artisans, made considerable gains.

This tendency toward economic advancement at the expense of political activism was present in an even more exaggerated form in the Lower South, particularly the port cities of Charleston, Mobile, and New Orleans. These areas were largely untouched by the egalitarian thrust of the American Revolution. Free Negroes there were a product not of ideologically inspired manumission but of paternalistic relations between masters and slaves. Almost all free Negroes were drawn from the small group of privileged slaves who had lived in close contact with their owners. Often these connections bespoke family ties. As a result, former slaves were overwhelmingly urban and light skinned, earning them the title "free people of color," or in New Orleans *gens de couleur*. Although comparatively few in number, most were far more skilled than free Negroes in the Upper South. In some places, like Charleston and New Orleans, over three-quarters of the free men of color practiced skilled crafts, and they monopolized some trades. A handful of wealthy free people of color purchased slaves and moved into the planter class.

As in the Upper South, the presence of slavery prevented Lower South free people of color from translating their higher economic standing into social and political gains. Denied suffrage and proscribed from office, they found a political voice only by acting through white patrons — their manumittors, customers, and occasionally fathers. Their own organizations remained private, exclusive, and often shadowy, especially in comparison to the robust public institutions created by black people in the North. Although some were well traveled and highly educated, as much at home in Paris and Glasgow as in New Orleans and Charleston, they dared not attack slavery or racial inequality publicly. Many feared to identify with slaves in any fashion. Rather, they saw themselves — and increasingly came to be seen by whites — as a third caste, distinct from both free whites and enslaved blacks.

With the general emancipation of 1863, free Negroes carried their diverse histories into freedom. Although Civil War emancipation liquidated their special status, their collective experience continued to shape American race relations and Afro-American life.

Ira Berlin, *Slaves without Masters: The Free Negro in the Antebellum South* (1974); Leon F. Litwack, *North of Slavery: The Negro in the Free States, 1790–1860* (1965).

IRA BERLIN

See also Allen, Richard; Banneker, Benjamin; Cuffe, Paul; Delany, Martin R.; Douglass, Frederick; Jones, Absalom; Truth, Sojourner; Tubman, Harriet; Walker, David.

FREEPORT DOCTRINE

Senator Stephen A. Douglas enunciated this policy at Freeport, Illinois, on August 27, 1858, during one of his celebrated debates with Abraham Lincoln. Lincoln had asked in the wake of the *Dred Scott* decision, "Can the people of a United States Territory, in any lawful way, against the wish of any citizen of the United States, exclude slavery from its limits prior to the formation of a State Constitution?"

Lincoln knew how his opponent would reply because Douglas already had stated his position. Lincoln's purpose was to show antislavery voters that Douglas's position differed from their own. A longtime advocate of popular sovereignty, Douglas had broken with James Buchanan's administration over its preference for the proslavery Lecompton constitution in Kansas. Because this split had cost the "Little Giant" from Illinois his chance for southern support at the forthcoming Democratic presidential convention in 1860, Douglas could repeat his previous statements in the form of the Freeport Doctrine: "Slavery cannot exist a day in the midst of an unfriendly people with unfriendly laws." In appealing to a middle ground on slavery, Douglas restated his stand in behalf of popular sovereignty and defied the *Dred Scott* ruling. Thus, Douglas went too far for the South, which began to push harder for a territorial slave code, but not far enough for northerners who opposed slavery.

See also Douglas, Stephen A.; Lincoln-Douglas Debates; Popular Sovereignty.

FREE-SOIL PARTY

This short-lived organization affected and was affected by the second party system. Several related events produced it. New York Democrats had split between the Hunkers, who were ambivalent about or supported slavery, and the Barnburners, who opposed the institution. The national party divided in 1844 when southern Democrats pushed through the presidential nomination of Tennessean James K. Polk over the nominally antislavery Martin Van Buren, the party's leader and Andrew Jackson's protégé. Meanwhile, the antislavery Liberty party had twice nominated slaveholder-turned-abolitionist James G. Birney for president; in 1844 he diverted enough of New York's votes from Whig Henry Clay, who had waffled over the slavery issue, to throw the election to Polk.

When Democrats denied Van Buren the nomination in 1848, his supporters teamed with many Liberty men and antislavery Whigs and Democrats to form the Free-Soil party. It nominated Van Buren for president and Charles Francis Adams of Massachusetts for vice president. In 1852, the party chose abolitionist senator John P. Hale for president. It never won an electoral vote, but it garnered enough popular votes to help throw the 1848 election to Zachary Taylor, and in 1852 it reflected the divisions in the Whig party. With the Kansas-Nebraska Act of 1854, many former Free-Soilers, such as Salmon Chase and Charles Sumner, joined the Republicans, helping build the party and forming part of its radical branch.

See also Elections: 1848, 1852; Sumner, Charles; Van Buren, Martin.

FRENCH AND INDIAN WAR

See Colonial Wars; Seven Years' War.

FRENCH AND SPANISH SETTLEMENTS

The European colonization of North America did not begin at Jamestown or Plymouth Rock. Norse sagas suggest, and recent archaeology seems to confirm, that Viking explorers spent several years in "Vinland" (probably Newfoundland) shortly after A.D. 1000. Five centuries later the Spaniards who followed Christopher Columbus to the "Indies" began venturing outward from the Caribbean islands in search of gold, slaves, and a route to Cathay. In 1513 Juan Ponce de León, sailing from Puerto Rico, encountered and named Florida, which he assumed to be another island. His voyage marks the beginning of continuous European contact with North America.

Within the next decade the Europeans learned that the Gulf of Mexico offered no westward passage, that the Aztecs possessed great wealth, and that Ferdinand Magellan's southwestern passage to the Far East was long and arduous. All this prompted a generation of probing north of Mexico, by sea and land. In 1524 Giovanni da Verrazano cruised the Atlantic Coast, failing to find any Northwest Passage to the Pa-

cific but establishing a claim for the French king, who sent Jacques Cartier on similar missions to explore the St. Lawrence a decade later. In 1541 Cartier returned to establish the colony of Charlesbourg-Royal. The site near modern Quebec lay south of Paris in latitude, but the winters proved far colder and the French withdrew.

At the same time the rival Spanish were penetrating the continent from the south, hoping to find rich cities or a sea lane to China. Francisco Coronado, spurred on by the report of Álvar Cabeza de Vaca, explored the southwest as far north as Kansas (1540–1542), and Juan Cabrillo and Bartolomé Ferrelo sailed north along the California coast (1542–1543). Simultaneously Hernando de Soto led a large expedition through the southeastern interior, spreading disease and destruction but finding no immediate wealth (1539–1542). When France later placed a colony of Huguenot exiles at Fort Caroline on Florida's St. Johns River, the Spanish promptly wiped out these anti-Catholic refugees in 1565 and founded their own outpost at St. Augustine that same year.

This first permanent settlement of Europeans and Africans provided protection for the gold fleet that sailed from Havana to Spain each spring. It also provided a base for missionaries and traders who explored as far north as Appalachia and Chesapeake Bay, establishing outposts in the Sea Islands and across northern Florida. With England's creation of Carolina in the 1660s and Georgia in the 1730s, St. Augustine became a launching site for attacks on these Protestant rivals and a refuge for Indians fleeing English slaving raids and Africans escaping plantation slavery. A massive stone fort was constructed and a sizable garrison community evolved in its vicinity, exchanging goods with Caribbean ports and receiving occasional coastal traders from the English colonies eager to obtain hard currency from the Spanish. But even including the western outposts at San Marcos de Apalache and Pensacola, the multiracial Florida colony remained small; it had fewer than four thousand inhabitants when ceded to the English in 1763. (Florida was returned to Spain twenty years later and finally sold to the United States in 1819.)

Although Spain held onto Florida, it could not prevent rival powers from creating settlements to the north. Besides the English, the Dutch controlled the Hudson River Valley for much of the seventeenth century, and a Swedish colony occupied Delaware Bay for a shorter time. But the greatest domain was that of the French, who asserted control over the St. Lawrence Valley. Samuel de Champlain founded Quebec in 1608, and Montreal was created farther upstream in 1642; New France had more than five thousand colonists by 1672. The next year Father Jacques Marquette and Louis Joliet located the Mississippi, and by 1682 Sieur de la Salle had descended the river to the Gulf of Mexico and claimed its entire watershed for Louis XIV.

La Salle's effort to found a colony on the Mississippi failed, and the French did not gain a foothold on the gulf until Sieur d'Iberville brought colonists to Biloxi in 1699. This new French presence not only challenged the Spanish in Florida and New Spain; it also anchored a line of posts from Detroit to Mobile that encircled British coastal settlements. Plantations were carved out along the Lower Mississippi with black labor imported from the Caribbean, and interior trading posts were established at Fort Toulouse in Alabama and at Natchitoches on the Red River. But the colony never became fully self-sufficient, and by the 1760s Louisiana still contained scarcely ten thousand settlers. This included more than five thousand enslaved Africans and the earliest Cajuns, or Acadians — recent refugees from Nova Scotia.

French Canada also remained thinly populated, with most inhabitants farming on long narrow *seigneuries* stretching back from the St. Lawrence between Montreal and Quebec. Others traveled far into the interior as *coureurs du bois* to bargain with Indians for furs, a trade that proved profitable enough to shape the region's economy. England's seaboard colonies, in contrast, developed more diverse economies and much larger populations, and after mid-century the English victory over France in the Seven Years' War forced the French to give up Canada to the British and Louisiana to the Spanish in 1763. Though Napoleon regained the vast Loui-siana Territory for France in 1800, Jefferson purchased it for the United States in 1803.

Spain's southwestern colonies, from Texas to California, endured longer than the colonies of France and had an equally lasting influence upon North American culture. The earliest and largest involved New Mexico, founded in the upper Rio Grande Valley by Juan de Oñate in 1598, after the brutal suppression of the Pueblo Indians. The Spanish established Santa Fe as the capital in 1610, and a small contingent of soldiers, priests, and settlers held sway over the much larger Native American population in the region until the Pueblo Revolt of 1680. This uprising, the largest successful rebellion against European domination in North American history, drove the Spanish south for more than a decade and prompted the rapid dissemination of Spanish horses among Indians of the Great Plains during the next three generations.

Before 1700 the Spanish had reconquered New Mexico and were extending their explorations on both sides of the Rio Grande. In the east, troubled by the French incursion into Louisiana, the Spanish sent Franciscans into Texas, where they founded San Antonio in 1718 — the same year the French founded New Orleans. In the west the Jesuit Father Eusebio Kino explored Arizona and demonstrated that California was not an island, as many Europeans had thought. But it was not until 1768, the year the Jesuits were expelled from New Spain, that plans were finalized to occupy Alta California above the peninsula. While the English colonies struggled for their independence on the Atlantic Coast, Spanish soldiers and Franciscan missionaries (under Father Junípero Serra) established a string of outposts on the Pacific, including San Diego (1769), Monterey (1770), San Francisco (1776), San Jose (1777), Los Angeles (1781), and Santa Barbara (1782).

Fear of rival encroachment motivated this thrust, for Vitus Bering had claimed Alaska for Russia in 1741. Besides the Russians, the English too had designs on the Northwest Coast, especially after Capt. James Cook, making a final search for the western end of the fabled Northwest Passage in 1778, discovered that sea otter pelts purchased from Nootka Indians on Vancouver Island could be sold in China at great profit. Although the Spanish claimed Nootka Sound for themselves, they could not defend the claim against British and American fur traders. Nor, farther south, could they sustain their hold on the vast American West, giving it up piece by piece to American soldiers and settlers over the course of the nineteenth century.

John Francis Bannon, *The Spanish Borderlands Frontier, 1513–1821* (1970); W. J. Eccles, *France in America* (1972).

PETER H. WOOD

See also Colonial Wars; Exploration of North America; Indians; Missionaries; Serra, Junípero; Slavery; Southern Colonies.

FRICK, HENRY CLAY

(1849–1919), industrialist and art collector. Born in Westmoreland County, Pennsylvania, the son of an impecunious farmer, Clay was determined to escape the poverty of his unambitious father and sought to emulate his maternal grandfather, Abraham Overholt, a successful whiskey distiller and the wealthiest man in the county. Nor did Frick have far to look to find a source for the wealth he desperately wanted, for under the thin topsoil of this region lay thousands of acres of soft coal, ideally suited for making coke, an essential ingredient in the production of Bessemer steel.

After a few years of schooling, Frick became a grocery clerk and then a bookkeeper in his grandfather's distillery. Every penny he could save or borrow was invested in the purchase of land and the building of coke ovens. Taking advantage of low prices during the 1870s depression and with the financial backing of Thomas Mellon, Frick by 1880 had emerged as the Coke King of Pennsylvania.

He had also attracted the attention of Andrew Carnegie, the acknowledged Steel King of America. On a wedding trip to New York in 1881, Frick and his bride, Adelaide Childs, met Carnegie at a dinner. Carnegie surprised the guests by proposing a partnership with Frick, which the latter quickly accepted. From that moment, the two men's destinies were joined, and

both were to profit immensely from the union. Carnegie gained control of the coke his steel mills needed and in Frick found the able general manager of operations he had long sought. Frick, in turn, now had a partnership in Carnegie Steel and the capital he needed for further expansion.

Both shared the same views in building an industrial empire: cut costs and reinvest profits in plant expansion rather than pay out big dividends. Frick proved to be even more daring than Carnegie in seeking vertical integration. It was he who persuaded his reluctant senior partner to seize an opportunity to lease the rich Mesabi iron range lands owned by John D. Rockefeller.

In temperament, however, the two men were polar opposites. Frick was as taciturn and antisocial as Carnegie was voluble and gregarious. Frick scorned Carnegie's frequent pronouncements on the rights of labor and the social responsibility of wealth as foolish, if not hypocritical. A break between the two was inevitable.

It began with the Homestead strike of 1892. Although Frick was simply carrying out Carnegie's instructions to break the union at that plant, Carnegie never forgave him for the bloodshed that resulted when Pinkerton strikebreakers were brought in. Carnegie tried to shift the blame for the massacre onto Frick, but the latter won public sympathy by being nearly assassinated by the anarchist Alexander Berkman.

The final break occurred in 1900 when Frick sought to end the special pricing agreement between Carnegie Steel and the Frick Coke Company. In retaliation, Carnegie demanded that Frick sell his 11 percent interest in Carnegie Steel at its grossly undervalued book value. Frick fought back and won. He kept his steel stock, and when Carnegie the following year sold out to a syndicate headed by J. P. Morgan, Frick played a prominent role as director of the newly created United States Steel Corporation.

Although generally regarded as a tough entrepreneur whose only interest was in business, Frick was far more complex than most associates realized. Within his family he was warm and affectionate, and in his avid collecting of European art, he expressed a surprising appreciation for aesthetic values. He left to the American people one of the country's finest art collections, housed in his mansion on Fifth Avenue and richly endowed for its maintenance.

George Harvey, *Henry Clay Frick: The Man* (1936); Joseph Frazier Wall, *Andrew Carnegie* (1989).

JOSEPH FRAZIER WALL

See also Carnegie, Andrew; Homestead Strike; Iron and Steel Industry.

FRIEDAN, BETTY

(1921–), catalyst and leader in the second feminist movement. Friedan graduated summa cum laude from Smith College in 1942 and settled in New York City. During the ten years after her marriage to Carl Friedan in 1947, she was a housewife, mother of three children, and free-lance magazine writer.

Friedan's role as catalyst of the second feminist wave began with her book, *The Feminine Mystique.* For her fifteenth college reunion in 1957 she sent questionnaires to members of her class asking them to describe their lives since college. From their answers and other research came the book, which she published in 1963. It was an instant best-seller, was excerpted in major women's magazines, and made Friedan a celebrity. Its thesis that suburban middle-class housewives were not necessarily fulfilled by housewifery and childbearing engendered hundreds of letters from unhappy, dissatisfied women who realized that Friedan had identified their "problem with no name." She called it the "feminine mystique," the theory that women's fulfillment could be found only in motherhood and family. She criticized psychiatrists, social scientists, educators, and businesspeople who used the mystique to encourage women to live segregated lives in the suburban ghettos of the postwar world.

In 1966 she helped found the National Organization for Women (NOW). As president during its first three years, she wrote NOW's founding statement demanding full equality for women in the mainstream of American life. She also led the organization in its decisions in 1967 to support the Equal Rights Amendment for women and legalized abortion. During her presidency, she traveled across the country publicizing the new feminism and NOW and encouraged its older members to listen to the younger, more radical feminists. When she stepped down from the presidency in 1969, she suggested that NOW sponsor a national strike on August 26, 1970, to commemorate the fiftieth anniversary of women's obtaining the vote. An attempt to broaden the feminist movement, it succeeded far beyond her expectations: the New York rally alone attracted fifty thousand women.

Initially Friedan and other feminists criticized women's role as primary caretaker of the family because they believed that status and success could be achieved only through work outside the home. But by the 1980s, she and others had come to believe that women *and* men desire both the prestige and fulfillment that come from work outside the home and the love and identity gained through marriage and children. In *The Second Stage* (1981) Friedan argued that feminism had become too woman-centered in the 1970s and had polarized the relationship between the sexes. She urged feminists to move away from this stance and join with men and even conservatives on these new family issues.

Betty Friedan, *The Feminine Mystique* (1963) and *The Second Stage* (1981).

FRANCES ARICK KOLB

See also Equal Rights Amendment; Feminist Movement; National Organization for Women.

FROST, ROBERT

(1874–1963), poet and critic. Although Frost is closely linked with the New England region, it was in England that he published his first collections, *A Boy's Will* (1913) and *North of Boston* (1914). He and his wife and children had moved there in 1912 after Frost had been unable to make a living in a variety of occupations or to find a publisher for his poems in the United States.

The son of an alcoholic and sporadically brutal father who died early, leaving his family in poverty, Frost had had a difficult childhood, and this was reflected in his financial and emotional problems after his school years. Clearly a depressive, he funneled his energies into his art.

While living in England, he found companionship among the post-Georgian poets there and was admired by such critics and poets as Ezra Pound, Amy Lowell, and Ford Madox Ford. His work, distinctive in its combination of traditional form with a unique, recognizable voice, coincided with the aesthetic movement known as imagism, and young experimental poets were glad to claim his work as a corollary to theirs.

Most readers responded more readily to Frost's poetry, however, because it was still sonorous and presented a meaning, a moral. His poetry was not simple, nor did it oversimplify the problems of the twentieth century. It spoke of despair, of endurance, of failure — of life as many readers had experienced it. And it was accessible. It played by poetic rules that readers recognized; it often had rhyme, rhythm, stanza organization that reinforced meaning, and key symbols that expressed more than the literal sense of the poem. It was art that readers could meditate on. Such poems as "Mending Wall," "After Apple-Picking," "The Road Not Taken," "An Old Man's Winter Night" (with its chilling opening line, "All out-of-doors looked darkly in at him"), "Birches," "Fire and Ice," "Stopping by Woods on a Snowy Evening," "Desert Places," "Acquainted with the Night," "The Need of Being Versed in Country Things," "Design," "Nothing Gold Can Stay," "The Death of the Hired Man," and others became a permanent part of America's literary heritage.

When Frost returned to the United States in 1915, he was a significant modern poet. The life he then led in New England — farming, teaching, giving readings, in spite of what was still a difficult family life because of children's illnesses and death — enabled him to become one of America's most important poets. No other writer has received four Pulitzer Prizes for poetry or the number of accolades from universities and foundations that Frost did. The public Frost — humorous, witty, nonintellectual — was quite different from the real Frost — well educated, cynical, and sometimes cruel — but the tensions and conflicts of his life seem to have been resolved in the high polish of his distinctive poems.

Frost taught at Amherst, Harvard, and the University of Michigan, and won his Pulitzers for *New Hampshire* (1923), *Collected Poems* (1930), *A Further Range* (1936), and *A Witness Tree* (1942). His poems reflect his move toward the universal, toward a fuller understanding as a person as well as a writer. Among his last works were two blank-verse plays, *A Masque of Reason* (1945) and *A Masque of Mercy* (1947) (a form that allowed more complete statements of the problems of life and death), and his 1962 collection, *In the Clearing*. In 1961, John F. Kennedy invited Frost to read a poem at his inauguration; Frost also served as consultant in poetry to the Library of Congress and was awarded a Senate resolution on his eighty-fifth birthday. In 1963 he received the Bollingen Prize for poetry.

James M. Cox, ed., *Robert Frost: A Collection of Critical Essays* (1962); Richard Poirier, *Robert Frost* (1989); Lawrance Thompson, *Robert Frost: The Early Years, 1874–1915, Robert Frost: The Years of Triumph, 1915–1938,* and, with R. H. Winnick, *Robert Frost: The Later Years, 1938–1963* (1966–1976).

LINDA WAGNER-MARTIN

See also Expatriates and Exiles; Literature.

FTC

See Federal Trade Commission.

FUGITIVE SLAVE LAW

This measure was the most controversial part of the Compromise of 1850. It called for federal commissioners to be appointed and given authority to issue warrants, gather posses, and force citizens to help catch runaway slaves under penalty of a fine or imprisonment. Accused runaways were denied both a jury trial and the right to testify in their own behalf. They could be sent to the South on the basis of a supposed owner's affidavit. Also working against the accused's chances for freedom was the fee to be paid to the commissioners to decide each case: they received ten dollars for returning the fugitive to the claimant, five dollars if they freed the person.

The Fugitive Slave Law of 1850 served to inject the reality of slavery more forcefully into the everyday lives of many northerners. Abolitionists decried the cases of blacks, long free, who were torn from their families and forced into slavery. Mobs in several northern cities cowed federal commissioners into ruling in favor of accused fugitives or stopped slave owners and their agents from returning to the South with their human cargo. Some northern states passed new personal liberty laws designed to prevent state officials from enforcing the act. The Supreme Court upheld the law's constitutionality and, in the Wisconsin case of *Ableman* v. *Booth,* ruled that states had no right to circumvent or contradict a federal law.

See also Ableman v. *Booth;* Slavery.

FULLER, MARGARET

(1810–1850), author and revolutionary. Born into a politically prominent Massachusetts family, Fuller was educated at local academies and became a teacher at an early age. She took over as head of the family upon the death of her father in 1835 and postponed her plans for European travel, a dream from her childhood years. In 1836 she met Ralph Waldo Emerson who became a close friend and introduced her to a wide circle of intellectuals, including the transcendentalists. In 1839 she launched a new career by holding "Conversations," as she called her discussion forums attended by prominent bluestockings at a Boston bookstore. These meetings earned her a formidable reputation, and in 1840 she was invited by Emerson, Henry David Thoreau, and other prominent New England literati to edit their journal, the *Dial.* She also taught at an experimental academy run by fellow transcendentalist Bronson Alcott.

When she published her first book, an account of travel through the Great Lakes and Wisconsin, she caught the attention of editor Horace Greeley, who in 1844 hired her for his *New York Tribune.* Fuller became the first female journalist for a major newspaper.

In 1845 her book, *Woman in the Nineteenth Century,* gained her a wide audience and became a classic interpretation of women's lives during this era. Fuller's argument that women had a universal sacred right to develop their individual natures stemmed from transcendental philosophy, but her radical call to collective action, her attack upon the sexual double standard, and her endorsement of women's entrance into the public sphere earned her a feminist reputation.

In 1846 Greeley sent Fuller to Europe to cover the revolutions in the making; she was thus one of the first official foreign correspondents for the American press. Fuller worked in England, France — where she became friends with George Sand — and Italy, which became her adopted homeland. In her dispatches to New York she chronicled events, sketched portraits of leaders, reported the pulse of the people, and clarified the political conflicts of the time for her American audience.

In 1847, while in Rome, she became involved with an Italian revolutionary, Giovanni Ossoli, and her reports became more partisan. By 1848 with movements for revolution sparking uprisings across the continent (Paris in February, Venice in March), Fuller found herself committed to the cause of a free Roman republic and, what was more, pregnant by Ossoli. She withdrew from the city to give birth to a son in September 1848 and then left the infant behind to join Ossoli on the barricades in November. When Rome fell to invading French troops sent to restore the pope's authority, Ossoli, Fuller, and their child moved to Florence. Fearful of police surveillance, the couple set sail for America in May of 1850, with Fuller determined to stir up support for Italian liberation with a manuscript she was preparing, her history of the revolution. Within sight of America, the ship sank off the coast of Fire Island. Fuller, Ossoli, and the manuscript disappeared; only her son's body was recovered.

Canonized by her transcendentalist circle and celebrated by American feminists, Fuller has been the subject of intense debate. The assessment of her legacy varies from generation to generation and scholar to scholar, but her vision of a life fully lived clearly was well ahead of her time.

Bell Gale Chevigny, *The Woman and the Myth: Margaret Fuller's Life and Writings* (1976); Robert N. Hudspeth, ed., *The Letters of Margaret Fuller,* 4 vols. to date (1983–).

CATHERINE CLINTON

See also Feminist Movement; Transcendentalism.

FULTON, ROBERT

(1765–1815), engineer and artist. Fulton did not invent the steamboat, but he designed and built the first commercially successful one. His genius lay in putting the ideas of others to practical use.

Fulton was born in New Britain, Pennsylvania, not far from Lancaster. He early showed a marked mechanical and artistic aptitude, building a skyrocket in his teens to celebrate Independence Day and designing a human-powered paddle-wheel boat to make fishing expeditions with his friends easier.

Fulton learned the art of gunsmithing but was apprenticed to a Philadelphia jeweler. In 1785 he went into business for himself as a "miniature painter and hair worker," at which he succeeded so well he was able to buy his mother a farm before setting off for England in 1786. There, like many aspiring American artists, he studied painting under Benjamin West but abandoned art for engineering a few years later.

In 1796 he published his *Treatise on the Improvement of Canal Navigation* and tried unsuccessfully to interest the American government, and then the French, in his canal proposals. He moved to France in 1797, where he submitted plans for a submarine by which, he argued, France could overcome Britain's naval supremacy. He built the *Nautilus* in 1800, and it worked better than any previous submarine, although in many ways it was modeled on one designed by David Bushnell in 1776. The *Nautilus* was reconstructed and improved the following year, but the French government still rejected the project.

Fulton turned his energies then to steamboats and, with financing from Robert Livingston, the American minister to Paris, built an experimental vessel in 1803 that operated on the Seine. The following year the British government, well aware of Fulton's activities (having been kept informed by Fulton himself), invited him to return to Britain and experiment there. But after winning the Battle of Trafalgar in 1805, the British Admiralty lost interest in new naval weapons, and Fulton returned to the United States.

His friend Robert Livingston had also returned by that time and had been granted a monopoly of steamboat navigation in New York waters. The pair ordered a boat powered by a twenty-eight-horsepower steam engine manufactured by James Watt's firm in England. It was launched on August 9, 1807, and on August 17 it made the trip from New York City to Albany in thirty-two hours, far faster than a sailing vessel could travel with any regularity. The vessel was rebuilt the following year, lengthened to 149 feet and named *The North River Steamboat of Clermont.* The press promptly shortened this to *Clermont,* by which name the vessel is known to history.

Fulton and Livingston built several other steamboats for the Hudson as well as ferries to connect Manhattan with New Jersey and Long Island. Fulton also designed the first steamboat to operate on the Mississippi.

Fulton's last major project was a floating fortress for New York Harbor. It was launched shortly before the end of the War of 1812, but never saw action. Fulton died in New York City.

James T. Flexner, *Steamboats Come True* (1944).

JOHN STEELE GORDON

See also Transportation Revolution.

FUNDAMENTAL CONSTITUTIONS OF CAROLINA

The Fundamental Constitutions of Carolina were adopted in March 1669 by the eight proprietors of Carolina, a patent from Charles II comprising most of the land between present-day Virginia and Florida. Carolina was first governed under a document entitled Concessions and Agreements (1665), which granted an elected assembly, freedom of conscience, and substantial land distribution (subject to payment of an annual quitrent to the proprietors). In 1669, however, the proprietors issued the more elaborate Fundamental Constitutions.

This document is believed to have been drafted, though not conceived, by John Locke, who served for many years as physician and secretary to one of the proprietors, Sir Anthony Ashley Cooper (later earl of Shaftesbury). The new document guaranteed religious freedom (though a 1670 revision established the Church of England), and it assured the use of militia rather than a standing army for defense. But its basic tendency was aristocratic, since it proposed to create a quasi-feudal structure of hereditary nobility, freeholders, serfs, and slaves. Under the initial plan, all legislative power would reside in the nobility; a later revision proposed a bicameral legislature, but the upper house, controlled by the nobility, would retain sole power to initiate legislation.

The proprietors revised the Fundamental Constitutions several times, but the plan was never accepted by the assembly, and none of the designed seignories or baronies was ever created. The colonists continued to resist proprietary direction. By 1700 the Constitutions had been abandoned, and within twenty years the last proprietary governor had been overthrown.

See also Southern Colonies.

FUNDAMENTALISM

See Evangelicalism.

G

GADSDEN PURCHASE

This land acquisition of the 1850s marked the end of continental expansion in America. It helped settle the direction of a proposed southern route for a transcontinental railroad, but it also became caught up in the sectional conflict.

James Gadsden, who had long promoted a transcontinental route from the South to the Pacific, had been President Franklin Pierce's choice as minister to Mexico. A railroad executive from South Carolina, Gadsden was instructed to obtain land in the Gila River region in present-day New Mexico and Arizona for the southern route. He also could negotiate for Lower California, a port on the Gulf of California, and what remained of northern Mexico after the Mexican War. The Pierce administration authorized Gadsden to offer Antonio Santa Anna, Mexico's dictator, up to $50 million for the 250,000 square miles.

Gadsden was partly successful. The Senate first turned down the treaty; some southerners felt the United States received too little land, whereas many northerners opposed buying potential slave territory. The Gadsden Purchase passed the Senate only after administration supporters cut the acquisition by 9,000 square miles. For $15 million, Mexico gave up 55,000 square miles in what are now southern New Mexico and Arizona. The nation had completed what became the forty-eight contiguous states, and the Pierce administration had its only expansionist victory. But the sectional conflict had compelled the Senate for the first time to turn down a purchase of land.

See also Expansion, Continental and Overseas.

GAG RULE

Gag rule is a parliamentary device that permits legislative bodies to suppress or shorten debate. This rule was used by the House of Representatives from 1836 to 1844 to avoid debating the thousands of antislavery petitions being sent to northern congressmen. Southern legislators had come to interpret any debate of slavery as a hostile act, and many northerners, though personally opposed to slavery, were prepared to avoid the topic, either out of a belief that Congress had no rights in the matter or simply in the interests of political harmony. The petition movement, sponsored by the American Anti-Slavery Society, enraged the southerners and made it more difficult for northern politicians to remain silent. In addition, because the petitions focused on the District of Columbia, where Congress was the sole authority, the argument that slavery was a matter for the states to decide did not apply.

The Senate rejected the southerners' proposal that petitioning be prohibited but preserved harmony by denying each petition as it arrived. The House, however, adopted a gag rule on May 18, 1836, whereby all petitions related to slavery would automatically be tabled. This rule, which required renewal at each session, was allowed to lapse briefly when Congress opened in December 1837, but the immediate presentation of petitions on the House floor led to an even stricter gag rule, which was renewed annually for the next six years. Former president John Quincy Adams (now a congressman) had fought the gag rule from the first, and widespread public protests reinforced his arguments. Gradually, more and more northern congressmen came to feel that, whatever one's position on slavery, limiting citizens' right of petition was indefensible. In December 1844, the gag rule was rescinded.

In fact, the abolitionists had gained more from the gag rule than they had lost. They had frequently warned that the "slave power's" growing control of the federal government would ultimately destroy all Americans' liberties. By its demonstration of how efforts to placate the South led directly to the abridgment of constitutional rights, the gag rule made converts even among those who did not favor abolition.

See also Abolitionist Movement; House of Representatives.

GALARZA, ERNESTO

(1905–1984), labor organizer, historian, professor, and community activist. Galarza was a quintessential man of all seasons. He filled his diverse roles with a sense of responsibility and commitment. When once asked how he was able to do so much, his response was both practical and existential: "When I felt the need to be involved in labor organizing, I did that. When I wanted to write, I wrote."

Galarza's life, although atypical of the Mexican-American experience, also reflected various aspects of that experience. Like millions of other Mexican-Americans, Galarza was a child of an immigrant family. He was born near Tepic, the capital of the state of Nayarit, at the beginning of a great upheaval in Mexico that resulted in the Mexican Revolution of 1910. Dislocated by the revolution, the Galarza family migrated to the United States. After settling in Sacramento, Galarza began the process of acculturation into American life. The history of the young Ernesto was set down years later in his marvelous autobiography, *Barrio Boy* (1971). More fortunate than other Mexican-American children in his ability to adapt to the American public school system, Galarza became a successful "scholarship boy." After graduating from high school, he earned a B.A. from Occidental College in Los Angeles and then an M.A. in history from Stanford in 1929. He later received a Ph.D. from Columbia University with honors in history.

Galarza might easily have pursued a career as a scholar, but his commitment to social causes led him instead to work with the Pan-American Union from 1936 to 1947 where he dealt with education and labor in Latin America. In the post–World War II period, Galarza, seeing the plight of poor farm-working families in the United States and no doubt remembering his own family's labor in the fields of Sacramento, joined the National Farm Labor Union and returned to California. For the next several years, he worked at the difficult task of organizing farm labor in the face of bitter opposition from the large California growers. During this period he also researched the condition of the braceros, the Mexican contract workers in the California agricultural industry. This led him to write his most significant book, *Merchants of Labor* (1964), an exposé of the exploitation of braceros.

During the 1960s Galarza turned his attention to urban Mexican-Americans and the effort to organize community-based groups to deal with the many social problems in the barrios. A teacher at various universities, he was always concerned about education. During the last year of his life he worked in San Jose to improve the public school education provided to Mexican-American children.

Galarza's decision to address educational issues was perhaps the result of his awareness of how much his own educational success was, for the most part, an anomaly within the Mexican-American community. Historically, for most Mexican-Americans, public school education via the so-called Mexican schools had been a bad experience. These segregated schools in the barrios were characterized by inferior physical conditions, congestion, insensitive teachers, limited access to high school education until the 1930s, more emphasis on a vocational as opposed to an academic curriculum, and an unwillingness to relate to the culturally different child. By his own example, Galarza hoped to obtain for other Mexican-Americans the sort of education he had had.

Ernesto Galarza, *Barrio Boy* (1971); Ernesto Galarza, *Merchants of Labor: The Mexican Bracero Story* (1964); Ernesto Galarza, *Spiders in the House and Workers in the Field* (1970).

Mario T. García

See also Labor; Mexico-U.S. Relations.

GARBO, GRETA

(1905–1990), actress. Born Greta Lovisa Gustafsson in Stockholm, Sweden, Garbo as a child lived in poverty. After the death of her father, when she was fourteen, she went to work as a barber's assistant, lathering faces. Later she became a salesgirl at PUB, a Stockholm department store. Because of her exquisite features she modeled hats for a PUB catalog and in 1921 appeared in a short film promoting the store's clothes. In 1922 she made another short film advertising bakery products, played the female lead in a low-budget comedy film *Luffar-Petter* (Peter the Tramp), and won a scholarship to Stockholm's Royal Dramatic Theatre Academy.

While she was there, Sweden's foremost filmmaker, Mauritz Stiller, cast her as the female lead in his movie *Gösta Berling's Saga* (1924). Stiller took over her life in a relationship described as "Svengali and Trilby all over again" and changed her name to Garbo. Following the failure of a German-financed Turkish project, Stiller and Garbo went to Berlin where she played a lead in director G. W. Pabst's stark view of post–World War I Vienna, *Die Freudlose Gase* (The Joyless Street). Meanwhile, MGM signed Stiller and, at his insistence, Garbo, too. They arrived in Hollywood in 1925, but he floundered and returned to Sweden. She flourished, making twenty-four films (ten silent) before retiring in 1941.

Invariably, as in her first MGM film, *The Torrent* (1926), she played passionate, sensual, insecure women. Among her silents *Flesh and the Devil* (1927) especially thrilled audiences because of the apparently uninhibited romantic scenes with John Gilbert, with whom she was having a well-publicized affair. Garbo made the transition to sound successfully when MGM carefully packaged her in a well-received version of Eugene O'Neill's *Anna Christie* (1930). During 1931–1932, at the height of her American box-office power, MGM produced five Garbo films. But the profitability of her films increasingly depended on overseas earnings, and MGM allowed sixteen months to pass between the release of *Anna Karenina* (1935) and *Camille* (1937). Both roles won her New York Critics' Best Actress Awards and Academy Award nominations.

The outbreak of World War II in 1939 adversely affected Garbo's career because the markets supporting her movies were cut off. Her last films were the anticommunist satire *Ninotchka* (1939), which won her another Academy Award nomination, and the lackluster comedy *Two-Faced Women* (1941), a disastrous attempt to change her screen persona. Garbo never made another movie despite the many projects offered her. In the 1920s, MGM, unsure of how to promote her, had dubbed her "the Swedish Sphinx"; she turned P.R. into reality by becoming an increasingly private person. Although the press reported various romances, she never married. The frugal Garbo had been among MGM's highest paid stars (getting $250,000 a film in the mid-1930s), and having invested her money wisely, she had a comfortable retirement.

Garbo remains an icon from another era. Regarded, in Alistair Cooke's words, as "an unapproachable goddess," she retained her following and won new admirers as her films were shown on television and made available on videocassettes. Through her long retirement, she remained the prototypical movie star and in 1954 received a special Oscar for "her unforgettable screen performances."

John Bainbridge, *Garbo* (1971); Mark Ricci, *The Films of Greta Garbo* (1968); Frederick Sands and Sven Broman, *The Divine Garbo* (1979).

Daniel J. Leab

See also Movies.

GARFIELD, JAMES A.

(1831–1881), twentieth president of the United States. The once bright image of Garfield has dimmed with time so that now he seems merely another figure in that gray procession of bearded politicos that novelist Thomas Wolfe called "the lost Americans." This obscurity is compounded by the brevity of his administration — only two hundred days from his inauguration to his death at the hands of Charles J. Guiteau, an unhinged religious fanatic (*not* the "disappointed office seeker" of the familiar catchphrase). Yet to Garfield's contemporaries his sudden loss seemed a tragedy unmatched since the Civil War and they responded with an extravagant outburst of public mourning.

In so doing, they were commemorating not only the president but the man, whose life seemed to embody nineteenth-century American values. Born in a log cabin on the outskirts of Cleveland, Ohio, he was the last president to be blessed with that politically potent symbol of humble origins. Reared in rural poverty, he escaped by means of religion and education, becoming a minister in the Disciples of Christ church, the president of what would become Hiram College, and then a lawyer. When the Civil War broke out, he became the youngest major general in the Union army and then resigned his commission in midwar for a seat in the U.S. Congress. Touching as it did the familiar chords of Home, School, Church, Flag, and Country, his career encapsulated and even justified the most cherished values of his day. Horatio Alger himself was moved to write one of Garfield's campaign biographies.

Garfield brought to public life the moral fervor and scholarly discipline he had learned from the pulpit and the classroom, applying them especially to his crusade on behalf of hard money. An intellectual in politics, he also possessed a warm, amiable personality that commanded friendship and respect from most elements of his Republican party and even many Democratic opponents.

Despite being touched by the Crédit Mobilier and other scandals, he had become, by 1880, his party's leader in the House of Representatives and was ready to move on to the U.S. Senate to which he had just been elected, when his career took an unexpected turn. When the Republican National Convention deadlocked between the Stalwart supporters of Ulysses S. Grant and his rivals, the delegates turned to Garfield, nominating him on the thirty-sixth ballot. In November he defeated the Democratic candidate, Winfield Scott Hancock, by less than ten thousand popular votes.

Garfield's brief presidency was marred by a patronage struggle with Senator Roscoe Conkling, the embittered leader of the Stalwart faction. But victory in that struggle gave prestige not only to Garfield but to the institution of the presidency itself. There are indications that Garfield was planning to use that prestige to reorient the Republican party away from its preoccupation with the issues of Civil War and Reconstruction to a fresh emphasis on the new problems of an industrialized America when death intervened.

H. Wayne Morgan, *From Hayes to McKinley* (1969); Allan Peskin, *Garfield* (1978).

ALLAN PESKIN

See also Elections: 1880.

GARRISON, WILLIAM LLOYD

(1805–1879), abolitionist leader. Garrison rose from an impoverished childhood in Newburyport, Massachusetts, to national prominence as an advocate of the immediate abolition of slavery. Trained as a printer, Garrison was converted to "the cause of the slave" by Quaker Benjamin Lundy in 1828. A deeply religious Baptist, Garrison denounced slaveholding as an abomination in God's sight and demanded immediate, unqualified emancipation. After being jailed for libeling a slave trader, Garrison first published his famous *Liberator* in Boston on January 1, 1831. The *Liberator* through 1865 served as Garrison's personal vehicle for waging war against both slavery and his many critics, including abolitionists who questioned his zealous approach.

Garrison was a founder of the American Anti-Slavery Society in 1833. He wrote its *Declaration of Sentiments,* which demanded immediate emancipation and racial equality. The society took a nonviolent approach based on "moral suasion" — an appeal to the religious conscience of Americans. In the early 1830s Garrison developed an alliance with Great Britain's highly successful abolitionist movement. By the mid-1830s, he had gained a reputation for his scathingly denunciatory style and moral absolutism. He and his coworkers became the target of violence and political repression. Mobs broke up abolitionist meetings, and Andrew Jackson's administration did nothing when southerners removed antislavery materials from the federal mails. But this repression, in turn, brought publicity and sympathy to the abolitionist cause.

In the late 1830s, as the issue of slavery's westward expansion divided the nation's politicians, the American Anti-Slavery Society split over issues raised by Garrison's leadership. Many abolitionists objected to his growing advocacy of women's rights, Christian nonresistance, and a theology of Christian perfectionism. He, in turn, rejected the ideas put forward by many of his opponents that women should not be given political equality within the movement, and that abolitionists should become active in electoral politics. In 1840, after Garrison's opponents failed to purge him and his supporters from the American Anti-Slavery Society, they seceded to form their own organizations, the American and Foreign Anti-Slavery Society and the Liberty party.

From 1840 until 1865, Garrison retained control of a society much reduced in numbers but with women as full participants. By 1843, he had led the society to adopt the doctrine of "No Union with Slaveholders," insisting that abolitionists peacefully renounce their moral allegiances to an allegedly proslavery U.S. Constitution and political system. Concurrently, he and many of his followers cultivated a strident anticlericalism, condemning all religious denominations and ordained clergy as apologists for slaveholding. As leader of an unpopular minority of agitators, Garrison's measurable impact on the nation's politics was probably negligible in the 1840s and 1850s, and his symbolic status as the embodiment of abolitionist extremism and idealism continued to grow. But when the Civil War broke out, Garrison foreswore his disunionist pacifism and was soon hailed in the North as a prophet whose warnings had been confirmed by events.

A supporter of President Abraham Lincoln and the Republican party, Garrison parted company during the war with many of his colleagues, led by Wendell Phillips, who insisted that true emancipation of the slave required legal guarantees of suffrage and full civil rights. In 1865, when the Thirteenth Amendment secured the formal abolition of slavery, Garrison declared that his crusade had concluded in triumph and resigned from the American Anti-Slavery Society. The society carried on until 1870 under Phillips's direction.

James Brewer Stewart, *William Lloyd Garrison and the Challenge of Emancipation* (1991); John L. Thomas, *The Liberator William Lloyd Garrison: A Biography* (1963).

JAMES BREWER STEWART

See also Abolitionist Movement.

GARVEY, MARCUS

(1887–1940), black nationalist leader. Born in Jamaica, Garvey aimed to organize blacks everywhere but achieved his greatest impact in the United States, where he tapped into and enhanced the growing black aspirations for justice, wealth, and a sense of community. During World War I and the 1920s, his Universal Negro Improvement Association (UNIA) was the largest black secular organization in African-American history. Possibly a million men and women from the United States, the Caribbean, and Africa belonged to it.

Garvey came to New York in 1916 and concluded that the growing black communities in northern cities could provide the wealth and unity to end both imperialism in Africa and discrimination in the United States. He combined the economic nationalist ideas of Booker T. Washington and Pan-Africanists with the political possibilities and urban style of men and women living outside of plantation and colonial societies. Garvey's ideas gestated amid the social upheavals, anticolonial movements, and revolutions of World War I, which demonstrated the power of popular mobilization to change entrenched structures of power.

Garvey's goals were modern and urban. He

sought to end imperialist rule and create modern societies in Africa, not, as his critics charged, to transport blacks "back to Africa." He knitted black communities on three continents with his newspaper the *Negro World* and in 1919 formed the Black Star Line, an international shipping company to provide transportation and encourage trade among the black businesses of Africa and the Americas. In the same year, he founded the Negro Factories Corporation to establish such businesses. In 1920 he presided over the first of several international conventions of the UNIA. Garvey sought to channel the new black militancy into one organization that could overcome class and national divisions.

Although local UNIA chapters provided many social and economic benefits for their members, Garvey's main efforts failed: the Black Star Line suspended operations in 1922 and the other enterprises fared no better. Garvey's ambition and determination to lead inevitably collided with associates and black leaders in other organizations. His verbal talent and flair for the dramatic attracted thousands, but his faltering projects only augmented ideological and personality conflicts. In the end, he could neither unite blacks nor accumulate enough power to significantly alter the societies the UNIA functioned in.

Finally, the Justice Department, animated by J. Edgar Hoover's Federal Bureau of Investigation and sensing his growing weakness, indicted Garvey for mail fraud. He was convicted in 1923, imprisoned in 1925, and deported to Jamaica in 1927. Unable to resurrect the UNIA, he moved to London, where he died in 1940.

Garvey's movement was the first black attempt to join modern urban goals and mass organization. Although most subsequent leaders did not try to create black economic institutions as he had, Garvey had demonstrated to them that the urban masses were a potentially powerful force in the struggle for black freedom.

Robert Hill, ed., *The Marcus Garvey and Universal Negro Improvement Association Papers*, 10 vols. projected (1983–); Judith Stein, *The World of Marcus Garvey: Race and Class in Modern Society* (1986).

JUDITH STEIN

See also Africa-U.S. Relations; Black Nationalism; Black Power; Expatriates and Exiles; Washington, Booker T.

GATLING GUN

The Gatling gun is a machine gun that consists of multiple barrels revolving around a central axis and is capable of being fired at a rapid rate. Gen. Benjamin F. Butler of the Union army first used the gun at the siege of Petersburg, Virginia, in 1864–1865.

The gun is named for its inventor, Richard Jordan Gatling, a physician. Gatling neatly divided his sympathies during the Civil War. While trying to sell machine guns to the Union, he was an active member of the Order of American Knights, a secret group of Confederate sympathizers and saboteurs.

The conservatism of the Union army chief of ordinance and the unreliability of early models of the gun frustrated efforts to sell it to the U.S. Army. But Gatling soon improved on the original six-barrel, .58 caliber version of the gun, which fired 350 rounds a minute, by designing a ten-barrel, .30 caliber model, which fired 400 rounds a minute. The U.S. Army adopted the Gatling gun in 1866, and it remained standard until it was replaced in the early twentieth century by the Maxim single-barrel machine gun.

The Gatling gun played an important role after the Civil War, giving small numbers of U.S. troops enormous advantages in firepower over the western Indians. In newly colonized portions of Africa and Asia, the Gatling gun provided the Europeans' margin of victory over local forces.

A modern, helicopter-mounted version of the Gatling gun, the Vulcan minigun, was widely used by the U.S. Army in the Indochina war. The minigun, popularly known as "Puff, the Magic Dragon" for the flames and smoke emitted from its muzzle, fires at the staggering rate of 6,000 rounds per minute, enough to decimate an entire village in one burst. The minigun continues to be used as a counterinsurgency weapon in Central America. A larger version, the 20mm Vulcan is used for antiaircraft defense.

See also Guns and Gun Control.

GAYS

See Homosexuality.

GENERAL FEDERATION OF WOMEN'S CLUBS

The General Federation of Women's Clubs (GFWC) was founded in Chicago in 1890. Starting with a few thousand members, the organization grew rapidly, reaching a membership of over a million in 1910. The clubs began, like most similar organizations of the day, by offering self-improvement and recreation to middle-class women — for whom, according to contemporary custom, paid work was both unnecessary and inappropriate. Gradually, however, the GFWC was caught up in the enthusiasm for reform that was sweeping the country at the end of the nineteenth century. Turning to social betterment, the clubs within the GFWC started nursery schools and children's clinics, supported health and welfare programs, and lobbied for conservation, pure food and drugs, the abolition of child labor, and other progressive programs, especially those related to maternal and child welfare.

After World War I, the members' enthusiasm for social change slackened, and by the early 1920s they had retreated to the less controversial grounds of fighting pornography and promoting home economics. Even in its activist days, the GFWC had never ventured beyond the mainstream of progressivism — it made no effort to join hands with black women's clubs or with working-class women's organizations. It did not endorse woman suffrage until 1914. But it had provided formidable support for a broad range of social reforms in the years before the First World War.

See also Women's Voluntary Associations.

GENTLEMAN'S AGREEMENT

The Gentleman's Agreement between the United States and Japan in 1907–1908 represented an effort by President Theodore Roosevelt to calm growing tension between the two countries over the immigration of Japanese workers. A treaty with Japan in 1894 had assured free immigration, but as the number of Japanese workers in California increased, they were met with growing hostility. In August 1900, Japan agreed to deny passports to laborers seeking to enter the United States; this, however, did not stop the many workers who obtained passports to Canada, Mexico, or Hawaii and then moved on to the United States. Racial antagonism intensified, fed by inflammatory articles in the press. On May 7, 1905, a Japanese and Korean Exclusion League was organized, and on October 11, 1906, the San Francisco school board arranged for all Asian children to be placed in a segregated school.

Japan was prepared to limit immigration to the United States, but was deeply wounded by San Francisco's discriminatory law aimed specifically at its people. President Roosevelt, wishing to preserve good relations with Japan as a counter to Russian expansion in the Far East, intervened. While the American ambassador reassured the Japanese government, Roosevelt summoned the San Francisco mayor and school board to the White House in February 1907 and persuaded them to rescind the segregation order, promising that the federal government would itself address the question of immigration. On February 24, the Gentleman's Agreement with Japan was concluded in the form of a Japanese note agreeing to deny passports to laborers intending to enter the United States and recognizing the U.S. right to exclude Japanese immigrants holding passports originally issued for other countries. This was followed by the formal withdrawal of the San Francisco school board order on March 13, 1907. A final Japanese note dated February 18, 1908, made the Gentleman's Agreement fully effective. The agreement was superseded by the exclusionary Immigration Act of 1924.

See also Asia-U.S. Relations; Immigration.

GEORGE, HENRY

(1839–1897), economist and social reformer. One of the last serious, nonacademic scholars, George fashioned a powerful critique of the capitalist marketplace and then fought for his ideas in the public arena where he developed a genuinely mass, even international, following. The very homespun quality of his insights and his commitment to the "single tax" as a panacea for social inequality and poverty proved both his peculiar strength and his weakness as a representative of his times.

George's struggle in the 1860s to find a place for himself in California as a typographer or writer equipped him with insights into and sympathy for the dark underside of America's Industrial Revolution. His family's evangelical bent echoed in his alternating visions of social apocalypse and millenarian redemption. Exposure to the high cost of California land and shock at the coexistence of wealth and destitution in New York City inspired his pursuit of a basic riddle: how could poverty expand and deepen amid the most prosperous civilization in the world?

George first sketched his answer in the pamphlet *Our Land and Land Policy* in 1871, which he expanded into his masterpiece, *Progress and Poverty* (1877–1879). In this book he argued his basic propositions: all men have the right to apply their labor to natural resources; economic rent is mere parasitism on labor and industry; as population increases, land values soar, creating economic monopoly; therefore, the market value of land (or economic rent) should be confiscated by public taxation; this land tax (called by others the single tax) would ensure the orderly working of the economic marketplace. This antimonopoly critique was delivered in pungent prose: "The 'tramp' comes with the locomotive, and the almshouses and prisons are as surely the makers of 'material progress' as are costly dwellings, rich warehouses, and magnificent churches." Resonating with a traditional American reverence for free land and egalitarian opportunity unhampered by bureaucratic control, George's solution challenged other contemporary remedies, including socialism, workers' trade union organization, and the populist resort to cooperatives and an inflationary currency.

George was first championed by the American partisans of the Irish Land League, who facilitated his immensely successful tour of the British Isles in 1881–1882. His following grew in consonance with the broad-gauged reform ag-

itation surrounding the Knights of Labor, which George joined in 1883. As industrial unrest crested in the 1880s, workers adopted George as a tribune of the people — as much for his general sympathies and power of expression as for his theories. He ran for mayor of New York City on a United Labor party ticket in 1886, but narrowly lost to Democratic candidate Abram S. Hewitt while soundly defeating Republican Theodore Roosevelt.

Amid factional discord in labor's ranks and his insistence on the single-tax nostrum, George's influence fell off dramatically after 1886. His ideas met with near-universal rejection from academic economists. Still, he remained a powerful symbol of egalitarian and republican principles in a corporate age, with devoted apostles including antimonopoly Cleveland mayor, Tom Johnson. When he died in 1897, some 100,000 Americans filed past his casket in Grand Central Palace.

Edward J. Rose, *Henry George* (1968); John L. Thomas, *Alternative America: Henry George, Edward Bellamy, Henry Demarest Lloyd and the Adversary Tradition* (1983).

LEON FINK

See also Labor; Radicalism.

GERMANY-U.S. RELATIONS

The United States' relations with a German state officially began in September 1785 when it negotiated a commercial treaty with Prussia. The more important immigration and cultural connection had started a century earlier when Germans settled in colonial Pennsylvania. By the time America achieved independence, Germans, who were scattered throughout the nation, comprised about 9 percent of the population. In the nineteenth century they continued to arrive by the thousands. Although these immigrants frequently encountered nativist animosity, their industriousness and frugality generally made a favorable impression. Americans who studied at German universities also helped create an admiration for German thought and culture. During the Civil War many people in the German states were friendly toward the Union cause, and

Americans favored Prussia in its nineteenth-century wars.

Following Germany's unification in January 1871, economic, colonial, and naval rivalry often replaced the earlier cordiality. There were periodic conflicts over trade and tariffs and colonial rivalry over Samoa, which Germany sought to annex. The latter dispute did not end until 1899 with the partition of Samoa, but American distrust of Germany remained strong. A year earlier, during the Spanish-American War, an American naval force in the Philippines had faced a stronger German fleet seemingly poised to take the islands if the United States did not. No clash occurred, but again American suspicion of Germany mounted.

The United States' closeness to Great Britain was a key ingredient in the growing antagonism. British and American leaders both viewed Germany, the possessor of Europe's strongest army and a powerful fleet, as autocratic and militaristic. The extent of U.S.-British cordiality was illustrated when Germany and Britain in 1902 punished Venezuela for reneging on its debts: Americans criticized Germany, not Britain, for violating the Monroe Doctrine.

In August 1914, when the First World War started, President Woodrow Wilson proclaimed neutrality, but he and most Americans favored the Allied side. When Americans received news of Belgium's violation and other military high-handedness, it confirmed their negative perception of imperial Germany. The most critical friction between the two countries arose out of maritime issues. Early in 1915 Germany used submarines to break a British blockade and destroy shipments of American military supplies sent to the Allies. Wilson protested, saying that the United States would hold Germany accountable for any loss of American lives and property.

The first major confrontation occurred on May 7 with the sinking of the British passenger liner *Lusitania*. Nearly 1,200 people died, 128 of them American. Backed by an aroused public, the president demanded that Germany abandon its U-boat attacks on civilian vessels. That crisis passed with a partial German retreat. But more sinkings, revelations of German spying in the United States, and the renewal of unrestricted submarine warfare in January 1917 led the president to ask for a declaration of war against Germany, which Congress voted on April 6. Anti-German sentiment rose to a fever pitch with many Americans violently attacking the German language, music, and culture.

Fresh American troops in Europe proved crucial in turning the tide in favor of the Allies, and in 1918 Germany sued for an armistice on terms outlined in Wilson's Fourteen Points. Fearing harsh treatment from the French and British, the Germans at Versailles pinned their hopes for a mild settlement on Wilson. To a degree the tactic worked: he blocked French plans for dismembering Germany.

In the postwar era, as anti-German sentiment in the United States subsided, the relationship between the two countries revolved around economics and culture. Under the Dawes Plan of 1924 American loans provided Germany with funds for reparations to Allied nations, which in turn used the money to repay debts owed to the United States. This system, which scaled down both reparations and debts, contributed to an economic revival in Germany that ended with the Great Depression.

In January 1933 Adolf Hitler became Germany's chancellor, and soon thereafter the brief spell of cordiality with the United States ended. Hitler rearmed Germany in defiance of treaty restrictions, and when in October 1937 President Franklin D. Roosevelt urged a quarantine of aggressors, official German-American relations became minimal. The Third Reich's annexation of Austria the following March inaugurated eighteen months of almost constant crises. In November the Nazis launched a pogrom against Jews, and the United States in protest recalled its ambassador.

When in September 1939 the Nazis invaded Poland, Roosevelt, although outraged, proclaimed neutrality. But since he regarded Nazi Germany as a threat to national security, he aided the Allied cause in any way he could. In September 1940 Hitler countered with the Tripartite Treaty, an alliance with Italy and Japan aimed at the United States. All the while the American government was shipping vast amounts of war matériel to Britain and, after

June 1941, to the Soviet Union then under assault by the Nazis. On December 11, four days after the Japanese attacked Pearl Harbor, Hitler cast aside caution and declared war on the United States.

All through the Second World War Roosevelt insisted on a policy of unconditional surrender because he wanted the German people this time to taste the full reality of defeat. They did in May 1945. The victors divided Germany into four zones of occupation, but soon the country's fate became the most important issue in the cold war rivalry between the United States and the Soviet Union. In 1948 the Western powers integrated their zones and brought West Germany into the European Recovery Program backed by the American Marshall Plan. The Soviets countered with a blockade of the Western sections of Berlin, which the United States and its allies then supplied by air until the Russians backed down. In September 1949 American initiative shaped the Federal Republic of Germany and a month later the Soviets formed the German Democratic Republic. Two Germanys had come into existence, one hostile to the United States, and the other a client state. In May 1955 the Western powers brought the Federal Republic into the North Atlantic Treaty Organization (NATO), overcoming fears of a revived German militarism by tying the country to the Western European community.

As West Germany benefited from American aid and trade, the relationship between Germans and Americans became friendly once again. Beginning with John F. Kennedy's administration, the United States promoted off and on a policy of détente with the Soviets, which implied de facto acceptance of Germany's partition. In 1974 the United States established formal relations with the German Democratic Republic.

During these decades West Germany became one of the world's most prosperous nations. It possessed Western Europe's largest army and became a bastion of NATO and America's major Continental ally. Americans admired German achievements in science, engineering, and industry as well as its music, philosophy, and literature. American political ideas, popular music, and movies, in turn, influenced German society. Americans also rejoiced over the dismantling in 1989 of the wall built by the Soviets that divided Berlin. In public opinion polls in 1990, Americans — unlike many Europeans — approved of Germany's reunification. On the other hand, many Americans were still haunted by the memory of two great wars and the Holocaust.

Thus, over the years Americans have regarded Germans with ambivalence. Nevertheless, those with German blood in their veins form the second largest ethnic group in the United States. In recent decades the theme of cordiality in the German-American relationship has prevailed over that of animosity.

Hans W. Gatzke, *Germany and the United States: A "Special Relationship"?* (1980); Manfred Jonas, *The United States and Germany: A Diplomatic History* (1984); Frank Ninkovich, *Germany and the United States: The Transformation of the German Question since 1945* (1988).

ALEXANDER DeCONDE

See also Berlin Blockade; Cold War; Dawes Plan; Holocaust, American Response to the; Versailles Treaty and League of Nations; World War I; World War II.

GERONIMO

(1829–1909), Apache Indian chief. When Geronimo died, he had been a legend for more than a generation. But his courage and determination did more than provide a battle cry for paratroopers of another day. It helped sustain the spirits of his people, the Chiricahua Apaches, in the last desperate days of the Indian wars.

Geronimo was born in the upper Gila River country of Arizona. He came to maturity in the final years of Mexican rule of the region. His antagonism toward the Mexicans was as deep-rooted as it was understandable. In one fateful encounter, Mexican soldiers killed his mother, his wife, and his three small children. This tragic event steeled the young man for a long life of frequent conflict.

In 1848, soon after the signing of the Treaty of Guadalupe Hidalgo, in which Mexico ceded extensive lands in the Southwest to the United

States, the Anglo-Americans made it clear they intended to restrict the old patterns of raiding and territorial use by the different Apache bands. The Anglo-American mines, ranches, and communities disrupted established Apache lifeways. The intruders set limits on where the Apaches could live and how. The Apaches, of course, had other ideas.

The initial reservation established for the Chiricahua Apaches in 1872 included at least a portion of their homeland. The Chiricahuas were unhappy with the prospect of any reservation life, but their dismay turned to anger when they were evicted from this reserve and forcibly gathered with other Apache groups on the San Carlos Reservation in Arizona in the mid-1870s. Geronimo bitterly resented the move, and he especially disliked San Carlos. For the next decade he and his followers repeatedly broke out from what they saw as imprisonment. Once clear of San Carlos, they were difficult to locate and bring back, for they knew well the country of southern Arizona and northern Mexico. Time after time, Geronimo sought a more unfettered existence, despite the best efforts of the U.S. Army.

Geronimo's repeated escapes embarrassed and provoked politicians, army officers, and the non-Indian populace of the Southwest. His very name brought terror to the people who continually heard of his evading capture and occasionally killing Anglo-Americans and Mexicans. Territorial newspaper headlines blared his name, time and again.

His final surrender to Gen. Nelson Miles in Skeleton Canyon, Arizona, just north of the Mexican border, on September 4, 1886, truly marked the end of a chapter in Apache and western American history. It meant exile for himself and almost four hundred of his fellows. They were sent by train to incarceration at Fort Pickens, Florida; Mount Vernon Barracks, Alabama; and finally, in 1894, Fort Sill, near Lawton, Oklahoma. Geronimo spent more than fourteen years at Fort Sill, although he was allowed sporadically to appear at world's fairs and other gatherings. He was a celebrity in defeat but still a captive when he died and was buried at Fort Sill in the new state of Oklahoma.

Angie Debo, *Geronimo: The Man, His Time, His Place* (1976).

PETER IVERSON

See also Indians.

GERRYMANDER

Gerrymander refers to the drawing of boundaries of legislative districts to benefit one party or group and handicap another. Although the practice dates back to the colonial period, its name is derived from Elbridge Gerry, a signer of the Declaration of Independence, a nonsigning delegate to the Federal Convention of 1787, and a leader of the Jeffersonian Republican party.

In 1812, while Gerry was governor of Massachusetts, the Republican-dominated legislature redrew district lines to weight representation in favor of Republicans and against Federalists. The Federalists attacked the redistricting, specifically blaming Gerry although he had nothing to do with the project and, in private, opposed it. A Federalist newspaper published a political cartoon depicting the oddly shaped district covering Essex County as a salamander; the cartoonist dubbed his creation a "Gerry-mander." The word quickly passed into common parlance.

Since the 1950s, the federal courts have been increasingly willing to examine states' defining of representative districts to determine their adherence to the principle of "one man, one vote," as enunciated in *Baker* v. *Carr* (1962). Ironically, in light of the term's New England origins, most gerrymanders examined by the Supreme Court have come from southern states, where local legislatures sought to dilute the representation of urban residents and African-Americans.

See also Baker v. *Carr;* Suffrage.

GERSHWIN, GEORGE

(1898–1937), songwriter, pianist, and composer. Although best known as a composer of popular songs, Gershwin (born Jacob Gershvin) also wrote music for orchestra, piano, and the musical theater. After early piano study in his native Brooklyn, he left high school to become a song plugger for Jerome H. Remick and Co., a Tin Pan Alley publishing company. He soon began writing his own songs, and his first full-scale Broadway revue, *La La Lucille,* opened in May of 1919. Between 1920 and 1924, Gershwin composed five of the *George White's Scandals* revues. In 1920, Al Jolson's recording of "Swanee," the composer's first hit, established Gershwin as a popular songwriter.

Gershwin's interest in both romantic and modern music, along with his skill as a composer in popular genres, contributed to his development of a symphonic jazz style in the 1920s and to his later use of African-American music on the operatic stage. On November 1, 1923, Gershwin accompanied soprano Eva Gauthier in a concert of vocal music that ranged from Purcell to Hindemith and also included some of his own songs. Critics praised his pianistic technique and the sophisticated arrangements of popular songs.

In 1924, the premiere of Gershwin's *Rhapsody in Blue* by the Paul Whiteman Orchestra, billed as "An Experiment in Modern Music," brought him instant fame. The piece offered a synthesis of jazz and symphonic music. Familiar jazz riffs in the context of the late-nineteenth-century romantic concerto style pleased the public, if not the critics, many of whom felt that popular music had no place in the concert hall. Gershwin nevertheless continued to use the sounds of American popular music in his compositions, including the Concerto in F (1925), Three Preludes for piano (1923–1926), *An American in Paris* (1928), and the "I Got Rhythm" variations (1934).

Gershwin integrated the music of African-Americans most effectively in his American folk opera, *Porgy and Bess,* which was first performed on the Broadway stage in 1935. The work was based on a play by DuBose Heyward and included lyrics by the composer's brother, Ira Gershwin. It was not financially successful, although the use of black characters in leading operatic roles and African-American musical styles contributed to the work's importance in the history of American musical theater. *Porgy and Bess* has reached a broad international audience in numerous stage productions and a film version (1959). Gershwin's original operatic setting has been faithfully revived in recent years, most notably by the Houston and Metropolitan Opera companies.

Gershwin's melodic gift and sensitivity to the fit of music and lyrics provided him with an extraordinary reputation as a songwriter. From 1918 until his death of a brain tumor in 1937, he collaborated often with his brother, Ira, a talented lyricist. They composed numerous songs and Broadway shows, including *Of Thee I Sing,* which won a Pulitzer Prize in 1931, *Funny Face* (1927), *Strike Up the Band* (1927), and *Girl Crazy* (1930). But George Gershwin's role in American musical history as a songwriter is rivaled by his parallel careers as pianist and composer in the orchestral and theatrical genres. He brought together disparate musical traditions and contributed to the recognition of American folk and popular music as legitimate sources of national culture.

David Ewen, *A Journey to Greatness: The Life and Music of George Gershwin* (1956); R. Kimball and A. Simon, *The Gershwins* (1973).

BARBARA L. TISCHLER

See also Jazz; Music; Musical Theater.

GETTY, JEAN PAUL

(1892–1976), oil executive and art collector. Born in Minneapolis to a lawyer who turned a lease bought on a gamble into a successful oil company, J. Paul Getty, through his autocratic rule and skillful manipulation of the stock market, brought the Getty Oil Company to the status of an "eighth sister" among the giants in the business. But eight years after his death, the company became the subject of a fierce takeover battle and was eventually absorbed by Texaco.

The young J. Paul worked in the oil fields during school vacations as a general laborer, acquiring the hands-on experience he later found useful in his management of the company. After his father's death in 1930, he and his eighty-year-old mother battled for control of the family wealth. Sarah was skeptical of her son's practice of buying the stock of companies in shaky financial condition during the depression. To control his spending, and to preserve some of the wealth for future generations, his mother created the Sarah Getty Trust, which later became the subject of litigation among its beneficiaries. J. Paul's stock market speculation, however, proved to be a sound business strategy. It laid the foundation of what eventually became the billion-dollar Getty Oil empire, which included holdings in oil and natural gas, as well as gold and uranium mines, a copper deposit, vineyards, orchards, grazing lands, timberlands, refineries, and chemical plants.

As shrewd a businessman as Getty proved to be, he was unsuccessful in his personal life. Though he tried to emulate the Rockefellers and Kennedys, his own family was too fragmented and embattled to invite comparison. He had five sons by four wives and never invited his parents to any of his weddings. Similarly, he failed to attend his sons' weddings and even missed the funeral of his youngest son, Timothy. All of his surviving sons did a stint in the family business, but none lived up to his expectations. He changed his will twenty-one times, using it as a weapon to punish filial "disloyalty."

Getty spent the final twenty-five years of his life at his Sutton Place estate twenty miles from London, surrounded by double barbed-wire fences and patrolled by plainclothes guards and twenty-five German shepherd attack dogs. Yet he maintained firm control of his company, though fear of flying kept him from visiting the Los Angeles headquarters. Declared the richest man in the world by *Fortune* magazine in 1957, he was nevertheless tight with money: he installed a pay phone in his home, saved bits of string and was delighted when he had enough to tie up a parcel, and throughout his life washed his own underwear. Perhaps the most notorious example of his penny-pinching was his refusal to pay ransom for his grandson, J. Paul III, until finally the kidnappers cut off the boy's right ear.

Always an avid art collector, Getty left virtually his entire estate to the J. Paul Getty Museum Trust. Designed as a replica of a Roman villa, the Malibu museum houses paintings, sculpture, and eighteenth-century French furniture. Though the endowment has grown to $3

billion since Getty's bequest, making the collection one of the world's richest cultural institutions (its budget is roughly twenty-five times the New York Metropolitan Museum's), it has failed to monopolize the art market in the way many feared. Critics charge that the museum has not been aggressive in broadening its mediocre collection to include modern art, or pieces from periods other than what its founder collected, although its acquisition of van Gogh's *Irises* in 1990 was an important exception. The museum has also come under intense public scrutiny with questions about the authenticity of some of its recent purchases.

Robert Lenzner, *The Great Getty* (1985); Russell Miller, *The House of Getty* (1985).

Susan Keselenko Coll

See also Libraries and Museums; Oil Industry.

GETTYSBURG ADDRESS

This speech, regarded as one of Abraham Lincoln's finest works, was delivered at Gettysburg, Pennsylvania, on November 19, 1863. Ceremonies were held to dedicate a cemetery for those killed in the battle of July 1–3 between George Gordon Meade's Army of the Potomac and Robert E. Lee's Army of Northern Virginia. The main speaker was Edward Everett, a renowned orator.

When the board in charge of the event extended invitations to various national figures, it was expected that Lincoln would not be present, but he made his attendance a priority. Contrary to legend, he did not write his speech on the back of an envelope as he traveled to the ceremonies aboard a train. He had made two drafts of the remarks he planned to deliver. After Everett's two-hour oration, Lincoln spoke for only a few minutes. He began, "Four score and seven years ago our fathers brought forth, upon this continent, a new nation, conceived in Liberty, and dedicated to the proposition that all men are created equal." He concluded, "government of the people, by the people, for the people, shall not perish from the earth."

The ten sentences composing the speech received little attention at the time. Everett himself, however, appreciated Lincoln's eloquence, writing him, "I should be glad if I could flatter myself that I came as near to the central idea of the occasion in two hours as you did in two minutes." Through the years, the address, considered a model of its kind, has been much studied, proving one of his predictions wrong: "The world will little note, nor long remember, what we say here, but can never forget what they did here."

See also Lincoln, Abraham.

GHETTOS

See Black Ghettos.

GIBBONS V. OGDEN

In *Gibbons* v. *Ogden* (1824) the Supreme Court defined Congress's constitutional power to regulate interstate commerce. Rival steamboat ferries were operating between New Jersey and New York. Aaron Ogden operated his ferry under a monopoly granted by the New York state legislature. Thomas Gibbons, formerly Ogden's partner, secured a license to ferry under the Federal Coasting Act of 1793 and competed with him. When Ogden sued Gibbons in New York State, the court confirmed his monopoly and ordered Gibbons to stop his service. Gibbons appealed to the U.S. Supreme Court.

Gibbons's federal license was valid, Chief Justice John Marshall wrote in delivering the Court's opinion. National law had to be considered superior to state law when the two conflicted. If state powers were broad and Congress's narrow, it would leave the Constitution "a magnificent structure, indeed, to look at, but totally unfit for use." Marshall's interpretation rested on the federal government's constitutional power to regulate interstate commerce, which Marshall defined broadly as intercourse. Thus *Gibbons* became the basis in later years for Congress's regulation of all interstate communication, from navigation to radio and television.

See also Interstate Commerce Commission.

G.I. BILL

The G.I. bill, officially the Servicemen's Readjustment Act of 1944, provided many benefits to veterans of World War II. It established veterans' hospitals, provided for vocational rehabilitation, made low-interest mortgages available, and granted stipends covering tuition and living expenses for veterans attending college or trade schools. Subsequent legislation extended these benefits to veterans of the Korean War, and the Readjustment Benefits Act of 1966 extended them to all who served in the armed forces even in peacetime.

From 1944 to 1949, nearly 9 million veterans received close to $4 billion from the G.I. bill's unemployment compensation program. The education and training provisions existed until 1956, providing benefits to nearly 10 million veterans. The Veterans' Administration offered insured loans until 1962, and they totaled more than $50 billion. The economic assistance provided by the G.I. bill and the Veterans' Administration accelerated the postwar demand for goods and services.

GIDEON V. WAINWRIGHT

This case (1963) established the right of defendants in felony trials to have legal counsel. Clarence Earl Gideon was charged with breaking into a poolroom intending to commit a misdemeanor, a felony in Florida. Being indigent, he asked the trial judge to appoint an attorney to defend him but was denied such counsel. Florida law required the appointment of lawyers only in capital cases. Gideon therefore conducted his own defense and was convicted. After the Florida Supreme Court denied an appeal of the conviction, Gideon wrote a letter to the U.S. Supreme Court from jail saying he had been denied a fair trial; the Court agreed to hear his case.

In a previous decision, *Betts* v. *Brady* (1942), the Court was unwilling to find that the Constitution's Sixth Amendment guarantee of legal counsel applied to state trials. It held that a right to an attorney existed only when a capital crime was charged or in "certain circumstances." In virtually every case reviewed by the Court subsequently, as Justice John Marshall Harlan later observed, "circumstances" required a court-appointed attorney. A clear rule for representation was needed.

The Court overturned *Betts* in *Gideon.* It found the Fourteenth Amendment's due process clause required states to guarantee legal representation. Justice Hugo Black wrote the majority opinion, adopting the "noble idea" that every defendant stands equal before the law. "Reason and reflection require us to recognize that in our adversary system of criminal justice, any person hailed into court, who is too poor to hire a lawyer, cannot be assured a fair trial unless counsel is provided for him." In 1972 the Burger Court guaranteed an attorney to every person facing a possible prison term.

GILMAN, CHARLOTTE PERKINS

(1860–1935), feminist, author, and lecturer. Gilman achieved international fame as a feminist-socialist theorist with the publication of *Women and Economics: The Economic Factor between Men and Women as a Factor in Social Evolution* in 1898. The book was translated into seven languages and is still in print today (the latest edition was published in 1975). She was a major critic of society who sought to create a cohesive, systematic body of thought that combined socialism (she was ideologically close to the English Fabians) and feminism (she described herself as a humanist, not a feminist, asserting that the world was masculinist and that she wished to redress the balance).

In her vast body of work, which included book-length studies in history, anthropology, sociology, philosophy, and ethics, as well as novels, poetry, and short stories, Gilman tried to define a humane social order built upon what she called female values — life giving and nurturing. She constructed a worldview to explain human behavior, past and present, and to project her visions for the future. In her sociological and historical works she analyzed the past from the perspective of gender; in her fiction she illustrated the human drama embodied in contemporary social relations; and in her utopian works she suggested the kind of world we could have if we were persuaded to remake it. The place to begin, she argued, was in the ideological sphere; thus she saw herself as engaged in a struggle for the minds of women.

Gilman had an enormous reputation in her own time, but dropped into neglect thereafter. She was brought back to public attention by the revitalization of the women's movement. Today she is best known as the author of the chilling short story "The Yellow Wallpaper" (1892), about a woman's descent into madness, and the witty and trenchant utopian novel *Herland,* serialized monthly in the *Forerunner,* a magazine she wrote and edited between 1909 and 1916. *Herland* was not published in book form until 1979.

Gilman argued that women's subordination, which began with the expropriation by men of the agricultural surplus women produced, limited women's autonomy and therefore dehumanized them. It was the model for all subsequent exploitation, she said. Beginning with recorded history, women were forced to depend economically on male authority, so that by the nineteenth century it was believed to be "natural" that one sex should function as the domestic servants of the other. At one time, Gilman believed, the involuntary sacrifice of women's equality had been necessary because masculine traits of assertiveness, combativeness, and display were essential for the growth of society. But civilization now requires the restoration of the original balance to include female qualities of cooperation and nurturance.

The most important fact about men and women, she said many times in many ways, is the common humanity we share, not the differences that distinguish us and that are magnified in contemporary culture. Subordination of women will end, she asserted, only when women lead the struggle for their own autonomy and equality, thereby freeing themselves from bondage and freeing men from the distortions that come from dominance.

Polly Wynn Allen, *Building Domestic Liberty: Charlotte Perkins Gilman's Architectural Feminism* (1988); Charlotte Perkins Gilman, *The Living of Charlotte Perkins Gilman: An Autobiography,* new ed. (1990); Ann J. Lane, *To*

"Herland" and Beyond: The Life and Work of Charlotte Perkins Gilman (1990).

ANN J. LANE

See also Feminist Movement.

GINSBERG, ALLEN

(1926–   ), poet. Along with Robert Lowell, Ginsberg was the writer most responsible for a great shift in American poetry in the late 1950s. Poetry in the forties and fifties was dominated by formal, metrical, often rhymed verse, densely impacted with wit, irony, and allusion, as in Lowell's early poems. By the mid-fifties, however, both Ginsberg and Lowell had come under the spell of William Carlos Williams, who had worked for decades to bring his poems closer to the supple rhythms of prose and the transparency of spoken language. Ginsberg was also influenced by the jazzlike flow and immediacy of his friend Jack Kerouac's as-yet unpublished fiction.

Ginsberg's breakthrough came in his long poem "Howl" (1956), written directly at the typewriter in imitation of Kerouac's methods of spontaneous composition. In it, he boldly revived an impassioned biblical rhetoric of the sublime. Borrowing the kind of heightened yet prosaic long line that had been used by outcast poets like Christopher Smart, William Blake, and Walt Whitman, Ginsberg hallucinated a hipster's dream world of drugs, madness, and homosexuality as a counterpoint to "Moloch," the straight world dominated by money, machinery, and war, which he saw as a prison house of the spirit.

When Ginsberg read the poem aloud first at the Six Gallery in San Francisco in 1955 and again at readings across the country, the impact on the younger generation was enormous. Though attacked or ignored by most critics, accused of obscenity, incoherence, and sensationalism, the work of Ginsberg and Kerouac, along with the writings of friends like Gregory Corso, Lawrence Ferlinghetti, and William Burroughs, became a flashpoint of cultural rebellion, the seedbed of the counterculture of the 1960s.

To some the Beat movement was merely the triumph of public showmanship over literary values. Like earlier avant-gardes, the Beats tended to mythologize each other and aimed to provoke middle-class outrage. Their antinomianism could lead them to idealize the addict, the criminal, and the madman as "angelheaded hipsters" or doomed victims of society. Yet Ginsberg's work had a long literary ancestry, from the incantations of the Hebrew prophets to the rolling catalogs of Whitman and the fantastic imagery of the surrealists. Some of his best short poems, like "America," shared the mocking humor of the surrealists. Ginsberg also continued to grow as a writer. His next long poem, "Kaddish" (1957–1959), a tormented elegy for his mad communist mother, was a wrenching piece of autobiography in a class with Lowell's cooler, more fragmentary *Life Studies*. It remains one of the most moving works in contemporary poetry.

Ginsberg was the only Beat writer to sustain a full career. During the sixties he was a ubiquitous figure, an icon for the young and a pacifying presence; he was a key link between the counterculture and the anti–Vietnam War movement. His poems of the 1960s were collected in one of his best volumes, *Planet News* (1968). Later Ginsberg even became a member of the American Academy of Arts and Letters, a professor of English at Brooklyn College, and a scholar and archivist of his own work, publishing volumes of letters and journals and annotated collections of his earlier poetry, managing the transition from Beat rebel to elder statesman with surprising aplomb. In spite of his blunt homosexuality and his long sojourn in the underworld, itself an accepted literary conceit, Ginsberg's radical direction had been literary and traditional from the outset.

Morris Dickstein, *Gates of Eden: American Culture in the Sixties* (1989); Lewis Hyde, ed., *On the Poetry of Allen Ginsberg* (1984); Jane Kramer, *Allen Ginsberg in America* (1969).

MORRIS DICKSTEIN

See also Literature.

GLORIOUS REVOLUTION

In England's bloodless Glorious Revolution of 1688, James II was overthrown, and Parliament replaced him with his daughter Mary and her husband, William of Orange. American colonists greeted the news with enthusiasm because James II had sought to check the growing American trend toward self-governance. Besides using the Navigation Acts to reduce colonial economic independence, he had revoked many privileges granted in the early colonial charters. The chief target of this "reform" was Puritan New England, which had refused to allow freedom of religion and had enacted many laws that conflicted with English practice. In 1686 all the colonies from New Jersey to Maine had been incorporated into the Dominion of New England with the autocratic Sir Edmund Andros as governor.

With the ascension of William and Mary, the Americans mistakenly believed that England would reverse this policy of reducing local authority. But Parliament's displeasure with James II had arisen from the fear that he sought absolute power in England itself, not from his colonial policies. Under William and Mary the restrictions on colonial autonomy continued. Uprisings in several colonies followed, and these were harshly repressed. Although most Americans remained loyal to England, disillusionment resulting from the Glorious Revolution led in the future to the idea that perhaps the American colonies had more in common with one another than with England.

See also America in the British Empire; New England Colonies; Revolution.

GOLDBERG, ARTHUR

(1908–1990), labor lawyer, secretary of labor, associate justice, U.S. Supreme Court, and ambassador to the United Nations. Although best remembered for his service on the Supreme Court and his extraordinary decision to resign from it, Goldberg enjoyed his greatest influence as a leading figure within the American labor movement and the Kennedy administration. The son of immigrant Jews from the Ukraine, he was born and raised in Chicago. Quite poor, Goldberg worked his way through Northwestern University Law School, where he compiled an outstanding record. Five years after opening his own law firm in 1933 he took his first union cli-

ent, a local of the fledgling Congress of Industrial Organizations (CIO). He soon added the emerging steelworkers' union, which became his power base within the federation. The growing rift between its social democratic and more radical wings propelled Goldberg to the CIO's top ranks. He belonged to the former group, which after 1945 gave the highest priority to preserving the American working class's gains of the New Deal period. When the two factions finally broke apart in 1948, Goldberg's wing prevailed, and he succeeded radical Lee Pressman as the CIO's and the Steelworkers' general counsel.

In those capacities, Goldberg played a leading role in negotiating labor's postwar agreement with management. Under its terms, unions gave up trying to win control over the management of large enterprises, leaving the decisions about capital investment, marketing, plant location, and overall output in the hands of employers. Unions also pledged to link their wage demands to improvements in worker productivity, oust radicals from the labor leadership, allow the government to supervise their compliance with the agreement's terms, and support the Truman administration's anti-Soviet policies. In return, managers agreed to abandon their efforts to regain prerogatives lost during the 1930s and 1940s, grant fringe benefits that supplemented the government's limited social welfare system, and pursue investment and output policies that would help promote full employment for union workers.

Goldberg figured prominently in labor's efforts to promote that set of ideas over the next fifteen years. His most enduring achievements include winning a 1949 court ruling that helped establish a private social insurance scheme within the steel industry, a plan that quickly spread to other major manufacturing firms, and negotiating the 1955 AFL-CIO merger. When a managerial revolt against the postwar agreement arose during the late 1950s, Goldberg's efforts to contain it led him to support John F. Kennedy's presidential candidacy in 1960. Kennedy later appointed him secretary of labor. During his twenty months in that job, he tried unsuccessfully to negotiate a redefinition of the postwar agreement that would have preserved it.

Goldberg accepted a Supreme Court appointment in 1962, just as that social bargain began to come apart. As an associate justice, he provided the crucial fifth vote for a series of decisions aimed at extending the postwar agreement to the South, where it enjoyed the least viability. Although the rulings did help dismantle the system of legalized segregation, they did not spark the larger social transformation he had hoped for.

In July 1965 Goldberg came under pressure from President Lyndon B. Johnson to leave the Court and accept the much less important post of U.N. ambassador. Although the two men had never been close, Johnson urged Goldberg to make the change, saying that only he could negotiate an end to the Vietnam conflict and implying that once the task had been accomplished he would be reappointed to the Court. Moved by patriotism, an exaggerated sense of his own abilities, an unwillingness to incur Johnson's enmity, and the knowledge that Chief Justice Earl Warren planned to retire before Johnson's term expired (thus assuring Johnson of at least one future appointment), Goldberg reluctantly agreed to leave the Court. After spending three years fruitlessly seeking a diplomatic solution to the Vietnam War, he left the Johnson administration in June 1968 and two years later ran unsuccessfully for the New York governorship. Goldberg's rise to prominence and return to relative obscurity after 1970 reflected the changing fortunes of the labor movement he represented and of its social democratic faction in particular.

Dorothy Goldberg, *A Private View of a Public Life* (1975); Robert Shaplen, "Peacemaker," Parts 1, 2, *New Yorker,* April 7, 14, 1962, pp. 49–112, 49–105.

DAVID L. STEBENNE

See also Labor; Supreme Court.

GOLDMAN, EMMA

(1869–1940), anarchist and feminist. Opponent of established authority, war, and totalitarian government, Emma Goldman was the most famous rebel of her day. A passionate activist and charismatic speaker, she committed her life to radical causes in Europe and America. Born in a Jewish ghetto in Lithuania, Goldman immigrated to the United States when she was sixteen. Reared in a Jewish tradition of prophecy and opposition to injustice, her early experience molded by Russian anti-Semitism and reading in Russian nihilist literature, Goldman was destined to become a critic of her newly adopted country, just as she was of the Old World she left behind. But it was the hanging in 1887 of four Chicago anarchists accused of murdering policemen in the Haymarket affair that led her to dedicate her life to political radicalism.

A sewing machine operator in a corset factory, she concluded that she and other workers were exploited by factory owners. She was attracted to anarchism not only because it promised to replace capitalism with worker cooperatives but because anarchism espoused atheism, free speech, and freedom from sexual inhibition. Like many other anarchists of her day, Goldman also flirted with the idea of political violence. During the Homestead strike of 1892 she helped her lover, Alexander Berkman, plan the attempted assassination of steel mill owner Henry Clay Frick. A year later Goldman spent a year in prison for telling unemployed workers to steal bread if they had to. She was also implicated in President William McKinley's assassination.

From 1908 to 1917 Goldman spoke throughout the United States on behalf of the anarchist cause and edited the anarchist journal *Mother Earth* until 1916. Through her lectures and writing, she helped introduce American audiences to Henrik Ibsen, Bernard Shaw, August Strindberg, and other European playwrights, whom she admired for their advanced social ideas and spirit of rebellion.

Goldman believed that birth control would alleviate human misery by reducing the burden of large families on the poor and giving women of all classes sexual freedom. She was a pioneer lecturer on the subject. The decision not to bear children was a woman's right, she argued, and women should have the means to prevent conception. Having practiced as a midwife and a nurse, and attended a conference in Paris where condoms, douches, and diaphragms were discussed frankly, Goldman was familiar with modern birth-control methods. In 1916 she was arrested for violating a law that forbade giving out information about contraceptives. Goldman also advocated "free love," defined as a spiritual as well as sexual union between two people outside the bounds of matrimony, for marriage, she believed, made women lifelong dependents and sexual objects. To many Goldman embodied the "New Woman" — independent, unmarried, and sexually emancipated.

During World War I, Goldman was arrested and sent to prison for having organized an anticonscription campaign. Afterward, along with other anarchists, she was deported to Russia in 1919. Although an early supporter of the Bolshevik Revolution, Goldman became disillusioned with party rule and the suppression of free speech she encountered there. Her book, *My Disillusionment with Russia* (1923), was one of the first serious critiques of the Soviet system. She left Russia and spent the rest of her life in Europe and Canada. In the 1930s she made three trips to Catalonia during the Spanish civil war and enlisted support in England on behalf of the Spanish Republic.

Richard Drinnon, *Rebel in Paradise: A Biography of Emma Goldman* (1976); Candace Falk, *Love, Anarchy, and Emma Goldman* (1984).

Elizabeth H. Pleck

See also Birth Control; Conscientious Objection; Expatriates and Exiles; Radicalism.

GOLD RUSHES

For fifty years, from 1849 to 1899, news of gold discoveries and astonishing reports of miners digging their fortunes lured scores and eventually hundreds of thousands of Americans (and foreigners) to boomtowns and born-overnight mining camps, first in the mountains of California and finally on the frigid shores of the Bering Sea. Only the magnetism of gold (often with its geologic ally silver) could have attracted so many greenhorns from their settled lives in cities and on farms to forbidding wilderness regions previously known only to roving fur trappers and indigenous Indian tribes.

Decade by decade new mining excitements promised opportunities to strike it rich — in California in 1849, and then at Gold Hill, Colorado, 1859; Virginia City, Nevada, 1860; Orofino, Idaho, 1861; Virginia City, Montana, 1863; Deadwood, South Dakota, 1876; Tombstone, Arizona, 1877; Cripple Creek, Colorado, 1892; and Nome, Alaska, 1899. These were the places where fathers and sons, husbands and brothers, might make a fortune in a few weeks or months.

The first of the many gold rushes proved to be the most important, for it attracted the greatest number of people over the longest period of time and established the pattern for all that followed; and, too, it had the greatest psychological impact, for what happened in California gave birth to the dream that was pursued for half a century.

It all began in September 1848 when newspapers in New York and other eastern cities published letters from California's newly discovered goldfields, telling of nuggets "collected at random and without any trouble." Through the fall, the news spread across the thirty states. In December 1848 President Polk's message to Congress corroborated "the accounts of the abundance of gold" in that territory so recently acquired (February 1848) by the treaty ending the war with Mexico.

By spring 1849 "Californians" by the tens of thousands had set out for El Dorado. With few exceptions, wives and families stayed at home, comforted by their men's promises to return with "a pocket full of rocks." So many Americans rushed to California (and, too, men from Mexico, Europe, Australia, and China) that, although an average of 30,000 returned each year to their homes, the state's population by 1852 totaled more than 250,000 — this in an area where there had been at most 14,000 non-Indians before the discovery of gold at Sutter's Mill, January 24, 1848.

Without gold and its corollary industries, California would have evolved slowly, as a territory competing with Oregon for an annual few thousand immigrants. Instead, the Golden State's economy boomed, with industrial and agricultural growth stimulated by the great consumer markets of San Francisco and Sacramento and by thousands of miners in camps and towns demanding basic food supplies and lumber for boardinghouses and flumes, as well as luxuries from champagne to billiard tables.

During the years of California's rambunctious growth, far from the judgments of wives, in-laws, parents, grandparents, cousins, and neighbors, the masculine society felt free to be guided by ambition, even greed; safe to drink and swear and gamble and violate the Sabbath. With San Francisco its dominant image, California seemed to the rest of the nation to be a wild, dangerous place that scorned cherished standards and values. Letters sent back East confirmed families' anxieties: "The independence and liberality here and the excitement attending the rapid march of this country make one feel insignificant at the prospect of returning to the old beaten path at home."

The expectation that each subsequent mining site would be another California greatly strengthened the attraction of later discoveries. In 1859 many thousands from the Midwest hurried to Gold Hill in the mountains of Colorado, near a supply center to be known as Denver. After the initial flush times, however, the area's gold production depended on deep mining that required far greater expense and more advanced technology than the rich placers that had started the rush. In the 1870s silver discoveries, new smelting techniques, and railroads supported a boom that centered at Leadville where silver production continued through the 1880s.

Gold and silver discoveries on the eastern slope of the Sierra Nevada set off a wild rush to Virginia City, Nevada, in 1859–1860. Most of the men hurrying to what would soon be known to the world as the Comstock Lode came from the declining placer camps of California. They soon found their capital and skills insufficient to meet the demands of mining at depths that reached several thousand feet. Through the years thousands of miners labored for wages and hoped to make their fortunes by speculating in mining stocks while a few "bonanza kings" reaped millions from the output of the Comstock's fabulous mines.

More rewarding for men without capital, discoveries in Idaho in 1860–1862, and Montana, 1862–1864, offered the best chances of fulfilling the dream of finding gold placers like those in the early days of California. Veteran miners discouraged in Colorado and Nevada joined thousands of new gold seekers and rushed to Orofino and then Florence and Boise. Gold discovered in the gulches and mountain valleys of Montana drew some of Idaho's pioneers and many newcomers from far and wide to populate Virginia City and Helena. Later discoveries, new technologies, and railroads combined to develop these regions despite their isolation and severe climate.

In the next frenzied rush, thousands of veterans and greenhorns in 1876 pushed into the Black Hills of Dakota Territory where rich gold placers and later quartz mines supported boisterous boomtowns like Deadwood. A year later in the southeast corner of Arizona a silver strike at Tombstone created a national sensation that continued through the 1880s, with copper mining soon producing major profits as well.

Then in 1892 an astonishing gold discovery created another El Dorado at Cripple Creek, Colorado, where rich but complex ores yielded years of profit owing to advances in geology, engineering, and metallurgy.

The final gold rush came at a time of national despair, after the calamitous depression of the mid-1890s. On July 16, 1897, word flashed across the nation that an unbelievably rich gold discovery had been made on the Klondike River in the remote Canadian Yukon Territory. Two days later a ship docked at San Francisco with two tons of gold from "the golden Mecca of the North." Despite the distance and dangers, an estimated 100,000 Americans set out for Dawson City on the Klondike in 1897–1898. Exploration quickly led to new gold discoveries in U.S. territory in Alaska, culminating in the summer of 1899 with coarse gold found on the beach at Nome. The dozen miles along that shore of the Bering Sea proved to be the richest tidewater diggings ever known.

And so it ended, except for a postscript in the deserts of southern Nevada where gold and silver mines at Tonopah and Goldfield produced a few boom years between 1900 and 1918 reminiscent of earlier flush times.

Gold rushes in the Far West generated the founding of cities where wilderness would otherwise have prevailed for many decades; the building of railroads to connect the industrial islands in the midst of deserts, mountains, and forests; the creation of governments and the establishment of territories and states where none would have evolved for who knows how long; and the advance of technical knowledge and capital investment far and wide. And not least, gold in California and other wild places offered every man a chance to make his fortune.

J. S. Holliday, *The World Rushed In: The California Gold Rush Experience* (1981; paperback ed., 1983); Rodman Paul, *Mining Frontiers of the Far West, 1848–1880* (1963); T. H. Watkins, *Gold and Silver in the West* (1971).

J. S. HOLLIDAY

GOLD STANDARD

See Coin's Financial School.

GOMPERS, SAMUEL

(1850–1924), cofounder and first president, American Federation of Labor. Born into a Jewish working-class family in London, Gompers migrated with his family to New York City in 1863. Taught both the cigar trade and union principles by his father, Gompers thrived in the heady atmosphere that surrounded New York's labor movement during the 1870s. Advocates of Marxist and utopian socialism, anarchism, communalism, and a host of other reform programs jostled for support. Influenced by British trade union principles and by the Marxist emphasis on the primacy of economic organization of workers, Gompers favored the creation of strong, centralized trade union institutions that would foster the growth and direct the activity of local unions. In conjunction with Adolph Strasser and others, Gompers restructured the Cigar Makers International Union along such lines.

Although never an avowed Marxist himself, Gompers's approach to organizing workers owed much to two ideas advanced by Marxists. He agreed with them that it was only through the trade union that awareness of a broad class interest among workers could emerge. And it followed from this that Gompers and such early American Marxist labor leaders as Friedrick Sorge and J. P. McDonnell looked upon political activity with suspicion. The state had proved hostile to workers in both Europe and America; any gains won through political reform, they argued, could be enforced only by the concentrated power of organized workers in the factories and shops across the nation. In an era when craft workers still controlled important aspects of production, Gompers and his associates insisted upon craft organization as the foundation for the Federation of Organized Trades and Labor Unions (1881) and its successor organization, the American Federation of Labor (AFL; 1886).

The AFL grew over its first two decades until in 1904 it accounted for some 10 percent of all nonagricultural wageworkers. But the emphasis on skilled craft workers created a de facto exclusion of the less skilled at a time when these workers were becoming an increasingly important sector of the work force. This resulted in an organization of workers deeply divided along racial, gender, and ethnic lines. The weak position of the president of the AFL (its constitution ensured the autonomy of the constituent unions) largely precluded Gompers from broadening organizing efforts.

As government regulation of industrial relations grew, the AFL felt compelled to seek political alliances and in 1912 actively supported the successful Democratic candidate for president, Woodrow Wilson. During Wilson's two terms, Gompers helped shepherd through Congress the Clayton Anti-Trust Act and the Seamen's Act. With the advent of World War I, the Wilson administration pressured business to negotiate with union leaders in order to guarantee production, and the union's membership grew impressively. During the postwar years, however, neither governmental nor business connections (developed largely through Gompers's leadership position in the National Civic Federation) defended labor during the steel strike of 1919, the machinists' strike of 1922, or the nationwide anti-union campaign known as the "American Plan."

At Gompers's death the AFL's weakened membership and narrow organizational structure underscored both the fragility of labor's position in American society and the necessity of expanding organizing efforts. In the following decade the AFL and recently formed industrial unions would address those problems anew.

Samuel Gompers, *Seventy Years of Life and Labor,* 2 vols. (1925); Stuart Kaufman, *Samuel Gompers and the Origins of the American Federation of Labor, 1848–1896* (1973).

NICK SALVATORE

See also American Federation of Labor; Labor.

GOODMAN, BENNY

(1909–1986), jazz clarinetist, bandleader, and concert performer. The music of Benny Goodman, the "King of Swing," is most closely identified with the years 1935–1945, when big bands played at dances and on the radio. The swing band functioned like an orchestra, with a leader and carefully arranged musical parts. Many had elaborate costumes and "signature" tunes that were especially popular on radio. But Goodman was more than a bandleader and soloist; he also contributed to American musical history as a jazz clarinetist, composer, and performer of concert works for the clarinet.

Born in Chicago, Benjamin David Goodman received his earliest musical training in his synagogue and at Hull-House, the settlement house established by Jane Addams. As a high school student, he immersed himself in the jazz style that had become popular in New Orleans the previous decade, and clarinetists Leon Roppolo and Johnny Dodds and trumpeter Bix Beiderbecke were major influences on his early performance style.

Goodman made his professional debut in Chicago in 1921 and then left four years later to play with the Ben Pollack band in Los Angeles. He subsequently followed Pollack back to Chicago and then to New York, where, between 1929 and 1934 he was a popular free-lance player at a time when Fletcher Henderson and other bandleaders were developing swing band music. Goodman formed a twelve-piece band in 1934, which performed for the National Biscuit Company's weekly program on NBC radio, "Let's Dance." In August of 1935, the Goodman band performed live at the Palomar Ballroom in Los Angeles. The dancers were so moved by the virtuosity of the arrangements and solos that they crowded around the bandstand to listen to a performance that has since been characterized as a high point in the history of swing.

Goodman's band was most successful from 1936 to 1939. His January 16, 1938, Carnegie Hall concert brought together a wide range of jazz soloists and contributed to the growing respectability of jazz as a performance art. He formed other, larger performing groups in the 1940s and experimented with be-bop, but these bands were never as popular as his earlier one. Goodman also recorded with jazz chamber groups, first a trio with pianist Teddy Wilson and drummer Gene Krupa, and later a quartet with Wilson, Krupa, and vibraphonist Lionel Hampton.

During World War II, Goodman recorded for the army's "V disc" program and performed for Armed Forces Radio. After the war, he became a musical ambassador, touring the Far East for the State Department in 1956–1957 and playing at the Brussels World's Fair in 1958.

Goodman continued recording into the 1980s and also achieved success as a performer of the traditional clarinet repertoire. He played and recorded with many orchestras and commissioned pieces by Béla Bartók, Paul Hindemith, and Aaron Copland.

One of Goodman's most significant contributions to American culture was his bringing black and white musicians together in his performing and recording groups. He presented the best musical talent, regardless of the musician's race, at a time when segregation prevailed in the music world.

D. Russell Connor, *Benny Goodman: Listen to His Legacy* (1989); Benny Goodman and Irving Kolodin, *The Kingdom of Swing* (1939); F. Kappler and G. Simon, *Giants of Jazz: Benny Goodman* (1979).

BARBARA L. TISCHLER

See also Jazz; Music.

GOOD NEIGHBOR POLICY

The Good Neighbor policy refers to the Hoover-Roosevelt policy of refraining from armed intervention in Latin America. Franklin D. Roosevelt is usually credited with setting the policy, but President Herbert Hoover coined the phrase and put the policy into practice.

When Hoover was elected in 1928, U.S. relations with Latin America were at a low point. At the Sixth Pan-American Conference in Havana that year, Latin Americans angrily criticized the Coolidge administration's armed interventions in Haiti and Nicaragua. To mend relations, Hoover after the elections immediately set out on a goodwill trip to Latin American capitals. In Honduras he announced, "We have a desire to maintain not only the cordial relations of governments with each other but also the relations of good neighbors."

Relations further improved with other Hoover administration policies. In the Clark Memorandum of 1930, the State Department repudiated Theodore Roosevelt's Corollary to the Monroe Doctrine. The Corollary had declared that only the United States could enforce collections of debts owed to foreigners by countries in the Western Hemisphere. (The Clark Memorandum, however, did not repudiate the right to intervention itself.) The Hoover administration's withdrawal of troops from Nicaragua and a planned withdrawal from Haiti also helped ease tensions between Latin America and the United States.

When Roosevelt succeeded to the presidency, he adopted the Good Neighbor rhetoric, but his intentions were unclear at first. In 1933 his administration pointedly refrained from sending troops to shore up the conservative Machado regime in Cuba. But when the leftist government of Ramón Grau San Martín took power, Washington helped topple it by stationing warships offshore and withholding recognition.

The Good Neighbor policy came into its own, however, in a series of measures taken during the thirties. Secretary of State Cordell Hull, in a surprise move, voted for a nonintervention resolution at the Seventh Pan-American Conference held at Montevideo in December 1933. Hull's low-tariff policy also eased relations with countries whose exports had been hurt by the protective Smoot-Hawley Tariff of 1930. In 1934 the Platt Amendment, which gave the United States the right to intervene in Cuba, was repealed, and in 1936 the Panama Canal Treaty was renegotiated. The United States' restraint when Mexico nationalized its oil industry in 1938 also helped improve relations.

As World War II approached, the United States found itself competing for influence with Germany in Latin America. Just before and during the war the administration went to great lengths to ensure Latin American cooperation in the war effort, both to keep strategic raw materials flowing and to deny the Axis any base of operation against the Panama Canal or the United States itself. With the notable exception of Argentina, the United States was successful — the Good Neighbor policy had borne fruit.

See also Caribbean-U.S. Relations; Latin America–U.S. Relations; Mexico-U.S. Relations.

GOULD, JAY

(1836–1892), railroad financier. Christened Jason, Jay Gould was born on a farm near Roxbury, New York. He taught himself the rudiments of surveying, and by the age of twenty-one, the undersized, quick-witted youth had prepared several county maps, written a local history, and saved five thousand dollars. Between 1856 and 1860 Gould operated a tannery but gave it up to join a Wall Street brokerage house. Following the panic of 1857 he had made modest and profitable investments in several short railroads.

In 1867 Daniel Drew, treasurer and long-time director of the Erie Railroad, added Gould and James Fisk to the Erie board of directors. When Cornelius Vanderbilt, of the New York Central, sought to buy control of the Erie a spectacular battle ensued. Gould, Fisk, and Drew promptly issued thousands of shares of new, watered stock. When the angry Vanderbilt obtained an arrest warrant for the three, they ferried company headquarters to Jersey City, and Gould rushed to Albany where a pliable New York legislature authorized the stock issue. Eventually peace was made with Vanderbilt, but that gentleman was reported to have muttered that his trouble with the Erie "has learned me it never pays to kick a skunk." Later in the fall of 1869 Gould and Fisk conspired with the brother-in-law of President Ulysses S. Grant to corner the gold market, causing the panic of "Black Friday," September 24, 1869. Gould continued to loot the Erie until his departure in 1872. His role in the Erie War and the attempted gold corner gave him a reputation as the prime financial predator of the age.

Possessing a fortune, Gould turned to western railroads. In the twenty years after 1872 he was a director of seventeen major lines and the president of five. He purchased much Union Pacific stock and controlled that road until 1878. At first Gould improved the management of the Union Pacific but later blackmailed the company by threatening to have the Gould-controlled Kansas Pacific build a nuisance line to Utah. During the 1880s Gould controlled about half the mileage southwest of St. Louis and Kansas City and tried unsuccessfully to expand his western holdings into a transcontinental rail empire to the Atlantic Coast. He also owned the *New York World* for a time and held major investments in New York City's elevated railways and several large telegraph companies, including Western Union. In his last years Gould suffered from tuberculosis and died of that disease at the age of fifty-seven, leaving a fortune of $77 million to his six children.

Gould was a man of many faults and virtues. He was cold and unscrupulous but courteous and unassuming, and in his private life, devoted to his family, flowers, and books. He could not be trusted but nonetheless helped build more efficient regional rail systems. He was a wrecker of values but a railway leader who helped achieve major rate reductions. Gould remains the prototype robber baron of the late nineteenth century, although his defects probably have been exaggerated because he was never comfortable with the press.

Robert L. Frey, ed., *Railroads in the Nineteenth Century* (1988); Maury Klein, *The Life and Legend of Jay Gould* (1988).

JOHN F. STOVER

See also Railroads; Robber Barons.

GOVERNMENT, CITY

See City Government.

GOVERNMENT, COLONIAL

See Colonial Government.

GOVERNMENT AND THE ECONOMY

In the relationship between government and the economy, ideas influence policies and policies shape outcomes. This three-way connection is sometimes direct, sometimes tenuous, sometimes perverse. Of the three elements, the easiest to evaluate historically is outcomes. By almost any measure, the American economy is the most successful the world has ever known. Even in colonial times the standard of living was generally better in America, at least for whites, than in Europe or Asia. In the decades following the American Revolution, economic growth remained high and remarkably steady. By the end of the nineteenth century, the United States surpassed all other countries in both agricultural and industrial output.

For most of the twentieth century, gross national product per capita has remained higher in the United States than in any other country, with the occasional exception of small advanced economies such as Switzerland and Denmark or oil-rich nations such as Kuwait. Only in the 1980s was the United States overtaken by countries such as West Germany and Japan, and even then only by the measurement of GNP per capita at exchange rates favorable to the deutsche mark and yen. By any other index of quality of life, the American standard of living was still the highest in the world.

If this outcome of unique affluence is clear, the ideas and policies behind it remain open to interpretation. How much did American economic success derive from laissez-faire ideas and policies, how much from governmental intervention? How much did it stem from neither of these but from the simple fact of a wealthy, isolated, and sparsely inhabited continent ready for exploitation? Assuming, for the sake of argument, that the early policies can be characterized as laissez-faire, then how much of the letting alone originated in the reasoning of Adam Smith and Thomas Jefferson, how much in the practical impossibility of effective public administration over a far-flung country?

In tracing the ideas behind American economic policies, the colonial period is the proper starting place. As the historian Carl Degler once remarked, "Capitalism came in the first ships." The English settlers of North America brought with them clear convictions about the nature of sovereignty and the rights of property. These ideas, and the resulting policies, then interacted with the circumstances of a rich and underpopulated continent to set the context of economic activity.

During most of the colonial period, the hand of government lay lightly on the economy. This was true even allowing for such exceptions as the harshness of Puritan rule in early New England, the heavy taxation of Chesapeake tobacco by the English Crown, and the odious institution of slavery. When the colonists did revolt in 1775, it was in large measure against Britain's new revenue policies of the 1760s and 1770s, which conveyed to American shores a fresh corps of administrative officials. This new regime brought taxation without representation, together with other violations of the "rights of Englishmen."

The intellectual contours of the American Revolution suggest that the United States was born in a broad outburst of anti-authoritarianism that transcended any temporary disaffection from George III, the British monarch. This anti-authoritarianism is plainly reflected in the texts of contemporary documents: the scores of revolutionary pamphlets calling upon Americans to throw off the British yoke, the Declaration of Independence, the Constitution, the Federalist Papers, and the Bill of Rights. All of these late-eighteenth-century documents express the deep-seated aversion to absolute authority, the hostility to centralized power in which the Union was born. Even though the Constitution seemed to many revolutionaries to imply an unduly centralized government, it still vested ultimate sovereignty in "the people" and divided governmental power among three branches, each possessing the power to check the other two. In still another balancing act, the federal government as a whole both checked and was checked by state governments. As Charles Evans Hughes once remarked, the Founding Fathers had designed "the most successful contrivance the world has ever known for preventing things from being done."

Given these institutional limitations on authority, can it be said that the government of the United States historically followed a policy of laissez-faire? Perhaps, but only as measured against Soviet-style command economies or the statist developmental policies of Napoleonic France, Bismarckian Germany, or Meiji Japan. Compared with liberal regimes such as that of Victorian Britain, the American government violated laissez-faire as often as it practiced it.

Broadly speaking, both federal and state governments were active in the economic sphere during the first half of the nineteenth century, passive in the second half, and then active again throughout the twentieth century. In the first half of the nineteenth century, state governments chartered numerous banks and expended public funds liberally for internal improvements such as canals, turnpikes, and railways. Meanwhile, the federal government promoted agricultural exports, protected domestic industry through tariffs, subsidized commerce through a generous postal rate structure, and encouraged the building of railways. Equally important, and often overlooked in analyses of government-business relations, the national government pursued an energetic and relentless policy of land acquisition and development. During the nineteenth century, more individual Americans made their fortunes from the exploitation of newly annexed lands than from any other source. "Manifest destiny" was an operative economic policy as well as a slogan of nationalism and empire, as the geographical extent of the United States was multiplied severalfold by the addition of the Old Northwest, the Louisiana

Purchase, the Florida Cession, the Mexican Cession, the Gadsden Purchase, the Oregon Territory, and the acquisition of Texas, Alaska, and Hawaii.

In less visible ways, the legal order of the United States was shaped so as to lubricate the operations of private enterprise. Decade by decade, the states relaxed requirements for the privilege of incorporation, far in advance of parallel developments in Europe. In bankruptcy law, incentives were fashioned so as to favor debtors more than creditors, a reversal of common European practice. Similarly, contract law became highly refined in America, facilitating commerce among the disparate populations of strangers who came to American shores and pushed ever westward. Meanwhile, taxation remained light, a circumstance made possible by ample revenues from the sale of public lands and from customs duties on goods imported from Europe. All of this added up to a situation uncommonly hospitable to what the legal historian Willard Hurst has called "the release of energy." Policymakers had systematically designed a fertile setting for private entrepreneurship — a greenhouse for business. So long as individual companies stayed small, no real conflict between the welfare of the American people and that of its business units became serious. Unfortunately, that happy situation endured only until the 1880s.

Big business (trusts) appeared in the United States during that decade, a good deal earlier than in most other countries. Once established, it grew faster and to a larger size than it did elsewhere. One reason was the absence of any countervailing force in America. A new country made up entirely of immigrants (except for the Native Americans), the United States had no established church, no standing army, no hereditary aristocracy, no mandarin class, no feudal tradition. Because of the nation's individualistic ideology, almost no government ownership of business enterprise existed, in contrast to substantial public undertakings even in other market economies, let alone socialist ones. The exceptions to this rule became famous largely because they *were* exceptions: the Erie Canal in the nineteenth century, the Panama Canal Company and the Tennessee Valley Authority in the twentieth. Throughout American history, in-

cluding the present time, the total tax bite of all governmental units has typically been less than in comparable industrial countries such as Britain, France, and Germany. Until the twentieth century, the absolute size of the national government remained minuscule, and even today it is relatively smaller than those of other countries. In 1871, at the dawn of the age of big business, the federal government employed only fifty-one thousand civilians, of whom thirty-seven thousand were postal workers. The remaining fourteen thousand constituted the entire national government of a country with a population of 41 million. This amounted to one federal worker per twenty-nine hundred inhabitants in contrast to about one per hundred in the late twentieth century.

Of all major market economies, the rise of big business preceded that of big government only in the United States. And when big business came, no countervailing force resisted its initial impact. Thus, the manifold problems it raised provoked a powerful public response that immediately moved into the realm of politics. In the closing years of the nineteenth century, the United States became the only major industrial power to enact legislation explicitly designed to curb the power of large corporations. Congress passed the Interstate Commerce Act in 1887, the Sherman Antitrust Act in 1890, and the Federal Trade Commission and Clayton acts in 1914. The United States was the only country to attempt such a thoroughgoing regulation of railroads as that embodied in the Hepburn Act of 1906, which gave new teeth to the Interstate Commerce Act of 1887. In other nations, railroads were either publicly owned or smaller than the gigantic American companies, several of which employed more than 100,000 persons. Although many other countries eventually adopted antimonopoly laws, the Sherman Antitrust Act remains the most stringent in the world.

American regulatory practice during the twentieth century was shaped by three outbursts of legislation: during the Progressive Era (1901–1914), the New Deal (1933–1938), and the later period of focused concern for safety, social justice, and environmental protection (1964–1971). Although several exceptions might be noted, this legislation and the agencies it created generally were designed to restrain the power of business. An appropriate symbol is the giant statuary outside the Federal Trade Commission building in Washington, which depicts powerful, unruly horses being held in check by the hand of a man. American agencies with direct authority over business practices, such as the Securities and Exchange Commission, remain far stronger than their foreign counterparts.

In the United States, then, regulatory behavior in the twentieth century was typically restrictive. In other countries it was more often promotional. In some ways this represents a reversal of nineteenth-century practice, when the United States was the most hospitable of all countries to the conduct of business enterprise. The more precise point is that during the twentieth century, the promotional activities of the American government differed in kind from those elsewhere. In other countries, such measures focused on industrial planning, sectoral growth, and targeted key industries. Seen most clearly in the post–World War II activities of Japan's Ministry of International Trade and Industry, industrial planning had many counterparts elsewhere: in French indicative planning of the 1950s and 1960s, in the corporatist interlocks of German banks, labor unions, and large firms, even in the experiments under Labour governments in Britain. None of these practices, all of which fall under the general rubric of "industrial policy," took firm root in America, with the sole exception of what pejoratively has been called "Pentagon capitalism."

In America, nearly all promotional management of the macroeconomy was a post–New Deal phenomenon and was Keynesian in outlook. It looked not to individual firms, industries, or sectors but to aggregates of the major national income accounts: consumption, investment, and government spending. It operated primarily on the demand side through management of fiscal policy. Its general aim was to counteract violent swings of the business cycle such as those that brought severe depressions in the 1890s and 1930s. The ideas that motivated it were complex, involving such Keynesian arcana

as equations designed to compute the "autonomous spending multiplier" as a tool for setting tax policy. At the height of its influence in the 1960s, some Keynesians spoke confidently of fine-tuning the entire national economy. Subsequent events, including the Vietnam War, the combined high inflation and high unemployment of the 1970s, and the soaring fiscal and trade deficits of the 1980s, brought an embarrassed silence on the subject of fine-tuning.

Yet the fact remained that in the decades after World War II, the American state explicitly accepted the principle of a mixed economy and with it governmental responsibility for national economic well-being. This became evident starting with the Employment Act of 1946, an avowedly Keynesian measure, and it continued through all postwar presidencies — even that of Ronald Reagan, who, though no Keynesian, oversaw the most drastic (and hazardous) changes in fiscal policy since World War II. This overt acceptance of responsibility for economic performance epitomized the revolution in thinking about the connections among ideas, policies, and outcomes in the relationship between government and the economy.

J. R. T. Hughes, *Social Control in the Colonial Economy* (1976); Thomas K. McCraw, *Prophets of Regulation* (1984); Glenn Porter, ed., *Encyclopedia of American Economic History* (1980).

THOMAS K. MCCRAW

See also American System; Antitrust Movement; Economic Growth; Expansion, Continental and Overseas; Federal Trade Commission; Gramm-Rudman Act; Interstate Commerce Commission; National Debt; National Recovery Administration; New Deal; Reconstruction Finance Corporation; Securities and Exchange Commission; Slavery; Tariff.

GRAHAM, BILLY

(1918–   ), preacher and evangelist. Perhaps no figure is more fixed in popular consciousness as the embodiment of conservative Protestantism in the twentieth century than William Franklin ("Billy") Graham. His evangelistic crusades around the world, his television appearances and radio broadcasts, his friendships with presidents, and his unofficial role as spokesman for America's evangelicals have made him one of the most recognized religious figures of his time.

Graham, born near Charlotte, North Carolina, went to a revival service in 1934 and there experienced a religious conversion that shaped the direction of his life. After attending Bob Jones University, a hotbed of fundamentalism, he transferred to Florida Bible Institute near Tampa, where he became a Southern Baptist and began to develop the perspicuous and persuasive preaching style for which he would become famous. He then went to Wheaton College in Illinois, where he continued his preaching and enlarged his circle of evangelical contacts. Upon graduation, he skipped seminary, became pastor of a small congregation in Chicago, and started a weekly radio program. In 1946, Graham joined the staff of Youth for Christ and embarked on his evangelistic campaigns.

He conducted a successful Los Angeles crusade in 1949, which brought him national attention, in no small measure because newspaper magnate William Randolph Hearst, impressed with his preaching and his virulent anticommunist rhetoric, instructed his papers to "puff Graham." If the Los Angeles campaign made him a celebrity, his New York City crusade in 1957, which filled Madison Square Garden for four months, defined his place within the evangelical subculture. To many of the more militant fundamentalists, Graham's willingness to cooperate with mainline Protestant clergy was an act of betrayal. Indeed, throughout his career, Graham's refusal to be sectarian placed him at odds with many who regarded him as a liberal.

By any reasonable standard, of course, Graham has been no liberal, either theologically or politically. He has preached all the tenets of evangelical orthodoxy, including the necessity of spiritual rebirth and the expectation of an imminent apocalypse as predicted in the book of *Revelation*. His well-publicized friendships with American presidents have nudged him into the political arena, although, with one exception, he has stopped short of making endorsements. The exception turned out to be a major embarrass-

ment: Richard Nixon in 1972, the year of the Watergate scandals. Since then, Graham has shied away from politics, although he has spoken occasionally in favor of nuclear disarmament.

Throughout his career, Graham's appeal lay in his forceful preaching and a simple, homespun message that harks back to Charles Grandison Finney: repent of your sins, accept Christ as savior, and you shall be saved. Behind that simple message, however, stood a sophisticated organization, the Billy Graham Evangelistic Association, which provided extensive advance work and a follow-up program for converts. During the 1980s, when other television preachers were embroiled in sensational scandals, Graham remained above the fray.

For millions of American evangelicals, Graham is a kind of elder statesman and an exemplar of both Christian piety and ethical propriety. To the public, he is the most respectable symbol of American evangelicalism.

Marshall Frady, *Billy Graham: A Parable of American Righteousness* (1979); William G. McLoughlin, *Billy Graham: Revivalist in a Secular Age* (1960).

RANDALL BALMER

See also Evangelicalism; Religion.

GRAHAM, MARTHA

(1894–1991), dancer, choreographer, and pioneer in the development of American modern dance. Born in Allegheny, Pennsylvania, Graham discovered her vocation as a teenager in southern California when she witnessed a performance by Ruth St. Denis. Enrolling at the Denishawn school in Los Angeles, Graham studied the exotic styles popularized by St. Denis and other "art" dancers of the period and eventually joined the Denishawn company as a soloist.

Discontented with exoticism, Graham broke with Denishawn in 1923 and settled in New York. With composer Louis Horst, who became her accompanist and longtime collaborator, she now set out on the journey that established her as the leading figure of modern dance. The dances she began to create in the 1920s were spare, stark, angular, and abstract — movement stripped of inessentials, an art engaged with modernity. A recurring theme, masterfully captured in *Heretic,* pitted the outsider against society; other dances stressed ritual (*Primitive Mysteries*), the American experience (*Frontier*), and antifascism (*Deep Song*). Her stagecraft was as uncompromising as her vision; until 1935, she used no sets and only the simplest of dresses — long jersey "tubes" of her own design. Equally uncompromising was her technique, which she based on the principles of "contraction" and "release" and developed into the most influential system of training in modern dance.

From 1927 until 1938, Graham choreographed exclusively for women. But with the appearance of men in her society of vestals, the focus of her work changed. The anxiety of female desire now became her great theme, and in works based on ancient myth like *Night Journey* and *Clytemnestra,* she treated it as an archetypal dilemma of the human condition — a measure of Jung's powerful influence over artists of the 1940s and 1950s. Her treatment of design also changed; working with sculptor Isamu Noguchi, who created most of her sets between 1944 and 1967, she remade the stage as a timeless landscape of the mind — minimalist, erotically suggestive, and visually arresting.

Although Graham continued to choreograph, the 1960s brought a waning of her creative powers and the end of her influence over younger choreographers. With each passing season, however, her legend grew, as did that of her company, which has outlived all other modern dance groups since its founding in the late 1920s. This remarkable longevity, a tribute to Graham's vision, tenacity, and willpower, has kept her greatest works before the public, establishing her preeminent position among the makers of what is today called "historic" modern dance.

Just as Graham's technique influenced modern dance training for decades, so her company was the breeding ground for numerous modern dance choreographers, from Anna Sokolow, May O'Donnell, Jane Dudley, Sophie Maslow, Erick Hawkins, Pearl Lang, and Robert Cohan, who largely followed in her direction, to Merce Cunningham and Paul Taylor, who went their own ways to become the outstanding figures of the subsequent generation.

Don McDonagh, *Martha Graham: A Biography* (1973); Ernestine Stodelle, *Deep Song: The Dance Story of Martha Graham* (1984).

LYNN GARAFOLA

See also Dance.

GRAMM-RUDMAN ACT

This act, actually the Gramm-Rudman-Hollings Act, was passed on December 11, 1985. It set a series of targets for eliminating the federal budget deficit by October 1, 1990. If Congress and the president failed to agree on voluntary spending reductions, the law called for automatic cuts of the necessary percentage from each item in the budget. One-half of the cuts were to come from domestic spending and one-half from defense spending.

On July 7, 1986, the Supreme Court struck down the automatic-cut provision, on the ground that the act improperly delegated authority to the controller-general, an agent of Congress designated to implement the cuts. Congress restored the automatic cuts in 1987, avoiding constitutional problems by assigning the power to make the cuts to the president and the director of the Office of Management and Budget.

See also National Debt.

GRANGER MOVEMENT

The Granger movement began on December 4, 1867, in Washington, D.C., with the formation of a secret fraternal society for farmers called the National Grange of the Patrons of Husbandry. At first most of the local branches, called Granges, were in Minnesota, the home of the founder, Oliver Kelley. During the 1870s, however, the movement spread rapidly, fed by agrarian desperation over hard times, high railroad shipping rates, and tight money. By 1875, the membership had passed 850,000. During these years, the Grangers placed growing emphasis on the extent to which farmers were being victimized by railroads, merchants, and banks. The Patrons of Husbandry stood at the head of a nationwide agrarian movement — involving many non-Grange farmers' clubs and political parties — that created hundreds of cooperatives, founded banks, pushed through legislation regulating railroads and grain elevators, and campaigned for political candidates.

During the 1880s, agricultural conditions improved in the Midwest, and the Granger membership dropped to 150,000. But the agrarian revolt moved south and west, where the new Farmers' Alliance movement mushroomed as the Grange had a decade earlier. After the failure of the Populist party, which grew out of the Alliance in the 1890s, the Grange began to grow again, but it never regained the central position in agrarian politics it had held in the 1870s. Because of opposition from local businesses as well as the Grangers' own inexperience, few of their economic initiatives succeeded. Nevertheless, they set important precedents with their legislation, particularly those regulating railroads (as affirmed by the Supreme Court in *Munn* v. *Illinois,* 1877). More important, the Granger movement marked the beginning of an aggressive and self-conscious effort by the nation's farmers to define their problems in economic terms and to address those problems through economic and political action.

See also Agriculture; *Munn* v. *Illinois.*

GRANT, ULYSSES S.

(1822–1885), Civil War general and eighteenth president of the United States. Born in Point Pleasant, Ohio, Grant was a plain, unassuming product of the Midwest. His life was one of pathetically ordinary failure in everything save the waging or writing of war. The son of a tanner, he had no taste for his father's trade. He graduated from West Point in 1843 and compiled a solid record of service in the Mexican War, but his army career collapsed in the peacetime boredom of a long isolated tour of duty in northern California and Oregon. A drinking problem has-

tened his resignation from the army in 1854. Next he tried farming and real estate ventures without success. When the Civil War broke out in the spring of 1861, he was working as a clerk for his father in Galena, Illinois.

Grant found his calling in the Civil War. The conflict energized him and restored his confidence. First commissioned as a colonel of the Twenty-first Illinois Volunteer Infantry, he was promoted in August 1861 to brigadier general of volunteers. He commanded the land forces that captured Fort Henry on the Tennessee River and Fort Donelson on the Cumberland River in February 1862. This was his first important battle and the first major Union victory of the war. Confederate armies counterattacked at the Battle of Shiloh in April 1862. Aided by timely reinforcements, a surprised and initially outgeneraled Grant was able to hold his position and force a Confederate retreat into Mississippi.

Grant's most stunning victory in the West came out of the Vicksburg campaign in the spring of 1863. In a brilliant display of strategic audacity, he outflanked the Confederate defenders of Vicksburg by using the Union navy to run his army downriver from the city. He then defeated surprised and scattered Confederate armies and successfully besieged Vicksburg from the east. The city, the last major Confederate position on the Mississippi River, surrendered on July 4, 1863. Having been given the top Union command in the West in October, Grant lifted the Confederate siege of Chattanooga the next month and routed Braxton Bragg's Confederate Army of Tennessee. The way was now open for the Union campaign against Atlanta.

Congress revived the rank of lieutenant general specifically for Grant, and President Abraham Lincoln appointed him supreme commander of the Union armies in March 1864. In a series of bloody, grinding encounters Grant finally wore down Robert E. Lee's Army of Northern Virginia between May 1864 and April 1865. Lee surrendered to Grant at Appomattox Court House on April 9, 1865.

Grant's postwar career was decidedly anticlimactic. To be sure, he was elected as a Republican to two terms as president (1869–1877), but his administrations were marred by indecisive leadership, an inconsistent policy on southern Reconstruction, and massive corruption. Coupled with a severe economic depression that began in 1873, administration scandals cost Grant much of his popularity. Nonetheless, his presidency did have some solid accomplishments. The Treaty of Washington in 1872 resolved a major dispute with Great Britain over damages inflicted on American shipping by Confederate raiders built in British shipyards during the Civil War. The Enforcement Acts of 1870–1871 broke the power of the Ku Klux Klan in the Reconstruction South, and the Civil Rights Act of 1875 marked an unprecedented attempt to extend federal protection of black civil rights to areas of public accommodations.

After returning to the United States from a world tour in the late 1870s, Grant went bankrupt as a result of foolish investments in the fraudulent banking firm of Grant & Ward. Though once again a failure in civilian life, Grant did much to redeem his place in history by writing his *Personal Memoirs.* Finished just before his death from throat cancer in 1885, his memoirs stand as one of the clearest and most powerful military narratives ever written.

Ulysses S. Grant, *Personal Memoirs of U. S. Grant,* 2 vols., reprint ed. (1982); William S. McFeely, *Grant: A Biography* (1981).

WILLIAM L. BARNEY

See also Civil War; Elections: 1868, 1872. *For events during Grant's administration, see Alabama* Claims; Civil Service Reform; Corruption; Crédit Mobilier of America; Legal Tender Cases; Reconstruction; *Slaughterhouse* Cases; Tweed Ring.

GREAT AWAKENING

From the late 1730s to the 1760s a great wave of religious enthusiasm swept over large parts of Britain's North American colonies. This outburst of religious fervor, known as the Great Awakening, set the precedent for what became a recurrent and distinctive feature of American religious life: revivalism.

As far back as the 1720s Theodore Frelinghuysen, influenced by German Pietism, led a renewal of religious enthusiasm among New Jer-

sey congregants of the Dutch Reformed church. About the same time, William and Gilbert Tennent spurred a similar revival among New Jersey Presbyterians. And in 1734 Jonathan Edwards began preaching a powerful but gloomy message of revival to Congregationalists in the Connecticut River valley.

These isolated sparks of religious enthusiasm caught fire when George Whitefield, an English associate of John Wesley, arrived in Georgia in 1738. During his fifteen-month tour of the colonies, Whitefield preached in Charleston, Philadelphia, New York, and Boston. Employing a highly emotional speaking style, Whitefield made audiences shed tears of despair and joy. Thousands flocked to his sermons. His impact was enormous, his method and style widely imitated.

After initially welcoming Whitefield and his fellow revivalists, many clergymen began having second thoughts. Trained in theological seminaries and attached to churches and parishes, they perceived itinerant revivalists — many of whom had no theological training and did not depend on written texts for their sermons — as unorthodox, disruptive to regular churchgoing, and threats to clerical authority. As a result, Presbyterians, Congregationalists, and other denominations split into "Old Light" and "New Light" factions, and new sects like the Baptists and Methodists gained many adherents. Such schisms reinforced the divisions in American society between established elites and newer arrivals, town and country, debtors and creditors, and the growing tensions engendered by the spread of the market economy.

Revivalists themselves differed in emphasis, some dwelling on the consequences of eternal damnation, others on the observable effects of sinfulness; some on personal salvation, others on the collective transformation that would occur as a result of the events that would culminate in the Second Coming of Jesus. But the core of revivalism was belief in the sinfulness and helplessness of humankind and the possibility of redemption. To cleanse oneself of sin, to avoid eternal damnation and win eternal salvation, one had to surrender to God's will, to identify completely with Jesus Christ. This decision had to be accompanied by an emotionally wrenching conversion. Such conversion experiences were elicited by itinerant preachers in traveling revivals, called camp meetings, under tents or in open fields or often in churches provided (sometimes grudgingly) by regular clergy.

The Great Awakening extended the reach and scope of religion to the poor, to blacks who had been spurned by the established sects, to people in newly settled areas, and to women who were attracted to the new style of preaching. From the initial wave of fervor in the 1740s, religious enthusiasm ebbed and flowed in the colonies, finally peaking in Virginia in the 1760s. But the disruptions surrounding the Revolution to a large extent displaced religious obsessions in the mind of the public. Revivalism never completely disappeared, however. It would surface again in the nineteenth century in a Second Great Awakening.

See also Edwards, Jonathan; Evangelicalism; Religion; Second Great Awakening.

GREAT BRITAIN–U.S. RELATIONS

A famous comment about Anglo-American relations, attributed to Winston Churchill, asserts that the United States and Great Britain are two nations divided by a common language. Certainly there has been an ambiguity in their relations right from the start. In the twentieth century, the term *special relationship* has often been used to describe the conjunction of interests between the two nations. But while there is little doubt that there are many shared assumptions on both sides of the Atlantic, it would be misleading to minimize the differences. Their original relationship was defined by the tension between the mother country's colonial policies, eventually evolving into the system called mercantilism, and the desire in the colonies for increasing "home rule."

Colonists were also torn, however, between wishing to see themselves as English citizens, with all the rights and cultural advantages of such a status, and more specific ambitions for the prosperity of Massachusetts or Pennsylvania or Virginia. It was not until the middle of the eighteenth century that the latter feeling began to dominate, as various schemes of colonial unification were discussed in local taverns and political gatherings.

Benjamin Franklin, for example, took a leading part in drafting the Albany Plan of 1754, a proposal for a central colonial authority that could deal with Native Americans and the French threat. Neither London nor the colonial assemblies were ready for such a bold departure, and the plan died — but not the restless spirits behind the plan. At the end of the Great War for Empire (1754–1763), several new forces came into play that further stimulated the growth of an American "nationalism." Among these, of course, were the various levies and taxes that London sought to impose on the colonies.

From King George's point of view the need to pay for the war against the French justified the taxes, but they had a special ideological meaning in the colonies. It was now possible for protesting colonists to finesse the issue of rebellion or treason by seeing themselves as English citizens deprived of the rights of their forebears by a corrupt ministry. Franklin, who represented the colonies in England on various issues, came to a portentous conclusion in 1767 — one that reflected a dramatic shift for him personally and that captured a general developing mood. "Every man in England," he wrote a Scottish friend, "seems to consider himself as a Piece of a Sovereign over America; seems to jostle himself into the throne with the King, and talks of *OUR Subjects in the Colonies.*"

Neatly combined in Franklin's complaint were many of the themes that characterized Anglo-American relations, not only in the last years before the Revolution but well into the early years of American independence: Anglophobia, a sense of cultural inferiority, and outraged pride. These became particularly acute in the last decade of the eighteenth century, when protests against Jay's Treaty rocked the Washington administration. Popular outrage spread rapidly against supposedly humiliating terms that England imposed on the new nation if Americans were to gain access to empire markets. It was said that one could travel at night by the light of burning effigies of its negotiator, the abominable John Jay!

As much an ideological issue as a political or economic question, criticism of the treaty became a rallying point for a new political party, the Democratic-Republicans, which split the Federalist alliance. All the unresolved matters left over from the revolutionary war — economic, political, ideological — later came to a head in the disputes over the rights of neutral nations during the wars of the French Revolution. President Thomas Jefferson attempted to use economic coercion to bring England to abandon its infringement of those claimed rights through the novel method of a self-imposed embargo in 1807. The list of grievances this remedy was supposed to cure included the British practice of impressment of American sailors and London's continued aid to Native Americans opposing the westward march of settlers driving out into the Ohio Valley and beyond.

Not surprisingly, Jefferson failed in his mission and President James Madison finally opted for war as the only solution. The War of 1812 was arguably the least glorious episode in American military history. Attempted invasions of Canada failed miserably, and the British burned Washington. New England states — damaged economically by the embargo — opposed the war as quixotic, and even threatened to secede. Only Andrew Jackson's belated victory in the Battle of New Orleans offered a measure of solace for President Madison. Politically, however, the war marked the end of the period of intense Anglo-American antagonism. In that sense it perhaps deserves the title it is sometimes given — the Second War for Independence.

For the first time, American and British economic interests merged in other areas of the world, particularly Latin America. Both countries, for example, supported the independence of Latin America against any effort by Spain or France to reconquer the new nations. Secretary of State John Quincy Adams could even take some credit for one-upping British diplomacy by insisting that President James Monroe turn down an overture for a joint statement on Latin America. Since British interests dictated support for the new nations, he argued, there was no reason for the United States not to declare its own policy — and take the credit.

In the 1830s and 1840s there was, however, a strong feeling that America needed a third declaration of independence, an intellectual separation from England. Men of letters, especially, worried that Americans must find a new voice for themselves and not be tied to the European past. Ralph Waldo Emerson declared for "self-reliance" in all things, a theme taken up in one way or another by American writers down through Herman Melville and Walt Whitman, and even Henry James, who made American "innocence" a central core of his novels of transatlantic confrontation.

During the Civil War, careful diplomacy avoided what could have been a dangerous situation for both countries. British policymakers were pulled in two directions. On the one hand, the American conflict suggested a not unwelcome outcome of permanent division of the United States into two nations, forever rivals with one another, and therefore less a threat to Britain — especially since that outcome would ensure cheap cotton supplies for British industry. On the other hand, if that did not happen, and a victorious Lincoln administration and its successors harbored deep resentments against London for attempting to take advantage of the Civil War, a very bad situation could develop. For a time, the issue of Anglo-American relations hung in the balance. When it appeared that London would allow British shipbuilders to supply the Confederacy with armored rams that could break the Union blockade, the American minister, Charles Francis Adams, warned the British foreign secretary, Lord Russell, that if the rams sailed, "it would be superfluous in me to point out to your Lordship that this is war." The rams did not sail, and after the Civil War Britain paid the United States $15.5 million to settle the *Alabama* claims, compensation for damages done by a ship that had been allowed to sail before Russell intervened.

The last serious crisis in which war was an actual possibility came in the 1890s. In the middle of the decade Great Britain and Venezuela were at a dangerous point in a dispute over the boundaries of British Guiana. The matter was more than a question of territory and border markers because it involved control of the mouth of the Orinoco River, a crucial entrepôt for trade in the hinterland. The Cleveland administration, partly for domestic political reasons and partly to ensure its right to have a say on such questions in terms of its own political and economic interests, fired off a note that declared American wishes to be paramount in the Western Hemisphere. Britain would have to accept the proposed remedy of arbitration or face a crisis in Anglo-American relations. Faced with threats from Germany and Japan, London backed down.

The ensuing years of rapprochement saw the beginning of what would be called in the twentieth century the special relationship between England and the United States. It was based upon both an unwritten understanding that Britain would not challenge American policy in the Western Hemisphere and the two nations' growing commonality of interests in other areas — for example, China where the Continental powers and Japan sought exclusive spheres of influence. Secretary of State John Hay's famous Open Door notes (1899–1900), which called for equal treatment of foreign commerce throughout China, were only the latest additions to a policy long supported by British diplomats. London leaned over backward, on the other hand, to secure American goodwill in another famous issue, the Alaskan boundary dispute — even at the cost of alienating Canadian opinion. When gold was discovered in 1896, the boundary between Alaska and Canada became a vital issue. Infuriated by Canadian claims, President Theodore Roosevelt sent troops to Alaska. He eventually accepted a proposed solution of an arbitration commission; but instead of the impartial jurists called for in the agreement, he appointed three politicians committed to his position. The deciding vote, cast by England's lord chief justice, was in favor of Alaska, stranding the two Canadian appointees on a sacrificial altar to Anglo-American "friendship."

Nevertheless, when President Woodrow Wilson asked Congress to declare war on the Central Powers in April 1917, he was careful not to say he had joined the "Allies" in their struggle for victory. Instead, he formulated the awkward-sounding phrase the "Allies and Associated Powers" to describe America's arm's-length relations with England, France, and Russia. Although Wilson was himself a close student and admirer of British political institutions, the president was determined that American principles should replace European institutions if the world were to be made safe for democracy. And at the Paris peace conference, Anglo-American differences over many questions, including reparations from Germany, surfaced to disrupt Anglo-American harmony.

But the relationship had fundamentally changed. When America entered World War I it owed Europe several billions of dollars; at the time of the armistice, the situation was reversed. London agreed to pay an annual sum toward final settlement of a war debt to America that it naturally resented: in its eyes, Britain had endured great sacrifice on behalf of the interests of both English-speaking nations while America was still at peace and enjoying the profits of the war trade.

American pressure was also intense at the Washington Naval Conference of 1921–1922. At that gathering of the major sea powers, the United States insisted, before it would agree to limit naval construction, that the British abandon plans to renew the Anglo-Japanese alliance.

In the decade that followed the Washington Naval Conference, however, Anglo-American economic relations became closer than ever before, as American corporations like the Ford Motor Company and Hoover Vacuum Cleaners worked a small revolution in the way Britons traveled and took care of their homes. American films and jazz brought dramatic new changes to the way the British viewed the United States and the world. There were protests against the "Americanization" of British lifestyles and values, but the Americans were there to stay.

World War II completed the cycle. Thousands of American airmen and soldiers spent much of the war in England, to both the satisfaction and the dismay of the citizenry. When the Lend-Lease Act passed Congress in 1941, Prime Minister Winston Churchill called the aid program for England the most unsordid act in history. Washington attached conditions to Lend-Lease, however, that required the British to participate in the formation, largely on American terms, of a postwar economic system to replace the now-failed gold standard of Victorian days.

There was no question now but that the special relationship was a very one-sided affair. American policymakers soon came to believe that England should abandon dreams of its lost empire and join closely with Europe in the problems of reconstruction and the cold war. Annoyed by British reluctance to see things quite that way, an American statesman, Dean Acheson, declared in a public address that Great Britain had lost an empire but had not found a suitable role in the postwar world.

The formal "transfer of power," if that is a reasonable way to describe it, came in 1947, when British diplomats informed Washington that His Majesty's government could no longer support Western interests in Greece and Turkey. It now fell to the Americans to take up the responsibility, said London. On March 12, 1947, President Harry S. Truman asked Congress to appropriate $500 million for aid to Greece and Turkey, the first step in a policy soon to be called the Truman Doctrine. Henceforth Great Britain would play a supporting role in American cold war policy, abandoning its primacy in the Middle East in the 1950s and retreating from east of Suez in the next decade. With a sigh, Britons took up the burden of playing the Greeks to the new Roman Empire.

The Lion's last roar — the ill-fated 1956 attempt to reverse Egypt's nationalization of the Suez Canal — offered conclusive evidence that the special relationship did not protect London against Washington's anger if the two capitals disagreed about ways of meeting nationalist upsurges in the third world. During the 1960s and 1970s British policymakers and the public, on the other hand, were often disturbed about American policies in the third world, especially the Vietnam War. Some critics, indeed, saw joining Europe as a way of detaching Britain from the questionable benefits of the special relationship.

In the 1980s, however, something of a resurgence in Anglo-American relations took place, in large part because both nations were led by conservative parties and strong-minded individuals,

Margaret Thatcher and Ronald Reagan. Cultural ties between the two countries remained strong throughout the entire postwar era, as Americans adopted the Beatles for their own and British musical theater learned from Broadway the mysteries of the smash hit. With the end of the cold war, however, neither nation was too sure of its future role in European affairs.

David Dimbleby and David Reynolds, *An Ocean Apart: The Relationship between Britain and America in the Twentieth Century* (1988); Christopher Hitchens, *Blood, Class, and Nostalgia: Anglo-American Ironies* (1990).

LLOYD C. GARDNER

See also Alabama Claims; America in the British Empire; Civil War; Colonial Wars; Embargo Act of 1807; Impressment Controversy; Jay's Treaty; Lend-Lease Act; Middle East–U.S. Relations; Monroe Doctrine; North Atlantic Treaty Organization; Open Door Policy; Paris, Treaty of (1783); Revolution; War of 1812; World War I; World War II.

GREAT DEPRESSION

See Depressions.

GREAT RAILROAD STRIKE OF 1877

See Railroad Strike of 1877.

GREAT SOCIETY

Lyndon B. Johnson, early in his unexpected presidency, called on the federal government to create a "great society" in America. That phrase has since become synonymous with the domestic record of the two Democratic administrations of the 1960s. Many Great Society programs had their origins under John F. Kennedy but came to fruition after (and in part because of) Kennedy's untimely death. Others were responses to the particular social crises of Johnson's own troubled administration. Whatever their beginnings, however, the programs of the Great Society constituted the most important expansion of the American state since the New Deal.

Unlike the New Deal, which was a response to a severe economic crisis, the Great Society emerged in a period of unprecedented prosperity. Its first and most important programs emerged largely from within the government itself, a result of optimistic planning by policymakers who believed that American economic growth would make possible bold new public efforts. But some later Great Society initiatives were a result of social pressure from below, a response to the increasing militancy and intermittent violence of the black struggle for equality and to the conviction of many liberals that only a major public effort to fight urban poverty could prevent continuing social disorder.

The most important domestic achievement of the Johnson administration may have been the president's success in translating some of the demands of the civil rights movement into law. Two major civil rights acts were passed in the first two years of his presidency. The 1964 act forbade job discrimination and the segregation of public accommodations; the 1965 law guaranteed black voting rights. A third civil rights act in 1968 banned housing discrimination and extended constitutional protections to Indians on reservations. But when historians refer to the Great Society, they usually mean the remarkable array of initiatives launched between 1964 and 1967 designed to expand the social welfare system and eliminate poverty.

Johnson had begun his political career as a disciple of Franklin D. Roosevelt, and his fondest dream was to create a record of domestic achievement comparable to that of the New Deal. Indeed, several of his administration's most important achievements fulfilled pledges that Roosevelt and Harry S. Truman had made a generation before. The Medicare program, which Congress approved in 1965, was a first step toward creating the system of national health insurance that liberals had been advocating since World War II. It provided federal funding for many of the medical costs of older Americans; and it overcame the bitter resistance to the idea of "socialized medicine" by making its benefits available to everyone over sixty-five, re-

gardless of need, and by linking payments to the existing private insurance system. A year later, the government extended the system to welfare recipients of all ages through the Medicaid program.

But the Johnson administration also moved into areas that few New Dealers had contemplated. It shattered a long-standing political taboo by providing significant federal aid to public education. The Elementary and Secondary Education Act of 1965 offered assistance to underfunded public school districts throughout the country; the Higher Education Act of the same year provided aid to needy college and university students. Other Great Society initiatives included the creation of the Department of Housing and Urban Development and the Department of Transportation, the establishment of the National Endowments for the Humanities and the Arts and the Corporation for Public Broadcasting, a dramatic expansion of federal housing subsidies, and environmental legislation to protect air and water.

The most ambitious and controversial part of the Great Society was a federal effort the Kennedy administration had been contemplating since at least early 1963. Johnson launched it publicly in the first months of his presidency: an "unconditional war on poverty" designed finally to eliminate hunger and deprivation from American life. The centerpiece of the War on Poverty was the Economic Opportunity Act of 1964, which created an Office of Economic Opportunity (OEO) to oversee a variety of community-based antipoverty programs. The OEO reflected a fragile consensus among policymakers that the best way to deal with poverty was not simply to raise the incomes of the poor but to help them better themselves through education, job training, and community development. Central to its mission was the idea of "community action," the participation of the poor themselves in framing and administering the programs designed to help them.

The War on Poverty began with a $1 billion appropriation in 1964 and spent another $2 billion in the following two years. It spawned dozens of programs, among them the Job Corps, whose purpose was to help disadvantaged youths develop marketable skills; Volunteers in Service to America (VISTA), a domestic version of the Peace Corps, which sent middle-class young people on "missions" into poor neighborhoods; the Model Cities program for urban redevelopment; Upward Bound, which assisted poor high school students entering college; legal services for the poor; the Food Stamps program; and Project Head Start, which offered preschool education for poor children.

In the end, however, the War on Poverty had only a modest impact. Controversial from the beginning, always without funding adequate for its goals, it scored some significant local successes and helped create several programs of lasting value (including Head Start and Food Stamps). But mounting political opposition to the community action programs as well as budgetary pressures caused by the expansion of the Vietnam War brought the War on Poverty to a premature end after 1967. American poverty did decline in the 1960s (although probably as much because of economic growth as of government programs), but it remained an intractable problem precisely where the War on Poverty had attempted to end it: in the inner cities, in rural America, and above all in the growing number of female-headed households in the nation's black communities.

The War on Poverty, and the Great Society of which it was a part, left a mixed legacy. They were responsible for the most important legal protections of civil rights since the 1860s; they permanently expanded the American welfare and social insurance system; and they gave the federal government important new responsibilities in such areas as the environment, education, and the arts. But the largest Great Society programs — Medicare and Medicaid — proved to be highly inefficient and unwieldy; they ultimately became two of the most costly items in the federal budget. And the gap between the expansive intentions of the War on Poverty and its relatively modest achievements fueled later conservative arguments that government is not an appropriate vehicle for solving social problems.

Michael B. Katz, *The Undeserving Poor* (1989); Allen J. Matusow, *The Unraveling of America* (1984); James T. Patterson, *America's Struggle against Poverty, 1900–1980* (1981).

ALAN BRINKLEY

See also Affirmative Action; Black Ghettos; Civil Rights Movement; Johnson, Lyndon B.; Medicaid; Medicare; Poverty; Welfare and Public Relief.

GREELEY, HORACE

(1811–1872), editor and political leader. The son of a New Hampshire farmer, Greeley grew up in poverty. He had little formal schooling, but, encouraged by his mother, he learned to read at home. Apprenticed to a newspaper editor at fourteen, he learned the printing trade and read widely in newspapers and books.

At the age of twenty he arrived in New York City with "a decent knowledge" of printing, ten dollars in his pocket, and a "rustic manner," as he recalled. An ardent Whig he acceded in 1838 to Thurlow Weed's request to edit a weekly paper backing William H. Seward for governor. For the next sixteen years Weed, Seward, and Greeley formed "a political firm" that ended only when Weed turned a deaf ear to Greeley's political ambitions.

After successfully editing another Whig weekly supporting William Henry Harrison for president in 1840, Greeley launched a daily newspaper. He conceived of the *New York Tribune* as a journal that would be neither extremely partisan nor politically neutral but loyal to its Whig editor's convictions.

Greeley by this time had developed a clear, vigorous literary style and a broad range of interests. The course he followed often seemed as eccentric as his personal appearance. A frail figure whose blue eyes set in a moon-shaped face peered through glasses resting low on his nose, he spoke in a high-pitched whine and dressed in ill-fitting clothes. An ardent champion of nationalism, he urged during the secession crisis that the government let the "wayward sisters," the cotton states, "depart in peace," but only after a popular vote. He became a strident foe of the Confederacy, although after the war he signed Jefferson Davis's bail bond. A lifelong supporter of a protective tariff, he nevertheless accepted the presidential nomination of the Liberal Republicans who favored tariff reduction. But despite these contradictory stances, he was a strong shaper of public opinion.

At the *Tribune*, Greeley surrounded himself with a brilliant staff that included Charles A. Dana, Margaret Fuller, James S. Pike, Bayard Taylor, and George Ripley. His influence, however, sprang chiefly from his faith in the common man and his championship of causes that would free Americans from political, class, and racial injustices. Over the years he supported homestead legislation, westward expansion, government aid to railroads, labor unions, cooperatives, vocational education, women's rights (but not suffrage), temperance, and free speech. He opposed land monopoly by railroads and capital punishment.

During the 1850s the *Tribune* extended its influence throughout the North, especially through its weekly edition. The paper took a vigorous antislavery stand, favoring the Wilmot Proviso and opposing the Fugitive Slave Act, the Kansas-Nebraska Act, and the *Dred Scott* decision.

But his course during the Civil War was less steady. He continued to exert some weight but puzzled many readers and lost influence. He urged imprudent military action with the cry, "Forward to Richmond!" but then became involved in an injudicious peace mission in 1864. He opposed Lincoln's renomination until September 1864. His campaign for emancipation climaxed in his famous editorial "The Prayer of Twenty Millions," which prompted Lincoln's equally famous defense of his emancipation policy.

During Reconstruction Greeley backed the Fourteenth and Fifteenth Amendments, the impeachment of President Andrew Johnson, and at the same time a general amnesty for Confederates. His early support of President Ulysses S. Grant soon soured. Lukewarmly sustained by the parties that nominated him for the presidency in 1872, he suffered vituperative abuse and was pilloried by the Republican press and cartoonist Thomas Nast. Voters resoundingly rejected him at the polls.

In the last days of the campaign Greeley kept vigil at the bedside of his sick wife, who died a few days before the election. Broken in spirit by his losses, he himself died a few weeks later.

Glyndon G. Van Deusen, *Horace Greeley: Nineteenth-Century Crusader* (1953); Horace Greeley, *Recollections of a Busy Life* (1868; reprint, 1970).

JAMES A. RAWLEY

See also Elections: 1872; Magazines and Newspapers.

GREENBACK PARTY

The Greenback party (also called the National Greenback party) was organized in 1876 to campaign for expansion of the supply of paper money — "greenbacks" — first issued by the federal government in 1862 to help pay for the Civil War. The idea that maintaining a flexible supply of paper money served the interests of working people, whereas paper money backed by specie (hard money, like gold or silver) benefited only the rich, had been advanced by Edward Kellogg as early as 1841. In the 1860s, Alexander Campbell popularized Kellogg's ideas, but greenbackism did not develop a significant following until the panic of 1873, when low prices and tight credit gave Campbell's writings new appeal, especially to farmers. Many people, however, passionately opposed greenbackism, arguing that an inflated supply of paper money was immoral. In addition, of course, creditors as a group stood to lose from inflation, since debts could be repaid with less valuable dollars than those originally borrowed.

Greenbackers had tried unsuccessfully to prevent passage of the 1875 Specie Resumption Act, the law that put the nation back on hard money; in 1876 they formed a political party to demand that the law be repealed and that more paper money be issued. The Greenback party won only 80,000 votes in its first year, but its strength increased as the labor troubles of 1877 left more and more workers prepared to blame hard times on the manipulations of business leaders and bankers. In the congressional elections of 1878, the newly formed Greenback party polled nearly a million votes, sending fourteen Greenbackers to Congress and electing many to local office. As prosperity returned in the late 1880s, however, and as it became clear that the Specie Resumption Act would not be repealed, greenbackism lost its following; the party mounted its last national campaign in 1884. Still, the Greenbackers' emphasis on the political implications of monetary policy left its mark on future reform programs like populism; indeed, in 1892 the Populists chose as their presidential candidate James B. Weaver of Iowa, one of the Greenback congressmen of 1878.

See also Elections: 1880, 1884; Government and the Economy; Third Parties.

GRIFFITH, D. W.

(1875–1948), screenwriter and film director. Contemporary journalists often write as if the impact of the mass media on American life came about in the last two decades. Nowhere are the shortcomings of that assessment more evident than in the career and work of D. W. Griffith, America's first great director. Born in La Grange, Kentucky, Griffith came from an impoverished southern farm family and barely attained a grade school education. He entered the struggling film industry in 1907 and found a market for his short one-reel melodramas among the immigrant working classes of the cities.

Over the next thirteen years the director made over four hundred films that drew on earlier innovations — the close-up, parallel editing, backlighting, location shooting — to create a coherent cinematic form. By 1914, Griffith's work had become associated with the birth of a new art form and the rise in popularity of movies among middle-class audiences, creating within the large cities a mass medium that appealed to diverse groups across the older Victorian barriers of class, sex, and ethnicity.

Throughout these years, Griffith and his contemporaries saw his films as an unprecedented agency for transforming modern society and politics. Griffith's films were praised by contemporary reformers because they taught moral lessons in an effort to Americanize the immigrants and revitalize Anglo-Saxon culture. He saw his stories as metaphors for the rescue of the people from the social dangers of the day: corrupt politicians, lusty foreigners, and greedy monopolists. Drawing on the themes of nineteenth-century melodrama and dime novels, the great director emphasized the struggle of pure heroes and heroines, bathed in soft light in contrast to dark villains.

Yet like many middle-class reformers, Griffith's antagonism toward those outside the Anglo-Saxon mainstream surfaced in numerous films, and dramatically so in his most famous movie, *Birth of a Nation*. Upon its release in 1915, the film aroused protests from civil rights groups for celebrating the restoration of white rule over African-Americans in the Reconstruction era. Deeply hurt by the criticism, Griffith defended white supremacy and antimiscegenation laws, displaying his reluctance to seek allies outside his own race and class in the struggle against industrial power. By 1920, he and his fellow progressives were bereft of support and helplessly watched a new corporate order rise to unprecedented power. Unsympathetic to the themes of moral emancipation espoused by Hollywood filmmakers, Griffith found by the early twenties that his career was virtually over.

Upon his death in 1948 many observers of the film industry tried to explain his tragic final years. Some claimed that the director's dream of progressive reform alienated him from the large corporation studios in Hollywood. Others, best exemplified by the noted critic, James Agee, observed that his forward-looking film techniques were yoked to revitalizing the old moral world that had informed the Victorian theater. But "all of it, good and bad, was dying when Griffith gave it a new lease on life. . . . it died soon after and took him down with it." The filmmaker's efforts to save the old Anglo-Saxon vision of purity ended in defeat, but, ironically, his technical innovations gave birth to a modern art.

Robert Henderson, *D. W. Griffith: His Life and Work* (1972); Lary May, *Screening Out the Past: The Birth of Mass Culture and the Motion Picture Industry* (1984); Richard Schickel, *D. W. Griffith: An American Life* (1984).

LARY MAY

See also Movies.

GRIMKÉ, ANGELINA, and GRIMKÉ, SARAH

(Angelina: 1805–1879; Sarah: 1792–1873), abolitionists and advocates of woman's rights. The Grimké sisters, born and raised in South Carolina, were the daughters of a slave-owning judge and planter and the only white southern women to become leading abolitionists. Unwilling to accommodate to life in a slave society, they moved to Philadelphia and joined the Society of Friends.

Angelina became publicly associated with the abolitionist cause in 1835, when a letter she had written to William Lloyd Garrison supporting his views was published in Garrison's paper, the *Liberator*. Her *Appeal to the Christian Women of the South* (1836) was a unique attempt to draw southern white women into the antislavery cause. As a result of its wide distribution in the North by the American Anti-Slavery Society, she was invited by that group to give public lectures to antislavery women.

Having converted Sarah to an organizational commitment, Angelina with her sister moved to New York City, where they became the first female agents of the American Anti-Slavery Society; their lectures drew large "mixed" audiences of men and women. They played a leading role in the Anti-Slavery Convention of American Women in 1837, especially in introducing resolutions against race prejudice. Their early pamphlets, Angelina's *Appeal to the Women of the Nominally Free States* and Sarah's *Epistle to the Clergy of the Southern States* (both 1836), were published by the American Anti-Slavery Society. The sisters undertook a lecture tour in New England in 1837–1838, which culminated in Angelina's testimony before the Massachusetts legislature. The first American woman to address a legislative body, she presented tens of thousands of antislavery petitions that had been collected by women. The tour resulted in the formation of dozens of female antislavery societies and in the launching of a mass petitioning campaign by women, which prepared the ground for later antislavery political organization.

The sisters were attacked in the press and from the pulpit, and even by many male abolitionists for daring, as women, to speak in public; but they persisted. Angelina's *Letters to Catharine Beecher* (1838) was a spirited defense of abolitionism and women's moral responsibility for leadership. Sarah's *Letters on the Equality of the Sexes and the Condition of Women* (1838) was the first comprehensive feminist argument presented by an American woman, ten years before the Seneca Falls convention. A highly original contribution to the development of feminist thought, it marks Sarah Grimké as an important theorist and pioneer of feminism.

After Angelina's marriage to the abolitionist Theodore Weld, the couple and Sarah, who made her home with them, moved to Raritan Bay, New Jersey. They collaborated on a documentary indictment of slavery, *American Slavery as It Is: Testimony of a Thousand Witnesses* (1839), which was the most important antislavery publication before *Uncle Tom's Cabin,* for which it served as a source. Raising the Welds' three children, the sisters devoted the rest of their lives to schoolteaching, first in a communal settlement at Raritan Bay and then in Hyde Park, Massachusetts. Both remained active in the causes of abolition and woman's rights. Late in life, after discovering the existence of two black nephews, sons of their brother Henry and one of his slaves, the sisters adopted the young men into their family and helped finance their education.

Contemporaries acclaimed them primarily as abolitionists, but Sarah and Angelina Grimké's significance as pioneers of woman's rights, both in theory and in practice, assured them a place of honor in the struggle for woman's rights as well.

GERDA LERNER

See also Abolitionist Movement; Feminist Movement.

GRISWOLD V. CONNECTICUT

In this 1965 decision, the Supreme Court expanded the constitutional right of privacy. An 1879 Connecticut law forbade any use of contraception or the assisting of anyone seeking contraception. Under this statute two officers of the Planned Parenthood League were convicted of providing contraceptive information to married couples. On appeal, the Supreme Court overturned the convictions, ruling that the law was unconstitutional.

Justice William O. Douglas's majority opinion identified ways in which the First, Third, Fourth, and Fifth Amendments to the Constitution provided degrees of privacy. Further, Douglas maintained that married people's right of privacy predated the Bill of Rights; laws invading this right were unconstitutional on their face. He also raised the specter of police raids on marital bedrooms for contraception evidence if the law were allowed to stand. A concurring opinion by Justice Arthur Goldberg, joined by Justices Earl Warren and William Brennan, located the right to marital privacy in the rarely invoked Ninth Amendment, which states that the fact that a particular right is not mentioned in the Constitution does not mean that it can be curtailed by government.

See also Birth Control; Constitution.

GUGGENHEIM, PEGGY

(1898–1979), art dealer and collector. Born into one of New York's elite Jewish families, Guggenheim spent her life embracing the avant-garde in art and literature.

In the 1920s Guggenheim became acquainted in expatriate Paris with the leading literary figures of her generation including James Joyce and Ernest Hemingway. In 1938 she opened the Guggenheim Jeune Gallery on London's Cork Street, enlisting Marcel Duchamp to help her outline the course her gallery should take and to introduce her to the artists she should exhibit. In the two years she ran Guggenheim Jeune, she exhibited such artists as Jean Cocteau, Wassily Kandinsky, Yves Tanguy, and Henry Moore. Guggenheim made it a point to buy one work from each exhibition.

Although the gallery was losing money, she decided to start a museum for modern art in London. Her adviser in this venture was the art historian Herbert Read. But with the outbreak of World War II in 1939 her plans for the museum were abandoned. Finding herself in Paris,

however, she declared her intention of buying a "picture a day." Because of the war, many artists were eager to sell their works even at bargain prices in order to leave France. Between September of 1939 and the fall of France in 1940 Guggenheim bought the bulk of what would become the Peggy Guggenheim Collection including works by Constantin Brancusi, Pablo Picasso, Duchamp, and Max Ernst, all for approximately forty thousand dollars.

As the situation in Europe worsened, Guggenheim, too, was forced to return to America. In October 1942, she opened her gallery, Art of This Century, in New York. This was to be her greatest achievement. Designed by the Viennese architect Frederick Kiesler, the gallery had curved gumwood walls and pictures mounted on baseball bats. Here Guggenheim exhibited her newly acquired collection of modern masters and, more important, promoted the work of undiscovered talents — this at a time when only a handful of New York galleries showed any modern art, let alone modern American art.

At Art of This Century, Guggenheim gave solo shows and first exhibitions to many of the artists known today as the New York school — Mark Rothko, Hans Hofmann, Clyfford Still, and others who changed the face of American art. She particularly promoted the career of Jackson Pollock. In her house and gallery Guggenheim played hostess to the European artists who made New York their wartime home, including André Breton, Salvador Dali, Tanguy, and Duchamp.

When the war ended, Guggenheim returned to Europe. She made Venice her new home, buying the Palazzo Venier dei Leoni on the Grand Canal, where she installed her fabulous modern art collection. There she continued to play hostess to the illustrious and to exhibit her now priceless collection to a growing public for modern art. When she died, the Solomon R. Guggenheim Foundation took over the collection.

Guggenheim appears to have been lucky in everything but love. She had two failed marriages — to Ernst and to the writer Laurence Vail — and many celebrated affairs including ones with Tanguy and Samuel Beckett.

Guggenheim's exhibition and promotion of

abstract expressionism and the New York school energized the movement. Without her flair for publicity and her championship of Jackson Pollock the New York school would not have been the same.

Peggy Guggenheim, *Out of This Century* (1979); Jacqueline Bograd Weld, *Peggy: The Wayward Guggenheim* (1986).

JACQUELINE BOGRAD WELD

See also Abstract Expressionism; Painting and Sculpture; Pollock, Jackson.

GULF OF TONKIN RESOLUTION

The Gulf of Tonkin Resolution (August 7, 1964) gave broad congressional approval for expansion of the Vietnam War. During the spring of 1964, military planners had developed a detailed design for major attacks on the North, but at that time President Lyndon B. Johnson and his advisers feared that the public would not support an expansion of the war. By summer, however, rebel forces had established control over nearly half of South Vietnam, and Senator Barry Goldwater, the Republican nominee for president, was criticizing the Johnson administration for not pursuing the war more aggressively.

On August 2, shortly after a clandestine raid on the North Vietnamese coast by South Vietnamese gunboats, the U.S. destroyer *Maddox* (conducting electronic espionage nearby) was fired on by North Vietnamese torpedo boats. Two days later, in the same area, the *Maddox* and another destroyer reported that they were again under attack. Although these reports now appear to have been mistaken, Johnson proceeded quickly to authorize retaliatory air strikes against North Vietnam. The next day he gathered congressional leaders and, without divulging the circumstances that might have helped provoke the torpedo attack, accused the North Vietnamese of "open aggression on the high seas." He then submitted to the Senate a resolution that authorized him to take "all necessary measures to repel any armed attack against the forces of the United States and to prevent further aggression." The resolution was quickly approved by Congress; only Senators Wayne Morse of Oregon and Ernest Gruening of Alaska voted against it. Later, when more information about the Tonkin incident became available, many concluded that Johnson and his advisers had misled Congress into supporting the expansion of the war.

Six years later, amid mounting criticism of President Richard M. Nixon's Cambodian incursion, the resolution was terminated (December 31, 1970). But in fact, the war had been sustained by Congress's continued military appropriations, not by the Tonkin Resolution. Nevertheless, Johnson had frequently cited the resolution as evidence of congressional support, and to critics of the war it had become a symbol of the escalation they opposed.

See also Vietnam War.

GUNS AND GUN CONTROL

The right to keep and bear arms originated in the common law right of self-defense. As Colin Greenwood has written, "The Common Law right to keep arms and the tradition of owning arms for protection, was built up during a period when there was no effective police, when the individual was compelled to see to his own protection."

Traditionally, Americans considered each person responsible both for self-protection and for the defense of the state. Well into the nineteenth century, people needed guns to protect themselves against hostile Indians. In addition, hunting was a major source of food. People legally carried guns as a matter of course, a practice accepted as both necessary and politically desirable.

Alexander Hamilton, replying to accusations that the military power granted to the federal government in the Constitution would lead to tyranny, pointed to the armed citizen as a counterweight: "that army [the Regular Army] can never be formidable to the liberties of the people while there is a large body of citizens, little if at all inferior to them in discipline and the use of arms, who stand ready to defend their own rights and those of their fellow citizens." The private bearing of arms, then, was seen by the Founding Fathers as a positive good. The new government could not oppress the people because a citizenry "properly armed and equipped" would protect their own rights. Citizens were even required to have guns. States enforced ownership at yearly militia musters when all men were required to present their guns and ammunition for inspection.

The Second Amendment to the Constitution — "A well regulated Militia, being necessary to the security of a free State, the right of the people to keep and bear Arms shall not be infringed" — simply asserts and protects this right, and Americans have traditionally exercised the right with few restrictions. Travelers in earlier years routinely went armed. Men's pants and women's dresses were made with built-in holsters. At times, however, a few trail towns in the West required that cowboys check their guns with the sheriff before getting drunk, and most western states prohibited carrying *concealed* weapons by 1850. But in the urban East there were few places where even this restriction existed. In New Jersey, until 1927, the only gun law was a prohibition on dueling.

Gun control, in the modern sense, was a fixture of the pre–Civil War Slave Codes designed to prevent a rebellion. These laws restricted all blacks both slave and free. Immediately after the war, laws were passed in the South to prohibit freedmen from owning firearms. But in response, civil rights legislation during Reconstruction made prohibition of black gun ownership impossible, so southern laws were rewritten to restrict pistols to the expensive "Army pistol." The effect was similar to a poll tax — it discriminated against both blacks and poor whites.

There are no reliable data on gun ownership or production in the nineteenth century or even the first half of this century. Millions of guns were manufactured, imported, or sold as surplus after wars, but no one kept track until the Bureau of Alcohol, Tobacco, and Firearms was reorganized in 1968.

In 1911, after an attempt to assassinate the mayor of New York City, the New York legislature passed the Sullivan Law, which required a police permit for *both* owning and carrying a pistol. Support for the law ranged from the *New York Times* and idealistic reformers to Tammany Hall political hacks like its author, Tim Sullivan. (He was trying to give police a way to frame his enemies. One political opponent had all his pockets sewn closed after three arrests for carrying guns without a permit.) Few states, however, followed New York's lead. In forty-five of them, unlicensed pistol ownership remains legal except for persons with criminal records or the insane.

Over the next thirty years most states adopted various forms of the National Revolver Act, a law largely drafted by the National Rifle Association. It established a permit system to regulate carrying concealed weapons. In some states, the law allowed the issuing authority to reject applications without a reason. Their guidelines were vague phrases such as "good character, public safety, or need." Elsewhere, license denial must be for clearly defined causes, such as a history of crime, alcoholism, insanity, or drug abuse.

In the late 1930s federal controls were imposed on machine guns, sawed-off guns, and other dangerous devices by the National Firearms acts. The Gun Control Act of 1968 forbade the sale of guns by mail or to out-of-state residents and placed restrictions on ammunition sales. The Firearms Owner's Protection Act of 1987 repealed federal restrictions on ammunition sales and out-of-state sales of rifles and shotguns because they had proven to have no crime reduction value. It also provided for the legal transportation by interstate travelers of "unloaded and inaccessible" guns regardless of local restrictions.

Approximately half the families in the United States own a gun; estimates on the number in the country range from 60 million up to 200 million. About one American in twenty (7.5 million) carries a gun for self-protection. Fourteen percent of the gun-owning households in the United States (about 14 million people) report that they have used a gun for protection of person or property exclusive of military or police work. In 60 percent of these cases, the gun was not fired but was used as a threat, and in only 9 percent of the instances was anyone injured or killed.

There is much debate between those who would ban guns as a danger to society and those who regard them as a necessary protection for the citizen. The major parties in the debate are the National Rifle Association and Handgun Control Inc.

The National Rifle Association (NRA) has 3 million members, and sponsors and encourages target shooting, hunting, safety training, and shooting sports. The NRA has been active in lobbying on gun control issues since the 1930s. Its lobbyists try to influence federal, state, and local legislators, and its many members inundate legislators with mail. The NRA asserts the right of citizens to own and use guns and advocates strict penalties for the criminal misuse of them. It supports carry permit laws that are clear in their requirements and do not allow arbitrary denial.

Handgun Control Inc. (HCI) has about 150,000 members who lobby against gun ownership. It focused originally on pistols but has recently lobbied against ownership of semiautomatic guns of all types. The group asserts that guns are a major cause of crime and accidents, and it aims ultimately at ending gun ownership by anyone except police and the military. It has adopted a step-by-step strategy of achieving gradually increasing restrictions. As first steps, HCI supports waiting periods and police background checks before a gun can be purchased.

The United States contains millions of guns, so many, in fact, that it would probably be impossible to collect them all. Whether one approves or disapproves of them, guns seem to be a permanent part of the American scene.

Don B. Kates, Jr., ed., *Restricting Handguns* (1979); James D. Wright, Peter H. Rossi, and Kathleen Daly, *Under the Gun* (1983).

EDWARD F. LEDDY

See also Dueling; Gatling Gun.

GUTHRIE, WOODY

(1912–1967), folksinger, folk songwriter, folk poet, and novelist. "Grass roots" and "nothing artificial" best describe the songs, poems, and stories that rolled from the mind and pen of Woody Guthrie in the 1930s and 1940s. His song "This Land Is Your Land" is still one of the most widely sung songs in the country, and his children's songs, such as "Put Your Finger in the Air," are thought to be old folk songs by millions of parents, grandparents, and teachers. Using humor and vivid description, he documented the Dust Bowl decade and the problems that stalked migrant agricultural workers. He wrote peace and war songs, cowboy and hobo songs, union and work songs, love songs — songs that made people feel good and take pride in themselves.

Guthrie grew up in Oklahoma in a culturally diverse area, among cowboys, farmers, coal miners, and railroad and oil workers. There were communities of blacks and Creek Indians nearby. Farmers argued about socialism and the Green Corn Rebellion. His parents were popular and prosperous until Huntington's disease altered his mother's behavior and tore the family apart. When he was fourteen, she was taken to a mental asylum and his father to Pampa, Texas, to recuperate from severe burns. In his autobiographical novel *Bound for Glory*, Guthrie tells about those years, which shaped his wanderlust spirit.

In 1929 he joined his father in Pampa, and there experienced the Dust Bowl years. In 1937 he moved to California where he became active in left-wing activities and in late 1939 went to New York City where he met Alan Lomax, Pete Seeger, and others involved in the growing folk-topical song movement. He believed that songs could change social conditions.

Lomax recorded lengthy interviews with him in 1940 for the Library of Congress, and that same year RCA Victor issued his *Dust Bowl Ballads*. Guthrie's largest body of recordings was made for Moses Asch and Folkways Records (the Folkways collection is now owned by the Smithsonian Institution).

Guthrie wrote over a thousand songs, some of which were given away during his hoboing years and subsequently lost. He also wrote novels, short stories, newspaper columns, magazine articles, and hundreds of letters. Words flowed onto paper as easily as speech from his mouth; his style was natural and unpretentious.

Huntington's disease hospitalized him for the last fifteen years of his life. He fought his illness with humor and courage, and during those years was visited by a growing number of admirers, of whom one was the young Bob Dylan. The 1960s' years of social change were accompanied and sometimes facilitated by songs and singing, and Guthrie's songs became part of the growing urban folk revival. His influence on Dylan and the folk-rock movement earned him a place in the Rock and Roll Music Hall of Fame, and the list of singers, songwriters, and literary figures who credit him as a major source of inspiration is a long one. Equally important, but often overlooked, is his massive repertoire of traditional folk songs learned in childhood and during his travels.

Woody Guthrie is said to have had "an influence on America as strong as Walt Whitman." As critic Clifton Fadiman wrote in 1943, he and his songs are "a national possession, like Yellowstone and Yosemite."

Woody Guthrie, *Bound for Glory* (1943); Joe Klein, *Woody Guthrie: A Life* (1980).

GUY LOGSDON

See also Music.

H

HALF-WAY COVENANT

The Half-Way Covenant was an attempt by New England Puritans to confront a serious religious crisis, a crisis of faith.

Puritans had made the arduous journey to the New World in order to establish a pure community of like-minded Christians, a "City on a Hill." Although all members of a Puritan community were expected to attend church, membership carried with it the right to vote in church matters and to take communion, and it was considered a strong indication that one would receive eternal salvation. Individuals demonstrated their worthiness for membership by testifying before the congregation that God had "sanctified" them, describing a conversion experience, or moment of revelation, that the congregation then evaluated. At the start, most Puritans had had such experiences. But as time passed, fewer and fewer of the subsequent generation of settlers could qualify for church membership.

In an attempt to shore up the decline in church membership, synods debated the questions: Who is qualified for baptism? Should the children of the saved be granted church membership as well?

In 1662 a Massachusetts synod agreed that, for all churches, a "half-way" membership status would be recognized. Adults who had been baptized as children but who had not yet experienced the conversion necessary for full membership could nonetheless have their children baptized. The parents in return were to agree to maintain the church's standards of moral conduct. Until conversion, however, these parents and their children were ineligible to vote in church affairs or take communion.

Despite the Half-Way Covenant, controversy over the issue would continue for more than a century.

See also Puritanism.

HAMILTON, ALEXANDER

(1755–1804), revolutionary, politician, and statesman. Hamilton, who fought in the American Revolution as an aide-de-camp to George Washington, was a driving figure in the Federalist movement and the first secretary of the treasury. In his public and private life he combined nationalist commitment, elitist politics, and a vision of dynamic capitalist development.

Born in the West Indies, Hamilton moved to the mainland in 1772 and entered King's College (now Columbia University) the following year. By 1774 he was speaking at public meetings and writing revolutionary essays, and in 1776 he became a captain of artillery. After taking part in the Battle of Long Island and the retreat from New York City, he joined Washington's staff in 1777, where he remained until February 1781. He commanded a battery of artillery at the Battle of Yorktown.

In 1780 he married Elizabeth Schuyler, daughter of the major general and Hudson Valley landlord Philip Schuyler. He was already close to the Livingston family, and the marriage cemented his social position and his political, elitist point of view. He argued throughout the 1780s for strengthening the national government in *The Continentalist* essays, the two *Letters from Phocion,* and *The Federalist,* written with James Madison and John Jay. He served in Congress and the New York state legislature and was a delegate to the Federal Convention of 1787. Although he had been central to the movement that led to the convention, his role was relatively minor and he was privately critical of the Constitution it produced. He nonetheless devoted his full energy to ratification in 1787 and 1788.

As secretary of the treasury Hamilton's great achievement was funding the federal debt at face value, which rectified and nationalized the financial chaos inherited from the Revolution. But he accomplished still more. He was responsible for creating the First Bank of the United States on the model of the Bank of England, and his *Report on Manufactures* fostered commercial and industrial development in the new nation. He also played a significant role in generating the Washington administration's policy of unfriendly neutrality toward the French Revolution and in establishing a rapprochement with Britain.

Hamilton's policies and actions provoked intense opposition, led by Thomas Jefferson and James Madison. Just as Hamilton and Madison had collaborated in the Federalist movement during the 1780s, so Jefferson and Madison now collaborated against Hamilton's Federalist party in the 1790s. The result was division, both within the Washington administration and in the country as a whole. After Hamilton left the Treasury in 1795 to practice law, he continued to be active in Federalist politics, but he was deeply critical of the presidency of John Adams. Nonetheless, at Washington's insistence, he was made inspector general of the army during the Quasi War with France in 1798.

Despite his personal and political dislike of Jefferson, Hamilton was instrumental in securing his victory over Aaron Burr in the presidential election of 1800. That and his subsequent opposition to Burr's bid to become governor of New York led to his death at Burr's hands in a duel in 1804.

Broadus Mitchell, *Alexander Hamilton,* 2 vols. (1957, 1972); Clinton Rossiter, *Alexander Hamilton and the Constitution* (1964).

EDWARD COUNTRYMAN

See also Bank of the United States; Burr, Aaron; Dueling; Federalist Papers; Federalist Party; National Debt; *Report on Manufactures;* Revolution.

HAMILTON, ALICE

(1869–1970), physician and reformer. Hamilton, a founder of the field of occupational health, was America's foremost specialist in industrial toxicology during the first third of the twentieth century. She received her medical degree from the University of Michigan in 1893 and did postgraduate work in Germany and at Johns Hopkins University. She became interested in industrial diseases at Chicago's Hull-House, where she lived full- or part-time from 1897 to 1935. While establishing herself professionally, first as professor of pathology at the Woman's Medical School of Northwestern University and then as a bacteriologist at Memorial Institute for Infectious Diseases, she found herself less interested in laboratory work than in Hull-House, where she encountered a world of immigrants, trade unions, radical talk, and social action far removed from the classical liberalism of her privileged Indiana family. (Edith Hamilton was her sister.)

Through the Hull-House connection, Hamilton became a member of the Illinois Commission on Occupational Diseases. In 1910 she conducted a pioneering survey of lead poisoning that demonstrated shockingly high morbidity and mortality rates and prompted passage of the state's first industrial disease law. This experience, which permitted her to integrate the ideals of science and service, finally brought her the cause she had been seeking. Working subsequently for the U.S. Department of Labor, Hamilton documented the prevalence of poisoning (typically denied by manufacturers) in the lead and munitions industries. In the absence of federal regulations, she assumed personal responsibility for persuading owners to improve plant conditions and also alerted medical colleagues and the public to the dangers of industrial diseases. Her ability to combine the attributes of scientist and crusader was the hallmark of her career.

Hamilton joined Harvard's new industrial hygiene program in 1919, thereby becoming the university's first woman professor. There she found new ways to protect workers' health. In addition to her own efforts, she prodded the U.S. surgeon general and other authorities to take up the broader problem of controlling industrial diseases. Hamilton's emphasis on practical achievement rather than laboratory research made her an anomaly at Harvard, as did her gender and her commitment to social reform. Returning to the Department of Labor as a consultant in 1935, she remained professionally active until she was eighty. The revised edition of her 1934 textbook, *Industrial Toxicology,* coauthored with Harriet Hardy, appeared in 1949.

Although never a political infighter, Hamilton was a public figure whose positions on domestic and foreign policy counted. Her experiences with Jane Addams in the international women's peace movement during World War I made her a pacifist, a position she modified after the U.S. entry into World War II because of her abhorrence of Hitler. An active member of the women's reform and peace network, she endorsed child labor reform and other welfare measures. In 1952, she withdrew her longstanding opposition to the Equal Rights Amendment, once convinced that it would not threaten protective labor legislation. An opponent of the cold war, she remained an outspoken advocate of civil liberties during a long and graceful old age; in her nineties, she protested the Vietnam War. To the end she retained the faith in progress that she had shared with a generation of reformers.

Alice Hamilton, *Exploring the Dangerous Trades* (1943); Barbara Sicherman, *Alice Hamilton: A Life in Letters* (1984).

BARBARA SICHERMAN

See also Hamilton, Edith; Settlement Houses.

HAMILTON, EDITH

(1867–1963), writer, classicist, and educator. Edith Hamilton, a popular and influential interpreter of ancient civilizations, grew up with the classics. Born into a cultured Fort Wayne, Indiana, family, Hamilton started studying Latin at seven, memorized poetry and long passages from the Bible, and even as a girl was a "natural storyteller." (Physician and reformer Alice Hamilton was her sister.) After receiving her B.A. and M.A. from Bryn Mawr College (1894), she studied classics in Germany. From 1896 to 1922 she was headmistress of the Bryn Mawr School in Baltimore, a rigorous college preparatory school for girls that she built into a thriving institution. To her students, she seemed "a figure of high, mysterious power." They were awed by her standards of excellence, dramatic interviews, and her senior class in Virgil.

Encouraged to write by friends whom she had electrified with her readings and interpretations of Greek tragedies, Hamilton published *The Greek Way* in 1930 (revised 1942) at the age of sixty-two. It was the first of nine books, which included a volume of translations (*Three Greek Plays* [1937]), the popular *Mythology* (1942), and the coedited Bollingen *Collected Dialogues of Plato* (1961). *The Greek Way* set the pattern for all her work: personal readings of ancient texts that highlighted what she considered eternal "truths of the spirit" and the contemporaneity of the past. To Hamilton, the Greeks were "the first Westerners," the "discoverers" of freedom who combined mind and spirit and whose achievements had never been surpassed. After publishing *The Roman Way* (1932), a less congenial subject, she moved on to the Bible. In *The Prophets of Israel* (1936, revised in 1949 as *Spokesmen for God*) and *Witness to the Truth* (1948), she praised the moral insights of the Old Testament prophets and "the living Jesus"; these unconventional seekers after truth rather than the orthodox were her heroes.

Hamilton catapulted to celebrity status in her nineties. In 1957 she was made an honorary citizen of Athens in a dramatic ceremony in the Theatre of Herodes Atticus, which was followed by a reading of her translation of Aeschylus' *Pro-*

metheus Bound. Book-of-the-Month Club editions, admiring articles in the press, and television interviews followed. Her late writings, with their low-keyed critique of mass education, proclaimed the relevance of ancient history "for the Atomic Age." *The Echo of Greece* (1957) depicted fourth-century Athens as a waning civilization in which liberty degenerated into license and the desire for security overcame the will to defend freedom, themes that also appeared in essays and talks posthumously collected in *The Ever-Present Past* (1964). Hamilton herself seemed as ageless as the Greeks she portrayed, no doubt a large part of her appeal as a public figure.

Although praised during her lifetime for their lucidity and wisdom, her books are dismissed by modern scholars because of her unsubstantiated personal and anachronistic interpretations of ancient texts. But her fan mail and enormous sales attest to the great pleasure they gave readers, to some of whom she became a virtual cult figure. She was taken seriously by many writers, intellectuals, and politicians, including the Kennedy family. Hamilton was essentially an inspirational writer whose enthusiasm for the past was contagious. Her personal conviction and intimate style — "She talks about Aeschylus exactly as though he were her eldest son!" — demystified the classics for readers who no longer knew them firsthand.

Alice Hamilton, *Exploring the Dangerous Trades* (1943); Doris Fielding Reid, *Edith Hamilton: An Intimate Portrait* (1967).

BARBARA SICHERMAN

See also Hamilton, Alice.

HANCOCK, JOHN

(1737–1793), merchant and American revolutionary political leader. Although best known for his bold signature on the Declaration of Independence, Hancock's historical importance rests chiefly on his leadership of Massachusetts before, during, and after the Revolution. Descended from two generations of Congregational clergymen, Hancock was taken in after his father's death by his uncle, a prominent Boston merchant, who put him through Harvard, sent him to London, and then made him his partner and principal heir. When his uncle died in 1764, John Hancock became one of Boston's richest men.

Hancock's public career began with election to the office of Boston selectman in 1765. He then aligned himself with Samuel Adams and the Patriot opposition to the Stamp Act. When his sloop, *Liberty,* was seized for smuggling during the opposition to the Townshend Acts in 1768, Hancock stood up as a champion of resistance to British measures. The following year Boston elected Hancock as one of its representatives to the Massachusetts legislature. Thereafter he was reputed to be the chief financial backer of the Patriot group, and in 1774 he delivered a rousing oration commemorating the Boston Massacre (1770). When, following the Coercive Acts, the Massachusetts legislature transformed itself into a Provincial Congress (1774), Hancock was elected its president and chairman of the Committee of Safety, a body empowered to call out the militia against the British. Consequently, he was charged with treason. When the British troops marched to Lexington and Concord on April 19, 1775, one of their missions was to capture Hancock and Samuel Adams.

Hancock's steadfast service to Massachusetts led to his being sent in 1775 to the Second Continental Congress, where he was elected its president but, to his dismay, passed over as commander of the Continental army in favor of George Washington. Hancock then served the American cause at both state and national levels, spending over two years in Baltimore and Philadelphia laboring at supplying the American forces and creating a navy.

In 1780 he was elected the first governor of Massachusetts under its new constitution and thereafter was easily reelected whenever he chose to run. Hancock's gubernatorial career was marked by his inability to prevent a fiscal and currency crisis in the mid-1780s. Faced with poor health and a political stalemate, he declined to run in 1785 and again in 1786 when Shays' Rebellion shook Massachusetts. In 1787, however, he was persuaded again to seek the governorship, which he won in a landslide. His policy of moderation toward the former followers of Shays and his gesture of donating part of his salary to the state helped restore public confidence.

When the time came to ratify the U.S. Constitution (1788), Hancock played a crucial role. Elected to preside at the state convention, he kept his own counsel until, near the end of the proceedings, he offered his qualified support for the Constitution, urging that it be ratified with the addition of a bill of rights. His leadership and conciliatory speech resulted in a narrow victory for the Constitution. When Hancock died in office at the age of fifty-six, he was the foremost popular politician in Massachusetts.

Herbert S. Allen, *John Hancock* (1948); William M. Fowler, Jr., *The Baron of Beacon Hill: A Biography of John Hancock* (1980).

RICHARD D. BROWN

See also Boston Massacre; Continental Congresses; Ratification of the Constitution; Revolution; Shays' Rebellion; Stamp Act.

HANNA, MARCUS ALONZO

(1837–1904), U.S. senator; the greatest of the businessmen-in-politics who rose to power hand in hand with machine politicians in late-nineteenth-century America. Mark Hanna was a representative figure as well as a prime mover. His ancestry, region, occupation, and lifestyle put him solidly within the cultural core of Republicanism, thus preparing him to play a pivotal role in the turn-of-the-century transformation of the GOP.

There was nothing up-from-the-bottom about Hanna the businessman. His was a family steeped in entrepreneurship. Investment reverses and a declining local economy drove the Hannas from New Lisbon, Ohio, to Cleveland in the 1850s, and it was in that city that he established his business and began his political careers. He married the daughter of Cleveland's leading coal and iron merchant, and his talent and connections enabled him to make M. A. Hanna and Company one of the city's leading enterprises.

From the early 1880s on, Hanna had the money and the time to devote himself to politics. He was strategically located to do so, for Ohio in those years was the party's keystone state. The presidential aspirants to whom Hanna attached himself — James A. Garfield in 1880, John Sherman in 1884 and 1888, William McKinley thereafter — were Ohio politicians.

At first Hanna contented himself with money raising and campaign managing. In this he followed in the footsteps of other businessmen turned president-makers such as the Republican Stephen B. Elkins, who managed James G. Blaine's 1884 campaign, or the Democrat William C. Whitney, who served Grover Cleveland. But the campaign of 1896 — that emblematic confrontation between the new world of corporate wealth and urban middle-class America, on the one hand, and rural discontent in the South and West, on the other — forced Hanna (as well as American politics at large) into a new mold. He became the Republican national chairman after McKinley won the nomination and ran the most highly centralized, ideological, abundantly financed (in great part by corporations) campaign to that time.

Hanna's money and power — and his exceptional personal and managerial skills — won him the U.S. senatorship from Ohio in 1897. He had no taste for large policy, though he did show an interest in conservation and a distaste for the primitive anti-unionism of many of his business peers. But the same qualities of intelligence and personality that made him successful in business and GOP politics thrust him into the leadership of the Senate. At the same time, for much of the country he was "Dollar Mark" (as the Hearst political cartoonist Homer Davenport so devastatingly portrayed him) — the prototype of plutocracy turned to politics. In fact he was neither ogre nor kindly paternalist but one of those uninhibitedly strong and self-confident men of affairs who strode across the American business and political scene around the turn of the century: embodiments of a newly imperial nation. The question of where Hanna might eventually have wound up — in the White House? in disgrace? — became moot with his death in 1904.

Thomas Beer, *Hanna, Crane, and the Mauve Decade* (1941); Herbert D. Croly, *Marcus Alonzo Hanna: His Life and Work* (1912).

MORTON KELLER

See also Elections: 1896; McKinley, William.

HARDING, WARREN G.

(1865–1923), twenty-ninth president of the United States. Harding presided over an administration marred by scandal but successful in reducing political acrimony and establishing policies pursued throughout the 1920s.

Born near Blooming Grove, Ohio, Harding attended Ohio Central College (1879–1882) and in 1884 became owner-editor of the *Marion Star*. In 1891 he married Florence Kling DeWolfe, who helped him make the newspaper a commercial success. Politically, he affiliated with Ohio's Old Guard Republicans and with their support was elected to two terms in the state senate (1900–1904) and one as lieutenant governor (1904–1906). He lost the gubernatorial contest in 1910 but was elected to the U.S. Senate in 1914. As senator, he was noted for his affability, party regularity, and skills as a political harmonizer. But he demonstrated few leadership qualities and had no important legislation identified with his name.

In 1919 Ohio political leader Harry M. Daugherty opened a campaign to make Harding president; and in 1920, following a deadlock between the leading contenders at the Republican National Convention, Harding was nominated on the tenth ballot. Urging a return to "normalcy," he easily defeated Democrat James M. Cox, receiving 61 percent of the popular vote and 404 electoral votes to Cox's 127. In constructing his cabinet, he found places for longtime political associates like Daugherty but also redeemed his pledge to make use of the nation's "best minds," particularly in appointing Herbert Hoover, Charles Evans Hughes, and Andrew Mellon. The policies that followed were conservative, especially in the areas of taxation and spending, tariff protection, immigration restriction, labor rights, and business regulation. But his administration also pushed moderate measures of farm aid, efforts to improve business management, freedom for wartime political prisoners, and limited social legislation. In foreign policy, Harding repudiated Woodrow Wilson's World War I peace settlement but sought to create a safer system of international treaties and adjustment mechanisms, the leading example being the treaties that emerged from the Washington Armament Conference of 1921–1922.

Most of the scandals besmirching Harding's reputation — the Teapot Dome oil leasing scandals, fraudulent transactions in the Veterans Bureau and Justice Department, and his extramarital affairs involving Nan Britton and Carrie Phillips — came to light only after his death. He had, however, learned enough about the corruption associated with his administration to be deeply worried, and this probably contributed to the stroke that killed him while he was returning from a speaking tour of Alaska.

Most historians have regarded Harding as the nation's worst president, not only a man flawed by bad personal habits but one basically unfitted for the office and manipulated by others. Recent revisionist scholarship, however, has shown that contrary to myth Harding was hardworking, conscientious, and nobody's puppet. He might well be credited with facilitating national passage through a painful transitional period.

Robert K. Murray, *The Harding Era* (1969); Francis Russell, *The Shadow of Blooming Grove* (1968); Andrew Sinclair, *The Available Man* (1965).

ELLIS W. HAWLEY

See also Conservatism; Elections: 1920; Mellon, Andrew; Teapot Dome Affair.

HARLAN, JOHN MARSHALL

(1833–1911), associate justice of the U.S. Supreme Court. Born into a slaveholding Kentucky family, Harlan imbibed strong nationalist views from his father, a two-term Whig congressman and an ally of Henry Clay. Entering law practice and politics during the turbulent 1850s, young Harlan became a staunch Unionist and, when war finally erupted, he became colonel of a

Union regiment. Nevertheless, although strongly opposed to secession, he remained a defender of slavery, denouncing Lincoln and wartime emancipation policies. Reconstruction, however, transformed Harlan's views on race. As an aspiring politician with an inbred hostility toward Democrats, he soon became a leading figure in the state's fledgling Republican party. With the zeal of the recent convert, he embraced the party's support for civil equality, advocating vigorous use of national power on behalf of the freedmen.

Republican politics brought Harlan to the national stage. In 1876, he played a crucial role in securing the presidential nomination for Rutherford B. Hayes, and in 1877 Hayes rewarded him with an appointment to the Supreme Court. Although affable and well liked by his colleagues, Harlan, a devout Presbyterian, viewed judging as a moral act. He was inflexible on matters of principle and refused to be swept along by the Court's drift to the right. As a member of the Court for thirty-four years (only three justices have served longer), he distinguished himself principally by passionate, often eloquent, dissents that forcefully challenged the new conservative orthodoxy.

During Harlan's tenure, a wide range of important economic issues came before the Court. In these cases, Harlan was no radical. He interpreted the contract clause as protecting out-of-state investors from state governments and used the due process clause to void legislation favorable to unions. Nevertheless, he demonstrated little of his conservative colleagues' fear that increasing government regulation would undermine private property and lead to socialism. An expansive nationalism and hostility to monopoly led him to support federal statutes regulating the railroads (*Texas and Pacific Railway Co.* v. *Interstate Commerce Commission,* 1896), curbing trusts (*Standard Oil Company* v. *United States,* 1911), and establishing an income tax (*Pollock* v. *Farmers' Loan and Trust Co.,* 1895).

Harlan's most important contribution to American jurisprudence came in the area of civil rights. He clung tenaciously to Radical Republican orthodoxy while his colleagues adopted a narrow view of national power under the Re-

construction amendments, gutted much of the civil rights legislation passed during Reconstruction, and upheld state segregation and disfranchisement measures. His dissent in *Plessy* v. *Ferguson,* the 1896 case that sustained a Louisiana segregation statute, offered a powerful defense of equal rights that the Court would echo fifty-eight years later in *Brown* v. *Board of Education of Topeka* (1954). "Our Constitution is color-blind, and neither knows nor tolerates classes among citizens," he wrote. "In respect of civil rights, all citizens are equal before the law." Harlan also took an expansive view of the rights protected by the Fourteenth Amendment, arguing that it incorporated the guarantees of the Bill of Rights and applied them to the states, a view that was rejected during his life but that in substance had been adopted by the end of the 1960s.

G. Edward White, *The American Judicial Tradition,* rev. ed. (1988).

DONALD NIEMAN

See also Plessy v. *Ferguson;* Reconstruction; Supreme Court.

HARLEM RENAISSANCE

Spanning the 1920s to the mid-1930s, the Harlem Renaissance was a literary, artistic, and intellectual movement that kindled a new black cultural identity. Its essence was summed up by critic and teacher Alain Locke in 1926 when he declared that through art, "Negro life is seizing its first chances for group expression and self determination." Harlem became the center of a "spiritual coming of age" in which Locke's "New Negro" transformed "social disillusionment to race pride." Chiefly literary, the Renaissance included the visual arts but excluded jazz, despite its parallel emergence as a black art form.

The nucleus of the movement included Jean Toomer, Langston Hughes, Rudolf Fisher, Wallace Thurman, Jessie Redmon Fauset, Nella Larsen, Arna Bontemps, Countee Cullen, and Zora Neale Hurston. An older generation of writers and intellectuals — James Weldon Johnson, Claude McKay, Alain Locke, and Charles S. Johnson — served as mentors.

The publishing industry, fueled by whites'

fascination with the exotic world of Harlem, sought out and published black writers. With much of the literature focusing on a realistic portrayal of black life, conservative black critics feared that the depiction of ghetto realism would impede the cause of racial equality. The intent of the movement, however, was not political but aesthetic. Any benefit a burgeoning black contribution to literature might have in defraying racial prejudice was secondary to, as Langston Hughes put it, the "expression of our individual dark-skinned selves."

The Harlem Renaissance influenced future generations of black writers, but it was largely ignored by the literary establishment after it waned in the 1930s. With the advent of the civil rights movement, it again acquired wider recognition.

See also Literature.

HARRIMAN, W. AVERELL

(1891–1986), businessman, diplomat, and politician. A significant figure in Soviet-American relations during World War II and the cold war, Harriman, a wealthy businessman, served as an administrator and diplomat as well as adviser to Democratic presidents from Franklin D. Roosevelt through Lyndon B. Johnson. Son of the financier and railroad magnate Edward H. Harriman and educated at Groton School and Yale University, he was chairman of the board of two major railroads and a Wall Street banker when he entered public service.

Despite his Republican background and some misgivings over New Deal economic policies, Harriman became a supporter of Roosevelt. At the urging of Harry Hopkins he served in the National Recovery Administration and was chairman of the Business Advisory Council in the Department of Commerce for three years.

With the coming of World War II, Harriman, associated with Hopkins, utilized his economics expertise in foreign affairs, becoming one of the president's major advisers. In February 1941, Roosevelt dispatched him to London as Lend-Lease expediter "to keep the British Isles afloat," instructing him to report directly to the White House, thus bypassing the American ambassador and the State Department. Harriman acted on this personal level for several years, attending all of the wartime conferences and twice going on missions to arrange increased aid to the Soviet Union. In October 1943 Roosevelt appointed him ambassador to Russia.

During the war Harriman worked directly with both Winston Churchill and Joseph Stalin, coming to know them well. While ambassador, he insisted upon obtaining the Russian specialist George Kennan as minister counselor, and he himself became one of the most influential experts on Russian policy.

Upon the death of Roosevelt, Harriman returned to Washington to brief President Harry S. Truman, advocating the firm but friendly restraint of Stalin. (Truman became rather firmer than Harriman wished, terminating Lend-Lease after VE-day.) Harriman served under Truman as ambassador to Great Britain and then in the fall of 1946 became secretary of commerce. His involvement with foreign affairs continued. He chaired a committee that prepared proposals for the Marshall Plan to stimulate the economic recovery of Europe and in 1948 became special representative in Europe for the Economic Cooperation Administration. During the Korean War he was Truman's special assistant on national security affairs and in 1951 became head of the Mutual Security Agency, responsible for foreign aid.

In 1954, during Dwight D. Eisenhower's presidency, Harriman was elected governor of New York, but when he sought reelection in 1958 he lost to Nelson Rockefeller.

When John F. Kennedy took office, Harriman again became a molder of foreign policy. In 1963 as under secretary of state for political affairs, he negotiated a nuclear test ban treaty with the Soviet Union, the first move toward arms reduction since the onset of the cold war. Much of his attention then shifted to Vietnam. As assistant secretary of state for Far Eastern affairs under Kennedy he had negotiated in 1962 the Geneva accords ending the civil war in Laos. In 1963 he helped arrange the overthrow of Ngo Dinh Diem, head of the South Vietnamese government. Harriman disliked President Lyndon

B. Johnson's escalation of the Vietnam War, but served as ambassador-at-large at the Paris peace talks with North Vietnam until the close of the Johnson administration.

W. Averell Harriman and Elie Abel, *Special Envoy to Churchill and Stalin, 1941–1946* (1975); George C. Herring, Jr., *Aid to Russia, 1941–1946* (1973); Walter Isaacson and Evan Thomas, *The Wise Men: Six Friends and the World They Made* (1986).

FRANK FREIDEL

HARRINGTON, MICHAEL

(1928–1989), writer and political activist. The author of sixteen books and an indefatigable organizer, Harrington was the most prominent socialist in the United States from the 1960s until his death in 1989.

Harrington was born into a middle-class Irish Catholic family in St. Louis and was educated, through college, at Jesuit institutions. After brief stints as a law student at Yale, as a graduate student in English at the University of Chicago, and as a social worker in St. Louis, he commenced his activist career by joining the Catholic Worker organization in New York in 1951. Two years later, he left the Catholic church and the Catholic Worker movement but remained involved with progressive organizations, joining the anticommunist, civil libertarian Young Socialist League in 1954.

Throughout the following decade he was an active supporter of the civil rights and trade union movements, as well as other liberal and leftist causes. A member of the League for Industrial Democracy (an affiliate of the Socialist party), he became an adviser to Martin Luther King, Jr., in 1965 as well as an outspoken critic of the Vietnam War. Dismayed by the conservative drift of the Socialist party, Harrington resigned its national chairmanship in 1972 and a year later founded the Democratic Socialist Organizing Committee (DSOC), a group devoted to building a progressive coalition within the Democratic party. In 1981, DSOC merged with the New America Movement to form the Democratic Socialists of America, which, though small, became the largest socialist organization in the United States since the 1930s.

Harrington's best-known contribution to American politics was his book *The Other America: Poverty in the United States* (1962). This volume of statistics, straightforward analysis, and simply told narratives attracted an extraordinary amount of attention. Appearing at a time when most politicians and commentators were celebrating the achievements of the postwar American economy, the book argued that tens of millions of Americans remained desperately poor and trapped in a culture of poverty. Despite its capabilities, Harrington argued, the United States had not solved the problem of poverty; it was instead turning a blind eye to the large minority of Americans who remained poor. The attention the book received led to its being read by President John F. Kennedy and helped to prompt and shape the War on Poverty (which included an expansion of existing social programs as well as new initiatives in housing and health care) sponsored by the Kennedy and Johnson administrations. Harrington himself became a participant in a presidential antipoverty task force and a highly visible spokesman for liberal policies and programs.

Harrington also played an important role in unifying the American Left and shaping its policies during the decades that followed the McCarthy era. He served as something of a bridge between the Left of the 1930s and the New Left of the 1960s (although in 1962, in an act he later regretted, he bitterly denounced the founders of the Students for a Democratic Society for being insufficiently anticommunist). Similarly, he served as a point of contact and a channel of communication between Democratic party liberals, such as John and Robert Kennedy, and left-wing activists and organizers who were wary of mainstream politics. ("I want to be on the left wing of the possible," he once said.)

Although many disagreed with his political views, Harrington, over the course of decades, earned great respect, nationally and internationally, for his consistent championing of a socialism that included political democracy and civil liberties. His extraordinary energy, dedication to principles, and humane personal style rendered him an admired symbol of progressive politics even during the politically conservative decades of the 1970s and 1980s.

Michael Harrington, *The Long-Distance Runner: An Autobiography* (1988) and *The Other America: Poverty in the United States* (1962).

ALEXANDER KEYSSAR

See also Liberalism; New Left; Poverty; Socialism; Socialist Party.

HARRISON, BENJAMIN

(1833–1901), twenty-third president of the United States. After graduating from Miami University in Ohio, his birthplace, this grandson of President William Henry Harrison became a lawyer in Indianapolis. A staunch Republican, he fought for the Union and emerged from the Civil War a brigadier general. Despite an iceberg-like personality and the loss of the gubernatorial campaign of 1876, he became Indiana's leading Republican. Although undistinguished during a term in the U.S. Senate, Harrison, as an inoffensive war hero from a crucial state, won the Republican nomination in 1888 with the help of James G. Blaine's endorsement. Because his supporters were strategically located, Harrison was elected by a majority in the electoral college even though the incumbent, Grover Cleveland, received more popular votes.

Harrison influenced legislation and was an efficient executive, but his lackluster personality made his administration seem colorless. In conjunction with the Republican-controlled "Billion Dollar Congress" of 1890, his administration was remarkably productive. To wipe out the $100 million surplus of revenues over expenditures, Congress passed a generous Dependent and Disability Pension Act and the protectionist McKinley Tariff, which raised rates higher than ever before. Responding to pressure from the West, Congress approved the Sherman Silver Purchase Act, which required that the government buy 4.5 million ounces of silver each month and pay for it with Treasury certificates.

Harrison managed the inflationist tendency of this legislation by redeeming the certificates in gold. At his request and to make good a plank in the Republican party's 1888 platform, Congress also passed the Sherman Antitrust Act, which was by far the most influential law passed during his administration.

With the State Department in the hands of Blaine, the administration pursued a vigorous foreign policy. Harrison favored a naval buildup, the acquisition of bases in the Caribbean and the Pacific (he secured a protectorate in Samoa), and an isthmian canal. He supported the first modern Pan-American Conference (1889), which was designed to expand American political and economic influence in Latin America at the expense of Great Britain. He also fought for the novel reciprocity feature in the McKinley Tariff, and his administration negotiated eight treaties that mutually reduced tariff rates. Harrison's greatest disappointment in foreign affairs was his failure to convince the Senate to annex Hawaii.

Despite a falling-out with Blaine and other party leaders, Harrison was renominated for the presidency in 1892, but this time he lost decisively to Cleveland. The dissatisfaction of New York Republicans, the anger of civil service reformers over his appointment policies, the alienation of western farmers favoring inflation and opposing protection, and labor unrest were responsible for his defeat. He was able, but his accomplishments and his personality offended more supporters than they attracted. In retirement, Harrison lectured and served as chief counsel for Venezuela in its boundary dispute with Great Britain.

Harry Joseph Sievers, *Benjamin Harrison, Hoosier Warrior, 1833–1865* (1952), *Benjamin Harrison, Hoosier Statesman: From the Civil War to the White House, 1865–1888* (1959), and *Benjamin Harrison, Hoosier President: The White House and After* (1968); Homer E. Socolofsky and Allan B. Spetter, *The Presidency of Benjamin Harrison* (1987).

ARI HOOGENBOOM

See also Blaine, James G.; Elections: 1888, 1892. *For events during Harrison's administration, see* Antitrust Movement; People's Party; Tariff.

HARRISON, WILLIAM HENRY

(1773–1841), ninth president of the United States, western military hero, territorial administrator, congressman, and diplomat. Born into a distinguished Virginia family, Harrison sought an army career and took part in Anthony Wayne's successful expedition against the Indian tribes of the Northwest that had defeated two American armies. He was present when the western tribes at the Treaty of Greenville ceded millions of acres of land to the United States.

Anxious to explore the opportunities he saw in the West, Harrison resigned his commission in 1798 to become secretary of the entire Northwest Territory. Appointed a delegate to represent the territory in Congress, Harrison drafted the first land law that opened up the West to pioneers and by this action added significantly to his political reputation. Following this service, he was named governor of what was called the Indiana Territory. In this capacity he negotiated a number of treaties with the Indian tribes that increased the original cessions. He also secured a division of the eastern portion of the territory that created the new territories of Ohio and Indiana. As governor of the Indiana Territory, Harrison negotiated other grants from the Indians that virtually secured a peaceful frontier in the Northwest and thus opened up these rich farmlands to white settlement.

As territorial governor, Harrison proved to be an able administrator, but it was as military commander that he gained wide popular support in the Northwest. In 1811 he marched against the forces of an Indian confederation that the Shawnee chief Tecumseh had put together. His militia force fought an inconclusive battle with the Indians at Tippecanoe, a creek in northwestern Indiana, but it led to the breakup of the Indian confederation. During the War of 1812 Harrison gained his greatest fame as a military commander. Ably supported by skillful subordinates, he defeated the British and the Indians at the Battle of the Thames. Tecumseh was killed during this engagement. In a second Treaty of Greenville, Harrison enlisted the Indian tribes as allies in the war against Great Britain.

Always a supporter of Henry Clay, Harrison ran on the Whig ticket in 1836 and almost won the election. To astute political leaders such as Thurlow Weed who had copied Martin Van Buren's methods of organization in New York State, Harrison embodied many of the features that had made Andrew Jackson such a popular figure. Largely through Weed's influence the Whig party again nominated Harrison for the presidency in 1840.

Although scarcely a person of humble background, he was pictured as the epitome of the common man of the West, the adventurous individualist who had built his own log cabin and farmed his own acres in Ohio. The Whigs outdid themselves in image building with coonskin caps, facsimile log cabins, popular tunes, slogans, and badges that added a theatrical dimension to the emerging two-party system. Their campaign also profited from economic depression. Harrison defeated Van Buren, the Democratic candidate, by a wide margin, but died of pneumonia after only one month in office.

Roger A. Fischer, *Tippecanoe and Trinkets Too* (1988); R. G. Gunderson, *The Log Cabin Campaign* (1957).

JOHN NIVEN

See also Elections: 1836, 1840; Whig Party.

HARTFORD CONVENTION OF 1814

The Hartford Convention (December 15, 1814–January 5, 1815) grew out of New England Federalists' opposition to the War of 1812. Because of their close mercantile ties to Great Britain, the New England states had tried to prevent the declaration of war in June 1812, and that summer, both Massachusetts and Connecticut refused to contribute militia to the federal government. In spite of an embargo enacted by Congress in December 1813, New Englanders continued to sell supplies to British troops in Canada and to British vessels offshore. This lively demand for wartime provisions benefited New England, as did the enhanced market for domestic manufactures, but the overall loss of trade offset these benefits and came to symbolize for the local Federalists their loss of national power in relation to the southern-dominated Republican party.

Early in 1814, several Massachusetts towns urged that a regional convention be held to formulate their grievances. That December, at the suggestion of the Massachusetts legislature, twenty-six Federalists representing Connecticut, Rhode Island, Massachusetts, New Hampshire, and Vermont met in Hartford, Connecticut. Although a number of Federalists had urged that the convention threaten secession, that proposal was defeated by the delegates. The final resolutions reflected the moderates' view. The convention proposed a number of changes (including several constitutional amendments) that they hoped would increase states' autonomy and restore the national power of New England Federalists. A committee of three was appointed to negotiate with the national government, but New England's effort to trade support of the war for greater influence in national councils was made irrelevant by news of the treaty ending the war (ratified by the Senate in February 1815).

Many critics poked fun at the convention, whereas others interpreted it as a forum for treasonous plotting; both views helped speed the demise of the convention's already weakened sponsors, the Federalists. The fact that the delegates had discussed secession, though they ended by rejecting it, set an early precedent for the idea that secession was an available choice for states dissatisfied with national policies.

See also Federalist Party; War of 1812.

HATCH ACT

The Hatch Act, August 2, 1939, was designed to "prevent pernicious political activities," primarily by regulating the relationship between federal agencies and political campaigns. It prohibited using for electoral purposes any public funds designated for relief or public works. It also forbade officials paid with federal funds from using promises of jobs, promotion, financial assistance, contracts, or any other benefit to coerce campaign contributions or political support.

In one sense, the Hatch Act grew out of a general tradition of electoral reform. But another significant influence, affecting both its timing and its content, was the widespread allegation that Works Progress Administration (WPA) funds had been misused by staff members and local Democratic politicians during the congressional elections of 1938. Although criticism of WPA workers centered on Kentucky, Tennessee, and Maryland, the political clout of federal dollars nationwide in the midst of the depression was undeniable; even without malfeasance, programs like the WPA attracted votes. Many Republicans, however, were convinced that WPA workers had gone further, intimidating staff members, pressuring clients, and using public funds for political purposes. This concern explains the Hatch Act's most restrictive provision — that persons below the policymaking level in the executive branch of the federal government must not only refrain from political practices that would be illegal for any citizen but must abstain from "any active part" in political campaigns. An amendment (July 19, 1940) extended coverage to state and local employees whose salaries included any federal funds. This amendment also set an annual ceiling of $3 million for political parties' campaign expenditures and $5,000 for individual campaign contributions.

The Hatch Act was appealed to the Supreme Court in 1947 and 1974 and was upheld both times. A proposed amendment to permit federal workers' participation in political campaigns passed the House but not the Senate in 1987; in 1990 a similar bill passed both houses but was vetoed by President George Bush.

See also Corruption.

HAWAII ANNEXATION

The U.S. annexation of the Hawaiian Islands on July 7, 1898, was the culmination of more than fifty years of growing U.S. commercial interests in Hawaii. During the second half of the nineteenth century, American investors in the sugar industry gradually increased their control over the islands' economic and political life. In 1887 they arranged to overthrow the local rulers and establish a government more favorable to their interests. But in 1891 they suffered a setback, when the new queen, Liliuokalani, replaced the liberal constitution they had secured with one giving her extensive personal powers.

A revolutionary "committee of safety," organized by Sanford B. Dole and apparently supported by the U.S. minister to Hawaii, called in U.S. Marines from a nearby cruiser (ostensibly to protect American lives) and established a new government with Dole as president. The U.S. minister, on his own authority, recognized the new provisional government and proclaimed Hawaii an American protectorate on February 1, 1893.

Dole's representatives submitted a draft treaty of annexation to the U.S. Senate, but Democratic opponents managed to delay approval until Grover Cleveland became president in March. Cleveland immediately ordered an investigation, which revealed that the revolution had been imposed by the sugar planters and that most Hawaiians did not want annexation. A new U.S. minister was sent to Hawaii, instructed to restore Queen Liliuokalani to the throne on condition that she reinstate the liberal 1887 constitution. President Dole, however, refused to step aside; he continued to rule and in 1894 proclaimed the independent Republic of Hawaii. Unwilling to dislodge the government by force, Cleveland reluctantly recognized it, but he refused to approve annexation.

His successor, President William McKinley, however, negotiated a new treaty in 1897. Although Democrats and anti-imperialists delayed its ratification for more than a year, the use of the U.S. naval base at Pearl Harbor during the Spanish-American War dramatized Hawaii's strategic importance. When it became clear that the administration still could not get the two-thirds vote necessary for ratification, annexation was approved instead by joint resolution of Congress, which required only a majority vote. In 1900, Hawaii was made a territory, with Dole as governor. In 1959, it was admitted as the fiftieth state in the Union.

See also Expansion, Continental and Overseas.

HAWTHORNE, NATHANIEL

(1804–1864), novelist and short story writer. Descended from a Puritan family that included one of the judges at Salem's witchcraft trials, Hawthorne became an explorer of the New England soul in his works. After his father was lost at sea, his mother became a recluse and encouraged a similar tendency in her son. He struggled against this heritage all his life. After graduating from Bowdoin, he settled in his native Salem and set out to become a writer. He read widely in the history of New England and spent summers tramping the countryside and filling notebooks with shrewd observations.

In 1828 he published an undistinguished novel, *Fanshawe,* which was hardly noticed by anyone except a Boston publisher named Goodrich, whose *New England Magazine* became Hawthorne's chief outlet. Two volumes of his short stories, *Twice-Told Tales,* appeared in 1837 and 1842 to mild approval. They reveal Hawthorne's preoccupation with the power of the past, particularly its relationship to guilt and secrecy, intellectual and moral pride, and the corrosive effects of these spiritual dilemmas on the personality. Badly in need of money, Hawthorne edited and wrote almost all the material for another Goodrich magazine as well as children's books under the name Peter Parley, part of a popular series that Goodrich had launched. With the help of his college friend Franklin Pierce, a rising power in the Democratic party, he spent two years as a political appointee in the Boston Custom House.

For a while he lived with the transcendentalists at Brook Farm near Boston but found no affinity with them. After his marriage to Sophia Peabody he settled in Concord and was similarly unimpressed by Bronson Alcott, Ralph Waldo Emerson, and the other worthies of that village at the height of its intellectual fame. Only Henry David Thoreau won his wary friendship. Otherwise Hawthorne's personal happiness revolved around his wife and growing family. His book of tales, *Mosses from an Old Manse,* subtly reflects his rejection of Emersonian optimism.

Still in need of money, he became surveyor of customs at Salem with Pierce's help, but when the Democrats lost power in 1850, he was dismissed — to his eternal gratitude. He moved to western Massachusetts, vowing to make a living with his pen, and produced his masterpiece of the historical imagination, *The Scarlet Letter,* a penetrating dramatization of the contradictions of seventeenth-century Puritanism. He followed this triumph with two more novels, *The House of the Seven Gables* and *The Blithedale Romance.* After returning to Concord with enough money to buy a fine house, he wrote a campaign biography for his friend Pierce, who astonished everyone by becoming the dark horse Democratic presidential candidate in 1852. After his election, Pierce rewarded Hawthorne with the lucrative consulship of Liverpool.

After four years in that post, Hawthorne resigned, complaining of boredom, and toured England and the Continent for two years. A sojourn in Italy produced *The Marble Faun,* a novel about European sensuality and American guilt that anticipated much of Henry James. Hawthorne's wry view of the English, "sodden in strong beer," was apparent in his last book, *Our Old Home* (1863). He dedicated it to Pierce, ignoring the Civil War which had made the former president's prosouthern views loathsome to most New Englanders. Hawthorne died profoundly pessimistic about the industrial America that was emerging from the gunsmoke. More than any other fiction writer of his time, Hawthorne combined high artistry and intellectual power. He also helped establish the short story as a uniquely American literary form.

Frederick C. Crews, *The Sins of the Fathers: Hawthorne's Psychological Themes* (1966); James R. Mellow, *Nathaniel Hawthorne and His Times* (1980).

Thomas Fleming

See also Literature.

HAYES, RUTHERFORD B.

(1822–1893), nineteenth president of the United States. Born in Ohio, Hayes graduated from Kenyon College at the top of his class in 1842 and three years later from Harvard Law School.

After beginning law practice in Lower Sandusky, Ohio, Hayes in 1850 moved to Cincinnati, where he married Lucy Ware Webb, an ardent abolitionist who helped make him a moderate reformer. Beginning in 1853 he defended captured runaway slaves. Later he joined the Republican party, entered politics, and from 1858 to 1861 was Cincinnati's city solicitor.

Outraged by the South's attack on Fort Sumter, Hayes volunteered for the Union army in 1861, served with conspicuous gallantry throughout the war, and emerged a major general and member-elect of Congress. In Congress from 1865 to 1867, he supported Radical Republican Reconstruction measures before resigning to run successfully for governor of Ohio. Reelected in 1869, Hayes counted as his greatest achievements Ohio's ratification of the Fifteenth Amendment and the establishment of Ohio State University. After retiring briefly, Hayes ran successfully for a third term as governor in 1875 and became Ohio's favorite-son candidate for the presidential nomination in 1876.

Hayes won the Republican nomination over his more prominent rivals because his record as a war hero, a Radical Republican congressman, and a reform governor would help him carry his crucial state. Hayes defeated the Democratic nominee, Samuel J. Tilden, after Congress, through an electoral commission, resolved a four-month dispute (pitting Democratic violence against Republican fraud) over who had carried South Carolina, Louisiana, and Florida. Tilden always believed that in a fair election he would have carried those and other southern states, although there is no way of knowing if he was correct.

By applying his principles pragmatically, Hayes as president strengthened his party. With northern public opinion no longer supporting Radical Reconstruction, he ordered federal troops to cease protecting the last two Republican governors in the South but only after he extracted promises (which proved empty) from incoming Democrats to protect the civil rights of blacks. Hayes courageously vetoed popular legislation to prevent Chinese laborers from migrating to the United States and to expand the currency (although Congress passed the Bland-Allison Silver Act over his objections). He enhanced the power and prestige of the presidency by defeating congressional attempts to dictate his appointees and to force him to accept obnoxious legislation (designed to destroy the voting rights of blacks) added as riders to appropriation bills. During the great railroad strike of 1877, he resisted pressure to operate the railroads and avoided a confrontation between strikers and federal forces, thereby saving lives and property. Hayes insisted that the merit system be applied in the New York Customhouse and Post Office and demonstrated the practicality of civil service reform.

Despite his growing popularity, Hayes refused to run for a second term. In retirement he worked to improve the quality of education for poor black and white children and, in keeping with his liberal use of the pardoning power, served as president of the National Prison Reform Association.

Harry Barnard, *Rutherford B. Hayes and His America* (1954); Ari Hoogenboom, *The Presidency of Rutherford B. Hayes* (1988).

ARI HOOGENBOOM

See also Compromise of 1877; Elections: 1876. *For events during Hayes's administration, see* Civil Service Reform; Greenback Party; Railroad Strike of 1877; Reconstruction.

HAYMARKET AFFAIR

The Haymarket affair began when a bomb exploded among a squad of policemen at a workers' rally in Haymarket Square, Chicago, on May 4, 1886. Since May 1, a loosely organized national strike for the eight-hour day had been gaining momentum in Chicago. On May 3 strikers had come to the support of an already-existing strike at the McCormick Harvesting Machine Company; police had fired on the crowd and four people had been killed. The Haymarket rally, organized by a small anarchist group, was one of many called to protest the killings. Only thirteen hundred people attended, and most left when it began to rain. About three hundred remained when 180 police arrived and demanded that they disperse. Suddenly a bomb exploded among the policemen, killing one and wounding many more, including seven who died later. The police responded with wild gunfire, killing seven or eight people in the crowd and injuring about a hundred, half of them fellow officers.

The Haymarket bombing triggered a national wave of fear; public officials, civic leaders, the press, and some union leaders joined in equating foreign birth with anarchism and terror. In Chicago hundreds of socialists, anarchists, and other radicals were rounded up. Eight anarchists (all but one of them German immigrants) were indicted for conspiracy, though none was charged with throwing the bomb. After a conspicuously biased trial, seven were condemned to hang; the eighth was given a long prison sentence. The convictions were upheld in September 1887, and the executions set for November 11. On November 10 one of the condemned men, Louis Lingg, hanged himself; a few hours later, Governor Richard J. Oglesby commuted two of the men's sentences to life imprisonment. The remaining four, Albert Parsons, August Spies, Adolph Fischer, and George Engel, were executed on schedule.

On June 26, 1893, Governor John Peter Altgeld pardoned the three survivors, Samuel Fielden, Michael Schwab, and Oscar Neebe. This action, though applauded by many, was also widely criticized and probably contributed to Altgeld's defeat for reelection. The nativistic fear of immigrants and radicals aroused by Haymarket lingered for years, preparing the ground for further red scares in the future.

See also Nativism; Radicalism.

HAYWOOD, WILLIAM

(1869–1928), labor leader and radical. Born in Salt Lake City, Utah, Haywood experienced a rude early life, losing his father at the age of three, obtaining minimal formal education, and working for wages as an adolescent. At fifteen he became an underground miner and in 1896 joined the Western Federation of Miners (WFM) in Silver City, Idaho, the era's preeminent radical labor union. He served as secretary and president of his local and in 1900 was promoted to the union's General Executive Board. In 1901 he moved to Denver where he served as editor of the WFM's journal and as secretary-treasurer. Within the radical milieu of the Denver headquarters, Haywood received an education in class struggle and socialism.

Between 1903 and 1905, Haywood participated in one of the most violent incidents in American labor history. The WFM waged a bitter conflict with mining and smelting corporations in Colorado that degenerated into a war between miners and state militia. Haywood's experiences with "class warfare" in Colorado convinced him that American workers must unite into "one big union." Thus in 1905 he presided at the founding convention of the Industrial Workers of the World (IWW, or Wobblies). That convention made Haywood one of the nation's best-known labor radicals, a man described as possessing two rare qualities, "genuine power and genuine simplicity." In 1906 Idaho imprisoned Haywood for complicity in the murder of former governor Frank Steunenberg. The ensuing sensational trial ended with the acquittal of Haywood and two codefendants.

After his acquittal, he became a leader of the Socialist party of America. But in a party opposed to violence and dedicated to respectability, Haywood advised socialists and workers to practice sabotage and risk imprisonment to foster revolution. In 1912 he was recalled from the Socialist National party's Executive Committee by a vote of its members.

More in touch with the mood of the IWW and its preference for direct mass action, Haywood returned to active labor leadership. In 1911–1912, he began the most significant phase of his career. At mass strikes in Lawrence, Massachusetts, in 1912, Paterson, New Jersey, in 1913, Akron, Ohio, in 1913, and elsewhere, he acted as an effective leader of unskilled immigrant workers. In 1915, he succeeded to the highest office in the IWW and directed the organization's enormous growth among western agricultural, timber, and mine workers during World War I. Because strikes in those sectors threatened the war effort, the federal government arrested all the leaders of the IWW in 1917 and charged them with violating espionage and

sedition acts. In 1918, Haywood and a hundred others went on trial in Chicago. The jury found them all guilty, and the judge sentenced them to long terms in prison.

Released on bail while his case underwent appeal, Haywood collapsed into a shell of his former self, a victim of alcohol and diabetes. In 1921, after the Supreme Court rejected his appeal, Haywood jumped bond and fled to the Soviet Union. There he led an unhappy life, an alien in Lenin's and Stalin's Russia, and on May 18, 1928, he died in a Moscow hospital. Half of his ashes were placed in the Kremlin Wall and the remainder shipped to Chicago. Haywood's life and career graphically exemplified the indigenous roots of American working-class radicalism as well as the savage treatment the rulers of a liberal democracy accorded their most contentious domestic adversaries.

Peter Carlson, *Roughneck: The Life and Times of Big Bill Haywood* (1983); Melvyn Dubofsky, *"Big Bill" Haywood* (1987).

MELVYN DUBOFSKY

See also Industrial Workers of the World; Labor; Radicalism; Socialist Party.

HEALTH

See Birthrate and Mortality; Epidemics; Medicine.

HEARST, WILLIAM RANDOLPH

(1863–1951), newspaper publisher. George Hearst, a mining millionaire and U.S. senator from California, gave his only son the *San Francisco Examiner* in 1887 in hopes that he would settle down. The young man, who had been expelled from Harvard University for raucous behavior, had worked briefly for Joseph Pulitzer's *New York World*. In the next decade Hearst spent more than $8 million of his family's money making the San Francisco paper a success. He then challenged Pulitzer by buying the *New York Journal*. In their battle over Richard Outcault's comic strip "The Yellow Kid" (the first to be printed in color), these publishers acquired the epithet "the yellow press," referring to their sensationalism.

Hearst's papers catered to urban working people, many of whom were recent immigrants. His papers favored labor unions, progressive taxation, and municipal ownership of utilities. They featured abundant pictures, advice to the lovelorn columns, and sentimental stories. Favoring Irish and German readers in particular, the papers condemned British influence and spread fears about the "yellow peril" of Asian immigration.

In 1898, Hearst championed the Cuban rebels and welcomed the U.S. declaration of war against Spain. At the height of the crisis more than a million copies of the *Journal* were sold each day. Hearst ordered a reporter to scuttle a ship in the Suez Canal to stop the Spanish fleet and waded ashore in Cuba to accept the surrender of a group of Spaniards. In Hearst's mind, a publisher and a president had equal right to act for the nation.

He wanted personally to lead the Democratic party to the White House, but the radicalism of his papers was a liability. They had endorsed political assassination as a "mental exercise" and printed a poem by Ambrose Bierce that joked about the death of the president. When William McKinley was assassinated by an anarchist in 1901, Hearst was blamed. Nevertheless, he was twice elected to the House of Representatives from New York City and won 40 percent of the votes for the presidential nomination on one ballot at the Democratic National Convention in 1904. He lost contests to become mayor of New York and governor of the state by narrow margins.

Had Hearst died at about the age of fifty, he would have been remembered as a man who transformed a fortune based on natural resources into an information and entertainment empire. He owned seven dailies, five magazines, two news services, and a film company. His obituary would have called him an important American on the left. In 1903 the trade unions of Los Angeles asked Hearst to begin a paper there so that workers would have a voice. He was praised by many socialists, including Upton Sinclair who compared him to Abraham Lincoln.

But Hearst ultimately failed both as an entrepreneur and as a leader. He had rarely been an innovator in publishing, and others now beat him at his own game with more pictures, livelier writing, and more appealing politics. He lost touch with his blue-collar readers, denouncing the New Deal and mounting quixotic assaults on communists. He had overexpanded in the 1920s and spent recklessly on art and real estate. By 1937 he had lost control of his holdings. He sold part of his art collection and stopped construction on his fabled San Simeon estate in California. Of the forty-two papers he had bought or established, seventeen remained by 1940.

At the end of his life, Hearst still headed the largest news conglomerate in America, but this was a measure of his capital, not of his business acumen or the quality of his journalism. The 1941 film *Citizen Kane* suggests that Hearst was the victim of psychological trauma, had suffered for his abuses of power, and had outlived his time. The historical record supports only the last observation.

Pauline Kael, *The Citizen Kane Book* (1971); W. A. Swanburg, *Citizen Hearst* (1971).

THOMAS C. LEONARD

See also Magazines and Newspapers.

HEMINGWAY, ERNEST

(1899–1961), novelist and adventurer. Born in Oak Park, Illinois, Hemingway influenced a generation of American writers and perhaps two generations of American men with his lean prose style and macho ethics. Revolting against an oppressively genteel mother and a stern doctor father, he declared himself a free soul, with allegiance to no country or creed except courage. After a brief stint on the *Kansas City Star,* he volunteered for the Red Cross ambulance corps in 1918. On the Italian front he was severely wounded after only a few weeks service. Upon recovering, he transferred his activities to Paris, where he reported for the *Toronto Star* and hobnobbed with writers such as Gertrude Stein. He began writing short stories set largely in northern Michigan where he had spent his boyhood summers.

His first novel, *The Sun Also Rises* (1926), won him international acclaim. A plotless tale about disillusioned expatriates in Paris who escape their ennui with drinking, brawling, and lovemaking, it became the bible of those whom Gertrude Stein christened "the lost generation." Hemingway followed this book with a far stronger story, *A Farewell to Arms* (1929), based on his wartime experiences in Italy. He also began cultivating a public persona as a sportsman and adventurer that became almost as important as his literary career. He hunted in the American West and in Africa, fished the Gulf Stream off Cuba, and wrote an essay on bullfighting, *Death in the Afternoon* (1932). Although he had proclaimed himself apolitical, Hemingway threw himself into supporting the Loyalist side in the Spanish civil war. He covered it as a corrrespondent and drew from the experience another fine novel, *For Whom the Bell Tolls* (1940).

Although Hemingway remained a public personality, his literary career went downhill, in part because of his alcoholism. He recovered some ground with a novella, *The Old Man and the Sea*, in 1952. An elemental tale about a heroic Cuban fisherman, the book won the Pulitzer Prize and positioned Hemingway for the Nobel Prize for literature, which he won in 1954. Thereafter he slipped into illness and depression, eventually killing himself with a favorite shotgun. Several works published posthumously have added little to his reputation. But his memoir of 1920s Paris, *A Moveable Feast* (1964), is full of rich observation and telling detail, including some savage attacks on fellow writers.

War was Hemingway's element. Although he stripped it of its glory, he remained profoundly fascinated by its brutality and violence — and the way it challenged men's traditional values. Oddly, he was unable to write successful fiction about World War II, which he also covered as a correspondent. Hemingway was at his best portraying men enduring defeat stoically, with grace and courage. A victorious war apparently left him artistically baffled. His attempt to create a philosophy out of his love of violence and danger was a failure. But his unforgettable prose style, the concentrated power of his best stories and novels, guarantee him a secure niche in American literature.

Carlos Baker, *Ernest Hemingway: A Life Story* (1969); Scott Donaldson, *By Force of Will* (1977).

THOMAS FLEMING

See also Expatriates and Exiles; Literature.

HENRY, PATRICK

(1736–1799), leader and orator in the American Revolution. Patrick Henry of Virginia, one of the great figures of the revolutionary generation, was both typical of his age and an enigma. He was first a failure as a planter and storekeeper, but then a brilliant success as a lawyer and politician. In the events that led to the Revolution he took a radical stance, most famously in his denunciation of George III after the passage of the Stamp Act. He opposed the tariffs imposed by the Townshend Acts and the British attempt to collect them by using the Royal Navy and naval courts-martial to apprehend and punish smugglers. He stood in the vanguard of those calling for united action by all the colonies against British "tyranny." In the Continental Congress he backed such actions as the general boycott of British goods and the raising of a Continental army. He was a firebrand demanding national independence, as seen in his Give Me Liberty or Give Me Death speech at an extralegal session of the Virginia Assembly in March 1775. He took the lead in raising troops to overthrow the royal governor. During the war and its immediate aftermath he was five times governor of Virginia.

Yet after the war Henry urged restoration of the property and rights of Loyalists, arguing that they would make good citizens of the new Republic, and he bitterly opposed the Constitution as a threat to the liberties of the people and the rights of the states.

Actually, Henry had seen the union of the rebellious colonies as a marriage of convenience, a kind of defensive alliance to protect already achieved liberties. He believed that once the war had been won a strong central authority was no longer needed. Times were hard in Virginia and he favored tax cuts and the issuance of paper money by the state as a way of providing relief for debtors and small farmers, policies that Virginia nationalists like James Madison and George Washington opposed. When their concerns resulted in the calling of the Constitutional Convention in 1787, Henry was elected as a delegate, but he refused to serve. After the new Constitution was published he dismissed it as an affront to "the spirit of republicanism" and the "genius of democracy." The preamble, beginning "We the *people*," particularly offended him. "Who authorized them to speak the language of We the people?" he asked. "If the states be not the agents of this compact, it must be one great consolidated national government."

Yet Henry's negativism had a positive result, probably his most significant contribution to American development. He demanded that the Constitution be amended to protect the liberties that the people had won by breaking free of the British Empire. In speech after speech he denounced the absence of a bill of rights in the document, arguing that the checks and balances stressed by people like Madison were "specious" and "imaginary" protection, mere "contrivances."

Virginia ratified the Constitution despite Henry, but his arguments and those of Samuel Adams and other Antifederalists were persuasive. Madison soon introduced in the new Congress the constitutional amendments that became the Bill of Rights. This satisfied Henry; indeed in his later years he became a Federalist.

Robert D. Meade, *Patrick Henry*, 2 vols. (1957, 1969).

JOHN A. GARRATY

See also Antifederalists; Bill of Rights; Constitution; Revolution.

HIGHER EDUCATION

See Education.

HIROSHIMA

See Nuclear Weapons: Origins and Legacy; World War II.

HISTORY AND HISTORIANS

In their writings about the American past, the nation's historians have identified and distinguished the American people. They have spelled out American ideals and institutions and explained how they originated and evolved. They have narrated America's collective memory. Because historians speak from and for the present, every age writes a different history. But American historians have over the years shared key perspectives about their past because American society, more than many others, has rested on certain premises that have been fairly consistently held. This does not mean that there have been no significant conflicts over American principles but rather that the conflicts did not mark radical changes and that, however redefined, the principles seemed to flow from one age into the next.

American historians have always said that their aim was to follow the dictates of historical science and to record the truth about the past, but in the decades after World War I some of the nation's leading historians came to believe that objective historical truth is unattainable and that in looking at the past everyone is in fact his own historian. For the larger part, American historians have not been overly preoccupied with the philosophical question of whether the past *as it actually was* can be retrieved. Every generation, from the Puritans' to our own, has claimed for its study the ideal and authenticity of science, but the definition and practice of historical science have regularly changed. Always guided by new methods of natural and social science, historians have consistently adapted their methods to accord with the changing paradigms of the sister sciences. The most important of these changes came, as we shall see, with the professionalization of history in the late nineteenth century.

Certain closely interwoven themes run through American historical writing, though they have been differently sounded from one age to the next. The men and women who peopled English North America were led by freedom-seeking Protestants moving under divine Providence. Trying to break away from a Catholicized English church, they wished to offer a model, a "city on a hill," for Protestant revolutionaries everywhere in Europe, and particularly in England. Providence moved the course of English Americans' moral and material condition steadily onward and upward. The principles of liberty and democracy were the pillars of their institutions. When the principles were violated by their mother country, Americans fought for and achieved their independence. Ever guided by Providence, they regularly reaffirmed these principles: in their westward expansion, in the War of 1812, in the war with Mexico, and in the Civil War. Their affinities with the Anglo-Saxon peoples, particularly the British, formed a continuous basis of their institutions. Though not riven by class warfare, American society often witnessed intense rivalries among economic interests. In the decades after World War II, the forces of history, if not necessarily the will of Providence, made the United States a commendable model for the nations of the world to contemplate. But in the course of these decades, the role their country was playing in world affairs caused many younger American historians to question the model. Others, giving up a unifying vision of the past, went their various ways in trying to understand it.

Two factors above all explain why American historians have in successive ages shifted perspective on the central themes of the nation's past: the transit, over centuries, from a religious view of the world to an increasingly secular one, and the impact of the critical developments of their own time. Significant shifts of perspective took place during major periods of American history: the Puritan years, the age of the Revolution, the early national years, the late nineteenth century, the Progressive Era, and the decades after World War II. We shall consider how, in the light of the major developments of their age, each generation of historians perceived and recorded the American past.

American historical writing begins with the early-seventeenth-century colonization of the eastern seaboard. New England was the principal habitat of the historians of the colonial age and Puritanism the informing element of their view of the past. First at Plymouth and Massachusetts Bay, and spreading from there throughout New England, they practiced their own brand of Calvinism, or what they called the reformed or true religion. The major historians were leaders in colonial society: William Bradford was governor of Plymouth Colony; John Winthrop was governor and deputy-governor of Massachusetts Bay; Edward Johnson occupied several offices in the Bay Colony; Cotton Mather and Thomas Prince were prominent Boston pastors. They did not doubt that the settlers of New England had been sent by Providence on a special errand into the American wilderness to found a new Zion, a model for Old England to emulate. As they saw it, they had fled the depraved Christianity of Europe, and of episcopal England in particular, to seek religious and civil liberty and to practice "a pure and exemplary Christianity." They wrote history as annals rather than as a continuous narrative because they believed that Providence directed the events of their lives and that their role was to record these events as an edifying account of God's wonder-working governance of his chosen people in their new Zion. The title of Mather's massive history, the most important of this genre, indicates its nature: *Magnalia Christi Americana* (or "The Great Achievements of Christ in America"). The Puritan premises of these historians were recast in more secular terms in the eighteenth century. Benjamin Franklin's *Autobiography* is a neo-Puritan's didactic account of his moral struggle for success through individual perfection.

The historians of the age of the American Revolution conducted a running debate over the justifiability of the War of Independence. Those who defended the colonies criticized George III and monarchical institutions. Providence still governed history, as they saw it, but by natural laws rather than by extraordinary intercessions. Depending heavily on *The Annual Register* edited by Edmund Burke, the leading English political philosopher of the time, the "patriotic" historians — William Gordon, David Ramsay, Mercy Otis Warren, and a whole school of biographers of George Washington who catered to the new nation's desire for a hero — presented the colonies' triumph as clear evidence of a favoring Providence. The most notable of those who differed was Thomas Hutchinson, the last royal governor of Massachusetts, who argued that it was an error to break with Britain, although even Hutchinson approved of New England's values and institutions.

The peace that followed the turbulent decades of the French Revolution and the War of 1812 signaled the need for American historians to ponder where their nation stood in the larger transatlantic world. They were sure that the United States stood at the high point of human progress. The lines of that progress could be traced as a westward march. Spain had opened the New World to the Old, said William Hickling Prescott, and rose to prominence by virtue of its principle of nationalism. The Netherlands had achieved greatness, said John Lothrop Motley, by fighting Spain for the principles of national independence and religious freedom. In the mid-eighteenth-century struggle over North America, said Francis Parkman, the French ideals of absolutism and Catholicism had fallen before the superior English ideals of liberty and Protestantism. It remained for George Bancroft to sum up, for his generation, the larger meaning of America for Europe. His *History of the United States* showed how the Americans had realized the most progressive ideas of that age: personal freedom, civil rights, democracy. He shared with his contemporaries the sense that Americans were an Anglo-Saxon people and, as such, particularly oriented to these ideas. But more than the other notable historians of his age, he insisted that Providence was guiding America in its historical role on a universal stage.

The wreckage of the Civil War left the United States with large and complex problems. Trained in new schools of higher education and organized in chartered associations, professional classes emerged in all walks of life who could lend their expertise to help anatomize the nation's institutions and solve its problems. The special role of the new professional historians was to achieve a more informed and disinterested understanding of the historical background of the transformed American world. Unlike the patrician or "amateur" historians of earlier generations, the professionals went through a course of formal training. They studied in seminars under master historians, did research in archives and libraries on materials contemporary with the age they were studying, and published monographs that presented the product of their researches in order to help advance historical knowledge. The doctoral degree was a testimony to their expertise and professional status. Opening its doors in 1876, The Johns Hopkins University led the way in graduate studies in history and the social sciences under the direction of Herbert Baxter Adams. Woodrow Wilson summed up the role of Adams and indeed the nature of the new professionalism by calling Adams "a captain of industry." Other major centers of professional history were organized at Columbia, Harvard, and Wisconsin.

The new historians did not differ significantly in ideas from the patrician historians who continued writing in the late nineteenth century. Both sounded themes of an earlier age, but in an altered key. For them the United States was yet a special, exemplary nation, but Providence was now secularized, working its wonders in more mundane, material ways. That the Civil War had validated the key American principles of freedom and national growth was a central idea of the major historians: James Ford Rhodes, Moses Coit Tyler, Edward Channing. Stimulated by their interest in the nation's growth, which they now perceived in terms of the new Darwinian science, historians paid particular attention to the colonial origins and evolution of American institutions. An increasing rapprochement with Britain encouraged a newer view of the Anglo-American relation. Some, like Herbert Baxter Adams, argued that Anglo-Saxon political institutions, transported from England, had been directly reproduced in America's early settlements. Others, while resisting this argument, nonetheless agreed that England had been central in the colonial age. The so-called imperial school of American colonial history made it doctrinal that the age could best be understood only as an interwoven Anglo-American experience and only through a study of English public and private records. The leaders of this school were Herbert Levi Osgood, George Louis Beer, Charles McLean Andrews, and, somewhat later, Lawrence Henry Gipson.

Progressive reform and historiography responded to the problems of early-twentieth-century American industrial society. Progressive historians widened the scope of historical study. James Harvey Robinson called for a new history that would relate the past to the issues of the present, highlight change rather than continuity, and focus less on institutions and more on the daily lives of people. One significant result of Robinson's prompting was the multivolume *History of American Life,* edited by Arthur M. Schlesinger, Sr., and Dixon Ryan Fox.

Two progressive historians dominated the age: Frederick Jackson Turner and Charles Austin Beard. What both said signified that America's guiding Providence had been further secularized and domesticated. History could best serve, said Turner, by "holding the lamp to conservative reform." He rejected Anglo-Saxonism as the matrix of popular institutions, insisting that America's ever-moving westward frontier had a democratizing impact on eastern settlements. The essential American past could therefore be found, he urged, in the changing sectional interests and conflicts produced by an ever-mobile and altering frontier.

Beard sounded more clearly than most the progressive theme that the American story was one of perennial conflict between the privileged few and the democratic many. In *An Economic Interpretation of the Constitution* (1913) he argued that, far from resting on high-flown abstract principles, the Constitution in fact reflected the property concerns of groups of creditors and businessmen. And in his *Rise of American Civilization* (1927) he presented the nation's history as an epic of conflicting economic interests.

The U.S. triumph in World War II led to what has been called the age of consensus in American historical writing. With their nation at the center of world events and compelled to compare it with the European powers who were now under its sway, historians sought to explain America's centrality and history. Most useful for that explanation was Alexis de Tocqueville's *Democracy in America* (1835, 1840), which analyzed U.S. institutions in terms of the nation's two basic principles: liberalism and democracy. Finding validation for their own ideas in Tocqueville, historians read the American past as one of a relatively homogeneous and conservative culture, essentially free of social conflict. America's past was unlike Europe's, which they regarded as having been riven by class warfare and revolution.

The new generation of scholars challenged the premises of progressive historiography and above all those of Beard, who had perceived politics as having been regularly managed by small self-serving business interests. Robert E. Brown insisted that colonial politics was essentially democratic, Edmund S. Morgan rehabilitated the patriotic view of the American Revolution, and both Brown and Forrest McDonald rejected Beard's argument that the Constitution catered to special economic interests. Many writers in the postwar era — among them Daniel J. Boorstin, David M. Potter, and Louis Hartz — sounded the theme of an American consensus.

Historical writing took a new turn in the 1960s. To many younger historians, the United States seemed to have been a land of conflict rather than consensus. Others replaced consensus with pluralism. Why did perceptions of the American past change so significantly? Four reasons suggest themselves. One was that, if they had earlier been sustained by the idea of a beneficent Providential role in world affairs, Americans were now doubtful about their continuing involvement in overseas conflicts, particularly the Vietnam War. Moreover, the American civil rights revolution that began in the 1950s made historians wonder about the condition and status of all disadvantaged groups. In addition, the extensive exchange programs among American and European scholars that began in the 1950s made it almost inevitable that American ideas about the study of society should be Europeanized. Finally, research and writing responded to the revolution in electronic technology, particularly the use of computers.

These reasons help explain some of the

principal themes and features of recent American historical writing. First: Many recent historians, particularly those of a New Left or neo-Marxist persuasion, questioning the consensus historians, found movements of class consciousness and conflict in America that they regarded as broadly analogous to those in Europe. They were dubious about the managers of the nation's social politics and of its diplomacy. Among those who advanced a newer, radical viewpoint were Sean Wilentz, writing on the New York working-class movement in the early Republic; Eugene Genovese, on the world the slaves made for themselves in the antebellum South; Eric Foner, on the class relations and class conflict of the Civil War and Reconstruction eras; Herbert Gutman, on the working class in the industrial age; Gabriel Kolko, on progressivism and the regulation of industry; and Kolko and Walter LaFeber, on the mainsprings of American diplomacy.

Second: The civil rights revolution aimed initially at the inequalities burdening American blacks, but it soon widened to include other groups that, in a changing ethos, appeared to have been treated unfairly: Native Americans, Hispanics, other ethnic minorities, children, the laboring poor, the mentally ill, individuals of divers sexual preferences, and, in particular, blacks and women. From having been effectively screened off from active politics, these groups became increasingly visible in all walks of public life. New curricula emerged at many universities that undertook the study of several of these groups, and an interest in all of them spawned a vast literature that now came rolling off the university presses.

If blacks dug into their past more certainly at first, it was because their agencies of historical research — largely the work of Carter G. Woodson some decades before — were already in place. The exploration of the black role in American life — in antebellum slavery, in the Civil War, in Reconstruction, in the New South, in the Harlem Renaissance, to name but a few subjects — now became a massive historiographical effort, in which white historians worked zealously along with black. In the 1970s began the remarkable enterprise of women's history. In an ever-growing number of books, articles, journals, courses, and associations, women (with occasional contributions by men) showed how significantly women had figured in shaping American institutions and values: domestic, communal, associational, and public. They were particularly concerned with women's role in family life, education, the work force, reform movements and social work, religion, the nation's wars, and indeed in struggling for an equitable, meaningful role for themselves in a public life that had been almost exclusively a male domain. Wanting to extend their angle of vision yet wider, other historians sought to examine American life "from the bottom up," with the intent of correcting the earlier view of society from the top down, which, they claimed, had given an elitist perspective to American historiography.

Third: A new social history was thus emerging. It was the product not merely of the egalitarian sentiments of the younger historians but also of the lessons afforded by European historiography, and particularly by the French *annalistes,* led by such men as Marc Bloch and Fernand Braudel, who regarded every aspect of life and every social group as worthy of study. American historians now wrote about prisons, churches, hospitals, mental institutions, mobility, kinship systems, social structure, public places, private places, sexuality, food, the bedroom, and the nursery — indeed every aspect of family life.

Fourth: They were helped in these studies by the computer. Quantitative investigations afforded them a more secure ground than the general tenets of consensual history. From the quantification made possible by computers came a new political history, a new economic history, and in rapid sequence, a new social history.

Fifth: The focus of the newer tendencies of thinking about the past was the locality. In centering on a town, a village, a community, the historian could follow the precepts of the newer history: study the daily lives of ordinary people; concentrate on sources that had hitherto gone largely untapped; use the computer to tabulate large bodies of information; and resist the practice of letting the premises guide the facts rather than the reverse. Examples of the new local history are the works of Philip Greven, Robert A. Gross, Anthony F. C. Wallace, Willie Lee Rose, and Stephan Thernstrom.

What then are this generation's historians saying about the major themes that have run through American historical writing? They have retreated from celebrating America's Providential role among the nations, its mission as a city on a hill, and the singularity and exceptionalism of its society. Although some have stressed the interwoven American principles of liberty and democracy, most have turned away from a larger vision, focusing instead on different aspects of society and on localities rather than the nation as a whole. In lieu of their earlier concentration on a mainstream, essentially Anglo-American politics and culture, they have been increasingly concerned with racial, ethnic, religious, generational, and sexual groups striving for civic and legal equity. If they seem to have no unifying vision of their past, that may very well be because they are too close to their own time to gain its overall measure.

John Higham, *History: Professional Scholarship in America* (1965; rev. ed., 1989); Michael Kraus and David D. Joyce, *The Writing of American History*, rev. ed. (1985).

ABRAHAM S. EISENSTADT

See also Adams, Henry; Bancroft, George; Beard, Charles A., and Beard, Mary R.; *Democracy in America;* Hofstadter, Richard; Hutchinson, Thomas; Mather, Increase, and Mather, Cotton; Turner, Frederick Jackson; Winthrop, John; Woodson, Carter G.

HOFFMAN, ABBIE

(1936–1989), cultural revolutionary. Hoffman's life is inextricably linked with the history of contemporary American radicalism. A civil rights, antiwar, and ecology organizer, he merged his own identity with social movements and used the mass media to publicize himself and his causes. The struggle against segregation signaled his initiation into politics, and he felt abandoned when the Student Non-Violent Coordinating Committee, of which he had been a part, asked

whites to leave. Hoffman, however, instinctively recognized the potential in the emerging hippie phenomenon of the sixties and quickly made a niche for himself in the counterculture. He encouraged youth to rebel against their parents, reject the Protestant work ethic, and experiment with drugs and sex. Utopian and apocalyptic, profoundly serious and intensely funny, he forged a revolutionary style all his own. At the New York Stock Exchange, the House Un-American Activities Committee, and the Pentagon, he staged theatrical protests that helped dismantle the paralyzing mind-set of the cold war. He was banned from speaking in a dozen states and censored by network television, but he thrived on his notoriety.

Influenced by Herbert Marcuse and Marshall McLuhan, he challenged traditional Marxism and argued that generational, not class, conflict propelled social change, and that changing America meant transforming the mass production of images, not manufactured goods. These notions were tested when he and the yippies disrupted the 1968 Democratic National Convention in Chicago. Charged and tried for conspiracy to riot, he and Jerry Rubin rejected traditional legal strategies and made the trial a cultural happening that polarized the nation and generated rebellion on campuses.

Like other radicals, Hoffman lost his sense of direction when the movement fragmented. Always looking for a hustle, he ventured into the realm of crime. Arrested during a cocaine deal, he went underground and in the guise of a modern outlaw taunted the FBI. As a fugitive Hoffman experienced an identity crisis, but he found a road back to political activity under the alias of Barry Freed, a grass-roots organizer for ecology. Fighting to save the St. Lawrence River, he saved himself and arranged a deal with authorities. He waged cultural warfare against Ronald Reagan's foreign and domestic policies but never regained the stature he had achieved during the sixties. The conservative climate exasperated him, and he fought rearguard actions, insisting that neither he nor his generation had compromised their values.

Unable to reconcile his buoyant persona with his lonely private life, and unable to cope with manic depression — a medical condition he kept secret — he committed suicide. His tragic death revealed his dark side, his divided self, and a moral confusion about his individual responsibility to social movements. At his best Hoffman brought to the American Left a riotous sense of humor, an irreverent iconoclasm, and a brilliant sense of strategy. In a world of competing media celebrities he had crafted himself into an original pop icon of revolution.

Daniel Simon and Abbie Hoffman, eds., *The Best of Abbie Hoffman* (1990).

JONAH RASKIN

See also Chicago Seven; New Left; Radicalism; Student Non-Violent Coordinating Committee.

HOFSTADTER, RICHARD

(1916–1970), historian. Hofstadter was once referred to by another historian of distinction, John Higham, as "the finest and also the most humane historical intelligence of our generation." Such a judgment, which has had a wide measure of concurrence both during Hofstadter's lifetime and in the years following his death, derives from what has been seen as a fresh and essentially new way of perceiving historical events, tendencies, and persons, and of writing about them.

The range of his interests was unusual, extending from the earliest phases of the American experience down to the concerns of his own time. Unlike most of his professional contemporaries, Hofstadter was not a "specialist," though his mastery of the many subjects to which he gave his attention was widely acknowledged and respected. It was "a telling fact," as one commentator on his work has observed, "that no two of his books closely resemble each other." If any one theme could be said to unite all his writings, it was the importance of ideas in history; more precisely, it was the relation between the way people behaved, in politics and other realms of effort, and the use they made of their minds. The historian, as he himself wrote, must "think of history as being not only the analysis but the expression of human experience," the search be-

ing "for clues not simply as to how life may be controlled but as to how it may be felt, and he realizes more fully than before how much history is indeed akin to literature."

Hofstadter was born in Buffalo, New York, of a Jewish father and Protestant mother, was educated in the public schools there, and attended the University of Buffalo and Columbia University, where he received his doctorate in 1942. His first book, *Social Darwinism in American Thought* (1944), was awarded the A. J. Beveridge Prize of the American Historical Association. His first academic position was at the University of Maryland, which he left in 1946 to join the history faculty at Columbia. Over the next twenty-four years at the university, he — along with such figures as Lionel Trilling and Robert K. Merton — helped create a climate of exceptional vitality in the realms of historical, literary, and social thought.

During his student years in the metropolis Hofstadter had been attracted to leftist politics, attending meetings of the Communist party and perhaps becoming for a brief time a party member. But an inherent skepticism and a pervading sense of irony in his temper served to limit the appeal of comprehensive theories of social change, and he tended to drift away from these early attachments. Although he did not remove himself from public causes — he took an active part in the Stevenson campaign of 1952 and in the Selma civil rights march of 1965 — he had little faith in radical solutions, from right or left, for anything.

His last significant public act occurred at the height of the campus uprisings at Columbia in the spring of 1968, at which time a general respect for his detachment and moderation made him the logical choice to deliver the commencement address of that year. He closed it with the question of how the university could go on after what had just happened. "I can only answer: How can it not go on? . . . What kind of people would we be if we allowed this center of our culture and our hope to languish and fail?"

Hofstadter's most influential books were *The American Political Tradition* (1948); two Pulitzer Prize winners, *The Age of Reform* (1955) and *Anti-Intellectualism in American Life* (1963);

The Progressive Historians: Turner, Beard, Parrington (1968); and *The Idea of a Party System* (1969). At the time of his death from leukemia in 1970 he was at work on a comprehensive historical portrait of American society from the mid-eighteenth century to the recent past, of which a completed fragment was posthumously published in 1971, *America at 1750.*

Stanley Elkins and Eric L. McKitrick, eds., *The Hofstadter Aegis: A Memorial* (1974); Daniel J. Singal, "Beyond Consensus: Richard Hofstadter and American Historiography," *American Historical Review* 89 (October 1984): 976–1004.

ERIC L. MCKITRICK

See also History and Historians.

HOLMES, OLIVER WENDELL, JR.

(1841–1935), associate justice, U.S. Supreme Court. Holmes was the son of an important Boston family. Through his father, a distinguished doctor and writer-poet, he was brought into contact with leading New England thinkers, drawing from them not only ideas but also the desire to achieve great things intellectually.

Holmes graduated from Harvard College in 1861, but the most formative influence on his life was his service in the Civil War. He was seriously wounded three times, experiences that led him to develop a harsh, unsentimental view of life as endless conflict, with an individual's destiny in the hands of an almost whimsical Fate.

After graduating in 1866 from the Harvard Law School (which he found a notably uninspiring institution), Holmes briefly practiced law and then devoted the next decade to the preparation of lectures on the history and structure of the common law. These lectures, published as *The Common Law* in 1881, brought him lasting fame. He emphasized both that the "life of the law has not been logic: it has been experience" and that the law develops according to the "felt necessities of the time" rather than according to any set of deductive premises.

After teaching briefly at the Harvard Law School, Holmes was appointed in 1882 to the Supreme Judicial Court of Massachusetts where he served until President Theodore Roosevelt appointed him to the U.S. Supreme Court in 1902. He served on that Court until 1932. Although many of his most notable opinions were written as dissents, he was probably the most important member of the Court during his long tenure because these opinions reflected and shaped the consciousness of the time. Although he was far more a social Darwinist than a social reformer, his very respect for brute power led him to give state legislatures and Congress vast discretion to legislate in behalf of their visions of the general welfare. He wrote powerful dissents in cases such as *Lochner* v. *New York* (1905), in which the Court struck down a New York law limiting the workweek of bakers, and *Hammer* v. *Dagenhart* (1918), in which the Court ruled invalid a congressional statute prohibiting child labor. Political progressives cited his views, which would become settled law after his death with the appointment by President Franklin D. Roosevelt of Felix Frankfurter and others who had drunk deeply from Holmes's well.

Also contributing to his influence was his talent for the pithy aphorism. Thus, in *Lochner*, Holmes attacked the economic laissez-faire position of the majority by noting that "the Fourteenth Amendment does not enact Mr. Herbert Spencer's *Social Statics*," and he went on to say that "the Fourteenth Amendment is perverted when it is held to prevent the natural outcome of a dominant opinion." Perhaps his best-known phrase is from *Schenck* v. *United States*, where he introduced the "clear-and-present-danger" test as a means of limiting the power of the state to restrict speech and illustrated it by reference to a person's "falsely shouting fire in a theater." His later development of this test, coupled with his emphasis on a basically unregulated "marketplace of ideas," was seminal for the development of modern free-speech law.

His retirement in 1932 was a national event, and he has remained, along with John Marshall, among the best known of all those who have served on the Supreme Court.

Gary J. Aichele, *Oliver Wendell Holmes, Jr.: Soldier, Scholar, Judge* (1989); Mark DeWolfe Howe, *Justice Oliver*

Wendell Holmes: The Shaping Years (1957) and *The Proving Years* (1963); Sheldon M. Novick, *Honorable Justice: The Life of Oliver Wendell Holmes* (1989).

SANFORD LEVINSON

See also Lochner v. New York; *Supreme Court.*

HOLOCAUST, AMERICAN RESPONSE TO THE

The systematic persecution of German Jewry began with Adolf Hitler's rise to power in 1933. Facing economic, social, and political oppression, thousands of German Jews wanted to flee the Third Reich but found few countries willing to accept them.

America's traditional policy of open immigration had ended when Congress enacted restrictive immigration quotas in 1921 and 1924. The quota system allowed only 25,957 Germans to enter the country every year. After the stock market crash of 1929, rising unemployment caused restrictionist sentiment to grow, and President Herbert Hoover ordered vigorous enforcement of visa regulations. The new policy significantly reduced immigration; in 1932 the United States issued only 35,576 immigration visas.

State Department officials continued their restrictive measures after Franklin D. Roosevelt's inauguration in March 1933. Although some Americans sincerely believed that the country lacked the resources to accommodate newcomers, the nativism of many others reflected the growing problem of anti-Semitism.

Of course, American anti-Semitism never approached the intensity of Jew-hatred in Nazi Germany, but pollsters found that many Americans looked upon Jews unfavorably. A much more threatening sign was the presence of anti-Semitic leaders and movements on the fringes of American politics, including Father Charles E. Coughlin, the charismatic radio priest, and William Dudley Pelley's Silver Shirts.

Although the quota walls seemed unassailable, some Americans took steps to alleviate the suffering of German Jews. American Jewish leaders organized a boycott of German goods, hoping that economic pressure might force Hitler to end his anti-Semitic policies, and prominent American Jews, including Louis D. Brandeis, interceded with the Roosevelt administration on the refugees' behalf. In response, the Roosevelt administration agreed to ease visa regulations, and in 1939, following the Nazi annexation of Austria, State Department officials issued all the visas available under the combined German-Austrian quota.

Responding to the increasingly difficult situation of German Jewry, Roosevelt organized the international Evian Conference on the refugee crisis in 1938. Although thirty-two nations attended, very little was accomplished because no country was willing to accept a large number of Jewish refugees. The conference did establish an Intergovernmental Committee on Refugees, but it failed to devise any practical solutions.

The extermination of European Jewry began when the German army invaded the Soviet Union in June 1941. The Nazis attempted to keep the Holocaust a secret, but in August 1942, Dr. Gerhart Riegner, the representative of the World Jewish Congress in Geneva, Switzerland, learned what was going on from a German source. Riegner asked American diplomats in Switzerland to inform Rabbi Stephen S. Wise, one of America's most prominent Jewish leaders, of the mass murder plan. But the State Department, characteristically insensitive and influenced by anti-Semitism, decided not to inform Wise.

The rabbi nevertheless learned of Riegner's terrible message from Jewish leaders in Great Britain. He immediately approached Under Secretary of State Sumner Welles, who asked Wise to keep the information confidential until the government had time to verify it. Wise agreed and it was not until November 1942 that Welles authorized the release of Riegner's message.

Wise held a press conference on the evening of November 24, 1942. The next day's *New York Times* reported his news on its tenth page. Throughout the rest of the war, the *Times* and most other newspapers failed to give prominent and extensive coverage to the Holocaust. During World War I, the American press had published reports of German atrocities that subsequently turned out to be false. As a result, journalists during World War II tended to approach atrocity reports with caution.

Although most Americans, preoccupied with the war itself, remained unaware of the terrible plight of European Jewry, the American Jewish community responded with alarm to Wise's news. American and British Jewish organizations pressured their governments to take action. As a result, Great Britain and the United States announced that they would hold an emergency conference in Bermuda to develop a plan to rescue the victims of Nazi atrocities.

Ironically, the Bermuda Conference opened in April 1943, the same month the Jews in the Warsaw ghetto were staging their revolt. The American and British delegates at Bermuda proved to be far less heroic than the Jews of Warsaw. Rather than discussing strategies, they worried about what to do with any Jews they successfully rescued. Britain refused to consider admitting more Jews into Palestine, which it administered at the time, and the United States was equally determined not to alter its immigration quotas. The conference produced no practical plan to aid European Jewry, although the press was informed that "significant progress" had been made.

Following the futile Bermuda Conference, American Jewish leaders became increasingly involved in a debate over Zionism. But the Emergency Committee to Save the Jewish People of Europe, led by Peter Bergson and a small group of emissaries from the Irgun, a right-wing Palestinian Jewish resistance group, turned to pageants, rallies, and newspaper advertisements to force Roosevelt to create a government agency to devise ways to rescue European Jewry. The Emergency Committee and its supporters in Congress helped publicize the Holocaust and the need for the United States to react.

President Roosevelt also found himself under pressure from another source. Treasury Department officials, working on projects to provide aid to European Jews, discovered that their colleagues in the State Department were actually undermining rescue efforts. They brought their concerns to Secretary of the Treasury Henry Morgenthau, Jr., who was Jewish and a longtime supporter of Roosevelt. Under Morgenthau's direction, Treasury officials prepared

a "Report to the Secretary on the Acquiescence of This Government in the Murder of the Jews." Morgenthau presented the report to Roosevelt and requested that he establish a rescue agency. Finally, on January 22, 1944, the president issued Executive Order 9417, creating the War Refugee Board (WRB). John Pehle of the Treasury Department served as the board's first executive director.

The establishment of the board did not resolve all the problems blocking American rescue efforts. For example, the War Department repeatedly refused to bomb Nazi concentration camps or the railroads leading to them. But the WRB did successfully develop a number of rescue projects. Estimates indicate that the WRB may have saved as many as 200,000 Jews. One WRB operative, Raoul Wallenberg, technically a Swedish diplomat in Budapest, provided at least 20,000 Jews with Swedish passports and protection. One can only speculate how many more might have been saved had the WRB been established in August 1942, when Gerhart Riegner's message reached the United States.

The American public discovered the full extent of the Holocaust only when the Allied armies liberated the extermination and concentration camps at the end of World War II. And as historians struggled to understand what had happened, attention increasingly focused on the inadequate American response and what lay behind it. It remains today the subject of great debate.

Aaron Berman, *Nazism, the Jews and American Zionism, 1933–1948* (1990); David S. Wyman, *Paper Walls: America and the Refugee Crisis, 1938–1941* (1968) and *The Abandonment of the Jews: America and the Holocaust, 1941–1945* (1984).

AARON BERMAN

See also Brandeis, Louis D.; Coughlin, Father Charles E.; Jews; Middle East–U.S. Relations; World War II.

HOMER, WINSLOW

(1836–1910), painter. Homer, essentially a self-taught artist, began his career as a magazine illustrator in the Boston area. In 1859 he went to

New York and attended classes at the National Academy of Design. When the Civil War broke out in 1861, *Harper's Weekly* sent him to Washington. He drew for the magazine a variety of subjects in the capital city and nearby theaters of war, working in a clear, direct style that commanded a significant audience. But he was not a mere realist, and his drawings conveyed a clear sense of their subjects' characters.

Most young American artists of his time went abroad to enroll in European art schools for formal technical training, but Homer went his independent way. He visited France briefly in 1866, but the trip did not alter his style. In the next few years he painted genre scenes, people at work and play, and individual character studies. His view was usually simple, often romantic if not sentimental, and executed in a direct manner without the suavity of the highly trained artists who commanded public attention.

In 1881–1882 while living near Tynemouth on the north coast of England, he became deeply interested in the types of people who lived by the sea and in the immense forces of the sea itself. By 1883 he had settled permanently at Prout's Neck, Maine, where he worked in isolation. He sensed that this contact with elemental life would strengthen his work and prevent him from becoming merely another successful artist.

"If a man wants to become an artist," Homer once said, "he should never look at paintings." Now his work changed fundamentally, as he focused on human confrontations with an unrelenting sea and on basic natural forces. In *The Life Line* (1884), he depicted a rescue at sea, with dramatic if idealized human types. *Eight Bells* (1886) shows two sailors calmly taking readings at a ship's rail while beyond them nature displays its powers on the water and in the sky. In *Lost on the Grand Banks* (1886), he caught a fisherman's anxiety as fog obscures the way home.

By the late 1880s, Homer was recognized as a preeminent marine painter, a reputation he enhanced with a variety of subjects drawn from the Caribbean where he often wintered. His most famous painting may be *The Gulf Stream* (1899), which shows a black man in a battered boat, who has survived a storm. He was equally effective in portraying the struggle for existence and the confrontations with nature in the snowy woods of his harsh winter environment. Homer was doubtless a Darwinist, but he focused on the heroic struggles of men and animals with a powerful regard for individuality, whatever the outcome.

Although Homer did not move among artists or figure in the social scene, he was honored in his last years. His skills steadily sharpened to accommodate his great views of human beings and nature. Homer continued to work in oil and helped make watercolor a major art medium in America.

Homer embodied many national ideals. He was self-made, independent, stubbornly committed to truth as well as to the facts of appearance, always determined not to submit to any popular taste that demanded easy or pretty solutions. Both the man and his works have become national icons.

James Thomas Flexner, *The World of Winslow Homer* (1969); Lloyd Goodrich, *Winslow Homer* (1959).

H. WAYNE MORGAN

See also Painting and Sculpture.

HOMESTEAD ACT

The Homestead Act (May 20, 1862) set in motion a program of public land grants to small farmers. Before the Civil War, the southern states had regularly voted against homestead legislation because they correctly foresaw that the law would hasten the settlement of western territory, ultimately adding to the number and political influence of the free states. This opposition to the homestead bill, as well as to other internal improvements that could hasten western settlement, exacerbated sectional conflicts. Indeed, the vision of independent yeomen establishing homesteads on the prairies was offered in the political rhetoric of the 1850s as a vivid contrast to the degradation of slave labor on southern plantations. A homestead bill passed the House in 1858 but was defeated by one vote in the Senate; the next year, a similar bill passed both houses but was vetoed by President James Buchanan. In 1860, the Republican platform included a plank advocating homestead legislation.

After the southern states had seceded, homestead legislation was high on the Republican agenda. The Homestead Act of 1862 provided that any adult citizen (or person intending to become a citizen) who headed a family could qualify for a grant of 160 acres of public land by paying a small registration fee and living on the land continuously for five years. If the settler was willing to pay $1.25 an acre, he could obtain the land after only six months' residence.

By the end of the Civil War, fifteen thousand homestead claims had been established, and more followed in the postwar years. But the law did not provide the new beginning for urban slum dwellers that some had hoped; few such families had the resources to start farming, even on free land. The grants did give new opportunities to many impoverished farmers from the East and Midwest, but much of the land granted under the Homestead Act fell quickly into the hands of speculators. Also, over time, the growing mechanization of American agriculture led to the replacement of individual homesteads with a smaller number of much larger farms.

See also Agriculture; Housing; Public Land Policy.

HOMESTEAD STRIKE

The Homestead strike, 1892, in Homestead, Pennsylvania, pitted one of the most powerful new corporations, Carnegie Steel Company, against the nation's strongest trade union, the Amalgamated Association of Iron and Steel Workers. An 1889 strike had won the steelworkers a favorable three-year contract; now Andrew Carnegie was determined to break the union. His plant manager, Henry Clay Frick, stepped up production demands, and when the union refused to accept the new conditions, Frick began locking the workers out of the plant; on July 2 all were discharged. The union, limited to skilled tradesmen, represented less than one-fifth of the thirty-eight hundred workers at the plant, but the rest voted overwhelmingly to join the strike. An advisory committee was formed, which directed the strike and soon took over the company town as well. Frick sent for three hundred Pinkerton guards, but when they arrived by barge on July 6 they were met by ten thousand strikers, many of them armed. After an all-day battle, the Pinkertons surrendered and were forced to run a gauntlet through the crowd. In all, nine strikers and seven Pinkertons were killed; many strikers and most of the remaining Pinkertons were injured, some seriously.

The sheriff, unable to recruit local residents against the strikers, appealed to Governor William Stone for support; eight thousand militia arrived on July 12. Gradually, under militia protection, strikebreakers got the plant running again. Frick's intransigence had won sympathy for the strikers, but an attempt on his life by anarchist Alexander Berkman on July 23 caused most of it to evaporate. Meanwhile, the corporation had more than a hundred strikers arrested, some of them for murder; though most were finally released, each case consumed much of the union's time, money, and energy. The strike lost momentum and ended on November 20, 1892. With the Amalgamated Association virtually destroyed, Carnegie Steel moved quickly to institute longer hours and lower wages. The Homestead strike inspired many workers, but it also underscored how difficult it was for any union to prevail against the combined power of the corporation and the government.

See also Labor.

HOMOSEXUALITY

Since the seventeenth century, homosexuality has been the target of condemnation and discriminatory laws, public policies, social customs, and cultural beliefs. By making gay men and lesbians the object of scorn, this hostility has kept much homosexual behavior hidden.

Religion has been of central importance in shaping this climate. Until the thirteenth century, the Christian tradition was ambiguous in its attitude toward homosexuality. But with the recodification of canon law under the influence of Thomas Aquinas, new attitudes set in. Homosexual behavior was thereafter excoriated as a heinous sin. The English carried these beliefs to North America, and the power of religion in early America guaranteed that such beliefs would shape colonial attitudes.

Colonial ministers spoke out frequently against the "sin of Sodom," castigating its appearance and warning of its dangers. For seventeenth-century settlers, with a precarious foothold on the edge of an unknown continent, the metaphor of an angry God destroying Sodom and Gomorrah must have been potent. The language of colonial sodomy statutes was drawn from the Bible. In Connecticut, the wording was taken from *Leviticus* 20:13: "If a man also lie with mankind, as he lieth with a woman, both of them have committed an abomination: they shall surely be put to death; their blood shall be upon them." The statute remained so worded until the 1820s. Colonial statutes severely punished homosexual activity. In every colony, sodomy was a capital offense — at least five men were executed during this era — and other homosexual acts, from "sodomitical practices" to lewdness between women, were punished with whippings and fines. To be sure, many other sexual acts, such as adultery and fornication, were also subject to punishment. But officials tended to single out homosexual offenses for especially severe treatment.

After the American Revolution, although the states reformed their criminal codes in the spirit of Enlightenment philosophy, revision of the sodomy statutes and the "crimes against nature" laws came very slowly; North Carolina did not eliminate capital punishment until 1869. Thomas Jefferson proposed that death be replaced by castration. Moreover, as time went on, legislatures and courts broadened the statutes to include a wider range of acts, such as oral sex between men and sexual activity between women. And even though the ties between religion and the state had become attenuated, religious language continued to surface. In 1897, for example, an Illinois court described sodomy as a crime "not fit to be named among Christians."

In the late nineteenth century, medical science added to the negative evaluation of homosexuality. The medical profession grew in influence, and almost without exception, American physicians diagnosed homosexuality as a form of illness. At first, opinion varied as to whether it was acquired or congenital; with the ascendance of Freudianism the acquired model became dominant.

A prolific medical literature, as well as records of treatment, suggest that many doctors viewed homosexuality with dread. Remedies included castration, hysterectomy, lobotomy, electroshock, and aversion therapy. Moralistic judgments permeated the "scientific" study of homosexuality. One physician described a case of homosexuality as "shocking to every sense of decency, disgusting and revolting," phrases that he surely would not have applied to a case of pneumonia or yellow fever.

The medical model gathered still more force in the mid-twentieth century. The immigration of German and Austrian psychoanalysts during the 1930s and the widespread use of psychiatrists by the military during World War II gave the profession more influence. In the years after World War II, more than half the states enacted "sexual psychopath" laws. Studies of their application reveal patterns of selective enforcement that singled out male homosexuals. In Sioux City, Iowa, for instance, in the late 1950s, the district attorney, employing a psychopath law, committed twenty-nine male homosexuals to asylums. Under these laws, homosexuals were often given indeterminate sentences in mental institutions as punishment. By the middle of the century only murder, rape, and kidnapping elicited heavier penalties of any sort than did private consensual sexual activity.

The shifting definitions of homosexuality, from sinful criminal act to diseased condition, have pointed historians toward important theoretical formulations, especially the distinction between homosexual acts, which can be documented across history and culture, and homosexual identities. In the United States it seems apparent that an important change occurred in the late nineteenth and early twentieth centuries, when a modern gay identity began to take shape.

In the colonial era, some individuals experienced homosexual desire. But given the era's system of family-based subsistence agriculture, marriage and procreation was central to survival, and such desires could hardly form the basis for structuring one's personal life. "Heterosexuality," as yet undefined, was as critical to individual survival as planting the crops in the spring. Indeed, much of the evidence of homosexual behavior that survives in court records points to its coexistence with marriage. Nicholas Sension of Windsor, Connecticut, for instance, who was brought to trial in the 1670s on charges of sodomy, was a married man. His case was not unique.

In the nineteenth century, as American life was restructured in part around the separation of female and male spheres, and as sexuality came to be understood in romantic, spiritualized terms, homosexual desire often occurred in the context of intense, passionate friendships in which physical intimacy was expressed un-self-consciously. These relationships frequently coexisted with marriage, and little connection was made between the passionate embracing of friends or their sharing of beds and the dreaded "crime against nature."

Late in the century, as large cities allowed for greater anonymity, as wage labor apart from family became common, and as more women were drawn out of the home, evidence of a new pattern of homosexual expression surfaced. Among men and women and across the spectrum of class and occupation, individuals were organizing their personal lives around their homosexual attractions. The doctors who wrote about homosexuality during these decades developed their theories through case histories of men and women whose lives exhibited these new patterns.

At first, these individuals developed ways of meeting one another and institutions to foster a sense of identity. Certain parks, streets, and bathhouses became meeting places for men. Bars and clubs appeared in or near the red-light districts of major cities. Women in female-dominated occupations formed private friendship networks. By 1915, one participant in this new gay world was referring to it as "a community distinctly organized." For the most part hidden from view because of social hostility, an urban gay subculture had come into existence by the 1920s and 1930s.

World War II served as a critical divide in the social history of homosexuality. Large numbers of the young left families, small towns, and closely knit ethnic neighborhoods to enter a sex-segregated military or to migrate to larger cities for wartime employment. It became easier for gay men and women to meet others, explore the gay world, and form extensive friendship networks. As one young gay man, Donald Vining, described it in his diary, "The war is a tragedy to my mind and soul, but to my physical being, it's a memorable experience." In many ways, the war was something of a nationwide "coming out" for gays.

After the war, many of them made choices designed to support their gay identities. Pat Bond, a woman from Iowa who first met other lesbians while in the military, decided to stay in San Francisco after her discharge. Vining remained in New York City rather than return to his small hometown in New Jersey. They, along with countless others, sustained a vibrant gay subculture that revolved around bars and friendship networks. Many cities saw their first gay bars during the 1940s. The publication of Alfred Kinsey's studies of human sexual behavior, moreover, confirmed for this generation that their sexuality was neither rare nor aberrant but a widespread pattern in society.

This new visibility provoked latent cultural prejudices. During the cold war era, as the nation searched for scapegoats, homosexuals were labeled a danger to society. Senate investigations portrayed a homosexual menace that was as threatening to American strength and security as communism. Firings from government jobs and purges from the military intensified in the 1950s; President Dwight D. Eisenhower issued an executive order in 1953 barring gay men and lesbians from all federal jobs. Many state and local governments and private corporations followed suit. The FBI began a surveillance program against homosexuals.

The lead taken by the federal government encouraged local police forces to harass gay citizens. Vice officers regularly raided gay bars, sometimes arresting dozens of men and women on a single night. In the 1950s, arrests in Washington, D.C., exceeded one thousand per year; in Philadelphia, misdemeanor charges against gay men and lesbians averaged one hundred a month. Wichita, Dallas, Memphis, and Seattle were among the cities that witnessed extensive antigay offensives. In some cities, such as Boise, Idaho, the fear of homosexuality led to a virtual witch-hunt.

Under these conditions, some gays began to organize politically. In November 1950 in Los Angeles, a small group of men led by Harry Hay and Chuck Rowland met to form what would become the Mattachine Society. Mostly male in membership, it was joined in 1955 by a lesbian organization in San Francisco, the Daughters of Bilitis, founded by Del Martin and Phyllis Lyon. In the 1950s, these organizations remained small, but they established chapters in several cities and published magazines that were a beacon of hope to their readers.

In the 1960s, influenced by the model of a militant black civil rights movement, the "homophile movement," as participants dubbed it, became more visible. Activists, such as Franklin Kameny and Barbara Gittings, picketed government agencies in Washington to protest discriminatory employment policies. In San Francisco, Martin, Lyon, and others targeted police harassment. By 1969, perhaps fifty homophile organizations existed in the United States, with memberships of a few thousand.

Then, on Friday evening, June 27, 1969, the police in New York City raided a Greenwich Village gay bar, the Stonewall Inn. Contrary to expectations, the patrons fought back, provoking three nights of rioting in the area accompanied by the appearance of "gay power" slogans on buildings. Almost overnight, a massive grassroots gay liberation movement was born. Owing much to the radical protest of blacks, women, and college students in the 1960s, gays challenged all the forms of hostility and punishment meted out by society. Choosing to "come out of the closet" and publicly proclaim their identity, they ushered in a social change movement that has grown substantially. By 1973, there were almost eight hundred gay and lesbian organizations in the United States; by 1990, the number was several thousand. In 1970, 5,000 gay men and lesbians marched in New York City to commemorate the first anniversary of the Stonewall

Riots; in October 1987, over 600,000 marched in Washington to demand equality.

The changes were far-reaching. Over the next two decades half the states decriminalized homosexual behavior, and police harassment was sharply contained. Many large cities included sexual orientation in their civil rights statutes, as did Wisconsin and Massachusetts, first among the states to do so. In 1974, the American Psychiatric Association eliminated homosexuality from its list of mental illnesses; the following year, the Civil Service Commission eliminated the ban on the employment of homosexuals in most federal jobs. Many of the nation's religious denominations engaged in spirited debates about the morality of homosexuality, and some, like Unitarianism and Reformed Judaism, opened their doors to gay and lesbian ministers and rabbis. The lesbian and gay world was no longer an underground subculture but, in larger cities especially, a well-organized community, with businesses, political clubs, social service agencies, community centers, and religious congregations bringing people together. In a number of places, openly gay candidates ran for elective office and won.

These changes spawned opposition. In 1977, the singer Anita Bryant led a campaign to repeal a gay rights ordinance in Dade County, Florida. Her success encouraged others, and by the early 1980s, a well-organized conservative force had materialized to target the gay rights movement. Politicians, such as Senator Jesse Helms of North Carolina, and fundamentalist ministers, such as Jerry Falwell of Lynchburg, Virginia, who formed Moral Majority, Inc., joined forces to slow the progress of the gay movement.

The onset of the AIDS epidemic in the 1980s, although it intensified the antigay rhetoric of the New Right, also stimulated further organizing within the gay community. AIDS made political mobilization a matter of life and death. With a large majority of the cases striking male homosexuals, the gay community in short order created a host of organizations, such as the Gay Men's Health Crisis in New York City, to provide services and assistance to those infected. Local and national gay civil rights groups also grew in size and number, as the community sought to increase funding for research and education and to win protection against discrimination. A personal and social tragedy of immense proportions, AIDS paradoxically strengthened the political arm of the gay movement.

One result of the changes wrought by the gay movement was the gradual recognition that gay men and lesbians had made important contributions to American society, culture, and politics in previous eras. The work of such literary figures as Walt Whitman, Willa Cather, and Langston Hughes was reinterpreted in the light of their homosexuality. Major figures in the history of women's education, such as M. Carey Thomas of Bryn Mawr, Mary Woolley of Mount Holyoke, and Katherine Lee Bates of Wellesley, lived in communities of women with longtime partners. The civil rights leader Bayard Rustin, the songwriter Cole Porter, the depression era journalist Lorena Hickok, and many other notable Americans of the past were gay men and lesbians whose homosexuality, though hidden, deeply influenced their sensibility, their values, and their careers.

John D'Emilio, *Sexual Politics, Sexual Communities: The Making of a Homosexual Minority in the United States, 1940–1970* (1983); Jonathan Katz, *Gay American History* (1976).

JOHN D'EMILIO

HOOVER, HERBERT

(1874–1964), engineer, philanthropist, and thirty-first president of the United States. Born in West Branch, Iowa, into a Quaker family, Hoover was orphaned at the age of nine and was reared by relatives in Iowa and Oregon.

Although Hoover's religious training was quite rigorous, he retained few outward signs of his Quaker upbringing, aside from his style of dress. His personal and professional aggressiveness (which made him a millionaire by the age of forty) was inconsistent with Quaker ideas of moderation, and he could swear with the roughest of the miners he directed as an engineer. Moreover, he was a habitual smoker, enjoyed a drink, and often fished on Sundays, albeit in a high collar and necktie. But he exhibited his early Quaker training as president by relying more on the power of negotiation than on force (especially in Central America and the Caribbean) and by supporting arms limitation, international arbitration, and moral suasion in foreign relations.

Hoover is still remembered primarily as a heartless depression president despite his philanthropic and government work during the First World War as head of the Commission for the Relief of Belgium, then as director general of the postwar American Relief Administration, and finally as President Woodrow Wilson's U.S. food administrator and director general of relief for Europe. These activities had made him such a popular figure by 1920 that both parties courted him as a presidential nominee. He refused to run but did serve as secretary of commerce in the administrations of Presidents Warren G. Harding and Calvin Coolidge, transforming his department into one of the most important and well-publicized agencies of the federal government. As commerce secretary Hoover helped develop some advanced economic theories on business cycles and industrial standardization, and he supervised regulation of the nascent radio and aviation industries.

In 1927 when Coolidge enigmatically "did not choose to run" again, Hoover decided to run for the presidency against the seasoned New York Democratic governor, Al Smith. Hoover's popularity and reputation and the prevailing prosperity in major areas of the country helped the Republicans win in this classic confrontation between two self-made men.

After he entered the White House, Hoover's previous business, philanthropic, and public relations skills seemed to fail him in the face of the worst depression in the country's history. Nevertheless, some of his ideas for combating the depression, such as the Reconstruction Finance Corporation, aid to agriculture, and long-term public works and relief appropriations, were adopted and popularized by his successor, Franklin D. Roosevelt. "We didn't admit it at the time," FDR's aide Rexford Tugwell recalled in a 1974 interview, "but practically the whole New Deal was extrapolated from programs that Hoover started." Hoover proved to be his own worst enemy as president, often clinging publicly to his least rather than most advanced economic thinking, approving, for example, the Smoot-Hawley protectionist tariff in 1930.

After he left office, he often attacked the New Deal on grounds that, ironically, were echoed in New Left criticisms in the 1960s. He was largely ignored by his own party, however, until Democratic president Harry S. Truman and later Republican president Dwight D. Eisenhower put his organizational skills to work. They appointed him to head the Commissions on Organization of the Executive Branch of Government, known as the Hoover Commissions.

George H. Nash, *The Life of Herbert Hoover,* 2 vols. (1983, 1988); Joan Hoff Wilson, *Herbert Hoover: Forgotten Progressive* (1974).

JOAN HOFF

See also Depressions; Elections: 1928, 1932.

HOOVER, J. EDGAR

(1895–1972), director of the Federal Bureau of Investigation. Born in Washington, D.C., the son of a low-level federal bureaucrat, Hoover earned a bachelor of laws (1916) and a master of laws (1917) from George Washington University. He was an assistant in the alien registration section of the Department of Justice during World War I, where he monitored alien radicals in what became a lifetime antiradical crusade.

Appointed head of the General Intelligence Division in 1919, Hoover continued to monitor radical activities, culminating in the series of deportation raids subsequently dubbed the red scare of 1919–1920. Because Attorney General A. Mitchell Palmer purposefully exploited these raids to promote his unsuccessful candidacy for the Democratic presidential nomination, Hoover was untarnished by the public's subsequent reaction to revelations of the bureau's abuses of power, which focused on Palmer. Following Warren Harding's election, Hoover's administrative skills and diligence won him promotion to assistant director of the Bureau of Investigation (renamed the Federal Bureau of Investigation in 1935), a post he held until appointed director by Attorney General Harlan Stone in 1924. Hoover held that post until his death in 1972.

A lifetime bachelor with few nonprofessional interests, Hoover devoted his considerable talents to furthering the power of the FBI. Having inherited an agency beset by scandal, Hoover moved quickly to restore public confidence by improving the quality of bureau employees and by ostensibly working within the limits of a powerful states' rights tradition. A more professional organization evolved and, responding to the seeming crime wave of the 1930s, the public came to accept the need for a federal law enforcement role. But while publicly opposing the creation of a national police force and emphasizing the limits to the bureau's responsibilities, Hoover remained committed to monitoring what he considered immoral and dissident activities. Because this was risky and contradicted his public posturing, the director proceeded cautiously and secretively.

Hoover's keen sense of public relations and careful cultivation of reporters, members of Congress, civic leaders, and conservative organizations won him a powerful constituency. An administrative genius, he devised sophisticated records procedures to preclude the discovery either of his authorization of illegal investigative techniques (break-ins, wiretaps, bugs) or the accumulation of derogatory personal information. Finally, Hoover willingly serviced the political and policy interests of presidents from Franklin D. Roosevelt to Richard Nixon to obtain their issuance of secret executive directives expanding FBI authority. As a result, the bureau not only increased in size (from 890 agents in 1940 to 7,002 in 1952, and 10,000 in 1970) but became an autonomous agency operating independently of executive, congressional, or judicial oversight.

Hoover successfully neutralized demands for independent investigations of the bureau's conduct and his administration during his forty-eight-year tenure as FBI director. His power, however, moved Congress in 1968 to enact legislation requiring Senate confirmation of future FBI directors and limiting their tenure to ten years. Because Hoover's death coincided with the furor created by the Watergate affair, it marked the end of an era. Thereafter, Congress and the media became more vigilant in monitoring the powerful agency Hoover had helped forge and legitimize.

Richard Gid Powers, *Secrecy and Power: The Life of J. Edgar Hoover* (1987); Athan Theoharis and John Stuart Cox, *The Boss: J. Edgar Hoover and the Great American Inquisition* (1988).

ATHAN G. THEOHARIS

See also Federal Bureau of Investigation.

HORNEY, KAREN

(1885–1952), psychoanalyst and writer. In the 1920s Horney was a leading light of the Berlin Psychoanalytic Institute, then the center of the psychoanalytic movement, and sufficiently self-confident to challenge even Sigmund Freud himself. When provoked by his newly published theories of female sexuality, Horney responded with characteristic boldness. In a series of essays she took issue with his contention that the psychology of women is organized around penis envy. Working within the Freudian framework of the libido theory, she constructed ingenious counterarguments from the perspective of German feminism with its belief (and pride) in woman's essentially maternal nature. She further suggested that psychoanalytic theory about women was a masculine ideology designed to obscure the "power struggle between the sexes" with assertions that women were inherently inferior. She attempted to explain in psychoanalytic terms the masculine "tendency to depreciate woman" in order to clear the way for a more objective theory of femininity. Despite her efforts, Freud was unmoved, and after a flurry of debate, psychoanalytic theory about women remained unchanged in its essentials for some time. The issue of masculine bias in psychoanalytic theory remained largely unexplored.

Horney later observed that her doubts about Freud's theories about women were the opening wedge to doubts about his theory as a whole. After she immigrated to the United States in the 1930s, these doubts received full expression in *The Neurotic Personality of Our Time* (1937) and *New Ways in Psychoanalysis* (1939), in which she jettisoned the libido theory and attempted to wed psychoanalysis to the cultural determinism of American anthropology. Their theses can be summarized by Horney's assertion that "when we realize the great impact of cultural conditions on neuroses, the biological and physiological conditions, which are considered by Freud to be their root, recede into the background." These books were successful with a broad public, but within psychoanalysis their critique of Freud precipitated "a landslide of anger," as one of her friends later recalled. To many of her colleagues, Horney had abandoned the essence of psychoanalysis.

Horney spent the last decade of her career outside the psychoanalytic mainstream. After a brief attempt at collaboration with fellow "culturalists," she became the leader of her own psychoanalytic school and devoted the rest of her life to theory building. The progress of her thinking can be traced in such books as *Our Inner Conflicts: A Constructive Theory of Neurosis* (1945) and *Neurosis and Human Growth: The Struggle toward Self-Realization* (1950). These books reflect a third phase in Horney's thinking; leaving behind the interpersonal emphasis of her culturalist period, she became preoccupied with her noninstinctual theory of intrapsychic processes. She combined an almost Freudian insistence on individual responsibility with an un-Freudian emphasis on the present as the basis of analytic technique.

Horney was a thinker of undeniable originality, and many of the issues she raised can now be seen to be crucial to the psychoanalytic enterprise. Her questions, if not in every case her answers, have been vindicated.

Karen Horney, *Feminine Psychology,* ed. Harold Kelman (1967); Susan Quinn, *A Mind of Her Own: The Life of Karen Horney* (1987).

ELIZABETH CAPELLE

HOUSE OF REPRESENTATIVES

The House of Representatives, created as the "popular" branch of government, was intended to counterbalance the more elitist Senate and presidency. Giving meaning to the principle "no taxation without representation," the Framers of the Constitution provided that House members be elected directly by the people and enjoy exclusive authority to initiate tax and spending legislation. Members are elected for two-year terms and apportioned among the states according to population. In the First Congress only sixty-five members from thirteen states sat in the House. The size of the chamber is set by law, and it steadily increased throughout the nineteenth century. Apart from a brief interlude following the admission of Alaska and Hawaii to the Union, the number of members has held constant at 435 since 1913.

The history of the House of Representatives has been shaped by three developing institutions: the committee system, the legislative party, and the office of the Speaker. In the late eighteenth and early nineteenth centuries, most legislation was considered in the full House or in temporary committees appointed for the purpose of perfecting individual bills. During these early decades the pace of congressional deliberations was slow, and the small size of the chamber permitted leisurely consideration of legislation. The rapid rise of permanent standing committees began after the War of 1812, and the system was well established by 1848 when the Mexican-American War broke out. By this time each committee held exclusive jurisdiction over some area of government policy. Although some of these panels, such as the Committee on the Library, had so little to do that they rarely met, others, such as the Committee on Ways and Means, became so powerful that their control by one or the other of the major party organizations could determine the course of government. For example, as the expansion of slavery increasingly threatened national unity in the antebellum period, control of the Committee on the Territories became an important factor in whether territories would come into the Union as slave or free states and, thus, was a fundamental issue in the election of the Speakers who appointed its membership. The balance of free trade and protectionist forces on the Ways and Means Committee was a similarly decisive factor in the legislative design of tariff policy. From the middle of the nineteenth century until just after World War I, the tariff was a major issue in American politics, and the Ways and Means chairmanship was usually considered the second-ranking post within the majority party.

The rise of party organizations in the House roughly coincided with the development of the committee system. At first, party influence was felt most directly through control of nominations for Speaker, the policy positions hammered out in party caucuses, and the appointment of officials to patronage positions within the federal government. Aside from the Progressive Era and a brief period during the 1970s, the major parties have not attempted to bind the voting decisions of their members on major legislative issues. Periods of "party government" have, instead, been associated with increasing authority over committee assignments. When either the Speaker or party organizations have exercised wide discretionary power over committee memberships, as was the case until the end of World War I and since 1975 (for the Democrats), the major parties have been a powerful force in legislative deliberations. During the halcyon years of the seniority system from the middle twenties until 1975, on the other hand, most committee assignments were allocated according to the length of service of individual members, and parties largely became hollow shells that rarely caucused.

Resting on influence over committee assignments and control of floor deliberations, the power of the Speaker's office has evolved in tandem with the rise and fall of both the committee system and party government. From the emergence of the standing committee system until 1910, the Speaker exercised decisive influence over the composition of legislative panels, and candidates for the post often bartered away assignments in return for the support of powerful members. Growing authority over the recognition of members during House deliberations was consolidated with other procedural powers in the 1890 adoption of the "Reed Rules," named for their author, Speaker Thomas B. Reed of Maine. For the next twenty years, both assignment and procedural preeminence coincided and the Speaker of the House of Representatives was an almost imperial figure whose influence over national policy rivaled, if not exceeded, that of the president. During these years deviance from party positions was routinely punished by demotion within or outright removal from prestigious panels.

Henry Clay of Kentucky was the single most important influence upon the Speaker's office during the early history of the House of Representatives. Elected to the chair in his first term, Clay served off and on as Speaker from 1811 to 1825. During this period Clay turned the chair into a highly partisan post from which succeeding Speakers of lesser ability led increasingly cohesive party organizations. Even so, the second most powerful member of the House during the nineteenth century was probably Thaddeus Stevens of Pennsylvania — a member never elected to the Speaker's office. Stevens owes his place in history to his chairmanships of the Ways and Means and Reconstruction committees during and just after the Civil War. A fierce, acerbic opponent of slavery and the southern plantation system, Stevens used his committee posts to promote northern industrial development and weaken the influence of southern planters in national politics. Eclipsing Speakers Galusha Grow of Pennsylvania and Schuyler Colfax of Indiana, Stevens became the foremost Republican leader through his handling of tariff and Reconstruction policies in legislative combat on the floor of the House. In this and many other respects, his career presaged the emergence of the modern post of majority party leader.

"Czar" Joseph G. Cannon (also called "Uncle Joe") was probably the most powerful Speaker in history. From 1903 when he ascended to the speakership until the revolt in 1910 in which the House of Representatives ended his iron rule, Cannon's rough-hewn personality and autocratic tendencies came to personify Republican opposition to progressive reform. By removing the Speaker from the Rules Committee, the panel that controls the flow of most legislation from committees to the floor, the 1910 revolt worked a permanent diminution in the power of the Speaker. This blow was almost immediately followed by loss of authority to make committee assignments. Other than Cannon, the most influ-

ential Speaker in the twentieth century has been Democrat Sam Rayburn of Texas who, except for four years when the Republicans organized the House, served from 1940 until he died in 1961. Rayburn's influence rested on his understanding of the collegial requirements of the committee system that then dominated the House. Repeated to many a freshman member, his motto was "to get along, go along." Although the Democrats almost always held a majority of the seats during this period, Rayburn's party was deeply divided over civil rights, agricultural subsidies, labor legislation, and other policy questions. "Mr. Sam," as he was affectionately called, saw his role as Speaker as using the committee system to decentralize power throughout the chamber in order to prevent these disputes from erupting into open political combat on the floor. After his death, the civil rights movement and opposition to the Vietnam War pressured the Democratic party into a series of reforms that have again strengthened both the speakership and the caucus.

Viewed in the broadest historical perspective, the House of Representatives was never more powerful as a force in national government than when under one-man, authoritarian rule at the turn of the century. The chamber was never weaker than during the 1940s and 1950s when decentralization brought unparalleled influence to individual committee chieftains but left the House and the major parties without a coherent legislative agenda.

Major reforms adopted during the 1970s have moved the House of Representatives in two potentially contradictory directions. On the one hand, the legislative process has become even more decentralized as rule changes have enhanced the power of subcommittees at the expense of the standing committees of the House. As a result, subcommittee chairs often play a decisive role within an increasingly fragmented institution. On the other hand, changes in the Democratic party rules and the formal powers of the office have greatly strengthened the speakership. In many respects the office has regained the authority (but not the stature) that it had at the turn of the century. But as long as the Speaker's powers are exercised in a highly decentralized chamber, the House will continue to play a distinctly secondary role in national politics.

George B. Galloway, *History of the House of Representatives* (1976); James H. Hutson, *To Make All Laws: The Congress of the United States, 1789–1989* (1990).

RICHARD BENSEL

See also Blaine, James G.; Clay, Henry; Constitution; Gag Rule; House Un-American Activities Committee; Philadelphia Convention; Senate; Stevens, Thaddeus.

HOUSE UN-AMERICAN ACTIVITIES COMMITTEE

The House Un-American Activities Committee (HUAC) was formed May 26, 1938. Although HUAC investigated disloyalty among fascists as well as communists, it concentrated almost exclusively on the latter. In the 1940s under Chairman Martin Dies, HUAC focused on labor unions and New Deal agencies, pioneering many of the techniques later used by Senator Joseph R. McCarthy: sweeping accusations, hearings in which being questioned or even mentioned became an indication of guilt, pressure on witnesses to name their former associates, and an assumption that association with a suspect organization proved one's disloyalty. Critics deplored HUAC's methods from the first, but the committee's political power was awesome, bolstered by broad popular support and by every representative's awareness that a vote against HUAC could be publicized as a vote for communism. In 1945 the House voted to make HUAC permanent, and in 1947 a federal appeals court upheld its power to cite uncooperative witnesses for contempt of Congress.

In 1948, HUAC investigated Alger Hiss, a former high-level State Department adviser. This case, which ended with Hiss's 1949 conviction for perjury, stirred tremendous controversy and won Congressman Richard M. Nixon his first national notice. More typical were the 1947 hearings on communism in Hollywood. The committee found ample evidence of leftist sympathies (a group of screenwriters, who came to be known as the Hollywood Ten, refused to co-operate and were cited for contempt), but it uncovered none of the systematic subversion it had alleged. Even so, film executives soon started refusing to hire suspected leftists; this blacklist — which spread to radio, television, and the stage — lasted for more than ten years.

In the 1950s, HUAC was overshadowed by Senator McCarthy's activities, but it outlasted him, making new allegations of subversion in universities and among the clergy and then in the civil rights, black power, student, and peace movements. Only in the 1970s, with the waning of the cold war, did the committee (renamed the Internal Security Committee in 1969) begin to lose ground. It was finally abolished in January 1975.

See also Anticommunism.

HOUSEWORK

In the preindustrial culture of colonial America, most unpaid household labor produced goods and services to be used by household members. Few households produced everything they used; most made occasional purchases of ironware, pottery, and salt, and wealthier families bought imported textiles, tea, and other luxuries. But the fundamental household chores — cleaning, food preparation, the manufacture and maintenance of clothing, the care of children, the aged, and the infirm — involved a considerable amount of productive labor. Women spun wool and flax, wove cloth, sewed it into clothing, grew food and prepared it for eating or storage, and made soap and candles. Other family members shared those tasks and (usually according to a gendered division of labor) worked in adjoining fields and small crafts shops. The colonial household, then, served as the central institution of economic production.

During the ensuing centuries, much of the production work of the household was subsumed by private industry and moved from the domestic realm to the public one. Unpaid work in the home abetted industrial production by preparing workers to go to work daily and by feeding, clothing, and caring for the children who would eventually join their parents in the factories. Increasing numbers of households had to adapt to industrial workers' new schedules; natural cycles of light and dark could not dictate routine when some family members lived by the clock. Factories began to produce goods that helped people adapt to urban life — soap for urban dwellers who had no reserves of fat left from slaughtering, lamps and lamp oils to brighten the time left after work. Manufactured textiles were ubiquitous by the eve of the Civil War.

Still, because only the wealthy could afford gas or plumbing until late in the century, the major daily tasks of housework continued to represent a substantial burden, and even small households required the labor of at least one adult working full-time. Nearly every chore demanded fire building and water hauling. Cast-iron stoves, widespread during the last half of the century, represented a substantial advance over fireplaces but still entailed fuel hauling, fire tending, and ash sifting and disposal. Oil and kerosene lamps required frequent cleaning and wick trimming. Heavy pails of hot water had to be carried for dishwashing and laundry, the latter task followed by hanging clothes on the line to dry and ironing them with heavy flatirons that had to be heated on the stove. Spring housecleaning was a necessity because of the soot deposited by heating and cooking with wood and coal. Nor did the production work disappear entirely: most men wore ready-made clothes at the end of the century, but most women's and children's clothing was still made at home.

All this labor was performed by unpaid married women, although others also worked in the home. Indentured servants did housework before the Industrial Revolution, and slaves were used in the South before the Civil War. Women often enlisted the help of their children. Upper-class and some middle-class households employed servants, especially for particularly burdensome tasks like laundry and those requiring special skills.

As the new industrial order developed and increasing numbers of men and single women went to work in factories and offices during the nineteenth century, work in the home became separate from the rest of society. Married women labored alone without pay, supervising themselves, isolated from the dominant trends of the new culture. Factory workers left home to work; most women worked at home. Factory workers had bosses; married women decided what needed to be done according to the task and not the clock, controlling their own work process. Around 1825, popular writers began to codify these distinctions in an ideology of separate spheres for men and women that, though not totally accurate, reflected the reality of industrial society. Even midcentury domestic writers like Catharine Beecher, who denounced the degradation of unpaid domestic labor that had gone along with the steady expansion of the money economy, held to that ideology.

Between about 1890 and 1920, mass production and mass distribution brought new products — gas, electricity, running water, prepared foods, ready-made clothes, factory-made furniture and utensils — to large numbers of American families. Even energy could now be consumed at the flick of a switch or the turn of a knob. The new utilities literally connected the household to the public sphere with wires and pipes. Standardized uniform goods that cost money replaced the various makeshifts most people used. This dealt a blow to the satisfactions of home production but brought about a general end to the arduous labor of the household and a rise in the standard of living. Some poor farm families, however, still produced most of what they used, did without plumbing or electricity, and consumed few industrial products other than tools. Housework increasingly assumed the new economic function that Beecher had noticed among the urban and suburban upper classes around the end of the Civil War: no longer primarily producers, American housewives became consumers.

Despite new cleaning products and technologies, houses, bodies, and clothes still got dirty. The vacuum cleaner and electric washing machine, both within the means of the middle class by the 1930s, had to be operated. (The washing machine substituted not only for hand laundering but for work done at the commercial laundry, and represented an unusual but important instance of a task being returned to the home after having been substantially commercialized.) Despite canned, packaged, and later frozen foods, and even through the development of the restaurant industry in the 1970s and 1980s, and the prevalence of fast food, regular daily meal preparation remained central. Finally, the care of small children, the elderly, and the infirm continued to require substantial labor and to present a significant concern to individual households as increasing numbers of married women entered the paid labor force.

Ruth Schwartz Cowan, *More Work for Mother: The Ironies of Household Technology from the Open Hearth to the Microwave* (1983); Susan Strasser, *Never Done: A History of American Housework* (1982).

SUSAN STRASSER

See also Beecher, Catharine; Cookery; Domestic Work; Women and the Work Force.

HOUSING

The production of housing is a central part of American economic history, involving the development of construction technologies, the organization of building trades, the ownership of real estate, the availability of capital and credit, and the marketing of units. At the same time, the design and use of housing is an important part of social and cultural history: the design usually reflects existing family patterns and may symbolize ideals of home and family as well. Aspects of the material history of class and ethnicity can be revealed by a careful study of housing conditions. The material history of gender is also closely tied to the design and use of housing because the home has been a major workplace for women.

Both individual houses and multifamily housing complexes always function as part of larger environments. Because piped water, gas and electric lines, sewers, paved streets, and garbage collection affect the healthfulness and quality of housing, the extension of these services is part of the history of housing as well as that of public works and sanitation. These services must be present for important household technologies such as indoor plumbing, gas and elec-

tric stoves, central heating, electric lights, and refrigeration to be used. Dwellings themselves offer the best evidence of past conditions, but building and zoning laws, building permits, deeds, insurance maps, and mortgage-lending records are some other specialized sources useful to the historian.

The history of North American house forms begins with Native American dwellings — such as tipis, pueblos, and longhouses. Colonizers brought British, French, Dutch, and Spanish dwelling forms and construction techniques with them, although at first they often needed help from Native Americans to build basic shelter. These European forms evolved into the heavy timber-framed houses of New England, the Dutch gabled houses of New Amsterdam, and the courtyard adobes of the Southwest. Slaves sometimes re-created house forms (or parts of forms) from Africa or the Caribbean. During the last half of the nineteenth century, immigrants from Europe introduced German, Irish, Polish, and Swedish house and farmstead types, bringing more layers of ethnic diversity to American rural and urban housing.

Early in the nineteenth century, an American national style began to evolve in the brick row houses of eastern cities and then in the wooden Greek Revival houses created by country builders in New England. With the help of popular carpenters' pattern books, these modest, well-proportioned houses were copied widely. By the 1840s, writers such as Andrew Jackson Downing and Catharine Beecher were adding advice about horticulture and housework to their housing sketches, promoting the ideal of a rural or suburban cottage with a garden tended by a "Christian" housewife. Some feminists, such as Melusina Peirce and Charlotte Perkins Gilman, later disparaged the model Christian home as sentimental and offered counterproposals for neighborhoods of kitchenless houses, community work centers, and kindergartens organized to support women's public lives. The proposals and experiments that feminists organized had a broad ideological influence on the housing policies later developed by socialist feminists in Europe, such as Lily Braun and Alva Myrdal.

An alternative approach to housing was developed in industrial towns. The Lowell mill owners constructed dormitories for their young women workers, just as earlier mining and logging enterprises offered bachelor accommodations for their male employees. Other industrial operations provided housing for entire families on the condition that all members — husband, wife, and children — work in the owner's mills. By the late nineteenth century industrial towns such as Pullman, Illinois, were renting housing to skilled male workers whose families did not work for the company. In every case, the household form was determined by the corporation, which owned the town and shaped the housing to define and control its labor force.

The tenement house appeared in American cities in the mid-nineteenth century. At first a word used to describe subdividing and subletting properties, *tenement* came to mean a densely inhabited apartment building, often on a twenty-five-by-hundred-foot lot, with four families or more per floor. Tenants shared sinks on the landings and privies in the basement. There were many windowless rooms, with light and air entering these structures only at the narrow ends. This kind of housing existed in industrial cities from 1870 to about 1930. Into such cramped units crowded grandparents, parents, children, in-laws, cousins, and boarders. Reformers attacked the tenements as unhealthful and proposed regulations to improve light, air, and plumbing. In New York City, legislation of this kind was passed in 1867, 1879, and 1901.

The second half of the nineteenth century also saw the introduction of better apartment houses. "French flats" (so called to distinguish these multiple dwellings from tenements) were succeeded by residential hotels and other apartment houses of both plain and ostentatious construction. (The Dakota, designed in 1882 by architect Henry Hardenberg of New York City, was one of the most elaborate.) Apartments became more respectable as family habitations as the nineteenth century gave way to the twentieth, but they were never as popular as individual houses.

The residents of the tenements and of most apartment houses were renters, as were most inhabitants of the early company towns. But after 1919, some employers provided opportunities for home ownership to skilled white male workers, seeing it as a way to reward employees and discourage worker mobility and strikes. Patterns of suburban home ownership were also influenced by the extension of streetcar lines in the late nineteenth century and by the availability of cheap bungalows and mail-order cottages. In the 1920s, Better Homes in America, Inc., an association of bankers, builders, realtors, and manufacturers, worked closely with the Department of Commerce under Secretary Herbert Hoover to promote home building and ownership. Over seven thousand chapters of this organization were operating by 1930.

During the Great Depression and World War II, federal support of private suburban housing development increased. The income tax deduction for mortgage interest (1939) was a powerful stimulus. Federal mortgage insurance for developers and G.I. mortgages for veterans after the war made purchasing a suburban house cheaper than renting an urban apartment. In addition, automobiles made the suburbs more accessible, and federal funds for road building encouraged low-density development.

Suburbs were increasingly segregated after the 1920s because of restrictive covenants and the federal Home Owners Loan Corporation, established in 1933, which had included the ethnicity and religion of residents among indicators of the creditworthiness of neighborhoods. The Federal Housing Administration continued this as part of an elaborate credit rating system ("red-lining"). Female-headed families and the elderly also had difficulty obtaining mortgage loans. As a result, most federal subsidies for housing, concentrated in the form of mortgage interest deductions, went to young white families headed by men. Families with bigger mortgages on bigger houses were more heavily subsidized than families with smaller mortgages on more modest houses.

One alternative for some of those in need was public housing. During World War I a small amount of federally sponsored housing was constructed for war workers in shipyard towns like Bridgeport, Connecticut. In response to lobbying efforts under the leadership of Catherine Bauer and Edith Elmer Wood, two housing specialists, the Wagner-Steagall Act was passed in 1937, creating the U.S. Housing Authority. Public housing projects after World War II, however, were built in urban locations often thought undesirable and construction standards were sometimes low. Many older public housing projects need extensive renovation today. By 1980 only a tiny proportion of American housing was publicly owned, in contrast to Western European countries where a third to a half might be.

Other federal programs of the 1960s and 1970s involved leases or pay-back arrangements to private developers designed to house poorer families in privately owned mixed-income rental projects subsidized by the government. In some cities, rent control legislation kept units affordable, but often landlords retaliated by attempting to turn rental units into condominiums. In the 1980s the Reagan administration cut federal assistance to all low-cost housing, which contributed to a growing problem of homelessness.

The history of housing in the United States, then, can only be described as uneven. The nation was reluctant to establish shelter as a right of all citizens. Although tens of millions of tract houses transformed the American landscape in the last half of the twentieth century, not all Americans had access to them, especially minorities, the poor, and female-headed families. As most federal subsidies were funneled to private owners through banks and builders, the dreams of the real estate lobby of the 1920s were realized, but not the larger goal of affordable housing for all Americans.

Dolores Hayden, *The Grand Domestic Revolution: A History of Feminist Designs for American Homes, Neighborhoods, and Cities* (1981); Kenneth Jackson, *Crabgrass Frontier: The Suburbanization of the United States* (1985); Gwendolyn Wright, *Building the Dream: A Social History of Housing in America* (1981).

DOLORES HAYDEN

See also Architecture; Balloon-Frame House; Black Ghettos; City Planning; G.I. Bill; Homestead Act; Levittowns; Suburbanization; Urbanization.

HOUSTON, SAM

(1793–1863), soldier and politician. The traits that distinguished Sam Houston in Texas would be evident well before he settled there. He spent time among the Cherokee as a youth in East Tennessee, acquiring his distinctive familiarity with Indians. His service during the War of 1812 demonstrated his military ability and attracted the attention of Gen. Andrew Jackson. Houston became a Jackson protégé and, later, a Jacksonian politician. He represented Tennessee's Seventh District in Congress for two terms before being elected governor in 1827. Resigning suddenly in 1829 after the collapse of his marriage, Houston spent several years with the Cherokee in Indian Territory.

Houston journeyed to Texas in 1832. Interested in land speculation and negotiating with Texas Indians on behalf of both the Cherokee and the United States, he was at the time and afterward accused of also intending to promote, with Jackson's encouragement, a Texan insurrection against Mexican rule. Whatever his original motives, Houston quickly became involved in the growing protest against Mexico. After armed struggle commenced in 1835, a provisional government appointed Houston commander of its army. He was at Washington on the Brazos when independence was declared on March 2, 1836. Shortly thereafter, the fall of the Alamo compelled the small force Houston led to retreat eastward from Gonzales, trailed by panicked civilians. But at San Jacinto on April 21 his men secured Texas independence by destroying a Mexican army and capturing its commander, Mexican president Santa Anna.

The politics of the Texan republic revolved largely around Houston. Texans elected him to nonconsecutive presidential terms (1836–1838, 1841–1844). In the interim he served in the legislature. As president, Houston avoided open warfare with Mexico, despite provocations on both sides, and reduced governmental expenditures. He halted warfare upon Indians. The degree to which Houston shared many Texans' enthusiasm for American statehood is unclear. After the United States spurned annexation in 1837, Houston courted England and France, hoping either that American anxieties over European encroachment would encourage annexation or that Europe would guarantee Texas independence. The Tyler administration finally moved to annex Texas during Houston's second term.

The annexation of Texas and the winning of territory in the consequent war with Mexico accelerated divisions over the future of slavery in America. But, as Texas senator (1846–1859), Houston was a leading voice against sectional agitation. Although an unapologetic slave owner, Houston, like his mentor Jackson, insisted that the Union in all cases be preserved. He was the only southern senator to vote for every measure of the Compromise of 1850 and was one of only two to oppose the Kansas-Nebraska Act. Increasingly at odds with other southern Democrats, even in Texas, Houston gravitated toward the Know-Nothings. Attracted by their unionism, he also endorsed their nativism. Houston's fortunes hit bottom in 1857 when his gubernatorial bid failed and the legislature voted not to return him to the Senate.

Houston managed to win the governorship in 1859. But his hope that sectional tensions might be diffused and his own career advanced by the establishment of a protectorate over Mexico came to naught, as did an effort to secure the Constitutional Union party's presidential nomination. Over Houston's opposition, a state secession convention met in January 1861. After a popular vote endorsed secession, Houston accepted Texas's leaving the Union but rejected any affiliation with the Confederacy. The convention deposed him and, rather than accept federal military support, Houston retired. He died in Huntsville, Texas.

Llerena Friend, *Sam Houston: The Great Designer* (1954); Marquis James, *The Raven: A Biography of Sam Houston* (1929).

PATRICK G. WILLIAMS

See also Mexican War; Texas Revolution and Annexation.

HOWELLS, WILLIAM DEAN

(1837–1920), novelist, critic, and editor. At no period in its history did American literary cul-

ture have so widely acknowledged a spokesman as in those decades from the 1870s to 1920 when Howells edited literary journals and championed realism in critical essays and the novels he produced at the rate of almost one a year. He discovered and promoted young writers as different as Hamlin Garland, Stephen Crane, Paul Laurence Dunbar, and Abraham Cahan. He also created an American readership for such European masters as Émile Zola and Leo Tolstoy and served as valued adviser and friend to Mark Twain and Henry James. Among other things, it was he who suggested a way out of the impasse that had caused Twain to put *Huckleberry Finn* aside and it was he who published the work of the young James and served as the model for the mature James's characterization of Lambert Strether in *The Ambassadors*.

Although critical opinion has elevated the works of Twain and James above those of Howells, he has never wanted for an appreciative readership. *The Rise of Silas Lapham* (1885) and *A Hazard of New Fortunes* (1890) are probably his most significant works, but the artistry he brought to everything he wrote (some thirty works of travel, criticism, biography, and memoirs in addition to his many volumes of fiction) still serves to make it accessible to interested readers.

Born in Ohio, the son of a printer and country journalist, Howells received his most important schooling in the print shop where he learned the journalist's craft and after hours taught himself German, Italian, and Spanish, shaping his taste by reading in those literatures as well as English and American works. While working as a reporter at the state capital he wrote a campaign biography of Abraham Lincoln and his running mate Hannibal Hamlin that resulted in his being awarded the U.S. consulship in Venice upon their election. En route to his post in 1860 he stopped off in Boston to visit James Russell Lowell who had accepted a poem of his for publication in the *Atlantic* and through Lowell met the famous literati of New England.

In 1871 Howells became editor-in-chief of the *Atlantic.* During his tenure he wrote more than four hundred book reviews and began his long career as a novelist. When in 1886 he accepted the editorship of *Harper's Monthly,* his move was seen as the definitive sign that New York had succeeded Boston as the nation's literary capital.

Howells supplied continuity to a culture too often fragmented in terms of the East versus the West, elite versus popular tastes, and cosmopolitanism versus nationalism. His doctrine of literary realism also bridged the centuries. In the 1870s his refutation of the orthodox belief that fiction was wicked unless it portrayed an idealized world purified of the grit and ambiguity of everyday life drew heavy fire from sentimentalists. And in the 1900s the naturalists were angered by his contention that although realism entailed the faithful depiction of everyday life, the fictional portrayal of an amoral universe was not justified. Rather than diminishing Howells, however, these opposing viewpoints define the nature of his achievement.

George Arms and William M. Gibson, *A Bibliography of William Dean Howells* (1948); Kenneth S. Lynn, *William Dean Howells: An American Life* (1971).

LARZER ZIFF

See also Literature; Magazines and Newspapers.

HUAC

See House Un-American Activities Committee.

HUDSON RIVER SCHOOL

A group of realist landscape painters, the Hudson River school (1820–1880) was characterized by exacting observation of nature and interest in distinctively American scenery. The artists portrayed the unspoiled wilderness of the Hudson valley, the New England coast, and the Catskill, Adirondack, and White mountains, with a few painters venturing to the West for subject matter. Niagara Falls and panoramic views of the Hudson were favorite scenes. The precise rendering of a particular glimpse of American geography, sketched directly from nature, became the school's hallmark.

Although its most prominent early member, Thomas Cole, imbued his landscapes with allegory and didactic content, and the leader of the school's later years, Frederick Church, chose dramatic moments in nature that invited a metaphysical reading, the majority of the Hudson River school believed that a faithful recording of nature would speak for itself. The association of America with its land — the timelessness and lyricism of the wilderness — reflected a growing sense of national pride. In addition to Cole and Church, the best known of its large membership included Thomas Doughty, Asher B. Durand, Jasper F. Cropsey, John Frederick Kensett, Albert Bierstadt, Worthington Whittredge, Henry Inman, and George Inness.

Popular in its heyday, the school fell in and out of favor in the twentieth century and was sometimes cited as an example of the tedious conventionality of genre painting.

See also Painting and Sculpture.

HUGHES, CHARLES EVANS

(1862–1948), chief justice of the U.S. Supreme Court. Hughes had an extraordinary public career. In addition to serving as chief justice in 1930–1941, he was New York governor (1907–1910), Supreme Court justice (1910–1916), Republican presidential candidate (1916), secretary of state (1921–1925), and World Court judge (1928–1930). His rise in public life was due largely to his intelligence, sense of duty, capacity for hard work, and self-sufficiency.

A precocious child, Hughes learned to read at the age of three and a half. Before he was six, he was reading and reciting verses from the New Testament, doing mental arithmetic, and studying French and German. After only three and a half years of formal schooling, he graduated from high school at the age of thirteen. After graduating Phi Beta Kappa from Brown University, Hughes went to Columbia Law School, where he ranked first in his class. When he took the New York bar examination in 1884, he received the highest grade given up to that time, 99½ percent. He had a photographic memory and could read a paragraph at a glance, a treatise in an evening. These abilities made Hughes a formidable opponent at the bar — he practiced law for almost thirty years — and contributed to his success as a politician, judge, and negotiator.

To Hughes, duty meant doing worthy things and doing them well. He drove himself mercilessly. His sense of duty led him to public service and enabled him to excel in almost everything he undertook. Hughes had no personal or political advisers, no favorites, no confidants. Herbert Hoover once said that he was the most self-contained man he had ever known. He made his own judgments based on his own analyses. At work, he was organized, intense, and serious, and had little time for pleasantries. That side of him gave rise to an aloof, cool, and humorless public image. At home, however, he showed warmth and humor; he was a sensitive husband and a caring father of three children.

Hughes came close to being elected president in 1916. A shift of less than four thousand votes in California would have given him that state's electoral votes and the presidency. If Hughes had not projected such an austere public image (or if he had secured the support of Governor Hiram W. Johnson), he would probably have been elected.

As secretary of state in the Harding and Coolidge administrations, Hughes negotiated a separate peace treaty with Germany when the Senate failed to ratify the Treaty of Versailles. He also chaired the Washington Disarmament Conference in 1921–1922, supported U.S. participation in the World Court, and withheld American recognition of the Soviet Union. Although he served two presidents who made political capital of rejecting Woodrow Wilson's vision of internationalism, he conducted a foreign policy that recognized the international responsibilities of the United States. In Latin America he sought a means to reduce U.S. intervention while defending a traditional conception of the national interest. In Europe he asserted a constructive role for the United States while avoiding formal commitments that would have involved Congress or excited public opinion.

As chief justice, Hughes led the Supreme Court during one of its most difficult periods. He presided over the Court's transformation of its basic role from defender of property rights to protector of civil liberties, writing the period's landmark opinions on freedom of speech and press — *Near* v. *Minnesota, Stromberg* v. *California,* and *DeJonge* v. *Oregon.* He also successfully opposed President Franklin D. Roosevelt's plan to "pack" the Supreme Court in 1937.

David J. Danelski and Joseph S. Tulchin, eds., *The Autobiographical Notes of Charles Evans Hughes* (1973); Merlo J. Pusey, *Charles Evans Hughes* (1951).

DAVID J. DANELSKI AND
JOSEPH S. TULCHIN

See also Elections: 1916; Supreme Court.

HUGHES, LANGSTON

(1902–1967), African-American poet, playwright, novelist, and journalist. Because his father immigrated to Mexico and his mother was often away, Hughes was reared in Lawrence, Kansas, by his grandmother Mary Langston, whose first husband had died at Harpers Ferry fighting under John Brown and whose second (Hughes's grandfather) had also been a fierce abolitionist. She helped inspire in Hughes a devotion to the cause of social justice.

A lonely child, he turned to reading and writing, publishing his first poems while in high school in Cleveland, Ohio. In 1921, after a failed reunion with his father, he entered Columbia University but left after an unhappy year. Even as he worked as a delivery man, a messman on ships to Africa and Europe, a busboy, and a dishwasher, his verse appeared regularly in such magazines as *Crisis* (NAACP) and *Opportunity* (National Urban League). As a poet, Hughes was a pioneer in the fusion of traditional verse with black artistic forms, especially blues and jazz.

He was a leader in the Harlem Renaissance of the twenties and thirties, publishing two verse collections, *The Weary Blues* (1926) and *Fine Clothes to the Jew* (1927), as well as a novel *Not without Laughter* (1930) and an embittered short-story collection *The Ways of White Folks* (1934). Mainly because of the depression and disillusionment with a wealthy patron, Hughes became a socialist in the 1930s. He never joined the Communist party, but he published radical verse and essays in magazines like *New Masses* and *International Literature* and spent a year (1932–1933) in the Soviet Union. Several of his plays also appeared in this decade, the most successful, *Mulatto,* a tragedy about miscegenation, reaching Broadway in 1935.

Around 1939, Hughes moved away from the political Left, as the apolitical tone of his autobiography *The Big Sea* (1940) suggests. During the war he supported the Allies with patriotic songs and sketches and published a verse collection, *Shakespeare in Harlem* (1942). He vigorously attacked segregation, especially in his column in the black weekly *Chicago Defender,* where he created a comic but incisive black urban Everyman, Jesse B. Semple, or "Simple." Simple's popularity over twenty years resulted in five published collections.

In 1947, as lyricist with Kurt Weill and Elmer Rice on the Broadway opera *Street Scene,* Hughes achieved a major critical success. After buying a house in Harlem, he lived there the rest of his life, although, as his book-length poem *Montage of a Dream Deferred* (1951) revealed, he feared for the future of urban blacks. His output became prodigious and included another book of verse, almost a dozen children's books, several opera libretti, four books translated from French and Spanish, two collections of stories, another novel, a history of the NAACP, and another volume of autobiography, *I Wonder As I Wander* (1956). He also continued his work in the theater, pioneering in the gospel musical play.

By the time of his death Hughes was widely recognized as the most representative of African-American writers and perhaps the most original of black poets. What set him apart was the deliberate saturation of his work in the primary expressive forms of black mass culture as well as in the typical life experiences of the mass of African-Americans, whom he viewed with near-total love and devotion. Despite his humane interest in other cultures and peoples, he saw blacks as his primary audience. As a result, his vast body of work, uneven in quality as it is, nevertheless rings with almost unrivaled authority and authenticity as an inspired portrait of black American culture and consciousness.

Faith Berry, *Langston Hughes: Before and beyond Harlem* (1983); Arnold Rampersad, *The Life of Langston Hughes,* 2 vols. (1986, 1988).

ARNOLD RAMPERSAD

See also Harlem Renaissance; Literature.

HULL-HOUSE

See Addams, Jane; Settlement Houses.

HUNDRED DAYS

The Hundred Days is the title often given to the first congressional session of President Franklin D. Roosevelt's administration, March 9 to June 16, 1933. To address the crisis of the worsening depression, the president convened Congress in special session and launched the New Deal with an avalanche of bills designed to stabilize the economy, create jobs, and bolster flagging local relief efforts.

Among the acts passed — most with hardly any debate — were the following: Emergency Banking Act (March 9), expanding assistance to and regulation of the nation's banks; Economy Act (March 20), reducing federal costs through reorganization of and cuts in salaries and veterans' pensions; Beer-Wine Revenue Act (March 22), legalizing and taxing wine and beer; Civilian Conservation Corps Act (March 31), creating work camps for 250,000 men ages eighteen to twenty-five; Federal Emergency Relief Act (May 12), creating a federal agency to distribute $500 million to states and localities for relief; Agricultural Adjustment Act (May 12), creating a federal agency to reduce crop surpluses by subsidizing farmers to curtail production; Thomas Amendment to the Agricultural Adjustment Act, permitting the president to inflate the currency in various ways; Tennessee Valley Authority Act (May 18), permitting the federal government to construct dams and power plants in the Tennessee Valley, to produce and sell the power, and to engage in area development; Federal Securities Act (May 27), tightening regulation of the securities business; joint resolution abandoning the gold standard (June 5); National Employment System Act (June 6), establishing the U.S. Employment Service; Home Owners Refinancing Act (June 13), creating the Home Owners Loan Corporation to refinance nonfarm home mortgages; Glass-Steagall Banking Act (June 16), instituting various banking reforms, including creating the Federal Bank Deposit Insurance Corporation; Farm Credit Act (June 16), providing for the refinancing of farm mortgages; Emergency Railroad Transportation Act (June 16), enhancing federal regulation of railroads; and the National Industrial Recovery Act (June 16), creating the National Recovery Administration and the Public Works Administration.

See also New Deal.

HURSTON, ZORA NEALE

(1891?–1960), folklorist, anthropologist, and novelist. Outspoken, spirited, and gifted, Hurston was the most prolific African-American woman writer of the 1930s. She was born and raised in all-black Eatonville, Florida, the major shaping influence of her affirmative vision of African-American rural folk culture. Inspired as a child by the advice of her dying mother to "jump at de sun" and to be her mother's voice, she achieved success under the guidance of Franz Boas as a prize-winning folklorist, anthropologist, and writer. Industry, intelligence, ingenuity, and white patrons facilitated her education as a writer and anthropologist at Morgan Academy, Howard University, Barnard College, and Columbia University, where she studied with Boas.

When she arrived in New York in 1925, Hurston's genius for storytelling, drama, and flamboyance helped her make friends quickly. In addition to Boas, the most important were Fannie Hurst, who employed her as a secretary and confidant, Carl Van Vechten, and Charlotte Mason, the patron of several black artists. Much of Hurston's folklore research in the South, the Bahamas, Haiti, and Jamaica was sponsored by these individuals; she also received a Guggenheim Fellowship in 1936.

Hurston drew on the tension between her folk and formal education for the ethnic material and double-voiced manner of short stories and articles that won her acclaim in the 1920s and 1930s. But many black contemporaries of the Harlem Renaissance and depression eras criticized her willingness to play the minstrel role for whites, and some criticized her books for being pastoral and apolitical. Her most controversial political act was to express opposition to the 1954 Supreme Court school desegregation decision, which she resented for portraying southern blacks as inferior to whites. She died in penniless obscurity.

Her literary revival began a decade after her death with poet and novelist Alice Walker's essay "Looking for Zora" (1971), which movingly describes her discovery of Hurston as a literary ancestor. Following the publication in 1977 of Robert Hemenway's Hurston biography, critics reclaimed from literary obscurity her two books of folklore (*Mules and Men*, 1935, and *Tell My Horse*, 1938), three romances (*Jonah's Gourd Vine*, 1934, *Their Eyes Were Watching God*, 1937, and *Moses, Man of the Mountain*, 1939), and autobiography (*Dust Tracks on a Road*, 1942).

More important, literary critics have reassessed Hurston's significance in the canons of European-American, African-American, and women's literatures. *Mules and Men* and *Tell My Horse*—the first based on materials collected in Florida and Louisiana, the second on materials gathered in Jamaica and Haiti—are distinctive for the lively, unorthodox manner in which Hurston integrates and dramatizes herself as ethnographer with her black informants, the tales they tell, and the folk culture they live. Both books are important resources for the bicultural belief systems and ritual practices of peoples of African descent in the Americas. *Mules and Men* provides useful descriptions of hoodoo, and *Tell My Horse* provides detailed accounts of voodoo.

Hurston's most commercially successful book was *Dust Tracks on a Road,* though critics agree that its dazzling black idiom and formal rhetoric conceal more than they reveal about the details of her life. Her most critically acclaimed book is *Their Eyes Were Watching God.* Janie Crawford's quest is the prototypical black love story and account of a woman's search for identity. Its mixture of formal rhetoric and black idiom is poetic without being folksy; its retrospective narrative structure is loose without being disjointed; its dynamic characters are stylized without being exotic; and its romantic quest for personal wholeness and female autonomy is centered on egalitarianism without exploitation in living and loving.

Robert E. Hemenway, *Zora Neale Hurston: A Literary Biography* (1977); Karla F. C. Holloway, *The Character of the Word: The Texts of Zora Neale Hurston* (1987); Alice Walker, *In Search of Our Mothers' Gardens: Womanist Prose* (1983).

BERNARD W. BELL

See also Harlem Renaissance; Literature.

HUTCHINS, ROBERT MAYNARD

(1899–1977), educator and author. Hutchins, born to a line of college-trained clergymen, excelled in his studies at Oberlin College and Yale. Tall, handsome, witty, and self-assured, he did not wait long for opportunity and recognition. After graduating from Yale with honors in 1921, he was named secretary of the Yale Corporation, found time amid his duties to complete a law degree in 1925, and two years later was named dean of the Yale Law School — at age twenty-eight.

Here began his career as an educational reformer. Associating himself with the younger "legal realist" school of jurisprudence and bringing in new faculty such as William O. Douglas, Hutchins in two years changed the course of the law school's development. In 1929, taking a "gamble on youth and brilliancy," the trustees of the University of Chicago appointed Hutchins president.

The gamble brought Chicago a twenty-year season of educational ferment that kept the university at the forefront of American education and established Hutchins as the nation's most audacious, innovative, and controversial university executive. He held strong views on the importance of a core undergraduate curriculum built around the "great books" of the Western tradition and was an outspoken critic of vocational emphases and narrow specialization. He engaged in public debate with educational philosopher John Dewey and published (during his lifetime) over three hundred essays on education, including most notably *The Higher Learning in America* (1936). He abolished football at Chicago, though most of his proposed curricular reforms were modified or blocked. Nevertheless, Chicago was in Hutchins's day a place of remarkable intellectual ferment.

Outspoken on many public issues and liberal in his politics, Hutchins was rumored to be in line for several New Deal posts in the late 1930s. He yearned only for a seat on the Supreme Court where his independence would be assured and his analytical powers given full scope, but this prospect faded when he opposed President Franklin D. Roosevelt's rearmament policies in 1940–1941.

Hutchins left Chicago in 1951 and with Ford Foundation support established the Fund for the Republic in 1954 and, as its operating arm, the Center for the Study of Democratic Institutions in Montecito, California, in 1959. Here he would establish his "great academy," a place where intellect could accomplish what modern universities could not — address the fundamentals of democratic institutions, serve as an "early warning system" for problems just over the societal horizon, and join social theory with social action. The center adopted no official stands, but its meetings and publications scrutinized the nuclear arms race, the errors of American foreign policy, and the failings of the press, and asserted the nation's vital stake in freedom of inquiry. The center's impact has not yet received adequate assessment; it closed in 1979, two years after Hutchins's death.

Harry S. Ashmore, *Unseasonable Truths: The Life of Robert Maynard Hutchins* (1989).

OTIS L. GRAHAM, JR.

See also Education.

HUTCHINSON, ANNE

(1591–1643), New England religious leader and midwife. Hutchinson is known chiefly for her role in the antinomian controversy in Massachusetts Bay Colony. Her participation in so public an event, though rare for premodern women, was not unique. From the early Christian era, female activism in religious life gave some women high visibility, thus preserving their voices in the historical record. The splintering of the Puritan movement in seventeenth-century England gave women broader scope for leadership as lay preachers, visionaries, and petitioners.

Like many of her contemporaries, Hutchinson left no correspondence, journal, or published works. Only the documents of the antinomian controversy, principally the record of her two trials before the General Court (November 1637) and the Church of Boston (March 1638), provide the primary source material for interpreting her mental world. Close readings of these documents have enabled historians to understand the political, theological, and gender issues at the root of this colonial crisis.

Several factors contributed to Hutchinson's social authority in early Boston. Born in Alford, Lincolnshire, England, she was the daughter of Bridget Dryden and the dissenting Anglican clergyman Francis Marbury. As the second daughter of the Marburys' thirteen children, Anne developed her talents for domestic leadership and the use of herbal medicines early in life. From her father she received an education in theology and conscientious dissent. The Marburys moved to London in 1605, but when Anne married the merchant William Hutchinson in 1612 the couple returned to Alford to live. They began traveling to St. Botolph's in Lincolnshire to hear the charismatic preaching of John Cotton. During these years, too, Hutchinson gave birth to twelve children; another would be born in Boston, Massachusetts. Following Cotton's suppression for his Puritan views, he migrated to the Massachusetts Bay Colony in 1633. Bereft at the loss of his inspiring ministry, Hutchinson persuaded her husband to remove their family to Boston, Massachusetts, in September 1634, where their gentry status and piety assured them a prominent position in the Puritan colony. Two years later, however, Anne Hutchinson and John Cotton found themselves at the center of a religious and political contest.

The antinomian controversy of 1636–1638 broke out in the waning months of a religious revival led by Cotton when a spiritual malaise gripped the colonists. Hutchinson had been holding biweekly devotional meetings to discuss Cotton's sermons at her home, which drew as many as sixty people. She brought attention to Cotton's spirit-centered theology, championing

him and her brother-in-law John Wheelwright as true Christian ministers against the "legal" preachers who taught that a moral life was sufficient grounds for salvation. With Cotton and Wheelwright, Hutchinson believed that redemption was God's gift to his elect and could not be earned by human effort: the soul remained passive to the work of divine grace in the drama of salvation.

The effect of Hutchinson's meetings was divisive, and her supporters composed a significant faction in the colony. A ministerial synod examined Cotton and cleared him from the charge of heresy; the investigation then focused on Hutchinson and Wheelwright. In contrast to Cotton, Hutchinson and her brother-in-law took their radical spirituality to an extreme position. Cotton's style was mediative; theirs was adversarial. Consequently, Hutchinson and her supporters were banished by the General Court of Massachusetts; and the result of her trial by the Church of Boston was excommunication. The Hutchinsons went to Aquidneck in Narragansett Bay. In 1642 when William Hutchinson died, his widow and the six youngest children moved to New York where all but one daughter were killed in an Indian raid in 1643.

The domestic setting for Hutchinson's leadership is key to understanding the role of premodern women in religious life. It was among her female neighbors in need of her medical skills that she first communicated her controversial religious ideas. Her devotional meetings were also common practice among the early Puritans. Like many religious movements, early Puritanism was a household religion. With its institutionalization, women lost the authority they had exercised in the formative domestic phase. Such was the case in Massachusetts where John Winthrop and company were intent on building a godly society protected by the coordinate powers of church and state. The enterprise demanded a new emphasis on outward morality, or sanctification, that would bolster the authority of both ministers and magistrates. But Hutchinson's prophetic stress on the indwelling Holy Spirit, although an authentic strain of Puritan belief, empowered the laity at the expense of the ministry. Moreover, her claim to immediate revelation was especially threatening to the advocates of law and order. A generation later a similar contest would be waged against the Quakers, some of whom had been among Hutchinson's supporters.

Francis J. Bremer, ed., *Anne Hutchinson: Troubler of the Puritan Zion* (1981); David D. Hall, ed., *The Antinomian Controversy, 1636–1638: A Documentary History,* rev. ed. (1990); Amy Lang, *Prophetic Woman: Anne Hutchinson and the Problem of Dissent in the Literature of New England* (1987).

BARBARA RITTER DAILEY

See also New England Colonies; Puritanism.

HUTCHINSON, THOMAS

(1711–1780), American colonial politician, judge, and historian. The last civilian royal governor of Massachusetts, Hutchinson was born in Boston, a great-great-grandson of the seventeenth-century nonconformist, Anne Hutchinson. His well-to-do merchant father sent him to Harvard College, where he took his degree at sixteen. Thereafter, he engaged in maritime commerce and trading.

Hutchinson's political career began in 1737, when he was elected a Boston selectman. Three months later, he became a member of the provincial legislature, where he served intermittently over the next two decades. He was also selected six times to participate in Indian conferences, and in 1746 was chosen Speaker of the Massachusetts House of Representatives. His most conspicuous service during this period came when the British government agreed to reimburse Massachusetts in gold for the cost of the successful 1745 military expedition against Louisbourg. Hutchinson, who, even his bitter enemy John Adams acknowledged, "understood the subject of coin and commerce better than any man I ever knew in this country," persuaded the legislature to use the specie to retire the province's degraded paper currency.

In 1754, Hutchinson played a major role in the Albany Congress, where representatives from seven colonies, besides negotiating still an-other Indian treaty, seriously debated and eventually drafted a plan of union.

In 1752, Hutchinson began amassing public offices, provoking hatred and envy. Although not trained as a lawyer, he became judge of the Suffolk County Probate Court and simultaneously took a seat on the Inferior Court of Common Pleas. Eight years later, he received a royal appointment as chief justice of the Superiour Court of Judicature, the highest judicial position in Massachusetts.

Intelligent, skilled in getting to the heart of a case and in weighing competing legal arguments, Hutchinson would have been better off limiting himself to judging and to historical writing (he published two volumes of an uncompleted *History of Massachusetts Bay*). Unfortunately, he retained not only his position as lieutenant governor, but also a seat on the Governor's Council and took an active role in the turmoil that bubbled after 1763. His position made him a natural supporter of royal (and parliamentary) authority, although he opposed the Stamp Act. Nonetheless, in 1765, the worst mob in Boston history gutted his home and destroyed its contents. Thereafter, he became less and less able to understand not only the political currents but his (and the home government's) inability to control them. As the violence escalated, culminating in the Boston Massacre (1770) and the Boston Tea Party (1773), Hutchinson, appointed governor in 1771, vainly tried to work out an imperial policy that could accommodate London's insistence on control and the radicals' increasingly overt resistance to parliamentary oversight.

The radicals obtained and published some of Hutchinson's private letters to an English correspondent, thus permanently destroying his political effectiveness. Replaced as governor by Gen. Thomas Gage, Hutchinson went to England in 1774, where, lacking all influence, reviled in America yet desperately homesick, he died suddenly in 1780.

Bernard Bailyn, *The Ordeal of Thomas Hutchinson* (1974).

HILLER B. ZOBEL

See also Albany Congress; Revolution.

HYDROGEN BOMB

When it became known in 1949 that the Soviet Union had developed the atomic bomb, thus pulling abreast of the United States in weapons capability, physicist Edward Teller, head of the Atomic Energy Commission Lewis Strauss, and other important government and military figures urged that the United States study the feasibility of producing a "superbomb" — the hydrogen bomb. They were opposed on moral and technical grounds by a group of other scientists, including J. Robert Oppenheimer. But President Harry S. Truman, spurred by the growing cold war, ordered a crash program to build the hydrogen bomb in February 1950.

After more than a year of work at Los Alamos, Teller, mathematician Stanislaw Ulam, and other scientists solved the technical problems involved and scheduled a test of a prototype hydrogen bomb at Eniwetok Atoll. Oppenheimer and other scientists, who had been appointed to a Panel of Consultants on Disarmament, recommended that the test be postponed. They suggested that the United States approach the Russians with a proposal that both sides cease testing nuclear weapons and urged that the public be made more aware of the implications of such weapons. But Truman, told that a postponement this far in the countdown under way at the atoll would adversely affect the weapon's development, disregarded the panel's recommendation and ordered the test to proceed. The explosion on November 1, 1952, caused an island to disappear and created in its place a crater a mile wide and 175 feet deep. A deliverable bomb was subsequently developed and successfully tested in 1954. The Soviet Union tested a hydrogen bomb on August 12, 1953, and the British followed on May 15, 1957.

The hydrogen bomb is a thermonuclear weapon capable of devastating 150 square miles by blast, with searing heat effects and radioactive fallout for more than 800 square miles, depending on the size of the weapon. Its explosions are much larger than those of atomic (fission) bombs. The hydrogen bomb explosion is produced by nuclear fusion — the collision of neutrons with the nucleus of an unstable isotope of hydrogen, either deuterium or tritium, under high temperatures. Usually an atomic bomb inside the thermonuclear device triggers the fusion reaction.

See also Cold War; Nuclear Power; Nuclear Weapons: Origins and Legacy; Oppenheimer, J. Robert.

I
★

ICC

See Interstate Commerce Commission.

IMMIGRATION

I. Immigration to 1965

America was built by immigrants. From Plymouth Rock in the seventeenth century to Ellis Island in the twentieth, people born elsewhere came to America. Some were fleeing religious persecution and political turmoil. Most, however, came for economic reasons and were part of extensive migratory systems that responded to changing demands in labor markets. Their experience in the United States was as diverse as their backgrounds and aspirations. Some became farmers and others toiled in factories. Some settled permanently and others returned to their homeland. Collectively, however, they contributed to the building of a nation by providing a constant source of inexpensive labor, by settling rural regions and industrial cities, and by bringing their unique forms of political and cultural expression.

The volume of immigration before the 1960s was staggering. Figures for the colonial period are imprecise, but by the time of the first census of 1790 nearly 1 million Afro-Americans and 4 million Europeans resided in the United States. The European population originated from three major streams: English and Welsh, Scotch-Irish, and German.

After 1820, the data became exact enough to document the volume of immigration more reliably. From 1820 to 1975 some 47 million people came to the United States: 8.3 million from other countries in the Western Hemisphere, 2.2 million from Asia, and 35.9 million from Europe. The stream was relatively continuous from 1820 to 1924 with only brief interruptions caused by the Civil War and occasional periods of economic downturns such as the depression of the 1890s, the panic of 1907–1908, and the Great Depression of the 1930s. World War II, of course, also greatly reduced the numbers emigrating. In fact, 32 million of the 35.9 million Europeans who came to the United States between 1820 and 1975 came prior to 1924.

Immigration on such a large scale resulted in greater ethnic diversity from the earlier colonial structure. In the century prior to World War I, the major sources of immigrants were Germany, Italy, Ireland, Austria-Hungary, Russia, and Great Britain, but Canada also supplied 4 million newcomers, including a large number of French-Canadians, and Mexico sent some 2 million. These emigrant centers supplied the largest ethnic concentrations in American society before the 1960s.

Immigrants to colonial America were welcomed because of its acute need for inexpensive labor. Proprietors seeking to develop large colonies and planters in such areas as the Virginia Tidewater trying to grow crops for a world market needed a constant stream of settlers and workers. Probably over half of all white laborers drawn to the colonies before 1776 were indentured servants, impoverished English persons

533

who worked in the colonies for a fixed period of years to pay off their debts and gain their freedom. But indentured servants, if they didn't die because of bad living conditions, eventually completed their obligations and left their employers. Thus, the need for labor was continuous. African labor was one solution that Virginia planters turned to in 1619. Although most Afro-Americans were not legally slaves when they first arrived, a system of slavery had been imposed upon these involuntary immigrants by the 1660s.

The English and Afro-Americans were quickly joined by Scotch-Irish, Scots, and German settlers. As many as 250,000 Scotch-Irish immigrated to the colonies before 1776. Although their decision to move was influenced by Protestant ministers in Ulster, they began leaving in 1717–1718 primarily because of a dramatic increase in their rents. They were joined after the 1760s by artisans and laborers from the Scottish Lowlands who, facing hard times at home, moved to the tobacco colonies as indentured servants. Germans started to arrive in Philadelphia in 1683, owing in part to William Penn's promises of religious toleration. By the 1760s over 60 percent of Pennsylvanians were of German origin. Other religious sects seeking religious toleration included Quakers, who settled in Pennsylvania, Moravians in Georgia and Pennsylvania, and Catholics in Maryland.

Immigrant streams to America often grew as extensions of European population movements. In the century between 1650 and 1750, rural workers were constantly on the move because of poverty and land shortages. Agents hired by land speculators and proprietors in the colonies could tap into these migratory streams and entice these mobile individuals to move across the ocean. This is essentially what happened between 1630 and 1642 when twenty-one thousand emigrants moved out of the migratory patterns of the East Anglia region of England and sailed to Puritan New England.

But the levels of colonial immigration were dwarfed by the figures of the nineteenth century. From 1815 to the start of the Civil War, 5 million people moved to the United States, about half from England and 40 percent from

Ireland. Between the end of the war and 1890 another 10 million came, mostly from northwestern Europe — England, Wales, Ireland, Germany, and Scandinavia. And finally, about 15 million immigrants arrived in the relatively brief period between 1890 and 1914 when the outbreak of war in Europe temporarily arrested the flow. This later group came mostly from eastern and southern Europe and consisted of new immigrant groups — Poles, Russian Jews, Ukrainians, Slovaks, Croatians, Slovenes, Hungarians, Romanians, Italians, and Greeks.

Leading Sources of Immigrants to the United States, 1820–1975

Country of Origin	Numbers (approx.)
Germany	6.9 million
Italy	5.2 million
Ireland	4.7 million
Austria-Hungary	4.3 million
Canada	4.0 million
Soviet Union/Russia	3.3 million
England	3.1 million
Mexico	1.9 million
West Indies	1.4 million
Sweden	1.2 million

These people came largely for the same reasons that colonials had. The American economy had needed both unskilled and skilled workers through much of the nineteenth century. But after the 1880s, the demand was almost exclusively for unskilled workers to fill the growing number of factory jobs. Coinciding with this were conditions in some areas of Europe, which were undergoing substantial economic changes in the 1880s. Southern and eastern Europeans, dislocated from their land and possessing few skills, were attracted to the burgeoning industries in the United States.

Four major factors had altered their society in Europe: a dramatic population increase, the spread of commercial agriculture, the rise of the factory system, and the proliferation of inexpensive means of transportation such as steamships and railroads.

Agricultural regions, the crucibles in which these factors were mingled, had become linked to cities by the new transportation routes. The increasing need of growing cities like London, Budapest, and Berlin for foodstuffs encouraged farmers to acquire more land in order to expand production for distant markets. But commercial rather than mere subsistence farming stimulated the rise of large estates and increased the overall price of land. Small owners or aspiring owners found it increasingly difficult to acquire sufficient land to support themselves. The problem for these smaller owners and tenants was compounded by the dramatic rise in Europe's population after the Napoleonic Wars. Food supplies became more plentiful, diets improved, and life expectancy increased. Population pressures were further heightened because, with less land to transmit, young people had less reason to wait for the landed inheritance once needed to start a family. Many simply went ahead and married. Earlier family formations, in turn, meant that women gave birth over a longer portion of their lives and more children were born. People of modest means then began to move in search of opportunities at home and in the United States.

The crisis in agriculture produced movement not only among farmers but also among craft workers. Skilled artisans such as Bavarian clock makers in southern Germany were destroyed economically: the transportation lines that took foodstuffs from their regions to the cities returned loaded with factory-made goods that could be sold more cheaply than their products. So Scottish weavers, Swedish potters, and British textile workers also joined the exodus to America.

Immigrants who were modest farmers in Europe had often attempted to become farmers in the United States prior to the 1880s, although some did settle in cities. But immigrants from southern and eastern Europe, especially Jews, Italians, and Slavs, almost invariably settled in cities. Regardless of their point of origin or their destination, they all developed a set of strategies that would facilitate their settlement and adjustment in a new land. Ethnic differences aside, immigrants were usually pragmatic people who acquired much information about America before they arrived. Letters from relatives in the United States told them something about land costs, wages, and job openings. Promotional literature from railroads and states unfortunately offered exaggerated descriptions of opportunities.

It took a great deal of planning to start an agricultural enterprise over again, and those going into farming, such as Swedish, German, and Norwegian farmers in the upper Middle West, had little intention of returning to their homeland. Between 1868 and 1873, when crop failures devastated their country, over 100,000 Swedes, hearing of the Homestead Act and its promise of virtually free land in America, moved across the ocean. Other Scandinavians were equally informed and adaptable and quickly learned what crops would bring a greater profit. Thus, Norwegians in Wisconsin in the 1860s reaped rewards by planting wheat, and Mennonite arrivals in Kansas brought with them from Russia hardy wheat strains that would flourish on the plains.

Those moving to cities exhibited a similar degree of advance knowledge of conditions and a fair amount of flexibility in adjusting to their new life. Jews, Slavs, Italians, Romanians, and Greeks, all of whom concentrated in industrial cities such as New York, Chicago, Cleveland, Detroit, and Boston where the number of unskilled jobs was increasing, moved to the United States within well-established family and ethnic networks that provided transportation fees, wage information, access to jobs, and housing. Italians heard of the harsh conditions in meat-packing plants in Chicago and shunned them in favor of outdoor work that was more seasonal and would allow them to return to Italy periodically. Similarly, large Irish immigrant families who needed their children's income as well as that of the parents to survive moved to textile towns that employed large numbers of young women. The existence of networks that supplied this type of information and access to work resulted in ethnic clustering throughout the American economy. By 1920 Jewish women were concentrated in garment trades in New York and 93 percent of the females doing hand embroidery were Italians. Sixty-nine percent of Slovak males were coal miners.

But the ability to move into urban economies and create institutions did not ensure that adjustment to a new society would be smooth. Immigrants tended to hold dangerous jobs that could result in injury or death. Steelworkers, for instance, readily contracted pneumonia from the daily move between the extremes of intense heat in the mills to the cold of a winter evening. Immigrant women had high rates of infant mortality stemming partially from their need to work incessantly at home for their families and boarders. All suffered from both poor nutrition and cramped and unsanitary housing. Labor protests often resulted in bloody retribution at the hands of law enforcement officials such as those at Lattimer, Pennsylvania, in 1897 and Ludlow, Colorado, in 1914.

American society reacted to the foreign-born in a variety of ways. During the Progressive Era, settlement house workers such as Lillian Wald and Jane Addams operated centers in urban neighborhoods to teach newcomers domestic and civic lessons and help them with problems of adjustment. Other Americans, however, were less humane. Fearing the newcomers would destroy American institutions or take away land and jobs from those already in the United States, many tried to restrict the rights of immigrants as well as the numbers entering the country. The American Federation of Labor, for example, supported immigration restriction. In 1920 Californians denied Japanese newcomers the right to own land, and in Illinois native-born citizens turned on Italian settlers, beating them and burning their homes.

Reflecting this bias was the Johnson-Reed Act of 1924, which curtailed immigration by establishing annual quotas that favored newcomers from northern Europe over those from the continent's southern and eastern regions. The Great Depression and World War II also kept immigration rates low; some 500,000 Mexican workers were deported during the early 1930s because it was thought that they took jobs away from the native-born.

Between the end of World War II and the passage of important immigrant reform legislation in 1965, most newcomers to the United States consisted of Europeans displaced by war and Mexican agricultural workers. In 1948 Congress passed the Displaced Persons Act that eventually admitted some 400,000 Europeans uprooted by war, although displaced people from Palestine, China, and India were ignored. Congress also responded to the requests of agricultural interests in the Southwest and allowed "braceros," or temporary workers from Mexico, into the country after 1952.

But regardless of the varying climate awaiting them in America, immigrants made lasting contributions to their new society. They gave the country its major religious strains — Protestant, Catholic, Jewish — and, in the case of British coal miners and German, Italian, and Jewish socialists, brought traditions of social justice that resulted in better wages and improved working conditions for millions. Major American business ventures, such as the Bank of America and Steinway Pianos, were founded by immigrants. And important works of American literature, often about the immigrant experience, were written by foreign-born authors such as Ole Rölvaag and Mary Antin. Immigrant groups brought such a variety of foods with them that ethnic restaurants constituted one of the key ways in which newcomers entered the American economy. Despite their contributions, however, the immigrant encounter with America produced uneven results. Although some were rewarded for their labor, others found economic stability and cultural adjustment more elusive.

Bernard Bailyn, *The Peopling of North America: An Introduction* (1986); John Bodnar, *The Transplanted: A History of Immigrants in Urban America* (1985); Maldwyn Allen Jones, *American Immigration* (1960).

JOHN BODNAR

II. Immigration from 1965 to the Present

The character of American immigration underwent a significant transformation with the passage of the Immigration Act of 1965. The legislation abolished the discriminatory quotas based on national origins that had favored northwestern Europeans and substituted a system based on family preference. Only 170,000 people would be allowed to enter from the Eastern

Hemisphere and 120,000 from the Western, but close relatives of individuals already in the United States would be exempt from these quotas. Thus, once immigrants became citizens, they could bring their relatives and reconstitute their families. This provision resulted in a much larger number of newcomers than legislators had imagined. Skilled workers and refugees stood in line after kin, but they also gained ready admittance.

Congress had anticipated that most immigrants would continue to be Europeans. But a general improvement in the European economy, worsening conditions in Latin America, the war in Vietnam, and the system of family preference resulted in a drastic shift. Newcomers from Asia and Latin America quickly began to outnumber Europeans, with 3 million of 4 million immigrants coming from those areas in the 1970s. Between 1951 and 1965, 53 percent of all immigrants came from Europe and only 6.6 percent from Asia. In the twelve-year period after 1966 Europeans represented only 24 percent of the total, and Asians, 28.4 percent. The Philippines, for instance, sent 6,093 people in 1965 and 41,300 in 1979. Legal Mexican immigrants totaled 37,969 in 1965 but over 92,367 in 1978, an amount that exceeded the annual Mexican quota of 20,000 because of the family preference rule.

Although there had always been some immigrants with strong educational and skill backgrounds, their numbers increased after 1965. Many urban professionals now immigrated to the United States with skills that were in demand. Between 1965 and 1974, 75,000 foreign-born physicians entered the country in response to an increased need for medical services resulting from the establishment of Medicare programs. After newspapers in Korea published discussions of the 1965 law, over 13,000 Korean medical professionals, a majority of them female nurses, entered the United States. Thousands of other Koreans also came and opened shops and small businesses in the cities. These immigrants were doing what immigrants to America had always done: entering niches in the economy abandoned by better-established residents. By 1977 over 4,500 Korean-Americans operated small businesses in southern California. Finally, skilled newcomers from Central and South America, especially El Salvador and Argentina, entered but had difficulties finding skilled work, and many returned home.

Not all immigrants after 1965 possessed skills or the inclination to become entrepreneurs. Large numbers of Arabs entered Detroit auto plants; Mexicans in southern California moved primarily into the service economy; but Haitian immigrants in southern Florida in the 1980s encountered more serious problems of adjustment. Fleeing poverty and political repression, these Haitians, most of them under thirty, were kept in government detention centers by Florida officials who feared they would become public charges. Even those who were free found it difficult to secure jobs with few relatives to help and little in the way of skills or education. By 1985 about one-third of Haitian men in southern Florida were jobless. To survive in a strange land, they were forced to rely heavily on female household members who could earn a minimal wage or secure some form of public assistance.

Leading Sources of Immigrants to the United States, 1976–1986

Country of Origin	Numbers (approx.)
Mexico	720,000
Vietnam	425,000
Philippines	379,000
Korea	363,000
China/Taiwan	331,000
Cuba	258,000
Dominican Republic	211,000
Jamaica	200,000
United Kingdom	150,000
Canada	129,000

A sizable portion of the immigrants after 1965 were refugees — people with widely diverse skills and educational and cultural backgrounds. The largest refugee group, the Cubans, came in three stages. About 200,000, mostly well educated and middle class, fled the island after the assumption of power by Fidel Castro in 1959. A second, more socially diverse wave of over 360,000 came when they were allowed to leave the island in 1965. And finally about 130,000 — the "mariel group" — left when Castro let many working-class Cubans emigrate in 1980–1981. Some came to Florida in boats operated by relatives already in the United States. By 1980, Cuban-Americans made up the largest single nationality of the post–World War II refugee stream.

Indochina was the second major source of refugees after 1965. After the fall of Saigon in 1975, the United States immediately accepted 130,000 Vietnamese. As communist power spread through Southeast Asia, sharply increased numbers of ethnic Chinese, Cambodians, and Laotians sought asylum in the United States as well. By 1985 over 700,000 Indochinese had entered the country, many of them resettled with the help of churches and other sponsoring agencies rather than relatives and friends. Although large numbers of Vietnamese possessed skills and strong educational backgrounds, many Cambodians and Laotians were peasants who could not enter the American economy as easily. By 1985 Indochinese refugees in southern California, where most of them settled, were 15 percent less likely to be employed than the population as a whole and were relying on low-wage jobs and public assistance to survive.

The largest immigrant group after 1965 came from Mexico, averaging over 60,000 a year in the 1970s. After Congress in 1964 eliminated the "bracero" program, which had allowed the hiring of temporary workers from Mexico, there was a large increase in the number of undocumented (illegal) workers migrating to Texas and California to enter manufacturing jobs. In the 1970s employment expanded by 645,000 jobs in Los Angeles County, and about one-third of those openings were filled by Mexicans. By 1980 nearly 1 million aliens from Mexico were apprehended annually by the Immigration and Naturalization Service. But the influx continued in large part because of the willingness of employers to ask the Mexicans no questions. In an attempt to stop this practice, the Immigration Reform Act of 1986 was passed. It imposed penalties on employers who hired illegal immigrants, but offered amnesty to those immigrants who had been in the United States continuously since 1982.

By the 1980s the pattern of immigrant adjustment was a mixed one. Those with skills, education, and family connections frequently did reasonably well. The median family income of Cubans was nearly 30 percent higher than that of other Latin-American immigrants because they entered the well-developed Cuban-American economy in southern Florida. Asian immigrants arriving between 1970 and 1980 earned incomes that nearly equaled those of the native-born. On the other hand, Mexican-Americans forced into unskilled jobs in the service sector of the economy earned mean family incomes well below those of Asians and native whites.

Nathan Glazer, ed., *Clamor at the Gates: The New American Immigration* (1985); David M. Reimers, ed., *Still the Golden Door: The Third World Comes to America* (1985).

JOHN BODNAR

See also Alien and Sedition Acts; Chinese Exclusion Act; Ethnicity; Homestead Act; Immigration Restriction League; Indentured Servitude; Internal Migration; Know-Nothing Party; Nativism; Radicalism; Roman Catholic Church; Settlement Houses; Slavery.

IMMIGRATION RESTRICTION LEAGUE

This organization was founded in 1894 by a group of Boston lawyers, professors, and philanthropists who were alarmed by the large number of immigrants entering America each year. The league urged that immigrants be required to demonstrate literacy in some language. In theory a literacy test would not discriminate against the people of any particular race, creed, or color. But in reality it would keep out many of the "new" immigrants from southern and eastern Europe — whom league members considered inferior beings, likely to become criminals or public charges if admitted.

A literacy bill was passed by Congress in 1897, but President Grover Cleveland vetoed it. In 1917, however, as wartime hysteria fed American xenophobia, another literacy bill was signed into law by President Woodrow Wilson. After 1917, as key members lost interest or passed away, the Immigration Restriction League declined in influence.

See also Immigration; Nativism.

IMPEACHMENT

Impeachment, the process specified in Article I, Sections 2 and 3, of the Constitution for trial and removal from office of federal officials accused of misconduct, has two stages: (1) the House of Representatives brings a formal accusation, known as "articles of impeachment," against the official, and (2) the Senate tries the impeached official on these articles. A two-thirds vote is required for conviction. The sole penalties after conviction are removal from office and disqualification from future officeholding under the Constitution.

The Framers of the Constitution borrowed impeachment from the English constitutional system; the seventeenth-century parliamentary opponents of the Stuart kings used impeachment as a powerful political weapon against officials allied with the Crown, and colonial legislatures in the seventeenth and eighteenth centuries followed their example.

Article II, Section 4, of the Constitution defines only "Treason, Bribery, or other high Crimes and Misdemeanors" as impeachable offenses. The exact meaning of "high Crimes and Misdemeanors" is a perennial source of controversy. One school of thought maintains that the phrase covers only crimes for which one can be indicted under federal or state law. Others insist that impeachable offenses also include offenses against the basic principles of the Constitution and the rule of law, including acts not indictable by a federal or state grand jury.

Other controversies focus on whether the government may prosecute a federal official for charges that are also the subject of an impeachment; whether an official may be tried by the Senate after he or she is acquitted in a criminal trial; and whether the Senate may delegate to a committee the tasks of examining evidence and hearing witnesses in an impeachment trial.

The House of Representatives has impeached fifteen officials since 1789. The Senate has convicted and removed seven, all of them federal judges.

See also Johnson, Andrew; Nixon, Richard M.

Impeached Federal Officials

William Blount, senator from Tennessee; charges dismissed for want of jurisdiction, January 14, 1799

John Pickering, United States district judge, District of New Hampshire; removed from office, March 12, 1804

Samuel Chase, associate justice, United States Supreme Court; acquitted March 1, 1805

James H. Peck, United States district judge, District of Missouri; acquitted January 31, 1831

West H. Humphreys, United States district judge, Middle, Eastern, and Western Districts of Tennessee; removed from office, June 26, 1862

Andrew Johnson, president of the United States; acquitted, May 26, 1868

William W. Belknap, secretary of war; acquitted, August 1, 1876

Charles Swayne, United States district judge, Northern District of Florida; acquitted, February 27, 1905

Robert W. Archbald, associate judge, United States Commerce Court; removed from office, January 13, 1913

George W. English, United States district judge, Eastern District of Illinois; proceedings dismissed upon resignation, November 4, 1926

Harold Louderback, United States district judge, Northern District of California; acquitted, May 24, 1933

Halsted L. Ritter, United States district judge, Southern District of Florida; removed from office, April 17, 1936

Harry E. Claiborne, United States district judge, District of Nevada; removed from office, October 9, 1986

Alcee L. Hastings, United States district judge, Southern District of Florida; removed from office, October 20, 1988

Walter L. Nixon, Jr., United States district judge, Southern District of Mississippi; removed from office, November 3, 1989

IMPERIALISM

See Expansion, Continental and Overseas.

IMPRESSMENT CONTROVERSY

The impressment controversy of the early 1800s grew from the British navy's long-standing practice of augmenting its crews with sailors forcibly taken from coastal towns and merchant ships. After the American Revolution, the British no longer sent "press gangs" onto American soil in search of crews, but they continued to stop American merchantmen at sea, insisting on their right to search for deserters from the British navy. America made frequent protests during the 1790s, but its continuing economic dependence on Great Britain as well as Britain's overwhelming naval preeminence made the United States hesitate to protest more forcefully.

With the revival of the Napoleonic Wars in 1803, the pace of impressments — along with other encroachments on America's maritime rights as a neutral — began to increase. In retaliation, Congress passed the Nicholson Non-Importation Act in April 1806, excluding a long list of British goods. President Thomas Jefferson persuaded Congress to suspend the act while James Monroe and William Pinkney attempted to end impressment (as well as other violations) by treaty, but by March 1807 it was clear that their mission had failed. Two months later, the captain of the British frigate *Leopard* set a disturbing precedent when he fired on the American warship *Chesapeake* for refusing to let him come aboard and search for deserters. He then boarded the damaged ship and removed four men. By the end of 1807, the British had impressed over six thousand American sailors.

In response, the Embargo Act (December 22, 1807) stopped nearly all U.S. trade with foreign nations. Wide popular opposition, especially in commercial centers, led Congress to substitute a law permitting resumption of trade with either France or Britain if it stopped violating neutral rights. But when trade was reopened with France in February 1811, the British responded with a blockade of New York Harbor and a rapid increase in impressments. On June 1, 1812, President James Madison asked Congress to declare war on Britain, citing impressment as one of his reasons. Meanwhile, the British were initiating a more conciliatory policy, but they were too late; war was declared on June 19.

See also Embargo Act of 1807; War of 1812.

INCOME, DISTRIBUTION OF

See Wealth and Its Distribution.

INCOME TAX

The personal income tax in its present form was first levied by the federal government in 1913. The rate was 1 percent on taxable net income above $3,000 ($4,000 for married couples), less deductions and exemptions. It rose gently to a top rate of 7 percent on incomes above $500,000. The law was class legislation and deliberately so.

The idea was not new. The biblical tithe was an income tax payable in commodities. The British introduced the modern form of the tax during the Napoleonic Wars, and the U.S. Treasury considered an income tax at the time of the War of 1812. The Civil War brought a tax on personal income for the first time, with rates ranging from 3 to 5 percent. This was a historic step in the development of the American federal tax system, but it was phased out by 1872. From then until 1913 the major support of the government came from import duties and excise taxes. Collection of these taxes was entrusted to the Bureau of Internal Revenue, which had been established in 1862. After evidence of irregularities in the bureau surfaced in 1953, the agency underwent a sweeping reorganization and the name was changed to the Internal Revenue Service (IRS).

Rising farm and labor discontent had culminated in 1894 in an attempt to write a peacetime tax into law. Although hard times returned in the nineties, the Congress, under pressure from important trade associations, passed the Wilson-Gorman tariff bill in 1894, which included an income tax. Personal exemption was high at four thousand dollars, and the 2 percent rate of the income tax was not graduated. Several months after the tax was enacted, a conservative Supreme Court declared the tax unconstitutional in the *Pollock* v. *Farmers' Loan and Trust Company* on the basis that it posed a "communistic threat" to property. Sentiment favorable to the tax gathered such momentum during the Progressive Era, however, that President William Howard Taft in 1909 proposed submitting the question of amending the Constitution to the states. An amendment was drafted giving Congress the authority to impose taxes on the proceeds of any lawful business without apportionment according to population or equal treatment of all taxpayers. By February 1913 the tax amendment — the Sixteenth — had the approval of the required three-fourths of the states. Three years later the word *lawful* was dropped from a new revenue law. Since 1916 the Treasury has collected on unlawful gains whenever possible.

Support for the amendment came from a coalition of those reluctant to force another Court review, of progressives alarmed by the rapid concentration of industrial wealth, and of some conservatives who felt that the government needed an elastic and reliable system of revenue to cope with national emergencies. From 1913 to the present both major political parties have accepted the desirability of a progressive tax on individuals, although the proper degree of graduation remains a source of intense debate and has led to adjustments and technical corrections in the U.S. Tax Code, which now runs to more than two thousand pages.

During World War I rates rose in an almost vertical ascent to 77 percent. During the prosperous 1920s the tax structure was scaled down, only to be reversed by huge Treasury deficits during the depression years. With the entry of the United States into World War II, taxation once again became directly connected with national survival and the top rate reached 91 percent. In 1943 Congress imposed a withholding system on income tax payers, making collections easier and doubling the government's yield in the first year, an important revenue boost during the war. Although Roosevelt vetoed the withholding bill as neglectful of the welfare of the low- and medium-income groups, the bill became law without his signature. At the same time, however, exemptions were lowered and the base broadened so that what had been a class tax became a mass tax. This can be seen in the numbers of people required to pay in two significant years: in 1939, 4 million people and in 1945, 42.7 million. Today the reach of the tax is shown in figures for 1989 indicating that the IRS processed 107.7 million individual returns. This number will rise, the agency estimates, to 118.3 million in 1995. By a wide margin, the income tax is the largest single source of federal receipts.

After World War II income taxes were moderately reduced, only to rise again during the Korean War. Laws enacted during the 1960s and 1970s increased the progressiveness of income tax through reforms designed to achieve equality of sacrifice. This is not a precise concept, however. Abstract justice becomes hard to discern in the thicket of deductions, credits, subsidies, and exemptions, all of which were patched into the Tax Code for the best of reasons — to balance colliding interests fairly. The result: a vast accumulation of precedents, administrative rulings, and case law. Moreover, the code must be framed complexly to counter the machinations not merely of average citizens but of the cleverest adversaries the law schools can produce, many of whom are alumni of the IRS itself. As a result, some 40 percent of all who file seek the services of professional tax preparers and simplification remains a distant and probably unattainable goal.

During the 1980s and especially after the passage of the Tax Reform Act of 1986, the progressive feature of the income tax was sharply curtailed. Yet the idea of taxation based upon the theory that the wealthy should contribute not proportionately but according to their ability to pay appeals intuitively to most people. An opposing view, however, is advanced vigorously by conservative economists and high-income taxpayers. It holds that the general welfare is best promoted when the affluent are lightly taxed and so are encouraged to save and invest. For more than seven decades this proposition has been articulated in hearings held before the House Ways and Means Committee where revenue bills originate. The weight of such testimony is evident in the present attrition of the principle of graduation.

Taxation is a political act involving controversial decisions arrived at through the democratic process. Fairness at any given time is what the law says it is. We shall never be certain that we are not paying too much and someone else too little. That is why, as Edmund Burke reminded the British Parliament in his famous speech on taxing the colonists, "to tax and to please, no more than to love and be wise, is not given to men."

David F. Bradford, *Untangling the Income Tax* (1986); Gerald Carson, *The Golden Egg: The Personal Income Tax: Where It Came from, How It Grew* (1977).

GERALD CARSON

INDENTURED SERVITUDE

The Virginia Company devised the system of indentured servitude in the late 1610s to finance the recruitment and transport of workers from England to the colony. Those unable to afford an Atlantic passage could "borrow" the needed funds. In return for their passage, maintenance during their service, and certain "freedom dues" at the end of the term, servants signed contracts or "indentures" to work for their masters for a fixed number of years. Servitude played a major role in the settlement of the colonies. During the colonial era, some 200,000 to 300,000 servants came to British mainland North America, accounting for one-half to two-thirds of all European immigrants.

Indentured servitude is sometimes thought of as an adaptation of apprenticeship, but it more closely resembled "service in husbandry," a major source of agricultural labor in early modern England. Typically, farm servants were boys and girls from poor families who left home in their early teens to work for more prosperous farmers until they married. They usually lived in their master's household, agreed to annual contracts for wages, food, and lodging, and changed places frequently, often every year. Given the pervasiveness of this form of life-cycle service, it is a likely antecedent for the indenture system

and was a major source of recruits for American plantations.

But indentured servitude was harsher and more restrictive than apprenticeship or service in husbandry. It was not, however, a form of slavery. Servants entered into their labor contracts voluntarily, and they retained some legal rights: they could bring suit and testify, own property, and turn to colonial courts for protection against abusive masters. On the other hand, they could not marry without their master's consent, and they had little control over the terms or conditions of their labor and living standards, although custom and local law did set limits and provide for certain minimums. Terms varied substantially, from four years for skilled adults to a decade or more for unskilled minors. And all could find their terms extended if they ran away or became pregnant. Servants could be sold without their consent, a necessity given the distance and terms involved. To sell an English youth "like a damn'd slave" at first shocked some contemporaries, but it was essential to the success of the indenture system.

That servants were willing to serve so long under such restrictive conditions testifies to their expectations of the opportunities in America. We do not know whether most did better than they would if they had stayed at home. A few joined the ranks of the colonial elite; more died in poverty, often while still servants. For most, a modest "competence" and a respectable position defined the limits of possibility. How many reached those limits is uncertain, but the high wages, cheap land, and rapid growth of the colonial economy remained sufficiently enticing to persuade successive generations of migrants to take the chance and endure the hardships.

There were four forms of immigrant servitude, three of them voluntary. Under the most common, servants signed an indenture before departure, which was sold to a master when the servant reached the colonies. Many servants arrived without written contracts, however, and they were to serve according to "the custom of the country." Customary servants were usually younger than those with indentures, and they served longer terms. The third form of voluntary servitude appeared in the eighteenth century with the German migration to the Mid-Atlantic colonies. "Redemptioners" agreed to pay passage upon arriving in the colonies, thus shifting much of the risk in the trade from merchants to the migrants. If unable to pay, they were sold as servants to satisfy their debt. In addition to these voluntary systems, penal servitude became an important source of labor in the eighteenth century when some fifty thousand convicts were shipped to the colonies.

The types of people who came to the colonies as servants varied over time and by region, although the several migrant streams shared a few common characteristics. Most were male, young, in their late teens and early twenties, and single, traveling alone rather than with family members. In the seventeenth century they were also chiefly English, although as opportunities and wages in England improved, more came from Scotland, Ireland, Wales, and Germany. Details of the individual migrations are now largely lost, but most seem to have entered the national labor market at home before signing on as servants, hitting the road in search of work and better prospects. Once on the road, detached from home and family, they became candidates for migration overseas in a process that made America an extension of the labor markets first of England and later of Britain and the Rhine Valley.

Servants played a critical role in the colonial economy. Although they worked in all regions at a wide range of tasks throughout the colonial period, there were clear patterns. Initially, servants were concentrated in the staple-producing colonies, working as field hands to produce sugar in the West Indies and tobacco along the Chesapeake Bay. As demand for labor grew and servant prices rose, planters found that they could employ African slaves more profitably in their fields but continued to use servants as plantation craftsmen and domestics and in supervisory positions. As slaves learned English and plantation work routines, they eventually displaced servants in those positions as well. By the early eighteenth century, indentured servants played only a marginal role in the plantation districts. Thereafter, they were concentrated in a few industries in the Mid-Atlantic region demanding particular skills — chiefly iron making, shipbuilding, and construction — and in the several colonial towns where they worked in various service trades and at precision or semiartistic crafts.

Isolated cases of indentured servitude among European immigrants appear as late as the 1830s, but the institution was unimportant in the United States after 1800. It flourished in the British West Indies after the abolition of slavery in the 1830s, when planters used indentures to finance the migration of Asians to work the sugar crop. And echoes of it appear in subsequent movements to the United States, especially in the debt contract schemes that financed Chinese and Japanese migration to California. Why such arrangements were rarely used to finance European migration after 1800 is unclear. Perhaps falling transatlantic passenger fares simply made indentured servitude unnecessary. Perhaps, too, a growing racism and the identification of blacks with bondage made any type of servitude seem inappropriate for whites. As so often happened in America, freedom and slavery progressed together.

Bernard Bailyn, *Voyagers to the West: A Passage in the Peopling of America on the Eve of the Revolution* (1986); David W. Galenson, *White Servitude in Colonial America: An Economic Analysis* (1981); Abbot Emerson Smith, *Colonists in Bondage: White Servitude and Convict Labor in America, 1607–1776* (1947).

RUSSELL R. MENARD

See also Colonial Economy.

INDEPENDENT TREASURY

The Independent Treasury Act, passed in 1840, removed the federal government from involvement with the nation's banking system by establishing federal depositories for public funds instead of keeping the money in national, state, or private banks. The act was proposed by President Martin Van Buren in 1837, partly in response to the fact that public funds had been lost when many state banks failed during the panic of 1837. Passage was delayed, however, until southern Democrats could be persuaded to join northern Democrats in approving the measure.

Under the Independent Treasury Act, bank notes were to be gradually phased out for payments to and from the government; by June 30, 1843, only hard money was to be accepted. The bill also established subtreasuries for federal funds in New York, Boston, Philadelphia, St. Louis, New Orleans, Washington, and Charleston — hence its alternative title, the subtreasury bill.

The Whigs, led by Henry Clay and Daniel Webster, opposed the Independent Treasury; they were committed to the reestablishment of a national bank like the one defeated by President Andrew Jackson in 1832. After winning a congressional majority in the election of 1840, the Whigs succeeded in repealing the Independent Treasury Act (August 13, 1841), although they were unable to gain President John Tyler's support for their national bank proposals. For the rest of Tyler's term, in spite of repeated Democratic efforts to reestablish the subtreasury system, the secretary of the treasury was left free to manage public funds according to his discretion, usually by depositing them in state banks. The return of the Democrats to power after the election of 1844 led to the passage in 1846 of a new Independent Treasury Act, nearly identical to that of 1841. This legislation remained substantially unchanged until passage of the Federal Reserve Act in 1913. The subtreasuries were finally abolished in 1920.

See also Banking.

INDIANS

I. Origins of American Indians

All human societies have versions of their own origins, and the American Indians are no different. Stories of natural or supernatural creation in the Americas or emergence from another world exist among all Indian tribes and, like the biblical narrative in *Genesis,* are regarded as matters of faith.

Apart from them, and not competing with them, is what is known from the evidence of science and scholarship. Since no remains of a pre–Homo sapiens type have ever been found in the Americas, it is assumed that humans did not evolve in the Western Hemisphere but entered it after the development of modern humans. It is also generally agreed — from the findings of archaeology in Mongolia, Siberia, and North America and studies in physical anthropology, linguistics, and other disciplines — that they came from eastern Asia in one or more migrations, crossing a land bridge that from time to time during the Ice Age connected Siberia with Alaska.

The time of the first arrivals is still in question. During the Wisconsin glacial stage, the last seventy thousand or so years of the Ice Age, the periodic formation of glaciers caused the sea levels to fall as much as three hundred feet. At such times, the retreating waters exposed a vast, flat landmass of tundra and grass (which scholars call Beringia) that extended north and south for up to a thousand miles across the area now covered by the Bering Strait and adjacent seas and provided passage between Asia and North America to migrating animals and humans. Conversely, during periods when the glaciers melted and withdrew, the seas rose again, covering the land bridge and preventing movement by land between the continents.

It is believed that the bridge existed sometime between seventy thousand and thirty thousand years ago; again, continuously, from twenty-five thousand to fifteen thousand years ago; and, once or twice, between approximately fourteen thousand and ten thousand years ago. At any of these times, it is presumed that small hunting bands from Asia, pursuing migrating herds of Ice Age megafauna across Beringia or along its coasts, could have reached Alaska. Whether these first Americans came at one time or in separate migrations at different periods during the Ice Age, once in Alaska, they and their descendants continued to pursue the Pleistocene big-game animals, following them along ice-free routes on the Alaskan coasts, up the Yukon and other river valleys, and gradually south through corridors that existed from time to time between the Laurentian and Cordilleran ice sheets. Eventually, south of the glaciers, the hunting bands spread to the Atlantic Coast and through Central and South America.

From archaeological discoveries, it is certain

that human beings were living in almost all parts of North and South America by at least twelve thousand years ago. Still controversial, though gaining increasing acceptance, are various finds from Alaska and the Yukon to Brazil and Chile and from California to Pennsylvania that suggest that humans were present thirty-five thousand years ago or earlier.

Although population at first was sparse, here and there bands undoubtedly met one another, combined, divided into new groups, or drove one another into less hospitable and accessible areas. Until the end of the Ice Age, about ten thousand years ago, the people on both continents lived essentially by hunting mammoths, mastodons, outsized bison, and other now-extinct animals and by fishing and gathering wild foods. After the disappearance of the big Pleistocene fauna, deer and other small game were hunted, and the gathering of nuts, berries, grass seeds, and wild vegetables and fruits became more important.

With the passage of time, physical and cultural variations began to appear as people adapted to the different environments in which they lived. Population increased, and weapons and tools became more sophisticated and varied. A basic Clovis-type, chipped-stone spear point, named for the New Mexican site in which it was first found but used by big-game hunters in many parts of the hemisphere about eleven thousand years ago, was succeeded by numerous specialized regional and local types.

In the millennia following the Ice Age, evolutionary processes and continued migrations within the Americas accelerated the differentiation among the peoples and their developing cultures. Those living along the coasts developed maritime-oriented cultures with economies based largely on harvesting fish and collecting shellfish. In the eastern half of the present-day United States, vigorous Woodland cultures of hunters, gatherers, and fishers emerged, and in the arid West, gatherers of wild foods developed a long-lived Desert Culture. At the same time, more arrivals from Asia, including the ancestors of the Eskimos and Aleuts, seem to have reached North America by crossing the open water in boats.

Less likely, but not to be ruled out, is the possibility of accidental contacts from the Old World — boats blown by winds or carried by ocean currents from Japan, China, Polynesia, Africa, or the Mediterranean. No proof has yet been offered of such an occurrence or of its influence on American Indian cultures. More fanciful claims that Indians are descendants of the Egyptians, the Phoenicians, the Welsh, a Lost Tribe of Israel, or refugees from the lost continent of Atlantis can be dismissed.

The invention of agriculture in the Western Hemisphere — occurring separately in Mexico and the Andean and the northern lowland regions of South America about nine thousand years ago — led to the settling down of the horticultural peoples to tend their gardens. Spreading through large parts of both continents, the growing of corn, squash, beans, manioc, and other crops allowed the storage of surplus food, the concentration and growth of populations, the stratification of societies under religious and secular leaders, and a flourishing of arts and crafts.

The last three thousand years before the arrival of Columbus saw the rise of advanced, agriculturally based Indian civilizations, with true urban centers, monumental public works, and ruling classes. Many, like the civilizations of the Mayas in Mesoamerica and the Chacoan peoples in the present-day American Southwest, fell before the Europeans came. But some, including the empires of the Aztecs and Incas and a few towns of the resplendent temple mound–building Mississippians in the U.S. Southeast still existed in 1492.

Alvin M. Josephy, Jr., *The Indian Heritage of America* (1968); Russell Thornton, *American Indian Holocaust and Survival* (1987).

ALVIN M. JOSEPHY, JR.

II. Societies and Cultures

During the period of European colonization, Native American societies within the present continental United States varied markedly. Despite this diversity, however, almost all the tribes were integrated through interconnecting political, economic, social, and religious obligations provided by extended families or kinship groups. During the next three centuries some of these societies were forced to alter many of their original structures, but others were able to preserve some of their traditional forms. All, however, retained considerable kinship ties, and within both the traditional and the acculturated modern societies, the extended family structures still form the basis for tribal cohesion.

In the Northeast most Indian people lived in small bands that came together in the summer to form larger villages. The people planted corn and other vegetables, which were cultivated by women, and they enjoyed a series of ceremonies marking the ripening of crops and the rhythm of the seasons. Some tribes (such as Senecas and Hurons) relied heavily upon agriculture, whereas others (Ottawas, Kickapoos) depended more upon hunting or fishing. During the seventeenth and eighteenth centuries almost all became dependent upon the fur trade, and by 1750 much of their economic activity focused upon procuring pelts for the Europeans. Their growing association with Europeans and colonists also encouraged a centralization of political power, since whites preferred to deal with a single "chief" rather than a series of band or kinship leaders. Protestant and Catholic missionaries proselytized among the tribes, and some groups were converted. Others integrated Christian doctrines with their traditional beliefs to form new syncretic faiths.

By the early nineteenth century most of these northeastern tribes had been forced to sell their lands, and during the 1830s and 1840s they were moved to new territory west of the Mississippi. Today many of their descendants live in Oklahoma where they have continued the acculturation process. Others (Senecas, Chippewas, Menominees) remain on reservations or tribal lands within their old homelands, where they retain many of their cultural patterns.

The southeastern tribes were more dependent upon agriculture, and many had been heavily influenced by the Mississippian culture, a complex, pre-Columbian way of life characterized by considerable political stratification, culturewide religious organizations, large burial mounds, and relatively large population centers. Although most adherents of the Mississippian culture were gone by the early 1700s, the southeastern tribes remained a sedentary village people held together through a network of primarily matrilineal clans. Like the northeastern tribes, they marked their calendar with a series of feasts and religious ceremonies. Although many southeastern people (Creeks, Cherokees, Choctaws) participated in the British deerskin trade, their adherence to agriculture and later herding (Choctaws) made them less dependent than the northeastern tribes upon the Anglo-Americans.

By 1800 intermarriage between white traders and members of the Five Southern, or "Civilized" Tribes (Cherokees, Choctaws, Chickasaws, Creeks, Seminoles — called "civilized" by whites because they had adopted many white cultural patterns) had produced mixed-blood leaders who championed further acculturation. By the 1820s, for example, many mixed-blood Cherokee leaders were raising cotton or other cash crops on large farms or plantations worked by black slaves. The Cherokees had a tribal government modeled after the federal system, with a bicameral council, an elected chief, and tribal courts. Sequoyah, a Cherokee living in Arkansas, had developed a Cherokee syllabary, and the tribe published a newspaper and books in the language. Although the other southern tribes were less acculturated than the Cherokees, they too had adopted many facets of white culture.

During the 1830s and 1840s, however, the southern tribes were forced to relinquish their lands and remove to Oklahoma. Intratribal arguments over the removal treaties created political divisions within the tribes, and this fragmentation continued to plague the tribes in the West. There the Five Southern Tribes reestablished their tribal governments, and for some the pace of acculturation quickened. Today, many Cherokees, Choctaws, Creeks, Chickasaws, and Seminoles continue to adhere to traditional values, but others, while maintaining their tribal identities, have become integrated into the American mainstream.

In the early contact period two types of tribal societies shared the Great Plains. Ensconced along the banks of major rivers, sedentary tribes such as the Mandans, Pawnees, and Hidatsas lived in villages of large earthen lodges. They tended fields of maize, beans, squash, and sunflowers, supplementing their diet with bison and other animals hunted on the plains. The village people followed a rich ceremonial life that included such rituals as the Okipa (Mandan) and the Morning Star ceremony (Pawnee), which involved the personal sacrifice of the individual for the benefit of the tribe. Kinship networks entailing a series of obligations and support systems provided the village people with social and political cohesion. Since these communities produced and stored agricultural surpluses, their villages prior to the mid-eighteenth century were major trading and political centers.

The plains during this early period were also inhabited by small numbers of wandering pedestrian hunters who would form groups to stalk bison or combine to drive herds of the animals over cliffs or "kill-sites." Carrying their small skin lodges with them, they lived a nomadic existence in search of the herds and may have spent the winter camped on the fringes of the plains or in sheltered river valleys.

The introduction of the horse in the eighteenth century had a profound impact upon both societies. For the nomads, the effect was beneficial. Horses enabled them to cover great distances, and hunters could locate and kill the bison more easily. Women's tasks were made easier, too, since horses served as beasts of burden. Because horse-drawn travois could drag heavier lodge skins and longer tipi poles, lodges increased in size and larger quantities of food and household possessions could be kept. More time was now available for creative activity, and skin painting, beadwork, and other artistic endeavors flourished. In addition, the tribes' ceremonial life was enlarged and elaborated; the Sun Dance became the most important communal religious experience on the plains.

The sedentary village people accepted horses, but they refused to adopt a nomadic way of life and now became the target of raids by the bison hunters. As the nomadic tribes (Sioux, Kiowas, Arapahoes, among others) flourished, the village people declined, and by the first decades of the nineteenth century the nomads dominated the plains. Indeed, this was their golden era, and their rich and abundant way of life became a cultural magnet, attracting other tribes to share in their lifestyle.

Tragically, by the last quarter of the nineteenth century, most of these Plains Indians were confined to reservations and subjected to forced acculturation programs by the federal government. Encouraged to abandon their traditional way of life and to become yeoman farmers in a region that would not sustain agriculture, most of the Plains tribes, like other Indian peoples of this period, suffered from disease and a declining birthrate. Recently their populations have increased, and although many of the reservation communities remain economically depressed, they are wellsprings of traditional culture. Many groups have resurrected tribal languages and religious traditions. Others are active in the Native American Church, a pan-Indian religious organization that has incorporated religious traditions from several tribes with Christian doctrines and the use of peyote. Tribal identities among the Plains peoples remain particularly strong.

Many of the Native American people living in the desert Southwest have also been able to retain much of their traditional culture. In the seventeenth century, Spanish immigrants into the region were welcomed by pueblo-dwelling villagers who had built adobe settlements along the Rio Grande watershed. Descendants of the Anasazi people, a widespread pre-Columbian cultural complex extending across the Southwest, the pueblo dwellers were agriculturists steeped in a religious ceremonialism that permeated their lives and was closely associated with the geographic features that marked their homelands. Their villages were governed by gender- and age-graded religious societies whose leaders formed a theocracy. Their followers were admonished to live in harmony both with their gods and with their fellow villagers. They wove cotton cloth and produced an abundance of highly decorated earthen pottery. Their villages attracted Spanish missionaries, and some of the Pueblo people converted to Christianity. But their steadfast adherence to many traditional beliefs forced the priests to incorporate them into

Roman Catholic ritual. Still residing in their ancestral villages, the modern Pueblo communities remain cohesive units retaining much of their rich ceremonialism. Although many residents work outside their communities, others produce traditional patterns of jewelry and ceramics that are much in demand. Among the Pueblo tribes, the Hopis of northern Arizona remain one of the most traditional Native American communities in the continental United States.

The Athabascan-speaking people, Apaches and Navajos, compose the other major southwestern group. Unlike the Pueblos they originally were a hunting and gathering people who supplemented their food supply through horticulture. Ranging across the Southwest, the Apaches lived in brush- and hide-covered wickiups. In the seventeenth century, their acquisition of horses increased mobility and probably diminished their already limited reliance upon horticulture.

The Navajos, their close relatives, lived in a similar fashion until they acquired horses and sheep in the same period. Adopting a more sedentary mode of life, the Navajos developed transhumant economic patterns: they followed their flocks and herds into the uplands during the summer and removed them to protected valleys during the winter. They erected hexagonal, dirt-covered hogans as residences and began to plant larger fields of beans and corn and small orchards of peach trees. After migrating westward into the canyon and mesa lands of northeastern Arizona, the Navajos grazed their animals on lands radiating out from Canyon de Chelly, a long, Y-shaped, steep-sided canyon near the modern Arizona–New Mexico border. Prospering in their new environment, the Navajos became successful herdsmen, harvesting wool to be woven into cloth. They also became skilled silversmiths. During the nineteenth century they acquired a very large reservation in their homeland where they still reside, scattered across the desert in small communities or individual dwellings. Clan identification remains important and many Navajos still follow traditional cultural patterns. Most are bilingual (Navajo and English), and in recent decades the question of energy development upon the reservations has stirred considerable interest in Navajo politics. The Navajos are the nation's largest Indian tribe.

During the early colonial period California held a larger Indian population than any other region, with the population concentrated along the coast and in the great interior valleys. Characterized by relatively small tribes or political units, the native peoples spoke many tongues and manifested a variety of cultural patterns. Most, however, were hunters, fishers, and gatherers, who often relied heavily upon the seasonal catches of salmon or the gathering of acorns. In the eighteenth century the tribes along the southern coast were forced into the Spanish mission system, and during the latter half of the nineteenth century the interior tribes were almost annihilated by the influx of Anglo-American settlers. During the twentieth century, however, economic opportunities in California attracted large numbers of Indian migrants, with both the Los Angeles basin and the San Francisco Bay region supporting relatively large urban Indian communities.

North of California, along the coast of Washington and Oregon, seafaring fishermen, Chinook and Salish, harvested a large variety of marine life and developed one of the most successful hunting and gathering cultures in the world. They lived in large wooden plank structures amid such material abundance that they developed institutional mechanisms, like the potlatch, for the redistribution of wealth. (Potlatches were ceremonies in which individuals gave away much of their wealth in return for the esteem and veneration of their fellow tribespeople.) Skilled woodworkers, they exhibited a fine artistry in intricately carved masks, wooden beams, and totem poles, the last reflecting the clan affiliation of the inhabitants in the extended family residences. These coastal dwellers suffered considerably from diseases introduced during the nineteenth century, but many small reservation communities persisted. Some still rely upon fishing while others have relocated in Seattle, Portland, and other cities in the region.

Although Native American cultures and societies underwent many changes after the period of initial European and American contact, most

ARCTIC OCEAN

Bering Strait

ARCTIC

SUB-ARCTIC

ARCTIC

NORTHWEST
COAST

SUB-ARCTIC

PLATEAU

GREAT
PLAINS

PRAIRIES

NORTHEAST

GREAT
BASIN

CALIFORNIA

ATLANTIC
OCEAN

SOUTHEAST

SOUTHWEST

NORTHEAST
MEXICO

CARIBBEAN

MESO-AMERICA

PACIFIC OCEAN

tribes retained at least some of the parts of their culture that they considered most important. Government-defined blood quotas aside, within the tribal communities "being Indian" is still defined in cultural terms. Each tribe remains unique, and the definition of tribal identity continues to reflect their diversity.

Jules B. Billiard, ed., *The World of the American Indian* (1974); Harold E. Driver, *Indians of North America* (1961).

R. DAVID EDMUNDS

See also Missionaries; Serra, Junípero.

III. Warfare

In spite of many differences, the universality of the art of war is demonstrated by a study of the causes of conflict and the battle methods used by American Indian tribes. As in all armies, hierarchy of rank was important, and rank was determined by demonstrated bravery and proficiency. Most of the tribes had a war leader with lieutenants to aid him. Dress and insignia indicated rank and experience in battle. Accompanying the warriors on long marches or during sieges was a commissary force of hunters to supply food and other requirements. Rituals and dances fanned the martial spirit and celebrated victories. And like many soldiers the world over, warriors carried some sort of amulet into battle to guard them from harm.

Occasionally they raided neighboring tribes for stores of food or for women or slaves. Early in the eighteenth century, for example, Creek Indians, serving as mercenaries for British colonists, attacked and captured several villages of Yamasee and other tribes who were sent to slavery in the Carolinas.

Causes of war varied from tribe to tribe, but usually involved territorial rights, retaliation for aggressive acts, or rituals marking young males' coming to manhood through the performance of brave deeds. If the rituals resulted in the slaying of members of another tribe, a revenge attack was almost certain, and this could escalate into tribal warfare.

When Europeans brought the horse to North America early in the sixteenth century, that animal became the most prized object for raiders and made it possible for a young man to prove himself by capturing an enemy's horse rather than having to kill the man. The capture of horses often resulted in running fights, in which other deeds could be performed that added to a warrior's status. An individual's standing in a tribe was also measured by the number of captured horses in his possession.

Territorial disputes between tribes had little to do with land ownership; rather, they concerned the wild game and food plants on the land. For example, food shortages during the seventeenth century brought the Pequot into conflict with the Niantic, Narragansett, and other tribes of southern New England. Fearing the presence of the Pequot, the colonists in the area supported the opposition tribes, including a dissident branch of the Pequot — the Mohegan led by the legendary Uncas. So many Pequot were killed or scattered that the tribe virtually ceased to exist.

Any tribe occupying territory with particularly rich food resources was liable to attack by other tribes wandering in search of the essentials of life. From the beginning of European colonization to the ceding of the last tracts in the Far West, Indians had difficulty comprehending the Euro-American concept of ownership of land. But after their living space was taken by artful treaties and removal was forced upon them, they often resorted to war. Examples include the uprising during the 1670s that was planned for almost a decade by Metacom in New England and is known as King Philip's War. Two hundred years later, the Sioux and Cheyenne on the northern plains were fighting to recover their holy Black Hills. Red Cloud of the Teton Sioux succeeded in holding for almost a decade lands claimed by them along tributaries of the Yellowstone River, but military expeditions and rapid settlement eventually forced the Plains Indians onto reservations.

Efforts by some chiefs to unify tribes for war did little to slow the spread of European settlement. In the seventeenth century, Popé brought the Pueblos together to fight for independence from Spanish rule. During the revolt they killed hundreds of Spaniards and forced the survivors out of their towns. But because of dissension among the Pueblos and attacks from other tribes, the alliance collapsed. Within a dozen years the Spaniards had returned. In the 1760s Pontiac, an Ottawa chief, organized an alliance to drive the British from his people's Ohio valley homeland, but it failed. Early in the nineteenth century, Tecumseh persuaded warriors from at least fifteen distantly separated tribes to join his confederacy, but they too could not stop the onrush of settlement across Ohio and Indiana.

Only the Iroquois League, a highly advanced combination of tribes in New York State, was able to withstand, for almost two centuries, the efforts of Europeans to seize their living space. The Mohawks, Cayugas, Oneidas, Onondagas, and Senecas — and later the Tuscaroras — were agricultural peoples, living on land rich in crops, venison, and furs. Long before the coming of Europeans, they had put together a federation (similar to the confederation that created the United States). This provided them with a central government that was peaceful in intent but if necessary could apply military pressure to defend against their neighbors, the Hurons and Algonquins. After colonization began, the French, English, and Dutch learned to respect the fierceness of Iroquois resistance.

The Iroquois were among the first Indians to obtain firearms by trading furs and corn. But they overextended their range in search of furs for trading, and the resulting conflicts gradually weakened the league. After the outbreak of the revolutionary war, the Iroquois split into factions. Neutrality failed, and many allied with the British. Their lands became battlegrounds; fields and granaries were destroyed. After the war, those who had not fled to Canada or westward were confined to reservations.

Even with a strong government, the Iroquois civil leaders were never able to control their warriors or change their ancient manner of fighting. To Iroquois warriors, war was individual combat. They did not concentrate their forces on command, as the Europeans had since the days of the Romans. Nor did any of the tribes maintain a standing army as European nations did. Service as a warrior was voluntary,

and although there were long-standing enmities between certain tribes, protracted wars were almost unknown. War parties varied greatly in size, but most of them were not much larger than a modern-day platoon. After the warriors and their leaders made a decision to organize a war party, volunteers were called for, and the war chief selected his lieutenants. Four or five days of fasting or feasting, prayer, dancing, singing, and other rituals might follow, and then after weapons were carefully inspected, paint applied to the body, and the proper amulets collected, the warriors departed.

Scouts went out two to four miles ahead of the party, reporting back to the war chief if they found wild game or traces of the enemy. When scouts sighted an enemy village, they quickly brought back information about its location, the number of lodges and horses, and the existence of suitable cover for an attack. If for some reason the party lost the element of surprise, or someone observed a bad luck sign or reported having a warning dream, the attack might be abandoned. But when the war chief decided upon an attack, the time most likely was at daybreak. Various signals directed the advance of the warriors — movements of hands, lances, or guns, or the sounding of eagle-wing or turkey-bone whistles. For signaling over long distances on the spacious plains, the warriors used smoke signals and flashing mirrors.

The Woodland Indians in the East fought mostly on foot, faithfully obeying their war leaders as they silently set ambushes or prepared for surprise assaults upon villages. But from the moment of the signaled attack, each warrior fought independently, seeking honors for himself. In the West, after the introduction of horses, the Plains Indians fought mostly mounted, and although sometimes described as the finest light cavalry in the world, they seldom charged in shock formations. Each horseman attacked as he pleased, often recklessly daring the fire of soldiers by seeking close combat in order to win honors by "striking coup." Warriors of the plains made their coup sticks from wooden poles, usually willow, about six feet long, and decorated with eagle feathers or bits of animal skins. Striking an enemy with a coup stick or weapon was the highest symbol of bravery, ranking above killing or scalping. George Grinnell, who lived with and studied the war customs of several Plains tribes, believed that the ceremony of counting coup was a survival of the times before Indians used arrows, when they fought hand-to-hand with clubs and sharpened sticks.

Scalping is a war practice that dates from antiquity. Before colonization, some North American tribes scalped their war victims, and some did not. The coming of Europeans undoubtedly accelerated the custom. In the struggle for control of North America, various nations offered bounties for the heads of enemy Indians or soldiers. Scalps were easy to remove with European metal knives and easier to transport than heads.

Before they had access to muskets and other firearms, the warriors' weapons were arrows, clubs, tomahawks, knives, and lances. Arrows were as varied as the tribes, but the heads were generally of two types — narrow and tapering like a lance or triangular. The latter were used in war, the heads often being loosely attached to the shafts so they would remain in the wound when the shaft was withdrawn. Some tribes cut grooves down the shafts to facilitate the flow of blood from the wound. In close encounters, a warrior trained from youth as a bowman could fire far more rapidly and accurately than an enemy armed with a muzzle-loader. After the introduction of breech-loaders and more rapidly firing rifles, arrows could be used effectively only in surprise attacks followed by swift withdrawals.

The war club was in general use across America and differed in material, shape, and decoration. A length of wood with a knob at the end was common among tribes of the forest. Sharp bits of stone or bone were added to the head; as metal became available blades and spikes were used. In the East war clubs developed into tomahawks, a hatchet-shaped weapon that was originally made of stone. After the Europeans came, the blades were metal, some actually made in Europe. Because of its war symbolism, the tomahawk was buried to represent peace and dug up for war.

To obtain greater range, especially on the plains, warriors used lances — poles as long as twelve feet or more with large stone or metal points shaped like arrowheads. Usually they were decorated with fur, eagle feathers, and strips of beads.

During the Civil War, tribes from Indian Territory fought on both sides. This experience, combined with years of observing uniformed soldiers in battle, gradually brought on modifications in their own comportment. In 1834, while approaching a Comanche village with a company of dragoons, George Catlin witnessed the maneuvers of several hundred warriors who galloped out at full speed to meet them. "As they wheeled their horses," he reported, "they very rapidly formed in a line, and 'dressed' like well-disciplined cavalry."

In 1867, George Armstrong Custer was similarly impressed with the defensive posture of a Cheyenne force outside a tipi village on the Kansas plains: "Most of the Indians were mounted; all were bedecked in their brightest colors, their heads crowned with the brilliant warbonnet, their lances bearing the crimson pennant, bows strung, and quivers full of barbed arrows. . . . In the line of battle before us there were several hundred Indians, while farther to the rear and at different distances were other organized bodies acting apparently as reserves."

Such developments in warfare came too late to have any substantial effects, although they played some part in the Indian victories in 1876 at the Rosebud and the Little Bighorn.

Angie Debo, *A History of the Indians of the United States* (1974); Thomas E. Mails, *The Mystic Warriors of the Plains* (1972); William C. Sturtevant, gen. ed., *Handbook of North American Indians*, 20 vols. (1977–).

DEE BROWN

See also Uncas.

IV. Indian-White Wars

Suspicion and hostility, stemming from technological and cultural differences as well as mutual feelings of superiority, have permeated relations between Indians and non-Indians in North America. Intertribal antagonisms among the Indians, and nationalistic rivalries, bad faith, and expansionist desires on the part of non-Indians exacerbated these tensions. The resulting white-Indian conflicts often took a particularly brutal turn and ultimately resulted in the near-destruction of the indigenous peoples.

Warfare between Europeans and Indians was common in the seventeenth century. In 1622, the Powhatan Confederacy nearly wiped out the struggling Jamestown colony. Frustrated at the continuing conflicts, Nathaniel Bacon and a group of vigilantes destroyed the Pamunkey Indians before leading an unsuccessful revolt against colonial authorities in 1676. Intermittent warfare also plagued early Dutch colonies in New York. In New England, Puritan forces annihilated the Pequots in 1636–1637, a campaign whose intensity seemed to foreshadow the future. Subsequent attacks inspired by Metacom (King Philip) against English settlements sparked a concerted response from the New England Confederation. Employing Indian auxiliaries and a scorched-earth policy, the colonists nearly exterminated the Narragansetts, Wampanoags, and Nipmucks in 1675–1676. A major Pueblo revolt also threatened Spanish-held New Mexico in 1680.

Indians were also a key factor in the imperial rivalries among France, Spain, and England. In King William's (1689–1697), Queen Anne's (1702–1713), and King George's (1744–1748) wars, the French sponsored Abnaki and Mohawk raids against the more numerous English. Meanwhile, the English and their trading partners, the Chickasaws and often the Cherokees, battled the French and associated tribes for control of the lower Mississippi River valley and the Spanish in western Florida. More decisive was the French and Indian War (1754–1763). The French and their Indian allies dominated the conflict's early stages, turning back several English columns in the north. Particularly serious was the near-annihilation of Gen. Edward Braddock's force of thirteen hundred men outside of Fort Duquesne in 1755. But with English minister William Pitt infusing new life into the war effort, British regulars and provincial militias overwhelmed the French and absorbed all of Canada.

But eighteenth-century conflicts were not limited to the European wars for empire. In Virginia and the Carolinas, English-speaking colonists pushed aside the Tuscaroras, the Yamasees, and the Cherokees. The Natchez, Chickasaw, and Fox Indians resisted French domination, and the Apaches and Comanches fought against Spanish expansion into Texas. In 1763, an Ottawa chief, Pontiac, forged a powerful confederation against British expansion into the Old Northwest. Although his raids wreaked havoc upon the surrounding white settlements, the British victory in the French and Indian War combined with the Proclamation of 1763, which forbade settlement west of the Appalachian Mountains, soon eroded Pontiac's support.

Most of the Indians east of the Mississippi River now perceived the colonial pioneers as a greater threat than the British government. Thus northern tribes, especially those influenced by Mohawk chief Thayendanegea (Joseph Brant), generally sided with the Crown during the American War for Independence. In 1777, they joined the Tories and the British in the unsuccessful offensives of John Burgoyne and Barry St. Leger in upstate New York. Western Pennsylvania and New York became savage battlegrounds as the conflict spread to the Wyoming and Cherry valleys. Strong American forces finally penetrated the heart of Iroquois territory, leaving a wide swath of destruction in their wake.

In the Midwest, George Rogers Clark captured strategic Vincennes for the Americans, but British agents based at Detroit continued to sponsor Tory and Indian forays as far south as Kentucky. The Americans resumed the initiative in 1782, when Clark marched northwest into Shawnee and Delaware country, ransacking villages and inflicting several stinging defeats upon the Indians. To the south, the British backed resistance among the Cherokees, Chickasaws, Creeks, and Choctaws but quickly forgot their former allies following the signing of the Treaty of Paris (1783).

By setting the boundaries of the newly recognized United States at the Mississippi River and the Great Lakes, that treaty virtually ensured future conflicts between whites and resident tribes. In 1790, Miami chief Little Turtle routed several hundred men led by Josiah Harmar along the Maumee River. Arthur St. Clair's column suffered an even more ignominious defeat on the Wabash River the following year; only in 1794 did Anthony Wayne gain revenge at the Battle of Fallen Timbers. Yet resistance to white expansion in the Old Northwest continued as a Shawnee chief, Tecumseh, molded a large Indian confederation based at Prophetstown. While Tecumseh was away seeking additional support, William Henry Harrison burned the village after a stalemate at the Battle of Tippecanoe in 1811.

Indian raids, often encouraged by the British, were influential in causing the United States to declare war on Great Britain in 1812. The British made Tecumseh a brigadier general and used Indian allies to help recapture Detroit and Fort Dearborn (Chicago). Several hundred American prisoners were killed following a skirmish at the River Raisin in early 1813. But Harrison pushed into Canada and won the Battle of the Thames, which saw the death of Tecumseh and the collapse of his confederation. In the Southeast, the Creeks gained a major triumph against American forces at Fort Sims, killing many of their prisoners in the process. Andrew Jackson led the counterthrust, winning victories at Tallasahatchee and Talladega before crushing the Creeks at Horseshoe Bend in 1814.

Alaska and Florida were also the scenes of bitter conflicts. Native peoples strongly contested the Russian occupation of Alaska. The Aleuts were defeated during the eighteenth century, but the Russians found it impossible to prevent Tlingit harassment of their hunting parties and trading posts. Upon the Spanish cession of Florida, Washington began removing the territory's tribes to lands west of the Mississippi River. But the Seminole Indians and runaway slaves refused to relocate, and the Second Seminole War saw fierce guerrilla-style actions from 1835 to 1842. Osceola, perhaps the greatest Seminole leader, was captured during peace talks in 1837, and nearly three thousand Seminoles were eventually removed. The Third Seminole War (1855–1858) stamped out all but a handful of the remaining members of the tribe.

In the United States, the removal policy met only sporadic armed resistance as whites pushed into the Mississippi River valley during the 1830s and 1840s. The Sac and Fox Indians were crushed in Black Hawk's War (1831–1832), and tribes throughout the region seemed powerless in the face of the growing numbers of forts and military roads the whites were constructing. The acquisition of Texas and the Southwest during the 1840s, however, sparked a new series of Indian-white conflicts. In Texas, where such warfare had marred the independent republic's brief history, the situation was especially volatile.

On the Pacific Coast, attacks against the native peoples accompanied the flood of immigrants to gold-laden California. Disease, malnutrition, and warfare combined with the poor lands set aside as reservations to reduce the Indian population of that state from 150,000 in 1845 to 35,000 in 1860. The army took the lead role in Oregon and Washington, using the Rogue River (1855–1856), Yakima (1855–1856), and Spokane (1858) wars to force several tribes onto reservations. Sporadic conflicts also plagued Arizona and New Mexico throughout the 1850s as the army struggled to establish its presence. On the southern plains, mounted warriors posed an even more formidable challenge to white expansion. Strikes against the Sioux, Cheyennes, Arapahos, Comanches, and Kiowas during the decade only hinted at the deadlier conflicts of years to come.

The Civil War saw the removal of the Regulars and an accompanying increase in the number and intensity of white-Indian conflicts. The influence of the Five Southern, or "Civilized" Tribes of the Indian Territory was sharply reduced. Seven Indian regiments served with Confederate troops at the Battle of Pea Ridge (1862). Defeat there and at Honey Springs (1863) dampened enthusiasm for the South, although tribal leaders like Stand Waite continued to support the confederacy until the war's end. James H. Carleton and Christopher ("Kit") Carson conducted a ruthlessly effective campaign against the Navahos in New Mexico and Arizona. Disputes on the southern plains culminated in the Sand Creek massacre (1864), during which John

M. Chivington's Colorado volunteers slaughtered over two hundred of Black Kettle's Cheyennes and Arapahos, many of whom had already attempted to come to terms with the government. In Minnesota, attacks by the Eastern Sioux prompted counterattacks by the volunteer forces of Henry H. Sibley, after which the tribes were removed to the Dakotas. The conflict became general when John Pope mounted a series of unsuccessful expeditions onto the plains in 1865.

Regular units, including four regiments of black troops, returned west following the Confederate collapse. Railroad expansion, new mining ventures, the destruction of the buffalo, and ever-increasing white demand for land exacerbated the centuries-old tensions. The mounted warriors of the Great Plains posed an especially thorny problem for an army plagued by a chronic shortage of cavalry and a government policy that demanded Indian removal on the cheap.

Winfield S. Hancock's ineffectual campaign in 1867 merely highlighted the bitterness between whites and Indians on the southern plains. Using a series of converging columns, Philip Sheridan achieved more success in his winter campaigns of 1868–1869, but only with the Red River War of 1874–1875 were the tribes broken. Major battlefield encounters like George Armstrong Custer's triumph at the Battle of the Washita (1868) had been rare; more telling was the army's destruction of Indian lodges, horses, and food supplies, exemplified by Ranald Mackenzie's slaughter of over a thousand Indian ponies following a skirmish at Palo Duro Canyon, Texas, in 1874.

To the north, the Sioux, Northern Cheyennes, and Arapahos had forced the army to abandon its Bozeman Trail forts in Red Cloud's War (1867). But arable lands and rumors of gold in the Dakotas continued to attract white migration; the government opened a major new war in 1876. Initial failures against a loose Indian coalition, forged by leaders including Crazy Horse and Sitting Bull, culminated in the annihilation of five troops of Custer's cavalry at the Little Bighorn. A series of army columns took the field that fall and again the following spring. By campaigning through much of the winter, harassing Indian villages, and winning battles like that at

Wolf Mountain (1877), Nelson A. Miles proved particularly effective. The tribes had to sue for peace, and even Sitting Bull's band returned from Canada to accept reservation life in 1881. Another outbreak among the Sioux and Northern Cheyennes, precipitated by government corruption, shrinking reservations, and the spread of the Ghost Dance, culminated in a grisly encounter at Wounded Knee (1890), in which casualties totaled over two hundred Indians and sixty-four soldiers.

Less spectacular but equally deadly were conflicts in the Pacific Northwest. In 1867–1868, George Crook defeated the Paiutes of northern California and southern Oregon. In a desperate effort to secure a new reservation on the tribal homelands, a Modoc chief assassinated Edward R. S. Canby during an abortive peace conference in 1873. Canby's death (he was the only general ever killed by Indians) helped shatter President Ulysses S. Grant's peace policy and resulted in the tribe's defeat and removal. Refusing life on a government-selected reservation, Chief Joseph's Nez Percés led the army on an epic seventeen-hundred-mile chase through Idaho, Wyoming, and Montana until checked by Miles just short of the Canadian border at Bear Paw Mountain (1877). Also unsuccessful was armed resistance among the Bannocks, Paiutes, Sheepeaters, and Utes in 1878–1879.

To the far southwest, Cochise, Victorio, and Geronimo led various Apache bands in resisting white and Hispanic encroachments, crossing and recrossing the border into Mexico with seeming impunity. Many an officer's record was scarred as repeated treaties proved abortive. Only after lengthy campaigning, during which army columns frequently entered Mexico, were the Apaches forced to surrender in the mid-1880s.

The army remained wary of potential trouble as incidental violence continued. Yet, with the exception of another clash in 1973 during which protesters temporarily seized control of Wounded Knee, the major Indian-white conflicts in the United States had ended. Militarily, several trends had become apparent. New technology often gave the whites a temporary advantage. But this edge was not universal; Indian warriors carrying repeating weapons during the latter nineteenth century sometimes outgunned their army opponents, who were equipped with cheaper (but often more reliable) single-shot rifles and carbines. As the scene shifted from the eastern woodlands to the western plains, white armies found it increasingly difficult to initiate fights with their Indian rivals. To force action, army columns converged upon Indian villages from several directions. This dangerous tactic had worked well at the Battle of the Washita but could produce disastrous results when large numbers of tribesmen chose to stand and fight, as at the Little Bighorn.

Throughout the centuries of conflict, both sides had taken the wars to the enemy populace, and the conflicts had exacted a heavy toll among noncombatants. Whites had been particularly effective in exploiting tribal rivalries; indeed, Indian scouts and auxiliaries were often essential in defeating tribes deemed hostile by white governments. In the end, however, military force alone had not destroyed Indian resistance. Only in conjunction with railroad expansion, the destruction of the buffalo, increased numbers of non-Indian settlers, and the determination of successive governments to crush any challenge to their sovereignty had white armies overwhelmed the tribes.

Francis Paul Prucha, *The Sword of the Republic: The United States Army on the Frontier, 1783–1846* (1969; reprint, 1977); Robert M. Utley, *Frontier Regulars: The United States Army and the Indian, 1866–1891* (1973).

ROBERT WOOSTER

See also Bacon's Rebellion; Black Hawk; Black Hawk War; Colonial Wars; Crazy Horse; Custer, George Armstrong; Geronimo; Joseph (Chief Joseph); King Philip's War; Philip (King Philip); Pontiac; Sitting Bull; Tecumseh.

V. Indian-White Relations

Indian-white relations in the period following the arrival of Columbus can be seen variously as the continuation of a normal process of migration by humans from one part of the world to another, as a genocidal assault by more powerful intruders upon weaker, more "primitive" peoples, or as the process by which Western civilization and Christianity were transferred from the Old World to the New. Whichever perception is adopted will be in accordance with one's cultural, epistemological, and emotional preconceptions.

The Europeans who followed Leif Eriksson's Norsemen at the turn of the tenth century (and gave us the first recorded account of European relations with the native peoples of North America) and those who followed Columbus at the end of the fifteenth century were greeted warily by the native population (in a friendly fashion in the case of Columbus's first voyage), but relations soon turned to hostility and war. In the Spanish case at least, the source of the hostility was Spanish cruelty and greed spurred by the realization that those living in the Caribbean basin were unable to defend themselves from the technologically superior newcomers. This conclusion derives from the evidence provided by the Spanish themselves, however much these accounts were exploited by Spain's rivals in the New World, whose hypocrisy often concealed similar cruelty and greed.

Spain and Portugal had a century's head start on France, England, Holland, and Sweden in establishing relations with the peoples of the newfound world; thus the two countries had first choice of which lands to conquer, colonize, and exploit. Although we tend to think of Latin America today as a poor third world area, in the sixteenth century these lands were considered the richest and most desirable because of their valuable resources and their extensive populations who were soon forced to serve the Europeans as slaves, servants, or dependent trading partners. The present areas of the United States and Canada were considered by the Iberian powers the least desirable portions of the New World, hardly worth colonizing except to prevent northern European nations from establishing bases from which to harass the Spanish and Portuguese.

Because of the absence of both mineral wealth and subservient populations in the areas north of Mexico, the English, French, Dutch, and Swedish set up colonies at the beginning of the seventeenth century that were primarily extensions of their own societies and dealt only intermittently with the surrounding native populations. The natural growth of these colonies provided increasing military and economic power vis-à-vis the Indians, whose numerical superiority in the first half-century in almost every colony was lost in the second half-century as European diseases and warfare took their toll.

Cruelty and greed were prevalent in the early history of all the northern European nations' dealings with the Indians, but the picture was not entirely one-sided: treachery and cunning existed on both sides. Cultural differences — the failure of each side to understand the assumptions of the other — led to frequent misunderstandings that in turn led to warfare. One of the most elementary forms of misunderstanding, for example, was the anger felt by the Indians over the colonists' allowing their cattle and hogs to roam in unfenced freedom. The consequence was often the destruction of the Indians' corn, which led to the Indians' killing the offending animals, which led to retaliation by the settlers upon the Indians who had killed the animals, and so on. And too often those retaliating failed to discriminate between the Indians who were responsible for the "offense" and those who were not.

While Spain and Portugal exploited the labor (through slavery and serfdom) of the large populations of the areas they settled, the northern Europeans made only limited use of Indian labor. Rather, they wanted land; if it had not been acquired through war or simple occupation, they sought to purchase it. But often the Indians assumed they were conferring on Europeans only the right to use the land without losing their own right to continue to use it for hunting, fishing, or gathering food. Northern European governments soon prohibited their colonists from making such purchases for fear that the contracts would compromise the royal assertions of ultimate sovereignty over all the lands.

With the destruction or subordination of most of the coastal tribes, England and France, the two most successful of the northern European colonial powers, extended their jurisdiction into the interior, the English across the Appalachian Mountains hemming in their coastal settlements, and the French down the St. Lawrence River and up the Mississippi. The French, from their interior position, hoped to confine their English rivals to the coastal regions. The French were more adept at forging alliances with the powerful Indian nations in the interior, though they were not averse to wars of extermination, such as that against the Natchez in the Mississippi valley. Because the French had fewer settlers than the English, they tended to rely on a network of military and trade alliances with the Indians rather than developing agricultural and commercial settlements to match those of the English.

With the destruction of French power in the great war for empire that raged across North America and Europe during the 1750s and 1760s, the situation of the Indians was weakened. They were no longer able to play off one European power against another but had to confront England directly. Only with the coming of the American Revolution did they recover the opportunity to play a balancing role. But, unfortunately, most tribes chose to side with the loser, and the victorious Americans treated the Indian nations who had fought with the British as defeated foes. Great Britain made no attempt to secure Indian rights in treaty negotiations with the Americans, and even the objections of Spain (America's wartime ally) that the area between the Appalachians and the Mississippi River remained Indian territory were dismissed by the victorious revolutionaries. But treating the Indians as defeated enemies was not an entirely successful tactic. After the tribes of the Old Northwest had inflicted a number of stinging setbacks upon the U.S. Army, the new American nation formulated a more moderate policy toward the Indians. The United States recognized the right of the Indian nations to exist as autonomous entities but sought to buy as much of their land as possible. Even the Indian allies of the Americans were pressured to sell off large portions of their lands.

As the United States grew in power in the early nineteenth century, several Indian nations such as the Cherokee were overwhelmed and sent on forced marches to the so-called Indian

Territory (later Oklahoma) with significant loss of life. The "Trail of Tears" of the Cherokee migration to the Indian Territory in the 1830s became an enduring symbol of white injustice toward the Indians, particularly since the removal was carried out despite the Cherokee Nation's legal victory over the state of Georgia in the Supreme Court. Most of the Indians in the eastern United States now moved West, either voluntarily or under duress, with a few remaining in small pockets near their original homelands.

The health and longevity of the Indians had suffered a steady decline since the arrival of the Europeans, for the whites carried diseases, such as smallpox and measles, for which the Indians had no immunity. The diseases and the numbers affected by them is a subject of intense debate among scholars. Estimates of Indian population before the arrival of whites have increased over the years, sometimes by as much as ten times the earlier estimates. Henry Dobyns put the number at some 10 to 12 million in North America north of Mexico and 90 to 112 million for the entire Western Hemisphere. Most scholars have discounted such high estimates, although conceding that earlier estimates (such as the traditional figure of about 1 million for the present area of the United States) were probably too low. In any event, the steady decline of the Indian population in the United States reached its low point of 228,000 in 1890.

This decline coincided with the loss of tribal lands and tribal authority, particularly under the General Allotment Act (Dawes Severalty Act) of 1887. This act imposed a system of individual land ownership upon many of the Indian tribes with the government selling off the surplus lands to white settlers for the presumed benefit of the tribes (some western tribes were exempted or not forced to comply). Contemporary Indians often cite the Dawes Act as legislation that could and should have been avoided, but that is probably an unrealistic assessment. The vast landholdings of small impotent tribes simply could not have been maintained against the millions of well-armed whites moving west. The land rush in 1889 into the Indian Territory (which became Oklahoma as a result) is an example. Even the staunchest friends of the Indian

were convinced that the tribes could not survive unless they gave up much of their land claims and secured a portion in severalty (individual allotments) with the security of a "white man's [fee simple] title."

Although the popular impression during those years was that the Indians were a "disappearing race," the twentieth century saw a dramatic reversal of almost all indexes of decline. Health problems came under increasing control, and diseases like tuberculosis were nearly eliminated. But alcoholism, or alcohol-related events such as car accidents, became the principal cause of death among Indians: no one has determined why Indians seem to be so susceptible to alcoholic stress, and the debate between those favoring a genetic explanation and those a cultural one continues.

The gradual loss of Indian tribal authority was suddenly reversed in 1934 with the passage of the Indian Reorganization Act, which addressed the strengthening of tribal life and government with federal assistance. Although it was subject to bitter debate both at the time and later, the evidence is conclusive that the act, the product of the thinking of John Collier, commissioner of Indian affairs, put Indian communities, then nearing political and cultural dissolution, on the road to recovery and growth. Collier, struck by the strength and viability of Indian communal societies in the Southwest (e.g., the Hopis) and appalled by the destructive effects on tribal societies of the allotment system, sought to restore tribal structures by making the tribes instrumentalities of the federal government. In this way, he asserted, tribes would be "surrounded by the protective guardianship of the federal government and clothed with the authority of the federal government." Indian tribal governments, as Collier foresaw, now exist on a government-to-government basis with the states and the federal government. Although they are financially and legally dependent upon the federal government, they have been able to extend their political and judicial authority in areas nineteenth-century politicians would have found unimaginable.

American Indians, now a rapidly growing minority group, possess a unique legal status (based on treaties and constitutional decisions) and are better educated, in better health, and more prosperous than ever before (despite the persistence of high levels of unemployment, poverty, and disease). The causes of this "Indian Renaissance" have been the subject of much dispute, some attributing it to the well-publicized activities of Indian radicals, others to the commitment and decency of the larger society. Nevertheless, the popular stereotype of the impoverished, drunken, abused Indian has continued to cloud Indian life.

Contemporary issues being fought out in the courts, legislatures, and tribal councils have concerned Indian religious freedom, water rights, and land claims. Demands in the 1980s and 1990s for the return of Indian skeletal remains in museum collections pitted some white museum administrators and archaeologists against Indian religious and political leaders. The Indians seemed to be winning, as the Smithsonian Institution, Stanford University, and other groups promised the repatriation of Indian remains and accompanying grave goods to the tribes claiming them. Water rights continued to be a bitter issue affecting western tribes, but Supreme Court decisions in the 1980s dampened the more optimistic Indian hopes for an increased portion of the limited water resources in the West. Land claims, although settled for the most part by the defunct Indian Claims Commission, were occasionally reasserted in specific instances in the 1980s, as among the Iroquois of New York State.

It has often been assumed that acculturation was a one-way street — that Indians were shaped by whites and not the other way around. But it is clear that the process was one of "transculturization," as the anthropologist Irving Hallowell put it. Not only did whites adopt aspects of Indian material culture (e.g., maize, moccasins), but spiritually and psychologically the transplanted European society acquired an Indian cast, particularly a taste for individual freedom and a distaste for the constraints of civilization, as D. H. Lawrence, James Adair, Carl Jung, and James Fenimore Cooper all noted. It was not because Indians were despised but because they were admired that their symbolic powers were often appropriated and celebrated by their former foes.

James Axtell, *The European and the Indian: Essays in the Ethnohistory of Colonial North America* (1981); Francis P. Prucha, *The Great Father: The United States Government and the American Indians,* 2 vols. (1984); Wilcomb E. Washburn, *The Indian in America* (1975).

WILCOMB E. WASHBURN

See also Bonnin, Gertrude; *Cherokee Nation* v. *Georgia;* Columbian Exchange; Dawes Severalty Act; French and Spanish Settlements; Internal Migration; McGillivray, Alexander; Montezuma, Carlos; Pocahontas; Public Land Policy; Trail of Tears; Wounded Knee, Battle of.

INDUSTRIAL REVOLUTION

The term *Industrial Revolution* is used to describe profound economic transformations resulting from the introduction of new technologies of production. Although technological innovation has been a continuous process, in the transformation of societies from agricultural, commercial, and rural to industrial and urban, two revolutionary periods stand out.

The First Industrial Revolution began in Great Britain in the last decades of the eighteenth century. It resulted from the rapid adoption of three new technologies — the steam engine, relying on the energy of the fossil fuel, coal; machines for spinning thread and weaving cloth and increasingly driven by steam rather than water power; and furnaces — blast, puddling, and rolling — to make iron ore into finished metal by using coal. The Second Industrial Revolution began about a century later and was centered in the United States and Germany. It resulted from a wave of innovations in the production of metals and other materials, machinery, chemicals, and foodstuffs. The First Industrial Revolution altered the direction and hastened the growth of the American economy. The Second transformed that economy into its modern urban industrial form.

The coming of the First Industrial Revolution in Britain had as significant an impact on American economic life as did the contemporary political revolution that brought the country's independence. The significance of the economic transformation, however, became clear only after more than two decades of warfare between Britain and France ceased in 1815. Then the United States became the major source of cotton for Britain's yarn and the foremost market for Britain's finished yarn and cloth as well as a major market for its iron and hardware industries. The voracious demand of British mills for raw cotton drove the slave plantation westward, and the marketing and shipping of textiles and hardware into the country through New York quickly made that city the nation's largest commercial center.

Finally, the transfer of the new technologies across the Atlantic gave the United States its first industrial factories, large mills that integrated spinning and weaving machinery in a single building. Their output far surpassed that of the small water-powered spinning mills in Rhode Island and southeastern Massachusetts built between 1792 and the War of 1812. The first integrated factory was built in 1814 for the Boston Manufacturing Company by Francis Cabot Lowell who had brought from Britain plans for an improved power loom. Soon capitalized at $600,000, the corporation employed more than three hundred workers, mostly young women recruited from nearby farms. In 1822 Lowell's associates began to build on the Merrimack River an industrial town named for Lowell (who had died in 1817). A number of integrated mills owned by different corporations were soon operating in Lowell, as were similar groups of mills built at other locations on the Merrimack, the Connecticut, and smaller rivers. Then as coal became available in quantity with the opening of canals into the anthracite region of Pennsylvania in the late 1820s, steam-powered integrated mills appeared in Providence, Fall River, New Bedford, and other New England coastal towns.

The availability of coal permitted the use of British techniques of making iron, and the first anthracite coal furnace went into blast in 1840. By 1854, 45 percent of the iron made in the United States was being produced by coal-fired furnaces rather than by charcoal furnaces and water-powered forges. The new supplies of coal and iron permitted American manufacturers to produce their own machine tools and machinery. By the 1850s they were making firearms, sewing machines, and agricultural equipment through the fabrication and assembly of standardized parts — a technique that was soon called the "American system" of manufacturing.

By the time of the Civil War the technologies on which the First Industrial Revolution were based were fully rooted in the United States. In the years after the war, the nation's industrial energies were concentrated on completing the railroad and telegraph networks of the North, rebuilding those of the South, and expanding those of the West. Once the harsh depression of the 1870s was over, the stage was set for the Second Industrial Revolution.

That revolution rested on three major developments. Most important was the completion of the nation's modern transportation and communication networks — the railroad, telegraph, steamship, and cable — that made possible the high-volume flow of goods essential for the creation of modern industrial economies. The second was the coming of electricity in the 1880s, which provided a more flexible source of power than steam for industrial machinery, a new means of urban transportation (the trolley and the subway), and brighter, cheaper, and safer illumination in factories, offices, and homes. Electricity also transformed chemical and metallurgical processes. The third development was the beginning of the application of science to industrial processes and to the creation of new and improved consumer and industrial products.

The new industries of the Second Industrial Revolution employed new or greatly improved processes to turn out new or greatly improved products that included steel and other metals, light and heavy machinery, oil, chemicals, and in addition, packaged food, drug, and tobacco products bearing brand names. These industries were capital-intensive — that is, the ratio of capital to labor was much greater than in the older industries such as textiles, apparel, furniture, lumber, and shipbuilding. They were also the first whose technologies of production enjoyed the cost advantages of economies of scale or scope; the larger plants had substantially lower unit costs than smaller ones. Such economies, however, could be achieved only if the works steadily operated at close to full capacity. To exploit fully the cost advantages of scale and scope, entrepreneurs in the new industries had to build plants of optimal size (based on the minimum efficient scale of the technology and the extent of the market) and to create national and international sales and distribution organizations to sell the output. And they had to recruit teams of salaried managers to coordinate and monitor the flow of materials through the processes of production and distribution.

The first entrepreneurs who made such investments in manufacturing, marketing, and management quickly dominated their industries. In oil, John D. Rockefeller and his managers reduced the cost of producing a gallon of kerosene from five cents in the early 1870s to less than half a cent in the mid-1880s. In steel, Andrew Carnegie brought the price down from sixty-seven dollars a ton in 1880 to seventeen dollars at the end of the century. In both cases, as cost (and price) went down and volume went up, profits soared, creating two of the world's largest industrial fortunes. So too the entrepreneurs who introduced the new electrolytic processes in refining and smelting copper and aluminum achieved comparable cost reductions. The Aluminum Company of America reduced the cost of what had once been a precious metal to thirty-five cents a pound.

In light machinery produced by the American system of manufacturing, the first entrepreneurs to create large enterprises in office machinery (Remington in typewriters, Burroughs in adding machines, National Cash Register in its industry, and the forerunners of International Business Machines in time clocks and punch cards), in agricultural machinery (McCormick Harvester and its successor International Harvester), and in sewing machines (Singer) quickly dominated global as well as American markets. In 1913, for example, the two largest commercial enterprises in Imperial Russia were Singer and International Harvester. The pattern was much the same in the new food processing and packaging industries where Borden in canned milk and Heinz and Campbell in canned

vegetables and soups achieved positions of comparable dominance, as did the American Tobacco Company in cigarettes.

In electrical equipment the earliest companies in the field in the 1890s, General Electric and Westinghouse, are still global leaders. And in chemicals, Du Pont, Dow, Monsanto, and the enterprises that became Union Carbide and Allied Chemical all dominated their different technologies. In both the chemical and electrical industries the leading companies from the beginning of the century recruited engineers, physicists, and chemists to concentrate on improving their products and processes. During most of the twentieth century close to half of the scientific personnel employed in American manufacturing worked in these two industries.

These capital-intensive and technologically advanced industries became, as Simon Kuznets points out in *Economic Growth of Nations,* the drivers of economic growth. Before World War II they helped make Germany the most powerful industrial nation in Europe and the United States the largest producer of industrial goods in the world. In the late 1920s the United States accounted for over 40 percent of the world's industrial output. In those industries most central to the growth and transformation of modern economies, the managers of a small number of large enterprises made operating decisions on output, product design, price, and services for a major share of their industry, and also the decisions on investment in facilities and research and development that determined the direction of the industry's future growth and its competitiveness in international markets.

In the interwar years the primary engine for economic growth and transformation was the automobile industry, and after World War II, the computer. The impact of these technologies was so profound that they seemed to contemporaries to be as revolutionary as the industries of the First and Second Industrial Revolutions. But their creation and growth followed a pattern strikingly similar to those that had made up the Second Industrial Revolution. In 1913, a little more than a decade after automobiles began to be sold commercially in the United States, two firms — Ford and General Motors — produced over half the annual output of passenger cars (Ford, 40 percent, and General Motors, 12 percent). In the 1920s Ford was successfully challenged by General Motors and then Chrysler. In 1929 the United States accounted for 85 percent of the world's output of automobiles with the Big Three enjoying the lion's share. And of the 15 percent produced abroad, subsidiaries of Ford and General Motors were responsible for a substantial amount.

The pattern in the postwar computer industry differed only in that many of the creators of that industry were established enterprises, not entrepreneurs like Ford, Rockefeller, or Carnegie. Business machine companies were the pioneers in establishing the industry's earliest product line, the mainframe computer. These included Remington Rand, Burroughs Adding Machine, National Cash Register, and Honeywell. International Business Machines, or IBM, made a massive investment in production, distribution, and management for its System 360 and became and remained the industry's dominant company. By 1980 these firms accounted for over 80 percent of all mainframe production. The entrepreneurial firms that appeared were those whose founders developed new types of computers for new markets and then made the three-pronged investment in production, marketing, and management. But these companies, which included Digital Equipment in minicomputers and Apple in microcomputers, were soon challenged by IBM and other established firms. The products of these relatively few enterprises transformed production, distribution, and management throughout the American economy, much as the motor vehicle and electrical equipment industries had done in earlier years.

Computers, in fact, brought as many changes in the workplace and work force as had the technological innovations of the Second Industrial Revolution. In the older labor-intensive nineteenth-century industries — particularly those that relied on a male work force such as printing, shoe making, cigar making, specialized machinery, and metal making — the workers' skills gave them bargaining power. In the latter part of the century these workers successfully organized local and national unions that bargained with owners and managers on wages, hours, and working conditions.

In the new capital-intensive industries of the Second Industrial Revolution, machines replaced craft skills, and the work force became largely one of semiskilled workers carrying out simple routine tasks that required little training. The workers were unable to organize in the new mass production industries, and existing craft unions disintegrated. It was not until the Great Depression of the 1930s that the workers in the new industries, supported by the Roosevelt administration, began to organize along industrial rather than craft lines. In 1937 John L. Lewis's CIO began unionizing the automobile, steel, electrical equipment, rubber, and other capital-intensive industries.

The computer-driven information revolution again replaced employees with machines. This time electronically controlled automated equipment operated by white-collar workers reduced both the number of semiskilled blue-collar workers and the influence of the unions in many industries.

With automation and the continuing growth of the labor-intensive service sector of the economy, the capital-intensive manufacturing industries provided a smaller proportion of jobs and of business profits than they had in the past. They remained, nevertheless, the central core of modern industrial economies, providing a constant and increasing flow of existing products and playing an essential role in the commercialization of new processes and products. Major new industries of the mid and late twentieth century — radio, television, man-made fibers, computers, pharmaceuticals, biogenetics — were developed and their products brought into everyday use by long-established enterprises in the older machinery and chemical industries.

This is why the Second Industrial Revolution had an even more profound impact on the evolution of modern economies than did the First. It set patterns of industrial operations and growth that the later transforming industries closely followed.

Alfred D. Chandler, Jr., *The Visible Hand: The Managerial Revolution in American Business* (1977); Peter Mathias, *The First Industrial Nation: An Economic History of Britain*, 2nd ed. (1983).

ALFRED D. CHANDLER, JR.

See also Cotton; Economic Growth; Iron and Steel Industry; Lowell System; Textile Industry.

INDUSTRIAL WORKERS OF THE WORLD

The Industrial Workers of the World (IWW, or Wobblies), a radical labor organization, was formed in June 1905 by a diverse lot of socialists and militant unionists, including William Haywood of the Western Federation of Miners, Eugene V. Debs, and Daniel De Leon. From the beginning, it was split by differences over philosophy and tactics. In general, however, Wobblies preferred on-the-job action, such as strikes and sabotage, to politics. They hoped to organize all workers in an industry into a single union and all unions into "one big union" in order to build labor solidarity and prepare for a mass strike that would topple capitalism.

Despite its revolutionary goals and violent reputation, the IWW is remembered chiefly for organizing women, blacks, "new" immigrants, and unskilled, semiskilled, and migratory laborers, all of whom American Federation of Labor craft unions tended to shun. Wobblies led strikes in the mines of the Rocky Mountain states, the lumber camps of the Pacific Northwest and the South, the textile mills of Lawrence, Massachusetts, and Paterson, New Jersey, and the steel mills of Pennsylvania. Typically, IWW locals dwindled soon after strikes ended; though some 3 million persons joined over the years, the IWW could never claim more than 150,000 members at any one time.

During the First World War, the IWW was subjected to vigilante attacks and prosecution under federal and state espionage, sedition, and criminal syndicalism statutes. By 1919, the communists had emerged as powerful rivals for the allegiance of radicals. The IWW was all but defunct by 1920, although it continues to maintain general headquarters in Chicago.

See also Labor; Radicalism.

INDUSTRY

See Automobiles; Cotton; Industrial Revolution; Iron and Steel Industry; Labor; Lowell System; Oil Industry; Textile Industry; Tobacco.

INTEGRATION

See Racial Desegregation.

INTERNAL MIGRATION

Internal migration has shaped the development of the North American continent since the first permanent European settlements were established on American shores. The availability of undeveloped land drew colonists inland and westward from the beginning. Although initially the frontier beckoned would-be migrants, the closing of that frontier did not still the flow. In the early twentieth century, northern cities attracted black and white farm laborers and sharecroppers fleeing the South, and since World War II a new stream of migrants has abandoned cities in the Northeast and Midwest for the Sunbelt cities of the South and West.

The first English colonists did not remain long confined to the seacoast settlements where they first landed. Puritan authorities in Plymouth and Massachusetts Bay were apprehensive about permitting widespread settlement, but in the end they could only regulate migration, not forbid it. New settlements spread first into the Connecticut and Merrimack river valleys and then into interior sites between New England rivers. Massachusetts, Rhode Island, and Connecticut saw the first movement into new towns, but in the eighteenth century migration shifted into Maine, New Hampshire, and Vermont, steadily approaching and occasionally spilling over the Canadian border.

Internal migration, of course, was not limited to New England. It was common in all regions and everywhere served much the same purposes. Chesapeake Bay and numerous sizable rivers into the interior provided waterways that facilitated migration from coastal towns. In Virginia, in particular, population flowed steadily from the Tidewater into the Piedmont.

Colonial expansion, whether in New England or the Chesapeake, engendered Native American resistance. In Virginia tribes of the Powhatan Confederacy rebelled against English expansion with uprisings in 1622 and 1646. In New England periodic skirmishes at frontier outposts gave way to King Philip's War in 1675–1676. The defeat of the Wampanoags and the Narragansetts led to the sale of many into West Indian slavery and drove the remaining Native Americans farther from English settlement.

Tensions between English colonials and Native Americans along the frontiers of settlement continued throughout the eighteenth century. At the conclusion of peace after the French and Indian War, the English government enacted the Proclamation of 1763, drawing a line that followed the Appalachians, reserving lands west of the line for Native Americans and ordering English colonials to remove to areas east of the line. This policy aimed at barring continued migration westward and proved to be one of the grievances that contributed to the American Revolution.

By the late eighteenth century, the former colonies had a population of almost 4 million, and given existing agricultural technology, rural areas were "filling up." Undeveloped land within the original states often consisted of marginal tracts that offered little in the way of future prospects. With the end of the American Revolution, renewed internal migration opened up new territories across the Appalachian Mountains. Settlers moving into Pennsylvania and western New York, the Ohio River valley, and Tennessee established a new American frontier.

In the North the greatest migrant stream in the last decades of the eighteenth century was directed toward western New York. The "Genesee Fever," as it was called by contemporaries, was contagious. Albany saw a peak traffic of five hundred sleighs one winter's day in 1795 and averaged twenty boats of migrants a day heading westward the next summer. Residents of Massachusetts and Connecticut towns led this migration, and the numerous homes and churches built in "the New England manner" testify to their influence. Timothy Dwight, a Connecticut native who toured the region and published an account of his travels in 1821, viewed it as a "colony from New England."

The expansion of New England continued into Ohio where funds from the sale of land in townships in the northeastern part of the state known as the Western Reserve went to the state of Connecticut. Settlers from Massachusetts and Connecticut once again dominated these new towns, though more diverse sources of migrants were evident along the Ohio River in the southern third of the state.

The remainder of the old Northwest Territories — Michigan, Illinois, Indiana, and Wisconsin — were settled by migrants from a broader range of states, including a sizable proportion of German, English, and Scandinavian immigrants. These states often received newcomers who themselves had migrated previously to western New York, Pennsylvania, or Kentucky. In this fashion, internal migrants commonly settled in a community, developed their lands, sold out, and migrated once again. This population movement dwarfed earlier migrations. Between 1800 and 1860 the population of the nonslave states west of the Appalachians increased by almost 8.5 million. The line of the frontier moved steadily westward at a rate that averaged seventeen miles a year in these decades.

While large numbers of New England farming families joined the migrant streams to western New York and the midwestern states, others migrated much shorter distances to the region's rapidly growing urban centers. Between 1810 and 1860, the proportion of New Englanders living in cities increased from 7 to 36 percent. Single men and women commonly migrated to mill towns or larger, commercial cities to work for a number of years. Many married and remained in these cities rather than return to their rural hometowns. Still other rural families gave up their farms and migrated together to cities. This internal migration was far shorter than the move to new lands in the West but made an equally significant contribution to the changing character of American life in the nineteenth century.

Internal migration within the South in the antebellum years differed in several ways from that in the North. In both regions, internal migration led to a diffusion of population and the expansion of the agricultural economy into new areas. In the South, however, such expansion also played a crucial role in the economic development of the settled areas of the region. As whites from Virginia, the Carolinas, and Georgia moved to Mississippi, Louisiana, Arkansas, and Texas, this process involved the involuntary migration of more than 800,000 slaves. Virginia, in particular, became a source for the interstate slave trade, and agricultural improvements in that state depended on the income planters derived from such sales. In addition, the westward expansion of slavery affected more than the economy of the South. As northern free farmers and southern slave owners competed to expand into the territories, the sectional conflict heated up and eventually led to the Civil War.

American expansion across the Mississippi had by 1840 begun to reach the Great Plains. Explorers and traders, moreover, had for some time opened up links to the Pacific Coast. War and diplomacy in the 1840s secured for the United States title to lands stretching to the Pacific, and migrants began to settle in the new territory almost immediately. Between 1840 and 1870 more than 350,000 Americans traveled by covered wagon across the overland trail to Oregon or California. Still others sailed by clipper ship around the Horn.

As settlers migrated westward, federal troops systematically subdued Native American tribes and by successive treaties required that they reside on reservations isolated from American settlers. Eastern tribes were forced to resettle west of the Mississippi by legal chicanery and military force. The Cherokees of Georgia, for instance, were forcibly removed in 1837 and 1838, in a migration known as the "Trail of Tears." The post–Civil War years saw continued pressure on Native Americans, this time in the plains and mountain states. Despite armed resistance, Native Americans found themselves increasingly relegated to reservations on the least desirable western lands.

Although military confrontation played a lesser role in anglicizing California and New Mexico, migrant Americans steadily encroached upon the lands and rights of Hispanic-Americans in these states. Military superiority, questionable legal practices, and the sheer force of numbers soon integrated these former Mexican provinces into the larger United States.

In 1890 the Bureau of the Census formally announced the closing of the American frontier. Pockets of unoccupied land remained, but no longer was there a distinct line separating settled from unsettled areas. Internal migration for more than 250 years had been in large part a response to the opportunities available on the frontier. Still, internal migration continued in succeeding years, though its changed character reflected the changed circumstances.

The years between 1910 and 1930 saw a mass movement of southern black farmers, sharecroppers, and farm laborers to the urban North. This migration built upon earlier precedents. With emancipation, large numbers of freedmen and women had moved to reunite families separated under slavery. Moreover, with the end of Reconstruction, there had been a sizable black exodus to Kansas beginning in the late 1870s and to Oklahoma in the 1890s. In the twentieth century, the lure of higher wages in the North, economic setbacks in the South, and the sting of growing racial discrimination motivated what came to be known as the Great Migration. New opportunities for blacks in northern industry during the labor shortages of World War I attracted 400,000 black migrants during the war period. The attraction did not abate at war's end, however, as more than 600,000 southern blacks migrated north in the 1920s.

The Great Depression set off yet another migrant stream — or perhaps we should say streams. With declining farm prices, mounting farm foreclosures, and the onset of drought, thousands of midwestern and southern farmers packed their possessions and headed westward. The Dust Bowl migrants found their way to California's cities and migrant labor camps during the thirties. With the coming of World War II, agricultural conditions improved considerably, but the lure of expanding defense-related jobs in California kept the migrants streaming.

During the depression, a second migration flow partly offset the exodus from the countryside. Faced with plant closings, massive layoffs, and extended unemployment, some families deserted cities and returned to the countryside where they could at least raise their own food. This stream of urban-rural migration temporarily stemmed the shift cityward in the nation's population. The 1920s saw a gain of more than 4 percent in the proportion of Americans residing in cities. In the depression decade, the comparable increase was less than 0.4 percent. With the resurgence of war-stimulated manufacturing after 1939, however, rural families were on the move again, and the proportion of urban residents increased by another 4 percent in the 1940s.

Internal migration persisted in the postwar decades. Three streams can be identified, though their relative importance varied over time. Expanding agribusiness displaced the family farm and led to a steady migration from the countryside into cities. By 1980, for instance, members of farming families composed less than 3 percent of the nation's population. Second, within metropolitan areas there was a significant suburbanization of the population as residents shifted from city cores to outlying communities. Finally, there was an evident increase in interurban migration, as Americans responded to the demands of a changing national economy. Since 1960 this latter migration has been chiefly from declining industrial cities of the Midwest and the Northeast to the growing Sunbelt cities of the South and West. Between 1940 and 1984, the proportion of the nation's population found in the South and West increased from 42 to 54 percent. Moreover, the urban population of these regions increased much more rapidly than did the rural. A shift from manufacturing to service employment, the aging of the American population, the influence of improved air conditioning and transportation, and differential government spending across regions fueled the shift in resources and population evident in these decades.

Internal migration has been a decisive influence over the entire course of the development of the United States. From the first modest moves inland of groups of settlers in Jamestown or Plymouth to the flight of inner-city residents to the suburbs in the 1950s, Americans have been on the move. Internal migration has shaped the landscape, promoted and reflected major shifts in the nation's economic life, and, through its contribution to shifts in regional population and voting strength, changed the balance of power in American politics. It has been a force for change whose significance can hardly be overstated.

John Mack Faragher, *Women and Men on the Overland Trail* (1979); James R. Grossman, *Land of Hope: Chicago, Black Southerners, and the Great Migration* (1989).

THOMAS DUBLIN

See also Black Exodus, 1879; Black Migration; Dust Bowl; Expansion, Continental and Overseas; Indians; Oregon Trail; Suburbanization; Sunbelt; Trail of Tears; Transportation Revolution; Urbanization; World War I.

INTERNATIONAL COMMERCE

I. From 1790 to the Civil War

Historians have long debated the relative importance of international commerce and internal economic development upon American economic growth during the years from the Revolution to the Civil War. Did the undeveloped state of the country, combined with the rapid increase of foreign commerce (both exports and imports) and foreign financing of development, prove the trade-driven origins of American growth? Or did the rapid growth of the internal economy in the vast continental common market and surging interregional trade show that American growth was internally generated?

American policymakers at the time argued over the relative importance of trade and domestic industry, with the result that American international commercial policy was ambiguous. Northeastern congressmen, who wanted to protect infant industries in their region, insisted upon — and sometimes passed — high tariff barriers. But southerners (and to a lesser degree westerners) wanted to encourage external commerce in foodstuffs and cotton by reducing trade barriers, believing that the prosperity of their regions depended upon it. An examination of the changing level and composition of international commerce helps determine which group had the better argument.

Between 1770 and 1800, the ratio of the value of exports to the gross national product fell from perhaps a fifth to a tenth; from the 1830s to 1860, it amounted to only 6 percent of the nation's output. This low, and diminishing, ratio of exports to gross national product suggests that the domestic economy had become increasingly more important than international commerce. In fact, the home market did grow dramatically, as farm specialization increased and cities grew. The vast majority of grain produced in the country, for example, remained on the farm, was traded locally, or entered the interregional trade. Midwest grain and flour was transported on canals to hungry workers in the cities.

Declining ratios of exports to gross national product, however, obscure large increases in foreign trade. The value of American merchandise exports exploded after 1790, growing from $22 million annually in the early 1790s to $81 million by 1800. It declined in war years, fluctuated between 1815 and 1830, and then resumed rapid growth after 1830, reaching $360 million on the eve of the Civil War. Merchandise imports grew in a similar way, rising from $30 million per year in the early 1790s to almost $360 million by 1860. Growing foreign trade may have had substantial linkage effects, sustaining growth in the domestic economy.

Americans financed part of their development through foreign commerce. Except during the depression of 1837–1844, the United States experienced a negative balance of merchandise trade, one that grew from an annual average of $10 million in the 1790s to $41 million in the 1850s. Much of this deficit was made up by short-term foreign commercial credit and long-term foreign loans and investments (such as purchases of canal or railroad bonds), especially from England. Such credit may have reached a total of $125 million outstanding by 1837. But when debtors defaulted on loans during the 1837–1844 depression, wiping out much British investment, new credit almost disappeared; foreigners lent only about $40 million between 1838 and 1849. The booming American economy of the 1850s encouraged new foreign investment totaling about $190 million.

Foreigners invested in the United States because of the high returns to investment in its transport and other companies and because its citizens produced grain and meat needed in urbanizing countries and cotton needed in textile manufacture. In return, Americans imported foreign manufactured goods. As late as 1869, the United States exported only 4 percent of locally produced manufactured goods, but imports provided 14 percent of manufactured goods consumed. In contrast, it exported 10 percent of agricultural production, but imported just 6 percent of agricultural goods consumed.

Farm products dominated American exports and became ever-more important to American farmers. The share of exports in agricultural gross product rose from about a tenth in 1810 to a sixth by 1860. Heavy and growing demand for cotton by English textile manufacturers led more and more southern planters to grow the crop. Cotton quickly became the key American export, constituting by 1816–1820 two-fifths of the value of American exports. After 1820, such exports made up from almost half to nearly two-thirds of the value of exports. Accelerating demand for cotton led English and New York capitalists to lend cotton planters money to expand their plantations and buy slaves in the interstate market. At the same time, tobacco and rice, the other plantation commodities, declined in significance from a fifth of the value of exports in 1816–1820 to only 7 percent by the 1850s. Notwithstanding domestic consumption of grain and livestock, the rapid growth of the Midwest produced such great surpluses of grain that the value of wheat and corn exports doubled during the 1840s. By the eve of the Civil War, grain, flour, and livestock constituted about a fifth of exports.

In contrast, Americans imported large quantities of finished manufactured goods, mostly from Great Britain, the first industrial nation. Between 1820 and 1860, a little over half of all imports were manufactured goods. Cotton, woolen, and silk textiles, used for making clothing, and hammered and rolled iron (including rails) dominated these imports. Demand was voracious; whenever foreign credit was available, huge quantities of these goods entered the country.

Despite these increasing imports, American industry developed rapidly during the antebellum decades. As large factories in New England and the Mid-Atlantic states replaced small shops in the textile and shoe industries, output of cloth and shoes accelerated. Most of these goods fed the home market, traveling via ship and railroad to the South, Midwest, and West. Without this growing domestic output, imports of textiles would have been much greater. Moreover, small but increasing quantities of manufactured goods reached export markets: the proportion of American finished goods that were exported rose from a twentieth in 1820 to an eighth by 1850.

Although the impact of commerce on economic development cannot be determined with any precision, clearly, the domestic market in this continental nation was quantitatively far more important than foreign trade in triggering growth. Nevertheless, the growth of the domestic market was related to international trade. The growing demand for cotton in England led southerners to specialize in cotton, increasing their needs for midwestern grain and northeastern manufactures. Moreover, foreign investment helped build canals and railroads, and foreign manufactured goods allowed American farmers to stay on the land and feed an increasingly urban nation.

Douglass C. North, *Economic Growth of the United States, 1790–1860* (1966); George Rogers Taylor, *The Transportation Revolution, 1815–1860* (1951).

ALLAN KULIKOFF

II. From the Civil War to the Present

In 1866 America was a net importer of merchandise, as it had been in most years before the Civil War. During the war, tariffs had risen, and the depreciation of the dollar had offered an added barrier to imports. On the other hand, America's major export, raw cotton, had fallen off dramatically.

The tariffs imposed during the Civil War

were retained, and throughout the late nineteenth and into the twentieth century (to 1913), the pattern was one of still higher duties. Behind a tariff wall, American industry flourished. Goods formerly imported were now made in America, and imports changed from manufactured goods to the raw materials needed to make them (such imports typically came in duty-free). Tariffs notwithstanding, total imports rose as the American population grew and demand increased.

In the aftermath of the Civil War, raw cotton resumed its traditional role as America's largest export good (from 1803 to 1937, the Civil War and two other years excluded, unmanufactured cotton was America's largest merchandise export). The country was also an important exporter of grain and mineral products. Yet, what most characterized the growth of American exports in the late nineteenth and early twentieth centuries was the rise of manufactured goods exports: *refined* petroleum, machinery, and other manufactured goods. Some exports were goods that had previously been imported, but usually they were mass-produced products made by methods not yet used abroad (such products included sewing machines, harvesters, and then, automobiles). Exports increased rapidly as American goods became highly competitive in world markets.

Indeed, as imports rose, exports rose even faster with the consequence that (at first sporadically and then consistently after 1889) exports always exceeded imports until 1971. When the balance of trade remained consistently positive, Americans gradually recognized that a high tariff policy was no longer necessary or even desirable. In 1913, with traditionally low-tariff Democrats in control of Congress, the Underwood Tariff lowered duties substantially. International commerce expanded faster in the late nineteenth and early twentieth centuries than did worldwide output, the gold standard aiding in the growth.

American exports soared in the aftermath of World War I, as Europe depended on the United States for aid in recovery. In 1919 U.S. exports reached a level that would not be exceeded until 1943. There was another change of importance.

Most U.S. trade had been financed before the war with sterling acceptances (credits denominated in pounds sterling). During World War I, dollar acceptances came into use. This meant Americans were financing their own trade. A third change was that with Republicans in power in the 1920s, the notion of reduced protectionism floundered (in 1922, the Fordney-McCumber Tariff raised duties, especially to protect new "infant" industries such as chemicals). When, after the 1929 crash, Congress was trying to deal with the downturn, it was easy to blame imports, and the 1930 Smoot-Hawley Tariff was exceptionally high.

In the 1920s, country after country that had abandoned the gold standard during World War I had sought to restore it, but the restoration proved temporary. In 1929–1933 world output declined; countries devalued their currencies to encourage exports, yet world trade plummeted. The 1930 Smoot-Hawley Tariff provoked retaliation: it reduced American imports, but owing to new foreign duties on U.S. products, American exports fell faster. In the 1930s, new barriers to U.S. exports proliferated — not only foreign tariffs but exchange controls, quotas, and a whole range of other impediments to trade. Currencies fluctuated against one another, creating unpredictable conditions. In 1933 the United States devalued the dollar and in 1934 attempted to spur exports with reciprocal trade legislation. But by then the world economy was in such disarray that these efforts did little good. In the second half of 1940 the United States, in response to Japanese militarism, started to restrict U.S. exports to Japan and in August 1941 sharply curtailed the flow of crude oil and gasoline to that country. Many believe that these trade sanctions provoked the Japanese attack on Pearl Harbor.

World War II requirements revived international trade and, specifically, American exports. In the aftermath of that war, America emerged as the world's economic leader, dedicated to developing a world of greater and freer trade. Its exports exceeded imports, because its goods were highly competitive in world markets. America was strong and physically unimpaired by the war; other industrial countries were in ruins. The United States was committed to lead and to shape a postwar world where trade could serve as a generator of economic growth. The United States was active in the formation of the International Monetary Fund, designed to provide a basis for the return to stable currency rates and to facilitate international payments; international trade could not resume if there were not adequate payment mechanisms. Likewise, the United States participated in the General Agreement on Tariffs and Trade (GATT), to assist countries in eliminating the then ubiquitous obstructions to international commerce. The Marshall Plan assisted both European recovery and American exports to Europe.

In 1962 Congress passed a major trade law, and the United States sharply lowered its tariffs. The United States as the world's leader believed that it had little to fear from imports and everything to gain from demonstrating its dedication to freer trade. The nation continued to participate in GATT, and the Kennedy round of trade negotiations (completed in 1967) was particularly successful in encouraging worldwide tariff reductions.

Yet as trade barriers fell in the 1960s, America began to experience balance of payments deficits; goods exports still exceeded goods imports (the trade balance), but the net exports did not offset U.S. foreign aid, military expenditures abroad, and large foreign investments. In 1971, when it appeared that America would have its first twentieth-century trade deficit, President Nixon devalued the dollar. After 1973, worldwide currencies floated. Consistently, American imports began to exceed exports, and the country was now importing a wide range of manufactured products. For the first time in its history, on a mass market basis, Americans were buying foreign cars, foreign hi-fi sets, and foreign steel. And the nation's dependence on high-cost oil imports made the trade deficit even worse. By the 1980s there were few product categories where American exports exceeded imports (these exports included wheat, chemicals, aircraft, and parts).

Most economists thought the fluctuating dollar would in time eliminate the trade deficit (as the American dollar fell, U.S. exports would become cheaper and thus more competitive; more costly imports would be reduced). The trade deficits, however, continued, and the dollar fluctuated wildly. Finally in the 1980s many economists recognized that floating exchange rates were not the answer, but attempts at currency stabilization proved difficult. Foreign markets for American agricultural products had been lost in periods of the strong dollar and were hard to recapture. As U.S. imports of manufactured goods increased, numerous discussions focused on America's competitive position. Demands mounted for protectionism — to save jobs. The 1988 Omnibus Trade and Competitiveness Act allowed the president to impose sanctions on individual nations that engaged in unfair trade practices.

In the 1970s and 1980s, Americans groped for ways to become more competitive in the world economy and, in turn, to deal with the persistent excess of goods imports over exports. The continuing trade imbalance, particularly with Japan, spurred controversy. Was it the fault of Americans: low productivity increases, absence of goods desired abroad, lack of attention to exports? Was it that the dollar had not declined sufficiently to make U.S. goods attractive to foreign buyers? Or, was it that America's trading partners acted in ways that were prejudicial to U.S. exports? Perhaps it was all of these. Clearly, however, American producers and consumers chose to buy imports, often preferring goods made abroad to those manufactured at home. The rise of imports relative to exports was critical to the trade deficit.

MIRA WILKINS

See also Agriculture; Cotton; Economic Growth; International Investment; Tariff; Textile Industry; Tobacco; Transportation Revolution.

INTERNATIONAL INVESTMENT

From the colonial era to 1914, the United States was a debtor nation in international accounts; that is, Americans owed more to foreigners than foreigners owed to Americans. From roughly 1917–1918 to the mid-1980s, this relationship was reversed: the United States became a creditor country. In the mid-1980s, another major transformation occurred as the nation moved from net creditor back to net debtor, at least as officially measured.

The American government had borrowed in Europe to help finance the Revolution, to assist Alexander Hamilton in his funding of national and state debts, and to purchase the Louisiana Territory. By year-end 1803, more than half of the U.S. public debt was held abroad, and 62 percent of the stock of America's largest business, the Bank of the United States, was in the hands of nonresident foreigners.

Thereafter, foreign interests in America grew, following an uneven path; although the importance varied over the years, until 1875 the bulk of foreign holdings was in government securities (federal, state, city, county). In the 1830s and in the post–Civil War years, state government bonds were highly popular in Europe. In the early 1840s and the mid-1870s, major defaults on these securities soured European investors.

When Americans started to build railroads, it became necessary to raise added moneys abroad because U.S. savings were inadequate. New mines and cattle ranches also attracted European (especially British) moneys, as did mineral processing, meat packing, and flour making. In the early twentieth century, British, German, Dutch, French, and other foreign investors produced a variety of goods and services in America (including rayon, the first synthetic fabric, Mercedes cars, oil by Royal-Dutch Shell, and Michelin tires). With the large inflow of capital, America became the world's greatest debtor nation.

Meanwhile, American businesses began to move abroad. In the colonial era, merchants had set up overseas units. During the nineteenth century, the number of enterprises abroad mounted slowly. Then, from the 1870s onward, as American companies grew at home, they also expanded over national borders. By the late nineteenth and early twentieth centuries, modern American multinational enterprises had emerged. Standard Oil of New Jersey, Singer, International Harvester, Western Electric, and by

1914, Ford Motor Company had major producing facilities outside the United States. Although foreign investment *in the United States* was of both a portfolio nature (investment in bonds and shares and bank lending that did not carry control) and of a direct investment nature (investment that carried management and control), the former was predominant; U.S. stakes abroad also consisted of both types, but foreign direct investment was supreme. The reason was that surplus capital in America was used at home. Thus, even while America was the great recipient of capital from abroad, its businesses were entering and growing in foreign lands, seeking new markets and sources of supply.

World War I was the watershed. The British sold American assets to finance the war, and German investments in America ended when the United States entered the war. The demand for capital abroad rose, and now Americans supplied it. American banks, once intermediaries in bringing capital *to* the United States, had developed the skills and contacts to play the opposite role — to dispatch U.S. moneys worldwide. Europe looked to America for loans to buy weapons. In 1917–1918 U.S. government lending became very important. Latin America attracted new U.S. business investments. Overnight, as it were, America was transformed into a creditor nation.

Businesses continued to expand in the 1920s and so did American lending. Excluding the U.S. intergovernmental credits, and with 1929 possibly an exception, American direct investment abroad always exceeded portfolio investment until the 1970s. During the 1930s, American lenders abroad faced major defaults and multinationals encountered difficulties. In 1934 the Johnson Act made it unlawful for U.S. bankers to lend to countries in default on U.S. government loans. World War II posed added hazards for international investors. In its aftermath, America emerged as economically strong and as the great creditor nation, the only economic giant in the world. Marshall Plan aid was vital to European recovery. Soon, American multinationals were spreading worldwide on a scale that dwarfed their past history. During the 1960s the American challenge — American investment accompanied by American technology — seemed unmatched.

While America was a creditor nation, foreign stakes in the United States were overshadowed. Yet they never entirely disappeared. Some foreign companies that had investments in the United States before 1914 remained and grew in size, and there were new entries. Certain portfolio holdings persisted and others were newly made. Indeed by the time of World War II, foreign investment had attained its 1914 level, even though the amounts were exceeded by U.S. investment abroad. After the Second World War, foreign investment in the United States was very much in the background.

In the 1970s, as the Organization of Petroleum Exporting Countries (OPEC) pushed oil prices up, its government members had capital surpluses that could not be absorbed into their domestic economies; these moneys were placed with U.S. banks and recycled into third world debt. With the new sources of funds, the character of American investment abroad changed. From being overwhelmingly investment by multinationals, it became increasingly made up of bank loans.

Americans, for balance of payments reasons, had sought to encourage foreign investment in the United States in the 1960s; by the 1970s and early 1980s, an awareness emerged of rising inward investment. America was both politically stable and provided a formidable market. While much of the new investment came from European (especially British, Dutch, and German) sources — often stimulated by the decline in the dollar after 1971–1973, which made American assets cheaper to foreign buyers — what attracted special concern was the newly conspicuous holdings of Arab investors and later of the Japanese.

Suddenly, in the mid-1980s, seemingly overnight, the United States had switched from net creditor to net debtor status in international accounts. And once again, by the end of the decade, America had become the world's greatest debtor nation. The transitions of 1914–1918 and the mid-1980s had been rapid, yet in each case the foundations had been laid in prior years. Despite much unhappy talk about "foreign multinationals in America" — especially the Japanese "invasion" — foreign investors still had their holdings mainly in liquid assets, portfolio investments. And, as during most of American history, it was still the British who had the largest investments. Moreover, as foreign investment in America grew, U.S. investment abroad persisted and direct investments expanded.

Historically, Americans were always ambivalent about foreign investment. This was true before 1914 when, on the one hand, there was the wish for foreign capital to finance the railroads and, on the other, a deep resentment against British investors. So, too, in many parts of the world, American investment over the years provoked a "can't live with it and can't live without it" state of mind — hated for its symbolic "alien" implications and yet desired for its positive contributions. As sizable foreign investment in the United States took place in the 1970s and 1980s, it was both courted by state governments that wanted more employment within their jurisdictions and lambasted by critics who saw "America for Sale." Despite economic integration worldwide, nations, the United States included, retained — as in times past — a mixed response toward outsiders' investments.

Mira Wilkins, *The Emergence of Multinational Enterprise: American Business Abroad from the Colonial Era to 1914* (1970); Mira Wilkins, *The History of Foreign Investment in the United States to 1914* (1989); Mira Wilkins, *The Maturing of Multinational Enterprise: American Business Abroad from 1914 to 1970* (1974).

MIRA WILKINS

See also Expansion, Continental and Overseas; International Commerce; Marshall Plan.

INTERSTATE COMMERCE COMMISSION

The Interstate Commerce Commission (ICC), the nation's first independent regulatory agency, was established in 1887 after more than a decade of mounting complaints over railroad rates and practices. A Supreme Court decision in 1886 ruling that states could not regulate interstate railroads made federal action more urgent; by then the railroads themselves had come to believe that federal legislation would be more consistent and perhaps more moderate than the growing patchwork of state laws. The number of members was set first at five, then seven, then nine, and finally eleven in 1920; members serve six-year terms and are appointed by the president, but may not be dismissed by him. Unlike most regulatory agencies, the ICC elects its own chairperson.

Initially, the ICC regulated only railroads, but its scope has gradually been extended to cover all surface common carriers, including buses and trucks (1935), barges (1940), and freight forwarders (1942). Its primary focus has been to ensure that rate setting is not used to suppress competition. Starting with the Hepburn Act in 1906, the ICC's power regarding rate setting has been steadily expanded, both through legislation and through broader court interpretations of the commerce clause. One important milestone was the Transportation Act of 1920, written when the government was returning to private hands the railroads it had taken over during World War I. Under this law, the ICC moved from approving railroad rates to actually setting them; it also was empowered to determine appropriate profit levels and organize mergers. Since then, the ICC has presided over a succession of programs designed to ensure the railroads' continuing survival and profitability. The ICC also regulated telephone, telegraph, and cable communication from 1910 until the establishment of the Federal Communications Commission in 1934 and monitored safety standards for railroads and trucks until the creation of the Department of Transportation in 1966. During the 1980s, the administration of President Ronald Reagan tried several times to abolish the ICC, on the ground that deregulation had made it unnecessary, but Congress refused to approve the proposals.

See also Railroads.

INVENTIONS

See Cotton Gin; Science and Technology.

INVESTMENT

See International Investment.

IRAN-CONTRA AFFAIR

The Iran-Contra affair grew out of a series of covert actions in foreign policy undertaken by officials of President Ronald Reagan's National Security Council (NSC) in the mid-1980s. The affair surfaced in November 1986 after reports in Lebanese newspapers forced President Reagan and Attorney General Edwin Meese III to disclose secret arms deals between the United States and Iran, one of the nation's principal adversaries. Officials of the NSC joined with private arms dealers to sell (at inflated prices) weapons and replacement parts to Iran for use in its war with Iraq. The apparent purpose of these sales — although it was repeatedly denied by the president — was to obtain Iranian assistance in securing the release of Americans held hostage in Lebanon by pro-Iranian terrorist groups. The excess profits generated by these sales were diverted to fund the American-backed Contra movement in Nicaragua, which was trying to overthrow the Marxist Sandinista government of that nation.

Between 1987 and 1989, congressional, journalistic, and prosecutorial investigations unearthed a pattern of secret activities by the NSC to assist the Contras by raising financial and logistical aid from private citizens and friendly foreign governments. Critics of the Reagan administration charged that these activities violated both federal laws barring officials from aiding the Contras and the Constitution — specifically, its provisions defining the congressional power of the purse and Congress's role in making foreign policy. Defenders of the president rejected the charges of illegality and unconstitutionality, maintaining that the executive branch was forced to take these measures in the face of unwarranted congressional interference with the president's authority to conduct foreign policy.

See also Middle East–U.S. Relations; Reagan, Ronald.

IRAN HOSTAGE CRISIS

The Iran hostage crisis began November 4, 1979, when a mob of Iranians seized the U.S. embassy in Tehran, taking a large group of employees hostage. Eleven months earlier, a revolution led by the Islamic fundamentalist Ayatollah Ruholla Khomeini had overthrown Mohammad Reza Pahlavi, the shah of Iran. Relations between the two countries had been strained since that time, as Iran's new leaders denounced the United States for its longtime support of the shah. When the exiled shah entered the United States in October for medical care, many Iranians feared a repetition of the U.S.-assisted coup that had put the shah on the throne in 1953. The hostage taking followed.

Nineteen hostages were released within a few weeks; the remaining fifty-two were held for 444 days. When it became clear that the Iranian government was not going to resolve the problem, President Jimmy Carter moved to freeze Iranian assets, both in the United States and abroad. Diplomatic efforts were launched through the United Nations and various private intermediaries, but by March 1980 it had become clear that none of the rival political groups in Iran was willing to risk the unpopularity of letting the hostages go. This impasse led Carter to order a rescue effort by helicopter, but three of the eight helicopters failed before reaching Tehran, and the mission had to be aborted. Eight men died in the operation.

News of the failure aggravated the American public's mounting frustration over the crisis, providing a focus for broader criticism of Carter's administration (sharpened by the fact that this was an election year) as well as more general distress over America's waning ability to control world events. These issues undoubtedly contributed to Carter's defeat by Ronald Reagan in November. Nevertheless, by then a new Iranian government had been formed, and serious negotiations began soon after, with Algeria as mediator. The United States agreed to unfreeze most Iranian assets in exchange for the hostages. Finally, on January 20, 1981 — only a few hours after Carter left office — all fifty-two hostages were released and landed safely in West Germany.

See also Carter, Jimmy; Middle East–U.S. Relations.

IRON AND STEEL INDUSTRY

Iron has been a vital material in technology for well over three thousand years. But until the Industrial Revolution, its mining, smelting, and working were largely done by individuals and small groups. Each mine, forge, and blacksmith usually employed only a few dozen men at most.

Iron mining and working began in British North America almost as soon as settlement began, the first ironworks being set up at Jamestown, Virginia, in 1621. John Winthrop, Jr., established an ironworks on the Saugus River in Lynn, Massachusetts, as early as 1646. It was an elaborate enterprise for its time and place, but it was never a profitable business and soon collapsed into bankruptcy.

As late as the year 1700, mines in the colonies were producing less than 2 percent of the world's iron. The eighteenth century, however, saw a great increase in American production of pig iron, the crude product that comes from the blast furnace. In 1750 Britain passed the Iron Act, one of the first of the Trade and Navigation Acts that were to be a major cause of the Revolution. The act forbade the building of mills in the colonies but admitted American pig iron into Britain duty-free under some circumstances. After 1757, as British demand grew quickly, American pig iron was admitted duty-free in all cases.

Soon the American colonies had more blast furnaces and forges than England and Wales, and the export of pig iron increased accordingly. In 1723 only fifteen tons were exported, all from Virginia and Maryland. In 1771 more than five thousand tons were shipped abroad, about half from Virginia and Maryland and most of the rest from Pennsylvania and New York. By the time of the outbreak of the Revolution, the colonies were producing thirty thousand tons of pig iron a year, one-seventh of the world's supply. When the war ended, the manufacture of iron products increased markedly, and mills producing nails, hinges, plows, and other products were established in several states.

Steel, however, was another matter. Known since ancient times, steel is made by alloying iron with carbon to produce a harder, stronger metal that will take a much keener edge. But steel was very expensive to manufacture by the primitive methods then available, and its use was largely confined to high-value specialty products such as swords and precision instruments. The United States imported almost all its steel until after the Civil War.

The coming of the steam age transformed the iron industry. The demand for rolled iron for boilers increased exponentially. And between 1830 and 1861 more than thirty thousand miles of railroad were built in the United States, providing an enormous market for iron rails and allowing the creation of a national market for manufactured goods. This vast increase in demand caused iron mills to grow quickly into major enterprises.

Pennsylvania had been a leader in the American iron industry since revolutionary days. With the discovery of very large deposits of anthracite coal in that state and its substitution for charcoal in smelting after 1840, Pennsylvania solidified its position as the nation's leading state in the iron industry.

In 1844 U.S. government surveyors discovered the first of the great iron ore deposits in the Great Lakes states. By the late 1850s these were being aggressively exploited. The abundance of rich iron ore around Lake Superior, the anthracite of Pennsylvania, and the cheap water transport available on the Great Lakes ensured that this area would be the center of the American iron and steel industry thereafter. As the production of iron and steel became the driving force of the Industrial Revolution, the Midwest became the center of American heavy industry.

In 1856 the British engineer Henry (later Sir Henry) Bessemer developed the Bessemer process for making steel. Two years later the Siemens-Martin open-hearth method was developed. Once perfected, these processes greatly lowered the cost of steel production and allowed the increasingly lavish use of steel for railroads, construction, and other industrial purposes.

The first Bessemer converter in the United States was established in 1864. Four years later Abram S. Hewitt built the first open-hearth furnace, which was better suited to most American iron ore. Steel production increased rapidly thereafter. In 1873 the United States, which had produced no steel rails before the Civil War, produced nearly 115,000 tons, one-eighth of all American rail production. As the price of steel continued to drop, iron rails, brittle and requiring frequent replacement, disappeared. The iron age was over.

In the years after the Civil War, the American steel industry grew with astonishing speed as the nation's economy expanded to become the largest in the world. Between 1880 and the turn of the century, steel production increased from 1.25 million tons to more than 10 million tons. By 1910 America was producing more than 24 million tons, by far the greatest of any country.

The industry also consolidated during this era as mill owners sought economies of scale, guaranteed sources of raw materials, and stable market conditions. Andrew Carnegie, Henry Clay Frick, Charles Schwab, and others shaped the modern industry in these years. The period was also often wracked by violent labor disputes such as the Homestead strike in 1892, and the industry would not be fully unionized until the 1930s.

In 1901, under the leadership of J. Pierpont Morgan and Elbert H. Gary, the United States Steel Corporation, the largest industrial enterprise on earth, was established. Capitalized at $1.4 billion, it controlled more than 60 percent of the American market.

The steel industry continued to be the measure of the size and strength of national economies until well after World War II. American steel production peaked in 1969 when the country produced 141,262,000 tons. But new, more efficient steel plants with much lower labor costs were being built abroad, and these, helped by a sharp drop in transportation expenses, began to give American steel companies increasing competition.

A major shakeout of the industry ensued. By 1975 American steel production had plunged by 37 percent to only 89 million tons. The industry, however, still employed 457,000 workers at very high wages. By 1988 production had rebounded to 102,700,000 tons, but the number of steelworkers had declined to 169,000. Annual steel production per worker had more than tripled in thirteen years.

American steel was once again competitive on world markets. But steel would never again hold the central place in the economy it had held for a hundred years. The age of steel had ended; the age of the computer had begun.

JOHN STEELE GORDON

See also Carnegie, Andrew; Frick, Henry Clay; Homestead Strike; Industrial Revolution; Morgan, J. Pierpont; Railroads.

ISOLATIONISM

Isolationism is the pejorative twentieth-century term used for America's traditional noninvolvement in European wars and avoidance of "entangling alliances." It assumed the United States' interests and values were different from and superior to those of Europe and held that America could lead the world toward freedom and democracy more effectively through example than through military action. Isolationists, however, never favored cutting off the United States from the rest of the world, nor did they rule out the possibilities of American expansion — territorial, commercial, financial, ideological, or military — particularly in the Western Hemisphere, the Pacific, and East Asia.

The roots of isolationism extended back to the colonial period. Settlers came to escape religious persecution, economic hardship, wars, or personal problems in Europe. From the beginning there was the assumption (or the hope) that the New World would be better than the Old. The long and dangerous journey magnified the geographic (and moral) separateness of America. Despite the alliance with France during the American Revolution, the attitudes undergirding isolationism were well established long before independence.

When George Washington in his Farewell Address asserted that Europe had "a set of primary interests which to us have none or a very remote relation" and advised America "to steer clear of permanent alliances," he was advancing views that were already old and widely accepted. The United States ended its alliance with France in time for its third president, Thomas Jefferson, to warn against "entangling alliances."

During the nineteenth century the United States expanded across North America and began to build an overseas empire in the Caribbean and the Pacific without departing from those traditional policies. It waged the War of 1812, the Mexican War, and the Spanish-American War without intervening in Europe or entering alliances. Nonetheless, forces were building at home and abroad that would undermine and then destroy those policies in the twentieth century. Fundamental were socioeconomic and political changes within the United States, along with power and security changes abroad.

If experiences had alienated Americans from Europe, other experiences and the Western heritage provided bonds with the Continent. Improved transportation and communication facilities — steamships, cable, radio — linked the two. The growth of foreign trade and shipping gradually built bases for America's world role. Within the United States the triumph of urban industry and finance and the decline of rural and small-town America were fundamental to the demise of isolationism. Traditional policies began to encounter more critical judgments in leadership circles.

Externally the growing German challenges to British power led some to see the British fleet as "free security" for the United States. German challenges to Anglo-French dominance in two world wars were turned back, but they led American leaders increasingly to recognize the significance of European power relationships to American security. The country's participation in World War I against the Central Powers was the first major break with traditional policies. Nonetheless, isolationism was by no means dead. Some, particularly Western agrarian progressives such as William Jennings Bryan of Nebraska, Robert M. La Follette of Wisconsin, and George W. Norris of Nebraska, spoke earnestly against involvement. It was significant that the immediate precipitant for the American declaration of war was unrestricted German submarine warfare and the resulting loss of ships and lives on the high seas, not developments on the European continent. The United States fought in World War I as an associate power, not as an ally. Despite President Woodrow Wilson's leadership the Senate rejected the Versailles treaty ending that war, and the United States never became a member of the League of Nations.

In the 1920s and 1930s the term *isolationism* came into widespread denigrating use, but the majority continued to oppose involvement in European wars and alliances. The Senate Investigation of the Munitions Industries in 1934–1936 and adoption of the Neutrality Acts of 1935, 1936, and 1937 marked a high point in the political defense of those policies. Isolationism was strongest in rural and small-town America in the Midwest and Great Plains and among Republicans more than among Democrats. It won a substantial following among Irish-Americans and German-Americans. Among its most prominent spokesmen were Western agrarian progressives such as William E. Borah of Idaho, Hiram Johnson of California, Burton K. Wheeler of Montana, Gerald P. Nye of North Dakota, Henrik Shipstead of Minnesota, and Robert M. La Follette, Jr., of Wisconsin. They denounced eastern urban business, financial, ideological, and political elites for involvement in European affairs.

The year 1940 marked a turning point for isolationists. German military triumphs in Europe and the Battle of Britain forced widespread American reconsideration of its relation to the war. Many worried that if Germany and Italy triumphed in Europe and Africa, and Japan triumphed in East Asia, the Western Hemisphere could be the next target. Even if America withstood assaults, its democracy, freedom, and economy could be traumatized in the "fortress America" it might have to maintain to guard its security. Given that frightening worst-case scenario, the majority, by the autumn of 1940, believed it important to ensure the defeat of the Axis even at the risk of war.

But in 1940–1941 many still supported the noninterventionist America First Committee. Isolationists failed to block proposals by the Roosevelt administration to aid victims of Axis aggression with methods short of war. Nonetheless, 80 percent of Americans opposed any declaration of war against the Axis states. Not until after Japan attacked Pearl Harbor on December 7, 1941, and Germany and Italy declared war on the United States on December 11 did America turn to full-scale war against the Axis.

Isolationist perspectives did not completely disappear, but never again did they dominate American attitudes and policies. During World War II the Roosevelt administration and leadership elites led Americans to support the creation of a United Nations Organization, and after the war the challenges posed by the Soviet Union under Joseph Stalin argued against the resumption of isolationism.

Within the United States the growth of urban industry and finance, expanded educational and informational facilities, and leadership by internationalists overwhelmed remnants of isolationism. Some still wished to return to America's traditional policies of nonintervention. But the world environment, military technology, and conditions within the United States had changed too drastically. In practical terms, traditional American isolationism was dead.

Wayne S. Cole, *Roosevelt and the Isolationists, 1932–1945* (1983); John Milton Cooper, Jr., *The Vanity of Power: American Isolationism and the First World War, 1914–1917* (1969); Ralph Stone, *The Irreconcilables: The Fight against the League of Nations* (1970).

WAYNE S. COLE

See also America First Committee; Borah, William E.; Bryan, William Jennings; La Follette, Robert M.; Neutrality Acts; Versailles Treaty and League of Nations.

ISRAEL-U.S. RELATIONS

See Middle East–U.S. Relations.

IVES, CHARLES

(1874–1954), composer and businessman. Ives was an American original in the tradition of the eighteenth-century composer William Billings, who declared that every composer "should be his own carver." Ives's music was imbued with the spirit of his New England forebears, and the ideas of the nineteenth-century transcendentalists provided the inspiration for many of his compositions. His strong belief in self-reliance and devotion to family and community appear in the pamphlets he issued on American democracy and business enterprise. (Ives earned his living in the insurance business and composed in private without recognition or approval from the larger musical community.)

Ives received his early musical training from his father, an unconventional bandmaster and choir director who encouraged original thought along with technical precision. His years at Yale (1894–1898) included composition study with Horatio Parker, who did not share the young composer's enthusiasm for unresolved dissonances. After graduation, Ives continued composing and embarked on his insurance career. He suffered a major heart attack in 1918 but was able to complete his *Concord* Sonata and a book, *Essays before a Sonata,* two years later.

Ives's compositions were difficult and demanded more preparation than many performers were prepared to devote to them. Nor did listeners always appreciate his music. But critic Henry Bellamann recognized the "lofty" qualities of the *Concord* Sonata in the early 1920s, and pianists Henry Cowell and Nicholas Slonimsky performed his music in the latter half of the decade. Seven of his songs were presented at the first Yaddo festival in 1932, which sparked an interest in his music among young American composers. Ives was awarded a Pulitzer Prize for his Third Symphony (1901–1904) in 1947, by which time he was a seventy-three-year-old recluse who had not composed for more than twenty-five years.

Ives's music harks back to the nineteenth century but also anticipates the sounds and techniques of modern composition. In his use of the orchestra, piano, voice, and chamber ensembles to paint evocative musical pictures of nineteenth-century New England towns, Ives can be considered a romantic. His interest in transcendentalist thought is reflected in the Second Pianoforte Sonata, *Concord, 1840–1860,* with its movements entitled "Emerson," "Hawthorne," "The Alcotts," and "Thoreau." But despite his nostalgic vision of an earlier New England and the echoes of familiar hymns and patriotic and popular songs that recur in his works, he used sounds that belong to the language of modern music, including polytonality, polyrhythms, and quarter tones. Thus, he brought the everyday music of an earlier era into the twentieth-century concert hall.

Recent debate over whether Charles Ives may have predated a number of his compositions to make them appear uninfluenced by European modern music has not detracted from his successful evocation of small-town nineteenth-century America.

Vivian Perlis, *Charles Ives Remembered: An Oral History* (1974); Rosalie Sandra Perry, *Charles Ives and the American Mind* (1974); Frank Rossiter, *Charles Ives and His America* (1975).

BARBARA L. TISCHLER

See also Music; Progressivism.

IWW

See Industrial Workers of the World.

J

JACKSON, ANDREW

(1767–1845), seventh president of the United States. A forceful, at times violent personality, Jackson continues to provoke controversy among historians, who see in him reflections of both the best and the worst tendencies of the new Republic.

Jackson was a southwestern parvenu who combined a sense of rough-hewn egalitarianism with the gentlemanly honor typical of his class. Born in the Carolina backwoods to an immigrant farming family from Ireland, he fought in the Revolution and was captured and imprisoned by the British. By war's end, all but one member of his immediate family had died in connection with the conflict. A teenager alone and adrift, Jackson eventually decided to study law and then to head farther west. Although immensely ambitious, he would never lose touch with his plebeian roots.

Jackson's rise, helped along by some fortunate contacts, was mercurial. Starting out as a prosecuting attorney for the western district of North Carolina (what is now Tennessee), he went on to serve as a delegate to the Tennessee constitutional convention, Tennessee's first elected congressman, and (briefly) U.S. senator, before he returned to Nashville in 1798 and won a seat on the state supreme court. He also set himself up as a slaveholder on a modest estate he would build into a major cotton plantation, the Hermitage.

Jackson won national fame, however, in the military. During the War of 1812, he and his troops crushed the Creek Indians after a lengthy campaign in the Mississippi Territory. Rewarded with a U.S. Army commission, he led the American forces to victory at the Battle of New Orleans, emerging as the war's greatest hero. In 1818, he ruthlessly pursued the government's war with the Seminoles into Spanish Florida, and provoked controversy by summarily executing two British subjects suspected of aiding the Indians. In 1821, he was named military governor of the Florida Territory.

By now, Jackson had gained a huge popular following as an Indian fighter and foe of British tyranny — and at the urging of friends he returned to politics. He reclaimed his Senate seat in 1823 and then ran for the presidency the following year in a four-man race, collecting a plurality of the popular tally but insufficient electoral votes to win. When the House of Representatives decided in favor of John Quincy Adams, Jackson thundered that he was the victim of a "corrupt bargain" between Adams and Henry Clay. But building a fresh coalition of southern strict constructionists, western expansionists, and antiadministration forces in the Mid-Atlantic states, he defeated Adams in 1828, believing he had vindicated his principle that "the majority is to govern."

It soon became clear that Jackson's ascent marked a change in the nation's political direction. Early on, he established the principle of rotation in office, on the premise that any plain and simple man could do the people's business. He checked the program of federal internal improvements proffered by Adams and Clay, believing it a dangerous expansion of federal power favorable to established wealth. On Indian affairs, he ran roughshod over his critics and proclaimed a policy of forced relocation of eastern tribes west of the Mississippi River, opening fresh lands for settlers. As antislavery agitation mounted — a danger, he thought, to national tranquillity and his own democratic political project — he condemned the abolitionists and backed efforts to curtail their activities. At the same time, he angrily defeated those emerging southern nationalists (led by his former ally, John C. Calhoun) who defied federal authority in the name of states' rights.

But it was Jackson's war on the Second Bank of the United States that consolidated his reputation as a champion of the common man. A hard-money advocate, suspicious of personal debt, Jackson viewed the Bank as a monstrosity that gave power over the people's money to a few unelected private bankers. After vetoing the Bank's recharter in 1832 — a move that helped secure his reelection — he ordered the removal of U.S. funds, tried to put the nation's economy on a hard-money footing, and revived populist, anticapitalist sentiments latent since Thomas Jefferson's presidency.

By the close of his second term, Jackson and his supporters had transformed his following into an effective national party, fashioned more or less in his own image. After seeing his protégé Martin Van Buren elected as his successor, he returned to the Hermitage, where he lived out his final years as a country gentleman and elder statesman.

Jackson's career exemplified, and in many ways molded, the contradictory forces at work in the democratization of the early Republic. In his appeals to the common man, his attacks on privileged wealth, and his help in building a new sort of mass political party, he advanced the causes of equal rights and majoritarian democracy. Yet those advances went hand in hand with the continued subjugation of Native Americans and a determination not to disturb the slavery issue. Jackson stood for a more egalitarian America, but his vision of democracy stopped squarely at the color line.

Robert V. Remini, *Andrew Jackson and the Course of American Empire, 1767–1821* (1977), *Andrew Jackson and the Course of American Freedom, 1822–1832* (1981), and *Andrew Jackson and the Course of American Democracy, 1833–1845* (1984).

SEAN WILENTZ

See also Corrupt Bargain; Elections: 1824, 1828, 1832; Indians; Jacksonian Democracy; War of 1812. *For events during Jackson's administration, see* Anti-Masons; Banking; Bank of the United States; Black Hawk War; *Cherokee Nation* v. *Georgia;* Kitchen Cabinet; Nullification Controversy; Specie Circular; Texas Revolution and Annexation; Webster-Hayne Debate; Whig Party.

JACKSON, JESSE

(1941–   ), political and civil rights leader. Once a follower and associate of Martin Luther King, Jr., Jackson emerged during the 1970s and 1980s as the most dynamic African-American leader of the post-King era. Born to an unwed mother in Greenville, South Carolina, he was raised in modest circumstances with his stepfather and lived near his more affluent father, witnessing and resenting the privileged circumstances of his half brother. Jackson's success as a student and an athlete led to a scholarship to the University of Illinois, but when he was not allowed to play quarterback, he transferred to North Carolina Agricultural and Technical College. Jackson then attended Chicago Theological Seminary and was ordained a Baptist minister in 1968.

Jackson met his future wife, Jacqueline Davis, at A&T in 1963, and both became active in the civil rights protests that spread throughout the South. In 1965, Jackson began working with King, and he demonstrated his effectiveness as an organizer when King assigned him to expand the Southern Christian Leadership Conference's (SCLC) operations in Chicago. He was present when King was assassinated in April 1968. Jackson later became active in numerous efforts, serving as national director of Operation Breadbasket and then leading his own organization, Operation PUSH (People United to Serve Humanity), formed in 1971 to pressure large corporations to provide jobs and economic opportunities for blacks and other minorities.

Responding to the increasing shift to the

right in American politics, Jackson began to emphasize economic empowerment rather than traditional civil rights issues. During the late 1970s, he started PUSH-Excel, designed to motivate black students. His rousing oratory, which combined elements of uplift ("I *am* somebody!") and militancy ("It's nationtime!"), attracted a large popular following. He also made several controversial ventures into international politics, including a meeting in 1979 with the head of the Palestine Liberation Organization. In 1983 he secured the release of a captured navy pilot during a trip to Syria.

By the early 1980s, he had become the black leader most capable of staging an effective campaign for the presidency. In his campaign, Jackson sought to appeal to all races and helped form the Rainbow Coalition, which became a base for his 1984 campaign. Hurt politically when a journalist overheard and reported his use of the term *Hymies* to refer to Jews (he later apologized for the slur), he nevertheless surprised observers when he ran a strong third in the Democratic primaries, garnering over 3 million votes. In 1988, he staged an even more successful campaign, winning 6.7 million votes in the primaries. Although he failed in his quest to gain the vice-presidential nomination, he remained the nation's most prominent black political leader.

Roger D. Hatch and Frank E. Watkins, eds., *Reverend Jesse L. Jackson: Straight from the Heart* (1987); Adolph L. Reed, *The Jesse Jackson Phenomenon* (1987).

CLAYBORNE CARSON

See also Civil Rights Movement; Democratic Party.

JACKSON, THOMAS J. (STONEWALL)

(1824–1863), Confederate general. Jackson grew up a poor orphan in western (now West) Virginia. In his youth he adopted the motto "You may be whatever you resolve to be." Young Jackson's resolve was firm enough to secure his appointment to West Point and to help him overcome miserably poor academic preparation. He began below the bottom of his class and graduated in 1846 seventeenth among fifty-nine graduates.

As a junior officer, Jackson served with distinction in the Mexican War, but afterward chafed at the pettiness of peacetime service. In 1851 he resigned from the army to accept an appointment as a professor of natural and experimental philosophy (essentially physics) at Virginia Military Institute (VMI). He attacked his new career with characteristic intensity, but he possessed little or no background in the subject he taught and, worse, seemed capable of neither patience nor humor. A zealous Presbyterian Calvinist, Jackson drilled his students "by the book" and appeared to believe that he was God's agent sent to separate the saved from the damned in his classroom.

Jackson's dour rigidity softened somewhat when he was away from his official duties. He married in 1856 and, after his first wife died, married again in 1857. At home and among his few close friends, Jackson relaxed a little, debated theological points for fun, and planted a garden.

When the Civil War broke out, Jackson volunteered his services to Virginia and initially drilled raw recruits at Harpers Ferry. An Alabama private described Jackson as "a large, fat, old fellow; looks very much like an old Virginia farmer." But when battles replaced parades, Jackson emerged as a fierce warrior. At First Bull Run/Manassas he earned his nickname "Stonewall" by standing like one with his brigade against Union assaults.

During the fall of 1861 Jackson led an ill-fated campaign against Romney, (West) Virginia. He feuded with fellow officers and even resigned from the Confederate army over a procedural quarrel with Secretary of War Judah P. Benjamin. Wisely, Benjamin refused to accept his resignation.

Jackson's campaign in the Shenandoah Valley during the spring of 1862 established his military genius. A series of brilliant maneuvers, sharp battles, and record marches established Jackson's Valley Army as "foot cavalry," while the Confederates battled and defeated a combined Union force nearly three times their numbers.

Then Jackson saddled his "foot cavalry" to join Robert E. Lee for a showdown against George B. McClellan's Union troops before Richmond. The Seven Days' Battles (June 25–July 1) defeated McClellan but failed to destroy his army as Lee had planned. The fault was largely Jackson's. He was uncharacteristically slow and passive, possibly the victim of the "fog of war" — stress fatigue brought on by extended marching and fighting.

Still Lee trusted Jackson, giving him semi-independent commands, and Jackson responded. He was again "Stonewall" at Second Bull Run/ Manassas August 27–30, 1862; he recaptured Harpers Ferry and saved Lee's army at Antietam; and he fought well at Fredericksburg on December 13, 1862.

At Chancellorsville on May 3, 1863, Jackson led his corps on a forced march to the Union rear and struck with awesome fury. In what was possibly Lee's greatest battle, Jackson was the hero. He planned to press his attack that night by moonlight. But in some dark woods a body of Confederates mistook their general for enemy cavalry and shot him. Jackson died of pneumonia a week later — Puritan martyr in the land of Cavaliers.

Robert G. Tanner, *Stonewall in the Valley: Thomas J. "Stonewall" Jackson's Shenandoah Valley Campaign, Spring, 1862* (1976); Frank E. Vandiver, *Mighty Stonewall* (1957).

EMORY M. THOMAS

See also Civil War.

JACKSONIAN DEMOCRACY

An ambiguous, controversial concept, Jacksonian Democracy in the strictest sense refers simply to the ascendancy of Andrew Jackson and the Democratic party after 1828. More loosely, it alludes to the entire range of democratic reforms that proceeded alongside the Jacksonians' triumph — from expanding the suffrage to restructuring federal institutions. From another angle, however, Jacksonianism appears as a political impulse tied to slavery, the subjugation of Native Americans, and the celebration of white supremacy — so much so that some scholars have dismissed the phrase "Jacksonian Democracy" as a contradiction in terms. Such tendentious revisionism may provide a useful corrective to older enthusiastic assessments, but it fails to capture a larger historical tragedy: Jacksonian Democracy was an authentic democratic movement, dedicated to powerful, at times radical, egalitarian ideals — but mainly for white men.

Socially and intellectually, the Jacksonian movement represented not the insurgency of a specific class or region but a diverse, sometimes testy national coalition. Its origins stretch back to the democratic stirrings of the American Revolution, the Antifederalists of the 1780s and 1790s, and the Jeffersonian Democratic Republicans. More directly, it arose out of the profound social and economic changes of the early nineteenth century.

Recent historians have analyzed these changes in terms of a market revolution. In the Northeast and Old Northwest, rapid transportation improvements and immigration hastened the collapse of an older yeoman and artisan economy and its replacement by cash-crop agriculture and capitalist manufacturing. In the South, the cotton boom revived a flagging plantation slave economy, which spread to occupy the best lands of the region. In the West, the seizure of lands from Native Americans and mixed-blood Hispanics opened up fresh areas for white settlement and cultivation — and for speculation.

Not everyone benefited equally from the market revolution, least of all those nonwhites for whom it was an unmitigated disaster. Jacksonianism, however, would grow directly from the tensions it generated within white society. Mortgaged farmers and an emerging proletariat in the Northeast, nonslaveholders in the South, tenants and would-be yeomen in the West — all had reasons to think that the spread of commerce and capitalism would bring not boundless opportunities but new forms of dependence. And in all sections of the country, some of the rising entrepreneurs of the market revolution suspected that older elites would block their way and shape economic development to suit themselves.

By the 1820s, these tensions fed into a

many-sided crisis of political faith. To the frustration of both self-made men and plebeians, certain eighteenth-century elitist republican assumptions remained strong, especially in the seaboard states, mandating that government be left to a natural aristocracy of virtuous, propertied gentlemen. Simultaneously, some of the looming shapes of nineteenth-century capitalism — chartered corporations, commercial banks, and other private institutions — presaged the consolidation of a new kind of moneyed aristocracy. And increasingly after the War of 1812, government policy seemed to combine the worst of both old and new, favoring the kinds of centralized, broad constructionist, top-down forms of economic development that many thought would aid men of established means while deepening inequalities among whites. Numerous events during and after the misnamed Era of Good Feelings — among them the neo-Federalist rulings of John Marshall's Supreme Court, the devastating effects of the panic of 1819, the launching of John Quincy Adams's and Henry Clay's American System — confirmed a growing impression that power was steadily flowing into the hands of a small, self-confident minority.

Proposed cures for this sickness included more democracy and a redirection of economic policy. In the older states, reformers fought to lower or abolish property requirements for voting and officeholding, and to equalize representation. A new generation of politicians broke with the old republican animus against mass political parties. Urban workers formed labor movements and demanded political reforms. Southerners sought low tariffs, greater respect for states' rights, and a return to strict constructionism. Westerners clamored for more and cheaper land and for relief from creditors, speculators, and bankers (above all, the hated Second Bank of the United States).

It has confounded some scholars that so much of this ferment eventually coalesced behind Andrew Jackson — a one-time land speculator, opponent of debtor relief, and fervent wartime nationalist. By the 1820s, however, Jackson's personal business experiences had long since altered his opinions about speculation and paper money, leaving him eternally suspicious of the credit system in general and banks in particular. His career as an Indian fighter and conqueror of the British made him a popular hero, especially among land-hungry settlers. His enthusiasm for nationalist programs had diminished after 1815, as foreign threats receded and economic difficulties multiplied. Above all, Jackson, with his own hardscrabble origins, epitomized contempt for the old republican elitism, with its hierarchical deference and its wariness of popular democracy.

After losing the "corrupt bargain" presidential election of 1824, Jackson expanded upon his political base in the lower and mid-South, pulling together many strands of disaffection from around the country. But in successfully challenging President John Quincy Adams in 1828, Jackson's supporters played mainly on his image as a manly warrior, framing the contest as one between Adams who could write and Jackson who could fight. Only after taking power did the Jacksonian Democracy refine its politics and ideology. Out of that self-definition came a fundamental shift in the terms of national political debate.

The Jacksonians' basic policy thrust, both in Washington and in the states, was to rid government of class biases and dismantle the top-down, credit-driven engines of the market revolution. The war on the Second Bank of the United States and subsequent hard-money initiatives set the tone — an unyielding effort to remove the hands of a few wealthy, unelected private bankers from the levers of the nation's economy. Under the Jacksonians, government-sponsored internal improvements generally fell into disfavor, on the grounds that they were unnecessary expansions of centralized power, beneficial mainly to men with connections. The Jacksonians defended rotation in office as a solvent to entrenched elitism. To aid hard-pressed farmers and planters, they pursued an unrelenting (some say unconstitutional) program of Indian removal, while backing cheap land prices and settlers' preemption rights.

Around these policies, Jacksonian leaders built a democratic ideology aimed primarily at voters who felt injured by or cut off from the market revolution. Updating the more democratic pieces of the republican legacy, they posited that no republic could long survive without a citizenry of economically independent men. Unfortunately, they claimed, that state of republican independence was exceedingly fragile. According to the Jacksonians, all of human history had involved a struggle between the few and the many, instigated by a greedy minority of wealth and privilege that hoped to exploit the vast majority. And this struggle, they declared, lay behind the major problems of the day, as the "associated wealth" of America sought to augment its domination.

The people's best weapons were equal rights and limited government — ensuring that the already wealthy and favored classes would not enrich themselves further by commandeering, enlarging, and then plundering public institutions. More broadly, the Jacksonians proclaimed a political culture predicated on white male equality, contrasting themselves with other self-styled reform movements. Nativism, for example, struck them as a hateful manifestation of elitist puritanism. Sabbatarians, temperance advocates, and other would-be moral uplifters, they insisted, should not impose righteousness on others. Beyond position-taking, the Jacksonians propounded a social vision in which any white man would have the chance to secure his economic independence, would be free to live as he saw fit, under a system of laws and representative government utterly cleansed of privilege.

As Jacksonian leaders developed these arguments, they roused a noisy opposition — some of it coming from elements of the coalition that originally elected Jackson president. Reactionary southern planters, centered in South Carolina, worried that the Jacksonians' egalitarianism might endanger their own prerogatives — and perhaps the institution of slavery — if southern nonslaveholders carried them too far. They also feared that Jackson, their supposed champion, lacked sufficient vigilance in protecting their interests — fears that provoked the nullification crisis in 1832–1833 and Jackson's crushing of extremist threats to federal authority. A broader southern opposition emerged in the late 1830s, mainly among wealthy planters alienated by the disastrous panic of 1837 and suspicious of Jackson's successor, the Yankee Martin Van Buren. In the rest of the country, meanwhile, the Jacksonian leadership's continuing hard-money, anti-bank campaigns offended more conservative men — the so-called Bank Democrats — who, whatever their displeasure with the Second Bank of the United States, did not want to see the entire paper money credit system dramatically curtailed.

The oppositionist core, however, came from a cross-class coalition, strongest in rapidly commercializing areas, that viewed the market revolution as the embodiment of civilized progress. Far from pitting the few against the many, oppositionists argued, carefully guided economic growth would provide more for everyone. Government encouragement — in the form of tariffs, internal improvements, a strong national bank, and aid to a wide range of benevolent institutions — was essential to that growth. Powerfully influenced by the evangelical Second Great Awakening, core oppositionists saw in moral reform not a threat to individual independence but an idealistic cooperative effort to relieve human degradation and further expand the store of national wealth. Eager to build up the country as it already existed, they were cool to territorial expansion. Angered by Jackson's large claims for presidential power and rotation in office, they charged that the Jacksonians had brought corruption and executive tyranny, not democracy. Above all, they believed that personal rectitude and industriousness, not alleged political inequalities, dictated men's failures or successes. The Jacksonians, with their spurious class rhetoric, menaced that natural harmony of interests between rich and poor which, if only left alone, would eventually bring widespread prosperity.

By 1840, both the Jacksonian Democracy and its opposite (now organized as the Whig party) had built formidable national followings and had turned politics into a debate over the market revolution itself. Yet less than a decade later, sectional contests linked to slavery promised to drown out that debate and fracture both major parties. In large measure, that turnabout derived from the racial exclusiveness of the Jacksonians' democratic vision.

The Jacksonian mainstream, so insistent on

the equality of white men, took racism for granted. To be sure, there were key radical exceptions — people like Frances Wright and Robert Dale Owen — who were drawn to the Democracy's cause. North and South, the democratic reforms achieved by plebeian whites — especially those respecting voting and representation — came at the direct expense of free blacks. Although informed by constitutional principles and genuine paternalist concern, the Jacksonian rationale for territorial expansion assumed that Indians (and, in some areas, Hispanics) were lesser peoples. As for slavery, the Jacksonians were determined, on both practical and ideological grounds, to keep the issue out of national affairs. Few mainstream Jacksonians had moral qualms about black enslavement or any desire to meddle with it where it existed. More important, they believed that the mounting antislavery agitation would distract attention from the artificial inequalities among white men and upset the party's delicate intersectional alliances. Deep down, many suspected that the slavery issue was but a smokescreen thrown up by disgruntled elitists looking to regain the initiative from the real people's cause.

Through the 1830s and 1840s, the mainstream Jacksonian leadership, correctly confident that their views matched those of the white majority, fought to keep the United States a democracy free from the slavery question — condemning abolitionists as fomenters of rebellion, curtailing abolitionist mail campaigns, enforcing the congressional gag rule that squelched debate on abolitionist petitions, while fending off the more extremist proslavery southerners. In all of this fighting, however, the Jacksonians also began to run afoul of their professions about white egalitarianism. Opposing antislavery was one thing; silencing the heretics with gag rules amounted to tampering with *white* people's equal rights. More important, Jacksonian proexpansionism — what one friendly periodical, the *Democratic Review,* boosted as "manifest destiny" — only intensified sectional rifts. Slaveholders, quite naturally, thought they were entitled to see as much new territory as legally possible opened up to slavery. But that prospect appalled northern whites who had hoped to settle in lily white areas, untroubled by that peculiar institution whose presence (they believed) would degrade the status of white free labor.

It would take until the 1850s before these contradictions fully unraveled the Jacksonian coalition. But as early as the mid-1840s, during the debates over Texas annexation, the Mexican War, and the Wilmot Proviso, sectional cleavages had grown ominous. The presidential candidacy of Martin Van Buren on the Free-Soil ticket in 1848 — a protest against growing southern power within the Democracy — amply symbolized northern Democratic alienation. Southern slaveholder Democrats, for their part, began to wonder if anything short of positive federal protection for slavery would spell doom for their class — and the white man's republic. In the middle remained a battered Jacksonian mainstream, ever hopeful that by raising the old issues, avoiding slavery, and resorting to the language of popular sovereignty, the party and the nation might be held together. Led by men like Stephen A. Douglas, these mainstream compromisers held sway into the mid-1850s, but at the cost of constant appeasement of southern concerns, further exacerbating sectional turmoil. Jacksonian Democracy was buried at Fort Sumter, but it had died many years earlier.

There was a grim, ironic justice to the Jacksonians' fate. Having tapped into the disaffection of the 1820s and 1830s and molded it into an effective national party, they advanced the democratization of American politics. By denouncing the moneyed aristocracy and proclaiming the common man, they also helped politicize American life, broadening electoral participation to include an overwhelming majority of the electorate. Yet this very politicization would ultimately prove the Jacksonian Democracy's undoing. Once the slavery issue entered the concerns of even a small portion of the electorate, it proved impossible to remove without trampling on some of the very egalitarian principles the Jacksonians were pledged to uphold.

None of this, however, should be a source of self-satisfaction to modern Americans. Although the Jacksonian Democracy died in the 1850s, it left a powerful legacy, entwining egalitarian aspirations and class justice with the presumptions of white supremacy. Over the decades after the Civil War, that legacy remained a bulwark of a new Democratic party, allying debt-ridden farmers and immigrant workers with the Solid South. The Second Reconstruction of the 1950s and 1960s forced Democrats to reckon with the party's past — only to see party schismatics and Republicans pick up the theme. And at the close of the twentieth century, the tragic mix of egalitarianism and racial prejudice so central to the Jacksonian Democracy still infected American politics, poisoning some of its best impulses with some of its worst.

Robert V. Remini, *Andrew Jackson and the Course of American Democracy, 1832–1845* (1984); Michael Paul Rogin, *Fathers and Children: Andrew Jackson and the Subjugation of the American Indian* (1975); Harry L. Watson, *Liberty and Power: The Politics of Jacksonian America* (1990).

SEAN WILENTZ

See also Democratic Party; Jackson, Andrew; Jeffersonian Democracy; Nullification Controversy; Republicanism; Whig Party.

JACKSON STATE INCIDENT

See Kent State Incident.

JACOBI, MARY PUTNAM

(1842–1906), physician, women's rights advocate, and medical educator. Of all the women physicians who achieved distinction in the nineteenth century, Jacobi was easily the most highly respected by her male colleagues. Indeed, her professional achievements were equaled by few of either sex. Her family supported her in her career decision in spite of their reservations about the field. Her father, the publisher George Palmer Putnam, considered medical science to be a "repulsive pursuit" but nevertheless took great pride in Mary's success. He begged only that she shun the company of "strong-minded women." "Be a lady from the dotting of your i's to the color of your ribbons," he wrote to her in 1863, "and if you must be a doctor and a philosopher, be an attractive and agreeable one."

Jacobi, who appreciated her parents' remarkable tolerance of her plans, spent many long years pursuing her goals. After receiving a degree in 1863 from the New York College of Pharmacy, she attended the Woman's Medical College of Pennsylvania, graduating a year later. She then studied clinical medicine at the New England Hospital for Women and Children. Dissatisfied with the level of training in the United States, she left for France, where after much perseverance, she was admitted to the Ecole de Médecine. She received her degree in 1871 (only the second woman to do so) and was awarded high honors and a bronze medal for her thesis.

Jacobi vacillated between research and clinical medicine before she returned to New York in 1871. She set up a practice and joined the Woman's Medical College of the New York Infirmary as professor of therapeutics and materia medica. Although she considered New York medicine inferior to that in Paris, Jacobi continued to develop as a first-rate physician and scientist. She was the first woman to be admitted to the New York Academy of Medicine and later chaired its section on neurology. She gained admission to numerous other medical societies as well and nurtured her sustained interest in research by publishing 9 books and over 120 medical articles. One of the books, *The Questions of Rest for Women during Menstruation,* won Harvard's esteemed Boylston Prize in 1876 in spite of its culturally charged subject.

In 1873 she married Dr. Abraham Jacobi, a German refugee who had already made a profound impact on New York medicine and is considered to be the father of the specialty of pediatrics. They formed a lively and stimulating intellectual and professional partnership.

A male member of the Pathological Society remembered Jacobi as a woman "whose knowledge of pathology was so thorough, whose range of the literature was so wide and whose criticism was so keen, fearless and just that in our discussions, we felt it prudent to shun the field of speculation to walk strictly in the path of demonstrated fact." She was especially supportive of women students, believing that high standards and rigorous training were essential if they were to find a place in the profession. Her status in the male professional world never deterred her from participating in the women's medical movement, and she remained active with the New York Infirmary and the Woman's Medical College of Pennsylvania in several capacities. One of her last scientific works was a detailed and remarkably insightful clinical account of the onset and progress of the meningeal tumor that led to her death in 1906.

Regina Morantz-Sanchez, *Sympathy and Science: Women Physicians in American Medicine* (1985); Rhoda Truax, *The Doctors Jacobi* (1952).

REGINA MORANTZ-SANCHEZ

See also Feminist Movement; Medicine.

JAMES, HENRY

(1843–1916), novelist, essayist, and critic. Born in New York City, James was the son of an eccentric Swedenborgian philosopher, who had inherited enough money to devote his life to his children's "sensuous education": the senior James hauled all five children back and forth between Europe and America in the 1850s, exposing them to ideas, books, music, theater, and art in several languages and cultures. It was an education, recalled Henry, in which "the literal played as small a part as it perhaps ever played in any. . . . we wholesomely breathed inconsistencies and ate and drank contradictions." Wholesome or not, these early years provided the future novelist with an acute sense of human inconsistencies and contradictions. His brother, the philosopher and psychologist William James, later wrote that Henry was really "a native of the James family, and has no other country."

Henry James published his first piece of writing (a critical essay in the *North American Review*) at the age of twenty-one; by the time he was thirty-eight he had moved to London, immersed himself in the works of Balzac, Thackeray, George Eliot, and Turgenev, published essays on literature, travel, and art, and made his mark as a fiction writer on both sides of the Atlantic with *Roderick Hudson* (1876), *The American* (1877), *The Europeans* (1878), *Daisy Miller* (1879), and *Washington Square* and *The Portrait of a Lady* (both 1881). He kept up this prodigious pace for the rest of his life. The works of his middle period, darker than the early books,

take up more specific political, social, and psychological questions; they include *The Bostonians* and *The Princess Casamassima* (both 1886), *The Aspern Papers* (1888), *The Spoils of Poynton* and *What Maisie Knew* (both 1897), *The Turn of the Screw* (1898), and *The Awkward Age* (1899). James tried writing plays in the 1890s, principally in hope of financial success, and suffered a prolonged depression after he was booed off the stage at the opening of his *Guy Domville* in 1895.

James's great theme, in his adult work, was the confrontation between two worlds, America and Europe: one fresh, innocent, eager, relatively simple, full of energy and curiosity; the other rich, dense, layered, knowing, infinitely subtle and complex. He wrote his finest and most difficult works on this international theme in the early 1900s — *The Wings of the Dove* (1902), *The Ambassadors* (1903), and *The Golden Bowl* (1904).

James's style grew more mannered and labyrinthine as he aged, as is evident not only in the late novels but in nonfiction works as well — *The American Scene* (1907, written after a long return visit to his native land) and two volumes of autobiography, *A Small Boy and Others* (1913), and *Notes of a Son and Brother* (1914). Beginning in 1907, he revised and wrote new prefaces to all the novels and tales he wanted to preserve and published them in the uniform New York Edition. He became a British citizen in 1915 and received the Order of Merit from King George V just before he died in 1916.

Leon Edel, *Henry James: A Life* (1985); Henry James, *A Small Boy and Others* (1913) and *Notes of a Son and Brother* (1914), in *Autobiography* (1956).

JEAN STROUSE

See also Expatriates and Exiles; James, William; Literature.

JAMES, WILLIAM

(1842–1910), psychologist, theologian, and philosopher. James's family background and his travels, wide interests, and friendliness combined with his scholarly work to make him internationally famous. His Irish immigrant grandfather, also named William, had made the family fortune in Albany, partly from the Erie Canal. His father, Henry, a man of leisure, was well known in American and English literary and theological circles, and his younger brother, Henry, was the famous novelist.

William himself was a polyglot cosmopolitan. He studied in Bonn, Boulogne, Geneva, London, and Paris. Throughout his life he often returned to Europe to visit friends, give lectures, receive honors from universities, or seek health cures. (He was slight, easily fatigued, and often ill; at twenty-eight, he suffered a prolonged, almost suicidal depression.)

James was also a polymath. His first serious ambition was to be a painter, but he turned from that to the study of chemistry, anatomy, and physiology, receiving an M.D. at age twenty-seven. He went up the Amazon with Louis Agassiz in 1865 to collect zoological specimens. As a Harvard professor, he started by teaching physiology and then, in turn, anatomy, psychology, and philosophy. Other strong interests included religion, psychic research, self-help psychotherapy, and education.

Principles of Psychology (1890), ten years in the writing, was his magnum opus. Written in his typical concrete, humorous, colloquial, and metaphoric style, it was interesting to both students and professionals. It became the most widely used text in the field and is still by far the best summary of the science of psychology at that time. *The Varieties of Religious Experience* (1902) became and remains his most popular book. It is filled with case studies of people whose lives were changed by mystical experiences. Although his intent was scientific, it still brings to many readers a confirmation of their own religious faith. James himself was noncommittal about mystical phenomena, but the skepticism of orthodox scientists regarding the subject aroused his sympathy. He was a founder of the American Society for Psychical Research and president of the English society.

Pragmatism (1907) was James's major contribution to philosophy. He viewed pragmatism as a means of moderating the conflicts between those with religious and those with scientific values. Pragmatism stresses the importance of evaluating ideas not by their origins but by their consequences. James did not mean by this worldly success, as is often assumed, but rather psychological, artistic, and moral consequences. Thus, for example, in the argument over abortion, pragmatism would advocate looking away from the origins of the prolife and prochoice principles and considering the actual consequences of enacting them into law.

Some thought that James had an excessive sympathy for lonely souls and lost causes. His earnestness, however, was softened by his love of fun and absence of self-righteousness. And the attention, affection, and recognition he lavished on others was repaid in kind by his friends in the arts and sciences. John Dewey called him "the greatest of American psychologists, a case of James first and no second"; Bertrand Russell considered him "the most widely known of contemporary philosophers"; and the *Boston Evening Transcript* said he was "the greatest of contemporary Americans."

William James, *The Letters of William James,* edited by his son Henry James (1920); R. B. Perry, *The Thought and Character of William James* (1954).

HENRY CLAY SMITH

See also James, Henry.

JAPANESE-AMERICAN RELOCATION

The relocation of thousands of Japanese-Americans into internment camps during World War II marked an ignoble chapter in American history. In 1941 when the Japanese bombed Pearl Harbor, there were 127,000 persons of Japanese ancestry in America, the majority residing on the West Coast. For years they had been denied the right to vote or own land. After Pearl Harbor, rumors spread that a Japanese plot to sabotage the American war effort was afoot. In early 1942, the Roosevelt administration was pressured to remove Japanese-Americans from the West Coast by agricultural interests seeking to eliminate Japanese competition, a public fearing sabotage, and politicians hoping to gain by aligning against this unpopular group.

In February 1942, the federal government

forced all Japanese-Americans regardless of loyalty or citizenship to evacuate the West Coast, which was perceived as a vulnerable military area. To justify this move against Americans only of Japanese — not German or Italian — descent, the government claimed that racial ties inclined the Japanese to disloyalty. When neighboring states resisted the incoming refugees, the government established ten internment camps in California, Idaho, Utah, Arizona, Wyoming, Colorado, and Arkansas to receive them. By September, 100,000 people had been moved. The camps resembled prisons, with cramped quarters, communal facilities, and poor food. Generational conflict beset the internees: older Issei (immigrants) were deprived of their traditional respect when their children, the Nisei (American-born), were alone permitted authority positions within the camps. Ultimately, 5,766 Nisei renounced their American citizenship. When internees were given the opportunity to leave the camps by joining the U.S. Army, only 1,200 did so.

The U.S. Supreme Court upheld the government's position in two cases challenging the relocation, *Hirabayashi* v. *United States* and *Korematsu* v. *United States*. Only after his reelection in 1944 did Franklin D. Roosevelt finally rescind the evacuation order, and by the end of 1945 the camps were closed. In 1968, the Japanese-Americans were reimbursed for property they had lost, and in 1988, Congress enacted legislation awarding restitution payments of twenty thousand dollars each to the 60,000 surviving internees.

See also World War II.

JAPAN-U.S. RELATIONS

See Asia-U.S. Relations.

JAY, JOHN

(1745–1829), member of the Continental Congress, diplomat, and first chief justice, U.S. Supreme Court. The descendant of French Protestant refugees who came to New York in the late seventeenth century, Jay began a distinguished career in national politics with his election to the First Continental Congress in 1774. A lawyer by training and a cautious politician by temperament, Jay was one of a group of moderate delegates who resisted independence until all hopes for reconciliation with Britain were gone. In the New York provincial convention in 1777, Jay was the principal author of a state constitution that limited legislative domination of government far more effectively than the charters that had just been written in other states.

In 1778 Jay was elected president of Congress. In this capacity he became deeply involved in a bitter dispute about foreign policy that disrupted Congress through much of 1779. In the autumn of that year, he accepted appointment as the American minister to Spain, which had entered the war against Britain as an ally of France but not the United States. Jay's more notable accomplishment came when he joined the American peace commission. In the crucial negotiations of 1782, he and John Adams prevailed on Benjamin Franklin to ignore their formal instructions from Congress and to seek the best terms they could obtain from Britain without relying on guidance from France.

Jay returned to America in 1784 to learn that Congress had appointed him to the position of secretary of foreign affairs. His most important actions again involved relations with Spain. In 1786 Jay asked Congress to allow him to surrender American claims to the free navigation of the Mississippi — which Spain controlled from New Orleans — in exchange for a satisfactory commercial treaty. This request met intense opposition from the southern states and precipitated a dispute within Congress that led many national leaders to wonder about the durability of the American union.

Although not a member of the Constitutional Convention of 1787, Jay strongly supported ratification of the Constitution and would have contributed far more than the five essays he wrote for *The Federalist* had ill health not sapped his strength.

President George Washington nominated Jay to be the first chief justice of the Supreme Court. Although the Court reached several notable decisions under his leadership, it was again as a diplomat that he exerted his greatest influence. In 1795 he was sent as special envoy to Great Britain to resolve the crisis that had erupted in 1794 when the Royal Navy seized hundreds of American merchantmen carrying contraband from the French West Indies. The treaty Jay negotiated resolved many of the outstanding issues of Anglo-American relations, but by the standards of those who opposed the administration's foreign policy, it failed to secure adequate British recognition of American neutral rights. The public controversy over Jay's Treaty was the single most important factor leading to full-scale political competition between the Federalist and Democratic-Republican parties.

Jay resigned from the Supreme Court after his return to America. After serving two terms as governor of New York, he retired from politics and sought a deeper consolation in religion. He died in 1829, one of the last of the revolutionary patriarchs.

Richard B. Morris, *John Jay: The Nation and the Court* (1967); Richard B. Morris, *The Peacemakers: The Great Powers and American Independence* (1965).

JACK N. RAKOVE

See also Federalist Papers; Jay's Treaty; Paris, Treaty of (1783); Ratification of the Constitution; Revolution.

JAY'S TREATY

This pact between the United States and Great Britain was negotiated in London by Chief Justice John Jay in 1795. Hoping to ease tensions caused by British seizures of American ships and restrictions on trade with the British West Indies, President George Washington sent Jay to England to seek the withdrawal of British troops from American territory in the West, the payment of reparations to American shippers, compensation for slaves abducted during the Revolution, and the right to trade freely with the British West Indies.

Jay proved to be a poor negotiator. Great Britain agreed to evacuate the western posts and pay reparations to American merchants. But though it opened the West Indies to American vessels, it did so under extremely restrictive terms. More important, Jay agreed to a clause giving up the right of neutral ships to trade freely with belligerents in wartime. He also accepted the British Rule of 1756, which held that in times of war, neutrals could not trade with ports closed to them in peacetime by mercantilistic regulations. Moreover, the treaty committed the United States to pay outstanding prerevolutionary debts to British merchants — although that issue was still being contested in American courts.

Despite widespread feeling that the treaty was humiliating to the United States, President Washington signed it and persuaded the Senate to ratify it on the ground that further conflict with England was not in the public interest.

See also Great Britain–U.S. Relations.

JAZZ

Jazz is a style of African-American music that developed in the southern United States around the turn of the twentieth century. Its roots lie in other forms of post-Reconstruction vernacular American music: ragtime, fife and drum bands, stringbands, and spirituals. Although New Orleans became the undisputed focal point for early jazz, this music probably emerged simultaneously in nearby cities such as Mobile, Alabama.

The pioneering jazz groups often consisted of several trumpets, saxophones, and even string instruments supported by a deeper brass bass, piano, and percussion. The early jazz musicians such as Ferdinand "Jelly Roll" Morton (piano) and Charles "Buddy" Bolden (cornet) performed at functions as diverse as house parties and funerals. Many of them also had regular jobs performing at the clubs of the notorious Storyville district where gambling, prostitutes, and drugs were readily available.

Within twenty years this syncopated, polyphonic music had spread far beyond its birthplace. Traveling musicians transported jazz across the South and north to Indianapolis, St. Louis, Chicago, and other river cities. By the early 1920s seminal figures such as trumpeters

Joe "King" Oliver and Louis Armstrong had migrated from New Orleans to Chicago. Their music was captured on the early "race records," which were marketed to a black audience, and by the late 1920s jazz could be heard anywhere in the United States. The Gennet recordings by King Oliver's Creole Jazz Band and the OKeh sessions of Louis Armstrong's Hot Five and Hot Seven are acknowledged masterpieces of early jazz. These and similar bands often accompanied the "classic" blues singers like Gertrude "Ma" Rainey, Bessie Smith, and Ida Cox on their live stage shows and recordings.

In 1927 Edward "Duke" Ellington moved from Washington, D.C., to New York City and shortly thereafter began his famous stand at Harlem's Cotton Club. He quickly emerged as a major innovator in jazz, and his large ensembles of twelve to fourteen pieces foreshadowed the swing craze of the middle 1930s. Ellington was distinguished by his ability to compose creative pieces, such as "East St. Louis Toodle-oo," "Black and Tan Fantasy," and "Take the A Train," with individual members of his orchestra in mind. Many of these compositions have become jazz standards that are performed all over the world. Other important orchestras, including those organized by Fletcher Henderson and Cab Calloway, emerged in the light of Ellington's work and performed in the sophisticated clubs of northern cities. From the Southwest came the rowdier, bluesier territory bands of Benny Moten and Count Basie.

In the middle 1930s jazz began to reach the masses as a result of the swing craze that made the Casa Loma Orchestra and the bands of Glenn Miller and Jimmy Dorsey household favorites. These white bands reduced the music of the more innovative black bandleaders to a formula that appealed to millions because of its swinging 4/4 beat, well-blended saxophone sections, and pleasant singers. The popularity of swing helped boost the careers of black bandleaders, too, but it also led to a creative slump that disheartened many of the musicians who were tiring of swing's predictability.

During the early 1940s a new style of jazz, called bop, was fermenting in the New York City clubs, and by the close of World War II many of the younger black musicians had embraced its vitality. This jazz was rhythmically vigorous and explored new melodic possibilities based on familiar harmonic changes. Small ensembles came back into vogue, led by young rebels like Charlie Parker (alto sax), Dizzy Gillespie (trumpet), and Thelonious Monk (piano) who had fled the stifling big bands. Singers such as Ella Fitzgerald, Sarah Vaughan, Betty Carter, and Eddie Jefferson soon began emulating the new ideas of the bebop stylists. They were also notable for their instrumental-like vocal phrasing. By the late 1940s even veteran swing artists had begun to accept bop as legitimate music, though it also triggered a revival of New Orleans jazz that led to renewed interest in veterans like clarinetist George Lewis and trombone-playing Kid Ory.

During the 1950s jazz all but slipped out of the commercial mainstream. Most of the big bands folded for lack of work, and bop evolved into new permutations. First came the cool school, a relaxed approach to small-group improvisation that gained favor on the West Coast. Gerry Mulligan (baritone sax) and Dave Brubeck (piano) are two of the best-known practitioners. In the late 1950s a fusion of jazz and classical music known as third stream, pioneered by composer and French horn player Gunther Schuller and the Modern Jazz Quartet, carved out a small following but never gained wide popularity. Finally, there was hard bop or soul jazz featuring short, concise blues themes. Art Blakey's Jazz Messengers and the Horace Silver Quintet emerged at the forefront of hard bop.

Another approach began to be heard in the very late 1950s in the groups fronted by Miles Davis (trumpet), Ornette Coleman (saxophone, trumpet, and violin), and John Coltrane (saxophone). Some of the music's standard notions of harmony and melodic improvisations were downplayed in favor of sound textures and modes.

Within six years both the United States and jazz were embracing radical new ideas, including black nationalism and protesting American military action in Vietnam. Saxophone players Archie Shepp, Pharoah Sanders, and Sam Rivers were playing fierce, sometimes angry music that wailed and lamented. Instead of the predictable format of small groups (theme, solos, theme), free jazz emphasized group improvisation, lengthy solos, and static harmonic development.

During the 1970s and early 1980s jazz and rock combined in a new fusion. Weather Report, Herbie Hancock's Headhunters, and Chick Corea's band spearheaded this movement toward an expanded audience. Electric pianos and guitars playing fast and long unison lines dominated the sound. The audience for the music increased as rock enthusiasts came to appreciate its sound and the improvisational skill it required.

Most recently the trend in jazz has been toward a neoclassical approach. Trumpeter Wynton Marsalis and other musicians in their twenties and thirties have moved back to the more harmonically predictable and sweetly melodic songs of Cole Porter, Jerome Kern, Irving Berlin, and the Gershwin brothers.

Mark Gridley, *Jazz Styles* (1985); Martin Williams, *Jazz in Its Own Time* (1989).

KIP LORNELL

See also Armstrong, Louis; Baker, Josephine; Berlin, Irving; Ellington, Duke; Fitzgerald, Ella; Gershwin, George; Goodman, Benny; Music; Porter, Cole; Sinatra, Frank.

JEFFERSON, THOMAS

(1743–1826), intellectual, statesman, and third president of the United States. Although Jefferson served as governor of Virginia, minister to France, secretary of state, vice president, and president, he is remembered in history less for the offices he held than for what he stood for: his belief in the natural rights of man as he expressed them in the Declaration of Independence and his faith in the people's ability to govern themselves. He left an impact on his times equaled by few others in American history. Introduced to the ideas of the Enlightenment as a student at the College of William and Mary, Jefferson displayed throughout his life an optimistic faith in the power of reason to regulate human affairs.

As a young member of the Virginia House of Burgesses, Jefferson questioned British colonial policies and was an early advocate of American rights. His forceful pamphlet *A Summary View of the Rights of British America* (1774) gained him the reputation that placed him on the committee of the Continental Congress charged with drafting the Declaration of Independence. As its principal author, Jefferson gave eloquent expression to the principles of the natural rights of man, among which, he affirmed, was self-government.

Jefferson's intellectual prowess led some political opponents to dismiss him as a visionary, but he was remarkably successful in politics. As leader of the opposition to the Federalist policies of Alexander Hamilton and John Adams, Jefferson was put forward by his supporters to run against Adams in the election of 1796 to succeed George Washington as president. He lost that contest but four years later defeated Adams to preside over the first transfer of political power from one party to another in the history of the young Republic. In his inaugural address in 1801, he set the ship of state on a republican course based on faith in majority rule, simplicity and frugality in government, limited central authority, and protection of civil liberties and minority rights. Alexis de Tocqueville, visiting America five years after Jefferson's death, declared Jefferson to be "the greatest democrat whom the democracy of America has as yet produced."

On the eve of his inauguration as vice president in 1797, Jefferson had been elected president of the American Philosophical Society, a post he retained until 1815. In many ways he found more pleasure in holding that office than in being president of the United States. A boundless intellectual curiosity fueled his interests in science and natural history, the classics, music, and the arts. He once reflected: "Nature intended me for the tranquil pursuits of science, by rendering them my supreme delight. But the enormities of the times in which I have lived have forced me to take a part in resisting them, and to commit myself on the boisterous ocean of political passions."

Jefferson translated his intellectual pursuits into action. His study of natural law and political thought informed his commitment to republican government. His devotion to science inspired numerous agricultural pursuits. His interest in architecture and the arts was manifest in the design of his home at Monticello. His concern about education led to proposals for public education in his state and to the founding of the University of Virginia, for which he was champion, architect, and academic planner.

The most versatile intellectual to occupy the presidential office, Jefferson was a complex man. He opposed an aristocracy and slavery, yet he enjoyed a life of privilege and owned slaves, optimistically hoping that the next generation would end that violation of natural law.

Jefferson's sense of priorities was strikingly revealed when he instructed that his tombstone be inscribed only with the words that he was the author of the Declaration of Independence and the Statute of Virginia for Religious Freedom, and the father of the University of Virginia.

Noble E. Cunningham, Jr., *In Pursuit of Reason: The Life of Thomas Jefferson* (1987); Merrill D. Peterson, *Thomas Jefferson and the New Nation: A Biography* (1970).

NOBLE E. CUNNINGHAM, JR.

See also Constitution; Declaration of Independence; Deism; Elections: 1796, 1800, 1804; Jeffersonian Democracy; Republicanism; Revolution; Virginia and Kentucky Resolutions. *For events during Jefferson's administration, see* Barbary Wars; Embargo Act of 1807; Impressment Controversy; Lewis and Clark Expedition; Louisiana Purchase; *Marbury* v. *Madison.*

JEFFERSONIAN DEMOCRACY

Looking back on the election of 1800, Thomas Jefferson described it as being "as real a revolution in the principles of our government as that of 1776 was in its form; not effected indeed by the sword, as that, but by the rational and peaceable instrument of reform, the suffrage of the people." Jefferson saw his election as reversing an earlier trend away from republicanism. The departure from true republican principles, as he judged it, had begun with the economic policies of Alexander Hamilton favoring financial and manufacturing interests and the strengthening

of the national government at the expense of the states. During John Adams's presidency, Jefferson was further alarmed by the threats to civil liberties posed by the Alien and Sedition Laws restricting freedom of speech, assembly, and the press. Under the administrations of both George Washington and Adams, Jefferson was also concerned that the rituals of the presidency resembled too closely the monarchical models of Europe, which he detested.

By 1800 Jefferson was convinced that the government must be put on a more republican tack if the new Republic were to succeed, and he directed his efforts in the election of 1800 toward that end. In a nation of farmers, Jefferson's belief in the virtues of an agrarian republic of independent farmers won wide support. The Republicans also drew support from artisans and workers in towns and cities, where Jefferson's opposition to an aristocracy of privilege gained him the image of a man of the people. The Jeffersonian Republicans found little support among the banking, manufacturing, and commercial interests attracted to Hamilton's vision of an industrial America. As a slaveholder who nevertheless opposed the institution of slavery, Jefferson drew support from both slaveholders and opponents of slavery; the Jeffersonian Republicans, however, did not include emancipation in their democratic agenda.

The philosophical roots of Jeffersonian Democracy are to be found in the ideas of the Enlightenment and in natural law that Jefferson expounded in the Declaration of Independence. In an address in 1790, he reiterated his faith in "the sufficiency of human reason for the care of human affairs" and stressed that "the will of the majority, the Natural law of every society, is the only sure guardian of the rights of man." This faith in the people was basic to the creed he enunciated in the election of 1800 and implemented as president. He wished to keep the government close to the people. "I am not for transferring all the powers of the States to the general government, and all those of that government to the Executive branch," he wrote at a time when a Federalist Congress had given the president extraordinary power over aliens. With civil liberties threatened by the Alien and Sedition Acts,

Jefferson reaffirmed his commitment to the Bill of Rights. In a period of rising military expenditures and mounting debt, he promised a government "rigorously frugal and simple," reducing the army and navy and applying the savings to discharging the national debt. The desire to decrease the army also reflected a republican fear of standing armies that had roots in radical English thought.

Jefferson restated these principles in his inaugural address on March 4, 1801. That speech provides the best and most succinct statement of Jeffersonian Democracy. Reaffirming his commitment to an "absolute acquiescence in the decisions of the majority" as a vital principle of republicanism, Jefferson added the "sacred principle that though the will of the majority is in all cases to prevail, that will, to be rightful, must be reasonable; that the minority possess their equal rights, which equal laws must protect, and to violate would be oppression." In responding to Federalists' efforts to suppress minority opinions, Jefferson more clearly defined a basic tenet of American democracy.

Intermingling general principles and specific policies, Jefferson promised "equal and exact justice to all men, of whatever state or persuasion, religious or political," and pledged a vigilant protection of civil liberties. He also vowed to protect the rights of states while preserving the general government in its whole constitutional vigor. The new president declared that he favored reliance on a well-disciplined militia for defense, the supremacy of civil over military authority, economy in public expenditures, the payment of debts, and the encouragement of agriculture and of commerce as its "handmaid." Though an agrarian republic was Jefferson's ideal, he recognized the necessity of commerce, and as president he was committed to its protection.

President Jefferson promptly initiated simplicity and frugality in government. With a Republican majority in Congress, government expenditures were reduced, taxes cut, and progress made in paying off the national debt. The Republicans also reduced the army and the navy and the diplomatic establishment abroad. Altered circumstances, however, led to the modification of many of these policies before the end of his second term. Renewed war in Europe and interference with American commerce led to the imposition of an embargo and increased military expenditures. The purchase of Louisiana required alterations in the schedule to pay off the national debt and also posed a challenge to his strict construction of the Constitution. Initially inclined to push for a constitutional amendment, he yielded to the opinion of advisers that the treaty-making power provided adequate constitutional grounds. But strict construction remained a tenet of Jeffersonian Democracy.

Jefferson reduced the ceremonial role of the presidency that had developed under Washington and Adams. Setting a more democratic tone for the executive, he began by walking to his inauguration. His dress was that of an ordinary citizen, "without any distinctive badge of office," one reporter noted. That was a sharp contrast to Washington and Adams, who had dressed elegantly and worn swords at their inaugurations. Instead of appearing in person to deliver an annual address to Congress, as had been the practice of Washington and Adams, Jefferson sent a written message to be read by a clerk. He also eliminated formal presidential receptions, or levees, which his predecessors had held, and he ignored the formal European rules of diplomatic etiquette by receiving foreign diplomats informally and offering no seating by rank at diplomatic dinners.

Despite earlier expressions of concern about executive power, Jefferson exerted strong presidential leadership, and with the enactment of an embargo in 1807 the federal government became more intrusive than Jeffersonian principles envisioned. But the embargo was repealed before Jefferson left office, and when he retired from political life, he left a legacy of faith in the people and a widening popular participation that continued to shape the development of American democracy.

Lance Banning, *The Jeffersonian Persuasion: Evolution of Party Ideology* (1978); Noble E. Cunningham, Jr., *The Process of Government under Jefferson* (1978).

NOBLE E. CUNNINGHAM, JR.

See also Alien and Sedition Acts; Bill of Rights; Jefferson, Thomas; Republicanism.

JEWS

The 6 million Americans of Jewish origin, 2.5 percent of the population, are the descendants of immigrants who arrived in waves from different parts of Europe from colonial times to the present. Despite dissimilar cultural backgrounds and political experiences in their countries of origin, Jews share a sense of being one people. They possess a past that extends back to biblical times, and a common religion, Judaism, that sanctifies that history. In addition, the experience of being a persecuted minority in a hostile world has left an indelible mark on Jewish consciousness.

Immigration and Settlement

The first Jews arrived on American shores in 1654. They had escaped from the Dutch settlement of Recife, in Brazil, following its conquest by the Portuguese, and found a haven in New Amsterdam. (They were descendants of Jews expelled from Spain and Portugal in the late fifteenth century.) By 1800, two thousand Jews, largely merchants, lived in port cities from New York to Savannah, Georgia.

In the 1830s, a large influx of Jews began arriving from German-speaking central Europe. They came as a result of anti-Jewish legislation and the disruption of the peasant economy. Because the United States was expanding westward, many Jews became peddlers and prospered by serving as links between the larger cities and rural areas. In a relatively short time, large numbers of German Jews had acquired the means to become small merchants. The more successful became wholesalers and bankers. A few gained prominence by establishing department stores or manufacturing ready-made clothing.

By 1880 there were 250,000 Jews in America, and over the next forty years, 2.5 million more arrived, nearly all from eastern Europe. This mass exodus was the result of several factors: rapid industrialization, which displaced many Jewish artisans and petty merchants; an enormous growth in the Jewish population, which exacerbated economic conditions; harsh discriminatory laws imposed by the czarist government; and the sporadic outbreak of pogroms. The great majority of these immigrants — 60 percent of whom were skilled workers — settled in the large cities of the East and Midwest, especially in places where the clothing industry was important. New York, the largest center of the industry, contained 45 percent of the nearly 3.5 million Jews in the United States in 1920, forming a quarter of the city's population.

The immigration restriction laws of 1924 severely limited Jewish immigration for some years, but from 1935 to 1941, about 150,000 refugees from Nazi Germany entered the country. Of middle-class background, often professionals, these immigrants included scores of internationally famous scientists, social scientists, and artists. The most distinguished among them was the Nobel laureate in physics, Albert Einstein. Most of the refugees settled in New York, Chicago, and Los Angeles.

During the years following the end of World War II, a similar number, survivors of the Holocaust, arrived. A remnant of the Jewish communities of Europe, they were assisted by relatives and American Jewish welfare agencies to begin life anew. From the 1960s to the 1990s, about 350,000 Jews came from Hungary, Israel, the Soviet Union, South Africa, and Iran because of political turmoil or economic distress.

Religious, Cultural, and Communal Life

Like all immigrants, the Jews were profoundly influenced by the culture of their new home. Those of German origin began reforming their synagogue services to comply with American Protestant norms in the 1850s. They deviated from Orthodox Judaism by replacing Hebrew prayers with English translations, removing the prohibition of men and women sitting together, allowing an organ to be used during services, and changing the rabbinical function from the traditional role of religious judge to preacher. Rabbis influenced by German Reform Judaism began arriving in America about this time and provided spiritual direction. They defined American Judaism as dedicated to bringing the universal prophetic ideals of social justice and moral behavior to the world. They rejected the notion that Jews were a people in exile waiting to return to the ancient homeland.

By the 1880s, Jews of German origin, most of whom belonged to Reformed temples and were quite affluent, created an impressive network of philanthropic and cultural institutions — Young Men's Hebrew Associations, agencies to aid the Jewish poor, and fraternal orders like B'nai B'rith, the largest of its kind. These institutions helped meet the needs of the impoverished immigrants from eastern Europe.

The East European Jewish immigrants, who crowded into the poorer neighborhoods of the big cities around the turn of the century, created their own culture in the Yiddish language. Eleven Yiddish dailies were published in America in 1916. Dozens of literary and political weeklies, Yiddish theaters (seven in New York alone in 1918), lectures on political and cultural topics, and a stream of belles lettres of high quality were expressions of a vital culture that lasted for a generation and left behind a rich legacy. The immigrants also formed a vast network of mutual aid societies and Orthodox congregations based on town of origin. Composing another part of the community were the garment industry trade unions organized and led by Jewish radicals and containing a majority of Jewish workers well into the 1920s. Socialism had many followers. Zionism — the belief that rebuilding Palestine as a Jewish state was necessary as a haven for persecuted Jews and as a guarantee of ethnic cultural survival — became an influential movement only after World War I.

As these Jews rose economically and socially, which they did with relative speed, they moved to better neighborhoods and underwent a process of rapid acculturation. The second generation saw education as the path to upward mobility. Many entered the professions of teaching, law, medicine, dentistry, and accounting, but the majority achieved middle-class status through commerce. This process of acculturation affected the Jewish community in a number of ways. Conservative Judaism, which maintained only selected traditional practices, accommodated itself to both the social and the religious needs of its middle-class members and grew quickly. Modern Orthodoxy made only minor modifications in religious customs and grew at a slower pace. Jewish community centers provided recreational, cultural, and social activities and attracted Jews with no synagogue affiliation. To meet communal needs and to aid Jews in distress in Europe, federations of Jewish philanthropies were created in nearly every Jewish community. They coordinated communal policy and undertook annual campaigns to raise funds for many activities, including Zionist colonization work in Palestine. Another concern that elicited much communal activity was the discrimination American Jews encountered in higher education, employment, and housing.

After World War II, American Jewry found itself the largest, most affluent, and most politically influential Jewish community in the world. Almost without exception, American Jews joined the efforts to alleviate the plight of those who had survived the Holocaust by supporting the establishment of a Jewish state in Palestine as a home for them. They lobbied vigorously for government support for the establishment of a Jewish state and then for economic and military assistance to Israel. American Jews also contributed large sums of money to support the resettlement of refugees there. Financial and political support for Israel, which still serves as an asylum for Jews from Europe and Muslim countries, continues to be of paramount concern to American Jews.

In their political preference, most Jews, beginning with the New Deal, have supported the liberal wing of the Democratic party. They have favored strong social welfare, civil rights and equal opportunity legislation, strict separation of church and state, and an activist foreign policy.

The postwar period also witnessed strong cultural advances among American Jews. The numbers receiving a college education were extraordinarily high. Novelists of Jewish origin — like Norman Mailer, Philip Roth, and Bernard Malamud — have been widely acclaimed. Saul Bellow and Isaac Bashevis Singer each won the Nobel Prize in literature. The social integration of Jews into American society was indicated by the rate of intermarriage, which rose from about 6 percent in 1950 to over 30 percent in 1990. For Jews committed to maintaining Jewish group identity, the rising incidence of intermarriage became a matter of much concern. The various denominations have been striving to deepen the spiritual content of Jewish ethnic identity, with Jewish religious education more extensive than ever. And Jewish studies have been introduced at hundreds of Jewish and secular colleges and universities.

America's Jews at the end of the century have retained their sense of community through their shared group identity, their concern for Israel's future, the still painful memories of the Holocaust, and the ever-present need to guard against anti-Jewish discrimination.

Irving Howe, *The World of Our Fathers* (1976); Abraham J. Karp, *Haven and Home: A History of the Jews in America* (1985).

ARTHUR A. GOREN

See also Holocaust, American Response to the; Literature; Middle East–U.S. Relations; Religion.

JIM CROW LAWS

See Segregation.

JOHN BIRCH SOCIETY

The John Birch Society, an organization of the radical Right, was established in Indianapolis in 1958 to combat what was perceived to be the infiltration of communism into American life. Its founder, Robert H. W. Welch, a Massachusetts businessman, named the society after a Baptist missionary who had been killed by Chinese Communists in 1945. Starting with only eleven members, the John Birch Society grew rapidly, drawing considerable support from rich conservatives; by the early 1960s it had an estimated annual income of $5 million and a membership of 60,000 to 100,000. John Birchers placed their principal emphasis on the extent to which communism had established control over the U.S. government; among those they accused of being

"dedicated, conscious agents of the Communist conspiracy" were President Dwight D. Eisenhower, CIA director Allen Dulles, and Chief Justice Earl Warren. The society has produced an extensive list of publications, offered cash prizes for college essays on topics like the impeachment of Warren, and maintained that the United States must become as conspiratorial as the communists in order to combat their subversion of American society.

See also Anticommunism.

JOHNS, JASPER

(1930–   ), painter and sculptor. A celebrated member of the generation succeeding the artists who established the abstract expressionist New York school, Johns, together with Robert Rauschenberg, injected a note of defiant irony concerning the nature of painting. After a stint in the U.S. Army, Johns settled in New York in 1952 where he soon met Rauschenberg. Shortly after, Johns began producing blunt encaustic paintings simulating flags, targets, numbers, and letter types with the express intention of challenging the assumptions of the older and more romantic abstract expressionists. He declared that such objects as flags, targets, and maps were things the mind already knows and as such, gave him room to work on other levels. By 1958, when he had his first one-man exhibition at the Leo Castelli Gallery, Johns had elaborated his emphasis on the conundrums presented by real things known to the mind when they are presented in the unreal contexts of painting, and he had begun to make three-dimensional effigies of such objects as light bulbs and flashlights.

Johns's views were undoubtedly influenced by the iconoclasm of the earlier dada movement and particularly by his idol, Marcel Duchamp, whom he sought out in 1960. After their initial meeting, Johns made a gesture worthy of Duchamp when he cast two beer cans in bronze and then painted them to look precisely like ordinary beer cans. This triple entendre clearly indicated how deeply Johns was engaged in the criticism of orthodox aesthetics, particularly the aesthetics of gestural painting, which he often parodied. His close friendship with Rauschenberg and his work with the composer John Cage and the dancer Merce Cunningham stimulated his desire to challenge the lofty views of the abstract expressionists. He deliberately raised questions concerning the meaning of painting by basing his own on direct experiences with the vernacular vocabulary of daily life (using objects such as cups, spoons, rulers, and maps as subjects) and the most banal encounters with literature and news. His viewers were meant to be galvanized into questioning the very nature of painting itself. A hint of his purpose occurs in his admiring assessment of Duchamp who, he said, had moved art past retinal boundaries "into a field where language, thought and vision act upon one another."

In Johns's paintings, sculptures, and prints of recent years, there are tantalizing allusions in fragments of words, in mysterious titles, and in a kind of subtext of literal images inserted in abstract fields. His use of the cross-hatch, for instance, with its venerable history as the draftsman's means of indicating shadow and depth, is basically ironic, yet another thrust at convention, undermining its real purpose. Johns's interest in paradox, endless ambiguity, and subversion of tradition has been expressed in both small works and vast, mural-like paintings, which, in their perplexing deviations from the established modes of identifying painting and its subjects, have brought him the attention and admiration of connoisseurs throughout the world. The "other levels" on which he professes to work are still shrouded in mystery, piquing curiosity and commentary, as once Duchamp's work had done.

Michael Crichton, *Jasper Johns* (1977); Irving Sandler, *The New York School: The Painters and Sculptors of the Fifties* (1978).

DORE ASHTON

See also Painting and Sculpture.

JOHNSON, ANDREW

(1808–1875), seventeenth president of the United States. Johnson, the only president ever to be impeached, was born in Raleigh, North Carolina, into very moderate circumstances. Apprenticed to a tailor as a youth, he ran away from his employer and settled in Greeneville, Tennessee, where he established himself as a tailor.

Johnson soon turned to politics, rising to governor and U.S. senator. He became a spokesman for the Jacksonian Democrats of his state, favoring populist measures, particularly a homestead bill. In 1860–1861, he remained loyal to the Union, the only senator from a seceding state to do so, and in 1862, Abraham Lincoln appointed him military governor of Tennessee.

In 1864 Johnson was elected vice president. Inaugurated as president after Lincoln's assassination, he announced his hatred for "traitors," but in reality embraced a lenient Reconstruction policy. A firm believer in states' rights, he held that blacks were innately inferior. Consequently, he asserted that the southern states had never left the Union and ought to be restored quickly, without regard to the safety of the freedmen. This was the rationale for his granting amnesty to all but a few ex-Confederates and appointing provisional governors charged with calling on white voters to reestablish loyal governments. The resulting administrations enacted Black Codes that virtually remanded the freedmen to slavery.

Congress, however, refused to seat the newly elected southern members and broke with the president when he vetoed the Freedmen's Bureau and civil rights bills and opposed the Fourteenth Amendment. His attempt to create a new conservative party and his "swing around the circle," a national tour during which he delivered unbecoming harangues, contributed to the defeat of his supporters in the 1866 midterm elections. Congress then curtailed his powers by passing the Tenure of Office Act to protect radical appointees and a measure to restrict his authority as commander in chief of the army. His objections proved unavailing, as was his bitter opposition to the Reconstruction Acts.

Because Secretary of War Edwin M. Stanton opposed his policies, Johnson sought to replace him with Gen. Ulysses S. Grant. Not only did the House attempt to impeach the president, but the Senate refused to concur in the secretary's suspension and ordered his reinstatement. After Grant refused to cooperate with Johnson, the president decided to rid himself of Stanton once and for all, this time in defiance of the Tenure of Office Act. In February 1868 he announced the appointment of Lorenzo Thomas as secretary ad interim, whereupon the House passed a resolution of impeachment. In the trial that followed, Johnson's opponents failed to obtain the necessary two-thirds for conviction, and the Senate acquitted him by one vote.

After his retirement, Johnson was reelected to the Senate in 1875. He served only briefly, for he died soon thereafter.

Although not successful as president, Johnson was a shrewd politician who repeatedly defeated both Whigs and Democrats in his home state. But by failing to take advantage of the opportunity of remaking the South in the months after Appomattox and by undermining Congressional Reconstruction, he contributed materially to its failure and kept the South a "white man's country."

James E. Sefton, *Andrew Johnson and the Uses of Constitutional Power* (1980); Hans L. Trefousse, *Andrew Johnson: A Biography* (1989).

HANS L. TREFOUSSE

See also Elections: 1864. *For events during Johnson's administration, see* Black Codes; Freedmen's Bureau; Granger Movement; Impeachment; Reconstruction; Tenure of Office Act.

JOHNSON, JAMES WELDON

(1871–1938), writer, civil rights leader, and promoter of African-American arts. Johnson was a central figure in the development of African-American cultural and political life during the first part of the twentieth century. He played a major role in articulating goals, devising strategies, and organizing constituencies in the struggle for racial equality. After graduating from Atlanta University in 1894, he forged an amazing patchwork of pursuits into a brilliant career.

Johnson's ideas and actions — often contradictory and inconsistent — reflected his ambivalent, complex personality. A product of the black middle class, he was widely traveled and multilingual. He expanded educational opportunities for blacks in his native Jacksonville, Florida, and taught in Harlem and at Fisk University. His training in law helped prepare him for tours as U.S. consul to Venezuela and Nicaragua (1906–1912) and equipped him for distinguished leadership (1916–1930) in the National Association for the Advancement of Colored People (NAACP).

As NAACP field secretary (1916–1920), Johnson worked tirelessly to increase the group's membership and expand its geographic representation, transforming a fledgling interracial civil rights group into a visible, vocal, and credible national force. His investigations of lynchings, peonage, and race riots raised public awareness and won the attention of national leaders. During Johnson's tenure as NAACP executive secretary (1920–1930), the organization defined the black agenda largely in legal and political terms, focusing on publicity, lobbying, and litigation in such areas as lynching, criminal justice, and residential segregation.

Johnson rejected both the vocational self-help philosophy of Booker T. Washington and the more radical economic measures advocated by W. E. B. Du Bois. He believed that African-Americans could advance their position in American society by demonstrating "intellectual parity . . . through the production of literature and art." Johnson himself helped shape the corpus of African-American literature during the Harlem Renaissance of the 1920s. He reached wide interracial audiences with his own poems and edited an important poetry anthology. His monumental *God's Trombones* — with its unforgettable Aaron Douglas illustrations — epitomized the period's literary and visual energy. Encouraging others, Johnson promoted art competitions and secured major sources of patronage for artists and writers who were black. During his lifetime he founded, edited, and wrote for various influential black periodicals and wrote books and articles on racial topics and contemporary issues. His novel, *The Autobiography of an Ex-Coloured Man,* remains a classic. Its protagonist, a light-skinned black pianist, tragically abandons his dream of creating racially conscious compositions. Succumbing to racism, he passes for white, choosing an artistically compromised but less restricted musical career.

Like his novel's protagonist, Johnson was also a musician. His songwriting spanned popular and high culture. He translated a libretto for the Metropolitan Opera and, collaborating with his brother, J. Rosamond Johnson, wrote lyrics for Broadway musicals, popular tunes, and comic opera, as well as a song known as the "Negro national anthem," "Lift Every Voice and Sing." During the Harlem Renaissance the brothers published two best-selling collections of traditional spirituals, documenting and spotlighting an overlooked but important American musical tradition. Writing during a period of overtly racist fascination with exotic African stereotypes, they asserted to black and white audiences the cultural legitimacy and vitality of African-American music.

James Weldon Johnson, *Along This Way* (1933; reprint, 1961); Eugene D. Levy, *James Weldon Johnson: Black Leader, Black Voice* (1973).

LINDA L. NIEMAN

See also Harlem Renaissance; Literature; Music; National Association for the Advancement of Colored People.

JOHNSON, LYNDON B.

(1908–1973), thirty-sixth president of the United States. Johnson was an extraordinarily energetic and ambitious politician. A native of the hill country of Texas, he appeared to his enemies as a stereotypical Texan: large, crude, egotistical, manipulative, and overbearing. Although a remarkably resourceful congressional leader, he could not shake the popular view that he was a wheeling-dealing political operator. When as president he greatly expanded American involvement in the Vietnam War, he polarized the nation and badly damaged his standing with the American people.

Contrary to myth, Johnson grew up in fairly comfortable circumstances. He earned a degree from South West Texas State Teachers College in 1930, taught school in Houston, served as a congressional aide in Washington, and became Texas director of the National Youth Adminis-

tration, a New Deal agency. Elected as a Democrat to the House of Representatives in 1937, he served until 1949, and then moved to the Senate.

Johnson rose quickly in the upper chamber, becoming majority leader in 1955. In that capacity he developed a well-earned reputation for hard work, attention to detail, and great skill at reconciling varied interests. As John F. Kennedy's vice-presidential running mate in 1960, Johnson helped his ticket to victory. He became president when Kennedy was assassinated in November 1963.

Thanks mainly to profitable investments in radio and television, Johnson was wealthy, but he identified with poor people, including African-Americans and Hispanics, and he greatly admired the liberal programs of President Franklin D. Roosevelt. When he reached the White House, he resolved to broaden and expand the New Deal — to create what he called the Great Society. Using all his political talents to the full, he secured approval in 1964 of the War on Poverty program and the first significant civil rights legislation since the 1870s. After a landslide victory over Republican Barry Goldwater in the 1964 presidential election, he pressed successfully for a wide range of liberal programs, including Medicare (health insurance for the elderly), Medicaid (care for the welfare poor), federal aid to elementary and secondary education, a more liberal immigration law, creation of the National Endowments for the Arts and Humanities, and a federal guarantee of voting rights. Thanks in good part to Johnson's extraordinarily able leadership, much of the agenda of modern American liberalism finally became law of the land.

Many of these programs, however, have evoked criticism. Medicare and Medicaid, although important to millions of people, proved to be much more expensive than proponents had anticipated. Partly because of cutbacks in funding, the War on Poverty fell far short of expectations. The civil rights laws, while promoting legal equality, did not address the socioeconomic problems of African-Americans. Aggressive neoconservatives counterattacked in the 1970s and 1980s, keeping American liberalism on the defensive.

Johnson's most troublesome problems as president stemmed from his escalation of the American military presence in Vietnam, which was in the throes of civil war. Intervening massively — with bombing raids and ultimately more than 500,000 American troops — Johnson grew increasingly stubborn and secretive. But his policies failed to turn the tide of battle. At home antiwar activists protested angrily, and bitter debates overwhelmed the hopeful, liberal mood of the early 1960s.

In 1968 Johnson began at last to listen to new advisers. He announced that he would not run again for president and that he was encouraging peace talks in Paris. But he refused to make significant concessions, and the war continued. When Johnson left office in January 1969 he was tired, despondent, and unpopular with the majority of the American people. He returned to his ranch in Texas, where he died four years later.

Paul K. Conkin, *Big Daddy from the Pedernales: Lyndon Baines Johnson* (1986); Allen J. Matusow, *The Unraveling of America: A History of Liberalism in the 1960s* (1984).

JAMES T. PATTERSON

See also Elections: 1960, 1964. *For events during Johnson's administration, see* Civil Rights Movement; Great Society; Medicaid; Medicare; Vietnam War.

JOHNSON, PHILIP

(1906–), architect. Although Johnson has been a successful designer of both commercial and prestige buildings, his greatest influence has been as a pundit on design issues, a curator and historian of architecture, and an encourager of new design ideas.

With his ground-breaking 1932 exhibition of modern architecture for the Museum of Modern Art, and his book *The International Style* (1932; written with Henry-Russell Hitchcock), the wealthy young enthusiast set the rules for modernism in the United States for a generation. His 1947 exhibition and monograph on Mies van der Rohe helped make Mies's austere yet classical steel-and-glass architecture the norm for corpo-

rate building. From the 1950s on, however, he led those who felt the International Style left too little room for beauty and dignity in architecture. His style and ideas have changed constantly over the years, and he has always worked to find and publicize the next important movement in design.

In his designs and lectures Johnson presents himself as a rebel intellectual, passionately devoted to architecture as a fine art. He insists that architecture has no moral or social mission beyond beauty and that style is a value-free (albeit necessary) quality. Telling architectural students in the 1950s that "you cannot not know history," Johnson reminded them of modernism's debts to past styles and of how architecture is constantly adapting to changes in society. His dissent from functionalist modernism encouraged those working for a more humane environment, from the historic preservation movement to the postmodernist architects.

Johnson did not begin professional practice until 1946. As an architect, he has made other designers' concepts more elegant and accessible to upper-class clients. His buildings are marked by careful planning and frequent references to past, usually classical, architectural masterpieces. In the landmark Glass House he designed for himself in New Canaan, Connecticut (1949), an adaptation of Mies's idiom, Johnson made subtle but encyclopedic use of the past to comment on the roots of modern design. His A.T.&T. Building in New York (1978–1984, with John Burgee, his partner from 1968 to 1987) openly mimicked past architectural styles, making it an acceptable practice again.

Johnson's prestige (he received the AIA Gold Medal in 1978) made him one of the most successful postmodern designers of the 1980s. But his later buildings disappointed earlier admirers. Their weaknesses — critics have called them overly large and visually disturbing — owe something to developer clients' demands, but more to Johnson's wish to shock modernists by playing with old and new styles.

Nonetheless, Johnson's iconoclasm, and his introduction of new design ideas to his clients over the years, helped keep architects and the public aware of the complex issues involved in creating good architecture. He has been largely responsible for making Americans conscious of architecture as a fine art.

John Jacobus, *Philip Johnson* (1962); Nory Miller and Richard Payne, *Johnson/Burgee: Architecture* (1980) and *Philip Johnson/John Burgee: Architecture, 1979–1985* (1985).

MILES DAVID SAMSON

See also Architecture.

JONES, ABSALOM

(1746–1818), African-American religious leader and reformer. Jones, an African-American who gained his freedom in the revolutionary era, contributed greatly to one of the first large free black communities in the United States. Born a slave in Sussex County, Delaware, Jones grew up on the estate of the merchant-planter Benjamin Wynkoop. He was brought by his master to Philadelphia in 1762, where he learned to read at a night school for blacks while working in Wynkoop's store. After long efforts, he purchased freedom for his wife and himself in 1784. He soon became one of the main leaders of the emerging free black community in Philadelphia — the largest urban gathering of emancipated slaves in the postrevolutionary period.

Within a few years, Jones became an important figure in the Free African Society of Philadelphia, probably the first independent black mutual aid society in the United States. From this society came the impulse for creating the African Church of Philadelphia, an impulse that was emblematic of the striving for dignity, self-improvement, and autonomy of a generation of mostly northern African-Americans released or escaped from bondage. Independent black churches became centers of social and political as well as religious activities in many northern cities in the early national era.

Jones's African Church of Philadelphia, planned in conjunction with black minister Richard Allen and with the assistance of Benjamin Rush and other white Philadelphia Quakers, was designed as a racially separate, nondenominational, and socially oriented church. But in order to gain state recognition of its corporate status, it affiliated with the Protestant Episcopal Church of North America and later took the name St. Thomas's African Episcopal Church. Jones was its first minister, serving from 1794 until his death in 1818.

While at St. Thomas's Jones coauthored with Allen *A Narrative of the Proceedings of the Black People, during the Late Awful Calamity in Philadelphia* — a defense of black contributions in the yellow fever epidemic of 1793 and an attack on slavery. In 1797 he helped organize the first petition of African-Americans against slavery, the slave trade, and the federal Fugitive Slave Law of 1793. Three years later, he organized another petition to President Thomas Jefferson and the Congress deploring slavery and the slave trade. From his pulpit, he preached against slavery and was responsible for informally establishing January 1 — the date on which the slave trade ended in 1808 — as a day of thanksgiving and celebration, an alternative to the Fourth of July for black Americans.

Like many nineteenth-century black clergymen, Jones also functioned outside his pulpit. As a teacher in schools established by the Pennsylvania Abolition Society and by his church, he helped train a generation of local black youth. As grand master of Philadelphia's Black Masons, a founder of the Society for the Suppression of Vice and Immorality (1809), and a founder of the literary Augustine Society (1817), he struggled to enhance the self-respect and skills of the North's largest free black community.

Gary B. Nash, *Race, Class, and Politics: Essays on American Colonial and Revolutionary Society* (1986).

GARY B. NASH

See also Abolitionist Movement; Black Churches; Free Negroes, 1619–1860.

JONES, JOHN PAUL

(1747–1792), naval officer. Jones was born in Scotland and was apprenticed in 1761 to a merchant. At thirteen years of age he began his career at sea, as a ship's boy on the *Friendship* sailing between Britain and Virginia and the West

Indies. Over the next fourteen years he learned the ways of the sea, sailing on merchant ships, including slavers. By age twenty-one he was the captain of a merchantman sailing between the West Indies and British ports. On one of these voyages in 1769, he had the ship's carpenter whipped; not long afterward the carpenter died and Jones faced a charge of murder but was later freed. In 1773, he put down a mutiny, running his sword through the ringleader in the process, and fled to America to avoid trial in a civil court.

Shortly after the Revolution began, he was in Philadelphia and through the friendship of Joseph Hewes, a delegate to the Continental Congress, was commissioned as first lieutenant on the *Alfred* in the Continental navy. Jones proved himself a capable officer in action on the *Alfred* and on the sloop *Providence* which he commanded in 1776. The next year Congress sent him to France as captain of the *Ranger* with orders to attack enemy commerce in British waters. His greatest success on the *Ranger* came in April 1778 when he sailed from Brest for the Irish Sea and then to Whitehaven. This superb foray saw him fail in his attempt to abduct the Earl of Selkirk, whom he intended to exchange for Americans held by the British, but he captured the sloop of war *Drake* in a fierce struggle. By May 8, the *Ranger* was back at Brest with seven prizes and many prisoners, having created a furor in the British press.

The French now took note of Jones and sent him off in August 1779 in command of a fleet of five naval vessels and two privateers. This voyage carried Jones and his ships clockwise around the British Isles. Jones's ship was the *Bonhomme Richard,* around nine hundred tons and slow, but the most heavily armed vessel he had commanded. Prizes were taken, but an attempt to extort ransom from Leith, Edinburgh's seaport, failed. The fleet sailed on until September 23, when Jones fought one of the great battles of the Revolution off the Yorkshire coast. The enemy was the *Serapis,* one of the British escorts of a large convoy. In the battle, mostly fought in moonlight, the *Bonhomme Richard* grappled with the *Serapis.* With the two vessels lashed together, the British captain asked Jones if he wished to surrender and received the famous reply, "I have

not yet begun to fight." Indeed Jones had not, and when the night's work was done, he accepted the surrender of his enemy.

This victory was the high point of John Paul Jones's war — and life. After the war, he served in the Russian navy in the Black Sea in a war with the Turks. He died in Paris, still an American citizen and one of the great heroes of the U.S. Navy.

Samuel Eliot Morison, *John Paul Jones: A Sailor's Biography* (1959).

ROBERT MIDDLEKAUFF

See also Revolution.

JONES, MARY HARRIS (MOTHER JONES)

(1837–1930), labor organizer. In addition to her organizing activities among coal miners and others, chiefly on behalf of the United Mine Workers of America, Mother Jones was a popular speaker for social and political causes ranging from the abolition of child labor to the 1910 campaign to free Mexican revolutionaries jailed in the United States. Her political views evolved from 1890s populism to socialism, and from socialism to support for Woodrow Wilson and the Democratic party in 1916.

Mother Jones began organizing coal miners in Pennsylvania sometime in the 1890s. During the 1900 anthracite (hard coal) strike, she was pictured in newspaper accounts as a colorful figure whose grandmotherly looks belied her sharp wit and militant pronouncements. Her strategy during that strike — organizing miners' wives to march over the mountains late at night banging on tin pans with the idea of blocking strikebreakers coming in for the morning shift — characterized her style. She had a knack for organizing public events designed for dramatic effect.

As she began to attract more attention, she skillfully used the news media to further the causes for which she worked. In one effective political pageant in 1903, she organized a highly publicized, week-long march of child mill workers from Pennsylvania to the New York home of

President Theodore Roosevelt. The children were physically stunted and mutilated, walking evidence of the abusive conditions of their labor. This was public theater designed to increase general awareness of the need for social justice.

A charismatic speaker, Mother Jones was revered by coal miners and their families, who called her "the miner's angel." Officers of the United Mine Workers of America found her persuasive abilities particularly useful at the inception of strikes, and she played a prominent role in virtually all the important coal strikes of the period. Her physical courage was legendary — stories abounded of how she would wade through freezing creeks or walk up to a mine guard who was threatening to shoot and put her hand on the muzzle of his gun.

Coal operators and their supporters tended to blame her for their labor troubles and for any violence that occurred, but she was not that powerful. Moreover, following union policy, she typically urged strikers to abstain from violence even in the face of provocation. She became familiar with the insides of various jails in West Virginia and Colorado, but her incarcerations generated so much public protest (owing to her age, gender, wit, and ability to attract newspaper attention) that she was able to serve the cause quite as well in jail as out.

She lived a nontraditional life, declaring that she made her home wherever there was a "good fight against wrong." Indeed, she had no permanent home, traveling from region to region to organize coal miners, whom she called "her boys." She often expressed herself in rough, "unwomanly" language. Yet her views on women's roles were entirely traditional: she believed their important work was in the home. (Her own husband and children had died in the Memphis yellow fever epidemic of 1867.) She opposed woman suffrage and looked upon her own activism as that of a mother.

When Mother Jones died in 1930, she quickly faded from public memory, except in coal mining communities. She was at once exceptional and quite typical — of the militant, pro-union coal miner's wife who might curse out a mine guard or beat up a strikebreaker but who also cherished her traditional role in the family.

Priscilla Long, *Where the Sun Never Shines: A History of America's Bloody Coal Industry* (1989); Edward M. Steel, ed., *The Speeches and Writings of Mother Jones* (1988).

PRISCILLA LONG

See also Labor; Radicalism.

JOSEPH (CHIEF JOSEPH)

(c. 1840–1904), Nez Percé Indian chief. The surrender speech of Chief Joseph has become perhaps the most famous statement in American Indian history:

> I am tired of fighting. Our chiefs are killed. . . . The old men are all killed. . . . It is cold and we have no blankets. The little children are freezing to death. My people, some of them, have run away to the hills and have no blankets, no food; no one knows where they are, perhaps freezing to death. I want time to look for my children and see how many of them I can find. Maybe I shall find them among the dead. Hear me, my chiefs, I am tired; my heart is sick and sad. From where the sun now stands, I will fight no more forever.

This speech came at the conclusion of a remarkable effort by the Nez Percé tribe to escape to Canada in 1877. They had traveled a circuitous route of about fifteen hundred miles and had nearly reached their destination before being forced to surrender just south of the Canadian border. Most historians believe that Joseph's role in the retreat has been exaggerated; he was only one of several leaders. Nonetheless he remains an enduring symbol of Indian resistance.

A reluctant general in an extraordinary campaign, Joseph belonged to a group victimized by a familiar series of events. The Nez Percé reservation had been greatly reduced in size after the discovery of gold in eastern Oregon. Although the Nez Percés had not agreed to the loss of their lands, the government insisted they be confined within the new boundaries. When young Nez Percés along the Salmon River killed people they deemed intruders, they knew retribution would come. Their tribe first hid them and then decided to flee.

Joseph at this time was in his late thirties;

he had succeeded his father as chief in 1871. A tall, dignified man, he had appeared well suited to lead in times of peace, but the times now demanded a different role. He and other Nez Percé men waged a series of battles during the summer of 1877. Making their way through the mountainous terrain of Idaho, Wyoming, and Montana, they frustrated the efforts of the U.S. Army to capture them.

The Nez Percés crossed the Missouri River in northern Montana on September 23. Soon thereafter, thinking they had outlasted and outwitted their pursuers, they stopped to rest in the vicinity of the Bear Paw Mountains, about forty miles south of the Canadian border. With no bluecoats in sight and suffering from hunger and exhaustion, they prepared for the final push into Canada. But there they were surprised by Gen. Nelson Miles on September 30. On October 5 they ended what had already become a famous flight.

Joseph had been assured that the Nez Percés would be permitted to return to their home country in the Wallowa Valley in eastern Oregon. But political pressure from the Northwest dictated another fate: exile to far-off Indian Territory (now Oklahoma). In 1885 some of the Nez Percés were allowed to move to the Lapwai Reservation in Idaho, not far from the Wallowa Valley, but Joseph and others were sent to the Colville Reservation in northeastern Washington.

For the remainder of his life, Joseph tried unsuccessfully to convince federal authorities that he and others from his tribe should regain a place in the valley "where most of my relatives and friends are sleeping their last sleep." But he died at Colville and was buried there. In 1905 a monument was erected in his honor at Nespelem on the reservation. On that occasion, a Nez Percé, Yellow Bull, rode Joseph's horse and spoke about him while on horseback. "Joseph is dead," the old man said, "but his words will live forever."

Alvin M. Josephy, Jr., *The Nez Percé Indians and the Opening of the Northwest* (1965).

PETER IVERSON

See also Indians.

JOURNALISM

See Magazines and Newspapers.

JUDAISM

See Jews.

JUDICIAL REVIEW

Judicial review refers to the power of American courts to determine whether the acts of all branches of government and government officials comply with the Constitution. An American innovation, judicial review is the basic institution by which the Constitution has become the supreme law of the land rather than a hortatory document like the Declaration of Independence.

Exercised by both the state and federal judiciary, judicial review is most identified with the U.S. Supreme Court. Although the Constitution does not expressly provide for judicial review, the Founding Fathers anticipated that the Court would exercise some control over the other branches of government. Chief Justice John Marshall's famous assertion of judicial review in *Marbury* v. *Madison* (1803) was not a brash departure but a crystallization of a nascent tradition.

That tradition was an amalgam of three somewhat contradictory strands of the young Republic's political and legal culture: popular sovereignty, fundamental law, and judicial independence. Popular sovereignty meant that the people were the paramount lawgiver and that they had ordained a Constitution allowing each branch of government only limited power. Fundamental law meant that there were divinely ordained and traditionally respected moral principles that should remain in force. Judicial independence meant that the Court's view of the Constitution could not be controlled by any other branch of government.

Some of the Court's specific decisions and doctrines have provoked intense debate, but since *Marbury,* the propriety of judicial review has rarely been controverted. Instead, arguments have centered on the Court's use of its power. On occasion, the Court's decisions have raised controversies concerning judicial review itself.

In the nineteenth century these controversies focused on whether the Court is the Constitution's ultimate expositor; in the twentieth, on how the Court is to interpret the Constitution. These controversies present the enduring problems of "constitutional" versus "judicial" supremacy, and judicial "restraint" versus "activism."

"Constitutional supremacy" is the doctrine that the Constitution, not the Court's rulings, is the supreme law of the land, and consequently, that every government official is entitled to act according to his or her understanding of that document. It means that the Court is entitled to abide by its interpretation of the Constitution in cases that come before it, but that the interpretation does not bind any other branch of government. "Judicial supremacy" is the opposite doctrine — that both the letter and spirit of the Court's constitutional determinations bind all branches of government and government officials. The premises that Marshall drew from in establishing judicial review speak ambiguously with regard to judicial supremacy. Indeed, the argument that the Supreme Court is an independent branch of government is reversible: other branches of government are also independent, and the Court cannot dictate its constitutional views to them.

Accordingly, all that *Marbury* clearly established was that in cases before it, the Court would abide by *its* understanding of the Constitution. Furthermore, extremely contentious litigation (*Martin* v. *Hunter's Lessee*, 1816, and *Cohens* v. *Virginia*, 1821) established that the Supreme Court's constitutional determinations bind state courts. *Martin* and *Cohens* represented the limits of the Court's acknowledged supremacy in the nineteenth century.

Throughout the pre–Civil War period, however, state courts took the position that Supreme Court rulings governed only the cases it actually determined, and they felt free to apply different principles to other cases, no matter how closely analogous to Supreme Court precedent. Nor did the other branches of the national government regard themselves as bound by Supreme Court determinations. President Thomas Jefferson advocated this view. President Andrew Jackson acted upon it when he vetoed a bill rechartering the Bank of America and indicated that he would not enforce the Court's mandate in *Worcester* v. *Georgia* (1832). President Abraham Lincoln, too, refused to comply with a variety of Court writs and mandates.

Yet, in the century following the Civil War, the Court's views on constitutional issues acquired a special status. Public opinion came to associate a stable constitutional order with respect for the Court's determinations. Drawing from this well of public support, the Court, since the mid-twentieth century, has spoken of itself as the "ultimate" and "supreme" expositor of the Constitution.

Nonetheless, the extent to which judicial review means judicial supremacy remains unclear. President Dwight D. Eisenhower federalized the Arkansas National Guard to prevent the state from interfering with federal court orders stemming from *Brown* v. *Board of Education of Topeka* to desegregate the Little Rock school system. On the national level, recent presidents and Congresses generally have obeyed direct Court orders.

Yet compliance with specific rulings has not been coupled with respect for the principles the Court adopts in its decisions. Frequently, government officials obey the Court's mandate in a given case, but continue to pursue the policy the Court had declared unconstitutional. At times, state legislatures enact clearly unconstitutional laws when it seems politically beneficial to do so. Thus, though the contemporary Court may be accorded more "supremacy" than its nineteenth-century predecessors, the doctrine of constitutional supremacy remains unresolved.

"Judicial restraint" and "judicial activism" refer to the extent to which the Court defers to the constitutional determinations of other branches of government and the extent to which it refuses to impose affirmative obligations upon government. Throughout its history, the Court has claimed to exercise judicial review with restraint, but it has always actively pursued its chosen policies of the moment.

The disparity between the Court's claims and its actions attracted little comment until the 1890s, when James Thayer published an article that moved the issue of judicial restraint to the center of constitutional debate. He argued that the Constitution has a range of possible meanings and that the Court should void only those acts of the national government that are beyond the pale of permissible meaning. Whenever it voids an act that is not "clearly mistaken," it is overturning an interpretation that a coequal branch of government prefers and substituting an interpretation it prefers. Nondeferential review, he concluded, is discretionary lawmaking that usurps the executive and legislative functions.

After Thayer, judicial review began to be conceived as a device by which nine unaccountable officials impose their opinions upon the nation. With the rise of pragmatic jurisprudence and legal realism in the early twentieth century, the view that judges make law when they interpret the Constitution became a truism. And the central issue of judicial review has become what, if anything, justifies their doing so. The Court responded by engaging in restrained or active review according to principles first sketched by Justice Harlan Fiske Stone in *United States* v. *Carolene Products Co.* (1938). Those principles spurned active review except when necessary to guard freedoms specifically protected by the Bill of Rights, rights considered fundamental to the functioning of the political process, or the rights of "discrete and insular" minority groups. Under these principles, the Court began in *Brown* v. *Board of Education of Topeka* (1954) a course of review that changed the face of American society by enforcing the civil rights of minority groups and the poor and enlarging the civil liberties of all citizens. This course frequently required the judiciary to impose remedial measures that redirected the activities of the states. Indeed, in the "one person, one vote" decisions that followed *Baker* v. *Carr* (1962), the Court remodeled state government itself.

These developments provoked controversy, which coalesced around the Court's defense of the unenumerated right of privacy in *Griswold* v. *Connecticut* (1965) and its development into the right to an abortion in *Roe* v. *Wade* (1973). Because of the controversy, and eight years of conservative Republican appointments, the Court in the mid-1980s reversed its course and began to abandon the *Carolene Products* model of judicial review. In its place, the Court has claimed to be developing a model of judicial review premised upon judicial restraint. The new Court has said it will defer to the decisions of democratically accountable officials and overturn only those acts that clearly violate specific constitutional text or traditions. Yet the Court's protection of property rights in *Nollan* v. *California Coastal Commission* (1987) and its condemnation of a municipal affirmative action plan in *City of Richmond* v. *J. A. Cronson Co.* (1989) intimated more active review of some constitutional claims. Thus it is unclear whether the Court's recent rulings portend a triumph of judicial restraint or merely another shift in the focus of judicial activism.

Judicial review, then, remains firmly established but subject to limitations. The controversies over judicial review may be interminable because, as Robert McCloskey pointed out, they attempt to resolve America's contradictory commitment to popular sovereignty and judicially enforceable fundamental law.

John Ely, *Democracy and Distrust* (1980); Robert McCloskey, *The American Supreme Court* (1960).

STEPHEN A. SIEGEL

See also Baker v. *Carr; Brown* v. *Board of Education of Topeka;* Constitution; *Griswold* v. *Connecticut; Marbury* v. *Madison;* Marshall, John; *Roe* v. *Wade;* Stone, Harlan Fiske; Supreme Court.

JUDICIARY ACT OF 1789

This act of the First Congress established the structure of the federal judiciary, the basic structure of which has remained intact. The Constitution stipulated only that the federal court system should consist of (1) a Supreme Court having original jurisdiction in certain cases and (2) "such inferior Courts as the Congress may . . . establish." Congress could have declined to create lower courts, making state courts rule first on almost all federal issues. Such cases would then appear before the single federal court. Instead, the 1789 act created two lower levels of courts. Federal district courts, each with a district judge, composed the lowest level.

Their district boundaries generally matched state lines. Every federal district also fell within the circuit of one of the three second-level courts, the circuit courts. Two Supreme Court justices and one district judge composed each circuit court bench; they traveled to each district to hear cases twice a year. When cases involved parties from differing states, they usually received their first hearing in the circuit courts. Occasionally, circuit courts also heard appeals from district courts. In addition to creating courts, the 1789 act granted the Supreme Court a controversial power to order federal officials to carry out their legal responsibilities.

See also Supreme Court.

JUDICIARY BRANCH

See Supreme Court.

JUNGLE, THE

Upton Sinclair's novel *The Jungle* tells the epic tragedy of a Lithuanian immigrant Jurgis Rudkus and a group of his friends and relatives. Penniless and unable to speak English, they are mercilessly exploited by employers, foremen, police, political bosses, and others with access to power in Packingtown. Women are forced into prostitution; older men, unable to work, are left to starve. Jurgis loses his wife in childbirth, and his infant son drowns in a pool of stinking water outside their shack. The novel also includes gruesome descriptions of food production: tubercular beef, the grinding up of poisoned rats, and even workers falling into vats and emerging as Durham's Pure Leaf Lard.

Published in January 1906, *The Jungle* unleashed a storm of public indignation. The scene had already been set by the "embalmed beef" scandal in the Spanish-American War of 1898 (concerning the quality of food supplied to U.S. troops) and the muckraking exposés of journalists like Samuel Hopkins Adams on patent medicines and Charles Edward Russell on the "Beef Trust." But the impact of *The Jungle* was probably decisive. Within six months of its publication a Pure Food and Drug Act and a Meat Inspection Act had been passed.

The irony is that Sinclair included the horrific details on meat production only in order to bolster his main theme, the exploitation of immigrant labor and the need for socialism. As he later wrote: "I aimed at the public's heart and by accident hit it in the stomach." Undeterred, Sinclair invested the proceeds from his masterpiece in the Helicon Hall colony, an experimental socialist community at Englewood, New Jersey.

See also Progressivism; Pure Food and Drug Act.

K

KANSAS-NEBRASKA ACT

This 1854 bill to organize western territories became part of the political whirlwind of sectionalism and railroad building, splitting two major political parties and helping to create another, as well as worsening North-South relations.

On January 4, 1854, Stephen A. Douglas, wanting to ensure a northern transcontinental railroad route that would benefit his Illinois constituents, introduced a bill to organize the territory of Nebraska in order to bring the area under civil control. But southern senators objected; the region lay north of latitude 36°30′ and so under the terms of the Missouri Compromise of 1820 would become a free state. To gain the southerners' support, Douglas proposed creating two territories in the area — Kansas and Nebraska — and repealing the Missouri Compromise line. The question of whether the territories would be slave or free would be left to the settlers under Douglas's principle of popular sovereignty. Presumably, the more northern territory would oppose slavery while the more southern one would permit it.

Although initially concerned about the political fallout, President Franklin Pierce gave Douglas and his southern allies his support. The "Appeal of the Independent Democrats," signed by such Free-Soilers as Salmon P. Chase and Charles Sumner and published in many northern newspapers, attacked Pierce, Douglas, and their supporters for breaking a sacred compact by repealing the Missouri Compromise.

The act passed Congress, but it failed in its purposes. By the time Kansas was admitted to statehood in 1861 after an internal civil war, southern states had begun to secede from the Union. The Independent Democrats and many northern Whigs abandoned their affiliations for the new antislavery Republican party, leaving southern Whigs without party links and creating an issue over which the already deeply divided Democrats would split even more. The railroad was eventually built but not along the route Douglas wanted and with funds voted by a Republican Congress during a Republican Civil War administration.

See also Douglas, Stephen A.; Missouri Compromise.

KELLER, HELEN

(1880–1968), author, lecturer, and crusader for the handicapped. Born physically normal in Tuscumbia, Alabama, Helen Keller lost her sight and hearing at the age of nineteen months to an illness now believed to have been scarlet fever. Five years later, on the advice of Alexander Graham Bell, her parents applied to the Perkins Institute for the Blind in Boston for a teacher, and from that school hired Anne Mansfield Sullivan. Through Sullivan's extraordinary instruction, the little girl learned to understand and communicate with the world around her. She went on to acquire an excellent education and to become an important influence on the treatment of the blind and deaf.

Keller learned from Sullivan to read and

write in Braille and to use the hand signals of the deaf-mute, which she could understand only by touch. Her later efforts to learn to speak were less successful, and in her public appearances she required the assistance of an interpreter to make herself understood. Nevertheless, her impact as educator, organizer, and fund-raiser was enormous, and she was responsible for many advances in public services to the handicapped.

With Sullivan repeating the lectures into her hand, Keller studied at schools for the deaf in Boston and New York City and graduated cum laude from Radcliffe College in 1904. Her unprecedented accomplishments in overcoming her disabilities made her a celebrity at an early age; at twelve she published an autobiographical sketch in the *Youth's Companion,* and during her junior year at Radcliffe she produced her first book, *The Story of My Life,* still in print in over fifty languages. Keller published four other books of her personal experiences as well as a volume on religion, one on contemporary social problems, and a biography of Anne Sullivan. She also wrote numerous articles for national magazines on the prevention of blindness and the education and special problems of the blind.

In addition to her many appearances on the lecture circuit, Keller in 1918 made a movie in Hollywood, *Deliverance,* to dramatize the plight of the blind and during the next two years supported herself and Sullivan on the vaudeville stage. She also spoke and wrote in support of women's rights and other liberal causes and in 1940 strongly backed the United States' entry into World War II.

In 1924, Keller joined the staff of the newly formed American Foundation for the Blind as an adviser and fund-raiser. Her international reputation and warm personality enabled her to enlist the support of many wealthy people, and she secured large contributions from Henry Ford, John D. Rockefeller, and leaders of the motion picture industry. When the AFB established a branch for the overseas blind, it was named Helen Keller International. Keller and Sullivan were the subjects of a Pulitzer Prize–winning play, *The Miracle Worker,* by William Gibson, which opened in New York in 1959 and became a successful Hollywood film in 1962.

Widely honored throughout the world and invited to the White House by every U.S. president from Grover Cleveland to Lyndon B. Johnson, Keller altered the world's perception of the capacities of the handicapped. More than any act in her long life, her courage, intelligence, and dedication combined to make her a symbol of the triumph of the human spirit over adversity.

Helen Keller, *The Story of My Life* (1903); Joseph P. Lash, *Helen and Teacher: The Story of Helen Keller and Anne Sullivan Macy* (1980).

DENNIS WEPMAN

KELLEY, FLORENCE

(1859–1932), social reformer. Born into a patrician Quaker family in Philadelphia, Kelley combined a tradition of female political activism inherited from her great-aunt Sarah Pugh, a leading abolitionist, with traditions inherited from her father, William Durrah Kelley, abolitionist, founding member of the Republican party, Radical Reconstructionist, and U.S. congressman from Philadelphia. Those traditions merged for her in 1891, when she joined Jane Addams and other women reformers in Chicago at one of the nation's first social settlements, Hull-House. From 1898 until her death in 1932, she served as head of the National Consumers' League (NCL), the single most effective lobbying agency for protective labor legislation for women and children.

Kelley's prodigious intellectual energy became evident when, at an early age, she systematically read through her father's extensive library. In 1882 she exemplified her generation's increasing access to higher education by graduating from Cornell, but in her wanderings during the next decade she also embodied the difficulty for educated women to locate work commensurate with their talents. Establishing her independence of her father's tradition, Kelley came into contact with European socialism while studying government and law at the University of Zurich; her translation into English of several major works by Karl Marx and Frederick Engels gave her a solid grounding in

European socialist thinking. (Her translation of Engels's *Condition of the Working Class in England in 1844* is still the preferred scholarly version.) In Zurich she also met and married Lazare Wischnewetzky, a Polish socialist medical student, and gave birth to three children in three years. Physically abused by her husband, she fled with her children to Chicago after their return to New York in 1886, where at Hull-House her potential as a social reformer finally found fertile soil.

Kelley exerted an immediate and dramatic influence on the generation of women reformers who clustered within the social settlement movement during the Progressive Era. Her understanding of the material basis of class conflict and her familiarity with American political institutions, combined with her spirited personality, placed her in the vanguard of a generation of reformers who sought to make American government more responsive to what they saw as the needs of working people. In this way they were critical components in the process by which American governments, state and national, shifted from liberal laissez-faire policies to positive regulatory programs.

Kelley summarized her reform strategy in the phrase "investigate, educate, legislate, and enforce." These tactics drew on her talents as a social scientist, a publicist, a lobbyist, and an attorney. As secretary-general of the NCL, Kelley helped establish sixty-four local consumers' leagues throughout the United States, traveling extensively among them each year to promote policies agreed upon by the national board. She and the Oregon league orchestrated the successful defense of the ten-hour-working-day legislation for women in the 1908 U.S. Supreme Court decision *Muller* v. *Oregon*. This was the legal innovation of the "Brandeis brief," which argued on the basis of sociological evidence rather than legal precedent. Kelley also introduced the social experiment of the minimum wage to the United States in 1909 and campaigned against child labor on a number of fronts. She herself thought her most important social contribution was the passage in 1921 of the Sheppard-Towner Maternity and Infancy Protection Act, which for the first time allocated federal funds for health care.

Kathryn Kish Sklar, "Hull House as a Community of Women Reformers in the 1890's," *Signs: Journal of Women in Culture and Society* 10 (Summer 1985): 657–677; Kathryn Kish Sklar, ed., *Florence Kelley, Notes of Sixty Years: The Autobiography of Florence Kelley* (1986).

KATHRYN KISH SKLAR

See also Child Labor; *Muller* v. *Oregon;* Progressivism; Settlement Houses.

KELLOGG-BRIAND PACT

In this treaty, signed on August 27, 1928, the United States, France, Great Britain, Japan, Italy, Belgium, Poland, and Czechoslovakia renounced war as an instrument of national policy.

French foreign minister Aristide Briand first suggested a treaty between the United States and France renouncing war as a method of settling disputes between the two countries. Secretary of State Frank Kellogg was furious because Briand proposed the treaty in a speech made directly to the American people, rather than going through diplomatic channels. If he accepted Briand's offer, he feared it would drag the United States into alliance with France in the event of another European war — which was what Briand had in mind. But if Kellogg declined, groups favoring such a treaty would attack him in Congress and in the press. Support for the treaty came from opposite ends of the political spectrum. For example, Nicholas Murray Butler, the internationalist president of Columbia University, believed a treaty would move America closer to the League of Nations, whereas isolationist senator William E. Borah, a pacifist, simply hoped that the treaty would end war.

Kellogg turned the tables on Briand by picking up an idea of Senator Borah's for a *multilateral* treaty. Both Kellogg and Briand knew that such a treaty lacked force, but Briand, already a Nobel Peace Prize winner, could hardly ignore public demand for an antiwar treaty. (Kellogg, too, was awarded a Nobel Peace Prize in 1929 for his role in formulating the pact.)

Great celebrations accompanied the signing of the Kellogg-Briand Pact, but diplomats did not take the pledge seriously. In the United States, for example, the next order of business on the Senate floor after ratification was a bill appropriating $274 million to build warships. The treaty is considered a diplomatic failure because a mere fourteen years after it purported to outlaw war, all the signatories had become belligerents in World War II.

KENNAN, GEORGE

(1904–   ), diplomat and historian. Kennan, one of the few outstanding American public intellectuals of the twentieth century, is best known as "the father of containment" and therefore as a key figure in the emergence of the cold war. This is not a wholly undeserved reputation, although he only articulated more eloquently than others what was taking place. But his "long telegram" from Moscow in 1946 and the article he wrote the next year under the pseudonym "X" have rightly been seen as foundational texts of the cold war, expressing and legitimating Washington's new and vigorously anti-Soviet policy.

Kennan, who played a leading role in the formulation of many crucial policies of this period, most notably the Marshall Plan, assumed that the Soviet regime was inherently expansionist and had to be "contained" — stopped from expanding in places of vital importance to the West. Since the Russians were thought to be fanatics, they were impossible to talk with. Stopping them therefore meant the abandonment of real diplomacy — in effect, a period of deep freeze coupled with tit-for-tat moves until frustration either broke the Soviet regime or mellowed it to the point where it could be made to see Western reason. Insofar as no "real diplomacy" was indeed the characteristic mark of the cold war, Kennan was its most sophisticated originating spirit.

By mid-1948, however, Kennan had become convinced that the situation in Western Europe had improved to the point where negotiations could be initiated with Moscow with a view to creating a unified Germany outside the power configurations of East and West. The suggestion did not resonate within the Truman administration, in part because the idea of a divided Europe had come to seem a useful arrangement. Kennan was thus increasingly marginalized.

In 1950 he left the State Department, except for two brief ambassadorial stints in the Soviet Union and Yugoslavia, and became a leading "realist" critic of American foreign policy. Intelligent pursuit of the national interest seemed to him impossible given such a decentered system of government, such an ingrained need to moralize by projecting American values on the world, such a basic lack of a sense of limits. His long-standing disenchantment with the mass culture of consumerism also surfaced. In the 1960s, he was, oddly, a celebrated critic of both the Vietnam War *and* the student revolt.

Throughout these years he wrote voluminously, publishing several important historical works on the Soviet Union and Soviet-American relations and, more recently, a multivolume treatise on the origins of the First World War. His *Memoirs* is a work of lasting literary value and one of the great American autobiographies. In the 1970s and 1980s he joined in the public debate as a profound and unbending critic of the arms race.

Walter Hixson, *George F. Kennan: Cold War Iconoclast* (1989); George F. Kennan, *Memoirs,* 2 vols. (1967, 1973); Anders Stephanson, *Kennan and the Art of Foreign Policy* (1989).

ANDERS STEPHANSON

See also Cold War.

KENNEDY, JOHN F.

(1917–1963), thirty-fifth president of the United States. Kennedy was born into an Irish-American family with aspirations resembling those of the British gentry. Overcoming limitations of health and doubts about his personal ambitions, he achieved the presidency by battling simultaneously on several fronts. Kennedy coasted to the inevitable first-ballot nomination at the Democratic party's Los Angeles convention in July 1960 and then pulled off what proved to be an essential political coup by selecting Senator Lyndon B. Johnson of Texas as his running mate. Kennedy's electoral college margin of 303–219 was won with little more than a 100,000-vote plurality out of nearly 69 million cast. At the age of forty-three, he became the youngest man to reach the White House via the electoral college. Most significant was his ability to demonstrate that a Roman Catholic could win.

John F. Kennedy left two different legacies. The first was best communicated through his lofty, inspiring rhetoric, his youth and personal elegance, and his glamorous wife. He also appealed to the aspirations of ordinary people through such programs as the Peace Corps. His Alliance for Progress, despite its inability to bring democratic reforms to Latin America, helped further his association with human rights. Much more electrifying was his promise to send an American to the moon by the end of the decade. Kennedy's delicate carrot-and-stick maneuvering with the Soviet Union and Nikita Khrushchev overcame a crisis over the future of the divided city of Berlin and the potential of a nuclear holocaust during the Cuban missile crisis of 1962, enabling him to conclude an agreement with the Soviet Union to ban nuclear tests in the atmosphere. His sudden martyrdom on November 22, 1963, by suspected assassin Lee Harvey Oswald quickly became the inspiration for President Johnson's Great Society program of social reforms, especially major civil rights legislation.

The second Kennedy legacy, more arguable and tentative, involved the contention that his objectives were myopic to begin with, and that he encouraged inflated expectations, both at home and abroad. His misguided effort to topple Fidel Castro's Cuban regime during the Bay of Pigs fiasco triggered a chain of events that helped lead to the later showdown over Russian missiles in Cuba. His continuation of the American commitment to the South Vietnamese government of President Ngo Dinh Diem intensified the escalation in Southeast Asia. That policy became virtually irreversible when Kennedy became an accomplice in Diem's subsequent overthrow. Those who had expected a more activist presidency found him too timid about pressuring the still-powerful congressional conservatives. Fear of political retribution inhibited requests for additional civil rights legislation until violent resistance to Rev. Dr. Martin Luther King, Jr.'s, desegregation efforts removed his options.

By then, Kennedy's reputation, together with the opening of a more hopeful dialogue with the Soviets, had made him an international hero. A transitional presidency became better remembered as a model for future White House leadership and for its reaffirmation of American humanitarian values. There had been other assassinations, but only Kennedy's resembled Lincoln's in helping create a new legend. To millions all over the world, John F. Kennedy continued to embody an almost mythical view of the ideal American president.

Herbert S. Parmet, *J. F. K.: The Presidency of John F. Kennedy* (1983); Arthur M. Schlesinger, Jr., *A Thousand Days* (1965).

HERBERT S. PARMET

See also Elections: 1960; Roman Catholic Church. *For events during Kennedy's administration, see* Bay of Pigs Invasion; Civil Rights Movement; Middle East–U.S. Relations; Peace Corps; Space Program; Vietnam War.

KENNEDY, ROBERT F.

(1925–1968), attorney general of the United States and senator from New York. Kennedy grew up in the spirited, closely knit, and highly competitive family of Joseph P. Kennedy. Educated at Harvard College and the University of Virginia Law School, he made his political debut in 1952 as manager of his older brother John's successful campaign for the U.S. Senate from Massachusetts.

In 1953 he went to work for the Senate Subcommittee on Investigations, chaired by Senator Joseph McCarthy, already notorious for reckless accusations of disloyalty. Belatedly disturbed by McCarthy's tactics, Kennedy resigned after six months. The next year, as Democratic counsel for the committee, he wrote the minority report condemning McCarthy's investigation of the army. His later work as chief counsel for the Senate Rackets Committee in 1957–1959 increased his reputation as an able and relentless prosecutor.

In 1960 he ran his brother's successful campaign for the presidency. His subsequent appointment as attorney general provoked criticism, but in time he won respect for his cogent, humane, and nonpartisan administration of the Department of Justice.

Challenged by the rising demand of black Americans for their constitutional rights, the Kennedys intervened to protect black students at the Universities of Mississippi and Alabama, though activists criticized the department's reluctance to assume local police power in protecting civil rights workers. Robert Kennedy saw voting as the key to racial justice and proposed the most far-reaching civil rights statute since Reconstruction, the Civil Rights Act of 1964, passed after President Kennedy's assassination.

Robert Kennedy's relationship to the president gave him a watching brief in foreign affairs. For a time he promoted an ill-conceived campaign of CIA covert action against Fidel Castro's Cuba, but during the missile crisis of 1962 he led the opposition to a surprise military attack on Cuba and played a key role in bringing about a peaceful resolution.

Devastated by his brother's death, he remained for some months in Lyndon Johnson's cabinet. But his relations with the new president were prickly, and he soon resigned to run for the Senate from New York. As senator, Kennedy applauded Johnson's Great Society but increasingly disagreed with the administration over foreign policy, especially in Vietnam.

The sixties were a turbulent decade, and Robert Kennedy responded to that turbulence with unusual directness and sensitivity. He had evolved from the rigid prosecutor of a decade earlier into a popular leader who combined political realism with social idealism and passion with humor. He identified increasingly with the dispossessed and powerless of America — the poor, the young, racial minorities. In 1968, after much hesitation, he struck out for the Democratic presidential nomination. A whirlwind campaign culminated in victory in the California primary. Later that night he was assassinated.

Robert Kennedy's brusque challenge to the complacencies of American society brought hope to many Americans, fear to others. His insistence that anyone who "stands up for an ideal, or acts to improve the lot of others, or strikes out against injustice" can make a difference to the world struck a moral nerve, especially among the young, and kept him alive in folk memory long after his death.

Arthur M. Schlesinger, Jr., *Robert Kennedy and His Times* (1978).

ARTHUR M. SCHLESINGER, JR.

See also Kennedy, John F.

KENT STATE INCIDENT

On April 30, 1970, President Richard M. Nixon appeared on national television to announce the invasion of Cambodia by the United States and the need to draft 150,000 more soldiers for an expansion of the Vietnam War effort. This provoked massive protests on campuses throughout the country. At Kent State University in Ohio, protesters launched a demonstration that included setting fire to the ROTC building, whereupon the governor of Ohio dispatched nine hundred National Guardsmen to the campus. During an altercation on May 4, twenty-eight guardsmen opened fire on a crowd, killing four students and wounding nine. Following the killings, the unrest across the country escalated even further. Almost five hundred colleges were shut down or disrupted by protests.

Despite the public outcry, the Justice Department initially declined to conduct a grand jury investigation. A report by the President's Commission on Campus Unrest did acknowledge, however, that the action of the guardsmen had been "unnecessary, unwarranted, and inexcusable." Eventually, a grand jury indicted eight of the guardsmen, but the charges were dismissed for lack of evidence.

In their coverage of the events at Kent State, the media used a photo, taken by a fellow student, of a woman kneeling in anguish, arms upraised, beside one of the slain students. This Pulitzer Prize–winning image soon became a symbol of the social upheaval of the time.

Another, similar incident took place ten days later, on May 14, at Jackson State University, an all-black school in Mississippi. During a student protest, police and state highway patrolmen fired automatic weapons into a dormitory, killing two students and wounding nine others. No warning had been given and no evidence was ever found of student sniping that might have justified the shootings. Nevertheless, unlike the Kent State episode, this incident evoked little national attention, embittering many blacks who felt that the killing of black students was not taken as seriously as that of whites.

See also Vietnam War.

KENTUCKY AND VIRGINIA RESOLUTIONS

See Virginia and Kentucky Resolutions.

KEROUAC, JACK

(1922–1969), novelist. Kerouac was an unlikely figure to become a patron saint of the Beat movement of the 1950s, which his novel *On the Road* made famous, or of the 1960s counterculture, which he eventually came to despise. He was born Jean-Louis Lebris de Kerouac to French-Canadian parents in Lowell, Massachusetts, a mill town where his father worked as a printer. A shy, introspective child with a deep religious streak, he achieved local fame as a high school athlete, which enabled him to attend Columbia University on a football scholarship.

But Kerouac, who had long wanted to be a writer, was restless. He dropped out of Columbia to become a merchant seaman and then enlisted in the U.S. Navy. When he returned to New York he met Allen Ginsberg and William Burroughs, whose friends, ranging from Columbia students and jazz musicians to petty thieves, formed the nucleus of the Beat legend that would be exhaustively chronicled by both Kerouac and Ginsberg. The circle was completed when Kerouac met a hypnotic character named Neal Cassady in 1946. Their cross-country travels between 1946 and 1950 became the subject of *On the Road,* his most accessible and widely read book, and *Visions of Cody,* his daring, at times unreadable experiment in free-form, spontaneous prose. (It was not published in its entirety until after his death.)

Kerouac's first and most conventional novel, *The Town and the City* (1950), was heavily indebted to another seemingly formless autobiographical writer, Thomas Wolfe, but it made little impact. *On the Road,* written in three weeks in 1951 on a single roll of printer's paper, did not find a publisher for six years. During this interval he wrote nearly a dozen books that appeared only after *On the Road* had caused a sensation.

To the public, Kerouac was associated with the flamboyant characters in *On the Road,* especially Dean Moriarty, who was based on Cassady. Yet Kerouac (as Sal Paradise) plays a largely passive role in the book: he's the inhibited observer looking for excitement, fascinated by people like Cassady and Ginsberg who seem more self-assured and wildly abandoned. Magnetic to men and women alike, the dexterous Cassady was a con man and sexual virtuoso who was above all intensely alive. Kerouac turned Cassady's complicated life into a dream of irresponsibility, a myth of cool, hip energy and impulsive mobility that sharply rebuked the conservative social values of the 1950s, which stressed home, family, stability, work, and success.

Often confused with his characters, alternately repelled and attracted by the adulation he received, Kerouac was destroyed by his new fame. He lost his fluency as a writer, grew increasingly tied to his domineering mother, suffered a nervous breakdown, which he described in *Big Sur* (1962), and withdrew into a cocoon of bitterness and alcohol. Pathetically isolated even from his friends, he drank himself to death, adding to the legend he had tried to escape.

Kerouac's messy, self-destructive life was redeemed by his honesty as a writer. Rarely inventing anything, he had remarkable powers of recollection and extraordinary tenderness toward everything he had experienced. His writing begs to be read aloud: the run-on cadences, inspired by jazz, influenced by Cassady's verbal riffs, were written for the ear rather than the page. Eschewing the constraints of formal prose, his kinetic language experiments often achieved an immediacy that helped make works like Ginsberg's "Howl" and Burroughs's *Naked Lunch* possible.

Ann Charters, *Kerouac: A Biography* (1973); Tim Hunt, *Kerouac's Crooked Road: Development of a Fiction* (1981); John Tytell, *Naked Angels: The Lives and Literature of the Beat Generation* (1976).

MORRIS DICKSTEIN

See also Literature.

KEY, FRANCIS SCOTT

(1779–1843), lawyer and author of the words of "The Star-Spangled Banner." Key was born in what is now Carroll County, Maryland, into a prosperous family. After graduating from St. John's College in Annapolis in 1796, Key trained as a lawyer. (An early friend was Roger B. Taney, later chief justice of the U.S. Supreme Court, who married Key's sister.) Key began the practice of law in Frederick in 1801 and by the time of the War of 1812 had established a successful law practice in Georgetown, D.C. He was also an amateur poet and was extremely active in the Episcopal church.

Key's chance for more than local fame came as a result of the War of 1812. As one phase of a series of attacks on the United States in 1814, the British landed troops in the Chesapeake Bay area. In August, after defeating the Americans at the Battle of Bladensburg, they temporarily occupied Washington, D.C., burned the public buildings, withdrew, and sailed up the Chesapeake to attack Baltimore. In the course of their withdrawal, the British arrested and took with them a local physician, Dr. William Beanes.

Beanes's friends asked Key to intervene with the British to secure his release. Accompanied by an American agent for prisoners of war, Key sailed out to the British fleet in Chesapeake Bay and arranged for Beanes to be freed. The British, however, were about to launch their attack on Baltimore, and they detained the Americans until after the attack. On the night of September 13–14 the British bombarded Fort McHenry, one of the American forts guarding Baltimore. In the morning, when "by dawn's early light" Key saw the American flag still flying over the fort, he was inspired to write the poem that became known as "The Star-Spangled Banner." He quickly jotted down the lines and that night on shore wrote out a fair copy. It was

printed immediately and issued in Baltimore as a handbill with the title "Defence of Fort M'Henry" and was quickly reprinted in Baltimore and elsewhere. Set to the music of the English drinking song "To Anacreon in Heaven," Key's composition soon achieved national popularity, although Congress did not adopt it as the official national anthem until 1931.

Key continued to practice law and from 1833 to 1841 served as U.S. district attorney for Washington, D.C. He was sent to Alabama to settle a dispute with that state over Creek Indian lands in 1833. Key was not a serious poet but wrote verses from time to time, a collection of which was published posthumously in 1857.

F. S. Key-Smith, *Francis Scott Key* (1911); *Poems of the Late Francis S. Key* (1857).

REGINALD HORSMAN

KING, BILLIE JEAN

(1943–   ), champion tennis player and outspoken advocate of equality for girls and women in sports. King's battle against elitism and sexism in competitive tennis has often reflected and sometimes helped shape significant changes in American society. At various times, King's words and actions have placed her in the center of debate over equality between the sexes, amateurism versus professionalism in sports, abortion rights, and gay and lesbian rights.

Billie Jean Moffitt learned to play tennis on the public courts of California. Her entry into the competitive ranks in 1955 at the Southern California Junior Championships gave her her first taste of the country club atmosphere and snobbishness endemic to tennis and its governing body, the United States Lawn Tennis Association (USLTA). Throughout her career, she devoted much of her energy to democratizing tennis. In 1967, with six Wimbledon titles under her belt, she attacked the USLTA in a series of press conferences. King strongly denounced "shamateurism," the USLTA's practice of paying top players under the table to guarantee their entry into USLTA-sponsored tournaments. According to King, this corrupt system, by preventing the professionalization of tennis, kept the game elitist and seriously limited opportunities for players who were not independently wealthy.

The advent of open tennis in 1968, only a few months after King had turned professional, presented a new set of problems, especially for women players on the tour. As under-the-table payments were replaced by prize money, the pay differential between men and women became a matter of heated public discussion. Defying male players, USLTA officials, and tournament promoters, most of whom argued that women should be paid less because the women's game was inferior and drew fewer spectators, King was a central figure in the formation of the Virginia Slims Tour in 1971. The tour offered women players a more lucrative alternative to USLTA-sponsored tournaments and, ultimately, commanded enough loyalty from top women players to force the USLTA to revise its sexist practice.

King's many campaigns on behalf of women in sports have earned her many accolades from devotees of feminism; nonetheless, she has often displayed a certain ambivalence toward the women's movement. In the early 1980s, she was unconvinced that the Equal Rights Amendment was necessary or desirable. King was also placed on the defensive by negative publicity surrounding her private life. The press often focused on the unconventional nature of the Kings' marriage, asking in postgame interviews if her husband Larry had seen the match, how often they saw each other, and if they wanted children. A publicized abortion in 1971 and a palimony suit in 1981 stemming from a lesbian affair with her personal secretary further fed the fires of speculation concerning her relationship to traditional femininity.

Billie Jean King, a militant, highly visible, and effective proponent of equality for women athletes, was named *Sports Illustrated*'s first Sportswoman of the Year in 1972. In 1973 she shattered the myth that the best women tennis players are inferior to even the most mediocre men players by decisively defeating Bobby Riggs before a television audience of 37 million people. In 1979, King won her twentieth Wimbledon title, thus breaking the all-time record. Upon retirement from competition in 1984, she held title to nine U.S. championships and one singles title

each in the Australian Open, the French Open, and the German Open.

Billie Jean King, with Kim Chapin, *Billie Jean* (1974); Billie Jean King, with Frank Deford, *Billie Jean* (1982).

CINDY HIMES

See also Feminist Movement; Spectator Sports.

KING, ERNEST

(1878–1956), World War II U.S. chief of naval operations. King saw action as a midshipman during the Spanish-American War and graduated near the top of the U.S. Naval Academy class of 1901. He served on the staff of Adm. Henry Mayo, the commander in chief of the Atlantic Fleet, during World War I. Following the armistice, King organized the Naval Postgraduate School and then went into the submarine service. In 1927 he won a Navy Cross for the salvage of the sunken submarine *S-51.*

At forty-nine, King turned his hand to naval aviation, commanded the carrier *Lexington,* and served as chief of the Bureau of Aeronautics from 1933 to 1936. He was in large measure responsible for the huge expansion of naval aviation in that decade and for the development of naval aircraft used in World War II. He took command of the Neutrality Patrol in 1940 and, a few months later, became commander in chief of the Atlantic Fleet. He handled this complex task by revamping his style of command and granting his subordinates enormous latitude. He was responsible for organizing and training a new amphibious force and for convoying transatlantic merchant shipping. Days after Pearl Harbor, Secretary of the Navy Frank Knox named him commander in chief of the U.S. Fleet, and in March 1942, he became chief of naval operations as well.

As a member of the Joint Chiefs of Staff, King played a major role in shaping Allied strategy in World War II. He had the widest command experience and the sharpest mind among the Allied chieftains, but his temper and disdain for those who did not possess his gifts made him a poor military statesman. King relied not on tactful persuasion but on logic and forceful presentation to get his ideas across, and the results were often not what he sought. He was instrumental in developing the escort carrier task forces that won the Battle of the Atlantic, and he provided the landing in Normandy with the landing craft and naval gunfire that ensured its success. King was the prime mover behind Operation Anvil, the landing in southern France in 1944 that provided logistics support to Gen. Dwight D. Eisenhower's drive across northern Europe.

But the bulk of the U.S. Navy was in the Pacific, and it was there that King's contribution was the greatest. He employed the carrier-launched raids that threw Japan's offensive off balance and led to the decisive victory at Midway in June 1942. King then remorselessly fed the South Pacific air campaign until attrition had destroyed the enemy's air arm. In 1944, after eight months of heavy fighting, the Japanese fleet was virtually destroyed in the Philippine Sea. King intended to bypass the Philippines and occupy Formosa, but President Franklin D. Roosevelt vetoed this strategy on political grounds. King supported preparations for an invasion of Japan, although he believed that the naval blockade and bombardment might make an invasion unnecessary. When the atomic bomb appeared as an alternative in mid-1945, King and army chief of staff Gen. George C. Marshall urged Harry S. Truman to use the device to end the war quickly. King retired in 1945 as a five-star fleet admiral.

Most naval historians agree that King was the greatest naval commander of the twentieth century. His powers of reason were first-rate, and his professionalism and understanding of the complexities of modern warfare were without parallel. Although he was too unrestrained a personality to succeed as a military diplomat, he was intelligent, dynamic, and merciless, widely respected for exacting outstanding results from his ships and his men. He was also feared and hated, but his grasp of strategy and his ability to impose his will on the enemy were major factors in the defeat of the Axis navies in World War II.

Thomas Buell, *Master of Sea Power* (1979); Ernest King, *Fleet Admiral King: A Naval Record* (1952); Robert W. Love, Jr., "Ernest J. King," in Robert W. Love, Jr., ed., *The Chiefs of Naval Operations* (1980).

ROBERT W. LOVE, JR.

See also Armed Forces; World War II.

KING, MARTIN LUTHER, JR.

(1929–1968), civil rights leader. One of the world's best-known advocates of nonviolent social change, King was born in Atlanta. As a student at Morehouse College in Atlanta, at Crozer Theological Seminary in Pennsylvania, and at Boston University, he deepened his understanding of theological scholarship and of Mahatma Gandhi's nonviolent strategy for social change. He received a Ph.D. in theology in 1955 and became pastor of Dexter Avenue Baptist Church in Montgomery, Alabama.

In December 1955, after Montgomery civil rights activist Rosa Parks refused to obey the city's policy mandating segregation on buses, black residents launched a bus boycott and elected King as president of the newly formed Montgomery Improvement Association. As the boycott continued during 1956, King gained national prominence for his exceptional oratorical skills and personal courage. His house was bombed, and he and other boycott leaders were convicted on charges of conspiring to interfere with the bus company's operations. But in December 1956 Montgomery's buses were desegregated when the Supreme Court declared Alabama's segregation laws unconstitutional.

In 1957, seeking to build upon the success in Montgomery, King and other black ministers founded the Southern Christian Leadership Conference (SCLC). As president, King emphasized the goal of black voting rights when he spoke at the Lincoln Memorial during the 1957 Prayer Pilgrimage for Freedom. He traveled to West Africa to attend the independence celebration of Ghana and toured India, increasing his understanding of Gandhi's ideas. At the end of 1959, he resigned from Dexter and returned to Atlanta where SCLC headquarters were located.

Although increasingly portrayed as the preeminent black spokesman, King did not mobilize mass protest activity during SCLC's first few years. Then southern black college students launched a wave of sit-in protests in 1960. Although King sympathized with their movement and spoke at the founding meeting of the Student Non-Violent Coordinating Committee (SNCC) in April 1960, he soon became the target of criticisms from SNCC activists. Even King's joining a student sit-in and his subsequent arrest in October 1960 did not allay the tensions. (After the arrest presidential candidate John F. Kennedy's sympathetic telephone call to King's wife, Coretta Scott King, helped attract crucial black support for Kennedy's campaign.) Conflicts between King and the younger militants were also evident when SCLC and SNCC assisted the Albany (Georgia) movement's campaign of mass protests in 1961–1962.

After achieving few of their objectives in Albany, King and his staff initiated a major campaign in Birmingham, Alabama, where white police officials were notorious for their antiblack attitudes. In 1963, clashes between unarmed black demonstrators and police with attack dogs and fire hoses generated newspaper headlines throughout the world. Subsequent mass demonstrations in many communities culminated in a march on August 28, 1963, attracting more than 250,000 protesters to Washington, D.C. Addressing the marchers from the steps of the Lincoln Memorial, King delivered his famous I Have a Dream oration.

During the year following the march, King's renown as a nonviolent leader grew, and, in 1964, he received the Nobel Peace Prize. Despite the accolades, however, King faced strong challenges to his leadership. Malcolm X's message of self-defense and black nationalism expressed the anger of northern urban blacks more effectively than did King's moderation, and in 1966 King encountered strong criticism from "black power" proponent Stokely Carmichael. Shortly afterward, white counterprotestors in Chicago physically assaulted King during an unsuccessful effort to transfer nonviolent protest techniques to the North. Nevertheless, King remained committed to nonviolence. Early in 1968, he initiated a "poor people's campaign" to confront economic problems not addressed by civil rights reforms.

King's ability to achieve his objectives was also limited by the increasing resistance he encountered from national political leaders. As urban racial violence escalated, FBI director J. Edgar Hoover intensified his efforts to discredit King, and King's public criticism of American intervention in the Vietnam War soured his relations with the Johnson administration. When he delivered his last speech during a bitter sanitation workers' strike in Memphis, he admitted, "We've got some difficult days ahead, but it really doesn't matter with me now, because I've been to the mountaintop." The following evening, April 4, 1968, he was assassinated by James Earl Ray.

After his death, King remained a controversial symbol of the civil rights struggle, revered by many for his martyrdom on behalf of nonviolence and condemned by others for his insurgent views. In 1986 King's birthday, January 15, became a federal holiday.

Taylor Branch, *Parting the Waters: America in the King Years, 1954–1963* (1988); David J. Garrow, *Bearing the Cross: Martin Luther King, Jr., and the Southern Christian Leadership Conference* (1986); David L. Lewis, *King: A Critical Biography* (1970).

CLAYBORNE CARSON

See also Civil Rights Movement; Southern Christian Leadership Conference.

KING PHILIP

See Philip (King Philip).

KING PHILIP'S WAR

King Philip's War of 1675–1676 (also known as Metacom's Rebellion) marked the last major effort by the Indians of southern New England to drive out the English settlers. Led by Metacom, the Pokunoket chief called "King Philip" by the English, the bands known today as Wampanoag Indians joined with the Nipmucks, Pocumtucks, and Narragansetts in a bloody uprising. It lasted fourteen months and destroyed twelve frontier towns.

Although the sequence of events leading to the outbreak of war is unclear, the Indians' resentment of the English had been building since the 1660s. They had become increasingly dependent on English goods, food, and weapons, and their bargaining power diminished as the fur trade dried up, tribal lands were sold, and Metacom and other leaders were forced by the colonists to recognize English sovereignty. Rather than accommodate further, some of the Indians took up arms. Others, including the Mohegan, Pequot, Massachusetts, and Nauset Indians, sided with the English.

The war ended in August 1676, shortly after Metacom was captured and beheaded. Some of his supporters escaped to Canada; those who surrendered were shipped off as slaves to the West Indies. The Puritans interpreted their victory as a sign of God's favor, as well as a symbolic purge of their spiritual community. The Indians who remained faced servitude, disease, cultural disruption, and the expropriation of their lands.

See also Indians; New England Colonies; Philip (King Philip).

KISSINGER, HENRY A.

(1923–   ), foreign policy specialist, national security adviser, and secretary of state. A German-Jewish refugee from Nazi Germany, Kissinger rose to prominence as a Harvard University professor of government in the 1950s and 1960s. He then became the most celebrated and controversial U.S. diplomat since the Second World War in the administrations of Richard M. Nixon and Gerald Ford. As Nixon's national security adviser he concentrated power in the White House and rendered Secretary of State William Rogers and the professional foreign service almost irrelevant by conducting personal, secret negotiations with North Vietnam, the Soviet Union, and China. He negotiated the Paris agreements of 1973 ending direct U.S. involvement in the Vietnam War, engineered a short-lived era of détente with the Soviet Union, and opened frozen relations with the People's Republic of China. As secretary of state he shuttled among the capitals of Israel, Egypt, and Syria after the 1973 Middle East war.

A gregarious but manipulative man, Kissinger, seeking power and favorable publicity, cultivated prominent officials and influential reporters. For a while he achieved more popularity than any modern American diplomat. The Gallup poll listed him as the most admired man in America in 1972 and 1973. He received the Nobel Peace Prize in 1973 for his negotiations leading to the Paris peace accords that ended U.S. military action in Vietnam. Journalists lauded him as a "genius" and the "smartest guy around" after his secret trip to Beijing in July 1971 prepared the way for Nixon's visit to China in February 1972. Egyptian politicians called him "the magician" for his disengagement agreements separating Israeli and Arab armies.

Kissinger's reputation faded after 1973. During the Watergate scandal, congressional investigators discovered that he had ordered the FBI to tap the telephones of subordinates on the staff of the National Security Council, a charge he had denied earlier. Congress also learned that he had tried to block the accession to power of Chile's President Salvador Allende Gossens in 1970 and had helped destabilize Allende's Socialist party government thereafter.

Some of Kissinger's foreign policy achievements crumbled in 1975 and 1976. The Communists' victory in Vietnam and Cambodia destroyed the Paris peace accords, and détente with the Soviet Union never fulfilled the hopes Kissinger had aroused. By 1976 the United States and the Soviet Union had not moved beyond the 1972 Interim Agreement limiting strategic arms to conclude a full-fledged Strategic Arms Limitation Talks.

Kissinger became a liability for President Ford during the 1976 presidential election. Ronald Reagan, challenging Ford for the Republican nomination, and Democrat Jimmy Carter both assailed Kissinger's policy of détente with the Soviet Union for ignoring Soviet abuses of human rights and Moscow's greater assertiveness in international relations. Reagan complained that Kissinger's program offered "the peace of the grave." Carter accused him of conducting "lone ranger diplomacy" by excluding Congress and foreign affairs professionals from foreign policy matters.

Kissinger's flair for dramatic diplomatic gestures brought him fame, and it encouraged diplomats in the Carter, Reagan, and George Bush administrations to try to emulate his accomplishments. He failed, however, to create the "structure of peace" he had promised. By 1977 he had lost control over American foreign policy, and no one after him ever dominated the process as he had from 1969 to 1974.

Seymour Hersh, *The Price of Power: Kissinger in the Nixon White House* (1983); Henry Kissinger, *White House Years* (1979) and *Years of Upheaval* (1982); Robert D. Schulzinger, *Henry Kissinger: Doctor of Diplomacy* (1989).

ROBERT D. SCHULZINGER

See also Détente; Elections: 1976; Middle East– U.S. Relations; Nixon, Richard M.; Strategic Arms Limitation Talks; Vietnam War.

KITCHEN CABINET

The "Kitchen Cabinet" was a group of unofficial advisers with whom President Andrew Jackson regularly consulted, particularly during his first years in office, 1829 to 1831. During this period, Jackson's official cabinet was riven with factionalism, much of it due to the personal rivalry between the vice president, John C. Calhoun, and the secretary of state, Martin Van Buren. Jackson soon stopped holding cabinet meetings altogether and instead formed his Kitchen Cabinet. The most influential member was Amos Kendall, a newspaper editor from Kentucky for whom Jackson arranged an appointment as fourth auditor of the Treasury; two others were Andrew J. Donelson, the president's secretary, and William B. Lewis, a close associate from his military days. Only two members of the official cabinet joined the informal group: Martin Van Buren and the secretary of war, John H. Eaton. Duff Green, editor of the administration's favored newspaper, *United States Telegraph,* served in the Kitchen Cabinet at first, but his partiality to Calhoun led to a rift in 1830, whereupon Francis J. Blair, like Kendall a Kentucky journalist, was persuaded to come to Washington and start a new paper, the *Washington Globe.* Blair then became an important member of the Kitchen Cabinet.

Relations between Jackson and his official cabinet reached a new low in the spring of 1831, when all the members except Van Buren opposed the president and supported their wives in ostracizing Secretary Eaton's new wife, a former barmaid. Eaton and Van Buren chose to resign over the matter, permitting Jackson to request resignations from the rest of the cabinet, most of whom were Calhoun supporters. After the formation of a wholly new cabinet in the summer of 1831, the role of the Kitchen Cabinet was considerably diminished.

See also Jackson, Andrew.

KNIGHTS OF LABOR

The Knights of Labor began as a secret society of tailors in Philadelphia in 1869. The organization grew slowly during the hard years of the 1870s, but worker militancy rose toward the end of the decade, especially after the great railroad strike of 1877, and the Knights' membership rose with it. Grand Master Workman Terence V. Powderly took office in 1879, and under his leadership the Knights flourished; by 1885 the group had 110,000 members. Powderly dispensed with the earlier rules of secrecy and committed the organization to seeking the eight-hour day, abolition of child labor, equal pay for equal work, and political reforms including the graduated income tax.

Unlike most trade unions of the day, the Knights' unions were vertically organized — each included all workers in a given industry, regardless of trade. The Knights were also unusual in accepting workers of all skill levels and both sexes; blacks were included after 1883 (though in segregated locals). On the other hand, the Knights strongly supported the Chinese Exclusion Act of 1882 and the Contract Labor Law of 1885; like many labor leaders at the time, Powderly believed these laws were needed to protect the American work force against competition from underpaid laborers imported by unscrupulous employers.

Powderly believed in boycotts and arbitration, but he opposed strikes. He had only marginal control over the union membership, however, and a successful strike by the Knights against Jay Gould's southwestern railroad system in 1884 brought a flood of new members. By the beginning of 1886, there were 700,000 Knights of Labor. But when the workers struck the Gould system again in the spring of 1886, they were badly beaten. Meanwhile, other members of the Knights participated — again, over Powderly's objections — in the general strike that began in Chicago on May 1, 1886. When a bomb explosion at a workers' rally in Haymarket Square May 4 triggered a national wave of arrests and repression, labor activism of every kind suffered a setback, and the Knights were particularly — though unfairly — singled out for blame. By 1890, the membership had fallen to 100,000. Although Powderly's somewhat erratic leadership and the continuing factionalism within the union undoubtedly contributed to the Knights' demise, the widespread repression of labor unions in the late 1880s was also an important factor.

See also Haymarket Affair; Labor.

KNOW-NOTHING PARTY

The American party of the 1850s derived its informal name from its members replying, when asked about their role, "I know nothing." The party was anti-Catholic and anti-immigrant. It grew out of the Order of the Star-Spangled Banner, a secret society apparently founded in New York City in 1849. In the wake of the collapse of the Whigs and the Democratic split over the Kansas-Nebraska Act in 1854 and 1855, its supporters won several offices, including mayor of Philadelphia and control of the Massachusetts legislature. Some northern Know-Nothings also sought to cooperate with antislavery forces not yet prepared to join an official Republican party.

When the Know-Nothing party endorsed the Kansas-Nebraska Act at its presidential nominating convention in 1856, northern members bolted. Southern members nominated former president Millard Fillmore of New York for president and Andrew J. Donelson of Tennessee for vice president. Most northern Know-Nothings tenuously supported the Republican candidate, John C. Frémont. Fillmore tried to distance himself from the party's nativist tendencies but carried only Maryland. The Know-Nothing party soon dissolved.

See also Elections: 1856; Nativism.

KOREAN WAR

Among the wars of the United States the Korean conflict was the last to utilize conventional strategies, tactics, and weapons. Simultaneously it was the first limited, inconclusive conflict to mix the antagonists of the cold war in the cauldron of a civil war.

Until the mid-1960s, most American interpretations of the United States' entry into the war supported the Truman administration's position that the United States had become involved because its honor and credibility were at stake, it felt compelled to contain the Moscow-directed global expansion of communism, and it saw tolerance of North Korean aggression as Munich-like appeasement. But the Vietnam War brought challenges to established views on American foreign and defense affairs, including the Korean War. Most revisionists blamed America and South Korea for precipitating hostilities, argued that the conflict was basically a civil war, and charged that ethnocentrism and economic imperialism had influenced American policymakers on Asia.

War erupted in Korea on June 25, 1950, along the thirty-eighth parallel that separated North and South Korea. As North Korean units pushed deep into South Korea, the U.N. Security Council, at the instigation of the United States, condemned the North Korean invasion and later called on members to assist South Korea. That first week, President Harry S. Truman, without seeking congressional approval, committed American forces to the conflict. On July 7, the U.N. Command was established, with General of the Army Douglas MacArthur appointed as its head. The nearest U.S. forces were already under his Far East Command, including in Japan alone four army divisions, the Fifth Air Force, and units of the Seventh Fleet. Eventually nearly 1.8 million Americans would serve in Korea, of whom 54,200 were killed, 103,300 wounded, and 8,200 missing in action. Besides the preponderant American and South Korean forces, military units from fifteen other members of the

United Nations fought in the conflict.

Military operations evolved in four phases during the initial, or MacArthur, period. First, the North Korean offensive of June to September 1950 drove from the thirty-eighth parallel to the Naktong River. MacArthur's forces succeeded in holding the southeast center of the Korean peninsula because of the rapid reinforcement of his command and the crippling interdiction of the North Korean supply lines by American air power. In the second phase, the United Nations–South Korean offensive of September to November 1950 began with a brilliant amphibious assault at Inchon and advanced north toward the Yalu River border. Next, Communist China intervened, launching an offensive (November 1950 to January 1951) that thwarted the United Nations' attempt to "liberate" North Korea and pushed MacArthur's forces below the thirty-eighth parallel. From January to April 1951, the Chinese were hurled back above the parallel in a counteroffensive by the rejuvenated U.S. Eighth Army of Gen. Matthew Ridgway.

Meanwhile MacArthur became increasingly vociferous and allegedly insubordinate in demanding a blockade of the Chinese coast, naval and air bombardments of Chinese industrial centers, and employment of Generalissimo Chiang Kai-shek's Taiwan troops in Korean operations and against the Chinese mainland. President Truman and the Joint Chiefs of Staff disagreed, however, and in April 1951 Truman named Ridgway to replace MacArthur as head of the U.N. Command, the U.S. Far East Command, U.S. Army Forces in the Far East, and the Allied occupation in Japan.

The next period of the war, April 1951–July 1953, fell into two major phases: operations and negotiations. The front lines became virtually stalemated, but hard fighting continued, primarily in the Iron Triangle and Punch Bowl regions just north of the thirty-eighth parallel. The two most savage battles of the period, both communist defeats, were Heartbreak Ridge in September-October 1951 and Pork Chop Hill in April 1953. The U.N. naval and air forces maintained firm control of the seas and skies of the combat zone, with the American strategic bombing campaign reaching a zenith in mid-1952. The U.N. Command was led by Ridgway until May 1952 and thereafter by Gen. Mark Clark. The U.S. Eighth Army, which was the principal ground force of the U.N. Command, was headed by Gen. James Van Fleet and then by Gen. Maxwell Taylor.

In the acrimonious truce negotiations, which began in July 1951, the U.N. delegation was led by Adm. Turner Joy and later by Gen. William Harrison, both Americans. The armistice, signed on July 27, 1953, resulted in a cessation of hostilities and a prisoner exchange, but it left the peninsula divided close to the thirty-eighth parallel and actually satisfied none of the belligerents.

Because of their appalling human and property losses in the war, both Koreas underwent slow rehabilitation. North Korea remained a staunchly communist state, though more closely aligned after 1953 to Peking than to Moscow. South Korea developed into a prosperous, if politically divided, country with strong economic and security links to the United States.

The consequences of the war for the United States were manifold. Desegregation of the Eighth Army during the Korean operations was a milestone for blacks in the American military establishment. McCarthyism fed on public discontent with the conduct of the war. Dissent grew as the war became protracted and indecisive, contributing to the 1952 presidential triumph of General of the Army Dwight D. Eisenhower, the first Republican in the White House in two decades. The Korean hostilities prompted the United States to strengthen its military commitment to NATO. The war also hastened the signing of the Japanese peace treaty, the formation of SEATO, and the creation of American security pacts with Japan, Australia, New Zealand, and the Philippines.

From the start of the Korean fighting, the Truman administration escalated military assistance to the French in the Vietnam War and then sent aid and advisers to the fledgling Republic of South Vietnam. Washington assumed that global communism was monolithic and that Moscow was dictating the aggression both in Korea and in Vietnam. In the later American involvement in Vietnam, as in Korea, the U.S. government was never able to delineate clearly the currents of nationalism, communism, and imperialism that seemed to flow into one another.

Clay Blair, *The Forgotten War: America in Korea, 1950–1953* (1987); Burton I. Kaufman, *The Korean War: Challenges in Crisis, Credibility, and Command* (1986).

D. Clayton James

See also Asia-U.S. Relations; Cold War; MacArthur, Douglas; Truman, Harry S.

KROC, RAY

(1902–1984), fast-food restaurant franchising pioneer. By developing the McDonald's Corporation (1955), the world's largest restaurateur changed public eating habits and the franchising industry.

A franchisor licenses others to (a) sell its products or (b) use its business format (name and operating methods). Product franchising has a long history, having been used by Isaac Singer in appointing sewing machine agent-dealers in the mid-nineteenth century. Product franchisors profit primarily from the sale of their wares to the franchisees. Ray Kroc was a leader in strict business-format franchising, whereby licensees must conform to detailed operating rules, normally pay the franchisor licensing fees and royalties on sales, and, often, buy merchandise from approved suppliers.

Raymond Albert Kroc, born in Chicago, never finished high school. He became a volunteer ambulance driver in World War I, a dance-band musician, a salesman and district sales manager for Lily-Tulip paper cups and plates, and a promoter of a milk shake mixing machine. This modest career taught him much about the low-price food service market, apparently fostered a strong drive for achievement when the opportunity emerged in his fifties, and probably reinforced such traits as persistence, optimism, and hard work, an ability to select and nurture ambitious associates, and an intuitive sense of mainstream American culture. An ardent political conservative, Kroc vigorously espoused an antiregulatory philosophy and particularly sought a modification of the minimum wage law to permit payment of lower wages to teenage and student workers. He contributed to the development of management practices by example rather than by theoretical writing.

In 1954, wondering why the McDonald brothers' small San Bernardino, California, hamburger stand needed so many of his milk shake mixers, he discovered they had developed a high-volume factory-like mass production (labor-specialization, task-routinization) system that produced good sandwiches at a low price. The brothers had already attracted much attention and had lackadaisically franchised some other restaurants, but with little guidance, control, or success.

Kroc persuaded the brothers to make him their exclusive agent in licensing others to use the McDonald name and methods and established McDonald's Corporation for the purpose. At the time few potential licensees anticipated how McDonald's would grow. Kroc also opened his own McDonald's drive-in in Des Plaines, Illinois, to demonstrate the format's profitability. Since he received only a small portion of the relatively low franchise royalty rate established by the McDonalds, his own restaurant earnings exceeded his income from franchising for a number of years. But he continued enthusiastically recruiting and supervising franchisees. He insisted on meticulous cleanliness and constantly improved the operating system. Under a plan he and an associate, Harry Sonnenborn, created, the Kroc-dominated corporation bought the real estate for new locations and then rented it to the franchisees on long-term leases. This increased revenues to support a field staff to work with franchisees and made the corporation more appealing for banks and other major lenders of capital funds. In 1961, the corporation bought out the brothers' interest at a price they themselves proposed but later regretted. In 1977, Kroc assumed the title of senior chairman. McDonald's had sold 65 billion hamburgers by 1987, the year before it opened its ten thousandth store.

The emphasis on cleanliness continued, but many of his (and the McDonalds') original ideas were ultimately modified. The store duties remained minutely divided and easily learned by large numbers of part-time, low-wage, teenage workers. But by the late 1980s, a dwindling teenage population had forced recruitment of senior citizens and others, and in some areas wages (and costs) increased. Fish, chicken, salad, and breakfast items were added to the original hamburgers to meet changing tastes and the need for higher sales volume. These changes complicated operations, slowed service, and increased costs. Tables and chairs finally appeared at most locations, without attracting the loungers Kroc feared.

Most early stores were located in small towns and suburbs to seek the family trade Kroc desired and were highly standardized in appearance with the ubiquitous "golden arches" outside. Subsequent units in city centers, airports, and other sites required exterior design changes. "Americanism" was a central theme in early McDonald advertising, but the corporation expanded to approximately fifty countries, including finally even the Soviet Union. The growing corporation acquired direct ownership of 25 to 30 percent of its restaurants, including many of the most profitable ones. Thus both the restaurants and the corporation became far more complex than Ray Kroc had originally envisaged, yet they retained much of his style and business philosophy.

Max Boas and Steve Crain, *Big Mac: The Unauthorized Story of McDonald's* (1977); John Love, *McDonald's behind the Arches* (1986).

STANLEY C. HOLLANDER

KU KLUX KLAN

There have been three Ku Klux Klan movements, which, despite a clear line of descent and strong family resemblances, were separate from one another in time, organization, and purpose.

The first Klan flourished during the Reconstruction era and was all but exclusively southern in its membership and concerns. Its objective was to perpetuate white supremacy following emancipation and the conferral of civil and political rights on blacks. It was founded at Pulaski, Tennessee, in 1866 as a social fraternity, but rapidly became a local regulator or vigilante organization similar to others at the time. Perhaps intrigued by its secrecy, disguises, and

unique name (derived from a Greek word for "circle" or "band"), former Confederates including Gen. Nathan Bedford Forrest converted the Klan in 1867 into a paramilitary force to oppose the Republican state government under William G. Brownlow. The order quickly spread across the South in the spring of 1868 as other Republican state governments came into being under the Congressional Reconstruction acts. A similar group in southern Louisiana called itself the Knights of the White Camellia.

Klansmen were drawn from every walk of life, but the leaders often were from the landholding and professional elite. After a brief flurry of practical joking and pretending to be ghosts, the Klan emerged as a terrorist group dedicated to defeating the Republican party and keeping blacks in "their place" socially and economically.

Most southern counties saw little of the Klan, but others were overrun by it for months or years at a time. It tended to thrive where the two parties or races were relatively evenly balanced; in such places, terrorism was most apt to change election results. In the worst-affected counties, disguised night riders ranged the countryside on a regular basis, dragging people from their homes, whipping, shooting, or otherwise assaulting them, destroying their property, or driving them away. Most of the victims were black, but white Republicans were also targets.

The Reconstruction Klan was largely rural; its victims fled to the towns for safety. It was also predominantly local, differing from place to place and with little or no central control. Members went their own way and few dared stop them. Most southern whites sympathized with the Klan's objectives if not its methods, and those who liked neither were often intimidated by it. As a result, few southerners opposed it, and the Klan often paralyzed the law enforcement process.

In a few states, such as Arkansas and North Carolina, white Republicans organized militia units and broke up the Klan. In most states, however, federal intervention was required, in the form of congressional legislation, military arrests, and trials in federal courts. By these means the Klan was virtually destroyed in 1871–1872.

Around the turn of the century the Klan, and the Confederate "lost cause" generally, took on a retrospective romantic appeal for southerners that had been lacking amid the suffering immediately after the conflict. This appeal was greatly stimulated by Thomas Dixon's 1905 novel, *The Clansman,* and D. W. Griffith's 1915 motion picture based on it, *Birth of a Nation.* The second Klan was born in that environment in 1915, which encouraged the superpatriotism of World War I. After the war its membership and geographic range expanded dramatically.

During its heyday in the early 1920s this Klan numbered over 3 million members nationwide, and it won political power in Indiana, Oklahoma, Oregon, and a number of other states. Unlike its predecessor it was mainly an urban phenomenon, reflecting the demographic changes in the nation. It drew members and leaders from all ranks of white society, but chiefly from lower-middle-class people, largely religious fundamentalists who felt threatened by a national drift away from the small-town Protestant culture they had grown up with.

The 1920s Klan fed on a variety of frustrations and fears: fear of the immigrants who were entering the country in large numbers, of communists and other radicals spawned by the Russian Revolution, of blacks who were moving into northern cities in increasing numbers, of Jews and Catholics who were rising in the economic and social order, and of labor unions demanding a larger share of the pie for their members.

Some of these Klansmen resorted to violence as in the days of old. But, in a membership exceeding 3 million, the vast majority were nonviolent. They marched in parades, paid dues, and bought regalia (this Klan was, for some of its organizers, a financial bonanza). They voted for Klan-endorsed political candidates and attended rallies where crosses were burned. (The original Klan did not burn crosses; the idea seems to have originated in Dixon's novels.) The organization dwindled away in the late 1920s, the result of its own legal, financial, and political excesses, though a remnant persisted until its final disbandment in 1944.

Only two years later the third Klan emerged. It was fueled by the fear of communism abroad and at home, but the civil rights movement provided its major stimulus. Organized in many parts of the country, it is primarily southern- and urban-based. Membership is still drawn disproportionately from undereducated people with relatively low social and economic status. The peak in membership came during the civil rights demonstrations of the 1960s, when it approached seventeen thousand.

The modern Klan is small, chronically fragmented, and prone to internal conflict over matters of policy and personal rivalry. Groups differ in their readiness to embrace violence. Some have accumulated substantial arsenals and have even manufactured and sold weapons to raise funds. They have sometimes forged alliances with like-minded organizations, as happened in 1979 when North Carolina Klansmen briefly formed a United Racist front with the state's tiny Nazi party. Klansmen have also had ties to such white supremacist organizations as the National States' Rights party, the Aryan Nations, and the Skinheads.

For all their power to make newspaper headlines, the three Klans historically failed to accomplish their major objectives. The first did not end southern Reconstruction in the 1870s; that was more nearly the work of organized rioters and Red Shirt campaigners. The second did not significantly deflect the nation's progress toward a pluralistic, democratic society in the 1920s. And the major effect of the third on the civil rights movement was to hasten the triumph of that cause when the Klan's violence helped mobilize public support for passage of landmark civil rights legislation in the 1960s.

David Chalmers, *Hooded Americanism: The History of the Ku Klux Klan,* 3d ed. (1987); Allen W. Trelease, *White Terror: The Ku Klux Klan Conspiracy and Southern Reconstruction* (1971); Wyn Craig Wade, *The Fiery Cross: The Ku Klux Klan in America* (1987).

ALLEN W. TRELEASE

See also Civil Rights Movement; Lynching; Reconstruction.

L

LABOR

I. Labor Movement

The origins of the labor movement lay in the formative years of the American nation, when a free wage-labor market emerged in the artisan trades late in the colonial period. The earliest recorded strike occurred in 1768 when New York journeymen tailors protested a wage reduction. The formation of the Federal Society of Journeymen Cordwainers (shoemakers) in Philadelphia in 1794 marks the beginning of sustained trade union organization among American workers. From that time on, local craft unions proliferated in the cities, publishing lists of "prices" for their work, defending their trades against diluted and cheap labor, and, increasingly, demanding a shorter workday. Thus a job-conscious orientation was quick to emerge, and in its wake there followed the key structural elements characterizing American trade unionism — first, beginning with the formation in 1827 of the Mechanics' Union of Trade Associations in Philadelphia, central labor bodies uniting craft unions within a single city, and then, with the creation of the International Typographical Union in 1852, national unions bringing together local unions of the same trade from across the United States and Canada (hence the frequent union designation "international"). Although the factory system was springing up during these years, industrial workers played little part in the early trade union development. In the nineteenth century, trade unionism was mainly a movement of skilled workers.

The early labor movement was, however, inspired by more than the immediate job interest of its craft members. It harbored a conception of the just society, deriving from the Ricardian labor theory of value and from the republican ideals of the American Revolution, which fostered social equality, celebrated honest labor, and relied on an independent, virtuous citizenship. The transforming economic changes of industrial capitalism ran counter to labor's vision. The result, as early labor leaders saw it, was to raise up "two distinct classes, the rich and the poor." Beginning with the workingmen's parties of the 1830s, the advocates of equal rights mounted a series of reform efforts that spanned the nineteenth century. Most notable were the National Labor Union, launched in 1866, and the Knights of Labor, which reached its zenith in the mid-1880s. On their face, these reform movements might have seemed at odds with trade unionism, aiming as they did at the cooperative commonwealth rather than a higher wage, appealing broadly to all "producers" rather than strictly to wageworkers, and eschewing the trade union reliance on the strike and boycott. But contemporaries saw no contradiction: trade unionism tended to the workers' immediate needs, labor reform to their higher hopes. The two were held to be strands of a single movement, rooted in a common working-class constituency and to some degree sharing a common leadership. But equally important, they were strands that had to be kept operationally separate and functionally distinct.

During the 1880s, that division fatally

eroded. Despite its labor reform rhetoric, the Knights of Labor attracted large numbers of workers hoping to improve their immediate conditions. As the Knights carried on strikes and organized along industrial lines, the threatened national trade unions demanded that the group confine itself to its professed labor reform purposes; when it refused, they joined in December 1886 to form the American Federation of Labor (AFL). The new federation marked a break with the past, for it denied to labor reform any further role in the struggles of American workers. In part, the assertion of trade union supremacy stemmed from an undeniable reality. As industrialism matured, labor reform lost its meaning — hence the confusion and ultimate failure of the Knights of Labor. Marxism taught Samuel Gompers and his fellow socialists that trade unionism was the indispensable instrument for preparing the working class for revolution. The founders of the AFL translated this notion into the principle of "pure and simple" unionism: only by self-organization along occupational lines and by a concentration on job-conscious goals would the worker be "furnished with the weapons which shall secure his industrial emancipation."

That class formulation necessarily defined trade unionism as the movement of the entire working class. The AFL asserted as a formal policy that it represented all workers, irrespective of skill, race, religion, nationality, or gender. But the national unions that had created the AFL in fact comprised only the skilled trades. Almost at once, therefore, the trade union movement encountered a dilemma: how to square ideological aspirations against contrary institutional realities? As sweeping technological change began to undermine the craft system of production, some national unions did move toward an industrial structure, most notably in coal mining and the garment trades. But most craft unions either refused or, as in iron and steel and in meat packing, failed to organize the less skilled. And since skill lines tended to conform to racial, ethnic, and gender divisions, the trade union movement took on a racist and sexist coloration as well. For a short period, the AFL resisted that tendency. But in 1895, unable to launch an interracial ma-

chinists' union of its own, the Federation reversed an earlier principled decision and chartered the whites-only International Association of Machinists. Formally or informally, the color bar thereafter spread throughout the trade union movement. In 1902, blacks made up scarcely 3 percent of total membership, most of them segregated in Jim Crow locals. In the case of women and eastern European immigrants, a similar devolution occurred — welcomed as equals in theory, excluded or segregated in practice. (Only the fate of Asian workers was unproblematic; their rights had never been asserted by the AFL in the first place.)

Gompers justified the subordination of principle to organizational reality on the constitutional grounds of "trade autonomy," by which each national union was assured the right to regulate its own internal affairs. But the organizational dynamism of the labor movement was in fact located in the national unions. Only as they experienced inner change might the labor movement expand beyond the narrow limits — roughly 10 percent of the labor force — at which it stabilized before World War I.

In the political realm, the founding doctrine of pure-and-simple unionism meant an arm's-length relationship to the state and the least possible entanglement in partisan politics. A total separation had, of course, never been seriously contemplated; some objectives, such as immigration restriction, could be achieved only through state action, and the predecessor to the AFL, the Federation of Organized Trades and Labor Unions (1881), had in fact been created to serve as labor's lobbying arm in Washington. Partly because of the lure of progressive labor legislation, even more in response to increasingly damaging court attacks on the trade unions, political activity quickened after 1900. With the enunciation of Labor's Bill of Grievances (1906), the AFL laid down a challenge to the major parties. Henceforth it would campaign for its friends and seek the defeat of its enemies.

This nonpartisan entry into electoral politics, paradoxically, undercut the left-wing advocates of an independent working-class politics. That question had been repeatedly debated within the AFL, first in 1890 over Socialist Labor party representation, then in 1893–1894 over an alliance with the Populist party, and after 1901 over affiliation with the Socialist party of America. Although Gompers prevailed each time, he never found it easy. Now, as labor's leverage with the major parties began to pay off, Gompers had an effective answer to his critics on the left: the labor movement could not afford to waste its political capital on socialist parties or independent politics. When that nonpartisan strategy failed, as it did in the reaction following World War I, an independent political strategy took hold, first through the robust campaigning of the Conference for Progressive Political Action in 1922, and in 1924 through labor's endorsement of Robert La Follette on the Progressive ticket. By then, however, the Republican administration was moderating its hard line, evident especially in Herbert Hoover's efforts to resolve the simmering crises in mining and on the railroads. In response, the trade unions abandoned the Progressive party, retreated to nonpartisanship, and, as their power waned, lapsed into inactivity.

It took the Great Depression to knock the labor movement off dead center. The discontent of industrial workers, combined with New Deal collective bargaining legislation, at last brought the great mass production industries within striking distance. When the craft unions stymied the AFL's organizing efforts, John L. Lewis of the United Mine Workers and his followers broke away in 1935 and formed the Committee for Industrial Organization (CIO), which crucially aided the emerging unions in auto, rubber, steel, and other basic industries. In 1938 the CIO was formally established as the Congress of Industrial Organizations. By the end of World War II, more than 12 million workers belonged to unions, and collective bargaining had taken hold throughout the industrial economy.

In politics, its enhanced power led the union movement not to a new departure but to a variant on the policy of nonpartisanship. As far back as the Progressive Era, organized labor had been drifting toward the Democratic party, partly because of the latter's greater programmatic appeal, perhaps even more because of its ethnocultural basis of support within an increasingly "new" immigrant working class. With the coming of Roosevelt's New Deal, this incipient alliance solidified, and from 1936 onward the Democratic party could count on — and came to rely on — the campaigning resources of the labor movement. That this alliance partook of the nonpartisan logic of Gompers's authorship — too much was at stake for organized labor to waste its political capital on third parties — became clear in the unsettled period of the early cold war. Not only did the CIO oppose the Progressive party of 1948, but it expelled the left-wing unions that broke ranks and supported Henry Wallace for the presidency that year.

The formation of the AFL-CIO in 1955 visibly testified to the powerful continuities persisting through the age of industrial unionism. Above all, the central purpose remained what it had always been — to advance the economic and job interests of the union membership. Collective bargaining performed impressively after World War II, more than tripling weekly earnings in manufacturing between 1945 and 1970, gaining for union workers an unprecedented measure of security against old age, illness, and unemployment, and, through contractual protections, greatly strengthening their right to fair treatment at the workplace. But if the benefits were greater and if they went to more people, the basic job-conscious thrust remained intact. Organized labor was still a *sectional* movement, covering at most only a third of America's wage earners and inaccessible to those cut off in the low-wage secondary labor market.

Nothing better captures the uneasy amalgam of old and new in the postwar labor movement than the treatment of minorities and women who flocked in, initially from the mass production industries, but after 1960 from the public and service sectors as well. Labor's historic commitment to racial and gender equality was thereby much strengthened, but not to the point of challenging the status quo within the labor movement itself. Thus the leadership structure remained largely closed to minorities — as did the skilled jobs that were historically the preserve of white male workers — notoriously so in the construction trades but in the industrial unions as well. Yet the AFL-CIO played a crucial role in the battle for civil rights legislation in 1964–1965. That this legislation might be directed against discriminatory trade union practices was anticipated (and quietly welcomed) by the more progressive labor leaders. But more significant was the meaning they found in championing this kind of reform: the chance to act on the broad ideals of the labor movement. And, so motivated, they deployed labor's power with great effect in the achievement of John F. Kennedy's and Lyndon B. Johnson's domestic programs during the 1960s.

This was ultimately economic, not political power, however, and as organized labor's grip on the industrial sector began to weaken, so did its political capability. From the early 1970s onward, new competitive forces swept through the heavily unionized industries, set off by deregulation in communications and transportation, by industrial restructuring, and by an unprecedented onslaught of foreign goods. As oligopolistic and regulated market structures broke down, nonunion competition spurted, concession bargaining became widespread, and plant closings decimated union memberships. The once-celebrated National Labor Relations Act increasingly hamstrung the labor movement; an all-out reform campaign to get the law amended failed in 1978. And with the election of Ronald Reagan in 1980, there came to power an anti-union administration the likes of which had not been seen since the Harding era. Between 1975 and 1985, union membership fell by 5 million. In manufacturing, the unionized portion of the labor force dropped below 25 percent, while mining and construction, once labor's flagship industries, were decimated. Only in the public sector did the unions hold their own. By the end of the 1980s, less than 17 percent of American workers were organized, half the proportion of the early 1950s.

Swift to change the labor movement has never been. But if the new high-tech and service sectors seemed beyond its reach in 1989, so did the mass production industries in 1929. And, as compared to the old AFL, organized labor is today much more diverse and broadly based: 40 percent of its members are white-collar workers, 30 percent are women, and the 14.5 percent who

are black signify a greater representation than in the general population and a greater rate of participation than by white workers (22.6 percent compared to 16.3 percent). In the meantime, however, the movement's impotence has been felt. "The collapse of labor's legislative power facilitated the adoption of a set of economic policies highly beneficial to the corporate sector and to the affluent," wrote analyst Thomas B. Edsall in 1984. And, with collective bargaining in retreat, declining living standards of American wage-earning families set in for the first time since the Great Depression. The union movement became in the 1980s a diminished economic and political force, and, in the Age of Reagan, this made for a less socially just nation.

Foster R. Dulles and Melvyn Dubofsky, *Labor in America: A History*, 4th ed. (1984); Robert H. Zieger, *American Workers, American Unions, 1920–1985* (1986).

DAVID BRODY

See also American Federation of Labor; Brotherhood of Sleeping Car Porters; *Commonwealth* v. *Hunt*; Congress of Industrial Organizations; Industrial Workers of the World; Knights of Labor; National Labor Relations Act; National Labor Relations Board; Southern Tenant Farmers' Union; Taft-Hartley Act; Textile Industry; Triangle Shirtwaist Fire; United States Women's Bureau; Women and the Work Force; Women's Trade Union League; *and entries for individual labor activists.*

II. Strikes

Strikes have played a significant role in the economic, political, and social life of the United States throughout its history. From strikes by shoemakers, printers, bakers, and other artisans in the era of the Revolution through the bitter airline strikes two centuries later, workers repeatedly tried to defend or improve their living and working conditions by collectively refusing to work until specific demands were met.

Since the early 1880s, when reliable statistics were first compiled, American workers have struck with a frequency roughly equal to that of their peers in Europe. Strikes in the United States, however, have tended to last longer than elsewhere, with a mean duration between 1881 and 1974 of twenty days. Accordingly, the total number of workdays lost in strikes proportionate to the size of the work force has been higher in the United States than almost anywhere else in the world.

The United States also has had the bloodiest labor history of any industrial nation. The first strike fatalities were two New York tailors, killed in 1850 by police dispersing a crowd of strikers. Since then, according to one estimate, well over seven hundred people — mostly strikers — have died in strike-related violence, and the total may be much higher. Some died in famous incidents, such as the 1913 Ludlow Massacre, when National Guardsmen attacked a tent colony of striking Colorado miners, or the 1937 Memorial Day Massacre, when ten supporters of a steel strike were killed by Chicago police. Most, however, died in little-noted confrontations with company guards, private detectives, scabs, or police.

Although wage disputes have been the single most common cause of strikes, workers have walked off their jobs for many reasons, including efforts to win union recognition, shorten the workday, gain or defend control over the work process, improve working conditions, and protest the disciplining of unionists. Strikes have been called to exclude nonwhites or women from jobs and, more rarely, to protest racial discrimination. Unlike elsewhere, political strikes over non-work-related issues have been uncommon.

Strikes have played a major role in both the rise and fall of unions (though many have occurred without union involvement). Often strikes have stimulated the formation of new unions or union federations. The first citywide labor federations, formed in the 1820s and 1830s, grew out of strikes by artisans seeking to shorten their workday. Over a century later, the Congress of Industrial Organizations (CIO) was indirectly an outgrowth of a wave of strikes by industrial workers. Conversely, failed strikes have destroyed many unions. The American Railway Union, for example, was unable to survive the defeat of its 1894 strike against the Pullman Car Company. More recently, the mass firing of striking air traffic controllers by the Reagan administration led to the demise of the Professional Air Traffic Controllers Organization.

American strikes have tended to come in waves, usually linked to the business cycle. Their frequency usually has risen whenever unemployment has been low. Unions have been strongest during such periods and workers less fearful about losing their jobs. Many of the bitterest strikes, though, occurred at the beginning of economic downturns, when companies slashed wages. Political and legal developments also have influenced the pattern of work stoppages. For instance, the passage of the National Industrial Recovery Act in 1933 stimulated a wave of strikes, as workers sensed a new sympathy for unionism on the part of the federal government.

The first American strikes, in the late eighteenth and early nineteenth centuries, were conducted by journeymen artisans, such as shoemakers, printers, and carpenters, often acting through local trade societies. Typically these "turn-outs" or "stand-outs" began when a group of workers decided on a scale of "prices" for their labor, pledging not to work for any employer paying less. Walkouts were almost always peaceful, since strikers simply stayed home until they could find a job paying the agreed-upon wages. Usually if within a few days employers did not meet the proposed prices, the strike collapsed.

Strikes by the early trade societies were effective because the supply of skilled workers within local labor markets was limited. Employers tried to counteract these stoppages through the courts. Starting in 1806 a series of criminal conspiracy cases was brought against workers for combining to raise wages and injure others (by refusing to work with nonunionists). These successful prosecutions inhibited the spread of strikes and trade societies, which were then dealt a devastating blow by the depression of 1819.

An economic upturn in the 1820s revived strike activity. Male artisans, and less commonly laborers, conducted most of the walkouts, but, unlike the earlier period, female craft workers and factory operatives of both sexes also struck. Most strikes were about wages or working hours. Out of them arose local federations of craft unions, and ultimately the Working Men's parties that for a while shifted the focus of the labor movement from strike action to electoral politics.

The failure of the Working Men's parties and a drop in the standard of living led to a larger wave of strikes during the 1830s. In Philadelphia sixteen trade societies simultaneously struck, demanding the ten-hour day. In New York strikes brought on another round of conspiracy prosecutions. An economic downturn in 1837, however, led to a near-total collapse of the union movement, and it did not reemerge until the 1850s, when there was a brief but intense renewal of strike activity. In 1853 and 1854 alone there were some four hundred strikes. In 1860 came the largest to date, a six-week walkout of over ten thousand shoe workers on the North Shore of Massachusetts.

After the Civil War the labor movement grew rapidly, as did the volume of strikes. But with improvements in transportation and the growing size of cities, unions found it difficult to prevent employers from recruiting scabs, leading to both strike defeats and violence. To avoid strikes many unions abandoned the system of unilaterally establishing wage scales and working hours, embracing instead "arbitration," the negotiation with employers of wages, work rules, and grievances. Written contracts became more common, and many unions transferred the power to call strikes from the rank and file to elected officers. The Knights of Labor, the most important nineteenth-century labor organization, generally disapproved of strikes, and some unions rejected them altogether.

In spite of the union retreat from the strike weapon, the 1870s saw a series of strikes of unprecedented size, violence, and national impact. Amid a severe depression that began in 1873, workers waged long, bitter strikes to resist wage cuts in the New England textile industry, the anthracite coal mines, and on the Pennsylvania Railroad. In 1877 the first nationwide strike paralyzed railroads throughout the East and Midwest, idled some 100,000 workers, led to over a

hundred deaths, and terrified the propertied classes. The strike began in West Virginia as a spontaneous protest by Baltimore and Ohio trainmen against a series of pay cuts. As it spread to Baltimore, Pittsburgh, Chicago, and St. Louis, it became a vast demonstration against the railroads and their allies; the railroad men were joined by farmers, coal miners, craft workers, and the unemployed in efforts to stop rail traffic. When local militiamen refused to attack strikers, state and federal troops from other regions were brought in, leading to massive clashes. The strike was defeated, but it had been, in the eyes of many, the American equivalent of the Paris Commune.

In the mid-1880s, as the economy underwent a modest recovery, the number of strikes soared, tripling from under five hundred a year in the early 1880s to some fifteen hundred in 1886. Well over half a million workers struck that year, and the volume of strikes remained high for the next decade. During this period over half of all strikers were in the coal, construction, or garment industries. Wages, working hours, union recognition, and work rules were the most important issues, and many strikes — over a third in the 1880s — were not initiated by unions. In the early 1890s sympathy strikes accounted for about 10 percent of all walkouts.

Employers unreconciled to unionism increasingly sought and received government assistance in defeating strikes. Between 1875 and 1910 state troops were called out nearly five hundred times to deal with labor unrest. In 1892, for example, after armed strikers at Andrew Carnegie's Homestead, Pennsylvania, steel mill repulsed an attack by Pinkerton guards, eight thousand state troops were sent to the town, leading to the defeat of the strike. When state authorities were unable or unwilling to provide troops, the U.S. Army was used, as occurred during the 1894 Pullman strike and a series of metal mining strikes in the Rocky Mountain region. State and federal court injunctions were also used frequently and effectively against strikers.

Although workers won roughly half of all strikes in the 1880s and 1890s, many leaders of craft unions affiliated with the American Federation of Labor (AFL) questioned their efficacy. In the early twentieth century, to avoid or settle strikes, many unions turned to private mediation groups or, after 1914, the Federal Mediation and Conciliation Service. Nonetheless, after a brief respite the volume of strikes rose sharply in the years just before World War I. Notable during this period was the increased number of female, unskilled, and immigrant strikers, evident in the Lawrence, Massachusetts, textile strike, several exceptionally bloody transit strikes, and a series of large garment strikes. In these and other contests, unions introduced new tactics, including mass picket lines, multilingual strike committees, and sophisticated public relations.

During World War I the AFL pledged to avoid strikes, but their volume nonetheless continued to rise as workers took advantage of a labor shortage to seek higher wages, union recognition, and control over the work process. The strike wave peaked in 1919, when workers sought to consolidate and extend their wartime gains and employers sought to reverse them. That year 4 million workers, one-fifth of the work force, went on strike, a higher proportion of workers than in any other year in the nation's history. In Boston policemen struck; in New York, garment workers and actors; in New England, textile workers and telephone operators; and in Seattle a general strike paralyzed the city for five days. Late in the year 400,000 coal miners walked off their jobs in defiance of a federal court injunction, winning a large wage increase. In the steel industry a strike by over 300,000 workers was defeated, dooming organizing efforts in the oligarchic basic industries for another fifteen years. Although the volume of strikes remained high through 1922, labor's postwar offensive was checked by government repression, a red scare that equated labor militancy with foreign radicalism, and a short but sharp economic downturn in 1921. By 1923 the number of strikers had declined dramatically, as had the number of unionists. Strike volume remained low for the rest of the decade and fell further during the early years of the Great Depression.

The revival and vast expansion of the union movement in the 1930s was closely linked to a new burst of strikes. The beginning of the New Deal, coming after four years of depression, sparked rising worker militancy. In 1934 striking Toledo auto workers, Minneapolis truckers, and West Coast longshoremen won important concessions after surviving police and vigilante attacks, although massive violence crushed a walkout of East Coast textile workers. These strikes helped stimulate in 1935 the passage of the National Labor Relations Act (NLRA) and the formation of the Committee for Industrial Organization (which became the Congress of Industrial Organizations in 1938). The key test for the CIO came in 1937, a six-week strike against General Motors. During the conflict thousands of strikers remained *inside* the company's plants. The success of the strike gave an enormous impetus to industrial unionism and spawned a wave of more sit-down strikes. Half a million workers took part in sit-downs before they were declared illegal by the Supreme Court in 1939. The overall volume of strikes remained very high until the United States entered World War II, as unions penetrated such previously unorganized industries as auto, steel, rubber, electrical equipment manufacturing, meat packing, and over-the-road trucking.

During World War II virtually all unions pledged not to strike, but despite this and government sanctions against striking, walkouts were frequent. Typically, they were small, short, and not union-initiated. Exceptional was a series of very large, union-led coal strikes. When the war ended, unions and employers jockeyed to maximize their power in postwar collective bargaining. As a result, in 1946 more workers went on strike and more workdays were lost than in any other year. Some strikes were very long, but in sharp contrast to the prewar years, most were peaceful. The NLRA was in part responsible: employers were now legally obligated to bargain with unions that could demonstrate majority worker support, and strikers were given legal protection. As labor relations became routinized during the 1950s, the volume of strikes dropped sharply, with unions almost always involved in those that did occur.

A large number of public employee strikes

— previously very unusual — contributed to an increase in strike activity during the 1960s. Most public-sector strikes involved local government employees, such as teachers or transit workers, but the largest public employee walkout in the nation's history was a 1970 wildcat strike of 180,000 postal workers.

Strike volume decreased during the 1970s and remained low during the 1980s. A severe recession, a conservative political climate, and declining union membership all contributed to this development. For the first time since World War II, it became not unusual for struck companies to attempt to resume operations using scab workers. The defeat of hard-fought strikes in the intercity bus, copper-mining, meat-packing, and airline industries convinced some observers that strikes were a thing of the past. Given their historically cyclical pattern and the lack of well-developed alternatives, however, it seemed unlikely that strikes would lose their central role in American labor relations in the future.

P. K. Edwards, *Strikes in the United States, 1881–1974* (1981); Richard B. Morris, ed., *The U.S. Department of Labor Bicentennial History of the American Worker* (1976).

JOSHUA B. FREEMAN

See also Homestead Strike; Lawrence Strike; Paterson Silk Strike; Pullman Strike; Railroad Strike of 1877; Sit-Down Strikes.

LA FOLLETTE, ROBERT M.

(1855–1925), Progressive Era political leader and reformer. "Democracy is a life," wrote La Follette in 1911, "and involves continual struggle." His own intense seventy years fully confirmed that faith. Born into a poor but respectable farming family in pioneer Wisconsin on the eve of the Civil War, La Follette ranks high among those progressives who tried to bring the twentieth century into harmony with the Republican ideal of a self-ruling republic of independent producers. At the University of Wisconsin his first loves were theater and declamation, but ambition and the need to make a living led him into law and elective office. From district attorney of Dane County he moved up to Con-

gress, serving three terms in the House (1885–1891) as a more or less orthodox Republican, but one who shone in debate.

Although his district unseated him in 1890, the defeat only led to his insurgency and fame. During his eight years of private practice in Madison, where echoes of agrarian revolt were loud, La Follette claimed to see in full profile at last a sinister alliance between the "interests" (Wisconsin's lumber and railroad corporations) and the "bosses" (the major-party leaders, predominantly Republican) who worked together to cheat "the people" — the farmers, small businessmen, and workers. He became the popular champion of these groups as he set out on a series of statewide speaking campaigns that led finally to his election as governor in 1900. The elements of his platform were open nominating primaries, equal and fair taxation of corporate property, state regulation of railroads and public utilities charges, and management of public resources in the public interest. Administration was to be entrusted to nonpartisan civil servants drawn largely from the Wisconsin faculty. Journalists publicized the "Wisconsin Idea," and La Follette's continual struggle to implement it soon marked him as a rising star in the nationwide progressive firmament. In 1905 he was elected to the U.S. Senate, where he remained until his death.

La Follette never became a successful Senate insider despite his long tenure. He gave his name to only one major law, the 1915 act protecting merchant seamen from exploitation. His role instead was to push uncompromisingly for progressive legislation on the floor and on the nationwide lecture circuit. So well did he play it that by 1912 he was considered the standout among the Senate group of Republican insurgents challenging conservative party regulars.

La Follette sought to take the presidential nomination away from the incumbent William Howard Taft that year, but his bid was preempted by that of Theodore Roosevelt (whose progressive credentials La Follette had always doubted). When Woodrow Wilson won the election as a Democratic progressive, La Follette supported his domestic programs but broke decisively with him in 1917 by heading up the opposition to American entry into the First World War. For this unpopular stand he was punished by widespread public vilification and ostracism during 1917–1918 (and nearly expelled from the Senate). But in the postwar period he was forgiven and assumed a new part — the aging, respected conscience of a progressive movement in eclipse under Warren G. Harding and Calvin Coolidge.

In 1924 he ran as an independent Progressive candidate for president, polling nearly 6 million votes out of some 30 million cast, but winning only Wisconsin's electoral votes. After his death the following June, his older son, Robert M. La Follette, Jr., followed him in the Senate and served until 1946. His younger son, Philip F. La Follette, served as governor of Wisconsin in the thirties.

David Thelen, *Robert La Follette and the Insurgent Spirit* (1976).

BERNARD A. WEISBERGER

See also Elections: 1912, 1924; Progressivism; Third Parties.

LA GUARDIA, FIORELLO

(1882–1947), congressman and mayor of New York City. Although born in Lower Manhattan, La Guardia was raised in the West where he shaped his personal credo: you did not complain about pain, you did not give in to fear, you carried on like a man. Just over five feet tall and with a high-pitched voice, this son of an Austrian Jewish mother and Italian agnostic father learned to fend for himself and accept no other identity than that of an American.

La Guardia was elected to Congress in 1917 and except for a short interval remained there until 1932, representing working-class districts in New York. By the end of the twenties La Guardia was leading House progressives in fighting against Prohibition, racism, and the prevailing doctrine of laissez-faire. Then the depression came, and as the number of unemployed and needy grew, his ideas influenced New Deal programs. The largest difference between La Guardia and the New Dealers was that the New

Yorker was a Republican, and in the landslide that brought Franklin D. Roosevelt into office in 1932, La Guardia was defeated.

He then turned to municipal politics. Reluctantly, reform elements settled on the mercurial La Guardia to defeat the city's bosses and on January 1, 1934, he took office as New York's ninety-ninth mayor.

La Guardia became the father of modern New York. Before him, the city was in the thrall of graft. Divided into political fiefdoms, it was haphazardly administered, with skimpy social and health services, decaying parks, and rusting bridges. With massive funding that he was able to attract from a friendly administration in Washington, La Guardia constructed bridges over the waters and dug tunnels under them, and built reservoirs, sewer systems, parks, highways, schools, hospitals, health centers, swimming pools, and airports. For the first time, New York offered its poor public housing, its working class a unified transit system, and its artists and musicians training and subsidies.

La Guardia wanted New Yorkers to enjoy a sense of ease and security, to live in decent quarters and raise healthy children. He also wanted them to be good: he declared war on gamblers, closed burlesque houses, and cleared racy magazines from the newsstands (under his powers of "garbage collection"). Always colorful, La Guardia, in what became the best-remembered act of his mayoralty, one Sunday during a newspaper strike asked radio listeners to bring the kiddies around and then proceeded to give a dramatic reading of the Dick Tracy comic strip that would have run that day.

Previous mayors had dealt with aldermen and state politicians; La Guardia took up local needs with the White House. He understood that the modern city could no longer be self-sufficient, and as president of the U.S. Conference of Mayors for close to a decade, he led a national coalition that fought for a generous federal urban policy.

La Guardia's practice had shortcomings. He undermined his reputation as a civil libertarian with his campaigns against smut and gambling. He instructed his police to "muss up" racketeers and "chiselers" with chilling abandon. He failed to consider sufficiently the long-term effects of his progressive policies. By the time he left office the colossal metropolis he helped build was saddled with debt, an infrastructure too expensive to maintain, dangerously expanding citizen expectations, and a snowballing bureaucracy.

Yet for all this, La Guardia thrust New York into modernity. He provided determined, honest leadership and managed in the words of Felix Frankfurter to "translate the complicated conduct of [New York] City's vast government into warm significance for every man, woman and child."

After he left office, he served briefly as director general of the United Nations Relief and Rehabilitation Administration before his death in 1947.

Thomas Kessner, *Fiorello H. La Guardia and the Making of Modern New York* (1989).

THOMAS KESSNER

LAND

See Entail; Expansion, Continental and Overseas; Homestead Act; Married Women's Property Acts; Morrill Land Grant Act; Primogeniture; Public Land Policy.

LANGE, DOROTHEA

(1895–1965), photographer. Lange's pictures of migrant families dramatized the plight of agricultural workers during the Great Depression and lent support for New Deal legislation.

Born in Hoboken, New Jersey, she early decided on a photography career and worked for portrait photographer Arnold Genthe before studying for a year with pictorialist Clarence White at Columbia University. She settled in San Francisco, married an artist, and opened a chic photography studio in 1919. Ten years later, while walking alone one day in the California hills, a sudden violent storm provoked a spiritual crisis. "It came to me that what I had to do," she recalled later, "was concentrate on people, all kinds of people, people who paid me and people who didn't." Within months, after the stock market crash, she began by turning her camera on the plight of the uprooted, homeless, and unemployed.

Drawn first to the streets of San Francisco, Lange was hired to photograph migrant workers for California's Emergency Relief Administration. She also joined such photographers as Ansel Adams and Edward Weston in the f.64 group, so named because members used the smallest possible lens opening to obtain depth and sharpness in their pictures. By 1935, her photographs came to the attention of Roy Stryker, then organizing his celebrated photographic section of the Resettlement (later Farm Security) Administration in Washington. Photographer and artist Ben Shahn recalled later that "Dorothea's work was sent in or brought in by somebody and this was a revelation, what this woman was doing." Lange soon joined Shahn, Walker Evans, Carl Mydans, Arthur Rothstein, and others in the organization. Their photographs marked the first time in American history that the government used art directly for propaganda purposes. Newspapers, magazines, exhibition rooms, and movie theaters were encouraged to display these images. Some 250,000 of their negatives are preserved in the Library of Congress Prints and Photographs Division.

Lange later photographed the internment of U.S. Japanese-Americans and contributed photoessays to *Life* magazine (where she was known as "Bourke-White West," referring to photojournalist Margaret Bourke-White). Although plagued by ill health, she traveled to Ireland, Asia, Egypt, and South America after World War II.

Her biographer David Scherman described Lange as "endowed with most of the acceptable stigmata of the certified genius, photography division." She was also, he contended, "alternately (but always theatrically) kindhearted and inconsiderate, implacably egotistical, domineering, contentious, apparently humorless, self-analytical *ad nauseum*," and "hardworking to the point of exhaustion." For Lange, her mission was the thing. "Among the tools of social science — graphs, statistics, maps, and text — documentation by photograph," she wrote in 1940, "now is assuming place." Documentary photography, she added, "invites and needs participation by amateurs as well as by professionals. Only through the interested work of amateurs who choose themes and follow them can documentation by the camera of our age and our complex society be intimate, pervasive, and adequate."

Milton Meltzer, *Dorothea Lange: A Photographer's Life* (1978); Karin Ohrn, *Dorothea Lange and the Documentary Tradition* (1980).

WILLIAM WELLING

See also Photography.

LANGUAGE

The history of American English can be divided into the colonial (1607–1776), the national (1776–1898), and the international (1898–present) periods. During nearly four hundred years of use in North America, the English language changed in small ways in pronunciation and grammar but extensively in vocabulary and in the attitude of its speakers.

English settlements along the Atlantic Coast during the seventeenth century provided the foundation for English as a permanent language in the New World. But the English of the American colonies was bound to become distinct from that of the motherland. When people do not talk with one another, they begin to talk differently. The Atlantic Ocean served as an effective barrier to oral communication between the colonists and those who stayed in England, ensuring that their speech would evolve in different directions.

On the one hand, changes in the English of England were slow to reach America, and some never made the crossing, so American English became in certain respects old-fashioned and eventually archaic, from the standpoint of the British. But on the other hand, the colonists were forced to talk about new physical features, flora, and fauna. For example, an Americanism early noted (and objected to) by British travelers was the use of *bluff* for the steep, high bank of a river. British rivers usually do not have such banks but are nearly level with the surrounding land, so when the colonists encountered the new fluvial topography, they had no name for it. Consequently, they pressed into service a word that means "steep" in naval jargon.

Americans also came cheek-to-jowl with Amerindians of several linguistic stocks, as well as French and Dutch speakers. They had to talk in new ways to communicate with their new neighbors. Moreover, the settlers had come from various districts and social groups of England, so there was a homogenizing effect: those in a given colony came to talk more like one another and less like any particular community in England. All these influences combined to make American English a distinct variety of the language.

Despite such changes, the norm of usage in the colonies remained that of the motherland until the American Revolution. Thereafter American English was no longer a colonial variety of the English of London but had entered its national period. Political independence was soon followed by cultural independence, of which a notable Founding Father was Noah Webster. As a schoolmaster, Webster recognized that the new nation needed a sense of linguistic identity. Accordingly he set out to provide dictionaries and textbooks for recording and teaching American English with American models. The need Webster sought to fill was twofold: to help Americans realize they should no longer look to England for a standard of usage and to foster a reasonable degree of uniformity in American English. To those ends, Webster's dictionary, reader, grammar, and blue-backed speller were major forces for institutionalizing what he called Federal English.

The language preserved its unity through the challenge of the Civil War (1861–1865); it assimilated immigrant languages and dialects, such as Spanish, German, and Irish, and replaced aboriginal Amerindian languages. The extension of American English and the preservation of its relative uniformity as the country expanded westward were aided by the railroads spanning the continent, the invention of the telegraph and telephone, and the explosion of journalism and popular education, all of which broadened communication.

By the end of the nineteenth century, the Manifest Destiny of American English had been achieved, along with that of the territorial expansion of the nation. Because the domestic frontier had been exhausted, the nation had to look abroad if it was to continue to expand, territorially and linguistically. The Spanish-American War in 1898, though lasting barely four months, was a turning point in the history of the language. Before that war, American English played no more than a walk-on role on the world stage; foreign influences usually had to come to it. Afterward, international activity sharply increased, and the prominence of American English around the globe became proportionately greater.

In the course of war or commerce American English spread to Hawaii, Puerto Rico, the Philippines, China, Panama and other countries in Latin America, the Virgin Islands, and nations throughout the world. To the consternation of some, American popular culture followed. Through music, films, recordings, television, computers, aeronautics, multinational companies, and the military, the second half of the twentieth century became the Age of America, for good or for ill. The linguistic consequences have been profound — both on the use of English internationally and on the language itself.

As American English has been institutionalized and used internationally, the nature of its relationship to British English has changed. From the national period until the present day, there have been two opposing attitudes: Americanizing and Briticizing. The Americanizing attitude recognizes American usage as independent of British, not inferior to it; at its most extreme it seeks to exaggerate the differences. The Briticizing attitude emphasizes the connections between American and British; at its most extreme it regards American as subordinate to British. Exemplifications of the Americanizing versus Briticizing are Noah Webster's dictionary versus Joseph Worcester's; Mark Twain versus Henry James; H. L. Mencken's *The American Language* versus George Philip Krapp's *The English Language in America,* and Robert Frost versus T. S. Eliot.

If Americans have been divided on their view of the relationship between American and British English, few Britishers have had any doubt, and their confidence is widely shared by continental Europeans. To them *English* means British English, and American is a dialect, if not an aberration. The international prestige of British English has been maintained by both the geographical proximity of continental Europe to the British Isles and the residual influence of the British Empire around the world. It is also supported by England's reputation as a source of high culture. America, in contrast, is seen as a source of technology, commercialism, and pop culture.

Today, however, there are two main branches of English in the world, both including several national varieties: British English in the United Kingdom, Ireland, Australia, New Zealand, South Africa, and elsewhere; and American English in the United States, Canada, and elsewhere. Although British English is more widely distributed, American English is spoken by nearly three times as many persons. That numerical preponderance has as an inevitable consequence that American English is now the principal representative of the English language and the major determinant of its future.

American English, although remarkably uniform considering that over 230 million people speak it, is by no means monolithic. It varies by location, social level, ethnic group, and other factors. There are four primary regional dialects in the United States: Southern or Coastal Southern, South Midland or Southern Mountain, North Midland or Lower Northern, and Northern or Upper Northern. The boundaries between them, which are traceable to the earliest settlements, are clearest in the eastern part of the country, where settlement came first. They become less distinct and more overlapping in the West.

The dialect regions are distinguished mainly by differences of pronunciation and vocabulary and only to a small extent by grammar. Pronunciation differences include the sounding or non-sounding of r in words like *mother* and *mirth;* the quality of the "aw" vowel in words like *lawn* and *caught;* the use of an "s" or "z" sound in *greasy;* and many other such features. Vocabulary differences include choices among *faucet, spigot* (*spicket*), and *tap; downtown* and *uptown* for a main business district; *soda, pop, Coke, tonic,* and *soft drink* for a carbonated beverage; and many other variations, including more restricted ones, such as *schlepp* for "mosey" or "lug" in the New York area or *arroyo* in the Southwest.

Ethnic dialects have phonological and grammatical characteristics, but they are most easily recognized by vocabulary. Many ethnic communities have contributed to the general American word stock: Louisiana creole *gumbo* and *lagniappe,* New York Dutch *cookie* and *boss,* Yiddish *schnook* and *chutzpa,* Mexican-Spanish *lasso* and *ranch,* Irish *shebang* and *blarney,* African-American *jazz* and *goober,* and many others.

Black English, one of the most prominent ethnic dialects, is the subject of great controversy concerning its history and present use. There are two opinions about its origin. One holds that slaves came from many tribes in Africa; they had no common language and therefore learned English from whites. In this view, Black English is a historical evolution of forms of nonstandard English that can be traced to the British Isles. The other holds that sailors and natives along the African coast used an English-based pidgin (or reduced language used for communication among persons speaking no other common tongue). Slaves brought to America knew this pidgin or soon learned it, and on the plantations it developed into a creole (a full language of mixed origins). In this view, Black English is a remnant of an independent language that has been gradually assimilating to general English, so that it now appears to be only a dialect. There is evidence for both opinions; it is impossible to say which is nearer to the historical reality.

The other controversy over Black English concerns its use and social status today. Some view it as a "home dialect" whose speakers need also to learn standard English to live effectively in the dominant society. Others regard that position as linguistic imperialism. They believe that the dominant society should respect minority cultures, including dialects, instead of expecting minorities to do the adapting. In practical terms, those who hold the second view would use Black English as a medium of instruction in the schools and would provide pedagogical materials written in it. Among the strong opponents of the second view are older-generation, middle-class African-Americans, who believe this would limit opportunities for social and economic advancement among blacks.

Hispanic English, another major ethnic dialect in the United States, exists in several subvarieties, notably Puerto Rican English in New York City, Cuban English in south Florida, and Chicano English in the Southwest. The main issue about Hispanic English (and other immigrant languages with sizable numbers of speakers) is that of bilingualism. It is parallel to the issue of the use and status of Black English. Specifically, the question is, should those who do not speak English be provided with schools, public services, legal proceedings, and so on in their native languages or should they be expected to learn English quickly and be linguistically disadvantaged until they do? In a larger sense, the question is whether non-English ethnic cultures should be preserved and fostered in Anglophone America or assimilated as quickly and completely as possible.

Both Black English and bilingualism are highly emotional issues with political overtones. The English First movement, which arose in opposition to other languages' achieving official status within American life, seeks the constitutional establishment of English as the only official language. Although seen by its opponents as xenophobic, the movement is a contemporary version of Noah Webster's Federal English — that is, an effort to provide a distinctive standard language for all citizens of the United States.

The very existence of a standard language has been called into question, but several things are clear. First, there is a standard written form of the language, extensively described in dictionaries and grammar books and used for most printed matter and public discourse. Second, this written standard is by no means monolithic but has a good deal of variation in it. Third, most arguments about what is or is not "good" English are concerned not with differentiating standard from nonstandard use but with variations within the standard. Fourth, standard English is chiefly a matter of grammar, spelling, and word choice; being primarily a matter of written English, it has little to do with pronunciation. Fifth, there is no standard pronunciation in the United States comparable to the Received Standard (or BBC English) of the United Kingdom.

Some particular pronunciations have low prestige ("ax" for *ask* or "liberry" for *library*), but pronunciation has not been institutionalized — there is no standard American accent. Recent presidents have spoken the easily identifiable regional accents of Massachusetts, Texas, and Georgia. What is called "General American" is a myth. Persons who deal with those from other regions may modify their pronunciation to eliminate phonetic features that are most readily identified as local dialect, but the result is not a unified, consistent accent. Rather, it is a pronunciation that has been "smoothed out" by avoiding easily recognized regionalisms.

Today English is an international language, widely used as a second and foreign language as well as a primary one. Although British English is more prestigious, American English is increasingly used. But in fact, the differences between them, especially in their written forms, are not great. In the foreseeable future, the unity of English — internationally and nationally in the United States — seems assured.

Dennis E. Baron, *Grammar and Good Taste: Reforming the American Language* (1982); Charles A. Ferguson and Shirley Brice Heath, eds., *Language in the USA* (1981); H. L. Mencken, *The American Language,* ed. Raven I. McDavid, Jr. (1963).

JOHN ALGEO

LATIN AMERICA–U.S. RELATIONS

The histories of the United States and Latin America are intimately related. Consider both that St. Augustine (the oldest city in the United States), Pensacola, New Orleans, San Antonio, Santa Fe, and many others were once Spanish towns and that citizens of Hispanic background now form the second largest minority in the United States. The relationship has been accompanied by cultural and demographic exchanges that have profoundly influenced all of its participants.

British colonization after 1607 was part of a "grand design" to wrest all the New World realms from Spain. The British soon converted their Caribbean colonies into sugar plantations worked by African slaves. The North American colonies were of less economic significance to this mercantilist development, participating mainly as suppliers of foodstuffs and lumber to the Caribbean and as its competitors in the production of cotton and tobacco. Continental militia, sharing the same goals as the British, took part in wars with Spain. One of the benefits was the conquest of Spanish Florida in 1763, resolving years of border struggles with Georgia.

But when the British continental colonies declared independence, it was with Spanish aid, and independence inspired Spanish colonials to revolt later. There were several uprisings, largely fueled by resentment over taxes levied to pay for Caribbean defense. The desire of Spanish colonial elites to separate was attenuated, however, when the 1791 Haitian Revolution was captured by its slaves. The loss of the strategic Haitian ports forced Napoleon Bonaparte to sell Louisiana for a trifle to the United States. The Americans, far from acknowledging their Haitian benefactors, joined the other slave powers in refusing to recognize Haitian independence.

Other independence movements broke out in the South American colonies soon after Napoleon invaded Spain in 1807. The United States did not recognize these insurgencies, much less offer them aid. It was becoming evident that these aristocratic "revolutionaries" were still less democratic than the monarchies of Europe. But opportunism was also at work: the United States did not want to endanger negotiations with Spain to acquire Florida (which that country had regained from Great Britain in the peace of 1783) and to draw a western boundary that would strengthen U.S. claims to Oregon. Only in 1823, when Latin American independence was already assured, did President James Monroe threaten sanctions should European powers attempt to recolonize. This "Monroe Doctrine" was also designed to discourage Russian expansion in the Pacific Northwest. In effect the declaration of a sphere of influence, it avoided challenging the legitimacy of remaining European colonies and renounced intervention in European affairs.

The Spanish viceroyalties soon broke up into small, weak, and often quarreling states (there were sixteen by 1839), and Portuguese Brazil became a unified empire under a Portuguese prince. Simon Bolivar, the most important independence leader, failed to form a regional organization at a congress he gathered at Panama in 1826. This suited the United States: it saw an advantage in Latin American fragmentation and pressed on these states most favored nation treaties whose intent was to forestall a common market among them.

America's belief in its "manifest destiny" resulted in the 1840s in the annexation of Texas and the defeat of Mexico and the absorption of half its territory in the Mexican War. In Central America, the United States achieved by midcentury an agreement with Great Britain that amounted to a joint sphere of influence. From Colombia it obtained the right to build a railroad across the isthmus of Panama (then part of Colombia). Private expeditions attempted to overthrow governments in Nicaragua and Cuba, a naval expedition was dispatched to landlocked Paraguay but was prevented from sailing upriver by Argentina, and a scientific expedition was sent down the Amazon to scout its potential for settling Virginia planters and their slaves.

Civil War in the United States offered European powers an opportunity to attempt recolonization. In 1863, Napoleon III, urged on by Mexican conservatives, enthroned a European prince in that country. But harried by the forces of the legitimate government under Benito Juárez and uneasy at the prospect of assistance from the northern army after the defeat of the Confederacy, Napoleon allowed his puppet to fall by 1867. Meanwhile, the Dominican Republic, fearing invasion by Haitian armies, invited the Spanish to reestablish colonial rule, but after a few years of mismanagement, expelled them again. A group of speculators close to President Ulysses S. Grant nearly persuaded the Senate to annex the Dominican Republic, failing by one vote.

Economic development in the United States magnified its power relative to the rest of the hemisphere. By 1880 its population was greater than all of Latin America's. Trade increased and stimulated a flow of capital. Latin America became a major source of foodstuffs and industrial raw materials and an important outlet for American goods — kerosene, lumber, grain, ice, and coal — and for manufactures such as barbed wire, sewing machines, rifles, windmills, and locomotives. American entrepreneurs went to the southern continent to build railroads, buy plantations, and open trading houses. The first multinational companies — United Fruit, Standard Oil, and W. R. Grace among them — invested there. In the 1880s, a modest statistical and cultural exchange bureau, the Pan-American Union, was created.

Cubans began fighting for independence in 1868. The United States had earlier considered annexing the island, but usually it supported Spanish control, lest its slaves rebel or the island fall under the influence of the British. In 1898, however, when Spain already wanted to abandon its colony, the United States intervened in behalf of the revolutionaries. The pretext was the mysterious blowing up of the battleship *Maine* in Havana harbor, but the impulse for war with Spain was broad and deep, fanned by newspaper accounts of Spanish atrocities and by a desire to emulate the European imperialist powers. Spain was easily defeated. The U.S. Congress had sworn to respect Cuban independence, but the insurgent government was barred from the peace conference and Cuba was subjected to military occupation. Spain turned over Puerto Rico, Guam, and the Philippines, which joined Hawaii and Samoa as U.S. colonies. Cuban legislators meeting to draft a constitution were given to understand that the U.S. Army would not withdraw until they ratified the Platt Amendment, which granted the United States the right to intervene and to build naval bases there.

In 1903, Panamanian businessmen, chafing against control by the strife-ridden central government of Colombia, and with U.S. naval support, declared independence. A treaty allowing the United States to build and operate a canal across the isthmus was hurriedly negotiated. The treaty and subsequent arrangements reduced Panama to the status of a protectorate, provided a windfall for investors in the rights of the earlier canal company, and incurred the enmity of Colombia. But the canal, completed in 1914 with West Indian labor, demonstrated U.S. engineering prowess and was strategically and commercially vital. Control of its sea approaches was a major reason for U.S. military occupations, for varying periods over the next two decades, of Nicaragua, the Dominican Republic, Cuba, and Haiti. Anxieties over imperialist competition also led the United States to purchase the Virgin Islands from Denmark and grant U.S. citizenship to Puerto Ricans.

The United States was much involved in the Mexican Revolution, which began in 1910. American investments had weakened the dictator Porfirio Diaz. Rebels were funded by Texan capitalists seeking advantage, as Diaz had been when he had come to power in 1876. The revolution, fueled by resentment of foreign influences, became even more xenophobic when, in 1914, President Woodrow Wilson ordered the capture of the port of Veracruz in a bungled attempt to make amends for U.S. complicity in the assassination of the elected president. In 1916, an unsuccessful expedition to capture Pancho Villa, a general who had raided Columbus, New Mexico, further incurred Mexican resentment.

World War I ruined European trade and investment in Latin America and correspondingly favored the United States, whose manufactures flooded the region. American multinational companies now produced petroleum and other raw materials there, and U.S. bankers became Latin America's principal creditors. This preeminence made it easier for the United States to abandon military occupations in the region. Nonintervention, the keystone of President Franklin D. Roosevelt's Good Neighbor policy, was in fact extracted from U.S. delegates at a Pan-American meeting in 1933 by the Latin Americans, who feared a new intervention in Cuba. (Nevertheless, the United States did encourage Gen. Fulgencio Batista to overthrow the Cuban government.)

As World War II became imminent, the Roosevelt administration sought broader cooperation with Latin America, fearing the consequences of a hostile continent on its southern flank. Thus, when Mexico expropriated foreign oil companies in 1938, an amicable settlement was arranged. The United States aligned the Latin American governments in behalf of its war aims, even though most of them were at the time ruled by generals who admired European fascism. After Pearl Harbor the U.S. military discouraged Latin American armed participation, but Brazil sent an infantry division to Italy, Mexico dispatched an air squadron to the Pacific, and naval units of various Latin American countries saw action. Soon after the war the United States persuaded them to sign mutual defense treaties and to participate in the Organization of American States, a regional organization under the United Nations based in Washington and funded largely by the United States.

By war's end, the military had abandoned power in most of Latin America, partly under pressure from the United States, which would have been embarrassed at the presence of fascist-inspired clients at the founding of the United Nations. But postwar U.S. policy disappointed Latin Americans. The Marshall Plan funded European reconstruction, and a new global economic structure restored the monetary and financial strength of the industrial powers, but ignored Latin America. The special relationship implied by the Good Neighbor policy and the Pan-American war propaganda were abandoned. The United States turned aside free trade overtures and saw the Latin Americans merely as suppliers of raw materials and tropical foodstuffs. The largest of these countries therefore undertook to restrict imports and to subsidize domestic industries. One result of these measures was to draw foreign companies to invest in Latin America, thereby paradoxically increasing friction with the United States as control of these economies appeared to escape even more rapidly from the hands of their citizens.

The United States, preoccupied with the cold war, worried that the region, suffering from poverty and a severe maldistribution of wealth, might fall to communism. To avert such a possibility in Guatemala, the CIA intervened there secretly in 1954. When Fidel Castro came to power in Cuba in 1959 and installed a government backed by the Soviet Union, the United States tried to subvert the revolution, culminating in the unsuccessful Bay of Pigs invasion by Cuban exiles in 1961. The following year Castro allowed the Soviets to install missiles to defend the island from continuing U.S. threats. In the consequent confrontation between the Soviet Union and the United States, the missiles were removed, but Cuba continued to receive Soviet economic and military assistance and served as an inspiration to radical movements all over Latin America. The United States reacted by greatly increasing loans and technical assistance through the Alliance for Progress program and by subsidizing secret police and armies throughout the region. In 1965, President Lyndon B. Johnson ordered the invasion of the Dominican Republic on slender evidence of communist penetration. Elsewhere, elites, fearing communist revolutions, allowed civilian governments to be taken over by the military.

The brutal methods of these regimes largely succeeded in crushing subversion. Washington's preoccupation with the region thereupon declined, except for Nicaragua and Grenada where leftist movements had come to power. In 1982, the United States invaded tiny Grenada, and Nicaragua was subjected to harassment by U.S.-funded guerrillas based in Honduras. The Salvadoran army, under siege by Marxist guerrillas since 1979, was provided with arms.

Latin America was stunned by the oil price rises of the 1970s and a subsequent decline in foreign investment. Government-owned sectors were expanded to take up the slack, borrowing the necessary capital from international banks. Their expenditures, however, were largely ill advised or corrupt, and the result was immense foreign debts that by 1980 were unpayable. At that point most of the military governments resigned in disgrace, restoring power to hapless civilians. Although these debts were the main reason for a decline in U.S. trade and investment in the region and the greatest threat to democracy there, the United States did little to deal with the problem.

Nontraditional issues, notably massive illegal immigration to the United States, the drug trade, and environmental degradation, none of which appeared manageable, complicated relations. The bonds with Latin America nevertheless became closer as the cultural and political presence of Americans of Latin American descent grew. Meanwhile, as the United States found itself less competitive in foreign markets, there was a return to discussion of a free trade area that might eventually encompass the hemisphere.

Alonso Aguilar, *Pan-Americanism from Monroe to the Present* (1969); John J. Johnson, *A Hemisphere Apart: Foundations of U.S. Policy toward Latin America* (1990); Robert F. Smith, *The United States and the Latin American Sphere of Influence* (1981).

WARREN DEAN

See also Bay of Pigs Invasion; Caribbean-U.S. Relations; Dollar Diplomacy; Good Neighbor Policy; Mexican War; Mexico-U.S. Relations; Monroe Doctrine; Panama Canal; Platt Amendment; Puerto Rico; Roosevelt Corollary; Spanish-American War; Texas Revolution and Annexation.

LATTER-DAY SAINTS

See Mormons.

LAWRENCE, ERNEST

(1901–1958), physicist. Lawrence, born in South Dakota, received his doctorate from Yale University, where he was appointed assistant professor. In 1928 he became an associate professor at the University of California in Berkeley. The subsequent rise of its physics department to world eminence was to a considerable extent based on Lawrence's contributions.

The most important among them was his invention of the cyclotron, a circular high-energy accelerator in which particles approach the speed of light as they travel in a spiral path from the center to the rim, where they are deflected toward a target and produce nuclear disintegrations. For a time Berkeley had a near monopoly of the new field of high-energy physics as important results kept pouring in from its new Radiation Laboratory, of which Lawrence was the first director. (It is now the Lawrence Berkeley Laboratory, not to be confused with the Lawrence Livermore National Laboratory, where basic and weapons research is carried on.) In 1939, Lawrence received the Nobel Prize in physics.

During World War II Lawrence worked on the development of the atomic fission bomb. His laboratory devised a way to obtain fissionable materials by an electromagnetic separation method that was later used at the Y-12 laboratory at Oak Ridge, Tennessee, where the atomic bomb was produced.

After the war, Lawrence became involved in the affair that resulted in the revocation of the security clearance of his former colleague J. Robert Oppenheimer because of alleged security infractions; Lawrence did not side with his old friend. (An underlying cause was Oppenheimer's opposition to the development of the more powerful hydrogen fusion bomb, whose proponents, led by Edward Teller, carried the day.) Meanwhile, partly because of its activities in nuclear research, the Berkeley laboratory continued to flourish under the sponsorship of the U.S. Atomic Energy Commission and its successor, the U.S. Department of Energy. It increased the size and energy of its accelerators and set the pattern for government support of large, near-autonomous laboratories on or close to university campuses. Lawrence also became increasingly active as a high-level government consultant.

Any assessment of Lawrence's significance must take into account his contributions as physicist, research leader and director of large-scale projects, university professor, and government adviser. A recurrent theme is his ingenuity in achieving significant results by simple means. This was true from his graduate work on photoelectricity, through his epochal invention of the cyclotron, and on to his devising of a novel way to display color television images that was a major contender among the methods under consideration in the 1950s. The Berkeley laboratory became the prototype for what has come to be known as "big science," the large-scale agglomeration of projects grouped around a central theme, employing thousands and managed by government contractors (often universities). Because of his opting for Berkeley over Yale and his subsequent status as the first American public university professor to win the Nobel Prize, he drew attention to the rising importance of such institutions vis-à-vis the better established private universities, a trend that has placed vast new resources at the nation's disposal.

At the laboratory, Lawrence is especially remembered for his innovative approach to the solution of technical problems. He was also an inventor of note, as witness his excursion into television technology. Finally, he was a major force in helping to resolve problems of international import. His last assignment, in 1958, was to participate in a conference to study ways of detecting violations of nuclear test agreements, a major obstacle to international pacts.

Herbert Childs, *An American Genius: The Life of Ernest Lawrence* (1968); N. P. Davis, *Lawrence and Oppenheimer* (1968); M. S. Livingston, *Particle Physics: The High Energy Frontier* (1968).

CHARLES SÜSSKIND

See also Nuclear Weapons: Origins and Legacy; Oppenheimer, J. Robert; Science and Technology.

LAWRENCE, JACOB

(1917–), artist. Lawrence's distinguished career has earned him a National Medal of Arts, election to the National Academy of Arts and Letters and the National Academy of Design, a National Council of the Arts commissionership, Guggenheim and Fulbright appointments, and dozens of honorary degrees and awards, including the NAACP's Spingarn Medal. His painting has been featured in several major retrospective exhibitions and numerous one-person shows at many of America's most prestigious museums.

The son of southern migrants, Lawrence grew up in Harlem during the Depression. New Deal programs afforded him extraordinary educational opportunities as well as his first employment as an artist. In the studio of his mentor, Charles Alston, young Lawrence painted while Harlem Renaissance luminaries and a younger generation of artists and writers gathered there, discussing ideas that would shape his art. He studied at the Harlem Art Workshop (1932–1937) and the American Artists School (1937–1939).

The 1930s art world was sharply divided between two competing schools: realism and abstractionism. Lawrence rejected both, charting his own course. His distinctive style evolved out of his subject matter, borrowing elements from several aesthetic traditions. His paintings are alive with human figures — usually African-Americans — engaged in all manner of activity. Without excess of emotion, they bear themselves and their circumstances with a transcendent dignity and grace. Lawrence's unique style of collage cubism — employing flat shapes, controlled outlines, and busy yet forceful compositions — simplifies and stylizes the human form. Patches of vivid, flat color juxtaposed upon layered planes of bold, repetitive patterns suggest the jumble of color and design found in a patchwork quilt or an African textile.

In dramatic narrative series of as many as sixty paintings, Lawrence documents and celebrates human triumph over oppression and injustice. Although each painting is complete in itself, an assembled series assumes epic force. Although they often relate the history and experience of black people (*Toussaint L'Ouverture, Migration of the Negro, Harlem*), their themes are universal. Lawrence also employs murals for his storytelling.

Throughout most of the twentieth century, institutions within the black community provided the only places for exhibiting the work of artists who were black. If occasionally invited to exhibit in galleries or museums, they were singled out as "Negro artists" and their work labeled "Negro art." Without gallery exposure, they could rarely reach influential patrons or command appropriate prices. But in 1941 Alain Locke introduced Edith Halpert, the perspicacious owner of New York's Downtown Gallery, to Lawrence's *Migration* series. Halpert immediately organized an exhibition, and Lawrence joined the select group of artists she represented, which included Stuart Davis, Charles Sheeler,

and Ben Shahn. *Migration* was purchased and divided between the Museum of Modern Art and the Phillips Collection, and *Fortune* magazine featured color reproductions of twenty-six of the panels. Lawrence's paintings had broken the art world's color line.

Also in 1941, Lawrence married painter Gwendolyn Knight. Except for service in World War II and frequent sojourns to paint and teach art, he worked in New York until joining the faculty of the University of Washington in 1971. Retired from teaching since 1983, he continues to create major new works and remains one of the few African-Americans to win recognition as a major American artist.

Ellen Harkins Wheat, *Jacob Lawrence: American Painter* (1986).

LINDA L. NIEMAN

See also Harlem Renaissance; Painting and Sculpture.

LAWRENCE STRIKE

This strike against the textile mills in Lawrence, Massachusetts, began in January 1912, when the owners of one mill lowered workers' pay in response to a new state law shortening the workweek. Within a few days, ten thousand men and women were out on strike. The American Federation of Labor (AFL) had long maintained that cohesive unions could not be built among the predominantly unskilled and ethnically diverse mill workers, but the Industrial Workers of the World (IWW) had been trying to organize them for more than a year. When the walkout occurred, two IWW representatives, Joseph Ettor and Arturo Giovannitti, assumed leadership of the strike. They were soon joined by two more of the IWW's best-known organizers, William Haywood and Elizabeth Gurley Flynn.

For weeks, the workers held rallies, paraded, and picketed. At the request of the mill owners, an AFL union — the United Textile Workers of America — tried to break the strike, but they were unsuccessful. Another effort to end the strike failed when a cache of dynamite discovered on mill premises turned out to have been planted by persons seeking to frame the strike leaders. Local police clashed repeatedly with the workers; when a young woman was killed in one of these confrontations, Ettor and Giovannitti were arrested for her murder. (Both were subsequently acquitted.) In an effort to save money as well as to dramatize the workers' plight, Flynn arranged to send a group of strikers' children to be cared for in other cities. The children's exodus evoked great public sympathy, especially when Lawrence police were photographed beating several women and children at the train station.

On March 1, the owners granted a 5 percent pay raise. The workers continued to hold out, however, and two weeks later, all four of their original demands were met. The outcome was hailed as a union triumph, but within a year, the owners had managed to regain most of the ground they had lost. Nevertheless, the strike stands as testimony to the fact that thousands of the least skilled, ethnically diverse workers could submerge their differences in a common expression of working-class solidarity.

See also Labor; Textile Industry.

LEAGUE OF NATIONS

See Versailles Treaty and League of Nations.

LEAGUE OF WOMEN VOTERS

The League of Women Voters was founded in Chicago in 1920 by Carrie Chapman Catt and other leaders of the National American Woman Suffrage Association (NAWSA) who had led the campaign for the recently ratified Nineteenth Amendment. Now that it was illegal for states to deny the vote on the basis of gender, Catt and her associates hoped that women voters would become a potent force in national politics. From the first, however, League members were divided on whether women should exercise their new power independently or through existing political parties. Catt argued for the latter. "Success can only be found on the inside," she said. "You won't be so welcome there, but that is the place to be." Other leaders, including Jane Ad-

dams, argued that women's special voice would be lost in the world of party politics. Members of this group further disagreed among themselves, however, some arguing that women should form their own party, and others that they should remain above all partisan politics. Finally it was agreed that the League would remain nonpartisan, supporting general programs of reform rather than functioning as an independent political organization for women.

Dissension continued within the women's movement during the 1920s and 1930s, especially between the League and the small but highly visible National Woman's party (NWP). The NWP focused exclusively on women's rights, to be realized through a constitutional amendment guaranteeing equal rights for both genders. The League opposed the amendment as harmful to the special needs of women and continued to work for a broad range of social reforms, only some of which were specifically intended to benefit women. "We are not feminists primarily," wrote one leader; "we are citizens."

In succeeding decades, the League continued its efforts to educate and mobilize public opinion on issues of general interest, gradually expanding its scope of concern to include nearly every aspect of public affairs — local, state, and national. While other organizations arose to carry on the traditions of feminism, the League sought to articulate the highest interests of both sexes. Starting in 1974, men were admitted as full members.

See also Suffrage; Women's Voluntary Associations.

LEE, ANN

(1736–1784), charismatic and visionary, called Mother Ann. Lee founded the United Society of Believers in Christ's Second Coming, known as the Shakers, by emigrating with eight followers from Manchester, England, to New York in 1774. Earlier, in 1770, her frenzied religious zeal, which included dervishlike dancing and crying out in strange tongues, had led to her imprisonment and the persecution of her followers. Accused by the Manchester magistrates of blasphemy, she had confounded church scholars examining her by speaking in seventy-two separate tongues. The millennium she envisioned had arrived.

In one of her visions Christ informed her that sexuality was depraved; she must endorse celibacy. She was hailed as the Female Christ. Believing in a just and nonsexist Mother/Father God, her followers thought that since Christ had already appeared as a man, the next manifestation would be female.

In another vision, a burning tree directed Ann to transport her church to America. The journey, which lasted three months in the brig *Mariah,* was fraught with difficulties, including a violent storm. But after fervent prayers, a miraculous wave accompanied by effulgent angels secured the ship.

In the band of immigrants were Ann's husband, a blacksmith, Abraham Standerin (known to the Shakers as Stanley); her brother William; a niece, Nancy; James Whittaker, a relative who later succeeded her as head of the sect; and John and James Hocknell who underwrote the journey and the purchase of land at Niskeyuna, New York, a few miles from Albany.

After nearly two years of misery in New York City, Ann joined her followers in upstate New York. During the revolutionary war period Shakers were thought to be spies since they refused to fight or to take oaths. The sect grew slowly until 1780 when charismatic New Light Baptists appeared. In 1781, Ann Lee began a missionary tour of the East, acquiring new followers and further incurring thereby the loathing of "the World." Shakers were whipped, clubbed, stoned, and dragged behind horses. In 1784, Ann Lee died as the result of beatings.

Under her successors, James Whittaker and James Meacham, the faith flourished. Meacham eventually founded some fifty communities and codified Shaker laws, which included celibacy, public confessions of sin, the common possession of property, the equality of the sexes, codes for dress and daily living, and an emphasis on the practical that was exemplified in their architecture and their renowned functional furniture. They also started international garden seed and herb industries and were responsible for such inventions as the circular saw and the first industrial washing machine. Their productive farms and orchards were models for area farmers. In 1784, there were twenty-five hundred Shakers, with the figure later swelling to about five to six thousand. Orphans were brought to the villages and many impoverished families arrived, attracted by the group's material security. But by 1908, as America grew more prosperous, the Shakers had shrunk in numbers to about a thousand.

Today, the communities at Pleasant Hill, Kentucky, Pittsfield, Massachusetts, Canterbury, New Hampshire, and Sabbathday Lake, Maine, are living museums. Only Sabbathday Lake, with a handful of aging Shaker sisters, functions as a productive, viable community, a continuing testimony to Ann Lee's vision.

Marguerite Fellows Melcher, *The Shaker Adventure* (1986); Robert L. Peters, *The Gift to Be Simple: A Garland for Ann Lee* (1988); Robert L. Peters, *Shaker Light: Mother Ann Lee in America* (1987).

ROBERT PETERS

See also Shakers.

LEE, ROBERT E.

(1807–1870), Confederate general. Lee was born in Virginia, the son of Ann Carter Lee and Henry ("Light-Horse Harry") Lee, who had earned fame as a cavalry commander in the American Revolution. The elder Lee, however, suffered financial reverses, and Robert grew up primarily in the care of his mother. In 1829 he graduated from the U.S. Military Academy second in his class and received a commission in the Engineer Corps. Two years later he married Mary Custis, heir to Arlington Plantation.

Lee served in the Engineer Corps at various posts until the Mexican War broke out, when he joined the staff of Winfield Scott in the campaign against Mexico City. His skill and daring at Cerro Gordo and Chapultepec won for him Scott's lasting admiration and a promotion to brevet colonel.

From 1852 to 1855 Lee was superintendent of West Point. Then he commanded a regiment in Texas, where in 1857 he learned of the death of his father-in-law. He took protracted leave to settle the snarled estate and was still living at Arlington when news of John Brown's raid on Harpers Ferry reached Washington in October 1859. In command of a detachment of marines, Lee captured Brown and several of his followers with no harm to Brown's thirteen hostages.

During the secession crisis in 1861, Lee declined an offer of principal field command from Scott and followed Virginia into the Confederacy. That fall he presided over a failed campaign in western (now West) Virginia and spent the winter overseeing coastal defenses in Georgia and South Carolina. Recalled to Richmond in March 1862, Lee advised Confederate president Jefferson Davis as the peninsular campaign of Union general George B. McClellan developed. Then in the Battle of Seven Pines/Fair Oaks, Confederate general Joseph E. Johnston suffered serious wounds, and on June 1, 1862, Davis appointed Lee to command what became the Army of Northern Virginia.

Lee plotted a brilliant campaign that resulted in the Seven Days' Battles (June 25–July 1) and drove the federals from the outskirts of Richmond. On August 30, 1862, he led the army to victory over John Pope in the Second Battle of Bull Run/Manassas. Lee then launched an invasion of Maryland that came to grief in the bloody stalemate at Antietam on September 17, 1862. But at Fredericksburg on December 13, his troops defeated Ambrose E. Burnside's Union troops and stabilized the Virginia front.

During the spring of 1863 Lee became ill, probably with the onset of the heart disease that plagued him thereafter. He recovered in time to confront Joseph Hooker's federal offensive at Chancellorsville, May 1–4, 1863. Lee daringly divided his inferior numbers and dispatched Thomas J. ("Stonewall") Jackson on a day-long march to the Union rear. Chancellorsville may have been Lee's greatest battle. Jackson, however, sustained accidental wounds that proved fatal.

Lee reorganized his high command and in June 1863 sent dispersed elements of his army through Maryland and into Pennsylvania. Union troops followed, and they met at Gettysburg,

July 1–3. On the final day Lee sought victory with a desperate charge at the center of the Union line. Gen. George G. Meade rendered "Pickett's charge" a grand disaster.

The following spring Ulysses S. Grant assumed command of all Union armies, and his men confronted Lee's southerners in the Wilderness, at Spotsylvania Court House, and at Cold Harbor. Grant then appeared south of Richmond and the James River and attacked a crucial railroad junction at Petersburg. But Petersburg held, and Lee made brilliant use of trenches to compensate for his dwindling numbers. The siege persisted through the winter, until on April 2, 1865, Lee's lines broke, and he evacuated Richmond. Grant's forces overtook and surrounded Lee's remnant army, and on April 9 Lee surrendered at Appomattox Court House, Virginia.

After the war Lee counseled reconciliation and served as president of Washington College (later Washington and Lee University) in Virginia. Called the American Napoleon, Lee displayed audacity and initiative in his zeal to "strike a blow" as an offensive commander. His use of trenches to offset his inferior numbers proved his genius on the defense. He has remained an American hero — revered for the strength of his character and the brilliance of his battles.

Thomas L. Connelly, *The Marble Man: Robert E. Lee and His Image in American Society* (1977); Douglas S. Freeman, *R. E. Lee: A Biography,* 4 vols. (1934–1935).

EMORY M. THOMAS

See also Civil War.

LEGAL TENDER CASES

These two cases decided by the Supreme Court in 1871 upheld the constitutionality of paper money issued by the U.S. Treasury. The Legal Tender Acts of 1862 and 1863 made paper money a legal substitute for gold and silver, including for the payment of preexisting debts.

In 1870, Chief Justice Salmon P. Chase, who as Treasury secretary during the Civil War sponsored the legal tender program, had written the opinion of the Court in *Hepburn* v. *Griswold,* which divided, 5–3, in finding the acts unconstitutional. In *Hepburn,* Chase had written that such laws were inconsistent with the spirit of the Constitution, which prohibited the states from passing "any . . . law impairing the obligation of contracts." Further, an act compelling holders of contracts that called for payment in gold or silver to accept as legal tender "mere promises to pay dollars" was unconstitutional because it deprived "such persons of property without due process of law" under the Fifth Amendment. The Court until this time had rarely found an act of Congress unconstitutional. This decision also interpreted "due process of law" to apply to the *substance* or *effect* of a law, not just to the procedure followed in adopting it.

In 1871, the Court, with two new justices on the bench, reversed itself with the legal tender cases, *Knox* v. *Lee* and *Parker* v. *Davis,* and declared the Legal Tender Acts constitutional. It said Congress had the power "to coin money and regulate its value" with the objects of self-preservation and the achievement of a more perfect union. As to the argument that the acts indirectly impaired the obligation of contracts, the Court said that "no obligation of a contract can extend to the defeat of legitimate government authority." Since the acts were within the spirit of the Constitution, Congress had not exceeded its authority.

LEGISLATURE

See House of Representatives; Senate.

LEISLER'S REBELLION

Leisler's Rebellion, 1689, was a briefly successful attempt by merchant Jacob Leisler to seize control of the colony of New York. Upon hearing that the Glorious Revolution in England had driven King James II off the throne, groups of colonists in New England and the Mid-Atlantic colonies deposed their royal governors and turned control over to elected assemblies. But in New York, after deposing Lieutenant Governor

Francis Nicholson, Leisler named himself governor. He was backed by Dutch laborers and artisans, who disliked the Anglo-Dutch elite group that had run the colony. But New York merchants were not so pleased and sought to unseat him.

In 1691, in order to reassert English control over the colony, King William appointed a royal governor. When Leisler refused to step down, he was charged with treason. On May 16, 1691, he and his son-in-law were hanged.

See also Middle Colonies.

LEND-LEASE ACT

The Lend-Lease Act of March 11, 1941, was the principal means for providing U.S. military aid to foreign nations during World War II. The act authorized the president to transfer arms or any other defense materials for which Congress appropriated money to "the government of any country whose defense the President deems vital to the defense of the United States." Britain, the Soviet Union, China, Brazil, and many other countries received weapons under this law.

By allowing the president to transfer war matériel to a beleaguered Britain — and without payment as required by the Neutrality Act of 1939 — the act enabled the British to keep fighting until events led America into the conflict. It also skirted the thorny problems of war debts that had followed World War I.

Lend-Lease brought the United States one step closer to entry into the war. Isolationists, such as Republican senator Robert Taft, opposed it. Taft correctly noted that the bill would "give the President power to carry on a kind of undeclared war all over the world, in which America would do everything except actually put soldiers in the front-line trenches where the fighting is."

See also World War II.

LESLIE, FRANK

(1821–1880), publisher. Born Henry Carter in England, the son of a glove manufacturer, he placed the pseudonym "Frank Leslie" on his early drawings to conceal his plans to break free of the family business. At age twenty-two he was head engraver for the upstart *Illustrated London News,* the first systematic effort to provide pictures and texts in journalism. Leslie, however, was not fitted to be anyone's employee, and he came to New York in 1848 to take advantage of the opportunities it offered. He acquired capital as an illustrator, principally through work for P. T. Barnum, the promoter.

In 1854 Leslie brought out the first magazine under his own name. In the next quarter century he worked his name into periodical mastheads twenty-two times and published seventy books under the Frank Leslie imprint. *Frank Leslie's Illustrated Newspaper* (1855–1922) was the first successful American venture to bring pictures and news together in a weekly. Leslie's career coincided with the rise of photography, a technological achievement that increased the public appetite for pictures. But the camera was little help for publishers during Leslie's life since there was no mechanical way to bring a photograph to the printing press. Thus magazine illustrations were done by hand. Leslie's breakthrough was in dividing the engraving into as many as thirty-two sections for individual engravers and then fitting the woodblocks together so that the seams fit. He could accomplish in a day what a single artisan had taken weeks to produce. Using these teams of engravers, he published pictures of events only a week old, a speed new to popular journalism.

Frank Leslie put his name atop his publishing house in New York and named his yacht and a private rail car after himself, but his achievements ranged beyond self-promotion. His newspaper covered the opening up of Japan, the Crimean War, and expeditions to the Arctic. He gave Americans their first pictures of striking workers and crusaded against unsafe milk. By turns, he celebrated and condemned the sport of bare-knuckle prize fighting. The *Illustrated Newspaper* published some three thousand pictures of the Civil War. More, it contained political gossip, fashion plates, and lurid coverage of crime. As Frank Leslie made the news pictorial, exciting, and kaleidoscopic, he anticipated what popular journalism would become.

Leslie's personal life was similarly colorful. In the 1860s he brought simultaneous suits against his son and his first wife. He lived in the home of his trusted editors, Ephraim and Miriam Squier. Stories of adulteries in the household spread through the rumor mills and enlivened the courts and the press of the 1870s; he married the ex–Mrs. Squier in 1874. The publisher was not without honors. He was the nation's commissioner at the Paris Universal Exposition (1867) and the representative of New York State to the Centennial Exposition at Philadelphia (1876). The economic panic of 1877 forced Leslie into bankruptcy because of losses outside his publishing empire. The courts left him in charge of editorial policy. Mrs. Leslie took the name "Frank Leslie" by court order after his death and revived his publishing business by the end of the century.

Budd L. Gambee, *Frank Leslie and His Illustrated Newspaper, 1855–1860* (1964); Madeleine B. Stern, *Purple Passage: The Life of Mrs. Frank Leslie* (1953).

THOMAS C. LEONARD

See also Magazines and Newspapers.

LEVITTOWNS

Levittown was the name given to three suburban developments constructed in the post–World War II decades by Levitt and Sons, the most important private builder of this period. Using mass production techniques, William Levitt turned home building from a cottage industry into a major manufacturing process, and his methods were emulated by builders nationwide.

The Levitts had entered the construction business in 1929, catering mainly to a wealthy market. During World War II they received government contracts to build homes for war workers. Under deadline pressure, they developed mass production methods to build houses quickly. These techniques were carried over to their postwar suburban developments. From 1947 to 1951, the company built the first Levittown, a community of 17,450 homes for 75,000 people in Hempstead, New York. The simply designed houses were built by crews, each performing one job in a twenty-seven-step construction process and using prefabricated materials. At the peak of production, over thirty houses were built per day. To cut costs at every level, Levitt and Sons hired only nonunion labor and produced most of its own materials, from concrete slabs to kitchen appliances. The company also planted trees on each plot and built community pools, parks, and playgrounds to create the ambience of a garden community.

In the face of a national housing shortage, public response to Levittown was overwhelming. Advances from the Federal Housing Administration and Veterans Administration enabled the Levitts to offer lenient credit terms, including no down payment. Thousands of middle-class families bought in quickly, as home prices were cheap; fourteen hundred contracts were signed in one day in 1949. As in most postwar suburban developments, blacks were excluded.

In the 1950s, the second Levittown was built near Philadelphia, and the third went up in New Jersey in the 1960s. Some observers criticized the monotonous uniformity of the Levittowns, charging that they promoted listless personalities, conformity, and escapism. But Herbert Gans's sociological study, *The Levittowners* (1967), found that homeownership gave the residents a viable sense of pride and more privacy and space, which they valued greatly.

See also Housing.

LEWIS, JOHN L.

(1880–1969), labor leader and president of the United Mine Workers (UMW) and the Congress of Industrial Organizations (CIO). Born in Cleveland, Iowa, the son of Welsh immigrants, Lewis, between 1898 and 1907, tried coal mining, farming, construction work, and small business before settling in 1907 on a career in the labor movement. Joined by his family in the coal-mining community of Panama, Illinois, Lewis built a local power base among immigrant coal miners. He rose quickly within the trade union hierarchy and became a national organizer for the American Federation of Labor (AFL) in 1909.

In 1917 he returned to the UMW as its statistician and editor.

As president of the UMW, the largest trade union in the United States, during the 1920s, Lewis dominated a declining union in a sick industry. Admired by businesspeople and other Republicans (he served as chair of the Republican party's National Labor Committee), he won a reputation as a "labor statesman." To critics, however, Lewis appeared to be "merely a labor boss of the most conventional kind," an autocratic "per capita counter" and "power seeker."

During the 1930s, Lewis was the nation's most imaginative and creative labor leader. He joined the Democratic party in 1932, hoping that the national government would help stabilize industrial relations in the coal industry. Working closely with Franklin D. Roosevelt and other New Dealers, Lewis rebuilt the UMW and successfully organized previously nonunion coal regions. When the AFL failed to seize the opportunity to organize mass production workers, Lewis resigned his AFL vice presidency and established the Committee for Industrial Organization (1935), which became the CIO. After the Roosevelt landslide of 1936, the CIO wrested union recognition and collective bargaining from the nation's two greatest mass production enterprises, General Motors and U.S. Steel. By 1937, Lewis had attained his greatest stature as a labor leader, but thereafter his power declined. Between 1937 and 1939, Lewis lost influence in the White House, and public sentiment turned against him. In 1940 he broke openly with Roosevelt because he felt that the president took labor for granted and that a Republican candidate elected with labor votes might repay the unions (and Lewis specifically). Lewis called upon workers to vote for Republican Wendell Willkie; when union voters rejected his advice, he resigned as president of the CIO.

After 1940 Lewis's power flowed solely from his absolute control of the UMW. In 1941, on the eve of America's entrance into World War II, Lewis took his miners out on strike, and in 1943, in the middle of the war, he again called them out. Those strikes won enormous gains for coal miners but further damaged Lewis's reputation with the public and fellow labor leaders.

Not without cause did the military newspaper *Stars and Stripes* in 1943 damn Lewis's "coal-black soul." But Lewis seemed to relish the guerrilla war he was waging against other labor leaders, Congress, and the White House. Between 1945 and 1950 he led four national coal strikes, rejoined and impetuously left the AFL, and fought aggressively against the antilabor Taft-Hartley Act.

After 1950, however, Lewis brought labor peace to a declining coal industry, steadily improved the material conditions of union members, and won esteem as an apostle of "cooperative capitalism." Lewis cooperated with mine operators because such cooperation stabilized the industry, increased union power, and guaranteed working miners high wages and greater fringe benefits. But Lewis's new brand of labor relations satisfied mine operators at the expense of miners who became the victims of technological change.

Lewis thus enjoyed great success and abysmal failure: he had served as "the great emancipator" for industrial workers during the 1930s and as their "great betrayer" for repudiating Roosevelt in 1940. A man whose life focused on accumulating power, he was that rare labor leader who left office voluntarily. In his own words, Lewis always behaved as "something of a man."

Melvyn Dubofsky and Warren Van Tine, *John L. Lewis: A Biography* (1986); Robert H. Zieger, *John L. Lewis: Labor Leader* (1987).

Melvyn Dubofsky

See also Congress of Industrial Organizations; Labor.

LEWIS, SINCLAIR

(1885–1951), novelist, satirist of middle-class values. Born in Sauk Centre, Minnesota, the son of a stern hardworking doctor, Lewis matured slowly, writing a number of minor novels and working as a publicist and editor. In 1920 he found his voice with *Main Street*, a devastating portrait of the American small town, its dullness, mindless prejudices, and lonely stultified women. He followed this book with *Babbitt* (1922), an equally vigorous assault on a typical small-town businessman and his narrow, contradictory values.

Lewis was more than a critic of American culture, however. In his next novel, *Arrowsmith* (1925), which he wrote in collaboration with the bacteriologist Paul de Kruif, he revealed his admiration for the heroic side of the American dream. Martin Arrowsmith is a brilliant medical researcher who struggles against the temptations of irresponsible women, unethical opportunists in the medical profession, and his own human impulses, which threaten his professional integrity. The novel won the Pulitzer Prize, but Lewis created a literary sensation by rejecting it. In 1920 the Pulitzer judges had awarded the prize to *Main Street*, but the trustees of Columbia University had declined to confirm the choice. In a stinging letter, Lewis claimed this kind of tacit censorship would emasculate American literature.

Next, Lewis returned to satiric assault with his most controversial novel, *Elmer Gantry* (1927), the story of a hypocritical evangelist. Although it created another sensation, it now seems among the weakest of Lewis's novels. One critic has called it a work of "pure revulsion." In *Dodsworth* (1929) Lewis returned to his favorite subject, the American businessman — but with far more sympathy and understanding. Sam Dodsworth is no George Babbitt. He goes abroad to expand his cultural and intellectual horizons, and there he realizes that his frivolous wife, Fran, sums up the emptiness he feels. He divorces her and marries a calm, perceptive woman who encourages him to launch a new business, building well-designed, artistically superior homes. *Dodsworth*'s contrast of European and American values and its international setting helped Lewis become the first American writer to win the Nobel Prize in 1930. Lewis's acceptance speech attacked the genteel tradition in American literature and praised such writers as Theodore Dreiser, Ernest Hemingway, and William Faulkner.

For the next twenty years, Lewis continued to search for problems in American life and to dramatize them in his fiction. *It Can't Happen*

Here (1935) described the rise of fascism in the United States, *Gideon Planish* (1943) exposed organized philanthropy, and *Kingsblood Royal* (1947) explored race prejudice. The best of these later novels is *Cass Timberlane,* about a thoughtful Minnesota judge who divorces his pushy wife and marries a younger playgirl. Since his death, critics have handled Lewis roughly, some calling him the literary equivalent of George Babbitt. But others have pointed out this criticism ignores the most salient fact. Only Lewis saw Babbitt and created him. Lewis's artistic reach may have exceeded his grasp, but he led the way in urging writers to use the novel to confront America critically, without illusions.

Mark Schorer, *Sinclair Lewis: An American Life* (1961); Vincent Sheean, *Dorothy and Red* (1963).

THOMAS FLEMING

See also Literature.

LEWIS AND CLARK EXPEDITION

Early in 1803, President Thomas Jefferson commissioned Meriwether Lewis and William Clark, both experienced soldiers, to explore what is now the northwestern United States. He requested detailed observations about natural resources and transcontinental routes, also instructing the leaders to contact Indian tribes. The Louisiana Purchase soon gave the expedition new urgency; almost nothing was known about the vast addition of land west of the Mississippi River.

In May 1804, Lewis and Clark's party of nearly fifty men set out from St. Louis. They headed up the Missouri River and at the onset of winter reached the site of present-day Bismarck, North Dakota, where they constructed a fort. At this time Sacagawea, a Shoshone woman, joined the expedition as a guide and translator. In 1805, the group followed the Missouri westward to its headwaters and then crossed the Rocky Mountains and proceeded along the Salmon, Snake, and Columbia rivers to the Pacific Ocean. On their return in 1806, Clark and Lewis separated and found two more passes over the Rockies. Once reunited, they continued down the Mis-

souri to St. Louis, arriving with abundant painstaking notes and drawings of the geography of the region and the wildlife and inhabitants they had encountered.

See also Exploration of North America; Louisiana Purchase and map.

LIBERALISM

Before the New Deal gave the term *liberalism* its modern American meaning, it was a little-used word that referred to a belief in laissez-faire economics and limited government. Franklin D. Roosevelt, the president who defined liberalism for most Americans, came to power in the midst of blinding economic misery at home and barbarism abroad. A month before Roosevelt took office in March 1933, Adolf Hitler took power in Germany and Joseph Stalin was liquidating millions of peasants in the Ukraine. Democracy, according to the "best" minds of the age, was a pleasant nineteenth-century myth out of place in a world where, as World War I had demonstrated, mass sentiment could be manufactured like bicycles. Democracy, said Benito Mussolini in Italy, was insufficiently dynamic. "All the experiments of our time," he crowed, "are antiliberal."

Overwhelmed by the collapse of the economy, bankers and businesspeople urged the president to take extraordinary powers. The respected liberal journalist Louis Fischer spoke for many when he argued that given the collapse of capitalist democracy, the country had to choose between "capitalistic dictatorship and white terror on the one hand and Soviet dictatorship on the other."

On the right, laissez-faire economists argued that the depression had been brought on by the trade unions which had undercut capitalism by reducing profit margins. The depression could be ended only if Roosevelt seized the emergency powers necessary to restrict democracy and restore profit margins. From the left came the assertion that prosperity could be restored only through a command economy that would necessarily restrict individual liberties. There was, said Roosevelt's 1936 presidential opponent, Alf

Landon, "no half-way house between these two systems."

But in a nation ravaged by depression and doubt, Roosevelt chose not to choose. He neither rolled back democracy nor expropriated the expropriators. Instead, through word and deed, he made democracy a fighting faith again. Roosevelt seized on *liberal,* until then a word of minor importance in the American political vocabulary, to describe his New Deal, his attempt to temper economic individualism with social democratic safeguards. For millions of Americans those safeguards — such as Social Security and bank deposit insurance — would become synonymous with the liberalism they repeatedly supported at the ballot box from 1932 to 1964.

Roosevelt's use of the term *liberal* angered those like Herbert Hoover who associated the word with limited government and laissez-faire economics, but its connotations of tolerance helped ward off those who labeled FDR's policies "communistic" or "fascist." "My friends," said Roosevelt, turning the tables on Hoover, "I am not for return to that definition of liberty under which for many years a free people were gradually regimented into the service" of big business. Yet, Roosevelt's liberalism was, in its unprecedented challenge to American individualism, more radical than anything the nation has seen before or since.

Many of FDR's specific programs drew on earlier reforms, but New Deal liberalism as a whole broke with its predecessors like progressivism by giving up on the hope of reconstructing the Jeffersonian ideal. The Great Depression had decimated the independent middle classes, the small businesspeople and farmers who had been the bulwark of self-government. Roosevelt redefined democracy for a mass society of industrial workers. He incorporated the wage-earning masses into the nation's political life by supporting the growth of trade unionism. Government, through New Deal laws like the Wagner Act which enabled labor to organize, became the guarantor of the independence once supplied by property ownership.

New Deal liberalism, Roosevelt explained, "is plain English for a changed concept of the duty and responsibility of government toward economic life." That responsibility, New Dealers argued, could be carried out only by a leadership capable of circumventing America's time-honored traditions of checks and balances. American government, said New Dealer Louis Brownlow, writing in a frankly utilitarian vein, should rest "on the truth that the general interest is superior to and has priority over any special or private interest." And said Roosevelt, paraphrasing John Dewey, the philosopher of liberalism, "The man who seeks freedom from responsibility in the name of individual liberty is either fooling himself or trying to cheat his fellow man."

"Private interest" for Rooseveltian liberals was represented not only by big business but by the Republican-dominated federal bench, which justified its defense of economic privilege by the due process clause of the Fourteenth Amendment. Given the liberal majorities in both houses of Congress, the primary opposition to the New Deal came from the federal courts. The New Dealers challenged the "word-magic" of the conservatives' legal formalism with an alternative form of expertise based on social scientific "knowledge."

In sum, New Deal liberalism distrusted both "the aristocracy of the bar" and the excesses of free-market individualism. It drew instead on "scientifically" oriented intellectuals to try to create in property-rights-oriented America something along the lines of a European social democracy. Its concentrated power, guided by academic expertise, was legitimated by a democratic majoritarianism that cut against the grain of American individualism. The "one great difference that has characterized the division [between liberals and conservatives]," said FDR, "has been that the liberal party — no matter what its particular name was at the time — believes in the efficacy of the will of the great majority of the people as distinguished from the judgment of a small minority."

After Roosevelt's death and the end of World War II, American liberalism became characterized by a defense of the mildly redistributive welfare state that emphasized equalizing, at least for whites, the possibilities of opportunity. Driven by Keynesian assumptions, it required leadership by expert economists manipulating aggregate demand (which angered businesspeople, who felt politically displaced), but it imposed only a limited regimen of administrative control.

Liberalism in the Truman era seemed to be simple self-interest to most families who benefited from the G.I. bill and veterans' mortgages. Campaigning in 1948 on the slogan "All I ask you to do is vote for yourself, vote for your family," Harry S. Truman not only defeated challenges from his left and right, but triumphed despite drawing only limited support from the top tiers as measured by wealth, education, or occupation.

New Deal liberalism's final political victory came in 1964 when Lyndon Johnson once again defeated Hoover's ghost in the form of the outspoken economic libertarian Barry Goldwater. Johnson went on, in effect, to complete much of the New Deal's agenda by expanding its social and health benefits for the poor, the elderly, and African-Americans who had earlier been ignored.

Civil rights aside, however, post-Truman liberalism was increasingly driven not by a popular mandate but by professional reformers. Liberalism in the 1960s rested in large measure on the newly acquired prestige of the social sciences, particularly economics and sociology. But the empire of science collapsed, its prestige consumed in the flames of Vietnam and the burning ghettos.

By the middle of the decade, New Deal liberalism was in retreat, routed initially not so much by its conservative opponents as by new forms of liberalism, which had emerged in response to the cataclysms of those years. In the next quarter century, its reputation declined until in the 1988 presidential race "liberal" became the "L word," an epithet.

New issues, such as racial justice and the misuse of a now powerful presidency to fight a morally untenable war in Vietnam, destroyed the New Deal political coalition. At the same time a renewed fear of government as a threat to individual moral autonomy, defined in terms not of property but of lifestyle, undermined the social and cultural assumptions of the New Deal's mild collectivism and authoritative institutions. Both civil rights and lifestyle liberalism were moral critiques of meat-and-potatoes majoritari-

anism and both pursued their goals through the courts, the "undemocratic" branch of government the New Deal had, in large measure, defined itself against.

The New Deal, dependent on the support of southern Democrats, had done little to confront racial injustice. Because an entire people cannot "rise above itself," wrote Alexis de Tocqueville, only a "despot" could free the African-American from the shackles of prejudice. The Supreme Court now became that benevolent "despot."

The Warren Court's 1954 *Brown* v. *Board of Education of Topeka* decision declaring school segregation unconstitutional transformed the very nature of American government. The Court's determination to define moral issues as beyond the boundaries of popular decision making as well as the moral challenge posed by the courage of the civil rights movement helped redefine liberal politics. *Brown* became the inspiration for women, gays, Hispanics, environmentalists, and others who saw that their interests could be vindicated outside of the ordinary legislative process.

In the 1970s, legal crusaders like Ralph Nader, famous for exposing the safety hazards of General Motors cars, filed class action suits to fill the vacuum created by the collapse of social science. The NAACP, the American Civil Liberties Union, the Legal Services Corporation, or one of the many "Naderite" public interest law firms was as likely to sue government on behalf of aggrieved minorities as to defend it. Liberalism became increasingly associated not with a broad majoritarian politics but with a court-imposed politics, whether dealing with racial and gender quotas or with pollution control standards.

Legal reformers initiated what, in regulatory terms, was almost a second New Deal between 1964 and 1977. Ten new regulatory agencies were created. Regulatory battles over everything from product safety to energy conservation took the shape of class conflict but — fatally for post–New Deal liberalism — without mass support. Without that support, the new liberalism, an alliance of lawyers and other professionals with minorities, was politically vulnerable.

Charles Reich captured the essence of the new liberalism in his 1971 book *The Greening of America*. Deeply critical of the bureaucratic state built by the New Deal, Reich wanted the courts to expand simultaneously individual freedoms by protecting the nonconformist against social mores and, in the name of rights, the social services that disadvantaged minorities were entitled to receive from their neighbors' tax dollars. It was a politically untenable mix that left the average citizen with a larger tax bill but little in the way of new services, while legitimating individuals' pursuance of their own interests.

Reich had stumbled on to what Simon Lazarus, the theorist of Naderism, described as "the philosophical crisis of American liberalism." New Deal liberalism had been erected on the understanding that it was the job of government to protect the virtuous people from the rapacious interests. But, asked the new politics liberals of the 1960s, what if the people themselves were corrupted by materialism, imperialism, racial bigotry, and a variety of other malignancies? Their answer, inspired in large measure by the civil rights movement, was to return to a pre–New Deal definition of democracy based largely on court-generated rights. Denuded of its democratic drive, liberalism had become minoritarian.

Beginning with Richard Nixon, the Republicans picked up the "common man" theme and ran with it to victories in five of six presidential elections between 1968 and 1988. Where FDR had spoken of the "forgotten man," Republicans like Nixon and Ronald Reagan spoke of the "silent majority" imperiled by crime and court-ordered "social engineering." Conservatives played on the opposition to social policies like busing for racial integration to argue that government, not big business, was the great danger to the average American. By the 1988 presidential election, twice as many voters defined themselves as conservatives than as liberals. Liberals, members of the party of court-protected minorities, had themselves become a minority.

Steve Fraser and Gary Gerstle, eds., *The Rise and Fall of the New Deal Order, 1930–1980* (1989); William E. Leuchtenburg, *In the Shadow of FDR: From Harry Truman to Ronald Reagan* (1983; rev. ed., 1989); Fred Siegel, *Troubled Journey: From Pearl Harbor to Ronald Reagan* (1984).

FRED SIEGEL

See also Civil Rights Movement; Dewey, John; Fair Deal; Great Society; Labor; Nader, Ralph; New Deal; New Left; Progressivism; Supreme Court.

LIBERTY LEAGUE

The American Liberty League was founded in August 1934 by conservative political and business leaders who opposed the policies of President Franklin D. Roosevelt. After supporting anti–New Deal candidates of both parties in the 1934 congressional elections, the League moved on in 1935 to attack the whole New Deal program. Its pamphlets, widely distributed, described the previous two years' legislation as extravagant, socialistic, and unconstitutional. Roosevelt's style of governance was compared to that of Stalin, Hitler, and Mussolini. Industrialists, particularly members of the du Pont family, provided the League with ample financial backing, and conservative Democrats like John W. Davis added their support. But the movement lacked a compelling political spokesperson. Former governor Alfred E. Smith of New York was persuaded to come out of retirement to support the League, but his keynote speech at a fundraising dinner on January 25, 1936, was so extreme and embittered that it harmed both his image and that of the League.

League leaders like John J. Raskob and the du Ponts briefly supported Governor Eugene Talmadge of Georgia, who was trying to rally grass-roots Democrats against the New Deal and at the same time further his own presidential ambitions, but this effort won little public support. Equally unsuccessful were the League's efforts to create new political organizations like the Farmers' Independence Council and the Southern Committee to Uphold the Constitution. By the time of the election in 1936 the League had little political standing, and Roosevelt's overwhelming victory completed its defeat.

See also Conservatism; New Deal.

LIBERTY PARTY

The Liberty party, organized in 1840, succeeded in placing slavery on the national political agenda. The party was founded in Albany, New York, by abolitionists, including the philanthropists Lewis and Arthur Tappan and Ohio clergyman Theodore Dwight Weld. At first, the Liberty party attracted few supporters. Its candidate for the 1840 presidential election, James G. Birney, a "reformed" slaveholder, received only 7,000 votes. But by 1844 the party had gained the backing of such leading abolitionists as Senator Salmon P. Chase, and this time Birney received 62,000 votes. The Liberty party held the balance of power in many closely contested local elections, which forced other candidates to take antislavery stances.

By 1848, disagreements over its future agenda caused a split in Liberty party ranks, and it was unable to agree on a presidential nominee. Many of its supporters joined with other antislavery groups, including the "Barnburners," a radical Democratic faction in New York, and the "Conscience" Whigs, to form the Free-Soil party, which nominated ex-president Martin Van Buren. In the election Van Buren received almost 300,000 votes, approximately 10 percent of the total.

See also Abolitionist Movement; Elections: 1840, 1844, 1848.

LIBRARIES AND MUSEUMS

The American passion for self-improvement and talent for voluntary association, commonly noted features of the national character since the early Republic, have found particular expression in the creation of libraries and museums. These institutions are two of the most admired features of American cultural and intellectual life. Both libraries and museums, aggressive and ingenious developers of user services, have attracted a blend of private and public support and much foreign imitation. Both have also betrayed tensions between populist educational aims and narrower research and collecting ideals. But though parallels link their foundation and oper-

ation, their histories are different enough to merit separate consideration.

Libraries

Books formed part of the material culture brought to the New World by European colonists and were particularly valued by some of the first English settlers of North America. Libraries constituted the cornerstone of higher educational institutions; the naming of Harvard College, for example, was linked to John Harvard's gift of books. Through the early eighteenth century American libraries fell into several types: private collections formed by amateur historians, scientists, philosophers, and classicists; college and university collections; and subscription libraries, created by groups of the mobile and ambitious, like the young men Benjamin Franklin gathered around him in Philadelphia, an enterprise that led to the formation of that city's Library Company in 1731.

During the late eighteenth century circulating libraries increased in number, and the social library, developed by groups of clerks, artisans, merchants, and mechanics, became a popular form in the following decades. In the mid-nineteenth century states permitted school districts and cities to levy taxes for library support. Easy accessibility to books was considered a necessity for both responsible political participation and widespread economic advancement, so the dream of free public libraries became part of the democratic litany.

It was not until the late nineteenth century, however, that a national stamp was put upon library expansion, and this through three components. The first was the professionalization of library service and the self-conscious creation of a corps of specialists, followed by the invention of new systems of classification and equipment. They were all brought together by the charismatic figure of Melvil Dewey, inventor of the most popular classification method (his *Decimal Classification* first appeared in 1876), distributor of library equipment, leader of the first great library school at Columbia University, and an active force in the founding of the American Library Association.

The second was the expansion of the Library of Congress — its rise to leadership among the research libraries of the world and its increasing acceptance of responsibility for standardizing library practices and strengthening bibliographical tools. The great building constructed for the Library of Congress in the 1890s, with its murals, mosaics, and statuary, symbolized a religion of the book that was national in character and reflected cosmopolitan scholarly goals.

The third component was the role of Andrew Carnegie, who gave away tens of millions of dollars in the early twentieth century for the establishment of public libraries. The Carnegie gifts were earmarked for construction and made conditional on community support (through tax revenues) for library operation. So enthusiastic and widespread was the eventual response that the Carnegie Foundation provided architectural plans for municipal imitation and the Carnegie Library became a recognizable landmark in cities and towns across the United States.

In the twentieth century American libraries expanded their traditions of service. Specialized libraries appeared for children, the blind, and foreign language speakers, and mobile units met the needs of populations scattered in rural areas. Public librarians preached the importance of library cards for children and turned their central branches into informal educational institutions for the ambitious and industrious. Research collections, formed from the legacies or collections of philanthropists like Walter Newberry of Chicago, J. Pierpont Morgan of New York, Henry E. Huntington of California, and Henry Clay Folger of Detroit and Washington, allowed American scholars to examine rare books and manuscripts. In the years after World War II American university libraries, helped by public funds as well as private gifts, expanded their holdings significantly.

Access to these collections was facilitated by the creation of elaborate bibliographical guides, one of the most notable being the enormous National Union Catalog begun by the Library of Congress in the 1950s. Quick to exploit the latest technologies, from microfilming in the 1930s and 1940s to computers in the 1960s and 1970s, American public libraries have competed with the lure of electronic mass media by aggressive advertising, by incorporating slides, films, and videotapes into their collections, and by declaring themselves to be information centers, geared to the needs of their diverse constituencies. They have also been campaigners for literacy and defenders of a libertarian reading tradition. Research libraries, on the other hand, although exploiting computerization, have remained the refuge of more traditional users, many of whom have been slow to accept the new technologies and upset by the adoption of decentralization as a means of coping with the immense growth of materials. Although in the 1970s and 1980s massive new structures were added to universities and public systems as well as to the Library of Congress, they have not been sufficient to meet the trials of overcrowding and congestion.

Library management in the United States has become increasingly a matter for information specialists and data managers, and the institution seems poised between two eras, one in which the printed book serves as the primary instrument of collected knowledge, the other, in which videodiscs, computer printers, and fax machines have begun to challenge the book for primacy. In the process of redefining their social and intellectual roles, American libraries remain vulnerable if triumphant symbols of the modern information revolution.

Museums

By the time European colonization of North America had begun, the systematic collecting of art, scientific curiosities, and historical relics was already well established. Cabinets of curiosities could be found in England and on the Continent. But there were few major collecting efforts in America until the late eighteenth century when patriotic, scientific, and pedagogical motives combined to stimulate a series of ambitious enterprises.

The most influential among them was probably that of the Philadelphia painter Charles Willson Peale. His American Museum, founded in 1784, was organized to display its art and scientific specimens as an object lesson in "the harmony of the universe." This high-minded experiment in Enlightenment argument was furthered by other museum foundations of the early nineteenth century, some by members of Peale's own family and others by civic boosters, scientists, and entrepreneurs. The creation of several art academies and learned societies, notably Boston's Athenaeum, New York's American Academy of Design and later National Academy of Design, and the Philadelphia Academy of Fine Art, added to the variety of museum installations available to Jacksonian Americans.

But the thrust of museum activities in the 1840s and 1850s was toward heterogeneous mixtures of art, science, and history, and commercial institutions run for profit and entertainment as well as enlightenment. The most successful museum manager in America at this time was Phineas T. Barnum, who had purchased Scudder's American Museum on Broadway in New York in 1841 and turned it into an immensely popular mix of genuine specimens, dubious mementos, "freaks" (as they were called then), and dramatic exotica. His exaggerated if highly successful publicity techniques and quest for financial return did not wholly deflect from the scientific and educational value of Barnum's efforts, but they did represent a devolution from earlier ideals. More serious efforts could be found before the Civil War in several university and college museums and in a few art and historical associations.

In the 1870s, the same decade that saw the professionalization of library service, American museums of art, history, and science began to assume some of their modern features. Located usually in large cities and founded by enterprising philanthropists, institutions like the Museum of Fine Arts in Boston, the Metropolitan Museum of Art and the American Museum of Natural History in New York, and the Art Institute of Chicago were financed through a blend of private and public funds. Often located on or adjacent to municipal parks, the museums derived their maintenance and occasionally their construction moneys from taxes, but the collections and staffing usually became the responsibility of private benefactors.

American museums were stimulated also by local interest in hosting international expositions. These impressive assemblages of art and industry, which dotted the United States between 1876 and 1915, served in effect as temporary museums and whetted local appetites for more permanent establishments. In a number of cases — Philadelphia, Chicago, St. Louis, and Buffalo among others — fair buildings and collections became the basis for museum developments.

Museum buildings (and libraries as well) were aided also by the City Beautiful movement of the 1890s and after, which was an extensive planning effort to give American cities elegant and highly finished centers. These often boasted immense neoclassical structures that featured art, history, science, and literature. Concern about the natural world, debates about evolutionary theory, and urban growth spurred creation of more specialized institutions like zoos and aquariums, all of them representing a profound commitment to popular education.

Although American art museums at first suffered a comparative lack of extensive old master holdings, by the early twentieth century the growth of private fortunes had begun to make possible the formation of extraordinary collections. J. Pierpont Morgan, Henry Clay Frick, Henry O. and Louisine Havemeyer, Bertha Palmer, Charles T. Yerkes, and Peter A. B. Widener took great satisfaction in art collecting, helped by dealers and galleries on both sides of the Atlantic. Although some of the art was dispersed by sale and auction, a very large portion of it found its way into local museums, turning them into treasure houses.

Americans not only collected the traditional fine art of Europe; they organized archaeological expeditions into the Middle and Far East and scientific expeditions to Africa and the South Seas, purchased art and antiques from Japan and China, and after World War I, demonstrated an interest in modern art and design as well. Museums became more specialized in character during the interwar period, featuring modern, medieval, or Far Eastern art in several instances, or focusing on American history and traditions, as in the reconstructed settings of Williamsburg, Virginia, and Dearborn, Michigan. Historic houses and shrines became popular as automobile tourism began its remarkable ascent.

The educational traditions established in the late nineteenth century flourished in the 1920s and 1930s. Most major American museums presented extensive lecture programs, formed close relationships with public school systems, hosted concerts and story hours, issued interpretive publications, and set up classrooms and lecture halls. Many of these museums relied heavily on membership groups to support their programs.

With the Great Depression came a crisis in museum management. Both private and public levels of support fell, forcing steep cuts in hours, staffing, and levels of service. Some standards of accessibility never returned. But after World War II an unprecedented period of expansion and prosperity emerged for museums of almost every type. These years saw the creation of two national endowments and the Institute of Museum Services, a federal indemnification program, as well as blockbuster exhibitions on an international scale, great gifts and dramatic purchases, innovative and rather startling structures, and thousands of new establishments. All combined to make the American museum an increasingly important source of popular events and instruction. Both new and old museums experienced tremendous increases in attendance, surpassing even sports spectatorship in numbers. Museums used sophisticated promotional techniques and glamorous shops to extend interest and raise funds for expansion.

But in the 1980s, on the crest of this prosperity, some wondered about the meaning of this growth, pointing to the overrepresentation of the prosperous and well educated within the museum audiences, and the failure to learn more about exhibition impact upon public taste and knowledge. Others challenged the canonized taste of these institutions, their ideological biases, and their patterns of staffing.

At the end of the decade foundation and governmental grants were supporting research into museum-going, and education departments were becoming more active. There was an increasing interest in the character and quality of the exhibition experience itself. Like American libraries, museums were exploiting the new mass media, using films, videotape, and interactive techniques to supplement stationary exhibi-

tions. And, in a reassertion of their service traditions, many museums began to conceive of their displays as instruments of social commentary, raising questions about conventional wisdom and pervasive values. The intensity of the debates testified to the vigor of the museum presence as well as the persistence of unresolved problems.

Libraries: Sidney Ditzion, *Arsenals of a Democratic Culture* (1947); Michael H. Harris, *Reader in American Library History* (1971). **Museums:** Nathaniel Burt, *Palaces for the People: A Social History of the American Art Museum* (1977); Laurence V. Coleman, *The Museum in America*, 3 vols. (1939).

NEIL HARRIS

See also Carnegie, Andrew; Frick, Henry Clay; Library of Congress; Philanthropy; Smithsonian Institution; World's Fairs.

LIBRARY OF CONGRESS

The oldest cultural institution in the nation's capital, the Library of Congress occupies a unique place in American civilization. Established as a legislative library in 1800, it grew into a national institution in the nineteenth century, a product of American cultural nationalism. Since World War II, it has become an international resource of unparalleled dimension and the world's largest library. In its three massive structures on Capitol Hill, the Thomas Jefferson Building (1897), the John Adams Building (1938), and the James Madison Memorial Building (1980), the Library of Congress brings together the concerns of government, learning, and librarianship — an uncommon combination, but one that has greatly benefited American polities, scholarship, and culture.

The history of the Library of Congress is the story of the accumulation of diverse functions and collections. As a repository of information and knowledge, its collections now number in all formats over 97 million items — books, film, maps, photographs, music, manuscripts, and graphics — from all over the world. The scope of these collections is universal; materials in more than four hundred languages have been acquired. The Library is open to everyone over high school age, and more than 2 million researchers, scholars, and tourists visit it annually.

The Library of Congress has been shaped primarily by the philosophy and ideas of its principal founder, Thomas Jefferson, who believed that a democratic legislature needed information and ideas in all subjects in order to do its job. It was established by Congress on April 24, 1800, with an appropriation of five thousand dollars, as the government prepared to move from Philadelphia to the new capital city of Washington. From the beginning, however, the institution was more than a legislative library, for an 1802 law made the appointment of the librarian of Congress a presidential responsibility. It also permitted the president and vice president to borrow books, a privilege that eventually was extended to the judiciary, officials of government agencies, and members of the public. Originally located in the Capitol, it moved into its first separate building in 1897. At the same time Congress gave the librarian of Congress sole responsibility for making the library's rules and regulations and invested in the Senate the authority to approve a president's nomination of a librarian of Congress.

Jefferson took a keen and continuing interest in the Library. In 1814, when the British invaded Washington, they destroyed the Capitol, including the Library of Congress. By then retired to Monticello, Jefferson offered to sell his personal library of over six thousand volumes to Congress. The purchase was approved in 1815, doubling the size of the Library. It also expanded the scope of the collections. Anticipating the argument that his collection might be too wide-ranging and comprehensive for use by a legislative body, Jefferson argued that there was "no subject to which a Member of Congress may not have occasion to refer." The Jeffersonian concept of universality is the philosophy and rationale behind the comprehensive collecting policies of today's Library.

The individual responsible for transforming the Library of Congress into an institution of national significance was Ainsworth Rand Spofford, librarian from 1864 to 1897. Spofford applied Jefferson's philosophy on a grand scale. He linked the Library's legislative and national functions, building a comprehensive collection for both the legislature and all citizens. In obtaining greatly increased support from Congress, Spofford employed a combination of logic, flattery, and nationalistic rhetoric. In 1867 his acquisitions made the Library of Congress the largest library in the United States. Spofford's other principal achievements were the centralization in 1870 of all U.S. copyright activities at the Library, which ensured the continuing growth of the collections by stipulating that two copies of every book, pamphlet, map, print, and piece of music registered for copyright be deposited in the Library, and the construction of a separate building, a twenty-six-year struggle not completed until 1897. The largest library building in the world at the time, it was immediately hailed as a monument to civilization, culture, and American achievement.

Spofford's concept of the Library of Congress as both legislative library for the American Congress and national library for the American people has been wholeheartedly accepted by his successors. Herbert Putnam, librarian of Congress from 1899 to 1939, extended this philosophy still further. To Putnam a national library was more than a comprehensive collection housed in Washington. It was "a collection universal in scope which has a duty to the country as a whole." He defined that duty as service to scholarship, both directly and through other libraries.

The first experienced librarian to fill the position, Putnam felt that a national library should actively serve other libraries, and he immediately began such a service. Through the sale and distribution of printed catalog cards, union catalogs, interlibrary loan, and other innovations, he "nationalized" the Library's collections and established the patterns of service that exist today. During his tenure, the Library helped systematize American scholarship and librarianship through the widespread sharing of its bibliographic apparatus, thus encouraging a national view of scholarship and research collections and establishing pioneering partnerships between the federal government and the private sector.

Balancing its legislative, national, and, after World War II, international roles, the Library of

Congress has grown steadily. Its major problem has been lack of space, not lack of support. Librarian Archibald MacLeish (1939–1944) stressed the Library's roles as a symbol of democracy and a cultural institution. Luther H. Evans (1945–1953) pushed forward the Library's international activities. L. Quincy Mumford (1954–1974), the only graduate of a professional library school to hold the job, greatly expanded all the Library's roles, but particularly its bibliographic activities and foreign acquisitions. By 1971, the Library of Congress had thirteen overseas offices for acquisitions and cataloging.

A new public role for the Library began to emerge under the leadership of historian Daniel J. Boorstin, librarian of Congress, 1975–1987. Emphasizing the Library as a national cultural resource, he greatly increased the institution's visibility. Boorstin's successor, historian James H. Billington (1987–   ) has employed new technology to share the Library's resources and pursue a new educational role for the institution. As it approaches its bicentennial in the year 2000, the Library of Congress is still guided by Thomas Jefferson's belief that all subjects are important to the library of the American legislature — and therefore to the American people.

Charles A. Goodrum, *The Treasures of the Library of Congress* (1980; rev. ed., 1991).

JOHN Y. COLE

See also Libraries and Museums.

LINCOLN, ABRAHAM

(1809–1865), sixteenth president of the United States. Lincoln summarized his early life as "the short and simple annals of the poor." He was born in a Kentucky log cabin, the son of a typical pioneer family. Never prosperous, the family moved several times, and he grew up in Kentucky and Indiana. He later reckoned that his total schooling did not exceed one year, but being unusually ambitious he pursued self-improvement through reading and longed for a better life. Lincoln's identification with the Whig party and its program to promote economic op-

portunity grew out of his hard lot as a youth.

When he came of age, Lincoln moved to New Salem, Illinois, where he held a variety of jobs, served in the legislature, and studied law. After receiving his attorney's license, he moved to the new capital of Springfield. He retired from the legislature after four terms, served one term in Congress (1847–1849), and then devoted himself to his legal practice and became an important and prosperous attorney.

The repeal of the Missouri Compromise in 1854 rekindled Lincoln's political ambition. He spoke eloquently against the expansion of slavery in the West, became a leader of the new Republican party, and gained national attention in 1858 from his debates with Stephen A. Douglas. In 1860, aided by the facts that he came from a doubtful state, had a reputation as a moderate on the slavery question, and was acceptable to both the Germans and the nativists, he won the Republican presidential nomination and was elected.

Shortly after Lincoln entered office the Civil War began. Taking a broad view of the president's war powers, he proclaimed a blockade, suspended the writ of habeas corpus for disloyal activity, spent money without congressional authorization, and controlled the war effort. On most legislative matters he yielded to Congress, but he carefully preserved his independence on questions that he considered executive responsibility. Despite his military inexperience, he displayed a shrewd grasp of military strategy, recognizing from the beginning the importance of the western theater and the necessity of taking advantage of the Union's superior resources. It took him several years, however, to find competent generals to implement this strategy.

On the issue of emancipation, Lincoln moved cautiously, insisting that his main priority was to save the Union. As the war continued, however, he became convinced that undermining slavery would weaken the Confederacy, and on January 1, 1863, he issued the Emancipation Proclamation. The proclamation applied only to areas under Confederate control, and its legal impact was uncertain, but it redefined the nature of the war and was of great symbolic significance.

Nevertheless, Lincoln seemed certain to be defeated in 1864. His record on civil liberties provoked protests, public opinion remained divided over emancipation, even Republicans lacked confidence in him, and most important, no end to the war was in sight. Sherman's capture of Atlanta in September, however, revived northern spirits and Lincoln was easily reelected. A few months later, in the hour of the Union's victory, he was cut down by an assassin's bullet.

Lincoln is justly considered our greatest president. He was a masterful politician, sensitive to and yet constantly shaping public opinion, skilled at balancing competing considerations, and extraordinarily adept at getting rival groups to work together toward a common goal. His leadership qualities were demonstrated in his brilliant handling of the border slave states at the beginning of the fighting, in his defeat of a congressional attempt to reorganize his cabinet in 1862, and in his defusing of the peace issue in the 1864 campaign when he maneuvered the Confederacy into rejecting negotiations. Never losing sight of the larger aims of the war, he remained flexible in his approach to problems, as evidenced by his evolving policies on emancipation and Reconstruction. Nevertheless, the toll of the war was visible in his haggard face: he stoically endured more than any other president personal slights, public ridicule, and criticism beyond the bounds of all decency, had his hopes dashed by one humiliating military defeat after another, and suffered deep personal anguish over the mounting casualty lists. Yet he never faltered in his resolve to persevere to victory.

Uncorrupted by power, Lincoln enunciated the nation's loftiest ideals during its darkest moment. The Gettysburg Address ranks as the supreme statement of the meaning of the war, and his second inaugural is testimony to his humane spirit. For the American people, his life from log cabin to White House epitomizes the American experience, and he has become the national symbol of democracy.

Stephen B. Oates, *With Malice toward None: The Life of Abraham Lincoln* (1977); James G. Randall, *Lincoln the President*, 4 vols. (1945–1955; vol. 4 completed by Richard N. Current).

William E. Gienapp

See also Elections: 1860, 1864; Lincoln-Douglas Debates; Republican Party; Slavery; Whig Party. *For events during Lincoln's administration, see* Civil War; Confederate States of America; Copperheads; Draft Riots; Emancipation Proclamation and Thirteenth Amendment; Gettysburg Address; Homestead Act; Morrill Land Grant Act; Secession; Wade-Davis Bill.

LINCOLN-DOUGLAS DEBATES

Historians have traditionally regarded the series of seven debates between Stephen A. Douglas and Abraham Lincoln during the 1858 Illinois state election campaign as among the most significant statements in American political history. The issues they discussed were not only of critical importance to the sectional conflict over slavery and states' rights but also touched deeper questions that would continue to influence political discourse. The issues, Lincoln said, would be discussed long after "these poor tongues of Judge Douglas and myself shall be silent."

What is often overlooked is that the debates were part of a larger campaign, that they were designed to achieve certain immediate political objectives, and that they reflected the characteristics of mid-nineteenth-century political rhetoric. Douglas, a member of Congress since 1843 and a nationally prominent spokesman for the Democratic party, was seeking reelection to a third term in the U.S. Senate, and Lincoln was running for Douglas's Senate seat as a Republican. Because of Douglas's political stature, the campaign attracted national attention. Its outcome, it was thought, would determine the ability of the Democratic party to maintain unity in the face of the divisive sectional and slavery issues, and some were convinced it would determine the viability of the Union itself. "The battle of the Union is to be fought in Illinois," a Washington paper declared.

Although senators were elected by the state legislatures until 1913, Douglas and Lincoln took their arguments directly to the people. The timing of the campaign, the context of sectional animosity within which it was fought, the volatility of the slavery issue, and the instability of the party system combined to give the debates a special importance. Not long before, Douglas had defied President James Buchanan and the southern Democratic leadership when he opposed the admission of Kansas as a slave state under the controversial Lecompton constitution, a stand for which he received support from Republicans in Congress as well as their interest in his reelection. At the same time, Buchanan and the southern slave interests gave tacit (and in some instances explicit) support to Lincoln's candidacy because of their hostility to Douglas. As a result of this strange alignment, Lincoln's principal task was to keep Illinois Republicans from supporting Douglas by exposing the moral gulf that separated them from the senator and to win the support of radical abolitionists and former conservative Whigs. A relative newcomer to the antislavery cause (before 1854, he said, slavery had been a "minor question" with him), Lincoln used the debates to develop and strengthen the moral quality of his position.

The groundwork for the campaign was laid in Lincoln's famous House Divided speech in Springfield on June 16, 1858. Douglas opened his campaign on July 9 in Chicago. By mid-August, the two candidates had agreed to a series of debates in seven of the state's nine congressional districts.

Lincoln opened the campaign on an ominous note, warning that the agitation over slavery would not cease until a crisis had been passed that resulted either in the extension of slavery to all the territories and states or in its ultimate extinction. "A house divided against itself cannot stand," he declared. Lincoln's forecast was a statement of what would be known as the irrepressible conflict doctrine. The threat of slavery expansion, he believed, came not from the slaveholding South but from Douglas's popular sovereignty position — allowing the territories to decide for themselves whether they wished to have slavery. Furthermore, Lincoln charged Douglas with conspiring to extend slavery to the free states as well as the territories, a false accusation that Douglas tried vainly to ig-

nore. Fundamental to Lincoln's argument was his conviction that slavery must be dealt with as a moral wrong. It violated the statement in the Declaration of Independence that all men are created equal, and it ran counter to the intentions of the Founding Fathers. The "real issue" in his contest with Douglas, Lincoln insisted, was the issue of right and wrong, and he charged that his opponent was trying to uphold a wrong. Only the power of the federal government, as exercised by Congress, could ultimately extinguish slavery. At the same time, Lincoln assured southerners that he had no intention of interfering with slavery in the states where it existed and assured northerners that he was opposed to the political and social equality of the races, points on which he and Douglas agreed.

Douglas rejected Lincoln's notion of an irrepressible conflict and disagreed with his analysis of the intentions of the Founding Fathers, pointing out that many of them were slaveholders who believed that each community should decide the question for itself. A devoted Jacksonian, he insisted that power should reside at the local level and should reflect the wishes of the people. He was convinced, however, that slavery would be effectively restricted for economic, geographic, and demographic reasons and that the territories, if allowed to decide, would choose to be free. In an important statement at Freeport, he held that the people could keep slavery out of their territories, in spite of the *Dred Scott* decision, simply by withholding the protection of the local law. Douglas was disturbed by Lincoln's effort to resolve a controversial moral question by political means, warning that it could lead to civil war. Finally, Douglas placed his disagreement with Lincoln on the level of republican ideology, arguing that the contest was between consolidation and confederation, or as he put it, "one consolidated empire" as proposed by Lincoln versus a "confederacy of sovereign and equal states" as he proposed.

On election day, the voters of Illinois chose members of the state legislature who in turn reelected Douglas to the Senate in January 1859. Although Lincoln lost, the Republicans received more popular votes than the Democrats, signaling an important shift in the political character of the state. Moreover, Lincoln had gained a reputation throughout the North. He was invited to campaign for Republican candidates in other states and was now mentioned as a candidate for the presidency. In winning, Douglas further alienated the Buchanan administration and the South, was soon to be stripped of his power in the Senate, and contributed to the division of the Democratic party.

Paul M. Angle, ed., *Created Equal? The Complete Lincoln-Douglas Debates of 1858* (1958); Richard Allen Heckman, *Lincoln vs. Douglas: The Great Debates Campaign* (1967); Harry V. Jaffa, *Crisis of the House Divided: An Interpretation of the Issues in the Lincoln-Douglas Debates* (1959; reprint, 1973).

ROBERT W. JOHANNSEN

See also Civil War; Douglas, Stephen A.; Freeport Doctrine; Lincoln, Abraham.

LINDBERGH, CHARLES A.

(1902–1974), aviator, adviser to the airlines and the military, and environmentalist. Always a "Lone Eagle," Lindbergh was a young airmail pilot in 1927 when he ordered and configured a small monoplane to his own design, christened it the *Spirit of St. Louis,* and then flew it from a rainy airstrip on Long Island to Paris nonstop in 33½ hours. It was a feat that electrified the world and galvanized public acceptance of the airplane and commercial aviation. A month later, *Aviation* magazine observed: "Some deeds are marked by an inherent nobility that lifts them above other feats. . . . [But] there is something leveling, as well as elevating, about aerial adventure. The substitution of the pilot's helmet for the diplomat's high hat, the leather jacket for the frock coat, and the greasy mitten for the kid glove, appear[s] to breed mass camaraderie that tramples down political barriers and official punctilios between nations."

Before his historic flight, Lindbergh had met Harry Guggenheim, another flyer and head of the Daniel Guggenheim Fund for the Promotion of Aviation. It was on Guggenheim's estate that he wrote his autobiographical *We* before embarking on a goodwill tour of Mexico and Central and South America, during which he met and afterward married Anne Morrow, daughter of the U.S. ambassador to Mexico. In 1931 the couple flew to the Orient via the great circle route used by airlines today. In 1933 they conducted a pioneering survey flight for Pan American Airways to Greenland, Europe, Russia, Africa, and South America. To one historian, Lindbergh progressed naturally from the "hands-on tinkering" of a mechanic to "the incisive methodical research" of a scientist. After he was hired as technical adviser to Transcontinental Air Transport (forerunner of Trans World Airlines), it quickly became known as "the Lindbergh line." It was he who prevailed upon TWA to require single-engine takeoff power on the DC-1, forerunner of the legendary DC-3. For PAA, he supervised the introduction of blind flying as well as the designs for PAA's first transocean clippers. Earlier, he had prevailed upon the Guggenheims to fund research by rocket pioneer Robert H. Goddard.

Writer Brendan Gill called Lindbergh "a very dark person" to whom "the horror was the fame he had secured by accident." The kidnapping and murder of his infant son in 1932 made him even more reclusive, and in 1935 the Lindberghs moved almost secretly to England.

There followed three visits to Nazi Germany, flight-testing of Luftwaffe aircraft, and receipt of a medal from Hermann Goering. After returning to the United States in 1939, Lindbergh became a prominent advocate of American isolationism. But when war came, he secretly flew fifty combat missions in the Far East, shot down a Japanese fighter, and proved that the combat radius and bomb-load capacity of several U.S. fighter aircraft could be increased.

President Dwight D. Eisenhower made Lindbergh a reserve brigadier general in 1954, and Lindbergh thereafter joined in selecting sites for air bases overseas and in the deliberations of the Air Force Scientific Advisory Board. His commitment to environmentalism came late, but by 1970 he was again a Lone Eagle opposing development of a supersonic transport on environmental grounds.

Two years later, after building a home in a jungle a mile from a missionary church he helped restore on Hawaii, he died of cancer and was buried on a knoll overlooking the Pacific. Today his gravesite continues to draw several hundred visitors daily.

Kenneth S. Davis, *The Hero: Charles A. Lindbergh and the American Dream* (1959); Walter S. Ross, *The Last Hero: Charles A. Lindbergh* (1964).

WILLIAM WELLING

See also America First Committee; Aviation; Conservation and Environmental Movements; Isolationism.

LIPPMANN, WALTER

(1889–1974), journalist and author. Lippmann was unique among twentieth-century writers in combining a career as an editor and syndicated columnist with that of an intellectual. Symbolic of this life were his many books, most of them edited versions of his columns on contemporary issues.

Lippmann was brought up in comfortable circumstances in New York by his businessman father. He graduated from Harvard in 1909 in a class that included such future notables as T. S. Eliot and journalist-revolutionary John Reed. His disciplined intellectual style and gift for lucid exposition of complicated ideas were apparent early in life. At Harvard he became an assistant to philosopher George Santayana and was known for the precision with which he planned his career. This orderliness verged on rigidity. He once refused to change the time of an appointment with Nikita Khrushchev because his schedule was filled.

Although his political views shifted during his life from an early attachment to socialism to the carefully contrived conservatism of his mature years, a consistent, skeptical core of beliefs ran through these changes. A brief spell as an assistant to the socialist mayor of Schenectady, New York, seems to have convinced him of the tediousness of political activism. Over the course of his life he became increasingly skeptical about the capabilities of the masses, and his social theories grew to depend on the intervention of experts. His work in propaganda during World War I left him pessimistic about the ability of the public to discern complex political issues.

Throughout his life he combined the careers of editor and publicist. He was a founder and an associate editor of the *New Republic* from 1914 to 1921. During the next decade he worked for the *New York World* and, after 1931, joined the *Herald Tribune,* where he wrote a column that was syndicated in over two hundred papers. He joined the *Washington Post* in 1961 in the same capacity.

Influenced by the writings of Sigmund Freud, Lippmann came to feel that humanity, ill-informed and subject to partiality, is driven by irrational impulses. His most influential book *Public Opinion* (1922) consolidated these ideas into an analysis said by Edward Bernays to have launched the profession of public relations. *The Phantom Public* (1925) was even more pessimistic.

Lippmann came to believe that civil society depended on the capacity of people to sublimate their aggressive impulses through the adoption of a rule of law. Although a lifelong religious skeptic, he recognized the void created by the absence of religious faith in *A Preface to Morals* (1929). He accepted as unavoidable the role of business organizations and their dominant place in industrial societies. He adopted a form of corporate collectivism: a state with a strong executive composed of private corporate entities managed by experts. He never wavered from these elitist ideas and continued to view popular government dependent on legislative procedures with skepticism, a view developed in *The Public Philosophy* (1955).

Throughout his career Lippmann retained a strong interest in foreign affairs. At the close of World War I he broke with Woodrow Wilson over the issue of ethnic self-determination, which he predicted would precipitate chaos in Central Europe. The rise of totalitarian governments during the thirties led him to develop his conception of a Western alliance based on Anglo-American solidarity. World War II confirmed his belief in collective security. Early in the cold war he opposed George Kennan's containment policy as a costly policy "of shifts and maneuvers" by fair-weather allies and puppets, which would risk war and undermine American prestige. He recommended instead consolidating the Atlantic community by helping through the Marshall Plan to reconstruct its economies. And during the Vietnam era he viewed the conflict as a dangerous strategic consequence of the cold war and urged caution in dealing with it.

John Morton Blum, ed., *Selected Letters of Public Philosopher Walter Lippmann* (1985); Ronald Steel, *Walter Lippmann and the American Century* (1980).

WILLIAM R. TAYLOR

LITERATURE

I. American Literature to 1860

According to one version of American cultural history, there was no American literature until the second third of the nineteenth century, when, in Ralph Waldo Emerson's phrase, "men grew reflective," and at long last "mind had become aware of itself." Explanations for the literary barrenness of early America were offered then and have been reiterated since, but all such arguments finally arise from the unexamined premise that what writing there was does not deserve the dignity of being called literature.

Colonial America was in fact very much a culture of the book, but for more than a century after the founding, especially in New England, the books were overwhelmingly religious, and the values the postromantic age would associate with literary production — originality, individual voice, the adversarial imagination — were incomprehensible at best or versions of heresy at worst. Early American literary expression arose partly from an oral tradition whose passing Emerson himself came to lament. This sense of loss marks one of his differences from his Concord contemporary Henry David Thoreau, who believed that "there is a memorable interval between the spoken and the written language" and that writing is "maturity" while speech is "transitory" and "almost brutish." It is a revealing irony that Emerson (who began as a preacher, and whose later essays were developed through the process of oral public delivery) devoted so much of his effort to recapturing the rhythms of inspired speech. Nearly a century after the Revolution, when the elderly Emerson thought that the "American mind . . . [was finally] beginning to show a quiet power . . . proper to a continent and an educated people," its literature was also losing some of its spontaneity and its sense of groundedness in a community that knew the sound of its own collective voice. The arrival of a truly national literature — celebrated in the early decades of the nineteenth century with proclamations of its tardiness by William Cullen Bryant (*Lectures on Poetry,* delivered 1826, published 1884), William Ellery Channing (*The Importance and Means of a National Literature,* 1830), and Emerson himself (The American Scholar address, 1837) — was accompanied by a sense of the urgent need to record the passing of an earlier America.

In the New England of Emerson's forebears, literature had been spoken. "Faith cometh by hearing" was the Apostle Paul's most frequently quoted injunction, and the ministry poured forth immense numbers of sermons — Sabbath sermons, lecture-day sermons, election-day sermons — many of them transcribed by a devoted lay member of the congregation and prepared for the press as a means of preserving the original experience of hearing the gospel word. From the New England presses there also came inventories of biblical types, chronicles of New England history as part of God's work of redemption, memoirs recording conversions, almanacs containing seasonal poetry and practical advice. Poetry was regarded as suspiciously ornamental, though one of the best-sellers of the seventeenth century, Michael Wigglesworth's chiliastic "The Day of Doom," was cast in an insistent, rhyming tetrameter. Anne Bradstreet's lyrics, composed and published in *The Tenth Muse* (1650), and the "preparatory meditations" written late in the century by Edward Taylor, minister of Westfield, as a means to prepare himself for administering the Lord's Supper, were the most enduring poetic achievements of Puritan civilization in America.

If we take the view that literature is the record of experience formulated within the terms made available by the culture, then all these writings — however occasional or restricted by the generic conventions of their mainly religious function — constitute literature. But if, in the words of the critic Richard Poirier, literature should furnish "an occasion for . . . amazement," whereby we are awakened to the world-creating power of words, the body of early American writing that can be called literature grows smaller. It does not, however, disappear. The greatest colonial preachers and historians — William Bradford, John Cotton, Thomas Hooker, Cotton Mather — recognized their challenge to employ an Old World language to express New World experience. The biblical accents of Bradford's great *Of Plymouth Plantation, 1620–1647* (written 1630–1650), or the exquisite mapping of the soul that "soul-physicians" like Cotton conducted in early New England, transformed the English language into a New England idiom that was saturated with biblical symbols and irresistibly drawn into the patterns of biblical narrative.

In the southern colonies, which had been settled by men with different aspirations who were often uncertain about the likely duration of their stay, the earliest public writings were largely promotional tracts intended to attract unpropertied young Englishmen into a New World apprenticeship or to allay the doubts of prospective investors. In the early eighteenth century, some significant historical works, notably Robert Beverley's *History of the Present State of Virginia* (1705), emerged. Perhaps the most remarkable document from the colonial South was William Byrd of Westover's candid diary (1709–1741), containing in raw form themes that would obsess southern writers for centuries to come: the contradictions of a genteel life built on the labor of slaves, the temptations to indolence inherent in the natural fertility, the perilously thin boundary between civilization and savagery.

Distinctions between the northern and southern imagination began to blur in the eighteenth century, as the spread of the Enlightenment modified the religious inheritance of New England and created a southern intellectual class that would eventually produce a group of political writers — Thomas Jefferson (the Declaration of Independence, 1776; *Notes on the State of Virginia,* 1787), James Madison (chief author of the Federalist Papers, 1787), John Taylor of Caroline (*Arator,* 1813), and much later John C. Calhoun (*A Disquisition on Government,* 1851) — whose articulation of the rationale for independence, and then for nationhood, reached a high level of eloquence, complexity, and prescience. The most powerful expressions of the New England mind remained religious, notably in the works of Jonathan Edwards, a latter-day Calvinist who fused the innovations of Lockean psychology with his Puritan inheritance and created an entirely new description of moral and religious experience (especially in his *Treatise on Religious Affections,* 1746, and in the posthumously published dissertations on *The Nature of True Virtue,* 1765, and *The End for Which God Created the World,* 1765). But the project of nation-building became the focus of literary energy in New England as well. In the 1740s, long before political independence was a thinkable idea, a vision of a new unity among the colonies began to be felt in the controversial writings of the Great Awakening and burst out with full force in the pamphlets of the 1760s and 1770s, of which the culminating example was Thomas Paine's *Common Sense* (1776).

After the Revolution, American writing — North and South — inevitably became more self-conscious. The common literary project was to furnish the new nation with a living mythology through which it might achieve a sense of positive identity as it rejected its function as a subsidiary part of the British Empire and sought to suppress its regional distinctions. One feature of this search for a common *American* history was the growing awareness (which had been sporadically expressed by certain dissident Puritans) of the brutalization and virtually inevitable extinction of the Native Americans — whose voices were represented in Jefferson's *Notes;* whose ancestors were evoked in Bryant's poem "The Prairies" (1832); who held the stage as the doomed opponents of imperial Britain in numerous "Indian plays," including the perennially popular *Metamora, or the Last of the Wampanoags* (1829) by John August Stone; and who appeared, as both sinister heathen and noble savage, in the Leatherstocking saga of James Fenimore Cooper beginning with *The Pioneers* (1823) and closing with *The Deerslayer* (1841).

A more usable mythic history was at work in the immensely popular *Life of Washington* (1800) by Parson Mason Weems, which appeared in many editions under the imprint of the entrepreneurial Philadelphia printer Mathew Carey and became one of the first American works to rival British literary productions in sales. It marked the onset of what has been called "the legend of the Founding Fathers." An American public with a taste for American themes had already begun to support indigenous comedy and melodrama in the theater (in such plays as Royall Tyler's *The Contrast,* 1787, and William Dunlap's *André,* 1798), and now, with the rise of a middle-class, female readership, the novel began to gain an audience too. Although more obliquely than in the didactic poetry of the Connecticut Wits or of the Jeffersonian poet Philip Freneau, the theme of the destiny of the young nation occupied the novel as well. Devoted to the epistolary form and to imitations of Samuel Richardson (as the drama was to Richard Brinsley Sheridan), the early American novel put forth its public theme of the tested virtue of the citizenry with a kind of sexual allegory, exploiting the titillating possibilities of the seduction plot. Books like William Hill Brown's *The Power of Sympathy* (1789), Susanna Rowson's *Charlotte Temple* (1791), and Hannah Foster's *The Coquette* (1797) have a threatened woman at the center, who, faced with a tempter's charms, undergoes an internal struggle between passion and restraint that strikingly resembles the national debate over radical Republicanism versus Federalist conservatism.

Before the turn of the century, a number of regional literary styles had begun to emerge — centered in Philadelphia around the *Port-Folio* of Joseph Dennie, in Boston around the *Monthly Anthology,* and in New York, somewhat later, around the Knickerbocker group that included James Kirke Paulding and Washington Irving. Irving's *Sketch-Book* (1820) was the most elegant expression of American nostalgia for the class hierarchy of preindustrial England and the elusive pastoral tranquillity that it seemed to represent.

Such literary societies, especially those of the Boston Unitarians, began to make possible a genuine critical discussion of what kind of literature would be appropriate for a democracy. This was the debate in which Emerson climaxed with his American Scholar address to the Harvard Phi Beta Kappa chapter in 1837, and despite all the literary ferment that had preceded him, he was right to announce — in *Nature* (1836) — that a new age was at hand. The critical debate and the tentative, derivative forays into fiction, drama, and neoclassic epic poetry now gave way to an explosion of creative energy that F. O. Matthiessen has memorably called the "American Renaissance." The decades following Emerson's prophecies of the late 1830s witnessed the greatest outpouring of literary genius in American history, before or since — the romances of Edgar Allan Poe, Nathaniel Hawthorne, and Herman Melville; the poetry of Walt Whitman and Emily Dickinson; the prose inventions of Emerson and Thoreau. Lesser writers also began to produce a literature of real social and aesthetic consequence — the exploratory social and psychological analyses of Margaret Fuller and Orestes Brownson; the beginnings of an African-American narrative tradition with the autobiographies of Frederick Douglass (*Narrative of the Life of an American Slave,* 1845) and Harriet Jacobs (*Incidents in the Life of a Slave Girl,* 1861); and the immensely influential fictional attack on slavery, *Uncle Tom's Cabin* (1852), by Harriet Beecher Stowe.

By the 1850s it was no longer possible to speak of American literature as provincial or submissive to English models. But as it matured it also modulated what Emerson called its optative mood; it became elegiac (as in Whitman's *Democratic Vistas,* 1871), and its greatest achievements remained uncomfortable within the traditional structures of literary expression. American literary genius, as in the case of Melville's *Moby-Dick* (1851), broke utterly away from the conventional prescriptions of the novel. To catch the American voice at its grandest, in what Melville called its "Vesuvian" register, one still needs to range beyond the customary boundaries of the "literary," since perhaps the greatest master of English prose in mid-nineteenth-century America was neither a novelist nor a poet, but a politician, Abraham Lincoln.

With the coming of the Civil War, as Melville had intimated in his straitened stories of the 1850s, there occurred what Edmund Wilson has called "the chastening of American prose style." This was a kind of evacuation of the symbolic density that had characterized literary language in America since the prophetic writings of the colonial period. With the advent of the large social novels of William Dean Howells, Henry James, Theodore Dreiser, and Edith Wharton, American literature may be said to have come of age. But with this triumph of the discursive language of realism, the great age of the American literary imagination may also be said to have passed. If its characteristic voice had once been extreme, self-obsessed, and extravagant, it now became measured, subdued, and controlled. In this change there was loss as well as gain. The extraordinary literary moment of what Melville called, near the end of his life, "the time before steamships," was over.

Lawrence Buell, *New England Literary Culture: From Revolution through Renaissance* (1986); Cathy Davidson, *Revolution and the Word: The Rise of the Novel in America* (1986); Emory Elliott, ed., *The Columbia Literary History of the United States* (1988); F. O. Matthiessen, *American Renaissance: Art and Expression in the Age of Emerson and Whitman* (1940).

ANDREW DELBANCO

II. American Literature from 1860 to 1914

The Civil War radically changed the pace of economic and social change in the United States, but minds changed slowly. Over the years between the Civil War and the First World War, a sense of small-town security and of an idyllic past coexisted with booming industrialization, the triumph of commercialized farming at the expense of the yeoman-farmer ideal, vast migrations from Europe and from the country to the city, the emergence of new fortunes and new slums on a scale never dreamed before. The distance between cultural habit and social actuality, which did not seem great in the 1870s and

1880s, gradually widened, bringing about that split between "highbrow" and "lowbrow" that Van Wyck Brooks was to proclaim in *America's Coming of Age* in 1915. The cultural split was reinforced by the widespread assumption of gender-related difference, sensibility and cultivation allegedly being "feminine" and practicality and tough-mindedness "masculine." (A curious blend of stereotype and subversion was Louisa May Alcott's *Little Women* [1868–1869], in which domestic survival depends on female practicality and is endangered by male incompetence.)

Class and gender divisions were compounded by a split between generations. Against the increasingly unstable official culture, the young were making ready a radical insurgency. By 1914, Ezra Pound, the most flamboyant of the insurgents, had published over half a dozen books of poetry and criticism; he had appointed himself advisory editor of *Poetry,* founded by Harriet Monroe in 1912; and he had discovered, among others, Robert Frost and T. S. Eliot. The revolution commonly associated with the 1920s began before the First World War.

The old regime that was to collapse in the twentieth century — the "genteel tradition," as it came to be called — had been strengthened by the Civil War. Old radicals, tamed by time, laid down their weapons. Ralph Waldo Emerson, who had once been accused of "the latest form of infidelity," became a mainstay of the Boston literary establishment. In 1866 John Greenleaf Whittier, the onetime abolitionist, published *Snow-Bound: A Winter Idyl* and took his place beside Henry Wadsworth Longfellow and James Russell Lowell as one of the household poets of the nation. At a time before movies and radio split off the audience for entertainment from the institutions of literate culture, these long-lived demigods set standards of taste, both popular and educated, that virtually stifled the emergence of new major talent.

Other poets whose careers continued past the Civil War were practically unrecognized. Two great monuments of the national ordeal, Walt Whitman's *Drum-Taps and Memories of President Lincoln* (1865) and Herman Melville's *Battle-Pieces and Aspects of the War* (1866), had to wait until the twentieth century to win the critical esteem that the nineteenth century bestowed on Lowell's "Commemoration Ode" (1865), which is hardly read today. Whitman had only a small cult following in the seventies and eighties, though by the 1890s he had won the esteem of poets in England and the United States. Melville had to subsidize publication of his poetry; his modern reputation is generally dated from 1915 when an English biographer began the renewal of interest. Emily Dickinson had written well over half her 1,775 poems by 1865 and she continued to write until her death in 1886, but she did not publish. Her posthumous volumes — heavily emended — won a fair-sized audience in the 1890s, but her work was not properly edited until the 1950s and her recognition is still in progress. E. A. Robinson began publishing in the 1890s, but his work was too plainspoken and somber for the prevailing taste. He did not begin to win a regular audience until his fifth volume, *The Man against the Sky* (1916). Robert Frost also began writing in the 1890s, but he went virtually unpublished until, with some help from Pound, he brought out *A Boy's Will* in London in 1913.

For the greatest prose master of the period there was no such delay of recognition. Mark Twain became a national figure with "The Notorious Jumping Frog of Calaveras County" in 1867, and he remained one until his death in 1910. As Samuel Clemens of Hannibal, Missouri, he had been brought up to the ways of the small-town middle class and he had absorbed the oral traditions of the Middle West and the South. As a Mississippi steamboatman, a would-be bonanza miner, and a frontier journalist, he shared in the newly released energies of his expanding country. In *The Innocents Abroad* (1869) he developed the contrast between unpolished, plain-thinking figures who spoke in the lowdown vernacular and the conventional creatures of polite society. Modulating the raciness of local speech with the flow and clarity of standard plain prose, he created an American idiom. The comic interplay between vernacular character and thoughtless conventionality, when slavery and freedom were at issue in *Adventures of Huckleberry Finn* (1885), became enlarged to the theme of nature versus civilization and disclosed subversive and tragic possibilities.

Mark Twain's recognition by the educated middle class dates from 1875 when William Dean Howells published *Old Times on the Mississippi* in the *Atlantic Monthly*. His conversion from newspaper humorist and popular lecturer into an *Atlantic* author bespoke an intellectual hospitality on the part of editors and readers. The widening of public taste paralleled a widening of audience — high school education was spreading to towns all over the country. Monthly magazines, supported by advertisers and national circulation, became the dominant medium, creating a seemingly limitless need for new material.

Local-color writers of sketches and tales helped satisfy the demand of the new literary market. Regional fiction had begun before the Civil War. Harriet Beecher Stowe started the first of her New England novels even before writing *Uncle Tom's Cabin;* the most famous of these, *Oldtown Folks,* came out in 1869 when the new movement was well under way. The brevity of the magazine piece lent itself to cottage industry and brought many women into professional writing. (Their numbers do not negate the difficulty of a woman's becoming a writer, especially a middle-class married woman, as Charlotte Perkins Gilman bore witness in her brilliant story of 1892, "The Yellow Wallpaper.") The magazine story provided a structure for the loosely related sketch-tales of Sarah Orne Jewett's masterly *Country of the Pointed Firs* (1896), and it did not obstruct the passing of some of Jewett's qualities to a similarly austere writer, Willa Cather. Cather's very different career was well launched before the First World War — her early novel *O Pioneers!* came out in 1913.

At the least, local color — that is, regional difference — allowed minor writers to vary the content of their work. At their best, writers caught local language and folkways that were in danger of disappearing beneath a uniform national culture. Southern writers often elaborated a plantation legend of magnolias, crinoline, and sweet sentiment, such as can be seen in the frame narrative of Joel Chandler Harris's Uncle Remus stories (first collected in 1880). But the

Brer Rabbit stories that Uncle Remus tells preserve West African animal tales that American slaves had modified and developed. The racist condescension of the outer story protected readers who did not wish to see the liberation animus of the fables within.

The tensions of southern culture did not always work out well. George W. Cable went on from magazine stories to write *The Grandissimes* (1880), a novel in which deep conflicts of race and status outgrow conventional narrative and take on tragic power. Cable was so ostracized in his native Louisiana that he moved to New England. Similarly, Kate Chopin won a following for her Louisiana local-color tales, but her masterpiece *The Awakening* (1899), a searching treatment of sex and gender in middle-class life, lost her audience and effectively ended her career. Most poignant of all, perhaps, was the case of Charles W. Chesnutt. Born a free Negro in Ohio, he had lived in the South, and he found that he could best get at the African-American experience in southern settings. Encouraged by Howells, who suggested without evident embarrassment that success would come easier if he concealed the fact that he was black, Chesnutt was to encounter even more directly the limits of Howells's intellectual openness. His novel of racial violence, *The Marrow of Tradition* (1901), was deplored by Howells as too bitter; loss of critical support foretold a loss of audience that soon brought Chesnutt's career to an end. For all three writers, the laws of the standardized market were to prove stronger than the ability of critics or readers to move beyond ruling convention. Their novels won recognition only in a later age.

These three writers are also exemplary in their turning from the short story to the novel: even in the monthly magazines, the novel became the dominant genre. Entertainment fiction then as now focused on love and adventure, sentiment and sensationalism, but a serious novelist of manners like Howells imported the term *realism* to support his concern for plausible psychology, rational canons of personal conduct, and what he regarded as the "average" circumstances of middle-class American life. The early career of Henry James seemed to conform to the same standards, though James conveyed an awareness that wealth was the usual condition in which the drama of personal consciousness could be enacted. A high point in the history of realism occurred in 1884–1885 when *Huckleberry Finn,* Howells's *The Rise of Silas Lapham,* and James's *The Bostonians* overlapped as serials in *Century* magazine.

By 1890 a profound change had set in. In *A Connecticut Yankee in King Arthur's Court* (1889), Mark Twain's sense of vernacular character and democratic possibility had turned into an apocalyptic vision of industrial and imperial power gone out of control. In *A Hazard of New Fortunes* (1890), Howells tried to deal with industrial strife and the modern city. James, having largely alienated his American audience with the political and cultural satire of *The Bostonians,* turned to other forms in the nineties. In the next decade he returned to the full-length novel, beginning with *The Ambassadors* (1903), and showed how far a sensitive and demanding fiction of consciousness could go beyond the simple psychology and prudent ideals of early realism. Only in the 1940s did his three late novels come to be termed his "major phase."

The novel of manners still had life in it: in the 1890s, Henry Blake Fuller proved as much in novels of old and new Chicago, and after the turn of the century Edith Wharton did so in novels of old and new New York. But other, younger writers who began their careers in the nineties, though they built on the work of their elders, seemed to leave them behind. The term *naturalism,* often applied to these new writers, implies that they saw human experience as subject to biological or environmental determinism, but that suggestion is rarely supported by what they wrote. Frank Norris, who had read the great French naturalist Émile Zola, came close to fitting this rubric. In *McTeague* (1899), he showed how thin was the veneer of civilization on his non-middle-class characters. And in *The Octopus* (1901), he showed how even educated, middle-class characters were enlarged by their involvement with natural, economic, and historic forces that were greater than themselves. Interpersonal relations were no longer seen as the sum of human experience.

Change of subject matter implied not only a new genre but new institutions of marketing the printed word. In the 1890s, Stephen Crane and Theodore Dreiser served their literary apprenticeship on city newspapers. Instead of writing for the magazine audience of middle-class families with daughters, they wrote for hardheaded, unsqueamish, presumptively male readers. They covered violent headline stories; they sketched life among the poor and homeless; they took up subjects that were taboo. Crane's *Maggie: A Girl of the Streets* (1893) and Dreiser's *Sister Carrie* (1900) are about "fallen women" who are scarcely aware of the moral world where that term is used, but who feel pain and elicit serious dramatic interest nonetheless.

The breakout from the constricted world of the *Atlantic* and the *Century* went deeper than the violation of sexual taboos. Howells critically welcomed Crane's *Maggie*, but he choked on his *Red Badge of Courage* (1895). The world of contingency and violence that Crane presented had too much in common with the adventure novel that Howells deplored. In such a world of flux, life is not conducted under the canons of security, rationality, and prudence.

The intellectual world into which Crane and Dreiser were born was described by William James, the philosopher and psychologist, as a world of inner and outer flux. Inventor of the term "the stream of consciousness," he explored its meanings in *The Principles of Psychology* (1890). James's student in the 1890s, Gertrude Stein, applied the concepts of Jamesian psychology to her writing. In the "experimental" *Three Lives* (1909) and *Tender Buttons* (1914), she showed how the conventions of sequential narrative and discursive description could be demolished and remade. Her breakout from the past, unlike Pound's, was to win an audience only slowly.

Thorstein Veblen applied similar concepts to social organization and social psychology in *The Theory of the Leisure Class* (1899). Describing social institutions as "habits of thought," adaptations to past circumstances and therefore necessarily out of date, he turned conventional wisdom upside down: "Whatever is, is wrong." He analyzed the new consumer culture in which "conspicuous consumption" — his coinage — served social status, and waste was paradoxically useful.

The literary audience gradually changed, as Dreiser's relation to the market suggests. Reversing Cable, Chopin, and Chesnutt, whose careers were ended by work that was too daring, Dreiser began with a disaster. *Sister Carrie* was virtually suppressed: the publisher, whose editors had accepted the book in his absence, simply withheld the usual marketing services. Dreiser barely survived the blow, and it was almost a decade before he turned his hand again to fiction. With the publication of *Jennie Gerhardt* (1911) and *The Financier* (1912) he found an audience.

The overlap of generations, the emergence of shared interests that defined new audiences, and a slow shift from cultural uniformity toward modern multiplicity — these fell into a recognizable pattern. Among historians, the slow sustained work of scholarly research meant that writers whose careers began before the Civil War were productive for decades thereafter. George Bancroft published the last revised volumes of his *History of the United States* in 1885, and Francis Parkman completed his series on France and England in North America in 1892. Like the household poets, these historians were taste-makers.

Henry Adams, the most important historian of the period, was connected to the pre–Civil War past by his family's deep engagement with the history of the nation. He helped professionalize historical writing as a Harvard professor from 1870 to 1877, while doubling as editor of the *North American Review,* a quarterly of long tradition. He worked more than a dozen years on his *History of the United States during the Administrations of Thomas Jefferson and James Madison* (1889–1891). As the dry, antiromantic title was meant to convey, this was serious institutional history — establishing the facts and critically analyzing the conduct of government in the widest sense. It was also more than that: without flourishes, Adams dramatized the rise of a democratic and technological American society as the great event of modern times even as he raised ironic questions about "progress."

After a decade of retirement, Adams in his

sixties resumed writing *about* history, though with different kinds of argument that required new forms. In *Mont-Saint-Michel and Chartres* (1913), he presented the imaginative world of the French Middle Ages, seeing the culture that built the great Gothic cathedrals as so strong that it could compel attention despite the violence, cruelty, and suffering of that same past. In *The Education of Henry Adams* (1907), he dealt with his own time. All the ideas of stability that a nineteenth-century education had given to the young, when put to the test, he found wanting. Disjunction rather than coherence seemed the rule in human affairs: "Chaos is the law of nature, Order is the dream of man." The only demonstrable progress was technological progress, and that was being channeled into military and imperial power more obviously than into the service of peace, security, or freedom; ironically he invited the future to prove him wrong. These two privately printed books steadily gathered readers: in 1911 he allowed the *Chartres* to be "pirated" for publication; when the *Education* was published posthumously in 1918, it became a best-seller. He helped create a twentieth-century audience for whom simple, secure, complacent notions of progress were untenable.

Of the generation born after the Civil War, one professional historian found a more than academic audience in his own time. W. E. B. Du Bois, a black scholar, taught at the segregated Atlanta University. Beginning with *The Suppression of the African Slave Trade* (1896), he pursued the study of African-American history, which had been either ignored or warped in conventional historiography. In *The Souls of Black Folk* (1903) he combined chapters on institutional history, folk culture, and individual reflections. While Adams was laying bare the disjunction between consciousness and events, Du Bois was showing the necessity that souls *and* facts be brought together to create a vital past for those who had largely been banished from white middle-class consciousness. As editor from 1910 to 1934 of *Crisis,* the magazine of the National Association for the Advancement of Colored People, he published many of the writers who were to create a Harlem Renaissance after World War I. After World War II, having struggled against racism and imperialism over his long life and seen no victory at home, he became an expatriate in Ghana and joined the Communist party. But even such strong gestures of insurgency could not deprive him of his increasingly important place in the American past.

The relative uniformity of the reading public of the 1860s slowly gave way under pressures of enlarged scale and unforeseen diversity until, in the second decade of the twentieth century, the "genteel tradition" seemed to cave in. But writing had been changing faster than publicists and scholars were always aware. The later work of Mark Twain, Howells, James, and Adams disclosed forces and ideas that the established norms could not contain. New writers as different as Dreiser, Cather, Frost, and Pound kept coming on the scene. Moreover, once the canons of gentility were dropped, readers began discovering that the older culture was richer and more various than its official spokesmen had surmised.

Warner Berthoff, *The Ferment of Realism: American Literature 1884–1919* (1965); Henry F. May, *The End of American Innocence: The First Years of Our Own Time, 1912–1917* (1959); Alan Trachtenberg, *The Incorporation of America: Culture and Society in the Gilded Age* (1982).

J. C. LEVENSON

III. American Literature since 1914

In the second decade of the century the new literary insurgencies on the American scene, however much they may in one particular or another have been uncertain of their aim, knew that at least their mission needed to involve the subversion of what George Santayana in 1911 had called the "genteel tradition." The generation of such writers as Edwin Arlington Robinson and Theodore Dreiser, of Robert Frost and Sherwood Anderson, of H. L. Mencken and William Carlos Williams, was convinced that it needed to distance itself from the timidities and pieties that had for too long subdued and tamed the major voices of American tradition. A milieu increasingly shaped by Darwin, Marx, Nietzsche, and Freud had to be reckoned with in ways that *Harper's* and the *Atlantic* and *Scribner's* and the

Century could not be expected to approve of. So new forums began to appear — *Poetry* in 1912, the *Little Review* and the *New Republic* in 1914, *Others* in 1915, the *Seven Arts* in 1916, and *Contact* and the *Dial* in 1920; and it was such periodicals that undertook to provide a hearing for the avant-garde that came to the fore in these years.

In *The Spirit of American Literature* (1913) the socialist critic John Macy had declared, "The whole country is crying out for those who will record it, satirize it, chant it." Just two years later in *America's Coming of Age,* a book that was to have enormous influence in the period immediately before and following the First World War, Van Wyck Brooks also sounded a call for the reinvigoration of the national culture. As Brooks argued, however, no "true revolution" would be realized until "a race of artists, profound and sincere, have brought us face to face with our own experience." And it was indeed toward the end of a newly enlivened sense of the complicated actualities making up American culture that the more significant writers of the time bent their energies — critics such as Lewis Mumford, Paul Rosenfeld, and Waldo Frank; novelists such as Dreiser, Sherwood Anderson, and Sinclair Lewis; poets such as Frost, William Carlos Williams, Edgar Lee Masters, and Carl Sandburg; and in the theater, the playwright Eugene O'Neill.

By the early 1920s some American writers were moving to France because, as Gertrude Stein said, Paris was "where the twentieth century was" and because there they would have direct access to the literary and artistic ferment that was shaping the consciousness of the age. But this exodus was by no means so general as myth suggests. John Dos Passos was in and out of Paris as a visitor in these years, but his status was never that of an expatriate; nor was any sort of exile elected by Willa Cather, Wallace Stevens, William Faulkner, Marianne Moore, and numerous others. And even extended periods of residence abroad, as in the case of Glenway Wescott, F. Scott Fitzgerald, and Ernest Hemingway, often did not at all signal any slackening in commitment among these people to their native culture. But the great thing that was

happening in the 1920s was an internationalization of the American writer's sensibility. As myth has it, the period of the twenties was the jazz age, the "gaudiest spree in history." Yet in deep and important ways American writers were entering into the full tide of the modernist movement, submitting to its exacting disciplines of skepticism and technical experimentation. The decade produced a remarkable array of classics: Hart Crane's *White Buildings* (1926), Dos Passos's *Manhattan Transfer* (1925), T. S. Eliot's *The Waste Land* (1922), Faulkner's *Sartoris* (1929), *The Sound and the Fury* (1929), and *As I Lay Dying* (1930), Fitzgerald's *The Great Gatsby* (1925), Hemingway's *The Sun Also Rises* (1926) and *A Farewell to Arms* (1929), Marianne Moore's *Poems* (1921) and *Observations* (1924), Ezra Pound's *Hugh Selwyn Mauberley* (1920) and *A Draft of XXX Cantos* (1933), Wallace Stevens's *Harmonium* (1923), Jean Toomer's *Cane* (1923), and Glenway Wescott's *The Grandmothers* (1927). The decade also produced the Harlem Renaissance, marked by Langston Hughes's *The Weary Blues* (1926), James Weldon Johnson's *God's Trombones* (1927), and Claude McKay's *Harlem Shadows* (1922).

But so great an efflorescence of talent and achievement was not matched in the 1930s. Although Faulkner's *Light in August* (1932) and *Absalom, Absalom!* (1936) were major accomplishments, Fitzgerald, after *Tender Is the Night* (1934), became a casualty of alcoholism. Nor is Hemingway's work of the period marked by any high distinction. His novel on the Spanish civil war, *For Whom the Bell Tolls* (1940), is an impressive book, but thereafter he wrote nothing of the first rank. And, otherwise, the scene in fiction during the thirties was, apart from the windy fustian of Thomas Wolfe, largely dominated by the kind of documentary naturalism represented by Erskine Caldwell, James T. Farrell, John O'Hara, John Steinbeck, and Richard Wright, for whom, as Alfred Kazin once said, "artistry was something one *added* to the concern" with the issues arising out of disorders in American society and out of the enormities perpetrated by the Nazi regime.

Nor did the literary scene brighten much in the period immediately after the Second World

War. Apart from a few fine novels that were devoted to the war experience — John Horne Burns's *The Gallery* (1947), James Gould Cozzens's *Guard of Honor* (1948), Norman Mailer's *The Naked and the Dead* (1948) — and Robert Penn Warren's distinguished novel on Louisiana politics, *All the King's Men* (1946), the representative fiction of the postwar years — Carson McCullers's *The Member of the Wedding* (1946), Jean Stafford's *The Mountain Lion* (1947), Truman Capote's *Other Voices, Other Rooms* (1948), Paul Bowles's *The Sheltering Sky* (1949), Mary McCarthy's *The Groves of Academe* (1952) — tended to be an affair of (as critic Malcolm Cowley phrased it) "a tidy room in Bedlam." Its personae were usually uninvolved in any sort of public scene. It was a literature wanting to do little more than register the tremors of the self's experience of its own inwardness in an adverse world.

In only a little more than another decade, though, it was apparent that, however lackluster the surfaces of literary life might have seemed in the 1940s, immense vitalities had been at work, and they were manifesting themselves in ethnic and regional configurations that had not won so high a visibility in an earlier time. In the years before World War II such figures as Ellen Glasgow, James Branch Cabell, DuBose Heyward, Stark Young, and John Peale Bishop had been noticeable as avatars of a kind of southern renascence, but the sudden recognition in the late forties of Faulkner's towering genius was accompanied by an equally sudden realization that he was surrounded by a vanguard of younger southerners representing enormous richness of talent — Warren, Eudora Welty, Peter Taylor, Flannery O'Connor, and William Styron in fiction; Tennessee Williams in theater; Allen Tate and Cleanth Brooks in criticism; and many others.

Similarly, whereas Ludwig Lewisohn, Paul Rosenfeld, Henry Roth, Daniel Fuchs, and Nathanael West had contributed a Jewish presence to the literary scene of the twenties and thirties, it was not till the late fifties that the awareness began to be unavoidable of a large and puissant Jewish movement having come to the fore by way of critics like Lionel Trilling, Alfred Kazin, and Irving Howe and such novelists as Mailer, Saul Bellow, Bernard Malamud, J. D. Salinger, Philip Roth, Herbert Gold, and others.

Among black writers, also, extraordinary vitality began to burst forth. Ralph Ellison's great novel *Invisible Man* appeared in 1952. In the following year James Baldwin's beautifully written first novel, *Go Tell It on the Mountain,* made its appearance. And by the end of the 1970s a flood of work by other black writers had reached full tide. Novelists like William Melvin Kelley, John Williams, Ishmael Reed, Clarence Major, John Wideman, Leon Forrest, Toni Morrison, and Alice Walker; poets like Melvin Tolson, Gwendolyn Brooks, Robert Hayden, and Michael Harper; and playwrights like LeRoi Jones (Imamu Amiri Baraka), Lorraine Hansberry, Ed Bullins, and August Wilson were all gifted rhetoricians who, in dramatizing the multifaceted world of black experience, added a new dimension to American literature.

It remains to be remarked that one of the glories of America's achievement in literature since 1914 has been its poetry. One knows not quite how, of course, to define T. S. Eliot's relation to the American scene, since (apart from "The Dry Salvages" and two or three of his early minor poems) his work is so little informed by his American background and his entire poetic career was lived out in England. Nor does one quite know how to measure the enigmatic legacy of Ezra Pound, since, for all the occasional brilliance and beauty of *The Cantos,* they are so much an affair of disjointed fragments.

But, even after Eliot and Pound are bracketed off, America's poetic literature demands to be acknowledged as something massive in its eloquence and ambitiousness and variety. By the early 1950s Robert Frost, Wallace Stevens, and William Carlos Williams, through the labors of a lifetime, had firmly established their position among the great poets of the modern West. And they were not alone. Marianne Moore's *Collected Poems* of 1951, for example, confirmed what many had long felt — that she, too, was a major poet. And the dazzling virtuosity of the work published by W. H. Auden after his emigration from England in 1939 made him seem a not unfair exchange for Eliot. Moreover, though Robert

Penn Warren's *Selected Poems: 1923–1943* (1944) had already guaranteed him a significant place in the annals of American poetry, it was that phase of his work extending from *Promises* (1957) to his late collections of the 1980s that definitively established his high status among the writers of his generation. Then, behind these leading figures (among whom needs to be included Stanley Kunitz) there came the talented Theodore Roethke, Delmore Schwartz, Robert Lowell, John Berryman, Elizabeth Bishop, Richard Wilbur, Anthony Hecht, Howard Nemerov, A. R. Ammons, Anne Sexton, Denise Levertov, James Merrill, Sylvia Plath, John Ashbery, Rita Dove, and fifty or sixty others.

The American imagination, then, as revealed in its literature, has had an extraordinary vigor and fecundity. As the English commentator Alan Pryce-Jones observed in the 1960s, "it is not anything as close-knit as the imagination of a European civilization," for the people whom it reflects do themselves form, as the old saw puts it, a great melting pot into which things European and African and Asian have been poured. And thus it is not surprising that the real genius of the national imagination, Pryce-Jones remarked, "has only come to fruition since the age of large-scale immigration."

Emory Elliott, ed., *Columbia Literary History of the United States* (1988).

NATHAN A. SCOTT, JR.

See also Expatriates and Exiles; Harlem Renaissance; Magazines and Newspapers; Publishing; Theater; Transcendentalism; *and entries for individual writers*.

LOCHNER V. NEW YORK

The Supreme Court dealt a blow in 1905 to efforts to regulate labor conditions in a 5–4 decision stating that states could not restrict ordinary workers' hours. Previously, in 1898, the Court had allowed to stand a Utah law that limited miners to eight-hour workdays. Because long hours led to mining accidents, the justices had accepted the measure as a protection of public health, and thus within the states' regulatory powers.

But now in 1905 the Court reviewed a New York State law restricting bakers to ten-hour workdays. Labor leaders and reformers argued that baking was a hazardous occupation. Bakers had a short life expectancy because they breathed in flour and worked at night for long hours. Nevertheless, the Court struck down the law as unconstitutional. Justice Rufus W. Peckham's majority opinion held that the law was not justified on health grounds. Its real intention, he wrote, was to regulate the hours of labor in private business. "The freedom of master and employee to contract with each other . . . cannot be prohibited or interfered with without violating the Fourteenth Amendment's guarantee of liberty."

Justice Oliver Wendell Holmes, Jr., dissented, claiming that the majority decision defended capitalism, not the Fourteenth Amendment. Defending capitalism was not the Court's role, he said; "a constitution is not established to embody a particular economic policy." John Marshall Harlan also dissented, emphasizing the dangers of long hours for bakers. Two other justices concurred with him that states could regulate hours in the interests of health. Harlan's reasoning later became the basis for *Lochner*'s partial reversal in *Muller* v. *Oregon* (1908).

See also Muller v. Oregon.

LONDON, JACK

(1876–1916), author. London's life and writing played a major role in reshaping the ideas of authorship and of literary expression in early twentieth-century America. Out of a San Francisco childhood of extreme poverty and hard manual labor — he was cannery worker, oyster pirate, and seaman while still in his teens — London burst on the literary scene at the turn of the century with fresh subject matter and iconoclastic beliefs. He achieved almost immediate success. Drawing upon his year in the Klondike during the Alaskan gold rush of 1897–1898, his initial and probably still most significant body of work consisted of short stories and novels set in the Far North. In them men and beasts test their strength and knowledge against the elemental forces of nature and the rapaciousness of other men. London's best Klondike fiction was collected in his first book, *The Son of the Wolf* (1900), and other volumes and reached its peak in the short novels *The Call of the Wild* (1903), his most famous novel, and *White Fang* (1906).

As London revealed in his powerful autobiographical novel *Martin Eden* (1909), he read widely but with little guidance as a young man. His early enthusiasm for the ideas of Karl Marx and Herbert Spencer produced an uneasy mix, as in one of his most popular novels, *The Sea-Wolf* (1904). In this book the central narrative of the initiation of a young aesthete during a sealing voyage into the reality of brute force in the world is leavened by a love story in which commitment to a common good is triumphant. London's personal life had something of the same mixed character. He abruptly left his first wife, Bess Maddern, and their children in 1903 for a new love, his second wife, Charmian Kittredge. And throughout his career — principally in his firsthand report of London slum life, *The People of the Abyss* (1903), and in his antiutopian novel, *The Iron Heel* (1908) — he preached a form of socialistic reform while pressing his publishers for increasingly large sums in order to acquire a baronial estate in Sonoma County, north of San Francisco.

Following a disastrous voyage to the South Seas during 1907–1909 on his yacht, the *Snark,* London's health and work began to decline. By the time of his death, he was worn out. He had published over forty books in seventeen years, had traveled — often under extreme conditions — throughout the world, had experienced periods of alcoholism, and had undergone a series of major accidents and illnesses. Although it was rumored at his death that he took his own life, it is now generally accepted that he died of acute uremia.

Long one of the most popular American writers, especially abroad and among the young, because of his "masculine" subject matter, direct narrative style, and personal code of honesty and courage, London in recent years has attracted, both as a writer and as an American life story, serious attention. His fiction, it is now re-alized, touches upon some of the central myths of Western experience. And his life epitomizes a distinctive moment in American cultural history (reflected as well in the career of Theodore Roosevelt) when the idea that it was necessary to engage all ranges of experience vigorously and with passion again became, as in the age of Emerson, a moral imperative.

Earle Labor, *Jack London* (1974); Andrew Sinclair, *Jack: A Biography of Jack London* (1977).

DONALD PIZER

See also Literature.

LONG, HUEY

(1893–1935), governor of Louisiana and U.S. senator. Long had two political careers, both of them extraordinary. The first was in his native Louisiana. There he rose from modest beginnings in the poor hill country to become a successful lawyer, a public service commissioner, and, in 1928, the most powerful governor in the history of the state, perhaps in the history of any state. Capitalizing on widespread public discontent with years of corrupt, myopic, conservative rule, Long developed a fervent popular following. He used it to build a power structure through which he dominated virtually every institution of government. In time, the legislature, the state bureaucracy, the courts, even local governments fell firmly under his control. He used that power to expand the state's underdeveloped infrastructure and social services, building bridges, roads, hospitals, and schools. He also revised the tax codes to place a larger burden on corporations. But power was for him an end in itself — a point made particularly vivid in Robert Penn Warren's 1946 novel *All the King's Men,* whose central character, Willy Stark, was inspired by Long. Within a few years, Long had developed a national reputation as the "dictator" of Louisiana. At home, he was known simply as the "Kingfish."

Beginning in 1932, when he resigned the governorship to enter the U.S. Senate, Long began a national political career that at times appeared boundless. He took little interest in the Senate, using it principally to advance his larger national ambitions. At first, he was an energetic supporter of Franklin D. Roosevelt. But by the middle of 1933, he had broken with the president and struck out on his own. Long voiced populist resentments that many depression-era Americans felt toward "wealthy plutocrats" and "bloated fortunes." He promised, through his implausible Share-Our-Wealth Plan, a radical redistribution of wealth: confiscatory taxes would scale down large fortunes, and the revenue would be used to guarantee everyone a minimum annual income of twenty-five hundred dollars. By 1935, he had launched his own national political organization (the Share-Our-Wealth clubs) and was talking openly of running for president the next year against Roosevelt. The crude public opinion polls of the time indicated that he could not win, but that he might tip the balance in a close race. In fact, the "Long threat," as Democratic politicians described it, was probably less serious than it appeared. Long's national organization was flimsy and decentralized, and he showed no ability to form effective alliances with the many other dissident leaders of the time, whose support he would have needed for an effective national campaign.

In any case, Long never had a chance to demonstrate his national potential. In September of 1935, he returned to Baton Rouge to supervise a special session of the state legislature (which, like the rest of the Louisiana government, he continued to control as completely while serving in the Senate as he had while governor). As Long walked down a marble corridor in the new state capitol he had built several years before, the son-in-law of one of his ruined political opponents stepped from behind a pillar and shot him. He died several days later, talking politics to the end.

Alan Brinkley, *Voices of Protest* (1982); T. Harry Williams, *Huey Long* (1969).

ALAN BRINKLEY

LONGFELLOW, HENRY WADSWORTH

(1807–1882), poet and translator. The most popular poet of his day and the first American poet to make an adequate living at his profession, Longfellow is now largely dismissed as a writer of little depth, whose work was rendered artificial and sentimental by his alliance with the privileged society of Victorian Boston and Cambridge.

A professor of modern European languages first at Bowdoin College in his native Maine and, after 1836, at Harvard, he established himself as a lyric poet with *Voices of the Night* (1839), which contains one of his most famous poems, "The Psalm of Life." This volume was followed by *Ballads and Other Poems* (1841), which includes such well-known works as "The Wreck of the Hesperus," "The Skeleton in Armor," "The Village Blacksmith," and "Excelsior." His *Poems on Slavery* (1842), a nod to the antislavery movement prompted by his liberal Unitarian values, was dedicated to William Ellery Channing. For the most part, however, unlike John Greenleaf Whittier, he kept his poetical vocation separate from matters of conscience and wrote most often and compellingly on nostalgic and picturesque themes. In 1847 he published *Evangeline, A Tale of Acadie,* the first in a series of popular narrative poems on American historical subjects, which he continued after his resignation from Harvard in 1854; these include *The Song of Hiawatha* (1855), *The Courtship of Miles Standish* (1858), and the verse dramas of *The New England Tragedies* (1868). His early prose works, *Outre-Mer* (1833–1835) and *Hyperion* (1839), imitate Washington Irving and exploit the popular interest in romantic travel literature; *Kavanagh* (1849), a New England tale, was his last venture in prose fiction.

Longfellow, who commanded a dozen languages, was an accomplished translator, eager to instruct American audiences in the riches of European literature. His *Poets and Poetry of Europe* (1845), the first anthology of its kind in America, and his translation of Dante's *Divine Comedy* (1867), were the most significant results of this cultural retailing.

His immense popularity was a complex phenomenon, resulting partly from his own shrewd marketing of his literary wares but rather more from the fact that his well-crafted, usually mellifluous poems challenged no one's prejudices. In many subtle ways he was perfectly attuned to the needs of his middle-class American audience, both in the Unitarian stoicism of his overt moralizing and in the unquestioning (and apparently unconscious) support that he gave to some central myths of his culture. His celebration of female fidelity and subservience ("the beauty and strength of woman's devotion") in such works as *Evangeline* and *The Golden Legend* (1851) authoritatively romanticized what the women's movement was rejecting. Similarly, Longfellow's picturesque rendition of the passing of Indian culture in *Hiawatha* arguably made the plight of Native Americans seem, to his white audience, comfortably inevitable. Much the same could be said of his treatment of Jews in "The Jewish Cemetery at Newport."

Longfellow's historical importance may lie in his having legitimized the writing of poetry as a profession in America, in his having assisted the career of Nathaniel Hawthorne, his Bowdoin College classmate, with an influential review of *Twice-told Tales,* and in a dozen or so minor poems of lasting value, including "Seaweed," "The Fire of Driftwood," "The Ropewalk," "Palingenesis," and a number of fine sonnets.

Newton Arvin, *Longfellow: His Life and Work* (1963); Edward Wagenknecht, *Henry Wadsworth Longfellow: His Poetry and Prose* (1986).

Albert J. von Frank

See also Literature.

LOUIS, JOE

(1914–1981), boxer. The son of Alabama sharecroppers, Joe Louis, during his reign as heavyweight champion of the world from 1937 to 1949, stood as a shining symbol of mythical and real American traits like racial unity, national strength, and unlimited opportunity. Through a rare combination of shattering events, an acceptable demeanor, expert handling, sympathetic press coverage, great pugilistic talent, the American obsession with sports, and the peculiar symbolism of the heavyweight boxing champion, Louis became the most popular black in America and one of the most popular of all Americans.

Although Louis established a phenomenal fistic record — he successfully defended his championship twenty-five times in twelve years (four of which were spent in the army) — what

helped immortalize him was the context in which his fights took place. In his 1935 defeat of the giant former heavyweight champion Primo Carnera, who was viewed as Benito Mussolini's emissary, Louis represented blacks who identified with "little" Ethiopia in its struggle against the bullying Italian aggressor. By becoming the first black to hold the heavyweight championship in twenty-two years with his victory over James J. Braddock in 1937, Louis lifted the spirits of the black masses in the midst of the Great Depression. At the same time he gained white acceptance because of his "humility" and willingness to avoid the provocative behavior of the previous black champion, Jack Johnson, who had antagonized white America by not "knowing his place." By "destroying" German Max Schmeling in their second encounter in 1938, as Adolf Hitler and the Nazis rose to power, Louis provided some assurance that America's best could beat the best that Germany had to offer. Louis continued to win white approval thereafter by joining the army, although he never saw combat.

Despite his remarkable achievements and tremendous popularity, Louis may be as important for what he did not accomplish as for what he did. Like many heroes he has been credited for much that he did not do. Commentators, for example, have overstated his impact on racist attitudes and practices. There is little evidence that Louis's success or that of other black athletes translated into a general acceptance of blacks or recommended them for roles outside sport.

Where Louis did change attitudes was among blacks. His position at the top of his sport, his celebrity status, and his public image helped bolster the confidence of a people whose heroes were rarely accorded white attention or respect. In the difficult time of war his decision to cooperate with and become a symbol of a government that was far from fair to him and his people offered a constructive, albeit imperfect, course of action.

In the end, Joe Louis was another edition of the American myth of the self-made man — that anyone who is industrious, patriotic, and moral can rise from the very bottom to the top of society where wealth, power, and fame await him. As with Louis, not all self-made men are as they appear to be. Not only did he have a lot of help; his wealth was more illusory than real.

For all his greatness as a boxer and a symbol, Louis, in reality, was simply human. Two words best describe his personal life, excessive and irresponsible. Louis lived far beyond his means, supported far too many charities, and lost a small fortune to golf hustlers alone. Worse was his notorious penchant for adultery, which cost him a loyal and loving wife. At the end of his boxing career, Louis had neither money nor family and faced an insurmountable federal tax debt, which the IRS forgave after considerable legal and political pressure. In his twilight years Louis struggled with a drug problem and served as a "greeter" at Caesar's Palace in Las Vegas, where he shook hands with common folk, gambled with house money to lure others, and played golf with high rollers before failing health incapacitated him. Yet, Louis's interment at Arlington National Cemetery indicates his place in myth and history; for, right or wrong, this is the public record on which society judges its heroes.

Lawrence Levine, *Black Culture and Black Consciousness: Afro-American Folk Thought from Slavery to Freedom* (1977); Chris Mead, *Champion-Joe Louis: Black Hero in White America* (1985); Jeffrey T. Sammons, *Beyond the Ring: The Role of Boxing in American Society* (1988).

JEFFREY T. SAMMONS

See also Spectator Sports.

LOUISIANA PURCHASE

With the Louisiana Purchase in 1803, the United States bought from France most of the land between the Mississippi River and the Rocky Mountains. Since achieving independence, the United States had repeatedly sought free access down the Mississippi to the Gulf of Mexico. Terms had been negotiated in 1795 with the Spanish, who then held the territory, but in 1801 President Thomas Jefferson learned that Spain had secretly ceded Louisiana to France.

Louisiana Purchase

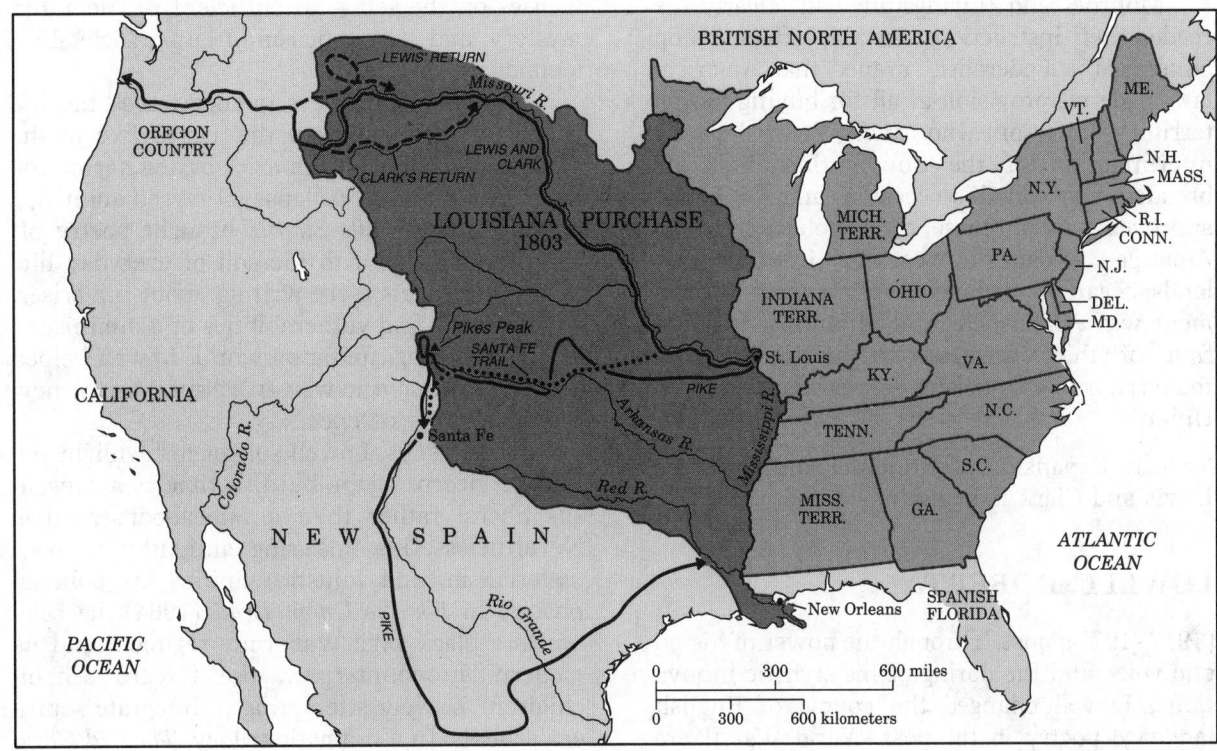

Jefferson instructed the American minister in Paris, Robert R. Livingston, to negotiate either for a port at the mouth of the Mississippi or, as a second choice, for permanent trading rights in New Orleans. In January 1803, James Monroe was sent to join Livingston, armed with an appropriation of $2 million to buy New Orleans and West Florida (the southern portions of Alabama and Mississippi); secretly, Monroe was told he could go as high as $10 million.

Napoleon had acquired Louisiana in hopes of building an empire in North America, but a Haitian slave revolt and an impending war with England had led him to abandon his plans. On April 11, Livingston and Monroe were offered all of Louisiana. The price agreed upon was $15 million. For approximately four cents an acre, the United States acquired about 828,000 square miles, doubling the size of the nation. The Mississippi River formed the eastern boundary, and the Gulf of Mexico, the southern; subsequent treaties defined the northern boundary as reaching to Canada, and the western, as running generally northwest to the middle of present-day Montana.

Monroe and Livingston had clearly exceeded their instructions. Indeed, Jefferson's opponents, the Federalists, argued that American law made no provision at all for buying foreign territory. Jefferson, who usually favored a strict interpretation of the Constitution, took the broadest view on this occasion, and the Senate approved the purchase on October 20, 1803. American expansion westward into the new lands began immediately. A territorial government was established in 1804, and in 1812 the first of thirteen states to be carved from the territory — Louisiana — was admitted to the Union.

See also Expansion, Continental and Overseas; Lewis and Clark Expedition.

LOWELL, ROBERT

(1917–1977), poet. Through the power of his poetic voice and the daring of his stylistic innovations, Lowell changed the course of English-language poetry in the post–World War II era.

From 1946, the date of his first major volume, to 1977, the year of his death, Lowell was the preeminent American poet of his generation.

In the Pulitzer Prize–winning *Lord Weary's Castle* (1946), Lowell perfected a style traditional in its metrical complexity and verbal ambiguity. He used that style to inveigh against modern civilization, war, materialism, and misused authority. The volume combined traditional values (e.g., a yearning for Christian transcendence) with a disaffected critique of American history and national policy (e.g., the war against Germany). Almost every poem expresses an apocalyptic rage that subverts any possibility of affirmation: "The scythers, Time and Death, / Helmed locusts, move upon the tree of breath."

In 1959, Lowell published his most important single volume, the revolutionary *Life Studies.* Here he perfected what has come to be called "confessional poetry." Banished were the intensity and artificiality, the Christianity and fury, of the earlier volume. Instead, *Life Studies* takes on the narrative power of fiction and the psychological insight of autobiography. Unable to save or even to understand the world, the poet focuses on the self — as sufficient problem and mystery, and as microcosm of larger societal dilemmas.

The volume's title sequence traces the life course of the poet from the age of five to the present and concludes in a celebrated harrowing depiction of mental collapse: "I myself am hell; / nobody's here." *Life Studies* brought poetry off its stilts and down to the soil of everyday life. Soon other poets were writing about the crises, complexities, and vulnerabilities of a diminished "I" in a baffling, unhappy world. Lowell helped poetry discover a new way of speaking, a new reason for its existence.

In the 1960s, Lowell sought to highlight political concerns again, but this time as a consensus liberal rather than a radical-conservative. Nevertheless, his enduring antipathy to war, materialism, and injustice unifies his political phases. In *For the Union Dead* (1964), he celebrates a black Civil War army regiment and its modern-day counterpart, the "Negro school-children" bravely attempting to integrate southern schools. In a dramatic trilogy, *The Old Glory*

(1965), he excoriates the anti-Indian, antiblack racism central to American history. And in *Near the Ocean* (1967), he eloquently laments the Vietnam War and other political ills.

After a politically active period during which he joined the peace movement and campaigned for Senator Eugene McCarthy, Lowell in the 1970s retreated to a meditational mode in which he reflected on his involvement with history (in *Notebook* and *History*), on his divorce and remarriage late in life (in the Pulitzer Prize–winning *The Dolphin*), and on the ambiguous relationship of writing to life (in both *The Dolphin* and his last volume, *Day by Day*). He asked whether "art" could be "a way to get well," either for the artist or for society. His career suggests that art, when imbued with the "grace of accuracy," can indeed foster social health. Lowell revived poetry in his time by exploring the endless complexities and interpenetrations of language, self, and community.

Steven Gould Axelrod, *Robert Lowell: Life and Art* (1978); Jeffrey Meyers, ed., *Robert Lowell: Interviews and Memoirs* (1988).

STEVEN GOULD AXELROD

See also Literature.

LOWELL SYSTEM

The Lowell system was a method of factory management that evolved in the textile mills of Lowell, Massachusetts, owned by the Boston Manufacturing Company. In 1814, the Boston Company built America's first fully mechanized mill in Waltham, Massachusetts. Nine years later, the company built a complex of new mills at East Chelmsford, soon renamed Lowell in honor of the company's founder, Francis Lowell. With the production process fully mechanized, the principal limitation on the firm's output was the availability of labor, and here the company made its second innovation: it began to recruit young farm girls from the surrounding countryside. In order to attract these women and to reassure their families, the owners developed a paternalistic approach to management that became known as the Lowell system.

The mill workers were housed in clean, well-run boardinghouses, were strictly supervised both at work and at home, and were paid unusually good wages. The farm girls responded with enthusiasm. They soon became renowned as excellent employees, and their lively self-improvement program (including a literary magazine) drew international attention. Few of the Lowell women worked more than a few years, but for every one who returned home to marry, two new ones appeared. By the 1830s, the Lowell system had become a national symbol of the fact that in America, humanity could go hand in hand with industrial success.

Even at the pinnacle of its renown, however, conditions in Lowell had begun to deteriorate. In 1834, an economic downturn led to the mills' first wage cuts. In the 1840s, managers instituted a speedup, requiring higher and higher output for the same hourly wage. The women formed the Lowell Female Labor Reform Association and tried to appeal to their employers and then to the state legislature through petitions. These led to state investigations in 1845 and 1846, but little changed. After 1848, conditions deteriorated further, as New England's textile industry began to suffer from overexpansion. Seeking cheaper labor, the mill owners turned increasingly to Irish immigrants and in the process discontinued the management policies they had devised to attract workers from the farms. By the 1850s, the Lowell system had been abandoned.

See also Labor; Textile Industry.

LUCE, HENRY

(1898–1967), journalist and publisher. Luce, the son of a Presbyterian missionary in China, felt an outsider among the well-to-do students at Hotchkiss and Yale. His answer in 1923 was to create *Time* magazine in an effort to make himself the arbiter of America's taste and destiny. The magazine was a distillation of twenties' journalism, but not a copy, for no one had ever thought of briskly summarizing the week's news. By the end of the decade the experiment was making money, and the untimely death of his partner, Briton Hadden, left Luce in charge.

He built up the staff and led them to stories that had seldom been written about before. He subsequently launched *Fortune* (1930), *Architectural Forum* (1934), and *Life* (1936), which was the first successful weekly magazine of photojournalism. *Sports Illustrated* (1954) was the last magazine developed under his leadership. Luce also did innovative work for radio, newsreels, and television, and his Time-Life Books became a major publishing house. Until 1964, he supervised all of his enterprises personally.

Both the style and substance of Luce journalism was under constant attack. "Backward ran sentences until reeled the mind," Wolcott Gibbs wrote in a parody of *Time*. Adjectives in Luce magazines were regarded warily by people in public life. Luce's objectives were clear enough. He believed in figures of destiny — politicians, entrepreneurs, spiritual leaders — and put them on the covers of his magazines and sought their company. Like his missionary father, he saw Christian purpose in global change and never doubted his ability to shape the outcome. (On the other hand, he never mastered simpler tasks such as driving a car or ordering in a restaurant.) Luce was attracted, at least for a time, by strong men, such as Benito Mussolini and Francisco Franco, and he was loyal to weak men he hoped to make strong, such as Chiang Kai-shek of China and Ngo Dinh Diem of South Vietnam. He fought the Democratic party domestically and, as a fierce anticommunist, counted on ex-radicals to spread his message. Luce exerted his greatest influence on U.S. policy toward China. His determination not to recognize the Chinese Revolution was not balanced by any comparable force in the American media and helped immobilize a generation of policymakers.

He liked the intellectual excitement of dissenters on his staff, but what they reported seldom got into his magazines. Theodore H. White, who lost his job with *Time* when he disagreed with Luce about China, admitted that "it was exhilarating to be working for a man who could discuss, all at the same time, the Bible, Confucius and the itchy gossip and color which sells readers on a magazine." No critic of Luce has underestimated his achievement on two points.

He said that journalism should take in the full cultural life of the times (the "back of the book" in *Time*) and that America's reach was global: the "American Century" had begun. Luce made his fellow journalists accept both premises.

Robert T. Elson, *Time Inc.: The Intimate History of a Publishing Enterprise, 1923–1941* (1968) and *The World of Time Inc.: The Intimate History of a Publishing Enterprise, 1941–1960* (1973).

THOMAS C. LEONARD

See also Magazines and Newspapers.

LYCEUMS

In 1826 in Millbury, Massachusetts, Josiah Holbrook organized a program of adult education courses he called a lyceum, named after Aristotle's school in ancient Athens. The popularity of Holbrook's program spread, and five years later, the National American Lyceum was established in New York City. In the years that followed, organizations all across the country began establishing their own lyceums; by 1834, there were several thousand.

Under these auspices, audiences heard lectures and concerts, watched scientific demonstrations and dramatic performances, and participated in debates and discussion groups. Institutions such as the Lowell Institute in Boston and Cooper Union in New York City were initially established as lyceums. Many of the best-known artists, writers, politicians, and journalists of the day appeared on the lyceum circuit, often scheduled through central booking offices like the Boston Lyceum Bureau, organized by James Redpath, a leader in the movement.

During its most active years — the 1830s to 1860s — the lyceum movement played an important role in American public education and social reform. Its influence began to wane after the Civil War, but its activities were carried on later by the chautauqua movement.

See also Chautauqua Movement; Education.

LYNCHING

Lynching is the practice whereby a mob — usually several dozen or several hundred persons — takes the law into its own hands in order to injure and kill a person accused of some wrongdoing. The alleged offense can range from a serious crime like theft or murder to a mere violation of local customs and sensibilities. The issue of the victim's guilt is usually secondary, since the mob serves as prosecutor, judge, jury, and executioner. Due process yields to momentary passions and expedient objectives.

Vigilantism, or summary justice, has a long history, but the term *lynch law* originated during the American Revolution with Col. Charles Lynch and his Virginia associates, who responded to unsettled times by making their own rules for confronting Tories and criminal elements. "Lynching" found an easy acceptance as the nation expanded. Raw frontier conditions encouraged swift punishment for real, imagined, or anticipated criminal behavior. Historically, social control has been an essential aspect of mob rule.

Opponents of slavery in pre–Civil War America and cattle rustlers, gamblers, horse thieves, and other "desperadoes" in the South and Old West were nineteenth-century targets. From the 1880s onward, however, mob violence increasingly reflected white America's contempt for various racial, ethnic, and cultural groups. African-Americans especially, and sometimes Native Americans, Latinos, Jews, Asian immigrants, and European newcomers, felt the mob's fury. In an era when racist theories prompted "true Americans" to assert their imagined superiority through imperialist ventures, mob violence became the domestic means of asserting white dominance. Occasionally, this complemented the profit motive, when the lynching of a successful black farmer or immigrant merchant opened new economic opportunities for local whites and simultaneously reaffirmed everyone's "place" in the social hierarchy. Sometimes lynching was aimed at unpopular ideas: labor union organizers, political radicals, critics of America's role in World War I, and civil rights advocates were targets.

African-Americans suffered grievously under lynch law. With the close of Reconstruction in the late 1870s, southern whites were determined to end northern and black participation in the region's affairs, and northerners exhibited a growing indifference toward the civil rights of black Americans. Taking its cue from this intersectional white harmony, the federal government abandoned its oversight of constitutional protections. Southern and border states responded with the Jim Crow laws of the 1890s, and white mobs flourished. With blacks barred from voting, public office, and jury service, officials felt no obligation to respect minority interests or safeguard minority lives. In addition to lynchings of individuals, dozens of race riots — with blacks as victims — scarred the national landscape from Wilmington, North Carolina, in 1898 to Tulsa, Oklahoma, in 1921.

Between 1882 (when reliable statistics were first collected) and 1968 (when the classic forms of lynching had disappeared), 4,743 persons died of lynching, 3,446 of them black men and women. Mississippi (539 black victims, 42 white) led this grim parade of death, followed by Georgia (492, 39), Texas (352, 141), Louisiana (335, 56), and Alabama (299, 48). From 1882 to 1901, the annual number nationally usually exceeded 100; 1892 had a record 230 deaths (161 black, 69 white). Although lynchings declined somewhat in the twentieth century, there were still 97 in 1908 (89 black, 8 white), 83 in the racially troubled postwar year of 1919 (76, 7, plus some 25 race riots), 30 in 1926 (23, 7), and 28 in 1933 (24, 4).

Statistics do not tell the entire story, however. These were *recorded* lynchings; others were never reported beyond the community involved. Furthermore, mobs used especially sadistic tactics when blacks were the prime targets. By the 1890s lynchers increasingly employed burning, torture, and dismemberment to prolong suffering and excite a "festive atmosphere" among the killers and onlookers. White families brought small children to watch, newspapers sometimes carried advance notices, railroad agents sold excursion tickets to announced lynching sites, and mobs cut off black victims' fingers, toes, ears, or genitalia as souvenirs. Nor was it necessarily the handiwork of a local rabble; not infrequently, the mob was encouraged or led by people prominent in the area's political and business circles. Lynching had become a ritual of interracial social control and recreation rather than simply a punishment for crime.

In an expression of racism and sexism, apologists claimed that lynching protected white women from black rapists, but actually, only one-quarter of lynching victims were accused of rape or attempted rape. In the 1890s, black journalist Ida B. Wells-Barnett publicized evidence refuting this rape myth, as did the later Association of Southern Women for the Prevention of Lynching, a white organization mobilized on a county-by-county basis throughout the 1930s to put an end to mob violence.

From the 1890s to the early 1930s, sixteen southern and border states had laws dealing with lynching and mob violence, but enforcement was uneven and ineffectual. With race as the issue, officials simply declined to apprehend and prosecute lynchers, even when their identities were no secret. Coroners' inquests regularly found that death had occurred "at the hands of parties unknown." Consequently, from 1918 to the 1960s, the National Association for the Advancement of Colored People (NAACP) sought federal intervention, usually through a statute designed to stiffen local resolve by punishing an officer whose delinquency contributed to a lynching or by fining the county or municipality involved. The bill would also have utilized federal prosecutors and judges relatively immune to local political pressures. The measure passed the House of Representatives three times (1922, 1937, 1940) but failed in the Senate because of real or threatened filibusters by southern Democrats aided by northern conservative Republicans. Nonetheless, this extended lobbying did alert the nation to the need for reform and placed the NAACP at the center of an emerging twentieth-century civil rights coalition.

Although Congress never passed an anti-lynching statute, portions of the 1968 Civil Rights Act provided for federal intervention in the event of injury to a person seeking constitutional rights. The last recorded lynching occurred in 1964 with the murder of three civil rights workers, James Chaney, Andrew Goodman, and Michael Schwerner, in Mississippi.

Modernizing trends in American life helped account for lynching's decline. With steady migration from the rural South, blacks shed their isolation and vulnerability and acquired, instead, a degree of political power and visibility throughout the nation; the results in legislative terms included the passage of five civil rights statutes and the ratification of two constitutional amendments from 1957 to 1968. Worried about its image among third world nations, cold war America sought to resolve its domestic racial tensions. Meanwhile, southern business and political leaders realized that the Sunbelt could not attract industrial investments and a skilled white-collar populace unless it lost its reputation for violence and civil disruptions.

Nonetheless, American culture still exhibits a vigilante spirit and a tendency to impose local conformity, as when, for example, self-appointed guardians invoke extralegal tactics to harass Asian boat people, firebomb abortion clinics, promote gay bashing, prevent "outsiders" from joining the neighborhood, or mobilize Aryan skinheads against social pluralism.

Walter White, *Rope and Faggot: A Biography of Judge Lynch* (1929); Robert L. Zangrando, *The NAACP Crusade Against Lynching, 1909–1950* (1980).

ROBERT L. ZANGRANDO

See also Civil Rights Movement; Ku Klux Klan; National Association for the Advancement of Colored People; Wells-Barnett, Ida B.; World War I.

M

★

MacARTHUR, DOUGLAS

(1880–1964), U.S. Army general. Son of a top-ranking army general, MacArthur was leader of his West Point class and commissioned as a lieutenant in 1903. He became a brigade commander and, near the end of World War I, commander of the famed Forty-second Division. In 1919, he returned home to head the U.S. Military Academy. His service in the 1920s was marked by two tours of duty in the Philippines. As army chief of staff from 1930 to 1935, he struggled to keep the army intact in a period of decline and economic depression.

At the conclusion of his Washington service, he accepted the post of military adviser to the government of the Philippines. Growing problems with Japan led President Franklin D. Roosevelt in mid-1941 to appoint him commander of U.S. Army forces in the Far East. After Pearl Harbor MacArthur conducted the defense of the Philippines until approaching defeat led Roosevelt to award him the Medal of Honor and order him to Australia. Some weeks later he became supreme commander of the southwest Pacific area. Choosing to attack Japan by way of New Guinea and the Philippines rather than by the navy's central Pacific approach, he was able in 1944 to keep his promise to return to the Philippines. After the atomic bomb ended Japanese resistance, MacArthur accepted the enemy's surrender on board the USS *Missouri* in Tokyo Bay, September 2, 1945. As supreme commander of the Allied powers in Japan, MacArthur (a five-star general since late 1944) assumed command

of a highly successful occupation of Japan from 1945 to 1950. He disarmed Japan, imposed a democratic constitution, and paved the way for economic reconstruction of the country.

When North Korea invaded South Korea in late June 1950, he became supreme allied commander of all U.S., Korean, and U.N. forces committed to the South Korean cause. To counter an enemy drive that had pushed Korean and American troops to the South Korean coast, MacArthur decided, in the face of general skepticism, on an amphibious landing at Inchon in mid-September 1950. Success of this maneuver led MacArthur to pursue the retreating enemy toward the Yalu River that lay between North Korea and China. Thrown back by Red Chinese forces pouring across the Yalu late in 1950, MacArthur demanded that the Chinese end of the Yalu bridges be bombed. When Washington and U.N. supporters of the American effort warned against expansion of the conflict in the Far East, MacArthur's public criticism of such strictures led President Harry S. Truman to remove him from command and order him home, where the general received a hero's reception. An effort by Republican presidential hopeful Senator Robert A. Taft to use MacArthur's support to halt Gen. Dwight D. Eisenhower's 1952 fight for the nomination was thwarted when Eisenhower won. MacArthur subsequently faded from public prominence.

A glittering figure and gifted soldier, capable of planning and conducting bold operations, MacArthur's belief in his own military judgment led to his public disagreement with the administration. His recall by the president was backed by the secretary of defense and the Joint Chiefs of Staff. In the congressional inquiry that followed, a majority of the Senate Armed Services and Foreign Relations committees supported the right of the president to dismiss the general, but a few antiadministration critics filed individual statements of condemnation of Truman's Far Eastern policy.

D. Clayton James, *The Years of MacArthur,* 3 vols. (1970–1985); Douglas MacArthur, *Reminiscences* (1964).

FORREST C. POGUE

See also Armed Forces; Korean War; World War II.

MACHINE POLITICS

See Urban Bosses and Machine Politics.

MADISON, JAMES

(1751–1836), fourth president of the United States and political theorist. One of the less colorful but most important of America's Founding Fathers, Madison may rightly be considered the principal architect of the political system defined by the U.S. Constitution. His extraordinary career in public life extended over forty years, intersecting every major phase of the history of the American Revolution and the early Republic. Although he served in a number of high offices, including secretary of state (1801–1809) and president (1809–1817), he is best remembered for his accomplishments as a political theorist and for his related role in launching the Constitution during the late 1780s and early 1790s.

Historians generally recognize the soft-spoken, diminutive, and scholarly Madison as the best prepared and most influential of the delegates to the Constitutional Convention of 1787. Drawing on his extensive study of past republics, as well as his recent experience as a delegate to both the Virginia legislature and the national Congress under the Articles of Confederation, Madison led the search at Philadelphia for what he later called "a republican remedy for the dis-

eases most incident to republican government." He hoped that by creating a new national government that rested directly on the people rather than on the states, the delegates could overcome the factional disorder, confusion, and injustice that prevailed during the postrevolutionary years without endangering liberty or compromising the American commitment to representative government.

Although the document that emerged from the convention disappointed Madison in some respects, he worked tirelessly for its ratification. He coauthored the brilliant collection of essays explaining and defending the Constitution, *The Federalist,* that is today still studied as a masterpiece of political theory. And in the Virginia ratifying convention he outdebated and outmaneuvered a formidable antagonist, Patrick Henry, to win narrow acceptance of the Constitution in that critical state.

Elected to the First Congress under the new regime, Madison, who initially enjoyed the trust and respect of President George Washington, immediately became the pivotal figure in drafting laws and establishing precedents that gave tangible shape and force to the new Constitution. Most important, following the advice of his close friend Thomas Jefferson, he guided the process that would produce the first ten amendments, now known as the Bill of Rights. Then, fearful that the new government might be corrupted by aggressive nationalists — principally his collaborator on *The Federalist* Alexander Hamilton — Madison joined Jefferson in opposing the Federalist administrations of both Washington and his successor John Adams. Most modern historians see significant discontinuity in his career, but Madison defended this apparent retreat from his earlier nationalism as necessary to preserve the Constitution as it had been understood during the ratification process.

After 1800, when the Jeffersonians defeated the Federalists in a watershed election, Madison served eight years as Jefferson's secretary of state. His two terms as president followed. Most historians consider Madison to have been a weak chief executive, citing his leadership during the War of 1812 as particularly inept. Nevertheless, the young nation emerged from that

"Second War for Independence" with a new measure of unity and self-confidence. Madison thus enjoyed tremendous popularity during his last years as president and his nineteen years in retirement, when he was widely revered for his role both in founding and in securing the first great modern republic.

Drew R. McCoy, *The Last of the Fathers: James Madison and the Republican Legacy* (1989); Robert A. Rutland, *James Madison: The Founding Father* (1987).

DREW R. MCCOY

See also Bill of Rights; Conservatism; Constitution; Elections: 1808, 1812; Federalist Papers; Philadelphia Convention; Ratification of the Constitution; Revolution. *For events during Madison's administration, see Fletcher* v. *Peck;* Hartford Convention of 1814; Impressment Controversy; Tecumseh; War Hawks; War of 1812.

MAGAZINES AND NEWSPAPERS

American printers had been circulating news for a century when George Washington took office as president, but the new nation's provincial press faced an uncertain future. "The expectation of failure is connected with the very name of a Magazine," Noah Webster said in the first days of the Republic. Of the more than two hundred papers in 1800, only about a dozen had published during the American Revolution, and not one of the twenty-four dailies was that old.

The weekly newspaper was the first form of journalism to adapt to an expanding democratic society. The flatbed press, not much changed since Gutenberg's time, was ideal for the frontier. Loaded onto a wagon or boat, set up in a tent or under a tree, the press became one of the earliest marks of community, both purveying news and boosting the town. Cincinnati got its first newspaper in 1793 when it had fewer than five hundred citizens. The first newspaper west of the Mississippi came to St. Louis in 1808 when the population was less than fifteen hundred. Leavenworth, Kansas, had a newspaper in 1854 when the town consisted of four tents. These papers relied on government subsidies through printing contracts and special postal rates. Editors received exchange papers, the source of most news, for free. Local papers could be sent free by post in the publisher's home territory throughout most of the nineteenth century. The pattern of settlement and government subsidies created the most decentralized press in the world.

These diverse papers, with names such as *Porcupine's Gazette, Huntress,* and *Live Giraffe,* were charged with many sins, but never dullness. The drama of politics was the center of almost every newspaper, but readers expected to be informed about wonders and horrors, too. In 1843, the *Illinois Statesman* tried to avoid this, saying "If our readers will for the present just have the goodness to imagine a certain due proportion of fires, tornadoes, murders, thefts, robberies and bully fights, from week to week, it will do just as well, for we can assure them they actually take place." The paper lasted less than a year, a lesson ignored by later publishers at their peril.

Mass circulation did not become the key to political influence until the middle of the nineteenth century. In the age of Andrew Jackson, powerful editors such as Amos Kendall, Thurlow Weed, and Thomas Ritchie owed their power to their parties, not their subscription lists. It was local editors who inspired voters and made electoral politics work.

The main-line press was not the pioneer of mass circulation. Evangelicals and social movements stemming from the religious impulse led the way in providing news for all. In the 1830s the American Tract Society alone produced five pages of religious information each year for every adult and child in America. Reform movements such as abolitionism broadened the audience for journalism to include women, children, and blacks. In the middle of the 1830s, for example, the American Antislavery Society flooded the mails with its publications.

Some commercial dailies in the largest cities, however, were becoming masters of mass circulation. They commanded capital just as the technological changes in printing demanded large investments. In the 1840s, big-city publications began to take advantage of the railroad and telegraph, and journalists reached an audience undreamed of earlier.

The newspaper became an impulse item in the 1830s when the "penny press" was born in eastern cities. Benjamin Day and James Gordon Bennett, unsatisfied with subscription sales, sent newsboys out to hawk papers. These dailies sold for a penny or two rather than the standard six cents. They mixed crime and adventure with news of politics and trade. Bennett's *New York Herald,* begun in 1835, had sales of 77,000 on the eve of the Civil War, the largest daily circulation in the world. Bennett, a cantankerous Democrat, published news for every taste, from the common reader to the elite. Horace Greeley's *New York Tribune,* also catering to a broad readership, published a weekly edition of 200,000 that circulated in the countryside. Greeley was a hero to urban artisans and entrepreneurs. A cross section of American radicals had their say in his paper, and Karl Marx was one of his European correspondents.

No American magazine had comparable influence before the Civil War. The Jacksonian *Democratic Review,* however, provided an attractive forum for writers such as Nathaniel Hawthorne and Walt Whitman. *Niles' Weekly Register,* a compendium of newspapers, had a grasp of the whole nation that was unmatched by other periodicals. Northern magazines dominated the flow of information and the definition of culture. Even *DeBow's Review,* targeted to southern readers and espousing secession, was published in New York City for about three thousand subscribers. Most contributors to these magazines were either poorly paid or not paid at all.

Magazines came to play a larger role when they published stories and articles directed at readers whom newspapers overlooked. *Godey's Lady's Book,* edited by Sarah J. Hale, and *Peterson's Ladies' National Magazine* helped create the nineteenth-century cult of domesticity. These Philadelphia journals each had 150,000 subscribers by the 1860s. Some of the earlier general interest magazines featured pictures and cartoons. Millions of Americans followed the Civil War in the woodblock prints of *Harper's Weekly* and *Frank Leslie's Illustrated Newspaper.*

After the war, a new breed of powerful dailies appeared. Immigrants and their offspring controlled many of the most influential papers: Joseph Pulitzer ran the *St. Louis Post-Dispatch* and the *New York World;* Adolph S. Ochs, the *New York Times;* Edward W. Scripps, the first great chain of newspapers. A millionaire from California, William Randolph Hearst, followed Pulitzer and Scripps in creating dailies that caught the imagination of working-class Americans. The *Appeal to Reason* of Girard, Kansas, was the one radical publication in modern America to break through to a mass audience. This weekly had a circulation of 750,000 in 1912, and an "appeal army" of eighty thousand subscription agents was busy in every state.

Ethnic newspapers thrived as well; many newcomers found more newspapers printed in their language in the United States than in their homeland. At the turn of the century, for example, there were six Yiddish dailies in New York City. African-Americans founded some forty papers before 1865 and responded to the end of slavery by starting more than one thousand by 1900.

Overall, the United States began the twentieth century with more varied sources of news in print than it had ever had or would have again. The number of daily newspapers alone peaked by 1910 at about twenty-six hundred.

News edited for a particular geographical, ethnic, or political community is limited in its appeal. Magazines of the Gilded Age had sought to bridge these divides, but rarely succeeded. Editors of the *Nation,* the *North American Review,* and the *Atlantic Monthly* had been grateful for ten thousand subscribers. But truly popular magazines capable of setting the national agenda appeared in the 1890s. Publishers cut their prices from the standard thirty-five cents to a nickel, took advantage of printing improvements such as the halftone engraving process, and sought out the best writing of the time.

New entrepreneurs such as S. S. McClure hit upon what Theodore Roosevelt dubbed as "muckraking." The term was taken as a compliment by the men and women who exposed corruption in politics and greed in business. Some of the most celebrated muckraking series were an exposé of patent medicines by Samuel H. Adams, a study of the Senate by David Graham Phillips, a report on urban government by Lincoln Steffens, and a history of the Standard Oil Company by Ida Tarbell. Several muckraking magazines had more than half a million subscribers, and overall, some 20 million American homes followed these investigations. In 1910 Senator Albert J. Beveridge called muckraking a "people's literature" amounting to "almost a mental and moral revolution." No permanent revolution of this type changed the American press, however. Cheap cover prices meant a heavier dependence on advertisers, who objected strongly to such journalism. Moreover, the exploitation of reform themes by so many magazines eventually made the formula stale in a culture attuned to novelty. Finally, as Roosevelt had feared, muckraking made political participation itself seem unappealing.

World War I gave popular journalism a fresh set of ideals as well as villains, and when it ended, few tried to return to the crusades of the prewar era. Several magazines appeared that were targeted at sophisticates: the *Smart Set* and *American Mercury,* edited by newspaperman H. L. Mencken, and the *New Yorker,* founded by Harold Ross in 1925. The general circulation magazines dropped the theme of reform and celebrated a culture of consumption. In the 1920s the *Saturday Evening Post* and *Ladies' Home Journal* became fixtures in middle-class homes and attracted some of the best young writers such as F. Scott Fitzgerald and William Faulkner. The new tabloid newspapers of the 1920s, notably the *New York Daily News,* achieved large circulations by covering crime, sports, and scandal. The most successful effort to win readers to serious topics in the interwar years was the family of magazines begun by Henry Luce: *Time* (1923), *Fortune* (1930), and *Life* (1936), a brilliant exercise in photojournalism.

Luce thought the duty of journalists was to see the world the way he saw it, an outlook shared by such publishers as Robert McCormick of the *Chicago Tribune* and the aging Hearst. But most of the press was no longer a pulpit for owners. As Walter Lippmann observed, professional staffs were exerting more control. The Newspaper Guild, for example, founded during the New Deal, challenged the authority of management over editorial employees. But if owners grew less important, the corporate organization of the press now acquired a greater influence on what Americans read. Newspaper chains, such as those founded in the 1920s by Frank E. Gannett and Samuel I. Newhouse, helped standardize local papers. At the end of World War II, four out of five newspapers were locally owned; in 1990 four out of five were controlled by outside corporations. The United States had more than sixteen hundred daily papers, but just fifteen chief executive officers were responsible for the majority of the circulation. About eleven thousand magazines were published, but with only six corporations accounting for the bulk of the business.

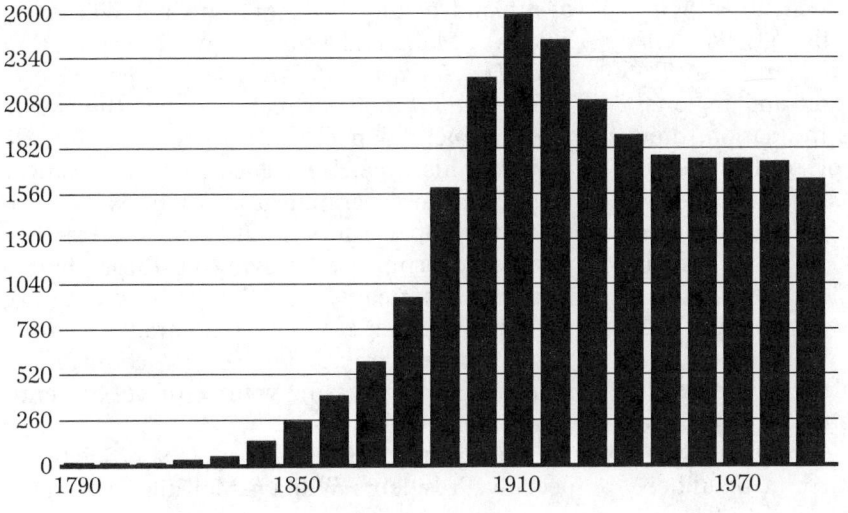

Number of Daily Newspapers in the United States, 1790–1990

Only in folklore were newspapers and magazines in a race for circulation. This competition was real enough when Ben Hecht and Charles MacArthur wrote *The Front Page* (1928), the classic account of journalists who would do anything to beat a rival and sell more papers. In the 1920s more than five hundred cities had competing dailies; sixty years later, there were forty and in only about half of these cities were the papers separately owned. The Newspaper Preservation Act of 1970 exempted failing newspapers from antitrust laws, allowing them to divide up their market. Ninety-eight percent of daily papers had no local competition for readers. General interest magazines found that large circulations could be a disadvantage. The *Saturday Evening Post* died in 1969 with 7 million paying readers; *Life* had even more when it folded in 1972. Individual copies of these weeklies sold for as little as half of what they cost to produce, so publishers had to rely on advertising to make a profit. But many readers were too isolated, too poor, or too old to be an attractive audience for advertisers. Television had eclipsed newspapers and magazines as a general advertising medium.

The age of print journalism as a common denominator providing news for all at a profit was over by the last quarter of the twentieth century. Most dailies were edited to appeal to upscale readers and the advertisers who wanted access to them. Hearst and Pulitzer had believed that everyone should read their papers, and Luce had had the same dream for his magazines. But in 1990, no publication was edited with such an audience in mind. Although the *New York Times,* the *Wall Street Journal,* and *USA Today* used satellite communication and regional printing plants to reach across the nation, they targeted only special groups of readers. Similarly, most successful magazines aimed at desirable consumers, not the public at large.

The press has never lacked critics. Presidents George Washington and Thomas Jefferson were outraged by lies in the newspapers of their times. In the nineteenth century, pictures in the press were condemned as frivolous and misleading. When Upton Sinclair compared the press establishment to a brothel in *The Brass Check* (1919), H. L. Mencken accused him of under-statement. The persistence of such criticism draws attention to an enterprise where the rules have never been clear but expectations have always been high. News in print has never lost the power to shock and worry Americans. The rise of new media has not dulled this concern. The consolidation of the press among fewer owners and narrower readerships means that the criticism has never been more necessary.

Thomas C. Leonard, *The Power of the Press: The Birth of American Political Reporting* (1987); Frank Luther Mott, *A History of American Magazines,* 5 vols. (1930–1968).

Thomas C. Leonard

See also Bennett, James Gordon, and Bennett, James Gordon, Jr.; Bok, Edward; Freedom of the Press; Greeley, Horace; Hearst, William Randolph; Howells, William Dean; Leslie, Frank; Luce, Henry; Mencken, H. L.; Muckrakers; Nast, Thomas; Pulitzer, Joseph; Wallace, DeWitt; Zenger Trial.

MAHAN, ALFRED THAYER

(1840–1914), naval strategist and historian. At a time when he was drifting "aimlessly" as a forty-five-year-old naval officer, Mahan recalled, his life was transformed in a Lima, Peru, library; he interpreted Theodor Mommsen's history of Rome to mean that the Roman Empire had been shaped by its control of the sea. Invited to the new U.S. Naval War College to lecture (because of a bland history he wrote on Civil War naval battles), Mahan developed his interpretation into *The Influence of Sea Power upon History, 1660–1783* (1890), which became the single most influential book on strategy and foreign policy in his time. He argued that naval power resulted from geographical position, excess production, proper national character, and a supportive government. Enjoying all these characteristics, Americans, "whether they will or no, . . . must now begin to look outward," he wrote. "The growing production of the country demands it. An increasing volume of public sentiment demands it."

He strongly influenced key U.S. officials, especially Presidents William McKinley and Theodore Roosevelt (a close friend), to follow the policies dictated by his insight: continual expansion overseas; the taking of Caribbean islands, Hawaii, the Philippines, and other Pacific territory for bases the navy needed to protect commerce; building an isthmian canal so the fleet and freighters could quickly move ocean to ocean; and, of course, constructing the great navy. The fleet, he preached, must be built around giant battleships that could score decisive victories, not small hit-and-run cruisers on which U.S. naval tactics had long depended. A navy that had ninety small ships (thirty-eight wooden) in 1882 became in the 1890s the Great White Fleet of steam-driven, armor-plated battleships that won the war of 1898 and fought in World War I.

Mahan's history and strategy, spelled out in half a dozen major books after 1890, had other far-reaching implications. Such an expansive policy required a powerful president. Mahan worried that the Constitution's restraints were "a lion in the path" of expansion, and he urged that those limits on presidential power be ignored. Believing that the world was dividing between naval powers (the United States, Great Britain, and Japan) and land powers (especially Russia), he urged the former to unite and defeat the latter, especially in Asia. He was even more admired in Great Britain, Japan, and Germany than in the United States. But when Japan dominated East Asia after defeating Russia in 1905, the Japanese discriminated against U.S. interests. Mahan could only urge Americans to pull back to Hawaii. That was an especially bitter decision, because as a hardened conservative he wanted overseas expansion, not "socialist" redistribution measures (which he hated) to solve the problem of excess U.S. production.

Finally, Mahan believed that modern arms were to prevent war, not wage it: "war now not only occurs more rarely . . . [but is] an occasional excess, from which recovery is easy." British historian Charles Webster observed that "Mahan was one of the causes of the First World War." Mahan helped spark a fatal British-German naval race, believing that great bloodshed would never occur. He died just as that bloodshed began.

William E. Livezey, *Mahan on Seapower* (1980); Robert Seager III, *Alfred Thayer Mahan: The Man and His Letters* (1977).

WALTER LaFEBER

See also Armed Forces; Expansion, Continental and Overseas.

MAILER, NORMAN

(1923–   ), novelist and filmmaker. At the climax of Mailer's fourth novel — titled, with bitter irony, *An American Dream* — the hero, who has murdered his wife, walks, drunk, around the parapet of a penthouse on a dare from his millionaire father-in-law. It is a foolish, even a childish thing to do, exhibitionistic and suicidal. And yet, as narrated by the hero, it also moves us as an authentic, existential, even religious validation of the self against the repressive forces of orthodoxy and the establishment.

Much of Mailer's unique, disturbing, and exhilarating presence in American letters is caught in that scene: an awkward tightrope-walk between the abyss and the luxury of success (another kind of abyss, really) that somehow, miraculously, comes off. Mailer *is* the drunken walker on the edge, taking wild risks with his art and his career for over forty years and somehow winning more often than he loses, and, most important, convincing us that this sort of risk-taking is crucial not just to his own self-definition but also to *our* imaginative survival in the big business, high-tech, soul-eating mindscape of post–World War II America. *Advertisements for Myself* he titled his 1965 collection of essays, poems, and stories: he has in fact not just advertised himself but made himself into a metaphor for the complex fate of the modern American imagination.

His first novel, *The Naked and the Dead* (1948), was an immense success and immensely misunderstood. There are still critics who speak of the "realism" of this war novel as if it were a standard from which his later work declined. In fact, there are no conventional battle scenes in the book. It is really not a "war novel" at all, as much as it is Mailer's prophetic vision of the America that will *follow* the war, an America divided between the spiritually "naked," who insist upon living life as a romantic quest for ultimate values, and the spiritually "dead," who embrace the killing blandishments of wealth and power. To see this is to see that Mailer has always been a moral allegorist, a legitimate heir of Henry Thoreau, Ralph Waldo Emerson, and Walt Whitman, and to see why his own career has been a constant flight from predictability, why for him "success" has to be a continual reinvention of himself against the very literary establishment that wants to canonize him, a "success" that only he can prove and that must be proved anew with every book.

No wonder, then, that in the fifties he was aligned with the antiestablishment Beat movement (though never quite fully a part of it) or that in the sixties and seventies his influence as well as his voice was strong among the writers of the new political and literary left (e.g., Thomas Pynchon, Kurt Vonnegut, Don DeLillo). As novelist and as essayist, his voice is a consistent and wryly radical one. He admits that he has made it, become a permanent and permanently salable member of the literary establishment, and yet he resolutely refuses to settle for that. "History as a Novel" and "The Novel as History" are the subdivisions of his great 1970 book on the Vietnam War, *The Armies of the Night*. For this blustering, sometimes buffoonish man, politics and fiction are, at a very deep level, a single visionary act, an act of moral urgency for writer and readers alike. His novels of the eighties, *Ancient Evenings* (1982) and *Tough Guys Don't Dance* (1984), show nothing as much as the undiminished quality of his energy, the one a meditation on the morality of warfare set in pharaonic Egypt, the other an exploration of American sexual confusion cast as a hard-boiled detective novel. A self-made insider whose sympathies are all with the outsiders — the losers, bums, killers, and poets — Mailer has kept himself heroically on the edge and in doing so inspired a great deal of very good writing by others. If his talent is enormous, his influence and importance are likely to loom even larger.

Peter Manso, *Mailer: His Life and Times* (1985); Frank D. McConnell, *Four Postwar American Novelists* (1977).

FRANK D. MCCONNELL

See also Literature.

MAIL-ORDER HOUSES

Although goods could be purchased by mail since colonial times, what could properly be called modern mail-order houses were first established in the 1870s and 1880s. They were developed to tap the vast market for goods among isolated American farmers who did not have access to good-quality merchandise at reasonable prices. Local merchants with whom farmers did business often offered only a limited choice of goods, and these were relatively expensive.

In 1872, A. Montgomery Ward organized the first mail-order house. With headquarters in Chicago, Montgomery Ward and Company began supplying goods to members of the Grange, the largest farm organization of the time. The firm was soon selling goods ordered by catalog to tens of thousands of midwestern farmers. By the early 1890s, Montgomery Ward was distributing a 280-page catalog advertising some ten thousand items.

It was Richard W. Sears, however, who established the most successful mail-order house. In 1886 Sears began selling watches by mail from Redwood Falls, Minnesota, and hired A. C. Roebuck as a watch repairman. He sold this business in 1889 and organized another mail-order firm to sell jewelry and watches. In 1894 he incorporated Sears, Roebuck and Company, a general mail-order house, and set up business in Chicago.

Sears was a master advertiser and salesman. In the pages of his catalog, sent to thousands of farm homes, he emphasized the variety, style, and low prices of his goods. The Sears catalog in 1897 contained 786 carefully indexed pages of a seemingly endless variety of food, apparel, hardware, machinery, household, and other items. Farmers could order a hammer, harness, wagon, or plow, and their wives could buy a corset, hat, sewing machine, or cook stove. In 1900 Sears was selling about $10 million worth of merchandise by mail a year, surpassing Montgomery Ward.

Farmers found that mail-order houses had several advantages over local merchants. The larger selection of goods included the latest models and styles, and many items in the catalog were not available at all in country stores. Farmers also liked the convenience of shopping by mail. A trip to town, often ten or more miles away, took several hours by horse and buggy; ordering by mail saved time that could be better spent working in the field. But the most attractive feature of buying from a mail-order house was the cheaper prices. Sears boasted in his 1897 catalog that the company could provide "the best goods at lower prices than they can be had elsewhere." Improved selection, convenience, and better prices combined to win Sears and Montgomery Ward a huge volume of farm business in the late nineteenth and early twentieth centuries. By 1915 the two companies were selling nearly $200 million worth of merchandise annually. And not surprisingly, local merchants strongly objected to the competition.

Rural free delivery of mail, begun in the 1890s, and parcel post, inaugurated in 1913, made it even more convenient to order by mail, and Sears and Montgomery Ward profited accordingly. Farmers and small-town residents could place their order in the mail box and have all but the largest items delivered by carrier in a matter of days. In 1925 Sears alone sold about $243 million worth of goods, over 95 percent of it by mail.

Other mail-order houses in the late nineteenth century included the National Cloak and Suit Company, which sold women's clothing out of New York, and the Chicago Mail Order House. Spiegel began selling by mail in 1904. But none of these companies approached the success of Sears and Montgomery Ward.

The mail-order houses had an important influence on farm and rural living. Farmers, often portrayed as poorly dressed and living under backward conditions, could now turn to mail-order houses for stylish goods and modern conveniences. This contributed not only to their comfort but to their self-esteem. The ability to buy goods by mail helped break down farm isolation and played a major role in homogenizing American society.

But the relative importance of mail-order houses began to decline in the late 1920s. Automobiles and improved roads made it easy for rural residents to travel long distances to shop. To adjust to this development, Sears and Montgomery Ward began establishing retail stores in 1925 and 1926, respectively, to tap the growing business in larger towns. Sears catalog sales had dropped to only 54 percent of the firm's total business by 1930. Fast and cheap transportation changed farm and small-town buying habits so drastically that though Sears has continued to sell by mail, Montgomery Ward in 1985 quit the mail-order business altogether.

Following World War II, however, a large number of specialty mail-order houses were established. Some of these companies sold only by mail; others used catalog sales to supplement business at their stores. By 1988 it took 312 pages just to list the hundreds of companies selling a great variety of products directly to consumers by mail. One could order food, electronic equipment, auto parts, clothing, and thousands of other items.

The mail-order catalogs that flooded American homes in the late twentieth century filled the public's changing needs. Millions of women had joined the work force, and by shopping by mail, they saved time and avoided crowds at shopping malls and department stores. This method of shopping was made even easier by toll-free telephone ordering and the growing use of credit cards. In the 1980s telemarketing provided yet another way to purchase goods by mail. The prospective buyer could see the merchandise and the price on the television screen, phone in an order, and pay with a credit card.

Over a century after Montgomery Ward and Sears, Roebuck had begun doing business, mail-order houses were still going strong. But now farmers had become a tiny minority of the nation's population, and the business catered to urbanites hard-pressed for time.

Boris Emmet and John E. Jeuck, *Catalogues and Counters: A History of Sears Roebuck and Company* (1950); Cecil C. Hoge, Sr., *The First Hundred Years Are the Toughest: What We Can Learn from the Century of Competition between Sears and Wards* (1988).

GILBERT C. FITE

MALCOLM X

(1925–1965), black leader. Born Malcolm Little in Omaha, Nebraska, Malcolm was the son of a

Baptist preacher who was a follower of Marcus Garvey. After the Ku Klux Klan made threats against his father, the family moved to Lansing, Michigan. There, in the face of similar threats, he continued to urge blacks to take control of their lives.

Malcolm's father was slain by the Klan-like Black Legionaries. Although he was found with his head crushed on one side and almost severed from his body, it was claimed he had committed suicide, and the family was denied his death benefit. Its disintegration quickly followed: welfare caseworkers sought to turn the children against each other and against their mother, from whom Malcolm, then six, was taken and placed in a foster home. Mrs. Little underwent a nervous breakdown from which she never recovered.

After the eighth grade, Malcolm dropped out of school, headed for a life of crime. He wore zoot suits, straightened his hair to affect a white look, and became known as "Detroit Red." When twenty-one, he was sentenced to prison for burglary and there encountered the teachings of Elijah Muhammad, leader of the Lost-Found Nation of Islam, popularly known as the Black Muslims. Muhammad's thesis that the white man is the devil with whom blacks cannot live had a strong impact on Malcolm. Turning to an ascetic way of life and reading widely, he began to overcome the degradation he had known. The argument that only blacks can cure the ills that afflict them confirmed for Malcolm the power of Muhammad's faith. He became a loyal disciple and adopted X — symbolic of a stolen identity — as his last name.

After six years Malcolm was released from prison. Later, he became the minister of Temple No. 7 in Harlem, his indictments of racism and his advocacy of self-defense eliciting admiration, as well as fear, far beyond the New York black community. Whites were especially fearful, recoiling from his sustained pronouncements of crimes against his people. While most contrasted him with Martin Luther King, Jr., with whose philosophy they were much more at ease, white college students found ugly truths in his searing rhetoric of condemnation. Malcolm, however, grew increasingly restive as the Nation of Islam failed to join in the mounting civil rights struggle and became convinced that Elijah Muhammad was lacking in sincerity, a view painfully validated by corruption at the highest level of the organization. For his part, Muhammad seemed threatened by the popularity of Malcolm, whose influence reached even into the respected Student Non-Violent Coordinating Committee (SNCC).

Malcolm's assertion that President John F. Kennedy's assassination amounted to "the chickens coming home to roost" led to his suspension from the Black Muslims in December 1963. A few months later, he left the organization, traveled to Mecca, and discovered that orthodox Muslims preach equality of the races, which led him to abandon the argument that whites are devils. Having returned to America as El-Hajj Malik El-Shabazz, he remained convinced that racism had corroded the spirit of America and that only blacks could free themselves. In June 1964, he founded the Organization of Afro-American Unity and moved increasingly in the direction of socialism. More sophisticated than in his Black Muslim days and of growing moral stature, he was assassinated by a Black Muslim at a rally of his organization in New York on February 21, 1965. Malcolm X had predicted that, though he had but little time to live, he would be more important in death than in life. Foreshadowings of his martyrdom are found in *The Autobiography of Malcolm X*. The almost painful honesty that enabled him to find his way from degradation to devotion to his people, the modest lifestyle that kept him on the edge of poverty, and the distance he somehow managed to put between himself and racial hatred serve, in that volume, as poignant reminders of human possibility and achievement.

Influenced largely by Malcolm, in the summer of 1966 members of SNCC called for black power for black people. Their lack of power was the foundation of Malcolm's charge that they were denied human rights in America. His clarity on this matter, as America continues its retreat from its commitment to full freedom for his people, has guaranteed for him pride of place among black leaders.

George Breitman, ed., *Malcolm X Speaks* (1965); Peter Goldman, "Malcolm X," in *Dictionary of American Negro*

Biography (1982); Malcolm X, *The Autobiography of Malcolm X* (1965).

STERLING STUCKEY

See also Black Nationalism; Civil Rights Movement.

MANHATTAN PROJECT

America's development of the atomic bomb was called the Manhattan Project because it was administered after 1942 by a section of the army code-named the Manhattan District. Pressure for the project began in 1939, when two scientists in Berlin accomplished atomic fission in uranium. Believing that Germany might successfully develop an atomic bomb, Albert Einstein and other physicists persuaded President Franklin D. Roosevelt to establish a small research program.

In June 1941 the Office of Scientific Research and Development (OSRD), headed by Vannevar Bush, was created to coordinate all government-sponsored scientific efforts, including the work on atomic fission. Under OSRD the fission project expanded, involving teams at a number of universities, including Columbia, Princeton, California, and Chicago. By the spring of 1942, these teams had confirmed that atomic fission was possible through a chain reaction in uranium, and Dr. Ernest Lawrence in California had shown that rather than their requiring the very scarce uranium isotope U-235, they could convert a more common one, U-238, into a new fissionable element, plutonium.

In June 1942, Bush and his colleagues reported to the president that creating an atomic bomb appeared to be feasible, and that although the project would be extraordinarily demanding — scientifically, logistically, and financially — it could be accomplished in time to affect the course of the war. Roosevelt gave his approval to proceed, and the Manhattan District was established within the Army Corps of Engineers to coordinate resource mobilization and production.

Dr. Arthur Compton's team in Chicago produced the first chain reaction in uranium in December 1942. Thereafter, actually building the bomb became the primary focus. In 1943, after a new laboratory for the purpose was established in Los Alamos, New Mexico, under the direction of J. Robert Oppenheimer, the Army assumed full control of the project. Over the next two years, researchers worked furiously to solve a myriad of scientific problems. Gen. Leslie R. Groves supervised the vast project, keeping its intricate phases synchronized, establishing huge plants in Oak Ridge, Tennessee, and Hanford, Washington, to produce the needed materials, setting and enforcing production schedules, and maintaining security. In all, development of the bomb involved the labors of 125,000 people and cost nearly $2 billion.

The first test explosion took place July 16, 1945, at Alamogordo, New Mexico; its stunning success filled those present with both jubilation and awe. By order of the new president, Harry S. Truman, the first atomic bomb was dropped on Hiroshima, Japan, on August 6, 1945, followed by a second on Nagasaki three days later. The Japanese surrender followed on August 14. The successful conclusion of the Manhattan Project marked the beginning of the nuclear age.

See also Nuclear Weapons: Origins and Legacy; World War II.

MANIFEST DESTINY

The term *manifest destiny* originated in the 1840s. It expressed the belief that it was Anglo-Saxon Americans' providential mission to expand their civilization and institutions across the breadth of North America. This expansion would involve not merely territorial aggrandizement but the progress of liberty and individual economic opportunity as well.

The phrase was first employed by John L. O'Sullivan in an article on the annexation of Texas published in the July-August 1845 edition of the *United States Magazine and Democratic Review*, which he edited. It was, O'Sullivan claimed, "our manifest destiny to overspread the continent allotted by Providence for the free development of our yearly multiplying millions." The term and the concept were taken up by those desiring to secure Oregon Territory, California, Mexican land in the Southwest, and, in the 1850s, Cuba. Originally a partisan Democratic issue, "manifest destiny" gained Republican adherents as time passed. By the end of the century, expansionists were employing quasi-Darwinist reasoning to argue that because its "Anglo-Saxon heritage" made America supremely fit, it had become the nation's "manifest destiny" to extend its influence beyond its continental boundaries into the Pacific and Caribbean basins.

See also Expansion, Continental and Overseas.

MANN, HORACE

(1796–1859), educator and reformer. Mann is well known as "the father of the American common school." A successful lawyer and member of the Massachusetts state legislature from 1827 to 1837, Mann was elected first secretary of the Massachusetts Board of Education in 1837. His willingness to give up a successful career in law and politics to become secretary of the board astonished many of his contemporaries. But the state's schools were in poor condition, and Mann, who was depressed following the recent death of his wife, was eager to absorb himself in a challenging benevolent cause. He found in the post a moral vocation and became what he later described as a "circuit rider to the next generation." As secretary of the board, he had little power to effect change, but he approached his responsibilities with passion and used the power he did have to maximum advantage.

As secretary of the board for twelve years, Mann traveled across the state, visiting schools and giving lectures. He started a biweekly *Common School Journal* for teachers, wrote stirring and informative annual reports to the state legislature, and published articles and essays about education in a wide range of newspapers and journals. As a result of his great skill in developing arguments that appealed to the particular interests of different constituencies, he turned school reform into one of the most popular campaigns of the reform movements of the era. When addressing audiences of manufacturers, Mann spoke of the importance of public schooling in the development of an educated and virtuous work force; when speaking before audiences of working people, he stressed the

necessity of public schooling in the furtherance of social and economic equality. He convinced many among his contemporaries that "the common school, improved and energized, . . . may become the most effective and benignant of all the forces of civilization." By the time he left office, the state legislature had more than doubled its school appropriations, teachers' salaries had risen (62 percent for men, 54 percent for women), the school year had been extended, and the state had established its first normal school for teacher training. Mann's annual reports circulated widely throughout the United States and in some Latin American and European nations as well. The example set by school reform in Massachusetts helped make the common school movement a popular cause nationwide.

In 1848, Mann resigned from the secretaryship, having been elected to John Quincy Adams's seat in the U.S. House of Representatives as an antislavery Whig. He was associated with a wide range of midcentury reforms and enthusiasms. In addition to opposing slavery, he supported temperance and advocated the establishment of a hospital for the insane in Massachusetts. In 1852, he ran for the governorship of Massachusetts as a Free-Soil candidate but was defeated. The following year, he became president of Antioch College in Yellow Springs, Ohio, a college established to provide equal opportunity to all students regardless of race, sex, or creed.

Lawrence A. Cremin, ed., *The Republic and the School: Horace Mann on the Education of Free Men* (1957); Jonathan Messerli, *Horace Mann: A Biography* (1972).

ELLEN CONDLIFFE LAGEMANN

See also Education.

MANUFACTURING

See Automobiles; Industrial Revolution; Iron and Steel Industry; Labor; Lowell System; Model T Ford; Textile Industry.

MAPP V. OHIO

In this 1961 case the Supreme Court ruled that the Fourteenth Amendment applied Fourth

Amendment protections against unreasonable searches and seizures to citizens in their dealings with individual states. The state of Ohio prosecuted Dollree Mapp for possessing illegal materials that officials had seized from her home without a search warrant. In *Wolf* v. *Colorado* (1949) the Court had denied that this "exclusionary rule" applied to the states, but the *Mapp* decision overturned *Wolf.* The opinion, written by Justice Tom C. Clark, eliminated the double standard. The requirement that all evidence be obtained legally "may appear as a technicality" benefiting a guilty party in a particular case, Clark wrote, but "tolerance of shortcut methods in law enforcement impairs its enduring effectiveness."

The number of search warrants issued increased dramatically following the decision. Supreme Court rulings in 1983 and 1984 narrowed *Mapp* by accepting evidence secured by warrants that were flawed but executed in good faith.

See also Bill of Rights; Constitution; Police Forces; Warren, Earl.

MARBURY V. MADISON

In *Marbury* v. *Madison* (1803) the Supreme Court announced for the first time the principle that a court may declare an act of Congress void if it is inconsistent with the Constitution. William Marbury had been appointed a justice of the peace for the District of Columbia in the final hours of the Adams administration. When James Madison, Thomas Jefferson's secretary of state, refused to deliver Marbury's commission, Marbury, joined by three other similarly situated appointees, petitioned for a writ of mandamus compelling delivery of the commissions. Chief Justice John Marshall, writing for a unanimous Court, denied the petition and refused to issue the writ. Although he found that the petitioners were entitled to their commissions, he held that the Constitution did not give the Supreme Court the power to issue writs of mandamus. Section 13 of the Judiciary Act of 1789 provided that such writs might be issued, but that section of the act was inconsistent with the Constitution and therefore invalid.

Although the immediate effect of the decision was to deny power to the Court, its long-run effect has been to increase the Court's power by establishing the rule that "it is emphatically the province and duty of the judicial department to say what the law is." Since *Marbury* v. *Madison* the Supreme Court has been the final arbiter of the constitutionality of congressional legislation.

See also Supreme Court.

MARCHES ON WASHINGTON: 1941, 1963

Twice in American history, more than twenty years apart, a March on Washington was planned, each intended to dramatize the right of black Americans to political and economic equality.

The first march was proposed in 1941 by A. Philip Randolph, president of the Brotherhood of Sleeping Car Porters. Blacks had benefited less than other groups from New Deal programs during the Great Depression, and continuing racial discrimination excluded them from defense jobs in the early 1940s. When President Franklin D. Roosevelt showed little inclination to take action on the problem, Randolph called for a March on Washington by fifty thousand people. After repeated efforts to persuade Randolph and his fellow leaders that the march would be inadvisable, Roosevelt issued Executive Order 8802 in June 1941, forbidding discrimination by any defense contractors and establishing the Fair Employment Practices Committee (FEPC) to investigate charges of racial discrimination. The March on Washington was then canceled. Nearly 2 million blacks were employed in defense work by the end of 1944. Order 8802 represented a limited victory, however; the FEPC went out of existence in 1946.

As blacks faced continuing discrimination in the postwar years, the March on Washington group met annually to reiterate blacks' demands for economic equality. The civil rights movement of the 1960s transformed the political climate, and in 1963, black leaders began to plan a new March on Washington, designed specifically to advocate passage of the Civil Rights Act then stalled in Congress. Chaired again by A. Philip Randolph and organized by his longtime associate, Bayard Rustin, this new March for Jobs and Freedom was expected to attract 100,000 participants. President John F. Kennedy showed as little enthusiasm for the march as had Roosevelt, but this time the black leaders would not be dissuaded. The National Association for the Advancement of Colored People and the Southern Christian Leadership Conference put aside their long-standing rivalry, black and white groups across the country were urged to attend, and elaborate arrangements were made to ensure a harmonious event. The growing disillusion among some civil rights workers was reflected in a speech planned by John Lewis of the Student Non-Violent Coordinating Committee, but in order to preserve the atmosphere of goodwill, leaders of the march persuaded Lewis to omit his harshest criticisms of the Kennedy administration.

The march was an unprecedented success. More than 200,000 black and white Americans shared a joyous day of speeches, songs, and prayers led by a celebrated array of clergymen, civil rights leaders, politicians, and entertainers. The Reverend Dr. Martin Luther King's soaring address climaxed the day; through his eloquence, the phrase "I Have a Dream" became an expression of the highest aspirations of the civil rights movement.

Like its predecessor, the March on Washington of 1963 was followed by years of disillusion and racial strife. Nevertheless, both marches represented an affirmation of hope, of belief in the democratic process, and of faith in the capacity of blacks and whites to work together for racial equality.

See also Civil Rights Movement; Racial Desegregation; Randolph, A. Philip.

MARÍN, LUIS MUÑOZ

See Muñoz Marín, Luis.

MARINE CORPS

See Armed Forces.

MARRIAGE

For people of European origin in colonial America, marriage was an act of practicality. Although a respectful love was supposed to develop in the course of the union, neither sexual attraction nor romantic love was the basis for wedlock. Marriage, as in England, was a form of alliance between families, stemming from considerations of property, religion, and complementary abilities. The fathers of the couple had the legal right to give or withhold consent, and they frequently entered into economic negotiations before the engagement was formally concluded. The bride usually brought with her a dowry of household goods, clothing, and money; the groom provided land, house, and tools. Marriage, in the tradition of English law, subsumed the legal being of the wife into that of the husband. Under this system, called coverture, when a woman married she lost her right to own property or enter into contracts.

In seventeenth-century New England, marriage took place and endured in a tight network of family and community control. It was a central institution in a society that defined the family as a major source of stability and order. But in the Chesapeake region, marriages were highly unstable. In the first generation of settlement, there were approximately four men to every woman in contrast to the New England ratio of three to two. As a result, it was difficult for men to marry and form families. Both illegitimacy rates and rates of premarital intercourse were high — approximately one-third of all women were pregnant when they wed, compared to about one-tenth of women in New England. This rate reflected the looser family and community controls in the South and the weaker status of religion, but the shortage of women may also have been a factor: chastity was a less important qualification for marriage when there were fewer women. An extremely high death rate was another cause of marital instability. About half of all marriages were broken by the death of one of the partners within seven years.

By the mid-eighteenth century, marriage had come to be based increasingly on love and affection. Married couples now referred to each other by first names or terms of endearment in their correspondence, replacing the impersonal "Sir" and "Madam" of the previous era. This trend intensified steadily, and by the nineteenth century the sentimental doctrines of romantic love had come to prevail. Nonetheless, Victorian marriages demanded strict fulfillment of gender-specific roles that were centered around family responsibilities and were based far more on ideals of duty than on self-fulfillment.

Slaves were prohibited from legal marriage, but most did enter into formal unions solemnized either in church weddings before black or white preachers or through simple ceremonies such as jumping over a broomstick. Because most African-Americans in bondage lived on small plantations with fewer than twenty slaves, many had to seek partners elsewhere, in what were called "broad marriages." Slaves had to have their owners' permission to marry, and about one in six marriages was broken by the sale of one of the partners. This happened so often, in fact, that one slave preacher married members of his community with the phrase "until death or distance do you part." Up to 20 percent of slave women had an "outside child" before marrying. Although this practice was at odds with the mores of the slave-owning class, it was probably in line with the practices of poor southern whites.

Many nineteenth-century utopian and religious movements considered the transformation of the institution of marriage to be fundamental to their particular visions of a reordered society. Members of the Oneida community, for example, practiced "complex marriage," in which all members of the community were married to all others, and sexual contact was regulated by the group. Advocates of "free love" argued that monogamous marriage oppressed women. Mormons adopted a polygamous system, which outraged many Americans. Utah was not admitted to the Union until the Mormon church renounced the practice. It was outlawed by the Supreme Court in 1878 on the ground that marriage is a civil contract regulated by law.

During the early decades of the twentieth century a sexual revolution took place. Premarital intercourse became more common, and this contributed to changing ideas about marriage. A new "companionate marriage" promised individual fulfillment, with couples bound together by mutual love and sexual attraction, not concepts of duty. This was essentially a middle-class ideal, however, that did not extend to many immigrants, rural folk, poor whites, or African-Americans.

During the Great Depression marriage rates plummeted, as it became economically difficult for young people to form new households. The marriage rate dropped almost 13 percent between 1930 and 1932, and by the end of the decade the average age at marriage had risen from 24.3 to 26.7 for men and from 21.3 to 23.3 for women. The divorce rate also fell, for many couples could not afford a legal divorce. Separation and desertion rates were high, however.

World War II brought economic recovery but also uncertainties about the future, and for both reasons, the marriage rate boomed. Between 1940 and 1942, one thousand servicemen and their brides married each day. Marriage rates remained high through the 1950s, and the average age at marriage dropped until by 1959, 47 percent of all brides were under nineteen. The staging of weddings became a small industry, and marriage was celebrated throughout popular culture. According to a 1957 poll, only 9 percent of Americans thought a single person could be happy. The ideal marriage was said to be a "partnership," centered around children and devoted to "togetherness."

But this decade-long celebration masked many tensions over men's and women's roles within marriage, and as the women's movement developed in the 1960s and 1970s, feminists began criticizing the institution. A second twentieth-century sexual revolution and the advent of the birth-control pill weakened the connection between sex and marriage. Average age at marriage began to rise again, and the divorce rate soared. "Living together" became commonplace, and the percentage of households composed of two unrelated members of the opposite sex tripled between 1970 and 1980 and rose another 14 percent between 1981 and 1982. This prompted the U.S. Census Bureau to coin the term POSSLQ, meaning "persons of the opposite sex sharing living quarters." Gay and lesbian couples claimed the right to legal marriage and won limited recognition in some cities. Marriage, however, remained a central institution in American society, although it had changed dramatically in both practice and ideology over the course of American history.

Elaine Tyler May, *Homeward Bound: American Families in the Cold War Era* (1988); Steven Mintz, *Domestic Revolutions: A Social History of American Family Life* (1988).

BETH BAILEY

See also Birth Control; Childhood; Divorce; Family.

MARRIED WOMEN'S PROPERTY ACTS

Before the middle of the nineteenth century, the property rights of American married women followed the dictates of common law, under which everything a woman owned became her husband's property upon her marriage. Married women could not hold, buy, or sell property, sue or be sued, enter into contracts, or retain their own wages. Between 1839 and 1895, this tradition was gradually reversed by a series of Married Women's Property Acts, passed in varying forms by every state in the Union.

In some states, the acts were limited in scope, shaped primarily to serve the interests of fathers wishing to protect their estates from improvident sons-in-law and husbands seeking to sequester their own property from seizure for debts. Typical of this pattern was America's first Married Women's Property Act, passed in Mississippi in 1839. This law (most of which dealt specifically with slaveholdings) guaranteed the right of married women to receive income from their property and protected it against being seized for their husbands' debts, but the law left husbands in sole charge of buying, selling, or managing the property.

In other states, especially where women's rights movements took a leading role in the campaigns, more ambitious property reform laws were passed, usually during the decade before the Civil War. In New York State in 1860, for instance, the lobbying of women's rights advocates like Elizabeth Cady Stanton helped win passage of one of the nation's most comprehensive Married Women's Property Acts. This law guaranteed wives' right to own, buy, and sell property, to sign contracts, to sue and be sued, to keep their own wages, and to be joint guardians of their children. By the mid-1870s, almost all the states in the North had passed Married Women's Property Acts, and by the end of the century, the southern states had as well. Although the scope of these laws varied widely from state to state, taken together they represented a sweeping transfer of property rights and a historic improvement in the status of American married women.

See also Feminist Movement; Marriage.

MARSHALL, GEORGE C.

(1880–1959), U.S. Army general, secretary of state, and secretary of defense. Commissioned lieutenant of infantry in 1902 after graduation from the Virginia Military Institute, Marshall won armywide recognition in World War I as training and planning officer of the first (American) division to go into action in France, as a planner at Gen. John J. Pershing's headquarters, and as chief of operations of the First Army. His vital contributions between the wars came in the five years he served as assistant commandant in charge of instruction at the Infantry School, Fort Benning, Georgia. Named chief of staff of the army in 1939, Marshall assumed command of the army and its air forces on the day war began in Europe. Holding this position for more than six years, Marshall increased his combined forces from 200,000 to more than 8.5 million. Winston Churchill pronounced him "the true organizer of victory" for his work as trainer, planner, and strategist. More than any other military leader, he was known for his advocacy of a cross-channel attack as the quickest way to defeat Germany.

He retired from the army in November 1945 only to be sent as head of a mission to China to make peace there between the Nationalists and Communists. After the failure of that mission, in early 1947 President Harry S. Truman appointed him secretary of state. Soon Marshall attended a conference in Moscow with British, French, and Soviet counterparts, trying futilely to make treaties with Germany and Austria. He saw the growing economic collapse of Europe and the obvious intent of Soviet Russia to benefit from that collapse, and he returned from the conference in April determined to seek a solution to this problem.

In a June 5 address during Harvard University's commencement observances, Marshall proposed that European countries take the initiative and suggest a plan for American economic aid for their recovery. When that proposal, dubbed by Truman "the Marshall Plan," was debated in Congress early in 1948, Marshall worked with congressional committees and made speeches throughout the country to guide the legislation through a Republican-controlled Congress. At the end of a year of crises and confrontations with the Soviets in central Europe, Marshall entered a hospital for removal of a diseased kidney and resigned early in the new year. When he recovered, Truman asked him that fall to head the American Red Cross.

A year later when North Korean troops had invaded South Korea, Truman urged Marshall to become secretary of defense. During the year that he agreed to stay in that post, the aging Marshall augmented army strength, secured U.N. military aid, and strengthened the North Atlantic Treaty Organization that he had helped foster in 1948. He retired for the last time in September 1951, after nearly fifty years of military and civilian public service. For his efforts toward European political and economic reconstruction he received the Nobel Peace Prize in 1953.

Often aloof and austere in manner in wartime, Marshall was remembered by friends as a man of warmth and compassion and of absolute integrity. Associates have placed him in the company of George Washington and Robert E. Lee as one who served his country selflessly, without thought of ambition or reward. Nonpartisan to the extent of never voting, he firmly believed that a democratic society required complete military subordination to civilian control.

Larry Bland, ed., *The Papers of George C. Marshall,* 2 vols. to date (1981–); George C. Marshall, *Memoirs of My Service in the World War* (1976); Forrest C. Pogue, *George C. Marshall,* 4 vols. (1963–1987).

FORREST C. POGUE

See also Armed Forces; Korean War; Marshall Plan; North Atlantic Treaty Organization; World War II.

MARSHALL, JOHN

(1755–1835), chief justice of the U.S. Supreme Court. Marshall, who had almost no formal schooling and studied law for only six weeks, nevertheless remains the only judge in American history whose distinction as a statesman derived almost entirely from his judicial career. Combat experience during the Revolution helped him develop a continental viewpoint. After admission to the bar in 1780, he entered the Virginia assembly and rose rapidly in state politics. He had good looks, a charismatic personality, and a debater's gifts. A Federalist in politics, he championed the Constitution in his state's ratification convention. Following a diplomatic mission to France, he won election to Congress, where he supported President John Adams. Adams appointed him secretary of state and in 1801 chief justice, a position he held until death.

John Jay, the first chief justice, who had resigned, described the Court as lacking "weight" and "respect." After Marshall no one could make that complaint. In 1801 he and his colleagues had to meet in a tiny room in the basement of the Capitol because the planners of Washington, D.C., had forgotten to provide space for the Supreme Court. Marshall made the Court a prestigious, coordinate branch of the government. In 1824 Senator Martin Van Buren, a political enemy, conceded that the Court attracted "idolatry" and its chief was admired "as the ablest Judge now sitting upon any judicial bench in the world."

During Marshall's thirty-four years as chief justice, he gave content to the Constitution's omissions, clarified its ambiguities, and added breathtaking sweep to the powers it conferred. He set the Court on a course for "ages to come" that would make the U.S. government supreme in the federal system and the Court the Constitution's expositor. He acted as if he were the enduring Framer whose constituency was the nation; he knew the true meaning of the Constitution and he meant it to prevail; he made his position a judicial pulpit to foster the Union of his dreams and to compete, if possible, with the political branches in shaping public opinion and national policy.

Marshall's judicial energies were as indefatigable as his vision was broad. Although he cast but a single vote and was eventually surrounded by colleagues appointed by a party he deplored, he dominated the Court as no one has since. He scrapped seriatim opinions in favor of a single "opinion of the Court" and during his long tenure wrote nearly half the Court's opinions in all fields of law and two-thirds of those involving constitutional questions. He exercised judicial review, firmly over state statutes and state courts, prudently over acts of Congress. *Marbury v. Madison* (1803) remains the fundamental case. Marshall read principles of vested rights into the contract clause and expanded the Court's jurisdiction. Notwithstanding judicial rhetoric conjuring up the bugles of Valley Forge, his judicial nationalism, which was real enough and helped emancipate American commerce in *Gibbons v. Ogden* (1824), sometimes constituted a guise to block regulatory state legislation that limited property rights. He linked the Constitution with national supremacy, capitalism, and judicial review.

Leonard Baker, *John Marshall: A Life in Law* (1974); Albert J. Beveridge, *The Life of John Marshall*, 4 vols. (1916–1919).

LEONARD W. LEVY

See also Constitution; Federalist Party; *Gibbons v. Ogden*; *Marbury v. Madison*; Supreme Court.

MARSHALL, THURGOOD

(1908–), associate justice, U.S. Supreme Court, and civil rights advocate. Marshall earned an important place in American history on the basis of two accomplishments. First, as legal counsel for the National Association for the Advancement of Colored People (NAACP), he guided the litigation that destroyed the legal underpinnings of Jim Crow segregation. Second, as an associate justice of the Supreme Court — the nation's first black justice — he crafted a distinctive jurisprudence marked by uncompromising liberalism, unusual attentiveness to practical considerations beyond the formalities of law, and an indefatigable willingness to dissent.

Marshall was born in Baltimore, Maryland, attended that city's racially segregated public schools, and graduated from Lincoln University. He received his law degree from Howard University where he came under the influence of Charles Hamilton Houston, dean of the law school and a pioneer in the use of litigation as a mode of social reform.

Between 1934 and 1961, as an attorney for the NAACP, Marshall traveled throughout the United States, representing all manner of clients whenever a dispute involved questions of racial justice — from trials for common crimes to appellate advocacy raising the most intricate matters of constitutional law. His exploits earned him the appellation "Mr. Civil Rights." He argued thirty-two cases before the Supreme Court, prevailing in twenty-nine of them. These cases include *Smith v. Allwright* (1944), which invalidated the so-called white primary (the practice of barring blacks from the Democratic party primary in a state where that party controlled state government), *Shelley v. Kraemer* (1948), which prohibited state courts from enforcing racially restrictive real estate covenants, and *Brown v. Board of Education of Topeka,* which invalidated state-enforced racial segregation in the public schools.

The next stage in Marshall's career consisted of a series of high-level appointments. In 1961, President John F. Kennedy appointed him to the U.S. Court of Appeals. In 1965, President Lyndon B. Johnson appointed him solicitor general, another racial "first." And in 1967, President Johnson appointed Marshall to the Supreme Court, declaring that it was "the right thing to do, the right time to do it, the right man and the right place."

Justice Marshall was an outspoken liberal

on a Court dominated by conservatives. In his twenty-four year tenure, he voted to uphold gender and racial affirmative action policies in every case in which they were challenged. He dissented in every case in which the Supreme Court failed to overturn a death sentence and opposed all efforts to narrow or burden the right of women to obtain abortions. No justice has been more libertarian in terms of opposing government regulation of speech or private sexual conduct. Nor has any justice been more egalitarian in terms of advancing a view of the Constitution that imposes positive duties on government to provide certain important benefits to people — education, legal services, access to courts — regardless of their ability to pay for them.

Randall Bland, *Private Pressure on Public Law: The Legal Career of Justice Thurgood Marshall* (1973); A Tribute to Justice Thurgood Marshall, special issue, *Harvard Blackletter Journal* 6 (Spring 1989).

RANDALL KENNEDY

See also Brown v. *Board of Education of Topeka;* National Association for the Advancement of Colored People; Supreme Court.

MARSHALL PLAN

The Marshall Plan, also known as the European Recovery Program, channeled over $13 billion to finance the economic recovery of Europe between 1948 and 1951. The Marshall Plan successfully sparked economic recovery, meeting its objective of "restoring the confidence of the European people in the economic future of their own countries and of Europe as a whole." The plan is named for Secretary of State George C. Marshall, who announced it in a commencement speech at Harvard University on June 5, 1947.

At the time, Americans perceived the plan as a generous subvention to Europe. The Soviet Union, however, viewed the Marshall Plan as an attempt to interfere in the internal affairs of other states and refused to participate. Ultimately, the Soviets prevented Poland and Czechoslovakia from taking part, despite their eagerness to do so.

Revisionist historians have challenged the assertion that the plan represented American altruism. They have argued that the export of dollars to Europe kept the United States from backsliding into depression by providing a market for U.S. capital goods. The Marshall Plan, according to revisionists, allowed the United States to remake the European economy in the image of the American economy. The plan promoted European economic integration and federalism, and created a mixture of public organization of the private economy similar to that in the domestic economy of the United States. This reorganization of the European economy provided a more congenial environment for American investment.

See also Marshall, George C.

MASON, GEORGE

(1725–1792), Virginia planter and political leader during the revolutionary era. Born and reared in the genteel plantation society that produced a generation of extraordinary leaders, Mason was unique in preferring public duties that did not bring the fame and glory sought by many of his contemporaries. From Gunston Hall in Fairfax County, Virginia, Mason watched the crisis between the North American colonies and Britain become critical, and he helped his neighbor, George Washington, prepare the influential Fairfax Resolves of July 1774. The resolves, carried by Washington to the Virginia House of Burgesses, clearly asserted colonial rights, called for an economic boycott of English goods, and denounced the slave trade, demanding an end "to such a wicked cruel and unnatural Trade." The resolves helped cement a close alliance among Mason, Patrick Henry, Richard Henry Lee, Washington, and other leading Virginians, as the tensions between the colonies and England escalated.

After April 1775 Mason was drawn into the vortex of the resistance movement in Virginia. He refused to take a place on the Virginia delegation to the Continental Congress but was active on the county Committee of Safety (procuring weapons for the militia) and replaced Washington on the county delegation elected to the Virginia Convention. Widowed in 1773, Mason carried on extensive tobacco cultivation at Gunston Hall while attending to his nine children's upbringing. He was saddened when the break with England made his participation on revolutionary councils urgent.

In May 1776 the Virginia Convention took the first step in severing the colony from the British Empire, and Mason's plans for a declaration of rights and a constitution "swallowed up all the rest." Printed in a Williamsburg newspaper and widely circulated, Mason's stirring rhetoric and systematic catalog of human rights, prefaced by an affirmation of every freeman's right to "life and liberty . . . and pursuing and obtaining happiness and safety," had an electrifying effect on other state assemblies. Thereafter, as most states cut the bonds with England they adopted similar declarations, often borrowing Mason's articles verbatim.

Mason continued to avoid public service outside Virginia, but he was active in the state legislature, and his intellectual grasp of political problems won the admiration of Thomas Jefferson and James Madison. Mason threw his support behind Jefferson's bill establishing religious freedom, which became law in 1786.

When the crisis in national affairs came to a head in 1786, Mason set aside his reservations and agreed to serve on the Virginia delegation at the Philadelphia Constitutional Convention of 1787. He was one of the most active speakers and consistently advocated liberal provisions for national elections, safeguards for majority rule, and limitations on presidential power. Mason urged schemes to give states power in the Senate and to control their exports, but was disappointed when his suggestion for a bill of rights was voted down.

Somewhat embittered by this rejection, Mason was one of three delegates at Philadelphia who refused to sign the finished Constitution on September 17, 1787. He wrote a critique of it that appeared in pamphlet form as his "Objections." His first sentence — "There is no Declaration of Rights" — became a rallying point for the Antifederalist opposition to the ratification of the Constitution. In June 1788 Mason served at the Virginia ratifying convention but was bested in the debate by Madison. He would not back down, however, calling even in defeat for a bill of rights in the Constitution — a concession finally made after a close vote (89 to 79).

With the new government in operation, Mason found that his opposition had somewhat alienated his old friend Washington. But he maintained his relationships with Jefferson and Madison, and the latter introduced the set of ten amendments that became part of the Constitution in December 1791. Mason then let his wartime associates know he was ready to "chearfully put my Hand & Heart to the new Government." He refused a proffered seat in the Senate, however, falling back on his old excuses of ill health (he suffered from gout) and family matters. Jefferson visited him on September 30, 1792, and they talked of political matters past and future in friendly fashion. A week later, Mason was dead.

Helen Hill Miller, *George Mason: Gentleman Revolutionary* (1975); Robert A. Rutland, *George Mason: Reluctant Statesman* (1980).

ROBERT ALLEN RUTLAND

See also Bill of Rights; Constitution; Philadelphia Convention; Ratification of the Constitution; Revolution.

MATHER, INCREASE, and MATHER, COTTON

(Increase: 1639–1723; Cotton: 1663–1728), prominent Puritan ministers and leaders. Increase Mather, son of Richard Mather, first pastor of the Dorchester Church, assumed his father's position of prominence in the Massachusetts Bay Colony and became an effective ambassador for the colony's interests at the courts of James II and William III when its original charter was being renegotiated. At first opposed to the Half-Way Covenant, which loosened the requirements for baptism, he reversed his position and in 1675 published an influential book, *The First Principles of New England,* asserting the founders' latitude on the question of who was entitled to be baptized. Author of more than one hundred works—sermons, political tracts, chronicles of the Indian wars, ecclesiastical treatises— Increase played a moderating role during the Salem witchcraft crisis, reflecting on the events in his *Cases of Conscience concerning Evil Spirits* (1692). In later years he was involved in the founding of Yale College, which he hoped would become the bastion of orthodoxy that Harvard had ceased to be.

Cotton Mather, an even more prolific writer and controversialist than his father, published nearly five hundred works, of which the most important is the *Magnalia Christi Americana* (1702), a massive history of New England under the aspect of divine providence. Though born to the Puritan purple (he was a grandson of John Cotton on his mother's side), Mather was in some respects more an Enlightenment figure than an orthodox Calvinist. He played an important role in disseminating scientific knowledge to the New England community (he wrote a treatise on medicine, *The Angel of Bethesda*, that remained unpublished in his lifetime), and, with Increase, he was at the forefront of the battle for acceptance of the smallpox vaccine. He also shared the pulpit of Boston's Old North Church with his father. The two fought against ecclesiastical innovation as New England was forced into toleration and some of the basic practices of the founders' generation (such as restricted communion and public profession of faith) came under attack. He remains best known, however, for his support of the witchcraft persecution, which he explained in his *Wonders of the Invisible World* (1693), a book that can be read—more sympathetically now than then—as a poignant assertion of New England's continuing centrality as the battleground between God and Satan.

Michael G. Hall, *The Last American Puritan: The Life of Increase Mather, 1639–1723* (1988); Robert Middlekauff, *The Mathers: Three Generations of Puritan Intellectuals, 1596–1728* (1971); Kenneth Silverman, *The Life and Times of Cotton Mather* (1984).

ANDREW DELBANCO

See also Half-Way Covenant; New England Colonies; Puritanism; Religion; Salem Witch Trials.

MAYER, LOUIS B.

(1885–1957), motion picture producer. "This is the end of a volume, not a chapter," said the rabbi in his eulogy at Mayer's funeral. Mayer was the first to die of that pioneering generation of movie moguls whose careers spanned both the silent and the sound eras.

Born in Minsk, Russia, Louis was not yet four when his family immigrated to North America. Louis, his father, and two brothers rose from ragpicking to ship salvage, and in 1904, they opened an office in Boston, with Louis in charge.

His arrival coincided with the nickelodeon craze that was sweeping the United States. Enthralled by the potential of these "flickers," Louis opened a theater in Haverhill, Massachusetts, and announced that it would be "the home of refined entertainment devoted to Miles Brothers moving pictures and illustrated songs," all to the accompaniment of an organ. For his Christmas attraction, Mayer secured Pathé's hand-tinted *Passion Play,* whose overwhelming success convinced him that the future of motion pictures was in mass-appeal dramas in which "virtue sorely tried" is in the end richly rewarded. Years later, he said, "I will make only pictures that I won't be ashamed to have my children see."

Capitalizing on his success in Haverhill, Mayer developed a chain of nickelodeons throughout New England and founded the American Feature Film Company to serve as his distributor. His most notable acquisition was D. W. Griffith's *Birth of a Nation* in 1915. This film demonstrated to Mayer that the moviegoing public was ready for feature-length motion pictures. He then founded the Metro Pictures Corporation of New York City, but, soon dissatisfied with the films Metro was producing, he moved to Los Angeles and opened Louis B. Mayer Productions.

A pending merger in 1924 between Metro Pictures and the Goldwyn Company was broadened to include Mayer Productions. Although it was initially viewed as a desperate move by his rivals, MGM, under the tutelage of Mayer and his young protégé Irving Thalberg, evolved into the most elaborate and profitable studio system in the history of motion pictures.

Mayer's career was now linked with Thalberg's. But their relationship was strained almost from the outset by disagreements and the perception in Hollywood that Thalberg, not Mayer, was the animating spirit at MGM. In

1927, for example, Warner Brothers released *The Jazz Singer*. Thalberg strongly argued the case for "talkies," while Mayer, just as strongly, doubted their practicality. When introduced to television twenty years later, Mayer dismissed it as a passing novelty.

One characteristic common to both men, however, was the recognition and nurturing of new talent. Separately or together, Mayer and Thalberg were responsible for the careers of Greta Garbo, Lon Chaney, Clark Gable, Jean Harlow, Greer Garson, Spencer Tracy, Wallace Berry, Joan Crawford, Judy Garland, Charles Laughton, and the Marx Brothers, plus countless writers, directors, and producers, including Lois Weber, Hollywood's first woman director. Beginning with *He Who Gets Slapped* in 1925, the team of Mayer and Thalberg produced such films as *Camille, Ben-Hur, The Good Earth,* and *A Night at the Opera*. After Thalberg's untimely death in 1936, Mayer maintained this tradition in *The Wizard of Oz* and *An American in Paris.*

World War II and its aftermath rendered the studio system and Mayer's cherished ideas of entertainment obsolete and prohibitively expensive. The war brought about a darkening view of the human condition, which he steadfastly ignored in approving projects for MGM, preferring to continue with the escapist tone of Andy Hardy. Mayer got his way as long as MGM turned a profit. But in August 1951, after several years of losses, the most powerful figure in Hollywood for nearly a quarter of a century was forced to resign from the company he had founded.

A brief tenure as chair of the fledgling Cinerama Production Corporation followed, during which Mayer waged an unsuccessful proxy fight to regain control of his former studio. Mayer died of leukemia soon after this final setback.

Bosley Crowther, *Hollywood Rajah: The Life and Times of Louis B. Mayer* (1960); Samuel Marx, *Mayer and Thalberg: The Make-Believe Saints* (1975).

R. FRANCE

See also Movies.

MAYFLOWER COMPACT

The Mayflower Compact, signed by English colonists on the ship *Mayflower* in November 1620, was the first written framework of government established in what is now the United States. The *Mayflower* carried not only the Pilgrims but a few other settlers as well. When it arrived at Cape Cod, several hundred miles north of its planned destination in Virginia owing to storms at sea, the passengers realized they were outside the bounds of the governmental authority they had contracted with in England.

William Bradford, the Pilgrim leader, was alarmed to learn that some of the others felt no obligation to respect the rules of the Pilgrims. In his words, they wanted to "use their owne libertie." The male heads of Pilgrim and non-Pilgrim families therefore drew up a compact that bound all signers to accept whatever form of government was established after landing. The compact created a "Civil Body Politic" to enact "just and equal Laws, Ordinances, Acts, Constitutions and Offices." Every adult male had to sign the agreement before going ashore. The compact remained in effect until Plymouth was incorporated into the short-lived Dominion of New England in 1686 and subsequently absorbed into the Massachusetts Bay Colony in 1691.

See also Bradford, William; New England Colonies.

MAYS, WILLIE

(1931–   ), baseball player with the New York Giants (1951–1957), San Francisco Giants (1958–1971), and New York Mets (1972–1973). Mays is almost universally regarded as one of the half dozen or so greatest baseball players of all time. Among all the ball players who ever played in the major leagues, Mays ranked third in number of home runs, fifth in runs scored, seventh in runs batted in, and tenth in slugging percentage, as of the end of the 1989 season. But statistics alone do not begin to tell the story of his greatness. One had to see him play.

Mays, who was born to a black working-class family in Alabama, was a baseball prodigy. On finishing high school, he joined the formidable Birmingham Black Barons of the Negro American League. In 1950 the New York Giants signed him to play with their minor league Trenton club. When, during the following season with Minneapolis in the Triple A American Association, Mays was hitting a startling .477, the Giants called him up to play center field during their pennant-winning year of 1951. After returning from army service in time for the 1954 season, Mays proceeded regularly to climb walls in the outfield, score from first base on singles, hit with awesome power, and do those things that rightly earned him the title, the Amazing Mays.

The astute baseball executive Branch Rickey, sportswriters like Dan Daniel and Leonard Koppett, and the leading managers and players of the past sixty years regarded Mays as peerless. Ted Williams once said that they invented baseball for Willie Mays. Certainly he played with a zest and enthusiasm that distinguished him from other great stars, who demonstrated their skills in a more subdued, methodical manner. Fans delighted in the sight of Mays running out from under his cap, whether pursuing a ball hit to the outfield or tearing around the bases, and they cheered happily as he made his unique "basket catch" of routine fly balls. Few players so palpably manifested their joy in the game as did Mays. And he did so not by overt gestures or facial expressions but by his every move.

Mays's greatness, however, rests above all on his unsurpassed combination of skills in the bedrock fundamentals of baseball. No one matched him in what Leo Durocher called "the five things you look for in a player": hitting, hitting with power, fielding, throwing, and base running. The aging Ty Cobb believed that Mays had "restored the art of base running to the game." In his prime years, his throwing arm was unsurpassed. Willie himself believed that his fielding was always his "greatest contribution." Nor was it merely a matter of his penchant for making amazing catches, such as his fabled "robbery" of Vic Wertz's drive in the 1954 World Series or the several times he dove headlong along the turf to catch a line drive in his bare right hand. The greatest thing about his fielding was his ability, demonstrated day in and day out, to turn doubles into singles and triples into doubles by his positioning, his lightning quickness, his superbly accurate throws.

Mays was chosen the player of the sixties in a *Sporting News* poll, and he was probably even

better in the 1950s. In the all-star games of those two decades, he towered above all other stars not only by his unsurpassed measurable — or statistically quantifiable — achievements at the bat but by what is perhaps best described as his unrivaled baseball intelligence, on the bases as well as in the field.

His career extended through the 1973 season, making him one of the most durable players in the history of the game, although the quality of his play had diminished by the late 1960s. In 1972 and 1973, he finished out his career as a part-time player with the New York Mets.

Charles Einstein, *Willie's Time* (1979); Willie Mays, as told to Charles Einstein, *My Life In and Out of Baseball,* rev. ed. (1972).

EDWARD PESSEN

See also Baseball; Spectator Sports.

McCARTHY, JOSEPH R.

(1908–1957), U.S. senator. McCarthy entered history when, during a speech in Wheeling, West Virginia, on February 9, 1950, he announced that he had in his hand a list of 205 communists in the State Department. The numbers were to fluctuate over the next few days, but the specificity of McCarthy's groundless charges as well as his genius for publicity quickly transformed the previously unknown senator from Wisconsin into the most notorious American politician of the 1950s.

Opportunism rather than ideological fervor marked McCarthy's career from the start. Initially a Democrat, he had switched parties and lied about his military service to parlay a local judgeship into Wisconsin's Republican senatorial nomination in 1946. Elected as part of the national GOP sweep of that year, he compiled an undistinguished and slightly shady record before latching onto anticommunism.

McCarthy's uniqueness was his lack of concern about the veracity of his accusations. In most other respects, however, he resembled his fellow conservative politicians who were then exploiting the issue of communism to embarrass the Truman administration. His early speeches echoed the right-wing Republican complaint that the Democratic administration had "lost" China to the communists.

McCarthy's charges, in particular his denunciation of Owen Lattimore, a leading China expert, as the "top Russian spy" in America, caused such an uproar that the Senate appointed a special investigating committee under Maryland's Millard Tydings. The hearings kept McCarthy on the front pages, and though the committee's majority found little substance in his charges, the partisan nature of the inquiry and the outbreak of the Korean War in June 1950 heightened the controversy.

Encouraged by his growing notoriety and the support of his party's leaders, McCarthy continued his attacks. During the following two years, he made increasingly wilder accusations, even attacking the respected secretary of defense, Gen. George C. Marshall. After the Republicans won the White House and control of Congress in the 1952 elections, McCarthy, as chair of the Subcommittee on Investigations of the Senate Committee on Governmental Operations, launched a highly publicized investigation of the Voice of America and the Army Signal Corps. Unlike other congressional investigators, McCarthy seemed unaware that the administration had changed; he continued his campaign against subversion in government even though he was now attacking his own party. As a result, he soon became a liability to the Eisenhower administration.

The denouement occurred in the spring of 1954 after McCarthy took on the U.S. Army, ostensibly because it had promoted a dentist accused of communism. With President Dwight D. Eisenhower's behind-the-scenes encouragement, a special congressional committee investigated the attempt by McCarthy and his chief counsel, Roy Cohn, to make the army grant special treatment to another McCarthy aide. The televised hearings revealed McCarthy as a blustering bully. By December 1954, when the Senate voted to censure him for his conduct, his power had evaporated.

Within three years, he was dead, the victim in part of the heavy drinking that may have caused his bizarre behavior. But the word *McCarthyism* lives on, its definition as controversial as the man himself. For some, it simply describes the senator's outrageous political style of reckless accusation and guilt by association; for others it also encompasses the anticommunist furor he personified. Either way it is a pejorative.

Robert Griffith, *The Politics of Fear* (1970); David M. Oshinsky, *A Conspiracy So Immense: The World of Joe McCarthy* (1983).

ELLEN W. SCHRECKER

See also Anticommunism; Army-McCarthy Hearings.

McCLELLAN, GEORGE B.

(1826–1885), Civil War soldier and political leader. In 1861, at the outbreak of the Civil War, George B. McClellan was considered the most promising general in the Union ranks and by training and experience ideally suited for the role of military executive. His subsequent erratic military conduct made him instead the most controversial general of the war. A West Point graduate, ranked second in the class of 1846, he had performed creditably in the Mexican War. His antebellum service was climaxed by an assignment in 1855 to study European military establishments and to observe the Crimean War, which cemented his reputation for military scholarship. He resigned from the army in 1857 to become one of the nation's leading railroad executives.

A month into the Civil War McClellan was appointed major general in the Regular Army and commander of the Department of the Ohio. After efficiently managing a campaign in western Virginia, he was summoned to Washington late in July 1861, following the Bull Run debacle, to take command of the main Union army in the East. Over the next eight months he trained and organized the Army of the Potomac, serving for four of those months as general-in-chief of all the Union armies.

In April 1862 McClellan took the field to direct the largest campaign of the war, an advance against Richmond via the Virginia peninsula. For three months he inched his way cautiously toward the Confederate capital, but in the Seven Days' Battles (June 25–July 1) he was driven into retreat by Robert E. Lee's smaller Army of Northern Virginia. Ordered to evacuate the peninsula in August, McClellan was slow to send reinforcements to the embattled Union forces at Second Bull Run, and Lee was again victorious. When the Confederate army invaded Maryland early in September, President Abraham Lincoln reluctantly turned once again to McClellan, a general stained by defeat but the only general capable of restoring shattered Union morale. On September 17, along Antietam Creek near Sharpsburg, McClellan finally brought Lee to battle. Despite his greatly superior force, McClellan's cautious generalship gained only a draw in the bloodiest single day's fighting of the war. He refused to pursue Lee back into Virginia and was reluctant to renew the campaign in the weeks that followed. On November 5, 1862, Lincoln ordered him relieved of command.

McClellan's failings stemmed from deeply rooted insecurities that led him to clothe reality in delusions — delusions that in battle he was invariably outnumbered, that his government conspired to see him defeated, that he bore no responsibility for his actions. He was a general afflicted with "the slows" (as Lincoln put it), too fearful of losing to risk winning.

During the next eighteen months McClellan, a conservative Democrat, became increasingly involved in political opposition to the Lincoln administration. At their convention in August 1864 the Democrats named him their presidential candidate but saddled him with a peace-at-any-price platform. Although he campaigned as a War Democrat, he could not overcome this handicap and was defeated in November by over 400,000 votes. McClellan did not return to national politics in the postwar years but instead earned a comfortable living as an engineering consultant and traveled widely. His last public service was as governor of New Jersey in 1878–1881.

Stephen W. Sears, *The Civil War Papers of George B. McClellan* (1989); Stephen W. Sears, *George B. McClellan: The Young Napoleon* (1988).

STEPHEN W. SEARS

See also Civil War; Elections: 1864.

McCORMICK, CYRUS

(1809–1884), inventor, businessman, and philanthropist. Born on a farm in Rockbridge County, Virginia, McCormick was raised in a conservative Presbyterian home.

At an early age he became interested in machines that would lighten the burden of farm labor and in 1831 built a mechanical reaper in his father's farm workshop. Most of the principles he incorporated had been tried earlier, but he integrated them into a workable, horse-drawn reaper. The machine included a cutting bar, a reel, a divider, guards over the reciprocating knives, a platform on which the grain fell after being cut, and a gear wheel. The next year he made improvements and demonstrated his reaper's capabilities on several nearby farms. He patented the machine in June 1834.

McCormick further improved his reaper in the late 1830s and marketed a few in the early 1840s. At first he contracted with manufacturers to produce machines to his specifications, but that arrangement did not prove satisfactory because he could not control quality. In 1847 he moved to Chicago, closer to the nation's main grain-producing areas, and set up his own factory. Meanwhile, he had become involved in litigation with Obed Hussey who had patented a reaper in 1833. The courts confirmed Hussey's patents in 1843, which left McCormick without overall patent protection for his machine.

Nevertheless, McCormick's business expanded and prospered. By 1856 his factory in Chicago was producing forty reapers a day, and he had become a millionaire. He began to sell reapers in Europe in the early 1850s and eventually sold thousands of machines there. McCormick improved his reapers by adding such refinements as a self-rake device to move the grain off the platform. In 1875 he produced a wire binder and in 1881 a twine binder. Although intense competition existed among reaper manufacturers, McCormick came to lead the field. He was an ambitious, aggressive, and persevering man who successfully combined an inventive talent with shrewd business practices. He united standardized procedures, mass production, aggressive advertising, and the extension of warranties and credit to expand his business throughout the country.

McCormick's achievement was to invent, manufacture, and distribute a machine that greatly reduced the amount of farm labor needed in grain production. It took twenty hours to harvest an acre of wheat in 1830 compared to less than one hour in 1895. Thus, he made a major contribution to the revolution in agricultural productivity in the nineteenth century.

McCormick married Nancy Fowler in 1858, a strong, practical woman with good business instincts who proved to be a great help to her husband. A wealthy man for his time, McCormick made substantial gifts, mainly to Presbyterian schools and seminaries. His strong interest in, and support of, the Presbyterian Seminary of the Northwest in Chicago prompted a renaming of that institution to the McCormick Theological Seminary after his death.

William T. Hutchinson, *Cyrus Hall McCormick: Seed-Time, 1809–1856* (1930) and *Cyrus Hall McCormick: Harvest, 1856–1884* (1935); Cyrus McCormick, *The Century of the Reaper* (1931).

GILBERT C. FITE

See also Agriculture; Philanthropy; Science and Technology.

McCULLOCH V. MARYLAND

This case, decided by the Supreme Court in 1819, asserted national supremacy vis-à-vis state action in areas of constitutionally granted authority. Maryland had placed a prohibitive tax on the bank notes of the Second Bank of the United States. When the Maryland courts upheld this law, the Bank, in the name of its Baltimore branch cashier James W. McCulloch, appealed to the Supreme Court. Daniel Webster, with William Pinkney, argued the case on behalf of the Bank.

Chief Justice John Marshall wrote the unanimous opinion of the Court. He stated first that the Constitution gave Congress the power to make "all laws . . . necessary and proper" to carry out the specific powers conferred on Congress in Article I, Section 8. Incorporating Alexander Hamilton's doctrine of "broad construction" of the Constitution, Marshall wrote, "Let the end be legitimate, let it be within the scope of the constitution, and all means which are appropriate, . . . which are not prohibited, . . . are constitutional." Since the Bank was a lawful instrument of specific federal authority, the law creating the Bank was constitutional.

Marshall then pointed to Article VI of the Constitution, which says that the Constitution is the "supreme Law of the Land; . . . any Thing in the . . . Laws of any State to the Contrary notwithstanding." Stating that "the power to tax involves the power to destroy," he said that the states "have no power, by taxation or otherwise, to retard, impede, or . . . control" the laws of the federal government, and thus the law "imposing a tax on the Bank of the United States, is unconstitutional and void."

See also Bank of the United States; Constitution.

McGILLIVRAY, ALEXANDER

(1759?–1793), Creek Indian leader. McGillivray, a major figure in Creek Indian history, played an intriguing role in the first years of the United States. The son of a Scottish trader and a Creek woman, he came to maturity at a time when the great tribes of the Southeast were facing unprecedented challenges. These communities often turned for leadership to people of mixed ancestry, because they spoke English well and understood Anglo-American ways and yet culturally remained Indians.

After a childhood spent near present-day Montgomery, Alabama, McGillivray was sent to Charleston, South Carolina, for additional schooling. In 1777 he returned home to work in the British Indian department. During the final years of the American Revolution, he rose to a prominent place in Creek political life, his rise fueled by his knowledge of English and his determination to defend Creek lands and ways.

Those writing the Treaty of Paris in 1783 disregarded Indian claims of independence and separate status within the new United States.

McGillivray contended that the Creeks would have to achieve an unprecedented degree of unity if they were to maintain their autonomy. As Britain had relinquished Florida to Spain, the Creeks signed a treaty with the Spaniards in June 1784. In the short run, this Treaty of Pensacola benefited both sides: the Creeks received Spanish recognition and ammunition and the Spaniards gained the pledge of Creek support.

The state of Georgia soon challenged Creek independence, however. McGillivray's political rivals, Hoboithle Mico and Eneah Mico, signed treaties with Georgia sanctioning the loss of a considerable amount of Creek territory. The state then tried to claim the land, but McGillivray and his followers denied the legality of the treaties.

McGillivray spurned the federal government's efforts to force the Creeks to recognize the treaties with Georgia. Instead he accepted an invitation from George Washington to come to New York to negotiate a better agreement. The Treaty of New York of August 7, 1790, appeared to be a triumph for McGillivray. In exchange for some of the land claimed by Georgia, the Creeks gained the promise of federal protection, the denial of Georgia's right to make further treaties, and the power to evict trespassing whites from their territory. There were also secret articles in the treaty. McGillivray received a salary of twelve hundred dollars and a commission as a brigadier general in the U.S. Army. And at his discretion, the Creeks could import goods without duty through an American port if necessary.

The Creek leader did not live long enough to enjoy these provisions or to achieve his objective of Creek unity. As internal divisions grew within the Creek nation, McGillivray fell ill and died at the age of thirty-four.

Michael D. Green, *The Politics of Indian Removal: Creek Government and Society in Crisis* (1982); J. Leitch Wright, *Creeks and Seminoles: The Destruction and Regeneration of the Muscogulge People* (1986).

PETER IVERSON

See also Indians.

McGUFFEY'S *READER*

This series of schoolbooks teaching reading and moral precepts, originally prepared by William Holmes McGuffey in 1836, had a profound influence on public education in the United States. McGuffey was a professor at Miami University in Oxford, Ohio, and a Presbyterian minister. A Cincinnati publishing firm asked him to compile a series of graded readers adapted to the values, beliefs, and way of life of "Western people." As a young schoolmaster, McGuffey had used the eighteenth-century Puritans' *New England Primer,* Noah Webster's *American Spelling Book,* and the Bible. His *Eclectic First Reader* and *Eclectic Second Reader* were published in 1836, the *Third* and *Fourth* in 1837. They contained stories of widely varied subject matter appealing to youngsters and taught religious, moral, and ethical principles that reflected both McGuffey's personality and society at the time. McGuffey's brother Alexander produced the *Fifth Reader* in 1844, a spelling book in 1846, and a *Sixth Reader* in 1857.

In 1841 the original publishing partnership dissolved. The books passed through a series of seven owners while their content evolved during almost a hundred years of publication. Although the revised texts issued in 1857 added the name "McGuffey" to the title, they moved away from the Calvinist values of salvation, righteousness, and piety and reflected the morality and cultural values of a broader American society that had incorporated religion within the civil structure. The 1879 editions taught morality and good character to the emerging middle class and provided children with a common knowledge and worldview. The first editions sold 7 million copies. By 1879 more than 60 million had been sold, and by 1920 over 122 million. In 1978 they were still in use in some school systems.

See also Education.

McKINLEY, WILLIAM

(1843–1901), twenty-fifth president of the United States. Born in Ohio, McKinley attended Allegheny College in Pennsylvania until his ill health forced him to return to Ohio, where he taught school. When the Civil War came, McKinley, who was eighteen, joined Rutherford B. Hayes's regiment as a private and after four years of fighting was breveted a major. After the war, he studied law and was admitted to the bar in 1867.

A staunch Republican and good campaigner, McKinley owed his rapid rise in Ohio politics to his friend Hayes. Although his district was strongly Democratic, McKinley was elected to serve in Congress from 1877 to 1883 and from 1885 to 1891, losing only in the Democratic landslide years of 1882 and 1890. In Congress he became the most conspicuous champion of protectionism and the primary author of the McKinley Tariff of 1890; he included in it (at the behest of James G. Blaine) a novel feature authorizing reciprocal trade agreements designed to enhance American exports abroad.

Elected governor of Ohio in 1891 and 1893, McKinley was by 1896 a leading Republican, and aided by his political lieutenant Marcus Alonzo Hanna, he easily secured the presidential nomination. The Democratic party, led by William Jennings Bryan, was discredited, demoralized, and divided by the depression following the panic of 1893. Whereas Bryan wished to inflate the currency by the unlimited coinage of silver, McKinley stressed protection and prosperity, defended the gold standard, and triumphed decisively.

McKinley's amiable personality, his pragmatic approach to issues, his willingness to compromise, and his patient, unobtrusive maneuvering toward his objectives masked his strength of character and his capacity to deal with Congress and dominate his advisers. After his inauguration McKinley called for a special session of Congress to revise the tariff. With rates higher than the McKinley Tariff, the new Dingley Tariff (1897) also included the reciprocity feature. Not a doctrinaire supporter of gold currency, McKinley initially favored international bimetalism, but when the British rejected that system, he abandoned it and in 1900 approved the Gold Standard Act.

Questions of war and empire, however, not domestic problems, dominated McKinley's pres-

idency. In Cuba a bloody rebellion against Spain, which began in 1895, outraged many Americans who clamored for war with Spain. Using diplomacy and the threat of military intervention, McKinley secured some concessions from Spain, but when it would not give up Cuba, he led the nation into war in 1898. He personally directed the war effort and made the crucial decisions that brought the United States a colonial empire in the Caribbean and the Pacific. His administration suppressed armed Philippine resistance to American rule with tactics similar to those Spain had employed in Cuba, established an American protectorate in Cuba, negotiated the Hay-Pauncefote treaties (1900, 1901), which allowed the United States to construct unilaterally an isthmian canal, and circulated the Open Door notes (1899, 1900), which opposed the dismemberment of China.

McKinley, who had done much to enhance the power and prestige of the presidency, was reelected in 1900, but his second term ended abruptly when he was assassinated by an anarchist, Leon Czolgosz, the next year.

Lewis L. Gould, *The Presidency of William McKinley* (1980); H. Wayne Morgan, *William McKinley and His America* (1963).

Ari Hoogenboom

See also Elections: 1896, 1900; Hanna, Marcus Alonzo; Tariff. *For events during McKinley's administration, see* Caribbean-U.S. Relations; Hawaii Annexation; Open Door Policy; Panama Canal; Philippines; Platt Amendment; Spanish-American War.

MEAD, MARGARET

(1901–1978), anthropologist. Mead, who turned the study of primitive cultures into a vehicle for criticizing her own, was born in Philadelphia. Both her father, Edward Mead, an economist at the Wharton School, and her mother, Emily Mead, a sociologist of immigrant family life and a feminist, were devoted to intellectual achievement and democratic ideals.

Mead discovered her calling as an undergraduate at Barnard College in the early 1920s in classes with Franz Boas, the patriarch of American anthropology, and in discussions with his assistant, Ruth Benedict. The study of primitive cultures, she learned, offered a unique laboratory for exploring a central question in American life: how much of human behavior is universal, therefore presumably natural and unalterable, and how much is socially induced? Among a people widely convinced of the inferiority of women and the immutability of gender roles, clear answers to this question could have important social consequences.

Selecting the peoples of the South Pacific as the focus of her research, Mead spent the rest of her life exploring the plasticity of human nature and the variability of social customs. In her first study, *Coming of Age in Samoa* (1928), she observed that Samoan children moved with relative ease into the adult world of sexuality and work, in contrast to children in the United States, where lingering Victorian restraints on sexual behavior and the increasing separation of children from the productive world made youth a needlessly difficult time. Westerners' deep-seated belief in innate femininity and masculinity served only to compound these troubles, Mead continued in *Sex and Temperament* (1935). Describing the widely varying temperaments exhibited by men and women in different cultures, from the nurturing men of the Arapesh tribe to the violent women of the Mundugumor, Mead maintained that social convention, not biology, determines how people behave. A decade later she qualified her environmental stance somewhat in *Male and Female* (1949), in which she analyzed the ways in which motherhood serves to reinforce male and female roles in all societies. She continued nevertheless to emphasize the possibility and wisdom of resisting traditional gender stereotypes.

By the 1950s Mead was widely regarded as a national oracle. She served as a curator at the Museum of Natural History from 1926 until her death and as an adjunct professor of anthropology at Columbia from 1954, but she devoted the greater part of her professional life to writing and lecturing. Married three times and the mother of only one child at a time when both divorce and only children were uncommon,

Mead nevertheless achieved fame as an expert on family life and child rearing. In such books as *Culture and Commitment* (1970) and her autobiographical *Blackberry Winter* (1972), in magazine articles for *Redbook,* and in her lectures, Mead tried to persuade Americans that understanding the lives of other people could help them understand their own, that a greater ease with sexuality (homosexual as well as heterosexual) could enrich them, that motherhood and careers could and should go together, and that building support networks for the overburdened nuclear family would bring greater well-being for all.

Jane Howard, *Margaret Mead: A Life* (1984).

ROSALIND ROSENBERG

See also Social Sciences.

MEDIA

See Magazines and Newspapers; Publishing; Radio and Television.

MEDICAID

Medicaid, a program of publicly funded health insurance for the poor, was established under the Social Security Amendments of 1965. Health insurance was excluded from the original Social Security Act of 1935 because of the opposition of the medical profession and private insurance interests. Similar pressure kept the program from being enacted during the 1940s and 1950s. Public support for the concept grew during these years, however, leading to the Kerr-Mills Act of 1960, which provided federal support for state medical programs serving the aged poor.

By 1965, there was a growing consensus that a broader program was needed, with a stronger federal role and wider eligibility. Thus, when the Medicare legislation creating health insurance for the elderly and the disabled was being worked out, Senator Wilbur Mills added another section establishing Medicaid, a similar program for the poor of all ages. Medicaid was designed to serve both those eligible for public assistance and those whose incomes fell just above that level but were judged to be "medically indigent." Like Medicare, Medicaid permits those who are eligible to purchase health care from the same hospitals and physicians as the general public, with the fees paid by the program. Unlike Medicare, however, which is run by the federal government, Medicaid is administered by the individual states, with a combination of state and federal funding.

Medicaid was passed by Congress with little debate, but it has developed into a highly important aspect of the nation's social welfare system. Program data show that millions of poor people have gained access to regular health care because of Medicaid. The program has weaknesses, however, including the wide variation in the quality and range of services in the different states. Furthermore, since the program was designed to have recipients purchase their health care in the private market at whatever fee the providers customarily charge, Medicaid has had little control over the cost of the services given to its clients. When health-care costs soared during the 1970s and 1980s, so did the Medicaid budgets. Various efforts have been made at the state and federal levels to limit eligibility, regulate providers' fees, and restrict the range of services covered, but program costs remain a major concern. In spite of these problems, however, Medicaid represents a historic step forward in America's system of services for the poor.

See also Medicine.

MEDICARE

Medicare is a program of national health insurance for persons who are over the age of sixty-five or seriously disabled. Administered by the federal Social Security Administration, it was established under the Social Security Amendments of 1965. Opposition by the medical profession and private insurance interests kept health insurance out of the Social Security Act of 1935 and its various amendments of the 1940s and 1950s. The Kerr-Mills Act of 1960 was an effort to forestall more radical action by providing federal support for state medical programs that served the aged poor. But few states participated, its coverage was extremely limited, and

the matching-grant formula meant that the poorest states tended to receive the least assistance. The inadequacies of this law, in fact, increased the demand for a more comprehensive program.

Even after it became clear that some form of health insurance would be enacted, advocates disagreed bitterly over whether the program should be compulsory or voluntary, serve all incomes or just the poor, and be run by the federal government or the states; also at issue was how public and private agencies would be balanced. As finally enacted, the 1965 amendments represented a compromise. Medicaid, adopted at the same time, served only the poor and was administered by the states; Medicare served the elderly and disabled of all incomes and was run by the federal government. Furthermore, under Part A of the Medicare legislation, hospital insurance was made compulsory; under Part B, recipients were permitted to choose whether or not to participate in a government-assisted insurance program to cover doctors' fees. A major role was guaranteed to the private sector by essentially limiting Medicare to a financing system. Program recipients would purchase all their health services in the open market; the government's only involvement would be in relation to payment.

A threatened boycott of Medicare and Medicaid by the American Medical Association did not materialize, and Medicare went into effect in 1966. The effects of the program were far-reaching. Most important, it gave millions of elderly and disabled people new access to medical care. But by arranging for program recipients to purchase their care from private providers at whatever fee those providers customarily charged, Medicare maintained relatively little control over the quality and cost of the services they received. In fact, the program proved to be far more expensive than its framers anticipated. Among the factors involved were the expanded market for health services that Medicare created, the growing number of elderly people in the population, and the increasing use of expensive medical technology. The rising cost of all health care during the 1970s and 1980s, dramatically reflected in growing Medicare budgets, provoked widespread debate. In response, state and federal officials initiated various schemes to control program costs, most notably the initiation of a "prospective payment" system in 1984, under which Medicare payment rates were set in advance for each medical diagnosis. There was even some discussion of giving Medicare only to the poor. At present, cost control remains an unsolved problem. Nevertheless, Medicare has become an established element in the nation's social welfare system.

See also Medicine.

MEDICINE

Until the early decades of the twentieth century, methods of treating disease were rooted in local customs and beliefs, not in a professional or scientific consensus. The medicine practiced in one area or by one group was often quite different from medicine elsewhere.

In rural America, laypeople combined local folk custom with information gleaned from medical dictionaries and popular texts to treat injuries and illnesses. Similarly, doctors, not yet an elite professional group, were usually trained through a combination of schooling and apprenticeship. A large number of medical schools were business institutions organized for the profit of local practitioners. Students, often from lower-middle- or working-class backgrounds, paid to attend lectures of dubious worth. Formal medical education, largely unregulated, could vary in length, content, and structure, and after 1847, when the American Medical Association (AMA) was formed, its lack of standardization was much criticized.

Few during the nineteenth century agreed on what constituted appropriate practice. Furthermore, most doctors and educated people were skeptical of those who sought to unify medicine under any one therapeutic umbrella. Calls for uniformity were perceived as little more than a political ploy to gain a measure of legitimacy for a particular medical interest group. Throughout much of the century, the disparate demands of different groups created a diverse body of therapeutic knowledge and practice. Accordingly, training differed for rural doctors, urban doctors, homeopaths, allopaths, eclectics, Thomsonians, and a host of others. Those treating different classes and ethnic groups were forced by the realities of the medical marketplace to adjust their practice.

Each group of practitioners identified with a particular "school" or "sect" of medicine. Rural doctors depended mostly on herbal treatments. Thomsonians and later the eclectics were among the botanical schools that developed throughout rural New England, the South, and the Midwest; these groups incorporated local folk customs into their therapeutics. In cities regular practitioners, homeopaths, and many others competed with one another for patients. Thus, unlike today, when patients have little control over the types of therapies used, patients in nineteenth-century America could choose among a wide variety of therapies.

Doctors, by and large, were "family" or "community" practitioners engaged in general medicine; only a small number specialized in surgery, ophthalmology, or other areas. Family doctors, the bulk of the profession, lived in the communities where they practiced, making house calls or treating patients in offices located in their homes. Often they and their patients were members of the same church or club. The family doctor would preside at the significant events in people's lives, tending to births as well as deaths. He saw it as his role to comfort the family, and it was not unusual for him to move into a patient's house for the duration of an illness.

This relationship between doctors and patients was not necessarily a product of a deep-seated belief in democracy or in the importance of trust and understanding in the therapeutic process. Rather, it was an outgrowth of the professional environment. These doctors were working in an era of great uncertainty concerning medical procedures and outcomes, and they were in severe competition with one another for clients. A large number of medical schools combined with loose licensure requirements produced an oversupply of practitioners. Without the options of research positions in universities, hospitals, or institutes, and without specialized forms of practice, doctors depended on the goodwill of their patients for their economic survival. Competition for patients was fierce by the end of the century, and familiarity, a pleasant demeanor, courteousness, and understanding were essential qualities for the successful doctor.

Because medical knowledge was sketchy and doctors depended on their patients for a living, they tended to practice in familiar ways that were accepted by their patients. This does not mean that they did not believe in their treatments, but that in many ways their knowledge was not much more sophisticated than that of their patients. Most doctors employed bleeding, cupping, purging, and other seemingly draconian measures to treat their patients. Because illness was often equated with moral failings, what we see as cruelty was viewed then as an appropriate consequence of transgressions.

Those who rejected regular therapeutics could turn to other, milder forms of practice. Appealing to merchants and other urban groups, homeopathy provided milder therapies and perhaps more elegant rationales. What might have been lacking in scientific rigor was made up for by the intimacy of practice itself. The authority of the practitioner rested as much on his social relationship to his patient as it did upon scientific fact.

Around the turn of the century a significant movement arose devoted to reforming medical education. By standardizing the training of physicians and controlling entry into the profession through licensure, reformers hoped to make medical practice itself more uniform. The movement culminated in the now-classic Carnegie Bulletin Number Four, or the "Flexner Report," which called for the reorganization of medical school curricula.

The report, named for its author, Abraham Flexner, illustrates some of the divisions within the medical community during these years and the centrality of arguments regarding standardization to those who sought to influence the health system. First, it called for the establishment of a common medical education built around laboratory science and two years of clinical experience as well as lectures. Second, it asserted that the guiding principles of professional behavior should be determined by the "science" of medical practice rather than the "art" of individual attention. Like the busy machine shops and industrial factories that were proving so successful in turning the country into an industrial power, medicine would be turned into a technically exact scientific enterprise. Finally, it called for the exclusion of women, blacks, and the poor from practice.

The Flexner Report, the product of a long, rancorous struggle among educators on the AMA's Council on Medical Education, achieved only some of its aims. Medical practice would remain a field filled with uncertainties and nonstandardized procedures, but the standardization of the social background of doctors would be realized. By the end of the nineteenth century, the eclectic nature of medical practice and the unregulated environment in which it had developed had created a large, diverse set of educational institutions that catered to women, black, and poorer students. In fact, there were sixteen women's medical schools by 1900 and ten black medical colleges, primarily in the southern states, by the same year. Also, the majority of students attending the various medical colleges were lower or lower middle class. But, by 1916, only two female women's colleges and two black schools remained in existence, and many of the proprietary institutions that had catered to part-time and working students had closed.

Reformers saw little need to protect these poorly endowed institutions in part because they believed that the future of scientific medicine would make social diversity within its ranks unimportant. If the physician of the future was to be a scientist treating patients regardless of social class or race, then there was little need to protect certain groups in medicine; doctors were to treat organs rather than people. In Flexner's model, white upper-middle-class male physicians would add to the social status of the profession without sacrificing the quality of care. Flexner's discussion of the future of the "Poor Boy," "Women," and "Negros" in medicine showed a simplistic, naive belief in the ability of medical science to resolve the issues of equity and equality that became the central concerns of health planners in the 1960s and 1970s.

Although the effect of the reform movement had profound implications for the social characteristics of American physicians, it had less of an impact on their practices. By and large, doctors were still tied to their private offices and were very defensive about "interference" from those seeking to standardize or evaluate their treatments. With no central organization capable of oversight, doctors adopted the mantle of science and the aura of scientists while maintaining their autonomy over treatment and procedure.

In recent years, however, the medical profession has faced a series of crises that have undermined its autonomy and undercut its authority. The staggering increase in the costs of basic health services and the growing skepticism of Americans with regard to professional dominance have produced a variety of movements to find alternatives to traditional forms of care. The 1960s saw a critique of medicine that emphasized the maldistribution of physicians, their extraordinary incomes, and the elitist, conservative nature of the AMA. Further, the dearth of hospital and physicians' services for the nation's poor added an obvious political dimension to the arguments over the medical profession.

These critiques spurred broad efforts to reform the health system. First, the long-standing struggle to enact a national health insurance plan culminated in the 1965 passage of Medicaid for the poor and disabled and Medicare for the elderly. Second, the argument that there were too few physicians provided a rationale for rapidly expanding the number of medical schools. Third, the argument that existing services were badly distributed and unable to address the pressing needs of the nation's poor led the Office of Economic Opportunity (OEO) within the Department of Health, Education, and Welfare to organize innovative programs to provide services to the urban poor. The OEO, for example, funded such efforts as the Urban Corps, which awarded scholarships to medical students in return for a commitment to serve poor communities and neighborhood health centers.

Another criticism during the 1960s and 1970s grew out of the women's movement. Critics attacked the male dominance of the profession and pressed for greater participation of women. As a result, the numbers of women entering the medical profession increased dramatically.

All these complaints reflected a growing sense that medicine had become far too removed from the population it served and that the sensitivity of medical practice to patient needs had been sacrificed on the altar of science and technology. By the late 1960s, some had begun to question the efficacy of medicine itself; critics contended that despite its increased costliness, it had done little or nothing to improve the overall health of the nation. Some even argued that medicine could be harmful — that it could cause iatrogenic (physician-caused) diseases. By the 1980s, the negative perceptions of medicine and its practitioners had had a strong impact: malpractice lawsuits skyrocketed in number and more restrictions were placed on educational subsidies for specialist training and undergraduate medical education.

Moreover, in the 1980s, lawyers, courts, ethicists, and philosophers began to explore questions that had previously been the preserve of the medical community alone. When should medical procedures be used to terminate pregnancies? Should physicians be allowed to use technology indefinitely to prolong life? Who should provide care and what type of care should be provided for the terminally ill? Only twenty years before, the general critique of medicine had argued that there were too few physicians and that more services were needed. The assumption was that medicine was a universal good that should be readily available to everyone. But the deep questioning of the efficacy of medicine and of the system had led to profound ethical and political debates that are still being argued.

Charles Rosenberg, *The Care of Strangers* (1987); David Rosner, *A Once Charitable Enterprise: Hospitals and Health Care in Brooklyn and New York* (1981); Rosemary Stevens, *In Sickness and in Wealth* (1988).

DAVID ROSNER

See also Abortion; Birth Control; Birthrate and Mortality; Epidemics; Medicaid; Medicare; Midwives; Sanitary Commission.

MELLON, ANDREW

(1855–1937), financier and secretary of the treasury (1921–1932). Mellon played leading roles in shaping American industrial development and the federal financial policies of the 1920s.

Born in Pittsburgh, Pennsylvania, Mellon left college before graduating to start a lumber business. In 1874 he entered his father's bank, T. Mellon and Sons, and in 1902 became president of its successor, the Mellon National Bank. As a financier, he showed exceptional ability to select, back, and acquire shares in promising business ventures, with the result that the Mellon interests came to include such major enterprises as the Aluminum Company of America, the Gulf Oil Corporation, and the Pittsburgh Coal Company. Regarded by some as America's greatest venture capitalist, he accumulated one of its largest fortunes and was actively involved in directing numerous corporations.

Mellon, a staunch conservative, entered politics through connections with such Pennsylvania Republican leaders as Boies Penrose and Philander C. Knox; through their influence he was appointed secretary of the treasury by Warren G. Harding in 1921. He brought business methods to government and succeeded, with the aid of an able group of subordinates, in implementing a conservative program of fiscal reforms. His chief legacies were liquidation of the war period's progressive tax structure, establishment of federal budgeting machinery, and a one-third reduction in the national debt. In addition, he chaired a commission responsible for war debt settlements and left the country a better designed and more convenient paper currency, much smaller in size. To the public at large he became, in spite of his frail appearance and retiring manner, a financial wizard whose accomplishments made him the greatest secretary of the treasury since Alexander Hamilton.

In 1929, Mellon's theory of prosperity through upper-bracket tax cuts, as set forth in *Taxation: The People's Business* (1924), seemed vindicated. But the Great Depression undermined his prestige and made him the subject of political attacks. In 1932 Herbert Hoover appointed him ambassador to Great Britain, a post from which he resigned after Franklin D. Roosevelt's election. Subsequently, he was charged with income tax evasion but was eventually cleared. In 1937 he donated his art collection to the nation along with money to build the National Gallery of Art. Also benefiting from his philanthropies were the Mellon Institute of Industrial Research and the Carnegie Library of Pittsburgh.

Of Mellon's life and work two widely divergent views still exist, one seeing him as a business genius who built great industries and great institutions of education, research, governance, and cultural enrichment, the other regarding him as a ruthless wielder of private power and formulator of public policies that widened economic disparity and helped produce the Great Depression. The latter view long dominated historical writing but has been moderated by recent revisionism and by Mellon's reemergence as a prophet and hero in conservative circles.

Burton Hersh, *The Mellon Family* (1978); Harvey O'Connor, *Mellon's Millions* (1933).

ELLIS W. HAWLEY

See also Conservatism; Harding, Warren G.; Philanthropy.

MELVILLE, HERMAN

(1819–1891), author. Although Melville has been regarded throughout most of the twentieth century as one of America's most powerful literary artists, particularly for his masterpiece *Moby-Dick,* he was largely unrecognized in his lifetime.

Born into a once-prominent family, Melville enlisted as a sailor on the whaler *Acushnet* in 1841. His experiences supplied him with raw materials for the sea narratives he later wrote. After four years at sea, Melville settled in New York and became associated with a group of editors and journalists seeking to foster a "home" literature. With the backing of editor Evert Duyckinck, Melville published his semiautobiographical sea adventure *Typee* in 1846, followed in 1847 by its sequel *Omoo.*

His critical reception was as favorable as it

would ever be. But even in these first reviews, critics condemned not only his enticing descriptions of Polynesian life and his attacks on American missionaries in the Pacific but less predictably, what they called his lack of "veracity" — a disinclination for realistic representation that suggested to some an intent to mislead his readers. Despite what he knew of his readership's intolerance for "flights of fancy," Melville then published a political allegory, *Mardi,* in 1849. Its lack of critical success led him to write the sea adventures *Redburn* (1849) and *White-Jacket* (1850), works he disdainfully referred to as "*jobs,* which I have done for money — being forced to it, as other men are to sawing wood."

With these novels, Melville's practical impulse was spent. Determined to convey a "Truth" for which his readership had no use, Melville, in a letter to Nathaniel Hawthorne, exuberantly described *Moby-Dick* (1851) as "a wicked book" that yet made him "feel spotless as the lamb." Although Melville's contemporaries found the novel frustratingly opaque, the tale of the tormented Captain Ahab, who unites his racially, ethnically, and nationally diverse crew in an apocalyptic quest for the white whale, has been valued by modern readers for its stylistic innovativeness and for the range of metaphysical, political, and cultural issues it addresses.

Moby-Dick was followed in 1852 by *Pierre,* a work on which Melville's reputation foundered. *Pierre* explored the plight of the aspiring American author caught in the maelstrom of competing definitions of the writer's role in relation to a culture anxious to discern in the new "democratic" literature a faithful — and flattering — self-portrait. *The Piazza Tales* (1853–1856), a collection of masterful short stories, and the short novel *Israel Potter* (1855), received scant critical notice. *The Confidence Man* (1857) was the last of his novels to be published while he was alive.

Melville then turned to poetry. His excellent Civil War poetry was published in 1866, although little critical notice was (or has been) taken of it. A poetic meditation on his visit to the Holy Land, *Clarel,* was published with family money in the centennial year, 1876. Melville apparently reworked two privately printed volumes of poetry, *John Marr and Other Sailors* (1888) and *Timoleon* (1891), into his uncompleted novel, *Billy Budd,* discovered in manuscript in 1924.

Melville's writings are so encyclopedic in subject matter and so far-ranging in their generic and stylistic experimentation that they have inspired a multitude of literary and historical theses on the preoccupations of antebellum America, from the theological crises of the post-Calvinist era to the political and cultural crises of American expansionism and slavery.

Wai-chee Dimock, *Empire for Liberty: Melville and the Politics of Individualism* (1989); Michael Paul Rogin, *Subversive Genealogy: The Politics and Art of Herman Melville* (1983).

NANCY RUTTENBURG

See also Literature.

MENCKEN, H. L.

(1880–1956), journalist, editor, author, and philologist. Mencken was born, lived, and died in Baltimore, and for all but about eight of his seventy-five years resided in one of the city's typical brick-front row houses. From this unlikely spot he radiated an enormous, indeed unique, influence on the intellectual and cultural life of the nation. In 1926 Walter Lippmann called him "the most powerful personal influence on this whole generation of educated people"; the *New York Times* claimed that he was the most powerful private citizen in America. His caustic wit and bludgeon-like style could evoke worshipful admiration or total loathing; it was impossible to be indifferent to him.

His career as journalist began in 1899 when he went to work as a reporter for the Baltimore *Morning Herald;* by the time the paper folded in 1906 he was its managing editor. Thereupon he transferred to the *Sun,* beginning an association that would last more than forty years. His simultaneous career as editor and critic started when he became book editor of the *Smart Set* in 1908. In 1914 he and George Jean Nathan became the magazine's coeditors, and in 1923 they left it to found the *American Mercury.* Between the *Sun* and the *Mercury* Mencken had a national audience for his attacks on the "genteel tradition" in American literature and on politicians ("a good politician, under democracy, is quite as unthinkable as an honest burglar"), bishops, Methodists, the English, the South, Prohibition, puritanism ("the haunting fear that somebody, somewhere, may be happy"), censorship, and all the beliefs and values of what he called the "booboisie." He became known as "the Sage of Baltimore."

Much of his critical writing was assembled in the six volumes of his *Prejudices* (1919–1927). *Notes on Democracy* (1926) was a scathing repudiation of the idea that all men are free and equal. *Treatise on the Gods* (1930) and *Treatise on Right and Wrong* (1934) set forth his skeptical opinions on religion and ethics. But during these years, too, he was producing the successive editions of his masterwork, *The American Language* (1919), an immense, scholarly study of the development of English in the United States.

With the coming of the depression and Franklin D. Roosevelt's New Deal, Mencken's popularity dwindled to the point where he was all but forgotten. But his reputation revived with the publication of the fourth edition of *The American Language* (1936) and its two *Supplements* (1945 and 1948), and three delightful, nostalgic volumes of autobiography: *Happy Days* (1940), *Newspaper Days* (1941), and *Heathen Days* (1943). However, his fanatical hatred of Roosevelt and his belief that the United States had no business being in World War II made him a lone dissonant voice in his later years.

Despite his fearsome reputation, Mencken in private life was a kind, gentle, considerate person who enjoyed playing music with a bunch of cronies every Saturday night for forty-four years and working in his backyard garden. In 1948 a massive stroke left him unable to read and write, and his career ended. The publication in 1989 of his *Diary,* with its anti-Semitic and racist comments, focused attention on him again. It has to be remembered, though, that such remarks were all too typical of the era in which he lived; he himself numbered scores of Jewish publishers, writers, physicians, and musicians among his good friends, and no man did more than he to encourage black writers and publish their work.

Carl Bode, *Mencken* (1969); Charles A. Fecher, *Mencken: A Study of His Thought* (1978); Vincent Fitzpatrick, *H. L. Mencken* (1989).

CHARLES A. FECHER

See also Literature; Magazines and Newspapers.

MEXICAN WAR

Although frequently simplified by students of the conflict, the causes of the Mexican War of 1846–1848 were complex. Relations between the two countries had been strained almost from the moment Mexico won its independence from Spain in 1821. Although a republican form of government was established in 1824, Mexico proved to be a republic in name more than in fact. Wracked by frequent revolutions, the nation remained weak and unstable and was often dominated by dictators.

As a result of the disorder, the United States, France, and Great Britain lodged claims against the government for damages inflicted upon their nationals and property. The American claims were submitted to a commission for arbitration, which settled on a figure of about $2 million. When the Mexican government defaulted, sentiment among Americans for collecting the claims by force increased, and some urged that war be declared.

Mexico's grievance against the United States focused on the issue of Texas. Already angered by America's aid to the Texas Revolution, the Mexican government became further alarmed when the movement to annex Texas to the United States gained momentum. Mexico had never recognized Texas's independence and made plans to recapture the area. As Congress debated the issue, Mexico made it clear that the permanent loss of Texas would be sufficient cause for war.

Events moved swiftly following the passage of an annexation resolution on March 3, 1845, the day before James K. Polk assumed the presidency. Fears for the safety of Texas and rumors that Mexico would transfer California to Great Britain in lieu of its debt payment, combined with a new sense of national identity and destiny, heightened American sensitivity to Mexico's threats and moved Americans closer to a war spirit. Mexico recalled its minister in Washington and broke off diplomatic relations. In response, U.S. troops commanded by Gen. Zachary Taylor entered Texas to protect the region until annexation was completed. Mexico countered by dispatching an army to the south bank of the Rio Grande. Hoping to avoid war with Mexico (conflict with Great Britain over the Oregon country loomed), President Polk sent an emissary, John Slidell, to the Mexican capital with instructions not only to negotiate a settlement of the claims and Texas issues but also to offer to buy New Mexico and California. Slidell arrived in early December amid a wave of anti-American feeling, and the government refused to receive him. The Mexican president, who it was said favored conciliation with the United States, was overthrown in a military coup. He was replaced by an officer who announced his intention to restore Texas to Mexico while he made overtures to European nations for the establishment of a monarchy in Mexico in return for aid against the United States.

Following the admission of Texas to the Union in December 1845, Taylor's army was ordered to the Rio Grande, the traditional boundary of the American claim to Texas dating back to the early years of the century. The opposing Mexican force received orders to attack the Americans, and in late April, the commanding general informed Taylor that hostilities had begun. An American patrol was ambushed north of the Rio Grande, followed quickly by a movement of the Mexican force across the river. The two armies clashed in the Battles of Palo Alto and Resaca de la Palma in early May 1846. Although outnumbered, Taylor's army was victorious in both engagements. Slidell's rebuff by the Mexican government and news of the first American losses along the Rio Grande persuaded President Polk and his cabinet to ask that Congress recognize a state of war with Mexico. The war resolution passed on May 13, with only token opposition.

The United States speedily mobilized its manpower and matériel. Congress authorized the enlistment of fifty thousand volunteers, assigning quotas to the states closest to the fighting. The government increased the size of the regular military forces, appropriated money for the production of equipment, and requisitioned ships to carry the troops to Mexico.

There were three areas of military operation. Taylor's army penetrated northern Mexico, occupied the important city of Monterrey, and defeated a larger Mexican army commanded by General Santa Anna at the Battle of Buena Vista on February 22–23, 1847. In the meantime, an army under the command of Stephen W. Kearny followed the Santa Fe Trail to New Mexico, occupied Santa Fe, and moved westward to the Pacific where it joined naval units in the occupation of California. Impatient to end the war, Polk opened a third operation against Mexico City itself. Commanded by Winfield Scott, an army made up largely of volunteers landed at Veracruz in March 1847 and marched inland, defeating the opposing forces in hard-fought battles at Cerro Gordo and in the Valley of Mexico. The capital was occupied in mid-September 1847.

The Treaty of Guadalupe Hidalgo, which ended the war, was signed early in February 1848. Mexico ceded New Mexico and California to the United States and, in recognition of the loss of Texas, agreed to the Rio Grande boundary. In return, the United States assumed the claims of its citizens against Mexico and paid Mexico an additional $15 million to help the country achieve long-needed fiscal stability.

The Mexican War was costly for the United States. Its military forces suffered almost thirteen thousand deaths, although only seventeen hundred were battle-related, the rest resulting from disease that swept through the army camps. Nevertheless, the war was popular. It was the first war covered by large numbers of correspondents, as the nation's press competed for war news. Some members of the Whig party and the abolitionists opposed the war, the former because they felt it was unconstitutional, the latter believing erroneously that it was part of a slaveholders' conspiracy to extend slavery. For many Americans, the war was a romantic venture in a distant and exotic land. The campaigns were often compared with the Spanish conquest of Mexico in the sixteenth century, which had recently been popularized by the historian William Hickling Prescott.

The reliance on volunteers gave the conflict a democratic cast, stimulating notions of an American mission to restore republican government to a people oppressed by military rulers. America's triumph seemed to confirm the superiority of democratic institutions, and literary figures like Walt Whitman and James Fenimore Cooper saw it as part of a worldwide mission to extend democratic ideals. Like most wars, however, this one left serious questions in its wake. The issue of whether slavery should be allowed in the lands taken from Mexico, first debated in 1846, set in motion a constitutional debate between the North and South that would dominate future political discourse, eventually dividing the Union itself.

K. Jack Bauer, *The Mexican War, 1846–1848* (1974); Robert W. Johannsen, *To the Halls of the Montezumas: The Mexican War in the American Imagination* (1985); David M. Pletcher, *The Diplomacy of Annexation: Texas, Oregon, and the Mexican War* (1973).

Robert W. Johannsen

See also Expansion, Continental and Overseas; Polk, James K.; Taylor, Zachary; Texas Revolution and Annexation.

MEXICO-U.S. RELATIONS

The border between the United States and Mexico represents the greatest division between the standards of living in neighboring countries. Yet, what was once a relationship easily dominated by the United States has developed into a bilateral relationship of increasing importance to both countries.

Early relations between the United States and what was to become Mexico were constantly troubled by border disputes. As a Spanish colony, Mexican territory was fought over and bartered for between the great powers of Europe. France had agreed, by treaty in 1800, to offer Louisiana to Spain if it were for sale, but in 1803 the territory was sold to the United States without consultation with Spain. The borders of that territory were never specified, and the United States interpreted them broadly to include what is now Texas.

Mexico declared its independence from Spain in 1821. Although free, Mexico found itself heavily in debt and the object of great power desires for expansion. The fragile condition of the new state caused the United States concern over possible invasion by a European power. In 1823 President James Monroe announced his famous doctrine, which stated that the United States would not tolerate any European attempts "to extend their system to any portion of this hemisphere." On October 4, 1824, Mexico became a federal republic based on a constitution similar to that of the United States. The republic was divided, however, between pro-British conservatives favoring a loose federation of states, and pro-American liberals seeking a strong central government.

American settlers in Texas agitated for annexation by the United States, and the increasingly murky status of that region led to the single most damaging event in U.S.-Mexican relations: the U.S.-Mexican War. But for sixty years after the war relations were relatively peaceful. To be sure, bitterness over the loss of Texas and fear of further territorial designs remained an important aspect of Mexico's view of the United States. Both countries, however, looked increasingly to domestic concerns and away from conflict with each other. In Mexico, liberals and conservatives struggled for control of government. The conservatives attempted to maintain control by allying with various European powers and instating dictators Antonio Santa Anna (1853) and Emperor Maximilian (1864). The liberal forces, led by Benito Juárez, were periodically successful in gaining control and establishing reforms. But the conservatives never accepted the reforms, and civil war ensued until 1876 when Porfirio Díaz took office.

During the 1850s, the United States had been inclined to deal with the conservatives and was pleased when Santa Anna's financial troubles led him to sell to the United States in the Gadsden Purchase what is now southern Arizona and New Mexico. This territory was valuable in order to secure for America a transportation route to the West Coast. Although American sentiment was largely with the liberals in 1855 when Juárez overthrew Santa Anna, the U.S. government was quick to recognize the conservative regime when it again seized power in 1857. Mexican conservatives, however, proved unwilling to sell off any more territory.

In the thirty-four years spanning the Díaz presidency, the country stabilized and the economy improved. Millions of U.S. investment dollars were attracted to Mexico's modernization plans, as Díaz promised protections and guarantees. American investments went a long way in building an effective railroad system as well as other public works, but caused alarm among Mexicans who believed modernization masked a growing inequality in Mexico's social organization and an increasing dependency on foreign powers, effectively undermining the nation's hard-won independence.

These resentments helped bring on the Mexican Revolution in 1910, which drastically changed the nature of relations between the two countries. Twice the United States sent military forces into Mexico. In 1914 Woodrow Wilson sent U.S. Marines into Veracruz following an incident involving an arrest of U.S. sailors, and in 1916, American troops entered Mexico, when Gen. John J. Pershing chased Pancho Villa back after his raids in New Mexico.

Foreign investment became a target of the revolutionaries who believed that national interests needed to guide modernization efforts. The new Mexican Constitution of 1917 gave the state the right to expropriate property, including that owned by foreign nations, when the property was deemed useful for improving social conditions.

In 1919 President Venustiano Carranza issued his doctrine, which outlined an antiforeign policy, including not permitting foreigners to attain a predominant position in relation to natives, disowning the Monroe Doctrine as constituting interference in the domestic affairs of Latin American countries, establishing solidarity among Latin American countries based on the principle of nonintervention, and gaining control over national resources and promoting industrialization.

The 1920s saw rising tensions as U.S. investors — particularly oil companies — feared expropriation. Mexico owned significant oil resources in which the United States and, to a lesser degree, Britain had invested heavily. Mexico and the United States agreed unofficially on how Mexico would apply oil and agrarian legislation to U.S.-owned property, which eased tensions, but Mexico was asserting its independence in foreign affairs as well as on its own soil.

In 1938 President Lázaro Cárdenas nationalized Mexican oil rights and created the state oil monopoly, PEMEX. Cárdenas became a national hero who had successfully defended Mexico from the Colossus of the North. Right-wing U.S. interests demanded that President Franklin D. Roosevelt intervene, but the Good Neighbor policy prevailed, and the United States finally accepted compensation, sending nothing more than a few angry notes. In the hope of deterring other Latin American countries from similar acts, the United States enforced a boycott of Mexican oil for thirty years, effectively undermining PEMEX operations. Nevertheless, the nationalization of oil companies may have established more equal and stable rules for U.S.-Mexican relations.

World War II brought the countries closer. In 1942, Mexico joined the Allies after repeated sinkings of its ships by German U-boats. Mexico provided an air force squadron trained in the United States and fought Japan in the Philippines. Mexico also supplied raw materials at government-controlled prices. Further, under the Bracero Agreement, the war years saw an increase of 300,000 Mexican laborers in the United States who filled job openings created by the draft.

The postwar years were generally stable, emphasizing the "special relationship" enjoyed by the two governments. The concord prevailed despite tensions created by the cold war, which cast suspicion on the Mexican emphasis on protectionism as a stimulus to industrialization. The simultaneous devaluation of the peso, however, made Mexico an attractive outlet for both tourists and foreign investors, and cold war concerns never dominated U.S.-Mexican relations. Although there was much popular outcry by Mexican nationalists against the U.S.-backed overthrow of Jacobo Arbenz Guzmán in Guatemala in 1954, the government kept silent beyond a restatement of the official policy of nonintervention. The Mexican government was more singular in its response to Fidel Castro's Cuba. In spite of U.S. pressure to censure Castro, Mexico was the only Latin American country to maintain relations with Cuba in the aftermath of the revolution. Yet Mexico backed the United States during the Cuban missile crisis and did not ally with other third world revolutionary movements.

The good relations lasted until the late 1960s, but then Mexico began to re-create its nationalist image. Operation Intercept, an antinarcotics program of the Nixon administration, unilaterally closed the border between the two countries and disrupted commercial traffic. Mexico saw this as an example of U.S. untrustworthiness. In 1971 Richard M. Nixon imposed a 10 percent duty on all imports, hurting Mexico, which sold almost 70 percent of its exports to the United States. These acts caused President Alvarez Echeverría to doubt that there was anything beneficially special about Mexico's relationship with the United States. Echeverría tried to orient Mexico away from the United States both economically and politically, but despite significant drops during the mid-seventies, Mexico was again sending 70 percent of its exports to the United States by 1980. In contrast, although trade with Mexico was larger than with any other Latin American country, it accounted for only 5 percent of U.S. foreign trade. Even a severe economic crisis in 1976, however, did not halt Mexico's bid for independence from U.S. influence.

Economic issues were coupled with political differences. In 1979 Mexico broke relations with Nicaragua's Somoza regime, sending a clear message of solidarity with the rebels against the U.S.-backed government. In 1981 Mexico gave similar support to the insurgents in El Salvador. Mexico's expressed support of nationalist movements in Central America and the Caribbean led to increased tensions between the two countries in the 1980s. But the end of the decade saw an increased mutual effort to establish a constructive relationship in the areas of trade agreements, migration, the drug war, and harmonious foreign policies.

Robert A. Pastor and Jorge G. Castañeda, *Limits to Friendship: The United States and Mexico* (1988); Josefina Zoraida Vázquez and Lorenzo Meyer, *The United States and Mexico* (1985).

NICHOLAS B. MAHER

See also Alamo; Caribbean-U.S. Relations; Gadsden Purchase; Good Neighbor Policy; Latin America–U.S. Relations; Mexican War; Monroe Doctrine; Texas Revolution and Annexation.

MICHELSON, ALBERT

(1852–1931), scientist. Although Albert Michelson was born in a Polish village to a Jewish father and a gentile mother, he became both a symbol and a star of American science as it stood in his time. He was three when his family immigrated to a California mining town, itself a symbol of American restlessness and hustle. Michelson graduated from the U.S. Naval Academy in 1873, ranking first among his classmates in optics. Unlike most Americans in the frenzied materialism of the Gilded Age, Michelson was attracted to science and found his métier in the sort of work most congenial to American scientists of his day: instrumentation and measurement. The ardent collection of discrete facts, rather than patient, long-range investigative projects, dominated American science in those years.

Michelson was a young physics instructor at Annapolis in 1877 when his department head urged him to open his lecture demonstrations with the French physicist Foucault's apparatus for measuring the speed of light. Michelson thereupon conceived an ingenious improvement on Foucault's device, simplifying it and significantly improving its accuracy. From then on, through almost half a century of university teaching, Michelson would pursue the holy grail of ultimate precision in measuring that fundamental physical constant. Early in the quest he confronted the problem of how light traveled. Scientists at the time generally accepted the theory that light traveled in the form of waves transmitted by a hypothetical substance they called the "ether," supposedly stationary and filling the entire universe. Michelson accepted that hypothesis and set out to determine the motion of the earth relative to the postulated ether.

In 1887, collaborating with a chemist friend,

Edward W. Morley, Michelson carried out an ingenious experiment with a negative result: the speed of light was the same regardless of its direction relative to the earth's motion in space. The ether, if it existed, evidently had no effect, at least at the earth's surface. This startling finding did not, as legend has had it, directly inspire Einstein's theory of relativity (which ruled out ether), though it did lead others to ideas that in turn played a part in that theory, and it gave experimental support to the theory, once formulated. Michelson himself, weak in mathematics like most American physicists of the period, continued to believe in the ether and grudgingly accepted Einstein's theory only after many years, on the pragmatic grounds that it accounted for certain measurable phenomena.

Although he neither claimed nor craved a share in Einstein's glory, Michelson found consolation and pride in the instrument he had developed for the classic experiment: the interferometer. He refined and improved it brilliantly over the years, adapting it to a dazzling array of scientific measurements. It became one of the basic instruments of physical science, in a class with telescopes, microscopes, and thermometers. It was for his instruments and measurements, not for any contribution to relativity, that Michelson in 1907 became the first American to win a Nobel Prize in science. The honor was a sign of American science's coming of age. Ironically, that meant going beyond the very kind of science that Michelson had so famously represented.

Dorothy M. Livingston, *The Master of Light* (1979); Loyd S. Swenson, Jr., *The Ethereal Aether: A History of the Michelson-Morley-Miller Aether Drift Experiments, 1880–1930* (1972).

ROBERT V. BRUCE

See also Science and Technology.

MIDDLE COLONIES

The region known as the Middle Colonies, which eventually encompassed New York, New Jersey, Pennsylvania, and Delaware, was the only part of British North America initially settled by non-English Europeans, a circumstance that did much to form the character of the section. An early-seventeenth-century Swedish toehold on the Delaware River was dislodged in 1655 by the Dutch, who in turn were ousted from their colony of New Netherland by the English in 1664. Only when these European claims to the Mid-Atlantic region were extinguished could English settlement begin in earnest.

By the conquest of 1664 the Restoration was in full stride in England, though the restored king, Charles II, confronted serious financial difficulties. To ease strains on the treasury, Charles turned to the recently acquired lands in America. By parceling them out to groups of proprietors, as they were called, the king not only discharged some of the Crown's debts but also attached a number of leading gentlemen to his rule.

Between 1664 and 1682, four proprietary colonies were carved from the conquered territory stretching from the Hudson River to the Delaware and then south along the Atlantic Coast to Chesapeake Bay. The entire region was initially granted to the king's brother, James, duke of York and Albany. The Dutch reconquered New York in 1673, only to surrender it again the following year. When the duke ascended the throne as King James II in 1685, New York was automatically converted from a proprietary to a royal colony.

New Jersey was granted to a series of proprietors, among whose leaders were John Lord Berkeley, Sir George Carteret, and William Penn. One-half of the colony, West Jersey, was purchased by Quakers in the 1670s. The other half, East Jersey, came under the control by 1682 of twenty-four proprietors, with Quakers, Scots, and Anglicans prominent among their number.

William Penn, meanwhile, had decided to form his own colony to provide a haven for Quakers and, as it turned out, other persecuted sects attracted by his policy of religious toleration. The proprietary charter he received from the Crown in 1681 designated Penn, or his deputy, as governor. The next year Penn was granted the three lower Delaware counties of Newcastle, Kent, and Sussex. Throughout the colonial era, these "Lower Counties" retained a separate legislature; in 1773 they broke off from Pennsylvania to form the colony of Delaware.

This fragmented and desultory beginning, as well as a late-seventeenth-century drop in English emigration, produced a complex middle-colony society composed of, among others, Dutch Calvinists, Scandinavian Lutherans, German Baptists, Swiss Pietists, Welsh Quakers, French Huguenots, Scots Presbyterians, and a large black slave population. In contrast to New England and the Chesapeake colonies, Englishmen and women composed the least part of early Mid-Atlantic society.

Because the seventeenth century was not a tolerant age, newcomers to the Middle Colonies tended to settle with their own kind in exclusive enclaves, a pattern facilitated by geography and the availability of land. Thus New York's Dutch Calvinists concentrated in King's County and the upper Hudson Valley, New England Puritans in eastern Long Island and Westchester County, French Huguenots at New Rochelle, and the later-arriving German Lutherans and Reformed in the Mohawk Valley. The English first congregated in Manhattan, later spreading out to nearby Queens and Westchester counties.

West Jersey, in turn, was dominated by adherents of the Society of Friends. Smaller numbers of Quakers lived in East Jersey, where they jostled for power with Scots, some Dutch, and a rising number of English Anglicans, the latter supporting the Crown's decision in 1702 to combine the Jerseys into a single royal colony. In Pennsylvania the early-arriving English and Welsh population settled along the Delaware River near Philadelphia and in the lower counties; many of the German Pietists and later-arriving German church people took up lands in Lancaster and surrounding northwestern counties, where the Scots-Irish joined them in the eighteenth century and then pushed on to the frontier. The slave population, laboring in nascent industries and on farms in New York and New Jersey, was widely scattered in towns and countryside.

With the middle-colony landscape dotted by clannish communities of the like-minded — their national origins still visible today in town names — the region came to be characterized by a cultural localism, or subsectionalism, that from the earliest years expressed itself in politics.

Each colony had a governor, either proprietary or royal, a council to advise him, and an assembly to represent the people — the last being the only elected part of provincial government. Owing to the diverse origins of the population, assemblymen were closely tied to and expected to reflect their constituents' cultural, religious, and economic concerns. Yet these local interests often clashed with the governors' imperial objectives, leading to a contentious politics that manifested itself in endemic factional strife. From New York's Leisler's Rebellion in 1689 to Pennsylvania's march of the Paxton Boys in 1764, middle-colony politics typically displayed an ethnoreligious edge.

In contrast to the atomized culture of the countryside stood the rising port cities of Philadelphia and New York, whose bustling commercial character became increasingly apparent. Once the seventeenth-century fur trade declined, local farmers turned their labor to the production of wheat, rye, fruits, beef, and the like. By the eighteenth century a strong market had developed for these staple products, which flowed from the hinterlands down the Hudson and Delaware rivers toward those ports' crowded roadways, there to be loaded on ships for distribution throughout the Atlantic world. The more metropolitan culture of New York and Philadelphia could be seen in the rising number of newspapers, large churches, libraries, and fraternal organizations. After mid-century each city chartered a college, Kings College (Columbia) in 1754 and the College of Philadelphia (University of Pennsylvania) the next year.

To be sure, in the more contained vessel of the cities, cultural and political pressures could rise dangerously. Yet over time toleration grew, if only because each group could secure its rights only by granting similar rights to others. Even in the volatile political arena compromises were achieved, as shifting parties of ins and outs weighed interests and struck bargains. Thus such protomodern political practices as ticket balancing, targeted propaganda, and voter roundups at election time found their most advanced expression in the Middle Colonies. By the mid-eighteenth century an ethos of pluralism, widening religious toleration, and a brokered politics of interest had come to characterize the Middle Colonies, forecasting in signal ways the future social configuration and political culture of the United States.

Patricia U. Bonomi, "The Middle Colonies: Embryo of the New Political Order," in Alden T. Vaughan and George A. Billias, eds., *Perspectives on Early American History: Essays in Honor of Richard B. Morris* (1973), 63–92; Douglas Greenberg, "The Middle Colonies in Recent American Historiography," *William and Mary Quarterly* 36 (1979): 396–427.

PATRICIA U. BONOMI

See also Colonial Culture; Colonial Economy; Colonial Government and Politics; Colonial Wars; Leisler's Rebellion; Stuyvesant, Peter.

MIDDLE EAST–U.S. RELATIONS

The first contacts between the United States and the Middle East occurred during late-eighteenth-century treaty negotiations with the states of North Africa and were interspersed with sporadic naval conflicts. The first sustained relations, however, resulted from American missionary efforts in various parts of the region, starting in 1819 and growing in importance throughout the nineteenth century. Aside from spreading Christianity, missionaries focused on creating educational institutions, primarily in Lebanon, Syria, and Palestine. One of the most important of these was the Syrian Protestant College established in 1866 (called the American University of Beirut after 1920). Similar efforts in Turkey led to the foundation of Robert College in 1863. Both institutions had a major impact on the Middle East because they educated members of local elites.

By World War I, decades of work by American missionaries and educators in these and other countries of the region had created an almost uniformly favorable view of the United States. It seemed the only Western power with no imperial designs on the region. This view was reinforced during World War I by President Woodrow Wilson's Fourteen Points, and by America's championing of the principle of self-determination at the Versailles peace conference. Countries of the Middle East that were resisting the encroachment of European powers hoped that the United States would serve as a counterbalance to traditional Western imperialism. This hope was expressed forcefully to the members of the King-Crane Commission, dispatched to Syria and Palestine at the behest of Wilson to ascertain the preferences of the populations regarding which mandatory power should be chosen to help them toward independence, as specified by the Covenant of the League of Nations.

The inquiry conducted by the King-Crane Commission showed the degree of sympathy for the United States that existed in Syria, Palestine, and Lebanon. An overwhelming majority of those polled expressed a desire for an American mandate in preference to a British or French one. But these results became a dead letter when the U.S. Senate repudiated the League's Covenant, and the mandates for Syria, Lebanon, Iraq, Palestine, and Jordan were soon afterward given to Britain and France. Nevertheless, Wilson's sending a commission to ascertain their wishes made a lasting positive impression on the people of these countries.

Aside from the activities of American oil companies, this was the last major American initiative in the Middle East until after World War II. Although the oil companies played a central role in the discovery of petroleum in Saudi Arabia in the late 1930s, they were generally restricted in their activities elsewhere by their British and French rivals, both of whom exploited the advantages provided by their countries' political dominance in the region. During the war large numbers of American troops fought in and traveled through the area, but only afterward did Middle East oil production grow in importance and the United States become a major power there.

Even after the Second World War, the United States initially tended to take a back seat to Britain in the region. But the United States was soon involved in either supporting or competing with Britain on issues related to the so-called Northern Tier of Middle Eastern states — notably Turkey and Iran — as well as Palestine.

In 1947 a financially straitened Britain was forced to halt its support for the governments of Greece and Turkey, creating a potential power vacuum on the southern flank of the Soviet Union. This the United States rushed to fill in keeping with the cold war atmosphere and its new role as a world power. The result was the Truman Doctrine, which proclaimed it a zone of particular American interest, the first of a series of presidential policies pertaining to the area.

In the early fifties, Britain and the United States opposed the government of Iranian prime minister Mohammad Mosaddeq, which had nationalized the country's mainly British-owned oil industry. The overthrow of Mosaddeq and the reimposition of the autocratic rule of Shah Mohammad Reza Pahlavi was in large measure a joint project of the American and British intelligence services. By associating itself with Britain in this episode, the United States came to be identified with that older imperial power against which Iranians had so many grievances dating back 150 years. In time, the American identification with the shah's regime became more and more of a liability, as Iranian nationalism, originally secular in nature, developed a much more religious cast.

But conflict, more than cooperation, characterized British-American relations in the case of Palestine. Britain was engaged in a bloody conflict with the Zionist movement, whose implantation in Palestine it had originally facilitated, but which was now strong enough to stand on its own. The capability of the Jewish *Yishuv* in Palestine — which had already developed into the embryo of the Israeli state — was greatly enhanced by the support it received from the United States, where the Jewish community was increasingly active in its behalf. The farsighted Zionist leader, David Ben-Gurion, had realized as early as 1942 that in the postwar international configuration the United States would be a more powerful patron than Britain. In that year, at his urging, the Biltmore Conference in New York committed the Zionist movement to an ambitious plan for an independent Jewish state in Palestine, which inevitably placed the movement on a collision course with Britain. Ben-Gurion risked this, against the inclinations of the movement's Anglophile elder statesman Chaim Weizmann, because of his confidence in the potential for American support, which in the event proved to be fully justified.

In 1946, the United States began to exert its influence over the question of Palestine with a proposal for an Anglo-American Commission of Inquiry. This group recommended the immediate entry into Palestine of 100,000 survivors of the Holocaust, who were still languishing in displaced-person camps long after the war's end, largely because of the refusal of European countries and the United States to admit them. This recommendation undermined the efforts of the British, who were struggling to maintain their commitments to their Arab clients in the region while confronting the growing insurrection of the Yishuv in Palestine. By 1947, Britain was forced to give up this impossible task and handed the question of Palestine over to the United Nations. In the U.N. General Assembly's consideration of the question in 1947, the United States played a decisive role in the passage of Resolution 181, which partitioned Palestine and allowed for the creation of Jewish and Arab states. When Israel came into existence in May 1948, the United States was the first country to extend recognition to it.

A consistent pattern in American relations with the Middle East thus emerged. The United States championed the cause of Israel while slowly replacing Britain as the major Western patron of conservative Arab regimes. The stresses of accommodating both an increasingly close relationship with Israel and ties with Arab states that were at war with Israel have marked American relations with the Arab world ever since. Relations became particularly acute during the Suez War of 1956, when the United States opposed the British-French-Israeli attack on Egypt in spite of Secretary of State John Foster Dulles's antipathy for the nationalist regime of Egyptian leader Gamal Abdel Nasser.

During this crisis, the desire to prevent the Soviet Union from exploiting the situation was probably uppermost in the minds of American policymakers, rather than the specifics of the Arab-Israeli conflict. American preoccupation with the growth of Soviet influence in the region became another consistent pattern during the next three decades, one that Israel increasingly benefited from, in the form of American financial, military, and diplomatic support. This support escalated particularly sharply following the June 1967 Arab-Israeli War, after which the United States became Israel's main supplier of advanced weaponry.

Enhanced American commitment to Israel was one of the major results of the growing polarization of the Middle East along cold war lines in the 1950s and 1960s. Several Arab states aligned themselves more closely with the Soviet Union, and other regional states, including Israel, Iran, Saudi Arabia, Jordan, and Morocco, grew closer to the United States. This trend transcended the boundaries of the Arab-Israeli conflict, however, as was evidenced by the Eisenhower Doctrine of 1957, which committed the United States to come to the aid of any state threatened by "international communism."

This doctrine became the basis for American support for conservative regimes against their radical local rivals. It was first put into practice with the landing of U.S. forces in Lebanon in 1958 to shore up the regime of President Camille Chamoun against his domestic opposition, which was supported by the Egyptian-dominated United Arab Republic. The Eisenhower administration also tried to incorporate the Middle East into its chain of regional pacts directed against the Soviet Union, but with only limited success. The fruit of this effort, the Baghdad Pact, which later evolved into the Central Treaty Organization, was highly unpopular in many countries and ultimately included only the non-Arab Muslim states of Turkey, Iran, and Pakistan.

The Kennedy administration initially tried to draw a distinction between Arab nationalist and "procommunist" regimes. Seeking to improve relations with Egypt, President John F. Kennedy initiated a personal correspondence with that country's President Nasser. But the outbreak of the Yemeni civil war in 1962, in which both Egypt and Saudi Arabia became deeply involved, and Kennedy's assassination the next year halted this process. The United States eventually ended up siding with Saudi Arabia and its clients, the Yemeni royalists, against Egypt and its clients, the Yemeni republicans, both backed by the Soviets.

In this highly polarized situation, the June 1967 Arab-Israeli War broke out, creating a set of problems for U.S. policy, most of which have persisted to the present day. Foremost among them has been the task of reconciling American sympathy and support for Israel with a desire to maintain a strong footing in Arab countries resentful of Israel's unwillingness to evacuate territories occupied during the 1967 war. This problem was partly alleviated by Egypt's shift from a pro-Soviet to a pro-American orientation after 1970 and by the Egyptian-Israeli peace treaty of 1979. But it persists because other aspects of the Arab-Israeli conflict, notably the Palestinian-Israeli dimension, have not been resolved.

While the United States was involved in efforts to resolve the Egyptian-Israeli aspect of this conflict in the wake of the October 1973 Arab-Israeli War, renewed importance was being attached to another American ally in the Middle East, Iran under the regime of the shah. Iran became the focus of the Nixon Doctrine of 1972, whereby in the wake of the Vietnam War experience, the United States laid greater stress on arming powerful regional allies. With American support, the shah embarked on a massive program to upgrade the Iranian military and turn his country into a regional superpower. This process both exacerbated tensions with Iran's neighbors, notably Iraq, and alienated elements among the Iranian public who were already highly critical of their nation's subordination to the United States and the shah's dictatorial rule over the country.

In 1979 a popular Islamic Revolution brought down the shah, throwing American policy in the Gulf region into disarray. The virulent anti-Americanism of the new regime, exemplified in the hostage crisis, angered Americans, arousing their concern about the Middle East as had nothing since the Arab oil boycott during the October 1973 war. The American public's long-standing lack of understanding of the region often complicated the task of U.S. policymakers. Diplomatic responses ranged from the

Carter Doctrine, which proclaimed the Gulf an area vital to American interests, to the Reagan administration's sending of American warships to protect the flow of Kuwaiti oil from Iranian attacks during the Iran-Iraq War, even while the administration was covertly trying to reestablish relations with Iran, as was revealed during the Iran-Contra scandal.

At the beginning of the 1990s, American relations with the Middle East continued to be dominated by the Arab-Israeli conflict and the question of oil. Israel and the Gulf became the major preoccupations of American Middle East policymakers, with alignment with the first and hostility toward the second overshadowing much else. Thus in Lebanon in 1982–1983, the Reagan administration initially went along with Israel's invasion of that country and later committed U.S. troops there while supporting a Lebanese government backed by only one of the country's sects. The objective was apparently support for Israeli objectives in Lebanon and opposition to its local rivals, the PLO and Syria; but the result was a defeat for the United States and Israel and the government they supported, at the cost of the lives of over three hundred American servicemen and diplomats, the kidnapping of many other Americans, and serious damage to American interests that had been built up over more than a century of missionary, educational, and medical efforts.

In the Gulf, the United States began the 1990s aligned with Iraq, a vestige of policymakers' obsession with the revolutionary Islamic regime in Iran. The Bush administration, however, turned against Iraq after its invasion, occupation, and annexation of Kuwait in August 1990, going to war with it at the head of a thirty-nation coalition in January of the following year. The allies smashed the Iraqi army and entire domestic infrastructure in a devastating campaign that lasted barely seven weeks and cost very low American casualties among its half million troops, but left 150,000 Iraqis dead, according to American military estimates. It was unclear at the war's end how the regional vacuum created by the defeat and eclipse of Iraq would benefit American or regional interests in the long term.

After two centuries, a relationship with the Middle East that began with aspects of both conflict and constructive endeavor had become one in which the United States was the preeminent power in the region, inextricably involved in its affairs in pursuit of access to oil and strategic advantage.

Seth P. Tillman, *The United States in the Middle East: Interests and Obstacles* (1982).

RASHID I. KHALIDI

See also Camp David Accord; Cold War; Great Britain–U.S. Relations; Iran-Contra Affair; Iran Hostage Crisis; Jews; Oil Industry; OPEC Oil Crisis; Truman Doctrine.

MIDDLETOWN

Middletown is the title of the classic sociological study of a typical middle-American city published in 1929 by Helen and Robert Lynd. The study was based on field research done in Muncie, Indiana, in 1924–1925. A sequel published in 1937, entitled *Middletown in Transition,* was based on the Lynds' return to Muncie in 1935. Muncie was referred to as Middletown to convey the representativeness of the city and their findings there.

The Middletown studies were influential in identifying and popularizing the idea of America as a consumer culture. By observing the day-to-day life of the city's residents, the Lynds showed how traditional values and customs were changing under the influence of industrialization. They contrasted Middletown in the 1890s and 1920s, portraying the shift from an active, civic-oriented citizenry to one embracing materialistic values. Since work and community life in the 1920s provided fewer satisfactions to Middletowners, they turned to consumerism to fulfill their social needs. *Middletown* depicted the dynamic conflict over this change, although most citizens believed it was inevitable and good. The Lynds implicitly criticized this emergent commercialism by successfully combining their moral critique with scientific analysis. The combination gave the study its power and originality.

Middletown in Transition focused on the power relationships in Muncie during the Great

Depression. The Lynds showed how the residents were subordinate to both a powerful, local business elite and the national consumer culture. This domination rendered Middletown citizens somewhat impotent, unable to change their society. The solution, the Lynds concluded, was for professional managers to mold social institutions for the greater public good.

MIDWIVES

In the seventeenth-century colonies, childbirth was the exclusive province of midwives — unschooled but respected women who learned their craft by observation and personal experience. Their role was to offer encouragement and reassurance to the woman, tie off the umbilical cord after delivery, be sure the placenta was expelled, and generally care for the mother and child. Since the great majority of births, then as now, were normal and uneventful, this was usually sufficient attention. In the case of difficult or lengthy labors, there was little the midwife could do, other than turn to a more experienced midwife. Women were not permitted to receive medical schooling, and though men were, they were never permitted in the lying-in chamber for reasons of modesty.

Gradually, midwives became licensed, which was merely a matter of the woman taking an oath to be "patient and caring," to report the "true father" to the authorities, to never "conceal a birth," to minister to the poor as well as the rich, and so on. The church also took an interest in a midwife's activities out of concern that she might be a witch who would practice her sorcery upon the infant — a child born with a deformity was a suspicious matter. (The first person executed in the Massachusetts Bay Colony was Margaret Jones, a midwife accused of witchcraft, in 1648.)

With the advent of the scientific revolution in the eighteenth century, the situation slowly changed. Young American men went to Europe to study medicine and the "new obstetrics," becoming men midwives as well as general practitioners on their return. But women were not admitted to schools and, moreover, did not have access to or training in the use of the new medical instruments like forceps. Thus, they found themselves relegated more and more to the practice of normal births and were expected to turn over difficult labors to the trained men. Middle- and upper-class women now gradually overcame their qualms about modesty, as the superiority of these men over untrained women became evident.

Competition between the two groups grew steadily between 1760 and 1800, with both advertising their services in newspapers and seeking to spread their reputation for safe births via word of mouth. But by 1820, Walter Channing, the first obstetrics professor at Harvard, could write with satisfaction, "Heretofore, where midwifery has been in the hands of women, they have only practised among the poorer and lower classes, . . . the richer and better informed preferring to employ physicians. . . . It was one of the first and happiest fruits of improved medical education in America, that . . . [women] were excluded from practice."

It was only when women in the course of the nineteenth and twentieth centuries gradually gained access to medical schools that they were able to compete on equal terms with male obstetricians.

See also Medicine.

MIGRATION

See Black Migration; Internal Migration.

MILITARY

See Armed Forces.

MILITARY ACADEMIES

See Armed Forces.

MILLER, ARTHUR

(1915–   ), playwright. Miller has said that the object of his plays is to discover "the ultimate judgment lying upon us all." Drama must examine "social and moral problems, not simply psychology." Miller's reputation, in fact, was built on this attempt to judge "man's rightful position" according to objective standards of fair play, moral sanity, and the welfare of the community. Ironically, however, his strongest plays deliver his verdict while exploring the psychological mechanisms of radical self-assertion. His most fluent language expresses the negative personal consequences of ego-centered "fanaticism" rather than the positive public consequences of selfless "sacrifice." It is the unstable tension between these two poles that has given energy to Miller's work.

Miller grew up during the Great Depression, which aroused his indignation over social inequities and their crushing impact on ordinary citizens. These reactions are reflected in his early plays, such as *All My Sons* (1947), his only novel, *Focus* (1945), and minor works, such as *The Misfits* (1961).

His more substantial plays, however, focus on the motivation of individuals demanding self-respect, not the challenges to self-respect delivered by irrational social conditions. *Death of a Salesman* (1949), *A View from the Bridge* (1955), and *After the Fall* (1964) illustrate that focus. In *The Crucible* (1953), *Incident at Vichy* (1964), and *The Price* (1968) he tried, with partial success, to balance the two themes. Whatever the emphasis, Miller's goal has remained constant: serious drama, he maintains, shows "an individual fulfilling his subjective needs through social action."

To project this model, Arthur Miller experimented with several styles. Probably the most important is the realistic mode made legitimate by Henrik Ibsen, whom Miller admires. Miller's only technical weakness, not uncommon in Ibsen's plays, arises from his eagerness to spell out his "judgment," resulting in overexplicit rhetoric that often interrupts the more subtle interplay between "social and psychological mechanisms."

Miller's life embodies the penchant for justice that animates the plays. For one thing, he has traveled widely in order to observe foreign systems of government and report upon them. He has also engaged in political activities — for example, as a delegate to and critic of the Democratic National Conventions of 1968 and 1972. And he served as president of PEN, an international activist association of poets, playwrights, essayists, and novelists (1965–1969).

He acquitted himself with honor during his interrogation in 1956 by the House Un-American Activities Committee, testifying that he had allied himself with liberal causes for many years but that he was not a communist and would not inform on others who might be. He was found guilty of contempt of Congress, but the verdict was reversed. Miller's belief that "you change society because you sharpen its consciousness" never wavered.

Miller's autobiography, *Timebends,* appeared in 1987. He has received many awards, including the New York Drama Critics Circle Award (*All My Sons*), the Pulitzer Prize (*Death of a Salesman*), the Antoinette Perry Award (*The Crucible*), and the Gold Medal for Drama, National Institute of Arts and Letters (1959). His wide social concerns and technical virtuosity, combining realistic, expressionist, and rhetorical styles, qualify him to be called America's most notable living dramatist.

Arthur Miller, *Timebends* (1987); Leonard Moss, *Arthur Miller* (1980).

LEONARD MOSS

See also House Un-American Activities Committee; Theater.

MINOR V. HAPPERSETT

In the case of *Minor* v. *Happersett* (1874) the Supreme Court decreed that the state of Missouri had been within its constitutional rights in denying a woman applicant, Virginia Minor, the right to vote. The feminist Victoria Woodhull had urged women to try to vote, arguing that the Fourteenth Amendment forbade the states to limit citizens' rights. This "new departure" was adopted by the National Woman Suffrage Association (NWSA), and Susan B. Anthony organized seventy suffragists nationwide — among them, Minor — to vote in the 1872 elections.

Minor was denied entrance to the Missouri polls by the registrar, Reese Happersett, on the ground that the state constitution limited voting to males. With her husband (because married women could not bring legal action on their own), she then sued the registrar, arguing that her rights of citizenship had been unlawfully abridged. When the case reached the Supreme

Court, however, the justices declared that voting was not among the privileges guaranteed to all citizens and was therefore not protected by the Fourteenth Amendment. This decision ended the "new departure," convincing the NWSA that woman suffrage could be won only by a new constitutional amendment.

See also Feminist Movement; Suffrage.

MIRANDA V. ARIZONA

Miranda v. *Arizona,* decided by the Supreme Court in 1966 by a 5–4 majority, held that the Constitution's Fifth Amendment prohibition against self-incrimination applied to an individual in police custody or "deprived of his freedom of action in any significant way." In order to safeguard this right, the Court ruled that prior to being questioned suspects have to be informed of their right to remain silent, that anything they say can be used against them in court, that they have the right to the presence of an attorney, and that if they cannot afford an attorney one will be appointed prior to questioning if they so desire. A statement obtained without compliance with these rules is inadmissible as is the fact that a defendant has chosen to exercise the right to remain silent "in the face of accusation." Although waiver of these rights is possible, the Court emphasized that "a heavy burden rests on the government" to prove that such a waiver has actually taken place.

The Court based its holding on an extensive review of actual police interrogation practices. In addition to outright physical abuse and the "third degree," the police had frequently obtained confessions through a variety of ploys and subterfuges, many of which were codified in police manuals and texts. The Court found that "the very fact of custodial interrogation exacts a heavy toll on individual liberty and trades on the weakness of individuals."

Hailed by civil libertarians as a victory for individual rights, the decision was attacked by conservatives as undermining the efforts of law enforcement officials. Meanwhile, a series of post–Warren Court decisions have significantly limited the applicability of *Miranda* while not overruling the case outright.

See also Bill of Rights; Police Forces; Warren, Earl.

MISSIONARIES

Missionaries of the Christian gospel throughout American history have been men and women who have determined to carry out what they take to be Jesus Christ's command to preach the message of God to all lands, seeking to win disciples and church members. They inherited an impulse and a practice that dates from first-century Christian communities.

When European Christians first came to the Americas, this missionary motive was interwoven with commercial intentions. The Iberian Catholics who dominated in parts of what became the American South and Southwest included missionaries who worked among American Indians. While they were often agents of conquistadores, they also sincerely believed that if they did not convert the "heathen" or "savages," these "creatures of God" would be lost and would suffer eternally in hell. So pioneers like Junípero Serra, who established missions along the California coast in the eighteenth century, built compounds where they offered work and rudimentary education, even as they disrupted the Indians' faith and practices.

In Canada and the American Northeast and Great Lakes region, missionary orders of friars and priests from France similarly set out to convert and minister to the native peoples. But in what became the United States, the missions were overwhelmingly in the hands of white Protestants, chiefly from the British Isles, although in the Middle Colonies substantial numbers were, among others, German- or Dutch-speaking Lutheran, Reformed, and Moravian church members.

The English missionaries justified colonization in part as an attempt to bring the unredeemed heathen into the Christian fold, but despite their expressed motives, most of them failed miserably. The Indians generally resisted, especially as conflicts developed with the Europeans. Or they found the stories missionaries told them complex and confusing, again disruptive of their own outlooks and practices. Doing "God's work" among the natives turned out to be dangerous, and most colonial missionaries lost all taste for risking their lives to convert what turned out to be only a small number of Indians. It is fair to say that by the time the United States was born, Protestants had all but abandoned their mission.

A second chapter for missionaries began on United States soil in the second decade of the nineteenth century. Collegians influenced by religious awakenings and revivals became convinced that it was their mission to bring about the millennium by making the world attractive for Christ's return and extending the sphere of the true Protestant faith. At such colleges as Williams and Amherst, students after their own conversion resolved to try again with the Indians on the frontier and in reservations in the West. They met with some success, but again there were great dangers, and because of the strife between the United States government and many Indian peoples, the Indians were not attractive as converts.

Many missionaries, therefore, set their sights on other parts of the world. Some scholars have seen their efforts as endeavors to reclaim the Christian commonwealth they were losing on the American Atlantic coast. Others have looked upon them as agents of the United States in its expansion as a colonial power. But many observers have come to understand that most of them found sustenance in their decision to risk their lives to win souls for Christ in the Sandwich Islands (Hawaii), the Middle East, and eventually Africa and Asia.

Missionaries often played a part in developing American foreign policy and changing the boundaries of expectations in religious life domestically. Thus when early missionaries arrived in the Sandwich Islands, later Hawaii, after 1820, they conflicted with commercial and naval interests. Poised between native peoples and aggressive exploiters, the missionaries interposed themselves as friends of the Hawaiians and tried to protect them from victimization. At the same time, they worked strenuously to supplant native religion with Christian faith. In both cases they played a large part in bringing Hawaii to United States' consciousness and eventually helped lead to its annexation in 1900.

Meanwhile, some religious movements did not restrict themselves to activity among the "heathen" or in the "pagan" worlds, but instead tried to reconvert already Christianized nations, particularly in Europe. The most celebrated of these ventures was the move by Mormons into Scandinavia and England within a decade after the founding in 1830 of the Church of Jesus Christ of Latter-day Saints. By 1840 Mormon converts in Europe had grown to sufficient numbers that they were migrating to the United States.

The missionary front also allowed for new roles for women. In a century when almost no denomination ordained women to the ministry, widows of missionaries often carried on full ministries overseas. Others found their vocations as nurses or teachers in missionary outposts, and thousands more developed organizational and rhetorical skills in auxiliaries and voluntary agencies in support of missions.

The missionary enterprise came to be an agency not only for conversion but also for education and charity. In company with European missionaries, the Americans effectively spread into most areas of the world. Yale missiologist Kenneth Scott Latourette, examining both Protestant and Catholic efforts, has called the nineteenth century "the Great Century" of Christian missions. But reaction set in in the next century among those whom missionaries sought to convert. As adherents to other religions perceived the disruption to their cultures, they offered more organized resistance. Asian and African nations increasingly rejected Western imperialism and grew suspicious of the missionaries whom they saw as chaplains of conquerors and exploiters. The leaders of indigenous Christian churches on historically non-Christian soil often welcomed spiritual or financial support, but they and their governments generally stopped welcoming personnel from the West. Anticolonialism, or the new nationalism, represented secular movements that came to reject the concept of missionaries from America.

For their part, moderate and liberal Protestants, as well as Roman Catholics after the Second Vatican Council (1962–1965), reappraised their relations to other religions (or, as their evangelical critics would say, experienced a failure of nerve). In 1933 prominent laypersons issued a report, *Rethinking Missions,* which questioned most features of the missionary enterprise. Nevertheless, although Catholics and mainstream Protestants have sent fewer missionaries overseas, they have continued to support indigenous churches in other countries and have engaged in efforts to improve the education and living conditions of peoples there.

Missionaries by the tens of thousands, however, continue to be sent from America, chiefly from more conservative or charismatic Protestant churches: evangelical, fundamentalist, and pentecostal. These missionaries and their supporters still believe that those of non-Christian faiths are damned, so that love for Christ and for other people impels them to evangelize the whole world. They work to attract converts who, in turn, will themselves become missionaries. Through their efforts and those of indigenous churches, Christianity continues to grow at impressive rates in sub-Saharan Africa, Latin America, the subcontinent of Asia, and the Pacific islands.

David B. Barrett, ed., *The World Christian Encyclopedia: A Comparative Study of Churches and Religions in the Modern World, A.D. 1900–2000* (1982); Henry Warner Bowden, *American Indians and Christian Missions: Studies in Cultural Conflict* (1981).

MARTIN E. MARTY

See also Evangelicalism; Middle East–U.S. Relations; Mormons; Serra, Junípero.

MISSOURI COMPROMISE

The Missouri Compromise was an effort by Congress to defuse the sectional and political rivalries triggered by the request of Missouri late in 1819 for admission as a state in which slavery would be permitted. At the time, the United States contained twenty-two states, evenly divided between slave and free. Admission of Missouri as a slave state would upset that balance; it would also set a precedent for congressional acquiescence in the expansion of slavery. Earlier in 1819, when Missouri was being organized as a territory, Representative James Tallmadge of New York had proposed an amendment that would ultimately have ended slavery there; this effort was defeated, as was a similar effort by Representative John Taylor of New York regarding Arkansas Territory.

The extraordinarily bitter debate over Missouri's application for admission ran from December 1819 to March 1820. Northerners, led by Senator Rufus King of New York, argued that Congress had the power to prohibit slavery in a new state. Southerners like Senator William Pinkney of Maryland held that new states had the same freedom of action as the original thirteen and were thus free to choose slavery if they wished. After the Senate and the House passed different bills and deadlock threatened, a compromise bill was worked out with the following provisions: (1) Missouri was admitted as a slave state and Maine (formerly part of Massachusetts) as free, and (2) except for Missouri, slavery was to be excluded from the Louisiana Purchase lands north of latitude 36°30′.

The Missouri Compromise was criticized by many southerners because it established the principle that Congress could make laws regarding slavery; northerners, on the other hand, condemned it for acquiescing in the expansion of slavery (though only south of the compromise line). Nevertheless, the act helped hold the Union together for more than thirty years. It was repealed by the Kansas-Nebraska Act of 1854, which established popular sovereignty (local choice) regarding slavery in Kansas and Nebraska, though both were north of the compromise line. Three years later, the Supreme Court in the *Dred Scott* case declared the Missouri Compromise unconstitutional, on the ground that Congress was prohibited by the Fifth Amendment from depriving individuals of private property without due process of law.

See also Dred Scott Case; Kansas-Nebraska Act.

MOBILITY, SOCIAL AND ECONOMIC

In a speech to the U.S. Senate on February 2, 1832, Henry Clay stated that almost all the successful property owners of his acquaintance were "self-made men, who have whatever wealth they possess by patient and diligent labor." Clay's fellow politicians, newspaper editors, lecturers, and men of great wealth ceaselessly reminded the nation that riches in America were won not by the well-born but by the hard-working. The New York merchant William E. Dodge made the precise claim that 75 percent of "our citizens of wealth" had risen from humble beginnings to their "present position." In *Democracy in America,* perhaps the most influential study of American society ever written, the French visitor Alexis de Tocqueville reported that in the United States "most of the rich men" had earlier in their lives known the "sting of want." Nor were such observations confined to the pre–Civil War decades.

The belief that anyone, of whatever origins, can attain worldly success in the United States, the "land of opportunity," is a central ingredient of what has been called the American Dream. But it was only after 1927, when the sociologist Pitirim Sorokin published his treatise *Social Mobility,* that scholars began to use that term to describe the "vertical movement" of individuals and groups from one social or economic level or class to another — whether above their starting point, as in upward mobility, or below, as in downward mobility.

Well before the American Revolution, the eminent New Yorker Cadwallader Colden wrote an English friend that "the most opulent families in our memory have arisen from the lowest rank of the people." At the end of the nineteenth century, millions of readers were regaled by the more than one hundred novels by Horatio Alger, all of them sounding variations on the theme that by hard work, honesty, and perseverance, abetted by a little luck, poor boys could attain great wealth in the United States. And the "Horatio Alger myth" persisted into the twentieth century.

These cheerful notions rested on evidence that some people had indeed risen from obscure and humble beginnings to great fame and fortune. Their numbers, however, were not legion. Historians and sociologists in the past quarter century have unearthed masses of data on Amer-

ican social mobility patterns over the past three centuries. Their evidence makes possible a historical overview of American social and economic mobility patterns that rests on something more solid than the random examples that in the past were construed as typical, apparently for no better reason than that they were upbeat and consoling to the national ego.

Before assessing the verdict offered by this evidence, a word of caution: for all its volume, it lights up only a small corner of the darkness. Many communities, individuals, groups, and lines of work remain unexamined. To begin with, scholars disagree as to what constitutes social or economic position and how to measure vertical mobility. Moreover, their judgments are not always persuasive. One historian counts as "successful" persons who after ten years have become richer, and as "unsuccessful" those who have grown poorer. By this standard, the pauper who amassed ten dollars over the decade is a success, and the millionaire who lost the same amount is a failure. Yet whatever their deficiencies, the recent studies of vertical mobility are invaluable. They have provided greater evidence than ever before on the early circumstances not simply of small numbers but of many thousands of successful individuals. More important, they go beyond accounts of rags to riches, which, for all their fascination, describe relatively few people, to investigations of the fates and career paths followed by hundreds of thousands of ordinary people over the course of their lives. A clearer light is thrown on the kind of opportunity a society provides by the extent to which masses of people experience modest but significant improvement in their circumstances than by the dramatic leap a few make from the bottom to the top of the social ladder.

Complexity best describes vertical mobility patterns in colonial America. In Maryland, for example, George Calvert offered vast land grants and the equivalent of aristocratic rank to those he anointed his ruling elite. These for the most part were men who in England had been regarded as of the "middling sort" and, if gentlemen, only gentlemen of the "fringe variety." Such men enjoyed what one scholar calls "shipboard mobility," moving a notch higher in the social scale merely by accepting Calvert's offer. Complicating the situation was the fact that high status in the colonies did not have quite the repute it had in the mother country. The poor men who came to Maryland as indentured servants in the first half of the seventeenth century thrived on attaining their personal freedom (after five to seven years of servitude), most of them becoming landowners and active in the affairs of their community. But the servants who came to Maryland in the latter half of the century fared poorly in freedom, victimized by the depression that overtook tobacco farming. In neighboring Virginia at the time, more than 40 percent of the members of the House of Burgesses had previously been servants. But Massachusetts, a land of small farms and hard work, offered few inducements to would-be aristocrats. In Salem, the socially emerging elite of the seventeenth century had considerable wealth to start with. For New England as a whole, those who achieved prominence had for the most part been successful in old England. Master craftsmen who came to America flourished; servants and journeymen "remained humble." A detailed investigation of the town of Dedham, Massachusetts, has revealed that during the seventeenth century "the average young man had little chance of growing rich." A century later his son's chances remained "bleak." Of course, this does not necessarily mean that "average young men" did not improve their lot at all.

In the eighteenth century the picture remained mixed. Opportunity to rise varied from place to place. Older, settled areas offered little chance of success to those of limited means. Opportunity in all geographical areas was greater in frontier counties than in developed eastern regions. One scholar is much impressed by the large proportion of young Bostonians who became taxpayers in the 1770s and 1780s. But another reads the evidence as proof of little vertical mobility in the 1770s and even less in the 1780s. The former finds upward movement in improvement or modest increase in property held; the latter dismisses as "trivial" changes in wealth or occupation unaccompanied by change in an individual's "position." On the one hand, abundance of land and shortage of labor made Amer-

ica the "best poor man's country"; on the other, the great majority of rich men were born to wealth or prominence, and wealth became more unequally distributed with the passage of time, particularly in towns and cities. African-Americans, who had, of course, come to America involuntarily, moved not upward but more firmly into enslavement after the mid-seventeenth century. Although a minority of skilled blacks did improve their economic lot, the status of all African-Americans was low, even those who became free.

The American Revolution had important social and economic as well as political consequences. Among other things, it resulted in the confiscation of Loyalists' estates and the appearance in the new state legislatures of many men of modest circumstances. The Loyalists' lands, however, most often wound up in the hands of substantial speculators, not those of small purchasers. The "new men" who thrived financially during the War for Independence did not supplant older wealth so much as supplement it.

In the first half of the nineteenth century the American economy took off. Booms in transportation, banking, commerce, and manufacturing enticed Europeans, mainly Germans and Irish, to come to the "fabled republic" in unprecedented numbers. The wealth of the nation increased dramatically and surely opened opportunities for at least modest gains to many. But the wealth was distributed more unequally than ever. Far from having suffered "the sting of want" as youngsters, the nation's richest men were almost invariably born to families of wealth and renown. The great majority of Americans, though by no means poverty-stricken, nevertheless owned few worldly goods and enjoyed little improvement in their condition during what used to be called "the era of the common man." Clever politicians and publicists outdid one another in praising "Tom, Dick, and Harry," but in fact ordinary people had little influence as well as little property other than a patch of land. The movement they experienced was more often geographical than vertical, as families facing poor prospects in their home communities moved to new locales. The depressions following the financial panics of 1837 and

1857 had disastrous effects on most families. But the well-to-do, whether in the urban Northeast or the rural West, not only survived but thrived. Detailed studies disclose that the rich got richer during hard times.

The post–Civil War decades saw the rise of big business, the emergence of the United States as the wealthiest and most industrialized nation in the world, and the appearance of vast fortunes, many of them attributed to social upstarts. But after observing that in fact no more than 3 percent of the nation's leading business tycoons had earlier been poor immigrant or farm boys, one historian wryly concluded that such poor lads who rose high had "always been more conspicuous in American history books than in American history."

If the top business leadership of the nation came inordinately from upper-class parents, studies of small communities have revealed a more fluid pattern. Thus, in Paterson, New Jersey, most metal industry manufacturers who opened small shops and factories had started out as workers. In late-nineteenth-century Newburyport, Massachusetts, the sons of blue-collar fathers remained in their class, but they did amass modest amounts of property and improved their lot. In the South, race and ethnicity significantly affected mobility rates, with blacks and Mexican-Americans lagging behind whites. In Michigan, whether rural or urban, an impressive upward movement during the decade after the Civil War had come to a halt by century's end.

Twentieth-century mobility has been intensively studied, above all by sociologists. They have traced the origins of the rich and successful, the occupational careers of entire city populations, the life histories of men and women in hundreds of occupations, the comparative chances of black and white youngsters, the characteristics of upwardly mobile women and downwardly mobile "skidders," and the effects on vertical mobility of people's emotional states, education, expectations, and religion, among other variables. The resultant social portrait is, unsurprisingly, complex, but it does not markedly modify earlier trends.

For the most part, the well-to-do and highly successful were born to advantage. What upward movement people experienced was usually "small-distanced": though they might hold a great variety of jobs in the course of a lifetime, most people in the end arrived at an occupational destination similar in prestige to the job they started out with. On the other hand, structural change, such as the sharp decline in agricultural work or the increasing replacement of blue-collar by white-collar work, gave many sons and daughters jobs that commanded greater prestige — if not higher real wages — than their parents had earned. After World War II, African-Americans in the North enjoyed a significant enhancement in work opportunities, and all Americans benefited from a remarkable increase in college enrollments. But differentiation in the standing and reputation of schools or professions was usually masked by the quantitative data that are the stuff of statistical studies. In life it mattered a great deal whether one attended a slum school or a prestigious prep school, or if one was a lawyer, whether one scratched out a living as a court-assigned attorney for the indigent or earned a large income as solicitor to the corporate mighty.

The complexity of the American situation is well revealed in a study of the composers of popular songs between the world wars. They appear to have been marvelously gifted, but abetting their success were their highly advantageous beginnings; almost all of them were born to parents occupying the upper tenth of the American social and economic structure. And not the least interesting finding of recent research is that vertical mobility rates in the twentieth-century United States are remarkably similar to those elsewhere in the industrial world.

Seymour M. Lipset and Reinhard Bendix, *Social Mobility in Industrial Society* (1959); Edward Pessen, ed., *Three Centuries of Social Mobility in America* (1974); Stephan Thernstrom, *Poverty and Progress: Social Mobility in a Nineteenth-Century City* (1963).

Edward Pessen

See also Democracy in America; Education; Wealth and Its Distribution.

MODEL T FORD

The Model T, according to Henry Ford, was available "in any color you choose, so long as it's black." This may be Ford's most famous statement about his most famous car, but it is not the most telling. The comment that most accurately reflects the nature of Ford's gift to the world is a little-known remark he made in October 1908, on the occasion of the birth of the Model T: "I will build a motor car for the great multitude."

That is exactly what the Model T was. With that vehicle, Ford revolutionized not only the automobile industry but American society, and arguably all of Western culture. With the introduction of the Model T, automobiles became available to everyone, not just the well-to-do.

Although the "Tin Lizzie," with its four-cylinder motor, magneto ignition, and planetary transmission, was a technically advanced automobile, it was by no means technically revolutionary. Rather, it was Ford's manufacturing process that revolutionized the industry. He was not the first to build a car on an assembly line, but he perfected the system. After Ford opened his new Model T plant in 1913, he produced one Model T every 93 minutes, a remarkable reduction from the 728 minutes per car that was previously required. By the time the last Model T was built in 1927, the company was producing an automobile every 24 *seconds*. In part because of this efficiency, the Model T's price dropped from its original 1908 cost of nearly $1,000 to under $300 in 1927. This was possible in spite of the fact that, beginning in 1914, Ford paid assembly-line workers $5.00 per day at a time when prevailing wages averaged about $2.35 per day.

Ultimately, this combination of efficiency and high wages led to the fulfillment of Ford's prediction. The Model T was, indeed, a motor car for the masses. Not only was it cheap, but thanks in part to Ford's wage scales, ordinary workers for the first time had the disposable income necessary to purchase one. With the Model T, the automobile, which had once been an expensive plaything for the wealthy, began its transformation into an everyday necessity.

See also Automobiles; Ford, Henry.

MODERN DANCE

See Dance.

MOLLY MAGUIRES

The Molly Maguires were members of a secret organization of miners in the anthracite-coal country of northeastern Pennsylvania in 1865–1875. These men (all of whom belonged to an Irish-American fraternal society, the Ancient Order of Hibernians) took their name, and to some extent their methods, from an extralegal association in Ireland organized to resist oppressive landlords. Angered by the grim conditions under which they lived and worked, frustrated by the mine owners' ability to prevent all union activity, and denied legal recourse by the owners' control of local police and politics, the Mollies turned to intimidation, arson, and murder.

In 1875, they finally succeeded in forming a miners' union and called a strike. At this point, the president of the Reading Railroad called in the Pinkerton Agency, and one of the Pinkertons, James McParlan, successfully infiltrated the Molly Maguires. Based on the testimony of McParlan and other agents, the organization was destroyed and twenty of its members hanged in 1877. Amid the bitter class conflict that characterized the last quarter of the nineteenth century, the Mollies were remembered by some as brutal terrorists, whereas others saw them as martyred heroes of the labor movement.

See also Labor.

MONROE, JAMES

(1758–1831), fifth president of the United States. Monroe, who succeeded James Madison as president of the United States in 1817, was the last of the dynasty of Virginia presidents that began with Thomas Jefferson in 1801. Much of Monroe's career was closely associated with his two presidential predecessors. After reading law with Jefferson, he retained close ties with his mentor, and through Jefferson, he became friends with Madison. Jefferson's and Madison's more brilliant minds, broader interests, and greater impact on their times have overshadowed Monroe's place in the history of the early Republic. Nevertheless, he achieved a high degree of success in public life and enjoyed wide popularity. For Monroe politics was a consuming interest; he was a pragmatic man keenly sensitive to political currents.

Though closely linked to Jefferson and Madison in his political career, Monroe had established his own identity early. Leaving the College of William and Mary in 1776, the eighteen-year-old Monroe enlisted in the Continental army and as a junior officer fought under Washington in the fierce engagements of that year, being wounded at the Battle of Trenton. After the war, Monroe served in the Continental Congress and favored reform of the Confederation, but he opposed the ratification of the Constitution in the Virginia ratifying convention, where Madison led the fight for adoption. Monroe broadly approved the basic structure of the new government, but he favored adding to the Constitution more republican provisions, such as the direct popular election of the president and senators. He also wanted a bill of rights added prior to ratification. Monroe's antifederalism did not prevent his election to the U.S. Senate, and he soon joined with Representative Madison in support of Secretary of State Jefferson's opposition to Alexander Hamilton. He was active in organizing the early Republican party. Governor of Virginia at the time of Jefferson's election to the presidency, Monroe later was sent on the successful mission to purchase Louisiana and was subsequently named minister to Great Britain.

As Jefferson's retirement from office approached, Monroe allowed his name to be brought forward by Virginia friends as an opponent to Madison for the Republican nomination for president in 1808. Despite Monroe's differences with Madison, Jefferson succeeded in keeping the circle of friendship from being permanently broken, and in 1811 President Madison brought Monroe into his cabinet as secretary of state. For a time during the War of 1812, Monroe also acted as secretary of war.

Elected president in 1816, Monroe faced challenges different from any of his predecessors. With the demise in national politics of the Federalist party, he sought to end party divisions in the United States and to be the head of the nation, not of a party. The absence of a strong party in Congress in support of the president necessitated the working out of new relationships with Congress and with members of his cabinet. The "era of good feelings," over which Monroe is commonly seen as presiding, lacked the bitter partisanship of earlier years, but the times were not lacking in controversy. Although settled by compromise, the divisions over the admission of Missouri as a state in 1820 provided disturbing evidence of underlying tensions. Monroe's presidency is often remembered for the doctrine that bears his name, but the Monroe Doctrine would become more important in later years than when it was announced in 1823. Still, Monroe's nearly unanimous reelection to a second term in 1820 testified to his successful management of the office and his popularity as president.

Harry Ammon, *James Monroe: The Quest for National Identity* (1971; reprint, 1990).

NOBLE E. CUNNINGHAM, JR.

See also Elections: 1816, 1820; Louisiana Purchase; Revolution. *For events during Monroe's administration, see* Adams-Onís Treaty; American System; *Dartmouth College* v. *Woodward;* Erie Canal; *Gibbons* v. *Ogden; McCulloch* v. *Maryland;* Missouri Compromise; Monroe Doctrine; National Road.

MONROE, MARILYN

(1926–1962), movie star. Born Norma Jean(e) Mortenson in Los Angeles, Monroe was the daughter of Gladys Baker, an unmarried movie technician. Her mother's mental instability resulted in a childhood marred by foster homes, neglect, and abuse. At sixteen she married James E. Dougherty, a defense worker. During World War II an army photographer took pin-up pictures of her, which attracted the attention of other photographers. She was signed by a modeling agency and bleached her light brown hair. In 1946 she divorced Dougherty.

The same year 20th Century–Fox signed her to a contract, and she became Marilyn Monroe. Her first bit part in *Scudda Hoo! Scudda Hay!* (1948) wound up almost entirely on the cutting room floor. The studio dropped her as did Columbia for whom she played a lead in the Grade B movie *Ladies of the Chorus* (1948). Then, in need of money, she posed nude for a calendar that upon her ascent to stardom became famous. With the help of various older men she got a series of small roles, most notably in *The Asphalt Jungle* (1950) as a crooked lawyer's "niece" and in *All about Eve* (1950) as a "graduate of the Copacabana School of Dramatic Art." Her rise was rapid, thanks to an intelligent, intensive publicity campaign orchestrated by Fox, which had signed her again and now recognized her box-office potential. She weathered revelations about the calendar and her mother's mental illness, and in 1952 appeared in her first starring role in the potboiler *Don't Bother to Knock*. It was followed by the equally ridiculous but equally successful *Niagara* (1953). Monroe had become a strong box-office attraction, and her breathless sexuality helped make hits of *Gentlemen Prefer Blondes* (1953) and *River of No Return* (1954), among other films.

A nine-month marriage to the baseball star Joe DiMaggio failed in 1954. In rebellion against her stereotyped blond sex symbol roles, Monroe moved to New York City, announcing she wished to play more serious parts. The success of *The Seven-Year Itch* (1955) led Fox to meet many of her demands. In 1956 she received critical accolades for her performance in the film version of the Broadway hit *Bus Stop,* married the playwright Arthur Miller, and went to England to make a movie with Sir Laurence Olivier. It flopped, but *Some Like It Hot* (1959), which followed, was her most successful film.

The marriage to Miller foundered, but he wrote her last movie, *The Misfits*. They were divorced in 1961 just days before it premiered to an indifferent response. Always a difficult performer to direct (she was noted for her lateness and indecision), she was fired by Fox from her last movie. Monroe now became increasingly unstable. She had tried to take her life several times before, and on the night of August 4, 1962, she succeeded. It is not clear, however, whether she really meant to kill herself.

Monroe was a sex goddess who yearned to be more. Whatever her shortcomings as an actress, in most of her films she exuded a blatant yet attractive sexuality that set her apart from the other screen personalities of her time. Although intelligent, hardworking, and determined, she could not escape her own image. She was, as her friend director Lee Strasberg noted in his eulogy, "a legend in her own lifetime."

Norman Mailer, *Marilyn* (1973); Randall Riese and Neal Hitchens, *The Unabridged Marilyn: Her Life from A–Z* (1987); Gloria Steinem, *Marilyn* (1986).

DANIEL J. LEAB

See also Movies.

MONROE DOCTRINE

On December 2, 1823, President James Monroe used his annual message to Congress for a bold assertion: "The American continents . . . are henceforth not to be considered as subjects for future colonization by any European powers." Along with such other statements as George Washington's Farewell Address and John Hay's Open Door notes regarding China, this "Monroe Doctrine" became a cornerstone of American foreign policy. Secretary of State John Quincy Adams had played the most important role in developing the wording of the declaration, and he also influenced the doctrine's overall shape.

Two things had been uppermost in the minds of Adams and Monroe. In 1821 the Russian czar had proclaimed that all the area north of the fifty-first parallel and extending one hundred miles into the Pacific would be off-limits to non-Russians. Adams had refused to accept this claim, and he told the Russian minister that the United States would defend the principle that the "American continents are no longer subjects of *any* new European colonial establishments."

More worrisome, however, was the situation in Central and South America. Revolutions against Spanish rule had been under way for some time, but it seemed possible that Spain and France might seek to reassert European rule in those regions. The British, meanwhile, were interested in ensuring the demise of Spanish colonialism, with all the trade restrictions that Spanish rule involved. British foreign secretary George Canning formally proposed, therefore, that London and Washington unite on a joint warning against intervention in Latin America. When the Monroe cabinet debated the idea, Adams opposed it, arguing that British interests dictated such a policy in any event, and that Canning's proposal also called upon the two powers to renounce any intention of annexing such areas as Cuba and Texas. Why should the United States, he asked, appear as a cockboat trailing in the wake of a British man-of-war?

In the decades following Monroe's announcement, American policymakers did not invoke the doctrine against European powers despite their occasional military "interventions" in Latin America. Monroe's principal concern had been to make sure that European mercantilism not be reimposed on an area of increasing importance economically and ideologically to the United States. When, however, President John Tyler used the doctrine in 1842 to justify seizing Texas, a Venezuelan newspaper responded with what would become an increasingly bitter theme throughout Latin America: "Beware, brothers, the wolf approaches the lambs."

Secretary of State William H. Seward attempted a bizarre use of the doctrine in 1861 in hopes of avoiding the Civil War. The United States, said Seward, in order to divert attention from the impending crisis, should challenge supposed European interventions in the Western Hemisphere by launching a drive to liberate Cuba and end the last vestiges of colonialism in the Americas. President Lincoln turned down the idea.

In the 1890s, the United States, once again by unilateral action, extended the doctrine to include the right to decide how a dispute between Venezuela and Great Britain over the boundaries of British Guiana should be settled. Secretary of State Richard Olney told the British, "Today the United States is practically sovereign on this continent and its fiat is law upon the subjects to which it confines its interposition. . . . its infinite resources combined with its isolated position render it master of the situation and practically invulnerable as against any or all other powers." The British, troubled by the rise of

Germany and Japan, could only acquiesce in American pretensions. But Latin American nations protested the way in which Washington had chosen to "defend" Venezuelan interests.

The greatest extension of the doctrine's purview came with Theodore Roosevelt's famous corollary. He announced that henceforth European nations would not be allowed to use force to collect debts owed to them by Latin American countries. In Roosevelt's mind, however, the biggest problem he faced was not European intervention but the need to establish governments in Latin America that would maintain "order within their boundaries and behave with a just regard for their obligations toward outsiders." But the Roosevelt Corollary soon became the justification for interventions in Central America and the Caribbean, and the creation of a series of semiprotectorates on the order of the American-imposed Platt Amendment to the Cuban-American Treaty of 1903. The United States had gone to war against Spain in 1898, ostensibly to free Cuba from colonial rule. With the Platt Amendment, however, Washington placed restrictions on Cuban freedom that lasted down to the Castro revolution of 1959.

Roosevelt's "Big Stick" Latin American policy became synonymous with the Monroe Doctrine, much to the chagrin of later American policymakers, who sought in various ways to change the image of the Monroe Doctrine. Franklin D. Roosevelt announced his intention to replace the Big Stick with the Good Neighbor. At his direction, for example, the United States renounced the right to intervene in Cuban affairs under the Platt Amendment. But it did not give up its naval base in Guantánamo Bay.

A variety of treaties signed in World War II and after attempted to turn the Monroe Doctrine into a multilateral undertaking, renamed the Inter-American System. When the United States dealt with the problem of Castro's Cuba, for example, or intervened in the Dominican Republic in 1965, Washington was always careful to declare that it was acting with, and even at the behest of, the Organization of American States.

This careful tiptoeing around the interventionist legacy of the Monroe Doctrine came to an end in the administration of Ronald Reagan.

Taking advantage of the backlash of the Vietnam War, and determined to affect the outcome of guerrilla wars and revolutions in El Salvador and Nicaragua, Reagan referred to the doctrine early in his first term. And Congress passed a resolution in 1982 declaring that arms should be used to prevent the spread of Marxism-Leninism in the Americas. In 1984, Defense Secretary Caspar Weinberger redefined the principles of the doctrine as meaning "that there should be no interference, no sponsorship of any kind of military activity in this hemisphere by countries in other hemispheres." Weinberger's pronouncement had an ironic tinge, however, for in the 1982 Falklands War, when Argentina attempted to "reclaim" the nearby islands it called the Malvinas, Reagan threw his support behind successful British military efforts to retain its colonial foothold in the hemisphere.

George Bush did not invoke the Monroe Doctrine in 1989 in order to justify his intervention in Panama and the hunting down of the dictator Manuel Noriega, but the groundwork had been laid by Reagan. Instead of European colonization, or even the spread of Marxism-Leninism, the doctrine now covered, by implication, almost anything that Washington felt should be removed from the hemisphere, or at least from Central America. Perhaps the territorial coverage had shrunk to that area. But what had begun in 1823 as a prohibition on European colonization — in practice, never used or needed — became in the twentieth century a fully generalized rationalization for American unilateralism.

Walter LaFeber, *Inevitable Revolutions: The United States in Central America* (1983); Dexter Perkins, *A History of the Monroe Doctrine* (1955).

LLOYD C. GARDNER

See also Caribbean-U.S. Relations; Good Neighbor Policy; Latin America–U.S. Relations; Mexico-U.S. Relations; Platt Amendment; Roosevelt Corollary; Spanish-American War.

MONTEZUMA, CARLOS

(c. 1865–1923), doctor and Indian spokesman. Montezuma (or Wassaja) was a Yavapai Indian whose career reflected many of the problems experienced by western American Indians in the late nineteenth and early twentieth centuries. Born in Arizona, he was kidnapped when he was a small boy by Pima Indians, who sold him to Carlos Gentile, a photographer. Gentile eventually gave up the boy, whom he christened Carlos Montezuma, to the guardianship of a Baptist church representative in Illinois.

Montezuma graduated from the University of Illinois and by 1889 had earned an M.D. from the Chicago Medical College. While in medical school he became acquainted with the founder of the Carlisle Indian School, Richard Henry Pratt, who influenced his early views on Indian policy. Also important in shaping his perspective were the years he spent working as a physician for the Bureau of Indian Affairs on western reservations.

Indian reservations, Montezuma argued, were prisons. For Indians to survive and prosper in urban industrial America, he believed, they had to learn English and find ways to adapt to modern society. After serving as a physician at Carlisle, Montezuma entered private practice in Chicago. He decided to be a missionary to white people in order to demonstrate that Indians could succeed if given the opportunity.

Montezuma traveled with the Carlisle football team to the Southwest at the turn of the century and became reacquainted with his Yavapai relatives, who in 1903 were given a small reservation, Fort McDowell, near Phoenix. In the final two decades of his life, Montezuma journeyed frequently to Fort McDowell and became more familiar with contemporary Yavapai life. He broke away from Pratt's simple assimilationist philosophy. Believing that Indians were entitled to both land and justice, he wanted to abolish the Bureau of Indian Affairs and railed against the way in which reservations were administered.

In the first two decades of the new century, Montezuma became a nationally recognized Indian spokesman. He helped establish the Society of American Indians in 1911 and, beginning in April 1916, published *Wassaja,* a newsletter about issues facing Indian peoples. Montezuma worked with the people at Fort McDowell to make sure they kept their land. He earned the enmity of local government agents, who referred to his followers as "the Bolsheviki element" or "the Montezuma bunch," but he gained the respect and affection of his fellow Yavapais.

In 1922, critically ill, Montezuma returned home to die with his relatives at Fort McDowell. He is buried in the tribal cemetery there. His memory continues to inspire the Yavapais, who are determined to stay on the land Montezuma could finally call home.

Peter Iverson, *Carlos Montezuma and the Changing World of American Indians* (1982).

PETER IVERSON

See also Indians.

MOON LANDING

See Space Program.

MOORE, MARIANNE

(1887–1972), poet, critic, translator, and literary magazine editor. Moore lived most of her life in New York City where she supported herself and her mother with income from free-lance writing; because it was difficult for a woman to earn a living in writing and publishing, she also taught business writing and held other odd jobs. Although at times patronizingly considered a "proper old maid" and a "precise" poet by her male contemporaries, she was an important figure in modern letters by the 1920s, having published her first collection, *Poems* (1921) and assumed the editorship of *Dial* magazine. In the latter role, from 1925 to 1929, she edited and published the fiction, poetry, and criticism of T. S. Eliot, I. A. Richards, William Carlos Williams, E. E. Cummings, Hart Crane, D. H. Lawrence and W. B. Yeats. She also wrote many reviews of contemporary poetry.

Her own poems, often drastically revised from one printing to another, are characterized by a mathematical or quantitative formalism by which the number of syllables and complex internal rhymes and rhythm, rather than stresses or end rhyme, determine stanzas. Undergraduate studies in biology at Bryn Mawr College (A.B., 1909) inform her many poems about animals, some of which were begun in notebooks and accompanied by fanciful or scientifically accurate sketches. (These notebooks are at the Rosenbach Foundation in Philadelphia, part of a major Moore collection.)

Her themes are ecological and aesthetic, her tone ironic, her vocabulary carefully descriptive. A favorite poetic topic and obsessively analyzed cultural phenomenon was baseball, particularly the Brooklyn Dodgers, whom she sadly watched move to Los Angeles. All her writings are subtle cultural analysis, written in at least two registers. While minutely depicting the bodies and habits of animals or their sometimes absurd human relatives, poems like "The Steeple-Jack," "Pangolin," "Marriage," and "Poetry" also reflect on art, the writing of poetry, and the graphic qualities of words. Fond of heaping up quotations from newspapers, poems, scientific publications, and sports and other statistics, Moore included these in poems at once cryptic and familiar. Her choice of costume (she once asked a tailor to design a cloak and hat "in the manner of Washington crossing the Delaware") further suggested her ironic and critical (im)posture as a self-declared historical figure, a player on the American cultural stage.

Characteristic of her interest in using animals for ironic social commentary is a major verse translation, *The Fables of La Fontaine* (1954). The brilliant and hilarious "Letters from Me to the Ford Motor Company"—concerning the choice of a product name for what became the Edsel when her suggestions were rejected—shows her semantic mastery and playfulness as well as a profound, multifaceted understanding of the "economy" of words and advertisement in social intercourse. Always honored by younger poets, Moore has recently attracted the wider critical attention of literary historians and feminists.

Charles Molesworth, *Marianne Moore: A Literary Life* (1990); Patricia Willis, ed., *Marianne Moore: Woman and Poet* (1989).

KATHRYNE V. LINDBERG

See also Literature.

MORENO, LUISA

(1906–   ), trade union leader and civil rights activist. Born into an upper-class Guatemalan family, Moreno attended schools in both the United States and Guatemala. As a teenager, she organized her affluent peers into La Sociedad Gabriela Mistral, a group that successfully lobbied for the admittance of women into Guatemalan universities. But she decided against pursuing a college degree herself and moved to Mexico where she worked as a journalist and wrote poetry. In 1927, she married a Mexican artist and the couple immigrated to New York City the next year. A few months later Moreno gave birth to her only child.

With the onset of the Great Depression, Moreno found work as a sewing machine operator in a Spanish Harlem sweatshop. Applying her organizing skills, she founded La Liga de Costureras, a Latina garment workers' union. Her talents did not go unnoticed, and in 1935 the AFL hired her as a professional organizer. Leaving her abusive husband and with daughter in tow, she moved to Florida where she unionized African-American and Latina cigar rollers. Within two years, she had switched to the CIO and in 1938 became an international representative of the United Cannery, Agricultural, Packing, and Allied Workers of America (UCAPAWA-CIO).

From 1938 to 1947, Moreno organized Mexican farm and food-processing workers throughout the Southwest. Her efforts, especially in California, helped bring thousands of cannery workers, 75 percent of whom were women, into the union. Under UCAPAWA, Mexican, Jewish, and Anglo women secured higher wages and innovative benefits including free legal advice and equal pay for equal work. A strong believer in grass-roots unionism, she encouraged people of color and women to run for local union offices. In 1943 Mexican women filled eight of fifteen elected positions within the Los Angeles local. Moreno herself was the first Latina vice president of a major U.S. trade union and the first Latina member of the California CIO Council.

Moreno also organized El Congreso de Pueblos Que Hablan Español (Spanish-Speaking Peoples' Congress), the first Latino civil rights assembly. In April 1939, delegates from across the nation gathered in downtown Los Angeles and called for an end to segregation in public facilities, housing, education, and employment. They also declared a boycott of consumer goods manufactured by Germany, Italy, and Japan. She and other Congreso leaders envisioned a national network of local chapters, but such groups never took root outside of California.

From 1945 to 1950, UCAPAWA slowly disintegrated, a target of red-baiting politicians and conservative trade unionists. After marrying a former labor organizer, Moreno retired from public life in 1947. A year later the Immigration and Naturalization Service initiated deportation proceedings against her. Journalist Carey McWilliams and newspaper editor Ignacio López headed her defense committee. She was offered citizenship in exchange for testifying at the deportation hearing of labor leader Harry Bridges, but she refused to be "a free woman with a mortgaged soul." In November 1950, she was deported on the grounds that she had once been a Communist party member.

An unsung heroine, Moreno helped lay the foundation for later generations of Latino activists. In reflecting on her life, she once remarked, "One person can't do anything; it's only with others that things are accomplished."

Mario T. Garcia, *Mexican Americans: Leadership, Ideology, and Identity, 1930–1960* (1989); Vicki L. Ruiz, *Cannery Women, Cannery Lives: Mexican Women, Unionization, and the California Food Processing Industry, 1930–1950* (1987).

VICKI L. RUIZ

See also Labor.

MORGAN, J. PIERPONT

(1837–1913), banker and art collector. Morgan headed J. P. Morgan and Company, the most important force in American finance in the quarter century before World War I, a time when the burgeoning American economy grew to be the largest and most powerful in the world.

Morgan was born into a wealthy family in

Hartford, Connecticut. In 1854, his father, Junius Spencer Morgan, became a partner of George Peabody's banking house in London and took over the firm when Peabody retired, renaming it J. S. Morgan and Co.

From his earliest days Morgan was exposed both to international banking at the highest levels and to the idea held by Peabody and his father that personal integrity was indispensable to success in that field; these were to dominate and characterize his life. In his last years Morgan was asked by a congressional committee if money was not the basis of commercial credit. "No sir," he replied, "the first thing is character. . . . a man I do not trust could not get money from me on all the bonds in Christendom."

After completing his education at the university at Göttingen, Germany, in 1857, Morgan went to work on Wall Street. In 1862 he opened his own firm and in 1871 joined forces with the Drexel firm of Philadelphia. The new firm, Drexel, Morgan and Co., opened its offices at the corner of Wall and Broad streets where the headquarters of the Morgan Bank have been located ever since.

American railroads expanded rapidly after the Civil War, but their profitability waned owing to rate wars and competitive overbuilding. Frequent mergers and bankruptcies often left railroads with bizarrely complex corporate structures. Morgan's firm did much to rationalize the companies in the eighties and nineties, reorganizing, among others, the Baltimore and Ohio, the Chesapeake and Ohio, and the Erie lines.

Morgan's success as a banker derived from his formidable physical presence and dominating personality almost as much as from his capital, expertise, and creativity. He looked and acted like a man of supreme authority and wisdom, and most people took him at face value. In 1890, when his father died, he took over J. S. Morgan and Co. in London and renamed it and the New York firm J. P. Morgan and Company.

About this time he began to collect art, an interest that soon became a sort of inspired mania. By the time of his death his collection was the largest in private hands the world has ever known and included paintings, drawings, jewelry, ceramics, sculpture, and manuscripts. Although somewhat dispersed after his death, the bulk of his collection is today at the Metropolitan Museum of Art and the Morgan Library in New York and the Wadsworth Atheneum in Hartford, Connecticut.

As industrial companies came to dominate the American economy, it was his firm that financed many of them, including General Electric and International Harvester. In 1901 Morgan was instrumental in the creation of U.S. Steel, the largest corporate enterprise in the world at the time, capitalized at $1.4 billion.

By the turn of the century Morgan had become the very symbol of Wall Street, the man the financial community looked to for leadership. In 1907, when a banking panic threatened to spin out of control, Morgan took command, rallied the other bankers, and restored confidence. This panic led to the creation of the Federal Reserve System in 1913, the same year Morgan died in Rome, Italy.

Frederick Lewis Allen, *The Great Pierpont Morgan* (1949); Ron Chernow, *The House of Morgan* (1990).

JOHN STEELE GORDON

See also Robber Barons.

MORMONS

The Church of Jesus Christ of Latter-day Saints (also called the Mormon church) was founded at Fayette, New York, on April 6, 1830, by Joseph Smith, Jr. Smith, the recipient of dreams and heavenly manifestations in the 1820s, dictated to scribes the translated text of a holy book he said had been engraved on gold plates by an American Indian historian about A.D. 400. The six-hundred-page *Book of Mormon* was published in the spring of 1830.

The Latter-day Saints church, as it is more accurately called, was intended to be a restoration of the primitive church established by Jesus and his apostles. God was a personal being, Jesus his literal son, and at the head of the church was a prophet, functioning under divine leadership and through an appointed, male, lay priesthood. The church accepted the Old Testament,

New Testament, *Book of Mormon,* and revelations of the prophet as sacred Scriptures.

Missionaries preached throughout New England, the Old Northwest, Canada, and England, and within five years there were more than eight thousand converts. The religious beliefs of the Mormons and their attempts to institute a government in which the godly ruled, however, ran counter to the democratic pluralism of American society, and the Mormons experienced repeated difficulties with their neighbors. Mormon settlers were driven by hostile mobs, in succession, from New York to Ohio, to Missouri, and to Nauvoo in Illinois. In these moves, the Mormons lost most of their property, and many were killed or died from illness.

In Nauvoo Mormons established a well-planned city and began building a temple, the University of Nauvoo, and a number of mills and shops. But once more the Mormons had difficulties with their neighbors, and in 1844 a mob, including members of the state militia, stormed the jail where Joseph Smith and his brother Hyrum were being held on the charge of inciting a riot and murdered them.

Within a few weeks, Brigham Young, leader of the Quorum of the Twelve Apostles, was "sustained" as the new prophet. Under his leadership preparations were made for removal of the church to the Great Basin in western America. Nauvoo was abandoned in 1846. A pioneer company of 148 persons reached the Salt Lake Valley in July 1847, where they made preparations for those to follow. About 2,000 wintered in the Salt Lake Valley in 1847–1848, and the remainder of some 16,000 exiles migrated to the Great Basin at a rate of about 3,000 per year. Meanwhile, the 30,000 or more converts in the eastern United States, Great Britain, and Scandinavia were arriving at a similar rate. By 1860 there were 40,000 Latter-day Saints in Utah; by 1900, more than 200,000.

Some believers who chose not to follow Brigham Young founded the Reorganized Church of Jesus Christ of Latter Day Saints in 1860 in Amboy, Illinois, with Joseph Smith III as their president. Headquarters were later removed to Iowa and still later to Missouri, where a large auditorium and other facilities were built. There were approximately 220,000 members of the Reorganized Church in 1990.

The Utah Mormons colonized 350 settlements in Utah, Nevada, Arizona, Wyoming, and Idaho and established industries required for their relatively self-sufficient agricultural economy. Community growth and welfare were supported by a system of voluntary "consecrations" and tithing.

Although the Mormons had hoped to establish a state government, Congress instead set up Utah Territory (which included present-day Nevada). This meant that Mormon settlers had to deal with officers appointed by the president. Although Brigham Young was the first governor, most of the federal appointees were hostile to the Mormons, and few, from any point of view, were competent.

Because the Mormons failed to cooperate with the "outsiders," President James Buchanan, accusing them of being in "a state of substantial rebellion" in 1857, sent the U.S. Army to occupy the territory. The troops remained until the outbreak of the Civil War in 1861.

Federal appointees and visiting journalists complained of three problems: the attempt of the Mormons to control the political life of the territory at the expense of the non-Mormon minorities; exclusivist economic practices, which inhibited the activities of "outside" businessmen; and the practice of plural marriage, even if by only a small minority. Federal legislation was directed at each of these practices during the 1860s and into the 1880s, culminating in the Edmunds-Tucker Act of 1887. This act disincorporated the Mormon church, placed regulation of elections in the territory in the hands of a commission appointed by the U.S. president, disfranchised Mormon women (who had been given the vote in 1870), and required the seizure by the territorial marshal of all assets of the church, except chapels and burial grounds. After Mormon leaders agreed in 1890 to refrain from performing plural marriages, to disband the church's political party, and to disengage from church-supported business enterprises, Utah was granted statehood in 1896.

Mormon religious beliefs have continued in the twentieth century essentially as promulgated by Joseph Smith and his successors. A worldwide network of forty thousand voluntary (unpaid) missionaries, usually young people, has continued to preach the gospel in some 110 countries and make conversions. The membership of the church rose from 300,000 in 1900 to 700,000 in 1930, 3 million in 1970, and 7 million in 1990. Approximately half the membership is in the United States.

Mormons emphasize strong family life, the work ethic, education and group progress, and abstinence from tobacco, harmful drugs, and alcoholic beverages. The church operates Brigham Young University in Provo, Utah; Ricks College, in Rexburg, Idaho; Brigham Young University (Hawaii Branch), in Laie, Hawaii; and other educational institutions in New Zealand, Mexico, and elsewhere. The church operates Institutes of Religion adjacent to most universities where college-level training in religious subjects is given, and seminaries adjacent to high schools where early-hour instruction is offered.

The local congregation, called a ward, consists of five to six hundred members in a given part of a city or settlement and is run by an appointed unpaid bishop. From five to ten wards make up a stake, with an appointed, unpaid stake president. The central church of the Latter-day Saints church, still headquartered in Salt Lake City, is headed by a president or prophet, with two counselors. The governing board of the church consists of the Council of Twelve Apostles, assisted by a Council of Seventies who hold various administrative posts. The Women's Relief Society is directed by a president and two counselors.

The church operates a daily newspaper, the *Deseret News,* a network of television and radio stations, a large printing establishment, and other enterprises to assist in its programs.

James B. Allen and Glen M. Leonard, *The Story of the Latter-day Saints* (1976); Leonard J. Arrington, *Great Basin Kingdom: An Economic History of the Latter-day Saints* (1958; paperback ed., 1966); Leonard J. Arrington and Davis Bitton, *The Mormon Experience: History of the Latter-day Saints* (1979).

LEONARD J. ARRINGTON

See also Missionaries; Religion; Smith, Joseph; Young, Brigham.

MORRILL LAND GRANT ACT

The Morrill Land Grant Act of 1862 gave to every state that had remained within the Union a huge tract of federal land, each state receiving a number of acres equivalent to the number of members in its congressional delegation multiplied by 30,000. (States that had insufficient federal acreage within their own borders were given land on the frontier.) The states were to sell the land and use the proceeds to endow at least one college that would offer courses in agriculture, engineering, and home economics, as well as regular academic programs.

This bill, which its sponsor, Congressman Justin Morrill of Vermont, had pressed for since 1857, represented a total grant of more than 17 million acres, from the sale of which the states received some $7 million. Over seventy land-grant colleges were established under the Morrill Act, laying the foundation for the development of higher education in the Middle and Far West. Another provision of the act required that military training be offered at each college, a program that ultimately became part of the Reserve Officers' Training Corps. A second Morrill Act in 1890 extended the land-grant provisions to sixteen southern states.

See also Education; Public Land Policy.

MORRIS, GOUVERNEUR

(1752–1816), politician, public official, and diplomat. Born into a New York family distinguished for its wealth, lineage, and political influence, Morris lost his leg in a carriage accident as a young man. He graduated from King's College (now Columbia University) and in 1771 was admitted to the bar. In 1775, he was elected to New York's provincial congress and in 1776 served on committees that drafted the state's new constitution and that instructed New York's delegates to the Second Continental Congress to support the Declaration of Independence. In 1778, as a New York delegate to the

Continental Congress, he signed the Articles of Confederation. Two years later Morris became the Confederation's assistant superintendent of finance under his political mentor, Robert Morris of Pennsylvania. In that post, he sought to expand the powers of the federal government and drafted a report to Congress recommending the first national currency — a decimal coinage based on the Spanish dollar.

In 1787, Robert Morris engineered an appointment for his protégé as a Pennsylvania delegate to the Federal Convention. Brilliant and irreverent, Gouverneur Morris spoke more often and at greater length than any other delegate. He supported the creation of a strong national government, favoring James Madison's proposals to grant Congress a veto over state laws and to create a council of revision comprising members of the national executive, legislature, and judiciary. Morris urged that senators be chosen for life and that they meet sizable property qualifications — but he advocated this measure as much to control the wealthy elite as to protect their interests, on the theory that the isolation of the elite in the Senate would make it easier to guard against their efforts to advance their own interests at the expense of the general good. He championed the direct election of the president and proportional representation for the states in Congress based on taxation. He opposed constitutional protection for slavery or the slave trade and disliked the Constitution's provision permitting new states to be admitted to the Union on an equal footing with the original thirteen. As a member of the convention's Committee on Style and Arrangement, he prepared the final draft of the Constitution.

Morris declined his friend Alexander Hamilton's invitation to contribute to *The Federalist* and played no role in the ratification of the Constitution. After travel in Europe on private business and a brief mission to Great Britain in 1790, Morris was named American minister to France (1792–1794). In that post he was critical of the French Revolution; his *Diary,* published in the 1880s, is a notable eyewitness account of the Terror. In 1794, after the United States demanded the recall of the French ambassador, Edmond Genet, the French in retaliation de-

manded Morris's recall. Genet had shown his contempt for the Washington administration by trying to foment American support for France in its wars with the rest of Europe, despite Washington's announced policy of neutrality. For his part, Morris had attempted a daring but impractical scheme to rescue Louis XVI and his family from the revolutionary authorities.

In 1800, Morris was elected a senator from New York, serving until 1803. In 1804, he helped found the New-York Historical Society and delivered the eulogy for Hamilton at Trinity Church. He was also the founding chairman of the Erie Canal Commission (1810–1816). In opposing the War of 1812, he went so far as to urge that New York and the New England states secede from the Union. When he died, his passing was regretted even by his political adversaries.

Max M. Mintz, *Gouverneur Morris and the American Revolution* (1970); Theodore Roosevelt, *Gouverneur Morris* (1888; reprint, 1981).

RICHARD B. BERNSTEIN

See also Articles of Confederation; Continental Congresses; Philadelphia Convention; War of 1812.

MORRIS, ROBERT

(1734–1806), merchant, member of the Continental Congress, and superintendent of finance. Brought to America in 1747 from his birthplace in Liverpool, England, Morris was orphaned by age sixteen. But his father, a tobacco agent, left him enough money to provide him with a substantial stake. Following an apprenticeship with the firm of Charles Willing, a Philadelphia merchant, Morris formed a partnership with Thomas Willing, his son, in 1754. The firm prospered, and both men became prominent members of the Philadelphia commercial community.

Although Morris supported American protests against British policies toward the colonies, his active political career began only with his election to the Continental Congress in 1775. Like other moderates from the Middle Colonies, Morris resisted the movement toward independence until he became convinced that the British government was committed to a policy of suppression. Whatever his doubts about the wisdom and costs of independence, Morris threw himself into organizing resistance to Britain and especially securing munitions and other vital supplies from overseas sources. A man whose stout girth mirrored his commercial ambitions, Morris used his far-flung connections for both public good and private profit — something that loose eighteenth-century notions of conflict of interest allowed. Although he regarded much of the business of Congress as "damn'd trash," even his detractors appreciated his efficiency and administrative skills.

Morris left Congress in November 1778 to concentrate on his private business. He returned to national politics in the spring of 1781 as the superintendent of finance, a position Congress had created in response to the near bankruptcy of the Treasury. In this capacity, Morris played a crucial role in sustaining the war effort in the climactic months leading to the decisive victory at Yorktown in October 1781. Simultaneously he began to develop an ambitious program to place the credit of the national government on a secure and durable foundation. In 1782 Morris recommended that Congress seek amendments to the Articles of Confederation that would allow it to collect customs duties and land and poll taxes. His heavy-handed efforts to manipulate public creditors and the army to support his program backfired, however, and Congress instead adopted a compromise revenue plan that fell well short of what Morris sought. Morris resigned his office in 1784, and Congress abolished the post. His many critics continued to regard him as overreaching and unscrupulous. Nevertheless, his financial program substantially anticipated many of the policies that Secretary of the Treasury Alexander Hamilton would pursue a decade later.

In 1787 Morris served as a member of the Pennsylvania delegation to the Federal Convention, but true to character, he did not participate actively in the debates. As a senator in the First Congress (1789–1791), he devoted his energies to efforts to make Philadelphia the national capital.

Morris remained in the Senate until 1795, but he increasingly engaged in massive land speculations in western New York, Pennsylvania, the projected District of Columbia, and elsewhere. These turned out disastrously, and by the mid-1790s he was near financial ruin. Confined to debtors' prison in 1798, he was released in 1801, and his former assistant, Gouverneur Morris (no relation), supported him until his death.

Clarence L. Ver Steeg, *Robert Morris: Revolutionary Financier* (1954).

JACK N. RAKOVE

See also Continental Congresses; Revolution.

MORSE, SAMUEL F. B.

(1791–1872), artist and inventor of the telegraph. Morse, one of the most versatile Americans of the nineteenth century, influenced American art, politics, and science. He grew up in Charlestown, Massachusetts, the son of a prominent minister. After graduating from Yale, Morse studied painting in England. He returned in 1815 to pursue the grand history painting much admired in Europe. Morse executed a monumental depiction of *The Old House of Representatives,* expecting that this would make his reputation. But there was little demand in America for history painting, and he reluctantly sought portrait commissions to support himself. Although Morse's works are now recognized as some of the most accomplished of the nineteenth century, he was often close to poverty during his career as an artist.

Morse returned to Europe in 1829, hoping that success on the Continent might boost his flagging career; instead, the trip led Morse to other undertakings. During a visit to Rome, a soldier knocked him down when he failed to kneel before a Catholic procession. Most Americans of the day harbored anti-Catholic sentiments, and Morse had often heard his father denounce "popery" in his sermons. So when Morse returned to the United States, he vented his newly intensified anti-Catholicism in a series of newspaper articles. Under the pen name "Brutus," Morse charged that the monarchies of Europe had enlisted the aid of the Catholic church to subvert American democracy by sending Catholic immigrants to take control of the underpopulated American West. According to Morse, a power base in the West combined with continuing Catholic immigration to the eastern United States would soon put America under the sway of Catholic despotism. Before Morse's articles appeared, Americans had considered immigration beneficial because it would help populate the nation's vast territories. But by linking immigration to Catholicism, Morse's articles (which went through many printings when republished as a book in 1835) helped spawn an anti-immigration movement that would persist for generations. Morse thus was recognized by contemporaries as a founding father of American nativism.

Morse's second voyage to Europe not only intensified his anti-Catholicism but also led to his invention of the electric telegraph. During his transatlantic voyage home, Morse became acquainted with Thomas Jackson, a scientist who had recently attended lectures on electricity in Paris. In the course of conversations with Jackson, the artist became convinced that an electrical current could be used for communication, and after his arrival home, he abandoned his artistic career to devote his full attention to the project. Morse convinced Congress to finance construction of his first telegraph line (from Washington to Baltimore), and on May 24, 1844, he inaugurated it with the message "What hath God wrought!" The telegraph revolutionized American life. Just ten years after the first line opened, twenty-three thousand miles of telegraph cable crisscrossed the country. Speedy communications made railroad travel safer, and businessmen could conduct their operations more efficiently and profitably. Not many inventions changed life as quickly as the telegraph did.

At his death, few remembered Morse for anything else. But his contributions to American art, politics, and science qualify him as one of the country's few "Renaissance men."

William Kloss, *Samuel F. B. Morse* (1988); Carleton Mabee, *American Leonardo: A Life of Samuel F. B. Morse* (1943).

TYLER ANBINDER

See also Nativism; Painting and Sculpture; Science and Technology.

MORTALITY

See Birthrate and Mortality.

MOTHER JONES

See Jones, Mary Harris (Mother Jones).

MOTT, LUCRETIA

(1793–1880), abolitionist and feminist. Born the daughter of a Nantucket sea captain, Mott was reared in a Quaker community that provided strong role models for the young girl. She attended a Quaker boarding academy in the Hudson Valley, New York, where she soon became a teacher. After her family moved to Philadelphia, a fellow instructor at the academy, James Mott, followed her there, and in 1811 the two were married. They had six children, five of whom survived infancy. The death of her first son deepened her spirituality, and in 1818, she became a member of the Quaker ministry.

Mott, like many Quakers, advocated antislavery and boycotted all products of slave labor. She helped found the Philadelphia Female Anti-Slavery Society in 1833 and served as its president. She also became prominent in the national organization after it admitted women. This sort of activity in reform groups was a radical departure for women of her era.

When denied a seat in 1840 at the World Anti-Slavery Convention in London on account of her sex, Mott preached her doctrine of female equality outside the conference hall. During her London visit, she befriended Elizabeth Cady Stanton, wife of abolitionist delegate Henry Stanton. During the summer of 1848 she and Stanton organized the meeting at Seneca Falls, New York, where the American women's rights movement was launched. Mott was elected president of the group in 1852.

Mott's feminist philosophy was outlined in her *Discourse on Women* (1850). She believed women's roles within society reflected limited education rather than innate inferiority. She advocated equal economic opportunity and supported women's equal political status, including suffrage.

After the Civil War, Mott, unlike many abolitionists who believed their work was done, threw herself into the cause of black suffrage and aid for freedpeople. She also helped establish a coeducational Quaker institution, Swarthmore College, in 1864. Two years later, despite increasing ill health, she was elected head of the American Equal Rights Association. Unfortunately the group broke into factions, the National Woman Suffrage Association (headed by Stanton and Susan B. Anthony) and the American Woman Suffrage Association (led by Lucy Stone, Julia Ward Howe, and others).

Although viewed as a peacemaker by both abolitionists and feminists, Mott did not thrive on her role as referee, suffering increasingly from severe stomach disorders. Nevertheless she pursued her own path as a champion of the unempowered — the poor, blacks, and women. Using her gift for oratory, Mott delivered hundreds of speeches and sermons, reached thousands of listeners, and was a strong force in effecting the reforms of her day.

Margaret Hope Bacon, *Valiant Friend: The Life of Lucretia Mott* (1980).

CATHERINE CLINTON

See also Abolitionist Movement; Feminist Movement; Seneca Falls Convention.

MOVIES

Although the United States has dominated commercial film production for much of the twentieth century, movies did not originate in America. Enterprising Europeans, such as the Lumière brothers in Paris, were already projecting motion pictures to paying audiences in 1895. The first important successful public exhibition in the United States of motion pictures was shown on April 23, 1896. Then, at Koster and Bial's Music Hall in New York City, Thomas Edison demonstrated the Vitascope. Although Edison later included movies on his list of inventions, his Vitascope merely refined the work of others.

Various other Americans contributed significantly to early cinema. Henry Heyl's Pharmatrope (first used in 1870) rapidly projected a series of photographs, giving the illusion of motion. Eadweard Muybridge's Zoopraxis (perfected in the 1870s) used a disc with serial pictures rotating in front of a light source to produce moving images. In the 1890s, W. K. L. Dickson, an associate of Edison, benefited from George Eastman's development of celluloid roll film during the 1880s and perfected the Kinetograph — a camera used to make fifteen-to-thirty-second movies — and the Kinetoscope — a peep-show device for individual viewing of such movies.

Kinetoscope "parlors" flourished briefly during the early 1890s, so much so that the country's first film studio (designed by Dickson) was built in 1893 at Edison's laboratories in West Orange, New Jersey. This studio turned out short films featuring dances, wrestling matches, and glimpses of popular personalities. The entrepreneurial Edison, realizing that one-viewer machines limited commercial possibilities, bought the rights to various projector systems including Thomas J. Armat's Phantoscope (perfected in 1895), which employed the first practicable intermittent-motion mechanism (necessary for projection) and served as the basis for the Vitascope.

It faced strong competition almost immediately. Within weeks the Lumière system debuted in New York, followed in October 1896 by the superior American Biograph system. Other firms quickly entered the field. All sold their movies cheaply to exhibitors; profits came from the sale of equipment. "Flickers" found a home in amusement arcades and vaudeville houses (which used them as "chasers" to turn over audiences). The American film industry grew rapidly despite excessive litigation over patent rights. In 1908, after a decade of court proceedings proved inconclusive, the exhausted litigants formed the Motion Picture Patents Company. The Edison and Biograph companies dominated the "Trust" (as it was called), which controlled all the important patents and through them aimed to control the industry.

The early films, a minute or so in length, were scenic views, glimpses of personalities, bits of daily life, one-gag jokes, and news items (often reenactments). Over time, story films were developed. Usually one reel (ten minutes, the length of a vaudeville turn), they were mostly chase melodramas and comedies. The most influential early film artist was Edwin S. Porter. In 1903 his *Life of an American Fireman* used crude but innovative editing to create a coherent narrative complete in itself; in *The Great Train Robbery* he used overlapping and parallel action to build to an exciting climax.

As story films proliferated and began to dominate production, purchase gave way to rental. "Exchanges" — middlemen who bought prints from companies and rented to exhibitors — made possible programs of greater variety. Over 150 exchanges operated across the country in 1908, servicing "nickelodeons." The first of these primitive theaters, whose name derived from the five-cent admission charge, opened in Pittsburgh in 1905. Three years later over eight thousand were in operation. Immediately and immensely profitable, the nickelodeons attracted over 25 million viewers a week, mostly working-class people for whom movies presented no linguistic, cultural, or social barriers.

The Trust's attempts at monopoly control foundered despite its vigorous use of the courts, questionable business practices, and strong-arm tactics. Its power had been broken well before 1915 when the Trust was found guilty of illegal practices in restraint of trade. The successful fight against Trust domination had important side effects. The anonymity of popular film performers ended. When in 1910 Florence Lawrence (known till then only as "the Biograph Girl") defected to an independent producer, he got her sensational publicity. She became the first star known to the public by name but almost immediately was joined by others as the box-office value of celebrity became obvious. Where movies were made changed, too. Southern California offered the independents more reliable sunshine as well as distance from the Trust's enforcers in the East. Hollywood, a rural suburb of Los Angeles, became a film production center.

Both the Trust's and its opponents' courting of the middle class, which could afford more than a nickel, sealed the fate of the nickelodeons. They gave way to more respectable, family-oriented theaters. This helped broaden film fare, as did the energy and vision of the independents, who in their fight for survival imported and made longer, more ambitious films. The Trust did likewise, and soon one- and two-reelers became program fillers.

During the patent wars American movies took significant creative strides. D. W. Griffith directed his first film for Biograph in 1908 and went on to direct hundreds of short films, revolutionizing filmmaking with his innovative use of narrative technique. His 1915 masterpiece *Birth of a Nation* established the feature film as a popular art form for all classes. Mack Sennett perfected his brand of zany slapstick comedy, developing a generation of screen clowns including Charlie Chaplin who made his film debut in 1914. Among other popular performers were Mary Pickford, who as "America's sweetheart" became world famous, and William S. Hart, who for years dominated that most typical of American genres, the western.

Between 1916 and 1926 the American film industry came into the hands of a few powerful companies, which controlled production, distribution, and exhibition. Their corporate headquarters were in New York City, but filmmaking took place mainly in Hollywood, which, thanks to the ravages suffered by the European film industry during World War I, had become the globe's undisputed movie capital. A constant supply of films was produced on an assembly-line basis for the companies' theaters. Permanent acting companies headed by a few stars appeared in these films, which were produced by an elaborately segmented labor force of creative and technical personnel. The ensuing economy of scale allowed the companies to buy up foreign talent that threatened their domination. Business refinements included the introduction of "block-booking," a practice instituted by Adolph Zukor of Paramount, which meant that unaffiliated exhibitors had to book a studio's inferior films in order to get the more desirable ones.

American films prior to World War I had often been preachy and sentimental, and set in a working-class milieu. Those made in the 1920s reflected changing social and moral standards. Some genres changed little. Comedy retained its traditional appeal of zaniness leavened with humanity, and westerns continued to emphasize archetypal themes. But the Pollyannish Victorian heroine found in earlier movies gave way to the "jazz baby." Cynicism and sensuality among the upper classes characterized many of the 1920s features, and democratic optimism gave way to rampant materialism. Among the new heroes were sexually aggressive "Latin lovers" such as those portrayed by Rudolph Valentino and his imitators. Among the new genres were gangster films that nihilistically glorified criminals. The new themes did not go unchallenged. In 1922 the increasing pressure for censorship and widely publicized scandals involving notable performers in rape, murder, and narcotics addiction led the industry to adopt a self-regulatory code of dos and don'ts, although it soon paid them little heed.

For all the industry's technical perfection and its production of some remarkable films, by 1927 box-office returns were not keeping pace with increasing costs, especially the continuing investment in "picture palaces," the splendidly appointed huge theaters that often seated thousands. "Talkies" helped delay the day of reckoning. Various attempts to combine pictures and sound had been made since the 1880s, but the problems of synchronization and amplification and the cost of converting theaters and studios were daunting. In 1926 financially hard-pressed Warner Brothers, owning fewer theaters requiring expensive conversion than the other companies, decided to gamble on a sound-on-disc system. It presented several programs of shorts as well as a feature with sound effects and recorded music. The studio on October 6, 1927, premiered *The Jazz Singer* (with songs and some dialogue) and in July 1928 the first all-talking feature. The public clamored for more, but the Warner system was cumbersome and unreliable. It was quickly superseded by sound-on-film, a system developed by Lee De Forest and first utilized in Hollywood by William Fox in newsreels. (De Forest earlier in the 1920s had tried to interest the industry in his system but failed because of the companies' unwillingness to invest in equipment.) In 1928 only thirteen hundred of the nation's twenty thousand movie houses

were wired for sound; by the end of 1930 almost half were. Sound helped the industry weather the 1929 Wall Street crash (the 57 million weekly admissions of 1927 had nearly doubled by 1930).

But sound also brought problems: production costs rose, foreign markets declined (until dubbing reopened them), many careers ended, and creativity stalled (until new sound techniques unfroze the camera). The industry's need for capital to take advantage of sound resulted in heavy outside investment and establishment of a studio hierarchy that lasted for a generation. It consisted of the five "majors" — Fox (later 20th Century–Fox), MGM (part of the Loew's empire), Paramount, RKO, and Warner Brothers — and the "little three" — Columbia and Universal, specializing in low-budget productions, and United Artists, a distributor for independent producers.

After 1931, as talkie enthusiasm waned, the industry felt the depression's impact. Ticket sales plummeted, theaters went dark, admission prices were slashed, and earnings declined; much of the industry faced receivership and bankruptcy. In 1934, at the behest of the Roman Catholic church's Legion of Decency, a much stricter Production Code went into effect: as administered, self-regulation governed not only morality but choice of subjects.

Hollywood, however, had fully recovered economically by the late 1930s and entered on an artistic golden age, producing annually over four hundred features for a broad-based audience of about 80 million people a week. Thriving studios with expansive rosters of players, directors, and supremely competent technicians developed distinct "house styles" that lasted for years (e.g., glossy MGM productions) and specialized in specific genres (e.g., Universal's horror films). Among the 1930s' most notable attractions were the child star Shirley Temple and the 1939 film *Gone with the Wind,* a spectacular epic that for decades remained the highest-grossing film. Creative and technical personnel overcame bitter industry opposition and unionized the studios.

The strong domestic market profitably sustained Hollywood during World War II when overseas markets closed down. With U.S. entry into the war Hollywood enlisted for the duration, coupling its traditional escapist fare with crude, mawkish propaganda (about 25 percent of the total feature output, 1942–1945). Wartime shortages and government restrictions resulted in fewer films being made, but profits rose as an entertainment-starved populace flocked to the movies (almost 90 million weekly). The industry reached its all-time peak of profitability in 1946.

During the next fifteen years the movies were displaced as the quintessential American mass medium. Immediately after the war the studios supplemented their usual product with more mature films dealing with controversial subjects such as prejudice. Audience response was positive, but the cold war climate resulted in a retreat from serious themes and a purge of "progressive" creative people that was institutionalized by a wide-ranging blacklist that slackened only in the late 1960s. Concurrently the movies were trying unsuccessfully to compete with television and were hampered by legally enforced changes in distribution. Federal antitrust actions resulted in court decisions ending such industry practices as block-booking and requiring that production companies divest themselves of their theaters.

With no guaranteed outlet for films, the studios limited production, making fewer films for an audience that steadily eroded as the public turned to television. The industry made some attempt to improve the content of its films. It emphasized aspects that television initially could not offer, spending freely on color, spectacles, wide-screen systems (Cinemascope debuted in 1953 with 20th Century–Fox's biblical epic *The Robe*), and short-lived novelties such as 3-D, "Smell-O-Rama," and Sensursound. But nothing worked for long. By 1968 the industry was producing fewer than 175 features annually for a weekly audience that had fallen below 20 million. And the increasing cost of production had led to much filming overseas, further diminishing Hollywood as a movie production center.

As the century drew to a close the American film industry went global. The studios, bought up by conglomerates during the merger fever of the 1960s and 1970s, became part of international multimedia giants: the Australian press lord Rupert Murdoch gained control in 1985 of 20th Century–Fox, and Japanese companies bought Columbia (1989) and Universal (1990). From the early 1960s onward "packagers" (especially a few important agents) increasingly assumed the production function as they put together "bankable" stars, important directors, and properties. The studios concentrated on financing, distribution, and making the property brought to them.

The replacement of the Production Code in the mid-1960s by an industry-regulated rating system (last revised in 1990) was supposed to lead to more mature treatment of serious themes, and this happened occasionally; but mainly it led to more nudity, sex, and on-screen gore. Most films were pitched at moviegoers aged sixteen to twenty-four, who had become the bulk of the audience in the heyday of the 1960s counterculture. Its demise led to rebellious-youth films being replaced by "slasher" movies, cheaply made sexual-initiation films, and big-budget juvenile fantasies (many the product of Steven Spielberg and George Lucas).

As the cost of making films soared (averaging by 1990 over $15 million each), producers played safe, rarely encouraging innovation and making frequent sequels of profitable films (*Rocky* was released in 1976; the fifth sequel, in 1990). A boom-or-bust pattern developed. Each year a few films grossed millions (1989's top-drawing *Batman* grossed over $200 million), and the rest depended for profit on ancillaries — foreign markets, sales to television, videocassette distribution, and spin-offs like T-shirts. By 1990 the gross from videocassettes nearly doubled that of ticket sales. As the possibility of profit increased, so too did the number of films made in the United States, though often outside Hollywood as state and city film commissions wooed productions for the money they would spend on location. But the movies continued to be an integral part of American culture, though one in a constant state of metamorphosis.

Kevin Brownlow, *The Parade's Gone By . . .* (1969); Garth Jowett, *Film: The Democratic Art* (1976); Thomas Schatz, *The Genius of the System: Hollywood Filmmaking in the Studio Era* (1988); Robert Sklar, *Movie-Made America: How the Movies Changed American Life* (1975).

DANIEL J. LEAB

See also Astaire, Fred; Chaplin, Charlie; DeMille, Cecil B.; Disney, Walt; Edison, Thomas A.; Garbo, Greta; Griffith, D. W.; Mayer, Louis B.; Monroe, Marilyn; Sinatra, Frank; Wayne, John; Welles, Orson.

MUCKRAKERS

In the early twentieth century, a group of journalists emerged who were committed to exposing the social, economic, and political ills of industrial life. In 1906 they were nicknamed "muckrakers" by President Theodore Roosevelt, who borrowed the word from John Bunyan's Puritan story *Pilgrim's Progress,* which spoke of a man with a "Muck-rake in his hand" who raked filth rather than look up to nobler things. Roosevelt recognized the muckrakers' key role in publicizing the need for progressive reform, but only as long as they knew when to "stop raking the muck" and avoid stirring up radical unrest.

Muckraking grew out of two related developments of the era — a changing journalism and the reform impulse. The muckrakers represented a new cadre of educated reporters, distinct from earlier journalists who wrote polemical, sensationalized news. They saw themselves as scientists objectively reporting the conditions and ills of modern industrial society. Most of their articles focused on business and political corruption, such as Ida Tarbell's series on Standard Oil, Lincoln Steffens's investigations of scandals in city and state politics, and Upton Sinclair's exposé of the meat-packing industry. Other subjects included insurance and stock manipulation, the exploitation of child labor, slum conditions, and racial discrimination. From 1902 to 1912, over a thousand such articles were published in magazines specializing in the genre, including *McClure's, Everybody's,* and *Collier's.*

These muckraking pieces heightened moral indignation among middle-class Americans over the corruption of big business and politicians. They rallied public support for several federal regulatory measures, including the Pure Food and Drug Act and Hepburn Act (for railroad regulation) of 1906. And finally, they were the impetus for uniting fragmented local and national reform movements into a single, more potent national political movement.

Although muckraking subsided with the demise of progressivism, some smaller political journals such as the *Nation* and the *New Republic* sustained the tradition. The muckraking style was revived after World War II in response to the government's increasingly frequent practice of managing the news, which infringed on the independence of journalists.

See also Jungle, The; Magazines and Newspapers; Progressivism.

MUGWUMPS

The mugwumps were a group of Independent Republicans who bolted their party in the presidential election of 1884 to vote for Grover Cleveland on the Democratic ticket. (The group was given its name, an old slang word for "kingpin," by the *New York Sun.*) The Independents, including men like George William Curtis, E. L. Godkin, and Carl Schurz, had hoped to win the Republican nomination for Cleveland, whom they championed (somewhat inaccurately) as a fighter in the cause of reform. Instead, the regulars at the June 1884 Republican convention easily overrode them and nominated Secretary of State James G. Blaine of Maine, a party stalwart whom the mugwumps regarded (with some justification) as politically corrupt. The anti-Blaine forces might have prevailed if they had been willing to renominate the incumbent president, Chester A. Arthur, but the mugwumps felt that he too was insufficiently reformist.

When the Democrats nominated Grover Cleveland in July 1884, the mugwumps deserted the Republicans and campaigned vigorously for him, raising funds and making speeches. Once in office, Cleveland proved to be a less aggressive reformer than his liberal backers had hoped, and a number of them deserted him during his unsuccessful campaign for reelection against Republican Benjamin Harrison in 1888. Four years of Republican rule, however, convinced them that Cleveland was their best hope, and many of them vigorously supported his successful return to office in 1892. Throughout these years, the mugwumps were useful members of the Democratic coalition, although neither their achievements, in terms of reform, nor their level of influence ever quite matched their aspirations.

See also Elections: 1884, 1888, 1892.

MULLER V. OREGON

This case, decided by the Supreme Court in 1908, upheld an Oregon law of 1903 limiting the number of hours women could work in certain commercial businesses. The law was one of many passed throughout the country for the protection of children, women, and those in hazardous occupations, such as mining. When laundry owner Curt Muller of Portland refused to obey the law, his case was selected for trial before the Supreme Court as a test of the constitutionality of such "social" legislation.

Muller's counsel relied on *Lochner* v. *New York* (1905), the "bakeshop case," in which the Court found that state legislation limiting hours of work "interferes with the right of contract between the employer and employees, concerning the number of hours in which the latter may labor.... The general right to make a contract... is part of the liberty of the individual" protected by the Fourteenth Amendment. In *Muller*, counsel argued that "women, equally with men, are endowed with the ... rights of liberty and property, and these rights cannot be ... destroyed by legislative action under the pretense of exercising the police power of the state."

Attorney Louis D. Brandeis was chosen to defend the state law and presented what became known as the "Brandeis brief," using sociological, medical, and other scientific data to illustrate the need for laws to protect laborers.

The Court found that the liberty of contract "is not absolute ... and that a State may ... restrict in many respects the individual's power of contract." Since "woman's physical structure and the performance of maternal functions place her at a disadvantage ... the physical well-being of woman becomes an object of public interest and care."

The Brandeis brief became the model for arguments upholding state social legislation directed at reform of labor conditions.

See also Labor.

MUNN V. ILLINOIS

This was a case decided by the Supreme Court in 1877, which, with related Granger railroad cases, upheld the power of states to regulate private property when it is used in the public interest. In 1873 the Illinois legislature had passed a Warehouse Act setting the maximum rates for storing grain in warehouses. The act was aimed at curbing price-fixing and other abuses harmful to farmers.

Although the firm of Ira Munn and George Scott, one of the largest grain storage businesses in Chicago, had already failed because of corruption, the successors to the property continued to defy the Warehouse Act. When the Illinois Supreme Court upheld the law, the new owners appealed to the U.S. Supreme Court, arguing that the Fourteenth Amendment to the Constitution forbids any state from depriving any person of life, liberty, or property without due process of law, and that the Warehouse Act destroyed private property by controlling rates and other business practices.

Chief Justice Morrison R. Waite wrote the majority opinion. In it he stated that private property becomes subject to regulation by the government through its "police powers" when the property is devoted to the public interest. And, he continued, "Common carriers exercise a sort of public office, and have duties to perform in which the public is interested.... Their business is, therefore, 'affected with a public interest.'" As to the argument that the law unconstitutionally destroyed private property, Waite wrote that the legislatures, which were elected by the people, were the proper judge of the wisdom of regulatory laws, thus enunciating a doctrine of "judicial self-restraint" in economic regulation cases.

MUÑOZ MARÍN, LUIS

(1898–1980), governor of Puerto Rico, 1948–1964, and writer. Luis Muñoz Marín embodied in his career the paradox of Puerto Rico. Long a colonial possession of Spain, Puerto Rico in 1898 was transferred to U.S. rule following the American victory in the Spanish-American War. Despite aspirations for independence, led by Luis Muñoz Marín's father, Puerto Ricans went from one subordinate status to another.

Muñoz Marín became a child of Puerto Rico's ambivalent position. He was raised mostly in the United States where his father represented Puerto Rican interests in Washington for many years. Hence, young Luis, in language and in culture, was more comfortable on the mainland than on the island. He made his name as a poet and essayist writing for such publications as the *Nation* in the United States, not Puerto Rico. Yet the lure of his father's homeland and of the Puerto Rican struggle for autonomy and identity, which paralleled his own search for identity, led him to return permanently to the island during the 1930s.

He immersed himself in New Deal–style reformist politics and became governor of Puerto Rico in 1948. He was reelected five consecutive times. His tenure as governor only furthered the paradox of Puerto Rico, however. His two most noted accomplishments — the establishment of commonwealth status for Puerto Rico in 1952 and the economic development strategy he originated known as Operation Bootstrap — led to both progress and poverty for Puerto Rico. Muñoz Marín and his supporters claimed that these strategies were realistic and improved Puerto Rico's fortunes, but others argued that the status of commonwealth was merely cosmetic and that under Muñoz Marín Puerto Rico had only slipped further into a colonial and dependent condition with respect to the United States.

Operation Bootstrap, for example, enticed American mainland investors to transfer industries to Puerto Rico or create new ones there by granting them tax concessions and other subsidies including access to a cheap labor market. Such investments did in fact bring some prosperity for certain sectors affiliated with these industries, but they also drained resources from the island, deprived Puerto Rico of tax revenues, prevented more native industries from developing, and limited the growth of a more highly trained and educated labor force. In time of recession, many of these industries, feeling little commitment to Puerto Rico, simply moved elsewhere. Although initially touted as an economic miracle, Operation Bootstrap by the 1960s was characterized more by large-scale, and what appeared to be permanent, unemployment on the island.

Despite these contradictions in his policies and the continued ambivalence of Puerto Rico's political status, Muñoz Marín throughout his tenure as governor maintained his charismatic personal leadership. Comfortable with both the rich and powerful and poorer citizens, Muñoz Marín as politician and intellectual was the most dominating figure in Puerto Rican politics in the twentieth century.

Thomas Aitken, Jr., *Poet in the Fortress: The Story of Luis Muñoz Marín* (1964).

MARIO T. GARCÍA

See also Caribbean-U.S. Relations; Puerto Rico.

MUSEUMS

See Libraries and Museums.

MUSIC

American Music to 1900

In traditional North American Indian cultures music is a part of everyday life. Chanting and singing accompany religious rites and festivals, and an oral tradition provides a record of history. The concept of music as a performance art is as unusual among Indians as it was among the seventeenth-century New England settlers who also placed music in the context of their religious observances by chanting psalms in the meetinghouse as an important communal activity.

By the close of the century, however, psalm

singing had become cacophonous, for worshipers could no longer read the metrical patterns in such sources as the *Bay Psalm Book*. Although the "correct" rendering of tunes was less important than religious fervor, many ministers and musical reformers supported the teaching of musical notation to restore order in the meetinghouse. "Regular singing" soon gave rise to the development of singing schools and the creation of music for secular entertainment.

The revolutionary war saw a flowering of musical creativity: supporters of the American cause often changed the words of British songs, such as "Yankee Doodle," to taunt their adversaries. William Billings, a Boston tanner, composed an anthem called "Chester" that expressed his confidence in the ability of the new nation to shake off the "iron rods" and "galling chains" of tyranny. The immediate postrevolutionary cultural climate was one of optimism that Americans could create their own culture free of English influence. Just as Noah Webster called for an American language that would serve the needs of an American people, Billings called for individual American creative voices.

Nevertheless, European influences dominated concert music after the Revolution. Alexander Reinagle of Philadelphia composed ballad operas on the English model; Benjamin Carr of New York edited a journal and ran a successful music business; and Johann Christian Gottlieb Graupner helped found Boston's Philharmonic Society and the Handel and Haydn Society. James Hewitt of New York composed a patriotic suite, *The Battle of Trenton,* which quoted "Yankee Doodle."

Religious music, which had occasionally deviated from European models with such American innovations as the fuguing tune, reverted to a more familiar style. Composers Andrew Law, Samuel Holyoke, and Oliver Holden advocated dignity in religious music and used melodies by Handel, Haydn, and Mozart for settings of religious texts. The emphasis on musical propriety continued throughout the nineteenth century. John Sullivan Dwight, a transcendentalist reformer and conservative cultural critic, argued that Associationists and other transcendentalist reformers should learn Handel's *Messiah* in or-

der to comprehend their mission. Dwight and other arbiters of good musical taste believed that popular music, especially military music, was a bad influence on citizens of the Republic. He felt that the lessons of democracy had to be learned and that the "right" music would have a salutary influence — good Beethoven would create better Americans.

Outside of the formal concert realm, Americans created their own music, sometimes for performance but often as an everyday activity. Stephen Foster's sentimental art songs were popular with audiences, and pianist and composer Louis Moreau Gottschalk was idolized prior to the Civil War for his good looks and astonishing technique. He used North and South American popular tunes in such works as "Creole Eyes," "Souvenir de Puerto Rico," "The Union" (which quotes the "Star-Spangled Banner"), "Hail Columbia," and "Yankee Doodle" — all rendered in a pianistic style reminiscent of the music of Franz Liszt; his "Le Banjo" imitates banjo strumming and quotes "Camptown Races."

The antebellum period also saw the continued development of African-American vocal music. Plantation slaves used the call-and-response style to tell stories in work songs, and individuals sang in the pre–blues style of the field holler. Music was an integral part of the religious life of slaves, and spirituals such as "My God Ain't No Lyin' Man" articulated their relationship with their faith.

In the 1850s, the call for an independent American music was heard again, this time from composer William Henry Fry, whose New York lectures in the early fifties inspired an interest in the development of an American musical language. But the drive for cultural independence fell short.

With the coming of the Civil War, marches and sentimental songs that spoke of home, sweethearts, and mothers became popular. Many of these were printed by composer-entrepreneurs such as George F. Root, whose Chicago publishing house was among many that thrived on the middle-class market of households with a piano in the parlor. By the second half of the century, many successful American composers had studied in Europe and saw no reason to abandon the romantic style despite the ongoing arguments for an American music. Three men who earned their livelihoods as professors — John Knowles Paine at Harvard, Horatio Parker at Yale, and Edward MacDowell at Columbia — achieved respectability with works that bore considerable resemblance to similar pieces being composed in Europe at the time.

By the end of the century, there were major orchestras in New York (the Philharmonic-Society was founded in 1842), Boston (1881), and Chicago (1891). In smaller communities, performances by local bands reflected the popular taste for dances, marches, and symphonic excerpts — a repertoire popularized by John Philip Sousa. In troupes throughout the country, vaudeville performers combined comedic episodes, scenes from Shakespeare's plays, dancing, and minstrel songs performed in black face. In a racially divided society, black vaudeville entertainers like Bert Williams could command high fees on the stage but could not enter restaurants near the theaters where they performed.

Concert music and opera were still the province of European, mainly German, conductors, performers, and managers. But a small group of composers — Henry F. Gilbert, Arthur Farwell, Charles Wakefield Cadman, and their colleagues — thought that the tools with which to compose American music lay in African-American culture, backwoods mountain or hill communities, and Indian tribal villages.

As these "Americanists by quotation" looked for materials to develop, new currents were stirring among black musicians. The cakewalk dance and the pianistic style known as ragtime emerged, with highly syncopated rhythms attractive to composers who thought these varieties of black music could be the material for a new American concert music. The stage was set for the emergence of jazz out of the marching-band traditions of New Orleans and its appearance in works for the concert hall. Debate still raged about whether there was an American music and what form it should take. But that debate would soon be subsumed under discussions about the utility of the many varieties of modern music for creating an American musical expression.

Gilbert Chase, *America's Music: From the Pilgrims to the Present*, 3rd ed. (1987); Charles Hamm, *Music in the New World* (1983); H. Wiley Hitchcock, *Music in the United States: A Historical Introduction* (1969).

BARBARA L. TISCHLER

American Music since 1900

Just as the United States did not leap forward into modernity at midnight on December 31, 1900, neither did the arrival of the twentieth century signal a turning point in the history of American music. The nation's major symphony orchestras and opera companies were still dominated by European performers and conductors. They received the support of the same wealthy patrons and provided the standard late-nineteenth-century repertoire to their audiences. American composers and performers continued to study in Europe, for a reputation won abroad often ensured acceptance at home.

In popular music, sentimental art songs, dances for the keyboard and concert band, and song-and-dance numbers for the vaudeville stage were among the entertainments patronized by middle- and working-class white audiences. In New Orleans, black marching bands played the syncopated rhythms that would soon become characteristic of early jazz, and in other black urban enclaves the cakewalk, a dance performed to music in "ragged time," was all the rage.

In the first decade of the century, a few composers sought to express a national identity in symphonic music. Henry F. B. Gilbert, Arthur Farwell, John Powell, and others looked to regional sources, using the melodies of Native Americans, plantation slaves and free blacks, and rural southern whites in works that otherwise sounded like late-nineteenth-century European romantic music. Edward MacDowell's *Indian Suite* typifies this approach to creating "American" music. Charles Ives made local materials a hallmark of his style, quoting and developing music he found around him, from popular hymns to patriotic airs. Ives, however, differed from his contemporaries because he placed familiar melodies in polytonal and polyrhythmic contexts. Later, his music was recognized as a significant contribution to American musical development.

In the concert hall and opera house, World War I raised the issue of culture versus patriotism. Where culture was presumed to be German, the demand for "100 percent Americanism" inspired the fear that orchestra and opera audiences would have no music at all. A furor developed when Karl Muck, the German-born conductor of the Boston Symphony Orchestra, refused to play the "Star-Spangled Banner" at a concert in 1917. Muck was arrested, and eventually deported, on suspicion of disloyalty, partly because of his denigration of the musical quality of the song (which did not become the national anthem until 1931) and his assertion that art and politics had no inherent connection. Popular tunes of German origin were torn from children's songbooks in California, and some organizations, such as New York's Metropolitan Opera, refused to perform any German music at all during the 1917–1918 season.

But by 1919 music by German, Austrian, and Hungarian composers had nearly resumed its dominant place on American orchestral programs, and the war had had a positive impact on programming, too. Many orchestras featured more "modern" music by French and Russian composers, and some even performed works by Americans. The Boston Symphony, because of wartime limitations on the employment of enemy aliens, hired its first American-born concertmaster in 1918.

The postwar period saw a wave of young American composers sailing to Europe, some to study with Arnold Schoenberg and other Vienna school composers who were experimenting with nontonal music. Aaron Copland and Virgil Thomson were among those who immersed themselves in French culture while studying under the rigorous Nadia Boulanger at the American Academy at Fountainebleau.

The war had brought American popular music to France with the arrival of James Reese Europe's dance band, and many French and German composers, inspired by American jazz, wrote compositions that employed muted brass instruments and the high hat cymbal and quoted familiar riffs, blue notes, and other jazz sounds. For these composers, including Darius Milhaud and Igor Stravinsky, the United States represented modernity, and jazz, with its African roots, was identified with the exotic.

After World War I, Americans heard the music of King Oliver's Creole Jazz Band, Louis Armstrong, and Jelly Roll Morton. The locus of jazz shifted from New Orleans north to Chicago, Kansas City, and New York and from the country, where vocal blues with harmonica and guitar accompaniment predominated, to the city, where the piano had a more important role in solo and ensemble jazz performance. Jazz also moved indoors and into the recording studio. The singing of Bessie Smith and Ma Rainey was preserved on so-called race records, as was the ragtime of Scott Joplin, the stride piano of James P. Johnson, and the boogie-woogie of such performers as Pine Top Smith. In 1924, the Paul Whiteman Orchestra performed George Gershwin's *Rhapsody in Blue,* an example of symphonic jazz. On stage, popular composers such as Gershwin, Jerome Kern, Irving Berlin, and Sigmund Romberg contributed to the musical spectacles of Florenz Ziegfeld, which ran every year from 1907 to 1925.

The Great Depression brought privation for musicians as it did for other Americans. Impoverished public schools often eliminated music from the curriculum, performers had fewer opportunities, and composers, who had never found it easy to attract an audience, had to find other ways to earn a living. The WPA's Federal Music Project created useful work for them. Performers were paid to play at free or inexpensive concerts, teachers returned to the schools, indexers discovered and cataloged American music, and copyists at the Fleischer Collection in Philadelphia made American music more accessible by creating playable scores. In the context of the depression, composers renewed their interest in the regional, ethnic, and folk musics of the United States. While Woody Guthrie and Hudie Ledbetter ("Leadbelly") composed and sang songs from white and black folk traditions, composers like Copland and Elie Siegmeister incorporated folk music into concert pieces and ballet scores, of which Copland's *Billy the Kid, Rodeo,* and *Appalachian Spring* are the best known. The composers who looked to the American scene for a usable musical past had all studied modern composition, and many had spent time in Europe after World War I. They were more successful in composing original music than the earlier "nationalists by quotation" because their musical sources formed the basis for thematic, harmonic, and rhythmic development using the techniques of modern rather than romantic composition.

For a brief period, composers of concert music looked to the tradition of workers' music for inspiration. Members of the Composers' Collective in New York (including Charles Seeger, Earl Robinson, Marc Blitzstein, Siegmeister, Copland, and others) wrote marching songs and workers' rounds for labor groups that were published in two *Workers Song Books* (1934, 1935). Some collective members also wrote articles for *New Masses* and *Modern Music,* published by the League of Composers.

The 1930s and 1940s was the age of swing. Big bands led by Fletcher Henderson, Benny Goodman, Glenn Miller, and Duke Ellington performed carefully arranged music in an orchestral style, with virtuoso improvisations by soloists. Singers like Frank Sinatra and Ella Fitzgerald set new interpretive standards in the 1940s. Swing music was dance music, and many of the most famous bands were heard regularly on radio, sponsored by soup and soap companies. Most of these groups had their own signature tunes and costumes that were replaced during World War II by army uniforms. The Glenn Miller Army Air Force Band was the most famous of these ensembles. This group offered sentimental tunes, dance numbers, and humorous pieces about military life to service personnel in Europe until Miller's disappearance in a plane crash in December 1944.

In the early 1940s, young jazz virtuosi, many of them black, found the conventions of swing stifling, and Charlie Parker, Dizzy Gillespie, Max Roach, Curly Russell, and other be-bop musicians developed a style antithetical to swing. In contrast to the large, tightly organized swing bands, be-bop ensembles were small groups of soloists who often improvised simulta-

neously, pushing their instruments and voices to the limits of their physical capabilities and audience tolerance. But be-bop demanded close audience attention, and few listeners could tap their feet or hum the tunes. Early reactions to bop were summarized in Louis Armstrong's disparaging remark that it was "Chinese music." Bop inspired its own reaction, and the 1950s "cool" jazz of Miles Davis, Lenny Tristano, and Thelonius Monk offered a less intense, but no less technically demanding, musical sound.

As be-bop had been a reaction to swing, the development of rock 'n' roll from African-American blues and southern hillbilly traditions was a reaction against the ballads, dance numbers, and novelty tunes of the early 1950s. With the coining of the term by Cleveland radio announcer Alan Freed in 1954, rock 'n' roll was young people's music, a rebellion against the standards of parents, schools, and authority in general. Ballads and speeded-up versions of the twelve-bar blues often contained vague sexual references, and performers like Elvis Presley became immensely popular as much for their audience appeal as the quality of their music. Throughout its history, rock has been attacked for its presumed contributions to juvenile delinquency, protest, and drug use, but it has remained an enduring and constantly developing aspect of American and international musical culture.

By the mid-1960s, rock music, along with ballads and talkin' blues pieces from America's folk traditions, had become an important part of the civil rights, anti–Vietnam War, and feminist movements. Starting with the early social commentary of Bob Dylan and Barry McGuire, performers as diverse as folk singers Joan Baez, Tom Paxton, and Pete Seeger and rock and soul musicians Country Joe MacDonald and James Brown used popular music to articulate a message of protest. By the end of the decade, rock music, whether or not it carried a specific protest message, was part of the counterculture.

Rock musicians, influenced by blues, jazz, and Indian music and philosophy, created eclectic works that were inappropriate because of their length and textual content for AM radio, where young people were accustomed to finding the latest music. A 1966 ruling by the Federal Communications Commission (FCC) opened large blocks of FM airtime to programmers who played music that was too long or too sexually or politically explicit for the AM radio band. Thus FM "alternative" radio became the medium through which new popular music reached its audience. Because it provides better reception, much classical music was also broadcast on FM.

The avant-garde of the 1950s and 1960s continued to search for new varieties of musical expression. Composers experimented with nontraditional instruments, such as the prepared piano used by John Cage, new instruments, such as those used by Harry Partch, and electronic sound, such as that generated at the Columbia-Princeton Electronic Music Center in New York. Groups like the Contemporary Chamber Ensemble presented to small but enthusiastic audiences compositions that sometimes included performers scattered through the hall, the use of noise and silence as part of the music, and tape recorders, speakers, and a stopwatch among the instruments. Early commercially recorded electronic records, such as *Switched-On Bach* released by Walter Carlos in 1969, were painstakingly generated, one line at a time, on a Moog synthesizer. Synthesizers, now smaller and able to play more than one note at a time, became performing instruments. Electronic music, uncommon in the concert hall, pervaded rock, popular music, and commercials.

Since the 1960s, composers and performers have felt less comfortable with stylistic labels and the boundaries they imply. For example, the compositional style of Leonard Bernstein, with its roots in jazz and the Broadway stage, Jewish liturgical music, and American ethnic music of many varieties, has long defied precise description. Composers such as Philip Glass and Steve Reich rejected the "minimalist" label in the early 1980s; they saw their works simply as individual creative expression rather than the product of any school or philosophy. Many musical artists fused elements of rock and jazz or jazz and concert music. Such "cross-over" artists found new ways to express themselves without being inhibited by stylistic boundaries, and performance artists utilizing music maintained a multidisciplinary focus.

Similarly, the debate over musical nationalism that seemed important early in the century became less relevant in an era of international study, performance, recording, and satellite broadcasts. In the 1950s and 1960s, Bernstein brought music to millions, and the symphony orchestra concert, opera performance, and ballet became staples on public television. Rap and contemporary protest singers owed a historical debt to the talkin' blues folk singers of earlier decades, and Americans heard electronic music everywhere. The blurring of boundaries contributed to an eclecticism in modern music that succeeded in large part in realizing Edgard Varèse's idea of music as "organized sound."

Irving Lowens, *Music in America and American Music* (1978); Virgil Thomson, *American Music since 1910* (1970); Barbara L. Tischler, *An American Music: The Search for an American Musical Identity* (1986).

BARBARA L. TISCHLER

See also Dance; Jazz; Musical Theater; Theater; *and entries for individual musicians.*

MUSICAL THEATER

Although English ballad operas and musical afterpieces were performed in many of the colonies, no native works appeared until the 1780s. They were called everything from "comic operas" to "oratorical entertainments." The first major star of the American musical stage was probably John Durang who performed hornpipes, jigs, and topical songs as interludes in plays and operas and later ran his own theater company. But it was not until *The Black Crook,* which opened in 1866 at Niblo's Gardens in New York, that song, dance, and spectacle were grafted onto an existing melodrama and the American musical was born. The story was rather wooden, but this was compensated for by lines of ballet girls dancing in precision formations while the chorus sang songs like "The Amazon March."

By the end of the nineteenth century the

American musical stage encompassed a number of genres. Operettas included Victor Herbert's *Babes in Toyland* (1903), with its famous "March of the Toys," and the Vienna import *The Merry Widow* by Franz Lehar, first seen in New York in 1907. There were also topical musicals such as *A Trip to Chinatown* (1891), which featured local color and geographical songs like "The Bowery," and revues with roots in minstrel shows, which were a sophisticated development of the burlesque and vaudeville format.

George M. Cohan, a key figure in the musical theater in the early twentieth century, wrote, produced, directed, and starred in shows that dealt with jingoistic and patriotic themes and made popular such songs as "Give My Regards to Broadway" and "Over There." After World War I Broadway entered one of its golden periods when "Cinderella" musicals (so called because usually the heroine starts poor and ends up rich and famous) like *Irene* (1919), *Sally* (1920), and *Sunny* (1925) dominated the stage, the last two tailor-made vehicles for the era's biggest star, Marilyn Miller. Tap dancing choruses regaled audiences in *No! No! Nanette!* (1925) or did the "Varsity Drag" in *Good News* (1927), and George and Ira Gershwin introduced a more sophisticated jazz style in such musicals as *Oh, Kay!* (1926) and *Funny Face* (1927).

Florenz Ziegfeld glorified the American girl in his famous annual *Follies,* which introduced Fanny Brice, Eddie Cantor, Will Rogers, and Bert Williams, the first black entertainer to become a major Broadway attraction. Ziegfeld's production of *Show Boat* (1927), written by Jerome Kern and Oscar Hammerstein II, pointed the way to a new form of musical play distinct from the fast-moving musical comedy and the flamboyant operetta.

During the Great Depression the revue format became less lavish; examples include *The Bandwagon* (1931), which showcased the talents of Fred and Adele Astaire, and Irving Berlin's *As Thousands Cheer* (1933), which introduced the hit songs "Heat Wave" and "Easter Parade." The composer who probably best personified the era was Cole Porter, whose wit and sophistication beguiled audiences in such musicals as *Anything Goes* (1934), *Red, Hot and Blue!* (1936), and

DuBarry Was a Lady (1939), all three written for Ethel Merman, famous for her clarion tone and spirited delivery.

Although dancing had always been a part of the musical, it became more closely linked to the story when Richard Rodgers and Lorenz Hart asked George Balanchine to choreograph the dances for *On Your Toes* in 1936. The importance of dance in the musical story was carried further by Agnes de Mille, choreographer in 1943 of Rodgers and Hammerstein's *Oklahoma!*, which banished dancing choruses and extraneous numbers and integrated song and dance with both plot and character development, especially in the "Dream Ballet" at the end of the first act, a dance making visual the heroine's personal dilemmas.

The Rodgers and Hammerstein format was employed successfully in productions from *South Pacific* (1949) to *The Sound of Music* (1959), both starring the popular Mary Martin, and was continued by Alan Jay Lerner and Frederick Loewe in *My Fair Lady* (1956) and *Camelot* (1960), among many others.

The next step in the Broadway musical was taken by Jerome Robbins who conceived, directed, and choreographed *West Side Story* (1957), written by Leonard Bernstein and Stephen Sondheim. This production made dance integral to the story (not just in a dream sequence) and demanded that performers sing, dance, and act — the triple-threat talent required for most subsequent shows.

During the 1960s the ascent of rock 'n' roll pushed Broadway out of its place as the trendsetter of American popular music. The Great White Way reacted in two ways: retreats into nostalgia in shows like Jerry Herman's *Hello, Dolly!* (1964) and *Mame* (1966) and spoofs of the rock craze, as in *Bye, Bye, Birdie* (1960). *Hair* (1967), billed as "the tribal love-rock musical," was the closest Broadway came to capturing the era, but there were no successful follow-ups. Black musicals such as *The Wiz* (1975) or *Ain't Misbehavin'* (1978) brought a more diverse audience to some theaters, but increasingly Broadway appealed to a more limited audience, as the high costs of producing a musical forced the price of tickets up — fifteen dollars for an orchestra seat in 1970, thirty-five dollars by 1980, sixty dollars by 1990. Stephen Sondheim was the most prominent American composer-lyricist of the era with his sophisticated approach that conceptualized the musical as a theme rather than a sequential story. This was first seen with *Company* in 1970 and continued twenty years later with *Into the Woods* (1989).

In contrast to the Sondheim musicals were director-choreographer shows, usually dealing with some form of show business. Examples include Gower Champion's *42nd Street* (1980), with its elaborate tap numbers, Bob Fosse's *Pippin* (1972) and *Chicago* (1974), which told their stories through a series of vaudeville numbers, and Michael Bennett's *A Chorus Line* (1974), which showed the grim prospects of a Broadway audition and became the longest-running musical in Broadway history, not closing until 1990. The director-choreographer tradition was continued by Tommy Tune whose unique style was first seen in *Best Little Whorehouse in Texas* (1978).

During the 1980s Broadway saw its leadership challenged by British musicals. Andrew Lloyd Webber was especially successful with such shows as *Evita* (1978), *Cats* (1982), and *Phantom of the Opera* (1987), all of which combined spectacle, special effects, and large casts accompanied by almost continuous music and little or no spoken dialogue. The American musical was not dead, however, and the acclaimed *City of Angels* (1990), in which Cy Coleman's jazz-inspired score accompanied a murder mystery set in Los Angeles during the 1940s, gave hope for a continuing vitality on the Broadway stage.

Gerald Bordman, *American Musical Theatre: A Chronicle,* enl. ed. (1986); Stanley Green, *Encyclopedia of the Musical Theatre,* rev. ed. (1980); Ethan Mordden, *Better Foot Forward: The History of American Musical Theatre* (1986).

FRANK W. D. RIES

See also Astaire, Fred; Balanchine, George; Berlin, Irving; Bernstein, Leonard; Dance; Gershwin, George; Music; Porter, Cole; Robbins, Jerome; Theater; Ziegfeld, Florenz.

N

NAACP

See National Association for the Advancement of Colored People.

NADER, RALPH

(1934–　), consumer advocate and activist. With unique vision and effectiveness, Nader invented and led a movement of Americans fighting for what he called "economic self-determination," using "citizen action against the growth of the corporate state and its political and economic disenfranchisement of the public."

Raised by immigrant Lebanese-American parents in Winsted, Connecticut, Nader graduated from Princeton in 1955 and then Harvard Law School. In 1963 he abandoned private practice in Hartford and with one suitcase hitchhiked to Washington, D.C., to open shop as a public crusader. After taking lodgings at the YMCA, he "walked across the street and had a hot dog, my last." He quickly researched what was in the hot dog and declared war on the meatpacking industry. Nader soon came to symbolize an unflagging commitment to consumer rights and participatory democracy.

In 1965 his *Unsafe at Any Speed* lambasted General Motors for producing a Corvair riddled with safety problems and for spending a mere $1 million of its $1.7 billion profits on safety research. GM promptly hired a detective in hopes of unearthing some blackmail material. But the private eye found nothing, and General Motors president John Roche was summoned before a Senate committee to apologize.

During the Corvair fracas, one corporate executive predicted the product safety movement would be a passing fad. But in 1969, riding a crest of Vietnam-inspired activism, Nader sent two hundred of his young "Raiders" into battle on issues ranging from the environment and auto safety to the rights of the disabled, insurance regulation, freedom of information in government, tax reform, public health, and control of Congress by moneyed interests.

"Naderism" soon became a credo for disgruntled consumers. His 1974 and 1975 "Critical Mass" conferences on atomic power, which he labeled a "technological Vietnam," launched a movement that helped reshape global energy policy. The ongoing Critical Mass Energy Project grew out of those conferences, taking its place alongside other Nader-inspired groups such as Congress Watch, the Center for Responsive Law, a nationwide network of Public Interest Research Groups, Public Citizen, the Center for Auto Safety, the National Insurance Consumer Organization, and the Health Research Group. The work of these and other Naderite organizations led directly or indirectly to the formation of the Occupational Safety and Health Administration, the Environmental Protection Agency, and the Consumer Product Safety Commission, deregulation of the airline and trucking industries, at least eight major federal consumer protection laws, and periodic recalls of millions of defective cars and trucks.

In the Reagan-dominated 1980s, Nader's critics argued that his activist credo had run its course. But in 1988 he helped win a California referendum mandating unprecedented insurance rate rollbacks and then used national radio talk shows to hold off a congressional pay hike.

Maintaining the same modest bachelor quarters throughout (his parsimony is legendary), Nader has thus far outlasted six presidencies and a dozen Congresses. "You've got to keep the pressure on, even if you lose," he said. "The essence of the citizens' movement is persistence."

As the 1990s began, Nader added to his agenda making his Connecticut hometown a model democracy. "The most important office in America for anyone to achieve," he said, "is full-time citizen." In a quarter-century of activism, he seemed to have virtually defined that exalted office for America's largest generation.

David Bollier, *Citizen Action and Other Big Ideas: A History of Ralph Nader and the Modern Consumer Movement* (1989).

HARVEY WASSERMAN

See also Liberalism.

NARCOTICS

See Drugs.

NAST, THOMAS

(1840–1902), political cartoonist. Nast may reasonably be judged the most powerful and influential political cartoonist that America has ever known. To a unique degree he both shaped and illuminated the political consciousness of his time. Nast's career was closely linked to the rise of illustrated magazines in the mid-nineteenth century. *Frank Leslie's Illustrated Newspaper*, America's first successful pictorial magazine, appeared in 1855, and the teenaged Nast was one of its artists. *Harper's Weekly*, the vehicle for Nast's greatest work, followed in 1857.

His medium was the woodblock engraving. His first important drawings, dealing with the course and character of the Civil War, relied appropriately enough on somber, fluid tones of gray and black. After the war he turned to vigorous political commentary, with drawings notable for their clarity of line. Part of the impact of his works derived from their size: his *Harper's* cover drawings were nine by ten inches, his inside double-spread cartoons more than thirteen

by twenty. But his real significance lay in what he had to say. As Daumier drew strength from his adversarial relationship to the France of the July Monarchy, so Nast gave pictorial form to the intense passions of the Civil War and Reconstruction. He was the great pictorialist (as Lincoln was the great wordsmith) of the crisis of nineteenth-century American nationalism.

Nast was born in Germany and brought to America in 1846. He came of age in antebellum New York City, part of a middlebrow literary-artistic community whose leitmotifs were romantic nationalism, classic liberalism, and anti-slavery. This was the worldview that gave form to Nast's brilliant comments on the great political drama of his time. During his peak productive years in the 1860s and 1870s, he created or popularized some of the most influential symbols of nineteenth-century American political life: the Tammany tiger, the Republican elephant, the Democratic donkey, the workingman with his cap and dinner pail, the Rag Baby of currency inflation. He also popularized the figure of Santa Claus as a round, cheery dispenser of gifts, exuding a gemütlichkeit that Nast drew from the folklore of his native land.

Nast's greatest work dealt with the politics and public policies of the post–Civil War decade. There is a notable correlation between the quality of his art and the force of personal conviction that lay behind it. When he commented on issues that stirred his liberal conscience — the struggle for the Union and against slavery, the plight of the freedmen during Reconstruction, the threat that Andrew Johnson and the Democrats posed to the war's results, the menace of the Tweed Ring, the danger (as he saw it) of Roman Catholicism to American mores and institutions — he did so with what has been called the "stark, focused style" of his artistic peak.

But his political commitments became muddied from the mid-1870s on, when postwar Radical Republicanism gave way to the scandals of the Grant administration, rising economic and social tensions, and a resurgent negrophobia. In pace with his growing disillusion, his art declined. He ended a pensioner of sorts, as the American consul in Guayaquil, Ecuador, where he died of yellow fever.

Morton Keller, *The Art and Politics of Thomas Nast* (1968); Albert B. Paine, *Thomas Nast, His Period and His Pictures* (1981).

MORTON KELLER

NATIONAL AMERICAN WOMAN SUFFRAGE ASSOCIATION

The National American Woman Suffrage Association (NAWSA), founded in 1890, united two suffragist organizations that had pursued opposing policies in the years after the Civil War. The National Woman Suffrage Association (NWSA), founded by Elizabeth Cady Stanton and Susan B. Anthony in 1869, had agitated for a federal constitutional amendment that would give women the vote, whereas the American Woman Suffrage Association (AWSA), organized the same year by Lucy Stone, Julia Ward Howe, and others, sought action through the state legislatures.

The two policies represented more than differing tactics. The NWSA's insistence on immediate federal action brought the women's movement into direct competition with the campaign for black male suffrage. The AWSA, on the other hand, recommended that women should not seek federal action until the campaign for black suffrage had been won. But after this goal was achieved with the ratification of the Fifteenth Amendment in 1870, it became clear that the Republican party would not take up the fight for woman suffrage as the AWSA had hoped. Residual bitterness between the two woman suffrage groups kept them apart for another twenty years, but the primary division over the Fifteenth Amendment no longer applied, and the two groups united in the NAWSA in 1890.

Under Cady and Stanton, the NWSA had expressed an assertive feminism, advocating a broad range of rights for women. With the amalgamation into NAWSA, the women's movement became both more focused and more conservative, seeking only the vote and often justifying it in terms of women's "purifying" influence rather than their inherent equality with men. Between 1890 and 1896, Wyoming and Utah entered the Union with woman suffrage in their constitutions, and Colorado and Idaho approved it by referenda. But over the next fourteen years, although suffragists launched 480 campaigns to get the question on other state ballots, they achieved only a handful of referenda and won none of them. But the situation began to change in 1910. Carrie Chapman Catt, former president of NAWSA, gave new life to the suffrage movement, aggressively organizing state campaigns that reached beyond NAWSA's traditional middle-class base to include immigrant and working-class women.

Between 1910 and 1912, half a dozen states gave women the vote, and more followed each year. At the same time, the suffrage movement was getting broader support from national reform groups, and in Washington the fiery Congressional Union, led by Alice Paul, was bringing the militant tactics of British suffragists to a campaign for a federal amendment. Although the Congressional Union's abrasiveness offended the NAWSA leadership, it also spurred them to action.

In 1915, Catt organized NAWSA's "Winning Plan," based on the principle that each state that gave women the vote could then be pressed to support the effort on the federal level. Catt herself cultivated President Woodrow Wilson, ultimately winning his support. In 1919, with twenty-six state legislatures petitioning Congress on behalf of woman suffrage, the Nineteenth Amendment passed by a large majority. It was proclaimed ratified in 1920. Thereafter, NAWSA disbanded, but many of its leaders were active in the founding of the League of Women Voters in the same year.

See also American Woman Suffrage Association; Anthony, Susan B.; Catt, Carrie Chapman; National Woman Suffrage Association; Paul, Alice; Stanton, Elizabeth Cady; Suffrage.

NATIONAL ASSOCIATION FOR THE ADVANCEMENT OF COLORED PEOPLE

The National Association for the Advancement of Colored People (NAACP) was founded in 1909–1910 in New York City by a group of white and black intellectuals. United in their opposition to the gradualism preached by Booker T. Washington, the NAACP leaders sought, first, to make whites aware of the need for racial equality. To do this, the organization launched a program of speechmaking, lobbying, and publicizing the issue. It also started a magazine, the *Crisis,* which was edited for years by the black leader W. E. B. Du Bois. At the same time, the NAACP attacked segregation and racial inequality through the courts. It won a Supreme Court decision in 1915 against the grandfather clause (used by many southern states to prevent blacks from voting) and another in 1927 against the all-white primary.

In 1916, a new field secretary, James Weldon Johnson, began expanding the organization's membership in the South. Johnson became the NAACP's first black executive secretary in 1920, by which time membership had grown to ninety thousand, of which nearly half was in the South. Under his leadership, followed by that of Walter White (who served as secretary from 1930 to 1955), the NAACP became the dominant civil rights organization in the country, noted particularly for its work in publicizing the evils of Jim Crow discrimination and for its leadership in the fight for a federal antilynching law.

In 1950, the NAACP began its campaign against the legal doctrine — first established in *Plessy* v. *Ferguson,* 1896 — that separate but equal schools for black and white children were constitutional. In a series of cases, it demonstrated that separate facilities provided to black students were not equal to those for whites. Then, drawing on extensive scholarly testimony showing the pernicious social and psychological effects of segregation, the NAACP set out to prove that facilities separated according to race were inherently unequal. Five desegregation suits were launched in different states (1950–1952). The 1954 Supreme Court decision on the case that reached it first — *Brown* v. *Board of Education of Topeka* (Kansas) — declared segregation in public schools to be unconstitutional. The decision was greeted with bitter hostility in the South, and among the reactions was a concerted attack — using both legal and illegal methods — on local NAACP branches. By 1957, its

membership in the South had dropped from nearly half of the organization to 28 percent.

Other civil rights groups attracted more members in the South during the 1960s, many using direct mass action instead of the legal strategies pioneered by the NAACP. The NAACP, however, remained active nationally both through its main organization and through its Legal Defense Fund. Although rivalry among civil rights groups was a continuous problem within the movement during those years, particularly at the leadership level, there were also innumerable instances of cooperation and mutual support, most notably the March on Washington in 1963. In the late 1970s, the NAACP broadened its scope by committing itself to the struggle for equal rights around the world.

See also Civil Rights Movement; Racial Desegregation.

NATIONAL DEBT

The national debt of the United States is the total of all the obligations of the Treasury to pay money to the federal government's creditors. It consists of bonds, notes, and bills issued to the creditors when they lend money to the government. When the national debt was created in its current form in 1791, it stood at $75 million, or about $18 per capita in dollars of 1791 purchasing power and $197 per capita in dollars of 1982–1984 purchasing power (see accompanying table). Nearly two centuries later in 1988, the debt stood at $2,600.8 billion, or $10,572 per capita in 1988 dollars and $8,937 in 1982–1984 dollars.

Such data, however, are not very informative. When a borrower applies for a loan, a lender usually appraises the borrower's income because that typically is the source of interest payments and repayments of principal. By analogy, in judging whether a national debt is large or small, one ought to compare it to the income (or product) of the national economy because that income, through taxation or further borrowing, is the ultimate source of interest and principal payments on the national debt. The accompanying figure presents the ratio of the national debt to the gross national product (GNP) of the United States from 1791 to 1988. It is apparent that the national debt has varied widely in comparison to the GNP over two centuries. Since we know that the GNP, the annual dollar value of all the goods and services produced by the American economy, has grown at relatively steady rates over long periods of time, most of the major fluctuations in the debt/GNP ratio have been caused by fluctuations in the national debt. Indeed, the history of the debt — its origins and its expansions and contractions over two centuries — reflects many of the key episodes of the American experience.

The national debt was born in the War of Independence. Within a week of the Battle of Bunker Hill in 1775, the Continental Congress, following colonial precedents, authorized an issue of $2 million of bills of credit called Continentals to finance the war. By the end of 1779, $241.6 million of Continentals had been authorized. U.S. loan certificates, foreign loans, state-issued bills of credit, and other evidences of public debt completed the stock of borrowing for the Revolution. The worst inflation in U.S. history resulted from the overissue of Continentals, and the bills became nearly valueless by 1780. The other evidences of revolutionary debt also depreciated greatly in value. After the war, starting in 1782, Congress authorized commissioners to travel around the country to examine claims against Congress and the Continental army and revalue them in terms of hard money. The revalued debt amounted to some $27 million.

Under the Articles of Confederation, Congress had no independent power to raise revenue. At the same time, the states, with debts of

| Year | Total Gross Debt (billions of dollars) | Debt per Capita | |
		Nominal (current dollars)	Real (1982–1984 dollars)
1791	.075	18	197
1804	.086	14	120
1811	.045	6	49
1816	.127	15	104
1835	.000	0	0
1845	.016	1	10
1851	.068	3	37
1860	.065	2	25
1866	2.756	75	475
1893	.961	14	160
1899	1.437	19	231
1914	1.188	12	119
1919	25.482	243	1,400
1930	16.185	132	787
1939	48.2	368	2,645
1946	271.0	1,917	9,824
1960	290.5	1,607	5,432
1970	380.9	1,857	4,783
1975	541.9	2,509	4,662
1980	908.5	3,989	4,841
1985	1,817.0	7,592	7,059
1988	2,600.8	10,572	8,937

National Debt of the United States, Selected Years, 1791–1988

Sources: U.S. Department of Commerce, *Historical Statistics of the United States* (U.S. Government Printing Office, 1975); *Economic Report of the President, 1989* (U.S. Government Printing Office, 1989); Thomas S. Berry, *Revised Annual Estimates of American Gross National Product, 1789–1889* (Bostwick Press, 1978).

their own, were reluctant to respond to Congress's requisitions for revenue. As a result, interest payments in the 1780s were met by issuing certificates of interest indebtedness. The Constitution of 1787 solved the revenue problem by giving the new federal government the power to tax, but by the beginning of 1790 the indebtedness of the United States, including arrears of interest, had increased to $13.2 million of foreign debt and $40.7 million of domestic debt, while state governments had outstanding debts of $18.3 million. In 1789, as the new government under the Constitution was being organized, the market priced the existing evidences of debt at only fifteen to thirty cents on the dollar because of uncertainties about if, how, and when they would be repaid. The new nation had a poor credit rating.

In January 1790, Alexander Hamilton, installed as the first secretary of the treasury, submitted his *Report on the Public Credit* to Congress. He called for funding nearly all the government's obligations, including the state debts, into long-term federal securities payable in specie — that is, hard money. After considerable debate Hamilton's proposals were adopted in August 1790. The foreign debt was fully funded, as was most of the domestic debt, although interest payments were deferred on part of the latter and another portion carried interest rates below the market rate. Only the depreciated Continental bills, nearly valueless, were funded at less than face value; one hundred dollars of Continentals were accepted as payment for one dollar of the new bonds. The most controversial part of Hamilton's plan, because some states had paid off the bulk of their debts while others had not, was the assumption of remaining state debts by the federal government. (To gain the support of Thomas Jefferson and his followers for the plan, Hamilton and the Federalists agreed to a compromise that located the future capital of the nation on the banks of the Potomac.)

Hamilton's refunding plan was generous to the government's creditors, who replaced securities selling for as little as fifteen cents on the dollar in 1789 with new federal bonds that soon rose toward par. How was such generosity jus-

tified? Hamilton argued in his report that his plan would restore faith in the government and public credit, attract foreign capital to the United States, and increase the effective stock of money, thereby stimulating the economy. Subsequent experience proved him correct. The U.S. government was nearly bankrupt in the 1780s; in 1803 it had no trouble borrowing $11.25 million on short notice, mostly from foreign subscribers, to finance the Louisiana Purchase, which doubled the size of the nation. By that time nearly 60 percent of the national debt had been purchased by foreigners, who in effect lent money to Americans in return for the government's promises to repay them in the future. Within the United States, debt owners could sell their federal securities for money or use them as collateral for bank loans. In retrospect, Hamilton's plan was a political and economic masterstroke for the new Republic. As Daniel Webster would later say, Hamilton "touched the dead corpse of the public credit, and it sprung upon its feet."

The subsequent history of the debt can be traced through the accompanying table and the figures' portrayal of the expansion and contraction of the debt/GNP ratio. A national debt of $75 million in 1791, when Hamilton's funding plan was implemented, may seem small to the modern observer. But it represented about 40 percent of the GNP then, and a debt/GNP ratio that high was not seen again in U.S. history until the 1930s when the Great Depression led to large federal deficits and increases in the debt at the same time the GNP was collapsing.

The national debt reached a high in 1804, when the Louisiana Purchase added $11.25 million to it in one transaction. But aside from this extravagance, the administrations of Jefferson and James Madison were noted for fiscal frugality. Although some of the old Federalist taxes were cut in those years, Treasury Secretary Albert Gallatin was nonetheless able to cut the debt nearly in half between 1804 and 1811. Another notable event in the history of the debt was its elimination in 1835 and 1836, an occurrence unprecedented in the history of modern nations. This was during the administration of Andrew Jackson who, like his Jeffersonian predecessors, was fiscally frugal. But the main reason was the rapid economic growth that swelled federal tariff and land-sale revenues.

Much of the rest of the history of the national debt before 1930 can be generalized as following a pattern of rapid expansion in times of war and gradual reduction in times of peace. Reliance on debt financing during wars can be justified in economic theory by treating war expenditures as investments (in national survival or territorial expansion, for example) benefiting later generations who ought to help pay for the benefits by servicing the debt. A more likely explanation is one of expedience: wars call for rapid increases in expenditures, but equally rapid increases in compulsory taxation would be less popular than borrowing.

The pattern of wartime debt expansion can be seen in the War of 1812 when the national debt nearly tripled between 1811 and 1816, in the Mexican War era when the debt more than

quadrupled between 1845 and 1851, in the Civil War when the debt increased forty-two-fold between 1860 and 1866, in the Spanish-American War era when the debt rose 50 percent between 1893 and 1899 (although the larger part of this increase occurred before the war), and in World War I when the debt increased twenty-one-fold between 1914 and 1919. World War II also fit the pattern: the debt increased nearly sixfold between 1939 and 1946.

The longest sustained period of debt reduction occurred after the Civil War, from 1866 to 1893, when the federal government ran a budget surplus every year and cut the debt to about a third of its initial value. On the whole, this was a positive development for the U.S. economy, as the government freed up funds for private investment and high levels of investment at some of the lowest interest rates in U.S. history fueled rapid economic growth. But debt reduction was controversial because it resulted from adminis-

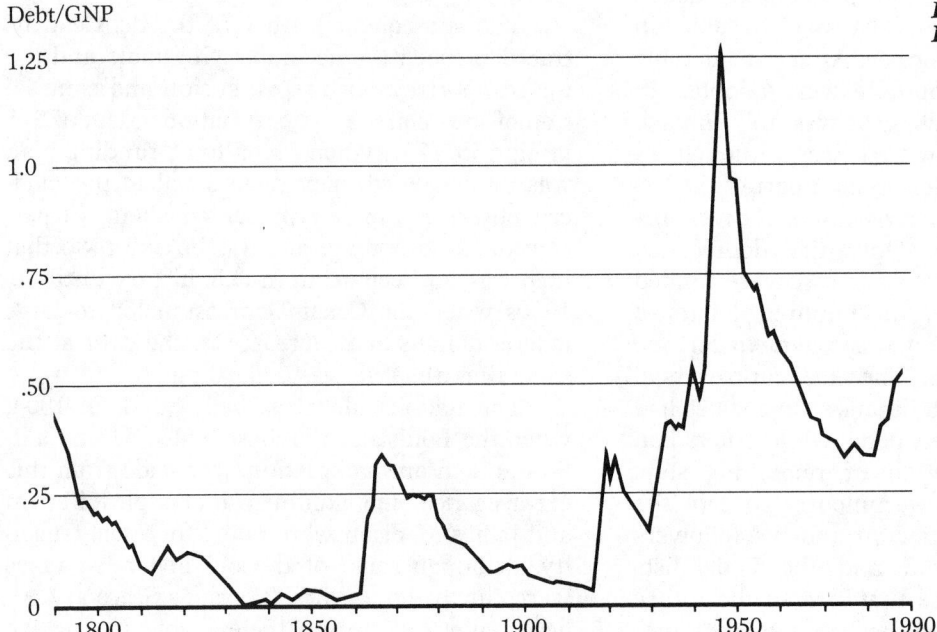

Ratio of the Gross Federal Debt to GNP, 1791–1988

Sources: U.S. Department of Commerce, *Historical Statistics of the United States* (U.S. Government Printing Office, 1975); *Economic Report of the President, 1989* (U.S. Government Printing Office, 1989); Thomas S. Berry, *Revised Annual Estimates of American Gross National Product, 1789–1889* (Bostwick Press, 1978).

trations, mostly Republican, that combined fiscal frugality with high tariff rates, producing revenue surpluses while protecting American manufacturers from foreign competition. The administration of Grover Cleveland was embarrassed in the late 1880s when, having retired all the callable federal bonds, it had to enter the market and buy up government debt at prices well in excess of par. Some modest debt reduction occurred between 1899 and 1914. The last sustained reduction came in the 1920s when the debt was reduced to less than two-thirds of its 1919 level. This was a favorite policy of Treasury Secretary Andrew Mellon, a conservative banker.

The year 1930 represented a watershed in the history of the national debt. Since that date the debt has never been reduced for more than a year or two in peacetime or, of course, in wartime. In the depressed 1930s the collapse of the GNP led to federal fiscal deficits and debt growth. World War II, as can be seen in the figure, saw the debt rise to by far its highest level in relation to GNP in previous or subsequent experience. The national debt peaked at 128 percent of GNP in 1946. After the war, although the debt continued to rise, the GNP until the 1980s rose much faster, so that by 1979–1981 the debt/GNP ratio was only 33 percent. From 1981 to 1988, the policies of the Reagan administration — tax cuts and increased defense spending — coupled with Congress's and the administration's reluctance to cut spending on inflation-swollen entitlement programs, produced large deficits that raised the debt/GNP ratio to 53 percent, its highest level in U.S. history apart from the World War II era, with no end to the rise in sight as of 1991. This trend disturbed many Americans, and federal deficits and rises in the national debt once again became major national issues. Even in 1988, however, the debt/GNP ratio was no larger than it was during the period 1943–1961.

Various strategies for marketing the debt have been followed through the years. The funded national debt of 1791 was created by exchanges of various Revolution era obligations for long-term bonds payable, principal and interest, in hard money. Before the Civil War, when new funds had to be raised, the Treasury usually relied on loan contractors to buy large amounts of new securities at negotiated prices and resell them to state and local governments, institutions, and wealthy individuals. Secondary trading markets emerged, allowing holders of the debt continuously to buy and sell their holdings of federal securities. Since much of the debt was held in Europe, arrangements were made to make it payable in European centers. Thus, $6.25 million of the Louisiana Purchase loan was made payable in London and $5 million in Amsterdam.

The Civil War brought sudden financial requirements and uncertainties that were too great for the old system of debt marketing. Jay Cooke, a private banker, contracted with the Treasury to place large war-debt issues with small investors throughout the Union. Cooke relied on heavy advertising expenditures and patriotic appeals to sell bonds. The newly created National Banks also bought large amounts of wartime issues, against which they could issue national currency. Jay Cooke's techniques of mass marketing Treasury debt within the United States introduced many Americans to ownership of paper wealth — a major development in the history of U.S. financial markets.

Cooke's techniques were employed again when the debt soared in World Wars I and II. Then, however, a central bank, the Federal Reserve System, was present to aid Treasury financing by creating new money to be exchanged for federal debt. Nonmarketable savings bonds were introduced, but they never became a major part of the total debt.

Today, the marketing of the national debt is almost continuous, with new issues of Treasury bills, for example, being sold every week. New notes and bonds are issued quarterly. Many new issues simply replace old ones, but in the 1980s a great deal of new money had to be raised to finance the large Reagan era federal deficits. In 1988, U.S. government agencies, trust funds, and Federal Reserve banks owned about 30 percent of the debt, private financial institutions held nearly 40 percent, and the remainder was owned by state and local governments (11 percent), U.S. individuals (7 percent), and foreign/international holders (13 percent).

Robert Heilbroner and Peter Bernstein, *The Debt and the Deficit* (1989).

RICHARD SYLLA

See also Banking; Depressions; Economic Growth; Government and the Economy; Gramm-Rudman Act; Hamilton, Alexander; Tariff.

NATIONAL INDEPENDENT PARTY

See Greenback Party.

NATIONALISM

See Black Nationalism; Nativism.

NATIONAL LABOR RELATIONS ACT

The National Labor Relations Act of 1935 is informally known as the Wagner Act, for its sponsor, Senator Robert Wagner of New York. It created the National Labor Relations Board (NLRB) and established workers' right to collective bargaining. (The right had been recognized in the National Industrial Recovery Act of 1933, but that act had been declared unconstitutional.)

In the spring and summer of 1934, half a million workers in many industries went on strike, spurring Congress to seek mechanisms for bringing greater labor stability to the nation. One of the NLRB's two functions was to supervise elections to determine if a union should represent a given group of workers. Its authority to decide which bargaining unit was appropriate for such an election — for example, a shop within a plant or the whole plant — came to be crucial. The American Federation of Labor (AFL), the expected beneficiary of the Wagner Act, lost many of the NLRB's early decisions to the newly forming Congress of Industrial Organizations (CIO). The second major function of the NLRB was to stop unfair labor practices on the part of employers, employees, or unions. Its tools were investigative powers, the means to encourage informal settlements, and quasi-judicial proceedings that could be enforced by the U.S. Court of Appeals.

The Wagner Act contributed substantially to the New Deal's popularity. Unions threw their support behind Franklin D. Roosevelt in the 1936 election and helped secure a Democratic landslide at every election level.

Ultimately, however, the Wagner Act's impact for labor was mixed. Instead of recognizing unions' legal status as organizations, the NLRB treated them as agents of workers, with no existence beyond employee-delegated power. Also, the board's role as mediator weakened the strike weapon. The 1947 Taft-Hartley Act hamstrung labor further by requiring anticommunist affidavits from unions and asserting that workers did not have to join the unions that represented them.

See also Labor.

NATIONAL LABOR RELATIONS BOARD

The National Labor Relations Board (NLRB) is a five-person federal agency charged with regulating the process of collective bargaining between American employers and their workers. The NLRB serves, in effect, as a court of appeals, investigating and resolving charges of unfair labor practices and disputes over the delineation of bargaining units and elections for union representation. Members of the board are appointed to five-year terms by the president, with the approval of the Senate.

A forerunner of the NLRB, the National Labor Board, was established in 1933 to enforce the collective bargaining provisions of the National Industrial Recovery Act (NIRA), but it had little power and was in any case invalidated when the Supreme Court struck down the NIRA in the spring of 1935. Senator Robert Wagner of New York had been pressing for some time for a more comprehensive labor law (including a strong three-person National Labor Relations Board), but had received little support from President Franklin D. Roosevelt. Then, in the summer of 1935, during a period of dramatic reform initiatives that came to be called the Second Hundred Days, Roosevelt suddenly announced his support for the Wagner-Connery Labor Relations Act. Despite conservative opposition, the bill passed both houses easily and was signed on July 5, 1935.

The NLRB, established under the Wagner Act, took an active role in supporting and extending labor's right to organize during the late 1930s. In earlier years, the Supreme Court had struck down a succession of New Deal laws; its upholding of the Wagner Act in *NLRB* v. *Jones & Laughlin Steel Corp.* (1937) marked the beginning of a series of decisions favorable to New Deal reforms.

The NLRB's role began to change after World War II. The Taft-Hartley Act (1947), in addition to expanding the board from three members to five, removed its power to prosecute, leaving it a solely judicial agency. And whereas the Wagner Act had focused exclusively on restraining unfair practices by employers, Taft-Hartley required the NLRB to examine unfair practices by unions as well. The Landrum-Griffin Act (1959) added further to the list of prohibited union actions the NLRB must investigate.

See also Labor.

NATIONAL ORGANIZATION FOR WOMEN

The National Organization for Women (NOW) both symbolized and spearheaded women's growing involvement in politics. Feminist leaders formed NOW in 1966, three years after the publication of Betty Friedan's *The Feminine Mystique* and two years after Title VII of the Civil Rights Act of 1964 had guaranteed women legal protection against discrimination. The organization's agenda included better education and employment and political opportunities for women. It also sought equal pay for equal work. In the liberal climate of the 1960s, NOW grew rapidly. It pioneered the use of "Ms." as a salutation and helped make two-career families more acceptable in middle-class society.

Pressure and activism from feminist groups like NOW continued to help women when the nation grew more conservative in the 1970s. It fought to preserve the Supreme Court's pro-choice ruling in *Roe* v. *Wade* (1973) and helped pave the way for women to take more active roles in science, sports, and politics. For example, Geraldine Ferraro became the first woman to run for vice president on a major party ticket. But NOW's agenda suffered, and it encountered failures and setbacks: the right-to-life movement gained momentum during the 1980s, and the Equal Rights Amendment failed to win the required three-fourths approval from state legislatures to become part of the Constitution.

See also Feminist Movement; Friedan, Betty.

NATIONAL PARKS

See Public Land Policy.

NATIONAL PROHIBITION ENFORCEMENT ACT

See Volstead Act.

NATIONAL RECOVERY ADMINISTRATION

The National Recovery Administration (NRA) was a New Deal agency designed to organize the stabilization and revival of the nation's economy; it was established under the National Industrial Recovery Act, June 16, 1933. Under NRA supervision, each sector of the economy was to develop an industrywide code, setting standards for production, prices, and wages. These codes would have the force of law and would be exempt from antitrust provisions.

The program received general support at first. Businesspeople saw it as a chance to formalize the trade association agreements that had flourished in the 1920s but were difficult to enforce under the economic pressures of the depression. Labor pinned its hopes on Section 7, which required that each code specify maximum hours, minimum wages, safe working conditions, and (under Section 7a) workers' right to organize. The program director, Gen. Hugh Johnson, launched the NRA with a dramatic publicity campaign, awarding a "Blue Eagle" to each participating company, and by September codes had been developed by most major industries. Criticism mounted, however, as it became clear that the largest firms were shaping the codes to suit their own priorities, with little input from labor, consumers, or the overextended NRA staff. At the same time, business was growing hostile to the provisions protecting labor and to the codes' administrative complexity.

During 1934 the NRA underwent several reorganizations; in September, Johnson was replaced by a five-man board. In May 1935, the Senate reluctantly approved a one-year extension of the NRA, but on May 27 the Supreme Court in *Schechter Poultry Corp.* v. *United States* declared the code system unconstitutional because of the quasi-legislative power granted to the executive branch. Although later legislation revived its labor provisions, the NRA's key feature, the industrial code system, was not repeated.

See also Government and the Economy; New Deal.

NATIONAL ROAD

The National Road (later called the Cumberland Road) was the first major federal response to the growing demand in the early nineteenth century for surfaced roads to facilitate westward travel. It ultimately ran from Baltimore, Maryland, through Pennsylvania, Virginia, Ohio, and Indiana, to Illinois. In 1806 Congress approved the route for the first section, largely along an Indian trail; it ran westward from the end of the Baltimore Turnpike in Cumberland, Maryland, to Wheeling, in western Virginia, where travelers could board ships on the Ohio River. Planning began in 1806, but contracts were not granted until 1811, and because of delays associated with the War of 1812, construction did not begin until 1815. The road reached Wheeling in 1818.

Sectional feelings on national road building ran high. Easterners had no particular interest in facilitating travel to and from the West, and the southern states were increasingly committed to state rather than federal action. But westerners pressed for improvements no single state could finance. Henry Clay of Kentucky became their champion in 1824 when he proposed the American System — a combination of protective tariffs and internal improvements intended to build a strong domestic network of industry and trade. Largely through Clay's efforts, the National Road was extended to Columbus, Ohio, in 1833.

From the start, some questioned whether federal involvement in such projects was constitutional. President James Monroe, who believed it was not, vetoed an 1822 bill to establish tolls and use the funds for repairs. President Andrew Jackson dealt with this controversy by turning the completed sections of the road over to the states, permitting them to finance repairs through tolls.

In 1850 the National Road reached Vandalia, Illinois, but before it could reach St. Louis, railroad construction had become the new national priority. In the years that followed, the road lost importance, until automobile travel brought it back into use as part of U.S. Route 40. Then in 1940, with the opening of the Pennsylvania Turnpike, Route 40, too, became less significant.

See also Transportation Revolution.

NATIONAL WOMAN'S PARTY

The National Woman's party (NWP) was an outgrowth of the Congressional Union, formed in 1913 by Alice Paul and other militant suffragists. Paul and her associates called for a federal amendment to give women the vote and pursued their goal with the aggressive methods used by their British counterparts, including parading, picketing, civil disobedience, and hunger strikes. This effort, combined with the passage of laws granting women suffrage at the state level, encouraged the larger and more conservative National American Woman Suffrage Association to join the campaign for federal action, culminating in the ratification of the Nineteenth Amendment in 1920.

With the vote won, many former suffragists believed that women should now abandon gender-specific efforts. Alice Paul disagreed, and, with other members of the Congressional Union, formed the NWP as an independent woman's party. Whereas organizations like the League of Women Voters (LWV) worked for generalized social and political reform, the NWP focused its energies on a single-minded struggle to win total equality for women. Its approach was embodied in its campaign, launched in 1923, for an Equal Rights Amendment. The LWV spoke for those who opposed the amendment, arguing that it would harm women by invalidating the various laws that gave them special rights and protection. This dispute became increasingly bitter and personalized over the years, further reducing the chances for compromise. Although the NWP had less than ten thousand members, the militance, energy, and persistence of Alice Paul and her followers succeeded in keeping the subject of an Equal Rights Amendment alive for decades, helping to lay the groundwork for a reinvigorated campaign in the 1970s.

See also Feminist Movement; Suffrage.

NATIONAL WOMAN SUFFRAGE ASSOCIATION

The National Woman Suffrage Association (NWSA) was founded in May 1869 by Susan B. Anthony, Elizabeth Cady Stanton, and other women exasperated at the collapse of an Equal Rights Association convention they attended in New York City. That convention split when former abolitionists, such as Frederick Douglass, accused Anthony and Stanton of racism because they campaigned for George Francis Train, a Democratic candidate for governor of Kansas who opposed votes for African-Americans but favored women's suffrage. Many women delegates also felt that demands for women's suffrage should be put aside until African-Americans received the right to vote. Other feminists, including Stanton and Anthony, had wanted the Equal Rights Association to concentrate its efforts on women's issues and formed the NWSA for that purpose.

The NWSA dealt with many issues of interest to women besides suffrage, such as the unionization of women workers. In 1872, it supported Victoria Woodhull, the first woman candidate for president of the United States. In contrast,

the American Woman Suffrage Association limited its efforts to securing the right to vote and tied itself closely to the Republican party.

After the 1872 election, the political differences between the two associations began to fade, but the acrimony was so great that they did not merge (becoming the National American Woman Suffrage Association) until 1890. Despite factionalism and changes in the political climate that both delayed the progress of the suffrage movement and undermined Radical Reconstruction, the NWSA set a precedent for women interested in organizing independently of male-dominated politics.

See also American Woman Suffrage Association; Anthony, Susan B.; Feminist Movement; National American Woman Suffrage Association; Stanton, Elizabeth Cady; Suffrage.

NATIVE AMERICANS

See Indians.

NATIVISM

Although the United States has always portrayed itself as a sanctuary for the world's victims of oppression and poverty, anti-immigrant sentiment — known as nativism — has pervaded most of the nation's history. In the seventeenth and eighteenth centuries, when much of America contained few inhabitants, colonists sought desperately to attract immigrants from Europe. In fact, the Declaration of Independence complained that King George III had "endeavored to prevent the population of these States" by "obstructing the Laws of Naturalization of Foreigners" and by "refusing to pass others to encourage their migration hither."

America's outlook toward immigration began to change after the Revolution. Realizing that most immigrants supported Thomas Jefferson's Republican faction, Federalists in Congress attempted to suppress the newcomers' political activity in 1798 by passing the Alien Acts, which curtailed the rights of unnaturalized immigrants. In the 1830s, however, nativists began focusing their attacks on Catholic immigrants, asserting that America's republican form of government could not be sustained with a large Catholic population. These Protestants insisted that republican governments require a virtuous, educated, and independent electorate, and they perceived Catholic immigrants to be superstitious, ignorant, and dominated by their priests. Such anti-Catholicism had a long history in America. The Puritans had journeyed across the ocean to escape the Church of England's "Romish" trappings, and southern colonists were known to have enjoyed a parlor game called "Break the Pope's Neck." So when pamphleteers such as Samuel F. B. Morse began linking immigration, which Americans had considered beneficial, with Catholicism, which most saw as a threat, American nativism found a larger audience.

Early nativists tried to transform their crusade into a political movement, but their principles initially influenced the workplace more than the ballot box. Artisans and laborers often complained that immigrants depressed wages because the newcomers would work for less pay than native-born workers. The frequency with which employers used immigrants to replace striking workingmen only deepened the animosity toward newcomers. Employers also practiced nativism: many help-wanted advertisements of the period ended with the proviso "No Irish Need Apply."

Aided by this persistent economic nativism, anti-immigrant sentiment soon entered politics. One of the first nativist political organizations, New York's Native American Democratic Association, nominated inventor Samuel F. B. Morse for mayor in 1836. He captured only 6 percent of the vote, but in 1844 a new nativist group, the American Republican party, elected six congressmen and dozens of local officials in New York, Philadelphia, and Boston. Nativism reached its political zenith ten years later with the meteoric rise of the "Know-Nothings." This secret fraternal organization, which sought to curtail the political power of Catholics and immigrants, probably derived its name from its members' pledge to feign ignorance if queried about the group.

The dramatic rise in immigration resulting from the Irish potato famine and German eco-nomic distress, disputes between Protestants and Catholics over the use of the Protestant King James Bible in public schools, and a disgust for conventional political parties that peaked after passage of the Kansas-Nebraska Act attracted more than 1 million members to the Know-Nothing party. By the end of 1855, the American party (as the Know-Nothings renamed themselves) had carried elections in a dozen states and elected more than one hundred congressmen. Many believed they would elect the next president, but divisions over the slavery issue drove many of its northern members into the new Republican party. Know-Nothings tried to attract new members by promising that the group would promote sectional harmony, but their 1856 presidential candidate, Millard Fillmore, carried only Maryland. This embarrassing performance hastened the party's decline, and by 1860, the Know-Nothings had disappeared.

Although no nativist political organization comparable in size to the Know-Nothings appeared after the Civil War, nativists often found that the existing parties were willing to enact their proposals. A central item on the Know-Nothings' agenda, a law banning the immigration of paupers and convicts, passed Congress in 1882. Registration and literacy tests for voters (which Know-Nothings had supported as a way to prevent immigrant voting) also became common.

By the late nineteenth century, however, antiradicalism had replaced anti-Catholicism as the cornerstone of nativism. Many believed that immigrants brought European radicalism with them to America, and they especially blamed the newcomers for fomenting the labor unrest that characterized much of the period. The role immigrants played in the communist, socialist, and anarchist movements also helped convince many Americans that unless the country restricted immigration, radicals from abroad might soon dominate the United States.

The first laws enacted to restrict immigration affected only Asians. Congress prohibited immigration from China for ten years starting in 1882 and banned it permanently in 1902. President Theodore Roosevelt concluded a "gentleman's agreement" with Japan in 1907 that excluded immigrants from that country.

Efforts to restrict non-Asian newcomers soon gained momentum as well. Northwestern Europe had provided most of America's immigrants in the nineteenth century, but by 1900 a majority hailed from Russia, Poland, Hungary, and Italy. Reinforcing their racial prejudices by misinterpreting findings made in the new field of genetics, many Americans concluded that immigrants from these countries lacked the intelligence and motivation that purportedly characterized northwestern Europeans, so the "new immigration" provided renewed impetus to the nativist movement.

The aftermath of World War I gave restrictionists more ammunition. Fear of foreign agitators (especially communists) reached epidemic proportions and culminated in the red scare that swept the United States. The Ku Klux Klan also revived at this time, and the group's new agenda, which added anti-Catholicism, anti-Semitism, and antiforeignism to the traditional hatred of blacks, attracted 5 million members. The labor movement called for immigration restriction as well, arguing that the newcomers' willingness to work for substandard wages depressed the earnings of all laborers. Finally, many feared that with immigration having fallen off because of the war, millions of refugees would now flock to America and spoil the prosperity of the Roaring Twenties.

Congress responded to these pressures by passing the National Origins Act (1924), which reflected prevailing prejudices by setting immigration quotas that blatantly discriminated against southern and eastern Europeans. For example, the law (as eventually amended) permitted 65,721 immigrants from Great Britain annually, but only 5,802 from Italy and 2,712 from the Soviet Union. Asians were almost completely excluded. The movement to restrict immigration, initiated nearly a century earlier, had finally achieved its goal.

It is difficult to assess the extent to which nativism still pervades American society. Organized nativism as epitomized by the Know-Nothings or the Klan has no great following. Yet this may reflect the lack of large-scale immigra-tion to the United States, because the quota system set up in the 1920s remains intact today, and attempts to prevent illegal immigration reflect public support for this system. Contemporary outbreaks of hostility toward Asian-Americans, motivated in part by the impression that Japan has surpassed the United States economically, also indicate that nativism continues to influence American thought. Whatever the case, it is clear that though immigration played an important role in almost every period of American history, nativism pervaded its past with equal persistence.

Ray A. Billington, *The Protestant Crusade, 1800–1860: A Study of the Origins of American Nativism* (1938); John Higham, *Strangers in the Land: Patterns of American Nativism, 1860–1925,* 2nd ed. (1963).

Tyler Anbinder

See also Alien and Sedition Acts; Chinese Exclusion Act; Haymarket Affair; Immigration; Immigration Restriction League; Know-Nothing Party; Ku Klux Klan; Morse, Samuel F. B.

NATO

See North Atlantic Treaty Organization.

NAVY

See Armed Forces.

NAWSA

See National American Woman Suffrage Association.

NEUTRALITY ACTS

The four Neutrality Acts of the late 1930s represented an effort to keep the United States out of "foreign" wars, an effort resulting in part from widespread questioning of the reasons for and results of America's participation in World War I. These laws, unlike U.S. policy in 1916–1917, limited the exercise of neutral rights as a way of protecting that neutrality. A characteristic of the acts was that they made no distinction between aggressor and victim; both sides were simply characterized as "belligerents."

The first Neutrality Act (August 1935), passed after Italy's attack on Ethiopia in May 1935, empowered the president, on finding a state of war, to declare an embargo on arms shipments to the belligerents and to announce that U.S. citizens traveling on belligerents' ships did so at their own risk. This act set no limits, however, on trade in materials useful for war, such as copper, steel, and oil. The 1935 act was replaced by the Neutrality Act of 1936 (February 29), which added a prohibition on extending loans or credits to belligerents.

The Spanish civil war, which broke out in July 1936, was not covered by existing neutrality legislation, which applied only to wars between nations; accordingly, Congress by joint resolution on January 6, 1937, forbade supplying arms to either side. When the 1936 law expired, the Neutrality Act of 1937 (May 1) included civil wars, empowered the president to add strategic materials to the embargo list, and made travel by U.S. citizens on belligerents' ships unlawful. The practical difficulties of maintaining neutrality became clear, however, when Japan's incursions into China led to the outbreak of fighting there on July 7, 1937. Since invoking the Neutrality Act would penalize China, which was more dependent than Japan on American assistance, President Franklin D. Roosevelt chose not to identify the fighting as a state of war.

The Neutrality Act of 1939 (November 4) contained a "cash and carry" formula devised by Bernard M. Baruch. Belligerents were again permitted to buy American arms and strategic materials, but they had to pay cash and to transport the goods in their own ships. This provision, it was believed, would prevent the United States from being drawn into war either by holding debt in some belligerent countries or by violating blockades while transporting supplies. In addition, the president was empowered to designate a "combat zone" in time of war, through which American citizens and ships were forbidden to travel.

On November 17, 1941, after repeated confrontations with German submarines in the North Atlantic and the torpedoing of the destroyer *Reuben James,* Congress amended the act

to permit merchant vessels to arm themselves and to carry cargoes to belligerent ports. But three weeks later, Japan bombed Pearl Harbor and the United States was at war.

See also Isolationism; World War II.

NEVELSON, LOUISE

(1900?–1988), artist. Nevelson became one of the world's best-known woman artists and the pioneer of environmental sculpture. Born Louise Berliawsky in Kiev in the Ukraine, she immigrated as a young child to Rockland, Maine, with her family. She moved to New York in 1920 to marry and initially explored dance, theater, and music. Dissatisfied with family life, she searched for a vocation. She turned to painting and drawing and studied at the Art Students League with Kenneth Hayes Miller, Kimon Nicolaides in 1928–1929, and briefly with Hans Hofmann in 1932. That same year she separated from her husband and took an extended trip to Europe. When she returned, they divorced and she dedicated herself to her work.

Although she had been exhibiting since the late 1930s, Nevelson arrived at a mature style only in her fifties. The twenty-five-year period of exploration before she arrived at her signature style (1933–1958) coincided with the development of New York City as the new center of the international art world. Working as an assistant to Diego Rivera on the Rockefeller murals and as an art teacher with the New Deal's WPA, Nevelson partook of contemporary trends and events. She was influenced in the thirties by the powerful forms of African, American Indian, and pre-Columbian art, and in the forties by the iconoclasm of dada and surrealism as well as the elements of dream and mystery represented in those movements.

Nevelson had the first of five one-woman shows between 1941 and 1946 at the prestigious Nierendorf Gallery in New York. Her most daring and prophetic works from this period were wood sculptures showing the effect of surrealist whimsy and her penchant for collage. They were included in her first thematic exhibition, The Circus, the Clown Is the Center of His World, at the Norlyst Gallery in 1943. She was prodigiously productive during the next fifteen years, and her style evolved from chunky terra-cottas to the evocative collages made of discarded wood scraps that became her specialty. During this period she also began her work as a printmaker.

In 1958, after four annual thematically designed exhibits, she mounted a show, Moon Garden + One, in which walls of boxed black wood collages surrounded the viewer in darkened rooms. This dramatic exhibition established Nevelson as the pioneer environmental American artist and an artist of the first rank. Although she produced some striking work in white-and-gold-painted wood, it was the black sculpted walls in wood and metal with their aura of mystery that captured the public imagination for the next thirty years. She also came to be celebrated for her unique flamboyant style of clothing and her forceful public personality.

Major shows in New York followed her success of 1958: at the Museum of Modern Art in 1959 and the Whitney Museum of American Art in 1967. From 1964 on she showed regularly at the Pace Gallery and eventually at galleries and museums in most of the world's art capitals including London, Milan, Paris, Brussels, Stockholm, Tokyo, Turin, and Zurich. In 1962 she represented the United States at the Venice Biennale. She received many public commissions, and in 1979 the Louise Nevelson Plaza, an entire outdoor environment of her black sculptures, was created in Lower Manhattan.

Louise Nevelson, *Dawns and Dusks,* ed. Diana MacKown (1976); Laurie Wilson, *Louise Nevelson: Iconography and Sources* (1981).

LAURIE WILSON

See also Painting and Sculpture.

NEW DEAL

Franklin D. Roosevelt accepted the Democratic nomination for president in 1932 by promising "a new deal for the American people," a phrase that has endured as a label for his administration and its many domestic achievements. The New Deal consisted of many different efforts to end the Great Depression and reform the American economy. Most of them failed, but there were enough successes to establish it as the most important episode of the twentieth century in the creation of the modern American state.

Roosevelt entered office with no single ideology or plan for dealing with the depression, but his programs were not without precedents. The New Deal reflected progressive ideas that Roosevelt and most of his original associates had absorbed in their political youths early in the century: an impatience with economic disorder; an opposition to monopoly; a commitment to government regulation of the economy; a belief that poverty was usually a product of social and economic forces, not a personal moral failure. The New Deal also drew heavily on the experiences of its leaders in the economic mobilization for World War I and on the policy experiments of the 1920s, both of which involved efforts to harmonize the economy by creating cooperative relationships among its constituent elements. The New Deal was eclectic, pragmatic, and frankly experimental. What many considered its incoherence, however, was a result not of an absence of ideology but of the presence of several competing ones.

The major domestic achievements of the New Deal took shape during three distinct periods. In 1933 the administration moved energetically to stop the economic panic that had engulfed the nation in 1932 (and had led to Roosevelt's decisive electoral victory). In the period from early 1935 to mid-1936, as the president prepared for reelection, the administration launched a second series of reforms, which historians have often called the "second New Deal." A third and less productive period of activism began in mid-1937 and continued through 1938 as the administration searched for ways to make the federal bureaucracy more efficient and to make the president more powerful within it. It tried as well to find a solution to a serious new recession. By 1939 the domestic political climate had become hostile to further reform, and the administration was turning its attention to the growing international tensions that would soon lead to war.

The desperate economic situation, combined with the substantial Democratic victories in the 1932 elections, gave Roosevelt unusual influence over Congress in the first months of his administration. He used his leverage to win rapid passage of a series of measures to prop up the tottering banking system, reform the stock market, aid the unemployed, and induce industrial and agricultural recovery. The celebrated first Hundred Days of the new administration produced a federal program to protect American farmers from the uncertainties of the market through subsidies and production controls, the Agricultural Adjustment Administration (AAA). It created a new federal regulatory agency to oversee the stock market, the Securities and Exchange Commission (SEC); a reform of the banking system that included a system of insurance for deposits, the Federal Deposit Insurance Corporation (FDIC); and a series of relief measures to aid some of the 15 million unemployed Americans, among them the Civilian Conservation Corps (CCC), the Civil Works Administration (CWA), and the Federal Emergency Relief Administration (FERA). The early New Deal also began the Tennessee Valley Authority (TVA), an unprecedented experiment in flood control, public power, and regional planning.

The National Industrial Recovery Act (NIRA), the most important undertaking of the first Hundred Days, contained a guarantee to workers of the right of collective bargaining and helped spur major union organizing drives in many industries. It created a substantial federal public works program, the Public Works Administration (PWA). Most important, and least successful, was the National Recovery Administration (NRA), which attempted to stabilize prices and wages through cooperative "code authorities" involving government, business, and labor.

These and other early initiatives created broad popular support for the Roosevelt administration and halted the rapid unraveling of the financial system. They did not, however, end, or even significantly abate, the Great Depression. Several crucial New Deal programs, moreover, violated conservative constitutional theory; the NRA, the AAA, and others were invalidated by the Supreme Court, which was dominated by conservatives with a narrow view of the interstate commerce clause of the Constitution, the basis of much New Deal legislation. In the meantime,

the administration was coming under increasing popular pressure to do more. Among those pressures were the increasing militancy of the trade union movement and the growing influence of such dissident challengers as Huey Long and Father Charles E. Coughlin.

In the spring of 1935, responding to the setbacks in the Court, restiveness in Congress, and the growing popular clamor for more dramatic action, the administration proposed or endorsed several important new initiatives. The National Labor Relations Act, also known as the Wagner Act, revived and strengthened the protections of collective bargaining contained in the original (and now invalidated) NIRA. New relief programs, of which the most prominent was the Works Progress Administration (WPA), created hundreds of thousands of jobs for the unemployed. Highly publicized, if largely symbolic, measures — a tax on large fortunes and an assault on utilities holding companies — established the New Deal's antimonopoly credentials. But the most important achievement of 1935, and perhaps of the New Deal as a whole, was the Social Security Act, which established a system of old-age pensions, unemployment insurance, and welfare benefits for such protected groups as dependent children and the handicapped. It established a framework that shaped the American welfare system through the remainder of the century.

Roosevelt's landslide reelection in 1936 produced large Democratic majorities in both houses of Congress and predictions (from the president's supporters) of great new achievements and (from his opponents) of an executive dictatorship. Instead, the administration encountered a long string of frustrations. They were partly a result of the president's own political errors. Emboldened by his triumphs and angry at the obduracy of his opponents (the Supreme Court among them), Roosevelt set out in 1937 to consolidate his authority within the government in ways that provoked powerful opposition. Early in the year, he proposed a "reform" of the judiciary designed to stop the series of reverses his programs had been suffering in the Supreme Court. He asked Congress to expand the number of justices so as to allow him to appoint members sympathetic to his ideas and hence tip the ideological balance of the Court. In one sense the proposal succeeded; two of the existing justices, almost certainly in response to the threat, switched positions and began voting to uphold New Deal measures, which created an effective liberal majority. But the "Court-packing plan," as it was known, did lasting political damage to Roosevelt and was finally rejected by Congress. At about the same time, the administration proposed a plan to reorganize the executive branch in ways that would significantly increase the president's control over the bureaucracy. Like the Court-packing plan, executive reorganization evoked strong opposition from those who feared a Roosevelt "dictatorship" and failed in Congress; a watered-down version of the bill finally won passage in 1939.

The biggest domestic event of Roosevelt's second term, however, was the severe recession that began in the fall of 1937 and continued through most of 1938 — a result, at least in part, of a premature effort by the administration to balance the budget by reducing federal spending. The New Deal responded in two ways. First, it launched a new rhetorical campaign against monopoly power, which many liberals believed was the cause of the recession. The centerpiece of this effort was a great public investigation of the issue by a special body, the Temporary National Economic Committee, composed of members of both the executive branch and Congress. By the time the committee completed its work, however, the nation was at war and the antimonopoly fervor had cooled. At about the same time, the president appointed an aggressive new director of the antitrust division of the Justice Department — Thurman Arnold, who greatly expanded the division's staff and launched prosecutions unprecedented in their number and range. Arnold, too, lost his effectiveness once World War II began and resigned in 1943, but not before achieving a permanent expansion of the bureaucratic capacities of the antitrust division.

The administration's second response to the 1937 recession was ultimately more significant. Responding to the urgings of liberal economists and others in his administration (and ignoring the impassioned pleas of the Treasury Department), Roosevelt abandoned his efforts to balance the budget and launched a $5 billion spending program in the spring of 1938 whose purpose was to increase mass purchasing power as an antidote to the recession. Few Americans were much aware yet of the ideas of John Maynard Keynes, whose theories would soon transform economic thought throughout much of the world. But the spending program of 1938 helped legitimize an approach to policy that would later become known as Keynesian economics.

The last major domestic achievement of the Roosevelt administration was the passage in 1938 of the Fair Labor Standards Act, which established a national minimum wage and set limits on hours of work. By the end of the year, the New Deal had effectively come to an end. Roosevelt went on to win an unprecedented third term in 1940 and a fourth in 1944, and to lead the nation through a great world war. But his efforts to reform the American economy no longer generated broad congressional or popular support. By 1939 he was turning increasingly to the great international crises that would dominate the last five years of his life.

In retrospect, the New Deal has often seemed as significant for the things it did not do as for the things it achieved. It did not end the Great Depression and the massive unemployment that accompanied it; only the enormous public and private spending for World War II finally did that. It did not, the complaints of conservative critics notwithstanding, transform American capitalism in any genuinely radical way; except in the field of labor relations, corporate power remained nearly as free from government regulation or control in 1945 as it had been in 1933. The New Deal did not end poverty or effect any significant redistribution of wealth. Nor did it do much to address some of the principal domestic challenges of the postwar era, among them the problems of racial and sexual inequality.

Even so, the achievements of the Roosevelt administration rank among the most important of any presidency in American history, for at least three reasons. First, the New Deal created a series of new state institutions that greatly, and permanently, expanded the role of the federal government in American life. The government was now committed to providing at least minimal assistance to the poor and unemployed; to protecting the rights of labor unions; to stabilizing the banking system; to building low-income housing; to regulating the financial markets; to subsidizing agricultural production; and to doing many other things that had not previously been federal responsibilities. As a result of the New Deal, American political and economic life became much more competitive than before, with workers, farmers, consumers, and others now able to press their demands upon the government in ways that in the past had been available only to the corporate world. (Hence the frequent description of the government the New Deal created as a "broker state," a state brokering the competing claims of numerous groups.) Second, the New Deal produced a new political coalition that sustained the Democrats as the majority party in national politics for more than a generation after its own end. Finally, the Roosevelt administration generated a set of political ideas — known to later generations as New Deal liberalism — that remained a source of inspiration and controversy for decades and that helped shape the next great experiment in liberal reform, the Great Society of the 1960s.

Anthony Badger, *The New Deal* (1988); Frank Freidel, *Franklin D. Roosevelt: A Rendezvous with Destiny* (1990); William E. Leuchtenberg, *Franklin D. Roosevelt and the New Deal* (1963); Arthur M. Schlesinger, Jr., *The Age of Roosevelt*, 3 vols. (1957–1960).

ALAN BRINKLEY

See also Brain Trust; Civilian Conservation Corps; Court-Packing Plan; Depressions; Federal Theatre Project; Federal Writers' Project; Government and the Economy; Hundred Days; National Labor Relations Act; National Labor Relations Board; National Recovery Administration; Public Works Administration; Roosevelt, Franklin D.; Securities and Exchange Commission; Social Security; Tennessee Valley Authority; Welfare and Public Relief; Works Progress Administration.

NEW ENGLAND COLONIES

Their opponents ridiculed them as "Puritans," but these radical reformers, the English followers of John Calvin, came to embrace that name as an emblem of honor. At the beginning of the seventeenth century, England faced a gathering storm in religious life — the Puritan movement. Before the storm abated, the Puritans had founded the first permanent European settlements in a region that came to be known as New England.

The Puritans believed that God had commanded the reform of both church and society. They condemned drunkenness, gambling, theatergoing, and Sabbath-breaking and denounced popular practices rooted in pagan custom, like the celebration of Christmas. They deplored the "corruptions" of Roman Catholicism that still pervaded the Church of England — churches and ceremonies they thought too elaborate, clergymen who were poorly educated.

The refusal of English monarchs to attack these "besetting evils" turned the Puritans into outspoken critics of the government. This King James I would not endure: he decided to rid England of these malcontents. With some of the Puritans, known as the Separatists, he seemed to have succeeded.

The Separatists, a tiny minority within the Puritan movement, were pious people from humble backgrounds who concluded that the Church of England was too corrupt to be reformed from within. In 1608 one Separatist congregation at Scrooby decided to flee to Holland. That move afforded them religious freedom, but they found only low-paying jobs and were distressed by desertions from within their ranks to other religions.

Some decided to move again, this time to North America. In December of 1620, eighty-eight Separatist "Pilgrims" disembarked from the *Mayflower* at a place they called Plymouth on the coast of present-day southeastern Massachusetts. But misfortune followed the Separatists to the New World. The hardships of the crossing and inadequate provisions left many vulnerable to a "starving time" during the winter. The Plymouth colony would have failed entirely if the Pilgrims had not received assistance from local Indian tribes.

The Pilgrims had received permission from England to settle farther south in the New World, but they had sailed off course and lacked any legal sanction for their land claims or their government in Plymouth. English authorities, however, distracted by more pressing problems, left the tiny colony alone. Among these distractions were other Puritans who were still striving to reform church and society in England. By the 1620s, Charles I, James's son and successor, had undertaken even more stringent measures for suppressing dissent. Compounding the religious crisis were mounting political tensions between the king and Parliament and continuing economic problems of recession and unemployment.

Many Puritans concluded that England was slipping toward the Apocalypse. Some, from the ranks of the Congregationalists, became interested in colonization, and in 1629, a group of merchants, landed gentlemen, and lawyers organized the Massachusetts Bay Company. Unlike the Separatists, these Puritans were imbued with a strong sense of mission; they claimed that they were neither separating from the church nor abandoning the cause of reform but, rather, regrouping for another assault on corruption on the other side of the Atlantic.

The Massachusetts Bay Company procured a royal charter confirming its title to most of present-day Massachusetts and New Hampshire and securing its rights to govern the region. Then the stockholders voted to transfer the company itself to Massachusetts Bay and elected as their first governor John Winthrop, a pious, tough-minded Puritan lawyer and landed gentleman. Winthrop sailed from England in 1630, declaring to his fellow passengers that "we shall be as a city on a hill." Once settled, Winthrop and the other stockholders transformed their royal charter for a trading company into the framework of government for a colony, which enabled them to shape state, society, and church to their liking.

The character of the initial migration itself gave New England settlers a unique opportunity to fashion an orderly society. Most of the immigrants, some twenty-one thousand, came in a cluster between 1630 and 1642, a movement of families from the middling ranks of English society known as the "Great Migration." The settlement of New England within the short span of twelve years meant that the colonies there escaped the strain of having to absorb a steady stream of newcomers throughout the seventeenth century. Rapid settlement also made for solidarity, because immigrants were unified by their persecution and their sense of religious mission. After the English Civil War and until the American Revolution, immigrants from throughout the British Isles trickled into New England at the rate of only a few hundred each year. The region was peopled largely by the descendants of members of the Great Migration.

Not only their like-mindedness but also their long lives fostered a sense of continuity for New England immigrants and their progeny. Probably because of their healthful climate, seventeenth-century New Englanders lived on average nearly twice as long as Virginians and about ten years longer than men and women in England itself. That longevity, combined with relatively low rates of infant mortality and roughly equal numbers of men and women, resulted in rapid population growth. While the people of Europe and the Chesapeake colonies barely reproduced themselves, the number of New Englanders doubled about every twenty-seven years; a typical family raised seven or eight children to maturity.

As the immigrants arrived in the colony after 1630, they quickly planted a ring of small villages around Massachusetts Bay. Others settled in Connecticut and Rhode Island, which received separate charters from Charles II in the 1660s. In the 1640s, Massachusetts successfully asserted its claim to New Hampshire, which did not become a separate colony until 1679. In 1658 the handful of families who had settled along the coast of present-day Maine also accepted rule by the Massachusetts Bay colony.

The settlement of New England towns proceeded in a pattern that laid the groundwork for a coherent organization of local life. Townspeople gradually parceled out among themselves the land granted by the colony. The distribution of land was remarkably even, allotting an average family about 150 acres. The first farmers left much of their acreage uncultivated, and it became a legacy for future generations. But as succeeding generations subdivided family lands, the legacies became smaller, and a growing number of young families moved on to found new communities on the frontiers of western Massachusetts, Maine, and New Hampshire.

New England Colonies, 1650

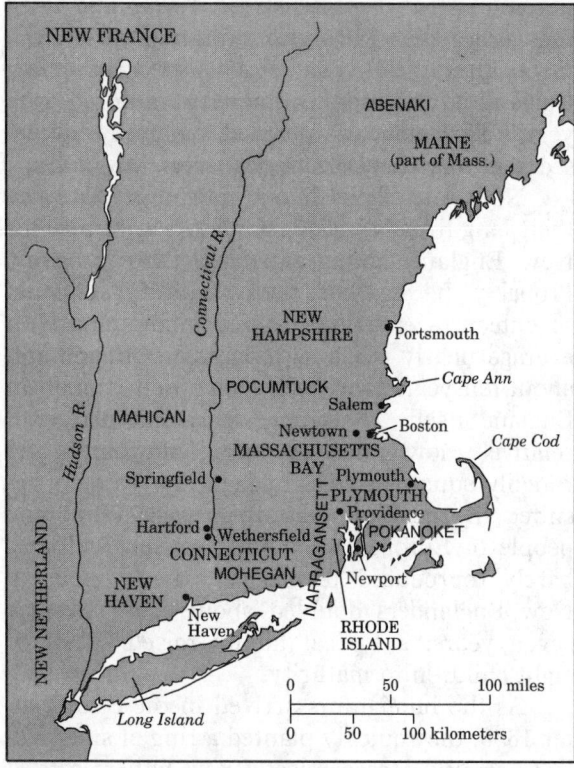

Early New Englanders established other institutions that contributed to the coherence of social life. First and foremost was the family, headed by fathers who exacted strict obedience from their children, even after they had reached maturity. Wives were also subordinated to their husbands' authority: by law, married women surrendered to their husbands any property they possessed before marriage, and divorce was almost impossible to obtain until the late eighteenth century. Only widows and the few single women had the same legal rights as men, and even they could not vote in colony elections.

To ensure the hierarchy that was regarded as essential to a stable society, each town also developed a group of village leaders. The heads of certain families — usually men with university degrees or craftsmen with some practical skill — received a little more than the average land allotment. These "town fathers" took the lead in directing local affairs, and their sons and grandsons often inherited their power and influence. But though only a handful of families monopolized local offices, the decisions of the town meeting, the basis of local self-government, required the unanimous agreement of the entire body of townsmen.

Equally important in maintaining order was the church. Ministers accompanied the immigrants to the colonies, and they formed churches as quickly as they founded towns. Although ministers exerted much informal influence over public and private life, they did not serve as officers in the civil government, and in the churches, the laity claimed ultimate power. Each village church conducted its own affairs, answerable to no higher authority. Church membership was voluntary, but in every colony except Rhode Island inhabitants were bound by law to attend Sabbath worship and to contribute to the support of the Congregationalist clergy. Membership was not available to anyone merely for the asking. Candidates had to give evidence that they had experienced "conversion" — a turning of the heart and soul toward God that was betokened by a disciplined life. After the middle of the seventeenth century, however, full church membership declined, especially among men.

Although many aspects of life in early New England enhanced order, perfect harmony proved elusive. A few fishing villages and fur-trading centers on the periphery of settlement during the seventeenth century departed dramatically from Puritan norms. These "company towns" were financed and developed by merchants who recruited crews of free and indentured laborers from the ports of England, Ireland, and the Channel Islands. Extreme inequality among classes deprived such settlements of any stability until the beginning of the eighteenth century.

But such inequality was not a source of strain in most early New England communities, because the region offered few opportunities to amass great wealth. Farmers could coax enough from the land to feed their families, but outside of the fertile Connecticut River valley, the climate and soil did not yield a large surplus. Since their farms could not sustain a profitable commercial agriculture, most farmers had no incentive to import large numbers of servants and slaves. Trade, fishing, and shipbuilding brought greater returns for the minority of New Englanders — about one in ten — who lived in seaports like Boston, Salem, Newport, and Gloucester, and over time, as these commercial centers expanded, class divisions became more clearly etched.

Most conflicts, however, were occasioned by other tensions. When immigrants from several English villages settled in the same New England community, variations in English local customs produced disagreement among townspeople about the proper way to distribute land, regulate livestock, or plant crops. As the first generation passed from the scene, disagreements of this sort died with them, but other quarrels arose to take their place. As local populations expanded and the centers of towns became overcrowded, many families moved to outlying districts and then petitioned the town meeting to create schools and churches of their own or to split off as a separate town. Reluctant to lose taxpayers, the town meeting often resisted, and a running battle between the two factions would ensue.

While such local controversies were little more than petty quarrels among people who agreed on fundamentals, religion triggered far more serious conflicts. Most of the men and women who settled in New England called themselves Puritans, but the name did not imply a uniform code of belief and practice. For example, the Pilgrims of Plymouth believed that religious purity required renouncing the Church of England, whereas most other New England Puritans clung to the hope of reform while remaining within the Anglican communion. During the earliest years, religious diversity led to the spread of settlements beyond Massachusetts Bay. In 1636, Thomas Hooker's more liberal standards for church membership prompted him to establish the first English outpost in Connecticut. Rhode Island served as a haven for the most radical religious outcasts from Massachusetts Bay, among them its founder, Roger Williams, Anne Hutchinson and some of her antinomian followers, and many members of the Society of Friends, called Quakers.

Even the inhabitants of Massachusetts Bay differed among themselves about religion. Congregationalism fostered a growing diversity of opinion and practice, because each local church was free to go its own way. By the end of the seventeenth century, many churches had adopted more liberal standards for admission to membership or to the sacraments of baptism and communion. Divisions among New England's Congregationalists became even more pronounced after the 1730s because of the first Great Awakening, a major religious revival. Some welcomed it, but others disliked the emotionalism and disorder that attended the new religious enthusiasm. Competing denominations gained from the Congregationalists' disputes: disgruntled conservatives deserted to the Anglicans and Quakers, and the most radical advocates of revivalism formed "Separate" churches or joined the Baptists.

By the middle of the eighteenth century, New England had become a more mobile, commercialized, stratified, and diverse society. But for most of the region's inhabitants, earlier patterns of life persisted. The majority remained an insular, rural folk, their lives defined by the seasonal rhythms of agriculture, the bonds of family, church, and local community, and a fundamentally religious outlook.

Francis Bremer, *The Puritan Experiment* (1976).

CHRISTINE LEIGH HEYRMAN

See also Bradford, William; Colonial Culture; Colonial Economy; Colonial Government and Politics; Colonial Wars; Edwards, Jonathan; Great Awakening; Hutchinson, Anne; Indians; Mather, Increase, and Mather, Cotton; Mayflower Compact; Puritanism; Quakers; Salem Witch Trials; Williams, Roger; Winthrop, John.

NEW FREEDOM

The presidential election of 1912 marked the culmination of a twenty-year struggle against political and economic privilege. Most Progressives sought to replace rampant individualism with collective organization in the public interest, but by 1912 the nature and extent of federal economic and social intervention had become the subject of fierce debate. President William Howard Taft represented old guard conservatism. Former president Theodore Roosevelt, running on the Progressive party ticket, advocated a "New Nationalism," a coherent platform of social and economic regulation.

In response, the Democratic candidate, Woodrow Wilson, formulated what he called the "New Freedom." Federal power, he argued, should be used only to sweep away social, economic, and political privilege and to restore business competition. Corporate monopolies, which were the great bugbear of the age, should be dismantled rather than regulated. Wilson also denounced Roosevelt's social and labor policies as paternalistic, arguing that the New Nationalism would sap entrepreneurial initiative and that it was potentially despotic. Untrammeled free enterprise had to remain the basis of American freedom. The irony is that Wilson, in office, came to see the New Freedom as increasingly anachronistic, and by 1915 his administration had enacted the principal tenets of Roosevelt's 1912 platform.

See also Elections: 1912; Wilson, Woodrow.

NEW FRONTIER

The New Frontier was the legislative program John F. Kennedy announced when he ran for president in 1960. It called for economic reforms to counter the inflation of the Eisenhower years and to "get the country moving again." But in office Kennedy proved unable to win passage of many of the items on his agenda, including Medicare to provide medical help for the elderly, programs to rebuild the inner cities, and an increase in federal funding for education. Congress did raise the minimum wage from $1.00 to $1.25 an hour and added 3.6 million workers to the rolls of those eligible to receive it. Kennedy also won support for expanding Social Security benefits and made $4.9 billion available in federal grants to cities for mass transit, open spaces, and middle-income housing.

Nevertheless, Kennedy could not, in the main, overcome a congressional coalition of Republicans and conservative, mostly southern Democrats. Only after his assassination in 1963 were many of his proposals enacted. His successor, Lyndon B. Johnson, building on the national feeling over Kennedy's death, declared a "war on poverty" and pushed much of the New Frontier program through Congress. Expanding it into his Great Society program, Johnson won passage of Medicare, the Job Corps, VISTA, Head Start, and several major civil rights laws.

See also Kennedy, John F.

NEW LEFT

The *New Left* was a term applied to a generation of Americans who came of age in the 1960s and were radicalized by social injustices, the civil rights movement, and the war in Vietnam. The New Left was made up largely of college students. The first major group to embody its principles was Students for a Democratic Society (SDS), which was formed in Michigan in 1962. Its Port Huron Statement attacked social injustice and the values of the so-called Affluent Society. The New Left grew in 1964 with the onset of the free-speech movement at the University of California at Berkeley, which was a protest against restrictions on student involvement in political demonstrations on campus. It also won followers by denouncing American involvement in Vietnam and deploring the failure of Lyndon B. Johnson's Great Society programs to eradicate poverty.

The New Left was prominent in countless university demonstrations, the best known of which took place at Columbia University in 1968, Harvard University in 1969, and Kent State University in 1970, when the National Guard killed four students after being called out to stop antiwar protests. The New Left was also active in the counterculture of the 1960s.

See also Chicago Seven; Hoffman, Abbie; Kent State Incident; Students for a Democratic Society.

NEW NATIONALISM

Frustrated by the conservatism of Republican president William Howard Taft, Theodore Roosevelt, Taft's predecessor, decided to seek a third term as president in 1912. Because he was a Republican and Taft was running again, Roosevelt ran as an independent candidate on the Progressive party ticket. Drawing much of his inspiration from Herbert Croly's *The Promise of American Life* (1909), Roosevelt formulated a platform called the "New Nationalism," which argued that the federal government had a positive interventionist role to play in the advancement of progressive democracy. The Democratic candidate, Woodrow Wilson, insisted that government should be used only for the negative purposes of sweeping away privilege and restoring unfettered competition. He called for the dismantling of trusts and monopolies. Roosevelt denounced this as anachronistic, arguing that large corporations had become indispensable in the modern age. They should not be dismantled but should be controlled and regulated in the public interest. Roosevelt also proposed a comprehensive program of labor and social legislation. Wilson (who won the election) denounced the New Nationalism as elitist and detected in it the seeds of despotism.

Despite elements of chauvinism and elitism, the New Nationalism was in essence a hard-headed attempt to come to terms with the modern corporate age. It was also by far the most progressive platform proposed by the three presidents of the Progressive Era.

See also Elections: 1912; Roosevelt, Theodore.

NEW SOUTH

Although often used by historians simply to designate the post-1877 period, the term *New South* is most prominently identified with a program of regional industrialization and agricultural diversification promoted by southern publicists, businesspeople, and politicians in the late nineteenth century.

The Civil War and Reconstruction had given certain antebellum southerners' dreams of a business-oriented, manufacturing South a new significance. The vision of a New South described by Edwin De Leon in magazine articles in the early 1870s was taken up by skillful propagandists like Henry Grady of the *Atlanta Constitution,* Henry Watterson of the *Louisville Courier-Journal,* and Richard Edmonds of the *Manufacturers' Record* and became a favored prescription for a rejuvenated Dixie. Instead of cultivating a few staple crops, the South, with the aid of northern investment, could become a land of industry, entrepreneurship, and scientific farming. In addition, although insisting upon white supremacy, the New South should devote itself to sectional reconciliation.

Southern industry, notably textile milling, did boom after the end of Reconstruction. Grady and his peers proclaimed their vision to have been realized. But, in fact, the region remained disproportionately poor, characterized by staple-crop monoculture, low-wage industry, and external ownership of much of its resources.

The catchphrase "New South" has not been the exclusive property of the Grady movement, however. Groups ranging from Union occupying forces in Confederate South Carolina to the twentieth-century Communist party issued publications entitled *New South.*

NEWSPAPERS

See Magazines and Newspapers.

NIAGARA MOVEMENT

This was a major step on the road to black militancy. Its beginnings may be traced to the publication in 1903 of *The Souls of Black Folk* by W. E. B. Du Bois, the first black American to earn a doctorate from Harvard. That book included an essay, "Of Mr. Booker T. Washington and Others," which attacked Washington's Atlanta Compromise speech and accused him of abandoning the fight for black political rights and accepting segregation in exchange for illusory economic gains.

In 1905, Du Bois and several other black supporters wishing to meet gathered at Niagara Falls, but on the Canadian side since no hotel on the American side would allow them to register. They drafted a list of demands that included an end to segregation and to discrimination in unions, the courts, and public accommodations, as well as equality of economic and educational opportunity.

Although the Niagara movement attracted the attention of like-minded whites, it had little impact on legislative or popular opinion. But after race riots in Springfield, Illinois, in 1909, a group of white progressives — including the social worker Jane Addams, the philosopher John Dewey, the novelist William Dean Howells, and the editor Oswald Garrison Villard, a grandson of abolitionist William Lloyd Garrison — formed the National Association for the Advancement of Colored People (NAACP). They adopted many of the goals of the Niagara movement and hired its leader, Du Bois, as director of publicity and research, and editor of their journal, *Crisis*.

See also Du Bois, W. E. B.; National Association for the Advancement of Colored People; Racial Desegregation.

NIEBUHR, REINHOLD

(1892–1971), professor of Christian social ethics. For four decades, Niebuhr taught at Union Theological Seminary in New York City. His teaching drew upon themes of the Bible and the history of political philosophy to illumine the moral issues of contemporary society.

From his student days at Yale in 1915 to his death, he wrote on international relations and U.S. foreign policy. His writing and political activism led Hans Morgenthau, himself a distinguished philosopher of international relations, to call Niebuhr "the greatest living political philosopher of America."

Niebuhr's roots were in the Evangelical Synod, a small German-speaking denomination in which his father was a minister. His mother, who would assist Reinhold in his parish work,

was the daughter of an Evangelical Synod pastor. Born in Wright City, Missouri, Niebuhr graduated from Elmhurst College, Eden Theological Seminary, and Yale University. He helped lead his small midwestern denomination into a merger with the Reformed church to create the Evangelical and Reformed church, which then merged with the Congregational church to create the United Church of Christ.

As a young pastor at Bethel Church in Detroit from 1915 to 1928, he was involved in the issues of racial conflict, economic justice, and international relations. The story of those early years is recorded in *The Leaves from the Notebook of a Tamed Cynic* (1929), which is still studied in seminaries. The chairmanship of the Mayor's Committee on Race after the 1925 race riots involved him in local politics, and his writing for the *Christian Century* won him a reputation as a critic of the Ford Motor Company's labor policies.

He joined the faculty of Union Theological Seminary in 1928 and served until retirement in 1960. As a democratic-socialist thinker and activist he joined with his friend Norman Thomas in reforming the Socialist party in which he served as vice chairman. His most famous book, *Moral Man and Immoral Society* (1932), reflects both his philosophy and his commitment to socialism. But in 1940 he supported Franklin D. Roosevelt for the presidency, later worked with Americans for Democratic Action, and was vice chairman of the Liberal party in New York.

His most important theological work, *The Nature and Destiny of Man* (two volumes, 1941, 1943), was written for the Gifford Lectures in Edinburgh, Scotland. It explores the themes of Christian anthropology and theology of history. In both cases he considers alternative philosophies and defends the theological understandings of the church on human nature and history. He stresses both the grandeur and the misery of the human condition and criticizes the facile optimism of liberal culture. These volumes established Niebuhr as a major theologian and as the founder of a school of social analysis called Christian realism. His founding of the journal *Christianity and Crisis* gave practical political expression to his theology. He used a neo-

Augustinian perspective to ground social ethics and political action on new foundations for mainline American Protestantism.

His other books on the theology of history or Christian philosophy of history include *Faith and History* (1949), *The Irony of American History* (1952), *The Self and the Dramas of History* (1955), *Pious and Secular America* (1958), and *The Structure of Nations and History* (1959). Arthur Schlesinger, Jr., once said that "Reinhold Niebuhr was the greatest man I knew," and Hubert H. Humphrey as vice president spoke for many: "No preacher or teacher, at least in my time, has had a greater impact on the secular world. No American has made a greater contribution to political wisdom and moral responsibility."

June Bingham, *Courage to Change: An Introduction to the Life and Thought of Reinhold Niebuhr* (1972); Charles Kegley, ed., *Reinhold Niebuhr: His Religious, Social, and Political Thought* (1984).

RONALD H. STONE

See also Religion; Socialism.

NIMITZ, CHESTER

(1885–1966), World War II admiral. Born in Fredericksburg, Texas, Nimitz graduated from the U.S. Naval Academy in 1905. He entered the submarine service, commanded the experimental submarine *A-1,* and became an expert in the new field of diesel engineering. In World War I he wrote a study of U-boat operations that influenced American naval strategy in 1918.

Between the wars Nimitz's career followed a conventional course until, in 1939, he was named chief of the Bureau of Naval Personnel. Nimitz failed utterly to persuade President Franklin D. Roosevelt to greatly increase navy manpower before Pearl Harbor, and his detailing of flag officers was disastrous. But this was not evident at the time, and the post brought Nimitz into frequent contact with Navy Secretary Frank Knox, who placed him in command of the Pacific Fleet after the Pearl Harbor debacle.

Nimitz presided over the immense expansion of the Pacific Fleet after 1942 and oversaw the great south and central Pacific offensives that destroyed the Japanese navy and brought American forces to Japan's doorstep by the summer of 1945. Strategy was conceived in Washington by the dynamic, hard-driving chief of naval operations, Adm. Ernest King, who kept a close watch on Nimitz's work during bimonthly conferences held throughout the war. Nimitz's main contribution was to make into a winning team such different personalities as the overly aggressive Adm. William "Bull" Halsey, the extremely conservative Adm. Raymond Spruance, and Marine Corps Gen. Holland M. Smith, whose demeanor was well expressed in his nickname, "Howlin' Mad."

Although Nimitz was jealous of his perks and prerogatives as a theater commander, his ceremonial dignity, personal warmth, and common sense were great strengths. On the other hand, he was bitterly criticized by naval aviators who correctly observed that he repeatedly allowed the Pacific Fleet carriers to be mishandled by the "battleship admirals." King's answer was to surround Nimitz with a strong staff, headed by Rear Adm. Forrest Sherman, his chief planner, with the result that Nimitz made few major mistakes. Nimitz, who always functioned best in an all-navy environment, was mostly blind to the grand politics of the war he was managing and to the enormous forces it was unleashing.

In late 1945, King forced Navy Secretary James V. Forrestal to appoint Nimitz to succeed him as chief of naval operations, but within six months King and others were agitating for his ouster. Nimitz lacked the drive needed to master the new political and strategic problems of the cold war, and he was incapable of waging the bare-knuckle public brawl necessary to preserve American naval power against the new U.S. Air Force in the early days of defense unification. He retired in 1947. Unlike other wartime leaders, Nimitz was never recalled to government service.

Edwin Hoyt, *How They Won the War in the Pacific: Nimitz and His Admirals* (1970); E. B. Potter, *Nimitz* (1976); Clark Reynold, *The Fast Carriers* (1967).

ROBERT W. LOVE, JR.

See also Armed Forces; World War II.

NINETEENTH AMENDMENT

See Suffrage.

NIXON, RICHARD M.

(1913–   ), thirty-seventh president of the United States. Nixon's youth was marked by hard work in a family store and the death of two brothers as well as by academic success. Except for Herbert Hoover, no president elected in this century grew up in more difficult circumstances. Following graduation from Whittier College (1934) and Duke University Law School (1937), he practiced law in California and married Thelma (Pat) Ryan. He served as a navy supply officer during World War II and was elected to the House of Representatives in 1946.

An ambitious, intelligent, disciplined loner, Nixon cultivated no hobbies and had few close friends. His political shrewdness was often undermined by his vindictiveness and capacity for self-deception. His rise was largely the product of the post–World War II red scare. He convinced the House that Alger Hiss, a second-level New Dealer, had been a Soviet spy and, in 1950, persuaded California voters to send him to the Senate to battle against subversives and "pink" Democrats. Elected vice president in 1952, he served President Dwight D. Eisenhower dutifully for eight years, despite occasional humiliations. He tried to present himself as a statesman-like "new Nixon," but, partly because memories of the old Nixon lingered, he lost races for president in 1960 and governor of California in 1962.

During the next four years, while prospering as a corporate lawyer, he rebuilt his political base. His successful campaign for president in 1968 raised a central question: would he govern as a responsible conservative, in the fashion of his mentor Eisenhower, or as an irresponsible demagogue, in the mold of the old Nixon? He proved to be both. In domestic affairs, his record included, on the one hand, creation of the Environmental Protection Agency, expansion of the Social Security system, and advocacy of a Family Assistance Plan that guaranteed an annual in-

come to the working poor, and, on the other hand, a weak civil rights record, sabotage of his political opposition, and emotional appeals to a "silent majority" who shared his resentment of the cosmopolitan elite. His foreign policy record was similarly mixed. Nixon accepted modest curbs on the nuclear arms race, pursued détente with the Soviet Union, and opened relations with the People's Republic of China. He also undermined the Marxist Chilean government and widened the Vietnam War by invading Cambodia before accepting truce terms in 1973 that he could have had in 1969.

The Watergate scandal was part of a broad campaign to sabotage political opposition. Although Nixon apparently had no advance knowledge of a break-in at Democratic National Committee headquarters in 1972, he subsequently obstructed an investigation of the crime. After fighting a two-year holding action, he faced impeachment by the House of Representatives and resigned on August 9, 1974. He accepted a pardon from President Gerald Ford and sank briefly into depression.

Then, characteristically, he began to rebuild his reputation, primarily through books combining memoirs and foreign policy advice. As memories of Watergate faded, some commentators emphasized Nixon's intelligence, domestic reforms, and foreign policy successes. Never very penitent about Watergate, he grew persistently less so and in 1990 described the scandal as "one part wrongdoing, one part blundering, and one part political vendetta" by his foes. Even in semiretirement Nixon remained the most fascinating American politician of his time.

Stephen E. Ambrose, *Nixon: The Education of a Politician, 1913–1962* (1987) and *Nixon: The Triumph of a Politician, 1962–1972* (1989); Stanley L. Kutler, *The Wars of Watergate: The Last Crisis of Richard Nixon* (1990).

Leo P. Ribuffo

See also Alger Hiss Case; Anticommunism; Elections: 1952, 1956, 1960, 1968, 1972. *For events during Nixon's administration, see* Asia-U.S. Relations; Détente; Kent State Incident; Middle East–U.S. Relations; OPEC Oil Crisis; *Roe* v. *Wade;* Space Program; Strategic Arms Limitation Talks; Vietnam War; Watergate Scandal.

NLRA

See National Labor Relations Act.

NLRB

See National Labor Relations Board.

NOGUCHI, ISAMU

(1904–1988), sculptor. An innovative and exceptionally versatile sculptor, Noguchi is often credited with having resurrected the lost art of designing great public spaces. His sculptured gardens — such as the marble court for the rare book library at Yale University, the sunken water garden for Chase-Manhattan Plaza in New York, the fountain and plaza in Detroit, the Japanese-style garden at UNESCO headquarters in Paris, and the remarkable sculpture garden and terraces carved from a mountain at the Jerusalem Museum — established new environmental practices that have instructed artists and architects throughout the world.

Noguchi's aesthetics were influenced by the unusual circumstances of his birth. His father, Yone Noguchi, was an ambitious Japanese poet who visited America before the turn of the century, and his mother was an aspiring American writer. Noguchi, born in Los Angeles, spent his childhood in Japan, but was sent to America when he was thirteen where he completed high school in a small Indiana town. His mixed parentage and early displacements contributed to his pronounced internationalism. The recognition he received at the age of twenty as an academic sculptor in New York encouraged his restless spirit of research.

Several clear sources can be cited in the formation of his artistic philosophy. In high school he was exposed to the writings of Emanuel Swedenborg and Ralph Waldo Emerson, both of whom suggested that the universe constituted a vast rhyming scheme. During the late 1920s, Noguchi spent several months as apprentice to the great modern sculptor Constantin Brancusi whose example as a direct carver finding essences in stone and wood greatly affected him. In 1930–1931, Noguchi began his lifelong wandering by traveling to China, where he learned traditional calligraphic brush drawing, and thence to Japan, where he sought both his father and the other half of his artistic heritage. In the mid-1930s Noguchi established his extended collaboration with the pioneer modern dancer Martha Graham by designing a spare set for *Frontier,* which became a classic in theater history. At the same time, he was investigating radical new methods and materials for sculpture, stimulated by his close friend the visionary R. Buckminster Fuller. Noguchi's extensive experience in theater was decisive in forming his viewpoint of sculpture as a symbolic theater of life and the world. Finally, in 1950, Noguchi made a close study of ancient Japanese meditation and stroll gardens that clarified his vision. He fused modern European and American developments in sculpture with ancient Japanese insights concerning time and space.

Although Noguchi won recognition for many undertakings, ranging from individual sculptures to commercially produced tables and lamps, his greatest achievements were the inspired works creating a total public space, which he thought of as a single sculpture. His use of water, flora, carved and natural stones, was singularly attuned to the modern idea of a total work of art that addresses all the senses and honors both nature and culture. In one of his last comments, Noguchi urged his viewers: "Call it sculpture if it moves you so."

Isamu Noguchi, *A Sculptor's World* (1968); Isamu Noguchi, *The Isamu Noguchi Garden Museum* (1987).

DORE ASHTON

See also Painting and Sculpture.

NORTH ATLANTIC TREATY ORGANIZATION

The North Atlantic Treaty Organization (NATO), formed in 1949 in response to the cold war, consisted of twelve Western nations — Great Britain, France, Belgium, the Netherlands, Denmark, Portugal, Italy, Luxembourg, Norway,

Iceland, Canada, and the United States. Greece and Turkey joined in 1952 and West Germany in 1955. Its members pledged to consider an attack on one an attack on the others and to maintain a force to defend the West against a possible Soviet invasion.

The organization increased American influence in Western Europe. The commanders of NATO forces included Gen. Dwight D. Eisenhower and Gen. Alexander Haig, and a large percentage of NATO's money and troops came from the United States. But NATO also prompted the Soviet Union to create the Warsaw Pact of nations friendly to — or controlled by — the Soviets, thus exacerbating cold war tensions. The organization was also a model for SEATO in Southeast Asia and CENTO in the Mediterranean region, both created by President Eisenhower and Secretary of State John Foster Dulles.

The end of the cold war in 1989, the reunification of the two Germanys in 1990, and the formal dissolution of the Warsaw Pact in 1991 raised questions about the future purpose of NATO.

See also Cold War.

NORTHWEST ORDINANCE

The Northwest Ordinance, approved by Congress on July 13, 1787, delineated rules for governing the Old Northwest, the area lying north of the Ohio River and east of the Mississippi. Thomas Jefferson had written the first ordinance for the territory three years earlier, calling for a division of the region into states. Each was to have the same political powers as the original thirteen states and was to prohibit slavery after 1800. The ordinance was adopted in April 1784, but it had not been instituted because no settlers held legal title yet.

Pressure from land speculators, particularly the well-connected Ohio Company, induced Congress to issue a revised Northwest Ordinance in 1787 providing for interim federal control while local governments were being developed. The new law, primarily written by Rufus King and Nathan Dane of Massachusetts, called — as Jefferson's had — for dividing the

area into several territories, but specified that each would be administered initially by a governor, a secretary, and three judges, all appointed by Congress. Whenever a district reached a population of five thousand free males, it could elect a bicameral legislature and send a nonvoting member to Congress. When its population reached sixty thousand free inhabitants (Jefferson had set the figure at twenty thousand), the district would be eligible for statehood. The ordinance guaranteed freedom of religion, trial by jury, and public support for education. It also provided that slavery was to be prohibited in the territory.

The Northwest Ordinance was one of the most important acts passed by Congress under the Articles of Confederation. It laid out the process through which a territory could move to statehood, it guaranteed that new states would be on an equal footing with the old, and it protected civil liberties in the new territories. This ordinance was also the first national legislation that set limits on the expansion of slavery.

See also Expansion, Continental and Overseas.

NOW

See National Organization for Women.

NRA

See National Recovery Administration.

NUCLEAR POWER

In the mid-1950s, nuclear physicists confidently predicted that nuclear energy would usher in a golden age for humanity: the cost of energy would be so low it would be "too cheap to meter." They predicted that, by the year 2000, there would be one thousand commercial reactors and one thousand "breeder" reactors producing unlimited amounts of power. Like the horse and buggy, oil and coal would become little more than historical curiosities.

Nuclear power has exceeded some of these early predictions. Its safety record, when compared, say, to the airline industry, is vastly superior. Compared to the air pollution and acid rain caused by the coal industry, its environmental record is admirable. It currently generates over 15 percent of the nation's electricity and has thus reduced the dependence on scarce fossil fuels. Some claim it may also reduce the impact of the greenhouse effect.

Ironically, however, this same industry is also teetering on the verge of collapse. Contrary to previous expectations, the United States now has over one hundred commercial reactors, the breeder reactor program is defunct, and there has not been a single reactor order since 1978, one year before an accident at Three Mile Island. Over one hundred reactor orders have been canceled, and costs have escalated so that the Nine Mile Point reactor in upstate New York will soar beyond $6 billion, or about six times the cost of a coal plant of similar power.

Never in modern history has a major technology, with the full backing of industry and the government, come to such an abrupt halt. Well over $100 billion has been invested in nuclear energy, yet the people of California voted to close down an operating reactor, and the people of Long Island, New York, are closing down the fully completed $5 billion Shoreham reactor before it opens.

Utilities that invested heavily in nuclear power have been driven to the wall by its mounting costs; the Washington Public Power Supply System went bankrupt, and the Long Island Lighting Co. incurred billions in losses. What went wrong?

Although the reasons for this unprecedented collapse are complex, many of the problems can be traced to unwise decisions made in the 1950s. Specifically, when the Nautilus nuclear submarine sailed effortlessly beneath the North Pole, it touched off a stampede among corporations interested in the commercial development of nuclear energy. The 1960s marked the "gold rush" in reactors, when General Electric, Westinghouse, Combustion Engineering, and Babcock-Wilcox scrambled to bring this technology to the marketplace. In fact, Con Edison even applied for a license to build its Ravenswood reactor in the heart of New York City opposite the United Nations.

Because large plants are more economical than small ones, designers started with the small (40-megawatt) Nautilus reactor and essentially scaled it up many times to the current 1,000-megawatt design, without clearly thinking through the consequences. Decades later, this would lead to three serious problems. First, in retrospect, scaling up the Nautilus design was a poor choice to begin with because the light-water Nautilus reactor is highly susceptible to a rapid melting of the uranium core. Alternate designs (e.g., gas-cooled high-temperature gas reactors) were much more stable against a meltdown but were ignored. Second, this meant that elaborate and expensive emergency core cooling systems had to be installed, which would later add hundreds of millions of dollars to the cost of the reactor and delay construction for several years. Third, no attention was paid to how reactors would be decommissioned after thirty to forty years of use or where the radioactive nuclear waste would be disposed of.

In 1957, a prophetic, but secret, report was issued by the Brookhaven National Laboratory, called WASH-740. It estimated that a meltdown, a Class 9 accident, could cause $7 billion in property damage, kill several thousand people, and contaminate fifty thousand square miles of real estate. (Many physicists in the Atomic Energy Commission even argued that reactors are so unstable they should be placed underground.) Unfortunately, this report was kept classified until released under the Freedom of Information Act in the 1970s.

Since it takes ten years to bring a reactor to completion, those ordered during the rush of the 1960s came on line in the 1970s. Upon further examination the apparent safety record of nuclear power actually masked deep systemic problems that were largely unknown to the public:

□ In 1966, Detroit Edison's Fermi I reactor suffered a disastrous accident and 2 percent of its core melted down. The accident was concealed from the public.

□ In 1970, GE's Dresden reactor suffered a serious steam-pipe break, which gutted many of its safety systems.

□ In 1975, the Brown's Ferry reactor in Alabama almost went out of control when a large fire destroyed most of the reactor's safety systems.

□ In 1979, during the Three Mile Island accident, the core came within thirty minutes of large-scale melting, almost reaching 5,000 degrees.

The risks of nuclear energy, in fact, are so great that it takes an act of Congress (the Price-Anderson Act) to artificially keep down the cost of insurance against a meltdown.

In the 1980s, the problems multiplied. Soaring interest rates meant that construction delays added billions to the final price tag of a reactor. Also, consumer demand for electricity flattened owing to conservation, so that utility companies found themselves with an embarrassing glut of electricity. Last, the falling price of oil led to decreased pressure to convert to nuclear power.

Most experts predict that orders for nuclear energy will remain at zero in the 1990s and well into the next century. Both Wall Street and the public remain skeptical about its viability. Historians may conclude that nuclear fission was an unfinished technology brought prematurely to the marketplace, and the question remains: will it be finished in the next century, or will newer advances — in nuclear fusion or solar/hydrogen power — render it obsolete? Only time will tell, but some would argue that fission power is a technology whose time has come and gone.

Michio Kaku and Jennifer Trainer, *Nuclear Power: Both Sides* (1982).

Michio Kaku

See also Atomic Energy Commission; Nuclear Weapons: Origins and Legacy; Science and Technology; Three Mile Island.

NUCLEAR REGULATORY COMMISSION

See Atomic Energy Commission.

NUCLEAR WEAPONS: ORIGINS AND LEGACY

Armed with tens of thousands of nuclear weapons capable of being launched from land, sea, and air, the United States and the Soviet Union became prisoners of a cold war process that neither controlled. Locked into a nuclear arms race justified by national security, they increased their peril, diminished their economies, and promoted an international atmosphere of impending catastrophe. While each government held the population of the other hostage to annihilation, both engaged in conventional wars on the territories of other nations. Occasionally, as in the Berlin crisis of 1961 and the Cuban missile crisis of 1962, they pushed each other to the nuclear brink. Living in the nuclear bull's-eye became a way of life.

How to prevent the nuclear system from becoming a way of death was the question that dominated the debate over nuclear weapons from their inception. Most responses to it promoted the nuclear arms race, including the massive retaliation doctrine, limited nuclear war plans, the concept of mutual assured destruction (MAD), the Strategic Defense Initiative, and even the SALT and START arms control negotiations.

In the United States the expectations and assumptions that led to these policies were formulated during World War II as policymakers debated whether to commit scarce resources to develop atomic bombs and, later, whether to use those bombs against Japanese cities. The answers to these questions not only led to the wartime destruction of Hiroshima and Nagasaki; they also established the attitudes and assumptions that rationalized the postwar nuclear arms race.

Nuclear fission was discovered late in 1938 in Germany. Yet it was not until the autumn of 1941 that scientists in Britain developed a theory that explained how an atomic bomb could be developed within a few years. Immediately after that information was transmitted to America, the U.S. government established an atomic bomb program, the Manhattan Project. This delayed beginning had a powerful influence on the end result. Fearing that German scientists had a head start in the race for the atomic bomb, scientists in Britain and America strove to convince Franklin D. Roosevelt and Winston Churchill that the war could be lost if Germany got the bomb first. The importance of the atomic bomb, they also argued, transcended the war, for its unprecedented power would profoundly affect the peace.

By 1944 "the bomb" began to take on a life of its own. Attention increasingly focused on the potential impact of the "ultimate weapon" on the postwar world. Although a small group of scientists proposed initiatives that could be taken during the war to avoid a nuclear arms race, Roosevelt became increasingly attracted to the advantages he and Churchill anticipated would result from an American-British atomic monopoly.

Roosevelt died on April 12, 1945, three months before an atomic weapon was ready to be tested. He left his successor, Harry S. Truman, who was completely uninformed about the bomb, with two atomic legacies: that the bomb would be used against Japan and that after the war it would be used as an instrument of diplomacy to limit Soviet ambitions. The transition from Roosevelt to Truman resulted in a subtle transformation during the final months of the war, as the two legacies merged. Increasingly angry and frustrated by Soviet behavior, Truman and his close advisers were drawn to the idea that the military use of the bomb against Japan would reinforce the weapon's diplomatic value in postwar negotiations with the Soviets. As the difficulties associated with peace loomed larger, the recommended alternatives to the wartime use of the bomb appeared less attractive.

The least imaginative alternative, the invasion of Japan, requires historical clarification. Truman recorded in his memoirs that such an invasion would have cost "half a million American lives," and he cited Gen. George C. Marshall as the source of this estimate. But recently declassified documents indicate that no such official estimates existed. The casualties projected by the army for the planned invasion in November 1945 ranged from a high of forty-six thousand Americans killed to a low of about twenty-five thousand. "The claim of a half million

American lives [saved by the atomic bombings]," historian Barton Bernstein has written, "was a postwar creation."

Two other options held out the possibility of ending the war against Japan in July or August 1945 without use of the bomb. Late in May of that year Acting Secretary of State Joseph C. Grew, the American ambassador to Japan in the 1930s, informed Truman that intercepted Japanese messages indicated that the unconditional surrender doctrine was undermining the peace advocates in the Japanese cabinet. If the United States guaranteed the emperor's personal safety and a constitutional monarchy, the Japanese would soon surrender, Grew believed.

The second alternative relied on the Soviets. In February 1945 at the Yalta Conference, Joseph Stalin renewed an earlier pledge to Roosevelt to enter the war against Japan within three months after Germany surrendered. Germany's capitulation on May 8 placed the deadline for Soviet entry into the Pacific war at August 8 (and on that day Stalin declared war on Japan). A recently declassified intelligence study, completed on April 30, 1946, concludes that "the dropping of the bomb was the pretext seized upon by all leaders as the reason for ending the war, but . . . [even if the bomb had not been used] the Japanese would have capitulated upon the entry of Russia into the war."

On August 6 and 9, atomic bombs were dropped on Hiroshima and Nagasaki, causing over 200,000 deaths. The destruction of the two cities resulted not from a lack of alternatives but from the belief that the nuclear option would both end the war and help organize the peace.

The role of nuclear weapons in postwar American national security policy was grounded on that expectation. As relations with the Soviets worsened, the Truman administration became increasingly convinced that the American atomic monopoly would pressure the Soviets to be more cooperative. But in August 1949, when the Soviet Union unexpectedly broke the atomic monopoly, a crash program was initiated to build the "Super," the hydrogen bomb, which the United States first tested in 1952.

In the 1950s the nuclear arms race acquired a momentum and internal logic of its own. In

1957 the Soviets' orbiting of *Sputnik* gave added impetus to the acceleration of the American nuclear weapons program, and in turn the Kennedy administration's extensive nuclear buildup in the early 1960s accelerated the Soviet program. In the following decades new warheads begot new delivery vehicles, and new technologies led to new systems that were faster, more accurate, and often more dangerous to stability.

As the nuclear bull's-eye expanded, criticism of nuclear weapons increased. In response, nuclear deterrence was transformed from a flawed theory into a cold war mantra that continues, despite the end of the cold war, to be chanted by some in Washington and Moscow. Mikhail Gorbachev's initiatives may have temporarily stayed the arms race between the superpowers, but because the assumptions that led to the destruction of Hiroshima and Nagasaki have proliferated, too, there are other nuclear arms races that will be even more difficult to bring under control.

Ronald Powaski, *March to Armageddon: The United States and the Nuclear Arms Race, 1939 to the Present* (1987); Martin J. Sherwin, *A World Destroyed: Hiroshima and the Origins of the Arms Race* (1987).

MARTIN J. SHERWIN

See also Hydrogen Bomb; Manhattan Project; Nuclear Power; Oppenheimer, J. Robert; Strategic Arms Limitation Talks; World War II.

NULLIFICATION CONTROVERSY

The famous nullification confrontation of 1832–1833, pitting President Andrew Jackson against South Carolina senator John C. Calhoun over whether a state could nullify federal law, was an important step in a long series of attempts to define the proper powers of the states. Behind all these controversies lay the peculiar American version of republicanism: the assumption that no government or branch thereof was the ultimate sovereign. The final arbiter was the people, in their capacity to make constitutions and dissolve governments. The American people had always met to exercise this absolute power in *state* conventions. It was state conventions that had dissolved the connection with England, created

state constitutions, and ratified the federal Constitution. These all-powerful state conventions, so states' righters conceived, would never render themselves powerless by giving what they saw as their mere agency, the federal government, limitless authority to pass anything in the "general welfare." Instead, unlimited state conventions gave limited federal agencies only powers strictly enumerated in the U.S. Constitution.

But how could theoretically limitless state conventions, lacking bureaucratic means of enforcing edicts, stop a theoretically limited federal government, possessed with powerful governmental machinery? Most states' righters usually answered that the U.S. Supreme Court, albeit a branch of the mere governmental agency, would protect states' rights from nationalistic seizure of nonenumerated powers. The great states' rights crises came when this restriction seemed insufficient. Then states' righters, driving their position to its logical conclusion, *denied* that the Supreme Court, as part of the mere agency, could be final judge of constitutional issues. The ultimate sovereign, the state convention, must be judge of last resort as to whether its agency acted within the powers it had granted.

This extreme position first found its expression in the Thomas Jefferson–James Madison Virginia and Kentucky Resolutions of 1798–1799. These edicts declared the Federalists' Alien and Sedition laws, restricting the right to dissent in an international crisis, unconstitutional. The drift of the Jefferson-Madison position was that state conventions, by threatening to withdraw the people's consent to be governed, would force the federal government to live within the powers they had granted it.

In 1832–1833, Calhoun and his fellow nullifiers also threatened to secede if the federal agency trampled on states' rights. But the nullifiers added the notion that a state convention, while remaining in the Union, could use its absolute sovereignty to render a law of the federal agency null and void within that particular state's limits.

The occasion for this addendum to states' rights polemics was an escalation of anxiety within the South's most extreme state, South Carolina. As the first southern state to plunge into widespread cotton cultivation in the early nineteenth century, South Carolina was the first to see its soil lose its fertility. The consequence of worn-out soil — poor yields — paralleled a disastrous decline in cotton prices in the 1819–1835 period. The simultaneous passage of progressively higher American tariffs in 1816, 1824, and 1828 to protect American industry from more advanced European competitors at least temporarily boosted the prices American farmers had to pay for industrial products. Carolina cotton producers blamed all their woes on these tariffs. They also claimed that the federal agency could not use its power to pass tariffs, a constitutionally enumerated, revenue-enhancing act, in order to protect industry, a manufacture-enhancing act nowhere explicitly authorized in the Constitution. In 1832, a Carolina convention declared the tariff null and void in the state and warned it would secede if President Andrew Jackson tried to enforce the tariff in South Carolina.

Behind the explicit assault on the tariff lay another implicit concern — protecting slavery. The South Carolina coastal plains, largely a rice-producing region, was the most densely enslaved southern area and thus particularly sensitive to America's first antislavery stirrings. The first confrontation over slavery, which led to the Missouri Compromise of 1820, had helped inspire the unsuccessful slave revolt in Charleston led by Denmark Vesey in 1822. South Carolina rice planters feared nationalistic tariffs, bad enough in themselves, would furthermore lead to assaults on slavery. They thus joined their cotton-producing upland cousins in defying Jackson.

Southerners outside of South Carolina, though they also suffered from low cotton prices and disliked high tariffs, did not have the nullifiers' angry edge, partly because cotton yields were not as poor on virgin southwestern soil, partly because their fears of an imminent challenge to slavery were less acute since their region had fewer blacks. These less distressed southerners clung to Jefferson's old position that states' rights allowed a state to secede. But they rejected Calhoun's addendum that a state could remain under a general government and still nullify its laws.

President Jackson pleased the antinullification southern majority by urging lower tariffs. But he angered many of his southern states' rights followers by denouncing not only Calhoun's addendum but also the essence of Jefferson and Madison's original position. Jackson's notion that states' rights justified neither state nullification nor state secession, stated most powerfully in his Nullification Proclamation of December 10, 1832, precipitated the defection of a fraction of his states' rights followers over to the opposition, which became the Whig party. Until 1832, Jackson had possessed almost monopoly control of the Deep South. Now a two-party struggle swept over the region, with both parties claiming that they could save states' rights and slavery.

Calhoun himself rendered nullification unnecessary by joining with Henry Clay in early 1833 to devise and push through Congress the Compromise Tariff, which very slowly lowered the duties. Congress also passed the "Force Bill," giving Jackson theoretical power to force compliance with the tariff. In March 1833, the South Carolina convention nullified the now theoretical Force Bill and ended the nullification episode by accepting the Compromise Tariff.

Antebellum southerners would never try to nullify another law, although the nullification controversy would reecho in the George Wallace–led "interpositions" of southern states against federal desegregation edicts in the 1960s. Instead, in the pre–Civil War years, most southerners worked within the two-party system to shore up slavery and states' rights. For many years, southern two-party politicians succeeded in this enterprise. In 1860, when Abraham Lincoln's election marked their temporary failure, southerners would turn Thomas Jefferson's threats of secession into reality — and thus move the last states' right step *beyond* Calhoun's step past Jefferson.

Richard E. Ellis, *The Union at Risk: Jacksonian Democracy, States' Rights and the Nullification Crisis* (1987); William W. Freehling, *Prelude to Civil War: The Nullification Controversy in South Carolina, 1816–1836* (1965).

WILLIAM W. FREEHLING

See also Calhoun, John C.; Clay, Henry; Cotton; Jackson, Andrew; Secession; Tariff; Virginia and Kentucky Resolutions; Webster-Hayne Debate; Whig Party.

NUREMBERG TRIALS

In the Nuremberg trials (1945–1946), an International Military Tribunal tried high Nazi officials for actions committed during World War II that contravened the accepted laws of war. Among the practices condemned were plotting and waging aggressive war, using slave labor, looting occupied countries, and abusing and murdering civilians (especially the Jews) and prisoners of war. The Allies' decision to try major Axis officials for war crimes had been announced in October 1943, when the American, British, and Russian foreign ministers met in Moscow. Planning for the trials began soon after V-J Day, and the tribunal opened in Nuremberg, Germany, on November 20, 1945, before a board of distinguished judges from the Allied countries. Adolf Hitler, Heinrich Himmler, and Josef Goebbels had committed suicide by that time, but Hermann Goering, Joachim Ribbentrop, Wilhelm Keitel, Alfred Jodl, Ernst Kaltenbrunner, Julius Streicher, Hjalmar Schacht, Martin Bormann (in absentia), and sixteen others were tried one by one for individually specified crimes.

Twenty-one of the 24 were convicted; of these, 12 were sentenced to hang and the remainder were sent to prison. Two of those condemned to death escaped execution — Goering by committing suicide and Bormann by remaining at large; the rest were hanged on October 16, 1946. Lesser officials were also tried, including officers and guards from the Dachau prison camp and civilians who had murdered American aviators. In all, 24 defendants were executed as a result of the Nuremberg trials, 128 were sent to prison, and 35 were acquitted. Similar trials in Tokyo (1946–1948) resulted in the hanging of 7 Japanese leaders and the imprisoning of 16.

The trials were criticized by many for retroactively criminalizing actions that had been legal, and even required under orders, at the time they occurred; to these critics, the trials appeared more like vengeance than impartial justice. But Robert Jackson, chief justice of the U.S. Supreme Court and chief U.S. prosecutor in the Nuremberg trials, maintained that the Kellogg-Briand Pact of 1928 had outlawed aggressive warfare; holding individuals accountable for their actions, he argued, would deter future aggression. This argument prevailed at Nuremberg and was subsequently supported by the United Nations.

See also World War II.

NWSA

See National Woman Suffrage Association.

O

O'CONNOR, SANDRA DAY

(1930–), associate justice, U.S. Supreme Court. O'Connor was born in Arizona and completed both her undergraduate and law degrees at Stanford University. Before her appointment to the Supreme Court, she practiced law and served in the Arizona state senate (1969–1974) and on the Arizona bench (1974–1981). President Ronald Reagan nominated her as the first female justice of the United States in 1981, to replace retiring justice Potter Stewart.

O'Connor began her tenure on the Court as a conservative, voting with Justice William Rehnquist more than 90 percent of the time. But in her first decade on the federal bench, she proved herself an independent thinker. By 1990, she had become the pivotal center vote on a Court made up during those years of four liberals and four conservatives.

Her central role is best illustrated by cases involving the establishment clause of the First Amendment. Her view of that clause, which prohibits any law "respecting an establishment of religion," is that it prohibits any government action that is intended to send, or actually sends, a message endorsing religion. On the basis of this idiosyncratic test, she voted to uphold a public Christmas display including a crèche, but to strike down a public Christmas display of a crèche alone. In each case, her vote determined the outcome. She also provided the crucial fifth vote to strike down a state-mandated moment of silence at the beginning of the public school day.

Another example of her role as the center of the Court is affirmative action. Not only did she often cast the determining vote on the legality of a particular affirmative action program; she also fashioned the constitutional test that gained majority support in 1989. For fifteen years the Court was unable to produce a majority opinion in any constitutional case involving affirmative action. In 1989, in a case involving a "set-aside" program for minority businesses adopted by the city of Richmond, Virginia, Justice O'Connor wrote an opinion accepted almost in its entirety by a majority of the Court. Her opinion trod a middle course, validating affirmative action programs designed to combat prior governmental discrimination, but invalidating those designed to combat merely prior discrimination by the society at large.

O'Connor also provided the determinative vote in a series of cases on the still-developing question of the execution of juvenile or mentally retarded offenders. She voted twice to uphold such convictions and twice to strike them down. In each case her vote was the determinative one, and in each she wrote a separate concurrence to stress that her resolution of the case depended on the particular facts, not on any per se rule, again treading a middle course.

The Court's gender discrimination decisions have also been influenced by O'Connor. Since her appointment, the Court has declared both sexual harassment and sexual stereotyping to be forms of illegal gender discrimination and has upheld various state and local efforts to increase women's opportunities to participate in the labor force. O'Connor has always voted with the majority in these cases, often providing the necessary fifth vote. On one of the most important constitutional issues for women, O'Connor has generally voted to uphold restrictions on abortion, but she has simultaneously provided a moderating influence by refusing to overturn *Roe* v. *Wade*.

Thus O'Connor's propensity to make independent and politically moderate judgments gave her significant influence during her first decade on an increasingly polarized Court. As the Court moves further to the right, it remains to be seen whether she can continue to provide a moderating influence or will find herself more often in dissent.

Richard M. Cordray and James I. Vradelis, "The Emerging Jurisprudence of Justice O'Connor," *University of Chicago Law Review* 52 (1985): 389; Barbara C. S. Shea, "Sandra Day O'Connor — Woman, Lawyer, Justice: Her First Four Terms on the Supreme Court," *University of Missouri at Kansas City Law Review* 55 (1986): 1; Suzanna Sherry, "Civic Virtue and the Feminine Voice in Constitutional Adjudication," *Virginia Law Review* 72 (1986): 543.

Suzanna Sherry

See also Supreme Court.

OIL INDUSTRY

Many of the early explorers of America encountered petroleum deposits in some form. They noted oil slicks off the coast of California in the sixteenth century. Louis Evans located deposits along the eastern seaboard on a 1775 map of the English Middle Colonies.

Settlers used oil as an illuminant for medicine, and as grease for wagons and tools. Rock oil distilled from shale became available as kerosene even before the Industrial Revolution began. While traveling in Austria, John Austin, a New York merchant, observed an effective, cheap oil lamp and made a model that upgraded kerosene lamps. Soon the U.S. rock oil industry boomed as whale oil increased in price owing to the growing scarcity of that mammal. Samuel Downer, Jr., an early entrepreneur, patented "Kerosene" as a trade name in 1859 and licensed its usage. As oil production and refining in-

creased, prices collapsed, which became characteristic of the industry.

The first oil corporation, which was created to develop oil found floating on water near Titusville, Pennsylvania, was the Pennsylvania Rock Oil Company of Connecticut (later the Seneca Oil Company). George H. Bissell, a New York lawyer, and James Townsend, a New Haven businessman, became interested when Dr. Benjamin Silliman of Yale University analyzed a bottle of the oil and said it would make an excellent light. Bissell and several friends purchased land near Titusville and engaged Edwin L. Drake to locate the oil there. Drake employed William Smith, an expert salt driller, to supervise drilling operations and on August 27, 1859, they struck oil at a depth of sixty-nine feet. So far as is known, this was the first time that oil was tapped at its source, using a drill.

Titusville and other towns in the area boomed. One of those who heard about the discovery was John D. Rockefeller. Because of his entrepreneurial instincts and his genius for organizing companies, Rockefeller became a leading figure in the U.S. oil industry. In 1859, he and a partner operated a commission firm in Cleveland. They soon sold it and built a small oil refinery. Rockefeller bought out his partner and in 1866 opened an export office in New York City. The next year he, his brother William, S. V. Harkness, and Henry M. Flagler created what was to become the Standard Oil Company. Flagler is considered by many to have been nearly as important a figure in the oil business as John D. himself.

Additional discoveries near the Drake well had led to the creation of numerous firms and the Rockefeller company quickly began to buy out or combine with its competitors. As John D. phrased it, their purpose was "to unite our skill and capital." By 1870 Standard had become the dominant oil refining firm in Pennsylvania.

Pipelines early became a major consideration in Standard's drive to gain business and profits. Samuel Van Syckel had built a four-mile pipeline from Pithole, Pennsylvania, to the nearest railroad. When Rockefeller observed this, he began to acquire pipelines for Standard. Soon the company owned a majority of the lines, which provided cheap, efficient transportation for oil. Cleveland became a center of the refining industry principally because of its transportation systems.

When product prices declined, the ensuing panic led to the beginning of a Standard Oil alliance in 1871. Within eleven years the company became partially integrated horizontally and vertically and ranked as one of the world's great corporations. The alliance employed an industrial chemist, Hermann Frasch II, to remove sulfur from oil found at Lima, Ohio. Sulfur made distilling kerosene very difficult, and even then it possessed a vile odor — another problem Frasch solved. Thereafter, Standard employed scientists both to improve its product and for pure research. Soon kerosene replaced other illuminants; it was more reliable, efficient, and economical than other fuels.

Eastern cities linked to the oil fields by rail and boat boomed also. The export trade from Philadelphia, New York, and Baltimore became so important that Standard and other companies located refineries in those cities. As early as 1866 the value of petroleum products exported to Europe provided a trade balance sufficient to pay the interest on U.S. bonds held abroad.

When the Civil War interrupted the regular flow of kerosene and other petroleum products to western states, pressure increased to find a better method of utilizing oil found in such states as California. But Standard exhibited little interest in the oil industry on the West Coast before 1900. In that year it purchased the Pacific Coast Oil Company and in 1906 incorporated all its western operations into Pacific Oil, now Chevron.

Edward L. Doheny located Los Angeles's first well in 1892, and five years later there were twenty-five hundred wells and two hundred oil companies in the area. When Standard entered California in 1900, seven integrated oil companies already flourished there. The Union Oil Company was the most important of these.

Operating difficulties plus the threat of taxation on its out-of-state properties led to the creation of the Standard Oil Trust in 1882. In 1899 the trust created Standard Oil Company (New Jersey), which became the parent company. The trust controlled member corporations principally through stock ownership, an arrangement not unlike that of the modern-day holding company.

The tremendous growth of Standard did not occur without competition. Pennsylvania producers engineered the creation of an important competitor, the Pure Oil Company, Ltd., in 1895. This concern endured for more than a half century.

In 1901 one of the largest and most significant oil strikes in history occurred near Beaumont, Texas, on a mound called Spindletop. Drillers brought in the greatest gusher ever seen within the United States. This strike ended any possible monopoly by Standard Oil. One year after the Spindletop discovery more than fifteen hundred oil companies had been chartered. Of these, fewer than a dozen survived, principally the Gulf Oil Corporation, the Magnolia Petroleum Company, and the Texas Company. The Sun Oil Company, an Ohio-Indiana concern, also moved to the Beaumont area as did other firms. Other oil strikes followed in Oklahoma, Louisiana, Arkansas, Colorado, and Kansas. Oil production in the United States by 1909 more than equaled that of the rest of the world combined.

Many smaller companies developed outside the Northeast and the Midwest where Rockefeller and his associates operated. Oil found at Corsicana, Texas, in the 1890s attracted a remarkable Pennsylvanian, Joseph S. ("Buckskin Joe") Cullinan, who organized several small companies. He later moved to Spindletop where he became instrumental in the organization of the Texas Company, soon a major competitor of Standard. Henri Deterding, creator of the Royal Dutch-Shell Group in Holland and Great Britain, moved into California in 1912 with his American Gasoline Company (Shell Company of California after 1914).

As Standard Oil grew in wealth and power, it encountered great hostility not only from its competitors but from a vast segment of the public. Standard fought competition by securing preferential railroad rates and rebates on its shipments. It also influenced legislatures and Congress through tactics that, though common in that era, were unethical. Nor was the company's handling of labor any better.

The Industrial Revolution had harmful effects on many farmers and residents of small-town America. Led by a number of charismatic leaders, those people demanded industrial, railroad, and labor reforms. They focused their spleen on Standard Trust and the railroads. This led in 1887 to a semblance of railroad regulation, the Interstate Commerce Act, and in 1890 to the relatively ineffective Sherman Antitrust Act.

In 1911 the Supreme Court declared that the Standard Trust had operated to monopolize and restrain trade, and it ordered the trust dissolved into thirty-four companies. That the trust's share of the industry had declined from 33 to 13 percent the Court held to be of little consequence. The splitting-off of the Standard affiliates proved difficult. Some marketed, some produced, some refined, and these concerns quickly moved toward vertical integration of their businesses. But the 1911 decision ensured that though the industry might have giants, they at least competed with one another.

Increasing sales of gasoline first for automobiles and then for airplanes in the early 1900s came as oil discoveries across the United States mounted. The oil industry had a vast new market for what had been for many years a useless by-product of the distilling process. As soon as the internal combustion engines created demand, refiners sought better methods to produce and improve gasolines.

Before its entry into World War I, the United States contributed oil to the Allies, and in 1917 the oil companies cooperated with the Fuel Administration. At war's end executives who had served with that agency created the American Petroleum Institute (1919), which in time became a major force in the economy and the business.

Although the U.S. oil industry had marketed abroad extensively before the war, it owned few foreign properties. Judging from government surveys, many producers believed that a major oil shortage would soon occur. Both Secretary of Commerce Herbert Hoover and Secretary of State Charles Evans Hughes began to pressure American companies to seek oil abroad. These firms invested in the Middle East, Southeast Asia, and South America and searched for oil everywhere while they continued to export quantities of oil from the United States.

The individual who focused attention back on the United States was Columbus Marion ("Dad") Joiner. Joiner became convinced that some flatlands in an East Texas basinlike structure contained oil. He obtained a lease near Tyler, Texas, and on October 5, 1930, after having drilled two dry holes, struck perhaps the largest oil pool ever found in America. It lay beneath 140,000 acres and contained 5 billion barrels. H. L. Hunt, an oil entrepreneur, bought Joiner's leases and later sold them to oil companies at a profit of $100 million, thereby adding to his already substantial fortune.

In a sense the Joiner strike came at an inopportune time; it was the onset of the Great Depression. The price of oil plummeted to ten cents a barrel in 1931, creating chaos in the industry. But some New Deal measures restored a modicum of prosperity, and then World War II stimulated the oil business enormously.

The various oil strikes focused attention on a legal situation unique to the United States. Land ownership carried with it rights to all subsoil minerals, termed the common law "right of capture." Oil companies, like other mineral companies, negotiated with each landowner for drilling rights. This right of capture continued for years despite the efforts of such industry giants as conservation-minded Henry L. Doherty of Cities Service Oil Company, who sought to institute oil field unitization. The right of capture ensured early exhaustion of oil fields and tragic waste of a valuable energy source. Wallace E. Pratt, a geologist and longtime Jersey Standard leader, has estimated that by releasing the natural gas that often underlies petroleum pools and by using poor production techniques, oil producers have wasted at least 75 percent of the oil and natural gas found to date in the United States.

World War II made the oil industry a key American resource. Oil company research and executive leadership played major roles in the conflict. Research increased the number of products made from petroleum and natural gas, including the explosive TNT and artificial rubber.

The Jersey-Dupont jointly owned product, tetraethyl lead, upgraded gasoline to improve airplane speed. Oil tankers supplied gasoline for the Allies at great risk from submarine attacks. The government rationed gasoline and controlled prices during the war. In the last analysis the war ended the delusion that American supplies of crude were unlimited, so that the industry and the securing of oil became a top priority for both foreign and domestic policy.

When the war ended, the United States faced the problem of stabilizing the peace. Over the next forty-five years numerous major crises occurred, in many of which oil played a key role. Europe underwent a coal shortage, the first energy crisis, immediately after the war. The Marshall Plan, created to solve that and other problems, was hampered by the first Iranian crisis of 1950–1954. From the 1956 Suez crisis to the Iraqi invasion of Kuwait in 1990, oil proved to be the most important consideration in America's Middle Eastern policy. The United States sought to balance support for the new state of Israel against the pressures of the oil producers, mostly Arab, united in 1960 as the Organization of Petroleum Exporting Countries (OPEC). This proved increasingly difficult as the United States became steadily more dependent on imported oil. In the United States the standard of living based on cheap oil continuously rose and the public, accustomed to this way of life, resisted all conservation measures. The United States continues to consume about two-thirds of the world's oil production. Oil should be considered the keystone of the standard of living in the United States and to a large degree its rank as a world power.

Part of the energy problem after 1940 resulted from the depletion of domestic oil reserves during World War II — around 6 billion barrels. In the Vietnam struggle experts contend the United States supplied about 5 billion barrels of oil, although great quantities of that came from Middle Eastern properties owned by American companies. Certainly the total for both wars represents a quantity larger than either that of the great East Texas oil field or possibly that discovered on Alaska's North Slope in 1967. After the 1960s, as domestic production declined and demand soared, the oil industry had to import vast quantities from the Middle East and Venezuela. The nation's key energy source increasingly hinged on balancing diplomatic relations with Arab oil-producing nations while continuing its aid to Israel.

While the United States was blessed with plentiful supplies of oil its growth to the rank of a great power accelerated. In today's world as an oil-dependent power it must find alternate sources of energy or accommodate drastic changes in its way of life and position in the world.

Paul H. Giddens, *The Birth of the Oil Industry* (1938); Ralph W. and Muriel E. Hidy, *Pioneering in Big Business, 1882–1911* (1955); Bennett H. Wall et al., *Growth in a Changing Environment: A History of Standard Oil Company (New Jersey), 1950–1972, and Exxon Corporation, 1972–1975* (1988); Daniel Yergin, *The Prize: The Epic Quest for Oil, Money, and Power* (1990).

BENNETT H. WALL

See also Getty, Jean Paul; Middle East–U.S. Relations; OPEC Oil Crisis; Rockefeller, John D.; Teapot Dome Affair.

O'KEEFFE, GEORGIA

(1887–1986), artist. Born on a farm in Wisconsin, O'Keeffe studied representational art at the Art Institute of Chicago (1905–1906) and the Art Students League in New York (1907–1908). She worked as a commercial artist in Chicago for several years and then came under the influence of Arthur Wesley Dow, head of the fine arts department at Columbia Teachers College in New York. His teaching concerning the importance of patterning and other principles of abstraction freed O'Keeffe from the dicta of realism and inspired her to return to fine art. In 1912 she became the art teacher for the Amarillo, Texas, public school system, where her painting became deeply imbued with the western light and landscape. She was also influenced by radical European ideas about art gleaned from books and journals, and letters from friends in New York.

After she had begun to develop her own expressionistic style, photographer Alfred Stieglitz exhibited her charcoal drawings and watercolors at his small avant-garde gallery in New York in 1916 and 1917. He was a strong advocate of the first generation of American modern artists, including John Marin, Arthur Dove, and Marsden Hartley, and he brought O'Keeffe into this circle, convinced that she expressed a female sensibility in a new, original, and bold manner. In 1923, the year before their marriage, he sponsored her first one-artist exhibit, followed by others virtually every year. O'Keeffe won early acceptance: the Brooklyn Museum exhibited her work in 1927 and the Museum of Modern Art in 1929; the Whitney Museum of American Art first purchased her work in 1932 as did the Metropolitan Museum of Art two years later. Her first retrospective was at the Art Institute of Chicago in 1943.

During the late teens and early twenties, O'Keeffe painted pure abstractions derived from imagined forms and intense feelings, many of which pivot on a central vertical axis and consist of sensuous colors; they are characterized by highly controlled and almost invisible brushwork. Along with a brief period of portraying New York skyscrapers, she also painted oversized views of natural objects — flower blossoms, leaves, rocks, shells, feathers, animal bones — in which she frequently integrated abstract and objective imagery. Many of these paintings were influenced by photographic techniques, especially close-ups and cropping. She tended to exaggerate sizes, simplify forms, eliminate middle distances, and employ surrealistic techniques, such as a floating animal skull against a distant mountain range.

Profoundly inspired by nature, O'Keeffe was an aesthetic descendant of the nineteenth-century Hudson River school, expressing her ecstatic feelings for nature in vibrant colors, organic forms, and uninhabited, dramatic vistas. After a visit to northern New Mexico in the summer of 1929, her work reflected its mesas, mountains, arroyos, and badlands and was invested with as much feeling as another artist might portray in the human body. She returned to the state almost every summer and moved permanently to the village of Abiquiu after Stieglitz's death in 1946. After her first trip to Europe in 1953, the aerial views she had seen inspired her to paint the large-scale, ethereal Sky above the Clouds series. She, in turn, influenced the work of the minimalists and color field abstract expressionists of the 1950s and 1960s. O'Keeffe was elected to the National Institute of Arts and Letters in 1949 and to the American Academy of Arts and Letters in 1962.

Laurie Lisle, *Portrait of an Artist: A Biography of Georgia O'Keeffe* (1986); Roxana Robinson, *Georgia O'Keeffe: A Life* (1989).

LAURIE LISLE

See also Painting and Sculpture.

O'NEILL, EUGENE

(1888–1953), dramatist. In 1920, O'Neill's *Beyond the Horizon* was acclaimed as America's first native stage tragedy. Thirty-six years later audiences were stunned by the Greek-sized passions of his posthumously produced masterpiece, *Long Day's Journey into Night*. Almost literally autobiographical (unlike his earlier works, in which he disguised the members of his family), it was written, he said, "in tears and blood." It revealed his father to have been a miser, his mother a morphine addict, and his brother an alcoholic.

O'Neill's mother, Ella Quinlan — beautiful, shy, convent-educated — fell in love with James O'Neill, a popular touring actor, who was haunted by his impoverished youth. Eugene was born in a Broadway hotel room, and his difficult birth, coupled with the rigors of accompanying James on his cross-country theatrical one-night stands, drove Ella to morphine addiction. Eugene's brother, Jamie, older by ten years — clever, cynical, an unsuccessful actor — combined all the weaknesses and none of the strengths of his parents.

O'Neill's art was influenced by what he proudly called his "life experience." He briefly attended Princeton, failed as an actor, fathered a child out of wedlock, shipped out to sea, lived as a derelict on the New York waterfront — where he drank himself senseless and attempted suicide — worked as a reporter in New London, Connecticut, recovered from tuberculosis, and lived a bohemian life among aspiring artists and writers in Provincetown, Massachusetts, and Greenwich Village.

O'Neill turned these experiences into artistic triumphs. In his most prolific period (1920–1933) O'Neill saw thirteen of his plays produced, all of them tragedies except the sunny *Ah, Wilderness!* (1933). They were often experimental (masks, stage asides, densely novelistic technique) and turned on such themes as poisoning, incest, infanticide, suicide, terminal illness, insanity, betrayal, drunkenness, blasphemy, adultery, and lechery. His protagonists were sailors, pimps, whores, stevedores, petty crooks, gamblers, and — occasionally — men and women who were educated but soul-sick. Most were hailed by the critics: *The Emperor Jones* (1920), *Anna Christie* (1921), *The Hairy Ape* (1922), *Desire under the Elms* (1924), the double-length *Strange Interlude* (1928), and the triple-length *Mourning Becomes Electra* (1931).

His masterworks were written between 1935 and 1943, despite persistent illness, depression, and marital problems with his third wife, Carlotta Monterey. In addition to *Long Day's Journey into Night,* these plays were *The Iceman Cometh* (produced 1946), *A Moon for the Misbegotten* (which closed out of town in 1947 but was successfully revived on Broadway after his death), and *A Touch of the Poet* (part of an unfinished play cycle, produced posthumously in 1958).

O'Neill believed, with the Greeks, that tragedy always brings exultation. "To me, the tragic alone has that significant beauty which is truth," he said. "It is the meaning of life — and the hope."

O'Neill is the only American playwright to have won the Nobel Prize for literature (1936); he also won four Pulitzer Prizes. He paved the way for such contemporary playwrights as Tennessee Williams and Arthur Miller, who said of him, "The theater will forever need the towering rebuke of O'Neill's life and his work and his agony."

Arthur and Barbara Gelb, *O'Neill* (1987); Eugene O'Neill, *Complete Plays,* ed. Travis Bogard, 3 vols. (1988).

ARTHUR AND BARBARA GELB

See also Theater.

OPEC OIL CRISIS

On October 17, 1973, the Organization of Arab Petroleum Exporting Countries (OPEC) declared an embargo on the shipment of oil to those countries that had supported Israel in its conflict with Egypt. With one stroke, the total dependence of the industrialized world on oil, much of which happened to reside beneath the sands of the Arab countries, became painfully clear.

Before the embargo, the industrialized West, especially the United States, had taken cheap and plentiful petroleum for granted. Oil consumption in the United States had more than doubled between 1950 and 1974. With approximately 6 percent of the world's population, the nation was consuming 33 percent of the world's energy.

The effects of the embargo were immediate. The retail price of a gallon of gasoline rose from a national average of 38.5 cents in May 1973 to 55.1 cents in June 1974. With the onset of the embargo, U.S. imports of oil from the Arab countries dropped from 1.2 million barrels a day to a mere 19,000 barrels. Daily consumption dropped by 6.1 percent from September to February, and by the summer of 1974, by 7 percent.

The U.S. government response to the embargo was quick, but of limited effectiveness. A national speed limit of 55 miles per hour was imposed to help reduce consumption. (This, incidentally, caused traffic fatalities to drop by 23 percent between 1973 and 1974.) President Richard M. Nixon named William Simon as an official "energy czar," and in 1977 a cabinet-level Department of Energy was created.

Some long-term effects of the embargo are still being felt. Public suspicion of the oil companies, who were thought to be profiteering or even working in collusion with OPEC, continues unabated (seven of the fifteen top Fortune 500 companies in 1974 were oil companies, with total assets of over $100 billion). But the initial moves toward more efficient automobiles and alternate sources of energy ended as oil prices fell and memory of gasoline lines faded. Ultimately, little of substance changed. Americans continue to use energy in amounts far out of proportion to their numbers, automakers continue to oppose legislation that would force them to increase the efficiency of cars, and the United States continues to respond to any threat to the supply of oil as a threat to national security.

See also Middle East–U.S. Relations; Oil Industry.

OPEN DOOR POLICY

By the late nineteenth century, Japan and the western European powers had carved much of China into separate spheres of influence. Within each, one nation held economic dominance. The United States, coming late to imperialism, advocated the Open Door policy (first proposed by a British customs official in China, Alfred E. Hippisley) under which all nations would have equal trading and development rights in China. This recommendation was communicated in notes sent by Secretary of State John Hay in 1899 to France, Germany, Great Britain, Italy, Japan, and Russia. Although Japan challenged the policy and the European powers replied evasively that they would comply if others would, Hay announced in March 1900 that his proposal had been approved.

Actually, few nations — including the United States — adhered to it in practice. The secret Taft-Katsura memorandum between Japan and the United States in 1905, for instance, set the stage for the establishment of a Japanese protectorate over Korea, and a number of Allied powers signed secret treaties during World War I assuring Japan of access to German colonies in or near China. Also, the Lansing-Ishii agreement between Japan and the United States in 1917, though reiterating the Open Door policy, acknowledged Japan's "special interests" in China.

An international Conference on the Limitation of Armament in Washington, D.C., in 1921–1922 was convened, in part, out of concern over continuing violations of China's territory. At this conference, the Open Door policy was again affirmed. Nevertheless, in 1932, when Japan seized Manchuria and established a pup-

pet state there, the United States was the only power to protest. Although Secretary of State Henry L. Stimson's doctrine of nonrecognition, supported by the League of Nations, did persuade Japan to withdraw from its next target, Shanghai, Japanese incursions resumed shortly thereafter, and on November 18, 1938, the Japanese asserted that the Open Door was "inapplicable" to the conditions "of today and tomorrow." With the beginning of World War II, the debate over the Open Door policy ended.

See also Asia-U.S. Relations.

OPPENHEIMER, J. ROBERT

(1904–1967), physicist and father of the atomic bomb. A charismatic leader of rare good qualities and commonplace flaws, Oppenheimer brought an uncommon sensibility to research, teaching, and government service. Ushered into the American pantheon as "the father of the atomic bomb" in 1945, he was ejected during the McCarthy era as a security risk for having opposed the escalation of the nuclear arms race. His life reveals how war and politics altered science in the twentieth century.

Raised in an environment of wealth and culture, Oppenheimer was educated at Harvard University. Equally brilliant in the humanities and sciences, he graduated summa cum laude in 1925, after only three years. Following an unhappy year studying experimental physics at Cambridge University, he moved to Göttingen, Germany, where he earned a Ph.D. in theoretical physics in 1927.

In 1929, already internationally recognized as a brilliant theoretical physicist, Oppenheimer returned to the United States to accept a unique joint appointment at both the University of California at Berkeley and the California Institute of Technology. In less than a decade he established Berkeley as the major American center for the study of quantum physics.

Languages, literature, music, art, and especially physics filled Oppenheimer's life until the mid-1930s when fascism in Europe and the Great Depression in America drew him into progressive politics. Although never a member of the Communist party, he was active in and contributed to many of the causes supported by the party — desegregation, better working conditions for migratory farm workers, and the Loyalist side in the Spanish civil war.

In 1939, the discovery of nuclear fission and Adolf Hitler's invasion of Poland linked science and Oppenheimer to the military. In 1942, overriding the protests of intelligence officers, Gen. Leslie R. Groves, the officer in charge of the Manhattan Project, appointed Oppenheimer director of the Los Alamos Scientific Laboratory. His assignment: to direct the design and construction of atomic bombs for use during the war. On August 6, 1945, the destruction of Hiroshima confirmed Groves's judgment of Oppenheimer's ability, although history will forever debate the wisdom of the result.

In 1947 Oppenheimer moved to Princeton, as director of the Institute for Advanced Study. Commuting to Washington, D.C., he served on numerous government committees, including the General Advisory Committee to the Atomic Energy Commission (AEC), which he chaired. In 1949, after the Soviet Union's successful test of an atomic bomb, he urged President Harry S. Truman to reject Edward Teller's proposal for a crash program to build a hydrogen bomb. He believed that instead the United States should seek an arms control agreement with the Soviet Union. Although Truman rejected this advice, resentment of Oppenheimer's continuing influence spread among Teller and his allies.

As the cold war developed, science and scientists were profoundly affected by the emerging political culture of conformity. Oppenheimer's opposition to the hydrogen bomb and his former communist associations were cited by his enemies as evidence of his unreconstructed sympathy for the Soviet Union. In 1954, an AEC security hearing, distorted by illegal FBI telephone taps and a biased hearing board, led to the revocation of his security clearance.

Nevertheless, Oppenheimer continued to direct the Institute for Advanced Study and to lecture throughout the world on science and education until his death. With respect to the most important issue of the day, the nuclear arms race, however, he had been silenced.

Peter Goodchild, *J. Robert Oppenheimer: Shatterer of Worlds* (1980); Philip Stern, *The Oppenheimer Case: Security on Trial* (1969).

MARTIN J. SHERWIN

See also Anticommunism; Hydrogen Bomb; Manhattan Project; Nuclear Weapons: Origins and Legacy; Science and Technology.

OREGON TRAIL

The Oregon Trail was an overland route from the Missouri River to the Willamette Valley in Oregon, which was followed by thousands of migrants to the West in the 1840s and 1850s. The route had been used since early in the century by trappers and traders, but the first wagon train of settlers reached Oregon by way of the trail in 1842. The next year came the "great migration," during which about a thousand people and more than a thousand head of stock followed the trail west. Within two years the number of migrants had tripled, and over the next decade, more and more families seeking homes in Oregon made the trek.

Francis Parkman's *The Oregon Trail* (1849) describes his trip along the eastern section of the trail. Most groups began the six-month trip in Independence, Missouri; from there the wagon trains traveled west along the Santa Fe Trail and then followed the Platte and North Platte rivers to South Pass, where they crossed the Rocky Mountains. A few days later they picked up the Snake River, which they followed to the point where they made a difficult climb through the Blue Mountains. From there the trail took them west to Fort Walla Walla and then down the Columbia River to their destination, the Willamette Valley, more than two thousand miles from where they had begun. In open country, the wagon trains would diverge widely, but at river fords and mountain passes, the trail would narrow to a single rutted path.

The trail remained in steady use until the coming of the railroads provided a less arduous way of traveling west. The Oregon Trail was finally abandoned in the 1870s.

See also Expansion, Continental and Overseas; Internal Migration.

OSTEND MANIFESTO

This document, signed in 1854 by three American diplomats in Ostend, Belgium, reflected the continuing belief in manifest destiny and the growing importance of the sectional conflict. Minister to Great Britain James Buchanan, Minister to France John Y. Mason, and, especially, Minister to Spain Pierre Soulé urged the purchase of the Spanish colony of Cuba for as much as $120 million.

Secretary of State William L. Marcy, who had authorized Soulé to set up the meeting of the envoys, instructed Soulé to negotiate for Cuba, allowing him to offer Spain up to $130 million. If that failed — which it did — Soulé, known for his hot temper and proslavery views, could "detach that island from the Spanish dominion." He met with Buchanan and Mason. They issued the manifesto, which stressed Cuba's importance to the nation and how well it would fare under American control.

The Ostend Manifesto, however, attracted criticism for its ideas and its tone, and Marcy repudiated it, forcing Soulé's resignation. It also became part of the sectional impasse: Cuba was expected to become slave territory. Also, Soulé and Mason resided in slave states, and Buchanan, bereft of his customary caution, had long steered clear of his native Pennsylvania's opposition to slavery.

See also Caribbean-U.S. Relations; Manifest Destiny.

OWENS, JESSE

(1913–1980), track and field athlete. In three outstanding meets, Owens gained international fame by establishing long-standing world or Olympic records and challenging Adolf Hitler's conception of Aryan supremacy.

Owens was born in Alabama as the tenth child of sharecroppers and moved with his family to Cleveland in the 1920s as part of the massive migration of blacks from the rural South to the urban North.

In junior high school, Owens was befriended by Charles Riley, a white teacher and coach, who saw talent in the small, slight black youth. He developed his sprinting, hurdling, and long-jump skills at Cleveland East Tech High School where he dominated Ohio high school track and field. Owens first came to national attention when he tied the world record of 9.4 seconds in the 100-yard dash and long-jumped 24 feet 9½ inches at the 1933 National High School Championship meet in Chicago. In college, Owens continued to excel in track and field, winning a record eight individual NCAA championships. His greatest collegiate performance occurred at the 1935 Big Ten Conference Championship where he tied or established world records in the 100-yard dash, long jump, 220-yard dash, and the 220-yard low hurdles.

Owens is most famous for his performance during the 1936 Olympic Games in Berlin, Germany. Adolf Hitler had planned to use the games to showcase German prosperity amid the worldwide depression and to demonstrate Aryan physical supremacy by fielding a strong German team. Although Germany did win more medals than any other nation, Owens's brilliant individual performance overshadowed its achievement. He won four gold medals, tying the 100-meter dash record and establishing new Olympic records in the 200-meter dash, long jump, and 4 X 100-meter relay. His records in the relay and the 200-meter dash were not broken until the 1956 games, and the others stood until 1960.

Following the games, Owens returned to the United States and attempted to cash in on his newfound fame by exploiting the offers telegraphed to him in Berlin. He reportedly received ten thousand dollars for supporting Republican presidential candidate Alf Landon in 1936, but few of the other offers materialized. He was reduced to performing in exhibitions such as running races against horses and touring with a band and basketball and baseball teams. These appearances were lucrative, but a laundry he owned failed because of poor management. Owens was taken to court for not paying his income taxes, and he eventually declared bankruptcy.

Through the 1950s and 1960s, however, Owens prospered by working in public relations for major corporations. His modesty, patriotism, and sincerity made him an excellent public speaker, much in demand. He remained a hero to black Americans and was acceptable to white people because of his conservative position on race issues. Ironically, he was criticized by many black Americans because he was a spokesman for the U.S. Olympic Committee during racial protests at the 1968 Mexico City Olympic Games. Nevertheless, he remained America's most popular and famous track and field athlete until his death from cancer in 1980.

William J. Baker, *Jesse Owens: An American Life* (1986); Richard D. Mandell, *The Nazi Olympics* (1971); Jesse Owens, as told to Paul Neimark, *The Jesse Owens Story* (1970).

C. ROBERT BARNETT

See also Spectator Sports.

P

PACIFISM

See Conscientious Objection.

PACT OF PARIS

See Kellogg-Briand Pact.

PAINE, THOMAS

(1737–1809), political philosopher and writer. "I know not whether any man in the world has had more influence on its inhabitants or affairs for the last thirty years than Tom Paine." So wrote John Adams in 1805. In an age of political pamphleteering, Paine had become the most influential pamphleteer of all. His writings remain classic statements of the egalitarian, democratic faith of the Age of Revolution.

Paine's origins lay among the lower orders of eighteenth-century England. The son of a Quaker corset maker, he practiced his father's trade and then worked as an excise tax collector. His father's religion undoubtedly influenced Paine's humanitarianism, and a strong interest in Newtonian science helped him develop a hatred for governments that rested on hereditary privilege.

Paine immigrated to Philadelphia in 1774 and soon became acquainted with advocates of political change. In January 1776, he published *Common Sense,* the first pamphlet to advocate American independence. It outlined ideas that would remain central to Paine's thought: the superiority of republican government over a monarchical system, equality of rights among all citizens, and the world significance of the American Revolution. Paine transformed the struggle over the rights of English people into a contest with meaning for people everywhere. In a world "overrun with oppression," America would be "an asylum for mankind."

Common Sense sold perhaps 150,000 copies in 1776, a tribute to both the persuasiveness of Paine's argument and the clarity and power of his literary style. Addressing a mass audience unfamiliar with legal precedents, classical learning, and complex rhetoric, Paine strove for simplicity. The message conveyed by his style was of a piece with his democratic politics: to understand the nature of politics, all it takes is common sense.

For the next several years, Paine threw himself into the struggle for independence, writing the *Crisis* papers (which begin with the famous phrase, "These are the times that try men's souls") to bolster the morale of Washington's army. He also took part in the movement that produced in Pennsylvania the era's most democratic state constitution.

Returning to Europe in 1787, Paine soon entered the political debate launched by the French Revolution. His *Rights of Man* defended the revolution against the attacks of Edmund Burke and proffered a new vision of the republican state as a promoter of the social welfare, advocating such policies as progressive taxation, retirement benefits, and public employment. An even greater success than *Common Sense, Rights of Man* transformed English radicalism, linking demands for political reform with a social program for the lower classes.

Charged with seditious libel for advocating an end to monarchy in Britain, Paine fled to France, where he became one of a handful of foreigners elected to the National Convention. His opposition to the execution of the king alienated the Jacobins, and when they came to power, Paine found himself in prison. After his release in 1794, he produced his last great pamphlets: *The Age of Reason,* an exposition of deism and an attack on the basic principles of Christianity, and *Agrarian Justice,* a call for land reform.

After his return to America in 1802, Paine came under constant assault by evangelical Christians for his deist writings. Only six mourners attended the funeral of the man who had once inspired millions to think in new ways about the world. But Paine's writings became part of the intellectual foundation for nineteenth-century radicalism.

Eric Foner, *Tom Paine and Revolutionary America* (1976); David F. Hawke, *Paine* (1974).

ERIC FONER

See also Common Sense; Deism; Radicalism; Revolution.

PAINTING AND SCULPTURE

I. Beginnings to 1913

During much of the two and a half centuries in which the visual arts in America developed from a primitive to a sophisticated state, there hung over artists a sense of debilitating provincialism. The arts, they believed, were European, and it was European mannerisms that set the standards of artistic etiquette. From the seventeenth century, when now unidentified limners were painting tavern signs and overmantels and portraits at a few shillings a head, to the end of the nineteenth century, when French impressionists and German and Dutch realists were the mentors of young American artists, American art almost never ran free of European harnesses.

What is remarkable is that during these centuries there emerged so many independent creative talents who produced a native art that, though influenced by Europe, was distinctly and inescapably American. Painting and sculpture reflected fashions in Europe, usually somewhat late. But there were times when American artists took off on their own, as did the landscapists of the Hudson River school, some of the genre painters, and a few explorers of fauna like the great painter of birds and small beasts John James Audubon (1785–1851). The sources of their subjects and their delight in them were the land, the creatures, and the people they knew, not European models.

The colonial New England limners took their styles, much simplified, from Elizabethan artists: linear and two-dimensional with special care paid to textiles. Clothes were a measure of social position; faces were less important. Mothers and children appear in these pictures as dressed-up dolls and the men as wooden-featured, static lay figures. They were not, to be sure, without considerable charm and stern probity.

Early in the eighteenth century a few professionally trained painters arrived from Europe to set up their easels wherever they might find customers — in Charleston, Annapolis, Philadelphia, Boston, and other cities whose prosperity depended on the commerce of the sea. Among them were Gustavus Hessalius (1682–1755), a portraitist who tried his hand at mythological scenes, and John Smibert (1688–1751), a pupil of the distinguished English portraitist Sir Geoffrey Kneller. Smibert painted and sold imported engravings, the only access in America other than inept copies to the masterpieces of Europe. Furthermore he trained a more gifted artist than himself, Robert Feke (c. 1705–c. 1750), who outdid him in elegance and the mastery of portraying character.

After the middle of the century it became the ambition of most young American painters to go to Europe to feast on the arts of the past and refine their skills. America's two most eminent artists were among them, Benjamin West (1738–1820) and John Singleton Copley (1738–1815). Copley's reputation as an artist of the first rank has outlasted West's, though West's fame in his lifetime exceeded Copley's. West's promise as a boy prompted a group of Philadelphia merchants to pay his way to Europe to study, possibly the earliest example of what we now call "business sponsorship of the arts." West prospered in London, becoming history painter to George III and president of the Royal Academy. His studio became a mecca for young American painters. Copley prospered in Boston where his most distinguished portraits were painted, far superior to any made before in America. But he longed for greener pastures and took off for London in 1774, where he eventually succumbed to the seduction of fashion and the quality of his work declined. He too took to history painting, scenes of battles and other events in a baroque manner that were momentarily popular successes.

Portraits were the artists' mainstay until photography stole a large part of their livelihood in the mid-nineteenth century. The reputations of Charles Willson Peale (1741–1827) of Philadelphia, Gilbert Stuart (1755–1828) who arrived in Boston from London in 1793, Ralph Earl (1751–1802) of Connecticut, and Samuel F. B. Morse (1791–1872), best known as an inventor of the telegraph, are fixed primarily by portraits they painted — Peale and Stuart of George Washington, for example, and Morse of Marquis de Lafayette. Peale at heart was as much a scientist as Morse was. He founded America's first museum of art and natural history in Philadelphia. Col. John Trumbull (1756–1843), one of the young Americans who haunted West's London studio, devoted himself almost entirely to history painting, the most famous of which was his depiction of the signing of the Declaration of Independence, reproduced by the millions on postage stamps. Trumbull founded the American Academy of Fine Arts in New York in 1802.

Two quite different painters, John Vanderlyn (1775–1852) and Washington Allston (1779–1843), took off for Europe in the early nineteenth century. What they brought back was unlike anything that had been seen before in America. Vanderlyn shocked the public with a voluptuous nude, *Ariadne Asleep on the Island of Naxos,* which was denounced as an example of French depravity. Allston, an intellectual romantic and dedicated aesthete, brought back cool Italian landscapes peopled with small mythological and biblical figures.

The flight of painters to Europe was followed in the 1830s by a flock of stonecutters bent on becoming sculptors. In colonial days the only sculpture galleries were the cemeteries where tombstones were often ornamented with distorted skeletons and winged death's heads. Craftsmen produced elegant weathervanes and wood-carvers decorated chests and turned out splendid, brightly polychromed figureheads for merchant ships and frigates. Although they were admired in ports around the world, their creators were considered mere wood-carvers. Nevertheless, one of the so-called fathers of American sculpture was William Rush (1756–1833), a Philadelphia wood-carver who was in every aesthetic sense a sculptor, producing figureheads and nymphs and occasional portrait figures (one a life-size Washington).

What Henry James called "the White Marmorean Flock" streamed to Italy in the 1820s and 1830s, determined to bring the noble art of sculpture back to America in a sophisticated (which meant neoclassical) manner. The most eminent of these, the Bostonian Horatio Greenough (1805–1852), was commissioned by Congress to create a heroic sculpture of George Washington. The statue, half-clad in marble draperies, was greeted with ridicule when it was installed in the rotunda of the Capitol. "Will it not be worth thirty thousand dollars," Greenough argued, "to be able to point to the figure and say, 'there was the first struggle of our infant art.'" Thomas Crawford (1813?–1857), whose *Armed Victory* is the spike on the dome of the Capitol, followed Greenough to Rome, as did William Wetmore Story (1819–1895) of Boston, as much a poet as a sculptor and short of genius at either. Story was, however, the urbane pivot around whom American artists in Rome revolved. Among them were a number of women sculptors, most notably Harriet Hosmer (1830–1908) of Boston and Edmonia Lewis (1845–?), daughter of an African-American father and a Chippewa Indian mother.

It was a time when fashion impelled sculptors to depict American politicians as Roman senators. None was more expert at this than Hiram Powers (1805–1873), America's most famous stonecutter at midcentury. His fame, however, derived primarily from his *Greek Slave,* a daring nude female, her hands fastened with a chain that somehow made her nakedness respectable. Powers settled in Florence and operated a sort of sculpture factory there, turning out reproductions of the maiden and portraits for a thousand dollars a head. But compared with two sculptors who stayed at home, Erastus Dow Palmer (1817–1904) of Albany and the anatomist Dr. William Rimmer (1816–1879), he was a mere statue maker. Powers worked from the outside in; Palmer and Rimmer from the inside out.

While sculptors flirted with neoclassicism, a group of painters, inspired by Thomas Cole (1801–1848), was capturing on canvas the romantic American landscape. They were the painters of the Hudson River school, the first indigenous school of American painting. They thrived from the 1830s until late in the century, when they were supplanted by the impressionists. Among them were Asher B. Durand (1796–1886), Frederick Church (1826–1900), Worthington Whittredge (1820–1910), Sanford R. Gifford (1824–1860), Albert Bierstadt (1830–1902), and John Frederick Kensett (1818–1872). They have also been called luminists because of their effective rendering of atmospheric subtleties and brilliance. Their landscapes were by no means limited to the Hudson valley; they painted the Rockies, the Andes, the western plains, the Berkshires, and the White Mountains.

It was not until the 1830s and 1840s that a new breed of artists painted people in places doing things people do. There appeared in those years a number of genre painters. William Sidney Mount (1807–1868) portrayed his farmer neighbors on Long Island, and George Caleb Bingham (1811–1879) in Kentucky and Missouri painted small-town and river scenes. They were considered unartistic by contemporary sophisticates but were popular with "the people." Bingham, forgotten for fifty years, was recognized as an American master only in the twentieth century.

Every aspect of the visual arts occupied American artists during the second half of the nineteenth century — sculpture, both monumental and sentimental (sometimes both at once), still life, illustration, reportage, portraits, fantasy, landscape, genre, social commentary, mural decoration. After the Civil War sculpture "escaped" from Rome and took to celebrating politicians, preachers, generals, admirals, pioneer women, and other favorites in bronze. War memorials appeared on village greens and in city parks, and small anecdotal sculptures, like the justifiably popular groups by John Rogers (1829–1904), appeared on parlor tables everywhere. Of these sculptors three stand out: John Q. A. Ward (1830–1910), Daniel Chester French (1850–1931), and, foremost, Augustus Saint-Gaudens (1848–1907). All were portrait sculptors who worked on both small and monumental scales. Ward is probably best known for his *Henry Ward Beecher* in Brooklyn, French for his seated *Lincoln* in the Lincoln Memorial in Washington, and Saint-Gaudens for his *General Sherman* in New York and the *Robert Gould Shaw Memorial* in Boston.

Most painters of any prominence still studied in Europe. One of those who went briefly but thought better of it was Winslow Homer (1836–1910) of Boston. During the Civil War he had been an artist-reporter for *Harper's Weekly,* but he gave up illustration to devote himself primarily to the out-of-doors and above all to the sea. He was arguably America's finest seascapist and watercolorist and most subtle genre painter, a master of light, a truth-teller free of sentimentality. His friend Eastman Johnson (1824–1906) went to Düsseldorf, Germany, to study, as did many young American artists then, and worked in Emanuel Leutze's studio on that painter's *Washington Crossing the Delaware,* a critically derided national icon. Johnson had a very successful career as a portrait and genre painter.

Thomas Eakins (1844–1916) of Philadelphia, like Homer, found little to his taste or temperament in Paris. He pursued a quiet, financially unsuccessful career as a portraitist of scrupulous veracity, a painter of poetic, albeit matter-of-fact, genre; he left a body of work that is one of the miracles of American painting. His portraits are as different in spirit and manner from those of his contemporary John Singer Sargent (1856–1925) or of William Merritt Chase (1849–1916) as probity is from panache. Few painters have enjoyed the popularity and acclaim in their day as Sargent and Chase did, and few deserved it more. Sargent was a muralist and portraitist as was John La Farge (1835–1910). James McNeill Whistler (1834–1903) was only marginally American. Like Benjamin West a century before, he made his reputation in Europe and saw no reason to return to the States. He deserves better than to be known as *Whistler's Mother*'s son. (His portrait of his mother is the only American painting in the Louvre.)

Two more modest talents of this period were William Harnett (1848–1892) and John F. Peto (1854–1907), who painted eye-foolers (trompe l'oeil) and made magic out of commonplace objects. Both were working in a long tradition of delightful foolery dating back to Raphaelle Peale (1774–1825), one of Charles Willson Peale's many painting progeny.

Toward the end of the century impressionism, born in France, permeated much of American painting. Mary Cassatt (1844–1926), a Philadelphian, went to Paris as a young woman and fell in with Edgar Degas and his circle and became one of them artistically. The many young artists flocking to Paris now were transformed by the visions of Monet and Renoir and Pissarro, and they saw the landscape in colors that the Hudson River school painters never glimpsed. Childe Hassam (1859–1935) was one of these, the best known of them today, but no painter of landscapes in America since has been untouched by the impressionists' discoveries. One, Albert Pinkham Ryder (1847–1917), stands darkly apart, however. He was in his time an abstract expressionist, but he threw his soul rather than his paint at his canvases full force and defiantly. A nineteenth-century spirit, Ryder was a twentieth-century discovery.

In the last years of the century, led by a painter who called himself Robert Henri (1865–1929), though his name was Cozad, there evolved a school of social realists with an aesthetic but not a political ax to grind. They believed in "the importance of life as the primary

motive of art" and threw aside the polite preoccupations of what has been called the genteel tradition of Sargent, Chase, and others. They would "tell it as it is." These artists — William Glackens (1870–1938), George Luks (1867–1933), Everett Shinn (1876–1953), John Sloan (1871–1951), principally — became known as the Ashcan school: they painted urban life with its underwear showing on laundry lines and its snowy streets blackened with soot. The time had come, they believed, to paint America not as a land of milk and honey but as a place where people live with all their faults and frustrations and escape hatches, their crowded streets and thronged beaches and honky-tonk.

When they closed the book on the nineteenth century, the first chapter of the volume they opened was called the Armory Show.

Wayne Craven, *Sculpture in America* (1968); E. P. Richardson, *A Short History of Painting in America: The Story of 450 Years* (1963).

Russell Lynes

See also Ashcan School; Audubon, John James; Cassatt, Mary; Copley, John Singleton; Eakins, Thomas; Folk Art; Homer, Winslow; Hudson River School; Morse, Samuel F. B.; Sargent, John Singer; Whistler, James McNeill.

II. Since the Armory Show

The 1913 Armory Show, which gave American artists and the public their first comprehensive look at the art produced by the modernist movement in Europe, had a profound effect on the way painting and sculpture in the United States were subsequently created. It also changed the way art was thought about. The American art world promptly divided into modernists and traditionalists, and their conflict often took the form of a fierce rivalry between an artistic minority that embraced the ideas of the European avant-garde and the majority who remained loyal to more familiar conservative styles. Although at first outnumbered, the minority that found in modernism its principal source of inspiration set the pace in artistic achievement for the remainder of the century.

The history of American painting and sculpture since 1913 is therefore, in large part, the history of American modernism and of the varying responses it met with in the course of the century. This history divides itself into two distinct periods. During the first, which began in 1913–1914 and ended in the early 1940s, the modernists worked under severe handicaps. With few exceptions, the public tended to be either hostile or indifferent to their work. Patronage was scarce and public ridicule common. Museums, the galleries, the collectors, the critics, and the academy generally regarded modernist art as aesthetic heresy, a betrayal of established standards if not indeed a threat to public morality. As a result, modernist artists were condemned to live and work in bohemian coteries and isolated enclaves outside the mainstream of American cultural life.

During the second period, which commenced with World War II and continues to the present day, the modernists acquired an ever-increasing measure of public recognition and artistic influence. By the end of the 1950s, their work had achieved a position of dominance in American cultural life. It now enjoyed widespread support from the institutions that had formerly spurned it, and these institutions were now more numerous and more powerful than before. For the first time, moreover, American modernist art occupied a prominent place in world esteem. Several modernists of the post–World War II period — Jackson Pollock, Mark Rothko, Willem de Kooning — became international celebrities.

This change paralleled a larger change in the relation between Europe and America. Until the beginning of World War II, Paris remained the unrivaled artistic capital of the Western world, the place where seminal art movements, from impressionism and postimpressionism in the nineteenth century to fauvism, cubism, and surrealism in the twentieth, were born and developed. It was thus to Paris that the first generation of American modernists looked for artistic leadership. It was to Paris that a significant number of the outstanding talents of that generation — Marsden Hartley, Max Weber, Man Ray, Morgan Russell, Patrick Henry Bruce, John Marin, and Alfred Maurer, among

others — traveled in order to establish contact with the art and the artists who were definitively altering the way painting and sculpture would henceforth be thought about. To meet the challenge of the new pictorial ideas to be found in the work of Paul Cézanne, Henri Matisse, Pablo Picasso, and others now became the irresistible imperative for this first generation of American modernists. Although their art remained in many ways American in fundamental outlook and character, Paris was nonetheless indispensable to their aesthetic orientation and to the standards by which this generation judged its achievements.

In the early 1940s, however, New York emerged for the first time as the artistic capital of the West. The Nazi occupation of Paris in 1940 marked the end of the reign that French art had enjoyed on the world scene for well over a century. In Nazi-occupied Europe, modernism — now stigmatized by Adolf Hitler as "degenerate" — was officially banned, and the United States became a refuge for many of the Europeans who had devoted their lives to it. It was to New York, in particular, that important representatives of the European avant-garde — not only artists but art dealers, art historians, museum curators, collectors, and writers on art — now expatriated themselves.

Their presence in New York during the war years had a powerful catalytic effect on American art and the whole cultural scene. European modernism still exerted an immense influence on the thinking of this emerging American vanguard, but with Europe itself in a state of political chaos and the future of its civilization in doubt, it seemed possible for American modernists to seize the artistic initiative, and they did. The result was the abstract expressionist movement — later dubbed the New York school — that catapulted American painting into a position of international dominance in the postwar era.

This development would have seemed unimaginable even a few years earlier. Between the two world wars, modernist art in America was very much on the defensive. New and important modernists came to prominence; Stuart Davis and Milton Avery were the most accomplished among the painters, and Gaston Lachaise, Elie Nadelman, and Alexander Calder, among the sculptors. Yet in the 1920s, the older generation of modernists had to some extent retreated from its avant-garde ambitions, seeking to entrench its art in a more recognizably American subject matter.

In the depression era of the thirties this nativist impulse acquired added political momentum with the emergence of two popular movements adamantly opposed to modernism and to the cosmopolitan culture it encompassed. One of these movements was called the American scene, which had its headquarters in the Midwest and specialized in idealized depictions of American rural, frontier, and small-town life. Its leading representatives were Thomas Hart Benton, Grant Wood, and John Steuart Curry, and its driving spirit was populist, isolationist, and xenophobic. Its regionalist outlook proscribed modernism and the metropolitan centers that fostered it as alien intrusions into the purity of American life.

The other antimodernist movement was the school of social realism that was tethered to the cultural and political program of the Communist party and its Popular Front. Social realists championed social consciousness in art under the banner of an antifascist crusade. The leading representatives of this school were Ben Shahn, Jack Levine, Jacob Lawrence, and William Gropper, and its principal focus was on class conflict, the plight of the poor and the dispossessed, and idealized depictions of the working class and rural poverty.

With the American economy in collapse in the thirties, both of these movements — the one essentially nativist, the other leftist — exerted a tremendous influence; the modernists were shunted off to the margins of American cultural life. Even the institution that was founded in 1929 to champion the cause of modernism — the Museum of Modern Art in New York — offered little support to the struggling American representatives of vanguard painting and sculpture. Although the museum was making its successful pioneering effort to introduce the American public to the classics of European modernism — Cézanne, Matisse, Picasso — its

first acquisition for its permanent collection was a railway landscape by the American realist Edward Hopper. It wasn't until the 1940s that the museum took up the cause of American modernism with real conviction.

A major element in the rise of the abstract expressionist movement in the early forties was its rejection of the social art of the thirties. Both the American scene painters and the school of social realism were shunned as too folksy, superficial, and propagandistic. There was a general turn toward a more inward, subjective, and psychological view of art. Psychoanalysis supplanted socialism and populism as a source of inspiration. In the early phase, abstract expressionism emphasized symbolism and myth; psychological archetypes replaced history and politics as appropriate subject matter for art.

This turn toward a more subjective and psychological art was greatly abetted by the influence of the French surrealists, who formed a significant part of the exiled European artists' community in New York during the war. It was one of the central beliefs of the surrealists that art should attempt to draw upon the unconscious depths of the psyche for its subjects, and toward this end they advocated a technique known as automatism as the most effective means of gaining access to the unconscious. This involved the temporary suspension of consciously planned composition in favor of improvisation and free association.

Automatism, both as an idea and as a technique, was seized upon by the abstract expressionists as a means of liberating their art from the obligation to deal with social and political subjects. Where they differed from the surrealists, however, was in their tendency to carry this automatist method into the realm of pure abstraction. As abstract expressionism developed in the late forties and fifties, Pollock, Rothko, Robert Motherwell, Adolph Gottlieb, and others removed the last traces of legible symbolism from their canvases. Painting became completely abstract. It was as a movement in large-scale abstract painting — and as a mode of abstraction based largely on the automatist method — that the New York school made its international impact from the fifties onward.

The sculpture of the New York school did not have an impact equal to that of its painting. It was generally true of American art in the twentieth century that sculpture lagged behind painting in setting the pace of aesthetic innovation and artistic achievement. If Gaston Lachaise and Elie Nadelman, both European-born, were exceptions to the rule in the period between the wars, it was because of their special ability to revitalize the classical tradition of European figurative sculpture and give it an American accent.

The most original sculptor in the interwar period, however, was Alexander Calder, who had been trained as an engineer and developed his artistic gifts only after he moved to Paris in the late twenties. Drawing his inspiration from Joan Miró, Piet Mondrian, and other Parisian exponents of abstract art, Calder applied his engineering skills to the creation of a new sculptural genre called the mobile. It was an audacious innovation that won the artist a good deal of popularity in America after World War II. Another important sculptor to emerge in the early thirties was Isamu Noguchi, whose highly simplified abstract stone carvings reflected both his Japanese heritage and the influence of Constantin Brancusi, the leading modernist sculptor of his generation in Paris.

The preeminent sculptor of the abstract expressionist generation was David Smith. Beginning as a painter who looked to cubism, surrealism, and abstraction for his artistic ideas, Smith seized upon the methods of cubist collage as a means of creating open-form sculptural construction. Following the example of Picasso and Julio González, he adopted welded metal as his principal material, and it was he, more than any other sculptor of his generation, who made open-form welded sculpture — sometimes called "drawing in space" — a major genre. Although at times employing symbolic images in the manner of the abstract expressionist painters, Smith's sculpture was largely abstract. His achievement was immense; his was the most important body of modernist sculpture produced by an American in this century. But recognition of that achievement came more slowly to Smith than to the painters of the New York school. To the world at large, the New York school has always been identified with painting.

The United States had never before produced an art movement that had such an impact on the international art world, and it was inevitable that so powerful a movement would meet with opposition. The first attempt to supplant the authority of the abstract expressionists — and of abstraction itself as a mode of artistic expression — came in the late fifties in the work of Jasper Johns and Robert Rauschenberg, painters who reintroduced recognizable images and objects into paintings and collage-like constructions that still owed something to abstract expressionist methods. The images that were now incorporated into art — commonplace items like flags, targets, and maps in Johns's work, and junk materials like rubber tires and stuffed animals in Rauschenberg's — had a facetious quality that mocked the psychological and metaphysical gravity of abstract expressionism. This impulse toward mockery and irony proved to be the basis of one of the principal movements of the 1960s: pop art.

The pop art movement that erupted in New York in the early sixties in the work of Andy Warhol, Roy Lichtenstein, Claes Oldenburg, James Rosenquist, and others specialized in making the iconography of popular culture — advertising, comic strips, media images — the basis of painting and sculpture. This movement marked a decisive shift away from the inwardness and subjectivity of abstract expressionism, and it became immensely popular and influential. Yet it did not mark the end of abstraction as a dominant strain in American art, for there also emerged in the sixties two new schools of abstraction: color-field painting — notably in the work of Helen Frankenthaler — which refined and simplified the legacy of abstract expressionism in a style that focused on pure color; and minimalist painting and sculpture that favored more geometrical and impersonal forms.

As a result of these diverse and conflicting art movements of the sixties, no single style or movement any longer enjoyed a position of historically sanctioned dominance. American art was more openly eclectic than it had been at any time since the war, and no single school enjoyed the position of unrivaled leadership that had characterized the abstract expressionists in the fifties. Not only pop art and minimalism and color-field abstraction but a broad range of representational styles, including a revival of realism, now competed in an open field. New fashions in art turned up with increasing regularity — neoexpressionism, for example, was one of the sensations of the 1980s — but the American art scene was too big, too varied, too crowded with competing ideas, styles, and claims, for any single group or movement to prevail.

What had been permanently altered, too, was the notion of the modernist artist as an isolated and rejected figure in American cultural life. The visual arts had entered the cultural mainstream with an impact that gave every sign of being irreversible.

Dore Ashton, *Modern American Sculpture* (1968); Milton W. Brown, *American Painting from the Armory Show to the Depression* (1955); Irving Sandler, *The Triumph of American Painting: A History of Abstract Expressionism* (1970).

HILTON KRAMER

See also Abstract Expressionism; Armory Show; Calder, Alexander; de Kooning, Willem; Guggenheim, Peggy; Johns, Jasper; Lawrence, Jacob; Nevelson, Louise; Noguchi, Isamu; O'Keeffe, Georgia; Pollock, Jackson; Pop Art; Warhol, Andy.

PANAMA CANAL

In the 1840s, as American settlers began pouring into Oregon and California, the United States sought a way of facilitating ocean travel to the Pacific Coast. The government therefore negotiated an agreement with New Granada (a nation composed of present-day Colombia and Panama) for transit rights from the Caribbean Sea to the Pacific across the narrow Isthmus of Panama. When the discovery of gold in California in 1848 vastly increased westward migration, the United States funded the construction of the Panama Railroad. But both America and Great Britain dreamed of building a canal across either Panama or Nicaragua, with the two countries agreeing (Clayton-Bulwer Treaty, 1850) that neither would seek independent rights over such a canal. The United States, however, became increasingly intent on exclusive control, particularly after the Spanish-American War (1898) brought the nation new territory in both the Caribbean and the Pacific. The British were persuaded to relinquish their claim in the Hay-Pauncefote Treaty (1901).

The next question was where to locate the canal. A French company under Ferdinand de Lesseps had started construction of a sea-level canal in Panama in 1881, but the project went bankrupt after a few years. In 1901, a U.S. commission recommended that the canal go through Nicaragua rather than Panama. But representatives of the New Panama Canal Company (which had taken over the French rights in Panama) lobbied vigorously for the Panama route, and President Theodore Roosevelt settled on it when the company reduced its asking price from $109 million to $40 million. The U.S. commission then reversed itself in January 1902, and in June, Congress authorized construction of the canal through Panama.

Early the next year, Congress ratified the Hay-Herrán Treaty, which granted the United States a strip of land ten miles wide across the isthmus for $10 million in cash and an annuity of $250,000 per year. But the senate of Colombia, hoping for a higher price, refused to approve the treaty. Shortly thereafter (November 3, 1903), a Panamanian uprising was engineered by Philippe Bunau-Varilla (a representative of the New Panama Canal Company), other canal supporters, and some local residents. The United States provided indirect support and promptly recognized the new Republic of Panama. Within a week the Hay-Bunau-Varilla Treaty was signed, granting the United States a renewable ninety-nine-year lease on the Canal Zone in exchange for the same payment that had been offered to New Granada. The treaty was ratified by the U.S. Senate in February 1904.

Various logistical problems, indecision about whether to build a sea-level or a lock canal, and the devastations of tropical disease delayed construction until 1906. A lock canal was decided upon, and work began on surveys and construction of the necessary facilities. Col. William Gorgas made a crucial contribution with his eradication of yellow fever and malaria. Col. G. W. Goethals of the U.S. Army Corps of Engineers directed most of the actual construction, which cost well over $300 million and involved the excavation of 240 million cubic yards of earth. The canal, forty miles in length, opened to shipping in August 1914 and was formally dedicated on July 12, 1920. In 1921, the United States paid Colombia $25 million as redress for the loss of Panama; in exchange, Colombia formally recognized Panama's independence.

In the 1960s and 1970s resentment mounted in Panama over the terms of the original agreement. Negotiators, working in an increasingly hostile atmosphere involving demonstrations and sometimes violence, tried to resolve the sticking points and arrive at a new treaty. At issue were the treaty's duration, economic benefits to be accorded Panama, and the right of the United States to expand canal facilities. The matter became a campaign issue in the 1976 presidential elections.

Finally on September 7, 1977, President Jimmy Carter and Panama's chief of government, Brig. Gen. Omar Torrijos Herrera, signed two treaties in the presence of twenty-six representatives of Western Hemisphere nations. The United States agreed to turn the canal over to Panama on December 31, 1999. The treaties included provisions protecting America's interests in the canal and increasing Panama's economic benefits.

See also Expansion, Continental and Overseas.

PARIS, TREATY OF (1783)

The Treaty of Paris of 1783, negotiated between the United States and Great Britain, ended the revolutionary war and recognized American independence.

The talks began in April 1782, after the American-French victory at Yorktown led to the toppling of Lord North's Tory government and the naming of a Whig, Lord Rockingham, as prime minister and Lord Shelburne as foreign

minister. The Continental Congress named a five-member commission to negotiate a treaty — John Adams, Benjamin Franklin, John Jay, Thomas Jefferson, and Henry Laurens. Laurens, however, was captured by a British warship and held in the Tower of London until the end of the war, and Jefferson did not leave the United States in time to take part in the negotiations. Thus, they were conducted by Adams, Franklin, and Jay.

The French foreign minister, the Comte de Vergennes, expected the Americans to coordinate their diplomatic strategy with the French, but the Americans distrusted the French attachment to their cause and pursued an independent course. Among the team's notable achievements were British recognition of American independence (a point pressed most strongly by Jay); the securing (by Adams) of American fishermen's right of access to the Grand Banks off the coast of Newfoundland and other traditional fisheries in Canadian waters; and Great Britain's ceding to the United States all territory between the Allegheny Mountains on the east and the Mississippi River on the west, thereby doubling the size of the new nation. For its part, the United States agreed to use its powers to end the persecution of Loyalists by state and local governments and to restore their property confiscated during the war. Both countries agreed not to block creditors from seeking to recover debts owed to them.

The preliminary articles of peace were signed by Adams, Franklin, and Jay for the United States and David Hartley for Great Britain on November 30, 1782. The final treaty was signed on September 3, 1783, and ratified by the Continental Congress early in 1784.

See also Revolution.

PARTY CONVENTIONS

The American party convention is a distinctive institution, with no exact counterpart in other Western democracies. For much of the nineteenth century, and in a vestigial form down to the present, conventions made up of delegates selected by subunits of the state and national parties chose nominees for elective offices. In their full vigor, they also adopted platforms that set forth the party's position on salient issues, created agencies to manage party affairs, and stimulated unity and enthusiasm within the ranks.

Before the invention of the delegate convention, parties in many states relied on their members in the legislature to nominate candidates for statewide offices. At the national level, the Democratic-Republicans utilized a congressional caucus between 1800 and 1824 to choose candidates for president and vice president. After the repudiation of the congressional caucus in 1824, presidential candidates in that year, and in 1828, were placed in nomination in various ways: by state legislatures, state party conventions, and legislative caucuses. But by 1844 most state parties had adopted the convention system.

The distinction of holding the first national convention fell to a third party, the Anti-Masons. Originating in New York in 1827, the party acquired formidable strength there and in adjacent states by 1830. Its imaginative leaders aspired to build the Anti-Masons into the major opponents of the dominant Jacksonians. A preparatory convention, held in Philadelphia in September 1830, issued a call for a second convention to meet in Baltimore on September 26, 1831. There the delegates nominated William Wirt of Maryland, a former attorney general under Presidents James Monroe and John Adams, for the presidency, with Amos Ellmaker of Pennsylvania as his running mate. They also adopted an "Address to the People," appointed a national committee, and scheduled a future convention to meet in December 1835.

The two major parties also held national conventions in preparation for the 1832 election. The adherents of Henry Clay, newly mobilized under the National Republican label, met in Baltimore in December 1831. Delegates from eighteen states attended. Clay was nominated with only one dissenting vote, together with John Sergeant of Pennsylvania. The Democrats convened in Baltimore in May 1832. Over three hundred delegates represented every state except Missouri. Because it was universally accepted that Andrew Jackson would run for a second term, the main purpose of the convention was to select a nominee for the vice presidency. After adopting a rule that a two-thirds vote would be required for any nomination (a rule that held until 1936 and that greatly enhanced the South's power in the Democratic party), Martin Van Buren of New York was placed on the ticket with Jackson.

Over the next few decades, the national convention evolved forms and rituals that were to persist down to the mid-twentieth century. A temporary chairman delivered a rousing keynote speech, designed to promote party harmony and lambaste the opposition. On occasion, disputes over the credentials of rival delegations from a state required tactful settlement. Then the platform would be debated and adopted. Next came the florid nominating speeches, followed by boisterous demonstrations staged by the nominee's adherents. This phase of the proceedings was often protracted when state delegations put forward favorite sons, usually to enhance their bargaining positions. The climactic event was the balloting, when each state delegation was called upon to announce its votes. On about one-half of such occasions, a single ballot sufficed, but at other times the roll calls might continue until exhaustion (and back-room deals) produced a victor. In 1924 the Democrats required 103 ballots to select John W. Davis in the lengthiest of all conventions. With rare exceptions, the most memorable of which was Franklin D. Roosevelt's flight to Chicago in 1932, the nominees did not deliver acceptance speeches until after the advent of television.

The old-style conventions were arenas where the chieftains of rival factions met in "smoke-filled rooms" to negotiate the choice of nominees. When deadlocks developed between preconvention favorites, they were broken by the selection of a dark horse. The first such outcome occurred in 1844, when the Democrats settled on James K. Polk. The adoption of party platforms, initiated by the Democrats in 1840, occasionally engendered extensive controversy. The Democrats, in particular, engaged in some notable wrangles. Most divisive were those in 1860 over the slavery issue, in 1896 over the plank endorsing "free silver," and in 1948, when the convention's stand on civil rights produced serious defections in the South.

Twice national conventions were unable to resolve factional feuds. In 1860, when the Democrats met in Charleston, numerous southern delegates bolted after losing a platform fight. A second convention in Baltimore failed to heal the schism. The rump convention then nominated Stephen A. Douglas of Illinois; the seceders chose John C. Breckenridge of Kentucky. In 1912 Theodore Roosevelt belatedly challenged the renomination of his one-time protégé William Howard Taft. After a bitter wrangle over the seating of contested delegates, the Roosevelt supporters withdrew, formed the Progressive party, and hailed the militant ex-president as their standard-bearer.

In the post–World War II era, many new influences undermined the importance and altered the character of the national conventions. The direct primary (first introduced in 1912, but of minor importance until the 1950s) enabled party members to vote directly for delegates pledged to particular candidates and thus greatly reduced the convention's decision-making role. Increasingly after 1952, success in winning primary contests determined the nomination. Since that year, only single ballots have been needed to select nominees.

With the advent of television coverage, the format of the conventions was tailored to accommodate the new medium. Key events were carefully staged for prime-time audiences, fewer candidates were placed in nomination, demonstrations were curtailed, and television commentators prowled the floor to reveal what lay behind the scene.

After 1968, elaborate measures to reform delegate-selection procedures in order to reduce the influence of bosses and make the conventions representative of the rank and file of the parties completed the transformation of the national conventions. They became quadrennial media events, where the results of the primaries were ratified and the prize was awarded to the individual who had won the most delegates. The victor, in turn, was now accorded the privilege of naming his running mate. The conventions survive, but they bear only a superficial resemblance in form and function to those that held sway from the Age of Jackson through the era of the New Deal.

Richard C. Bain and Judith H. Parris, *Convention Decisions and Voting Records*, 2nd ed. (1973); James S. Chase, *Emergence of the Presidential Nominating Convention, 1789–1832* (1973).

RICHARD P. McCORMICK

PATERSON SILK STRIKE

In 1913, a six-month general strike by 25,000 workers shut down the textile mills of Paterson, New Jersey. The strike began in January with a walkout at Doherty and Company, the largest mill, after the introduction of new looms that allowed a worker who had formerly tended one or two looms to work three or four simultaneously. Workers feared that employers producing more silk with less labor would begin layoffs.

The Industrial Workers of the World (IWW) played a key role in the strike, organizing a strike committee with representatives from each mill. The committee exercised considerable independence; the IWW leaders, Bill Haywood, Elizabeth Gurley Flynn, and Carlo Tresca, acted primarily as advisers. The press blamed the strike on IWW "agitators," most of whom spent at least part of the strike behind bars, as did 1,850 strikers. Employers refused to discuss the workers' demands for an eight-hour day, a daily minimum wage of twelve dollars, and the abolition of the four-loom system.

The strike continued through late spring. John Reed, a left-wing journalist, organized a pageant at Madison Square Garden to raise funds. On June 7, 1,000 workers performed a six-part reenactment of the strike's most dramatic moments, including orations delivered by Tresca, Flynn, and Haywood at the funeral of a murdered worker. A spectacular success as theater, the pageant failed as a fund-raising event.

Employers infiltrated scabs into the mills, and skilled ribbon weavers reached shop-by-shop settlements in early July. Having broken the unity of the strike, employers announced that only those who agreed to work under pre-strike conditions could return to their jobs. On

July 28, the strike ended with no gains for the workers. The defeat forced the IWW to abandon its attempt to organize workers in the Northeast, beginning a long period of retrenchment and consolidation for the union.

See also Labor; Reed, John; Textile Industry.

PAUL, ALICE

(1885–1977), feminist and suffragist. Born into a Quaker family in Moorestown, New Jersey, Paul was raised in an intellectual and religious environment. Her forebears included on her mother's side William Penn and on her father's side the Winthrops of Massachusetts; her maternal grandfather was one of the founders of Swarthmore College. Paul graduated from Swarthmore in 1905 and then attended the New York School of Philanthropy (later Columbia University School of Social Work), the University of Pennsylvania, and a training school for Quakers in Woodbridge, England. She remained in England from 1907 to 1910.

It was during those years that Paul, while studying and working as a case worker for a London settlement house, served her apprenticeship for what became her vocation: the struggle for women's rights. She was enlisted by England's militant suffragists Emmeline and Christobel Pankhurst. Her education as an activist was acquired through a series of arrests, imprisonments, hunger strikes, and forced feedings. She learned how to generate publicity for the cause and how to capitalize on that publicity.

Paul enrolled again at the University of Pennsylvania on her return to the United States in 1910. There she earned a Ph.D. in sociology and began to situate herself in the American suffrage movement. In 1912 she launched her full-time suffrage career. Working first within the National American Woman Suffrage Association (NAWSA), Paul gathered about her a group of young women, many of whom had also worked with the Pankhursts in England and who were willing to depart from the association's conservative tactics.

Paul broke with the NAWSA in 1914 and co-founded the Congressional Union, dedicated to seeking a federal constitutional amendment for woman suffrage. In 1916, she founded the National Woman's party. She led pickets at the White House and Congress and despite America's entry into World War I refused to abandon these tactics. She and her colleagues were arrested and imprisoned; they engaged in hunger strikes and endured forced feedings at the hands of authorities. Ultimately her tactics, as well as persuasion from Carrie Chapman Catt, induced President Woodrow Wilson to make a federal suffrage amendment a war measures priority, a stand he had previously refused to take. Paul was a pivotal force in the passage and ratification in 1920 of the Nineteenth Amendment.

In 1923, Paul proposed an Equal Rights Amendment to the Constitution. Overcoming the opposition of women's organizations who feared the loss of protective legislation, she helped gain acceptance of an ERA plank in the platforms of both major political parties in 1944. She continued to work actively out of the National Woman's party headquarters in Washington, D.C., until failing health forced her to relocate to the Connecticut countryside in 1972. Even then she continued to provide inspiration to new generations of women's rights activists until her death in 1977.

Throughout her life, Alice Paul remained personally conservative and professionally demanding of both herself and her colleagues. She did not relinquish power readily nor could she be easily persuaded to depart from the methods and tactics she had learned from the Pankhursts in England. But her vision for women always transcended her conservatism and rigidity. "I think if we get freedom for women, then they are probably going to do a lot of things that I wish they wouldn't do," she said shortly before her death. "But it seems to me that isn't our business to say what they should do with it. It is our business to see that they get it."

Inez Haynes Irwin, *Up Hill with Banners Flying* (1964); Christine A. Lunardini, *From Equal Suffrage to Equal Rights: Alice Paul and the National Woman's Party, 1910–1928* (1986); Doris Stevens, *Jailed for Freedom* (1920).

CHRISTINE A. LUNARDINI

See also Feminist Movement; National American Woman Suffrage Association; National Woman's Party; Suffrage.

PEACE CORPS

The Peace Corps sends volunteers abroad to aid developing countries in fields such as education, agriculture, and health care. Founded in 1961 during the administration of President John F. Kennedy, it was especially popular in the late 1960s among individuals interested in adventure, philanthropy, and political activism. Volunteers were typically recent college graduates.

After the Vietnam War and Watergate, the Peace Corps fell out of style and suffered from a lack of recruits and financial support. It was incorporated into a larger agency, ACTION, in 1971 but was revived in 1983 by the Reagan administration, which attempted to use it to advance a conservative ideology.

Today, some see the Peace Corps as a proper vehicle for expressing various versions of American values or as a way to promote peace and understanding between peoples. Others charge that it is a form of American interventionism or a means by which Americans assuage guilt caused by their relative affluence and political dominance. Because of its status as a government agency, its budget and agenda have often been a focus of partisan disputes.

The opening of Eastern Europe to American interests in 1990 increased the Peace Corps' membership and funding. More recent volunteers have been on average older than their predecessors and more experienced in specialized fields. The organization is characterized by a concentration on environmental issues and increasing presence in nontraditional urban settings.

See also Kennedy, John F.

PEARL HARBOR, ATTACK ON

The Japanese air attack on Pearl Harbor (on the Hawaiian island of Oahu), December 7, 1941, was the climax of a decade of rising tension between Japan and the United States. Throughout the 1930s, Japan had been steadily encroaching on China, and the United States had been trying to contain Japan's expansion. Since America supplied more than half of Japan's iron, steel, and oil, Japan was reluctant to push the United States too far, but it was also intent on getting control of its own sources of raw materials. On September 27, 1940, Japan joined the Triple Alliance with Italy and Germany and began to expand into northern Indochina. The United States, in response, placed an embargo on aviation gasoline, scrap metal, steel, and iron. After Japan's seizure of the rest of Indochina in July 1941, President Franklin D. Roosevelt closed the Panama Canal to Japanese shipping and added oil to the embargo list. In October 1941 Gen. Hideki Tojo, leader of the Japanese pro-war party, became premier.

Negotiations seeking a peaceful settlement went on in Washington, but both sides seem to have decided that war was inevitable. On November 25, 1941, though continuing the discussions, the Japanese dispatched aircraft carriers eastward toward Hawaii and began massing troops on the Malayan border. American military leaders, expecting a Japanese attack on Malaya, gave only general warnings to U.S. forces in Pearl Harbor. Adm. Husband E. Kimmel and Gen. Walter C. Short, in command on Oahu, took few precautions; there was no effective air patrol, and neither ships nor planes were safely dispersed.

Japanese planes attacked Pearl Harbor at 7:55 A.M., December 7; a second wave hit an hour later. By the time the planes returned to their carriers at 9:45, most of the American planes on Oahu were wrecked; eight battleships, three destroyers, and three cruisers had been put out of action; and two battleships, *Oklahoma* and *Arizona,* were utterly destroyed. A total of 2,323 U.S. servicemen had been killed. The next day President Roosevelt spoke for the American people when, before a joint session of Congress, he proclaimed December 7 a "date which will live in infamy." With only one dissent, Congress granted Roosevelt's request to recognize the state of war that existed between the United States and Japan. With that vote, America entered World War II.

See also World War II.

PEI, I. M.

(1917–   ), architect. I. M. Pei has based a successful worldwide career on the modernist dictum that abstract forms, derived from technology and function, can be used sensitively in workaday commercial buildings, large urban schemes, and monuments. The son of an important Chinese family, Pei was a student in Walter Gropius's master classes in architecture at Harvard in the mid-1940s and has never parted from the spare aesthetic vocabulary developed by Gropius at the German Bauhaus. At the same time, he has always insisted that the architect's obedience to modernism does not preclude culturally sensitive, even romantic, architectural design.

Pei's career is unusual for a high-profile architect because of its origins in commercial development. From 1948 to 1955 he headed the design staff of Webb & Knapp, the contracting division of William Zeckendorf's real-estate empire. In his large-scale redevelopment work for Zeckendorf, Pei showed a sensitivity to architectural form and urban design that made him a leader in the government-supported urban renewal schemes of the 1960s. His master plan for Boston's Government Center area (1959–1963), though perhaps too drastic in its effect on the cityscape, created a striking complex of buildings and spacious plazas in a decayed area. His 1964 commission for the John F. Kennedy Memorial Library in Boston (completed 1979) and the 1978 East Wing of the National Gallery of Art in Washington gained him an international reputation, which was capped by a commission from the French government to restore and replan the Louvre in Paris (1989–   ). His design for the museum, centering around a glass pyramid in the courtyard as a new main entrance, is both his most controversial and his most prestigious creation to date.

Pei is renowned for buildings that turn abstract shapes, elegantly if monochromatically finished, into breathtaking monuments. His cultural edifices, especially the East Wing, are known for exquisite siting and romantically expansive interior spaces.

The commercial buildings designed by Pei and his partners, Henry Cobb and James Ingo Freed, are equally striking transformations of modern materials into great minimalist sculptures. The elegant prism of the John Hancock Building in Boston (chiefly by Cobb) was first reviled as inhuman for its size and materials, especially when a design miscalculation made its windows fall out into the street at random; with that problem corrected, the building has since been embraced as a city landmark.

Neither a utopian planner nor a devotee of beauty above all, which sets him apart from most of Gropius's other protégés, Pei can be faulted for a preoccupation with high-prestige, large-scale work that slights more modest visions of architecture. But within the terms set for modern architecture by Gropius and its other early masters — the building as abstract form; the architect as collaborator with partners, investors, planners, and other experts; the idea of using the same technology-oriented design means to reshape both private and public realms — I. M. Pei has been a masterful and humane demonstrator of the uses of modernism.

Carter Wiseman, *I. M. Pei* (1990).

MILES DAVID SAMSON

See also Architecture.

PEOPLE'S PARTY

The People's (Populist) party was organized in St. Louis in February 1892 to speak for small producers, especially farmers, against the entrenched interests of railroads, bankers, corporations, and the politicians they influenced. Many Populists were veterans of earlier reform movements, but the party's most significant forerunner was the Farmers' Alliance, which had led the agrarian revolt of the 1880s. The alliance had first tried to influence the two major parties, but by 1892 those in favor of establishing a third party had prevailed.

In Omaha on July 4, 1892, the Populists nominated James B. Weaver, a former Union general, for president and James Field, an ex-Confederate from Virginia, for vice president. The Omaha Platform, written by Ignatius Donnelly and adapted from the earlier alliance program, called for government ownership of communication and transportation, the free coinage of silver, a progressive income tax, paper currency, the direct election of senators, the eight-hour day, and a new "Subtreasury" scheme for creating agricultural credit. Weaver received a million votes, carrying five western states, but the Populists made little headway among non-farm workers. Nor did they attract much support in the South, where sectional loyalties, white solidarity, widespread electoral irregularities, and some violence kept the Democratic party solidly in control.

By 1894, a split had developed between those Populists still committed to the Omaha Platform and those (including the national chairman, Herman E. Taubeneck) who advocated dropping the platform and building a new coalition with the Democratic party on the issue of the free coinage of silver. The latter view prevailed, and in 1896 the Populists accepted the Democratic nominee for president, William Jennings Bryan, as their candidate. An effort to maintain their independence by nominating a different vice presidential candidate, Tom Watson of Georgia, brought only bitterness and confusion.

When Bryan lost, the Populists were left with neither their former third-party significance nor a winning coalition. Rising farm prices in the late 1890s completed the party's dissolution. Nevertheless, their proposals were remembered, and many were instituted in the years that followed.

See also Elections: 1892, 1896; Farmers' Alliance; Populism; Third Parties.

PERKINS, FRANCES

(1880–1965), social reformer and U.S. secretary of labor. Perkins grew up in Worcester, Massachusetts, where her father ran a stationery business. She was raised in comfortable, middle-class, Republican circumstances. Perkins attended Worcester Classical High School, a largely male institution, and then went to Mount Holyoke College, graduating as president of the class of 1902. (She cherished the Holyoke experience for the rest of her life, serving on the college's board of governors and remaining involved in decisions affecting the school.) She taught physics and biology for several years, moving to Lake Forest, Illinois, in 1904. There she became involved in the social settlement movement, which kindled the interest in social reform that was to govern her life.

In 1907, Perkins moved to Philadelphia and then to New York City where she worked for social reform groups and simultaneously earned a master's degree in sociology and economics from Columbia University. In 1910 she became secretary of the New York Consumers' League where she investigated labor conditions and successfully lobbied the state legislature for a law to restrict the hours of women workers to fifty-four hours a week. Her association with Al Smith during those years led eventually to her appointment in 1918 as the first woman to serve on the New York State Industrial Commission. She became chair of the commission in 1926 and industrial commissioner of the state of New York in 1928. She was reappointed to that office by Governor Franklin D. Roosevelt in 1929 and retained it until her appointment by him as secretary of labor in 1933.

When she married Paul Caldwell Wilson in 1913, Perkins successfully fought to retain her own name. Until her husband lost much of his inheritance in 1918, Perkins was involved with volunteer work. Thereafter, she worked to support her husband and child, a task that was to become increasingly important as Wilson began exhibiting the mental irrationality that was to keep him institutionalized for much of his later years.

The first female cabinet member in U.S. history and one of only two Roosevelt cabinet appointees to serve throughout his tenure, Perkins brought to the job an unwavering devotion to social reform. She demanded, and got from Roosevelt, a commitment to support federal initiatives in the areas of unemployment relief and public works, insurance to guard workers from the hazards of old age and unemployment, and efforts to regulate child labor as well as wages and hours for adults. These became the cornerstones of the New Deal's policies for depression relief and reform. Carefully conceived under Perkins's watchful eyes and shepherded by her through the intricacies of the political process, the Social Security Act and the Fair Labor Standards Act remain monuments to her ability to make progress through incremental steps and to her mastery of the art of compromise.

Although Roosevelt leaned heavily on her, Perkins's strong attachment to social justice rendered her an unpopular figure in Congress and the press. She alienated business but won over the leaders of organized labor by resisting pressure from industrialists to intervene in strikes. She refused to succumb to threats of impeachment when right-wing congressional leaders urged her to deport Harry Bridges, leader of the Longshoremen's Union and a suspected communist, without appropriate legal action.

Perkins resigned her position after Roosevelt's death in 1945. Thereafter, she wrote a best-selling book, *The Roosevelt I Knew,* lectured widely, and accepted a professorship in the School of Industrial and Labor Relations at Cornell University.

George Martin, *Madam Secretary: Frances Perkins* (1976); Susan Ware, *Beyond Suffrage: Women in the New Deal* (1981).

ALICE KESSLER-HARRIS

See also Labor; New Deal; Settlement Houses; Social Security.

PERSHING, JOHN J.

(1860–1948), army commander. Pershing became the most famous American soldier of the World War I era because of his successful command of the American Expeditionary Forces (AEF) in France.

Pershing was born in Missouri and graduated from West Point in 1886. Prior to his baptism of fire at San Juan Hill in the Spanish-American War, he saw frontier duty as a cavalry officer, taught at and earned a law degree from the University of Nebraska, and served briefly at West Point. Although he impressed superiors with his bravery in Cuba, it was not until his

service in 1899–1903 against the Moros on Mindanao in the Philippines that he distinguished himself as a commander. Because of this, he won a rare promotion from captain to brigadier general in 1906. His next great opportunity came in 1916 when he led an eleven-thousand-man punitive expedition into Mexico in pursuit of the Mexican leader Pancho Villa, who had raided an American outpost in New Mexico. Although the expedition did not catch Villa, it probably deterred similar raids, at least during the eleven months the troops were in Mexico.

When the United States entered World War I in April 1917, Pershing was a major general and the only officer of that rank who had held a semi-independent command. When Secretary of War Newton D. Baker selected him to command an expedition to France, no one knew how large the army would be or how it would coordinate with the Allied forces. Pershing, accompanied by a small staff, sailed for France in May 1917. In his talks with the Allied leaders, he quickly grasped the desperation of the French situation after a great defeat that spring and called for a much larger force than the War Department had deemed possible. With the failure of a British offensive and the collapse of Russia in the fall, the Allies realized that more American troops would be necessary, and the British offered to supply the required shipping. But they wanted the Americans to serve as replacements in their ranks. Pershing argued forcefully with both the British prime minister David Lloyd George and the French premier Georges Clemenceau that the American troops should fight as a separate army under its own flag. In several conferences, the argument continued until the great German offensives in the spring of 1918 forced the issue.

Ultimately 2 million Americans served under Pershing's command in the AEF. It is a tribute to Pershing that the foundation he and his staff had so carefully laid was able to sustain such a huge force. In the summer of 1918, the AEF went on the offensive. From September 26 to November 11, it fought the greatest battle in American history to that point in the Meuse-Argonne campaign; it proved to be a major contribution to the Allied victory. Pershing's achievement rested on his ability to pick and command the loyalty of good subordinates, his organizing and managerial skills, and his iron will.

After the war, Congress promoted him to the unique rank of general of the armies, and he served as chief of staff of the army from 1921 to 1924. His memoir, *My Experiences in the World War* (1931), won the Pulitzer Prize for history in 1932.

Donald Smythe, *Pershing: General of the Armies* (1986); Frank E. Vandiver, *Black Jack: The Life and Times of John J. Pershing,* 2 vols. (1977).

EDWARD M. COFFMAN

See also World War I.

PERSONAL LIBERTY LAWS

Personal liberty laws, 1780–1861, were statutes designed to prevent slave owners from reclaiming slaves who had escaped to the free states. Although the Constitution granted owners the right to reclaim runaways, nearly all the free states thwarted them by passing antikidnapping and noncooperation laws. Ohio, Pennsylvania, and New York, for example, required claimants to obtain search warrants and assured accused blacks of jury trials. In 1842, however, this strategy was crippled when the Supreme Court, in *Prigg* v. *Pennsylvania* (1842), ruled that state laws obstructing the right of slave owners to reclaim slaves were unconstitutional.

Undeterred, in 1843 Massachusetts passed a new type of personal liberty law, which banned the use of state officials and facilities to catch runaways. This forced claimants to rely solely on federal officials, who were in short supply. In 1850, Congress reacted by passing the Fugitive Slave Act, which required all citizens to help apprehend runaways or face imprisonment and fines. Nonetheless, northern states continued to pass laws intended to protect runaways.

See also Abolitionist Movement; Fugitive Slave Law.

PETROLEUM INDUSTRY

See Oil Industry.

PHILADELPHIA CONVENTION

The Philadelphia Convention of 1787 (also known as the Federal Convention or the Constitutional Convention) was a landmark in American and world history. Both its handiwork, the Constitution of the United States, and its example of a people's representatives using reason and experience to decide how to govern themselves had profound influence on subsequent experiments in government.

The convention met in the State House (now called Independence Hall) in Philadelphia from May 25 to September 17, 1787. Fifty-five delegates from twelve of the thirteen states (Rhode Island did not send delegates) took part in its deliberations.

The convention was the result of a campaign to reform the first charter of government of the United States, the Articles of Confederation. Throughout the 1780s, politicians who thought in national terms worried that the Confederation faced problems its government was too weak to solve. Former allies, such as France and Spain, and its former adversary, Great Britain, restricted trade with the new nation and hampered America's development of its western territories. The Confederation Congress lacked the power to resolve boundary disputes between the states, to prevent states from imposing tariffs and other restrictions on interstate commerce, or to compel the states to meet requisitions issued to finance the Confederation. The Confederation even lacked an independent source of revenue, and plans in 1781 and 1783 to grant Congress authority to levy a 5 percent tax on imports had failed. Because all thirteen states had to ratify amendments, one state's refusal could block any attempt to amend the Articles.

Advocates of reform exchanged correspondence to muster support for a convention to revise the Articles, laying the foundation for interstate conferences and conventions seeking similar goals. In 1785, delegates from Maryland and Virginia, meeting in the Mount Vernon Conference, set a precedent for interstate conferences on reform. In 1786, hoping to extend this success, some proposed that the states meet in a convention on commercial matters at Annapolis,

Maryland. Twelve delegates from five states gathered there in September; their report, written by Alexander Hamilton of New York, urging a general convention spurred the calling of the Federal Convention.

On February 21, 1787, the Confederation Congress adopted a resolution authorizing the convention but limited its mandate to revision of the Articles. Several states already had named their delegates and, citing the Annapolis Convention's report, authorized them to take any measures "to render the constitution of government adequate to the exigencies of the Union." The convention thus began with an inconsistent mandate.

The convention consisted of states' governors, chief justices, attorneys general, and many delegates to the Confederation Congress, as well as several distinguished Americans who had agreed to come out of retirement to participate one last time in American politics. Although they followed a wide range of callings — lawyers, physicians, soldiers, clergymen, merchants, and farmers — most of the delegates were well-to-do members of their states' elite; one historian called them the well-bred, well-fed, well-wed, and well-read. They fell into several groups:

1. *National political figures:* Benjamin Franklin of Pennsylvania and George Washington of Virginia composed this group. Their willingness to place their prestige at risk by attending the convention testified to its legitimacy and to the severity of the problems facing the United States.

2. *Senior statesmen of American politics:* John Dickinson of Delaware, William Livingston of New Jersey, George Mason of Virginia, John Rutledge of South Carolina, and Roger Sherman of Connecticut were among these men. Veterans of colonial politics, they had helped lead the struggle against Great Britain. They brought with them an ability to compromise and a sensitivity to the clashing interests of the several states.

3. *Advocates of state and local interests:* These included John Lansing, Jr., of New York, Luther Martin of Maryland, William Paterson of New Jersey, Charles C. Pinckney of South Carolina, and Robert Yates, Jr., of New York. Because

they spoke for particular interests, they made it necessary at least to consider localist views and interests in framing the new charter of government.

4. *Architects of national government:* Alexander Hamilton of New York, James Madison of Virginia, Charles Pinckney of South Carolina, and James Wilson of Pennsylvania formed this group. Each of these men hoped to make his ideas the basis of the convention's deliberations.

5. *Quiet men:* Among these were John Blair of Virginia, Jacob Broome of Delaware, Jared Ingersoll of Pennsylvania, and James McHenry of Maryland. They provided the votes needed to build consensus and to establish grounds for compromise.

Some leading figures were not present: John Adams and Thomas Jefferson were the American ministers to London and Paris, John Jay was the Confederation's secretary for foreign affairs in New York City, and Patrick Henry was too interested in Virginia politics.

The convention elected Washington as its president and appointed a committee to prepare rules. Two of these were vital to the convention's success. First, as was customary among legislatures in the Anglo-American world, the convention met in secret, which would permit full and free discussion. Second, the delegates were free to change their minds and reopen any matters for further debate.

The delegates rotated between sessions in full convention and meetings of the Committee of the Whole House, the latter a useful parliamentary procedure permitting informal debate, freedom in stating views, and flexibility in reaching and reconsidering decisions. Select committees worked out compromises, prepared drafts, or formulated a range of solutions to a given problem. The delegates attacked questions piecemeal, debating and deciding on individual aspects. Often a decision on one issue would require them to reconsider other decisions they had reached. They traced a tortuous, crisscrossing route, at times pausing in dismay as they realized that a vote they had just taken had undone the accomplishments of hours or even days of grueling debate.

The convention discarded the Articles and

framed an entirely new constitution. They based their work on a set of resolutions known as the Virginia Plan, largely the work of James Madison. These resolutions proposed the creation of a supreme national government with separate legislative, executive, and judicial branches.

The convention's principal task was the design of the national legislature. The delegates agreed on the powers they wished to lodge in the new Congress, but disagreed about how the states and the American people would be represented in it. Under the Virginia Plan, population or some other proportional measure would determine representation in both houses of Congress. To protect the principle of state equality, small-state delegates rallied behind William Paterson's New Jersey Plan, which would have preserved each state's equal vote in a one-house Congress with augmented powers. Although the delegates rejected the New Jersey Plan on June 19, it took them nearly a month of further argument before they adopted on July 16 what has been called the Great Compromise, under which the House of Representatives would be apportioned based on population and each state would have two votes in the Senate.

Other difficulties facing them included the method of electing the chief executive, or president — solved by the invention of the electoral college; the counting of slaves in the ratio for apportioning representation and taxation among the states — resolved with the "three-fifths" ratio, under which three-fifths of the slave population would be added to the free population; and the dispute over the need for a bill of rights, a proposal rejected by the convention in its last week. But the delegates devoted little attention to the powers of the president and almost none to the structure of the judiciary or the executive branch, leaving these matters to the new Congress.

The document approved on September 17, the Constitution of the United States, was a terse outline of government — seven articles of four thousand words. In framing it, the delegates drew on their accumulated experience and memories of colonial, state, and national politics, their familiarity with English constitutional history and classical civilization, and the political

ideas of the Age of Enlightenment. Thirty-nine delegates signed the Constitution; the convention sent it to the Confederation Congress for submission to the states, which were to refer it in turn to ratifying conventions chosen by the people.

James Madison took detailed notes of the convention's debates to educate future generations about the difficulties and challenges of constitution making. Together with convention documents, the notes kept by Madison, John Lansing, Jr., Robert Yates, James McHenry, and other delegates form the basis for the modern understanding of the convention's work. Although these documents had little influence on the workings of the Constitution in its first decades, modern constitutional lawyers use them in preparing arguments about the "original intent" of the Framers.

Richard B. Bernstein with Kym S. Rice, *Are We to Be a Nation? The Making of the Constitution* (1987); Max Farrand, ed., *The Records of the Federal Convention of 1787* (1911; rev. ed., 4 vols., 1937; supplement, ed., James H. Hutson, 1987); Clinton L. Rossiter, *1787: The Grand Convention* (1966).

RICHARD B. BERNSTEIN

See also Articles of Confederation; Bill of Rights; Constitution; Electoral College; Ratification of the Constitution.

PHILANTHROPY

"In works of beneficence, no country has surpassed, perhaps none has equaled the United States," James Bryce, the British journalist, wrote in 1888. One hundred years later Americans had given $104.3 billion to charity. They did not invent philanthropy, but for a variety of reasons they have always stressed the importance of private giving.

The word *philanthropy* is Greek in origin and the American concept owes much to Jewish, Catholic, and Protestant tradition as well as to the English experience. Cotton Mather, a Puritan minister, argued in 1710 that everyone should engage in "a perpetual endeavor to do good in the world." But even earlier, the colonists had given private funds to establish Harvard and Yale, a variety of hospitals, and several institutions to help the worthy poor. In many ways Benjamin Franklin epitomized the American philanthropic spirit. Devoting the last part of his life to public service, he left a legacy that included the Library Company of Philadelphia, the school that became the University of Pennsylvania, and the Pennsylvania Hospital, and in his will, he established Franklin Funds in Boston and Philadelphia to lend money to "young married artificers of good character."

Although the tradition of private giving was established early in American history, the word *philanthropy* gradually changed its meaning. Originally it meant love of humanity, charity, and benevolence, but late in the nineteenth century it began to mean the social control and instruction of the lower classes. It also became something that could be taught. The School of Philanthropy was established in New York and the School of Civics and Philanthropy in Chicago. Social workers talked of "scientific philanthropy," by which they meant the organization of charity in order to eliminate waste and prevent the poor from cheating.

At the same time, *philanthropy* meant large-scale giving by the Rockefellers and other wealthy Americans (the most common definition today). Documenting this philosophy was the essay "Wealth" written in 1889 by Andrew Carnegie, in which he argued that the wealthy had a responsibility to give away a portion of their assets. This "gospel of wealth" was controversial. Washington Gladden, the social gospel minister, defined the gifts of the very wealthy as "tainted money" because of the exploitative way it had been earned. On one occasion, late in the nineteenth century, Jane Addams of Hull-House returned an anonymous gift of twenty thousand dollars because she suspected it came from the Rockefellers. But most Americans became accustomed in the late nineteenth century to the rich bestowing large private gifts on universities (Duke and Stanford, for example), medical centers, churches, and other local and national institutions.

Two developments early in the twentieth century helped ease the controversy over such gifts: the philanthropic foundation and the fed-

erated fund drive. The Peabody Fund, established in 1867 by George Peabody to assist southern education, is often credited with being the first foundation, but it was not until the twentieth century that this method of directing money to good causes became popular. The Rockefeller Institute for Medical Research (1901) was the first foundation with a director and a board to manage the business of benevolence. It was quickly followed by the Russell Sage Foundation (1907), the Carnegie Corporation (1911), the Rockefeller Foundation (1913), and then thousands of others (there were seventy-five hundred by one count in 1950 and over twenty thousand in 1990). The federated fund drive, whereby one campaign managed by professionals raises money from large and small donors for a great many institutions, was first tried in Denver in 1888, perfected in Cleveland before World War I, and adopted by most cities in the 1920s. The Red Cross and the National Tuberculosis Association borrowed a Danish idea for raising money in 1910 when they sold stamps to "stamp out TB." Benevolence had become organized and efficient.

Philanthropic giving reached a peak in 1928 when more than $2.5 billion was raised for charity, and individuals gave five hundred gifts of $1 million or more. The stock market crash and the depression reduced the amount of benevolent giving, however, and convinced many that private gifts alone could not alleviate suffering and want. The federal income tax, when initially passed in 1913, was so low that it had little impact on philanthropy, but with increasing tax rates and a steep inheritance tax, especially in the 1930s, the tax code came to exert a significant influence on giving. The wealthy could deduct up to 15 percent of their taxable income for charitable gifts, and, perhaps more important, they could avoid capital gains taxes by giving appreciated stock to a foundation and then, as trustees, retain the voting rights to the stock. Steeply rising tax rates during World War II made giving to charity even more important for the well-to-do.

Despite periodic investigations by Congress, which revealed that many foundations were more concerned with the interests of the founders than with society at large, foundations continued to proliferate, and many tried to promote social action and to improve the quality of life in the United States. The Ford Foundation, through its Public Affairs Program, gave grants in the 1960s to minority-owned businesses, supported low-income housing, promoted legal aid for the poor, and subsidized experimental programs to help juvenile delinquents. The Ford Foundation even gave grants to street gangs and to voter registration projects. It was not alone. One survey in 1968 discovered that 18 percent of all foundation grants were directed toward improving race relations and solving urban problems. The Reagan and Bush administrations sought to replace federal programs with private benevolence, but they were suspicious of the Ford Foundation and other philanthropies that seemed to advocate social action.

Large foundation gifts received most of the attention but in the 1960s foundations accounted for only 8 percent of all giving while individuals contributed 75 percent. In 1988 the foundation share had shrunk to 6 percent while individuals contributed over 83 percent (corporations and bequests made up the rest). Almost half the total gifts went to religious institutions, and higher education received about 8 percent, and the arts, culture, and the humanities just over 6 percent. The 1986 law that prohibited the deduction of the appreciated value of stocks or art objects on tax returns seemed to reduce the contribution of art to museums.

If James Bryce returned to the United States at the end of the twentieth century, he would probably once again be impressed by American benevolence.

Robert Bremner, *American Philanthropy,* 2nd ed. (1988); Merle Curti, *American Philanthropy Abroad* (1963).

ALLEN F. DAVIS

See also Carnegie, Andrew; Frick, Henry Clay; Mellon, Andrew; Rockefeller, John D.

PHILIP (KING PHILIP)

(1639?–1676), Wampanoag tribal sachem. Philip (Indian name, Metacom or Metacomet) was the son of Massasoit (Ousamequin) and brother of Alexander (Wamsutta) whom Philip succeeded as sachem in the summer of 1662. He was promptly coerced by the Plymouth General Court into signing an agreement that he would sell no land without the court's consent. Philip understood his promise to be for seven years' duration, but the written document, which he could not read, made it perpetual.

Being allied to Plymouth, Philip was caught in that settlement's territorial ambitions, as well as those of Massachusetts Bay and Rhode Island, whose new charter included within its bounds his homeland of Pokanoket (Bristol). Massachusetts's missionary John Eliot sent the "praying Indian" John Sassamon as ostensible secretary to Philip, but Philip caught Sassamon in forgery and chased him away.

In 1667, Plymouth founded the town of Swansea on land also claimed by Rhode Island, and in 1671 Philip sold land to Rhode Islanders, apparently believing that the seven years of his promise to Plymouth had expired. Plymouth in retaliation forced him to submit, ending his status as a "free" sachem, and the Commissioners of the United (Puritan) Colonies of New England confirmed his subjection.

In January 1675, John Sassamon emerged again to inform Plymouth's governor Josiah Winslow that Philip was preparing for war. Sassamon was murdered on his return journey. By questionable processes, a Plymouth jury convicted three of Philip's men of the murder, and Plymouth mobilized to "conform" the sachem (i.e., to subject him completely to Plymouth's control).

When an Indian was killed by encroaching Swansea settlers, Philip's Pokanokets retaliated by killing seven Swansea men. Plymouth then sent in an army, and the Pokanokets fled. They were joined by Nipmuck praying Indians of John Eliot's missions in assaults on Massachusetts towns. That colony in turn hired mercenaries who attacked any Indians they could reach, including the Narragansetts who were trying to stay neutral.

Philip sought refuge and aid among the upper Hudson River Mahicans. But New York's governor Sir Edmund Andros incited the Mohawks to attack them, whereupon Philip's band returned to Massachusetts where they conducted futile raids and were harried by Plymouth's Capt. Benjamin Church. After Philip executed a warrior for advocating peace, the victim's brother "Alderman" led Captain Church to Philip's hideout and killed him. Philip's head was exhibited on the fort at Plymouth town for twenty-five years.

Actually, Philip had become almost insignificant in the bloody war that bears his name. Troops from Connecticut and Massachusetts vied for "rights of conquest" over the territory of the large Narragansett tribe, which lay within a protesting Rhode Island's chartered bounds. Fire and massacre raged all over New England. The war produced the heaviest losses in proportion to population that the region has ever experienced. In addition to the loss of life, Massachusetts's charter was rescinded and the United Colonies of New England confederation dissolved.

Francis Jennings, *The Invasion of America: Indians, Colonialism, and the Cant of Conquest* (1975); Douglas Edward Leach, *Flintlock and Tomahawk: New England in King Philip's War* (1958).

Francis Jennings

See also Indians; King Philip's War; New England Colonies.

PHILIPPINES

Once a Spanish colony, the Philippine Islands came into American hands as a result of the Spanish-American War of 1898. Assistant Secretary of the Navy Theodore Roosevelt ordered Comdre. George Dewey in Hong Kong to move against Manila Bay if war began. Dewey took Manila with an impressive naval victory and the aid of rebels led by Emilio Aguinaldo. In the Treaty of Paris of 1899, the United States annexed the Philippines.

But the United States faced serious problems in the islands. Anti-imperialists opposed to taking over a foreign people without their consent and holding them in a colonial condition objected bitterly; nevertheless, the Senate ratified the treaty. In addition, Aguinaldo rebelled against American control, waging a guerrilla war until his capture in 1901. Peace was restored at war's end in 1902 with the help of a commission headed by an Ohio judge, William Howard Taft.

Thereafter, the United States poured aid into the archipelago for decades. During World War II, the Philippines were conquered by Japan, but they were liberated in February 1945. The next year the United States granted the Philippines their independence, though still maintaining bases and political influence there.

See also Expansion, Continental and Overseas; Spanish-American War.

PHILLIPS, WENDELL

(1811–1884), abolitionist, labor reformer, and orator. Born in Boston to a wealthy family of distinguished lineage, Phillips received his LL.B. from Harvard in 1834 and was admitted to the bar. But urged on by his wife, Ann Terry Greene Phillips, he soon abandoned his legal career for the cause of immediate slave emancipation. The attack by a proslavery mob in Boston on abolitionist William Lloyd Garrison in 1835 and the 1837 killing of abolitionist editor Elijah Lovejoy in Alton, Illinois, sealed his commitment to the cause, and he soon emerged as one of the nation's most accomplished and well-known public speakers.

Garrison served as Phillips's model of abolitionism and became his closest friend. Both rejected the idea of participating directly in electoral politics, embraced the imperative of northern disunionism, and insisted on the equality of women. When these issues split the American Anti-Slavery Society in 1840, Phillips emerged as a powerful spokesperson for "Garrisonism" and became regarded as radical abolitionism's most able expositor of legal theory and social reform. He also displayed considerable independence of mind, rejecting Garrison's beliefs in religious millennialism, nonresistance, and human perfectibility. He developed a highly politicized version of republican ideology that justified abolitionist agitators as heroic guardians of popular liberty, demanded state legislation in favor of social justice, and was prepared to meet oppression with violence.

Throughout the 1840s and 1850s, Phillips's

radical republicanism and Garrison's Christian perfectionism harmonized to supply their followers with inspirational leadership. At the same time, Phillips's republican ideology put him in close touch with beliefs that were widely shared. By the mid-1850s, he had become one of the nation's most popular public lecturers, traveling the Lyceum circuit and seeing his speeches reprinted in northern periodicals.

Phillips's influence extended far beyond the confines of organized abolitionism, making him a major force in the larger political struggles over slavery that led to the Civil War. He opposed the Mexican War and the Compromise of 1850, and called for defiance of the Fugitive Slave Law. In 1859–1860, his eloquent defense of the insurrectionist John Brown and his vehement insistence on northern disunion during the secession crisis aroused controversy, as did his criticism of Abraham Lincoln's emancipation policies during the course of the war. In 1864, he opposed Lincoln's reelection, arguing that the federal government owed the former slaves not only freedom but also land, education, and full civil rights. This demand led him to split with Garrison in 1865 when Garrison proposed to dissolve the American Anti-Slavery Society on the grounds that the Thirteenth Amendment had fulfilled its mission. Phillips became president of the society while many of his colleagues chose retirement, keeping the organized abolitionist movement alive until the adoption of the Fifteenth Amendment enfranchised black males.

Thereafter, Phillips pursued the causes of temperance, woman suffrage, the prohibition of capital punishment, and labor reform, a crusade he linked to demands for racial equality for African-Americans. In 1870, Phillips ran unsuccessfully for the Massachusetts governorship as a Labor and Prohibition party candidate and remained active as a public speaker and social agitator until the late 1870s. As an orator, Phillips is best remembered for breaking free of the formal classical traditions of American rhetoric in favor of an informal, colloquial delivery.

James Brewer Stewart, *Liberty's Hero: Wendell Phillips* (1986).

JAMES BREWER STEWART

See also Abolitionist Movement; Garrison, William Lloyd.

PHOTOGRAPHY

In the first history of photography published in New York in 1849, there is the tantalizing story of an Indiana youth, James M. Wattles, trying unsuccessfully in 1828 to secure survivable pictures on writing paper placed dry in a camera obscura (precursor to the camera) after he had soaked it in potash. But, so the story goes, his parents laughed at him and bade him attend to his studies and forget about such "moonshine" thoughts.

Only a few years later, W. H. Fox Talbot, a member of the English landed gentry, made what he called "photogenic drawings" — images of leaves, lace, and feathers secured on silver nitrate paper exposed in a camera obscura, the paper afterward being washed in a strong solution of salt to fix the images. The process gave Talbot what we now call a negative, and in a patent awarded in 1841, his improved process — calotype — called for contact printing the negatives on silver chloride paper for positives. Talbot's calotype process was thus the forerunner of photography's mainstream negative-positive systems that evolved ultimately to the roll film systems we know today.

But in 1826 or 1827, a Frenchman, Joseph Niepce, had secured the world's earliest surviving photograph (now in the Gernsheim collection at the University of Texas at Austin) on a pewter plate sensitized with bitumen and exposed for eight hours in a camera obscura. He called the direct positive image of a pigeon house and barn next to his home a heliograph. From 1829 until his death in 1833, Niepce worked in partnership with another Frenchman, Louis J. M. Daguerre, who in 1839 invented a means of taking photographs on copper plates lightly coated with sensitized silver (similarly exposed without a negative in a camera of new design) and "developed" over mercury fumes. That same year, the French government purchased the rights to the new "daguerreotype" process and donated them freely to the world. A daguerreotype, such as might be found today among old family possessions or in antique stores, was covered with glass and placed in a wood or leather case (usually about 3½ by 4 inches in size), both to protect it and to mimic the manner in which miniature oil portraits were packaged. Millions of daguerreotypes (mostly portraits) were made the world over from 1840 to about 1860. There followed cheaper methods of securing a cased image photo on glass, ambrotype, and on iron plates, tintype, the latter process remaining popular until well into the twentieth century at seaside resorts and amusement parks. In a sidelight to daguerreotype history, the first U.S. camera patent was awarded in May 1840 for a more primitive version of Daguerre's camera to New Yorker Alexander S. Wolcott, a manufacturer of instruments and dental equipment. But his camera was not equipped with a lens. Instead, sunlight was directed through an opening and reflected on the image plate by an internal concave mirror, restricting picture size to 2 by 2½ inches.

Photography's formative years in America followed a pattern similar to the American experience in art. Many who took up the daguerreotype process were house, sign, or carriage painters. Some, like their contemporaries in folk artistry, traveled the back roads of the nation as itinerant photographers. Much credit is due the American painter and inventor Samuel F. B. Morse, who visited Daguerre in 1839 and afterward not only taught the daguerreotype process to Mathew Brady and a host of Brady's peers but instilled in his students an appreciation for the rudiments of traditional art techniques. Although daguerreotype cameras were carried on several expeditions to the Canadian border, the American West, and the Yucatan, the process was ill suited to outdoor use. In 1849, American rights were secured to Talbot's calotype process, but by then, both a better (but short-lived) French paper negative and three newly invented glass negative modes were taking center stage. The process adopted after 1855 by most photographers called for sensitizing the glass negative with collodion (ether mixed with gun cotton) and exposing the plate in the camera while it was still wet. It is understandable that during the subsequent thirty-year wet-plate era, photography continued to remain largely in the hands

of professionals. There is no recorded manual for amateurs, for example, prior to one published by a wealthy Baltimorean, George B. Coale, in 1858, and it is doubtful that even this pocket-size booklet achieved wide distribution.

Just as landscape painting in America lagged behind oil portraiture, so American landscape photography developed slowly. The United States at mid-century lacked a leisure class to adopt photography as a hobby, as did many amateurs in Europe. In addition, Americans appear to have preferred scenic lithographs rather than photographs, whereas abroad, noted photographers and publishers sold numerous editions of large photographs of cityscapes and tourist meccas in Europe, the Middle East, and Asia. Public excitement with the opening of the American West probably had much to do with the success of such photographers as Eadweard Muybridge, Carlton E. Watkins, William H. Jackson, Timothy O'Sullivan, and Andrew J. Russell in selling large prints made with new "mammoth-plate" cameras of scenes in the wilds of today's Yosemite, Yellowstone, and other national parks and territories. Some of these photographs were offered in the same galleries that handled paintings by artists of the Hudson River school.

The introduction in 1860 of portrait photographs mounted on cards — the *carte de visite,* or visiting-card style upped to a larger *cabinet* size in 1866 — ended the reign of daguerreotype photography. It also led to the creation of the family photo album and to a new public taste for flamboyantly posed portraits of celebrities, using dramatic lights and period props. As the name Brady dominated the daguerreotype era, Napoleon Sarony became the undoubted American master of the card portrait era (1860s to the turn of the century). Nevertheless, it was a pioneer Brady carte de visite of Abraham Lincoln, widely reproduced and distributed in the 1860 presidential campaign, that Lincoln later said helped elect him president.

Of equal and perhaps greater significance was the concurrent proliferation of card stereographs — double pictures mounted side by side for viewing in three dimensions in handheld or newly manufactured home console viewing devices. The card stereoview format provides the world today with its most complete record of the transition from an agrarian to an industrial and urban way of life. Card stereoviews aroused public interest not only in views (domestic and foreign) but in fashion, genre, and news events photographs (a stereocard series, for example, portrayed the 1871 Chicago fire). Public viewing of card stereographs in the home is often characterized as a nineteenth-century form of American television.

Photographers who attended their national convention in Chicago in 1880 literally witnessed the birth of photography's modern era. A variety of reliable dry-plate glass negatives was shown, which could be sold to the public as well as the professional, ready-made for use at any time. A revolution in the medium and its practice was at hand. Eight years later when George Eastman brought out the Kodak (followed shortly by the first roll film), an estimated 84 million of the new dry plates had been sold. The manufacture of cameras designed for the new plates further doubled during the years 1895–1900.

But like many revolutions, this one, too, became fragmented. In the early 1880s, while photographers such as William Kurtz were specializing in taking portraits at night with flash powder, the journalist and social reformer Jacob Riis seized on flashlight photography as a means of better conveying the misery of slum life in New York City's tenements. This attracted the attention of a young civil service commissioner, Theodore Roosevelt, who as police commissioner (1895–1897) frequently took Riis with him on unannounced nighttime checks of city enforcement of health and safety regulations. At the turn of the century, other documentary photographers focused their cameras on the "vanishing race" of American Indians (Edward Curtis and Joseph Dixon were two), street life in New York (Percy Byron), Chicago (Sigmund Krausz), San Francisco's Chinatown (Arnold Genthe), and the arrival in New York of a new generation of immigrants (Lewis Hine). But there was little or no professional or fraternal interplay between any of these now celebrated documentary photographers and those of an emerging new school of art photographers. The works of the latter were individually printed and reproduced separately from text in a new publication, *Camera Notes,* edited by Alfred Stieglitz. To the Japanese-German dramatist, poet, and critic Sadakichi Hartmann, artistic photography, Stieglitz, and the New York Camera Club were "three different names for one and the same thing." But Hartmann also noted that the public at large never saw *Camera Notes* and that "ninety-nine persons out of a hundred [were] not yet familiar with the term 'artistic photography,' much less with its aspirations and aims."

The New York Camera Club was one of many such clubs established at the close of the nineteenth century. On their first outing in 1890, photographers in the New England club filled a yacht, which then "sailed down Narragansett Bay" with wealthy amateurs carrying some thirty view cameras and fifty or more Kodaks and Hawk-Eyes. But in launching the Photo-Secession movement in art photography a decade later, Stieglitz broke away from the camera club element. In a new publication, *Camera Work* (published from 1903 to 1917), he included the soft-focus pictorial, and more avant-garde works of a new elite group of photographers, among them Edward Steichen, Clarence White, Gertrude Käsebier, Alvin Langdon Coburn, F. Holland Day, Rudolph Eickemeyer, and Paul Strand. It was a time, internationally, of great artistic innovation (the cubist explosion in France, for example). Paul Strand, at age twenty-five, caught the spirit in 1915 when he produced his first abstract photographs. Stieglitz thereupon gave Strand a one-man exhibition and devoted the final issue of *Camera Work* to his works. During the 1920s, Stieglitz himself abandoned exhibiting pictorial photographs in favor of works by Picasso, Rodin, Marin, and other painters and sculptors. New York's famed Julien Levy Gallery (1931–1949) opened with an exhibition of surrealist works by George Platt Lynes and other photographers before mounting the works of "modern" artists such as Salvador Dali and Jean Cocteau.

A new realism became the vogue at this time when some of the best photographers — Strand, Steichen, Edward Weston, and later Ansel Adams — sought to make "straight" photographs — pictures unmanipulated, unsentimental, and sharply focused. The appearance of three new landmark cameras — the 35-mm Leica I, wide-aperture-lens Ermanox, and twin-lens-reflex Rolleiflex — greatly enhanced the new format. In the hands of Steichen and Irving Penn, these and other new small cameras provided appropriate tools for yet another new vogue, fashion photography. But more important, news photographers could abandon their bulky Graflex cameras, flash guns, and fast tank development in the darkroom. Using the new cameras and available light, such photographers as Eric Salomon in Europe and Albert Eisenstaedt, Margaret Bourke-White, and others in the United States became the pioneers of modern photojournalism. Socially concerned photographers such as Aaron Siskind made an early record (1928) of slum conditions in Harlem — even as his older and then unknown contemporary James Van Der Zee recorded in his studio, and sometimes in street scenes, the last vestiges of the black community's earlier social fabric.

Before 1900, the manufacture of cameras, emulsion-coated dry plates, photographic paper, and so on, was conducted by small firms. But the arrival on the scene of George Eastman and the dawn of a new era of business trusts and chain-store retail merchandising changed all this. By the turn of the century, photography, like the horse and buggy, was poised for a coming age of mechanization. At the outset, photography was clearly in the lead; there were, by 1900, 100,000 Kodak cameras alone in the hands of a new generation of amateurs, whereas only some 8,000 horseless carriages were registered by this time. During the years 1889–1909, production of photographic apparatus and materials grew at an annual rate of 11 percent, as against a growth rate of only about 4.7 percent annually by U.S. industrial production in general. In the latter years of the twentieth century, photography remained well ahead in the race, if there was one, with the horseless carriage, reaching an annual level of 10.7 billion in the number of photographs made by amateurs at the outset of the 1980s.

Until Kodachrome color film reached the market in 1935, no successful mode for combining color screens in a camera to produce color photographs had been perfected, although by the 1890s screens could be combined for three-dimensional viewing like card stereographs and could be projected on a wall or screen by a magic lantern. Polaroid introduced its first instant-picture camera in 1947, and the following year the manufacture of Nikon cameras began, leading after the Korean War to Japan's "invasion" of the U.S. camera market. The rudiments of camera automation appeared just before the outbreak of World War II with the development of prototype exposure control and flash synchronization systems.

The Metropolitan Museum of Art accepted its first collection of photographs (personal photographs belonging to Stieglitz) in 1926, fourteen years before the trend-setting department of photography was established at New York's Museum of Modern Art. When the J. Paul Getty Museum in California mounted a year-long series of five exhibitions to commemorate the 150th anniversary of the daguerreotype invention, the title chosen for the series was Experimental Photography, which allowed subjective illustration of early daguerreotype, calotype, and wet-plate-era works; photographs by painter photographers such as Thomas Eakins and Charles Sheeler; industrial and commonplace scenes artistically rendered by Strand, Weston, Walker Evans, and others; and a new subjectivity from the 1940s to the 1960s when realism yielded to a new ambiguity and introspection in photographs by André Kertesz, Harry Callahan, and W. Eugene Smith. Over the years, other exhibitions have categorized the motivations and achievements of great American photographers in other ways. The first comprehensive published study was completed by Time-Life Books in the 1970s.

Several critics have contended that every decade, in effect, imposes its own aesthetic. But one can find books of photographers' works covering the New Deal era that, on the one hand, suggest an "unbounded belief in the potential of growth," and on the other, portray works by Farm Security Administration photographers of the dust bowl conditions that led to John Steinbeck's The Grapes of Wrath. The immediacy of repeated crime, warfare, and other shocking scenes on television may also have dulled the public's ability to appreciate or respond to documentary photographs as in former times. Would photographs by Alexander Gardner of dead soldiers on the battlefield at Gettysburg today inspire a Gettysburg address?

Robert Taft, *Photography and the American Scene* (1989); William Welling, *Photography in America: The Formative Years 1839–1900* (1987).

WILLIAM WELLING

See also Bourke-White, Margaret; Brady, Mathew; Eastman, George; Lange, Dorothea; Steichen, Edward.

PIERCE, FRANKLIN

(1804–1869), fourteenth president of the United States. Born in New Hampshire and trained as a lawyer, Pierce was the successful builder and operator of his state's Democratic party. He served as a state legislator, congressman, and U.S. senator most of the time between 1827 and 1841, but his forte was political management. He epitomized much about the new style of political leadership that developed in the Jacksonian era. Like Martin Van Buren and James K. Polk, two other state Democratic leaders who became president, Pierce functioned best as an inside operator, planning and promoting his party's electoral success. The political convention, party headquarters, and campaign trail were his métier. Ideologically, he was a traditional Democrat, devoted to limiting the power of the national government in domestic affairs, hostile to social reformism including abolitionism, a nationalist in foreign affairs, a territorial expansionist, and celebratory of the egalitarian impulses that had been unleashed in the United States.

Pierce's devotion to the Democratic party, his success in the middle reaches of American politics, and his brief service in the Mexican War were all useful credentials at the faction-ridden, stalemated Democratic National Convention in 1852. Nominated for president, he was elected after a campaign based on traditional Democratic policies, coupled with a strong commitment to maintaining peace between the recently quarreling North and South. But Pierce was almost immediately faced by a renewal of the sectional crisis, this time over the right of southerners to bring their slaves into Kansas. His handling of the conflicting forces and of the extreme tensions provoked in Congress and throughout the country by Stephen A. Douglas's Kansas-Nebraska bill, which opened the area to slavery, was inept, and led to a period of disastrous political turmoil.

Pierce's role in the controversy suggested the limits of the kind of political leader he and others of his generation were. Believing strongly in maintaining party cohesion above all else, they resisted disruptive issues when they could, and when they could not, they negotiated and compromised in pursuit of the unity they sought. But the traditional political arts failed in the face of massive electoral turmoil at the local level and the bitter divisions within Congress. Many northern Democrats were under intense constituency pressure to resist the South's encroachment into nonslave territories. Pierce, though recognizing their difficulties, still sought a formula promoting compromise and unity — but that proved to be a chimera. The result was crisis and party disintegration. Although Pierce had won office at the Democrats' electoral high tide, a political revolution, much of it stimulated by a virulent nativism, the rest by sectional antagonisms, exploded in 1854 and reshaped the political landscape.

Despite his failures, Pierce sought nomination for a second term in 1856. His administration had had several foreign policy successes, and he had kept the partisan faith against attempts to increase the national government's involvement in economic affairs. The Democratic leaders, however, preferred someone unconnected with the recent disruptions as the only way to regain the electoral initiative. Defeated at the national convention, Pierce returned to New Hampshire in 1857, emerging briefly at the outset of the Civil War as part of an effort by elder statesmen to find one more compromise to prevent the Union's breakup.

William E. Gienapp, *The Origins of the Republican Party, 1852–1856* (1987); Roy F. Nichols, *Franklin Pierce: Young Hickory of the Granite Hills* (1958).

JOEL H. SILBEY

See also Elections: 1852.

PINKERTONS

The Pinkerton National Detective Agency was the first nationwide investigative organization. It was started in 1850 by Allan Pinkerton, a Scottish immigrant who had been Chicago's first police detective, and E. H. Rucker, a Chicago attorney who left the partnership after a year. The Pinkerton trademark was an open eye, with the slogan below, "The Eye That Never Sleeps." Besides working with local police, the Pinkertons were hired by railroads to patrol their trains and set up security systems — including the Illinois Central Railroad, through which Pinkerton met its lawyer, Abraham Lincoln. After Lincoln was elected president, Pinkerton helped plan his trip through Maryland en route to Washington, D.C., in February 1861, since there had been rumors of a "Baltimore Plot" to assassinate the president-elect.

Gen. George B. McClellan, whom he also knew from the Illinois Central, added Pinkerton to his staff under the name "Maj. E. J. Allen" to handle intelligence for the Army of the Potomac. Pinkerton and his men, who included fugitive slaves, gathered information on Southern spies and slipped behind Confederate lines to learn Southern military plans. But they also significantly overstated the number of Confederate soldiers, confirming McClellan's chronic belief that he faced overwhelming numbers. His slowness to attack for fear he was seriously outnumbered harmed his reputation and ultimately cost him his command.

After the war, the agency again concentrated on railroad robberies and security and "rode shotgun" on stagecoaches in the West, helping pursue the James and Reno gangs. The agency built a huge file of pictures and facts on criminals that was the only such repository until the creation of the Federal Bureau of Investigation. But the Pinkertons also helped industrialists battle labor, countering strikes and violence by the Molly Maguires of the Pennsylvania coal country and often initiating violence themselves, as in the Homestead strike of 1892 against Carnegie Steel Company.

In later years the Pinkerton agency concentrated on providing guard service for individuals and detectives for corporations.

See also Espionage; Homestead Strike; Molly Maguires; Police Forces.

PLANTATION SYSTEM

Plantations dominated southern agriculture from the mid-eighteenth century to the Civil War. These large farms, employing twenty or more slaves, produced staple crops (cotton, rice, tobacco) for domestic and foreign markets. Planters owned both the means of production — the land and tools — and the labor force. Such a system was not inevitable, however, even in an era before mechanization. Wage laborers, sharecroppers, and family farmers could also grow these staples, as the post–Civil War era clearly attested.

The plantation system, begun in the late seventeenth century (long after its appearance in Brazil and the West Indies), expanded through the coastal and Piedmont South during the eighteenth and early nineteenth centuries. With the end of slavery, the system collapsed because former slaves refused to work in gangs or to accept labor discipline; planters therefore divided their land into small sharecropped farms. A new plantation system based upon wage labor, however, briefly appeared in the 1930s and 1940s, when planters consolidated their units to take advantage of New Deal agricultural policies.

Before 1865, staple production, slavery, and the plantation system were intricately intertwined. Using their land as collateral, planters bought slaves in order to increase production. The more slaves a master could work, the larger his output and the greater his profits. By the mid-eighteenth century, the slave population was growing by natural increase, thereby permitting owners to increase their labor force without buying more Africans.

The plantation system originated in the tobacco economy of the seventeenth-century Chesapeake colonies. To meet the exploding European demand for tobacco, planters required more labor than their families could provide. They employed indentured servants, who, in return for transportation from England, agreed to work for a planter for a certain term of years.

Since servants were relatively inexpensive, a substantial minority of planters could afford them, thus creating a widespread distribution of relatively small agricultural units. But labor conditions were so oppressive that the flow of servants began to decline, especially after economic conditions began to improve in England in the late seventeenth century.

The growing scarcity of servants led planters to experiment with slave labor. Since men of wealth bought many Africans and enjoyed the consequent increase in production, their plantations grew larger. Although only about a tenth of Chesapeake tobacco cultivators were large planters, by the late eighteenth century close to half the slaves in the area were working on their holdings.

The plantation system spread throughout the South during the eighteenth and early nineteenth centuries. By 1720, it had appeared in the rice country of the Carolina and Georgia coasts, where great planters owned most of the slaves. The greatest diffusion of the plantation system occurred, however, between 1790 and 1860. Accelerating demand for cotton in England led wealthy southerners to move to the new Southwest — Alabama, Mississippi, Arkansas, and Texas — where they established cotton plantations. Although many yeomen grew cotton, aided by sons and a slave or two, plantations with many slaves produced most of the cotton grown in America. Wherever the plantation system became entrenched, white farmers who relied on family labor were marginalized and forced from the best land.

The plantation labor system was complex. Slaves planted, weeded, and harvested crops; kept fences and plantation structures in order; built slave cabins; and made products like shoes and barrels for the plantation. In order to achieve high levels of production, planters divided their slaves into specialized gangs and set overseers and slave drivers to compel sustained labor. But such productivity required compromises with slave workers. Slaves demanded the right to form families, create kin networks, and use their spare time in their quarters as they saw fit (visiting, attending religious services, or growing crops in their own plots). Since planta-

tion profits were tied to productivity, discipline of slaves became a crucial issue. Some masters used incentives (money, better jobs) to keep slaves reasonably content; others (especially on rice plantations) permitted slaves to work on their own after their daily tasks were completed. But positive incentives were rarely sufficient; to gain the greatest production, slaves often had to be driven and whipped.

The emancipation of slaves by the federal army, President Abraham Lincoln, and most important, by the actions of slaves themselves, destroyed the plantation system. Freedmen and freedwomen refused to accept plantation discipline, become permanent wage laborers, live in the old slave quarters, or even stay on the plantation. They wanted land of their own, where they could feed their families and perhaps produce small surpluses.

The end result of struggles between the planters (who wanted a docile labor force) and the freedpeople was the creation of a new labor system, one that provided some autonomy to former slaves while turning them into a kind of wage laborer. Planters refused to sell land to ex-slaves; instead they agreed to permit them to farm independent units, paying them a share of the crop at the end of the year. The planter still owned the land, tools, and crops; the share became the equivalent of a wage; moreover, the former slaves usually owed money at the end of the year to planters and local storekeepers, and were thereby kept in a form of debt peonage.

This sharecropping system lasted for about a half century. New Deal agricultural policies, especially payment to owners for not planting cotton, allowed planters to evict sharecroppers, consolidate their holdings, and then hire workers as they needed for wages. Lack of mechanization, especially of the cotton harvest, was long an obstacle to a completely successful wage-labor plantation system, but cotton harvesters, perfected by the late 1940s, resolved that problem. As plantations converted to a mechanized operation, hundreds of thousands of former sharecroppers and wage laborers migrated to cities. But this new, machine-intensive plantation environment lasted barely until 1960 in the old cotton South; it was far more productive to use the machinery in the flat land of the Southwest.

Robert William Fogel, *Without Consent or Contract: The Rise and Fall of American Slavery* (1989); Gavin Wright, *Old South, New South: Revolutions in the Southern Economy since the Civil War* (1986).

ALLAN KULIKOFF

See also Agriculture; Chesapeake Colonies; Colonial Economy; Cotton; Slavery; Southern Colonies; Tobacco.

PLATT AMENDMENT

The Platt Amendment to the Cuban Constitution was based on a clause in a bill drafted by Senator Orville H. Platt. The Teller Amendment (1898) had disclaimed any intention of annexation of Cuba as a result of the Spanish-American War of 1898, but American policymakers feared the imperial designs of Germany. Platt forged a compromise by introducing the amendment that bears his name to an army appropriation bill in 1901. It barred Cuba from making a treaty that gave another nation power over its affairs, going into debt, or stopping the United States from imposing a sanitation program on the island. Also, the United States could intervene in Cuban affairs to keep order or maintain independence, and could buy or lease sites for naval and coaling stations (the main one was Guantánamo Bay).

Later in 1901, under American pressure, Cuba included the amendment's provisions in its Constitution. After President Theodore Roosevelt withdrew federal troops from the island in 1902, Cuba signed a treaty with the United States that outlined American power in the area.

The United States exercised that power. Roosevelt sent American troops to Cuba in 1906, at the Cuban president's invitation, to restore order out of what they considered revolutionary chaos. The United States also refused to recognize revolutionary governments and dispatched its warships to Cuban waters. Finally, in 1934, as part of Franklin D. Roosevelt's Good Neighbor policy toward Latin America, the United States signed a treaty abrogating the Platt Amendment.

See also Caribbean-U.S. Relations.

PLESSY V. FERGUSON

In this case, the Supreme Court in 1896 upheld the constitutionality of social segregation of the "white and colored races" under the "separate but equal" doctrine. The case came from Louisiana, which in 1890 adopted a law providing for "equal but separate accommodations for the white and colored races" on its railroads. In 1892, passenger Homer Plessy refused to sit in a Jim Crow car. He was brought before Judge John H. Ferguson of the Criminal Court for New Orleans, who upheld the state law. The law was challenged in the Supreme Court on grounds that it conflicted with the Thirteenth and Fourteenth Amendments.

By a 7–1 vote, the Court said that a state law that "implies merely a legal distinction" between the two races did not conflict with the Thirteenth Amendment forbidding involuntary servitude, nor did it tend to reestablish such a condition.

The Court avoided discussion of the protection granted by the clause in the Fourteenth Amendment that forbids the states to make laws depriving citizens of their "privileges or immunities," but instead cited such laws in other states as a "reasonable" exercise of their authority under the police power. The purpose of the Fourteenth Amendment, the Court said, was "to enforce the absolute equality of the two races before the law. . . . Laws . . . requiring their separation . . . do not necessarily imply the inferiority of either race." The argument against segregation laws was false because of the "assumption that the enforced separation of the two races stamps the colored race with a badge of inferiority. If this be so, it is . . . solely because the colored race chooses to put that construction upon it."

The lone dissenter, Kentuckian and former slave owner Justice John Marshall Harlan, denied that a legislature could differentiate on the basis of race with regard to civil rights. He wrote: "The white race deems itself to be the dominant race," but the Constitution recognizes "no superior, dominant, ruling class of citizens." Harlan continued: "Our Constitution is colorblind. . . . In respect of civil rights all citizens are equal before the law." The Court's majority opinion, he pointed out, gave power to the states "to place in a condition of legal inferiority a large body of American citizens."

Following the *Plessy* decision, restrictive legislation based on race continued and expanded steadily, and its reasoning was not overturned until *Brown* v. *Board of Education of Topeka* in 1954.

See also Segregation.

POCAHONTAS

(c. 1596–1617), Indian "princess." Reputedly the favorite daughter of the Algonquin chief Powhatan, Pocahontas contributed significantly to the early survival of the Jamestown colony and played a brief but dramatic role in English imperial propaganda. Her untimely death cut short her successful mediation between the Powhatan Indians and the colony. Both before her intercession and long after her death, Jamestown — the first permanent English outpost in North America — was precarious, largely because of Indian hostility to the colony and its expansion.

Pocahontas's contributions to Jamestown date from her early acquaintance with Capt. John Smith after his capture by Powhatan's men in 1607. Her legendary rescue of the English captain on the verge of his execution was probably part of a traditional Indian adoption ceremony (misinterpreted or misunderstood by Smith), though it is possible that without her intercession he would have been killed. In any event, relations between Powhatan and the fledgling colony improved, and Pocahontas, then about twelve years old, became a frequent visitor at Jamestown and an important supplier of food for the colonists. She also became an informer for the colony, warning Smith of her father's belligerent plans.

After Smith's return to England, Pocahontas disappears for several years from the historical record. She may have married an Indian, resumed her proper name of Matoaka ("Pocahontas" was a nickname), and shunned the English, who, under Sir Thomas Dale, were at war with Powhatan. To force Powhatan's submission, Capt. Samuel Argall in 1613 lured Pocahontas on board a ship and held her hostage. During a prolonged captivity, she was converted to Christianity by the Reverend Alexander Whitaker and baptized as "Rebecca." In 1614 she married John Rolfe, a prominent colonist and recent widower. Powhatan grudgingly agreed to a truce with the colony that lasted until 1622.

The Virginia Company of London quickly recognized Pocahontas's enormous propaganda value as an example of Anglo-Indian harmony, of missionary success among the natives, and of the prospect that Indians could be persuaded to adopt English ways. To attract new settlers and fresh investments, the company in 1616 brought the Rolfes, their son, Thomas (b. 1615), and an entourage of a dozen or so Indians to England. She met many of the era's major figures, was presented at court, and had her portrait painted. She also took ill, probably from diseases that had no American counterpart. Pocahontas died in March 1617, after boarding ship for a return to Virginia, and was buried in Gravesend, England. With the death of Pocahontas and, soon after, of Powhatan, the fragile peace between colonists and Indians eroded. Ironically, the Indians' major grievance was the colonists' insatiable demand for land, triggered principally by windfall profits from the tobacco species introduced by John Rolfe.

In the public mind, Pocahontas is linked especially, and often romantically, with Smith. The rescue episode did not appear in Smith's accounts of Virginia published in 1608 and 1612 but surfaced in his *Generall Historie of Virginia, New England, and the Summer Isles* (1624). Doubts have been cast ever since on its authenticity and, if true, its meaning. Ethnographers and historians now generally agree that the event could well have taken place and that Smith's reasons for suppressing the story until 1624 had more to do with Pocahontas's early obscurity than with literary invention.

Philip L. Barbour, *Pocahontas and Her World* (1970); Frances Mossiker, *Pocahontas: The Life and Legend* (1977).

ALDEN T. VAUGHAN

See also Indians; Smith, John.

POE, EDGAR ALLAN

(1809–1849), short-story writer, poet, and critic. The son of itinerant actors, Poe was orphaned at two and was adopted by John Allan, a Richmond, Virginia, merchant and his wife. They gave Poe his middle name and a genteel childhood but eventually became the source of profound unhappiness. Allan was unfaithful to his wife, and when Poe took her part, Allan turned on him savagely. Although Allan violently opposed Poe's literary career, he unwittingly encouraged it. His firm imported many foreign books and magazines, which Poe read assiduously, giving him a literary sophistication far beyond his Richmond peers. Allan sent Poe to the University of Virginia with no spending money; when the boy ran up heavy gambling debts, his foster father refused to pay. After a bitter quarrel, Poe left home to seek literary fame.

Poe moved to Boston in 1827 where he published a book of poems but almost starved. He enlisted in the army and soon became sergeant major of his regiment. A reconciliation with Allan, motivated largely by Poe's hope of an inheritance, led to an appointment to West Point. There he began brilliantly, but another falling out with Allan plunged him into depression. He stopped attending classes and drills and was dismissed in 1831. His cadet friends helped finance a book of poems containing some of his best lyrics, "Israfel" and "The Doomed City," but the book was hardly noticed.

Poe spent the next years living in Baltimore with his aunt, Mrs. Maria Clemm, and her daughter, Virginia. One of his best stories, "A MS. Found in a Bottle," won him a job on the *Southern Literary Messenger* in Richmond. He proved an able editor, greatly increasing circulation. But he had begun drinking heavily, and he soon parted company with the magazine.

In 1836 he married Virginia Clemm, who was only thirteen, and departed with her and Mrs. Clemm for the North. For the next several years he alternated between editing and writing, publishing both poetry and prose, in particular *The Narrative of Arthur Gordon Pym*, a tale of shipwreck and picturesque horrors in the South Seas. As literary editor of *Graham's Lady's and Gentleman's Magazine,* which had a large circulation, Poe became a major figure in American letters, making enemies by the score with his trenchant criticism. But alcohol cost him this job, too.

He continued to write, however, producing "The Murders in the Rue Morgue," "The Gold Bug," and "The Mystery of Marie Roget" in a cool style that was the polar opposite of his romantic poems and horror stories. If he did not invent the detective story with these tales, he perfected it.

In 1842, inspired in part by a talk with Charles Dickens, Poe wrote "The Raven," his best-known poem. It was an immense success and almost instantly won Poe the fame for which he hungered. But money did not come with it: he still earned as little as four dollars for an article, fifteen dollars for a story. Tormented by poverty, Poe watched his wife die of tuberculosis. He became more and more unstable, drinking and taking opium, at one point attempting suicide with the drug. He published a grandiose prose poem, "Eureka," which combined half-baked science and dubious cosmogony. Returning to Richmond, he swore off liquor and became engaged to one of his youthful loves, now a rich widow. But a trip to Baltimore led to a fatal drinking bout.

As an editor Poe struggled to raise American literature to the level of his own formidable intelligence and talent. His instability doomed this ambition to failure, but his own artistry somehow survived his impulse for self-destruction. Poe added the concept of professionalism to the role of the writer in America. For him language and its artful use was virtually an end in itself, transcending ideology.

Julian Symons, *The Tell-Tale Heart: The Life and Works of Edgar Allan Poe* (1978); Edward Wagenknecht, *Edgar Allan Poe: The Man behind the Legend* (1963).

THOMAS FLEMING

See also Literature.

POETRY

See Literature.

POLICE FORCES

The early police forces in nineteenth-century America were modeled in part on the Metropolitan Police of London, formed in 1829 by Robert Peel (hence the nicknames "peelers" and "bobbies"). But American police came to differ from the police of other Western nations in several important ways. First, they have always been a part of local government, unlike other countries where the local police are a part of a nationally administered force. Second, because of their local roots, police departments appeared at different times throughout the nation. In general, big eastern cities created police forces first, with smaller cities lagging well behind. Third, as a part of the executive office of the city, police departments have been administered separately from state and county systems of criminal justice. Historian Wilbur Miller has argued that this final difference accounts for some of the more obvious contrasts between American and English police: American police have seen themselves as administering justice on the street; the English, as representing law, or the unwritten English Constitution.

The kind of police Americans knew in the early nineteenth century was descended from the medieval police of England — a constable and watch system composed of a volunteer night watch, who patrolled the city, and a daytime constable, who supervised the watch and charged fees for his services. Most night watchmen, however, were actually paid substitutes for volunteers and traditionally were drawn from society's unemployables. When Dogberry in Shakespeare's *Much Ado about Nothing* selects a night constable from among the watchmen, he picks "the most senseless and fit man," whom he orders, "You shall comprehend all vagrom men." As for sleeping on the job, Dogberry offers that he "cannot see how sleeping should offend; only, have a care that your bills [weapons] be not stolen." In this scene, Shakespeare ridiculed the notorious failings of the watch, which persisted through the nineteenth century: they drank, slept, and ran from any sign of danger. And constables were venal, illiterate Dogberries, intervening in crimes only when there was the promise of a good fee. In the United States, similar complaints were voiced about the watch and constables, but cities managed to survive under this loose system until they were quite large. New York had over a half million people before it got a permanent police in 1853, Boston about 175,000 (1859), and Philadelphia about 250,000 (1856).

Cities created their police forces for a variety of reasons, not the least of which was simply imitativeness: in the post–Civil War era, a city with any pretensions had to have modern police officers. This, however, is not to deny the usefulness of the new police. First, they were hierarchically organized and relatively accountable. The wearing of uniforms ensured that citizens could recognize police officers, and the city could try to keep them out of bars and on patrol. The latter innovation — regular patrol beats — incorporated the new organizational mode: patrolling in uniform, it was thought, would deter crime by scaring off criminals.

A second useful feature of the new police derived from their receiving regular salaries from the city government: they no longer needed to extract fees for their services, making them far more helpful to the poor. Salaries also provided a means for politicians to support their supporters; political machines hoping to mobilize the Irish vote would hire Irish police officers. Thus, early on, the ethnic and racial composition of the police force became a mirror of local politics. Police officers were also partisan workers for incumbent political parties, working to get out the vote or, sometimes, to prevent people from voting. Until their jobs became subject to civil service rules in the late nineteenth century, the police were intimately tied to city politics. And it was this tie that sometimes caused police to support strikers, say, or to refuse to implement morality legislation such as Sunday closing laws. In both cases, the police were partisans of the city government; when majority state governments enacted laws not supported by a local party, then police might well be on the minority side. Thus partisan conflicts became entangled with issues of ethnicity and working-class politics; states often tried to make the local police responsible to a state-level board in order to undercut city politicians.

Another, and unexpected feature of the new

uniformed police came from the opportunistic use of their presence on the streets. They helped strangers find their way, took in lost children, boarded and sometimes fed the homeless (called "station house lodgers"), enforced health ordinances, and directed traffic. They became the front line in a long series of urban services that ultimately landed in specially created city departments.

Toward the end of the nineteenth century, police departments began to hire blacks and women. Blacks were often employed to patrol black neighborhoods (the City Guard of New Orleans hired free blacks as early as 1814), but their chances of movement into white neighborhoods were negligible. By the mid-1960s most police departments had some black officers; Washington, D.C., had the most, with blacks composing about 20 percent of the force. Women were hired as "matrons" to oversee lost children, women's lodging rooms, and women prisoners. These matrons were sometimes funded by social welfare organizations rather than by the city, suggesting their status as social workers rather than law enforcement officers. Not until 1968 did women move full time into patrol, the city of Indianapolis leading the way. As a consequence of pressure from the civil rights movement and, later in the 1970s, the women's movement, police departments across the United States began to change their recruitment patterns.

The nature of the patrol officer's task was in part preventive and in part to provide on-the-spot service. But both duties kept officers from following up on complaints, and within twenty years after founding a police department, most cities added detectives to the force. Until now, the organization of the police had been modeled on the military, with officers' titles and similar uniforms (after the Civil War, blue became the color of choice). But detectives wore citizens' clothing, which helped some fall prey to police corruption. The lack of a uniform meant difficulty in supervision — something early police reformers had feared.

Police corruption followed and still follows certain structural faults in policing, faults present since the eighteenth century when Jonathan Wild claimed the title of "thief taker–general" in England. Wild, for a fee, would return stolen property to its owners, who would rather have their property than see someone go to prison. Obviously, the more involved he was in the original theft, the better able he was to "find" and return the stolen items.

Although there is some evidence of this sort of activity in the pre-police American constabulary, the structural corruption more common in the United States has come from so-called victimless crimes — vice. As criminologist Jerome Skolnick has demonstrated, it is very difficult for detectives to make arrests for these crimes: the "victims" — the buyers of drugs, sex, or gambling — are unwilling to complain. Therefore the detective must present other forms of evidence, which all too often is obtained by illegal means — bribery, threats, actual involvement in the crime. For instance, a prostitute might be persuaded to testify against a pimp for a bribe of heroin; or a drug dealer might have a drug planted on him by a narcotics detective ("framing a guilty man").

Sometimes when this form of corruption spread beyond a single police officer and became systematic, exposés and prosecutions followed. One such was that of the Lexow committee in 1894, which exposed police corruption in New York City. But such investigations, and the growing use of internal police investigation units in recent times, have never been able to attack the root cause of this kind of corruption: crimes in which the victim does not exist as an individual but is the larger society, as in prostitution, drugs, and gambling. Major investigations of police malpractice came about every twenty years after the Lexow investigation — in the Progressive Era, during the 1930s (the Wickersham Commission), in individual cities in the early 1950s, and most notably in the mid-1960s with the President's Commission on the Causes of Violence.

There is also a structural feature of policing unique to the United States — its multiple criminal codes and literally thousands of police departments. When, in the nineteenth century, crime or conflict ranged across jurisdictions, there was no single agency to turn to. Early forms of crime, for example, occurred on railroads, by their nature spread across policed cities, unpoliced countrysides and villages, and often across states, each with a different criminal code. Catching and prosecuting anyone stealing from a train conductor, or a conductor stealing from his employer, was difficult for local police, whose jurisdiction ended at the city limits. Similarly, a criminal operating across a broad district, such as counterfeiters, could easily avoid the local police.

Private detective companies — Allan Pinkerton's was the most famous — offered a solution to this problem for those with the money to hire them. Pinkerton exploited and gave a public relations spin to his operations in a series of thrillers, which he started publishing in 1874. Highlighting his radical activities in Scotland and his service to the Union during the Civil War, Pinkerton created a dramatic image of the intelligent detective versus the evildoer. But, as Frank Morn has shown, Pinkerton's business was much more mundane than the image he presented and less honorable. Since his time the essence of detection has been duplicity: a successful detective lies his or her way into the confidence of those with criminal knowledge and then turns them in. Working most often for large corporations and "testing" the honesty of employees by trying to get them to cheat (for example, offering a bribe to a train conductor in exchange for a free ride), Pinkerton's company earned itself a decidedly bad name by the 1880s and 1890s in its paralegal attacks on organized labor.

Just as employers found the police inadequate in labor incidents, public authorities could not always rely upon them in riots. One of the most famous riots in American history, the New York City draft riot of 1863, illustrates why. This eruption against New York City blacks raged for two days, with the police ineffectively trying to quell the mobs and their superintendent sustaining injuries to which some attributed his death a few years later. The police were unable to coordinate their maneuvers and lacked the training and discipline to confront moving bands of angry men. The riot was brought under control only with help from Union army troops from Pennsylvania.

The difficulties riots caused for police were most notable a century after the draft riots, over a four-year period from 1964 to 1968, when blacks in most major U.S. cities rioted. These riots, first in New York in 1964, followed by one in Los Angeles in 1965, focused attention on brutal police practices in minority communities. Almost inevitably, the police looked bad, both racist (even though by this time some forces were on their way to being integrated) and incompetent. The Left and the Right criticized the police, and the decade saw a series of federal initiatives aimed at making the police more efficient and more just.

In the Progressive Era, police were often the focus of reformers' efforts to end their corruption and their use of torture (calling it "the third degree" somehow made it seem less nasty) and to increase their efficiency. It is surprising to realize that prior to the period 1890–1920, there was no national coordination of identification other than through picture magazines like the *Police Gazette* and the *Detective;* nor did fingerprinting come into vogue until the first decade of the twentieth century. When a centralized National Identification Bureau was finally created at the turn of the century, it was only with voluntary funding from individual city police departments.

All of these historic elements culminated in the mid-1960s. A series of Supreme Court rulings on evidence (for instance, *Mapp* v. *Ohio,* 1961, and *Miranda* v. *Arizona,* 1966) placed more control on police discretion in gathering evidence and ensured that suspects had access to attorneys. Federal legislation funded additional, nonlocal support of policing via the Law Enforcement Assistance Administration (1968). The LEAA transferred millions of dollars to local police for training, communications technology, and weapons. It also funded a small amount of research, which resulted by the 1970s in growing sophistication in criminal justice research.

Yet, by the end of the 1980s, some of the tensions initially present in policing remained. Increased technological competence still left an open mesh rather than a dragnet for criminal catching; police officers retained considerable discretion; minority neighborhoods complained about police brutality and at the same time about inadequate policing; and nonalcoholic drugs troubled the society and the police as much as alcohol enforcement had a half-century earlier. Most of the discussion of these issues took place at the national level, as did most proposed solutions. Yet the distinguishing historical feature of American police, their local funding and control, added a special character to the national problems: they remain local, independent, and a part of city government.

Roger Lane, *Policing the City: Boston, 1822–1985* (1967); Eric H. Monkkonen, *Police in Urban America, 1860–1920* (1981); Samuel Walker, *Popular Justice: A History of American Criminal Justice* (1980).

ERIC H. MONKKONEN

See also Crime; Draft Riots; Haymarket Affair; *Mapp* v. *Ohio; Miranda v. Arizona;* Pinkertons; Prohibition and Temperance; Prostitution.

POLITICAL PARTIES

See American Independent Party; Communist Party; Constitutional Union Party; Democratic Party; Dixiecrat Party; Federalist Party; Free-Soil Party; Greenback Party; Know-Nothing Party; Liberty Party; National Woman's Party; Party Conventions; People's Party; Republican Party; Socialist Party; Third Parties; Whig Party.

POLITICS, COLONIAL

See Colonial Government and Politics.

POLK, JAMES K.

(1795–1849), eleventh president of the United States. Polk was the son of a prosperous Tennessee farmer. His mother, a devout Presbyterian, made an indelible impression on his character, instilling Calvinistic virtues of hard work, self-discipline, individualism, and a belief in the imperfection of human nature.

After graduating from the University of North Carolina, he took up the practice of law. In 1825 he won a seat in the U.S. House of Representatives, where as a Jacksonian Democrat he distinguished himself as an advocate of states'

rights. He served as Speaker of the House (1835–1839) and governor of Tennessee (1839–1841).

Subsequently twice defeated for reelection to the governorship, he seemed in eclipse until a deadlocked Democratic convention in 1844 unexpectedly nominated him for president. He prevailed over Henry Clay, the Whig nominee, and James G. Birney, the Liberty nominee, becoming a minority president but enjoying majorities in both houses of Congress. The election marked the beginnings of party realignment, and Polk's administration denoted factionalism.

Describing himself as "the hardest working man in this country," Polk displayed a quality of leadership that has won for him a high rating by historians. His success is attributable to a well-formulated set of goals, the dexterous use of his cabinet, frequent consultation with congressmen, the establishment of an administration press, and his conception of himself as representative of the whole people.

The election of 1844 was virtually a referendum on westward expansion, the Democrats championing "the reannexation of Texas" and "the reoccupation of Oregon." Combining belligerency and tact, Polk arrived at a compromise with Great Britain that set the forty-ninth parallel as the northern boundary of the Oregon Territory, thus securing an excellent harbor on the northwest coast.

Texas had been annexed before Polk's inauguration. Wishing to acquire California and New Mexico also, Polk seized on a skirmish between Mexican and U.S. troops as a pretext and in 1846 asked Congress to declare war. His handling of the dispute, his message blaming Mexico for the war, and his zeal for adding territory in the Southwest badly divided the nation. But the Treaty of Guadalupe Hidalgo ending the war gained for the United States the southwestern territory Polk coveted. Polk's negotiations regarding Oregon and military actions in Mexico added 522 million acres to the public domain.

Jacksonian principles marked Polk's economic policy. The Walker Tariff of 1846 lowered duties, and the Independent Treasury law restored a federal depository designed to keep public money out of private banks. But the Democrats lost control of the House in 1846, and his aggressive war policy provoked the Wilmot Proviso aimed at excluding slavery from the territories taken from Mexico. Although the proviso was not passed by the Senate, the principle that Congress could exclude slavery from the territories became the focus of the Republican party.

By 1848 Polk, myopic about the immorality of slavery and the modernization of the nation, was cursing "southern agitators and northern fanatics." His policies led eventually to disintegration of both major parties and the sectional crisis of 1849–1850, although his achievements in adding territory and securing the tariff and banking laws were considerable.

Paul H. Bergeron, *The Presidency of James K. Polk* (1987); Milo Quaife, ed., *The Diary of James K. Polk during His Presidency, 1845 to 1849,* 4 vols. (1910; abridged edition, 1 vol., ed. Allan Nevins, 1929).

JAMES A. RAWLEY

See also Elections: 1844. *For events during Polk's administration, see* Expansion, Continental and Overseas; Independent Treasury; Mexican War; Wilmot Proviso.

POLLING

See Public Opinion Polling.

POLLOCK, JACKSON

(1912–1956), abstract expressionist painter. A pioneering leader of the New York school, Pollock is almost as well known for the myths about his chaotic life as he is for his drip and stain works. Although his departure from painting conventions left him open to criticism, the moment was right for cultural breakthroughs after World War II. The Old World looked to the New, and here was this very American son of the romantic West. Both outsider and seeker, Pollock was unsophisticated, intellectually uncluttered, straightforward, and imaginative. He read little, spoke seldom in company when sober, and was a good listener to those he respected. His unique contribution was to express emotion through abstraction.

As much phenomenon as genius, Pollock was born not on a sheep ranch as myth has it but in Cody, Wyoming. In 1930 he became a student of the regionalist artist Thomas Hart Benton at New York's Art Students League. He was soon a Benton family intimate, taking the feisty, hard-drinking Benton as a role model, artistically and behaviorally. He was also influenced by his museum visits and studies of Rubens and El Greco. As he moved on from Ryder, Miró, Matisse, and finally Picasso, he worked his way through cubism and surrealism, extending them to form his own statement as a master of "direct" painting.

Pollock's attempts at therapy for alcoholism were not effective ultimately, but he was sober from 1948 through most of 1950. Two of his therapists were Jungians and influenced his work, which he saw as coming directly from the unconscious. Discarding easel and palette, Pollock laid his unprimed canvas flat. This allowed him to work it from all sides, even to be *in* the painting, or "arena" of action, to use critic Harold Rosenberg's word.

The physical movements, which created broad sweeps of line, gave rise to the terms *gestural* and *action painting,* and Pollock's use of the canvas totality — "all over" — made for a creative continuum. This had to do with his need to break limits, freeing the work to join its life to that of space. To pour and drip not as accident but as technique had been done by others, but he developed a control that eliminated the accident. He used hard brushes and sticks, even basters, without contacting the canvas. If foreign matter worked — perhaps a cigarette butt — it joined the painting.

He worked without preliminary sketches, and though abstract, his paintings still had a sense of image. In the early fifties, the image began to reappear, notably in his drawings and stain works, which many viewers thought represented regression. To others they are among the most moving of Pollock's works, articulate to a degree he himself never managed.

Pollock also worked "direct" at the experimental graphics studio of Stanley William Hayter, Atelier 17. Hayter influenced Pollock even more than did John Graham, who included him in a 1941 show with the painter Lee Krasner whom he married in 1945. His relationship with her was to be as vital to Pollock's survival as a person as was the promotion of his art by the critic Clement Greenberg.

The collector and dealer Peggy Guggenheim had given Pollock a contract the previous year, as well as commissioning *Mural,* and in his studio in Long Island he was able to do large works, such as the Accabonac series. He joined the Betty Parsons Gallery in 1947, but discouraged by the disaster of his 1951 Black and White show, he moved to the Sidney Janis Gallery in 1952. Such works as the 1952 *Blue Poles* and *Portrait of a Dream* (1953) did better, but in his last year he was little richer in either pocket or spirit. In 1956 his speeding car overturned near his home, killing him and a passenger.

Pollock's breakthrough work, which helped move the avant-garde capital from Paris to New York, has been of incalculable influence and in more than the graphic arts. Expression for all of us has been freed, part of the beauty of his work being in the beauty of our seeing. "In him," Clement Greenberg said, "we had truth."

B. H. Friedman, *Jackson Pollock: Energy Made Visible* (1972); Ellen G. Landau, *Jackson Pollock* (1989); Jeffrey Potter, *To a Violent Grave* (1985; paperback ed., 1988).

JEFFREY POTTER

See also Abstract Expressionism; Guggenheim, Peggy; Painting and Sculpture.

PONTIAC

(c. 1720–1769), Ottawa Indian chief. Pontiac came to symbolize Indian resistance to the spread of white influence and power in the eighteenth century. The subject of Francis Parkman's *The Conspiracy of Pontiac* (1851), he emerged from its pages as a brilliant and determined "Satan of this forest paradise." From the vantage point of the late twentieth century, however, he appears as one of many Indian leaders who sought desperately but ultimately unsuccessfully to limit European dominance in the 1700s.

Pontiac grew up in a time of particularly rapid cultural and technological change. In early adulthood he did not seem an especially noteworthy figure among the Ottawas, a tribe that had lived for several generations in the Great Lakes region. Like many other tribes, the Ottawas had gained materially from their association with the French, but the arrival of British traders in the 1730s ushered in a period of conflict. In the early 1760s the British victory over the French in North America in the French and Indian War signaled altered circumstances for all the Indians of the Midwest.

The British had little patience with the French tradition of gift giving and even less interest in continuing the French practice of donating ammunition, food, and other items to the tribes. The British triumph thus brought confusion and anger that escalated into war. It was in this context that Pontiac, now middle-aged, emerged from obscurity.

As happened occasionally in times of despair in Indian cultures, a visionary appeared, in this case an Indian called the Delaware Prophet who had been living in upper Ohio. He preached to the tribes, exhorting them to turn away from European goods and holding out the dream of the whites' disappearance. Pontiac apparently used his words for his own purposes, challenging the Ottawas and other peoples to unite to drive the British out of the region. In the spring of 1763 he spearheaded a campaign that, though ultimately unsuccessful, achieved some dramatic victories and made clear the degree of Indian discontent with the new order.

Ottawa men joined with allies from the Hurons, Potawotomis, Miamis, Delawares, Senecas, Shawnees, Kickapoos, Chippewas, and other tribes to mount an assault aimed at ridding the area of the British. In the spring and summer of 1763, they attacked a string of British forts, capturing eight and forcing the abandonment of a ninth. But an extended siege of Fort Detroit finally undermined Pontiac's broad but fragile coalition. By late October 1763 Pontiac had been forced to accept the dreary news that the French would not assist him and that the British could not be driven out.

Although he persisted for a time in attempts to reinvigorate his faltering alliance, Pontiac's time had passed, and he gave up altogether the following year. In 1769, now living in peace and relative obscurity, he was murdered by a Peoria man in Cahokia, Illinois.

Howard H. Peckham, *Pontiac and the Indian Uprising* (1947).

PETER IVERSON

See also Colonial Wars; Indians.

PONY EXPRESS

The Pony Express was a system of delivering mail to the American West. Although short-lived and unprofitable, it captivated the popular imagination. It was developed by William H. Russell, who handled promotion, William B. Waddell, in charge of finances, and Alexander Majors, founder of an important freighting business between Independence, Missouri, and Santa Fe, New Mexico. Seeking publicity and federal aid for an overland mail service, Russell induced his partners to go along with his plans for the Pony Express, which would operate between St. Joseph, Missouri, and San Francisco.

The first run was on April 3, 1860, and the Pony Express functioned on a semiweekly basis for nearly two years. A rider would cover two hundred miles a day for ten days, changing horses approximately every ten miles. The route followed a settlers' trail across the present-day states of Kansas, Nebraska, Wyoming, Colorado, Utah, and Nevada to California, carrying mail as well as some small freight for the young Wells Fargo Company.

The Pony Express contributed to the economy of the towns on its route, especially Salt Lake City. But Russell, Waddell, and Majors made no money from it and went bankrupt in 1862. After originally advancing money to the firm, Ben Holladay, who operated a freight business and was later a power in stagecoaches, steamships, and railroads, took over the Pony Express at a foreclosure sale in 1862. Although it had served a need by providing mail service, the Pony Express was rendered obsolete by the Western Union Telegraph Company and the coming of the transcontinental railroad.

POP ART

Pop art's subject matter was the slick, formulaic images of mass culture and its medium the stylized graphics of commercial art. Although originating in England, the movement flourished in America during the mid-1950s and 1960s. Glorifying everyday objects and visual clichés, it served as witty commentary on the materialism and banality of mid-twentieth-century America.

Among its famous examples are Jasper Johns's American flags, the packaged sexuality of Tom Wesselman's *Great American Nude* series, Andy Warhol's canonization of the Campbell's soup can, and Roy Lichtenstein's blowups of comic strip details. Other artists associated with the movement included Claes Oldenburg, Robert Rauschenberg, James Rosenquist, Robert Indiana, and Jim Dine.

Pop art was a reaction against the introspective and rarefied sensibility of abstract expressionism. Surface appearance replaced inner vision, humor substituted for high seriousness, and the impersonality of silk screen and the benday dot subsumed painterly expression. Like dada, its European forerunner, it challenged the concept of art by elevating the vulgar and ordinary to the status of art object. Yet pop art shared none of dada's vitriol; typically presenting the appearance of impervious neutrality toward its subject matter, it rarely betrayed outright satire. Detractors lamented that pop art merely imitated rather than transcended its content; supporters countered that by serving up the commonplace as icons, it invited examination of the numbing pervasiveness of secondhand experience.

See also Painting and Sculpture.

POPULAR SOVEREIGNTY

Also known as "squatter sovereignty," this was one of several suggested answers to the question of slavery in the territories. In the wake of the Wilmot Proviso, Senator Lewis Cass of Michigan wrote in the "Nicholson letter" of December 1847 that whether or not Congress had the power to decide the issue, it should actually be left to the territory's citizens. Popular sovereignty became Democratic policy, and Cass was the party's nominee for president in 1848. He was defeated, however, by Whig Zachary Taylor, in part because antislavery Democrats bolted to the Free-Soil party. Thus, the 36°30′ line created by the Missouri Compromise of 1820 remained in place. After the Compromise of 1850, if the issue remained open, the debate over it quieted.

Senator Stephen A. Douglas of Illinois again raised the question of popular sovereignty in 1854 in the Kansas-Nebraska Act, which repealed the Missouri Compromise. The measure ostensibly represented another sectional trade-off — Nebraska would be free, and Kansas slave. Instead, it reopened the debate over slavery, split the Democratic party, and led to the collapse of the second party system, to "Bleeding Kansas," and to the birth of the Republican party. When the Supreme Court ruled in the *Dred Scott* case that Congress had no power to ban slavery in the territories, Douglas countered by enunciating what became known as the Freeport Doctrine during his debates with Abraham Lincoln: "Slavery cannot exist a day in the midst of an unfriendly people with unfriendly laws." By supporting popular sovereignty over the *Dred Scott* ruling, Douglas lost most of his support among southerners.

See also Democratic Party; Douglas, Stephen A.

POPULATION

See table on facing page.

POPULISM

As a term of political description, *populism* is one of the most frequently misused words in the English language. It signals a politics of resentment — mean-spirited and incipiently violent. As commonly employed, *populism* appears as a term of condescension, vague and formless but no less evocative in the disdain it projects.

In recent years, this characterization has undergone full-scale revaluation in the wake of a broad array of new evidence as to who the original populists were, what they believed, and how they acted. In the process, our sense of the intricacies involved in popular politics has been deepened in ways that enrich the modern understanding of politics itself.

In strictly historical terms, Populism refers to a third-party movement that materialized in America in the 1890s, generating a spirited energy that also caused a certain alarm near the seats of the mighty. The Populists engaged in a social analysis of contemporary American society that yielded a range of proposed economic reforms. Foremost among them was the Subtreasury Land and Loan System, which reconceptualized American banking and proposed a restructured monetary system that would fundamentally alter the power relationships between bankers and everyone else. The Populist concern about "concentrated capital" extended beyond banks to include large-scale business organizations generally. Populist reformers felt that business domination of the political process — through massive campaign contributions to friendly officeholders and persistently effective lobbying in the national Congress and the state legislatures — had proceeded to the point that the practice had begun to undermine the democratic idea itself.

In an effort to restructure American politics, Populists formed the People's party, which was free of corporate influence. The new party polled over a million votes in its initial campaign in 1892, made sizable gains in 1894, and then joined with the free-silver wing of the Democratic party to support William Jennings Bryan's unsuccessful presidential candidacy in 1896. Having lost much of its distinctive identity in the course of its "fusion" with the Democrats, the third party suffered an abrupt decline thereafter.

For many years, the scholarly verdict on populism was fairly patronizing, for it was considered an "alarmist" response to the growth of industrial America. The remedies suggested by the reformers, though doubtless well-meaning, were taken to be "excessive." Beyond this, scholars, digesting the mountain of social and economic analysis generated by the Populists, focused on certain colorful characters, such as Mary Elizabeth Lease of Kansas and Thomas Watson of Georgia, and quoted selected purple passages to emphasize the "primitive" or "demagogic" elements that seemed to animate the movement. The final blow to the Populists' reputation came in the form of suggestions that some were racists, nativists, anti-Semites, anti-Catholics, or a combination thereof. The movement, therefore, could be understood as a behavioral manifestation of deep-seated prejudices and "status anxieties," not a sensible product aimed at correcting unbalanced or generally exploitative economic practices pervading American society.

Over the past generation, social historians have sharpened their penetration into voluntary social formations such as the one the Populists constructed and, in so doing, have unearthed evidence of democratic advocacy that has fundamentally altered the understanding of the relevance of the nineteenth-century movement. The parent institution of populism, the National Farmers Alliance and Industrial Union, set up

Population of the United States, 1790–1990

Census Year	Population	% Change from Last Census
1790	3,929,214	—
1800	5,308,483	35.1
1810	7,239,881	36.4
1820	9,638,453	33.1
1830	12,866,020	33.5
1840	17,069,453	32.7
1850	23,191,876	35.9
1860	31,443,321	35.6
1870	39,818,449	26.6
1880	50,155,783	26.0
1890	62,947,714	25.5
1900	75,994,575	20.7
1910	91,972,266	21.0
1920	105,710,620	14.9
1930	122,775,046	16.1
1940	131,669,275	7.2
1950	151,325,798	14.5
1960	179,323,175	18.5
1970	203,211,926	13.3
1980	226,504,825	11.5
1990	249,632,692[a]	10.21

a. Preliminary figure.

an elaborate lecturing system that turned some forty thousand "suballiances" into a veritable schoolroom of economic and political inquiry. The Populist reforms were not only broadly egalitarian and democratic but workable as well. Instead of appearing as mindless provincials, the reformers were regarded as humanistic advocates who numbered within their ranks prominent reform editors and organizers — Catholic, Jewish, and African-American as well as white, Anglo-Saxon, and Protestant. Historian Walter T. K. Nugent summarized matters in the title of his book: *The Tolerant Populists.*

Beyond the issue of historical accuracy, the restructured view of the Populists is of increasing interest to political scientists for the light the research casts upon categories of analysis that have long been used by theorists to interpret and project social possibility. The Populist experience shows how easily election campaigns and the legislative process are made vulnerable to powerful economic influences and how these malpractices can be brought into public view through critical appraisals generated by self-organized popular constituencies. There is a third, rather unwanted, discovery — the multiple hazards to popular democracy that persist in highly stratified and socially isolated modern populations. As the Populist experience clarifies the interrelationship of these dynamics, a series of long-standing assumptions about political conduct in the modern state have come under sustained revaluation.

For generations, many scholars took the sudden appearance of citizen politics in any society as some sort of "spontaneous" happening through which the routine "apathy" of "ordinary people" was somehow temporarily overcome. As the enormous practical difficulties involved in creating organized citizen advocacy have become better understood, it is increasingly apparent that serious political movements are laboriously constructed by human hands and are in no sense "spontaneous." Indeed, the term is used by scholars to describe moments of political organization they have not otherwise researched. As such, the word *spontaneous* routinely conceals the social relations it purports to describe.

Moreover, given the powerful economic and

cultural authority invested in prevailing forms of elite governance, the hesitancy of average citizens to expose themselves to retribution and ridicule by opposing sanctioned authority clearly involves an intelligent (if cautious) response that cannot accurately be described as "apathetic." The process through which social fear is, on occasion, overcome stands as an important and neglected question that bears directly on the long-term durability of democratic substance in any society.

In the aggregate, what a clear reading of populism and other large-scale popular movements reveals is that, as a category of political science, democratic movement building has been centrally overlooked. Abstract description has substituted for sustained research. What scholars mean to imply when they use the term *political consciousness* is similarly ephemeral and thus stands in need of detailed elaboration and redefinition. In the contemporary period when the savings and loan crisis and attendant structural problems in the banking system itself have once again forced the populist concern for the "financial question" upon the stage of national politics, the paucity of systematic analysis of the nation's banking system has brought all these matters of social and political interpretation to the surface with transparent power. As scholars seek more precise categories of analysis with which to interpret "reform politics," new questions arise as to the way "mainstream politics" is understood as well. The dynamics that underlay the appearance of nineteenth-century populism thus turn out to be quite "modern."

Lawrence Goodwyn, *Democratic Promise: The Populist Movement in America* (1976); Walter T. K. Nugent, *The Tolerant Populists: Kansas Populists and Nativism* (1963).

LAWRENCE GOODWYN

See also Elections: 1892, 1896; People's Party; Subtreasury Land and Loan System.

PORTER, COLE

(1891–1964), songwriter. A new kind of popular song was heard in the United States after World War I, its lyrics earthy, sophisticated, and altogether un-Victorian, its melody and rhythm influenced by black jazz and European impressionism. One of the leading composers of the new music was Cole Porter of Peru, Indiana, Yale University, and a "smart set" that made London, Paris, Biarritz, Venice, and Manhattan its playground. Although he is best known for the cleverness, double entendres, and sexual suggestiveness of his lyrics and for melodies that pulse with a Latin or tropical beat, Porter in fact created dazzlingly diverse poems and tunes, some classically romantic, others the delight of jazz musicians.

Born to wealth and indulged by an adoring mother, Porter early on displayed remarkable talent for musical composition, deft phrasemaking, and high living. When he wrote in "I Get a Kick Out of You," "I get no kick from cocaine," he wrote from personal experience, as he did, also, in "Anything Goes," in which he observed that, when "every night the set that's smart is intruding in nudist parties in studios, anything goes!" As a composer, however, Cole was as disciplined and hardworking as any Calvinist, and fortunately, he was blessed with a genius for songwriting that transcended his personal experiences. Only George Gershwin, Jerome Kern, Richard Rodgers, and Irving Berlin could match him in the quality and quantity of enduring songs they created — and of this nonpareil group only Berlin and Porter wrote both the words and the music of their songs.

Most of Porter's finest works were written for the musical comedies that flourished on Broadway between the two world wars. Among these were *Gay Divorce; Anything Goes; Jubilee; Red, Hot and Blue!; DuBarry Was a Lady; Panama Hattie; Something for the Boys; Kiss Me, Kate; Out of This World;* and *Can-Can.* He also wrote the scores for such films as *Born to Dance, Rosalie, Broadway Melody of 1940, Something to Shout About, High Society, Les Girls,* and, of course, those of his Broadway musicals that Hollywood produced.

Porterian naughtiness is nicely displayed in "Let's Do It" (to which censors insisted he add the politic subtitle: "Let's Fall in Love"), "My Heart Belongs to Daddy," and "Always True to You in My Fashion." Cole's gift for satiric realism is revealed in "Love for Sale" and "Anything Goes." He is an unblushing romantic in "I Concentrate on You," "In the Still of the Night," and "All through the Night," a cheerful lover in "It's De-Lovely," "You're the Top," and "At Long Last Love," wistful in "Why Shouldn't I?" and "Every Time We Say Goodbye," and obsessed in "Night and Day" and "I've Got You under My Skin."

Although not all of Porter's songs were popular or artistic hits, his successes were many and remarkable, appealing to mass audiences as well as to urbane showgoers on Broadway. A heroic feature of Cole Porter's life was his refusal to permit a near-fatal horseback-riding accident that caused him great pain every day of his life after 1937 to interfere either with the quantity of his creative output or the often droll and carefree mood characteristic of so many of his songs.

George Eells, *The Life That Late He Led* (1967); Charles Schwartz, *Cole Porter: A Biography* (1979).

EDWARD PESSEN

See also Jazz; Music; Musical Theater.

POTSDAM CONFERENCE

The Potsdam Conference, held near Berlin, July 17–August 2, 1945, was the last of the Big Three meetings during World War II. It was attended by Premier Joseph Stalin of the Soviet Union, the new American president, Harry S. Truman, and Prime Minister Winston Churchill of Great Britain (replaced on July 28 by his successor, Clement Attlee). On July 26, the leaders issued a declaration demanding "unconditional surrender" from Japan, concealing the fact that they had privately agreed to let Japan retain its emperor. Otherwise, the conference centered on postwar Europe. A Council of Foreign Ministers was agreed upon, with membership from the Big Three plus China and France.

Military administration of Germany was established, with a central Allied Control Council (the requirement that ACC decisions be unanimous would later prove to be crippling). The leaders arrived at various agreements on the German economy, placing primary emphasis on the development of agriculture and nonmilitary industry. The institutions that had controlled the economy under the Nazis were to be decentralized, but all of Germany would be treated as a single economic unit. War criminals would be brought to trial. Stalin's request to define the Polish-German border was put off till the peace treaty, but the conference accepted his transfer of the land east of the Oder and Neisse rivers from Germany to Poland. Regarding reparations, a compromise was worked out, based on an exchange of capital equipment from the Western zone for raw materials from the East. It resolved a dispute but set the precedent of managing the German economy by zone rather than comprehensively as the Western powers had hoped.

Although postwar Europe dominated the Potsdam agenda, the war in the Pacific lurked offstage. Truman received word of the successful atomic bomb test soon after he arrived at Potsdam; he told Churchill the news but mentioned "a new weapon" only casually to Stalin. Truman continued to solicit Stalin's assistance against Japan, but he knew that if the bomb succeeded, Russian help would not be needed. Indeed, the bomb would give the United States unprecedented power in the postwar world.

See also Truman, Harry S.; World War II.

POUND, EZRA

(1885–1972), poet. Until age twenty-two Pound lived and attended schools in New York and Pennsylvania. In 1901 at the University of Pennsylvania he began a lifelong friendship with William Carlos Williams. He transferred to Hamilton where in 1905 he received a Ph.B. — a degree the school invented for him (and never offered before or since) to fit the assortment of courses he insisted on taking. He then returned to Penn. Money problems in 1907 forced him to take a job at Wabash College, Indiana, but after four months he was fired for being "a Latin Quarter type." The next year he went by cattle boat to Spain, crossed to Venice, stayed for three months, and then went to London where William Butler Yeats was and the action should be. There he became a catalyst for all serious artists who fought to realize their élan and "make it new": T. S. Eliot, James Joyce, Ford Madox Ford, Wyndham Lewis, and H. D., among others. In 1914 he married Dorothy Shakespear. She had a small income; he supported himself by writing.

His major works include, in poetry: *A lume spento* (1908), *Cathay* (1915), *Lustra* (1916), *Quia pauper amavi* (1919), and *The Cantos* (1917–1961); in prose: *The Spirit of Romance* (1910), *Noh* (1916), *Instigations* (1920), *ABC of Reading* (1934), *Guide to Kulchur* (1938), and *The Classic Anthology Defined by Confucius* (1954). Concurrently, he translated volumes of poetry, prose, and drama from Greek, Latin, Provençal, Japanese, and Chinese. Tirelessly, he fought Western provincialism and celebrated the great art of China, Japan, and Africa.

From Rapallo, Italy, where he lived after 1924, he conducted a worldwide correspondence with all who sought his help. But he became increasingly controversial, partly because his critics didn't know what he meant by words such as *illumination*. That word, which he said he used "in a technical sense," is the key to his life and his work and marks him as a visionary and a mystic in the Neoplatonic-Blake-Whitman tradition.

Pound's major work, *The Cantos,* expresses this tradition, as did all his acts and opinions. According to Pound, *The Cantos* was a poem containing history and concerning humanity's progress out of tribal darkness toward the light of *paradiso terrestre* to come in the future. All mystics find that the major world religions manifest tribal darkness, which they express by war and dogma, and "dogma" is the "bluff" of "tax-gathering priests" based on "ignorance." Of Christ himself he said, "He is hardly to be blamed for the religion that has been foisted upon him." The coming of paradiso terrestre is deterred mainly by the love of money, for money is power and power corrupts. Thus avarice was a central theme of *The Cantos,* in which bankers and munition makers create wars. He became known as anti-Semitic though he wrote, "Inasmuch as the Jew has conducted no holy war for nearly two millennia, he is preferable to the Christian and the Muhammadan." His anti-Semitism was due not to his opinions on race or religion but to what Pound saw as the corrupting force of money and power.

In 1945 he was arrested for treason because of radio broadcasts he made from Italy in 1941. He spent six months at the Disciplinary Training Center in Pisa and was then flown to the United States. Being found unfit to stand trial, he was remanded to St. Elizabeths where, before his release and return to Italy, he stayed for thirteen years. Being thus relieved of the need to make a living, he practiced his art and produced his greatest work. All his life, he had said the state should provide its artists with a "competence": money enough to exist on so they could create. Ironically, at St. Elizabeths the state provided that competence. Even better, Congress founded the National Endowment for the Arts, which brought us a little closer to the light of paradise-on-earth when, as the final lines of *The Cantos* say, we will enter "arcanum" "To be men not destroyers."

Hugh Kenner, *The Pound Era* (1971); Peter Makin, *Pound's Cantos* (1985).

CARROLL F. TERRELL

See also Expatriates and Exiles; Literature.

POVERTY

Although Americans have long celebrated their nation's wealth and the abundance of its resources, poverty has been omnipresent in American history. From the colonial period to the present day, large numbers of Americans have been poor: they have lacked the resources to feed, clothe, and shelter themselves adequately according to socially defined standards. Just how many Americans have lived in poverty over the course of more than three centuries is impossible to gauge; not only are data scarce, but the definition of poverty has changed too often (and is too subject to debate) to permit precise measurement. Nonetheless, there can be no doubt that poverty, as a personal condition and as a social problem, has long been a prominent feature of the economic and social landscape.

Poverty was certainly widespread during the

settlement decades of the seventeenth century. Most settlers in the New World had to contend with at least periodic material scarcity, and unfree laborers (slaves and indentured servants) always lived near the margins of subsistence. Seventeenth-century society also recognized the enduring presence of dependent and destitute individuals; by 1685, for example, the city of Boston had constructed an almshouse. Both the poor and the outright destitute (often the aged or infirm) were regarded as natural and inevitable components of an inherently hierarchical social order.

In the course of the eighteenth century, poverty became a more visible social problem, particularly in the port cities of the North. While farmers who lived on marginal lands continued to inhabit a world of scarcity, the urban centers witnessed a significant growth in the number of wage earners who became destitute whenever commerce flagged or serious economic dislocations occurred. In Boston, New York, and Philadelphia, for example, the number of people needing public assistance rose dramatically during and after the Seven Years' War. By the end of the century, according to some national estimates, virtually all African-Americans (slave and free) and between one-fifth and one-third of all whites lived in poverty.

Despite economic growth fueled by agricultural expansion and the Industrial Revolution, the problem of poverty did not become any less acute in the nineteenth century. Rural poverty persisted, particularly in the South; at the same time, the nation witnessed enormous population growth, rapid urbanization, and the formation of a large industrial working class most of whose members were either poor or could easily become so during hard times. It was in this century, particularly after 1870, that the social problem of poverty began to be identified primarily with urban society and crowded urban ghettos. In 1904, in his pioneering study, *Poverty,* Robert Hunter, citing Jacob Riis, noted that 10 percent of the people who died in New York City between 1885 and 1890 had been given a pauper's burial; he also claimed that 20 percent of the population of Boston lived in actual distress. In the nation as a whole, Hunter estimated that 10 million people, roughly 12 percent of the population, were poor at the turn of the century. More recent analysts have concluded that Hunter's estimates — distressing as they may have been to contemporaries — were far too low, that, in fact, a broader definition of poverty would have embraced roughly 40 percent of all Americans in 1900.

The twentieth century witnessed a significant, yet unsteady, decline in the overall incidence of poverty (as well as a dramatic improvement in the acquisition of data bearing on the issue). Increases in real wages permitted many blue-collar Americans to cross the poverty line during the first quarter of the century, but the Great Depression reversed the gains that had been made. When Franklin D. Roosevelt proclaimed, in 1937, that "one-third" of the nation was "ill-housed, ill-clad, ill-nourished," he was understating the problem: in fact, the poverty rate was probably closer to 40 or 45 percent. After the Great Depression, however, the proportion of Americans living in poverty dropped sharply: according to government statistics, the figure stood at 30 percent in 1950, 20 percent in 1960, 13 percent in 1968, and 11 percent in 1973. Although these percentages meant that millions of people remained poor (23 million lived in official poverty in 1973), they suggested that the extraordinary growth of the economy between 1940 and the early 1970s was gradually eradicating the problem. Unfortunately, this benign statistical trend came to a halt in the 1970s and reversed itself after 1980. During the depression of the early 1980s, the poverty rate rose above 15 percent; in 1988, well after the depression had ended, it stood at 13 percent, reflecting the poverty of 32 million people — 8 million more than had been officially poor a decade earlier.

Throughout these years, poverty afflicted some segments of the population far more than others. During the eighteenth and nineteenth centuries, more poor people lived in rural areas than in cities; although less visible and perhaps less dramatic, rural poverty was just as debilitating as its urban counterpart, and there were millions of rural families who experienced chronic or periodic distress well into the twentieth century. Many of these families eventually responded to their plight by migrating to the cities; indeed, after 1940, when technological transformations in agriculture precipitated a massive exodus from the land, the number of poor people living in rural areas declined substantially.

This exodus was most pronounced in the South, which had always been the nation's poorest region. In the late nineteenth century, poverty was far more widespread in all the southern states than in any others; as late as 1930, one-fourth of the population of the South lived in housing that typically lacked indoor plumbing, electricity, or running water. Only after World War II did the gap between the South and the rest of the country narrow noticeably, as a result both of the diversification of the Sunbelt economies and of the migration of poor southerners to other regions. This migration, indeed, symbolized the most pronounced cluster of changes that has occurred in the social history of poverty in the United States: the problem has moved northward and from the countryside to the cities.

In both urban and rural America, poverty has always been more common among nonwhites than among whites; from the eighteenth century through the mid-twentieth century, most African-Americans were among the rural poor. And during key periods, poverty was also much more common among immigrants than among the native-born, particularly in cities: the poor, in nineteenth-century cities, tended to be disproportionately Irish, Italian, eastern European, or French Canadian. In key respects, these tendencies have proved to be durable; as recently as 1988, the poverty rates for African-Americans and for people of Hispanic background were roughly triple the rate for whites.

Two other dimensions of the distribution of poverty warrant mention. First, throughout the eighteenth and nineteenth centuries, the elderly constituted a relatively high percentage of the poor or, at least, the dependent poor. But in the mid-twentieth century, as a result of both private pension plans and the Social Security system, the incidence of poverty among the elderly declined. And second, at roughly the same time, the problem became increasingly rampant among women and children. In 1988, more than half of all poor families were headed by women, and nearly 40 percent of the nation's poor were children.

Public perceptions and understandings of poverty have changed considerably over the years. In the seventeenth-century world where scarcity was commonplace, the existence of poverty was regarded as natural, inescapable, and divinely sanctioned. The poor — meaning the overtly needy and dependent — were to be helped and pitied, but their poverty did not necessarily reflect on their characters, nor was their presence an emblem of societal failure. Only in the nineteenth century did a more secular, moralistic view of poverty become widespread; as urban industrial poverty became more common, so too did the conviction that people became poor because of personal flaws. As more and more able-bodied men and women began to show up in the ranks of the poor, public attitudes hardened: paupers were regarded as improvident, drunken, lazy, or promiscuous. Poverty, in most but not all cases, was construed as a sign of individual failure; the distinction between the "worthy" and the "unworthy" poor became an important one in middle-class perceptions of the working class.

In some circles, at least, this moralistic view was succeeded by a structural understanding of poverty in the late nineteenth and early twentieth centuries. Social reformers, Robert Hunter among them, launched numerous investigations of the problem and concluded that the causes of poverty, in the vast majority of cases, were societal rather than personal: unsteady employment rather than sloth, according to Hunter, was the most common source of poverty among urban workers. (This fact — and indeed the structural understanding of poverty — was already well known among workers themselves.) These reformers also transformed the definition of the social problem of poverty: they argued that pauperism or dependence was merely the tip of the iceberg, that the real poverty problem in the United States was the far more widespread inadequacy of food, clothing, shelter, medical care, and education. In addition, turn-of-the-century progressives put forward the notion that the

American nation had become sufficiently wealthy for poverty to be eradicated. Throughout the twentieth century, this structural understanding — with changes in some of its details — has coexisted with the more moralistic view; the poor consequently have been regarded both as victims of societal shortcomings and as lazy or immoral perpetrators of their own plight.

Not surprisingly, these shifts in understanding and attitudes, coupled with the changes that occurred in the composition of the poor population, led to a succession of public responses to the problem. In the seventeenth and eighteenth centuries, local communities or counties assumed responsibility for caring for their own poor (or at least the dependent poor, who were most commonly either the aged or the infirm). Poor people lacking a legal residence were "warned out" of town, but those who did belong either were given "outdoor" relief (while they remained in their own homes) or were cared for in individual households or almshouses, with the cost shared by the community. The nineteenth century, however, witnessed a series of reforms in these customary practices, reforms that were often aimed at lowering the cost of poor relief as well as helping the poor. Large public poorhouses, designed both to rehabilitate and isolate the indigent, were institutionalized during the first half of the century. And in subsequent decades the "scientific charity" movement successfully promoted the abolition, or diminution, of public outdoor relief; the new charity experts also insisted that private agencies carefully investigate and screen the poor to weed out the able-bodied and to separate the "worthy" from the "unworthy."

The most significant policy changes to occur in modern American history were those promulgated during the New Deal. Responsibility for providing aid to the poor was, to a considerable degree, shifted from municipalities and states to the federal government; the unemployed and the elderly were provided with social insurance; public assistance for some of the disabled and infirm, as well as dependent children, became an "entitlement." These programs vastly enlarged the support available to the poor and, coupled with the rapid economic growth that began in 1940, led many Americans to conclude that poverty was a problem of the past. The rediscovery of poverty amidst great plenty in the 1960s came then as a shock to middle-class Americans, a shock that helped launch attacks on poverty by the Kennedy and Johnson administrations. Lyndon B. Johnson's War on Poverty — an assembly of large-scale federal programs targeted at a variety of subpopulations — achieved some tangible results, but it did not come close to its widely publicized goal of conquering the problem. In its aftermath, few innovative or significant public policies were put into place; indeed, one of the central tenets of the Republican administrations of the 1970s and 1980s was that the problem of poverty was best addressed by promoting private-sector economic growth.

Just why poverty has been so persistent — why more than 30 million people remain poor — is a much-debated issue. Some analysts have argued that the rate of economic growth has been insufficient to eradicate poverty, whereas others maintain that the cause resides more in the maldistribution of income. Some see the poor as lacking the skills or the will to escape their condition; others see the economy as dependent upon the poor to provide a low-wage labor force for industry and agriculture. Some critics have argued that government programs have not been sufficiently extensive or adequately funded to achieve their goals; others have claimed that such programs were always designed not to cure the problem but to discipline and regulate the poor. This lack of agreement, about the diagnosis and the prescription, has long been characteristic of twentieth-century public discourse about poverty. Yet, as the century drew to a close, both policy experts and the citizenry as a whole seemed to be less optimistic than they once were that the problem could, or would, be eradicated at all.

Robert H. Bremner, *From the Depths: The Discovery of Poverty in the United States* (1956); Gary B. Nash, *The Urban Crucible: Social Change, Political Consciousness, and the Origins of the American Revolution* (1979); James T. Patterson, *America's Struggle against Poverty, 1900–1980* (1981).

ALEXANDER KEYSSAR

See also Depressions; Great Society; Harrington, Michael; Internal Migration; Mobility, Social and Economic; New Deal; Settlement Houses; Townsend Plan; Unemployment; Wealth and Its Distribution; Welfare and Public Relief.

PRESIDENCY

Established under Article 2 of the Constitution, the office of the president was unique and without precedent, although some of its features, including the designation "president," were foreshadowed in several state constitutions. The principal architect was James Wilson of Pennsylvania, head of the faction at the Constitutional Convention calling for a strong executive on the ground that in a country as large as the United States only such a one could have influence in distant parts. As chairman of the Committee of Detail, he proposed a single rather than a plural head, who would have control of foreign affairs and be able to exercise a legislative veto. Wilson's view that the president must be a man of the people carried the day, though his desire that the president be elected directly by the people did not.

The question of how to choose the executive was commingled with the question of how to keep the office independent of the legislature. The outcome was the creation of an electoral college chosen by the state legislatures exclusively for the purpose of naming a president. The assumption that George Washington would be the first president and willing to serve indefinitely informed the decision that there should be no limit on the reeligibility of the president. The length of the president's term, much discussed, was fixed at four years by the committee appointed late in the convention to deal with unfinished business. Charged to see that the laws are faithfully executed, the president is head of the executive branch and commander in chief of the armed forces. Through the veto he also exercises legislative power, and through his power to appoint judges and the requirement that he execute the laws, he exercises judicial power, too.

In practice the presidency has been an evolving office. Each chief executive has put his stamp on it through the force of his personality and the requirements of the day. The president is now the central American political figure, a constant source of news and symbol of the nation. He has become the de facto head of his political party, and the chief shaper of foreign policy, including the initiation of treaties. Through the device of executive agreements a president may make international arrangements for the life of his term in office that dispense with the need to obtain the approval of Congress. Congress, moreover, has by statute conferred extraconstitutional powers upon the president that include such matters as the management of trade relations, the protection of natural resources, and the right to intervene in labor-management disputes.

The recruitment of presidents has been a source of fascination, wonderment, and entertainment for Americans almost from the beginning of the Republic. George Washington in 1789 (and again in 1793), and John Adams in 1797 were chosen chief executive by the electoral college, as the Constitution intended. Adams was succeeded in turn by Thomas Jefferson (1801), James Madison (1809), and James Monroe (1817) — all from Virginia. This so-called Virginia Dynasty came to an end as new states farther to the west entered the Union and made claims requiring satisfaction.

Meanwhile, by 1800, divergent political factions were coalescing into the Federalist and Democratic-Republican parties, and these loosely organized entities, through their leaders in Congress assembled in caucuses, selected the candidates for the office. After 1824, when John Quincy Adams was elected in a canvass so close that it had to be decided by the House of Representatives, "King Caucus," increasingly criticized as "undemocratic," gave way to popularly chosen nominating conventions, which had already found favor in many states. By 1832, the major parties, now the National Republicans and the Democrats, were nominating their presidential candidates in national conventions.

Andrew Jackson, an icon of the frontier, was elected handily in 1828. He was the first "man of the people" and the creator of a new kind of president, a man with a national rather than merely sectional constituency and responsive to newly emergent public opinion. The death of William Henry Harrison in 1841, the first president to die in office, settled the problem of presidential succession. Despite some argument that the vice president was only acting president, John Tyler's insistence that he was indeed the president prevailed. Still, it was not until Theodore Roosevelt, who had succeeded to the presidency on the death of William McKinley in 1901, was subsequently nominated for the top place (in 1904) that an "accidental" president was so honored.

The election of Abraham Lincoln in 1860, which provoked secession and brought on the Civil War, opened yet another era in the history of the office. The Republican party, recognized as the savior of the Union, became for two generations the party of the presidents. Between 1860 and 1932 only Grover Cleveland and Woodrow Wilson carried the Democratic banner to victory. But the Great Depression that led in 1932 to the election of Franklin D. Roosevelt, a Democrat, not only shattered the spell of the Republicans but once more altered the character of the office. Under Roosevelt, it became a dynamo of social experimentation aimed at providing for the needs of the deprived. The Second World War, which began in the middle of Roosevelt's unique four-term presidency, gave the office immense cachet as the voice of democracy and the free world. By that time, presidents were elected following campaigns of nationwide barnstorming, after the pattern set by William Jennings Bryan, the Democratic candidate in 1896. Candidates' positions earlier were conveyed to a few newspapers in carefully wrought letters. Beginning in 1932 radio was a principal means of reaching the public, followed after 1948 by television.

The coming of the cold war in 1945 placed new responsibility on the presidency as the energizer of opposition to communism. That long struggle ended with the collapse of the Soviet empire in the late 1980s. In the same period, the presidency had not flourished uniformly. After Dwight D. Eisenhower's two terms ended in 1961, no chief executive left office amid the cheers of the people for almost thirty years: John

F. Kennedy was assassinated in 1963 (the fourth assassination in the history of the office, after Lincoln, 1865; James A. Garfield, 1881; William McKinley, 1901); Lyndon B. Johnson's presidency was devastated by the nation's growing opposition to the war in Vietnam; Richard M. Nixon's tenure was terminated by his resignation (the first in White House history) when he was about to be impeached for obstruction of justice, abuse of power, and contempt of Congress — all charges growing out of the Watergate affair. Vice President Spiro T. Agnew, having been forced to resign under threat of indictment for income-tax evasion, was replaced by Nixon under the terms of the Twenty-fifth Amendment with Representative Gerald Ford of Michigan. When Ford became president upon Nixon's departure, he named Nelson A. Rockefeller to be vice president, thus giving the country for the only time both an unelected chief executive and an unelected vice president.

The election in 1976 of Jimmy Carter and in 1980 of Ronald Reagan, whose main experience had been as governors, seemed to show a popular desire to have a president who arose outside the "intrigues" of Washington, D.C. But in 1988, when George Bush became president, the public opted for a person well acquainted with politics in the nation's capital.

From the start of the presidency, the president's wife has been a public figure in her own right. Although the label "First Lady" was not commonly used until after the Civil War, the wife of the president has always been accorded uncommon respect. Martha Washington was often referred to as "Lady Washington," and the titles "Mrs. President" and "Presidentress" were familiar appellations until the Civil War, a recognition that in significant ways the presidency is a two-person office. James Buchanan remains the only bachelor president.

Among presidents' wives, a number have stood out in the public eye in addition to Mrs. Washington: Dolley Payne Madison (who served as hostess for Jefferson, a widower, and then for her husband, 1801–1817), Sara Childress Polk (1845–1849), Mary Todd Lincoln (1861–1865), and Eleanor Roosevelt (1933–1945). Although no woman has yet been elected to the White

Presidents of the United States

No.	Name	Born–Died	Years in Office	Political Party	Home State	Vice President
1	George Washington	1732–1799	1789–1797	None	Va.	John Adams
2	John Adams	1735–1826	1797–1801	Federalist	Mass.	Thomas Jefferson
3	Thomas Jefferson	1743–1826	1801–1809	Republican[a]	Va.	Aaron Burr
						George Clinton
4	James Madison	1751–1836	1809–1817	Republican	Va.	George Clinton
						Elbridge Gerry
5	James Monroe	1758–1831	1817–1825	Republican	Va.	Daniel D. Tompkins
6	John Quincy Adams	1767–1848	1825–1829	Republican	Mass.	John C. Calhoun
7	Andrew Jackson	1767–1845	1829–1837	Democratic	Tenn.	John C. Calhoun
						Martin Van Buren
8	Martin Van Buren	1782–1862	1837–1841	Democratic	N.Y.	Richard M. Johnson
9	William Henry Harrison	1773–1841	1841	Whig	Ohio	John Tyler
10	John Tyler	1790–1862	1841–1845	Whig	Va.	—
11	James K. Polk	1795–1849	1845–1849	Democratic	Tenn.	George M. Dallas
12	Zachary Taylor	1784–1850	1849–1850	Whig	La.	Millard Fillmore
13	Millard Fillmore	1800–1874	1850–1853	Whig	N.Y.	—
14	Franklin Pierce	1804–1869	1853–1857	Democratic	N.H.	William R. King
15	James Buchanan	1791–1868	1857–1861	Democratic	Pa.	John C. Breckinridge
16	Abraham Lincoln	1809–1865	1861–1865	Republican	Ill.	Hannibal Hamlin
						Andrew Johnson
17	Andrew Johnson	1808–1875	1865–1869	Republican	Tenn.	—
18	Ulysses S. Grant	1822–1885	1869–1877	Republican	Ill.	Schuyler Colfax
						Henry Wilson
19	Rutherford B. Hayes	1822–1893	1877–1881	Republican	Ohio	William A. Wheeler
20	James A. Garfield	1831–1881	1881	Republican	Ohio	Chester A. Arthur
21	Chester A. Arthur	1830–1886	1881–1885	Republican	N.Y.	—
22	Grover Cleveland	1837–1908	1885–1889	Democratic	N.Y.	Thomas A. Hendricks
23	Benjamin Harrison	1833–1901	1889–1893	Republican	Ind.	Levi P. Morton
24	Grover Cleveland		1893–1897	Democratic	N.Y.	Adlai E. Stevenson
25	William McKinley	1843–1901	1897–1901	Republican	Ohio	Garret A. Hobart
						Theodore Roosevelt
26	Theodore Roosevelt	1858–1919	1901–1909	Republican	N.Y.	—
						Charles W. Fairbanks
27	William Howard Taft	1857–1930	1909–1913	Republican	Ohio	James S. Sherman
28	Woodrow Wilson	1856–1924	1913–1921	Democratic	N.J.	Thomas R. Marshall
29	Warren G. Harding	1865–1923	1921–1923	Republican	Ohio	Calvin Coolidge
30	Calvin Coolidge	1872–1933	1923–1929	Republican	Mass.	—
						Charles G. Dawes
31	Herbert Hoover	1874–1964	1929–1933	Republican	Calif.	Charles Curtis
32	Franklin D. Roosevelt	1882–1945	1933–1945	Democratic	N.Y.	John Nance Garner
						Henry Wallace
						Harry S. Truman
33	Harry S. Truman	1884–1972	1945–1953	Democratic	Mo.	—
						Alben W. Barkley
34	Dwight D. Eisenhower	1890–1969	1953–1961	Republican	Kans.	Richard M. Nixon
35	John F. Kennedy	1917–1963	1961–1963	Democratic	Mass.	Lyndon B. Johnson
36	Lyndon B. Johnson	1908–1973	1963–1969	Democratic	Texas	Hubert H. Humphrey
37	Richard M. Nixon	1913–	1969–1974	Republican	Calif.	Spiro T. Agnew
						Gerald Ford

Presidents of the United States (continued)

No.	Name	Born–Died	Years in Office	Political Party	Home State	Vice President
38	Gerald Ford	1913–	1974–1977	Republican	Mich.	Nelson A. Rockefeller
39	Jimmy Carter	1924–	1977–1981	Democratic	Ga.	Walter F. Mondale
40	Ronald Reagan	1911–	1981–1989	Republican	Calif.	George Bush
41	George Bush	1924–	1989–	Republican	Texas	J. Danforth Quayle

a. The Republican party of the third through sixth presidents was not the modern party, which was founded in 1854.

House, Edith Galt Wilson, President Wilson's wife, performed so many duties during his incapacity from a massive stroke that she has been called the "first woman president." Jimmy Carter's wife, Rosalynn, sometimes attended cabinet meetings and conducted diplomacy unofficially. She and Betty Ford expressed the opinion that the First Lady ought to be a paid position. Nancy Reagan was widely known to help make her husband's calendar and to influence the choice of staff members.

Indubitably the presidents have tended to be what the people want them to be. Some part of James Monroe's appeal, for instance, was that he *looked* like George Washington. Some part of Abraham Lincoln's appeal was that he could be both "Honest Abe," a rail-splitting frontiersman, and "Father Abraham," a biblical figure battling the sin of slavery. Some part of Franklin D. Roosevelt's appeal was that, unable to walk, he symbolized an entire nation paralyzed and needing help to get going again. And time and again, the electorate has chosen the chief executive because he triumphed on the battlefield. Indeed, each victorious war has produced a hero who became president. Jackson ("Old Hickory") and William Henry Harrison ("Old Tippecanoe") had been heroes of the War of 1812, Zachary Taylor ("Old Rough and Ready") was a conquering hero of the Mexican War, and the Civil War yielded a whole series of chief executives. Theodore Roosevelt, who came to the White House via the vice presidency, owed his place on the ticket chiefly to his derring-do in the Spanish-American War. Herbert Hoover, though not a military figure, was widely revered as the man who had helped feed the Allies in World War I. And Dwight Eisenhower ("Ike") was the "liberator of Europe" in World War II.

In recent years presidents have had to wrestle with questions that hitherto were dealt with on the municipal or state levels. They are now involved with public health matters, homelessness, child care, and innumerable other issues never dreamed of by the Founding Fathers. A consequence is that presidents have become, after a fashion, "super mayors" and "super governors," drawing political fire they formerly were spared. To meet the nation's myriad needs, the president must rely on an array of advisers, whom he selects on the basis of personal and political preference that is as varied as the presidents themselves. The cabinet, an extraconstitutional body that came into existence in 1791, is the president's "official family." Originally consisting of the heads of the Departments of State, Treasury, and War, and the Office of the Attorney General, today it has fourteen members, making it an unwieldy body for the making of decisions. The president relies heavily on his in-house staff and particularly on his chief of staff, who is effectively his main consultant in generating policy.

As the president has become the political pivot of the country, the citizenry has evidenced an inclination to tinker with the office, proposing such changes as limiting the chief executive to a single six-year term (which Jackson advocated) and adopting a system more like the British parliamentary arrangement with a prime minister. Aside from the Bill of Rights and the Civil War amendments, most of the amendments to the Constitution have modified the presidency, although the alterations have not affected its powers. The changes attest to the incompleteness of the Constitution on the subject deriving from the understandable inability of the Founding Fathers to foresee future contingencies and to a continuing public concern over the choice of the president and other details of his service.

The Twelfth Amendment (1804) provided that the president and vice president be chosen on separate ballots — to prevent a recurrence of the disarray caused in 1800 when Jefferson and Aaron Burr were tied for president in the electoral college and the choice had to be made by the House of Representatives, with the loser, Burr, becoming vice president. The Twentieth Amendment (1933) moved Inauguration Day from March 4 to January 20 and provided that if the president-elect fails to qualify by that day, the vice president–elect becomes president. The Twenty-second Amendment (1951) declared that no person may be elected president more than twice — a posthumous slap at Franklin D. Roosevelt. The Twenty-fifth Amendment (1967) created an arrangement of wide scope to cover presidential disability — prompted by Eisenhower's major illnesses while in office and by Kennedy's assassination. The line of succession to the presidency after the vice president was established by statute in 1947, placing the Speaker of the House of Representatives after the vice president, followed by the president pro tempore of the Senate, and then the members of the cabinet, beginning with the secretary of state, in the order of the creation of the departments. An earlier law of 1886, now superseded, had placed the members of the cabinet after the vice president.

At the end of the twentieth century, the presidency more than ever was what Theodore Roosevelt called it, a "bully pulpit" for the exercise of moral leadership and the preachment of national values. It remained the richest political prize in the world, quested after like no other. Those who would occupy this august office, as well as the student who would understand it, must accept the pronouncement of Calvin Coolidge: the presidency "does not yield to definition. Like the glory of the morning sunrise, it can only be experienced — it cannot be told."

Betty Boyd Caroli, *First Ladies* (1987); Henry F. Graff, ed., *The Presidents: A Reference History* (1984); Joseph Nathan Kane, *Facts about the Presidents: A Compilation of Biographical and Historical Information* (1989); Louis W. Koenig, *The Chief Executive*, 5th ed. (1986).

HENRY F. GRAFF

See also Constitution; Elections; Electoral College; Impeachment; Kitchen Cabinet; Party Conventions; Public Opinion Polling; Vice Presidency.

PRESIDENTIAL ELECTIONS

See Elections.

PRESLEY, ELVIS

(1935–1977), rock singer. The most revolutionary figure in the history of pop music, the "king of rock 'n' roll" was born in Tupelo, Mississippi, the only child of poor sharecroppers; the family moved to Memphis in 1948. After graduating from high school, Presley worked as a truck driver.

In 1954 Sam Phillips, president of Sun Records in Memphis, recognized his talent as "a white man who had the Negro sound and the Negro feel." Phillips released Presley's "That's All Right, Mama," an up-tempo blues song sung with an exuberant sense of freedom; it was followed by four other singles. Many critics regard these early records, recorded in 1953–1955, as his best. His country songs, like "Tryin' to Get to You," expressed affection and respect for the traditions of poor white southerners; his blues, like "Good Rockin' Tonight," conveyed rebellion against and defiance of those traditions. This pattern of respect and rebellion gave Presley's early music its remarkable emotional complexity and power.

The years 1956–1959 marked Presley's triumph: "Heartbreak Hotel" (1956) held the number 1 spot on the charts for eight weeks, followed by "Don't Be Cruel," backed by "Hound Dog," number 1 for eleven weeks — a record for the rock era. With these songs Elvis initiated a cultural rebellion of young people against an adult world they saw as conservative and trivial. In his 1956 television appearances Elvis, shaking his hips and swiveling his knees, shattered the world of bland family entertainment with his raw, unruly power. Adults were outraged over the "vulgarity" of "Elvis the Pelvis," and most programs showed him only from the waist up when he was performing. Elvis now exemplified the rock 'n' roll rebel with his potent fusion of white teenage exuberance and the pulsating beat and frank sexuality of black rhythm and blues.

Presley was drafted into the army in 1958. After his release in 1960 he entered a period of steady decline. Although he was more popular than ever, his music lost its rebellious energy; under his domineering manager, Colonel Tom Parker, he adapted to pop formulas. He retreated from rock 'n' roll to make movies — thirty in all. They made a great deal of money, but the stories, the acting, and the sound tracks got steadily worse, trivializing everything he had come to represent. In 1968, however, he made a stunning comeback in a Christmas television special in which he performed live with a small combo, singing with immense passion and intensity, equaling if not surpassing the best of his early work. After that Presley returned to live performances, but his singing again became careless and shallow.

His final years brought revelations of a miserable personal life consumed by drugs. He died of an accidental overdose. With his death came an immense outpouring of grief: Graceland, his Memphis home, became one of the most popular national shrines in the country, attracting far more visitors annually than Mount Vernon. The man who embodied the classic American success story — poor country boy makes good — and fulfilled the American fantasy of freedom had found it hollow.

Peter Guralnik, "Elvis Presley," in Jim Miller, ed., *Rolling Stone Illustrated History of Rock & Roll* (1980); Greil Marcus, *Mystery Train: Images of America in Rock 'n' Roll Music* (1990); *This Is Elvis*, produced by David Wolper, written and directed by Malcolm Leo and Andrew Solt (available on video).

Jon Wiener

See also Music.

PRIMOGENITURE

This form of land transfer was a holdover from medieval times that affected American colonization and ended in the wave of reforms that swept the newly created United States in the wake of the Revolution. In Britain, under primogeniture, a family's land was inherited entirely by the oldest male child, a system that served to keep estates intact and perpetuate the aristocracy. As a result, often lacking land or the means to buy it, many younger British sons turned to careers in the military or clergy, or sought marriage with the daughter of a wealthy family.

Another alternative was to leave England for the New World, and this possibility attracted many settlers to what became the thirteen colonies along the Atlantic seaboard. They brought the institution of primogeniture with them, but it began to fade as colonization continued, for, unlike Great Britain, America offered enough land to go around, and it was more easily acquired. The principle of primogeniture was followed only when a landowner died without a will.

The American Revolution ended the practice. During and after the war, the new states abolished such feudal holdovers as entail (which also kept land within a family) and quitrents (a tax paid to the land grantor). Primogeniture met a similar fate: Georgia was the first to end it in 1777, and the other states followed suit.

See also Entail.

PROCLAMATION OF 1763

After the conclusion of the French and Indian War in America, the British Empire began to tighten control over its rather autonomous colonies. This royal proclamation, which closed down colonial expansion westward, was the first measure to affect all thirteen colonies. In response to a revolt of Native Americans led by Pontiac, an Ottawa chief, King George III declared all lands west of the Appalachian Divide off-limits to colonial settlers. The edict forbade private citizens and colonial governments alike to buy land from or make any agreements with natives; the empire would conduct all official relations. Furthermore, only licensed traders would be allowed to travel west or deal with Indians. Theoretically protecting colonists from Indian rampages, the measure was also intended to shield Native Americans from increasingly frequent attacks by white settlers.

Although the proclamation was introduced as a temporary measure, its economic benefits for Britain prompted ministers to keep it until the eve of the Revolution. A desire for good farmland caused many colonists to defy the proclamation; others merely resented the royal restrictions on trade and migration.

See also America in the British Empire.

PROGRESSIVE PARTIES: 1912, 1924, 1948

Although these parties were related only in name, their supporters were similar in their liberalism and their dissatisfaction with the Republicans and Democrats.

In 1912, Senator Robert M. La Follette of Wisconsin led a movement of voters opposed to the reelection of Republican president William Howard Taft. Theodore Roosevelt also opposed Taft but failed to defeat him at the party's convention. Most Progressives then abandoned La Follette for the popular ex-president, who won the new party's nomination. Roosevelt received more than a quarter of the popular vote and 88 electoral votes to 435 for Democrat Woodrow Wilson and 8 for Taft. In 1916, Republican Progressives returned to their old party and generally supported the presidential nominee, Supreme Court Justice Charles Evans Hughes.

La Follette finally had his chance in 1924, when he led a revolt of Republicans unhappy with stand-pat president Calvin Coolidge and Democratic nominee John W. Davis of South Carolina. This Progressive party won one-sixth of the popular vote and 13 electoral votes but was swamped by Coolidge.

The 1948 Progressive party nominated Henry A. Wallace, who had been Franklin D. Roosevelt's agriculture secretary and third-term vice president and President Harry S. Truman's commerce secretary. Wallace resented Truman's assumption of the New Deal mantle and objected to his anti-Soviet policies. In the election he faced Truman, Republican Thomas Dewey, and Dixiecrat Strom Thurmond, who had bolted

the Democratic party because of its liberal civil rights policy. Wallace won only 2 percent of the popular vote and no electoral votes, as Truman won reelection.

See also Elections: 1912, 1924, 1948; La Follette, Robert M.; Roosevelt, Theodore.

PROGRESSIVISM

Like romanticism or Victorianism, progressivism is one of those words people frequently use but rarely define with precision. Both at the time and in subsequent histories, a person seemed progressive who supported one or more reforms popular after the turn of the twentieth century. Any political activity that pretended to make the American economic or political system fairer in some way qualified. Although the term applied most obviously to the short-lived Progressive party of former president Theodore Roosevelt in the 1912 elections, progressivism as a general stance clearly applied to many members of the Republican, Democratic, Socialist, and Prohibition parties as well.

Progressivism in this context was a blanket term for many political movements: on the local level, it included efforts to reform the structure of city governments, to grant them home rule, to lower transit fares, to regulate or socialize natural monopolies such as electricity and natural gas, and to rid politics of the stench of the saloon and the open control of politicians by those engaged in dubious business practices. At both state and local levels, progressives argued for the right of citizens to initiate legislation, to nominate candidates in open primary elections, to vote on laws directly, to elect and recall judges, to have secret ballots, and to revise the tax system to spread burdens more justly.

At the national level, progressive movements supported antitrust laws, the establishment of the Federal Reserve System of currency management, lower tariffs, imposition of an income tax, the right of women to vote and of all voters to elect senators directly, and the prohibition of the sale of alcoholic beverages. This list is long but hardly exhaustive.

Scholars have viewed the period in conflicting ways. Some have assumed that progressivism was the form liberalism took for the first fourteen years of the century, a firm if inadequate step toward the welfare legislation of the New Deal. Others have countered this view with the observation that many elements of the movement were reactionary, pointing out the fundamentalist religion, the puritanical legislation in morals, and the nostalgia for a yeoman farmer past clearly evident in so eminent a leader as William Jennings Bryan. They have stressed the middle-class nature of the reformers and the fear many seemed to have that they were losing status in economic and social life to those from untraditional backgrounds. Radicals have argued that because some businessmen were involved in the enactment of reforms and in the machinery of their administration, progressive legislation actually fended off true reform. Social scientists have stressed the way modernization affected the class structure and accelerated the shift from rural to urban living patterns. Many analysts have asserted that amid such a tangle of factors, generalization becomes meaningless and clear definition impossible.

The "progressive movement" lingers as a term but should disappear. It is too precise and insistently political, too redolent of Whig assumptions of inevitable progress, to fit the larger picture now available. "Progressivism" fits better, as a climate of creativity, an ethos, a persuasion, making the events of the thirty years between 1889 and 1920 cohere as everyone assumed they did at the time. Progressivism in this broader context was political only on its surface. At its core it was religious, an attempt by Americans from all social classes, but chiefly the middle class, to restore the proper balances among Protestant moral values, capitalistic competition, and democratic processes, which the expansion of business in the Gilded Age seemed to have changed in alarming ways. Having lost the literal faith of their ancestors, progressive leaders still wanted religious values to dominate political and economic life; they wanted better and fairer competition; and they wanted every citizen to participate in the polity. Such views could be either reactionary or enlightened, depending on context, and among themselves progressives disagreed on practically every specific proposal. In other words, they agreed on the need to remoralize society, but disagreed about how to accomplish it.

Religious thinkers were prominent in ways they never were again in American history. Conscious that many influential citizens were leaving their churches, both for reasons of belief and reasons of residence in outlying suburbs, clergy in most Protestant faiths began to apply Christian doctrine to policy concerning the poor who often lived close by. Washington Gladden preached largely to his local congregation; George D. Herron taught college students and then spoke across the country; Walter Rauschenbusch redefined the Christian mission from his quiet study in a theological seminary. Gladden's autobiography, Herron's collected speeches, and Rauschenbusch's *Christianity and the Social Crisis* (1907) and *Christianizing the Social Order* (1912) formulated the essential elements of Christian progressivism: work in this world to establish a Kingdom of God with social justice for all.

Progressives were primarily members of a post–Civil War generation that had to master a world very different from that of their parents. They were children of religious homes, and their autobiographies repeat the tales of discipline, of long Sundays with two or three church services, and of the duty everyone had of choosing a calling in which to work. But these children grew up in an age of Darwinism and big business; they did not have the religious fervor of their parents, nor did they have any special desire to grow rich. Farming bored them, the ministry was no longer attractive, and other professional opportunities few. Young progressives channeled Protestant energies into the forming of new professions, which they pursued with the same zeal their parents had displayed in converting sinners and fighting slavery. They went to the new graduate schools founded along the lines of Johns Hopkins University; they created modern journalism and social work; they went into teaching and the law; and a few entered politics, finding in statesmanship the best outlet for Christian stewardship. Jews and Roman Catholics occasionally worked on the edges of progressivism, but those who set the tone and wrote the manifestos were Protestants.

Considered on this broad scale, progressivism began with the founding of Hull-House by Jane Addams and Ellen Gates Starr in the fall of 1889. These pioneers of social work in Chicago soon became role models for young men and women in other cities, attracting such figures as John Dewey and George Herbert Mead to study what they were doing and to work their insights into a pragmatic philosophy that would solve the problems of democracy. A new breed of journalists soon appeared, often referred to as "muckrakers," who publicized the problems social workers faced and illuminated the business and political conditions that made social work important in the modern city. No one spoke of "networking" in the years around 1900, but social workers, intellectuals, and journalists all quickly came to know of each other. Journalists such as Lincoln Steffens and Ida Tarbell, social scientists such as Richard Ely and Woodrow Wilson, and politicians such as Brand Whitlock and Robert La Follette were soon in touch through letters and occasional meetings. With the inauguration of President Theodore Roosevelt in 1901, they had a national hero capable of dramatizing issues and providing leadership insofar as he was willing.

Progressivism produced three presidents, and their achievements comprise the most important legacy in the eyes of many analysts. Roosevelt moved against the trusts and backed railway regulation, pure food and drug laws, and the conservation of natural resources. William Howard Taft compromised on several issues, such as the tariff and conservation, but pursued a policy of vigorous judicial progressivism in his efforts to break up trusts, strengthen the Interstate Commerce Commission, and facilitate the workings of the courts. Woodrow Wilson lowered the tariff, reformed the currency, and toughened the trust laws yet again. He then carried progressive ideals into World War I, seeing it as a fight for democracy; at Versailles, however, he failed to work out a treaty capable of maintaining a free and peaceful world. Progressivism died twice: at Versailles itself, where Wilson compromised his position repeatedly in the face of European pressures, and in the U.S. Senate, which refused to ratify the treaty or permit American participation in the League of Nations.

But politics was only one discipline in which progressivism flourished; even the inclusion of journalism and social work in no way exhausts the scope of its influence. In literature, many novelists wrote about prison conditions, political corruption, prostitution, and other evils; the best-known volume is *The Jungle* (1906), Upton Sinclair's socialist examination of Chicago's Packingtown, its savage working conditions and unsanitary products. Painters entered the slums, the sporting halls, and the circuses to produce the Ashcan school of realistic portrayal that, in many cases, held manifest political content: Robert Henri was an anarchist, for example, and John Sloan a socialist. The poetry of Vachel Lindsay recalled William Jennings Bryan and William Booth, founder of the Salvation Army, and that of Carl Sandburg celebrated Chicago. Charles Beard and Frederick Jackson Turner wrote progressive histories, reinterpreting the past so it would be "useful" and "relevant" to democratic citizens and legislators. John Dewey's pragmatism entered the public schools and dominated pedagogy for three generations, making "progressive education" perhaps the most enduring, both for better and for worse, of the achievements of those years.

The two most eminent of the creative personalities whom progressivism produced, ironically and untypically, were in the fine arts. In music, Charles Ives looked back at the transcendentalists to create an aesthetic of innovative nostalgia; by trying to recapture the lost paths of Emerson and Thoreau, the romances of Hawthorne, and the antiabolitionist riots of his forebears, he made so many experiments in dissonance, polytonality, and polyrhythm that he emerged after World War II as the most important pioneer in American musical history. Architect Frank Lloyd Wright exceeded even Ives's achievements. Sharing an affection for the organic ideas of the American Renaissance before the Civil War and asserting that form and function were one, Wright developed the Prairie school of architecture, which sought to integrate the design of housing and the land it used and forced Americans to think more carefully about rapid urbanization. In terms of impact abroad, perhaps the most useful yardstick of achievement, Wright's work still influences architects and city planners.

For a climate that began with optimism, progressivism ended with extreme pessimism. President Wilson's foreign policy lay in rubble, and few politicians or publicists dared to recommend intervention in world affairs for the next generation, thus preventing Franklin D. Roosevelt from taking proper steps against the Japanese and the Germans in the 1930s. The political reforms worked no miracles. Women used their new right to vote to help elect Presidents Warren G. Harding, Calvin Coolidge, and Herbert Hoover and did little to purify the political process. Race relations, never a progressive priority, went from bad to worse. The initiative, referendum, and recall had only minor impact. Only in financial matters did any important legacy remain: the Federal Reserve System, despite changes, remained at the heart of the economy, and the income tax paid many of the bills for important welfare measures and the fighting of World War II. Surviving progressives themselves often grew disillusioned, and a majority opposed the more significant New Deal measures. The largest exception to this generalization was the group that identified with social settlement work: from Jane Addams to Eleanor Roosevelt, these progressives supported the New Deal and helped usher the welfare state into the American system.

Robert M. Crunden, *Ministers of Reform: The Progressives' Achievement in American Civilization, 1889–1920* (1982); Richard Hofstadter, *The Age of Reform* (1955).

ROBERT M. CRUNDEN

See also Ashcan School; Beard, Charles A., and Beard, Mary R.; Dewey, John; Ives, Charles; *Jungle, The;* Muckrakers; Progressive Parties: 1912, 1924, 1948; Roosevelt, Theodore; Settlement Houses; Taft, William Howard; Turner, Frederick Jackson; Wilson, Woodrow.

PROHIBITION AND TEMPERANCE

The Prohibition era usually refers to the period from January 1920 until April 1933 when the National Prohibition Enforcement Act forbade the manufacture and sale of beverages with an alcoholic content greater than 0.5 percent. Supporters of this law (commonly called the Volstead Act) believed that it would quickly bring an end to the apprehensions of most Americans for more than a century about the social problems associated with alcoholic intoxication.

A useful historical signal of such problems has been the annual per capita consumption of absolute alcohol by the drinking-age population. (Spirits bottled at 80 proof — the "ardent spirits" or "hard liquor" of historical literature — are 40 percent absolute alcohol; most beers are from 3 to 8 percent; most wines, 10 to 20 percent.) During the 1830s, this per capita figure was 7.1 gallons. Considering that at this time there were many abstainers and that women, children, and slaves probably did not consume their per capita share, that stark statistic pointed to what some called an "alcoholic republic." Thus Thomas Jefferson had hoped that viniculture might provide a safe alternative to ardent spirits, and James Madison, in his old age, urged that for the "good of the country" young men abstain. In 1842 Abraham Lincoln sadly recalled that during his youth intoxicating liquors had come forth "like the Egyptian angel of death, commissioned to slay, if not the first, the fairest born in every family."

Temperance became a social movement when large numbers of people urged upon themselves and others a reasonable sort of individual discipline — usually abstention from hard liquor and a moderate use of wine and beer — to protect individual health and family well-being. Prohibition — like the prohibition of slavery, dueling, gambling, and prostitution — became a political movement when large numbers of voters began to demand of government what churches could no longer provide: a strong sense of moral stewardship.

It was in the 1840s that a businessman named Neal Dow in Portland, Maine, discovered in his hometown an astonishing range of moral delinquencies — family violence, poverty, crime, disorder, and incompetence in shops and factories — all of which he attributed to the "excessive use" of alcohol encouraged by local custom and competition among grog shops. Dow, like Jefferson, at first hoped to persuade individuals to become temperate. But when this failed, he and many others became convinced that the state legislature should abolish the sale of alcohol. Dow's achievement, the "Maine Law" of 1851, prohibited the manufacture and sale of intoxicating liquors. Thirteen of the thirty-one states had such laws by 1855.

Such laws were especially vulnerable to the turbulent realignment of political loyalties then sweeping through these states. The emerging Republican leaders, inclined toward Prohibition but fearful that their stand against the extension of slavery might be compromised by other moral issues, removed Prohibition from their platforms. This bound to the party many opponents of Prohibition who, wet or dry, held religious persuasions emphasizing the role of the church, not the state, in matters of moral stewardship. These people were often, but not exclusively, recent immigrants: Irish and German Catholics, some German and Scandinavian Lutherans.

This unity did not long survive the Civil War. In the 1870s groups of women — in the first such movement in American history — began to march from church meetings to the streets, where they halted traffic with their demands that the saloons close their doors. Spreading from Ohio in 1873, these protests demonstrated that women had found in the saloon both a symbol and an active agent of the threats raised by a new industrial society to what Frances Willard called the purity of the American home. Among these threats Willard could see drunkenness, prostitution, crime, and ignorance. As president of the Woman's Christian Temperance Union (WCTU), she urged women in their role of home protectors to move to the streets and the legislative halls committed to direct action. In their protests, disrupting almost every major city in the North, her followers were at first asking not for the franchise but only for "home protection," though many of them did indeed want to vote so they could vote

against the saloon. Republicans responded in 1888 by bringing into their platforms a delicate approval of "purity of the home" and "temperance and morality."

In 1895, the leaders of the Anti-Saloon League of America (ASL), then holding their first national convention, were confident that these matters were at the center of middle-class consciousness. Enlisting Protestant congregations as basic organizational units, the ASL was strikingly successful in guiding Prohibition sentiment through a sequence of political reforms that in many states were changing fundamental democratic procedures. Early in the 1900s, direct primary laws opened the selection of political candidates to the influence of ASL leaders, who then identified for their membership those candidates — Democratic or Republican — who were safely "dry."

Within a few years, dry legislatures were favoring women's suffrage and allowing popular referenda on the question of whether states should prohibit saloons. To many voters — frightened by the common knowledge that increasing competition among saloons encouraged crime and political corruption, and by the psychologists and neurologists whose research indicated that alcohol was in fact an addictive poison — there was then no more important political question. By 1916, twenty-one states had banned saloons. National elections that year returned a Congress in which dry members outnumbered the wets two-to-one. In December 1917, Congress submitted to the states the Eighteenth Amendment, which, when ratified in 1919, placed in the Constitution a nationwide ban on the "manufacture, sale, or transportation of intoxicating liquors." By that time most of the states had been dry for years. In 1920, the Volstead Act was to most Americans a belated confirmation of an earlier reality.

For several years after 1920, the illicit manufacture and sale of alcohol, if not entirely eliminated, was at least inconspicuous. Many people who regarded themselves as victims of a bewildering law and expected regularly to violate it nevertheless praised it as a high-minded achievement for the next generation. But most people probably wanted to obey the law and were curious about the emerging character of the dry rather than the alcoholic republic. They rejoiced that arrests for drunkenness declined sharply, along with the cost of maintaining prisons, and that medical statistics recorded a drop in the number of treatments for diseases associated with alcoholic psychoses. It is reasonably certain that many drinkers drank considerably less — especially if they were wage earners — if only because of the high cost of bootleg beers and liquors. (Between 1916 and 1928, the price of whiskey in most places rose by an average of 520 percent.)

Although determining the extent of drinking by any group at that time is difficult, Prohibition was at least partly effective. Records show that annual per capita consumption stood at 2.60 gallons for the period 1906 to 1910, before state dry laws had much impact. In 1934, when accurate statistics were again available, the figure was less than a gallon, and even as late as 1945, it was only 2 gallons. Not until 1975 did per capita consumption rise again to what it had been before Prohibition.

But at some time near the middle of the 1920s it became abundantly clear that "Volsteadism" was presenting enormous, if not intolerable problems. Stopping the illegal traffic seemed impossible. Few political leaders had realistic plans for funding a naval blockade of the coasts or for closing the thousands of miles of borders along Canada and Mexico. Nor were elected officials inclined to pay for the huge police forces necessary to restrict the bootlegging that became pandemic, or to monitor the distillation of medical alcohol, which flowed easily into illicit outlets, or to track the production of sacramental wines, which so easily found secular markets. Token raids on speakeasies by federal agents usually encouraged colorful newspaper stories rather than respect for federal law. In fact, after 1925, more and more citizens seemed to resent the cynicism with which the federal government (whose Founding Fathers had left murders, lynchings, adulteries, and other moral transgressions to the disciplines of the state legislatures) was so inconsistently pursuing an intrusive interest in whatever it was they might be tempted to drink.

Congress had placed the matter within the jurisdiction of the Treasury Department, whose untrained Prohibition officers faced challenges that would have defeated entire armies and navies. They operated with ineffective budgets — if any at all could have been effective — and only slight approval by the public. Even their friends in the Anti-Saloon League began to feel that, having made Prohibition the law of the land, they should employ their lagging energies and resources in the interest of propaganda and education, not law enforcement. Congress seemed to agree: it allowed Prohibition for the most part to live or die in the public conscience.

To some voters, this seemed adequate. Many in the rural areas, especially the farm counties, had voted dry early in the century and had remained happily so ever since. In such areas few people ever saw a bootlegger or visited a speakeasy. But in the major urban areas the failures of Volsteadism became both obvious and notorious. The ease with which beer and liquor flowed in such cities as New York, Chicago, Detroit, New Orleans, and San Francisco could easily convince observers that the Eighteenth Amendment was destroying respect for law and order throughout the nation.

Yet before 1930 few people called for outright repeal of the amendment. No amendment to the Constitution had ever been repealed, and it was clear that few Americans were moved to political action yet by the partial successes or failures of the Eighteenth. Newspaper polls did reveal that large numbers of readers approved of some revision in the Volstead Act to allow light beers and wines but would not accept outright repeal. Most of these readers voted in 1928 for Herbert Hoover, who during the campaign had called Prohibition "a great social and economic experiment, noble in motive and far-reaching in purpose." He had, of course, also promised to uphold the Constitution.

Thus the repeal movement, which since the early 1920s had been a sullen and hopeless expression of minority discontent, astounded even its most dedicated supporters when it suddenly gained political momentum. What had not been articulated in 1928 was that the nation had been moving away from the concerns that from the beginning had lay at the heart of Prohibition. The postwar industrial society and the new lifestyles of individualism and personal freedom — apparent in Europe and America — were making the protection of the Victorian home and family seem less and less urgent. The powerful accelerators of change were mass production, the automobile, the telephone, the radio, the new literature, the movies — all with their stunning potential for broadening individual freedoms, including the freedom to use intoxicating beverages. But the most powerful accelerator was the Great Depression, which for many people everywhere marked the end of a cultural and social era, an era that had embraced Prohibition.

The Association Against the Prohibition Amendment (AAPA), which had supported wet candidates since 1922, was an organization of wealthy industrialists who shared the view that Prohibition was at best an eruption of sheer lunacy that had without warning ruined their leisure and increased their taxes, and at worst a dark victory of rural ignorance and prejudice over civil liberty and urban sophistication. They also feared the augmented powers that Prohibition had given the federal government. After 1929 these men argued that repeal would increase the number of wage-earning jobs the country so desperately needed and that reviving the manufacture and sale of alcohol would provide vast profits to be tapped for taxation. The AAPA found widespread support, including that from the Women's Organization for National Prohibition Reform, a remarkable group of wealthy women who were prepared to speak from caravans of expensive automobiles about the rights of women to individual freedom — in striking contrast to the dimly remembered antisaloon parades thirty years earlier when prominent women had campaigned for a woman's right to protect home and family with a vote for Prohibition. In 1932 the critical issue before the AAPA and its supporters was the election of a sympathetic Congress and president.

At that moment, the AAPA had a daring plan: this was to validate the Twenty-first Amendment, repealing the Eighteenth, in such a way as to circumvent the traditional process of ratification by the state legislatures, in some of which, AAPA attorneys feared, the entrenched powers of dry legislators presented a threat far out of proportion to their actual representation. According to this plan, Congress — for the first time since the Constitution itself had been ratified — was to call for ratifying conventions in each state, whose delegates would be elected in 1933 for the specific purpose of saying yes or no to the Twenty-first Amendment. The plan worked. Two-thirds of the conventions quickly voted yes, and when the delegates' voting was complete on December 5, 1933, the nationwide total favoring ratification was almost 73 percent. With this vote, the states were again in control of liquor legislation.

Although it is true that some simply rejected the moral and economic premises of repeal and steadfastly held to Prohibition (Kansas did not accept state repeal until 1948, Oklahoma until 1957, and Mississippi until 1966), the great question before most legislatures in 1934 concerned liquor laws for states that were now anti-Prohibition but still antisaloon: what would define the next phase in the historical movement toward protecting American society from drunkenness?

There were, almost immediately, efforts to prevent what earlier had been called the "drunkard-making business" — laws that, following examples in Canada and Sweden, created state monopolies of liquor sales to prevent free-market competition. Fifteen states had such laws by 1936. Others allowed taverns, hotels, and restaurants to serve beer and wine but banned barrooms and service of liquor by the drink. Still others created various forms of county local option. Liquor advertising fell under close scrutiny almost everywhere, and taxation on all alcoholic beverages — computed to raise revenues as well as to discourage drinking — assumed a gratifyingly moral dimension. During this time, many medical researchers were encouraging the view that addiction to alcohol was not so much a moral flaw as a disease, one open to study and perhaps receptive to new therapies. As alcohol studies progressed in university laboratories, many states began introducing the findings into public school curricula. The new phase of protection thus variously emphasized coercion, education, research, and treatment.

The years since 1960, however, have seen ambiguously ironic developments. Coercive measures, especially those directed against drunken driving, have become increasingly harsh and, in many areas, effective. American drinking habits, perhaps in response to education, seem to have been moving away from ardent spirits and toward light wines and beers. But at the very time when alcohol studies and curricula were becoming mandatory and treatment centers based upon the disease theory of alcohol addiction were popular and profitable, leading researchers in the field were questioning the validity of the theory itself.

This most recent phase has been called one of "neotemperance," and it probably anticipates future phases. It seems clear that most Americans have rejected the controlling idea of prohibitionists since the victories of Neal Dow — the notion that alcohol is without qualification an evil substance, an inevitably addictive poison, a relentless threat to the innocent. And most Americans seem to have accepted as the lesson of Prohibition that alcohol cannot be abolished outright. Yet they just as surely do not share the early Puritans' full confidence that alcohol is the "water of life," the "good creature of God," that only the eternally degenerate abuse. The language of neotemperance is rich in words like *stability, responsibility,* and *prudence.*

Mark Moore and Dean Gerstein, eds., *Alcohol and Public Policy: Beyond the Shadow of Prohibition* (1981); W. J. Rorabaugh, *The Alcoholic Republic* (1979).

NORMAN H. CLARK

See also Anti-Saloon League; Volstead Act; Willard, Frances; Woman's Christian Temperance Union.

PROSTITUTION

Prostitution was a European import to North America, for the concept was foreign to Native American culture. Compared to England, the American colonies had few prostitutes, and most of them were confined primarily to the water-front neighborhoods of seaports. During the eighteenth century, Boston and New York had the most prostitutes owing to the large numbers of soldiers stationed in those ports, the economic dislocations resulting from colonial wars, and the presence of many impoverished unmarried women.

Prostitution became a social and political issue only after 1810. In the ensuing century, virtually all American cities and numerous towns experienced noticeable increases. Rapid, unplanned urbanization, an expanding transient male population, low female wages, and discrimination against women contributed to the rise. In addition, landlords often preferred to rent their properties to prostitutes because they were more lucrative and stable than working-class tenants. Common law tradition never implicated the owners of houses of prostitution. Indeed, until the twentieth century, no statutory definition of prostitution existed in most American communities. It was treated as a form of vagrancy and a simple misdemeanor. Because of arbitrary, weak, or corrupt municipal law enforcement, most prostitutes plied their trade unpunished. The Victorian ideologies of women's separate sphere and the double standard for sexuality divided females into two groups: "respectable" women, supposedly passionless and sexually repressed, and "unrespectable" women, irredeemable and available for purchase.

Nineteenth-century prostitution was structured around three subcultures. First, about 5 to 10 percent of young females in large cities engaged in prostitution at some point, earning twice as much in an evening as factory or service employment would bring in a week. Most were single, in their teens or early twenties, native-born, and recently arrived in the city. The majority worked only for short periods, eventually securing more socially acceptable employment or marrying.

Second, a prominent "sporting male" subculture encouraged men to hire prostitutes. As factory work replaced the craft system, and the unregulated boardinghouse replaced the hierarchical artisan household, young males enjoyed greater freedom, and rigid sexual controls quickly vanished. Male leisure institutions after

1820 provided a social niche separate from the family and more "feminized" entertainments. Prizefighting, heavy drinking, and sexual aggression were admired. This rough masculinity and the increasing commercialization of leisure produced a distinct male world with its own promiscuous sexual norms. The worst elements in this fraternity were the pimps, who first appeared in New York after 1835.

The third subculture, part of an underground economy, was that of the brothels, which numbered in the hundreds in Chicago, Philadelphia, and St. Louis. By the time of the Civil War, New York had over five hundred, many advertising in newspapers and guidebooks. There were proportionate numbers in Austin, Louisville, Omaha, Richmond, San Antonio, and Spokane. Periodic arrests and raids everywhere were so common that they constituted a form of taxing and licensing. This de facto regulation of prostitution extended to other leisure institutions. Antebellum theater proprietors routinely permitted prostitutes to solicit in the "third tier" of their establishments. Concert halls, saloons, cigar stores, restaurants, and cabarets supported prostitution to attract patrons.

Sex, or "red-light," districts were well known before 1850 and later. New York's Five Points and the Tenderloin, San Francisco's Barbary Coast, New Orleans's Basin Street and Storyville, Chicago's Levee, and even the Alley in Boise, Idaho, were nationally known for the promiscuous sexuality they promoted. By the late nineteenth century, prostitution was a multi-million-dollar business, with organized networks of madames, landlords, doctors, and municipal officials.

The growth of prostitution was countered throughout the century by antiprostitution movements frequently linked to temperance and "moral purity" crusades. Reformers, church leaders, and women's societies sought to assist prostitutes and close down brothels, but their efforts were sporadic and ineffective.

After 1890, urban antivice crusades grew increasingly popular, with ministers decrying municipal tolerance of prostitution. Progressive reformers and federal officials followed, attacking "white slavery," proposing programs of protection and prevention, and sometimes recasting prostitutes into public enemies. Between 1900 and 1918, more than forty vice commissions recommended eliminating urban sex districts. In 1909, Iowa was the first of some thirty states that passed red-light abatement laws permitting citizens to obtain injunctions and close buildings promoting commercial sex. Prostitutes were treated more coercively with the creation of special courts, police vice squads, and the introduction of social workers in prisons.

Congressional legislation in 1903 and 1907 outlawed the importation of prostitutes and permitted the deportation of immigrant prostitutes. The Mann Act of 1910, which made the transport of women across state lines for "immoral purposes" illegal, resulted in 1,537 convictions by 1916. The Commission on Training Camp Activities led by Raymond Fosdick during World War I closed the sex districts in the nation's leading ports.

By the 1920s, the era of the brothel and open prostitution had ended, and significant changes emerged over the next four decades. Municipal officials grew less tolerant of the sporting male subculture. Prostitution became a clandestine activity; prostitutes no longer advertised but conducted their business in tenements, dance halls, massage parlors, "call houses," and even taxicabs. During Prohibition, prostitution developed closer ties with the alcohol trade and organized crime. The famous New York madame Polly Adler, for example, was protected by gangsters. Finally, increasing state repression and bureaucratic intervention ranging from the FBI in World War II to the congressional Kefauver committee in 1950 and 1951 forced many prostitutes to work alone.

None of this, however, suppressed America's appetite for the subject. Public titillation was fed by the periodic attention given to celebrity madames, like Polly Adler and San Francisco's Sally Stanford, who was even elected mayor of Sausalito, California, in 1976.

After 1965, prostitution entered a new period of openness and publicity. One study in 1968 found 95,550 arrests for prostitution nationwide and estimated that every day 286,650 men visited prostitutes. Sporadic attempts have been made over the years to legalize prostitution on various grounds, and in 1971 Nevada became the first state to do so (in its smaller counties).

Prostitutes themselves grew more assertive. In 1973, San Francisco's Margo St. James, a college-educated prostitute, founded the first labor organization for prostitutes known as COYOTE (Call Off Your Old Tired Ethics). Similar organizations followed in other states. St. James and her supporters defended prostitution as a privacy issue, demanding that it be accepted as legitimate women's work, but feminist and other groups attacked this libertarian view, charging that prostitution was an exploitative extension of women's dependency on men. By the end of the 1980s, however, growing fears regarding the AIDS epidemic threatened prostitutes with even greater regulation and discrimination.

Timothy J. Gilfoyle, *City of Eros: New York City, Prostitution, and the Commercialization of Sex, 1790–1920* (1991); Barbara Meil Hobson, *Uneasy Virtue: The Politics of Prostitution and the American Reform Tradition* (1987); Ruth Rosen, *The Lost Sisterhood: Prostitution in America, 1900–1918* (1982).

TIMOTHY J. GILFOYLE

PROTESTANT CHURCHES

See Black Churches; Evangelicalism; Religion.

PUBLIC HEALTH

See Epidemics; Medicine.

PUBLIC LAND POLICY

The great abundance of land in the area that eventually became the United States was the most important factor in determining national land policies. In 1790 the new nation contained 568,839,040 acres, but as a result of the Louisiana Purchase (1803), the Mexican Cession (1848), and other acquisitions, including Alaska and Hawaii, the United States by 1970 extended over 2,271,343,000 acres of land and water. Of this vast area, 1,511,140,000 acres were privately owned, and 760,204,000 were held by the federal government.

The availability of so much unoccupied land

required the British colonies, as well as individual proprietors who had received large grants from the king of England, to adopt liberal land policies to attract settlers. It took population to increase the value of land. Virginia and other colonies adopted the headright system, which gave a quantity of land to those who paid their own way to America or who completed an indenture. Proprietors such as William Penn also gave land to those who transported themselves and their families to Pennsylvania. Other settlers simply went to the frontier and occupied unsettled land. By the time of the Revolution there was a widespread belief among Americans that they should have easy access to land, meaning that it should be cheap or even free to honest settlers who wanted to establish family farms.

Under the Articles of Confederation and later the Constitution, land not included within the boundaries of the original thirteen states became public domain, owned and administered by the national government. Congress provided for surveying and selling public lands in the Land Ordinance of 1785. This law established the rectangular system of survey, which divided land into townships six miles square, sections a mile square containing 640 acres, and quarter sections of 160 acres. The law also set the least amount of land one could buy from the government at 640 acres for a minimum price of $1.00 an acre. Land had to be offered at public auction before it could be sold directly to individuals, a provision that endured until 1841. The ordinance was more favorable to speculators than to ordinary farmers because the average settler did not have $640.00 for the minimum purchase. Speculators took advantage of the law, buying large quantities of land and reselling it in small plots to individual purchasers at higher prices.

During the 1790s, controversy arose over whether policies should be directed at using public lands mainly as a source of revenue or at helping actual settlers easily obtain land. Those who favored the principle of using land for revenue won out in the Land Act of 1796. This law raised the minimum price of government land to $2.00 an acre.

The policy of making it easier for settlers to acquire land, however, soon prevailed. In 1800

Congress passed the Harrison Land Law that reduced the amount that could be purchased directly from the federal government to 320 acres and permitted payment over four years. Even at $2.00 an acre, a settler could obtain 320 acres with a down payment of only $160.00. Four years later the minimum purchase was lowered even further to 160 acres. In 1820 Congress abolished the credit provision, but lowered the price to $1.25 an acre and cut the minimum purchase to 80 acres. Now a settler could buy a piece of public land for as little as $100.00. Congress was moving toward the democratic policy of widespread private ownership of land.

Many settlers moved ahead of government surveys and occupied parts of the public domain as squatters. When the land was surveyed and put up for sale, they would insist they had prior rights. Congress recognized this position when it passed the Pre-emption Act of 1841, which assured squatters they would have first chance to purchase 160 acres at the minimum price of $1.25 an acre. Since the quality of land varied, many western leaders proposed that poorer land be sold at reduced prices if it remained on the market for an extended time. In 1854 Congress passed the Graduation Act, which permitted land that had remained unsold for as long as thirty years to be bought for as little as 12½ cents an acre.

Meanwhile, there was a growing demand, especially from westerners, for the federal government to give land to individuals who would settle on it and cultivate it. Supporters of free homesteads argued that land ownership would give people a strong economic stake in society and an interest in good government and political stability. Many Americans held the Jeffersonian view that farmers were more democratic, honest, hardworking, independent, virtuous, and patriotic than city residents. Thus to increase the number of family farmers would benefit and strengthen the nation. The homestead principle, however, had strong opponents. Eastern manufacturers feared that free land would draw away their workers, and southerners believed that western lands would be occupied by free farmers, which might ultimately reduce the power of the slave states.

Bills offering free land to actual settlers were considered regularly by Congress after 1840, and in 1848 the Free-Soil party made homesteads a national political issue. Four years later the first homestead bill passed the House of Representatives, but it failed in the Senate. Nevertheless, the idea continued to gain support. Congress passed a weakened homestead bill in 1860, but President James Buchanan vetoed it. It was not until May 10, 1862, after Abraham Lincoln and the Republicans came to power and the southern states had seceded, that Congress passed the Homestead Act. The law provided for granting 160 acres of land to qualified individuals who agreed to build a residence and live on the land for at least five years. The only cost was a small filing fee.

Other laws designed to place public lands into private ownership soon followed. In 1866 Congress passed the Southern Homestead Act to help black freedmen acquire land, but few entries were made and the law was repealed in 1876. The Timber Culture Act of 1873 granted 160 acres to qualified persons in certain western states if they planted one-fourth of the land with trees, a requirement later reduced to 10 acres. The Desert Land Act of 1877 offered 640 acres of land in parts of the West for $1.25 an acre with only 25 cents an acre down, providing the buyer promised to irrigate part of it. A year later the Timber and Stone Act permitted the purchase of 160 acres that were valuable only for timber and stone. The price was only $2.50 an acre, less than the value of one tree on some forest land disposed of in this manner.

As settlers pushed into the far western states, new problems emerged. Farmers needed irrigation water in many areas and larger acreages for dry-land farming and ranching. The Reclamation Act of 1902 provided that revenue from the sale of public lands in sixteen western states be placed in a national fund to be used for constructing dams and irrigation works. This law was designed to encourage the settlement of bona fide farmers on small farms throughout the arid West by making irrigation water available at reasonable prices. Although many problems emerged in this program, it helped establish thousands of small irrigated farms.

When settlers reached the semiarid Great Plains, it became clear that 160-acre homesteads were too small for successful farming or ranching in such an environment. In 1909 Congress passed the Enlarged Homestead Act, which authorized 320-acre homesteads in several western states. In 1916, 640-acre stock-raising homesteads were permitted in some parts of the West.

Except for the Homestead Act of 1862, none of these laws did much to help actual settlers. Large ranchers were the main beneficiaries of the Desert Land Act, and timber and mining companies profited most from the Timber and Stone Act. A great deal of graft and corruption surrounded disposal of the public domain in the late nineteenth century. The goal of assisting settlers was compromised by poorly drawn laws, inefficient administration of the land offices, and outright fraud. Nevertheless, in some western states the Homestead Act was a major factor in farm building; between 1868 and 1904 final homestead entries totaled 718,819.

Although helping farmers acquire land was a primary objective of national land policy, the federal government disposed of millions of acres for other purposes. During the nineteenth century, Congress granted land to the states for canal and road construction, for river improvements, and for public buildings. To encourage enlistments and reward soldiers for their wartime service, veterans of the War of 1812 and the Mexican War received bounty warrants redeemable in land. The states were also awarded land to help fund schools and colleges. Many states received sections 16 and 36 in each township for the support of common schools. The Morrill Land Grant Act of 1862 gave the states 30,000 acres of land for each of their congressmen and senators to endow agricultural and mechanical colleges. The largest grants went to railroads to encourage construction of the transcontinental lines. Altogether, between 1850 and 1871, when the railroad land grant policy ended, railroads received 175,350,000 acres from the public domain, although they later had to forfeit some 35 million acres for failure to meet construction agreements.

During the rapid occupation of the public lands in the nineteenth century, American Indians were pushed into ever smaller areas. Although the federal government recognized some Indian rights to the lands they occupied, there were strong efforts to acquire the lands by agreement, treaty, or force. Removal of the "Five Civilized Tribes" from the Southeast to Oklahoma in the 1830s illustrates that policy at its worst. During the late nineteenth century, Indians were forced onto reservations and their surplus lands opened to white settlement. In 1887 Congress passed the Dawes Act, which provided for individual allotments to Indians of most tribes.

Around 1890, national land policy, which had focused on getting public land into private hands quickly, easily, and cheaply, began to change, and by World War I it had become national policy to maintain permanent federal control over some lands. The shift was toward conservation. The Forest Reservation Act of 1891 permitted setting apart timberland from private entry. Even earlier Congress had begun to turn areas of unusual natural beauty into national parks — Yellowstone National Park had been established in 1872. President Theodore Roosevelt was an ardent conservationist, and by the end of his administration in 1909 forest reserves totaled some 194,505,000 acres. He also set aside land for parks, dam sites, and other public purposes, and the federal government reserved oil, coal, and grazing lands.

By the 1930s there was general acceptance that the national government would reserve and administer millions of acres in a permanent public domain. The Taylor Act of 1934 provided for improved administration and conservation of some 80 million acres of federally held grazing land. This law reflected a desire for more careful and efficient administration of the public domain in order to preserve valuable natural resources. Executive orders in November 1934 and February 1935 withdrew all public lands from private entry. These actions ended homesteading, although a few exceptions were subsequently approved. Most of the public lands were administered by agencies within the Departments of Interior and Agriculture.

Private individuals and companies were not denied use of resources on the public domain, but users had to operate under rules laid down by Congress and administrative agencies. By the middle of the twentieth century more ardent conservationists were demanding that some parts of the public domain be permanently set aside as wilderness areas. They argued that timber cutting, oil drilling, and other economic activities should be completely prohibited and urged preserving the designated areas in their pristine state. Responding to these demands, Congress passed the Wilderness Act of 1964, which set aside millions of acres as wilderness with very restrictive rules on their use. Many westerners bitterly criticized this law, insisting that more resource development should be permitted on federal lands. Conservationists, however, won the day. The Federal Land Policy and Management Act of 1976 emphasized the principle of permanent ownership of the public domain and gave the secretary of interior greater powers to enforce restrictive policies on use of public lands. There were strong countervailing pressures in the 1980s to permit greater economic development in parts of the public domain, including Alaska. For the most part, however, these forces were unsuccessful in changing basic federal policy. In the last half of the twentieth century, administration of federal lands shifted from a custodial role to a much more positive and intensive administration of the more than 700 million acres of public lands. There was heavy emphasis on conservation with uses directed to recreation and wildlife preservation, as well as diminished economic development.

Public land policies achieved a number of goals during the nation's first two hundred years. The sale and leasing of land raised millions of dollars in revenue. Second, and much more important, was the fact that the land laws, especially the Homestead Act, encouraged private ownership of family farms. Federal land policies also promoted and supported internal improvements, education, and general economic development. In the second century of the nation's history, federal policy aimed at preserving a permanent public domain in the form of forests, grazing districts, parks, national monuments, and other lands for the general benefit of all Americans.

Marion Clawson, *The Federal Lands Revisited* (1983); Paul W. Gates, *History of Public Land Law Development* (1968).

GILBERT C. FITE

See also Ballinger-Pinchot Controversy; Conservation and Environmental Movements; Homestead Act; Indians; Internal Migration; Louisiana Purchase; Morrill Land Grant Act.

PUBLIC OPINION POLLING

Although the systematic collection of information about society and social issues can be traced to eighteenth-century England, it was not until the early nineteenth century in the United States that public opinion became the subject of empirical study.

Among the earliest soundings of opinion on record are those of the *Harrisburg Pennsylvanian* and the *Raleigh Star* in connection with the 1824 presidential election. In July, the *Pennsylvanian* reported that Andrew Jackson received 335 of more than 500 votes cast in a poll it conducted in Wilmington, Delaware. A month later the *Star* reported Jackson the heavy favorite in canvassing it did at political meetings in North Carolina.

Concurrent with these early soundings of opinion was the independent development of the theoretical underpinnings of sampling. In 1848, the Belgian mathematician Adolphe Quetelet advanced the idea of the "average man" by arguing that the concept of the normal distribution of observations around a mean could be applied to analysis of society as well as to the physical world.

This fundamental conception was the link to more rigorous forms of sampling and the measurement of opinion that took place in the 1920s. Techniques of consumer and audience research were refined as Archibald M. Crossley pioneered the measurement of the American public's radio listening habits, and George H. Gallup developed techniques to assess reader interest in newspaper articles.

The presidential election of 1936 brought the new "science" of polling to prominence when three independent polls (by Crossley, Gallup, and Elmo Roper) predicted Franklin D. Roosevelt's victory over Alf Landon. These polls stood in stark contrast to the prediction of the *Literary Digest* that Roosevelt would receive only 40.9 percent of the vote. As in its widely publicized reports about public opinion over the preceding decade, the *Digest* rested its 1936 prediction on a tally of ballots returned from millions that had been mailed out across the country. That Crossley, Gallup, and Roper had the audacity to base predictions on relatively small samples (compared to the 2 million ballots on which the *Digest* based its claim) was itself newsworthy. But when their projections were borne out by the election returns, the validity of modern polling had been established. The point had been made that the *way* a sample is drawn is more important than its *size*. Bias toward the affluent inherent in the lists from which the *Digest* had drawn names — telephone subscribers and owners of automobiles — could not be offset by large numbers.

Confidence in the potential of the new polling technique abounded for the next decade. Gallup and Roper found journalistic sponsors for their polls, Gallup through syndication to newspapers and Roper in a relationship with *Fortune* magazine. Opinion research also demonstrated its usefulness for government. In 1939, Rensis Likert developed polling for the U.S. Department of Agriculture, the first such operation within an agency of government.

Polls by Hadley Cantril provided President Roosevelt with valuable information on American public opinion throughout World War II. The Office of Public Opinion Research he established in 1940 at Princeton University conducted research into the methodology of polling and became a central archive for polling data. In 1941, the National Opinion Research Center, now at the University of Chicago, was established.

These were also years in which practitioners from commercial and academic research came together in an awareness that their new field had intellectual merit and a legitimate public purpose. The *Public Opinion Quarterly,* now the principal journal in the field was founded in 1937, and the American Association for Public Opinion Research was organized in 1947.

But in 1948 President Harry S. Truman's defeat of Governor Thomas E. Dewey by almost five percentage points stung the pollsters, all of whom had predicted a Dewey victory. Credibility was on the line as newspapers canceled subscriptions to the Gallup Poll and Roper reported a drop in business. A panel of the Social Science Research Council reviewed polling procedures that had been employed and urged the pollsters to improve their sampling methods and continue interviewing until the closing days of future election campaigns.

From the 1948 debacle until the mid-1970s the field was preoccupied with technique and issues of data *reliability*. The focus was on measurement issues, improved sampling procedures, and increasingly complex forms of data analysis. Particular emphasis was placed on the importance of repeated efforts ("callbacks") to contact hard-to-find respondents in order to protect against overrepresentation of those who happen to be at home when interviewers first call. Much of opinion research since the mid-1970s can be described as a quest for *validity*. Researchers, seeking to ensure that the conclusions they draw from poll data are appropriate, have paid close attention to nonsampling error, including the many ways question wording, question order, and the interviewing process itself may affect the results a poll yields.

The election of 1988 was regarded by many in the polling community as a watershed in terms of the *legitimacy* of polling. Concern about the quality of electoral politics was voiced by political observers and picked up in the polls. Some pollsters worried that their craft had become part of the problem by providing the insights upon which political consultants cynically framed campaign issues and targeted their negative television commercials.

Only recently (1984) have polls themselves been shown to have an impact — though limited — on public opinion. Some voters may be influenced by poll results early in a presidential primary campaign when they have little information about any of the candidates and the outcome of the primary is in doubt. But it has been shown that such "bandwagon" effects dissipate as the election approaches.

News organizations are the primary sponsors of election polls and many now conduct their own. One result is tension between journalistic criteria of what is newsworthy and research criteria of how reliable the data are and whether reports of a poll portray its results accurately and fully. The matter is high on the agenda of contemporary polling as it strives to raise standards of professional competence and devise more effective forms of accountability to the public.

Norman M. Bradburn and Seymour Sudman, *Polls and Surveys: Understanding What They Tell Us* (1988); Albert H. Cantril, *The Opinion Connection: Polling, Politics, and the Press* (1991).

ALBERT H. CANTRIL

PUBLIC RELIEF

See Welfare and Public Relief.

PUBLIC TRANSPORTATION

Prior to 1825, no city in the world possessed a public transportation system — which may be defined as transportation operating along a fixed route, according to an established schedule, for a single fare. In the United States, horse-drawn carriages for hire called hackneys carried the public on short trips, and stagecoaches served a similar function for more distant journeys.

The Omnibus

The first transit system anywhere was developed in Nantes, France, in 1826, by a retired army officer who set up a short stage line between the center of town and his public baths on the outskirts. When he discovered that passengers were more interested in getting off at intermediate points than in patronizing his baths, he shifted his focus. His new "omnibus" combined the functions of the hackney and the stagecoach. Word of his success spread quickly, and by 1832, the idea had been copied in Paris, Bordeaux, Lyons, and London.

In the United States, omnibus service began in 1829 with Abraham Brower's route along lower Broadway in New York City; others took the idea to Philadelphia in 1831, Boston in 1835, and Baltimore in 1844. Typically the city government granted a private company — usually a small businessman already in the livery or freight business — an exclusive franchise to operate coaches along a given street. In return, the company agreed to maintain certain minimum levels of service.

Although the omnibus represented an obvious improvement over walking, the unpadded benches, poor ventilation, and slow speed provided an uncomfortable ride. Moreover, the heavy, twelve-passenger vehicles were hampered by the condition of city streets, which at best were paved with uneven cobblestones. Not surprisingly, even in New York City, which had the most extensive omnibus network, only about twenty-five thousand persons, or one resident in twenty-five, used this form of transportation on a daily basis in 1850.

The Horsecar

Placing the omnibus on iron rails was the next major innovation. Initially developed by John Mason on regular railroad tracks between Prince and Fourteenth streets in Manhattan in 1832, the horse-drawn streetcar, popularly known as the horsecar, combined the low cost, flexibility, and safety of animal power with the efficiency, smoothness, and all-weather capability of a rail right-of-way.

The great expansion of horse-drawn railways came after 1852, when Alphonse Loubat developed a grooved rail that lay flush with the pavement. This was an essential improvement because the earliest horsecars had used rails that protruded six inches or more above street level, seriously interfering with coach and wagon traffic. By 1855, the horsecar had forced the omnibus off the major thoroughfares and onto secondary routes in New York; by 1860, the same process was taking place in Baltimore, Philadelphia, Pittsburgh, Chicago, Montreal, and Boston.

The great advantage of the horsecar obviously lay in its use of rails, which made possible a much smoother ride at a speed (six to eight miles per hour) almost twice as fast as the omnibus, an important consideration if one lived at a distance from work. Moreover, the reduced friction enabled a single horse to pull a thirty- to forty-passenger vehicle that had more inside room, an easier exit, and more effective brakes than the typical omnibus. All these advantages lowered operating costs, ultimately reducing the average fare for a single ride from fifteen cents on the omnibus to ten cents on the horsecar. The only person whose ride was not noticeably improved was the driver, who sat unprotected from the weather on an open platform. It was thought that if the platform were enclosed, the driver's attention and alertness might be compromised.

By the mid-1880s, there were 415 street railway companies in the United States operating over six thousand miles of track and carrying 188 million passengers per year, or about twelve rides for every man, woman, and child who lived in a city of at least twenty-five hundred persons. Horsecar railways were built much more slowly in Europe. As late as 1875, the total ridership of Paris, London, Vienna, and Berlin combined was much less than that of New York City alone. In Tokyo, the largest city in Asia, the horsecar was not even introduced until 1882.

The Cable Car

In 1867, a maverick New York City inventor, Charles T. Harvey, developed an overhead vehicle connected by a releasable grip to a constantly moving cable and installed a primitive prototype over a three-block run in Greenwich Village. The effort ultimately failed, however, and it was left to Andrew Smith Hallidie, a Scottish immigrant who had found wealth in San Francisco as a wire-rope manufacturer, to attempt an urban duplication of the English mining technique of hauling cars by large cables. Passenger vehicles ran along tracks similar to those of the horse railways, but the power came from giant steam engines that moved the cable. Easily adaptable to the broad, straight avenues of American cities, as opposed to the narrow, sinuous streets of European urban centers, the cable car was particularly suited to Nob Hill and other perilous inclines of the City by the Bay. Chicago, however, quickly developed the world's most extensive cable system, particularly to its South Side, and by 1894, the city boasted more than fifteen hundred grip and trailer cars operating on eighty-six miles of track. Philadelphia opened its first cable line in 1883, followed by New York and Oakland in 1887. By 1890, when cable transportation reached its peak, there were five hundred miles of track in twenty-three cities carrying 373 million passengers per year.

But since cable car construction costs were several times those of the horsecar, cable operations had to be restricted to the most heavily traveled routes where passenger revenues would be sufficient to recover the investment. Not surprisingly, the popularity of cable systems soon waned, and most cities remained with the horsecar. Only San Francisco retains Hallidie's invention, primarily for nostalgia and tourism.

The Steam Railroad

The first American railroads were designed for long distance rather than local travel. But they sought ridership wherever they could find it and very early on built stations whenever their lines passed through rural villages on the outskirts of the larger cities. In the nation's largest metropolis, rudimentary commuter travel by steam railroad began in 1832, and by 1837 the New York and Harlem Railroad was offering regular service to 125th Street. Meanwhile, the New York and New Haven Railroad along Long Island Sound reached New Haven in 1843, and the Harlem River line toward Albany reached Peekskill in 1849. Similarly, the Long Island Railroad and the New York and Flushing Railroad enabled former Manhattanites to commute from the east. Over the next half century population growth along these tracks was substantial, and by 1898 the three major passenger lines to the north of the city were alone disgorging 118,000 daily commuters into Grand Central Terminal. This pattern was duplicated elsewhere, and by 1900 railroad commuting was well established in Philadelphia, Boston, and Chicago.

Relative to other forms of public transportation, however, railroad travel was both expensive and time consuming. Steam engines were difficult to start and stop; unlike the horsecar or the electric streetcar, the steam engine generated speed slowly. The practical result of this limitation was that railroad suburbs were usually discontinuous and located at least a mile or two from each other. Typically, they developed like beads on a string; the towns were connected by the railroad line but were not initially contiguous either to each other or to the central city.

The Electric Streetcar

The trolley — called a tram in Europe — was born in the United States. The first practical applications were by Leo Daft in Baltimore in 1885, Charles J. Van Depoele in Montgomery, Alabama, in 1886, and Frank Julian Sprague in Richmond in 1887. Sprague in particular demonstrated the feasibility of moving many cars simultaneously by means of an overhead electric wire. By the turn of the century, half the streetcar systems in the United States were equipped by him, and 90 percent were using his patents.

The typical trolley resembled a nineteenth-century railroad car. It had metal wheels, open platforms front and rear, and large windows all around. About half the size of a modern bus, it swayed and clanged down the small railroad tracks that were especially designed for its use. With its constantly humming motor controlled by a driver in a glassed-in cubicle, the vehicle ordinarily had no front or back because it could not be turned around at the end of the line.

Pollution-free electric traction possessed many advantages. Faster than either the cable car or the horse-drawn streetcar, it raised the potential speed of city travel to twenty miles per hour (the average was ten to fifteen miles per hour) and was capable of additional acceleration in low-density areas. Similarly, it achieved substantial economies over other forms of transit. It required neither the extensive underground paraphernalia of the cable car nor the heavy investment in animals, feed, and stables of the horsecar. Because trolleys tended to be larger than horsecars, the cost per passenger mile was reduced by at least half. The average fare dropped from a dime to a nickel.

The American people embraced the trolley with extraordinary rapidity and enthusiasm. In 1890, when the federal government first canvassed the nation's rail systems, it enumerated 5,700 miles of horsecar track, 500 miles for cable cars, and 1,260 for the trolley. By 1893, only six years after Sprague's successful Richmond experiment, more than 250 electric railways had been incorporated in the United States, and more than 60 percent of the nation's 12,000 miles of track had been electrified. By the end of 1903 America's 30,000 miles of street railway were 98 percent electrified. It was one of the most rapidly accepted innovations in the history of technology. By comparison, the automobile, which was invented at about the same time, was a late bloomer.

The rapidity of the American adoption of the trolley was especially striking in comparison with Europe. In 1890, for example, the number of passengers carried on American street railways (including cable and elevated systems) was over 2 billion per year, or more than twice that of the rest of the world combined. In cities of more than 100,000 inhabitants, the average number of rides per person each year was 172, a figure that included children and other persons who rarely traveled. Berlin, which then had the best system in Europe, would have ranked no higher than twenty-second in the United States. At the turn of the century, when the horsecar had virtually disappeared from American streets, it was still the dominant form of urban transport in Britain. In Tokyo, the electric streetcar did not appear until 1903, and in 1911 its system was less than one-tenth as large as that of New York City.

Rapid Transit

Because the streetcar, whether powered by an animal or an electric wire, could not eliminate congestion on the streets, transit experts turned early to the notion of a public right-of-way for their busiest lines. Two methods were possible — elevated trains and subways. The elevated was the older mode, the first line in New York having opened in 1870. Faster and more capital-intensive than the horsecars with which it initially competed, the "els" were noisy, unsightly, and dirty, even after electrification began to replace the small steam engines after 1900. A better solution was underground transit, which became necessary when the elevated structures themselves became an impediment to the smooth flow of traffic. The first American subway opened in Boston in 1897, long after London (1863) and shortly after Glasgow (1896) and Budapest (1896). But New York City, when its initial underground line opened in 1904, became the world pacesetter for two reasons — its immense size and technological innovation. Gotham's competing transit companies built new lines and extended old ones with unmatched vigor, and by 1937 the region had 308 route miles (and more than 700 track miles) of rapid transit service and was handling 4.2 million passengers per day, exclusive of bus and streetcar patronage. As designed by Chief Engineer William Barclay Parsons, New York's subway was the first in the world with a fully integrated express and local system. Parsons chose the cut-and-cover method of digging, and his underground became a model for the construction of rapid transit elsewhere.

The Twentieth Century

The public transportation system of the United States, easily the best in the world in 1900, slipped badly in the following decades, and by 1920 it had been overtaken by the government-subsidized systems of Germany, France, Holland, and Britain. The number of American streetcar riders peaked in 1923 at 15.7 billion. Patronage declined slowly in the 1920s (to 14.4 billion in 1929) and precipitously in the 1930s (to 8.3 billion in 1940). By 1990, the clang of the trolley could be heard on only a few lines in Boston, New Orleans, Pittsburgh, Philadelphia, and Newark. Initially, the streetcars were replaced by gasoline-powered buses, but this method of conveyance also proved unable to compete with the private automobile. In the last decade of the twentieth century, America's public bus lines offered poor service at high prices in comparison to transit systems elsewhere in the world.

Commuting by steam railroad survived automotive competition better than did the trolleys and subways. Indeed, the golden age of railroad commutation was during the 1920s, when every major eastern and midwestern city benefited from frequent rail service. The depression years saw a sharp drop in patronage, but the demise of the once magnificent passenger railroad system of the United States did not come until the 1950s, when bankruptcy and deteriorating service were the inevitable result of a national transportation policy that subsidized air and automobile travel and taxed the railroads. By 1990, only a handful of cities — including New York,

Boston, Chicago, and Philadelphia — could boast of impressive railroad commuter traffic.

Meanwhile, the private automobile became the primary form of transportation in the United States. Led by Henry Ford and his moving assembly line, American automobile registrations climbed from 1 million in 1913 to 10 million in 1923, when Kansas alone had more cars than France or Germany, and Michigan counted more than Great Britain and Ireland combined. By 1927, when the American total had risen to 26 million, the United States was building about 85 percent of the world's automobiles, and there was one motor vehicle for every five people in the country.

The triumph of the private automobile was greatly aided by federal policy. Unlike European governments, Washington treated public transportation as if it were a private business, while regarding the motorcar as worthy of immense public subsidies. Indeed, Senator Gaylord Nelson of Wisconsin reported that between 1945 and 1980, 75 percent of government expenditures on transport went for highways, and only 1 percent went to public buses, trolleys, or subways. The inevitable result of the bias in American policy, a bias that began even before the Interstate Highway Act of 1956 and one that has no counterpart in either Europe or Asia, was that by 1991 the United States had the world's best road system and very nearly its worst public transit offerings.

Harry J. Carman, *The Street Surface Railway Franchises of New York City* (1919); Kenneth T. Jackson, *Crabgrass Frontier: The Suburbanization of the United States* (1985); John P. McKay, *Tramways and Trolleys: The Rise of Urban Mass Transport in Europe* (1976).

KENNETH T. JACKSON

See also Automobiles; National Road; Railroads; Transportation Revolution.

PUBLIC WORKS ADMINISTRATION

The Federal Emergency Administration of Public Works, created by Title II in the National Industrial Recovery Act of June 1933, became the first national peacetime effort to create jobs.

Eventually known as the Public Works Administration (PWA), this New Deal program spent over $6 billion to shore up the nation's infrastructure while combating unemployment. Under Secretary of the Interior Harold Ickes's direction, the PWA constructed or refurbished highways, dams, low-cost housing, airports, warships, and other public projects. States and municipalities provided supervision in some cases, but all had to respect PWA guidelines. No PWA projects could use convict labor or work employees more than thirty hours a week. Congress required that human labor be used "in lieu of machinery whenever practicable" to maximize employment. By the close of 1933, thirteen thousand federal projects and twenty-five hundred locally supervised projects were under way.

The PWA earned a near spotless reputation for good management, and Ickes used every avenue to guarantee Afro-Americans their share of positions at all levels. Critics, however, complained that Ickes planned too cautiously, thereby delaying projects and new jobs.

See also New Deal.

PUBLISHING

As the Gilded Age publisher Henry Holt once observed, a "book is a thing by itself. There is nothing like it, as one shoe is like another, or as one kind of whiskey is like another." Part commodity and part cultural artifact, often subject to the whims of popular taste, books have variable social and economic values that make their planning, printing, and merchandising a volatile and uncertain business. Yet the history of American book publishing is closely tied to commercial and industrial development in the nation at large.

American publishing, well into the nineteenth century, retained features of the original colonial trade. The Anglo-American book market developed within a provincial network of family and religious ties. Patronage was weak, religious and political censorship frequent, and capital in short supply. Seventeenth-century printers, such as Cambridge's Samuel Green, Philadelphia's William Bradford, and Maryland's William Nuthead, engaged in a local and inconstant trade. Their books were few and expensive, and their output confined largely to primers, catechisms, Psalters, almanacs, and the Bible; the last, in the early 1800s, was printed in twenty-four locations in Massachusetts alone. Even in the eighteenth century, the term *publisher* — exemplified by entrepreneurs like New England's Isaiah Thomas and Philadelphia's Matthew Carey — could refer variously to an editor, printer, author, or compiler. Authors, under the subscription systems that began to appear in the 1760s, were commonly paid in kind — that is, with copies of their books. Titles originating in America still constituted less than half of the books sold. Because of the lack of an international copyright law, steady sellers like Daniel Defoe, Henry Fielding, and Samuel Richardson were habitually pirated.

Local printing continued to flourish in the early national era. In 1755 there had been about 50 printing houses; by 1860, there were over 380. But starting in the 1830s with the founding of such firms as John Wiley & Sons and the House of Harper, the trade was becoming more centralized and the village printer-bookseller a thing of the past. Technological and transportation improvements (stereotype plating, cylinder steam presses, railroads) made for larger printings, cheaper publications, and wider distribution. Children's literature, fiction, and magazines and newspapers challenged the popularity of devotional literature and almanacs. Meanwhile, penny press entrepreneurs like Frank Leslie, and dime novel houses like Beadle Brothers and Street & Smith, provided young, working-class audiences with a steady diet of sensational stories. Although data on audiences are fragmentary, the business of book publishing seems to have been conducted on three levels: the mass dime novel industry, cheap reprint companies that often supplied home subscription libraries in the West and South, and a group of genteel, northeastern houses that also published magazines. These last firms maintained an uneasy hegemony over elite and middle-class family reading. Victorian publishers like George Palmer Putnam, Charles Scribner, and Henry Houghton saw themselves as gentleman publicists and cultural gatekeepers; Boston's James T. Fields, for example, promised to "manufacture" Nathaniel Hawthorne "into a classic" while also maintaining a small literary salon.

The establishment of international copyrights in 1891 (whose effects were not entirely foreseen) altered the structure of the publishing industry. Initially backed by authors and major houses hoping to outlaw piracy, the copyright law in one blow doomed reprint houses, made the prices of U.S. authors competitive with those of Europeans, and — through a protectionist manufacturing clause — brought new prosperity to the American printing industry. As lawmakers had hoped, books written, printed, and published by Americans now outsold those of European rivals. But instead of the predicted stability, what followed was a period of intense competition, as U.S. houses competed heavily for both foreign and native-born authors.

A new breed of entrepreneur — Frank N. Doubleday, Walter Hines Page, George P. Brett of Macmillan's American wing — displaced the Gilded Age gentlemen publishers. Theirs was the top-down management style taking hold in other industries. Best-sellers were first recorded in the 1890s, as the newly founded trade organ *Publishers Weekly* began to keep track of sales. Authors were now commissioned to write books in advance, and even radical works like Upton Sinclair's *The Jungle* (1906) were given full-scale promotion. The dime novel, which had succumbed to the competition of Sunday newspaper supplements, was replaced by other experiments in mass publications like Haldeman-Julius's Little Blue Books.

In the twentieth century, the pattern was mixed. Successive waves of commercial concentration, retrenchment, and publishers' claims to cultural patronage occurred. Major publishers often subsisted by sustaining a back list of recurrent favorites and classics, by cross-subsidizing weak titles with best-sellers, and by developing increasingly elaborate subsidiary rights (by 1922, over a hundred novels had been made into motion pictures). Literary agents, grudgingly accepted after 1900, became commonplace. The twenties witnessed a virtual explosion of American fad books, historical outlines, and self-help texts. The Book-of-the-Month Club was founded

(1926) as well as important firms like Simon & Schuster, Random House, Viking, and Boni & Liveright. Publishers and editors varied from patient patrons of authors (like Scribner's Maxwell Perkins) to ingenious publicists (like Bennett Cerf of Random House). The Great Depression forced many firms to experiment with covers, cheap popular novels, and ultimately paperback editions, the prototype being Robert de Graff's Pocket Books (1939).

Meanwhile, university presses, often begun on a small scale during the Gilded Age, capitalized on the expansion of scholarly publication following World War I. The Association of American University Presses (AAUP), after tentative organization in the twenties, formally adopted a constitution in 1937. Academic publishers served the nation's cultural life by publishing scholarly monographs, anthologies, textbooks, periodicals, encyclopedias, and standard editions of classics. After decades of surging growth, university presses faced tighter budgets and stricter management in the 1970s; some formed consortiums like the University Press of New England (1971) or sought external philanthropic funding. In the 1980s, although individual sales of traditional scholarly books tended to decline, many academic presses expanded their annual lists, often aggressively marketing books in general interest categories previously offered only by commercial houses. By the mid-1980s, the membership of the AAUP had expanded to over seventy-five publishing houses. Academic presses now accounted for nearly 10 percent of books published in the United States.

After World War II, paperbacks and, later, chain bookstores like B. Dalton's and Waldenbooks often dictated the merchandising horizons of the industry. Now book publishing attracted the interest of large conglomerates like RCA and MCA. To some, these takeovers brought greater efficiency, more direct access to specialized buyers, and skyrocketing royalties; to others, they meant severely trimmed back lists, overemphasis on "blockbuster" best-sellers, and even possible censorship. Despite the magnitude of the changes in publishing, it remained what colonial printer William Bradford had called an "Art and Mystery."

John Tebbel, *A History of Book Publishing in the United States,* 4 vols. (1978).

Christopher P. Wilson

See also Literature; Magazines and Newspapers.

PUERTO RICO

Puerto Rico became an American colony as a result of the war with Spain in 1898. American troops occupied the island in July of that year virtually without opposition, and the Treaty of Paris in December gave the United States control of the island. Expansionists and anti-imperialists hotly debated whether the nation could "Americanize" the Puerto Ricans, most of whom appeared willing to accept American rule.

In 1900, Congress passed the Foraker Act, which established civilian government there and set up a locally elected lower house in the legislature but gave the president the power to appoint the governor and the upper house. Tariffs were placed on Puerto Rican products entering the United States. This provision raised a legal question: how could tariffs be imposed if Puerto Rico was part of the United States? The Supreme Court decided this issue in the so-called Insular Cases (especially *Downes* v. *Bidwell* in 1901). The Court distinguished between "unincorporated" territory — insular possessions where the U.S. Constitution was not binding — and "incorporated" lands — such as federal territories where it was.

The United States has ruled Puerto Rico ever since. Its residents were granted citizenship in 1917, and Puerto Rico was granted status as a commonwealth in 1952, meaning that it would be U.S. territory but would govern itself under its own constitution. Many Puerto Ricans have immigrated to the U.S. mainland, which as citizens they can do freely, in search of better economic opportunities. Movements both for statehood and for complete independence flourish on the island.

See also Expansion, Continental and Overseas; Muñoz Marín, Luis; Spanish-American War.

PULITZER, JOSEPH

(1847–1911), journalist. Pulitzer founded the most influential newspapers of America's industrial age. At seventeen he fled from his prosperous home in Hungary, a would-be soldier of fortune. This thin, gawky man with weak eyes came to America because the Union army was the only armed force that would take him. Having little English, he migrated to the German community of St. Louis at the end of the Civil War. He began reporting in German for the *Westliche Post* and was a reliable party worker for the liberal Republicans. But by the time he was thirty, Pulitzer had embraced the Democratic party and English-language journalism. In 1878 he brought together two struggling afternoon dailies, the *Post* and *Dispatch,* and sought to wake up St. Louis.

This river town, inebriated by dreams of commercial supremacy, had lost out to Chicago and its rail network. Pulitzer reported what had gone wrong: the corruption of government, the pretensions of the upper class, the despair of the tenements. The *Post-Dispatch* featured exposés and gossip, albeit with protestations of moral seriousness. Readers were drawn to a paper that was at once sensational and reliable, and circulation rose from two thousand to thirty thousand in the first five years. Pulitzer appealed to the urban working class, but he did not drop his price as low as did all his competitors and he had no socialist leanings. He was a classical liberal who believed that a newspaper should actively seek to right injustices so that government could remain small. "More crime, immorality and rascality is prevented by the fear of exposure in the newspapers than by all the laws, morals and statutes ever devised," he told readers.

Pulitzer wanted to be at the center of power and in 1883 he purchased the *New York World.* He paid for the best talent and set to work ridiculing the American plutocracy and reporting on the struggles of the poor. He was marked as an outsider. The *Journalist,* aware of his father's religion, printed the newcomer's name "Jewish Pulitzer." Through illustrations and cartoons he helped broaden interest in the newspaper. One of his cartoonists, Richard Outcault, drew the "Yellow Kid" and inspired the epithet "the yellow press." "In using the word masses I do not exclude anybody," Pulitzer said. Indeed, his ideal was stories and editorials so compelling that every American would read his paper. Rising to do battle with a young challenger, William Randolph Hearst, in 1895, Pulitzer spread the gaudiest stories put forward by Cuban insurgents during the crisis that led to the Spanish-American War. As a result the *World* sold a hundred copies for every one sold when Pulitzer had bought the paper.

Eventually Pulitzer turned away from mere crowd pleasing. At the turn of the century, the *World* was set on a course that would make it the most admired paper among journalists. Pulitzer fled the roaring cities his paper had done so much to amplify. Nearly blind, he grew reclusive and spent most of his final years sailing the oceans of the world. He edited his papers by telegram and filled his life with classical literature. He wanted to control journalism from the grave, and so his will sought to perpetuate the *World* as an exemplary paper, set up the Graduate School of Journalism at Columbia University to further professionalism, and endowed the prizes for excellence that bear his name.

W. A. Swanberg, *Pulitzer* (1967).

THOMAS C. LEONARD

See also Magazines and Newspapers.

PULLMAN STRIKE

The Pullman strike of 1894 demonstrated late-nineteenth-century business and government attitudes toward labor and did much to chart the course of American socialism. In the wake of the highly profitable Chicago World's Fair of 1893 and the panic that struck the world economy the same year, George Pullman, the inventor of the railroad sleeping car, fired one-third of his workers and cut the wages of those who remained by 30 percent. But he would not cut prices for homes or food in Pullman, the company town near Chicago that he had built to house his employees.

In 1894, Eugene V. Debs, president of the American Railway Union (ARU), ordered a strike when Pullman refused to negotiate with the ARU over the cuts. The owners and management of other lines backed Pullman, providing replacement workers while Debs organized his rank and file, who refused to work on any trains that used a Pullman car. President Grover Cleveland also sided with Pullman, contending that strike-related violence and boycotts interrupted mail service. On July 2, Debs defied a federal injunction to return to work, prompting his arrest and the use of federal troops.

An investigating committee appointed by Cleveland later revealed the abuses of the strikers by the courts. The troops effectively broke the strike, and Debs was eventually sentenced to six months in prison for contempt. He served the term and came out of jail widely known for his activities and in demand as a speaker. He also came out a socialist and was the most prominent and popular leader of the Socialist party into the 1920s, running several times as its presidential candidate.

See also Debs, Eugene V.; Labor; Socialist Party.

PURE FOOD AND DRUG ACT

By 1900 most American states had enacted food laws, but they were poorly enforced. The effort to enact a federal law was led by Dr. Harvey W. Wiley, head of the Bureau of Chemistry in the Department of Agriculture. Wiley enlisted the support of the more responsible food producers and pharmaceutical manufacturers, the American Medical Association, the General Federation of Women's Clubs, and other consumer groups. He faced the entrenched opposition of the politically powerful "Beef Trust," small producers of patent medicines, and southern congressmen concerned with the constitutional validity of the proposed law.

The tide was turned in Wiley's favor by a series of sensational articles by muckraking journalists. Following the "embalmed beef" scandal of the Spanish-American War in 1898 (this concerned the quality of food supplied to U.S. troops), Charles Edward Russell produced a series of articles exposing the greed and corruption of the Beef Trust. Samuel Hopkins Adams demonstrated that patent medicines were often pernicious compounds of alcohol and other drugs. Then, in January 1906, Upton Sinclair published his best-selling novel *The Jungle,* replete with hair-raising descriptions of the manner in which meat products were prepared in the Chicago stockyards.

Amid a storm of public indignation, a Pure Food and Drug Act was passed on June 30, 1906. The act forbade foreign and interstate commerce in adulterated or fraudulently labeled food and drugs. Products could now be seized and condemned, and offending persons could be fined and jailed. The first of a series of consumer protection laws passed in the twentieth century, the Pure Food and Drug Act of 1906 was a triumph of progressive reform.

See also Jungle, The; Muckrakers; Progressivism.

PURITANISM

Puritanism was a religious reform movement that arose within the Church of England in the late sixteenth century. Under siege from church and crown, it sent an offshoot in the third and fourth decades of the seventeenth century to the northern English colonies in the New World — a migration that laid the foundation for the religious, intellectual, and social order of New England. Puritanism, however, was not only a historically specific phenomenon coincident with the founding of New England; it was also a way of being in the world — a style of response to lived experience — that has reverberated through American life ever since.

The roots of Puritanism are to be found in the beginnings of the English Reformation. The name "Puritans" (they were sometimes called "precisionists") was a term of contempt assigned to the movement by its enemies. Although the epithet first emerged in the 1560s, the process through which Puritanism developed had been initiated in the 1530s, when King Henry VIII repudiated papal authority and transformed the Church of Rome into a state Church of England. But the Church of England retained much of the liturgy and ritual of Roman Catholicism and

seemed, to many dissenters, to be insufficiently reformed.

Well into the sixteenth century many priests were barely literate and often very poor. Employment by more than one parish was common, and the resulting itinerancy of priests, along with their immunity to certain penalties of the civil law, fed anticlerical hostility and contributed to their isolation from the spiritual needs of the people.

Through the reigns of the Protestant King Edward VI (1547–1553), who introduced the first vernacular prayer book, and the Catholic Queen Mary (1553–1558), who sent some dissenting clergymen to their deaths and others into exile, the Puritan movement — whether tolerated or suppressed — continued to grow. Some Puritans favored a presbyterian form of church organization; others, more radical, began to claim autonomy for individual congregations. Still others were content to remain within the structure of the national church, but set themselves against the doctrinal and liturgical vestiges of Catholic tradition, especially the vestments that symbolized episcopal authority. As they gained strength, Puritans were portrayed by their enemies as hairsplitters who slavishly followed their Bibles as guides to daily life; or they were caricatured as licentious hypocrites who adopted a grave aspect but cheated the very neighbors whom they judged inadequate Christians. They appeared in drama and satire as secretly lascivious purveyors of feigned piety.

Yet the Puritan attack on the established church gained popular strength, especially in East Anglia and among the lawyers and merchants of London. The movement found wide support among these new professional classes, in part because it was congenial to their growing discontent with mercantile economic restraints. During the reign of Queen Elizabeth I, an uneasy peace prevailed within English religious life, but the struggle over the tone and purpose of the church continued. Many men and women were more and more forced to contend with the dislocations — emotional as well as physical — that accompanied the beginnings of a market economy. Subsistence farmers were called upon to enter the world of production for profit.

Under the rule of primogeniture, younger sons tended to enter the professions (especially the law) with increasing frequency and seek their livelihood in the burgeoning cities. With the growth of a continental market for wool, land enclosure for sheep farming became an attractive alternative for large landowners, who thereby disrupted centuries-old patterns of rural communal life. The English countryside was plagued by scavengers, highwaymen, and vagabonds — a newly visible class of the poor who strained the ancient charity laws and pressed upon the townsfolk new questions of social responsibility.

Puritanism was a response to these new social and psychological conditions as well as a strictly religious movement. It stressed the pastoral responsibility of the clergy and thus placed an unprecedented emphasis on the sermon as the central rite of religious life. Puritans attacked relentlessly whatever seemed to them the vestiges of popery; some put an end to kneeling at communion, to the ceremonial marriage ring, to crossing the child in baptism. In ecclesiastical matters, Puritans did not believe that the preaching ministry drew its legitimacy from superior church officers, who, in turn, claimed theirs through the chain of apostolic succession. They believed, instead, that a true church was a continually renewed collective act of "edification" — a mutually committed group of believers from whose ranks arose a mandate for a pastoral minister to serve them. God spoke primarily through the preaching ministry, not through the sacraments.

Doctrinally, Puritans adhered to the Five Points of Calvinism as codified at the Synod of Dort in 1619: (1) unconditional election (the idea that God had decreed who was damned and who was saved from before the beginning of the world); (2) limited atonement (the idea that Christ died for the elect only); (3) total depravity (humanity's utter corruption since the Fall); (4) irresistible grace (regeneration as entirely a work of God, which cannot be resisted and to which the sinner contributes nothing); and (5) the perseverance of the saints (the elect, despite their backsliding and faintness of heart, cannot fall away from grace).

But the real novelty and force of the Puritans was neither doctrinal nor ecclesiological. What most stirred the exasperation of the Anglican establishment was their devotion to sermons, "not Sermons read neither ... but sermons without book, sermons which spend their life in their birth and may have public audience but once." So that the "meanest understanding" could grasp them, these sermons were increasingly delivered in a "plain style"; they were long, frequent, and likely to stray from traditional biblical subjects and raise such questions as the mutual obligations of debtors and creditors. At heart, Puritan sermons were passionate appeals for conversion. They stressed a process of self-examination by which the inner corruption of the soul could be exposed and for which God, at his own pleasure, might forgive the penitent sinner. The great paradox for Puritan believers — which was raised to even higher pitch in New England — was their simultaneous striving for self-knowledge and acknowledgment of the infinity of their ignorance. A Puritan might hear, in a pious lifetime, hundreds of sermons proclaiming God's inscrutability and the futility of human effort to do anything to affect God's will. Yet virtually the only hope for salvation was to submit to this auditory form of the saving word and to pray that the holy spirit would enter the soul through the imprecatory voice of the minister.

In the early decades of the seventeenth century some groups of worshipers began to separate themselves from the main body of their local parish church where preaching was inadequate and to engage an energetic "lecturer," typically a young man with a fresh Cambridge degree, who was a lively speaker and steeped in reform theology. Some congregations went further, declared themselves separated from the national church, and remade themselves into communities of "visible saints," withdrawn from the English City of Man into a self-proclaimed City of God.

One such faction was a group of separatist believers in the Yorkshire village of Scrooby, who, fearing for their safety, moved to Holland in 1608 and thence, in 1620, to the place they called Plymouth in New England. A decade later, a larger, better-financed group, mostly from East Anglia, migrated to Massachusetts Bay. There they set up gathered churches on much the same model as the transplanted church at Plymouth (with deacons, preaching elders, and, though not right away, a communion restricted to full church members, or "saints"). These Puritans called themselves "nonseparating congregationalists," by which they meant that they had not repudiated the Church of England as a false church. But in practice they acted — from the point of view of Episcopalians and even Presbyterians at home — exactly as the separatists were acting. By the 1640s their enterprise at Massachusetts Bay had grown to about ten thousand persons, and through the inevitable centrifugal pressures of land scarcity within the borders of the swelling towns, ecclesiastical quarreling, and sheer restlessness of spirit, they had outgrown the bounds of the original settlement and spread into what would become Connecticut, New Hampshire, Rhode Island, and Maine, and eventually beyond the limits of New England.

The Puritan migration was overwhelmingly a migration of families (unlike other migrations to early America, which were composed largely of young unattached men). The literacy rate was high, and the intensity of devotional life, as recorded in the many surviving diaries, sermon notes, poems, and letters, was seldom to be matched in American life. The Puritans' ecclesiastical order was as intolerant as the one they had fled. Yet, as a loosely confederated collection of gathered churches, Puritanism contained within itself the seed of its own fragmentation. Following hard upon the arrival in New England, dissident groups within the Puritan sect began to proliferate — Quakers, Antinomians, Baptists — fierce believers who carried the essential Puritan idea of the aloneness of each believer with an inscrutable God so far that even the ministry became an obstruction to faith.

The ensuing religious history of early New England is a tale of conflicts between congregational and synodical authority; between those who stressed the utter helplessness of the individual in the process of salvation and those who began to allow a place for human initiative; between those who believed that the Lord's Supper was a sacrament reserved for the regenerate and those who believed that it could be a "converting ordinance"; and perhaps most divisively as time went on, between those who regarded baptism as a rite due only to the children of full communing church members and those who believed it could be safely extended to the children of "half-way" members — second-generation Puritans who had never stepped forward to make the profession of faith that the founders had required for entrance into the true church.

These sorts of disputes — which have a certain inevitability in any community where the quality of true faith is the only value worth disputing — make the history of American Puritanism seem a story of family rancor and, ultimately, of disintegration. But Puritanism as a basic attitude was remarkably durable and can hardly be overestimated as a formative element of early American life. Among its intellectual contributions was a psychological empiricism that has rarely, if ever, been exceeded in categorical subtlety. It furnished Americans with a sense of history as a progressive drama under the direction of God, in which they played a role akin to, if not prophetically aligned with, that of the Old Testament Jews as a new chosen people. Perhaps most important, as Max Weber profoundly understood, was the strength of Puritanism as a way of coping with the contradictory requirements of Christian ethics in a world on the verge of modernity. It supplied an ethics that somehow balanced the injunction to charity and the premium on self-discipline; it counseled moderation within a psychology that virtually ensured exertion toward worldly prosperity as the best sign of divine favor. Such an ethics was particularly urgent in a New World where opportunity can be as obvious as the source of moral authority is obscure.

By the beginning of the eighteenth century, Puritanism had both declined and shown its tenacity. Every New England generation, especially through the characteristic rhetoric of the jeremiad, sorrowfully proclaimed the end of "the faith once delivered to the saints." If we measure the purity of Puritanism by its fidelity to its covenant of faith untainted by a covenant of works or to its original principles of restricted baptism and communion, then we must go even further than its severest internal critics and say that Puritanism never really existed in America at all. The burden of its American experience was its discovery that it had been, in essence, an oppositional movement; that life "in the free air of the New World" posed insuperable dangers to its coherence and survival. But if we regard Puritanism as a way of seeing the world, as an excruciating but exquisite program of self-scrutiny by which the stirrings of grace might be acknowledged and the divinely sanctioned energies of the soul put to use — in both benevolent and violently destructive ways — then we must account it the dominant spiritual regimen of early America.

Though "the New England Way" evolved into a relatively minor system of organizing religious experience within the broader American scene, its central themes recur in the related religious communities of Quakers, Baptists, Presbyterians, Methodists, and a whole range of evangelical Protestants. More recently, the word "Puritan" has once again become a pejorative epithet, meaning prudish, constricted, cold — as in H. L. Mencken's famous remark that a Puritan is one who suspects "somewhere someone is having a good time." Puritanism, however, had a more significant persistence in American life than as the religion of black-frocked caricatures. It survived, perhaps most conspicuously, in the transmuted secular form of self-reliance and political localism that became, by the Age of Enlightenment, virtually the definition of Americanism. And in its bequest of intellectual and moral rigor to the New England mind, it established what was arguably the central strand of American cultural life until the twentieth century.

Alan Heimert and Andrew Delbanco, eds., *The Puritans in America* (1985); Perry Miller, *The New England Mind: The Seventeenth Century* (1939) and *The New England Mind: From Colony to Province* (1953).

ANDREW DELBANCO

See also Half-Way Covenant; Hutchinson, Anne; Mather, Increase, and Mather, Cotton; New England Colonies; Religion; Salem Witch Trials; Winthrop, John.

PWA

See Public Works Administration.

Q

QUAKERS

Because the Protestant reformers of the sixteenth century attempted to eliminate intermediaries between God and people, the Society of Friends, or Quakers, may be regarded as the fullest expression of the Reformation. Most reformers rejected some sacraments and priestly offices of the Roman Catholic church, but the Quakers omitted them all, including baptism, the Lord's Supper, and any ordained, paid clergy. Quakers instead relied upon the direction of what they called "Christ within" or the Inner Light. Their worship consisted of waiting in silence until the Inner Light led members to share their religious concerns with the brethren.

To most Protestants, this primary reliance on inward inspiration depreciated the authority of the Bible, the centrality of the historical Jesus and the Atonement, and hierarchy within church, state, and family. The earliest Quakers (in England, 1651–1660) seemed to confirm the worst suspicions of their critics by proselytizing with abandon and adding thousands to their numbers. Then and later, they were persecuted as "ranters" or anarchists. Even within the Society of Friends the significance of the Atonement and the Bible remained an unsettling question, causing schisms, especially in the nineteenth century. But Quakers enjoyed a complementary freedom from biblicism that permitted the Society uniquely to innovate and change radically over the centuries. Quaker abolitionism was one such innovation.

The missionary efforts of the earliest Friends, including founder George Fox, took them to North America where, as in England, they were persecuted. Massachusetts Bay Colony executed four. Quaker colonization of America, however, offered the prospect of a refuge and more. In contrast to other radical offspring of the Reformation, such as the Amish, Quakers believed that government was divinely instituted and virtuous men and women must help make it operate as God intended. No Quaker did more to enlist his brethren into public service than William Penn. In Pennsylvania, a responsive government of virtuous men would encourage peace, justice, charity, spiritual equality, and liberty for the benefit not just of Quakers but also of Native Americans and non-English refugees from Europe. It was to be a "Holy Experiment" and, in its way, as much a "City on a Hill" as New England.

Although the reality fell short of Penn's utopian hopes, it still succeeded mightily in the opinion of immigrants and posterity. Ambition, envy, and avarice produced thirty years of tumultuous politics in the new province and left Penn convinced that his experiment had failed. But at the same time, Pennsylvania gained a reputation as the "best poor man's country," free of feudal elites, established churches, tithes, discriminatory oaths, high taxes, compulsory military service, and war. While Pennsylvania prospered, Quakers prospered more than others. They always composed the majority of the elite merchants of colonial Philadelphia as well as the most prosperous farmers of the eastern counties.

Although at odds with each other politically,

Quakers nevertheless dominated the government of Pennsylvania. By 1740 Quaker politicians had become sufficiently anxious about their ever-declining proportion of the population and their more aggressive political enemies that they closed ranks and formed possibly the most formidable Whig political organization in colonial America, the Quaker party.

Ironically, political hegemony and social and economic preeminence raised dissenting voices among Friends, and in the 1750s they determined to reverse the direction the Society had taken since 1682. They believed that Quaker participation in government had brought with it intolerable compromises in such Quaker beliefs as pacifism and that many Friends, especially wealthy ones, had assimilated "worldly" secular behavior. After another generation there would be nothing left of Quakerism but the name, lamented one dissenter. To restore the integrity of the Society, reformers insisted on strict enforcement of all its mores, especially endogamy, and in the violence brought to Pennsylvania by the French and Indian War, they demanded that Quakers resign from public office rather than become bellicose. On the social front they moved quickly against deviancy, expelling more than one in five Friends by 1775, but not until the more intense public crisis of the Revolution did all Friends leave public office and the Holy Experiment completely end.

This sectarian revival in the Society brought with it an outburst of philanthropy and testimonies that have become synonymous with Quakerism. From 1755 to 1776, the Society became the first organization in history to ban slaveholding, and Quakers created abolition societies to promote emancipation. In the next century, Quakers populated the abolitionist movement in numbers far exceeding their proportion of all Americans. Some labored for such gradual solutions as the colonization of freedmen, while more conspicuous Quaker abolitionists espoused immediate emancipation. The latter were critically important to organizations like the American Anti-Slavery Society, the Philadelphia Anti-Slavery Society, and the Female Antislavery Society, and to active resistance such as the "underground railway" in Pennsylvania and the

Midwest. Following the example of eighteenth-century abolitionist Anthony Benezet, Friends showed an interest in the education and social progress of blacks. During Reconstruction, American and English Quakers raised hundreds of thousands of dollars for freedmen's relief and established scores of schools for freedmen.

Penn's legendary friendship with Native Americans partly underlay Quakers' renewed pacifism during the French and Indian War and their concurrent departure from government. Thereafter they continued to pursue justice and charity for Native Americans and in the post–Civil War era lobbied and cooperated with the federal government in the administration of Indian affairs in the trans-Mississippi West.

Women Friends shared in all these testimonies and philanthropies. Since the 1650s when Margaret Fell invaluably aided George Fox, whom she later married, women's role and status in the Society of Friends more closely approached equality with men's than in any other Christian church. Preaching and ministering to mixed audiences, traveling extensively unaccompanied by men, regulating the lives of fellow Quaker women without men's assistance (such as in church discipline and marriage arrangements), Quaker women knew a sphere of activity and attained a range of skills that surpassed those of their non-Quaker cohorts. Not surprisingly, historian Mary Maples Dunn found that in nineteenth-century America Quaker women comprised 40 percent of female abolitionists, 19 percent of feminists born before 1830, and 15 percent of suffragists born before 1830.

Although Quakers never returned to public office in any great number after 1776, they never retreated from politics. They believed that out of office, immune to the verdict of the ballot box, they could serve as democracy's conscience better than ever before.

Although a more regimented Society emerged from the eighteenth-century reformation, the Society almost never disciplined a Friend over theology. That tolerance ended in the nineteenth century, however. In 1827 the venerable Philadelphia Yearly Meeting of Friends split into an evangelical group (called the "orthodox") and a liberal group (called

"Hicksite"). In succeeding years, divisions increased, spreading to other areas and yearly meetings of America and also subdividing already fractured meetings. Anxiety over Unitarian theology, languishing membership, industrialization, and the disciplinary powers of meetings, among other things, contributed to the splits. Quaker energies and voices, which had been better focused since the 1750s, became dissipated in intramural recriminations. Quakers continued to practice antislavery, pacifism, and their traditional philanthropies, but not as one body.

Twentieth-century Quakerism has been surprisingly diverse. In the northeastern United States silent worship and quietism often prevailed, whereas in the Midwest and beyond (where two-thirds of Quakers lived) evangelical Friends were most common and resembled typical Protestants. The philanthropic spirit flourished and appeared especially in the American Friends Service Committee, which was created to support wartime pacifists in 1917 but became a world-renowned agency for relief and development. In the mid-twentieth century, Friends moved toward more cooperation and reunion.

Hugh Barbour and J. William Frost, *The Quakers* (1988).

JACK D. MARIETTA

See also Abolitionist Movement; Conscientious Objection; Religion; Woolman, John.

QUARTERING ACTS

In the decade before the American Revolution, a series of Quartering Acts were passed by Parliament to provide for the housing and provisioning of British troops in the American colonies. The first act, which took effect in March 1765, required the colonies to provide barracks for the troops and to keep them supplied with free bedding, firewood, cooking utensils, and certain staple provisions, as well as a daily allowance of cider. A second act in 1766 required billeting the troops in inns, alehouses, and unoccupied dwellings.

In January 1766, the members of the New York Assembly argued that because the British commander had his headquarters in New York, they carried a disproportionate burden under the Quartering Act; they therefore agreed to provide some but not all the supplies specified in the bill. Their defiance mounted until in December 1766 they refused to make any provisions at all for the troops. As punishment, the Board of Trade in October 1767 declared all acts of the New York Assembly to be null and void until the colony complied with the Quartering Act. In the meantime, the assemblymen had given in (June 1767) and voted a grant of three thousand pounds. The matter was thus resolved, but ill-feeling remained on both sides.

In 1774, Parliament passed a group of laws entitled the Coercive Acts (the colonists called them the Intolerable Acts) designed to restore imperial control over the American colonies. All the Coercive Acts dealt specifically with Massachusetts, except one, a new Quartering Act, which applied to all thirteen colonies. This Quartering Act extended the provisions of the earlier legislation; it required that troops be housed not only in commercial and empty buildings but in occupied dwellings as well. The law was bitterly protested, symbolizing as it did to the colonists the potential dangers and abuses of standing armies.

The quartering of troops in America was specifically cited as a grievance in both the Resolves of the First Continental Congress (October 1774) and the Declaration of Independence (July 1776).

See also Coercive Acts; Revolution.

QUEBEC ACT

In 1774 Parliament passed an act annexing the Ohio region to Canada; that and other Canadian provisions helped propel the lower thirteen colonies into revolution. Colonists called the Quebec Act one of the Intolerable Acts. The Continental Congress complained of it prominently in several petitions, and Richard Henry Lee, when introducing the motion for American independence in the Congress, called it "the worst grievance."

Colonial outrage was triggered by several aspects of the measure. Americans had been barred from the Ohio territory by the Proclamation of 1763, but they hoped eventually to be allowed to move there. Those who defied the proclamation would now become Canadians. The provisions for Ohio's government were much more authoritarian than those of any previous charters. American colonists saw in the Ohio plan a glimpse of their fate if the English limitations on colonial self-government were not resisted.

The Quebec Act also alarmed Protestant American colonists when it assured the French-Canadian residents of Quebec that they could continue to practice Catholicism. This aspect may have disturbed Americans most of all. Intolerance of Catholics was virtually universal in the thirteen colonies, reflecting religious biases and a century-old political ideology that linked Roman Catholicism to corruption.

See also Revolution.

R

RACIAL DESEGREGATION

Racial desegregation refers to controversial, complicated, and ongoing efforts to erase racial stratification — "the color line" — from American society. Although desegregation has touched every aspect of social life — from employment to public accommodations to marriage — public schooling is the context in which desegregation has attained its most salient position as a national issue.

Throughout the history of the United States, reformers have challenged laws and customs that compelled the separation of racial groups, separation that typically stigmatized people of color and relegated them to facilities decidedly inferior to those reserved for whites. In 1850, for instance, in *Roberts* v. *City of Boston,* the nation's first school desegregation case, a black parent unsuccessfully sued public school officials in Boston, Massachusetts, who refused to change their policy of educating black children in schools separate from those for whites.

Despite the massive changes wrought by the Civil War and Reconstruction, it was not until the twentieth century that reformers began to succeed on a wide scale in uprooting segregationist practices. One difficulty reformers faced has been that laws imposing segregation sometimes reflected an advance in the actual living conditions of people of color and almost always promised a certain form of equality. By creating "separate but equal" facilities, states promised to provide to blacks public goods that had previously been denied to them altogether. These states also promised to treat whites and people of color alike insofar as both groups were promised equal, albeit separate, facilities.

One antisegregationist strategy consisted, ironically, of demanding that states actually fulfill their segregationist promises. In *Missouri ex rel Gaines* v. *Canada* (1938), for instance, a black denied admission to the University of Missouri Law School successfully argued that if a state provided its white citizens with a law school, it must provide its black citizens with one as well. Similarly, some state and lower federal courts ruled in favor of black plaintiffs who sought the equalization of resources allocated to racially segregated institutions. Black teachers, for instance, working in "black" schools successfully argued that they were entitled to the same pay offered to white teachers working in "white" schools. Some reformers believed that, eventually, the sheer expense of maintaining redundant facilities would drive states to scrap segregation.

A more far-reaching attack consisted of the proposition that, even when equal financial resources were allocated to black and white institutions, government-imposed (de jure) separation of the races necessarily violated the Constitution's requirement of racial equality. In *Brown* v. *Board of Education of Topeka* (1954), the U.S. Supreme Court unanimously embraced this argument, concluding that "in the field of public education the doctrine of 'separate but equal' has no place. Separate educational facilities are inherently unequal."

Segregationists resisted *Brown* in a wide variety of ways. Many southern white members of Congress signed the "Southern Manifesto," which condemned *Brown* as illegitimate and asserted the right of states to ignore it. Some officials closed all public schools rather than desegregate them. Others resorted to tokenism as a way of minimizing the actual effects of *Brown,* instituting policies that provided, for instance, that schools would be desegregated a grade per year.

For nearly fifteen years, the Supreme Court largely avoided the many difficulties created by segregationist recalcitrance. Only on occasions when officials blatantly defied the Court did the justices intervene. In *Aaron* v. *Cooper* (1958), for instance, the Court ordered the immediate desegregation of a public high school in Little Rock, Arkansas, at which state National Guard troops, under instructions from Governor Orval Faubus, had prevented the admission of nine black youngsters. "Law and order," the Court declared, "are not here to be preserved by depriving the Negro children of their constitutional rights." Despite the Court's brave rhetoric, however, little progress was made; by 1964, only 2.3 percent of all southern black children attended desegregated schools.

Yet, over the course of the decade, the situation in the South changed dramatically. The success of the civil rights movement in stigmatizing racism encouraged all branches of the federal government to apply pressure against segregationist-inspired delays and evasions. In *Greene* v. *County School Board* (1968), the Supreme Court invalidated desegregation plans that allowed students to choose the schools they wished to attend when such "freedom of choice" plans failed to erase the color line in districts that had previously been subject to de jure segregation. The Court required a system "without a 'white' school and a 'Negro' school, but just schools." To transform racially identifiable dual school systems into unitary systems of "just schools," the Court ordered a wide range of remedies, including extensive busing of students.

In the 1970s, the Supreme Court began to adjudicate school desegregation cases arising from northern jurisdictions. The Court recognized constitutional violations and ordered re-

medial reforms when plaintiffs could demonstrate that officials had purposely sought to segregate the races. Over time, however, it became increasingly difficult to persuade the Court that officials had acted wrongly or that the federal judiciary could appropriately intervene extensively in the running of local schools. Indicative of this trend was *Miliken* v. *Bradley* (1974), a Supreme Court decision that reversed a lower court ruling, which had ordered predominantly white suburbs of Detroit, Michigan, to enter into a desegregation plan with the predominantly black core of that city. The flagging commitment of a reconstituted Supreme Court, largely staffed by conservative appointees of Republican presidents, reflected a broad-based impatience with the egalitarianism loosed by the civil rights movement, solicitude for potential white "victims" of judicial decrees, and anxieties about the practical value of desegregation.

Although the struggle to desegregate public schools in the United States is often portrayed as a triumph of principle over prejudice, the reality is more complicated and sobering. In some areas, desegregation attained widespread public support and became an accepted part of daily life. But in others, an intense and unyielding resistance continued. A haunting reminder of the troubled history of desegregation in public schooling is that *Brown* v. *Board of Education of Topeka* remained an ongoing case thirty-five years after the Supreme Court's landmark ruling. Linda Brown, the little girl for whom the case is named, herself became a parent alleging that her children's constitutional rights were violated by a state's failure to desegregate fully its public schools.

Public education is but one of many arenas in which reformers have sought to desegregate American society. Since the Civil War, scores of state and federal statutes have been enacted to eliminate racial segregation in all spheres of social life including public accommodations, employment, and housing. Many of these laws apply to private individuals as well as government officials and have undoubtedly improved the status and living conditions of racial minorities. The mixed record that characterizes racial desegregation in schooling, however, also describes the fate of desegregation more generally. Despite statutory and judicial reforms, the race line in American life remains a powerful, vexing, and ubiquitous presence.

Donald G. Nieman, *Promises to Keep: African-Americans and the Constitutional Order, 1776 to the Present* (1991); Gary Orfield, *Public School Desegregation in the United States, 1968–1980* (1983).

RANDALL KENNEDY

See also American Dilemma, An; Brown v. *Board of Education of Topeka;* Civil Rights Movement; Niagara Movement; *Plessy* v. *Ferguson;* Segregation.

RACIAL SEGREGATION

See Segregation.

RADICALISM

Radicalism — political and social movements and ideologies that aim at fundamental change in the structure of society — has been a persistent feature of U.S. history. Radical movements have challenged Americans to live up to their professed ideals and have developed penetrating critiques of social and economic inequality.

Two distinct, although often overlapping, radical traditions have coexisted in America. Some radical movements accept the society's prevailing emphasis on the ideal of the "free individual" (often linked with ownership of property as the guarantor of personal autonomy) and seek to eliminate obstacles to its fulfillment or extend it to excluded groups. Much of nineteenth-century labor radicalism fitted this pattern, as have many expressions of feminism and black radicalism. Other movements, based on a collectivist outlook, reject individualist values and see private property as an obstacle to genuine freedom. Various socialist and communitarian movements have exemplified this type.

Traditions transplanted from Europe helped shape radicalism in colonial America. The concept of the "freeborn Englishman" postulated that government did not possess the right to interfere with basic individual liberties and justified resistance to overbearing authorities. The tradition of "moral economy" asserted that government had a responsibility to protect the basic well-being of all citizens. According to this view, economic life should be governed by the noneconomic consideration of equity rather than the vagaries of the free market. In addition, the religious revivalism of the Great Awakening in the 1740s stimulated the idea that devout men and women should strive to purge a corrupt society of sin. Although not necessarily linked to any specific political program, this sensibility fostered the notion that American society was in need of fundamental change.

These customary values and popular traditions helped produce and legitimize the colonial resistance to British rule that culminated in the American Revolution. And during the Revolution, along with other political and social ideas, they were absorbed into the comprehensive ideology of republicanism that came to dominate American political culture. In republican thought, stable democratic government rested on a citizenry possessing political "virtue" — that is, the ability to place the good of society above selfish concerns. This quality stemmed from "independence," especially that economic self-reliance that derived from ownership of productive property.

Much of nineteenth-century American radicalism came directly from the Revolution. The Declaration of Independence, which posited the equality of all humankind and the right to resist unjust authority, inspired later generations of radicals. Nineteenth-century radicals, moreover, feared that the evolution of American society was imperiling the republican heritage of independence and broad social equality, and they searched for ways to restore the virtue and independence central to republicanism. But some radicals, such as participants in communitarian experiments, rejected altogether the individualism and commitment to private property of the society at large. Hundreds of such communities, mostly short-lived, were established before the Civil War; their appeal rested on widespread dissatisfaction with the intense competitiveness of American life and on the premise that far-reaching social change could be brought about without violent conflict by building a model of the new society within the old.

Most nineteenth-century radicals, however, sought to preserve individual independence rather than submerge it in a cooperative social order. Throughout the century, for example, the labor movement searched for ways to restore the ideal of the independent citizen in the face of the spread of factory production, the loss of the artisan's autonomy, and growing social inequality. From the Workingmen's parties of the late 1820s to the Knights of Labor in the 1880s, labor spoke the republican language of social harmony and economic independence rather than the Marxist language of unavoidable class conflict. Its characteristic goals were shorter working hours (to enable laborers to fulfill their responsibilities as republican citizens), the establishment of producer cooperatives (to counteract the spread of wage labor and the erosion of economic independence), and access to western land for eastern workers. The Industrial Revolution, labor radicals insisted, was leading Americans toward a society of fixed, hostile, and unequal classes. As in Europe, "nonproducers" reaped economic benefits while ordinary laborers struggled to make ends meet.

The Populists of the 1890s also spoke this republican language, although Populism, more than previous movements, looked to the national government to end the subservience of the small producer to a transportation and credit system that made a mockery of the idea of economic independence. Drawing on an idea developed by Greenbackers earlier in the century, Populists called on the government to take control of the currency from private bankers and directly finance the marketing of small farmers' crops. Henry George, author of the single most influential work of nineteenth-century radicalism, *Progress and Poverty,* stood squarely within this tradition of small-producer radicalism. His proposal to nationalize the land promised to restore republican equality and social harmony at a time of bitter labor conflict and a widening gap between rich and poor.

A similar emphasis on individual freedom, but in this case based on the idea of ownership of one's self rather than ownership of property,

inspired nineteenth-century movements like abolitionism and feminism, which aimed to extend the idea of equal rights to subordinated groups. Antebellum abolitionism, the greatest radical movement of that era, established the pattern by which most future movements would operate in America's democratic political culture. It was open rather than secretive and relied on moral suasion (the widespread dissemination of pamphlets, newspapers, and speeches) rather than violence or coercion. Abolitionism, moreover, was the nation's first racially integrated radical movement, and northern blacks and fugitives from bondage like Frederick Douglass became prominent leaders. The movement drew on the impulse for social change unleashed by the Second Great Awakening early in the century and traditional American democratic values to argue that slavery was a gross violation of human rights. And out of abolitionism emerged nineteenth-century feminism, which demanded for women the same legal and political equality the crusade against slavery sought for blacks. Not until after the Civil War, in the wake of a dispute over whether the struggle for women's rights should temporarily be laid aside in order to concentrate on obtaining the vote for male former slaves, did an independent feminist movement emerge, one that did not rest on the abolitionist constituency.

The 1890s and the early twentieth century, which witnessed so many changes, saw a fundamental shift in American radicalism. The American Federation of Labor (AFL), which replaced the Knights as the major labor organization, adopted a less far-reaching set of goals than its predecessor. Its "bread-and-butter unionism" concentrated on improving the wages and hours of its members within the existing system rather than challenging the organization of the economy. Yet the AFL was the first major labor organization to accept the reality that the wage-earning class was a permanent feature of American life rather than an aberration caused by a departure from republican principles.

Other groups at the time built upon a frank acceptance of class conflict to seek more radical outcomes. Socialism, a minor presence in American life since its transplantation by German immigrants in the mid-nineteenth century, suddenly became a mass movement. With its greatest strength among Jewish and German immigrants, in the former Populist strongholds of the Southwest, and among native-born miners and skilled workers, the Socialist party polled nearly a million votes in 1912 for its presidential candidate, Eugene V. Debs. Although its ideology ultimately derived from Karl Marx's critique of capitalism and his vision of a proletarian revolution, the Socialist party adopted an evolutionary, electoral approach to social change. More radical in tactics was the Industrial Workers of the World (IWW), which sought to organize unskilled industrial workers, women, and racial and ethnic minorities — all groups excluded from the AFL. In its call for labor solidarity and its aim of superseding capitalism by worker-controlled production, the IWW harked back to the Knights. The organization was destroyed by the wave of repression that followed World War I, which also fatally weakened the Socialist party.

Although both the Socialist party and the IWW were open to black membership, neither developed a special program regarding racism or an analysis of blacks' distinctive position in American society. Since blacks were part of the working class, the liberation of the proletariat would liberate them as well. With most white radicals blind to blacks' unique experience, black radicals tended to turn not to integrated organizations but to nationalism. The largest black mass movement of the early twentieth century was that organized by Marcus Garvey, whose message on pan-Africanism and racial pride appealed to tens of thousands who had migrated from the rural South to northern ghettos only to encounter pervasive racism.

The 1930s and World War II saw the final flowering of American socialism, embodied this time in the Communist party, which reached a membership of 100,000 and exerted an influence beyond its numbers in the labor movement, civil rights organizations, and intellectual circles. Unlike their socialist predecessors, the communists did not focus on electoral politics, but took the lead in militant struggles of numerous kinds in depression America — union organization, un-employment relief, civil rights activism. Their connection with the Soviet Union gave the communists the prestige of association with the world's only socialist society while at the same time making them vulnerable to abrupt changes in party policy geared to Soviet rather than American realities.

The advent of the cold war turned the Soviet connection from an asset into a severe liability, unleashing a period of political repression that drove the party underground, victimized many of its members, and destroyed its influence. But the 1950s and 1960s witnessed new expressions of American radicalism. The drive for civil rights, the largest mass movement since the depression, mobilized southern blacks and black and white allies throughout the country in a successful assault on the South's system of segregation and disfranchisement. Like the abolitionists, civil rights advocates drew on mainstream values of equality and individual self-determination to pose a powerful challenge to entrenched racism. And like abolitionism, the movement's tactics were grounded in nonviolence and moral suasion, in the belief that white America could be persuaded to live up to the national creed.

Meanwhile, partly inspired by civil rights activism, a New Left arose among white youth. For the first time in American history, the torch of radical leadership passed to college students, before World War II a tiny, largely conservative portion of the population. The New Left was new in its conscious rejection of the belief that the working class was the predestined agent of social change, in its identification with revolutionary movements of the third world rather than the Soviet Union, and in its focus on the spiritual crisis of a society of abundance rather than on widespread economic misery. But it drew upon radical ideas dating back to the abolitionists and communitarians — a distaste for competitiveness and materialism in American life, a desire for individual autonomy and authenticity, a belief in direct action by morally pure individuals.

By the end of the 1960s, with the Vietnam War inspiring massive opposition on college campuses, the New Left had turned into a full-fledged generational revolt, complete with its own counterculture avowedly hostile to middle-class respectability. But in the early 1970s, the movement splintered. Some participants went underground into a self-destructive crusade of violence; others moved on to different issues, ranging from the second wave of feminism to environmentalism and the peace movement; still others abandoned it altogether, rejoining the American mainstream.

As the nation entered the 1990s, there were many radical organizations and issues, but no coherent radical outlook or movement to serve as a focal point for demands for far-reaching change, like abolitionism in the nineteenth century and socialism and communism in the twentieth. One thing, however, seemed certain. Every generation of Americans since the Revolution has seen the emergence of one kind of radical movement or another, and the future is not likely to be different.

Sidney Lens, *Radicalism in America,* rev. ed. (1969); Staughton Lynd, *Intellectual Origins of American Radicalism* (1968).

ERIC FONER

See also Abolitionist Movement; Civil Rights Movement; Communist Party; Debs, Eugene V.; Feminist Movement; Garvey, Marcus; Haymarket Affair; Industrial Workers of the World; Knights of Labor; New Left; Populism; Socialism; Students for a Democratic Society; Utopian Communities.

RADIO AND TELEVISION

Of all the major inventions of the twentieth century, few have had a more profound impact on people's lives than radio and television. By 1933, two-thirds of American homes had at least one radio, twice as many as those with telephones. Forty-five years later, 97 percent of all households had at least one television set. But the numbers cannot convey the contradictory roles that broadcasting has played in American society as it has reshaped the country's politics, economy, and culture.

The broadcast media have allowed Ameri-cans to listen to and watch candidates for public office in order to decide for themselves who merits their support. But television has also triv-ialized politics, overemphasizing appearance and style while too often serving as gatekeeper for the flow of information about the political pro-cess. Radio and television have exposed Ameri-cans to an unprecedented amount of news and information. But they have also promoted anti-intellectualism and elevated mindless entertain-ment over the pursuit of knowledge. Broadcast-ing provides free entertainment in the home, which is often a godsend for the ill, the confined, parents of small children, and those simply ex-hausted after a day's work. But in exchange, the audience has become a commodity sold to adver-tisers, who in turn try to persuade everyone, in-cluding children, to buy their products. Radio and television, then, have both expanded and narrowed people's horizons. But as we review their enormous impact on American life, we should keep in mind that they are not a sort of hypodermic needle, injecting an unsuspecting culture with alien messages. They are the prod-uct of American history, having themselves been shaped by the trends and events of the twentieth century.

When Guglielmo Marconi, the Irish-Italian inventor, came to the United States in 1899 to demonstrate how his wireless telegraph might expedite press coverage of the America's Cup races, the concept of broadcasting had not en-tered his mind at all. He thought his device, which sent Morse code messages without con-necting wires, would be useful for corporate clients who needed a rapid, mobile communica-tions system. His American competitors, how-ever, sought to expand the invention's applica-tions and to use it to transmit music and voice. On Christmas Eve, 1906, Reginald Fessenden, who developed the first sophisticated radio transmitter, the high-frequency alternator, sent out a program of music and speech. Lee de For-est, inventor of the radio tube, attempted to broadcast synthesized music and opera in New York City between 1907 and 1909. By the next decade, amateur operators were broadcasting speech, music, and coded messages in dozens of cities. This activity, interrupted by World War I, resumed in the early 1920s, and the radio boom began. The number of broadcasting stations soared, from 30 in 1922 to 556 in 1923, and by the next year, the number of homes with radios had tripled. This explosion produced chaos in the airwaves, and broadcasters wrestled with how to avoid interference and how to pay for programming.

The solutions to these problems established commercial and regulatory precedents that determined how broadcasting would be managed. Owners of radio stations, seeking to reduce competition and maximize profits, organized stations into networks to broadcast the same show at the same time. And they began experimenting with on-air advertising as a way to finance programming. Radio advertising was, in the 1920s, only one of several proposals for financing radio, and it was controversial. Critics felt that sending ads over the airwaves constituted an invasion of privacy, sabotaging people's ability to keep the marketplace out of the home. So sponsors who wanted to sell their products over radio began with "indirect advertising." The merits of a product, its price, or where it could be purchased were not mentioned. Instead, singing groups, comedians, or bands assumed the name of the sponsor, giving rise to such radio celebrities as the Cliquot Club Eskimos and the A&P Gypsies. Because corporate sponsorship provided money to increase the quality and variety of programming, companies found they generated goodwill with listeners, and resistance to advertising (although not resentment of it) gradually broke down. During the depression, as advertisers gained more financial clout, direct sales pitches became the norm.

What made radio so attractive to advertisers was the formation of networks: NBC (National Broadcasting Company, 1926), CBS (Columbia Broadcasting System, 1927), and MBS (Mutual Broadcasting System, 1934) offered advertisers instant access to a national audience. Thus, networks and advertisers helped accelerate and consolidate the emergence of a highly profitable national market for products.

Yet advertisers, in the early 1930s, knew almost nothing about this vast audience. Who listened to what, and when? Why might they buy one product over another? And which ads were the most effective? To answer such questions, audience research became an important component of the broadcasting industry. Ever since the mid-1930s, advertisers have relied on ratings of shows and demographic breakdowns of audiences to decide which programs to sponsor. Thus began the analysis and packaging of the public as audiences for sale to advertisers, who exerted increasing influence over the content and form of the shows they supported.

With radio relying on a limited natural resource, the electromagnetic spectrum, various interests pressed for government regulation. The Radio Act of 1912 had initiated the licensing of stations and introduced a crude allocation of wavelengths. The law was revised and expanded in 1927 and revamped again in 1934, when the Federal Communications Commission (FCC) was established. Fearing that a radio czar would have too much power, Congress established a commission of seven to consider license applications and renewals. Licensees had to demonstrate, every three years, that they were serving the "public interest, convenience and/or necessity." The FCC periodically investigated charges of monopoly, and though it did not have censorship powers, it issued guidelines on obscenity, fraudulent and excessive advertising, and other controversial issues. To reduce interference and improve the quality of reception, the government allocated most of the spectrum, and certainly its preferred portions, to those with the most powerful and sophisticated transmitting equipment. This approach, begun in 1927, automatically gave preference to business interests and discriminated against the poorer educational stations, whose numbers dropped from ninety-eight in 1927 to forty-three in 1933, and continued to decline.

By the late 1930s, radio was woven into the fabric of American life. Public events, from political rallies to sporting events and vaudeville routines, were now enjoyed by millions in private. And, increasingly, Americans got their news from radio, especially news of the expanding war in Europe. The immediacy and drama of the war news tied people more intimately to unfolding events; it also, apparently, put some on edge. When Orson Welles broadcast his "War of the Worlds" on Halloween, 1938, he had no inkling that the mock terror of the play would resonate with a real terror of invasion among some listeners, prompting them to clog highways as they sought to flee the Martians.

The war also catapulted broadcast journalism into a powerful, and often superior, competitor to the newspaper. Edward R. Murrow, whose wartime broadcasts from London established a new level of eloquence and courage in radio newscasting, brought the war into people's living rooms. So did Eric Sevareid, Howard K. Smith, and Charles Collingwood, among others.

Although experimentation with television broadcasting began in the late 1920s, technical difficulties, corporate competition, and World War II postponed its introduction to the public until 1946. Television constituted a revolutionary change from radio, but its introduction was not as chaotic as that of radio, for an institutional framework already existed. The television boom occurred between 1949, when 940,000 households had a set, and 1953, when the number soared to 20 million.

The rapid integration of television into American life coincided with the explosive rise of a consumer culture after the war. Pent-up demand fueled by the privations of the depression and the war, coupled with prosperity, was exploited by advertisers who turned to television to sell their products. In the early 1950s, many corporations produced and sponsored entire shows, and ads were at least one minute in length. But as programming became more expensive, and advertisers discovered that thirty-second spots were as effective as longer ones, shows were sponsored by several products, increasing dramatically the sheer number of commercials. As the pace and intensity of advertising increased, the images on television became more homogenized, portraying in such programs as "Leave It to Beaver" and "Bonanza" idealized white middle-class families and norms. Advertisers' desires to appeal to the broadest possible audience, coupled with an atmosphere of conformity fueled by McCarthyism, blacklisting, and cold war paranoia, made programmers extremely cautious, and they pandered to the lowest common denominator. Television excluded diversity and elevated consumerism into a national obsession.

Yet the voices of those ignored or betrayed broke through on television in the 1960s, primarily on the nightly news. The often horrifying footage of the civil rights movement, followed by John F. Kennedy's assassination, brought a new primacy to network news, which expanded from fifteen-minute to half-hour broadcasts in 1963. Soon television was bringing the Vietnam War, antiwar demonstrations, and the women's movement into the nation's homes. Television in the 1960s was an agent both of conformity and of rebellion, providing some images that unified America and others that reflected, and sometimes exacerbated, the country's deep racial, class, and gender divisions.

Television has had both a salubrious and a corrupting effect on politics. Congressional investigations from the Army-McCarthy hearings in 1954 to Watergate in 1973 and the Iran-Contra hearings in 1988 exposed the wrongdoings of government officials. But politicians also learned to be cautious and calculating in their use of television. They emphasized appearances, exploited visual symbols, and stage-managed the news whenever possible. Television journalists, dependent on highly placed sources and government handouts, were not inclined to challenge official versions of reality. Network news executives, increasingly drawn from the ranks of the business community rather than from journalism, believed that the public did not want analyses of complex issues but simply entertainment. The symbiotic relationship between politicians and television journalists led to an emphasis on style over substance in the coverage of presidential campaigns so that, in 1988, the Pledge of Allegiance was a major campaign topic while the nation's huge deficit was virtually ignored.

Because television brings images, as well as sound, into the home, it has been more criticized than radio for squandering its potential to educate and inform. Newton Minow, the FCC chairman in 1961, called television "a vast wasteland." Others worried about the levels of violence in programming and its effects on children.

Spurred by such criticisms, Congress in 1967 established the Corporation for Public Broadcasting and, in 1969, the Public Broadcasting System (PBS), which received some federal money to support noncommercial and educational programs. But PBS must still rely on viewer support and corporate sponsorship to survive.

Criticism of the medium has intensified, and many of the nation's problems, from widespread illiteracy to political apathy, have been attributed to television. Critics on the right charge that television news is infused with a liberal bias and that programming contains too much sex. Critics on the left counter that news programs serve to legitimize the status quo and marginalize any proposals for far-reaching social change. Cultural critics lament the privatization of American life, with viewers staying home glued to the tube instead of participating in political or social activities. And though television continues to provide viewers with common stories and scenes of events that help construct a sense of national unity, the ideology of television programming, especially the message that limitless consumerism is the most important freedom, has alarming political and cultural implications.

Television has intensified the commodification of people's deeply felt aspirations and fears, and has turned private matters, from reproductive decisions to mourning the loss of loved ones, into public spectacles. And as the networks confront the competition from cable and VCRs that is making inroads in their audiences, their executives resort to conflating nonfiction television with entertainment, producing "infotainment" like tabloid television. Although there is still much debate over whether television contributes to violent behavior, low educational attainment, or political corruption, there seems to be common agreement among most people that the enormous potential of this medium is yet to be realized.

Erik Barnouw, *A History of Broadcasting in the United States,* 3 vols. (1966, 1968, 1970); Christopher Sterling and John Kittross, *Stay Tuned: A Concise History of American Broadcasting* (1990).

SUSAN J. DOUGLAS

See also Advertising; Federal Communications Commission.

RAILROADS

In the optimistic years following the Treaty of Ghent (1814) major eastern cities sought to capture the trade of the expanding West. Taverns across the country heard the arguments of merchants, politicians, and farmers as they voiced the rival claims of turnpikes and canals, of steamboats and railroads. Businesspeople in New York City and Philadelphia favored canals and river steamboats, but the merchants of Baltimore, Charleston, and Boston sought to reach expanded western markets with railroads, which first appeared in America in the 1820s. The Baltimore & Ohio Railroad by 1831 had completed a line to Frederick, Maryland, and replaced horses with steam locomotives.

The acceptance of railroads came quickly in the 1830s, although there was some opposition: divines preached against the "iron horse," doctors warned of the excessive speed, and canal, turnpike, and coaching companies, of course, were hostile. But most Americans agreed with the French economist Michel Chevalier, who wrote, "The Americans have a perfect passion for railroads." By 1840 the New England and Mid-Atlantic states had 2,083 miles of track, seven southern states had a total of 636 miles, and the Old Northwest had 89 miles. The nation had almost 3,000 miles of railway, whereas all of Europe had only 1,800 miles. In 1847, Daniel Webster claimed the railroad "towers above all other inventions of this or the preceding age."

The iron network expanded quickly during the 1840s. Trackage increased over 150 percent in the Northeast, more than tripled in the South, and grew a dozenfold in the Old Northwest. In the 1830s many lines had more passenger revenue than freight, but the next decade saw freight traffic dominate. By 1850 the typical freight train consisted of a dozen cars, each of about ten-ton capacity. The double truck eight-wheel passenger coach had long since replaced the original stagecoach design. The typical locomotive was a wood-burning American type (a swiveled four-wheeled truck ahead of four drivers), bright with brass and paint, with a functional cowcatcher, large headlight, and balloon stack.

American railroads, a broken skein of 9,000 miles in 1850, became a national network of 30,000 miles in 1860. Iowa, Missouri, Arkansas, Texas, and California built their first lines during the 1850s, and by the end of the decade the network had reached the frontier. Northern and western lines were usually built in the English 4-foot-8½-inch track gauge, and most southern roads in the 5-foot gauge.

Four important Mid-Atlantic lines reached Lake Erie or the Ohio River early: predecessor lines of the New York Central, the Erie, the Pennsylvania, and the Baltimore & Ohio. Chicago saw its first locomotive in 1848, had rail service to the East in 1853, and was served by eleven railroads with a hundred daily trains in 1860. Shippers welcomed year-round rail service — it was faster than the competition, cheaper than turnpikes, and more direct than canal packets and steamboats.

Railroads were big business in mid-century. Few other concerns employed so many men so varied in skill, did business on so vast a scale, had operations so intricate, or financed themselves in such a variety of ways. The total investment in American railroads grew from $300 million in 1850 to $2.5 billion in 1870. Most of the investment was private, but many state and city governments also helped finance early railroads. The thousands of miles of east-west lines built across Illinois, Indiana, and Ohio during the 1850s had strengthened commercial and political ties between the industrial East and the agricultural West by the eve of the Civil War.

That war was the first American conflict in which railroads played a major role. In mileage, equipment, employees, and the ability to build and repair rails and equipment, the South was much weaker than the North. Moreover, since most of the fighting was in the South, Confederate railways were in a shambles by 1865, while Yankee railroads had grown stronger.

During the war and after, Cornelius Vanderbilt of the New York Central, John Edgar Thomson of the Pennsylvania, and John W. Garrett of the Baltimore & Ohio continued to push their lines to the major cities of the Old Northwest.

The most dramatic construction, however, was west of the Mississippi; European railroads usually served established communities, but American railroads often created new centers of population. As the Union Pacific and Central Pacific track crews raced each other to their 1869 "golden spike" ceremony in Utah marking the meeting of the east-west rails, they were building through territories still years away from statehood.

Many western lines received federal land grants to aid their construction. Between 1850 (when the Illinois Central–Mobile & Ohio route obtained the first grant) and 1871 the railroads received more than 131 million acres of land for nearly 19,000 miles of line. All land-grant roads were required to give reduced rates for federal traffic, and these savings to the government were roughly equal to the value of the land grants.

The national rail network grew from 35,000 miles in 1865 to 93,000 miles in 1880, and the railroads enjoyed a golden age of rapid growth and development between then and World War I. During the 1880s more than 70,000 miles of line were built, with 164,000 miles in operation by 1890. Most of the construction was in the trans-Mississippi West, and four Granger lines continued to expand in the northern central plains region. Several Pacific roads were completed in the early eighties and James Hill's Great Northern a decade later.

Railroad construction declined in the 1890s after the panic of 1893, just as it had during the panic of 1873. Labor trouble accompanied each depression — the railroad strike in 1877 and the Pullman strike in 1894. Labor lost both times since it was not well organized except for the big four brotherhoods (engineers organized in 1863, conductors in 1868, firemen in 1873, and trainmen in 1883). Because of the depressions, a quarter of the lines were in receivership by 1894, although many later reorganized under J. P. Morgan & Co. or Kuhn, Loeb, & Co. Mergers and consolidations followed, and by 1906 about two-thirds of the nation's mileage was controlled by seven rail groupings under the leadership of such magnates as James J. Hill, Edward H. Harriman, and J. P. Morgan. Mileage continued to expand and by 1916 the national network was at a record high of 254,000 miles.

In the late nineteenth century railroads achieved many technical advances that greatly improved the efficiency and uniformity of operation. The use of heavier rails, bridges built across the Ohio, Mississippi, and Missouri rivers, and the introduction of block and interlocking signals all led to improved service. Standard time zones were adopted in 1883, and three years later the last of the five-foot gauge lines in the South were changed to standard gauge. Automatic couplers and air-brakes had appeared by 1870. After the Civil War most locomotives burned coal instead of wood, and fuel oil was first tried in 1887. As engines became heavier and more powerful with extra drivers and a wider firebox, average train loads grew from one hundred tons in 1870 to five hundred or more tons by 1915. Labor productivity in freight services more than doubled between 1880 and 1916. Passenger travel became safer and more comfortable with the introduction of dining cars in 1868, steam heat in 1881, solid vestibule trains and electric lights in 1887, and all-steel coaches in 1904.

These many innovations permitted a decline in average freight rates from about two cents a ton-mile in 1865 to .75 cents a ton-mile by 1900. With such low rates Texas cattle, Chicago packed meat, New England shoes, Pittsburgh steel, Moline plows, and Twin City flour could all be moved economically greater and greater distances. American industry boomed and local or regional markets became national. The nation's rail freight grew from 10 billion ton-miles in 1865 to 366 billion ton-miles in 1916, and the per capita rail freight from 285 ton-miles per year to 3,588 ton-miles. In 1916 the nation's railways were carrying 77 percent of the intercity freight traffic and 98 percent of the intercity passenger business.

But these years were also years of corruption, discrimination, and increased regulation. In the South railroad carpetbaggers were milking many a railroad exchequer, and western builders were making extra profits from "false front" construction companies like the Crédit Mobilier of America. In the East, Jim Fisk, Jay Gould, Tom Scott, and Commodore Vanderbilt were rigging the stock market, issuing watered stock, engaging in rate wars, or building nuisance lines in a competitor's territory. Western farmers protested freight rate discrimination, railroad pooling, rebates, and free passes, and through Grange-sponsored legislation created state regulatory commissions. In 1887 the federal government established the Interstate Commerce Commission (ICC) to ensure "reasonable and just" freight rates, although early rate cases were usually decided in favor of the railroads. During the Progressive Era the Elkins Act (1903), the Hepburn Act (1906), and the Mann-Elkins Act (1910) prohibited free passes and rebates, and gave the ICC greater control over freight rates. Tougher regulation came at the very time that new competition was appearing by highway, air, and pipeline.

American Railroads in Their Golden Age

Year	Mileage	Total Investment (billions)	Operating Revenues (millions)	Railroad Employees	Average Annual Wages		Annual Freight Ton-Mileage per Employee
					Current Dollars	1880 Dollars	
1880	93,000	$ 5	$ 614	419,000	$465	$465	88,000
1890	164,000	9	1,006	749,000	572	602	101,000
1900	193,000	11	1,372	1,018,000	567	591	138,000
1916	254,000	21	3,353	1,701,000	886	620	215,000

Sources: John F. Stover, *American Railroads* (University of Chicago Press, 1978); *Railroad Facts* (Association of American Railroads, 1988).

In April 1917, when the United States entered World War I, the railroads were not well prepared for the rush of traffic. Many lines were short of locomotives, cars, and proper maintenance since the ICC had denied rate hikes to meet higher operating costs. Severe winter weather increased record car shortages, and in December 1917, President Woodrow Wilson placed the railroads under federal operation, a control that continued for twenty-six months. The federal operation was both necessary and inevitable, but rail managers believed that director-general of railways William G. McAdoo had excessively increased wages and created work rules that would imperil operating efficiency. The Transportation Act of 1920, which returned the lines to their owners, was intended to ensure the railways a fair rate of return of about 6 percent on the investment. The actual return from 1921 to 1930 averaged under 4.5 percent. In the 1920s the railroads faced new competition from interurbans, buses, trucks, private cars, airlines, and pipelines. This competition would grow worse, but already by 1930 the rail share of commercial traffic had dropped to 75 percent for freight and 68 percent for passenger traffic.

Traffic, wages, and profits dropped sharply during the depression. The average rate of return was only 2.25 percent for the decade, and in 1938 about 31 percent of the nation's mileage was bankrupt or in receivership. But World War II revived the railroads and they outdid themselves in a cooperative effort to avoid federal operation. Using nearly a third fewer locomotives, cars, and workers than in World War I, they provided freight and passenger services from 1942 to 1945 that were 50 percent above the peak World War I year of 1918. The wartime prosperity enabled the railroads to retire $2 billion of bonds, or nearly a fifth of their funded debt.

Of the many technical advances appearing in the postwar years the diesel locomotive was the most important. Diesel units were not cheap, but their low consumption of fuel and water, modest maintenance costs, and long hours of service made them popular. First used in freight service in 1941, diesel units were providing more than 92 percent of all switching, passenger, and freight service by 1957. New types of freight equipment, heavier rail, longer trains, and the use of radio and improved traffic control all helped upgrade freight service.

After the war some lines improved their passenger service with new streamliners, including vistadome cars and slumber coaches, but this did not slow the sharp decline in passenger traffic. Between 1940 and 1965 the rail share of intercity commercial passenger traffic had fallen from 64 percent to 17 percent, and that of freight from 61 percent to 44 percent. In the sixties, seventies, and eighties the use of welded rail, microwave communication, computers, mechanized track maintenance equipment, unit trains, and greater piggyback and container service slowed the decline somewhat, but by 1987 railroads provided only 36 percent of intercity freight traffic and 3 percent of passenger service.

American Railroads in Decline

| Year | Mileage | Total Investment (billions) | Operating Revenues (millions) | Railroad Employees | Average Annual Wages | | Annual Freight Ton-Mileage per Employee |
					Current Dollars	1920 Dollars	
1920	253,000	$20	$ 6,310	2,076,000	$ 1,820	$1,820	199,000
1933	246,000	25	3,138	991,000	1,445	2,225	253,000
1945	227,000	24	8,986	1,439,000	2,720	3,019	475,000
1965	212,000	26	10,425	655,000	7,490	4,719	1,076,000
1987	163,000	47	26,622	247,000	37,716	6,713	3,919,000

Sources: John F. Stover, *American Railroads* (University of Chicago Press, 1978); *Railroad Facts* (Association of American Railroads, 1988).

In 1971 Congress created Amtrak passenger service over a 24,000-mile network, ending nearly all other rail passenger service, and five years later, it created Conrail to provide freight service for six northeastern bankrupt railroads. Both Amtrak and Conrail were government subsidized, but Amtrak was paying 69 percent of its way by 1988, and Conrail, in the black by 1981, was sold to private interests in 1987. The Staggers Rail Act of 1980 liberalized much of the federal railroad regulation and helped provide a rate of return of 5.5 percent in the mid-1980s, well above the 2 to 3 percent of earlier years. Even with the major reduction both in work force and total mileage American rail freight ton-mileage in the late 1980s was a third larger than that of World War II. Railroad managers still complained of featherbedding by labor but had to admit that labor's efficiency in handling freight was doubling every fifteen years. In the late 1980s the nation's railways could look back proudly on a century and a half of service to the American Republic. The inherent economy of the flanged wheel running on a steel rail is so great that American railroads remain a viable form of transport.

Alfred D. Chandler, Jr., *The Railroads: The Nation's First Big Business* (1965); Oliver Jensen, *Railroads in America* (1975); John F. Stover, *The Life and Decline of the American Railroad* (1970).

JOHN F. STOVER

See also Brotherhood of Sleeping Car Porters; Crédit Mobilier of America; Gould, Jay; Interstate Commerce Commission; Morgan, J. Pierpont; Railroad Strike of 1877; Transportation Revolution; Vanderbilt, Cornelius.

RAILROAD STRIKE OF 1877

What came to be called the great railroad strike of 1877 began on July 17 in Martinsburg, West Virginia, after the Baltimore & Ohio Railroad had cut wages for the second time in a year. Protesting workers refused to let any trains move until the pay cut was restored. Militia units were sent in by the governor to restore train service, but when the soldiers refused to use force against the strikers, the governor called for federal troops, the first time such troops had been used for strikebreaking since the 1830s. In the meantime, the strike had spread to Baltimore, triggering bloody street battles between workers and the Maryland militia; when the outmanned soldiers fired into an attacking crowd, ten people were killed. In Pittsburgh, as in Martinsburg, local law enforcers refused to fire on the strikers, and soldiers brought in from outside were routed by a ferocious crowd, which took control of the city until federal troops imposed order.

By then, sympathy strikes had spread out along the railroads in every direction, from line to line, from city to city, from railroad workers to other industries. In Chicago, demonstrations organized by the Workingmen's party drew crowds of twenty thousand; in St. Louis, a general strike put the city in the workers' hands for nearly a week. In towns throughout the country, streets were thronged with strikers and their supporters; there were battles and arrests, injuries and deaths. The struggle seemed to align all workers against all employers. To some, this was a hopeful sign, bearing the promise of future labor victories, but others saw it as a threat to the very foundation of American society. Federal troops were rushed from city to city, putting down strike after strike, until finally, a few weeks after it had begun, the great railroad strike of 1877 was over.

In the aftermath, union organizers planned future campaigns, and politicians and business leaders took steps to ensure that such chaos could not recur. Many states enacted conspiracy statutes. New militia units were formed, and National Guard armories were constructed in many cities. For workers and employers alike, the strikes had dramatized the power of workers in combination to challenge the most established structures of American life.

See also Labor; Railroads.

RANDOLPH, A. PHILIP

(1889–1979), labor and civil rights leader. Randolph was the most important civil rights leader to emerge from the labor movement. Throughout his long career, he consistently kept the interests of black workers at the forefront of the racial agenda. Whereas W. E. B. Du Bois argued that the problem of the twentieth century was "the color line," Randolph concluded that it was the question of the "common man."

Randolph's politics were rooted in the World War I era. A child of hard-working parents who respected learning, he left Crescent City, Florida, for New York City in 1911. Working during the day and studying at the City College at night, Randolph broadened his intellectual horizons as he read modern economic and political writers, including Marx. This theoretical grounding predisposed him to view the black working class, not the black elite, as the major hope for black progress. His associations with socialists and the continuing urbanization of the black population strengthened his working-class orientation.

In 1917, Randolph and his friend Chandler Owen founded the *Messenger*. The magazine's intelligent and spirited prose criticized President Woodrow Wilson as readily as Booker T. Washington and Du Bois. Its approval of the Bolshevik Revolution was cited by various government watchdogs during the red scare of 1919, although Randolph always resisted the appeal of the communists.

The postwar reaction limited the possibilities of working-class organization, but after a few false starts, Randolph in 1925 became general organizer of the Brotherhood of Sleeping Car Porters. Following a long struggle, the porters, an overwhelmingly black group, won an election and then a contract with the railroads in 1937.

The victory made Randolph the leading black figure in the labor movement. He headed the new National Negro Congress, an umbrella movement of mass organizations, but resigned in 1940, believing the group was controlled by communists. Striking out independently, he organized the March on Washington movement in 1941, which succeeded in pressuring President Franklin D. Roosevelt to issue Executive Order 8802 banning discrimination in defense industries. After the war, a similar technique led to President Harry S. Truman's order desegregating the army.

While expanding his targets, Randolph never forgot the interests of black workers and was a constant critic of discrimination in some unions. The originator of the March on Washington in 1963, Randolph aimed to obtain government sponsorship of black jobs. Although his goal was overshadowed by the demands of the southern civil rights movement, Randolph's understanding of the economic needs of blacks predated the riots that drew the nation's attention to them. He also became a critic of the black power movement, which he believed was programmatically bankrupt.

Despite his concern for ordinary workers, Randolph's style was intellectual and aloof. Perhaps because he believed in the controlling force of self-interest, he could not fully comprehend the social and psychological impetus for the black power movement. But his theoretical bent and rationality enabled him to construct political alliances and to choose and win significant labor and civil rights objectives.

Jervis Anderson, *A. Philip Randolph: A Biographical Portrait* (1972); William H. Harris, *Keeping the Faith: A. Philip Randolph, Milton P. Webster, and the Brotherhood of Sleeping Car Porters, 1925–1937* (1977).

JUDITH STEIN

See also Black Power; Brotherhood of Sleeping Car Porters; Civil Rights Movement; Labor; Marches on Washington: 1941, 1963; Racial Desegregation; Socialism.

RANKIN, JEANNETTE

(1880–1973), suffragist, pacifist, and congresswoman. Rankin, the first woman elected to the U.S. Congress, served two terms in the House of Representatives, in 1917–1919 and in 1941–1942. Born on a ranch near Missoula in Montana Territory, she became a restless, extraordinarily energetic person and a fighter for altruistic, demanding, and sometimes highly unpopular causes.

Rankin graduated from the University of Montana in 1902. After trying elementary schoolteaching and other occupations, she studied social work at the New York School of Philanthropy but found this profession also insufficiently rewarding. In 1910 she entered the University of Washington where she joined the state suffrage organization. For the next four years, she traveled back and forth across the continent, speaking and lobbying for women's right to vote. She was the moving force behind the organization that secured Montana women the franchise in 1914.

Two years later Rankin was elected to Congress on the Republican ticket. Soon after taking her seat she cast an anguished vote against the declaration of war on Germany, stating, "I want to stand by my country, but I cannot vote for war." During her term she supported the federal woman suffrage amendment, measures to protect women workers, mothers, and children, and efforts to abolish prostitution near army camps. She voted for Prohibition and against the Espionage Act of 1917 and sought to end a strike in a copper field owned by the Anaconda company, the dominant political and economic power in Montana, by having the federal government nationalize the mine.

In 1918 she ran unsuccessfully for the U.S. Senate as an independent. Then, while serving as a field secretary for the National Consumers' League, she campaigned for legislation to promote maternal and child health care and to regulate the hours and wages of women workers. She served as an officer of the Women's International League for Peace and Freedom during the early 1920s and, as a lobbyist for the Women's Peace Union, campaigned to outlaw war. Rankin became a part-time resident of Georgia where she founded the Georgia Peace Society in 1928. The following year she joined the National Council for the Prevention of War as its chief Washington lobbyist and field organizer.

Ten years later, Rankin left the National Council and was again elected to Congress, where she opposed conscription, Lend-Lease, and the repeal of neutrality laws. In December 1941 she cast the only vote against the declaration of war on Japan. After her term ended, she traveled between her homes in Montana and Georgia. Deeply interested in the nonviolent methods of Mohandas K. Gandhi and in the liberation of third world peoples, she made several visits to India. She captured the attention of the public for the last time in 1968 by leading the Jeannette Rankin Brigade, some five thousand feminists, pacifists, radicals, students, and others, to Washington, D.C., to demonstrate against the Vietnam War.

Hannah G. Josephson, *Jeannette Rankin, First Lady in Congress: A Biography* (1974).

RONALD SCHAFFER

See also Suffrage.

RATIFICATION OF THE CONSTITUTION

The ratification, or adoption, of the Constitution took place between September of 1787 and July of 1788. The Federal Convention, which had drafted the Constitution between May and September 1787, had no authority to impose it on the American people. Article VII of the Constitution and resolutions adopted by the convention on September 17, 1787, detailed a four-stage ratification process: (1) submission of the Constitution to the Confederation Congress, (2) transmission of the Constitution by Congress to the state legislatures, (3) election of delegates to conventions in each state to consider the Constitution, and (4) ratification by the conventions of at least nine of the thirteen states.

The procedure reflected the political realities and principles of 1787–1788. Putting the Constitution in the hands of specially elected conventions would avoid the hostility of state officials jealous of their state's sovereignty, as would the nine-states requirement (the Articles required all thirteen states' consent for ratification of an amendment). The delegates also viewed the Constitution as a fundamental law requiring a form of adoption more solemn and significant, and less vulnerable to shifts of public opinion, than approval by state legislatures. The ratification process itself would induce Americans to think of themselves as a nation, encouraging them to look beyond their state's borders in deciding whether to support the Constitution and disposing them to adopt a new government for the American nation. Finally, the Constitution's proponents hoped, a series of quick ratifications by the first state conventions might generate momentum that would be difficult to resist.

Ratification was not guaranteed, however. The Confederation Congress might reject the Constitution, rewrite it, or refer it to a second general convention, claiming that the first had violated its limited mandate to suggest amendments to the Articles. For the same reason, the states might refuse to elect ratifying conventions. Enough state conventions might spurn the Constitution (whether as an illegitimate proposal or on its merits) to prevent its implementation. Finally, rejection by the legislatures or conventions of any or all of four key states — Massachusetts, New York, Pennsylvania, and Virginia — might cripple the Constitution, even if the necessary nine states did approve it. These possibilities dominated American politics of the time.

On September 28, 1787, after three days of bitter debate, the Confederation Congress sent the Constitution to the states with neither an endorsement nor a condemnation. This action, a compromise engineered by Federalist members, disposed of the argument that the convention had exceeded its mandate; in the tacit opinion of Congress, the Constitution was validly before the people. The state legislatures' decisions to hold ratifying conventions confirmed the Constitution's legitimacy.

The ratification controversy pitted supporters of the Constitution, who claimed the name "Federalists," against a loosely organized group known as "Antifederalists." The Antifederalists denounced the Constitution as a radically centralizing document that would destroy American liberty and betray the principles of the Revolution. The Federalists urged that the nation's problems were directly linked to the frail, inadequate Confederation and that nothing short of the Constitution would enable the American people to preserve their liberty and independence, the fruits of the Revolution.

The Federalists — led by Alexander Hamilton, James Madison, John Jay, John Marshall, James Wilson, John Dickinson, and Roger Sherman — had several advantages. In a time of national political crisis, they offered a clear prescription for the nation's ills; they were well organized and well financed; and they were used to thinking in national terms and to working with politicians from other states. They also had the support of the only two truly national political figures, George Washington and Benjamin Franklin.

The Antifederalists — led by Patrick Henry, George Mason, Richard Henry Lee, James Monroe, John Hancock, Samuel Adams, Elbridge Gerry, George Clinton, Willie Jones, and Melancton Smith — counted among their advantages the support of most state politicians and the American people's distrust of strong central government. Their most potent argument against the Constitution was that it lacked a bill of rights.

The lively newspaper and pamphlet war over the Constitution was a key element of the ratification controversy. Federalists and Antifederalists published hundreds of essays praising or denouncing the document. They often signed these essays with pseudonyms drawn from classical sources such as Plutarch's *Lives* or from the seventeenth-century English struggles against the tyranny of the Stuart kings. Notable Antifederalist pamphlets included the *Letters of Brutus*, attributed to Robert Yates; Luther Martin's *Genuine Information*; Mercy Otis Warren's *Observations on the New Constitution . . . by a Columbian Patriot*; and the *Letters from the Federal Farmer to the Republican*, whose authorship is still disputed. Leading Federalist writings included John Jay's *Address to the People of the State of New York* (the most popular and influential pro-Constitution publication) and *The Federalist*, a series of eighty-five newspaper essays by Alexander Hamilton, James Madison, and John Jay under the name Publius. Although *The Federalist* was the most thorough and intellectually challenging of these works, citizens in 1787–1788 did not share modern readers' deep respect for Publius' arguments and rhetorical skills. *The Federalist* served mainly as a debater's handbook for Federalist delegates in the Virginia and New York conventions, becoming a classic work of American political thought and the foremost commentary on the Constitution only after the ratification controversy.

Every state but Rhode Island elected a ratifying convention in 1787–1788, and only North Carolina's adjourned (August 2, 1788, by a vote of 185–84) without voting on the Constitution. (Rhode Island submitted the Constitution to its town meetings; on March 24, 1788, in a vote boycotted by most Federalists, the voters rejected it, 2,708–237.) The first five ratifications took place in quick succession: Delaware, December 7, 1787 (unanimous); Pennsylvania, December 12, 1787 (46–23); New Jersey, December 18, 1787 (unanimous); Georgia, January 2, 1788 (unanimous); and Connecticut, January 9, 1788 (128–40).

In Massachusetts, however, the Constitution ran into serious, organized opposition. Only after two leading Antifederalists, Adams and Hancock, negotiated a far-reaching compromise did the convention vote for ratification on February 6, 1788 (187–168). Antifederalists had demanded that the Constitution be amended before they would consider it or that amendments be a condition of ratification; Federalists had retorted that it had to be accepted or rejected as it was. Under the Massachusetts compromise, the delegates recommended amendments to be considered by the new Congress, should the Constitution go into effect.

The Massachusetts compromise determined the fate of the Constitution, as it permitted delegates with doubts to vote for it in the hope that it would be amended. All subsequent state conventions but Maryland's recommended amendments as part of their decisions to ratify: Maryland, April 28, 1788 (63–11); South Carolina, May 23, 1788 (149–73); New Hampshire, June 21, 1788 (57–47); Virginia, June 25, 1788 (89–79); and New York, July 26, 1788 (30–27). By that date, eleven states had ratified, including all four critical states.

The lists of recommended amendments and the Federalists' promise to work for amendments (particularly a bill of rights), set in motion the process by which the Bill of Rights was added to the Constitution in 1789–1791. In turn, the First Congress's proposing of amendments in 1789 induced the hold-out states to elect conventions that ratified the Constitution — North Carolina, November 21, 1789 (195–77) and Rhode Island, May 29, 1790 (34–32).

The struggle for ratification of the Constitution was both a direct, unabashed contest for votes and a complex, impressive argument about politics and constitutional theory. It was the first time that the people of a nation freely determined their form of government. It was also the first national political controversy in American history; the people of all thirteen states for the first time debated and decided the same issue. Ratification was a catalyst for the creation of a national political community, transforming the ways Americans thought of themselves and encouraging the growth and popularity of national loyalties. The political discourse generated by the ratification controversy continues to this day within the matrix of the Constitution; the argument in 1787–1788 is one of the finest chapters of that discourse.

Patrick T. Conley and John P. Kaminski, eds., *The Constitution and the States* (1989); Merrill Jensen, John P. Kaminski, Gaspare J. Saladino, and Richard Leffler, eds., *The Documentary History of the Ratification of the Constitution and the Bill of Rights, 1787–1791* (1976–).

RICHARD B. BERNSTEIN

See also Antifederalists; Articles of Confederation; Bill of Rights; Constitution; Federalist Papers; Philadelphia Convention.

REAGAN, RONALD

(1911–   ), fortieth president of the United States. Reagan, an ex-liberal, built what was probably the most successful conservative coalition of the twentieth century. Born in Tampico, Illinois, he cultivated an optimistic personality despite — or because of — his father's intermittent unemployment and heavy drinking. After graduating from Eureka College in 1932 and briefly working as a radio broadcaster, he went to California and quickly established himself in the movies. Little affected by Hollywood glamour, Reagan aptly described himself as "Mr. Norm." He was during these years a staunch Democrat who voted four times for Franklin D. Roosevelt.

Following World War II (during which he acted in government films), a near-fatal bout with pneumonia, a painful divorce from actress Jane Wyman, and a declining film career, Reagan turned to a new career as spokesman for General Electric. He soon changed his political views, leaving the Democratic party and becoming a conservative Republican. In 1966, he was elected governor of California and in office verbally assailed big government but enlarged the state budget and often compromised with Democratic legislators. Reagan won the presidential nomination in 1980 and defeated President Jimmy Carter in the election.

Intelligent but intellectually lazy, Reagan was prone to making groundless assertions that he often rendered as quips. More than any other modern president, he enunciated broad themes and then left day-to-day governance to subordinates. Personally he exuded friendliness and optimism, and, after an attempted assassination in 1981, grace and bravery. These qualities deflected criticism and facilitated negotiations with Congress, enabling him to hold together a coalition of Republican regulars, recently politicized evangelical Protestants, and disenchanted Democrats. Though affable to everyone, Reagan felt close only to a few old friends and his wife, Nancy Reagan. Indeed, she was said by White House watchers to have exerted greater influence on government operations than any previous First Lady.

Reagan reshaped American politics. While leaving intact such popular New Deal programs as Social Security, his administration gutted Great Society antipoverty programs, accepted a deep recession in order to curb inflation, and sharply reduced income taxes in the higher brackets. Initially Reagan supported the largest military buildup in American history and denounced the Soviet Union as an "evil empire," but in his second term he reached a détente with Soviet leader Mikhail Gorbachev.

His administration intervened briefly yet disastrously in the multisided Lebanese civil war, invaded Grenada, bombed Libya, and sponsored the Nicaraguan Contras, who were trying to overthrow the leftist government in that country. In 1985, Reagan authorized the sale of arms to Iran in an unsuccessful effort to free Americans held hostage in Lebanon, but he claimed not to know that subordinates were illegally diverting the proceeds to the Contras.

Reagan left office as the most popular president since Dwight D. Eisenhower. But the future of his coalition, the long-term impact of his economic policies, and thus his place in history remained uncertain.

Laurence I. Barrett, *Gambling with History: Ronald Reagan in the White House* (1984); Lou Cannon, *Reagan* (1982); Jane Mayer and Doyle McManus, *Landslide: The Unmaking of the President, 1984–1988* (1988).

LEO P. RIBUFFO

See also Anticommunism; Conservatism; Elections: 1980, 1984; Republican Party. *For events during Reagan's administration, see* Cold War; Gramm-Rudman Act; Iran-Contra Affair; Middle East–U.S. Relations; National Debt.

REBELLIONS

From early colonial times foreign observers have marveled at the richness of the American environment, the absence of the extreme social and economic distinctions that existed in Europe, and the opportunities for advancement available to ordinary people. Yet at various times, numbers of Americans have been so dissatisfied with their lot that they have even taken up arms in an effort to improve it.

During the colonial period settlers in frontier districts were often at odds with eastern-dominated governments over Indian policy. The best-known example is Bacon's Rebellion, which erupted in Virginia in 1676. The Virginia House of Burgesses was dominated by the royal governor, Sir William Berkeley, and the Tidewater planters who supported him. Planters in the western part of the colony resented the uppity attitude of the easterners, but their main grievances were their lack of equal representation in the Burgesses and the refusal of the government to help them kill Indians. Led by Nathaniel Bacon, they organized a small army and murdered some inoffensive local Indians. Then they headed east, burned Jamestown, and forced Berkeley to flee across Chesapeake Bay to the safety of the Northern Neck. Before the year was out, however, Bacon died of "the flux," and when a contingent of Redcoats arrived from England, the rebellion collapsed.

A similar uprising occurred in 1763 in Pennsylvania, when westerners known as the Paxton Boys, angered by Indian attacks that the Quaker-dominated legislature, safe in Philadelphia, refused to do anything about, marched on that city. But no actual rebellion took place. The Boys disbanded peacefully when a delegation headed by Benjamin Franklin promised that the legislature would place a bounty on Indian scalps.

These were democratic protests in the sense that the westerners were not fairly represented in the Virginia and Pennsylvania legislatures. A few years later a more serious conflict known as the Regulator War broke out in North Carolina. Again, eastern domination of the legislature was the primary cause. The protesters, known as "regulators," committed many local acts of violence while protesting against high taxes and other forms of legislative mistreatment. In 1771 the governor, William Tryon, sent more than a thousand militia west. They routed two thousand regulators at the Battle of the Almance. The leading regulators were then executed and the movement collapsed.

Despite its democratizing aspects, the American Revolution did not put an end to conflicts of this type. The Dorr Rebellion of 1841–1842 in Rhode Island was a protest against that state's antediluvian constitution, which disfranchised roughly half the adult males. An extralegal convention organized by Thomas Dorr drafted a new constitution, which was ratified overwhelmingly in an equally unofficial election. The legal governor then called up the state militia, and after a few minor clashes, the Dorrites gave up. Dorr was sentenced to life imprisonment but was soon released.

Another type of rebellion involved minorities resisting particular economic policies of the majority. Shays' Rebellion (1786–1787), the best known of these, was an uprising by Massachusetts farmers protesting strict foreclosure laws and high taxes. In itself it was a mere flurry — in Jefferson's famous phrase, "a little rebellion." When confronted by militia, Daniel Shays and his followers fled the state. But their use of force to prevent foreclosures and their demand for the large-scale printing of paper money to ease their debt problems frightened conservatives in all the states and had much to do with the calling of the convention that drafted the Constitution. In a way this reaction to Shays' Rebellion reflected a new public attitude. Because of the Revolution, "the people" now ruled. Therefore extralegal activities were illegitimate and those who rebelled against the people's government were traitors of a sort.

The Whiskey Rebellion of 1794, a protest against a tax on whiskey imposed by Congress, provides a better example. Farmers in western Pennsylvania were accustomed to distilling much of the grain they raised into liquor because corn and rye were too bulky to be transported long distances; the new tax hit them hard in the pocketbook. President George Washington, however, raised an enormous force (larger than any army he had commanded during the Revolution), and the "rebels" quickly dispersed.

In 1799 John Fries, a militia captain who had helped overawe the Whiskey rebels, found himself on the other side of the fence. Once again a federal tax (this one on property) was the reason. Fries and his followers chased a few assessors out of Bucks County, Pennsylvania, but federal troops easily put an end to their activities. Fries was captured, tried, and sentenced to death for treason, but President John Adams pardoned him.

The so-called Anti-Rent War in New York's Hudson Valley was another rebellion of this type. It began in 1839 when the heirs of Stephen Van Rensselaer set out to collect $400,000 in "rent" owed him by several thousand farmers. The rents were feudal-like obligations based on a seventeenth-century charter granted to Van Rensselaer's great-great-great-grandfather. When the Van Rensselaer heirs instituted foreclosure proceedings, "debtors," who insisted that they were freeholders, not tenants, reacted so violently that the militia had to be summoned. Later, in 1844, a legislative committee determined that the rents were legal. Because of the resulting uproar, martial law was declared again, but the farmers held on to their lands. Finally, in 1846, a new state constitution formally abolished the old feudal obligations.

Northerners at the time of the Civil War called it "the war of the rebellion," but from the southern point of view secession was a legal way of separating from the United States, not a rebellion at all. On the other hand, John Brown's raid on Harpers Ferry in October 1859 was rebellious both in fact and in intent. Brown believed that by seizing the government arsenal at Harpers Ferry and commandeering its weapons he could arm the local slaves (whom he expected to rush forward to join him) and eventually invade the South and put an end to slavery. The Civil War draft riots, the most important of which occurred in New York City in July 1863, were violent protests against conscription, with powerful overtones of negrophobia, but they were brief explosions, probably not organized efforts to force the government to change the law. This was less true of the socialist-led Green Corn Rebellion in Oklahoma against the 1917 conscription act. In August of that year a group of German-Americans, blacks, and Indians rallied behind the slogan "Now is the time to rebel against this war with Germany." Although they dispersed quickly when confronted by an angry posse, some were arrested and sent to prison.

Most Indian rebellions — Pontiac's "conspiracy" of 1763–1766 and Tecumseh's confederacy of 1811 are examples — were really wars. The Indians were seeking to drive the whites out of their homelands, not demanding changes in systems of which they were a part. The Indian "wars" of the post–Civil War era were, however, more rebellions against the policies of the federal government than true wars, and after the passage of the Dawes Act of 1887, expelling the whites or even obtaining true sovereignty in limited areas was no longer a viable objective for the tribes.

Slave uprisings — Nat Turner's 1831 rebellion being the best known and bloodiest — were desperate protests aimed at punishing particular oppressors, and only indirectly attempts to abolish the institution. The efforts of American slaves to obtain their freedom were largely individual attempts to escape; no large-scale slave social revolution, such as Toussaint-L'Ouverture's uprising in Haiti, took place in the United States. Nevertheless, slave uprisings were ruthlessly repressed when they occurred, and even

when they did not. Nat Turner and some twenty of his followers were executed because of their rebellion, but they had slaughtered fifty-seven whites. When an 1822 uprising planned by Denmark Vesey, a South Carolina black who had managed to purchase his freedom, was betrayed before it could be carried out, Vesey and thirty-five other blacks were nonetheless executed.

Today's rebels usually seek to discommode rather than actually overpower their oppressors. Such is the force available to modern authorities that armed resistance is not a viable alternative. When organized violence has erupted it has been begun by the authorities, as when Gen. Douglas MacArthur used federal troops to disperse the Bonus Marchers in Washington in 1932. The infamous Chicago police riot during the 1968 Democratic National Convention is another example. Race riots, such as the six-day uprising in the Watts section of Los Angeles in 1965 and the havoc wreaked by blacks in Washington, Detroit, and a dozen other cities after the assassination of Martin Luther King, Jr., have produced violence aplenty. But these outbursts were spontaneous and undirected, although the underlying causes of black discontent were real and plain to see.

JOHN A. GARRATY

See also Bacon's Rebellion; Brown, John; Draft Riots; Indians; Leisler's Rebellion; Shays' Rebellion; Slavery.

RECONSTRUCTION

I. Political Aspects

Reconstruction, the period that followed the Civil War, is perhaps the most controversial era in American history. Traditionally portrayed as a sordid time when vindictive Radical Republicans fastened black supremacy upon the defeated Confederacy, Reconstruction has come to be viewed more sympathetically, as a laudable if unsuccessful experiment in interracial democracy.

Reconstruction witnessed far-reaching changes in America's political life. At the national level, new laws and constitutional amendments permanently altered the federal system and the nature of American citizenship. In the South, a politically mobilized black community joined with white allies to bring the Republican party to power, and with it a redefinition of the purposes and responsibilities of government.

The national debate over Reconstruction began during the Civil War. On what terms should the defeated Confederacy be reunited with the Union? Who should establish these terms, Congress or the president? What should be the place of blacks in the political and social life of the South? These were the questions on which Reconstruction persistently turned, and they acquired increasing urgency as emancipation became a Union war aim in 1863.

In December of that year, President Abraham Lincoln announced the first comprehensive program for Reconstruction, the Ten Percent Plan. This offered a pardon to all southerners, except Confederate leaders, who took an oath affirming loyalty to the Union and support for emancipation. When 10 percent of a state's voters had taken such an oath, they could establish a new state government. To Lincoln, the plan was more an attempt to weaken the Confederacy than a blueprint for the postwar South. Although it was put into operation in Union-occupied Arkansas, Louisiana, Tennessee, and Virginia, none of the new governments achieved broad local support or was recognized by Congress. Many Republicans deemed Lincoln's plan too lenient. In 1864, Congress enacted (and Lincoln pocket vetoed) the Wade-Davis bill, which proposed to delay the formation of new southern governments until a majority of voters had taken a loyalty oath. Some Republicans, moreover, were already convinced that equal rights for the former slaves must accompany the South's readmission to the Union. In his last speech, in April 1865, Lincoln himself expressed the view that some southern blacks ought to enjoy the right to vote.

Thus, Gen. Robert E. Lee's surrender in April 1865 found the Union without a settled Reconstruction policy. With Congress out of session, it fell to Lincoln's successor, Andrew Johnson, to outline plans for the South's readmission. In May, he issued a series of proclamations that inaugurated the period of Presidential Reconstruction (1865–1867). Johnson offered a pardon to all southern whites except Confederate leaders and wealthy planters (although most of these subsequently received individual pardons), appointed provisional governors, and outlined steps whereby new state governments would be created. Apart from the requirements that they abolish slavery, repudiate secession, and abrogate the Confederate debt — all inescapable corollaries of southern defeat — these governments were granted a free hand in managing their affairs. Johnson offered blacks no role whatever in the politics of Reconstruction. Having long identified himself as a tribune of the South's (white) common people, Johnson assumed that ordinary yeomen would replace in office the planters who had led the South into secession. But when southern elections restored members of the old elite to power, he did not modify his Reconstruction program.

The course adopted by the new southern governments turned much of the North against Presidential Reconstruction. Alarmed by the apparent ascendancy of "rebels," northern Republicans were further outraged by the Black Codes enacted by southern legislatures. These laws required blacks to sign yearly labor contracts, declared unemployed blacks vagrants who could be hired out to white landowners, provided for the apprenticing of black children to white employers without the consent of their former owners, and in other ways sought to limit the freedmen's economic options and reestablish plantation discipline. Blacks strongly resisted the implementation of these measures, and the evident inability of the white South's leaders to accept emancipation fatally undermined northern support for Johnson's policies.

When Congress assembled in December 1865, Radical Republicans like Thaddeus Stevens and Charles Sumner called for the abrogation of the Johnson governments and the establishment of new ones based on equality before the law and manhood suffrage. But the more numerous moderate Republicans hoped to work with Johnson while modifying his program. Congress refused to seat the congressmen and senators elected from the southern states and in early 1866 passed and sent to Johnson the Freedmen's Bureau and civil rights bills. The first extended the life of an agency Congress had created in 1865 to oversee the transition from slavery to freedom. The second defined all persons born in the United States as national citizens and spelled out rights they were to enjoy equally without regard to race — making contracts, bringing lawsuits, and enjoying "full and equal benefit of all laws and proceedings for the security of person and property."

As the first statutory definition of the rights of American citizenship, the civil rights bill embodied a profound change in federal-state relations. Traditionally, citizens' rights had been delineated and protected by the states. Less than a decade earlier, Chief Justice Roger A. Taney, in the *Dred Scott* decision, had announced that a black person could not be a citizen of the United States. Now Congress proposed that the federal government guarantee the principle of equality before the law, regardless of race, against state violation.

A combination of personal stubbornness, fervent belief in states' rights, and deeply held racist convictions led Johnson to reject the bills. His vetoes caused a permanent rupture between the president and Congress. The Civil Rights Act was the first major piece of legislation in American history to become law over a president's veto. Shortly thereafter, Congress approved the Fourteenth Amendment, which forbade states from depriving any citizen of the "equal protection of the laws," barred many Confederates from holding state or national office, and threatened to reduce the South's representation in Congress if black men continued to be kept from voting.

Not until 1867, however, was Congress prepared to endorse black suffrage directly. This happened after two developments further strengthened the Radical Republicans. First, northern voters overwhelmingly repudiated Johnson's policies in the fall 1866 congressional elections. Then, the southern states, with the exception of Tennessee, rejected the Fourteenth Amendment. Congress now decided to begin Reconstruction anew. The Reconstruction Acts of 1867 divided the South into five military dis-

tricts and outlined how new governments, based on manhood suffrage, were to be established. Thus began the period of Radical or Congressional Reconstruction, which lasted until the fall of the last southern Republican governments in 1877.

By 1870, all the former Confederate states had been readmitted to the Union, and nearly all were controlled by the Republican party. These groups made up southern Republicanism. Carpetbaggers, or recent arrivals from the North, were former Union soldiers, teachers, Freedmen's Bureau agents, and businessmen, most of whom had come south before 1867, when the possibility of obtaining office was remote. But they leapt at the opportunity to help mold the "backward" South in the image of the North.

The second large group of Republicans — scalawags, or native-born white Republicans — included some Old Whig planters who hoped to lead a "harnessed revolution" in which whites would recognize blacks' civil and political rights but retain control of state government. Most, however, were nonslaveholding small farmers from the southern up-country. Loyal to the Union during the Civil War, they saw the Republican party as a means of keeping "rebels" from regaining power in the South.

In every state, blacks formed the overwhelming majority of southern Republican voters. Composed mainly of those who had been free before the Civil War and slave ministers, artisans, and Civil War veterans, an articulate black political leadership emerged during Reconstruction to press for the elimination of the nation's racial caste system and the economic uplifting of the former slaves. Although blacks did not obtain office in proportion to their numbers in the party, and "black supremacy" never existed, some sixteen served in Congress during Reconstruction, over six hundred in state legislatures, and hundreds more in local offices, from sheriff to justice of the peace, scattered across the South. The presence of sympathetic local officials, black or white, made a real difference in southern life, ensuring that those accused of crimes would be tried before juries of their peers and enforcing fairness in such prosaic aspects of local government as road repair, tax assessment, and poor relief.

In many ways, Reconstruction at the state level profoundly altered traditions of southern government. Serving an expanded citizenry and embracing a new definition of public responsibility, Reconstruction governments established the South's first state-funded public school systems, adopted measures designed to strengthen the bargaining power of plantation laborers, made taxation more equitable, and outlawed racial discrimination in public transportation and accommodations. They also embarked on ambitious programs of economic development, offering lavish aid to railroads and other enterprises in the hope of creating a New South whose economic expansion would benefit black and white alike. But the program of railroad aid did much to undermine support for Reconstruction. Spawning corruption and rising taxes, it alienated increasing numbers of white voters.

The essential reason for the growing opposition to Reconstruction, however, was the fact that southern whites could not accept the idea of former slaves voting and holding office or the egalitarian policies adopted by the new governments. Increasingly, Reconstruction's opponents turned to violence. The Ku Klux Klan launched a campaign of terror that targeted for beatings or assassination local Republican leaders as well as blacks who asserted their rights in dealings with white employers. The Klan decimated the Republican organization in many localities. Increasingly, the new southern governments looked to Washington for survival.

By 1869, the Republican party was firmly in control of all three branches of the federal government. After attempting to remove Secretary of War Edwin M. Stanton, in apparent violation of the new Tenure of Office Act, Johnson had been impeached by the House of Representatives in 1868. Although the Senate, by a single vote, failed to convict him, his power to obstruct the course of Reconstruction was gone. Republican Ulysses S. Grant was elected president that fall. Soon afterward, Congress approved the Fifteenth Amendment, prohibiting states from restricting the franchise because of race. Then it enacted a series of Enforcement Acts authoriz-

ing national action to suppress political violence. In 1871, the administration launched a legal and military offensive that destroyed the Klan. Grant was reelected in 1872 in the most peaceful election of the period.

Nonetheless, Reconstruction soon began to wane. Democrats had never accepted its legitimacy, and during the 1870s, many Republicans retreated from both the racial egalitarianism and the broad definition of federal power spawned by the Civil War. Southern corruption and instability, Reconstruction's critics argued, stemmed from the exclusion of the region's "best men" — the old planters — from power. As the northern Republican party became more conservative, Reconstruction came to symbolize both misgovernment and a misguided attempt to use state power to uplift the lower classes of society. The depression that began in 1873 pushed economic questions to the forefront of politics, eclipsing Reconstruction. And when Democrats, for the first time since the Civil War, won control of the House of Representatives in 1874, it was clear that southern Republicans could expect little further help from Washington. When violence again erupted in the South in the mid-1870s, Grant failed to intervene.

By 1876, only South Carolina, Florida, and Louisiana remained under Republican control — the remaining southern states had been "redeemed" by white Democrats. The outcome of the presidential election of 1876 between Republican Rutherford B. Hayes and Democrat Samuel J. Tilden hinged on the disputed returns from these states. After negotiations between southern political leaders and representatives of Hayes, a compromise was reached: Hayes would recognize Democratic control of the remaining southern states, and Democrats would not block the certification of his election by Congress. Hayes was inaugurated, federal troops returned to their barracks, and Reconstruction came to an irrevocable end.

The collapse of Reconstruction deeply affected the future course of American development. Except in a few areas, the southern Republican party all but disappeared, and the South long remained a one-party region under the control of a reactionary ruling elite who used the same violence and fraud that had helped defeat Reconstruction to stifle internal dissent. Despite its expanded authority over citizens' rights, the federal government stood by indifferently as the South effectively nullified the Fourteenth and Fifteenth Amendments and stripped blacks of the right to vote. Not until the 1960s would the nation again attempt to come to terms with the political agenda of Reconstruction.

ERIC FONER

II. Economic and Social Aspects

For all Americans, the Civil War and the postwar era of Reconstruction brought far-reaching economic and social changes. As Allan Nevins observed over fifty years ago, the period witnessed the "emergence of modern America." In the victorious North and West, these years saw the completion of the national railroad network, the creation of the modern steel industry, the settlement of the trans-Mississippi West and final subduing of the Plains Indians, and the expansion of the mining frontier. The world of small farms and artisans' shops inexorably gave way to a rapidly industrializing economy, as the wage earner replaced the independent small producer as the typical member of the laboring class. Even though the depression of the 1870s brought an abrupt halt to the heady economic expansion of the immediate postwar years, by the end of Reconstruction in 1877 the nation's industrial production stood 75 percent above its 1865 level. Many issues that galvanized postwar northern politics — from the fate of the greenback currency to labor's demand for the eight-hour day and farmers' calls for railroad regulation — arose from the economic changes unleashed during the war and Reconstruction.

Because of the destruction of slavery, the South's social and economic transformation proved even more far-reaching than the North's. The central institution of antebellum southern life, slavery was simultaneously a system of labor, a form of race relations, and the foundation of a distinctive regional ruling class. Its demise led inevitably to conflict between blacks seeking to breathe substantive meaning into their freedom and planters seeking to retain as much as possible of the old order. Out of this conflict arose new systems of labor and new kinds of relations between black and white southerners. But these developments took place in a context that severely limited the region's prospects for economic growth. A war-torn, capital-scarce region, whose level of per capita income continued to lag far behind the rest of the nation, the South lacked the institutional base for sustained economic development.

To blacks, freedom meant independence from white control, autonomy both as individuals and as members of a community itself being transformed as a result of emancipation. This aspiration was reflected in the consolidation and expansion of the institutions of black life. Under slavery, most blacks had lived in nuclear family units, although they faced the constant threat of separation from loved ones by sale. Reconstruction provided the opportunity for blacks to solidify their family ties. Freedpeople made remarkable efforts to locate loved ones from whom they had been separated under slavery, and many black women, preferring to devote more time to their families, refused to work any longer in the cotton fields. Continuing resistance to planters' efforts to bind black children for involuntary labor through court-ordered apprenticeship revealed that control over their family life was a major preoccupation of the former slaves.

At the same time, blacks withdrew almost entirely from white-controlled religious institutions. On the eve of the war, forty-two thousand black Methodists worshiped in biracial South Carolina churches (where they were excluded from a role in church governance); by the end of Reconstruction only six hundred remained. At the same time, blacks established a network of independent fraternal, benevolent, and mutual aid societies. And although aided by northern reform societies and the federal government, the freedmen often took the initiative in establishing schools, pooling their meager resources to construct buildings and hire teachers.

Thus, race relations during Reconstruction had a contradictory quality. In social life, there was separation, as both races retreated into their own institutions. Despite Reconstruction civil rights laws, segregation was also the rule in many public facilities and private businesses. Almost all the new public school systems educated black and white children in separate schools, and many railroads, hotels, and theaters either excluded blacks altogether or relegated them to inferior accommodations. But the polity was color-blind. Blacks and whites sat together on juries, school boards, and city councils, and the Republican party provided a meeting ground for like-minded men of both races. Politics and government were the most integrated institutions in southern life during Reconstruction.

The appalling loss of life in the Civil War, and the widespread destruction of work animals, farm buildings, and machinery, ensured that the South's economic revival would be slow and painful. Between 1860 and 1870, while farm output expanded in the rest of the nation, the South experienced precipitous declines in the value of farm land, the number of farm animals, and the amount of acreage under cultivation. But economic reconstruction required more than rebuilding shattered farms and repairing broken bridges. An entire social order had been swept away, and on its ruins a new one had to be constructed.

In the postwar South, as in every nineteenth-century society that abolished slavery, emancipation was followed by a comprehensive struggle over access to the land and the forging of a new labor system. The conflict between former masters aiming to re-create a disciplined labor force and blacks seeking to carve out the greatest degree of economic autonomy helped shape the transition from slave to free labor. Planters were convinced that their own survival and the region's prosperity depended on their ability to resume production using disciplined gang labor, as under slavery. It was an article of faith that the freedmen, naturally indolent, would work only under compulsion. When they found that their personal authority over black laborers had vanished, planters turned to the new state governments of Presidential Reconstruction, which enacted the Black Codes in an unsuccessful attempt to stabilize the plantation labor force.

To blacks, economic autonomy rested on ownership of land. Many freedmen in 1865 and 1866 refused to sign labor contracts, expecting the federal government to provide them with farms of their own, to which their past labor, they believed, entitled them. In some localities, as an Alabama overseer reported, they "set up claims to the plantation and all on it." But President Andrew Johnson in the summer of 1865 ordered land in federal hands to be returned to its former owners. Most rural blacks remained propertyless and poor, as did those who flocked to southern towns and cities after the Civil War in an unsuccessful search for better employment opportunities.

Most blacks were thus compelled to go to work as laborers on white-owned farms and plantations, although they continued to resist white supervision of their work routines and daily lives. Nearly all former slaves refused to work in gangs under an overseer's direction, and most preferred to rent land for a fixed payment rather than work for wages. Out of the conflict on the plantations, new systems of labor emerged in the different regions of the South. Sharecropping came to dominate the cotton South. A compromise between blacks' desire for land and planters' for labor discipline, sharecropping allowed each black family to work its own plot, with the crop divided with the landowner at year's end. In the rice kingdom of coastal South Carolina and Georgia, planters were unable to acquire the large amounts of capital necessary to repair irrigation systems and threshing machinery destroyed by the war, and blacks clung tenaciously to land they had occupied in 1865. In the end, the great plantations fell to pieces, and blacks were able to acquire small parcels of land and take up self-sufficient farming. In the Louisiana sugar region, gang labor survived the end of slavery, with blacks paid wages and allowed access to garden plots to grow their own food.

In all these cases, blacks' economic opportunities were limited by whites' control of credit and by the vagaries of a world market in which the price of agricultural goods suffered a prolonged decline. In the late 1860s, some blacks managed to accumulate enough money to move from sharecropper to renter, and a few purchased land of their own. But many farmers who obtained supplies on credit from merchants found themselves still mired in debt after their portion of the crop was marketed at year's end.

The South's postwar economic transformation also affected the position of the white yeomanry. Wartime devastation set in motion a train of events that permanently altered their previous self-sufficient way of life. Plunged into poverty by the war, many yeomen in up-country areas saw their plight exacerbated by successive crop failures in early Reconstruction. In the face of this economic disaster, yeomen clung tenaciously to their farms. But needing to borrow money for the seed, implements, and livestock required to resume farming, many fell into debt and were forced to take up the growing of cotton, a process accelerated as new railroads linked yeomen areas to the national market. By the mid-1870s, white farmers, who cultivated only one-tenth of the South's cotton crop in 1860, were growing 40 percent of the crop, and a region in which a majority of small farmers had once owned their land was increasingly trapped in a cycle of tenancy and cotton overproduction, and unable to feed itself.

The rise of up-country cotton farming was only one part of a wholesale reorientation of southern trading patterns and a shift in regional economic power. As railroads penetrated the interior, they enabled merchants in rapidly developing market towns like Atlanta to trade directly with the North, bypassing the coastal cities that had traditionally monopolized southern commerce. In the up-country emerged a new bourgeoisie composed of merchants, railroad promoters, and bankers. Nationally, this class wielded little economic power, for it depended for credit and supplies on northern financiers and merchants. But within the South, it reaped the benefit of the spread of cotton agriculture.

In the plantation belt, the planter still stood atop the social pyramid. In a few areas, such as the sugar region, large numbers of planters saw their lands pass into the hands of northern investors. Generally, however, the majority of planter families managed to retain control of their land. Yet Reconstruction altered their world. Stripped of political influence at Washington and often at the state level, and lacking the ability to control their volatile labor force, many planters found themselves reduced to poverty.

The South's economic problems were exacerbated by the depression that began in 1873. Within four years, the price of cotton fell by nearly 50 percent, plunging farmers into poverty and drying up the region's already inadequate sources of credit. The depression shattered what hopes remained for the early emergence of a modernizing New South, and forced long-established businesses into bankruptcy. It facilitated the penetration of northern capital, as outside corporations bought up bankrupt southern railroads and other enterprises. Hard times accelerated the spread of tenancy among white farmers, ruined many planters, and reversed much of the modest economic progress blacks had made in the postemancipation years.

By 1877, the contours of the South's new social order were apparent. A new class structure was well on its way to being consolidated, with a rural proletariat composed of the descendants of the former slaves and white yeomen and a new owning class of planters and merchants, itself subordinate to northern financiers and industrialists. And the end of Reconstruction sharply reduced blacks' bargaining power and opportunities for organization. Laws limiting the options of plantation laborers, impossible to enact while blacks retained a significant role in politics, now appeared on southern statute books. Planters succeeded in stabilizing the plantation system, but only by blocking the growth of alternative enterprises, like factories, that might draw off black laborers, thus locking the region further into a pattern of economic underdevelopment. Long into the twentieth century, the South would remain the nation's foremost economic problem — a legacy not only of slavery but of the social and economic changes that began during Reconstruction, and of Reconstruction's political failure.

Eric Foner, *Reconstruction: America's Unfinished Revolution* (1988; abridged edition, *A Short History of Reconstruction*, 1990); Gerald D. Jaynes, *Branches without Roots: Genesis of the Black Working Class in the American South*,

1862–1882 (1986); Leon F. Litwack, *Been in the Storm So Long: The Aftermath of Slavery* (1979).

ERIC FONER

See also Black Codes; Bruce, Blanche K.; Carpetbaggers; Civil War; Cotton; Douglass, Frederick; Emancipation Proclamation and Thirteenth Amendment; Freedmen's Bureau; Grant, Ulysses S.; Johnson, Andrew; Ku Klux Klan; Lynching; Plantation System; Redeemers; Republican Party; Scalawags; Slavery; Stevens, Thaddeus; Suffrage; Sumner, Charles; Truth, Sojourner; Wade-Davis Bill; Washington, Booker T.

RECONSTRUCTION FINANCE CORPORATION

The Reconstruction Finance Corporation (RFC) was established by President Herbert Hoover on February 2, 1932, to make emergency loans to banks and railroads in danger of defaulting at the outset of the Great Depression. The RFC dispensed $1.5 billion in its first year and was credited with contributing to the reduction in bank failures during the first half of 1932. Although five thousand financial institutions, railroads, and life insurance companies received loans, however, it became clear when the first accounting was published in July 1932 that most RFC money was going to a few large firms; a more equitable distribution was achieved thereafter.

As the financial situation worsened again in the second half of 1932, Hoover's congressional opponents argued for direct federal grants to states, municipalities, or individuals, but Hoover opposed all such programs, convinced that bolstering the nation's businesses was the only appropriate and effective role for the federal government. The Emergency Relief Act of July 21, 1932, did authorize the RFC to lend nearly $300 million to states that had exhausted their own relief funds, but less than $30 million had been given out by the end of 1933.

Under President Franklin D. Roosevelt's New Deal, the RFC's role was widened to include (under the Emergency Banking Act of March 1933) the purchase of banks' stock in order to provide them with liquid capital. The RFC also continued to make loans — $11 billion to more than seven thousand banks and trust companies during Roosevelt's first term. With the approach of war, the RFC became a major source of financial backing for the nation's military buildup. Beginning June 25, 1940, the agency was empowered to make loans for buying and producing strategic raw materials and for constructing and operating defense plants. It also began lending money to foreign governments. After the war the RFC reverted to its former role of financing American business ventures. Scandals arose in the early 1950s when Senator J. William Fulbright's Senate Banking and Currency Committee revealed evidence of favoritism and influence-peddling at the RFC. Reorganization followed, but the agency stopped operating in 1956.

See also Government and the Economy; New Deal.

REDEEMERS

The Redeemers, a loose political coalition in the post–Civil War South, consisted of prewar Democrats, Union Whigs, Confederate army veterans, and individuals interested in industrial development. They sought to "redeem" the South by undoing the changes brought about by the Civil War. Although the various groups had widely different visions of the South, they shared a commitment to reduce the scope of state government and institute stricter economic and political control of blacks.

In the late 1870s Redeemers won many state and local offices by vowing to dismantle the "corrupt" Reconstruction system. In power they cut government spending, shortened legislative sessions, lowered politicians' salaries, scaled back public aid to railroads and corporations, and reduced support for public education. They also passed laws requiring blacks to sign labor contracts and imposing poll taxes and taxes on tools and farm animals — measures that placed an added burden on tenant farmers and sharecroppers, black and white alike. The Redeemers' policies inhibited regional economic development and exacerbated the class strife and racial violence that followed the war.

See also Reconstruction.

RED SCARES

See Anticommunism.

REED, JOHN

(1887–1920), journalist and political radical. Reed's life was filled with excitement, courage, and contradictions. Born into a middle-class family in Portland, Oregon, he attended private schools and graduated from Harvard University in 1910, determined to make a name for himself as a poet. He settled in Greenwich Village where he found a job with a magazine. By 1912 he became associated with the radical periodical, the *Masses*. A year later he published a witty verse portrait of Village life, *The Day in Bohemia, or Life among the Artists.*

While observing striking silk workers in Paterson, New Jersey, Reed was arrested, and his subsequent article for the *Masses,* "War in Paterson," not only suggested an awakened social conscience and made him an immediate Village celebrity; it also changed his life. The article was the first example of the participatory journalism that remained his trademark.

Radicalized by the Paterson experience, he directed the Paterson Pageant at Madison Square Garden on June 7, 1913, to raise money for the strikers. Using striking workers, short dramatic scenes, and audience participation, Reed anticipated several innovative techniques employed by pageantry and radical theater in the 1920s and 1930s.

In late 1913, Reed was sent by *Metropolitan* magazine to report on the Mexican Revolution. His fame grew as he rode with revolutionaries, interviewed their celebrated leader, Pancho Villa, and merged personal experiences with dramatic events in an impressionistic analysis, *Insurgent Mexico* (1914). Reed wrote best about events to which he was personally committed. Unlike his Mexican reporting, his articles on World War I were less than brilliant because he opposed the war. His journalistic career seemed to be unraveling when he was barred from the western front because of a foolish prank. Yet the most important part of his life was just beginning when he and his wife, Louise Bryant, a fel-

low writer, went to Russia after the czar's overthrow.

Reed discovered in revolutionary Russia a working class determined to control its own destiny. In Petrograd when the Bolsheviks seized power, he sympathetically described the events in *Ten Days That Shook the World* (1919). Reed subordinated his persona to the book's central character, the Russian working class. He anticipated the new journalism of the 1960s by actively participating in the events he was describing and by exploring the meaning of the revolution by trying to capture the emotions of its participants.

In Russia, as in Paterson and Mexico, Reed was committed to the events he reported. This commitment went further in the case of Russia than ever before, however; he tried to help the revolution succeed by working for the Bureau of International Revolutionary Propaganda in Moscow and later by helping found an American communist party. Neither doctrinaire nor systematic in his thinking, he tried to ensure that this party would conform to unique American needs. He was instrumental in helping found the Communist Labor party, a body distinct from the Communist party of the foreign-language federations, which he believed did not understand the psychology of the American working class. At the Second Congress of the Communist International in Moscow, he also unsuccessfully campaigned for the creation of an industrial union in the United States along the lines of the IWW rather than following party doctrine of trying to control from within the more conservative unions like the AFL.

After his death of typhus in 1920, he was buried within the Kremlin walls. At the time of his death he was still deeply committed to the revolution but willing to question the application of its ideals to the United States.

Granville Hicks, *John Reed: The Making of a Revolutionary* (1937); Robert A. Rosenstone, *Romantic Revolutionary: A Biography of John Reed* (1975).

DAVID C. DUKE

See also Communist Party; Expatriates and Exiles; Paterson Silk Strike; Radicalism.

REFORM

See Civil Rights Movement; Feminist Movement; Great Society; Muckrakers; New Deal; Populism; Progressivism; Prohibition and Temperance; Women's Voluntary Associations.

REHNQUIST, WILLIAM

(1924–), chief justice, U.S. Supreme Court. Rehnquist was born in Milwaukee, Wisconsin. He received M.A. degrees in political science from both Stanford and Harvard and graduated from the Stanford Law School, where he was first in his class, in 1951. He was serving as law clerk to Supreme Court Justice Robert Jackson when the Court first heard arguments in *Brown* v. *Board of Education of Topeka,* the school segregation case. Rehnquist wrote a memorandum suggesting that "separate but equal" schools were constitutional. The Court, of course, unanimously ruled otherwise in 1954. Rehnquist later insisted that the memorandum was written simply to test a line of reasoning and was not an indication of his personal views.

Following his clerkship, Rehnquist practiced law in Phoenix, Arizona, and became active in local Republican politics. Upon Richard Nixon's becoming president in 1969, Rehnquist returned to Washington to join the Justice Department as assistant attorney general for the Office of Legal Counsel. In 1971 Nixon unexpectedly nominated him, together with Lewis Powell, to the Supreme Court. Largely because of his "schools" memorandum, the nomination was extremely controversial, but the Senate confirmed him on December 10, 1971.

Rehnquist quickly became the most conservative member of the Court presided over by Chief Justice Warren Burger. One thread of his philosophy was skepticism about claims of individual rights against state regulation. Thus, he dissented in *Roe* v. *Wade,* the 1973 case that ruled unconstitutional the criminalization of abortion. Another was sympathy for claims of states objecting to what they deemed overregulation by the national government. Perhaps his most important opinion during his first five years on the Court was in *National League of Cit-*

ies v. *Usery,* in which the Court, by a 5–4 vote, struck down a congressional statute that applied minimum wage laws to state and city employees. (This decision was overruled by the Court in 1985, with Rehnquist writing a dissent indicating his hope for a return in the future to his views in *Usery.*) Finally, Rehnquist rarely expressed sympathy for criminal defendants challenging the validity of the procedures used against them, nor was he supportive of the legal claims of prisoners objecting to the conditions of their incarceration.

During Ronald Reagan's presidency the Court moved substantially toward Rehnquist's views. In 1986, upon Chief Justice Burger's resignation, Reagan nominated Rehnquist as his successor. Once again Rehnquist proved an unusually controversial nominee, and he was confirmed over the opposition of thirty-three senators. In contrast, the equally conservative Antonin Scalia, nominated at the same time, was confirmed unanimously by the Senate.

The Rehnquist Court became markedly more conservative in regard to the rights of criminal defendants and the administration of the death penalty as well as far more skeptical about so-called affirmative action programs based on race, but there were few explicit reversals of major Warren and Burger Court precedents.

Sue Davis, *Justice Rehnquist and the Constitution* (1989).

Sanford Levinson

See also *Brown* v. *Board of Education of Topeka; Roe* v. *Wade;* Supreme Court.

RELIGION

"Upon my arrival in the United States," Alexis de Tocqueville wrote in 1835, "the religious aspect of the country was the first thing that struck my attention." Throughout American history visitors have remarked on the religious character of the United States. G. K. Chesterton, for instance, concluded that America thought of itself in religious terms and that the United States was "a nation with the soul of a church."

Indeed, the statistics are staggering. Gallup

poll data tell us that 94 percent of Americans believe in God or a universal spirit, as compared with 76 percent of the British, 62 percent of the French, and 52 percent of the Swedes. In addition, 65 percent of Americans claim membership in a church or synagogue, and 42 percent attend religious services in any given week.

Thus, Americans are undeniably a religious people. To a remarkable degree, many seek to fashion their conduct around religious principles, and their religious communities very often define their social networks. Extolling the unique religious character of the United States has become a staple of political discourse. Throughout their history Americans have believed that their country occupies a special place in the divine plan. When Thomas Prince sat down early in the eighteenth century to write his history of New England, he felt compelled to begin his narrative with the *Genesis* account of creation, so confident was he of America's special place in providential history. The Puritans saw themselves as the New Israel, fleeing the Egypt of England for the Promised Land of Massachusetts. Even Benjamin Franklin, so much a man of the Enlightenment, proposed that the seal of the United States depict Moses leading the children of Israel across the Red Sea.

In addition to historical identifications with ancient Israel, millennial notions have also shaped American self-identity and its hopes for the future. No less a thinker than Jonathan Edwards believed that the millennium would begin in Northampton, Massachusetts. Joseph Smith taught his followers that the center stake of Zion would be in Jackson County, Missouri. Countless religious visionaries have decided that America would provide the most fertile soil for constructing one sort of utopia or another. America's sense of destiny has also filtered into political rhetoric. One has only to chart the political slogans through the centuries — John Winthrop's "Citty upon a Hill" in the seventeenth century, "the sacred cause of liberty" during the revolutionary era, "manifest destiny" in the nineteenth century, "making the world safe for democracy" in the twentieth — to get a sense of America's belief in its divine mission.

Undeniably, the hyperbole of political rhet-oric notwithstanding, religion has played an important role in America's history. Spanish conquistadors bore the standard of Christianity to the New World, although they were clearly not averse to filling the king's coffers and lining their own pockets with booty. The Pilgrims, exiled from England and uneasy with their new lives in the Netherlands, sought religious refuge across the Atlantic. The Puritans, who followed a decade later, had a more ambitious agenda — to demonstrate to the world the workings of a true church purified of all vestiges of Roman Catholicism — but by the close of the seventeenth century their quest for profits had unmistakably compromised their professions of piety. The religious motivations of other settlers — the Dutch, the Swedes, the Scots-Irish, the Anglicans — are considerably less obvious, although it is clear that the Huguenots fled religious persecution in France after the revocation of the Edict of Nantes in 1685. Roger Williams, Lord Baltimore, and William Penn all envisioned havens of religious toleration in the New World.

The religious pluralism that characterized colonial America demanded some kind of unique accommodation in the polity of the new nation. Indeed, religious establishment — the designation of a particular religious group or denomination as favored by civil authorities and therefore eligible to receive public revenues — had proved impractical in most of the colonies outside of New England. Protestant leaders such as Isaac Backus and William Livingston joined Thomas Jefferson and Enlightenment deists in an unlikely alliance to ensure religious toleration and disestablishment. Far from crippling religious expression, as the Congregationalists of New England had feared, disestablishment instead created a salubrious religious climate in America. The First Amendment, with its proscription against religious establishment and its guarantee of religious freedom, has set up a kind of free market of religion in America, where religious "entrepreneurs" of all stripes — Joseph Smith, Ellen Gould White, Mary Baker Eddy, Elijah Muhammad, Jimmy Swaggart, Robert Schuller — have competed for popular followings in the marketplace of ideas.

This playing to popular tastes has doubtlessly compromised religious orthodoxy and rigor. Indeed, another peculiar characteristic about religion in America is its latitudinarianism. With the exception of Jonathan Edwards and Reinhold Niebuhr, Americans have rarely distinguished themselves as theologians; they tend to be rather eclectic in their beliefs, with little regard for consistency. But *what* you believe is less important than belief itself, or at least the trappings of spirituality. One has only to glance in the direction of the vitiated religious establishments in other Western nations to understand the contrast. Whereas other peoples become passionate about politics, Americans are passionate about religion, and in any priority of personal disclosure most Americans would divulge their religious views before their political affiliations.

No era of American history better demonstrates the influence of religion on public life than the nineteenth century, particularly the antebellum period. The revival fires of the Second Great Awakening unleashed an unprecedented reforming impulse in the new nation, much of it directed toward the establishment of a millennial kingdom in America. Americans were so steeped in optimism about the perfectibility of individuals and the amelioration of society that they organized benevolent and reform societies — temperance reform, abolitionism, female suffrage, prison reform — with a zealotry unmatched in American history. Religious sensibilities pervaded American culture, often mixing with nationalism and xenophobia — witness the nativist sentiment directed against non-Protestant immigrants, as well as McGuffey's *Reader* of the nineteenth century, with its unabashed celebration of Protestantism and patriotism.

But if Protestantism's influence on American culture has been pervasive, its hold has never been hegemonic. Indeed, Americans' religious imagination has been limitless, giving rise to all manner of permutations and innovations — restorationism, Mormonism, Christian Science, transcendentalism, Jehovah's Witnesses, the Moorish Science Temple, Jewish Reconstructionism, the Nation of Islam, and countless others. All are indigenous American religions, and all have won a place — and at least a mea-

sure of respectability — in the marketplace of ideas. Indeed, the challenge facing Americans over the last century has been the accommodation of the nation's religious pluralism, a concession that some of the more conservative Protestants have been reluctant to grant, especially to non-Christian traditions such as Hinduism, Buddhism, and Islam.

Religious sensibilities have shaped American culture beyond the realm of politics. Sunday blue laws persisted well into the twentieth century, and the Methodist township of Ocean Grove, New Jersey, managed to ban automobiles from its streets every Sunday until a court decision in 1979 declared the law unconstitutional. United States coins and currency bear the inscription, "In God We Trust." Sunday schools began in the late eighteenth century to provide a rudimentary education for children of the working poor, but as common schools grew in popularity during the succeeding decades, Sunday schools provided religious instruction and served as a significant means of recruitment for Protestant churches. Public schools, however, shed their Protestant biases only slowly, and this reluctance prompted the great school wars in New York and Philadelphia over what amounted, Roman Catholics charged, to Protestant catechetical instruction in the public schools. At the Third Plenary Council in 1884, Catholics responded with an ambitious program of parochial schooling to educate and socialize Catholic children in the faith. The "school wars" of the twentieth century placed conservative Protestants on the defensive. Ever since the Supreme Court's 1963 decision banning prayer in public schools, fundamentalists have urged a reversal of that decision, and they have launched desultory efforts either to ban the teaching of evolutionary theory or, once that battle was lost, to insist that public schools teach the *Genesis* account of creation alongside of Darwinism.

Historically, religion has shaped higher education in America as well. A large portion of the nation's most prestigious universities trace their origins to confessional or sectarian motivations: Harvard, Yale, and Dartmouth (Congregational); the College of William and Mary and Columbia (Anglican); Princeton (Presbyterian); Brown

(Baptist); Georgetown (Jesuit). Although many of these institutions have slipped their religious moorings, others — Notre Dame, Southern Methodist, Brigham Young — have remained rather more faithful to their origins. In addition, hundreds of colleges throughout the country were begun by religious groups in an effort to expand their influence on American culture — Colby (Baptist), Connecticut Wesleyan (Methodist), Davidson (Presbyterian), Gettysburg (Lutheran), Kenyon (Episcopal), to name only a few.

Indeed, the aggregate influence of religion upon American culture is so great as to be incalculable, but the reverse is true as well: religion in America bears a distinctive cultural stamp. More than anything else it is marked by a disregard for tradition and precedent. The New World attracted adventurers, people disenchanted in one way or another with the existing order, many of whom fled the institutional constraints of the Old World. They brought with them a willingness to experiment and even a passion for novelty. The United States was the first modern, Western nation founded by Protestants, not Catholics. Protestantism, which by its very definition defies tradition, did not have to overcome the ossified European institutions of churches and universities; instead, the New World allowed Protestants to start anew.

The other peculiar characteristic of religion in America derives from its populist character. Lacking confessional boundaries and institutional constraints, religious groups very often coalesce around a charismatic individual who defines the faith, beliefs, and practices of his or her followers. In the twentieth century, the media have allowed a number of religious figures to exploit that circumstance to their advantage and build large empires of radio and television stations, colleges, seminaries, and even, however briefly, an amusement park.

Religion in America has had oddly divergent influences on American life, in some cases challenging and in other cases defending the status quo. Northern Protestants of the antebellum period pushed a comprehensive agenda of social reform. The Social Gospel movement at the turn of the century sought to redress the ravages of urban life. Dorothy Day and the Catholic Worker movement advocated workers' rights and even socialism. The "peace churches" — Quakers, Mennonites, and others — have faced censure, ridicule, and even the distraint of goods in times of war. Jews and Christians cooperated in the civil rights struggle against Jim Crow laws and against the mores of southern culture.

Religion, however, has generally exerted a conservative influence on American life — witness the unabashed celebration of patriotic values in McGuffey's *Reader,* the identification of capitalism with Christianity by powerful churchmen such as John D. Rockefeller, the fundamentalist political resurgence since 1975, and the fierce conservatism of the Mormons, despite their persecution at the hands of federal authorities in the nineteenth century. Religion in America rarely challenges the political or social order; when it does, it usually does so only to champion so-called traditional values or to evoke a halcyon past when America was purportedly even more religious. On such occasions it calls upon and thereby perpetuates the enduring mythology of America as a Christian nation and Americans as God's chosen people.

Twenty, fifty, and even a hundred years ago, the conventional wisdom of modernization and secularization theorists was that as any nation modernizes and industrializes, religion would be pushed to the periphery. America's persistent spirituality, however, has confounded those experts. In the United States, surely among the most modern and industrialized nations on earth, religion remains very much a part of both private life and public discourse.

Sidney E. Ahlstrom, *A Religious History of the American People* (1972); Mark A. Noll, *One Nation under God? Christian Faith and Political Action in America* (1988).

RANDALL BALMER

See also A.M.E. Church; Black Churches; Blue Laws; Christian Science; Church and State; Deism; Evangelicalism; Great Awakening; Jews; Missionaries; Mormons; Puritanism; Quakers; Roman Catholic Church; Second Great Awakening; Shakers; Social Gospel; Transcendentalism; *and entries for individual religious figures.*

REPORT ON MANUFACTURES

The third major state paper of Alexander Hamilton, America's first secretary of the treasury, the *Report on the Subject of Manufactures* (1791) revealed the full range of Hamilton's plan for industrializing the United States. Rejecting the common assumption that America could prosper with an agricultural base, Hamilton argued that the new Republic should concentrate on developing industry. To nurture American industry in its formative years, he proposed the imposition of protective tariffs and the prohibition of imported manufactured goods that would compete with domestic products. Other suggestions included prohibiting the exportation of raw materials, inspecting manufactured goods to ensure high standards of quality, and encouraging inventions. Hamilton sought more than the alteration of America's economic base, however. He hoped to change the very nature of the people — to instill in them a new spirit of industriousness, energy, and innovation.

Of great help to Hamilton in the preparation of his report was Assistant Secretary of the Treasury Tench Coxe. Although Coxe's contributions have been underestimated in the past, discoveries of drafts in his hand have proved that he added a great deal to the final version.

The report was submitted to Congress on December 5, 1791, a period when Hamilton's political enemies were particularly active. Because of their opposition and the far-reaching implications of the plan, Congress failed to act on it. But many of the specific tariffs he called for were enacted the next year, and his overall vision of the importance of industry to America proved prescient in the years to come.

See also Hamilton, Alexander.

REPUBLICANISM

Republicanism was the ideology of the leaders of the American Revolution, and it still determines much of what Americans believe. In the monarchy-dominated world of the eighteenth century, republicanism was not simply a form of government; it was a form of life, a way by which dissatisfied people could criticize the patriarchy, luxury, and corruption of eighteenth-century monarchy.

Its deepest origins lay in the great era of the Roman republic. The world of the eighteenth century learned most of what it wanted to know about the Roman republic from the writings of the celebrated Latin writers flourishing from the middle of the first century B.C. to the establishment of the empire in the middle of the second century A.D. — Cicero, Sallust, Tacitus, and Plutarch among others. These men lived after the greatest days of the republic had passed, and they contrasted the stratification, corruption, and disorder they saw around them with an imagined earlier world of rustic simplicity and pastoral virtue. Roman farmers had once been hardy soldiers devoted to their country, but they had become selfish, corrupted by luxury, and torn by struggles between rich and poor; they had lost their capacity to serve the public good. In their pessimistic explanations of the republic's decline, these writers left a legacy of beliefs and values — about the good life, about citizenship, about political health, about social morality — that have had an enduring effect on Western culture.

This body of classical literature was revived and updated by Renaissance writers, especially the Italian philosopher Machiavelli. It was blended into a tradition of "civic humanism" — a tradition that stressed the moral character of the independent citizen as the prerequisite to good politics and disinterested service to the country. To be good citizens people had to be free of control by others and free of the influence of selfish interests.

This classical republican tradition passed into the culture of northern Europe. In England it inspired the writings of the great seventeenth-century republicans, John Milton, James Harrington, and Algernon Sidney, and was carried into the eighteenth century by scores of popularizers and translators. This republican tradition had a decisive effect on the thinking of the American revolutionary leaders.

Republicanism in 1776 meant more than eliminating a king and instituting an elective system of government; it set forth moral and social goals as well. Republics required a particular sort of egalitarian and virtuous people: independent, property-holding citizens who were willing to sacrifice many of their private, selfish interests for the res publica, the good of the whole community. Equality lay at the heart of republicanism; it meant a society whose distinctions were based only on merit. No longer would one's position rest on whom one knew or married or on who one's parents were.

Such dependence on a relatively equal and virtuous populace, it was thought, made republics very fragile and often short-lived. Monarchies were long-lasting; they could maintain order from the top down over large, diverse, and even corrupt populations through their use of patronage, hereditary privilege, executive authority, standing armies, and religious establishments. But republics, such as the American states were, had to be held together from below, from virtue, from the consent and sacrifice of the people themselves. The only republics left in the eighteenth century — the Netherlands and the city-states of Italy and Switzerland — were small and compact. Larger heterogeneous states that tried to establish republics — as England had in the eighteenth century — were bound to end up in chaos resulting in some sort of military dictatorship, like that of Oliver Cromwell. If it were too large and embraced too many diverse interests, a republic would fly apart.

The Americans' new extended republic in 1787 flew in the face of these traditional assumptions and made their experiment in republicanism a highly risky venture indeed. A national republic that encompassed a huge society of diverse interests and sprawled over half a continent demanded new explanations. Much of the originality and creativity of the Framers' political thought accompanying the creation of the Constitution in 1787–1788, including *The Federalist,* came from their need to justify the republicanism of the new federal government in opposition to the conventional wisdom of the day. The Founding Fathers ultimately recognized the reality of an American society composed of many conflicting private interests, but they hoped that these would neutralize themselves and allow enlightened leaders who were free of selfish marketplace concerns and local partisan interests to promote the general good. To that extent they clung to classical republicanism.

The democratic revolution of the subsequent decades, at least in the North, virtually destroyed this classical dream of republican leaders acting as disinterested umpires over the economic and political struggles of the society. Political parties emerged to reestablish patronage and to promote partisan interests, and countless individuals took off in pursuit of their private happiness. By the middle of the nineteenth century America gave as much free rein to commercial activity and the self-interestedness of the people as any society in history.

But much of the republican tradition has remained alive, even to this day. Republicanism tempers the scramble for private wealth and happiness and accounts for many of the Americans' ideas and aspirations: for their belief in equality and their dislike of pretension and privilege; for their relentless yearning for individual autonomy and freedom from all ties of dependency; for their periodic hopes, expressed, for example, in the election of military heroes and in the mugwump and progressive movements, that some political leaders might rise above parties and become truly disinterested umpires; for their long-held conviction that farming is morally healthier and freer of selfish marketplace concerns than other occupations; for their preoccupation with the fragility of the Republic and its vulnerability to corruption; and, finally, for their remarkable obsession with their own national virtue — an obsession that still bewilders the rest of the world.

J. G. A. Pocock, *The Machiavellian Moment: Florentine Political Thought and the Atlantic Republican Tradition* (1975); Gordon S. Wood, *The Creation of the American Republic, 1776–1787* (1969).

GORDON S. WOOD

See also Federalist Papers; Jeffersonian Democracy; Mugwumps; Progressivism.

REPUBLICAN PARTY

The Republican party has been a major political force in the United States since it first appeared on the presidential ballot in 1856. Following the 1854 Kansas-Nebraska Act, the Whig party disintegrated, and mass meetings in the upper midwestern states led to the formation of a new party opposed to the spread of slavery into the western territories. One such meeting, at Ripon, Wisconsin, on March 20, 1854, is usually credited as marking the birth of the Republican party.

The Republicans rapidly became established as the dominant political force in the North. In 1856 their presidential candidate, John C. Frémont, carried eleven of the sixteen northern states. By 1860 the Republicans had also absorbed the support of the nativist Know-Nothing party, and their candidate, Abraham Lincoln, was elected president, an outcome that precipitated the outbreak of the Civil War. The war firmly identified the Republican party as the party of the victorious North. As such, the Republicans became anathema to the white South for almost a century, with the exception of several antislavery redoubts in the mountain areas. That loss was more than counterbalanced in other parts of the country, however, by the Republicans' reputation as the party that had freed the slaves and saved the Union.

After the war, the Republicans continued the Whig tradition of promoting industrial development through high tariffs, while their popular base lay among the freedmen and the white, Protestant population of the northern states (the party began to be referred to as the "Grand Old Party," or GOP, during this period). Western farmers had supported the Republicans in resisting the spread of slave agriculture, but in the 1865–1900 period the laissez-faire ideology of the eastern, corporate wing of the party predominated. The tension between the Republicans' "Wall Street" and "Main Street" wings would become an abiding feature of Republican party politics.

Immediately after the Civil War, Republicans in Congress passed the Thirteenth, Fourteenth, and Fifteenth Amendments to the Constitution and promoted a Radical Reconstruction policy regarding the southern states. But in order to secure the disputed electoral votes of four southern states in the 1876 presidential election, the Republicans abandoned Radical Reconstruction and the cause of black civil rights. By doing so they virtually surrendered the South to the Democrats.

The scandals of President Ulysses S. Grant's administration (1869–1877) provoked a revolt in the 1872 election by Republican civil service reformers known as the Liberal Republicans. This issue was kept alive by a group of patrician Republicans in New York — the so-called mugwumps — who agitated against the widespread corruption of the time.

After the critical election of 1896 the nature of the party conflict changed. The close competition between the parties in the post–Civil War period was replaced by Republican dominance, as the Democrats became associated with agrarian radicalism. The Republican grip was reinforced by the return of prosperity under William McKinley and by the Spanish-American War. McKinley's defeat of William Jennings Bryan in 1896 and 1900 was followed by Republican victories in every presidential election until 1932, except for Democrat Woodrow Wilson's victories in 1912 (when the Republicans were split) and 1916. They also controlled Congress from 1896 to 1930, save for the 1910–1918 period. In every region of the country outside the solidly Democratic South, the Republicans were dominant.

The party's western agrarian radicals and eastern upper-middle-class reformers became more prominent after 1896. The latter tendency was most clearly exemplified by President Theodore Roosevelt who identified the Republicans with the cause of progressivism — in particular the idea of a vigorous executive regulating the economy and society in the public interest. The 1912 election (when Roosevelt emerged from retirement to challenge his successor, William Howard Taft) demonstrated the factional divisions within the Republican party. Western agrarian progressivism was represented by the candidacy of the radical senator from Wisconsin, Robert M. La Follette, the more urbane progressivism of the East by Roosevelt, and the party's conservative business mainstream by President Taft. In disgust at Taft's renomination, Roosevelt bolted from the Republicans and launched his own Bull Moose candidacy, thereby guaranteeing defeat for the GOP.

Widespread disillusionment with Woodrow Wilson and with progressivism in general after World War I allowed the Republicans to reassert their electoral dominance during the 1920s. Three Republican presidents — Warren G. Harding, Calvin Coolidge, and Herbert Hoover — were elected with comfortable margins, and the GOP retained a firm grip on Congress. After Roosevelt's death in 1919, eastern urban progressivism lay dormant temporarily, and the party's corporate establishment, epitomized by Treasury Secretary Andrew Mellon, was in control. The western tradition of radical Republicanism was sustained by continuing economic hardship in the agricultural states, but its spokesmen in the Senate — La Follette of Wisconsin, William Borah of Idaho, George Norris of Nebraska, and Hiram Johnson of California — were regarded derisively as the "Sons of the Wild Jackass" by the party elite.

The Republicans returned to the laissez-faire probusiness policies of the late nineteenth century in the domestic sphere. In foreign affairs, the Senate Republicans were instrumental in defeating Wilson's League of Nations in 1919–1920, and the party ostensibly became committed to a policy of isolationism. This was particularly true of the western radicals in the Senate, but the dominant Wall Street Republicans were less strident and did not pursue an isolationist economic policy vis-à-vis Europe. Republican foreign policy from the time of Theodore Roosevelt has emphasized robust defense of American interests within an international balance of power rather than "making the world safe for democracy." It was thus not so much isolationist as unilateralist, in contrast to the Democrats' Wilsonian universalism.

The Great Depression brought an end to the era of Republican dominance, as Herbert Hoover was overwhelmed by Franklin D. Roosevelt in 1932. After supporting the Roosevelt administration's initial emergency measures, the Republicans became unremittingly hostile toward the New Deal. As a result the Republican presidential candidate in 1936, Alfred M. Landon, carried only Maine and Vermont, and the GOP

was reduced to a paltry seventeen senators and eighty-nine representatives in Congress.

From the nadir of 1936, however, the Republicans recovered as the tone of their opposition became less strident. In Congress, they formed alliances with conservative southern Democrats against FDR's more radical proposals (particularly his 1937 Court-packing bill). This so-called conservative coalition generally controlled both houses of Congress until the early 1970s.

While the western radical Republicans either merged with the New Deal Democrats or turned conservative, progressive Republicanism revived in the metropolitan Northeast. Led initially by corporate lawyer Wendell Willkie and later by New York governor Thomas E. Dewey, the new Republican progressivism accepted the need for some government intervention in economic and social policy. Progressive Republicans also emphasized a commitment to civil rights and advocated a more Atlanticist foreign policy.

After Willkie's defeat by FDR in 1940, the leadership of the party fell upon Dewey, who was nominated in 1944 and 1948. During this period the progressive wing (also referred to as the moderate or even liberal wing of the party) was able to control the party's national convention because of its strength in the large delegations of the northeastern states and support from the progressive states of the Pacific Coast. The financial power of Wall Street over Republican elites in the western and midwestern states and over the shadow Republican organizations of the South was also decisive.

The party's isolationist, midwestern, Main Street tradition did not disappear, however. Inspired by the candidacy of Ohio senator Robert A. Taft, members of this wing bitterly contested the party's presidential nomination at every convention during the 1940–1952 period. On each occasion, Taft was thwarted by the eastern Republican establishment, primarily because of his lack of enthusiasm for America's post–World War II global commitments.

Although the progressives consistently won the presidential nomination, they equally consistently failed to win the White House. The Republicans managed to regain control of Congress in 1946, but two years later Dewey unexpectedly lost the presidential election to Harry S. Truman. In desperation after 1948, the Republicans at last discovered several issues they could use effectively against Truman's administration. They attributed the "fall of China" and the outbreak of the Korean War to the Truman–Dean Acheson foreign policy and to domestic communist "subversion." The Republican congressional leadership encouraged Wisconsin senator Joseph R. McCarthy to attack the Democrats on the latter issue, and anticommunism also became a means by which previously isolationist Republicans could justify international commitments by the United States. This "new nationalism" was particularly evident in the approach of the junior California senator, Richard M. Nixon.

In 1952 with Gen. Dwight D. Eisenhower at the head of their ticket (and Nixon as the vice-presidential nominee), the Republicans at last regained the White House. They also won control of Congress, and Eisenhower was able to make inroads in the Democratic South. Yet though Eisenhower was overwhelmingly re-elected in 1956, his administration did not strengthen the Republicans' electoral position significantly. No major changes were made in domestic or foreign policy, and after the anticommunist issue had exhausted its electoral potential, the Republicans lost control of Congress in 1954. Nixon also lost the 1960 presidential election narrowly to Democrat John F. Kennedy.

During the Eisenhower years a new species of conservatism began to emerge within the party. This new Republican Right was composed of stalwart conservatives alienated by Eisenhower's failure to defeat communism and reverse the New Deal, the emerging Republican party in the South, and Catholics in the North who identified with McCarthy's anticommunist crusade. Organized into a network of intellectuals, interest groups, and journals, the conservatives defeated the moderate eastern establishment in 1964 and secured the party's presidential nomination for Arizona senator Barry M. Goldwater, who confirmed the moderates' worst fears by losing in a landslide to Democrat Lyndon B. Johnson.

The New Right had become so powerful within the Republican presidential party, however, that former vice president Nixon had to accommodate them to win the party's nomination in 1968. The movement toward the right within the GOP reflected a broader shift of economic power and population away from the party's old northeastern base and toward the South and West, as well as the Republican mobilization of conservative white southerners in the wake of the civil rights revolution. With that movement the balance of power shifted from the moderate eastern establishment to southern and western conservatives.

Nixon's administration repeated the moderation of Eisenhower both at home and abroad; only rhetorically did it reflect Nixon's alliance with the New Right. The Watergate scandal during his presidency reflected badly on all elements of the party and retarded the progress the Republicans had hoped to make in the 1970s with the Democrats torn apart by Vietnam, race, and various social issues. In 1976, President Gerald Ford only narrowly defeated former California governor Ronald Reagan (who had succeeded Goldwater as the hero of the Republican Right) for the presidential nomination.

The years in opposition during Jimmy Carter's presidency reinforced the New Right's hold on the Republican party. This was largely due to the continuing Republican mobilization of formerly Democratic white southerners and northern, white, middle-class, Catholic, ethnic voters concerned about crime, inflation, and American "weakness" abroad. A further addition to the Republican ranks at this time were many formerly apolitical evangelical and fundamentalist Christians antagonized by Supreme Court decisions proscribing prayer in public schools and the national Democrats' association with the sexual revolution of the 1960s. Reagan easily won the party's nomination in 1980 and triumphed over President Carter in November, perhaps helped to some extent by an independent candidacy by liberal Republican congressman John B. Anderson. The Republicans also took control of the U.S. Senate for the first time since 1954.

Reagan's administration pursued the New Right agenda more zealously than had those of Nixon and Ford. The impact was greatest in the economic sphere as Reagan's 1981 tax and spending cuts reversed the direction of policy since the New Deal. In addition, the administration achieved a massive increase in defense spending and adopted a much more aggressive American posture vis-à-vis the Soviet Union and communist insurgencies in the third world. Finally, the Reagan administration was also committed to a social agenda of opposition to recent Supreme Court rulings on abortion, school prayer, and civil rights. The most significant legacy of the Reagan presidency, however, was the unprecedented federal budget deficit engendered by the combination of sweeping tax cuts and large increases in defense spending. The deficit precluded any short-term expansion of federal government programs and changed the whole context of political debate.

Although the Republicans won their third consecutive presidential election victory in 1988 under Reagan's vice president, George Bush, they had lost the Senate in the 1986 elections and had little prospect of taking control of the House. In elections for statewide offices and in state legislatures also, the Democrats retained a clear advantage.

The Republicans hoped they could realign the party system in their favor during the 1990s, because of the continuing shift of population to the South and West where they had recently been dominant in presidential elections and also because of indications that younger voters favored them over the Democrats. But any decline in the economic prosperity of the Reagan years could severely retard their progress, and the ending of the protracted American-Soviet conflict threatened to deprive the GOP of the defense issue, which had been so electorally advantageous for them. Moreover, Court decisions in favor of the New Right social agenda could alienate upper-middle-class business Republicans and the younger voters whom the party had been assiduously wooing in recent years.

Regardless of the electoral balance between the parties in the 1990s, the powerful constraints that exist to maintain the two-party system in the United States, such as ballot access and the plurality voting system, would likely ensure that the Republican party, formed in the heat of the slavery crisis of the 1850s, would remain a major political force into the twenty-first century.

George H. Mayer, *The Republican Party, 1854–1964* (1964); Nicol C. Rae, *The Decline and Fall of the Liberal Republicans: From 1952 to the Present* (1989).

NICOL C. RAE

See also Anticommunism; Civil War; Conservatism; Isolationism; Liberalism; Mugwumps; Progressive Parties: 1912, 1924, 1948; Progressivism; Reconstruction; Whig Party; *and entries for individual party figures.*

RESORTS

See Vacations and Resorts.

REVERE, PAUL

(1735–1818), silversmith, industrialist, and American Revolution figure. Although most familiar as the hard-riding hero of Longfellow's poem, Paul Revere's claims to historical significance rest even more on his talent as a craftsman and on his industrial perspicacity.

The son of a Huguenot silversmith, Apollos Rivoire, and Deborah Hitchbourn, Revere received a rudimentary "writing-school" education before turning to his father's trade. Upon the latter's death, Paul at nineteen assumed artistic responsibility for the family's shop. Over the next twenty years, he became one of the preeminent American goldsmiths — a term that encompassed every phase of the eighteenth-century precious-metals craftsman's art. Besides silver bowls, utensils, pots, and flatware (many of which are museum pieces today), Revere and his apprentices and journeymen turned out a variety of engravings: pictures, cartoons, calling cards, bookplates, tradesmen's bills, and even music. As a sideline, he practiced what passed for dentistry in his day, developing as well a rudimentary form of orthodontia.

From the beginning, Revere participated in public affairs. During the French and Indian War, Richard Gridley (who had commanded the artillery at the siege of Louisbourg and was later to direct the American digging-in at Bunker Hill) organized an artillery regiment. Commissioned a second lieutenant, Revere participated during 1756 in the failed expedition against Crown Point.

Revere became a Freemason in 1760, and soon joined two more overtly political groups — the Sons of Liberty and the North End Caucus. Through them, he participated in Samuel Adams's gradually accelerating movement toward independence, serving primarily as a courier and an engraver of propaganda pictures, the two best-known examples of which are a "view" of British ships landing troops in 1768 and a wildly inaccurate cartoon depicting the Boston Massacre of 1770.

The highlight of his Whig activity came the night of April 18–19, 1775, when on Joseph Warren's orders he crossed the Charles River and rode to Lexington to warn Samuel Adams and John Hancock that British troops were coming through on their way to Concord. Revere got the word to the radical leaders, but a British patrol prevented any further progress. Once hostilities began, Revere once again joined the artillery, serving without note until the disastrous expedition to Castine, Maine. In the aftermath of the American rout there, he faced charges of disobedience and incompetence that, although ultimately refuted, permanently ended his service.

Thereafter, Revere turned his energies to commerce. Developing a profitable foundry and hardware business, he planned and established the nation's first successful sheet-copper mill. The navy could now copper-bottom all its ships, including the frigate USS *Constitution,* with American-rolled copper. In his later life, Revere served as grand master of the Masonic Grand Lodge, as one of the organizers of Boston's first successful mutual fire insurance company, as Suffolk County coroner, and as the first president of the Boston Board of Health.

Esther Forbes, *Paul Revere and the World He Lived In* (1942; reprint, 1962).

HILLER B. ZOBEL

See also Revolution.

REVIVALS

See Great Awakening; Second Great Awakening.

REVOLUTION

I. Outbreak of the Conflict

When George III came to the throne in 1760 scarcely anyone in England or America foresaw independence for thirteen of the British colonies in North America. Colonists were proud of their affiliation with Great Britain and satisfied with the prosperity they enjoyed as part of Britain's commercial empire. Only in retrospect do the irritations that arose in the course of Britain's management of its vast empire appear to point toward revolution.

From the seventeenth century on, colonists bridled under the governance of royal officials sent to protect the Crown's interests in North America. The policies themselves were not at issue, since for the most part they harmonized well enough with the colonists' interests. The colonists worried more about bureaucratic avarice. They suspected that the officials, whether governors, customs officers, or surveyors of the woods, pursued their personal interests under the guise of enforcing royal policy. It seemed all too likely that fees, taxes, and fines collected in the name of the king would end up in the pockets of the officials rather than the royal treasury. These suspicions persisted throughout the eighteenth century, but against this ever-present danger the colonists erected a "hedge" to keep them, as they said, "from the wild Beasts of the field." The hedge was the right of their local legislatures to pass laws, raise taxes, authorize military operations, and audit accounts, free from official intimidation. The colonists' success in establishing the rights of their legislative assemblies, always in the face of complaints of their obstinacy, gave a measure of confidence that their liberty was secure. Everywhere in 1760 the colonists enthusiastically celebrated the ascent of the new king to the throne.

Imperial officials in London, though always uneasy about the assertiveness of the colonial legislatures, had no concerted plan for reform at the end of the French and Indian War in 1763. The events that led to revolution in 1776 did not grow out of a British resolve to bring the loosely governed empire under control at last. That came to be a secondary goal of policy, but initially Parliament naively stumbled into the American controversy in pursuit of other ends. They were looking in another direction entirely when in 1765 the colonies exploded in rage at parliamentary taxation.

The Crown's ministers were simply seeking a way to finance the king's military policy. During the French and Indian War the British government had taken financial responsibility for the defense of the colonies as well as provided military leadership and many of the troops. Rather than demobilizing at the end of the war, George III with his minister William Pitt's backing chose to keep the army at near wartime strength of eighty-five regiments to be ready in the event of renewed hostilities with France. The problem was how to pay for them. England was financially exhausted after the lengthy and costly war that had nearly doubled the national debt, and the country could not bear additional taxes. The solution was to station large portions of the army in Ireland and America and require local support for the troops in each location. The Sugar Act, the Stamp Act, and the Townshend Duties were intended to help finance the £359,000 needed annually to sustain the troops in America.

The American Revenue Act of 1764, or Sugar Act, confused the Americans. It was in the first place not a new tax but an alteration of an old customs duty. To prevent trade with the French West Indies, Parliament in 1733 had passed a prohibitive tariff on sugar, molasses, and other goods imported from those islands. The colonists lived with these annoying customs duties by evading them through smuggling. They could scarcely object in principle to duties they had long acknowledged as legitimate. In the second place, the Sugar Act reduced the duty, from 6d. on a gallon of molasses, for example, to 3d. The difference was, of course, that mechanisms were put in place to collect the duty and American shippers faced having actually to pay it.

There were objections heard to the Sugar Act on grounds that it was intended for revenue, not regulation, and so was illegitimate, but the ambiguities were sufficiently great to blunt American opposition.

The Stamp Act presented no such ambiguities. It was a tax laid directly on the people for the express purpose of raising revenue. To collect the tax the British ministry embossed stamps of varying values in sheets of paper and sold the paper to the colonists for use as legal documents, newspapers, and pamphlets. No document written on unstamped paper had legal standing, and so the colonists were compelled to buy the stamps and pay the tax. In Britain stamp taxes were considered inoffensive and easy to collect, but if Whitehall officials expected the colonists to acquiesce for that reason, they were soon disabused of their illusion.

The colonists at virtually every level of society, including many who later became Loyalists, rose in protest. The colonial legislatures and a specially called Stamp Act Congress submitted complaining petitions to Parliament. Urban crowds made public spectacles of the men chosen to distribute the stamps and sometimes attacked them. The actions of the crowds provide a clue to the reasons for the outrage. They did not merely excoriate the Parliament that enacted the Stamp Act; they attacked the stamp distributors, virtually all of them local citizens. The charges brought in newspapers and pamphlets against these men reflected the old suspicion about British colonial officials. The people feared that the "Stamp Men" were benefiting from the tax. Moreover, it was Parliament that had enacted the Stamp Act, not the colonial legislature, thus breaking down the hedge that had contained the wild beast. Without that defense there was no protection against the avarice of men in power.

What could the colonists do but reassert the rights on which they had long based their opposition to royal governors and all the other officials who threatened to oppress them? They claimed as British subjects the right to tax themselves, and since the colonists could not be represented in Parliament, the taxes had to originate in their colonial assemblies. This was the major constitutional question at issue throughout the conflict. The British believed that Parliament was sovereign over all the empire; everyone in it had to yield to its authority. True, the colonists did not elect members to Parliament, but Parliament nonetheless represented the colonists as it did other groups — large cities in England among them — that did not have the right to elect members. But the colonists could not acknowledge this notion of being "virtually" represented. The trouble was that members of Parliament were not themselves affected by taxes laid on the colonists. In fact, they and their associates stood to benefit from increased colonial taxation because it would reduce the tax burden in England. In the ensuing debate, neither side would budge.

Then suddenly in 1766 the controversy seemingly dissolved. In the House of Commons William Pitt, the hero of the French and Indian War, made an eloquent if somewhat inconsistent plea for the colonies' right to tax themselves while affirming Parliament's supremacy in all other legislative matters. Pitt's speech carried the day and the Stamp Act was repealed.

On the same day, however, Parliament passed a Declaratory Act that reasserted the right of Parliament to legislate "in all cases whatsoever." In their rejoicing the colonists paid no heed to the merely verbal assertions. In the long struggle with royal governors, they had become accustomed to such compromises; they knew they had won this one. A few months later the duty on molasses was reduced to 1d. The colonists calculated that smuggling cost them about 1½d. per gallon, so they willingly paid the lesser fee. The new duty brought substantial revenues to the Crown and all parties were content.

Unfortunately, however, Britain still needed funds to sustain its American regiments. In 1767 the chancellor of the exchequer, Charles Townshend, proposed a new revenue measure that tried to make the most of American compliance with trade regulation such as the Sugar Act. Since the Americans objected to internal taxes like the stamp duties, Townshend proposed import duties on glass, lead, paints, paper, and tea similar to those on sugar and molasses. To his dismay, the Americans would have none of it.

John Dickinson, in his *Letters from a Farmer in Pennsylvania,* warned Americans that the Townshend Duties were every bit as much a revenue measure as the Stamp Act and should be repudiated. His fellow citizens agreed. At considerable loss to themselves, merchants in one port after another agreed not to import British goods — not just items subject to duties but a broad range of other goods. By 1769 only New Hampshire merchants had failed to enter a nonimportation pact. When American imports fell by nearly a third, the ministry in London took notice. The new head of government, Lord North, led the way, and in 1770 the Townshend Duties were repealed. This time the assertion of principle took the form of retaining the duty on tea. Americans objected but could not sustain the painful nonimportation agreements. As the news of repeal spread, the merchants resumed trade with Britain except for the importation of tea.

Again as in 1766 a reconciliation seemed to have been achieved, and for two years political life returned to normal. There was a tragic incident in 1770 when troops fired on a civilian crowd that was harassing them. Some called it the Boston Massacre, but more levelheaded citizens recognized the deaths were an accident. John Adams, a leader of the resistance to the British measures, defended the soldiers in court. For the most part it seemed that good sense had prevailed and a compromise had been reached in the dispute with Parliament.

But once again the British ministry inadvertently stumbled into controversy while looking in another direction. The East India Company had fallen on hard times, and Parliament in an attempt to bail out the lumbering giant granted it privileges with grave implications for America. The company's inventory of imported tea had built up in British warehouses. In 1773 Parliament decided that when tea was reexported to the colonies, the import duties paid when it was first brought into England would be remitted, enabling the company to retail the tea at a reduced price. The company still had to pay the old Townshend Duty of 3d. a pound when the tea arrived in America, but there would be enough of a price differential to give the company a substantial marketing advantage even against smuggled Dutch tea. Furthermore the company was allowed to sell through its own American agents rather than through middlemen, further reducing the price.

It is a little difficult to understand the American reaction to the Tea Act. No new duty had been imposed. Americans were no more obligated to buy the tea than before the act was passed. But at all four major ports where tea shipments arrived — Boston, New York, Philadelphia, and Charleston — people resisted. They interpreted the act as an attempt to bribe Americans into buying tea and paying the duty, thus opening the door to still more oppressive taxation. In three ports the tea shipments were halted or sent back; in Boston Governor Thomas Hutchinson seemed resolved to land the tea at whatever cost. To stop him, townspeople on December 16, 1773, dumped 342 chests of tea into the harbor. The Tea Act had brought the resistance movement back to life.

The Boston Tea Party was the beginning of the end. All of England was outraged. In willfully destroying valuable private property the Americans had gone too far. Parliament responded in March 1774 by closing the port of Boston to all trade and in May passed the Coercive Acts intended to restrict Massachusetts government. The governor was authorized to appoint members of the Governor's Council rather than letting the lower house nominate them; he similarly was empowered to appoint judicial officials without the necessity of council approval; and town meetings were forbidden except to elect selectmen.

The ministry had hoped to isolate Massachusetts with these measures and show by example the fate that awaited other colonies that carried resistance too far. Instead the colonies interpreted Massachusetts's fate as the doom that awaited them all if they failed to resist. In September 1774 the First Continental Congress met in Philadelphia to protest the Coercive Acts and to organize a new nonimportation movement. In Massachusetts itself the new governor, Gen. Thomas Gage, decided not to keep the assembly in session, knowing it would do nothing but protest Britain's actions. But in a truly revolutionary act, the assembly refused to disband and continued to meet as a Provincial Congress to take measures against the exercise of arbitrary power. The Congress's main purpose was to declare the colony's rights and to enforce the nonimportation agreement, but it soon assumed the form of a shadow government. Tax revenues were diverted from the official treasury to the Congress. Fearing reprisals, it urged the town militias to make themselves ready and provided for the collection of arms.

Governor Gage, a mild man who hoped to calm the aroused colonists, saw a revolutionary government forming before his eyes. He tolerated many of the resolves issuing from the Provincial Congress; he could not tolerate the organization of a military force. When he heard that a cache of arms had been stored at Concord twenty-one miles from Boston, he felt obligated to send troops to destroy it. On the evening of April 18 the troops embarked from Boston Common to cross the Charles River to Cambridge. At Lexington in the early morning hours they encountered a small, confused band of militiamen and shots were fired. A few miles farther at Concord, militia from the surrounding towns put up more resistance. Seeing they were outnumbered, the British began their retreat under heavy fire. The Revolution had begun.

Merrill Jensen, *The Founding of a Nation: A History of the American Revolution, 1763–1776* (1968); Pauline Maier, *From Resistance to Revolution: Colonial Radicals and the Development of Opposition to Britain, 1765–1776* (1972).

RICHARD L. BUSHMAN

See also Adams, John; Adams, Samuel; America in the British Empire; Association (1774); Boston Massacre; Boston Tea Party; Coercive Acts; Colonial Wars; Committees of Correspondence; Continental Congresses; Hancock, John; Henry, Patrick; Hutchinson, Thomas; Quartering Acts; Revere, Paul; Sons of Liberty; Stamp Act; Sugar Act; Townshend Acts.

II. War of Independence

For years the great question about the revolutionary war was how the Americans managed to win. How did the inexperienced, poorly armed, badly trained forces of an infant nation made up of thirteen independent and mutually jealous states come to defeat one of the world's greatest military powers? Was it American marksmanship, unfamiliar New World guerrilla tactics, British blunders, French aid, or the intervention of Divine Providence that made the difference? The debate went on until American and French experience in Indochina in the 1950s and 1960s took the life out of the question. There were clearly significant differences between the Vietnamese conflict and the American revolutionary war, but after Vietnam it no longer seemed improbable that a great military power could bog down in a struggle with a smaller but tenacious enemy amid a civilian population whose loyalties could not be relied upon, especially when the costs of the war and uncertainty about its purposes undermined the great power's domestic support. All those conditions existed in Britain's war with its American colonies, and post-Vietnam Americans know firsthand why Britain at last might choose to withdraw its forces — even though it was not completely defeated — rather than to prolong a debilitating struggle.

In subsequent years it has been possible to assess more sympathetically than before the problems Britain faced in devising an effective strategy for ending American resistance and to mark the alterations in British conceptions of how to conduct a difficult war. Initially the British conceived of the conflict as discipline of the unruly. After the clash at Concord on April 19, 1775, the British believed they might end rebellion by isolating and punishing the rebels at Boston through a show of force. By crushing the center of resistance, the British hoped to bring the rest of the colonies into line. But this strategic plan did not last long. At the Battle of Bunker Hill on June 17, 1775, the British launched a reckless frontal assault on the American positions on Breed's Hill in an attempt to demonstrate the invincibility of trained troops against untrained militia. The demonstration was a failure. Apart from the high casualties, the refusal of the Americans to give way until they exhausted their ammunition compelled the British to reassess American strength. It was no longer certain that the rebels could be intimidated. Fur-

thermore, the outpouring of support from other New England towns and the promises of aid from the other colonies weakened the conviction that the rebellion centered in Boston alone. With initial assumptions about the Revolution collapsing, the British were in need of a new strategy.

On June 15, 1775, the Continental Congress commissioned George Washington to lead the army, and on July 3 he took command at Cambridge. After capturing cannon and mortars at Fort Ticonderoga, the Americans occupied Dorchester Heights south of Boston where they could command the city. Recognizing the vulnerability of his position, Sir William Howe, now commander of British forces in America, evacuated Boston on March 7, 1776, and transported his army to New York. Recognizing the altered conditions of the war, Howe shifted his strategy. For the next two years he waged war on classical European lines with the aim of engaging the enemy army and destroying it, thus breaking the back of the resistance. He drove the American army from Long Island in August and occupied New York City, which was to remain British headquarters for the remainder of the war. He then pursued Washington's army up the east side of the Hudson until the American general escaped with his troops and retreated across New Jersey toward Pennsylvania with the British at their heels. With the Americans in retreat, Howe seemed to have demonstrated the superiority of British forces and routed the rebels. The Patriot militia in New Jersey disintegrated after the British occupation, and three thousand Americans took an oath of allegiance to the king.

But in the long run, classical warfare of army against army proved no more successful than the intimidation and discipline strategy of the first year of war. Howe discovered that his outposts were vulnerable when Washington came back across the Delaware River from Pennsylvania to New Jersey to attack the Hessians at Trenton on December 26, 1776, and a British main force near Princeton on January 3, 1777. Forced to pull back, Howe discovered that New Jersey quickly reverted to the Patriots. The British maintained control only in the immediate vicinity of New York City. He learned the same lesson with the attack on Philadelphia. Bringing his troops by sea from New York up Chesapeake Bay, Howe defeated Washington at every encounter and occupied Philadelphia on September 26, 1777, while the Congress fled to Lancaster and York. But the victory of the army proved hollow when the countryside could not be subdued. The lesson was brought home first in the North. Gen. John Burgoyne, descending from Canada to Lake Champlain in an effort to cut off New England from the other colonies, found himself swamped amid a hostile population and ultimately surrendered at Saratoga, New York, on October 17, 1777. British intelligence had severely underestimated civilian hostility, and an army far from its supply base simply could not survive. It was little better for Howe and his successor, Sir Henry Clinton, in Philadelphia. Pennsylvania farmers supplied them with food for a price, and Philadelphia society enjoyed the officers' company for the winter, but the colony and city were no more loyal after the occupation than when the Americans controlled the city. Fearing the approach of the French fleet, Clinton evacuated Philadelphia on June 18, 1778, and headed back to New York having accomplished nothing toward defeat of the American cause.

It now seemed apparent that the British had paid too little heed to "pacifying" the civilian population. Though many Americans flocked to the British side when the army occupied American territory, the long-term effect of the British presence was more often to alienate neutral citizens and convert them to the Revolution. The British themselves were conscious of the "licentiousness of the troops, who committed every species of rapine and plunder," frequently without regard for the political sympathies of the civilian population. Such offenses necessarily made Patriots out of potential friends of Britain. Moreover, with the approach and retreat of the British army as it moved from one region to another, the Patriot militia compelled the citizenry to take a stand. Seeing the impermanence of British occupation, otherwise disinterested people threw in their lot with the Patriots if only to avoid harassment. By a variety of routes, the war recruited civilians for political and military action, more frequently to the advantage of the Americans than the British.

The war moved to the South in 1778 on the strength of reports of a Loyalist population there. The British commanders now turned their attention to mobilizing support among the civilian population. When Savannah fell to the British on December 29, 1778, twenty Loyalist militia companies were recruited and fourteen hundred Georgians took the oath of allegiance. During 1779 campaigns were conducted in Georgia and South Carolina. In May 1780 Clinton captured Charleston. In accord with the concern for the civilian population, he ordered the Loyalist militia to refrain from inflicting violence on innocent civilians and to protect "the aged, the infirm, the women and children from insult and outrage." When Clinton left Charleston in June 1780 he was confident he had won South Carolina for the Crown.

But in the long run the British attempt to cultivate Loyalist citizens was no more successful than the other strategies. Despite the attention to civilian needs, the Patriot militia once again sprang to life as soon as the British army departed. If anything the swing of the pendulum was more extreme because of the retribution the Patriots sought against the Loyalist militia. Instead of pacifying the Carolina and Georgia countryside, British policy had left it more severely divided. Moreover, the British could never perfectly discipline their own troops. Col. Banastre Tarleton was as famed for his harsh treatment of the populace as for his slashing military tactics. He left in his wake hundreds of formerly neutral Americans committed to active rebellion.

The failures in the South along with the approach of the American army from the North compelled the British to change their strategy once more, this time reverting to classical warfare of army against army. Gen. Charles Cornwallis, commander of British forces in the South, moved north from Wilmington, North Carolina, in May 1781 to attack the supply and training bases in Virginia that were supporting Patriot forces in North Carolina. He met little resistance as he marched deep into Virginia; Tarleton nearly captured Governor Thomas Jefferson and the Virginia legislature at Charlottesville. But as American forces collected to resist his advance, he returned to the coast to establish contact with the British fleet. At Yorktown he established a base from which he could keep in touch with Clinton in New York. Then his fortunes reversed. Cornwallis knew he was in trouble when he discovered that the French fleet rather than the British controlled the mouth of the Chesapeake. With the American armies closing in, he found himself in a trap.

In this final battle of army against army, Washington won one of his few major victories of the war. American forces under Marie Joseph, Marquis de Lafayette, aided by French troops landed from Adm. François Joseph Paul de Grasse's fleet controlling the Chesapeake, laid siege to Cornwallis's encampment. After de Grasse brought Washington's army down the Chesapeake to Williamsburg, the allied forces of over sixteen thousand men heavily outnumbered Cornwallis's eight thousand. Every avenue of escape closed to him, Cornwallis surrendered on October 19, 1781.

The defeat at Yorktown ended British desires to prosecute the war. In March 1782 the House of Commons voted to abandon the effort. Lord North's government fell, and the new ministry under Lord Rockingham opened negotiations with the American peace commissioners. Talks began in April in Paris and the preliminary articles of peace were signed November 30, 1782. After acceptance by Britain and the U.S. Congress, the final peace treaty was signed September 3, 1783.

The war has been refought innumerable times in an attempt to identify the crucial British mistakes. Probably no strategy was equal to the task of quelling American resistance. Despite their superior numbers, the British operated in a hostile environment that repeatedly defeated all efforts to put down rebellion. As much as anything that fact accounts for their defeat. It is true that as the war dragged on Americans were slow to enlist, reluctant to pay for still more provisions, and heartily tired of the conflict, but in the final analysis it was the refusal of the civilian population to capitulate and the determination of hundreds of ill-trained, poorly supplied militia companies to harass the enemy that weighed most heavily in the defeat of the British forces in America.

Charles Royster, *A Revolutionary People at War: The Continental Army and American Character, 1775–1783* (1979); Willard M. Wallace, *Appeal to Arms: A Military History of the American Revolution* (1951).

RICHARD L. BUSHMAN

See also Arnold, Benedict; *Common Sense;* France-U.S. Relations; Franklin, Benjamin; Jay, John; Paine, Thomas; Paris, Treaty of (1783); Washington, George.

III. Social and Cultural Change

The revolutionary movement began as a defense of the status quo. All the colonists asked for in their first protests was the continuance of their traditional right as English subjects to consent to their own taxes. They were not impelled by a vision of a new social order or the repudiation of a burdensome ancien régime. Had Britain pulled back at nearly any point before 1775, the resistance would have died away.

Was it possible for a revolution that began so conservatively to effect significant changes in society once it reached full flood? What would propel change? What would come under attack? The conservative revolution became radical as conflict with the imperial government compelled the colonists to search to the roots of their allegiance. As the government became increasingly oppressive, the colonists had to ask why they obeyed at all. Jefferson summed up a decade of thought in the Declaration of Independence when he wrote about "equality" and "inalienable rights." When a government fails in its duty to protect those rights, the people may organize a new government. It was a simple line of thought, but unlike the initial protest against parliamentary taxation, the thinking was radical.

Equality is the most perplexing word in the Declaration of Independence. What could the wealthy planters and slaveholders of the Chesapeake or the rich merchants of the North have meant when they subscribed to the Declaration of Independence with that word in it? They surely could not have meant equality of property when differences in wealth were so blatant. We commonly say the word implied equality before the law or equality of opportunity. Probably in part it meant both. But the most prominent eighteenth-century meaning of *equality* was stated by John Locke: it meant no one had by nature the right to rule another human being without that person's consent. Creatures of the same species, Locke said, "should also be equal one amongst another without Subordination or Subjection." People might differ in wealth, education, or manners, but no one had the right to govern another because of these advantages. There was to be no separate rank above freeman with special privileges in the state. After the Revolution, for the first time, the word *aristocrat* became a term of political opprobrium.

That was the radical idea that propelled social change in the aftermath of independence. It made people deeply suspicious of the Society of Cincinnati, the club of military officers that many believed aspired to aristocratic status. It made it difficult to justify an upper house in the legislature, because senates were traditionally assemblages of aristocrats. But most important it made slavery untenable. Following the Revolution, antislavery societies were formed in virtually all the northern states from Massachusetts to Virginia, abetting a movement already strong among the Quakers. By legislation or judicial decision slaves were manumitted in most states from Pennsylvania north before 1800. In 1787 Congress prohibited slavery in the Northwest Territory. The southern delegates had insisted that the federal Constitution forbid interference with the slave trade for twenty years, and in 1808, when the prohibition expired, Congress stopped the importation of slaves. But there progress halted. Slavery remained an institution in the states from Maryland south and spread into new states in the Southwest. The revolutionary idea had run up against the vested interests of planters whose economy and way of life were founded on slavery.

The limited impact of revolutionary ideals on slavery was a story repeated in other areas of reform. The principle of equality lacked the strength to achieve full realization in the face of opposing interests. The revolutionaries understood, for example, that property and liberty were interrelated. In theory the Revolution might have effected reforms in the economy. "Dominion is founded in property," said Ezra Stiles, the president of Yale College. People dependent on others for their livelihood were under their dominion, as a child or a woman was dependent on the father of the family. Tenants, it was believed, would inevitably vote as their landlords directed. Wherever large amounts of property accumulated, the danger arose of owners dominating their employees, destroying the equality of dominion that was the republican ideal. "Equality of property," wrote Noah Webster, the dictionary man, "is the very soul of a republic."

If carried to its limit, this line of thinking might have radically disrupted the American social order. But the countervailing notion of rights of property stopped the progress of equality along this line. Confiscation of large properties, except for Tory lands, was unthinkable. Moreover, radical reform of property holdings could not build up momentum because landed property was already so widely distributed that dependence seemed more the exception than the rule. Stiles and Webster both thought New England had largely achieved the required equality of property. The real enemy of independence, they thought, was primogeniture, the practice of passing all the landed estate to the eldest son, allowing large tracts to remain in a very few hands. Virtually all the states ended primogeniture for intestate estates before 1800. It was a mild reform, considering that most people distributed their property among all their children anyway. But it advanced the revolutionary belief in equality a step or two without seriously disturbing property rights as they existed.

One other institution came under attack in the name of revolutionary equality — the church. Americans did not bear a grudge against the established church as the French or the English did, mainly because the American religious establishments exercised so few privileges and so generously tolerated dissenters. Nevertheless, established churches here came under attack because they were believed to threaten freedom of conscience. As children of the Enlightenment, the American revolutionaries believed that the will to resist tyranny originated in the mind. People claimed their rights because they understood what they were. As the Americans understood history, churches had entered into an unholy alliance with tyrannical governments to crush these ideas. Priests of established churches taught passive obedience and unthinking subservience to governments in order to receive in return state-enforced tithes. To ensure freedom of conscience and the free circulation of ideas, this alliance had to be broken and establishments ended. The Anglican church in Virginia was anything but an overpowering intellectual influence in the state, yet Jefferson counted among his greatest achievements passage in 1786 of the Bill for Establishing Religious Freedom. The New England states were slower to disestablish their Congregational churches (Connecticut in 1818 and Massachusetts in 1833), but the principle enunciated in the First Amendment that Congress should make no law respecting an establishment of religion eventually prevailed.

Social and cultural change growing out of the Revolution was thus halting and incomplete. It was for the most part a time of planting rather than harvest. Despite considerable agitation, slavery continued to the Civil War. Women, in another instance of blatant inequality, were not allowed to vote until 1920. A few women began to question the customary subordination to husbands, contributing possibly to a rising number of divorces. Women's role as "Republican Mothers," with responsibility for training their children to be citizens, also received recognition. But women's sphere of influence was still the home, not business or politics, and no one advocated suffrage. The great changes came later when the implications of revolutionary principles were more fully recognized. It was no different with other oppressed groups. Alterations in their lives were modest. The power of the idea of equality lay more in its enduring strength than in its immediate effect. Although usually haltingly, the principle of equality has been altering American society for two centuries and continues today as an ongoing consequence of the American Revolution.

J. Franklin Jameson, *The American Revolution Considered as a Social Movement* (1926); Winthrop Jordan, *White over Black: American Attitudes toward the Negro, 1550–1812* (1968); Linda K. Kerber, *Women of the Republic: Intellect and Ideology in Revolutionary America* (1980).

RICHARD L. BUSHMAN

See also Abolitionist Movement; Bill of Rights; Declaration of Independence; Feminist Movement; Freedom of Speech; Freedom of the Press; Hamilton, Alexander; Jefferson, Thomas; Madison, James; Primogeniture; Republicanism; Suffrage.

IV. World Impact

The United States began as a lonely democratic experiment in a world of monarchies. At the time of the nation's founding, the only democracies that existed were tiny places — Swiss cantons, for example — that offered no assurance that democratic government would work for a large nation. The Dutch, who had once enjoyed a republic, were fast slipping back toward monarchy. In classical antiquity, Athens, Sparta, and the Roman republic provided examples of democracy at work. But they were not as inspiring as might be wished, for they had been notoriously unstable, deteriorating into mob rule until a strong leader restored order. The Americans had little reason to believe from the study of history that their experiment would succeed.

The Founders could take courage, however, from the interest of advanced political thinkers throughout the civilized world. The United States came into existence in an age when hopes were high that tyranny could be overthrown and rational government based on liberty and equality established in its place. In actual fact the monarchies of Europe were not toppling; indeed they seemed to be growing stronger. But that did not dampen the hopes of the French philosophes or the English radical Whigs for more enlightened regimes. America even before independence had attracted the attention of these intellectuals. Socially and economically the colonies were far advanced: land was widely distributed and there was no feudal aristocracy. J. Hector St. John Crèvecoeur's *Letters from an American Farmer,* though published in 1782 after American independence was secured, drew on the author's earlier experiences in America and expressed his admiration for the simple, egalitarian, and free life of its people. Thomas Hollis, an English radical Whig, sent shipment after shipment of libertarian literature to America before the Revolution because he believed there was a better chance to preserve liberty in this fresh new land than in his own.

After the Revolution, these intellectuals observed events in the United States with greater interest than ever. The Americans were engaged in an experiment in democratic government that had powerful implications for their own countries. In 1786 the French philosopher Condorcet argued that the United States was living proof that enlightened ideas were the source of human happiness:

> It is not enough that the rights of man be written in the books of philosophers and inscribed in the hearts of virtuous men; the weak and ignorant must be able to read them in the example of a great nation. America has given us this example. (*The Influence of the American Revolution on Europe*)

The Americans, of course, greeted the French Revolution with joy and relief. The establishment of a constitutional monarchy and subsequently a republic sustained the American experiment in many ways. It assured them that the United States led the way in the pursuit of freedom and that it was not alone in its commitment to republicanism. Now the United States and one of the most powerful nations on earth were joined in the grand experiment. French diplomats, French culture, French news, were welcomed everywhere.

In the course of the 1790s the rejoicing turned to horror as the French Revolution moved rapidly from constitutional monarchy to republic to Terror to chaos to a dictatorial directorate and finally to Napoleon. The course of the French Revolution fulfilled to the letter the classical predictions of the fate of a democracy. From being a source of strength, the French example became a powerful critique and prophecy of doom for the United States. Troubled by their own disorders in the 1790s, American conservatives felt that every effort must be made to prevent the United States from following the same mad course. The extremes of the Alien and Sedition Acts of 1798, which severely limited freedom to criticize government, reflected the anxieties many American leaders felt.

The first half of the nineteenth century repeated, less dramatically, the cycle of hope and despair that Americans had passed through with the French revolutions. A few successful revolutions in Latin America and Greece shored up confidence in the general applicability of republican government, and Americans honored the heroes of those revolutions as successors to their own Washington. But more characteristically attempted revolutions in the major European nations began with expectations of establishing democracy and ended with a restoration of monarchy. A series of revolts in 1830 failed, and the more ambitious revolutions of 1848 were followed by even sterner repression. On each occasion the example of the United States initially gave courage to the revolutionaries, but the subsequent failure disheartened Americans.

As late as the Civil War, the United States still stood as a lonely beacon of republican government. Although democracy had made great progress in England under constitutional monarchy, repressed peoples in Latin America and Europe looked to the United States for inspiration. Abraham Lincoln had these facts in mind as the nation entered the Civil War. America was, he said, the "last best hope" of democracy. If the United States divided against itself and was allowed to splinter, it would demonstrate conclusively the long-standing predictions of the skeptics: a nation founded in liberty could not survive. Lincoln believed that America fought to preserve the Union not for its own sake alone but so that "government of the people, by the people, for the people, shall not perish from the earth."

Government by the people did not perish from the earth; in the century after the Civil War democratic government spread through Europe and elsewhere through the world, with the American example ever present as a reserve of experience on which other nations could draw.

The U.S. Constitution offered a practical model for constitution-makers everywhere. In the twentieth century, a new kind of revolution, typified by the Soviet Union and China, emphasized social and economic equality above political democracy, making the American Revolution appear incomplete, even conservative. But even the socialist nations framed written constitutions for the organization of their governments, following the American example.

In the years after World War II, the American Revolution became more relevant than ever as countries throughout the third world sought independence from the European colonial powers. The wars of colonial liberation in Southeast Asia and Africa inevitably led to comparisons with the American War of Independence in 1776. In both instances, the primary urge was nationalistic — to achieve liberty for the local population by repudiating outside rule. The similarities were strong enough to compel leaders in the emerging nations to think seriously about the American Revolution as a precedent for their own wars. A central question for many was how far to depend on the American model as contrasted to the Soviet Union.

Asian nations particularly were conscious of the American precedent — on some occasions to the embarrassment and confusion of the United States. The ruler of North Vietnam, Ho Chi Minh, could claim during the Vietnam War that his people were simply fighting another American Revolution to rid themselves of outside control and create a united Vietnamese nation. Despite the obvious differences, the similarities were one reason for the reservations of Americans in fighting North Vietnam. If the Vietnamese revolutionaries were a modern version of American revolutionaries, why was the United States their enemy? These latter-day revolutions compelled Americans to look again at their own Revolution in search of the traits that distinguished it from the wars of liberation sweeping the globe.

In the late 1980s and 1990s American democracy was receiving attention in unlikely quarters — among the nations of Eastern Europe and in the Soviet Union where people for decades had been living in the aftermath of so-cialist and Stalinist revolutions or occupation. The form of their emerging governments as they sloughed off socialism would doubtless be shaped by their peculiar circumstances, but the American Constitution, with two hundred years of stable government to its credit, continued to be a point of reference. In the late twentieth century, the American Revolution was once more serving as an inspiration and a source of ideas for people aspiring to democracy.

Durand Echeverria, *Mirage in the West: A History of the French Image of American Society to 1815* (1957); Richard B. Morris, *The Emerging Nations and the American Revolution* (1970).

RICHARD L. BUSHMAN

See also Constitution; Foreign Views of America.

RFC

See Reconstruction Finance Corporation.

RICKEY, BRANCH

(1881–1965), major league baseball executive. After a brief stint as a teacher in his native Ohio, Rickey graduated from Ohio Wesleyan University in 1906. His love of philosophy, which he taught briefly and which owed something to the pious Methodism in which he was reared, was intertwined with his love of sports, particularly baseball. He became a catcher with the Cincinnati Reds in 1904, but hobbled by injuries and by his religious objections to playing on Sundays, he was dropped. After unsuccessful turns with the St. Louis Browns and the New York Highlanders, he ended his playing days.

Following a long bout with tuberculosis, he earned an LL.B. in 1911 at the University of Michigan, where he also coached baseball. After practicing law for a short while, Rickey became an assistant to the owner of the Browns and manager of the team. To help it compete with wealthier clubs, he created a farm system — formal and informal arrangements with minor league teams to take on their players as they developed them. Shortly, he became manager and president of the other team in town, the Cardinals. There he so perfected the farm system that the Cardinals for a quarter of a century never had to buy a player. The far-flung minor league operation he conducted, which included tryout and instructional camps, made him wealthy; he had an agreement with the Cardinals that netted him a percentage of the price of any player he sold — and the surplus was large.

After he was forced out of the Cardinal organization by a jealous associate, he joined the Brooklyn Dodgers in 1945 as president and general manager; soon he was a co-owner. Now he widened his search for talent beyond the farm system to include black and Latin American players. Greatly influenced by the writings on race of Professor Frank Tannenbaum of Columbia University's Department of History, among others, Rickey had decided to breach the all-white barrier in organized baseball. He selected and groomed Jackie Robinson, an outstanding college athlete from the University of California at Los Angeles, assigning him in late 1945 to a Dodger farm team, the Montreal Royals of the International League. Robinson led the league in batting in 1946 and Rickey promoted him to Brooklyn the next year. Robinson's luminous achievements as a Dodger and his notable restraint in facing the bigotry rampant in the game, on and off the field, opened the door to a steady stream of black players.

In 1950 Rickey once again broke with associates and left for the Pittsburgh Pirates, hoping to build there yet another championship team. Dismissed in 1955 for failing, he took the presidency of the new Continental League, which aimed to bring baseball of major league quality to cities lacking a big league franchise. The league failed, but in its wake owners of the majors were persuaded that the time had come to expand their sixteen teams to include long-neglected urban communities.

Rickey, this remarkable baseball innovator, was short and stocky, and looked and sounded like a professor. A shrewd businessman, his integrity (critics sometimes read it as self-righteousness) seemed a telltale of his stern upbringing. His warm encouragement of young players must be measured against his artful manipulation of some of the players in the farm system, which stunted many careers. Still, he was the "Man Who Emancipated Baseball," helping stimulate the modern civil rights movement in the process.

Harvey Frommer, *Rickey and Robinson: The Men Who Broke Baseball's Color Barrier* (1982); Murray Polner, *Branch Rickey: A Biography* (1982).

HENRY F. GRAFF

See also Baseball; Robinson, Jackie; Spectator Sports.

RIOTS

See Draft Riots; Rebellions; Slavery.

ROBBER BARONS

This disapproving term was used to describe late-nineteenth-century industrialists, especially those who ostentatiously displayed their wealth. The phrase gained widespread popularity as the title of a history published in 1934 by Matthew Josephson in the depths of the Great Depression. It was applied to industrial leaders and corporations of the late nineteenth century, such as Andrew Carnegie and Carnegie Steel, John D. Rockefeller and Standard Oil, and Cornelius and William Vanderbilt and their railroads. Emphasizing efficiency, these men used increasingly modern practices like large-scale, specialized production in place of decentralized methods. They also practiced "vertical integration," controlling not only the manufacturing and sale of the final product but also the raw resources. Thus, Carnegie Steel was involved in coal and iron, and Standard Oil owned wells and refineries, and controlled railroads that transported the oil to market. The term *robber barons* also has been applied to financiers such as Jay Gould and J. Pierpont Morgan, who set up large trusts and provided loans for these industrialists.

Their defenders have described Carnegie, Rockefeller, Vanderbilt, and their peers as "industrial statesmen" because they enhanced and modernized the American capitalist system by making the nation more productive and thus stronger economically and internationally. But the term *robber barons* suggests a different view that puts more emphasis on their indifference to the public welfare and their display of wealth at the expense of their workers: huge mansions, for example, in contrast to the company towns or urban squalor in which their employees lived. Such comments as William Vanderbilt's "The public be damned!" expressed the scornful attitude that earned the robber barons their unsavory reputation.

See also Carnegie, Andrew; Gould, Jay; Morgan, J. Pierpont; Rockefeller, John D.; Vanderbilt, Cornelius.

ROBBINS, JEROME

(1918–), choreographer and dancer. Robbins is widely considered to be the greatest American choreographer. Born Jerome Rabinowitz in New York and raised in New Jersey, he began his career acting in Yiddish theater. He joined Ballet Theatre when it was founded in 1940, quickly becoming celebrated as an interpreter of great character roles, especially Petrouchka in Fokine's ballet of that name.

The turning point in his life came in 1944 when he conceived the idea for the ballet *Fancy Free* and, with Leonard Bernstein, brought it to fruition with Ballet Theatre on the Metropolitan Opera House stage. It was the greatest popular and critical success in American ballet up to that time. Depicting three sailors on shore leave who meet up with two girls on a bittersweet summer evening in New York City, the ballet was vernacular in style (the women wore high heels rather than pointe shoes; the men, sailor suits rather than tights). It drew on popular dance forms of the 1940s, such as the Lindy and the Samba, and touched a deep vein of American optimism, wistfulness, and naïveté. These were to become Robbins's hallmarks as a choreographer, as he interwove classical traditions with a contemporary sensibility.

The transformation of *Fancy Free* into a musical — *On the Town* — and ultimately a movie launched the varied nature of Robbins's career, as he moved between the theater, an occasional film, and ballet. In the theater, an ex-

traordinary number of hits are attached to his name as choreographer and director, among them *The King and I* (1951), *Peter Pan* (1954), *Bells Are Ringing* (1956), *West Side Story* (1957), *Gypsy* (1959), and *Fiddler on the Roof* (1964), an exploration of his Russian-Jewish roots. The culmination of this side of his talent was seen with the production, in 1989, of *Jerome Robbins' Broadway,* a compilation of highlights from eleven of his shows. As a theater man, Robbins stayed true to his roots as a dancer, always presenting the image of the dancer as the highest ideal and the embodiment of humanistic values.

In 1953 during the red scare, Robbins experienced profound difficulties with the House Un-American Activities Committee. When called to answer questions about his membership, from 1943 to 1947, in the Communist party, he implicated eight others as party members.

Associated first with Ballet Theatre as a dancer and choreographer, Robbins later worked in that double capacity with New York City Ballet (NYCB), where he became a legendary interpreter of the title role in *Prodigal Son*. He later had his own company, Ballets U.S.A., from 1958 to 1961. In 1964 he returned to work again with NYCB, where his career as a choreographer was conducted alongside, and inevitably to some degree in the shadow of, the giant of twentieth-century ballet George Balanchine. Robbins recognized Balanchine's preeminence and said he chose to work with NYCB in order to be close to his genius. Certainly dance critics rank Robbins second only to Balanchine overall, but as the finest American-born classical choreographer. Following Balanchine's death in 1983, Robbins served with Peter Martins as NYCB's co–ballet master in chief and was the subject of a two-week-long festival devoted to his ballets in the spring of 1990.

Robbins created ballets in many styles and atmospheres. Some, such as *Interplay* (1945), *Fanfare* (1953), *Mother Goose* (1975), and his comic triumph *The Concert* (1956), are light and effervescent. But he is also known for works that are probing, dark, preoccupied with contemporary themes such as neurosis and alienation. Among the stand-out works in this mode were *Age of Anxiety* (1950), *The Cage* (1951), and

N.Y. Export: Opus Jazz (1958). Robbins has perhaps been most acclaimed for his masterpieces of lyrical dance theater, among them Afternoon of a Faun (1953), In the Night (1970), Other Dances (1976), and especially the landmark Dances at a Gathering (1969), whose impact was as explosive and transforming as Fancy Free.

Robbins has always been open to experiment within the classical framework. Notable among these works are The Goldberg Variations (1971), the Noh-inspired Watermill (1972), encounters with Philip Glass (Glass Pieces, 1983) and Steve Reich (Eight Lines, 1985), and the films of Fred Astaire (I'm Old-Fashioned, 1983). After Balanchine's death, Robbins produced a series of elegiac ballets expressive of mourning and loss: In Memory of . . . (1985), for Suzanne Farrell; Quiet City (1986), widely seen as a tribute to Joseph Duell, an NYCB dancer who committed suicide that year at age twenty-nine; and Ives, Songs (1988), a leave-taking to youth and spring. Robbins left NYCB in 1990 to embark upon new projects.

ANITA FINKEL

See also Dance; Musical Theater.

ROBESON, PAUL

(1898–1976), actor, singer, and political radical. A man of remarkable talents, Paul Robeson achieved a string of successes, unprecedented for a black American, in sports, on the stage, and as a concert artist. By the early 1940s he was one of the country's most beloved figures. But during the McCarthy era he paid a heavy price for his outspoken criticism of racial injustice in the United States and his close ties to the Communist party and the Soviet Union.

Born in Princeton, Robeson was only the third black student to attend Rutgers, New Jersey's state university. He became an all-American football player, excelled at other sports, and was class valedictorian. After graduation, he enrolled in Columbia Law School and married Eslanda Goode, a descendant of a South Carolina free black family. Partly at her urging, he launched a career as an actor and singer in which he achieved spectacular success. On Broadway and in films, Robeson appeared in roles previously off limits to black actors, including the leads in works by Eugene O'Neill, America's foremost playwright. During World War II, he gave a memorable performance as Othello in the longest-running Shakespeare production ever to appear on Broadway, and his recording of Ballad for Americans reached the top of the popular music charts. Robeson was perhaps best known for his concerts of Negro spirituals, in which his magnificent bass voice electrified audiences.

Yet Robeson could not escape the realities of American race relations. Even at the height of his fame, he was denied service at hotels and restaurants throughout the North. The praise lavished upon him often stressed his supposed "instinctive state of emotion" rather than the disciplined work underlying his stage triumphs.

His father, a Presbyterian minister born a slave, taught Robeson to endure affronts without surrendering his dignity. But racism produced within him a deep anger. Increasingly, he turned to politics for a definition of black identity and an understanding of the sources of racism. His political involvement began with his discovery of Africa, via Jomo Kenyatta, C. L. R. James, and other pan-Africanists in London, where Robeson lived for much of the 1930s. Then, after a series of visits to the Soviet Union, where for the first time he felt free from the burden of racism, Robeson formed close ties with American Communists. Although he never actually joined the party, he established friendships with many of its leaders and threw himself into its campaign for equal rights for black Americans.

Robeson's outspoken criticism of the Truman administration's cold war policies — especially a widely publicized prediction that black Americans would not fight in a war against the Soviet Union — brought down upon him the full weight of McCarthy-era repression. He was driven from radio, television, and the concert stage, and the State Department, branding him "one of the most dangerous men in the world," revoked his passport. The black establishment joined in the assault (the NAACP even excising Robeson's name from a published list of recipients of its Springarn Medal).

Separated from the audiences, at home and abroad, on whose adulation he thrived, Robeson suffered a series of mental breakdowns. By the time he died, he had been all but forgotten. Although he is now recognized as one of the greatest figures in Afro-American history, Robeson's life remains, as a black newspaper put it shortly after his death, "a challenge and a reproach to white and black America."

Martin Bauml Duberman, *Paul Robeson* (1989).

ERIC FONER

See also Expatriates and Exiles; Radicalism; Segregation.

ROBINSON, JACKIE

(1919–1972), professional baseball player with the Brooklyn Dodgers (1947–1956); first African-American to play in major league baseball in the twentieth century. Intensely proud of his talents and his blackness in a white-dominated world, Robinson created drama throughout his life. He fought racism viscerally — in his California childhood, at college, and in the army, where he faced a court-martial for defying illegal segregation on an army bus.

When general manager Branch Rickey of the Brooklyn Dodgers offered Robinson the chance to break organized baseball's powerful but unwritten color line, the fiery ballplayer not only accepted, he also agreed to Rickey's condition: that he not respond to the abuse he would face.

Jackie Robinson's debut in organized baseball is a legend (April 18, 1946, with the Montreal Royals of the International League, the Dodgers' best farm club). In five at-bats he hit a three-run homer and three singles, stole two bases, and scored four times, twice by forcing the pitcher to balk. Promoted to the Dodgers the following spring, Robinson thrived on the pressure and established himself as the most exciting player in baseball. His playing style combined traditional elements of black sports — the opportunistic risk taking known as "tricky baseball" in the Negro Leagues — with an aggressiveness asserting his right to be at the plate or on the basepaths. According to his manager Leo Durocher, "This guy didn't just come to play. He come to beat ya."

In their response to Jackie Robinson, African-Americans rejected "separate but equal" status and embraced integration. Robinson's presence in baseball electrified them, and they flocked to see the Dodgers in huge numbers and from great distances. African-American sportswriters, many of whom had advocated baseball integration for years, focused their attentions on Robinson and the black players who followed him. His success encouraged the integration of professional football, basketball, and tennis, while the Negro Leagues, which in a sense depended on segregation, began an irreversible decline, losing ballplayers, spectators, and reporters.

During his first two years with the Dodgers, Robinson kept his word to Rickey and endured astonishing abuse amid national scrutiny without fighting back. His dignified courage in the face of virulent racism — from jeers and insults to beanballs, hate mail, and death threats — commanded the admiration of whites as well as blacks and foreshadowed the tactics that the 1960s civil rights movement would develop into the theory and practice of nonviolence.

Robinson, however, finally broke his emotional and political silence in 1949, becoming an outspoken and controversial opponent of racial discrimination. He criticized the slow pace of baseball integration and objected to the Jim Crow practices in the southern states where most clubs conducted spring training. Robinson led other ballplayers in urging baseball to use its economic power to desegregate southern towns, hotels, and ballparks. Because most baseball teams integrated relatively calmly, the "Jackie Robinson experiment" provided an important example of successful desegregation to ambivalent white southern political and business leaders.

Having watched baseball integrate through a combination of individual black achievements, white goodwill, economic persuasion, and public outspokenness, Robinson, when he retired from baseball in 1957, sought to bring the same tactics to bear on increasing African-American employment opportunities.

His lifelong struggle continued to his last public appearance nine days before he died: he told television viewers of an Old-Timers' Game, "I'd like to live to see a black manager." Fittingly, his eulogy was delivered by the outstanding advocate of African-American self-help and employment opportunity — the Reverend Jesse Jackson. "When Jackie took the field," Jackson declared, "something reminded us of our birthright to be free."

Jules Tygiel, *Baseball's Great Experiment: Jackie Robinson and His Legacy* (1984).

WARREN GOLDSTEIN

See also Baseball; Racial Desegregation; Rickey, Branch; Spectator Sports.

ROCKEFELLER, JOHN D.

(1839–1937), industrialist and philanthropist. Rockefeller was the primary force behind the establishment of the Standard Oil Company and thus of the American petroleum industry.

Rockefeller was born in Richford, New York, and moved with his family to Cleveland, Ohio, where he finished high school in 1855. He began his business career as a bookkeeper-clerk in a commission house the same year. The first successful drilling for oil took place in western Pennsylvania in 1859, and Rockefeller realized that Cleveland was ideally suited to exploit this new resource. He built his first refinery in 1863 in partnership with others.

The early oil business was chaotic and hazardous, with barrel prices rising as high as $13.75 and falling as low as ten cents during the 1860s, but Rockefeller, a born executive, kept his firm consistently profitable and growing. In 1870 he, Henry Flagler, and others formed the Standard Oil Company, with Rockefeller owning 26.7 percent of the stock. Using such then-legal tactics as railroad rebates and predatory pricing, Standard Oil steadily increased its hold over the American oil industry until by 1880 it controlled fully 90 percent of it.

The corporate structure of this expanding enterprise had become unwieldy, and state corporation laws made it difficult to rationalize what had become a nationwide company. In 1882, Standard Oil's legal counsel devised the trust form of organization. Standard Oil thus became both the first and the largest of the "trusts," one of the great bogeymen of American politics ever since.

As such, it necessarily became a major target of reformers. Although he played the game hard, Rockefeller never operated outside the law or sought an absolute monopoly. Rather, he wanted Standard Oil to be large enough to enforce "order" in the oil business and prevent a return to the chaos that had marked the industry's early years. And despite Standard's near monopoly position, the price of oil and oil products fell drastically between 1870 and 1900. In 1883, Rockefeller moved the company's headquarters to New York.

Always active in the Baptist church, Rockefeller early began the practice of making substantial charitable contributions. As his resources grew, so did his philanthropy. He had largely retired from Standard Oil by 1897 and devoted much of his energy to looking for creative ways to give his money away. He was often guided by Baptist ministers and others, and he established an organization to investigate carefully before giving. Once he had made up his mind, however, he gave with wholly unprecedented generosity. In 1889 he gave $600,000 to establish the University of Chicago (the family would ultimately give it more than $80 million), and in the final decades of his long life he gave away an estimated $550 million to worthy causes. He also established the Rockefeller Institute, the General Education Board, the Rockefeller Foundation, and the Laura Spelman Rockefeller Memorial Foundation.

Peter Collier and David Horowitz, *The Rockefellers: An American Dynasty* (1977); Allan Nevins, *Study in Power* (1953).

JOHN STEELE GORDON

See also Oil Industry; Philanthropy; Robber Barons.

ROE V. WADE

This 1973 Supreme Court ruling proved to be one of the most controversial in the Court's history. "Roe" was Norma McGorvey, who was denied the right under Texas law to abort a fetus she did not want to bear. She sued the state, and the case came before the U.S. Supreme Court. The Court had turned increasingly conservative after the retirement of Chief Justice Earl Warren, the deaths of liberal Hugo Black and moderate John Marshall Harlan II, and President Richard M. Nixon's appointments of Chief Justice Warren Burger and Justices Harry Blackmun, Lewis Powell, and William Rehnquist. Nonetheless, the Court ruled 7–2 that women had an unrestricted right to abort a fetus during the first trimester of pregnancy, but that the state had an interest in protecting the fetus after that, when it became "viable" or able to live outside the womb.

The opinion extended the "right to privacy" enunciated in *Griswold* v. *Connecticut* (1965), in which the Court ruled that a state could not prohibit married couples from using contraceptives; this right to privacy was implied in the First Amendment guarantee of free speech, the Ninth Amendment's reference to "certain rights," and the Fourteenth Amendment's guarantee of due process of law. Blackmun wrote the majority opinion, with Rehnquist and Justice Byron White dissenting.

The ruling continues to cause controversy. Early in the 1980s, the "right-to-life" movement, with help from politicians such as President Ronald Reagan, pushed for a constitutional amendment prohibiting abortion except in cases of rape, incest, or a threat to the mother's life. Although antiabortionists were unable to pass the amendment, they did secure a ban on federal and, in many cases, state financing of abortions. The Roman Catholic church and many Protestant fundamentalist groups strongly opposed abortion. In response, women's groups such as the National Organization for Women stepped up their efforts to elect prochoice candidates. The abortion issue had evolved into a "litmus test" for both liberals and conservatives and had become a trying issue for many political candidates and judicial appointees.

See also Abortion.

ROMAN CATHOLIC CHURCH

With some 50 million members, the Roman Catholic church is much the largest religious organization in America. Yet at the time of the American Revolution, there were only a few American Catholics: mostly people from Spanish and French colonies, along with a handful of English-speaking Catholics who lived mainly in the Middle Colonies, especially Maryland.

Neither Catholic Europe nor the overwhelmingly Protestant United States anticipated then that the new nation would prove hospitable to the emergence of a strong American Catholicism. For one thing, the church was proudly *Roman,* and the new nation was manifestly committed to developing *American* institutions — in religion as well as in politics and economics. Throughout the nineteenth century, furthermore, the church became increasingly ultramontane, concentrating ever more authority in Rome and skeptical of adaptations to national folkways. The Vatican Council of 1869–1870 endowed the popes with ordinary jurisdiction in every Catholic diocese.

Second, American religious culture, almost from the start, was pluralistic; even in those few colonies that attempted to establish the one true religion, dissenting faiths soon were granted considerable freedoms. The First Amendment to the Constitution stipulated that there would be no established religion in the new nation, and no state tried for very long to maintain an establishment. In fact, Protestants quickly came to acknowledge that most other religious groups were legitimate "denominations" of the true church. In contrast, Catholics were obliged by their faith to insist that theirs was the one true church. Catholics could accept the separation of church and state only as an unfortunate necessity in a culture where so many erroneous churches flourished.

Finally, American culture, in religion as in politics and economics, was deeply individualistic, antihierarchical, and anti-authoritarian. Laypeople, speaking for themselves or in concert with a congregation, were accustomed to judge the clergy as functionaries expected to give a moving sermon, preach up a revival, or meet other lay needs. In contrast, the trend in Catholicism, since the Council of Trent, had been to emphasize hierarchy and the authority of priests, bishops, and popes. (Not until the middle of the twentieth century — when Catholics began to stress the "mystical body of Christ," which included both laypeople and clergy, and in the Second Vatican Council, the "people of God" — was the celebration of unqualified clerical authority reconsidered.) Much of the drama in the history of the American Catholic church centered around attempts to transcend these seeming contradictions between Americanism and Catholicism.

The first leader of an American Roman Catholic church was John Carroll (1735–1815), a member of a prominent Maryland family. Carroll, chosen the first bishop of the American church in 1790, endorsed the separation of church and state because he believed it essential to Catholic freedom in a pluralist society like America and because he felt that established churches in Europe had suffered gravely from state control. He argued that the church in America should be headed by a bishop nominated by the American clergy. He wanted also to avoid overclose supervision of the young American church by the Roman Curia.

Carroll believed that American Catholics would be best served by American-born, American-trained priests and hoped that the laity would play an active role in managing their parishes. In his early years as bishop, he endorsed the use of English in the liturgy, believing that free men and women would place a high value on intelligibility. He seems to have favored a private, internal piety more than public, clerically led, devotional exercises. In his later years, however, Carroll was troubled by the lengths to which republicanism had been carried in France and was distressed by the unwillingness of some laypeople to accept the leadership of priests or bishops. Increasingly, he stressed tradition and the virtue of laypeople submitting to the clergy, the clergy to the bishops, and the bishops to Rome. These later attitudes would dominate the American church for the next century and more.

The earlier vision was never completely abandoned, however. Toward the end of the century, a group of Americanist churchmen, inspired by Isaac Thomas Hecker (1819–1888), the founder of the Paulist Fathers, and led by Archbishop John Ireland of St. Paul (1838–1918), proclaimed the perfect harmony of Catholicism with the individualism and activism of American life.

But from the early nineteenth century until the middle of the twentieth, the experience of the Roman Catholic church in America was shaped less by episcopal preferences than by the fact that it had become the "Church of the Immigrants." The huge influx of Catholics — from Ireland and Germany in the middle of the nineteenth century; from Italy, Poland, and the Balkans between 1880 and 1924; and from Latin America beginning in the 1920s — was the major reason for the church's spectacular growth. It also defined many of the tasks the church had to assume.

Until the 1920s, America did not limit the numbers of immigrants, but its welcome was qualified by the expectation that immigrants would speedily Americanize. To some Americans, Catholicism was one of those foreign traits that immigrants should cheerfully renounce. But most of the newcomers, uprooted from their native culture, clung to their ancestral religion not only because of its spiritual claims but also because it served as surrogate for their personal, familial, and ethnic identity. Catholicism was valued and defended for what made it distinctive, not for those characteristics that might be shown to resemble the traits of American denominations. That European Catholicism was, increasingly in these years, stressing the contradictions between modern culture and genuine Catholicism ensured that the immigrant strain in the American church would generally be supported by European church leaders and especially by Rome. As a consequence, the Church of the Immigrants redoubled its efforts to protect Catholics against an American culture, which, one editor wrote, "exhales an atmosphere filled with germs poisonous and fatal to Catholic life." Catholics needed an array of separate institutions — churches, asylums, schools — to shelter them.

Most strikingly, they needed schools. In

nineteenth-century America immigrants encountered a culture that wholeheartedly believed that children could not be satisfactorily educated in the home, the neighborhood, or the church. State after state passed laws requiring all children to attend schools. And state after state established public schools that reflected the values supposedly common to all its citizens. Inevitably, in a largely non-Catholic culture, many of the schools were oblivious to the special heritage, present needs, and future aspirations of Catholics, and some may even have been designed to "grind the Catholicity" out of Catholic children. As a result, Catholics undertook, sometimes reluctantly, to build a separate but equal school system. One bishop after another declared that "a parish without a parochial school is not a Catholic parish" — indeed, that a parish should build a school before it built a church. The fact that at no time did more than half the Catholic children of school age attend parochial schools does not diminish the church's remarkable achievement in providing a school system that would, as far as possible, educate their children in the ways, and to the ends, that *they* — not American society — desired.

The parish also assumed an increasing number of other obligations. Spiritual societies organized a new, more intense, and more public devotionalism. A Rosary Society or a Confraternity of the Sacred Heart required the regular recitation of certain prayers, regular attendance at Mass, regular reception of Communion. By the end of the nineteenth century, large urban parishes frequently sustained a myriad of additional societies designed to meet "spiritual, recreational, educational, and charitable" interests. For a large proportion of Catholics, the parish was the center of their lives.

A common characteristic of all these activities in the immigrant parish was the dominant role of the priest, who, as one observer wrote, was expected to be "cult leader, confessor, teacher, counselor, social director, administrator, recreation director . . . and a social worker." Not surprisingly, priests claimed and were granted enormous authority. Whereas in earlier years, laypeople had sometimes been allowed to help manage parish life, by the mid-nineteenth century priests were roundly condemning lay in-

itiatives as a "trusteeism" contrary to the right ordering of a hierarchical church. In the same spirit, bishops asserted their unqualified right to assign or reassign priests. Taking advantage of American law, bishops constituted themselves "corporations sole," which enabled them to hold all church property in a diocese in their own names. American Catholics, readily deferring to priestly authority, had little difficulty accepting the most extravagant interpretations of papal infallibility.

Most resistance to the exercise (if not the principle) of authority in nineteenth-century Catholicism derived from the presence in many dioceses of a large number of diverse nationalities. Bishops had frequently been willing to create "national parishes," to which all Catholics speaking the same foreign tongue could repair. But when it was not possible to assign a priest of the same nationality, controversies were likely to ensue. German Catholics were less disposed to yield trusting obedience when an Irish Catholic priest was assigned to "their" parish. Bishops almost invariably backed up priests against "disloyal" laypeople. And Rome made clear that in appointing a bishop it would not compromise its authority by deferring to the ethnic predilections of the priests and people in the diocese.

The two dominant notes of the nineteenth-century church — the Church of the Immigrants — were a heightened authority of the clergy and hierarchy and a pronounced public, communal devotionalism for the laity, both of them conducing to a preoccupation with specifically Catholic culture. It is hardly surprising, therefore, that Catholics in this era participated only gingerly in the American society of which they were an increasingly numerous part. They publicly celebrated their patriotism. In New York City, parochial schools installed an American flag in their classrooms before the public schools did. They did probably more than their share of the fighting in the Civil War, World War I, and even the Spanish-American War (which some Europeans saw as an assault on Catholic Spain). But they took no active role, *as Catholics,* in politics. Priests and bishops in large cities with substantial concentrations of Catholic voters no doubt benefited from the deferential attention paid them by machine bosses. But the clergy generally abstained from public partisanship. Most of them recognized that Catholic political action was all too likely to engender anti-Catholic outbursts. They also sensed that the political process was likely to require compromises.

In a century when many Americans were enthusiastic reformers, most Catholics chose to remain on the sidelines. Contemporary culture was undoubtedly sinful, but it was unlikely to be redeemed by social action. Although consistently preaching the virtue of temperance, Catholic leaders were disenchanted when the temperance crusade focused increasingly on political measures. The church sympathized with the plight of the disproportionately large numbers of Catholics in the working class, but it was the exceptional priest or bishop who condoned unions or supported labor legislation. Pope Leo XIII, in 1891, issued an encyclical on the condition of labor, but for a generation American Catholics pointed more enthusiastically to his criticism of socialism than to his demand that the church support the legitimate aspirations of the workers. When the National Catholic Welfare Conference (formed to foster the war effort in 1917) sponsored a program of postwar social reconstruction, the response of the bishops was lukewarm. The Church of the Immigrants would not easily abandon its traditional social conservatism.

By the middle of the twentieth century, however, the Catholic church in the United States had changed considerably. Although new Catholic immigrants continued to flood in — particularly from the Caribbean and Latin America — most American Catholics were no longer immigrants in fact, in memory, or in outlook. By the criteria of wealth, education, and occupational status, they outdid, as a group, American Protestants. They no longer had to fear discrimination; the election of John F. Kennedy, a Catholic, as president in 1960 corroborated the growing conviction that American culture was not innately hostile; the church need not be preoccupied with sheltering Catholics from the age. And American Catholics found in the papacy of John XXIII and in many of the conclusions of the Second Vatican Council reason to believe that Rome would not disapprove

of a more confident, more activist stance in the American church.

The laity was encouraged to participate in new ways in the life of the parish. With much of the liturgy in English and with the priest facing the congregation and praying *with* them, not *for* them, laypeople were invited to sing hymns and exchange greetings of peace with each other. Increasingly the devotional spirit found expression less in parish missions than in meetings where Catholics could respond more personally and individually to the leadings of the spirit.

Fears of trusteeism abated sufficiently for many parishes to establish councils in which lay members could help shape policy. A sharp decline in vocations to holy orders made it almost inevitable that the laity would take on more responsibilities in the work of the church. The traditional conception of the priesthood was sometimes challenged by proposals — not yet accepted by the hierarchy — that women or married men be consecrated as priests. These developments did not constitute a challenge to the authority of the church, but rather an assertion that laypeople were, as much as the clergy, "people of God" with gracious freedoms as well as duties. Although the popes, generally supported by the American hierarchy, continued to proclaim that artificial birth control was a sinful violation of natural law, increasing numbers of American Catholics claimed, as Catholics, the right to act as their consciences dictated.

Many Catholics came to feel not only free but obliged on occasion to call on the nation to reform. Invoking both American traditions and Catholic principles, clergy and laity gave strong support to the civil rights movement, and a few were prominent critics of the Vietnam War. Many were particularly outspoken in demanding social justice, even to the point of casting doubt on the essential morality of the American capitalist system. And Catholics, deploring abortion, have taken a leading role in demanding that the government guarantee "the right to life."

It is no doubt premature to conclude that these striking developments of the latter part of the twentieth century defined the contours of a "new Catholicism." Considerable numbers of American Catholics did not welcome the new departures in liturgical practice, or the new roles of clergy and laity, or the provocative witness of the church against some of the failings of American culture. And the American church's options continued to be limited by its loyal membership in the world church. The pontificate of John Paul II made it clear that the plans of American Catholics remained subject to authoritative criticism (as well as endorsement) from Rome.

Jay P. Dolan, *The American Catholic Experience: A History from Colonial Times to the Present* (1985); James Hennesey, S.J., *American Catholics: A History of the Roman Catholic Community in the United States* (1981).

ROBERT D. CROSS

See also Abortion; Birth Control; Coughlin, Father Charles E.; Day, Dorothy; Ethnicity; Missionaries; Religion; Serra, Junípero.

ROOSEVELT, ELEANOR

(1884–1962), social reformer, Democratic politician, and First Lady (1933–1945). Roosevelt overcame personal adversity and a sheltered upper-class background to become one of the twentieth century's most passionate advocates of social justice and international cooperation. Marriage to her cousin, Franklin Delano Roosevelt, in 1905 brought together two strong-willed personalities whose lack of personal intimacy was more than compensated for by shared values and political goals. Their marriage represents one of the greatest political partnerships in American history.

At the very least, Eleanor Roosevelt expanded, if she did not revolutionize, the role of the political wife. Her genius was to take a position that had no institutional responsibilities or duties and turn it into a base for independent political action. Throughout her husband's public career, Eleanor Roosevelt spoke out forcefully on issues that she believed in and then followed up her public advocacy with behind-the-scenes prodding. As New Deal politician Molly Dewson recalled, if she ever wanted help on some point, Eleanor would seat her by the president at dinner and the matter would be settled before they had finished their soup. The First Lady's support gave an individual or cause instant credibility, and civil rights activists, youth leaders,

WPA administrators, urban planners, and labor reformers were among the beneficiaries. Although Eleanor Roosevelt remained controversial throughout the 1930s, she often won people's respect for having the courage of her convictions even if they did not share her views. The New Deal would have been a far less humane undertaking without Eleanor Roosevelt in the White House.

Eleanor Roosevelt's public image shifted after World War II as she became more identified with international cooperation and world peace. Confounding her critics who hoped she would fade from public view after Franklin's death in 1945, she played a central role in the adoption of the Declaration of Human Rights by the United Nations in 1948, one of her proudest accomplishments. After she retired from the U.N. delegation in 1953, she continued her active support for internationalism. Yet to remember her as a gray-haired elder stateswoman of the postwar world fails to do justice to her influence as one of the most effective politicians the twentieth century has produced. Her wide-ranging involvement in Democratic politics throughout the 1950s continued the pattern set in the 1920s and New Deal years.

Throughout her life, Eleanor Roosevelt supported movements for social change that presented radical challenges to prevailing attitudes and institutions: civil rights for black Americans, full equality for women, liberation for the world's subject peoples, a vision of the federal government as a positive, caring force for the betterment of its citizens' lives. A person of enormous energy and curiosity, she touched millions of individual lives through her extensive travels, lectures, and writings. At her death in 1962, she was widely recognized as the twentieth century's most influential woman, and her reputation has continued to rise ever since. Few politicians, male or female, can match such a legacy.

Joseph P. Lash, *Eleanor and Franklin* (1971) and *Eleanor: The Years Alone* (1972); Eleanor Roosevelt, *This Is My Story* (1937) and *This I Remember* (1949).

SUSAN WARE

See also Roosevelt, Franklin D.

ROOSEVELT, FRANKLIN D.

(1882–1945), thirty-second president of the United States. Born in Hyde Park, New York, the only child in an affluent patrician family, Roosevelt was educated at such citadels of the northeastern establishment as Groton School, Harvard College, class of '04, and Columbia Law School. Law practice bored him, and he early embraced a career in politics, entering with relish into the reform tumult of the Progressive Era.

Two influences shaping his public career were his distant kinsman Theodore Roosevelt, whose niece Eleanor he married in 1905, and Woodrow Wilson, whom he served as assistant secretary of the navy during the First World War. In 1920 Roosevelt was the Democratic candidate for vice president in a Republican year. Struck down by poliomyelitis in 1921, he never recovered the use of his legs, though with braces and cane, buoyant determination, and the cooperation of the press, he managed in subsequent years to convey the illusion of mobility. Encouraged by his wife, he returned to politics and in 1928 was elected governor of New York.

In 1932, at the bottom of the Great Depression, Roosevelt defeated Herbert Hoover in the presidential election. A quarter of the labor force was out of work, the economy in collapse, and the nation in despair. Confronted by an emergency to which no one knew the answer, Roosevelt saw the national government as the instrument of the general welfare and experiment as the method of democracy. Theodore Roosevelt's New Nationalism, with its emphasis on federal regulation of big business, was reborn in Franklin Roosevelt's first term, and Wilson's New Freedom, with its emphasis on antitrust policy, reemerged in his second term.

The New Deal, though sometimes contradictory in detail and uneven in impact, restored national morale and remolded the landscape of American life. In particular, it established the responsibility of government to maintain a high level of economic activity, to provide for the unemployed and the elderly, to guarantee workers unions of their own choosing, to prohibit antisocial business practices, to protect natural re-

sources, and to develop the Tennessee Valley and other undeveloped regions.

Though some, especially in the business community, hated "that man in the White House" as a "traitor to his class," the voters returned him to office by a landslide in 1936. An ill-advised effort in 1937 to overcome judicial vetoes of New Deal legislation by enlarging the Supreme Court broke his political stride, and the forward thrust of the New Deal had come to an end by 1938.

After a sharp recession in 1937, Roosevelt turned to Keynesian deficit spending policies to revive the economy. Despite his reputation as a profligate spender, his largest peacetime deficit — $3.5 billion in 1936 — was insufficient as economic stimulus. Not until war overcame business opposition to government spending were deficits large enough to soak up unemployment, thereby ending the depression and proving the case for compensatory fiscal policy.

In foreign policy Roosevelt combined Theodore Roosevelt's balance-of-power realism with Wilson's idealistic vision of an organized common peace. Concerned from an early point by German and Japanese aggression, he began a long campaign to awaken Americans from isolationist slumber. When war broke out in 1939, he made the United States, over vociferous opposition, the "arsenal of democracy." International crisis led to his unprecedented reelection to third and fourth terms.

After Pearl Harbor, Roosevelt proved a highly effective commander in chief. He also, through the Four Freedoms, the Atlantic Charter, the Bretton Woods arrangements, and the United Nations, prepared the United States for leadership of the postwar world. Agreements made with Joseph Stalin at Yalta provoked subsequent criticism; but it is to be noted that Stalin had to break the agreements to achieve his purposes.

Roosevelt died of a massive cerebral hemorrhage on April 12, 1945. As controversy faded after his death, he came to be seen as a gallant, joyous, and eloquent, if sometimes crafty and devious, president who led the nation greatly through two of its deepest crises — the Great Depression and the Second World War — and reshaped its domestic polity, its role in the international order, and the office of the presidency itself.

James MacGregor Burns, *Roosevelt: The Lion and the Fox* (1956) and *The Soldier of Freedom* (1970); Frank Freidel, *Franklin D. Roosevelt: A Rendezvous with Destiny* (1990); Robert E. Sherwood, *Roosevelt and Hopkins* (1948).

ARTHUR M. SCHLESINGER, JR.

See also Democratic Party; Elections: 1920, 1932, 1936, 1940, 1944; Roosevelt, Eleanor. *For events during Roosevelt's administration, see* Atlantic Charter; Court-Packing Plan; Depressions; Expansion, Continental and Overseas; Four Freedoms; G.I. Bill; Good Neighbor Policy; Government and the Economy; Isolationism; Labor; Lend-Lease Act; Manhattan Project; Marches on Washington: 1941, 1963; Neutrality Acts; New Deal; Pearl Harbor, Attack on; Progressivism; *Scottsboro* Case; Sit-Down Strikes; Welfare and Public Relief; World War II; Yalta Conference.

ROOSEVELT, THEODORE

(1858–1919), twenty-sixth president of the United States. The most dynamic of American presidents, Roosevelt was at once a realist and a romanticist in foreign affairs and a progressive in domestic policy. He was also a fervent nationalist and a consummate moralist.

Born in New York City, Roosevelt graduated from Harvard in 1880. He emerged as the leader of reform Republicans in the New York State Assembly in the early 1880s. Thereafter, he pushed practical reforms as head of the U.S. Civil Service Commission (1889–1895), president of the New York City police commission (1895–1897), assistant secretary of the navy (1897–1898), and governor of New York (1899–1900). He vigorously advocated war against Spain in 1898 and then performed heroically in Cuba as colonel of a volunteer cavalry unit, the "Rough Riders."

Elected vice president of the United States in 1900, Roosevelt became president after the assassination of William McKinley in September 1901. For seven and a half years, Roosevelt strove to balance the interests of farmers, workers, and businesspeople. Despite his image as a trustbuster, he preferred continuous regulation of giant corporations to dissolution under the antitrust laws, and to that end he drove through Congress legislation creating the Bureau of Corporations and strengthening the regulation of railroads. He also supported regulation of the food and drug industries. But his most significant accomplishment was probably the transfer of 125 million acres of public land into the forest reserves, the doubling of national parks, the creation of sixteen national monuments such as California's Muir Woods, and the establishment of fifty-one wildlife refuges.

In 1904 Roosevelt won a full term by decisively defeating Democrat Alton B. Parker. He became increasingly progressive thereafter and by 1909 had endorsed proposals for graduated income and inheritance taxes and other concepts then deemed radical.

In foreign affairs, Roosevelt willingly shouldered the responsibilities of world power. He broke precedents, acted independently of Congress, and held himself ready to invoke force in defense of the national interest if necessary. He arranged to construct a canal through Panama. ("I took Panama," he boasted, with some cause.) He faced down the kaiser over German involvement in Venezuela. He assumed in the Roosevelt Corollary to the Monroe Doctrine the right to intervene in the affairs of Latin American states. And he facilitated, and to some extent mediated, the end of the Russo-Japanese War in 1905. That same year he secretly recognized Japanese suzerainty in Korea and, in 1908, implicitly accepted Japan's economic ascendancy in Manchuria.

Roosevelt's views continued to evolve in retirement, and in 1910 he urged President William Howard Taft to abandon commercial ambitions in North China. Roosevelt also moved beyond the advanced progressive themes of the last years of his presidency. His commitment to an expanded regulatory and welfare program (the "New Nationalism") made conflict between him and Taft virtually inevitable; in 1912, running as the candidate of the Progressive, or Bull Moose party, Roosevelt outpolled his successor in the presidential campaign, which, however, Woodrow Wilson won. An ardent proponent of military preparedness and American entry into World War I, Roosevelt returned to the Republican party in 1916. He strenuously supported the war effort but opposed the League of Nations as conceived by Wilson.

Theodore Roosevelt was the first president of the modern era to react broadly to the challenges raised by the industrial and technological revolutions. In so doing, he contributed substantially to the enlargement of federal power.

Lewis L. Gould, *The Presidency of Theodore Roosevelt* (1990); William H. Harbaugh, *Power and Responsibility: The Life and Times of Theodore Roosevelt* (1961).

WILLIAM H. HARBAUGH

See also Elections: 1900, 1904, 1912; New Nationalism; Progressive Parties: 1912, 1924, 1948; Progressivism; Spanish-American War. *For events during Roosevelt's administration, see* Antitrust Movement; Asia-U.S. Relations; Brownsville Affair; Caribbean-U.S. Relations; Conservation and Environmental Movements; Interstate Commerce Commission; Latin America–U.S. Relations; *Lochner* v. *New York;* Muckrakers; *Muller* v. *Oregon;* Panama Canal; Pure Food and Drug Act; Roosevelt Corollary.

ROOSEVELT COROLLARY

This was Theodore Roosevelt's "amendment" to the Monroe Doctrine. In 1904, the government of the Dominican Republic was bankrupt, and Roosevelt feared that foreign nations, especially Germany, might intervene forcibly to collect their debts. To keep other powers out and ensure financial solvency, Roosevelt issued his corollary: "Chronic wrongdoing . . . may in America, as elsewhere, ultimately require intervention by some civilized nation," he announced in his annual message to Congress in December 1904, "and in the Western Hemisphere the adherence of the United States to the Monroe Doctrine may force the United States, however reluctantly, in flagrant cases of such wrongdoing or impotence, to the exercise of an international police power." Roosevelt tied his policy to the Monroe Doctrine to win public acceptance.

The Dominicans then "invited" American help. The United States took over customs collections and used the money to pay Santo Domingo's foreign debts. Roosevelt and later presidents cited the corollary to justify intervention in the Dominican Republic, Cuba, Nicaragua, Mexico, and Haiti. In 1934, however, Franklin D. Roosevelt renounced interventionism and established his Good Neighbor policy, prompting one commentator to say, "A Roosevelt gave and a Roosevelt hath taken away."

See also Dollar Diplomacy; Latin America–U.S. Relations; Monroe Doctrine.

ROSENBERG CASE

Julius and Ethel Rosenberg were a husband and wife executed in 1953 for allegedly providing atomic secrets to the Soviet Union at the height of the cold war. The case began with the arrest of Klaus Fuchs, a British atomic scientist who confessed to providing secrets about the atomic and hydrogen bombs to the Soviet Union. The FBI soon arrested Harry Gold, a Philadelphia chemist, as an accomplice. Further investigation found that David Greenglass, who had been stationed near the atomic testing site at Los Alamos, New Mexico, during World War II, had provided Gold with information about the atomic bomb.

On July 17, 1950, federal authorities arrested Greenglass's brother-in-law, Julius Rosenberg, a thirty-two-year-old machine shop owner who was accused of serving as a go-between. His wife, Ethel Rosenberg, Greenglass's sister, was also arrested. The Rosenbergs were indicted, along with a former Soviet consular official, for conspiring with Gold, Greenglass, and his wife to obtain national defense information for the Soviet Union because of their communist leanings. The Rosenbergs pleaded innocent, but the Greenglasses testified against them, and a U.S. Court of Appeals jury found them guilty. Greenglass was sentenced to fifteen years in prison and served ten of them. Justice Irving Kaufman sentenced the Rosenbergs to die.

The Rosenbergs and their attorneys appealed the decision to the Supreme Court, which declined their appeal. But in June 1953, Justice William O. Douglas, doubtful of Kaufman's power to issue a death sentence, granted a stay of execution. The Supreme Court held a special session and voted 6–3 (Justices Douglas, Hugo Black, and Felix Frankfurter dissented) to allow the Rosenbergs to be executed. They were, on

June 19, 1953. But the executions did not stop the questions and arguments about the case, which critics have attributed to hysteria surrounding the cold war and McCarthyism. The sentence is now viewed as a miscarriage of justice even by many who believe they were guilty.

See also Anticommunism; Cold War; Espionage.

RUSSIA-U.S. RELATIONS

See Cold War; Soviet-American Relations, 1917–1945.

RUTH, BABE

(1895–1948), baseball player with Boston Red Sox (1914–1919), New York Yankees (1920–1934), and Boston Braves (1935). George Herman ("Babe") Ruth was the greatest player in baseball history and one of the outstanding American celebrities in the years between the two world wars. Ruth's personality merged with his extraordinary baseball skill and the public demands of the new consumer culture to create a larger-than-life figure — a hero of popular mythology.

Within baseball Ruth's legend has four sources. First, he is the only player in history to have mastered completely the two antagonistic sides of the game: pitching and hitting. Thus Ruth was already a marvel when he further astounded the baseball world in 1920 by hitting not only more home runs than any previous player but more than any other team in the American League. Prior to Ruth's home run explosion, baseball strategy had been built around single runs: "scientific" batting (bunts, hit-and-run plays, place hitting), the stolen base, and the careful calculations of "inside baseball." By demonstrating the potential of a baseball offense centered on power, Ruth pioneered a reshaping of the game itself in the 1920s — and the rest of the twentieth century.

Third, the daily drama of Ruth's home run hitting in 1920–1921 and beyond helped deflect public attention from the sordid, unfolding "Black Sox" betting scandal and focus it on baseball's playing fields, so that the game's popularity grew enormously in the decade. The legend that Ruth "saved" baseball is overstated, but it does carry some truth.

Finally, Ruth's sheer baseball skill, and the apparent ease with which he played, amazed his contemporaries and still astonishes historians who have only the statistical record. Baseball has always been such a difficult game that those few who play it well and joyfully and gracefully — players such as Ruth and Shoeless Joe Jackson and Willie Mays — are lifted by fans into the realm of myth.

Ruth's fame spread far beyond baseball. In his trademark camel's hair coat and touring cap he was as well known as he was in uniform. Unlike the heroes of the "scientific" game — most notably the nasty, sharp-featured, intensely calculating Ty Cobb — Babe Ruth was large, broad, round-featured, and easygoing. Writers described him as a child-man, a genial natural who played by instinct and wielded a primitive force through his clublike bat. Boys idolized him and Ruth both basked in their admiration and returned the sentiment to those he called "the kids." Known universally as "the Babe," Ruth himself seemed an oversized child in the delight with which he played the game and lived his life.

Ruth's image was consumed by the American public as that of perhaps no one else of his time. The country's new mass culture, which both invited and represented a loosening of individual self-control, fed on celebrities, and the nourishment Babe Ruth offered to that culture was matched only by his own gargantuan hungers. His appetites were an advertisement for consumption itself. He earned and spent ostentatiously more money than any previous ballplayer. He devoured immense quantities of food and drink; his sexual appetites approached insatiability, and he went through women almost as quickly as he went through silk shirts. On a grand but personal scale, he helped create, and then exemplified, the culture of consumption.

Robert W. Creamer, *Babe: The Legend Comes to Life* (1983); Lawrence S. Ritter and Mark Rucker, *Babe: A Life in Pictures* (1988).

WARREN GOLDSTEIN

See also Baseball; Spectator Sports.

S

SACCO-VANZETTI CASE

Nicola Sacco and Bartolomeo Vanzetti were self-proclaimed anarchists and Italian aliens whose trial and execution in the 1920s earned them international attention as victims of prejudice. Many believed their conviction was based less on evidence than on bias against their radical political views.

In May 1920, Sacco, a shoemaker, and Vanzetti, a fish peddler, were arrested and charged with robbing and murdering the paymaster and guard of a shoe company in South Braintree, Massachusetts. They were found guilty on the basis of evidence that hinged on witness identification and "consciousness of guilt" — despite Sacco's testimony, which was corroborated, that he was at the Italian consulate in Boston inquiring about a passport on the day of the murder. The defendants' radicalism became an issue during the trial, and it was charged that their political views prompted the guilty verdict. Repeated motions for a new trial were denied by Judge Webster Thayer and later by the Massachusetts Supreme Judicial Court.

Finally, in 1927, Judge Thayer sentenced them to death. Their impending execution stirred mass demonstrations and appeals for clemency from around the world. But Massachusetts governor Alvan T. Fuller denied these petitions after a fact-finding committee found no legal grounds for a retrial. Sacco and Vanzetti were executed by electric chair on August 23, 1927, at Charlestown State Prison.

Because the powers that convicted Sacco and Vanzetti were of the upper class, the execution appeared to be class-based. It eventually provided symbolic pathos, ideological justification, and martyrs for a generation of 1930s radicals, and the case was still being written about and debated in the 1990s.

See also Anticommunism; Radicalism.

SALEM WITCH TRIALS

Many colonists in late-seventeenth-century New England combined their Puritan faith with a belief in witchcraft, and charges that one or another person was one of Satan's agents, bent on bringing harm to the community, were common. By far the greatest concentration of these charges occurred in Salem Village, Massachusetts, in 1692. In February, a group of teenaged girls in Salem began experiencing spectacular fits, during which they thrashed about, wincing and shrieking. At first the girls blamed no one, but under repeated questioning by adults, they began to identify a widening circle of local residents as witches and wizards — mostly middle-aged women but also men and even one four-year-old child. Arrest followed arrest, but the fits increased. By the end of the summer, hundreds had been accused, twenty-seven put on trial, and nineteen executed.

Meanwhile, however, discomfort over the trials had been growing, both within Salem Village and in the wider community, including, among others, the Boston clergyman Increase Mather and the new governor, William Phips.

Although few questioned the reality of witchcraft, many were troubled with the chaotic proceedings in Salem. In early October, the governor forbade further trials. In January 1693, he formed a new court, which, working under stricter evidentiary guidelines, acquitted forty-nine out of fifty-two prisoners; the rest were discharged by spring. Accusations of witchcraft decreased dramatically thereafter throughout New England.

A number of historians have linked the witch trials to the painful changes that Puritan society was experiencing at the time. Torn between the communal asceticism of their original goals and the commercial individualism fast overtaking them, some Puritans, the historians argue, responded with guilt and fear, seeking scapegoats on whom they could blame their sense of moral loss. Within Salem Village, a history of bitter factionalism (as well as resentment toward the more prosperous Salem Town, which controlled the village politically and ecclesiastically) may have helped make the witch-hunt in Salem Village the most virulent in New England.

See also New England Colonies; Puritanism.

SALK, JONAS

(1914–   ), developer of the first polio vaccine. Salk's childhood ambition was to study law, but by the time he entered college his interests had turned to the laws of nature that could be deciphered through medical research. He graduated from New York University Medical School in 1939.

While still a student, Salk became interested in vaccines. At the time it was acknowledged that bacterial vaccines could be made from a preparation of *dead* bacteria, which would immunize without inducing an infection. But scientists believed that a *live* vaccine had to be used in order to immunize against a virus. These ideas seemed contradictory to Salk. After his internship he joined Dr. Thomas Francis's influenza vaccine project at the University of Michigan. As a result of Salk's efforts, the influenza vaccine became the first killed-virus vaccine.

Salk then moved to the University of Pittsburgh to direct his own viral research laboratory, where he began developing a polio vaccine under the sponsorship of the March of Dimes Foundation. Because the polio virus is highly unstable and mutates very rapidly, Salk was convinced that only a killed-virus vaccine could be both effective and safe. In 1954 national field trials were conducted for the vaccine he created; on April 12, 1955, the vaccine was declared safe and effective. Salk became an international hero as millions of parents were relieved of the anxiety each summer brought: the fear that their child might be struck down by polio and die or be crippled for life.

At the same time, however, older and more established researchers — some of whom had tried unsuccessfully for years to develop a live-virus vaccine — resented Salk's success. In 1957 the release of one batch of faulty vaccine due to the Cutter Laboratory's failure to follow the correct procedures became fuel for the argument that a killed-virus vaccine was not adequate. Five years later when Dr. Albert Sabin completed his live-virus vaccine, he persuaded the medical establishment to change to his version, administered orally on sugar cubes — despite the fact that a few people every year contract polio from the live vaccine itself. As a result the United States still reports a few cases of polio every year, whereas in countries that use only the Salk vaccine, such as Sweden, Denmark, and Norway, polio has been eradicated.

In 1960 Salk founded the Salk Institute for Biomedical Sciences in La Jolla, California, housed in a much-admired building designed by the architect Louis Kahn with Salk's collaboration. In the 1970s he published five books of essays on human life and the nature of evolution. He also became involved in philanthropy through his appointment as a director of the MacArthur Foundation.

In the early 1980s Salk joined the search for a vaccine for AIDS, and by 1987 he had developed a postinfection, immunotherapeutic vaccine, which is currently undergoing tests.

The brilliance of Salk's contribution as a research scientist has never been fully acknowledged by the American medical community. His insight that viral vaccines do not need to infect in order to immunize was radical when he proposed it, but it has been borne out. His work made possible the modern array of viral vaccines made from killed viruses or parts of viruses, such as that for hepatitis B. Salk's observation that the cells of the immune system resemble those of the central nervous system led him to hypothesize that disease may involve interrelationships among the genetic system, the nervous system, the immune system, and behavior — and that the nervous and immune systems may follow similar patterns of development. In this respect, Salk is one of the founders of the field of psychoneuroimmunology — the study of how mind, nervous system, and immune system work together.

Richard Carter, *Breakthrough: The Saga of Jonas Salk* (1966); Jane S. Smith, *Patenting the Sun* (1990).

D. LYDIA BRONTË

See also Epidemics; Medicine.

SALT

See Strategic Arms Limitation Talks.

SANGER, MARGARET

(1879–1966), pioneer birth-control advocate. Sanger was born in Corning, New York, one of eleven children of Irish-American parents. Her mother was Catholic, her father a radical follower of freethinker Robert Ingersoll and single-taxer Henry George. Sanger later attributed the family's lack of prosperity and her mother's death at forty-nine to her parents' having had so many children. The inequality she observed between them stimulated her lifelong social activism.

Margaret, with help from her sisters, attended Claverack College, after which she went to nursing school. She did not immediately use her medical training because, she later wrote, William Sanger "pressured" her into marrying and leaving school in 1902. Sanger, an artist and architect, moved the family (soon to include three children) to suburban Westchester. While

he commuted to New York, Margaret grew restless as a result of her isolation and full-time housekeeping.

In 1910 the Sangers moved back to Manhattan, and Margaret began working as a visiting nurse on the Lower East Side. She became active in radical politics, joining the Socialist party and working with the Industrial Workers of the World in supporting several militant strikes. From this network she absorbed feminist ideas and came to agree with Emma Goldman that women had a right to control their sexual and reproductive lives. Her work as a nurse with the poor further convinced her that birth control was vital to women's health and freedom.

In 1912 she began to write and speak on sexual and health issues under socialist auspices and was encouraged by her enthusiastic reception. The censorship of one of her columns by the U.S. Post Office in 1913 brought her more publicity. In 1914 she published several issues of the *Woman Rebel,* a radical feminist newspaper, and *Family Limitation,* a pamphlet intended for mass distribution and containing explicit instructions for contraception. A warrant was issued for her arrest, and she fled to Europe, where she studied with Havelock Ellis and Dutch feminist physician Aletta Jacobs.

She returned to the United States in 1915 to find a nationwide birth-control movement under way; the charges against her were dropped. In 1916 she and her sister Evelyn Byrne established a birth-control clinic in Brooklyn as an act of civil disobedience, since providing birth control remained illegal. Such clinics were opening throughout the country, in defiance of laws against them, and attracted many clients.

Sanger became increasingly angered by the Left's refusal to make birth control a priority and decided on a strategy of making legalization of contraception a single-issue campaign. Distancing herself from her left-wing friends, she now sought support from physicians and academic eugenicists. Their influence replaced that of the feminist and socialist movements, then in retreat, and Sanger sometimes used eugenic arguments for birth control — that it could help reduce the birthrate of "inferiors." In 1921 she established the American Birth Control League, a national lobbying group, which became Planned Parenthood in 1942. Very much needing personal recognition, Sanger came to think of birth control as virtually her own invention and her leadership as irreplaceable. Her aggressive campaigning, however, did play a large part in the legalization of contraception by many states between the 1920s and 1960s, though the success was qualified in that contraception became understood not as a woman's right but as a medical matter requiring a doctor's prescription.

After World War II, fears of overpopulation renewed political support for birth control, and Sanger was then instrumental in securing funding for research into hormonal contraception.

Sanger today is still controversial. Planned Parenthood regards her as a modern hero, the founder of birth control, downplaying its longer history as a women's rights issue dating from the early nineteenth century. In contrast, anti-abortionists in the 1980s have cited her use of racist and eugenic arguments for birth control in their efforts to discredit the contemporary movement.

Linda Gordon, *Woman's Body, Woman's Right: A Social History of Birth Control in America* (1976; rev. ed., 1990); James Reed, *From Private Vice to Public Virtue: The Birth Control Movement and American Society since 1830* (1978).

LINDA GORDON

See also Birth Control.

SANITARY COMMISSION

This private organization sought to provide aid and comfort to Northern soldiers during the Civil War. An outgrowth of the Women's Central Association of Relief for the Sick and Wounded in the Army, it was founded in New York in 1861. With the approval of President Abraham Lincoln, it became the "Commission of Inquiry and Advice in respect of the Sanitary Interests of the United States Forces." The Sanitary Commission had to overcome opposition from the Army Medical Bureau, whose leadership resented civilian involvement and questioned the use of women as nurses.

Led by such luminaries as diarist and lawyer George Templeton Strong and the landscape architect Frederick Law Olmsted, the commission inspected sanitary conditions at army camps and provided — and provided for — nurses, ambulances, hospitals, and food. As it gained power in the wake of its success, the commission helped induce Congress to approve changes in the Medical Bureau to promote younger, more progressive surgeons. But the commission also led to disputes with similar groups such as the Christian Commission, whose members felt that their counterpart was less interested in sympathizing with the plight of soldiers than in providing something for the upper classes to do in the war, aside from fighting. In turn, pointing to its record, the Sanitary Commission accused its critics of being too sentimental about the war effort.

The commission had several long-term effects. At the grass roots, most of its workers were Northern women, who thereby developed an involvement in public affairs and some of whom were later active in the movement for women's suffrage. Besides its obvious medical benefits, the Sanitary Commission demonstrated the usefulness of philanthropic groups. It also influenced one of its nurses, Clara Barton, to start the American Red Cross after the war.

See also Civil War.

SARGENT, JOHN SINGER

(1856–1925), portrait painter. Born in Florence, Italy, Sargent was the son of moderately well-to-do American expatriates. Constantly traveling and with enthusiastic parental encouragement, Sargent and his sisters imbibed the art, music, and culture of Europe.

After brief study at the Accademia delle Belle Arti in Florence, Sargent moved in 1874 to Paris, the international art center. He studied with the fashionable portraitist Emile Auguste Carolus-Duran and, after strenuous examinations, gained entrance to the prestigious Ecole des Beaux-Arts.

Early artistic achievements assured the precocious Sargent of a promising career within the Parisian art scene: the Salon of 1877 accepted his *Frances Sherburne Ridley Watts,* and the 1878

Salon accepted *The Oyster Gatherers of Cancale;* in 1879, his portrait of *Carolus-Duran* received honorable mention. Other critically acclaimed works included *El Jaleo* and *The Daughters of Edward D. Boit.* In these years he also sought to establish his reputation in America by sending pictures to the New York exhibitions of the Society of American Artists, a group of younger, Paris-trained painters then challenging the older American academicians.

Portrait commissions began to come his way, but dropped off with the scandal of his 1884 Salon entry, *Madame X (Madame Pierre Gautreau).* This portrait of an American society beauty married to a successful French banker attracted criticism because of what seemed to be the subject's eccentric exhibitionism. Sargent retreated to England where portrait commissions still awaited him. Patrons and friends, including the expatriate American novelist Henry James, urged him to stay, and the following year he established permanent residence in London.

A highly complimentary article by James in 1887 for *Harper's New Monthly Magazine* boosted Sargent's reputation just as he arrived in America for exhibitions of his work in Boston and New York. During his next trip to America (1889–1890), portrait commissions almost overwhelmed him, but he also agreed to paint murals for the new Boston Public Library. Over the next three decades Sargent spent much time in Boston while he finished this commission as well as murals for Harvard University and the Museum of Fine Arts.

On both sides of the Atlantic the celebrated Sargent was sought after to paint portraits of American businessmen and financiers, English manufacturers and their wives, fashionable Edwardian aristocrats, and the English gentry. The international art community admired his style of seemingly effortless, bravura brushwork and dashing likenesses. But he tired of portrait requests and increasingly turned his attention to painting his sisters Emily Sargent and Violet Ormond and Violet's family, and, more and more, holiday subjects in watercolor and oil.

History will remember Sargent as a portraitist in the grand tradition of Van Dyck, Reynolds, and Gainsborough. He captured the poise and authority of the prominent and influential in an era when the British Empire reached its zenith and America had arrived as a dominant international power.

Patricia Hills, *John Singer Sargent* (1986); Stanley Olson, *John Singer Sargent: His Portrait* (1986).

PATRICIA HILLS

See also Painting and Sculpture.

SCALAWAGS

During the period of Congressional Reconstruction after the Civil War (1867–1876), southern white Republicans were called "scalawags" by their political opponents. The scalawags were considered traitors by many white southerners for supporting the party that had led the fight against the Confederacy and had now placed the defeated South under military rule. The fact that the majority of southern Republicans were former slaves and free blacks and that others in the party were newcomers from the North (whom the southern conservatives called "carpetbaggers") made the scalawags' behavior seem even more disloyal.

For many years, historians accepted the conservatives' view that most scalawags were corrupt opportunists, the dregs of southern society. More recent analysis, however, has shown that they represented a much broader variety of backgrounds and motivations. Some undoubtedly were careerists; some were up-country yeoman farmers who had contested the domination of the planter aristocracy for decades; others were planters themselves, often former Whigs who had opposed secession but fought for the South once war was declared. And though many scalawag officials were guilty of corruption, their political practices do not appear to have differed significantly from those of their opponents or of their contemporaries in other sections of the country.

With many former Confederates disfranchised and with freedmen hesitant at first to assert political leadership, the scalawags took the lead initially in establishing and administering the Republican state governments. Factionalism soon grew within the party, however, setting blacks against whites, carpetbaggers against scalawags, planters against men from the upcountry, and businessmen against farmers. In general, the scalawags supported a policy of moderate reform, which they hoped would win over white southern Democrats. They stressed economic development and advocated only the most gradual increase in blacks' political and civil status. The freedmen, on the other hand (often supported by the carpetbaggers), pressed for more rapid social improvements, for enhanced civil rights provisions, and, most notably, for appointing more blacks to public office.

Convinced that such policies would doom the Republicans, the scalawags began to withdraw from the party. As their numbers diminished, the pressure on the remainder to leave became even greater. Their departure was speeded as well by widespread intimidation and violence aimed at both black and white Republicans. The most flagrant of these actions were often carried out by groups like the Ku Klux Klan, but the increasing emphasis on white supremacy within the Democratic party exerted its own pressure, ranging from threats of social and economic ostracism to the most naked demands for racial solidarity. Beset by factionalism, economic crises, and white hostility, the southern Republicans were further weakened by the fact that they received hardly any support from the federal government. Within a few years, many of the scalawags had withdrawn from politics or returned to the Democratic party. By 1876 the Democrats had regained control of every southern state.

See also Reconstruction.

SCANDALS

See Corruption; Crédit Mobilier of America; Iran-Contra Affair; Teapot Dome Affair; Watergate Scandal.

SCHOOL DESEGREGATION

See Civil Rights Movement; Racial Desegregation.

SCHOOLS

See Education.

SCIENCE AND TECHNOLOGY

Two forces shaped the development of American science and technology: internal logic and external circumstance. The first, in the United States as elsewhere, led from individual, small-scale, amateur efforts to organized, large-scale, professional undertakings. The second, arising from the physical and social environment, gave a distinctive national character to those pursuits.

The environmental influence dominated at first. Seventeenth-century scientists, short of books, instruments, public support, and contacts with fellow workers, largely confined their endeavors to mining the New World's immense lode of raw material for natural history and sending their data to Europe for processing. Only Boston, encouraged by the Royal Society of London and benefited by New England's concern for general literacy, developed anything like a scientific community. After the 1720s, as rapid population growth gave rise to towns, libraries, colleges, and newspapers, other scientific centers formed at Philadelphia, Charleston, and New York. Intercolonial and transatlantic communication quickened. Americans began contributing ideas as well as data, starting with Cotton Mather and peaking with Benjamin Franklin. Nevertheless amateurs, chiefly physicians, predominated, depending on Europe for instruments and theoretical guidance.

Americans assumed that science would yield material benefits, but they added little to the English technology they imported, other than adapting it, as in ax design, to their abundance of wood. Their small, dispersed, largely self-sufficient farms held them to handicrafts, though this did foster an ingenious versatility.

Friction with England generated a cultural nationalism that quickened American scientific growth in the 1760s. The Revolution weakened ties with British scientists, disrupted colleges, subjected scientific centers to sporadic enemy occupation, and impoverished, distracted, or commandeered scientists. But the Revolution also broadened intellectual and cultural horizons and challenged Americans in the 1780s to prove that freedom nurtured science. New museums, journals, societies, and colleges sprang up. Although the initial postwar fervor soon cooled, the vision persisted. With little help from science, postwar technology flourished. England's Industrial Revolution pointed the way, and an elastic market freed from class inhibitions called for labor-saving machinery. Transplanted British engineers, mechanics, and artisans added a leaven. The patent system, economic expansion, and natural resources encouraged homegrown tinkerers, and American distances induced a transportation revolution that in turn brought forth native engineers and technical schools in the early years of the nineteenth century.

Meanwhile, under the science-minded President Thomas Jefferson, the federal government entered the picture with the Lewis and Clark Expedition and the Coast Survey. By 1830 states were sponsoring geological surveys, college teaching was providing livelihoods, and public interest was being kindled. Still, American science, concentrated in the Northeast, progressed slowly. Not until Joseph Henry's electrical researches in the 1830s did an American approach Franklin's scientific stature. Under army auspices, exploration of the vast western territories acquired during the 1840s prolonged the emphasis of American science on descriptive natural history and confirmed its tilt toward discrete, short-term, line-of-sight researches — targets of opportunity — a characteristic that would tincture it for at least another century.

Despite those persistent imbalances, modern American science took shape between the mid-1840s and the mid-1870s. Europe demonstrated the new ways of professionalism, specialization, graduate education, governmental and philanthropic support, and collective organization. Americans returning from European study and immigrants like Louis Agassiz carried the gospel back and preached it with nationalistic fervor. An inner circle of leading scientists, jokingly dubbing themselves "the Lazzaroni," or beggars, and including Agassiz, Alexander Dallas Bache of the Coast Survey, and Joseph Henry of the new Smithsonian Institution promoted the Eu-

ropean ways and crusaded against amateurish and sloppy science. They strove for national organization and better communication, especially through the American Association for the Advancement of Science (AAAS), which they helped found in 1847 and dominated for a decade, though the members eventually rebelled against them in the name of democracy.

A major Lazzaroni goal was support without strings, since science was growing too complex and expensive for part-time amateurs. Half of the leading midcentury scientists lived by teaching and a quarter by state or federal employment, but routine chores left them little time for research. Henry wanted his Smithsonian to be a pilot project for unfettered, full-time research, but natural history collections inescapably engrossed it. The Lazzaroni ardently promoted the new German concept of research as a proper function of college faculties. The growing need for advanced university training gave impetus to the idea, and by 1876, when The Johns Hopkins University was founded as a research-oriented school, several colleges were awarding the Ph.D. in science.

To rally public support, scientists artfully encouraged the notion that all technology came out of science, but in fact, most nineteenth-century technology developed on its own. Still, technologists were increasingly adopting the norms and tactics of scientific research and emulating the scientists' examples of higher education, professional associations, and professional journals.

The Civil War, by sweeping aside southern obstructionism, enabled farmers to win federal subsidies for agricultural and technological colleges and let the Lazzaroni wangle a charter for a National Academy of Sciences, ostensibly to advise the federal government. (The government, however, largely ignored the academy until the twentieth century.) Otherwise the Civil War, like the Revolution, sucked scientists into military service or war work, distracting them and diverting support for their projects to war purposes. The AAAS was suspended for the duration, other societies died, and southern science, already weak before the war, was devastated physically and financially. The Civil War was the first major conflict to make significant use of a number of peacetime advances in military technology, but it did not mobilize science or technology to develop more. The South lacked the foundations; hence the North lacked the challenge. Belief that the war would be short, along with pressure for immediate production, discouraged technological research and development by both government and private industry.

The half century that followed the war, however, saw the United States rise to world leadership in technology. Independent inventors like Thomas A. Edison and Alexander Graham Bell became household words, their creations household necessities. Tools of great precision and speed permitted mass production on an unprecedented scale. Some inventors, from Edison to Henry Ford, created elaborate technological systems. The increasing sophistication and urgency of technology compelled the pooling of talents and expertise in industrial research laboratories. Foreshadowed by Edison's famous Menlo Park laboratory of 1876, these matured at the turn of the century under such corporate giants as General Electric and AT&T, overshadowing the independent inventors who had planted their seeds. The new scale and tempo of technology also increased the numbers, specialization, and professional consciousness of college-trained engineers, some of whom even dreamed of engineering a social utopia.

Although the Civil War had tended to centralize government, postwar American science moved toward pluralism. By 1900 the growing state universities were following private institutions in supporting research. Yale had already nurtured the greatest American physicist of the time, Josiah Willard Gibbs. The new universities improved geographic balance by stimulating science in the Midwest and Far West. The federal government remained another locus of support and power, although a congressional commission in the 1880s rejected a call for a consolidated Department of Science. The age of military and naval explorations ended, but the army sponsored notable western surveys in the seventies and won a famous victory over yellow fever in Cuba and Panama at the turn of the century. Beginning in the eighties, the Department of Agriculture conducted scientifically and economically rewarding researches on plants, animals, and insects. Even before the stimulus of the world wars, the burgeoning of government scientific bureaus raised the stature of Washington, D.C., as a major scientific center. Still other centers of scientific power emerged when the vast private fortunes of the Gilded Age underwrote research foundations like the Rockefeller Institute and the Carnegie Institution, both endowed in 1901. And within the scientific community itself polycentrism became the rule. The AAAS reawakened and grew, the National Academy survived and eventually enlarged its role, and specialization gave rise to national associations like the American Chemical Society (1876).

As the twentieth century began, the inner logic of scientific development had superseded physical environment in shaping American science. To be sure, earlier influences had left their mark. The only two American Nobelists in science during the first twenty years of the prizes, Albert Michelson in physics (1907) and Theodore W. Richards in chemistry (1914), won for characteristically American feats of precision in measurement. The British and the Germans still outpaced the Americans, but the Americans were now in the running and bent on taking the lead. Many took up the rallying cries of the departed Lazzaroni: more basic theory, more long-range strategy, less insistence on quick payoffs, more autonomy in research, more balance in fields. The growing weight of university research and private foundations furthered those ends. The growing interdependence of science and technology in both theory and instrumentation made science's claims to public favor more persuasive. And the expansion and democratizing of higher education broadened the base of the scientific community.

Natural history no longer dominated. Chemistry remained strong, though still heavily weighted toward practical application. Astronomy kept its hold on the public's imagination and purse strings. Thanks in part to the rise of bacteriology and foundation-backed research, medicine became more scientific. Thomas H. Morgan brilliantly applied the American quantitative approach to revolutionize understanding of genetics. American physics, once a weak field, had come up to Europe's in quantity if not quality by 1900, though the shift from classical to modern physics subsequently handicapped the mathematically unsophisticated Americans.

World War I aroused public and governmental interest in the enlistment of science and technology, now ripe for the assignment. The resulting agencies had no time to achieve much, but the National Research Council (1916) survived to dispense postwar fellowships, and the National Advisory Committee for Aeronautics (1915) ultimately evolved into the National Aeronautics and Space Administration (NASA) of 1958.

The 1920s saw private support of science at its relative peak. Foundations increased their funding, minor in dollars but significant as seed money for unconstrained research. Herbert Hoover's Commerce Department promoted industrial research, and academic physics developed strong ties with industry. American technology now captivated the mind of Western civilization. "Fordism" and Frederick Winslow Taylor's "scientific management" reverberated not only in art, architecture, and cinema but also in political doctrine from benevolent progressivism to the savage utopianism of Lenin and Stalin and the hideous visions of Hitler. (Ford was the only American Hitler admired.) American scientists still fretted about their international standing and social status at home and about professional elitism in a democratic society. But revolutionary developments in Europe excited the physicists, now braced by more advanced training in mathematics. The same excitement, dramatized by Albert Einstein, reached the public mind and kept support coming even through the depression of the 1930s. Ernest Lawrence moved physics toward "big science" with his cyclotron. Chemists also grew more confident in their theory, and astronomy, already big science, prospered further. And in the 1930s brilliant Europeans, fleeing the rising tide of tyranny, significantly enriched American science.

Thus invigorated, American science in the late 1930s began a half century of preeminence in Nobel Prizes. Not coincidentally, those were the years of World War II and the cold war, an external influence as powerful as that of the natural environment had once been. Scientists were mustered in force for World War II, mainly un-

der government contract at universities or in affiliated establishments like MIT's Radiation Lab. The Office of Scientific Research and Development (OSRD; 1941) overshadowed the older federal agencies. Although the OSRD gave scientists much say in conceiving and developing new weapons, the old issue of scientific self-rule still troubled them, as well as new issues of secrecy and the ethics of mass destruction. The most notable new weapons — radar, the proximity fuse, the atom bomb — sprang from prewar breakthroughs. And it was not basic research nor even applied science but applied technology, the stupendous production of existing weapons and matériel, that decided World War II. Nevertheless the awesome revelation of the atom bomb project at war's end convinced the nation that science could win the next war — or better yet, prevent it.

So a massive, government-sponsored, postwar research and development (R&D) program gathered force from Soviet-American rivalry, fired up periodically by the Korean conflict (1950–1953), the shock of the first Soviet earth satellite, *Sputnik* (1957), and the Vietnam War (1964–1973). The *Sputnik* scare inspired the National Defense Education Act (1958), strengthening the educational underpinnings of science, and led to NASA and the triumphant moon landing of 1969. Serving the cold war arms race, longer-lived government R&D agencies succeeded the wartime OSRD, and the new federal activism extended beyond military concerns to the National Science Foundation and the National Institutes of Health. Federal wealth supported a new age of big science, not only in high-energy physics but also in astronomy and biomedicine, culminating in the nineties with the Hubble Space Telescope, the human genome mapping project, and the superconducting supercollider, as grandiose in scale as in name. And big technology armed science with space vehicles, computers, lasers, and other wonders. Although big science made headlines, smaller-scale science, even in physics, also flourished. In the late eighties Americans produced more than a third of the world's scientific papers.

Not least, Americans led in the postwar computer revolution, springing from a marriage of science and technology and offering each of its progenitors a tool of epochal versatility and power. Although the computer's early theoretical development owed much to European mathematicians from Blaise Pascal through Charles Babbage to William Thomson (Baron Kelvin), Americans dominated the crucial transition from mechanical analog machines to electronic digital machines in the 1940s. The first large-scale automatic digital computer was conceived by Howard Aiken of Harvard in 1937 and completed in 1944. An army team, including J. Presper Eckert, John W. Mauchly, Herman H. Goldstine, and John G. Brainerd, developed the first all-electronic, general-purpose computer, ENIAC (1943–1945). In those years also the ENIAC group, joined by John von Neumann, formulated objectives basic to further development, such as stored programs, random-access memories, and conditional branching. And Americans led in the practical realization of those concepts.

By 1951 Eckert and Mauchly had developed a commercially available line of computers. Industry assumed a major role in extending computer speed and power. American advances in solid-state technology, notably the transistor, and integrated circuits in the fifties and sixties greatly reduced size and cost and increased reliability and speed. Microminiaturization in the seventies and eighties carried those trends to astounding lengths. The new instruments themselves gave new scope and power to both science and technology. Not only in storing, processing, and interpreting immense quantities of numerical data in astronomy, meteorology, physics, chemistry, genetics, and other sciences, but also in furnishing tools for scientific observation, such as space-probe guidance systems, image transmission and enhancement, and noninvasive medical scanning, computers became indispensable. In industry, computers gave new scope to automation, industrial design, business transactions, quality control, air and rail traffic control, stock market operations, and economic modeling. They entered the home in personal computers, word processors, video games, and household appliances. And these lists are far from exhaustive.

Yet all was not glory, gold, and gloating. Although still pluralistic, American science had become a tighter web of universities, government, foundations, industry, and the military; and the weight of government tended to warp that web, tilting university research away from the earth sciences toward microbiology, physics, and other fields. Worse, it herded much of American science and technology into the barrens of weapons development. It also raised fears of political constraints and stultifying secrecy. Polls showed scientists second only to physicians in public esteem, yet much of the public was ambivalent. Creationists, pacifists, environmentalists, antiabortionists, antinuclear protesters, antielitists, and believers in the supernatural pelted scientists and technologists from all sides. The scientists' long-standing ambition to rank first in the world had been realized in absolute terms. Yet the nation ranked fifth in percentage of gross national product spent on civilian R&D, and its students lagged behind those of other nations in math and science. In some areas the technological efficiency and quality of the Japanese, Germans, and others put Americans to shame. The space program, a symbol of big science and technological prowess, suffered a series of humiliating failures and hitches attributable to faulty management and human error, most notably the tragic destruction of the space shuttle *Challenger* with its crew of seven in 1986 and the error in grinding a mirror that crippled the Hubble Telescope in 1990. American science and technology both approached the third millennium uneasily looking over their shoulders.

Robert V. Bruce, *The Launching of Modern American Science, 1846–1876* (1987); Thomas P. Hughes, *American Genesis* (1989); Sally Gregory Kohlstedt and Margaret W. Rossiter, eds., *Historical Writing on American Science* (1985).

ROBERT V. BRUCE

See also Automobiles; Aviation; Cotton Gin; Education; Industrial Revolution; Lewis and Clark Expedition; Medicine; Nuclear Power; Smithsonian Institution; Space Program; Taylorism; Transportation Revolution; *and entries for individual scientists, inventors.*

SCIENTIFIC MANAGEMENT

See Taylorism.

SCLC

See Southern Christian Leadership Conference.

SCOPES TRIAL

In 1925, John T. Scopes was arrested in Dayton, Tennessee, for teaching evolution in his high school biology class. He was charged with violating a state law that prohibited the teaching in public schools of any theory that conflicted with the biblical story of the Creation. In the trial, often called the Monkey Trial, William Jennings Bryan argued the state's case, and Clarence Darrow led the defense team, which was financed by the American Civil Liberties Union.

The case, which received national attention, was the first jury trial brought to the public by live radio broadcasts. Hordes of spectators converged on Dayton, which took on a carnival-like atmosphere that included vendors selling Bibles, toy monkeys, and hot dogs and lemonade.

Judge John Raulston, who opened each day of the trial with a prayer, did not allow any expert scientific testimony about evolution for the defense. Darrow's sole witness was Bryan himself, who agreed to provide testimony concerning the Bible. Darrow proceeded to discredit Bryan, leading him to say, under oath, that he believed Jonah had been swallowed whole by a "big fish"; that the first woman's name was Eve and that she had literally been made from Adam's rib; and that in 2348 B.C. the world had been flooded and all living things inundated except fish and the animals in Noah's ark.

Nevertheless, the jury found Scopes guilty, and the judge fined him one hundred dollars. The Tennessee Supreme Court overturned the decision on a technicality, leaving the constitutional issues unaddressed until 1968, when the U.S. Supreme Court overturned a similar Arkansas law. Bryan, however, had been publicly humiliated (he died a few days later), and the fundamentalist cause had been dealt a severe blow. The antievolution law remained on the books, but it was never again enforced, and evolution continued to be taught in Tennessee schools.

See also Bryan, William Jennings; Darrow, Clarence.

SCOTTSBORO CASE

The *Scottsboro* case involved nine African-Americans, ages thirteen to twenty-one, who were taken from a freight train in Alabama, March 25, 1931, and charged with the gang rape of two white women who had been in the same boxcar. The evidence was questionable, but within two weeks the defendants had been tried by an all-white jury and found guilty; all were sentenced to the electric chair. The Communist-backed International Labor Defense (ILD) took up the case, gained the trust of several defendants' parents, and appealed the case to the Alabama Supreme Court. The ILD also organized protests across the country, dramatizing the "Scottsboro Boys" experience as an example of American racism. The National Association for the Advancement of Colored People (NAACP), after some initial hesitation, tried to get control of the case, but by late summer 1931, all nine defendants had committed themselves to the ILD, causing the lawyers recruited by the NAACP (including the renowned Clarence Darrow) and finally the NAACP itself to withdraw. The Alabama Supreme Court upheld the convictions in March 1932, but in November the U.S. Supreme Court ordered a new trial on the ground that the defendants had not received adequate counsel.

The new trials began in March 1933, with Samuel Liebowitz, an eminent criminal lawyer recruited by the ILD, defending the accused. When the first defendant was quickly sentenced to death again, the Communists organized renewed protests, gaining support from a broad political spectrum that included the NAACP, though the alliance continued to be strained. The U.S. Supreme Court reversed the second set of convictions April 1, 1935, on the ground that excluding Negroes from Alabama juries denied the defendants due process. In 1936–1937, five of the defendants were again tried and found guilty. Charges against the remaining four were dismissed. None of the Scottsboro defendants was executed, but the five who were convicted served long prison terms, the last one not being paroled until 1950.

SCULPTURE

See Painting and Sculpture.

SDS

See Students for a Democratic Society.

SEC

See Securities and Exchange Commission.

SECESSION

Secession, as it applies to the outbreak of the American Civil War, comprises the series of events that began on December 20, 1860, and extended through June 8 of the next year when eleven states in the Lower and Upper South severed their ties with the Union. The first seven seceding states of the Lower South set up a provisional government at Montgomery, Alabama. After hostilities began at Fort Sumter in Charleston Harbor on April 12, 1861, the border states of Virginia, Arkansas, Tennessee, and North Carolina joined the new government, which then moved its capital to Richmond, Virginia. The Union was thus divided approximately on geographic lines. Twenty-one northern and border states retained the style and title of the United States, while the eleven slave states adopted the nomenclature of the Confederate States of America.

The border slave states of Maryland, Delaware, Kentucky, and Missouri remained with the Union, although they all contributed volunteers to the Confederacy. Fifty counties of western Virginia were loyal to the Union government, and in 1863 this area was constituted the separate state of West Virginia. Secession in practical terms meant that about a third of the population with substantial material resources had withdrawn from what had constituted a single nation and established a separate government.

The term *secession* had been used as early as 1776. South Carolina threatened separation when the Continental Congress sought to tax all the colonies on the basis of a total population count that would include slaves. Secession in this instance and throughout the antebellum period came to mean the assertion of minority sectional interests against what was perceived to be a hostile or indifferent majority. Secession had been a matter of concern to some members of the Constitutional Convention that met at Philadelphia in 1787. Theoretically, secession was bound up closely with Whig thought, which claimed the right of revolution against a despotic government. Algernon Sidney, John Locke, and the British Commonwealth Men argued this theme, and it played a prominent role in the American Revolution.

Any federal republic by its very nature invited challenge to central control, a danger that James Madison recognized. He sought at the convention a clause that would prohibit secession from the proposed union once the states had ratified the Constitution. In debate over other points, Madison repeatedly warned that secession or "disunion" was a major concern. The Constitution as framed and finally accepted by the states divided the exercise of sovereign power between the states and the national government. By virtue of the fact that it was a legal document and in most respects enumerated the powers of the central government, the division was weighted toward the states. Yet much of the charter was drawn up in general terms and was susceptible to interpretation that might vary with time and circumstance.

The very thing that Madison feared took on a concrete form during the party battles of the Washington and Adams administrations. And paradoxically, Madison found himself involved with those who seemed to threaten separation. In their reaction to the arbitrary assumption of power in the Alien and Sedition Acts, Thomas Jefferson and Madison argued for state annulment of this legislation. Jefferson's response in the Kentucky Resolution advanced the compact interpretation of the federal Constitution. Madison's Virginia Resolution was far more moderate, but both resolutions looked to state action against what were deemed unconstitutional laws. The national judiciary, they felt, was packed with their opponents. Neither resolution claimed original sovereignty for the states, but both argued for a strict reading of enumerated powers. During the War of 1812, a disaffected Federalist majority in New England advanced the compact theory and considered secession from the Union.

As modernization began to take hold in the United States, differences between the two major sections grew more pronounced: a plantation cotton culture worked by slave labor became concentrated in the South and industrial development featuring free labor in the North. A wave of reform activity in Europe and the United States made the abolition or at least the restriction of slavery a significant goal in the free states. Since abolition struck at the labor system as well as the social structure of the slave states, threats of secession punctuated the political dialogue from 1819 through 1860.

John C. Calhoun, the leading spokesman of the slave states, charged frequently and eloquently that the South and its way of life were under assault from an industrializing North. Like other proponents of endangered minorities, he looked to the Virginia and Kentucky Resolutions and their assertion of the federal compact for the basis of his defense. He argued that a state or a group of states could nullify a federal law that was felt to be against a particular interest. But Calhoun made a fundamental extension of the Jeffersonian concept of states' rights and claimed original undivided sovereignty for the people acting through the states. Although always seeking an accommodation for the South and its slave plantation system within the Union, Calhoun had hoped that nullification was a proper, constitutional alternative to disunion. But he eventually invoked secession with particular vehemence after the territorial acquisitions of the Mexican War and the formation of the Free-Soil party in 1848. Nationalists like John Marshall, Joseph Story, and Daniel Webster countered the Calhoun argument. They declared that the Constitution operated directly through the states on the people, not upon the states as corporate bodies, and their view gained wide acceptance in the free states.

Calhoun was instrumental in fostering southern unity on a sectional basis and in formulating the call for a convention of delegates from the slave states to be held at Nashville, Tennessee, in 1850. There is little doubt that had he lived, Calhoun would have been a formidable force for secession as the ultimate weapon. His death and the working out of a compromise that strengthened moderate opinion in both sections kept the secessionist element at bay temporarily.

But the territorial issue flared up again, this time with renewed fury over the question of whether Kansas should enter the Union as a free or slave state. By now antislavery sentiment had grown significantly in the free states. And opinion leaders in the slave states drew closer together in defense against what they saw as an impending attack on their institutions. The Kansas question created the Republican party, a frankly sectional political organization, and it nominated John C. Frémont for president on a Free-Soil platform in 1856. Although the Democrats, still functioning along national lines, managed to elect James Buchanan president by a slim margin, the slave states threatened secession if the Republicans should win the election in 1860.

The South was committed to an agrarian way of life. It was a land where profitable and efficient plantations worked by slave labor produced cotton for the world market. It was also a land where a majority of its white population was made up of subsistence farmers who lived isolated lives on the edge of poverty and whose literacy rates were low compared with those in the more densely populated North.

The South nevertheless was beginning to industrialize, a factor that added to the social tensions surfacing during the 1850s between the haves — plantation owners and professional groups in the few urban centers — and the have-nots — an increasingly restive yeoman or small-farmer group. But the issue of black servitude provided cohesion for the white bloc and contributed greatly to a patriarchal system wherein the masses of the whites still looked to a planter-professional elite for political and social guidance. Although the northern masses might also defer to the opinions of the powerful and living conditions among the urban poor were precarious, educational levels were far higher than in the South. The ethic of free capital and free labor was deeply ingrained in the cities and in farm communities as well. It was this ethic that formed the ideological basis for a broad antislavery movement.

Southern leaders were concerned over internal stresses in their society and were increasingly aware of the moral and social repugnance the slave system engendered not only in the North but also in Western Europe. Southern leadership, though surely not unified in its response to a political victory of antislavery forces in 1860, began as early as 1858 to prepare its section for separation from the Union.

Even though the Republican platform of 1860 disavowed any move that would interfere with slavery where the custom and the law of a given state upheld it, many of the more extreme opinion makers in the South promoted the idea that a Republican victory meant eventual emancipation and social and political equality for their black population. So inflamed were the voters in South Carolina that before the election of Lincoln, they had chosen a convention that was committed to secession on news of a Republican victory. The situation of other states in the Deep South was more complicated. Elections were held promptly, but the results showed considerable division on secession. Three factions emerged: those for immediate secession, those who sought delay until the policy of the new administration toward the slave states became clear, and those who believed they could bargain with the new administration. All these groups, however, were united in support of the doctrine of secession. With this idea as a basic commitment, the better organized immediate secessionists were able to prevail.

The close connection between the right to revolution and separation from the governing power in the spirit of 1776 was an early theme in the provisional Confederacy. To be sure, the revolution was posited as a peaceful one. Separation from a Union perceived to be under the control of a tyrannical power that would destroy southern institutions was the objective.

Confederate leaders at this early date thought that the North would not fight to preserve the Union. But the provisional government nevertheless began purchasing arms and munitions, and seceded states started to equip and train their militias.

State and Confederate government authorities seized federal forts, arsenals, and other national property within their jurisdiction. When Abraham Lincoln was inaugurated on March 4, 1861, federal troops held only Fort Sumter in Charleston Harbor, Fort Pickens off the Florida coast, and one or two other outposts in the South.

Concerned about the loyalty of the border states of Virginia, Maryland, Missouri, and Kentucky, the new administration went so far as to offer the slave states an amendment to the Constitution that would guarantee slavery where it legally existed. Lincoln himself in his inaugural address pledged only to hold federal property that was in the possession of the Union on March 4, 1861.

The provisional Confederacy likewise sought vigorously to stimulate secession sentiment in the border states. Had all the border slave states thrown in their lot with one or the other government, there might not have been a war, or conversely, separation might well have become an accomplished fact. As it was, however, the prompt action of the Lincoln administration after the bombardment and surrender of Fort Sumter secured Maryland and Delaware for the Union. Kentucky proclaimed its neutrality but eventually remained loyal to the Union. Missouri, too, though a major battleground for the contending forces, contributed most of its resources in men and matériel to the Union.

Once the war was joined, waves of patriotic sentiment swept over North and South. Vocal political opposition would exist on both sides, but it was never strong enough to overthrow either government. Secession as revolution, an early theme in southern rhetoric, was not emphasized after the formation of the Confederacy. Rather, Jefferson's compact theory was enshrined in its Constitution. A nation could not have been formed, nor a war fought, if the states were wholly independent of any central authority.

Behind it all, of course, was the unity of a minority geographical section defending a distinct set of institutions that were thought to be under attack. The original federal Union that shared the exercise of power with the states strengthened the concept of secession. It also supplied a pretext for southern leaders to seize the initiative and form a separate nation.

Bernard Bailyn, *The Ideological Origin of the American Revolution* (1965); Kenneth M. Stampp, *And the War Came: The North and Secession Crises, 1860–1861* (1950).

JOHN NIVEN

See also Calhoun, John C.; Civil War; Confederate States of America; Nullification Controversy; Virginia and Kentucky Resolutions.

SECOND GREAT AWAKENING

In the late 1820s and 1830s a religious revival called the Second Great Awakening (a reference to a similar revival that had swept the colonies in the previous century) had a strong impact on antebellum American religion and reform. It grew partly out of evangelical opposition to the deism associated with the French Revolution and gathered strength in 1826, when Charles Grandison Finney, a charismatic lawyer-turned-itinerant preacher, conducted a revival in Utica, New York. Finney argued against the belief that a Calvinist God controlled the destiny of human beings. He told congregations throughout the northern United States that they were "moral free agents" who could obtain salvation through their own efforts — but, he admonished, they must hurry because time was short.

Finney achieved his greatest success in New York State's "burned-over district," especially in the winter of 1830–1831 in Rochester, where prayer meetings were crowded almost every night, and conversions and confessions of sin were frequent. Finney and other preachers, such as Theodore Weld, tried to be entertaining and to appeal to the average citizen. Their approach

and the new techniques of evangelizing — protracted meetings, communitywide campaigns, the "anxious bench" for those wrestling with the decision to convert, testimony meetings for the converted — worked: in 1831, for example, church membership grew nationally by 100,000.

The Second Great Awakening had effects that extended beyond American Protestantism. The period has been called a "shopkeeper's millennium" because nascent capitalists used church membership and the admonition to work and avoid sin as a means of instilling discipline in workers accustomed to being independent artisans. And by spreading the belief that "heaven on earth" was possible, the revival movement inspired or contributed to many secular reform movements, including sabbatarianism, temperance, abolition, antidueling, moral reform, public education, philanthropic endeavors, and utopian socialism. It especially appealed to women, many of whom were encouraged to become missionaries and lay preachers.

See also Evangelicalism; Great Awakening; Religion.

SECURITIES AND EXCHANGE COMMISSION

The Securities and Exchange Commission was established in 1934 to regulate the commerce in stocks, bonds, and other securities. After the October 29, 1929, stock market crash, reflections on its cause prompted calls for reform. Controls on the issuing and trading of securities were virtually nonexistent, allowing for any number of frauds and other schemes. Further, the unreported concentration of controlling stock interests in a very few hands led to the abuses of power that the free exchange of stock supposedly eliminated.

To bring order out of chaos, Congress passed three major acts creating the Securities and Exchange Commission (SEC) and defining its responsibilities. The Securities Act of 1933 required public corporations to register their stock sales and distribution and make regular financial disclosures. The Securities Exchange Act of 1934 created the SEC to regulate exchanges, brokers, and over-the-counter markets, as well as to monitor the required financial disclosures. The 1935 Public Utility Holding Company Act did away with holding companies more than twice removed from the utilities whose stocks they held. This "death sentence" ended the practice of using holding companies to obscure the intertwined ownership of public utility companies. Further, the act authorized the SEC to break up any unnecessarily large utility combinations into smaller, geographically based companies and to set up federal commissions to regulate utility rates and financial practices.

The business community, wary of New Deal reforms, was mollified by the efficient chairmanships of Joseph P. Kennedy and William O. Douglas.

See also Government and the Economy; New Deal.

SEGREGATION

Segregation is the physical separation of categories of individuals, usually on the basis of gender, race, religion, or class. It can be de jure or de facto — sanctioned by law or custom. Although the word normally connotes an involuntary situation, segregation can also reflect voluntary behavior or some mixture of voluntary and involuntary circumstances. Various types of segregation have been common in American history, but the term usually refers to a systemic pattern that has historically affected blacks more than other Americans.

Prior to the Civil War, blacks in the North and in southern cities were much more likely to experience segregation than those in the southern countryside where there were few opportunities or incentives for segregation. In the North, an influx of European immigrants and the spread of universal white male suffrage between the mid-1820s and the 1840s were largely responsible for the end of an earlier period of less restrictive race relations. Whether owing to custom or — less often — to law, white-initiated segregation became common in schools and public accommodations at the same time that blacks

lost jobs to whites and new limits were placed on black voting. Demonstrating a combination of protest and accommodation, blacks responded to segregation within white churches by founding African Methodist Episcopal, African Methodist Episcopal Zion, and independent local Baptist churches; they countered exclusion from white fraternal orders by establishing black Masonic and Odd Fellow lodges. Although growing segregation in housing was partly due to the desires of blacks, it was mostly the result of white hostility. Blacks prevailed upon the Massachusetts legislature to bypass that state's supreme court endorsement of separate but equal schools and had some success in desegregating train travel, but even in Massachusetts they lost most other challenges to segregation.

White fears of slave rebellions and what were called "uppity" free Negroes produced a slightly different situation in antebellum southern cities. Although black sections of town were beginning to take shape, most slaves lived behind their masters' houses. Some free Negroes and slaves were allowed to organize independent black churches, but most were segregated within white congregations. Blacks also had segregated access to certain theaters and other places of amusement, but most whites preferred a policy of total exclusion. As a result, blacks were barred from the few public schools and social welfare institutions and most places of public accommodation.

The North's triumph in the Civil War initially produced a system of largely de facto but occasionally de jure segregation in the South. Although the first postwar governments led by former Confederates sought to minimize the break with the past, the Thirteenth, Fourteenth, and Fifteenth Amendments, and various civil rights acts, abolished slavery, made blacks citizens with equal rights before the law, and prohibited racial discrimination in voting. Yet the new Republican-controlled Reconstruction governments generally sought to replace the old publicly supported policy of exclusion with one of separate but equal access. With the notable exception of New Orleans, the region's new school systems were segregated, as were poorhouses, institutions for the blind, deaf, dumb, and insane, cemeteries, and most prison facilities. Segregation also existed in militia units, public accommodations, on most trains and boats, and to a lesser extent, streetcars. Segregation thus became the rule throughout most areas of the South's public life, but blacks and their white Republican allies viewed it as an improvement — the separate treatment was to be equal and what it replaced was not integration but total exclusion. Meanwhile blacks were forming their own political and voluntary associations. After initiating an exodus from white churches, they established their own congregations, leaving behind only a handful of blacks in the segregated sections of a few churches. Housing segregation also increased as former slaves left their masters' compounds and joined other blacks on the outskirts of cities in the remnants of antebellum free black enclaves or of freedmen's camps set up earlier by the victorious Yankees.

With the return of the former Confederates to power in the South during the 1870s, the triumph of the Democrats in Congress, and the withering of northern determination to protect the rights of blacks, conditions for southern blacks deteriorated. The new Redeemer governments accepted the shift from total exclusion to segregation but quickly abandoned all but the pretense of equal treatment. Then beginning in the late 1880s, the region's race relations entered a new phase. Amid increased lynchings and anti-black political rhetoric, a coalition of Black Belt planters, elite townspeople, and agrarian radicals disfranchised blacks and passed state and local statutes that extended segregation to cover such new facilities as phone booths and water fountains, legalized long customary discriminatory practices in public accommodations, and eliminated whatever flexibility had survived in public conveyances. In *Plessy* v. *Ferguson* (1896), a case that grew out of a Louisiana statute requiring segregation on the state's railroads, the U.S. Supreme Court held that such separation was constitutional as long as both races received equal treatment. That rarely occurred, but only in *Buchanan* v. *Warley* (1917), a decision that declared legally enforced residential segregation unconstitutional, was any form of segregation

successfully challenged in court. A combination of white discrimination and, to a lesser extent, black choice produced widespread de facto segregation in southern housing. An occasional facility remained integrated into the twentieth century (normally where the lower classes of both races intermingled), and vestiges of exclusion persisted, but by the turn of the century the policy of separate but *unequal* treatment of the races had become firmly entrenched in the South.

Southern blacks sought to make the best of the situation. Long before Booker T. Washington proclaimed in his 1895 Atlanta Compromise speech that blacks and whites should be like the separate fingers of the same hand, a new middle class of black ministers, teachers, and businesspeople had emerged with a vested interest in segregation. Until the middle of the twentieth century, despite sporadic opposition to segregation, most black leaders preferred to attack instances of exclusion or unequal separate treatment.

Reconstruction posed a greater challenge to segregation in the North where, down to the 1890s, the new black vote was often crucial. Although the Civil Rights Act of 1875 (which had already become a dead letter in the South) was declared unconstitutional in 1883, northern state governments not only passed their own civil rights legislation but eliminated antimiscegenation statutes at the same time that southern states were reenacting theirs. Although segregated schools and public accommodations persisted in many places, they were now against the law.

But increased migration of blacks northward after the turn of the century and post–World War I competition with immigrants and white veterans for jobs and housing — sometimes marked by violence — led to the creation of large-scale black urban ghettos with their own schools, community institutions, and businesses. These ghettos had become a fixture of northern urban life by the 1920s, as conditions for blacks in the North and South came to resemble each other more closely, especially with regard to the centrality of segregation.

Prior to the 1950s, northern blacks were more likely than their southern counterparts to challenge segregation per se. But during the so-called Second Reconstruction of the mid-twentieth century the federal government intervened partly in response to demands for change from blacks and white liberals and partly out of concern for world opinion. The North's de facto segregation, however, proved more entrenched, more difficult to overcome than the South's primarily de jure–based system. Today, de jure segregation is a thing of the past, but in many areas, especially housing and public education, de facto segregation persists in the nation's cities.

Howard N. Rabinowitz, *Race Relations in the Urban South, 1865–1890* (1978); C. Vann Woodward, *The Strange Career of Jim Crow,* 3rd ed. (1974).

HOWARD N. RABINOWITZ

See also Black Ghettos; *Brown* v. *Board of Education of Topeka;* Civil Rights Movement; *Plessy* v. *Ferguson;* Racial Desegregation; Reconstruction; World War I.

SENATE

The Framers of the Constitution created the U.S. Senate as a safeguard for the rights of states and minority opinion in a powerful national government. They modeled the Senate on colonial governors' councils and on the state senates that had evolved from them. James Madison explained that the Senate's role was "first to protect the people against their rulers [and] secondly to protect the people against the transient impressions into which they themselves might be led."

To balance power between the large and small states at the Constitutional Convention, the Framers agreed that states would be represented equally in the Senate and in proportion to their populations in the House. Further preserving the authority of individual states, the Framers provided that state legislatures would elect senators. To guarantee senators' independence from short-term political pressures, the Framers assigned them a six-year term, three times as long as that of popularly elected House members. Madison reasoned that longer terms would provide stability. "If it not be a firm body," he concluded, "the other branch being more numerous, and coming immediately from the people, will overwhelm it." Responding to fears that a six-year Senate term would produce an untouchable aristocracy capable of conspiratorial behavior, the Framers specified that one-third of the terms would expire every two years, thus combining the principles of continuity and rotation in office.

In the early weeks of the Constitutional Convention, the Framers had tentatively decided to give the Senate sole power to make treaties and appoint federal judges and ambassadors. As the convention drew to a close, however, they moved to divide these powers between the Senate and the president, following Gouverneur Morris's reasoning that "as the president was to nominate, there would be responsibility, and as the Senate was to concur, there would be security." Consent to the ratification of a treaty would require a two-thirds vote, reflecting the concern of individual states that other states might combine against them, by a simple majority vote, for commercial or economic gain. In dealing with nominations, senators as statewide officials would be uniquely qualified to identify suitable candidates for federal judicial posts and would confirm them, along with cabinet secretaries and other key federal officials, by a simple majority vote.

The First Senate convened on March 4, 1789, in an elegant second-floor chamber of New York City's newly remodeled Federal Hall. Present were only eight of the twenty-two members from the eleven states that had then ratified the Constitution. On April 6 the twelve members necessary to provide a quorum answered the roll call and got down to business. The Senate elected New Hampshire's John Langdon president pro tempore and invited the House of Representatives to its chamber to count the electoral ballots for president and vice president. On April 21 John Adams took his oath as vice president, thereby assuming his responsibility under the Constitution to serve as the Senate's president. Nine days later, House members again crowded into the Senate chamber to witness George Washington's inauguration.

In its first session the Senate cautiously engaged its constitutional responsibilities, mindful of the precedent-setting nature of its every action. Senators gave serious attention to their duty to provide advice and consent to the president's nominations and treaties. A Georgia senator's objection to an appointment of a naval officer in his state resulted in the first Senate rejection of a presidential nominee. This reflected the understanding that senators were the best judges of appointees from their states to which other members would defer as a matter of "senatorial courtesy." When President Washington visited the Senate in August 1789 to consult about a recently negotiated Indian treaty, he expected an immediate response. To his frustration, the Senate referred the issue to committee for further study. After Washington received Senate approval, he vowed that he would never again seek the chamber's advice and consent in person.

The Senate's work load increased greatly during the final weeks of the 1789 session. This accorded with the Framers' notion that the House would serve as the principal workshop for crafting legislation, while the Senate would pass on the representatives' handiwork, polishing and reworking in consideration of what were presumably the nation's broader and longer-term interests. In a second session convened in January 1790, the Senate turned to legislation that would place the nation on a firm financial footing and provided for a permanent seat of government in a special federal district along the Potomac River. While that site was being prepared, Congress agreed to move the government to Philadelphia, where the final session of the First Congress met between December 1790 and March 1791.

During its ten-year residence in Philadelphia, the Senate conducted its proceedings in the second-floor chamber of that city's recently reconstructed "Congress Hall." That chamber witnessed the rise of political parties as the principal determinants of legislative debate and accomplishment.

A clash in 1794 between Federalists and Antifederalists over the seating of newly elected Pennsylvania Antifederalist senator Albert Gallatin brought a partial abandonment of the Senate's closed-door policy. Like the Constitutional Convention, but in contrast to the House, the Senate in 1789 had decided to conduct its sessions behind closed doors. In 1794 members of the Federalist majority feared that their planned rejection of Gallatin on questionable constitutional grounds would trigger charges of arbitrary behavior if done in secret. Opposition to the closed-door policy came principally from the state legislatures, whose members argued that they could not effectively assess the conduct of the senators they had elected if they operated in secret. Press coverage of open sessions in the House of Representatives helped popularize that body's role. The Senate was in danger of becoming the forgotten chamber. (The same attitude played a part when the Senate decided to allow its proceedings to be televised in 1986, seven years after the House.) Consequently, the Senate opened its doors for all legislative business, although the doors would remain closed for executive business related to presidential nominations and treaties until 1929.

On November 21, 1800, the Senate took up residence in basement quarters in the unfinished Capitol at Washington. In the following decade, the Senate moved to a grander chamber on the Capitol's second floor, where it remained until 1859. This large, semicircular room, with its plain walls and low-vaulted domed ceiling, provided an ideal setting, both acoustically and dramatically, for the Senate as it moved into its so-called golden age. Although the Senate operated in the shadow of the larger and more boisterous House of Representatives for the first three decades after its move to Washington, it dominated the House and the presidency, with the exception of the Civil War years, for the remainder of the nineteenth century.

In 1833 the Senate's membership had risen to only 48, compared with 242 in the House of Representatives. With fewer numbers and equal balance between slave and free states, the Senate offered a forum better suited to lively and discursive debate. In the face of growing national tensions associated with federal authority versus states' rights and the extension of slavery into the nation's territories, the Senate served as a workshop for fashioning major compromise agreements. In this era Daniel Webster most dramatically articulated northern interests; John C. Calhoun those of the South; and Henry Clay, Thomas Hart Benton, and Stephen A. Douglas those of the West. The sectional accords they vigorously debated bought time for a maturing nation. When civil war could no longer be held back, the national government had amassed the experience, balance, and strength to guarantee its survival under the Constitution.

The nation's territorial expansion in this era produced five new states between 1845 and 1850, and new quarters were needed to accommodate the additional members. On January 4, 1859, the Senate's sixty-four members moved to a larger chamber in the Capitol's newly completed north wing. This room, in which the Senate has met since that day, witnessed the crisis of the Civil War. In 1868, amid the turmoil of postwar reconstruction, it provided the setting for President Andrew Johnson's impeachment trial. (Seven years later Johnson would become the only former president to return to serve in the Senate.)

The Republican party controlled the Senate's majority from 1861 to 1913, with the exception of the 1879 and 1893 Congresses. During the final decades of the nineteenth century, chairmen of major committees exercised great power on the Senate floor. Most members, viewing the Senate as a way station in a political or business career, served only a single term. In an institution that had come to assign power on the basis of seniority, a few long-term senators, through the newly developed party caucus system, controlled key legislative strategy decisions.

In 1913 the Democrats won control and established the position of majority floor leader to push through the party's legislative agenda. Within a decade the post of party floor leader achieved the primacy in conducting the Senate's business that it possesses in modern times. A second major change in the Senate's structure occurred in 1913 with the ratification of the Constitution's Seventeenth Amendment, providing for direct popular election of senators. Selection of senators by state legislatures had worked reasonably well for half a century, but eventually deadlocks began to occur between the upper

and lower houses of those bodies. This delayed state legislative business and deprived states of their full Senate representation. By the start of the twentieth century, direct popular election of senators had become a major objective for progressive reformers who sought to remove control of government from the influence of special interests and corrupt state legislators. Although this amendment did not significantly affect the quality of persons subsequently elected to the Senate, its passage marked the only structural modification of the Framers' original design of the institution.

The Constitution's Framers would likely recognize several of the modern Senate's roles, particularly its unique constitutional responsibility to provide advice and consent to nominations and treaties. During the Senate's first two centuries it objected to few cabinet nominees and rejected only eight. This reflected an attitude that presidents were entitled to choose their own advisers, unless those officials clearly demonstrated unfitness to serve. The Senate gave greater scrutiny, however, to judicial nominees with lifetime tenure. Directing particular attention to the Supreme Court, the Senate rejected approximately 20 percent of those nominated to the nation's highest tribunal. Of the thousands of treaties submitted, the Senate turned down fewer than two dozen, but it routinely influenced treaty negotiations with threats of modification through the addition of amendments, reservations, or understandings.

The Framers would also find much in the Senate, as in modern America, that would surprise them. They would surely be amazed that the Senate has grown to one hundred members, with seven thousand staff members housed in immense office buildings, or that members tend to view service as a long-term career. And they would be surprised at the importance the Senate accords to its committee system. In its earliest years, the Senate relied on temporary committees to draft specific legislative language after the entire body had reached a consensus regarding a measure's general objectives. The War of 1812 demonstrated the need for consistently available expertise based in permanent, or standing, committees. In 1816, the Senate established permanent committees organized according to the broad categories of the president's annual message. Throughout the late nineteenth and early twentieth centuries, Senate committees proliferated. At a time when only committee chairmen had staff and office space, the number of committees nearly equaled the number of members. In 1920 and again after World War II, the Senate eliminated many committees. Since the 1950s the Senate has provided committees with significant professional staff resources and has enacted reforms to minimize the autocratic control by chairs that had existed earlier.

Since the 1920s Senate committees have taken on a greater investigative role. Among the most notable special investigations have been those of oil leasing in the 1920s, securities regulation in the 1930s, war profiteering in the 1940s, organized crime in the 1950s, Vietnam in the 1960s, Watergate in the 1970s, and covert intelligence operations in the 1980s. Through its combined investigative and legislative powers, the Senate has sought to preserve its balance with the presidency, supporting presidential initiatives while maintaining vigilant oversight of executive branch operations.

In retrospect, the Constitution's Framers would appreciate the Senate's passion for deliberation, its untidiness, its aloofness from the House of Representatives, and its suspicion of the presidency. Neither they nor most of the eighteen hundred persons (including sixteen women) who served as senators during the first two hundred years would be surprised at the continuing calls for reform. Viewed over the broad sweep of its history, the U.S. Senate has demonstrated the ability to balance faithfulness to the Constitution's principles with requirements for measured change in response to the complex demands of a diverse society.

Richard Allan Baker, *The Senate of the United States: A Bicentennial History* (1988); Robert C. Byrd, *The Senate, 1789–1989: Addresses on the History of the United States Senate,* 2 vols. (1988, 1990).

RICHARD ALLAN BAKER

See also Calhoun, John C.; Clay, Henry; Constitution; Douglas, Stephen A.; House of Representatives; McCarthy, Joseph R.; Philadelphia Convention; Sumner, Charles; Webster, Daniel.

SENECA FALLS CONVENTION

The Seneca Falls Convention, held in Seneca Falls, New York, on July 19–20, 1848, was the first public political meeting in the United States dealing with women's rights. It issued the "Seneca Falls Declaration of Sentiments" (modeled on the Declaration of Independence), enumerating the ways in which men had oppressed American women, including depriving them of the vote, of equal property rights, of equal access to employment and education — in short, of the full rights and privileges of citizens. The "Resolutions," which accompanied the "Declaration of Sentiments," were unanimously approved, except for one demanding the vote. Some participants felt this demand was too extreme; others believed women should avoid being drawn into politics. The suffrage plank did pass, but by a narrow majority.

The Seneca Falls Convention was organized by Lucretia Mott and Elizabeth Cady Stanton, two Quakers whose concern for women's rights was heightened when Mott, as a woman, was denied a seat at an international antislavery meeting in London. In 1848, at Stanton's home near Seneca Falls, the two women, working with Martha Wright (Mott's sister), Mary Ann McClintock, and Jane Hunt, sent out a call for a women's conference to be held a week later at the Wesleyan Chapel in Seneca Falls. The meeting attracted 240 people, including — unexpectedly — 40 men (among them, Frederick Douglass, the ex-slave abolitionist). Daunted by the size of the gathering, the organizers persuaded Mott's husband, James, to chair the meeting. In spite of the men's participation, however, the resolutions approved at the meeting explicitly blamed men for the injustices women were suffering and made clear that women must rely on themselves to achieve their emancipation.

The convention was followed two weeks later by an even larger meeting in Rochester, New York. Thereafter, national women's conventions were held annually, providing an important focus for the growing women's rights movement.

See also Feminist Movement.

SERRA, JUNÍPERO

(1713–1784), Franciscan missionary and founder of Spanish missions in California. Born on the island of Mallorca, Spain, Serra became a Franciscan novice at age sixteen. He chose as his confirmation name and patron Brother Juniper, the legendary friend of Saint Francis of Assisi, who was known for his good-spiritedness and self-abnegation.

After his ordination, Serra taught theology and was awarded his doctorate in 1742. Among his first students at the Convent of San Francisco in Mallorca was Francisco Palou, who later became a fellow missionary in Mexico and California and served as Serra's chronicler and first biographer. In 1748, setting aside a comfortable career as a recognized theologian and priest, Serra, along with Palou, traveled to Mexico to take up a foreign mission.

In the New World, Serra quickly became an important figure. Noted for his religious enthusiasm and self-discipline, he amazed Native Americans and religious Spanish alike by flagellating himself during sermons, persistently following the Franciscan injunction to travel on foot despite crippling ulcerations in his foot and leg, and facing threats of death with equanimity. Moreover, he was an able administrator and advocate for church interests to the Spanish government. In 1767, after the Jesuits were expelled from Spain and Mexico by Carlos III, Serra was appointed to head up a Franciscan missionary effort in northern California. He dreamed of establishing fifty missions and eventually founded nine, from San Diego to San Francisco, overseeing their administration to the time of his death.

Serra was appointed to the tribunal and commissary of the Inquisition for the Sierra Gorda region in 1752. Although Palou records his "zealous" reputation, he only vaguely suggests the scope of Serra's role in the Inquisition. The handful of documents that have been located by scholars portray only marginal involvement.

From his first mission assignment at Sierra Gorda (1750), Serra established a pattern of interceding on behalf of the land interests of converted Native Americans. When Spanish settlers and soldiers tried to dispossess the Pames Indians of their mission lands, Serra petitioned the Mexican viceroy to disband the Spanish settlement — and won. Later, in similar conflicts — for instance, that between the Santa Clara Mission Indians and the Pueblo San Jose — Serra did not prevail over local Spanish colonial interests.

Serra was more consistently successful in his lifelong goal of converting Native Americans to Catholicism. Late in life, after establishing nine missions, he obtained a grant from the pope allowing him to confirm Native American Catholic novitiates in 1778. For the next six years, Serra traveled tirelessly on foot, making roughly fifty-three hundred confirmations. He died just months after his patent expired.

Junípero Serra has been a controversial figure in the Catholic church. He was designated "venerable" by John Paul II in 1985 and subsequently considered for sainthood. This honor, however, was protested by Native American and other Catholic activists, who questioned this move as a general endorsement of the exploitative colonization of Native Americans. Although Serra was known to have argued on behalf of the property rights and economic entitlement of converted Native Americans, he consistently advocated against their right to self-governance. He was, further, a staunch supporter of corporal punishment, appealing to the Spanish government for an extension of friars' jurisdiction to flog Indians.

Daniel Fogel, *Junípero Serra, the Vatican, and Enslavement Theology* (1988); Maynard Geiger, O.F.M., *The Life and Times of Junípero Serra, O.F.M.: The Man Who Never Turned Back (1713–1784)* (1959).

DANA D. NELSON SALVINO

See also French and Spanish Settlements; Missionaries.

SETTLEMENT HOUSES

The settlement movement was part of a broad attempt to preserve human values in an urban and industrial age. Samuel A. Barnett, an Anglican clergyman, founded Toynbee Hall, the first settlement in the slums of East London in 1884. The settlement idea, as formulated by Barnett, was to have university men "settle" in a working-class neighborhood where they would not only help relieve poverty and despair but also learn something about the real world from the people of the slums.

Several Americans were independently influenced by the English experiment including Stanton Coit who founded Neighborhood Guild, the first American settlement, on the Lower East Side of New York City in 1886. In 1889 Jane Addams and her Rockford College classmate, Ellen Starr, founded Hull-House (soon to be the most famous settlement) in a run-down mansion on the West Side of Chicago. Just a week earlier, with no knowledge of the Chicago project, a group of young college women, many of them graduates of Smith, had opened the College Settlement in New York.

The settlement idea spread rapidly in the United States. There were seventy-four settlements in 1897, over a hundred in 1900, and more than four hundred in 1910. Most of these were in large cities (40 percent in Boston, Chicago, and New York), but most small cities and many rural communities boasted at least one settlement. In the early years the settlements were financed entirely by donations, and the residents themselves paid for their room and board. Some settlements were associated with religious groups. Many were little more than missions, but Hull-House in Chicago, Henry Street Settlement in New York, and several others had an important impact on the reform movements of the Progressive Era.

The American settlement movement diverged from the English model in several ways. More women became leaders in the American movement, and there was a greater interest in social research and reform. But probably the biggest difference was the presence around the American settlements of a diverse ethnic population. Working with recent immigrants, trying to ease their adjustment to the new country, and acting as their advocate in the neighborhood and the nation became a primary function of the American workers. They did not escape the prejudice nor completely overcome the ethnic stereotypes common to their generation, however, and they tried consciously to teach middle-class values, often betraying a paternalistic attitude toward the poor. Yet they also organized immigrant protective associations, sponsored festivals and pageants, and tried to preserve each group's heritage. On the other hand, and this was typical of progressivism, most settlements were segregated. Although Hull-House and other settlements helped establish separate institutions for black neighborhoods, pioneered in studying black urban communities, and helped organize the National Association for the Advancement of Colored People, blacks were not welcome at the major settlements.

To serve their neighborhoods, most settlement workers started with clubs, classes, lectures, and art exhibitions. They usually had better luck attracting women and children. Some men would come to play basketball, but no settlement ever replaced the local saloon as a male social center. The settlements added programs as they discovered a need. They pioneered in the kindergarten movement, taught English, and established theaters, courses in industrial education, and music schools (Benny Goodman learned to play the clarinet at Hull-House).

The settlement program often led the residents outside their neighborhoods. They became housing reformers, campaigned for anti–child labor laws, and established parks and playgrounds. They also wrote reports, prepared statistical studies, and described their personal experiences in memoirs (*Hull-House Maps and Papers,* Robert Woods's *City Wilderness,* Jane Addams's *Twenty Years at Hull-House,* and Lillian Wald's *House on Henry Street* all became classics).

Settlements had an impact on only a small percentage of the immigrant community, though an immigrant like Francis Hackett said simply, "Life began for me in a social settlement." A Catholic church a few blocks from Hull-House and a Jewish club down the street from Henry

Street Settlement probably had a greater influence on their communities. But the settlements and their residents had a larger impact on the nation. The settlements not only led a variety of reform movements but also influenced the lives and attitudes of the young men and women who spent a year or two in residence. In the beginning those at the settlements were not trained social workers; many were recent college graduates and they often held other jobs while living at the settlement. Especially for unmarried women the settlement provided an acceptable alternative to living alone or with family. The maid service and the public kitchen freed them from the task of keeping house. But more important, the living arrangements often provided stimulating companionship and close personal relationships and encouraged cooperative reform efforts.

The settlements became training grounds for new careers in government, industry, and the universities. Jane Addams, Lillian Wald, Robert Woods, and a few others spent their working lives in the settlements, but others moved on to careers that were largely invented there. Florence Kelley left to become director of the National Consumers' League. Julia Lathrop became the first head of the Children's Bureau. Grace Abbott was the director of the Immigrants' Protective League before replacing Lathrop at the Children's Bureau. Alice Hamilton left Hull-House to become the first woman professor at the Harvard Medical School and an expert on industrial medicine. Sophonisba Breckinridge and Edith Abbott were leaders in the new professional field of social work. In addition many settlement graduates played important roles in the New Deal. Frances Perkins and Harry Hopkins were the most prominent, and Eleanor Roosevelt, a settlement volunteer in her early years, was strongly influenced by the movement.

Settlements began to change in the 1920s as social work became more professional and concerned with psychiatric adjustment rather than with changing society. Because of financial problems, many settlements became dependent on the United Fund and thus lost some of their independence. Shifting populations and urban renewal in the period after World War II forced many to move. In 1980 there were at least eight hundred settlements in the country, but most called themselves neighborhood centers, and all had given up the requirement that workers should live in the settlement. Still, many provided needed services for senior citizens, disadvantaged youths, and battered women and children. The settlement movement was no longer in the vanguard of a national reform movement, but in many cities it still represented a measure of hope in a time of despair.

Mary Lynn McCree Bryan and Allen F. Davis, eds., *One Hundred Years at Hull-House* (1990); Allen F. Davis, *Spearheads for Reform: The Social Settlements and the Progressive Movement, 1890–1914*, 2nd ed. (1984); Judith Ann Trolander, *Professionalism and Social Change: From the Settlement House Movement to Neighborhood Centers, 1886 to the Present* (1987).

ALLEN F. DAVIS

See also Addams, Jane; Hamilton, Alice; Kelley, Florence; Perkins, Frances; Progressivism; Roosevelt, Eleanor.

SETTLEMENTS

See French and Spanish Settlements.

SEVEN YEARS' WAR

The Seven Years' War (called the French and Indian War in the colonies) lasted from 1756 to 1763, forming a chapter in the imperial struggle between Britain and France called the Second Hundred Years' War. In the early 1750s, France's expansion into the Ohio River valley repeatedly brought it into conflict with the claims of the British colonies, especially Virginia. During 1754 and 1755, the French defeated in quick succession the young George Washington, Gen. Edward Braddock, and Braddock's successor, Governor William Shirley of Massachusetts. In 1755, Governor Shirley, fearing that the French settlers in Nova Scotia (Acadia) would side with France in any military confrontation, expelled hundreds of them to other British colonies; many of the exiles suffered cruelly. Throughout this period, the British military effort was hampered by lack of interest at home, rivalries among the American colonies, and France's greater success in winning the support of the Indians. In 1756 the British formally declared war (marking the official beginning of the Seven Years' War), but their new commander in America, Lord Loudoun, faced the same problems as his predecessors and met with little success against the French and their Indian allies.

The tide turned in 1757 because William Pitt, the new British leader, saw the colonial conflicts as the key to building a vast British empire. Borrowing heavily to finance the war, he paid Prussia to fight in Europe and reimbursed the colonies for raising troops in North America. In July 1758, the British won their first great victory at Louisbourg, near the mouth of the St. Lawrence River. A month later, they took Fort Frontenac at the western end of the river. Then they closed in on Quebec, where Gen. James Wolfe won a spectacular victory on the Plains of Abraham, September 1759 (though both he and the French commander, the Marquis de Montcalm, were fatally wounded). With the fall of Montreal in September 1760, the French lost their last foothold in Canada. Soon, Spain joined France against England, and for the rest of the war Britain concentrated on seizing French and Spanish territories in other parts of the world.

At the peace conference in 1763, the British received Canada from France and Florida from Spain, but permitted France to keep its West Indian sugar islands and gave Louisiana to Spain. The treaty strengthened the American colonies significantly by removing their European rivals to the north and south and opening the Mississippi Valley to westward expansion.

See also Colonial Wars.

SEWARD, WILLIAM H.

(1801–1872), New York politician and secretary of state. Seward was one of the major political figures of the mid-nineteenth century. Born in New York, he graduated from Union College and was admitted to the bar, afterward setting up a law office in Auburn, New York. But politics quickly became Seward's main interest. He served in the state senate as an Anti-Mason and in 1838 was elected governor as a Whig. His two terms in office were controversial: he proposed a costly internal improvements program, advocated tax support for parochial schools, and endorsed antislavery principles.

In 1848, he was elected to the U.S. Senate, where he opposed Henry Clay's compromise proposals in 1850 and promoted Winfield Scott's nomination in 1852 over his state rival President Millard Fillmore. When the Kansas-Nebraska bill reignited the slavery issue in 1854, Seward opposed the repeal of the Missouri Compromise, but wishing to maintain the Whigs' national organization, he held aloof from the Republican party and denounced the nativist Know-Nothing organization. Only in 1855, after he had been reelected, did he embrace the Republican movement.

From 1855 to 1860, Seward was the most prominent Republican leader in the country. Filled with presidential ambitions and underestimating the power of his words, he pursued an erratic course. He called for the immediate admission of Kansas as a free state and denounced the *Dred Scott* decision as a proslavery conspiracy, yet urged an alliance with Stephen A. Douglas in 1858 after the Illinois Democrat opposed Kansas's admission under the proslavery Lecompton constitution. In a speech that year he proclaimed there was an irrepressible conflict between slavery and freedom; two years later, in an unsuccessful bid for the Republican nomination, he insisted that the party posed no threat to the South. Passed over by the Republican convention because of his radical antislavery reputation (largely undeserved) and the bitter hostility of the nativists, he faithfully campaigned for Abraham Lincoln. During the secession crisis, his invincible optimism blinded him to its true nature, and he continued to believe that the Union could be peacefully restored.

In recognition of Seward's stature in the party, Lincoln named him secretary of state. Laboring under the mistaken assumption that he would be the real leader of the administration, Seward initially made some serious missteps, but before long he emerged as Lincoln's closest adviser in the cabinet. He conducted diplomatic affairs with a firm and steady hand, helped rally northern public opinion, and adroitly parried Confederate efforts to gain diplomatic recognition in Europe. After the war, he induced the French to leave Mexico and purchased Alaska (called at the time "Seward's icebox") from Russia. He remained in office under Andrew Johnson and supported the president's lenient Reconstruction program. When he retired in 1869, his health had deteriorated, and he died three years later.

Seward was a complex personality. At heart a conservative, he nevertheless had a reputation for radicalism, and although he was often courageous and independent, he tended to take up the latest cause in a bid for popularity. He was at times inconsistent, yet he remained flexible in pursuing political goals. He ranks as one of the greatest secretaries of state in American history.

David P. Crook, *The North, the South, and the Powers, 1861–1865* (1974); Glyndon Van Deusen, *William Henry Seward: Lincoln's Secretary of State* (1967).

WILLIAM E. GIENAPP

See also Alaska Purchase; Anti-Masons; Civil War; Compromise of 1850; Kansas-Nebraska Act; Lincoln, Abraham; Missouri Compromise; Nativism; Republican Party; Whig Party.

SHAKERS

The Shakers, a perfectionist utopian movement, originated in Manchester, England, after Ann Lee, a member of the Shaking Quakers, had a visionary experience. She claimed to have seen Adam and Eve in sexual intercourse, after which Jesus enjoined her to teach others that lust was the source of sin. Her ideas about lust and corruption were intensified by the death of her four children. Thereafter, she suffered a dread of sexual relations and formed a religious order based on celibacy.

In 1774 Lee moved her group to America. They settled first near Albany, New York, but after Lee's death in 1784, they moved to New Lebanon, New York. By 1822 there were four thousand Shakers in more than a dozen communities.

In the 1780s leaders initiated a cooperative economic system and organized communes composed of extended "families." Shaker communities abolished private property, regulated all behavior, and imposed mandatory confessions. Organized around the concept of celibacy, Shaker communities kept men and women carefully segregated. Children were raised communally. Their religious services provided emotional release through trembling, speaking in tongues, and falling into trances — hence, the name Shakers.

Membership turnover was always high, but before 1830 many members stayed for decades. Often whole families joined. Shaker population reached its peak of about five to six thousand during the 1830s but then dropped dramatically. Shakers were renowned for their original styles of vocal music, crafts, and architecture. Adhering to the idea that form follows function, they created furniture designs that are highly prized for their simple lines and functionality. Shakers invented an impressive array of devices from the common clothespin and the flat broom to a revolving oven and a folding stereoscope. They pioneered the industry of herbal medicines and the selling of garden seeds in packets.

See also Lee, Ann; Religion; Utopian Communities.

SHARECROPPING

See Plantation System; Reconstruction.

SHAYS' REBELLION

Shays' Rebellion is the name given to a series of protests in 1786 and 1787 by American farmers against state and local enforcement of tax collections and judgments for debt. Although farmers took up arms in states from New Hampshire to South Carolina, the rebellion was most serious in Massachusetts, where bad harvests, economic depression, and high taxes threatened farmers with the loss of their farms. The rebellion took its name from its symbolic leader, Daniel Shays of Massachusetts, a former captain in the Continental army.

The uprising in Massachusetts began in the

summer of 1786. The rebels tried to capture the federal arsenal at Springfield and harassed leading merchants, lawyers, and supporters of the state government. The state militia, commanded by Gen. Benjamin Lincoln, crushed the rebels in several engagements in the winter of 1787. Shays and the other principal figures of the rebellion fled first to Rhode Island and then to Vermont.

Although it never seriously threatened the stability of the United States, Shays' Rebellion greatly alarmed politicians throughout the nation. Proponents of constitutional reform at the national level cited the rebellion as justification for revision or replacement of the Articles of Confederation, and Shays' Rebellion figured prominently in the debates over the framing and ratification of the Constitution.

See also Rebellions.

SHERMAN, WILLIAM TECUMSEH

(1820–1891), Civil War general. Second in importance only to Ulysses S. Grant among Union generals of the Civil War, Sherman was born in Lancaster, Ohio. Orphaned by the death of his father in 1829, he was raised in the home of a neighbor, Thomas Ewing. After graduating from West Point in 1840, he was assigned to various garrisons in the South before serving in the Mexican War. He resigned from the army in 1853 to pursue a banking career in San Francisco, but the collapse of his bank in the commercial panic of 1857 and an unsatisfactory stint as a lawyer in Kansas convinced Sherman to return to the military. He became the superintendent of the state military academy in Alexandria, Louisiana. When that state seceded from the Union in January 1861, Sherman resigned and rejoined the U.S. Army as a colonel.

Appointed a brigadier general of volunteers after Bull Run in July 1861, Sherman's first command in Kentucky did not go well. Amid allegations that he had exaggerated the weakness of his position, he was relieved as head of the Department of the Cumberland in November 1861. Struggling with the apparent symptoms of manic depression and stung by criticism in the press that he was "crazy," Sherman redeemed himself at the Battle of Shiloh in April 1862. Although caught badly off guard at the beginning of the battle, he rallied his troops and thereby regained his confidence. Now promoted to major general, he commanded the Union occupying forces in Memphis during the summer and fall of 1862. As Grant's most trusted corps commander, he played a key role in the Union campaign that secured the surrender of Vicksburg in July 1863, after which he was promoted to brigadier general in the Regular Army and placed in command of the Army of the Tennessee. Sherman led the Union forces at Missionary Ridge in the rout of the Confederates at Chattanooga in November 1863, and when Grant was called east as commander in chief, Sherman took over the top command in the West.

Sherman's Atlanta campaign in May to September 1864 won the Confederate prize that ensured Lincoln's reelection that year. Sherman ordered a civilian evacuation of Atlanta, burned everything of any military value, and in November headed out of the city on his famous "march to the sea." More than any other Civil War commander, Sherman grasped the brutal logic of total war. In such a war, civilian morale and economic resources are just as much military targets as the enemy's armies. For Sherman, war unleashed the fury of hell, and he refused to sentimentalize the killing and pillaging required for victory. After capturing Savannah on December 21, 1864, he swung his army north and led another devastating march through the Carolinas. On April 26, 1865, Gen. Joseph Johnston, the commander of the last major Confederate army in the East after Lee's capitulation at Appomattox, surrendered to Sherman in North Carolina.

Although radical in his concept of total war, Sherman was quite conservative in racial matters. He believed that blacks were incapable of becoming good combat soldiers, and he consistently opposed the Union policy of enlisting black troops in the last half of the war. Wishing to free his army of the encumbrance of several thousand refugee blacks, he issued Special Field Order No. 15 in January 1865. This order set aside for the exclusive use of freed slaves a coastal strip of land from Charleston, South Carolina, to Jacksonville, Florida. Blacks quickly settled on this land, but before they could secure legal title President Andrew Johnson returned that land to its former rebel owners in the fall of 1865.

In 1869 Sherman succeeded Grant as commander of the U.S. Army. He now applied precepts of total war to the military subjugation of the Plains Indians. After retiring in 1883, he refused to be drawn into politics as the Republican presidential nominee in 1884. His memoirs, published in 1875, rank with those of Grant's as classics of military literature.

B. H. Liddell Hart, *Sherman: Soldier, Realist, American* (1960); William T. Sherman, *Memoirs of General William T. Sherman,* reprint ed. (1984).

WILLIAM L. BARNEY

See also Civil War.

SINATRA, FRANK

(1915–   ), singer and actor. Sinatra, probably the greatest singer of American popular music, was born in working-class Hoboken, New Jersey, the only child of Italian immigrants. His singing with Tommy Dorsey's popular orchestra from 1940 to 1942 made him a star. Sinatra's records of "All or Nothing at All" and "In the Blue of the Evening" topped the charts in 1943. His fans in the World War II era, dubbed "bobby-soxers," set a new standard for female hysteria over pop stars, especially in 1944 when thirty thousand of them rioted outside Manhattan's Paramount Theater.

Sinatra quickly developed a distinctive singing style. His voice, a supple baritone, ranged from brash arrogance to intimate tenderness. He could sing romantic ballads that built to a dramatic climax and swinging up-tempo songs. In both, he emphasized a personal interpretation of the lyrics through his subtle phrasing and rhythmic variation.

The House I Live In, a short film made in 1945, featured Sinatra speaking out against racial and religious discrimination; the title song celebrated America's working people. Made at the peak of his popularity, the film won Sinatra a special Academy Award in 1945 and summed up his commitment to racial justice and progressive political causes. But in the late forties, as McCarthyism spread in the entertainment industry, he came under attack by right-wing gossip columnists who portrayed him as a communist sympathizer. The charges succeeded in destroying his career; by 1950 he was a has-been at thirty-four.

In 1953 he made an extraordinary comeback as a dramatic actor in *From Here to Eternity,* which won him the Academy Award for best supporting actor. His thirty-one subsequent films included comedies and musicals, notably *Guys and Dolls* (1955) and *Pal Joey* (1957), and dramatic films, like *The Man with the Golden Arm* (1955) and *The Manchurian Candidate* (1962).

Sinatra reached a new musical peak in the late fifties with what is regarded as his best album, *Only the Lonely* (1958), composed of ravishing and vulnerable ballads, and *Songs for Swingin' Lovers* (1956), which consists of up-tempo songs sung with a strong rhythmic punch. But his new fame was accompanied by a stormy personal life involving nightclub brawling, widely publicized womanizing, and venomous denunciations of rock 'n' roll.

In 1960 his version of "High Hopes" served as the official song of John F. Kennedy's presidential campaign, and he starred in the inaugural gala. *September of My Years* won the Grammy Award for best album in 1967. "My Way" (1969), his signature song, spoke of a man at the end of his life looking back at his achievements.

Sinatra announced his retirement in 1971 and shifted his political affiliations from left to right. President Richard M. Nixon invited him to perform at the White House in 1973, and he presided at the 1981 inaugural festivities for President Ronald Reagan.

Kitty Kelley, *His Way: The Unauthorized Biography of Frank Sinatra* (1986); John Rockwell, *Sinatra: An American Classic* (1984).

JON WIENER

See also Jazz; Movies; Music.

SIT-DOWN STRIKES

Sit-down strikes, in which employees stopped working but continued to occupy the workplace, were more effective than traditional walkouts in preventing lockouts or the use of strikebreakers by management. They were first practiced on a mass scale in America in job actions by Akron, Ohio, rubber workers in early 1936.

By year's end, the technique had been taken up by workers in the automotive industry seeking to end speedups and to win recognition for their fledgling union, the United Automobile Workers (UAW). In late December sit-downs hit General Motors' Fisher Body Plant in Cleveland and then spread to the crucial Fisher plants in Flint, Michigan. By January 1937 they had spread to other of the firm's plants in Michigan, Indiana, Ohio, and Wisconsin. Because Michigan governor Frank Murphy was unwilling to use state forces to evict the Flint strikers, General Motors was eventually forced to grant the UAW exclusive bargaining rights in a number of strategic plants. Sit-down strikes continued, though, in the auto industry (at Chrysler in March 1937, for example) and among other workers.

The Bureau of Labor Statistics estimated that some 400,000 Americans engaged in sit-downs in 1937 alone. In 1939, however, the Supreme Court, in *N.L.R.B.* v. *Fansteel Metallurgical Corp.,* declared sit-down strikes to be illegal seizures of property.

See also Labor.

SITTING BULL

(c. 1834–1890), Hunkpapa Teton Sioux leader. Born in the Grand River Valley in what is now South Dakota, Sitting Bull, or Tatanka Yotanka, received early recognition from his tribe as a warrior and man of vision. During his youth he joined in the usual tribal raids for horses against traditional enemies such as the Crow and Assiniboin.

Because the Hunkpapa lived and hunted north of the early routes of western travel, Sitting Bull had little contact with whites until the Santee Sioux uprising in Minnesota in 1862. When the defeated Indians were driven west to the plains, he heard from them what life was like on a reservation. In July 1864, he was one of the defenders when Gen. Alfred Sully used artil-

lery against a Teton encampment at Killdeer Mountain. It was during this period that Sitting Bull formed his resolve to keep his people away from the white man's world and never to sign a treaty that would force them to live on a reservation.

With other Sioux leaders he soon took his followers to the pristine valleys of the Powder and Yellowstone rivers where buffalo and other game were abundant. He continually warned his followers that their survival as free Indians depended upon the buffalo. During this time, Red Cloud of the Oglala subtribe was the leader of the Tetons, but Sitting Bull's influence as a holy man was steadily growing.

Beginning in the summer of 1865 columns of U.S. soldiers repeatedly invaded the Powder River country. Sitting Bull had occasional encounters with them, learning their ways of fighting, their strengths and weaknesses.

After Red Cloud signed the Fort Laramie treaty of 1868, and then agreed to live on a reservation, his influence waned. Sitting Bull's disdain for treaties and reservation life soon attracted a large following not only from the Sioux but from the Cheyenne and Arapaho. In 1873, he and Lt. Col. George Armstrong Custer skirmished briefly while Custer was guarding surveyors for the Northern Pacific Railroad in Montana Territory.

Three years later they met again on the Little Bighorn in the battle that made both men famous. Sitting Bull was not a war leader in that fight, but he had predicted that many soldiers would fall, and his followers believed that his magical powers had brought the victory. Although Sitting Bull survived, an aroused and vengeful army forced him to flee to Canada.

In 1881 he returned to the United States, surrendered, and was held as a prisoner of war at Fort Randall, South Dakota Territory. After two years he was permitted to live on Standing Rock Reservation where he continued to use his influence to keep Sioux lands from being taken by the government. In 1885 he traveled for a season with Buffalo Bill Cody's wild west show. The rise of the Ghost Dance, a tribal religion that proclaimed that all whites would disappear and dead Indians and buffalo would return, brought him into disfavor with government officials in 1890 because he made no effort to stop the dancing at Standing Rock. When Indian police were sent to arrest him on December 15, 1890, Sitting Bull was killed in a melee outside his cabin.

Alexander B. Adams, *Sitting Bull: An Epic of the Plains* (1973); Stanley Vestal, *Sitting Bull, Champion of the Sioux* (1957).

DEE BROWN

See also Cody, Buffalo Bill; Crazy Horse; Custer, George Armstrong; Indians.

SLAUGHTERHOUSE CASES

This Supreme Court ruling in 1873 had profound effects on the interpretation of the Fourteenth Amendment, passed originally to protect the freedoms of former slaves. In 1869, Louisiana chartered a meat-packing company and gave it a monopoly over butchering in New Orleans in order, it was said, to protect peoples' health. A group of white butchers sued, claiming that the law violated the Fourteenth Amendment, which provided that states could not deprive any person of life, liberty, or property without due process of law. In a 5–4 decision, the Court held that the Fourteenth Amendment protected only the ex-slaves, not butchers, and that it affected only those rights related to *national* citizenship, not the right of the states to exercise their regulatory powers.

The dissent by Justice Stephen J. Field, however, had a more profound effect on how future justices would view the amendment. A Lincoln appointee, Field was nonetheless a Democrat who opposed Radical Reconstruction. He argued in his dissent that the amendment gave the federal government broader powers than Justice Samuel F. Miller's majority opinion claimed. Field was not trying to involve the federal government in protecting black civil rights; rather, he wanted the federal government to be able to stop the states from regulating such economic interests as railroads, actions that groups like the Grange were urging. Field's opinion became the center of conservative judicial views of the Constitution into the next century, giving the Four-

teenth Amendment a meaning different from the one its authors intended.

See also Constitution.

SLAVERY

I. The Institution of Slavery

Slavery has been of signal importance in American history. During the antebellum period, it undergirded the nation's economy, increasingly dominated its politics, and finally led to civil war between North and South. After that war, the legacy of slavery continued to shape much of American history, from the struggle over Reconstruction in the 1860s and 1870s to the struggle over civil rights a century later.

Forced labor emerged in the American colonies, as it did elsewhere in the New World, to meet a pervasive labor shortage that resulted when settlers sought commercial exploitation of agricultural staples (primarily tobacco in the Upper South and rice in the Lower South) in areas of low population density. Although twenty Africans were sold to settlers in Virginia as early as 1619, throughout most of the seventeenth century white indentured servants were far more numerous in the English mainland colonies than African slaves. Only after 1680, when the flow of indentured migrants from Europe diminished, did European servitude increasingly give way to African slavery. By the middle of the eighteenth century, slavery existed in all thirteen colonies and formed the heart of the agricultural labor system in the southern colonies.

In the years following the American Revolution, slavery, which had never been so prevalent or economically important in the North as in the South, became the South's "peculiar institution." Between 1774 and 1804 all the northern states undertook to abolish slavery. In some states emancipation was immediate, but more often — as in New York and New Jersey — it was gradual, freeing slaves born after passage of the state's emancipation act when they reached a given age (usually in their twenties). But despite widespread questioning of its morality and a proliferation of private manumissions in the Upper South during the revolutionary era, bondage actually expanded in the southern states. The spread of cotton production following the invention of the cotton gin in 1793 sharply increased the demand for slave labor and made possible the emergence of a vast new slave empire as southerners moved west. At the outbreak of the Revolution, the United States contained about half a million slaves, North and South; on the eve of the Civil War the country held almost 4 million slaves, confined entirely to the South.

Slave Population, 1790–1860

Year	Total Population
1790	697,624
1800	893,602
1810	1,191,362
1820	1,538,022
1830	2,009,043
1840	2,487,355
1850	3,204,313
1860	3,953,760

Source: A Century of Population Growth: From the First Census of the United States to the Twelfth, 1790–1900 (Baltimore: Genealogical Publishing Co., 1970).

Southern slavery was highly diverse. Slaveholdings varied according to size, location, and crops produced. Slavery in cities differed substantially from that in the countryside. Masters exhibited varying temperaments and used diverse methods to run their farms and plantations. Slaves served as skilled craftsmen, preachers, nurses, drivers, and mill workers, as well as field hands and house servants.

Despite these variations, southern slavery displayed some distinctive features. Unlike slavery in the rest of the New World, which depended on the continued importation of Africans, that in the southern United States was self-sustaining: during the half century after the end of legal importation in 1808, the slave population more than tripled. One consequence of this natural population growth was an equal ratio of males to females that — in contrast to the male preponderance in slave societies heavily dependent on imports from Africa — facilitated the formation of strong families. Another was the emergence of a slave population that, despite its

distinctive cultural norms, was increasingly American in birth and character. Slaves adopted the religion of their masters, for example, but adapted it to their own particular needs. In short, Africans became African-Americans.

Equally important was the moderate ratio of slaves to nonslaves, which set the South off both from societies in which slavery was legal but slaves were few and from Caribbean countries like Haiti and Jamaica, where slaves formed over 90 percent of the population, lived on immense estates with hundreds of other slaves, and rarely saw their owners. Throughout the antebellum period, slaves constituted about one-third of the southern population. Most lived on large farms and small plantations — three-quarters on holdings with fewer than fifty slaves — with resident masters who took an active role in directing them and were committed to slavery not just as an economic investment but as a way of life.

The slave-master relationship was intense and unstable. Slaves strove mightily to improve their conditions, sometimes by running away or striking back at hated individuals but more often by focusing on their families, friends, and churches. Although slaves were able to secure a measure of social autonomy in their quarters, that autonomy was severely limited by the masters' pervasive interference in their lives. Owners held Bible readings, nursed the sick, provided material conditions that were relatively high by international standards, and prided themselves on caring for their "people." But they (and their overseers) subjected the slaves to countless arbitrary regulations, resorted frequently to the lash, took sexual liberties with slave women, separated family members more often than they admitted, and strove to keep their human property in a state of complete dependence.

The unique sectional nature of antebellum slavery led to an increasingly bitter political struggle between North and South that culminated in civil war. A militant abolitionist movement, predicated on the sinfulness of slaveholding, emerged in the 1830s. Far more persuasive to most northerners was the "free-labor" argument that slavery was backward, inefficient, and socially degrading and must not be allowed to expand. Southern spokesmen responded with elaborate arguments in defense of slavery, including pseudoscientific demonstrations that blacks were unfit for freedom, reminders that the nation's economic well-being depended on slave labor, assertions that the Bible itself sanctioned the enslavement of the "sons of Ham," and claims that slavery produced a more humane and harmonious social order than the exploitative free-labor system of Great Britain and the North. From the late 1840s, the controversy over slavery increasingly dominated national politics. Finally, Abraham Lincoln's election to the presidency in 1860 on a free-labor Republican platform plunged the country into a secession crisis and civil war as southern politicians defended to the end their peculiar institution.

The chief casualty of the war to preserve slavery was slavery itself. Under the combined pressure of military necessity, growing northern antislavery sentiment, and the self-liberation of slaves who deserted in droves as federal troops neared, northern war aims, originally limited to preserving the Union, evolved to include the destruction of slavery. After Lincoln issued the Emancipation Proclamation that took effect on January 1, 1863, it became clear that northern victory would mean the end of slavery. The Thirteenth Amendment to the Constitution, ratified in 1865, provided legal confirmation. What should replace slavery, however, remained unanswered and would emerge as the primary issue of Reconstruction.

John B. Boles, *Black Southerners, 1619–1869* (1984); Eugene D. Genovese, *Roll, Jordan, Roll: The World the Slaves Made* (1974); Kenneth M. Stampp, *The Peculiar Institution: Slavery in the Ante-Bellum South* (1956).

PETER KOLCHIN

II. Economic Aspects

From the middle of the seventeenth century to the start of the Civil War, slavery and commercial agriculture were intimately associated. During the colonial period, slaves grew much of the tobacco in Virginia and the Carolinas, rice in the low country of South Carolina and Georgia, and sugar on the Caribbean islands — all crops that found their way into world markets. Neither southerners, who used slaves as field laborers and servants, nor northerners, who supplied slaves and food to the southern and Caribbean plantations and consumed the products of slave labor, questioned the economic value of slavery. By the late eighteenth century, however, some southern slaveholders began to have doubts. Deteriorating tobacco lands and declining prices for southern crops seemed to be transforming valuable slaves into what George Washington in 1794 called "a very troublesome species of property."

Ironically, Washington wrote just as Eli Whitney began production of his cotton gin, an innovation that would begin the expansion of cotton production and end any slaveholders' doubts about the economic value of slavery. The growing demand for cotton from European and northern mills drove prices up and drew settlers west seeking new lands on which to grow the staple. Cotton rapidly became far and away the nation's most valuable commercial crop during the antebellum years. Although cotton was grown on family farms, the amount was small, limited by the labor force of family members and their need to produce food also. Those using slaves could increase output and their income, which allowed them to buy more and better land and more slaves to increase production even further. As a result, slaves grew most of the cotton (as well as the other southern staple crops — tobacco, rice, and sugar), the largest proportion on plantations with a slave labor force that numbered in the tens or hundreds.

Slavery seemed enormously profitable. Cotton exports alone constituted 50–60 percent of the value of the nation's total exports, helping pay for imports from abroad. And slave labor provided the raw material for New England's textile mills, helping stimulate the nation's early industrialization. Slave-produced commercial crops required a host of middlemen to sell and transport them to markets and to finance and supply the slave-owning planters. Southern cities such as New Orleans, Mobile, Savannah, Charleston, and Memphis and northern ports such as New York, Boston, and Philadelphia depended heavily on the southern trade. Northern farmers and manufacturers found ready markets for their products in southern towns and cities, but especially on the southern plantations.

If the products of slave labor stimulated the nation's economic development, the slave South itself remained primarily agricultural and did not experience the urban and industrial growth that took place in the North. Some blamed slavery for fastening a backward, inefficient agrarian economy on the South. Theorists could find support for their views in the works of Adam Smith and other classical economists who argued that slave labor was inherently less efficient than free labor, and the more practical-minded charged that slavery absorbed the South's resources, allowing northern and foreign bankers, merchants, and manufacturers to reap the benefits from the South's production. Others, however, argued that the South lagged behind the North only because southerners failed to take advantage of available opportunities. They called for economic diversification, saying that slaves could be profitably employed in industry and other urban jobs, as indeed they sometimes were. But the planters ignored such advice and continued to invest their profits in more land and more slaves to grow more of the staple crops.

Although many southerners got rich by using slave labor to produce agricultural staples, northerners were clearly demonstrating that trade, commerce, banking, shipping, and manufacturing could be equally or even more rewarding. Southern slave owners largely ignored these investment opportunities in the South and continued to invest in slaves because earning maximum profits was not their primary motivation. The most ardent proslavery advocates admitted that slave labor was not as efficient as free labor but then insisted that the slave system had advantages that outweighed this deficiency. It united all whites on the basis of race, thereby avoiding the class antagonisms and labor unrest that characterized northern society. Unlike northern employers who discharged workers when they were old, sick, or no longer needed, slaveholders protected their slave workers throughout their entire lives, not merely because they were valuable property but also because they were part of what the planters called their "families," and deserved and needed this protection. Such reasoning provided proslavery advocates with a response to those who condemned slavery on economic and moral grounds.

"We want no manufactures; we desire no trading, no mechanical or manufacturing classes," an Alabama politician told an English visitor. He and the planters who dominated southern society recognized that to adopt northern economic practices would be to destroy the slave system. Even the limited use of slaves in manufacturing posed a danger; urban slaves escaped close supervision and control and were, as some put it, "half free." Large-scale commercial and industrial development would bring to the South masses of free workers, who would object to competing with slaves, and would create rich and powerful industrialists, bankers, and others, who would have little reason to protect the interests of slave owners when these interests clashed with their own. As a result, planters paid little heed to calls for economic diversification and maintained their control over a slave society that lagged behind the growing North. If some grew rich, the three-quarters of the white population that did not own slaves and, of course, the slaves themselves did not share in the wealth.

Northerners who depended upon cotton and other staples and who served the southern market strenuously opposed those who would destroy the system that undergirded their livelihood. But when southerners threatened to expand their system at the expense of free labor and when the very economic development that had depended so heavily on slave-produced staples and on the southern trade produced new and increasingly more important markets in the North and abroad, opposition to slavery grew stronger. Southerners, convinced that cotton was king and could command the world, found when they attempted to secede that other, more powerful forces had usurped the power of their monarch.

Robert William Fogel and Stanley L. Engerman, *Time on the Cross: The Economics of American Negro Slavery* (1974); Eugene D. Genovese, *The Political Economy of Slavery* (1965).

HAROLD D. WOODMAN

III. Slave Trade

The Atlantic slave trade began in the fifteenth century incidental to the Portuguese exploration of the African coast. Although trade in slaves dates back to ancient times, the Atlantic trade was marked by its westward direction, huge volume, long duration of the crossing, and racial character. Europe and the Iberian islands made the first imports; not until the second half of the sixteenth century did Latin America become the major market.

Dutch, French, and English colonization in America opened new markets for slave traders. The practice of importing labor from distant Africa sprang from the colonists' failure to develop a work force among Native Americans and white immigrants. Colonists, finding that Africans were cheap and relatively immune to tropical diseases, rationalized slavery on grounds that blacks were racially inferior.

Although the Dutch introduced the first Africans in North America in 1619, only about 20,500 had arrived by 1700. But the expansion of staple agriculture in the eighteenth century, especially tobacco, rice, and indigo, created a rising demand for slave labor: these crops required the performance of many manual tasks and a force that could be relied on to work through the long growing season.

Importation of Africans into the present United States occurred during a relatively short span of time. Only about one-third of the total arrived before 1760, more than one-half in the next half century, and a large influx — over one-sixth — in the decade before importation was abolished in 1808. Perhaps a thousand a year were brought in illegally over the next half century. Total imports, including those into Louisiana after 1761, amounted to some 600,000 persons — about 6 percent of the whole transatlantic traffic.

West Africa, stretching from the Senegal River through the Congo region, provided most of the slave trade's victims. Contrary to some historians, the West Indies did not ship many slaves to North America. A study of Virginia imports, 1727–1769, found that only about a tenth arrived from the West Indies, and another study,

of South Carolina imports, 1735–1775, found that a seventh came from there. Most slaves entering the American mainland came directly from Africa, without the "seasoning" in the West Indies described by some writers.

The antebellum argument that New England slavers fastened the practice on the South is a myth. To the contrary, British ships from London, Bristol, and Liverpool introduced most of the slaves, with New England vessels contributing only in a small way to mainland trade.

The leading North American carrier was Newport, the fifth largest colonial port. Rhode Islanders, who were at a disadvantage competing with the more advanced economies of Europe in textiles, metalwares, and guns, had one product of superior quality — the rum they distilled. Often trading the liquor directly with Africans instead of Europeans, Rhode Islanders successfully plied the trade for a century, transporting over 106,000 Africans by 1808.

Rhode Island slavers supplied West Indian markets in far greater proportion than those on the mainland. Before the American Revolution Barbados was their most important destination, and after 1783 Cuba took half of their slave cargoes. The mainland market never averaged more than a third of the Rhode Island trade. New York, which sent out 151 voyages, and other ports, including Boston, Philadelphia, and Charleston, shared in transporting slaves. In general, southerners did not engage in the carrying business.

South Carolina and Virginia were the main markets, the first receiving about seventy thousand slaves between 1735 and 1775, and the second about the same number between 1699 and 1775. The trade virtually ceased during the American Revolution, but South Carolina afterward intermittently imported slaves in large numbers until 1808.

The Middle Passage, as the trip across the Atlantic was called, was undoubtedly horrible, with the frightened Africans mercilessly shackled, stowed, and sometimes cruelly handled and driven to suicide. Modern investigators, however, have lightened a little the grim picture painted by abolitionists by pointing out that traders had a financial stake in delivering slaves alive and healthy. It has been shown that white mortality on ocean voyages, especially in the tropics, was also heavy. Rhode Island averaged a 12 percent loss of slaves, higher than the English rate.

The slave trade came under attack in the egalitarian and anti-British atmosphere of the American Revolution. But in deference to certain objectors, drafters of the Declaration of Independence dropped a proposed condemnation of the practice in that document, and the Framers of the Constitution compromised on the issue. It was agreed that the trade could be abolished as early as 1808, an agreement that was fulfilled with a minimum of dissent. Efforts to end the subsequent illegal traffic were hampered for over half a century by southern objections as well as friction with the British, some of whom were crusading to suppress the traffic entirely. During the Civil War, with southerners out of Congress and an antislavery administration in power, the United States signed a treaty with Great Britain that led to ending the traffic.

The Constitution did not contemplate a ban on interstate slave trading, leaving the issue to the states. The federal government, however, prohibited trade in the District of Columbia and set regulations regarding the size of ships used in coastal trade. The exhaustion of soil in the older states, expansion of the cotton kingdom, and suppression of the foreign trade combined to encourage domestic trading. Many slaves migrated westward with their masters, and others were sold through a system that was well established by the early nineteenth century. The seaboard and border states exported an estimated twenty-five thousand slaves a year, with Virginia the largest source.

Large-scale traders in the Upper South maintained agencies and representatives in the Lower South. Although water transport was used, slaves more commonly were marched overland, in coffles, to markets where they commanded prices that at least quadrupled between 1800 and 1860. At first only erratically regulated by the states and then unregulated altogether by 1850, the trade led to the breakup of families, which became the particular target of antislavery writers like Harriet Beecher Stowe.

Frederic Bancroft, *Slave Trading in the Old South* (1931); Jay Coughtry, *The Notorious Triangle: Rhode Island and the African Slave Trade, 1700–1807* (1981); James A. Rawley, *The Transatlantic Slave Trade: A History* (1981).

JAMES A. RAWLEY

IV. Slave Rebellions

From the earliest days of the peculiar institution, resistance was a constant feature of American slavery. It took many forms, from individual acts of sabotage, poor work, feigning illness, or committing crimes like arson and poisoning to escaping the system altogether by running away to the North. There were also "maroons" — groups of fugitive slaves who formed independent communities in inaccessible areas like Virginia's Great Dismal Swamp and the Florida Everglades.

But the most dramatic instances were outright slave rebellions. Because American plantations were far smaller than those in other parts of the Western Hemisphere and because in the United States, unlike other areas, whites outnumbered slaves, slave rebellions were smaller and less frequent than in Brazil and the West Indies. (The most massive rebellion outside the United States was the slave insurrection of the 1790s that overthrew slavery and French rule in Saint Domingue and established the nation of Haiti.) Nevertheless, one scholar, Herbert Aptheker, has counted over two hundred plots, conspiracies, and actual uprisings between the early seventeenth century and the Civil War.

The colonial era witnessed two significant slave rebellions. In 1712, some twenty-five slaves armed themselves with guns and clubs and set fire to houses on the northern edge of New York City. They killed the first nine whites who arrived on the scene and then were killed or captured by soldiers. In the aftermath, eighteen participants were executed in the most brutal manner (individuals were burned alive, broken on the wheel, and subjected to other tortures). The event set a pattern for subsequent uprisings — the violence of the retribution far exceeded the mayhem committed by the rebelling slaves.

A second uprising, Cato's Conspiracy, originated in Stono, South Carolina, in 1739. England at this time was at war with Spain, and a group of about eighty slaves took up arms and attempted to march to Spanish Florida, where they expected to find refuge. A battle ensued when they were overtaken by armed whites. Some forty-four blacks and twenty-one whites were killed.

Two years later, fear of a slave conspiracy swept New York City. After a rash of suspicious fires, a white female servant claimed to have knowledge of a slave conspiracy; those she named implicated others to avoid execution. In the end, thirty-one slaves and four whites were hanged. To this day, no one is certain whether a conspiracy actually existed or whether a cycle of fears, unfounded accusations, and coerced confessions had resulted in the death of innocent men and women.

In addition to a Louisiana uprising in 1811 about which very little is known, three major slave plots took place in the nineteenth century. The first was Gabriel's Rebellion, organized in 1800 by a Richmond blacksmith, Gabriel Prosser, and his brother Martin, a slave preacher. Gabriel Prosser was, in a sense, a typical Virginian of Jefferson's day — he couched his opposition to slavery in the language of the rights of man and the Declaration of Independence. Martin Prosser organized slaves at funerals and secret religious meetings, employing the biblical story of the Israelites escaping Egyptian bondage to justify rebellion. The rebels planned to march on Richmond from surrounding plantations, seize the city arsenal, and kill all the white residents except Quakers and Methodists (many of whom were opposed to slavery) and the French (the United States was engaged in an undeclared war with France). No one knows how many slaves the plot involved, for on the night the rebels were to gather, a storm washed out the roads to Richmond and caused those who had gathered at the meeting place to scatter.

Like Gabriel's Rebellion, Denmark Vesey's conspiracy drew inspiration from both democratic and Christian beliefs. Vesey was a resident of Charleston, a slave carpenter who had acquired the money to purchase his freedom in 1800 by winning a lottery. A leading figure in the city's black church life, he "studied the Bible a great deal," a follower later remarked, "and tried to prove from it that slavery and bondage is against the Bible." But he also knew of the rebellion in Haiti and followed closely debates in Congress over the expansion of slavery into Missouri. In 1821 and 1822, along with a group of Charleston house servants and artisans, he recruited rural slaves for an armed attack on the city. But the plot was betrayed, and Vesey and other leaders were tried and executed.

The most celebrated slave rebellion in American history, organized by Nat Turner, took place in Southampton County, Virginia, an area of small farms rather than large plantations. Born in 1800, Turner was a slave preacher and something of a mystic. In the 1820s, he began to see visions in the sky: black and white angels fighting, the heavens running red with blood. He became convinced that he had been chosen by God to lead his people to freedom.

In August 1831 Turner and five followers met and, without a plan or a clear objective, launched their rebellion. For twelve hours, they moved from farm to farm, killing every white person they encountered (nearly all women and children, for most of the area's adult males had gone off to a nearby religious revival). By the time the militia suppressed the uprising, nearly eighty slaves had joined the rebellion, and sixty whites lay dead. A wave of terror swept over the area. Scores of innocent blacks were murdered by bands of vigilantes. Turner himself escaped, remained at large for several weeks, and was finally captured and executed. In the aftermath of the rebellion, Virginia's legislature debated proposals for the gradual abolition of slavery as a threat to public order. But in the end, it chose to tighten the slave codes, further limiting blacks' freedom of movement and making it illegal for black preachers to conduct services without a white being present.

Slavery in the United States was so carefully policed that rebellion became a near-impossibility. It is instructive that the three major plots occurred outside the plantation belt — in two cities and a small farming area. Here, controls on slaves were often lax, and the conspirators could move about relatively freely. The leaders of the three plots were, compared to ordinary slaves, skilled, privileged individuals — a blacksmith (Prosser), a free black (Vesey), and a preacher (Turner). Such men had greater opportunities to learn to read and write and greater knowledge of the outside world than plantation field hands. In all three uprisings, religion played a significant role, reflecting its status as a pillar of the slave community and a source of antislavery values among the blacks. When asked whether he regretted what he had done, Turner replied, "Was not Christ crucified?"

If slave rebellions were not nearly so common as individual, day-to-day acts of resistance to slavery, they did keep alive the hope of freedom and expressed in the most dramatic form the discontent that lay just beneath the apparently placid surface of southern slavery.

Herbert Aptheker, *American Negro Slave Revolts* (1943); Eugene D. Genovese, *From Rebellion to Revolution* (1979).

ERIC FONER

See also Ableman v. *Booth;* Abolitionist Movement; *Amistad* Case; Bleeding Kansas; Chesapeake Colonies; Civil War; Colonial Economy; Compromise of 1850; Cotton; Crittenden Compromise; *Dred Scott* Case; Emancipation Proclamation and Thirteenth Amendment; Fugitive Slave Law; Kansas-Nebraska Act; Missouri Compromise; Personal Liberty Laws; Plantation System; Southern Colonies; Tobacco; Triangular Trade; *Uncle Tom's Cabin;* Underground Railroad; Wilmot Proviso.

SMITH, JOHN

(1580–1631), colonizer and publicist. During his two years in America, Smith was principally responsible for the survival of England's first permanent colony in the New World. His bold leadership, military experience, and determination brought a measure of discipline to the dissolute colonists; his negotiations with the Indians prevented starvation; and his dispersal of the colony from unhealthy Jamestown lowered mortality. After his return to England, his promotional writings contributed significantly to English efforts for an American empire.

Smith's early career had prepared him for Virginia's challenges. As a teenager he fought in the Low Countries ("that university of warre") and survived several remarkable escapades in western Europe before joining a Christian army fighting the Turks in Hungary. After more improbable episodes, including three victories in duels, he was captured and enslaved. Smith killed his master and then wandered through eastern Europe and sailed briefly to Morocco before returning to England in 1604. His years abroad predisposed him to military solutions. "The Warres in *Europe, Asia,* and *Affrica,*" he later boasted, "taught me how to subdue the wilde·Salvages in . . . *America.*" Smith's military exploits also provided the necessary social distinctions for a position of colonial leadership — a captaincy and a coat of arms.

The promoters of the Virginia enterprise appreciated Smith's value to a garrison outpost likely to be attacked by Spanish or French forces and sure to be on uneasy terms with neighboring natives. In 1607–1608, as a member of the colony's council, he explored the Chesapeake's geography and ethnology and sent home a detailed account of the colony's first year. Included was the story of his capture by Indians of the Powhatan Confederacy, but he neglected to mention his timely rescue by the chief's daughter, Pocahontas — a tale that would become a staple of American folklore.

As the colony's president from the summer of 1608 to the fall of 1609, Smith ruled firmly but fairly. Regardless of rank or occupation, everyone worked for the common good or suffered Smith's wrath, which earned him the enmity of the local gentry. He dealt with the Indians more brazenly, using threats and sometimes force to get corn, which annoyed the Virginia Company of London as well as Chief Powhatan. In October 1609, under pressure from his enemies at Jamestown and wounded by a gunpowder explosion, Smith relinquished the presidency and returned to England.

Smith's literary achievements in the next two decades were probably more important to England's imperial aspirations than were his actions in Virginia. After a voyage along the northern American coast in 1614, he insisted that the area he named "New England" had immense potential in fish, furs, and other mundane resources and that England's imperial future lay in people committed to hard work and realistic rewards.

From 1608 until the eve of his death, Smith was British America's most prolific and insistent champion. His publications offered practical advice on seamanship and colonization, but mostly he advocated British imperial vigor: "be it by *Londoner, Scot, Welch,* or *English,* that are true subjects to our King and Countrey . . . there is more then enough [in America] for all." By the time of his death in 1631, he had published nearly a dozen tracts, including a comprehensive *Generall Historie of Virginia, New England, and the Summer Isles* (1624), which mixed (and often repeated) his earlier writings with reports by others of events after 1609. He also published an account of his *True Travels, Adventures, and Observations* (1630). Along with the Pocahontas rescue (belatedly recounted in his *Generall Historie*), *True Travels* instigated the skepticism about his veracity that flourished in seventeenth-century England and revived in mid-nineteenth-century America. Since about 1950, however, the essential accuracy of Smith's autobiographical writings has been established by several scholars.

Philip L. Barbour, *The Three Worlds of Captain John Smith* (1964); Alden T. Vaughan, *American Genesis: Captain John Smith and the Founding of Virginia* (1975).

ALDEN T. VAUGHAN

See also Chesapeake Colonies; Pocahontas.

SMITH, JOSEPH

(1805–1844), founding prophet of the Church of Jesus Christ of Latter-day Saints (Mormon). This charismatic and controversial religious leader was born in Sharon, Vermont, fourth in a family of nine children. His parents worked on rented farms before moving to Palmyra in western New York State in 1816, when Joseph was ten.

The Smith family was religious; young Joseph read the Bible, attended religious revivals, and pondered which church to join. In the spring of 1820, when he was fourteen, he went to a clearing in the nearby woods to pray and had a vision of God in which, he reported to his parents, he was forgiven his sins and instructed to keep a pure heart.

Three years later, he informed his family that during a nighttime prayer, he was visited by an angel named Moroni who told him about a sacred history engraved on gold plates, which gave an account of the religious and other experiences of former inhabitants of the Western Hemisphere who had migrated from the Near East. Young Joseph, however, was not permitted to take the plates until September 1827, after he had married and established a home on a farm in Manchester, New York. Over the next two years, in between farming and other enterprises, Smith dictated to his wife and other scribes the contents of the book, and it was published as the *Book of Mormon* in the spring of 1830. The six-hundred-page work was equivalent to a Bible for the Chosen People of ancient America.

Shortly after the book appeared, Smith gathered a few believers and organized the Church of Christ (later called the Church of Jesus Christ of Latter-day Saints) on April 6, 1830, in Fayette, New York. Smith, who claimed to be in communion with God, established a lay priesthood of all worthy adult males, revealed doctrines and practices, and set up gathering places for believers on the Western Reserve in northeastern Ohio; in Jackson and Caldwell counties, Missouri; and Nauvoo in western Illinois.

A superb organizer, Smith ordained deacons, teachers, priests, elders, "seventies," and high priests and gave each appropriate tasks. As leader of the Latter-day Saint communities he also laid out cities, organized cooperative farms and industries, founded a university, built temples in Ohio and Illinois, and founded a woman's auxiliary, the Women's Relief Society.

Smith was a controversial personality. Ministers and members of other faiths refused to accept the *Book of Mormon* and his revelations as emanating from divine sources. Because of his claims of heavenly instruction and his leadership of an exclusivist community, Smith was subjected to kidnappings, tarrings and featherings, threats on his life, and vexatious lawsuits. There were also disputes among his followers over some of his precepts and policies. Nevertheless, Smith was able to attract and retain the loyalty of a large, diverse, and talented group of associates.

On June 27, 1844, an anti-Mormon mob, including many members of the Illinois state militia, broke into the jail in Carthage, Illinois, where he was being held on a charge of inciting a riot, killed Smith and his brother Hyrum, and injured two others who were in jail with them. At Smith's death there were approximately thirty-five thousand Latter-day Saints.

Richard L. Bushman, *Joseph Smith and the Beginnings of Mormonism* (1984); Donna Hill, *Joseph Smith: The First Mormon* (1977); Lucy Mack Smith, *Biographical Sketches of Joseph Smith, the Prophet* (1853).

LEONARD J. ARRINGTON

See also Mormons; Religion; Young, Brigham.

SMITHSONIAN INSTITUTION

This complex in Washington, D.C., has been variously called "America's Castle" and "America's Attic." Its beginnings can be traced to the death in 1829 of British scientist James Smithson, who left $500,000 to the United States with the proviso that it be used to promote the "increase and diffusion of knowledge." Robert Dale Owen of New Harmony, Indiana, a Democratic representative and son of the utopian socialist Robert Owen, wrote the bill to set up the Smithsonian Institution, which was to include a library, art gallery, museum, and lecture and scientific research facilities.

In 1846, the Board of Trustees, including Owen, approved the Victorian-style plans by New York architect James Renwick, Jr., who designed that city's Grace Church, for a building to include eight towers and a chapel on the Mall between Twelfth and Fourteenth streets in the nation's capital. Eight years later, when the building was finished, the trustees hired as secretary Joseph Henry, a professor of natural philosophy at Princeton, who wanted the Smithso-

nian to be used only for scientific research. He largely managed to enforce his ideas until his death in 1878.

The Smithsonian Institution since has become more as Owen and his fellow trustees envisioned it, although it has remained strongly oriented toward science. It has long been an important tourist attraction and cultural center. In 1964, the Smithsonian began a long-term major restoration after years of deterioration; in 1970, it opened the Woodrow Wilson International Center for Scholars to promote all forms of research. Today the Smithsonian is still America's Castle or Attic, serving as a storehouse for artifacts of American culture ranging from classical music through Lindbergh's plane, the *Lone Eagle,* to the chair in which Archie Bunker sat on television's "All in the Family."

See also Libraries and Museums; Science and Technology.

SNCC

See Student Non-Violent Coordinating Committee.

SOCIAL DARWINISM

Social Darwinism was an application of Charles Darwin's theory of evolution to the field of social relations. Throughout human history, wrote the English philosopher Herbert Spencer, society had operated like a jungle, in which only the strongest and best adapted — the "fittest" — survived. Although the process was a cruel one, it promised long-term benefits, for humans were gradually evolving toward a wholly just and peaceful society. He emphasized, however, that this evolutionary process must proceed at its own slow pace; efforts to improve social conditions along the way would be both misguided and futile.

When Spencer's works became popular in the United States in the 1870s, the American business world had itself come to exemplify the struggle for existence that he described. Corporate leaders seized on Social Darwinism as "scientific" justification for their actions. Businessmen like Andrew Carnegie argued that unrestrained competition was simply natural selection at work, steadily improving the national economy by weeding out the unfit. Social Darwinism also appealed to those who opposed social legislation. Exponents of Spencer's work like Charles Sumner of Yale University quoted him to show that human intervention could not hasten the pace of evolution or ease the merciless struggle for existence dictated by natural law.

Throughout the 1870s and 1880s, Social Darwinism provided a powerful defense for the status quo, but toward the end of the century, its influence on domestic policy waned as dissatisfaction with the effects of unlimited economic and social laissez-faire began to spread through American society. At the same time, however, the United States was beginning its imperialist adventures abroad, and soon the Darwinian arguments were being used, with a new racist tinge, to justify the conquest of weak countries by strong ones. Social Darwinism was rarely cited after about 1914, but it had helped shape the pattern of American thought, and its influence is still recognizable, even today.

SOCIAL GOSPEL

Social gospel, also known as Christian socialism, was a moral reform movement of the late nineteenth century that helped pave the way for the progressive movement. Rapid urbanization and industrialization in the 1880s and 1890s aroused the interest of many Protestant clergymen in the need to secure social justice for the poor. They aimed to expand their appeal in the cities, where the Roman Catholic church was especially popular among the large immigrant population. The leaders of the social gospel movement were Washington Gladden, who sympathized with workers and urged them to seek unity in Christianity, William Dwight Porter Bliss, who worked with the Knights of Labor and the Socialist party, and especially Walter Rauschenbusch, a Baptist minister in New York City who called for a democratic cooperative society to be achieved by nonviolent means.

The social gospel movement had mixed results. It attracted a number of followers and

helped liberalize organized religion and link Christianity with progressivism. It contributed to the efforts of political and social reformers like Theodore Roosevelt, Woodrow Wilson, and Jane Addams, and economist Richard Ely, all of whom were moved to look at reform in moral terms. But it failed to win over many urban immigrants, and it proposed few lasting solutions to urban problems.

See also Progressivism; Religion.

SOCIALISM

Socialism, as concept and social movement, has played a vital role in American society as a voice of opposition to class and sex exploitation, to race or ethnic hatreds, to imperial cupidity, and to the acquisitive mentality of the dominant classes at large. Judged by the standard of the ordered class movements of other (especially European) societies, it has been relatively weak in the United States. Yet faced with the monolith of modern capitalism, it has been surprisingly versatile, at times actually threatening the system or forcing major institutional improvements through the promulgation of a popular alternative worldview and the organization of widespread social resistance.

The origins of American socialism lay in the mostly (but not entirely) religious communal settlements of the late eighteenth and nineteenth centuries. Especially notable in the Radical Reformation's diaspora to Pennsylvania, but also scattered throughout other colonies and then the newly emerging nation, these sought to offer models of social cooperation. Characteristically, the colonists engaged in nongenocidal relations with nearby Native Americans, practiced a greater degree of sexual equality than the outside world (a pattern often maintained through celibacy), and undertook agrarian or small-crafts production.

These colonies made notable contributions to American crafts and culture. The Ephrata Colony, for instance, served as a major publication and educational center in the early eighteenth century, establishing a substantial tradition of German-American literature. The Shakers, famed for their "plain ways" and their furniture, popularized communitarianism for generations. Utopian intellectuals Frances Wright, Robert Dale Owen, and John Humphrey Noyes, among others, participated in national debates over sexual egalitarianism and "free love." For all their inner strengths, however, the colonies lacked the capital and — especially if secular — the inner cohesion to establish themselves permanently. With the rise of heavy industry following the Civil War, they gave way to immigrant socialist movements and to utopianism of another type, more cultural or intellectual than practical.

German-American immigrants, along with Jewish immigrants at the end of the century and a scattering of other groups, established a roughly Marxian socialist presence within labor organizations (which they frequently founded), ethnic newspapers, mutual benefit societies, and cultural associations in large cities and small industrial towns. At two points they had a major impact. During the national railroad strike of 1877, the few thousand organized socialists contributed speakers, leaflets, and in the case of St. Louis (governed briefly by a strike committee), insurrectionary political leaders. In the working-class drive of the middle 1880s for an eight-hour day and for local labor parties, socialists (and "revolutionary socialists," or anarchists) often took a leading regional or local role — and suffered the brunt of the murderous repression following the Haymarket Square incident in which a bomb thrown by persons unknown killed a number of Chicago policemen.

A second wave of utopianism, following the publication of Edward Bellamy's novel *Looking Backward* (1888), briefly organized hundreds of study circles or clubs seeking a peaceful route to the classless society. This initiative, along with the waning populist movement, the catastrophic 1890s depression, and a widespread disillusionment with increasingly corporate control of nominally democratic institutions, prompted an education-minded political socialism among the native-born. Eugene V. Debs, erstwhile champion of the American Railway Union, had become by 1900 the personal symbol of this sentiment, linked to the varied immigrant socialist movements.

The Socialist party, although it elected hundreds of candidates to local office and obtained nearly a million votes for Eugene Debs's 1912 presidential candidacy, failed nevertheless to bridge the gaps between skilled and unskilled workers, and native-born whites, blacks, and immigrants. Unlike their European counterparts who encompassed a more homogeneous mass and led the working class into modern political participation, American socialists offered only a philosophy of brotherhood and the resistance of particular groups at the rough edges of all-powerful American capitalism.

For a while, the Industrial Workers of the World (IWW) seemed to pose another alternative. Organized in 1905, the IWW promulgated the vision of "one big union" for all workers. By the lights of socialist ideologue Daniel De Leon, the new union constituted nothing less than the basis of a new civilization, ready to substitute a purely functional economic cooperative coordination for state-dominated political rule. Although mounting great strikes among the unskilled, the IWW could not overcome the combined hostility of employers, the state, and craft labor movements. With U.S. entry into World War I and the collaboration of the American Federation of Labor's leader with government aims, socialists and IWW activists suffered beatings, jailings, deportations, and the suppression of their publications.

One section of the socialist movement thereafter allied itself with newly founded communist factions, amid much destructive internecine warfare, government infiltration, and antiradical propaganda. Another section joined in emerging farmer-labor movements or became largely quiescent. The rollback of labor organizations in the 1920s sealed the Left's isolation, but enjoined socialists of all kinds (particularly Christians and communists) to address otherwise virtually unchallenged racism and imperialism. In a subtle but decided reorientation, radicals became the often lonely champions of a multiracial democratic American society.

The depression years saw a revival of socialist movements not so much in a directly political sense as in activity within labor and reform causes. The struggles of the unemployed, the victims of racism, the Spanish Republicans, and above all the unskilled workers enabled the Left to mount one fairly impressive political effort (Norman Thomas's 1932 bid for the presidency) and many dramatic campaigns. Industrial unions and progressive ethnic movements, by the end of the 1930s, fairly radiated a socialistic consciousness, even as they leaned upon the presence of the New Deal for political legitimation. Leftish political figures, such as New York congressman Vito Marcantonio, wove immigrant aspirations with a militantly democratic internationalism. Intellectual influences from the Left meanwhile fairly dominated a generation of writers and artists. Leaders of the communist Left, Earl Browder the most prominent among them, briefly gained, if not respectability, at least a wide hearing.

The approach of World War II, and the political obeisance of communists to Moscow's direction, permitted a powerful engine of political repression to surface within Congress and to utilize the infiltration and intimidation the FBI had already set in motion. The outbreak of the cold war brought with it a heresy-hunting national mood. The president, Congress, the Justice Department, the commercial press, the Catholic church, employers, compliant labor leaders, and a wing of prestigious liberals joined to isolate dissent and dissenters. Socialists of all kinds faded away, and only scatterings of radicals openly opposed the arms race, U.S. foreign adventures, and neocolonialism in the 1950s and early 1960s.

The Vietnam War, and the unwillingness of institutional authorities to redress adequately the full consequences of racism, brought a new socialist movement into being, but only briefly. Student opposition to the war met with tenacious institutional resistance by campus authorities and wide public denunciation by opinion leaders — conservative and liberal alike — effectively containing the transformational potential of "the movement." Racial protests, where not deflected by ameliorative social programs, were uprooted through massive government infiltration, harassment, and arrest of known leaders. Thus hampered, the New Left could propose only the *possibility* of a new and better society, free of class, sexual, racial, and imperial depredations.

With the presidential victory of Richard Nixon in 1972, and the end of the Vietnam War, that socialist movement disappeared as well. In the decades since, its traces could best be found in resistance movements against continued U.S. aggression in Latin America, in feminist and homosexual causes, and in ecological opposition to globe-depleting economics.

Paul Buhle, *Marxism in the United States: Remapping the History of the American Left* (1987).

PAUL M. BUHLE

See also Debs, Eugene V.; Elections: 1912; Haymarket Affair; Industrial Workers of the World; New Left; Populism; Radicalism; Railroad Strike of 1877; Shakers; Socialist Party; Utopian Communities.

SOCIALIST PARTY

This group, in its various American forms, has combined its European ancestry with uniquely American characteristics. It can be traced to the utopian socialism of such Europeans as Robert Owen and Charles Fourier and the communist theories of Karl Marx. Its first American manifestation was the Socialist Labor party, founded in 1877. Its leader, Daniel De Leon, broke with the American Federation of Labor over Samuel Gompers's rejection of political action. In 1901, a merger of several socialist groups created the Socialist party in Indianapolis, which had about 10,000 members at the start.

Its perennial presidential candidate was Eugene V. Debs, a labor organizer who had led the Pullman strike of 1894. Debs advocated an Americanized socialism that anticipated much of the legislation of the New Deal and the modern welfare state rather than government ownership of the means of production. In 1912, Debs received about 900,000 votes, 6 percent of the total, in the presidential election, and twelve hundred Socialists won various state and local offices.

The nationalism of World War I hurt the Socialist party, which split between those opposing and those supporting the war. Debs was jailed for his opposition to the war. After Debs's death in 1926, Norman Thomas became the party's major figure and led a party revival during the Great Depression. But neither Thomas nor those who followed him approached the electoral popularity of Debs and the party early in the twentieth century. In short, the party has achieved little electoral success, but, in the words of one of its modern leaders, Michael Harrington, "its most significant accomplishments were made indirectly, and not in the party's own name."

See also Debs, Eugene V.; Elections: 1912, 1920; Harrington, Michael; Haywood, William; Socialism.

SOCIAL MOBILITY

See Mobility, Social and Economic.

SOCIAL SCIENCES

The idea that human society could be studied "scientifically" gained prominence throughout the Western world during the nineteenth century largely as a result of the triumphs of the sciences of nature, especially physics and biology. If the application of scientific method to the natural order increased our knowledge and enabled us to create new industries and technologies, might not the application of this method to human beings enable us to understand ourselves and bring our affairs under more rational control? Although the hope implied in this question was given its earliest and most influential formulations by European thinkers — especially Auguste Comte of France and John Stuart Mill of Great Britain — the United States proved to be the primary national setting in which the project of developing a "science of society" flourished. American intellectuals created a formidable complex of professional organizations, journals, and attendant institutions designed to advance this project. The history of social science, while in large part an episode in international history, is also a major episode in the intellectual history of the United States.

European social scientists have often claimed to possess more philosophical sophistication than do their American colleagues, to have pursued projects of greater theoretical significance, and to have maintained a more critical perspective on the power structure of their own societies. Although these comparisons have sometimes been overdrawn, it is true that American social scientists have excelled in datagathering, in the development of research institutions, and in the volume of research completed. It was by means of a creativity more institutional than intellectual that American social science established itself decisively between about 1880 and World War I. During those years American scholars created a variety of specialized professional organizations (e.g., the American Economic Association, founded 1885; the American Political Science Association, 1903; and the American Sociological Society, 1905) and coordinated the activities of these organizations with the operation of two other vital institutions developed simultaneously: the journals in which social science research could be published (e.g., the *American Journal of Sociology* and the *American Political Science Review*) and the discipline-defined departments (e.g., economics, sociology, and psychology) in universities around which both doctoral and undergraduate programs were organized. No individual American social scientist of this era made intellectual contributions remotely as original or as enduring as those made in Germany by Max Weber, in England by Alfred Marshall, or in France by Émile Durkheim. Nevertheless, in America the enterprise of specialized, professional social science was firmly and extensively in place.

A major source of the growth of social science in the United States was the widespread hope of middle-class reformers that "experts" would be able to solve many of the social problems that had become manifest in an urban, industrial society with a largely immigrant labor force. Could poverty, corruption, crime, monopoly, and inefficiency be contained by new knowledge and by expert administration? Not only might the social sciences help legislatures and philanthropists address these problems; they might produce a class of "social engineers" ready to manage human affairs. Especially during the Progressive Era, public discussion of social science emphasized this potential contribution to public policy and administration.

Although this technocratic impulse remained prominent within American social science and in the outlook of many people who supported it, two rather different impulses gained strength in the 1920s and proved equally enduring. One was the conviction that the business of social scientists was simply to advance knowledge. In this view, knowledge might be put to good use by politicians, journalists, and everyday citizens, but the role of social scientists themselves was strictly research and theoretical analysis. This "pure science" perspective was evident, for example, in *Recent Social Trends* (1933), a massive analysis of American society and its problems commissioned by President Herbert Hoover. This perspective became more sharply etched in what came to be called the "behaviorist" and "empiricist" movements of the post-World War II era, as exemplified in quantitative studies of voting behavior. The classic study of this sort was *The American Voter* (1960), by Angus Campbell, Philip Converse, William Miller, and Donald Stokes.

The second nontechnocratic impulse installed the social scientist in the role of public moralist previously filled by the clergy and by men and women of letters. Margaret Mead's *Coming of Age in Samoa* (1928) combined an anthropologist's report of fieldwork in the South Pacific with a social critic's opinions concerning the basic values that ought to inform the lives of Americans. Mead developed a genre of social scientific writing for a large public that was later adopted by a great many of her contemporaries and successors, including the psychologist B. F. Skinner, the economist John Kenneth Galbraith, and the sociologists David Riesman and Daniel Bell. Some of these scholars were said to be too journalistic by their pure science contemporaries within American social science, but the latter, in turn, were accused of being narrowly scientistic and of exaggerating their own methodological affinities with physicists.

Although the distinctions among technocrats, pure researchers, and public moralists cut across disciplinary lines, it is those lines between disciplines that have most defined the work and self-image of American social scientists since the Progressive Era. By that time, the sociologists, political scientists, and economists had sorted themselves out from one another and from the historians, with whom the political scientists especially had been closely associated. By that time, also, the psychologists were becoming more sharply set apart from the philosophers, with whom they often continued to share university departments. Anthropology had always been a distinctive enterprise in America, having begun with museums rather than with universities and reform organizations as its primary institutional home. Yet by 1920 the anthropologists were advancing quickly into academia, even if by means of departments shared with sociologists. Hence much of the history of American social science is a history of specific disciplines, each of which has maintained its own agendas for research and its own shifting theoretical premises. Each of these disciplines, moreover, has become increasingly specialized into subdisciplines, each possessed of its own journals and national professional societies. This is especially true of psychology: some university departments of psychology have become little more than administrative devices for the management of what amounts to four or five distinctive, departmentlike programs in undergraduate education as well as graduate training and research.

Some of these American social scientific disciplines became known throughout the world for distinctive intellectual orientations that endured for decades. American anthropologists, for example, were distinguished by their practice of cross-cultural analysis, which undermined the claims to absolute validity made on behalf of the norms of any particular culture. This anthropology of the Boasian school (so called for its leader, Franz Boas) supplanted an "evolutionary" school dominant in the nineteenth century. The Boasians largely controlled American anthropology from the era of World War I until the 1960s. Even thereafter, the most widely discussed American anthropologist of the 1970s and 1980s, Clifford Geertz, worked in the Boasian tradition.

American psychologists were sharply divided into several competing schools, the most prominent of which from the 1930s through the 1970s was the anti-introspective behaviorist school led by Clark Hull and B. F. Skinner. Many of the advances made by the behaviorists resulted from research carried out on laboratory animals, especially rats.

American economists have excelled in the refinement and mathematical modeling of laws believed to operate in capitalist economies. Although the maverick Thorstein Veblen is a famous counterexample, most leading economists in modern America have been called neoclassical because of their broad affinities with the highly rationalist classical theorists (e.g., Adam Smith and David Ricardo) of the early era of capitalist development. Among the most influential of these American neoclassical theorists in the period since World War II have been the Nobel laureates Paul Samuelson, Kenneth Arrow, and Herbert Solow.

Sociology and political science have been more intellectually diverse than the other social scientific disciplines in the United States. Between the 1930s and the 1970s, however, the functionalist orientation of Talcott Parsons and Robert K. Merton defined a large portion of the work done by American sociologists. The functionalists tended to see society as an equilibrium of forces and interests, subject to change through adaptation to novel conditions. The diversity of American political scientists was narrowed in the 1960s by the behaviorist revolution of which *The American Voter,* cited above, was an exemplary agent. Traditionalists committed to the study of political theory and political institutions sometimes resisted the behaviorists' emphasis on quantitative, large-data-base research with the result that political science became the most contentious of the disciplinary communities within American social science.

Yet for all their disciplinary identity, American social scientists carried out two cross-disciplinary projects of considerable public importance during the third quarter of the twentieth century. The first was the critique of the theoretical and empirical bases for racial discrimination in the United States. Some of the relevant social scientific research was cited by the U.S. Supreme Court in its pivotal 1954 ruling against segregated public schools, *Brown* v. *Board of Education of Topeka.* In the ensuing era, intensive public discussion of race in American life drew upon the work of social scientists of every discipline. Sociologists were especially successful in demonstrating the falsity of many traditional ideas about race, and their work charted the destructive effects of racism on the lives of black Americans.

The second major cross-disciplinary project was directed at what were often called the developing nations of the third world. The experience of postcolonial societies in Asia, Africa, and Latin America was interpreted within the terms of a theory of modernization, according to which every society passes successively through the stages already seen in the modern history of the industrialized West. In this view, the basic social structural, economic, and cultural transformations that took place in Great Britain, Germany, France, and the United States could be expected to unfold in Ghana, Kenya, Indonesia, and other modernizing nations. This theory was articulated in the shadow of the American-Soviet rivalry and was sometimes offered frankly as the basis for an anticommunist program of world economic development. This was true, for example, of one of the most widely cited formulations of the theory, *The Stages of Economic Growth* (1959) by the economist Walter W. Rostow. The refinement and critical revision of modernization theory was carried out by the political scientist David Apter, the sociologist Daniel Lerner, and a host of scholars in many disciplines.

The intellectual diversity that always characterized social science in America remains more pronounced than ever and renders more difficult any effort to generalize about it as a single entity. Although the concept of social science was originally a means of encouraging and enabling what was once a novel and specific set of projects devoted to the scientific study of society, this set of projects, once firmly established and elaborated by several generations of energetic and creative scholars, outgrew the late nineteenth century's notion of what it meant to be scientific. By the late twentieth century individuals and groups within many of the social science disciplines were doing work very similar to that being carried out simultaneously by historians, philosophers, and other humanistic scholars, even literary critics. The line between science and nonscience that meant so much to early sociologists and political scientists, especially, seemed less portentous to their well-established successors. That "blurred genres" were a prominent feature of the 1970s and 1980s was suggested by Clifford Geertz, and many people came to regard the concept of social science as little more than a convenient administrative category for dealing with a sprawling expanse of enterprises not easily absorbed into natural science, nor into the even more multitudinous humanities.

DAVID A. HOLLINGER

SOCIAL SECURITY

Social Security has two distinct meanings in American life. Specifically it refers to the old age insurance system established by the Social Security Act of 1935. It also describes a much broader goal: protection for all citizens against a wide range of suffering, including poverty, homelessness, disability, and ill health. The considerable difference between the two meanings says much about America's approach to social deprivation.

The Social Security Act represented a sharp departure from previous American practice. The United States had traditionally celebrated individualism and voluntarism, and except for war veterans the national government prior to 1929 did not provide old age pensions, unemployment compensation, health insurance, or public assistance. The Great Depression of the early 1930s, however, created widespread suffering and provoked an organized popular movement for old age pensions led by Francis Townsend, an elderly California physician. The administration of President Franklin D. Roosevelt responded to such pressures by securing the Social Security Act in 1935.

The old age insurance provisions of the law

were conservative. Funding for the pensions (for workers who reached the age of sixty-five) was to be raised entirely through taxes on employers and employees — and not, as in other countries, subsidized by general public revenues. The size of individual pensions was to reflect the amount of worker contributions — the higher one's earnings, the higher one's pension. The original program did not cover survivors of pensioners or nonworkers who could not make regular contributions. It exempted from coverage agricultural laborers and domestics, many of whom were poor people of color. Pensions were not to be paid before 1942. These provisions reflected Roosevelt's fiscal conservatism and the historic American suspicion of governmental social programs. Contemporary activists were highly critical of the result.

In the long run, however, the old age insurance system grew to become America's most important social program. As early as 1939, Congress amended the act to provide survivors' insurance and to authorize the paying of pensions in 1940. Later amendments between 1950 and 1972 greatly broadened coverage, sizably increased the real value of benefits, and indexed them against future inflation. Medicare (health care for eligible retirees) was added to the system in 1965; like the pensions, it is financed through contributions. By 1989 Social Security covered 38 million people (virtually all the elderly) and accounted for nearly a quarter of the federal budget of more than $1 trillion. Although income inequality among the aged remains higher in the United States than in most other industrialized nations, the average income security of the elderly (many of whom receive company pensions as well as Social Security benefits) is considerably greater than it was in the 1930s and 1940s. The poverty rate among the aged in the late 1980s was slightly below that of the population as a whole. Moreover, the linking of individual contributions and benefits has proved politically astute. Contributors, convinced that they are entitled to their pensions, have zealously protected the program from conservative assaults. Old age insurance in the United States is a sacred cow.

The broader meaning of Social Security in

America also stems in part from the Social Security Act, which introduced other programs. Two have become especially important. One is unemployment insurance, which is financed by taxes on employer payrolls. The other is means-tested public assistance, originally to categories of needy people such as the blind, the handicapped, the elderly poor, and dependent children in single-parent families (Aid to Dependent Children, or ADC). In 1950 Congress amended ADC to authorize grants to single parents as well as to their children, and the program was renamed Aid to Families of Dependent Children (AFDC).

Since 1935 the government has added other programs aimed at promoting a broader Social Security. National minimum wage and child labor laws, on the books since 1938, seek to protect against exploitation. Federal disability insurance was added to Social Security in 1956. Medicaid, approved in 1965, is a federal-state program that subsidizes health care for the poor on public welfare. Public housing and rent supplements help a small proportion of the needy find shelter. A food stamps program, which grew rapidly in the late 1960s and 1970s, assists many poor people to purchase groceries. A Supplemental Security Income system (SSI), enacted in 1972, established a national system of means-tested assistance for the elderly and disabled poor. Amendments to AFDC have extended coverage to many poor two-parent families with children, and court decisions have helped broaden eligibility. From an initially small program intended to help only a small number of "deserving" families (mostly headed by widows), AFDC has become a much expanded — and highly controversial — welfare effort affecting more than 3 million poor American families.

In all these ways the United States has made considerable strides toward the broad provision of Social Security. Between 1960 and the mid-1970s — a period of considerable expansion of programs — the percentage of Americans officially defined as poor declined from around 21 percent to less than 12 percent. Although general economic growth was vitally important in producing this improvement, government programs contributed substantially. These were the result of overwhelming need, as in the 1930s; of

organized pressures, as in the case of the Townsend movement; of responses by liberal activists, who designed and passed most of the programs in the 1930s and 1960s; and, perhaps most important in the unprecedentedly affluent postwar era, of broadening popular expectations from life.

In comparison to other industrialized nations, however, the United States offers relatively little Social Security. It and South Africa are the only such countries without a system of national health insurance. In 1989 an estimated 37 million Americans, almost one-sixth of the population, had no medical insurance. There is no nationally financed program providing assistance to nonelderly, nondisabled poor people without dependent children. These Americans, including millions of the working poor, must look to better wages, help from private charity, or general assistance payments financed, often very frugally, by states and municipalities. Many programs, such as AFDC, Medicaid, and unemployment insurance, give individual states considerable leeway in establishing eligibility and benefits. Great local variations have followed. Because they are often poorly financed, public assistance programs nowhere bring incomes near the poverty line.

The result of these gaps and inequities is a hodgepodge of social programs that make no serious effort to redistribute wealth or income, that often vary substantially from state to state, and that fall well short of providing a safety net for all needy citizens. Roughly 15 percent of Americans were poor in each year of the late 1980s, including 33 percent of African-Americans, 29 percent of Hispanics, and nearly 40 percent of all children under eighteen.

The reasons for such gaps are varied and powerful. Well-established lobbies, such as the American Medical Association, have often blocked legislation expanding Social Security. Corporate groups have frequently resisted programs, such as the minimum wage or generous unemployment compensation, that add to payroll costs. Fiscal conservatives have tried to hold the line on public spending. Many Americans still cling to historically powerful attitudes, among them hostility to "handouts," distrust of the state, attachment to the work ethic, and racism. Contributory social insurance, they have come to believe, is an entitlement; means-tested public welfare is not. For all these reasons, Social Security, broadly conceived, remains elusive for millions of Americans.

Michael Katz, *In the Shadow of the Poorhouse: A Social History of Welfare in America* (1986); James T. Patterson, *America's Struggle against Poverty, 1900–1985* (1986).

JAMES T. PATTERSON

See also New Deal; Welfare and Public Relief.

SOCIETIES

See Fraternal Societies; Women's Voluntary Associations.

SOCIETY OF FRIENDS

See Quakers.

SONS OF LIBERTY

The Sons of Liberty was a loose affiliation of colonial Patriot groups, organized during the Stamp Act resistance of 1765. The term *son of liberty* had been used earlier to designate any supporter of freedom, and individual groups under various names had formed in many of the colonies in previous years; but the Sons of Liberty was the first formal intercolonial organization of such groups.

The movement began in New York City, where a Sons organization was established in January 1765. This group initiated correspondence with Sons of Liberty in New England and then established ties with the Carolinas, Virginia, and Georgia. In many cities, the new name was given to a preexisting club or association; in other places, a specific episode of resistance gave birth to the group. Most members were middle or upper class, but (though the movement was initially organized as a secret society) they usually tried to build a broad base of political support. Cooperation with less disciplined extralegal groups frequently triggered violence, and though the Sons rarely sought such

outbursts (and sometimes worked with local officials to restrain them), they also continued the political agitation that tended to precipitate crowd action. Although British officials widely suspected them of plotting to overthrow the government, the Sons' official aims were narrower; they focused specifically on organizing — and sometimes compelling — resistance to the Stamp Act. Indeed, they insisted on their loyalty to the king and stressed that they were upholding the Constitution against the usurpation of royal officials.

With the repeal of the Stamp Act in 1766, the movement dissolved. It revived, however, in 1768 in response to the Townshend Acts. From then until the Revolution, Sons of Liberty groups remained in active correspondence with one another and took the lead in organizing and enforcing resistance movements within their respective colonies.

See also Revolution.

SOUTH AMERICA–U.S. RELATIONS

See Latin America–U.S. Relations.

SOUTHERN CHRISTIAN LEADERSHIP CONFERENCE

The Southern Christian Leadership Conference (SCLC) was led by the Reverend Dr. Martin Luther King, Jr., and was the backbone of the civil rights movement of the 1950s and 1960s. The group was formed in the wake of the Montgomery, Alabama, bus boycott of 1955–1956. King and two other ministers, Charles K. Steele and Fred L. Shuttlesworth, issued a call for clergymen who wanted to press for civil rights to meet in Atlanta early in 1957. Sixty black ministers from ten states came to set up the coordinating group for the regional movement; they elected King SCLC's first president, with the Reverend Ralph Abernathy as treasurer.

The organization accomplished little in the next three years but was galvanized into action by the spreading movement, mostly among college students, to conduct sit-ins at cafeterias and lunch counters that would not serve blacks. King and his organization then took a leading role in the Freedom Rides challenging segregation on buses and other public accommodations and in the Freedom Summer program to register rural Mississippi blacks to vote. The group also planned and conducted demonstrations in southern cities to fight discrimination and to keep attention focused on southern racism. In Birmingham, the violence inflicted on civil rights activists by Sheriff Eugene ("Bull") Connor's policemen and dogs angered all who saw the events unfold on television. President John F. Kennedy was forced to take more active steps on behalf of civil rights, including supporting the 1963 March on Washington where King delivered his I Have a Dream speech. And the Selma, Alabama, demonstrations SCLC set up helped induce Congress to approve the Voting Rights Act of 1965.

Although SCLC played a major role in organizing the civil rights demonstrations, it lost influence as the movement continued. Many blacks, especially younger ones, rejected the nonviolent tactics King and SCLC preached and resented what they perceived as King's willingness to compromise with whites. King added to the controversy by opposing the escalating war in Vietnam, angering President Lyndon B. Johnson. After King's assassination in 1968, the SCLC leadership was deeply divided over the organization's future. Nevertheless, led by King's family and friends — most recently, the Reverend Joseph Lowery — SCLC has continued fighting segregation and discrimination.

See also Civil Rights Movement; King, Martin Luther, Jr.

SOUTHERN COLONIES

Colonization of the North American coast might have evolved differently if the English expedition sent to Roanoke Island by Sir Walter Raleigh in the 1580s had established a lasting foothold on the Outer Banks. When that colony was "lost," English attention turned to better harbors farther north, postponing colonization between Chesapeake Bay and Spanish Florida. Since nothing came of Charles I's grant of "Carolana" to Sir Robert Heath in 1629, Charles II bestowed the same region on some of his loyal supporters soon after the English Restoration of 1660.

On paper, the eight lords proprietors claimed the coast from the Outer Banks to the vicinity of St. Augustine, plus the whole interior as far as the Pacific. But in fact English settlement was confined to the coastal low country for another generation. From 1670 onward, a trickle of colonists, mostly from Barbados, staked out claims, establishing Charles Town at the confluence of the Ashley and Cooper rivers in 1680. South of this port, small groups of Dissenters from New England settled; to the northeast, Huguenot refugees from France took up residence near the Santee River.

Labor was scarce among these early immigrants, and they lacked an immediate staple crop. But hogs and cattle multiplied rapidly on the coastal savannahs, and their meat could be sent to West Indian planters in exchange for enslaved Africans. The colony's headright system allowed a planter to claim more land for each person imported, slave or free, and these workers could cut trees and make barrel staves until land was cleared for agriculture. Some of these first black arrivals understood the cultivation of rice, a grain well known in West Africa but unfamiliar to northern Europe. Ironically, this crop was quickly adopted by their white owners, who used the profits to buy more African workers. By 1708 there was a black majority in the colony, and plantation agriculture was beginning to expand.

All along the coast, expansion met Indian resistance. More than a century of contact with Spanish explorers and missionaries had spread European diseases among Native Americans. The devastation had already been enormous, obliterating small coastal tribes and continuing to reach farther inland. In the 1690s, smallpox decimated the Cherokees in southern Appalachia, cutting in half a nation of more than thirty thousand persons. After 1670 English slaving raids compounded Indian loss to disease. As their numbers declined, Piedmont inhabitants elected to fight, beginning with the Iroquoian tribe known as the Tuscaroras.

Along Carolina's northern border, Virginia

settlers had begun to drift south in the 1650s and 1660s. The first arrivals settled along Albemarle Sound, and others continued south to the Pamlico and Neuse rivers. Known initially as Albemarle, the portion of Carolina north of Cape Fear had a separate governor designated by the proprietors and by 1712 was known as North Carolina. A year earlier the powerful Tuscaroras had waged war on the European newcomers but were defeated in 1713. Many of the tribe's survivors then moved north to rejoin the Iroquois League. Two years later, the Yamasees and their Creek allies attacked South Carolina; only the refusal of the Cherokees to join in the conflict saved the colony from total destruction.

The two Carolina colonies evolved in very different ways over the next half century, owing in large measure to their different geography. North Carolina lacked a major deep-water port for drawing new immigrants and exporting the tar and pitch the settlers made from local pines. Only the Cape Fear River flowed directly into the Atlantic, and it became the entry point for Welsh and Scottish immigrants who traveled upstream to establish farms in the backcountry. A much larger flow of newcomers arrived overland from the north. Thousands of Scots-Irish and German settlers traveled south down the Great Wagon Road from Pennsylvania through the Shenandoah Valley into the North Carolina Piedmont.

This large influx shaped the distinctive character of the colony. These farmers seeking fertile land differed in their ethnic and religious backgrounds from the Anglican planters along the coast. Unlike the eastern elite, they lacked a strong commitment to the institution of slavery. Tensions quickly developed along regional and class lines, which led to the Regulator movement, an uprising in the 1760s of well-organized backcountry farmers who resented being overtaxed and underrepresented in the colonial legislature in New Bern.

South Carolina grew almost as rapidly as North Carolina; its population had reached 180,000 by the time of independence, compared to 210,000 farther north. But the composition differed markedly; by 1776 Europeans made up 75 percent of North Carolinians but only 40 per-

cent of South Carolinians. The enslaved workers who cleared the low-country swamps produced ever-increasing quantities of rice and, after 1740, indigo. No other mainland English colony generated so much wealth or distributed it so unequally. In 1739, black Carolinians at Stono tried to escape southward to St. Augustine, where Spanish authorities had promised them freedom, but local planters brutally suppressed the rebellion.

Georgia, England's final mainland colony, came into being in the 1730s partly to provide a buffer between Carolina and Spanish Florida. In 1732 philanthropist James Oglethorpe and twenty other trustees obtained from George II a charter for a colony between the Savannah and Altamaha rivers, stretching west to the Pacific, that would avoid the economic divisions and racial conflicts of its neighbor. Originally conceived as a haven for English debtors, the colony emphasized "liberty of conscience" and quickly recruited Lutheran Salzburgers, Scottish Presbyterians, and Jews, though Roman Catholics were excluded. African-Americans were also excluded by the trustees, who passed idealistic acts forbidding slavery, prohibiting rum, and regulating the Indian trade.

For Georgia's founders, as for Carolina's, the gap between expectation and reality proved considerable. Oglethorpe, who established Savannah in 1733, could not conquer St. Augustine as hoped, nor could he retain the ban on slavery. Faced with incessant pressure from would-be planters, the trustees repealed their Negro Act in 1751, a year before they gave the colony over to royal control. By the eve of the Revolution, some fifteen thousand of Georgia's thirty-three thousand colonial inhabitants were African-Americans, forced to work tracts owned by others. What had started as a settler colony for independent farmers comparable to backcountry North Carolina had evolved into a planter-dominated domain more similar to low-country South Carolina.

Verner W. Crane, *The Southern Frontier, 1670–1732* (1928; reprint, 1981); Robert M. Weir, *Colonial South Carolina: A History* (1983).

PETER H. WOOD

See also Bacon's Rebellion; Colonial Culture; Colonial Economy; Colonial Government and Politics; Colonial Wars; French and Spanish Settlements; Fundamental Constitutions of Carolina; Indians; Plantation System; Slavery.

SOUTHERN TENANT FARMERS' UNION

The Southern Tenant Farmers' Union (STFU) was formed in July 1934 in the cotton country of eastern Arkansas. Although founders H. L. Mitchell and Clay East were socialists, the STFU was a broad-based, indigenous protest movement. While advocating "land for the landless" and cooperative farming communities, it concentrated on challenging the way the Agricultural Adjustment Administration's (AAA) crop-reduction programs were administered. Many tenants had been driven off the land or forced into day labor as cotton production was cut under the law. Others were deprived by landlords of their portion of AAA subsidy payments. The STFU protested evictions and called strikes to raise farm labor wages. Their efforts, though of limited success, were impressively interracial. Separation of the races was permitted in locals, but the STFU boasted both talented black organizers and some integrated local units. Blacks composed from one-half to two-thirds of the membership, which came to number between twenty-five thousand and thirty-five thousand in six southern states.

The STFU drew national attention to the plight of sharecroppers. It quickly won the moral and financial support of reform organizations, radicals, and liberal clergy and gained powerful allies in New Deal Washington. But official action on sharecropper issues was taken only after socially prominent white supporters became targets of the widespread anti-STFU violence and harassment in Arkansas. Farm tenancy commissions were formed at the federal and state levels, but the Bankhead-Jones Farm Tenancy Act of 1937 provided only a limited program of loans to tenants, administered by the new Farm Security Administration.

The union's influence declined soon after that year. Factional battles between socialists and communists and black dissatisfaction with the white leadership of the STFU increased after its affiliation with a CIO agricultural union in 1937. The STFU survived under various names until 1960, but it scored few successes as farm mechanization thinned the ranks of southern sharecroppers.

See also Agriculture; Labor.

SOVIET-AMERICAN RELATIONS, 1917–1945

Prolonged competition and confrontation, with brief periods of cooperation and conciliation, have marked Soviet-American relations. When the preeminent capitalist nation and foremost communist country have had shared interests, as in the late 1980s and early 1990s, they have practiced accommodation and détente. More characteristic of their historical relationship, however, have been sharp differences, especially evident in the period 1917–1945, as their empires and ideologies have clashed. Virulent anticommunism has coursed periodically through domestic American politics, just as a deep suspicion of the "West" has typified the Soviet leadership. If the Soviets have feared "capitalist encirclement," Americans have feared an "international communist conspiracy." Each side, in mirror image, has seen the other as intransigent and aggressive.

In early 1917 Americans applauded the Russian Revolution that ousted the czar. But when the Bolshevik, or October, Revolution rocked Russia, Americans grew wary. Adherents of Marxism, the Bolsheviks (Communists or Soviets), vowed to mount an anticapitalist world revolution. President Woodrow Wilson's goal of a liberal, capitalist international order seemed threatened by what he called the "poison of Bolshevism." He pursued several policies to topple or at least contain the Soviets: nonrecognition, economic blockade, aid to non-Bolshevik forces, exclusion of Soviet Russia from the postwar peace conference in Paris, and military intervention (1918–1919 in northern Russia and 1918–1920 in Siberia). At home the Wilson administration's antiradicalism manifested itself in the red scare.

During the 1920s the Republican administrations continued Wilson's nonrecognition policy. They complained that the Union of Soviet Socialist Republics (USSR) refused to pay Americans about $600 million for confiscated property and repudiated debts, and they objected to communism's hostility to religion. Still, in the early 1920s, the American Relief Administration sent food to famine-stricken Russia. During the decade American businesses like General Electric and International Harvester began to enter the centrally planned Soviet marketplace; Henry Ford signed a contract to build an automobile factory. By 1928 a quarter of all foreign investment in the Soviet Union was American, and trade in American agricultural and industrial equipment was substantial.

President Franklin D. Roosevelt reasoned in 1933 that nonrecognition had failed and that improved relations might stimulate trade to help pull America out of the Great Depression and deter Japanese expansion in Asia. He extended formal diplomatic recognition to the Soviet Union and agreed to settle the debts issue at future meetings. But as General Secretary of the Communist party Joseph Stalin's bloody purges terrorized his people and five-year plans, including forced labor and the collectivization of agriculture, transformed the Soviet economy, U.S. relations with the USSR deteriorated.

Especially upsetting to Americans was the 1939 Nazi-Soviet pact. Now the Soviet Union seemed just another aggressor, especially after it seized part of Poland and attacked Finland. Americans did not appreciate the Soviet viewpoint: that Great Britain and the United States, by practicing appeasement toward Nazi Germany, had left the Soviet Union no choice but to make peace with Berlin in order to buy time to get ready for an expected German attack. That attack came in June 1941. Roosevelt sent Lend-Lease aid (by war's end a total of $11 billion), calculating that the Soviets could hold down scores of German divisions in the East to ease German pressure against Great Britain in the West.

When the United States entered the war in December 1941, it formed a Grand Alliance with the Soviet Union and Great Britain. Although always tension-ridden, the alliance was held together by the common objective of defeating the Axis. The Allies differed most vigorously over the timing for the opening of a second, or western, front. Stalin frequently urged a British-American assault against German-occupied France, and Roosevelt repeatedly promised and then delayed the cross-channel landing. At the Tehran Conference of December 1943, Roosevelt met with Stalin and Winston Churchill and they agreed to open the second front (code-named Operation Overlord) in early 1944. Later in 1944, at Dumbarton Oaks in Washington, D.C., the Allies mapped plans for the United Nations Organization, with the United States, the Soviet Union, and three others holding veto power in the Security Council. Both Washington and Moscow sought a postwar world dominated by the great powers.

The three leaders met again at the Yalta Conference in February 1945, a time when the Red Army was fighting through Eastern Europe and into Germany. In a series of trade-offs, they agreed to create a "more broadly based" coalition government in Soviet-dominated Poland, to draw a boundary line favorable to the USSR in eastern Poland, and to transfer certain Asian territories to the Soviets. They also divided Germany into zones and required it to pay reparations. The Soviet Union agreed to negotiate a treaty with America's ally Chiang Kai-shek (Jiang Jieshi) in China and to enter the war against Japan two to three months after the defeat of Germany.

The hopes for continued Soviet-American accommodation inspired by the Yalta compromises were soon dashed as the Allies jockeyed for international influence at the close of the war. The Potsdam Conference in July 1945, after the defeat of Germany, saw as much disagreement as accord. The Soviet Union fulfilled its Yalta pledge to declare war against Japan in August, but it came after the American atomic bombing of Hiroshima, when U.S. leaders no longer wanted Soviet participation in the Pacific theater. The traditional Soviet-American friction — intensified in the postwar period through rival military alliances, propaganda wars, competing reconstruction programs, interventions in weaker states, and a dangerous and expensive nuclear arms race — soon took a new name: the cold war.

John Lewis Gaddis, *Russia, the Soviet Union, and the United States: An Interpretive History,* 2nd ed. (1990); Joan Hoff Wilson, *Ideology and Economics: U.S. Relations with the Soviet Union, 1917–1933* (1974).

THOMAS G. PATERSON

See also Anticommunism; Potsdam Conference; World War II; Yalta Conference. *For Soviet-American relations after 1945, see* Cold War.

SPACE PROGRAM

The 1950s witnessed the birth of the modern era of space exploration. A milestone in this process was the inauguration of the National Aeronautics and Space Administration (NASA) on October 1, 1958, as the successor to the National Advisory Committee for Aeronautics. The latter, founded in 1915, had played a key role in the development of the nation's aeronautical industry through research and related activities. The new agency had a similar mandate and was also delegated the task of overseeing the civilian space program.

It was born in the midst of a space race between the United States and the Soviet Union. Russia had become the first nation to successfully launch an artificial satellite, *Sputnik 1,* on October 4, 1957, and the United States followed with *Explorer 1* in January 1958. Russia soon reached another plateau in its program and initiated the era of manned space flight on April 12, 1961, when Yuri Gagarin became the first human in space during a one-orbit mission.

The U.S. manned program, at that time, centered about Project Mercury and its seven astronauts. On May 5, 1961, Alan Shepard became the first American in space during a fifteen-minute suborbital flight, and John Glenn made the first orbital flight nine months later.

While the six manned Mercury missions provided NASA with invaluable experience, Project Gemini, its successor, was a bridge to the up-

coming lunar program. On May 25, 1961, President John F. Kennedy committed the nation to landing an astronaut on the moon before the end of the decade. The manned Gemini missions, which were initiated in March 1965, played an important role in this endeavor. Program highlights included the first U.S. space walks, docking maneuvers in space, and flights of longer duration. Gemini 12, the final mission, was completed in November 1966.

The next phase, the Project Apollo moon program, suffered a serious setback on January 27, 1967, when a fire in the Apollo command module killed three astronauts. Manned flights were delayed until October 1968, and on July 20, 1969, Neil Armstrong and Edwin Aldrin of Apollo 11 became the first humans to walk on the moon. They arrived on the lunar surface via *Eagle,* a module designed for this operation, while their comrade Michael Collins orbited overhead in the command module *Columbia.* Armstrong and Aldrin were reunited with Collins in *Columbia* after a lunar lift-off, and all three returned safely to earth.

Apollo 11 was followed by other successful missions that supported extended lunar walks and the deployment of a lunar roving vehicle. But the program came to an abrupt end after the Apollo 17 mission in December 1972, owing to financial considerations and the changing U.S. social and political climate.

Beyond the lunar missions, the 1970s and early 1980s witnessed the launching of *Skylab* (1973), America's first space station; the Apollo-Soyuz Test Project (1975), in which a Soviet and an American spacecraft docked in orbit; and the development of the space shuttle. The shuttle was a winged reusable manned spacecraft that could support scientific missions and carry payloads in its cargo bay. After a mission, the shuttle orbiter returned to earth to be refurbished for its next flight. The goal of this design was to make space flight a routine and cost-effective operation.

The first space shuttle, *Columbia,* lifted off from the Kennedy Space Center on April 12, 1981. It was flown by astronauts John Young and Robert Crippen. This mission, as well as subsequent flights of the shuttle fleet, demonstrated the spacecraft's operational capabilities.

Yet, despite numerous mission successes, the shuttle program was beset by problems, such as long delays in the refurbishing process. Ultimately, a combination of factors led to an explosion and the loss of the space shuttle *Challenger,* along with its crew of astronauts and mission specialists, on January 28, 1986. The explosion was traced to a failure of an O-ring, a seal in a solid rocket booster used during the launch. The accident was also attributed to design flaws of other shuttle components and to program mismanagement.

The *Challenger* disaster triggered governmental and private investigations and eventually led to design and program modifications. It paralyzed the program until September 1988 when flights resumed with the launch of *Discovery.*

In the post-*Challenger* era, NASA has continued its support of the shuttle program and has proposed various future missions. These include constructing the space station *Freedom,* landing astronauts on Mars, and developing a permanent lunar base.

An important support element of the space program has been the use of unmanned satellites and space probes to explore the earth, the solar system, and the universe at large. The first of the Explorer satellites, for instance, detected the Van Allen belts surrounding the earth, and the Landsat remote sensing satellites have imaged the earth for agricultural and geological purposes. Pictures from the Ranger, Surveyor, and Lunar Orbiter probes paved the way for the Apollo moon landings, and the Mariner series of probes explored Mars, Venus, and Mercury. Farther away, *Voyager 2,* launched in 1977, examined Jupiter, Saturn, Uranus, and Neptune during its extended planetary tour. Other missions will include an intensive investigation of Jupiter and its moons by the Galileo probe in the 1990s. On the astronomical front, the Hubble Space Telescope, launched in 1990, will explore the depths of the universe from its vantage point of a low earth orbit. Yet, postlaunch tests have determined that the telescope's performance is far below design specifications in key areas. An investigation subsequently revealed that the telescope's optical system was never fully tested on earth, probably to save time and money, and a manufacturing error went undetected. But it may be possible to enhance the telescope's performance at a later date by using modified instruments installed by astronauts.

Although the future of the U.S. space program is promising, NASA must tackle several issues before its agenda of both unmanned and manned missions can be fully implemented. Some of these issues have, in fact, influenced the space program for a number of years. For example, economic, social, and political forces have had an impact on NASA's ability to sustain a broad-based program with multiple long-range objectives. An ever-shrinking budget, in addition to the loss of *Challenger,* contributed to the dearth of unmanned planetary missions from the late 1970s until the late 1980s.

The nation's focus on the Vietnam War and other social and political questions similarly had an impact upon the Apollo program in that the number of missions was curtailed. The space race also helped dictate the program's overall profile. Although the primary objective of landing the first astronaut on the moon was achieved, the program did not, to the bitter disappointment of many, directly lead to the establishment of a permanent lunar base.

Factors of this nature may have a similar impact on NASA's ability to initiate future agenda items, such as a manned Mars expedition. And another debate was rekindled by the *Challenger* disaster: should the U.S. space effort focus on unmanned rather than manned missions in order to save money and possibly lives? Finally, the development of a sophisticated technology base to support new missions and the implementation of stricter engineering and management policies to prevent another *Challenger*-like disaster are other key issues that NASA must continue to address.

Robin Kerrod, *The Illustrated History of NASA* (1988); Clayton R. Koppes, *JPL and the American Space Program* (1982); National Commission on Space, *Pioneering the Space Frontier* (1986).

MICHAEL M. MIRABITO

See also Science and Technology.

SPANISH-AMERICAN WAR

The Spanish-American War — that "splendid little war," as John Hay characterized it to Theodore Roosevelt — has undergone several changes of meaning as an event in American history. At the time, and for long thereafter, it was generally regarded as an unsullied instance of applied idealism: a precursor of the American crusades to make the world safe for democracy in World War I and to defeat fascism in World War II. Then in the disillusioned wake of the First World War, and again in the era of Vietnam, the war came to be seen as an ugly instance of imperialism: the overture to the expansion abroad of twentieth-century American capitalism and military power.

A more accurate perspective would avoid the exaggerations of both the idealist and the imperialist views. The war can most usefully be seen as the product of a particular historical moment, of a distinctive combination of external pulls and internal pushes.

The most immediate cause was the crisis in Spanish-American relations emerging from the Cuban rebellion against Spanish rule and Spain's brutal but ineffective response. The leaders of the Cuban revolt used the United States as their base of operations and received a good deal of their financial and material support from American sympathizers — much as many other nationalist revolutionaries did in decades to come. Modern, too, was the scale and immediacy of the coverage by the surging American press, alert to the circulation-building potential of a popular insurrection so close to U.S. shores. American opinion was inflamed as well by the undeniably brutal consequences of the Spanish military's concentration of masses of Cuban civilians in areas under their control: about 100,000 of them died between 1896 and 1898.

Presidents Grover Cleveland and William McKinley sought both to give voice to the popular distaste for Spain's Cuban policy and to avoid war. Sending the battleship *Maine* on an ostensibly friendly visit to Cuba in January 1898 was part of this strategy. But the battleship blew up in Havana harbor at the cost of 266 lives, the consequence, it now seems clear, of spontaneous combustion in one of its magazines, not because of a Spanish or Cuban mine. The resulting domestic outcry probably made war inevitable, particularly so since the weak monarchy in Spain, feeling the force of an inflamed Spanish public opinion of its own, could not do the one thing that might have avoided war: grant Cuba its independence.

This, then, was the immediate cause of war. But the readiness of Americans to react as they did still needs to be explained. Most often noted by historians is the widespread influence of the ideology of imperialism: the sense of Anglo-Saxon superiority and the "white man's burden," the belief that a strong nation needed overseas markets, coaling stations, and colonies to play its proper role in the "great game" of international power politics. Politicians Theodore Roosevelt and Henry Cabot Lodge, naval strategist Alfred Thayer Mahan, and geopolitical theorists Brooks Adams and Homer C. Lea were major exponents of this view.

But this limited (though influential) group would not have had its way without other elements of public opinion, those that saw in war with Spain not the road to empire but an expression of American idealism and national purpose. And in the 1890s various Americans wanted a spur to their sense of national identity.

Many southern ex-Confederates were ready to enact a final rite of reunion. Many western agrarians, battered by the bruising politics of populism, Bryanism, and free silver, had their own particular need for national reconciliation. And many new immigrants in the large cities welcomed an emotive way of expressing their identity with their adopted country — a need amply met by the pro-Cuban, anti-Spanish sensationalism of the Hearst and Pulitzer press.

Indeed, the one group decidedly reluctant to go to war was composed of big businessmen and financiers and their political spokesmen such as Senators Mark Hanna, Nelson W. Aldrich, and Orville H. Platt. American banks held Spanish securities; as long as the Cuban revolt went on, investors in Cuban sugar would suffer. It is not surprising that hotbloods like Theodore Roosevelt and Henry Cabot Lodge decried "the money power" and the cautious McKinley as the major obstacles to war.

The war itself lasted only four months, from mid-April to mid-August 1898. There were 379 American combat deaths, but more than 5,000 servicemen died of disease.

The navy scored smashing successes in two major actions, destroying the Spanish fleets in Manila Bay in the Philippines and outside Santiago harbor on Cuba's northern coast. It is hard to judge the level of American competence, given the decrepitude and inadequacy of the Spanish forces. But these almost costless victories satisfied the popular yearnings that did so much to bring about the war.

The army's experience in Cuba was more problematic. The Puerto Rican campaign was a cakewalk, but hard and costly fighting preceded the capture of Santiago. Unsettling tales spread of the incompetence of Secretary of War Russell Alger and Gen. William R. Shafter, who headed the expeditionary force in Cuba. But in compensation, Theodore Roosevelt and his Rough Rider regiment of cowboys and Ivy Leaguers engaged in some authentic (and thoroughly reported) heroics at San Juan Hill outside Santiago.

What of the war's consequences? Most immediately it produced the nation's first overseas empire, a modest one by contemporary European standards, but sufficiently at odds with the national self-image to lead to bruising political controversy. The decision to take, and keep, the Philippines set off an ugly guerrilla war with the islands' nationalists, who had been fighting the Spaniards, and thus began an ongoing story of domination and involvement that has not yet ended. The acquisition of Puerto Rico, the other major territorial gain, produced its own complex saga of cultural assimilation and conflict. And although the United States forswore the annexation of Cuba, its relations with that island have remained contentious and difficult. This rather tatterdemalion and halfhearted venture into empire aside, the war's chief legacy lay in the part it played in the emergence of a new popular nationalism around the turn of the century — the nationalism of an urban, mass-culture, industrial society.

Frank Freidel, *Splendid Little War* (1958); Gerald B. Linderman, *Mirror of War: American Society and the Spanish-American War* (1974).

MORTON KELLER

See also Expansion, Continental and Overseas; Mahan, Alfred Thayer; McKinley, William; Philippines; Puerto Rico; Roosevelt, Theodore.

SPANISH AND FRENCH SETTLEMENTS

See French and Spanish Settlements.

SPECIE CIRCULAR

The Specie Circular issued by President Andrew Jackson and his treasury secretary, Levi Woodbury, on July 11, 1836, required payment in gold or silver for all purchases of government lands. The Jackson administration believed that the Circular would check the boom in speculative land purchases that had resulted from Jackson's "war" against the Second Bank of the United States. The president had withdrawn government deposits from the Bank and then deposited the money in numerous state "pet banks." Distribution of the deposits allowed these banks to lend more money, based on their new reserves. With easy credit available, sales of government lands skyrocketed from $2.6 million in 1832 to $24.9 million in 1836. Large speculators rather than homesteaders bought most of this land.

Many state banks, however, loaned more money than their newfound reserves could justify and were threatened with bankruptcy. Jackson, who had once lost his fortune in a bank failure, wanted to bring the situation under control by promulgating the Specie Circular. He chose a poor method. The deflationary Circular contracted the money supply too rapidly, leading in part to the panic of 1837.

See also Banking; Jackson, Andrew.

SPECTATOR SPORTS

Spectator sports as we know them in America date from roughly the late nineteenth century.

Before that time, Americans held contests of skill and prowess witnessed by interested observers. But professional athletes, rules, leagues, teams, regular schedules, paid admissions, sports entrepreneurs, and governing bodies such as the National Collegiate Athletic Association and the baseball leagues are little more than a hundred years old.

Before the modern era, pastimes inherited from England predominated in American sports. Horse racing, stick fighting (cudgeling), animal baiting (trained dogs were set against a bear or bull), cockfighting, informal ball games, and lawn bowling were popular in the colonies and early Republic. These events often took place at rural inns and urban taverns, where publicans sponsored sports and other entertainments to stimulate business. Another important context for early sports were the annual holidays and market days held throughout the colonies, events at which the buying and selling of goods were part of a round of festive activities. Here, early sports reinforced social hierarchies. Various classes might mingle at a horse race or cockfight, whereas those who owned the animals, put up the prizes, and wagered the most money were often prominent citizens, whose social prestige was enhanced by displays of wealth. In all these contexts, however, the line between spectators and participants was thin; the man cheering one heat of a quarter-horse race might be riding in the next.

This division began to sharpen in the 1800s. First, the scale of sporting events increased dramatically. Running races (called pedestrianism) and horse races occasionally attracted crowds in the tens of thousands. Rivalries were regional or even national in significance, and the newspapers devoted increasing space to such events. Although it was illegal, boxing became the preeminent sport among working-class men by midcentury. Brutal bare-knuckle matches attracted a rough crowd of young, usually single men who enlivened their working lives with gambling, drinking, and carousing. Harness racing was a more respectable sport, one popular with the middle class. Advocates of the trotters like Oliver Wendell Holmes, Sr., argued that trotting matches were properly democratic, for

any good work animal might also race well, and the matches improved American livestock. Harness racing was a harbinger of what was to come in other sports: detailed records were kept; organizations were formed to regulate competition; rules of competition were standardized; and an ideology was articulated to defend the pastime against charges that it promoted idleness.

By midcentury the old folk game of baseball was being played by clubs of young men eager for recreation and fellowship. New York City was the center of baseball (as it was for most sports of this era), for here men gathered in sufficient numbers to form clubs, sometimes based on occupation or social status. Here too were large numbers of potential spectators. By the 1860s and 1870s, teams were spread throughout the Atlantic seaboard and into the Midwest, and competition had raised the level of play sufficiently that some teams charged admission and paid the players. This was a crucial step toward the professionalization of sports.

When the National League was formed in 1876, many of the trappings of the modern game were in place, including private ownership of clubs, their affiliation with particular cities, the establishment of standardized rules and schedules, the keeping of statistics, and extensive coverage in the newspapers (separate sports pages did not appear until late in the century). Above all, the National League was an organization of *clubs;* it operated as a cartel to limit players' ability to sell their services to other teams. In their quest for profits, and to expand baseball's appeal to the respectable middle class, owners forbade playing on the Sabbath, as well as drinking, swearing, and gambling at ballparks. In important respects, then, the National League was the prototype for contemporary sports organizations.

By the turn of the century, the most prominent spectator sports of today were well on the way to their present forms. In 1892, the first heavyweight championship prize fight was held under the Marquis of Queensberry rules, which mandated the use of padded gloves and timed rounds. John L. Sullivan lost his title to challenger James J. Corbett under the new regime;

the fight was legal (unlike bare-knuckle battles) and was held in an indoor arena before some ten thousand fans. In other words, boxing was no longer the exclusive province of an urban bachelor subculture; it had become a profitable business affiliated with the entertainment industry.

Football's path to acceptance was a different one. From colonial times, college boys had engaged in informal interclass games, some vaguely resembling modern soccer or rugby, others more akin to mass brawling. By late in the nineteenth century, college students — who increasingly came from newly wealthy families or from upwardly mobile middle-class backgrounds — were demanding a more flexible academic curriculum, as well as a range of extracurricular activities, including athletics. Football quickly became the preeminent sport in the eastern colleges. By the end of the century, rules had been standardized, and the game had spread to the Midwest and the Far West. The annual Yale-Harvard game, held on Thanksgiving Day, became an important social event, and elites came from far away to see and be seen at the round of balls, parades, and parties. Football in these years, incidentally, was an extraordinarily violent sport: fractured limbs, broken necks, and even deaths were not uncommon.

Baseball and football dominated the college schedule, and these sports were also played in private men's clubs. But this left the winter months without an organized sport for athletes. Thus, basketball, a fully modern and synthetic sport, was invented in the 1890s at the YMCA in Springfield, Massachusetts, by James Naismith to give men an indoor game to play between the end of the football season and the beginning of baseball. (The YMCAs, it should be noted, had become important places where urban middle-class men could exercise in what was regarded as a wholesome Christian atmosphere, apart from the drinking, gambling, and swearing of pool halls, bowling alleys, and similar places.)

At the end of the nineteenth century, not only were sports commonplace, but an ideology of athletics had displaced old Victorian doubts that games made men slothful or unleashed base passions. Early in the twentieth century, sports advocates like football coach Walter Camp ar-

gued that athletics were part of the nation's success ethic; that team games taught corporate cooperation; that athletes upheld the values of hard work and self-discipline; that men who competed learned about fair play and following rules. The use of the word *men* here is important, for sports were seen as primarily a male preserve; athletics, it was said, taught manliness. Even today, for many men, playing sports or displaying expertise as a spectator is still a critical part of their self-image as males; sports remain central to how American culture defines masculinity. For women, however, those who participated in sports were often considered unfeminine. They were segregated into their own games and received little remuneration or recognition. Not until the women's movement of the late twentieth century was the definition of femininity reshaped to accommodate athleticism.

The 1920s were a cultural watershed, for during those prosperous years spectator sports moved to the center of American consciousness. The golden age of sports was part of the flowering of the entertainment business, the growth of a leisure-oriented consumer ethic, and the rise of the cult of celebrity. During the 1920s, radio knit together the entire nation with live broadcasts of such events as the World Series or championship fights. Meanwhile, newspapers gave page after page of coverage to these great national affairs (the first Dempsey-Tunney fight in 1926, for example, received over a dozen full pages of coverage in the *New York Times*). And the movies kept sports stars' images before the public with replays of important games and dramatized versions of their lives. Like movie stars, athletes became celebrities whose faces appeared in countless advertisements and whose salaries were reported in the press and marveled at by adoring fans. Babe Ruth and Lou Gehrig in baseball, Red Grange in football, and Jack Dempsey and Gene Tunney in boxing were the most celebrated in a pantheon of heroes whose public lives exemplified glamour, fame, and the good life.

The twentieth century brought other fundamental changes. Sports became big business. By midcentury, stadiums had been built by municipalities seeking to attract or retain teams, but the clubs themselves were privately owned, worth millions of dollars, and usually quite profitable. Most team owners were very wealthy men who held other large business interests. Old prejudices against professionalism — pro athletes, after all, were usually men of common origins, not genteel amateurs who could afford "sport for sport's sake" — continued to give way, and after midcentury, professional football and basketball competed with baseball in popularity. Players benefited from this state of affairs, and though they had little control over how leagues or teams were run, their salaries rivaled those of chief executive officers of large corporations.

Perhaps the most important change after midcentury was the advent of television in big-time sports. Television contracts involved millions, even billions of dollars, and the medium's requirements affected the timing of events, the status of players, and the rules of games. College teams, like professional ones, craved media exposure, sometimes at the expense of academic standards. Television also had an impact on which events became most prominent. Certain sports, such as tennis, can be seen well on the small screen, whereas a defensive game like soccer, spread over an enormous field, is difficult to cover. Television also expanded the potential audience for sports. Those that appealed to an affluent clientele — golf and tennis, for example — became especially important for the networks because they attracted precisely the audience that sponsors wanted.

Television's potential for reaching new spectators also aided the growth of women's sports. The women's movement in the 1960s and 1970s helped make women's athletics much more popular than ever before. Feminist ideals insisted that women could be strong, competent, and competitive, and sports provided a vehicle for the demonstration of women's physical skills and their ability to succeed under pressure. Moreover, increasing numbers of women as well as men became physically active in the second half of the twentieth century as medical evidence mounted that exercise prolonged life, and as American culture glamourized youth and vigor. Millions of Americans took up jogging,

tennis, golf, and other sports; as the numbers of participants grew, so did the audience for professional-level competitions. Marathons, tennis matches, and golf tournaments became enormous media events, and women grew particularly prominent as participants and spectators. Perhaps most important, our very definition of femininity changed to encompass such traits as vigor, physical strength, and competitiveness. As women participated more actively in the worlds of work and politics, athletics became an increasingly important expression of their sensibilities and values.

Finally, the twentieth century saw new ethnic groups grow increasingly prominent in sports, though the particular groups changed over the years as other avenues of social mobility opened. Irish and English immigrants during the nineteenth century succeeded as boxers and baseball players, Scots brought to America their Caledonian events (forerunners to modern track and field), and German immigrants brought gymnastics' antecedents to these shores in their Turner societies. In the twentieth century, Jews became prominent in boxing and basketball, but African-Americans and Hispanics came to dominate the former, and blacks alone the latter.

It is often remarked that sports are a sort of idealized version of the American social structure, offering equality of opportunity purely on the basis of merit. Although this concept is central to sports ideology, the reality is more complex. Amateur athletic clubs were designed in the late nineteenth century specifically to exclude lower-class people and "undesirable" ethnic groups. The most telling example of exclusion, of course, was that of blacks from major league baseball until after World War II. Yet it would be a mistake to say that once Jackie Robinson broke in with the Brooklyn Dodgers, the integration of sports was on the road to completion. On the contrary, blacks became so prominent as players in part because other doors of opportunity in the larger society remained closed; sports were perceived as one of the few ways out of the ghetto. Equally important, the sports business structure paralleled that of American society in the sense that the openings it offered minorities tended to be on the bottom rungs of the ladder. Jobs in management and the front office remained largely closed at the end of the century to blacks and other minorities.

ELLIOTT J. GORN

See also Ali, Muhammad; Baseball; Football; King, Billie Jean; Louis, Joe; Mays, Willie; Owens, Jesse; Rickey, Branch; Robinson, Jackie; Ruth, Babe; Sports, Popular Participation in; Thorpe, Jim; Tilden, Bill.

SPIES

See Espionage.

SPOCK, BENJAMIN

(1903–   ), pediatrician, author, and political activist. For decades after its publication in 1946, Dr. Benjamin Spock's child-rearing manual, *Baby and Child Care*, remained a national bestseller. Almost immediately, "Dr. Spock" became a household name, and by 1972 his book had sold 24 million copies — a record exceeded only by Shakespeare and the Bible. His reassuring message to parents — that they should trust themselves as they attend to their children's physical and psychological needs — appealed to a generation of parents who reared the children of the baby boom in the years after World War II.

After graduating from Yale University in 1924, Spock attended medical school at Yale and Columbia. After a one-year pediatric internship in Hell's Kitchen in New York City, he took a year's residency in psychiatry, wanting to apply its principles in his practice of pediatrics, which he began in 1933.

Spock began work on *Baby and Child Care* in 1943, at the request of Donald Porter Geddes of Pocket Books. He intended the book to combine "sound pediatrics and sound psychology." While serving in the navy as a psychiatrist from 1944 to 1946, he continued work on the manuscript, which he dictated to his wife, Jane Cheney. The first edition, illustrated by Dorothea Fox, was published in 1946, just as the postwar baby boom began.

Spock's book, an ideal guide for a nation preoccupied with children and family life, was written for mothers, who he correctly assumed would be the primary caretakers of children in middle-class homes. *Baby and Child Care* appeared at a time when the average age at marriage was dropping rapidly, and millions of middle-class women were leaving college and jobs to devote themselves full-time to caring for their homes and children. "Expertise" was in fashion, too, and Spock became one of the most trusted experts in the nation by telling parents to "trust themselves."

At the time of its publication, *Baby and Child Care* appeared to emphasize permissiveness in child rearing, in striking contrast to earlier child-rearing guides that stressed harsh discipline. His advice fit the mood of the time, which was geared toward a pleasurable domestic life. In the years since his book became a bestseller, he has been lionized for having made child rearing more professional and for providing new parents with self-confidence. On the other hand, critics have blamed him for contributing to an unhealthy child-centeredness that they felt produced guilt-ridden mothers and spoiled children. Since the 1960s, feminists have assailed him for making women believe that they were fully responsible for their children's development and that full-time mothering was essential; conservatives have held him responsible for what they have believed to be the misbehavior of the youth of the sixties who were reared according to his "permissive" formulas.

Spock became politically active because of his opposition to the Vietnam War and to the nuclear bomb. He has been a spokesperson for the National Committee for a Sane Nuclear Policy (SANE). Although he retired in 1967, he has continued to write books and to speak out on political issues that identify him with the youth movements of the 1960s.

In the 1970s, Spock revised his book in response to feminist criticisms: *Baby and Child Care* now discusses the participation of fathers, sitters, and day-care centers in child rearing and alternates the pronouns *he* and *she* when referring to children. That child rearing should be both professional and natural remains central to his message.

Lynn Z. Bloom, *Dr. Spock: Biography of a Conservative Radical* (1972); Benjamin Spock, *Spock on Spock: A Memoir of Growing Up with the Century* (1989).

ELAINE TYLER MAY

See also Childhood; Family.

SPOILS SYSTEM

The spoils system was the name given by its critics in the 1830s to the policy of filling government offices with adherents of the winning political party. The practice of discharging officials appointed by one's predecessor and replacing them with those who had rendered service to one's own party had been common in the United States ever since political parties became well established during the presidency of Thomas Jefferson.

The spoils system, however, became most closely associated in the public mind with President Andrew Jackson, partly because his administration practiced it so widely and partly because he so explicitly endorsed it. In his first inaugural address in 1829, Jackson offered "rotation in office" as a way of democratizing government, arguing that men of ordinary common sense could administer public affairs as effectively as the more aristocratic men who had previously dominated public office. In large part, the policy of rotation in office represented a genuine effort at reform, applicable to officeholders of both parties. Nevertheless, it also provided justification for the incoming Democrats to replace officials of the Adams administration with their own party faithful. Senator William Learned Marcy of New York gave the practice a harsher rationale (as well as a name) when he stated in 1831: "To the victor belong the spoils." Although the Democrats were bitterly criticized by their political opponents for their use of patronage, no more than 10 to 20 percent of federal positions changed hands during Jackson's two terms. In fact, his critics, the Whigs, proved at least as enthusiastic spoilsmen once they took office.

Over the next forty years, the system became more and more associated with corruption, and public dissatisfaction mounted. In 1881, a man said to be a disappointed office seeker assassinated President James A. Garfield. The Pendleton Act was passed two years later, establishing the Civil Service Commission. This law started the process of separating federal appointments from considerations of political loyalty. In succeeding decades the spoils system was increasingly constrained by reform legislation, but patronage did not disappear. Even today, it remains a significant factor in political life.

See also Civil Service Reform; Corruption.

SPORTS

See Baseball; Football; Spectator Sports; Sports, Popular Participation in.

SPORTS, POPULAR PARTICIPATION IN

During the colonial period recreation took many forms, but exercise as an end in itself was not for most people a priority. Society was overwhelmingly rural. Clearing land, plowing — indeed, all agricultural activity — supplied enough exercise for nearly everyone. Another restraining factor in some areas was the injunction against "profaning" the Sabbath, the only time working people had to relax.

Hunting had its recreational aspect, but for most people its primary purpose was utilitarian. As one historian put it, "The master hunted for the fun of it, the servant for the meat of it." Getting from place to place on horseback was good exercise and could be pleasurable, but it too was mostly of this character. In seventeenth-century Virginia a judge declared that it was "contrary to law for a labourer to make a race" because horse racing was "a sport only for gentlemen."

Children, of course, engaged in all sorts of games and physical activities. "I spent my time," John Adams recalled in his *Autobiography*, "driving hoops, playing marbles, playing Quoits, Wrestling, Swimming, Skaiting and above all in shooting." Square dancing was popular in some regions and foot racing, bowling, and wrestling were other ways adults employed whatever energy they could muster when the day's work was done.

By the eighteenth century communal projects like barn raisings and clearing land had become occasions for dancing and for racing and other informal athletic contests. In winter skating and sledding were common in northern climes. Crude copies of English-style fox hunts occupied southern planters and some upper-class northern groups.

City people are likely to feel they need more exercise, and this may explain why sports became more popular as cities multiplied and expanded in the nineteenth century. The Reverend Sylvester Graham, inventor of the graham cracker, wrote and lectured widely on the benefits of diet, fresh air, and exercise in the 1830s. German immigrants introduced gymnastics to America in the decades before the Civil War, among them Francis Lieber, later a professor of history and political science, who ran a gymnastics and swimming school in Boston in the 1820s.

How effective hortatory works like Graham's were in changing people's habits is not clear. A writer in *Harper's Monthly* described Americans as "a pale pasty-faced, narrow chested spindle-shanked dwarfed race." But scattered evidence suggests that many people became more conscious of the value of physical activity. Crowds of fifty thousand ice skaters jammed the lakes of Central Park in New York while it was still under construction. "The Autocrat of the Breakfast Table," the senior Oliver Wendell Holmes, could regularly be seen rowing on the Charles River.

Organized sport competitions were rare until midcentury. Young Abraham Lincoln's famous pinning of Jack Armstrong made him the wrestling champion of New Salem, Illinois, but did not lead to a statewide contest. By midcentury, however, team sports were beginning to appear. Except for basketball and lacrosse (the latter first played by American Indians), all the team sports were of European origin. Colleges organized rowing crews, and a rudimentary form of baseball evolved. Competition between teams followed, in rural areas at fairs and revival meetings, in cities on a regular basis. The games attracted crowds, which exposed more people to the fun and excitement of participation, tempted players and entrepreneurs to charge admission fees, and in turn led to professionalism.

The Civil War contributed greatly to the interest in sports. When not engaged in battles or maneuvers, soldiers spent long boring periods in camp with little to do. A lot of their energy went into horseplay and rough-and-tumble, but they also organized foot races, wrestling contests, and team sports, especially baseball.

After the war individual athletic activity and spectator sports advanced in concert. Tennis was imported from England in 1875, golf in the 1880s. For many years both were upper-class activities; people gathered to watch the better athletes, but the crowds were small, the players amateurs, the locations private. Yet these sports (and most others) became *organized,* nearly all in the 1880s, a time when most of the professions and scholarly disciplines were going through a similar process. A Canoe Association was formed in 1880 as was a group of bicyclists, the League of American Wheelmen. The next year a National Lawn Tennis Association sponsored a "championship" tournament at the posh Casino in Newport, Rhode Island. Norwegian-Americans in Red Wing, Minnesota, created a ski association in 1883. Hockey, a Canadian invention organized there in 1883, was introduced in America a decade later. Professionalization came to these sports only to the degree that some athletes became teachers, instruction being much in demand as the popularity of the sports increased.

Around the turn of the century the tennis and golf associations ran local, regional, and national tournaments. Being easy to play but difficult to master, golf produced large numbers of professional teachers as golf clubs expanded in number and size. The first national open championship, in which amateurs and professionals competed, was held in 1894. But like tennis, golf remained primarily a sport of the elite well into the twentieth century. Most players of ordinary means who learned the game did so by serving as caddies. The first golf "national hero," Francis Ouimet, winner of the 1913 open, got his start in this way. Ouimet remained an amateur, as did the most remarkable of all golfers, Robert "Bobby" Jones, whose grand slam sweep of the American and British open and amateur championships in 1930 has never been equaled. But most outstanding golfers have been professionals. Tennis, however, remained steadfastly amateur for decades, although even before World War II some of the best players turned professional while still in their prime and made large sums playing exhibitions. The upper-class character of tennis and golf eroded during the 1920s and 1930s as public facilities for these sports multiplied, and large crowds attended their national championships.

In the 1960s and after, several trends combined to increase popular participation in sports. People had more leisure time and in a service economy were more in need of exercise. Awareness of the health benefits of athletics produced millions of new bicyclists, joggers, and power walkers, all activities that could be performed at any time and required little special equipment. Even that ultimate test of fitness, the marathon, attracted runners by the thousands — the annual New York race regularly drew twenty thousand or more. The number of women participants in sports of all kinds also increased greatly, partly because of the concern for physical fitness, partly because of feminists' insistence on equal opportunity in all fields.

Finally there was the pervasive impact of television. Spectator sports, of course, were revolutionized by the medium. But it is important to remember that most spectator sports also involved mass participation. Golf and tennis were played by more people than any other game, but millions participated avidly in all the major spectator sports except boxing. If so many people had not, they would not have troubled to watch these sports so often, in stadiums or on television.

John R. Betts, *America's Sporting Heritage, 1850–1950* (1974).

JOHN A. GARRATY

See also Spectator Sports.

STAMP ACT

The Stamp Act, passed by Parliament in March 1765, was designed to help defray the costs of maintaining British troops in the American colonies by requiring tax stamps for an extensive range of public documents, including newspapers, customs documents, legal papers, and li-

censes. The Seven Years' War had left Britain with a large national debt, and the government felt that since the colonies had benefited from the war — most notably from the expulsion of France from Canada — they should contribute to imperial expenses. The colonies, however, responded with outrage. They pointed to the expenses they had already incurred in the war and predicted that the new tax would exhaust their meager supply of hard money; their objections particularly focused on the constitutional issue. Few denied Parliament's right to regulate the colonies' external trade, but with the Stamp Act — as with the previous year's Sugar Act — Parliament was trespassing on the domain the colonial legislatures had long claimed as their own: the power to tax.

Throughout the summer of 1765 waves of protest swept the colonies, involving everyone from street mobs to civic leaders, often organized by secret organizations called the Sons of Liberty. Pressure — and sometimes violence — centered on the men selected as stamp agents; by fall, all had resigned their posts and the new law was being almost universally defied. In October, a Stamp Act Congress held in New York City (representing nine colonies) petitioned Parliament for repeal and reiterated the colonists' right to be taxed only by their own elected representatives. Merchants agreed not to import British goods until the law was repealed, and soon Parliament was bombarded by petitions from English merchants suffering the effects of nonimportation. Simultaneously, the colonies' London agents as well as many English political leaders were arguing that the law — whether just or unjust — was unenforceable.

Finally in March 1766, with the king's support, the Stamp Act was repealed. The news of repeal was jubilantly received in America, but the colonies had been close to armed rebellion, and the protest had given life to ideas and methods of organization that resurfaced in later clashes between Britain and the colonies.

See also Revolution.

STANTON, ELIZABETH CADY

(1815–1902), women's rights leader. Born in Johnstown, New York, Elizabeth Cady received the best female education available at the time, at Emma Willard's Academy, but regretted not having a full-fledged college education. She spent her postacademy years like other young women of leisure, in visiting and social activities, primarily at the home of her cousin, the abolitionist Gerrit Smith. There she fell in love with another abolitionist, Henry B. Stanton. An older, romantic figure, Henry was part of the exciting world of reform and politics to which she was drawn. Despite her father's opposition, they married in 1840 and for their honeymoon went to London to attend the World's Antislavery Convention. There Cady Stanton met Lucretia Mott, the leading American female abolitionist, and began to study the Anglo-American traditions of women's rights.

In 1847, the Stantons moved to rural Seneca Falls, New York, where Elizabeth bore the last three of their seven children and grew resentful of her domestic confinement. In 1848, with the help of Mott, she organized the world's first women's rights convention. Despite Mott's reluctance, she insisted on including the right to woman suffrage in its resolutions. In 1851, Cady Stanton met Susan B. Anthony, with whom she formed a lifelong partnership based on their common dedication to women's emancipation. Three years later, she addressed the New York legislature on an omnibus women's rights bill. In 1860, most of the legal reforms she sought in women's status, with the notable exception of enfranchisement, were secured.

Cady Stanton threw herself into the political drama of the Civil War and with Anthony formed the National Women's Loyal League on behalf of the constitutional abolition of slavery. After the war, the two created deep conflicts among reformers by attempting to link woman suffrage to black suffrage and, when their efforts failed, by criticizing the Fourteenth and Fifteenth Amendments for ignoring woman suffrage. Determined to use the Constitution to enfranchise women, they established in 1869 the National Woman Suffrage Association, forerunner of the organization that eventually secured the Nineteenth Amendment.

Cady Stanton's interests extended far beyond the vote. She had always advocated divorce law liberalization, and in 1860 she precipitated a heated debate among women's rights advocates by urging women to leave unhappy marriages. In the late 1860s, she began to advocate what she called the "right to self-sovereignty" — women should take deliberate measures to avoid becoming pregnant. These beliefs led her in the early 1870s into association with the notorious "free lover," Victoria Woodhull. Because of Cady Stanton's advocacy of liberalized divorce laws, reproductive self-determination, and greater sexual freedom for women, hers became an increasingly marginalized voice among women reformers in the 1880s.

Cady Stanton also diverged from the mainstream women's movement over religion. Her deep dislike of organized religion grew out of a traumatic youthful conversion experience. In the 1880s, she visited England, where she was influenced by freethinkers and biblical critics. Back in the United States, she learned that Christian political activists were attempting to close public institutions on the Sabbath, undo divorce law liberalization, and even establish Christianity as the state religion. Determined to oppose them, she found herself on a collision course with the Woman's Christian Temperance Union, a new generation of suffrage leaders, and even Anthony. In 1898 she published *The Woman's Bible*, a scholarly but irreverent feminist commentary, for which the National American Woman Suffrage Association censured her. Although embittered, she continued her independent course on behalf of women's emancipation until her death in 1902.

Elisabeth Griffith, *In Her Own Right: The Life of Elizabeth Cady Stanton* (1984); Elizabeth Cady Stanton, *Eighty Years and More: Reminiscences, 1815–1897* (1898).

ELLEN CAROL DuBois

See also Abolitionist Movement; Anthony, Susan B.; Birth Control; Divorce; Feminist Movement; Mott, Lucretia; National Woman Suffrage Association; Seneca Falls Convention; Suffrage.

STATES

See table and map, pages 1025–1027.

States of the Union

Order of Admission	State	Date of Admission	Capital	Population[a]
1.	Delaware	Dec. 7, 1787	Dover	668,696
2.	Pennsylvania	Dec. 12, 1787	Harrisburg	11,924,710
3.	New Jersey	Dec. 18, 1787	Trenton	7,748,634
4.	Georgia	Jan. 2, 1788	Atlanta	6,508,419
5.	Connecticut	Jan. 9, 1788	Hartford	3,295,669
6.	Massachusetts	Feb. 6, 1788	Boston	6,029,051
7.	Maryland	Apr. 28, 1788	Annapolis	4,798,622
8.	South Carolina	May 23, 1788	Columbia	3,505,707
9.	New Hampshire	June 21, 1788	Concord	1,113,915
10.	Virginia	June 25, 1788	Richmond	6,216,568
11.	New York	July 26, 1788	Albany	18,044,505
12.	North Carolina	Nov. 21, 1789	Raleigh	6,657,630
13.	Rhode Island	May 29, 1790	Providence	1,005,984
14.	Vermont	Mar. 4, 1791	Montpelier	564,964
15.	Kentucky	June 1, 1792	Frankfort	3,698,969
16.	Tennessee	June 1, 1796	Nashville	4,896,641
17.	Ohio	Mar. 1, 1803	Columbus	10,887,325
18.	Louisiana	Apr. 30, 1812	Baton Rouge	4,238,216
19.	Indiana	Dec. 11, 1816	Indianapolis	5,564,228
20.	Mississippi	Dec. 10, 1817	Jackson	2,586,443
21.	Illinois	Dec. 3, 1818	Springfield	11,466,682
22.	Alabama	Dec. 14, 1819	Montgomery	4,062,608
23.	Maine	Mar. 15, 1820	Augusta	1,233,223
24.	Missouri	Aug. 10, 1821	Jefferson City	5,137,804
25.	Arkansas	June 15, 1836	Little Rock	2,362,239
26.	Michigan	Jan. 26, 1837	Lansing	9,328,784
27.	Florida	Mar. 3, 1845	Tallahassee	13,003,362
28.	Texas	Dec. 29, 1845	Austin	17,059,805
29.	Iowa	Dec. 28, 1846	Des Moines	2,787,424
30.	Wisconsin	May 29, 1848	Madison	4,906,745
31.	California	Sept. 9, 1850	Sacramento	29,839,250
32.	Minnesota	May 11, 1858	St. Paul	4,387,029
33.	Oregon	Feb. 14, 1859	Salem	2,853,733
34.	Kansas	Jan. 29, 1861	Topeka	2,485,600
35.	West Virginia	June 20, 1863	Charleston	1,801,625
36.	Nevada	Oct. 31, 1864	Carson City	1,206,152
37.	Nebraska	Mar. 1, 1867	Lincoln	1,584,617
38.	Colorado	Aug. 1, 1876	Denver	3,307,912
39.	North Dakota	Nov. 2, 1889	Bismarck	641,364
40.	South Dakota	Nov. 2, 1889	Pierre	699,999
41.	Montana	Nov. 8, 1889	Helena	803,655
42.	Washington	Nov. 11, 1889	Olympia	4,887,941
43.	Idaho	July 3, 1890	Boise	1,011,986
44.	Wyoming	July 10, 1890	Cheyenne	455,975
45.	Utah	Jan. 4, 1896	Salt Lake City	1,727,784
46.	Oklahoma	Nov. 16, 1907	Oklahoma City	3,157,604
47.	New Mexico	Jan. 6, 1912	Santa Fe	1,521,779
48.	Arizona	Feb. 14, 1912	Phoenix	3,677,985
49.	Alaska	Jan. 3, 1959	Juneau	551,947
50.	Hawaii	Aug. 21, 1959	Honolulu	1,115,274
	District of Columbia			609,909
			Total	249,632,692

a. U.S. Bureau of the Census, 1990 figures (preliminary).

STATES' RIGHTS

See Nullification Controversy.

STATES' RIGHTS PARTY

See Dixiecrat Party.

STATUE OF LIBERTY

A gift from France to celebrate republicanism, the Statue of Liberty has been an inspiration to millions of immigrants to the United States. In 1865, French republican Édouard de Laboulaye conceived the idea of a giant statue to honor the two nations' commitment to liberty and formed the French-American Union to raise money for it. Eventually, France provided $400,000 for the 151-foot statue, and a fund-raising drive in the United States netted $270,000 for the 89-foot pedestal.

Sculptor Frédéric Auguste Bartholdi combined elements of the Egyptian pyramids he admired with his mother's face to serve as a model for the statue, which he finished early in 1884. It was shipped across the Atlantic in 214 crates and was reassembled on a pedestal designed by Gen. Charles Stone and a group of engineers. The Statue of Liberty was dedicated on October 28, 1886, on Bedloe's Island, now Liberty Island, in New York Harbor near Ellis Island, the arrival point for European immigrants. Catching sight of it for the first time was a moving experience for millions who crossed the Atlantic by ship.

The statue soon became a major tourist attraction, and its heavy use, combined with the effects of water, led to its deterioration. Early in the 1980s, French engineers studied the structure and concluded that climate control was required for the interior and that holes should be covered, the twenty-one-foot torch rewired, and the rusted skeleton repaired. In 1982 President Ronald Reagan set up the Statue of Liberty–Ellis Island Centennial Commission, under Chrysler executive Lee Iacocca, to raise the $230 million needed for restoration. The statue was closed to the public for two years while undergoing the repairs and reopened in 1986 with a centennial celebration.

The Statue of Liberty still inspires millions who read the poem on its base by Emma Lazarus, which concludes with the lines:

> "Give me your tired, your poor,
> Your huddled masses yearning to breathe free,
> The wretched refuse of your teeming shore.
> Send these, the homeless, tempest-tost to me,
> I lift my lamp beside the golden door!"

See also France-U.S. Relations.

STEEL INDUSTRY

See Iron and Steel Industry.

STEICHEN, EDWARD

(1879–1973), photographer. Born in Luxembourg, Steichen became America's most celebrated and highest-paid photographer. His career spanned three-quarters of a century and embraced two radically differing styles: impressionism and hard-edged realism. Exploring photography as a fine art, he created a breathtaking gallery of perceptive portraits, landscapes, still lifes, theater scenes, and war pictures. In 1955, while director of photography at the Museum of Modern Art, he organized the most widely acclaimed exhibit in the history of photography, The Family of Man.

Steichen was three years old when he immigrated with his parents to Hancock, Michigan. After his father's health failed, the family moved to Milwaukee, where Edward left school at fifteen to become an apprentice in a lithography house. Wielding a four-by-five-inch folding view camera, he photographed pigs and wheat fields to use as models for posters and show cards for local brewers, flour mills, and pork packers. In his free time, he experimented with impressionistic photography, bathing his lens in water or jiggling the tripod as he tripped the shutter to achieve a misty, painterly effect. In 1899 his soft-focus print *The Lady in the Doorway* attracted national attention at the second Philadelphia Salon exhibition.

While in Paris to study painting and photography, Steichen photographed many European notables including August Rodin. His portrait of the sculptor won first prize in a competition at The Hague. When he returned to New York in 1902, he helped found the Photo-Secession movement dedicated to art photography. At the Photo-Secession Galleries on Fifth Avenue, he arranged the first American exhibitions of modern art by Cézanne, Matisse, and Picasso. From 1906 until the beginning of World War I, Steichen lived again in France, painting, photographing, and gardening; he returned to New York two days before an advance patrol of German troops arrived at his farmhouse. After America entered the war, he volunteered for service as a photographic reconnaissance officer with the American Expeditionary Force.

After the war, Steichen became chief photographer for Condé Nast Publications. His slick portraits of such people as Garbo, Gish, Valentino, Dietrich, and Chaplin appeared regularly in *Vanity Fair,* and his sophisticated fashion photography adorned *Vogue.* He also did advertising work for the J. Walter Thompson agency. Reportedly, he commanded a six-figure salary, and he charged a thousand dollars for private portraits.

During World War II, Steichen was placed in command of navy combat photography and appointed director of the U.S. Navy Photographic Institute. He supervised the film *The Fighting Lady,* wrote and illustrated the book *The Blue Ghost,* and mounted two photo exhibitions for the Museum of Modern Art. The museum named him director of its photography department in 1947, a position he held until 1962, and it later established the Edward Steichen Photography Center.

Christopher Phillips, *Steichen at War* (1981); Edward Steichen, *A Life in Photography* (1963).

PATRICIA CONDON JOHNSTON

See also Photography.

STEIN, GERTRUDE

(1874–1946), writer. Stein was born in Allegheny, Pennsylvania, the last of five children of a German-Jewish family, and grew up in Oak-land, California. In 1903, she moved to France where she lived until her death from stomach cancer, a painful illness for a sociable woman who liked good food. America provided her with subject matter; Europe, with the freedom to write and make herself into one of the most original figures of twentieth-century literature.

Stein was a celebrity who frequently examined the tension between an authentic identity and a public image. She regretted that she was less well known for her serious experiments than for an apparently willful obscurity, such lines as "Rose is a rose is a rose," and her art collection and salon. Much of her work (nearly six hundred plays and opera librettos, poems, portraits and biographies, novels, lectures and essays, film scripts, autobiographies, philosophical meditations, and a mystery story) was published in little magazines or privately, some of it posthumously.

Stein could be judgmental and some of her judgments were bad. But her magnitude and influence are now clear. From 1893 to 1897, she had studied at Radcliffe College, most notably with William James. From 1897 to 1901, she had attended The Johns Hopkins School of Medicine, but left without a degree. Her formal education shows her independence, fascination with consciousness and perception, and ability to look rigorously at phenomena if they interested her.

After 1901, Stein answered two questions that haunted educated modern women. First, whom would she love? After her adolescence, when both parents had died, Stein's closest companion had been her brother Leo. In 1907, she met another American, Alice B. Toklas. Their lifelong relationship, a happy marriage, is a persistent theme.

The second question was that of vocation. Around 1902, Stein committed herself to writing. Initially fearful that genius was a masculine trait, she later claimed it for women and herself. Within ten years she had produced *Q.E.D.,* a study of a lesbian triangle; *Three Lives,* novellas about poor women; *The Making of Americans,* a psychological and family epic; a number of early portraits; and *Tender Buttons,* a re-seeing of ordinary objects that has shaped the decentered, fragmented narratives of postmodernism. She next investigated love poetry and drama; her theatrical innovations ended in her last major work, about Susan B. Anthony, *The Mother of Us All* (1945–1946). In the 1920s, she explored landscape and criticism, which led to such explanations of her mind and method as *Lectures in America* (1935) and *The Geographical History of America* (1936). In the 1930s, she took up autobiography, most famously *The Autobiography of Alice B. Toklas* (1933), and, once again, narrative.

A modernist, Stein focused on the "continuous present" and its relation to the permanent. Relentlessly but playfully she deconstructed and reconstructed history and culture, literary forms (genre, for example, or voice), theories of representation, and language, which she construed as the re-creation, not the imitation, of reality. Toklas says that Stein's last words were, "What is the question?" She is among America's powerful askers and answerers.

Harold Bloom, ed., *Gertrude Stein: Modern Critical Views* (1986); James R. Mellow, *Charmed Circle: Gertrude Stein and Company* (1974).

C A T H A R I N E   R .   S T I M P S O N

See also Expatriates and Exiles; Literature.

STEINBECK, JOHN

(1902–1968), author. Steinbeck's place in American literature is assured by his late 1930s novels about the plight of the working class: *In Dubious Battle* (1936), *Of Mice and Men* (1937), and the Pulitzer Prize–winning *The Grapes of Wrath* (1939).

Growing up in agrarian Salinas, California, Steinbeck felt both empathy for the weak and scorn for the middle-class complacency of his hometown. At fourteen, he decided to write romances, but after a long apprenticeship, he found his voice in more realistic stories about ordinary people trying to achieve dignity in a repressive society. His short stories of the early 1930s, collected in *The Long Valley* (1938), tell of the misplaced, the lonely, and the misunder-

stood, their frustration conveyed in prose that, like Hemingway's, is terse and suggestive.

That compact style also served humorously to expose the stifling norms of the middle class. The rollicking *Tortilla Flat* (1935), his first commercial success, relates the misadventures of a group of drunken, finagling paisanos whose uninhibited zest for life and loyalty to one another are contrasted favorably with bourgeois sensibilities, a theme and tone he later adopted when he wrote about Monterey's *Cannery Row* (1945). Steinbeck's symbolic realism and sociopolitical convictions achieve their fullest expression, however, in his masterpiece, *The Grapes of Wrath*. This saga of the Joad family — "tractored out" of Oklahoma, exiled to California, and oppressed as migrant laborers — focused national attention on the plight of the homeless. The popularity of the book and of John Ford's classic film version brought Steinbeck the fame that, in fact, he scarcely relished.

To escape publicity, Steinbeck turned to seemingly unrelated projects. In 1941 he and marine biologist Edward Ricketts published *Sea of Cortez*, an account of their expedition cataloging marine life and a philosophical record of their ecological perspective. Steinbeck's decision to become a serious student of science was characteristic of his career. He was among the first major twentieth-century writers to view his characters with scientific detachment, focusing on what is, not on what could or should be. Steinbeck and Ricketts called this "nonteleological" or "is" thinking. Steinbeck's *Sea of Cortez* and *Cannery Row* give full expression to this ecological and holistic awareness.

Steinbeck's shift from politics to biology was but an occasion of his constant experimentation with genres. In the 1940s and 1950s he composed screenplays, a musical, journalistic pieces, travel narratives, fables, an epic, and play/novelettes — his term to describe short fiction that could be performed directly from the text. Perhaps because of this diversity, his later work is uneven. Although some of his journalistic pieces reflect the clarity and sympathy of his earlier work, others are unmistakably slight. That same unevenness is reflected in his experiments with fabulist fiction. Whereas the symbolic play/novelette *Burning Bright* (1950) was a critical failure, the tight fable *The Pearl* (1947) occupies a high place in his canon. Undoubtedly his most impressive fictional experiment after *Grapes,* however, is *East of Eden.* In this epic novel, he intertwined realistic family history with a symbolic rendering of the Cain and Abel story. Technically flawed and again uneven, the novel is nevertheless riveting. Its importance lies in Steinbeck's efforts to come to terms with individual ethical responsibility rather than social dynamics.

At the end of his career, Steinbeck recorded with increasing dismay the problems of a materialistic culture. After publishing an incisive critique of America's moral decline, *The Winter of Our Discontent* (1961), he was awarded the Nobel Prize for literature. Taken together, his works are remarkable in their diversity and their power to articulate the dreams and frustrations of average Americans within quintessentially American landscapes.

Jackson J. Benson, *The True Adventures of John Steinbeck, Writer* (1984); Elaine Steinbeck and Robert Wallsten, eds., *Steinbeck: A Life in Letters* (1975).

SUSAN SHILLINGLAW

See also Literature.

STEINEM, GLORIA

(1934–   ), feminist editor, writer, and speaker. A popular media figure, a writer, and an editor of *Ms.* magazine from 1972 to 1987, Steinem has been active politically since 1969 as an advocate for women in their struggle for equality and self-determination, as well as for those excluded from full participation in American society because of race or poverty.

Steinem's emergence as a public figure coincided with the media's discovery that the women's movement was news. Her glamour, wit, and forthright manner made her a popular television interviewee and a symbol of modern feminism. (The mother of Sally Ride, the first American woman astronaut, is said to have exclaimed, "God bless Gloria Steinem.")

Through her work as a journalist, particularly when working on an exposé of the Playboy Clubs' exploitation of "bunnies," Steinem had become aware of women's powerlessness. ("Pretend you are a woman and read this," an editor of the *Ladies' Home Journal* once said to her, thus revealing his contempt for his readership.) But it was not until New York State appointed a commission to investigate abortion that her ideas coalesced. The makeup of the commission — fourteen men and a nun — aroused the ire of many women and made Steinem aware of herself as a feminist and a defender of women's right to control their own bodies. She was soon delivering feminist speeches around the country, often several times a week. She was always accompanied by a black woman speaker — Dorothy Hughes Pitman, Flo Kennedy, and Margaret Sloan in turn — in an attempt to change the popular conception of feminism as a strictly white middle-class movement.

In 1972 Steinem became a cofounder and editor of *Ms.* magazine, which for fifteen years under her editorship was the chief popular medium for American feminism. In the end, the demands of advertisers for control over copy defeated the magazine, and it was sold. But in 1990, a new *Ms.* without advertising was started, with Steinem as consulting editor. For the first issue, she wrote an analysis of the control advertisers have over the editorial content of women's magazines.

Steinem, who began her journalistic career as a free-lance writer, published *Outrageous Acts and Everyday Rebellions* in 1983, a collection of her articles. It included a highly praised and moving memoir of her mother and of her own impoverished childhood as her mother's sole caretaker.

In addition to her work on behalf of feminism, Steinem has been active in civil rights and peace campaigns, including the United Farm Workers, the Vietnam war tax protest, and the Committee for the Legal Defense of Angela Davis, and in the political campaigns of Adlai Stevenson, Robert Kennedy, Eugene McCarthy, Shirley Chisholm, and George McGovern. She also cofounded and served on the board of directors of the Women's Action Alliance and was a member of the National Advisory Committee of the National Women's Political Caucus, co-founder and president of the board of directors of the Ms. Foundation for Women, founding member of the Coalition of Labor Union Women, and member of the International Women's Year Commission, 1977.

As one of the best-known U.S. public figures who is neither a politician nor a television, movie, sports, or rock star, she has always placed her talents at the service of women and the dispossessed.

CAROLYN G. HEILBRUN

See also Feminist Movement.

STEVENS, THADDEUS

(1792–1868), political leader. In the traditional view of Reconstruction, Thaddeus Stevens was the evil genius who wrecked President Andrew Johnson's lenient policy and turned the South over to the depredations of "black rule." Today, he is seen more sympathetically, as an outspoken foe of slavery who sought to accord blacks the rights of American citizenship and to provide an economic underpinning for their freedom.

Born and educated in New England, Stevens moved as a young man to the Lancaster area of Pennsylvania, where he practiced law and entered the business of iron manufacturing. Born with a clubfoot — then considered a mark of evil — he felt at home among the dissenters and outsiders (most notably the Amish) who peopled the region. He never married, but lived for years with a black housekeeper and showed no interest in either confirming or denying rumors about their relationship.

Successively an Anti-Mason, Whig, and Republican, Stevens served several terms in the Pennsylvania legislature, where he won renown as an advocate of free public education. He also emerged as an outspoken foe of slavery and defender of the rights of the state's black population. He served as a delegate to Pennsylvania's constitutional convention of 1838 but refused to sign the final document because it limited the suffrage to whites. He served in Congress be-

tween 1849 and 1853 and was reelected in 1858, in time to argue against northern concessions to the South in the secession winter of 1860–1861.

During the Civil War and Reconstruction, Stevens came into his own as the most radical of the Radical Republicans. His personal qualities — honesty, imperviousness to criticism or flattery, willingness to use daring means to achieve his ends — won the respect even of political foes. A master of parliamentary tactics, he knew when to bully the House and when to compromise. His quick wit and sarcastic tongue were legendary — "I would sooner get into difficulty with a porcupine," one colleague remarked.

During the war, as chairman of the House Committee on Ways and Means, Stevens urged the administration to emancipate and arm the slaves. He opposed as too lenient President Abraham Lincoln's Ten Percent Plan for readmitting Confederate states to the Union during Reconstruction, and by the end of the war he was advocating black suffrage in the South and the disfranchisement of former Confederates.

To Stevens, Reconstruction offered an opportunity to create a "perfect republic," shorn of racial inequality. As Republican floor leader, he shepherded to passage key measures of Congressional Reconstruction — the Civil Rights Act of 1866, the Fourteenth Amendment, and the Reconstruction Act of 1867 — even though none of these was as radical as he desired. He was one of President Johnson's fiercest congressional critics and an early advocate of his impeachment.

Stevens was most closely identified during Reconstruction with his plan for the division of planters' land among the former slaves, which, he insisted, would make them "small independent landholders, . . . the support and guardians of republican liberty." "The whole fabric of southern society," he declared, "*must* be changed, and never can it be done if this opportunity is lost." But Stevens's plan was too radical for most Republicans, and after the passage of the Reconstruction Act, his influence waned.

When he died in 1868, Stevens one last time challenged Americans to rise above their prejudices, for he was buried in an integrated Pennsylvania cemetery, with an epitaph written by himself: "I have chosen this that I might illustrate in my death the principles which I advocated through a long life, Equality of Man before his Creator."

Fawn Brodie, *Thaddeus Stevens: Scourge of the South* (1959); Ralph Korngold, *Thaddeus Stevens* (1955).

ERIC FONER

See also Abolitionist Movement; House of Representatives; Reconstruction.

STEVENS, WALLACE

(1879–1955), poet, aesthetician, and insurance lawyer. Stevens's poetry has been the subject of more books of formalist, rhetorical, psychological, and poststructuralist criticism than that of any other modern American poet, though he published relatively little and mostly cryptic lyrical poetry. His first book, *Harmonium* (1923), appeared when he was forty-four. His major poems are collected in two volumes, *Collected Poems* (1954, which won the Pulitzer Prize and National Book Award) and *Opus Posthumous* (1957); he also published a slim volume of essays on aesthetics, *The Necessary Angel* (1951).

His early short lyrics and several mature epic-like lyrics are characterized by stunning verbal mastery and what might be called a "unified field theory" of poetry, which was for him all of philosophy and experience, the ordinary mystified and magnified.

Stevens generally kept aloof from the political turbulence of the 1930s, although his unfortunate attraction to the romantic individualism of Benito Mussolini and his reactionary politics emerge in his personal correspondence. His measured stand on the artistic battles of the day appears in his stylized and precise poetic meditations about the act of writing poetry. Stevens's distance from the literary wars of his time is explained in part by his career as an insurance lawyer in Hartford, Connecticut. After winning many literary awards in three years at Harvard and a year as a paid journalist, he earned a law degree at New York University in 1903. He had many friends among the New York cognoscenti and was a serious modern art collector. In later

years, in public readings and lectures, he spoke of the power of figurative language to transform the world.

Stevens's longer poetic meditations do not answer all the metaphysical and psychological questions they pose; rather, they engage the reader in speculations that echo the music and ideas encrypted in the Western tradition. Figurative complexity, semantic texture, and interpretive richness leave his poems open, ready to be finished by critics engaged in the quest for personal meaning. Such ambitious and ambiguous poems as *Notes Toward a Supreme Fiction* raise poetry to the status of a secular religion, a monistic philosophy. Nevertheless, Stevens wrote in an insistently American idiom, constructing a poetics based in national cultural ambitions and anxieties that had been earlier registered by Emerson and Whitman.

Stevens has been much emulated by recent poets for the rich sensuousness of his language, the haunting, festooned vocabulary with its double-register of suggestion fanning out, through endless metaphors, into philosophical speculation and psychological rumination. Many of Stevens's poems probe the source and extent of poetry, of the poet's mind, and the relationship of fragments of thought and vision to an elusive perfection beyond language.

Recently criticized for irrelevance to political and economic issues and for excluding nonwhite, nonmale, and other alleged minority interests, Stevens's powerful style nevertheless continues to attract disciples and detractors from across wide poetic and political spectra.

Frank Doggett and Robert Buttel, eds., *Wallace Stevens: A Celebration* (1980).

KATHRYNE V. LINDBERG

See also Literature.

STIMSON, HENRY L.

(1867–1950), statesman. Stimson served in high government positions from the administration of Theodore Roosevelt to that of Harry S. Truman. President William Howard Taft appointed him secretary of war, Herbert Hoover made him secretary of state, and on the eve of World War II, Franklin D. Roosevelt reappointed him secretary of war, correctly believing that his reputation for integrity and his Republican party affiliation would help build support for the war effort.

Whether inspecting water projects in the California wilderness or administering the largest military expansion in U.S. history, Stimson combined rugged individualism with the urbanity of a Wall Street lawyer educated at Yale and Harvard. Like his mentor, Elihu Root, he was a conservative modernizer striving to stabilize American capitalism through regulation "in the public interest." The idea of a neutral public interest was a distinguishing trait of his philosophy whether he was governing the Philippines, as he did in the twenties, or agonizing over the implications of the atomic bomb.

Stimson's close friend President Theodore Roosevelt appointed him to his first public office, U.S. attorney in New York City. During this time, he made fundamental, but little-known, contributions to the strengthening of federal power and the reshaping of American capitalism. He created the first modern, professional federal prosecutor's office, which engaged in high-profile enforcement of trade regulation laws. Among the bright young lawyers he brought into public life was Felix Frankfurter, who later ascended to the Supreme Court.

As secretary of state at the beginning of the Great Depression, Stimson hoped to maintain American power without resorting to war. Though a strong partisan of army reform and military preparedness prior to both world wars, he energetically negotiated arms limitation treaties and took a hard line against perceived violations of international law, such as the Japanese invasion of Manchuria in 1931. Under the Stimson Doctrine the United States refused to recognize any territorial change effected by conquest, but lacking British support, the doctrine remained a paper declaration.

As Franklin D. Roosevelt's secretary of war, Stimson had his greatest impact on American life. During the pre–Pearl Harbor days of World War II he worked closely with Chief of Staff George C. Marshall to secure congressional approval for conscription, promote the growth of war industries, and reorganize the War Department, a necessity in a military establishment about to expand to 12 million men and women.

Stimson valued technological innovation. He pushed for the development of radar and played a central role in the administration of atomic bomb development. When Roosevelt died, Stimson was the person who informed Truman of the existence of the weapon. Though Stimson never doubted that atomic weapons should be used against Japan, he vetoed the selection of the old imperial capital of Kyoto as the first target, arguing that destruction of a major cultural treasure would violate the norms of civilized behavior.

A committed internationalist, Stimson favored an early sharing of atomic technology with other nations, including the Soviet Union, with the objective of limiting further military development of the technology. In the Truman cabinet, he fought against punitive treatment of Germany and Japan. Stimson envisioned a stable, American-dominated postwar order that would permit free trade throughout the world.

Elting E. Morison, *Turmoil and Tradition: A Study of the Life and Times of Henry L. Stimson* (1960); Henry Stimson and McGeorge Bundy, *On Active Service in Peace and War* (1948).

JONATHAN SOFFER

STONE, HARLAN FISKE

(1872–1946), lawyer, teacher, and chief justice, U.S. Supreme Court. Born in New Hampshire and raised in western Massachusetts, Stone entered Columbia Law School at a time of great intellectual ferment in the 1890s. On graduation he taught at the law school and engaged in private practice, primarily with the Wall Street firm of Wilmer and Canfield. From 1910 to 1923 he served as dean of the law school.

Stone's tenure at Columbia was marked by frequent battles with the dictatorial president of the university, Nicholas Murray Butler. The faculty usually supported Stone, who was able to improve the school's standards and faculty significantly.

In early 1924 President Calvin Coolidge, attempting to restore public confidence after the scandals of the Harding administration, named Stone attorney general. Stone cleaned up the Justice Department, especially its investigative branch, and named J. Edgar Hoover to head the FBI.

The following year, an appreciative Coolidge named Stone to the Supreme Court, where he joined Oliver Wendell Holmes and Louis D. Brandeis in the Court's liberal bloc. Like them, he believed in judicial restraint and was willing to defer to legislatures despite any personal qualms about the wisdom of their policies.

Stone emerged as the leader of the liberal bloc during the fight over New Deal legislation. He wrote a number of vigorous dissents upholding Congress's exercise of the commerce and tax powers to meliorate the economic effects of the depression. His most famous dissent came in *United States* v. *Butler* (1936), in which he methodically tore apart the majority opinion and charged the conservatives with substituting their judgment for that of Congress.

Following the constitutional crisis of 1937, in which President Franklin D. Roosevelt unsuccessfully tried to pack the Supreme Court, the Court abandoned close review of economic policy and began to focus more on individual rights. Stone made what was possibly his most important contribution to modern jurisprudence in *United States* v. *Carolene Products Co.* (1938). He held that henceforth the Court would apply only a minimal level of scrutiny to economic legislation but suggested in a famous footnote that laws affecting individual rights and liberties would require more careful review — the basis for the modern doctrine of strict scrutiny. Stone demonstrated what this meant in his lone dissent in the first flag salute case, *Minersville School District* v. *Gobitis* (1940), in which he argued that the Court should not defer to the legislature when it violated civil liberties.

When Charles Evans Hughes retired in 1941, President Franklin D. Roosevelt elevated the Republican Stone to be chief justice, an appointment applauded in both parties and in legal and academic circles. His tenure, however, disappointed his admirers. Stone had the misfortune of heading the Court in wartime, when

even the cautious often gave in to war hysteria. Stone himself delivered the Court's opinion in the leading Japanese relocation case, *Hirabayashi* v. *United States* (1943), which upheld the government's actions.

Moreover, although possessing a fine legal mind, Stone did not have the tough political skills necessary to keep one of the most fractious benches in history in line. The number of dissents and split opinions increased sharply as the Court divided between a conservative faction headed by Felix Frankfurter and devoted to judicial restraint and the more activist group centered around Hugo Black, which plunged ahead with the logic of Stone's *Carolene Products* footnote.

Alpheus T. Mason, *Harlan Fiske Stone: Pillar of the Law* (1956).

MELVIN I. UROFSKY

See also Supreme Court.

STOWE, HARRIET BEECHER

(1811–1896), author. Born in Litchfield, Connecticut, Harriet Beecher was the seventh child of the Reverend Lyman Beecher, a Congregational minister and moral reformer, and Roxanna Foote Beecher. She was schooled at the Pierce Academy and at her sister Catharine Beecher's Hartford Female Seminary, where she also taught. She moved with the family to Cincinnati in 1832, when her father was appointed president of Lane Theological Seminary. The spectacle of chattel slavery across the Ohio River in Kentucky and its effects on the acquiescent commercial interests of white Cincinnati moved her deeply.

In 1836, she married Calvin Ellis Stowe, professor of biblical literature at Lane. The death of a son in 1849 led her away from her father's Calvinism and gave supremacy in her views to the redemptive spirit of Christian love. By 1850, the family had moved to Maine, where, in response to the Fugitive Slave Act of that year, Stowe wrote *Uncle Tom's Cabin* (1852), her most celebrated work. Sentimental and realistic by turns, the novel explored the cruelties of chattel slavery in the Upper and Lower South and exposed the moral ironies in the legal, religious, and social arguments of white apologists.

The immense impact of the novel (it sold 300,000 copies in its first year) was unexpected. Antislavery fiction had never sold well; Stowe was not an established writer, and few would have expected a woman to gain a popular hearing on the great political question of the day. Some female abolitionists had shocked decorum in the 1840s by speaking at public gatherings, but they were widely resented. The success of *Uncle Tom's Cabin* went far toward legitimizing, if not indeed creating, a role for women in public affairs.

To the dismay of many northern radicals, *Uncle Tom's Cabin* casually endorsed colonization rather than abolition. In fact, Stowe was unconcerned about the tactics that made slavery a political issue: for her, the problem was religious and emotional, and one that women were best equipped to confront. Her stated purpose, "to awaken sympathy and feeling for the African race" and to urge that readers "feel right" about the issue, belongs to a feminist and utopian agenda that contemporary readers were slow to recognize. In the South, the book was read as sectional propaganda; in the North, it was read as a compelling moral romance. Although Stowe blamed the slave system itself as "the essence of all abuse" rather than the slaveholders and deliberately made its chief villain, Simon Legree, a displaced New Englander, the novel's effect was to exacerbate regional antagonisms. Indeed, *Uncle Tom's Cabin,* which called forth anti-Tom novels from southern writers, so raised the temperature of the dialogue that Lincoln would later, half-seriously, apportion to Stowe some responsibility for starting the Civil War.

Notable among Stowe's subsequent works are *A Key to Uncle Tom's Cabin* (1853), documenting her case against slavery; *Dred: A Tale of the Great Dismal Swamp* (1856), also on slavery; and *The Minister's Wooing* (1859), a historical novel that attacks Calvinism. Stowe also wrote realistic regional fiction, including *The Pearl of Orr's Island* (1861), which influenced Sarah Orne Jewett and Mary E. Wilkins Freeman. Her miscellaneous writings include *Lady Byron Vin-*

dicated (1870), which created an international sensation by charging Lord Byron with incest, and *Palmetto Leaves* (1873), written at her winter home in Florida, which encouraged a Florida land boom.

Thomas F. Gossett, *Uncle Tom's Cabin and American Culture* (1985); Eric J. Sundquist, ed., *New Essays on Uncle Tom's Cabin* (1986); Forrest Wilson, *Crusader in Crinoline: The Life of Harriet Beecher Stowe* (1941).

ALBERT J. VON FRANK

See also Abolitionist Movement; Literature; *Uncle Tom's Cabin.*

STRATEGIC ARMS LIMITATION TALKS

These negotiations helped thaw Soviet-American relations during the cold war. With help from National Security Adviser Henry A. Kissinger, President Richard M. Nixon and Soviet premier Leonid Brezhnev completed the first Strategic Arms Limitation Talks (SALT) in 1972. (Contrary to popular impression, the "T" stands for "Talks," not "Treaty"; the acronym was coined originally to serve as a file heading for material related to the talks.) Both sides agreed to limit their offensive intercontinental ballistic missiles. The United States ended up with fewer missiles (710 submarine and 1,000 land missiles to 950 submarine and 1,410 land missiles for the Soviets), and Nixon would not cut other weapons, especially MIRVs (Multiple Independently Targetable Re-entry Vehicles), which put several warheads on one missile. But he and Brezhnev agreed to limit the amount of defensive antiballistic missiles (ABMs). The Senate approved the treaties 88–2.

Nixon's successors met mixed results in negotiating SALT II. President Gerald Ford and Secretary of State Kissinger met with Brezhnev and agreed to reduce the number of missiles, but disputes over Soviet treatment of Jews chilled relations. When President Jimmy Carter proposed more cuts, Brezhnev refused. Then, with the United States opening diplomatic relations with China and the Soviets needing economic help, Brezhnev met with Carter in Vienna in 1979 and agreed to SALT II, which limited strategic nuclear launching missiles to 2,400 (later cut to 2,250) per side, with a maximum of 1,320 to be MIRVs. But the treaty ran into opposition in the Senate, and the Soviet invasion of Afghanistan in December 1979 again harmed Soviet-American relations. The treaty was not approved, and in 1982, President Ronald Reagan announced that SALT was being replaced by a new round of negotiations, START (Strategic Arms Reduction Talks), which led to subsequent agreements to reduce nuclear weapons.

See also Cold War; Nuclear Weapons: Origins and Legacy.

STRAVINSKY, IGOR

(1882–1971), composer. Stravinsky earned fame as a composer for Sergei Diaghilev's Ballets Russes, a Russian company based from 1909 to 1929 in Paris. Three ballets — *The Firebird* (1910), *Petrushka* (1911), and *The Rite of Spring* (1913) — secured his reputation both as continuator of the traditions of the Russian national school and as fearless modernist. After World War I, his prestige in Paris was enhanced by his advocacy of a smart neoclassical aesthetic that accorded well with the ideals of the reigning intellectual and creative avant-garde. The vogue for American popular music in Europe is reflected in a number of his compositions of the period. By the 1930s he was widely regarded as being (with Arnold Schoenberg) one of the two greatest living composers.

Stravinsky first toured the United States in 1925. He received commissions for two major compositions: the ballet *Apollon musagète* (1927–1928; revised 1947 as *Apollo*) and the *Symphony of Psalms* (1930).

While on his second American tour in 1935, he received a commission from Lincoln Kirstein for the ballet *Jeu de cartes*, first performed under the composer's baton at the Metropolitan Opera House in 1937. Other American commissions of the thirties included his Concerto in E-flat for chamber orchestra (1938, known as the *Dumbarton Oaks* Concerto) and the Symphony in C (1939–1940).

In 1939–1940 he was the Charles Eliot Norton professor of poetry at Harvard University. The six lectures he delivered in French were translated into English as *The Poetics of Music* and remain a major enunciation of modernist musical aesthetics.

Stravinsky was in America at the outbreak of World War II (he had resided in neutral Switzerland in World War I) and decided to stay put — a decision partly motivated by a wish to start life anew in the aftermath of personal tragedy (he had lost a daughter, his wife, and his mother the preceding year). He remarried and settled in Hollywood, where he lived until 1969. Despite several attempts, Stravinsky never succeeded in getting his music accepted by the Hollywood studios; some of the music he wrote "on spec" for the movies wound up in his scores from the forties. Another ill-starred early project was his arrangement of "The Star-Spangled Banner," which became a cause célèbre and was banned in Boston in 1941.

Stravinsky had an enormous influence on young American composers despite the fact that he rarely took pupils. Partly thanks to the presence in Boston at that time of Nadia Boulanger, a Stravinsky disciple, a virtual "Stravinsky school" of American neoclassical composition grew up in that city. There was little in the way of reciprocal American influence on Stravinsky; the only composition of his that clearly reflects the impact of his new environment was the *Ebony* Concerto (1945) for jazz ensemble (plus harp and French horn), written for the Woody Herman band.

In 1947 Stravinsky collaborated with W. H. Auden on an opera in English, based on Hogarth's series of engravings *The Rake's Progress*. Because of his discomfort with the language, he engaged the young American conductor Robert Craft to read the libretto aloud to him. The relationship with Craft became a quasi-filial one, with profound consequences for Stravinsky's work.

It was Craft's enthusiastic involvement with the music of Schoenberg and his pupils Berg and Webern that piqued Stravinsky's interest in their techniques of serial composition. His gradual approach to the twelve-tone system can be surveyed in works like the Cantata (1952), the ballet *Agon* (1957), and *Threni* (for chorus and orchestra, 1957–1958), his first fully twelve-tone work. Stravinsky evolved his own twelve-tone methods over the next decade or so, achieving a remarkable synthesis of the serial approach with his earlier habits of rhythm, articulation, and harmonic structure.

Robert Craft, *Stravinsky: Chronicle of a Friendship, 1948–1971* (1972); Eric Walter White and Jeremy Noble, "Stravinsky," in *The New Grove Modern Masters* (1984).

RICHARD F. TARUSKIN

See also Music.

STRIKES

See Labor.

STUDENT NON-VIOLENT COORDINATING COMMITTEE

The Student Non-Violent Coordinating Committee (SNCC), formed to give younger blacks more of a voice in the civil rights movement, became one of the movement's more radical branches. In the wake of the early sit-ins at lunch counters closed to blacks, which started in February 1960 in Greensboro, North Carolina, Ella Baker, then director of the Southern Christian Leadership Conference (SCLC), helped set up the first meeting of what became SNCC. She was concerned that SCLC, led by the Reverend Dr. Martin Luther King, Jr., was out of touch with younger blacks who wanted the movement to make faster progress. Baker encouraged those who formed SNCC to look beyond integration to broader social change and to view King's principle of nonviolence more as a political tactic than as a way of life.

The new group played a large part in the Freedom Rides aimed at desegregating buses and in the marches organized by King and SCLC. Under the leadership of James Forman, Bob Moses, and Marion Barry, the Student Non-Violent Coordinating Committee also directed much of the black voter registration drives in the South. Three of its members died at the hands of the

Ku Klux Klan during the Mississippi Freedom Summer of 1964. Events such as these heightened divisions between King and SNCC. The latter objected to compromises at the 1964 Democratic National Convention, where the party refused to replace the all-white Mississippi delegation with the integrated Freedom Democrats.

In 1966, Stokely Carmichael was elected head of SNCC and popularized the term *black power* to characterize the new tactics and goals — including black self-reliance and the use of violence as a legitimate means of self-defense. He also drew attention to the plight of blacks in the inner cities. Carmichael's successor, H. Rap Brown, went further, saying "Violence is as American as cherry pie." But the fires and disorders that followed in the summer of 1967 led to Brown's arrest for incitement to riot, and SNCC disbanded shortly thereafter as the civil rights movement itself splintered.

See also Baker, Ella; Black Power; Civil Rights Movement.

STUDENTS FOR A DEMOCRATIC SOCIETY

Students for a Democratic Society (SDS), founded in 1960, was the institutional mainstay of the New Left. In June 1962, fifty-nine SDS members and sympathizers met in Port Huron, Michigan, to draft a sixty-three-page political platform. A thoughtful critique of the cold war and the materialistic complacency of postwar American life, the Port Huron Statement proposed that universities should be the locus of a new movement for "participatory democracy." That goal, never precisely defined, animated SDS and aimed generally toward transferring power from representative institutions to individuals and communities. In September 1963, SDS formed the Economic Research and Action Project to put participatory democracy into practice. In the summer of 1964, 125 SDS organizers in nine cities tried to mobilize poor people for "the new insurgency." In Newark and Chicago they acquired some influence. But their efforts never resolved the conflict between an increasingly revolutionary outlook and the fact that most concrete gains came from cooperation with the government.

The group then turned to antiwar activism. On April 17, 1965, SDS held the first of several mass demonstrations against the Vietnam War, drawing fifteen thousand people to Washington, D.C. In November, it cosponsored a demonstration that drew thirty thousand.

In 1968, SDS achieved a level of power and prominence unprecedented for a student organization. To protest Columbia University's participation in war-related research and its appropriation of a public park as the site for a new gymnasium, students occupied campus buildings in April. The university brought the occupation to an end by calling in the New York City police who injured over 200 students and arrested 712. Similar occupations spread to some forty other campuses across the country.

By that year, however, the rapid growth of SDS had created chaos and divisions within the organization. When the Progressive Labor party, a tiny remnant of the Old Left, took it over in June 1969, SDS collapsed. What remained became a small revolutionary sect known as the Weathermen.

See also New Left; Radicalism.

STUYVESANT, PETER

(c. 1610–1672), director general of New Netherland from 1647 to 1664. Stuyvesant was responsible for enacting the directives of the Dutch West India Company, which sought to exploit the commercial potential of the New World for the United Provinces. By 1664, his administration had resulted in a promising venture, with his surveyor able to report the existence of two cities (one, New Amsterdam, had 342 houses and 14 public buildings), thirteen villages, two forts, and three colonies. In addition, a strong influx of colonists had begun in 1657, and transatlantic trade, though favoring the home-country merchants, was bringing increased stability.

Stuyvesant, born in Friesland, was the son of a minister of the Reformed Church, whose piety may have influenced Peter's own inflexible religious nature. Young Stuyvesant began his ca-

reer with the West India Company, where he learned the skills needed by its resident overseas directors: the ability to command its marines at sea and in fortified trading stations and the capacity to direct a small bureaucracy of accountants and clerks.

By 1639, Stuyvesant was serving as the company's commissary of stores on the island of Curaçao. When the director suddenly died, Stuyvesant was selected to replace him. Immediately, he committed himself to the island's careful governance but also pursued the aggressive policy of previous directors. In 1644, he attacked St. Martin, an island lost by the Dutch to the Spaniards in 1633, and sustained a severe wound, resulting in the amputation of his right leg below the knee. To recover his health, he returned to Rotterdam.

In 1646 Stuyvesant was commissioned director of New Netherland and arrived on Manhattan Island the next year. Under Willem Kieft, his predecessor, the colony had seriously deteriorated. Residents were factious and unconcerned for the settlement's prosperity. Although Stuyvesant attacked this disorder aggressively — placing himself above the factions, tightening trading regulations, and slowly restoring confidence in the company — enmities lingered until 1652.

The unrest exacerbated the long struggle during which the burghers contended with Stuyvesant for New Amsterdam's independence as a city. He yielded the most important of his rights in 1653, when the burghers won a court of inferior jurisdiction. After that time, Stuyvesant was forced to bargain with the city's officials on such issues as the collection of excise taxes and defenses. He was a tough negotiator but always understood how the delicately balanced decentralization of power fit into the republicanism of the Low Countries.

Stuyvesant also inherited unstable relations with nearby Indian tribes because of Kieft's brutal policies. His own was a pragmatic program of amicable relations. Although quick to use violence in 1655 against the Esopus Indians (near present-day Kingston), he usually promoted legislation to exploit the natives as a cheap work force — as hunters, for example, who could bring furs from distant tribes.

In 1655, Stuyvesant received orders to eliminate competition from the Swedes trading along the Delaware River. He subsequently captured New Sweden and incorporated its population into New Netherland. His insoluble problem, however, concerned the colony's English neighbors. Relations with those to the south (Virginia) were good, partly because of the mutual profits to be had in the exchange of tobacco for household wares. But colonists to the north — New Englanders and English-speaking Long Islanders — routinely pressed upon Dutch lands and disregarded intercolonial agreements. In 1664, a squadron sent by King Charles II of England forced Stuyvesant to surrender New Netherland to the British.

Stuyvesant returned home to defend his decision to surrender and then traveled back to New Netherland — now New York — where he lived quietly on his farm until his death.

Henry H. Kessler and Eugene Rachlis, *Peter Stuyvesant and His New York* (1959); Hendrik Van Loon, *Life and Times of Peter Stuyvesant* (1928).

DONNA MERWICK

See also Middle Colonies.

SUBTREASURY LAND AND LOAN SYSTEM

The Subtreasury Land and Loan System was a plan advocated by the National Farmers' Alliance and Industrial Union and the People's party in the early 1890s. It proposed a federal solution to the problem of agricultural credit. Depressed staple prices and tight money had forced many farmers into debt. In order to secure the credit necessary to see them through the agricultural year, farmers had to execute liens on crops or land on most unfavorable terms. In 1889, Charles Macune of the Farmers' Alliance proposed that the federal government establish "subtreasury" offices and storage facilities in counties selling more than $500,000 worth of agricultural products annually. Farmers could deposit "imperishable" commodities — cotton, wheat, corn, oats, barley, rye, rice, tobacco, wool, or sugar — and in return be loaned government legal tender notes, at 1 percent interest, for up to 80 percent of their crops' value. The proposal was later amended to provide similar loans secured by land.

The system had several advantages. Farmers would be able to mortgage crops or land to the federal government at nominal interest rates rather than to profit-seeking individuals or companies. They could store their crops in government warehouses until supplies were low and prices high. Advocates argued that the legal tender notes would create a flexible monetary system responsive to the public's needs.

The Subtreasury idea helped prompt the formation of Populist parties, especially in the South. Through 1890, Southern Alliance members had generally renounced third-party efforts, preferring to work within the Democratic party. But with the major parties opposed to the plan, many of its advocates concluded that the Subtreasury plan could be won only through independent action. The plan was never enacted, however, though many of its elements appeared in later federal legislation.

See also Farmers' Alliance; Populism.

SUBURBANIZATION

"The United States," observed historian Richard Hofstadter, "was born in the country and has moved to the city." In fact, he was only half correct. Having moved to the city, Americans kept going and wound up in the suburbs. This shift was so profound and so enormous that by 1990 more than 45 percent of the population, or more than 120 million people, lived in suburban areas, a far higher proportion than resided either in rural regions or in central cities. Quite simply, the United States had become the world's first suburban nation.

Although the term *suburb* is vague and many different types of places are often labeled suburban, one may generalize about the American experience, especially in comparison with patterns elsewhere in the world. Indeed, the United States has thus far been unique in four important respects that can be summed up in the following sentence: affluent and middle-class

Americans live in suburban areas that are far from their workplaces, in homes that they own, and in the center of yards that by international standards are enormous.

The first distinguishing element of metropolitan areas in the United States is their low residential density and the absence of sharp divisions between town and country. The outer boundaries of Tokyo, Paris, Moscow, Cologne, Stockholm, and Vienna, to take only a few obvious examples, abruptly terminate with groups of apartment buildings. But American cities blend into communities with broad streets and expansive lawns, which sprawl over hundreds and sometimes thousands of square miles. This dispersal results from the privatization of American life and the tendency of people to live in fully detached homes. Of the more than 90 million dwelling units in the nation in 1990, fully two-thirds consisted of a single family living in a single dwelling surrounded by an ornamental lawn.

The second distinguishing residential feature of American culture is a strong penchant for homeownership. In 1990, about two-thirds of all families in the United States owned their dwellings, a proportion approximately double that of Germany, France, Britain, Japan, Norway, and Switzerland. Only New Zealand, Australia, and Canada, all with strong frontier traditions, small populations, and a British-induced cultural dislike of cities, share the American home-owning experience.

The third and most important characteristic of the housing pattern is the socioeconomic distinction between the center and the periphery. In the United States, status and income correlate with suburbs, the area that provides the homes for an overwhelming proportion of those with college educations, those engaged in professional pursuits, and those in the upper-income brackets. Despite hopes and claims of a recent revival in American cities, the 1990 census revealed a widening disparity between residents of central cities and those of their surrounding suburbs not only in income but also in housing and family structure.

The situation in other nations again offers a striking contrast. The highest socioeconomic sections of Rome, Barcelona, Paris, Amsterdam, and Vienna are near the business districts; suburban areas are usually lower income in character. In Cairo, the affluent Garden City section lies along the Nile River almost at the center of the metropolis; the major slums are on the southern and northeastern fringes. In Calcutta and Bombay, the only areas with a passable water supply are at the core, where the wealthy live. The depths of squalor can be found in the thousands of legally defined slum districts, known as *bustees,* around the rim of the cities. Similarly, in São Paulo and Rio de Janeiro, the concentration of the poor on the outskirts is so deeply rooted in the culture that the pastel-colored squatter settlements are called *favelas* after the name of a flowering tree that grows in profusion on the hillsides.

The final distinguishing characteristic of the American residential experience is the length of the average journey to work, whether measured in miles or minutes. According to the 1980 census, typical American workers traveled 9.2 miles and expended twenty-two minutes each way in reaching their places of employment. In larger metropolitan areas, the figures were much higher. Precise statistics are unavailable for Europe, Asia, and South America, but one need only think of the widespread practice of going home for lunch, often for a siesta as well, to realize that an easier connection between work and residence is more valued and achieved in other cultures.

How and why have living patterns in the United States become so different from those of the rest of the world? No single answer can account for such an important phenomenon, but it is clear that American suburbanization began even before the Civil War, by which time influential architects like Andrew Jackson Downing and Alexander Jackson Davis had already touted the cottage as the solution to social ills, and important authors like Catharine Beecher and Henry David Thoreau had extolled the virtues of yards and meadows to an audience that was coming to see cities as too large, too noisy, and too fearsome to raise children in. By 1900, suburbs had begun to sprout around every city. In New York City, a hundred thousand commuters were daily passing through Grand Central Terminal; in Philadelphia, the suburban Main Line was famous in European capitals; in Boston, affluent Brookline was resisting annexation and thumbing its nose at the Hub; in Chicago, a vast rail network was opening new suburbs to the north, south, and west. If the particular circumstances were everywhere different, the basic pattern was everywhere the same — a new kind of metropolis was emerging that was very different from the walking city of a century earlier. By 1900, the center of every American city had become an area of office and commercial uses that was almost devoid of residences. Nearby were the grimy factories, and just beyond them the first tenement districts of the poor, the recent immigrants, and the unskilled, persons unable to afford good housing. Along these same streets, the well-to-do had lived only two generations earlier.

Beyond the compact confines of the walking city lay the new streetcar suburbs. The residential structures that filled them were not elegant, but they were spacious and affordable by European standards and they represented an attainable goal in 1900.

Farther out, the railroad commuters lived in houses that sprawled in ample yards, thick with trees and shrubbery behind iron or wooden fences. These residences represented a new American ideal. Unlike the in-town residences of the English gentry, the structures were uniquely American; with their pseudo-Gothic cupolas and mansard roofs, they set a suburban rather than an urban standard for achievement-oriented Americans.

How to account for the residential deconcentration of the United States? Why did a rich, powerful, and technologically sophisticated nation neglect its cities and concentrate so much of its energy, creativity, and vitality in the suburbs? Two factors — racial prejudice and cheap housing — were paramount.

In comparison with the relative homogeneity of Germany, Japan, Britain, and France, the cities of the United States, and particularly the larger metropolises, have long been extraordinarily diverse. In suburban terms, this has provided an extra incentive — fear — for persons to move away from their older domiciles. After the mass migration of African-Americans from the South gained momentum during World War I, and especially after the Supreme Court decision in 1954 outlawing school segregation as unconstitutional, millions of families moved out of the city "for the kids" and especially for the educational (as measured by standardized test scores) and social (as measured by family income) superiority of smaller and more homogeneous suburban school systems. The sprawling, single-story public schools of outlying towns, surrounded by playing fields and parking lots, became familiar symbols of suburban life and educational manifestations of tract developments.

Economic causes have been even more important than skin color in the suburbanization of the United States, however. Contrary to popular impression, the real cost of American houses has been relatively low and affordable over the past century and a half, especially in comparison with other nations of the world. There are essentially five reasons for this. The first has been per-capita wealth. With its vast middle class, the United States was the first society in history in which the distribution of wealth did not resemble a pyramid. As a "people of plenty," Americans could afford the wastefulness of low-density housing on the metropolitan fringe.

The second component of low cost has been inexpensive land. Building lots in North America have typically been priced from one-fourth to one-half of comparably sized parcels in Europe and about one-tenth of those in Japan. This is largely because the United States is a land of spaciousness and openness in contrast to its industrial rivals. Abundant land has meant cheap land.

The third component has been inexpensive transport, which has brought home sites within easy commuting range of workplaces. Although the omnibus, the steam railroad, the subway, and the automobile were all developed first in Europe, it was in the United States that they were most enthusiastically adopted and where they most immediately affected the lives of ordinary citizens. Especially before World War I, the subways, commuter railroads, elevated trains, and electric trolleys of American cities were faster, more frequent, more efficient, and more cost-effective than transportation options elsewhere in the world. The mass production of automobiles reinforced the pattern because for the first seventy years of the twentieth century the real price of both cars and fuel fell. Even in 1990, the cost of operating an automobile remained cheaper in the United States than in other advanced nations.

The fourth component of low cost has been the balloon-frame house. The development of an inexpensive and peculiarly American method of building houses with two-by-four-inch wooden studs simplified construction and brought the price of a private dwelling within the reach of most citizens. Whether the exterior material is brick, stucco, or clapboard, more than 90 percent of all single-family homes are made of wood at their core. Such structures are uncommon in other countries, in part because their citizens regard the balloon frame as flimsy, and in part because they lack the timber resources of the heavily forested United States.

And finally, government, particularly at the federal level, has played a central role in promoting affordability. Particularly important has been the unusual American practice of allowing taxpayers to deduct mortgage interest and property taxes from taxable income. The size of this subsidy to homeownership is staggering and typically exceeds by five or six times all the direct expenditures Congress grants to housing. Simply put, the Internal Revenue Code finances the continued growth of suburbia. Similarly, FHA and VA mortgage insurance, the highway system, the financing of sewers, the placement of public housing at the center of ghetto neighborhoods, and the locational decisions of federal agencies, to name only the most obvious examples, have encouraged scattered development into the open countryside.

These economic factors, combined with racial prejudice and a pervasive fondness for grass and solitude, have made private detached houses affordable and desirable to the middle class. They have produced a suburban pattern of work, residence, and consumption that has thus far been more pronounced in the United States than elsewhere.

Robert Fishman, *Bourgeois Utopias: The Rise and Fall of Suburbia* (1987); Kenneth T. Jackson, *Crabgrass Frontier: The Suburbanization of the United States* (1985).

KENNETH T. JACKSON

See also Automobiles; Balloon-Frame House; Housing; Levittowns; Public Transportation.

SUFFRAGE

The history of the right to vote in the United States suggests an inevitable progress toward democracy. In colonial America property qualifications limited the right to vote, whereas suffrage today is open to all citizens at the age of eighteen. The colonists regarded the suffrage as a privilege; Americans today consider it a right. But this interpretation obscures long periods in which various groups — women, black men, and paupers — were disfranchised.

The history of American suffrage begins in England in 1430, when Parliament restricted the vote in county parliamentary elections to persons owning land that generated an annual income of at least forty shillings. English boroughs had a hodgepodge of criteria for their elections. Laws also excluded aliens, servants, non-Anglicans, and women.

The colonies initially established suffrage requirements that resembled the rules of the boroughs, but by the early eighteenth century lawmakers came to emulate the spirit of the law of 1430. For example, Massachusetts at first enfranchised all male adult Congregational church members, but excluded Anglican property owners. Pressure in post-Restoration England compelled the colony to allow propertied Anglicans over the age of twenty-four to vote alongside twenty-one-year-old propertyless Congregational church members.

After the Glorious Revolution, the charter of 1691 established a modified version of the election act of 1430. Elsewhere in New England and in New York, the forty-shilling freehold was reproduced; frequently it involved a freehold of a certain size (often fifty acres) or value (usually forty or fifty pounds). Several New England colonies also allowed a personal estate of forty pounds as a substitute.

Because land was readily available, the application of English standards created a large electorate. Eligibility ranged from about 50 to 80 percent of free males. Moreover, because most free men eventually acquired land, the landholding qualification functioned most often only as an age requirement.

Voters also had to meet religious, racial, and residency requirements. Some colonies disfranchised dissenting Protestants, Catholics, and Jews until 1689; thereafter, most excluded only non-Protestants. Free blacks were disfranchised in every southern colony during part of the colonial era, and ten colonies established residency requirements.

Colonial and revolutionary Americans believed that a man's economic independence earned him membership in the political community. His autonomy supposedly enabled him to make independent political decisions; his economic stake in society would impel him to act in the public interest. The disfranchisement of propertyless males grew partly out of the related belief that economic dependence encouraged corruption, and that economic grievances endangered property rights.

During the crises leading to the Revolution, quarrels about representation caused a reconsideration of relations among property, taxation, and voting. Americans insisted that Parliament lacked the authority to tax unrepresented subjects. Extending this argument, many claimed that taxpayers, not only property holders, needed the vote to protect themselves against excessive taxation. By 1790, five states permitted all male (in some states only white male) taxpayers to vote for all or some offices. The states also relied increasingly upon residency, not land ownership, as evidence of one's attachment to the community. Virtually all set one to two years as the required length of residency.

The Revolution itself and the subsequent turmoil in the states threatened to sever political rights from their economic moorings. During the war many Americans argued that the polity should include those men who supported the Revolution, without reference to property. Tories, no matter how much property they possessed, were denied the vote. After the war, residency requirements took the place of loyalty oaths.

For all the alterations in political rights wrought by the Revolution, far more than half the adult population remained disfranchised. Among them were many propertyless men, women, slaves, some free black men, apprentices, indentured laborers, felons, and those considered mentally incompetent. Slaves and indentured servants were excluded because of their legal dependence upon a master, felons and the mentally impaired because they showed no attachment to the community or were considered incompetent.

Women were excluded because of a presumed incapacity for sound reasoning. Only in New Jersey were women enfranchised. The New Jersey Constitution of 1776 granted the vote to all inhabitants "worth" fifty pounds who had resided in a voting place for one year. In subsequent years, election officials interpreted the provision literally and permitted propertied women to vote. New Jersey, however, was the exception.

But the revolutionary struggle had significantly expanded the electorate. During the Revolution states with poll taxes and taxpayer franchises (such as North Carolina and New Hampshire) established nearly universal free male suffrage. When suffrage qualifications were tied to the value of an estate, wartime inflation eroded barriers. All states ended religious restrictions on voting. At war's end, the eligible electorate numbered from 60 to 90 percent of free males, with most states edging close to the high end of that range.

Between the Revolution and the Civil War, politically active Americans carried forward the Revolution's ambiguous legacy. Because property ownership was widespread, it no longer served as a benchmark for citizenship. Political incapacity continued to be linked to gender. Most men thought of women as politically incompetent and thus connected civic virtue with masculinity. But white Americans also linked civic virtue to race. Blacks were seen as incapable of civic virtue, white men as naturally virtuous. Between 1790 and 1860 almost every state, old and new, disfranchised free blacks while expanding the electorate to include almost all white adult male citizens.

The suffrage requirements of the frontier states were more democratic than eastern ones. Beginning with Kentucky in 1792, all but two western states embraced white male adult suffrage; in the East, all but two states retained either a property or taxpaying qualification for all or part of the period from 1820 to 1860. Several western states even enfranchised aliens who had established permanent residence and Indians who had given up tribal citizenship. The new West's rapid movement toward universal white manhood suffrage was facilitated by insecure land titles, the erosion of social distinctions, the desire to attract new settlers, and the belief that Indians could eventually become enough like whites to exercise political rights intelligently. Electoral competition everywhere also encouraged politicians to lower suffrage qualifications so they could portray themselves as champions of popular democracy.

With the advent of the second American party system, Democrats and Whigs hotly disagreed about the scope of political rights. The Democrats, worried less about civic virtue and more about each man's need to defend himself against governmental tyranny, viewed the suffrage as an inherent right of white males. The Whigs largely accepted republican notions of a hierarchical organic society and therefore treated the suffrage as a privilege. But by 1850, electoral pressure had converted most Whigs to the idea of white male democracy.

Only in the state of Rhode Island did politicians resist the trend. The state's requirement that a man own a $134 freehold in order to vote became increasingly restrictive as the Rhode Island economy shifted from agriculture toward industry. By the early 1840s more than half of the state's male population was disfranchised. But a reform effort led by Thomas Dorr, after holding an extralegal constitutional convention in 1841 and an extralegal gubernatorial election, sparked some liberalization of suffrage requirements.

In Seneca Falls, New York, in 1848 three hundred female and male reformers asserted the right of women to vote. The idea of woman suffrage grew in response to the nearly universal enfranchisement of white males and female participation in abolitionism after the 1820s. But in a culture that exalted the domestic role of women, few people argued the merits of female enfranchisement.

Although suffrage had always been regulated by state constitutions and statutes and local ordinances, woman suffragists after the Civil War hoped for national enfranchisement alongside newly freed black men. But they lost as traditional notions of woman's place predominated in Congress: the Fourteenth Amendment tacitly endorsed suffrage restrictions based upon sex.

Congress, in an act unique among postemancipation societies, admitted freedmen to membership in the political community. In so doing, congressmen imagined that the suffrage would give the freedmen the ability to protect themselves and their families from exploitation. The Republican-dominated Congress also enfranchised black men to strengthen Republican control in the southern states. Black male suffrage became national in 1870 when the Fifteenth Amendment prohibited states from discriminating against potential voters because of race or previous condition of servitude (but not sex).

The amendment was partially successful. For most of Reconstruction, blacks voted and often used their resulting political power to protect their other rights. Although white Democrats overthrew Reconstruction by forcibly keeping blacks from the polls, thereafter they generally eschewed violence. Instead, they relied upon discriminatory apportionment and election laws to limit black and poor white political influence, and in the 1890s and 1900s, imposed poll taxes and literacy and property requirements through constitutional revisions. Thus they disfranchised virtually all black men and many poor whites, and thereby ensured Democratic hegemony.

At the same time, northern ballot reformers sought to "purify" the election process, thereby reducing the size of the electorate. The secret ballot eliminated vote-buying, but also voters who were illiterate in English. Formal literacy tests were adopted in a dozen northern states by the early twentieth century. Strict voter registration laws placed the burden of proving eligibility on citizens.

The disfranchisement of growing numbers of blacks and immigrants was applauded by many woman suffragists, who argued that the enfranchisement of native white women would secure the social order, whereas undesirable black and immigrant male voters endangered it. This conservative turn did not appreciably help their cause. Neither did the reunification of the movement in 1890 under a new organization, the National American Woman Suffrage Association. Despite the changing role of women in American society (as more women entered the workplace, became educated, bore fewer children, and spent less time caring for them), the movement met increased resistance from the liquor industry (which feared female support for prohibition) and the textile industry (which feared female support for restrictions on child labor). Beneath such practical concerns lay a more deeply felt anxiety about changing sex roles.

But the adoption of more vigorous tactics and the triumph of progressive reforms throughout the country (which made woman suffrage appear to be less radical) stimulated massive support for woman suffrage. In 1916, the Democratic and Republican parties endorsed female enfranchisement; in 1919 Congress approved, and a year later the states ratified, the Nineteenth Amendment, which granted women the right to vote.

As women were gaining the suffrage, blacks sought its restoration in the South. The NAACP, established in 1909, pursued reenfranchisement through litigation. At first, it successfully closed loopholes in southern disfranchisement that had permitted some poor, illiterate whites to vote. But its most important early success was the Supreme Court's 1944 decision prohibiting the white primary. The Court ruled that Texas had made the party primary part of the public electoral process; therefore the white-only primary violated black rights under the Fifteenth Amendment.

Despite that victory, poll taxes, literacy tests, and the manipulation of election laws by local registrars effectively excluded the vast majority of black adults. The struggle for southern enfranchisement (a major goal of the civil rights movement) accelerated after World War II for several reasons, among them the belief that the United States was hypocritical in claiming that it was defending freedom against Soviet communism while oppressing African-Americans at home. But the most important reason was the migration of millions of black southerners to the North, where blacks already voted. That circumstance gave blacks political leverage on both parties. But because Democrats hoped to retain the allegiance of southern white voters and Republicans wished to attract those voters, weak compromises resulted in the form of the Civil Rights Acts of 1957 and 1960, which ineffectually authorized federal protection of black voting rights.

The civil rights struggle intensified in the early 1960s. After passage of the Civil Rights Act of 1964, activists focused increasingly on the suffrage. The Mississippi Freedom Summer in 1964 registered few black Mississippians but drew national attention to black disfranchisement. Then, in March 1965, the Alabama State Troopers' assault on marchers outside the town of Selma generated so much support for national protection of black voters that President Lyndon B. Johnson demanded passage of an effective voting rights act, which he signed into law in August. When combined with prohibition of the poll tax in federal elections by the Twenty-third Amendment and a sweeping Supreme Court decision in 1966, the Voting Rights Act of 1965 sparked the registration of the vast majority of eligible black southerners.

Thus, amendments to the U.S. Constitution and federal law enfranchised virtually all male and female citizens at the age of twenty-one. But U.S. involvement in the Vietnam War revived a claim made since the Revolution that men old enough to fight were also old enough to vote: in 1971 the Twenty-sixth Amendment lowered the voting age to eighteen.

Steven F. Lawson, *Black Ballots: Voting Rights in the South, 1944–1969* (1976); Anne Firor Scott and Andrew MacKay Scott, *One Half the People: The Fight for Woman*

Suffrage (1982); Chilton Williamson, *American Suffrage from Property to Democracy* (1960).

MARC W. KRUMAN

See also American Woman Suffrage Association; *Baker* v. *Carr;* Civil Rights Movement; Feminist Movement; Freedom Summer; *Minor* v. *Happersett;* National American Woman Suffrage Association; National Association for the Advancement of Colored People; National Woman Suffrage Association; Reconstruction; Seneca Falls Convention.

SUGAR ACT

The Sugar Act (formally titled the American Revenue Act) was passed by Parliament in April 1764 at the recommendation of George Grenville, chancellor of the exchequer. This law, the first ever passed by Parliament specifically to raise revenue from the colonies, was part of a broader effort to strengthen imperial control after the Seven Years' War and at the same time help reduce the large national debt Britain had incurred during the fighting. Specifically, Grenville hoped to use the revenues from the act to help defray the expenses of the British troops in America. Designed as an extension of the generally unenforced Molasses Act of 1733, the Sugar Act imposed new or higher duties on sugar, textiles, coffee, indigo, and wine from non-British territories; it also added to the list of "enumerated goods" that the colonies could ship only to English ports. It discouraged the sending of foreign goods first to England and then to the colonies (a familiar way of evading import regulations) by doubling the duty on reshipments. Finally, the Sugar Act established a rigorous structure of documentation and inspection to support its provisions.

The colonists maintained that the Sugar Act constituted "taxation without representation," since their elected representatives sat in the colonial legislatures, not in Parliament. Furthermore, Grenville's overall program to extract more revenue from the colonies was perceived by them as an economic threat, in view of the business decline America had experienced since the war. The colonies began corresponding with one another over the issue, and in a number of cities agreements were made not to import British goods. These protests set the stage for the more extensive resistance movements that arose the following year over the Stamp Act.

See also Revolution.

SULLIVAN, LOUIS H.

(1856–1924), architect. Sullivan developed a unique system of ornament, which he applied as the first architect to define a rational skyscraper aesthetic and bring bank design into the twentieth century. He pioneered the attempt to remove historical reference from American architecture, the creation of which he saw as a social as opposed to an artistic act. Sullivan was the teacher of Frank Lloyd Wright, whom he employed from 1888 to 1893.

Born in Boston of Irish and Swiss/French lineage, Sullivan studied architecture at the Massachusetts Institute of Technology in 1872–1873, worked briefly in Philadelphia for the eccentric design genius Frank Furness and in Chicago for William Le Baron Jenney, an innovator in high-rise metal frame construction, and then studied in Paris (1874–1875) at the École des Beaux-Arts.

Settling in Chicago, Sullivan established a partnership in 1879 with Dankmar Adler, a brilliant acoustical and structural engineer. So successful was their collaboration that for the next twelve years their firm represented the cutting edge of American design.

The partners achieved fame before 1886 for their theater designs and concert hall renovations, Sullivan attracting attention for his bold use of color and his luxurious, organically based ornamentation within which he placed lighting and ventilating fixtures. Their acoustical, aesthetic, and lighting successes led in 1886 to their grandest commission, the Chicago Auditorium Building, a $3.2 million theater, hotel, and commercial complex, at the time the largest building in volume in the United States. Sullivan's theater, banquet hall, dining room, and other interior spaces were applauded as masterpieces, and he was regarded as the premier ornamentalist, if not architect, in the nation.

The building's fame generated major commissions of all sorts from around the country, but after 1890, Adler and Sullivan's reputation was primarily based on skyscrapers. In the Wainwright Building (St. Louis, 1890), the Schiller Building (Chicago, 1891), and the Guaranty Building (1894–1895, Buffalo), Sullivan developed a "vertical aesthetic" in which windows and horizontals were inset slightly behind columns and piers, creating what he called "a proud and soaring" image that was noticeable in the work of other architects — at Rockefeller Center, for example — as late as the 1930s, and even in 1965 on Eero Saarinen's CBS Building, also in New York. On the other hand, in the Chicago Stock Exchange (1893), the Schlesinger and Mayer (now Carson Pirie Scott) department store (Chicago, 1898, 1902), and several unrealized but well-publicized 1890s projects, Sullivan developed a frame-expressing aesthetic that allowed the directionally neutral network of steel members to determine façade composition, an organizing principle still evident in much modernist work of the 1960s. Although Sullivan actually built only seven of his twenty-five or so high-rise schemes, his influence was lasting.

By 1895, when Adler and Sullivan dissolved their partnership, they had collaborated on 180 commissions. Barely 30 stand today. For a variety of personal and professional reasons, Sullivan's career declined not in design brilliance but in his ability to get work. After 1895, he procured a mere 57 projects, of which 33 were built and only 19 remain. Seven of these were small-town midwestern banks, the best known of which — the National Farmers' (Owatonna, Minnesota, 1906–1908), Merchants' National (Grinnell, Iowa, 1913–1914), and the People's Savings and Loan (Sidney, Ohio, 1917) — exemplify Sullivan's dictum, "form follows function," by expressing interior program on the exterior and by imposing a new banking image — the strongbox — on the façade. The banks are still praised for their artistic elegance, their excellent climate controls, and their efficient internal organization.

Although Sullivan died in poverty, he re-mained for many a "Lieber Meister," in Wright's words, inspiring later generations with his lush ornament, his commitment to architectural consistency, and his refusal to compromise philosophical principle.

Louis Sullivan, *The Autobiography of an Idea* (1924); Robert Twombly, *Louis Sullivan: His Life and Work* (1986).

ROBERT TWOMBLY

See also Architecture.

SUMNER, CHARLES

(1811–1874), U.S. senator. Known for his powerful oratory and deep commitment to the cause of civil rights, Sumner emerged as an antislavery leader in the late 1840s. The Harvard-educated lawyer had previously engaged in disarmament efforts and prison and school reforms. In 1849, in the *Roberts* case, Sumner argued for integrated public schools in Massachusetts. He also became active in political protests against Texas's annexation and the Mexican War. In 1848, he joined with other disenchanted Whigs and Democrats to form the Free-Soil party, which opposed the extension of slavery into newly acquired territories.

Despite the Free-Soil defeat in 1848, and especially after the passage of the odious Fugitive Slave Law in 1850, Sumner persevered in his antislavery activities. In 1851, he was elected to the U.S. Senate as a Free-Soiler, where he campaigned against what he saw as southern aggression on the slavery issue. In 1855 he endorsed the Republican party, which had been organized primarily to oppose slavery interests.

As North-South tensions heightened, so did Sumner's rhetoric. In his Crime against Kansas speech, delivered in May 1856, he lambasted southern efforts to extend slavery into Kansas and attacked his colleague, Andrew P. Butler of South Carolina. Shortly after that speech, Butler's cousin, Congressman Preston Brooks, assaulted Sumner on the Senate floor. He spent three and a half years recovering from the beating.

When Sumner returned to the Senate in 1859, the North-South rift had intensified, but he, like most other Republicans, did not realize or perhaps care that Republican ascendancy would bring on civil war. From the war's beginning Sumner argued that it should be waged to abolish slavery, not solely to preserve the Union. He regularly pressed President Abraham Lincoln to sponsor legislation to free the slaves, grant them civil rights, and enlist them in the Union army. He also argued for stringent conditions for readmission of Confederate states to the Union.

Throughout Reconstruction Sumner urged that Congress play a predominant role in the process. He saw Reconstruction as the opportunity to establish civil rights for blacks, first in the South where Congress had explicit authority and gradually in the North. In 1865 he insisted that suffrage be granted to all black males. At the time of his death, Sumner was still vainly agitating for federal legislation repealing all discriminatory laws.

As chairman of the Senate Foreign Relations Committee, 1861–1871, Sumner sought to control U.S. foreign policy. He blamed Great Britain for the prolongation of the Civil War, because he thought Britain had favored the Confederacy. His strong stand on the *Alabama* claims issue created a rift with Ulysses S. Grant's administration. When Sumner refused to support Grant's treaty to annex the Dominican Republic (1870), the rift widened. Finally, in 1871, Senate leaders removed him from his powerful chairmanship.

Sumner's determination and drive, when devoted to a cause like that of antislavery, were admirable; yet his self-righteous, unyielding personality led to conflicts not only with presidents but with friends and family (his wife left him after eight months of marriage). Sumner believed in the power of his words, and their power often yielded results. He also believed in *what* he uttered, so much so that he could rarely see another side to the argument.

David Herbert Donald, *Charles Sumner and the Coming of the Civil War* (1960; paperback ed., 1989) and *Charles Sumner and the Rights of Man* (1970); Beverly Wilson Palmer, ed., *Selected Letters of Charles Sumner*, 2 vols. (1990).

BEVERLY WILSON PALMER

See also Abolitionist Movement; *Alabama* Claims; Civil War; Free-Soil Party; Reconstruction; Senate.

SUNBELT

After World War II a region comprising fifteen states along the southern part of the United States became known as the Sunbelt. Extending from Virginia to southern California below the thirty-seventh parallel, this territory experienced rapid population and economic growth during the postwar decades, shifting the regional balance of the country and reversing the century-old movement of population from South to North. One of the greatest population shifts in American history, it occurred at the expense of the older manufacturing regions of the Northeast and Midwest, known as the "Frostbelt."

The Sunbelt is characterized by high rates of in-migration by retirees and highly skilled professionals from the Frostbelt, an accelerated rate of economic growth, and aggressively conservative politics. Between 1940 and 1980, the population increased by 112.3 percent, as compared to a 41.9 percent increase in the Frostbelt. The growth has been concentrated in urban areas, several of which experienced spectacular increases, such as Phoenix's 1,137.8 percent and San Diego's 626 percent between 1940 and 1980. The population is distinguished by high mobility, middle-class values, and leisure-oriented lifestyles.

The Sunbelt's economic expansion was stimulated by four main factors: federal defense spending for weapons systems and military installations, particularly those instigated during World War II; other federal spending, such as interstate highway construction and Social Security, the latter enabling stable retirement for more Americans; a favorable business climate, apparent in tax incentives and low unionization rates; and an attractive quality of life, enhanced by the home air conditioner. Other influences played key roles in specific areas, such as oil and gas exploration in Texas and Oklahoma, the growth of retirement centers in Florida and Arizona, and recreation and tourism in southern

California and Florida. The Sunbelt economy is driven by high-technology chemical, electronics, and aerospace industries and bolstered by vast natural energy resources and highly productive agriculture.

See also Internal Migration.

SUPREME COURT

Although the Supreme Court is the most important judicial body in the world in terms of the role it plays within the political order, no one could have predicted this at the time the Constitution was written in 1787. The first chief justice, John Jay, resigned in 1795 to run for governor of New York. Nominated as his successor by President George Washington was John Rutledge, who had been named to the initial Court in 1789, but resigned in 1791, without ever sitting, to go to what was considered the more prestigious South Carolina Supreme Court. Because Rutledge failed to receive Senate confirmation, Oliver Ellsworth was nominated and confirmed in 1796 as chief justice, but he too resigned to accept a diplomatic post in France in 1800. Few decisions of this period were of great significance. The most important, a 1793 decision upholding federal jurisdiction in a suit brought by South Carolina land speculators against the state of Georgia, was met by a storm of protest that resulted in the quick proposal and ratification of the Eleventh Amendment effectively overruling the decision.

The rise in importance of the Supreme Court began with the appointment by President John Adams in 1801 of John Marshall, his secretary of state, to succeed Ellsworth. This appointment was widely interpreted as the symbol of the desire of the Federalists who had lost the recent election to retain control of the judicial branch after Thomas Jefferson and his supporters took over the presidency and Congress. This illustrates the extent to which the institutional mechanisms of checks and balances can help a repudiated political party. Given the lifetime tenure of justices, the Supreme Court is almost by definition a "conservative" force, even if what is being "conserved" is the liberal vision of an earlier party.

Not the least important of Marshall's contributions to the power of the Supreme Court was his establishment of the notion of a single "opinion of the Court" and his efforts, usually successful, to discourage the expression of any dissent from this opinion. Previously, the justices, like members of English courts, delivered separate opinions, with none being designated as the view of the institutional Court.

Marshall's opinion in *Marbury* v. *Madison* (1803) is famous for exemplifying the Court's power to invalidate even a congressional statute thought to violate the Constitution. Far more important, however, were a number of decisions upholding congressional power or limiting state power.

Most important was *McCulloch* v. *Maryland* (1819), which upheld the power of Congress to charter the (Second) Bank of the United States even though the Constitution contains no language specifically authorizing such an act. (This lack of authorization had led Representative James Madison, when the First Bank of the United States was chartered in 1791, to oppose the act as unconstitutional.) Moreover, the Court invalidated an attempt by Maryland to tax the Bank, viewing such a tax as an impermissible attack on the powers of the national government. What *McCulloch* illustrates is the crucial ability of the Supreme Court to legitimize the decisions made by other branches of government by reassuring the public that they are, indeed, "constitutional."

Although "judicial review" is analyzed most often in terms of the ability of the Court to invalidate unconstitutional legislation, in fact the Court rarely finds legislation unconstitutional. Most often challenges, especially to federal legislation, fail, and the disputed legislation gains legitimacy from having survived judicial scrutiny.

Also more important than *Marbury*, practically speaking, was the 1810 decision in *Fletcher* v. *Peck,* in which for the first time the Court struck down state legislation as constitutionally invalid. Over the half century following *Marbury,* the combination of the Court's upholding federal legislation and invalidating state legislation deemed offensive to one or another constitutional principle (most often the contract clause or the commerce clause) served to bolster the power of the national government and to provide reins on state powers.

Marshall was succeeded as chief justice in 1836 by Andrew Jackson's close associate, Roger B. Taney. Never again would it make quite so much sense to name a Court after its chief justice, because fragmentation, rather than unity, increasingly characterized future Courts. Broadly speaking, the so-called Taney Court did not deviate too sharply from the paths established earlier. On two occasions it upheld Fugitive Slave Acts, even though Congress was nowhere specifically authorized to pass such legislation. Taney bitterly opposed use of the contract or commerce clause to limit state regulatory power, though he did not always prevail and could only indicate his opposition in dissents.

The most notorious case of this period was *Dred Scott* v. *Sanford* in 1857. Taney ruled that blacks could not be citizens of the United States (he viewed the founding generation of Americans to have been so racist that they could not have intended that blacks would be part of the political community). He went on to declare that Congress was without power to limit the taking of slaves into new territories being opened. Inasmuch as the newly formed Republican party argued in behalf of Congress's right to make the territories "free soil," the majority of the Court, over sharp dissent, in effect declared the Republican platform unconstitutional. Although the majority may have been motivated by a desire to resolve the tremendous political hostilities generated by the slavery issue, it clearly failed, and many historians view *Dred Scott* as contributing to the outbreak of war four years later.

The Court had varying numbers of members in its first seventy-five years, for the number of justices is not specified in the Constitution. Beginning with six members, it rose to a high of ten in the Lincoln administration, as Congress was eager to make sure that the new administration could in fact control the Court. When Taney died in 1864, he was succeeded by Salmon P. Chase, Lincoln's secretary of the treas-

ury and a noted abolitionist lawyer during the 1850s. Thereafter, when Lincoln was succeeded by Andrew Johnson and open conflict broke out between Congress and the new president, Congress limited membership to eight justices to prevent the president from filling any vacancies. It then increased the membership to nine after the election of President Ulysses S. Grant, where it has stayed since. President Franklin D. Roosevelt, however, frustrated by the hostility of the majority to New Deal legislation, proposed that the number rise to as many as fifteen. But he suffered an overwhelming defeat, and the number nine now seems firmly established as part of what might be termed the "unwritten" Constitution.

During much of the nineteenth century, certain associate justices had more impact on legal development than did the chief justices. In the last quarter of the century, the most important members of the Court were Stephen J. Field, Joseph P. Bradley, and, from the perspective of a later generation, John Marshall Harlan. The first two led the Court to monitor, and often rule invalid, state economic regulation and to use the new Fourteenth Amendment to strike down some of the regulation as an illegitimate infringement of "liberty." Enforcement of "freedom of contract" became most extensive in the early twentieth century, reaping a field well sown by these earlier justices. Similarly, these and other justices refused to grant sweeping powers to Congress under the commerce clause.

Justice Harlan is noted for two great dissents. The first was delivered in the 1883 civil rights cases, in which the Court struck down the Civil Rights Act of 1875 prohibiting racial discrimination in hotels and other public accommodations. The majority declined to read the Fourteenth Amendment as authorizing such a statute as a means of providing the "equal protection of the laws" promised in its first section. Justice Harlan denounced the majority for refusing to recognize that such racial discrimination was a "badge and incident" of slavery and thus prohibited under both the Fourteenth and the Thirteenth Amendments. Later, in 1896, Harlan wrote an equally eloquent lone dissent denouncing the majority's toleration of racial segregation in the infamous case of *Plessy* v. *Ferguson.*

The laissez-faire doctrines linked with Justice Field were subjected to withering criticism by Justices Oliver Wendell Holmes, Jr. (appointed in 1902), and Louis D. Brandeis (appointed in 1916), both of whom preached deference to the decisions of Congress and state legislatures in matters of legislation involving the public interest. Although these justices inspired a generation of lawyers, their critiques would not prevail until the so-called Revolution of 1937. Then the Court, after first rejecting the constitutional legitimacy of many New Deal measures, sharply reversed itself and became extraordinarily deferential to the wishes of the other branches of government.

The relative capitulation of the Court to legislative bodies in regard to social and economic regulation did not mean that a time of concord had arrived. Indeed, the great disputes since 1937 have involved the extent to which the Court should construe the Constitution to protect racial and religious minorities, and persons with unpopular political views, from majority-backed regulation. Harlan Fiske Stone, who became chief justice in 1941, had, as an associate justice in 1938, suggested that the Court, however deferential in most circumstances, might have some special role to play in regard to "discrete and insular minorities" or where legislation made it more difficult for political outsiders to make their views felt.

Certainly the most dramatic example of this role was the Court's 1954 decision in *Brown* v. *Board of Education of Topeka* invalidating racial segregation in the schools (and, it would soon become apparent, everywhere else as well). That decision was written by Chief Justice Earl Warren, appointed by President Dwight D. Eisenhower in 1953.

Warren was certainly a significant figure, though the "Warren Court" might, on occasion, as easily have been called the "Hugo Black Court" or the "William Brennan Court," to name two especially important associate justices. However named, this Court delivered many important decisions challenging aspects of the political and legal status quo, such as the reapportionment decisions in the 1960s requiring one person—one vote in electing state legislatures. The Court became significantly more protective of freedom of speech as well.

President Richard M. Nixon was elected in 1968 in part as an avowed opponent of the Warren Court. Indeed, his first appointment was that of Warren's successor, Warren Burger, in 1969. The Burger Court did reverse the Warren Court in important ways, particularly in regard to such areas as the rights of criminal defendants. Yet three of Nixon's four appointees — Warren Burger, Lewis Powell, and Harry Blackmun — joined in what is certainly the most controversial decision of the past twenty-five years, *Roe* v. *Wade* (1973), invalidating almost all laws prohibiting abortion early in pregnancy.

With the ascent of William Rehnquist to the chief justiceship in 1986 (he had dissented in *Roe* v. *Wade*) and the appointment of conservatives Antonin Scalia in 1986, Anthony Kennedy in 1988, and (the presumably conservative) David Souter in 1990, some commentators saw the possibility of changes in the Court's approach equal in importance to those of the "Revolution of 1937."

For roughly the first 135 years of its history, the key role assigned itself by the Supreme Court was to be what was sometimes called the "umpire of the federal system." Over the past fifty years or so, the formalities of federalism have dropped into the background, to be succeeded by concern with the limits of governmental power on individual rights or, more recently, the duties of government to provide resources necessary to the individual's full enjoyment of these rights. What has remained constant throughout this period is the controversial status of the Court whenever it has attempted to resolve the great issues of the time.

Archibald Cox, *The Court and the Constitution* (1987); Robert McCloskey, *The American Supreme Court* (1960).

SANFORD LEVINSON

See also Constitution; Court-Packing Plan; Judicial Review; Judiciary Act of 1789; *and entries for individual justices, cases.*

*Supreme Court
Chief Justices*

Chief Justices	Term of Service[a]	Years of Service	Life Span
John Jay	1789–1795	5	1745–1829
John Rutledge[b]	1795	—	1739–1800
Oliver Ellsworth	1796–1800	4	1745–1807
John Marshall	1801–1835	34	1755–1835
Roger B. Taney	1836–1864	28	1777–1864
Salmon P. Chase	1864–1873	8	1808–1873
Morrison R. Waite	1874–1888	14	1816–1888
Melville W. Fuller	1888–1910	21	1833–1910
Edward D. White	1910–1921	11	1845–1921
William H. Taft	1921–1930	8	1857–1930
Charles E. Hughes	1930–1941	11	1862–1948
Harlan F. Stone	1941–1946	5	1872–1946
Fred M. Vinson	1946–1953	7	1890–1953
Earl Warren	1953–1969	16	1891–1974
Warren E. Burger	1969–1986	17	1907–
William H. Rehnquist	1986–	—	1924–

a. Term of service refers only to years as chief justice. Any previous service as associate justice appears below.
b. Appointed and served one term, but not confirmed by the Senate.

*Supreme Court
Associate Justices*

Associate Justices	Term of Service	Years of Service	Life Span
John Rutledge	1789–1791	1	1739–1800
William Cushing	1789–1810	20	1732–1810
James Wilson	1789–1798	8	1742–1798
John Blair	1789–1796	6	1732–1800
Robert H. Harrison	1789–1790	—	1745–1790
James Iredell	1790–1799	9	1751–1799
Thomas Johnson	1791–1793	1	1732–1819
William Paterson	1793–1806	13	1745–1806
Samuel Chase	1796–1811	15	1741–1811
Bushrod Washington	1798–1829	31	1762–1829
Alfred Moore	1799–1804	4	1755–1810
William Johnson	1804–1834	30	1771–1834
Henry Brockholst Livingston	1806–1823	16	1757–1823
Thomas Todd	1807–1826	18	1765–1826
Joseph Story	1811–1845	33	1779–1845
Gabriel Duval	1811–1835	24	1752–1844
Smith Thompson	1823–1843	20	1768–1843
Robert Trimble	1826–1828	2	1777–1828
John McLean	1829–1861	32	1785–1861
Henry Baldwin	1830–1844	14	1780–1844
James M. Wayne	1835–1867	32	1790–1867
Philip P. Barbour	1836–1841	4	1783–1841

Associate Justices	Term of Service	Years of Service	Life Span
John Catron	1837–1865	28	1786–1865
John McKinley	1837–1852	15	1780–1852
Peter V. Daniel	1841–1860	19	1784–1860
Samuel Nelson	1845–1872	27	1792–1873
Levi Woodbury	1845–1851	5	1789–1851
Robert C. Grier	1846–1870	23	1794–1870
Benjamin Curtis	1851–1857	6	1809–1874
John A. Campbell	1853–1861	8	1811–1889
Nathan Clifford	1858–1881	23	1803–1881
Noah H. Swayne	1862–1881	18	1804–1884
Samuel F. Miller	1862–1890	28	1816–1890
David Davis	1862–1877	14	1815–1886
Stephen J. Field	1863–1897	34	1816–1899
William Strong	1870–1880	10	1808–1895
Joseph P. Bradley	1870–1892	22	1813–1892
Ward Hunt	1873–1882	9	1810–1886
John M. Harlan	1877–1911	34	1833–1911
William B. Woods	1880–1887	7	1824–1887
Stanley Matthews	1881–1889	7	1824–1889
Horace Gray	1882–1902	20	1828–1902
Samuel Blatchford	1882–1893	11	1820–1893
Lucius Q. C. Lamar	1888–1893	5	1825–1893
David J. Brewer	1890–1910	20	1837–1910
Henry B. Brown	1890–1906	16	1836–1913
George Shiras, Jr.	1892–1903	10	1832–1924
Howell E. Jackson	1893–1895	2	1832–1895
Edward D. White	1894–1910	16	1845–1921
Rufus W. Peckham	1895–1909	14	1838–1909
Joseph McKenna	1898–1925	26	1843–1926
Oliver W. Holmes	1902–1932	30	1841–1935
William R. Day	1903–1922	19	1849–1923
William H. Moody	1906–1910	3	1853–1917
Horace H. Lurton	1910–1914	4	1844–1914
Charles E. Hughes	1910–1916	5	1862–1948
Willis Van Devanter	1911–1937	26	1859–1941
Joseph R. Lamar	1911–1916	5	1857–1916
Mahlon Pitney	1912–1922	10	1858–1924
James C. McReynolds	1914–1941	26	1862–1946
Louis D. Brandeis	1916–1939	22	1856–1941
John H. Clarke	1916–1922	6	1857–1945
George Sutherland	1922–1938	15	1862–1942
Pierce Butler	1923–1939	16	1866–1939
Edward T. Sanford	1923–1930	7	1865–1930
Harlan F. Stone	1925–1941	16	1872–1946
Owen J. Roberts	1930–1945	15	1875–1955
Benjamin N. Cardozo	1932–1938	6	1870–1938
Hugo L. Black	1937–1971	34	1886–1971
Stanley F. Reed	1938–1957	19	1884–1980

Supreme Court Associate Justices (continued)

Supreme Court Associate Justices (continued)

Associate Justices	Term of Service	Years of Service	Life Span
Felix Frankfurter	1939–1962	23	1882–1965
William O. Douglas	1939–1975	36	1898–1980
Frank Murphy	1940–1949	9	1890–1949
James F. Byrnes	1941–1942	1	1879–1972
Robert H. Jackson	1941–1954	13	1892–1954
Wiley B. Rutledge	1943–1949	6	1894–1949
Harold H. Burton	1945–1958	13	1888–1964
Tom C. Clark	1949–1967	18	1899–1977
Sherman Minton	1949–1956	7	1890–1965
John Marshall Harlan	1955–1971	16	1899–1971
William J. Brennan, Jr.	1956–1990	34	1906–
Charles E. Whittaker	1957–1962	5	1901–1973
Potter Stewart	1958–1981	23	1915–1985
Byron R. White	1962–	—	1917–
Arthur J. Goldberg	1962–1965	3	1908–1990
Abe Fortas	1965–1969	4	1910–1982
Thurgood Marshall	1967–1991	24	1908–
Harry A. Blackmun	1970–	—	1908–
Lewis F. Powell, Jr.	1972–1987	15	1907–
William H. Rehnquist	1972–1986	14	1924–
John P. Stevens III	1975–	—	1920–
Sandra Day O'Connor	1981–	—	1930–
Antonin Scalia	1986–	—	1936–
Anthony M. Kennedy	1988–	—	1936–
David Souter	1990–	—	1939–

T

TAFT, WILLIAM HOWARD

(1857–1930), twenty-seventh president of the United States and chief justice, U.S. Supreme Court. A native of Cincinnati and a graduate of Yale, Taft was an able administrator and an intelligent, if unimaginative, lawyer and jurist. He was, however, a poor politician.

Taft served as U.S. solicitor general from 1890 to 1892 and as a federal circuit court judge from 1892 to 1900. He became head of the Second Philippine Commission in 1901 and the first governor-general of the Philippines the year following. In both posts he did much to advance civil government and to reconcile the Filipinos to American rule. Appointed secretary of war in 1904, he faithfully executed President Theodore Roosevelt's policies. In 1908, at Roosevelt's urging, he ran for president, handily defeating the Democratic candidate, William Jennings Bryan.

Conservative in temperament but moderately progressive in intellect, Taft deemed it his mission as president to consolidate rather than expand the Roosevelt reforms — to give them "the sanction of law," as he privately phrased it. But he surrounded himself with conventional-minded lawyers and allowed Old Guard Republican leaders to control his lines to Congress. Partly in consequence, he compromised on the tariff after a courageous initial call for reform. He also suffered the resignation of Roosevelt's intimate, Chief Forester Gifford Pinchot, because he believed that some of the Roosevelt-Pinchot conservation practices had been "exercised far beyond legal limitation." Yet Taft instituted twice as many antitrust proceedings as Roosevelt had, and he signed a number of long-deferred measures, including a corporation tax, into law. Constitutional amendments for an income tax and direct election of senators were also approved during his administration, though they owed more to a coalition of progressive Republicans and Democrats than to the president.

Taft's performance in foreign affairs was similarly mixed. A strong proponent of international law, he strove unsuccessfully to win Senate support of a series of arbitration treaties, but he also sent marines into Nicaragua. Nevertheless, he much preferred economic to military action, and he supported an unproductive program of "dollar diplomacy" in the Caribbean and the Far East. Taft failed to be reelected in 1912 because of the defection of progressives to Roosevelt, who ran on the Bull Moose ticket, and to Woodrow Wilson, the successful Democratic candidate.

From Yale University, where he became a professor of law after leaving the White House, Taft gave measured support to Wilson's neutrality policies before the United States entered World War I. In 1915 he became president of the League to Enforce Peace, an organization of largely Republican internationalists, and he subsequently influenced Wilson to modify his proposed Covenant of the League of Nations. Convinced that qualified American membership in the League was better than nonparticipation, Taft reluctantly supported proposed Republican reservations. He hoped, in vain, that the internationalist wing of the GOP would control foreign policy following the election of Warren G. Harding in 1920.

During the war, Taft had performed yeoman service as joint chairman of the quasi-judicial War Labor Board. After his appointment as chief justice of the Supreme Court in 1921, he modernized the judiciary system somewhat and exercised an influential voice in appointments. A genial and considerate man who weighed three hundred pounds, Taft frequently persuaded the Court's minority to refrain from dissent in order to convey an impression of unity. Although historians continue to regard Taft as politically maladroit, they tend to agree that, both as president and as chief justice, he was somewhat more progressive than conservative.

Paola Coletta, *The Presidency of William Howard Taft* (1973); Alpheus T. Mason, *William Howard Taft: Chief Justice* (1965); Henry F. Pringle, *The Life and Times of William Howard Taft*, 2 vols. (1939).

WILLIAM H. HARBAUGH

See also Elections: 1908, 1912; Philippines; Progressivism; Supreme Court. *For events during Taft's administration, see* Antitrust Movement; Asia-U.S. Relations; Ballinger-Pinchot Controversy; Caribbean-U.S. Relations; Dollar Diplomacy; Income Tax; Tariff.

TAFT-HARTLEY ACT

The Taft-Hartley Act, passed in 1947 by a Republican-controlled Congress over the veto of President Harry S. Truman, was designed to roll back the gains made by labor during the New Deal. Known officially as the Labor-Management Relations Act, it was sponsored in the House by Fred Hartley, Jr., of New Jersey and in the Senate by Robert A. Taft of Ohio.

Its provisions made the closed shop illegal and outlawed secondary boycotts. Section 14(b), the most controversial, allowed states to pass right-to-work laws, which would enable them to regulate the number of union shops. But its most important provision gave the president the power to order a "cooling-off" period to stop strikes that threatened national safety or health. It also required unions to register and file financial reports with the Department of Labor, and union leaders had to swear under oath that they were not communists.

The Taft-Hartley Act hurt smaller unions, but the labor movement as a whole was not seriously weakened by the law. It did galvanize labor politically to battle Republicans in 1948, the year of Truman's upset victory over Thomas E. Dewey.

See also Labor.

TAMMANY HALL

Tammany Hall was a political force in New York City from its 1789 inception as a benevolent association to mayoral campaigns in the 1950s. Frequently its leadership was identical to the Executive Committee of the local Democratic party, and it was a major or controlling faction in the party in 1821–1872 and 1905–1932. Key Tammany bosses through the years included William M. Tweed, Richard F. Croker, and Charles F. Murray.

Although its name was synonymous with corruption to many, Tammany Hall's popularity and endurance resulted from its willingness to help the city's poor and immigrant populations. Irish émigrés forced Tammany Hall to admit them as members in 1817, and the Irish thereafter never lost their tie with it. Because in the 1820s Tammany successfully fought to extend the franchise to all propertyless white males, it was popular with the working class. A close association with the Democratic party was also forged in the Jacksonian era.

Tammany's decentralized organization enabled ward leaders to act as advocates for individuals when they had difficulties with the law. A criminal judge, for example, appointed or kept in office by Tammany Hall would have to listen carefully to a local ward leader asking for a suspended sentence in a particular case. Later, the hundreds receiving Tammany Hall assistance with problems or baskets of food on holidays would show their gratitude at the polls.

"Reform" administrations periodically took power away from the Hall, but for many years it always made a comeback. Then anti-Tammany mayor Fiorello La Guardia (1934–1945), with the help of Franklin D. Roosevelt, was able to weaken the machine's power permanently. It retained some strength, however, until John V. Lindsay's mayoralty (1966–1973).

See also Corruption; La Guardia, Fiorello; Tweed Ring; Urban Bosses and Machine Politics.

TANEY, ROGER B.

(1777–1864), chief justice of the U.S. Supreme Court. Born to a wealthy Maryland slaveholding family, Taney was admitted to the bar in 1799. An active Federalist and defender of the landed gentry in his early years, he supported Andrew Jackson in the 1820s. As Jackson's attorney general and then secretary of the treasury, Taney played a central role in the president's struggle against the Bank of the United States. He helped draft Jackson's Bank veto message (contributing the passage that denied that the Supreme Court's interpretation of the Constitution bound the president) and, as treasury secretary, carried out the removal of federal funds from the Bank.

When John Marshall died in 1835, Jackson rewarded his loyal ally with the chief justiceship. Although denounced as a "political hack" by Senate Whigs who delayed confirmation for eight months, Taney proved a distinguished chief justice and made lasting contributions to American constitutional law. Nevertheless, he lacked his predecessor's power of persuasion and failed to dominate the Court as Marshall had.

Suspicious of corporations and concerned about federal interference with slavery, Taney was much more inclined than Marshall to support state power and to emphasize the states' role in the federal system. His landmark opinion in the *Charles River Bridge* case (1837) struck a balance between private rights and state regulatory authority. In commerce clause cases, he helped persuade the Court to accept state power over local matters that fell within the realm of interstate commerce. Moreover, he skillfully employed the concept of dual sovereignty to reserve to the states broad authority within their borders.

Taney nevertheless enlarged the role of the federal courts in American government. During his tenure, the Court extended federal admiralty jurisdiction to inland waterways, broadened the federal courts' jurisdiction over corporations, and allowed them to create a uniform body of federal commercial law. In *Ableman* v. *Booth* (1859), a case involving fugitive slaves, Taney's masterful opinion shielded federal courts from encroachments on their jurisdiction by state tribunals.

But Taney proved unable to navigate the treacherous shoals of the slavery controversy. As sectional conflict intensified during the 1850s, he attempted to use the Court to protect the South and its peculiar institution. In *Dred Scott* v. *Sanford* (1857), he ruled that blacks were not citizens (even if they were free), denied Congress authority to prevent the expansion of slavery by excluding it from the territories, and even suggested that Congress had an obligation to protect slavery within its jurisdiction. Taney's opinion — polemical in nature, resting on a strained interpretation of the Constitution, and blind to the limits of judicial power — brought the Court and its author into disrepute and ultimately proved unenforceable.

Remaining on the bench until his death in 1864, Taney privately supported secession and opposed Republican war measures. He declared Abraham Lincoln's suspension of habeas corpus unconstitutional in a circuit court opinion that the president ignored. He also wrote private memoranda striking down the Emancipation Proclamation and the conscription and legal tender acts. Because no cases concerning these matters came before him, however, these opinions remained unpublished, silent memorials to the antebellum constitutional order shattered by the war.

Don E. Feherenbacher, *The Dred Scott Case: Its Significance in American Law and Politics* (1978); Carl Brent Swisher, *Roger B. Taney* (1935).

Donald Nieman

See also *Ableman* v. *Booth;* Bank of the United States; *Charles River Bridge* v. *Warren Bridge; Dred Scott* Case; Nullification Controversy; Secession; Supreme Court.

TARIFF

A customs duty is a tax on commodities crossing a political boundary. A tariff, technically, is a schedule of such taxes, but the terms are often used interchangeably. In American politics the "tariff question" was a major, often passionate, political issue from the dawn of the Republic until modern times.

A tariff can serve several purposes: like all taxes, it can raise money to pay the costs of government; it can protect domestic goods from foreign competition; and it can seek to force a foreign country to change a policy.

A primary reason for calling the Constitutional Convention in the summer of 1787 was the fact that the central government under the Articles of Confederation lacked the power to lay taxes. It was thus dependent on the states for revenues, and these were usually late or not forthcoming at all.

The new Constitution gave the federal government the power to tax and the sole power to lay tariffs, but it required that taxes be uniform throughout the United States. Further, Article I, Section 9, forbade the federal government to tax the exports of any state. Therefore customs duties could be laid only on imports from abroad. The tariff would be the most important tax laid by the federal government until the First World War, providing the majority of the government's revenue throughout that time, except during the Civil War years.

Even before Alexander Hamilton was appointed the first secretary of the treasury, Congress established a tariff on various commodities. It was immediately evident that everyone in Congress felt the burden of the tariff should fall on someone else's constituents.

Since New England imported large quantities of molasses from the West Indies to make rum, that region's representatives and senators sought to ensure that any duty on molasses would be as low as possible. Pennsylvania, before the new Constitution came into force, had passed a protective state tariff to foster its nascent iron industry, and it wanted this tariff to be duplicated by the federal government. Southern states, with no comparable industries, wanted no such duty. Virginia, with a surplus slave population, favored a ten-dollar-a-head tax on imported slaves. The more southerly states, slave importers, opposed it.

On December 5, 1791, Hamilton submitted to Congress his *Report on Manufactures* in which he set forth his systematic vision of how the country should develop economically. In it he called for protective tariffs to foster American industry. Although this report, in retrospect, was the work of a man who saw the economic future more clearly than any of his contemporaries, Congress ignored it at the time and continued to set tariffs based solely upon the ebb and flow of political pressure.

The first tariff, enacted on July 4, 1789, called for specific duties on thirty commodities such as steel, molasses, and hemp. It also provided for an ad valorem tariff on other goods that varied for each but averaged 7.5 percent. All other goods were taxed at 5 percent. To encourage American shipping, the law provided for a 10 percent reduction in tariffs on goods that arrived in American bottoms.

After the War of 1812, using the tariff for protective purposes began in earnest. A duty of twenty-five cents per yard on cheap cotton cloth, enacted in 1816, virtually excluded it from entering the American market and sheltered the burgeoning New England mills from English competition. Protectionism rose steadily in the next decade, over the fierce opposition of New England shipping interests and southern planters, leading finally to the so-called Tariff of Abominations in 1828.

This measure was deeply resented in most of the South and led directly to the concept of nullification, the idea that individual states could decide for themselves if acts of the federal government were constitutional. This in turn led to one of the many grave sectional confrontations that threatened the Union in the pre-Civil War era. After the nullification crisis had ended in compromise, the tariff trend was downward until the Civil War forced sharp increases.

Following the war, American industry grew very rapidly in the North, traditionally favorable to a high tariff, and pressure for increased tariff protection grew. Moreover, the South, traditionally hostile, steadily lost political power as a result both of the war and of slower population growth. As a result, the tariff climbed steadily in the thirty years after the Civil War. In 1896, William McKinley's slogan for his presidential campaign was "Peace, Prosperity, and Protectionism." He won by a landslide.

The following year, the tariff was raised to an average of 57 percent on the value of imported goods in the Dingley Tariff of 1897, the highest in the nation's history. But high tariffs at home tended to generate high retaliatory tariffs abroad, crimping American exports. As American industry matured, it did not need to fear foreign competition as much, and tariffs were moderated beginning in 1909, when the Payne-Aldrich Tariff lowered rates to an average of 38 percent.

After the First World War, American agricultural prosperity declined markedly, and duties on agricultural products were raised in hopes of helping American farmers. In 1930 the Smoot-Hawley Tariff raised rates sharply to protect the rest of the American market from foreign competition as the depression deepened. The Smoot-Hawley Tariff proved to be one of the most disastrous pieces of legislation ever enacted in America, for other nations had no choice but to follow suit with beggar-thy-neighbor tariff hikes of their own. This caused a general collapse of world trade, which in 1939 was less than it had been in 1914, greatly exacerbating the depression.

After the Second World War, the United States, having learned its lesson, used its overwhelming economic dominance to lead the fight for lower tariffs and the lessening of other barriers to world trade. This highly successful policy continues to the present day, including the 1989 free-trade agreement with Canada, which when fully implemented will amount to a North American common market.

In the 1990s the tariff has provided only about 1.5 percent of federal revenues, and the protection of inefficient American industries, perhaps most notably automobiles and sugar, was far more often accomplished with such devices as quotas rather than the tariff. For 140 years the tariff was one of the leading political issues facing the Union. With the passion now wholly spent, the tariff was quietly fading into oblivion as the world edged toward a truly global market.

JOHN STEELE GORDON

See also Government and the Economy; International Commerce; *Report on Manufactures.*

TAXATION

See Income Tax; Social Security.

TAYLOR, ZACHARY

(1784–1850), twelfth president of the United States. Taylor grew up in Kentucky, where his father was a moderately prosperous planter. Despite his family's social standing, he received little formal schooling; as a result, his writing was ungrammatical, and he found reading difficult all his life.

Aided by his family's political connections, he received an army commission in 1808. Prior to the Mexican War, most of his service was spent on the frontier dealing with Indian affairs. His informal attire and indifference to physical hardship led his troops to nickname him Old Rough-and-Ready. During these years, Taylor successfully speculated in land. Eventually he purchased cotton plantations in Louisiana (which he made his home) and Mississippi and became a wealthy slave owner.

When relations with Mexico deteriorated following the annexation of Texas, the Polk administration ordered Taylor to move his army of four thousand men to the Rio Grande. War commenced shortly after his arrival in March 1846 when Mexican forces attacked units of Taylor's army. In May, Taylor defeated the Mexican army at Palo Alto and quickly won another victory at Resaca de la Palma. His subsequent capture of Monterrey and his victory at the Battle of Buena Vista (February 22–23, 1847), where he was outnumbered three to one, firmly established his popular reputation as a military hero.

He was a brave commander who remained calm in the heat of battle, but not a brilliant military leader: he was excessively cautious, failed to plan campaigns adequately, and displayed limited tactical ability. His successes stemmed more from his opponents' blunders, effective leadership by his subordinates, and his own dogged determination.

Up to this point in his life, Taylor, who harbored moderate Whig sympathies, had evidenced only limited interest in politics. As his popularity increased, however, a number of Whig leaders, looking for an available candidate, boomed Taylor for president. He was nominated without a platform and elected in November 1848.

Taylor's political inexperience caused him to oversimplify complex problems as president. This quality was most apparent in his response to the growing controversy over the expansion of slavery. Although a defender of slavery, he nevertheless believed that lack of rainfall would exclude the institution from the territory acquired from Mexico, and thus he dismissed the issue as pointless. He proposed to bypass the territorial phase and organize the entire Mexican Cession into two huge free states, California and New Mexico.

Taylor's proposal exacerbated the sectional controversy. Southern Whigs angrily denounced the president and threatened secession, while Henry Clay introduced a more extensive compromise plan early in 1850. Habitually suspicious of other men's motives, Taylor stubbornly clung to his plan, and his saber-rattling against Texas in its boundary dispute with New Mexico did nothing to defuse tensions. Matters were at a stalemate when the president died suddenly on July 9, 1850, from an attack of cholera.

Taylor was honest and well intentioned, but his blunt manner and unsophisticated mind handicapped him as president. An ardent nationalist, he did not appreciate southerners' fears, and his inflexible will, which had served him well in the military, was less useful in working with Congress. Under different circumstances, he might have been a successful president, but he lacked the intellectual subtlety or political tact necessary to handle the sectional crisis.

K. Jack Bauer, *Zachary Taylor: Soldier, Planter, Statesman of the Old Southwest* (1985); Elbert B. Smith, *The Presidencies of Zachary Taylor and Millard Fillmore* (1988).

WILLIAM E. GIENAPP

See also Elections: 1848; Mexican War. *For events during Taylor's administration, see* Compromise of 1850; Gold Rushes.

TAYLORISM

Taylorism, a system originated by Frederick Taylor and publicized in his book *The Principles of Scientific Management* (1911), was designed to increase industrial output by rationalizing the production process.

Over the course of the nineteenth century, unskilled workers and then machines had begun to replace skilled craftsmen. Yet because of their specialized knowledge, the more skilled workers continued to exert considerable control over the pace of work, the methods used, and the levels of output. Taylor, working as a foreman in the Midvale Steel Company in the 1880s, concluded that to increase production, managers must take control of the process, starting by doing time studies of each factory job. This involved observing workers meticulously, analyzing each step in terms of time spent and energy expended, and using the results to determine the best method for each task. This standard method would be required of every worker, with scaled piecework rates providing incentives for higher output.

After his methods had increased production significantly at Midvale, Taylor became a pioneer management consultant, publicizing his system and advising the nation's burgeoning corporations on how to use it. For workers, Taylorism brought a marked loss of autonomy, as managers supervised more and more closely the activities of the shop floor. Many workers felt that they knew more about production than the managers, planners, and experts now in charge; some asserted that the gains in incentive pay were a poor exchange for the increasing pressure and regimentation of working in a scientifically managed factory. But Taylorism fit with the trend to larger-scale, more mechanized production, and it appealed to the growing class of corporate managers who were distrustful of labor and intent on maximizing efficiency and profits. Other consultants, like Lillian and Frank Gilbreth and H. L. Gantt, pursued similar ideas. Taylor's doctrine was not always followed precisely by his converts, but by the 1920s his emphasis on standardization, close accounting, and managerial control had had a profound effect on industrial management throughout the United States.

See also Industrial Revolution; Science and Technology.

TEAPOT DOME AFFAIR

Teapot Dome, Wyoming, was one of two naval oil reserve sites improperly leased to private interests by Secretary of the Interior Albert B. Fall in 1922. The incident was one of numerous examples of corruption and malfeasance during the administration of President Warren G. Harding. Teapot Dome and Elk Hills, California, had been set aside before World War I for naval use. Soon after Harding's inauguration in 1921, Fall persuaded the secretary of the navy to turn over the administration of both sites to the Department of the Interior. Then, in the spring of 1922, he secretly leased Elk Hills to the Pan-American Petroleum Company and Teapot Dome to the Mammoth Oil Company.

Some questions were raised at the time the sites were transferred to Interior, and more arose when news of the leases leaked out. But the full story did not emerge until after Harding died in August 1923. That October, the Senate Public Lands Committee, at the urging of Thomas J. Walsh of Montana, launched an investigation. It revealed that at the time the leases were signed, Edwin Doheny, president of Pan-American, had presented Fall with a $100,000 unsecured interest-free loan, and Harry Sinclair, president of Mammoth Oil, had given him more than $300,000 in government bonds and cash. As a result of these findings, Congress agreed by joint resolution on February 8, 1924, to sue for cancelation of the leases; the suit was finally won in 1927. Meanwhile, Doheny, Sinclair, and

Fall were all acquitted of conspiracy to defraud the government, but Sinclair was imprisoned for contempt of Congress and jury tampering, and Fall paid a large fine and served a year in prison for bribery.

See also Corruption.

TECHNOLOGY

See Science and Technology.

TECUMSEH

(1768–1813), Shawnee political leader and war chief. Born at Old Piqua, on the Mad River in western Ohio, Tecumseh grew to manhood amid the border warfare that ravaged the Ohio Valley during the last quarter of the eighteenth century. In 1774, his father, Puckeshinwa, was killed at the Battle of Point Pleasant, and in 1779 his mother, Methoataske, accompanied those Shawnees who migrated to Missouri. Raised by an older sister, Tecumpease, he accompanied an older brother, Chiksika, on a series of raids against frontier settlements in Kentucky and Tennessee in the late 1780s. He did not participate in the defeat of Gen. Josiah Harmar (1790), but led a scouting party that monitored Gen. Arthur St. Clair's advance (1791) and fought at Fort Recovery and Fallen Timbers (1794). Embittered by the Indian defeat, he did not attend the subsequent negotiations and refused to sign the Treaty of Greenville (1795).

By 1800 Tecumseh had emerged as a prominent war chief. He led a band of militant, younger warriors and their families located at a village on the White River in east-central Indiana. There in 1805 Lalawethika, one of Tecumseh's younger brothers, experienced a series of visions that transformed him into a prominent religious leader. Taking the name Tenskwatawa, or "The Open Door," the new Shawnee Prophet began to preach a nativistic revitalization that seemed to offer the Indians a religious deliverance from their problems.

Tecumseh seemed reluctant to accept his brother's teachings until June 16, 1806, when the Prophet accurately predicted an eclipse of the sun, and Indians from throughout the Midwest flocked to the Shawnee village at Greenville, Ohio. Tecumseh slowly transformed his brother's religious following into a political movement. In 1808 Tecumseh and the Prophet moved their village to the juncture of the Tippecanoe and Wabash rivers, where the new settlement, Prophetstown, continued to attract Indians. After the loss of much Indian land at the Treaty of Fort Wayne (1809), Tecumseh gradually eclipsed his brother as the primary leader of the movement. He traveled throughout the Midwest urging tribes to form a political confederacy to prevent any further erosion of their lands. In November 1811, while Tecumseh was in the South attempting to recruit the Creeks into his confederacy, U.S. forces marched against Prophetstown. In the subsequent Battle of the Tippecanoe they defeated the Prophet, burned the settlement, and destroyed the Indians' food supplies.

After returning from the South Tecumseh tried to rebuild his shattered confederacy. But when the War of 1812 broke out, he withdrew to Michigan where he assisted the British in the capture of Detroit and led pro-British Indians in subsequent actions in southern Michigan (Monguagon) and northern Ohio (Fort Meigs). When William Henry Harrison invaded Upper Canada, Tecumseh reluctantly accompanied the British retreat. He was killed by American forces at the Battle of the Thames on October 13, 1813.

Tecumseh's political leadership, oratory, humanitarianism, and personal bravery attracted the attention of friends and foes. He was much admired by both the British and the Americans. After his death (his body was never recovered), a considerable mythology developed about him, and he has become an American folk hero.

R. David Edmunds, *The Shawnee Prophet* (1983); R. David Edmunds, *Tecumseh and the Quest for Indian Leadership* (1984).

R. DAVID EDMUNDS

See also Indians.

TELEVISION

See Radio and Television.

TEMPERANCE

See Prohibition and Temperance.

TENNESSEE VALLEY AUTHORITY

Created during the first Hundred Days session of Franklin D. Roosevelt's presidency in 1933, the Tennessee Valley Authority (TVA) brought power to rural areas along the Tennessee River in seven states. Progressive reformers long had argued for government ownership of municipal services, and the Great Depression and the resulting financial problems of private utilities gave them the chance to enact one such project. Roosevelt sought a coordinated plan involving industrialization, soil conservation, reforesting, and the provision of electricity in the seven-state area. The measure set up the TVA board to construct dams and power plants in Tennessee, Alabama, Mississippi, Kentucky, Virginia, North Carolina, and Georgia. The agency eventually built five dams, improved twenty others, and constructed a system of inland waterways. The TVA also became involved in local communities, selling fertilizers and electricity, building flood control projects, improving the navigation of the meandering river, and engaging in programs of reforestation and soil conservation.

The TVA was a success, but it provided neither the comprehensive planning the Roosevelt administration hoped for nor widespread prosperity. President Dwight D. Eisenhower later condemned it as an example of New Deal "creeping socialism." Nevertheless, the TVA enhanced the quality of life of many citizens along the Tennessee River by bringing electric power and better use of the soil to the region. It also enabled federal and state governments to determine how much electrical power actually cost. This helped them better to regulate private power companies, as the TVA became one of the nation's largest and cheapest suppliers of power.

See also New Deal.

TENURE OF OFFICE ACT

Congress used this controversial law as the legal basis for its impeachment case against President

Andrew Johnson in 1868. Seeking to limit his power to interfere with Radical (or even moderate) Reconstruction in the South, Congress passed it on March 2, 1867. The bill prohibited the president from removing officials appointed by and with the advice of the Senate without senatorial approval.

In theory, the Tenure Act was to protect low-level patronage appointees. In practice, it was to shield members of Johnson's cabinet who disagreed with him over Reconstruction — especially Secretary of War Edwin M. Stanton, who was closely tied to the Radical Republicans. When Johnson tried to oust Stanton in favor of General of the Army Ulysses S. Grant, the Senate disapproved of the president's actions, and when Johnson sought to replace Stanton with Adjutant General Lorenzo Thomas, the House impeached him. Nine of the eleven impeachment articles cited Johnson's removal of Stanton and appointment of Thomas. For the impeachers, the problem was the Tenure Act's murkiness: whether Stanton was protected was unclear. He had been a Lincoln appointee who simply remained in office, without being formally appointed, after Johnson became president. In any event, the effort to remove Johnson from office failed by one vote.

In 1878 the act initially prevented President Rutherford B. Hayes, as part of his effort at civil service reform, from removing Chester A. Arthur and Alonzo B. Cornell from their political patronage jobs at the New York customhouse. Eventually, with Democratic help in Congress, he circumvented the act and secured confirmation of his own appointments.

The Tenure of Office Act was repealed in 1887 after President Grover Cleveland challenged its constitutionality: the president, he said, had the sole power to remove appointees from office. The independence of the executive branch was thereby strengthened.

See also Presidency.

TERRITORIAL EXPANSION

See Expansion, Continental and Overseas.

TET OFFENSIVE

The Tet offensive, which began January 30, 1968, was a climactic battle of the Vietnam War, a coordinated surprise attack by the Viet Cong (the rebel forces, sponsored by North Vietnam) on hundreds of cities, towns, and hamlets throughout South Vietnam.

By late 1967, forces of the U.S. Army and the Army of the Republic of Vietnam (ARVN) had established themselves in the urban centers of South Vietnam and were reporting growing success in the countryside. Late in the year, however, a series of scattered diversionary attacks by the Viet Cong gradually drew more and more American and ARVN soldiers away from the cities. Then in late January 1968, on the first day of Tet (the lunar new year holiday previously observed with a truce), Viet Cong units attacked five of South Vietnam's six cities, most of its provincial and district capitals, and fifty hamlets. In Saigon they assaulted the airport, the presidential palace, and the ARVN headquarters and broke into the U.S. embassy compound. The U.S. and ARVN forces, though caught off guard, responded quickly and within a week had regained most of the ground the attackers had won. Only in Hue did the Viet Cong hold on; by the time that city was retaken on February 24, thousands had died, 100,000 Vietnamese had lost their homes, and there was little left of the ancient capital but rubble.

American spokespersons initially described the Tet offensive as a failure for the Viet Cong, pointing to their rapid retreat and terrible casualties (estimated as high as forty thousand). But when Gen. William C. Westmoreland reported that completing the Viet Cong's defeat would require 200,000 more American soldiers (necessitating a call-up of the reserves, a step President Lyndon B. Johnson had long avoided), even steadfast supporters of the war began to feel that changes, at least in strategy, were essential. To a growing segment of the American public, as well as a number of senior policymakers, Tet demonstrated the unimpaired resilience of the Viet Cong and the fragility of South Vietnam's control over its own territory.

See also Vietnam War.

TEXAS REVOLUTION AND ANNEXATION

The Alamo, a line drawn in the dust — the images of 1836 are almost as familiar to Americans as those of 1776. Many recognize the distinctiveness of Texas's experience — its revolt against Mexico, its life as an independent republic, and finally, its voluntary surrender of nationhood. But the causes and consequences of its unique course are less well understood.

After gaining independence from Spain in the 1820s, Mexico welcomed foreign settlers to sparsely populated Texas. Promised land on generous terms, some twenty thousand to twenty-five thousand Americans migrated there within a decade, far outnumbering the resident Mexicans (Tejanos). These immigrants clustered in relatively autonomous colonies along the lower Brazos and Colorado rivers and in the east. Alarmed at their reluctance to assimilate, Mexico passed laws in 1830 to slow American immigration. But rent by conflict between federalists and conservative centralists, the government could not enforce them. The regulations succeeded only in angering both settlers and those Tejanos interested in economic development.

Yet these laws were as much symptom as cause of friction. Some immigrants had never been reconciled to Mexican rule, citing putative U.S. claims to Texas by virtue of the Louisiana Purchase. Speculators counted on American annexation to raise the value of their land. Many Texans balked when earlier privileges, such as exemption from import duties, began to be withdrawn. The status of slavery rankled, too. The national government and the state government of Coahuila and Texas (in which Texans had little influence) passed various emancipation measures and banned the import of American slaves. Slaveholding Texans won exemption from some of these laws and evaded the others, and by 1835 slaves represented 10 to 15 percent of the non-Indian population. Though the laws did little except slow the immigration of slaveholders, they clearly worried those who believed rich but labor-scarce Texas could prosper only through slave cultivation of staple crops.

Mexico's ability to offend Texans without effectively regulating their behavior bespoke more general sources of trouble. The Mexican government presumed it could mold economic, social, even religious life in Texas. It allowed the military to intrude upon what Americans took to be civil affairs — trade, legal proceedings, the master-slave relationship. Yet this same government could not with any regularity provide such seeming fundamentals as speedy justice or trial by jury. Immigrants from Jacksonian America had certain expectations of republican government, expectations that involved government neither claiming so much nor delivering so little.

This failure of government to behave in accustomed ways provoked a crisis in 1835. Developments in Mexico had overshadowed political and legal reforms Texans had won in 1833 and 1834. Political turmoil allowed Gen. Antonio López de Santa Anna to amass an increasingly authoritarian power. Like colonists in prerevolutionary America, Texans perceived in the prospect of more strictly governed relations with the central government larger threats to their liberties and property. Santa Anna's triumph seemed also to dash the hopes of Tejanos for a democratic, decentralized Mexico. The coincidence of renewed trouble with the Mexican garrison at Anahuac and Santa Anna's march against various opponents in northern Mexico catalyzed resistance in the summer of 1835. A "war party" had been agitating for separation for some time, but the insistence of Mexican authorities that troublemakers be turned over to the military and, finally, an influx of Mexican troops in September convinced even the traditionally conciliatory Stephen Austin that "war is our only resource."

A chaotic rebellion ensued. Significant military action occurred well before the rebels officially declared for independence. A provisional government, established in November, called only for separate statehood within Mexico and the federalist constitution of 1824, hoping to win the aid of liberal Mexicans elsewhere. That government could barely rally support within its own ranks, however, as the governor and council vied for authority. No single, effective military authority existed either. Volunteers held the Alamo, for instance, despite orders to the contrary. The creation of a new government and a consolidated military command after Texas declared independence in early March 1836 did not immediately bring order. The fall of the Alamo and the retreat of Sam Houston's forces eastward provoked panic and mass flight among civilians. Perhaps only the overconfidence this bred in Santa Anna — and the anger of Texan volunteers over the massacres at the Alamo and Goliad — saved the day. In late April, Houston's men surprised a Mexican force at San Jacinto. Houston's victory and the capture of Santa Anna suddenly ended Mexico's effort to subdue Texas.

But apparently, independence was not what many Texans really desired. Voters elected Houston president, but also overwhelmingly endorsed union with the United States. The Jackson and Van Buren administrations spurned annexation, however. They feared both diplomatic trouble and the political consequences of pressing for the admission of a territory in which slavery, now constitutionally protected, was growing rapidly. A contributing factor to the Revolution, slavery had become the paramount consideration in annexation. As a result, the new republic struggled on alone. Presidents Houston, Mirabeau Lamar, and Anson Jones pursued various policies as to Mexican and Indian relations and the mounting debt, but none of them rendered Texas secure or solvent.

By 1844, American caution about issues that might divide national parties along sectional lines had diminished. Some hoped the increased enthusiasm for territorial expansion, or anxiety over possible European machinations in Texas, might eclipse northern concerns over slavery. Many southerners, eager to secure and expand America's slaveholding territory, worried that Britain intended to promote abolition in Texas. For Secretary of State John C. Calhoun, the well-being of the South overrode any commitment to the existing party system. The health of that system did not overly concern President John Tyler either. Having alienated both parties, he vainly hoped the Texas issue might win him a new following.

Initially, the traditional restraint regarding sectional issues seemed to prevail. The front-runners for the 1844 presidential nominations,

Democrat Martin Van Buren and Whig Henry Clay, announced against immediate annexation. A treaty admitting Texas as a territory failed to win a majority in the Senate, much less the required two-thirds. But southern Democrats blocked Van Buren's nomination, opening the way for dark horse James Polk who campaigned for the acquisition of both Texas and Oregon (which presumably would remain free territory). Clay's subsequent equivocations on Texas may well have hastened the defection of antislavery Whigs to the Liberty party, a defection that probably cost him the election. Annexationists heralded Polk's narrow victory as a mandate. In early 1845 Congress, employing its power to admit new states, simply annexed Texas by a majority vote. Texan leaders who had been coy on annexation, hoping to prod either Europe into guaranteeing Texas independence or America into admitting Texas on the most favorable terms, likewise yielded to public sentiment. In June 1845 the republic's Congress accepted U.S. statehood.

James Buchanan would later compare Texas to the Trojan horse. Its admission hastened the unraveling of the national parties. Many Van Buren Democrats, convinced that southerners had ridden roughshod over them in 1844, found their way into the Free-Soil or even the Republican movements. Annexation helped provoke war with Mexico, bringing America additional southwestern territory and fatally linking the politics of slavery and expansion.

Robert Calvert and Arnoldo De León, *The History of Texas* (1990); Andreas Reichstein, *Rise of the Lone Star: The Making of Texas* (1989).

PATRICK G. WILLIAMS

See also Alamo; Austin, Stephen F.; Calhoun, John C.; Clay, Henry; Compromise of 1850; Elections: 1844; Houston, Sam; Mexican War; Polk, James K.; Slavery; Tyler, John; Van Buren, Martin.

TEXTILE INDUSTRY

The American textile industry was in every sense a child of the British factory system. In

1790 Samuel Slater, a British mechanic, introduced the first successful American cotton-spinning mill in Pawtucket, Rhode Island. This event transformed New England from an agricultural to an industrial region and led to such modern forms as the corporation, the separation of ownership and management, and the development of big business. The system's emphasis on the individual rather than family or community was a major shift in American society and came to characterize the new nation's industrial and social development. It also meant that the federal government would only encourage industry; the actual operation of mills would be left to individuals.

Slater, while living in England, had worked for Jedediah Strutt, partner of Richard Arkwright, who was the progressive factory master and inventor of a revolutionary water-powered spinning machine. Strutt exposed Slater to every phase of textile production from the construction of machines to the management of a labor force. Because of limited opportunities in England, Slater immigrated to America in 1789. In New York, he answered an advertisement from Moses Brown who wanted a mechanic knowledgeable about the English system of production. After considerable negotiation, the men formed the firm of Almy, Brown, and Slater. With financial backing from the Brown family, Slater constructed machines based on the Arkwright model and employed young children to operate them. The business grew, and Slater constructed additional mills in Massachusetts, Rhode Island, and Connecticut.

Slater soon realized that British practices would have to be modified to meet the requirements of New Englanders. The family was an important institution in New England, and any system of production that disregarded its interests would be short-lived. Slater altered the British system to fit the local situation. The new system featured the partnership or single proprietorship form of ownership, personal management, small-scale production, the use of water power, and the employment of family labor. A division of labor based on gender and age emerged. Men were employed in supervisory capacities as farm hands and laborers or as skilled artisans. Adult women remained at home, and children and adolescents worked in the mills. The children, some as young as seven or eight, earned as little as twenty-five cents a week, and all wages went directly to the head of the household. Hundreds of manufacturers throughout New England and the Mid-Atlantic states emulated Slater, and his mode of operation became known variously as the Slater, Rhode Island, or British system.

During these years of industrial experimentation, the federal government was developing its strategy toward manufacturing. In his *Report on Manufactures* issued in 1791, Alexander Hamilton enumerated the advantages of industrial development for the United States and advocated government assistance for industrialization. What form that assistance should take was debated. Should the government subsidize industry, or decide the location of mills or towns or the type of product to be manufactured? In the case of the textile industry, agents for the Society for Establishing Useful Manufactures selected the site of Paterson, New Jersey, as a potential textile manufacturing center and encouraged its development. But the undertaking proved unsuccessful, and it folded in 1796. This ended direct government interest in the location and construction of textile mills. Thereafter, the federal government confined its support to passing tariffs and issuing patent protection. With the exception of the arms industry, private capital and individual entrepreneurs were to chart America's industrial future.

The Slater system was not the only factory form to develop during the early nineteenth century. Francis Cabot Lowell, a wealthy Boston merchant, introduced another form to New England. Known as the Lowell system, it differed markedly from Slater's. His Boston Manufacturing Company, capitalized at $400,000, built a factory in Waltham, Massachusetts, in 1813. Unlike Slater's, Lowell's early mills used power looms, and his operations combined the spinning of yarn and the weaving of cloth. To operate the equipment, Lowell employed women and girls. Historians have labeled the Lowell style the first form of big business in America. His enterprises were large-scale, integrated, incorporated ventures utilizing professional management. His eventual domination of the domestic market for coarse cloth was assisted by the passage of the tariff of 1816, which imposed a 25 percent tariff on imported cotton and woolen goods. The Lowell companies were an immediate financial success with profits reaching 20–24 percent annually.

In 1826 the town of Lowell was founded in Massachusetts and six firms established there. The company built boardinghouses to accommodate its labor force of twelve-to-twenty-five-year-old females. The twenty-five or so women residing in each house developed a sense of sisterhood, working, eating, and spending leisure time together. Although they enjoyed the cultural and economic advantages available in Lowell, they did not succumb to the popular notion that Lowell was a "finishing school for young ladies." They had come, mostly from New England farms, to work, and they expected to be paid for their labor and treated with respect.

When a downturn occurred in the textile industry beginning in 1829 and management sought to cut wages, these women reacted. They went out on strike in 1834 and 1836 and ran petition campaigns in the 1840s. They formed the Factory Girls' Association and joined the widespread ten-hour movement. Theirs were among the first forms of collective action taken by industrial workers. In response, mill owners there and elsewhere turned to immigrant labor, hiring French-Canadian and Irish workers to replace the native-born labor force.

By the time of the Civil War, the distinctions between the Lowell and Slater systems had begun to dissolve. Both utilized immigrant and family labor, constructed tenements to house workers, and sought to control their lives as well as their working hours. Both adopted the corporate form of ownership, professional management, and cost accounting.

But New England was not the only center of textile production. The Paterson, New Jersey, venture was successfully revived, and in Philadelphia, the textile industry flourished. Diversification was the key here with factories specializing in weaving, spinning, dyeing, or finishing.

The labor situation in Philadelphia, however, was volatile. Strikes and riots in the 1840s reflected disputes between labor and management as well as nativist anger over the hiring of immigrants. There was also a labor glut during the decade, and management played one group of workers against another: immigrants versus the native-born, men versus women, adults versus children. Given these conditions, along with the depression of 1836–1844 and scant experience with organization, labor won few victories during these years.

For much of the nineteenth century, the Northeast remained the center for textile production with cotton, woolen, linen, and thread output soaring. New mills were constructed in Connecticut, Massachusetts, New Hampshire, and New York; some of them were considered model operations, such as that at Hopedale, Massachusetts, but others, including mills at Lawrence and Fall River, were substandard.

In the 1880s a shift in location began to occur. Small textile mills moved south, many of them mirroring the earlier Slater system: town design based on rural villages, small-scale production, and paternalistic practices by owners. These southern mill towns were controlled by mill agents and superintendents, with the company providing jobs, houses, food, clothing, and goods. The work force was drawn from the countryside, and conditions were harsh. In the 1880s and 1890s the Knights of Labor and the National Union of Textile Workers organized southern mill workers, but strikes were ineffective with the national economy in trouble.

In the early twentieth century, conditions in the textile industry continued to deteriorate in the North. Major strikes organized by the Industrial Workers of the World (IWW) occurred in 1912 and 1913, with the IWW developing new tactics. One of the most successful was the "Children's Crusade." Workers in Lawrence sent their children dressed in rags to New York and other cities to parade through the streets and gain sympathy for the strikers. Although a settlement was reached in this case, overall, labor could do little to influence management's long-range operations. If labor got too powerful in one location, the firms simply moved.

Several new factors were entering the picture now, including the introduction of synthetic fibers like nylon, which began to replace cotton; changing fashions in the 1920s, which subjected textile producers to the whims of designers and consumers; and increasing international competition, especially from Japan. Tariffs on woolens and cottons had been drastically lowered in 1913. Although sporadic adjustments were made in the 1920s and 1930s, they were not enough to help, and many manufacturers shut down, left the industry, or moved south. By the 1920s New England textile towns were in a depression.

In the South the situation was equally precarious. Mill owners instituted the speed-up and the stretch-out (forcing workers to manage additional machines), initiated night work, and cut wages. Strikes occurred across the South, and the National Textile Workers Union moved in to organize the workers. Violence erupted and the strike it called was eventually lost. But it had foreshadowed the issues that were to preoccupy the nation in the 1930s: unemployment or low wages, long hours, night work, miserable factory conditions, and union ineptitude.

In 1934 the United Textile Workers called for a general strike of the textile industry, and again it failed. Broad economic circumstances did not favor collective action. Only the passage of the National Labor Relations Act in 1935 and the advent of World War II permitted unions to establish a foothold in the South.

In the decades following the war, the American textile industry lost ground to firms in Asia and Central and South America. In 1946 imports of cotton and woolen manufactures were worth $45 million and $41 million, respectively; within ten years they had risen to $161 million and $196 million. Textile communities throughout the nation were forced to develop new economic strategies. Lowell, Massachusetts, for example, became a center of high technology. But many textile towns continued to decay, reflecting the new realities of American industry in a global context.

Thomas Dublin, *Women at Work: The Transformation of Work and Community in Lowell, Massachusetts, 1826–1860* (1979); Jacquelyn Hall et al., *Like a Family: The Making of a Southern Cotton Mill World* (1987); Barbara M. Tucker, *Samuel Slater and the Origins of the American Textile Industry, 1790–1860* (1984).

BARBARA M. TUCKER

See also Child Labor; Cotton; Industrial Revolution; Labor; Lawrence Strike; Lowell System; Nativism; Paterson Silk Strike; *Report on Manufactures.*

THEATER

The American theater normally denotes a commercial enterprise in which performers mount a stage to entertain an audience. But this definition fails to convey the tremendous variety of entertainments the American stage has hosted nor does it suggest the diverse circumstances under which theater has been carried on. Of all the arts, none has labored under such severe strictures of economic necessity, cultural suspicion, and technological impact as has theater. A source of pleasure for its patrons, the theater also holds up a mirror to the changing nature of American society.

Colonial theater was a fitful institution, restrained by a limited urban patronage, a lack of trained actors, and periodic legislation to close down theaters. Although drama was staged in the few colonial urban centers earlier in the eighteenth century, professional American theater is traditionally dated from the arrival of Lewis Hallam's English troupe in Williamsburg in 1752. After a hiatus during the American Revolution (when the Continental Congress urged states to ban theatricals and other amusements as extravagant diversions from the serious business of war) the young Republic witnessed a slow expansion of the dramatic arts. Theaters were built in Charleston, Philadelphia, Newport, New York, and even that stronghold of Puritan resistance, Boston.

Theater became a more pervasive part of American life during the early nineteenth century, both in cities and in the hinterland. Playhouses in major cities had their own ensemble companies, which performed a varied repertory of plays. But popular interest was greatest when these stock companies supported a touring star, such as English actors Edmund Kean, George

Frederick Cooke, and William Charles Macready, or Americans Edwin Forrest and Charlotte Cushman. Resident companies — as well as most stars — also regularly embarked on tours of provincial America. Some of these were theatrical families, the Drakes and Chapmans notably, who made careers of barnstorming the Ohio River valley and California's Gold Coast. Performing on the road could be rugged, theaters frequently lacking heat or even the barest of props. In lieu of a theater, shows would sometimes go on in a dining room or barn.

Urban or rural, audiences were in command not only because of their power to attend or not but also because within the theater they expressed their favor or disfavor directly. Theater was a reflection of America's participatory democratic spirit. Audiences would call for favorite musical numbers, drum offending players off the stage with hisses or brickbats, and occasionally erupt into full-scale riot. Ongoing rivalry between Macready and Forrest fueled the anti-English and anti-aristocratic Astor Place riot in the New York of 1849, leaving twenty-two dead.

Americans' increasing fondness for theatrical amusements provoked repeated ministerial warnings against the "Synagogue of Satan" and its "almost universally vicious" actors. Sensitive to these charges of moral decadence, William Dunlap, manager of New York's Park Theatre early in the century, sought to provide a drama of republican uplift. But he discovered that public taste ran much more to the sensationalism and sentimentality of melodrama, especially the dramas extolling patriotic themes.

American dramatists borrowed the melodramatic formula from European playwrights and wove into it native themes and characters that evoked a spread-eagle enthusiasm. Royall Tyler's *The Contrast* (1787) introduced the homespun Jonathan, who became the archetypal stage American. John Augustus Stone's *Metamora* (1829) exemplified the drama of the heroic but ill-fated Indian. And the most enduring American melodrama of the century, Harriet Beecher Stowe's *Uncle Tom's Cabin* (1852), found inspiration in the slavery issue. Legends of literature and folklore, such as Rip Van Winkle and Davy Crockett, also became stage favorites.

Nineteenth-century American drama, it must be admitted, has not endured as compelling literature. Compared to notable accomplishments in other literary fields, drama was distinctly inferior. Dramatists, burdened by inadequate royalties, lack of copyright protection for their works (a problem shared with other writers and not adequately remedied until the end of the century), and the commercial imperatives of their art, enjoyed neither the respect nor the relative freedom of other writers. And limitations also resided in the inherent structure of melodrama, wherein gimmickry and contrived plots drove the action. Moreover, classics of nineteenth-century European drama (until the theatrical renaissance late in the century) are nearly as rare as American.

But a purely literary judgment of American drama misses an important point. Melodrama, perhaps better than any other dramatic genre, expresses theatricality itself in its tendency to heighten and externalize emotion and conflict. Moreover, American audiences, especially of the antebellum era, sought a drama that epitomized virtue and vice. The exaggerated gestures and thunderous declamation of Edwin Forrest, America's greatest tragedian, intended to embody the expansive greatness of Jacksonian America.

Whether attending an American play or one from the older European repertory (and Shakespeare — albeit in shortened form — continued to be the most performed playwright), audiences through midcentury also enjoyed between-act songs, novelty turns, such as acrobats or performing animals, and a short farce to finish off the evening. Low-comedy ethnic characters — the stage Irishman or Mose the fire boy, representative of the working urban audience — were character favorites. Another set of ethnic stereotypes fostered one of the most popular forms of midcentury theater: the minstrel show. First suggested by Thomas Rice's Jim Crow dance in 1828, minstrelsy appeared as a uniquely American theatrical genre in the 1840s. Minstrel songs, dances, and comedy routines exploited racial stereotypes, unconsciously serving to reassure white Americans about the suitability of blacks for slavery.

Theater in the second half of the nineteenth century became both more diverse and more specialized, with audiences choosing among legitimate theater, ballet, vaudeville, burlesque, and opera. The tendency toward consolidation in business inexorably affected the theater. By the 1880s New York City had become the organizing center for touring companies that performed on stages literally throughout the land. Within a few years theatrical bookings were likewise centralized by the infamous Theatrical Syndicate and then by the Shubert brothers.

These developments, although disturbing to some, in fact symbolized theater's arrival as mass entertainment. The two decades on either side of 1900 represented the golden age of American theater; at one point in 1904, 420 companies were touring. American audiences had come to expect more sophistication of plot and staging, and producer-directors such as Augustin Daly, Charles Frohman, and David Belasco offered updated melodramas for an urban taste.

If the hits of that age — *Girl of the Golden West* (1905), *Hazel Kirke* (1880), or *Trilby* (1895) — leave later audiences unmoved, we can readily appreciate the appeal of its stars, whose numbers proliferated in response to a growing demand. Theater had long known stars, but this age witnessed something new: the phenomenon of celebrity. More important than the play itself, the star — Maude Adams, Ethel Barrymore, Richard Mansfield, John Drew — became the focus of popular interest. The realism of gesture and word that predominated by late century bespoke a new relationship between player and public. Where traditional acting portrayed larger-than-life types who reinforced shared social convictions, realistic acting was based on the appeal of an individual personality. Acting styles were less grandiloquent, with audiences not looking for heroism as much as for models of success and a particular lifestyle. This change — indeed the whole phenomenon of celebrity — followed logically from both the urbanization of the country, which newly valued style and personality, and a growing mass media, which publicized actors' lives and attitudes in great detail.

Vaudeville's emergence also bespoke theater's response to urbanization. Beginning as the slightly disreputable variety shows of the post–Civil War era, vaudeville was first elevated by Tony Pastor and then given its distinctive format of continuous acts by B. F. Keith, who recognized the potentially huge middle-class audience for wholesome family amusements. From the 1880s through the 1930s (when movies and radio effectively killed it) vaudeville's fast-paced collage of music, comedy, dance, novelty numbers, and skits reflected the pace and variety of city life while offering informal lessons in the requisite values for success in modern society. The vaudeville palaces themselves were intended to envelop patrons in an atmosphere of splendor, heightening the audience's theatrical fantasies.

Theaters (legitimate and vaudeville) also utilized a stage design (particularly after the 1860s) that enhanced actors' sense of control. Where earlier players trod a stage that jutted out into the audience, actors now performed under the boxlike proscenium arch. This new design (accompanying the trend toward theatrical realism) also separated players from the patrons, endowing actors with a new sense of authority. At the same time, theater etiquette was becoming more constrained, audiences rarely expressing direct disapproval as in earlier days.

Vaudeville and the legitimate stage could coexist and thrive. But motion pictures proved less accommodating. By 1915 the large salaries and the chance for celluloid immortality were luring those stage actors who suited the scrutinizing lens of the camera. Moreover, the vivid realism of cinematic melodramas made the efforts of the stage less convincing. By the 1920s theater, although thriving on New York's Great White Way, had lost its national mass audience.

Hollywood's competition deprived live theater of a mass public but enabled it to play to its unique strengths: more sophisticated drama and musicals that the silent screen could not duplicate. The early twentieth century witnessed a turn to serious drama and innovative stagecraft. The imported plays of Henrik Ibsen, Bernard Shaw, and August Strindberg encouraged American dramatists to attempt similar plays of ideas. William Vaughn Moody and Edward Sheldon utilized native themes in a provocative manner early in the century. Serious drama found further advocates in the little theater movement and such experimental groups as the Washington Square Players (1915) and the Provincetown Players (1916). The Broadway production of Eugene O'Neill's *Beyond the Horizon* in 1920 is often considered American dramatic literature's coming of age.

The depression decade of the 1930s nurtured an unprecedented social and political consciousness on the stage. Plays such as Clifford Odets's *Waiting for Lefty* (1935) and Maxwell Anderson's *Winterset* (1935) castigated the oppression of workers and immigrants. The repertory Group Theatre championed this drama while also introducing Konstantin Stanislavsky's Method system of acting that shaped the upcoming generation of actors. The depression also brought the federal government into theater as never before through the Federal Theatre Project. Established in 1935 to provide work for the theater's unemployed, it staged such highly innovative (and politically controversial) productions as Sinclair Lewis's *It Can't Happen Here* (1935), Orson Welles's modern-dress interpretation of *Julius Caesar* (1937), and Elmer Rice's *The Living Newspaper* (1936). Following World War II came a remarkable flowering of American drama: Arthur Miller's *Death of a Salesman* (1949), Tennessee Williams's *A Streetcar Named Desire* (1947), and O'Neill's autobiographical reflection, *Long Day's Journey into Night* (1956).

The cultural upheavals of the 1960s and 1970s led to a new demand in some quarters that theater be a vanguard of reform. Off- and off-off-Broadway groups served up caustic political commentary (e.g., *MacBird,* 1967), and groups such as Julian Beck's Living Theatre combined radical politics with a revolutionary breakdown of the boundary between spectator and performer. Although some observers celebrated this trend as fulfilling the promise of a meaningful American theater, in retrospect it seemed (as with the drama of the thirties) more the temporary product of a contentious era. The hopeful American temper remained uncongenial to the tragic vision necessary for the most profound drama.

But if the American dramatic tradition was a thin one, the nation could lay claim to innovative genius in another realm of theater. The musical stage of the twentieth century might be said to constitute the American vernacular in theater, and it proved to be the country's most popular theatrical export.

Music had accompanied theatricals since colonial days, with European and native comic operas, entr'acte songs during melodramas, and minstrel tunes gracing antebellum stages. The sensation caused by *The Black Crook* (1866) showed the potent combination of music, dance, and female leg on stage, inspiring both burlesque and musical comedy. Musical extravaganzas continued being staged later in the century, notably the comic ethnic musicals of Edward Harrigan and Tony Hart and the most successful of all, Charles Hoyt's *A Trip to Chinatown* (1890), the longest running production on any New York stage in the nineteenth century.

Alongside the lavish extravaganzas of the early twentieth century appeared the operettas with their light plots and lilting waltzes. Victor Herbert's *Babes in Toyland* (1903) and *Naughty Marietta* (1910) constituted a notable American contribution to a European art form. A more indigenous American musical, however, was shaped by George M. Cohan. His *Little Johnny Jones* (1904) and *Forty-five Minutes from Broadway* (1906) introduced songs that have become part of the nation's musical repertory.

But even Cohan's musicals did not fully integrate plot and music into a cohesive whole. That remained for Jerome Kern's *Showboat* (1927), which, drawing explicitly upon vernacular themes, represented a marriage of plot and music that defined the book musical. A further landmark of the genre came in 1943 with Richard Rodgers and Oscar Hammerstein's *Oklahoma,* combining exuberant music and lyrics with a ballet choreography that reshaped the musical. Jerome Robbins and Leonard Bernstein's *West Side Story* (1957) reinterpreted *Romeo and Juliet* as urban sociology, setting romance and graceful ballet amid a backdrop of harsh tenements and violent action. Later popular musicals such as *A Chorus Line* (1975) and *42nd Street* (1981) further stressed the significance of dance while diminishing the book.

The American theater of the 1980s and 1990s might be divided into three categories. First, Broadway productions (and their few road shows) persisted — despite repeated predictions of doom — as lavish and increasingly expensive attractions for New York tourists and a limited number of faithful theatergoers. Second, many fine regional theaters (descendants of the earlier little theater movement) dotted urban centers across the country. Some of the best new drama found a stage at such places as the Tyrone Guthrie Theater in Minneapolis and the Actors Theatre of Louisville. Subsidized in ways previously unknown to the American stage — by corporations, foundations, and the government — regional theater, for some critics, represented the best hope of American drama. Finally, colleges and universities continued to support active theater programs. Gaining a place in the curriculum early in the twentieth century, drama in its many aspects was taught widely in the academy, sometimes accompanied by professional resident acting companies.

The theater, then, played an ongoing if modest part in the entertainment scene of most Americans. The oldest of the performing arts, drama was elbowed aside by the technologies of television and film. Nevertheless it endured and shall continue to do so as long as people value the human dimension offered only by the live stage.

David Grimsted, *Melodrama Unveiled: American Theater and Culture, 1800–1850* (1968); Mary Henderson, *Theater in America* (1986); Benjamin McArthur, *Actors and American Culture, 1880–1920* (1984).

BENJAMIN MCARTHUR

See also Federal Theatre Project; Miller, Arthur; Movies; Musical Theater; O'Neill, Eugene; Radio and Television; Robeson, Paul; *Uncle Tom's Cabin;* Williams, Tennessee.

THIRD PARTIES

Americans frequently refer to their two-party system, yet one-party politics long prevailed in southern states and third parties have repeatedly appeared. A national system of competitive ma-

jor parties had only begun to emerge in the later 1820s when what are regarded as America's earliest third parties formed — the Anti-Masons and the Workingmen's parties of the Northeast. Third-party challenges have continued into contemporary times, with John Anderson's independent candidacy garnering 6 percent of the 1980 presidential vote.

Third parties have been as diverse as the nation itself. Organizationally, they have ranged from those most active at the state or local level, like the Greenbackers, to those created primarily to campaign for the presidency, like Robert La Follette's Progressives of 1924. Even when working from regional strongholds, the latter sort generally failed to contest state offices or build enduring local organizations. The life spans of third parties have also varied enormously. Certain minor parties pursued some enduring goal like socialism or temperance for decades. Others, like the Populists, responding to more specific sets of economic and political circumstances, survived a shorter time. And some, like the 1980 Anderson campaign, have been fleeting efforts, leaving neither an organization nor an articulated set of principles behind. But third parties have differed most in their purposes. Some of them, like the antislavery Liberty party or New York's Right to Life party, have focused on a single issue, and others have emphasized the concerns of a single constituency — La Raza Unida, for instance, has represented Chicanos. But still others have emerged because major parties were failing to serve a number of interest groups on a whole range of issues. The Progressives of 1912, for example, seceded from the GOP when it became clear the party would embrace neither their concerns nor their candidate, Theodore Roosevelt.

These many parties have all been conspicuously unsuccessful in national campaigns. Free-Soil candidate Martin Van Buren won 10 percent of the 1848 popular vote. In 1856 and 1860, new parties scored better; but with the Whigs disintegrating and Democrats in disarray, it might be questioned whether the Republicans, Know-Nothings, and Constitutional Union party were truly *third* parties. Between 1864 and 1988, only five third-party candidates won electoral votes — James Weaver (Populist) in 1892, Theodore Roosevelt (Progressive) in 1912, Robert La Follette (Progressive) in 1924, Strom Thurmond ("Dixiecrat") in 1948, and George Wallace (American Independent) in 1968. Only six won more than 5 percent of the popular vote in those same years — Weaver, Roosevelt, La Follette, Wallace, Anderson, and Eugene Debs (Socialist, 1912). Of these, only Roosevelt outpolled a major party.

This dismal track record has been explained variously. Some cite factors, such as America's relative abundance or egalitarian ethos, that they say predispose citizens toward the classless, centrist politics the major parties typically embody. But third parties have more clearly been hindered by certain inertial qualities of the political system. Competing in a federal system, in which local, state, and national elections are held, requires resources and a thoroughgoing organization that new parties often lack. Third parties have been stymied, too, by the winner-take-all system. They do not win power or representation proportionate to the number of votes they receive, but only if they win a plurality of the votes cast in a district or state. Voters are thereby discouraged from supporting parties unable to outpoll all competitors. Third parties, frequently identified with specific regions or interests, have also stumbled in the coalition building required for victory in a large and diverse nation. For instance, southern and midwestern Populists, known as spokespersons for agrarian interests, found it difficult to attract labor votes. Coalition building itself carries risks. Third parties risk irrelevance if they fail, but loss of identity if they succeed too well — as happened in 1896 when Populists fused with Democrats on the basis of free silver. Third parties have faced state laws that have made it difficult for them to get on the ballot and have also encountered outright repression. Intimidation, fraud, and harassment weakened southern Populists and, during World War I, the Socialist party.

Third parties, however, have not been as ineffectual as their record in presidential campaigns might indicate. They have been able to reach voters and build coalitions in certain state and local elections. Even the Socialist party, which never topped 6 percent in a presidential vote, repeatedly elected mayors in several cities including Milwaukee and Bridgeport, Connecticut. And, from the 1850s through the 1940s, Congress typically included at least a scattering of third-party representatives — Free-Soil in the early 1850s, Greenback in the 1870s, Populist in the 1890s, Socialist in the 1910s, Farmer-Labor in the 1920s and 1930s, and American Labor party in the 1930s and 1940s. Third parties have usually done best where one of the major parties was historically weak — owing, for instance, to lingering Civil War era loyalties — or where neither party was addressing the concerns of some locally significant constituency. In parts of the post-Reconstruction South, Greenbackers and Populists could outpoll Republicans and, especially when they pooled efforts with Republicans, even outpoll Democrats. In midwestern and western states, where Democrats often lacked strength, agrarian and progressive third parties sometimes triumphed. Kansas, Colorado, and North Dakota elected Populist governors in the 1890s. During World War I, the Nonpartisan League conquered North Dakota by entering its own candidates in Republican primaries. In the following decades, Minnesota's Farmer-Labor party and Wisconsin's Progressive party elected both governors and senators.

Third parties' contributions to American politics have come not only when they won power. Many of them hardly expected victory but simply wished to agitate and educate. And in this, perhaps, third parties have had their greatest successes. They have often served as early advocates of causes later embraced by the nation — from emancipation or prohibition to government-sponsored loans for farmers. Although no direct link necessarily exists between a third party's espousal of a principle and its eventual enactment into law, it is certainly the case that abolitionist, Free-Soil, and Populist politicians focused contemporary public debate on issues of concern to them. Third parties, either as secessionist spin-offs or wholly new organizations, have also contributed to the formation or realignment of major parties. They organized constituencies that became the nuclei of new parties or that existing parties moved to incorporate. The forces rallied by the antislavery parties became a central element in the Republican party. The white southerners whose habit of voting Democratic was broken by the 1948 Dixiecrat and 1968 Wallace campaigns became prey for Republican coalition builders. Finally, third parties have played the role of potential spoiler. This can be exaggerated since third parties may mobilize those who otherwise would not vote as well as take votes away from other parties. Third parties' efforts to gain the balance of power in presidential elections by denying either party an electoral majority have always failed. But third parties probably have altered the outcome of certain elections. In 1844, for instance, the Liberty party siphoned off enough votes from the Whig Henry Clay to throw New York and the nation to a southern Democrat, James Polk.

Steven Rosenstone, Roy Behr, and Edward Lazarus, *Third Parties in America: Citizen Response to Major Party Failure* (1984); Arthur M. Schlesinger, Jr., and Fred Israel, eds., *History of American Presidential Elections, 1789–1968,* 4 vols. (1971).

PATRICK G. WILLIAMS

See also American Independent Party; Anti-Masons; Communist Party; Constitutional Union Party; Dixiecrat Party; Free-Soil Party; Greenback Party; Know-Nothing Party; Liberty Party; National Woman's Party; People's Party; Populism; Progressive Parties: 1912, 1924, 1948; Socialist Party.

THIRTEENTH AMENDMENT

See Emancipation Proclamation and Thirteenth Amendment.

THOMSON, VIRGIL

(1896–1989), composer and critic. As a composer, Thomson utilized a wide variety of musical materials, from Gregorian chant to Baptist hymns and popular tunes that are, in his words, "as ordinary as Dick's hatband," to reflect his own stylistic eclecticism as well as the diversity of the American landscape and its people. As a critic, he consistently recognized the importance of individual creativity for the American composer but also advocated learning from and using, rather than rejecting, European compositional models.

Thomson began his piano and organ study in Kansas City, where he was born. After brief service in the military in World War I, he began formal composition study at Harvard University with Edward Burlingame Hill. He studied organ and counterpoint with Nadia Boulanger in Paris in 1921–1922 and contributed reviews to the *Boston Evening Transcript.* After a brief return to the United States, Thomson settled in Paris, where he lived until 1940.

Thomson was introduced to the writings of Gertrude Stein during his Harvard career, and he set the American expatriate writer's "Susie Asado" to music prior to meeting her in 1926. Their collaboration produced the opera *Four Saints in Three Acts,* which Thomson completed with an orchestral score in 1933. Stein and Thomson worked together again in 1946 to produce *The Mother of Us All,* an opera about the nineteenth-century women's suffrage leader Susan B. Anthony. The historical setting gave Thomson the opportunity to refer in the score to popular songs and dances of the period. In both his instrumental and his stage pieces, Thomson was influenced by the ideas of simplicity, irony, and humor espoused by the French modernist Erik Satie. Thomson also adapted Stein's vocal cadence and use of repetition to good advantage.

Musical references to the United States were put to effective use in his scores for *The Plow that Broke the Plains* (1936) and *The River* (1937), two films directed by Pare Lorentz for the New Deal's Resettlement Administration. He used similar materials in the score for the ballet *Filling Station,* commissioned by Lincoln Kirstein for the Ballet Caravan and first performed in 1938. In 1949 Thomson's score for Robert Flaherty's film *Louisiana Story* won a Pulitzer Prize. Thomson composed his third opera, *Lord Byron,* working with librettist Jack Larson from 1961 to 1968.

An outspoken critic, Thomson brought wit and irony to his reviews for the *New York Herald-Tribune* from 1940 to 1954. His writing stood in marked contrast to the jargon-laden, wordy, and technical language of much music criticism of the period. Many of his reviews were collected and published in *The State of Music* (1939, rev. 1974), *The Musical Scene* (1945, rev. 1968), *Music Right and Left* (1951, rev. 1969), and *Music Reviewed, 1940–54* (1967). Thomson also wrote essays on music and a textbook, *American Music since 1910* (1971). He was elected to the National Institute of Arts and Letters in 1948 and to the American Academy of Arts and Letters in 1959. *A Virgil Thomson Reader* (1981) won a National Book Critics Circle Award in 1981, and in 1983 he was honored by the John F. Kennedy Center for the Performing Arts for his long and successful career.

Kathleen Hoover and John Cage, *Virgil Thomson: His Life and Music* (1959).

BARBARA L. TISCHLER

See also Music.

THOREAU, HENRY DAVID

(1817–1862), writer. Thoreau was of French Huguenot and Scottish ancestry, but accented his name on the first syllable. He was educated at Concord Academy and Harvard College, from which he graduated in 1837. He taught school, lectured, served as surveyor for the town of Concord, did odd jobs, worked as Ralph Waldo Emerson's handyman, and helped him edit the *Dial,* for which he wrote extensively. His major business always was writing undistinguished poetry and superb prose (most of it in his journal). Today he stands in the front rank of the classical American writers.

From July 4, 1845, to September 6, 1847, he lived in a cabin he had built near Walden Pond, and during the summer of 1846 he spent a night in jail because of his refusal to pay taxes as a protest against slavery and the Mexican War. His essay "Civil Disobedience" influenced both Gandhi and Martin Luther King, Jr.

His early reputation was as a nature writer, but he declined membership in a scientific society, saying he was "a mystic, a transcendentalist, and a natural philosopher to boot." He accumu-

lated a vast amount of Indian data but died without completing the "Kalender" that he had designed as a total, all-comprehending picture of life. "I went to the woods," he wrote, "because I wished to live deliberately, to front only the essential facts of life, and see if I could learn what it had to teach, and not, when I came to die, discover that I had not lived." His book about his life at Walden Pond is not a literal account but, rather, an elaborately structured work of art. In 1927 Vernon Louis Parrington inaugurated a new phase of Thoreau studies by calling him a "transcendental economist," perceiving clearly that his essential purpose was "to order life so that the primary things should not be lost amid the superfluities."

Thoreau's stance was always much less extreme than many of his individual, sometimes inconsistent statements suggest. Theoretically he believed that that government was best that governed least and that the ideal was no government, yet in practice he wanted the state to foster culture and education, build good roads, prevent crime, and protect wildlife. He was a pioneer ecologist and conservationist, one of the first Americans to perceive that the country's resources are not inexhaustible.

Mistrustful of institutionalism, Thoreau disliked churches and ignored most aspects of Christian theology, but he believed that "man flows at once to God when his channel of purity is open." He was a "panentheist," believing that though the entire universe exists in God, God transcends the universe and possesses consciousness and benevolence.

When Thoreau died in his native Concord on May 6, 1862, he had published only two books, *A Week on the Concord and Merrimack Rivers* (1849) and *Walden* (1854), both of which were out of print, and was little known outside the town.

Walter Harding and Michael Meyer, *The New Thoreau Handbook* (1980); Edward Wagenknecht, *Henry David Thoreau: What Manner of Man?* (1981).

EDWARD WAGENKNECHT

See also Conscientious Objection; Transcendentalism.

THORPE, JIM

(1888–1953), Olympic and professional athlete. Born in Indian Territory (now Oklahoma), Thorpe was the son of a farmer of Irish and Sac and Fox Indian descent; his mother was part French and part Potawatomi Indian. The tribal name given him at birth was Wa-tho-huck, which meant Bright Path. In 1904, he was sent to the Carlisle Indian School in Pennsylvania. Glenn S. "Pop" Warner, the legendary coach at Carlisle, "discovered" Thorpe in 1907 when he saw him high-jump six feet in street clothing. Thorpe became a star on the Carlisle track team and in 1908, a promising substitute on the football team.

Thorpe left Carlisle in 1909 to play baseball for two seasons in the newly formed East Carolina minor league. Unlike other "amateur" athletes who played in the league under aliases, Thorpe used his own name. After returning to Carlisle in 1911, he led the football team to an 11–1 record and was named to Walter Camp's All-American team.

Thorpe's most notable achievement came at the 1912 Olympic Games in Stockholm where he won two gold medals. He took four of the five track events in the Pentathlon and scored an astounding 8,412 points in winning the Decathlon, a score that was unsurpassed for fifteen years. King Gustav V of Sweden said to him, "Sir, you are the greatest athlete in the world." Thorpe replied, "Thanks, King."

The high point of the next football season for the Indians was a 27 to 6 massacre of the U.S. Military Academy. Thorpe scored a season record 195 points and was again named to the All-American team. But in January 1913, a sportswriter who had seen Thorpe play baseball in North Carolina, exposed him as a professional, and the Amateur Athletic Union stripped him of his Olympic records and medals.

Thorpe joined the New York Giants as an outfielder in 1913. He played six seasons in the National League but saw little playing time. Ironically, his best season was his last, 1919, when he played in sixty-two games for the Boston Braves and hit a respectable .327.

While Thorpe was playing major league baseball, he was also playing professional football. He joined the Canton, Ohio, Bulldogs in 1915 for the then exorbitant salary of $250 a game. He was so successful on the field and so popular with the fans that he remained with the Bulldogs through 1920 as a player-coach. He was named as the first commissioner of the new National Football League in 1920 and played for and coached a number of NFL teams in the 1920s, including the Oorang Indians of La Rue, Ohio. The team was made up of Indians and founded by dog breeder Walter Lingo to help promote the sale of his Oorang Airedales. The team was not very successful, because most of their games were played on the road and players often participated in pregame or halftime shows with the trained Airedales. Thorpe retired from professional football at age forty, following the 1928 season with the Chicago Cardinals.

From 1928 until his death, Thorpe worked as a laborer and actor. In 1950, he was voted both the greatest football player and the greatest athlete of the first half of the twentieth century by the Associated Press and was inducted into the College and Pro-Football Halls of Fame. In 1982, after years of appeals, the International Olympic Committee finally returned Thorpe's Olympic medals to his family.

Jack Newcombe, *The Best of the Athletic Boys: The White Man's Impact on Jim Thorpe* (1975); Robert W. Wheeler, *Pathway to Glory* (1975).

C. ROBERT BARNETT

See also Baseball; Football; Spectator Sports.

THREE MILE ISLAND

An unlikely series of mechanical and human errors in Unit 2 of the nuclear generating plant at Three Mile Island, near Harrisburg, Pennsylvania, in 1979 resulted in an accident that profoundly affected the utility industry. A complicated combination of stuck valves, misread gauges, and poor decisions led to a partial meltdown of the reactor core and a release of significant amounts of radioactive gases. The near-total devastation of the nuclear power industry resulted, because the disaster at Three Mile Island tipped the scales in the ongoing controversy over nuclear power in favor of those opposed to it. Massive demonstrations followed the accident, culminating in a rally in New York City that attracted upward of 200,000 people. By the mid-1980s, the construction of nuclear power plants in the United States had virtually ceased.

The radioactive gases released by the accident prompted the governor of Pennsylvania to evacuate pregnant women from the area. An investigation by the Nuclear Regulatory Commission claimed that the amount of radioactivity released was not a health threat, but antinuclear activists and many local citizens disputed this. The reactor itself remained unusable — in fact, virtually unapproachable — more than a decade later.

See also Nuclear Power.

TILDEN, BILL

(1893–1953), tennis player. Before or during his lifetime, no tennis player exceeded the importance of William T. ("Big Bill") Tilden. He not only brought to the game a new level of performance but was more responsible than any other person for the emergence of tennis as an important spectator sport. In the celebrity-oriented 1920s, he joined such athletes as Babe Ruth and Jack Dempsey as national sports idols.

Tilden was remarkably slow to develop into a championship player. Born into a patrician Philadelphia family, Tilden dabbled in the game as a youngster at the exclusive Germantown Cricket Club. He did not win an individual national title until 1920, when he was twenty-seven years of age. But from 1920 through 1925 he never lost a match of any consequence. He won the U.S. championship six times and the 1920 and 1921 All-England (Wimbledon) titles. He also led the U.S. team in capturing and retaining the Davis Cup. Between 1925 and 1930, Tilden continued to dominate American tennis, winning his seventh American title in 1929 and Wimbledon again in 1930 at the age of thirty-seven, though by then he no longer retained his world supremacy.

Although Tilden's feats were indeed phenomenal, the public acclaim accorded him sprang from something more than his championships. He brought to tennis a new, more flamboyant style of play. Prior to Tilden, players had specialized either on strokes executed from near the baseline or on trying to get close to the net as soon as possible so they could win the point with a "put-away" volley. Tilden was the first player to master both styles. Approaching the game as an art form, he tailored his shots to fit match circumstances and the strengths and weaknesses of his opponents. Tilden also made the tennis court a stage with himself as the leading actor. (He loved the theater and performed the lead in several shows, including one Broadway production.) In match after match, or so it seemed, he fashioned incredible comebacks while teetering on the brink of defeat. Finally, Tilden gave to tennis, a sport that had traditionally projected an effete upper-class image, an athletic and swashbuckling masculine style. To the American public, Tilden was colossal, a veritable giant who, for nearly a decade, single-handedly held off the tennis invaders from Europe.

Tilden was a celebrity off the tennis court as well. Tall, angular, egotistical, and fancying himself as something of an intellectual, he wrote nondescript plays, short stories, and novels. His articles and books on tennis, however, were authoritative and remain classics in tennis literature to this day. He hobnobbed regularly with Hollywood stars and starlets and frequently quarreled with the officials of the United States Lawn Tennis Association. Sadly, Tilden finished his days suffering from financial insecurity and was arrested and briefly jailed twice for misdemeanors arising from his homosexuality.

Frank Deford, *Big Bill Tilden: The Triumphs and the Tragedy* (1976).

BENJAMIN G. RADER

See also Spectator Sports.

TOBACCO

Tobacco, one of the most widely used addictive substances in the world, is a plant native to the Americas and historically one of the half-dozen most important crops grown by American farmers. From 1617 to 1793 tobacco was the most valuable staple export from the English American mainland colonies and the United States. Until the 1960s, the United States not only grew but also manufactured and exported more tobacco than any other country. Since 1964 conclusive epidemiological evidence of the deadly effects of tobacco consumption has led to a sharp decline in official support for producers and manufacturers of tobacco, in spite of its indisputably large contribution to the agricultural, fiscal, manufacturing, and exporting sectors of the economy.

By 1617 John Rolfe's experiments with Spanish tobacco (*Nicotiana tabacum*) had provided the English settlement in Virginia with a staple export of high value in proportion to the cost of its transportation across the Atlantic. As a result tobacco served as the chief incentive for the subsequent demographic and economic growth of the colonial Chesapeake. English merchants supplied colonists with manufactured goods and bound labor and took their profits primarily from the return cargoes of tobacco. Before the last quarter of the seventeenth century the bond servants who grew tobacco came primarily from the British Isles, but thereafter the laborers were principally black slaves from the West Indies and Africa. These laborers, settled on small plantations or quarters, swelled the population of the Chesapeake colonies from a few hundred in 1618 to perhaps thirty-five thousand by 1675 and well over half a million by 1776. The quantity of tobacco shipped to Great Britain rose from twenty thousand pounds in 1617 to over 40 million pounds in 1727, and even as the agricultural economy became diversified after 1700, colonists continued to produce ever larger crops of tobacco. Tobacco inspection systems enacted by Virginia in 1730 and by Maryland in 1747 improved the quality of Chesapeake tobacco exported to Britain and from there to the Continent. The huge crops (averaging 100 million pounds in the early 1770s) and low price of Chesapeake tobacco overwhelmed its European competitors. By 1775, not only England but much of Europe depended on the Chesapeake for tobacco.

The American and French revolutions and the Napoleonic Wars temporarily curtailed the European demand for Chesapeake tobacco. But a growing domestic market in the United States and a reviving European market after 1815 consumed ever larger quantities of tobacco, now extensively grown in North Carolina as well as in the new states of the Mississippi valley. Between the late eighteenth century and 1860, moreover, slave labor predominated in both the cultivation of tobacco and its manufacture into plugs and twists in southern factories. In the North, however, the manufacture of snuff and cigars remained largely the operation of whites. By 1860 the United States produced more than twice as much tobacco as in 1775, though a good half of it was now consumed domestically.

From the time of Elizabeth I until 1700, Europeans characteristically consumed tobacco in small-bowled clay pipes with long stems. In the eighteenth century the taking of snuff, known to the Indians but made fashionable by the French, largely displaced smoking among the aristocracy and the more cultivated city folk of Britain and Europe. In America the colonists, too, smoked clay pipes, but in the early nineteenth century the "chaw" became popular. The proclivities of American tobacco-chewers, whose amber streams seemed frequently to miss whatever cuspidor was available, often disgusted foreign visitors.

The Civil War gave a boost to the consumption of tobacco in the portable forms of cigars and the relatively new cigarettes. Within a decade after Appomattox, American production of tobacco had nearly doubled again, led by increased demand for smoking tobacco and cigarettes, at that time still made by hand. With slavery at an end, small independent farmers, mostly white, and tenant farmers, both black and white, grew most of the tobacco; their families assisted in cultivation. New centers for the manufacture of smoking tobacco and cigarettes followed the culture of bright leaf, flue-cured tobacco to Durham and Winston-Salem, North Carolina. There, in the next quarter century, James Buchanan Duke and R. J. Reynolds used aggressive advertising, the most efficient machinery available, and big-business techniques for eliminating competition to create multimillion-dollar corporations, among the largest and most profitable in the United States. Per capita consumption of chewing tobacco declined after 1890. By the 1920s annual per capita consumption of cigarettes in the United States approached one thousand, and advertisers began targeting women. The cigarette age had arrived.

Between 1929 and 1989, government, science, and technology transformed tobacco culture into agribusiness by legislation, invention, and mechanization. Tobacco farmers prospered from government price support programs from 1934 through 1981, but the advent in 1969 of a successful tobacco harvesting machine for bright leaf tobacco spelled the end of tobacco farming as a labor-intensive, family-farm operation. By the early 1980s almost 50 percent of flue-cured tobacco was harvested by machine. Burley tobacco (grown chiefly in Kentucky and Tennessee) enjoyed fewer economies of scale and mechanization, but high leaf yields kept it competitive for cigarette blending.

Between 1930 and 1979 per capita consumption of cigarettes in the United States almost tripled, increasing from 972 to 2,775. The 1930s also produced the first widely noted scientific studies associating smoking "with a definite impairment of longevity," but these early warnings left tobacco manufacturers free to market their cigarettes (albeit with cost-saving filter tips) to a largely uninformed public. Ignorance ended on January 11, 1964, when Luther L. Terry, surgeon general of the United States, issued the report of a blue-ribbon advisory committee, which condemned cigarette smoking "in such clear and concise language that it could not be misunderstood." Every surgeon general since Terry has campaigned against smoking. Governments in most of the industrialized nations adopted a variety of policies to curtail or prohibit cigarette smoking. In response to the worldwide decline in smoking among the better educated, the multinational manufacturers of cigarettes skillfully targeted advertising campaigns at specific groups among less well-educated Americans and increased exports of cigarettes to less-developed nations.

Pete Daniel, *Breaking the Land: The Transformation of Cotton, Tobacco, and Rice Cultures since 1880* (1985); Joseph C. Robert, *The Story of Tobacco in America* (1949).

JOHN M. HEMPHILL II

See also Chesapeake Colonies; Colonial Economy; Plantation System.

TOCQUEVILLE, ALEXIS DE

See Democracy in America.

TOWNSEND PLAN

The Townsend Plan was proposed by Dr. Francis Townsend in 1933 as a way of ending the depression while resolving the particular financial hardships of the elderly. It called for a pension of two hundred dollars per month to be paid to every person over sixty years of age who promised not to look for work and to spend the money promptly. The pensions were to be financed by a 2 percent sales tax. Townsend created a nonprofit corporation, Old Age Revolving Pensions, Ltd., on January 1, 1934, and began mailing out brochures. The response was overwhelming; within a year his plan was being promoted by 500,000 dues-paying members organized in Townsend Clubs all across the country. Although economists agreed that the Townsend Plan was unworkable and impossibly expensive, their criticisms made little difference; by 1936, membership was estimated at 2 million.

As the Townsend Clubs grew, so did their political power, especially in areas like California where they were most concentrated. Members of Congress were inundated with letters and petitions urging enactment of the Townsend Plan; many responded with proposed legislation, though none came close to passage. The Social Security Act, passed on August 14, 1935, ended any chance that the Townsend Plan would become law, but the clubs remained numerous and active throughout 1935 and 1936.

The parallel concerns and overlapping memberships of the Townsend Clubs, Senator Huey Long's Share-Our-Wealth Clubs, and Father Charles E. Coughlin's National Union for Social Justice made it almost inevitable that the three groups would join forces as the 1936 presidential election approached. Large numbers of Townsendites attended the coalition's Union party convention in Cleveland in July 1936. In the election, however, the party was soundly defeated, winning less than 2 percent of the vote. Enthusiasm for the Townsend Plan or Share-Our-Wealth, it became clear, did not necessarily mean opposition to the New Deal. After 1936 the national Townsend organization gradually disintegrated.

See also Coughlin, Father Charles E.; Elections: 1936; Long, Huey.

TOWNSHEND ACTS

The Townshend Acts were a series of measures introduced into Parliament by Chancellor of the Exchequer Charles Townshend in 1767. The acts imposed duties on glass, lead, paints, paper, and tea imported into the colonies and created a Board of Customs Commissioners to enforce customs laws without the accused having recourse to a trial by jury.

Townshend hoped the acts would defray imperial expenses in the colonies. Because Benjamin Franklin and other Americans in Britain had argued against Parliament's power to impose the Stamp Act on the ground that it was a direct tax, British leaders convinced themselves that the colonists would accept so-called indirect taxes such as import duties, a wishful misunderstanding of colonial opinion.

Many influential Americans believed that Parliament had no right to impose any taxes on the colonists, viewing taxation as an abuse of Great Britain's constitutional relationship with the colonies. As Samuel Adams, speaking for the Massachusetts legislature, put it: "In all free states, the constitution is fixed; it is from thence, that the legislature derives its authority; therefore it cannot change the constitution without destroying its own foundation." Governor Francis Bernard of Massachusetts dissolved the legislature when it issued a Circular Letter describing the measures it had taken against the Townshend Acts. The Circular Letter led to a series of Non-Importation Agreements, which reduced colonial imports from Britain in 1768–1769 by half.

In April 1770, Parliament repealed all the Townshend duties except the tax on tea, which it retained in order to assert its right to tax the colonies. This led to a sort of truce, which lasted until the burning of the British patrol boat *Gaspee* in 1772. In the years before the Revolution, resistance to the tea tax became a symbol of American patriotism.

See also Revolution.

TRADE

See International Commerce; Slavery.

TRAIL OF TEARS

The Trail of Tears refers to the route followed by fifteen thousand Cherokee during their 1838 removal and forced march from Georgia to Indian Territory (present-day Oklahoma).

In 1791, a U.S. treaty had recognized Cherokee territory in Georgia as independent, and the Cherokee people had created a thriving republic with a written constitution. For decades, the state of Georgia sought to enforce its authority over the Cherokee Nation, but its efforts had little effect until the election of President Andrew Jackson, a longtime supporter of Indian removal. Although the Supreme Court declared Congress's 1830 Indian removal bill unconstitutional (*Worcester* v. *Georgia,* 1832), the national and state harassment continued, culminating in the rounding up of the Cherokee by troops in 1838.

The Cherokee were forced to abandon their property, livestock, and ancestral burial grounds and move to camps in Tennessee. From there, in the midst of severe winter weather, they were marched another eight hundred miles to Indian Territory. An estimated four thousand people — over 25 percent of the Cherokee Nation — died during the march.

The Trail of Tears, the path the Cherokee followed, became a national monument in 1987, serving as a symbol of the wrongs suffered by Indians at the hands of the U.S. government.

See also Cherokee Nation v. *Georgia;* Indians.

TRANSCENDENTALISM

Transcendentalism is the term applied to the thought and style of a loosely associated group of romantic writers and reformers including Ralph Waldo Emerson, Henry David Thoreau, Margaret Fuller, Amos Bronson Alcott, and others who flourished in New England between 1830 and 1850. More broadly, it is the name given to a religious and spiritual movement of protest and revival that, especially through Emerson's work, has influenced American literature and society ever since. Because the term originally denoted the philosophy of Immanuel Kant and F. W. Schelling, it was applied in New England to those writers — principally essayists and poets — whose affirmation of philosophical idealism was influenced by German thought, either directly or through the mediation of Samuel Taylor Coleridge and Thomas Carlyle. This group, of which Emerson quickly became the center, first emerged as a distinctive intellectual force by developing a romantic critique of the Unitarianism in which most of its members had been trained and educated.

Unitarianism, which by 1825 had gained a secure ascendancy in eastern Massachusetts, represented a rationalist critique of Calvinist orthodoxy. Unitarians rejected as unscriptural such Puritan beliefs as innate depravity, predestination, and what they felt was the unreasonable mystery of a triune God. They offered in place of these dogmas a "rational" or "liberal" theology stressing self-culture and the human capacity for good. Yet a number of young men entering the ministry at this time, including Emerson, were deeply dissatisfied with this religion of the commercial class, so evidently accommodated to a diminished capacity for faith and so entirely predicated on the dry rationalism of John Locke's empiricism. For a time these young men would be mollified by the presence of the great Unitarian leader William Ellery Channing, who was receptive to European and romantic ideas, spoke of the human "likeness to God," admired the Catholic mysticism of Archbishop Fénelon, and resisted the drift of liberal religion into the formalism of a distinct sect. But it turned out that Channing had merely pointed the way to a confrontation between the younger generation and the conservative forces who defended the "corpse-cold Unitarianism of Brattle Street and Harvard College." Like their Puritan ancestors before them, the transcendentalists sought to replace a religion of forms and observances with a warmer, more intuitive life of the spirit.

The besetting sin of the times, the transcendentalists felt, was that when they believed at all, most people believed in the wrong things and deferred their own power to powers outside themselves — that, for example, they made an idol of historical Christianity, when the proper object of faith was surely the truth it conveyed. Indeed, the insurgents held that truth is truth only as it transcends particular times, places, institutions, and persons, a perception that was to motivate the watershed "miracles controversy" of the 1830s. This dispute sharply divided the transcendentalists from mainline Unitarians, led by Andrews Norton, who held that the New Testament miracles were proof of the special divinity of Christ and were therefore the indispensable guarantor of the truth of the Christian gospel. The transcendentalists held that truth needs no external support; it is always its own best evidence. The conviction, for example, that precepts about loving one's neighbor are divine arises from an intuitive recognition of their truth and value, not from a sense that their "inventor" had supernatural authority to impose rules. That the doctrines of Christianity would command assent only as they kept within the bounds of truth seemed to the transcendentalists to imply that Truth is a prior and superior category, timeless, spiritual, and independent of the valuations issuing from human institutions.

This argument, which W. H. Furness broached in his *Remarks on the Four Gospels* (1836), Emerson memorably set forth in his Divinity School address (1838), and Theodore Parker expounded in his *Transient and Permanent in Christianity* (1841), was thus at bottom an argument — democratic in spirit — about the nature of authority, and its implications extended well beyond the religious context. It followed, for example, that transcendentalists would encourage self-reliance as a means to authentic thought and action. The argument was also a calculated rebuke to what they regarded as a Unitarian idolatry, which by making so much of outward events eighteen hundred years before, seemed to privilege time and matter over the spiritual force of truth. Miracles, said the transcendentalists, happen continually.

In 1836, four years after resigning his pastorate at Boston's Second Church, Emerson published *Nature,* a central manifesto of the movement, which, though avoiding sectarian issues and relying more on poetic insight than logical argument, directly challenged the materialism of the age. At the same time, the Transcendental Club began to meet, attended by Emerson, Alcott, Fuller, Parker, Thoreau, George Ripley, Orestes Brownson, Jones Very, Frederic Henry Hedge, and others. James Freeman Clarke called it "the Club of the Like-Minded . . . because no two of us thought alike." Hedge, Ripley, and Fuller, for instance, were well versed in German literature; Alcott and Ripley were interested in educational and social reform; Brownson and Parker were able controversialists; Very was a poet. Emerson's central position in the movement was reflected in his sympathetic responsiveness to all these concerns.

Apart from their writings, the accomplishments of the transcendentalists included the famous Brook Farm experiment in communal living (1840–1847), organized in West Roxbury, Massachusetts, by Ripley, and Fruitlands, a more modest socialist experiment led by Alcott and his friend Charles Lane. These, like Thoreau's noncollectivist experiment at Walden Pond, were largely motivated by a sense of the social and moral distortions incident to a capitalist economy. The movement also spawned a number of small but important journals, including the *Western Messenger,* edited by Clarke, the *Harbinger,* published at Brook Farm in its Fourierist phase, and, most notably, the *Dial,* conducted between 1840 and 1844 by Emerson and Fuller.

The popular perception that transcendentalism was a radical, threatening, antiestablishment movement had faded considerably by 1850 when Fuller died in a shipwreck on her return from the revolution in Italy. Of all those associated with the movement, only Emerson still seemed capable of holding the attention of a national audience, and by 1850 he had become a familiar figure in the American cultural landscape, as much by virtue of his popular lectures as by his published writing. Others, like Hedge and Convers Francis, lapsed into relative conformity or, like Alcott and Brownson, mortgaged their reputations to a succession of eccentric causes. Thoreau was young and untried during the years of the Transcendental Club and the *Dial;* his great work, *Walden,* published in 1854, is perhaps the ripest fruit of the movement.

Born of discontent with the religious, social, and economic culture it confronted, New England transcendentalism was notoriously experimental and so sponsored its share of brave failures. But it was from its beginning a valuable source of cultural agitation, challenging religious complacency and orthodox theologies in the 1830s, supporting a wide variety of reform causes in the forties and, in the fifties, supplying considerable impetus to the antislavery movement. Ultimately, the significance of transcendentalism lay in its having gotten memorably on the literary record a vision of the universe in which God and the world, spirit and matter, existed in intimate symbolic relation. This vision of the universe and of humanity's central place in it served to nurture the artistic imagination in a predominantly materialistic society. It influenced such later figures as Walt Whitman, Emily Dickinson, Charles Ives, William James, Robert Frost, and Wallace Stevens, and it has remained central to a continuing element of romanticism in American culture.

Philip F. Gura and Joel Myerson, eds., *Critical Essays on American Transcendentalism* (1982); Perry Miller, ed., *The Transcendentalists: An Anthology* (1950).

ALBERT J. VON FRANK

See also Emerson, Ralph Waldo; Fuller, Margaret; Thoreau, Henry David.

TRANSCONTINENTAL RAILROAD SYSTEM

See Railroads.

TRANSPORTATION

See Public Transportation.

TRANSPORTATION REVOLUTION

For the early settlers on the North American mainland, the ocean was their only connection to sources of supplies and to markets for their products. To maintain that connection, those who ventured inland settled along the rivers that flowed to the ocean. Beginning in the late eighteenth century, as growing numbers of Americans crossed the Alleghenies, they clustered along the Ohio and Mississippi rivers and their tributaries. Bulky agricultural products could be floated downstream on rafts or boats, eventually reaching New Orleans and other gulf towns and then taken by ship to eastern cities or foreign markets. The trip was long and arduous and required pilots of the boats and rafts to return home over hundreds of miles on overland paths such as the Natchez Trace.

Bringing goods into the interior was even more difficult — and more expensive. Attempts to use sails or towing mechanisms to move boats upstream had limited success on short hauls and proved impossible for long distances. Instead, goods were purchased in the eastern cities, taken over the mountains on treacherous roads and paths by horse and wagon to the western rivers, floated to a river town, and then hauled overland to their final destination.

Because of the difficulty and high cost of moving goods, westerners remained relatively isolated from outside markets and had no choice but to maintain a high degree of self-sufficiency. Each town usually had a wide array of manufacturing establishments — mills that processed agricultural goods, sawed wood, spun thread, and wove cloth, and artisan shops that produced and repaired machinery and household items. Much like a tariff, high transportation costs protected the small local producers from competitors who might have been able to produce cheaper and better commodities but would find such advantages offset by the expense of transporting the commodities to markets.

But beginning in the first decade of the nineteenth century, a transportation revolution — improvements in roads, but, more important, the development of steamboats and the building of canals and railroads — rapidly diminished western isolation. In 1807 Robert Fulton demonstrated the feasibility of steam-powered boats on inland rivers when his paddle wheeler, the *Clermont,* made the trip on the Hudson River from New York to Albany and back in five days. Used initially on the deeper rivers, the steamboat was quickly adapted to carry large cargoes on shallower western rivers. Although rafts and riverboats continued to carry bulky agricultural products downstream, the steamboats easily moved against the current, and transportation costs for goods going upstream dropped precipitously. Westerners soon found an ample supply of eastern and foreign goods in local stores, the price of these products no longer burdened by high transport costs.

Those who lived a distance from the rivers remained relatively isolated. Dirt roads in good weather were dusty and rough; heavy rains made them impassable muddy quagmires. In a few places sawed wooden planks or unsawed logs covered the surface of dirt roads and ridges providing all-weather roads. But these roads were expensive — their builders charged high tolls to cover building costs — and they quickly deteriorated. It would take canals and railroads, rather than roads, to open interior regions.

The success of the Erie Canal, opened in 1825, initiated a canal-building frenzy in both the East and the West. By 1840 the United States had over three thousand miles of canals. Like the Erie, which ran from the Hudson River to Lake Erie, these artificial waterways linked interior areas to natural waterways, providing transportation facilities to places far from navigable rivers and lakes. Many canals provided access to more than one market; in Ohio and Indiana, for example, canals allowed shipments to go south to the Ohio and then by riverboat to the gulf, or north to the Great Lakes and then via lake boats and the Erie Canal to New York City. Except for the Erie, most of the canals were not commercially successful; they were hastily built at great expense and often inadequately maintained. These problems, however, might have been overcome had the canals not faced competition from a new, more efficient, and faster form of transport.

Railroads could reach interior areas, including places where an inadequate water supply or rough terrain made canals impossible. Unlike canals, which froze in winter or became impassable when water was low, railroads ran year-round, and they could easily ascend and descend hills and mountains. Initially financed by municipal governments and enterprising businessmen in river, lake, and ocean towns and cities, the first railroads extended short distances into the interior to tap potential markets in the surrounding countryside. Extension and connection of short lines soon provided uninterrupted transportation over long distances. By 1840, the United States had almost three thousand miles of track; by 1860, a network of thirty thousand miles linked most of the nation's major cities and towns.

Transportation innovations, by cutting the costs and increasing the speed of moving goods, helped create a national market and provided an impetus for an interregional division of labor. Westerners became important commercial producers and consumers of goods produced elsewhere; commercial opportunities drew masses of easterners and immigrants into western lands and stimulated the growth of marketing as well as manufacturing towns and cities. The movement of goods over long distances required a supporting infrastructure, stimulating the growth of market towns in which merchants, bankers, warehousemen, wholesalers, retailers, and other middlemen handled goods and provided the services necessary to move them from producers to consumers. More extensive markets increased competition and innovation as manufacturers, no longer saddled with high transportation costs, sought to produce a better and cheaper product in order to capture a larger share of the market.

The increase in the volume of trade was matched by an increase in the pace of business. Faster transportation meant faster dissemination of information via the mails about supplies of goods and price movements in various markets. The increasing use of the telegraph after the mid-1840s provided almost instantaneous information, first between larger cities in the East, but gradually throughout the settled areas of the nation as lines, strung along the railroads to co-

ordinate the movement of trains over long distances, also carried market information.

George Rogers Taylor, *The Transportation Revolution, 1815–1860* (1962).

HAROLD D. WOODMAN

See also Erie Canal; National Road; Railroads.

TREATY OF PARIS (1783)

See Paris, Treaty of (1783).

TRIANGLE SHIRTWAIST FIRE

One of the nation's worst industrial tragedies, the Triangle Shirtwaist fire had a profound impact on women's unionism and job safety and affected local and national politics in the process. On March 25, 1911, a fire swept through the Triangle Shirtwaist Company in the Greenwich Village section of New York City, a sweatshop where workers, mostly women, did low-paying piecework in a building with no safety precautions. The blaze killed 146 workers who were trapped by the lack of fire escapes and management's practice of locking all the exits to keep workers from leaving the job for breaks. The factory's owners were indicted, but a jury acquitted them, fanning the outrage over the tragedy.

The fire led to stepped-up efforts on the part of the International Ladies Garment Workers Union, which had been founded in 1900 to organize the women who worked in the Triangle factory and improve working conditions in sweatshops. The public outcry also prompted the creation of a state commission, which investigated both the factory in question and industrial working conditions generally. In 1914, its report called for widespread changes. New York's state legislature balked at first but finally acted under pressure from Tammany Hall and its boss, Charles Francis Murphy, and two lawmakers who would go on to prominence, State Senator Robert Wagner, later a U.S. senator, and Assemblyman Alfred E. Smith, later governor and a presidential candidate. New laws imposed tougher municipal building codes and more stringent factory inspections in New York and elsewhere.

See also Labor.

TRIANGULAR TRADE

Triangular trade is a simplified term for the trading patterns that developed among the American colonies, the West Indies, the coast of Africa, and the British Isles during the eighteenth century. One triangle began with New England merchants transporting flour, meat, and other provisions to the West Indies, whose commitment to staple crops required them to import food; the food would be exchanged in the West Indies for sugar, which the New Englanders would carry to England and exchange for manufactured goods to be brought back to the colonies. The advantage of this triangle was that it permitted the American traders to obtain English goods without spending their precious supplies of hard currency. Another triangle took the New Englanders first to the coast of Africa, where simple manufactured goods from America were exchanged for slaves. The slaves were then transported over the terrible Middle Passage to the West Indies, where they were traded for rum and molasses to be sold at home.

After the Seven Years' War, however, Britain's effort to reassert control of American trade somewhat constrained the colonies' international commerce, and after the Revolution, the United States had less access to British West Indian ports. The prohibition of slave imports after 1808 eliminated that element of the triangular trade.

In actuality, patterns of commerce were much more complicated than the term *triangular trade* suggests. Many trading voyages involved more than three exchanges of goods, and others were limited to two ports. Often the ships used for slaving were inappropriate for other ventures. In addition, European ports as well as other colonies frequently featured in the merchants' itineraries. The term *triangular trade* is most helpful, then, in suggesting the international and interactive character of American commerce at the time rather than describing a specific route.

See also Slavery.

TRUMAN, HARRY S.

(1884–1972), thirty-third president of the United States, remembered for his genial common touch and outspoken bluntness. Truman rose in politics as the result of an alliance with the notorious Pendergast machine of Kansas City. A failure in various business ventures, he was notably successful in other endeavors — as a combat artillery captain in World War I, a rising figure in the Reserve Officers Corps (1920–1939), an effective county administrator (1923–1924, 1927–1934), and a popular and industrious U.S. senator (1935–1945). Beneath a usually friendly manner, he harbored a thick layer of aggressiveness that occasionally discharged itself in angry outbursts.

Achieving the vice presidency in 1944 because of his acceptability to all wings of the Democratic party, he became president upon the death of Franklin D. Roosevelt, April 12, 1945. As a party leader, he hoped to maintain a grand coalition that would have room for all the diverse elements of Roosevelt's political coalition. Personally, however, he considered himself a bit to the left of center and possessed roots in the tradition of western and midwestern insurgency. As president, therefore, he pursued an aggressively liberal program (the Fair Deal) that roused the Democratic presidential party and helped him win election in 1948. Its major elements, however, were defeated by a conservative Congress and an indifferent postwar public concerned primarily with preserving the New Deal rather than with achieving new liberal breakthroughs.

In foreign policy, Truman had long been an aggressive internationalist who envisioned the United States as a world leader with the mission of spreading democratic political institutions and capitalist prosperity. As president, he adopted epochal measures (the Truman Doctrine, the Marshall Plan, the North Atlantic Treaty) designed to block Soviet expansion into Western Europe. Neither original nor subtle as a diplomatist, he nevertheless displayed good judgment in selecting his lieutenants, followed their advice on the large issues, and supported them loyally. His European policies were highly successful, but Asia was less amenable to U.S. intervention. Public frustration with the fall of China to communism in 1949 and with the limited Korean War (1950–1953) gave a strong boost to McCarthyism, disrupted the coalition Truman had largely preserved in 1948, and paved the way for the Republican victory of 1952.

Truman's greatest asset, an ability to identify with the ordinary American, was also his greatest liability. He could seem, at his worst, limited, undignified, erratic, and altogether incapable of dealing with the awesome responsibilities of the postwar presidency. He attempted to mask what appears to have been a certain discomfort with his high office by adopting a pose of decisiveness that too often appeared to be impetuosity. Widely unpopular when he retired in 1953, he enjoyed a subsequent upswing in public esteem as the American people increasingly remembered him for his frank commonness and contrasted him favorably with successors who appeared artificial and devious.

Robert J. Donovan, *Conflict and Crisis: The Presidency of Harry S. Truman, 1945–1948* (1977) and *Tumultuous Years: The Presidency of Harry S. Truman, 1949–1953* (1982); Robert Ferrell, ed., *Off the Record: The Private Papers of Harry S. Truman* (1980).

ALONZO L. HAMBY

See also Elections: 1944, 1948. *For events during Truman's administration, see Alger Hiss* Case; Anticommunism; Berlin Blockade; Cold War; Dixiecrat Party; Fair Deal; Hydrogen Bomb; Korean War; Marshall Plan; North Atlantic Treaty Organization; Nuclear Weapons: Origins and Legacy; Nuremberg Trials; Potsdam Conference; Progressive Parties: 1912, 1924, 1948; Racial Desegregation; *Rosenberg* Case; Taft-Hartley Act; Truman Doctrine; World War II.

TRUMAN DOCTRINE

This pronouncement and its uses expanded the nation's role in checking the spread of communism in the postwar era. In the early months of the cold war, as the atmosphere of wartime cooperation disintegrated, the British were propping up the Greek government against communist guerrillas believed to be receiving support from Moscow. In February 1947, facing financial problems and the end of its empire, Great Britain announced its plans to withdraw, prompting American fears that Greece and perhaps Turkey would fall under Soviet control.

After meeting with military and congressional leaders, President Harry S. Truman addressed Congress on March 12 and enunciated what became known as the Truman Doctrine: "It must be the policy of the United States to support free peoples who are resisting attempted subjugation by armed minorities or by outside pressures." He said that this support ideally would be mainly economic aid, and Congress acceded to his request to appropriate $400 million for the two Mediterranean nations.

The Truman Doctrine resulted from and played a large role in the cold war. The extent of the Soviet role in Greece is still debated, and Truman's critics have accused him of seeing communism as monolithic. The Truman Doctrine helped set the stage for the Marshall Plan, through which the United States did much to rebuild Western Europe and counter any communist threat there. But it also paved the way for the policy of containment that would form the backbone of the nation's cold war diplomacy in fighting communism throughout the world, especially in Vietnam.

See also Cold War; Middle East–U.S. Relations; Truman, Harry S.

TRUTH, SOJOURNER

(c. 1797–1883), evangelist, abolitionist, and feminist. Sojourner Truth is remembered for her unschooled but remarkable voice raised in support of abolitionism, the freedmen, and women's rights. Tales of her aggressive platform style, of her challenge to Frederick Douglass on the issue of violence against slavery ("Frederick! Is God dead?"), and of her baring her breasts before a crude audience who had challenged her womanhood grace the pages of abolitionist lore.

Truth was six feet tall, blessed with a powerful voice (she spoke English with a Dutch accent), and driven by deep religious conviction. Harriet Beecher Stowe attested to Truth's personal magnetism, saying that she had never "been conversant with anyone who had more of that silent and subtle power which we call personal presence than this woman." Truth was born of slave parents owned by a wealthy Dutch patroon in Ulster County, New York. Details of her early life remain cloudy. What is clear is that her name was Isabella and she served a household in New Paltz, New York, from 1810 to 1827, where she bore some five children by a fellow slave. At least two of her daughters and one son were sold away from her during these years.

Isabella escaped slavery in 1827, one year before mandatory emancipation in New York State, by fleeing to a Quaker family, the Van Wageners, whose name she took. She moved to New York City, worked as a domestic, became involved in moral reform, embraced evangelical religion, started her street-corner preaching career, and eventually joined a utopian community in Sing Sing, New York. Illiterate and a mystic, Isabella nevertheless acquired a wide knowledge of the Bible and emerged in the 1840s in Massachusetts, working among the Garrisonian abolitionists. A popular platform figure, she told stories and sang gospel songs that instructed and entertained. Adopting the name "Sojourner Truth" in 1843, she became a wandering orator. In the mid-1850s she settled in Battle Creek, Michigan, her base of operations for the rest of her life.

During the Civil War, Truth tramped the roads of Michigan collecting food and clothing for black regiments. She traveled to Washington, D.C., where she met with Abraham Lincoln at the White House, and immersed herself in relief work for the freedpeople. During Reconstruction, Truth barely supported herself by selling a narrative of her life as well as her "shadows," photographs of herself. She lent her unique skills to the women's suffrage movement and initiated a petition drive to obtain land for the freedpeople, even suggesting the idea of a "Negro state" in the West. She preached cleanliness and godliness among the freedpeople and dictated many letters about the land question, which provide rich details about that aspect of Reconstruction.

Truth's most important legacy is the tone and substance of her language. As an old woman she stumped the country providing emancipation with an eloquent epigraph: "Give 'em land and an outset, and hab teachers learn 'em to read. Den they can be somebody." Few modern activists have better described politicians or the purpose of a petition drive than Truth did: "Send *tons* of paper down to Washington for them spouters to chaw on." And when she was brutally knocked off of Washington's segregated streetcars, she denounced racism: "It is hard for the old slaveholding spirit to die, but *die* it must." She herself died of old age and ulcerated legs in 1883; her funeral and burial in Battle Creek was the largest that town had ever seen, testimony to her hold on America's historical imagination.

Jacqueline Bernard, *Journey toward Freedom: The Story of Sojourner Truth* (1967); Hertha Pauli, *Her Name Was Sojourner Truth* (1962).

DAVID W. BLIGHT

See also Abolitionist Movement; Feminist Movement; Free Negroes, 1619–1860; Reconstruction; Slavery; Suffrage.

TUBMAN, HARRIET

(1815?–1913), abolitionist, spy, and scout. Tubman became famous as a "conductor" on the Underground Railroad during the turbulent 1850s. Born a slave on Maryland's eastern shore, she endured brutal beatings by her master and the harsh regime of the field hand. Her life was a testimony to the fierce resistance of African-American people to slavery.

In 1849 Tubman fled Maryland, leaving behind her free husband of five years, John Tubman, and her parents, sisters, and brothers. "Mah people mus' go free," her constant refrain, suggests a determination uncommon among even the most militant slaves. She returned to the South at least nineteen times to lead her family and hundreds of other slaves to freedom via the Underground Railroad. Utilizing her native intelligence and drawing on her boundless courage, she eluded bounty hunters seeking a reward for her capture, which eventually went as high as forty thousand dollars. She never lost a fugitive or allowed one to turn back.

Two things sustained her: the pistol at her side and her faith in God. She would not hesitate to use the pistol in self-defense, but it was also a symbol to instruct slaves, making it clear that "dead Negroes tell no tales." Timid slaves seemed to find courage in her presence; no one ever betrayed her. She affirmed her faith in God in her statement, "I always tole God, I'm gwine to hole stiddy on to you, an' you've got to see me trou [through]."

Tubman collaborated with John Brown in 1858 in planning his raid on Harpers Ferry. The two met in Canada where she told him all she knew of the Underground Railroad in the East. Advising him on the area in which he planned to operate, she promised to deliver aid from fugitives in the region. Brown's admiration for her was immeasurable, and he wanted her to accompany him on the raid. Tubman planned to be present but was ill at the time and could not participate.

Tubman's resistance to slavery did not end with the outbreak of the Civil War. Her services as nurse, scout, and spy were solicited by the Union government. For more than three years she nursed the sick and wounded in Florida and the Carolinas, tending whites and blacks, soldiers and contrabands. Tubman was a short woman without distinctive features. With a bandanna on her head and several front teeth missing, she moved unnoticed through rebel territory. This made her invaluable as a scout and spy under the command of Col. James Montgomery of the Second Carolina Volunteers. As leader of a corps of local blacks, she made several forays into rebel territory, collecting information. Armed with knowledge of the location of cotton warehouses, ammunition depots, and slaves waiting to be liberated, Colonel Montgomery made several raids in southern coastal areas. Tubman led the way on his celebrated expedition up the Combahee River in June 1863. For all of her work, Tubman was paid only two hundred dollars over a three-year period and had to support herself by selling pies, gingerbread, and root beer.

After the war, Tubman returned to Auburn, New York, and continued to help blacks forge new lives in freedom. She cared for her parents and other needy relatives, turning her residence into the Home for Indigent and Aged Negroes. Lack of money continued to be a pressing problem, and she financed the home by selling copies of her biography and giving speeches. Her most memorable appearance was at the organizing meeting of the National Association of Colored Women in 1896 in Washington, D.C. Two generations came together to celebrate the strength of black women and to continue their struggle for a life of dignity and respect. Harriet Tubman, the oldest member present, was the embodiment of their strength and their struggle.

Sarah Bradford, *Harriet: The Moses of Her People* (1886); Earl Conrad, *Harriet Tubman* (1943); Dorothy Sterling, ed., *We Are Your Sisters: Black Women in the Nineteenth Century* (1984).

TIFFANY R. L. PATTERSON

See also Abolitionist Movement; Brown, John; Civil War; Free Negroes, 1619–1860; Slavery; Underground Railroad.

TURNER, FREDERICK JACKSON

(1861–1932), historian. Turner was educated at the University of Wisconsin and received his doctorate from Johns Hopkins University (1891). He taught at Wisconsin and at Harvard and then served as a senior research associate at the Huntington Library until his death. He was a gifted public speaker with a vibrant voice, and he loved the outdoors.

Turner made significant contributions to many fields in American history and also pioneered new methodologies. He challenged historians to utilize the research in cognate disciplines such as geography, statistics, economics, and sociology. His research, methods, and sources were often so different from those of traditional historians that some of them doubted that he was one himself, but he argued that historians should use whatever knowledge and tools would help them explain the past. He urged American historians to escape the parochialism of New England and the Seaboard South and to study immigration and assimilation, urbanization, diplomacy, economic history, political behavior, social and cultural history, and the frontier experience.

His nostalgic view of frontier Wisconsin led him to rebel against the conventional wisdom of his generation. He was trained by Herbert Baxter Adams at Hopkins, who endorsed German scientific methods of historical investigation and espoused the so-called germ theory, which held that all American institutions derived from early Germanic tribal practices. Turner's doctoral dissertation on the Indian trade in Wisconsin only partly accepted Adams's ideas.

His later essay, "The Significance of the Frontier in American History" (1893), which repudiated the germ theory altogether, was a turning point in American historical scholarship. Within a decade of the essay's publication, the "Turner thesis" — that the frontier experience had a lasting if not permanent impact on the American character and society — became the organizing principle of American historical studies and a subject of continuing controversy.

Another essay was less successful: "The Significance of the Section in American History" (1925), which integrated political and cultural attitudes with geographical units and economic interest groups. Although his subsequent book on the subject won a Pulitzer Prize, the sectionalism thesis has been of only marginal influence in organizing historical study, but it achieved healthy recognition among some economists, geographers, and political scientists.

Turner believed in the uniqueness of America and suggested that it offered a laboratory to study the evolution of society. But he accepted multiple causation and was neither a geographic nor an economic determinist.

Turner, along with historians Woodrow Wilson, Charles Homer Haskins, Max Farrand, and J. Franklin Jameson, made up a network that dominated the discipline and controlled appointments to major institutions and editorial boards for decades. Although sharply criticized almost from the start, his work and that of his disciples and students were important in most

American universities until at least the Great Depression. His ideas also enjoyed a renaissance after the Second World War, but in modified form. Today, historians, whether defenders or critics of Turner's ideas, still feel compelled to confront them. Moreover, his methodological concerns, especially his search for a means of correlating numerical data, made him a forerunner of contemporary quantitative social and political history.

R. A. Billington, *The American Frontier Thesis: Attack and Defense* (1971); R. A. Billington, *Frederick Jackson Turner: Historian, Scholar, Teacher* (1973).

MARTIN RIDGE

See also History and Historians; Progressivism.

TVA

See Tennessee Valley Authority.

TWAIN, MARK

(1835–1910), writer and lecturer. Under his pen name of Mark Twain, Samuel L. Clemens was an exceptionally popular author during his lifetime and is still regarded as one of America's best writers. Beginning as a journalist, he wrote travel books, an autobiography, and novels. The best of the latter, *The Adventures of Tom Sawyer* (1876) and *Adventures of Huckleberry Finn* (1884) were based chiefly on his childhood experiences in Hannibal, Missouri, and on the Mississippi River, where he was a riverboat pilot. (His pen name is derived from the Mississippi leadsman's call "Mark Twain," meaning two fathoms.)

Mark Twain's first humorous pieces were written while he was living in California and Nevada. His enormous following was based on his humorous manner, which some people found crude and irreverent, and on his appealing personality. He reached a wide audience with *The Innocents Abroad* (1869), an account of his travels in the Mediterranean and the Holy Land, and subsequent lectures and readings. But soon, because he had married into a wealthy, genteel family, he felt obliged to write what would be acceptable to his wife's social class. The results include *The Prince and the Pauper* (1882), a historical novel, and *Joan of Arc* (1896), a fictionalized biography. His most ambitious book, *A Connecticut Yankee in King Arthur's Court* (1889), was an attempt to celebrate the achievements of his own age, but many modern readers find the book to be a prophecy of the horrors of modern warfare, something different from what the author intended.

Mark Twain was an avid critic of American society. His novel *The Gilded Age* (1873, written with Charles Dudley Warner) satirizes the post–Civil War boom years and Washington politics. *Life on the Mississippi* (1883) is a highly critical account of middle-American society. *Huckleberry Finn* attacks racism, as Huck gradually comes to recognize the humanity that he shares with the escaped slave Jim. After a round-the-world lecture tour in 1895–1896, Mark Twain became an outspoken critic of imperialism. He attacked the actions of Western nations in Africa, China, and the Philippines in various works and served as vice president of the American Congo Reform Association. In his last years, when he thought of himself as a philosopher, he wrote but did not publish many works that expressed his deterministic, pessimistic, and anti-Christian views, a good example being *Letters from the Earth,* first published in 1962.

In Mark Twain, lust for wealth vied with his identification with the common man, the spontaneity of his writing with his inability to be a good judge of his own work, his dedication to literary realism with his fanciful imagination. Despite these contradictions, his writings are greatly admired, chiefly because of their good humor, charm, and nostalgic depiction of a lost America.

Everett Emerson, *The Authentic Mark Twain: A Literary Biography of Samuel L. Clemens* (1984); Justin Kaplan, *Mister Clemens and Mark Twain* (1966).

EVERETT EMERSON

See also Literature.

TWEED RING

In the late 1860s, Boss William Marcy Tweed created a network of city officials, Democratic party workers, and contractors in New York City, which his critics dubbed the Tweed Ring.

The network was a notorious instance of municipal corruption. Some historians claim it left a permanent smirch on New York City's image.

After terms in the 1850s as city alderman and congressman, Tweed was appointed a supervisor of city elections. He gained popularity by supporting labor unions and the Roman Catholic church. Tweed's associates in the state legislature secured a new city charter that gave New York control of its budget and police. He himself pushed for the overhaul of the city's infrastructure, funded mostly by municipal bonds. The city soon accumulated large debts while Tweed was making money on kickbacks from contractors. For example, he formed a printing company and saw that it received all city printing contracts. Railroads and other corporations found it worthwhile to pay the nonlawyer Tweed's "firm" extravagant "retainers."

Tweed's power declined dramatically once the city's financial peril became apparent. Cartoonist Thomas Nast of *Harper's Weekly* weakened Tweed's popularity through his caricatures of the politician; one depicted a large thumb crushing Manhattan. The costs of building a lavish courthouse, which became known as the Tweed Courthouse, aroused particular suspicion. In 1871 Tweed was arrested and prosecuted for failing to audit contractors' bills to the city for this building; his associates were not charged. He was convicted for the misdemeanor but never prosecuted for related felony charges; his sentence was one year. The state of New York sued him in the Supreme Court of New York County for over $6 million. Faced with exorbitant bail and rulings that prevented an effective defense in the suit, Tweed escaped from jail in 1875. The next year, however, he was identified in Spain and arrested. Returned to New York's Ludlow Street jail, he died before the suit was tried.

See also Corruption; Nast, Thomas; Urban Bosses and Machine Politics.

TYLER, JOHN

(1790–1862), tenth president of the United States. Tyler was the first to ascend from the vice presidency through the accident of a chief executive's death. "His Accidency" was also only the second politician to switch parties before attaining the White House and the first to be driven from his party before departing Pennsylvania Avenue. Yet this partisan without a party and chief executive with almost no followers scored a presidential triumph so portentous as to make him one of the most important American presidents.

Tyler believed that these paradoxes stemmed from his devout adherence to states' rights. Born and bred to be a Virginia gentleman of the old school, he was educated at William and Mary, studied law, and swiftly ascended in state politics. He served successively in the Virginia House of Delegates, the U.S. House of Representatives, and the governorship of Virginia before being elected to the U.S. Senate in 1827.

Tyler's senatorial tenure coincided with Andrew Jackson's presidency. Tyler, seeking a less imperial president and a stronger states' rights policy, joined a small group of Jacksonians who deserted the fold and eventually became known as southern states' rights Whigs. In 1836, the Jacksonian-controlled Virginia legislature demanded and secured the recreant's senatorial resignation.

Tyler soon received compensation for his losses. In 1840, the Whig party, seeking a southern states' righter to balance William Henry Harrison's more nationalistic views, nominated Tyler as Harrison's running mate. Tyler, swept into subordinate office in the famous "Tippecanoe and Tyler Too" campaign, became president when Harrison died a month after the inaugural.

His Accidency's greatest problem was that Whig nationalists, in command of the party, would take no commands from a states' righter like Tyler. Twice Henry Clay drove nationalistic bank bills through Congress. Twice Tyler vetoed them. The second time, the Whig congressional caucus drummed the president out of the party. Almost the entire cabinet then resigned.

But the seemingly powerless president still remained potent enough to take advantage of the emergence of the Texas annexation issue. In the early 1840s, both major parties' leaders opposed adding the Lone Star Republic as a slave state to the nation, fearing a possible war with Mexico and an escalation of North-South tension. But Tyler was afraid that Texas, if not annexed, would ally with England to secure protection against Mexico and would be forced to emancipate its relatively few slaves in order to seal the English bargain. Tyler, determined to protect the South and states' rights, secured an annexation treaty and demanded that southern states' righters come to his aid.

Southern Jacksonians answered the call. They forced the nomination of an annexationist, James K. Polk, at the Democratic convention and won the election of 1844. Although still lacking a two-thirds majority to ratify Tyler's treaty in the Senate, the Democrats admitted Texas to the Union by resolution (which required only simple majorities in House and Senate) in late February 1845. A few days later, Tyler retired to his Virginia plantation.

The ex-president could only watch as consequences of his Texas prize escalated: war with Mexico, the crisis of 1850, a decade of sectional controversy. Tyler would not serve his people or his creed again until 1861, when he was chairman of the failed peace convention during the secession crisis. He subsequently voted for disunion in the Virginia secession convention and was elected to the Confederate House of Representatives. But the old states' righter was not destined to fulfill this last responsibility. John Tyler, the accident who not-at-all-accidentally helped precipitate the near-destruction of a nation, died in 1862 before taking the oath to serve the Southern nation he had come to prefer.

Oliver Perry Chitwood, *John Tyler, Champion of the Old South* (1939); Frederick Merk, *Fruits of Propaganda in the Tyler Administration* (1971).

WILLIAM W. FREEHLING

See also Elections: 1840; Texas Revolution and Annexation; Whig Party.

U

---★---

U-2 AFFAIR

The U-2 affair refers to the downing of a high-altitude U.S. reconnaissance plane over the Soviet Union on May 1, 1960. The incident led to the cancelation of a summit conference between President Dwight D. Eisenhower and Soviet premier Nikita Khrushchev planned for two weeks later.

At first, American officials announced that the U-2 was a weather plane that had strayed off course. They were greatly embarrassed when the Soviets produced the pilot, Francis Gary Powers, who confessed to espionage and subsequently served about two years of a ten-year sentence in a Soviet prison.

On May 7 the State Department admitted that the U-2 had been engaged in intelligence activities but claimed that such flights were unauthorized. On May 25 President Eisenhower took "full responsibility for approving all the various programs undertaken by our government to secure and evaluate military intelligence." He refused to apologize for the overflights, arguing that the Soviets had known of the flights for years but had not protested.

See also Cold War; Espionage.

UNCAS

(c. 1588–c. 1682), Mohegan Indian sachem. Uncas is probably more famous as a character in James Fenimore Cooper's *The Last of the Mohicans* than as a real-life person. But he is significant in the context of seventeenth-century New England history.

Uncas was a member of the Mohegans, a splinter community of the Pequot Indians. He played a leading role in the Mohegan effort to avoid domination by the Pequot sachem Sassacus. The colonists, to be sure, encouraged such separatism, because a divided group of Indian nations naturally was to their advantage. At the same time, groups like the Mohegans seized upon the English presence as an opportunity to rid themselves of powerful Indian foes.

Uncas thus sided with the English in the bloody Pequot War of 1637. Indeed, he helped precipitate the conflict, realizing he would gain politically from its predictable outcome — the whites' victory. As part of the overall campaign, Uncas led seventy Mohegans and other Indians against Sassacus and his Pequot followers. (Sassacus lost only a few men in the battle, but soon thereafter he was killed in a clash with Mohawks.) The war destroyed the Pequots as a force in the region and transformed Uncas from a leader of a small band of dissidents to a commander of hundreds.

But a Pequot ally, the Narragansett sachem Miantonomi, then decided to fight Uncas, first obtaining formal English permission to do so. In the ensuing struggle, the Narragansett leader was captured by Mohegan forces. Members of his tribe offered a ransom of wampum if Miantonomi were handed over to the colonial authorities, who, they assumed, would release him. The authorities, however, concluded, as John Winthrop said, "that it would not be safe to set

1093

him at liberty, neither had we sufficient ground for us to put him to death."

The English thus allowed Uncas to take Miantonomi outside of English jurisdiction and with "justice and prudence" execute him. Although they did not doubt Uncas's intentions, they insisted "that some discreet and faithful persons of the English accompany" him to "see the execution for our more full satisfaction." Knowing that the Mohegans would feel the wrath of Miantonomi's people, they also pledged "a competent strength" of men to defend Uncas "against any present fury or assault." Uncas carried out the execution and in so doing removed a major obstacle to English hegemony in the region.

At the outbreak of King Philip's War in 1675, Uncas again allied with the whites and helped ensure the demise of the Wampanoag king. By then an old man, he was willing for younger Mohegans to do the fighting. He died a stubborn adherent to his particular agenda but an Indian whose actions had expedited the domination of New England by the white settlers.

Francis Jennings, *The Invasion of America: Indians, Colonialism, and the Cant of Conquest* (1975); Neal Salisbury, *Manitou and Providence: Indians, Europeans, and the Making of New England, 1500–1643* (1982).

PETER IVERSON

See also Colonial Wars; Indians; King Philip's War.

UNCLE TOM'S CABIN

This novel by Harriet Beecher Stowe did much to galvanize northern public opinion against slavery. *Uncle Tom's Cabin, or, Life Among the Lowly* began as a ten-month serial in the *National Era*, an abolitionist newspaper, on June 5, 1851. Published in book form in March 1852, it quickly sold 300,000 copies and eventually about 7 million throughout the world. It was also dramatized in 1852 by George Aiken (without Stowe's consent) and had a successful stage run.

The book tells the story of a Christian slave, Uncle Tom, who is sold by a Kentucky family burdened by debt. Finally, sold again, he dies under the lash of the henchman of a cruel overseer, Simon Legree, who wants Uncle Tom to accept him instead of God as his master. Stowe, a member of a family of abolitionists and ministers, also recounts the flight of a family of runaways on the Underground Railroad.

Many northerners were shocked into a hatred for the institution so melodramatically described. When introduced to Stowe during the Civil War, Abraham Lincoln is said to have called her the "little lady who made this big war." The novel also affected the American language: "Uncle Tom" became an epithet for passive, usually older blacks (paradoxically, considering that Tom will answer to no white man, only to God), and "Simon Legree" became a synonym for cruelty.

See also Abolitionist Movement; Stowe, Harriet Beecher.

UNDERGROUND RAILROAD

The *Underground Railroad* was the term used to describe a network of persons who helped escaped slaves on their way to freedom in the northern states or Canada. Although George Washington had commented upon such practices by the Quakers as early as the 1780s, the term gained currency in the 1830s, as northern abolitionists became more vocal and southern suspicions of threats to their peculiar institution grew.

The popular perception of a well-coordinated system of Quaker, Covenanter, and Methodist "conductors" secretly helping fugitives from "station" to "station" is an exaggeration. The practice involved more spontaneity than the railroad analogy suggests. By the time escapees reached areas where sympathetic persons might assist them, they had already completed the most difficult part of their journey. A successful escape was usually less the product of coordinated assistance and more a matter of the runaways' resourcefulness — and a great deal of luck.

The most active of the Railroad workers were northern free blacks, who had little or no support from white abolitionists. The most famous "conductor," an escaped slave named Harriet Tubman, reportedly made nineteen return trips to the South; she helped some three hundred slaves escape. A number of individual whites also aided runaways, as did "vigilance committees," often biracial in character, in northern cities.

Estimates of the number of slaves assisted vary widely, but only a minuscule fraction of those held in bondage ever escaped. Few, particularly from the Lower South, even attempted the arduous journey north. But the idea of organized "outsiders" undermining the institution of slavery angered white southerners, leading to their demands in the 1840s that the Fugitive Slave Laws be strengthened.

See also Fugitive Slave Law; Personal Liberty Laws; Tubman, Harriet.

UNEMPLOYMENT

The problem of unemployment appeared in the United States only in the nineteenth century. Although there had long been men and women who were involuntarily jobless and traditional rhythms of labor were unsteady in many trades, the modern phenomenon of unemployment was the child of industrial capitalism: only when large numbers of adults had become employees, dependent on their wages to survive, was the unsteadiness of economic activity translated into the chronic, and periodically widespread, presence of jobless individuals who needed and wanted to work. This phenomenon began to be visible in the urban centers of the Northeast during the trade depressions of the antebellum era, most notably those of 1837–1842 and 1857. The word *unemployed* acquired its modern definition between 1850 and 1880, and the term *unemployment* probably did not appear in print until 1887.

Once arrived, the problem proved to be tenacious and difficult to solve. Beginning in the 1870s, unemployment became a persistent feature of economic life in the Northeast and the Midwest, and it became a national phenomenon no later than the depression of the 1890s. From the Civil War until World War II, unemployment rates ranged from roughly 4 or 5 percent in good years to more than 15 percent during the troughs of the worst depressions. But such fig-

ures (which reveal only the percentage of labor force members *simultaneously* jobless) understate the breadth of the phenomenon. In all likelihood, between 20 and 25 percent of working Americans experienced some unemployment during the average year, and they tended to remain jobless for roughly three months. During depressions, up to 40 percent of the labor force was laid off in the course of each year for spells averaging more than four months. The problem was most severe during the downturns that began in 1893, 1907, and 1920, and it reached its nadir during the Great Depression of the 1930s — when roughly 25 percent of the labor force was simultaneously jobless, with many of the unemployed remaining out of work for a year or more.

But unemployment was not entirely, or even primarily, a depression experience. Even during prosperous years millions of workers experienced layoffs; only in wartime did the nation have "full employment" in the sense that every able-bodied and willing worker could find a job. The impact of unemployment was also shaped by chronic, yet shifting, variations in regional and local unemployment levels: unemployment, almost always, was high in some cities and states while low in others. During the national prosperity of the 1920s, for example, tens of thousands of workers struggled to cope with layoffs in the shoe and textile manufacturing cities of New England.

Despite its salience in the lives of working people, unemployment became a public policy issue only gradually. During the depressions of the late nineteenth century, labor unions and working-class political parties demanded public works programs, as well as relief, from municipal and state authorities; in 1894 the federal government received similar demands from protesting "armies" led by Jacob Coxey and others. But, with scattered and temporary exceptions, these demands met with little success: Coxey's army disbanded in failure, and in most locales, the only sources of aid for the unemployed remained private charities and traditional poor relief agencies. Similarly, workers and their organizations tried repeatedly to develop strategies to reduce unemployment levels, the most sustained of which was the drive for shorter hours.

(It was widely, if erroneously, believed that the eight-hour day would eradicate "involuntary idleness.") But these efforts bore few fruits, and the major political parties adhered to the view that the government neither could nor should assume responsibility for solving the problem — except insofar as solutions resulted from traditional "sound" economic policies on such matters as the tariff and currency questions.

These views began to change early in the twentieth century, as pressure from the working class mounted, middle-class reformers focused on the problem, and precedents of economic regulation and social welfare legislation were established. Nonetheless, it took the crucible of the Great Depression to produce new national policies and institutions. Massive public works programs were created as a part of the New Deal, and a joint federal-state unemployment insurance system was established through the Social Security Act of 1935. In the course of the 1930s the federal government tacitly assumed responsibility for the problem of unemployment, a responsibility formalized in the Employment Act of 1946; at the same time, the economic theories of J. M. Keynes seemed to offer governments tools with which they could control unemployment.

Without question, the New Deal and the Great Depression constituted a watershed in the history of unemployment, the beginning of an era of "managed" rather than uncontrolled unemployment. After World War II, both major political parties presumed that it was the duty of the federal government to minimize unemployment, and in the 1950s and 1960s, it appeared to many analysts that the problem was close to being solved: the business cycle was being tamed through Keynesian techniques, durable unemployment rates of 2–3 percent looked feasible, and the insurance system seemed capable of tiding over the unfortunate victims of technological change or the small, yet incessant, shifts in labor market conditions that produced what was called frictional unemployment.

Since the early 1970s, however, the picture has looked less rosy. Unemployment levels crept upward in the 1970s, and in 1982 the rate exceeded 10 percent for the first time since the 1930s. Although it fell back to the 5–6 percent range by the late 1980s, it was apparent that the business cycle had not been tamed and that 3 percent unemployment was no longer on the horizon. Of equal importance, teenage unemployment rates remained high, as they had been (increasingly) since World War II, and joblessness among blacks continued to be an acute problem, as it had been, in all likelihood, since World War I. (Reliable statistics regarding black unemployment do not exist for the years before 1940; ironically, unemployment levels among blacks before World War I may have been relatively low because blacks had great difficulty obtaining jobs in manufacturing and construction, where work tended to be particularly unsteady.) This uneven distribution of unemployment posed a challenge to policymakers — since economic growth alone seemed incapable of eradicating black or teenage unemployment — and raised the possibility that the earlier postwar job security of adult white males had been achieved (through a mixture of seniority systems and discrimination) at the expense of blacks and the young. For most years of the 1950s and 1960s, for example, unemployment rates for black males and for all males under the age of twenty-five tended to be double or triple the rates for white males over the age of thirty.

The regional distribution of joblessness also remained uneven and shifting. In the 1970s the most dramatic job losses came in the "smokestack" industries of the Midwest, and the collapse of the oil economies of Texas and Louisiana in the late 1980s made clear that the growing Sunbelt was not immune to unemployment. To make matters worse, there was also a sharp drop in the proportion of the jobless covered by unemployment insurance. Indeed, by the end of the 1980s, the American track record (reinforced by the specter of European trends) suggested that the problem of unemployment might, in the long run, be growing more, rather than less, severe. A century after the term first appeared in print, unemployment remained a significant problem for American society.

John A. Garraty, *Unemployment in History: Economic Thought and Public Policy* (1978); Alexander Keyssar, *Out of Work: The First Century of Unemployment in Massachusetts* (1986).

ALEXANDER KEYSSAR

See also Coxey's Army; Depressions; New Deal; Welfare and Public Relief.

UNIONS

See Labor.

UNITED FARM WORKERS

See Chavez, Cesar.

UNITED STATES V. E. C. KNIGHT CO.

In this 1895 decision, the Supreme Court drastically limited the power of the federal government to regulate big business. The Sherman Antitrust Act of 1890 had outlawed combinations "in restraint of trade." When the American Sugar Refining Company acquired four Pennsylvania sugar refineries, thus obtaining control of 98 percent of the nation's sugar-refining capacity, the government sought to break up the new combination. In the *Knight* case, however, the Supreme Court ruled that the Sherman Act did not apply to manufacturing per se. Chief Justice Melville Fuller's majority opinion declared that Congress had the authority to regulate only interstate commerce: "That which belongs to commerce is within the jurisdiction of the United States, but that which does not belong to commerce is within the jurisdiction of the state. . . . Doubtless the power to control the manufacture of a given thing involves in a certain sense the control of its disposition, but . . . affects it only incidentally and indirectly." Although the Sherman Antitrust Act was applied with limited success to combinations closely tied to transportation, *Knight* prevented Congress from directly regulating the American economy until the mid-1930s.

See also Antitrust Movement; Government and the Economy.

UNITED STATES WOMEN'S BUREAU

This federal agency has both informed and directed the continuing fight for women's rights. In 1920, Congress approved the creation of the Women's Bureau of the Department of Labor to create "standards and policies which shall promote the welfare of wage-earning women." Under the leadership of its first director, Mary Anderson, from 1920 to 1944, the bureau helped direct lobbying by such groups as the League of Women Voters, the Young Women's Christian Association, and the American Association of University Women. Anderson opposed an Equal Rights Amendment as a threat to legislation protecting women workers and emphasized alleviating the plight of working women over securing careers for middle-class women. Besides calling for protective legislation in the workplace and the home, the bureau also was an important disseminator and clearinghouse of information for and about women, which it used to assist its case for protective laws for them. It cited one finding, for example, that they usually worked not to provide luxuries but to help feed their families and that they faced the added burden of housework after their first workday was through.

The bureau achieved mixed results. Many continued to doubt its findings. Feminists divided over its longtime opposition to an Equal Rights Amendment. During World War II, it emphasized war production over helping women in general, and black women in particular, make significant inroads into the permanent work force; but it also urged employers to give women rest time and an eight-hour day. By 1969, with the appointment of Elizabeth Koontz as director, the Women's Bureau began to shift away from seeking protective legislation for working women toward supporting the Equal Rights Amendment.

See also Feminist Movement; Labor; Women and the Work Force.

UNIVERSITIES

See Education.

URBAN BOSSES AND MACHINE POLITICS

When Chicago mayor and political boss Richard J. Daley died in office in 1976, obituaries not only lamented his passing but commented on the demise of urban political machines. Thirteen years later when his son, Richard M. Daley, was elected mayor, critics warned of a "pin-striped machine," in which the Loop's politically connected lawyers would replace old-style precinct captains. But the father had once told the son, "I can put you on the ballroom floor, but you'll have to dance for yourself." To the critics' surprise, in the early days of the younger Daley's first administration, the music was that of reform.

The Daley family saga illustrates the complexity of urban politics. Call a politician a boss rather than a leader, label party structure a machine rather than an organization — either sends the voter a clear message. That is why the prototype of the political boss, William M. Tweed, proclaimed himself to be a "Statesman!" Whether Robin Hood or scoundrel, corrupter or modernizer of cities, omnipotent dictator or mere cog in the many-spoked wheel of municipal government, the boss is an urban institution that must be understood if one is to know the history of America's cities.

A century ago, when he wanted to reinforce his belief that local government in the United States was a conspicuous failure, James Bryce described the boss as "dominant among his fellows. . . . He dispenses places, rewards the loyal, punishes the mutinous, concocts schemes, negotiates treaties. He generally avoids publicity, preferring the substance to the pomp of power, and is all the more dangerous because he sits, like a spider, hidden in the midst of his web. He is a Boss." Reading Bryce's *The American Commonwealth*, one envisions an all-powerful chieftain controlling every aspect of urban political life. But more often, the power was dispersed. Neighborhood or ward bosses contended with one another for political control; they had to deal with bureaucrats and found themselves confronted with the conflicting desires of competing ethnic groups. Even in cities with one preeminent boss,

such as Tweed in New York, George Cox in Cincinnati, Thomas Pendergast in Kansas City, Daniel P. O'Connell in Albany, or Daley in Chicago, he was not so much Bryce's spider as a big fish in a large pool, who had to contend with sharks.

Incipient bosses, such as Joel Barlow Sutherland of Philadelphia, and machines like Tammany Hall existed in one form or another as early as the 1780s. But the classic age of the machine began after the Civil War and continued until the Great Depression. It is no coincidence that this was also the age of the rise of America's industrial cities. In the preindustrial city, politics was left to the amateur; just as labor specialized in other ways with the rise of industrialism, politics emerged as a distinct and full-time professional pursuit.

The boss and his machine helped cope with the enormous changes brought about by rapid urbanization. New York City's population increased by more than 800,000 between 1820 and 1870. By the latter year, the height of the Tweed Ring's activity, Irish and German immigrants composed almost half of the city's population. The growing numbers placed increasing pressure on the inadequate urban infrastructure — the streets, buildings, transportation — and what welfare services there were. Smaller cities like Cincinnati witnessed a similar breakdown in services during the 1880s and 1890s. That city's fire marshal, reflecting on the small size of his force, feared that if two fires erupted at once, it would mean disaster. The water supply ran short, and the lack of sewers created a health hazard. Because the structure of urban government incorporated the principle of the separation (and therefore fragmentation) of powers, it was difficult to respond to such needs.

One theory contends that the boss and the political machine arose to cope with the problems the official city government could not solve. According to this view, the machines were parallel governments that functioned to meet the needs of the public. In turn, a grateful community offered its allegiance and votes. The boss helped someone find a job, filled the coal bin in winter, brought a turkey to the table at Christmas, and performed many other useful functions. Businessmen, eager to build trolley lines or develop neighborhoods, turned to the bosses for assistance in winning monopolistic franchises or avoiding permit and licensing restrictions. Gamblers and racketeers sought the machine's help in being allowed to conduct their illegitimate businesses. In return, the recipients of favors contributed to the politicians' war chests.

The boss not only provided such services but did much to modernize American cities, for construction meant jobs and jobs meant patronage. As a consequence, the machine politician was willing to spend and borrow with abandon in order to pave and light streets, construct sewers, and generally improve the urban infrastructure. His motivation might have been self-interest, but the result was a better city environment despite the cost, which often was excessive. The famous Tweed Courthouse near New York's City Hall cost nearly twice as much to build as the price of Alaska, which was purchased around the same time. Similarly, in the twentieth century, Kansas City's Boss Pendergast devised a ten-year plan that involved a massive public works program — and lined many pockets as well.

It has been contended that the corruption that accompanied such building simply greased the wheels of urban growth and that the "big payoff" was necessary to get things done. For instance, machine politicians, especially between 1870 and 1920, were among the major promoters and facilitators of spectator sports. Political pull helped build ballparks and racetracks at the cheapest, most accessible sites and protected them and boxing clubs from competition and police interference. As politics promoted spectator sports, sports added luster to a politician's popularity.

"I work for my pocket all the time," testified Richard Croker, one of Tweed's successors, and the legendary ward boss George Washington Plunkitt unabashedly remarked, "I saw my opportunities and took 'em." Such men would have argued that they were doing well by doing good.

Defenders of the bosses usually play down their corruption. Instead, they stress that the political machine offered a vehicle of social mobil-

ity, especially for immigrants, and most particularly for the Irish. Tweed's Irish successors in Tammany Hall (Tweed himself was native-born of Scottish Protestant stock), as well as Frank Hague of Jersey City, Edward J. Kelly, Patrick A. Nash, and Daley of Chicago, C. A. Buckley of San Francisco, David L. Lawrence of Pittsburgh, and O'Connell of Albany were some of the leading figures in the Irish Machine Politics Hall of Fame. Blocked from more traditional activity by entrenched WASPs, the Irish went where the signs "Irish Need Not Apply" had not been raised. Hence, they, and after them other ethnic groups, flocked to politics, sports, and crime in an effort to make a living and climb the economic ladder.

Critics of the bosses and their place in American history counter that such an interpretation sentimentalizes machine politicians. Careful studies of urban fiscal politics have found scant evidence of the big spending required to establish a large-scale patronage organization. The pork in the pork barrel seems to have been paltry. Moreover, they contend that the voters didn't need patronage because of the broad occupational and property mobility that pervaded the American urban scene; nor did city dwellers want to pay the increased property taxes that accompanied escalating costs associated with bossism. Since the machines' coffers were more modest than they appeared, they did not serve many ethnic groups apart from the Irish, who jealously guarded the limited political resources. Electoral demand had to be balanced with resource supply.

Whichever interpretation one accepts, it cannot be denied that a *perceived* escalation in costs and corruption gave rise to many reform movements. One observer has suggested that American city dwellers are willing to tolerate a "reasonable" level of graft and corruption, but when it gets too high, they balk. It is at that time that urban reformers have the best chance to seize power from the machines. Cost, then, can act as a trigger for reform. On the other hand, successful reform movements did not always ensure more efficient and less expensive government. At the turn of the century during the Progressive Era, for instance, inflation often propelled increased costs, resulting in higher taxes under reform governments and government structures such as the city manager and commission. Moreover, once in control, the "goo-goos" (good-government advocates) often found that corporate efficiency could not easily be transplanted to the public sector.

Reformers, however, had other goals besides less expensive government and structural change. Frequently, they were concerned with the morals of the community and advocated changes that would limit or eliminate drinking, wipe out prostitution, or curtail commercial and leisure activity on Sundays. Occasionally, they promoted environmental improvements tied to the new profession of city planning. Some supported social reform such as factory safety laws, minimum-wage and maximum-hour laws, and protective legislation for women and children. It was not unusual, however, for the bosses to advocate many of the same changes. Although the machines seemed less concerned with their constituents' morality, it was to their advantage to improve the quality of urban life, for such action won them community support. The line between bosses and reformers was not always as sharp as the critics of machine politics contend.

Perhaps that is one of the reasons machines lasted long into the twentieth century despite the forces working against them. Many expected federal welfare measures stemming from the New Deal to weaken if not eliminate the need for the local political machine. It has been shown, however, that in many cities such as Pittsburgh and Kansas City federal largess actually strengthened them.

Nevertheless, a better-educated electorate, the acculturation of immigrants and their families into the American mainstream, civil service reform, and television campaigning all militated against the continuation of the classic political machine in post–World War II America. With the machine rooted in the nation's industrialization, the shift to a postindustrial economy further diluted its power. There were fewer unskilled jobs in a high-tech society and businesses moved farther and farther from city centers, robbing urban governments of their tax base and machine politicians of their resources.

The boss and his machine, however, is still perceived to exist and remains a staple of attack during political campaigns. When one considers the needs of today's urban ghetto population, there would seem to be room for a politician who offers quick and easy solutions to its problems. But the facts that resources have dwindled and many city dwellers are black are among the significant changes that have taken place since the classic age of bossism. For a time it did not seem unreasonable to assume that a new age of black bosses might emerge; the election of a large number of black mayors pointed in this direction. As, paradoxically, minorities composed urban majorities or came close to doing so, Wilson Goode in Philadelphia, Harold Washington in Chicago, and David Dinkins in New York City represented only the tip of the iceberg. In smaller cities, as well, demographic trends permitted the rise of black politicians to positions of prominence. But taking power in financially strapped cities weakened by crime, drugs, and a rotting infrastructure is not the same as assuming control in urban centers on the cusp of a dynamic economy.

When Richard M. Daley sat down at his father's old desk on the fifth floor of Chicago's City Hall after defeating a black candidate, he danced to his own tune. But as the twentieth century drew to a close, Americans looked at their cities and recognized that the days of Tweed had long passed, but urban politics retained a familiar quality.

John M. Allswang, *Bosses, Machines, and Urban Voters* (1986); Bruce M. Stave and Sondra Astor Stave, eds., *Urban Bosses, Machines, and Progressive Reformers* (1984).

BRUCE M. STAVE

See also City Government; City Planning; Corruption; Daley, Richard; Progressivism; Tammany Hall; Tweed Ring; Urbanization.

URBANIZATION

The United States, it has been aptly remarked, was born in the country and moved to the city. Few nations have urbanized more rapidly or more extensively. Starting its history under the

Constitution as a rural (95 percent) and agricultural society, the United States in the course of the nineteenth century developed a vast network of cities. By 1920 the urban population exceeded the rural.

Urbanization is by definition a process whereby the number of urban dwellers increases in relation to rural dwellers. By 1970 this process had been largely completed in the United States. Although in recent decades cities have continued to receive migrants, the pattern of migration has been within an urban system — from city to city, from city to suburb, from suburb to city, as well as from foreign to American city.

So much of the nineteenth-century history of the United States is associated with the western movement that one naturally wonders about the relation of urbanization to continental expansion. The two movements reinforced each other. Cities were "the spearhead of the frontier." Urban markets and marketing mechanisms gave value to agricultural land in the United States. The combination of local trade and an agricultural base enabled many cities, especially inland ones, to develop small-scale manufacturing.

Much nineteenth-century American development was fueled by urban rivalry. Boosters sought to make their cities regional centers by promoting transportation improvements and often encouraging investments in cultural institutions: a museum, a theater or opera house, a college, a scientific society, a large park.

Except in the case of the South under slavery, in the United States economic development and urban growth were intertwined. The result was an exceptionally dynamic economy and a dense network of cities. Unlike many developing countries in the post–World War II era, where a single overgrown metropolis dominates, in America large cities are to be found in every region, each in turn surrounded by networks of medium-sized cities.

Urbanization encompasses changes in form and social character that illuminate larger changes in American social and economic history. At the time of the American Revolution all major cities were seaports. The port provided the basis of the urban economy, and it supplied a principle of order for the social and physical organization of the city. Nearly all eighteenth-century views of New York, Boston, and Philadelphia place the harbor with its ships and wharves in the foreground. This idea of the city as a port dominated urban perception until the middle of the nineteenth century.

It is appropriate to call the late-eighteenth-century city a walking city. A comfortable walk represented the limits of human movement and, by implication, urban culture. Until the middle of the nineteenth century people and messages moved at the same speed. With such limits on communication, urban life was not easily managed over a territory extending more than a mile or two from the center.

Within the bounds of the compact walking city, various urban activities and social classes were situated cheek by jowl. In the wharf area there was some clustering of special functions: countinghouses, warehouses, and shipping-related artisans' shops around the docks. Nearby were homes for rich merchants. But that was the extent of differentiation. There was no strictly residential district, nor was there one exclusively devoted to business. Residential segregation by class and ethnicity was limited; employees often lived in the same houses as their employers or in a rear building.

But after the War of 1812 changes in the Atlantic economy and the development of internal transportation and a national market stimulated unprecedented growth. In 1790, the year of the first census, no American city had a population of 50,000 persons and only 5 had more than 10,000. In the middle decades of the nineteenth century changes in communication and transportation, especially the railroad, enhanced trade and urbanization, while the development of the steam engine enabled urban manufacturing to increase, drawing native migrants and foreign immigrants to the city. By 1870, 168 places had populations over 10,000, and 15 cities had populations over 100,000.

For most of this city building, the gridiron supplied the basic form. Although there had been a few earlier gridiron plans (Philadelphia and New Haven in the seventeenth century, Savannah and Los Angeles in the eighteenth), the gridiron became the norm in the nineteenth century. Of major American cities, only central Boston and Lower Manhattan exemplify the irregular pattern associated with the medieval street plans of European cities. And New York in 1811 adopted a gridiron for development above Houston Street.

Changes in the economy and in the scale of cities altered the organization of social life and the space within them. Ports were still important at midcentury, but cities no longer clustered so tightly about their harbors. They were becoming more extensive, partly because of the development of omnibuses and horse-drawn street railways. The separation of work and residence,

dating from this period, marks a watershed in the history of urban life. With the breakdown of the traditional apprentice system, work groups increased in size and most employees became wage earners for life. They formed a working class that sought out cheap housing of their own. Employers also tended to move away from the workplace to exclusively residential areas that better sustained a developing interest in domesticity. The full specialization of urban space would be achieved only in the twentieth century, but the future had become apparent by the middle of the 1800s: the places of work and residence had become distinguished in terms of location, architecture, and social experience.

Largest Cities by Population, 1700–1990

	1700 City	1700 Population	1790 City	1790 Population	1850 City	1850 Population
1.	Boston	6,700	New York	33,131	New York	515,547
2.	New York	4,937[a]	Philadelphia	28,522	Baltimore	169,054
3.	Philadelphia	4,400[b]	Boston	18,320	Boston	136,881
4.	—	—	Charleston	16,359	Philadelphia	121,376
5.	—	—	Baltimore	13,503	New Orleans	116,375
6.	—	—	Northern Liberties, Pa.[c]	9,913	Cincinnati	115,435
7.	—	—	Salem, Mass.	7,921	Brooklyn[d]	96,838
8.	—	—	Newport, R.I.	6,716	St. Louis	77,860
9.	—	—	Providence, R.I.	6,380	Spring Garden, Pa.[e]	58,894
10.	—	—	Marblehead, Mass.	5,661	Albany, N.Y.	50,763

	1900 City	1900 Population	1950 City	1950 Population	1990 City	1990 Population[g]
1.	New York[f]	3,437,202	New York	7,891,957	New York	7,322,564
2.	Chicago	1,698,575	Chicago	3,620,962	Los Angeles	3,485,398
3.	Philadelphia	1,293,697	Philadelphia	2,071,605	Chicago	2,783,726
4.	St. Louis	575,238	Los Angeles	1,970,358	Houston	1,630,553
5.	Boston	560,892	Detroit	1,849,568	Philadelphia	1,585,577
6.	Baltimore	508,957	Baltimore	949,708	San Diego	1,110,549
7.	Cleveland	381,768	Cleveland	914,808	Detroit	1,027,974
8.	Buffalo, N.Y.	352,387	St. Louis	856,796	Dallas	1,006,877
9.	San Francisco	342,782	Washington	802,178	Phoenix	983,403
10.	Cincinnati	325,902	Boston	801,444	San Antonio	935,933

a. Figure from a census taken in 1698.   b. Philadelphia population includes suburbs.   c. Annexed by Philadelphia in 1854.
d. Consolidated with New York in 1898.   e. Annexed by Philadelphia in 1854.   f. Population is for New York and its boroughs, consolidated in 1898.   g. Preliminary census figures.

The mid-nineteenth-century city was a five-story city, a crowded jumble of small buildings. A vast increase in population had occurred within tight constraints. Construction technology, as well as the lack of a safe passenger elevator or a way to get water above the fifth floor, limited the height of buildings. Adequate urban transit had to await the development of the electric streetcar in the late 1880s. The territory of the city had been slightly extended, but the increase in population was achieved mainly through unprecedented crowding.

For the urban dweller in 1850 the city was a multiplicity of environments, many of them unknown and even frightening. The slum, where the "other half" lived, became a part of the urban imagination. In retrospect, however, the midcentury city was more ordered than many contemporaries recognized. Distinct commercial areas, often extensions of the waterfront in coastal or river cities, had emerged. Nearby were small manufacturing enterprises, especially those associated with the port or likely to be organized by merchant capital. Farther out, toward the fringes but near a working-class neighborhood, were a few heavy industrial enterprises. Within the commercial district lay a cluster of major financial institutions, some retail blocks (forerunners of department stores), and entertainment establishments. Not far from the center would be at least one fashionable neighborhood (Beacon Hill in Boston was typical) and a slum (like Five Points in New York). Farther away were larger bourgeois and working-class quarters. The city extended perhaps three or four miles; at the edge was a ragged and mixed-use area marked by pockets of residential, commercial, and industrial structures.

After 1870, technology facilitating both vertical and horizontal movement provided the basis for a dramatic reorganization of urban form in America. The first elevator in an office building was installed in New York's Equitable Life Assurance Building. Elevators equalized the rental value of all floors, which raised land values in city centers. Between 1870 and 1930 the tall central-city office building and business block gave both a new appearance and a new function to the central business district, as it came to be called. By the 1890s it was apparent, first in New York and later in other large cities, that dense clusters of tall buildings had created a new kind of urban skyline.

The tall office building stood for a new era. Large cities — especially New York — became financial and administrative centers, directing national corporations with plants in a myriad of smaller cities. These changes in the economy, along with the new building technologies and the aesthetic visions of architects, gave birth to the skyscraper.

While the city was soaring upward, it was also extending outward, producing the familiar American pattern of central business core, close-in slum and working-class residential areas, and a ring of prosperous suburbs. The advent of electric streetcars and elevated railways extended the bounds of the city to a radius of ten miles or more. The streetcars, which typically converged at the center, in effect created a funnel that established the central business district as the locale for offices, places of entertainment, government facilities, department stores, and specialty shops.

This change in the physical form of cities was accompanied by changes in their social composition. Although blacks had lived in cities as early as the colonial period, after 1890 and particularly during World Wars I and II black migration to northern cities accelerated, driven by southern racism, by changes in the conditions and technology of southern agriculture, and by perceived opportunities in the North. Also in the 1890s, the volume and source of foreign immigration changed, as large numbers of migrants from eastern and southern Europe came to the United States, settling mainly in cities.

Neighborhoods defined by class, race, and ethnicity became arrayed along the streetcar lines. These residential neighborhoods had their own consumer businesses and with their distinctive qualities made the social landscape something of a mosaic. Manufacturing, which had once shared central city sites with other uses, now demanded more and different space, typically along transportation corridors.

The years from 1890 to 1945 were the classic years of the big city and its "downtown." It was this city that nourished the urban liberalism that was such an important component of the New Deal welfare state. The politics of the New Deal were in part a coalition of liberals in Washington and city machines, and they formed a progressive alliance. Their policies in turn enhanced urban life. Although the New Deal did not have a formal urban policy, the development of federally funded public housing programs provided significant low-income housing for cities, and the WPA employment program enabled cities to build schools, hospitals, parks, and other civic amenities.

After World War II, this city unraveled. The automobile and the freeway system, the development of which was made possible by the Federal Highway Act of 1956, encouraged a new kind of decentralization that undermined the central city. Concurrently, the Federal Housing Administration, the G.I. bill, and the tax system made purchasing a home easier, opening suburban living to large numbers of the middle and working classes. The central city, with an increasingly black population, lost political and social importance in relation to the overwhelmingly white subcenters within the metropolitan region. Urban liberalism was weakened, with grave consequences for the urban poor and the urban infrastructure.

The contemporary metropolis evokes mixed images — the glitter of massive postmodern office towers, convention and cultural centers, and shopping malls, on the one hand, and the despair of homelessness, failing schools, drug addiction, and poverty, on the other. But the starkness of such images, however painfully real, may distort what is actually happening. The large cities of the United States — especially New York, Miami, and Los Angeles — are being transformed by a new wave of immigration from Asia, Latin America, the Caribbean, and Africa. They have again become immigrant cities, and they are receiving newcomers from a wider variety of homelands than ever before. Both the postmodern office towers housing multinational corporations and these new, mostly nonwhite immigrants who are building middle-class neighborhoods with distinctive cultures are creating in the late twentieth century a new kind of city in the United States — the World City.

Christopher Tunnard and Henry Hope Reed, *American Skyline* (1956); David Ward, *Cities and Immigrants: A Geography of Change in Nineteenth-Century America* (1971); Sam Bass Warner, Jr., *The Urban Wilderness: A History of the American City* (1972).

THOMAS BENDER

See also Architecture; Black Ghettos; Black Migration; City Government; City Planning; Housing; Immigration; Internal Migration; Public Transportation; Suburbanization; Urban Bosses and Machine Politics.

URBAN RENEWAL

See City Government; City Planning.

USSR-U.S. RELATIONS

See Cold War; Soviet-American Relations, 1917–1945.

UTOPIAN COMMUNITIES

In 1663 a small group of Dutch Mennonites settled near what is now Lewes, Delaware, to form a community based on their religious principles. Although the English destroyed the settlement a year later, it marked the beginning of a communitarian tradition in North America that stretches forward to the urban collectives and rural communes of the late twentieth century. Over that long span of time, communitarian societies have differed greatly in ideology and structure (the Dutch Mennonites would be horrified at their 1960s descendants), and perhaps not all have been consistently utopian in the strict sense of trying to implement a plan for a perfect society on earth. Utopian communitarianism, however, appears to have stronger roots in the United States than in Western Europe, at least in terms of putting ideology into practice. That collective vision may seem out of place in a nation valuing individualism; but the persistence of the communities reveals much about deep currents in American culture, particularly about how men and women have imagined social change and their role in it.

Utopia-building proceeded in waves. Between 1663 and the Revolution approximately twenty communities were constructed by religious groups, mostly German. The great success story, however, was a sect, the Shakers, founded by an Englishwoman, Mother Ann Lee, and established in North America in 1774. By the 1840s it had approximately six thousand members scattered in various communities. From the time of the Shakers to that of the present-day Hutterite Brethren, whose numbers reached seventeen thousand in 1970, religiously based utopian communities have been the largest in scale and most long-lived. Indeed, the Mormon Church had aspects of a communitarian society in its early years and drew upon the same mixture of utopianism and revivalistic religion that drove men and women into the Shakers and other utopian ventures in the pre–Civil War decades. In that respect, the Mormons, not the Shakers (who are near extinction), stand as the most enduring monument to antebellum religious communitarianism.

Utopianism took a different turn in 1824 with the arrival of a British visionary, Robert Owen, whose ideology was secular and promised to transform property and labor relationships. He embodied his ideas in New Harmony, Indiana, on land sold by a German communitarian group (which moved to Pennsylvania and long outlasted Owen's experiment). Although Owen's initial settlement failed dismally, his ideas paved the way for a new outburst of secular communitarianism in the 1840s, this time drawing on the writings of another European, the Frenchman Charles Fourier. Like Owen, Fourier foresaw a harmonious world in which men and women would realize their true natures in communities of approximately twenty-five hundred people. The utopias he influenced — most notably Brook Farm in Massachusetts and the North American Phalanx in Red Bank, New Jersey — were neither as large nor as perfect as he anticipated, but his work, along with Owen's, helps explain a proliferation of utopian ventures in the pre–Civil War years. Over ninety appeared between 1800 and 1850, many religious in origin but a significant number rooted in secular ideologies as well.

Much of the utopian fervor had passed by 1850, but there was a renewal of interest in communitarian projects after the Civil War, particularly between the late 1870s and the mid-1890s, when another hundred or so communitarian ventures appeared. Interest declined again toward the end of the century, perhaps because of a depression in the 1890s, perhaps because it was difficult to believe that small-scale communities could be a model for humankind in the age of giant corporations, and perhaps because competing secular ideologies, like socialism, promised progress through political struggle rather than withdrawal from mainstream society.

Americans, nevertheless, continued to build utopian communities on into the twentieth century; they ranged from coast to coast and from the South to the North. The new century brought an even greater proliferation of secular ones. Some were based on pseudoscientific doctrines, exemplified by Estero, which was founded in Florida in 1900 on the ideas of Cyrus R. Teed, who believed that, despite appearances, the earth is a hollow sphere with the sun in the center.

The next great wave of utopian communities, far surpassing the first, came in a brief span of years, from 1965 to roughly 1973. During that period, perhaps as many as two thousand communes appeared, with a membership of 250,000 or more. Many of these were little more than a half-dozen or so people in unconventional living arrangements. Others were larger, serious attempts to find alternative ways of life in an America then waging war in Vietnam and torn apart with racial strife. The majority were rural, but urban collectives and communes also existed. Clearly a part of the counterculture of the 1960s, these utopian communities sometimes emphasized a relatively new element: the notion of collective living as a form of self-fulfillment and personal growth, even therapy. Earlier utopias usually stressed collective goals and transcendent ideologies. The number of utopian communities had declined by the mid-1970s. Prosperity had made them possible, even though, in the minds of many members, they stood as critiques of a materialistic society run amok. In the end, they were victims of disillusion and economic distress.

Explaining the communitarian impulse is no easy matter, given the diversity of forms it has taken. To some extent, communitarian societies have existed in America because it has been relatively easy for them to do so in a generally tolerant, prosperous nation with abundant land. Those factors, however, better explain the persistence of utopian societies than the fluctuations in their attractiveness. A key to understanding their appeal may lie in the fact that the greatest peaks of communitarian activity correspond to periods of religious and social ferment. The Shakers grew in the wake of religious revivalism; secular communities before the Civil War were part of a heady mix of reform activity; and the most recent outburst of utopian societies coincided with the student activism of the 1960s. Communitarianism has been both a product and a critique of these larger movements. It partook of their sense that the world could — and should — be transformed; but it promised to do so by constructing a model society rather than engaging in direct political or social action of the sort swirling around it.

In many ways, utopians were less radical than they seemed. Frequently, they envisioned either a nonviolent revolution or the more limited goal of personal salvation. But they often drew upon values, impulses, and tensions thoroughly embedded in American culture. Their rhetoric, and the communities they built, for example, expressed such traditional views as a belief that America might lead the way in redemption of humankind; a sense that change begins with individuals and small groups rather than with institutions; a conviction that it is better to act than merely to theorize; and a deeply seated hope that an orderly society can rest on voluntary action rather than coercion.

In addition to the political and social implications, utopianism has offered psychological satisfactions. For some, it promised alternatives to confining social roles, even before the hippie communes in the 1960s preached sexual and psychic liberation. Some nineteenth-century utopias, for instance, liberated women from the restrictions of normal family life by granting them positions of leadership (most notably among the Shakers) and unconventional choices concerning reproduction in celibate and "free love" communes. In spite of many unorthodox practices, however, one of the strongest appeals of utopian societies has been their attempt to answer a classic American question — how to find individual fulfillment and yet be part of a community.

One of the ironies of utopian communities — and a source of their recurring strength — is that of all forms of social action, they most starkly present an all-encompassing alternative to the way things are; yet they do so by withdrawing from, rather than directly confronting, the social order. Theirs is a peaceful revolution and, increasingly in the twentieth century, a personal one. Their power lies in their ability to stand as an alternative to America as it is while moving to the larger rhythms of society and, in often unperceived ways, mirroring some of its fundamental values.

Mark Halloway, *Heavens on Earth: Utopian Communities in America, 1680–1880* (1966); Rosabeth Moss Kanter, *Commitment and Community: Communes and Utopias in Sociological Perspective* (1972).

RONALD G. WALTERS

See also Mormons; Shakers.

V

VACATIONS AND RESORTS

Americans did not begin to vacation, in the sense that we understand the word today, until the mid-nineteenth century. During the colonial period most people, deterred from travel by the absence of good roads and comfortable transportation, looked for recreation close to their homes. A few spots, however, catered to those members of the aristocracy who had the resources and time to travel. Newport, Rhode Island, for example, was by the 1760s attracting wealthy southerners for the summer. But it was not until the 1820s that increasing numbers of the elite left home for trips that had some of the characteristics of a vacation. Wealthy Americans began to frequent the watering places, spas, and seaside resorts that were being established during these years, places like White Sulphur Springs in western Virginia, Cape May on the shore of southern New Jersey, Pine Orchard House (later called Catskill Mountain House) in the Catskills, and Saratoga in upstate New York.

During these years most Americans still lived on farms, and for them extended absence from home during the summer months was out of the question. Only those with substantial financial assets and accommodating work schedules could frequent these early resorts. Southern planters took their families to the springs, leaving their plantations in the hands of overseers. Wealthy merchants arranged their affairs in order to spend time at Newport or Saratoga. Those involved in literary pursuits — often in those days people of independent wealth — took their work with them to summer spots. And well-to-do urban men who could not spend the entire season away sometimes arranged to leave their families in country or seaside homes, near enough to the city to allow for frequent trips back and forth.

Many of these early "vacationers," however, would have denied that the primary purpose of their trips was recreation or pleasure. Health, most would have said, was the reason for their sojourns. Many of America's first vacation spots began as health resorts, often growing up around natural springs whose waters reputedly possessed health-giving qualities. Both medical and lay opinion held that drinking or bathing in such waters could cure a vast array of illnesses. If the promotional literature were to be believed, ailments ranging from constipation to sterility, from scrofula to gout, as well as female diseases, sleeplessness, chronic diarrhea, bilious complaints, and hair loss would all succumb to the powers of the mineral waters. Those resorts that could not boast of proximity to mineral springs promoted instead the health-giving properties of their geography or climate. Newport and Cape May made claims for the ameliorative effects of ocean breezes or sea bathing, and Catskill Mountain House touted the virtues of mountain air. Whether in the mountains, by the ocean, or near the springs, the resorts became havens from the frequent summer epidemics of cholera and yellow fever that plagued cities and low-lying areas in these years.

Nevertheless, if the ostensible purpose of these vacations was health, there is no doubt that clients sought relaxation and recreation as well. In the 1830s and 1840s much of the fun apparently stemmed from associating with the rich and famous who increasingly flocked to these resorts. Seeing and being seen were often primary attractions, since many of the resorts offered little else in the way of amenities. Visitors to these spots wrote in letters and diaries of the less than luxurious, even primitive, conditions — cramped and dirty accommodations, hard beds, flea-infested blankets, crowded dining rooms, surly staff, and horrible food. There were, however, compensations. Guests amused themselves playing cards or nine pins, dancing at balls, walking or riding in the mountains, enjoying the scenery, flirting, courting, and gambling.

The years around the Civil War brought alterations in the social and technological fabric of American life that contributed to the increase in the number of vacation resorts and to the growth of a large and more diverse vacationing public. Most important were changes in the nature of work. As the industrial economy matured it brought with it increasing numbers of people filling salaried, white-collar jobs. Employees of burgeoning corporate and government bureaucracies became part of a new middle class. These people could structure their activities to make time for vacations. By late in the century many firms were regularly giving their white-collar staff at least a week of paid vacation. Moreover, the fairly steady employment that such bureaucratic labor promised allowed these workers to budget time and funds in ways that made vacations possible.

Another impetus to the vacation industry was the expanding network of railroads, which brought vacation spots within the geographical and financial reach of more people. In the antebellum years it might have taken four or five days and considerable expense to travel from Washington, D.C., to one of the Virginia springs, but by the 1870s the trip could be accomplished in a day. The railroad brought travelers from New York City to Catskill Mountain House in six and a half hours in contrast to the day and a half it had taken by steamer and coach. The development of numerous rail lines encouraged the growth of resorts in a variety of areas, many of which drew middle-class patrons. These were the years, for example, when the New Jersey shore began to sprout beach communities that attracted growing numbers of city folk from New York or Philadelphia for a few weeks' stay in the summer. The first train brought visitors to Atlantic City in July 1854, although this resort did not really take off until the 1870s when the first boardwalk was built and a second railroad began to bring increasing numbers of vacationers from Philadelphia.

As more Americans took vacations during these years, they created a demand for more types of resorts. Those who could afford it sometimes tried to hobnob with the wealthy in the grand hotels of Saratoga or Long Branch. But most middle-class vacationers settled for more modest alternatives. Boarding at a country farmhouse or in a small hotel or private home at the seashore may not have offered the amenities or panache of a resort hotel, but it still afforded clerks or schoolteachers a way out of the hot city. On the other hand, many sought the city as a place to vacation, some, for example, visiting one of the expositions of those years — Philadelphia in 1876 or Chicago in 1893.

The sorts of resorts that became popular after the Civil War suggest that many Americans felt that vacations should be used for more than mere recreation. Indeed, religion apparently motivated some to found, develop, and visit resorts. Since the early nineteenth century Methodists had been holding revival camp meetings, and some of these sites were becoming permanent fixtures. In the summer of 1857, for example, over 250 families lived in tents and participated in a revival at Wesleyan Grove on Martha's Vineyard off the coast of Massachusetts. By the 1870s Wesleyan Grove and its neighboring town of Oak Bluffs were growing resort communities. In that decade another group of Methodists formed the Ocean Grove Camp Meeting Association on a site on the northern New Jersey shore. The association built a large auditorium where the faithful came together for religious meetings, lectures, and concerts throughout the summer. The association also established rules prohibiting not only the sale of liquor but Sunday swimming and carriage riding. Although these laws were strictly enforced, a thriving resort of hotels, boardinghouses, and cottages developed. By the turn of the twentieth century the summer population of Ocean Grove numbered thirty-five thousand. Rehoboth, on the Delaware shore, also began as a Methodist camp meeting in the 1870s and had become a seaside resort by the late nineteenth century. Resorts like these served two purposes. They provided sites for religious meetings, and they created vacation spots where God-fearing Christians could feel comfortable and enjoy themselves without fearing that recreation would degenerate into dissipation. The saloons and bawdy houses in places like Atlantic City would find no home in a Christian resort. Here families could pray, spend time together, and enjoy the sun and beach.

Methodists pioneered another sort of vacation venture. In 1874 minister John Vincent founded chautauqua on the banks of the western New York lake of that name. Originally envisioned as a school for Sunday school workers, chautauqua within a few years assumed a much broader educational purpose. Growing numbers of visitors spent a few days or a few weeks on the lovely grounds attending classes in art, music, and literature and listening to lectures on topics that ranged from science to temperance. Those who came to the shores of Lake Chautauqua to participate in the summer assemblies combined rest and recreation with moral and intellectual uplift. They attended classes but also enjoyed boating, swimming, beautiful scenery, and lively company. Chautauqua apparently captured the attention and imagination of the American people; by the turn of the century about two hundred other chautauquas were operating across the country.

Those with more adventuresome tastes had by that time other options. Yellowstone was made a national park in 1872 and became accessible to vacationers when the Northern Pacific Railroad was completed in 1883. Within a few years guests could find hotels there or choose, as did many, to camp out. Vacationers who wanted to visit the West without forgoing the conveniences of the East could book a packaged tour

with the Thomas Cook agency that would take them from New York to San Francisco in luxury. The Grand Canyon began to attract vacationers when the Sante Fe Railroad built a branch line directly to the canyon's rim in 1900.

Regardless of where Americans chose to vacation, until the 1920s it was primarily those from the middle or upper class who could afford the time or money for anything more than a one-day excursion. The 1920s and 1930s, however, witnessed an important change in vacation patterns. Social critics, economists, forward-thinking industrialists, and some union leaders began to debate the issue of vacations for factory workers. Many argued that paid vacations for workers might, in fact, prove profitable for their employers. A rested and refreshed work force, they said, would repay in increased productivity more than the investment in the workers' vacations. Slowly, American business began to offer industrial workers the same sorts of vacation privileges that the white-collar work force had been enjoying for half a century. As a result a new, larger group of Americans joined the vacationing public.

Among these new groups were Americans of various ethnic backgrounds, many of whom created their own resorts or vacation spots. Jews from New York City, for example, began in the early 1900s to take their families to the Catskill Mountains. Since most Catskill resorts refused to admit Jews, these vacationers boarded at farmhouses owned by other Jews. Many Jewish immigrants who had tried their hand at farming soon found that summer boarders provided a more lucrative income. As a result, many Jewish resorts grew from what had once been modest farms.

By the turn of the twentieth century blacks, as well, were vacationing at a variety of places. Readers of the *Indianapolis Freeman,* an important black newspaper, found advertisements for resort hotels in the New Jersey countryside and for excursion trains to Niagara Falls, Atlantic City, Cape May, and other beach resorts.

Another twentieth-century change in vacationing came from technology. Just as earlier the railroads had opened vacation spots to middle-class travelers, so now the automobile made new sorts of vacations possible. At first only the rich could afford automobiles, and a few wealthy and adventurous Americans motored off into the unknown — a hazardous and expensive undertaking. These vacationers sought independence and adventure, hoping to escape from the restraints of rail travel and to find an alternative to the crowded and often stuffy resort hotel.

During the 1920s, however, the price of automobiles fell, making it possible for people with more modest incomes to own them. Automobile owners soon discovered that cars provided one of the least expensive means of vacationing. Paved roads replaced the dirt paths that early motorists had followed, and campgrounds and motels sprang up along these routes to serve this new public. Whether the destination was seashore, mountain, lake, national park, or only relatives in another state, Americans could now reach them in their own cars. Moreover, by the mid-1930s the possibilities at each of these destinations had proliferated. One could rent a cabin in a national park for as little as $1 a day, board with a farmer in the country for $12 a week, spend a week on a Mississippi River boat for $47.50, or stay at a luxury dude ranch for as much as $75 a week.

The growth of the commercial airline industry following World War II also had an enormous impact on America's vacationing practices. Those who could afford to travel by air found that time constraints no longer limited vacation choices. It became possible to vacation on the opposite coast or in Europe, even if the vacationer could spare only a week from work. The decreasing time it took to reach destinations allowed Americans to split their vacations, taking two shorter breaks rather than one long one.

Although many mid-twentieth-century Americans chose the same sorts of seashore, mountain, or country resorts as had their counterparts half a century earlier, others sought new sorts of experiences. Disneyland, the first of America's theme parks, opened in Anaheim, California, in 1955, and by the 1980s more than 10 million people a year were visiting it. Millions more flocked to Walt Disney World in Orlando, Florida, and to the numerous other parks organized around a variety of themes — from country mu-

sic and Christianity to wildlife and the frontier. Winter vacations became increasingly popular as some sought to escape from the cold and others headed for the ski slopes. Time-sharing arrangements made it possible for people to "own" a home at the shore for one or two weeks a year, and excursion fares and charter flights opened air travel to people of more moderate means.

Vacationing, which had begun in the early nineteenth century as the preserve of the elite, had grown to include the white-collar middle class in the years after the Civil War and in the 1930s the working class as well. Today vacationing, though certainly not a universal phenomenon, is nevertheless an experience shared by a wide cross section of the American population.

Foster Rhea Dulles, *A History of Recreation: America Learns to Play* (1965); Alf Evers et al., *Resorts of the Catskills* (1977); Perceval Reniers, *The Springs of Virginia: Life, Love, and Death at the Waters, 1775–1900* (1941).

CINDY SONDIK ARON

See also Automobiles; Centennial Exposition; Chautauqua Movement; World's Fairs.

VAN BUREN, MARTIN

(1782–1862), eighth president of the United States, vice president, U.S. senator, governor of New York. Hardworking, quick at collecting and absorbing facts, and a good judge of character, Martin Van Buren was in his early career an exceptionally able trial lawyer who gained a reputation for his political skills.

Van Buren at first supported Aaron Burr in his efforts to break the influence of the great families that had ruled New York for several generations. But soon discovering that Burr was doomed to defeat, he changed sides and allied himself with DeWitt Clinton, then the rising star in New York politics. Constantly on the move attending sessions of the various courts, Van Buren widened his acquaintances among lawyers and officials throughout the state and utilized this network to build a political organization. For many years known as the "Albany Regency," it dominated the politics of the state. Van

Buren's novel tactics, his patronage policies, and his understanding of communication and discipline anticipated modern political practices. As such, he was the principle architect of the second American party system.

Van Buren's rise in the political affairs of New York soon brought him into conflict with his erstwhile patron, DeWitt Clinton. Between 1812 and Clinton's death in 1828, the rivalry between the two was a major force in New York and national politics. After Van Buren consolidated his hold on the state's Republican party, he was elected to the U.S. Senate in 1821 and reelected in 1827.

He supported William H. Crawford, James Monroe's secretary of the treasury, for president in the election of 1824. After Crawford was defeated in the House election of John Quincy Adams to the presidency, Van Buren switched to Andrew Jackson and helped secure his election in 1828. In an effort to improve his political image, Van Buren ran for and won election to the governorship of New York, but he served only four months in that post before resigning to become secretary of state. Through various maneuvers that included a cabinet reorganization, Van Buren resigned as secretary of state to become minister to Great Britain. When the Senate refused to confirm his appointment, he was nominated with Jackson's backing for the vice presidency and was elected in 1832.

After his election to the presidency four years later, he was faced almost immediately with a financial panic and depression. Van Buren did what he could within the limits of his laissez-faire philosophy to cope with the economic distress. His major remedy was the creation of an independent treasury system that divorced the federal government from the banking system. But this measure split what was now the Democratic party. Even in a political sense, he found it much easier to be elected president than to retain public confidence in his policies. Further depression, the political divisions, and a theatrical campaign put on by the newly created Whig party brought about his defeat in 1840.

He sought the nomination again in 1844, but was unable to overcome southern and expansionist opposition because of his stand against the immediate annexation of Texas. Van Buren once more entered the political arena briefly in 1848 as the candidate of the Free-Soil party. His willingness to head that ticket furthered the antislavery cause because of his national visibility and his political following in the key northern states.

John Niven, *Martin Van Buren: The Romantic Age of American Politics* (1983); Arthur M. Schlesinger, Jr., *The Age of Jackson* (1946).

JOHN NIVEN

See also Albany Regency; Depressions; Elections: 1832, 1836, 1840; Free-Soil Party; Independent Treasury; Texas Revolution and Annexation.

VANDERBILT, CORNELIUS

(1794–1877), steamship and railroad promoter and financier. Cornelius Vanderbilt, born in Port Richmond, Staten Island, New York, left school at the age of eleven to help his father. When he was sixteen, Vanderbilt purchased a small sailing vessel with a hundred dollars advanced by his parents and started a ferry service to New York City. Between 1814 and 1818 he acquired several schooners for service in Long Island Sound and the coastal trade from New England to Charleston. He sold his sailing vessels in 1818 and became a steam ferry captain for Thomas Gibbons who was challenging the Aaron Ogden steam navigation monopoly in New York State. Soon he was managing Gibbons's fleet and by 1828 had accumulated over thirty thousand dollars.

In 1829 Vanderbilt established a line of steamboats from New York to New Brunswick, New Jersey, with service on to Philadelphia. Soon he transferred his operations to the Hudson River, Long Island Sound, Providence, and Boston. Vanderbilt made his ships safe, comfortable, and fast. Before he was fifty he was a millionaire and was called "Commodore" because of his primacy among New York shipmasters. In 1846 Vanderbilt left Staten Island for New York City, where he built a town house on Washington Place. As traffic to California grew during the gold rush, Vanderbilt built fast steamers for service to Nicaragua, where he constructed roads to the Pacific Coast. This line prospered, and by 1853 Vanderbilt was worth $11 million. In 1854 he entered the Atlantic trade against the British Cunard Line. Vanderbilt vessels set speed records, but he found it difficult to compete against the heavily subsidized British ships. During the Civil War Vanderbilt offered several of his ships to the federal government to aid the Union war effort.

Commodore Vanderbilt was a hardheaded businessman, big, bumptious, loud, and coarse in speech but frank and faithful to his word once he had given it. He entered upon new ventures only after careful consideration. Certainly he was not hasty in entering railroading. In 1857 he invested in the New York & Harlem Railroad and in 1863 was its president. By 1865 he also controlled the Hudson River Railroad. Both lines connected New York and Albany. West of Albany the New York Central served Buffalo but used barges and steamboats on the Hudson River to reach New York City. In January 1867, with the Hudson thick with ice, Vanderbilt refused to accept any New York Central freight headed for New York. The New York Central capitulated, and Vanderbilt was soon in control of the line to Buffalo. Vanderbilt in 1869 merged the Hudson River and the New York Central and later acquired a long-term lease of the New York & Harlem. His eldest son, William H., who helped run the enlarged system, urged the addition of the Lake Shore & Michigan Southern in 1873 and the Michigan Central in 1875, lines that served Chicago.

Although Vanderbilt dealt in millions of dollars of watered stock, his rail system was efficiently managed and paid good dividends even during the long panic of 1873. Commodore Vanderbilt, oldest and perhaps the greatest of the nineteenth-century railroad barons, died the richest man in New York City. Wanting his fortune and railroad to remain intact, he left the bulk of his $100 million estate to his son William (one of his thirteen children) and William's sons. As an exemplar of the common person's shrewdness and dislike of social niceties, Vanderbilt became a folk hero as well as a major business figure.

Robert L. Frey, ed., *Railroads in the Nineteenth Century* (1988); Wheaton J. Lane, *Commodore Vanderbilt: An Epic of the Steam Age* (1942).

JOHN F. STOVER

See also Gould, Jay; Railroads; Robber Barons; Transportation Revolution.

VEBLEN, THORSTEIN

(1857–1929), economist and social critic. Veblen's criticisms of the accepted corpus of economic theory and his analyses of economic and social change helped form the basis of the institutionalist school of economic thought and earned for him a reputation as a skilled satirist and critic of capitalist society.

Veblen was born into the culturally isolated Norwegian immigrant community of the Upper Midwest. English was still his second language when he entered college. He remained somewhat of an outsider to mainstream American society throughout his life, and the descriptions of aspects of that society found in his books sometimes have the flavor of an anthropologist's account of an alien culture.

Veblen believed the economic theory of his day to be built on faulty assumptions about the nature of people and society. He argued that economics would not be a modern science until economists adopted an "evolutionary" viewpoint, recognizing and seeking to explain past and ongoing changes in customary patterns of economic and social interaction. Veblen's own theories focused on the role of technology in shaping a society's value system, which in turn influenced all other aspects of social organization. Social change occurred as technological innovations originally introduced to further ends consistent with one value system led to the formation of an alternative value system. Veblen incorporated into his theories aspects of William Graham Sumner's evolutionary social theory and John Dewey's instrumentalism, as well as strands of anthropological research. In many respects Veblen's ideas resembled those of Karl Marx, although he rejected the labor theory of value and the teleological elements of Marxism.

Veblen is best known for his first book, *The*

Theory of the Leisure Class (1899), which he presented as a scientific analysis of upper-class mores and behaviors. It portrayed the life of the well-bred individual as an unremitting quest for status in a pecuniary culture — that is, a culture in which status was based upon wealth. It was in this context that Veblen coined the phrase "conspicuous consumption" to describe spending undertaken mainly to demonstrate for others the spender's ability to pay. The book reached an audience far beyond the economics profession. (Most readers believed it to be as much satire as scholarship.)

A general theme in Veblen's many books and articles was that the system of private property was no longer compatible with the technological basis of modern industry. Veblen also elaborated on what he believed to be an unstable dichotomy in modern society, differentiating between industrial occupations, which were involved with the production of goods via machine-based processes, and business occupations, which were involved with the purchase and sale of goods in the pursuit of profit. Associated with these types of occupations were two antagonistic worldviews. Veblen insisted that a social upheaval was imminent, as those in industrial occupations were coming to question the social value of business activity and the system of private property upon which it was based.

Most of Veblen's career was spent in academe, where he acquired a reputation among colleagues as a brilliant intellect who could bring a great deal of knowledge and considerable wit to bear on the discussion of almost any subject. But his unwillingness to conduct his personal life in accordance with the prevailing norms of the academic community and his failure to show the expected deference toward constituted authority led to his dismissal from more than one university and kept him from ever achieving the rank of full professor.

The influence of Veblen's ideas peaked in the decade following his death, as the Great Depression and the rise of fascism in Europe seemed to bear out his predictions regarding the future of capitalism. Many prominent figures in the New Deal, including Rexford Tugwell and Jerome Frank, counted themselves as followers of Veblen. Some aspects of his worldview have entered the popular culture, including his characterization of the pecuniary culture and his unflattering portrayal of business employments. His ideas, however, have had little impact on the field of economics. Even at its height in the twenties and thirties the institutionalist movement he inspired involved only a small fraction of the economics profession, and mainstream economic theory retains today many of the characteristics that led Veblen to dismiss its turn-of-the-century counterpart as "pre-Darwinian" and thus obsolete.

Joseph Dorfman, *Thorstein Veblen and His America* (1934; reprint, 1961); Thorstein Veblen, *The Theory of the Leisure Class: An Economic Study of Institutions* (1899; reprint, 1934).

JEFF E. BIDDLE

See also Literature; New Deal.

VERSAILLES TREATY AND LEAGUE OF NATIONS

For the American people the making of peace after World War I proved one of the most baffling experiences in their national history. They could not understand why the Treaty of Versailles and the League of Nations produced so much contention between their president, Woodrow Wilson, and his opponents in the Senate and elsewhere. Eventually they decided simply to consign the controversy to oblivion, to forget about what seemed to be an impenetrable argument.

After the end of the war with Germany, with the armistice of November 11, 1918, Wilson made a series of errors that complicated his tasks but did not necessarily mean failure of the treaty and the League in the United States. He decided to attend the peace conference, which exposed him to foreign adversaries who proved adept at negotiation; he chose a weak group of peace commissioners, which included only a single Republican, Henry White, an inconsequential politician; and he allowed organization of a delegation staff in which he had no confidence. As the conference's first order of business the president insisted that the leading delegates form a committee to draw up the Covenant, the constitution of the League of Nations. That work completed, he went back to the United States for a month, leaving his friend Col. Edward M. House in charge, and returned to discover, he believed, that House had compromised on major issues. In part for this reason he reduced the conference's decisive group from plenary conferences and the Council of Ten (two representatives each for the United States, Britain, France, Italy, and Japan) to the Council of Four (himself, David Lloyd George, Georges Clemenceau, and Vittorio Orlando), which became the Council of Three when Orlando went back to Rome in a huff over Wilson's refusal to grant Italy's territorial demands.

At Paris the conferees arranged penalties against the Central Powers, mainly Germany, including loss of territory, reparations, and disarmament. Another task was to apply the principle of national self-determination, ensuring the independence of Poland, Czechoslovakia, Finland, and the Baltic states of Latvia, Lithuania, and Estonia. Self-determination elsewhere, in India and in Africa, failed at the Paris conference; the British refused to consider Indian independence, and the Allies parceled out to themselves German possessions in Africa and the Pacific as mandates — that is, territories controlled by them under varying degrees of supervision by the League of Nations. They reached no agreement about the so-called Russian problem, whether to try to break up the new Bolshevik government or allow it to go its way. The Japanese problem also proved awkward — what to do with Japan's claims of territory and concessions from China. To obtain those claims, and also to embarrass the British and Americans, the Japanese proposed a resolution of racial equality. Wilson and his colleagues went along with Japan's demands on China and finessed the proposed racial resolution by not voting on it.

As for the failure of the treaty in the Senate, it is necessary to point out, first, that at Paris the president had arranged for a Covenant that was neither fish nor fowl: it was a document that was exceedingly difficult to explain to the American people. It was not the sort of international agreement the United States had signed before, supporting world peace through mediation or arbitration or codifying international law. Nor was it an outright military alliance. The president said that the "heart of the Covenant" was Article 10, which asked League members to "respect and preserve" (whatever that meant — it clearly was not a guarantee) the territory of member nations. The president did not help matters by arguing that the Covenant was a moral rather than a legal document and that a moral pledge was more binding than mere legality.

Having taken this unusual stance, Wilson refused to compromise. There really was no deadlock between himself and the Senate: he could have obtained senatorial consent to the treaty and Covenant at any time, had he been willing to accept senatorial reservations. Instead he displayed a cavalier attitude. He said the Senate had to take its medicine; he exhibited Calvinistic certainty about the treaty he had helped to draw, basked in his oratorical abilities, and overestimated his prestige as a war leader, emboldened perhaps by his luck in avoiding blame for wartime failures with military and economic mobilization. Behind his intransigence could have been his imminent physical breakdown; he had a history of arteriosclerosis and strokes that went back to a seizure in 1896, and he suffered an illness while in Paris that was diagnosed as influenza but may have been a stroke.

Sensing victory in the 1920 presidential election, the Republicans stood their ground. The treaty failed in a vote on November 19, 1919, and again, with two more votes, on March 19, 1920. The architect of failure appeared to be the GOP majority leader, Senator Henry Cabot Lodge. The real architect was the president. A few reservations, even the fourteen Lodge reservations, would not have harmed the already ambiguous Covenant and might have clarified it. Lodge facetiously drew the issue in terms of campus rivalry. Wilson had been president of Princeton and Lodge had a Ph.D. in history from Harvard. The treaty, the senator said, "might get by at Princeton but not at Harvard." The Democrats lost the presidential election largely because the Republicans tarred the Democratic candidate, the Ohio newspaperman James M. Cox, with the brush of "Wilsonism."

In long retrospect it appears that two forces — one, a precipitating cause, the other, a deeper one — upset the Wilsonian world order imposed by the rest of the Allies after the United States refused to sign the Versailles treaty. The first was the Great Depression, the economic cataclysm that beset all the world's industrial nations beginning in 1929 and lasting through most of the 1930s. It crucially weakened the resolve of the former Allies and resulted in aggressive actions by Germany, Italy, and Japan. But behind the collapse of the Versailles settlement lay what President Wilson and others described as the "war psychosis," hatreds raised up in Europe by a war that lasted so long its participants staggered with weariness. Europe's leaders lost all perspective, and a generation of future leaders died on the battlefields. The cost in deaths (Germany, 1.8 million; Russia, 1.7 million; France, 1.4 million; Britain, .9 million) was too high for any treaty to resolve. The Americans did not suffer nearly as much (50,000 deaths) and could not understand the mindless national rivalries that would produce World War II.

Robert H. Ferrell, *Woodrow Wilson and World War I* (1985); John A. Garraty, *Henry Cabot Lodge* (1953).

ROBERT H. FERRELL

See also Elections: 1920; Isolationism; Middle East–U.S. Relations; Wilson, Woodrow; World War I.

VICE PRESIDENCY

When the Founding Fathers created the office of president they labored hard and long to define its powers and the manner in which its holders were to be chosen, but they had little to say about the vice presidency. This does not mean that they considered that office unimportant. The Founders expected vice presidents to be experienced and highly regarded men, for instead of providing for separate vice-presidential elections, they decided that the person receiving the second largest number of electoral votes for president should hold the office. They saw the vice president as a kind of understudy, a person capable of playing the leading role in the national drama in case the star should, as the Constitution explains, die, become incapacitated, resign, or be found guilty of treason, bribery, or "other high Crimes and Misdemeanors." To keep vice presidents occupied (as distinct from busy), they were to preside over the Senate, an occupation likely to keep them well informed about national affairs, but undemanding.

For nearly half a century, the expectations of the Founding Fathers were fulfilled. This was true despite the unanticipated development of political parties. In 1800 Thomas Jefferson, the presidential candidate of the Democratic-Republicans, and Aaron Burr, their vice-presidential choice, each received seventy-three electoral college votes, while John Adams, the Federalist presidential candidate, received only sixty-five. The tie caused a major political crisis and resulted in the passage of the Twelfth Amendment (1804) requiring members of the electoral college to vote separately for president and vice president.

Running separate candidates did not mean that men of no more than ordinary distinction quickly took over the second spot. From Adams and Jefferson to John C. Calhoun and Martin Van Buren, politicians of character and ability held the vice-presidential office. Even the apparent exception, Monroe's vice president Daniel Tompkins, who had serious drinking and financial problems in his later years, was serving his fourth term as governor of New York when nominated for the office in 1816.

But the increased importance of parties and the growing use of political office to reward loyal supporters eventually changed the way vice-presidential candidates were selected. The tactic of picking someone from a different section of the country in order to balance the ticket also played a part in the change. The turning point came in 1836 when the Democrats nominated Richard Mentor Johnson. Johnson had served extensively in Congress, but his major political asset was his claim to have killed the great Indian chief Tecumseh during the Battle of the Thames in 1813. He had, however, been an unswerving follower of retiring president Andrew Jackson. Jackson wanted to reward him — and Jackson's wish was all it took.

By 1840, however, even Jackson had had enough of Johnson, so after renominating Van Buren for a second term, the Democratic convention adjourned without picking any vice-presidential candidate. For the rest of the century and beyond, with few exceptions, men with no better than second-rate records ran for and held the office.

In 1841, only weeks after Richard Mentor Johnson's term ended, the death of President William Henry Harrison produced another political crisis. Was the vice president, John Tyler, now president of the United States or merely acting president? Many, including all of Harrison's cabinet, argued the latter designation. But Tyler boldly went to Supreme Court Justice William Cranch and took the oath required of presidents by the Constitution, and when Congress, after a brief debate, decided to recognize him as president rather than acting president, the matter was settled. This demonstration of the importance of the vice presidency did not, however, do much to change the way politicians treated the office.

Between 1850 and 1901 four more presidents died in office, the last three at the hands of assassins. Millard Fillmore, who succeeded upon the death of Zachary Taylor, had served three terms in Congress before being nominated for vice president, but a historian has described him as "bland in manner, loyal to party, and a natural compromiser." Andrew Johnson had had a long career in Tennessee and national politics, but few considered him presidential timber. He was chosen as Lincoln's 1864 running mate only because he was a Democrat from a border state and the only southern senator who had stayed with the Union in 1861. As for Chester A. Arthur, who became president when James A. Garfield was assassinated in 1881, he was a former collector of the port · in New York City — in other words, a political hack. He turned out to be a more creditable president than anyone had a right to expect, but he was a political hack nevertheless. Before 1880 he had never held or even run for an elective office.

In 1900 New York's youthful governor, The-odore Roosevelt, was widely recognized as a leader of potential national stature when he was picked as William McKinley's running mate in the 1900 election following the death of Vice President Garret A. Hobart. But if the party leaders who engineered his nomination had considered the possibility that McKinley might die in office, they would never have selected him. They did so only to oblige Thomas Collier "Boss" Platt, who was desperate to get Roosevelt, whom he considered radical and unstable, out of New York politics.

The power and influence of presidents have, of course, increased greatly since TR's day, and, alas, presidents have continued to die in office. Yet time after time, both parties selected their vice-presidential candidates with little or no thought of how effective they would be should the single heart between them and the White House cease to beat. Preserving party unity and adding strength to the ticket in a particular state or region (or in the case of the nomination of Congresswoman Geraldine Ferraro, with a type of voter), not the ability of the person selected, continued to be the determining factors in nearly every case. Still more disturbing, since television and the increase in the number of presidential primaries have diminished the role of national conventions in the selection of candidates, the choice of a running mate has become a prerogative of the person who wins the presidential nomination.

Presidential candidates have nearly always had a hand in choosing their running mates. But until the decline of the conventions' importance, they had to give some thought to how delegates would react to their selection. After nominating Warren G. Harding for president, the delegates at the 1920 Republican convention rejected Senator Irvine Lenroot of Wisconsin, who had been anointed by the leadership, and nominated Calvin Coolidge for vice president. As late as 1944, as powerful a president as Franklin D. Roosevelt felt obliged to obtain the approval of convention leaders before agreeing to the nomination of Harry S. Truman as his running mate.

The last time a nominating convention had a real say about who was to run for vice president was in 1956 when Adlai Stevenson, the

Vice Presidents of the United States

*John Adams (1789–1797)

*Thomas Jefferson (1797–1801)

*Aaron Burr (1801–1805)

George Clinton (1805–1812), delegate from New York to Second Continental Congress; revolutionary war general; seven-term governor of New York, 1777–1795, 1801–1804

Elbridge Gerry (1813–1814), member, Continental Congress, 1776–1781, 1782–1785; delegate, Constitutional Convention; congressman from Massachusetts, 1789–1793; governor of Massachusetts, 1810–1812

Daniel D. Tompkins (1817–1825), associate justice, New York State Supreme Court, 1804–1807; governor of New York, 1807–1817

*John C. Calhoun (1825–1832)

*Martin Van Buren (1833–1837)

Richard Mentor Johnson (1837–1841), congressman from Kentucky, 1807–1819, 1829–1837; colonel, Kentucky militia, in War of 1812; U.S. senator, 1819–1829

*John Tyler (1841)

George Mifflin Dallas (1845–1849), U.S. senator from Pennsylvania, 1831–1833; minister to Russia, 1837–1839

*Millard Fillmore (1849–1850)

William R. King (1853), congressman from North Carolina, 1811–1816; U.S. senator from Alabama, 1819–1844, 1848–1852; minister to France, 1844–1846

John C. Breckinridge (1857–1861), congressman from Kentucky, 1851–1855

Hannibal Hamlin (1861–1865), congressman from Maine, 1843–1847; U.S. senator, 1848–1861, 1869–1881

*Andrew Johnson (1865)

Schuyler Colfax (1869–1873), congressman from Indiana, 1855–1869; Speaker, 1863–1869

Henry Wilson (1873–1875), U.S. senator from Massachusetts, 1855–1873

William Wheeler (1877–1881), congressman from New York, 1861–1863, 1869–1877 (When suggested to Rutherford B. Hayes as a possible running mate, Hayes responded, "Who is *Wheeler?*")

*Chester A. Arthur (1881)

Thomas A. Hendricks (1885), congressman from Indiana, 1851–1855; U.S. senator, 1863–1869; governor of Indiana, 1873–1877

Levi P. Morton (1889–1893), Wall Street banker; congressman from New York, 1879–1881; minister to France, 1881–1885; governor of New York, 1895–1897

Adlai E. Stevenson (1893–1897), congressman from Illinois, 1875–1877, 1879–1881; assistant postmaster general, 1885–1889

Garret A. Hobart (1897–1899), New Jersey businessman; member, Republican National Committee

*Theodore Roosevelt (1901)

Charles W. Fairbanks (1905–1909), U.S. senator from Indiana, 1897–1905

James S. Sherman (1909–1912), congressman from New York, 1887–1891, 1893–1909

Thomas R. Marshall (1913–1921), governor of Indiana, 1909–1913 (Famous for the line: "What this country really needs is a good five-cent cigar.")

*Calvin Coolidge (1921–1923)

Charles G. Dawes (1925–1929), controller of the currency, 1897–1902; director, Bureau of the Budget, 1921–1924

Charles Curtis (1929–1933), congressman from Kansas, 1893–1907; U.S. senator, 1907–1929

John Nance Garner (1933–1941), congressman from Texas, 1903–1933; Speaker, 1931–1933

Henry A. Wallace (1941–1945), secretary of agriculture, 1933–1940; secretary of commerce, 1945–1946; candidate for president, Progressive party, 1948

*Harry S. Truman (1945)

Alben W. Barkley (1949–1953), congressman from Kentucky, 1913–1927; U.S. senator, 1927–1949; majority leader, 1937–1947

*Richard M. Nixon (1953–1961)

*Lyndon B. Johnson (1961–1963)

Hubert H. Humphrey (1965–1969), mayor of Minneapolis, 1945–1948; U.S. senator from Minnesota, 1948–1964; 1970–1978

Spiro T. Agnew (1969–1973), governor of Maryland, 1967–1969

*Gerald Ford (1973–1974)

Nelson A. Rockefeller (1974–1977), assistant secretary of state, 1944–1945; under secretary, Department of Health, Education, and Welfare, 1953–1954; governor of New York, 1959–1973

Walter F. Mondale (1977–1981), attorney general of Minnesota, 1960–1964; U.S. senator, 1964–1976

*George Bush (1981–1989)

J. Danforth Quayle (1989–), congressman from Indiana, 1976–1980; U.S. senator, 1980–1988

*See entry in this book for biography.

Democratic presidential nominee, turned the choice over to the convention, with the result that Senator Estes Kefauver defeated Senator John F. Kennedy in a close fight.

The Twenty-fifth Amendment (1967) requiring the president to nominate a successor "whenever there is a vacancy in the office of the Vice President" has eliminated the possibility that the country might have no vice president for an extended period, as was true not only after the deaths of Harrison, Lincoln, Garfield, McKinley, Harding, Roosevelt, and Kennedy but also after Vice President Calhoun resigned in 1832 and after the deaths of Vice Presidents William R. King in 1853, Henry Wilson in 1875, Thomas A. Hendricks in 1885, Garret A. Hobart in 1899, and James S. Sherman in 1912.

Under the amendment, when Vice President Spiro T. Agnew was forced to resign in 1973, President Richard M. Nixon chose Gerald Ford as vice president. Then, after Nixon's resignation in 1974, President Ford appointed Nelson Rockefeller to the post. This meant that for more than two years, both the president and the vice president were appointees rather than elected officials. Such a situation is unlikely to recur. But by placing the naming of the new vice president in presidential hands (albeit subject to congressional approval), the Twenty-fifth Amendment unofficially ratified the right of presidents to name their possible successors under normal circumstances as well.

Leaving the choice to the head of the ticket has not changed the reasons particular candidates are chosen. It may even with a few notorious exceptions have improved the quality of the persons selected. But despite all their hoopla and sordid dealing, the old-fashioned nominating conventions gave substance to the idea that the people, through their chosen delegates, were deciding who the party standard-bearers should be.

The primary system is undoubtedly a more effective way of discovering which candidates for president the voters prefer. The primaries practically compel candidates to describe what they intend to do if nominated, but they studiously avoid committing themselves as to whom they want as running mates. And there are no vice-presidential primaries.

Given the frequency with which fate has turned vice presidents into instant presidents, this is disturbing. That presidents should be able to pick their successors is undemocratic. It is also illogical. Since they must be dead, incompetent, or disgraced before the occasion can arise, they are the last persons who should have that power.

JOHN A. GARRATY

VIETNAM WAR

The Vietnam War, the nation's longest, cost fifty-eight thousand American lives. Only the Civil War and the two world wars were deadlier for Americans. During the decade of direct U.S. military participation in Vietnam beginning in 1964, the U.S. Treasury spent over $140 billion on the war, enough money to fund urban renewal projects in every major American city. Despite these enormous costs and their accompanying public and private trauma for the American people, the United States failed, for the first time in its history, to achieve its stated war aims. The goal was to preserve a separate, independent, noncommunist government in South Vietnam, but after April 1975, the communist Democratic Republic of Vietnam (DRV) ruled the entire nation.

The initial reasons for U.S. involvement in Vietnam seemed logical and compelling to American leaders. Following its success in World War II, the United States faced the future with a sense of moral rectitude and material confidence. From Washington's perspective, the principal threat to U.S. security and world peace was monolithic, dictatorial communism emanating from the Soviet Union. Any communist anywhere, at home or abroad, was, by definition, an enemy of the United States. Drawing an analogy with the unsuccessful appeasement of fascist dictators before World War II, the Truman administration believed that any sign of communist aggression must be met quickly and forcefully by the United States and its allies. This reactive policy was known as containment.

In Vietnam the target of containment was Ho Chi Minh and the Vietminh front he had created in 1941. Ho and his chief lieutenants were communists with long-standing connections to the Soviet Union. They were also ardent Vietnamese nationalists who fought first to rid their country of the Japanese and then, after 1945, to prevent France from reestablishing its former colonial mastery over Vietnam and the rest of Indochina. Harry S. Truman and other American leaders, having no sympathy for French colonialism, favored Vietnamese independence. But expanding communist control of Eastern Europe and the triumph of the communists in China's civil war made France's war against Ho seem an anticommunist rather than a colonialist effort. When France agreed to a quasi-independent Vietnam under Emperor Bao Dai as an alternative to Ho's DRV, the United States decided to support the French position.

The American conception of Vietnam as a cold war battleground largely ignored the struggle for social justice and national sovereignty occurring within the country. American attention focused primarily on Europe and on Asia beyond Vietnam. Aid to France in Indochina was a quid pro quo for French cooperation with America's plans for the defense of Europe through the North Atlantic Treaty Organization. After China became a communist state in 1949, the stability of Japan became of paramount importance to Washington, and Japanese development required access to the markets and raw materials of Southeast Asia. The outbreak of war in Korea in 1950 served primarily to confirm Washington's belief that communist aggression posed a great danger to Asia. And subsequent charges that Truman had "lost" China and had settled for a stalemate in Korea caused succeeding presidents to fear the domestic political consequences if they "lost" Vietnam. This apprehension, an overestimation of American power, and an underestimation of Vietnamese communist strength locked all administrations from 1950 through the 1960s into a firm anticommunist stand in Vietnam.

Because American policymakers failed to appreciate the amount of effort that would be required to exert influence on Vietnam's political and social structure, the course of American policy led to a steady escalation of U.S. involvement. President Dwight D. Eisenhower increased the level of aid to the French but continued to avoid military intervention, even when the French experienced a devastating defeat at Dien Bien Phu in the spring of 1954. Following that battle, an international conference at Geneva, Switzerland, arranged a cease-fire and provided for a North-South partition of Vietnam until elections could be held. The United States was not a party to the Geneva Agreements and began to foster the creation of a Vietnamese regime in South Vietnam to rival that of Ho in the North. Eisenhower enunciated the "domino theory," which held that, if the communists succeeded in controlling Vietnam, they would progressively dominate all of Southeast Asia. With support from Washington, South Vietnam's autocratic president Ngo Dinh Diem, who deposed Bao Dai in October 1955, resisted holding an election on the reunification of Vietnam. Despite over $1 billion of U.S. aid between 1955 and 1961, the South Vietnamese economy languished and internal security deteriorated. Nation building was failing in the South, and, in 1960, communist cadres created the National Liberation Front (NLF), or Vietcong as its enemies called it, to challenge the Diem regime.

President John F. Kennedy concurred with his predecessor's domino theory and also believed that the credibility of U.S. anticommunist commitments around the world was imperiled in 1961. Consequently, by 1963 he had tripled American aid to South Vietnam and expanded the number of military advisers there from less than seven hundred to more than sixteen thousand. But the Diem government still failed to show economic or political progress. Buddhist priests, spiritual leaders of the majority of Vietnamese, staged dramatic protests, including self-immolation, against the dictatorship of the Catholic Diem. Ngo Dinh Nhu, Diem's brother, led a brutal suppression of the Buddhist resistance. Finally, after receiving assurances of noninterference from U.S. officials, South Vietnamese military officers conducted a coup that ended with the murders of Diem and Nhu. Whether these gruesome developments would have led Kennedy to redirect or decrease U.S. involvement in Vietnam is unknown, since Kennedy himself was assassinated three weeks later.

Diem's death left a leadership vacuum in South Vietnam, and the survival of the Saigon regime was in jeopardy. With a presidential election approaching, Lyndon B. Johnson did not want to be saddled with the charge of having lost South Vietnam. On the other hand, an expansion of U.S. responsibility for the war against the Vietcong and North Vietnam would divert resources from Johnson's ambitious and expensive domestic program, the Great Society. A larger war in Vietnam also raised the risk of a military clash with China. Using as a provocation alleged North Vietnamese attacks on U.S. Navy vessels in the Gulf of Tonkin in August 1964, Johnson authorized limited bombing raids on North Vietnam and secured a resolution from Congress allowing him to use military forces in Vietnam. These actions helped Johnson win the November election, but they did not dissuade the Vietcong from its relentless pressure against the Saigon government.

By July 1965, Johnson faced the choice of being the first president to lose a war or of converting the Vietnam War into a massive, U.S.-directed military effort. He chose a middle course that vastly escalated U.S. involvement but that stopped short of an all-out application of American power. Troop levels immediately jumped beyond 300,000, and by 1968 the number exceeded 500,000. Supporting these ground troops was a tremendous air bombardment of North Vietnam that by 1967 surpassed the total tonnage dropped on Germany, Italy, and Japan in World War II.

Gen. William Westmoreland, the U.S. commander in Vietnam, pursued an attrition strategy designed to inflict such heavy losses on the enemy that its will to continue would be broken. By late 1967, his headquarters was claiming that the crossover point had been reached and that enemy strength was being destroyed faster than it could be replenished. But the communists' Tet offensive launched in January 1968 quickly extinguished the "light at the end of the tunnel." The Vietcong struck throughout South Vietnam, including a penetration of the U.S. embassy compound in Saigon. American and South Vietnamese forces eventually repulsed the offensive and inflicted heavy losses on the Vietcong, but the fighting had exposed the reality that a quick end of the war was not in sight.

Following the Tet offensive, American leaders began a slow and agonizing reduction of U.S. involvement. Johnson limited the bombing, began peace talks with Hanoi and the NLF, and withdrew as a candidate for reelection. His successor, Richard M. Nixon, announced a program of Vietnamization, which basically represented a return to the Eisenhower and Kennedy policies of helping Vietnamese forces fight the war. Nixon gradually reduced U.S. ground troops in Vietnam, but he increased the bombing; the tonnage dropped after 1969 exceeded the already prodigious levels reached by Johnson. Nixon expanded air and ground operations into Cambodia and Laos in attempts to block enemy supply routes along Vietnam's borders. He traveled to Moscow and Beijing for talks and sent his aide Henry A. Kissinger to Paris for secret negotiations with the North Vietnamese. In January 1973, the United States and North Vietnam signed the Paris Peace Agreement, which provided for the withdrawal of all remaining U.S. forces from Vietnam, the return of U.S. prisoners of war, and a cease-fire. The American troops and POWs came home, but the war continued. Nixon termed it "peace with honor," since a separate government remained in Saigon, but Kissinger acknowledged that the arrangement provided primarily for a "decent interval" between U.S. withdrawal and the collapse of the South. In April 1975, North Vietnamese troops and tanks converged on Saigon, and the war was over.

Why did the United States lose the war? Some postmortems singled out media criticism of the war and antiwar activism in America as undermining the will of the U.S. government to continue fighting. Others cited the restrictions placed by civilian politicians on the military's operations or, conversely, blamed U.S. military chiefs for not providing civilian leaders with a sound strategy for victory. These so-called win arguments assume that victory was possible, but they overlook the flawed reasons for U.S. involvement in Vietnam. Washington had sought to contain international communism, but this global strategic concern masked the reality that the appeal of the communists in Vietnam derived from local economic, social, and historical conditions. The U.S. response to Vietnamese communism was essentially to apply a military solution to an internal political problem. America's infliction of enormous destruction on Vietnam served only to discredit politically the Vietnamese that the United States sought to assist. Furthermore, U.S. leaders underestimated the tenacity of the enemy. For the Vietnamese communists, the struggle was a total war for their own and their cause's survival. For the United States, it was a limited war. Despite U.S. concern about global credibility, Vietnam was a peripheral theater of the cold war. For many Americans, the ultimate issue in Vietnam was not a question of winning or losing. Rather, they came to believe that the rising level of expenditure of lives and dollars was unacceptable in pursuit of a marginal national objective.

The rhetoric of U.S. leaders after World War II about the superiority of American values, the dangers of appeasement, and the challenge of godless communism recognized no limit to U.S. ability to meet the test of global leadership. In reality, neither the United States nor any other nation had the power to guarantee alone the freedom and security of peoples of the world. The Vietnam War taught Americans a humbling lesson about the limits of power.

The domestic consequences of the war were equally profound. From Truman through Nixon, the war demonstrated the increasing dominance of the presidency within the federal government. Congress essentially defaulted to the "imperial presidency" in the conduct of foreign affairs. Vietnam also destroyed credibility within the American political process. The public came to distrust its leaders, and many officials distrusted the public. In May 1970, Ohio National Guardsmen killed four Kent State University students during a protest over U.S. troops invading Cambodia. Many Americans were outraged while others defended the Ohio authorities. As this tragic example reveals, the war rent the fabric of trust that traditionally clothed the American polity. Vietnam figured prominently in inflation, unfulfilled Great Society programs, and the generation gap. The Vietnam War brought an end to the domestic consensus that had sustained U.S. cold war policies since World War II and that

had formed the basis for the federal government's authority since the sweeping expansion of that authority under Franklin D. Roosevelt.

George C. Herring, *America's Longest War: The United States and Vietnam, 1950–1975*, 2nd ed. (1986); Stanley Karnow, *Vietnam: A History* (1983).

DAVID L. ANDERSON

See also Asia-U.S. Relations; Cold War; Gulf of Tonkin Resolution; Kent State Incident; Kissinger, Henry A.; Tet Offensive.

VIRGINIA AND KENTUCKY RESOLUTIONS

The Virginia and Kentucky Resolutions of 1798 and 1799 raised the question of states rights' and nullification. They were drafted in response to the passage of the Alien and Sedition Acts of 1798 but were concerned with a larger and more deep-rooted problem. How was power to be divided between the federal government and the states, and who was to settle disputes between the two?

The first Kentucky Resolution, passed by the state legislature on November 16, 1798, stated that when the federal government exercised power not specifically delegated to it by the Constitution, each state could judge the validity of that action for itself. The Virginia Resolution of December 24, 1798, claimed that the states "have the right and are in duty bound to interpose for arresting the progress of the evil." Several northern states objected that the judiciary, not the states, should be the arbiter of constitutionality. The Kentucky legislature passed a second Resolution on November 22, 1799, arguing that a single state had the power to nullify a federal action it deemed unconstitutional.

Unknown to contemporaries, the Virginia and Kentucky Resolutions were drafted, respectively, by James Madison and Thomas Jefferson. The doctrines they enunciated were later cited by southern slaveholders in support of their right to secede from the Union. Yet it would be a mistake to conclude that either Jefferson or Madison truly wanted to dismantle the Union. The Resolutions are best understood in the context of the fierce political battles between Federalists and Jeffersonians in the 1790s and the prevailing theory of divided sovereignty. When John C. Calhoun evoked the Resolutions in the 1820s to support his own doctrine of nullification, he was solidly opposed by James Madison.

See also Calhoun, John C.; Jefferson, Thomas; Madison, James; Nullification Controversy; Secession.

VOLSTEAD ACT

The Volstead Act (National Prohibition Enforcement Act), passed on October 28, 1919, provided for enforcement of the recently ratified Eighteenth Amendment, which prohibited the manufacture, sale, or transportation of alcoholic beverages in the United States. The act, passed over President Woodrow Wilson's veto, affirmed and further specified the provisions of the Eighteenth Amendment, delineated fines and prison terms for violation of the law, empowered the Bureau of Internal Revenue to administer Prohibition, and classified as alcoholic all beverages containing more than one-half of 1 percent alcohol by volume.

The temperance movement had been active in the United States for most of the nineteenth century and since 1900 had placed increasing emphasis on legal prohibition rather than personal reform. By 1914, fourteen states had adopted prohibition; by 1919, the number had risen to twenty-six. Even many temperance advocates had opposed the extension of federal power necessarily involved in national prohibition, but with the outbreak of World War I, the Anti-Saloon League was able to win passage of various federal prohibitory laws as part of the war effort, either to protect the morals of servicemen or to conserve grain for nutritional purposes. Thus, the principal effect of the Volstead Act was to extend the wartime measures to peacetime.

Once passed, Prohibition proved extraordinarily difficult to enforce. Although overall drinking was generally thought to have declined, it continued uninterrupted in many parts of the country, particularly in large cities and in areas with large foreign-born populations. Critics pointed to the demoralizing effect of a law that was routinely violated by respectable citizens and maintained that the profitable business of supplying illegal liquor fostered the growth of organized crime and the corruption of public officials.

Calls for repeal of the Eighteenth Amendment began as early as 1923. Republicans continued to defend the "experiment noble in purpose" (as President Herbert Hoover called it), but division over the issue nearly sundered the Democratic party in 1928. An investigation ordered by Hoover in 1929 and completed in 1931 confirmed that the Eighteenth Amendment remained largely unenforced. In 1932, the Democrats came out for repeal of Prohibition. Their overwhelming electoral victory encouraged Congress to pass the Twenty-first Amendment, repealing the Eighteenth, on February 20, 1933. On March 22, the Volstead Act was amended to permit the sale of 3.2 percent beer and wine. Once the Twenty-first Amendment was ratified the following December, the Volstead Act became void.

See also Prohibition and Temperance.

VOLUNTARY ASSOCIATIONS

See Fraternal Societies; Women's Voluntary Associations.

VON NEUMANN, JOHN

(1903–1957), mathematician and technologist. Von Neumann is one of those individuals whose historical significance can be assessed adequately only by considering simultaneously several fields — in his case, pure mathematics, computer science, logical analysis, and the cold war. To many of his contemporaries von Neumann represented the paradigm of "the logical thinker"; one colleague wrote that his mind was "a perfect instrument whose gears were machined to mesh accurately to a thousandth of an inch." His logical powers were supplemented by unusual rapidity of thought, an extraordinary memory, and mathematical brilliance.

Von Neumann left a rich legacy of work in mathematics proper. Pure mathematics spans a number of subspecialties, and von Neumann, in work of a highly technical nature, made substantial contributions to several of them. He also applied mathematics to physics (formulation of quantum mechanics), economics (game theory, which provides criteria for choosing moves in a game, such as checkers or poker, against an intelligent opponent), and computers (automaton theory). He was a major figure in modern computer development, and his study of automata led him to explore analogies between computers and the human brain.

It was the tenor of his times to extol logic and neglect its limitations, an intellectual misjudgment that eventually manifested itself in connection with some of von Neumann's work. He had for years been working on a mathematical proof that all mathematics is free from contradiction, when Kurt Gödel (1931) showed that it is in principle impossible. He tried to settle a philosophical controversy concerning the interpretation of quantum mechanics by a neat mathematical proof (nonexistence of hidden variables) and indeed for a time stilled the controversy. But a critical reexamination of von Neumann's proof, particularly by John S. Bell (1964), reopened the debate. In his mathematical approach to weather prediction, which was widely adopted, he was also overoptimistic. But from America's perspective the most costly misjudgment derived from the use of von Neumann's game theory in formulating political policy and military strategy. For example, U.S. government strategists applied game theory to decide policies concerning the Vietnam War, instead of basing decisions on firsthand knowledge of the people of Vietnam and their history, which would have shown clearly that the policies were futile and self-defeating.

Von Neumann had grown up in Budapest at a time characterized, as he put it, "by an external pressure on the whole society, a subconscious feeling of extreme insecurity in individuals, and the necessity of producing the unusual or facing extinction." These conditions also made his generation of Hungarians highly sensitive to international politics. He produced the unusual in mathematics before World War II, when he became the foremost mathematical consultant on the building of the first atom bombs. After the war he became active in promoting U.S. government policies that would increase the destructive power of American weaponry. In contrast to most physicists, he favored speedy building of the hydrogen bomb. He headed the most influential government committee advising President Dwight D. Eisenhower on missiles and pressed urgently for the building of intercontinental ballistic missiles. Accordingly, Eisenhower reshuffled his priorities. During the last years of his life von Neumann served as an atomic energy commissioner.

Steve J. Heims, *John von Neumann and Norbert Wiener: From Mathematics to the Technologies of Life and Death* (1980); Stanislaw Ulam, *Adventures of a Mathematician* (1976).

STEVE JOSHUA HEIMS

See also Science and Technology.

VOTE, THE

See Suffrage.

VOTING RIGHTS ACT

See Civil Rights Movement.

W

WADE-DAVIS BILL

This Civil War measure, introduced by two Radical Republicans, Ohio senator Benjamin F. Wade and Maryland representative Henry Winter Davis, asserted congressional power over Reconstruction. It required that a majority of a seceded state's white men take an oath of loyalty to the Constitution and guarantee black equality. Then the state could hold elections for a constitutional convention, starting the readmission process. The Radicals were seeking an alternative to Abraham Lincoln's Proclamation of Amnesty and Reconstruction. Lincoln's plan called for creating new southern state governments when 10 percent of voters in the 1860 election pledged loyalty to the Union and agreed to abolish slavery but without enfranchising blacks. Congress passed the Wade-Davis bill in 1864, but Lincoln pocket-vetoed it. He then invited southerners to rejoin the Union under either plan, knowing they would prefer his easier terms.

Wade and Davis replied with a blistering manifesto, charging Lincoln with defying Congress and acting like a dictator. The widespread support for the Wade-Davis bill by congressional Republicans reflected their desire for a larger role in shaping Reconstruction.

See also Reconstruction.

WAGNER ACT

See National Labor Relations Act.

WALKER, C. J. (MADAME)

(1867–1919), entrepreneur. Born Sarah Breedlove, the daughter of Louisiana sharecroppers, Walker was orphaned at six, married at fourteen, and widowed at twenty with a two-year-old daughter to care for. She resettled in St. Louis and went to work as a laundress. Her early years reflected patterns all too common for black women of her generation.

In 1905 Walker, who had been losing her hair, sought a treatment for the condition. The method of beauty culture she developed revolutionized black hair care. The combination of scalp preparation, application of lotions, and use of iron combs became known as the "Walker system." She distinguished her products from the hair straighteners advocated by white cosmetic firms, arguing that her treatment was geared to the special health needs of blacks. She sold her homemade products directly to black women, using a personal approach that won her customers and eventually a fleet of loyal saleswomen.

Walker trained her "beauty culturalists" after establishing her business headquarters in Denver, with a branch in Pittsburgh managed by her daughter A'Lelia. Her second husband, Charles J. Walker, a journalist, helped promote his wife's flourishing enterprise. Her lectures and demonstrations won thousands of customers, and in 1910 she moved her headquarters to Indianapolis. Her business employed over three thousand workers, mainly door-to-door saleswomen. Her product line of nearly twenty hair and skin items was widely advertised in the black press.

Walker, whose talent for self-promotion made her one of the best-known black Americans during the first quarter of the century, was lauded as "the first black woman millionaire in America." Her largesse was legendary, and she spent extravagant sums on her Manhattan townhouse. When her daughter inherited the mansion in the 1920s, it became a salon for members of the Harlem Renaissance. Walker also owned a luxurious country home, Villa Lewaro, in Irvington-on-Hudson, designed by black architect Vertner Tandy.

Walker was as generous as she was successful, establishing a network of clubs for her employees and offering bonuses and prizes to those who contributed to their communities through charitable works. She promoted female talent: the charter of her company provided that only a woman could serve as president. She was a standard-bearer for black self-help, funding scholarships for women at Tuskegee Institute and donating large sums to the NAACP, the black YMCA, and dozens of black charities.

Madame Walker's plans for her headquarters, the Walker Building, were carried out after her premature death at fifty-one. The structure, completed in 1927, today is part of a historic renovation district in downtown Indianapolis.

CATHERINE CLINTON

WALKER, DAVID

(1785–1830), abolitionist. As the author of *An Appeal to the Coloured Citizens of the World* (1829), Walker was one of the earliest and most militant voices among black abolitionists. Widely regarded as a founding text of black nationalist thought, Walker's *Appeal* was an impassioned indictment of slavery and a cry of outrage against ignorance, Christian hypocrisy, and colonization. At a time when few could imagine an American future without slavery, the pamphlet challenged blacks, slave and free, to seize control of their lives, develop their own leadership and institutions, and shoulder the burden of their liberation. Walker shocked his readers by calling upon slaves to rebel and overthrow slavery by force.

Born a free black in Wilmington, North Carolina, Walker's early life is obscure. His father was a slave, who may have died before David was born, and his mother was free. Walker acquired books and a remarkable education and traveled widely throughout the South before moving to Boston during the mid-1820s. Thus he both witnessed the ravages of slavery and experienced the bitter, anomalous life of a free black in antebellum America. By 1827 Walker was operating a "slop shop" on Brattle Street in Boston, near the wharves, where he sold old clothes to sailors preparing to go to sea. In 1828, he became an agent of the first black weekly newspaper, *Freedom's Journal,* and a frequent street-corner and lecture hall speaker against slavery.

During 1829–1830, the seventy-eight-page *Appeal* went through three editions and gained widespread notoriety. Even fellow abolitionists such as Benjamin Lundy and Harriet Martineau disapproved of the incendiary quality of the pamphlet. A handsome price was placed on Walker's head in Georgia after some sixty copies turned up in Savannah. Among Walker's clandestine methods for distributing his pamphlet was to sew copies into the trousers and jackets he sold to sailors departing for the South. Only a few weeks after publication of the third edition in June 1830, Walker was found dead in the doorway of his shop, a victim of poison, a common theory had it.

Few have doubted that his eloquent voice met with other than a violent death in exchange for his challenge to the American conscience. Walker wrote with unsurpassed anger, evangelical zeal, scathing irony, and an uncompromising assertion of the philosophy of natural rights. The *Appeal* is nothing less than a jeremiad against slavery and racism. "Oh Americans," he wrote, "when God Almighty commences his battle on the continent of America, for the oppression of his people, tyrants will wish they were never born!" He invoked the Bible, the Declaration of Independence, and the spirit of pan-African unity in addressing his white audience. Although Walker viewed America as a land of brutal contradictions, he claimed the birthright of all blacks as Americans through their "blood and tears." He insisted that the nation live up to its creed or pay a terrible price. He will always be remembered for his brave use of the pen to forge black nationalist theory and to confront the American conscience with the consequences of unredeemed oppression.

Sterling Stuckey, *Slave Culture: Nationalist Theory and the Foundations of Black America* (1987); Charles M. Wiltse, ed., *David Walker's Appeal to the Coloured Citizens of the World* (1965).

DAVID W. BLIGHT

See also Abolitionist Movement; Black Nationalism; Free Negroes, 1619–1860; Slavery.

WALLACE, DeWITT

(1889–1981), magazine and book publisher. Born in the northwestern American heartland, nurtured in a firm Christian household, and uniquely gifted as a salesman, Wallace, founder of the *Reader's Digest,* is the perfect twentieth-century exemplar of self-made success in publishing. His story is rooted in a tradition that goes back to Benjamin Franklin, a more complex and sophisticated man, but an equally popular publisher. Franklin moved on to science, civic activism, and diplomacy. Wallace invested his energies, after his first triumph, in creating a print empire of uplift.

After graduating from the University of California at Berkeley, Wallace sold agricultural textbooks, calendars, and novelties, and then served in France in World War I. While recovering from battle wounds, he conceived of a compact magazine for busy people that would consist of short articles "of lasting interest" written in a basic English accessible to every level of readership. Originally he meant to sell the idea to a publisher, but his sample issue was uniformly rejected. So in 1922, with the help of his wife, Lila Acheson Wallace (whose Christian social service background resembled his own), he launched the *Reader's Digest* himself. The first printing consisted of five thousand copies in a pocket-sized format selling for a quarter and containing thirty-one articles — one for each day — condensed (with permission) from other magazines.

Wallace had struck gold. An expanding urban middle class wanted self-improvement and information quickly and without "highbrow" challenges. The *Digest* spoke to this audience. It stressed traditional strive-and-succeed themes, preached courage in the face of adversity, and extolled God, family, community, and country. It was not blindly uncritical, but it covered sports, science, history, and current affairs with a light touch and was seasoned with features like "Improve Your Word Power" and "Life in These United States," bite-sized chunks of piquant information. Wallace's sense of the popular mind, refracted through competent roving editors, matched that of two contemporaries in mass culture, Walt Disney and Henry Luce. By its seventh birthday in 1929 the *Digest* had achieved a circulation of 216,000.

In the early 1930s the magazine began to feature more "in-house" articles, sometimes planting them first in other journals. In a deliberately chosen, symbolic flight to suburbia, Wallace moved his growing staff to Pleasantville, New York, where he and his wife, an active partner in the enterprise, watched over it paternalistically. But expansion enlarged and depersonalized the "family." A British edition appeared in 1938, followed by Spanish and Portuguese versions and other foreign spinoffs until, by the middle of the 1950s, the *Digest* was being read in sixteen languages by over 30.5 million people. It portrayed an America that was kindly, religious, self-sufficient, neighborly, and staunchly anticommunist, as the *Digest* became a major voice of conservative cold war policies.

In the 1960s the company's sphere of influence was extended into hardcover publishing through Reader's Digest Books. The firm issued condensed books from other publishers, classic reprints, how-to books, encyclopedias, and informational-educational literature created by teams of editors and illustrators and marketed by mail order. By the time of Wallace's death at 92, he had become one of the major shapers of the American popular mind.

John Bainbridge, *Little Wonder* (1946).

BERNARD A. WEISBERGER

See also Magazines and Newspapers.

WALLACE, GEORGE C.

(1919–   ), Alabama governor, four-time candidate for president of the United States. Wallace began his political career as a moderate to liberal Alabama politician in the mold of his mentor, Governor James Folsom. When he lost his first run for the governorship in 1958 at the hands of an ultrasegregationist candidate, Wallace vowed he would "never be out-niggered again." Four years later he swept to victory.

In his 1963 inaugural address Wallace promised his white followers: "Segregation now! Segregation tomorrow! Segregation forever!" The promise lasted six months. In June of that year, he "stood in the schoolhouse door" at the University of Alabama but stepped aside to allow the enrollment of black students. When desegregation came to the public schools in the fall of 1963 he vowed resistance but eventually capitulated to federal court orders.

His defense of segregation, however, made him enormously popular among whites. During the 1960s he tightened his hold on his power base in the state, combining bellicose anti–civil rights rhetoric with a heavy dose of social spending. Rake-offs from state contractors and support from thousands of small contributors furnished a solid financial base for his political activities.

His testimony before congressional committees, appearances on national news and interview shows, and speaking tours outside the South made him a leading national spokesman for resistance to racial change. In 1964 he entered the Democratic presidential primaries in Wisconsin, Indiana, and Maryland. Religious, political, and community leaders in those states denounced him as a racist, but he drew 34 percent of the primary vote in Wisconsin, 30 percent in Indiana, and 43 percent in Maryland. The civil rights movement was at high tide, but Wallace's successful campaign showed the extent of "white backlash."

A strong run as the candidate of his American Independent party in 1968 proved his 1964 appeal was not a fluke. Despite state laws that often handicapped third-party candidates, Wallace managed to get on the ballot in all fifty states and in the election, he drew 10 million votes, half of them from outside the South.

In 1972, his political fortunes peaked when he returned to the Democratic party. Nixon operatives, welcoming Wallace as a divisive force among the Democrats, gave his campaign covert tactical support, but his appeal was all his own. Still running on a platform to "get tough with protestors," end court-ordered school busing (which had increasingly affected northern voters), and restore respect for "law and order," he rolled up wins and strong showings throughout the South and Midwest, culminating with victories on May 16 in Michigan and Maryland.

But twenty-four hours before the May 16 sweep, he was shot and seriously wounded by Arthur Bremner at an outdoor rally in Laurel, Maryland. This ended his presidential campaign.

George Wallace speaking softly from a wheelchair was never able to reignite the support that had carried him to national prominence. When he ran again in 1976, Jimmy Carter from Georgia trounced him in North Carolina and Florida, destroying his southern political base. He had nevertheless proved himself one of the major political figures of the 1960s and 1970s, shaping the agenda of social conservatism and white backlash that would dominate the politics of the 1980s.

Wallace served another term as governor in 1983–1987, winning with the overwhelming support of black voters. In an ironic conclusion to his career, the man who had promised segregation forever made more black political appointments than any figure in Alabama history.

Jody Carlson, *George C. Wallace and the Politics of Powerlessness* (1981); Marshall Frady, *Wallace* (1968).

DAN T. CARTER

See also American Independent Party; Civil Rights Movement; Elections: 1968; Third Parties.

WAR

See Barbary Wars; Bay of Pigs Invasion; Black Hawk War; Civil War; Colonial Wars; Indians;

King Philip's War; Korean War; Mexican War; Revolution; Spanish-American War; Vietnam War; War of 1812; World War I; World War II.

WAR CRIMES TRIAL

See Nuremberg Trials.

WAR HAWKS

The War Hawks (so named by Congressman John Randolph of Virginia, a political opponent) were a group of young Republicans from southern and western states who pressed for war against Great Britain in 1810–1811. Although opposed by both the Federalists and the "Old Republican" wing of their party, the War Hawks gained significant political power within the House of Representatives after the congressional elections of 1810. Henry Clay of Kentucky, who was elected Speaker, and John C. Calhoun of South Carolina, Felix Grundy of Tennessee, and Peter Porter of western New York, who dominated the Foreign Relations Committee, were among the group.

The War Hawks vigorously protested the incursions being made by Great Britain on the United States' maritime and commercial sovereignty — impressing sailors, blockading American ports, and violating American neutrality — but in fact these violations had relatively little impact on the communities the War Hawks represented. A more compelling reason for war with Great Britain, from the point of view of the War Hawks' home districts, was the possibility that such a war might result in American conquest of Canada, Florida, and Texas (the latter two controlled by England's ally, Spain). Indeed, protests against Britain's disregard of American sovereignty fit into the War Hawks' larger vision of an aggressive, expansionist republic insisting on its proper place in the world of nations.

The War Hawks' vigorous rhetoric undoubtedly contributed to the rising tension between Great Britain and the United States. Nevertheless, it was the maritime and commercial issues rather than the War Hawks' dreams of national expansion that seem to have played the larger

part in finally bringing the two nations to war in 1812.

See also Clay, Henry; Impressment Controversy; War of 1812.

WARHOL, ANDY

(1928?–1987), artist. When the most famous image in pop art, Warhol's *Campbell's Soup Can,* was first exhibited in 1962, a nearby gallery displayed actual soup cans with the sign, "Get the real thing for 29 cents." Underlying the humor was an acknowledgment that Warhol's work threatened the concept of art as serious and transcendent: the artist's intentions, devoid of satire, seemed as cheerfully vacuous as his subject matter. Pop art's celebration of the banal and its unapologetic dismissal of higher aims soon lost their original shock value, yet Warhol, its best-known figure, remained provocative.

Born Andrew Warhola in Pennsylvania, he graduated from Carnegie Institute of Technology (now Carnegie-Mellon University) in 1949 and moved to New York City, where he became a prize-winning commercial artist. His development as a fine artist began with wry, delicate drawings and culminated in the hard-edged graphic style that became instantly and ubiquitously recognizable. A solo show at New York's Stable Gallery in 1962 brought overnight fame. Calling his studio the Factory, Warhol used the glib impersonality of silk screen to produce mass market images by mass market means. His characteristic repetition of subjects — rows of Marilyn Monroes and stacks of soup cans — mimicked the effect of media saturation.

He identified America's vacant icons with his paintings of Coke bottles and Brillo pads and the lure of the meretricious in his celebrity portraits of Elvis Presley, Elizabeth Taylor, and others. Warhol's painting mirrored American consumer society but declined to judge it; any indictment of twentieth-century life was in the eye of the beholder. Even the disturbing "disaster" pictures of electric chairs, suicides, and car crashes suggest no more than the fascination of grisly tabloid scenes.

In 1963 he began making films (among them

Empire, featuring eight uninterrupted hours of the Empire State Building), which attracted a smaller following. But by this time Warhol's persona eclipsed his work. He turned products into art and himself into a product: silver-haired and ghostly, he became an image as recognizable as his celebrity portraits. At a retrospective, the gallery was so mobbed that the canvases had to be removed from the walls. The crowd, focused on Warhol, did not seem to notice — it was a triumph of superstardom over substance. After he was shot by a fan in 1968, he later posed for photographers with his scars displayed, transforming a dark human moment into an exhibitionistic media event. Dramatizing the disposable, surface quality of celebrity, he sent a Warhol impersonator as his stand-in on a college lecture tour. Warhol made being avant-garde fun and defiantly low-brow: his unabashed aspirations were money and fame, he surrounded himself with a glamourous retinue and rock group, and he entertained and scandalized the public with his deadpan proverbs. His democratic prediction that in the future everyone would be famous for fifteen minutes lent status to the ordinary and deflated the pretensions of celebrities (including himself). Preoccupied from the seventies onward with nightlife and the jet set, Warhol was increasingly criticized for selling out and social climbing — yet such behavior was true to his image of himself.

"If you want to know all about Andy Warhol," he said, "just look at the surface of my paintings and films and me, and there I am. There's nothing behind it." The question of whether to take him at face value, look behind the façade, or see his statement as the subterfuge of a cynic as manipulative as the commercial world he depicted underscores his complexity. Warhol, as one critic put it, was "relentlessly superficial," an oxymoron that embodied the difficulty of drawing conclusions about him, a quality that made his art continually arresting.

Carter Ratcliff, *Andy Warhol* (1983); Andy Warhol, *The Philosophy of Andy Warhol: From A to B and Back Again* (1977).

BORGNA BRUNNER

See also Painting and Sculpture; Pop Art.

WAR OF 1812

The War of 1812, sometimes called "the Second War of Independence," was fought between the United States and Great Britain from 1812 to 1815. Relations between the two countries had often been strained after the United States won its independence in 1783, but the greatest problems developed during the war between England and France that broke out in 1793. To prevent American neutral shipping from helping the French, the British instituted extensive maritime blockades of European ports. The resulting seizures of American merchant shipping quickly brought demands for retaliation in the United States. From 1794 on, however, tensions eased as the administrations of George Washington and John Adams worked to avoid diplomatic difficulties with the British.

In the years between 1803 and 1812 relations between the United States and Great Britain again deteriorated sharply. France was now ruled by Napoleon, and the European struggle became more widespread. Beginning in 1805 the British imposed much stricter maritime blockades, culminating in the Orders in Council of 1807. These orders severely restricted neutral trade with Europe. The effect of these blockades was compounded by the British practice of impressment. The British navy claimed the right to stop neutral vessels on the high seas to look for "deserters." In the course of searching American ships, mistakes were often made, and as a result many American seamen were impressed into the British navy.

From 1807 to 1811 the Democratic-Republican administrations of Thomas Jefferson and James Madison attempted to change British policies by economic coercion, restricting British imports as well as American exports to Great Britain. The most severe of these measures was the Embargo Act, passed in December 1807, which banned all exports and confined American shipping to the coastal trade. When neither economic coercion nor negotiation changed British policies, war sentiment built in the United States.

Beginning in 1810 young Democratic-Republican "War Hawks" from the West and the

South argued that the right to export American products without losing ships and men had to be defended. They also objected to the British inciting the Indians along the Great Lakes frontier and argued that the British would be forced to change their policies if the United States attacked Canada. Some believed that the future of republican government was in danger if the United States could not successfully defend its rights. Others hoped that if Canada was conquered it could be retained after the war.

In spite of bitter opposition from the Federalist party, centered in New England, the United States declared war against Great Britain on June 18, 1812. General American strategy called for an invasion of Canada on three fronts: along Lake Champlain toward Montreal, across the Niagara frontier, and from Detroit into upper Canada. The campaigns of the summer and fall of 1812 were disasters. Detroit surrendered to the British on August 18, and the Americans were defeated on the Niagara frontier at the Battle of Queenston Heights in October. The year ended with American forces on the Lake Champlain front withdrawing from an attempted invasion of Canada without seriously engaging the enemy.

The main consolation in the first year of the war was the unexpected performance of the small American navy. In a single-ship engagement the frigate *Constitution* defeated the *Guerriere* in August 1812. Later in the year the *United States* captured the British frigate *Macedonian* and brought it into port as a prize of war. Later the *Constitution* defeated the *Java* in a battle off the coast of Brazil. This run of successes came to an end in June 1813 when the *Chesapeake* lost to the *Shannon* in a bitterly fought engagement. But in spite of the morale-boosting victories of the frigates and successful forays by American privateers, the British navy effectively blockaded the American coast and laid it open to hit-and-run raids.

American attempts to invade Canada failed again in 1813. Although Capt. Oliver Hazard Perry's ships won the Battle of Lake Erie in October and Gen. William Henry Harrison defeated the British and the Indians at the Battle of the Thames in Canada in the same month, the Americans were unable to make major inroads into Canada.

In 1814, with France collapsing, the British were able to launch major attacks against the United States. In July, American forces resisted the British at the Battles of Chippawa and Lundy's Lane on the Niagara frontier, but in the next month the United States suffered a severe blow. When Washington was occupied in August, President Madison and Congress were forced to flee, and the White House and other public buildings were burned. American morale was at a low ebb: the country faced bankruptcy as a result of the British blockade and the Federalists of New England were in open opposition to the war.

But in the following months American fortunes suddenly revived. The British force that had occupied Washington failed in an attempt to take Baltimore, and on September 11 Thomas Macdonough's naval force won a decisive victory at the Battle of Plattsburg Bay on Lake Champlain. This victory forced an invading British army to retreat into Canada.

Since August 1814 the two sides had been negotiating a settlement at Ghent in Belgium. When the British heard of the retreat of their army in the Battle of Plattsburg Bay, they lost interest in continuing the war. On December 24 the Treaty of Ghent was signed. It provided for the mutual restoration of territory captured by both sides. With the ending of the European war, the problem of American neutral rights was no longer an issue.

One battle was still to be fought, however, for the British force proceeding against the Gulf coast could not be informed of the peace in time. On January 8, 1815, the American forces commanded by Andrew Jackson inflicted a crushing defeat on the British at New Orleans. Americans heard of Jackson's great victory and the Treaty of Ghent at about the same time. Once again the British had been successfully resisted, and a surge of national self-confidence swept the United States. A war that had begun with the object of defending American commerce and vindicating republican independence was viewed in the end as a victory only because British attacks on the United States had failed.

Harry Coles, *The War of 1812* (1965); Reginald Horsman, *The War of 1812* (1969).

REGINALD HORSMAN

See also Clay, Henry; Conscientious Objection; Embargo Act of 1807; Federalist Party; Great Britain–U.S. Relations; Hartford Convention of 1814; Impressment Controversy; Key, Francis Scott; War Hawks.

WAR OF INDEPENDENCE

See Revolution.

WAR ON POVERTY

See Great Society.

WARREN, EARL

(1891–1974), California governor and chief justice, U.S. Supreme Court. Warren, born and raised in California, was elected district attorney of Alameda County in 1925, California attorney general in 1938, and governor in 1942. In three terms as governor he reorganized the state government and secured major reform legislation — modernizing the state's hospital system, prisons, and highways, and expanding old-age and unemployment benefits. In 1953, President Dwight D. Eisenhower appointed him the fourteenth chief justice of the United States. He retired in 1969.

There have been two great creative periods in American public law. During the first, the Marshall Court laid down the foundations of the American system. During the second, the Warren era, the Court rewrote much of the corpus of constitutional law. Warren was the leader in his Court's work, actively exercising his authority to reach the results he favored. In terms of creative impact Warren's tenure can be compared only with that of Marshall.

As a successful chief executive, Warren developed leadership abilities that enabled him to guide his Court effectively. His fellow justices all stressed his forceful leadership, particularly at the conferences where cases are discussed and decided. Justice William O. Douglas ranked him

with John Marshall and Charles Evans Hughes "as our three greatest Chief Justices." Those behind the "Impeach Earl Warren" movement were correct in considering him the prime mover in the Warren Court's jurisprudence.

Warren's leadership can best be seen in the 1954 *Brown* v. *Board of Education of Topeka* decision — the most important by his Court. When the justices first discussed the case under Warren's predecessor, they were sharply divided. But under Warren, they ruled unanimously that school segregation was unconstitutional. The unanimous decision was a direct result of Warren's efforts. This and other Warren Court decisions furthering racial equality were the catalyst for the civil rights protests of the 1950s and 1960s and the civil rights laws passed by Congress, themselves upheld by the Warren Court.

Next in importance were the reapportionment decisions. The Court ruled that the "one-person, one-vote" principle controls in all legislative apportionments. The result has been an electoral reform shifting voting power from rural districts to urban and suburban areas.

In addition to racial and political equality, the Warren Court sought equality in criminal justice. The landmark here was *Gideon* v. *Wainwright* (1963), which required counsel for indigent defendants. Warren's emphasis on fairness in criminal proceedings also led to *Mapp* v. *Ohio* (1961), barring illegally seized evidence and *Miranda* v. *Arizona* (1966), requiring warnings to arrested persons of their right to counsel, including appointed counsel if they could not afford one.

Earlier Courts had stressed property rights. Under Warren the emphasis shifted to personal rights, placing them in a preferred constitutional position. This was particularly true of First Amendment rights. Protection was extended to civil rights demonstrators and criticism of public officials; the power to restrain publication on obscenity grounds was also limited. Moreover, the Court recognized new personal rights, notably a constitutional right of privacy.

Warren expressed disappointment that he had never become president, although he had actively sought the Republican nomination in 1948 and 1952. Yet, as chief justice, he was able to accomplish more than most presidents. He led his Court to what Justice Abe Fortas once termed "the most profound and pervasive revolution ever achieved by substantially peaceful means."

Bernard Schwartz, *Super Chief: Earl Warren and His Supreme Court — A Judicial Biography* (1983).

BERNARD SCHWARTZ

See also Brown v. *Board of Education of Topeka;* Gideon v. *Wainwright;* Mapp v. *Ohio;* Miranda v. *Arizona;* Supreme Court.

WASHINGTON, BOOKER T.

(1856–1915), educator. Across the landscape of the most anguished era of American race relations (1895–1915) strode the self-assured and influential Booker T. Washington. The foremost black educator, power broker, and institution builder of his time, Washington in 1881 founded Tuskegee Institute, a black school in Alabama devoted to industrial and moral education and to the training of public school teachers. From his southern small-town base, he created a national political network of schools, newspapers, and the National Negro Business League (founded in 1901). In response to the age of Jim Crow, Washington offered the doctrine of accommodation, acquiescing in social and political inequality for blacks while training them for economic self-determination in the industrial arts.

Born a slave on a small farm in western Virginia, Washington was nine years old when the Civil War ended. His humble but stern rearing included his working in a salt furnace when he was ten and serving as a houseboy for a white family where he first learned the virtues of frugality, cleanliness, and personal morality. Washington was educated at Hampton Institute, one of the earliest freedmen's schools devoted to industrial education; Hampton was the model upon which he based his institute in Tuskegee. Growing up during Reconstruction and imbued with moral as opposed to intellectual training, he came to believe that postwar social uplift had begun at the wrong end: the acquisition of po-

litical and civil rights rather than economic self-determination.

Washington's philosophy and the "Tuskegee machine" won him widespread support among northern white philanthropists as well as acclaim among blacks. In his Atlanta Compromise address, delivered at the Cotton States Exposition in 1895, he struck the keynotes of racial accommodationism: "Cast down your buckets where you are," Washington urged blacks. "In all things that are purely social," he announced to attentive whites, "we can be as separate as the fingers, yet one as the hand in all things essential to mutual progress." His thoroughly bourgeois, antilabor, antidemocratic appeal stood for years as an endorsement of segregation. He sustained his power as an educational statesman by some ruthless and duplicitous methods. Rival black newspapers, educators, and thinkers were frequently intimidated by his brand of boss politics. Black newspaper editors and aspiring young intellectuals risked ostracism and unemployment if they embraced political activism rather than Washington's accommodationist social policy. Such disputes surfaced especially in the famous debate between Washington and W. E. B. Du Bois over the aims of "industrial" as opposed to "classical" education among blacks.

Growing black and white opposition to Washington's acquiescence in disfranchisement and Jim Crow led to the formation of the Niagara Movement (1905–1909) and the NAACP, activist organizations working for civil and political rights as well as against lynching. Ironically, Washington also labored secretly against Jim Crow laws and racial violence, writing letters in code names and protecting blacks from lynch mobs, though these efforts were rarely known in his own time.

Washington was a pragmatist who engaged in deliberate ambiguity in order to sustain white recognition of his leadership. Such visibility won him international fame and the role of black adviser to Presidents Theodore Roosevelt and William Howard Taft. His widely read autobiography, *Up from Slavery* (1901), stands as a classic in the genre of narratives by American self-made men, as well as the prime source for Washington's social and historical philosophy. His racial philosophy did not long survive his death, but in theory and practice, his views on economic self-reliance have remained one of the deepest strains in Afro-American thought.

Louis R. Harlan, *Booker T. Washington,* 2 vols. (1972, 1984).

DAVID W. BLIGHT

See also Du Bois, W. E. B.; Fortune, T. Thomas; National Association for the Advancement of Colored People; Niagara Movement; Reconstruction; Segregation; Suffrage.

WASHINGTON, GEORGE

(1732–1799), Virginia planter, commander of the Continental army, and first president of the United States. Washington was the son of Augustine Washington, a Virginia planter of modest wealth. When he died in 1743, George went to live with his older brother at Mount Vernon.

As a youth, Washington worked as a surveyor and in 1754 was sent with a military expedition to maintain Virginia's claim to Ohio lands against the French. In a battle fought in the wilderness he and most of his men were forced to surrender. After his release, he was appointed head of Virginia's militia on the frontier and served until 1758.

In 1759, Washington married Martha Custis, a wealthy widow. Marriage and the responsibilities of running a plantation helped him mature emotionally and intellectually. By 1770 he was an experienced leader — a vestryman, a justice of the peace, and a member of the Virginia House of Burgesses. He was a delegate to the First and Second Continental Congresses, where John Adams remarked on his "soldier-like air" and, along with everyone else, thought he was the natural leader of the Continental army when it took shape in 1775.

As military commander, Washington's strategy grew from a clear vision of the large political objective of the Revolution: independence. His task was to hold the army together and maintain an armed resistance to the British forces in America while Congress sought foreign aid and recognition. The army had to remain intact to persuade Britain that the Americans were not going to surrender; only when that conviction pervaded British governing circles would independence be won.

During the war Washington suffered several defeats, but he held his forces together and won at Trenton and Princeton (1776–1777), and most important, at Yorktown (1781). His leadership and sense of strategy made him a superb commander in chief. His respect for civilian control, despite the weakness of Congress, proved especially important to the new Republic.

When the war ended, Washington returned to Mount Vernon and the life of a tobacco planter. But he was called out of retirement to preside at the Constitutional Convention in 1787 at Philadelphia. His great prestige supported the new government and made his election as the first president of the United States almost inevitable.

Washington's achievements as president were also enormous. He was creating a new government — its institutions, offices, and practices were not completely described in the Constitution — and he persuaded the American people that their future lay in a union under a strong central authority.

Cabinet members Alexander Hamilton and Thomas Jefferson soon disagreed over domestic and foreign policy. Washington backed Hamilton on key issues — the funding of the national debt, the assumption of state debts, and the establishment of a national bank chartered by the federal government — but he did not favor Hamilton's plan for the support of manufactures. Washington felt more confident of his knowledge of foreign affairs than he did of domestic policy. In 1790 when Spain seized three British ships in Nootka Sound, Vancouver Island, territory claimed by the Spanish, Washington maintained American neutrality and did the same in 1793 when war broke out between France and England. Jefferson objected, urging that the Treaty of Alliance with France be upheld, and left the government not long after. Washington settled outstanding issues with Britain through Jay's Treaty (1795) and with Spain through Pinckney's Treaty (1795). He put down

the farmers in western Pennsylvania who instigated the Whiskey Rebellion (1794) and dealt a
blow to the Indians of Ohio, after they were defeated by Gen. Anthony Wayne, in the Treaty of
Greenville (1795).

In Washington's first term, an opposition
began to make itself heard, and in his second
term, the outlines of the first party system, composed of the Democratic-Republican and Federalist parties, became clear. Washington never
understood the need for political parties, seeing
something sinister in them. Fatigued and somewhat discouraged, he retired to Mount Vernon
after he left the presidency.

Douglas Southhall Freeman, *George Washington: A Biography,* completed by J. A. Carroll and M. W. Ashworth, 7
vols. (1948–1957).

ROBERT MIDDLEKAUFF

See also Continental Congresses; Elections: 1789,
1792; Federalist Party; Philadelphia Convention;
Presidency; Revolution. *For events during Washington's administration, see* Bank of the United
States; Bill of Rights; *Chisholm* v. *Georgia;* Jay's
Treaty; Judiciary Act of 1789; *Report on Manufactures.*

WASHINGTON, MARCHES ON

See Marches on Washington: 1941, 1963.

WATERGATE SCANDAL

The Watergate affair signifies the web of political scandals that plagued President Richard M.
Nixon from 1972 until his resignation in 1974.

On June 17, 1972, during the presidential
campaign of that year, Washington, D.C., police
officers arrested seven employees of the Committee to Re-Elect the President (CREEP), as they
were breaking into the Democratic National
Committee's headquarters in the Watergate
apartment complex. Details of the gathering
scandal emerged after the election in news stories in the *Washington Post* and from a Senate select committee's televised hearings that grew out
of them. Not only had Nixon, his aides, and his

reelection campaign conspired to sabotage the
president's Democratic challengers, but they
were now attempting to impede the investigation of the Watergate case.

In May 1973, Nixon was forced to agree to
the naming of a special prosecutor for the case,
Archibald Cox. Working with a federal grand
jury presided over by Judge John Sirica, Cox
subpoenaed secret tape recordings of presidential meetings and telephone conversations;
Nixon refused to release them, citing the doctrine of executive privilege. In October 1973, the
president ordered Cox's firing. This was done,
but only after the Justice Department's two
highest officials resigned rather than carry out
the order. Public outrage forced Nixon to reacti-
vate the Watergate Special Prosecution Force. A
new special prosecutor, Leon Jaworski, resumed
the legal battle to obtain the tapes.

In July 1974, the House Judiciary Committee adopted three articles of impeachment,
charging the president with obstruction of justice. The Supreme Court rejected the president's
claim of executive privilege in *United States* v.
Nixon (1974), upholding Judge Sirica's order that
the tapes be produced. Responding to the
Court's decision and the committee's vote,
Nixon released eight transcripts of subpoenaed
tapes; they provided the "smoking gun" evidence
that he had violated the law and that he had
known about the cover-up, which he had steadfastly denied. Public reaction and the prospect of
an impeachment trial forced Nixon to resign
from the presidency on August 9, 1974. His successor, Gerald Ford, pardoned him the next
month for all offenses he had committed or
might have committed during his presidency.

Controversy persists as to the significance of
Watergate. Nixon and his defenders argue that
he did nothing that other presidents of both parties had not already done; they claim that Nixon
was hounded from office by his political enemies. Nixon's critics reply that he endangered
the constitutional system by corrupting the electoral process and that he had sought to expand
the powers of the presidency beyond constitutional limits.

See also Elections: 1972; Nixon, Richard M.

WATSON, JAMES D.

(1928–   ), scientist. Watson earned a B.S. degree in zoology in 1947 from the University of Chicago and a Ph.D. from Indiana University in 1950. A National Research Council Fellowship, supplemented by a grant from the March of Dimes Foundation, enabled him to do postgraduate research first in Copenhagen and then in Cambridge, England, at the Cavendish Laboratories. Here Watson began collaborative work on DNA (deoxyribonucleic acid) with Francis Crick; they were joined shortly by Maurice Wilkins of King's College, London, who had been working independently in the same field. Their efforts led to the deciphering of the structure of DNA in 1953.

The search for the structure of the DNA molecule, which holds the secret of life, was the ultimate treasure hunt of that era of microbiology. DNA's capacity to replicate itself suggested that anyone who could solve the puzzle of its structure would open the gates to a new universe of scientific discoveries. Watson and Crick defined that structure as a double helix: a form like a long, gently twisted spiral staircase. The steps of the staircase are composed of alternating units of phosphate and deoxyribose (a sugar), and each rung is made of a pair of nitrogen-containing nucleotides, bonded by hydrogen. When the DNA molecule reproduces itself, it divides along the center of the step pairs; each side replicates and the new halves join to form a second double helix identical to the first.

From 1953 to 1956 Watson was Senior Research Fellow at Cal Tech; in 1956 he moved to Harvard University. In 1962 Watson, Crick, and Wilkins were awarded Nobel Prizes in medicine and physiology for their discovery of the structure of DNA.

In the mid-1950s Watson decided to write the story of their discovery and circulated the manuscript in draft form among a number of people. It raised a storm of protest from many of those mentioned in the narrative because of his critical remarks about other scientists, including the late Rosalind Franklin, who had worked in Wilkins's laboratory and who some thought deserved more credit for her contributions than she had received. At the time, the public image of science was one of high-minded devotion to the good of humanity and the advancement of knowledge; but the manuscript portrayed the field as fiercely competitive and highly personalized — undoubtedly far closer to the everyday reality. Watson's trenchant comments about many of his colleagues, however, offended even those who admired his accomplishments. Harvard University Press withdrew from an agreement to publish the book, and subsequently it was brought out by Atheneum in a somewhat revised version under the title *The Double Helix* in 1968.

That same year Watson became the director of the Cold Spring Harbor Laboratory on Long Island, New York. Under his leadership the laboratory thrived, functioning as a major center of DNA research in addition to its scientists' work on plant molecular biology, cell biochemistry, and cancer.

In 1989 Watson was chosen as the director of the Human Genome Project, a national effort funded by Congress through the National Institutes of Health to map the human genome, recording the identity and position of every unit in a chemical chain 3 billion links long. The largest biomedical research project ever mounted in the United States, its cost is estimated at $200 million each year for ten to fifteen years.

James D. Watson, *The Double Helix: A Personal Account of the Discovery of the Structure of DNA*, ed. Gunther S. Stent (1980).

D. LYDIA BRONTË

See also Science and Technology.

WAYNE, JOHN

(1907–1979), actor. Born Marion Michael Morrison in Winterset, Iowa, Wayne moved with his family to southern California in 1913. It was here that he acquired the nickname "Duke." In 1925, he entered the University of Southern California on a football scholarship. His coach arranged summer jobs for several of the players at Fox Film Studios, among them Duke Morrison. "My wages were thirty-five dollars a week," he later recalled. "My job was to lug furniture and props around."

His screen debut, as an unbilled stunt man in *Brown of Harvard,* came in 1926. The following summer, he and his teammate Ward Bond appeared in *The Drop Kick.* But it was in his capacity as a prop man at Fox that he first attracted the attention of John Ford. Beginning with *Mother Machree* (1928), Ford directed him in fourteen films over the years, including *Stagecoach* (1939), *The Long Voyage* (1940), *The Quiet Man* (1952), and *The Searchers* (1956). A father-son relationship developed between them that endured until Ford's death in 1973.

In 1930, another Fox director, Raoul Walsh, was casting *The Big Trail.* When Gary Cooper refused the leading role, Ford suggested his protégé. "To be a cowboy star," Walsh contended, "you've got to be six-foot-three or over, have no hips, and a face that looks right under a sombrero." Another stipulation was a "manly" name, and for *The Big Trail,* Marion Michael Morrison was given the nom-de-film John Wayne.

The Big Trail launched Wayne as a leading man, but Fox did not renew his contract. For the next nine years, he toiled in a long succession of B-movies. In a 1932 serial, *Singing Sandy,* Wayne achieved a dubious distinction — he became Hollywood's first singing cowboy. But *Stagecoach* rescued his career. It was, he later said, "my passport to fame."

Although mainly identified with westerns (he made over eighty in all), Wayne made a significant contribution to yet another distinctly American genre: the war movie. From John Ford's *Men without Women* (1929) to his most propagandistic picture *The Green Berets* (1968), Wayne appeared in seventeen war movies. As a rule, the setting was World War II — America's last "good" war. Most of these films — and, beginning with *Red River* (1948), his westerns as well — are characterized by a generational plot: Wayne, as either charismatic leader or unabashedly patriotic role model, guides the younger generation through its rite of passage to responsible adulthood.

Wayne's portrayal of Rooster Cogburn in *True Grit* earned for him the 1970 Academy Award, and was, in the words of critic Richard Schickel, "the true climax of a great and well-beloved career, if not as an actor, then as an American institution." His last film, *The Shootist* (1976), was on the order of an epitaph. In it, he plays an aging gunfighter who is dying of cancer, an illness that Wayne himself succumbed to three years later.

Of all the tributes to John Wayne, perhaps the most fitting was Vincent Canby's in the *New York Times:* "Mr. Wayne's extraordinary physique, along with his particular grace of movement and self-assurance of style, gave weight to minor movies and certified the authenticity of the great ones, to such an extent that we eventually came to see the myth as the man."

Emanuel Levy, *John Wayne: Prophet of the American Way of Life* (1988); Mark Ricci, Boris Zmijewsky, and Steven Zmijewsky, *The Films of John Wayne* (1972).

R. France

See also Movies.

WCTU

See Woman's Christian Temperance Union.

WEALTH AND ITS DISTRIBUTION

For early years in America, more is known about aggregate wealth and its distribution among people than about income. Usually, individuals knew, and sometimes preserved in written records, what they held in land, housing, barns, livestock, and so on, as well as their financial assets such as currency, bank deposits, bonds, stocks, and loans, and details of their inheritances. In contrast, there are few data on individual incomes, particularly for farmers and independent employees, at least until the advent of the federal income tax. We can make some definite statements about the distribution of wealth in the eighteenth and nineteenth centuries, but we must bear in mind the serious weakness in these calculations — namely, that a large minority, if not the majority, of families and single people had few assets other than farm animals, clothing, cooking utensils, and some consumer goods. Records of wealth, then, are largely for people whose income was above the average.

Economic Growth in Wealth

Studies of deeds of sale for various counties show that real value per acre of land grew at least 1 percent a year during the eighteenth century. The age and average wealth of U.S. counties by 1798 imply a growth rate of .7 percent a year for the value of land and houses, and 2 percent for houses. Thus, lands valued at only a few cents at the time of settlement in the seventeenth century had become worth many dollars per acre by 1800. The number of acres in private hands grew at rates equivalent to those of population settlement, first in Pennsylvania and later in Ohio and lands farther west.

The level of per capita wealth in the United States was remarkably high by 1800, being almost as high as that in any country. Values of lands had risen steadily throughout the eighteenth century in real terms — that is, in terms of the commodities the money would buy. Part of this growth in value was due to clearing of additional land and to improvements in transportation, particularly the road system, and part was due to the *perceived* increased value of American land — by both Europeans and Americans — after 1775. That the United States had won the war, that the federal Constitution had been ratified, and that Congress and the nation's first presidents functioned successfully meant that the new country was viable. Its stability promised good long-run returns to investors.

This perception was borne out by the economic growth of the antebellum period. A census of real estate in the United States made in 1798, coupled with censuses of wealth from 1850 to 1870, indicates the extent of the growth. Wealth in real estate per adult free male grew from $708 in 1798 to $1,050 in 1850 and to $1,540 in 1860, implying real growth rates of 1.4 to 1.7 percent a year, when adjusted for consumer price changes.

Inequality of Wealth

But the kind of growth described above provided an impetus to inequality in the distribution of wealth. In general, families who had settled first accumulated more than those who settled at a later time. On the other hand, growth may redound to the benefit of lower middle classes, if not to the poorest. Durable consumer goods such as watches or clocks may at one time be a luxury available only to the affluent. But if their price declines or incomes rise relative to the price, they may become more widely owned.

A case demonstrating some narrowing of inequality is shown in the distribution of housing values. If we consider all housing values in the country, from the most expensive to the cheapest, we find that the top 1 percent constituted 19 percent of total dwelling value in 1798 but only 6 percent in 1980; moreover, the top 50 percent of houses constituted 94 percent of total value in 1798 and 76 percent in 1980. At the earlier time, mansions dominated the value range, relative to the multitude of frame houses, log cabins, and even shanties. Today's mansions, relatively speaking, are not the luxuries they were at the end of the eighteenth century.

Nevertheless, there is a strong feeling — and strong evidence — that aggregate wealth in tangible form changed little in the past, at least over long periods of time. Consider first the distribution of real estate among adult free males having wealth in 1774 and 1798, two years for which data for the entire country are available. Inequality in wealth appears to have remained roughly the same in the two years. The rich in the top groups held similar proportions of wealth at the end of the colonial period and a quarter of a century later. And studies for years before 1774 in some colonial regions demonstrate considerable inequality.

Next, consider the years 1798 and 1860, again years for which information is available. The top groups held shares of wealth almost the same in each year. The proportion of adult free males with wealth was 49 percent in 1798 and 46 percent in 1860 — evidence that inequality changed little. An analysis of shares of total estate among groups of free males in 1870 (and in 1860) and the net worth of families and single people in 1962 shows a little less inequality in 1962 than a century earlier. And a 1983 study of real estate distribution yields a pattern similar to that for real estate in Ohio in 1835; this, in turn, is consistent with results for the United States in 1798, 1850, 1860, and 1870.

The general conclusion is that comparisons

between the distributions of *relative* inequality of wealth at various times in U.S. history reveal little change between 1798 and 1980. Studies for 1771 and 1774 again show few differences. This does not mean that studies for years of cyclical peaks and troughs, such as 1820, 1890, 1929, or 1933, would not demonstrate cyclical change. Nor would an accounting that captures dynamic changes in wealth, defined in ever-widening aspects, necessarily uncover further constancy.

But surely one's wealth should include not only tangible assets but also an estimate of, say, the present value of future Social Security payments. In the future, will the value of public health benefits be included? The very definition of *wealth* must be considered carefully. The change toward equality was, in one sense, infinite between 1860 and 1870 when slaves became free. And the tenuous rights of wives to estates in earlier centuries surely have changed. As Alexis de Tocqueville remarked, "There is greater equality of condition in Christian countries at the present day than there has been at any previous time, in any part of the world, so that the magnitude of what already has been done prevents us from foreseeing what is yet to be accomplished."

Alice Hanson Jones, *Wealth of a Nation to Be* (1980); Lee Soltow, *Distribution of Wealth and Income in the United States in 1798* (1989).

LEE SOLTOW

See also Colonial Economy; Depressions; Economic Growth; Government and the Economy; Income Tax; Mobility, Social and Economic; Poverty; Socialism; Unemployment.

WEAPONS

See Dueling; Gatling Gun; Guns and Gun Control; Indians; Nuclear Weapons: Origins and Legacy.

WEBSTER, DANIEL

(1782–1852), statesman, lawyer, and orator. Webster gained fame for his championship of a strong federal government, though he had been a rather extreme advocate of states' rights at the beginning of his forty years in public life. As a congressman (1813–1817) from New Hampshire, he opposed the War of 1812 and hinted at nullification. As a congressman (1823–1827) and a senator (1827–1841, 1845–1850) from Massachusetts, he became a leading proponent of federal action to stimulate the economy through protective tariffs, transportation improvements, and a national bank. He won renown as the defender of the Constitution by denouncing nullification when South Carolina adopted it. Long an opponent of slavery extension, he spoke against annexing Texas and against going to war with Mexico. He held, however, that no law was needed to prevent the further extension of slavery when he urged the Compromise of 1850 as a Union-saving measure.

As secretary of state (1841–1843, 1850–1852), Webster earned a reputation as one of the greatest ever to hold the office. His most notable achievement was the negotiation of the Webster-Ashburton Treaty, which settled a long-standing dispute over the Maine and New Brunswick boundary and ended a threat of war between Great Britain and the United States.

The most highly paid attorney of his time, Webster exerted considerable influence on the development of constitutional law. The Supreme Court under Chief Justice John Marshall adopted Webster's arguments in a number of significant cases, among them *Dartmouth College* v. *Woodward, McCulloch* v. *Maryland,* and *Gibbons* v. *Ogden.* These decisions strengthened the federal government as against the state governments, the judiciary as against the legislative and executive branches, and commercial and industrial as against agricultural interests.

As an orator, Webster had no equal among his American contemporaries. With the magic of the spoken word he moved judges and juries, visitors and colleagues in Congress, and vast audiences gathered for special occasions. His great occasional addresses, commemorating such historic events as the landing of the Pilgrims and the Battle of Bunker Hill, gave dramatic expression to his nationalism and conservatism. He reached the height of his eloquence in his reply to the nullificationist Robert Y. Hayne, a reply that concluded with the words "Liberty *and* Union, now and forever, one and inseparable!"

In politics Webster along with Henry Clay and John C. Calhoun formed what was called a "great triumvirate," though the three seldom combined except in opposition to President Andrew Jackson. All were ambitious for the presidency. Webster rivaled Clay for leadership of the Whig party but never obtained the party's presidential nomination except in his own state of Massachusetts. Whigs generally considered him unavailable because of his close association with the Bank of the United States and with Boston and New York businessmen, from whom he received generous subsidies.

Although identified with the Boston aristocracy, Webster had come from a plain New Hampshire farm background. A college education, at Dartmouth, helped him to rise in the world. Despite his large income he remained constantly in debt as a result of high living, unfortunate land speculations, and expenses as a gentleman farmer.

Irving H. Bartlett, *Daniel Webster* (1978); Maurice G. Baxter, *One and Inseparable: Daniel Webster and the Union* (1984).

RICHARD N. CURRENT

See also Dartmouth College v. *Woodward; Gibbons* v. *Ogden; McCulloch* v. *Maryland;* Webster-Hayne Debate; Whig Party.

WEBSTER-HAYNE DEBATE

Senator Daniel Webster of Massachusetts and Robert Y. Hayne of South Carolina participated in this famous debate of January 19–27, 1830. The highly protective "Tariff of Abominations" of 1828 was the paramount sectional issue in the late 1820s. Southerners, who exported cotton and imported manufactured goods from Europe, paid higher prices on these manufactured items because of the tariff. Increasingly aware that it failed to promote local manufacturing but that it translated into profits for northeastern producers, southern politicians hoped to forge a sectional alliance to repeal the tariff. If westerners and southerners could agree to vote for low tar-

iffs and cheap federal land, both regions would benefit economically.

Hayne proposed such an alliance between the South and West after Senator Thomas Hart Benton of Missouri denounced a pending proposal to restrict the sale of federal lands. Webster, a powerful voice for the northeastern manufacturing interests, responded to Hayne first by goading him into making a passionate claim for states' rights. Hayne blamed the Tariff of 1828 for economic difficulties in South Carolina. He argued that the federal Constitution was a compact among the states and raised the specter of nullification as an option for states harmed by federal action.

Hayne's remarks set the stage for Webster's famous reply. For two days, Webster held the floor and the attention of his colleagues and packed galleries. The Constitution was not a mere agreement of states, he said, but a compact of the American people guaranteeing freedom. "Liberty *and* Union, now and forever, one and inseparable!" By his impassioned rhetoric, Webster made the states' rights position look like treason, temporarily diffusing its potency.

See also Nullification Controversy; Tariff; Webster, Daniel.

WELFARE AND PUBLIC RELIEF

The principle of public responsibility for those in need was observed by the earliest colonists in British North America. Although funds made available for public assistance, as well as the unit of government administering them, varied greatly over time, Americans never wavered from this fundamental acceptance of public responsibility.

The English Parliament laid down the legal framework for public assistance in a series of enactments from 1597 to 1601 that became known as the Elizabethan Poor Law. Settlers carried this set of arrangements with them to the New World, and it continued to define obligations well into the twentieth century in the United States. Central to the system was the declaration that primary responsibility for care rested within the family: parents were expected to care for their children, and adult children, for their aged parents; eventually in many regions the obligation covered grandparents and grandchildren and in some cases extended even to brothers and sisters. Only when the family was unable to care for its own did public responsibility become operative. In the colonies, and later in the states, the effective unit of government came to be the town or township, the parish, the city, or the county. With the passage of time the unit most often was the county, as evidenced in the tens of thousands of county departments of public welfare that still carry chief responsibility for the administration of general relief funds.

The initial legislation permitted local governments to provide assistance through "outdoor" relief — that is, to persons in their own homes — or through the establishment of "indoor" institutions — almshouses for infirm dependent persons and workhouses for the presumably able-bodied poor. To assist orphaned, neglected, or abandoned children, local government had the power to assign them to other families by apprenticeship or indenture contracts (a process that survives today as foster placement). A later addition, stated in the English Act of Settlement (1662) and implemented with various degrees of severity in the colonies, required that legal residency in town or county be a precondition of eligibility to receive assistance. Although this system did not establish a legal right to assistance on the part of needy citizens, it did create a powerful presumption of the obligation of local government to assist them.

Local officials in village and countryside knew firsthand the conditions and resources of families who might fall into need. When sickness, disability, old age, or death of a spouse rendered persons dependent, they could petition for assistance knowing that if they could still manage a household their basic needs would be supplied in kind (with grants of food, fuel, clothing) or with modest cash grants. If no longer competent to care for themselves, they could be placed in the households of others who, for their services, received a somewhat larger stipend than the sums accorded for regular outdoor assistance. Only rarely, until urbanization accelerated in the nineteenth century, did localities resort to the institution of poorhouses to shelter dependent people. The able-bodied were left to fend for themselves; but very old widows and widowers, the mentally ill or retarded, the physically handicapped, orphans, and dependent children were cared for at levels that local propertied taxpayers would tolerate — not generous amounts but enough to provide a bare subsistence. Persons without legal residence were "warned out" of the community or "passed along" on a journey back to their original legal residence.

Colonial governments at the provincial level supplemented local relief funds only in times of natural catastrophe or following the dislocations of war. With independence and ratification of the U.S. Constitution, the traditional assignment of responsibility for public assistance to local units of government was secured in the Tenth Amendment, which reserved for the states and their subdivisions broad powers to provide for the general well-being of the citizenry. Here lay the source of political resistance to the assumption by the nation of any responsibility for public assistance until widespread and deep human need during the Great Depression of the 1930s prompted a number of New Deal measures involving direct federal grants and subsidies to sustain families devastated by hard times. An earlier precedent for direct federal action — the Freedmen's Bureau, 1865–1870 — provided food, clothing, and medicine to recently freed slaves, but it was only a temporary measure.

Throughout the nineteenth and into the twentieth century, modifications in the administration of relief programs had to be made as industrialization, urbanization, and economic centralization transformed American society. In large urban centers, overseers of the poor could no longer know the circumstances of persons who petitioned for relief, and government in those years did not yet have the bureaucratic capacity to control the expenditure of relief funds. The values and norms of a bourgeois, capitalistic society, moreover, did not easily tolerate those who would "feed at the public trough." The Anglo-American Protestant tradition had always honored hard work, thrift, and self-reliance, but in the Victorian era those values took on a harshness provoked by a striving, competitive social economy. Social norms distinguished sharply between those needy persons who were perceived as being "worthy" — widows, orphans, respectable aged persons, the severely handicapped — and the "unworthy" — those whose need was perceived to be rooted in laziness, intemperance, profligacy, or vice.

In an economy hungry for investment capital, every dollar "squandered" on the poor subtracted from the national substance. As dictates of efficiency and rationalization of economic resources took command, moreover, substantial citizens increasingly objected to the inefficiency and corruption they thought characterized the expenditure of tax moneys on the poor. Respectable community leaders began to speak and write of the "dangerous classes" (not unlike today's "underclass") and the threat they posed to social order and established norms of morality. In such an environment, local governments throughout the nation rushed to establish almshouses or poor farms where the disorderly lives of the poor could, it was hoped, be ordered. Proponents believed that the discipline of the poorhouse could be made so punitive that potential clients would pursue every strategy to avoid incarceration, and that such deterrence would lead to financial savings. In fact, persons forced by circumstance to seek shelter in these institutions were rarely employable or able to do profitable work within their walls, and the poorhouses were quickly crowded with a pathetic lot of unfortunates. People voicing the rhetorical hope that almshouses would serve as "bettering" institutions were doomed to disillusionment in the United States as well as other countries.

Contrary to expectations, the elaboration of the poorhouse system did not lead to a reduction in overall expenditures for public relief. Assistance to families in their own homes continued in most regions of the country, but it was rendered haphazardly and at levels lower than the lowest standards prevailing among the working poor.

The nineteenth century also saw the proliferation of tens of thousands of private benevolent or charitable agencies, many rooted in religious conviction, some church-sponsored, others moved by humane or philanthropic sentiments. Intended primarily to provide services, not financial assistance, to those deemed to be "worthy" of moral support, these agencies initiated a variety of programs to protect and uplift their clients. Although they promised "not alms but a friend," many of them were driven in fact by the needs of those whom they served to offer relief in kind and even in cash. Serving quasi-public functions, they frequently received substantial capital grants from local and state governments, which found it more convenient to lay out funds through direct subsidies than to erect elaborate public agency bureaucracies. Here was a precedent picked up again in the 1960s through the 1980s, whereby social work agencies provided human services to diverse clienteles, using large grants from federal, state, and local governments mixed together with funds from individuals, corporations, United Ways, and foundations.

Although traditionally the burden of public assistance had fallen primarily upon local government, states began to assume a share of the obligation beginning in the late 1820s with the founding of asylums for the insane. Subsequent generations created other specialized institutions — houses of refuge for dependent or delinquent youngsters, homes for the blind, the "deaf and dumb," and the mentally retarded, and state orphanages. To oversee these institutions, states gradually created supervisory boards and agencies that in time evolved into state welfare commissions with vastly increased resources and powers.

From state initiative, beginning in the 1910s, came programs to provide "mothers' assistance," which later was designated as aid to dependent children. The declared objective was to enable mothers of young children suffering economic need owing to the death of husband and father to stay at home and provide maternal care. But whatever the motives and intended goals, programs were weighed down with eligibility criteria difficult to meet: there was a means test, of course, for only the "truly needy" were deserving; there was also a test of marital status, and mothers deserted, separated, or divorced rarely qualified; and finally there were morals tests in that recipients were to be of sound character, able and willing to provide a "suitable home" for their offspring. It is estimated that less than 10 percent of mothers eligible solely on economic grounds were ever able to qualify. Throughout the nation, but especially in the South, mothers of a minority race were all but automatically excluded. Hard times in the early 1930s led to the discontinuance of many of these programs. But as a part of the Social Security Act (1935), federal funds were offered on a matching basis to the states for reinstituting programs of assistance. It was not until the 1960s that relatively objective economic criteria crowded out morals testing of eligibility, and from that time, an expanded program of Aid to *Families* of Dependent Children (AFDC, 1961) came to constitute the largest single expenditure of funds for direct public assistance.

The 1930s had marked a watershed in public assistance. Beginning in 1933, as emergency measures, federal funds were provided for direct relief grants to individuals, through the Federal Emergency Relief Administration, for example. Through the Civil Works Administration, the Works Progress Administration, the Civilian Conservation Corps, and the National Youth Administration, unemployed persons were hired on works projects fully funded and directly administered by agencies of the federal government.

Passage of the Social Security Act (1935) initiated a two-track system of welfare: one path insured participating employees against unemployment and old age (dependents and disabled persons were later brought under the umbrella of secured income); the other track provided federal funds through dollar-matching arrangements with state governments for specific categories of the needy. Striking differences persisted between the two tracks. Categorical aid was means-tested; its benefits, awarded at levels below the lowest prevailing income standards in a given community, were perceived by the public as unearned benefits provided as charity, not as entitlements. They invariably carried a stigma. Programs blanketed under social insurance, on the other hand, provided benefits earned by contributions into the system over a lifetime of employment. They provided benefits

at levels roughly corresponding to a recipient's employment and income experience, and neither the payments nor the recipients were in any way stigmatized.

To these basic programs of assistance and insurance a number of additions were made: food stamps (1964), Medicare insurance for persons retired under Social Security (1965), Medicaid payments to providers of health care to persons otherwise unable to afford them (1965), and a Supplementary Security Income (SSI) benefit for income-needy aged, blind, and disabled persons (1972). By the end of the 1970s these programs together with vastly increased expenditures for families of dependent children had substantially enlarged the costs of welfare assistance at every level of government and thus provoked a fiscal reaction and a clamor for "reform" of the "welfare mess" in the 1980s.

The poverty programs initiated during the 1960s dealt far more with provision of services than with public assistance. Federal funds invested in local community action programs were used for preschool education (Head Start), for legal aid, for local medical clinics, and for family planning, but none involved the transfer of money directly to persons in need.

In conclusion it can be observed that many features that had characterized public assistance from earliest colonial days lost force after the 1930s. Although family responsibility still operated as a moral norm, it no longer enjoyed legal force; the eligibility requirement of residency fell, at long last, to court rulings in 1969; the federal government came to be a major source of funding for public assistance and social insurance. But some traditions survived into the present era: assistance programs for families of dependent children and for general assistance remained stigmatized; general assistance to persons not covered by AFDC or SSI remained the exclusive obligation of local government; such programs were means-tested and awarded grudgingly at relatively low benefit levels; federal funding assumed major importance, but the administration of categorical programs resided primarily at the level of county government; human service agencies in the private sector received funding not only from private subscriptions and foundation grants but from federal, state, and local subsidies, grants, and contracts as well. Public assistance today, then, is a patchwork system, in which past traditions and present circumstances each plays a part.

Blanche D. Coll, *Perspectives in Public Welfare: A History* (1969); Michael B. Katz, *In the Shadow of the Poorhouse: A Social History of Welfare in America* (1986).

CLARKE A. CHAMBERS

See also Civilian Conservation Corps; Dix, Dorothea; Freedmen's Bureau; Great Society; Medicaid; Medicare; New Deal; Philanthropy; Poverty; Public Works Administration; Settlement Houses; Social Security; Unemployment; Works Progress Administration.

WELLES, ORSON

(1915–1985), actor, writer, director. Welles was born in Kenosha, Wisconsin. Although he had little formal education, he was, fortuitously, enrolled in the Todd School for Boys in Woodstock, Illinois. There he came under the tutelage of its headmaster, Roger Hill, who introduced the young prodigy to his favorite author, Shakespeare, and encouraged his theatrical experiments. At the time of his graduation from Todd in 1931, Welles had already formulated many of the basic concepts that would inform his adult career.

He then embarked on a painting tour of Ireland. While there, he made his professional debut in the Dublin Gate Theatre production of *Jew Süss*. Unable to parlay his Irish success into either a London or a New York engagement, Welles returned to the Todd School in 1932, where he and Hill prepared for publication a series of acting editions, *The Mercury Shakespeare*.

The following year, Welles met Katherine Cornell and her husband, Guthrie McClintic, who invited him to join a national tour. In July 1934, during the summer hiatus, Welles appeared in and directed his first film, a silent one-reeler, *Hearts of Age*. He made his New York debut the same year, as Tybalt in *Romeo and Juliet*.

Thereafter, he divided his time between radio and the stage and within a year was one of an elite band of radio actors commanding the highest salaries. He also formed a partnership with John Houseman, who, in 1935, became head of the Negro Theatre Project for the Works Progress Administration, with a mandate that included producing Shakespeare in Harlem. After one production, the so-called Voodoo *Macbeth* (1936), Houseman and Welles set up their own WPA unit. One year and three productions later, they formed the Mercury Theatre. Despite an increasingly tenuous relationship, Houseman stood by Welles through the modern-dress *Julius Caesar* (1937), "The War of the Worlds" broadcast (1938), and the filming of *Citizen Kane* (1941). The half-dozen years of their collaboration represent Welles's only sustained success in the theater, as well as his major achievements in radio and film.

The rhetorical content of Welles's radio programs, theatrical productions, and films was based on the most heightened emotional appeal possible in each of these mediums. Despite disclaimers that clearly identified it as a dramatization (including several announcements), "The War of the Worlds" broadcast, which resembled a series of news bulletins, was mistaken for actual news flashes. But to audiences who, by 1938, had become conditioned to their favorite radio programs being interrupted by news from Europe of increasingly gruesome atrocities, "The War of the Worlds" was chillingly real. The broadcast, not the Halloween prank that Welles intended, resulted in nationwide panic. *Citizen Kane,* the most honored film of the sound era, included all of the visual and auditory devices that Welles had thus far employed in radio and theater. Characteristically, he minimized the film's rhetorical content, the tedious and banal story of Charles Foster Kane, and concentrated instead on its expressive qualities, so that there appears more to the unfolding of events in *Citizen Kane* than is readily apparent in its mélange of evocations of popular culture.

It was the failure in 1939 of his theatrical masterpiece, *Five Kings,* an amalgam of Holinshed with Shakespeare's history plays, that finally led Welles to heed the call of Hollywood. Welles himself questioned the wisdom of his defection from the theater shortly before his death.

Film, he said, "is the most expensive mistress that anyone could have, and I've been trying to support her ever since." Only with *Citizen Kane* did Welles enjoy the same dominating role in film that had marked his stage productions. Beginning with *The Magnificent Ambersons* (1942), his career as a filmmaker was plagued by fiscal constraints and studio interference. Nevertheless, films like *The Lady from Shanghai* (1947) and *Touch of Evil* (1957) managed to fulfill most of his original intentions.

The practice of hiring out as an actor in other people's films began in the 1940s, notably as Rochester in *Jane Eyre* (1944) and Harry Lime in *The Third Man* (1949). Throughout the 1950s and 1960s, Welles lent his name as an actor to increasingly dubious film and television projects in order to finance his productions.

In his final years, Welles, ironically, was showered with awards by the same Hollywood establishment that had previously ostracized him. In three mediums — radio, theater, and film — he had managed the seamless joining of high art and popular culture that is so sought after and so seldom attained.

Richard France, *The Theatre of Orson Welles* (1977); James Naremore, *The Magic World of Orson Welles* (1991).

R. FRANCE

See also Movies.

WELLS-BARNETT, IDA B.

(1862–1931), anti-lynching crusader, journalist, and advocate for racial justice and women's suffrage. For Wells-Barnett, overcoming racism and halting the violent murder of black men was a central mission among her wide-ranging struggles for justice and human dignity. Born in Mississippi, she was educated at Rust University, actually a high school and industrial school. From 1884 to 1891 she taught in a rural school near Memphis and attended summer classes at Fisk University in Nashville.

A pattern of resistance to racial subordination was set early in her life. In 1887 she purchased a railroad ticket in Memphis and took a seat in the section reserved for whites. When she refused to move, she was bodily thrown off the train. She successfully sued the Chesapeake and Ohio Railroad for damages. Upon appeal, however, the Supreme Court of Tennessee reversed the lower court's ruling.

Wells-Barnett cofounded in 1891 the militant newspaper *Free Speech* in Memphis. She wrote scathing editorials denouncing local whites for lynching black men ostensibly to protect the sanctity of white womanhood but actually to eliminate them as economic competitors. Her pieces provoked a mob to burn her press while she was on a lecture trip to Philadelphia and New York. With a death threat hanging over her in Memphis, Wells-Barnett decided to remain in the North. During her exile, she wrote the pamphlet *A Red Record* (1895), a statistical account and analysis of three years of lynchings.

Wells-Barnett then launched an international crusade against lynching. She lectured in England in 1893 and 1894. She implored churches and organizations like the Young Women's Christian Association and the Woman's Christian Temperance Union to lend support. In 1895 she married Ferdinand Lee Barnett, lawyer and editor of the *Chicago Conservator*. They raised four children, and she adeptly managed career, marriage, motherhood, and social protest work.

Given the fervor of her determination to end racial discrimination and sexual inequality, it is not surprising that Wells-Barnett played a pivotal role in the development of a local and national network of black women's clubs. President of the Ida B. Wells Club and founder of the Negro Fellowship League and the Alpha Suffrage Club of Chicago, Wells-Barnett greatly influenced black life during the Progressive Era. She worked with Jane Addams to block the establishment of segregated public schools in Chicago and served as probation officer from 1913 to 1917 for the Chicago municipal court.

When the National Association for the Advancement of Colored People (NAACP) was formed in 1909, Wells-Barnett insisted that the leadership take an unwavering stand against lynching and years later withdrew when the organization's leadership failed to adopt the militant posture she advocated. She was also unable to persuade leaders in the women's suffrage movement to speak out against racism and denounce lynching. The young white leaders of the National American Woman Suffrage Association — and especially its southern members — feared that too close an association with black issues would jeopardize their cause. It would not be until 1930, the year before Wells-Barnett's death, that black and white women joined forces to launch the Association of Southern Women for the Prevention of Lynching.

Alfreda M. Duster, *Crusade for Justice: The Autobiography of Ida B. Wells* (1970); Thomas C. Holt, "The Lonely Warrior: Ida B. Wells-Barnett and the Struggle for Black Leadership," in John Hope Franklin and August Meier, eds., *Black Leaders of the Twentieth Century* (1982), 39–62.

DARLENE CLARK HINE

See also Lynching; Suffrage.

WEST, THE

See Cowboys; Expansion, Continental and Overseas; Gold Rushes; Pony Express.

WHARTON, EDITH

(1862–1937), author and philanthropist. Wharton was born into the wealthy "old New York" society of the late nineteenth century, and the atmosphere of her world permeates most of her work. She married a wealthy Bostonian and ostensibly settled into the life of the comfortable. But the marriage was not successful and the Whartons divorced in 1913.

Partly to release the energies confined by the rigid social strictures and anti-intellectualism of her aristocratic world, and later to relieve the unhappiness of her marriage, Wharton turned to writing. She privately printed her first book of poems in 1878, when she was sixteen. Wharton wrote two collections of short stories, *The Greater Inclination* (1899) and *Crucial Instances* (1901), and a book on interior decoration, *The Decoration of Houses* (1897), before publishing her first novel, *The Valley of Decision,* in 1902. By this time, Wharton had also formed a close personal and literary friendship with Henry James, and their work continues to be compared for similarities in both style and theme.

All her works were favorably reviewed, but Wharton did not receive critical acclaim until *The House of Mirth* appeared in 1905. Set in old New York in the first years of the twentieth century, *The House of Mirth* is a complex study of the rise and fall of the tragic heroine, Lily Bart, as she moves downward through the intricate class system of aristocratic New York. The novel is valuable not only for its study of human psychology but also for its depiction of the changing social patterns of a country undergoing rapid economic growth, and the consequent invasion of the nouveaux riches into this bastion of culture and what had become moral corruption.

The themes evident in *The House of Mirth* — the moral decay of an indolent society, the waste of treating women as decorative objects, the need for the social order to protect the values of decency, honesty, and commitment, the belief that the true dramas of history are worked out within the soul — characterized Wharton's work throughout the sixty years of her career. At her death she had published seventeen novels, seven novelettes, eleven volumes of short stories, and numerous miscellaneous works. Included in the novels was another masterpiece, the work for which she is best known, *The Age of Innocence* (1920), for which she won a Pulitzer Prize in 1921.

In her lifetime, Wharton endured the social upheavals perpetrated by the robber barons, the tremendous physical and psychic wounds of World War I (she won the Legion of Honor in 1916 for her refugee work), the frenetic healing of the 1920s, and the Great Depression. During much of this time she lived in France, satirically chronicling — with the advantages and disadvantages of distance — the disappearing world of the 1870s through the 1920s. Her autobiography, *A Backward Glance* (1934), is emblematic of her crisp, reticent style, her interest in the past, and her ability to foreshadow a time when women as artists, and as players, would be taken more seriously.

Because of the focus on women in most of her major fiction, Wharton's career had a revival in the 1980s, as critics came to realize that this artist who so often focused on an earlier culture had also predicted the new. Wharton's canon, then, remains valuable to students of history for what it reveals about a particular time and place in American culture and about the expatriates who fled it to live in Europe. It is valuable, too, for its revelations of the tragic aspects of human nature. As the *New York Times* said in her obituary, "There can be no reading of human character without ethics, no tragedy without conflict between things that matter. This Edith Wharton knew and never forgot, and by that token we know her for the artist she was."

Elizabeth Ammons, *Edith Wharton's Argument with America* (1980); R. W. B. Lewis, *Edith Wharton: A Biography* (1975).

MARLENE A. SPRINGER

See also Expatriates and Exiles; Literature.

WHIG PARTY

In 1834 political opponents of President Andrew Jackson organized a new party to contest Jacksonian Democrats nationally and in the states. Guided by their most prominent leader, Henry Clay, they called themselves Whigs — the name of the English antimonarchist party — the better to stigmatize the seventh president as "King Andrew." They were immediately derided by the Jacksonian Democrats as a party devoted to the interests of wealth and aristocracy, a charge they were never able to shake completely. Yet during the party's brief life, it managed to win support from diverse economic groups in all sections and to hold its own in presidential elections.

Although unable to unite behind a single candidate in 1836, thus permitting Jackson's handpicked successor Martin Van Buren to obtain an electoral majority, the Whigs won a popular vote for their candidates that was close to the popular tally for the Democrats. And in 1840 and 1848, the party captured the White House. Their only loss in a presidential election during the decade occurred in 1844 when Clay lost by a hair to the Democrats' dark horse James K. Polk, who had greater appeal to voters favoring the ex-

pansion both of territory and slavery. But in 1852, as slavery's expansion became the great issue of American politics, the Whigs suffered a drastic decline in popularity. And by 1854 they had given up the ghost, no longer able to hold the support of "cotton Whigs," who found a more congenial political home in the Democratic party, or of "conscience Whigs," who helped form the new Republican party.

Historians have interpreted the Whigs in strikingly different ways. They have been seen as champions of banks, business, corporations, economic growth, the positive liberal state, humanitarian reform, and morality in politics, and as opponents of expansionism, executive tyranny, states' rights, labor, and the democratic suffrage, among other things. These dissimilar assessments are unsurprising given the heterogeneity of the party itself, in its leaders, policies and programs, political style, and rank-and-file supporters.

The Whig party was founded by individuals united only in their antagonism to Jackson's war on the Second Bank of the United States and his high-handed measures in waging that war and ignoring Supreme Court decisions, the Constitution, and Indian rights embodied in federal treaties. Beyond that, however, there were Whigs and Whigs. Some played the demagogic anti-Catholic game; others scorned it. Some spoke critically of working people; others, admiringly. Detailed studies of the Whig party in the states and biographies of such Whig leaders as Clay, William Seward, Daniel Webster, and Horace Greeley reveal dissimilar policies from one state to another and important differences in the character, beliefs, and actions of the leaders. Thurlow Weed was much more opportunistic than his New York State colleague Seward. Thaddeus Stevens of Pennsylvania was more high-minded and not nearly as pragmatic as Clay of Kentucky. For all Clay's political flexibility and his lust for the presidency, he could still inspire the young congressman from Illinois, Abraham Lincoln.

The tendency of Whig officeholders to vote as a bloc on certain issues, in opposition to Democratic blocs, helps account for the tendency of some historians to exaggerate the extent and depth of Whig single-mindedness. In Congress, Whigs supported the Second Bank of the United States, a high tariff, distribution of land revenues to the states, relief legislation to mitigate the effects of the great depression that followed the financial panics of 1837 and 1839, and federal reapportionment of House seats (a "reform" likely to enlarge Whig representation in Congress). Studies of voting patterns in the states reveal Whig support of banks, limited liability for corporations, prison reform, educational reform, abolition of capital punishment, and temperance. Although the Whig party was hardly an antislavery party, free blacks and abolitionists overwhelmingly preferred it to more ardently proslavery Jacksonian Democrats.

The old notion propagated by the party's enemies — that the Whigs drew their support primarily from the rich and the well-to-do — has been sharply modified by modern scholarship. The relatively few rich men in the country did prefer Whigs to Democrats, but by a modest margin. Whigs fared well at the polls among people of all classes in economically dynamic communities heavily engaged in commerce. Jacksonian propaganda did induce many people to regard the Whigs as an upper-class party (not organized working men, however, whose leaders dismissed both Democrats and Whigs as "humbugs"). Yet Whigs could win presidential elections, governorships, and state legislature majorities only because they attracted mass support. Although they received the votes of many small farmers, shopkeepers, clerks, and artisans, they appear to have appealed particularly to what some modern historians call distinctive ethnocultural groups: evangelical as opposed to liturgical Protestants; moralists and abstainers; persons unhappy with brutal treatment of blacks and Native Americans. In some states Whig leaders seemed so critical of political parties that they appeared to be religious zealots rather than party leaders. Yet for all their antiparty rhetoric, Whigs were as realistic and efficiently organized as their Democratic opponents.

American major parties develop their own distinctive auras that are no less real for being intangible and unmeasurable. Whig and Democratic leaders were strikingly similar in such significant characteristics as wealth, occupational prestige, a fundamentally conservative social ideology, materialism, and opportunism. These similarities help explain why both major parties were attractive to moneyed men. But it is unwise to discount the significance of the unique blending of moral values and social philosophies that some imaginative historians have recently discerned in Whig leaders, a blending that helps account for the Whigs' special appeal to one rather than another kind of individual.

Ultimately, however, the Whigs are best understood as an American major party trying to be many things to many men, ready to abandon one deeply held "conviction" for another in the drive for political power. The party died not because its unique aura no longer appealed to voters but because it could not cope effectively or persuasively with what after the Compromise of 1850 became the great issue of American politics, the expansion of slavery.

Ronald P. Formisano, *The Transformation of American Political Culture* (1983); Daniel Walker Howe, *The Political Culture of the American Whigs* (1979); Edward Pessen, *Jacksonian America: Society, Personality, and Politics,* rev. ed. (1985).

EDWARD PESSEN

See also Bank of the United States; Clay, Henry; Democratic Party; Elections: 1836, 1840, 1844, 1848, 1852; Greeley, Horace; Harrison, William Henry; Jackson, Andrew; Republican Party; Seward, William H.; Stevens, Thaddeus; Taylor, Zachary; Webster, Daniel.

WHISTLER, JAMES McNEILL

(1834–1903), artist. Following an unsuccessful career at the U.S. Military Academy at West Point, Whistler worked for the U.S. Coast and Geodetic Survey where he strengthened his skills in the graphic arts, particularly in the medium of engraving.

In 1855 he moved to Europe to pursue an artistic career. He settled permanently in London in 1859, traveling frequently to Paris to visit friends and keep abreast of developments in French art. Whistler associated himself with that circle of artists espousing the avant-garde theories of the realists. Through Henri Fantin-Latour he met such artists as Gustave Courbet, Édouard Manet, and Edgar Degas.

After Whistler exhibited his painting *The White Girl* (1862) in the famous Salon des Refusés of 1863 (which coincidentally featured Manet's controversial *Le déjeuner sur l'herbe*), critics and artists alike began to take notice of his work. This painting, later given the additional title *Symphony in White No. 1,* is a curious work that evokes, on one hand, the portraits of Diego Velázquez and, on the other, the suppressed sensualism of Pre-Raphaelite paintings. It was one of the first works in which he flirted with a seminal impressionistic oriental vocabulary.

Whistler rejected the high-keyed palette of the impressionists, but his continued interest in the two-dimensional nature of Japanese prints led him, in the early 1870s, to a series of paintings close in spirit to the works of Manet. Among these are *Arrangement in Gray and Black No. 1: Portrait of the Artist's Mother* (1871; popularly known as *Whistler's Mother*) and *Arrangement in Gray and Black No. 2: Thomas Carlyle* (1872–1873). The 1870s were the years in which Whistler painted his most abstract and perhaps most successful canvases, works that are often stylistically referred to as tonal impressionism. Moved by the possibilities of intellectually equating painting with the more nonobjective realm of music, he employed such terms as *arrangement, nocturne,* and *symphony* for his titles. Often these paintings carry two titles — a musical one to evoke subjective thought and another, more traditional, objective one. One of the better examples is *Nocturne in Black and Gold: The Falling Rocket* (1874), a painting exhibited in 1877 and verbally attacked by the critic John Ruskin. This led to a celebrated court battle that ended in a moral rather than financial victory for Whistler.

The Peacock Room, now in the Freer Gallery in Washington, D.C., executed in London in 1866–1867 for the residence of Frederick R. Leyland, shows Whistler's inventiveness in incorporating oriental motifs into interior design. These ideas were to play a major role in the vocabular-ies of the art nouveau and symbolist movements. Whistler's lecture, "Ten O'Clock" (1885), eventually translated and published in France, and his book, *The Gentle Art of Making Enemies* (1890), found a receptive audience in Europe and America.

Roy McMullen, *Victorian Outsider: A Biography of J. A. M. Whistler* (1973); John Walker, *James Abbott McNeill Whistler* (1987).

KENNETH W. WALPUCK

See also Expatriates and Exiles; Painting and Sculpture.

WHITE, EDWARD D.

(1845–1921), chief justice, U.S. Supreme Court. Following service in the Confederate army, White read law in New Orleans and took some courses in what would later be the Tulane Law School. He passed the Louisiana bar in 1868, became active in state Democratic politics, and was elected to the state senate in 1874. When the Democrats swept back into power at the end of Reconstruction, Governor Francis T. Nicholls named White to the Louisiana Supreme Court. A few years later, however, another faction of the party gained control and rewrote the constitution to make the thirty-four-year-old White ineligible because of his age. The Nicholls faction regained power in 1890, and the governor appointed White to the U.S. Senate, where he defended states' rights as well as business interests against any encroachment by the federal government.

When Justice Samuel Blatchford of the U.S. Supreme Court died in 1893, tradition dictated that another New Yorker be named to his seat. But the two New York senators so despised President Grover Cleveland that they blocked his first two nominees. Although Cleveland had been opposed by White on the tariff issue, the president agreed with White's conservative views and named him to the Court, daring the Senate to reject one of its own. Although confirmed quickly, White refused to take his seat on the Court until he had secured high protective rates for sugar in the 1894 tariff.

White served as an associate justice from

1894 to 1911, when President William Howard Taft elevated him to the chief justiceship. Although generally conservative, he cannot be grouped with those who automatically opposed any reform measure that interfered with private property. He voted with the minority in the infamous 1905 *Lochner* decision, invalidating a maximum-hours law for bakers, yet he voted in favor of freedom of contract in voiding a federal ban against yellow-dog agreements (by which workers agreed not to join a union) in *Adair* v. *United States* (1908). He supported a state maximum-hours law for women in *Muller* v. *Oregon* (1908), yet a few years later voted against a similar law for men in *Bunting* v. *Oregon* (1917). Although he had been a strong champion of states' rights as a senator, once on the Court he voted consistently to uphold federal regulatory powers in cases such as *Champion* v. *Ames* (1903) and *Hipolite Egg Co.* v. *United States* (1911).

White's major doctrinal contributions came in the *Insular* cases and in antitrust decisions. The acquisition of overseas possessions raised the question of whether the Constitution followed the flag, so that American colonies enjoyed the same legal status as the mainland. White argued that the test should be the degree of "incorporation" or lack of it that Congress granted to these possessions through statute or treaty, and he ultimately saw the Court adopt this view in *Dowdell* v. *United States* (1911).

White also espoused the "rule of reason" in interpreting the Sherman Antitrust Act (1890). Almost from the time he came on the Court he believed that the statute did not outlaw all restrictions on competition, but only unreasonable ones. He spoke for the Court in *Standard Oil of New Jersey* v. *United States* (1911), in which it adopted this position. White voted with the majority to uphold segregation in *Plessy* v. *Ferguson* (1896), but he also voted with the majority to strike down southern peonage laws and to invalidate racially restrictive zoning ordinances.

White was not a "great" chief justice, but it was said that his "striking personality and his lovable human traits" made him well liked and well respected as head of the nation's highest Court, and Washington as well as the nation mourned his death.

Marie C. Klinkhamer, *Edward Douglass White, Chief Justice of the United States* (1943).

MELVIN I. UROFSKY

See also Antitrust Movement; *Lochner* v. *New York*; *Muller* v. *Oregon*; *Plessy* v. *Ferguson*; Supreme Court.

WHITE SUPREMACISTS

See Ku Klux Klan; Reconstruction; Segregation.

WHITMAN, WALT

(1819–1892), poet. Born on Long Island, New York, Whitman was the son of a house builder. Largely self-educated, he learned the printer's trade and taught school. Between 1838 and 1855 he edited papers in New York, Brooklyn, and New Orleans while turning out unremarkable poems, sketches, and stories and immersing himself in political and cultural life. He delighted in oratory and grand opera, became a devotee of phrenology, and mixed happily with urban crowds, relishing ferry-boat pilots, Broadway omnibus drivers, firemen, and Bowery roughs. His mind was "simmering" as he took in the kaleidoscopic scene — his reading Shakespeare, Carlyle, Goethe, George Sand, and, above all, Emerson brought it to a "boil."

Out of this chemistry came *Leaves of Grass.* What he called a "language experiment" exfoliated in successive stages from the 12 poems of the 1855 edition to the more than 350 poems of the "deathbed" edition of 1891. It was at once a ventilation of his mind and memory and a qualified celebration of American history, politics, geography, occupations, and speech.

Whitman's protean work was slow to win acceptance. Antebellum reviewers, shocked by his anatomical delineations of the "body electric," pronounced him the "dirtiest beast" of his age and mocked his neologisms and stylistic oddities. Today he is recognized as one of the most original and influential American poets and by some as a forerunner of homosexual liberation.

During the Civil War, as "wound-dresser" to the soldiers of both camps in military hospitals, Whitman witnessed the war's carnage. *Drum-*

Taps and Sequel (1865) commemorated the suffering and heroism of the common soldier. "When Lilacs Last in the Dooryard Bloom'd," the finest threnody on the war, elegized Abraham Lincoln, the emblem of Whitman's idealized republic.

Even before the war, he had been troubled by the money-mania of his fellow citizens and by signs of class polarization. In fact, *Leaves* can be read as Whitman's effort to stifle his apprehensions about America's future by creating a "Kosmos" in which national blemishes, if not denied, are overwhelmed by geographical space as much as by the energy and latent nobility of the people. The war severely tested that faith. Although the sundered Union coalesced, he could not expunge the memory of an entire nation seemingly "bandaged and bloody *in hospital*," and the sordidness of the Gilded Age further taxed his confidence.

The hollowness of much of his later verse — rhetorical prophecies churned out for ceremonial occasions — contrasts with the buoyancy and audacity of "Song of Myself," Whitman's most remarkable poem. His prose, however, such as the explosive jeremiad *Democratic Vistas* (1871) or recollections of a happier past like *Specimen Days* (1882), retains the old freshness and vigor.

Crippled by strokes, Whitman ended his days more honored abroad than at home. He acknowledged without bitterness "that I have not gain'd acceptance in my own times" and fell back "on fond dreams of the future — anticipations." They would be realized sooner than he supposed.

Justin Kaplan, *Walt Whitman: A Life* (1980); M. Wynn Thomas, *The Lunar Light of Whitman's Poetry* (1987).

DANIEL AARON

See also Literature.

WHITNEY, ELI

(1765–1825), inventor and manufacturer. Whitney exhibited mechanical skills and an entrepreneurial spirit at an early age. He mastered the use of the tools in the workshop on his father's farm in Westborough, Massachusetts, became a general mechanical handyman in the area, and organized a successful nail-making business.

After graduating from Yale, he moved to Georgia where he had been hired as a tutor, but quickly found an opportunity that was more to his liking and promised great rewards. Learning that the tedious and time-consuming task of picking the seeds out of cotton lint blocked the commercial production of short-staple, green-seed cotton, he decided to create a machine that would do the job. He wrote to his father in September 1793 that in ten days he produced a prototype gin that allowed one man to do the work of fifty. He declined an offer of "a Hundred Guineas" for his invention and decided instead "to relinquish my school and turn my attention to perfecting the Machine." He quickly improved his model, secured a patent, and in 1794, with a partner supplying financial backing, began manufacturing his gin. "It is generally said by those who know anything about it, that I shall make a Fortune by it," he noted optimistically.

Almost overnight the gin made cotton production economically feasible, breathing new life into a languishing slave system by providing the South with a new commercial crop and the world with relatively cheap, high-quality cotton. But Whitney did not benefit financially from his revolutionary invention. Others had succeeded in producing similar gins at about the same time, and Whitney's device was simple and easy to copy. When he decided to charge royalties for use of his gin, rather than to sell it outright, cotton planters bought competing gins or unauthorized copies of Whitney's. Whitney went to court to protect his patent and even managed to win a patent infringement suit, but rivals continued to produce and sell their machines. The competition, the legal costs, and finally, his inability to get his patent renewed deprived Whitney of most of his anticipated profits.

In the meantime, however, Whitney found a new opportunity. In 1798, the federal government granted him a contract to produce ten thousand muskets using what he promised would be a new process to make the various parts of the weapons interchangeable. Once again Whitney's mechanical talents led him to a revolutionary innovation; the manufacture of products with interchangeable parts became a key element in modern industrial production.

Although the concept of interchangeable parts did not originate with Whitney and did not become widespread until the later development of the machine tool industry, Whitney's factory at Mill Rock, near New Haven, Connecticut, was one of the earliest to use the method successfully. Whitney designed and built the necessary machinery and trained workers to use it, tasks that took longer than he originally expected. But, in the end, he produced the weapons with interchangeable parts. This time Whitney benefited financially from his innovation. Additional contracts from the federal government and from several states provided new work and income for his arms factory.

Although he lived through massive political and economic changes in the nation, Whitney showed little interest in such matters, except on the few occasions when policies directly affected his business. He retained little of the religious puritanism of his upbringing and was unconcerned with the religious ferment in the nation during his adult life. He single-mindedly devoted himself to his business affairs and died a wealthy man. His successful firm passed to his son and then to his grandson and was eventually sold to the Winchester Arms Company.

Constance McL. Green, *Eli Whitney and the Birth of American Technology* (1956); Jeanette Mirsky and Allan Nevins, *The World of Eli Whitney* (1952).

HAROLD D. WOODMAN

See also Cotton Gin; Industrial Revolution; Science and Technology.

WILLARD, FRANCES

(1839–1898), temperance activist and women's rights leader. Willard was born near Rochester, New York. In 1845 her father settled the family on a frontier farm in Wisconsin Territory. Frances grew up a tomboy (she preferred to be called "Frank") and did her best to get an edu-

cation, despite her father's opposition. As a young woman, she preferred women's company, and her one serious romance, to a Methodist minister, ended badly. She found the ideas of women's rights inspiring and determined to dedicate herself to the elevation of her sex. The life she chose was female-centered, economically and emotionally independent of men. After teaching for several years and working for women's benevolent societies, she became president of the Evanston College for Ladies in 1871. Two years later, the college was absorbed into Northwestern University, and Willard became its first dean of women. But the university's president was her former fiancé, and conflicts over her position and his authority soon led her to resign.

In 1874, temperance activism became the focus of her life and the medium through which she expressed her feminist intentions. The year before, a "crusade" of praying women had swept through New York and Ohio, shutting down saloons and reviving the dormant temperance movement. In 1874 the Woman's Christian Temperance Union (WCTU) was formed, and Willard was elected corresponding secretary. She saw in temperance a way to expand the public activities and civic awareness of conservative, middle-class, churchgoing women. Her sympathy with these women, coupled with her great organizational skills, made her the leading woman reformer of the era. She transformed women's rights, which had been hampered by its radical antebellum origins and New England roots, into a movement in tune with the conservatism of the Gilded Age.

Convinced that she could induce the WCTU to support woman suffrage, she campaigned for its presidency and, in 1879, was elected to that office, which she held for the rest of her life. She began her drive for suffrage by calling for a "home protection ballot," a limited form of votes for women on temperance matters. In 1881, she introduced Susan B. Anthony, America's leading suffragist, on the WCTU platform, and in 1882, she led the organization to endorse woman suffrage outright, decades before any other national women's association.

Willard transformed the WCTU from a Protestant benevolent society into a multi-issue reform organization. She declared a "Do-Everything Policy" and set up dozens of departments to reform everything from obscene literature to labor conditions. By rooting her organization in values held dear by her female constituency ("For God and Home and Native Land") and by appreciating their need for expanded public activity, she was able to prevail upon most WCTU members to follow her lead.

She attempted to use her considerable power as WCTU president to influence reform politics. In 1882, she joined forces with the Prohibition party and in 1890 plunged into the formation of a People's party. But she was unable to commit the populists to woman suffrage or the prohibitionists to populism, and the women of the WCTU found politics a final step they could not take.

In 1892, Willard went to live in England with Lady Henry Somerset. There, influenced by Fabian socialism, she decided that poverty rather than intemperance was the cause of social ills. These new beliefs, her many absences, and her failed political efforts eroded her organizational position, so that when she died at the age of fifty-eight, her vision for the WCTU died with her.

Ruth Bordin, *Frances Willard: A Biography* (1986); Mary Earhart, *Frances Willard: From Prayers to Politics* (1944).

ELLEN CAROL DuBOIS

See also People's Party; Prohibition and Temperance; Suffrage; Woman's Christian Temperance Union.

WILLIAMS, ROGER

(1603?–1683), religious dissenter and founder of Rhode Island (1636). During his fifty years in New England, Williams was a staunch advocate of religious toleration and separation of church and state. Reflecting these principles, he and his fellow Rhode Islanders framed a colony government devoted to protecting individual "liberty of conscience." This "lively experiment" became Williams's most tangible legacy, though he was best known in his own time as a radical Pietist and the author of polemical treatises defending his religious principles, condemning the orthodoxy of New England Puritanism, and attacking the theological underpinnings of Quakerism.

His lifelong search for a closer personal union with God forged his beliefs and ideas. Rejecting the moderate theology of Puritanism, Williams embraced the radical tenets of separatism, turned briefly to Baptist principles, but ultimately declared that Christ's true church could not be known among men until Christ himself returned to establish it. From his reading of the New Testament, in which Christ had commanded religious truth and error to coexist in every nation until the end of the world, Williams concluded that liberty of conscience — "soul liberty" as he called it — was necessary because no one could know for certain which form of religion was the true one God had intended.

These views, among others, kept him embroiled in protracted religious and political controversies throughout his life. His banishment from Massachusetts in 1636, when he fled into the wilderness and founded the town of Providence, was only the first of several disputes that consumed his energies. For Williams, the banishment became a kind of personal badge of courage. In his dealings with neighboring Puritans, he never missed an opportunity to remind them of the wrong they had committed against him. In numerous polemical writings, he engaged in a prodigious religious debate with John Cotton, the Boston minister, and referred often to his banishment as proof of the human injustice that resulted from intolerance.

In his own colony, Williams could not resolve the political conflicts that divided Rhode Islanders into contending factions. Attempting to protect Indian land from expropriation, he became involved in endless boundary disputes with neighbors and speculators from surrounding colonies. In the 1670s, as the Quakers were gaining political power in Rhode Island, Williams tried to discredit the teachings of George Fox; he succeeded only in raising public doubts about his sincere commitment to the idea of "soul liberty." Although his friendship with the Narragansett Indians helped sustain generally peaceful relations between the Indians and English settlers until the outbreak of King Philip's

War (1676), some Puritan leaders suspected his close ties with the Narragansetts had blurred his ability to see them objectively.

His death went mostly unnoticed. It was the American Revolution that transformed Williams into a local hero — Rhode Islanders came to appreciate the legacy of religious freedom he had bequeathed to them. Although he has often been portrayed by biographers as a harbinger of Jeffersonian Democracy, most scholars now conclude that Williams was less a democrat than a "Puritan's Puritan" who courageously pushed his dissenting ideas to their logical ends.

Glenn W. LaFantasie, ed., *The Correspondence of Roger Williams*, 2 vols. (1988); Edmund S. Morgan, *Roger Williams: The Church and the State* (1967).

GLENN W. LAFANTASIE

See also New England Colonies; Puritanism; Religion.

WILLIAMS, TENNESSEE

(1911–1983), playwright. Considered by some to be America's premier dramatist, Williams achieved popular and critical success with plays about fragile individuals trapped in desperate circumstances. His best-known works — among them *The Glass Menagerie* (1945), *A Streetcar Named Desire* (1947), *Summer and Smoke* (1948), *Cat on a Hot Tin Roof* (1955), and *Sweet Bird of Youth* (1959) — are characterized by decadent southern settings, beautifully cadenced dialogue, expressive stage pictures, bizarre humor, and an aura of sexuality. His greatest legacy is a set of legendary characters, including Blanche DuBois and Big Daddy. Their eccentric personalities and larger-than-life dimensions have appealed to star performers — Laurette Taylor, Jessica Tandy, Marlon Brando, and Vivien Leigh, to name a few — who have found them ideal acting vehicles.

Williams was himself a colorful and complex figure. Like his characters, he was restless and driven by contradictory impulses: he was both gentle and fiery, lonely and gregarious, optimistic and fatalistic. His homosexuality, detailed in *Memoirs* (1975), contributed certain values and sympathies to his plays. But of more significance was the influence of his sister Rose. His devoted companion during their childhood in Mississippi and St. Louis, she later became mentally unstable and withdrew from the world. Williams believed her condition was not helped by their parents' unhappy marriage and his own insensitivity to her. In 1937, Rose underwent a prefrontal lobotomy, then considered therapeutic, which necessitated lifelong care in an institution. So deeply did Williams empathize with her trauma that it shaped his master theme — the confining nature of human existence.

A prolific author, Williams wrote more than seventy plays, but his reputation rests largely on his first two Broadway hits. *The Glass Menagerie*, set in a cramped apartment, focuses poignantly on the escapist dreams of a destitute family. It features the unforgettable Amanda Wingfield, who avoids the hopeless present by living in her southern-belle past, when she was courted by "gentleman callers." Amanda's daughter seems modeled on Rose Williams: the fragile Laura who retreats from reality to play with glass figurines. In his next play, *A Streetcar Named Desire*, Williams created two now-famous characters, Blanche DuBois and Stanley Kowalski. The playwright's beloved French Quarter in New Orleans provides the setting for a tenacious struggle between high-strung, guilt-ridden Blanche and brutal Stanley. He crushes her spirit, and as Blanche leaves for a mental institution, she speaks movingly of her dependence on "the kindness of strangers." *Streetcar* earned Williams the first of his two Pulitzer Prizes.

After *The Night of the Iguana* (1961), Williams suffered a creative crisis and abandoned many of his techniques. Critics disliked the change. Although his later plays lack the memorable characters and rich, suggestive atmospheres of his earlier ones, several are noteworthy. *Out Cry* (1971), also called *The Two-Character Play*, is a nonrealistic drama about a brother and sister locked in a theater. The autobiographical *Vieux Carré* (1978) presents his initial stay in New Orleans during the 1930s from the perspective of his older self, who laments the waning of his imaginative powers.

An artist of international renown, Williams deserves to be ranked with Eugene O'Neill and Arthur Miller among American playwrights. At his best, he outshines both. His lyrical plays have also made a lasting impact on the work of a generation of younger dramatists, including Lanford Wilson and Beth Henley.

Donald Spoto, *The Kindness of Strangers: The Life of Tennessee Williams* (1985); Tennessee Williams, *Memoirs* (1975).

BRUCE J. MANN

See also Theater.

WILLIAMS, WILLIAM CARLOS

(1883–1963), poet, essayist, novelist, short-story writer, and physician. Educated at the University of Pennsylvania (M.D., 1906), Williams spent nearly all his professional life, both as an obstetrician–general practitioner and an insistently American experimental writer, in and around his hometown of Rutherford, New Jersey. More single-mindedly than many of his contemporaries, Williams looked to American literary and political revolutions, and to a common language and even the pained screams of his patients, for topics and inspiration.

A player in the New York art and poetry worlds, he frequented Alfred Stieglitz's 291 and other galleries and was an intimate friend of painters Charles Sheeler and Charles Demuth, whose well-known *Number 5,* an abstract portrait of Williams, is based on the short poem "The Great Figure." He contributed poems, stories, and reviews to numerous American and international literary, artistic, and political magazines (Harriet Monroe's *Poetry,* the Social Crediters' *New Democracy, Blast: A Journal of Proletarian Prose,* his own *Contact*). Less a partisan than a proponent of radical individualism and of the *new* in any form, he was a self-proclaimed heir of Walt Whitman and adopted father of the Beats, who especially prized his further loosening of Whitman's "free verse" in colloquial language and the flexible line, "the variable foot."

His New York City literary and artistic associates and influences were variously related to European traditions and the French avant-garde (especially to dadaism and cubism), but he positioned these *In the American Grain,* the title of his 1925 polemical account of the "American" imagination manifest in such figures as Whitman, Poe, Lincoln, Columbus, a mythic Eric the Red, and the noble Montezuma. Prizing his mother's Puerto Rican heritage as well as her painting, Williams refused to limit his definition of "America" to English and Puritan colonization of the United States. The revisionary, heterogeneous, or "pagan" (as in *Voyage to Pagany,* his autobiographical, novelistic send-up) American tradition that informs his response to contemporary artistic rivals is best exemplified by the "Prologue" to *Kora in Hell: Improvisations* (1920), a creative commentary on epistolary attacks by Wallace Stevens, Ezra Pound, H. D., and others, and by *Spring and All* (1923), the mixed genre, proto-epic, analytic prose-poems. These works, available in *Imaginations,* the best anthology of Williams's early writings in various genres, summarize his critical and historical positions.

His most important representative work is *Paterson,* an experimental or parodic "epic"; published in separate books (1946–1958), it is a long poem composed of personal letters, newspaper articles, and otherwise "original" verse. "Paterson" names the poem's locale (Paterson, New Jersey), central character (the partially autobiographical Dr. Paterson), and oedipal theme (eponymously in the pun, *pater*-son) of a renewed American poetics. As intended, *Paterson* bears aesthetic and historical comparison with other modern epics or epochal works: T. S. Eliot's *The Waste Land,* Gertrude Stein's *The Making of Americans,* Ezra Pound's *The Cantos,* H. D.'s *Trilogy,* and Wallace Stevens's *Notes toward a Supreme Fiction.*

Paul Mariani, *William Carlos Williams: A New World Naked* (1981); Joseph N. Riddel, *The Inverted Bell: Modernism and the Counterpoetics of William Carlos Williams* (1974).

KATHRYNE V. LINDBERG

See also Literature.

WILMOT PROVISO

This measure was designed to ban slavery within territory acquired as a result of the Mexican War. It was introduced on August 8, 1846, only a few months into the war, by Democratic representative David Wilmot of Pennsylvania as part of a bill to appropriate $2 million to negotiate a treaty with the Mexicans.

The antislavery declaration reflected the national political situation. The Democrats had divided over slavery and expansion during the 1844 election, but after his victory James K. Polk had pushed for the acquisition of the Oregon country and for a larger share of Texas from Mexico. Northern Democrats such as Wilmot, who feared the addition of slave territory, had resented Polk's willingness to compromise the Oregon dispute with Great Britain at the forty-ninth parallel — less territory than expected. More interested in northern free labor than in the plight of southern slaves, Wilmot had been an administration loyalist until he presented his proviso. Apparently, it may not even have been his idea. The language was taken from the Northwest Ordinance of 1787, and several antislavery congressmen had written similar measures.

Although the measure was blocked in the southern-dominated Senate, it helped widen the growing sectional rift, and it inspired such politicians of the time as James Buchanan, Lewis Cass, and John C. Calhoun to formulate their own plans for dealing with slavery as the nation expanded its territory.

See also Mexican War; Slavery.

WILSON, WOODROW

(1856–1924), twenty-eighth president of the United States and winner of the Nobel Peace Prize (1919). Born in Staunton, Virginia, Wilson received the Ph.D. degree from Johns Hopkins University in 1886. As a college professor, he was one of the founders of the discipline of political science in the United States and made significant contributions to the fields of comparative government and administration. Several texts he wrote are regarded as classics. He was also a prolific academic and popular historian. As president of Princeton, he transformed a venerable college into a world-class university, but conflicts over the reorganization of the social life of undergraduates and control of the graduate school caused him to resign in October 1910.

Meanwhile, Wilson had accepted the Democratic nomination for governor of New Jersey. After his election in November 1910, he pushed through measures that put the state in the forefront of progressive reform. This success catapulted him into national prominence and led to his election as president on the Democratic ticket in 1912.

Wilson transformed the presidency into the institution we know today by his strong leadership in foreign affairs, his command of public opinion, and his leadership of his party in Congress. Under his aegis, Congress from 1913 to 1916 enacted the most coherent, constructive, and comprehensive program to that time. It included measures for banking reorganization and control through the Federal Reserve System, tariff reduction, federal oversight of business, support of labor organizations, and federal aid to education and agriculture. In foreign affairs during his first term, Wilson acted most notably as an anti-imperialist and advocate of human rights. He defended and protected the Mexican Revolution begun in 1910, sought to protect the infant Chinese republic against Japanese aggression, and brought home rule to the Philippine Islands and Puerto Rico.

Wilson viewed the outbreak of war in 1914 as the result of European imperialistic rivalries and arms races and sought to protect American neutrality against both British and German violations of American rights on the high seas. His efforts to end the war through mediation failed, and, in April 1917, he asked Congress to declare war against Germany after it began all-out submarine war against American shipping.

Wilson mobilized the nation for total war for the first time in its history, with great success. American soldiers in France turned the tide and enabled the Allied and Associated powers to bring the war to an end on November 11, 1918. Wilson led the American delegation to the Paris

Peace Conference, which negotiated the Treaty of Versailles. His most notable accomplishment at Paris was to secure the incorporation of the Covenant of the League of Nations into the treaty with Germany.

But many Americans were not prepared to undertake such international obligations as the Covenant required. A healthy Wilson would undoubtedly have found common ground with the moderate Republicans in the Senate who had reservations about the League and would have achieved ratification of the treaty by the autumn of 1919. The president, however, after making a national speaking tour on behalf of the League, suffered a severe stroke on October 2, which paralyzed his left side and caused severe brain damage, leaving him unable to view the political situation realistically. He thus twice prevented Democrats in the Senate from making the treaty's ratification possible. After his term expired Wilson lived in retirement in Washington with his wife, Edith Bolling Galt Wilson, until his death in 1924.

Ray Stannard Baker, *Woodrow Wilson: Life and Letters,* 8 vols. (1927–1939); Kendrick A. Clements, *Woodrow Wilson: World Statesman* (1987); Arthur S. Link, *Wilson,* 5 vols. (1947–1964).

ARTHUR S. LINK

See also Elections: 1912, 1916; Progressivism. *For events during Wilson's administration, see* Antitrust Movement; Expansion, Continental and Overseas; Federal Trade Commission; Fourteen Points; Germany-U.S. Relations; Mexico-U.S. Relations; Middle East–U.S. Relations; New Freedom; Philippines; Prohibition and Temperance; Puerto Rico; Versailles Treaty and League of Nations; Volstead Act; World War I.

WINTHROP, JOHN

(1588–1649), founding governor of Massachusetts Bay Colony. Winthrop's contribution to the Puritan adventure in British North America would appear self-evident. He was governor of the Bay Colony almost continuously from 1630 to 1649, and in the interim years he also exerted a powerful influence over colonial affairs as a member of the Council of Assistants. Dedicating his personal funds as well as his administrative talents, Winthrop conscientiously advanced the Puritan standard of "nursing father" to the emergent wilderness theocracy.

He symbolizes the ambiguity of the Puritan mystique at the root of American national identity. Consider the importance ascribed to Winthrop's famous sermon, "The Modell of Christian Charity," which he wrote and possibly delivered on board the flagship *Arbella* when the Puritans were en route to America. More than the formulaic admonition that was customarily preached to shipmates at the launching of transatlantic voyages, it was the moral code for a godly society that Winthrop hoped would serve as a model for a reformed England. In later generations his prediction that "wee shall bee as a Citty upon a hill, the eyes of all people . . . upon us" evoked a self-conscious ideal against which the themes of each day were measured. Still later, the image would become a republican symbol of American exceptionalism and world mission, and ultimately an ideological touchstone for imperial diplomacy in the twentieth century.

Winthrop was a third-generation son of English landed gentry, whose religious aspirations were focused on the advancement of the Protestant Reformation in England and continental Europe. His migration to Massachusetts Bay was in response to "corruptions" he perceived in English society at a time when the Puritans were threatened with persecution as well as an unpromising economic future. His life and writings reveal a man caught in the broad overlap of the late medieval and early modern eras. His *Journal* is both an excellent source for early Massachusetts history and the chronicle of his personal efforts to secure the commonwealth as a gentry-dominated oligarchy.

Winthrop regarded the governorship as his lifetime position. But several defeats in colonial elections revealed a significant opposition to his arbitrary methods. His political ideal presupposed an interdependent community wherein all members had a prescribed place and function in the social hierarchy. Despite his legal training at the Inns of Court, he opposed the movement to curtail magistrates' authority by enacting a code of laws. Instead, he consistently defended discretionary rule and the magisterial veto over the resistance of the town deputies. In a famous speech to the General Court in 1645 he distinguished *civil* from *natural liberty* as that which "is maintained and exercised in a way of subjection to authority."

Winthrop's imperious treatment of dissenters may also be seen in the context of premodern social ideals that defined the religious mission of Massachusetts Bay Colony. To achieve a Puritan utopia, Winthrop and his colleagues committed themselves to a policy of intolerance. He played a leading role in prosecuting Anne Hutchinson and her supporters during the antinomian controversy (1636–1638); in ordering the capture of Rhode Island radical Samuel Gorton and his company at Shawomet to be tried and sentenced at Boston (1643); and in subduing the "Presbyterians" William Vassal, Robert Child, and Samuel Maverick for their "Remonstrance and Humble Petition" (1646), which called for a more liberal church membership policy. In each case, the possibility of English interference threatened the goals of Winthrop's godly society.

England accepted a limited toleration in the 1640s, but Massachusetts continued to punish dissenters, thus isolating itself from the mainstream of political culture abroad. Then, too, Boston's development into a seaport town was a process that made Winthrop's medieval standard of social relations anachronistic by the final decade of his life. Ironically, it was this transformation that refurbished Winthrop's "Citty upon a hill" imagery as an American emblem, one that related the themes of progress and declension in popular rhetoric.

Edmund S. Morgan, *The Puritan Dilemma: The Story of John Winthrop* (1958); Darrett B. Rutman, *Winthrop's Boston: Portrait of a Puritan Town, 1630–1649* (1965).

BARBARA RITTER DAILEY

See also New England Colonies; Puritanism.

WITCHCRAFT

See Salem Witch Trials.

WOBBLIES

See Industrial Workers of the World.

WOMAN'S CHRISTIAN TEMPERANCE UNION

This organization grew out of an aggressive women's temperance movement in Washington Court House, Ohio, in 1874 and became a national crusader for prohibition. After the Ohio women ended the local liquor trade with a combination of marches, negotiations, and axes wielded in saloons, they formed the Woman's Christian Temperance Union (WCTU). It was small and largely unsuccessful until Frances Willard became its president in 1879. A former schoolteacher, president of a women's college, and dean of women at Northwestern University, Willard took over the leadership of a group of mostly middle-class, Protestant women and tried at first to turn it into an organization advocating socialism. In this she failed, but the WCTU gained in membership — 150,000 by 1890.

Arguing that alcohol consumption was related to a poor environment, the group sought to improve the conditions of the working class — more than did most male temperance reformers. In some ways, too, the WCTU challenged patriarchy and the nuclear family, seeking more power for women inside the home and more opportunity outside it, as well as advocating equal pay for equal work. It also gave strong support to the national Prohibition party. (Some members, however, disagreed with this policy and split off to form the Non-Partisan WCTU.) Joining with other groups such as the Anti-Saloon League, the WCTU worked at first for prohibition at the state level before turning to the fight for a national constitutional amendment.

Although the WCTU proved stronger than its sister groups after Prohibition became a reality in 1919, the advent of women's suffrage the next year divided its members. Like many other women's groups, the organization debated the question of what women's new role in politics should be. With the subsequent failure of Prohibition, the WCTU's influence steadily declined.

See also Prohibition and Temperance; Willard, Frances; Women's Voluntary Associations.

WOMEN AND THE WORK FORCE

Long before the colonization of America by Europeans, Native American women were part of the work force, and when Europeans settled the territory, the colonists and their imported servants and slaves included large numbers of women. Thus, women have always been a crucial component of American labor. Their jobs, like the jobs of men, changed dramatically as the society moved from a largely agrarian to a predominantly urban culture. These shifts were accompanied by changing values and attitudes with regard to gender roles.

In preindustrial society, nearly everybody worked and almost no one worked for wages. The home, whether tipi, log cabin, or spacious house, was the center of production — the place where food, clothing, and furnishings were created. Most families produced nearly all their household goods. What they could not provide for themselves — such items as rum, coffee, tea, salt, sugar — they acquired by trading surplus grain or butter, yarn or cloth. Prosperous families might enlist the services of others to provide boots, pewter dishes, and tinware. But rudimentary carpentry, soap and candle making, spinning, weaving, and sewing were the province of every household.

Among the European colonists, a division of labor by sex, though common, was not rigid. Women's efforts usually focused on work in and around the house, but it was not unusual for a woman to help plow or pitch hay. Similarly, men spent twilight hours alongside their wives at the loom, and throughout the eighteenth century, both boys and girls were trained to spin and weave. Circumstances varied regionally. In the frontier family, for example, women frequently handled rifles, hunted, trapped, and defended themselves and their children against Indians and predatory creatures.

Differences of wealth sharply divided the labor force. The wealthiest women supervised slaves or servants who performed the tasks necessary to run a large household. Such a woman ran the dairy, supervised the vegetable gardens, managed and instructed servants, ordered supplies, and planned menus. She cared for the health of the family and sometimes of numerous servants or slaves as well. Often, she made decisions about the planting, harvesting, and sale of crops.

Indentured servants and slave women did the manual labor of the household. Some women worked in the fields, plowing, digging, and harvesting alongside the men. Others laundered, nursed, cleaned, and cooked. The work of both groups was physically taxing and often dangerous, and women were frequently subjected to the sexual abuse of masters. In the middle states and the North, free white women might start their working lives as hired servants. After marriage, they contributed to the household economy by raising cash crops, spinning and weaving at home, or perhaps running a tavern or a millinery shop. To widows and the never-married fell such hard and consistently underpaid work as teaching in dame schools, sewing, and laundering.

The onset of industrialization at the beginning of the nineteenth century highlighted differences among women just as it exacerbated those between men and women workers. At first, women in farming families brought cash into the household by participating in cottage industries. Typically, they accepted a consignment of goods from a merchant or factor, agreeing to complete it in a specified way and within a given time. They were sometimes paid in cash, but it was not unusual for them to receive instead some small portion of the goods they had made. This mode of production, called the putting-out system, could involve many members of a household in such activities as binding shoes or stitching gloves. It rarely provided an income either steady or sufficient enough to support a family.

As technology developed, merchants found it more profitable to consolidate their operations under a single roof. Spinning and weaving were the first of many activities to migrate from home to factory in the period from about 1800 to 1850. Widows and children, as well as young unmarried women, trying to cope with the difficulties of making a living on New England's stony farms, were tempted by the relatively high wages of factory work. These women and their families constituted the core of the first factory labor forces. In mill towns in New England, New York, Pennsylvania, and New Jersey, women could learn a skill that yielded sufficient income to support themselves in minimal comfort and that often provided an environment with congenial companions as well. But by the 1840s and 1850s, mill owners, facing rising pressures from competition, were cutting wages and increasing the intensity of work. Young single women with other options now found factory jobs less attractive. They were replaced by immigrant women and poor women from cities like New York and Boston. Less able to defend themselves than the earlier factory workers, these women found themselves caught in a process of immiserization that continued well into the twentieth century. Long hours, subsistence pay, and harsh working conditions undermined the health and well-being of women whose working days stretched to incorporate many hours of household labor as well.

To be sure, there were a few women in a great variety of other occupations, some of which paid reasonably well. Women worked as printers, cigar makers, teachers, and telegraphers. A handful ran their own businesses or earned their living as writers and lecturers. But until long after the Civil War most working women held such traditional jobs as domestic service, sewing, or laundering. In 1870, 60 percent of all female workers were engaged in some aspect of domestic service and another 25 percent earned their livings in factories and workshops. Except for janitorial work, factory jobs were off-limits to black women. As late as 1900, when the proportion of white women in domestic service had dropped below 50 percent, most women of color supported themselves and their families with various forms of domestic service. Others participated in the agricultural work that continued to sustain the majority of black families.

In the late nineteenth century, the lives of women were sharply bounded by economic, ethnic, and racial circumstances. Proscriptions against married women working outside the home prevented the most prosperous from engaging in paid work. The wives and daughters of skilled male workers might similarly hope that their husbands and fathers could earn a wage sufficient to support a family. This "family wage" would protect them from the harsh realities of the job market. But most women spent some portion of their lives before marriage at poorly paid, brutal work in the fields or factories or in someone else's kitchen. Lucky women and the well educated might teach or serve as governesses or companions. The poorest continued, even after marriage, to earn money by taking in boarders, washing, or sewing. Not until late in the century were these options significantly expanded by new jobs in retail stores and business offices.

In the labor force that emerged at the height of the industrialization process, virtually all skilled jobs and access to occupational mobility were reserved for male workers. Although about one-fifth of white women and more than a third of women of color worked for wages outside their homes, they usually occupied the least skilled and poorest paid jobs. Their efforts to improve their condition included attempts at collective action and unionization. In the nineteenth century, the most successful and enduring efforts at unionization included women shoe workers who organized the Daughters of St. Crispin, Irish collar ironers who started the Troy, New York, Female Collar Laundry Workers Union, and printers who founded the Women's Typographical Union in New York City in 1868. In the 1880s, about half a million women joined the Knights of Labor, a powerful national federation of unions. When the Knights faded away late in the decade, most women were left without unions. The American Federation of Labor, which succeeded the Knights as America's major umbrella organization for unions, consisted largely of skilled craftsmen reluctant to organize those they considered unskilled, much less women.

Only 3.3 percent of the 4 million women engaged in nonagricultural jobs in 1900 belonged to trade unions. That proportion doubled in the aftermath of a successful wave of strikes by young immigrant garment workers in the winter of 1909–1910. Nevertheless, in 1920 less than one in fifteen wage-earning women was a union member, and women accounted for less than 7 percent of organized workers. Limited organization among women is partly explained by their relatively low levels of skill, which made them vulnerable to replacement by employers bent on cutting labor costs. In addition, women tended to work in difficult-to-organize small shops and to move in and out of the work force more frequently than skilled men. Women's efforts to organize also challenged the paternalistic self-image of employers.

In the absence of union protection, many women began to look to state regulation to ameliorate the harsh conditions of their work. With the aid of middle-class allies in such groups as the Women's Trade Union League, they pushed for protective labor legislation, which began to take root shortly after the turn of the century and was widespread by World War I. Most of this legislation sought to provide safe and clean working conditions, minimize health hazards, put a floor under wages, and shorten hours. But almost every industrial state also passed restrictive laws that prohibited women from holding a wide variety of jobs and from working at night. This legislation tended to reflect the prevailing sense that women's primary role was that of the mother.

The practical effects of this protective legislation were mixed. The laws had the immense advantage of ameliorating the worst conditions of women's work, while offering to conserve their health and energy in the service of their families. At the same time, by reducing the economic advantages of female employees, the new laws institutionalized their secondary labor force positions. They provided both a practical and an ideological message that restricted women's ability to compete with males.

Fortunately for women, new job opportunities in white-collar areas emerged just at the time that protective legislation became widespread. Women had first entered offices during the Civil War, and their tenure in federal jobs had expanded steadily thereafter. The invention of the typewriter and other machines speeded their integration. Still, by 1900, less than 10 per-

cent of all employed women worked in offices. That number climbed dramatically after the turn of the century, so that by 1920, more than 25 percent of all employed women held jobs as office workers or telephone operators — a proportion that equaled that of factory workers and would soon surpass it. At the same time, the proportion of women employed in domestic work plunged. By 1920, less than one in five women had a job in domestic service, compared to three in five in 1870. Women also found jobs in new professional fields like nursing, library science, and social work, and a few broke into the ranks of medicine, journalism, and the law. By 1920, the proportion of professional women had climbed to 13 percent and it increased rapidly thereafter.

New job opportunities best explain why the rate at which women participated in the labor force rose during the 1920s and resisted the pressures of the Great Depression. These new openings were also accompanied by two major developments that conspired to encourage women to enter the labor force in ever-increasing numbers. The first was a change in the mode of production. Even before World War I, new managerial techniques embodying the principles of scientific management began to rationalize jobs so that they could be more readily learned. These techniques, which spread rapidly in the twenties, encouraged a reduction in working hours for all employees, and they were accompanied by efforts to enhance the loyalty and commitment of workers to their jobs by providing such amenities as paid vacations, night school classes, sports teams, and cafeterias. These techniques supported and sustained consumerism, the second major change. As consumer goods became less expensive, and families began to develop a taste for vacuum cleaners, automobiles, telephones, and better housing, married women were increasingly drawn to wage work to help meet the new needs. By 1930, approximately one of every six married women had a paid job — nearly triple the proportion of 1900; that was the first inkling of the revolution of attitudes toward women's work that was to come.

During the depression the high rate of unemployment led to demands that all women, especially those who were married, give up their jobs to men, but the number of employed married women rose inexorably thereafter. Pressures to reduce women's labor force participation did not succeed, partly because more and more families needed women to function as providers and partly because a sex-segregated labor market stabilized the demand for women.

World War II briefly transformed demands for exclusion into an insistence that women take jobs in war industries. It thus opened the possibility of a counteroffensive on the part of women who sometimes successfully fought for equal pay for equal work. Black women benefited from a brief respite in job segregation to move into skilled factory jobs. But at war's end, they, along with most newly hired women, were pushed out of desirable jobs to make way for returning veterans. Still, the lessons of the war were not forgotten as the economic demands of the consumer-conscious households of the fifties encouraged many women to continue wage work.

A new phase emerged in the 1960s. Sparked by the debates of President John F. Kennedy's Commission on the Status of Women and by the birth of a new women's movement, a spate of legislation supported women's efforts to overcome job discrimination. In 1963, Congress passed a long-sought Equal Pay Act. The 1964 Civil Rights Act forbade discrimination on the grounds of sex and created an Equal Employment Opportunity Commission that workers could use to bring suit against employers who did not comply with the law. As a result, a small number of women managed to inch their way into better jobs. By the seventies, medical and law schools, corporate and financial institutions, and political bureaucracies had increased equal access for women. Though many women complained of a "glass ceiling" that limited access to the most powerful and lucrative jobs, the barriers to managerial-level jobs had become more permeable.

Poor women, however, did not seem to benefit as much. Those who headed the expanding number of single-parent families searched for ways to combine family life with work. Many women found themselves confined to the pink-collar ghetto of retail sales, clerical, and service jobs where low wages and part-time work carrying no benefits proliferated. New immigrants could find jobs only in sweatshops that recalled the conditions of the early twentieth century. At the same time the rising cost of living locked many two-parent families into dual wage earning, with its concomitant problem of how to integrate work and family life. As attention shifted from workplace conditions, legislators and others increasingly advocated such reforms as subsidized child care, paid pregnancy and parental leaves, flextime, and more generous health care coverage. Most experts agreed that resolving these family-related issues would be the key to achieving equality for women in the workplace of the twenty-first century.

Claudia Goldin, *Understanding the Gender Gap: An Economic History of American Women* (1990); Alice Kessler-Harris, *Out to Work: A History of Wage-Earning Women in the United States* (1982).

ALICE KESSLER-HARRIS

See also Domestic Work; Feminist Movement; Indentured Servitude; Industrial Revolution; Labor; Slavery; Textile Industry; Triangle Shirtwaist Fire; United States Women's Bureau; Women's Trade Union League.

WOMEN'S EDUCATION

See Education.

WOMEN'S MOVEMENT

See Feminist Movement.

WOMEN'S TRADE UNION LEAGUE

This organization sought to organize working women into trade unions while introducing their everyday concerns about wages and working conditions to the growing women's rights movement. The Women's Trade Union League (WTUL) was formed in 1903. Modeled on a similar league in England, it faced problems in outlook from its beginnings. Its members included progressive reformers from settlement houses and the Young Women's Christian Association, who sought federal and state protective legislation, and working women from the trade union movement, who emphasized the need to organize labor. Both groups had to deal with the chauvinism of male reformers and the increasingly conservative American Federation of Labor. Thus, they turned to groups created inside and outside the league to promote education and better working conditions and to boycott companies guilty of bias or overpricing, looking to protective laws only when all other means had failed.

The WTUL did succeed in advancing women's education, better wages, job safety, and sexual and racial integration. Especially in its early years under the leadership of Margaret Robins, it helped women during strikes set up picket lines, counter police violence, build up public opinion behind their efforts, and support their families. The WTUL also joined other women's groups to lobby state and national politicians. But the organization broke up in 1950 amid antiunionism, McCarthyism, and the post–World War II baby boom that returned many wartime working women to the home. It declared — prematurely — that it had achieved its goals.

See also Feminist Movement; Labor; Women and the Work Force.

WOMEN'S VOLUNTARY ASSOCIATIONS

American women have cooperated with one another in voluntary associations since the time of the American Revolution, and their organizations continue to function as an important vehicle for exerting influence in the public arena. Throughout most U.S. history, popular belief held that "women's place was in the home," that their talents should be applied solely within the domestic setting. Until modern times women were unwelcome in most groups founded by men for civic action, self-improvement, or social interaction. Yet throughout history women routinely defied the proscriptions against their public role and met with one another to create a collective voice for change. In this way American

men have come to accept women's use of organizations to help shape the nation's political, social, and economic life.

During the War for Independence, the Daughters of Liberty raised funds for George Washington's army, setting a precedent that would be followed by future generations in wartime. Ladies Relief Societies and similarly named organizations provided material and moral support during every subsequent military conflict in which American soldiers were engaged. No doubt the toleration during wartime for women's activities outside the home arose from the fact that they were engaged in patriotic work during an emergency; moreover, war relief activities would have been viewed as an extension of what was seen as their normal caretaking function.

In peacetime, however, women generally faced constraints against collective action through association. Nevertheless, antebellum women founded a great number of associations to address the social issues of their day. These groups served as one of women's few outlets to express their opinions and to work for change. The period saw the emergence of women's temperance societies, which called first for the moderate use of alcohol and later for total abstinence. Temperance groups expanded their activities and took stands on other reform causes, including easier divorces for wives of alcoholics, the adoption of more comfortable clothes for women, and improved diets. The movement eventually evolved into one of the largest organizations of women in America, the Woman's Christian Temperance Union (WCTU), founded in 1873. This group, which catapulted its late-nineteenth-century president, Frances Willard, to a position of worldwide importance, worked also for such reforms as woman suffrage, free kindergartens, and social purity.

Women in the northern states in the 1830s founded groups in cities like Philadelphia, Boston, and Salem to seek the abolition of slavery. Protestant churches also generated many organizational efforts, including moral reform societies, missionary associations, and charitable enterprises. And numerous secular groups engaged in benevolent work, creating asylums, homes for the friendless, and schools for industrial education.

After the outbreak of the Civil War, women on both sides of the Mason-Dixon line applied their organizational experience to wartime relief activities. In the North, the U.S. Sanitary Commission enlisted the help of women to provide nursing care, raise funds for supplies, and prepare donated food and clothing for soldiers for the Union cause, and in the South, Confederate women provided similar social services.

After the war ended, women's organizational activities blossomed. Multitudes of local groups formed for a variety of social, educational, and civic purposes. They sprang up in large cities and small towns, and enrolled usually, although not exclusively, white, middle-class, middle-aged women — those with enough freedom from housekeeping and child-raising responsibilities to attend monthly or weekly meetings. The clubs, varying in size from half a dozen to several hundred, often allied with regional and national networks, thereby generating increased support for the projects they undertook. For example, churchwomen forged alliances to assist the goals of their religious institutions. National groups like the Woman's American Baptist Foreign Mission Society, Woman's American Baptist Home Missionary Society, Women's Relief Societies of the Church of Latter-day Saints, and later the National Council of Catholic Women, National Council of Jewish Women, and Hadassah, received support from branches in great numbers of communities. Their members worked for a multitude of worthwhile projects including the founding and supporting of schools, orphanages, and settlement houses, although appreciation by the men heading the religious institutions was sometimes grudging or lacking altogether.

The late nineteenth century also saw the emergence of women's auxiliaries to men's organizations. The Patrons of Husbandry, or the Grange, created a woman's division for the female relatives of its members. The Woman's Relief Corps was founded in 1883 as a counterpart to the Grand Army of the Republic, the Civil War Union Veterans Association, and the United Daughters of the Confederacy was created in 1903 as an outgrowth of the Grand Camp of Confederate Veterans. Similarly, the National Society of the Daughters of the American Revolution formed when the Sons of the American Revolution refused admission to female descendants of revolutionary soldiers. Secret societies, or fraternal orders, a phenomenon that boomed in the late nineteenth century, inspired wives and daughters of members to create parallel associations. Order of the Eastern Star, Order of the King's Daughters, Job's Daughters, Ladies of the Maccabees, Order of the Rainbow, and Daughters of Norway are examples of these.

A major development in the organizational history of American women was the so-called woman's club movement. Among its key founders was New York journalist and syndicated columnist Jane Cunningham Croly, who established the Sorosis club in 1868, and Julia Ward Howe, a Boston reformer and writer who started the New England Woman's Club in the same year. The women who attended these early gatherings were seeking social and intellectual exchange, unlike women in many of the other groups who were targeting specific causes. They constituted a who's who of leading nineteenth-century women in literature, science, reform movements, and other professions and included such notables as astronomer Maria Mitchell, physician Mary Putnam Jacobi, and author Sara Willis Parton. Women in large cities and small towns all over America were inspired to create similar groups for self-improvement, public service projects, and mutual support for ambitions that reached beyond their immediate households. The proliferation of these clubs was encouraged by the Association for the Advancement of Women, an alliance of public-minded women who sponsored an annual three-day conference in a different city every year from 1873 to 1897. At each conference the slate of speakers attracted large audiences for lectures concerning the capabilities of modern women, inspiring many in their audiences to form women's clubs.

By 1890, despite some complaints that members were neglecting their responsibilities to home and family, the nationwide woman's club phenomenon was well under way. In fact, it was sufficiently broad that delegates from sixty-three clubs in seventeen states met in New York City at the behest of Sorosis to form the General Federation of Women's Clubs. Among the clubs that sent representatives were the Woman's Club of Indianapolis, New Century Club of Philadelphia, Old and New of Malden, Massachusetts, and Century Club of San Francisco. The federation was to serve as an umbrella organization and a clearinghouse for the burgeoning numbers of women's clubs, although it came to influence even unaffiliated clubs. The federation's leaders urged members to formalize their groups: they should incorporate, write a constitution, follow parliamentary procedure, and hold an annual election of officers. They suggested study topics, provided bibliographies, and held biennial conventions to help clubs in their study of topics ranging from the plays of William Shakespeare to the history and art of other nations, current events, and modern women novelists. The federation also encouraged the membership to examine social issues of the day, including civil service reform, conservation of natural resources, immigration, public health, and improved education. Because clubs throughout the nation usually focused their lobbying on the same legislation, the woman's club movement was influential in securing many municipal, state, and federal reforms. The Home Teacher Act, Pure Food and Drug Act, well baby clinics, registration of nurses, inspection of milk, and protection of the redwood trees are a representative handful of the programs these clubwomen supported.

Black women, welcome in only a few of the white women's clubs such as the New England Woman's Club, formed a network of their own. The National Association of Colored Women (later National Association of Colored Women's Clubs) was formed in 1896 with the merging of the National Federation of Afro-American Women and the Colored Woman's League. Members undertook many projects of an educational, social, and reform nature, but they also addressed the issue of racial injustice in America.

With the advent of the twentieth century and a changing society, new organizations focused on modern women's concerns. Factory women created labor organizations to seek im-

proved working conditions, and the Women's Trade Union League linked the drive for woman suffrage with the improvement of industrial conditions. Businesswomen allied in the National Federation of Business and Professional Women's Organizations, Altrusa, and Soroptimist. Nurses, schoolteachers, music teachers, cosmeticians, home economists, anthropologists, lawyers, mothers — all formed groups to share their occupational concerns. Composers, writers, and painters founded the National League of American Penwomen.

The association movement encompassed girls and young women, too. This period saw the formation of working girls' clubs, Girl Scouts, Camp Fire Girls, Four-H Club Girls, the Young Women's Christian Association, and sororities, such as Alpha Chi Alpha, Delta Zeta, and Omicron Nu. Debutantes in major American cities joined the Junior League to engage in charitable works. Growing numbers of colleges invited graduates to join alumnae associations, which supported educational projects. Many institutions of higher learning allied their alumnae with the Association of Collegiate Alumnae, which later became the American Association of University Women.

Politics absorbed the attention of many women's groups. The National Woman Suffrage Association and American Woman Suffrage Association, rival groups dedicated to attaining the franchise for women, had been founded in the late 1860s. The two factions merged in 1890 as the National American Woman Suffrage Association (NAWSA). But Alice Paul, objecting to what she felt were ineffective strategies, created the Congressional Union in 1913 (later called the National Woman's party) and adopted more militant tactics to achieve woman suffrage. (Anti-woman suffrage associations were also formed.) Once women were granted the ballot in 1920, the new voters could join the League of Women Voters, the still-active National Woman's party, or the women's committees of the various political parties. Women seeking to use their newly won vote to shape public policies continued to work through organizations to increase their effectiveness. Women in every state created women's legislative councils, often sponsored by existing women's groups, to monitor the progress of acts under consideration by state legislators. At the federal level, women's groups lobbied Congress via the Women's Joint Congressional Committee and supported the creation of the Women's Bureau within the national government.

Those interested in specific reforms organized such groups as the Association of Southern Women for the Prevention of Lynching, the American Birth Control League, and the National Conference on the Cause and Cure of War. International alliances developed through the Women's International League for Peace and Freedom, the Inter-American Union of Women, and the International Council of Women.

The size and influence of many women's associations peaked in the mid-1920s but had begun to wane by the end of the decade. Some probably were frightened off by attacks from conservatives, who charged that certain of the groups advocated Bolshevik-style solutions for American social problems. Many women were simply unable to pay club dues after the stock market crash of 1929. On the other hand, the suffering caused by the Great Depression motivated many to redouble their charitable efforts. And in World War II, some club memberships surged briefly, as women once again performed wartime relief work. After the war, several women's organizations successfully pressured Congress to reconsider the inclusion of an Equal Rights Amendment in the Constitution.

The reawakening of the feminist movement, beginning in the late 1960s, plus the increased numbers of women entering the work force, drew contemporary women away from their traditional volunteer work in associations. But it also sparked the creation of new women's groups to address the new issues. Formed now were the National Organization for Women, the Coalition of Labor Union Women, informal consciousness-raising groups, and networks of career women. In the struggle over abortion rights, prochoice, Planned Parenthood, and right-to-life groups enlisted women on both sides of the question. So, too, the renewed push for sexual equality inspired some women to challenge the policies of male-only groups, notably the Rotary Club, and the courts increasingly supported their demand that women be admitted. Women's associations continue to serve a wide membership today, uniting women, as always, to address the social questions that touch their lives.

Paula Baker, "The Domestication of Politics: Women and American Political Society, 1780–1920," *American Historical Review* 89 (June 1984): 620–647; Karen J. Blair, *The History of American Women's Voluntary Organizations, 1810–1960: A Guide to Sources* (1989).

KAREN J. BLAIR

See also American Woman Suffrage Association; General Federation of Women's Clubs; League of Women Voters; National American Woman Suffrage Association; National Organization for Women; National Woman Suffrage Association; National Woman's Party; United States Women's Bureau; Woman's Christian Temperance Union; Women's Trade Union League.

WOODHULL, VICTORIA

(1838–1927), women's rights activist. Woodhull was one of the more remarkable figures on the late-nineteenth-century American scene. Flamboyant and unorthodox, she strained the boundaries of public discourse and private values, challenging gender roles, questioning sexual ethics, and demanding political rights for women. She lived the principles of women's emancipation and sexual equality. In doing so, she became the subject of public controversy and derision.

Woodhull was married three times, divorced twice, and included her lovers as well as her ex-husbands in her household. She bore two children with her first husband, Canning Woodhull, an alcoholic physician. Her son, Byron, fell from a window at the age of two and remained mentally impaired thereafter. Her daughter, Zulu Maud, born in 1861, became her constant companion, particularly during her later years.

Woodhull's public life resembled her domestic arrangements. Between 1870 and 1877 she often dominated the attention of reformers and newspaper reporters. With her sister, Tennessee Claflin, she opened the first female brokerage house on Wall Street (reputedly financed by the aging Cornelius Vanderbilt) and published the lively, controversial, and unorthodox newspaper *Woodhull and Claflin's Weekly*. Through the *Weekly* she became the leader of the New York section of Marx's Second International and published the first English translation of the *Communist Manifesto*. The *Weekly* also launched two campaigns promoting Woodhull for president on self-styled Progressive and Equal Rights platforms. Perhaps most significant, however, was the *Weekly*'s campaign for women's suffrage and equal rights. Woodhull was the first woman to address Congress on this or any other subject. Her outspoken advocacy of free love exacerbated divisions among suffrage activists, alarming more moderate reformers like Susan B. Anthony but winning the admiration of Elizabeth Cady Stanton because of her vision and ideals.

Woodhull's political positions challenged traditional public-private distinctions, most notoriously in her exposé of the Beecher-Tilton scandal. In 1872 the *Weekly* published details of an affair between the popular and respected reform preacher Henry Ward Beecher and the wife of his colleague and fellow reformer Theodore Tilton. The revelations shocked the reform community, raising contradictions between public respectability and private sexual ethics. Woodhull chastised Beecher's hypocrisy in preaching against free love while carrying on an affair with a married woman. Publicizing the scandal conveniently combined Woodhull's principles with her long-standing private resentments against Beecher and Tilton. Shortly after revealing the details of the affair, Woodhull and her sister were arrested under the Comstock laws, which prohibited sending obscene materials through the mails. Several months later, after a vociferous public debate and the collapse of Woodhull's health, the sisters were acquitted of all charges.

The Beecher-Tilton scandal and Woodhull's subsequent trial effectively ended her political career. Although she continued speaking and launched several other newspapers, she never regained political credibility. Still, she maintained a commitment to sexual equality and the emancipation of women. Her later years were spent in England as the widow of British banker John Biddulph Martin. She built schools and introduced new agricultural methods on her estate. One of her last projects involved renting small plots of land exclusively to women so that they might learn the skills of farming.

Woodhull's remarkable career and flamboyant lifestyle challenged an array of nineteenth-century political, social, and sexual assumptions. Her extreme positions often made other reform proposals appear more moderate and therefore more acceptable. Woodhull's demands for women's sexual and political equality and her refusal to distinguish between public behavior and private morality suggest an as yet unexplored dimension to the history of nineteenth-century American reform movements.

Susan Levine

See also Feminist Movement.

WOODSON, CARTER G.

(1875–1950), historian. Born in New Canton, Virginia, Woodson was the only black American born of slave parents to earn a Ph.D. in history. One of nine children of James Henry and Anne Eliza Woodson, the future historian worked on the family farm as a small child and as an agricultural day laborer in his teens. The family moved to West Virginia, where, at the age of twenty, Woodson enrolled in Frederick Douglass High School and completed four years of course work in two years. He then enrolled in Berea College and graduated in 1903, one year before Kentucky enacted the Day Law, which prohibited interracial education. In 1907 Woodson enrolled as a full-time student at the University of Chicago and earned another bachelor's degree as well as a master's in history; his thesis concerned French diplomatic policy toward Germany in the eighteenth century. He earned a Ph.D. in American history at Harvard University in 1912, completing a dissertation on the secession movement in western Virginia. He taught high school in Washington, D.C., and later served as a dean at Howard University and West Virginia State College.

Woodson founded the Association for the Study of Negro Life and History in 1915 and the following year began publishing the *Journal of Negro History*. Through the *Journal* Woodson challenged the racist bias of mainstream studies of slavery, Reconstruction, and African history. The association functioned as a clearinghouse and information bureau, providing research assistance in black history to scholars and the public. The annual celebration of Negro History Week, begun in 1926, was among Woodson's most important achievements. During his lifetime the idea, which attracted whites as well as blacks, spread to South America, the West Indies, Africa, the Philippines, and the Virgin Islands. In 1937 Woodson also began publishing the *Negro History Bulletin*, which was directed at black schoolchildren.

With the publication of his first book, *The Education of the Negro prior to 1861*, Woodson embarked on a scholarly career that, judged by output alone, few could match. Between 1915 and 1947, when the ninth edition of *The Negro in Our History*, appeared, he published four monographs, five textbooks, five edited collections of source materials, and thirteen articles, and collaborated on five sociological studies. The major objective of his research was to correct the racist bias implicit in the work of most white scholars of the time. Woodson investigated all aspects of the black experience in the United States from the colonial period through the 1920s, as well as that of blacks in the West Indies, South America, and Africa. Woodson pioneered in writing social history using new sources and methods. He moved away from interpreting blacks solely as victims of white oppression and racism, viewing them instead as major actors in American history. In recognition of his work the NAACP awarded Woodson its highest award, the Springarn Medal, in 1926.

August Meier and Elliott Rudwick, *Black History and the Historical Profession* (1986); Earle E. Thorpe, *Black History: A Critique* (1971).

JACQUELINE GOGGIN

See also History and Historians.

WOOLMAN, JOHN

(1720–1772), Quaker minister and essayist. Woolman was an early critic of slavery and materialism, whose *Journal* is an American classic. His essays against slaveholding were instrumental in awakening antislavery sentiment in the North American colonies and Great Britain.

Woolman's upbringing and education were in many ways unexceptional for an eighteenth-century Quaker. He was raised on a New Jersey farm, attended the local Quaker school, and was apprenticed to a tailor. In his late teens, he experienced a period of spiritual turmoil that eventuated in his becoming a lay Quaker minister. Unlike many members of the Society of Friends who immersed themselves in politics and commerce, Woolman limited his business in order to devote himself to the ministry. He took seriously the Quaker dictum to live simply and warned others that excessive worldliness would impede communion with the Holy Spirit. *A Plea for the Poor* (1793), which he wrote in the mid-1760s, addressed this concern.

Woolman's greatest work was his crusade against slavery. He was not the first to argue that slavery was inconsistent with the Quaker tenet that all people are equal before God, but he took up the challenge at a time of ferment among Friends. Many of the older generation of Pennsylvania and New Jersey Quaker leaders were dying; they had owned slaves and blocked earlier efforts to censure the practice. In the 1750s, new leaders, including Woolman and Anthony Benezet, promulgated a reform program that included opposition to slavery. Philadelphia Yearly Meeting was the first religious body to denounce slaveholding (in 1754) and prohibit members from buying and selling slaves (in 1758).

Woolman had first awakened to the evils of slavery during the early 1740s when he was asked to write a bill of sale for a black woman. In 1746, he made his first journey to Maryland, Virginia, and Carolina, returning home full of remorse because, as he explained in his *Journal*, he had eaten and "lodged free-cost with people who lived in ease on the hard labour of their slaves." He saw in the "southern provinces so many vices and corruptions increased by [the slave] trade and this way of life that it appeared to me as a dark gloominess hanging over the land." His essay *Some Considerations on the Keeping of Negroes* (1754) held that blacks had not forfeited "the natural right of freedom" and warned that slaveholders tested divine benevolence by treating slaves "with rigour, to increase our wealth and gain riches for our children."

Woolman made about thirty journeys to proselytize among slaveholders from New England to the Carolinas, and he was among the first to abstain from using products of slave labor. In 1762 he published *Considerations on Keeping Negroes: Part Second.* His *Journal,* which was published posthumously in 1774, has remained in print, providing to successive generations the example of a Quaker "saint" who sought to live according to the dictates of religion and his conscience.

Phillips P. Moulton, ed., *The Journal and Major Essays of John Woolman* (1971); Jean R. Soderlund, *Quakers and Slavery: A Divided Spirit* (1985).

JEAN R. SODERLUND

See also Abolitionist Movement; Quakers.

WORK

See Child Labor; Domestic Work; Housework; Indentured Servitude; Labor; Slavery; Women and the Work Force.

WORKS PROGRESS ADMINISTRATION

The Works Progress Administration (WPA) was established under the Emergency Relief Appropriation Act of April 1935 to create public jobs for the unemployed. Although responsibility for the unemployable (children, the aged, and the disabled) was returned to the states, the WPA under the direction of Harry L. Hopkins created millions of jobs for those who could work, averaging an enrollment of about 2 million during its seven-year history. Mandated to choose projects that would make a genuine contribution but would not compete with private business, the WPA concentrated on physical improvements: building streets, highways, bridges, public buildings, and airfields, clearing slums, restoring forests, and extending electrical power to rural areas. The WPA National Youth Administration (NYA) gave work to nearly a million students; the Federal Theatre, Arts, Music, and Writers' Projects brought music and drama to the smallest communities, commissioned public sculptures, paintings, and murals, sponsored surveys of national archives, and produced a series of state and regional travel guides.

Although the WPA never served more than a quarter of the nation's unemployed, its scale was unprecedented, and its public popularity contributed to Franklin D. Roosevelt's resounding electoral victory in 1936. At the same time, opponents of the New Deal attacked the program, charging waste, political manipulation, and even subversion; they moved quickly to cut back the program when unemployment dropped slightly in 1937. Funding was restored in 1938 when unemployment surged again, but 1939 brought more cuts: the Emergency Relief Appropriations Act (June 30) abolished the Federal Theatre Project, reduced WPA wages, and required that no one remain on program rolls more than eighteen months. In response to accusations of politicking by WPA workers in the 1938 congressional elections, the Hatch Act (August 1939) prohibited a wide range of political activities by federal employees. With growing prosperity in the 1940s, the WPA became increasingly difficult to defend, and in 1943 the agency was dissolved.

See also Federal Theatre Project; Federal Writers' Project; Hatch Act; New Deal.

WORLD'S FAIRS

American international expositions, like their counterparts in other countries, trace their origins to London's 1851 Crystal Palace Exhibition, the first world's fair. And like it, America's expositions drew on and reshaped an earlier tradition of agricultural and mechanical fairs.

In the aftermath of the Crystal Palace Exhibition, a group of prominent New Yorkers, including Horace Greeley and Phineas T. Barnum, organized America's first international fair in New York City in 1853. But the fair's financial failure together with the mounting sectional crisis postponed the emergence of a bona fide world's fair movement in the United States until 1876, when a group of Philadelphia civic leaders together with the federal government organized an international exhibition to celebrate the nation's centennial and its reunification after the Civil War. The success of the Philadelphia Centennial Exposition in attracting millions of visitors launched the first generation of American international fairs. By 1916, fairs organized in New Orleans (1884–1885), Chicago (1893), Atlanta (1895), Nashville (1897), Omaha (1898), Buffalo (1901), Charleston (1901), St. Louis (1904), Portland (1905), Jamestown (1907), Seattle (1909), San Francisco (1915), and San Diego (1915–1916) had attracted nearly 100 million visitors. The Chicago fair included a mile-long entertainment strip, and every subsequent fair incorporated a variant of the midway idea.

The purpose of these expositions was summed up by President William McKinley just before he was assassinated at the 1901 Buffalo fair. "Expositions," he declared, "are timekeepers of progress." Through the world's fairs held during the economic convulsions of the late Victorian era, organizers laid out blueprints for national progress that centered on technological advance, nationalism, imperialism, and white supremacy. All the fairs exhibited the latest in technological marvels, ranging from the Corliss engine at Philadelphia to an early motion picture camera at Chicago. The Pledge of Allegiance was written for the dedication ceremonies of the Chicago exposition, and the Liberty Bell journeyed to many of the fairs. During the prolonged economic depression that followed the panic of 1873, the fairs exhibited a cornucopia of agricultural surpluses as well as a variety of industrial products intended to foster the image of a healthy economy. The fairs also served as seedbeds for the emergence of modern advertising and the mass amusement industry.

Equally important to the promotion of a vision of American progress were displays of nonwhite people, frequently arranged by anthropologists from the Smithsonian Institution and universities. These so-called living ethnological exhibits of Africans, Asians, and American Indians, often arranged along exposition midways, introduced millions of Americans to Darwinian ideas about racial advance and lent legitimacy to the imperial ambitions of exposition organizers. St. Louis fair authorities, for instance, organized twelve hundred Filipinos into a "Philippines Reservation" that was intended to promote American colonial policies in that nation. Set against the backdrop of temporary but palatial "white cities" constructed on the main exposition grounds, these exhibits underscored the racist nature of turn-of-the-century American society.

When the First World War caused many Americans to call into question the ideas of progress and of science and technology acting as guarantors of the nation's future, industrialists and scientists launched a cultural offensive with a new generation of world's fairs. Just as the 1926 Philadelphia Sesquicentennial Exposition was faltering owing to the failure of many exhibitors to have their displays ready for opening day, business leaders in Chicago decided to organize a fair to commemorate the centennial birth of their city and turned to the National Research Council for scientific expertise in formulating a philosophy for their exposition.

With the stock market crash and the ensuing depression, however, the Century of Progress Exposition (1933–1934) took on unexpected importance and spurred the organization of expositions in San Diego (1935–1936), Dallas (1936), Cleveland (1936), San Francisco (1939–1940), and New York City (1939–1940). Fairs during the depression era drew audiences that nearly equaled the attendance at the earlier fairs and became a central part of New Deal efforts to demonstrate the government's concern for the economic and social welfare of Americans. The fairs provided thousands of jobs and gave countless fairgoers the opportunity to imagine a better future based on a partnership of government and corporation planners on the one hand and scientists and engineers on the other. Exhibits, ranging from an early display of television at the Chicago fair to General Motors's World of Tomorrow display at the New York World's Fair, radiated the gospel of technological utopianism and marked a significant shift in the structure of American society, as exhibition palaces devoted to agriculture, mining, fine arts, and the like, gave way to exhibition halls bearing the names of corporations. In short, these fairs played an integral role in adjusting Americans to a new, corporation-dominated economic order and actively promoted the development of a consumer culture as a way out of the depression.

Yet, while these fairs facilitated change in American life, they also fostered cultural continuity. These modern festivals of abundance once again practiced overt discrimination against African-Americans and included shows that degraded nonwhites. Imperial themes also persisted. San Francisco's 1939 fair, for instance, was organized, in part, to rekindle dreams of an American Pacific empire with California as its hub.

Between the close of the 1939–1940 fairs and the opening of the 1962 Seattle World's Fair, international expositions seemed destined to become cultural dinosaurs. The Second World War had raised new questions about the meaning of progress and a new technology, television, occupied the nation's living rooms, performing many of the functions of world's fairs. International expositions, however, continued to be organized in the wake of Seattle's exposition and New York's 1964–1965 extravaganza. San Antonio hosted HemisFair '68, Spokane held a fair in 1974, and Knoxville and New Orleans organized expositions in 1982 and 1984, respectively. Several of these expositions were financial disasters, which led critics to proclaim the end of world's fairs, a refrain dating back to the nineteenth century. Nevertheless, America's postwar fairs continued to address — with a view toward shaping — popular concerns about the role of new technologies and scientific discoveries (especially those involving nuclear energy) in American life.

For more than a century, world's fairs have influenced American life in many ways. Their imprint on architecture and urban planning has been lasting. They have inspired works of literature (for instance, William Dean Howells's *Letters of an Altruian Traveller* and E. L. Doctorow's

World's Fair) and served as occasions for congresses of intellectuals from around the world. They heralded momentous developments in national thinking and policies (e.g., Frederick Jackson Turner presented his famous paper "The Significance of the Frontier in American History" to a gathering of historians at the 1893 Chicago World's Columbian Exposition and Booker T. Washington delivered his Atlanta Compromise address at the opening of the 1895 fair). Fairs, moreover, played a critical role in the emergence and development of museums around the country, including the Smithsonian Institution in Washington, D.C., the Field Museum of Natural History and the Museum of Science and Industry in Chicago, and the Museum of Man in San Diego. Fairs, in short, have given form and substance to the way countless Americans have understood themselves and the world.

Burton L. Benedict, *The Anthropology of World's Fairs* (1983); Robert W. Rydell, *All the World's a Fair* (1984).

ROBERT W. RYDELL

See also Barnum, Phineas T.; Centennial Exposition; Libraries and Museums.

WORLD WAR I

When the guns of August 1914 shattered the peace of Europe, pitting Germany and Austria-Hungary (the Central Powers) against Britain, France, and Russia, President Woodrow Wilson on August 4 issued a proclamation of neutrality. Two weeks later he urged Americans to be "impartial in thought as well as in action." But in the realms of both official policy and public opinion, neutrality proved difficult to sustain. Wilson insisted, for reasons of both principle and economic advantage, on full neutral trading rights with all the belligerent powers. Britain and Germany had different ideas. Each tried to throttle American trade with the other. Britain, whose battle fleet controlled the surface of the Atlantic, succeeded spectacularly. American commerce with Germany had fallen by 1916 to less than 1 percent of its 1914 value. In the same period, American trade with Britain and its French and (after 1915) Italian allies tripled.

British restrictions on American trade elicited repeated American complaints, but the harm done by British commercial regulations and surface ships paled next to the damage inflicted by German submarines. The U-boat (*Unterseeboot*) ignored existing rules of naval warfare. Contrary to the traditional practice, submerged U-boats torpedoed merchant ships without warning. When sinkings resulted in the loss of American lives — as in the assault on the British passenger liner *Lusitania* on May 7, 1915, killing 128 Americans — Wilson's government protested vehemently. Germany restrained its submarine attacks thereafter, but on January 31, 1917, in a desperate move to end the two-and-a-half-year-old military stalemate in Europe, the German high command declared unrestricted submarine warfare against all shipping, neutral or belligerent, destined for Britain.

Wilson broke diplomatic relations with Berlin, but declined to ask Congress for a declaration of war in the absence of "actual overt acts" against American lives and property. He sought instead to arm American merchant vessels as a way of forestalling attacks and thus avoiding war. But the "overt acts" came with the sinking of several American ships in February and March 1917. At about the same time, newspapers published an intercepted telegram from German foreign minister Arthur Zimmermann, proposing a German-Mexican alliance against the United States. Mexico's reward would be the recovery of territory it had lost in Texas, New Mexico, and Arizona. Wilson, though reelected in November 1916 on the slogan "He kept us out of war," asked Congress on April 2 for a declaration of war. Four days later, Congress complied, with six senators and fifty representatives (including the first congresswoman, Jeannette Rankin of Montana) voting against the war resolution.

"It is a fearful thing to lead this great peaceful people into war," Wilson declared in his war message. It was fearful indeed. The war had already butchered millions of Europeans and shredded the social fabric of many of the belligerent states, and in the United States, many people still opposed America's involvement in the conflict.

Many factors fostered the American reservations, even after the U-boat attacks and the Zimmermann telegram. One was Wilson's own suspicions about the war aims of Britain and France, which precluded his becoming their formal ally. At his insistence, the United States officially fought as an "Associated Power." Others included America's historical isolation from European embroilments; the geographical remoteness of the fighting; the tangled and confusing causes of the war in noxious European imperial rivalries; the partisan contentiousness of the era of progressive reform over which Wilson and his predecessor, Theodore Roosevelt, had presided; and, above all, the deep ethnic divisions in early twentieth-century American society. The 1910 census revealed that one out of every three Americans was either foreign-born or the child of a foreign-born parent. Of those 32 million Americans with strong foreign ties, some 10 million came from what were now the enemy countries of Germany and Austria-Hungary. Neither their loyalty to the American cause nor even the enthusiasm for the war of millions of other Americans could be taken for granted.

Knowing this, the Wilson administration undertook an extraordinary propaganda campaign aimed at shaping American public opinion favorable to the war and mobilization efforts. The centerpiece of this campaign was the Committee on Public Information (CPI), formed in April 1917 and headed by progressive journalist George Creel. The CPI mobilized some seventy-five thousand speakers — "four-minute men" — who delivered patriotic exhortations in churches, schools, movie houses, and other public places. It distributed 75 million copies of pamphlets in several languages explaining America's relation to the war. It sponsored war expositions in nearly two dozen cities and produced films like *The Kaiser: The Beast of Berlin*.

Other government agencies, such as the Food Administration under Herbert Hoover and the Treasury under William Gibbs McAdoo, employed similar techniques. Hoover exhorted housewives in the name of patriotism to observe "meatless Mondays" and "wheatless Wednesdays" as food conservation measures. McAdoo sponsored gigantic rallies to urge the purchase of war bonds. These approaches typified the American mobilization effort, which relied less on the majesty of the law (food rationing or heavy taxation, for example) and more on aroused passion and voluntary compliance to accomplish its goals. Even the War Industries Board, usually considered the most potent of the wartime mobilization agencies, exercised its actually modest powers with reluctance. Its colorful chairman, lone-eagle stock speculator Bernard M. Baruch, doubted the statutory basis for many of the actions he wanted to take to orchestrate American industrial production. Accordingly, he relied instead on suasion, cajolery, and occasionally the threat of public humiliation to work his will. Even in the midst of a globe-girdling crisis, Americans thus expressed their historic preference for the principles of laissez-faire and their fear of a strong central government.

The crisis of war nevertheless pressed in with sufficient urgency that the Wilson administration had eventually to resort to the blunt exercise of governmental power, as when it took over the operation of the nation's railroads in late 1917. But in general, the government applied less naked force to the economy than it did to the suppression of dissenting political opinion. The Espionage Act of June 15, 1917, as amended by the so-called Sedition Act of May 16, 1918, provided the legal foundation for sundry prosecutions of pacifists and left-wing political groups opposed to the war, such as the Socialists and the Industrial Workers of the World (IWW). In the controversial case of *Schenck* v. *United States* in 1919, the Supreme Court upheld the constitutionality of the Espionage Act. Government propaganda also fueled the fires of popular passion and helped create an atmosphere in which an aroused vigilantism led to numerous atrocities. Especially victimized by these emotional outbursts were German-Americans. Though they had historically been among the most esteemed immigrant groups, they now found themselves the targets of a mindless fury that knew few restraints. Familiar German terms like "hamburger" and "sauerkraut" were replaced by "liberty sandwich" and

"liberty cabbage." Playing German music and teaching — or even speaking — the German language were prohibited. One German-American was stripped, bound with an American flag, and lynched by a mob of five hundred persons near St. Louis.

The Selective Service Act of May 18, 1917, helped raise the size of the American army from about 200,000 men in early 1917 to nearly 4 million by war's end. Some 2 million men served overseas in the American Expeditionary Force (AEF), of whom roughly three-quarters experienced combat. Gen. John J. Pershing, commander of the AEF, landed in France on June 14, 1917, and his troops began to arrive the following month. They came slowly at first and then in greatly accelerating numbers in the spring and summer of 1918.

As men left for the fighting front, employment opportunities opened up for women. Some prominent women like Jane Addams opposed American entrance into the war on pacifist grounds. But many other women leaders welcomed the chance, as a Women's Trade Union League speaker put it in 1917, to come "into the labor and festival of life on equal terms with men." About a million women entered the labor force during the war, but most quickly departed when peace returned.

Russia, under a new revolutionary government, concluded a separate peace with Germany and left the war in March 1918. (Wilson's famous Fourteen Points, announced on January 8, 1918, as the basis for a nonpunitive peace settlement with Germany, were prompted in part by an effort to keep reeling Russia in the war. But the effort was in vain.) The Germans thereupon began shifting troops from the Russian to the western front, preparatory to the mounting of a massive offensive on March 21, 1918. British and French officials now redoubled their demands that American troops be amalgamated into Allied units. All such requests Pershing, under orders to make the AEF a "distinct and separate component," had adamantly denied. Now he partially relented and allowed American soldiers and marines to be thrown in under foreign command to brace the buckling Allied lines. Green American troops fought at Cantigny in

May 1918 and at Chateau-Thierry and Belleau Wood in June. The German drive was halted. The American giant had arisen in the West, Winston Churchill later wrote, to replace the dying Russian titan in the East.

On August 10 the First U.S. Army was formed and assigned to a sector of the front stretching from the area around Verdun eastward to the Vosges Mountains. The American role in the counteroffensive of 1918 was twofold: to reduce the German salient behind the village of Saint-Mihiel to the southeast of Verdun, and then to attack the main German front to the northwest of Verdun, through the heavily fortified terrain bounded by the Meuse River on the west and the Argonne Forest on the east. The ultimate American objective was the important German railroad center at Sedan.

The Saint-Mihiel campaign, September 12–16, 1918, went smoothly, largely because the American attack happened to catch the Germans in the midst of a previously planned evacuation. The Meuse-Argonne offensive, launched on September 26, 1918, was a different matter. The Germans were deeply entrenched in formidable defenses. The terrain exposed the attackers to murderous enfilade as they proceeded up the two narrow valleys that flanked the first American objective, the strategic heights of Monfaucon. But the Americans had the advantage of numbers. Pershing hurled some 1.2 million "doughboys" into the Meuse-Argonne attack, and though their inexperience produced appalling casualties, their sheer quantity finally broke the German resistance. Germany quickly realized it could not hold out against the western Allies now that the huge weight of America's apparently inexhaustible manpower reserves had been thrown into the scales. Germany had initiated unrestricted submarine warfare on the calculated gamble that this would bring the Allies to their knees before the United States could field an effective fighting force. Germany lost that gamble, and the war ended with the surrender of the Central Powers on November 11, 1918. Total American war deaths were 112,432, more than half from disease. Government expenditures related to the war totaled some $26 billion during wartime, and eventually, with interest rates, veterans' benefits, and the like, the war's direct financial cost to the United States came to about $112 billion.

America's main contributions to the victory over the Central Powers had been foodstuffs, manpower, and money. The Allies depended neither on American armaments nor, in the last analysis, on American military victories in the field. They had sufficient weapons of their own and in fact supplied most munitions of war to the AEF, which sailed in British ships, fired British and French artillery, and flew Allied aircraft. But without American food and especially financial resources — some $10 billion in U.S. Treasury loans were extended to the Allied governments in the two years after April 1917 — Britain, France, and Italy would probably have had to sue for terms. Similarly, it was not so much American fighting prowess as the prospect of endless American reinforcements that tipped the scales against Germany in late 1918.

At home, the war had been too brief to have had a deeply transformative effect on American society. In this respect it differed from the Civil War as well as World War II. But the war did plant the seeds and provide the models for much future change. Wartime labor shortages, for example, drew hundreds of thousands of African-Americans out of the South and into industrial employment in the North, laying the foundations for large black communities in cities like Chicago and New York. The mass movement of African-Americans into what had been predominantly white communities provoked interracial friction and occasionally violence. Vicious race riots broke out in East St. Louis in July 1917, killing nine whites and a larger but undetermined number of blacks. Even worse rioting rocked Chicago in July 1919, leaving fifteen whites and twenty-three blacks dead. Blacks also served in the military, under conditions that reflected the segregationist practices common to American society at the time. They were brigaded in all-black units under white officers and mostly assigned noncombat roles in construction battalions and as stevedores. Four regiments of the Ninety-third Division were seconded to the French army and fought well enough to receive unit citations for bravery. Yet the poor record of the Ninety-second Division's 368th Regiment in the Meuse-Argonne offensive received more attention in the press and seemed to confirm racist opinions that blacks were unsuited for combat.

The war established many precedents for future political developments. The War Finance Corporation, established to help firms convert to military production, inspired the Hoover administration's chief antidepression tool, the Reconstruction Finance Corporation. The New Deal's National Recovery Administration was patterned on the War Industries Board. The National War Labor Board, charged with mediating wartime labor disputes, provided an important precedent for the Wagner National Labor Relations Act of 1935. And there were the more immediate and concrete achievements, at least partly facilitated by the war, of Prohibition, which was enacted by the Eighteenth Amendment in 1919, and women's suffrage, guaranteed by the Nineteenth Amendment in 1920. The war also introduced sufficient stresses into American society that Woodrow Wilson's Democratic party, despite its military victory, lost control of the Congress in 1918 and of the presidency in 1920, ushering in a decade of Republican dominance in national politics.

Robert H. Ferrell, *Woodrow Wilson and World War I, 1917–1921* (1985); David M. Kennedy, *Over Here: The First World War and American Society* (1980).

DAVID M. KENNEDY

See also Addams, Jane; Armed Forces; Baruch, Bernard M.; Black Migration; Conscientious Objection; Conscription; Dawes Plan; Fourteen Points; Germany-U.S. Relations; Isolationism; Pershing, John J.; Rankin, Jeannette; Segregation; Versailles Treaty and League of Nations; Wilson, Woodrow; Women and the Work Force.

WORLD WAR II

I. United States' Entry into the War

When the Japanese seized Manchuria and then invaded China and began a drive to the south, they put their country on the road to war with the United States. But this aggression was at least in part a result of the West's efforts to weaken Japan as an economic rival after World War I. The Great Depression, Japan's population explosion, and the need to find new resources and markets to continue as a first-rate power were other causes of the invasion.

Neither Japan nor America would have come to the brink of war except for the social and economic disruption of Europe after World War I and the rise of communism and fascism. These two sweeping forces brought about the tragedy of war between Japan and America. Unfortunately both countries were inept negotiators driven by paranoiac fear — Japan, fear of communism from both Russia and Mao Tsetung, and America, fear of the "yellow peril."

President Franklin D. Roosevelt brought their differences to a head on the night of July 26, 1941. After learning that the Japanese army had pushed into Indochina, he froze all Japanese assets in America. In consequence, not only did all trade with the United States cease, but the fact that America had been Japan's major source of oil imports now left Japan in an untenable position.

On September 6 an imperial conference was convened in Tokyo to decide on war or peace. Traditionally the emperor was supposed to remain silent. Instead Hirohito recited a poem of peace written by his grandfather. Startled, the military leaders promised to give first consideration to diplomacy. Prime Minister Fumimaro Konoye was forced to resign, and it was suggested that Gen. Hideki Tojo, the war minister, replace him. Only he could control the army. Tojo, although shocked by the offer, accepted and was ordered to "go back to blank paper," that is, to start with a clean slate and negotiate with America for peace.

Despite protests from the military, a new offer was sent to Washington on November 20. Japan promised not to make any more aggressive moves south, and once peace was restored with China or a general peace in the Pacific established, all troops would be pulled out of Indochina. In the meantime Japan would at once move all troops in southern Indochina to the north of that country. In return, America was to sell Japan a million tons of aviation gasoline. Roosevelt was so impressed that he wrote out a reply in pencil and sent it to Secretary of State Cordell Hull. The secretary passed on copies to Chiang Kai-shek and Winston Churchill. Both protested so forcefully that the message was never sent to the Japanese. On November 26 news came of another Japanese expedition to Indochina, and the president "fairly blew up" when informed by Hull. In place of Roosevelt's earlier message a harsh note was sent calling for Japan to withdraw all military forces from China and Indochina. It was regarded as an insult by the Japanese cabinet. It is possible that if Hull had sent Roosevelt's original note Japan would have either come to some agreement with America or been forced to debate the issue, thus compelling postponement of an attack until the spring of 1942 because of weather conditions. By this time it would have been obvious that Moscow would not fall. This would dangerously weaken the Axis and cause the Japanese leaders to reconsider a Pearl Harbor attack at such an inauspicious moment. Then the implausible series of chances and coincidences that led to December 7 might not have occurred.

A war that could possibly have been avoided now broke out because of mutual misunderstanding and language difficulties, along with Japanese opportunism, irrationality, pride, and fear and American racial prejudice, distrust, ignorance of the Orient, self-righteousness, and pride.

Bitter political controversy had clouded the issue of war or peace in America. The interventionists, convinced that the nation's future safety depended on its helping crush the aggressor nations, had pushed through Congress the Lend-Lease Act committing America to unlimited aid, "short of war," to the enemies of the Axis. The United States would be the "arsenal of democracy." The opponents of intervention included strange bedfellows: the right-wing America Firsters of Charles Lindbergh, Senator William E. Borah, and the German-American Bund, the "American peace mobilization" of the Communist and Labor parties, and the traditionally isolationist Midwest, which, though sympathetic to Great Britain and China, wanted no part of a shooting war.

The bombs at Pearl Harbor brought Americans together, but the honeymoon ended when Roosevelt put the blame for Pearl Harbor on the commanders in Hawaii, Adm. Husband Kimmel and Gen. Walter Short. To quell protests the president appointed Supreme Court Justice Owen Roberts to head a Pearl Harbor inquiry. It found Kimmel and Short the principal culprits. Rather than ending the dispute this stirred vigorous protests, which resulted in several minor inquiries followed by major army and navy inquiries in the summer of 1944. When a Naval Intelligence officer testified that key messages indicating a possible raid on Pearl Harbor had been destroyed, and two army officers revealed that they had been forced to change testimony concerning Gen. George C. Marshall, both the army and the navy courts concluded that the principal blame lay in Washington. These conclusions were kept from the public.

After the war Congress held public hearings that convinced the majority of Americans that Kimmel and Short *should* carry the burden of blame and that Roosevelt and Marshall had done their best to prevent war with a nation run by bandits. Most historians agreed with these findings, but there was evidence to suggest that the truth had been distorted by reversions of testimony, cover-ups, and outright lies. There was evidence, for instance, that President Roosevelt knew as early as December 2, 1941, that Japanese carriers were approaching Pearl Harbor. According to the testimony of Capt. Johan Ranneft, naval attaché of the Netherlands in Washington, he was informed by U.S. Naval Intelligence on December 2 that two Japanese carriers were halfway between Japan and Hawaii. Four days later they were some three hundred to four hundred miles from Pearl Harbor. He reported this to his government and wrote the details in his war diary. Of course, where the carriers were going and for what purpose was unclear.

Roosevelt had been assured by Marshall that Oahu was the strongest fortress in the world and any enemy task force would be destroyed. The president, therefore, took a calculated risk and lost. This was understandable, but if he instigated a cover-up, as some evidence indicates, that was a serious offense. Perhaps the whole truth will never be known.

J. O. Richardson, as told to George C. Dyer, *On the Treadmill to Pearl Harbor* (1973); John Toland, *Infamy* (1982).

JOHN TOLAND

See also America First Committee; Asia-U.S. Relations; Atlantic Charter; Four Freedoms; Isolationism; Lend-Lease Act; Marshall, George C.; Neutrality Acts; Pearl Harbor, Attack on; Roosevelt, Franklin D.

II. Events and Results

Adolf Hitler's plan to seize all of Europe was set into motion on March 7, 1936, when he sent troops into the demilitarized Rhineland in violation of earlier treaties. The British did not seriously consider taking action and the French feared to do so. Ironically, the fuehrer had given orders to retreat if challenged by the French; thus, his occupation of the Rhineland was accomplished by default. Then followed moves into Austria, where he was greeted with enthusiasm, and into Czechoslovakia. Finally on September 1, 1939, his forces invaded Poland. This at last brought a declaration of war from England.

As Poland was about to fall, the opportunistic Joseph Stalin occupied the eastern half of the country. On September 28, the two dictators signed a nonaggression treaty. With his rear thus protected, Hitler made plans to invade the West and in May 1940 sent troops across the borders of Belgium, Holland, and Luxembourg. Caught by surprise, the British and French were soon overwhelmed. The survivors of a British expeditionary force escaped across the English Channel, and the French capitulated on June 22.

Now Hitler prepared to turn on his ally, Stalin, and so become the master of all Europe. When massive air raids on England failed to subdue the stubborn British, he sought to bring them to the negotiating table by capturing Gibraltar. This would not only keep the Royal Navy out of the Mediterranean, thus ensuring Hitler's takeover of North Africa and the Middle East, but drastically lengthen England's lifelines to the Far East. Britain would be forced to surrender and become a silent partner in his crusade against Jewish Bolshevism.

All he needed was Francisco Franco's permission to transport troops through Spain. But to his dismay, the Spanish dictator, though he seemed to agree, kept stalling. He did nothing, thus saving Gibraltar for England. Besides fear of aligning himself with a possible loser, Franco had a compelling personal motive. He was part Jewish.

This setback was followed by another when Italy's Benito Mussolini, who so far had avoided going to war, attempted to seize the Balkans and failed. Hitler felt compelled to do so himself before his attack on Russia could safely be launched; this forced him to postpone that invasion for at least a month. It finally began on June 22, 1941. Great advances were made until early October, and then sleet turned into snow and the mud froze. The cold intensified, and Field Marshal Gerd von Rundstedt radioed Hitler that his troops must retreat or "they will be destroyed." Instead the fuehrer ordered the attack to continue and was caught completely off balance on the night of December 4 when the Soviets launched a massive counteroffensive. Hitler not only lost Moscow but appeared destined to suffer Napoleon's fate in the winter snows of Russia. Despondent, he admitted to Gen. Alfred Jodl that "victory could no longer be achieved."

On December 7 the Japanese attacked Pearl Harbor, whereupon Hitler made still another mistake. He declared war on America, thus saving President Roosevelt from the risk of incurring the opposition of German-Americans by asking Congress to declare war on Germany first.

Two hours after the first bombs fell on Pearl Harbor, Japanese planes hit Clark Field, the main U.S. base in the Philippines, wiping out half of Gen. Douglas MacArthur's Far East air force. Within three days he had little air defense, and soon forty-three thousand Japanese troops landed 135 air miles north of Manila. MacArthur withdrew the bulk of his U.S.-Filipino forces to Bataan Peninsula and the adjoining island of Corregidor. After a bitter struggle the defenders of Bataan were driven back, and MacArthur was ordered to fly to Australia. On April 7 more than seventy-six thousand survivors on Bataan surrendered, and a month later Gen. Jonathan Wainwright, MacArthur's replacement, surrendered the remaining troops in the Philippines.

With Indochina, Thailand, and the chain of islands from Sumatra to Guadalcanal occupied, Japanese naval leaders decided that operations should be started against Australia and Hawaii. The army protested, but a surprise bombing of Tokyo by Col. James Doolittle in mid-April allowed Adm. Isoroku Yamamoto to prevail. Preparations were made to attack Midway Island, fifteen hundred miles northwest of Pearl Harbor. It was thought that this would all but wipe out the U.S. Pacific Fleet and leave Hawaii open to invasion.

But the Americans had broken the Japanese code, and Adm. Chester Nimitz was ready. In the most crucial sea battle of the war, U.S. Navy and Marine airmen sank four carriers on June 4. America now controlled the Pacific. The Japanese commanders had fought the battle too carefully. In contrast, Rear Adm. Raymond Spruance, bold at the right moment, had launched his strike early. What gave Spruance the chance to win was Nimitz back in Pearl Harbor. He had made all the right decisions before a shot was fired.

The spring of 1942 saw almost no change in Germany's military situation. The eastern front remained stagnant, and Gen. Erwin Rommel was not quite ready for a new offensive in North Africa. Still determined to crush Russia, Hitler ordered a drive into the Caucasus, but rains held it up until June. Then, encouraged by an early success, the fuehrer made another mistake. He decided to mount a major attack on Stalingrad, an industrial city on the Volga, while continuing the drive to the Caucasus. By mid-September double victory seemed certain — and then the Soviets' defense abruptly stiffened.

November proved to be a month of disaster. Although Hitler had ordered him not to retreat "one inch" from North Africa, Rommel was forced to withdraw. An even more critical reversal occurred at Stalingrad. On November 22 two arms of a tremendous Soviet pincer movement encircled the entire Sixth Army, and more than 200,000 German troops along with a hundred tanks, eighteen hundred big guns, and more than ten thousand vehicles were caught in a giant trap. On February 2, 1943, the Germans capitulated.

In the Far East the Americans were advancing on two fronts. While MacArthur slogged across New Guinea toward the Philippines, Nimitz's amphibious forces were leapfrogging from island to island in the Pacific. On August 7, 1942, U.S. Marines landed at Guadalcanal, and after five months of deadly battle, the Japanese survivors were evacuated by ship. Nimitz's forces continued toward Japan and by February 4, 1944, had reached the western limit of the Marianas, a chain of volcanic islands.

The next target was the most strategic island of the chain, Saipan. On June 15, 1944, two Marine divisions landed on the west coast and began pushing across Saipan to link up with G.I.s of the Twenty-seventh Division. This brought swift reaction from the Japanese navy. Vice Adm. Jisaburo Ozawa was ordered to annihilate Admiral Spruance's Task Force 58, but in a savage air battle on June 19 Ozawa lost 346 planes while shooting down only 50 Americans. In a bold stroke Japan's naval power had been fatally crippled. This crushing defeat doomed the defenders of Saipan, and it was all over a month later. Close to 22,000 Japanese civilians — two out of three — perished, many of them by suicide. Almost the entire garrison — at least 30,000 — died. The Americans suffered 14,111 casualties. But the main island bastion protecting Japan's homeland had been won by the United States. More important, the lowlands of southern Saipan offered a base from which massive B-29 bombing raids could be launched at the heart of the Japanese empire, Tokyo.

While the Americans were taking Saipan, the Allies in Europe landed in Normandy on June 6. Hitler was taken by surprise, and within ten days the Allies had managed to land a million men and 500,000 tons of matériel. While the U.S. and British forces swept forward, an attempt to assassinate Hitler on July 20 almost succeeded. On August 25 Paris was liberated, and by late autumn the Germans were driven back to their own borders.

Faced with disaster, Hitler made one final attempt to win in the West. The plan was to drive through the Ardennes and reach the English Channel, thus splitting the Americans and British. On the night of December 15 three German armies moved secretly to the line of departure. The next morning they struck, taking the Americans off guard. But after retreating for eight days, the U.S. troops regrouped and stopped the Nazis. The Battle of the Bulge soon ended with the Germans in full retreat. Two weeks later they suffered another defeat, and the Red Army crossed the Vistula.

Now Hitler was being crushed from two sides. He had a momentary flash of hope on April 12 upon learning that President Roosevelt had died. But as the Soviets approached his bunker, he realized the end had come and shot himself. When he died so did National Socialism and the "Thousand-Year Reich."

Adolf Hitler was probably the greatest mover and shaker of the twentieth century. Certainly no other human disrupted so many lives in our times or incurred so much hatred. He was driven by a number of forces. Blinded by gas in 1918, he had resolved that if he recovered his sight, he would abandon his goal of becoming an architect and enter politics. One night, like Saint Joan, he heard voices summoning him to save his country. All at once, as he recorded in *Mein Kampf*, "a miracle came to pass." He could see! He vowed he would become a politician and "bring Germany from the depths of despair to the greatness she deserved."

Like millions of frontline troops, Hitler believed that they had been betrayed by those back home — strikers, malingerers, Jews, politicians, profiteers. They had forced the generals to surrender and accept the unjust and shameful Versailles treaty. Soon he became convinced that the greatest enemy to his crusade for a new Germany was communism, which he believed had been engendered by Jews. Anti-Semitism had

flourished throughout Europe for centuries, and Hitler found many adherents. Obsessed by his dream of cleansing the Continent of Jews, he became a warped archangel. He had intended the elimination of Jews to be his great gift to the world. Ironically, it would lead instead to the formation of a Jewish state.

In the Far East, also, there were impressive American victories. MacArthur, who had landed on Leyte in October 1944, had cleared the island of defenders by January 12, 1945. While he continued to advance toward Luzon, marines were wiping out the Japanese on the tiny but important island of Iwo Jima.

After Okinawa was occupied on July 12, the defeat of Japan was inevitable. Convinced that a direct attack on the four main islands of Japan would be too costly, President Harry S. Truman ordered the dropping of atomic bombs on Hiroshima and Nagasaki. At an imperial conference Emperor Hirohito announced that the time had come to bear the unbearable. On August 15 he informed his people over a nationwide radio hookup that Japan was surrendering.

World War II was, in fact, two separate wars. In the West Hitler had two aims: the first to seize all of Europe and North Africa so he could dominate the Mediterranean, and the second to wipe out communism and eliminate the Jews. His ally, Mussolini, had his own aims: domination of both the Mediterranean and the Balkans.

As for the Allies, both England and France fought to preserve their countries and stabilize Europe. Roosevelt's aim was broader: destruction of Nazism and establishment of democracy throughout Europe. The Soviet aim was to drive out the Nazis and emerge strong enough to continue communization of the world.

In the Far East the Americans fought to rid themselves of a foe who some thought threatened their Pacific island possessions and their own West Coast. In addition they were eager to aid Chiang Kai-shek's China. Some Americans also felt it was a good time to eliminate Japan as a serious economic rival.

As for the Japanese, they attacked Hawaii because it harbored the Pacific Fleet and was perceived as a spear aimed at their proposed conquest of Southeast Asia for oil.

The Allies won in Europe because of the blows inflicted on the Germans by the Russians, the endurance of the British, and the air and armaments superiority supplied by the might of American production. On the other hand, the victory in Europe resulted in a takeover of eastern Europe, despite Stalin's promises at Yalta, and a cold war between the Soviets and the democracies. In Asia victory resulted in the takeover of China and Manchuria by the People's Republic of China, chaos in Southeast Asia, and a division of Korea, with the Soviets in the North and the Americans in the South, that would lead to another war.

John Keegan, *The Second World War* (1990); John Toland, *Adolf Hitler* (1976); John Toland, *The Rising Sun* (1970).

JOHN TOLAND

See also Bradley, Omar; D-Day; Eisenhower, Dwight D.; Germany-U.S. Relations; Great Britain–U.S. Relations; Holocaust, American Response to the; Japanese-American Relocation; King, Ernest; MacArthur, Douglas; Manhattan Project; Nimitz, Chester; Nuclear Weapons: Origins and Legacy; Nuremberg Trials; Oppenheimer, J. Robert; Potsdam Conference; Soviet-American Relations, 1917–1945; Yalta Conference.

WOUNDED KNEE, BATTLE OF

The Battle of Wounded Knee on December 29, 1890, was, in fact, not a battle but a massacre, in which the U.S. Seventh Cavalry Division killed 146 Sioux men, women, and children, after the Sioux warriors refused to surrender their arms.

Two years earlier, on a reservation in Nevada, a Paiute named Wovoka (also known as Jack Wilson) had begun preaching that an Indian Messiah would soon arrive who would restore the American continent to the Indians and reunite them with their dead families. A cult grew from his teachings, centering on the mystical Ghost Dance, and within a year it had spread to dozens of other reservations. Its strength among the Sioux alarmed U.S. officials,

who made repeated efforts to suppress the new religion. These efforts culminated in the massacre at the Black Hills Reservation in Wounded Knee, South Dakota, ending the Ghost Dance (or Messiah) War. Wounded Knee was the last military encounter between American Indians and whites.

See also Indians.

WPA

See Works Progress Administration.

WRIGHT, FRANCES

(1795–1852), reformer. A freethinker, editor, orator, and lifelong rebel, Wright was one of the boldest radical reformers of her time. Born in Scotland to a prosperous family of democratic views, she was orphaned as a child and raised in London by rigid Tory relatives, whom she grew to despise. In 1813, she ran off to live with her uncle, James Mylne, a professor of moral philosophy at the University of Glasgow. Wright read widely in classical philosophy and began writing. At eighteen, she composed a competent treatise on philosophical materialism (published as *A Few Days in Athens* in 1822). But political ideas also gripped her, especially the egalitarian principles of the American Revolution. In 1818, she set sail for New York to learn more.

Accompanied by her sister Camilla, Wright mingled easily with Manhattan's intelligentsia before journeying through the northern and eastern states. After returning to Great Britain, she published her *Views of Society and Manners in America* (1821), the first serious study of the United States by a British woman. Openly sympathetic toward the new Republic, the book won Wright the admiration of several British luminaries (including Jeremy Bentham) and sparked a friendship with the Marquis de Lafayette.

In 1824, Wright joined Lafayette on his celebrated tour of the United States; he introduced her to James Madison and Thomas Jefferson, with whom she discussed the greatest anomaly in republican America, slavery. Influenced by the writings of the utopian socialist Robert Owen, she developed a communitarian emancipation scheme. Instead of returning with Lafayette, she used a large portion of her inheritance to purchase land in Tennessee, where she implemented her plan.

Wright's interracial community, Nashoba, made her notorious. Her original objective was to have slaves earn their freedom by working the land for five years and then moving to another country. Some of her recruits, however, also advanced the idea of free sexual unions within the community. Wright's defense of absolute racial and sexual equality outraged conventional (and even liberal) opinion. Although she eventually managed to resettle a handful of ex-slaves in Haiti, the Nashoba experiment collapsed, a victim of disastrous finances and Wright's own paternalist misperceptions.

Undaunted, Wright joined with Owen's son, Robert Dale Owen, in 1828 to edit a newspaper at the Owenite community at New Harmony, Indiana, and defied the limits on women by appearing widely as a public lecturer. She addressed the touchiest themes, attacking slavery, revealed religion, the rising influence of evangelical clerics, and existing forms of schooling. Above all, she railed against traditional marriage and the subjugation of women. An electrifying speaker and a hero to fellow freethinkers, Wright became the object of vitriolic abuse.

In 1829, Wright and Owen relocated their newspaper to New York City, where they established a new headquarters. They increasingly focused on the plight of urban workers and promoted a system of state-sponsored free education as the key to abolishing class inequality. Their ideas proved influential among some of the artisan radicals within New York's short-lived Workingman's party.

The rest of Wright's life tested her cruelly. In 1831, her beloved sister suddenly died. That same year, to the malicious amusement of her critics, Wright married a longtime political associate, William Phiquepal D'Arusmont, and moved to France, but the marriage proved emotionally empty. Wright returned to the United States in 1835 to resume her writing and lecturing, but her radical edge had dulled. Her ideas about gradual emancipation and colonization now seemed almost moderate amid the rise of immediatist abolitionism. And in 1836, she found herself oddly close to the political mainstream, campaigning on behalf of Martin Van Buren and the Jacksonians' banking policies. (The Jacksonian press, wishing no link to "the Red Harlot of Infidelity," ignored her.) She remained a champion of women's rights and published some powerful statements about the universality of women's oppression. Through the 1840s, though, her writings and speeches got tangled in abstract theorizing and self-justifications. In January 1852, having endured a bitter divorce battle with D'Arusmont, she slipped on ice and broke her thigh. After a year of pain, she died.

Wright formed an important transatlantic bridge between the drawing-room radicalism of the rationalist Enlightenment and the secularist reform and radical movements of the nineteenth century. Her main legacy has been to the causes of women's equality and sexual emancipation. More broadly, her life testifies to the radical potential of American egalitarian ideals — and to the difficulties confronting those who try to realize that potential in words and deeds.

Celia Morris Eckhardt, *Fanny Wright: Rebel in America* (1984).

SEAN WILENTZ

See also Feminist Movement; Radicalism; Utopian Communities.

WRIGHT, FRANK LLOYD

(1867–1959), architect. The most innovative and important architect in U.S. history, Wright is known for his pioneering private residences and his bold public buildings. During a seventy-two-year career, he produced over eight hundred designs, of which some four hundred were built and three hundred still stand. In his most creative periods (c. 1901–1909, 1935–1941), he revolutionized the suburban home, in the process acquiring international standing while generating unprecedented overseas interest in American architecture.

Wright was born in Richland Center, Wisconsin, and spent two unfruitful semesters at the University of Wisconsin. He then moved to

Chicago in 1887 to work with the architect J. L. Silsbee, soon shifting to Louis H. Sullivan's firm.

Wright rose quickly from renderer to chief draftsman to Sullivan's confidant, but their relationship ended prematurely in 1893 when Wright, who had taken his own commissions in violation of contract, was fired. In speeches, essays, and designs during the next eight years, his keen interest in new technologies, midwestern topography, middle-class family life, and the national search for an indigenous style were gradually but brashly synthesized into a design concept that in 1901 he labeled the "prairie house."

Frederick C. Robie's home (1906–1908, Chicago) is the most famous of these houses. They featured long, low, horizontal lines in harmony with the landscape, an open plan of interpenetrating group spaces, a heightened visual and physical association between indoors and out, and decorations functionally integrated with the structure. Wright also applied this style to nonresidential work, notably the Larkin Building (1904, Buffalo) and Unity Temple (1905–1906, Oak Park, Illinois). It was widely imitated, mostly in the Midwest, and exerted enormous influence in Europe, especially in Germany and the Netherlands.

In 1909 Wright left his wife and family and moved to Europe with Mamah Borthwick (Cheney), a client, ultimately settling with her on family land in Spring Green, Wisconsin. The accompanying scandal that almost ruined his career was exacerbated in 1914 by Borthwick's axmurder (along with six others including her children) and the destruction of Taliesin, their home, by arson. During the next twenty years, two love affairs and marriages, a child born out of wedlock, another fire at Taliesin, numerous lawsuits, an arrest and jailing, and a period in exile contributed to Wright's going bankrupt. In 1913–1914 he had built the massive Midway Gardens entertainment complex in Chicago and from 1913 to 1922 executed the even more massive Imperial Hotel in Tokyo, but overall, from 1915 to 1935, he completed few commissions. He lectured and wrote regularly but was considered finished as a practicing architect.

Then in a burst of creativity from 1935 to 1937, Wright designed Fallingwater in western Pennsylvania, widely considered the finest private house of the twentieth century; the Johnson Wax Administration Building in Racine, Wisconsin, a tour-de-force of aesthetic and structural innovation; and the Herbert Jacobs residence in Madison, the prototype "Usonian" house. Based on a thorough rethinking of the prairie house, the Usonian residence featured partial prefabrication, radiant heating, increased open planning and indoor-outdoor association, utility clustering, and site specificity. Influenced by the International Style of the 1920s, the Usonians erected by 1941 were important models for post–World War II suburban housing.

From 1945 until his death, Wright was extraordinarily prolific, writing and lecturing, campaigning endlessly for his deurbanization scheme, and building some 150 commissions. These were the years of his boldest large works — New York's Guggenheim Museum, the Marin County Civic Center in California, and many others — and hundreds of projects of every sort, ranging from a Baghdad cultural center to a mile-high skyscraper, hotels, churches, parking garages, and even a doghouse.

Aside from his innovations and popularizations — the carport, open and geometric grid planning, unframed corner windows, radiant heating, decorated concrete blocks, and many more — his greatest legacy may have been consistency, his steadfast adherence to his own principles resulting in his unwillingness to follow fashion. Unlike Mies van der Rohe, Wright left no disciples of note because his work was not reducible to formulae. But his reputation remains unmatched, and the fecundity of his ideas, still incompletely mined, continues to stimulate new generations of architects.

Robert Twombly, *Frank Lloyd Wright: His Life and His Architecture* (1979); Frank Lloyd Wright, *The Future of Architecture* (1953).

Robert Twombly

See also Architecture; Progressivism.

WRIGHT, RICHARD

(1908–1960), African-American novelist and social critic. His father's desertion of the family, coupled with his mother's crippling illness, which left her and her two sons in poverty, made Wright's early years unhappy ones. Growing up in Mississippi, Tennessee, and Arkansas, Wright felt isolated and rebellious against authority. Self-taught following his graduation from junior high school, and embittered by segregation and racism, he was drawn to the acerbic social criticism of H. L. Mencken and the naturalistic novels of Theodore Dreiser and Sinclair Lewis.

In 1927, he left the South for Chicago, where he entered the postal service. Attracted by communist organizers, he became executive secretary of the John Reed Club of Chicago and joined the party around 1933. He published radical poetry, essays, and short fiction in such leftist magazines as *Anvil* and *New Masses*. He also had other, often conflicting literary interests. Influenced by James Joyce, Gertrude Stein, and James T. Farrell, he completed in 1934 his first novel, "Cesspool" (published posthumously as *Lawd Today*), which offered a bleak and pessimistic view of humanity.

His first book, *Uncle Tom's Children: Four Novellas* (1938), won praise for its harsh depiction of the South, but led to his first disagreements with the party over the question of his freedom as a writer. The estrangement grew with the appearance of his landmark novel *Native Son* (1940), a story of crime and punishment that revolutionized the depiction of blacks in America by emphasizing their despair and the will to violence. His autobiography, *Black Boy* (1945), recounted his bitter childhood in the South and confirmed his reputation as the finest black writer in America.

By this time Wright had broken with the party, an episode he explored in 1944 in his *Atlantic Monthly* essay "I Tried to Be a Communist." After visiting France, he moved there in 1947 with his wife, Ellen Poplar, and their daughter. Welcomed by leading intellectuals, including Jean-Paul Sartre and Simone de Beauvoir, as well as by black writers such as Léopold Senghor, Aimé Césaire, and Alioune Diop, he developed strong interests in existentialism and in Africa and colonialism. The first led to his longest novel, *The Outsider* (1953), about an arrogant, godless black man fatally caught between

fascism and communism. The second resulted in *Black Power: A Record of Reactions in a Land of Pathos* (1954), written after a visit to Africa that confirmed his anticolonialism but left him critical of many African attitudes and practices. Wright also published provocative books on the 1953 Bandung conference of nonaligned nations (*The Color Curtain*, 1956) and on atavistic impulses in Spain (*Pagan Spain*, 1957), as well as a collection of hard-hitting essays on race and culture, *White Man, Listen!* (1957).

Wright's early and persisting radical estrangement from American culture, black or white, together with his exposure to Marxism and the techniques of naturalism in American fiction, enabled him to isolate and depict some of the harshest truths about the consequences of slavery, segregation, and racism in America — truths often evaded in more genteel approaches to literature. As a result, *Native Son* remains a major literary landmark in the racial history of the United States, and *Black Boy* one of the most compelling documents about the struggle of an artistic individual for identity and achievement on the American scene.

In his last novel, *The Long Dream* (1958), Wright returned to the issue of race and the South, but the book enjoyed only moderate success. Disillusioned about life in France, he tried to settle in England but was officially rebuffed. In 1960, following an attack of amoebic dysentery, he died in a Paris hospital.

Michael Fabre, *The Unfinished Quest of Richard Wright* (1973); Addison Gayle, *Richard Wright: Ordeal of a Native Son* (1980).

ARNOLD RAMPERSAD

See also Expatriates and Exiles; Literature.

WRIGHT, WILBUR, and WRIGHT, ORVILLE

(Wilbur: 1867–1912; Orville: 1871–1948), aviation pioneers. Wilbur and Orville Wright were the sons of a much admired bishop in the Church of the United Brethren in Christ. They were educated in local schools in Ohio, Iowa, and Indiana, and neither attended college. Their father was a self-assured man with a will of iron who regarded his home as a refuge against the evils that beset honest men and women in the world beyond the family doorstep. The result was an insulated, tightly knit, and loving family in which the five children were taught to think for themselves and place absolute reliance on one another. In commenting on the importance of his family background in later years, Orville Wright remarked, "We were lucky enough to grow up in a home environment where there was always much encouragement to children to pursue intellectual interests, to investigate whatever aroused curiosity. In a different kind of environment, our curiosity might have been nipped long before it could have borne fruit."

The brothers launched their first joint venture, a print shop, in 1889. In addition to job printing, they edited and published two short-lived neighborhood newspapers and issued a third paper edited by Paul Laurence Dunbar, a high school classmate of Orville's who went on to become an important poet and novelist. While continuing to operate the print shop, the brothers entered the bicycle trade in 1892. By 1896 they were manufacturing bicycles for sale on a small scale. Never more than moderately successful as small businessmen, the Wrights nevertheless enjoyed a modest prosperity during the years 1890–1905. They financed their flying machine experiments solely from the profits of their business enterprises.

The brothers became interested in flight as a result of newspaper articles reporting the death of the German aeronautical experimenter Otto Lilienthal in a glider crash in 1896. Between 1899 and 1905, Wilbur and Orville constructed seven aircraft: one kite (1899), three gliders (1900, 1901, 1902), and three powered airplanes (1903, 1904, 1905). The disappointing performance of the first two gliders led them to undertake a series of key experiments with a wind tunnel of their own design during the fall of 1901.

The wind tunnel tests, coupled with two years of gliding experience, opened the road to success. The Wrights made the world's first powered, sustained, and controlled flights with a heavier-than-air flying machine at Kitty Hawk, North Carolina, on December 17, 1903. They returned to Dayton and continued their experiments in the relative secrecy of a local cow pasture for two more years. By the close of the 1905 flying season, they had transformed the marginally successful machine of 1903 into the world's first practical airplane. They won world fame with their first public demonstration flights in Europe and America in the summer and fall of 1908.

The brothers founded the Wright Company to build and sell aircraft in the United States and licensed various manufacturers to produce their machines in Europe. With their business in the hands of professional managers, the Wrights devoted most of their time and energy to pursuing patent infringers in courts on both sides of the Atlantic.

Wilbur Wright died suddenly of typhoid fever in 1912, and Orville sold the Wright Company to a group of investors in 1915. Widely regarded as the elder statesman of world aviation, he served as a consulting engineer during World War I and was a member of several leading aviation committees, notably the governing boards of both the Daniel and Florence Guggenheim Fund for the Promotion of Aeronautics and the National Advisory Committee for Aeronautics.

Tom D. Crouch, *The Bishop's Boys: A Life of Wilbur and Orville Wright* (1989); Marvin W. McFarland, ed., *The Papers of Wilbur and Orville Wright* (1953).

TOM D. CROUCH

See also Aviation.

X

XYZ AFFAIR

The XYZ Affair is the name given to an incident that nearly brought the United States to war with France in 1798. America had signed a treaty with France in 1778, but relations had cooled thereafter. The Americans provided no assistance during the French revolutionary wars, and in 1793 the injudicious involvement in American politics by France's minister to the United States, Citizen Genet (Edmond Charles Genet), had further aggravated matters. The conclusion of Jay's Treaty between the United States and Great Britain in 1795 also angered the French, who found it biased in Britain's favor; they particularly objected to clauses that undid the American agreements with France. French privateers began seizing American ships, and in 1796 the French foreign minister, Charles Maurice Talleyrand, refused to receive Charles Pinckney, the new U.S. minister to France. President John Adams then appointed John Marshall and Elbridge Gerry to join Pinckney and negotiate a new treaty with France.

On their arrival in Paris in October 1797, the commissioners were put off by Talleyrand and were then visited by three of his agents, who suggested that before a treaty could even be discussed, the United States must loan France $12 million and pay a bribe of $250,000 to Talleyrand. (The agents were designated in the American commissioners' dispatches as X, Y, and Z.) The commissioners refused these terms, and in March 1798, President Adams reported to Congress that the mission had failed.

When the XYZ correspondence was released a month later, it inflamed public opinion, leading to calls for immediate war against France, a course that one faction within the president's Federalist party had long advocated. Two years of naval conflict between France and the United States followed, but the war remained undeclared. In 1800, Adams angered the prowar Federalists by negotiating the Treaty of Morfontaine, which restored peace between the two countries.

See also France-U.S. Relations.

Y

YALTA CONFERENCE

The Yalta Conference was a meeting of British prime minister Winston Churchill, Soviet premier Joseph Stalin, and President Franklin D. Roosevelt early in February 1945 as World War II was winding down. The leaders agreed to require Germany's unconditional surrender and to set up in the conquered nation four zones of occupation to be run by their three countries and France. They scheduled another meeting for April in San Francisco to create the United Nations. Stalin also agreed to permit free elections in Eastern Europe and to enter the Asian war against Japan. In turn, he was promised the return of lands lost to Japan in the Russo-Japanese War of 1904–1905. At the time, most of these agreements were kept secret.

Yalta became controversial after Soviet-American wartime cooperation degenerated into the cold war. Stalin broke his promise of free elections in Eastern Europe and installed governments dominated by the Soviet Union. Then American critics charged that Roosevelt, who died two months after the conference, had "sold out" to the Soviets at Yalta.

See also World War II.

YOUNG, BRIGHAM

(1801–1877), Mormon leader, American colonizer, and Utah's first governor. Born in Whitingham, Vermont, Young was the ninth of eleven children. His family moved to New York when he was three. Shortly after his mother's death in 1815, he left home to make his living as carpenter, joiner, glazier, painter, and landscape gardener.

Young was baptized a member of the Church of Jesus Christ of Latter-day Saints (Mormon) in 1832. He became an ardent missionary and disciple, and moved to Kirtland, Ohio, where he did carpentry work and undertook preaching missions. He was ordained an apostle in 1835 and became one of the Quorum of the Twelve, who directed missionary work, emigration and settlement, and construction projects. In 1838–1839, he directed the removal of the Mormons from Missouri to Illinois. He served as a missionary in Great Britain in 1840–1841, and upon his return he was placed in charge of the business operations of the church. After the assassination of Joseph Smith in 1844, Young was chosen leader of the Mormons and continued as president until his death.

Young not only directed the migration of sixteen thousand Mormons from Illinois to Utah in 1846–1852 but also established the Perpetual Emigrating Fund Company, which during the years 1852–1877 assisted approximately eighty thousand converts to migrate to Utah from Great Britain, Scandinavia, and continental Europe. Young also directed the colonization and development of some 350 settlements in Utah, Idaho, Wyoming, Nevada, Arizona, and California.

In 1861 Young contracted to build the transcontinental telegraph line from Nebraska to California and then erected the twelve-hundred-mile Deseret Telegraph line from Franklin, Idaho, to northern Arizona to connect all Mormon villages with one another and with Salt Lake City. He also contracted to prepare the roadbed for part of the transcontinental railroad line and then organized railroads to provide rail transportation for most Mormon communities in Idaho, Utah, and Nevada.

When Utah became a territory in 1851, Young was the first governor and superintendent of Indian affairs, serving until 1858. As governor, he had repeated difficulties with "outside" non-Mormon presidential appointees, especially judges and territorial secretaries, who were envious, if not fearful, of his power.

As president of the Mormon church, Young traveled to most settlements at least once a year, where he listened to grievances, discussed problems, and informed himself of local events and personalities. Under prodding from Young, Utah gave women the vote in 1870, thus recognizing their political equality and also adding to Mormon vote pluralities.

Young constructed the Mormon Tabernacle in Salt Lake City and began the erection of the Salt Lake Temple. He founded Brigham Young University; the University of Deseret, now University of Utah; and the Salt Lake Theatre, where major actors and actresses performed.

Young was a leading Western colonizer, energetic entrepreneur of new industry, astute politician, friend of Native Americans, and effective sermonizer. The more than five hundred recorded sermons he delivered over the thirty-three years of his leadership emphasize practical religion — the improvement of living conditions, correct behavior, and the achievement of harmonious social relationships.

Leonard J. Arrington, *Brigham Young: American Moses* (1985); Newell G. Bringhurst, *Brigham Young and the Expanding American Frontier* (1986).

LEONARD J. ARRINGTON

See also Mormons; Religion; Smith, Joseph.

Z

ZENGER TRIAL

In 1733, the royal governor of New York, William Cosby, suspended Lewis Morris, chief justice of the provincial court, for ruling against him in a salary dispute. Morris and a group of merchants and lawyers wanted to publicize their opposition to Cosby, but New York's only newspaper, the *New York Gazette,* was dependent on Cosby's patronage and would print no material critical of his policies. Morris and his friends therefore provided the financial backing for a New York City printer, John Peter Zenger, to start an opposition paper, the *New-York Weekly Journal.* Zenger had immigrated to America from Germany some twenty years earlier and, after serving an apprenticeship under a local printer, had established his own printing business. The *Journal* mounted a bitter attack on Cosby, accusing him of seeking to destroy the provincial courts and of flouting both English and American law.

In 1734, Zenger was arrested on a charge of seditious libel. Although his backers probably wrote most of the contested material, Zenger as publisher was held legally accountable for the paper's contents. For ten months Zenger was held incommunicado, and his wife kept his paper going. Brought to trial in 1735, he was brilliantly defended by Andrew Hamilton of Philadelphia, who argued that Zenger had not committed seditious libel because the material he printed was true. Although the court refused to accept the evidence submitted to prove the truth of the contested articles, the jury appears to have been moved by Hamilton's argument, and Zenger was acquitted. Within a few years, he became public printer for both New York and New Jersey.

The Zenger case did not bring an immediate end to prosecutions for seditious libel, but it was an early milestone in the struggle for freedom of the press. Its argument that true statements could not be defined as libelous was often cited in later years.

See also Freedom of the Press.

ZIEGFELD, FLORENZ

(1867?–1932), theatrical producer and creator of *The Ziegfeld Follies.* As the master showman of the early twentieth century, Ziegfeld brought a unique and sophisticated style, taste, and extravagance to the theater, popularizing a new form of entertainment called the revue.

Perhaps in reaction to his strict father's classical music career, Ziegfeld entered show business as a producer of variety entertainments, such as "dancing ducks" and later "Sandow, the Strongman." But not until his production of *A Parlor Match,* with French performer Anna Held, did Ziegfeld demonstrate his talent as an impresario by using beautiful women, lavish costumes, and elaborate scenery to create spectacle. Ziegfeld staged *A Parlor Match* so that the production emphasized Held's beauty and risqué charm; although she appeared in only one scene, she became the star of the show. Ziegfeld entered into a common law marriage with Held soon after this success; they divorced in 1912. Later he married Billie Burke, a musical comedy star who appeared as Glenda, the good witch, in the film *The Wizard of Oz.*

As a result of the success of *A Parlor Match,* the producing firm of Klaw and Erlanger approached Ziegfeld to mount a light musical entertainment for the summer season. He devised a show that combined European style with American topical humor. The result, *The Follies of 1907,* was so successful that Ziegfeld produced the show annually, eventually calling it *The Ziegfeld Follies.*

Twenty-one editions of the *Follies* were staged. Over the years, the productions developed from a modest topical review of current events with a chorus of women, staged during the slack summer season, to a complex spectacular presentation, lavish in style and grand in scale, serving as the regular season's premiere entertainment. In a two-act presentation of twenty-three scenes, Ziegfeld blended comedy sketches, dances, and specialty acts with costly costumes and innovative scenery into a carefully crafted production that emphasized the beauty of the sixty-woman chorus — the *Follies'* most noted feature. The shows were kaleidoscopic, for Ziegfeld was a master at blending these elements into an organic, spectacular whole. Called the "Great Glorifier," Ziegfeld created a theatri-

cal environment in which the chorus as well as the featured performers, such as Fanny Brice, Will Rogers, W. C. Fields, and Eddie Cantor, assumed a special and heightened star status.

Because of the *Follies'* emphases on opulence, spectacle, and beauty, the shows embodied the values of an America imbued with the notion of prosperity and the American Dream. Significantly, the names of the elite who attended on opening nights — the Vanderbilts, the Rockefellers, the Guggenheims, show business celebrities — were mentioned in newspaper reviews of the shows.

The *Follies* also represented the height of American show business, for Ziegfeld did not let financial considerations impinge upon artistic ones in the creation of his personal theatrical vision. With his death in 1932, at the height of the depression, the American theater lost not only a great showman but a form of entertainment never matched or duplicated since.

Randolf Carter, *The World of Flo Ziegfeld* (1962); Charles Higham, *Ziegfeld* (1972).

GERALDINE MASCHIO

See also Musical Theater.

ZIONISM

See Jews.

Appendix

DECLARATION OF INDEPENDENCE
JULY 4, 1776

The unanimous declaration of the thirteen United States of America

When, in the course of human events, it becomes necessary for one people to dissolve the political bonds which have connected them with another, and to assume, among the powers of the earth, the separate and equal station to which the laws of nature and of nature's God entitle them, a decent respect to the opinions of mankind requires that they should declare the causes which impel them to the separation.

We hold these truths to be self-evident: That all men are created equal; that they are endowed by their Creator with certain unalienable rights; that among these are life, liberty, and the pursuit of happiness; that, to secure these rights, governments are instituted among men, deriving their just powers from the consent of the governed; that whenever any form of government becomes destructive of these ends, it is the right of the people to alter or to abolish it, and to institute new government, laying its foundation on such principles, and organizing its powers in such form, as to them shall seem most likely to effect their safety and happiness. Prudence, indeed, will dictate that governments long established should not be changed for light and transient causes; and accordingly all experience hath shown that mankind are more disposed to suf-

fer, while evils are sufferable, than to right themselves by abolishing the forms to which they are accustomed. But when a long train of abuses and usurpations, pursuing invariably the same object, evinces a design to reduce them under absolute despotism, it is their right, it is their duty, to throw off such government, and to provide new guards for their future security. Such has been the patient sufferance of these colonies; and such is now the necessity which constrains them to alter their former systems of government. The history of the present King of Great Britain is a history of repeated injuries and usurpations, all having in direct object the establishment of an absolute tyranny over these states. To prove this, let facts be submitted to a candid world.

He has refused his assent to laws, the most wholesome and necessary for the public good.

He has forbidden his governors to pass laws of immediate and pressing importance, unless suspended in their operation till his assent should be obtained; and, when so suspended, he has utterly neglected to attend to them.

He has refused to pass other laws for the accommodation of large districts of people, unless those people would relinquish the right of representation in the legislature, a right inestimable to them, and formidable to tyrants only.

He has called together legislative bodies at places unusual, uncomfortable, and distant from the depository of their public records, for the sole purpose of fatiguing them into compliance with his measures.

He has dissolved representative houses repeatedly, for opposing, with manly firmness, his invasions on the rights of the people.

He has refused for a long time, after such dissolutions, to cause others to be elected; whereby the legislative powers, incapable of annihilation, have returned to the people at large for their exercise; the state remaining, in the mean time, exposed to all the dangers of invasions from without and convulsions within.

He has endeavored to prevent the population of these states; for that purpose obstructing the laws for naturalization of foreigners; refusing to pass others to encourage their migration hither, and raising the conditions of new appropriations of lands.

He has obstructed the administration of justice, by refusing his assent to laws for establishing judiciary powers.

He has made judges dependent on his will alone, for the tenure of their offices, and the amount and payment of their salaries.

He has erected a multitude of new offices, and sent hither swarms of officers to harass our people and eat out their substance.

He has kept among us, in times of peace, standing armies, without the consent of our legislatures.

He has affected to render the military independent of, and superior to, the civil power.

He has combined with others to subject us to a jurisdiction foreign to our constitution, and unacknowledged by our laws, giving his assent to their acts of pretended legislation:

For quartering large bodies of armed troops among us;

For protecting them, by a mock trial, from punishment for any murders which they should commit on the inhabitants of these states;

For cutting off our trade with all parts of the world;

For imposing taxes on us without our consent;

For depriving us, in many cases, of the benefits of trial by jury;

For transporting us beyond seas, to be tried for pretended offenses;

For abolishing the free system of English laws in a neighboring province, establishing therein an arbitrary government, and enlarging its boundaries, so as to render it at once an example and fit instrument for introducing the same absolute rule into these colonies;

For taking away our charters, abolishing our most valuable laws, and altering fundamentally the forms of our governments;

For suspending our own legislatures, and declaring themselves invested with power to legislate for us in all cases whatsoever.

He has abdicated government here, by declaring us out of his protection and waging war against us.

He has plundered our seas, ravaged our coasts, burned our towns, and destroyed the lives of our people.

He is at this time transporting large armies of foreign mercenaries to complete the works of death, desolation, and tyranny already begun with circumstances of cruelty and perfidy scarcely paralleled in the most barbarous ages, and totally unworthy the head of a civilized nation.

He has constrained our fellow-citizens, taken captive on the high seas, to bear arms against their country, to become the executioners of their friends and brethren, or to fall themselves by their hands.

He has excited domestic insurrection among us, and has endeavored to bring on the inhabitants of our frontiers the merciless Indian savages, whose known rule of warfare is an undistinguished destruction of all ages, sexes, and conditions.

In every stage of these oppressions we have petitioned for redress in the most humble terms; our repeated petitions have been answered only by repeated injury. A prince, whose character is thus marked by every act which may define a tyrant, is unfit to be the ruler of a free people.

Nor have we been wanting in our attentions to our British brethren. We have warned them, from time to time, of attempts by their legislature to extend an unwarrantable jurisdiction over us. We have reminded them of the circumstances of our emigration and settlement here. We have appealed to their native justice and magnanimity; and we have conjured them, by the ties of our common kindred, to disavow these usurpations, which would inevitably interrupt our connections and correspondence. They, too, have been deaf to the voice of justice and of consanguinity. We must, therefore, acquiesce in the necessity which denounces our separation, and hold them, as we hold the rest of mankind, enemies in war, in peace friends.

We, therefore, the representatives of the United States of America, in General Congress assembled, appealing to the Supreme Judge of the world for the rectitude of our intentions, do, in the name and by the authority of the good people of these colonies, solemnly publish and declare, that these United Colonies are, and of right ought to be, FREE AND INDEPENDENT STATES; that they are absolved from all allegiance to the British crown, and that all political connection between them and the state of Great Britain is, and ought to be, totally dissolved; and that, as free and independent states, they have full power to levy war, conclude peace, contract alliances, establish commerce, and do all other acts and things which independent states may of right do. And for the support of this declaration, with a firm reliance on the protection of Divine Providence, we mutually pledge to each other our lives, our fortunes, and our sacred honor.

JOHN HANCOCK *and fifty-five others*

CONSTITUTION OF THE UNITED STATES OF AMERICA

Preamble

We the people of the United States, in order to form a more perfect union, establish justice, insure domestic tranquillity, provide for the common defense, promote the general welfare, and secure the blessings of liberty to ourselves and our posterity, do ordain and establish this Constitution for the United States of America.

Article I

Section 1   All legislative powers herein granted shall be vested in a Congress of the United

---

Passages no longer in effect are printed in italic type.

States, which shall consist of a Senate and a House of Representatives.

Section 2   The House of Representatives shall be composed of members chosen every second year by the people of the several States, and the electors in each State shall have the qualifications requisite for electors of the most numerous branch of the State Legislature.

No person shall be a Representative who shall not have attained to the age of twenty-five years, and been seven years a citizen of the United States, and who shall not, when elected, be an inhabitant of that State in which he shall be chosen.

Representatives and direct taxes shall be apportioned among the several States which may be included within this Union, according to their respective numbers, *which shall be determined by adding to the whole number of free persons, including those bound to service for a term of years and excluding Indians not taxed, three-fifths of all other persons.* The actual enumeration shall be made within three years after the first meeting of the Congress of the United States, and within every subsequent term of ten years, in such manner as they shall by law direct. The number of Representatives shall not exceed one for every thirty thousand, but each State shall have at least one Representative; *and until such enumeration shall be made, the State of New Hampshire shall be entitled to choose three, Massachusetts eight, Rhode Island and Providence Plantations one, Connecticut five, New York six, New Jersey four, Pennsylvania eight, Delaware one, Maryland six, Virginia ten, North Carolina five, South Carolina five, and Georgia three.*

When vacancies happen in the representation from any State, the Executive authority thereof shall issue writs of election to fill such vacancies.

The House of Representatives shall choose their Speaker and other officers; and shall have the sole power of impeachment.

Section 3   The Senate of the United States shall be composed of two Senators from each State, *chosen by the legislature thereof,* for six years; and each Senator shall have one vote.

Immediately after they shall be assembled in consequence of the first election, they shall be divided as equally as may be into three classes. The seats of the Senators of the first class shall be vacated at the expiration of the second year, of the second class at the expiration of the fourth year, and of the third class at the expiration of the sixth year, so that one-third may be chosen every second year; *and if vacancies happen by resignation or otherwise, during the recess of the legislature of any State, the Executive thereof may make temporary appointments until the next meeting of the legislature, which shall then fill such vacancies.*

No person shall be a Senator who shall not have attained to the age of thirty years, and been nine years a citizen of the United States, and who shall not, when elected, be an inhabitant of that State for which he shall be chosen.

The Vice-President of the United States shall be President of the Senate, but shall have no vote, unless they be equally divided.

The Senate shall choose their other officers, and also a President *pro tempore,* in the absence of the Vice-President, or when he shall exercise the office of President of the United States.

The Senate shall have the sole power to try all impeachments. When sitting for that purpose, they shall be on oath or affirmation. When the President of the United States is tried, the Chief Justice shall preside: and no person shall be convicted without the concurrence of two-thirds of the members present.

Judgment in cases of impeachment shall not extend further than to removal from the office, and disqualification to hold and enjoy any office of honor, trust or profit under the United States: but the party convicted shall nevertheless be liable and subject to indictment, trial, judgment and punishment, according to law.

Section 4 The times, places and manner of holding elections for Senators and Representatives shall be prescribed in each State by the legislature thereof; but the Congress may at any time by law make or alter such regulations, except as to the places of choosing Senators.

The Congress shall assemble at least once in every year, and such meeting *shall be on the first Monday in December, unless they shall by law appoint a different day.*

Section 5 Each house shall be the judge of the elections, returns and qualifications of its own members, and a majority of each shall constitute a quorum to do business; but a smaller number may adjourn from day to day, and may be authorized to compel the attendance of absent members, in such manner, and under such penalties, as each house may provide.

Each house may determine the rules of its proceedings, punish its members for disorderly behavior, and with the concurrence of two-thirds, expel a member.

Each house shall keep a journal of its proceedings, and from time to time publish the same, excepting such parts as may in their judgment require secrecy; and the yeas and nays of the members of either house on any question shall, at the desire of one-fifth of those present, be entered on the journal.

Neither house, during the session of Congress, shall, without the consent of the other, adjourn for more than three days, nor to any other place than that in which the two houses shall be sitting.

Section 6 The Senators and Representatives shall receive a compensation for their services, to be ascertained by law and paid out of the treasury of the United States. They shall in all cases except treason, felony and breach of the peace, be privileged from arrest during their attendance at the session of their respective houses, and in going to and returning from the same; and for any speech or debate in either house, they shall not be questioned in any other place.

No Senator or Representative shall, during the time for which he was elected, be appointed to any civil office under the authority of the United States, which shall have been created, or the emoluments whereof shall have been increased, during such time; and no person holding any office under the United States shall be a member of either house during his continuance in office.

Section 7 All bills for raising revenue shall originate in the House of Representatives; but the Senate may propose or concur with amendments as on other bills.

Every bill which shall have passed the House of Representatives and the Senate, shall, before it become a law, be presented to the President of the United States; if he approve he shall sign it, but if not he shall return it with objections to that house in which it originated, who shall enter the objections at large on their journal, and proceed to reconsider it. If after such reconsideration two-thirds of that house shall agree to pass the bill, it shall be sent, together with the objections, to the other house, by which it shall likewise be reconsidered, and, if approved by two-thirds of that house, it shall become a law. But in all such cases the votes of both houses shall be determined by yeas and nays, and the names of the persons voting for and against the bill shall be entered on the journal of each house respectively. If any bill shall not be returned by the President within ten days (Sundays excepted) after it shall have been presented to him, the same shall be a law, in like manner as if he had signed it, unless the Congress by their adjournment prevent its return, in which case it shall not be a law.

Every order, resolution, or vote to which the concurrence of the Senate and House of Representatives may be necessary (except on a question of adjournment) shall be presented to the President of the United States; and before the same shall take effect, shall be approved by him, or being disapproved by him, shall be repassed by two-thirds of the Senate and House of Representatives, according to the rules and limitations prescribed in the case of a bill.

Section 8   The Congress shall have power

To lay and collect taxes, duties, imposts, and excises, to pay the debts and provide for the common defense and general welfare of the United States; but all duties, imposts and excises shall be uniform throughout the United States;

To borrow money on the credit of the United States;

To regulate commerce with foreign nations, and among the several States, and with the Indian tribes;

To establish an uniform rule of naturalization, and uniform laws on the subject of bankruptcies throughout the United States;

To coin money, regulate the value thereof, and of foreign coin, and fix the standard of weights and measures;

To provide for the punishment of counterfeiting the securities and current coin of the United States;

To establish post offices and post roads;

To promote the progress of science and useful arts by securing for limited times to authors and inventors the exclusive right to their respective writings and discoveries;

To constitute tribunals inferior to the Supreme Court;

To define and punish piracies and felonies committed on the high seas and offenses against the law of nations;

To declare war, grant letters of marque and reprisal, and make rules concerning captures on land and water;

To raise and support armies, but no appropriation of money to that use shall be for a longer term than two years;

To provide and maintain a navy;

To make rules for the government and regulation of the land and naval forces;

To provide for calling forth the militia to execute the laws of the Union, suppress insurrections, and repel invasions;

To provide for organizing, arming, and disciplining the militia, and for governing such part of them as may be employed in the service of the United States, reserving to the States respectively the appointment of the officers, and the authority of training the militia according to the discipline prescribed by Congress;

To exercise exclusive legislation in all cases whatsoever, over such district (not exceeding ten miles square) as may, by cession of particular States, and the acceptance of Congress, become the seat of government of the United States, and to exercise like authority over all places purchased by the consent of the legislature of the State, in which the same shall be, for erection of forts, magazines, arsenals, dockyards, and other needful buildings; — and

To make all laws which shall be necessary and proper for carrying into execution the foregoing powers, and all other powers vested by this Constitution in the government of the United States, or in any department or officer thereof.

Section 9 *The migration or importation of such persons as any of the States now existing shall think proper to admit shall not be prohibited by the Congress prior to the year 1808; but a tax or duty may be imposed on such importation, not exceeding $10 for each person.*

The privilege of the writ of habeas corpus shall not be suspended, unless when in cases of rebellion or invasion the public safety may require it.

No bill of attainder or ex post facto law shall be passed.

No capitation, or other direct, tax shall be laid, unless in proportion to the census or enumeration herein before directed to be taken.

No tax or duty shall be laid on articles exported from any State.

No preference shall be given by any regulation of commerce or revenue to the ports of one State over those of another; nor shall vessels bound to, or from, one State, be obliged to enter, clear, or pay duties in another.

No money shall be drawn from the treasury, but in consequence of appropriations made by law; and a regular statement and account of the receipts and expenditures of all public money shall be published from time to time.

No title of nobility shall be granted by the United States: and no person holding any office of profit or trust under them, shall, without the consent of the Congress, accept of any present, emolument, office, or title, of any kind whatever, from any king, prince, or foreign state.

Section 10 No State shall enter into any treaty, alliance, or confederation; grant letters of marque and reprisal; coin money; emit bills of credit; make anything but gold and silver coin a tender in payment of debts; pass any bill of attainder, ex post facto law, or law impairing the obligation of contracts, or grant any title of nobility.

No State shall, without the consent of Congress, lay any imposts or duties on imports or exports, except what may be absolutely necessary for executing its inspection laws: and the net produce of all duties and imposts, laid by any State on imports or exports, shall be for the use of the treasury of the United States; and all such laws shall be subject to the revision and control of the Congress.

No State shall, without the consent of Congress, lay any duty of tonnage, keep troops or ships of war in time of peace, enter into any agreement or compact with another State, or with a foreign power, or engage in war, unless actually invaded, or in such imminent danger as will not admit of delay.

Article II

Section 1 The executive power shall be vested in a President of the United States of America. He shall hold his office during the term of four years, and, together with the Vice-President, chosen for the same term, be elected as follows:

Each State shall appoint, in such manner as the legislature thereof may direct, a number of electors, equal to the whole number of Senators and Representatives to which the State may be entitled in the Congress; but no Senator or Representative, or person holding an office of trust or profit under the United States, shall be appointed an elector.

The electors shall meet in their respective States, and vote by ballot for two persons, of whom one at least shall not be an inhabitant of the same State with themselves. And they shall make a list of all the persons voted for, and of the number of votes for each; which list they shall sign and certify, and transmit sealed to the seat of government of the United States, directed to the President of the Senate. The President of the Senate shall, in the presence of the Senate and House of Representatives, open all the certificates, and the votes shall then be counted. The person having the greatest number of votes shall be the President, if such number be a majority of the whole number of electors appointed; and if there be more than one who have such majority, and have an equal number of votes, then the House of Representatives shall immediately choose by ballot one of them for President; and if no person have a majority, then from the five highest on the list said house shall in like manner choose the President. But in choosing the President the votes shall be taken by

States, the representation from each State having one vote; a quorum for this purpose shall consist of a member or members from two-thirds of the States, and a majority of all the States shall be necessary to a choice. In every case, after the choice of the President, the person having the greatest number of votes of the electors shall be the Vice-President. But if there should remain two or more who have equal votes, the Senate shall choose from them by ballot the Vice-President.

The Congress may determine the time of choosing the electors and the day on which they shall give their votes; which day shall be the same throughout the United States.

No person except a natural-born citizen, *or a citizen of the United States at the time of the adoption of this Constitution,* shall be eligible to the office of President; neither shall any person be eligible to that office who shall not have attained to the age of thirty-five years, and been fourteen years a resident within the United States.

In case of the removal of the President from office or of his death, resignation, or inability to discharge the powers and duties of the said office, the same shall devolve on the Vice-President, and the Congress may by law provide for the case of removal, death, resignation, or inability, both of the President and Vice-President, declaring what officer shall then act as President, and such officer shall act accordingly, until the disability be removed, or a President shall be elected.

The President shall, at stated times, receive for his services a compensation, which shall neither be increased nor diminished during the period for which he shall have been elected, and he shall not receive within that period any other emolument from the United States, or any of them.

Before he enter on the execution of his office, he shall take the following oath or affirmation: — "I do solemnly swear (or affirm) that I will faithfully execute the office of the President of the United States, and will to the best of my ability preserve, protect and defend the Constitution of the United States."

Section 2   The President shall be commander in chief of the army and navy of the United States, and of the militia of the several States, when called into the actual service of the United States; he may require the opinion, in writing, of the principal officer in each of the executive departments, upon any subject relating to the duties of their respective offices, and he shall have power to grant reprieves and pardons for offenses against the United States, except in cases of impeachment.

He shall have power, by and with the advice and consent of the Senate, to make treaties, provided two-thirds of the Senators present concur; and he shall nominate, and by and with the advice and consent of the Senate, shall appoint ambassadors, other public ministers and consuls, judges of the Supreme Court, and all other officers of the United States, whose appointments are not herein otherwise provided for, and which shall be established by law: but Congress may by law vest the appointment of such inferior officers, as they think proper, in the President alone, in the courts of law, or in the heads of departments.

The President shall have power to fill up all vacancies that may happen during the recess of the Senate, by granting commissions which shall expire at the end of their next session.

Section 3   He shall from time to time give to the Congress information of the state of the Union, and recommend to their consideration such measures as he shall judge necessary and expedient; he may, on extraordinary occasions, convene both houses, or either of them, and in case of disagreement between them, with respect to the time of adjournment, he may adjourn them to such time as he shall think proper; he shall receive ambassadors and other public ministers; he shall take care that the laws be faithfully executed, and shall commission all the officers of the United States.

Section 4   The President, Vice-President and all civil officers of the United States shall be removed from office on impeachment for, and on conviction of, treason, bribery, or other high crimes and misdemeanors.

Article III

Section 1 The judicial power of the United States shall be vested in one Supreme Court, and in such inferior courts as the Congress may from time to time ordain and establish. The judges, both of the Supreme and inferior courts, shall hold their offices during good behavior, and shall, at stated times, receive for their services a compensation which shall not be diminished during their continuance in office.

Section 2 The judicial power shall extend to all cases, in law and equity, arising under this Constitution, the laws of the United States, and treaties made, or which shall be made, under their authority; — to all cases affecting ambassadors, other public ministers and consuls; — to all cases of admiralty and maritime jurisdiction; — to controversies to which the United States shall be a party; — to controversies between two or more States; — *between a State and citizens of another State;* — between citizens of different States; — between citizens of the same State claiming lands under grants of different States, and between a State, or the citizens thereof, and foreign states, citizens or subjects.

In all cases affecting ambassadors, other public ministers and consuls, and those in which a State shall be party, the Supreme Court shall have original jurisdiction. In all the other cases before mentioned, the Supreme Court shall have appellate jurisdiction, both as to law and fact, with such exceptions, and under such regulations, as the Congress shall make.

The trial of all crimes, except in cases of impeachment, shall be by jury; and such trial shall be held in the State where said crimes shall have been committed; but when not committed within any State, the trial shall be at such place or places as the Congress may by law have directed.

Section 3 Treason against the United States shall consist only in levying war against them, or in adhering to their enemies, giving them aid and comfort. No person shall be convicted of treason unless on the testimony of two witnesses to the same overt act, or on confession in open court.

The Congress shall have power to declare the punishment of treason, but no attainder of treason shall work corruption of blood, or forfeiture except during the life of the person attainted.

Article IV

Section 1 Full faith and credit shall be given in each State to the public acts, records, and judicial proceedings of every other State. And the Congress may by general laws prescribe the manner in which such acts, records, and proceedings shall be proved, and the effect thereof.

Section 2 The citizens of each State shall be entitled to all privileges and immunities of citizens in the several States.

A person charged in any State with treason, felony, or other crime, who shall flee from justice, and be found in another State, shall on demand of the executive authority of the State from which he fled, be delivered up, to be removed to the State having jurisdiction of the crime.

No person held to service or labor in one State, under the laws thereof, escaping into another, shall, in consequence of any law or regulation therein, be discharged from such service or labor, but shall be delivered up on claim of the party to whom such service or labor may be due.

Section 3 New States may be admitted by the Congress into this Union; but no new State shall be formed or erected within the jurisdiction of any other State; nor any State be formed by the junction of two or more States, or parts of States, without the consent of the legislatures of the States concerned as well as of the Congress.

The Congress shall have power to dispose of and make all needful rules and regulations respecting the territory or other property belonging to the United States; and nothing in this Constitution shall be so construed as to prejudice any claims of the United States, or of any particular State.

Section 4 The United States shall guarantee to every State in this Union a republican form of government, and shall protect each of them against invasion; and on application of the legislature, or of the executive (when the legislature cannot be convened), against domestic violence.

Article V

The Congress, whenever two-thirds of both houses shall deem it necessary, shall propose amendments to this Constitution, or, on the application of the legislatures of two-thirds of the several States, shall call a convention for proposing amendments, which, in either case, shall be valid to all intents and purposes, as part of this Constitution, when ratified by the legislatures of three-fourths of the several States, or by conventions in three-fourths thereof, as the one or the other mode of ratification may be proposed by the Congress; provided *that no amendments which may be made prior to the year one thousand eight hundred and eight shall in any manner affect the first and fourth clauses in the ninth section of the first article;* and that no State, without its consent, shall be deprived of its equal suffrage in the Senate.

Article VI

All debts contracted and engagements entered into, before the adoption of this Constitution, shall be as valid against the United States under this Constitution, as under the Confederation.

This Constitution, and the laws of the United States which shall be made in pursuance thereof; and all treaties made, or which shall be made, under the authority of the United States, shall be the supreme law of the land; and the judges in every State shall be bound thereby, anything in the Constitution or laws of any State to the contrary notwithstanding.

The Senators and Representatives before mentioned, and the members of the several State legislatures, and all executive and judicial officers, both of the United States and of the several States, shall be bound by oath or affirmation to support this Constitution; but no religious test shall ever be required as a qualification to any office or public trust under the United States.

Article VII

The ratification of the conventions of nine States shall be sufficient for the establishment of this Constitution between the States so ratifying the same.

Done in Convention by the unanimous consent of the States present, the seventeenth day of September in the year of our Lord one thousand seven hundred and eighty-seven and of the Independence of the United States of America the twelfth. In witness whereof we have hereunto subscribed our names.

GEORGE WASHINGTON *and thirty-seven others*

Amendments to the Constitution

Amendment I

Congress shall make no law respecting an establishment of religion, or prohibiting the free exercise thereof; or abridging the freedom of speech, or of the press; or the right of the people peaceably to assemble, and to petition the government for a redress of grievances.

Amendment II

A well-regulated militia being necessary to the security of a free State, the right of the people to keep and bear arms shall not be infringed.

Amendment III

No soldier shall, in time of peace, be quartered in any house without the consent of the owner, nor in time of war, but in a manner to be prescribed by law.

Amendment IV

The right of the people to be secure in their persons, houses, papers, and effects, against unreasonable searches and seizures, shall not be violated, and no warrants shall issue but upon probable cause, supported by oath or affirmation, and particularly describing the place to be searched, and the persons or things to be seized.

The first ten Amendments (the Bill of Rights) were adopted in 1791.

Amendment V

No person shall be held to answer for a capital, or otherwise infamous crime, unless on a presentment or indictment of a grand jury, except in cases arising in the land or naval forces, or in the militia, when in actual service in time of war or public danger; nor shall any person be subject for the same offense to be twice put in jeopardy of life or limb; nor shall be compelled in any criminal case to be a witness against himself, nor be deprived of life, liberty, or property, without due process of law; nor shall private property be taken for public use without just compensation.

Amendment VI

In all criminal prosecutions, the accused shall enjoy the right to a speedy and public trial, by an impartial jury of the State and district wherein the crime shall have been committed, which district shall have been previously ascertained by law, and to be informed of the nature and cause of the accusation; to be confronted with the witnesses against him; to have compulsory process for obtaining witnesses in his favor, and to have the assistance of counsel for his defense.

Amendment VII

In suits at common law, where the value in controversy shall exceed twenty dollars, the right of trial by jury shall be preserved, and no fact tried by a jury shall be otherwise reexamined in any court of the United States, than according to the rules of the common law.

Amendment VIII

Excessive bail shall not be required, nor excessive fines imposed, nor cruel and unusual punishments inflicted.

Amendment IX

The enumeration in the Constitution, of certain rights, shall not be construed to deny or disparage others retained by the people.

Amendment X

The powers not delegated to the United States by the Constitution, nor prohibited by it to the States, are reserved to the States respectively, or to the people.

Amendment XI

[Adopted 1798]

The judicial power of the United States shall not be construed to extend to any suit in law or equity, commenced or prosecuted against one of the United States by citizens of another State, or by citizens or subjects of any foreign state.

Amendment XII

[Adopted 1804]

The electors shall meet in their respective States, and vote by ballot for President and Vice-President, one of whom, at least, shall not be an inhabitant of the same State with themselves; they shall name in their ballots the person voted for as President, and in distinct ballots the person voted for as Vice-President, and they shall make distinct lists of all persons voted for as President, and of all persons voted for as Vice-President, and of the number of votes for each, which lists they shall sign and certify, and transmit sealed to the seat of government of the United States, directed to the President of the Senate; — the President of the Senate shall, in the presence of the Senate and House of Representatives, open all the certificates and the votes shall then be counted; — the person having the greatest number of votes for President shall be the President, if such number be a majority of the whole number of electors appointed; and if no person have such majority, then from the persons having the highest numbers not exceeding three on the list of those voted for as President, the House of Representatives shall choose immediately, by ballot, the President. But in choosing the President, the votes shall be taken by States, the representation from each State having one vote; a quorum for this purpose shall consist of a member or members from two-thirds of the States, and a majority of all the States shall be necessary to a choice. And if the House of Representatives shall not choose a President whenever the right of choice shall devolve upon them, before *the fourth day of March* next following, then the Vice-President shall act as President, as in the case of the death or other constitutional disability of the President.

The person having the greatest number of votes as Vice-President shall be the Vice-President, if such number be a majority of the whole number of electors appointed; and if no person have a majority, then from the two highest numbers on the list the Senate shall choose the Vice-President; a quorum for the purpose shall consist of two-thirds of the whole number of Senators, and a majority of the whole number shall be necessary to a choice. But no person constitutionally ineligible to the office of President shall be eligible to that of Vice-President of the United States.

Amendment XIII

[Adopted 1865]

Section 1   Neither slavery nor involuntary servitude, except as a punishment for crime whereof the party shall have been duly convicted, shall exist within the United States, or any place subject to their jurisdiction.

Section 2   Congress shall have power to enforce this article by appropriate legislation.

Amendment XIV

[Adopted 1868]

Section 1   All persons born or naturalized in the United States, and subject to the jurisdiction thereof, are citizens of the United States and of the State wherein they reside. No State shall make or enforce any law which shall abridge the privileges or immunities of citizens of the United States; nor shall any State deprive any person of life, liberty, or property, without due process of law; nor deny to any person within its jurisdiction the equal protection of the laws.

Section 2   Representatives shall be apportioned among the several States according to their respective numbers, counting the whole number of persons in each State, excluding Indians not taxed. But when the right to vote at any election for the choice of Electors for President and Vice-President of the United States, Representatives in Congress, the executive and judicial officers of a State, or the members of the legislature thereof, is denied to any of the male inhabitants of such State, being twenty-one years of age and citizens of the United States, or in any way abridged, except for participation in rebellion, or other crime, the basis of representation therein shall be reduced in the proportion which the number of such male citizens shall bear to the whole number of male citizens twenty-one years of age in such State.

Section 3   No person shall be a Senator or Representative in Congress, or Elector of President and Vice-President, or hold any office, civil or military, under the United States, or under any State, who, having previously taken an oath, as a member of Congress, or as an officer of the United States, or as a member of any State legislature, or as an executive or judicial officer of any State, to support the Constitution of the United States, shall have engaged in insurrection or rebellion against the same, or given aid or comfort to the enemies thereof. Congress may, by a vote of two-thirds of each house, remove such disability.

Section 4   The validity of the public debt of the United States, authorized by law, including debts incurred for payment of pensions and bounties for services in suppressing insurrection or rebellion, shall not be questioned. But neither the United States nor any State shall assume or pay any debt or obligation incurred in aid of insurrection or rebellion against the United States, or any claim for the loss of emancipation of any slave; but all such debts, obligations, and claims shall be held illegal and void.

Section 5   The Congress shall have power to enforce, by appropriate legislation, the provisions of this article.

Amendment XV

[Adopted 1870]

Section 1 The right of citizens of the United States to vote shall not be denied or abridged by the United States or by any State on account of race, color, or previous condition of servitude.

Section 2 The Congress shall have power to enforce this article by appropriate legislation.

Amendment XVI

[Adopted 1913]

The Congress shall have power to lay and collect taxes on incomes, from whatever source derived, without apportionment among the several States, and without regard to any census or enumeration.

Amendment XVII

[Adopted 1913]

Section 1 The Senate of the United States shall be composed of two Senators from each State, elected by the people thereof, for six years; and each Senator shall have one vote. The electors in each State shall have the qualifications requisite for electors of [voters for] the most numerous branch of the State legislatures.

Section 2 When vacancies happen in the representation of any State in the Senate, the executive authority of such State shall issue writs of election to fill such vacancies: Provided, that the Legislature of any State may empower the executive thereof to make temporary appointments until the people fill the vacancies by election as the Legislature may direct.

Section 3 This amendment shall not be so construed as to affect the election or term of any Senator chosen before it becomes valid as part of the Constitution.

Amendment XVIII

[Adopted 1919; Repealed 1933]

Section 1 After one year from the ratification of this article the manufacture, sale, or transportation of intoxicating liquors within, the importation thereof into, or the exportation thereof from the United States and all territory subject to the jurisdiction thereof, for beverage purposes, is hereby prohibited.

Section 2 The Congress and the several States shall have concurrent power to enforce this article by appropriate legislation.

Section 3 This article shall be inoperative unless it shall have been ratified as an amendment to the Constitution by the legislatures of the several States, as provided by the Constitution, within seven years from the date of the submission thereof to the States by the Congress.

Amendment XIX

[Adopted 1920]

Section 1 The right of citizens of the United States to vote shall not be denied or abridged by the United States or by any State on account of sex.

Section 2 The Congress shall have power to enforce this article by appropriate legislation.

Amendment XX

[Adopted 1933]

Section 1 The terms of the President and Vice-President shall end at noon on the 20th day of January, and the terms of Senators and Representatives at noon on the 3d day of January, of the years in which such terms would have ended if this article had not been ratified; and the terms of their successors shall then begin.

Section 2 The Congress shall assemble at least once in every year, and such meeting shall begin at noon on the 3d day of January, unless they shall by law appoint a different day.

Section 3 If, at the time fixed for the beginning of the term of the President, the President-elect shall have died, the Vice-President-elect shall become President. If a President shall not have been chosen before the time fixed for the beginning of his term, or if the President-elect shall have failed to qualify, then the Vice-President-elect shall act as President until a President shall have qualified; and the Congress may by law provide for the case wherein neither a President-elect nor a Vice-President-elect shall have qualified, declaring who shall then act as President, or the manner in which one who is to act shall be selected, and such persons shall act accordingly until a President or Vice-President shall have qualified.

Section 4 The Congress may by law provide for the case of the death of any of the persons from whom the House of Representatives may choose a President whenever the right of choice shall have devolved upon them, and for the case of the death of any of the persons from whom the Senate may choose a Vice-President whenever the right of choice shall have devolved upon them.

Section 5 Sections 1 and 2 shall take effect on the 15th day of October following the ratification of this article.

Section 6 This article shall be inoperative unless it shall have been ratified as an amendment to the Constitution by the Legislatures of three-fourths of the several States within seven years from the date of its submission.

Amendment XXI

[Adopted 1933]

Section 1 The eighteenth article of amendment to the Constitution of the United States is hereby repealed.

Section 2 The transportation or importation into any State, Territory, or Possession of the United States for delivery or use therein of intoxicating liquors, in violation of the laws thereof, is hereby prohibited.

Section 3 This article shall be inoperative unless it shall have been ratified as an amendment to the Constitution by conventions in the several States, as provided in the Constitution, within seven years from the date of submission thereof to the States by the Congress.

Amendment XXII

[Adopted 1951]

Section 1 No person shall be elected to the office of President more than twice, and no person who has held the office of President, or acted as President, for more than two years of a term to which some other person was elected President shall be elected to the office of President more than once. But this article shall not apply to any person holding the office of President when this article was proposed by the Congress, and shall not prevent any person who may be holding the office of President, or acting as President, during the term within which this article becomes operative from holding the office of President or acting as President during the remainder of such term.

Section 2 This article shall be inoperative unless it shall have been ratified as an amendment to the Constitution by the legislatures of three-fourths of the several States within seven years from the date of its submission to the States by the Congress.

Amendment XXIII

[Adopted 1961]

Section 1 The District constituting the seat of Government of the United States shall appoint in such manner as the Congress may direct:

A number of electors of President and Vice-President equal to the whole number of Senators and Representatives in Congress to which the District would be entitled if it were a State, but in no event more than the least populous State; they shall be in addition to those appointed by the States, but they shall be considered for the purposes of the election of President and Vice-President, to be electors appointed by a State;

and they shall meet in the District and perform such duties as provided by the twelfth article of amendment.

Section 2 The Congress shall have the power to enforce this article by appropriate legislation.

Amendment XXIV

[Adopted 1964]

Section 1 The right of citizens of the United States to vote in any primary or other election for President or Vice-President, for electors for President or Vice-President, or for Senator or Representative in Congress, shall not be denied or abridged by the United States or any State by reason of failure to pay any poll tax or other tax.

Section 2 The Congress shall have the power to enforce this article by appropriate legislation.

Amendment XXV

[Adopted 1967]

Section 1 In case of the removal of the President from office or of his death or resignation, the Vice-President shall become President.

Section 2 Whenever there is a vacancy in the office of the Vice-President, the President shall nominate a Vice-President who shall take office upon confirmation by a majority vote of both Houses of Congress.

Section 3 Whenever the President transmits to the President pro tempore of the Senate and the Speaker of the House of Representatives his written declaration that he is unable to discharge the powers and duties of his office, and until he transmits to them a written declaration to the contrary, such powers and duties shall be discharged by the Vice-President as Acting President.

Section 4 Whenever the Vice-President and a majority of either the principal officers of the ex-ecutive departments or of such other body as Congress may by law provide, transmit to the President pro tempore of the Senate and the Speaker of the House of Representatives their written declaration that the President is unable to discharge the powers and duties of his office, the Vice-President shall immediately assume the powers and duties of the office as Acting President.

Thereafter, when the President transmits to the President pro tempore of the Senate and the Speaker of the House of Representatives his written declaration that no inability exists, he shall resume the powers and duties of his office unless the Vice-President and a majority of either the principal officers of the executive de-partment[s] or of such other body as Congress may by law provide, transmit within four days to the President pro tempore of the Senate and the Speaker of the House of Representatives their written declaration that the President is unable to discharge the powers and duties of his office. Thereupon Congress shall decide the is-sue, assembling within forty-eight hours for that purpose if not in session. If the Congress, within twenty-one days after receipt of the latter writ-ten declaration, or, if Congress is not in session, within twenty-one days after Congress is re-quired to assemble, determines by two-thirds vote of both Houses that the President is unable to discharge the powers and duties of his office, the Vice-President shall continue to discharge the same as Acting President; otherwise, the President shall resume the powers and duties of his office.

Amendment XXVI

[Adopted 1971]

Section 1 The right of citizens of the United States, who are eighteen years of age or older, to vote shall not be denied or abridged by the United States or by any State on account of age.

Section 2 The Congress shall have power to enforce this article by appropriate legislation.

Contributors Index

General Index

Page numbers in **boldface type** refer to the major article for an entry.